W9-DCY-220

ENCYCLOPAEDIA OF THE ARTS

Architecture
Sculpture
Applied Arts
Painting
Graphic Arts
Literature
Theatre
Cinema
Photography
Music
Opera
Ballet

Biographies
Titles
Styles
Schools
Movements and Groups
Technical Terms
Techniques and Materials

10,250 entries
3,550 illustrations
79 colour plates
984 pages

ENCYCLOPAEDIA OF THE ARTS

Consulting Editor HERBERT READ

MEREDITH PRESS · NEW YORK

MANAGING EDITOR
Geoffrey Hindley

ASSISTANT EDITOR
Nathaniel Harris

EDITORIAL RESEARCH
Philippa Le Hardy
Elspeth Evans
Mary Bainbridge

PICTURE RESEARCH
Richard Howard
Susan Bakker
Pamela Woods

To assist them in covering so wide a field the editors have called on the help of numerous writers and scholars, and the material supplied by them has constituted a most important element in the book. It is obvious that such a work as the present has been subject to stringent editorial requirements, and the editors acknowledge responsibility for any errors which may have crept into the text in pursuance of these requirements.

The following is a list of contributors with the areas in which they have made contributions.

Michael Archer (applied arts); Barry Argyle (Commonwealth literature); Diana Balden (ballet); Malcolm Bradbury (U.S. literature); Andrzej Busza (Polish literature); Geoffrey Butler (German literature); Patricia Butler (applied arts); Ian Cameron (cinema); Francis Carr (fine art); Renata Clewes (Italian literature); J. M. Cohen (Spanish literature); J. K. D. Cooper (applied arts); Czigany Lorant (Hungarian literature); J. C. Darracott (fine art); Colin Davies (fine art); Evelyn Davson (applied arts); Peter Dean (cinema); Michael Edwardes (non-Western cultures); Stephan Feuchtwang (Chinese art); A. C. Gibbs (English literature); Josephine Gilbey (English literature); Camilla Gray (Russian art); Lionel Grigson (jazz); Nathaniel Harris (Russian literature); Geoffrey Hindley (music); H. N. Hindley (classical literature); Louis James (English literature); Philippa Le Hardy (fine art); Sheila W. Masson (French literature); Michael Mott (fine art); Eric Mottram (U.S. literature); R. L. Ormond (applied arts); Brian Rowley (German literature); Raymond Rudorff (Spanish and Italian literatures); Julian Silverman (modern music); Ian Sutton (architecture); Geoffrey Tetlow (theatre); W. M. Tydeman (English literature); Nicholas Wadley (fine art); Ross Watson (applied arts); J. G. Weightman (French literature); John Winter (modern architecture).

PUBLISHED BY THAMES AND HUDSON LTD 1966

PUBLISHED IN THE UNITED STATES OF
AMERICA BY MEREDITH PRESS
DES MOINES AND NEW YORK, 1966
LIBRARY OF CONGRESS CATALOG CARD NUMBER 66–23883
PRINTED IN GREAT BRITAIN BY JARROLD AND SONS LTD, NORWICH

INTRODUCTION

'THE ARTS', in English usage, is a term that covers more than the single substantive word 'art'. Though this single word can be used to denote skill in any kind of human activity (such as surgery, boxing, acting) its proper use is restricted to spheres in which utility is not the first consideration. In this sense art is the application of skill to various modes of expression, where the intention is to please or perhaps to terrify, to effect some emotional response, to rouse some degree of feeling. In the past the products of skill in this restricted sense have been called the 'Fine Arts', and if that phrase now seems somewhat old-fashioned, it is only because the modern age has been responsible for the invention of a wide range of new materials and processes which greatly extend the range of art. We inevitably associate the phrase 'the Fine Arts' with the arts of painting, sculpture and architecture; we hesitate to include within its scope arts such as the film or works that have some claim to beauty but are produced by machine-tools rather than the hand. It is for this reason that a work such as the present one could not be called an Encyclopaedia of the Fine Arts; nevertheless, the underlying principles remain the same: skill is always involved, but so is the imagination.

Though an encyclopaedia must, if it is to be useful, have a defined scope, it must include every aspect of its subject-matter. Thus this encyclopaedia will be found to include entries for individual artists and for particular works of art (books, films, plays, operas, paintings, etc.); it will also be found to include more general articles on historical movements in the arts and groups of artists; others on techniques and materials. Always the aim is to be precise and specific, to give information rather than to express an opinion, and to avoid discursive articles on subjects (such as English Literature or Humour) which by their very nature cannot be made precise. An encyclopaedia is a work of reference, and though it may be enjoyed in moments of idle curiosity, speed of reference is the first consideration and must not be impeded by irrelevant chatter.

Though all encyclopaedias aim at universality, usefulness again dictates certain limitations. This particular encyclopaedia is designed for readers in the Western World, and though such readers have a natural curiosity about cultures outside their own world (such as those of China, Japan and Islam) the range of their interest in such cultures is less specific. Within the scope of one volume it would not be possible to list, for example, all the poets and painters who for three millennia have contributed to the arts of China and Japan. In such circumstances there is a criterion that can be easily applied–to restrict the entries to those artists in such civilizations who may have had some influence in the West. An entry will be found, for example, for Hokusai, though not for Soga Jasoku, though the latter may be a greater artist.

For the same reason, those cultures which have influenced the West have entries (China, Japan, Islam, primitive art, African art, etc.); the object in these is not so much to describe the culture itself as to analyse its influence on the West.

In general then, it may be said that the subject of this book is Western culture. There are no chronological limits, but a certain bias has been displayed towards the arts of the present century, for the simple reason that they are likely to evoke more curiosity than the arts of earlier periods. The inclusion or exclusion of any particular subject has always been determined by this criterion, and is not to be taken as expressing a critical judgement.

It has required more than 10,000 entries to give a comprehensive account of this vast field, and where it has seemed appropriate illustrations have been added to illuminate the text. Cross-references, indicated by asterisks (*), are provided where they would seem to be useful, but only to indicate where directly relevant material can be found. When the fame of a particular book, play, painting, opera or film, etc. would seem to merit such treatment, the title is entered as a cross-reference to the author, painter, composer, etc. Under works based on classical mythology we have taken the opportunity to outline the myths, since they have often been used and reinterpreted in art. It has also proved convenient to use the entries for plays by Shakespeare to give details of sources, production and publication. Unless otherwise stated, dates of books refer to publication, dates of plays, operas, ballets and other stage works to performance. Dates in other cases usually indicate the year of execution.

Titles of books, plays, etc., mentioned in an entry about their author are given in the original language, followed by the date of publication and the title and date of the first English translation, thus: *L'Assommoir* (1877; *The Dram Shop*, 1884). If the original language is not written in the Latin alphabet (as, for example, Russian) the familiar English title and dates of publication and translation only are given: *War and Peace* (1869; 1886). Musical items, paintings, etc., are also given their familiar titles.

Finally, the illustrations are functional as well as decorative: the wealth of picture material provided has been fully exploited by a system of cross-references in the captions. The principle of utility and the system of cross-referencing extends also to the colour plates. These have been carefully selected to form a section, complete within itself, which presents in terms of historical evolution the material treated analytically in the text.

The Encyclopaedia has been compiled by a team of research workers under the general editorship of Geoffrey Hindley and Nathaniel Harris. My own part in the enterprise was confined to the planning stages, to general advice about the treatment of subjects, and to a reading of the proofs.

HERBERT READ

ABBREVIATIONS

Most of the abbreviations in this book are in common use or are self-evident: e.g. the subject of an article is referred to by its first letter (Shakespeare becomes S.) in the text of the article. Abbreviations like trs. indicate various forms of the same word (translation, translator, translated), and are used wherever the meaning is clear from the context. We have followed the *Oxford English Dictionary* in using full stops only where the last letter of the abbreviation is *not* the last letter of the word in full. Thus trs. (translation); but trs (translations) and St (Saint).

A.	Art, Arte, etc.
Ac., Ak.	Academy, Akademie, etc.
anon.	anonymous
B.-A.	Beaux-Arts, Bellas Artes, etc.
Bibl.	Bibliothèque
B.M.	British Museum, London
Brera	Pinacoteca di Brera, Milan
c.	century
c.	*circa*
Civ.	Civic, Civica, etc.
coll.	collection, etc.
Com.	Communal, Comunale, etc.
ed.	edition, etc.
Fitz. Mus.	Fitzwilliam Museum, Cambridge
fl.	*floruit* (flourished)
G. or Gal.	Gallery
G. Gal.	Gemäldegalerie
Hermitage	National Museum of the Hermitage, Leningrad
Inst.	Institute
K.	Kunst
Lib.	Library
Louvre	Musée National du Louvre, Paris
M. or Mus.	Museum
maj.	major
Mauritshuis	Royal Picture Gallery (Mauritshuis), The Hague
M.B.-van B.	Museum Boymans-van Beuningen, Rotterdam
Met. Mus.	Metropolitan Museum, New York City
min.	minor
ms.	manuscript
N.	National, Nacional, etc.
N.G.	National Gallery
N.P.G.	National Portrait Gallery, London
N., S., E., W.	North, South, East, West
op.	opus
Pal.	Palace, Palazzo, etc.
Pina.	Pinacoteca, Pinakothek
Pitti	Galleria Palatina, Palazzo Pitti, Florence
posth.	posthumous
Prado	Museo Nacional del Prado, Spain
pseud.	pseudonym
publ.	published, etc.
R.A.	Royal Academy of Arts, London
R. Coll.	Royal Art Collections, Great Britain: Windsor Castle, Hampton Court, Holyrood House, Buckingham Palace, etc.
S., St, Sta, Ste	Saint, San, Santa, etc.
Soc.	Society
Stat., Staat., Stad.	State, Statens, Staatliche, Stadens, etc.
Tate	Tate Gallery, London
trs.	translation, etc.
Uffizi	Galleria degli Uffizi, Florence
Univ.	University
V. and A.	Victoria and Albert Museum, London
vol.	volume
W.-R. Mus.	Wallraf-Richartz Museum, Cologne

Aachen cathedral, view of the octagon

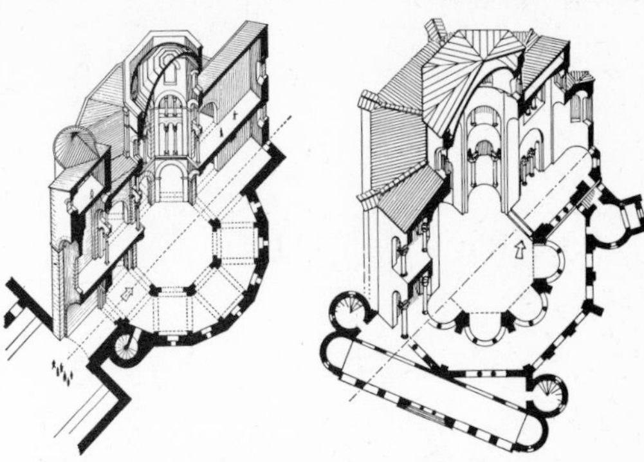

Aachen. Isometric drawings of Aachen cathedral (left) and S. Vitale, Ravenna

Aachen cathedral Germany. Originally the royal chapel of Charlemagne. It was built (795–805) on the model of S. Vitale, Ravenna, but lacks that church's subtleties. It is a domed octagon with 8 thick piers on the ground-storey; above that there is open arcading between the piers, but straight, not concave as at Ravenna. The octagon is surrounded by a circular groin-vaulted ambulatory. Charlemagne's throne is above the W. door at gallery level looking towards the altar. Columns are taken from classical and Byzantine buildings. In the 14th c. an elaborate Gothic choir was added at the E. end, and in the 17th an incongruous wooden roof was built over the dome.

Aakjaer Jeppe (1866–1930). Danish regional novelist and poet. The novel *Vreden's børn* (1904) is set in A.'s native Jutland and tells, with indignation, of the frustrations and injustices suffered by the peasantry. A.'s verse includes the songs *Rugens sange* (1906) and he also trs. Robert Burns, using the Jutland dialect in an attempt to reproduce Burns's idiom.

Aalto Alvar (1898–). Finnish architect, and furniture designer and one of the modern masters of functionalism. He makes imaginative use of new construction methods and of traditional raw materials such as timber. A. aims to build environments for human beings rather than mere geometrical designs. His 1st major building, the library at Viipuri, Finland (1927–35), was destroyed (1944) in the Russo-Finnish War before it was widely known and the Turun Sanomat newspaper building, Turku, Finland (1929) is the 1st important building surviving. Other major works are: the tuberculosis sanatorium, Paimio, Finland (1929–33); the Finnish pavilions at the Paris Exhibition (1937) and the New York World Fair (1939); the House of Culture for the Democratic People's Party, Helsinki (1956) and the art museum, Baghdad (1958–). His great achievement is the industrial complex, the Sunila plant, near Kotka, Finland; the 1st stage was completed in 1939, since when there have been extensions. In 1935 A., with his wife Aino A. and N. G. Hahl, founded the design shop Artek, in Helsinki.

Aaltonen Waïnö (1894–). Finnish sculptor and painter and a major force in modern Finnish sculpture. His work in granite is classical in line despite its monumental character. Besides a number of female torsos and portrait heads, A. has executed important public monuments.

Aarestrup Carl Ludvig Emil (1800–56). Danish poet unrecognized during his life, now regarded as a master of erotic verse. Works include *Erotiske Situationer* (1838) and many *ritournelles*. A.'s coll. works were publ. in 5 vols (1922–5).

Aasen Ivar Andreas (1813–96). Norwegian poet and philologist. From dialects, which he showed retained forms from Old Norse, he evolved the *landsmål* (now called *Nynorsk*, 'New Norse'), and publ. in it a grammar (1848), dictionary (1850) and folk-tales. NYNORSK, nationalistic in intent and a scholarly amalgam of ancient and scattered usages, is an official Norwegian language; it is taught in schools and used by some dialect writers but newspapers and almost all original literary work are in the other official language, BOKMÅL (formerly *riksmål*). This, the language used by Ibsen, is the literary version of the Dano-Norwegian language which evolved during the Danish rule in Norway.

abacus. Architectural term for the flat top of the capital of a column; it supports the entablature.

Abbate Niccolò dell' (*c.* 1512–71). A Modenese painter who, from 1552, worked in France and was, with Primaticcio, a leader of the school of *Fontainebleau. A. was stylistically influenced by the illusionism of Mantegna and the softness of Correggio, but more important was his characteristically mannerist treatment of landscape, as in the *Rape of Proserpine* (Louvre). There are similarities in his work, to Dosso Dossi and also Patenier and the Antwerp school, and A. himself introduced mannerism in landscape into France. A major picture is *The Death of Eurydice* (N.G., London).

Abbaye Group. Group of French writers who took 'L'Abbaye' (1906–7), an old house at Créteil, where they tried to support themselves by printing and selling books. The members included *Duhamel and *Romains; the A. press issued the latter's *Vie unanime*.

Abbey Edwin Austin (1852–1911). U.S. oil painter, watercolourist and book illustrator, who worked much in England, becoming an R.A. in 1898. He drew illustrations in pen for works by Robert Herrick, Oliver Goldsmith and Shakespeare, and painted the scenes of *The Quest of the Holy Grail* on the walls of the public library, Boston, Mass.

Abbate. *The Death of Eurydice* (detail)

Aaltonen. *Wader*

Aalto. Tuberculosis sanatorium, Paimio, Finland (1929–33)

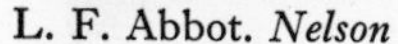

L. F. Abbot. *Nelson*

Abbey Theatre. G. B. Shaw's *Blanco Posnet*

Abelard and Héloïse. 14th-c. carved capital

Abbey Henry Eugene (1846–96). U.S. theatre manager, one of the first to engage European stars. In 1881 he introduced Bernhardt to New York and in 1893 engaged Irving and Ellen Terry to play in Tennyson's *Becket* at the opening of Abbey's Theatre, New York.

Abbey Theatre Dublin. Theatre acquired in 1904 with the financial help of Miss A. E. F. Horniman by the Irish National Theatre Society, led by Frank and William Fay, W. B. *Yeats and Lady Augusta *Gregory, as a centre for national drama. The Abbey Theatre Co. was formed, originally of amateur actors, and a repertory of new plays on Irish themes produced, e.g. *The Playboy of the Western World* (1907) by J. M. *Synge. Many Irish writers have been closely associated with the theatre: Lennox *Robinson, *A.E., Padraic Colum, George Moore and George Shiels. Standards declined in the 1930s because of government interference in the selection of plays and a decision by the theatre (1938) to produce plays in Gaelic–despite the lack of good playwrights or actors in this language.

Abbott Berenice (1898–). U.S. photographer. Recognizing the quality of *Atget's work she devoted herself to publicizing and preserving it. She returned to New York in 1929 to fulfil a commission from the Mus. of the City of New York, creating a valuable record of the city as it was in the 1930s.

Abbott Jacob (1803–79). U.S. clergyman and writer of children's books. Most famous were his didactic novels about the boy Rollo.

Abbott Lemuel Francis (*c.* 1760–1803). English portrait painter, known for his portraits of Lord Nelson and the poet Cowper.

Abbt Thomas (1738–66). German philosopher of the *Enlightenment and regarded as a forerunner of German classicism. He contributed to the *Literaturbriefe* (*Lessing).

abecedarius. A form of *acrostic in which the initial letters of the lines are the letters of the alphabet taken in order.

A'Beckett Gilbert Abbott (1811–56). English humorist and one of the original staff of *Punch*.

Abel Karl Friedrich (1723–87). German musician and last great virtuoso on the bass viol. Studied under J. S. Bach and composed chamber music and symphonies. In 1759 he settled in London, where, with J. C. Bach, he organized a series of concerts.

Abelard Peter (Pierre Abélard) (1079–1142). French philosopher, theologian and poet. As a teacher in Paris he attracted an immense following. When he was about 40, he fell in love with one of his pupils, *Héloïse. 5 of his letters to her have survived but his famous love-poems for her are lost. After the birth of their son they married. Nevertheless she retired to a convent and her enraged uncle, thinking A. had deserted her, had him castrated. A. tells the story in his famous letter, the *Historia Calamitatum.* The most celebrated of his religious lyrics is 'O qualia, qualia sunt illa sabbata', written for Héloïse's convent. His teaching was condemned by the Church in 1121 and again in 1140.

Abell Kjeld (1901–). Danish playwright. His comedy *Melodien der blev vaek* (1935; *The Melody that Got Lost*, 1936), an elegant satire on the bourgeoisie, was an immediate success. Other comedies include *Anna Sophie Hedvig* (1939) and *Silkeborg* (1946), about a Danish family during the German occupation.

Abercrombie Lascelles (1881–1938). English poet and critic and brother of Sir P. A. His poetry, mostly written between 1908 and 1914, gained limited recognition; after the war he concentrated on criticism, e.g. *Poetry: its Music and Meaning* (1932) and *An Essay towards a Theory of Art* (1922).

Abercrombie Sir (Leslie) Patrick (1879–1957). English architect and town planner, who held professorships at Liverpool (1915–35) and London (1935–46) univs. A. was famous for his *County of London Plan* (with J. H. Forshaw, 1943) and *Greater London Plan* (1944) produced for the London County Council. His proposals for improving working and housing conditions combined aesthetic with functional considerations. A. was also consulted on the replanning of other cities in England and abroad.

Abil(d)gaard Nicolai Abraham (1743–1809). Danish painter who studied in Italy (1772–9). His style was classical and he favoured heroic subjects. He painted little after 4 allegorical frescoes by him in the Royal Palace, Copenhagen, which he considered his best work, were burnt in 1794. Sketches of these together with many other works are preserved in the Royal Gallery, Copenhagen. B. Thorwaldsen was his pupil.

About Edmond (1828–85). French novelist and journalist. The capricious humour of his early stories, e.g. *Les Mariages de Paris* (1856) and *Le Roi des montagnes* (1856) was abandoned for realism, but resumed with *L'Homme à l'oreille cassée* (1862), *Le Nez d'un notaire* (1862) and others. He was liberal and anti-clerical, a witty and powerful controversialist. In 1871 he founded and ed. the periodical *Le XIXe Siècle.*

À Bout de Souffle (1960). Film directed by J.-L. *Godard.

Abraham Gerald (1904–). English musicologist. An authority on Russian music, e.g. *Studies in Russian Music* (1935), *Eight Soviet Composers* (1943), A. has also written on many other musical topics. He ed. the series 'Music of the Masters'.

Abramtsevo Colony. A group of Russian artists drawn together in the 1870s and 1880s by the railway tycoon S. Mamontov. They included V. Polenov, I. Levitan, the Vasnetsov brothers, I. Repin, V. A. *Serov, and M. Vrubel. A number were members of the *Wanderers group. The colony was nationalistic in outlook and Russian folk-art and the Russo-Byzantine tradition influenced their work. They were the 1st Russian artists to work as theatrical designers, most of them working in Mamontov's 'Private Opera'.

Abrantès Laure Permon, duchesse d' (1785–1835). French writer, the wife of Junot, one of Napoleon's generals, now remembered for her *Mémoires . . .* (1831–5; 1833–5) and *Histoire des Salons de Paris* (1837–8), which are exciting though unreliable. She also wrote novels.

Absalom, Absalom! (1936). Novel by William Faulkner.

Absalom and Achitophel (1681). Poem by *Dryden.

Abse Daniel ('Danny') (1923–). English poet. A.'s work is marked by its irony and it shows a consciousness of his situation as a Jew. His colls include *Tenants of the House* (1957).

Abstract art. Mondrian, *Composition London* (1940–2)

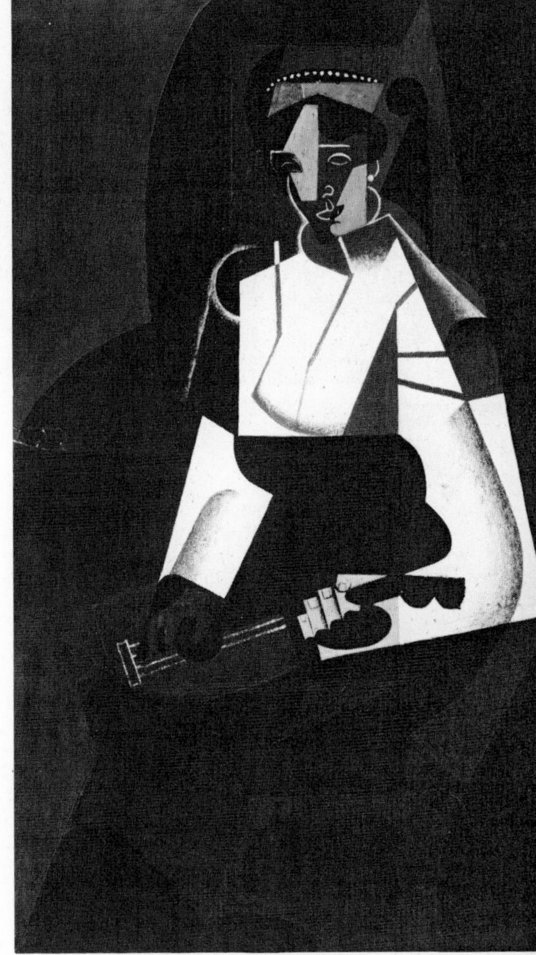

Abstract art. Juan Gris, *Woman with a Mandolin* (1916)

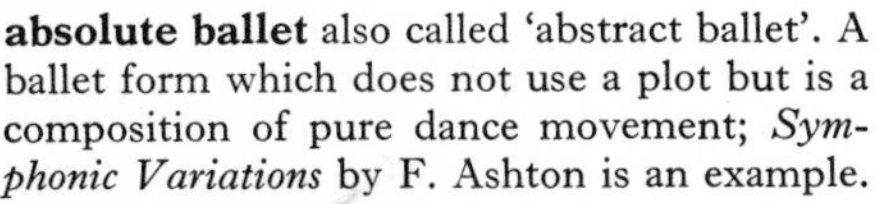

absolute ballet also called 'abstract ballet'. A ballet form which does not use a plot but is a composition of pure dance movement; *Symphonic Variations* by F. Ashton is an example.

absolute music. Music which does not attempt to represent natural phenomena, emotions, etc., or illustrate another work of art, e.g. poem, picture, etc. The opposite of *programme music.

'absolute pitch' sense of. In music this describes the ability to identify by name any note heard, or to sing any note asked for, without the aid of any reference note. Strictly speaking this sense of pitch can only be correctly described as absolute when its possessor can designate the vibrational frequency of the note (*pitch). In fact, in almost all cases, he unconsciously relates the note to a conventionally established system of pitch.

abstract art. Art which does not imitate or directly represent external reality: some writers restrict the term to non-figurative art, while others use it of art which is not representational though ultimately derived from reality. Various alternatives have been suggested (non-representational art, non-objective art, concrete art) but none has been generally accepted. 'Abstract' is frequently used as a relative term, paintings being more or less abstract in treatment. The visual inspiration of an abstract painting, say landscape or still-life, may be visible or decipherable: most cubist painting is of this sort. Simplified or geometric shapes may be used exclusively, as in Mondrian's art. In a 3rd type of abstraction, brush-strokes, the colour and textures of the material used suggest the development of the painting, as in Jackson Pollock's work.
The idea that forms and colour in themselves can move the spectator underlies all a. a. Much 20th-c. painting and sculpture has attempted to have, like music, no representational purpose. Sources and parallels for this art have been found in ceramic decorations, decorative patterns in manuscripts and the applied arts (especially Celtic art, e.g. The Book of Kells), Mohammedan art, primitive and tribal sculpture, and non-realistic elements in European painting (e.g. simplified architectural backgrounds in paintings by Fra Angelico).
20th-c. a. a. springs from Cézanne who treated some landscape motifs as geometric solids, and whose painting was much admired by the cubists. *Cubism, the 1st abstract style, had a decisive effect on other artists and groups.
The independent value of colour was not emphasized by cubism, but by other groups. Flat pattern design in pictures, used by Gauguin and the Pont-Aven painters, was taken up by the *nabis: the *fauves were particularly interested in colour. The 1st non-figurative painting was made by Kandinsky in 1910, but before this there are several painters in some of whose work the subject had become virtually indistinguishable, for example Hölzel and Gustave Moreau. The emotional impact of colour was also of the first importance for German expressionism. Cubism was followed and rivalled by futurism in Italy, vorticism in Britain, de stijl in the Netherlands, and various forms of abstraction in Russia, including the rayonism of Gontcharova and Larionov, constructivism, and the rigid geometric a. a. of Malevich (suprematism). Abstraction of various sorts became more common in the painting and sculpture of the 1920s, having for the most part a geometric basis: exceptionally Arp had made some chance compositions (e.g. with torn paper), and in surrealism there was some experiment with more informal types of abstraction. The main trend of a. a. in the 1930s was geometric, and the Abstraction-Création group was formed in 1932 to exhibit such art. This abstract salon was succeeded after the war by Salon de Réalités Nouvelles. In abstract painting since the war informal compositions and innovations in technique have been more frequent. Sculpture during the 20th c. has been frequently abstract, particularly in the work of several major figures like Brancusi, Arp and Calder, the inventor of mobiles.

Abstract art. Kandinsky, *Composition 6* (1913)

The French Academy under construction

Abstraction-Création. Auguste Herbin, *Articulate Flowers*

Abu Simbel. Entrance façade to the temple

Acanthus leaf capital

abstract dance. A form of ballet in which the movements of the dance are subordinated to the geometrical patterns established by the costumes. It arose from the work of O. *Schlemmer.

abstract expressionism: *expressionism

Abstraction-Création. School of non-figurative art founded in Paris in 1932 by A. Pevsner and N. Gabo. It has not attempted a full synthesis of the plastic arts but rather a merging of some of the techniques of painting and sculpture.

Abt Franz (1819–85). German composer and chorus master. His songs and male voice quartets were popular in Germany and some, e.g. *O Schwarzwald, o Heimat*, have now almost the status of folk-songs.

Abu Simbel. The site of 3 temples built by the Pharaoh, Rameses II (*c.* 1304–1237 B.C.), on the W. bank of the Nile and 164 miles S. of Aswan, Upper Egypt. The largest temple penetrates 180 ft into a sandstone cliff rising straight out of the desert. The entrance is flanked by 4 seated figures of Rameses, each 65 ft high, hewn out of the rock, and the rooms and columns are decorated with reliefs and inscriptions detailing the exploits of the Pharaoh. The rising level of the Nile above the great Aswan dam threatening to flood A. S. has led to a decision to remove the temples piecemeal to another site.

abutment. Architectural term for the part of a wall or pier which helps to support an arch, i.e. acts as a *buttress.

academic art. The term applies to art in a well-established, often realistic, tradition, showing expert command of draughtsmanship and other techniques. In the 19th c. the academies of painting became centres of opposition to new movements so that a. a. now generally has the pejorative overtones of 'conservative' and 'unimaginative'.

Academic Festival Overture (1881). Work by *Brahms using German student songs.

academies. Institutions which derive their name from Plato's Academy. In effect they originated in 15th-c. Italy, where humanist gatherings quickly attracted the official patronage–e.g. the famous *Accademia Platonica* founded by Cosimo I of Florence (*c.* 1542)–which became a frequent feature of subsequent bodies. Vasari's *Accademia di Disegno* (1562) aimed to establish the status of artists (a frequent motive of these foundations); but many were essentially teaching organizations. Examples are the famous academy of the *Carracci and, among present British institutions, the *Royal Academy of Music* (R.A.M.; 1822), the *Royal College of Music* (R.C.M.; 1873) and the *Royal Academy of Dramatic Art* (R.A.D.A.; founded in 1904 by Sir Herbert Beerbohm Tree). Literary academies have sometimes functioned as arbiters of language. In this respect the *Académie française*, founded by Richelieu in 1635, is pre-eminent. It has, however, been accused of undue conservatism, and has excluded many great French writers, including Molière, Balzac and Flaubert. In painting the same kind of criticism has been levelled at the British *Royal Academy* (R.A.; founded in 1768; many British painters were trained in its schools) and the French *Académie royale des beaux-arts* (founded by Louis XIV in 1648). The *British Academy* (1901) is devoted to scholarship in many fields.

Academy. Greek school of philosophy founded by *Plato; the name is derived from the grove of Academus where Plato taught. It continued to function until A.D. 529 (though not always expounding Platonic doctrines), when it was closed by Justinian.

acanthus. A plant whose bold fleshy leaves were first used as a decorative motif by the Greeks in metalwork and stone-carving and subsequently adopted in a conventional form in classical architecture, forming part of the capitals of the Corinthian and Composite orders. It is frequently found on late 17th- and 18th-c. furniture and silver.

a capella. A musical term from the Italian, 'as in church', meaning for unaccompanied voices.

accidentals. Musical term for sharps or flats or natural signs that are not in the *key signature but are put in front of the notes they refer to.

Accolti Bernardo: Unico *Aretino

Piano-accordion

Acropolis, Athens. See also colour plate 6

accordion. Musical instrument in which metal reeds are vibrated by bellows slung across the player's body. The reeds, set in boxes at the ends of the bellows, are selected by studs or keys operated by the player's fingers, as his hands work the bellows. On the piano-a., now the commonest type, both melody and harmony are possible.

Achebe Chinua (1931–). Nigerian novelist, whose *Things Fall Apart* (1958) indicates his concern with the gradual disintegration in the 20th c. of tribal organization in Eastern Nigeria. The conflict between tribal society and Western Christianity and law is personalized; contestants assuming heroic stature. The book shows A.'s appreciation of the connection between society and legend.

Ackermann Rudolf (1764–1834). German art publ. and bookseller who opened a shop in the Strand, London, in 1795. He introduced art lithography to England, 1817. A. publ. various illustrated magazines, e.g. *Repository of Arts, Literature, Fashions*, etc., topographical books, e.g. *History of the University of Oxford* (2 vols, 1814), *The Microcosm of London* (3 vols, 1808–11), and many travel books, employing artists such as T. Rowlandson, and A. Pugin. The illustrated annual *Forget-me-not* (begun 1825) was another of A.'s typographic and artistic successes.

acmeism. Russian literary movement founded in 1912 by N. S. Gumilyov as the 'Poets' Guild'. A., which attacked symbolism for mystical vagueness of imagery and for its use of symbolic imagery for metaphysical concepts, practised clear precise verse endeavouring to name themes and concepts accurately rather than evoke them allusively.

acoustic bass. In musical terms the *resultant note of a perfect 5th is the 8ve below its lower note. On an organ, the a. b. stop (sometimes called the 'quint') combines notes of 16 ft *register with the 5ths above them, thus giving the effect of a note of 32 ft register; e.g. 16 ft C sounding with the G above, gives 32 ft C.

acoustic jars. Pots found in the masonry of medieval churches (particularly in the chancel area) and placed there, it is supposed, to improve the resonance of the building.

acropolis (Greek, 'higher city' and hence 'citadel'). Name for the citadel of any ancient Greek town, but that at Athens is known as *the* Acropolis. It was the site of fortifications, palaces and temples from the early 6th c. B.C.; these were destroyed in the Persian sack of Athens in 480 B.C. The ruins of the temple of Athena and a number of *archaic statues of this 'pre-Persian' period have been discovered. Under Pericles, new buildings were erected under the supervision of the sculptor *Phidias, assisted by the architects Ictinus, Callicrates and Mnesicles. These buildings, which include the *Parthenon, the *Erechtheum, the *Propylaea and the temple of Athena Nike, make the A. one of the greatest sites of Greek architecture.

Across the River and into the Trees (1950). Novel by Hemingway.

acrostic. Verse in which letters in successive lines spell a word or form a pattern. Either the initial letters of each line are used, or, in a mesostich and telestich respectively, the middle and last letters, and in a 'cross a.' the initial letter of line one, the 2nd letter of line two and so on.

action. The mechanism of a musical, especially keyboard, instrument which transmits the player's operations on the keyboard to the strings or pipes of the instrument; e.g. tracker action on the *organ.

action painting. A method of painting widespread in the 1950s in which the paint is dropped or thrown on the canvas–hence the French term *tachisme* (*tache*, 'stain or spot'); some critics use both terms as interchangeable with abstract *expressionism. The term was first used about the work of Jackson Pollock but has also been applied to such European artists as Alan Davie, and particularly aptly to Georges Mathieu (who has painted a picture as a public performance in a Paris theatre). Characteristic a. p. effects are sometimes achieved with a brush.

Activists, The. Group of U.S. writers, mostly living in the San Francisco Bay district, which came into being in 1936. Following the lead of L. Hart they are concerned to ensure the effectiveness of words in poetry; to make language 'active' enough to convey emotion.

Ackermann. The Royal Institution; from *The Microcosm of London*

Action painting. Jackson Pollock working

H. G. Adam. *Tapisserie*

Lord Acton

L. S. Adam. *Neptune Calming the Waves*

Acton John Emerich Edward Dalberg, 1st Baron Acton (1834–1902). English historian. In 1895 he became regius professor at Cambridge and 1st ed. of *The Cambridge Modern History*. He planned a great 'History of Liberty' but failed to write this or any other book. Colls of his articles and lectures include *The History of Freedom . . .* (1907) and *Lectures on Modern History* (1906). He wrote the almost proverbial 'Power tends to corrupt and absolute power corrupts absolutely', in a letter (1887) to the historian M. Creighton.

Acts of the Apostles (*c.* A.D. 70). One of the books of the *Bible (New Testament), traditionally ascribed to St Luke. It deals with the expansion of Christianity, especially the apostolic activities of St Peter and St Paul.

adagio (Italian, 'at ease'). In music: (1) an indication of fairly slow tempo; (2) a composition or movement in that tempo.

Adam Adolphe-Charles (1803–56). French opera and ballet composer. He had early success and in 1847 opened a theatre but closed in the Revolution of 1848. A. is best remembered for his music to the ballet **Giselle* (1841) but his operas *Le postillon de Longjumeau* (1836) and *La Poupée de Nuremberg* (1852) are still performed.

Adam Henri-Georges (1904–). French designer, painter, from 1934 graphic artist and from 1940 sculptor, producing his 1st abstract work in the 1940s; he is head of the sculpture atelier at the École des Beaux-Arts. Important sculptures include *Le Gisant* (1944), *Seated Woman* (1948), *Horned Beast* (1947, bronze) and *Seated Stele* (1954, engraved sculpture). He has invented a new tapestry technique and has designed tapestries for the Unesco building, Paris.

Adam James (1730–94). Scottish architect, younger brother of Robert A. He succeeded him as architect to George III and was associated with him in many projects, particularly as a furniture designer.

Adam John. 18th-c. Scottish architect, elder brother of Robert A.

Adam Juliette (1836–1936). French writer. In the 1870s her *salon* became a centre for Republican leaders and in 1879 she founded and ed. the literary and political review *Nouvelle Revue*, contributing *Lettres sur la politique extérieure*. She wrote autobiographical books and the novel *Païenne* (1883).

Adam Lambert-Sigisbert (1700–59). French baroque sculptor, son of the sculptor Jacob-Sigisbert A. (1670–1747). In Rome (1723–33), he was strongly influenced by Bernini. His fountain *Triomphe de Neptune et d'Amphitrite* (1740) is at Versailles.

Adam Paul (1862–1920). French novelist. *Robes rouges* (1891) dealt with the legal, *La Force du mal* (1896) with the Bohemian world, and a group of 16 novels *Le Temps et la vie* (1899–1903) with French life, 1800–30. Despite a turgid style he was popular during his lifetime.

Adam Robert (1728–92). Scottish architect, the best known of 4 brothers, all architects and designers. In 1754–7 he studied the ruins of Roman architecture and in 1757 made a detailed examination of the palace of Diocletian at Spalato (Split, Yugoslavia), subsequently publ. (1764) with A.'s drawings. In 1762 he was appointed architect to George III, resigned in 1768 and became an M.P. In this year, in association with his brothers, he planned and built the Adelphi (Greek, *αδελφοι* 'brothers') off the Strand, London, as a piece of speculative building. During the last 20 years of his life he was unquestioned head of his profession. He was buried in Westminster Abbey.

The Adelphi was A.'s most ambitious project. The river front consisted of a long terrace raised on an immense sub-structure of vaults and arches. Behind it, between the Thames and the Strand, was a series of streets with classical façades, based on the Palace of Diocletian. The Adelphi was barbarously demolished, except for a few houses, in 1936. A. conceived his buildings as unities, making himself responsible for the interior décor, fireplaces, furniture, even the door-handles and carpets, and in fact his influence was far more powerful in domestic design, where he virtually

Robert Adam. Syon House interior. Also *Adelphi, *classicism

William Adams. Early 19th-c. stoneware vase

initiated a revolution, than in architecture proper. Using mostly late Roman motifs he achieved an entirely personal style–light, elegant and restrained–a typically English version of rococo. His work can be described with equal truth as the end of the English baroque or as the beginning of the classical revival. His rooms were beautifully proportioned, often with open columns and entablatures and niches for antique sculpture or plaster casts. He was especially fond of stucco and used also soft pastel 'Wedgwood' colours. Notable examples of his interiors are to be found at Kenwood House, London (especially the library); Syon House, Middlesex; Osterley Park, Middlesex and Kedleston Hall, Derbyshire.

Adam William, Sr. (1689–1748). Scottish architect and father of Robert A. and his brothers, of whom William, Jr., was the youngest.

Adam de la Halle also Le Bossu (*c.* 1240–*c.* 1285). French poet and musician. After studying at Paris, he became a **ménestrel* under Robert II, Count of Artois. In this post he went to Naples, where he joined the court of Charles of Anjou, King of Sicily. The violently satirical *Jeu de la feuillée* was an early work. At Naples A. composed his major work, *Jeu de Robin et Marion*, a remarkable formal innovation and essentially a precursor of the *opéra-comique*. The story is presented in dialogues between 10 'characters', interrupted by airs and dialogue duets often drawn from folk-melodies. A.'s **rondeaux* are the earliest known examples of this form; he also wrote numerous *chansons* and *jeux partis*.

Adamic Louis (1899–1951). U.S. writer of Yugoslav origin who, besides novels, wrote books about the U.S., stressing the contribution of non-Anglo-Saxons to its society, e.g. *A Nation of Nations* (1945).

Adamnan St (*c.* 625–704). Irish monk and abbot of Iona from 679. A Latin life of St Colomba, the fullest extant early medieval biography, and *Adamnan's Vision*, a poem in Old Irish, are attributed to him.

Adam of Fulda (*c.* 1445–1505). German composer and musical theorist. Wrote church music in the style of Busnois and the tract *De musica*, an important source on 15th-c. composers.

Adamov Arthur (1908–). Russian-born French playwright. A. has moved from dramas exposing the absurdity of existence (and related to those of *Ionesco) to social commitment; this development can be traced through *Ping Pong* (1955; 1962) and *Paolo Paoli* (1957; 1959) to *Le Printemps 71* (1963).

Adams. Family of English potters, a N. Staffordshire family with a long association with the industry. The 1st recorded as a potter was WILLIAM (1550–1617) of Burslem, where 4 generations of his descendants subsequently worked; it is from him that the family members of the firm of William Adams and Sons claim descent. WILLIAM (1745–1805) set up a manufacture of jasperware at Greengates which is said to equal the quality of *Wedgwood's production. At the end of the 18th c. a member of another branch of the family was associated with the introduction of underglaze blue decoration into Staffordshire.

Adams Abigail (née Smith) (1744–1818). Wife of the U.S. President John A.; she is remembered for her witty and learned letters.

Adams Ansel (1902–). U.S. photographer noted for landscapes. In 1931 he co-founded Group 64 with E. *Weston, whose credo was maximum detail and clarity in all parts of the photographic image. In 1940 he directed 'Pageant of Photography' at the San Francisco World's Fair and helped found the Department of Photography as an Art at the M.M.A. In 1941 he was appointed Photo Muralist to the Department of the Interior. In 1948 he began publishing an important series of basic photography books.

Adams Henry (Brooks) (1838–1918). U.S. historian, philosopher of history and novelist. His best-known work is *The Education of Henry Adams: a Study of Twentieth-Century Multiplicity* (privately printed, 1907; publ. posth.

Adam de la Halle. Ms. in the Bibliothèque, Arras

Ansel Adams. *Roots* (1948)

Joseph Addison: painting by Kneller

R. Adams. *Maquette for architectural screen* (1956)

Receiving Houses of the Spectator and Tatler.

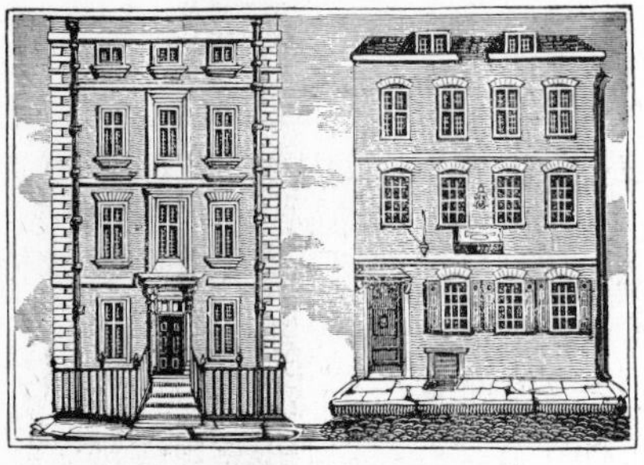

Trifles light as air, when connected with men of genius, and associated with hallowed literature, become interesting to every well-attuned mind. Hence many persons will feel gratified in having presented to them fac-similes of the premises so celebrated in the classic days of the Spectator and Tatler, when statesmen were either men of letters, or their patrons, and when nobility was dignified by the familiar association of genius. The house in Fulwood's Rents, Holborn, where letters were received for the Spectator,. at that time bore the name of Squire's Coffee House; and the Trumpet, in Shire-Lane, Temple Bar, whence the Tatlers were dated, still exists as the Duke-of-York public-house.

Joseph Addison. Receiving houses of *The Spectator* and *The Tatler*

Adam-Salomon. Portrait of Charles Garnier

1918); it expounds his dynamic theory of history and the 'acceleration' of historical forces which have created in the modern world a 'multiverse', to be contrasted with the unitary universe of the middle ages. The book exposes the inadequacy of his generation's education to cope with the diversity of 20th-c. life. *Mont-Saint-Michel and Chartres* (privately printed 1904; publ. 1913) is a study of the middle ages and analyses the forces which produced their cultural unity. A. wrote 2 novels, *Democracy* (1880), on U.S. politics, and *Esther* (1884), on New York society.

Adams Léonie (1899–). U.S. poet. Her 1st coll. *Those Not Elect* (1925) showed a sensitivity of expression characteristic of all her work; there are also echoes of the Jacobean, and similarities to the metaphysical poets. *High Falcon* (1929) contains abstract and intense poems, among them *The Mount*. The coll. *This Measure* (1933) emphasized A.'s affinities with the English 17th-c. lyrical and metaphysical poets. *Poems* appeared in 1954.

Adams Robert (1917–). English non-figurative sculptor working in various materials; he uses geometrical forms, producing works which are formally satisfying yet emotionally unagressive.

Adam-Salomon Antony-Samuel (1818–81). French portrait photographer and sculptor. His photographs with their use of heavy chiaroscuro effects were praised for their approximation to the 17th-c. Dutch paintings.

Adamson Robert (1821–48). Scots chemist and photographer. He worked (1830–48) with D. O. *Hill using a paper negative process called the *calotype. He was one of the first people to recognize the use of photography for journalistic and propaganda purposes.

Adam's Rib (1949). Film directed by G. *Cukor.

Adding Machine, The (1923). Play by Elmer *Rice.

Addinsell Richard (1904–). English composer of much film and theatre music. Whether his popular 'Warsaw' concerto for the film *Dangerous Moonlight* was intended as a parody of Rachmaninov's style or as an imitation, has been debated.

Addison John (1766?–1844). English double-bass player and composer of songs, operas and oratorios. His wife was a famous opera singer.

Addison John (1920–). British composer. Works include: sextet for woodwind (1949), film music, *3 Terpsichorean Studies* for orchestra (1948) and music for the review *Cranks* (1956).

Addison Joseph (1672–1719). English essayist, poet and playwright and with Richard Steele ed. of *The Spectator*. At Oxford he gained a reputation as a scholar and from 1699 to 1702, when his patron, Lord Halifax, was dismissed from office, he travelled on a government pension. In 1705 A. publ. *The Campaign*, a poem commissioned by the Whig ministry to celebrate Marlborough's victorious Blenheim campaign. The poem was such good propaganda for the Whigs that A. was made an under-secretary of state (1706). In 1709–10 he became secretary to the lord-lieutenant of Ireland, a post which brought him into contact with Jonathan Swift, and from this year sat in parliament as member for Malmesbury. A. was a contributor to *Steele's *Tatler* (1709) and with him founded *The Spectator* (1711–12). In 1715 A. became chief secretary to the lord-lieutenant of Ireland. In 1716 he received further offices, also marrying in this year, and in 1717 he was made secretary of state but resigned the following year. In his last years he was involved in both a literary dispute with Pope, who later satirized him in *The Dunciad*, and in a public dispute (1719) with Steele over a political issue.

A.'s writings include the celebrated hymn beginning, 'The spacious firmament on high', the verse *Letter from Italy* (1703), the opera libretto *Rosamond* (1706), a failure, and the 5 numbers of *The Whig Examiner*. His tragedy *Cato* (1713) was a great success at home and widely praised on the Continent for its classical form and obedience to the dramatic unities; Voltaire thought it the best English tragedy.

A.'s fame rests on his essays in *The Tatler* and *The Spectator*; to the latter he contributed more than half its 555 numbers and, in effect,

Adelphi Terrace

Adoration of the Lamb. Panel from the Ghent altarpiece

directed it. Each number was an essay on some social, moral, literary or scientific topic; politics were excluded. Other contributors were Steele, Alexander Pope, T. Tickell, E. Budgell, Ambrose Philips and L. Eusden. The paper was supposedly run by the fictional 'Spectator Club', of whose members Sir Roger de Coverley, the country squire, is the most famous. A.'s intention was didactic and typical of 18th-c. enlightenment. He aimed to 'banish vice and ignorance out of the territories of Great Britain', to 'enliven morality with wit, and to temper wit with morality' and to 'cultivate a taste of polite writing'. Inevitably he is sometimes condescending and priggish but despite this *The Spectator*, because it popularized serious subjects in an entertaining if sometimes superficial way, because of its strict, if restrictive, sense of moral fitness, because of its social satire and because of A.'s conversational easy-flowing style, made a huge impact on English and European life (there were French, Italian, Dutch and German trs and foreign imitations). In literature A. innovated with his extensive criticism of and praise for Milton's *Paradise Lost* and, more startling to his contemporaries, a serious critical study of *The Ballad of *Chevy Chase*. *The Spectator* was discontinued in Dec. 1712 and a continuation ended in 1714; from 1715 to 1716 A. ed. *The Freeholder*, a political magazine.

Ade George (1866–1944). U.S. writer best known for his *Fables in Slang*, written in conversational prose spiced with colloquialisms, sprinkled with capitals and concluded with a moral, sometimes serious; 3 colls appeared during 1900–1. A. also wrote plays and musicals, e.g. *Leave It to Jane* with J. Kern.

Adelphi, The. A site in London between the Strand and the Thames developed as a piece of speculative building by the architect R. *Adam and his brothers.

Adelung Johann Christoph (1732–1806). German grammarian and philologist, who helped to standardize the orthography and idiom of German. His major works are his dictionary, *Grammatisch-kritisches Wörterbuch* . . . (1774–86), and *Mithridates* . . . (1806–17; completed by J. S. Vater), a survey of world languages.

Adenet le Roi of Brabant. A 13th-c. poet called king of **ménestrels*. He rewrote several **chansons de geste*, using the *alexandrine in place of the earlier 10-syllable line, and wrote the romance *Cléomadès* in which he describes the life of a *ménestrel*.

Adler Jankel (1895–1949). Polish painter. His figure studies were influenced by Picasso and Léger. He travelled widely in Europe teaching for a time at the Düsseldorf Academy with Paul Klee and working with S. W. *Hayter at Atelier 17. In 1941 he settled in Great Britain. From near realism his work became increasingly abstract. It had considerable effect on several English painters, e.g. R. Colquhoun.

Adler Larry (1914–). U.S. harmonica virtuoso who has gained concert recognition for his instrument. Milhaud is one of the composers who have written for him.

ad libitum, ad lib (Latin, 'at will'). Indication on music giving the performer freedom: (1) to vary the tempo; (2) to omit a vocal or instrumental part so marked; (3) to provide his own cadenza at the place marked.

Admirable Crichton, The (1902). Play by J. M. Barrie.

Admiral's Men. Company of players active from about 1580 to 1625. The lead actor from the late 1580s to the early 1600s was Edward Alleyn and the manager Philip Henslowe; during this period they played mainly at the Fortune Theatre.

Adolphe (1816). Novel by Benjamin *Constant.

Adonais, An Elegy on the Death of John Keats (1821). Poem by *Shelley.

Adoration of the Lamb The. Alternative English name for the *Ghent Altarpiece* by the van *Eyck brothers.

Advancement of Learning, The (1605). Treatise by Francis Bacon.

Ady Endre (1877–1919). Hungarian poet. In 1904 he met and followed Adél Brüll, the 'Léda' of his poems to Paris where

J. Adler. *Woman with Hat* (1940)

Endre Ady

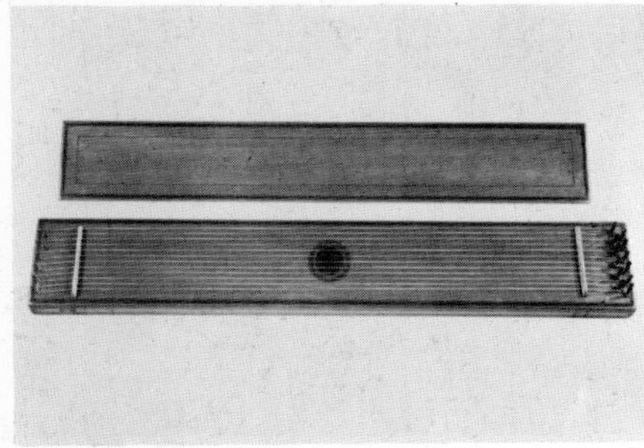

Aeolian harp

Aertsen. *Christ in the House of Martha and Mary*

Aelfric. From a Latin ms. *Book of Genesis*

A.E. Contemporary photograph of the first performance of *Deirdre*

contemporary French poetry stimulated his determination to break away from traditional Hungarian styles. His new poems *Új versek* (1906) caused fierce literary controversy in Hungary. A.'s followers rallied round *Nyugat*, a literary magazine influential on subsequent Hungarian literature. A.'s poetry lays bare the apocalyptic world of a great poet whose social responsibility and restless revolutionary spirit manifested itself in a powerful language rich in unexpected associative references.

A.E. (AE, Æ). Pseud. of George William Russell (1867–1935). Irish poet, journalist and painter, a leading figure in the *Irish Literary Renaissance. With W. B. Yeats, J. Eglinton and W. Larminie he contributed to *Literary Ideals in Ireland* (1899), an important discussion of the ideals of the revival and the function of a national literature. His play *Deirdre*, produced (1902) by F. and W. Fay with costumes and scenery designed by himself, was one of the earliest to be written for the Irish dramatic movement and showed that an Irish national school of dramatic writing had serious artistic potentialities. His poetry is mystical and incorporates themes from Irish mythology and ancestral tradition: *Homeward: Songs by the Way* (1894), *Collected Poems* (1913). He also wrote the dream story *On an Irish Hill* (in *The Mask of Apollo*, 1904) and his spiritual autobiography *The Candle of Vision* (1919).

Aelfric (*c.* 955–*c.* 1020). From 1005 abbot of Eynsham. A. was a major figure in Anglo-Saxon literature and the greatest Latin prose stylist of his time. His chief works were homilies and lives of the saints.

Aelst Willem van (1625/26–83?). Dutch still-life painter from Delft. He was a good draughtsman and vivid colourist. A.'s still-lifes are distinguishable from those of other Dutch painters, being frequently littered with the bric-à-brac of Renaissance antiquarianism.

Aeneid. Epic poem by *Virgil.

aeolian harp. Musical instrument, called after Aeolus, god of the winds, consisting of strings on a square frame and sounding-box and set in vibration by the wind. Invented in the mid 17th c., it was popular throughout the 18th c. and early 19th c., especially with English romantic poets, e.g. Thomson and Coleridge.

Aertsen (Aertszen, Aartsen, Aertsz) Pieter (Pier Lange) (1507/8–75). Dutch painter, working in Antwerp and Amsterdam, whose detailed and colourful genre and still-life paintings were highly popular and also stylistically influential on the 17th-c. Netherlands genre school. Many of his religious paintings have been destroyed.

Aeschbacher Hans (1906–). Swiss sculptor, self-taught. He began in 1936 with figurative work but has since developed an abstract style of great austerity.

Aeschylus (525–456 B.C.). A., who came of noble family in the ancient Athenian city of Eleusis, is the earliest of the Greek tragedians whose work has survived. But out of more than 80 plays only 7 are extant and these seem all to belong to the last 20 years of his life. In 490 he fought in the great battle against the Persians at Marathon and 10 years later in the battle at Salamis, which he describes in his play *The Persians*. His epitaph, possibly written by himself, conspicuously omits any reference to his work as a tragedian, but records his service against the Persians. After the war he visited the court of Hiero, the tyrant of Syracuse, in Sicily. There he presented *The Persians* and a new play, *The Etnaeans*, commissioned by Hiero to celebrate the founding of his new city of Etna. On a 2nd visit A. died at Gela, Sicily. It would be natural to assume that a member of a noble family at Eleusis would have been initiated into the mysteries of Demeter celebrated there and Aristophanes in *The Frogs* makes A. refer to Demeter as the nurse of his genius, but there is a 4th-c. story that A. was prosecuted for revealing the secrets of the mysteries and only escaped by claiming ignorance. A.'s profound piety perhaps owes more to Pythagorean sources, and his almost monotheistic theology to philosophical influence.

The Persians (472) is unique in dealing with a historical subject. A. invests the plot with the quality of myth by transferring the scene to the Persian capital and viewing the events as a Persian defeat rather than as a Greek victory. He presents Xerxes, the king, as a typical victim of Nemesis, and builds a climax

Aeschbacher. *Figure XI* (1960)

Aeschylus. Greek Art Theatre performance of *The Persians*

culminating in the return of the king, disgraced, in rags. *The Seven against Thebes* (467) is the last and single surviving tragedy of a trilogy dealing with the *Oedipus story: it shows the outcome of the last battle between Oedipus' 2 sons Eteocles and Polyneices. *The Suppliant Women* (461? or 463?) is the first of a trilogy on the Danaids. In spite of the late date now assigned to it on papyrological evidence, this play presents the most primitive form of tragedy in that the chorus plays the principal part in the action. The **Oresteia* (458), comprising the *Agamemnon, Choephori* and *Eumenides* (*Furies*), is the only complete trilogy extant. *Prometheus Bound* belongs to the last years of A.'s life. It presents the punishment of Prometheus, who according to Greek legend stole fire from the gods to give to man; on Zeus' command he is chained to a rock in the Caucasus. Zeus, whom A. elsewhere describes as the personification of divine justice, appears as an oppressor. As this is the only surviving play of the trilogy, we have no means of telling how A. resolved the apparent paradox: either Zeus must repent or Prometheus must recant. A.'s theology reflects the philosophical criticism of the Olympians which had been growing in the 6th c. But he incorporated the philosophers' approach to monotheism in a refined image of Olympian Zeus. Like Pindar he prefers to purify the traditional accounts of the gods rather than jettison the whole structure of religion. In the theatre he eagerly employed all the technical improvements of his time, e.g. the various mechanical devices for producing special effects. His language is grandiloquent and includes many original compound words. His theatrical technique appears chiefly in his ability to handle long tracts of legendary time and to spin out the thread of his argument even more richly than the staple of his discourse. Compared with Sophocles he appears diffuse and slow-moving, but his command of the other resources of his theatre, particularly choreography, was legendary.

Aesop. Greek fabulist. Nothing is known about him except a brief story in Herodotus and, although nearly 400 fables have survived under his name, we can identify none as definitely by him. Herodotus' account merely confirms what was generally accepted as fact in the 5th c. B.C., that A. was a slave from Asia Minor and died at Delphi some time in the 6th c. A. did not even invent the *fable, but after his time any anecdote tended to be attributed to him, particularly if it concerned animals. The characteristics of the Aesopic fable are brevity, the moral and the use of animals as interlocutors. Although none of these features originated with A., they represent what antiquity regarded as his peculiar properties.

aesthetic movement. English literary and artistic movement of the 1880s in protest against the idea that art must serve some ulterior purpose and also against the 'philistine' taste of the period. Walter *Pater was its most important member but Oscar *Wilde its most obviously aggressive. The a. m. was ridiculed by *Punch* and in Gilbert and Sullivan's operetta *Patience*.

aesthetics. The study of the concepts of 'beauty' and 'art'. A. attempts to give an account of the human reaction to beauty and art, to define the words, to explain how men perceive the 'beautiful' or the 'artistic', to decide whether the concepts have any other than a subjective meaning and to explain what happens when a man stands before a 'beautiful' sight or a work of 'art'–what kind of experiences he has and in what way he is able to 'experience' anything. Although the writings of *Plato and *Aristotle contain observations on the subject-matter of a., the word was first used by the 18th-c. German philosopher A. G. Baumgarten. The following writers have been the most important theoreticians in a.: *Plotinus, G. W. *Leibniz, J. J. *Winckelmann, G. E. *Lessing, I. *Kant, J. *Schiller, G. *Hegel, A. *Schopenhauer, J. *Ruskin, H. *Taine, B. *Croce, W. *Worringer. See also: 'Longinus', J. G. Herder, A. W. Schlegel, Novalis, F. T. Vischer, W. Pater, R. G. Collingwood.

Afinogenov Alexander (1904–41). Soviet playwright. *Fear* (1934; 1935), about an old scientist who becomes an anti-Soviet saboteur and then repents, had a wide success at home and abroad. So, also, did the Chekhovian *Distant Point* (1936; 1941). It describes a day in the life of a remote railway station, when an important official has been delayed there.

Aesop. Ed. of the *Fables*, Munich (1490)

Aestheticism. Lampoon of Wilde

African art. 20th-c. wooden dance mask; Bakota, Congo

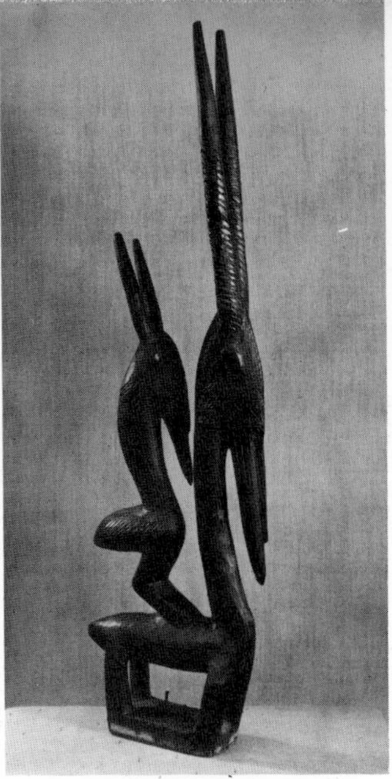

African art. 20th-c. wooden dance head-dress; Bambara tribe, W. Sudan

Agateware stag. Staffordshire

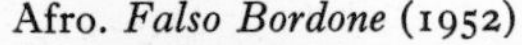

Afro. *Falso Bordone* (1952)

African art. The term refers only to Negro African art and particularly to sculpture and carving (mostly in wood) from the vast area surrounding the Niger and Congo basins. Ancient Egyptian art and bushman painting from southern Africa are thus excluded. Distinction must be made between the courtly art (especially from *Ife and *Benin) which tended to be naturalistic and commemorative, and made in durable materials (stone, terracotta, bronze, hardwood); and the conceptual, often abstract art consisting mainly of wood-carvings (masks, ancestor figures) used during religious ceremonies. It was work of the 2nd kind which made its impact on Western artists at the beginning of the 20th c.

All the tribal artists were inspired by similar beliefs. In African 'animist' religions 'being' is regarded as vital energy and not solely as the living state. Every existing thing has a vital force or energy and by understanding and correctly approaching these forces man can use them, but in order to ensure the continuance and increase of this vital energy in the tribe and in himself he must perform religious rituals at regular intervals and on set occasions. Masks and statues are used in communication with the spirit world, in the cult of the ancestors and as protective charms in the direct exploitation of the vital energy in the world.

The artist works within a formal convention to embody in his carving some concept related to the subject and to give his carving a dynamic power, so that it can be used to enlist and generate energy. He therefore does not aim to reproduce his subject realistically nor is his 1st intention to produce 'beautiful' forms. The head of the statue is often disproportionately large due to the belief that it is the seat of the life force and is therefore more important than the body. Statuettes are almost always made from a single block from a tree, thus leading to elongation of the body with the arms held close to the sides, and foreshortening of the features.

African Queen, The (1951). Film directed by J. *Huston.

Afro (Basaldella, Afro) (1912–). Italian painter who after an early post-impressionist period was influenced by the cubism of Braque and Picasso and since about 1945 has developed a personal style, combining vigorous colouring and sensuous handling of paint with abstract forms.

Agamemnon. 1st part of Aeschylus' dramatic trilogy, the **Oresteia*.

agate. A semi-precious stone, a form of quartz of variegated colour: white, brown and red or white and black. AGATEWARE in pottery is a type of *marbled ware, made in imitation of a.

Agathon (late 5th c. B.C.). Athenian tragic poet. His victory at the Lenaea festival (416) suggested to Plato the setting for his *Symposium* in which A. speaks in the manner of the sophist Gorgias. His tragedy *Antheus* is mentioned by Aristotle for its innovations which included the use of an original, not traditional, plot.

Âge d'Or, L' (1930). Film directed by L. *Buñuel.

Agee James (1909–55). U.S. novelist, film critic and script writer. Both his novels *The Morning Watch* (1954) and *A Death in the Family* (posth. 1957), dramatized in 1960 as *All the Way Home*, were set in his home state of Tennessee. His coll. film criticisms were publ. posth. as *Agee on Film* (1958).

Ageladas (*fl.* 520–460 B.C.). Greek sculptor said to have been the teacher of Myron, Phidias and Polycleitus. No known work of his survives.

Age of Reason, The (1946). Novel by *Sartre.

aglet (from French *aiguillette*, 'little needle or point'). Originally the pointed metal tags of a fastening lace; hence a metal or jewelled spiky tag worn ornamentally, especially in the 16th and early 17th c.

Agnolo Andrea d': *Andrea del Sarto

Agnus Dei: *mass

Agostino di Duccio (1418–81). Florentine sculptor mainly of reliefs, possibly a pupil of

Aigrette, 18th c.

Aglet. S. German (*c.* 1600)

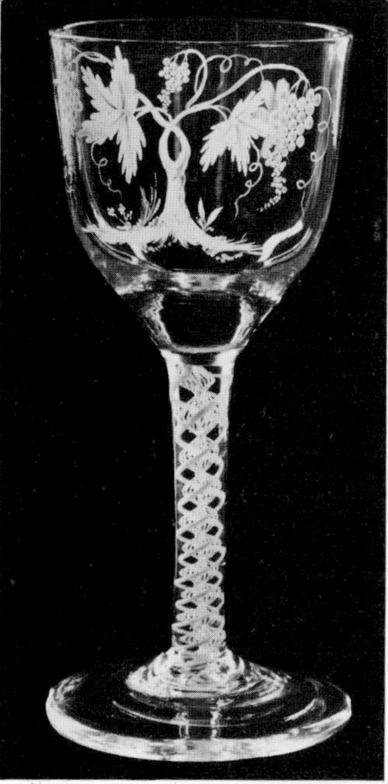
Air-twist stemmed glass, 17th c.

J. della Quercia. His earliest independent work was probably the altar (completed by 1442) in Modena cathedral. His major work is at the Tempio Malatestiano, Rimini (architect L. B. *Alberti, painter Piero della Francesca). A.'s style is essentially linear, his relief work is flat with no attempt at illusionism.

Agoult Marie de Flavigny, comtesse d' (1805–76). French writer of novels (under the pseud. 'Daniel Stern') and mistress of the composer *Liszt.

Agricola Alexander (d. 1506). Netherlands composer, of the school of J. Ockeghem, who worked in many court chapels in Europe. Died at Valladolid, Spain.

Agricola Martin (1486–1556). German composer and musical theorist. Settled about 1520 in Magdeburg. As well as many Latin works and trs he wrote in German 3 books on German music and also *Von den proportionibus* still informative because of its many examples. This and A.'s other writings on notation are important in the history of the subject.

Agricola Rodolphus. Latin name of Roelof Huysman (*c.* 1443–85), Dutch humanist whose influence was an important factor in the Renaissance in Germany. He lectured on classical literature at Heidelberg and Worms and was also highly regarded by Erasmus and the Italian humanists.

Aida (1871). Opera by *Verdi commissioned for the inauguration of the opera-house at Cairo.

aigrette. A feather-shaped ornament worn by women, generally on the head. Jewelled or enamelled, it was often completed with real feathers. Probably named after the egret, a bird which develops magnificent plumes.

Aiguier Louis-Auguste-Laurent (1819–65). French romantic landscape painter. He worked at Marseilles.

Aiken Conrad Potter (1889–). U.S. poet, short-story writer and critic. His 1st important vol. of poetry was *The Jig of Forslin* (1916); the next, *Nocturne of Remembered Spring* (1917), was so strongly influenced by T. S. Eliot that A. himself later criticized it for this in an anon. article; the most important early influence however, is Poe. A.'s early poem *Senlin: A Biography* in *The Charnel Rose* (1918) is one of his best known and one of his best. A.'s interest in psychology appears in the poems *Punch: The Immortal Liar* (1921) and in psychoanalysis, in the short stories, *Bring! Bring!* (1925) and the novels, *Blue Voyage* (1927), a stream of consciousness novel, and *King Coffin* (1935), the story of a criminal. Other works include: the poetry, *Brownstone Eclogues and other Poems* (1942) and *The Kid* (1947), and his autobiography, *Ushant* (1952) 'the autobiography of the creative spirit'.

Ainsworth William Harrison (1805–82). English author of once very popular romantic historical novels, e.g. *Jack Sheppard* (1839) and *Old Saint Paul's* (1871).

Air-Conditioned Nightmare, The (1945). Book by Henry *Miller.

air-twist and colour-twist. English glasses of the early 18th c. often have stems decorated with spirals done in white or coloured glass or sometimes with elongated air-bubbles. These are known as 'c.-t.' or 'a.-t.'. Opaque white twists are known as 'enamel-twists' and do not appear until the late 1740s. Large numbers of these 'twist' stem glasses were made, many combining coloured with plain twists, when they are known as 'mixed-twists'.

aisle. Term applied to a peripheral space in a church (or Roman basilica). The 2 main a.s run N. and S. of and parallel with the nave; the chancel and transepts, however, may also be aisled.

Ajanta cave paintings (Hyderabad state, India). A series of wall paintings, dating from the 1st to the 7th c. A.D., of which only parts now survive. They depicted scenes in the life of the Buddha and the Jataka stories of his former lives, scenes from contemporary life and animals and plants. The handling is sure and subtle, the line controlled, the colour vivid and

Agostino di Duccio. Angel; relief from the Tempio Malatestiano, Rimini

Ajanta. Detail from a 5th-c. fresco

well contrasted and the presentation, a somewhat stylized realism, ignores perspective. There are also carved pillars and sculptures.

Ajax (448?). Play by *Sophocles.

Akenside Mark (1720–70). English author and physician famous during his life for his didactic poem *The Pleasures of Imagination* (1744). His interest in ethics, psychological interpretation and the grandeur of nature anticipate Wordsworth. The best of his minor poems, *Hymn to the Naiads*, was publ. in R. *Dodsley's *Collection of Poems*.

Akhmatova

Akhmatova Anna (1888–). Pseud. of A. A. Gorenko, Russian poet and from 1910 to 1918 wife of the poet N. S. Gumilyov. Through him she joined the movement of *acmeism and her early and best poems have the vivid actuality and faculty for immediate statement characteristic of the acmeists. Her poems are short and compact and their theme is usually love; A. expresses her passion, her yearning, her pain and her happiness with a burning conciseness and accuracy which is very rare and very moving. Her books of poetry include *Evening* (1912), *The Rosary* (1914), *The White Flock* (1917), *Anno Domini MCMXXI* (1922) and also *Selections from Six Books* (1940). She has also written (1926–36) a series of critical essays on Pushkin. In 1946 A. was expelled from the Union of Soviet Writers.

Alabaster relief. *Descent from the Cross*. Selby abbey, Yorkshire

Aksakov Sergey Timofeyevich (1791–1859). Russian novelist. He was a member of the landed classes and served in the government service from 1807 to 1839. Although a conservative in politics and literature he was overwhelmed by the writings of Gogol, whom he met in 1832 and who became a frequent visitor at A.'s house. A.'s first writings included a short story (1834) obviously affected by Gogol and essays on sporting subjects, all publ. anon., but in 1840 he began to write the semi-autobiographical *Family Chronicle* (1856; 1871). The book brought him immediate recognition. It describes, with detached and objective realism, life on a Russian estate in the late 18th and early 19th c. and is famous for the sensitively observed and recorded scenes from A.'s childhood, the nostalgic evocation of the Baskiria steppe country and the simplicity of A.'s style.

Akutagawa Ryunosuke (1892–1927). Japanese short-story writer. Using modern psychology he retold, often in a macabre and fantastic way, medieval Japanese stories, with vivid imagination and stylistic precision. The most famous, *Rashomon* (1915; *Rashomon and other Stories*, 1952) has been filmed (1952) under the direction of A. Kurosawa. A bandit rapes a woman in front of her husband and then kills him. At the trial all 3 (the husband is recalled through a medium) give their versions of what happened and 'the truth' is never established. *Jigokuhen* (1918; *Hell Screen and other Stories*, 1948) is about an artist who must witness scenes of horror before he can paint a terrible masterpiece. In 1922 A. turned less successfully to autobiographical fiction. He committed suicide.

alabaster. A natural stone used for statues and ornamental carving. It is a granular form of gypsum, usually white, pink or yellowish in colour and very soft. The best sort is pure white and translucent but it can be made nearly opaque to resemble marble by heating it in almost boiling water. It was extensively used in the medieval and Renaissance periods. In the late 14th c. and 15th c. English work, particularly that of Nottingham, had a European reputation. Being soft, a. allows a more delicate style of carving than is possible in stone.

Aladdin and the Wonderful Lamp. Accepted as a supplementary tale to *The *Arabian Nights' Entertainments* but the only Arabic ms. is late and the origin of the story obscure.

Alain. Pseud. of Émile-Auguste Chartier (1868–1951). French intellectual and teacher of philosophy at the Henri IV *lycée*, Paris, whose work deeply influenced French thought in the 1st part of the 20th c. In a long series of brilliant essays or *propos*, first publ. in the newspaper *Dépêche de Rouen* and then in *Nouvelle Revue Française*, he treated such subjects as aesthetics, politics, philosophy and education using a clear, concise style; expounding his ideas provocatively. His thought, whose development can best be studied in *Histoire de mes pensées* (1936), is characterized by a rational humanism. He was opposed to all forms of tyranny found in the modern world, upheld the freedom of the individual, was anti-militarist and anti-clerical. Other colls of essays include: *Le Cent un propos d'Alain* (1908–14), *Système des beaux-arts* (1920), *Éléments d'une doctrine radicale* (1925), *Propos de littérature* (1933) and *Spinoza* (1949).

Alain-Fournier. Pseud. of Henri-Alban Fournier (1886–1914). French writer, a schoolmaster's son. A. was killed in World War I. *Le Grand Meaulnes*, publ. in the *Nouvelle Revue*

Alain-Fournier

Française (1913; *The Wanderer*, 1929; also called *The Lost Domain*) was his only novel. It relates the attempt by Augustin Meaulnes, a schoolboy, to rediscover a mysterious and delightful house he had stumbled on one night. The events of the story have a rational explanation, but the dream-like quality of the narrative evokes the enchanted world of childhood and gives M.'s quest a symbolic meaning. A coll. of A.'s sketches, *Miracles* (1924), and his correspondence with Jacques Rivière (1926) were publ. posth.

Alarcón y Ariza Pedro Antonio de (1833–91). Spanish author who began his career as a political revolutionary and journalist, but later became more conservative. His wit, racy dialogue and comment, lively action and genre scenes of Spain were best suited to short stories and short novels such as *El capitan Veneno* (1881; *Captain Venom*, 1914) or better still in the tragi-comic *El sombrero de tres picos* (1874; *The *Three Cornered Hat*, 1886).

À la recherche du temps perdu (1913–27). Novel by *Proust.

Alastor (1816). Poem by *Shelley.

Alas y Ureña Leopoldo (1852–1901). Spanish novelist and under the pseud. 'Clarín' a vigorous and polemical critic. He was strongly affected by French naturalism as a young man and his best novel, *La Regenta* (2 vols, 1884/5), is a vivid, exact and subtle presentation of life in Oviedo, where A. was professor of law at the univ.

Albani Francesco (1578–1660). Italian painter working at Bologna and Rome and popular with his contemporaries for graceful, if somewhat sentimental, religious and mythological paintings. He studied first under the Flemish painter D. Calvaert and then under the Carracci.

albarello (Italian, derivation uncertain). A small ceramic container for ointments, etc.; the slight waist, the foot and flanged neck, to take the parchment cover, were typical.

Albee Edward (1928–). U.S. playwright, author of the successful *Who's Afraid of Virginia Woolf?* (1962), an examination of inadequacy, malice and fantasy in marriage and social success. Works include *The Death of Bessie Smith* (1960) and *The American Dream* (1960).

Albéniz Isaac (1860–1909). Spanish composer-pianist. He entered the Madrid Conservatory aged 8; when 13 he ran away and gave a series of recitals in Spain. He then stowed away on a ship bound for Puerto Rico, made a coast-to-coast tour of the U.S. as performer-manager and in 1874 returned to Europe. In 1878 he took lessons from Liszt and in 1890 lessons in composition from V. d'Indy and P. Dukas. In London in 1891 he met the millionaire F. B. Money-Coutts, who paid him generously to set his libretti, e.g. *Pepita Jiménez* (1896). A.'s music was strongly nationalistic. His major work was the piano suite *Iberia* (1906–9).

Albers Joseph (1888–). German painter and designer. After an academic training in Berlin, Essen and Munich, he studied at the Bauhaus and was later invited by Gropius to teach there. His 1st work included pictures in glass and furniture and abstract work. In 1933 he went to America and developed a new free abstract style (*Étude in Red-Violet*, 1935) and later became interested in the manipulation of colour (his series of *Variantes* from 1947). He has always been an experimental artist, his work being closely related to his practice as a teacher. From 1955 he has been chairman of the Design Department at Yale Univ.

Albert of Saxe-Coburg-Gotha, Prince Consort of England (1819–61). He reorganized and enlarged the colls of old masters, e.g. Raphael, in the Royal Library, Windsor, and promoted interest in the Italian primitives. He favoured the picturesque in architecture and was largely responsible for designing Osborne, Isle of Wight, and Balmoral, Scotland, in Italian villa and Scottish baronial styles respectively. He was director of the Concerts of *Ancient Music and his compositions included anthems sung at Queen Victoria's jubilees (1887, 1897). It was largely owing to him that the Great Exhibition (1851) took place; the proceeds went to endow the South Kensington (later the V. and A.) Mus. In London the ALBERT MEMORIAL, designed by Sir G. G. Scott, and the Royal Albert Hall were erected in his memory.

Albert Heinrich (1604–51). German poet and composer of the 'Königsberg circle'; he set poems by other members to music.

Albertazzi Adolfo (1865–1924). Italian writer whose short stories about working-class people are written with precision and delicacy, e.g. *Il diavolo nell' ampolla* (1918). A. also wrote novels.

Alberti Domenico (*c.* 1710–40). Italian composer. Besides operas and motets he composed harpsichord sonatas. Because of his extensive

Albarello (*c.* 1480)

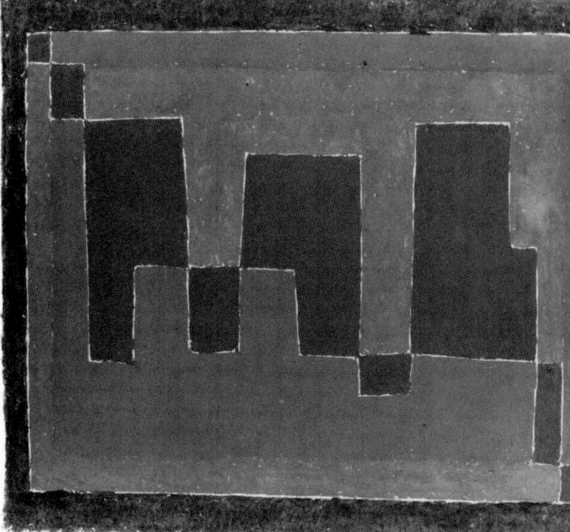

Albers. *Luftspiegelung A* (1940); painting

Prince Albert: portrait by Winterhalter

L. B. Alberti. Self-portrait on a medal

use of it, the type of broken chord accompaniment here illustrated is now called the A.

Bass;

Alberti Leone Battista (1404–72). Italian humanist, architect, writer and musician. The natural son of a wealthy Genoese patrician, A. had a rich and intensive education. From 1428 he travelled extensively and in 1432 he joined the papal chancellery, visiting Florence in this post. From 1443 he lived in Rome. His buildings included the Tempio Malatestiano (an unfinished restoration of the church of S. Francesco, Rimini), S. Sebastiano, Mantua, the most thoroughly centralized church plan up to that time, and the Rucellai Palace, Florence.

L. B. Alberti. Tempio Malatestiano, Rimini

A. was the 1st major art theorist of the Italian Renaissance and his influence on its painters and sculptors and above all architects was powerful. His theories are contained in *Della Pittura . . .* (written 1436), a treatise on painting dedicated to his friend Brunelleschi, and including one of the earliest discussions of perspective, *De Re Aedificatoria* (written *c.* 1450 with additions up to 1472) which provided the theoretical basis for Renaissance architecture and was the 1st book on architecture to be printed, and *De Statua* (written *c.* 1464), a pamphlet on sculpture. A. was the 1st Renaissance artist to make a thorough study of classical antiquity and particularly Roman architecture, which heavily affected his work. Unlike his predecessors, he worked as a designer rather than as a master-mason. He was the first to give a detailed and classified account of the classical orders and to use them systematically and the first to describe the architect as town planner. He outlined the design stages for building a new town, dealing with the choice of site, layout, width of streets, the need for interrelating the various kinds of buildings harmoniously and even proposing uniform façade design throughout a whole street. A. believed that art was based on reason and method and that there were fixed and understandable rules of beauty. The function of painting was to produce objects of beauty by the imitation of nature. To do this the artist had to select so as to avoid the imperfections which prevent perfect beauty in nature–an almost Aristotelian position. In *De Statua* A. lists the perfect proportions of the male body as discovered by comparing several bodies of good proportions and taking the average. Besides his treatises on art A. wrote *Philodoxeos*, a Latin comedy.

Alberti Rafael (1902–). Spanish poet who began his career as a cubist painter but then turned to poetry. His early poems *Marinero en tierra* (1925), *La amante* (1926), *El alba del alhelí* (1927), *Cal y canto* (1929) used folk-song rhythms or traditional forms but also showed receptiveness to the contemporary surrealist movement. His masterpiece *Sobre los Ángeles* (1929) is fully modern in technique, in some respects surrealist, and A.'s remarkable and characteristic control of form never weakens. The poem traces with convincing precision and deep self-analysis the crisis of self-confidence in a creative mind–the crisis, the despair, the readjustment to living. In 1930 A. became a Communist and in 1933 founded the Communist periodical *Octubre*. Like García Lorca he wrote a lament on the death of the bull fighter Sánchez Mejías, *Verte y no verte* (1936) in which A.'s 'intellectualism' is in contrast with Lorca's approach. In 1939 A. settled in Buenos Aires.

Albertinelli Mariotto (1474–1515). Florentine painter. Close friend of, and collaborator with, Fra *Bartolommeo, whom he met in the atelier of Cosimo Rosselli. Their partnership broke up about 1512, when A. became an innkeeper. With a technique sometimes indistinguishable from Bartolommeo's A.'s best independent work is his *Visitation* (1503, Uffizi).

Albi cathedral France. Fortified church begun in 1282. It is of brick, the interior a single large hall, furnished with battlements along the roof and a strong W. tower like the keep of a castle.

Albinoni Tommaso (1671–1750). Italian violinist and composer of about 50 operas and several orchestral works. J. S. Bach used certain of his themes and studied his works.

Albrechtsberger Johann Georg (1736–1809). Austrian composer and, more importantly, teacher of composition. His works on theory, notably *Gründliche Anweisung zur Komposition* (1790, 1818) were once widely used. Beethoven studied counterpoint under him.

Albertinelli. *The Visitation*

Albi cathedral

Albrecht von Halberstadt (*c.* 1180–1251). German writer of the 1st direct trs. into German of Ovid's *Metamorphoses*. In it he substituted dwarfs and elves for satyrs and fauns and germanized the poem in other respects. His work remained unnoticed until adapted (1545) by G. Wickram. 2 fragments of A.'s original survive.

Alcaeus (b. *c.* 620 B.C.). Lyric poet of Lesbos. Like Sappho A. wrote monodies which developed the simple style and subjective themes of Aeolian folk-songs. He wrote in dialect in an unusual range of metres including the 4-line ALCAIC stanza adapted by Horace to Latin verse.

Alcamenes (late 5th c. B.C.). Athenian sculptor, a pupil of Phidias. The group *Procne and Itys* in the Acropolis Mus., Athens, is attributed to him, and he may have collaborated in the sculptures for the Parthenon.

Alcestis (438 B.C.). Play by *Euripides based on myth. A. is the wife of Admetus, King of Thessaly, whom Fate promises to spare from death if somebody will go to Hades in his place. A. agrees, and dies; but she is rescued by Hercules. The story is used in a play by Alfieri and an opera by Gluck.

Alchemist, The (1610). Comedy by Ben *Jonson.

Alciphron (2nd c. A.D.). Athenian author of 4 groups of letters purporting to be from Athenian town and country types of the 4th c. B.C. The letters, particularly those from courtesans, contain material derived from writers of the *new comedy, e.g. Menander.

Alcman (7th c. B.C.). Lyric poet of Sparta. The fragmentary remains of his poems are the earliest surviving examples of Doric choral odes. His fragment on the sleep of nature was adapted by Goethe in *Über allen Gipfeln.*

Alcoforado Maria (1640–1723). Portuguese nun, long supposed the authoress of the popular *Lettres Portugaises* (1669; *Five Love Letters from a Nun to a Cavalier*, 1678) publ. in French and purporting to be a trs. from a Portuguese original. The author was finally identified (1962) as Gabriel de Lavergne, vicomte de Guilleragues.

Alcools (1913). Coll. of poems by Apollinaire.

Alcora. Town in Valencia, Spain. A factory here (founded 1726–7) produced, under Joseph Olerys and Edouard Roux, some of Europe's finest faïence, e.g. superb pictorial ware.

Alcott Louisa May (1832–88). U.S. writer, daughter of the famous educationalist AMOS BRONSON A. (1799–1888), remembered for her children's books, above all *Little Women* (1868–9).

Alcuin (*c.* 730–804). Anglo-Saxon churchman who was a driving force behind the *Carolingian renaissance. In 766 he had become head of the cathedral school at York but in 781 Charlemagne persuaded him to come to the Frankish court. A. founded the palace library and wrote manuals on grammar, rhetoric and dialectics and a number of homilies; more than 300 of his letters, mostly to Charlemagne, survive. He made revisions to the text of the Latin Bible. In 796 Charlemagne made A. abbot of Tours. Under him the abbey school attracted many students and the abbey produced important mss in the Carolingian miniscule script.

Aldeburgh. Village in Suffolk, England; the centre of a festival organized by Benjamin *Britten.

Aldine Press: Aldus *Manutius

Aldington Richard (1892–1962). British imagist poet and a novelist and biographer. Books of poetry include *Images – Old and New* (1916) and *Images of War* (1919); A.'s best-known novel is *Death of a Hero* (1929). His biography of T. E. Lawrence, *Lawrence of Arabia* (1955), denounced Lawrence as a near-charlatan.

Aldobrandini Wedding, The. A 1st-c. B.C. Roman wall painting after a Greek original; so called after a former owner. Now in the Vatican, Rome.

Aldrich Henry (1647–1710). English architect, composer and classical scholar. Most of his life he was connected with Christ Church, Oxford where he designed the Peckwater quadrangle. His compositions included the round 'Great Tom is cast' and much church music.

Louisa M. Alcott: daguerreotype

H. Aldrich. The Peckwater quadrangle, Oxford

Alcuin. Mid-9th-c. copy (from Tours) of Alcuin's revision of the Bible

The Aldobrandini Wedding (detail). See also colour plate 18

Aldrich. *Whatever Happened to Baby Jane?*

Alembert

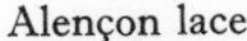

Alençon lace

Alessi. Courtyard of the Palazzo Marino, Milan

Aldrich Robert (1918–). U.S. film director. A.'s 1st important work was a western, *Apache* (1954), partly influenced by Losey, for whom A. worked on *The Prowler*. More personal was *Vera Cruz* (1954), a large-scale comic-heroic western. A.'s best film is *Kiss Me, Deadly* (1955) which presents extreme violence in an ornate post-Welles style and uses its Mickey Spillane hero to represent the American fascist. The baroque style survives in *The Big Knife* (1955), from a melodramatic Odets play and his shocker *Whatever Happened to Baby Jane?* (1962) which had great commercial success, partly due to the stars Joan Crawford and Bette Davis.

Aldrich Thomas Bailey (1836–1907). U.S. writer and (1881–90) ed. of *The Atlantic Monthly*. His autobiographical boys' book, *The Story of a Bad Boy* (1869), and poetry, technically skilful but 'genteel', were once widely read. He also wrote *The Stillwater Tragedy* (1880), an early detective story.

Alecsandri Vasile (1821–90). Rumanian poet, foreign minister (1859–60) and minister to France (1885–90). A. produced a quantity of melodious verse, made important colls of ballads and songs, and as playwright and director made a great contribution to the Rumanian theatre.

Aleichem Sholem. Hebrew greeting, 'Peace be with you', used as a pseud. by Solomon J. Rabinowitz (1859–1916), Russian-born Jewish humorous writer. As a young man he was for a time a rabbi but then devoted himself to writing. He wrote in Russian, Hebrew and Yiddish and insisted on the validity of the last as a literary language. His short stories in a colloquial idiom combined pathos with humour.

Aleixandre Vicente (1900–). Spanish poet associated with the modernist movement of the 1920s. His 1st vol. *Ámbito* (1928) was largely ignored but the complex surrealist imagery and free rhythms of *Espadas como labios* (1932) and the prose poems *Pasión de la tierra* (1935) made a great stir. Other works include: *La destrucción o el amor* (1935) and *Sombra del Paraíso* (1944). A. became a member of the Spanish Academy in 1950.

Alemán Mateo (1568–?). Spanish *picaresque novelist. His *Guzman de Alfarache* (2 parts, 1599, 1604; *The Rogue: or the Life of Guzman de Alfarache*, 1622) quickly gained a European reputation. It is in the form of a rogue's autobiography but is heavy with the moralizing popular with A.'s contemporaries. A. went to Mexico in 1608 and died there some time after 1613.

Alembert Jean le Rond d' (1717–83). A great French mathematician and philosopher. With D. Diderot he ed. the **Encyclopédie*, to which he contributed the introduction.

Alençon lace. Needle point *lace (from the French town of Alençon) of a thick and firm character, originally imitating Venetian lace. The net background was also made with the needle. The great period was in the 17th and 18th c.

Alessi Galeazzo (1512–72). Italian architect who became the chief exponent of mannerist architecture in Genoa and Milan. He built many palaces and churches including the Villa delle Peschiere and the Villa Cambiaso, Genoa, and the church of S. Vittoria, Milan.

Alexander mosaic (3rd c. B.C.) also called *The Battle of Issus*. The finest Roman mosaic known, which shows a battle between Greeks and Persians, including a combat supposedly between Alexander the Great and Darius; it may be a copy of a work by the Greek painter Philoxenus of Eretria (*c.* 300 B.C.). Found at Pompeii, it is now at the Gal. N., Naples.

Alexander Nevsky (1938). Film directed by S. M. *Eisenstein.

Alexandrian Quartet, The (1957–60). Name often used of a novel tetralogy by Lawrence *Durrell.

Alexandrian school. A school of Greek writers working at Alexandria from the 3rd to 1st c. B.C. The most distinguished writers of its golden age were Callimachus (*c.* 305–*c.* 240 B.C.), author of hymns and epigrams, short epics and the extended miscellany of mythology called *Aetia*, Apollonius Rhodius, second librarian at Alexandria and author of the epic *Argonautica*, Theocritus and Aratus (*c.* 315–*c.* 240), author of the astronomical *Phaenomena*. Their masters were Philetas of Cos (born before 320 B.C.) and Asclepiades of Samos (*fl.* 270 B.C.), their successors Euphorion, Nicander and Meleager. All these poets, with their scholarly

Alexander mosaic. For Alexander sarcophagus see colour plate 11

ideals of nicety and polish influenced the Roman poets of the 1st c. B.C.–Catullus, Propertius, Virgil, Horace and Ovid.

alexandrine. Line used in English and French poetry. In English it has 6 iambic feet and is chiefly used as the last line of a Spenserian stanza; in French it has 12 unstressed syllables and was once the most common poetic metre. Its name derives from the *Roman d'Alexandre*. (late 12th c.). In France it became very general in the 13th c., lapsed in the 15th c. and was revived in the 16th c. by the poets of the *Pléiade. It was subjected by N. *Boileau in the 17th c. to strict regulations, e.g. concerning the caesura, freely broken in the 19th c. by Hugo and later poets.

Alexandrov Grigori (1903–). Russian film director. Assistant to *Eisenstein from *Battleship Potemkin* to *Que Viva Mexico?* He also directed a number of films including *Volga Volga* (1938), a musical of great gusto and charm.

Alexeieff Alexandre (1901–). Russian-born film animator who with Claire Parker devised a novel method of animation using illuminated pins pushed into a screen. The process was capable of remarkable effects, e.g. *Night on the Bare Mountain* (1934) to music by Mussorgsky. A. also produced the titles for Welles's *The Trial*.

Alexis Paul (1847–1901). French writer passionately involved with the naturalist movement, a disciple of Zola. A. publ. the story *Après la bataille* in *Les *Soirées de Médan* (1880). Short story colls include *La Fin de Lucie Pellegrin* (1880); plays written in collaboration with O. Méténier include *Les Frères Zemganno* (1890), based on the novel by Edmond de Goncourt.

Alexis Willibald. Pseud. of Georg Wilhelm Heinrich Häring (1798–1871), German historical novelist who publ. his first 2 books as trs of Sir W. Scott. His best novels deal with Brandenburg.

Alfieri Count Vittorio (1749–1803). Italian tragic dramatist and poet. His 22 tragedies include *Saul*, generally considered his best, *Mirra* and several based on Greek tragedies, e.g. *Oreste*. He held that tragedy should describe man's noblest emotions in the simplest forms and, following classical tradition, he therefore excluded from his plays all secondary characters and episodes. He conceived the tragic hero as a victim of tyranny and his passionate hatred of oppression made him a precursor of the Italian *risorgimento*. In the *Misogallo* (1799), a polemical work against the French, A. appeals to Italians to recover their freedom. He also wrote several comedies and his autobiography *Vita di Vittorio Alfieri* (1790; 1803; 1810).

Alfieri. Scene from *Mirra*

Alfonso X 'el Sabio' ('the Learned') (1221–84), from 1252 king of Castile and Leon. Under his direction scholars, including Jews and Arabs, trs. Latin, Jewish and Arabic writings into Castilian. A. himself wrote a work on astrology compiled from Arabic sources. He wrote an unfinished universal history, and *Crónica general*, a history of Spain up to the reign of his father. The latter, for which A. drew upon chronicles and *chansons de geste*, was the most important historical work of the middle ages and inspired a series of historical chronicles. The trs together with A.'s own writings form the earliest corpus of Castilian prose. He was also responsible for a coll. of Galician lyrics, *Cantigas de Santa Maria*, a large and valuable coll. of medieval music.

Alfonso X. From the *Cantigas de Santa Maria*

Alfred (or Aelfred) (848–900), the 'Great'. King of the W. Saxons and scholar. At A.'s accession (871) all England was threatened with Danish occupation; by containing this threat A. assured the political and cultural future of Anglo-Saxon society. More than this he planned an 'educational reform' and the preface to his trs. of the *Pastoral Care* of Pope Gregory I, sent to each diocese, outlined his intentions. A trs. of the *Historia ecclesiastica* of Bede, for the study of national history, was supplemented by A.'s own trs. of the universal history and geography of Orosius, *Historia adversus paganos*; and The Anglo-Saxon Chronicle was begun during his reign. A.'s trs. of *De consolatione philosophiae* by Boethius, contains some additions which are clearly his own.

Alfven Hugo (1872–1960). Swedish composer. Influences from Wagner and R. Strauss are traceable in his work. He wrote 5 symphonies and also 3 rhapsodies including the well-known *Midsommarvaka* (*Midsummer Rhapsody*, 1903).

Algardi Alessandro (1602–54). Bolognese sculptor. After studying at the Carracci

King Alfred. Head on a silver penny

Algardi. *Tomb of Leo XI* (*left*) and *The Meeting of Attila and Leo I*

Alhambra vase

Alhambra. The Court of Lions

Academy he settled about 1525 in Rome, where his friends included Domenichino, N. Poussin and A. Sacchi. A. excelled as a portraitist, particularly in the depth of his character analysis, e.g. his *Francesco Bracciolini* (V. and A., London). Although A.'s approach was classical and although he was Bernini's chief rival, his statue of Innocent X (Palazzo dei Conservatori, Rome) was influenced by the latter's *Urban VIII* and above all his tomb for Leo XI (St Peter's, Rome, 1645/50) is the first of many to be modelled on Bernini's for Urban. From 1646 to 1653 A. was working on his relief of *The Meeting of Attila and Leo I* (St Peter's). With its modulation from the free-standing figures of the foreground to the shallow relief of the background, this was to be influential on later relief technique.

Algarotti Count Francesco (1712–64). Italian poet, writer and connoisseur of art and music and a friend of Voltaire and Frederick II of Prussia. In *Neutonianismo per le dame*... (1737; trs. 1739) he popularized Newton's optical theories, and the *Saggio sopra l'opera in musica* (1763; *An Essay on the Opera*, 1767) was a protest against the elaborate machinery of the 18th-c. stage.

Alger Horatio Jr. (1834–99). U.S. clergyman and writer of improving stories for boys, e.g. the *Ragged Dick* series (beginning in 1867), the *Luck and Pluck* series (1869) and the *Tattered Tom* series (1871). In these yarns poor yet virtuous lads repeatedly make good – i.e. money. A.'s name has become a byword for this naïve version of the American 'log cabin to White House' dream.

Algren Nelson (1909–). U.S. short-story writer and novelist who writes about Chicago's West Side slums. Books include *Never Come Morning* (1942), *The Man with the Golden Arm* (1949), made into a film (1956), describing drug addiction and violence among frustrated Chicago slum dwellers, and *A Walk on the Wild Side* (1956).

Alhambra (Arabic, 'red castle'). Fortified palace of the Moorish rulers of Spain built in the 13th and 14th c. at Granada, Spain; a fine example of Moorish architecture. Galleries and small rooms lead off arcaded courts, the most famous of which are the 'Court of the Lions' and the 'Court of Alberca'. Characteristic are the elaborate, geometrical patterns and the perspective effects achieved with delicate columns. Part of the castle was destroyed by Charles V and replaced by a Renaissance palace. In the A. is the famous Hispano-Moresque ALHAMBRA VASE (*c.* 1380–1400), possibly made in Granada, although similar vessels almost certainly came from Malaga. The large tin-glazed earthenware vase is decorated with arabesque patterns and gazelles.

Alhambra Theatre London. In the late 19th and early 20th c. this theatre and the Empire Theatre, London, were the only English theatres which attempted to produce serious ballets. Famous dancers appearing at the A. included P. Legnani, J. Espinosa and E. Cecchetti. In 1911 it changed to revue. It was demolished in 1936.

Aliamet Jean-Jacques (1726–88). French engraver. Executed engravings after C.-J. Vernet and 17th-c. Dutch painters, particularly N. Berchem. His brother, FRANÇOIS-GERMAIN (1734–88), also an engraver, worked in London under Sir Robert Strange.

Ali Baba and the Forty Thieves. An Arabic story and supplementary tale to *The *Arabian Nights' Entertainments*.

Alice B. Toklas, The Autobiography of (1933). Book by Gertrude *Stein.

Alice's Adventures in Wonderland (1865). Children's story by Lewis *Carroll.

Alkan Charles Henri Valentin. Pseud. of C. H. V. Morhange (1813–88). French pianist and composer for the piano and pedal-piano. His music, particularly the 'Études', demands

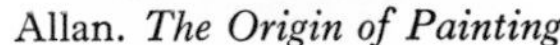
Allan. *The Origin of Painting*

Allegretto. *Three Saints*

Edward Alleyn

masterly technique and is notable for its chromaticism.

Alken Henry (*fl.* 1816–31). English painter and engraver of sporting subjects, chiefly fox-hunting.

All About Eve (1950). Film directed by J. L. *Mankiewicz.

Allan David (1744–96). Scottish genre and portrait painter. He worked in Rome (1764–77) and won a prize there for a history painting. Sometimes called the 'Scottish Hogarth', more as a measure of his fame than his style.

alla prima (Italian, 'at once'). Method of painting in which the colour is applied in one session and no subsequent modification is made. In oil painting any previous drawing or underpainting is obliterated so that it does not affect the final result.

allegory. A story, whether in verse or in prose, or a painting in which the literal account or presentation is intended to have, or is interpreted as having, another and parallel meaning. Bunyan's *The Pilgrim's Progress*, a comparatively simple example, describes a man's journey from one city to another but the city he leaves is called Destruction and the city he goes to is called Celestial. A. was most frequent and most subtle in the middle ages. Of the many a.s written then *Le *Roman de la Rose* was the most popular throughout Europe; *Langland's *Piers Plowman*, the great English religious a., is a uniquely subtle and complex use of the form.

Allegret Marc (1900–). French film director. A.'s early work was dominated by personalities other than his own–Gide, with whom he made *Le Voyage au Congo* (1926) and *Pagnol for whom he made *Fanny* (1932), one of the *Marius* trilogy. His own films have usually been comedies, like *Mam'zelle Nitouche* (1953) and *En Effeuillant la Marguerite* (or *Mam'zelle Striptease*, 1957), often of considerable charm. Yves A. is his brother.

Allegret Yves (1907–). French film director. A latter-day exponent of the fatalism which characterized French films of the 1930s. He was responsible for a series of heavily pessimistic films including *Dédée d'Anvers* (1948), *Une si jolie petite plage* (1948), *Manèges* (1950) and his most famous film, *Les Orgueilleux* (1953).

Allegretto Nuzi (di Nuzio) (1315/20–73). Italian painter working at Florence. He was affected by the Sienese school as well as by the work of Giotto. A. signed many of his pictures in full, which was unusual in the 14th c.

Allegri Gregorio (1582–1652). Italian composer of church music whose 9-part *Miserere*, once jealously reserved to the Sistine Chapel, is famous for its magical beauty. Not complex, it gains effect from the traditional ornamentations and from the acoustics of the chapel. Mozart, aged 14, copied it down after one hearing.

allegro (Italian, 'merry'). In music: (1) an indication of quick, lively tempo; (2) a composition or movement in that tempo.

Allegro, L' (1632). Poem by *Milton.

allemande (French, 'German'), early English equivalents ALMAN, ALMAND, ALMAIN. A dance in moderate 4-4 time *binary in form, each section usually beginning with a short note before the bar line. The classical dance suite opened either with a. or prelude.

Allen (Charles) Grant (Blairfindie) (1848–99). Canadian-born writer educated and domiciled in England. Besides the essay *Physiological Aesthetics* (1877) and many articles popularizing evolutionary theories, he wrote over 30 novels. These included *The Woman Who Did* (1895), whose heroine refused, on feminist principles, to marry, and the satirical *The British Barbarians* (1895).

Allen (William) Hervey (1889–1949). U.S. author of the best-seller *Anthony Adverse* (1933), a picaresque novel about the Napoleonic age. *Action at Aquila* (1938), about the U.S. Civil War, and later historical works were not so successful. He also wrote *Israfel* (1926), a biography of E. A. Poe, and poetry including *Wampum and Old Gold* (1921) and *Carolina Chansons* (with Du Bose Heyward, 1922).

Allen James Lane (1849–1935). U.S. novelist whose early books, e.g. *Flute and Violin . . .* (1891), *A Kentucky Cardinal* (1895) and *Aftermath* (1896), describe the romanticized ideal society of the southern states before the Civil War.

Allende (y Saron), (Pedro) Humberto (1885–). Chilean composer, the 1st modernist in Chile; teacher of composition (1928–46) at Santiago Conservatory. A.'s works include the symphonic poem *La voz de las calles* (1920) and he has made folk-song colls.

Alleyn Edward (1566–1626). English actor and only rival of R. Burbage. He was greatest in the title-roles of plays by Marlowe, e.g. *Jew of Malta*, *Doctor Faustus* and *Tamburlaine the Great*. Manager or proprietor of theatres and other places of entertainment, e.g. the Fortune Theatre, where he partnered P. Henslowe. In 1604 he retired and bought the manor of Dulwich, founding Dulwich College in 1619.

All for Love, or The World well lost (1678). Play by *Dryden.

Allingham William (1824–89). Irish poet; friend of D. G. Rossetti, Tennyson, Carlyle and Leigh Hunt. His poems, which affected the young W. B. Yeats, include *Poems* (1850) and *Irish Songs and Poems* (1887); his *Diary* was publ. in 1907.

alliteration and alliterative verse. A. is, strictly, the repetition or echo of the same initial sound, whether consonantal or vowel, in several words, e.g. 'Full fathom five thy father lies'. The term a. verse is used of the poetry of early Germanic languages, e.g. Old Norse,

Allori. *Judith with the Head of Holofernes*

Alphorn

ENGLANDS
Parnassus:
OR
The choysest Flowers of our Moderne
Poets, with their Poeticall comparisons.
Descriptions of Bewties, Personages, Castles,
Pallaces, Mountaines, Groues, Seas,
Springs, Riuers, &c.
*Whereunto are annexed other various discourses,
both pleasaunt and profitable.*
Imprinted at London for N. L. C. B.
and T. H. 1600.

Allott. *Englands Parnassus*

Icelandic, Old English, based on an a. line divided into half-lines by a caesura. The line contains a definite number of stressed syllables and the 2 half-lines are held together by the rhythmic and a. pattern. There is little use of end rhyme and in its earlier forms a. verse is rarely stanzaic. In England, a. verse survived in Middle English of the 14th c. in such poems as *Pearl*, *Syr Gawayne and the Grene Knight* and *Piers Plowman*. *Pearl* and *Syr Gawayne* both use stanza and rhyme. Strict a. was also the basis of Celtic verse, and has endured in classical Welsh poetry. Some 19th- and 20th-c. poets, e.g. G. M. Hopkins and W. H. Auden, have adapted Welsh or Old English a. verse in some of their work.

All My Sons (1947). Play by Arthur Miller.

Allori Alessandro (1535–1607). Florentine painter. Used the name Bronzino after the death of his uncle, Il Bronzino. Studied under Bronzino and in Rome under Michelangelo. Although his drawing was rigid and his colouring cold he was popular as a painter of decorative frescoes into which he inserted portraits of prominent contemporaries. CRISTOFANO (1577–1621), mannerist painter, son of Alessandro. His painting united the rich colouring of the Venetian with the careful drawing of the Florentine school. His best-known painting is *Judith with the head of Holofernes* (Pitti). Judith is a portrait of his mistress Mazzafirra, while Holofernes is supposed to be a self-portrait.

Allott Robert (*fl.* 1600). English ed. of 2 books, *Englands Parnassus* (1600), containing some valuable extracts of Elizabethan poetry and important for its identification of the authors of a number of books, and *Wits Theatre of the Little World* (1599) a prose anthology from pagan and Christian writers.

All Quiet on the Western Front (1928). Novel by *Remarque, made into a film (1930) directed by L. *Milestone.

Allston Washington (1779–1843). U.S. painter and writer. In Europe (1801–10, 1811–18), he studied under B. West in London and visited Paris and Rome, becoming a close friend of S. T. Coleridge, W. Irving and B. Thorwaldsen. As the 1st U.S. artist to paint romantic landscapes he was a precursor of the *Hudson River school; he also painted portraits, e.g. that of Coleridge (N.P.G., London), and large dramatic Biblical and classical subjects. His *Lectures on Art* were publ. in 1850.

All's Well that End's Well (publ. 1623). Comedy by *Shakespeare, perhaps a revised version (*c.* 1602) of an earlier play. Its source was a story by Boccaccio in *The *Palace of Pleasure.*

All the King's Men (1946). Novel by Robert Penn *Warren.

Alma-Tadema Sir Lawrence (1836–1912). Netherlands academic painter who settled in London (1870). He was immensely popular for his idealized, but accurately detailed and brilliantly coloured, scenes of Greek and Roman life.

Almayer's Folly (1895). Novel by Conrad.

Almeida-Garrett João Baptista da Silva Leitão, Visconde de (1799–1854). Portuguese writer and revolutionary politician; discovered romanticism when an exile in England; his poems, *Camões* (Paris, 1825) and *Dona Branca* (Paris, 1826) initiated Portuguese romanticism. A. inaugurated theatre reforms and wrote the 1st Portuguese historical novel *O Arco de Sanct' Anna* (2 vols, 1845–50). His plays include *Frei Luís de Sousa* (1843; *Brother Luiz . . .*, 1909).

Almogáver Juan Boscán de: Juan *Boscán de Almogáver.

Almqvist Carl Jonas Love (1793–1866). Swedish writer. He worked as a teacher, clergyman and journalist but fled from Sweden for the U.S. in 1857 to escape a murder charge. A. represents the transition from romantic introversion to realism in Sweden; important influences on him included Swedenborg and Fourier. A.'s work, apart from the *Songes*, fine lyrics, was mainly prose: short stories, historical novels and plays which appeared under the title *Tornrosens bok* (1832–51). His other

Allston. Portrait of Coleridge

works include the long short story *Det går an,* justifying extra-marital relations.

Alonso Alicia (1921–). Cuban dancer who joined Ballet Caravan in 1939 and Ballet Theater 2 years later. With this co. she created the role of Lizzie Borden in Agnes *de Mille's *Fall River Legend* (1948); the same year she formed a co. in Cuba. Returning to Ballet Theater, she became leading dancer in 1951.

Alonso Dámaso (1898–). Spanish poet, critic and philologist and historian of literature. His poems *Poemas puros, poemillas de la ciudad* (1921) were imagist but those in *Hijos de la ira* (1944) express the existentialist dilemma of modern man. Critical works included an important ed. of *Las Soledades* of Góngora publ. 1927.

alphorn. Musical instrument used by cowherds in the Swiss Alps. It consists of a straight conical tube about 6 to 7 ft long and is played with a mouthpiece similar to a brass instrument's.

Alsloot Denis van (d. *c.* 1626). Flemish painter who specialized in pageant and procession scenes.

Alsop Richard (1761–1815). U.S. poet and satirist, one of the Hartford Wits. He collaborated with others of the group to write *The Echo* (in *The American Mercury,* 1791–1805) and *The Political Greenhouse* (in *Connecticut Courant,* 1799), verse satires against anti-Federalist opinions.

Also sprach Zarathustra. Philosophical work by *Nietzsche (1883–4, 1892) and tone-poem (1895) based on it by R. *Strauss.

Altamira. Limestone cave in Santander province, northern Spain, where animal paintings of the upper palaeolithic or leptolithic era were first discovered (1879). A.'s famous roof frieze of naturalistic bison is now recognized as late Magdalenian art *c.* 10,000 B.C., belonging to the final phase of the ice age hunting cultures of western Europe. The paintings are executed in earth colours, mostly blacks and reds, straight on to porous rock; in some cases one painting is superimposed on another. Also *cave art.

Altdorfer Albrecht (*c.* 1480–1538). German painter and city architect and councillor of Regensburg, Bavaria. His *St George* (Alte Pina., Munich) is one of the first true landscape paintings in Europe. In it a mass of forest foliage soars above the tiny figures of St George and the dragon. Even in his early works, which show influences of L. Cranach and Dürer, landscape predominates, and a tour of the Danube and the Austrian Alps (*c.* 1511) confirmed his inclinations. An immediate result was the series of canvases, drawings and etchings of Danube landscapes (*Danube school). Other major works are *Alexander's Victory,* also called the *Battle of Arbela* (1529, Alte Pina.), and the *St Florian Altar.* This was 8 panels depicting the life of St Florian, painted for St Florian's church, near Linz, Austria. 7 of the panels are now in colls elsewhere; the Germanisches N.-Mus., Nuremberg; the Uffizi; and a private coll.

Altichiero da Zevio (*fl.* 1369–84). Italian painter from Verona. His figures are reminiscent of Giotto's style but show a greater awareness of one another suggestive of later painters. There are frescoes by him in Verona and Padua including a great *Crucifixion* in the church of Sant' Antonio, Padua.

alto (Italian, 'high'). In music: (1) the highest male voice (*counter tenor) and sometimes used of the lower female or contralto voice; (2) instruments of approximately this register, e.g. a. saxophone; (3) French term for the viola. The a. *clef is used for viola and, sometimes, for a. trombone parts.

Altona, Les Séquestrés d' (1959). Play by *Sartre.

Alunno di Domenico (Disciple of Domenico, i.e. Ghirlandaio). Name given by B. Berenson to a Florentine painter and illustrator (*fl.* late 15th–early 16th c.). His work included the predella for Ghirlandaio's *Adoration of the Magi* (1488) for the church of the Innocenti, Florence. Berenson later discovered a contract (1488) made for the execution of this predella

Altdorfer. *The Danube near Regensburg.* Also *Danube school

Altichiero. *The Crucifixion* at Padua (detail)

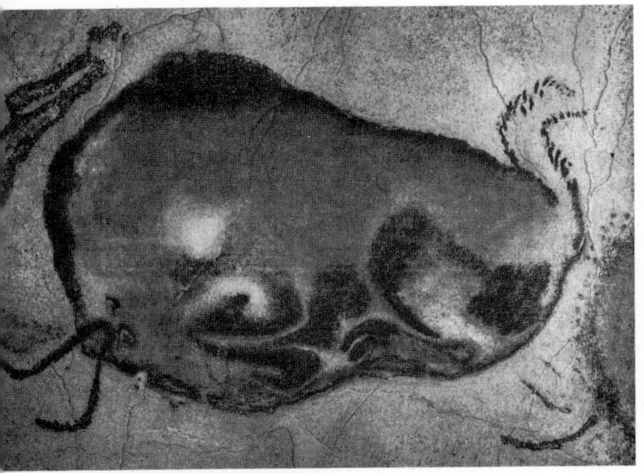

Altamira. Cave painting

Alunno di Domenico. *The Presentation in the Temple*

Amarna. Nefertiti

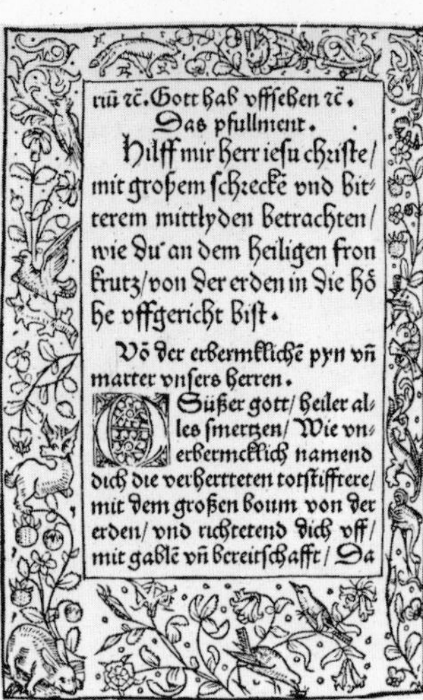

rū ꝛc. Gott hab vffseben ꝛc.
Das pfullment.
Hilff mir herr iesu christe/ mit großem schrecke vnd bitterem mittlyden betrachten/ wie du an dem heiligen fron krutz/von der erden in die hö he vffgericht bist.
Vō der erbermklichē pyn vñ marter vnsers herren.
O Süßer gott/ heiler alles smertzen/ Wie vnerbermcklich namend dich die verhertteten totstiffrere/ mit dem großen boum von der erden/ vnd richtetend dich vff/ mit gablē vñ bereitschafft/ Da

feit weg vnd vermögen begegnet/ dz du vnd iohannes/ dyne swesteren vnd gesippten/ mochtend zū dem herrē komen/ zū dē krütz/ A dyner großen vnd ver-

Amerbach. Two pages from a block-book, 1492

between the prior of the Innocenti and a Bartolommeo di Giovanni; he accepted this as the real name of his artist but retained the name A. as more instructive.

Álvarez Quintero the brothers Serafín (1871–1938) and Joaquín (1873–1944). Spanish playwrights from Andalusia who collaborated in more than 100 light comedies and *zarzuelas*, simple in plot and with sparkling dialogue. Their best-known plays include *El patio* (1900) and *Mariquilla terremoto* (1930).

Alwyn William (1905–). British composer, traditionalist in style. He has written music to over 50 films including *Odd Man Out* (1947). Other works include the oratorio *Marriage of Heaven and Hell* (1936), *Concerto Grosso* (1942), *Suite of Scottish Dances* (1946) and *Manchester Suite* (1947) and settings of songs by Louis MacNeice (1947).

Amadis de Gaula. A 14th-c. romance of chivalry of Spanish or Portuguese origin, first printed in 1508 (Books 1–4). Its publ. set a fashion for such books (of which it was much the best) which Cervantes satirized in *Don Quixote*.

Amarna (Tel-el-Amarna) in Upper Egypt, near the E. bank of the Nile, about 190 miles above Cairo. It is the ruined site of the city founded *c.* 1370 B.C. by the Pharaoh Akhenaten (Amenhotep IV) as his new capital. Excavations revealed 300 clay tablets of diplomatic correspondence and also outstanding works of art, remarkable in Egyptian art for their naturalism and animation. The most famous piece is the bust of Nefertiti, Akhenaten's queen, now in the N. Mus., Berlin.

Amasis painter. Greek potter and vase painter in the *black-figured style; his figures are lithe, vigorous and witty.

Amati a family of violin makers working at *Cremona. ANDREA (1505/10–1570/81) established the design characteristic of the family and essentially that of the modern violin; ANTONIO (1550–1638) and GIROLAMO (1551–1635), known as 'the brothers Amati', were his sons. NICOLO (1596–1684), Girolamo's son, is now the best known; A. Stradivari and A. Guarneri were his apprentices.

Carmen Amaya

Amaya Carmen (1920–). Spanish flamenco dancer who began her career in cabaret. She formed a co. mainly from members of her family and has toured in many countries. She first appeared in New York in 1941 and London in 1948.

Ambassadors, The (1903). Novel by Henry *James.

Amberger Christoph (*c.* 1500–*c.* 1561/2). German portrait painter whose work shows Venetian influence. Working in Augsburg he painted many famous people, including the Emperor Charles V (1532, Berlin).

Amberger. *The Emperor Charles V*

Ambler Eric (1909–). English writer of adventure books. He commands a powerful narrative style and psychological penetration which makes such books as *Passage at Arms* (1959) and *Mask of Dimitrios* (1939) more than mere adventure stories.

Ambros August Wilhelm (1816–76). Austrian musicologist, critic and author of *Geschichte der Musik* (4 vols, 1862–78; unfinished), still valuable on Renaissance and baroque music.

Ambrose St (340–97). Bishop of Milan. A style of *plainsong is associated with his name.

ambulatory (from Latin *ambulare*, 'to walk'). In a large church the processional aisle or walk round the E. end behind the high altar.

Amerbach Johann (1443–1513). The 1st printer of the great Basle tradition. His publ. house produced books which were both fine pieces of printing and scholarly works in the style of the new humanism; A.'s chief editorial adviser was his former teacher, the humanist Heynlin.

America, a Prophecy (1793). Prophetic poem by Blake.

American in Paris, An (1950). Film directed by V. *Minnelli.

American Mercury, The (1924–). Monthly literary magazine, founded by H. L. *Mencken (ed. 1924–33) and G. J. Nathan, celebrated for its iconoclastic editorials, which satirized U.S. culture and political institutions, and for its encouragement of 'real-life' writers such as T. Dreiser, Sherwood Anderson and Sinclair Lewis.

American Tragedy, An (1925). Novel by Theodore *Dreiser.

Amerika (1927). Novel by *Kafka.

Ames Joseph (1816–72). U.S. portrait painter, self-taught. Among the famous Americans he painted was Daniel Webster. A. worked quickly and his paintings are not highly finished.

Amiche, Le (1955). Film directed by M. *Antonioni.

Amicis Edmondo de (1846–1908). Italian writer. When a young man he resigned an army commission to write, modelling his style on A. Manzoni. A series of travel books was followed by books urging educational reform. The boys' book *Cuore* (1886; *Cuore: an Italian Schoolboy's Journal*, 1887), immensely successful and widely trs., was characteristic in its sentimentality.

Amico di Sandro (Italian, 'friend of Sandro', i.e. Botticelli). An 'artist' invented by B. Berenson as the painter of certain pictures attributed to Botticelli and Filippino Lippi, which seemed to show a uniform style midway between those artists. Berenson later decided that he was mistaken and the pictures have been reattributed.

Amiel Henri-Frédéric (1821–81). Swiss philosopher posth. famous for his journal publ. during 1883/4 as *Fragments d'un Journal intime* (Eng. trs: first 1885, best *The Private Journal of Henri Frédéric Amiel*, 1935). It reveals a sensitive and subtle mind whose creativity was stunted by habitual introspection.

Amiens cathedral France. One of the supreme creations of Gothic architecture. Coming towards the end of the development of the Île de France style, it was begun in 1220 and finished *c.* 1247. The proportions stress verticality (vault is 149 ft high); it has 8-light windows, bar-tracery, sophisticated flying buttresses and a wealth of fine sculpture. The compact plan is typically French, with transepts hardly projecting beyond the aisles.

Amigoni Jacopo (1675–1752). Venetian rococo painter who worked in various European countries and during his own lifetime was very popular.

Amis Kingsley (William) (1922–). English novelist, poet, critic and univ. lecturer in English. His novels include *Lucky Jim* (1954), the 1st widely known work of the *Angry Young Men, *That Uncertain Feeling* (1955), *Take a Girl like You* (1960) and *One Fat Englishman* (1963).

Amis and Amiloun. Middle English metrical romance depicting friendship as a knightly virtue.

Amleth. Alternative spelling of the name *Hamlet, the hero of a Danish legend recorded by Saxo Grammaticus and used by Shakespeare.

Amman Jo(b)st (1539–91). Swiss woodcut artist and painter who settled in Nuremberg (1561), where he became a prolific illustrator. He executed woodcut illustrations for S. Feyerabend's Bible (1564) and a set of 115 for a series on arts and trades.

Amman(n)ati Bartolomeo (1511–92). Florentine sculptor and architect. In Florence he carved the Neptune fountain (1563–77) in the Piazza della Signoria and built the famous Bridge of the Trinity (1567–9), destroyed in an air raid (1944), but since rebuilt, and extensions (1560–77) to the Pitti Palace. There are also buildings by A. in Rome and Lucca.

Amory Thomas (*c.* 1691–1788). British author of 2 eccentric and discursive books, *Memoirs of Several Ladies of Great Britain* (1755), which in fact deals with only one, an imaginary

Amico di Sandro. *Adoration of the Kings* (detail)

Amiens cathedral. Also *Gothic and colour plate 30

Amman. *Apocalypse*; woodcut

Kingsley Amis

Ammanati. The Neptune fountain, Florence

THE
ANATOMY OF
MELANCHOLY,
VVHAT IT IS.
VVITH ALL THE KINDES,
CAVSES, SYMPTOMES, PROG-
NOSTICKES, AND SEVE-
RALL CVRES OF IT.
IN THREE MAINE PARTITIONS
with their feuerall SECTIONS, MEM-
BERS, and SVBSEC-
TIONS.
PHILOSOPHICALLY, MEDICI-
NALLY, HISTORICALLY, OPE-
NED AND CVT VP.
BY
DEMOCRITVS Iunior.
With a Satyricall PREFACE, conducing to
the following Difcourfe.
MACROB.
Omne meum, Nihil meum.
AT OXFORD,
Printed by IOHN LICHFIELD and IAMES
SHORT, for HENRY CRIPPS.
Anno Dom. 1621.

The Anatomy of Melancholy, ed. of 1621

Hans Christian Andersen

Amphora, Attic, 9th c. B.C. (*above*); amphora, *c.* 520 B.C. (*below*)

Mrs Marinda Benlow, and the semi-autobiographical, *The Life of John Buncle Esq.* (2 vols, 1756–66).

Amos. One of the minor prophetic books of the *Bible (Old Testament).

amour courtois: *Provençal culture

Amour médecin, L' (1665). Play by *Molière.

amphibrach: *metre in verse

amphimacer: *metre in verse

Amphitryon. Comedy by Plautus based on the Greek legend that Zeus disguised himself as the absent A. in order to seduce his wife; the comedy rests on the confusions caused by A.'s return. The story is the basis of comedies by Dryden, Molière and Giraudoux.

amphora. The standard ancient Greek container for oil or wine. The pots are normally about 18 ins high with 2 handles attached to a narrow neck merging into the body, which has a moulded foot. Fine painted amphorae were sometimes used at funerals and weddings, while a wide-mouthed variety were used as decanters. The a. shape originated during the Mycenaean period.

Amsler Samuel (1791–1849). Swiss engraver who worked in Munich, Germany. His work includes good reproductions of Raphael's paintings and *Triumphal March of Alexander the Great* after a sculpture by his friend B. Thorwaldsen.

Amyot Jacques (1513–93). French scholar who rose from poor origins to be tutor of Charles IX and Henry III of France, and bishop of Auxerre. His vigorous and lucid trs. of Plutarch's *Lives* (1559) strongly influenced French prose and was trs. into English by Sir Thomas *North.

Anabase (1924). Poem by Saint-John *Perse.

Anabasis. Book by *Xenophon.

Anacreon (b. *c.* 570 B.C.). Greek lyric and elegiac poet. His surviving poetry deals for the most part with wine, women (boys) or song and was very popular with 17th-c. European, particularly English, poets. ANACREONTIC VERSE in other literatures has these themes and makes similar use of brief lines in trochaic tetrameter.

anapaest: *metre in verse

Anatomy of Melancholy, The (1621). Book by Robert *Burton.

Ancelot Mme Virginie (née Marguerite-Louise Chardon) (1792–1875). French literary hostess whose *salon* was frequented by many distinguished writers including Stendhal. She wrote *Un Salon de Paris, 1824–1864* (1865).

Anchieta José de (*c.* 1533–97). 'The Apostle of Brazil', Portuguese Jesuit missionary in Brazil, the first to exert any real cultural influence there. He opened a grammar school and compiled a Brazilian grammar and dictionary; he wrote poetry and a play in Portuguese with Brazilian interludes.

Ancient Mariner, The Rime of the (1798). Poem by *Coleridge.

Ancient Music, Concerts of (1776–1848). Concerts, organized by an aristocratic committee in London, at which no music composed in the previous 20 years could be performed. From 1785 they were also known as the 'King's Concerts'; the directors included George III and Prince Albert. 12 concerts a year were given plus a charity performance of Handel's *Messiah*.

Ancients and Moderns Controversy i.e. *Querelle des anciens et des modernes*. French literary controversy in the 2nd half of the 17th c. Boileau, supported by La Fontaine and La Bruyère, held that the literature of classical antiquity had achieved perfection in all forms, and could only be imitated; Desmarets, Charles Perrault and Fontenelle claimed that modern works were superior.

Ancren Wisse or **Riwle** (Guide for Anchoresses or Anchoresses' Rule) (*c.* 1200–50). Prose devotional manual of unknown authorship, written for the guidance of 3 ladies about to become recluses. The Middle English text is probably the original but there are also French and Latin versions. Its sensitivity of thought and balanced style make it the finest piece of prose literature of the period.

Sherwood Anderson: portrait by Steichen

Marian Anderson

Judith Anderson

andante (Italian, 'going'). In music: (1) an indication of a medium to fairly slow, flowing tempo; (2) a composition or movement in that tempo.

Andersen Hans Christian (1805–75). Danish writer of fairy-tales, poet, novelist and playwright. His father, a poor shoemaker, died in 1816, and A.'s childhood was spent in reading and working on a toy theatre. Ambitious to become an opera singer, he went to Copenhagen in 1819, but lived penniless until adopted by a director of the Royal Theatre. His 1st real success as a writer was the novel *Improvisatoren* (1835) based on his experiences during a 2-year stay in Italy. His series of fairy-tales (*Eventyr*) began in 1835, further colls appearing up to 1872. Not immediately popular, these nevertheless soon brought him a European reputation. The tales were based on sagas and folk-tales, freely reworked; A. affected to despise them and his novels and stories, often autobiographical, frequently have as their theme the struggle of genius for recognition.

Anderson Judith (1898–). Australian stage and film actress who went to New York in 1918 and became famous as a tragedienne. She played Lavinia in O'Neill's *Mourning Becomes Electra* (1931), Gertrude in Gielgud's *Hamlet* (New York, 1936), Lady Macbeth (Old Vic, 1937) and *Medea* in Robinson Jeffers's adaptation of Euripides produced by Gielgud (New York, 1947). In films she has played mainly secondary parts.

Anderson Lindsay (1923–). British film director. A left-wing 'committed' film critic, graduate from the magazine *Sequence*, who made a few documentaries like *Every Day Except Christmas* (1957). He worked as a stage director before making *This Sporting Life* (1963), produced by K. *Reisz, taken from the novel by David *Storey.

Anderson Marian (1902–). U.S. Negro singer, a contralto who has gained an international reputation as an opera-star, and in particular as a dramatic interpreter of *Lieder*, e.g. those of Schubert and Mahler.

Anderson Maxwell (1888–1959). U.S. playwright and poet. *What Price Glory?* (1924), about World War I and written with L. Stallings, was his 1st major play and was an overwhelming success. He wrote several historical plays including *Elizabeth the Queen* (1930) and *Mary of Scotland* (1933), both in verse and both dealing with British 16th-c. history, *Joan of Lorraine* (1946) about Joan of Arc and *Barefoot in Athens* (1951) about Socrates. *Both Your Houses* (1933), a prose satire on congressional corruption, and his verse tragedy *Winterset* (1935) on the Sacco-Vanzetti case, were among his works on social and political themes. The musical *Knickerbocker Holiday* (1938) with music by K. Weill, contains the lyric 'September Song'. In *The Essence of Tragedy* (1935) A. enunciated a systematic theory of drama; he insists on moral values, e.g. the protagonist must represent the forces of good in conflict against evil.

Anderson Michael (1920–). British film director. After making 2 financially successful films in Britain, *The Dam Busters* (1955) and *1984* (1956), he was employed by M. *Todd to direct *Around the World in 80 Days* (1956). Since then, he has worked mainly in Hollywood.

Anderson Robert Woodruff (1917–). U.S. playwright, author of *Tea and Sympathy* (1953, film, 1956).

Anderson Sherwood (1876–1941). U.S. writer whose books dealt with the frustrations and neuroses of the machine age. Without warning he left his job and family and settled in Chicago, where he began to write. His 1st success was *Winesburg, Ohio* (1919) about small town life; *Dark Laughter* (1925) contrasted the uninhibited Negro with the tense, neurotic, sterile White. A. hated the machine as a repressive and destructive force and described its rape of a small town's beauty and significance in *Poor White* (1920). He saw a mystical bond between man and nature, and sex as man's liberation from the prison of the machine world. A. also wrote poetry *New Testament* (1927), the novel *Beyond Desire* (1932) and his *Letters* (publ. posth. 1953).

andiron or fire-dog (derivation uncertain). A horizontal metal bar for the support of burning logs, raised on a foot at either end. The forward foot was frequently given an elaborate decorative form and by the 17th c. examples in brass, enamel and even silver are known. 'Creepers' are a smaller support.

Andokides painter. Greek vase painter in the *red-figured style.

Andirons, gilt-bronze, 18th c.

Andokides painter.
Heracles coaxing Cerberus (detail)

Andrea del Sarto.
Madonna delle Arpie (detail)

Ivo Andřic

Andromache. *Leavetaking of Hector from Andromache.* Chalcidian krater, *c.* 540 B.C.

Andrea del Castagno: *Castagno

Andrea del Sarto '*senza errori*', 'the faultless painter' (1486–1531). Florentine painter with feeling for tone and colour characteristic of the Venetian rather than the Florentine school. Invited by Francis I to Paris (1518) he returned to Florence (1519) to his wife. His life and works were much studied and admired in the 19th c. and Browning's poem *Andrea del Sarto* was a sensitive and acceptable picture of a gifted, irresolute and reflective man. A.'s frescoes *Birth of the Virgin* (1514) and *Madonna del Sacco* (1525), both in SS Annunziata church, Florence, are perfect examples of the high Renaissance. Other major works include *Madonna delle Arpie* (1517, Uffizi), classical in style, and the Holy Family was a favourite theme. Among his pupils were the mannerists J. da *Pontormo and G. B. Rosso.

Andres Stefan (1906–). German poet, playwright and novelist whose themes are inspired by his Catholicism. His short novel *Wir Sind Utopia* (1942; *We are Utopia*, 1955) was his 1st success, consolidated by the trilogy *Die Sintflut* (1949–59).

Andrewes Lancelot (1555–1626). English divine and from 1618 bishop of Winchester. He was distinguished as a scholar and preacher and is remembered for his *Private Devotions* written in Greek and Latin but publ. first in English (1647). One of the panel of trs for the Authorized Version of the Bible.

Andreyev Leonid Nikolayevich (1871–1919). Russian writer, notably of fantastic, macabre, and pessimistic short stories. He and Artsybashev replaced Gorki as the most popular and representative Russian authors between the revolutions of 1905 and 1917; their spiritual nihilism reflects the decline of optimism among the intelligentsia after the failure of the 1st revolution. A.'s best stories include *Thought*, *The Red Laugh* and *The Curse of the Beast.*

Andřic Ivo (1892–). Yugoslav writer, Nobel prizewinner, 1961. *Ex Ponto* (1918) draws on his experiences as a political prisoner in World War I. He spent the inter-war years in the Yugoslav diplomatic corps and wrote mainly poems and short stories. During World War II he publ., in Belgrade, his epic trilogy of the South Slavic Balkans. Its 1st vol. *Na Drini Cuprija* (1945; *The Bridge over the Drina*, 1948) brought international recognition.

Andriessen. Family of Dutch musicians: WILLEM (1887–) director of the Amsterdam Conservatory and composer; his brother HENDRIK (1892–) director of The Hague Conservatory and composer of much church music; and Hendrik's son JURRIAAN (1925–) whose compositions include the chamber work *Homage to Milhaud.*

Androcles and the Lion (1913). Play by G. B. Shaw.

Andromache. Play by Euripides; its sensational plot turns on the fate of A., widow of the Trojan hero Hector and now a Greek slave. Racine wrote a play on the subject.

Andrzejewski Jerzy (1909–). Polish novelist, author of *Popiól i diament* (1948; *Ashes and Diamonds*, 1962) a realistic novel dealing with the moral and political problems of post-war Poland. *Bramy raju* (1960; *The Gates of Paradise*, 1963) is both a deeply poetical account of the 13th-c. Children's crusade, and a philosophical parable.

Aneirin (Aneurin) (*fl. c.* A.D. 600) Welsh bardic poet and writer of the *Gododin*, which tells of the Saxon victory at Cattraeth over the Britons of Strathclyde. A.'s works survive in a 13th-c. ms.

Anerio Felice (*c.* 1560–1614) was Palestrina's successor in the post of composer to the papal chapel. Both he and his brother GIOVANNI FRANCESCO (1567–1630) wrote in the style of Palestrina.

Angel Exterminador, El (1962). Film directed by L. *Buñuel.

Angelico, Fra (Giovanni da Fiesole) (*c.* 1387–1455). Italian painter celebrated for his frescoes in the convent of S. Marco, Florence. In 1407 he entered the Dominican convent of S. Domenico, Fiesole, near Florence, of which he was later prior (1449–52). Papal politics forced the community to leave Fiesole (1409–18) and some time after their return A. began to paint; nothing is known about his early training but he shows the influence of such international Gothic painters as Lorenzo Monaco. He executed (*c.* 1428–33) an altarpiece (extensively

Fra Angelico. *Coronation of the Virgin*

altered by Lorenzo di Credi, *c.* 1501) and 3 frescoes (*sala capitolare* of the convent; Hermitage, Leningrad; Louvre) for his own convent and an *Annunciation* (Museo de Gesù, Cortona) for the church of S. Domenico, Cortona; these foreshadow the simplicity of his mature work. In 1433 he was commissioned to paint the 'Linaiuoli' or Linenworkers' triptych (Museo di S. Marco, Florence) particularly famous for the 12 angels playing on musical instruments which decorate the frame surrounding the central figures of the Virgin and Child. 2 triptychs, painted after this for the churches of S. Domenico, Cortona and Perugia (Gal. Nazionale, Perugia) in the Gothic style, show that A. was attempting to break with the conventions of this form of altarpiece. In 1436 Cosimo de' Medici commissioned A. to paint 3 altarpieces including the high altar for the Dominican convent of S. Marco, Florence–*Virgin and Child Enthroned with SS Cosmas and Damian* (1438–40; Museo di S. Marco, Florence). In these and the slightly earlier *Coronation of the Virgin* for Fiesole (Louvre) the figures of saints and angels recede towards the central figure, marking a step in the development of the *sacra conversazione* altarpiece. A. also uses single panels instead of the triptych and completely abandons the Gothic gold background; in the S. Marco altarpiece he introduces landscape background. The predella scenes for this altarpiece from the lives of SS Cosmas and Damian (N.G., Washington; Alte Pina., Munich; N.G., Dublin; Louvre; Museo di S. Marco) illustrate A.'s excellence as a colourist and are his most lively narrative paintings. A. began, about this time, to supervise the painting of 50 frescoes of scenes from the life of Christ for the cells of the convent of S. Marco; he himself probably painted not more than 10. Their setting and purpose, which was not decorative but to act as an aid to meditation, were ideally suited to the direct and simple piety characteristic of A.'s painting. Those by him are the most straightforward and hence most effectively fulfil their purpose. In 1447 he was in Orvieto where he painted *The Last Judgement* (Orvieto cathedral), finished by Signorelli, and in Rome executing decorative work in the Vatican for Pope Nicholas V. Only his frescoes in the chapel of Nicholas V (1447/8) survive. In keeping with their setting these are richer and more complex than any of A.'s previous work. A. died in Rome. Much of A.'s work refers back to Giotto and he took no part in the artistic experiments and secular interests of his contemporaries, although he utilized new visual techniques such as perspective if they served the devotional purpose of his painting. Benozzo Gozzoli was his pupil.

Fra Angelico. *Deposition*

Angel Pavement (1930). Novel by J. B. Priestley.

Angelus, The (1859). Painting by J.-F. Millet.

Angelus Silesius. Name adopted at his conversion to Catholicism by Johann Scheffler (1624–77), German poet and mystic. His *Cherubinischer Wandersmann . . .* (1674; *The Spiritual Maxims of Angelus Silesius*, 1914), influenced by Jakob Böhme, is a coll. of distichs epigrammatic in form and on mystical themes.

Angers David d': Pierre-Jean *David

Angerstein John Julius (1735–1823). British merchant and art coll. of Russian origin. 38 of his pictures, purchased for the nation in 1824, were the basis for the N.G., London.

Anges du Péché, Les (1943). Film directed by R. *Bresson.

Angiolini Gasparo (1731–1803). Italian composer and choreographer, ballet master in Vienna and St Petersburg. He was an exponent of *ballet d'action* and developed it in his choreography for Gluck's *Don Juan* (1761). He tried to revive ancient Roman ballet pantomime in *Sémiramis* (1765) by Gluck. A. opposed J.-G. Noverre's custom of summarizing ballets in programme notes and wrote the important *Lettere . . . a Monsieur Noverre* (1773).

Anglican chant. Method of psalm singing used in the Church of England.

Anglo-Saxon Chronicle. Old English historical record, recounting events in English history, from the 5th to 12th cs. Begun in the 9th c., it may have been inspired by Alfred the Great. The chronology of the earlier annals is disputed but from the 10th c. it is a basic source. Outstanding literary passages are the verse annal for 937 (*Battle of Brunanburh*) and the prose account of sufferings in the civil war under Stephen.

Anglo-Venetian glass. In the 16th and the earlier part of the 17th cs a number of emigrant Italian glass-workers set up houses in various

The Angelus

Anglo-Venetian glass, 16th c.

Fra Angelico. *San Lorenzo distributing alms*

Animal style. Part of a silver-gilt brooch from Galsted

Animal style. Ostrogothic gold cloisonné brooch (*c.* 500)

Animal style. Bronze belt-buckle (2nd c.) from Hontheim

Ansbach porcelain figure

Jean Anouilh

European countries, including England, where the Venetian Jacopo Verzelini (1522–1606) is said to have begun producing glass in 1571. These glasses in the Venetian style often had moulded knops, diamond-engraving and decorative 'wings' on the stems.

Angry Young Men. Term loosely applied to some British writers, including Kingsley *Amis, John *Osborne, John *Wain and Colin *Wilson, who became known in the 1950s and were felt to have in common a hostile attitude to existing society and institutions.

animal carpets: *hunting carpets

Animal Crackers (1930). Film with the *Marx Brothers.

Animal Farm (1945). Novel by George *Orwell.

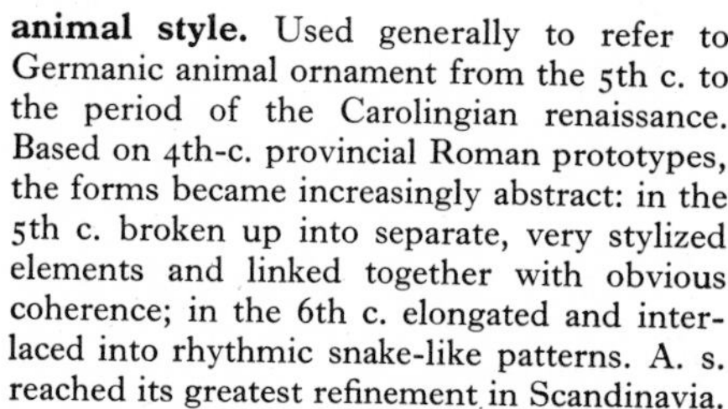

animal style. Used generally to refer to Germanic animal ornament from the 5th c. to the period of the Carolingian renaissance. Based on 4th-c. provincial Roman prototypes, the forms became increasingly abstract: in the 5th c. broken up into separate, very stylized elements and linked together with obvious coherence; in the 6th c. elongated and interlaced into rhythmic snake-like patterns. A. s. reached its greatest refinement in Scandinavia.

animated film. Any film in which the illusion of movement is artificially produced, whether with drawings (cartoons), figurines, cut-outs, or non-representational shapes and objects. *Disney, *Hubley, *Trnka, *MacLaren, *Reiniger, *Alexeieff, for various techniques of a. f.

Animuccia Giovanni (*c.* 1500–71). Italian composer; musical director at the Vatican and a friend of St Philip Neri, for whom he composed church music.

Anker Larsen Johannes (1874–1957). Danish writer. His novels reflect a love of the Danish countryside but also the religious crisis of their author; best known is *De Vises Sten* (1923; *The Philosopher's Stone,* 1924).

Anna Christie (1921). Play by Eugene *O'Neill.

Anna Karenina (1875–7). Novel by *Tolstoy.

Annales Cambriae. Ancient Latin annals of Welsh history, a source of the Arthurian legend. The compiler is unknown and the earliest extant ms. late 10th c.

annealing. Glass, when manufactured by hand or machinery, is subjected to much shaping and uneven cooling. This sets up internal strains and stresses which make the glass brittle and therefore impractical for normal use. To overcome these stresses the glass object, when finished, is annealed, i.e. placed in a heated chamber or tunnel called a 'lehr' or 'leer' and cooled gradually.

Année Dernière à Marienbad, L' (1961). Film directed by A. *Resnais.

Annensky Innokenti Fyodorovich (1856–1909). Russian poet; his restraint and precision influenced the *acmeist revolt against symbolism.

Annigoni Pietro (1910–). Italian painter and society portraitist, e.g. of British royalty.

Annonce faite à Marie, L' (1912) Poetic drama by Claudel.

Annual Register, The (1758–). English review of current affairs and the arts founded by R. *Dodsley and publ. by R. and J. Dodsley. Burke had close editorial associations with *The A. R.* for about 30 years after its inauguration.

Annus Mirabilis (1667). Poem by *Dryden.

Anouilh Jean (1910–). French playwright. A.'s comedies have a strong element of fantasy,

Ernest Ansermet

Antelami. *Adoration of the Kings*

e.g. *L'Invitation au Château* (1947; *Ring Round The Moon*, 1950) and *Valse des Toreadors* (1952; 1957). Of his 'black plays', many deal with the impossibility of the survival of integrity, and their protagonists–often girls–choose death rather than submit to the lies and compromises needed in life. This theme runs through *Eurydice* (1942; 1951) and *Antigone* (1943; 1951), reworkings of the classical stories; and *L'Alouette* (1953; *The Lark*, 1955), about Joan of Arc. Works include *Pauvre Bitos* (1956; 1958), revealing the elements of pride and resentment in 'incorruptibility'; *La Répétition* (1950; *The Rehearsal*, 1952) after Marivaux; and *Becket* (1959; 1960), a study loosely based on 12th-c. English history.

À nous la liberté (1932). Film directed by René *Clair.

Anquetil-Duperron Abraham Hyacinthe (1731–1805). French orientalist. His version of the *Zend-Avesta, Ouvrage de Zoroaster* (1771) was the 1st European trs. Schopenhauer derived his knowledge of Indian philosophy from *Oupnek'hat* (1801–2), A.-D.'s trs. of the 4 principal Upanishads.

Ansbach. Town in Bavaria. Factories here produced some of the best German faïence, especially *c.* 1730–50, when work in the **famille verte* style was made, and later fine porcelain *c.* 1765–85.

Ansermet Ernest (1883–). Swiss conductor and founder of the Orchestre de la Suisse Romande. A.'s major importance is as an interpreter and theorist of modern music, especially Stravinsky's. He did much work with Diaghilev's ballet co.

Anstey Christopher (1724–1805). English poet. His *New Bath Guide* (1766), verse letters mainly in anapaests, is a humorous description of manners.

Anstey Edgar (1907–). A key figure in the British documentary film movement. He worked for the GPO Film Unit, organized the Shell Film Unit (1934–5), was director of productions for *March of Time* (1936–8). During the war he produced documentaries for the government and he now runs British Transport Films. As a director, his most significant work is *Housing Problems* (1935), made with A. *Elton. This pioneered the interview form now the stock-in-trade of television.

Anstey F. Pseud. of Thomas Anstey Guthrie (1856–1934), English comic novelist relying on the fantastic and magical for many effects. Books include *Vice Versa* (1882), *The Man from Blankley's* (1893) and *The Brass Bottle* (1900).

answer: *fugue

Antelami Benedetto (12th c.). Northern Italian Romanesque sculptor. He executed a relief of the *Deposition* (1178) and other work in Parma cathedral.

Antheil George (1900–59). U.S. pianist and composer whose *Zingareska* (Berlin, 1922) was one of the 1st orchestral pieces to use jazz elements. Other works: 6 symphonies, including the 'Jazz' (1926), 6 operas including *Transatlantic* (1929) and *Volpone* (1950), the *Ballet mécanique* (Paris, 1926), scored for xylophones, electric bells, 10 pianos and player-piano, much film music and an autobiography *The Bad Boy of Music* (1945).

anthem. Short choral composition used in the services of the Anglican Church and in effect the English descendant of the *motet. Set to words, usually not a part of the liturgy, the a. may be accompanied or unaccompanied, with or without solo passages; with solo passages it is called a 'verse', without it is called a 'full' a.

Anthemius of Tralles (*fl.* 1st half of 6th c. A.D.). One of the architects of *S. Sophia, Constantinople.

anthology (from Greek, 'garland'). A selected coll. of verse or prose. The so-called Greek A., which reached its final form in the middle ages, is a coll. of Greek epigrams, etc. The pieces were selected from various earlier colls such as the *Garland* of Meleager (*c.* 90 B.C.) and the Palatine A. (10th c. A.D.).

anti-bacchius: *metre in verse

anti-cerne (French *cerne*, 'outline'). The opposite of a black outline; it is a contour effected by leaving a bare strip of ground between two or more areas of colour.

Antic Hay (1923). Novel by Aldous Huxley.

anti-climax. In the arts the term is used of a climax which fails to achieve its expected intensity either by reason of the author's calculated intention or his incompetence.

Antigone (441 B.C.). Tragedy by *Sophocles. A. is the daughter of *Oedipus. Her brother Polyneices has been killed in an attack on Thebes and denied burial by Creon, Oedipus' successor as king of Thebes. A. defies him by performing the funerary rites over Polyneices' body and is condemned to be buried alive. Under pressure Creon reverses his decision, but too late: A. kills herself, and her death causes that of her betrothed, Haemon, Creon's son, and Creon's wife Eurydice. A. is the subject of plays by Euripides (of which only fragments survive), Alfieri, Cocteau and Anouilh.

anti-hero. Critical term, which gained currency in the 1950s, for a protagonist of play or book who ultimately has the author's sympathy but not the traditional virtues of the 'hero'.

Antill John Henry (1904–). Australian composer of stage works, e.g. the ballet *Corroboree* (1947) and the opera *Endymion*. He also wrote a cantata *The Song of Hagar*.

antiphon. In the divine offices of the Roman Catholic Church, a brief passage, often from the psalms, intoned or sung before and after the

Antonello. *Portrait of a Young Man*

Antwerp mannerists. *The Calling of St Matthew* (attributed to Coninxloo)

psalm itself. The a. is sung as responses either between single voice and choir or opposing choirs, hence ANTIPHONAL used of music, instrumental or choral, performed thus.

Antiquary, The (1816). Historical novel by Sir Walter Scott.

Antiquities of Athens, The (1762). Book by James *Stuart and Nicholas Revett.

antistrophe (Greek, 'turning about'). That part of a Greek choral ode sung by the chorus as it turned and moved in the opposite direction in response to the *strophe. Both strophe and a. are in the same metre. A. in rhetoric can either mean the repetition of words in inverse order or the turning of an opponent's plea against him.

Antonio and Rosario

Antonello da Messina (*c.* 1430–79). Sicilian painter. In Naples he saw work by Netherlandish artists and may have studied under Colantonio, whose style was based on that of J. van Eyck. He learnt van Eyck's method of oil painting and achieved a delicate synthesis between the Northern and Italian styles. Working in Venice (1475) he passed his knowledge on to G. *Bellini, altering his manner of painting and through him exercising great influence on the development of the Venetian school. His paintings include *St Sebastian* (G. Gal., Dresden), *Crucifixion*, *Portrait of a Young Man*, *St Jerome in his study* (all N.G., London) and *Condottiere* (Louvre).

Antonio (born A. Ruiz Soler) (1922–). Spanish dancer who began his career in 1928 with his cousin Rosario as partner. They later toured the world, making their American début in 1940 and London in 1951. His finest dance is a *zapateado*; he formed his own co. in 1953.

Antonio Nicolas (1617–84). Spanish bibliographer. His *Bibliotheca Hispana vetus* (posth. 1696) and *Bibliotheca . . . nova* (1672), formed an exhaustive and scholarly catalogue of Spanish literature from the time of the Roman emperor Augustus to 1670.

Antonioni Michelangelo (1912–). Italian film director. A. is a N. Italian, ascetic rather than exuberant, whose aim has been to use the resources of the cinema systematically to demonstrate and analyse emotional situations. This has led him in his latest films, particularly *L'Eclisse* (1962), into a certain falseness through using action and camera to be expressive rather than convincing. Apart from his 7 short documentaries (1943–50), his work has been very uniform in direction. His best features are his first, *Cronaca di un amore* (1950), *Le Amiche* (1955) and *L'Avventura* (1960). The strong visual style and elliptical manner of these has been widely imitated. *Deserto Rosso* (1964) attempts to break away from his usual theme of the instability of normal emotions by dealing with mental illness. It is in colour, used non-realistically.

Anton Ulrich Duke of Brunswick-Wofenbüttel (1633–1714). The most gifted German prince of his time and friend of Leibnitz. He wrote odes, opera libretti and the novels *Die durchläuchtige Syrerin Aramena* (5 vols, 1669–73) and *Römische Octavia* (6 vols, 1677–85), the finest examples of the German baroque courtly novel.

Antony and Cleopatra (publ. 1623). Tragedy by *Shakespeare, written *c.* 1606. Its source was Sir Thomas *North's trs. of Plutarch.

Antwerp mannerists. Group of Antwerp painters of the early 16th c. whose work is characterized by Italianate ornamentation and affected attitudes. Unconnected with later *mannerism.

Anzengruber Ludwig (1839–89). Austrian playwright, short-story writer and novelist. Peasant life, his family background, formed the setting for many of his plays. He attacked bigoted conventional attitudes and his attempt to develop a form of dialogue suited to realistic drama influenced G. Hauptmann. Of his best plays *Der Pfarrer von Kirchfeld* (1870) attacks religious fanaticism, and *Das vierte Gebot* (1877) parental tyranny. His novels include *Der Sternsteinhof* (1885).

Aparajito (1957). Film directed by S. *Ray.

Apel Willi (1893–). U.S. musicologist of German origin (emigrated to America, 1936). A. has publ. much important work on medieval music and also *Historical Anthology of Music* (2 vols, 1947–50).

Apelles (*fl.* mid 4th c. B.C.). Greek painter who studied near Corinth under Pamphilos.

Antonioni. *L'Avventura*

Apocalypse tapestries

Apocalypse carvings at Rheims cathedral. Also *Amman

He became court painter to Alexander the Great, whose portrait he alone was permitted to paint. His reputation rests simply on literary references since none of his paintings nor his treatise on painting survive.

Apes of God, The (1930). Satirical novel by Wyndham *Lewis.

Aphrodite, Cnidian. Statue by *Praxiteles (originally at Cnidus in Asia Minor) of the Greek goddess of love, beauty and fertility.

ApIvor Denis (1916–). Irish composer of Welsh parentage. Most of his works employ the 12-note method; they include *Six Songs of . . . Lorca* (1946), the cantata (not 12 note) *The Hollow Men* (1939, revised 1946) after T. S. Eliot, the ballets *A Mirror for Witches* (1952), *Blood Wedding* (1953) and *Veneziana* (1953) and the opera *Yerma* (1957/8) based on Lorca.

Apocalypse, The i.e. *The Revelation of St John the Divine* (*c.* A.D. 96). The last book of the New Testament, written during the persecution of the Christians by Domitian and variously attributed. The book deals with what must soon take place at a time when the end of the world was thought to be imminent. There have been numerous subsequent interpretations. The imagery contains elements from Jewish apocalyptic, Persian and Babylonian mythology and Greco-Roman astrology. The writer sees the 7 seals of a scroll broken in the heavenly court by the Lamb (Christ). This is accompanied by other visions including that of the 4 horsemen: a victorious warrior on a white horse, War on a red horse, Famine on a black horse and Death on a pale horse with Hell following behind. The opening of the 7th seal ushers in a series of catastrophes–war in heaven, the appearance of a blaspheming beast (Antichrist) men are compelled to worship–before the establishment of a 'new heaven and a new earth'.

Most famous of the works of art illustrating The A. are the APOCALYPSE TAPESTRIES (begun 1376), a set of hangings commissioned by Louis I, Duke of Anjou, woven in wool by N. Bataille from cartoons by Hennequin of Bruges and now preserved in the château at Angers. The original size is estimated at 156 yds by 6 yds, of which survive about 70 scenes and fragments.

Other works include frescoes by Cimabue in the upper church at Assisi, Italy, a sculptured doorway in Rheims cathedral, and an altarpiece by Master Bertram (V. and A., London). From the 8th to the 14th c. cycles of illustrated mss of The A. were immensely popular in Europe; *Dürer did a series of 15 woodcuts (*c.* 1498).

apocalyptic literature. A type of Jewish, and later of Christian, literature *c.* 200 B.C.–*c.* A.D. 350, which claimed to reveal the divine purpose for the future. A. l. characteristically uses symbolic numbers or beasts, etc., to represent nations or persons and the device of pseud. authorship–contemporary events being described in the guise of prophetic utterances by a revered ancient, e.g. the canonical book of *Daniel* (written *c.* 165 B.C. but purporting to be by Daniel 400 years earlier). *The Assumption of Moses* (early 1st c. A.D.), *The Apocalypse of Peter* (*c.* 100–140) and of *Paul* (*c.* 388) are examples of the large extra-canonical a. l.

Apocrypha. The A. proper is a group of books written between 200 B.C. and A.D. 50 which were included by St Jerome in his Vulgate but are omitted from the Protestant Bible; controversy over their canonicity began in the 4th c. The A. throws light on the period between the end of the Old Testament and the beginning of the New. *The Wisdom of Solomon* and *Ecclesiasticus* are books of the A. The adjective apocryphal is also used of a large para-Biblical literature (accepted by no Biblical canon) which includes the Gospels of Peter and Thomas and the 'Teaching of the 12 Apostles'. This apocryphal literature was the source for much medieval folk-lore and art.

Apollinaire Guillaume. The adopted name of Wilhelm Apollinaris de Kostrowitsky (1880–1918). French poet (naturalized 1914) of Polish-Italian parentage. A. went to Paris in 1898, becoming a leader of the revolutionary artistic and literary movements there. In 1908 he joined the Groupe du *Bateau-Lavoir centred upon Picasso and Braque and the same year introduced Léger to the group. With publ. in 1913 of his poems *Alcools* and the essay *Les Peintres cubistes* (*Cubist Painters* in *Documents of Modern Art*, vol. i, ed. R. Motherwell, 1944) his importance as poet and publicist became obvious. His poetry broke with all traditions and disciplines, in subject-matter, style, punctuation and typography and *Les Peintres cubistes* helped define the new school in painting. Works include his collected poems

The Cnidian Aphrodite

Apollinaire: caricature by Picasso (1905)

Apollo Belvedere

Calligrammes (1918) and the play *Les Mamelles de Tirésias* (1917) which he described as '*une drame surréaliste*'. A. christened *orphism and A. Breton and P. Soupault adopted the term *surrealism in homage to him.

Apollo Belvedere. Roman copy of a 4th-c. B.C. Greek statue; it influenced Michelangelo and other Renaissance artists, and is the most famous statue of this Greek god, who is always represented as the ideal of manly beauty. Others are the Etruscan A. from Veil (*c.* 510 B.C.; Mus. N. di Villa Giulia, Rome) and the A. from the W. pediment of the temple of Zeus, Olympia (*c.* 460 B.C.; Mus., Olympia).

Apollodoros (5th c. B.C.). Greek painter famous for panel as opposed to wall paintings and called '*skiagraphos*' ('the shadow painter') because he introduced shading into his work to achieve more naturalistic effects. He also experimented with foreshortening.

Apollodorus of Damascus (*c.* 60–*c.* 130). Greek architect brought by Trajan to Rome where he designed the forum of Trajan (112–13). He also built baths and a circus in Rome. He was banished and put to death by Hadrian.

Apollonius Rhodius (3rd c. B.C.). Greek poet and librarian at Alexandria. His epic *Argonautica* is distinguished by its subtle adaptation of Homeric vocabulary and by the sensitive portrayal of Medea's love for Jason (book 3), but marred by excessive erudition. It provoked the dispute with *Callimachus over the viability of the epic form.

Apologia pro Vita sua (1864). Book by J. H. *Newman.

Apologie for Poetrie, The (1595). Essay by Sir Philip *Sidney.

apology (Greek απολογια, 'defence'). A written or spoken defence of the writer's or speaker's opinions or actions, e.g. Plato's *Apology*, an account of Socrates' defence before his judges, and J. H. Newman's *Apologia pro Vita sua*, an attempt to justify his conversion to Roman Catholicism.

Apostel Hans Erich (1901–). Viennese composer; an early disciple of Schoenberg's and a friend and pupil of Berg's. His work makes extensive but not rigorous use of 12-note methods.

apostle spoons. The end of the stem of a spoon was in England from the mid 14th c. to late Tudor times, frequently fashioned into such devices as acorns, lions sejant, owls, boars' heads, a female bust (known as a maidenhead), or geometric shapes. Sets of 13 spoons in silver with figure ends showing Christ and the Apostles, each bearing an identifying symbol, were especially popular, although no complete set is now known dating from before the 16th c. The modern a. s. is usually based on a simple cloaked masculine form without identifying symbol.

Appalachian Spring. Ballet with music by Copland and choreography by Martha Graham; 1st performance in Washington in 1944.

Appassionata (Italian, 'impassioned'). The name given by its publ. to Beethoven's piano sonata in F min. op. 57 (1804).

Appel Karel (1921–). Dutch painter. He travelled widely in Europe, becoming in 1948 a leader in the Amsterdam experimental group which, in 1949, became the international Cobra group. A. has been influenced by Picasso and primitive and naïve art which has contributed to the formation of his personal abstract style. He settled in Paris in 1950 and has had several important commissions, e.g. a fresco for the Stedelijk Mus., Amsterdam (1951) and a mural for Unesco in 1958.

Apple Cart, The (1929). Play by G. B. *Shaw.

appoggiatura. Motif in musical *ornamentation.

Après-Midi d'un Faune, L'. (1) Poem by S. Mallarmé written in 1876; (2) a piece of music by Debussy; (3) a 1-act ballet based on Debussy's music with choreography by Nijinsky, and décor by Bakst; 1st performance 1912.

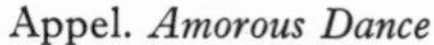

Appel. *Amorous Dance*

L'Après-Midi d'un Faune. Nijinsky

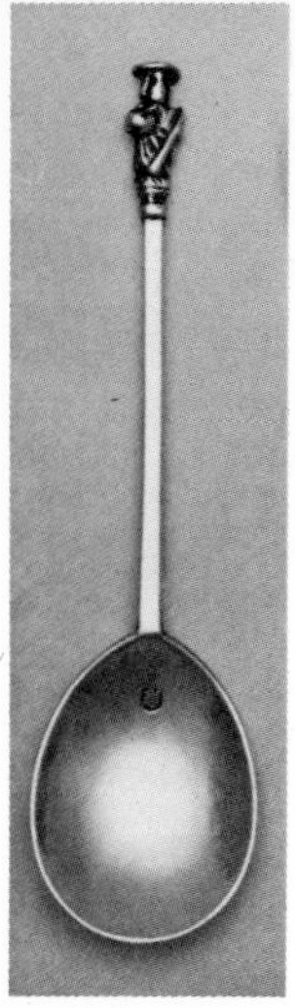

Apostle spoon. London, 1599

Apron stage. Copy of Jan de Witt's drawing of the Swan Theatre, 1596

Apuleius. Head from a 4th-c. medallion

Apuleius. From a 16th-c. ed. of *The Golden Ass*

Aprile Giuseppe (1732–1813). Italian castrato singer, composer and teacher; D. Cimarosa was for a time his pupil.

apron stage. An important feature of the *Elizabethan stage; now applied to any large forestage in a theatre, on which the action is thus seen without the frame of the *proscenium arch. 20th-c. experimental theatre design frequently seeks to adapt the a. s. and exploit its possibilities, and *theatre in the round is one outcome of this.

apse. In architecture, a sanctuary, semicircular or polygonal in plan and with a domed roof, at the end of choir or aisle in a church. Diagram *basilica.

Apt Ulrich or Abt, the Elder. Late 15th- to early 16th-c. German painter. His works include the *Matthäus Altarpiece* and the dramatic and experimental *Lamentation over the Dead Christ*, both in Munich. The *Portrait of a Young Man* (Berlin), discovered in the 19th c., was remarkably like A.'s work but showed the initials 'L.S.' on a piece of armour. A.'s best works were reattributed to 'L.S.' until it was recently shown that the initials were simply those of the armourer.

Apuleius (b. *c.* A.D. 125). Latin writer born in N. Africa. He wrote verse, philosophical tracts, an *Apologia* in his own defence against a charge of sorcery and the only complete surviving Latin novel, the *Metamorphoses* (*The Bookes of the Golden Asse*, 1566). This story of the adventures of a young philosopher magically turned into an ass contains, besides the famous story of *Cupid and Psyche*, much curious and hermetic lore which shows the cast of A.'s mind and the preoccupations of his age.

aquarelle (French, 'watercolour'). A painting executed in transparent watercolour. The term is sometimes applied to delicate music.

aquatint. Artistic technique: *engraving.

Aquinas Thomas (*c.* 1225–74). Canonized 1323. The greatest Catholic theologian, A., born in S. Italy, gave the Church a systematic, rationalistic account of theology in the light of the Aristotelian system. In *Summa contra Gentiles* and *Summa Theologica* he set out the celebrated 5 'proofs' of God's existence, the basic premise of which is the notion of a First Cause, itself an explanation of the apparently infinite chain of cause and effect. The late 19th c. witnessed a revival of Thomist philosophy under Leo XIII which developed into an important intellectual movement.

arabesque. A decorative pattern used, for example, in pilaster decoration, consisting of usually symmetrical intertwining foliage, scroll-work, figures and other motifs derived from Roman grotesques. In ballet the name is given to a number of positions resembling arrested flight. Sometimes also used of a short decorative piece of music.

Arabia Deserta, Travels in (1888). Book by C. M. *Doughty.

Arabian Nights' Entertainments, The or *The Thousand and One Nights* (Literal trs. 'A Thousand Nights and a Night'). A famous Arabic coll. of popular stories from India and the Middle East. Since at least the 9th c. A.D. tales have accumulated within the frame story. A king discovers that his wife has been regularly unfaithful; he thereafter marries and kills a new wife each day. Determined to stop the slaughter Scheherazade, the vizier's daughter, marries the king. She tells a tale each evening always promising to finish it if she is alive the following day; each time the king postpones her execution and finally relents. The French trs. of A. *Galland (d. 1715) was the 1st European version. The best-known English version was Sir Richard *Burton's (1885).

Aragon Louis (1897–). French poet, novelist and journalist. He was associated with dadaism, was joint ed. of the review *Littérature* and a pioneer of surrealism in literature, later expounding its theories in *Traité du style* (1928). In 1930 he became a militant Communist. In 1931 he wrote the insurrectionary poem *Front rouge* (*The Red Front*, 1933) and quarrelled with the surrealists. He began to write social realist novels, e.g. *Les cloches de Bâle* (1934; *The Bells of Basel*, 1938). During World War II he was a prominent member of the Resistance and

Aquinas: *Thomas Triumphant* by F. Traini (*c.* 1340)

Arabesque. Woodcarving at Claydon House, Buckinghamshire

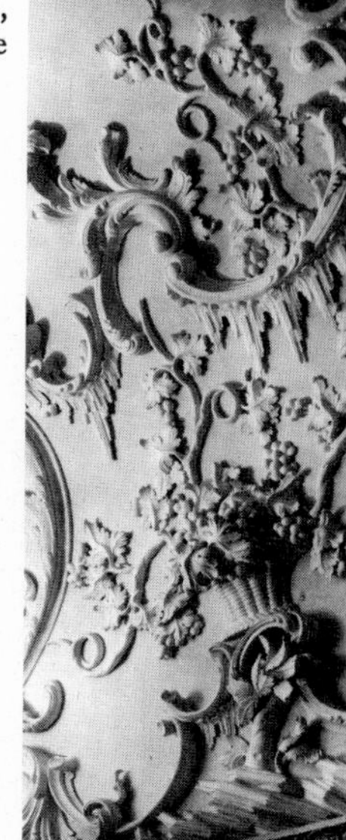

Louis Aragon

Archaic. A marble *kore*, *c.* 510 B.C., showing the characteristic 'archaic smile'. See also colour plate 3

CANTVS
IL TERZO LIBRO DE I MADRIGALI NOVISSIMI
di archadelt a quattro voci insieme con alchuni di constantio festa & altri dieci bellissimi
a voci mudare novamente ristampati con nova gionta & nova correctione.
.A. G.
M. D. XLIIII
Venetiis apud antonium gardane

Arcadelt. Title-page for a book of madrigals

Thomas Archer. St Paul's, Deptford

their representative poet; he wrote *Le Crève-cœur* (1941), *Les yeux d'Elsa* (1942) and *Le Musée Grévin* (1943). After the war he ed. the Communist newspaper *Ce Soir* until 1953.

Arany János (1817–82). One of the greatest Hungarian poets of the 19th c. A. raised 'naïve realism' to artistic perfection in his epic *Toldi* trilogy (1847–54; selections trs. 1914). His ballads possess a tragic, sometimes visionary atmosphere and dramatic expression. A. never wholly recovered from the shock caused by the failure of the 1848 War of Independence; the bulk of his works was written amidst struggles and discord. His vol. *Öszikék*, a fine lyrical account of his impressions in old age, was posth. publ. A.'s trs of Shakespeare's plays, e.g. *Hamlet* (1867), are among the best in the language.

Arblay Frances d': Fanny *Burney

Arbuthnot John (1667–1735). Scottish physician, satirist and poet who settled in London, where he became a friend of Swift and Pope. He created the figure of John Bull, the typical Englishman, in a series of pamphlets coll. as *The History of John Bull* (1712) and was the principal author of the satirical *Memoirs of Martinus Scriblerus*.

arcade. Architectural term for a row of arches carrying a roof and supported by columns or piers. BLANK OR BLIND ARCADING is used of rows of small arches built against a wall for decorative purposes.

Arcadelt Jakob (*c.* 1514–before 72). Flemish composer who worked first at the papal court but moved in 1555 to Paris. A. wrote fine church music but his 250 madrigals (1539–44), among the earliest examples of the form, were his greatest achievement. A. also cultivated the French *chanson*.

Arcadia. Geographically a district of the Peloponnese; in literature an ideal pastoral utopia which appears first in the works of Ovid and Virgil and came again to the fore in the Renaissance with the work of Poliziano and above all Sannazaro. Sir Philip Sidney's *Arcadia* (1590) continues the theme and in the 17th c. Poussin's famous painting of shepherds in an Arcadian landscape around a tomb inscribed *Et in Arcadia Ego* gave a new twist to the idea of A. The theme found its final, most exaggerated expression in the Swiss 'dairy' at the Versailles of Louis XVI.

arcanist (from Latin, *arcanum*, 'a secret'). In the 18th c. a title adopted by workmen who professed to know the secrets of *porcelain manufacture and other techniques. Many a.s were impostors but the term was also used of factory employees using the secret processes.

arch. Architectural term for a (usually) curved structure bridging an opening. The simplest kind of a. is the ROUND OR SEMICIRCULAR a. with a semicircle of *voussoirs; some other important types are the SEGMENTAL a., which has a curve lower than that of a semicircular a.; the HORSE-SHOE a., which may be round or pointed but has a diameter at some point wider than the opening to be spanned; the STILTED a., in which the impost is some way below the springing-line, giving the impression that the top parts of the supporting pillars or walls belong to the arch; the OGEE a., each side of which has 2 curves, the higher concave, the lower convex, i.e. the whole is roughly onion-shaped; and the SQUINCH a., which is used to erect a dome or octagonal spire over a rectangular space, the a. being thrown diagonally across the corners of the rectangle. Also *TRIUMPHAL a.

archaic. In Greek art, the period *c.* 700–480 B.C., especially in sculpture, e.g. the *kouroi* and *korai* (nude youths and draped girls) from the Acropolis. Figures are stiff and formalized (Egyptian influence) gradually becoming more naturalistic. In vase painting the a. period includes Corinthian, Attic black-figure and the earliest red-figure, in architecture early Doric (e.g. Paestum) and early Ionic (e.g. 1st temple of Artemis at Ephesus).

Archduke trio, The. Nickname subsequently given to *Beethoven's trio in B♭ op. 97, for piano, violin and cello (1811).

Archer Frederic Scott (1813–57). English photographer who in 1851 invented the *collodion negative, thereby replacing the *daguerreotype. He was also a sculptor.

Archer Thomas (*c.* 1668–1743). English architect, influenced by the baroque style of Borromini. His churches of St John, Smith Square, London (interior gutted in 1941) and St Paul, Deptford are among the boldest and most interesting of their time. His St Philip, Birmingham (now the cathedral) has been much altered.

Arcadia. Poussin's *Et in Arcadia Ego* (detail)

(*a*) Gothic pointed arch. (*b*) Romanesque rounded arch (showing a, voussoirs; b, springing-line; c, impost). (*c*) Arabic rounded horseshoe arch

Archer William (1856–1924). Scottish writer on the theatre, translator and the 1st important weekly dramatic critic in Britain, whose reviews from 1878 not only affected standards of production but revolutionized criticism. He was largely responsible for introducing Ibsen to England but his trs (coll. ed. 1906–12), although the first, missed the wit and poetry of the original. He also wrote the successful melodrama *The Green Goddess* (New York, 1921).

Archilochus (*fl.* 7th c. B.C.). Greek poet reputed to have introduced the elegiac couplet and the iambic and trochaic metres and their variations. Also the first to write freely about his personal feelings.

Archipenko Alexander (1887–1964). Russian-born sculptor. He went to Paris in 1908 and soon made contact with the cubists; his work was among the most important in the development of the new styles in 20th-c. sculpture. From essentially cubistic premises he evolved new approaches and techniques introducing (1912) for example, the collage in sculpture, i.e. using wood, metal and glass, etc., on the same work. His *Boxers* (1913) is an important landmark in the assimilation by modern sculptors of the vitalist nature of primitive art (*African art).

architectonic. Term used metaphorically of a work of art with a structural pattern reminiscent of architecture in its rhythm and balance. The term is often applied to contrapuntal music where repeated themes, references and recollections of earlier material accumulate to give an effect of balance and a sense of architectural structure. The themes themselves often have a similar kind of coherence.

architrave. Architectural term for the lowest section of an entablature, immediately above the capitals of the columns. *Orders.

Arch poet. The name given to a 12th-c. German poet, author of a well-known *Confession.*

archy and mehitabel (1927). Verse sketches by Don *Marquis.

Arcimboldi Giuseppe (1527–93). Milanese painter sometimes considered an ancestor of the *surrealists by virtue of his fantasy portrait heads; these are made up of fruit, vegetables, flowers, fragments of landscape, birds, animals, human bodies, tools, weapons, etc. Worked (in conventional style) at Milan cathedral and as painter to the Hapsburg court at Prague (1562–87).

Arden John (1930–). English playwright. A. treats public themes but gives his sympathies impartially – to the vagabonds as well as the respectable (*Live Like Pigs*, 1958), to the doctors as well as to the old people on whom they experiment (*The Happy Haven*, 1960). Works include *Sergeant Musgrave's Dance* (1960).

Arden of Faversham, The Tragedy of Mr (1592). Play sometimes attributed to Shakespeare; its subject is a murder actually committed in Faversham.

Arditi Luigi (1822–1903). Italian conductor and composer settled in England (1858). Wrote the widely popular waltz song 'Il Bacio' ('The Kiss').

Ardizzone Edward Jeffrey Irving (1900–). British artist in etching, lithography, pen drawing and watercolour. He was an official war artist (1940–5) and is known as a book illustrator and as author as well as illustrator of children's books, e.g. *Tim all Alone* (1956).

À rebours (1884). Novel by J.-K. *Huysmans.

Arensky Anton Stepanovich (1861–1906). Russian composer, pupil of Rimsky-Korsakov but closer in musical affinities to Tchaikovsky than the extreme nationalist school. Wrote operas and symphonies but his piano and chamber music and songs are most frequently performed.

Arentsz Arent (1585/6–before October 1635). Dutch landscape painter. Like H. Avercamp's, his landscapes are heavily populated with figure groups.

Areopagitica a speech: . . . for the Liberty of Unlicensed Printing . . . (1644). Pamphlet by *Milton.

Aretino Pietro, the 'scourge of princes' (1492–1556). Italian poet, playwright and prose writer of unexampled obscenity, and self-styled prophet. He was dreaded for his satire and was thus assured of praise and popularity. His works included pasquinades, saints' lives, the *giudizi*, annual prophetic almanacs, prose

Archipenko. *Seated Mother* (1911). Also *cubism

Arcimboldi. *Summer*

Pietro Aretino: painting by Titian

Aristophanes. Greek Art Theatre performance of *The Birds*

Pearl Argyle in *Cabriole Suite*

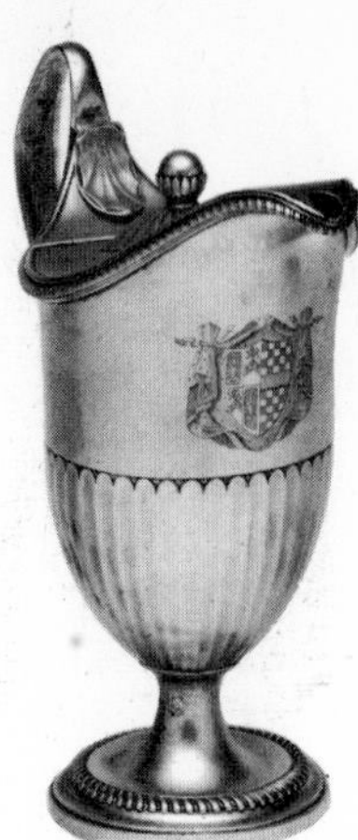
Argyle jug

dialogues, 5 comedies and a tragedy *Orazia* (1546). A. launched the publ. of 3,000 of his own letters–these are informative on contemporary life.

Aretino Unico (born Bernardo Accolti) (1458–1535). Italian poet whose surviving work does not justify the acclaim he received from his contemporaries. He is best known for his comedy *Virginia* (1494), based on a story by Boccaccio.

Argensola Bartolomé Leonardo de (1562–1631). Spanish poet and historian. A. opposed the exaggerations of Gongorism, and his poems –satires, epistles, sonnets, odes and trs of Horace–were sophisticated and restrained and looked to classical models. His history of the Spanish conquest of the Molucca Islands, Indonesia, was used by J. Fletcher for *The Island Princess.*

Argensola Lupercio Leonardo de (1559–1613). Spanish poet, dramatist and historian, brother of Bartolomé A. His tragedies, e.g. *Alejandra* and *Isabela*, imitations of Seneca, were admired by Cervantes. He urged King Philip II to suppress the theatre on moral grounds. His poems were less finished than his brother's but similar in type and style. Their poems were publ. together (1634).

Argentina, La (1888–1936). Argentinian dancer, taught Spanish dancing by her father; in 1899 she was appointed principal dancer at the Madrid Opera and in the 1920s formed her own co. in Paris. She was responsible for awakening public interest in Spanish dancing and establishing it as a theatrical form.

Argentinita, La (Encarnacio Lopez) (1898–1945). Spanish dancer who continued the popularization of Spanish dancing begun by La *Argentina. She excelled in classical Spanish dancing, sensitively retaining the national character without over-stylization. Sister of Pilar *Lopez, she danced in the 1930s with her own co. (Madrid Ballet) and later appeared with Ballet Theater.

Arghezi Tudor. The pseud. of Ion Teodorescu (1880–). Leading Rumanian poet and writer between the wars.

argyle. A deep, lidded sauce-jug in silver, etc., used for the serving of gravy and said to have been designed for an 18th-c. duke of Argyll. A hot iron or coal is inserted into a central compartment to keep the liquid hot, and the spout is set low on the body so that the meaty solids may be poured out.

Argyle Pearl (1910–47). The 1st entirely English-trained dancer to earn the title ballerina; she filled the void in the Vic-Wells Ballet when leading dancer Alicia Markova left the co. in 1935.

aria (Italian, 'song'). An operatic song; it has a clear formal structure (as distinct from *arioso or recitative), sections being repeated, the bass and treble lines having a composed melodic and rhythmic shape. The DA CAPO A. of the 18th c. repeats the 1st section after a contrasting section.

arioso. An operatic term for a passage for solo voice melodic but without the *aria's clarity of formal structure and having some of the rhythmic freedom of *recitative.

Ariosto Ludovico (1474–1533). Italian poet in the service of the d'Este family of Ferrara; he was a distinguished administrator and statesman. A.'s great work *Orlando Furioso* (1516; 1591) is an epic poem in 46 cantos in the tradition of Boiardo's *Orlando Innamorato.* Its subject is the war between Charlemagne and Agramante, King of the Saracens. The knight Orlando (English, Roland) has lost his mind for the love of the beautiful Angelica; Orlando's mind is found on the moon where all lost human attributes are said to be kept. Orlando, himself again, leads Charlemagne's armies to victory. A.'s poem tells other stories of love and chivalry, most outstandingly that of the warrior Bradamante and her love for Ruggiero. The epic is sustained by A.'s great narrative gift and distinguished by dramatic strength and psychological insight. Other work includes Latin elegies and epigrams and plays, which, although derivative from Latin models, assimilated and modernized rather than merely trs. them.

Aristides (4th c. B.C.). Greek painter renowned for the pathos of his figures. His most famous painting showed a dying mother in a conquered city shielding her baby from the blood on her breast.

Aristophanes (*c.* 450–*c.* 385 B.C.). Greek playwright and the most brilliant practitioner of the 'Old Comedy' at Athens. Born just as Periclean Athens was reaching the peak of her fortunes, he witnessed the whole course of the Peloponnesian War and the city's decline. To the traditional horseplay and bawdry of the comedy he added his own gifts of grace and wit, particularly his gift for lyric poetry. He admired both *Euripides and Socrates, but as his protagonist is commonly a rather stupid old man (perhaps part of the comic tradition), who presents the opinions of reaction, A. has earned the name of reactionary himself. His real hostility was reserved for the principles, policies and acts of Cleon, 'the most violent of the citizens', and for the war party. 11 out of 44 plays survive. In *The Acharnians* (425) Dicaeopolis, about to celebrate the private peace he has secured for himself, is set upon by the chorus for disloyalty, but with props and gags filched from Euripides, he wins them for the cause of peace. In *The Knights* (424) Cleon appears as the wily Paphlagonian slave who misleads the old man Demos. *The Clouds* (423) guys Socrates' 'think-shop'. *The Wasps* (422) appears to be an attack on the jury-courts, but the protagonist's name, Philocleon, probably reveals the true target. The *Peace* (421) appeals to all the Hellenes to stop the war, and almost coincided with the peace of Nicias, the first lull in the fighting. *The Birds* (414) concerns the fantasy utopia called 'cloud-cuckoo-land'. *Lysistrata* (411) deals with the plot led by the eponymous heroine to stop the war by withholding conjugal rights. *Thesmophoriazusae*

Aristotle. Roman bust

Armitage. *Figure lying on its side, no. 5* (1959)

(411) mocks Euripides for his characterization of women. *The Frogs* (405), A.'s most extended essay in literary criticism, finally settles Euripides' reputation. *Ecclesiazusae* (391) presents a feminist republic, perhaps a skit on Plato's *Republic*. The *Plutus* (380) belongs to the 'Middle Comedy' and looks very feeble beside A.'s earlier work. These last 2 plays were both produced after the war, when Athens was spent.

Aristotle (384–322 B.C.). Greek philosopher and scientist whose systems of physics, political philosophy, logic and metaphysics (surviving in the form of lecture notes) profoundly influenced the course of philosophy and dominated medieval European thought. His aesthetic doctrine, developed in the *Poetics* and the *Rhetoric*, is based on the common Greek belief that art is a form of imitation. Unlike Plato he considered the arts neither deceitful nor harmful; on the contrary he considered their emotive power useful. 'Tragedy is an imitation of a worthy action complete in itself . . . which by means of pity and fear achieves the *catharsis* of emotions of that kind.' The Greek word catharsis means: (1) ritual purification; (2) medical purging by an aperient; (3) a tempering or harmonizing of the body's humours by drugs. Discussion has raged about these meanings, but most probably the metaphor is to be interpreted with reference to the third. Tragedy improves the soul's well-being by tempering the elements of pity and fear in its composition. A. held that a tragedy should be a coherent whole, i.e. that it should maintain a 'unity of action' and observed that the events described in the tragedies of Sophocles usually took place within 24 hours (*unities).

Arland Marcel (1899–). French novelist, literary critic and reviewer on the *Nouvelle Revue Française* to 1939. His novels, heavily influenced by Gide, include *L'Ordre* (1929, Prix Goncourt), *Terre natale* (1938) and *Zelie dans le désert* (1944). A. has said, 'All problems can be reduced to the single problem of God.'

Arlequin: *Harlequin

Arlincourt Charles-Victor-Prévost, vicomte d' (1789–1856). French poet and novelist, best known for his romantic fantasy *Le Solitaire* (1821). He was nicknamed *'l'inversif vicomte'*, because of his excessive use of grammatical inversion.

armature. Metal framework used in modelling and sculpture to support the clay or other material and prevent it sagging or collapsing.

Armitage Kenneth (1916–). English sculptor, born in Leeds where he studied before entering the Slade School. In 1956 he won a competition for a war memorial at Krefeld. He was shown in the 1963 Darmstadt exhibition 'Evidences of Anxiety in Modern Art'. A. works almost entirely in plaster cast into bronze, concentrating on achieving an effect of movement and vitality in his figures, notable in the *Walking Group* (1951). His works include the *Figure lying on its side, no. 5* (1959; coll. the artist) and *Pandarus 8* (1963; Malborough Fine Art coll., London).

armorial glass. Any glass bearing a coat of arms can be so described but the term is normally applied, in a specialist sense, to glass made at Venice in the 16th c. and decorated there with the purchaser's coat of arms done in enamels. The decoration is often done with soft gilding and white and coloured dots.

Armory Show (Feb. 1913). International exhibition of over 1,100 works by 'modern' artists held in New York at the armoury of the 69th Regiment. Cubists, expressionists, fauvists and futurists received their first proper showing in the U.S. and the exhibition had a major impact on U.S. art and criticism. The A. S. was organized by the Association of American Painters and Sculptors and supported by the group The *Eight It subsequently moved to the Art Institute, Chicago.

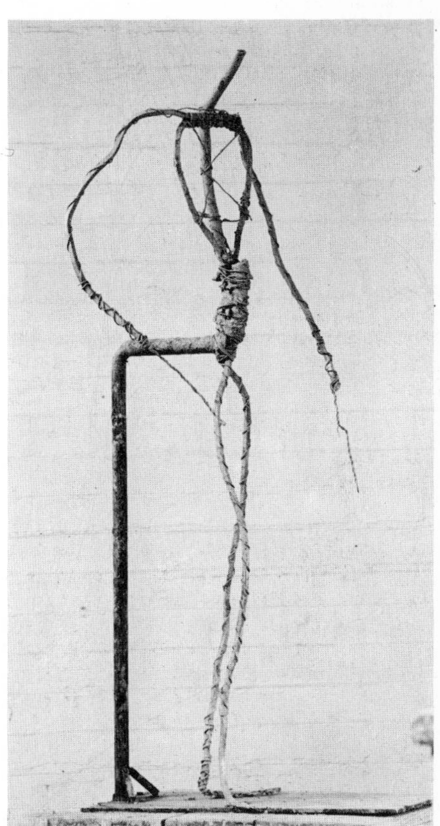

Armature

Bettina von Arnim

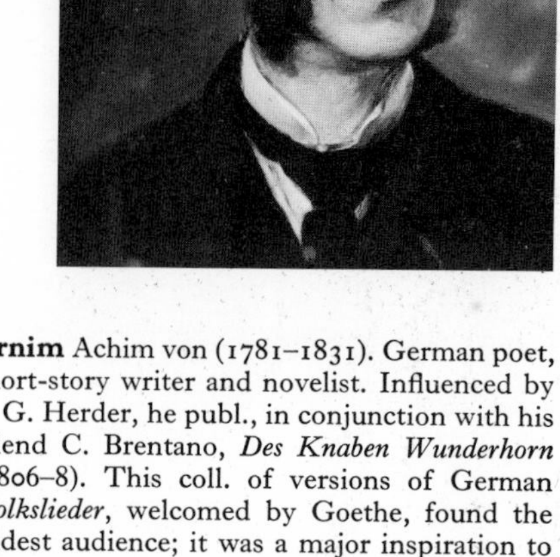
Matthew Arnold

Louis Armstrong

Arne: caricature by Bartolozzi

Arms and the Man (1894). Play by G. B. *Shaw.

Armstrong John (1709–79). Scottish doctor, author of the very popular poem *The Art of Preserving Health* (1744).

Armstrong (Daniel) Louis (1900–). U.S. trumpeter, usually called 'Satchmo' (Satchelmouth). He was the 1st jazz soloist to achieve world-wide recognition, and has remained one of the great creative forces in jazz. By the late 1920s, he had achieved a classic synthesis of instrumental virtuosity and melodic and rhythmic inventiveness, demonstrated in his Hot Five and Hot Seven recordings, that influenced a generation of trumpet players (Red Allen, Roy Eldridge, Buck Clayton *et al.*) and other instrumentalists of the 1920s and 1930s.

Armstrong Sir Thomas Henry Wait (1898–). English conductor, composer, especially of choral works, and organist at Christ Church cathedral, Oxford. Principal of the R.A.M. from 1955.

Arnault Antoine-Vincent (1766–1834). French writer of verse tragedies, e.g. *Marius à Minturnes* (1791) based on Roman history, and satirical verse *Fables* (1812), e.g. *La Feuille.*

Arndt Ernst Moritz (1769–1860). German poet, historian and patriot of the Napoleonic era. *Geist der Zeit* (vol. 1, 1806; *Spirit of the Times,* 1808), called for a united German resistance to Napoleonic pretensions. With the French advance he fled to Sweden where he continued to write patriotic songs, poems and pamphlets. He also wrote his autobiography (1840).

Arne Thomas Augustine (1710–78). English composer. Becoming a musician against his father's will, he produced his 1st opera *Rosamond* in 1733. The masque *Alfred* (1740) contained 'Rule Britannia' and A. is also remembered for his settings of Shakespearean songs, e.g. 'Where the bee sucks' and 'Blow, blow thou winter wind'. Of his 30 operas, masques and entertainments, the opera *Artaxerxes,* admired by Hadyn, was revived in 1962. A. also wrote 2 oratorios, symphonies, trio sonatas and organ concertos.

Arnim Achim von (1781–1831). German poet, short-story writer and novelist. Influenced by J. G. Herder, he publ., in conjunction with his friend C. Brentano, *Des Knaben Wunderhorn* (1806–8). This coll. of versions of German *Volkslieder,* welcomed by Goethe, found the widest audience; it was a major inspiration to later German romanticism, influencing poets and being drawn on by composers, e.g. Mahler. Other writing includes the historical romance *Die Kronenwächter* (2 vols, 1817; unfinished) and short stories.

Arnim Bettina (Elisabeth) von (1785–1859). German writer. She was the daughter of Maximiliane de la Roche, an early love of Goethe's, married the poet A. von Arnim (1811) and was a friend of and corresponded with Goethe and other great men. She is remembered for semi-fictional books based on her letters, e.g. *Goethes Briefwechsel mit einem Kinde* (1835; *Goethe's correspondence with a Child,* 1837), but also wrote on social and political questions.

Arnold Sir Edwin (1832–1904). English poet and journalist. Work in India (1856–61) inspired *The Light of Asia* (1879), a colourful, highly readable blank-verse epic about the life and teaching of the Buddha.

Arnold Jack (1916–). U.S. film director. A competent worker who has spent most of his career under contract to Universal, where he has tackled a wide range of subjects, particularly horror and science fiction films and westerns, like his best film, *No Name on the Bullet* (1959).

Arnold Malcolm (1921–). British composer and from 1946 principal trumpet, London Philharmonic Orchestra. Works include much film music, 5 symphonies, including the 'Toy' symphony (1957), a concerto for harmonica, the ballet *Homage to the Queen* (1953) and the overture *Tam O'Shanter* (1955). His orchestration is colourful, his style uncomplicated.

Arnold Matthew (1822–88). English poet and critic. Son of Thomas A. (1795–1842), the celebrated headmaster of Rugby. A. was professor of poetry at Oxford, and an inspector of schools from 1851 to 1883. His verse is mainly sombre, expressive of longing and frustration, somewhat academic and frigid, exemplifying his respect for classical models and enlightened

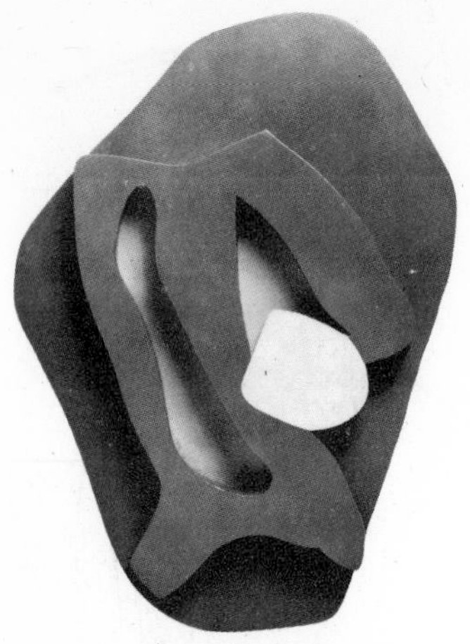

Arp. *Earth Forms*, painted wood (1916–17) (*far left*); and *Hybrid Fruit called Pagoda*, bronze (1949). Also *dada

by images of great beauty. As a critic A. proclaimed the central role of criticism in literary studies, the importance of achieving objective standards, the dangers of dogmatism, and the relevance of literary criticism to life. The last belief led him on to social criticism in *Culture and Anarchy* (1869), a major work, in which he discusses notions of unrestricted individualism and the way in which culture can contribute to the creation of a more unified society, in the face of materialism, bourgeois 'philistinism' and apathy. *The Strayed Reveller*, his 1st coll. of poems, appeared in 1849; *Empedocles on Etna*, a dramatic poem of disillusioned idealism followed in 1852. Both these vols A. withdrew from circulation, but issued in 1853, *Poems*, containing *The Scholar Gipsy* and *Sohrab and Rustum*, together with earlier pieces. *Poems, Second Series*, in which *Balder Dead* features, came out in 1855; *Merope*, a classical tragedy, in 1858. *New Poems* (1867) includes *Thyrsis*, an elegy for A. H. Clough. His critical works include: *On Translating Homer* (1861), an impressive series of Oxford lectures; *Essays in Criticism* (1865 and 1888); *The Study of Celtic Literature* (1867). A. also wrote on religion, e.g. *Literature and Dogma* (1873) and *God and the Bible* (1875).

Arnold Samuel (1740–1802). English composer of opera and church music and musical ed. He publ. an ed. of Handel's works (1787–97), a continuation (1790) to W. *Boyce's *Cathedral Music* and was a founder of the Glee Club.

Arnolfo di Cambio (*c.* 1232–1302). Italian sculptor and architect. Assistant to Nicola Pisano both on the shrine of S. Dominic in Bologna and the pulpit at Siena. His statue of Charles of Anjou (before 1277, Conservatori Gal., Rome) is the 1st modern portrait statue by a known artist and the design of his wall tomb of Cardinal de Braye (the cardinal lies on a bier beneath the Madonna and Child in glory) was a model for over a c. A. was an architect of the cathedral of S. Maria del Fiore and the church of S. Croce, both Florence, and also carved the sculptural decoration on the cathedral façade.

Arnoux Alexandre (1884–). French writer of short stories, e.g. *Le Cabaret* (1919), about World War I, and novels, e.g. *Algorithme* (1948), written with an atmosphere of rarefied introspection, *Paris-sur-Seine* (1939), portraying the chaotic aspects of a modern metropolis, and *Pour solde de tout compte* (1958). He has also written pieces for the theatre, e.g. *Huon de Bordeaux* (1923) and *L'amour des trois oranges* (1947) and has produced several film scenarios.

Arolas Juan (1805–49). Spanish monk and romantic poet who sought escape from monastic life in sensuous, highly imaginative poems about medieval and oriental life or in delicate love poetry. His best poem is the beautiful and resigned *A una bella* (publ. in *Poesías caballerescas y orientales*, 1840; *To a Beauty*) with its refrain 'Be happier than I'. He died in an asylum.

Around the World in 80 Days (1956). Film produced by M. *Todd; from the novel (1873) by Jules Verne.

Arp Bill. Pseud. of Charles Henry Smith (1826–1903). Southern U.S. humorist who during the Civil War satirized the North in a newspaper series of 'letters' to 'Mr Abe Linkhorn'. Colls include *Bill A., So-Called* (1866) and *Bill A.: from the Uncivil War to Date* (1903).

Arp Jean or Hans (1888–). Alsatian sculptor, graphic artist, painter and writer. He exhibited with Der Blaue Reiter artists and contributed to *Der Sturm*, and his interest in poetry inspired a great deal of his graphic work. In 1915 he moved to Zürich and, together with his wife, Sophie Taeuber, started to make *collages according to the 'law of chance'. In 1916/17 he made his 1st abstract sculptures; he participated in the dada movement and the 1st surrealist exhibition in 1925. In addition to sculptures, reliefs (one at the Unesco building in Paris), collages and drawings, A. has designed tapestries and written much, both poetry and prose in French and German. His works are usually abstract or near abstract but nevertheless identify themselves quite clearly with natural forms.

arpeggio (Italian *arpa*, 'harp'). Musical term for a broken chord in which the notes are played in rapid succession.

Arpino Guiseppe Cesari (called 'Chevalier d'Arpino') (1568–1640). One of the last and most conservative of Italian mannerist painters. He designed the mosaics for the dome of St

Arpino. *Annunciation*

Arnolfo di Cambio. *Charles of Anjou*

Arthurian legend; from a medieval ms.

Art nouveau. Vases by Emile Gallé (*left*) and Louis Tiffany

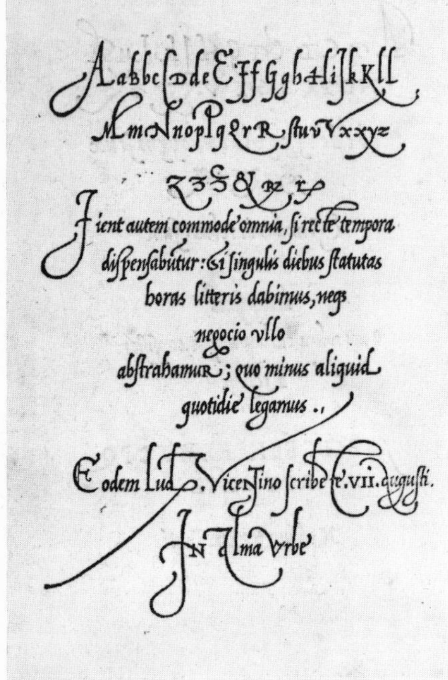

Fient autem commode omnia, si recte tempora dispensabitur: Si singulis diebus statutas horas litteris dabimus, neq; negocio ullo abstrahamur; quo minus aliquid quotidie legamus ..

Eodem Lud. Vicentino scribe

In alma urbe

Arrighi writing block

Ars moriendi. *Dying man tempted to show impatience*

Peter's, Rome and painted the frescoes in S. Martino, Naples (1589–91) and a series of large histories in the Conservatori Palace, Rome (1591–1636). Caravaggio was his pupil.

Arrau Claudio (1903–). Chilean pianist of world renown; his playing is distinguished by its power and bravura.

Arrighi Ludovico degli ('Il Vicentino') (d. *c.* 1527). Italian calligrapher and printer. He was a scribe in the papal chancellery and wrote and publ. (1522) the 1st copybook of writing for the layman, which he based on the cursive script of the chancellery. He had adapted this for printing (*c.* 1520) with the help of the Roman printer A. Blado, and the resulting type-face was an important step in the development of *italic calligraphy and type-faces, and was influential in Italy and France.

arris. The sharp angle edge where 2 surfaces meet, a term applied to architecture and silver. It was particularly popular in silver-work during the neo-classic revival.

Arrowsmith (1925). Novel by Sinclair Lewis.

Ars Amatoria. Poem by *Ovid.

ars antiqua. The style in music of the late 12th and 13th cs associated with Perotin and the school of Paris. It was primarily a style of embellished organum.

Arsenal (1929). Film directed by A. *Dovzhenko.

Ars moriendi (Latin, 'art of dying'). Title of a famous block-book of a popular devotional character printed in Germany *c.* 1465. The earliest English version *Ars moriendi, that is to saye the craft for to deye for the helthe of mannes sowle* was printed by Caxton *c.* 1491.

ars nova. The style in music of the 14th c. characterized by free part writing, 'discord' rather than euphony and the use of such forms as the *isorhythmic motet; composers included *Machaut and Philippe de *Vitry.

Ars Poetica. *Horace's last literary epistle.

Artaud Antonin (1896–1948). French poet and playwright, and an actor and director in plays and films. Works include the prose poems *L'Ombilic des limbes* (1925) and the influential *Le Théâtre et son double* (1938).

Arthur King. From brief references in the *Historia Britonum* of Nennius (*fl.* 796) and **Annales Cambriae* it is probable that there was an historical A., a British general of the 5th or 6th c. A.D. Together with *The *Black Book of Carmarthen* and the story *Kilhwch and Olwen*, these were the main literary sources for a huge corpus of romances, the ARTHURIAN LEGEND. According to *Geoffrey of Monmouth's *Historia Regum Britanniae* (*c.* 1135), the earliest literature to romanticize A., his parents were the British king, Uther Pendragon, and Ygaerne (Igraine), seduced by Uther with Merlin's help. As king, A. makes many conquests in Britain and on the Continent, marries Guanhamara (Guinevere) and holds his court at Caerleon (Camelot) where his most famous knights are Kay, Bedivere and Gawayne. He proceeds on an expedition against Rome leaving as regent his nephew Mordred, who seizes the kingdom and Guanhamara. Returning, A. defeats Mordred at the river Camel, Cornwall, but is fatally wounded and carried to Avalon. Both the belief that A. would return from Avalon and the Round Table were introduced by Wace.

Legends, probably oral, must have circulated widely before Geoffrey's *Historia Regum* as *William of Malmesbury in his *Gesta Regum* (1125) demands that they be discredited and there are early 12th-c. carvings of A. and his court in Modena cathedral, Italy. Geoffrey's work was loosely trs. into Norman French by *Wace, *Roman de Brut* (*c.* 1154), and on this were based the 1st English version by *Layamon and the first of the French **romans bretons*, that of Chrétien de Troyes. A mass of Arthurian literature followed in England, France and elsewhere (13th–15th c.). During this period other cycles, mostly French in origin, e.g. those about Lancelot, Perceval, Tristan and the Holy Grail, were incorporated into the original Arthurian legend. A. becomes overshadowed by his knights, his court merely a background for their feats. All this material was used by Sir Thomas Malory in *Morte d'Arthur* (1469/70) and the story was retold by Tennyson in *Idylls of the King* (1842–85).

Art nouveau. Métro station by Guimard; and staircase by Horta

Arup. Somerville College, Oxford

Arthur Jean (1908–). U.S. film actress coming from the stage to films in 1923; her 1st big break came with *Mr Deeds Goes to Town* (1936), after which she continued as a light comedienne in a variety of star parts culminating in *A Foreign Affair* (1948) and *Shane* (1952), the 1st psychological western.

art nouveau. A style of decoration and architecture current in the 1890s and early 1900s. The name derives from a gallery for interior decoration opened in Paris in 1896, called the 'Maison de l'Art Nouveau'; the same style in Germany is called 'Jugendstil' after a magazine called *Die Jugend* (Youth) and in Italy 'Floreale' or 'Liberty' after the London store. Characteristic decorative motifs are writhing plant forms, as in the wrought-iron entrances to Paris Métro stations (by Hector Guimard). Similar forms were used both in book illustrations and in the applied arts, for example furniture or glassware of the French artist Emile Gallé and of Louis Tiffany in the United States. The best-known graphic artist is Aubrey Beardsley, whose sinister line drawings were exceptionally well adapted to illustration. The architectural movement was widespread, leading figures being C. R. Mackintosh, and Anton Gaudí in Barcelona, whose work has a bold fantastic style. Interior decorators include Siegfried Bing (Germany), Victor Horta and Henri Van de Velde (Belgium).

Art of Fugue, The (publ. 1752) *Die Kunst der Fuge.* The name given by its publ. to J. S. *Bach's unfinished work consisting of fugues and canons of progressive complexity.

Art of Love, The. Poem by *Ovid.

arts and crafts movement. Name given, in the 1st instance, to a movement in late 19th- and early 20th-c. England whose leading figures included C. R. *Ashbee. Taking its inspiration from William Morris, the movement urged a return to the ideals of the medieval craftsman as a means to reviving standards of design and artistic integrity, threatened by the advance of industrialism. The movement contributed essentially to the beginnings of the European renaissance in design, but it lost influence because it rejected rather than attempted to shape machine-age developments.

Artsybashev Mikhail Petrovich (1878–1927). Russian novelist and playwright. A. was expelled from the Soviet Union in 1923. His novels *Sanine* (1907; 1915) and *Breaking Point* (1912; 1915) caused a sensation, though their popularity has been short-lived. A. asserted that sex and death were the only realities behind the veneer of civilization, and preached obedience to impulse.

Arundel 2nd Earl of: Thomas *Howard

Arup Ove (1895–). Danish architect, born in England of Danish parents and trained as an engineer in Denmark; he was a wartime consultant in London, designing air-raid shelters and marine works. Since 1949 his work has included administrative buildings, factories, laboratories, dwellings and academic buildings, e.g. the design for Somerville College, Oxford, including fellows' rooms and shops, which offers an unusual alternative to uniformity in a screen-wall façade, and the Kingsgate footbridge at Durham Univ.

Arzamas. Russian literary group founded in 1815. Its members included Zhukovsky, Batyushkov and Pushkin. They supported the literary reforms of Karamzin.

Asafiev Boris (1884–1949) Russian composer, a pupil of Liadov and Rimsky-Korsakov, and music theorist. His compositions include the ballets *The Flames of Paris* and *The Fountain of Bakkchisarai.*

Asam Cosmas and Egid, sons of the Bavarian painter Hans Georg (1649–1711), were church decorators and designers in whose work S. German baroque achieved its zenith. Cosmas Damian (1686–1739) was a painter and architect of the monastic church of Weltenburg (1717–21). In his painting illusionism is carried to its furthest extremes, e.g. his frescoes in the church of Maria Viktoria, Ingolstadt (1736) and the Alteglofsheim Palace in Břevnow (1730). His use of light colours tends to the style of rococo. Like his brother he held high positions in S. German courts. Egid Quirin (1692–1750) was stucco-worker, sculptor and architect; his churches include the collegiate church at Rohr (1718–25) and St Johann Nepomuk (called the Asam) church, Munich (1733–*c.* 1750) although Cosmas may have

E. Q. Asam. *Assumption of the Virgin*, altar at Rohr; and (*below*) *St George*, Weltenburg

Ashton. *Symphonic Variations.* Also **Cinderella*

Dame Peggy Ashcroft as Queen Margaret in *Henry VI*

Lo Inferno i. 1—42

COMINCIA LA COMMEDIA DI DANTE NELLA QUALE TRATTA DELLE PENE DE' VIZII & DE' PREMII DELLE VIRTU. CANTICA PRIMA APPELLATA INFERNO. CANTO PRIMO NEL QUALE SI PROEMIA A TUTTA L'OPERA.

NEL MEZZO DEL CAMMIN DI NOSTRA VITA
Mi ritrovai per una selva oscura,
Che la diritta via era smarrita.
E quanto a dir qual era è cosa dura
Questa selva selvaggia ed aspra e forte,
Che nel pensier rinnuova la paura!
Tanto è amara, che poco è più morte:
Ma per trattar del ben ch'i' vi trovai,
Dirò dell'altre cose ch'io v'ho scorte.
I' non so ben ridir com'io v'entrai;
Tant'era pien di sonno in su quel punto,
Che la verace via abbandonai.
Ma poi ch'io fui al piè d'un colle giunto,
Là dove terminava quella valle
Che m'avea di paura il cor compunto,
Guardai in alto, & vidi le sue spalle
Vestite già de' raggi del pianeta
Che mena dritto altrui per ogni calle.
Allor fu la paura un poco queta
Che nel lago del cor m'era durata
La notte ch'i' passai con tanta pieta.
E come quei che con lena affannata
Uscito fuor del pelago alla riva,
Si volge all'acqua perigliosa e guata;
Così l'animo mio che ancor fuggiva,
Si volse indietro a rimirar lo passo,
Che non lasciò giammai persona viva.
Poi ch'ei posato un poco il corpo lasso,
Ripresi via per la piaggia diserta,
Sì che il piè fermo sempre era il più basso;
Ed ecco, quasi al cominciar dell'erta,
Una lonza leggiera e presta molto,
Che di pel maculato era coperta.
E non mi si partia dinanzi al volto;
Anzi impediva tanto il mio cammino,
Ch'io fui per ritornar più volte volto.
Tempo era dal principio del mattino;
E il sol montava su con quelle stelle
Ch'eran con lui, quando l'amor divino
Mosse da prima quelle cose belle;
Sì che a bene sperar m'era cagione
Di quella fera alla gaietta pelle,

28

Ashendene Press ed. of Dante

Ashbee. 38 Cheyne Walk, London

helped in the latter. All his sculpture of any importance is designed for churches and his best works are his altarpieces, e.g. the *Assumption of the Virgin* at Rohr and the *St George* at Weltenburg. The brothers worked in such harmony that it is usually difficult to distinguish their work. They were employed to redecorate Romanesque or Gothic churches (as at Freising cathedral, 1723/4, or St Emmeram's church, Regensburg) but their masterpiece is the St Johann Nepomuk church, Munich where painting, sculpture, stucco and architecture serve the illusive confusion of the real and imaginary worlds (*baroque).

Asbjørnsen Peter Christen (1812–85). Norwegian folk-lorist and author, whose work was the foundation of a distinct Norwegian literary style and influential on the present *bokmål* (I. *Aasen). He was influenced by the brothers Grimm and with J. Moe coll. and retold many Norwegian folk-tales, e.g. *Norske Folkeeventyr* (1842–52; *Popular Tales from the Norse*, 1859). He himself wrote short stories of local life.

Ascent of F6, The (1936). Play by Auden and Isherwood.

Asch Sholem (Shalom) (1880–1957). Polish-Jewish novelist, from 1909 settled in the U.S., short-story writer and playwright in Yiddish and German whose work made Yiddish drama known in W. Europe and the U.S. and raised the standard of Yiddish writing. His plays combine naturalism with imaginative symbolism, e.g. *Der Got fur Nekome* (1907; *The God of Vengeance*, 1918). His novel *Der Tilim Yid* (1934; *Salvation*, 1934) expresses belief in the need for a faith. Other works include the trilogy *The Nazarene* (1939), *The Apostle* (1943) and *Mary* (1949).

Ascham Roger (1515–68). English writer, educationalist and diplomat. He stressed the place of sport in education, *Toxophilus* (1545), and condemned flogging in schools, *The Scholemaster* (publ. posth. 1570). His simple style noticeably influenced English prose.

Ashbee Charles Robert (1863–1942). British designer and architect, inspired by the ideals of William *Morris. He founded the Guild of Handicraft (1888–1907), distinguished especially for its printing; it moved in 1902 to Chipping Campden, and became known as the 'Campden experiment'. A. was secretary and adviser (1918–22) to the Pro-Jerusalem Society and initiated the cleaning and restoration of buildings in the city.

Ashcan School. Name given in the 1930s to early 20th-c. U.S. realist painters including some members of The *Eight–Bellows and Jerome Myers–because of their preference for painting the unattractive aspects of city life.

Ashcroft Dame Peggy (1907–). Leading English actress for over 30 years; she first made an impact in *Jew Süss* (1929). She is an extremely versatile performer and has played a variety of parts, her greatest triumph being *Hedda Gabler* in 1954. She has played many leading Shakespearean roles at the Old Vic, 1932/3 being her 1st season there, and recently at the Shakespeare Memorial Theatre. She has also appeared in films.

Ashendene Press. One of the English private presses which led to the revival of European typography; Emery *Walker and S. C. Cockerell designed the press's Subiaco type-face. The press operated from 1895 to 1915 and from 1920 to 1930, an ed. of Dante (1909) being considered its masterpiece.

Ashes and Diamonds (1958). Film directed by A. *Wajda.

Ashmole Elias (1617–92). English antiquary and astrologer. His coll. of curiosities, which he presented to Oxford Univ., formed the basis of the Ashmolean Museum, the 1st public museum in Europe. His memoirs were first publ. in 1717 and were re-ed in 1927.

Ashton Sir Frederick (1906–). English ballet dancer and choreographer. In 1926 and 1928–35 he worked with the Ballet Rambert and in 1935 became choreographer for Sadler's Wells Ballet. For this co. A. made 38 complete works including the skating ballet *Les Patineurs* (1937), a virtuoso exploitation of classical idioms, *Symphonic Variations* (1946), an example of pure neo-classical dance, *Ondine*

Assisi. Basilica of St Francis

Asplund. Entrance to Skogskyrkogård crematorium

Asselyn. *The Angry Swan*

(1958), the climax of his choreography for Fonteyn, and *La Fille Mal Gardée* (1960). In addition he has made new versions of traditional ballets and ballets for foreign companies, e.g. *Romeo and Juliet* for the Royal Danish Ballet. With some exceptions his work is classical in that he emphasizes the dance, not the drama, uses traditional dancing techniques and the 3-act ballet form, e.g. *Cinderella* (1948). He became director of the Royal Ballet in 1963.

As I Lay Dying (1930). Novel by William Faulkner.

Aspern Papers, The (1888). Long short story by Henry *James.

Asphalt Jungle, The (1950). Film directed by J. *Huston.

Asplund Erik Gunnar (1885–1940). Swedish architect and a leading exponent of functionalism in N. Europe. The neo-classicism of his early style developed into an abstract functionalism which made its 1st impact on the Swedish public at the Stockholm exhibition of 1930, A. being chief architect. A district was laid out in a consistent style so that modern architecture could be assessed as an environment for living. Other major buildings include the Skandia cinema (1923), city library (1927) and the Skogskyrkogård crematorium (1940), all Stockholm. This last is the culmination of A.'s development, the abstract rhythms of its lines echoing the lines of the surrounding landscape.

Asquith Anthony (1902–). British film director. A. has always preferred subjects with respectable literary origins. He has achieved commercial success with such adaptations as *The Importance of Being Earnest* (1952) fro Wilde, *The Millionairess* (1960) from Shaw and *The VIP's* (1963) from Rattigan.

Asselyn Jan (1610–52). Dutch painter. After visiting Rome he began to paint Italianate landscapes in the manner of Claude Lorrain, being one of the first in Holland to do so. His best-known, though not his most characteristic, work is *The Angry Swan* (Rijksmus., Amsterdam), an allegory of Dutch independence.

Assisi. Town in Perugia, Italy; the birthplace of Sextus *Propertius and St *Francis of A. On Monte Subasio are the Franciscan monastery and the lower and upper churches of St Francis, built 1228–53 in Gothic style. The lower contains frescoes over the high altar by Giotto, illustrating the vows of the Franciscan order, and others attributed to Cimabue; the upper, frescoes by Giotto and pupils showing scenes from the life of St Francis. The oratory (or *Porziuncola*) of St Francis and the cell in which he died are in the church of Santa Maria degli Angeli which was built round them (1569–79; rebuilt after 1832). The basilica at A. was begun *c.* 1132.

Assisi embroidery. A fashion of embroidery (worked in Assisi since the 16th c.) in which the background is embroidered in cross stitch and the pattern, outlined in double running (Holbein) stitch, is left blank.

Assommoir, L' (1877). Novel by *Zola.

assonance. The rhyming of words whose accentual and following vowels are the same, e.g. 'matin' and 'anvil'. Its most notable use is in the *Chanson de Roland.*

Astafieva Seraphina (1876–1934). Russian dancer and teacher, trained at the Imperial School, St Petersburg. As a teacher in London she was responsible for bringing the direct influence of the Russian school to such British dancers as Alicia *Markova, Margot *Fonteyn and Anton *Dolin.

Astaire Fred. Name adopted by Frederick Austerlitz (1899–). U.S. stage and film dancer, singer and actor. He had many successful shows in London and New York starring with his sister Adèle, e.g. *Over the Top* (1917) and *Apple Blossoms* (1919). In films he appeared with Ginger Rogers until 1939, e.g. *Top Hat* (1935) and was later partnered by Eleanor Powell, Rita Hayworth and Judy Garland.

Astbury John (1688–1743). English potter; little is known about him. He worked at Shelton and is credited with the production of white salt-glazed stoneware, having learned the secret from the Elers brothers. The pottery

Astbury figure

Atelier 17. Design by Hayter (1949)

Atget. *Basket and Broom shop, Paris*

Atelier 5. Siedlung Halen, 5 dwellings shown

Astruc. J.-C. Brialy and M.-J. Nat in *L'Éducation Sentimentale*

associated with A. is decorated with reliefs stamped from pads of white clay which were applied to the brown body of the pieces, but no specimens are known marked with his name. He is also credited with the production of 'image toys'; groups of musicians, soldiers, etc., in red and white clay under a lead glaze, sometimes crudely stained with oxides. The most important technical innovations attributed to him are the use of Devonshire white clay as a surface-wash on darker clays, and the introduction of calcined flint into the body of his wares to give a greater lightness and a whiter colouring.

astragal. A small circular half-round moulding, originally used at the top and bottom of classical columns. Later adapted as a decorative pattern on various fine wares, particularly silver.

Astrophel and Stella (1591). Sonnet sequence by Sir Philip *Sidney.

Astruc Alexandre (1923–). French film director. A brilliant film critic, whose 'camera-stylo' theory pointed to a new style of film making (a 'camera to write with': free, expressive and personal). *Le Rideau Cramoisi* (1952), a short, was greatly admired. A. is very much an aesthete; his work has a detachment often at odds with its content, e.g. *Une Vie* (1956), from Maupassant. *La Proie pour l'ombre* (1960) and *L'Éducation Sentimentale* (1961) are 'lyrical tragedies' in modern settings.

As You Like It (publ. 1623). Comedy by *Shakespeare, written *c.* 1599 and possibly performed before James I in 1603. Its main source was *Rosalynde, or Euphues golden legacie* (1590) by Thomas Lodge. It has been filmed several times, notably in 1936, featuring Elisabeth Bergner and Olivier.

Atala (1801). Story by *Chateaubriand.

Atalanta in Calydon (1865). Poetic drama by *Swinburne.

Atalante, L' (1934). Film directed by J. *Vigo.

atelier (French, 'studio'). Used of a painter's or sculptor's studio or collectively of the pupils gathered round a master. *Atelier libre* (or sometimes *académie*) is a studio in which a model is provided but no tuition given. Famous paintings of a.s are Courbet's *Atelier du peintre* (1855; Louvre), painted as an allegorical manifesto of realism, and Fantin-Latour's *L'Atelier des Batignolles* or *Hommage à Manet* (1869; Louvre) showing Manet with Renoir, Monet, Bazille, Zola and E. Maitre.

Atelier 5. Group of Swiss architects, Fritz, Gerber, Herterberg, Hostettler, Morgenthaler, Pini and Thormann, designers of concrete houses in the late manner of Le Corbusier. Their Siedlung Halen, Berne (1962), is 80 dwellings packed together on a wooded site, so designed that each dwelling has privacy and most have gardens; it is the best-known design in high-density, low-rise dwellings.

Atelier 17. Founded in Paris in 1927 by the English engraver S. W. Hayter for research into new graphic techniques. It became one of the most influential schools for graphic art.

Atget Eugène (1856–1927). French photographer who took straight but evocative pictures of life and architecture in Paris in the early 20th c. and is considered the father of documentary photography. His photographs were used as aids by painters such as Braque and Utrillo and he helped the surrealist painters by providing incongruously superimposed photographs.

Athalie (1691). Play by *Racine.

Athenaeum, The (1828). Literary periodical founded by James Silk Buckingham (1786–1855); most of the leading 19th-c. writers were contributors. In 1921 it became *The Nation and A.*; in 1931 it was incorporated into *The New Statesman and Nation.*

Aubusson carpet of the Empire period

John Aubrey

Attaignant part book

Atherton Mrs Gertrude F(ranklin) (1857–1948). U.S. novelist. Her many historical novels included *The Californians* (1898) and *The Conqueror* (1902), a fictional biography of Alexander Hamilton. Among her other light fiction was *Black Oxen* (1923), a tale of rejuvenation by glandular operation.

Atkins Robert (1886–). English actor at his best in Shakespeare, especially roles like Sir Toby Belch in *Twelfth Night*. He has worked at Stratford, was director of the Old Vic and gave the 1st English production of *Peer Gynt* and has also acted and directed frequently at the Regent's Park open-air theatre.

Atlantic Monthly, The. Leading U.S. literary magazine founded in 1857. Its contributors have numbered Emerson, Longfellow, Robert Frost and Virginia Woolf.

atonal music: *tonality

Atonement of Gosta Berling, The (1923). Film directed by M. *Stiller.

atrium. Architectural term for (1) the small central courtyard of a Greek or Roman house; (2) the open forecourt of an early Christian church.

Attaignant Pierre (d. *c.* 1553). 1st Paris music publ.-printer to use movable type. Numerous publs survive (earliest imprint 1528) of lute music, of songs (35 books), of dances, of masses (7 books), of motets (13 books). All the significant composers of the contemporary Franco-Flemish school were represented, notably J. Arcadelt, Clemens non Papa, C. Janequin, Josquin and A. Willaert.

Attenborough Riehard (1923–). English film and stage actor. Boyish looks cast him in juvenile roles, e.g. *Brighton Rock*, but his intelligent talent has recently flowered in films which he has co-produced, e.g. *The League of Gentlemen* (1959).

Atterberg Kurt (1887–). Swedish composer and music critic. Often used Swedish folk-music, e.g. the opera *Fanal* (1934). His 6th symphony in C maj. (written 1927) won an international Schubert commemoration prize (1928). Subsequently A. pointed out that it was largely pastiche. He has also written concertos, ballets and incidental music.

Atterbom Per Daniel Amadeus (1790–1855). Swedish romantic poet and leading figure of the Fosforister group, called after their periodical *Phosphoros* (1810–13). In its first ed. A. called for a new 'pure' poetry. His cycle *Blommorna* (1812–37) shows the influence of Schelling's nature philosophy but A.'s major works, the poetic dramas *Fågel Blå* (unfinished) and *Lycksalighetens ö* (1824–7) express a belief in unselfishness and suffering as a means to happiness.

Atticus Titus Pomponius (109–32 B.C.). Roman patron of letters famous for his friendship and correspondence with Cicero, whose letters A. himself ed and publ.; his own are lost.

Attiret Jean-Denis (1702–68). French painter who in the 1730s became a Jesuit and went as a missionary to China where he became court painter at Peking. His later work is in the Chinese manner.

Attwood Thomas (1765–1838). English organist and composer of church music. He was a pupil of Mozart in Vienna and produced operas, songs and keyboard music.

Atwood Thomas Warr (d. 1775). English architect who worked in Bath, under the strong influence of John *Wood the Elder. His best work is the Paragon (1769), Bath's 2nd crescent.

Auber Daniel-François-Esprit (1782–1871). French opera composer of *The Dumb Girl of Portici* (1828, also called *Masaniello*), *Fra Diavolo* (1830) and *Manon Lescaut* (1856). Most of his 40-odd operas, written in close partnership with the librettist E. Scribe, were in the *opéra-comique* genre but *Masaniello* was the earliest French grand opera.

Aubignac François-Hédelin, abbé d' (1604–76). French dramatic theorist. His *La Pratique du théâtre* (1657) defended the *unities and is now useful because of the light it throws on the theatre of the time. He questioned the existence of Homer in *Conjectures académiques sur l'Iliade d'Homère* (publ. posth. 1715).

Aubigné Théodore-Agrippa d' (1552–1630). French Protestant poet and historian. *Les Tragiques* (1616), a poem almost epic in scope, describes the wretchedness caused by the wars of religion, in which he fought, and looks forward to God's ultimate vindication of the Huguenots. His early love-poetry in the manner of Ronsard is coll. in *Printemps* (not publ. until 1874).

Aubrey John (1626–97). English antiquary, foundation fellow of the Royal Society and writer chiefly remembered for his 'Brief Lives' of 17th-c. figures. These consist largely of vivid anecdotes and were first publ. as *Lives of Eminent Men* in vol. 2 of *Letters written by Eminent Persons in the 17th and 18th centuries* (1813). His *Monumenta Britannica* (never publ. in full) contains the 1st description of the Avebury stone circle, the 1st account of the Aubrey holes at Stonehenge and the 1st (and mistaken) association of Stonehenge with the druids. He left unfinished *The Naturall Historie of Wiltshire* (begun 1656, first publ. 1847).

Aubusson. A centre of carpet manufacture in France established in the 16th c. but flourishing mainly in the 18th c. and early 19th c. In distinction to the carpets of the Savonnerie, which were pile carpets, those at Aubusson were *tapis ras* ('short napped') and woven like tapestry.

Auden W(ystan) H(ugh) (1907–). English poet. A. studied at Christ Church, Oxford, taught for a time and, on the publ. of *Poems* (1930), became the leader of a group of young poets of the Left (it included Louis MacNeice and Stephen Spender) who were influenced poetically by Eliot and Yeats and intellectually

W. H. Auden

Audubon. The whip-poor-will from *The Birds of America*

Augustin. *Portrait of a Young Lady*

by Marxian and Freudian theories. A. served as a stretcher-bearer in the Spanish Civil War. In 1938 he went to America, where he taught at various univs and colleges, eventually becoming a U.S. citizen. A.'s purpose in the 1930s was to make intellectuals and poets take cognisance of the new industrial society and adopt an attitude towards it. An assertive tone and grim industrial imagery were a necessity; originally A.'s, they became the badges of a school. A. was already experimenting with a variety of verse forms and submitting himself to many influences; in the early years these were Hardy, Old English and Middle English verse (especially Langland's *Piers Plowman* with its social content), and Rilke and Brecht. Since that time he has developed a more individual voice: the tight elliptical verse of the 1930s has given way to a more conversational style; and his socio-political concern has been replaced by a religious outlook based on Pascal and Kierkegaard, revealed, for example, in *The Quest: A Sonnet Sequence* and *For the Time Being: A Christmas Oratorio* (1944). He collaborated with Isherwood in 3 expressionist plays, among them *The Dog Beneath the Skin* (1935) and *The Ascent of F6* (1936).

Audran Edmond (1842–1901). French operetta composer whose *La Mascotte* had 1,700 performances in Paris alone between 1880 and 1897. *La Poupée* (1896) was almost as successful.

Audubon John James (1785–1851). U.S. naturalist and artist who painted from life 435 watercolours of birds, often in action, which were reproduced in coloured aquatint by Robert Havell Jr. and publ. in London as *The Birds of America* (4 vols, 1827–38); only these prints survive. The text, written with the help of William MacGillivray, was publ. separately as *Ornithological Biography* (5 vols, 1831–9). A.'s paintings have considerable artistic merit although their scientific accuracy varies.

Auer Leopold (1845–1930). Hungarian violinist and teacher; pupil of Joachim. From 1868 to 1917 he was violin professor at the Imperial Conservatory, St Petersburg. In 1918 he went to New York, where his pupils included J. Heifetz, E. Zimbalist and N. Milstein.

Auerbach Berthold (1812–82). German-Jewish writer. He began his 1st novel *Spinoza* (1837; 1882) in prison for student political activities. His widely imitated *Schwarzwälder Dorfgeschichten* (first 4 vols 1843–54; *Village Tales from the Black Forest*, 1846) had phenomenal European success. A. combined strong Jewish sympathies with fervent nationalism; wrote on Jewish questions and, in enthusiasm at the German empire (1871), the novel *Waldfried* (1874; *Waldfried*, 1874).

Auerbach Johann: Johannes *Froben

Auersperg Anton Alexander, Graf von: Anastasius *Grün

Augier (Guillaume-Victor) Émile (1820–89). French dramatist, one of the first to break with romanticism and write realistically, within the limits of his strict, 'bourgeois' morality, about social questions; a member of the *école du bon sens. His plays include *Le Gendre de M. Poirier* (with J. Sandeau, 1854), which contrasts aristocratic and bourgeois values, and *Le Fils de Giboyer* (1862).

augmentation. In music, describes the lengthening of the time values of the notes of a given theme. The lengthening is usually uniform and by some simple multiple (e.g. double, quadruple). Frequent in fugue where the subject, usually in its later entries, may be varied in this way. Diminution is the shortening of the note values usually by half or quarter.

Augustan age. The reign of the Roman emperor, Augustus (27 B.C.–A.D. 14), was the age of Horace, Virgil and Ovid; hence the term A. is used of the high classical periods in other literatures. In England it was the age of Addison and Pope (sometimes Dryden is included) or merely the reign of Queen Anne (1702–14); in France the age of Corneille, Racine and Molière.

Augustin Jacques-Jean-Baptiste (1759–1832). French miniaturist who revived the art in France; his paintings have strong, pure colours, certainty of execution and high finish.

Augustine of Hippo, St (354–430). Christian theologian and bishop of Hippo, tremendously influential on religious thought. His *Civitas Dei* (*City of God*) integrates some of the metaphysics of Greek philosophy with Christianity. The *Confessiones* (*Confessions*) is a spiritual autobiography recounting, from the time of his first, childish sins, his search for truth.

Aukrust Olav (1883–1929). Norwegian poet steeped in folk-culture, the author of 3 long poetic cycles in *Nynorsk* (*Aasen). Of these *Himmelvarden* (1916) and *Solrenning* (1930) are religious and nationalistic, symbolizing the development of the nation in the poet's own inner struggle; *Hamar i Hellom* (1926) traces the growth and continuity of Norse tradition.

Aumer Jean (1774–1833). French dancer and choreographer who created ballets for the Paris Opéra and in Lyons, Cassel and Vienna. He was choreographer of the 1st recorded production of *Sleeping Beauty* (1829) when he set the story to music by Hérold.

Auric Georges (1899–). French composer who studied under d'Indy, and was later a disciple of E. *Satie and one of the group The *Six. He was influenced by Stravinsky. His large output includes several ballets, *Les Matelots* (1925), orchestral and vocal music and much film music, e.g. René Clair's *À nous la liberté* (1932) and 2 Ealing comedies.

Ausonius Decimus Magnus (*c.* 310–*c.* 395). Latin Christian poet. A. was born in Bordeaux and taught there until appointed (*c.* 365) tutor to the future emperor, Gratian, who made him consul (379); the prose work *Gratiarum actio* was A.'s address of thanks. He wrote occasional epigrams, *centos and poems and the long poem *Mosella*, a description of the river Moselle. Some of A.'s letters survive, e.g. to his former pupil Bishop Paulinus of Nola, in which A. deplores his excessive Christian enthusiasm.

Austen Jane (1775–1817). English novelist. Youngest daughter of the rector of Steventon in Hampshire, she grew up in a lively, well-connected family, was educated briefly in schools, then at home, and passed a largely uneventful life, moving to Bath with her family in 1801, then (1805) to Southampton, finally to Chawton, near Alton, where she lived from 1809 to 1817. She died at Winchester. Apart from her brilliant wit and sense of comedy, A.'s novels are remarkable for their precise and elegant style and economy of construction.

Auric. Scene from *Les Matelots,* 1st production

Jane Austen

They deal with the limited social milieu of the English gentry but this does not detract from the value of their complex characterizations and subtle, often ironic, descriptions of human relationships. A.'s exposures of affectation, humbug, self-deception and pride are clear-sighted, but her humour and tolerance alleviate her censure. Apart from youthful fragments like the epistolary novels *Lady Susan* and *Elinor and Marianne*, a 1st draft of *Sense and Sensibility*, A.'s 1st work was the high-spirited comic novel of the love-affairs of the Bennet sisters, *Pride and Prejudice* (originally entitled *First Impressions*), begun in 1796 but declined for publ. the following year. *Sense and Sensibility*, which contrasts the emotional Marianne Dashwood with her more composed sister Elinor, was begun in 1797, but abandoned for some years; *Northanger Abbey* (publ. posth. 1818), partly a satire on the *Gothick novel, was started in 1798 and sold to a publ. who then withheld it. It was recovered in 1816. At Chawton, she began to write again after a gap of some years from which only a fragment, *The Watsons*, survives. In 1811 she publ. *Sense and Sensibility* at her own expense; *Pride and Prejudice* followed in 1813. Then came the more mature and serious story of Fanny Price and the Bertram family, *Mansfield Park* (1814), and the delightful and assured novel, *Emma* (1815; dated 1816), describing the growth to maturity of the self-satisfied Miss Emma Woodhouse. *Persuasion*, an autumnal work of great tenderness, appeared posth. in 1818. She was working on *Sanditon*, a more robust novel, when her last illness began.

Austin Alfred (1835–1913). English poet laureate (1896), novelist, critic and political writer. His huge output had little merit; a prose work *The Garden that I Love* (2 series, 1894 and 1907) was popular.

Austin George (1786–1848). English architect, appointed *c.* 1820 surveyor to Canterbury cathedral. He found the building in a bad state of repair and in addition to various interior restorations demolished the Norman N.W. tower and rebuilt it in perpendicular style to harmonize with the S.W. tower; this provoked much controversy.

Austin Mrs Mary (Hunter) (1868–1934). U.S. writer who spent many years among the Indians in New Mexico. She describes them with understanding in her autobiography *Earth Horizon* (1932), *The Land of Little Rain* (1903), a poetic description of the desert, and the play *The Arrow Maker* (1911); in *The American Rhythm* (1923), a treatise on poetry, A. included her own versions of Indian songs and poems. She also deals with problems of social adjustment, often from a feminist point of view, e.g. in *Santa Lucia: a common story* (1908), about marriage, and *A Woman of Genius* (1912).

Austin Richard. 18th-c. British typographer, punch-cutter at J. Bell's British Letter Foundry, who designed the Bell type (1788), a roman type-face derived from the French *Didot types. It was the 1st English *'modern' face and strongly influenced subsequent type design. It gradually lost favour in England in the 19th c. but was extensively used in the U.S.

Autant-Lara Claude (1903–). French film director. A. was associated with the French *avant-garde* cinema of the 1920s as designer for *L'Herbier and assistant to *Clair. Overshadowed during the 1930s by Clair and Carné, he reached his zenith, both of fame and achievement, in the late 1940s with *Le Diable au Corps* (1947) from Radiguet and *Occupe-toi d'Amélie* (1949) from *Feydeau.

Autocrat of the Breakfast Table, The (1858). Book by Oliver Wendell *Holmes.

automatism. In writing or painting, to suspend the control of reason and allow the release of subconscious imagery. It is chiefly associated with surrealism, which was defined in Breton's *Manifeste du Surréalisme* (1924) as 'pure psychic automatism'.

Autun cathedral France. Burgundian Romanesque church (*c.* 1100–35), with pointed arches throughout (an early use) and fluted pilasters showing the influence of Roman buildings. It is of outstanding importance in the history of sculpture for the work of *Gislebertus.

avant-garde (French, 'vanguard'). Term applied to the group of writers, artists, etc., thought at any given time to be most 'advanced' in their techniques or subject-matter.

Autun cathedral

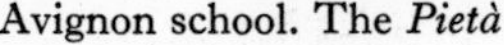

Avignon school. The *Pietà*

Avedon. Portrait of Stravinsky

Ayrton. *Icarus*; bronze

Avare, L' (1668). Comedy by *Molière.

Aved Jacques (1702–66). French portrait painter who studied in Amsterdam and unlike his French contemporaries usually painted his subjects in their normal dress and surroundings. He urged his friend J.-B. *Chardin to take up portraiture and their work has sometimes been confused.

Avedon Richard (1923–). U.S. photographer noted chiefly for his highly stylized fashion and advertising work which has appeared for many years in *Vogue* and similar magazines.

Ave Maria (Latin, 'Hail Mary!'). Prayer used in the Roman Catholic Church which has often been the subject of musical compositions, e.g. by *Gounod.

Avercamp Hendrik (1585–1634). Dutch landscape painter who specialized in winter landscapes with numerous tiny figures.

Averroes. Latinized form of Ibn Rushd (1126–98), Arab philosopher working most of his life at Cordova in Spain. His commentaries, especially those on Aristotle, were very influential in Christian Europe. Also *Islam.

Avianus Flavius (?4th, ?6th c. A.D.). Latin fabulist. Most of his 42 fables are elaborated versions of the Greek fables of Babrius. They were a popular textbook in medieval schools and were frequently imitated.

Avicenna. Latinized form of Ibn Sina (979–1037), Arab philosopher and physician. His medical treatises were influential in Western Europe. Also *Islam.

Avignon school. 15th-c. French school of painting of which the leading known master was Enguerrand *Quarton and the outstanding work the beautiful and austere anon. **Pietà*. The school represents the final flowering of Avignon's 14th-c. cultural ascendancy during the papal exile.

Avvakum (*c.* 1621–82). Leader of the persecuted Russian sect (often called 'old believers') which opposed the reforms in church ritual made in the 1650s; he was burned at the stake. A. wrote exhortatory letters to his followers and a vigorous autobiography (*c.* 1672), the 1st work of its kind in Russian, being written in colloquial language instead of the standardized rhetoric of church Slavonic.

Avventura, L' (1960). Film directed by M. *Antonioni.

Awake and Sing (1935). Play by Clifford *Odets.

Axel (1894). Play by *Villiers de l'Isle-Adam.

Axel's Castle (1931). Book by Edmund *Wilson.

Ayala Pero Lopez de: Pero *Lopez de Ayala

Ayala Ramón Pérez de: Ramón *Pérez de Ayala

Aymé Marcel (1902–). French novelist, playwright and writer of masterly short stories, e.g. *Le vin de Paris* (1947). Novels include *La Jument verte* (1933; *The Green Mare*, 1938), a Rabelaisian fantasy of country life; *Travelingue* (1941; *The Miraculous Barber*, 1950), a satire on bourgeois snobbery; *Le chemin des écoliers* (1946; *The Transient Hour*, 1948), on Paris during the German occupation, and *Uranus* (1948; *Fanfare in Blémont*, 1950), on Paris after the liberation. Other works include the fables for children *Les Contes du chat perché* (1939; *The Wonderful Farm*, selected tales, 1951).

Aymon, Les Quatre Fils: *Renaud de Montauban

Ayrer Jakob (1544–1605). German playwright in the tradition of Hans Sachs. His work, however, shows the impact of the English travelling players in Germany in the 1590s; his *Comedia von der schönen Sidea* (after 1600); is interesting in that Shakespeare's *The Tempest* shows close similarities. His **Singspiele* are important in the history of the form.

Ayrton Michael (1921–). Leading English figurative sculptor, painter and draughtsman. His major preoccupations are with Greek myths, e.g. Daedalus, the Minotaur and the Delphic oracle. A. is also a gifted writer, his main work being *Testament of Daedalus* (1962).

Ayto(u)n Sir Robert (1570–1637/8). Scottish poet at the court of James I of England. His love-lyrics are his best poetry. He is the reputed author of the lines on which Burns based 'Auld Lang Syne'.

Aytoun William Edmondstoune (1813–65). Scottish writer, author with Sir T. Martin of *Bon Gaultier Ballads* (1845), a coll. of parodies on Tennyson, Macaulay and others.

Azorín (José Martínez Ruiz) (1874–). Spanish critic, novelist, playwright and essayist, and brilliant representative of the 'Generation of '98'. His finest writings are his essays on the people, landscape, and traditions of Castile written in simple but magnificently evocative prose free from any sentimentality or affectation.

Aztec art: *Pre-Columbian art

Azuela Mariano (1873–1952). Mexican novelist best known for his books about the Mexican Revolution (1910–20) and its effects, e.g. *Los de abajo* (1916; *The Under Dogs*, 1929), a brutal account, the result of his experiences as an army doctor (1915). *Las moscas* (1918; *The Flies*, 1956) and *Los caciques* (1917; *The Bosses*, 1956) express his political disillusionment. Concern for social justice and stylistic experimentation characterize his work.

azulejos. Glazed earthenware tiles, elaborately patterned and brilliantly coloured, used in Moslem and Spanish buildings, notably on the inner walls of the *Alhambra.

B

Baalbek. Temple of Bacchus

Isaac Babel

B. In German musical nomenclature 'B' is the term for the note called in English 'B♭'; the German term for the note called in English 'B' is H. Thus the theme B-A-C-H is, in English nomenclature, the notes B♭-A-C-B♮. It was used by J. S. Bach himself and subsequently by other composers, notably Liszt.

Baal (1922). Play by Bertolt *Brecht.

Baalbek Lebanon. Roman temple complex from the 2nd–3rd c. A.D. It consisted of a monumental entrance, approached by steps, a hexagonal forecourt and square main court, all lined with Corinthian columns. The Great Temple or Temple of Bacchus (A.D. 131–61) stood at the far end, the Temple of Jupiter (A.D. 273) outside the main court to the left. The round Temple of Venus (A.D. 273) lay outside the complex altogether. Extensive ruins remain.

Baan Jan van (1633–1702). Dutch portrait painter who visited the court of Charles II of England.

Babbitt (1922). Satirical novel by Sinclair *Lewis.

Babbitt Irving (1865–1933). U.S. critic and philosopher of literature; a leader of the *new humanism. He held romanticism responsible for a collapse of aesthetic standards, in *The New Laokoön . . .* (1910), *Rousseau and Romanticism* (1919), and attacked *avant-garde* contemporary writers and their advocate H. L. *Mencken, as continuators of the decline. Major critical work: *The Masters of Modern French Criticism* (1912).

Babbitt Milton (1916–). U.S. composer. Outstanding theoretician of electronic and serial music who believes in consolidating the implications of Schoenberg's thought rather than relying (as is more usual) upon techniques derived from *Webern.

Babel Isaac Emmanuilovich (1894–1939). Soviet short-story writer, born in Odessa. B. joined the army and, after the Revolution, served with a Bolshevik Cossack regiment in the Polish campaign of 1920. He was arrested in 1937 and died in a concentration camp. B.'s stories and sketches are generally brief and laconic, vividly catching moments of human experience. *Odessa Tales* (1924; 1925) depicts the Jewish environment of B.'s youth. In *Red Cavalry* (1926; 1929) the descriptions of Cossacks at war, in appearance cold and impersonal, subtly convey B.'s conflicting emotions–the Jewish intellectual's admiration for the unthinking, passionate life of the body and his revulsion from its cruelty and stupidity. Many of the stories are humorous, however, and make liberal and skilful use of slang.

Babilée Jean (1923–). French dancer and choreographer who studied at the Paris Opéra and in 1945 joined the newly-formed Ballets des Champs-Élysées as its premier danseur. He made his London début with this co. in 1946 and later appeared in America with Ballet Theater. His most outstanding roles are in the Bluebird variation, *Le Spectre de la Rose* and *Le Jeune Homme et la Mort*, which he created in 1946. His 1st choreography was for *L'Amour et son Amour* (1948) to music by César Franck. His experimental ballet *Caméléopard* (1956) is about the last days of a decadent civilization.

Babits Mihály (1883–1941). Hungarian writer. A meditative poet with philosophical tendencies, he grew into a virtuoso of bold, unusual verse and diction, e.g. *Levelek Irisz koszorú jából* (1909) and *Recitatív* (1916); his last vol. *Jónás könyve* (1940) is of classical purity void of all superfluous adornment. His novels reveal his interest in the subconscious; *A halál fiai* (1927) portrays the fools' paradise of the Hungarian middle class.

Baburen Dirck van (*c.* 1590–1624). Dutch painter, one of the principal members of the *Utrecht school. For a short period he worked in Rome, where he was affected by the work of Caravaggio; he was one of the first to introduce

Jean Babilée. Also *Chauviré

Baburen. *Soldiers gaming*

J. S. Bach: contemporary painting

J. C. Bach: attributed to Gainsborough

C. P. E. Bach: contemporary pastel

Baccarat glass

Bacchiacca. *Mary returns to her home* (detail)

Caravaggio's chiaroscuro technique into the Netherlands (*tenebrosi).

baby ballerinas. The name given to *Baronova, *Toumanova and *Riabouchinska, who first appeared in Monte Carlo in 1932 with Col. de *Basil's co. Ballets Russes when aged 13, 14 and 15 respectively. This stunt launched ballet as a popular craze.

Baby Doll (1956). Film directed by E. *Kazan and scripted by Tennessee *Williams.

Bacall Lauren (1924–). U.S. film actress, who became famous as the slinky, blonde charmer working in perfect harmony opposite her husband Humphrey Bogart: Hawks's *To Have and Have Not* (1944) was her 1st success, followed by *The Big Sleep* (1946) and *Key Largo* (1948).

Baccarat and St Louis. French glass factories established 1765 and 1767 producing fine 'cristal' glass in the English manner, most of it indistinguishable from English glass of the same period. In the early 19th c. these French factories employed a technique of enclosing white porcellaneous medallions in cut-glass. This method of decoration, and also *millefiori* and naturalistic floral motifs, was sometimes used for paperweights.

Bacchae, The. Play by *Euripides.

Bacchiacca Francesco Ubertini (1494–1557). Florentine painter, probably a pupil of Perugino but with an eclectic style most heavily influenced by Andrea del Sarto. B. painted religious subjects and decorative panels for walls or furniture, and designed tapestries.

bacchic: *metre in verse

Bach. Family of musicians and composers, active in central Germany, whose earliest recorded ancestor was Veit B. (d. 1619) and whose last descendant died in the 19th c. Individual entries on the leading members follow in alphabetical order.

Bach Carl Philipp Emanuel (1714–88). 5th child of J.S.B., and to his contemporaries the great B. Court musician to Frederick II of Prussia from 1740, he took a church appointment in Hamburg in 1767; here he was the admired friend of Klopstock and Lessing. He was noted for his keyboard playing, his piano sonatas and his treatise on keyboard technique, *Versuch über die wahre Art das Clavier zu spielen* (2 parts, 1753, 1762), and also wrote symphonies, concertos, chamber and church music. He abandoned the polyphony of his father, tending towards the style of Haydn and Mozart, both of whom acknowledged his influence.

Bach Johann Christian (1735–82). 18th child of J.S.B., and known as the 'English B.'. He settled in London (1762), where he organized a series of concerts with K. F. Abel. Mozart met B. on his visit to London in 1764 and retained a high respect for his compositions.

Bach Johann Christoph (1642–1703). Second cousin to J.S.B.; an able composer whose motet *Ich lasse dich nicht*, known in English as 'I Wrestle and Pray', was formerly ascribed to J.S.B.

Bach Johann Sebastian (1685–1750). German composer and famous among his contemporaries as a keyboard virtuoso. His compositions, the grand culmination of the later polyphonic tradition, were not so admired; that tradition itself was giving way to newer forms. Born at Eisenach, B. was orphaned when 10 years old. His early musical education came from an uncle and his brother (with whose family he lived, 1695–1700). He was a chorister at St Michael's church, Lüneburg (1700–3); violinist in the court band at Weimar (1703–5); organist at Arnstadt (1703–7), Mühlhausen (1707–8) when he married his 2nd cousin Maria Barbara B., and Weimar (1708–17, from 1714 court concert master). At Weimar, already familiar with the German organ school, e.g. J. Pachelbel, G. Böhm and D. Buxtehude, he closely studied Italian composers, e.g. A. Vivaldi (many of whose works he arranged and whose music influenced him noticeably), A. Corelli and G. Frescobaldi. He was Kapellmeister to the court of Anhalt-Köthen (1717–23). From 1723 to 1750 he was cantor in the school of St Thomas's church, Leipzig where he directed the music of the city's 2 chief churches and the univ. and taught in the school. His 1st wife died in 1720, and in 1721 he married Anna Magdalena. Shortly before his death he went blind. B.'s influence on later composers, first significantly apparent in the late Mozart, has

J. S. Bach. On this last page of *The Art of Fugue* ms., C. P. E. Bach notes that his father died at the point where he had reintroduced as counter subject the theme *B-A-C-H

W. F. Bach: contemporary painting

increased and has most recently affected certain jazz musicians, e.g. The Modern Jazz Quartet. B. developed no new musical form but left supreme examples of existing forms, the *passion, the *chorale prelude, the *cantata, the *concerto, the orchestral suite. In all these he used fugal texture, demonstrating an unequalled mastery of *fugue. B.'s musical structures are composed of singing melodic lines, in all parts, punctuated with rich resultant harmonies and built up in grand units architecturally balanced. This architectonic structure is well shown in the D min. chaconne for solo violin–as the music proceeds, it grows with recollections and references which are seen to balance. The C min. organ passacaglia, the *Kyrie* of the B min. Mass, the final chorus of the *St Matthew Passion* and the ground bass of the 2nd movement of the D min. clavier concerto all exemplify B.'s mighty gift for architectural organization, and the harpsichord cadenza in the 1st movement of the 5th Brandenburg concerto shows his control of climax. In his instrumental music B. frequently develops exhaustively a melodic or harmonic motif to build a climax which depends not on crescendo or rhythmic variation but simply on an accumulation of musical images developed from the 1st motif; e.g. the great A. min. organ prelude. His enormous output (which includes over 200 cantatas alone) precludes adequate summarization but, briefly, his works are generally grouped in 3 periods. WEIMAR (1708–17). Sacred cantatas, *Orgelbüchlein*, great organ works, including the passacaglia and double fugue in C min. and the famous D min. toccata and fugue. KÖTHEN (1717–23). Sonatas and partitas for solo violin (*c.* 1720); suites for solo cello (*c.* 1720); the 6 *concerto grosso style Brandenburg concertos (1721) dedicated to the margrave of Brandenburg; D min. concerto for 2 violins; the *Well Tempered Clavier* (1722), 24 preludes and fugues in all the maj. and min. keys (*temperament), *Italian concerto.* LEIPZIG (1723–50). Sacred and secular cantatas, *St John Passion* (1723), *Magnificat* (1723), *St Matthew Passion* (1729); *Chromatic fantasia and fugue* (1730), *Christmas oratorio* (1734); D. min. clavier concerto (1729–36); *Goldberg variations (1742); a further 24 preludes and fugues called book II of the *Well Tempered Clavier* (completed 1744); *The Musical Offering* (1747), a sonata and a group of canons and ricercares on a theme said to be by Frederick II of Prussia, the dedicatee; *The Art of Fugue* (1749–50), a group of fugues and canons on a single group of subjects, which demonstrate with increasing complexity the techniques of counterpoint. Much of the music of the great Mass in B min. is reworking of earlier pieces: the *Kyrie* and the *Gloria* (constituting the Lutheran *missa*) were composed in 1733 but recent research suggests that the *Sanctus* was first written in 1724 and that this and the rest of the Mass was given its final form in B.'s last years.

Bach Wilhelm Friedemann (1710–84). Eldest son of J.S.B., who wrote some of his keyboard works for him. A gifted composer and musician, he held important posts, but because of his erratic character died in poverty. He was the subject of the romantic novel *Friedemann B.* (1858) by A. E. Brachvogel.

Bachauer Gina (1913–). Greek pianist, taught by A. Cortot and Rachmaninov. She excels in the concertos of Tchaikovsky and Rachmaninov.

Bachelors, The (1934). Novel by Henry de *Montherlant.

Bachianas Brasilieras. Group of works for instruments and voices by *Villa-Lobos.

Baciccia (Baciccio). Nickname of Giovanni Battista Gaulli (1639–1709), one of the finest Italian baroque portrait painters and decorators. His style was influenced by Rubens and Van Dyck. Working in Rome, where he was a friend of Bernini, he produced masterpieces of illusionist decorative work, notably the ceiling of the church of Il Gesù (1668–83).

backdrop. Scenic device in the theatre; a large sheet of painted canvas which can be lowered to cover the back of the stage.

Backer Jacob Adriaensz (1608–51). Dutch portrait painter and pupil of Rembrandt whose influence on him was strong. He was also influenced by the work of Hals.

Backhaus Wilhelm (1884–). German pianist, taught by A. Reckendorf and E. d'Albert. His reputation is greater abroad (especially in England and the U.S.) than in Germany, where he is considered an academic performer. B. is noted for his Beethoven interpretations.

Backer. *Portrait of a woman*

Baciccia. *Triumph of the Name of Jesus*, ceiling of Il Gesù

Backhuysen. *Boats in a storm*

Francis Bacon. *Study for the nurse in Battleship Potemkin* (detail; 1957)

Sir Francis Bacon: contemporary print

John Bacon. Chatham monument

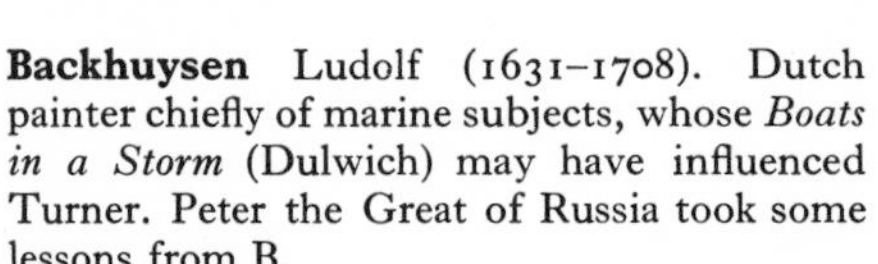

Backhuysen Ludolf (1631–1708). Dutch painter chiefly of marine subjects, whose *Boats in a Storm* (Dulwich) may have influenced Turner. Peter the Great of Russia took some lessons from B.

Backof(f)en Hans (d. 1519). German late Gothic sculptor, from 1505 active in Mainz. His work includes the tomb of Archbishop Uriel von Gemmingen (Mainz cathedral) and Crucifixion groups in the churchyards of St Peter's and the cathedral, Frankfurt.

Back to Methuselah (1922). Cycle of 5 plays by G. B. *Shaw.

Bacon Francis, 1st Baron Verulam and Viscount St Albans (1561–1626). English writer, and a distinguished statesman, whose career under Elizabeth I and James I ended in 1621, when he was found guilty of corruption. B. was the 1st philosopher to advocate confidently the practice of observation and experiment which was superseding medieval scholasticism. With the exception of *The Advancement of Learning* (1605) his most important works in this field are written in Latin. B.'s contributions to English literature include *The New Atlantis* (1626) and, above all, the *Essays, or Counsels, Civill and Morall* (1597; final ed. 1625), which are short disquisitions conveying a practical wisdom on many subjects, written in a compressed, vigorous and aphoristic style. The theory that B. wrote the plays commonly accepted as by Shakespeare, dates from the late 18th c. and is the most frequently advanced of about 60 similar theories.

Bacon Francis (1910–). Irish painter. His powerful images are largely based on photographs (e.g. the screaming nurse in the film the **Battleship Potemkin*), reproductions of paintings he admires (e.g. Velazquez's *Pope Innocent X* (Gal. Doria, Rome)), and 2 books, the *Human Figure in Motion* and *Animals in Motion*, both by E. Muybridge. One of his aims is to freeze fleeting transitional expressions and gestures in paint; most of his pictures show figures in motion, usually isolated and painted in violent colours. He is not interested in nature. He has said that 'painting is the pattern of one's nervous system being projected on canvas'.

Bacon John (1740–99). British porcelain modeller and sculptor. He began working in marble in 1763 and improved the method for transferring the design of the clay model to the stone. He became a fashionable society sculptor of tombs and monuments, e.g. the Chatham monument in Westminster Abbey.

Bacon Lloyd (1889–1955). U.S. film director. A specialist in musicals and comedies, B.'s most famous film is *Forty-Second Street* (1933), which gained its reputation, however, from the musical numbers which were directed by Busby *Berkeley.

Baczyński Krzysztof Kamil (1921–44). Polish lyric poet, killed in the Warsaw Rising. He wrote reflective and visionary poetry, expressing in dynamic and highly metaphorical language the tragedy of his generation. B. also produced some very fine love poems.

Badarzewska-Baranowska Telka (1838–61). Polish composer. She wrote the piano solo *The Maiden's Prayer* (1856), trite but fantastically successful everywhere except in Poland.

Badings Henk (Hendrik Herman) (1907–). Dutch composer, pupil of W. Pijper. B.'s 1st symphony was performed in 1930. From 1941 to 1945 he was director of The Hague Conservatory. His music, which has had wide international success, is marked by balance and complexity of form. Works include: 8 symphonies (*Psalm symphony*, no. 6, 1953), concerto for 2 violins (1954), saxophone concerto (1951), organ and carillon music, much chamber music, 3 operas and the radio opera *Orestes* (1954). Since 1956 he has worked with electronic music.

Baena Juan Alfonso de. 15th-c. Spanish poet remembered for an anthology, *Cancionero de*

Francis Bacon. *Pope II* (1951)

Bagpipe player; woodcut by Dürer

Baglione. *St John the Baptist*

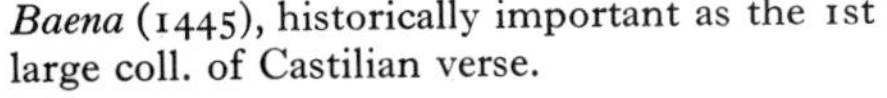

Baena (1445), historically important as the 1st large coll. of Castilian verse.

Bagehot Walter (1826–77). English critic and ed. of *The Economist* (1860–7), best known for his penetrating analysis of *The English Constitution* (1867). He wrote essays on literary and biographical subjects.

Baggesen Jens (1764–1826). Danish poet and prose-writer, whose travel book *Labyrinten* (2 vols, 1792–3), in the style of L. Sterne, is a model of Danish prose. The witty, elegant verse coll. *Comiske Fortaellinger* (1785) made his name. He wrote also in German and French, living in France for a time. After his return to Denmark (1806) he suffered a short conversion to romanticism but soon broke violently with the school and its leader A. G. Oehlenschlæger. He died poor and forgotten.

Baglione Giovanni (*c.* 1573–1644). Italian late mannerist painter and the author of a history of art in Rome during his lifetime, *Le vite de' pittori, scultori ed architetti* . . . (1642). In spite of the hostility he expressed towards Caravaggio, his own painting *c.* 1600 acquired a superficial likeness to Caravaggio's. He was one of the artists commissioned by Pope Paul V to paint frescoes in the church of S. Maria Maggiore, Rome.

bagpipes. Musical instrument common in folk-music of all European countries in various forms. A 'chanter' pipe gives the melody, additional pipes giving a drone accompaniment; usually these all lead from a bladder held under the player's arm and acting as a reservoir of air; sometimes the chanter is played by a separate performer. The air-supply is either the player's wind or is supplied by bellows. The French term for b. *musette* has given its name to a movement introduced to the suite in the 18th c.

Bagshot diamonds. Crystals used as imitation diamonds and exported from England especially in the period 1770–1800. In France crystals from Alençon or Chatellerault were similarly used.

Bähr Georg (1666–1738). German architect. City carpenter of Dresden, B. designed the Frauenkirche (1726), the greatest Protestant church in Germany (destroyed by bombs, 1945). It had an almost square plan surmounted by a huge dome and galleries arranged inside like an opera-house.

Bahr Herman (1863–1934). Austrian writer and, as a publicist rather than a creator, in the forefront of every literary movement 1890–1920. His play *Das Konzert* (1909) had European success.

Baïf Jean-Antoine de (1532–89). French poet and scholar. Member of the *Pléiade. His moral and satirical *Mimes* (1581) is remembered, but his poetic talent did not equal his learning or his tireless experimentation with language and versification; the '*baïfin*' was a 15-syllable line.

Bailey P(hilip) J(ames) (1816–1902). English poet whose 40,000-line *Festus* (1839; continuously enlarged until 1889), inspired by Goethe's *Faust*, was extremely popular and highly regarded in the 19th c.

Bailey-Adounard Georges (1903–). Guadeloupe-born French painter. His predominantly abstract canvases are inspired by the luxuriant landscapes of his native island, e.g. *Le Melon Sanglant*, but his occasional visits to Marseilles have introduced urban imagery to some of his later work.

Bailiff's Daughter of Islington, The. An English ballad, included in *Percy's *Reliques* . . . . A squire's son loves the bailiff's daughter, but is prevented from marrying her by being sent to London as an apprentice. 7 years later the lovers meet again and are united.

Baillie Isobel (1895–). Scottish soprano. She sang mainly oratorio and *Lieder*; her voice was distinguished by exceptional purity of tone.

Bähr. Frauenkirche, Dresden

Josephine Baker at a wartime concert in London

Balakirev

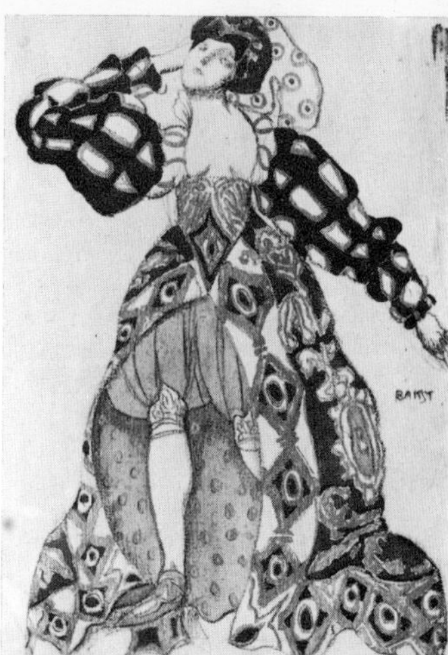
Bakst. Designs for *The Sleeping Princess* and *La Légende de Joseph*

Le Baiser

Bakema. Lynbaan pedestrian shopping centre

Baillie Joanna (1762–1851). Scottish dramatist and poet whose *Plays on the Passions* were admired by her friend Scott; the most successful was *The Family Legend* (1810).

Baillot Pierre-Marie-François de Sales (1771–1842). French violinist and composer. In 1791, after a period in Italy, he returned to Paris where he studied composition under Cherubini and gained a professorship of the violin at the Conservatoire. He had a great reputation as a performer but is remembered for his influential treatise *Art du violon* (1834).

Bainton Edgar (Leslie) (1880–1956). English composer. He was the principal of the State Conservatory of New South Wales, Sydney (1934–47). Works include the symphony *Before Sunrise* for contralto chorus and orchestra (1917), 2 operas, choral works and the symphonic poem *Paracelsus* (1921).

Bairstow (Sir) Edward Cuthbert (1874–1946). English organist, from 1913 at York Minster, and composer of church music.

Baiser, Le ('The Kiss', 1886). Sculpture by Rodin.

Bakema Jacob (1914–). Dutch architect in practice with Van den Broek since 1948; they designed the Lynbaan pedestrian shopping centre in Rotterdam (1953) and the civic centre at Marl now under construction. B. was a prominent member of Team X which caused the break-up of *CIAM.

Baker George Pierce (1866–1935). U.S. lecturer on all aspects of theatre and dramatic composition and, as the founder and director of the 47 Workshop (originated 1905), one of the major formative influences in the modern U.S. theatre. Writers who studied under B. included O'Neill, Howard, Behrman and Dos Passos.

Baker Josephine (1906–). American-born French entertainer and singer who has appeared in countless revues, most notably in Paris at the Folies-Bergères, Casino de Paris and La Créole. Her many films include *Zouzou* and *Princess Tam-Tam*. A Chevalier de la Légion d'Honneur, she now lives in Paris.

Baker Sir Richard (1568–1645). English historian. While imprisoned for debt through misfortune, B. wrote *A Chronicle of the Kings of England . . .* (1641). 9 eds appeared before 1700.

Bakic Vojin (1915–). Yugoslav sculptor, trained at Zagreb Academy of Fine Arts. After periods of realism and neo-cubism he has evolved a style of formal purity in the tradition of Brancusi and Arp.

Bakst Léon (1866–1924). Russian artist and stage designer. After studying in Paris (1893) he returned to St Petersburg, where with A. Benois and S. *Diaghilev he collaborated on the magazine *Mir Iskustva* ('World of Art'). In 1909 he went to Paris and joined Diaghilev's Ballets Russes. Here his sets for the ballets *Cléopâtre* (1909) and above all *Schéhérazade* (1910) caused a sensation. B.'s designs, characterized by throbbing colours and exotic line, were the first to integrate costumes and sets into a visual unity. Other designs were for Nijinsky's ballet *Le Spectre de la Rose* (1911), G. D'Annunzio's play *La Pisanella* and the ballet *The Sleeping Princess* (1921).

Balaguer Victor (1824–1901). Catalan poet, playwright, novelist, historian and nationalist politician. His history *Historia de Cataluña* (5 vols, 1860–3) and other work, e.g. *Poesías catalánas completas . . .* (2 vols, 1868) were important in the *Catalan renaissance.

Balakirev Mily (1837–1910). Russian composer and pianist; founder and mentor of the nationalistic group The *Mighty Handful. Friendship with Glinka from 1855 directed his enthusiasm for Russian folk-music. B. was conductor (1863), later director of the Free School of Music in St Petersburg, but poverty

Balanchine. Scene from *Apollon-Musagète*

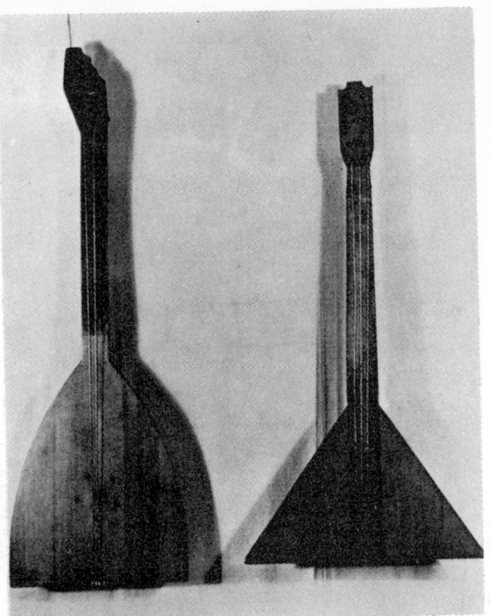

Balalaika

Baldovinetti. *The Virgin*, from the *Annunciation* fresco

and a phase of obsessive religion caused him to retire from music (1872–6). He was afterwards the director of the imperial chapel (1883–94). B. learnt much from Glinka in setting folk-melodies and integrated oriental idioms and romanticism (of Liszt especially) into a coherent style, e.g. in the piano fantasy *Islamey* (1869) and the symphonic poem *Tamara* (1867–82); he also wrote many songs and 2 symphonies.

balalaika. Plucked string instrument of the guitar type, very popular in Russia. The b. has a triangular body, a long fretted neck with 3 strings usually tuned in 4ths and plucked with a plectrum; it is made in various sizes. B. bands are common in Russia.

Balanchine George (1904–). Russian choreographer, naturalized U.S. citizen 1939. In 1924 he toured Europe with the Soviet State Dancers and from 1925 to 1929 worked for S. Diaghilev, e.g. producing *Apollon-Musagète* (1928). In 1934 he became director of the new School of American Ballet. He was a co-founder of the New York City Ballet (1948). B.'s abstract style is exemplified in *Ballet Imperial* (1941) and *Concerto barocco* (1941).

Balassi (or Balassa) Bálint (1554–94). Hungarian poet and soldier; the 1st great personality of Hungarian literature. His work broke through the conventional patterns of contemporary humanism.

Balbuena Bernardo de (1568–1627). Spanish poet who spent most of his life in Central America, becoming bishop of Puerto Rico (1620). *El Bernardo* . . . (written in B.'s youth, publ. 1624) is the best of a number of Spanish epics written in imitation of *Orlando Furioso*; B.'s *Siglio de Oro* . . . (1607), a pastoral novel, contains much good poetry.

Balcon Sir Michael (1896–). Film producer: B. started as a producer in British studios in 1922. His Ealing studios were responsible for the move of documentary film makers into feature films during World War II. This resulted in post-war successes like *The Overlanders*. He also produced the series of Ealing comedies, including *Kind Hearts and Coronets* and *The Man in the White Suit*. Unlike Korda, he worked on the principle that British films should be budgeted to succeed on the British market alone. Ealing studios were sold to television in 1956 but B. continued as an independent.

Baldi Bernardino (1553–1617). Italian poet whose chief work was *La Nautica*, a didactic poem in the style of Virgil's *Georgics*, dealing with navigation and ship-building.

Baldinucci Filippo (*c.* 1624–96). Florentine art historian. In the course of his studies he made a huge coll. of drawings (now in the Uffizi) and used documents more than Vasari had done. His chief work was *Notizie de' professori del disegno* . . . (1681–1728), which covered the period 1260 to 1670.

Baldovinetti Alesso (*c.* 1425–99). Florentine painter; studied under Domenico Veneziano. His surviving masterpiece, the fresco of the *Annunciation*, S. Annunziata, Florence, shows his interest in landscape, the serenity of his figures and the sensitivity of his colour. B. executed work in stained glass and mosaic. He influenced Ghirlandaio.

Baldung (Grien) Hans (*c.* 1480–1545). German painter and graphic artist. He was influenced by Dürer, under whom he probably studied, and indeed in his portraits he showed a psychological insight and mastery of drawing comparable to his master's. Besides portraits he painted allegorical subjects and, like Cranach, a series of female nudes; but his fame rested on his religious paintings, and the altarpiece *The Coronation of the Virgin* (1512–16), in the cathedral at Freiburg im Breisgau, is still considered his masterpiece. His paintings are characterized by their unusual colour combinations and his woodcuts by their inventiveness, fantasy and grotesque humour. He also designed for stained glass.

Baldung. *Harmony*

James Baldwin

Balla. *Dog on a Leash.* Also *futurism

Thomas Baldwin. The Guildhall, Bath

Baldwin James (1924–). U.S. Negro writer. His 1st novel, *Go tell it on the Mountain* (1953), about religious experience in Negro Harlem, established his reputation. Other books include essays, *Notes of a Native Son* (1955), the novel *Giovanni's Room* (1956), set in Paris, where B. lived for some years, and *Nobody Knows My Name* (1961), describing his return to the U.S. Other works on the colour question are *Another Country* (1962), *The Fire Next Time* (1963), and the play *Blues for Mr Charlie* (1964).

Baldwin Thomas (1750–1820). English architect who worked mainly in Bath. He designed the Guildhall (1766), with its sumptuous banqueting hall; the Pump Room; and many terraces and streets, including Bathwick, on the other side of the Avon–an ambitious attempt to rival *Wood's earlier scheme.

Bale John (1495–1563). English Protestant bishop, author of many vituperative anti-Catholic morality plays and hence nicknamed 'bilious Bale'. *Kynge Johan* marks a transition between the medieval miracle play and Elizabethan historical drama. B. also compiled a compendium of British authors of his day, noting the sources of his information.

Balen Hendrik van (1575–1632). Antwerp painter of small and charming landscapes, allegorical, Biblical and mythological scenes. He collaborated with J. Bruegel the Younger, Momper and Vrancx. Van Dyck and Snyders were his pupils.

Balestra Antonio (1666–1740). Italian late baroque painter, pupil of C. Maratta. He worked chiefly in Venice and Verona and was influential as a teacher.

Balfe Michael William (1808–70). British composer and theatre manager. B. studied in Italy, wrote *The Bohemian Girl* (1843) and produced his operas in London, Paris, Berlin and St Petersburg.

Ball Hugo (1886–1927). German painter and poet who went to Switzerland at the beginning of World War I. He was one of the founders of the *dada movement and ed. of the 1st dada review, *Cabaret Voltaire*. In 1917 he quarrelled with T. Tzara and left the movement.

Balla Giacomo (1871–1958). Italian painter, a founder of futurism and one of the signatories of the futurist manifesto (1910). On a visit to Paris (1900) he was strongly affected by the impressionist and divisionist painters. B.'s *Dog on a Leash* (1912; M.M.A., New York), as an attempt to present motion by superimposing several images, is a logical exposition of futurism; but his pictures developed towards abstract art, increasingly resolving into abstract lines of movement and force.

ballad. A type of traditional narrative poetry (perhaps originally sung) surviving as the end product of a modifying oral tradition. The form varies, but in English, a b. usually has a simple stanzaic form and rhyme scheme. In all countries, however, the b. tells of legendary events and heroes and the supernatural beings of folklore. One of the earliest and richest of European b. literatures is Danish, the 2 other main ones being Spanish and English. In all cases early colls survive. In late 16th-c. Spain there was a vogue for the b.: Lope de Vega occasionally used b. plots and G. de Castro's play, *Las Mocedades del Cid* is based on the b. The earliest English b. coll. is the 17th-c. ms., the Percy folio. This was the basis for the *Reliques* of T. Percy which influenced English romantic poetry and had an immeasurable influence on German romanticism (also A. W. *Schlegel). Poets who revived the b. included G. A. Burger, Uhland, Schiller and Goethe and in England Wordsworth, Coleridge, Scott and Keats. The rich b. literature of the U.S. contains many pieces of English origin as well as others on the Revolution, the Civil War, Negroes (e.g. John Henry) and the West (e.g. Billy the Kid).

ballade. Medieval French verse form; its main form consists of three 8-line stanzas rhyming

Ballet Russe de Monte Carlo.
La Boutique Fantasque (1934)

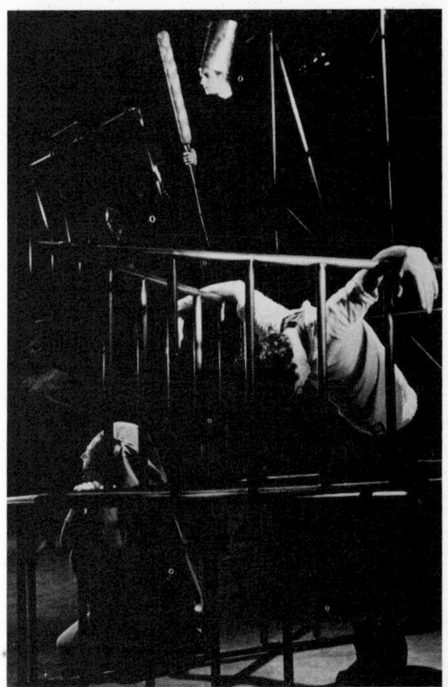

Ballet Rambert.
The Realms of Choice

ababbcbc, the last line being a repeated refrain, and an *envoi* rhyming *bcbc* and ending with the refrain. It was pre-eminent, with the *rondeau, during the 14th–15th c., Villon being a master of the form. It was revived in the 19th c. The medieval musical form of b. follows the verse form in structure.

Ballad of a Soldier (1959). Film directed by G. *Chukrai.

Ballad of Reading Gaol, The (1898). Poem by Oscar *Wilde.

Ballad of the Sad Café, The (1951). Novel by Carson *McCullers.

ballad opera. English form, in which spoken dialogue alternates with verses set to folk or popular tunes, so popular in London (1728–38) that Handel complained it was driving out Italian opera. The 1st and most famous was Gay's *The Beggar's Opera*.

Ballantyne Robert Michael (1825–94). Scottish author of popular stories for boys. He worked in Hudson Bay territories, Canada (1842–8) and travelled extensively in other parts of the world. *The Coral Island* (1857) is his most famous book.

ball clay. Clay of sedimentary origin, very fine and of high plasticity. It fires white or whiteish and withstands high temperatures. The name derives from the method of excavation, which produces squares of clay weighing 30–35 lb which are called 'balls' by the workmen. The clays are used in the production of earthenware.

ballerina. Technically a title of a female dancer who plays leading roles in classical ballets and loosely a term for any female ballet dancer. The title 'prima b. assoluta' was given in the Russian Imperial Ballet, to P. Legnani and M. Kschessinskaya. The term 'prima b.' is not used in the ballet world.

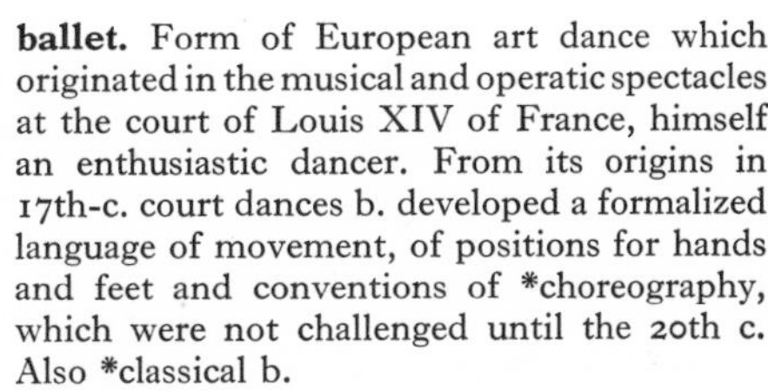

ballet. Form of European art dance which originated in the musical and operatic spectacles at the court of Louis XIV of France, himself an enthusiastic dancer. From its origins in 17th-c. court dances b. developed a formalized language of movement, of positions for hands and feet and conventions of *choreography, which were not challenged until the 20th c. Also *classical b.

ballet d'action. Term distinguishing ballets with a theme or story from ballets common in the 17th and 18th cs which were primarily suites of dances.

balletomane. A word originating in Tsarist Russia to describe ballet lovers who attended performances at the Imperial Theatre, St Petersburg and formed a type of fan club for individual dancers.

Ballet Rambert. Founded by Marie *Rambert.

Ballet Russe de Monte Carlo. Founded 1937 by R. *Blum with L. Massine as artistic director. In 1938 it moved to the U.S. where, after Massine's resignation and Blum's death, it continued, though as a predominantly U.S. co.

Ballets de Paris. (1948–50; 1953–4; 1955.) French co., formed by R. *Petit, whose members included R. Jeanmaire. Its productions were characterized by their acrobatic nature. Their *Carmen*, first produced in London, 1949, had a *succès fou* there and in Paris and New York.

Ballets des Champs-Élysées, Les. In Paris in 1945, dissatisfied splinter groups of young dancers from the Opéra and Opéra-Comique gathered round Roland Petit and Janine Charrat. With the encouragement of Jean Cocteau and others they formed a co. based on the Théâtre des Champs-Élysées (1945). This mostly teen-aged co. endowed French ballet with a new vitality and mounted such works as *Les Forains* (1945), *Jeu de Cartes* (1945), *Le*

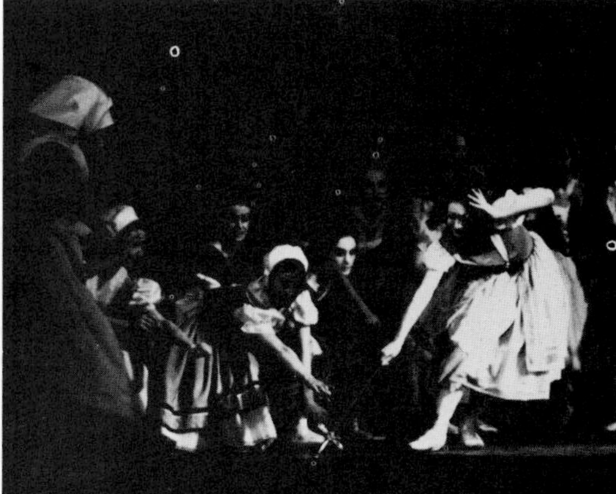

Ballet Rambert. The 'Mad Scene' from *Giselle*

Ballets des Champs-Élysées.
Petit and Vyroubova in *Les Forains*

Ballets Russes. Lifar in *Pastorale* (1926)

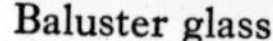
Baluster glass

Balusters

Ballets Russes. Danilova and Lifar in *Triumph of Neptune* (1927)

Balzac: watercolour by Boulanger

Rendez-Vous (1945), *Le Jeune Homme et la Mort* (1946), and *La Création* (1948). Dancers such as Jean Babilée, Renée Jeanmaire and Nina Vyroubova appeared with the co., but they dispersed gradually and finally disbanded in the early 1950s.

Ballet Society. Founded (New York, 1946) by L. Kirstein and G. Balanchine to present new ballet. It became the New York City Ballet in 1948.

Ballets Russes. The co., formed by *Diaghilev, whose 1st season (Paris, 1909), which included *The Dances from Prince Igor*, was a revolutionary break with ballet and theatre conventions and heavily influenced subsequent developments in the Western theatre. Its ballets were short, and the exotic costumes and sets and vivid music formed a dramatic whole. Members of the co. included the dancers A. *Pavlova, I. *Rubinstein, V. *Nijinsky, M. *Fokine as ballet master, A. *Benois as artistic director, and L. *Bakst as set designer. In the following season productions included **Schéhérazade*, Stravinsky's *The Firebird, Petrushka* and *The Rite of Spring* and M. Fokine's *Le Spectre de la Rose*. Personnel changed, the original novelty was lost and a new period opened with the stage sets of Picasso, Matisse and the music of Poulenc among others. On Diaghilev's death in 1929 the co. dissolved.

Ballets Russes de Monte Carlo (from 1936, COL. DE BASIL'S BALLET RUSSE; from 1939, ORIGINAL BALLET RUSSE). The immediate successor of Diaghilev's Ballets Russes. It was founded in 1932 under de *Basil with G. Balanchine as ballet master (1932–3 season) and R. Blum as artistic director. The co. continued under its various names into the late 1940s (1940–7 in the Americas).

Ballet Theater (from 1957 AMERICAN BALLET THEATER). Founded 1940. Some of its early productions were staged by M. Fokine. Among U.S. choreographers it introduced were A. de Mille and J. *Robbins. A. Dolin, A. Markova, L. Massine and A. *Tudor, artistic administrator from 1946, have all been associated with B. T.

ballon. Ballet term used to describe the springiness in a dancer's feet.

Balmont Konstantin Dmitrievich (1867–1943). Russian poet connected with the symbolists. After 1905 he lived mostly in exile. His work, including *Under Northern Skies* (1894) and *Let Us Be as the Sun* (1903), had a luxuriant word music, similar to Shelley, new in Russian poetry.

Balthazar (1958). Novel by Lawrence *Durrell.

baluster. A small column or pillar, slender at its top and bottom and usually swelling out at its middle; a supporting member of a balustrade. In furniture, a baluster also has a supporting function but can be variously straight, twisted, or tapered in shape. It has a similar application in metalwork, for example in the stems of wine-cups, candlesticks and similar objects.

Balzac Honoré de (1799–1850). French novelist. After 3 years in a law office and 2 years as a printer-publisher ending in bankruptcy (1816–21), B. turned to fiction. Stimulated by the works of Scott he wrote adventure stories anonymously from 1822 to 1825, to earn a living. In 1831 he found his true *métier* with *Le Peau de Chagrin* followed by short stories and a masterpiece, his novel *Eugénie Grandet* (1833). From then onwards with a creative exuberance rarely equalled in literary history, he wrote with a vigour, speed, marvellous breadth of outlook and grasp of detail, a succession of works that have established him as one of the world's greatest novelists.
In 1842 he grouped what he had written under the general title *La Comédie Humaine* (1842–8; *The Human Comedy*, 1895–9) dividing it into: STUDIES OF SOCIETY (*Études de Mœurs*).
Scenes from private life. 27 novels, including *Modeste Mignon* (1844) and *Le Père Goriot* (1834–5). The latter describes the initiation of Eugene Rastignac into the cruel ways of society and the callous impoverishment of the retired merchant Goriot by his ungrateful daughters.
Scenes from provincial life. 12 novels, including *Eugénie Grandet, Le Curé de Tours* (1832) and *Illusions perdues* (1837–43).
Scenes from Parisian life. 21 novels, including *Histoire . . . de César Birotteau* (1837) and *La Cousine Bette* (1846).
Scenes from political life. 4 novels, including *Une Ténébreuse Affaire* (1841).

Bandinelli. *Hercules and Caco*, Piazza della Signoria, Florence

Bandinelli. Pen and ink design for the monument of Pope Clement VII

Scenes from military life. 2 novels, including *Les Chouans* (1829).
Scenes from country life. 4 novels including *Le Médecin de campagne* (1833).
PHILOSOPHICAL STUDIES. 19 novels, including *Le Peau de Chagrin* (1830–1), *Louis Lambert* (1832) and *La Recherche de l'Absolu* (1834).
ANALYTICAL STUDIES. 4 novels.
More than 2,000 characters appear and re-appear, taking sometimes major, sometimes minor roles, and although the books were written at different times the whole *Comédie* is a developing chronicle of French society from the 1790s to the 1830s. It was said of B. that his work was less an observation of society than the creation of another, and his best characters, usually from middle-class or lower-class life, seem to be subjects of a biography rather than a novel. The pungent sense of reality comes from his vivid presentation of his characters' environment, occupations and way of life, based upon an intense study of the people he met in the streets of Paris and elsewhere, and his prodigious memory for minute detail. He was the forerunner of the realism exemplified in the novels of the brothers Goncourt. The nature of B.'s achievement makes irrelevant criticisms of his characterization as exaggerated and of his style as clumsy and inelegant by canons of classical French. Despite the almost incredible speed at which he wrote, he revised his work extensively, usually at proof stage, and frequently deprived himself of any income at all because of his printer's bills. He wrote a number of plays, some of which are still performed, and was twice an unsuccessful candidate for the French Academy.
Throughout his life B. was in debt: added to his working methods was a mania for speculation. He drove himself mercilessly and died largely of overwork, leaving detailed plans for much further writing. He had affairs with several women, among them Mme Hanska, a Polish countess, whom he married a few months before his death. Their correspondence was publ. as *Lettres à l'Étrangère* (2 vols, 1899, 1906).

Balzac Jean-Louis Guez de (*c.* 1595–1654). French writer, an important figure in the development of French prose, which by careful study he made lucid and sonorous. However, the content of his many essays and dialogues is no longer of much interest.

Bambini Ci Guardano, I (1942). Film directed by V. de *Sica.

bambocciata (Italian, 'jest'). A genre of painting which deals with peasant life and bawdy scenes. 17th-c. Dutch and Flemish artists were particularly given to it.

Bamboccio: P. van *Laer

Bandello Matteo (1485–1561). Italian writer. His coll. of short stories *Le Novelle* contains *Giulietta e Romeo*, from which Shakespeare wrote *Romeo and Juliet.*

Bandinelli Baccio (sometimes called 'Bartolommeo') (1493–1560). Florentine sculptor, painter and goldsmith. The well-hated rival of Benvenuto Cellini and in his own opinion the equal of Michelangelo. He executed a series of reliefs in Florence cathedral and founded 2 of the earliest *academies.

banding. In furniture, where an inlaid strip of contrasting wood or woods is made to form a border. In the neo-classical period of the 18th c. satinwood and other exotic hardwoods were widely used in broad banding. Varieties include straight b. where the wood has been cut along the length of the grain; cross-b. across the grain; and feather-b. at an angle between straight and cross. The term is used in architecture for walls, etc., decorated with layers of masonry alternating in colour or texture.

bandora. Plucked stringed musical instrument with frets using wire strings and having a flat back. It was evolved in England in the late 16th c.

Bandwagon, The (1953). Film directed by V. *Minnelli.

Bang Herman (1857–1912). Danish novelist and short-story writer. Both his masterly realist novel *Ved vejen* (1898) and the coll. of short stories *Stille Eksistenser* (1886) show his interest in insignificant and downtrodden people.

banjo. Instrument of guitar type plucked with fingers or plectrum. The round body is a metal frame over which is stretched the resonating

Banjo

Banding. Louis XVI secrétaire

Banks. Monument for Penelope Boothby

Tallulah Bankhead

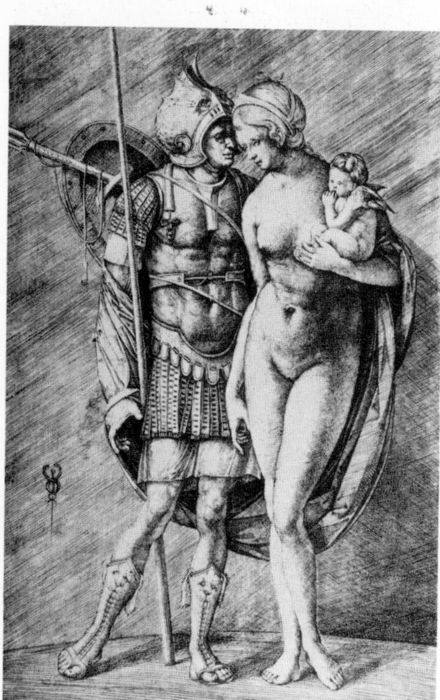

De' Barbari. *Mars and Venus*; engraving

table of vellum; the b. has a long fretted neck and 5 strings (4 on the plectrum b.) of which one is an 8ve string or '*chanterelle*'. The b. probably originated in Africa.

Bank Dick, The (1940). Film directed by E. *Cline.

Bankhead Tallulah (1903–). U.S. actress who became famous in London in *The Dancers* (1923) and *The Green Hat* (1925). Returning to New York (1933) she achieved the greatest of her many successes as Regina Giddens in *The Little Foxes* (1939). *Tallulah: My Autobiography*, was publ. in 1952.

Banks Sir Thomas (1735–1805). British sculptor who went to Rome (1772–9) and was among the 1st British sculptors of neo-classicism. His most famous works were the *Thetis* (V. and A.) and the monument to the dead child Penelope Boothby (Ashbourne, Derbyshire).

Bannister John (1760–1836). English comic actor. B. appeared at Drury Lane in such parts as Don Ferolo Whiskerandos in Sheridan's *The Critic*, Sir Anthony Absolute in his *The Rivals* and Tony Lumpkin in Goldsmith's *She Stoops to Conquer*. He retired in 1815.

Bantock Sir Granville (1868–1946). English conductor and composer largely for the voice, e.g. unaccompanied choral works, solo and part songs. He wrote the opera *The Seal Woman* (1924) and his orchestral music included the 'Hebridean' symphony. He was professor of music at Birmingham Univ. (1908–34).

Banville Théodore de (1823–91). French poet, dramatist and writer. His books of poetry include *Les Cariatides* (1842), *Le Sang de la coupe* (1857) and *Les Exilés* (1867). He was an early member of the *Parnassian school and in 1866 a contributor to the magazine *Le Parnasse contemporain*. B. revived the ballad form, wrote plays, short stories and a treatise on French versification.

bar. (1) In music, a division on the stave made by vertical 'b.-lines' and indicating a metrical unit; the b.s may be of 2, 3, etc., 'beats in the b.'. (2) In ballet, a rail in the studio which the dancer uses to balance himself in certain exercises.

John Bannister

Bara Theda (1890–1955). U.S. silent-film star and the original 'vamp', e.g. *The Eternal Sin* (1917).

Barabbas (1950). Novel by Pär *Lagerkvist; also the subject of films directed by A. *Sjöberg (1953) and R. *Fleischer (1962).

Baratier Jacques (1918–). French film director. From 1948 to 1955 B. made a series of gently lyrical shorts, mainly on Paris and Parisians. He carried the same qualities to Tunisia to film the fable of *Goha* (1956–7). The pantomime qualities of this found less successful expression in the politico-sexual fantasies written by Jacques Audiberti in *La Poupée* (1962). His satire on the cinéma-vérité of *Rouch *Dragées au Poivre* (1963) was spirited but unskilled.

Baratynsky Evgeny Abramovich (1800–44). Russian romantic poet, in his youth strongly influenced by Pushkin; his late verse, intellectual and deeply pessimistic, has great power and originality.

Barbara Allen. In the ballad *Bonny Barbara Allen*, B. A. ignores her lover's pining for her, but when she hears his death-knell tolling, she repents and dies of remorse. In the U.S., the most popular of the British ballads.

Barbari Jacopo de' (*c.* 1450–1515/16). Venetian painter and draughtsman, perhaps of German origin, chiefly remembered as an engraver of mythological and sacred subjects. He worked for some time in Germany and the Netherlands where he was known as 'Jacob Walch'. His work was a link between the Italian and northern schools. He is credited with instructing Dürer in the mathematical proportions of the human figure.

Barbatelli Bernardino: Bernardino *Poccetti

Barbellion W. N. P. Pseud. of Bruce Frederick Cummings (1889–1919). English writer, author of *The Journal of a Disappointed Man* (1919).

Barber Samuel (1910–). U.S. composer of the widely known *Adagio for Strings* (1938). He also wrote the overture *The School for Scandal*, the opera *Vanessa* (1958), 2 essays for orchestra and the *Capricorn* concerto for flute, oboe, trumpet and strings. His style is in the romantic tradition.

Barbotines from Roman Britain

Barbizon school. *Woodland scene* by Diaz

Barber of Seville, The. Opera by Rossini, 1st performance in 1816, based on *Beaumarchais's comedy *Le Barbier de Séville* (1775).

Barbey d'Aurevilly Jules-Amédée (1808–89). French novelist, critic and dandy (*dandyism). From 1829 to 1833 he was in Caen, where Beau Brummel was British consul, and wrote *Du Dandysme et de G. Brummel* (1845). After a breakdown caused by alcohol and opium, he became an ardent Catholic and his sometimes farsighted criticism (e.g. he was almost the only critic to encourage Baudelaire) suffered from Catholic and royalist prejudices. Novels include *L'Ensorcelée* (1854; *Bewitched*, 1928) and *Le Chevalier des Touches* (1864). B. gained a following among young writers and was known as *'le connétable des lettres'*.

barbican. Fortified outwork designed to protect the entrance to a castle or town.

Barbier Henri-Auguste (1805–82). French poet, author of *Iambes* (1831), a coll. of verse satires on political themes.

Barbieri Giovanni Francesco: Il *Guercino

Barbirolli Sir John (born Giovanni Battista), (1899–). British conductor. Originally a cellist, he turned to conducting after forming his own chamber orchestra in 1925. From 1937 to 1943 he was conductor of the New York Philharmonic-Symphony Orchestra; from 1943, of the Hallé Orchestra, Manchester, which he raised to international standing.

Barbizon school. Group of mid-19th-c. romantic landscape painters who, led by T. Rousseau and J.-F. Millet, settled in the village of Barbizon in the forest of Fontainebleau. In opposition to academic conventions they painted the *'paysage intime'*, undramatic details of the countryside or peasant life. They were influenced by 17th-c. Dutch landscapists and Constable, and were forerunners of the impressionists. Other members of the school included N.-V. Diaz, J. Dupré and G. Daubigny.

barbotine. In pottery a form of applied ornament in which a semi-liquid clay slip is laid on by piping with a tube. It appears to have been invented by Rhenish potters of the 1st c. A.D. who transmitted it to the potters of the Roman empire. It was much used in the provincial British ware made at Castor (Northamptonshire) in the 2nd c. for animal figures and foliation in white slip on a dark ground. B. is often used synonymously with *slipware to cover all forms of decoration in trailed slip. Examples of this ancient technique are to be seen in the work of the 17th-c. Staffordshire potters Thomas and Ralph Toft.

Barbour John (*c.* 1320–95). Scottish poet whose epic *The Brus* (*c.* 1375) celebrates the achievements of Robert the Bruce.

Barbusse Henri (1873–1935). French novelist. *Le Feu: Journal d'une escouade* (1916; *Under Fire*, 1917) was among the most read books of World War I. Other novels include *Les Suppliants* (1895), *L'Enfer* (1908) and *Clarté* (1919; *Light*, 1919).

Barchester Towers (1857). Novel by A. *Trollope.

Barclay Alexander (*c.* 1475–1552). Scottish poet and scholar who settled in England. B. is best known for *The Shyp of Folys* (1509) a satire trs. into English verse from S. Brant's *Narrenschiff* (1494) and adapted to English conditions. His *Eclogues* (*c.* 1515), based on Italian models, were the earliest English pastorals.

Barclay John (1582–1621). Scottish writer born in France, author of the novels (in Latin) *Argenis* and *Euphormionis Satyricon.*

Bardem Juan Antonio (1922–). Spanish film director. In view of the lamentable condition of the Spanish cinema at the time the post-*Welles technique of his *Death of a Cyclist* (1955) was welcomed internationally as a breakthrough. Since then, his films have progressively lost the peculiarities which were their main distinction.

Bardi Giovanni, Count of Vernio (1534–1614). This Florentine nobleman's palace was the meeting-place of the Camerata: Galilei, Caccini, Strozzi, Corsi, Peri and Rinuccini, the group which invented 'opera' in the modern sense. B. himself took an active part in the discussions and wrote short scenes set to music by Caccini.

Bardot Brigitte (1934–). French film actress. A blonde, pouting child became the sex symbol of the 1950s; her aggressive appeal plus a run of off-screen scandals, made her world famous.

Barbirolli conducts the Hallé in rehearsal

Brigitte Bardot in *Heaven Fell That Night*

Barlach. *The Beggar* and *Peasant Woman*, figures for St Catherine's, Lübeck; in position there since 1945

Barna da Siena. *The Kiss of Judas* (detail)

In *Et Dieu Créa La Femme* (1956) and *Vie Privée* (1961) she showed considerable acting ability.

bards and bardic verse. In the Celtic society contemporaneous with the Roman empire the b.s were the writers of eulogistic and satiric poetry. In ancient Ireland the b.s sank from the status of writers to that of mere reciters of verse. In Wales the b.s were a distinct and organized society with a code as early as the 10th c. A.D. The b.s' congress or *Eisteddfod lapsed in the 16th c. but was revived in the early 19th c. The term b. verse is now usually applied to the Irish eulogies and laments of the 13th to 17th c. and the Welsh occasional poetry of the 12th to 13th c. dealing with social rather than heroic subjects.

Barretti Guiseppe Marc' Antonio (1719–89). Italian writer, in England from 1751 to 1760. He was a friend of Samuel Johnson who prefaced B.'s *Dictionary of the English and Italian Languages* (1760). In the periodical *La Frusta letteraria* (1763–5) he attacked stale 'Arcadian' conventions under the pseud. 'Aristarco Scannabue'.

Barnaba da Modena. *The Coronation of the Virgin*

Barham Richard Harris (1788–1845). English humorous poet and churchman, best known as the author of the *Ingoldsby Legends*, a series of comic tales in verse, which appeared (1837 onwards) in *Bentley's Miscellany*. They were publ. collectively 1840–7. He also wrote the *Ingoldsby Lyrics* (posth. 1881) and a novel, *Some Account of My Cousin Nicholas* (1834).

baritone. (1) Man's voice of approximate range from the F at the bottom of the bass stave to the F above it; (2) used of musical instruments of about this range, e.g. b. saxhorn; (3) in brass bands the b. saxhorn is known simply as b.

Barker George (Granville) (1913–). English poet of emotional lyricism, once associated with Dylan Thomas. Works include *Thirty Preliminary Poems* (1933), *Eros in Dogma* (1944), *The True Confession of George Barker* (1950) and *A Vision of Beasts and Gods* (1954).

Barker Thomas (1769–1847). English landscape painter known as 'B. of Bath' (where he lived from 1793). Many of his paintings were reproduced on pottery.

Barlach Ernst (Heinrich) (1870–1938). N. German sculptor, wood-carver, draughtsman and writer associated with expressionism. He was at the Dresden Academy (1891–5), and Paris (1895–6); in 1906 he visited Russia, in 1909 Florence. Russia shaped him: it was, for him, a land where symbol met reality. The Russian beggar symbolized and presented the truth about man; B.'s statements on human suffering, humiliation, callousness, are in terms of peasant life. The medieval associations of his work gained him a commission for sculptures at St Catherine's church, Lübeck, but the Nazi government, which destroyed many of B.'s public statues, stopped the work. Between 1898 and 1902, he illustrated *Die Jugend* magazine. B.'s writings include the plays *Der tote Tag* (1912), *Die Sundflut* (1924) and his autobiography (1928).

Barlow Francis (1626?–1702). British painter of animal and sporting subjects. He illustrated Mrs Afra Behn's trs. of Aesop (1666).

Barlow Joel (1754–1812). U.S. writer and diplomat, one of the *Hartford Wits. In Europe B. met Tom Paine and French revolutionaries. He wrote *The Columbiad* (1807), intended as 'the great American epic', now forgotten, prose works containing his best writing, e.g. *A Letter to the National Convention of France*... (1792), and the mock-pastoral poem *The Hasty-Pudding* (1797) for which he is remembered.

Barna (da Siena). Mid-14th-c. Sienese painter influenced by Duccio and Simone Martini, and notable for his highly dramatic style. The frescoes on the life of Christ in the Collegiata at S. Gimignano are his main work; according to Vasari he was killed in a fall from the scaffolding while painting them.

Barnaba da Modena (*fl.* 1362–83). Italian painter of the Byzantine tradition whose work was affected, but only slightly, by Giotto.

Barnaby Rudge (1841). Historical novel by *Dickens.

Barnett Boris (1902–). Russian film director. B. was an actor who became a pupil of *Kuleshov. His films include the silent *The House on Trubnoi Square* (1927), notable for its use of trick effects, and *Okraina* (1933).

Barnfield Richard (1574–1627). English lyric poet influenced by Virgil and Spenser; his pastoral *The Affectionate Shepheard* (1594) was based on Virgil's 2nd Eclogue. His 2 songs 'If Musique and Sweet Poetrie agree' and 'As it fell upon a day' appeared in *The *Passionate Pilgrim* (1599).

Barocci Federico (1526–1612). Italian mannerist painter who worked mostly in his native town of Urbino but also in Rome and elsewhere. His style went beyond *mannerism and influenced 18th-c. French painters.

Baroja y Nessi Pio (1872–1956). Spanish novelist. At first a regional writer of the Basque provinces, e.g. in *Le mayorazgo de Labraz* (1903; *Lord of Labrez*, 1926), B. turned to more ambitious picaresque novels notable for their descriptive power, especially *Camino de perfección* (1913).

Baron Michel (1653–1729). French actor, a distinguished member of Molière's co.

Baronova Irina (1919–). Russian dancer who studied in Paris under *Preobrajenska and danced at the Paris Opéra. In her early teens she was one of the *baby ballerinas with Col. de Basil's Ballets Russes de Monte Carlo. With this co. she created roles in *Les Présages* (1933), *Le Beau Danube* in the same year and *Le Coq d'Or* (1937). She retired in 1946.

Baronzio Giovanni (mid 14th c.). Italian painter working at Rimini although there are also frescoes of his at Ravenna and Tolentino. B. was heavily influenced by Cavallini and Giotto.

baroque (perhaps from Portuguese *barroco*, 'a misshapen pearl'). A term, at first of abuse, applied to European architecture and painting of the period approximately 1600 to 1750. B. architecture was at its height in Rome under Bernini and Borromini (*c.* 1630–80) and in S. Germany (*c.* 1700–50) under Balthazar Neumann and Fischer von Erlach. The building was planned round a series of geometrically controlled spaces – circles, squares and ellipses, within, imposed upon, adjoining one another, rhythms of convex against concave curves, exterior lines contrasted or harmonized. The actual structure forced to conform to these patterns was heavily decorated with relief and stucco-work and free-standing sculpture, which burst in upon and receded from the interior space. All the arts were enlisted and impinged on each other, painting was highly illusionistic, sculptors such as Bernini made full use of the play of light on surface and contour. The ensemble made a theatrical and emotional assault on the spectator, enmeshing him in a spatial geometry whose lines are never still, leading him from one enclave to the next, involving him in the drama depicted in the picture or relief, confusing the spatial domains of art and reality. B. became more and more heavily ornate and gradually gave way to the lighter and more restful style of rococo; in Spain it lapsed into the extravagances of churrigueresque, called after the architect José de *Churriguera. B. art was intimately bound up with the Counter-Reformation and in particular the Jesuit order. The involvement of the spectator in the church fabric itself and the religious narratives portrayed on its walls had an intentionally evangelistic aim. Jesuit missionaries carried the style wherever they went and established it in S. America, particularly, as the dominant style in European architecture: a position it held there until the late 19th c. In music the term is used loosely of the period between Monteverdi (d. 1643) and J. S. Bach (d. 1750); a b. organ, in 20th-c. terminology, is one of this period. It has a more brilliant tone than 19th-c. organs, resulting from its reed and mutation stops.

Barrack-Room Ballads (1892). Poems in cockney dialect by *Kipling.

Barrault Jean-Louis (1910–). French theatre director and actor noted as a mime, e.g. in the film *Les Enfants du Paradis* (1945). He was the pupil of C. *Dullin. He acted with the Comédie-Française (1940–7), was co-director, with his wife M. Renaud, of Marigny Theatre (1947–57); and from 1959 director of Théâtre de France. His greatest productions have been *Hamlet* (1946) and *The Trial* (1947) by Kafka, in both of which he played the lead. His style as director is strongly influenced by mime techniques.

Barrès (Augustin) Maurice (1862–1923). French writer, a master of prose and an important intellectual influence in the early 20th c. From his early individualistic cult of the self (*moi*) he turned to an extreme nationalism, exalting the virtues of tradition, race and the soil. His works include *Du sang, de la volupté*

Baroque. Dome of the Capella della Sta Sindone, Turin; by Guarini

Baroque. Fischer von Erlach, Salzburg Trinity church

Barrault and G. Page in Racine's *Andromaque*

Barocci. *Madonna del Popolo*

Baroque. Bernini's *Ecstasy of St Teresa*

Sir Charles Barry. The Houses of Parliament

Lionel Barrymore (bottom) in *Grand Hotel*

Sir James Barrie

J. Barry. *Trinity of Modern Commerce* (detail)

et de la mort (1894) and the novels *Les Déracinés* (1898) and *Colette Baudoche* (1909).

Barret the Elder, George (d. 1784). Irish landscape painter and engraver who settled in England in 1762 and became a founder-member of the R.A. By painting picturesque scenes on private estates he ensured his success with noble patrons. His son GEORGE B. the Younger (d. 1842) was a watercolourist of ideal landscapes.

Barreto Lima (1905–). Brazilian film director. After making documentaries, B. was able to make a feature, *O Cangaceiro* (*The Bandit*) (1953), for the co. headed by *Cavalcanti. A violent film, strongly influenced by folk-ballads, it gave the Brazilian cinema its 1st international success.

Barrie Sir James Matthew (1860–1937). Scottish novelist and playwright, the creator of *Peter Pan* (1904). Other plays include *Quality Street* (1902), *The Admirable Crichton* (1902), *What Every Woman Knows* (1908) and *Dear Brutus* (1917). He wrote a biography of his mother *Margaret Ogilvy* (1896) and the novels *Auld Licht Idylls* (1888) in the style of the *Kailyard school and *Farewell Miss Julie Logan* (1931). His blend of the fey and whimsy has not proved very durable except in *Peter Pan*.

Barrili Anton Giulio (1836–1908). Italian writer of sentimental novels about aristocratic romance, including *Cuor di ferro e cuor d'oro* (1877). He also publ. memoirs of campaigning with Garibaldi, *Garibaldi alle porte di Roma* (1867).

Barrow Isaac (1630–77). English divine, classical scholar and mathematician; a teacher of Isaac Newton. His rich and lucid prose was praised by Coleridge.

Barry Sir Charles (1795–1860). British architect and designer of the Houses of Parliament (1836–52). This design with its classical proportions and medieval detail (executed by A. W. N. Pugin) combines his two styles. B. travelled in the Near East in early life and publ. some fine sketches made there. Other famous buildings include the Reform Club, London. He was also a brilliant landscape gardener.

Barry James (1741–1806). Irish history and portrait painter. Patronized by Burke, he studied in Italy and in 1782 became a professor at the R.A. He was expelled in 1799 for attacks on other members and on the memory of Reynolds, and died destitute.

Barry Philip (1896–1949). U.S. playwright, a student of G. P. Baker at the *47 Workshop, producing *You and I* (1922; New York production, 1923). Other plays include the comedies *In A Garden* (1925), *Paris Bound* (1927), *The Animal Kingdom* (1932), about marriage, and *The Philadelphia Story* (1939).

Barrymore. Family of U.S. stage and film actors. MAURICE (1847–1905), an Englishman, went to the U.S. in 1875. Besides acting, he wrote the play *Nadjeska* (1884) which, he claimed, V. Sardou plagiarized in *La Tosca*. LIONEL (1878–1954), his son, was a leading New York stage actor until he went into films, 1909. Among his best-known films were *A Yellow Streak* (1915), *Grand Hotel* (1932), *Captains Courageous* (1937) and *Duel in the Sun* (1947). ETHEL (1879–1959), L.'s sister, had one of the most brilliant careers of the U.S. stage and worked in films and broadcasting. One of her best roles was Miss Moffat in E. Williams's *The Corn is Green* (1940); her films include *None but the Lonely Heart* (1944). The E.B. Theater in New York is named after her. JOHN (1882–1942) was M.'s youngest child. His *Hamlet* (New York, 1922; London, 1925) placed him in the front of English actors but his stage career did not fulfil this high promise. He worked much in films, e.g. *Moby Dick* (1930).

Barstow Stan (1928–). English novelist whose realistic study of Yorkshire working-class life, *A Kind of Loving* (1960), was a best-seller. Works include *Joby* (1964).

Bart Lionel (1930–). English composer and writer of such musicals as *Oliver* (1960), *Blitz* (1962) and *Maggie May* (1964).

Bartas Guillaume de Sal(l)uste, sieur du (1544–90). French Protestant poet, author of *La Semaine où Création du Monde* (1578), an epic ostensibly describing the creation of the world and containing all contemporary scientific knowledge. Of the sequel, *La Seconde*

Ethel Barrymore in *Rasputin and the Empress*

John Barrymore and C. Horn in *Tempest*

Semaine (1548), he completed only 4 of the days. The trs. of J. Sylvester (1563–1618) had some influence in England.

Bartered Bride, The. Opera by *Smetana, text by K. Sabina; première in Prague 1866, revised and final version 1870.

Barthelmess Richard (1897–1963). U.S. film actor, his appealing yet virile hero remained popular; he retired after the introduction of sound, making only sporadic appearances. His pictures include *Broken Blossoms* (1919), *Way Down East* (1920) and Hawks's *Dawn Patrol* (1930).

Bartholin Birger (1900–). Danish dancer and choreographer who studied with Fokine and Legat. He danced abroad until 1931 when he returned to Denmark to form his own co. 4 years later he joined the Ballets Russes de Monte Carlo and in 1937 the Ballets de la Jeunesse.

Bartholomew Fair (1614). Play by Ben Jonson.

Bartók Béla (1881–1945). Hungarian composer, pianist and folk-musicologist. His father died in 1889. In 1894 he and his mother settled, after much travel in their district of Hungary, in Pozsony (now Bratislava, Czechoslovakia). Here B. took composition lessons, his early music being influenced by Brahms and Dohnányi. Between 1899 and 1903 he studied the piano at Budapest. The symphonic poem *Kossuth* (performed in 1904) shows the influence of the Hungarian nationalist school; the rhapsody for piano and orchestra (1904) that of Liszt. In 1905 B. began an intense study of peasant music (as opposed to the 'gipsy' music of Liszt) which, he said, liberated him from the traditional harmonic system. In 1906 B. publ. an ed. of 20 Hungarian folk-songs with Kodály. In 1907 he became professor of the piano at Budapest Academy. After the fall of Béla Kun (1919) he experienced continuous political difficulties. In 1923 he composed a dance suite for the concert commemorating 50 years' union between Buda and Pest (to which Kodály and Dohnányi also contributed). Between 1923 and 1926 he wrote little. In 1934 he resigned his teaching post to concentrate on researches into E. European folk-music. In 1940 he left Hungary because of the Fascist régime and migrated to the U.S. An honorary professor at Columbia Univ., he tried to maintain himself by piano recitals. He died in poverty.
B.'s writing for the piano was often violently percussive (1st piano concerto) and his music as a whole was heavily affected by his pianistic technique, being characterized in its middle period by great rhythmic complexity. It was identifiable with no 20th-c. school; influenced by Liszt, Wagner and Strauss, by peasant music and the techniques of Schoenberg and A. Berg, it was always unmistakably B., reflecting the integrity of its composer. B. widely extended 19th-c. harmony. Dissonances were used for effect, chords of remote keys juxtaposed without modulation, consonances used unexpectedly with heightened effect. He used the maj.-min. chord (where maj. and min. 3rds sound simultaneously) and when repeating a melody or phrase, freely interchanged notes and chords with their neighbours. B.'s melody showed some folk influence, especially in rhythm, and was also characterized by the use of small intervals and of a 'central' note. Above all B.'s orchestration and instrumentation had an unmistakable quality. He extracted from full orchestra and from strings alone, sonorities previously unheard. B.'s main works were the opera *Duke Bluebeard's Castle* (1911; 1918); the ballet *The Miraculous Mandarin* (1919; 1925); the *Cantata profana* (1930); the *Concerto for Orchestra* (1943); piano concertos no. 1 (1926), no. 2 (1931), and no. 3 (1945); a violin concerto (1937–8); the draft of a viola concerto which was left among his papers; the string quartets no. 1 (1908), no. 2 (1915–17), no. 3 (1927), no. 4 (1928), no. 5 (1934), and no. 6 (1939). The many piano works include *14 Bagatelles* (1908), the well-known *Allegro barbaro* (1911) and the *Mikrokosmos* (1926–37). This is a series of 153 graded piano 'exercises' in 6 books; above all they show a progressive complexity of rhythm.

Béla Bartók

Bartoli Taddeo: *Taddeo di Bartolo

Bartolo di Fredi. Sienese fresco painter, a pupil of A. Lorenzetti. His best 2 fresco cycles are at S. Gimignano, one dealing with Old Testament subjects in the Collegiata (1356) and one in the church of S. Agostino on the birth and death of the Virgin (1366).

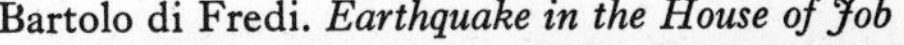
Bartolo di Fredi. *Earthquake in the House of Job*

Bartolommeo. *Adoration of the Child* (detail)

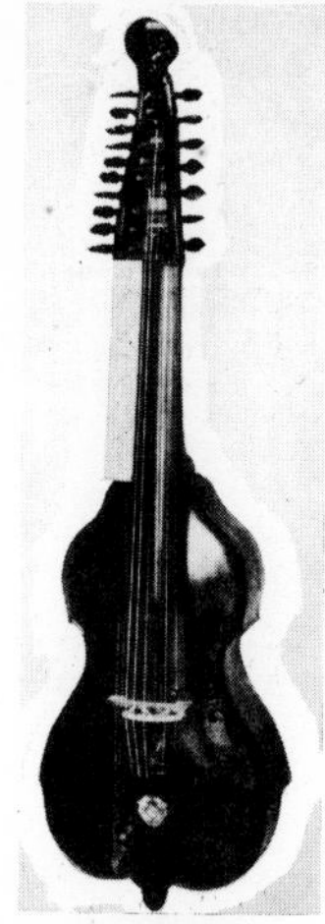

Baryton, dated 1785

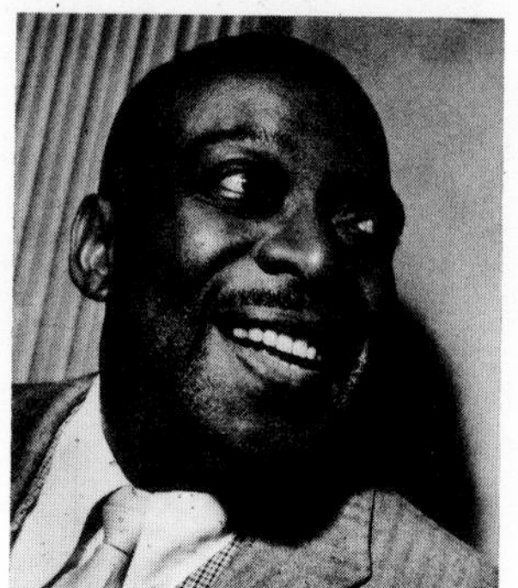

Count Basie

Basaiti. *Madonna and Child* (detail)

Barye. *Indian mounted on an elephant killing a tiger*

Bartolommeo Fra (1472–1517). Florentine painter and draughtsman. As student under Cosimo Rosselli he met M. Albertinelli with whom he later often collaborated. B. early inclined to mysticism and, impelled by the preaching of *Savonarola, publicly burnt many of his paintings. In 1500 he entered the monastery of S. Marco. He resumed painting in 1504, becoming a close friend of Raphael. He worked in Venice (1507), then with Albertinelli in Florence (*c.* 1509–12) when he went to Rome. Here he was so overwhelmed by Michelangelo and Raphael's work in the Vatican that he refused all entreaties to collaborate. B.'s work is distinguished by complex yet controlled composition and by his refined and delicate draughtsmanship and use of colour. One of his finest works is *Adoration of the Child* (N.G., London). Late in life he lost something of his delicacy of treatment.

Bartolommeo di Giovanni: *Alunno di Domenico

Bartolozzi Francesco (1728–1815). Italian mezzotint engraver, miniaturist and draughtsman who settled in England (1764) and was a founder-member of the R.A. In 1802 he became head of a school for engravers in Lisbon. Through mastery of stipple and crayon and allied techniques B. achieved great softness and luminosity of effect; this together with his elegant tenderness assured him great popularity.

Bartsch Rudolph Hans (1873–1952). Austrian author of sentimental period romances of provincial life. *Schwammerl* (1912) about Schubert's life, was the basis of the operetta *Lilac Time.*

Baruch. One of the books of the *Apocrypha.

Barye Antoine-Louis (1796–1875). French romantic sculptor and painter who was the son of a goldsmith. For a time he followed his father's profession producing statuettes of wild animals. This subject interested him all his life and his treatment has the violence of the romantics Delacroix, his friend, and Géricault, though it lacks the verve and panache of their work. He also produced *Napoleon dominating History and the Arts* (1855–7), on the Pavillon d'Horloge at the Louvre, and the equestrian statue of Napoleon at Ajaccio (1860).

baryton. Stringed musical instrument now practically obsolete. In effect it was a bass *viol with sympathetic strings and is remembered as the instrument of Haydn's patron Prince Esterházy for whom the composer wrote many pieces.

Barzun Henri-Martin (1881–). French poet closely associated with the *Abbaye group and founder of simultaneism, a movement which took elements from cubism, futurism and unanimism. B.'s works include the colls *La Trilogie des forces* (1908–14).

Basaiti Marco (*fl.* 1496–1530). Venetian painter, perhaps of Greek origin, and possibly a pupil of A. Vivarini. His early style sometimes resembles that of Giovanni Bellini, but one of his best pictures, *The Calling of the Sons of Zebedee* (Accademia, Venice) shows Vivarini's influence in the hard outlines of the figures and the unnatural lighting. The term 'Pseudo-Basaiti' was coined to describe paintings not definitely assignable to either Bellini or B., but is now considered an unwarranted invention.

basaltes: Josiah *Wedgwood

Basevi George (1794–1845). English architect of the Fitzwilliam Museum, Cambridge.

Bashkirtseff Marie (1860–84). Russian girl who came with her family to France in 1870. Her diary, written in French, records her reactions to her life of meaningless luxury, her ambition to be a great painter and her struggle against, and final resignation to the consumption which killed her.

Basie William 'Count' (1904–). U.S. *jazz pianist and band-leader.

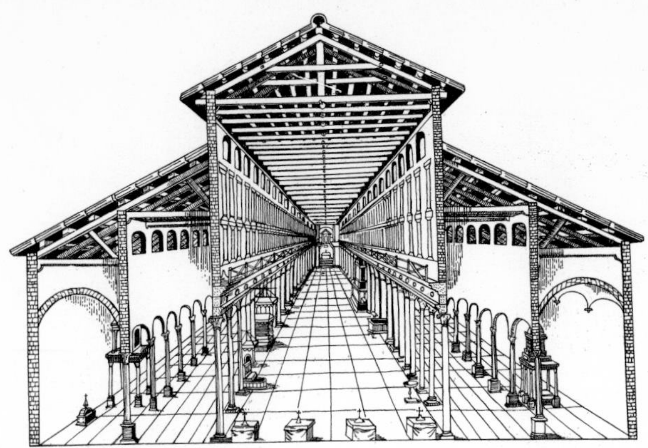

Basilica. Section of Old St Peter's, Rome

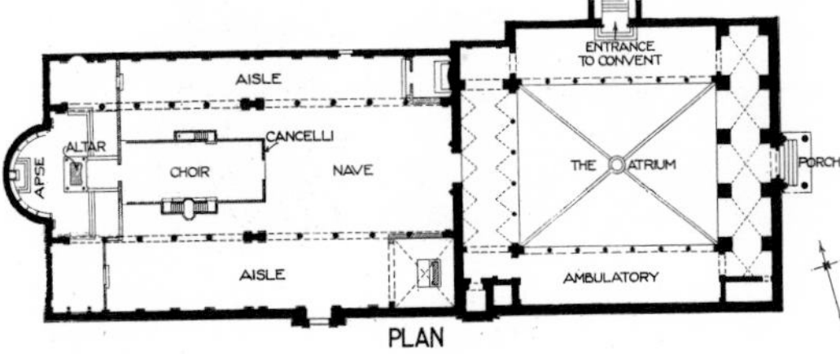

Basilica. Plan of the basilican church of S. Clemente, Rome

SATYRA III.

Umbritio, ob faſtidia et incommoda Urbis Cumas petenti, gratulatur.

QUAMVIS digreſſu veteris confuſus amici,
Laudo tamen vacuis quod ſedem figere Cumis
Deſtinet, atque unum civem donare ſibyllæ.
Janua Bajarum eſt, et gratum litus amœni
Seceſſus. Ego vel Prochytam præpono Suburræ.
Nam quid tam miſerum, tam ſolum vidimus, ut non
Deterius credas horrere incendia, lapſus
Tectorum aſſiduos, ac mille pericula ſævæ
Urbis, et Auguſto recitantes menſe poetas?
Sed dum tota domus rheda componitur una,
Subſtitit ad veteres arcus, madidamque Capenam:
Hic, ubi nocturnæ Numa conſtituebat amicæ.
Nunc ſacri fontis nemus, et delubra locantur
Judæis, quorum cophinus, fœnumque ſupellex.
Omnis enim populo mercedem pendere juſſa eſt
Arbor, et ejectis mendicat ſilva Camœnis.
In vallem Egeriæ deſcendimus, et ſpeluncas
Diſſimiles

Baskerville. From his ed. of Juvenal's *Satires*

Basil Col. Wladimir de (pseud. of Vasily Grigorevich Voskresensky) (1880–1951). Russian ballet impresario who did much to popularize ballet throughout the world. After the death of Diaghilev in 1929, Col. de Basil and R. Blum combined to revive the Diaghilev co. under the name of Ballets Russes de Monte Carlo (1932).

basilica. Architectural term for, (*a*) a civic hall in a Roman city, with the typical ground-plan shown in Fig. 1, (*b*) an early form of Christian church (Fig. 2), derived from it, in which the nave was lighted by a clerestory above the level of the aisles.

Basilica of Maxentius (also called, of Constantine), Rome. The last of the great Roman basilicas. It was built A.D. 310–13 (begun by Maxentius, finished by Constantine); the central 'nave', (365 × 83 ft) was vaulted in 3 bays with quadripartite groined vaulting supported on 8 monolithic columns. Between them, opening into the nave and providing the necessary abutment, were 6 compartments (3 on each side) covered by barrel-vaults at right angles to the nave. Much of the building still survives.

Baskerville John (1706–75). English printer, designer of one of the most readable, elegant and influential type-faces since the 16th c. and the man who restored typography as the basis of good book production. Working in Birmingham, B. produced some 50 masterpieces. His 1st book was a Virgil (1757), the greatest was his folio Bible of 1763, and among the most popular were the quarto eds of Latin authors (1772–3). From 1758 to 1768, B. was printer to Cambridge Univ. Finding no English buyer, his widow sold his types to Beaumarchais for his ed. of Voltaire.

ba(s)s-relief (in Italian *bassorilièvo*). A carved *relief projecting only slightly from its background.

bass. (1) Lowest line in a musical score. (2) The lowest male singing voice with a range beginning on the E or F below the bass stave, though specially trained Russian singers descend an 8ve below this. (3) Used of low-pitched musical instruments, e.g. b. trombone. For BASSO CONTINUO, THOROUGH BASS and FIGURED BASS *continuo.

Bass Saul. U.S. designer. B. is famous for his application of poster design graphics to the cinema. He pioneered the extended decorative title sequence.

Bassá Ferrer (*c.* 1290–after 1348). Painter of the Catalan school and 1st major painter of Spain. Until the early 20th c. the only records of him were in the criminal records of the kingdom of Aragon (for rape and other offences). The fresco series in the Franciscan convent at Predalbes (painted 1345/6) is now known to be by him. It shows that B. knew the work of the Sienese school, particularly that of Simone Martini.

Bassano. Family of Venetian painters working in Bassano. JACOPO (or Giacomo) da Ponte (1510/15–1592) first worked under his father, the painter Francesco the Elder (1475–1539), then studied in Venice. About 1530 he returned to Bassano where some of his finest work was done. His portraits and Biblical subjects are notable for their realistic landscape settings, which include animals and details of peasant life, and for their colour, influenced by Titian. The best known of his 4 sons are FRANCESCO the Younger (1549–92) and LEANDRO (1557–1622) whose work closely followed that of their father. Many paintings attributed to Jacopo are the work of his sons.

basset horn. A musical instrument suitably described as a tenor *clarinet.

bassoon. Wind musical instrument with a range upwards of three 8ves from the B♭ below the bass stave. Like the oboe it is a double *reed instrument of conical bore and it is used in orchestral music as the bass of the oboe family. DOUBLE B. or CONTRA B. has a range a full 8ve lower. RUSSIAN B. was in fact a form of *serpent.

Bassano. *Portrait of a Bearded Man*

Bassá. *Deposition*

Bath. Royal Crescent by John Wood the Younger

Batoni. Portrait of Peter Beckford

Baths of Diocletian

Baths of Caracalla

Bastien und Bastienne. One-act operetta by Mozart, libretto by F. W. Weiskern; first performed 1768.

Bastien-Lepage Jules (1848–84). French painter remembered for his peasant genre scenes such as *The Hayfield* (Luxembourg Mus., Paris). Although his technique was affected by impressionism, the sentiment of his work was in the tradition of G. Courbet and J.-F. Millet.

bastion. A projection from the *curtain wall of a fortress; from it those attacking the wall could be strafed.

Bataille Henri (1872–1922). French playwright widely popular in his lifetime. Works, which include *Maman Colibri* (1904), *L'Enfant de l'amour* (1911) and *La Tendresse* (1921), used psychological analysis but were somewhat factitious in their sentiments and plots.

Bataille Nicolas (d. 1400). Weaver of the *Apocalypse tapestries.

Bataille du Rail, La (1946). Film directed by R. *Clement.

Bate Stanley (1911–59). English composer and pianist. His teachers included Vaughan Williams, N. Boulanger and Hindemith. He established his reputation in N. and S. America (1942–9). His compositions include 4 symphonies, 2 sinfoniettas, concerto grosso for piano and strings (1952), instrumental concertos including 3 for piano, several ballets, chamber, incidental and film music and songs.

Bateau ivre, Le (1884). Poem by *Rimbaud.

Bateau-Lavoir, Groupe du. Group of painters and writers founded in Paris 1908 including Braque, Picasso, Apollinaire, Juan Gris and Gertrude Stein. The name means 'the floating laundry' and was the nickname of the tenement where Picasso lived.

Bates Herbert Ernest (1905–). British novelist and short-story writer. He has remarkable sense of 'mood'. Novels include: *A House of Women* (1936), *The Purple Plain* (1947) and *The Jacaranda Tree* (1949), both set in Burma, and *The Darling Buds of May* (1958).

Bath. The best example in England of 18th-c. town-planning and still in many ways a model of urban development. It became a centre of fashion in the 1st quarter of the 18th c. due mainly to the efforts of Ralph Allen (a rich businessman), Beau Nash (master of ceremonies from 1704) and the architect John *Wood. In 1725 Wood proposed a far-reaching scheme inspired equally by Palladio and by ancient Rome, to include a 'forum', a 'grand circus' and an 'imperial gymnasium'. He built Queen Square (1729–36), the Parades (begun 1754) and the Circus (begun 1754). The work was continued by his son; other architects include T. W. *Atwood, T. *Baldwin and J. Palmer. Pulteney bridge (1770) is by Robert Adam. Georgian Bath was complete by 1825; as a whole it is characterized by a unique consistency of style (English neo-classical), combining French formality (the vista) with English 'picturesque'.

Bath-house, The (1930). Play by *Mayakovsky.

bathos (Greek, 'depth'). In literature a sudden fall from the exalted to the ordinary, the ridiculous result of a writer striving beyond his powers to achieve the noble or pathetic. *Pope wrote an admirable funny treatise on b., *Peri Bathous, Or The Art of Sinking in Poetry* (1727).

baths. Roman baths were among the largest buildings ever created and in vaulting the great halls with brick Roman engineers achieved some of their greatest triumphs. Of those which remain the most important are: (1) Baths of Caracalla, Rome; they contained an area of 285,000 square ft, comprising 3 big halls (*calidarum*, *tepidarum* and *frigidarum*) surrounded by other halls, rooms, libraries and

Bauchant. *The Funeral of Alexander*

Baudelaire: photograph by Carjat

places of amusement. (2) Baths of Diocletian, Rome. The *tepidarum* remains largely intact and was connected with the church of S. Maria degli Angeli by Michelangelo (1563).

Bat(t)oni Pompeo Girolamo (1708–87). Italian painter, with A. R. Mengs the leading painter in Rome. His main output was portraits of travelling foreigners (particularly Englishmen on the Grand Tour) whom he often set in front of classical monuments, but he also painted many religious, historical and mythological subjects. He was ennobled by Maria Therese for his double portrait of the emperor Joseph II and the future Leopold II at their meeting in Rome (1769).

battement (French). A collective term describing ballet exercises with a beating movement, but always using 1 leg or foot to beat against a supporting leg or foot; it is to be distinguished from *batterie, where both feet engage in beating at the same time.

batter. Architectural term for a slight inward slope given to a wall, sometimes in order to strengthen the construction, more often to achieve pleasing optical effects.

batterie. French term, literally a series of beats, more broadly defined as steps in ballet which involve beating the feet together, either in grande batterie or petite batterie. These include large elevation steps such as grand brisé, tour en l'air batu and cabriole and small beaten steps such as entrechat. B. is a main feature of *Cecchetti's method.

Battishill Jonathan (1738–1801). English composer, harpsichordist at Covent Garden and later church organist. Wrote stage music, e.g. the opera *Almena* (1764) with M. Arne, and many anthems.

Battle of Issus, The. Alternative name for the *Alexander mosaic.

Battle of the Books, The (*An Account of a Battel Between the Ancient and Modern Books in St James Library*) (1704). Prose satire by *Swift.

Battleship Potemkin (1925). Film directed by S. M. *Eisenstein.

Battle Symphony (Vienna, 1813) also *The Battle of Vittoria* and *Wellington's Victory* are English names for *Beethoven's programmatic work (op. 91) commissioned by J. N. *Mälzel for his 'panharmonicon'.

Batyushkov Konstantin Nikolayevich (1787–1855). Russian poet. In 1821 he went insane. Following N. M. *Karamzin's reforms B. aimed to give Russian verse the fluency of Italian, taking such models as Tibullus, Tasso and Petrarch. His small output achieved a sometimes effeminate sweetness but works like the elegy *The Shade of a Dying Friend* and B.'s trs from the Greek Anthology are masterpieces.

Bauchant André (1873–1958). French 'primitive' painter commissioned by Diaghilev to design the décor for Stravinsky's *Apollon-Musagète* (1928). He was originally a gardener but began to draw while serving in World War I and became a full-time painter in the early 1920s. He first chose historical subjects but later painted genre scenes, landscapes and sensitive flower-pieces.

Baudelaire Charles-Pierre (1821–67). French poet and critic. He was born into the well-to-do middle class and, when he was 7, his widowed mother married a stern, upright soldier, the future General Aupick, whom B. was later to magnify into the typically repressive stepfather. As a young man B. was sent on a voyage to the Far East to cure him of his literary vocation, but the only effect was to supply him with exotic imagery which he was to use later in his verse. At 21 he came into his inheritance and proceeded to squander it by leading the life of an anti-conventional, literary dandy (*dandyism). His great love was a mulatto actress, Jeanne Duval, the 'black Venus' of his poems. For the rest of his career he was painfully short of money and suffered from the increasing effects of syphilis. Yet he produced in 1857 *Les Fleurs du mal* (selection *The Flowers of Evil*, 1909) which many critics consider to be the greatest single book of verse in the language. It was attacked on grounds of immorality, and in his lifetime B. did not receive the recognition he deserved. Besides his poetry, he wrote much influential criticism of literature, painting and music. He was a passionate admirer of Poe and De Quincey and trs. some of their works. His last years were clouded by poverty and illness and he lost the power of speech some months before he died. B. had a romantic view of the poet as an exceptional being born to exemplary suffering, but his verse has a density and power rarely found in his romantic predecessors. *Les Fleurs du mal* can be read as a history of the human soul, oscillating between extremes of horror and delight (*'l'horreur de la vie, l'extase de la vie'*). B. interprets both nature and man's creations–i.e. towns and works of art–as patterns of interlocking symbols. In this he was no doubt influenced by his reading of Swedenborg, and he was one of the originators of the literary movement later to be known as symbolism. It has been argued that *Les Fleurs du mal* is a carefully constructed whole, and that B. intended a final version of the cycle. Uncertainty surrounds his religious belief: was he really a Catholic or a God-defying atheist who sometimes wrote in a Catholic tone? Opinions may differ on these points, but it is agreed that many of his individual poems are amongst the most outstanding modern masterpieces and have influenced poets all over the world. He also left private diaries (*Mon cœur mis à nu*), a vol. of prose poems, and many critical articles coll. in *Curiosités esthétiques* (publ. posth. 1868) and *L'Art romantique* (publ. posth. 1868).

Baudouin Pierre-Antoine (1723–69). French painter, pupil and follower of F. Boucher.

Baudry Paul (Jacques Aimé) (1828–86). French painter known for his mural decorations, particularly those in the Opéra, Paris.

The Bauhaus building, Dessau

Bayeu: portrait by Goya

Bauhaus. 'Barcelona' chair by Mies van der Rohe (1929)

Bauhaus. Symbol designed by Schlemmer

Baumeister. *Polished stones*

Bauernfeld Eduard von (1802–90). Austrian playwright; the best of his comedies was *Aus der Gesellschaft* (1866). His work shows derivation from Kotzebue and Scribe.

Bauhaus. A teaching institution for the arts founded, in 1919, at Weimar, Germany by *Gropius. The aim was to reunify artistic disciplines and integrate them with constructional techniques. The visual arts and architecture were to be studied and applied as related activities, and any division between structural and decorative arts was denied. There were 2 parallel courses, one studying material and techniques and one studying form in the studio. A basic aim was to teach design suited to machine production and articles were produced by students as prototypes for a mass-production line. Teachers at the school included *Kandinsky, *Klee, *Feininger, *Schlemmer and Breuer. In 1925 the B. moved to Dessau where its building, by Gropius, exemplified its principles. Mies van der Rohe succeeded Gropius as director in 1928. The B. was closed in 1933 by the Nazi government. In 1937 L. *Moholy-Nagy became director of a new B. at Chicago and many other artists moved to the U.S. B. principles have deeply influenced subsequent developments in architecture and the visual arts.

Baum Vicky (1888–1960). Austrian light novelist; her books include *Menschen im Hotel* (1929; *Grand Hotel*, 1931; film, 1932).

Baumeister Willi (1889–1955). Leading German abstract painter and creator of murals. B. studied in Stuttgart under A. Hoelzel; he visited Paris in 1912, 1914 and in 1924 when he met F. Léger, and took a teaching post in Frankfurt from 1928 to 1933 when he was removed by the Nazis as a *'degenerate'. He became a professor at Stuttgart in 1946. B. publ. his theories of art in *Das Unbekannte in der Kunst* (1947). From early affinities to constructivism, e.g. the combination of relief and painting in his murals (1919–23), his art became increasingly abstract, but in the 1940s influenced by prehistoric art, he developed an ideogrammatic technique.

Bava Mario (1914–). Italian cinematographer and film director. His expertise with handling images, and particularly with the power of camera movement and lighting, enabled him to make 2 of the best recent horror films in *La Maschera del demonio* (1960) and *I Tre Volti della Paura* (1963). He has also made a couple of spectaculars and a thriller, *La Ragazza che sapeva troppo* (1962).

Bax Sir Arnold (1883–1953). English composer and from 1942 Master of the King's Music. His large output included 7 symphonies, the symphonic poems *The Garden of Fand* (1916), *Tintagel* (1917)and *November Woods* (1917), and the choral work *Mater ora filium* (1921). B. was influenced by the Celtic revival and was a professed romantic.

Baxter James (1926–). New Zealand poet, playwright and critic, representing a maturity in New Zealand literature that no longer defines itself in nationalistic terms. *The Fallen House* (1953) and *In Fires of No Return* (1958) assert lyrically and satirically personal integrity as the criterion of poetry.

Baxter Richard (1615–91). English Presbyterian minister. B. was famed for his eloquence, voluminous writings on practical Christianity and his autobiography *Reliquiae Baxterianae: or Mr Richard Baxter's Narrative* (1696), recording his life's work and persecution as a Nonconformist.

bay. Architectural term for the area between 2 columns or piers of a row, and including the wall and ceiling of the area; the term is applied by extension to any area of wall-surface divided (outside) by windows or (inside) by any large vertical features.

Bayeu Francisco (1734–95). Spanish neo-classical painter, particularly of frescoes, who worked under R. Mengs in the decoration of the Royal Palace at Madrid. Many of his works are now in the Prado, Madrid, where there is also a portrait of him by Goya, his brother-in-law and pupil.

Bayeux tapestry (probably late 11th c.). Not properly a *tapestry but a strip of linen 231 ft

Bayeux tapestry. See also colour plate 25

Bead and reel. Child's high chair (*c.* 1660)

long and 20 ins deep embroidered in coloured wools. It represents events in the life of Harold of England and the Norman Conquest (1066) in a series of scenes which are supplemented by a Latin commentary and decorative borders depicting, e.g. scenes from fables and everyday life. First mentioned (1476) in an inventory of Bayeux cathedral, where it was used occasionally to decorate the nave. It was probably commissioned by Odo, bishop of Bayeux, half-brother of William the Conqueror, but whether it is of Norman or Saxon design is uncertain; a totally unfounded tradition connects Mathilda, William the Conqueror's queen, with the B. t. It is the only work of its kind which survives and is now exhibited in Bayeux.

Bayle Pierre (1647–1706). French writer, a forerunner of the encyclopaedists. His famous *Dictionnaire historique et critique* (1697; *An Historical and Critical Dictionary*, 1710) contained many arguments against received opinions in theology and philosophy and was used by the **philosophes.*

Baylis Lilian (1874–1937). English theatre manager. In 1914, she took over the Royal Victorian Coffee Music Hall, which as the *Old Vic became the home of Shakespeare in London. Her choice of Ninette de Valois as ballet mistress when she founded the Sadler's Wells co. (1931) marks the beginning of English ballet.

Bay Psalm Book, The (1640). The 1st book printed in colonial America, originally titled *The Whole Booke of Psalmes Faithfully Translated into English metre. . . .* It was based on the Authorized Version but sacrificed elegance to accuracy.

Bayreuth. German town where Wagner (d. 1883) retired and designed the Wagner Festival Theatre (opened 1876) for the performance of his operas; B. has had regular Wagner festivals since that time. During the period 1886–1906 under Cosima Wagner, the composer's widow, productions at B. were a model for European opera-houses. They hold a leading position today under Wagner's grandsons Wieland and Wolfgang.

Bazaine Jean (1904–). French painter and theorist, author of *Notes sur la peinture d'aujourd'hui* (1948). He has also worked in stained glass, e.g. windows for the church at Assy (1930). Since 1945 his increasingly abstract and symbolic style has influenced younger painters.

Bazille Jean-Frédéric (1841–70). Early French impressionist painter. While a pupil under C. Gleyre he met Renoir (with whom he shared a studio), Monet and Sisley, and through them Manet. B. painted out of doors and was interested in the correlation between flesh tints and landscape tones. He was a painter of great promise but was killed in action in the Franco-Prussian War.

Bazin René (1853–1932). French novelist. B.'s novels of rural family life include *Les Oberlé* (1901; *The Oberlé Family*, 1933), *La Terre qui meurt* (1899; *Autumn Glory*, 1901) and *Le Blé qui lève* (1907; *The Rising Corn*, 1909).

B.B.P.R. An architectural partnership in Milan consisting of Banfi (died in a concentration camp during the war), Belgiojoso, Peresutti and Rogers. They achieved fame in the 1930s with flats in Milan and a sanatorium at Legnano. After the war they were in the vanguard of Milanese architecture, but have recently developed a more personal direction, outside the mainstream of the modern movement, as in their Torre Velasca, 1957.

Beach Amy Marcy, née Cheney (known as Mrs H. H. Beach) (1867–1944). U.S. pianist and composer whose 'Gaelic' symphony (1896) is considered the 1st important symphony by a U.S. composer.

bead and reel. A decorative border derived from classical architecture consisting of alternate beads and reels. Often used in the form of inlay in the 16th and 17th cs in furniture decoration.

Beale Charles (b. 1660). English painter and draughtsman. He was the son of Mary B. and worked as her assistant. His most individual work was a series of figure studies in red chalk

Bazille. *Young girl in a pink dress.* Also *Fantin-Latour

Beale. *Young Woman in a Fur Hat*; red chalk. Also *Flatman

Beaumarchais

Beardsley. *The Peacock Skirt* for Wilde's *Salome*

Beaton. Portrait of Diana Wynyard

which were previously attributed to his mother and resemble the work of Dutch artists such as G. Metsu and G. van Honthorst rather than anything in contemporary English art.

Beale Mary (1632/3–99). English portrait painter in the style of Sir P. Lely and after his death in 1680 she was frequently employed to make replicas of his portraits.

Beardsley Aubrey Vincent (1872–98). English artist in black and white whose work epitomized the 'decadence' of the 1890s. His illustrations to J. M. Dent's ed. of *Morte d'Arthur* (1892) are strongly influenced by Burne-Jones. In 1893, work of his, showing Japanese influences, was publ. in *The Studio* (the 1st *art nouveau magazine). In 1894 B. illustrated the English trs. of Oscar Wilde's *Salome* and became art ed. of *The *Yellow Book*, but following Wilde's fall in 1895 B. had to resign. In 1896 he became ed. of the new magazine *The Savoy*, where his illustrations of Pope's *The Rape of the Lock* and of his own fragment *Under the Hill* appeared. In these, the stark black and white masses are broken down and the effect shows B.'s interest in 18th-c. French illustration. In 1896 began the final onset of his consumption and in 1897 B. went to Mentone, where he died.

beast epic. Poetic genre developed in the middle ages: a story about animals is used for satirical comment on contemporary manners. The most famous is *Le *Roman de Renart*.

Beaton Cecil (1904–). English designer and photographer noted for the elaborate detail of his portrait studies.

beats. Term loosely applied to a U.S. group who reject the conventions and goals of ordinary society, using their own slang and often leading a wandering life. They originated *c.* 1940 but received wide publicity in the 1950s through the writers–including *Kerouac, *Ginsberg, *Corso and *Ferlinghetti–associated with them. Typical of their interests are the criminal and the drug-addict, jazz and Zen Buddhism.

Beattie James (1735–1803). Scottish poet, essayist and professor of moral philosophy, Aberdeen Univ., 1760. Works include *An Essay on . . . Truth* (1770), an attack on the sceptical philosophy of David Hume, and the poem *The Minstrel: or The Progress of Genius* (1771–4; unfinished), an Augustan imitation of Spenser.

Beau Geste (1924). Adventure novel, by P. C. *Wren; also the basis of films directed by H. Brennon (1926) and W. Wellman (1939).

Beaumarchais Pierre-Augustin Caron de (1732–99). Adventurer and comic dramatist. He was the son of a watchmaker but soon left the trade and lived on his wits. In 1757 he married a widow who died in 1758 and in 1768 another widow who also died; gave music lessons to Louis XV's daughter, engaged in somewhat dubious financial affairs and in resulting lawsuits, which he lost, despite his bribes: and for these he was imprisoned. He defended himself in 4 *Mémoires* (1774), masterpieces of special pleading, wit and invective, which rapidly became best-sellers. Now famous, he was able to produce his comedy *La Barbier de Séville* (written 1772) which, after drastic revision and reduction to 4 acts, was a great success. It brought new life to the French theatre, with its sparkling dialogue and was remarkable above all for the inimitable valet Figaro. B. attempted to repeat his success with *Le Mariage de Figaro* but the play was held back by the censorship until 1784. Three persons lost their lives in the crush on the first night. Less subtle and more brutal, direct and licentious than the *Barbier*, the new play was a brilliant and deadly satire on contemporary French society and a resounding manifesto against the *ancien régime*. Figaro represented B. himself, and in applauding him and his play the French ruling classes convincingly testified to their lack of faith in their own privileged social status. B. made and lost fortunes, became a royal secret agent, led a fleet of privateers against England and launched the Kehl ed. of Voltaire. He had a stormy time during the French Revolution, which ruined him. He returned from exile in Hamburg in 1796. Mozart's opera *Le Nozze di Figaro* and Rossini's *Il Barbiere di Siviglia* are based on B.'s plays.

Beaumont Sir Francis (1584–1616). English dramatist and collaborator with John *Fletcher from about 1606 to 1613, when B. married. In a coll. publ. in 1679, 53 plays were attributed to their joint authorship; a modern scholar has reduced the number to 7. B. was known as a master of plot and seems to have been more moralistic and conservative than Fletcher; he wrote *The Woman Hater* and most if not all of *The Knight of the Burning Pestle* (*c.* 1607, publ. 1613) burlesquing the contemporary heroic and romantic play.

Beaumont Sir George Howland (1753–1827). English patron and amateur landscape painter. B. knew many artists and writers including Dr Johnson, Reynolds, Wordsworth, Byron, Scott, Coleridge and Constable. His gift of pictures (1826) to the N.G., London was one of its major acquisitions.

Beau Serge, Le (1958). Film directed by C. *Chabrol.

Beauté du Diable, Le (1950). Film directed by R. *Clair.

Beautiful and the Damned, The (1922). Novel by F. Scott *Fitzgerald.

Beauvais cathedral (begun 1247). The last of the series of Île de France cathedrals which formed the Gothic style. It was to be the biggest cathedral in the world but only the choir and (much later) the transepts were ever built, and even these collapsed and had to be strengthened. The vault of the choir is 157 ft high (an openwork spire over the crossing was 500 ft high but fell down in 1573). The vaulting is sexpartite and there is a dazzling display of flying buttresses.
B. is also famous for its low-warp *tapestries. The tapestry factory established in 1664 was destroyed in World War II.

Beauvoir Simone de (1908–). French novelist, essayist and existentialist philosopher. Associated with Sartre in founding (1941) the periodical *Les Temps Modernes*. Like Sartre she uses the novel, e.g. *Le Sang des autres* (1945; *The Blood of Others*, 1948), or the theatre, e.g. *Les Bouches inutiles* (1945), to disseminate philosophical or political ideas. Her work deals with existential problems in relation to the individual and the state. She is an ardent feminist and states her case most fully in *Le deuxième sexe* (1949; *The Second Sex*, 1953). In the novel *Les Mandarins* (1954; *The Mandarins*, 1957) she portrays the intelligentsia of post-war Paris.

Beaux-Arts, École des. The school of art in Paris which replaced the school of the Académie royale des beaux-arts, suppressed during the Revolution. Most impressionist painters were taught there but rebelled against its teaching. The school became associated with reaction, and the fact that it controlled official commissions had a stultifying effect. The school is now rather more liberal.

Beaux' Stratagem, The (1707). Play by *Farquhar.

bebop. A form of *jazz.

Beccafumi called 'Il Mecarino', Domenico di Pace (*c.* 1485–1551). Sienese painter, took his patron's name, B., and studied under Mecarino. His masterpiece is the mosaic for S. Bernardino church, Siena. He also worked in Pisa and Genoa. His delicate early style, typical of the Sienese school, shows, in its compositional coherence, the influence of Raphael; it derived vigour and boldness from B.'s study of Michelangelo.

Beccaria Cesare, Marchese Bonesana (1738–94). Italian jurist who first urged, on rational and humane grounds, the abolition of capital punishment. B.'s great work *Dei delitti e delle peni* (1764), which Voltaire helped to popularize, argues his then revolutionary case against capital punishment, judicial torture, etc., with an epigrammatic loftiness and eloquence, in the spirit of the Enlightenment.

Becher Johannes R(obert) (1891–1958). German poet and novelist. He was a member of the Communist party from an early age and gradually abandoned the expressionism of *Verfall und Triumph* (1914) as his work became increasing political, e.g. *Gedichte für ein Volk* (1919), *Vorwärts, du rote Front!* (1924). He was an exile in Russia (1933–45).

Bechet Sidney (1897–1959). U.S. soprano saxophonist and clarinettist. His forceful style was characterized by a wide vibrato and sweeping melodic lines. After early experience as a clarinettist with some of the important figures of early New Orleans jazz, he toured Europe in 1919. In the late 1940s he settled in France, where he influenced many young French traditional jazz musicians.

Bechstein. World-famous German firm of piano and grand-piano makers founded by Friedrich Wilhelm Carl B. (1826–1900) in 1853. He incorporated the American iron frame and the English action into his instruments, which were praised by Liszt and others. From 1879 to 1915 there was a B. branch in London which in 1901 opened a concert hall, now the Wigmore Hall.

Beck Conrad (1901–). Swiss composer. In Paris from 1922 to 1923 he was a pupil of N. Boulanger; in 1938 he became musical director of Basle radio. His music has a strict contrapuntal pattern and is spare and austere in methods and effect. It includes an oratorio on texts from Angelus Silesius and *Der Tod zu Basel* a miserere for speaker, chorus and orchestra (1935).

Beauvais cathedral. The choir; 18th-c. engraving

Beauvais tapestry: *The Audience*

Beccafumi. *Birth of the Virgin*

Sidney Bechet

Simone de Beauvoir

Beckett. *Endgame*

William Beckford

Beck Hans (1861–1952). Danish ballet dancer and choreographer, ballet master of the Danish Royal Ballet, Copenhagen 1894–1915 and one of the greatest male dancers of his generation. He was mainly responsible for the preservation of A. Bournonville's ballets.

Becker Jacques (1906–60). French film director. B. was assistant to J. *Renoir (1932–8). His 1st completed film was *Dernier Atout* (1942). He attempted many genres, but his talent was for precise observation as in the modest, sensitive comedy *Goupi Mains Rouges* (1943) and *Édouard et Caroline* (1951). *Casque d'Or* (1952) was a period tragedy. *Touchez pas au grisbi* (1951) was a violent crime melodrama and *Le Trou* (1960) about a prison escape, was his last and most personal film.

Beckett Samuel (1906–). Irish poet, novelist and dramatist who settled in France 1937. His early work, poems and novels, e.g. *Murphy* (1938), influenced by James Joyce, were in English, but since 1945 B. has written in French, trs. some of his own works into English. Using much symbolism he presents his characters, often few in number, paralysed in will, physically decrepit and existing untouchable in their private desolation. Action is minimal, there is only boredom, human suffering and human cruelty which together constitute B.'s despairing but ultimately compassionate view of the human condition. Novels include *Malone meurt* (1951; *Malone Dies*, 1956), *L'Innomable* (1953; *The Unnamable*, 1958), *Molloy* (1955; English trs. publ. the same year), and *Watt* (1953) and numerous plays, e.g. *En attendant Godot* (1957; *Waiting for Godot*, 1956), *Fin de Partie* (1957; *Endgame*, 1958) and *Krapp's Last Tape* (1959).

Beckmann. *Odysseus and Calypso*

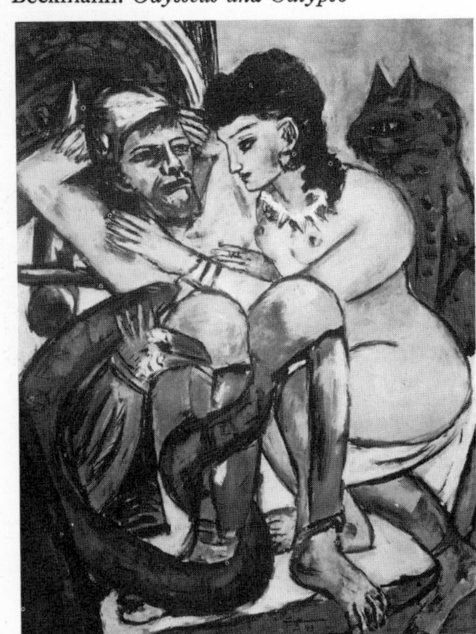

Beckford William (1759–1844). English writer and dilettante best known for his novel *Vathek* (written in French but publ. first in English, 1786), an oriental romance admired by Byron; and for his architectural extravagances at his mansion of Fonthill (J. *Wyatt), an early and influential example of the Gothic revival. He also wrote about his travels in Italy, Spain and Portugal.

Beckmann Max (1884–1950). German painter, lithographer and woodcut artist and one of the greatest 20th-c. figure painters. In World War I he served in a medical corps but was released following a nervous breakdown. A teacher at Frankfurt school of art (1915–33) he was dismissed by the Nazi régime and settled in Amsterdam in 1937 moving to the U.S. in 1947. He is identifiable with no one school but his army experiences radically affected him and his work passed through a period of expressionistic distortion and *new objectivity realism, using scenes from everyday life for subjects. B. left a large series of self-portraits. He was 'immersed in the problem of individuality' of people and objects; he greatly admired Cézanne and believed that the artist, out of an intuitive feeling for objects should attempt to give an expression of their inner nature.

Becky Sharp (1935). Film directed by R. *Mamoulian.

Becque Henri (1837–99). French dramatist who wrote *Les Corbeaux* (1882) and *La Parisienne* (1885; 1943), 2 of the earliest naturalistic dramas, in which he aimed to present an uncompromisingly honest picture of life. They were first performed by the *Théâtre Libre.

Bécquer Gustavo Adolfo (1836–70). Spanish romantic and lyrical poet. B. worked as a trs. and journalist in Madrid where he led a Bohemian existence, and died just as he was beginning to establish a literary reputation. A fine writer of prose, his fantastic series of tales *Leyendas* owed much to German romanticism, but his finest works were his lyric poems, *Rimas* (publ. posth. 1871). They dealt mainly with unrequited love in a gentle, melancholy style, used simple language and reverted to the old Spanish device of assonance instead of rhyme.

Bedbug, The (1929). Play by *Mayakovsky.

Beddoes Thomas Lovell (1803–49). English poet, son of a physician. In 1822 he publ. the dramatic poem *The Bride's Tragedy* and from 1825 lived in Germany and Switzerland studying medicine. His romantic morbidity is shown in *Death's Jest Book* (begun 1825; publ. posth. 1850) a 5-act dramatic poem in Elizabethan style. His works, many publ. after B.'s suicide, gradually gained reputation, particularly the lyrical poems, e.g. *Dirge for Wolfram* and *Dream Pedlary*.

Bede or Baeda (*c.* 673–735). 'The father of English history' and a scholar of European significance. B. was a monk at Jarrow where he spent a lifetime in study. He wrote, among other works, commentaries on the Scriptures, lives of St Cuthbert and the abbots of Wearmouth and Jarrow and his invaluable and unrivalled *Ecclesiastical History of the English People*. It remains the basic authority for events from 597 to 731. B. took great pains to achieve accuracy and a pleasant literary presentation. His reputation drew scholars to Jarrow which he made a centre of the revival of learning in N. England.

Bedells Phyllis (1893–). English dancer and teacher who studied under Cecchetti, Genée and Pavlova. She achieved success as a dancer and in 1935 opened a ballet school in Bristol, later moving to London where some of the most famous dancers of the Royal Ballet have passed through her studio.

Beecham Sir Thomas (1879–1961). English conductor and impresario and founder of the London Philharmonic (1932) and Royal Philharmonic (1947) orchestras. In 1906 he made his orchestral début and from 1909 to 1919 conducted and financed opera, introducing music of R. Strauss, popularizing Mozart, Berlioz, Verdi and Wagner in England and in 1911 introducing Diaghilev's Ballets Russes to London. From 1928 to 1933 he was chief conductor of the London Symphony Orchestra. B. was internationally known for the sensitivity and verve of his Mozart interpretations, and was champion of the music of Delius.

Beechey Sir William (1753–1839). English portrait painter. In 1793 he became official portrait painter to George III's queen, Charlotte.

Beer. Family of Swiss-Austrian architects, flourishing in the late 17th and early 18th cs. The chief member is Franz (1660–1726), architect of the churches of Irsee and Holzen in Germany and St Urbain, Switzerland.

Beer Jan de (1475–1536). Flemish painter, one of the *Antwerp mannerist school many of whose paintings were formerly ascribed to him.

Beerbohm Sir Max (1872–1956). 'The Incomparable Max.' English satirist, caricaturist and dramatic critic, succeeding G. B. Shaw as critic on *The Saturday Review* in 1898. He wrote sophisticated elegant fables of contemporary life, e.g. the novel *Zuleika Dobson* (1911) and the short stories *Seven Men* (1919), satire of surgical precision and brilliant criticism, e.g. *A Christmas Garland* (1912). His caricatures include *The Poet's Corner* (1904) and *Rossetti and his circle* (1922).

Beerstraten. Name of 2 Flemish landscape painters. Anthonie (*fl.* 1639–65) painted mostly snow scenes somewhat similar to those of H. Avercamp; Jan Abrahamsz (*fl.* 1622–66) used more conventional subject-matter.

Beethoven Ludwig van (1770–1827). German composer of Flemish extraction, his grandfather settling in Bonn, 1733. His father Johann B. was a musician at the electoral court there. B. studied under C. G. *Neefe (from 1781 court organist) and occasionally acted as his deputy, becoming assistant organist in 1784; he showed precocious but not astonishing gifts. At Bonn B. became a close friend of the Breuning family. In 1787, intending to become Mozart's pupil, he visited Vienna, but had to return to Bonn since his mother, whom he passionately loved, was dying. When his father was dismissed (1789) B. supported the family. In 1792 B. settled in Vienna. He took lessons with Haydn but sought more exacting teachers, among them J. G. *Albrechtsberger and A. *Salieri. In 1795, B. made his 1st public appearance as a pianist; in 1800 his 1st symphony was performed. For some years B. had had dysentery and this perhaps provoked his deafness which eventually became complete. At Heiligenstadt in 1802 he wrote the famous *Testament* in which he pours forth his miseries; a deaf composer and a naturally irascible man further cut off from his friends. From 1803 to 1804 he was working on the *'Eroica' symphony. In 1806 appeared op. 59, the 3 string quartets commissioned by Count A. K. Rasumovsky, the Russian ambassador in Vienna. In 1809, to prevent his leaving Vienna, 3 aristocratic friends, among them the Archduke Rudolph, guaranteed B. an annual income; in fact a monetary devaluation and the death and bankruptcy of 2 of the sponsors drastically reduced its value. B. longed for marriage and had many

Bede. From a 12th-c. ms. of B.'s *Life of Cuthbert*

Beechey. *Queen Charlotte*

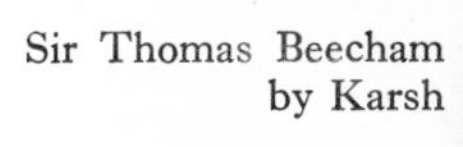

Sir Thomas Beecham by Karsh

F. Beer. St Urbain

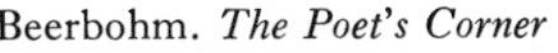

Beerbohm. *The Poet's Corner*

Beethoven. Pen sketch by J. P. Lyser

Beethoven. Ms. score of the 'Eroica' with the dedication to Napoleon scratched out by Beethoven

Beethoven. Engraved from a portrait by J. G. Waldmueller

The Beggar's Opera: painting by Hogarth

love-affairs, the letter to the 'Immortal Beloved' being his most famous surviving love-letter. He had a great admiration for Goethe and their meeting (1812) was, for him, a precious experience. In 1815 B. became guardian of his nephew Karl but a legal dispute with the mother dragged on for 5 years. B.'s overpowering affection and possessive concern and Karl's natural reaction of withdrawal and ingratitude imposed terrible strains on both of them, and Karl's attempted suicide in 1826 was B.'s last and greatest tragedy.

His working methods can be minutely studied because many of his sketchbooks have survived. These show long periods of gestation and repeated reworking of his ideas. The conversation books he used record the personality of this deaf musician.

B. was the 1st musician to live by royalties and commissions rather than by a salary from a church body or an aristocratic household; this involved him in negotiations with publs and musical societies and occasionally his own business dealings bordered on chicanery. He was frequently short of money but after 1815 he kept untouched a large investment intended for his nephew Karl.

Stylistically B.'s music is marked by sudden contrasts of mood, of dynamics and of instrumental densities, tutti passages abruptly give way to solo lines. He extensively develops fragmentary but astonishingly fertile themes and in a musical phrase is able to suggest an abstract idea. Although he extended the length of the symphony and gave the 1st movement sonata form a more dynamic evolutionary development he was no formal innovator, expanding, rather, the symphonic and quartet forms, stabilized in their essentials by Haydn. Nevertheless B. changed music irrevocably.

He was the 1st composer to use his music consistently to express extra-musical ideas: his own emotional and philosophical reaction to life, the grandeur and beauties of nature, the ideals of the heroic, the ideal of freedom. His music was the seminal force of the 19th c., deeply affecting if not initiating the romantic school. He became the subject of a cult of the demi-god artist, the superman mightily overmastering his environment.

The following is a list of some of B.'s major works with dates of composition. Opera: *Fidelio* (1803–5). Mass in D, *Missa solemnis* (1818–23). Symphonies: no. 1 in C (1799); no. 2 in D (1802); no. 3 in E♭, 'Eroica' (1803–4); no. 4 in B♭ (1806); no. 5 in C min. (1805–7); no. 6 in F, *Pastoral* (1807–8); no. 7 in A (1812); no. 8 in F (1812); no. 9 in D min. called 'The Choral' (1817–23). Also *Wellingtons Sieg, bei Vittoria*, the so-called *'Battle Symphony'. Overtures: 'Leonore no. 2' (1805); 'Leonore no. 3' (1806); 'Leonore no. 1' (1807); 'Coriolan' (1807); *Fidelio* (1814). Piano concertos: no. 1 in C (1797?); no. 2 in B♭ (1795, reworked 1798); no. 3 in C min. (1800); no. 4 in G (1805–6); no. 5 in E♭, called 'The Emperor' (1809). Violin concerto in D (1806). Chamber music: 6 string quartets (1798–1800); septet for clarinet, horn, bassoon, violin, viola, cello, double bass (1799–1800); 3 string quartets dedicated to Count A. K. Rasumovsky (1806); string quartet called 'The Harp' (1809); trio in B♭ for violin, cello, piano called 'The Archduke trio' (1811); string quartets ('the last quartets'): op. 127 in E♭ (1824), op. 132 in A min. (1825), op. 130 in B♭ (1825; new finale, 1826), *Grosse Fuge* op. 133 in B♭ (1825), op. 131 in C♯ min. (1826), op. 135 in F (1826). Piano music; sonatas: *Grande Sonate Pathétique* in C min. (1798); in C min. called 'The Moonlight' (1801); in D called 'The Pastoral' (1801); in C dedicated to Count von Waldstein (1804); in F min. called 'Appassionata' (1804); in B♭ called 'Hammerklavier' (1818). Violin sonata in A called *'Kreutzer' (1803); variations: 32 in C min. (1806); in C, 33 variations (1819–23) on a waltz by A. *Diabelli.

Beets Nicolaas (1814–1903). Dutch clergyman poet and short-story writer. Besides sermons and romantic verse he wrote, under the pseud. 'HILDEBRAND', the coll. of long short stories and essays *Camera Obscura* (1839).

before all letters. In engraving, a proof taken before the plate has had the title and dedication, etc., added. Such proofs are naturally rare.

Bega Cornelis (1620–64). Dutch painter. He was the pupil of Adriaen van Ostade and painted the same kind of peasant genre scenes, but his work is far inferior.

Beggar's Opera, The (1728). * Ballad opera by John *Gay, music arranged by J. C. Pepusch. The British film (1953) was directed by Peter Brook. Benjamin Britten has publ. a new version.

Beggarstaff brothers. Name used by Sir William *Nicholson and James *Pryde in their work together as poster artists.

Brendan Behan

Afra Behn

Behrens. Turbine factory, Berlin

Beham Hans Sebald (1500–50). This German etcher, engraver, painter and woodcut artist produced over 1,000 book illustrations. His work is distinguished by force and restraint of expression as well as technical mastery whether on copper or wood. Very few of his paintings are known. His brother, BARTHEL (1502–40), for a time painter to the Bavarian court at Munich, in 1535 moved to Italy where he died. His paintings at Munich include the *Miracle of the Cross* (1530). He also left engravings.

Behan Brendan (1923–64). Irish writer. B. was imprisoned 1939–47 for I.R.A. activity and utilized these experiences in his plays *The Quare Fellow* (1955), which deals with the reaction inside a prison to a man in the condemned cell, and *The Hostage* (1958), an extravaganza about Anglo-Irish relations. *Borstal Boy* (1958) is an autobiographical novel; *Brendan Behan's Island* (1962) is impressions of Ireland. His work is distinguished for its exuberance and pithy, colloquial dialogue.

Behn Afra (Aphra, Ayfara) (1640–89). English dramatist, novelist and the 1st English woman writer to make her living by writing. She served as a secret agent in the Netherlands 1666; on her return she was imprisoned for debt and began writing to clear herself. Her plays include *The Forc'd Marriage* (1671) and the most popular *The Rover* (2 parts, 1677, 1681). Her novel *Oroonoko: or The Royal Slave* (1688) anticipated the 18th-c. theme of the Noble Savage.

Behrens Peter (1869–1940). German painter, designer and architect, the first to exploit the aesthetic possibilities of industrial architecture. From 1903 to 1907 he was director of the Düsseldorf art school, under him the leading school in Germany, and from 1907 to 1912 chief architect and design adviser to the electrical firm of AEG; during this time W. Gropius was his pupil. In 1922 he was teaching in Vienna, in 1936 at Berlin. B.'s AEG appointment was a landmark in design history for he controlled design of products, advertising and factories. His 'Art Building' at an Oldenburg exhibition (1905) had presaged a return to classicism and was followed in 1909 by his turbine factory for AEG, 'the first modern building'. Here B. used modern materials of glass and steel fittingly, in a perfectly proportioned and efficient industrial unit.

Behrman S(amuel) N(athaniel) (1893–). U.S. dramatist. His plays, sophisticated comedies, include *The Second Man* (1927), *Serena Blandish* (1929) and *Biography* (1932); *Rain from Heaven* (1934) was one of the 1st plays against German Nazism, and he adapted his *Amphitryon 38* (1937) from Giraudoux.

Beiderbecke Bix (1903–31). U.S. jazz cornetist, the 1st outstanding white jazzman and a strong influence on later trumpet and cornet players.

Beijeren (Beyeren) Abraham Hendricsz van. 17th-c. Dutch still-life painter, specializing in all kinds of sea food.

Beilby William (1740–1819) and Mary (1749–97). Brother and sister, the 1st English artists to produce *enamelled glass. They produced much charming and accomplished work and their pieces, and those decorated by other members of their family, bear the surname alone. They are often done in a bluish white enamel in the rococo style. Work attributed to them is thought to have been done between about 1762 and 1774–8.

Beilby. Glass bowl

Belaiev Mitrofan Petrovich (1836–1904). Patron of Russian nationalistic composers, e.g. Rimsky-Korsakov and Borodin. B. organized concerts and founded a publ. house for their works.

Bel-Ami (1885). Novel by Guy de *Maupassant.

Bel and the Dragon. One of the books of the *Apocrypha.

Belasco David (1853–1931). U.S. playwright, producer and manager. U.S. theatre 1890–1914 was dominated by 'Belascoism', the cult of well-made but shallow dramas with sets meticulously reproducing reality. B. pioneered with experimental lighting effects. Wrote many plays including *The Heart of Maryland* (1895), *The Girl of the Golden West* (1905), and others with collaborators.

bel canto (Italian for 'beautiful song'). An Italian style of singing cultivated during the 18th c. and the 1st half of the 19th c. It was characterized by clarity of tone and enunciation, fine control of dynamics and technical agility. Post-Wagnerian opera demands a more 'declamatory' style.

Beham. Engraving from the *Seven Planets* series

Bellarmine bottle, *c.* 1660

Church-bell at Almería

Belinsky: portrait by G. J. Afanasiev

Vanessa Bell. Portrait of Iris Tree

Belgiojoso Lodovico (1909–). Italian architect *B.B.P.R.

Belgrade Theatre Coventry. English repertory theatre opened in 1958 and the 1st to be run by civic authorities. All the wood in the interior was the gift of the city of Belgrade (Coventry sent ambulances to Yugoslavia during the war), hence its name. Many of the plays of Arnold Wesker have had their première there.

Belinsky Vissarion Grigorievich (1811–48). Russian critic, a socialist and atheist whose work influenced 2 generations. After his expulsion–partly for political reasons–from Moscow Univ. (1832) he worked for several journals. His letter to Gogol (1847) became the accepted statement of radical belief. B.'s career marks the beginning of the literary ascendancy of a classless intelligentsia (the *raznochintsy*); his conviction that literature should deal with socially significant problems and ideas was reflected in most subsequent Russian writing (as was his inattention to stylistic and formal qualities), and anticipated the Soviet dogma of Socialist Realism. His judgement of contemporaries was generally accurate, though sometimes–as in the cases of Gogol and Dostoyevsky–based on incorrect interpretations of their 'civic' intentions.

bell. These instruments vary in size from the Great Bell of Moscow of 180 tons to a fraction of an ounce; they are cast from a bronze alloy and demand expert tuning to produce the 'strike-note', the 'hum-note' an 8ve below this, and persisting after the strike-note is no longer heard, and the major overtones. Apart from the b.'s use as an alarm, for celebration and in religious ceremonial, groups of b.s are used, in *carillons, for the performance of music and in 'rings', for change ringing. A 'ring' of b.s may have from 5 b.s upwards; they can be sounded successively in different sequences or 'changes'.

Bell (Arthur) Clive (Howard) (1881–1960). English writer on art, husband of Vanessa B. B.'s works were important in securing recognition for post-impressionist art; their emphasis was on 'significant form' rather than subject-matter. Works include *Art* (1914) and *Civilization* (1928).

Bell Currer, Ellis and Acton: the *Brontë family

Bell Gertrude Margaret Lowthian (1868–1926). English writer, traveller, archaeologist and alpinist. Her understanding of Arab society and travel in Arab countries gave her a wide reputation. *The Desert and the Sown* (1907), about Syria, is a classic of travel literature. The selection, *The Letters of Gertrude Bell* (1927), was widely read.

Bell John (1745–1831). English printer, publ., bookseller and journalist. He publ. attractive cheap eds of *Poets of Great Britain complete from Chaucer to Churchill*, was a founder of the daily newspaper *Morning Post* (1772) among others and revolutionized newspaper typography and display by breaking the page into columns and concentrating on the unit of the paragraph. The Bell type (R. *Austin) became popular in the U.S. and B. was the 1st printer to drop the long 's' from his fount.

Bell Marie (1900–). French stage and film actress. She was at the Comédie-Française (1921–53), has appeared in more than 30 films and now has her own theatre co.

Bell Vanessa (1879–1961). English painter and designer for the Omega Workshops, member of the Bloomsbury Group and the London Group; sister of Virginia Woolf. Between 1912 and 1918 she experimented with post-impressionist styles. She collaborated with Duncan Grant on various decorative projects.

Bellamy Edward (1850–98). U.S. novelist and journalist whose *Looking Backward: 2000–1887* (1888), a novel expounding his utopian socialist ideas, sold very widely and influenced U.S. politics. He wrote a sequel, *Equality* (1897).

Bellarmine bottle. A 16th–17th-c. type of German salt-glazed stoneware jug or bottle with a rounded belly and a handle, characterized by the applied moulded ornament on its neck or shoulder consisting of the mark of a bearded man (hence the popular name 'greybeard jug', German *Bartmann*). Ornament on the belly was, in the 16th c. an allover applied pattern of foliage, in the 17th c. a roundel in the centre.

Bellay Joachim du (1522–60). French poet, after Ronsard the most important member of the *Pléiade, to whose doctrines Ronsard introduced him during a casual but decisive meeting. B.'s greatest achievements were in the sonnet form (e.g. the long sequence *L'Olive*) which he employed for many purposes–to celebrate love, to evoke nostalgia, to satirize. Works include the colls *Antiquités de Rome* (1558) and *Regrets* (1558), and the treatise *Défense et illustration de la langue française* (1549). Spenser trs. some of his poems.

Belleau Remi (Remy) (1528–77). French poet of the *Pléiade. His delicate work included the prose and verse coll. *La Bergerie* (1565, 1572) with descriptions of the seasons and *Les Amours . . . des pierres précieuses* (1576) on the properties of precious stones.

Belle Dame sans Merci, La (written 1819). Poem by Keats.

Belle et la Bête, La (1946). Film directed by *Cocteau.

Bellegambe Jean (*c.* 1480–*c.* 1535). Flemish painter of altarpieces, known as 'the master of colour', working in Amiens. He was influenced by Italian painting in such works as the polyptych (Mus. Municipal, Douai).

Belle Helène, La. Operetta by Offenbach; 1st performance in Paris in 1864.

Belle Jardinière, La (*c.* 1520). Painting of a Madonna by Raphael.

belles-lettres (French, 'fine writings'). Used in English to describe light essays, particularly essays on literature in a wide sense, its beauties and subtleties. In earlier usage the term was used as a synonym for 'literature'.

Bellini. Family of Italian painters, Jacopo and his sons Gentile and Giovanni, who created the Venetian school of the Renaissance.

Bellini Gentile (*c.* 1429–1507). Italian painter famous for his narrative works in the *scuole* (confraternities) of Venice, e.g. the *Procession of the Relic of the Cross in the Piazza of San Marco* (1496), and for his portraits. He was chosen to paint the Sultan Mohammed II in Constantinople (*c.* 1480). In his works austere draughtsmanship and architectural composition are combined with rich colouring.

Bellini Giovanni (*c.* 1430–1516). Pupil of his father and first collaborated with him and Gentile on the great decorative works for the *scuole* (Gentile *B.), now destroyed. Having no interest in classical subjects, which were becoming popular, he chose predominantly religious themes, which he treated with much of the devotional restraint of earlier painters. Nevertheless, by adopting the technique of oil glazing and gradually abandoning the linear conception of form he revolutionized Venetian painting and substantially affected the future course of European painting through his most famous pupils, Giorgione and Titian. He was slow to find his own style and never ceased to develop it. In Padua (1458–60) he was strongly influenced by Mantegna, though his work was never as sculptural or severe as Mantegna's, e.g. their respective treatments of *The Agony in the Garden* (N.G., London), both based on a sketch by Jacopo B. B.'s version has a naturalistic landscape background (one of the earliest examples of landscape painting); it illustrates his ability to create a lyrical affinity between his figures and their settings. Other early works probably done at this time include several madonnas and pietàs. These madonnas have the serenity, tenderness and individuality typical of his later work; the suffusion of light and the presentation of half-length figures are also characteristic of his style. B. returned to Venice in 1460. 4 triptychs (1460–1) for the Carità church (Accademia, Venice) were his 1st major undertaking and these were followed by the *Altarpiece with St Vincent Ferrar* (1464), for the church of SS. Giovanni e Paolo, notable for the differences in style between the panels. In 1470 he was working on the decoration of the Scuola Grande di S. Marco with Gentile and visited Rimini and Pesaro. There he saw oil paintings by Rogier van der Weyden, which impressed him by their realism and tonal variations. He himself learnt the Flemish technique of oil glazing from Antonella da Messina in 1475, and his *Resurrection* (1475/6; Berlin) was the 1st Venetian painting executed in glazes of pure oil paint. He had been using a mixture of oil and tempera in Rimini while the brushwork of the *Pietà with St John* in the Brera, Milan, is typical of that used with oil. His work gradually lost its sharp contours, expressing form by a developing richness and variety of tone and colour, e.g. the altarpiece from S. Giobbe *The Virgin and Child with Saints and an Orchestra of Angels* (Accademia, Venice). This style was more fully exploited by Titian.

Bellegambe. *Glorification of the Holy Trinity* (detail)

Gentile Bellini. *Miracle of the Cross*

Giovanni Bellini. *The Agony in the Gardon.* Also *imago pietis

Giovanni Bellini. *The Feast of the Gods*

Vincenzo Bellini

Hilaire Belloc

Saul Bellow

Jacopo Bellini. *Madonna*

Bellotto. *The University Square, Vienna* (detail). Also *Dresden

Much of B.'s time after 1497 was occupied in restoring the frescoes of the hall of the great council in the Doge's Palace, Venice, a work begun by Gentile. Among B.'s portraits is the famous *The Doge Loredano* (*c.* 1503; N.G., London). He painted few mythological subjects, but the best known, *The Feast of the Gods* (*c.* 1514; N.G., Washington), painted for the *camerino* or study of Alfonso d'Este of Ferrara, was unusual for its time in its representation of deities as ordinary people, possibly members of the court of Ferrara. Titian, who completed the decoration of the room, repainted the landscape background of this picture and made minor alterations to the figures, though retaining B.'s composition.

Bellini Jacopo (*c.* 1400–*c.* 70). Follower of A. Pisanello and Gentile da Fabriano. His rare extant paintings show him to have been competent rather than outstanding, and his importance lies in his interest in the return to antiquity and the new scientific approach to the subjects of painting. Two valuable sketchbooks of his exist. Many of these sketches, which include figure studies for larger compositions and show an interest in landscape, architectural design and the problems of perspective, were used by his sons and his son-in-law Mantegna.

Bellini Vincenzo (1801–35). Italian opera composer. In his music harmonic and instrumental interests are subordinate to the melodic line; if sung by virtuosi, the solo parts are exhilarating displays of the emotional and technical range of the human voice. B.'s 3 major operas are *Norma* (1831), the tragedy of a druid priestess in love with a Roman soldier; *Sonnambula* (1831), about a village girl whose sleepwalking leads her in to situations which makes her fiancé doubt her faithfulness; and *I Puritani* (1835), set in the English Civil War.

Bellman Carl Michael (1740–95). Swedish poet. He drank heavily, lived in debt and died in penury. B. picturesquely described low life in old Stockholm, ignored classical poetic standards and was despised by most contemporary poets, though his best pieces achieve sensuous rapture. The verses of his entertainments, performed with lute accompaniments by himself, were publ. as *Fredmans Epistlar* (1790, preface by J. H. Kellgren) and *Fredmans Sånger* (1791).

Belloc Hilaire (1870–1953). English writer, and a fervent and aggressive Catholic apologist. *Verses and Sonnets* (1896) contains good serious poetry, but B. is remembered for his light verse *The Bad Child's Book of Beasts* (1897) and *Cautionary Tales* (1907). Other writings include *The Path to Rome* (1902); history, *Marie Antoinette* (1909), *Cromwell* (1934); the semi-autobiographical novel *The Cruise of the 'Nona'* (1925). B. was a close friend of G. K. Chesterton.

Bellotto Bernardo (1720–80). Italian landscape and townscape painter, also called Canaletto, whose nephew and pupil he was and whose style and name he adopted. In 1747 B. went to Dresden, where he became painter to the electoral court. In 1767 he settled in Warsaw, working for the Polish king until his death. His views of Warsaw are so exact that they were used when the city was reconstructed after World War II.

Bellow Saul (1915–). Canadian-born novelist, living in the U.S. since 1924. His theme is modern man's struggle for self-realization in a vast and frightened society. In *Dangling Man* (1944), a soldier finds orders to the front line in some way liberating because of their finality. *The Adventures of Augie March* (1953) is in the loose form of a Fielding novel. Augie learns that the unconnected events of his life could be used as a way to self-realization. In *Henderson the Rain King* (1959) the chaotic, explosive and naïve hero makes a solitary expedition into the African wilds hoping to resolve the stresses of his life. In *Herzog* (1964) the hero retreats from reality into fantasy.

Bellows George (1882–1925). U.S. painter of portraits, landscapes and urban life. He studied under R. Henri. His work provided an

Bellows. *Stag at Sharkey's*

Pietro Bembo: medallion

emotional, often bitter, comment on contemporary U.S. life, from which he drew his subjects with uncompromising realism. His series of 6 prize-fight paintings (1909) demonstrate his natural dashing style, which he later subjected to the theory of 'dynamic symmetry' to give a formal balance to his compositions. He turned with great success to lithography, e.g. a war series (1918), and book illustration.

Bells of St Mary's, The (1945). Film directed by L. *McCarey.

Belmondo Jean-Paul (1934–). French film actor who caught public attention in the 'improvised' *À Bout de Souffle* (1960). He has since starred in Peter Brook's psychological drama *Moderato Cantabile* (1960), and 3 films by *Melville, e.g. *Leon Morin, Prêtre* (1961).

Belper. Coarse brown pottery in the tradition of Nottingham stoneware was manufactured at Belper, near Derby, from the mid 18th c. until the early 19th c.

Bely Andrey. Pseud. of Boris Nikolayevich Bugayev (1880–1934). Russian symbolist poet and prose writer, a prolific author and close friend of Blok, of whom he wrote *Recollections* . . . (1922). B. was at the height of his influence in the years immediately following the Revolution, but emigrated in 1923. His verse was intensely musical and displayed great word virtuosity; his prose, e.g. the famous *Symphonies* (1902–8) and the novel *The Silver Dove* (1910), was rhythmical, harmonious and pure; but the interest of his mystical and spiritual themes has faded.

Bembo Pietro (1470–1547). Italian humanist, cardinal, historian of Venice and poet. In *Prose . . . della volgar lingua* (1525) he upheld Italian against Latin as a literary medium, successfully advocating the Tuscan of Petrarch and Boccaccio as the ideal norm. B. wrote *Gli Asolani* (1505) a prose dialogue on Platonic love. 'Bembo' is also the name now given to the type-face designed by F. Griffo and first used to print B.'s *De Aetna* (1495).

Bemelmans Ludwig (1898–1962). Writer, illustrator and artist born in Austria; emigrated to the U.S. in 1914 (naturalized 1918). His work is distinguished for its conscious *naïveté* and deadpan humour. His early books were for children, e.g. *Quito Express* (1938). Other books include *Hotel Bemelmans* (1946), stories based on his experiences of the hotel business, and *My War with the United States* (1937).

Benavente y Martínez Jacinto (1866–1954). Influential Spanish dramatist, best known for social satire, e.g. *Gente conocida* (1896), and Nobel prizewinner in 1922. His best play, *Los interéses Creados* (1907; *The Bonds of Interest*, 1917), uses **commedia dell'arte* conventions in its satire of the dualism of the human condition. *Señora ama* (1908), which B. considered his masterpiece, has for its heroine a wife whose tolerance of her husband's infidelities is lost when she becomes a mother. B. also wrote the powerful tragedy *La noche del sábado* (1903; *Saturday Night*, 1923), *La malguerida* (1913; *La Malguerida*, 1917), dealing with peasant life, and the children's play *El principe que todo lo aprendio en los libros* (1919; *The Prince who Learned Everything out of Books*, 1923).

Benda. Family of Czech musicians. Jiři (or Georg) Antonín (1722–95) worked in Germany and composed the early *melodramas *Ariadne auf Naxos* and *Medea* (both 1775), highly praised by Mozart.

Benda Julien (1867–1956). French philosopher and littérateur. Best known, of all his many books, for *La Trahison des Clercs* (1927; *The Great Betrayal*, 1928). B. described his early years in the novel *La Jeunesse d'un clerc* (1937). He sharply attacked Bergson and other 'traitors' who had abandoned intellectual discipline for mystical or intuitive interpretations of the world.

Benedek Laszlo (1907–). U.S. film director. B. made his name with an undistinguished adaptation of Miller's *Death of a Salesman*

Julien Benda

Benedek. Marlon Brando (pointing the bottle) in *The Wild One*

Arnold Bennett

Beni-Hassan. Wall painting of a foreign prince

(1952) and a Marlon Brando picture, *The Wild One* (1953). Recently he has worked in Europe.

Benedictus: *mass

Benét Stephen Vincent (1898–1943). U.S. writer whose epic poem *John Brown's Body* (1928; Pulitzer prize 1929; dramatized 1953) about the Civil War, was recognized as a classic; his story *The Devil and Daniel Webster* (1937), almost equally famous, was dramatized and was the basis of D. Moore's opera (both 1939). Other works include *Ballads and Poems, 1915–30* (1931) and *Western Star* (1943; posth. Pulitzer prize), a section of another (projected) epic, and novels. WILLIAM ROSE B. (1886–1950), the poet, novelist and playwright, was his brother.

Ben Hur: A Tale of the Christ (1880). Novel by Lew *Wallace; filmed by F. Niblo (1926), and by W. Wyler and A. Marton (1959).

Beni-Hassan. A village on the E. bank of the Nile in Middle Egypt opposite ancient Hermopolis. Renowned for tombs cut in the limestone cliffs above the river dating from the 12th dynasty (*c.* 2000 B.C.).

Benin. City and warrior kingdom of W. Nigeria; its greatest period was apparently during the 14th–17th cs A.D. The Portuguese reached B. in the late 15th c.; a British punitive expedition (1897) opened the BENIN ART treasures to Europe. These consist of naturalistic bronzes (cast by *cire perdue technique) and ivories; bronze reliefs, once decorations for the royal palace; human heads in the round, probably idealized, not actual portraits, of royalties; human and animal figures; implements. Sources and development are obscure but the surviving objects are the products of a court art, probably inspired by the art of *Ife and showing slight European influences.

Benito Cereno (1856). Story by Herman Melville.

Benjamin Arthur (1893–1960). Australian composer, from 1926 teacher at the R.C.M., London, where Britten was one of his pupils. He wrote the 1-act operas *The Devil Take Her* (1931) and *Prima Donna* (written 1933), the opera *The Tale of Two Cities* (1957) and much film music.

Benn Gottfried (1886–1956). German writer, a medical specialist who served in 2 World Wars. His powerful early expressionist poems, e.g. *Morgue* (1912), and stories, convey in clinical language B.'s conviction that life is meaningless; later, art and contemplation are increasingly regarded as the only activities of consequence, e.g. the poems in *Statische Gedichte* (1948).

Bennett Arnold (1867–1931). English novelist, dramatist, journalist, literary and dramatic critic; 1893 assistant ed., 1896–1900 ed. of the magazine *Woman.* His 1st novel, following the realism of George Moore, was *A Man From the North* (1898). His plays *What the Public Wants* (1909), *The Great Adventure* (1913) were very popular, but his reputation rests on his realistic novels portraying lower-middle-class life in the Staffordshire potteries, the 'five towns', e.g. *The Old Wives' Tale* (1908), which made him famous, *Clayhanger* (1910), *Hilda Lessways* (1911) and *These Twain* (1916). Other novels are *The Card* (1911), *Riceyman Steps* (1923), his last 'northern' novel, and *Imperial Palace* (1930), reflecting B.'s fascination with hotel life.

Bennett Richard Rodney (1936–). English composer, very prolific, who has composed in all styles from *serial to jazz. He has also written film music.

Bennett Sir William Sterndale (1816–75). English pianist, composer, teacher and conductor, and a friend of Mendelssohn and Schumann, who regarded him highly; he composed little. Works include the overture *The Naiads* and the oratorio *The Woman of Samaria.*

Benois Alexandre (1870–1960). Russian painter and theatrical designer, the founder of the St Petersburg *World of Art movement. B. belonged to a very cosmopolitan and cultured family, as did most of his friends; this many-streamed culture bridged the gap isolating Russia from the rest of Europe after the 19th-c. nationalist *Wanderers. From B. came the interest in ballet, to which he introduced *Diaghilev, a member of the group. *Le Pavillon d'Armide*, which headed the 1st Diaghilev season of ballet in 1909 in Paris, was an entirely B. conception. In B. were united interest in painting and music, and it was he who first gathered together the artists, writers,

Benin. Ivory pendant mask (16th c.?)

Benin. Bronze head of a Queen Mother (16th c.?)

Benois. Nijinsky's costume in the 1st version (1907) of *Le Pavillon d'Armide*

composers and poets who laid the foundation for the Ballets Russes.

Benoît de Sainte-Maure or Sainte-More. 12th-c. French poet whose *Roman de Troie* was widely popular in the middle ages. It deals with the story of Troy from the time of the Argonauts to the city's capture by the Greeks and contains the 1st version of the story of Troilus and Cressida (later used by Chaucer and Shakespeare) which was probably invented by B. He is possibly the 'Benoît' who wrote a chronicle of the dukes of Normandy (*c.* 1175) for Henry II of England.

Benoit-Levy Jean (1888–). French film director. During the 1930s, he made educational films and a few socially-slanted fiction films, of which the most famous is *La Maternelle* (1932) starring Madeleine Renaud, which he made with Marie Epstein.

Benozzo di Lese: *Gozzoli

Benserade Isaac de (1612–91). French writer of mediocre tragedies and highly successful court entertainments, e.g. masques and ballets, often using J.-B. Lully's music. His sonnet on Job caused a fierce literary debate as to whether it or V. Voiture's *Uranie* was superior.

Benson Ambrosius (d. 1550). Lombard painter who settled in Bruges (1519) and painted in a Flemish style particularly reflecting the influence of G. David. There are many of his pictures in Spain and he was formerly known as the 'Master of Segovia'.

Bentham Jeremy (1748–1832). English juridical reformer, political philosopher and constitution maker influential throughout 19th-c. Europe. In works like his *Introduction to the Principles of Morals and Philosophy* (1789), B. used his doctrine of utilitarianism – the criterion of usefulness in securing 'the greatest happiness of the greatest number' – to judge laws and institutions. He coined such words as 'maximize', 'codify' and 'international'.

Bentley Edmund Clerihew (1875–1956). English journalist, humorist and author of the 1st naturalistic detective story, *Trent's Last Case* (1913). B. publ. under the name E. Clerihew, *Biography for Beginners* (1905) a book of nonsense verse illustrated by his friend G. K. Chesterton. This introduced the 'Clerihew', a verse of 4 short rhyming lines, in no fixed metrical pattern, dealing with a famous subject.

Bentley John Francis (1839–1902). English architect and designer of church decorations. He worked in a neo-Gothic idiom, e.g. church of the Holy Rood, Watford (1887), until about 1894 when he was appointed architect of the proposed Westminster cathedral. This was required to be in a Byzantine style and B. made a study tour of Italy.

Bentley Richard (1662–1742). Brilliant but erratic English scholar, the first to employ scientific textual criticism combining philological with historical knowledge. He revised the texts of Horace, Terence and Manlius, and his *Dissertation on the Letters of Phalaris* (1699) inflamed the Ancients and Moderns Controversy by proving the spuriousness of the letters, which Sir W. *Temple had praised. Pope ridiculed him in *The Dunciad.*

Bentname. Nickname of the Dutch and Flemish painters in Rome who formed a group (also called 'Bentvueghels' – 'birds of a flock') in 1623. The centre of much scandalous behaviour, it was suppressed by the pope in 1720.

Benton Thomas Hart (1889–). U.S. regional painter who was one of the most voluble of those protesting against foreign influences and movements in U.S. art. *Roasting Ears* (Met. Mus.) and *Cattle Loading, West Texas* (Andover, Mass.) are typical in portraying U.S. rural scenes.

Benvenuto di Giovanni di Meo del Guasta (1436–*c.* 1518). Sienese painter, pupil of Vecchietta. His paintings include *Annunciation* (S. Girolamo, Volterra), *Nativity* (Volterra cathedral) and *Assumption of the Virgin* (Met. Mus.).

Ben Yehuda Eliezer. Pseud. of E. Perlman (1858–1922). Polish-Jewish scholar and journalist who settled in Palestine (1881). B. played an important part in the creation of a spoken Hebrew by his personal example, his editorship of the weekly *ha-Zebi*, and his *Complete Dictionary of Ancient and Modern Hebrew.*

Beowulf. The only surviving Old English epic poem of any length, the 1st major poem in English literature. It was probably written in the late 7th or early 8th c. A.D., drawing on earlier Scandinavian tradition. It celebrates

Jeremy Bentham

Benvenuto di Giovanni. *St Jerome*

Benois. Set design for *Les Noces de Psyche.* Also *Diaghilev

Benton. *Roasting Ears*

Alban Berg

Berg. The 'Bar Scene' from *Wozzeck*

Berchem. *Mountainous Landscape*

Gerrit Berckheyde. *The Grote Kerk, Haarlem* (detail)

with many digressions 2 heroic exploits by B. of the Geatas, a tribe in S. Sweden. B. visits the court of Hrothgar the Dane, where he slays the monster Grendel and its dam. He returns home, and having reigned 50 years, dies after fighting and killing a dragon; the dragon's treasure is laid on his funeral pyre. The tribal conflicts and chief characters described are partly historical, partly mythical. The poem, 3,200 lines long, survives in a ms. *c.* 1000; but since this version contains a Christian element which may not properly belong to the poem, it is not certainly the original version.

Béranger Pierre-Jean de (1780–1857). French writer of gay and witty verses. *Chansons* (1815) contained *Le Roi d'Yvetot*, a light satire on Napoleon's régime. *Chansons* (1821), satirizing the restored monarchy, gained him a short imprisonment and *Chansons . . . inédites* (1828), frankly Bonapartist, brought imprisonment and a fine; this was paid by public subscription.

Berceo Gonzalo de. 13th-c. Spanish poet of the lives of the saints and the Virgin, e.g. *Milagros de la Virgen.* His work is mostly monotonous and naïve, but he is the 1st Spanish poet whose name is known.

berceuse (French, 'cradle-song'). Instrumental, usually piano, piece with rocking accompaniment; Chopin's b. in D♭ maj. (1845) is the most famous.

Berchem (Berghem) Nicolaes (1620–83). Dutch Italianate painter. He toured Italy *c.* 1642–5 and thereafter his best pictures were of Arcadian landscapes, delicately painted and suffused with light after the manner of Claude Lorrain. He was sometimes employed by J. van Ruisdael and Hobbema to animate their landscapes.

Berchet Giovanni (1783–1851). Italian patriotic poet. In his *Lettera semiseria di Crisostomo* (1816), which accompanied a prose trs. of G. A. Bürger's ballads, B. urged that literature should be popular in approach and advocated that Italian writers should follow Mme de *Staël's advice to become acquainted with other literatures, particularly, B. said, the German which had found inspiration in folk-literature. B.'s frankly patriotic poems included *Romito del Censio* (1823), on the plight of Italy, and *Le Fantasie* (1829), 'visions' of Italy's ancient glories, written in exile in England.

Berckheyde Gerrit (1638–98). Dutch townscape painter, pupil of his brother Job, and imitator of the style of P. J. *Saenredam. In his paintings he frequently changed the actual relative positions of the buildings to suit the pictorial composition.

Berckheyde Job (1630–93). Dutch painter of townscapes. He was a more powerful colourist than his brother Gerrit.

Bérénice (1670). Tragedy by Racine.

Berenson Bernard (1865–1959). U.S. art critic, historian and art dealer; art adviser to the dealer Joseph Duveen. B.'s many works on the history and aesthetics of Italian painting, especially his *The Italian Painters of the Renaissance* (1952; first publ. as individual essays, 1894–1907), gained him a following as an expert on art and culture. Other important works are *Drawings of the Florentine Painters* (1903 and 1938) and *Aesthetics and History in the Visual Arts* (1948).

Berent Wacław (1873–1940). Polish novelist; many of his works are satirical in intention, e.g. *Fachowiec* (1895) and *Próchno* (1903). His best work, *Ozimina* (1911), describes a party at a fashionable Warsaw house; it has elaborate narrative technique and restricts the action to one place and a short period of time.

Berg Alban (1885–1935). Austrian *twelve-note composer. From 1904 to 1910 he was the pupil of Schoenberg. In 1921 he completed the opera *Wozzeck* (Berlin, 1925) based on the play by K. G. *Büchner. He began the unfinished opera *Lulu* in 1928. His grief at Manon Gropius's death directly inspired the violin concerto of 1935. B.'s music is characterized by impressionistic orchestration, mastery of form, e.g. the quartet op. 3 (1909/10), and lyricism, e.g. *Lulu* and the violin concerto. It is permeated by his semi-mystical views on the symbolism of music and of numbers in music; the chamber concerto for violin and piano with wind instruments (1923–5) revolves round the number 3, i.e. 3 instrumental units, 3 movements, themes whose bar lengths are multiples of 3; the violin concerto round the number 2. This concerto employs 12-note technique yet gives a distinct impression of tonality; the impression is reinforced in the 2nd movement, where B. exactly quotes a Bach chorale which uncannily conforms to the dodecaphonic framework. *Wozzeck* is the logical development of

Ingmar Bergman. *The Seventh Seal*

Van den Berghe. *Genealogie* (1929)

Wagnerian 'music drama', being an opera conceived in instrumental forms – the suite, air and variations and symphonic forms are all used. B.'s other works include the atonal *3 Pieces for Orchestra* (1914).

Berg Max (1870–1947). German architect whose long career produced the one great achievement, the Centenary Hall, Breslau (1913). A vast arena spanned with concrete ribs, it is one of the 1st great reinforced concrete structures.

Bergerac: Savinien de *Cyrano de Bergerac

Berghe Frits van den (1883–1939). Belgian expressionist painter and graphic artist, leader of the *Laethem-Saint-Martin group and co-founder of *Art Vivant*. His style developed from an early impressionism to an exaggerated expressionism verging on surrealism.

Bergman Bo Hjalmar (1869–). Swedish writer of verse lyric colls, e.g. *Marionetterna* (1903) and *Riket* (1944); short stories, e.g. *Valda noveller* (1950); the novel *Ett bokslut* (1942), and the critical essay on his friend Hjalmar Söderberg (1951). B.'s earlier work had Söderberg's pessimistic irony.

Bergman Hjalmar Fredrik Elgerus (1883–1931). Sweden's best-known dramatist after the death of Strindberg, novelist and short-story writer. His plays include *Marionettspel* (1917), *Ett Experiment* (1918), *Swedenhielms* (1925) and *Patrasket* (1928). Among his novels were *Markurells i Wadköping* (1919; *God's Orchid*, 1924) and *Chefen fru Ingeborg* (1924; *The Head of the Firm*, 1936).

Bergman Ingmar (1918–). Swedish film director. The son of a pastor, B. was a theatrical director (an activity which he has always continued) before writing the script for **Frenzy*. Since his early realist films like *Hamnstad* (1948), his work has become increasingly symbolic, veering at first towards expressionism, e.g. *Prison* (1948), in which it was combined with a complete pessimism that has been an intermittent feature of his work. His best films of the 1950s were much more elaborate than their predecessors – the comedy *Smiles of a Summer Night* (1955) in its décor and relationships, *Wild Strawberries* (1958) in its handling of time and memory. *The Seventh Seal* (1956), a film of characteristic pictorial clarity and beauty, captures the apocalyptic atmosphere of the medieval world afflicted by the plague. From *So Close to Life* (1958) B. has progressively stripped away all the elaboration of his previous films down to the completely ascetic style of his trilogy: *Through a Glass Darkly* (1961), *Winter Light* (1962) and *The Silence* (1963). *About all those Women* (1964) is a comedy in colour.

Bergman Ingrid (1917–). Swedish film and stage actress. Beautiful, with sound dramatic ability, she has filmed in Sweden, England, France, Italy, Germany and America – everywhere in the language of the country. Her films include: *Intermezzo* (1939), *Gaslight* (1944) – her 1st Oscar, *Joan of Arc* (1948), *Rossellini's *Voyage to Italy* (1953) and *Anastasia* (1957) – her 2nd Oscar. Her stage appearances in the U.S. included Eugene O'Neill's *Anna Christie* (1943).

Bergognone (Borgognone) Il (Ambrogio da Fossano) (active 1481–d. 1523). Italian painter of the Lombard school whose use of subdued and subtle colours led Berenson to nickname him the 'Whistler of the Renaissance'. He painted an altarpiece and frescoes for the convent of the Carthusians at Pavia (1514) and frescoes in the church of S. Simpliciano, Milan.

bergomask (Italian *bergamasca*). In the 16th c. a boisterous dance from the Italian town of Bergamo. In England a specific tune, frequently used for lute compositions, was associated with the b. The term is now vague but suggests the picturesque. An example is Debussy's *Suite bergamasque* (composed during 1890–1905) for piano.

Bergognone. *Crucifixion*

Bergson Henri-Louis (1859–1941). French philosopher whose work was strongly anti-mechanistic, emphasizing a life-drive (*élan vital*) in evolution, intuition in the apprehension of ultimate reality, and time as experienced by consciousness (*la durée*) distinct from time measured by the clock. His most famous book is *L'Évolution créatrice* (1907; *Creative Evolution*, 1911). Elegantly expressed and lucidly expounded, his ideas won him a large public following and influenced vitalists like Bernard Shaw (*vitalism).

Berio Luciano (1925–). Italian *serial composer. B. has worked at the electronic-music studio in Milan and taught in univs in the U.S.

Henri Bergson

Beriosova as Cinderella

Irving Berlin

George Berkeley

Berlage. The Bourse, Amsterdam

Busby Berkeley. *Dames* (1934)

Berlanga. *Placido*

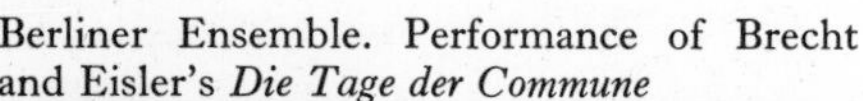
Berliner Ensemble. Performance of Brecht and Eisler's *Die Tage der Commune*

and Europe. In *Omaggio a Joyce* and *Cercles* (e.e. cummings) he uses techniques derived from experiments to find musical equivalents to vowels and consonants used in speech; in the one case electronically, in the other by 2 harps and percussion group. He has written other music for flute and tape, and for flute alone or with chamber orchestra.

Beriosova Svetlana (1932–). Lithuanian dancer, naturalized British (1955), who received her early training from her father, a member of R. Blum's co. She spent the war years in the U.S. and in 1950 joined the Sadler's Wells Theatre Ballet. She is now at Covent Garden, where she enjoys ballerina status.

Bériot Charles-Auguste de (1802–70). Belgian violinist who toured Europe with, and married (1836), the singer M. Garcia-Malibran. Professor at the Brussels Conservatoire (1843–52), he publ. an important manual of violin technique; his pupils included H. Vieuxtemps.

Berkeley Busby (1895–). U.S. film director and choreographer. B.'s regiments of dancers, grandiose sets and huge camera movements produced results that were often graceless and unexcitingly symmetrical, but which had considerable panache and set the style in musicals for nearly a decade.

Berkeley George (1685–1753). Irish philosopher and bishop; he became dean of Derry in 1724 and bishop of Cloyne in 1734. He spent a fruitless 3 years in America trying to establish a missionary college in Bermuda.
B.'s most important contribution to philosophy was perhaps his insistence on the use of clearly defined terms. In his most influential work, *A Treatise concerning the Principles of Human Knowledge* (1710), where he contradicts *Locke, B. expounds the theory that 'to exist' is 'to be perceived' and also 'to perceive'. Men perceive only 'ideas', themselves in the mind, not material substance; ideas are therefore dependent on a perceiver and 'all the choir of heaven and the furniture of earth' must be ideas in the mind of God. His *Essay towards a new theory of Vision* denies that contact with material objects alone causes and directs thought.

Berkeley Lennox (1903–). British composer, who studied under N. Boulanger in Paris (1927–33) and from 1946 was professor of composition at the R.A.M. B.'s music was influenced formally and harmonically by Stravinsky. He writes best for voices. His works include the oratorio *Jonah* (1935), *Serenade for Strings* (1939), 4 poems of St Teresa for contralto and strings (1947), the opera *Nelson* (1953) and 2 symphonies.

Berlage Hendrik Petrus (1856–1934). Dutch architect and one of the pioneers of the modern movement in architecture in Europe. His most famous building, the Bourse or New Exchange at Amsterdam (completed 1903), demonstrates his belief that traditional materials (in this case the Dutch brick architecture of the middle ages) could be developed in a modern way. On a visit to the U.S. in 1911 B. was strongly impressed by the work of Frank Lloyd Wright and his lectures and articles were important in introducing Wright to Europe.

Berlanga Luis (1921–). Spanish film director. B. is a director of comedies with marked social and topical preoccupations, starting with *Bienvenido Mr Marshall* (1952) and *Calabuch* (1956). His recent films have been more raucous – *Placido* (1961) – and blacker – *El Verdugo* (1963).

Berlichingen Gottfried (Götz) von (1480–1562). German knight and freebooting soldier. One of his hands, lost in one of many petty wars, was replaced by an iron one. He was a leader in the Peasants War, 1525. His autobiography (1st publ. 1731), one of the earliest in German, was used by *Goethe in his play *Götz von Berlichingen* (1773).

Berlin Irving (1888–). Russian-born composer (original name Israel Baline) living in the U.S. since 1893. His many popular works include 'Alexander's Rag Time Band' (1911), 'I'm Dreaming of a White Christmas' (1942) and the musical *Call Me Madam* (1950).

Berliner Ensemble. E. German theatrical co. founded in 1949 by the ministry of education and placed under the direction of Brecht and his wife, Helene Weigel, who became the chief

Berlin porcelain centre-piece (*The Temple of Bacchus*)

actress. The B. E. played first at the Deutsches Theater, then (1954) moved to the Theater am Schiffbauerdamm. Its use of *Brecht's theories and interpretations of his plays are famous.

Berlin porcelain. The 1st Berlin porcelain factory was established in 1752 with the encouragement of Frederick the Great, anxious to emulate Meissen; the venture died a few years later, but in 1763 Frederick bought a 2nd factory, founded by J. E. Gotzkowsky, and this as the Royal, later State, Porcelain Factory continued into the 20th c. The early B. p. is among the finest German 18th-c. porcelain.

Berlin, the Symphony of a Great City (1927). Film directed by W. *Ruttmann.

Berlioz Louis Hector (1803–69). French romantic composer, a pioneer of modern orchestration, whose life epitomized the romantic artist's. B. was born at Côte-Saint-André; as a doctor's son, he first studied medicine, coming to Paris in 1821. Determined on a musical career, he supported himself as a choral singer and journalist. At the Paris Conservatoire he was a pupil of A. *Reicha and J.-F. *Lesueur. In 1827 he became violently infatuated with an English actress, Henrietta Smithson. *Huit scènes de Faust*, completed 1829, he considered his 1st important work. After several rejections he won the 1st Rome prize in 1830. In 1833 he married Henrietta, who bore him a son. Passion soon died and in 1840 Berlioz left her to live with Marie Recio, a singer. From 1835 he was music critic to the *Journal des Débats*. B. also conducted, often his own music, on tour in Germany, Austria, Russia and London. In 1854 Henrietta died and B. married Marie. Her death in 1862 and his son's broke him and the meeting with Estelle, a childhood love, though completing the romantic cycle, did not relieve the depression of his last years.

B.'s music was the subject of abuse or acclaim throughout his life, and long caused controversy. His calculated dissonances and long-ranging, yet in fact coherent, melodies brought the charge of technical inadequacy. He was also criticized for the huge forces he often used; the *Grande Messe des Morts* (1837) requires, besides full orchestra and massive choir, 4 brass bands. His influential *Traité d'instrumentation et d'orchestration modernes* (1844) insists that a large varied orchestra allows a wide range of musical colour and not simply noise; the music shows B. a master of drama and a range of effects, whether solemn, terrifying or lyrical, once revolutionary and still unsurpassed.

The *Symphonie Fantastique: épisode de la vie d'un artiste* (1830, revised 1831), frankly autobiographical, had a written programme, regarded by B. as indispensable, describing the artist's infatuation and disillusionment with his beloved (Henrietta). It was followed by the symphony *Harold en Italie* (1834), also autobiographical, where the **idée fixe* was much used. The majestic *Grande Messe* used to celebrate the taking of Constantine, Algeria, was followed by the opera *Benvenuto Cellini* (1834/8). Its failure kept B. from opera for 18 years. In 1839, however, the 'dramatic symphony' (a new form) *Roméo et Juliette*, whose influence Wagner acknowledged, was a further success; the 'programme' (*programme music) was sung as an integral part of the work. In 1840 came the *Symphonie funèbre et triomphale* to commemorate the Revolution of 1830 and conducted by B. with a sword – it was a success. *La Damnation de Faust* (1846), despite its subsequent reputation outside France, failed at its 1st performance.

In 1852 B. attended a 'Berlioz week' at Weimar, organized by Liszt. *L'Enfance du Christ*, for which B. wrote both music and words, was performed in 1854. It is a pastoral gentle work, scored for small orchestra and chorus, interesting for its use of modal techniques, a significant return to archaic models found elsewhere in B.'s music. B. was again fêted at Weimar in 1855, but an estrangement with Wagner began which ended in open conflict in the *Journal des Débats* in 1860. *Béatrice et Bénédict*, based on Shakespeare's *Much Ado About Nothing*, was performed in 1862. *Les Troyens*, B.'s greatest opera both in musical grandeur and psychological interest, was finally performed, much against his will, in 2 sections, *La Prise de Troie* and *Les Troyens à Carthage*, in 1863. The libretto, 'Shakespeare Virgilianized' as he himself said, was again by B. and the music was more classical in mood than anything he had written.

Hector Berlioz

Berlioz: German caricature of a concert of 1846. Also **Harold in Italy*

Bermejo. *Pietà*

Sarah Bernhardt

Bernardin de Saint-Pierre

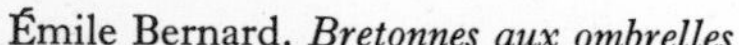

Émile Bernard. *Bretonnes aux ombrelles*

Bermejo Bartolomé (*fl.* 1474–95). Spanish painter whose work shows Flemish influences; active in and around Barcelona. His masterpiece is a *Pietà* in Barcelona cathedral.

Bernacchi Antonio Maria (1685–1756). Italian castrato singer (soprano) admired for his almost instrumental virtuosity. On his retirement he founded a singing academy in Bologna.

Bernanos Georges (1888–1948). French novelist and polemicist, famous for his *Journal d'un curé de campagne* (1936; *Diary of a Country Priest*, 1937). His polemical *Les Grands cimitières sous la lune* (1937; *A Diary of My Times*, 1938) was a sharp reaction to the Spanish Civil War. B. left France to live in Brazil (1938–45) where he wrote *Lettre aux Anglais* (1942; *Plea for Liberty*, 1944).

Bernard St, of Clairvaux (1090–1153). French Cistercian monk and mystic under whose influence the Cistercian order revived and expanded; 1st abbot of Clairvaux, canonized 1174, Doctor of the Church 1830. His devotional works, e.g. *de gradibus humilitatis et superbiae* and *de diligendo deo* influenced the development of 12th-c. devotional literature, which flourished particularly amongst the Cistercians. Other works include the theological treatise *de gratia et libero arbitrio*. In 1132 he undertook reforms in the music of the *gradual and *antiphon. He opposed submitting the tenets of the faith to reason, and condemned Peter Abelard. In 1145 he preached the 2nd crusade.

Bernard Émile (1868–1941). French painter and critic who claimed to have been the originator of the cloissoniste style used by Gauguin. He was a leader of the symbolist movement in painting and in his later years worked for the revival of religious art. He was a friend and correspondent of Van Gogh and of Cézanne, who wrote to him the famous letter about treating nature 'by means of the cylinder, the sphere and the cone'.

Bernard de Ventadour (*c.* 1130–95). Provençal *troubadour whose *cansos* were among the best and the most famous. About 1153–5 he was at the court of Henry II of England and his queen Eleanor of Aquitaine, to whom his most famous songs are addressed. B. later served Raymond V, comte de Toulouse; he retired to a monastery *c.* 1194.

Bernardes Diogo (1532?–*c.* 96). Portuguese pastoral poet whose eclogues were so good that some were attributed to Camoens. He acknowledged a debt to his friends Sá de Miranda and A. Ferreira. He wrote *Rimas várias, flores do Lima* (1597) and the devotional poems *Várias rimas ao Bom Jesus . . .* (1594).

Bernardin de Saint-Pierre Jacques-Henri (1737–1814). French writer and amateur naturalist; worked for a period as an engineer in Mauritius. His series *Études de la Nature* (1784–92; *Studies of Nature*, 1796), picturesque studies of nature, included in the 1787 ed. *Paul et Virginie* (*Paul and Mary, an Indian Story*, 1789). This Rousseauesque novel describes the romance and tragedy of a young couple brought up in poverty and innocence in a tropical paradise.

Bernardino de' Conti (*fl.* 1490–1522). Italian painter of the school of Milan, a follower and possibly an assistant of Leonardo.

Berners Lord Gerald (1883–1950). English composer, painter and novelist; his ballets include: *The Triumph of Neptune* (1926), for Diaghilev, *The Wedding Bouquet* (1937) and *Cupid and Psyche* (1939).

Berners John Bourchier, Lord (1467–1533). English nobleman whose trs from the French include an admirable version of Froissart's *Chronicles* (1523/5).

Bernhardt Sarah (real name Henriette-Rosine Bernard) (1844–1923). French tragedienne, 'The Divine Sarah', idolized for her voice and personality. She followed up her earliest triumph in Victor Hugo's *Ruy Blas* (1872) with her 1st appearance in Racine's *Phèdre* (1874). Some of her most popular repertory roles were those written for her by Sardou including *Fédora* (1882), *Théodora* (1884) and *La Tosca* (1887), though they encouraged a facility detrimental to her acting. She managed the

Bernini. *Self-portrait*; chalk drawing

Bernini. Bust of Louis XIV

Bernini. The Baldacchino

Bernini. Colonnade of St Peter's. Also *baroque

Théâtre de la Renaissance (1893–99) and Théâtre Sarah Bernhardt (1899–1923), where she appeared as Hamlet (1899) and in Rostand's *L'Aiglon* (1900). Her leg was amputated in 1915 but she continued to act. She publ. *Mémoires de ma vie* (1907).

Bernini Gian Lorenzo (1598–1680). Italian sculptor and architect born at Naples; son of a Tuscan mannerist sculptor who worked in Rome. B. was precociously skilful as a sculptor, and attracted the attention and patronage of Cardinal Scipione Borghese executing 4 groups for his garden, including *Aeneas and Anchises* (1618/19) and *Apollo and Daphne* (1622/4) (both in Gal. Borghese, Rome). During the pontificate of Urban VIII B. completed numerous large-scale commissions in and around St Peter's: the Baldacchino (1624–33), the Barberini Palace (1625–33), the Cathedra Petri (1657–65) and his layout of the square and colonnades in front of the basilica, his grandest and subtlest architectural achievement. Also notable is his layout of the Piazza Navona and the fountain there, as well as churches (S. Andrea al Quirinale) and numerous other fountains. B. gave Rome its predominantly baroque character.

He was a man of deep faith, and the supreme artist of the Catholic Counter-Reformation. Both as architect and sculptor he dazzled the 17th c., partly through genius and partly through skill in keeping rivals (e.g. Duquesnoy and Algardi) in the background. And this in spite of the fact that a tower which he built on the façade of St Peter's had to be rapidly demolished in 1646 when cracks appeared in the fabric of the church. In his series of portrait busts, of Cardinal Scipione Borghese (1632; Gal. Borghese), Duke Francis I d'Este (1650/1; Mus. Estense, Modena), Constanza Bonarelli (*c.* 1635; Mus. Nazionale, Florence), Charles I (now lost) and many others, B. revealed both his deep insight into character and his virtuosity of technique. In 1641 he made a bust of Cardinal Richelieu (Louvre) after the triple portrait by Philippe de Champaigne; this was so successful that he was invited to Paris to work for the king. He did not go until 1655. The only result of this visit was his superb bust of Louis XIV (Versailles). At the height of his fame B. had prophesied the decline of his reputation, a decline that lasted until the present generation. Indeed during his lifetime an equestrian statue of Louis XIV, completed in 1673, was so disliked that it was altered by Girardon in 1688 into a park ornament. B.'s sculptural style evolved partly from Michelangelo and partly from the expressiveness of Caravaggio and Annibale Carracci, whom he greatly admired. His emphasis on the unity of sculpture and its setting produced many fine tombs, in particular those of Pope Alexander VII (1671/8; St Peter's, Rome), with its marble draperies lifted by the skeleton figure of Death, and that of the Blessed Lodovica Albertoni (1671/4; Altieri chapel, S. Francesco a Ripa, Rome). The masterpiece of his religious sculpture, as well as the most brilliant example of his use of varied materials, is the *Ecstasy of St Teresa* (1645–52) in the Cornaro chapel in S. Maria della Vittoria, Rome. B.'s work freed sculpture from the classic concept of a block to be seen from one angle. The vitality of execution, as well as the restless poses of his works, at first demanded a multiple viewpoint, but this tension was often resolved into the clear-cut energy and movement of such a group as *Apollo and Daphne*. The un-classical involvement of the spectator in his response to the vigour and emotion of such figures show how B. was the seminal genius (and largely the creator) of the baroque style.

Bernstein Henri (1876–1953). French playwright whose technical skill and adaptability ensured the popularity of his works from *Le Marché* (1900) to *Evangeline* (1953). They are mainly domestic situation-dramas of violent passions.

Bernstein Leonard (1918–). American composer. He studied composition under W. Piston. He was conductor of the New York City Center Symphony Orchestra (1945–8), and has conducted all major European and U.S. orchestras on annual tours. He was professor of music at Brandeis Univ. (1951–6). Works include symphonies, no. 1 *Jeremiah* (1942), no. 2 *The Age of Anxiety* (1949), no. 3 (1957); the ballet *Fancy Free* (1944); the musicals *Candide* (1956) and *West Side Story* (1957).

Leonard Bernstein

Bestiary. Part of a page from *De Herba Vettonica* (mid 13th c.)

Alonso Berruguete. *The Sacrifice of Isaac*

Pedro Berruguete. *Appearance of the Virgin to a monastic community*

Béroul. Late 12th-c. poet who wrote an unusually direct and vivid Tristan romance in the Norman dialect. Only a part survives.

Berrettini Pietro: *Pietro da Cortona

Berruguete Alonso (*c.* 1488–1561). The greatest Spanish sculptor of the 16th c. and also a painter, working mainly in Valladolid. He lived in Italy (*c.* 1504–*c.* 1517) studying above all Michelangelo's work, the influence of which is reflected in B.'s *Resurrection* carved in relief in alabaster for Valencia cathedral. Other major works are the altars for the monastery of La Mejorada (1526), now in Valladolid Mus., and for the church of S. Benito (1527–32), also at Valladolid, and the 36 choir stalls in wood (1539–43) for Toledo cathedral. B. was the 1st Spaniard to react strongly against the high Renaissance ideals of perfection of form. He was affected by mannerism but used distortion or unbalanced composition to express the emotions of his mind or the agonies and ecstasies of the religious life.

Berruguete Pedro (*fl.* 1483–1503/4). Castilian painter, father of Alonso. He worked in Avila, in Toledo cathedral and as court painter to Ferdinand and Isabella of Spain. A tradition that he studied in Urbino, Italy, is supported by the style of some of his pictures.

Bersezio Vittorio (1828–1900). Italian playwright and novelist. The best of his comedies, written in the Piedmontese dialect, is *Le Miserie d'munssú Travet*, whose protagonist became the Italian byword for the downtrodden clerk.

Bertaut Jean (1552–1611). French court poet and bishop of Séez (1606). His poetry . . . *Oeuvres poétiques* (1601, 1605) and . . . *vers amoureux* (1602), polished, sensitive, yet somewhat weak, imitates the style of Ronsard.

Bertoldo di Giovanni (*c.* 1420–91). Italian sculptor; pupil and assistant of Donatello. As keeper of the Medici coll. of sculpture and head of the academy established in connection with it, he was a teacher of Michelangelo.

Bertram of Minden: *Master Bertram

Bertrand Louis called Aloysius (1807–41). French author of *Gaspard de la nuit*, 'fantasies in the manner of Rembrandt and Callot', written *c.* 1830, publ. posth. in 1842 with a preface by Sainte-Beuve. On medieval themes dear to the romantics, this coll. of prose poems contains vivid, sometimes grotesque, images alternating with naturalistic descriptions; Baudelaire acknowledged B.'s influence in the preface to *Petits poèmes en prose.*

Bertran de Born (*c.* 1140–*c.* 1215). Provençal troubadour and warrior, famous for his love-songs and **sirventes*. Placed by Dante (*Inferno*) in hell for intensifying the friction between Henry II of England and his rebellious sons. B. figures in ballads by the 19th-c. romantic poets Heine and Uhland.

Berwald Franz Adolf (1796–1868). Swedish romantic composer whose highly individual music, e.g. his 2nd symphony, the *Sérieuse*, has considerable imaginative power.

Besnard (Paul) Albert (1849–1934). French painter trained under J. Brémond in the romantic classicism of Ingres. From 1883 his work was influenced by the light and colour of the impressionists. The intense colours of his pictures of India (1912) attracted wide attention. He also executed frescoes, pastels and etchings.

Best William Thomas (1826–97). British organist. B. gave weekly popular recitals as organist at St George's Hall, Liverpool (1855–94), wrote 2 books on organ playing, and publ. an ed. of Bach's organ works.

bestiary. A type of natural history book in poetry or prose, very popular in the 12th–13th c., in which descriptions of the (usually fabulous) habits or qualities of animals are used to point moral or religious lessons. It was immediately derived from the *Physiologus* (i.e. *The Naturalist*) by an anon. writer, probably 4th–5th c. in Egypt, who was widely trs. Enlarged with material from other sources (e.g. Pliny and Isidore of Seville), systematized and illustrated, this grew into the b. The *Bestiaire d'amour* (*c.* 1250) of Richard de Fournival was the first to have love as its theme. B.

Bewick. *The Tame Goose*; from *History of British Birds*

Bethlehem. Cross-sections of the Church of the Nativity

Master Betty

illustrations influenced ecclesiastical decoration and heraldry.

Best Years of Our Lives, The (1946). Film directed by W. *Wyler.

Bête Humaine, La (1890). Novel by *Zola, made into a film (1938) directed by J. *Renoir.

Bethell Mary Ursula (1874–1945). English-born poet who spent her childhood and old age (from 1924) in New Zealand. She used the pseud. 'Evelyn Hayes' when publ. her 1st coll., *From a Garden in the Antipodes* (1929), which contained fresh and precise descriptions of her garden and the feelings it evoked. Later colls, in which the verse grew denser, were *Time and Place* (1936) and *Day and Night* (1939).

Bethlehem Church of the Nativity. Founded by Constantine and rebuilt in 527–65, it is a plain basilican church with double aisles, colonnade with straight entablature (not arches) and wooden roof.

Betjeman John (1906–). English poet, writer of guide-books and advocate of Victoriana. Works include *Mount Zion* (1931), *A Few Late Chrysanthemums* (1954), *Collected Poems* (1958), which made him for a time best-selling contemporary English poet, and the autobiographical *Summoned by Bells* (1960).

Betterton Thomas (1635?–1710). English actor considered without equal in tragic or comic parts. Dramatists, including Dryden, often accepted suggestions from him. B. also adapted Shakespearean plays to contemporary taste and arranged J. Fletcher's *The Prophetess* as an opera, with music by Purcell. His wife Mary Saunderson B. (d. *c.* 1712) was a well-known actress.

Betti Ugo (1892–1953). Italian dramatist, who was a lawyer by profession. He began writing stories and essays in an Austrian prison in World War I. His 1st play was *La Padrona* (1927) and thereafter he concentrated on the theatre, his work showing the influence of Pirandello. B. seems to search for the mysterious reasons for evil and its deep secret significance. Throughout the plays there is an insistence on the individual–individual responsibility, individual guilt, dangers to the individual. His works include *Frano allo scalo nord* (1936), *Il Vento notturno* (1945), *Ispezione* (1947) and *La Regina e gli insorti* (1951; *The Queen and the Rebels*, 1956).

Betty William Henry West (1791–1874). English actor, a child prodigy known as the 'Young Roscius'. He enjoyed tremendous popularity *c.* 1803–6–the House of Commons adjourned to see him on Pitt's motion–then fell into obscurity.

Between the Acts (1941). Novel by Virginia Woolf.

Beuckelaer Joachim (*c.* 1533–73). Flemish painter, most of whose career was spent as an assistant to other artists, e.g. A. Mor and possibly P. Aertsen, his uncle by marriage and also probably his master. B.'s few original pictures are mostly of market or kitchen scenes.

Beuves de Haumtone. 12th-c. French *chanson de geste*, a very popular story used in the 14th-c. English romance Bevis of Hampton and retold in Drayton's *Polyolbion*.

Bewick Thomas (1753–1828). English wood engraver and book illustrator, best known for his animal and bird studies. He made *wood engraving a medium of fine art, designing and cutting his own blocks. He used boxwood as making for a stronger block, and introduced techniques which greatly extended the tonal range. His work includes the engraving known as the 'Chillingham Bull', and illustrations for Goldsmith's poems *The Traveller* and *The Deserted Village* and R. Beilby's *A General History of Quadrupeds* (1790) and *History of British Birds* (2 vols, 1797, 1840), the 1st vol. amended, the 2nd vol. written by B. Among his best work are the numerous book tailpieces, studies of the English countryside. His autobiography, *Memoirs of Thomas Bewick, by Himself*, was publ. in 1862.

Beyle Henri-Marie: *Stendhal

Beyond Good and Evil (1886). Book by Nietzsche.

Betterton

Beuckelaer. *Christ in the House of Mary and Martha*

Théodore de Bèze

Bèze or Beza, Théodore de (1519–1605). French Protestant theologian, Calvin's successor as head of the Church of Geneva. He wrote the play *Abraham sacrifiant*.

bezel. A term in jewellery now used to describe the principal part or motif of a ring; but it originally only referred to the part bearing the stone.

Bhagavad-Gītā or 'Song of the Blessed One'. A Hindu religious poem incorporated early in the Christian era in the epic *Mahābhārata*. Also *India.

Biagio Vincenzo di: *Catena

Bianchi Francesco (1752–1810). Italian opera composer and teacher of H. R. Bishop. After working in Paris and Italy he came to London about 1795 and remained in Great Britain as theatre composer until his suicide. His *Aci e Galatea* (1792) was praised by Haydn.

Bianco Bartolomeo (before 1590–1657). Italian baroque architect who built for the Balbi family in Genoa the Univ. (1623), a magnificently unified design of a building on different levels, and the Durazzo-Pallavicini (begun 1619) and Senarega (after 1620) palaces.

Bianco. Palazzo Durazzo-Pallavicini

Biber Heinrich Ignaz Franz von (1644–1704). Bohemian-born composer and virtuoso violinist. His works, in an Italianate style with occasional German touches, include: 16 violin sonatas; 8 unaccompanied violin sonatas, seven 3-part partitas *Harmonia artificiosa-ariosa* (which use *scordatura) and operas.

Bib(b)iena Galli da. Italian family of high baroque architects and theatrical designers. They worked in most European courts and produced sumptuous and elaborate settings for operas and court festivities. Originally called Galli, they took the name B. from the birthplace of GIOVANNI MARIA (1625–65), painter and pupil of F. Albani. FERDINANDO (1657–1743), architect, writer on architecture and stage designer, son of Giovanni Maria. He worked for 28 years at Parma and then for the Emperor Charles VI in Vienna. He was the 1st to use diagonal perspective for stage design; it enabled the family to build their famous architectural settings. FRANCESCO (1659–1739), architect, son of Giovanni Maria. He built the theatre at Nancy and the Teatro Filarmonico at Verona. ALESSANDRO (1687–1769), architect, son of Ferdinando. GIUSEPPE (1696–1757), stage designer, son of Ferdinando, with whom he worked in Vienna. He introduced transparent scenery lighted from behind (1723) and publ. engravings of his stage designs in 3 vols (1716–44). ANTONIO (1700–74), architect of the Teatro Comunale, Bologna and son of Ferdinando, with whom he worked in Vienna. CARLO (1728–87), stage designer, son of Giuseppe. He travelled extensively; one of his sets is preserved in the old Royal Theatre, Drottningholm, Sweden.

Galli da Bibiena. Etching

Bible, The (from Greek, 'the books'). Coll. of religious books, believed to be divinely inspired and accepted as fundamental authority by Jews (the Old Testament) and Christians (Old and New Testaments). One canon of the Old Testament (written in Hebrew) was established by the Hebrew council of Jamnia (*c.* A.D. 90). The 3 main sections of this were the *Torah* ('Law') or *Pentateuch*, i.e. the 1st 5 books, including the story of the Creation, the Flood, Abraham, Moses and the laws the Hebrews received from God; the *Prophets*, containing historical and prophetic books; and the *Writings* or *Hagiographa*, a heterogeneous section including the Psalms, Proverbs, Song of Songs and Ecclesiastes. The **Apocrypha* was rejected; Christian churches, however, followed the *Septuagint*–a trs. of the Old Testament made by Hellenized Jews in the 3rd c. B.C.–in including it; after the Reformation, Protestant churches refused to recognize it. The canon of the New Testament (written in Greek) was established late in the 4th c. and consists of 4 *Gospels*, i.e. the 3 synoptic Gospels of SS Matthew, Mark and Luke, which agree closely, and the Gospel of St John, each narrating the life and teaching of Jesus; the *Acts of the Apostles*, describing the expansion of Christianity; 21 epistles, including 14 which have been attributed (the majority almost certainly wrongly) to St Paul; and the *Revelations of St John the Divine* ('Book of Revelations') or **Apocalypse*. Important trs of part or the whole of the Bible include the Vulgate of St *Jerome; the trs of *Ulfilas, *Wycliffe, *Tyndale, *Coverdale and *Luther; the (Calvinist) Geneva or 'Breeches' B. (1560); the Authorized Version (1611), the stately, elevated and musical style of which has had an enduring effect on the thought and language of English-speaking peoples; the (Catholic) Rheims-Douai B. (1582–1610); the Revised Version (1880–90) and its U.S. counterpart (the 'Gideon' B., 1901); and *The New English Bible* (1961) and other contemporary versions attempting to render the B. in the modern prose idiom. See also the articles on the separate books of the B.

Galli da Bibiena. *Fate carrying a distaff*

Bible in Spain, The (1843). Book by George *Borrow.

Bicci di Lorenzo (1373–1452). Florentine painter influenced by Lorenzo Monaco, Gentile da Fabriano and Fra Angelico. Many galleries have works by him and there are frescoes in S. Franceso, Arezzo and in several churches in Florence.

Biches, Les. 1-act ballet with choreography by Nijinska, music by Poulenc and décor by Marie Laurencin; 1st performance 1924.

Bickerstaffe Isaac (*c.* 1735–1812?). Irish dramatist. Among his works are the comedies *Love in a Village* (1762), *The Maid of the Mill* (1765), based on Richardson's novel *Pamela,* and *The Hypocrite* (1768), adapted from Molière and Cibber.

Bicycle Thieves (1948). Film directed by V. de *Sica.

Bidermann Jakob (1578–1639). One of the best of the *Jesuit dramatists in Germany. His themes were the transitoriness of human happiness and the conflict between worldly and spiritual values. He wrote in Latin, his best plays being *Cenodoxus* . . . (1609) and *Belisar* (1607).

Bidone, Il (1955). Film directed by F. *Fellini.

Biedermeier. Critical term used of the arts in Germany between *c.* 1815 and *c.* 1850; it implies a restrained romanticism. More broadly it is used as a synonym for 'bourgeois' or 'philistine' in describing attitudes towards the arts.

Bierbaum Otto Julius (1865–1910). German poet; author of the popular love-verse coll. *Irrgarten der Liebe* (1901) and founder of the literary magazine *Der Insel.*

Bierce Ambrose (1842–1914?). U.S. short-story writer, journalist, wit and satirist. As a young man he pursued the European cult of Bohemia. The stories, mostly about the U.S. Civil War, in *Tales of Soldiers and Civilians* (1891; retitled *In the Midst of Life,* 1892) and *Can Such Things Be?* (1893), show tight construction and a precise style; they emphasize the horror of war. *The Devil's Dictionary* (1911; 1st ed. *The Cynic's Word Book,* 1906) is a coll. of his most deadly and still quotable witticisms. The essays *The Shadow on the Dial* (1909), show B.'s despair of contemporary civilization and in 1913 he disappeared into Mexico. His death is the subject of many legends. Other works include the satirical verses *Black Beetles in Amber* (1895) and the *Fantastic Fables* (1899).

Bierstadt Albert (1830–1902). U.S. landscape painter of German extraction. After study in Europe (1853–7) he joined a surveying expedition of the Rocky Mountains (1858). From then on he painted large-scale pictures mostly of the Rockies and Far West, acquiring a fortune, a great reputation and decorations from several European states. His style reflects that of the German romantics.

Big Money, The (1936). Novel by *Dos Passos.

Big Parade, The (1925). Film directed by K. *Vidor.

Big Sleep, The (1939). Detective novel by R. Chandler, made into a film (1946) directed by H. *Hawks.

Bilderdijk Willem (1756–1831). Dutch poet whose style, romantic ideas expressed in Renaissance poetic forms, was used by many 19th-c. successors, among them I. Da Costa who ed. B.'s poetic works (1856–9). B. was a fiery polemicist and an impulsive man; his best works are poems of sombre religious fervour.

Bildungsroman. German critical term sometimes met with in English writing. Literally it means 'formation novel', i.e. a novel about the early formation and development of a character. Examples are *David Copperfield* by Dickens and *The Way of All Flesh* by S. Butler. *Erziehungsroman* ('education novel') is an alternative term.

Bill Max (1908–). Swiss sculptor, painter, architect, industrial designer and art theorist strongly influenced by the ideals of the Bauhaus. From 1951 to 1956 he was rector of the Hochschule für Gestaltung at Ulm, which he also designed. He gives support to van Doesburg's theory of concrete art in his painting and sculpture, in written work and in the organization of exhibitions such as 'Konkrete Kunst' (1944) at Basle. In *Die mathematische Denkweise in der Kunst unserer Zeit* (1949) he advocates a new approach to artistic creativity based on mathematical concepts.

Ambrose Bierce

Bierstadt. *Valley of the Yosemite*

Biedermeier interior

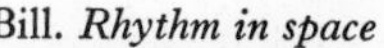

Bill. *Rhythm in space*

Les Biches. Design by Laurencin

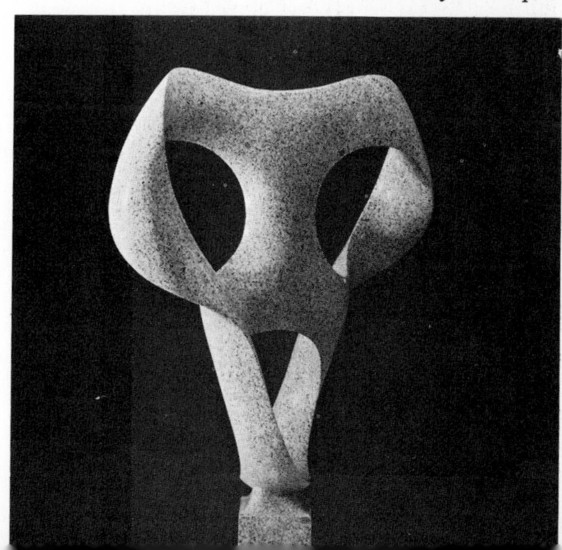

Billy Budd. Scene on the berth-deck in Britten's opera

Francis Bird. Monument to Dr Richard Busby

Binchois (right) and Dufay; from a 15th-c. ms. of Martin Le Franc's *Champion des Dames*

Bingham. *The Trapper's Return*

billet. A term principally applied to Gothic architecture, referring to an ornamental moulding, resembling small billets of wood, square or cylindrical, regularly spaced and sunk in a moulding. The term also refers to the thumb-piece on a tankard or similar object.

Billings Josh. Pseud. of Henry Wheeler Shaw (1818–85). U.S. writer, Yankee humorist and provider of intentionally misspelt homespun philosophy and sayings. A typical title is *Allminax* (1869–80).

Billings William (1746–1800). The 1st professional U.S. composer. B. wrote mostly church music including the hymn tune *Chester* which, set to militant verses by B. himself, was sung by the Revolutionary army.

Billy André (1882–). French novelist, critic and journalist, distinguished for his critical works, e.g. *Apollinaire vivant* (1923) and *Les frères Goncourts* (1954; *Goncourt Brothers*, 1960). His novels include *L'Approbaniste* (1937) and *Madame* (1954).

Billy Budd (1924). Short novel by Herman *Melville; the subject of an opera by *Britten (1951), with a libretto by E. M. Forster and E. Crozier; and a film (1962) directed by P. Ustinov.

binary form. A musical form in 2 sections unified by a simple harmonic pattern: the 1st section begins in the home key and moves into a related key, the 2nd section moves from this key back to the home key. The 2 sections use similar, not contrasted melodic material.

Binchois Gilles de Binche, called (*c.* 1400–60). Flemish composer. He began life as a soldier, was a chaplain of Duke Philip the Good of Burgundy and held a canonry at Mons, as did his friend G. *Dufay. B.'s works included masses, motets, hymns and a set of passions (now lost) 'in a new manner' but his greatness rests on his **chansons* of which over 50 survive. The best are unsurpassed in expressiveness and B.'s sensitivity is emphasized by his choice of poets – Charles d'Orléans, Alain Chartier and Christine of Pisa.

Bingham George Caleb (1811–79). U.S. painter. After a brief training at the Pennsylvania Academy of Fine Arts and travel in Europe and the U.S. he settled in his home state of Missouri. He painted scenes from frontier life, portraits of the wealthier Missouri citizens and many political subjects. He himself held state office.

Binyon (Robert) Laurence (1869–1943). English poet, writer on art and dramatist. His poems include the poem of remembrance *For the Fallen* (1914); he also wrote verse plays, co-operating with John *Masefield in his attempt to revive verse speaking and drama. He wrote on Blake, the English watercolourists and oriental art.

Biographia Literaria (1817). Book by S. T. *Coleridge.

bio-mechanics. A system of play-production created by V. Meyerhold in Russia in the early days of the October Revolution. It called for the complete elimination of personality in the actor, conventional and stylized gesture, a minimum use of scenery and considerable audience participation.

Bird Francis (1667–1731). English monumental sculptor trained in Brussels and Rome who carved most of the statuary on St Paul's cathedral. The monument to Sir Cloudesley Shovel in Westminster Abbey, formerly ascribed to B. was, in fact, probably by Gibbons.

Bird Robert Montgomery (1806–54). U.S. playwright and romantic novelist influenced by the work of J. Fenimore Cooper. Plays included *The Gladiator* (1831), *Oralloossa* (1832) and *The Broker of Bogota* (1834); novels, *Nick of the Woods* (1837), his best, whose hero has a split personality, and *The Hawks of Hawk-Hollow* (1835), about the last stages of the Revolution.

Birds, The. Comedy by *Aristophanes.

Birken Sigmund von (1626–81). German lyric poet and dramatist of the Nuremberg school. B.'s verse conformed to the Arcadianism of the school and he joined G. P. *Harsdörffer's Pegnitz Shepherds, adopting the name

Birolli. *Agricultural Machine* (1955)

Bissière. *Composition* (1957)

'Floridan'. He wrote many occasional pieces and also pastoral comedies, e.g. *Pegnesis* (1673–9) influenced by Harsdörffer.

Birmingham Repertory Theatre. Leading British provincial theatre (opened 1913), built at the personal expense of its director Sir Barry *Jackson. It has a high-raked auditorium and was one of the 1st theatres which encouraged close contact between actor and audience. In its distinguished history it has presented many new plays (especially by G. B. Shaw) and it was in this theatre that many leading players made their début.

Birney (Alfred) Earle (1904–). Canadian poet. He works within a 'vitalist' tradition and is more concerned with experience than with artistic possibilities of expressing that experience. The narrative poem *Canada: Case History* (1948), deals with the threats to national identity in British and especially American influence.

Birolli Renato (1906–59). Italian painter who consistently advocated the necessity of a European outlook in Italian art. He was a leading member of the Corrente group before World War II and was a prominent anti-Fascist. During the war he produced a series of drawings entitled *Italia 1944*, protesting against the horrors of war. In 1947 he went to Paris and on his return was a founder of the *Fronte nuova delle arte. He developed a personal abstract idiom of great emotional and colouristic intensity.

Birth of a Nation, The (1915). Film directed by D. W. *Griffith.

Birth of Venus, The. Painting by *Botticelli.

Birtwhistle Harrison (1934–). English composer, associated with A. *Goehr and Maxwell *Davies in Manchester. His music is concentrated and lyrical, e.g. *Refrains and Choruses* (wind quintet), *Monody for Corpus Christi* (soprano, violin, flute and horn), *The Worldes Blisse* (after *Isaak) for chamber ensemble.

Bischof Werner (1916–56). Swiss photographer whose reportages on the political upheavals of Central Europe and Asia strongly influenced present-day journalistic photography.

biscuit. Term used by potters for unglazed fired ware.

Bishop Sir Henry Rowley (1786–1855). English composer, and conductor. He composed and adapted over 100 operas, including *Aladdin* (1826), commissioned in competition with Weber's *Oberon*, adaptations of foreign operas, ballets, cantatas, and the song 'Home, Sweet Home'. His wife was ANN BISHOP (1810–84) the celebrated soprano; in 1839 she eloped with R.-N.-C. *Bochsa.

Bissière Roger (1888–). French painter and designer, and influential teacher (1925–38) at the Académie Ranson, Paris; collaborated on the periodical *Esprit Nouveau*. Although he was a notable supporter of *avant-garde* art movements between the World Wars, it was not until 1945 that B. developed his characteristic abstract style. His rich luminous compositions sometimes relate closely to his earlier landscapes.

bistre. An artist's pigment brown in colour and made from charred wood. It can be used as an ink, chalk or wash and was favoured as a drawing material by Rembrandt.

bitonality. In music, the using of 2 keys simultaneously in the same piece (*polytonality).

Bitter Sweet (1929). 'Operette' by Noël Coward.

bitumen. An artist's pigment, a richer brown than bistre, and made from asphaltum. It never fully dries out and, remaining chemically active, gradually damages the painting; this is noticeable in work of the 18th and 19th cs when b. was very popular.

Bizet Georges (1838–75). French composer. B., a precocious child, entered the Paris Conservatoire in 1848. Here he met Gounod, becoming his close friend and being heavily influenced at first by his music. When 17, B.

Bischof. *Hunger in Madras* (1951)

Georges Bizet

Black-figured style

Peter Blake. *Self-portrait with badges*

Blackman. *A Brisbane Dream* (1962)

David Blair

wrote his brilliant symphony in C (1st performed 1935) marked by ingenuity in structure and orchestration and great freshness. In 1857 he won the 1st Rome prize. From 1862 B.'s development was retarded by worries that his music lacked serious 'German' weight, and the operas *The Pearl Fishers* (1863), *The Fair Maid of Perth* (1867), the only piece well received in his lifetime except the overture *Patrie* (1874), and *Djamileh* (1872) were all unequal in quality. B.'s masterpiece *Carmen* was 1st performed at Paris in 1875. It is taken from Prosper Mérimée's *nouvelle* of a young man and his tragic passion for a wilful gipsy girl. B.'s incidental music to A. Daudet's *L'Arlésienne* (1872) is still performed as an orchestral suite, as is the symphony *Roma* (1868).

Björling Jussi (1907–60). Swedish tenor famous for his warm lyrical style, especially in Puccini, Verdi, Mozart and French opera.

Bjørnson Bjørnstjerne Martinus (1832–1910). Norwegian playwright, novelist, political orator and patriot poet; he wrote the words of the national anthem and had a great popular reputation. Besides novels he wrote short stories of peasant life, considered daringly realistic by contemporaries, in fact somewhat sentimental but still read. For some years he directed theatres at Bergen and Christiana and his most important work lies in his plays, which include: the historical *Sigurd Slembe* (1862; trs. 1888); plays on contemporary themes, such as journalism, business and masculine morality, e.g. *En Handske* (1883; *A Gauntlet*, 1912); comedies, e.g. *Geografi og Kjærlighed* (1885; *Love and Geography*, 1914); and the 2 fine plays *Over Ævne* (1895; *Beyond Human Might*, 1914), against fanaticism, and *Paul Lange og Tora Parsberg* (1898; 1899).

Black Beauty (1877). Children's classic by Anna Sewell.

Black Book, The (1938). Novel by Lawrence *Durrell.

Black Book of Carmarthen, The. 12th-c. ms. of Welsh poetry, some of it dating from a much earlier period. It is a chief source for legends about King *Arthur.

Blackburn Thomas (1916–). English poet. B. publ. his 1st coll., *Outer Darkness* (1952), when he was 35. Colls include *The Holy Stone* (1954), *In the Fire* (1956), *The Next Word* (1958) and *A Smell of Burning* (1960).

black-figured style. Style of Greek vase painting where the figures are painted in black on a red ground. It flourished from the late 7th to the late 6th c. B.C.; it was superseded by the *red-figured style.

Blackmail (1929). Film directed by A. *Hitchcock.

Blackman Charles (1920–). Australian painter. At first attracted by the expressionist school at Melbourne, he was one of the new humanist group of younger painters who turned to city life for subject-matter.

Black Mischief (1932). Novel by Evelyn Waugh.

Blackmore Richard Doddridge (1825–1900). English romantic novelist, author of *Lorna Doone*, set in 17th-c. Devon, and other novels of romance and adventure, including *Clara Vaughan* (1864), *Cradock Nowell* (1866) and *Springhaven* (1887).

Black Spring (1936). Book by Henry *Miller.

Blackton Stuart (1875–1941). British-born film director and producer; a pioneer of the U.S. cinema. B. founded the Vitagraph Co. in 1896. His films include an animated cartoon made in 1907 which pioneered the techniques of producing an animated image one frame at a time. From 1908, B. produced newsreels and from 1922 to 1926 he directed features in Great Britain.

Blackwood's Edinburgh Magazine. Well-known magazine begun by William Blackwood (1776–1834) as a rival to *The Edinburgh Review*.

Blair David (1932–). English dancer and Royal Academy of Dancing scholar who entered Sadler's Wells School in 1946. A year later he graduated to the Sadler's Wells Theatre Ballet and soon was taking leading roles, creating parts in *Pastorale* (1950) and *Pineapple Poll* (1951). In 1953 he moved to the Sadler's Wells Co. at Covent Garden as soloist and later partner to Margot Fonteyn.

Blair Eric: George *Orwell

Blair Robert (1690–1746). English Presbyterian minister and poet. His didactic poem on death, *The Grave* (1743), is in blank verse and is similar to Young's *Night Thoughts*; both were imitated by writers of the *Graveyard school. *The Grave* inspired a set of illustrations (1808) by Blake.

Blake Peter (1932–). Leading English pop artist; studied at the R.C.A. His paintings include the oil and collage *Drum Majorette* (1957).

Blake William (1757–1827). English poet, illustrator, draughtsman, engraver, writer and visionary. He completed (1779) his 7-year apprenticeship as an engraver with James Basire, and engraving remained his basic livelihood. B. also studied for a brief time at the R.A. In 1782 he married Catherine Boucher, his beloved and constant companion. Friends such as the sculptor Flaxman supported the publ. of *Poetical Sketches* (1783) but after *Songs of Innocence* (1789) B. printed his own works by a process (duplicated in experiments by Ruthven Todd, S. W. Hayter and Joan Miró) of relief etching of the text and the surrounding design, printing in coloured inks often with retouching in paint. Another very successful technique was colour printing by superimposed impressions from millboard. B. lived mainly in London, but between 1800 and 1803 worked at Felpham, the estate of William Hayley, for whom B. was engraving some poems. While he was at Felpham an argument with a soldier brought B. on trial on a sedition charge, but he was acquitted. The poverty of his last years was relieved by the discipleship of such young painters as Palmer and Calvert, and commissions from another young friend, John Linnel, for B.'s engravings of *Illustrations of the Book of Job* (1825) and 100-odd water-colours to Dante's *Divine Comedy*. All B.'s work is infused with his intense imagination and visionary experiences; he claimed regular visits from heavenly emissaries. The powerful images of his engravings and paintings display his admiration of Michelangelo (e.g. in their distorted anatomy), Raphael and Dürer; but he rejected the academic traditions represented by Reynolds and the R.A. and the Venetian colourists, as at once too vague and too material. His rebellion against accepted contemporary artistic theories parallels his political radicalism and religious unorthodoxy. He rejoiced in the French and American revolutions and his spiritual explorations, and his disgust with injustice and hypocrisy strengthened by his contacts with the radical circle of Paine and Godwin, are reflected in the prose satire *The Marriage of Heaven and Hell* (1790–3), the poem coll. *Songs of Innocence and Experience* (1789–94), and such poems as *The French Revolution* and *America, a Prophecy* (1793). In B.'s religious system, God is a vengeful terrible power (Urizen); Jesus the embodiment of humanity (Orc); and the virtues which derive from the human principle in its fullest and highest manifestation are Los, the male, Enitharmon, the female. B.'s works include the long poems *Milton* (1804–8) and *Jerusalem, The Emanation of the Giant Albion* (1804–20); the verse prophetic books *The Everlasting Gospel* (*c.* 1818), the *Book of Thel* (1789), *The Song of Los* and *Vala or the Four Zoas* (1797–1804).

Blakelock Ralph Albert (1847–1919). U.S. painter, self-taught. His landscapes of the American West were painted in rich dark colours, and reflected B.'s mood (usually melancholy) rather than realistically represented their subject. In 1899 B. had a mental breakdown and went into an asylum–his paintings meanwhile had begun to change hands at very high prices.

blanc-de-chine. Unpainted porcelain wares made at Te-hua in the Fukien province of China (17th–19th cs) and exported to Europe where they were often painted; they were sometimes made to order in European forms. The

Blakelock. *Moonlight*

William Blake. Engraved page from *Job*

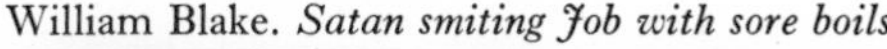

William Blake. *Satan smiting Job with sore boils*

Blanc-de-chine. Ch'ing dynasty figure of the goddess of compassion

The Countess of Blessington: painting by Sir Thomas Lawrence

Bles. *The Copper Mines*

best-known products of Te-hua were Buddhist figures whose highly plastic forms and flowing drapery were copied by European rococo potters. The favourite Chinese relief decoration of plum blossom on bowls and vases, etc., was also copied at Saint-Cloud, Meissen, Bow and other factories.

blank verse. English verse written in unrhymed lines of 5 iambic feet (i.e. of 10 syllables), and since its introduction in the 16th c. the most common English verse form; it was extensively used, e.g., by Marlowe, Shakespeare, Milton and Wordsworth.

Blasco Ibañez Vicente (1867–1928). Spanish novelist who made his name outside Spain with his highly coloured treatment of *costumbrismo* (*costumbristas) themes, in which he combined realism with striking descriptive passages. Best known of his novels abroad are his *Sangre y Arena* (1908; *Blood and Sand*, 1913) and *Los cuatro Jinetes del Apocalipsis* (1916; *The Four Horsemen of the Apocalypse*, 1918), on World War I.

Blasetti Alessandro (1900–). Italian film director; an ex-critic, whose 1st film, *Sole* (1929), has as its background Mussolini's scheme for draining the Pontine Marshes. After making Fascist propaganda films in the 1930s, he directed a peasant comedy, *Four Steps in the Clouds* (1942), one of the forerunners of neo-realism in the Italian cinema.

Blasis Carlo (1797–1878). Italian dancer, teacher and choreographer who studied in Milan and in 1837 was appointed director of the Imperial Academy of Dancing at La Scala, where he taught many famous dancers such as Brianza and Cerrito. His teaching methods, recorded in his books *Treatise on the Dance* (1820) and *The Code of Terpsichore* (1830), form the basis of classical ballet training today.

Blast (1914–15). English magazine publ. by Wyndham *Lewis; the organ of vorticism.

Blaue Reiter, Der (German, 'The Blue Rider'). A group of German expressionist painters, led by Marc, Kandinsky and Macke. Kandinsky, with a passion for blue, and Marc, enthusiastic about horses, invented the name. 2 major exhibitions were held at Munich in 1912 and 1913 with contributions from non-German artists such as Delaunay, the Burliuk brothers, the composer Schoenberg, Braque, de la Fresnaye, Malevich, Picasso and de Vlaminck; the German exhibitors included Klee. The movement also publ. the *B. R. Almanac* (1912) containing major essays by Marc and Kandinsky. The B. R. programme rested on primitivism, intellectual in concept but intuitive in application, a new emphasis on *child art as a source of inspiration, abstract forms and the symbolic and psychological aspects of line and colour. The group disbanded in 1914.

Blaue Reiter. *Above:* book-jacket for the *B. R. Almanac*; by Kandinsky. *Below:* Marc, *Fabeltier*; coloured woodcut, 1912

Blaue Vier, Die (German, 'The Blue Four'). From 1924, for about a decade, the painters Kandinsky, Jawlensky, Klee and Feininger exhibited their work jointly under this title in Europe and the U.S.

Bleak House (1853). Novel by *Dickens.

Bleibtreu Karl (1859–1928). German writer whose manifesto *Revolution der Literatur* (1886), showing the inevitable influence of Zola, proclaimed the principles of *naturalism in Germany. B. proposed the *storm and stress period and the plays of Lenz and Grabbe as German forerunners of the naturalist 'revolution'. In B.'s huge and mediocre output of original work, novels, e.g. *Dies irae* (1882), and plays, about war and great soldiers, predominate.

Bles Herri met de (*c.* 1480–after 1550). Antwerp painter of landscapes and religious pictures whose style was similar to Patenier's, but there was a fantastic element in his work, especially in his mining landscapes, e.g. *The Copper Mines* (Uffizi). He was probably related to Patenier and may have been identical with the Herri de Patenir recorded in the Antwerp Guild in 1535; Bles, meaning 'blaze of white hair', was possibly a nickname. In Italy he was known as 'Henrico Civetta', from the owl emblem with which he signed his pictures.

Blessed Damozel, The (1850). Poem by D. G. *Rossetti.

Blessington Marguerite, Countess of (1789–1849). Authoress and society hostess born in Ireland. She is chiefly remembered for her association with Count d'Orsay and for her *Conversations of Lord Byron* . . . (1834) which, with *The Idler in Italy* (1839–40) and *The Idler in France* (1841), became popular for their personal gossip, ease and humour. She also produced several novels.

Blicher Steen Steensen (1782–1848). Danish poet and short-story writer who trs. *'Ossian' into Danish (1807–9) and who was the founder of the Jutland dialect school.

Bloemaert. *Prodigal Son*

blind storey. Architectural term, an alternative for *triforium.

Bliss Sir Arthur (1891–). English composer who studied under Stanford, Vaughan Williams and Holst. He visited Paris and worked in California (1923–5); was musical director of the B.B.C. (1942–4), and from 1953 Master of the Queen's Music. His earlier works, e.g. *Rout* for soprano and chamber orchestra (1919) and *Rhapsody* for soprano and tenor and chamber ensemble (1922), showed influences of Ravel and Stravinsky. *Hymn to Apollo* for orchestra (1926) and the *Introduction and Allegro* (1926) showed a classicism developed in *Music for Strings* (1935). Other works include *Colour Symphony* (1922), *Morning Heroes* (1930) with orator and chorus, the opera *The Olympians* (1949), libretto by J. B. Priestley, the ballets *Miracle in the Gorbals* (1944) and *Checkmate* (1937).

Blithedale Romance, The (1852). Novel by *Hawthorne.

Blitheman (Blytheman) William (d. 1591). English organist of the Chapel Royal from 1585 and composer and teacher of John Bull. Two 4-part motets survive but more important are his keyboard compositions; 2 of his sets of variations were used as models by Bull and J. P. Sweelinck.

Blithe Spirit (1941). Play by Noël Coward.

Blitzstein Marc (1905–64). U.S. composer of theatre music who believed art to be propaganda and whose style has similarities with popular music so as to reach a larger audience. His 1st full-length opera, *The Cradle will Rock* (1937), was produced by Orson Welles at the Federal Theater. Other works include: the opera-oratorio *The Condemned* (1932), on the Sacco-Vanzetti case, the opera *No for an Answer* (1941), and the ballet *The Guest* (1949), choreography by J. Robbins.

Bloch Ernest (1880–1959). Swiss-born Jewish composer, naturalized U.S. citizen 1924. He studied under Jaques-Dalcroze, F. Rasse, I. Knorr and L. Thuille; also the violin under Ysaÿe (1897–9). He was an original composer employing techniques as they suited his purpose (e.g. the quarter tones in the piano quintet). His works are often rhapsodic in form, unrestricted in harmonic invention and have frequent rhythmic variations. His early work in particular, is often reminiscent of Jewish music. Among his most important works are the opera *Macbeth* (1909), *Trois Poèmes juifs* for orchestra (1913), *Schelomo* rhapsody for cello and orchestra (1915–16), the orchestral rhapsody *America* (1926), the 'Sacred Service' (1930–3), the well-known concerto grosso (1953), 5 string quartets and 2 piano quintets.

Bloch Jean-Richard (1884–1947). French novelist, Alsatian Jewish in origin. B.'s works, all strongly humanitarian in outlook, include *. . . et Cie* (1913; *. . . And Co.*, 1930) which describes the vicissitudes of a Jewish business family. His later books reflect his conversion to Communism.

block-book. Early type of illustrated book in which both text and illustrations were cut from the same wood block. No existing b.-b.s can be dated before *c.* 1455, i.e. after the invention of movable type, and they continued into the 16th c. Although produced in large numbers in Germany and the Netherlands they included only a few titles. The best known are *Ars Moriendi* and *Biblia pauperum.*

Blockx Jan (1851–1912). Belgian composer who studied under P. Benoît. An early local reputation came with Flemish songs and chamber music, a national reputation with operas, e.g. *Maître Martin* (1892) and *De Bruid der zee* (1901). Other works include a symphony and cantatas, e.g. *Op den stroom* (1875).

Bloemaert Abraham (1564–1651). Dutch painter of Biblical and historical subjects, portraits and still-lifes. After a period of travel, including Paris (1580–3) and Amsterdam (1591–3), he settled at Utrecht, where he played an important part in founding the Utrecht school. He had a great reputation, being visited by Rubens and Elisabeth, Queen of Bohemia, and was the master of J. G. Cuyp, G. Honthorst and H. Terbrugghen. Through the Dutch 'Italianizers' he was affected by mannerism and Caravaggio's use of chiaroscuro.

Bloemen Jan Frans van, called 'Orizonte' (1662–1749). Flemish painter who lived in Rome from *c.* 1681 and was influenced by G. Dughet. He painted classical landscapes of great charm.

Bloemen Pieter van (1657–1720). Flemish genre and landscape painter, brother of Jan Frans van B. and in Rome *c.* 1674–93.

Blois France. Royal château, containing architecture from all periods from the 13th to the 17th c. but remarkable for the juxtaposition of

Block-book: *Ars Moriendi*

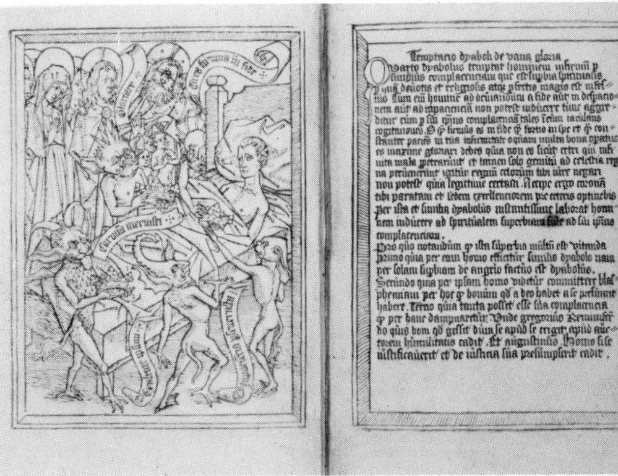

Sir Arthur Bliss

Ernest Bloch

Blois. Francis I's wing: the staircase

François Blondel. Porte Saint-Denis

very late Gothic (Louis XIII's wing, 1503) with early Renaissance (Francis I's wing, 1515), including the famous open spiral staircase. It marks the introduction of Italian Renaissance forms into France, and the chief influence is the *Certosa, Pavia.

Blok Alexander Alexandrovich (1880–1921). Russian poet. B. studied at the univ. of St Petersburg (1898–1906). Although he had been writing for several years, he publ. nothing until 1903, when he quickly became the acknowledged leader of the symbolists. B.'s early poems, including his 1st coll., *The Verses about the Beautiful Lady* (1904), are ethereal visions of Sophia, the feminine principle of Divine Wisdom (whose cult, derived from the writings of V. Soloviev, influenced several poets). After 1903 he became disillusioned and mocked his own mysticism in the verse plays *The Puppet Show* (1906) and *The Stranger* (1906). He expressed a growing love for Russia in the cycle *The Field of Kulikovo* (1908), the unfinished narrative poem *Retaliation*, and *The Scythians* (1918). At heart a mystic rather than a Marxist, B. nevertheless welcomed the Revolution and worked with the Bolsheviks, who are the heroes of *The Twelve* (1918; trs., in part, 1920), probably his masterpiece.

Alexander Blok

Blom Eric Walter (1888–1959). British musicologist and author; ed. of the 5th ed. of *Grove's Dictionary of Music and Musicians* (1954).

Blomfield Sir Arthur William (1829–99). English architect who worked mainly in the neo-Gothic style.

Blomfield Sir Reginald Theodore (1856–1942). English architect and writer on architecture. He adapted traditional styles to his diverse work, which included Lady Margaret Hall, Oxford, and the Menin Gate, Ypres.

Blondel François (1618–86). French architect who built the Porte Saint-Denis, Paris (1672/3) but devoted himself mainly to architectural theory, in which he followed Vitruvius. His best-known book is *Cours d'Architecture* (1675–83), lectures delivered at the Paris Academy of Architecture, of which he was the 1st director.

Blondel Jacques-François (1705–74). French architect, nephew of the architect Jean-François (1683–1756) and one of the 1st French architects to establish an atelier; Sir W. Chambers and C.-N. Ledoux were among his pupils. His *L'Architecture française* (1752–6), praising the classicism of French architecture, is valuable for its views of buildings since altered or demolished.

Blondel de Neele or de Nesles (*fl.* late 12th c.). French *trouvère*. According to a 13th-c. tradition B. was a close friend of Richard the Lionheart and identified the Austrian castle where Richard was imprisoned (1192) by singing outside many fortresses the 1st couplet of a song they had jointly composed until he heard the 2nd couplet sung by the king.

Blood Wedding (1933). Play by *Lorca.

Bloomfield Robert (1766–1823). English 'uneducated' poet, shoemaker and author of *The Farmer's Boy* (1800, with woodcuts by T. Bewick), a long poem in heroic couplets, immensely popular for 50 years. His verse, which includes *Rural Tales . . .* (1802) and *Wild Flowers* (1806), is mostly stilted and unsophisticated.

Bloomsbury Group. Circle of intellectuals who met at the 2 houses in Bloomsbury, London, of the Stephen family (which included Virginia Woolf and Vanessa Bell) from *c.* 1907. Among them were the philosopher G. E. Moore, the economist Keynes, the artist Duncan Grant and the writers E. M. Forster, Lytton Strachey, Roger Fry, Arthur Waley and Clive Bell.

Blore Edward (1787–1879). English architect, a leading figure of the Gothic revival. In 1816

Blore. Abbotsford

Blot drawing. Landscape in watercolour by Alexander Cozens

MR. WILLIAM
SHAKESPEARES
COMEDIES,
HISTORIES, &
TRAGEDIES.
Published according to the True Originall Copies.
LONDON
Printed by Isaac Iaggard, and Ed. Blount. 1623

Blount. Title-page of the Shakespeare 1st folio

Sir Walter Scott commissioned him to design his country house at Abbotsford. His best-known work was the main E. front of Buckingham Palace, later concealed beneath the façade of Sir A. Webb. He designed many undistinguished neo-Gothic churches and carried out often ill-judged restorations.

blot drawing. Name given by A. Cozens to his technique of developing a landscape composition out of ink blots allowed to fall at random on a sheet of paper. This method, which he described in a book publ. in 1785, is an extension of Leonardo's advice to artists to study the stains on a wall or the ashes of a fire to excite inspiration.

Blount Edward (*fl.* 1588–1632). English printer, publ. and trs. who, with Isaac Jaggard, produced the 1st folio of Shakespeare's plays (1623). Other notable publs were Florio's trs. of Montaigne's *Essays* (1603), J. Lyly's *Sixe Court Comedies* (publ. 1632), and *Hero and Leander* (publ. 1598) by Marlowe, who was B.'s intimate friend.

Blow John (1649–1708). English composer and organist, teacher of Purcell. He was organist at Westminster Abbey from 1668 to 1680 and again from 1695, surrendering the post to Purcell in the interim. Some of his large output of church music such as the motet for 6 voices 'Salvator Mundi', was outstanding. His great works are the *St Cecilia Ode* for 1684, the act song 'Awake, Awake my Lyre' and the *Ode on the Death of Mr Henry Purcell*. B.'s imagination was not sufficient for his productivity, but his best work, although less adventurous than Purcell's, sometimes approaches it.

blue-and-white. Chinese style of decoration on porcelain vessels, most often dishes and bowls, produced at its best in the Hsuan-te reign period (1426–35) of the *Ming dynasty. It is based on the use of cobalt-blue for painting decoration under the transluscent glaze–a technique introduced to China during the rule of the Mongols in the early 14th c. Cobalt was painted over the glaze in Mesopotamia and Persia from the 9th c.; under the glaze by Kashan potters in the 13th c. At the time of its introduction to China the technique became associated with the maturing of a mode of decoration, founded on the flower-and-bird tradition of *Sung dynasty painting, which demanded as much skill in painting as in glazing. Sacrificing its purely decorative value, it gradually became more figurative: by the late Ming and Ch'ing dynasties it included landscapes and cliché scenes from novels.
The ware of the late Ming dynasty, imported via Persia, became the model for European delftware and set the still persistent fashion for monochrome blue painting on porcelain. Blue-and-white imports to Europe reached their peak in the K'ang Hsi (Ch'ing) period (1662–1722) and were so popular that English delftware potteries copied even their defects.

Blue Angel, The (1930). Film directed by J. von *Sternberg; from the novel *Professor Unrat* (1905) by Heinrich *Mann.

Bluebeard's Castle, Duke. Opera by Bartók, libretto by B. Balázs; 1st performance in Budapest in 1918.

Blue Bird, The (1909). Play by *Maeterlinck.

Blue Boy, The. Portrait painting by *Gainsborough.

Blue Rose Group. Group of Russian artists which succeeded the *World of Art in 1907 as the leading movement of the Russian *avant-garde.*

blues, the. A vocal and instrumental idiom overlapping with and influencing jazz rather than forming part of it. The greatest of the 'classic' b. singers of the 1920s, Gertrude 'Ma' Rainey and Bessie Smith, frequently worked and recorded with jazz musicians such as Louis Armstrong and Fletcher Henderson. On the other hand, the singing and guitar playing

Blue-and-white Ming bowl

Blue Rose Group. *Grape Harvest* by Kusnetsov

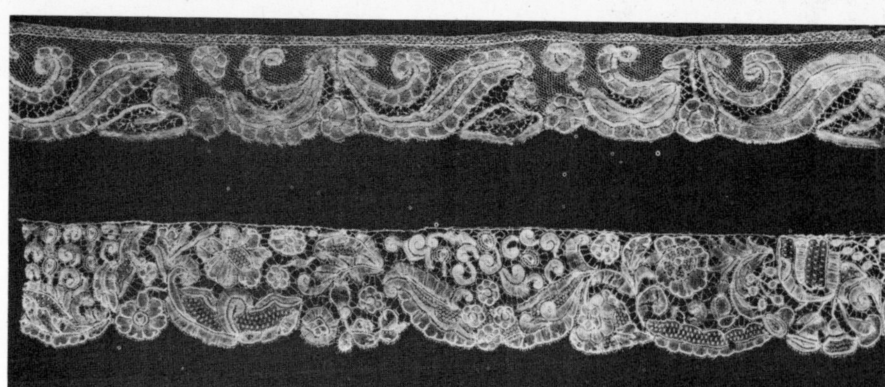

Bobbin lace bands, 18th-c. English

Boccaccino. *Gipsy Girl*

Boccaccio: painting by Andrea del Castagno

of such artists as Huddie 'Leadbelly' Ledbetter and William 'Big Bill' Broonzy represented a tradition of rural b. comparatively untouched by developments in jazz. An instrumental offshoot of the b. that gained popularity in the 1930s was the 'boogie-woogie' piano style, based on a rhythm of 8 beats to the bar. Today the 'rhythm-and-blues' style of the highly successful Ray Charles is an amalgam of urban b. and modern jazz.

blue stocking. A woman of, or affecting, intellectual tastes. In 18th-c. London, in the gatherings held at the houses of Mrs Montagu, Mrs Vesey and Mrs Ord, card games and gossip were replaced by literary conversation. Eminent men such as Dr Johnson and S. Richardson attended; dress was informal and Stillingfleet's use of blue worsted stockings, instead of the black silk usual for assemblies was the origin of the term b. s.

Blum Léon (1872–1950). French essayist, literary and dramatic critic and a major figure of French socialism. B.'s criticism appeared in the *Revue blanche* and in 1901 he publ. *Nouvelles Conversations de Goethe avec Eckermann* on literature, aesthetics and politics. His critical masterpiece was the study *Stendhal et le Beylisme* (1914).

Blum René (1878–1942). French ballet impresario who in 1932 combined with Col. de *Basil to re-form *Diaghilev's co., which had disbanded after Diaghilev's death 3 years earlier. The new co. was called Ballets Russes de Monte Carlo. In 1936 B. resigned and founded the René Blum Ballets de Monte Carlo (later called Ballet Russe de Monte Carlo) with *Fokine as ballet master. Blum took his group to the U.S. and it gradually became an American co.

Blunden Edmund (Charles) (1896–). English poet, critic and biographer. Deeply affected by World War I, he wrote a subtle and moving account of his experiences in *Undertones of War* (1928). His country verse is delicate and 'literary', and as a scholarly critic he has helped to re-establish the poetry of Christopher Smart and John Clare.

Blunt Wilfrid Scawen (1840–1922). English poet and political writer. His diaries are full of vivid and cruel characterizations of his contemporaries.

bobbin lace. Any *lace made with bobbins on a pillow, but used in England to distinguish coarse lace made with large wooden bobbins from bone lace made with light bone bobbins.

Bob le Flambeur (1956). Film directed by J.-P. *Melville.

Boccaccino Boccaccio (active 1493–d. 1524/5). Italian painter. After working at Genoa, Ferrara and Venice B. settled in Cremona and his masterpiece is a series of frescoes (1510–19) of the life of the Virgin in the cathedral there; he also did other frescoes in the cathedral. His work often shows the influence of Giovanni Bellini.

Boccaccio Giovanni (1313–75). Italian poet and prose writer, the natural son of a wealthy merchant. He was sent as a boy to study at Naples, where he met the woman he later immortalized as 'Fiammetta' and was introduced to classical literature by humanists at the court. In the 1340s he returned to Florence; he was engaged on minor diplomatic missions, became a friend of Petrarch, who helped him over a spiritual crisis in the early 1360s (during which B. proposed to destroy his own works) and retired to Certaldo (1374), where he died. B.'s great work is *The Decameron* (written 1348–53), 100 short stories told by a group of 7 girls and 3 young men gathered in a house near Florence to escape the Black Death of 1348. Each day one of the young people directs the games, dances and singing in the beautiful gardens of the villa; in the late afternoon each in turn tells a story. The stories vary in character and theme, but their technique is masterly, their prevailing tone gay, often bawdy, and their purpose to entertain; B. draws on traditional and classical sources but his tales are set with vivid realism in 14th-c. Italy. His prose style, characteristically periodic, strongly influenced Italian prose of the Renaissance, and *The Decameron* itself was a source-book for later writers outside Italy, including Shakespeare, Lope de Vega and La Fontaine. B., an

Boccioni. *Unique Forms of Continuity in Space* (1913)

Bodegón. Velazquez's *Old Woman Cooking Eggs*

ardent admirer of Dante as well as of his own friend Petrarch, wrote a commentary on the *Divine Comedy* and *Trattatello in Laude di Dante*. B.'s minor works include: *Il Filocolo*, a prose romance, based on a French original, which reveals B.'s sensuality; *Filostrato*, the story of Troilus and Cressida, as found in Benoît de Sainte-Maure, drawn upon by Chaucer; *La Fiammetta*, a prose romance (in which Fiammetta laments her desertion by Panfilo) which shows considerable psychological insight; *Il Ninfale Fiesolano*, a charming simply told idyll set in rural Tuscany; and *Il Corbaccio*, which B. wrote (1355) to avenge himself on a widow who had refused his love. B. also wrote numerous works in Latin and also, in search of forgotten classical texts, found works by Tacitus and Apuleius.

Boccherini Luigi (1743–1805). Italian cellist and composer. He studied in Rome (1757–61), won a great reputation in Paris (1767), and took up a court appointment at Madrid in 1769; between 1787 and 1797 he stayed at Berlin, but returned to Spain, where his fortunes gradually declined, and died in poverty. His chamber music can be compared with Haydn's for its originality of style and inventiveness, and it was widely popular with B.'s contemporaries. It fell out of favour during the 19th c. but B. is now regarded as a fine composer who influenced the development of early chamber music. His output includes 125 string quintets.

Boccioni Umberto (1882–1916). Italian *futurist painter, sculptor and writer who studied under G. Balla in Rome. Inspired by Marinetti's futurist manifesto (1909), B. issued the *Manifesto of Futuristic Painters* (1910). He contributed to an exhibition of futurist art in Paris (1912) and summarized its ideals in his book *Pittura, scultura futuriste* (1914). Characteristic works are the painting *The City Rises* (1910; M.M.A., Rome) and the sculpture *Unique Forms of Continuity in Space* (1913; M.M.A., New York).

Bochsa Robert-Nicolas-Charles (1789–1856). French composer and court harpist to Napoleon and Louis XVIII. Charged with forgery, B. fled to London (1817) where he and his instrument had a great vogue. In 1839 he eloped with H. R. *Bishop's wife touring the world with her and dying in Australia. His compositions were slight but he greatly developed harp technique.

Böcklin Arnold (1827–1901). Swiss romantic painter whose early works were sentimentalized, cliché-ridden classical landscapes; his later fantastic pictures of creatures from Germanic legend and classical mythology, e.g. *Triton and Nereid* (1873/4; Schackgal., Munich) were ponderous rather than dramatic. Imaginative landscapes, e.g. *Isle of the Dead* (1880; M.M.A., New York), following the tradition of C. D. Friedrich, have a supernatural, if theatrical, atmosphere.

bodegón (Spanish, 'tavern'). Kitchen picture with still-life as a major feature, a genre popular in Spain in the 17th c. A famous example is Velazquez's *Old Woman Cooking Eggs* (N.G., Edinburgh).

Bodenheim Maxwell (1893–1954). U.S. novelist and poet whose early verse, e.g. *Minna and Myself* (1918), was influenced by imagism. His novels, cynically directed against established traditions, include *Crazy Man* (1924), *Replenishing Jessica* (1925, originally banned) and *Sixty Seconds* (1929). He ended his bohemian life as a vagrant in Greenwich Village and was finally murdered.

Bodenstedt Friedrich von (1819–92). German writer. B. lived for several years in Moscow and Tiflis. In 1851 he publ. *Die Lieder des Mirza-Schaffy* (264th ed. 1917; *The Songs of Mirza Schaffy*, 1880), a coll. of pseudo-oriental poems supposedly containing the wisdom of a Tartar friend. B. also made excellent trs from the Russian and English classics, including a version of Shakespeare.

Bodley George Frederick (1827–1907). English ecclesiastical architect, pupil of Sir G. G. Scott and one of the best exponents of the *Gothic revival in England. He built St Michael's, Brighton (1859/62) and St Martin's-on-the-Cliff, Scarborough (1863). Other work includes All Saints', Cambridge (begun 1863), St Augustine, Pendlebury, Lancs. (1874) and the cathedral Washington, D.C.

Böcklin. *Isle of the Dead*

Bodley. St Michael's

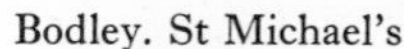

CORALE

Quousque tandem abutère, Catilina, patientià nostrà? quamdiu etiam furor iste tuus nos *eludet? quem ad finem sese effre-*

GRAVINA

Bodoni. Page from the *Manuale Tipografico*

Boethius. Medieval illuminated ms.

Boeckl. Fresco in the church at Seckau

Bodley Sir Thomas (1545–1613). English diplomat and man of letters, founder of the BODLEIAN LIBRARY at Oxford, opened 1602.

Bodmer Johann Jakob (1698–1783). German Swiss literary theorist, professor at Zürich Univ. and associated there with J. J. Breitinger (they are often called 'the Swiss critics'). He pioneered the revival of medieval German literature, proposed English poets as better models than French and with his *Critische Abhandlung . . .* (1740) provoked the criticism of Gottsched.

Bodoni Giambattista (1740–1813). Italian printer, typographer and type designer who worked at the Vatican press and then as head of the ducal press of Parma. In his early books, printed in French *Fournier or similar types, he used printer's ornaments and decorated capitals, doing some of his best work in this manner. In 1788 he produced some of the best specimens of roman and italic alphabets ever designed. His style changed *c.* 1800. He designed *modern faces, dispensed with decoration and left large areas of page unprinted. This was never widely popular though preferred by B., who thought Fénelon's *Télémaque* (1812), designed in this second manner, his greatest book. His types remain valuable; so do his books as typographical masterpieces but they are too full of printer's errors to be useful for scholarly purposes. His *Manuale Tipografico* (2 vols, 1788, 1818) contained specimens of roman, cursive, italic and foreign types, *Oratio Dominica . . .* (1806) specimens of foreign and ancient types.

body colour. An opaque watercolour, achieved by mixing with white and used to emphasize highlights, either in drawings on coloured paper or in watercolour paintings.

Boece (Boethius or Boyis) Hector (1465?–1536). Scottish historian who wrote the *Lives of the Bishops Mortlach and Aberdeen* (1522, trs. 1894) and the *History of Scotland* (1526, trs. 1536), both in Latin. The latter combines fact and fable and contains the story of Macbeth, made accessible to Shakespeare via *Holinshed's *Chronicles*.

Boeckl Herbert (1894–). Austrian expressionist painter whose religious paintings (e.g. frescoes in the Benedictine abbey church, Seckau) are an important contribution to 20th-c. religious art. By the mid 1940s increased simplification of forms and spiritualization had brought his work close to abstraction.

Boehm Theobald (1794–1881). German composer, flute player and maker. He aimed to increase the flute's volume of sound and revolutionized flute design by a new system of finger keys and by changing the traditional conical bore to a cylindrical one. The BOEHM SYSTEM (*flute) has been adapted to other woodwind instruments.

Boethius (*c.* 480–524). Statesman and philosopher, and an adviser of Theodoric, the Gothic king at Ravenna. Suspecting his loyalty, Theodoric had B. imprisoned and later executed. B.'s *De Consolatione Philosophiae* was written in prison. This great work, in the form of a dialogue between B. and philosophy, was much revered in medieval Europe; in England it was trs. by King Alfred and Chaucer.

Boetticher Budd (Oscar B. Jr) (1916–). U.S. film director. His 1st important film was *The Bullfighter and the Lady* (1951). In 1956 he teamed up with Randolph Scott (as star and usually co-producer) to make the series of westerns on which his reputation mainly rests, from *Seven Men from Now* (1956) to *Ride Lonesome* and *Comanche Station* (1959). After a viciously comic 1920s crime film, *The Rise and Fall of Legs Diamond* (1959), he returned to Mexico.

Boffrand Germain (1667–1754). French architect. After studying under J.-H. Mansard he worked in Germany and then in Paris. In 1711 he was appointed architect to the duke of Lorraine and for the next 30 years worked mostly in his capital at Nancy, designing numerous public buildings and private mansions, and giving Nancy much of the 18th-c. elegance that still marks it today.

Bogan Louise (1897–). U.S. poet and critic. Her slow calculated and melancholy verses, which are for the most part cast in traditional mould, are distinguished for their vivid metaphysical imagery. Publs include *Dark Summer* (1929) and *Collected Poems* (1954), and a selection of critical essays (1955).

Bogarde Dirk (1920–). British film actor, whose 1st success was as the young delinquent in *The Blue Lamp* (1949). Since a version of

Boffrand. Hôtel de Soubise, Paris

Humphrey Bogart (left) in *The Maltese Falcon*

Bohemian glass

Shaw's *The Doctor's Dilemma* (1959) he has extended his range, making a decisive impression as a serious actor in *The Servant* (1964).

Bogardus James (1800–74). U.S. engineer, one of the pioneers of the use of cast-iron in buildings. In 1848 he designed a 4-storey factory with the structure entirely of cast-iron (Center Street, New York).

Bogart Humphrey (1899–1957). U.S. film actor. Rock-faced gangster, cynical private eye, man of few words and dry humour. His career included *The Petrified Forest* (1936), *The Maltese Falcon* (1941), *The Treasure of Sierra Madre* (1947), *The African Queen* (1951), which won an Oscar, and *Sabrina Fair* (1954).

Bogusławski Wojciech (1757–1829). Polish actor and playwright, creator of the Polish national theatre; he also gave the 1st performance of *Hamlet* in Poland (1797). Among his numerous works, the most popular was a musical comedy, *Cud mniemany, czyli Krakowiacy i Górale* (1841).

Bohème, La. Opera by *Puccini, libretto by G. Giacosa and L. Illica after Murger; 1st performance in 1896 in Turin.

bohemian. Term used to describe a vagabond or unconventional life–usually that of the artist (*Murger); it derives from the French *bohémien*, applied to the gipsies (thought in the 15th c. to originate in Bohemia).

Bohemian glass. From the 15th c. onwards Bohemia was an important glass-producing area. In the late 16th and early 17th cs Bohemia became well known for its enamel-painted glass, which is often blue in colour; the style was much copied in Brandenburg and Prussia. In the 1st half of the 18th c. Bohemian glass engraving was particularly fine, and from this date every kind of glass, including an opaque white variety, was made in Bohemia. In the 19th c. Bohemian engraving again achieved a dominant place in German glass production.

Bohemian master (*fl.* mid 14th c.). Painter working in Prague at the court of the Emperor Charles IV. By him are *The Glatz Madonna* (Berlin) and *Death of the Virgin* (M. of Fine A., Boston), 2 of the finest examples of international Gothic style.

Böhm Georg (1661–1733). German organist and composer, transitional between the German tradition of J. J. Froberger and the style of J. S. Bach. B. became organist at St John's, Lüneburg in 1698; J. S. Bach's early organ music was much influenced by him. B.'s surviving work includes suites for clavier, preludes and fugues and chorale works for organ, and 5 cantatas.

Böhme Jakob (1575–1624). German nature mystic and philosopher whose writings, e.g. *Aurora* . . . (1613), influenced the poet Angelus Silesius, also Hegel and Schelling, and in England Coleridge and Wordsworth.

Boiardo Matteo Maria (1441–94). Italian poet and humanist. He was an accomplished classical scholar and trs. Among his finest poems are a series of lyrics (*Canzoniere*) in which Petrarch's influence can clearly be seen, and a magnificent but unfinished narrative poem, *Orlando Innamorato*, a chivalric romance written in epic form. Its theme is drawn from the legend of Charlemagne. Ariosto wrote his *Orlando Furioso* as a sequel.

Boïeldieu (François) Adrien (1775–1834). French composer. He was taught by the organist at Rouen, his home town; he came to Paris (1796), meeting Cherubini and Méhul among others. B.'s comic opera *Le Calife de Bagdad* (1800) was very successful. As court composer at St Petersburg (1803–11), he wrote nothing important. However *Jean de Paris* (1812), produced after his return to Paris, was well received, and *La Dame Blanche* (1825) had immense success. Besides operas, B. wrote some chamber music.

Boileau (-Despréaux) Nicolas (1636–1711). French poet, critic and literary arbiter. B.'s didactic poem *L'Art poétique* (1674) was strictly classical in its views and triggered off the *Ancients and Moderns Controversy. B. in effect originated French literary criticism and established canons for the use of the *alexandrine. Other works include the verse *Satires* and *Épîtres* and a trs. of the treatise *'On the Sublime'.

Boilly Louis-Léopold (1761–1845). Popular and prolific French portrait, history and genre painter. His work includes *Triumph of Marat* (*c.* 1794, Lille Mus.) and *The Arrival of the Stage-Coach* (1803, Louvre).

Bohemian master. *The Glatz Madonna*

Nicolas Boileau

Boilly. *Baron von Humboldt*

Bol. *Governors of the Leper Hospital*

School of Bologna. Guido Reni's *Lot and his daughters leaving Sodom*

Giovanni da Bologna. *Samson Slaying a Philistine*. Also *Doccia

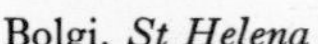

Bolgi. *St Helena*

Boito Arrigo (1842–1918). Italian composer, music critic, librettist and poet. His libretti included those for Verdi's operas, *Simone Boccanegra*, *Otello* and *Falstaff*; he also trs. Wagner's *Rienzi* and *Tristan*. As a composer B. was strongly influenced by Wagner; he wrote the operas *Mefistofele* (1868) and *Nerone* (1911, produced 1924). His poetry includes *Re Orso* (1865), late romantic in style, resplendent with extravagant 'medieval' settings and luxuriant word music.

Boker George Henry (1823–90). U.S. poet and romantic dramatist who specialized in verse plays on medieval themes. These include the comedy *The Betrothal* (1850) and the tragedies *Leonor de Guzman* (1853) and *Francesca da Rimini* (1855), his best work, based on Dante's story of Francesca and Paolo.

bokmål. A Norwegian language (Ivar *Aasen).

Bol Ferdinand (1616–80). Dutch painter, prior to 1640 a pupil of Rembrandt, to whom many of B.'s paintings were attributed, so well did he imitate his master. In the 1660s his work deteriorated as he pandered to popular taste and painted in a more elegant and decorative manner.

Boldrewood Rolf. Pseud. of Thomas Alexander Browne (1826–1915). Australian novelist brought from England when he was 4. *Robbery Under Arms* (1888), the best known of B.'s 13 novels, is 'a straightforward, thrilling story (with a veneer of moralizing) of bushrangers and their attractive, aristocratic leader Captain Starlight.

bolection moulding. A projecting moulding, S-shaped in section (*ogee), surrounding a panel. In furniture such a moulding may cover the joint of 2 parallel planes.

bolero. Spanish dance of 17th-c. origins in a moderate 3/4 time, originally accompanied by a voice and castanets. Chopin wrote a b. for piano solo (op. 19) and Ravel the famous B. for orchestra (1928), a display piece of virtuoso orchestration.

Bolgi Andrea (1605–56). Italian sculptor who worked in Bernini's studio in Rome from 1626 and executed the statue of St Helena (1629–49) in St Peter's. His style was not sufficiently vigorous to satisfy high baroque taste and he gradually fell out of favour in Rome.

Böll Heinrich (1917–). German writer. B. treats contemporary themes – war, its aftermath, life and mores in W. German society – satirically, earnestly, vividly. With sharp observation he combines masterly dialogue, simple, subtle, precise language, slightly mannered. His works include: the novels, *Wo warst du Adam?* (1951), *Das Brot der frühen Jahre* (1955; *The Bread of Our Early Years*, 1957), and *Ansichten eines Clowns* (1963).

Bolm Adolph (1884–1951). Russian dancer who trained at the Imperial School, St Petersburg. He appeared during the Diaghilev co.'s 1st Paris season (1910) and settled in the U.S. after touring in 1917. There he taught and did choreography for stage and films; his pioneer work greatly helped towards the development of American ballet tradition.

Bologna Giovanni da (Giambologna, Jean de Boulogne) (1529–1608). One of the greatest and most influential mannerist sculptors, born at Douai and settled in Florence. His most important works were undertaken for the Medici family and are in Florence, including *Flying Mercury* (Bargello), *Rape of the Sabines* (Loggia dei Lanzi) and fountains in the Boboli gardens; among his other works are the early fountain of Neptune at Bolgona and *Samson Slaying a Philistine* (V. and A., London). The Kunsthistorisches Mus., Vienna has a fine coll. of his small bronzes.

Bologna, school of. School of Italian painting which in the 16th and 17th cs was the centre of classicism as taught by the *Carracci Academy. Distinguished Bolognese painters include Albani, Reni, Domenichino, Guercino, Lanfranco and Sassoferrato; several of them were influential in the development of the baroque style in Rome.

Bolognini Mauro (1920–). Italian film director. His more famous films, *La Notte Brava* (1959) and *Il Bell'Antonio* (1960), comedies with marked social undertones, owe

Boltraffio. *Narcissus*

Bolshoi Ballet: performance of *Swan Lake*

their qualities to their scripts (by *Pasolini, etc.). His more recent work has gained notoriety from censor troubles. Although his origins lie in neo-realism, he has lately moved from the escapist, pseudo-realism of *La Notte Brava* to period reconstruction.

Bolshoi Theatre Moscow. Founded in 1776 for opera, ballet and a theatre group. It still has resident opera and ballet cos which produce contemporary and traditional works. The BOLSHOI BALLET was founded in 1780 and replaced the co. at the Maryinsky (St Petersburg) as the leading Russian co. after the capital was transferred to Moscow (1918). Today it is one of the outstanding cos in the world and has fostered many brilliant dancers. Although, as a previously provincial co., folk and national dancing were its mainstay, it now has a balanced repertoire of traditional and contemporary ballets. Among the latter are *Flames of Paris*, with choreography by Vainonen (1932), *Fountain of Bakhisaray*, choreography by Zakharov (1934) and *Laurencia*, choreography by Chabukiani.

Bolt Robert (Oxton) (1924–). English playwright, author of *Flowering Cherry* (1957), *A Man for all Seasons* (1960), about Sir Thomas More, and *The Tiger and the Horse* (1960).

Boltraffio (Beltraffio) Giovanni Antonio (1466/7–1516). Italian painter, a pupil of Leonardo da Vinci in Milan. His work includes *Virgin and Child* and *Narcissus* (both N.G., London); many of his paintings are in Milan.

bolus ground. A preparation of an artist's canvas (*oil painting). Bole is a reddish or dark brown earth; applied to the canvas as a ground or working surface, it eventually shows through the painting, producing characteristic effects.

bombardon. Brass-band term for the bass tuba; also the name of an organ stop.

Bombelli Sebastiano (1635–before 1716). Venetian history and portrait painter strongly influenced by Veronese. He also worked in Germany.

Bombois Camille (1883–). French 'primitive' painter, ex-wrestler and navvy. He was a 'Sunday painter' until 1923, when he began to paint full-time, becoming noted for his lively scenes of circuses and fairs with enormous fleshy women and muscle-bound men as side-show attractions.

Bonagiunta Orbicciani (*c.* 1220–*c.* 98). Italian poet who wrote in Tuscan. He was influenced both by the troubadour tradition and the school of Sicilian poets, but managed to avoid the defects of the latter, for his love-poems have an appealing freshness and sincerity of tone.

Bonanno of Pisa (*fl.* late 12th c.). Italian sculptor and architect. He made the bronze doors of the cathedrals of Monreale and Pisa (except on the S. side destroyed and replaced). The 'Leaning Tower' of Pisa was begun under his direction.

Bonaventura St (1221–74). Italian Franciscan theologian and writer and biographer of St Francis of Assisi. He was renowned as a teacher and worked closely with Thomas Aquinas for a time; he wrote numerous theological and mystical works, and is known as the 'Seraphic Doctor'.

bonbonnière. A small box, normally of gold, silver or enamel, used to contain sweetmeats and particularly fashionable in 18th-c. France. Larger than, but often confused with, snuff-boxes.

bond. Architectural term for the laying of bricks so that they overlap; this makes brick-work strong and secure. In FLEMISH b. each layer contains alternating 'headers' (bricks laid with the long side at right angles to the wall so that only the end of each brick is visible when the wall is finished) and 'stretchers' (bricks laid with the long side parallel with the wall); ENGLISH b. has alternating layers of headers and stretchers.

Bone Sir Muirhead (1876–1953). Scottish draughtsman and etcher who settled in London (1901) and specialized in architectural subjects, e.g. *Demolition of St James's Hall* and *Ruins of London from St Bride's* (World War II). He was an official war artist during World War I.

Bonanno of Pisa. *Adam and Eve with their Children*; Monreale cathedral

Bombois. *Fairground athlete*

Sir Muirhead Bone. *St Bride's and the City after the Fire, 29 December 1940*; pen drawing

Bonheur. *Horse Fair*

Bono da Ferrara. *St Jerome in a Landscape*

Bonington. *The Column of St Mark, Venice*

bone china. A hard-paste porcelain modified by the addition of calcined bone. Since the beginning of the 19th c. it has been the standard English porcelain paste. Josiah Spode is traditionally credited with its perfection, although bone ash as an ingredient had been used in Staffordshire and elsewhere in the 18th c. The special qualities of bone china are the ease and cheapness of manufacture, its translucency, and its suitability for coloured underglaze decoration.

bone lace: *bobbin lace

Boner Ulrich (mid 14th c.). German Dominican monk from Bern, author of *Der Edelstein*, a coll. of 100 Latin fables trs. into witty and fresh German dialect verse. It was one of the 1st books printed in the vernacular (by A. Pfister, 1461) and remained very popular into the 16th c.; it was next reprinted in 1757, the ed. used by Lessing in an essay on the fable.

Bonfigli Benedetto (active 1445–d. 1496). Italian painter strongly influenced by Gozzoli. He worked mainly at Perugia, where his work includes a series of frescoes in the prior's chapel in the town hall.

Bonheur Marie-Rosalie called Rosa (1822–99). French animal painter widely acclaimed in her lifetime. Her best pictures, often of horses, combine vigorous action with accurate detail and are frequently huge, one depicting 10 life-size horses. For her most important work, *Horse Fair* (1853; Met. Mus.; quarter-size copy, N.G., London) she disguised herself as a man to obtain correct 'local colour'.

bonheur du jour. A kind of writing-table popular in France from the mid 18th c. It was usually found in the boudoir and there are often small cupboards for books or accessories for the toilet.

Bonifazio di Pitati (1487–1553). Italian painter of the Venetian school whose paintings closely resemble those of Giorgione and Titian. Many paintings in the style of these artists have been attributed to B. but only one work signed by him survives, *Madonna and Child with Saints* (1553; Palazzo Reale, Venice).

Bonington Richard Parkes (1802–28). English painter and lithographer of great talent, living and working, however, mainly in Calais. B. was a friend of Delacroix and Lawrence. He was awarded a gold medal at the Paris Salon in 1824 at the same time as Constable. In his work the English tradition of topographical landscape combined with the spirit of French romanticism. His oil paintings and watercolours of marine subjects painted with a light palette and free handling are regarded as his best work. Though B. died young, he had a considerable influence over contemporary and later landscape painting, mainly in France. He was regarded as one of the first to break with the tradition of David.

Bonjour Tristesse (1954). Novel by Françoise *Sagan; made into a film (1957) directed by O. *Preminger.

Bonnard Pierre (1867–1947). French painter, lithographer and designer who studied at the École des Beaux-Arts (1888) and the Académie Julian (1889). While a student he met Sérusier, Vallotton, Vuillard and the other *nabis who first exhibited together at the Café Volpini in 1889. His early graphic work (*Revue Blanche* cover, 1895) combines acute and often humorous observation of a fleeting pose with an instinctive sense of design. He illustrated a number of books for Vollard including *Parallèlement* (1900) and the outstanding edition of *Daphnis et Chloé* (1902). His decorative use of silhouette reflects the widespread influence of art nouveau and of Japanese prints. He subscribed to the nabi doctrine of abandoning 3-dimensional modelling in favour of flat colour areas, but was never committed to the symbolist aspect of the movement.
After 1900 he concentrated more on painting and although he still worked more from his observation than his imagination, his early wit and charm gave way to a Matisse-like monumentality of design. Mature works like *La Baignoire* (1925; Tate) play off the considerable surface richness of paint and colour against a simple formal strength and his acute perception of light. After 1911 he worked either at Vernon or in S. France.

Bonnes Femmes, Les (1960). Film directed by C. *Chabrol.

Bono da Ferrara (*fl.* mid 15th c.). Italian painter influenced by Pisanello and Squarcione. His best surviving work is *St Jerome in a Landscape* (N.G., London).

Bonnard. *Interior with Boy*

Junius Brutus Booth

Edwin Booth

Bonomi Joseph (1739–1808). Italian architect who settled in England (1767), invited by the Adam brothers. He was a fashionable designer of country houses, mentioned in Jane Austen's *Sense and Sensibility* (1811), and was sponsored by Sir J. Reynolds for the R.A.

Bononcini Antonio Maria (1677–1726). Italian composer, son of G.M.B. In 1696 he produced the opera *Il trionfo di Camilla*, popular in Italy and England throughout the early 18th c. He toured Italian and European courts, sometimes with his brother G.B.B., with whose works B.'s are often confused.

Bononcini Giovanni Battista (1670–1747). Italian composer, son of G.M.B. After working in Rome he was court composer in Vienna and in 1720 was invited to London by the anti-Hanoverian faction, Handel being the royal favourite; B.'s London operas included *Astarto* (1720). After he left London (*c.* 1732) B.'s career is obscure; his reputation as a composer has been dimmed by Handel's brilliance.

Bononcini Giovanni Maria (1642–78). Italian composer working at Modena. He wrote much instrumental and vocal music, and a theoretical treatise, *Musico prattico* (1673).

Bonsignori Francesco (1455?–1519?). Italian portrait painter influenced by Mantegna. From *c.* 1490 he worked chiefly at the court of the Gonzagas in Mantua.

Bonvicino Alessandro: Il *Moretto

boogie-woogie: *jazz

Book of Nonsense, The (1846). Book by Edward Lear.

Book of Snobs, The (1847). Coll. of articles by *Thackeray.

Book of the Duchess, The (1369–70). Allegorical poem by *Chaucer.

Book of the Dun Cow. Irish ms., dating from before 1106, of several myths and including the *Cattle Raid of Cooley*; this was supposedly first recorded on the hide of a cow.

Booth family. Family of U.S. actors; the most important members were English-born Junius Brutus B. (1796–1852) and his son Edwin Thomas B. (1833–93), who founded his own theatre in New York (1869) and achieved an international reputation; his run of 100 performances as Hamlet was a record. His brother John Wilkes B. (1838–65) was the assassin of Lincoln.

Bor Paulus (*c.* 1600–69). Dutch painter, member of the *Utrecht school and while in Rome in the 1620s a leader of the *bentname.

Borchert Wolfgang (1921–47). German poet, dramatist and prose writer; he achieved sudden fame with *Draussen vor der Tür* (1947), a play depicting the reception and despairing reactions of a German soldier on his return home from Siberia in 1946. The keynote of B.'s writings–which reflect his love of Germany and, in particular, of his native Hamburg–is one of bitter, optimistic protest at the horror of war and its aftermath. His language, highly emotional in content yet restrained in style, is simple, colloquial, repetitious, staccato. Works include 3 colls of short stories and sketches: *Die Hundeblume* (1947), *An diesem Dienstag* (1948) and *Die traurigen Geranien* (1962).

Borck Caspar Wilhelm von (1704–47). Author of the 1st printed German trs. of a Shakespeare play; his version of *Julius Caesar*, in alexandrine verse, appeared in 1741.

Bordeaux Henri (Camille) (1870–). French novelist of provincial middle-class family life. Besides essays and a few early patriotic stories he wrote about 50 novels including *Les Roquevillard* (1906; *The Will to Live*, 1916), *La Robe de laine* (1910; *The Woollen Dress*, 1913) and *Les yeux accusateurs* (1949).

Bordone Paris (1500–71). Venetian painter, a pupil of Titian, whose style he followed closely. He worked in France for King Francis I and later in Augsburg and Milan, painting portrait, religious, allegorical and mythological subjects including *Fisherman presenting the Ring of St Mark to the Doge* (Accademia, Venice) and *Salvator Mundi* (N.G., London).

Borduas Paul Émile (1905–). Canadian *tachiste* painter, with Riopelle founder of the group Les Automatistes (1940) in Montreal and leader of the group of painters who publ. the manifesto *Refus Global* (1948). In the 1950s he lived in Paris.

Bordone. *Salvator Mundi*

Borduas. *Morning Candelabra* (1948)

Borissov-Mussatov. *The Reservoir*

Boris Godunov: performance of Mussorgsky's opera at the Bolshoi Theatre

Borrassá. *Christ and St Peter*

Alexander Porfirevich Borodin

Borel Pierre-Joseph called Pétrus (1809–59). French poet and leader of the 'bousingos', a group of rowdy young romantic writers and artists. His works included the poem colls *Rhapsodies* (1832) and *Champavert, contes immoraux* (1833) and the novel *Madame Putiphar* (1839); they proclaim defiance against society and are crowded with macabre incidents. He has been called a forerunner of A. *Jarry.

Borges Jorge Luis (1900–). Argentinian poet and writer of short stories. He was educated in Europe (Geneva and Madrid) but his subject is Argentina and the district round Buenos Aires in particular. His verse shows affinities with European *imagism.

Borghi Giuseppe (1790–1847). Italian poet and priest; his best work was the coll. of religious poems *Inni Sacri* (1829–31).

Borgognone, Il: Il *Bergognone

Boris Godunov. Play by *Pushkin (1831) and opera by *Mussorgsky, based on the play.

Borissov-Mussatov Victor (1870–1905). Russian painter. In Paris he worked in Gustave Moreau's studio; Puvis de Chavannes made a great impression on him. He returned to Russia (1899), working near Saratov painting melancholy scenes of derelict classical mansions peopled by sad, crinolined figures. A lonely figure, both as artist and man, he was influential on the *Blue Rose Group.

Born Yesterday (1950). Film directed by G. *Cukor.

Borne Ludwig (1786–1837). German writer and gifted journalist who settled in Paris in 1830. His *Briefe aus Paris* (1832–4), demanding German political reforms, was prohibited by the authorities and very popular; its easy and witty style was also influential on German prose. B.'s sketches, e.g. *Der Esskünstler*, lightly imitate Jean-Paul Richter.

Borodin Alexander Porfirevich (1833–87). Russian composer, one of the *Mighty Handful group and the illegitimate son of a Russian prince. Although he composed from childhood, he developed a passionate interest in chemistry and from 1862 was on the staff of the St Petersburg Medico-Surgical Academy. A meeting with M. *Balakirev (1862) decided him to begin his 1st symphony (finished 1867). Scientific teaching and research slowed up B.'s composition and his output was small. Despite this he is a major Russian composer. His style, although slightly influenced by Glinka and Russian folk-music, was highly original; his harmonies are often bold and his lyrical sense is outstanding. His music often has an oriental flavour and his symphony movements are characteristically monothematic. His great B min. symphony (no. 2) was written between 1869 and 1875, and in 1869 also he began the opera *Prince Igor*, from which come the famous 'Polovtsian Dances'. This opera, like his 3rd symphony (begun 1886), was left unfinished (both were completed by Rimsky-Korsakov and Glazunov). B.'s other important works are 2 quartets, the symphonic poem *In the Steppes of Central Asia*, and 14 songs. In 1877, at Weimar, B. met Liszt, who actively sponsored his music and in the 1880s B.'s reputation spread widely in Western Europe.

Borough, The (1810). Poem by *Crabbe.

Borowczyk Walerian (1923–). Polish film maker, collaborator of *Lenica. B. moved to France where he made an animated science-fiction burlesque, *Les Astronautes* (1959), with Chris *Marker. He has since worked for French television and made other animated films, including *Renaissance* (1963).

Borrassá Luis (1360–1426). Spanish painter who introduced the international Gothic style, the 3rd period of Spanish Gothic painting, into Barcelona. Of his many imaginative and richly coloured altarpieces the *Altarpiece of St Clare* is a fine example.

Borromini Francesco (1599–1667). Italian architect working in Rome; one of the 3 great masters of baroque. He was a difficult, neurotic man, envious of rivals and colleagues; he committed suicide. B.'s style was extremely personal, but he became the dominant influence on the next generation of architects, especially

Borromini. S. Agnese

Borromini. S. Ivo della Sapienza

Borromini. The Cupola of S. Ivo

in Piedmont (*Guarini), and so helped to form the baroque style of S. Germany and Austria. He himself described the sources of his art as 'Nature, Antiquity and Michelangelo.' All his designs can be reduced to fairly simple geometrical shapes (especially ovals and triangles, shapes not generally used before in architecture) but they are so closely integrated, overlapping and often interpenetrating each other, and in practice often so subtly disguised, that the final effect is of a freely moulded space. Architectural elements, instead of being kept clearly distinct, as in Renaissance and mannerism, merge into one another; nothing is unambiguous or stable. B.'s masterpiece is the tiny church of S. Carlo alle Quattro Fontane (1634). The plan is based on interpenetrating ovals, giving the interior elevations a complex swaying movement; it has an oval coffered dome over the centre, with a design based on a Roman pavement. The façade was designed 30 years later in 1662: there are 2 levels with conflicting convex and concave movement and plenty of sculpture. S. Ivo della Sapienza (1642) has a plan based on a 6-pointed star (i.e. superimposed triangles), the angles treated in alternating concave and convex shapes; the whole geometry is carried up into the vault and progressively simplified until it achieves its climax in a point; the exterior is concave, with a unique spiralling cupola. Other works include: part of the Palazzo Barberini; the Oratory of S. Filippo Neri; the Collegio della Propaganda Fide–a cramped façade with giant pilasters and a puny entablature (both these buildings use the convex-concave rhythm); S. Agnese, a centrally-planned church with a 2-tower façade and dome, altered by later architects; and part of S. Andrea delle Fratte.

Borrow George Henry (1803–81). English travel writer and novelist. B.'s works freely mix fiction with glamorized recollections of his wanderings, including an agency for the Bible Society in Spain and travels in Russia. The great success of his *The Bible in Spain* (1843) encouraged him to write the novels *Lavengro* (1851) and its sequel *The Romany Rye* (1857), drawing upon his vagabond youth in England and knowledge of gipsy ways. Works include *The Zincali, or . . . the Gypsies in Spain* (1841) and *Wild Wales* (1862).

Bortniansky Dmitry Stepanovich (1751–1825). Russian composer, the 'Russian Palestrina'; studied under B. Galuppi at St Petersburg and in Italy, where he produced a few operas. In 1796 he became musical director of the imperial chapel, writing much church music. A reaction against his Italianization followed B.'s death, but Tchaikovsky ed. his collected works.

Borup Marten (1446–1526). Danish poet, author of the fine Latin poem *Carmen vernale.*

Borzage Frank (1893–1961). U.S. film director. B. made features from 1918 until 1958 with a 10-year gap before his last two films, *China Doll* (1958) and *The Big Fisherman* (1959). B. was one of the cinema's few true romantics, with little taste for surface realism. His films include *A Farewell to Arms* (1932), *A Man's Castle* (1933), *Little Man, What Now?* (1934), *History is Made at Night* (1937) and *Moonrise* (1948).

Bosboom-Toussaint Anna Louisa Geertruida (1812–86). Dutch author of historical romances in the style of Sir W. Scott, such as *De Graf van Leycester in Nederland* (1845) and, in later life, some contemporary novels.

Boscán (Almugáver) Juan (*c.* 1495–1542). Spanish poet; a friend of Garcilaso de la Vega. His works (publ. posth.) include poems in the Castilian style and those using Italian forms which he and Garcilaso introduced into Spanish poetry. He also trs. Castiglione's *Courtier* into Spanish.

Bosch Hieronymus, also called van Aeken (*c.* 1450–1516). Netherlands painter. Documentary evidence connects him at various periods between 1480 and 1516 with his birthplace 's Hertogenbosch (Bois-le-Duc), where he belonged to the Brotherhood of the Holy Virgin; he designed the stained-glass windows and a crucifix for the Chapel of the Brotherhood (1511–12) and was presumably a highly respected member of the community. He was referred to at his death as the 'famous artist', which is borne out by a commission in 1504 for a *Last Judgement* by Philip the Handsome of Burgundy. B. was a religious painter with a

Bosch. *Last Judgement* (detail)

Bosch. *The Garden of Delights* (detail)

Bossuet: painting by Rigaud

James Boswell

strong bent towards satire, pessimistic comment and great interest in everyday life. This has made his work, a unity in form and content, one of the last profound expressions of the medieval world view. Landscape plays an important part in his compositions, it sets the mood and it is seen with directness. Religious iconography is reinterpreted freely in the mood of popular prints, and the unbridled fantasy of the artist explores, not so much the world of the subconscious but every thematic variation, allusion and symbol available to his contemporaries. These were not puzzle pictures in their time, but picture books which could be read and understood. Only when the tradition and the understanding were lost did they increasingly require interpretation of some kind, until in our own time, with the advent of surrealism, attempts have been made to 'explain' B. by means of dream analysis. He was also referred to as a heretic by later generations. It is impossible to date and arrange his work in chronological sequence as much of his original work is now lost, many copies were made in his lifetime and even his signature forged. *The Haywain* and *The Garden of Delights* (both Prado) are triptychs fully authenticated and so is the table panel of the Escorial (Prado), which once belonged to Philip II as one of his intimate possessions. Other important paintings by B. are: *Christ Mocked* (N.G., London), and a protrayal of the *Ship of Fools* (Louvre) a common contemporary theme (S. *Brant).

Boscoreale mural

Bosco Henri (1888–). French novelist of Provençal life and landscape. Primitive regional folk-lore and mystery figure prominently in such novels as *Pierre Lampédouze* (1924), *L'Âne culotte* (1937), *Le Jardin d'Hyacinthe* (1946) and *Malicroix* (1948). B. also wrote the brilliant and satirical *Monsieur Carre-Benoît à la campagne* (1947; 1956).

Boscoreale. In 1900 were discovered 1st-c. Roman murals in a villa at this site near Pompeii. The paintings are now divided between the Naples Mus. and the Met. Mus.

Boshier. *Vista City* (1964)

Boshier Derek (1937–). English hard edge abstract painter; studied at the R.C.A. (1958–61). He tries to identify his work with the age via the motifs of mass advertising, the package, the hoarding, etc. and the world of fashion.

Bossi (Marco) Enrico (1861–1925). Italian virtuoso organist and composer who revolutionized organ building and technique by his example, compositions and *Metodo di studio per l'organo moderno* (1893; co-author G. Tebaldini). Besides outstanding organ music, B. wrote operas, orchestral and chamber music, e.g. the violin sonata in E min. and oratorios including *Il Paradiso perduto* (1903) and *Giovanna d'Arco* (1914).

Bossuet Jacques-Bénigne (1627–1704). French churchman, bishop of Condom (1669) and of Meaux (1681), famous as a theologian. B. also publ. an exposition of the divine right of kings. He had a lyrical literary style; his sermons were simple and touching, his funeral orations combined eloquence with pomp.

boss up. To beat a sheet of metal from the rear into approximately the required shape.

Bostonians, The (1886). Novel by Henry James.

Boswell James (1740–95). Scottish writer. B. met Samuel Johnson while visiting London in 1763, and the association between them continued until the latter's death in 1784. The *Journal of a Voyage to the Hebrides* was publ. in 1785 and the *Life of Johnson* in 1791, enjoying an immediate success. B. studied and practised law, rather reluctantly, and travelled on the Continent, meeting many of the most famous people of the age. From about 1762 he kept detailed, semi-private journals written with considerable art, which have been discovered and ed. in recent years, e.g. *Boswell's London Journal, 1762–1763* (1950), 2 vols of *Boswell on the Grand Tour . . .* (1953, 1955) and *Boswell in search of a Wife, 1766–1769* (1957). The journals disarm by the naïve candour with which B. reveals his vanity and snobbery and his weaknesses for women and drink. They are a unique source of detail about the daily life of the mid 18th c. and share the precise recollection, dramatic presentation, and gift for organizing material which make the *Life of Johnson* a great biography. B.'s reverence and affection for Johnson did not make his observation less sharp. He does not probe the private depths of Johnson's character, but gives a vividly dramatic account of him in social life detailing his prejudices, his melancholy and his formidable goodness.

Botev Christo (1847–76). Bulgarian poet and revolutionary killed at the head of a small band of armed insurgents against the Turks. He wrote some of the earliest and still finest Bulgarian lyrics.

Both Andries (*c.* 1608–49) and Jan (*c.* 1618–52). Dutch painters, pupils of A. Bloemaert. Working in Venice and Rome they are reputed to have collaborated in their paintings, Jan executing the landscape backgrounds, Andries the figures, usually peasants in *bambocciata* style. Returning to the Netherlands after his brother's death, Jan became one of the leading Italianate landscapists.

bottega. This Italian word for 'shop' is used, technically, of a master artist's studio in which his assistants work under supervision.

Bottesini Giovanni (1821–89). Italian double bass virtuoso and composer. He worked in many countries: his opera *Cristoforo Colombo* was produced in Havana (1847) and he conducted the 1st performance of *Aida* in Cairo (1871). Besides operas he wrote music for his instrument.

Botticelli Sandro, born Alessandro Filipepi (*c.* 1445–1510). Italian painter. Born in Florence, B. lived at the time of the city's greatest intellectual and artistic flowering, which coincides roughly with the reign of Lorenzo the Magnificent (1449–92). He was trained or influenced by Fra Filippo *Lippi and by the two Pollaiuolo brothers. In 1470 he painted the figure *Fortitude*, one of 7 'Virtues', commissioned from P. Pollaiuolo (all now in the Uffizi). Another teacher or influence was unquestionably Verrocchio. Thus B. was prepared for his career by those masters who represented all that was most vital in Florentine painting. To this he brought a rare talent for draughtsmanship and a very unusual temperament. 19th-c. writers on art have been responsible for creating an almost legendary figure, making B. the very type of the Renaissance painter: in fact, he was by no means typical. The picture of B. as a lyrical painter, bringing back to life the myths of the Golden Age of Greece must also be modified. It relies on those paintings B. was commissioned to paint by patrons such as Lorenzo the Magnificent, and his cousin, Lorenzo di Pier Francesco de' *Medici who set the subjects from Poliziano, Marsilio Ficino and classical authors, and who restrained B.'s natural temperament. The most famous of these paintings of classical myths are *The Birth of Venus*, the *Primavera*, *Pallas Subduing a Centaur* (all Uffizi) and *Venus and Mars* (N.G., London). Thoughtful, but serene, they have coloured men's ideas about classical antiquity since they were painted. With the madonnas and such large works as *The Adoration of the Magi* (versions: Uffizi; N.G., Washington; N.G., Edinburgh; and N.G., London) they are the best known of B.'s works. B. probably reveals himself more fully, however, in such paintings as *The Calumny of Apelles* (Uffizi), another classical subject, where the story from Lucian is told with effects that are strained to the point of frenzy. The drawn and troubled figure of the Baptist in the *St Barnabas Altarpiece* (Uffizi) is obviously close in feeling to similar figures by A. Castagno, but there is something about it which disturbs the serenity of the whole picture. Such elements are even more pronounced in the *Deposition* (Brera, Milan) and in the same subject in the Alte Pina., Munich. We know that when Savonarola proclaimed his religious crusade against the vanities of Renaissance Florence at the end of B.'s life, B. became one of his followers. Very little is certain about his life that is not based upon Vasari, but it seems likely that in the *Mystic Nativity* (N.G., London) which is dated 1500/1501, and which has an inscription referring to the Apocalypse and the 'troubles of Italy', the reconciliation between the angels and the fallen angels at the birth of Christ gives a significant clue to the divisions in B.'s own personality.

However great his inner turmoil, his life seems to have been relatively tranquil for the times. He won early recognition for his talent. Between 1481 and 1482 he was in Rome painting

Jan Both. *Scene in Rome.*

Botticelli. *Fortitude*

Botticelli. *The Birth of Venus.* See also colour plate 43

Botticini. *The Apostle St Andrew*; tabernacle at the Collegiata, Empoli

Bouchardon. Fountain in the Rue de Grenelle

Bottle glass, mid-17th c.

frescoes in the Sistine Chapel with a number of the leading painters. Vasari claims that he lost much of the reputation he had built up after this by taking time from painting to illustrate Dante. These drawings show an incredible gift for draughtsmanship (*Beatrice and Dante in Paradise*, formerly Kupferstich Kabinett, Berlin). B. was prosperous enough by the end of the c. to be running a large workshop, but with the revolutions in painting brought about by Leonardo and Michelangelo, and his own ill-health in old age, B.'s popularity appears to have diminished. After his death he was often forged but seldom imitated.

Boucher. *Pan and Syrinx*

Botticini Francesco di Giovanni called (*c.* 1446–97). Florentine painter who imitated distinguished contemporary painters such as Verrocchio and Botticelli; critical opinion has differed considerably as to which works can be attributed to B. Definitely by him is a tabernacle (commissioned 1484) in the Mus. della Collegiata, Empoli.

bottle glass. The manufacture of glass wine-bottles began in England in the mid 17th c.; at first they were bulbous with long necks. There was often a pad of glass on the shoulder of the bottle bearing the date. The bottles were made of a dark green or brown b. g. The colour is characteristic of unrefined glass since natural silica often has traces of iron in it.

Bouchardon Edmé (1698–1762). French sculptor strongly influenced by classical sculpture during a stay in Italy. His works include the fountain in the Rue de Grenelle, Paris and the *putti* on the fountain of Neptune, Versailles. His brother and pupil JACQUES-PHILIPPE (1711–53) worked at the Swedish court.

Boucher François (1703–70). French court painter and decorative artist, the truest exponent of the rococo style. He studied under F. Lemoyne and first worked on engravings after Watteau. In Italy (1727–31) B. was influenced by Tiepolo. In the 1740s he obtained the patronage of Madame de Pompadour; he painted several portraits of her and through her influence became chief painter to Louis XV in 1765. His superficial but graceful, delicately coloured, frivolous and endlessly inventive variations on pastoral and mythological themes were exactly attuned to the artificiality of Louis XV tastes. He also executed delightful designs for Beauvais and Gobelins tapestries. J.-H. Fragonard was his pupil.

Nadia Boulanger

Boucicault Dion(ysius) (1820–90). Irish-born playwright and actor who went to the U.S. in 1853. His plays, often adaptations, included *London Assurance* (1841), *The Corsican Brothers* (1852), *Grimaldi* (1855), and the melodrama *Octoroon* (1859), about slavery. He also wrote several plays with Irish settings, e.g. *The Colleen Bawn* (1860) and *Arrah-na-Pogue* (1864). B. appeared with his wife AGNES KELLY ROBERTSON (1833–1916) in most of these plays.

Boudin (Louis) Eugène (1824–98). French painter. He worked mainly in and around Deauville and Trouville and is famous for his pictures of choppy seas, windy skies and fashionable visitors. He painted out of doors and introduced *Monet to this method. B.'s style marks the transition between that of Corot and the impressionists; he exhibited at the 1st impressionist exhibition (1874).

Bouffons, Guerre des. The war between the music of France (Rameau) and of Italy (Pergolesi and the *opera buffa*) which raged in Paris in the early 1750s.

Boughton Rutland (1878–1960). English composer, largely self-taught and much influenced by Wagner. With the poet R. Buckley, B. ran a series of operas and concerts at Glastonbury intending to establish an English *Bayreuth, for operas on the Arthurian legend. B.'s operas include *The Immortal Hour* (1914), libretto by Fiona Macleod, and *Alkestis* (1924). B. also wrote the choral drama *The Birth of Arthur*, symphonies, symphonic poems and chamber music.

Bouguereau (Adolphe) William (1825–1905). The most revered French academic painter of his day. His harmony of composition and technical skill, as displayed in his female nudes, were superb but his subjects banal.

Boulanger Lili (1893–1918). French composer and in 1913 the 1st woman ever to win the Grand Prix de Rome for music. Besides her winning cantata *Faust et Hélène* (1913) she wrote orchestral, incidental and chamber music, more choral works and songs. She was the sister of Nadia B.

Boulanger Nadia (1887–). French teacher of composition, conductor and composer and the sister of L.B. Through her very numerous

Boulle commode; made for the King's room in the Trianon. Also *ébénistes

Boulton. Silver sauceboat and cover

pupils she has exerted a great influence, particularly on U.S. composers. As a conductor she has popularized French music old and new in England and produced magnificent recordings of vocal works by Monteverdi in 1937, important in the revival of his music.

Boule-de-suif (1880). Short story by *Maupassant.

boulevard. Originally, a promenade laid out on the site of the demolished ramparts of a walled town (as, e.g., in Paris); hence the modern meaning–a wide, tree-lined street.

boulevard drama. A term deriving from the late 19th-c. French theatre and used to describe elegant, sophisticated, commercial comedies.

Boulez Pierre (1925–). French composer, a pupil of Messiaen. In 1945 he became musical director of J.-L. Barrault's theatre co. His music developed from a study of 12-note techniques, especially the music of Webern, and in its original instrumental colours has been affected by Indonesian *gamelan music, being also reminiscent of Debussy. Characteristic are frequent changes of time signature and complexity of rhythms, regulated on principles derived from an extension of 12-note theories (*serial music). His works include: *Polyphony X* (1951) for 18 solo instruments; *Le Soleil des Eaux* (1948), settings of words by R. Char; *Marteau sans maître* (1955), after texts by Char, for alto voice, flute, viola, guitar, vibraphone and percussion; *Doubles* (1958) for orchestra; 2 piano sonatas and *Structures* (1956) for 2 pianos. B. has also composed electronic music.

Boulle. A family of French ébénistes of whom the most famous was ANDRÉ-CHARLES (1642–1732). In his workshop the most characteristic technique (to which he gave his name) was an inlay of brass and tortoiseshell, sometimes with coloured foil behind. This gives 2 veneers: a positive or *première-partie* and a negative or *contre-partie*, the part in tortoiseshell in one being in brass in the other.

Boult Sir Adrian (Cedric) (1889–). British conductor. B. studied at Leipzig under A. Nikisch, conducted a season of Diaghilev's Ballets Russes, and toured the Continent with modern English music. In 1930 B. became conductor of the B.B.C. Symphony Orchestra, which under him acquired a European reputation; in 1950 he became conductor of the London Philharmonic Orchestra.

Boulting John and Roy (1913–). The B. twins have collaborated as film producers/directors (usually alternating roles) since 1937. Notable films: *Thunder Rock* (1942), *Brighton Rock* (1947) from Graham Greene; *Seven Days to Noon* (1950); *Private's Progress* (1955). In recent years they have concentrated on satirizing British institutions: *Lucky Jim* (1957); *I'm All Right Jack* (1959); *Heavens Above* (1962).

Boulton Matthew (1728–1809). One of the great 18th-c. manufacturers of fine ware, besides being a leading industrialist and engineer and the partner of James Watt. His silverware was mainly in the neo-classic style, and he employed designers like Adam, Flaxman and Chambers. B. also produced garnitures, clocks and other objects in Blue-John (Derbyshire fluorspar), marble and other stones, often elaborately decorated with ormulu. He also made extensive use of *Sheffield plate.

Bourdelle (Émile) Antoine (1861–1929). French sculptor, painter and designer, for several years Rodin's assistant. Rodin's influence can be seen in the strong lines and vigorous movement of B.'s work, e.g. *Hercules the Archer* (1909; M.M.A., Paris) but B. was also affected by his own study of ancient Greek and Egyptian art. His output includes frescoes and reliefs for the Théâtre des Champs-Elysées (1912), monumental work and many portrait busts.

Bourdichon Jehan (*c.* 1457–1521). French court painter and illuminator, a follower of J. Fouquet. Of his religious paintings and portraits only a triptych (Pinakothek, Naples) has been identified and his fame rests on his illuminated mss, e.g. *Hours of Anne of Brittany* (completed 1508; Bibliothèque Nationale, Paris). In part this follows the Gothic style of 15th-c. illuminators, but his scenes are often more naturalistic and sometimes show the marked influence of Italian paintings, particularly by Perugino; he was the 1st French artist to be influenced by the Italian Renaissance.

bourdon. A low-pitched, quiet-toned organ stop.

Bourdelle. *Hercules the Archer*

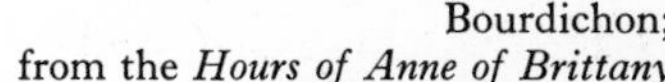

Bourdichon; from the *Hours of Anne of Brittany*

Bouts. *Last Supper*

Bourges cathedral

Bourdon Sébastien (1616–71). French painter of portraits, historical and religious subjects and landscape. In Rome (1634–7) he executed pastiches after Castiglione, P. van Laer, Claude and N. Poussin. Returning to Paris, he gained a great reputation and was one of the founders of the Paris Academy of Painting and Sculpture (1648). From 1652 to 1654 he was court painter to Queen Christina of Sweden.

Bourgeois Loys (b. *c.* 1510). French Huguenot composer who lived for a time in Geneva. He largely established the contents and notation of the Huguenot Psalter and also publ. harmonized psalm colls and a treatise on teaching music.

Bourgeois gentilhomme, Le (1670). Comedy by *Molière.

Bourges cathedral France. One of the largest of Gothic cathedrals (begun 1190) and remarkable for its double aisles (the inner aisles have a *triforium and *clerestory, features usually found in the nave only) and wealth of 13th-c. stained glass.

Bourget Paul (1852–1935). French critic and novelist. His psychological novels about the leisured classes revolve round some crisis of conscience; his later books were heavily affected by his Roman Catholic and monarchist beliefs. His criticism, e.g. *Essais de psychologie contemporaine* (1883) and *Nouveaux essais . . .* (1886), influenced by Taine, is now thought more valuable than his novels.

Bourke-White Margaret (1904–). U.S. photo-journalist. A star reporter for *Fortune* and *Life* since 1930, B.-W. has won world recognition for photo-essays covering such diverse subjects as Soviet Russia's 1st 5-Year Plan, the breaking of the sound barrier, and the Jesuits of America. Her books, *Dear Fatherland, Rest Quietly*; *Shooting the Russian War* and *Purple Heart Valley*, are classics of World War II.

Bournonville August (1805–79). Danish dancer and choreographer who studied at the Royal Danish Ballet School and under Vestris, who greatly influenced him. The most popular of his ballets, *Napoli* (1832), and others are still in the repertoire of the Royal Danish Ballet and his principles are generally followed in modern Danish classical ballet.

bourrée (French). Dance in quick duple time and beginning with an up beat. It was adopted by the court of Louis XIV and was often included in 18th-c. dance suites.

Boutens Pieter Cornelis (1870–1943). Dutch poet. His main theme was the beauty of ultimate reality, revealed through nature and responded to by man in solitude. Using an impressionistic idiom of great subtlety he combined strict and intricate stanza form with rhythmic freedom. B. also made trs from Aeschylus, Sophocles and Plato and trs. the *Odyssey* (1937).

Boutique Fantasque, La. 1-act ballet with choreography by Massine; music from Rossini, arranged by Respighi; and décor by Derain; 1st performance 1919.

Bouts Dirk (*c.* 1415–75). Early Netherlands painter who united in his work the influence of the brothers van Eyck and of Rogier van der Weyden, possibly his master. An objective painter, he was concerned with a detached observation of reality and an intellectual approach to spatial problems, to perspective and composition. This is evident in the *Eucharist* triptych (St Peter, Louvain) where a contemporary banqueting scene is transformed by an austere geometry into the pathos of the *Last Supper*. The *Hades* panel of the *Last Judgement* (Louvre) triptych reveals a more tender lyricism in expression and characterization of resignation and grace.

Bouvard et Pécuchet (1881). Novel by *Flaubert.

Bow. Soft-paste *porcelain from the factory at Stratford-le-Bow, London. At its best, between 1748 and 1759, Bow produced porcelain of a very high quality. It is best known for the many figurines which were produced from the earliest days; for table-wares, many of which were in the oriental tradition of decoration; and for fine flower paintings of a distinctive style and colouring. T. Frye, the principal patentee of the factory, made the 1st practical use of bone ash, in a porcelain recipe.

bow. Used to vibrate the strings of such musical instruments as the violin and viol families. It is a stick with horse hair stretched along its length between the tip and an adjustable nut which can be used to tighten the hair.

Bourke-White. *The Plantation* (1937)

Bourdon. *Martyrdom of St Peter*

The shape was standardized by the French violinist F. Tourte (1745–1835); before Tourte the stick was parallel to the hair and enabled, with the flatter *bridge then used, the playing of 3- or 4-part chords as written in Bach's unaccompanied violin sonatas. The so-called Bach bow is a 20th-c. invention. BOWING: the way the bow is used, e.g. how many notes on one stroke, whether up or down strokes, etc.; it affects the phrasing of the music.

Bow Clara (1905–65). U.S. film star. As Bardot stood for the 1950s, B. symbolized the Jazz age; the flapper girl of *It* (1927).

Bowdler Thomas (1754–1825). English man of letters. He rendered Shakespeare suitable for family reading by altering or deleting passages which he considered obscene or distasteful. He also prepared a similar ed. of Gibbon's *The History of the Decline and Fall of the Roman Empire*. Hence 'bowdlerize'.

Bowen Elizabeth (Dorothea Cole) (1899–). Anglo-Irish novelist and short-story writer, whose books include *The Death of the Heart* (1938), *The Heat of the Day* (1949), *A World of Love* (1955).

Bowen York (1884–). English pianist and composer. His music includes 2 symphonies and other orchestral music, 3 piano concertos (no. 1, 1904), violin and viola concertos, chamber music and much piano music.

Bowles Paul (Frederic) (1910–). U.S. writer and composer. B. has written much incidental music, film music, ballets, operas, e.g. *The Wind Remains* (1943), libretto by Lorca, orchestral and chamber music and songs. His music characteristically has heavy scoring for wind and percussion and original use of rhythm. Besides short stories and poems, B. has also written the novels *The Sheltering Sky* (1949) and *Let it come down* (1952).

Bowles Rev. William Lisle (1762–1850). English poet and critic. His *Fourteen Sonnets . . .* (1789) were simple and direct enough to excite the young Coleridge. In 1806 he publ. a critical ed. of Pope blaming him for neglecting natural images and emotions. For this he was attacked by Byron; Coleridge, Wordsworth and Southey rallied to B.'s support.

box-set. Theatrical term for a set (on a proscenium stage) in the form of a room with 3 walls; the audience see the action through the 'missing' 4th wall.

Boyce William (*c.* 1710–79). English composer and organist, a pupil of M. Greene. Among other posts B. was, from 1736, composer to the Chapel Royal and organist (1758–69), resigning because of encroaching deafness, and (1755–79) Master of the King's Band. B. wrote much church music, but his great work was his *Cathedral Music . . .* (3 vols, 1760–72) 'being a collection in score of . . . compositions . . . by . . . English masters of the last 200 years'. B. also wrote for the stage and his best music is instrumental. It includes 12 overtures, 12 trio sonatas and 8 symphonies. These last, originally overtures, were ed by C. Lambert.

Boyd Arthur (1920–). Australian painter, mainly self-taught. B. fought in the Australian army during World War II and has since established a considerable reputation. Since 1959 he has been working in London. His painting is romantic and sensual, using and creating myths, as Nolan does, but exhibiting a gentler and more personal flavour. Works include a huge sculpture for the Olympic Games pool, Melbourne, 1956.

Boydell Brian (Patrick) (1917–). Irish composer. His music, which shows a strong reaction against the folk-music influences important to his immediate predecessors, includes *Five Joyce Songs* (1946), *In Memoriam Mahatma Gandhi* (1948) and *Meditation and Fugue* (1956) for orchestra.

Boydell John (1719–1804). English engraver and printseller and publ. In 1786 he began to commission the best artists of the day, including Reynolds, Romney, Fuseli and A. Kaufmann, to paint pictures illustrating Shakespeare (engravings of these appeared in an ed. of Shakespeare publ. 1802) which he exhibited in his gal. in Pall Mall.

Boyer Charles (1898–). French-born film actor working mainly in the U.S. His fame as 'the Great Lover' stems from *The Garden of Allah* (1936) opposite Dietrich and *Marie Walewska* (1937) with Garbo; his other films include *Madame de . . .* (1953). He now plays character parts, with considerable skill.

Boyhood (1854). Novel by Tolstoy.

Elizabeth Bowen

Boyd. *Bride drinking from a pool* (1960)

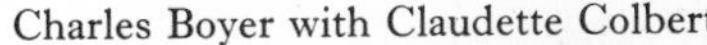

Charles Boyer with Claudette Colbert

William Boyce

Bow figure: *Spring*

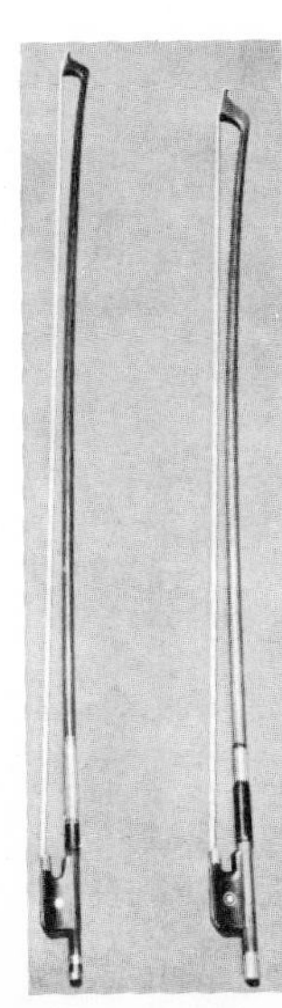

Modern viola and cello bows on the model standardized by Tourte

Bracket-clock; late 17th c.

Brady. *Northern artillery in action*

Cartoon of Brahms

Boyle Kay (1903–). U.S. novelist, short-story writer and poet. She was first interested as a novelist, in psychological analysis but later concentrated more on plot. Novels include *Death of a Man* (1936), *Primer for Combat* (1942), about Occupied France, *A Frenchman Must Die* (1946) and *Generation Without Farewell* (1959); short stories, *The White Horses of Vienna . . .* (1936); poems, *American Citizen* (1944).

Boyle Roger, Earl of Orrery (1621–79). One of the 1st English writers of heroic drama whose plays, which included *The Tragedy of Mustapha . . .* (1665) and *The Black Prince* (1667), influenced Dryden. He also wrote the prose romance *Parthenissa* (1654–69).

Boy with Green Hair, The (1948). Film directed by J. *Losey.

braccio: *gamba

Bracciolini Francesco (1566–1645). Italian poet. Works include the mock-heroic *Dello scherno degli Dei* (1618–26), in 20 cantos, and the serious heroic poem *Della croce racquistata* (1605, 1611). B. also wrote tragedies.

Bracciolini (Gian Francesco) Poggio (1380–1459). Italian humanist most important for his discovery, in monastic libraries, of copies of many lost classical works, including works by Lucretius and Quintilian. B. was also a first-class, if scurrilous, polemicist, e.g. the *Liber facetiarum*, largely against the clergy, which started a fashion for colls of satirical anecdotes. B. wrote excellent dialogues and letters, and a history of Florence.

Brachvogel Albert Emil (1824–78). German playwright and novelist whose melodramatic tragedy *Narziss* (1856; English adaptation *Narcisse the Vagrant*, 1877) gained European fame. Of his other plays and novels (also essentially theatrical) only *Friedemann Bach* (1858; English adaptation 1875), on J. S. Bach's eldest son, is still read.

Brackenridge Hugh Henry (1748–1816). U.S. clergyman and writer, author of the 4-vol. comic novel *Modern Chivalry* (1792–1815) satirizing politics and frontier life.

bracket. In architecture, a horizontal support projecting from a wall or pier.

bracket-clock. A 17th- or 18th-c. clock provided with its own matching bracket or wall-support. Portable clocks generally came to be known as both mantel- and bracket-clocks.

Bradbury Ray (1920–). U.S. writer of science fiction, plays and scripts for radio and film. He devises highly imaginative futuristic situations to analyse human behaviour in fantastic environments. Books include *The Illustrated Man* (1951), *The Golden Apples of the Sun* (1953), *Fahrenheit 451* (1953), *The October Country* (1955) and *A Medicine for Melancholy* (1959).

Bradstreet Mrs Anne (1612?–72). The 1st British-American colonist to publ. poetry. The coll. *The Tenth Muse lately sprung up in America . . .* (London, 1650) showed heavy dependence on F. Quarles, Spenser and the French Protestant writer Du Bartas. Later pieces, e.g. the reflective nature poem *Contemplations* (1678), are now considered her best.

Brady Mathew (1823–96). U.S. photographer who, with the assistance of A. *Gardener and Timothy *O'Sullivan photographed the American Civil War, producing a unique coll. of plates depicting the battlefields, the military leaders, the statesmen, and even the shabby soldiers themselves.

Brae June (1917–). British ballet dancer who became a principal with the Sadler's Wells Ballet in 1936. With them she created the roles of the Black Queen in *Checkmate* (1937) and the Woman in Helpmann's *Adam Zero* (1946).

Brahms Johannes (1833–97). German composer and also concert pianist of his own works. B. received his 1st music lessons from his father, a double bassist in Hamburg theatres. In his early teens he worked as a bar pianist but in 1853 was engaged for the Hanover court band by Joachim, who also gave B. an introduction to Liszt at Weimar. From there B. went to Düsseldorf, where he met the Schumanns, Robert acclaiming his genius in the *Neue Zeitschrift für Musik.* For a time B. was deeply in love with Clara, and their correspondence continued until her death. In 1863 B. settled in Vienna. In 1860, with Joachim and 2 others, he had publ. a manifesto against the neo-German school led by Liszt and Wagner and the feud between him and the neo-Germans was long and bitter. B. rejected their

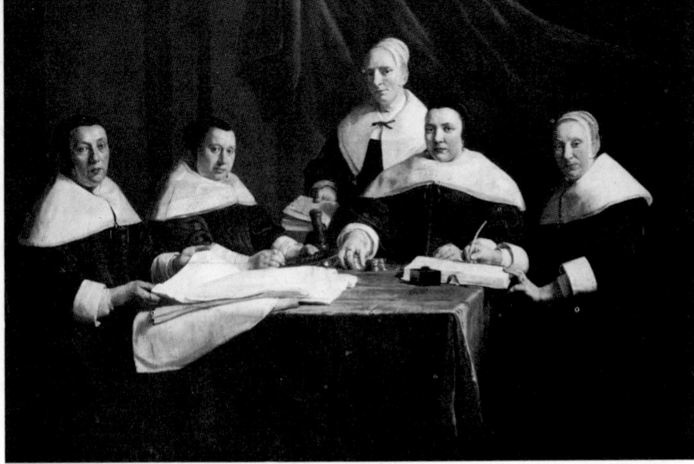

Jan de Braij. *Regentesses of the Haarlem Orphanage*

programmatic and literary approach and ignored Liszt's symphonic poem form, developing rather the classical forms as left by Beethoven, e.g. the sonata form and the variation, which B. used extensively. Up to 1876 (the completion after 20 years of B.'s 1st symphony) Beethoven's stylistic influence marks B.'s music but thereafter it gains independence. At its best B.'s music has rhythmic complexity, lyrical inspiration yet often rich sonorities, great fecundity in thematic development and transmutation yet strict formal organization.
The following are some major works. Orchestral: symphonies, no. 1 in C min. (1876), no. 2 in D maj. (1877), no. 3 in F maj. (1883), no. 4 in E min. (1885); *Variations on the St Anthony Chorale* or *On a theme by Haydn* (1873): *Academic Festival Overture* (1880), *Tragic Overture* (1880). Concertos: no. 1 in D min. for piano (1858), no. 2 in B♭ maj. for piano (1881); in D maj. for violin (1878); in A min. for violin (1878); in A min. for violin and cello (1887). Choral: *A German Requiem* (*Ein deutsches Requiem*, 1857–68), text from Luther's trs. of the Bible. Chamber music: piano quintet in F min. (1864), string quintet in G maj. (1890), clarinet quintet in A min. (1891) and 2 string sextets. Piano works: *Variations and fugue on a theme by Handel* (1861) and many sonatas. B.'s 200 songs, influenced by folk-music, show extreme sensitivity in the setting of poetry to music and the integration of accompaniment and melodic line; most famous are the *4 Serious Songs* (1896).

Braij (Bray) Jan de (d. 1697). Dutch portrait painter and architect, son and possibly pupil of SALOMON (1597–1664), also a painter and architect. Jan worked in Haarlem. His best paintings are of young women or groups such as *Regentesses of the Haarlem Orphanage* (Haarlem Mus.).

Brain Aubrey (Harold) (1893–1955). English horn virtuoso, father and teacher of Denis B; professor at the R.A.M., 1923–55. E. Smyth's concerto for violin, horn and orchestra (1927) was written for him. B. used a French type of *horn, not the more usual German instrument.

Brain Dennis (1921–57). English horn virtuoso, the most brilliant performer of this c. Like his father Aubrey he used a French-type horn, producing a full and powerful tone unusual for this instrument. Works written for him include a concerto by Hindemith and the serenade for tenor, horn and strings by Britten. B. was killed in a car crash.

Braine John (Gerard) (1922–). English novelist. B. produced in 1957 *Room at the Top* (filmed 1959), the story of a young man's ruthless determination to succeed. Other novels are *The Vodi* (1959): a man's surrender to a childhood fantasy in a fight against despair; *Life at the Top* (1962); and *The Jealous God* (1964).

Bramah Ernest. Pseud. of Ernest Bramah Smith (1869?–1942). English writer, author of story colls in a mock-Chinese idiom which humorously exploit Western notions of Chinese manners and speech (i.e. elaborateness, formality, understatement). The central figure is the mendicant story-teller Kai-Lung.

Bramante Donato (1444–1514). Italian architect, born near Urbino. He was a relation of Raphael and trained first as a painter. He epitomizes the high Renaissance; his distinguishing qualities are a real Roman grandeur and beauty of proportion. B. went to Milan *c.* 1482. He built there the church of S. Maria presso S. Satiro; the nave arcade is wholly Roman, with one big order supporting a flat entablature and a smaller order inside supporting arches, and a coffered vault. There was no room for a chancel so B. built a fake one in diminishing perspective. At Milan B. also built the E. end of S. Maria delle Grazie, with a dome over a square crossing, and the cloister of S. Ambrogio with a simple Doric arcade. In these works the structure is fundamentally Roman, the ornament florid Lombard Renaissance in style. B. had not yet studied Roman buildings at first hand. In 1491 he came to Rome to work for the pope. In Rome B. built the cloister of S. Maria della Pace (1500); the 'Tempietto' at S. Pietro in Montorio (1502), a tiny circular chapel with a hemispherical dome, surrounded externally by columns, accepted by later architects as the perfect classical building; the 'House of Raphael' (1509; demolished), a reconstruction of a Roman town house, the ground-floor being given over to shops, and the main rooms on the first-floor with paired pilasters on the façade; and the Cortile del Belvedere, Vatican (1505), a large courtyard with a staircase combining several Roman motifs, including the triumphal arch. When Pope Julius II demolished the thousand-year-old basilica of St Peter's, he

Bramante. Cortile del Belvedere, Vatican; 16th-c. print

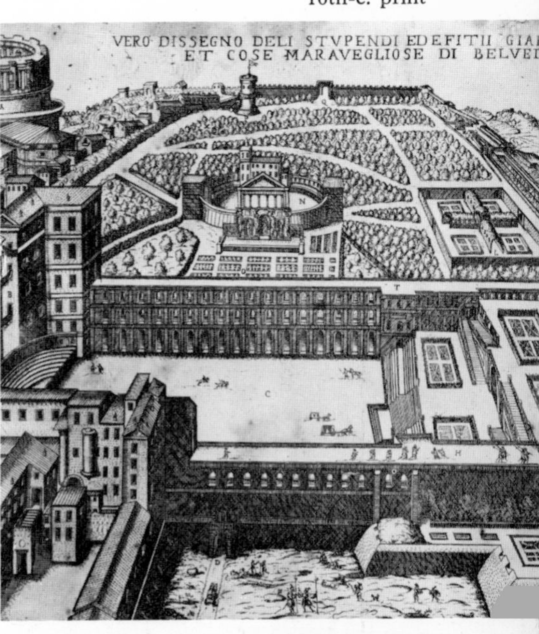

Bramante. 'Tempietto' at S. Pietro in Montorio

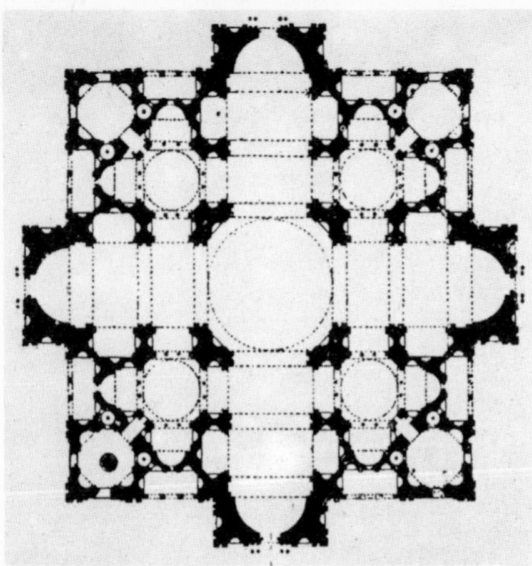

Bramante's plan for St Peter's

commissioned B. to design a new one (begun in 1506). B.'s plan has been obscured by later work, though Michelangelo used as much of it as he could. It was a Greek cross, with all the arms of equal length, and was to have had a classical portico, several sizes of order and a hemispherical dome, modelled on the Pantheon, over the central space. What the interior would have looked like can be seen in Raphael's painting of *The School of Athens*.

Bran, The Voyage of (8th c.). Early Irish work, partly prose, partly verse. Bran is summoned to 'The Happy Otherworld' in the Western Ocean, but is magically drawn to the Island of Women and kept there for, it seems, a year. However, he returns home to find himself a legendary hero. He tells his adventures and then magically disappears.

Brancusi. *Le Baiser* (1908)

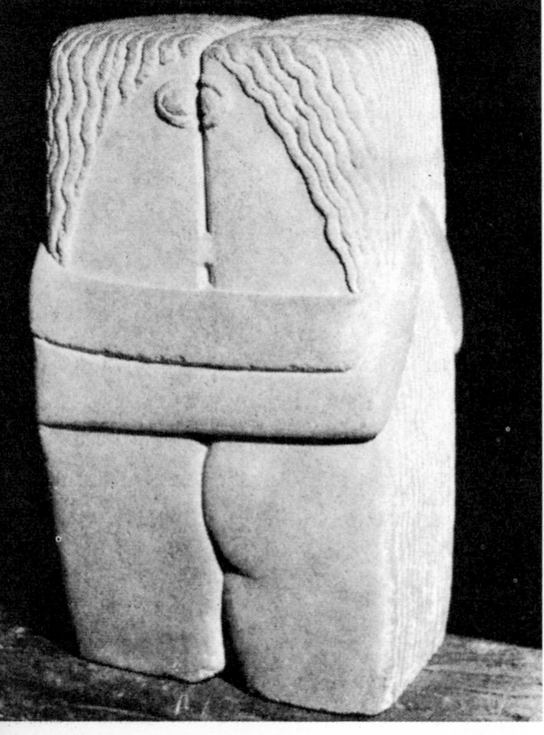

Brancusi Constantin (1876–1957). One of the outstanding sculptors of the 20th c., born in Rumania and trained initially as a carpenter and stonemason. He studied sculpture at Bucharest (1898–1902) and in 1904 settled in Paris for life. Here he soon shared the interest, common among Parisian painters, in African and other primitive arts, but the most absorbing influence on him was that of oriental art. Primarily a carver of wood and stone, he worked towards expressive strength through formal simplification, and *Le Baiser* (1908, Montparnasse) is in some ways a sculptural counterpart to Picasso's *Demoiselles D'Avignon* of 1907. But, unlike Picasso, B. always retained in his carvings something of the mystic symbolism of non-European art. *Le Nouveau-Né* (1915) and *Le Commencement du Monde* (1924) are universal symbols of life and fertility–simple but never symmetrical or geometrical.
His deep influence on 20th-c. sculpture is twofold. He brought about a revival of carving and had a craftsmanlike respect for the nature of his materials; his last years were devoted to polishing the surface of earlier works, e.g. *Fish* (1940s; New York). Secondly he endowed sculpture with an almost sacred significance: his carvings are objects for contemplation. 'B.'s mission was to make us shape-conscious.' (Henry Moore).

Brand (1866). Poetic drama by *Ibsen.

Brandenburg concertos. Instrumental works by J. S. *Bach.

Brandes Georg Morris Cohen (1842–1927). Danish-Jewish literary figure of great importance throughout Scandinavia as an apostle of such new European trends as *naturalism. A series of lectures delivered in Copenhagen during the 1870s, in which B. accused his contemporaries in Denmark of inbred insularity and attacked idealism in literature, provoked such antagonism towards him that he emigrated to Germany for a period. B. preached the doctrines of realism and advocated a new and more stringent criticism to be based on the antecedents and milieu of literary works and using principles of psychological analysis. With his friend Ibsen he was a principal figure in the modern breakthrough in Scandinavian literature. B.'s works include: trs of J. S. Mill, many important critical studies in European literature, and a series of biographies of great men, the result of the great influence which Nietzsche's work came to exert on B.

Brando Marlon (1924–). A disciple of the *Method school and undoubtedly the strongest, most individual player on the U.S. screen. He aims never to repeat a role, and since his début in 1950 he has substantially succeeded; his films include *A Streetcar Named Desire* (1951), *Viva Zapata!* (1952), Mark Antony in *Julius Caesar* (1953), *On the Waterfront* (1954), a musical and a western.

Brandt Bill (1906–). English photographer. B. was employed by the Home Office to document the life of Londoners during the Blitz. Since then he has devoted himself to the interpretation of scenes evoked in English literature. His recent works have been nude studies with perspective distortions, achieving abstract effects.

Brangwyn Sir Frank (1867–1956). British painter of detailed and brilliantly coloured murals, examples of which are to be found in the Royal Exchange, Skinner's Hall and Lloyd's Registry, London, and in Missouri State Capitol and the Rockefeller Center, New York. In addition to many drawings, paintings and etchings he also designed pottery, furniture and textiles.

branle. Round dance of French peasant origin popular in polite society in the 16th and 17th c.

Brant Sebastian (1457/8–1521). German writer. He was educated at the humanist univ.

Georg Brandes

Brandt.
Coal-searcher at East Durham (1936)

Brangwyn. *Bridge of Sighs, Venice*; pen drawing

of Basle and mixed with humanists at Strassburg, his home, from 1501, but his work is more medieval than Renaissance in tone. His famous *Das Narrenschiff* (1494; Eng. trs., 1509), in rhyming couplets, is a biting satire of contemporary follies (particularly clerical abuses) each one represented by a fool aboard the ship bound for Narragonia (the land of fools). The book's success, partly due to the woodcut illustrations (probably by Dürer) was immediate and European.

Braque Georges (1882–1963). French painter. He was born in Argenteuil, and served an apprenticeship to a painter-decorator in Le Havre in 1889. He moved to Paris in 1900 and then studied at the free Académie Humbert (1902–4). In 1905 he was deeply impressed by the room of fauve paintings at the Salon d'Automne (including Matisse, Derain and B.'s friends from Le Havre, Friesz and Dufy). The landscapes that B. painted (1906–7) at Antwerp (e.g. *Harbour Scene, Antwerp*, 1906; N.G., Ottawa), L'Estaque and Le Ciotat are in freely broken strokes of strong colour. B. considered these his 1st creative works.
In 1907, like so many of his generation, he was overwhelmed by the Cézanne Memorial Exhibition at the Salon d'Automne and this revelation was followed by his meeting with Picasso and the disconcerting distortions of the *Demoiselles d'Avignon*. B.'s ruthlessly simplified sombre-coloured landscapes and figures, e.g. *Nude* (1907–8; Cuttoli Coll., Paris), of the next 2 years show the extent of his change of direction and prepare the way for the development of cubism. B. is credited with the introduction into cubist painting of typography (in *Le Portugais*, 1911; K. mus., Basle) and of the decorator's techniques of wood-graining and marbling, but cubism was essentially the product of a remarkable partnership with Picasso ('marriage' was Picasso's word) which was broken by the war and B.'s call up in 1914. Cubism established above all the self-sufficient existence of the work of art, independent of reality, that was implicit in Cézanne's late landscapes. In looking beyond the superficial appearance of their subjects, Picasso and B. created a precedent which has contributed in one way or another to most subsequent developments in European painting and sculpture, both figurative and abstract.
Seriously injured in 1915, B. returned to Paris in 1917 where, apart from summers at Varengeville, he spent the rest of his life. His earliest post-war paintings returned to synthetic cubism with a stronger palette; *La Guitariete* (1917; K. mus., Basle).
From 1920, although still related to his cubist experience in their formal improvisation, his paintings are less obviously disciplined. The qualities which distinguished his cubist paintings from Picasso's–his fluent painterliness and his natural ability as a rich but subtle colourist–predominate in a work like *Guitar and Jug* (1927; Tate). The still-life has remained his principal theme from the *Gueridon* series (1927–30) to the climactic *Atelier* series (1949–55) in which the scope of the still-life extends to include the studio, the artist, his model and even the painting itself. The mysterious presence of the bird in flight is gently evocative in this as in other works by B., and the mood of his whole œuvre–apart from his short-lived excursion into surrealism in the early 1930s–is serene and harmonious.

Brasch Charles (1909–). New Zealand poet; his main work, done in the 1930s, explored the mythopoeic possibilities of his homeland. His poetry, even in *Disputed Ground* (1948), exhibits a search for national identity.

brass. An alloy consisting of copper and zinc, the colour varying according to the proportions. Harder than copper, b. wears better and can be cast easily. It is found in many forms both useful and decorative. Monumental brasses found in medieval churches are made of latten or sheet b. let into the pavement, walls or the top of a tomb. The details of the face, clothes, etc, are engraved on the surface; often they are not only of considerable fineness, but appear also to have been portrait likenesses.

Brassai Pierre. Originally Gyula Halasz (1899–). Hungarian-born photographer who documented the night-life of Paris in the 1920s and 1930s. His *Paris by Night*, publ. in 1933, presents a record of a vanished era.

brass instruments. Musical instruments made of metal, blown through a conical or cup-shaped mouthpiece and employing the principle of the *harmonic series. 2 features determine the tone colour of a b. i. The mouthpiece: either cup-shaped, as in the trumpet; or conical as in the horn. The bore: either cylindrical (trumpet), i.e. maintaining the same tube-diameter from mouthpiece to the flaring bell;

Braque. *Still-life with pitcher and bread* (1938)

Braque. *Violin and jug* (1910). Also *collage, *cubism

Brant.
Title-page of *Das Narrenschiff*

Brassai. *Tramp in the Street, Paris 1937*

Bertolt Brecht

Brecht. Berliner Ensemble performance of *Puntila*

or conical (horn), i.e. gradually widening in tube-diameter from mouthpiece to bell. The most important brass families of instruments are the trumpets, trombones, horns and tubas. The article on the harmonic series explains how a blown tube, e.g. a hunting horn, will give a series of notes which are widely spaced at the bottom of the series.

The natural horns and trumpets were simple tubes of fixed length and thus restricted to a certain harmonic series. Though it was possible, by adding crooks (lengths of tube) to change the pitch, i.e. the key of the instrument before playing, the large gaps between the lower harmonics were unbridgeable and a chromatic scale impossible. With the introduction of valves in the early 19th c., instantaneous alterations in length were made possible, and so, in effect, the player is able to select harmonics from other series. Mutes, i.e. stoppers of various shapes and sizes fitted into the bell, are used to produce different qualities of tone colour as well as to dampen the volume.

Bratby John (1928–). English painter of domestic interiors. B. was the most outspoken member of the short-lived New Realist group (the 'Kitchen Sink school') which emerged in London in the early 1950s as a reaction against contemporary abstraction. B. has also written novels.

Bratby. *Coach-house door* (*c.* 1959)

Brauner Victor (1903–). Rumanian painter working mainly in France and associated with the surrealist movement.

Brave New World (1932). Novel by Aldous *Huxley.

Brecht Bert(olt) (1898–1956). German playwright and poet. He emigrated in 1933, lived in the U.S. from 1941 but returned in 1948 to East Berlin, where he founded the theatrical group Berliner Ensemble. B. was a convinced if unorthodox Communist; his revolutionary anti-dramatic 'epic theatre' was intended to present man as 'the sum total of all social conditions'. The keynote of this purposive theatre–writing, staging and acting–is *Verfremdung* ('estrangement', 'alienation'), the breaking of illusion, the distancing of the audience from what is being enacted, the making strange of what is normally accepted, thereby drawing attention to its alterability. This is achieved by various types of commentary (e.g. intercalated songs, choruses), by word-play, by the use of masks, placards and projections, and by numerous other structural, linguistic and technical devices.

A master of language–deceptively simple, unaffected yet unorthodox, economical to the point of terseness, yet vivid and varied–B. has created memorable scenes (rather than closely knit plays) and memorable characters. His large output as a poet may well outlive his work for the theatre. With great formal versatility (and a particular penchant for balladry and the epigrammatic) he expresses a multiplicity of emotions and convictions in a strikingly casual, colloquial idiom, with the occasional aid of parody and profanity. After several turbulent, aggressively anti-bourgeois plays, notably the–in part–expressionistic *Baal* (1920) and *Trommeln in der Nacht* (1923), B. came to fame with *Die Dreigroschenoper* (1928, music by Kurt Weill; *The Threepenny Opera*, 1955), based on Gay's *Beggar's Opera*. Weill also wrote the music for B.'s next opera, . . . *Mahagonny* (1930), in which, as in the play *Die heilige Johanna der Schlachthöfe* (1932, music by Paul Dessau; *St Joan of the Stockyards*, 1956), American capitalism is bitterly satirized. In *Der gute Mensch von Sezuan* (1942; *The Good Woman of Setzuan*, 1948) 'badness' is seen as a product of capitalist society. . . . *Galileo Galilei* (1939; *The Life of Galileo*, 1952) contains a double-edged message concerning the scientist's responsibility towards science, society and self; *Mutter Courage* . . . (1939; *Mother Courage*. . . , 1941) is a graphic series of pictures illustrating the destructiveness of war. A like evangelism inspires the argument which rounds off *Der kaukasische Kreidekreis* (1944–5; *The Caucasian Chalk Circle*, 1948)–that things should belong to those who are good for them (children to the motherly, land to those who make it fruitful).

Bredero Gerbrand Adriaenszoon (1585–1618). Dutch poet and, in his youth, painter. His work resembles Dutch painting in its realism and his songs describe, with a genius for characterization, the kind of low life painted by D. Teniers the Elder. His comedies include *De Spaansche Brabander* (1618). B. also wrote excellent love-poetry, observing courtly conventions of diction but distinguished by spontaneity.

Breitinger Johann Jakob (1701–76). German-Swiss literary critic, professor at Zürich Univ. and associated with J. J. *Bodmer.

Clemens Brentano

Bresson. Florence Carrez in *Le Procès de Jeanne d'Arc*

Brett. *Val D'Aosta* (detail)

Bremer Fredrika (1801–65). Swedish novelist and feminist. Among her novels of upper-middle-class life *Grannarne* (1837; *The Neighbours*, 1842) is the best, the others suffering from sentimentalism and melodrama.

Brennan Christopher John (1870–1932). Australian poet. He was the first of the few Australian poets who have had an intimate knowledge of world literature, being influenced by French symbolists, particularly Mallarmé, with whom he corresponded. His poetry has an emotional and intellectual maturity and daring, comparable with any contemporaries abroad.

Brentano Clemens (Wenzel Maria) (1778–1842). German romantic poet. B. met the Schlegel brothers and L. Tieck at Jena Univ. With A. von *Arnim B. publ. *Des Knaben Wunderhorn* (1806–8). His own chief works were the 'unruly' ('*verwildert*') romantic novel *Godwi* . . . (1801), the fragmentary but delicate prose work *Aus der Chronika eines fahrenden Schülers* (1818) about the middle ages, short stories *Märchen* and the *Lore Lay* (1800), based on the Lorelei legend of a beautiful water nymph who lured sailors on to a rock in the Rhine.

Bresdin Rodolphe (1825–85). French graphic artist called 'Chien-Caillou'. He owed his nickname to Champfleury, who made him the subject of *Chien-Caillou* (1847), a story about an engraver. He led an eccentric restless life and created a curious visionary art appreciated by Murger and Baudelaire.

Bresson Robert (1907–). French film director. After his 1st feature, *Les Anges du Péché* (1943, dialogue by Giraudoux), B.'s films increasingly dispensed with environmental settings from *Les Dames du Bois de Boulogne* (1945, from Diderot, dialogue by Cocteau) through *Le Journal d'un Curé de Campagne* (1950) to *Un Condamné à Mort s'est Échappé* (1956) which used as a basis for its spiritual investigations a meticulously detailed account of a prison escape. A similar technique was employed in *Pickpocket* (1960) and *Le Procès de Jeanne d'Arc* (1962); the whole trial is shot in medium shots of the key participants without the luxury of general long shots or close-ups.

Breton André (1896–). French poet, leader and principal theorist of surrealism. He publ. 3 surrealist manifestoes (1924, 1930, 1934) and founded surrealist research laboratories which employed Freudian techniques in studying the subconscious. His works include: the poem colls *Mont de piété* (1919), *Les Pas perdus* (1924) and *Poèmes* (1948); he also wrote the partly autobiographical 'novel' *Nadja* (1928).

Brett John (1831–1902). English landscape painter who, after 1870, specialized in scenes of the Cornish coast. Under *Pre-Raphaelite influence, he aimed to achieve an exact detailed imitation of nature. *The Stone Breaker* (1858; Walker Gal., Liverpool) and *Val D'Aosta* (1859; Coll. Sir William Cooper) were much admired by Ruskin.

Brettingham Matthew (1699–1769). English Palladian architect who supervised the building of Holkham Hall, Norfolk, to the designs of William Kent, though he later described himself as architect. His own work includes Benacre Hall, Suffolk; several country-houses in Norfolk; N.E. wing of Kedleston Hall, Derbyshire; No. 5 St James's Square, London and other houses (now demolished) in St James's Square and Pall Mall. His son MATTHEW (1725–1803) was also an architect.

Breu Jörg (*c.* 1480–1534). Augsburg painter and draughtsman whose subjects included portraits, altarpieces and battle scenes. He travelled in Austria, where he executed his earliest signed work, an altarpiece in the monastery of Herzogenburg; he later visited Italy. The style he developed was close to that of Burgkmair.

Breuer Marcel (1902–). Hungarian-born architect and furniture designer, subsequently influential as a teacher. At the age of 22 he was teacher in charge of the carpentry shops at the Bauhaus, and during World War II he was again teaching with Walter Gropius, this time at Harvard.

He designed the furniture for the Bauhaus building at Dessau, introduced the chromium-plated tube into furniture design and pioneered the cantilever chair; later he designed the 1st successful aluminium furniture, and in 1935, with the Isokon co. in England he developed a range of very successful plywood chairs.

His practice as an architect was at first small, but his work was extremely elegantly designed and detailed. He practised in England (1935–7) in partnership with F. R. S. Yorke, designed some of the best modern houses in England

Brettingham. Norfolk House, St James's Square (demolished in 1938)

Breu. *Madonna with SS Barbara and Catherine*

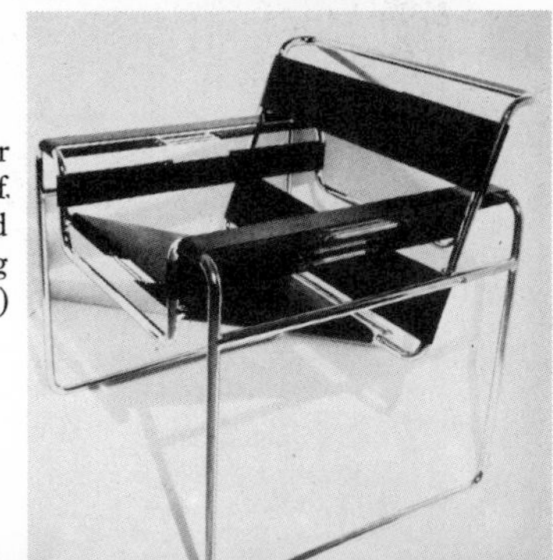

Breuer. Chair with frame of nickel-plated steel tubing (1925)

and then settled in the U.S. He designed many houses in New England in a pleasantly relaxed idiom. Then in the late 1950s, following his work on the Unesco building in Paris, he received large commissions, but these were rarely carried out with the verve of his small houses.

Breuil Abbé (Henri Édouard Henri Prosper) (1877–1961). French archaeologist who discovered (1902) the paleolithic cave paintings at Font-de-Gaume and Combarelles and made important copies there and in other places (including Altamira). He publ. a number of illustrated monographs.

Robert Bridges

Brian (William) Havergal (1876–). English composer, self-taught. His music, in a strongly individual romantic idiom, includes: symphonies, e.g. the 'Gothic' for large chorus and orchestra, performed 1962; 4 English suites for orchestra; 2 symphonic poems and *Prometheus Unbound* (based on Shelley) for solo voices, chorus and orchestra.

Brianza Carlotta (1867–?). Italian dancer, one of the *Blasis pupils responsible for bringing Italian influences to the Imperial School at St Petersburg. She first appeared there in 1887 and 3 years later created the title-role in *Petipa's *Sleeping Beauty* at the Maryinsky Theatre.

bride: *lace

Brideshead Revisited (1945). Novel by Evelyn *Waugh.

Paul Bril. *Scene in Rome*

bridge. That part of a stringed instrument which transfers the vibrations of the strings to the resonating body. Bowed instruments (e.g. violins) use a 'pressure bridge'; the strings, anchored at the tail-piece and peg, pass over the b., which is held in place on the instrument's belly by their pressure. Plucked instruments (e.g. the guitar) use a 'tension bridge'; this is stuck to the instrument's belly, serving as a tail-piece anchorage as well as transferring vibrations. In keyboard stringed instruments the b.s are the 2 bars between which the strings vibrate.

Bridge Frank (1879–1941). English composer, conductor and violist. His music, originally late romantic in tone, became in the late 1920s avowedly modernistic, showing particularly the influence of Scriabin. His chamber music includes the quartet in E min. (1906), piano quintet (1905), 3rd string quartet (1926). Orchestral works include the suite *The Sea* (1910–11), *Enter Spring* (1930). He wrote an opera, *The Christmas Rose.*

Brise-soleil. Le Corbusier: Supreme Court, Chandigarh

Bridge, The (1930). Poem by Hart *Crane.

Bridge of San Luis Rey, The (1927). Novel by Thornton *Wilder.

Bridge on the River Kwai, The (1957). Film directed by D. *Lean.

Bridges Robert Seymour (1844–1930). English poet; poet laureate 1913. Intimate friend and correspondent of G. M. *Hopkins, whose poems he publ. in 1918. B.'s longer poems, verse dramas such as *Prometheus the Firegiver* (publ. 1883), the narrative poem *Eros and Psyche* (publ. 1885), and the philosophic *Testament of Beauty* (publ. 1929) incline to frigidity. He is best in short poems marked by a lyrical realism, e.g. *London Snow* or 'The upper skies are palest blue'.

Bridget St (1303–73). Sweden's national saint. She was a noblewoman who in middle age took up religion. Her *Revelations*, dictated in Swedish but surviving only in Latin trs., are bold and racy in style.

Bridie James. Pseud. of Dr Osborne Henry Mavor (1888–1951), Scottish dramatist. He is best known for *The Anatomist* (1930); his many other plays include *Tobias and the Angel* (1930), *A Sleeping Clergyman* (1933) and *Mr Bolfry* (1943). His plays are often marred by weak conclusions, though his best work allies comedy and horror, fantasy and wit with an underlying seriousness of purpose.

Brief Encounter (1945). Film directed by D. *Lean.

bright-cut. A form of engraving found on silver and jewellery, dating from the late 18th c. and particularly associated with Birmingham. Instead of the narrow incision, the grooves were shallow and cut at different angles to produce a 'bright' effect.

Brighton Rock (1938). Novel by Graham *Greene.

Bril(l) Mattheus (1550–83) and Paul (1554–1626). Flemish landscape painters who worked in Rome and received papal patronage. They developed a style between the panoramic scenes of Flemish artists and the ideal landscapes of N. Poussin and Claude. Paul B.'s landscapes painted on copper exerted some influence on Elsheimer.

Brillat-Savarin Jean-Anthelme (1755–1826). French lawyer and gastronome who wrote *Physiologie du goût . . .* (2 vols, publ. anon. 1825; Eng. trs., 1884). B. was a good conversationalist and his famous book is a coll. of anecdotes and aphorisms related but not always relevant to the theme of good eating.

Bringing up Baby (1938). Film directed by H. *Hawks.

brise-soleil. Architectural term for a screen used to diminish the glare of the sun on windows; although now scientifically designed and of considerable complexity, fundamentally the b.-s. filters light through a semi-transparent material or consists of slats (sometimes adjustable) which deflect the light, i.e. in basically the same way as the Venetian blind.

Bristol. Centre of a number of English factories producing tin-glazed earthenware in the late 17th and the 18th c., at first 'maiolica', later often excellent delft. Soft-paste *porcelain was produced (*c.* 1750–2), and the *Plymouth hard-paste porcelain factory moved to B. (1770–81).

Bristol cathedral: the chancel vault

Bristol tea-caddy, *c.* 1760 (two views)

Bristol garniture of vases, mid-18th c.

Bristol cathedral England (1298–1330). One of the best examples of the decorated style. It is a *hall-church, the chancel vault (which has liernes but no transverse arches and no ridge-rib) being supported on flying struts across the aisles, forming a sort of skeleton vault. (The nave is 19th c. by *Street.)

Bristol glass. After London and Stourbridge, Bristol had the largest number of glass houses in England at the end of the 17th c., flint-glass being made there from the middle of the 18th c. Much opaque white glass was made at Bristol, often imitating the shape and decoration of Chinese porcelain, which was very popular at the time. Blue glass was also made there but the popular belief that all opaque white and blue glass comes from Bristol is false.

Bristol Old Vic. Leading English repertory co. It is based at the Theatre Royal, Bristol, which, built in 1778, is one of the only 2 surviving 18th-c. theatres. The other is at Richmond, Yorkshire.

Bristowes (corrupted from Bristols). Crystals from Bristol much used in early 18th-c. English and Flemish jewellery.

Britannia glasses. During the Seven Years War (1756–63) and to celebrate its close, a number of glasses were produced engraved with ships, portraits of Frederick the Great of Prussia and figures of Britannia seated with her shield and spear and sometimes an olive branch; they often bear such patriotic legends as 'Success to the British Fleet 1759.' These goblets and wine-glasses are sometimes faceted, a very early appearance of this technique used on drinking-glasses.

Britannia metal. An alloy of tin and regulus of antimony resembling silver. It was discovered by James Vickers in the late 18th c., and was chiefly produced at Sheffield.

Britannia standard. Introduced by an Act of Parliament in 1697; it increased the amount of silver in each troy pound by 8 dwts from 925 to 958 parts fine per thousand. The standard silver mark became a figure of Britannia seated and makers had to change their marks. In 1719 there was a reversion to the old standard, though the B. s. was retained and can still be used.

Britten (Edward) Benjamin (1913–). English composer, conductor and pianist, born at Lowestoft in Suffolk. He showed remarkable precociousness, composing his 1st 'Simple' symphony (revised 1934) when aged 12; his teachers were F. Bridge and J. Ireland for composition and A. Benjamin for piano. In 1933 B. left the R.C.M., in 1934 his *Fantasy Quartet* for oboe was performed at the Florence I.S.C.M. and in 1937 his *Variations on a Theme of Frank Bridge* at the Salzburg Festival. During this period he also wrote much music for plays and films (especially documentaries). From 1939 to 1942 B. was in the U.S., where his *Sinfonia da Requiem* (1940) was first performed. The opera *Peter Grimes*, given its première at Sadler's Wells in 1945, brought B. a huge European reputation. In 1947 he founded the English Opera Group and in 1948 inaugurated the Aldeburgh Festival.

Britannia glasses

Benjamin Britten. Also **Billy Budd*

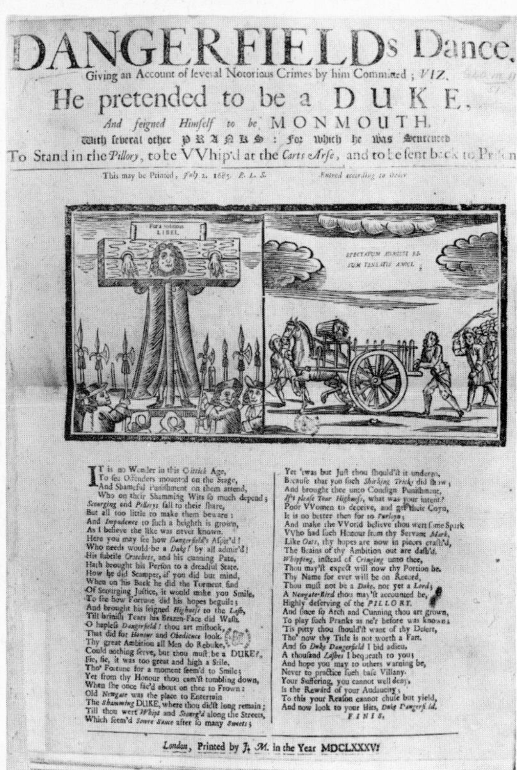

DANGERFIELDs Dance.

Giving an Account of ſeveral Notorious Crimes by him Committed; *VIZ.*

He pretended to be a DUKE.

And feigned Himſelf to be MONMOUTH.

With ſeveral other PRANKS: For which he was Sentenced

To Stand in the *Pillory*, to be VVhip'd at the *Carts Arſe*, and to be ſent back to Priſon

This may be Printed, *July* 2. 1685. *R. L. S.* *Entred according to Order*

IT is no Wonder in this *Gittick* Age,
To ſee Offenders mounted on the Stage,
And Shameful Puniſhment on them attend,
Who on their Shamming Wits ſo much depend;
Scourging and *Pillorys* fall to their ſhare,
But all too little to make them beware:
And *Impudence* to ſuch a heighth is grown,
As I believe the like was never known.
Here you may ſee how *Dangerfield's* Aſpir'd!
Who needs would-be a *Duke!* by all admir'd!
His ſubtile *Crotchets*, and his cunning Pate,
Hath brought his Perſon to a dreadful State.
How he did Scamper, if you did but mind,
When on his Back he did the Torment find
Of Scourging Juſtice, it would make you Smile,
To ſee how Fortune did his hopes beguile;
And brought his feigned *Highneſs* to the *Laſh*,
Till briniſh Tears his Brazen-Face did Waſh.
O hapleſs *Dangerfield!* thou art miſtook,
That did for *Honour* and *Obedience* look.
Thy great Ambition all Men do Rebuke,
Could nothing ſerve, but thou muſt be a DUKE?
Fie, fie, it was too great and high a Stile,
Tho' Fortune for a moment ſeem'd to Smile;
Yet from thy Honour thou cam'ſt tumbling down,
When ſhe once fac'd about on thee to Frown:
Old *Newgate* was the place to Entertain
The *Shamming* DUKE, where thou did'ſt long remain;
Till thou wert *Whipt* and *Scourg'd* along the Streets,
Which ſeem'd *Sowre Sauce* after ſo many *Sweets*;

Yet 'twas but Juſt thou ſhould'ſt it undergo,
Becauſe that you ſuch *Shirking Tricks* did ſhow;
And brought thee unto Condign Puniſhment,
If't pleaſe Your Highneſs, what was your intent?
Poor VVomen to deceive, and get their Coyn,
It is no better then for to *Purloyn*;
And make the VVorld believe thou wert ſome Spark
VVho had ſuch Honour from thy Servant *Mark*,
Like *Oats*, thy hopes are now in pieces craſh'd,
The Brains of thy Ambition out are daſh'd.
Whipping, inſtead of *Cringing* unto thee,
Thou may'ſt expect will now thy Portion be.
Thy Name for ever will be on Record,
Thou muſt not be a *Duke*, nor yet a *Lord*;
A *Newgate-Bird* thou may'ſt accounted be,
Highly deſerving of the *PILLORY*.
And ſince ſo Arch and Cunning thou art grown,
To play ſuch Pranks as ne'r before was known;
'Tis pitty thou ſhould'ſt want of thy Deſert,
Tho' now thy Title is not worth a Fart.
And ſo *Duke Dangerfield* I bid adieu,
A thouſand *Laſhes* I bequeath to you;
And hope you may to others warning be,
Never to practice ſuch baſe Villany.
Your Suffering, you cannot well deny,
Is the Reward of your Audacity;
To this your Reaſon cannot chuſe but yield,
And now look to your Hits, *Duke Dangerfield*.
FINIS.

London, Printed by *J. M.* in the Year MDCLXXXV.

Broadside, 1685

Broadwood. Piano used by Chopin (1848)

Broederlam. *Annunciation*: detail from the altar-wing at the Mus., Dijon

The sources of B.'s inspiration range from the Elizabethan composers and Purcell to Stravinsky but his idiom is unmistakably individual. His music is tonal and is characterized by economy, the ability to generate atmosphere with the sparest means, lyricism and an infallible sense for the setting of words to music. A fine pianist, B. is an outstanding accompanist, particularly of the tenor, Peter Pears, for whom B. has written many of his songs.
The most important works in his large output include the following. Operas: *Peter Grimes* (1945), libretto based on G. Crabbe's poem *The Borough*; *The Rape of Lucretia* (1946), a chamber opera; *Albert Herring* (1947), libretto based on a story by G. de Maupassant; the children's entertainment *Let's Make An Opera* (1949), libretto based on Blake's poem *The Chimney Sweep*; *Billy Budd* (1951), based on the story by Melville; *The Turn of the Screw* (1954), based on Henry James's story; the 1-act *Noye's Fludde* (1958) for children's voices, from the Chester mystery plays; and *A Midsummer Night's Dream* (1960), based on Shakespeare. Choral works: *A War Requiem* (1963) in which poems by Wilfred Owen, killed in World War I, are set in juxtaposition with the Latin requiem; the cantata *St Nicholas* (1948); the *Spring Symphony* (1949) for solo voice, chorus and orchestra; *Hymn to St Cecilia* (1942) for unaccompanied chorus; *A Ceremony of Carols* (1942) for treble voices and harp. Instrumental music: a violin concerto (1939); 4 sea interludes from *Peter Grimes*; *The Young Persons' Guide to the Orchestra* (1946), variations and fugue on a theme by Purcell (1945). Song cycles: *Les Illuminations* (1939), words from poems by Rimbaud, for high voices and strings; *Serenade* for tenor, horn and strings (1943), with words from English poets of the 15th–19th cs; *Seven Sonnets of Michelangelo* (1940) for tenor; *Holy Sonnets of John Donne* (1945); Canticle No. 3 *Still Falls the Rain*, words by E. Sitwell, for tenor, horn and piano; and settings of English folk-songs.

broad manner: *fine manner

broadside. A popular ballad, primarily of the 16th and 17th c., based on a news item. These b. ballads, dealt with political events or the latest sensation; they were printed on a single sheet of paper decorated with a woodcut, and the name of the popular tune they were to be sung to was given. B. ballads were sold on the streets of English towns from the late 16th c. up to the mid 19th c.

Broadwood (i.e. John Broadwood and Sons). The oldest firm of keyboard instrument makers in the world. Founded in London *c.* 1728 by the Swiss cabinet maker Burckhard Tschudi (anglicized as Burkat Shudi) whose daughter married John Broadwood (1732–1812), who had joined the firm in 1761. B.'s customers included the Empress Maria Theresa and Haydn. B. presented a piano to Beethoven.

Broca Philippe De (1933–). French film director. His first 3 comedies, built around the person of Jean-Pierre Cassel, *Les Jeux de L'Amour* (1959), *Le Farceur* (1960) and *L'Amant de Cinq Jours* (1960), revealed serious emotional truths behind the gay and cynical façade. Later films include *L'Homme de Rio* (1964).

Brockes Barthold Heinrich (1680–1747). German writer whose *Irdisches Vergnügen in Gott* (9 parts, 1721–48) was the 1st nature poetry in German. B. was influenced in his close observation and praise of nature by such English writers as J. Thomson, whose *The Seasons* he trs. (1745).

Brod Max (1884–). Austrian-Jewish novelist and playwright; friend, executor and biographer of Kafka (*Franz Kafka*, 1937; Eng. trs., 1947). Works include the novels *Tycho Brahes Weg zu Gott* (1916; *The Redemption of Tycho Brahe*, 1928), *Reubeni, Fürst der Juden* (1925; *Reubeni, Prince of the Jews*, 1928) and poetry *Neue Gedichte* (1949).

broderie anglaise (French, 'English embroidery') or eyelet work, A form of open embroidery in which holes of various shapes are cut or pierced in the ground fabric, usually white or pale blue. They are then overcast, and the borders of the work finished with a scallop. Modified types using surface stitches such as simple running and satin stitch are Ayrshire, Madeira or Swiss work.

Broederlam Melchior (active 1381–*c.* 1409). Painter born at Ypres. About 1385 he became painter to Philip the Bold, Duke of Burgundy, who commissioned from him 2 wings for an altar in the Carthusian monastery at Champmol (1392–9; Mus., Dijon). These depict the Annunciation, the Visitation, the Presentation

Charlotte Brontë

Emily Brontë: painting by Branwell Brontë

Anne Brontë: from a watercolour by Charlotte Brontë

in the Temple and the Flight into Egypt, and are an early example of international Gothic style.

Broken Blossoms (1919). Film directed by D. W. *Griffith.

broken chords. (1) In keyboard, lute or harp music, chords whose notes are sounded successively, the bass note usually coming first and on the beat, rather than simultaneously. This 'spreading' of chords is a form of *ornamentation and for various effects notes other than the bass are sometimes struck first. (2) On bowed instruments, chords executed as *arpeggios often because of the technical limitations of the instrument (*bow).

Bromfield Louis (1896–1956). U.S. novelist whose early books *The Green Bay Tree* (1924), *Possession* (1925), *Early Autumn* (1926) and *A Good Woman* (1927) showed sensitivity and descriptive powers. Other works: *The Strange Case of Miss Annie Spragg* (1928), *The Rains Came* (1937) and books about his Ohio farm, Malabar.

Bronston Samuel. U.S. film producer, Bessarabian-born and Sorbonne-educated. B. worked steadily as an independent producer, and made *A Walk in the Sun.* He started making the spectacular films for which he is famous, in 1959, and had his 1st big success with *El Cid.* The films he made in his Madrid studios largely lack the personal characteristics of their directors *Mann and *Ray.

Brontë Family, The. English writers. The 3 sisters Charlotte, Emily and Anne, and their brother Branwell, the children of the curate of Haworth, Patrick B., spent most of their lives at the lonely parsonage (their mother died in 1821) yet produced some of the most remarkable works in English literature. In 1846 they publ. *Poems by Currer, Ellis and Acton Bell*, pseuds they continued to use in their individual productions. ANNE (1820–49) wrote the novels *Agnes Grey* (1847) and *The Tenant of Wildfell Hall* (1848), the bulk of which is the story of an unhappily married woman. CHARLOTTE (1816–55) was the only one of the sisters who achieved contemporary success. Her novel *The Professor* was rejected by the publishers, and appeared only in 1857, over 10 years after it was written; but *Jane Eyre* (1847), received immediate and lasting appreciation of its sure characterization and simple, sincere 1st-person narrative. It is based on her humiliating experiences as a schoolgirl and governess, but centres on a fictional love-affair with the mysterious, irascible Mr Rochester. She also wrote *Shirley* (1849), in which the heroine is a portrait of her sister Emily, and *Villette* (1853), based on periods of study in Brussels with Emily (1842) and alone (1843). She married in 1854. EMILY (1818–48) was the only true poet in the family (e.g. *Last Lines*), a gift she expressed most successfully in the novel *Wuthering Heights* (1847). It surpasses her sisters' productions, achieving great emotional intensity and creating an almost supernatural atmosphere in a bleak Yorkshire moorland setting. The book is dominated by the demonic figure of Heathcliffe, the wild gipsy boy who exacts a terrible revenge for the wrongs done to him. (Patrick) BRANWELL B. (1817–48) became a drunkard and opium addict. He has often been proposed as the author of *Wuthering Heights*, perhaps because Emily described passion with an intensity unusual in 19th-c. woman writers. The theory was also plausible because the 4 children were very close and invented collective fantasies on which they drew as creative individuals.

bronze. An alloy of copper and tin, harder and more suitable for casting than copper; the qualities of an ancient b. are enhanced by the *patina which develops on it. From early times the virtues of the metal were realized and both the Greek and the Chinese sculptors achieved a standard that has never been excelled. With the fall of the Roman empire the secret of the casting of figures (*cire perdue) was largely lost but was revived at the Renaissance when working reached a new peak. Fine b.s have been found at the African centres of Benin and *Ife.

Bronze Horseman, The (1841). Poem by *Pushkin.

Bronzino, Il (1503–72). Florentine mannerist painter, pupil of J. da Pontormo. B. was painter to Cosimo I de' Medici, for whom he undertook decorative works and many court portraits, e.g. those of Eleanor of Toledo and her son, and Lucrezia Panciatichi (both Uffizi). He used fine rich colours but portrayed his sitters with unrelaxed posture and faces of inscrutable reserve. His allegorical paintings and religious subjects, which appear devoid of deep or religious feeling, show typical mannerist figure

Bronzino. *Venus, Cupid, Folly and Time*

Brook. *Lord of the Flies*

Brooks. Burt Lancaster in *Elmer Gantry*

De Brosse. S. Gervais

elongation and include *Christ in Limbo* (1552; Mus. di S. Croce, Florence) and *Venus, Cupid, Folly and Time* (N.G., London), remarkable for its harshly metallic flesh tones against a brilliant blue background. B. also wrote poetry.

Brook Peter (1925–). English theatre and film director. B. was director of Covent Garden Opera (1949–50) and (1962) appointed co-director of the Royal Shakespeare Co. Films include: *The Beggar's Opera* (1952), *Moderato Cantabile* (1960) and *Lord of the Flies* (1962).

Brook Kerith, The (1916). Historical novel by George Moore.

Brooke Rupert (Chawner) (1887–1915). English poet. Circumstances made him the most popular minor poet of the c. Writing with skill in the homely upper-middle-class mode of the Georgian movement, this young poet of charm, looks and undergraduate prestige (at Cambridge), died at sea in World War I and was buried on an Aegean island. Winston Churchill was instrumental in romanticizing him as the symbol of youth willingly sacrificing itself *pro patria*, partly on the strength of the patriotic sonnets in Brooke's posth. *1914 and other poems* (1915). The charm of his famous *Grantchester* was attuned by style and feeling to the nostalgia of the post-war years.

Brooks Richard (1912–). U.S. film director. B. was a reporter and worked in radio and theatre. He wrote 3 novels, including *The Brick Foxhole* (1945), which was filmed as *Crossfire*. He directed his 1st film in 1950, *Crisis*, about a South American dictatorship. *The Blackboard Jungle* (1955) had a great success for its treatment of high school violence and its introduction, as theme music, of the first rock'n roll number. His style allows much of the flexibility in genre of a younger Preminger. He was equally successful with a western, *The Last Hunt* (1955), and a Tennessee Williams adaptation, *Cat on a Hot Tin Roof* (1958). And if the colour experiments of *The Brothers Karamazov* (1958) failed they provided the foundation for his remarkable version of *Elmer Gantry* (1960), and for *Lord Jim* (1965).

Brooks Van Wyck (1886–1963). U.S. critic and biographer. In *The Wine of the Puritans* (London, 1908; New York, 1909), *America's Coming-of-Age* (1915), *The Ordeal of Mark Twain* (1920) and *The Pilgrimage of Henry James* (1925) B. developed the theory that American literature had been damaged and isolated from life by a dualism between aesthetic and material values produced by the Puritan tradition. In his 'Makers and Finders' including *The Flowering of New England, 1815–65* (1936), B. aimed to trace a valid tradition of U.S. literature.

Brorson Hans Adolf (1694–1764). Danish pietist clergyman and hymn writer. His hymn coll. *Troens Rare Klenodie* (1739) consisted largely of trs from the German but these were excellent Danish poetry in their own right.

Brosse Salamon de (1571–1626). French architect, grandson of Du Cerceau the Elder. He uses the classical elements in a massive, very French way. Chief works: Coulommiers (1613), a large château, never finished; the Palais du Luxembourg (1616), with rusticated garden-front to remind Marie de Medicis of the Pitti Palace; the Protestant 'Temple' at Charenton (1623) (demolished), based on Vitruvius's recipe for a basilica; S. Gervais, Paris (1616)–the W. front only–based on Anet.

Brothers Karamazov, The (1880). Novel by *Dostoyevsky.

Brouwer Adriaen (*c.* 1605–38). Flemish genre painter, mainly of low life, and landscape painter. He led a dissipated life and died of the plague at Antwerp. In his realistic, often dramatic, tavern scenes the vulgarities and rowdy emotions of the subjects are fully recorded. B. often used dark tones and thick, violent but economical brush-strokes; in his last years he painted sensitive impressionistic landscapes. B.'s genre pieces strongly influenced D. Teniers the Younger and A. van Ostade.

Brown Charles Brockden (1771–1810). 1st professional U.S. author. His best novels, *Wieland* (1798), *Ormond* (1799), *Arthur Mervyn* (2 parts, 1799, 1800) and *Edgar Huntly* (1799), relied more on pseudo-scientific phenomena and on analysing psychotic states than on the horror devices of the English *Gothic novel. B. was influenced by Godwin and his work was greatly admired by Shelley, Keats, Scott and Poe.

Rupert Brooke

Brouwer. *The Smokers*

Capability Brown.
Landscaped artificial lake at Blenheim Palace

Brown Clarence (1890–). U.S. film director. B. was one of M.G.M.'s most important contract directors. He made a number of *Garbo films including *Flesh and the Devil* (1927), *Anna Christie* (1930) from Eugene O'Neill and *Anna Karenina* (1935) from Tolstoy. He gained a certain critical acclaim for his film of Faulkner's *Intruder in the Dust* (1949).

Brown Ford Madox (1821–93). English painter, who was born in France and studied in Antwerp, Paris and Rome, where he met J. F. Overbeck. He settled in London, and in 1848 Rossetti became his pupil and introduced him to the *Pre-Raphaelites, who affected his work, e.g. *The Last of England* (1855; City Mus., Birmingham; small versions, Tate and Fitz. Mus., Cambridge), but he was never a member of the Brotherhood. He was a partner in the firm of Morris, Marshall, Faulkner and Co. (William *Morris).

Brown Lancelot (1715–83). English landscape gardener called 'Capability' through telling his clients that their estates had 'great capabilities'. He continued the reaction begun by Kent against the formal French garden. This English style, the greatest innovation in garden design in the 18th c., depended on the organization of natural landscape features, eliminating flower-beds, parterres, hedges, formal avenues, and walls. Ponds were drained to make fields or joined together to make a lake as at Blenheim. A reaction set in under H. *Repton.

Brown Thomas (Tom) (1663–1704). English writer whose satires gave rise to disputes with Dryden, R. Blackmore, J. Collier, and T. Durfey. He was author of the well-known rendering of a Martial epigram: 'I do not love thee, Dr Fell' (*Fell).

Brown Thomas Edward (1830–97). English poet, son of a clergyman in the Isle of Man. His best poems *Fo'c'sle Yarns* (1881) are partly dialect narratives of Manx life. He is unfairly known–and parodied–for his anthologized lyric *My Garden.*

Browne Sir Thomas (1605–82). English doctor and writer, the son of a mercer. He was educated at Winchester and Oxford and studied medicine at Montpellier, Padua and Leyden where he received his M.D. Oxford granted him another doctorate (1637). B. was a loyal though not active Royalist. He was knighted in 1671. Like many contemporaries B. combined scientific rationalism with superstition; on his testimony 2 women were executed for witchcraft. This combination of scepticism and faith appears in *Religio Medici* (authorized publ. 1643), a scientific man's religious credo.
His works contain a wealth of knowledge but are memorable chiefly for the baroque splendour and harmony of language which is latinized in construction and vocabulary. The last chapter of *Hydrotaphia, Urne-Buriall* (1658) is an example of flawless rhetorical prose. This treatise, arising from the discovery of burial urns in Norfolk, considers various burial customs and philosophizes on death.
Works include: *Pseudodoxia Epidemica* (*Vulgar Errors*) (1646), *The Garden of Cyrus* (1658), and the fascinating coll. *The Miscellaneous Writings . . .* (1946).

Browne William (1590/1–1643/5), commonly called 'W. B. of Tavistock'. English pastoral and lyric poet, friend of Jonson and Drayton. His chief work *Britannia's Pastorals* (3 books, 1613; 1616; 1852, unfinished) continues the mode established by Spenser, and associates Arcadia with his native Devonshire in verse of frequent beauty, appreciated by Milton, Keats and Tennyson. His lyrics, including *An Ode, Song of the Syrens*, and *Celadyne's Song* (in *Pastorals*, book 3), are often of the most subtle melodic brilliance.

Browning Elizabeth Barrett (1806–61). English poet. Elizabeth Barrett was already a poet of some repute when she met *Browning in 1846, and eloped with him the same year. She had publ. verse, essays and trs, including *Poems* (1844), containing the celebrated plea against child-labour, *The Cry of the Children.* She extolled the cause of Italian freedom in many poems, also writing *Aurora Leigh* (1856), the study of a modern love-affair, and *Sonnets from the Portuguese*, original love-poems addressed to her husband.

Elizabeth Barrett Browning: from a photograph

Browning Robert (1812–89). English poet. In 1846 he married Elizabeth Barrett (see above) and until her death they lived in Italy. B.'s recondite allusions, deliberate obscurity, and fondness for ellipsis earned him the reputation of a 'difficult' and daring poet, and his fame has since suffered. But his development of the colloquial manner, his human curiosity and energy, and the graphic power of his descriptions deserve to be remembered. His early

Robert Browning: painting by G. F. Watts

Brücke. *Painters of the Brücke Group* (1925) by Kirchner

Brücke. Kirchner: portfolio for Schmidt-Rottluff

works include: *Pauline* (1833), a shapeless love 'confession' influenced by Shelley, *Paracelsus* (1835), and *Sordello* (1840), an obscure study set in medieval Italy. W. C. Macready staged his historical tragedy, *Strafford*, in 1837. The 8 numbers of *Bells and Pomegranates* (1841–6), including *Pippa Passes*, and *Dramatic Romances and Lyrics*, established his literary reputation. *Men and Women* (1855) contains some of his best lyrics and dramatic monologues, a form which he made his own. His most ambitious work, *The Ring and the Book* (1868–9) is based on a 17th-c. Italian murder case. B.'s set of monologues presents the crime from different standpoints.

Browning Tod (1882–1944). U.S. film director. His *Dracula* (1931) is, with Whale's *Frankenstein*, the starting-point of the American horror film. He also directed the much-banned *Freaks* (1932), set in a circus and featuring grotesquely deformed but real human 'freaks'.

Browning Version, The (1948). Play by Terence Rattigan.

Bruant Libéral (*c.* 1635–97). French architect. He designed the Invalides (but not the church), on a grid-layout and with plain undecorated façades, and the chapel of the Salpêtrière Hospital–an ingenious building whose plan consists of a central octagon surrounded by 4 more octagons and 4 rectangles.

Bruce Patrick Henry (1880–1937). U.S. painter who worked in Paris (1907–30). He was first an adherent of fauvism, then of orphism, but abandoned this to make experiments in abstract structure with geometric shapes and pure colours. He finally left pure abstraction and constructed his pictures round recognizable motifs. He destroyed much of his work.

Bruch Max (1838–1920). German composer and conductor. Among other appointments he was conductor of the Liverpool Philharmonic Orchestra (1880–3) and professor in composition at Berlin (1891–1910). He is remembered for his 1st violin concerto in G min. (1868) and *Kol Nidrei* (1880) for cello and orchestra on a Hebrew melody, but in Germany his choral music was thought his best work. Folk-music of all nationalities fascinated B.; his own music, technically excellent, is highly eclectic.

Brücke, Die (German, 'The Bridge'). The 1st group of German *expressionist painters, founded at Dresden in 1905 and formally dissolved in 1913. Associated with it were E. L. Kirchner, the leading member, E. Nolde, K. Schmitt-Rottluf, M. Pechstein, E. Heckel and O. Mueller. The artists shared a common studio, cultivated the medieval guild ideal and also canvassed 'bourgeois' support with a lay membership scheme. The B. painters were inspired by Munch, Cézanne, Gauguin and Van Gogh, and by African and Pacific art. Their work was at first characterized by flat, linear, rhythmical expression and by simplification of form and colour, and their extensive use of the woodcut especially in posters, made it an important 20th-c. medium.

Bruckman Clyde (1894–1955). U.S. film director and script writer. B. worked with the famous silent comedy stars. He worked on the scripts of many Keaton films from 1923 and co-directed *The General*. He also directed 3 Harold Lloyd features and the 1st shorts starring Laurel and Hardy.

Bruckner Anton (1824–96). Austrian composer and organist born at Ausfelden. Appointed organist to Linz cathedral in 1856, he abandoned his career as a school-teacher for music. He was introduced to Wagner's music by his teacher O. Kitzer, met Wagner in Munich in 1865, and became his devoted admirer. In 1868 B. settled in Vienna as a teacher at the Conservatory. B.'s greatest work is in his 9 symphonies. In formal and thematic structure they extend the methods of Beethoven, in harmony and instrumentation they show strong Wagnerian influences, in their vast design these monumental works are magnificent formally coherent structures. B. himself reworked them and they were first performed in shortened versions; symphony no. 4 in E♭ is known as the 'Romantic' and no. 8 in C min. as the 'Apocalyptic'; no. 9 in D min. was unfinished. B. was a simple man with a simple Catholic faith; his church music (showing the impact of the 19th-c. movement to revive polyphonic methods) includes: 6 masses, among them *Missa Solemnis* in B min. (1854), a requiem, a Te Deum (1884), and motets; B.'s chamber music includes a string quintet (1879).

Bruegel. Family of Flemish painters flourishing in the 16th and 17th cs whose most

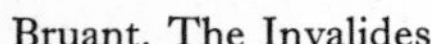

Bruant. The Invalides

Anton Bruckner

Jan Bruegel the Elder. *Flowers in a Vase*

important members are listed alphabetically below. Various spellings of the name have been used such as the later 'Breugel' and 'Brueghel'. The greatest of the family, Pieter B. the Elder, was also its founder.

Bruegel (Brueghel, Breugel) Jan the Elder (1568–1625). Flemish painter, the son of P. B. the Elder; he painted flowers, landscapes and Garden of Eden subjects in a highly-finished manner which won him the nickname 'Velvet B.'.

Bruegel (Brueghel, Breugel) Jan the Younger (1600/2–78). Flemish painter, the close follower of his father, Jan B. the Elder. He often painted his highly-finished flower studies and landscapes on copper.

Bruegel Pieter the Elder (active 1551–d.1569). The last and one of the greatest of the early Netherlandish artists. B. was named for his birthplace, but there is no general agreement which of 3 possible villages this was. Moreover, his name is variously spelt. He signed his work Bruegel and Brueghel, while he was nicknamed 'Bruegel the Droll' or 'Peasant Bruegel', by later writers on art to distinguish him from other members of the family of painters he founded. Even the date of B.'s birth is uncertain, as are details of his training. Obviously an early influence on him was the work of Bosch (d. 1516) and it is likely B. was apprenticed to P. Coecke van Aelst, whose daughter he married in 1563. He was a master of the Antwerp Guild in 1551. Shortly afterwards B. journeyed extensively in Italy, probably as far south as Sicily, returning through the Grisons and the Tyrol. After his marriage B. moved from Antwerp to Brussels. There is much conjecture but little evidence regarding his position and attitude during the early years of the rebellion against Spanish rule, the religious controversy and the horrors of civil war. When B. died he left a family of imitators. He had established almost all the categories of later Flemish painting and his own paintings were highly priced. Yet, despite the admiration of Rubens and the fact that most of his paintings were quickly acquired for royal colls, B.'s reputation declined until the great revival of interest in his work within the last 50 to 60 years. B. earned a living for many years with drawings for engravings publ. by the humanist printseller, Hieronymous Cock. He probably painted in watercolour technique, but this work has been lost. About 40 paintings in oil and a few in tempera on linen survive. Briefly, the outstanding feature of B.'s style is its independence of Italian models at the time when most of his contemporaries in the Netherlands were already Romanists. In colour he favoured a muted palette of blue-greens, blue-greys and a wide range of browns, frequently enlivening the picture with points of clear colour, often yellow or red. He extended painting to include the countryside in all seasons, moods and weathers, following medieval books of the hours and tapestries. He also showed much the same sympathetic but unsentimental interest in those who worked on the land. Between the labourers and their environment B. manages to establish a wholly original relationship in visual terms, e.g. between the lean hunters and the countryside locked in winter–*Hunters in the Snow* (K. Mus., Vienna); the feeling of well-being won from nature–*The Corn Harvest* (Met. Mus.); or a steel-cold winter's day providing the background to an act of human brutality–*The Massacre of the Innocents* (K. Mus., Vienna). At times the landscape almost overpowers the activities of men, as the dramatic Alpine settings do in both *The Suicide of Saul* and *The Conversion of St Paul* (both K. Mus., Vienna), or the turbulent water in *Storm at Sea* (same). *The Peasant Dance* and *Peasant Wedding* (also K. Mus., Vienna) provide 'close-ups' of the peasants' happier hours. Throughout his life B. used everyday sayings and proverbs to draw personal and highly sophisticated morals on the condition of man. The mastery he came to achieve over his vast material, observed and imagined, can nowhere be better seen than by comparing his early, over-crowded *Netherlandish Proverbs* (Dahlem, Berlin) with the brilliantly composed late work *The Blind Leading the Blind* (Mus. N., Naples). 2 works showing the power of his imagination at its greatest are *Dulle Griet* (Mus. Mayer van der Bergh, Antwerp) and *The Triumph of Death* (Prado). The first, a satanic landscape peopled by all the devils of medieval folk-lore, has been a stimulus to poets, painters and also film producers in the 20th c., while *The Triumph of Death*, with its almost mechanical destruction of human life by thousands, has appeared grimly appropriate to aspects of our times.

Bruegel (Brueghel, Breugel) Pieter the Younger (*c.* 1564–1638). Flemish painter, the son of Pieter B. the Elder, he imitated the fantasy subjects of his father, earning the nickname 'Hell B.'. F. *Snyders was his pupil and his son, Pieter B. III, was also a painter.

Pieter Bruegel the Elder. *Dulle Griet*

Pieter Bruegel the Elder. *Peasant Wedding*

Pieter Bruegel the Elder. *Massacre of the Innocents* (detail)

Bruges: the belfry

Brunelleschi. Loggia of the Ospedale degli Innocenti

Brunelleschi. Dome of Florence cathedral

Bruges Belgium. Flemish city which became commercially prosperous in the 14th and 15th c. producing a wealth of fine late *Gothic secular architecture which (unusually) still survives: notably the town hall and the Cloth Hall with its 400-ft-high belfry.

Bruhn Eric (1929–). Danish dancer trained at the Royal Danish School, where he is now principal dancer. He has made many guest appearances in the U.S. and other countries, and although he has successfully tackled demi-character roles, is one of the finest contemporary classical dancers.

Brummell George Bryan (known as 'Beau Brummell') (1778–1840). English arbiter of fashion who elevated sartorial elegance (quiet, seemingly casual but in reality carefully precise) into an artistic exercise–his views culminated in French *dandyism. An intimate of George IV, B. was also celebrated for his wit; he died in France, in penury and squalor.

Brunanburh, The Battle of. Old English prose poem, included in The Anglo-Saxon Chronicle under the year 937, which deals with a battle between King Aethelstan and the Vikings supported by Welsh and Scottish forces. It is a song of triumph recounting the deeds of Aethelstan and his brother Eadmund and the rout of the invaders. There is a version in modern English by Tennyson.

Bruneau Alfred (1857–1934). French composer; most of his operas were based on Zola's work and Zola himself wrote librettos for 3 early ones.

Brunel Isambard Kingdom (1806–59). English civil engineer of French extraction, chief engineer of the Great Western Railway from 1833. He designed the railway bridge (1838) at Maidenhead, Berks., one of the largest brick bridges in the world; the Clifton suspension bridge (begun 1836) and the Royal Albert bridge, Saltash (1853–9). B.'s magnificent and beautiful structures embody the pride of a pioneer age, express their engineering function and enhance their landscape setting.

Brunelleschi Filippo (1377–1446). Florentine architect who began his career as a goldsmith and sculptor. In 1401, having lost the competition for the Baptistery doors (*Ghiberti), he went with Donatello to Rome, where he spent 3 years studying Roman ruins, earning his living as a goldsmith. All B.'s buildings had an enormous influence on later architects up to and including Michelangelo. He was the first deliberately to model himself on ancient Roman architecture, though this does not account for everything in his work. His church plans are more early Christian than Roman and many of his favourite motifs (e.g. patterning in marble) derive from the Tuscan Romanesque of the 12th c. (so-called 'proto-Renaissance'), for instance S. Miniato al Monte. His works are all in Florence. The dome of the cathedral (designed 1407; the lantern 1437), the largest dome since S. Sophia, is built of brick and partly based on Roman examples; the technique, however, is still Gothic–it is pointed in section, where Roman would have been hemispherical. The Ospedale degli Innocenti (1419), an open arcade of classical columns, closely following Roman models–is usually counted as the 1st Renaissance building. The church of S. Lorenzo (designed 1425) has classical arcades in the nave and a system of simple ratios in the plan. S. Spirito (1432) is similar to S. Lorenzo, but with the system of ratios extended to the elevation as well as the plan; B. planned the aisles to go right round the building, including the west end. Both S. Lorenzo and S. Spirito are longitudinal basilicas with transepts, the traditional Romanesque-Gothic plan; neither of the façades was ever begun. The Pazzi Chapel (1430) in the cloister of S. Croce has an exterior colonnade, small plain interior with dome, the ratios being marked out by patterns on the stone. S. Maria degli Angeli (1434), only partly preserved, had a centralized plan, influenced by Roman circular temples. B. also designed the heavily rusticated lower storeys of the Pitti Palace (1440).

Bruni Leonardo, called 'Aretino' (1374–1444). Italian humanist writer; his Latin history of Florence is remarkable for its careful treatment of facts, use of documents, attempt to discover historical causes and its perspective. B. also wrote biographies of Dante and Petrarch; the former, often based on sources now lost, is especially important. He produced valuable Latin trs of Greek classics.

Brunot Ferdinand (1860–1938). French philologist, author of a monumental and important *Histoire de la langue francaise. . .*; subsequent workers have continued it.

Brunel. Clifton Suspension Bridge

Isambard Kingdom Brunel

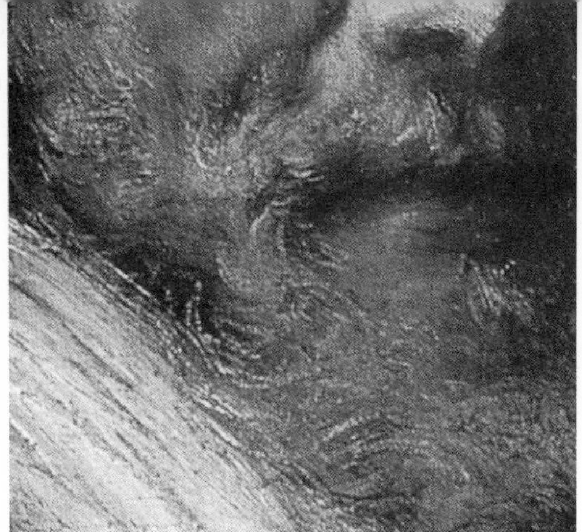

Brushwork:
detail from a Rembrandt portrait

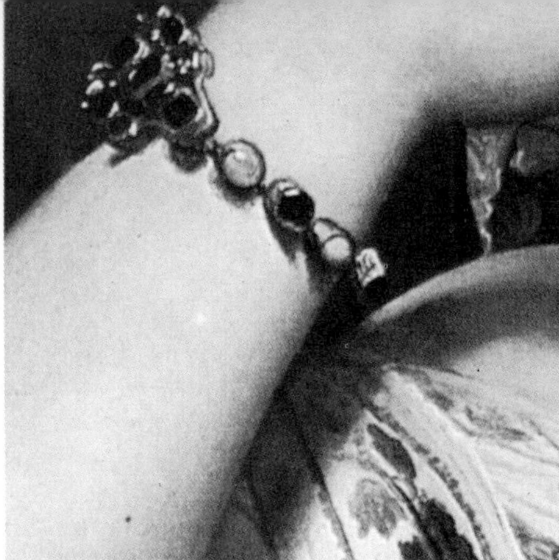

Brushwork: detail from Ingres's *Mme Moitessier seated*

Brushwork: detail from Van Gogh's *Pietà* after Delacroix

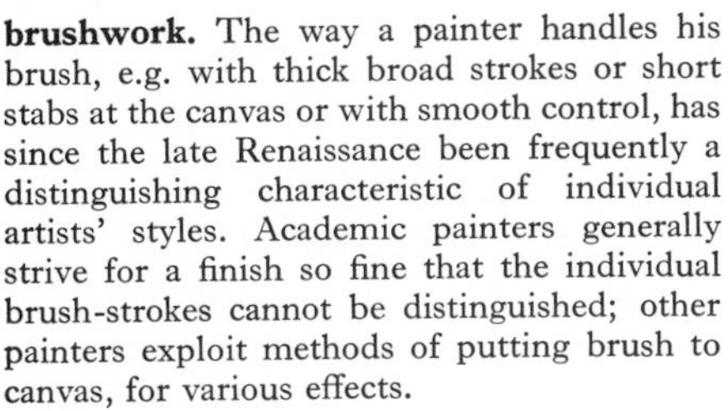

brushwork. The way a painter handles his brush, e.g. with thick broad strokes or short stabs at the canvas or with smooth control, has since the late Renaissance been frequently a distinguishing characteristic of individual artists' styles. Academic painters generally strive for a finish so fine that the individual brush-strokes cannot be distinguished; other painters exploit methods of putting brush to canvas, for various effects.

Brusselmans Jean (1884–1953). Belgian expressionist painter who moved from post-impressionism to severe formalized compositions which linked his work with primitive Flemish painting and gave him an isolated position among modern Flemish painters.

Brussels carpet. From the town of that name. A type of carpet, formerly hand-made but now universally machine-made, in which extra warp threads, longer than the foundation warp, are woven into the fabric to give a row of loops which project to give a pile. In the Wilton style of carpet the same technique is employed but the loops are cut open to form a thick pile.

Brussels lace. From the town of that name; it was first made in the 15th c. Motifs, usually floral, either needle point or bobbin made or both (*lace), are made separately from the net ground. In old B. l. the ground was worked with bobbins round the flowers: later the flowers were sewn to the net. Nets of various sized mesh are used together as background.

Brut. History by *Layamon.

brutalism. Architectural movement so called because of the emphasis it places on the unconcealed use of materials in modern building –steel girders remain exposed, concrete and brick walls are undisguised by stone facing or stucco–and by its aim of giving clear expression of structure and services, and insistence on the use of materials 'as found'. The movement originated in Britain in the work of Peter and Alison Smithson, who coined the term 'New B.' (1953); their school at Hunstanton (1954) was a landmark. The Park Hill Housing Estate at Sheffield (by Jack Lynn and Ivor Smith) is another example. Le Corbusier and Louis Kahn are taken as precursors.

Bruyn Bartholomaüs (1493–1555). German painter, chiefly of portraits of the wealthy bourgeoisie of Cologne, where he worked. His style of portraiture as exemplified in his portrait of Burgomaster Arnold von Brauweiler (Cologne Mus.) resembles that of Joos van Cleve. Some of his religious paintings show the Italianate influence of J. van Scorel.

Bryant William Cullen (1794–1878). U.S. poet. Early poems included one of his best, *Thanatopsis* in the style of Thomas Gray. In 1826 he joined the New York *Evening Post and* was ed. from 1829, becoming a major figure of New York's literary life. Most of his work was nature poetry and was influenced by Wordsworth.

Brygos painter, the. Unidentified Greek painter of the early 5th c. B.C. so called because 5 cups decorated by him have the potter's mark *Brygos epoisen*–'made by Brygos'. About 170 vessels have been identified as painted by him. Stylistic characteristics are violent movement, tenseness of line in drapery folds and economy of line in depicting nude figures. His style was much imitated. Later works show a decline in vitality.

Bryusov Valery Yakovlevich (1873–1924). Russian poet and novelist, one of the leading symbolists and important as a publ. of their work. B.'s writing was modelled on that of Verlaine and Poe. After the Bolshevik Revolution he was for a time in charge of the censorship.

Brzękowski Jan (1903–). Polish poet, critic and novelist, one of the founders of the Awangarda movement. Strong surrealist tendencies have set him apart from the main stream of the movement. B. has also publ. poetry in French.

Brzozowski Stanisław (1878–1911). Polish literary critic, novelist, dramatist and philosopher. In his critique of the Young Poland movement, he criticized the dissociation of life and art advocated by the movement, and stressed the social function of art.

Buchan John (1st Baron Tweedsmuir) (1875–1940). Scottish novelist, historian, biographer and statesman. Adventure stories such as *The Thirty-Nine Steps* (1915), *Greenmantle* (1916), *Prester John* (1910) are among his best work.

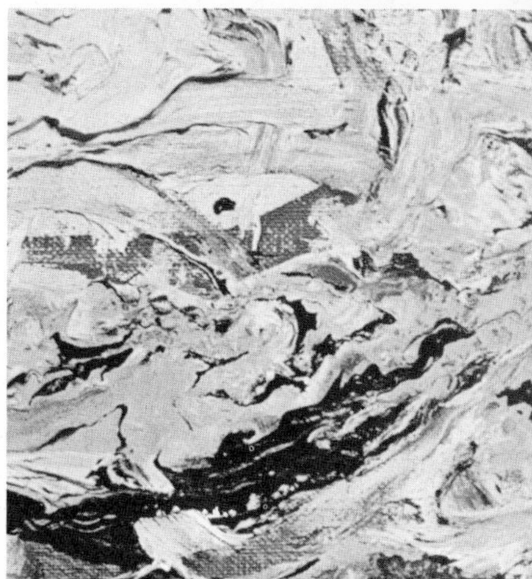

Brushwork: detail from a painting by Pollock

Brygos painter. *Priam ransoming Hector's body*

Brutalism. Hunstanton School

Buffet. *Self-portrait–T.4*

Bugle

Karl Georg Büchner

He wrote the biographies *Montrose* (1928), *Sir Walter Scott* (1932) and *Oliver Cromwell* (1934).

Buchanan George (1506–82). Scottish humanist. He studied and taught on the Continent (Montaigne was one of his pupils); became tutor to James VI of Scotland and I of England, to whom he dedicated his great *Rerum Scoticarum historia . . .* (1582; *The History of Scotland*, 1690); and wrote Latin poems and tragedies.

Buchanan Robert Williams (1841–1901). Scottish writer and critic who, under the pseud. 'Thomas Maitland', publ. the article *The Fleshly School of Poetry . . .* in *The Contemporary Review* (1871), an attack on moral grounds directed against Swinburne, D. G. Rossetti and the Pre-Raphaelites. This began a vague and protracted controversy foreshadowing more specific attacks on 'decadence'.

Buch(h)oltz Andreas Heinrich (1607–71). German author of 2 long, learned and didactic novels and a quantity of religious poetry.

Buen Retiro

Büchner Karl Georg (1813–37). German writer and scientist. Having written a revolutionary pamphlet, *Der Hessische Landbote* (1834), B. fled to Strassburg, later (1836) becoming lecturer in anatomy at Zürich. He wrote an ironic comedy *Leonce and Lena* (1836), but has gained his great 20th-c. reputation largely for the historical tragedy *Dantons Tod* (1835) and the social tragedy *Woyzeck* (written 1836–7, unfinished; publ. 1879). Both are studies in human isolation, powerfully presented in a 'slice-of-life' technique (highly colloquial prose, abrupt scene changes, sordid subjects) which looks back to the storm and stress and forward to naturalism. *Danton* deals with the powerlessness of the individual, however great, against historical forces; *Woyzeck* is the story of a private soldier, exploited by those around him, who is driven to murder his unfaithful mistress: it is the basis of Berg's opera *Wozzeck.* In both B. probes his character's minds, as he does in the unfinished story *Lenz* (posth. 1839), a study of the eponymous 18th-c. dramatist on the brink of madness.

Buck Pearl S(ydenstricker) (1892–). U.S. novelist and missionary to China. Of her many books on China *The Good Earth* (1931; Pulitzer prize) and *Dragon Seed* (1942) are among the best. She received the Nobel prize for literature in 1938.

Buckingham George Villiers, 2nd Duke of (1628–87). English courtier, son of George Villiers (1592–1628), the favourite of James I. B. wrote–perhaps in collaboration–the comedy *The Rehearsal* (1671), which parodies heroic drama and ridicules contemporary poets including Dryden. B. is satirized as Zimri in Dryden's *Absalom and Achitophel.*

Buddenbrooks (1901). Novel by Thomas *Mann.

Buen Retiro. Royal palace in Madrid; in its gardens Charles III established (1760) a royal porcelain factory which, under his patronage, produced much fine work influenced by the style of Sèvres but including many independent masterpieces. Many of the original craftsmen were brought by Charles from *Naples. After Charles's death (1788) the quality and inspiration of the work declined; the factory was closed in 1808.

Buffalmacco Buonamico di Cristofano, called (13th–14th c.). Painter of the early Florentine school best known for his contemporary reputation as practical joker. Vasari lists many paintings by him but none can now be attributed with certainty.

Buffet Bernard (1928–). French painter who trained at the École des Beaux-Arts, Paris. The expressive draughtsmanship of his early near-monochromatic paintings has become–under the pressure of his phenomenal public success–a mannerism. His *Self-portrait* (1954) is in the Tate.

bugle. Valveless treble-pitched *brass wind instrument with cup mouthpiece and conical bore. It uses the 2nd–6th harmonics of the harmonic series. Instruments of this type have been used since early times for military signals and hunting calls.

Bulfinch Charles (1763–1844). U.S. architect. He studied in Europe (1785–7) and practised in Boston. His State House, Boston (completed 1800) was modelled on Somerset House by Sir W. Chambers but most of his work including domestic architecture in Boston, Maine State House and the E. portico of the Capitol, Washington, was in the style of R. Adam. B.

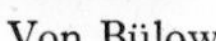

Von Bülow

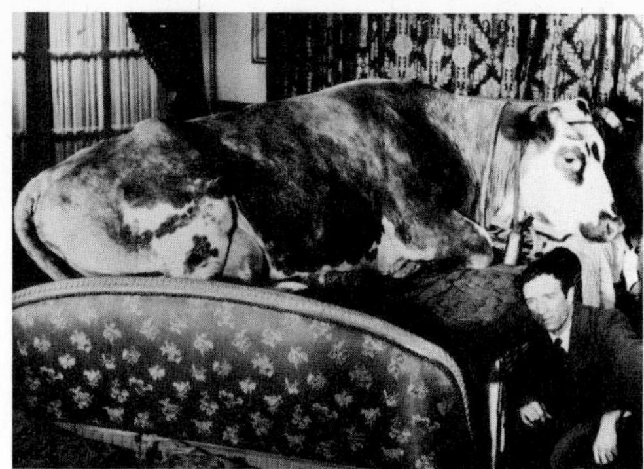

Buñuel. *L'Âge d'Or*

John Bull: anon. painting

was the first in America to design a row of houses with a unified street façade.

Bulfinch Thomas (1796–1867). U.S. writer, son of the above. His *Age of Fable* (1855) and *Age of Chivalry* (1858) retold ancient and medieval myths; they quickly became classics.

Bull John (1562–1628). English keyboard composer and virtuoso with a European reputation. He was the pupil of W. Blitheman at the Chapel Royal and became organist in the Chapel Royal (1591). On Queen Elizabeth I's recommendation, B. was made professor of music at Gresham's College (1596–1607). He left England in 1613, becoming organist first in Brussels and then in 1617 at Antwerp cathedral. B.'s 150 keyboard pieces show a sense of style and the purely instrumental possibilities of the keyboard which affected 17th-c. composers, e.g. J. P. Sweelinck, probably a friend, and the development of keyboard music. He also wrote church and viol music.

Bull Ole Bornemann (1810–80). Norwegian virtuoso violinist, basically self-taught. B. toured Europe and N. America, his arrangements of Norwegian folk-tunes and improvisations being particularly popular. He used a very flattened bridge (allowing 4-part chords) and a long heavy bow. B. was strongly patriotic, founded a short-lived Norse theatre at Bergen (1850) and tried to establish a Norwegian colony in the U.S.

Bullant Jean (*c.* 1510–78). French architect. He lived in Rome from 1540 to 1545 and evolved a style that combined classical elements with a rather arbitrary personal taste, e.g. entablature cut into by dormer-windows. Chief works: N. wing of the château of Ecouen, and the Châtelet at Chantilly.

Bülow Hans (Guido) von (1830–94). German pianist and conductor. An enthusiastic 'neo-German' (*Wagner) he studied piano under Liszt (1851–3) marrying (1857) Liszt's daughter Cosima. He was conductor at the Munich Opera (1864–9), producing the premières of Wagner's *Tristan and Isolde* (1865) and *Die Meistersinger* (1868). In 1869 Cosima left B. for Wagner. As a pianist B. had a vast repertoire and phenomenal memory; as a conductor and music journalist he became a champion of Brahms.

Bulwer-Lytton Edward George Earle Lytton (1803–73). English novelist whose many popular, well-constructed books include *Pelham* (1828), about a dandy, and the historical novels *The Last Days of Pompeii* (1834) and *Rienzi* (1835). His son EDWARD ROBERT (1831–91) publ. poems under the pseud. 'Owen Meredith'.

Bunin Ivan Alexeyevich (1870–1953). Russian novelist and poet. B. left the Soviet Union in 1920; he was the 1st Russian writer to receive the Nobel prize (1933). His best novels, including *Mitia's Love* (1925; 1926) and *The Well of Days* (1927; 1933) are closely-observed works of realism.

Bunning James Bunstone (1802–63). English architect. He designed Holloway Prison, London (with a castellated 'folly' gate-house) and the Coal Exchange, London (1847); its interior was one of the most elegant and original pieces of 19th-c. European architecture. It was demolished by the City Corporation in 1963. It was of cast iron, with no masonry visible – a large circular hall covered by a glazed dome and surrounded by 3 tiers of galleries.

Bunshaft Gordon (1909–). U.S. architect. Partner in charge of design in the New York office of Skidmore, Owings and Merrill. B. designed the Lever Building, New York (1952), a curtain-walled office building which has been copied all over the world, refined the design in the Pepsi Building (1959) and Chase Manhattan Bank (1961), both in New York, and has now abandoned this idiom for a more flamboyant style in concrete.

Bunting Edward (1773–1843). Irish musicologist. Publ. 3 vols of folk-tunes collected mainly from Irish harpists, such as D. Hempson, and wrote on the history of music in Ireland.

Buñuel Luis (1900–). Spanish-born film director. B.'s 1st films were surrealist, made with S. *Dali – *Un Chien Andalou* (1929) and *L'Âge d'Or* (1930), a savage attack on society and religion. *Las Hurdes* (1932), also known as *Land without Bread*, was a documentary set in Spain, where he directed the Republican film service (1936–9) before moving to the U.S. and then Mexico, where in 1945 he started directing features. Until 1957 his films were very uneven, dictated by repressive producers and minimal resources, but among them are a few which break out from their restrictions to have overall rather than incidental merit: *Los*

Bunning. The Coal Exchange

Bunshaft. Lever Building

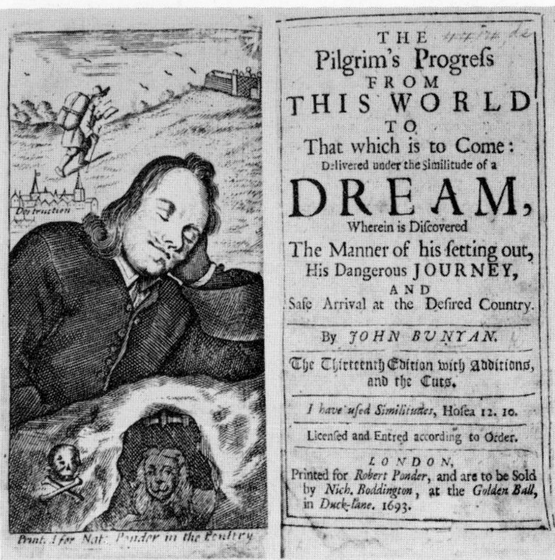
THE
Pilgrim's Progreſs
FROM
THIS WORLD
TO
That which is to Come:
Delivered under the Similitude of a
DREAM,
Wherein is Diſcovered
The Manner of his ſetting out,
His Dangerous JOURNEY,
AND
Safe Arrival at the Deſired Country.

By *JOHN BUNYAN.*

The Thirteenth Edition with Additions, and the Cuts.

I have uſed Similitudes, Hoſea 12. 10.

Licenſed and Entred according to Order.

LONDON,
Printed for *Robert Ponder*, and are to be Sold by *Nich. Boddington*, at the *Golden Ball*, in *Duck-lane.* 1693.

Bunyan. Frontispiece and title-page of *The Pilgrim's Progress*

Buontalenti. S. Stefano de' Cavalieri

Richard Burbage

Buon. Porta della Carta

Olvidados (1950), *El* (1953), *Robinson Crusoe* (1954). However, with only one exception all his films from *Nazarin* (1958) have been personal works. This and *Viridiana* (1961) express to the full B.'s fascination with moral and physical decay. *The Young One* (1960) is about racialism while *El Ángel Exterminador* (1962) is a strange social satire.

Bunyan John (1628–88). English sectarian preacher and writer. B. worked as a tinker and served in the Civil War between 1644 and 1646. After his marriage in 1648 he underwent the religious conversion described in *Grace Abounding to the Worst of Sinners* (1666), becoming a Nonconformist in 1653. A popular itinerant preacher, he refused to abandon preaching when it became illegal at the Restoration, suffering imprisonment from 1660 to 1672. While in Bedford gaol he continued to preach and to write religious works, of which the most famous is *Grace Abounding*. The 1st part of *The Pilgrim's Progress* was written later and publ. in 1678. On his release he was licensed to preach and became pastor of the Nonconformist congregation at Bedford.
B. had little education and his reading, although deep, was limited; the cadences of the Authorized Version can constantly be heard behind his simple and majestic style. He had an intensely vivid and concrete imagination and could express spiritual and moral concepts in an immediately telling manner, which was partly the result of temperament and partly of long experience of preaching to simple audiences. With these qualities he turned naturally to allegory; Christian's journey, in *The Pilgrim's Progress*, is a parable of the journey through life's temptations to eternal salvation, but encounters are observed with an acuteness, and sketched with a dramatic skill, which give the intellectual structure a life and human significance beyond the bounds of B.'s theology. Further books included *The Life and Death of Mr Badman* (1680) and part 2 of *Pilgrim's Progress* (1684).

Buon Bartolomeo (*c.* 1374–1464). Venetian sculptor. With his father Giovanni he was responsible for the Porta della Carta, one of the last additions to the exterior of the Ducal Palace, Venice. The style is still late Gothic, though a few Renaissance motifs appear.

Buonarroti Michelangelo: *Michelangelo Buonarroti

Buonconsiglio Giovanni (15th–16th c.) called 'Il Marescalco'. Italian painter influenced by Antonella da Messina and Giovanni Bellini. He worked in Vicenza and Venice. His masterpiece is the *Pietà* in Vicenza Mus.

Buontalenti Bernardo (1536–1608). Italian architect, sculptor and painter; a leading mannerist. His Casino di S. Marco (now the Palazzo dei Tribunali), Florence (1574) uses such features as: a doorway decorated with stone studs; a tympanum in the form of a shell; rustication that bends inwards; a keystone transformed into a coat of arms with stone 'drapery' rising from it to support a balcony; and windows with concave sills. He also had a hand in the façades of S. Trinità, Florence, and S. Stefano de' Cavaliere, Pisa. B., who was aptly named, produced spectacles of all sorts, scenery for plays, music and firework displays, and arranged a naval battle inside the Pitti Palace.

Burbage Richard (1567?–1619). English actor and rival of E. *Alleyn, the first to play Shakespeare's Hamlet, Lear, Othello, Richard III. He was also a painter; at Dulwich College there is a portrait of a woman by him. B. began his career with the co. The Admiral's Men at The *Theatre, built by his father JAMES (d. 1597) who also trained him. B. and his brother CUTHBERT (1566?–1636) built the *Globe.

Burchfield Charles Ephraim (1893–). U.S. painter of the U.S. scene. In early watercolours he evoked with expressionistic intensity the scenes and emotions of his childhood in Salem, Ohio. He then began to work in a more objective style applied to architectural subjects. In the 1940s there appeared an element of fantasy in his paintings which links them with the work of his earlier period.

Burckhardt Jakob (1818–97). Swiss historian, one of the first writers to study history in terms of the development of culture and trace the interaction of artistic and politico-social processes. His major work was *Die Kultur der Renaissance in Italien* (1860; *The Civilization of the Renaissance in Italy*, 1878).

Bürger Gottfried August (1747–94). German poet, connected with the Göttingen circle, whose romantic ballads, particularly *Lenore* (1773), vitally affected the development of

European romanticism. B. in turn was affected by Percy's *Reliques* . . . and also made direct trs of English ballads. B. wrote sonnets, started a version of the *Iliad* (1771–5), trs. *Macbeth* (1783) and produced the German version of the *Baron Münchausen* cycle (1786; R. E. *Raspe).

Burges William (1827–81). English neo-Gothic architect. His works include Cardiff Castle and Castell Coch, Wales (elaborate and expensive essays in recreating a glamorized middle ages). B.'s characteristics are a feeling for bold, massive effects and an unrestrained romanticism.

Burgkmair Hans (1473–1531). German painter of portraits and religious subjects and woodcut designer. He studied under his father Thomas and M. Schongauer and was a friend of Dürer. He was affected by Venetian painting and was one of the 1st Germans whose work showed Italian influence. He is best remembered for his striking woodcuts, e.g. the 2 series *Triumph of the Emperor Maximilian I* with 135 cuts and *The Wise King* with 327 cuts.

Burgos cathedral Spain. It was begun in 1220 and shows strong influence from French Gothic. It has a French chevet, stiff-leaf capitals and plate-tracery, but the plan and proportions are traditionally Spanish.

Burgundian school. Term misleadingly applied to a group of 15th-c. Flemish composers, chief among them G. *Dufay, G. *Binchois and A. *Busnois, who held appointments at the court of the dukes of Burgundy; their works do not show the close stylistic affinities expected of a 'school'.

Burial of Count Orgaz, The (1586). Painting by El *Greco.

burin (also called 'graver'). The tool used by the engraver for cutting the lines on block or plate. It is, essentially, a V-shaped cutting edge.

Burke Edmund (1729–97). Irish statesman and philosopher. His involved, rhetorical prose style was capable of impassioned pleading–his oratory in the same vein was famous, e.g. his speeches at the trial of Warren Hastings. *A Philosophical Inquiry into . . . the Sublime and Beautiful* (1756) was highly regarded by the aesthetic school in Germany; it was trs. by G. Lessing and probably inspired his *Laokoon.* Among B.'s many important political works were *Observations on . . . The Present State of the Nation* (1769) and the anti-Revolutionary *Reflections on the Revolution in France* (1790).

Burkhard Willy (1900–55). Swiss composer. B.'s music in its contrapuntal and imitative characteristics has affinities to 15th- and 16th-c. polyphonic compositions and also baroque music. Its harmonic idiom, however, is modern, affected by Stravinsky, Hindemith and Bartók, with an austerity peculiar to itself. Works include: the oratorio *Das Gesicht Jesajas* (1935) and the great mass (1951); also the cantata *Till Ulenspiegel* (1929), 'Musical Exercise' for chorus and orchestra (1934), a fantasia for strings (1934), the oratorio *Das Jahr* (1941), 2 symphonies and chamber music.

Burlador de Sevilla y convidado de piedro, El (publ. 1630). Play by *Tirso de Molina.

burlesque. Farcical treatment (literary or dramatic) of a serious work or subject, e.g. Buckingham's *The Rehearsal* (1671), parodying Dryden and the heroic style. Closely linked to the b. are the 'extravaganza', a fantastic, humorous work but with no direct object of satire, and the *'burletta', a comic opera or musical farce. In the U.S., b. (or 'burleycue') was *risqué* comedy entertainment for men, which led *c.* 1920 to the striptease.

burletta. 18th-c. English theatrical entertainment with music.

Burlington Richard Boyle, 3rd Earl of (1694–1753). English patron and amateur architect. He went to Italy in 1714 and again in 1719, when he made a special study of Palladio. On his return he gathered round him a circle of architects and painters including Kent, Campbell and Flitcroft. He also drew up designs of his own, e.g. Chiswick House, the Assembly Rooms, York, and Boynton Hall, Yorkshire. By the 1730s B.'s brand of Palladianism had largely replaced the native English baroque of Wren and Hawksmoor.

Burliuk the brothers David (1882–) and Vladimir (188?–1917). Prominent Russian futurists. They studied painting first in Odessa and then in Munich under Azbe. In 1907 in Moscow they came into contact with Larionov,

Burgkmair. *Maximilian I receiving the Russian ambassadors.* Also *drum

Burke: cartoon

Burlington and Kent. Chiswick House

Burgos cathedral

Burges. Castell Coch

David Burliuk. *My Cossack Ancestor* (*c.* 1908)

Burne-Jones. *Pygmalion and the Image*

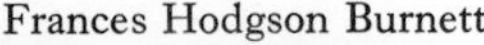

Goncharova and Exter with whom they organized a number of small exhibitions. In 1910 they contributed to the 1st anthology of Russian futurist poetry; they made friends with Kandinsky, subsequently contributing to Blaue Reiter exhibitions and *Almanac*. In 1911 David met Mayakovsky and encouraged him to write poetry; subsequently they together devoted themselves to writing and propaganda for the 'new art'. In 1918 David left Russia and later worked in the U.S. in a primitivist style. Vladimir was killed in action.

Burne-Jones Sir Edward (1833–98). English painter and decorative artist who became a painter under the influence of D. G. Rossetti and was associated with the second, 'romantic' phase of Pre-Raphaelitism. He was strongly affected by Botticelli and Mantegna when visiting Italy in 1859 and 1862. B. lacked the vigour and social ideals of the Pre-Raphaelites; based on literary themes, chiefly from Greek mythology, Chaucer and Malory, his mystic, romantic and unhistorical pictures represented a dream world of escape from 19th-c. industrialism. He worked in subdued tones and a linear manner which contributed to art nouveau. He made influential designs for stained glass for his friend W. Morris, for whom he also illustrated books, e.g. the *Kelmscott Press *Chaucer* (1897).

Burnet Gilbert (1643–1715). Scottish writer and bishop; his *History of His Own Time* (1724–34) is a classic of English literature both for its fine style and its vivid if slanted portrayal of people and events.

Burnett Frances Eliza Hodgson (1849–1924). English-born novelist who emigrated to the U.S. (1865), the author of the celebrated *Little Lord Fauntleroy* (1886), the story of a priggish child, who, by his beauty and charm, persuades his irascible grandfather into various good works on his estate and eventually into recognizing his American daughter-in-law, the child's mother. Other stories include *That Lass o' Lowrie's* (1877), *Sara Crewe* (1888), and the still deservedly popular *The Secret Garden* (1911).

Burney Dr Charles (1726–1814). English music historian, organist and composer. In 1770 he began his European tours to gather material for his great *A General History of Music* . . . (4 vols, publ. 1776 to 1789); this and Sir J. *Hawkins's (publ. 1776) were immediately regarded as rivals but B.'s had the strong advantage of being written by a practising musician and in a fine English style. B.'s accounts of musical Europe are still immensely valuable, e.g. *The Present State of Music in France and Italy* . . . (1771) and . . . *in Germany, the Netherlands and the United Provinces* . . . (1773). B.'s friends included Haydn; Fanny Burney was his daughter.

Burney Fanny (Madame D'Arblay) (1752–1840). English novelist, daughter of Dr Charles Burney, the musician, and a great favourite of Dr Johnson. Her *Diary and Letters* (vols 1–5 1842; 6 and 7 1846) are remarkable for their lively portraiture and natural dialogue. Her best novel, *Evelina* (1778), preceded *Cecilia* (1782) and *Camilla* (1796)–the heroines being progressive self-portraits.

burnisher. An implement fitted with a very hard polished surface, for example, agate, used for burnishing gold or silver.

Burns Robert (1759–96). Scottish poet. Though he was a skilled ploughman by the age of 15, B. received a sound basic education from his father and the village schoolmaster at Alloway. From his mother he learned the traditional Scottish songs and ballads. His 1st poem, *Handsome Nell*, was written at the age of 16. A farm which he and his brother Gilbert bought after his father's death in 1784 failed, and in desperation B. planned to emigrate to Jamaica. At this time Jean Armour was expecting his child, but her family's attitude to their marriage caused a bitter quarrel. B. began a romance with Mary Campbell, the 'Highland Mary' of his poetry, but she died from fever. In 1786 he publ. *Poems chiefly in the Scottish Dialect*, containing some of his best and most characteristic work; an Edinburgh ed. brought him £500 and the freedom of Edinburgh literary society. He acknowledged Jean Armour as his wife in 1788 and they settled at Ellisland Farm; B. became an exciseman to ensure some financial security. The farm was a failure and was given up in 1791. At about this time B. contributed, without payment, 200 songs to 2 miscellanies. Some of the songs were original, others traditional poems polished by B.
B. was heir to Scottish tradition in more than his use of vernacular Scots, which in any case was modified in the majority of his poems. 2

Frances Hodgson Burnett

Dr Charles Burney

Fanny Burney

Robert Burns

currents of Scottish writing met in him, that of folk-song and that of the rhymed epistle or satire, its rhythms calling upon those of the dance. To these elements and to the stanza form which he took from the earlier work of Ramsay and Fergusson, he brought an acute selective intelligence and taste; capable of bustling poems like the lively narrative *Tam O' Shanter* and *The Jolly Beggars*, and of vigorous abusive satires like *Holy Willie's Prayer*, B.'s truest genius was for short lyrics, love-lyrics above all. The many love-songs which he wrote or coll. are full of tenderness and a natural delicacy of taste.

Burnt-Out Case, A (1961). Novel by Graham *Greene.

burr. In *engraving, the fragments of copper left on either side of the channel cut by the burin.

Burra Edward (1905–). English painter and theatrical designer; member of Unit I (1933). The work of Signorelli and Goya, Grosz and the surrealists, influenced the development of his fantastic, richly imaginative art, which also mirrors his love of Spain and Mexico. B. first specialized in scenes of the underworld, exposing the decadence and disillusionment which existed between the wars but also indulging his taste for the flamboyant and bizarre. With the Spanish Civil War and World War II his work acquired menacing and tragic overtones. He works in watercolour, usually on a large scale.

Burroughs Edgar Rice (1875–1950). U.S. writer and millionaire through his *Tarzan* books, which began with *Tarzan of the Apes* (1914).

Burroughs William S. (1914–). U.S. author associated with the *beat generation, living mainly in Tangier. B. publ. his 1st book, *Junky* (1953), under the pseud. 'William Lee'. From experiences while taking drugs he has written *The Naked Lunch* (1959), *The Soft Machine* (1960) and *The Ticket that Exploded* (1962), novels crowded with hallucinatory images and containing perverse sexual fantasies.

Burt Francis (1926–). English composer, a pupil of H. Ferguson and B. Blacher, living in Germany. His works include the opera *Volpone* (1957) after Ben Jonson, *Iambics* for orchestra (1955) and a string quartet (1953).

Burton Decimus (1800–81). English architect of the classical revival, son of James B. In Regent's Park he designed Cornwall Terrace (1821), 'The Holme' (now part of Bedford College) and several of the zoo buildings; also in London the arch and screen at Hyde Park Corner (1825) and the Athenaeum Club. In Tunbridge Wells he designed the Calverley Park Estate (1828–48), in Hove part of Adelaide Crescent and with his father was responsible for the development of St Leonards-on-Sea. He built several neo-Gothic churches but never used this style easily or extensively.

Burton James (1761–1837). Scottish builder who practised in London; father of Decimus B. In Regent's Park he built many of Nash's houses and several designed by his son, as well as much of Bloomsbury including Burton Street (1807) and Russell Square (1800–14).

Burton Sir Richard Francis (1821–90). English writer, orientalist and explorer. He served in the Indian army and on the Sind survey and made a journey to Mecca in disguise. In his trs. of *The *Arabian Nights' Entertainments–The Book of a Thousand Nights and a Night* (1885–8) his attempt to render the Arabic idiom exactly resulted in a singular style, rich in archaisms and inventions. He also made a trs. (1883) of the **Kama Sutra* for private circulation.

Burton Richard (1925–). Welsh actor. With a wealth of theatre experience (especially in Shakespeare), B. has not had great scope for his talent in cinema. His starring role in the multi-million-dollar spectacular **Cleopatra* (1963) was followed by the title-role in *Becket* (1964); if allowed, his full flowering is still to come.

Burton Robert (1577–1640). English writer, author of the treatise *The Anatomy of Melancholy* (1621), which was constantly revised by B. It deals with the causes, symptoms and nature of the melancholy humour (i.e. morbid depression) and its cure, but ranges so widely as to be, in effect, an essay on human life and society. The writing, in a heavily latinized English style, has humour and irony and there are innumerable quotations from every branch of literature. It was regularly read by Dr

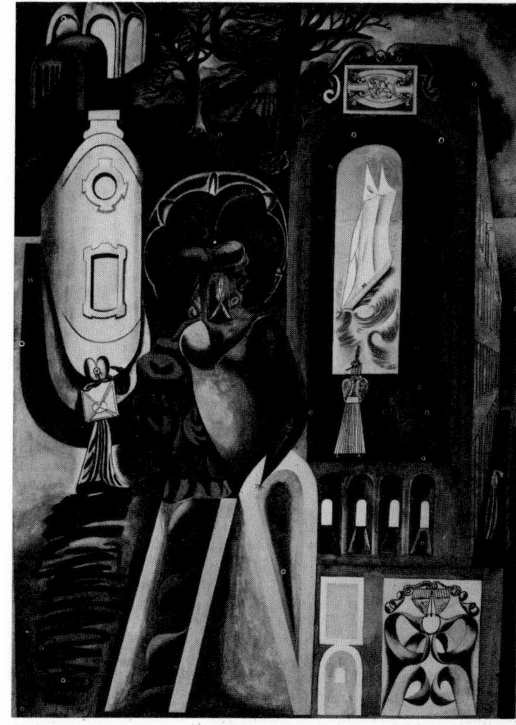

Burra. *Surrealist Composition* (1934)

Decimus Burton. The arch and screen at Hyde Park Corner

Wilhelm Busch. *Comic*; woodcut

Bustelli: porcelain figure

Ferruccio Busoni

Johnson, freely plagiarized by Laurence Sterne, parodied by Charles Lamb, annotated by Coleridge and praised by Byron. B. also wrote academic Latin verses and a Latin comedy, *Philosophaster.*

Busch Adolf (1891–1952). German-born Swiss violinist and also composer. He led a famous string quartet and also performed with the pianist R. Serkin. His brother FRITZ (1890–1951) was a distinguished conductor on the Continent, at the Glyndebourne Opera and the Metropolitan Opera House, New York (1945–50).

Busch Ernest (1900–). German actor, closely associated with the *Berliner Ensemble. He was imprisoned by the Nazis during World War II.

Busch Wilhelm (1832–1908). German graphic humorist and landscape and portrait painter best known for his rhymed picture stories, in particular *Max und Moritz* (1865; *Max and Moritz*, 1874) which remains popular. His satirical cartoons contributed to the comic paper *Fliegende Blätter* from 1871 expressed an essentially pessimistic view of life.

Bush Alan Dudley (1900–). English composer who studied under J. Ireland. From 1925 he was professor of composition at the R.A.M.; in 1936 he founded the Workers' Music Association. B.'s earlier work is characteristically cerebral in his 'thematic' method of composition: every note is thematically significant; Communist convictions produced after World War II a conscious simplifying of style. His works include: the operas, *Wat Tyler* (Leipzig, 1953), *Men of Blackmoor* (Weimar, 1956); symphony no. 1 in C maj. (1940), no. 2 'Nottingham' (1949); *Piers Plowman's Day* for orchestra (Prague Radio, 1947); *Dialectic* for string quartet (1929) and *Concert Piece* for cello and piano (1936).

Bushnell John (*c.* 1630–1701). English sculptor. He travelled in France and Italy where he executed the huge tomb (1660s) of Alvise Mocenizo in the church of the Mendicanti, Venice. Having returned to London, he gained many commissions because of his baroque style (a novelty in England) but his work is uneven in quality, often badly designed and tentatively expressed.

Busnois Antoine de Busnes or (d. 1492). Flemish composer at the court of Burgundy (1467–81?), considered by contemporaries the equal of J. Ockeghem. B.'s ingenious and elegant *chansons*, in the *rederijker tradition, reflect the sophistication of the Burgundian court, but his church music is often over-complex and lacks the spiritual depth of Ockeghem's; it includes 3 masses (one on *L'*homme armé*) and 7 motets. B. used imitation extensively, but not strictly, and canon.

Busoni Ferruccio Benvenuto (1866–1924). Italian composer and virtuoso pianist specially noted for his Liszt interpretations. B.'s music, eclectic rather than revolutionary, shows strong sense of form; his harmony, from 1910 on, extended and renovated traditional tonality rather than abandoned it. B. considered *Elegies* for piano (1907) his 1st mature work although the piano concerto with final male chorus was written in 1903–4 and 'Concert piece' for piano and orchestra in 1890. Other important works are: operas, *Die Brautwahl* (1912), *Turandot* (1917), *Doktor Faust* (completed by a pupil–Jarnach–and produced posth. in 1927); *Berceuse élégiaque* for orchestra (1909); much piano music, including the *Fantasia contrappuntistica* (1910, 4th version for 2 pianos 1913), piano arrangements of works by Bach. He published his theories in the book *Entwurf einer neuen Ästhetik der Tonkunst* (1907; *Sketch of a New Esthetic of Music*, 1911), which contains ideas for new scales, new instruments, etc., and a theory of continuous development which anticipates in some respects the aesthetic of *serial music. His essays on Mozart, etc., show him to have had an unusually creative understanding of earlier music.

Busser Henri (Paul) (1872–). French conductor and composer, pupil of Gounod; also influenced by Fauré and, in his operas, by Wagner; he won the 1st Rome prize (1893). His many works include symphonies, church music, incidental music and orchestration of piano pieces by Debussy.

Bussy-Rabutin Roger de Rabutin, comte de Bussy (1618–93). French author of *Histoire amoureuse des Gaules* (1665; *The Amorous History of the Gauls*, 1725), a set of scandalous anecdotes about ladies at the court of Louis XIV. For it B. was imprisoned and then exiled to his estates; the book was popular.

Bustelli Franz Anton (1723–63). Modeller in porcelain, born at Locarno, whose pieces are the finest expression of rococo in this medium; he worked at *Nymphenburg (1754–63). He produced a set of 16 *commedia dell'arte* figures (Bavarian State Mus., Munich) which, like his other work, are characterized by simplicity of form and graceful line, charming wit and rich colouring.

Butinone Bernardino (*fl.* 1484–1507). Italian painter, who worked in Treviglio and Milan. B. was early influenced by Mantegna, later by Vincenzo Foppa, but his work retains traces of Lombard Gothic. In collaboration with B. Zenale he painted frescoes in S. Pietro in Gessate, Milan (*c.* 1489–93) and an altarpiece at Treviglio. Other work includes a triptych (1484) now in the Brera, Milan.

Butler David (1894–). U.S. film director. A specialist in musicals, including the lively *Calamity Jane* (1953).

Butler Reg(inald) (1913–). British sculptor trained as an architect. He began to make sculpture in 1944 and held his 1st one-man exhibition in 1949. He held a Gregory Fellowship at Leeds Univ. (1950–3) and in 1953 won the major prize in the Unknown Political Prisoner international competition. Since 1950 he has taught sculpture at the Slade School. His earliest figure groups, e.g. *Boy and Girl* (1950; Arts Council Coll.) were purely linear constructions, but since then he has evolved a language of more sensual, robust but vulnerable figures, often delicately balanced like *Girl* (1956–7; Hanover Gal., London) or trapped within an angular network of lines.

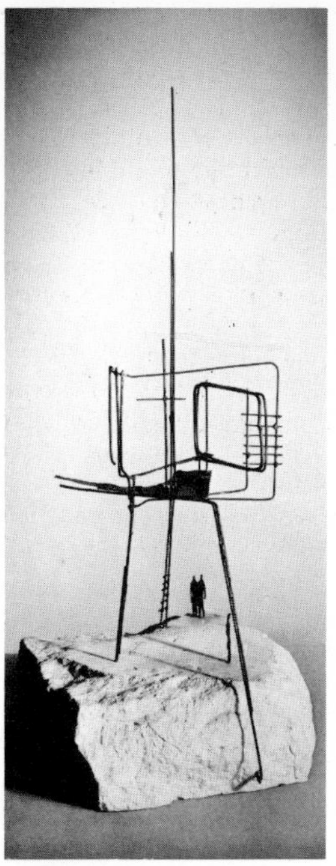
Reg Butler. Project for a monument to the Unknown Political Prisoner

Reg Butler. *Girl*

Samuel Butler (1612–80)

Samuel Butler (1835–1902)

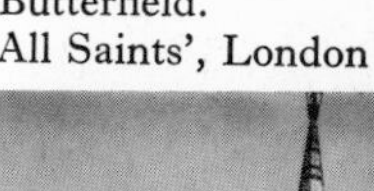
Butterfield. All Saints', London

Butler Samuel (1612–80). English poet; he spent most of his life as secretary to various patrons. B.'s long mock-heroic poem *Hudibras* (1663, 64, 78) satirizes the Puritans and gained him the favour of Charles II. It was written in a galloping metre (the octosyllabic tetrameter, now called the 'hudibrastic' when used satirically) and created a lasting vogue for mock-heroic verse (practised by, e.g., Dryden and Pope).

Butler Samuel (1835–1902). English author. His most famous book is *Erewhon* (anagram of nowhere) (1872) an anti-machine utopia satirizing English society and inspired by his visit to New Zealand; the sequel, *Erewhon Revisited . . .* , appeared in 1901. Works include the autobiographical novel *The Way of All Flesh* (publ. posth. 1903) which attacks Victorian education, personified by B.'s domineering father, and religion. A controversialist over a wide field, B. wrote *The Authoress of the Odyssey* (1897), *Shakespeare's Sonnets reconsidered . . .* (1899), etc., and contributed to the evolutionary controversy. His poems include the famous *A Psalm of Montreal*, his paintings *Mr Heatherley's Holiday* (Tate), and he also composed cantatas in a Handelian style.

Butor Michel (1926–). French novelist of the new realist school. His 3rd novel *Degrés* (1960; *Degrees*, U.S. 1961, U.K. 1962), acclaimed in France and abroad, tells of a French school-teacher endeavouring to write a novel which shall be an absolutely true account of the school and facing difficulties of definition and impartial, unclouded observation.

Butterfield William (1814–1900). English ecclesiastical architect of the *Gothic revival. His buildings are characterized by use of different coloured bricks on the same building, e.g. Keble College, Oxford (1868–70) and Rugby School chapel (1875). His churches include All Saints', Margaret Street (1849–59), one of his best, and the over-elaborate St Augustine, Queen's Gate (1861–71), both London.

Butterworth George (Sainton Kaye) (1885–1916). English composer. His interest in folk music influenced his work which includes 6 songs arranged from A. E. Housman's *A Shropshire Lad* (1911), 5 songs, also from Housman, including *In Summertime on Bredon* (1912). B. also wrote *The Shropshire Lad* rhapsody and *The Banks of Green Willow*. He was killed in action in World War I.

buttress. Architectural term for a mass of masonry projecting from and supporting the external face of a wall. It was particularly important in Gothic architecture, as was the FLYING BUTTRESS, in which the masonry is free-standing and a half-arch transfers thrust from the wall to the masonry below.

Buxheim organ book (Bavarian State Library, Munich). 15th-c. musical ms. in German keyboard tablature originally in the monastery of Buxheim. It contains over 200 pieces, most of them transcriptions of *chansons* and motets; these are mostly German but English, French, Netherlands and Italian composers are represented. There are also 2 large sections

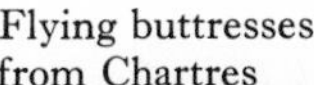
Flying buttresses from Chartres

Buttresses (Sherborne Abbey)

Buxheim organ book

Bylert. *Sutler*

William Byrd

illustrating the technique of keyboard extemporization and ornamentation.

Buxtehude Dietrich (*c.* 1637–1707). German composer and organist at St Mary's church, Lübeck. Musically he belongs to the N. German school, but was born a Danish subject (probably at Oldesloe, Holstein, then Danish). B. took over the *Abendmusik* concerts, which originated as weekday diversions for merchants visiting Lübeck Exchange, running 5 concerts on Sundays preceding Christmas. His best music was in cantatas (many now lost) composed for these concerts; in inventiveness, variety of form and lyrical expression they reveal B. as one of Bach's greatest predecessors. B.'s surviving works include 116 cantatas (composed between 1676 and 1687), a *missa brevis*, a *magnificat*, a 24-part motet; his chorale preludes, variations and fantasies, and also toccatas, for organ are fine examples of N. German keyboard style.

Buytewech Willem Pietersz (*c.* 1585–*c.* 1625). Dutch genre painter and one of the few significant landscape etchers before Rembrandt.

Bwana Devil (1953). 1st feature film in 3-D (stereoscopic).

Bylert Jan van (1603–71). Dutch painter, a pupil of A. Bloemaert. He began painting in the Caravaggesque style of the Utrecht school, but after 1630 his style changed and his pictures became lighter and prettier.

Byrd William (1543?–1623). English composer. He was probably a pupil of T. Tallis; became organist at Lincoln cathedral in 1563, was appointed gentleman of the Chapel Royal in 1570 but moved to London only in 1572, then sharing with Tallis the post of organist at the Chapel Royal. In 1575 he and Tallis received from Elizabeth I the effective monopoly, for 21 years, of music printing in England and publ. jointly in that year *Cantiones . . . sacrae*. . . . In 1593 B. settled near Ongar in Essex. From about 1580 to 1610 B. was frequently involved in law suits over property claims; he was a Catholic but appears to have been unmolested. B. is ranked with Europe's greatest composers. His polyphonic vocal music shows great contrapuntal ingenuity and the melodic shape of individual parts is subtly varied and at its best passionate and exalted. Added to this was B.'s use of dissonance to produce momentary tensions and bold modulation (e.g. the motet *Vide Domine*) to dramatic effect. This stylistic mastery was deployed in almost every known musical form.

Of B.'s Latin church music the masses (3, 4 and 5 voices) are outstanding not only contrapuntally but also for formal unity; the 2 books of *Gradualia . . .* (1605–7) contained motets for the major Catholic feast-days. But his greatest motets occur in the non-liturgical *Cantiones sacrae* (book I 1589; book II 1591), e.g. *Laudibus in sanctis* and *Haec dies* (both book II). For the Anglican service B. produced the 'Great Service' written for two 5-voice choirs; it is of great rhythmic and contrapuntal complexity and its sonorities are reminiscent of the school of Venice. Other English church music includes the 'Short Service', the 'Second Service' and the 'Third Service', full anthems, verse anthems, among the earliest examples of this form, and psalms.

Secular vocal music, anthems and some instrumental pieces appeared in 1588, 1589 and 1611. The madrigalian pieces of the 1588 set were intended for solo voice and 4 instrumental parts. B. greatly developed this form, making the accompanying parts clearly instrumental in character. B.'s viol fantasies and In nomines fully exploit the instrumental ensemble and in the same way, in his keyboard compositions, B. exploits the medium, developing the variation form, e.g. *The Carman's Whistle*, and using typically keyboard ornamentation. Like much of his music, B.'s keyboard compositions survive in ms. but he contributed 8 pieces to the vol. *Parthenia* (1611) publ. jointly with Bull and Gibbons.

Byrom John (1692–1763). English poet whose 1st poem, *Colin and Phebe*, a pastoral, was printed in Addison's *Spectator* (1714). He wrote unmannered light verse (*Contentment*, *Tom the Porter*, *Careless Content*), well-known hymns, e.g. 'Christians awake! Salute the happy morn', invented a system of shorthand and left the valuable *The Private Journal*.

Lord Byron

Byron George Gordon, Lord (1788–1824). English romantic poet who early developed a morbid sense of isolation, partly caused by his unhappy childhood and lameness. He attended Harrow and Trinity College, Cambridge, where he publ. a coll. of verse, *Hours of Idleness* (1807). The harsh criticism of *The Edinburgh Review* provoked *English Bards and*

Scotch Reviewers (1809), B.'s satirical rejoinder in the manner of Pope, in which he manifests his dislike of the Lake Poets. He travelled widely. In the House of Lords he opposed capital punishment of workers who, fearing unemployment, destroyed machines. Then *Childe Harold's Pilgrimage: a romaunt* (1812–18) enjoyed immediate and sensational success. Handsome and famous, B. was lionized; but his intrigue with Lady Caroline Lamb, the rapid failure of his marriage (1815), and his relations with his half-sister, Augusta, caused scandals which drove him from England (1816). He finally settled in Italy, becoming the lover of Teresa, Countess Guiccioli. B. died of fever at Missolonghi (April 1824) on an expedition to help the Greek revolt against Turkish rule.

B.'s importance is threefold–as a man and a poet and, above all, as a legend. Gloomy, meditative, burdened with a mysterious guilt, the Byronic hero was imitated throughout Europe in life as in literature; he influenced poets like Pushkin directly, and the whole literature of revolt against society owes something to him. In *Childe Harold* he wanders over Europe seeking distraction; in the oriental romances *The Giaour*, *The Bride of Abydos* (both 1813), *The Corsair* and *Lara* (both 1814) he becomes an outlaw in fact as well as spirit; and he rebels against the very scheme of the universe in the dramatic poems *Manfred* (1817) and *Cain* (1821). But B. had another side: the satirist and man of sense, temperamentally if not stylistically kin to the Augustans, appears in his letters, in *English Bards* and *Beppo* (1818). *The Vision of Judgement* (1822) satirizes Southey and George III. *Don Juan* (1819–24), often considered his masterpiece, is zestful, witty and irreverent, by turns an oriental romance of amorous intrigue, a satire on European society, a rollicking comedy of manners, a confession, and a virtuoso display of impudent rhymes and verbal effects. B.'s works include *The Lament of Tasso* (1817); *Marino Faliero*, *Sardanapalus* and *The Two Foscari* (all 1821); and *Heaven and Earth* and *Werner* (both 1823).

Byzantine art. Art produced in and under the influence of the E. Roman or B. empire; this is conveniently dated from the founding of Constantinople in A.D. 330 to its conquest by the Turks in A.D. 1453. Examples of B. a. survive in Ravenna in Italy, the Balkans, S. Russia and other areas which once belonged to the empire, as well as in Asia Minor proper. B. artists produced wall paintings, illuminated mss, panel paintings and above all *mosaics. The brilliant shining colours of these last, their conventions of iconography and powerful mystical religiosity embody the best and most characteristic of B. a., which enjoyed its golden ages in the 6th to 7th cs and 9th to 12th cs, and in the 13th c.–a renaissance marked by an increased realism of treatment. The impact of B. a. on medieval European art was of great importance and is especially clear in the work of 13th- and 14th-c. Italian painters.

The 2 most important elements in Byzantine architecture were the Roman brick vault and the dome, which probably originated in Persia. Byzantine architects fused these with the use of mosaic as developed in early Christian art into a powerful highly individual style which found its most magnificent expression in the church of *S. Sophia.

Byzantium (1929). Poem by W. B. Yeats.

Byzantine art. Mosaic of Christ the Almighty *c.* 1100; in the dome, Daphni, Greece

Byzantine art. Mosaic of the Empress Theodora and her suite, at S. Vitale, Ravenna

Byzantine art. S. Sophia

Stool with cabriole legs

George Washington Cable

James Branch Cabell

Cacoyannis. *Electra*

cabaletta (Italian, related to *cavatinetta*). A musical term. In 19th-c. Italian opera one type of aria was in several sections each one frequently faster than the preceding one; the c. was the final short section.

Caballero Fernán. Pseud. of Cecilia Böhl de Faber (1797–1877), Spanish novelist whose books deal with the people, customs, language and social manners of Andalusia. *La Gaviota* (1849) is generally considered to be her best novel, and her *Cuentos y poesías populares andaluces* (1859) was the 1st Spanish coll. of nursery-tales and folk-songs.

Cabanilles Juan (1644–1712). Spanish organist and composer. Appointed organist at Valencia cathedral in 1665, he held the post until his death, becoming the leading performer and teacher in Spain. C.'s surviving music shows a remarkable and advanced sense of form.

Cabell James Branch (1879–1958). U.S. writer. His early work was influenced by post-Civil War realism (Dreiser and Crane), but his own documentation was too weak for this genre. His true ability appeared in a series of escapist novels, supposedly medieval French and Spanish chronicles (1919–27), whose centrepiece is the life of Manuel, a 13th-c. prophet. The best of these is *Jurgen* (1919), a novel of fantasy, satire and Rabelaisian humour originally suppressed by the police and achieving a *succès de scandale.*

Cabezón Antonio de (*c.* 1500–66). Spanish composer and organist to Prince Philip (later Philip II) from 1548. C.'s keyboard music is remarkable for its true instrumental style and for its use of the variation form; the strong Spanish tradition of instrumental writing and the work of the *vihuela composers were major influences. C. had a brother Juan (d. 1566), a composer and member of the Royal Chapel, and 2 sons Agustín (d. before 1564) and Hernando (1541–1602), court musician to Philip II. In 1578 he publ. a coll. of his father's works but was a good composer in his own right.

Cabinet of Doctor Caligari, The (1919). Film directed by R. *Wiene.

cabinet picture. Small easel painting. The minor Netherlands painters specialized in this type of picture.

Cabiria (1913). Film directed by G. *Pastrone.

Cable George Washington (1844–1925). U.S. historian, novelist and short-story writer. Though a Southerner, C. was opposed to slavery and wrote various works on social problems. His novels are noted for their lively drawing of New Orleans society. Works include *Old Creole Days* (1879); the novel *The Grandissimes* (1880); the historical *The Creoles of Louisiana* (1884); and *The Cavalier* (1901), a story of the Civil War.

cabochon (from French *caboche*, 'big head'). A precious stone, especially a garnet, not cut or faceted but polished into a smooth semi-globular shape.

cabriole. An elevated step in ballet where the dancer springs from one foot with the working leg extended and brings up the supporting leg to meet the horizontal one, which he is raising at the same time. It is a step usually executed by male dancers.

cabriole leg. A type of leg much used in chair and table design in the 1st half of the 18th c. French in origin and typical of the rococo style, its main feature is an outward curving at the knee which is rounded (sometimes bearing a *cabochon), the leg then descending in an inward curve to curve outwards again at the foot.

caccia (Italian, 'hunt'). Medieval musical form; a piece for voices and instruments describing a hunt (sometimes also fishing scenes, etc.).

Caccini Giulio (*c.* 1550–1618). Italian composer, singer and lutenist; one of the *camerata. His *Euridice* (1600) was the 1st opera to be printed but more important was the coll. *Le Nuove musiche* (1601) containing monodies, madrigals and 1 chorus. The preface outlined the principles of this 'new music' which aimed at an emotional heightening of the text rather than mere descriptive word painting. C. criticized the dense structures of 16th-c. polyphony advocated *monody and *recitative and expounded a new style of singing which should express as naturally as possible the full emotion of the vocal line.

Cacoyannis Michael (1922–). Cypriot-born Greek film director. C. worked in British films before making *Windfall in Athens* (1953), a

The Ca' d'Oro

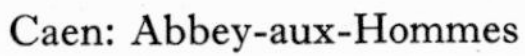

Caen: Abbey-aux-Hommes

post-*Clair comedy. Since then he has made melodramas, of which the best was *A Girl in Black* (1956). His other films are *Stella* (1955), *A Matter of Dignity* (1958), *The Wastrel* (1961) and *Electra* (1962) from Euripides.

cadence. In music a progression of chords which, coming at the end of a section or phrase, gives the effect of finality or closure. The main types of cadential chord progressions are as follows: the PERFECT, dominant to tonic; the IMPERFECT, tonic (or other chord) to dominant; the PLAGAL, subdominant to tonic; the INTERRUPTED, dominant to some chord other than the tonic, usually the submediant. In any of the preceding the final chord usually falls on a strong beat; when it comes on a weak beat we have a 'FEMININE' c.
In literature the term is used of either the natural rhythm of a language produced by the alternation of stressed and unstressed syllables, or the artificial organization of these rhythms in verse or prose.

cadenza (Italian, 'cadence'). Musical term for the section of an instrumental concerto given over to the solo instrument, primarily for the display of virtuosity. The c. was originally extemporized but since Mozart, composers have provided c.s for their concertos and famous performers have composed others; from the late 19th c. composers have left no part of the concerto to the will of the performer. The term was originally applied (18th c.) to the elaborate and extended passage of ornamentation before the penultimate chord of a cadence in a vocal aria.

Cadman Charles Wakefield (1881–1946). U.S. composer who made frequent use of American Indian themes. He composed many songs, e.g. 'From the Land of the Sky-Bluewater'. His compositions include the operas *Shanewis* (1918) and *A Witch of Salem* (1926) and the *Suite on American Folk Tunes* (1937) for strings.

Ca' d'Oro Venice (i.e. *Casa d'Oro*, 'House of Gold'). The most brilliant surviving Gothic palace on the Grand Canal, built 1424–36, the canal-front follows the normal pattern, with gondola-entrance at water-level and the main rooms, with highly decorated windows and balconies, on the first and second floors. The tracery makes lavish use of the favourite late Gothic motif, the ogee arch, and there is probably some Islamic influence.

Caedmon (*fl.* 7th c.). Anglo-Saxon poet. According to Bede he was an illiterate herdsman of the monastery of Whitby, who received the divine gift of song in a vision; he composed poetry from Scriptural passages trs. for him. Only the hymn recorded by Bede can be ascribed to him with certainty.

Caen France. Site of 2 of the most important churches in the Normandy-Romanesque style, from which English 'Norman' descends–the Abbaye-aux-Hommes and the Abbaye-aux-Dames. Both were built during the 3rd quarter of the 11th c., with long naves, transepts and 2-tower façades, and both were given sexpartite rib-vaults, *c.* 1130.

Caesar Gaius Julius (102/1–44 B.C.). Roman statesman, general and historian. C. conquered Gaul and made 2 expeditions to Britain. He defeated Pompey and his followers in a long and bloody civil war, and became dictator of Rome, paving the way for the creation of the Roman empire. He was assassinated by Brutus, Cassius and other republicans.
C.'s commentaries, *de bello Gallico* and *de bello civili*, written to justify his wars politically, were immediately recognized by Cicero as models of a new literary genre. 'Nothing is finer in historical writing than clear and perspicuous terseness.' C. was also a notable orator, second perhaps only to Cicero.

Caesar and Cleopatra (1899). Play by G. B. *Shaw, made into a film (1946) directed by G. Pascal.

caesura (from Latin, 'to cut'). In classical verse the break occurring in a foot between 2 words. In English verse a c. is a break in the line, usually about midway, and it usually coincides with a natural pause in the sense.

Caffarelli. Stage-name of Gaetano Majorano (1703–83), one of the greatest Italian male soprano *castrati singers. According to tradition his teacher, N. Porpora, kept him for 5 years at work on one page of exercises and then released him as 'the greatest singer in Europe'. C. amassed a fortune and bought a dukedom.

Cage John (1912–). U.S. composer. Using at first a percussion ensemble, and later 2 prepared pianos, he employed 'random' methods of composition–marking off staves round

Caedmon. Paraphrase of *Genesis* attributed to him; Junian ms. (10th c.)

Julius Caesar: coin

Calder. *Lobster Trap and Fish Tail* (1939); mobile

Calder. *Le Petit Nez* (1959); stabile

Caldecott. *The Fox jumped over the Parson's Gate*; coloured drawing

Maria Callas

Calderón de la Barca

smudges or scattered ink marks, or by throwing dice, etc. Appealing to Zen Buddhist principles, he claims that one should listen to the sounds (Nature) and not the idea (the Person). In his works single notes or bangs punctuate lengthy periods of silence, audience noise or the sound of radios tuned to random frequencies or of breaking glass, etc., or there is nothing but 'silence'. The audience, having questioned the absurdity of the performance should be forced into a new awareness of things outside the medium, which is the essence of the only communication possible for C.

Cagney James (1904–). U.S. film actor; in gangster roles, comedies, dramas and musicals. His star career was launched in *Public Enemy* (1931); other films include Dieterle's *A Midsummer Night's Dream* (1935), Walsh's *The Roaring '20s* (1939), *What Price Glory?* (1952), Ford's and Le Roy's *Mr Roberts* (1955) and Wilder's *One, Two, Three* (1963).

Cahiers du cinéma: *nouvelle vague

Caillebotte Gustave (1848–94). French impressionist painter and an early collector of impressionist paintings. He bequeathed his coll. to the Musée du Luxembourg and it is now in the Musée d'Impressionisme (Paris).

Caine Sir Thomas Henry Hall (1853–1931). English novelist. He became the secretary and close friend of D. G. Rossetti and produced his *Recollections* of Rossetti in 1882.

Cakes and Ale (1930). Novel by W. Somerset *Maugham.

Caldara Antonio (*c.* 1670–1736). Venetian composer. In Vienna he was, with J. J. Fux, in charge of music in the Imperial Chapel. He wrote over 70 operas, over 30 oratorios and motets, masses and string sonatas similar in style to Corelli.

Caldara Polidoro: *Polidoro da Caravaggio

Caldecott Randolph (1846–86). English illustrator and painter best known for his picture-books for children which were among the first to make use of colour wood engravings.

Calder Alexander (1898–). U.S. artist who first trained as an engineer. In Paris in the 1930s he was influenced by the work of Mondrian and Miró and broke new ground with his wire figure sculptures; these 'stabiles' gave place to C.'s new concept in sculpture, the mobile. C.'s mobiles, sometimes several feet from extremity to extremity, are carefully balanced constructions of metal plates, rods and wires which are activated by either air currents, mechanical means or the push of a hand. With their continually changing configurations they provide a new medium for the artist of space. C. has also produced book illustrations and stage sets.

Calderón Serafín Estébanez (1799–1867). Spanish writer whose reputation rests on his lively sketches of Andalusian scenes and customs, *Escenas andaluzas* (1847). His other works include a vol. of poetry, *Las poesías del solitario* (1830), and a novel, *Cristianos y moriscos* (1838).

Calderón de la Barca Pedro (1600–81). Spanish playwright and poet. He abandoned a theological training for writing and with the death of Lope de Vega in 1635 he was already the foremost Spanish playwright. In 1640 he enlisted as a cuirassier to fight against the insurgents in Catalonia where a rebellion had broken out, but had to retire 2 years later through ill-health. In 1651 he joined the order of St Francis as a priest. He began to write again, but most of his plays were *autos sacramentales* or allegorical scenes to be performed at Corpus Christi festivals and similar occasions. In 1663 he was appointed honorary chaplain to the king, holding the office until his death, but he seems to have been a poor man at the end of his life.

C., the last of the golden age of Spanish dramatists, was a prolific playwright. His best works (1628–40) show great skill in the elaborate construction of their plots (often based on Lope de Vega's). His most successful plays are mostly of the cloak-and-dagger type (*La dama duende*, 1629; *Mañanas de abril y mayo*), tragedies of honour and jealousy featuring the peculiarly fierce Spanish moral code in which the unfortunate heroine is usually sacrificed to the exigencies of an implacable convention (*El médico de su honra*, 1635). The 2 plays for which C. is now most renowned are his masterpieces *El alcalde de Zalamea* (*The Mayor of Zalamea*, before 1638) and the *La Vida es sueño* (1635). The former is one of the finest tragedies in Spanish literature and the most original and profound of all C.'s works. Based on a play by Lope, it deals with the honour of a peasant

Callot. *Robbers hanged from a tree*; from the *Misères*

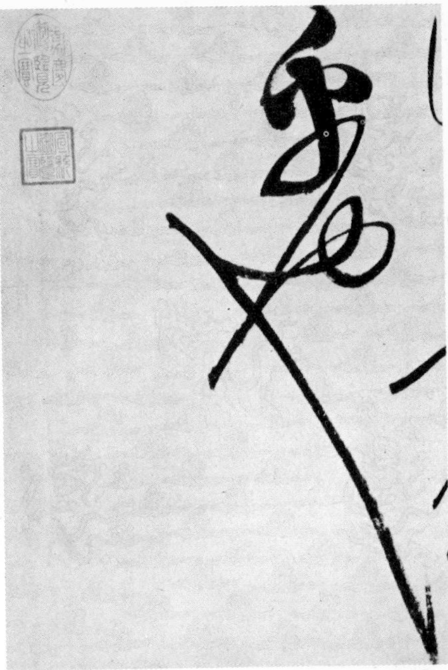

Calligraphy. Early 12th-c. Chinese characters

Calligraphy. Kline's *White Forms* (1955)

whose daughter has been raped by a captain of militia. It expresses C.'s views on the human condition in terms of a philosophical allegory, and dramatizes man's conflict with fate and the reality of life, which appears to be as fleeting as a dream.

Caldwell Erskine (Preston) (1903–). U.S. journalist, short-story writer, novelist and screen writer, whose works vehemently attack social inequalities and race hatred. Novels include *Tobacco Road* (1932), later dramatized by J. Kirkland, *God's Little Acre* (1933), *Place called Estherville* (1949), and short stories *Jackpot* (1940).

Caleb Williams, The Adventures of (1794). Novel by William *Godwin.

Caliari Paolo: *Veronese

calinda. A dance brought by Negro slaves to the Americas. Delius bases on it 'La Calinda', an orchestral piece in his opera *Koanga*.

Callaghan Morley Edward (1903–). Canadian novelist and short-story writer, a journalist colleague of Hemingway, whose influence is apparent in C.'s earlier work. Montreal and Toronto are his particular milieu. *The Loved and the Lost* (1951) represents an impressive departure from former realism and naturalism into symbolism.

Callas Maria (1923–). Soprano operatic singer of world fame. She was born in the U.S. of Greek parents (original name Calogeropoulos) but first made her name in Italy, where she married Meneghini (since divorced), adopting the name Meneghini-C. She specializes in Rossini, Donizetti and Bellini, and is remarkable not only as a singer but as a great actress.

Callicrates (*fl.* mid 5th c. B.C.). One of the architects of the *Parthenon, Athens.

Calligrammes (1918). The coll. poems of G. *Apollinaire.

calligraphy. This has been classified as a fine art in China since the 4th c. A.D. The brush is used both for writing and for painting, and the written word is a visual ideogram and not, as in the West, the equivalent of a sound by phonetic symbols. While brush-strokes in China must be life-containing and spontaneous, their execution and appreciation are bound by strict rules. Each character must distribute its ink-intensities and lines in a rectangular field of its own; it is both an abstract composition and part of the sentence's flow. The aesthetic concentration on brush-strokes has recently been taken up as a style in painting by modern Western painters, such as *Kline, Michaux, and *Tobey, under direct Japanese influence.

Callimachus (*fl.* 5th c. B.C.). Greek sculptor and architect to whom was ascribed (doubtless unhistorically) the invention of the Corinthian capital. He is said to have been inspired by seeing an acanthus plant growing through a basket.

Call of the Wild, The (1903). Novel by Jack *London.

Callot Jacques (1592–1635). French etcher, one of the masters of this technique who made it a respectable medium in its own right. He spent about 10 years in Rome and Florence but from 1622 worked mainly in Nancy. He drew court festivities, battle and crowd scenes, grotesque figures, etc., but is most famous for *Les Grandes Misères de la Guerre* (1633) illustrating the horrifying brutalities of the 30 Years War. His use of etching rather than line engraving enabled him to make extensive use of aerial perspective.

calotype process. Photographic negative process perfected by Fox Talbot in England in 1840; it became obsolete in 1851 when it was superseded by the *collodion negative which gave generally better and faster results.

Cals Adolphe-Félix (1810–80). French genre and landscape painter whose work gives a sympathetic, slightly melancholy portrayal of peasant life. In 1879 he exhibited with the impressionists.

Calvaert Dionisio or Denis (*c.* 1545–1619). Flemish painter of landscape and religious subjects who went to Italy in his early 20s. After studying in Bologna and Rome he opened an academy in Bologna which preceded that of the *Carracci; F. Albani, G. Reni and Domenichino were among his pupils. His work was eclectic, but popular for its brilliant colours and sensitive brushwork.

Calvaert. *Scourging of Christ* (detail)

Calvert. *The Ploughman, or the Christian Ploughing the Last Furrow of Life*; engraving

Jean Calvin

Camargo: painting by Vigée-Lebrun

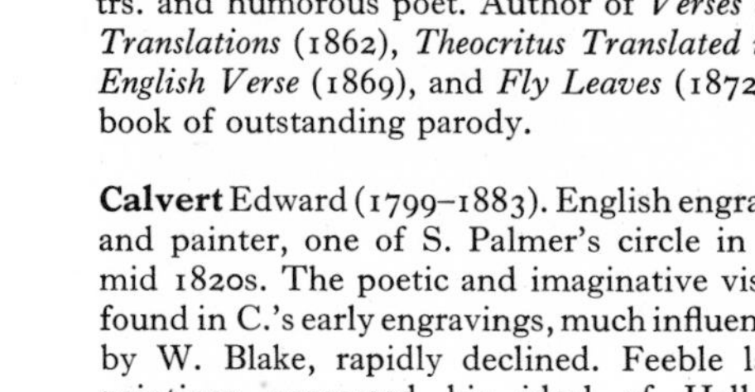

Calverley Charles Stuart (1831–84). English trs. and humorous poet. Author of *Verses and Translations* (1862), *Theocritus Translated into English Verse* (1869), and *Fly Leaves* (1872), a book of outstanding parody.

Calvert Edward (1799–1883). English engraver and painter, one of S. Palmer's circle in the mid 1820s. The poetic and imaginative vision found in C.'s early engravings, much influenced by W. Blake, rapidly declined. Feeble later paintings expressed his ideal of Hellenic paganism.

Calvin Jean (1509–64). French religious reformer and writer. When the Protestant clergy of Geneva established ecclesiastical government (1541), this was organized by Calvin, who thereafter ruled the city. His famous work, *L'Institution de la réligion chrétienne*, was condemned and burned in France. Calvin himself trs. his original Latin ed. (1536) into French (1541), thereby bringing a new literary dignity to the vernacular and setting a precedent for its future use, even in serious prose.

Camargo Marie Anne de Cupis de (1710–70). French dancer, chiefly remembered for her daring in shortening the dance skirt to just a few ins above the ground, thus making possible, for the 1st time, steps of elevation. She also introduced the heel-less shoe to give the dancer further freedom.

Camargo Society, The. Ballet company, named after Marie *Camargo, formed in London (1930) by P. J. S. Richardson and A. Haskell for the advancement of ballet in England. The society commissioned ballets from, among others, F. Ashton and N. de Valois. It was dissolved in 1933 and the repertoire and funds handed over to the newly established Vic-Wells Ballet.

Cambert Robert (*c.* 1628–77). French composer; he and his associate and librettist Pierre Perrin (*c.* 1620–75) were the forerunners of opera in France. Their *La pastorale d'Issy* (1659) was called the 'first French comedy in music'. In 1671 they produced *Pomone* with the 1st French recitative but in 1672 *Lully took over their theatre and C. went to London.

Cambridge. One of the 2 ancient univ. towns of England, notable for its college architecture. The most splendid single building is King's College Chapel (1446–1515), the last masterpiece of the Gothic style in England: a simple rectangle in plan with tall pinnacles at the corners; large windows filled with stained glass (still complete); perpendicular tracery on both windows and wall surfaces, with lavish deeply carved decoration and a superb fan-vault. Some other colleges contain medieval buildings (St John's, Jesus) and there are notable works by *Gibbs, *Wilkins, Sir G. G. *Scott, Leslie *Martin, Sir Basil *Spence and Denys *Lasdun.

Camden William (1551–1623). English antiquary and historian. He wrote in Latin the archaeological and topographical survey *Britannia . . .* (1586, trs. 1610), which served as a guide for Drayton when writing his *Polyolbion*; and a history of Elizabeth I's reign.

Camden Town Group, The. Inspired by *Sickert and formed in 1911 by English painters who introduced *post-impressionism into England, this group, which later merged with the London Group, included F. S. *Gore and Harold *Gilman.

cameo. Relief engraving of gems or hard stones; it derived from the Egyptian, Greek and Etruscan practice of carving scarabs. These stones, bearing the mystic symbol of a beetle in relief on the one side and an intaglio design on the other, were the primitives of the antique c. The material is usually a siliceous stone consisting of 2 or more bands of distinctive colour. Onyx describes a stone with a black and a white layer in which the design is normally cut into the white with the black layer forming the background. Sardonyx is richer, having layers of cornelian or sard in addition to the black and white. Antique c.s were much prized in the middle ages and the Renaissance and were often richly remounted. The art of engraving flourished again in 15th- and 16th-c. Italy and in the late 18th–early 19th c. when the c. style was used in interior and exterior decoration and in pottery, e.g. *Wedgwood's jasper ware.

Cameraman, The (1928). Film with B. *Keaton.

camera obscura ('dark') and **lucida** ('light'). Devices using light to throw an image of a landscape, portrait, etc., on to paper; the artist can then copy or trace it. The c. o. (in which

Cameo of agate; Italian; *c.* 1580. See also colour plate 17

Cambridge. King's College Chapel

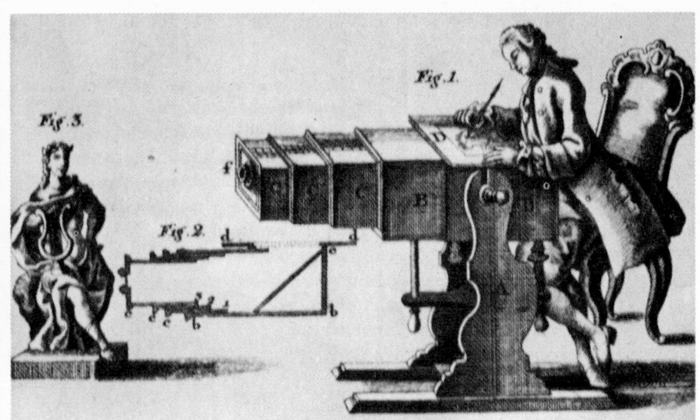

Table camera obscura, 1769

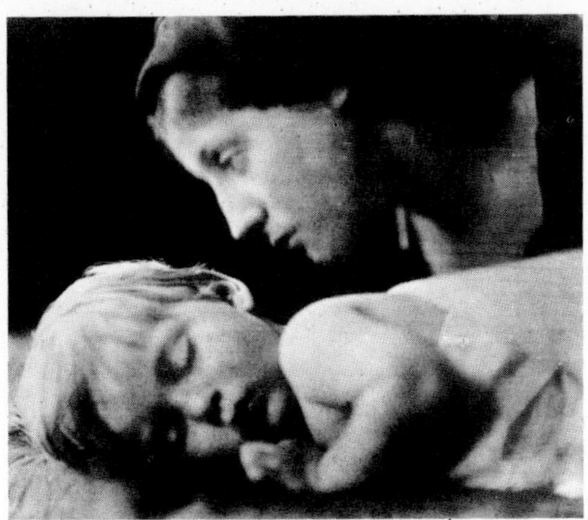
Julia Margaret Cameron. *Mother and Child.* Also *Carlyle

Camoens

an inverted image is thrown through a small opening on to a surface in a darkened room) uses an optical principle which makes photography possible. The c. l. uses a prism to throw an image on to a drawing surface.

camerata. The group of musicians, writers and amateurs, meeting in Florence during the 1590s, who developed the early opera. They included the composers G. *Caccini, E. de' Cavalieri, V. Galilei and J. *Peri, the poet O. *Rinuccini and the patron Count Bardi.

Cameron Charles (*c.* 1740–1812). Scottish architect who worked mainly in Russia. He built part of Tsarskoe Selo, the cathedral of St Sophia and the Agate Pavilion (all in or near Leningrad) for Catherine the Great. His style, a combination of Palladian and Adam brothers, was also influenced by C.'s early study of Roman baths.

Cameron Julia Margaret (1815–79). English photographer of the Pre-Raphaelite school. Her portraits of the literary, artistic and scientific celebrities of the day are characterized by their soft lines and psychological perception. In 1875 she went to Ceylon where she devoted her talents to documenting the native mores.

Cameron Norman (1905–53). English poet and trs. Most of his small output is in *The Winter House* (1935) and in *1957 Collected Poems.* It is distinguished for its rhythm, wit and verbal precision.

Camille (1926). Film directed by G. *Cukor.

Cammaerts Émile (1879–1953). Belgian poet and playwright, from 1908 living in England and writing studies of Belgian life, etc., in English. Verse colls include *Chants patriotiques* (1915; *Belgian Poems*, 1915).

Camoens Luis Vaz de (*c.* 1524–80). The greatest of Portuguese poets. As a young man he was a court favourite at Lisbon until, *c.* 1542, he was banished for an indiscreet amour. After exile in N. Africa, where he lost an eye on active service against the Moors, he returned to Lisbon only to suffer banishment once again (1553) this time to India, for an affray with a court official. Not until 1570 did C. finally return to Lisbon, his years of exile taking him to Goa and then to Macao in the capacity of a minor colonial official; he received a small government pension on the publ. of *Os Lusiadas* in 1572 (*The Lusiad*, 1655).

The Lusiads is a major formative work of Portuguese verse and a European masterpiece. Tasso addressed a sonnet to C., Lope de Vega rated *The Lusiads* above the *Aeneid* and the *Iliad*, and Voltaire greatly admired the work. It recounts in 10 cantos Vasco da Gama's voyage of discovery to India, and within this framework, using da Gama's conversations with the rulers he meets, prophecies by the Olympian gods, etc., narrates in detail the history of Portugal. The story is one of courage and man's intrepidity; C. describes the daring navigators as true heroes, and the sea, their element, is brilliantly presented in all its moods. C.'s poetry, both in *The Lusiads* and in his exquisite lyrical verse, is distinguished by its ease and transparency, by its passionate outbursts, sometimes achieving the greatest heights of poetic expression. His personal courage and fierce patriotism shapes his epic, and the flashes of wit and the moments of melancholy and of stoical endurance make it a work of universal significance, the forceful and precise style one of great poetic stature.

Campagnola Domenico (*c.* 1482–*c.* 1562). Painter and engraver of the Venetian school. He closely imitated Titian and Giorgione, and several works until recently believed to be by those masters are now attributed to C.

Campagnoli Bartolommeo (1751–1827). Italian violinist, composer and teacher. His system *Metodo per violino* (1797) was widely trs. and frequently re-publ.; among his compositions the 41 capriccios for viola are the best.

Campana Dino (1885–1932). Italian poet, whose wild and Bohemian life ended in a mental home. His main work, *Canti Orfici* (1914), has a remarkable hallucinatory power and a haunting dream-like quality combined with extremely original and expressive imagery. C. greatly influenced several of his contemporaries.

campanile. Architectural term for a bell-tower; it may be part of a church or, as in the famous 'Leaning Tower' of Pisa, a separate building. The most famous c. is that of St Mark's, Venice.

Charles Cameron. The Green Dining-room, the Catherine Palace, Tsarskoe Selo

The campanile of St Mark's

Mrs Patrick Campbell in *The Notorious Mrs Ebbsmith*

Albert Camus

Colin Campbell. Mereworth Castle

Campendonck. *Bavarian landscape*

Campbell Colin (d. 1729). Scottish architect. He was a Palladian before Lord *Burlington, who employed him on Burlington House. His books, *Vitruvius Britannicus* and a trs. of Palladio's *Quattro Libri*, had a great influence. C.'s best work is Mereworth Castle, Kent, a version of Palladio's Villa Rotunda.

Campbell Mrs Patrick (1865–1940). English actress; her friend, G. B. Shaw wrote the part of Eliza for her in *Pygmalion* (1914). Witty as well as beautiful, she was one of the most stylish actresses of her generation.

Campbell Roy (1901–57). South African poet. He lived most of his life as an expatriate in Spain and Portugal, where he was killed in a car crash.
The best of his poetry is in *Flaming Terrapin* (1931) and *Mithraic Emblems* (1936) and especially in 3 vols of coll. poetry publ. since his death. His exuberant sense of life is matched by an extraordinary technical excellence and virtuosity.

Campbell Thomas (1777–1844). Scottish poet, chiefly known for such patriotic pieces as *Hohenlinden* and *Ye Mariners of England.*

Campendonk Heinrich (1889–1957). German painter, woodcut artist and designer of stained glass; member of Der Blaue Reiter group. In 1935 he emigrated to Holland. He was influenced by Marc and Chagall and the Ravenna mosaics, and derived inspiration from folk-art, particularly Bavarian glass painting and African sculpture. In compositions expressing an ideal state of unification between man and nature he showed himself, particularly in his earlier work, a colourist of great imaginative charm and tenderness.

Campigli Massimo (1895–). Italian painter who has evolved an archaistic style based on Etruscan and Cretan art, modified by the cylindrical forms of cubism.

Campin Robert: *Master of Flémalle

Campion or **Campian** Thomas (1562–1620). English poet and composer, setting his own words, e.g. the exquisite 'There is a garden in her face'. His publs include 5 books of late ayres; the verses to *Songs of Mourning* (1613), on the death of Prince Henry, and *Observations in the Art of English Poesie* (1602) criticizing the use of rhyme in English poetry.

Campoamor Ramón de (1817–1901). Spanish poet who wished to reform the language of poetry and expel the inflated vocabulary of the romantics. His work, however, is trivial, sententious and flat, though gently ironical. The recent generation of 'realist' poets has endeavoured to rehabilitate him, but can find praise only for his poetic theories, not for his writing.

Campra André (1660–1744). French composer. After a career in provincial cathedrals he was director of music at Notre-Dame, Paris (1694–1700), thereafter writing for the stage. His were the leading French operas between Lully and Rameau; he endeavoured, he said, to combine the delicacy of French with the vivacity of Italian music.

Camus Albert (1913–60). French novelist, essayist and dramatist, awarded the Nobel prize in 1957. Born and bred in Algeria, C. thought of himself as a 'Mediterranean' writer. He was active in the Resistance movement, a prominent contributor to the post-war daily, *Combat*, and an associate of J.-P. Sartre until they quarrelled over the attitude to adopt towards Communism. C.'s development was from a pagan sense of the pointlessness and occasional beauty of existence, expressed in *L'Étranger* (1942; *The Outsider*, 1946) to an awareness of collective responsibility in face of evil in *La Peste* (1947; *The Plague*, 1948) and then to an almost religious sense of guilt in *La Chute* (1956; *The Fall*, 1957). He was at work on a further novel when he was killed in a car accident. His major theoretical statements are to be found in *Le Mythe de Sisyphe* (1942; *The Myth of Sisyphus*, 1955) and *L'Homme revolté* (1952; *The Rebel*, 1953). C. shares the notion of the Absurd with the existentialists and the post-existentialist dramatists, but he is distinguished both by his exceptional stylistic gift and by his search for a common-sense secular philosophy. His most considerable and perhaps most representative work is *La Peste*, a modern parable in which evil takes the form of an outbreak of bubonic plague in the N. African town of Oran. His plays, *Caligula* (1944), *L'État de Siège* (1948) and *Les Justes* (1949) treat similar themes, but less convincingly.

Canaletto Bernardo Bellotto: Bernardo *Bellotto

Canaletto. Name adopted by Giovanni Antonio Canale (1697–1768), Italian painter of the Venetian school. Trained by his father and by Pannini in Rome, C. became the painter of Venice, its canals, the Rialto, the Riva dei Schiavoni, the Salute. His pictures were sold to tourists, including Englishmen on the Grand Tour, with whom he became so popular that he placed most of his business through Joseph Smith, later British consul in Venice. In 1746 C. was in London, and for the next 10 or so years he painted English scenes, but he appears to have been less in demand when he came to his market than he was in Venice. C. gives his studies of buildings, sky and water a shimmering effect and the rapid, stylized drawings of small figures in landscapes and town scenes were to influence artists and illustrators in every part of Europe to the present day. The Royal Colls contain much of his best work, both of the Venetian and the English period. A number of outstanding Venetian studies are in the Wallace Coll., London, and the masterly *Stone Mason's Yard* is in the N.G.

can-can (also called 'chahut'). Parisian show dance of quadrille type developing about 1850; it is used by Offenbach in his *Orpheus in the Underworld*. The c.-c. is in quick 2/4 time; it demands high-kicking, good legs and nice frilly skirts.

Cancelleria ('Chancellery') Rome. An important and influential early Renaissance palace whose authorship is still uncertain. Bramante probably had some part in it, though it was begun in 1486, before he came to Rome. The façade shows the influence of the Colosseum and the Palazzo Rucellai.

cancrizans. For canon cancrizans, *canon.

Candeille Amélie-Julie (1767–1834). French actress, singer and composer. Her 1st opera was produced in 1792 and she also wrote piano music. Her father, Pierre-Joseph C. (1744–1827), was also a composer.

Candela Felix (1910–). Spanish engineer and architect who settled in Mexico in 1939. His use of thin warped planes of concrete has produced structures of lightness, elegance and daring, and enabled him to roof large spaces economically.

candelabra. A standard candle-holder with 2 or more branches and sockets. Early examples are on a small scale, usually less than 10 ins, but the introduction of weighted bases and Sheffield plate in the late 18th c. led to larger and more elaborate styles.

Candida (1895). Play by G. B. *Shaw.

Candide, ou l'Optimisme (1759). Satirical novel by *Voltaire.

Canfield (married name Fisher) Dorothy (1879–1958). U.S. novelist, short-story writer, critic and trs. Her fiction includes *The Squirrel-Cage* (1912), *The Brimming Cup* (1921) and *The Deepening Stream* (1930).

Cannabich Christian (1731–98). German composer of the *Mannheim school, conductor and violinist. Besides about 50 symphonies he wrote operas and chamber music.

Cannery Row (1945). Book by John *Steinbeck.

cannetille. French term used in jewellery of matted gold enriched further with coarse filigree imitating the raised gold embroideries worn in France in the Napoleonic Empire.

Canning George (1770–1827). English statesman and writer, prime minister in 1827. C. was noted for his witty contributions to the journal *The Anti-Jacobin* (1797–8) which he founded. His *Poetical Works* were publ. in 1823.

Cannon Robert (1901–64). U.S. animated-film director. C. was the leading director at Stephen Bosustow's U.P.A. in the 1950s and led the breakaway from the chocolate-box naturalism of latter-day Disney cartoons. His emphasis on line and areas of plain colour was taken up by Ernest Pintoff. He was responsible for the *Christopher Crumpet* and *Gerald McBoing Boing* series.

Cano Alonso (1601–67). Spanish court painter, architect and sculptor called, on account of his versatility, the 'Michelangelo of Spain'. Like Velazquez he studied under F. Pacheco. He painted portraits and religious subjects in soft golden brownish tones but often with hard contours. There is an excellent portrait of C. by Velazquez.

canon. In music a form of composition in which one part (the 'dux') leads off and is imitated, note for note, by the other parts (the

Cano. *Annunciation*

Candela and Gonzalez Reyna. Institute of Radiology (1954)

The Cancelleria

Canaletto. *Stone Mason's Yard*

Canopic jars; alabaster

Canova. *Pauline Bonaparte Borghese as Venus*

'comites') entering at fixed intervals and overlapping; the round 'London's Burning' is a simple example. The subsequent parts can enter either on the same note as the first or at the 8ve above or below or on any intervening note; hence c. at the 8ve, c. at the 5th, c. at the unison and so on. When each voice on finishing begins again (as in a round) we have PERPETUAL c. C. 'two in one' is simply a c. for 2 voices and c. 'four in two' in effect two 2-part c.s played simultaneously (e.g. soprano imitated by tenor, alto by bass). The varieties of c. are c. by DIMINUTION, by *AUGMENTATION, by *INVERSION, when the imitating voices handle the dux in one of these ways, and the CRAB c. (or retrograde c. or c. canzicrans or c. recte et recto) in which the 2nd part is the 1st given backwards.

canopic jars. The 4 jars used in ancient Egyptian burials to hold the entrails of the embalmed person, the stopper of each jar being decorated with a head of one of the sons of the god Horus.

Canova Antonio (1757–1822). Italian sculptor, the most celebrated exponent of neo-classicism in sculpture. In Rome he executed monuments of Popes Clement XIII (1787–92; St Peter's) and Clement XIV (1782–7; SS Apostoli) and in Vienna the tomb of the Archduchess Maria Christina (completed 1805; Augustinerkirche). Other work included *Pauline Bonaparte Borghese as Venus* (1807; Borghese Gal., Rome) and the charming *Amor and Psyche* (1793; Louvre); C. also executed 2 huge nudes of the Emperor Napoleon, one of which was captured by Wellington (Apsley House, London).

Cantarini Simone called 'Simone da Pesaro' or 'Il Pesarese' (1612–48). Italian painter of portraits and religious subjects in the style of G. Reni.

cantata. Musical form in which a lyrical, dramatic or religious text is set to instrumental accompaniment. The Italian chamber c. originated from the late 16th-c. Florentine *monody; it was for solo voice, with lute or keyboard accompaniment, handled a dramatic or narrative theme (generally secular) and consisted of a series of arias and recitatives; the later church c. differed only in having a religious theme. In the late 17th c. both the above forms came to be set for more than one voice; in the early 18th c. the chamber c. acquired a semi-theatrical character, a more complex structure and ensemble accompaniment, but gradually gave place to the sonata; the church c., however, was further developed by German composers, above all J. S. Bach. The German church c. was a work of several movements, usually opening with a chorus and closing with a chorale, on an explicitly religious text often written for specific days in the liturgical year. It usually involved soloists, chorus and orchestra, though solo c.s were occasionally written. German secular c.s had the same elaboration of form and musical resources.

cante hondo (Spanish, 'profound song'). A traditional song type, with guitar accompaniment, from Andalusia. It begins with a long vocalization; this is followed by a melodic section usually confined to the range of a 6th and characterized by modifications of the semitone interval, great play with repeated notes and very florid embellishments. CANTE FLAMENCO (Flemish (?), 'song') is a derivation from c. h. and is best known through the work of flamenco guitarists.

Cantelli Guido (1920–56). Italian conductor appointed principal conductor of La Scala, Milan, but killed a few weeks later in an air crash.

Canterbury. A small music-stand, usually under 3 ft in height, fitted with partitions to hold music-books and popular during the 1st half of the 19th c. Also a plate and cutlery stand with a semicircular end designed specially for supper-parties in the late 18th c.

Canterbury cathedral. One of the key buildings in the history of English architecture, since it marks the introduction of French Île de France Gothic. The Norman choir, destroyed by fire in 1170, was rebuilt by *William of Sens. Specifically French features are the alternation of supports (circular and octagonal piers) with a sexpartite vault, coupled columns (presumably imitated from William's native city) and crocket capitals. But some Norman features survive (chevron ornament, round arches) and the use of black Purbeck marble was to become traditional in England but not in France. From 1178 the work was continued by William the Englishman, who was responsible for raising the level of the extreme E. end by a 2nd flight of steps. In 1378–1400 the nave was rebuilt by Henry *Yevele, and in 1494–7

Canterbury cathedral. See also colour plate 34

Capelle. *Dutch yacht firing a salute*

the crossing tower ('Bell Harry') built by John Wastell.

Canterbury Tales, The. *Chaucer's masterpiece.

Cantigas de Sānta Maria. One of the most important coll. of medieval music, a coll. of monophonic airs made by King *Alfonso X of Castile.

cantilena (Italian). Musical term describing a smooth flowing melodic line or style or performance, whether vocal or instrumental.

cantilever. Architectural term for a beam or girder supported in the middle and weighted at one end (e.g. by a wall) in order to be capable of carrying a weight (e.g. a balcony) at the other end.

Cantiones sacrae (Latin, 'sacred songs'). Name often given to colls of motets in the 16th c.

canto (Italian, 'song'). A literary term for a major section of a long poem, e.g. the c.s in Dante's *Divine Comedy*, or Spenser's *The Faerie Queene.*

canto fermo. Italian version of the Latin *cantus firmus.

Canton enamels. Ware produced and shipped to Europe in the 18th and 19th cs at the S. China port of Canton. Plates, dishes, bowls, etc., were decorated with multi-coloured designs painted in enamel on a white ground over the basic copper. These designs were reproduced from porcelain wares of the same date painted in enamel at Canton, both probably being inspired by Limoges painted enamels.

cantor (Latin, 'chanter'). (1) Church official, in English now generally called 'precentor'; his stall is on the N. side (called 'cantoris') of the choir, the dean's on the S. side (called 'decani'). Formerly the c. was in charge of the music, now usually the organist's responsibility. (2) In a German Evangelical church the director of music is called *Cantor* or *Kantor.* (3) Synagogue official who leads and directs the music of the service. The c.s have maintained the tradition of Jewish synagogue music. During the 18th c. 'wandering c.s' from Russia and Poland brought chaos to Central European synagogue music with their 'improvisations' often heavily influenced by Western art music. The great c. S. Sulzer initiated a major reform of synagogue music.

Cantos, The. Poetic work by Ezra *Pound.

cantus firmus (Latin, 'fixed song'). Either a piece of plainsong or a secular melody used by medieval and early Renaissance composers as a unifying basis of a mass or other piece. This 'theme' (often rhythmically modified) was given in one part, while the polyphony weaved about it. The c. f. often gave its name to the mass, e.g. *L'*homme armé.* In a wider sense, a c. f. is any theme played in one part of a composition as a thread round which the counterpoint weaves.

canzone (or canzona) (Italian, 'song'). (1) An Italian lyric verse form, often providing the text for a *frottole, deriving from the 13th-c. Provençal *canzo.* (2) *Canzoni alla francese* was the name given by 16th-c. Italian composers to their instrumental arrangements, for ensemble, lute or keyboard (usually organ), of French **chansons.* (3) In the 17th c. a form of instrumental composition often with a fugal introduction, the English term for this being CANZONA. (4) In the 18th c. a song (not an aria) in an opera or a light instrumental piece.

canzonet. English abbreviation of the Italian *canzonetta*, 'little song'. Late 16th–early 17th-c. strophic choral song similar to the madrigal, originating in Italy but taken over by English composers such as T. Morley.

Capa Robert, born Andrei Friedman (1913–54). Hungarian photographer, generally considered the greatest war photographer of our time. His most memorable photographs were taken during the Spanish Civil War, the invasion of Normandy and the war in Indo-China, where he died in a minefield. His principal concern was with direct action and the decisive moment; technical considerations were secondary. He was, with *Cartier-Bresson and David Seymour, one of the original founders of *Magnum photos.

Čapek Josef (1887–1945). Czech author, who collaborated with his younger brother Karel in some of his early works including *Ze života hmyzu* (1921; *The Insect Play*, 1923).

Čapek Karel (1890–1938). Czech writer, who often used fantasy situations e.g. *Ze života hmyzu* (1921; *The Insect Play*, 1923), in which insects are made human, for satire and moral comment. He was much alive to the dangers of science, particularly regimentation by the machine, e.g. his play *R.U.R.* (1921; *R.U.R.*, 1923) which first gave English the word 'robot' (from Czech *robotit*–'to drudge'). C.'s novels, often affected by H. G. Wells's early books, include *Krakatit* (1924; *Krakatit*, 1925), *Továrna na absolutno* (1922; *The Absolute at Large*, 1927), *Válka s Mloky* (1936; *War With the Newts*, 1937) and *Hordubal* (1933; *Hordubal*, 1934); and the delightful, humorous sketches *Anglické listy* (1924; *Letters from England*, 1925).

Capelle Jan van de (1624–79). Dutch marine painter, follower of S. de Vlieger. Being a man of some means, he painted for pleasure and appears to have been self-taught. His works are notable for greyish brown tones, high blowy clouds and reflected sunlight. He also painted winter scenes.

capital. Architectural term for the broad top of a column; it supports the entablature, and may be carved or moulded in various distinctive ways, each of the classical *orders and other styles (*Romanesque, *Gothic, etc.) requiring different treatment of the c.s.

Caplet André (1879–1925). French composer and conductor, a close friend of Debussy, several of whose works he orchestrated or arranged for piano. C.'s own music is highly individual, impressionistic, poetic and, in his religious work, mystical. His works include *Le Pié Jésus* (1919) for voice and organ and *Le Miroir de Jésus* (1924) for string quintet, harp and 3 female voices.

Capogrossi Giuseppe (1900–). Italian painter who turned from a representational style to abstraction in 1950. He began to paint his *Surfaces* in which he works out an infinite number of variations on a simple motif.

Capote Truman (1924–). U.S. novelist, film-script and short-story writer. In his works, with their strong psychological interest, the dream world and reality are closely related. Works include *Other Voices, Other Rooms* (1948); *The Grass Harp* (1951; dramatized 1952); *Breakfast at Tiffany's* (1958; filmed 1961); *A Tree of Night* (1949), coll. short stories; and *House of Flowers* (1954) for the Broadway musical comedy.

Karel Čapek

Capa. *Dying Spanish rebel*

Capogrossi. *Composition, 1953*

Capra. Gary Cooper in *Mr Deeds Goes to Town*

Capra Frank (1897–). Italian-born U.S. film director. C. started by directing shorts (1921) and after working as a gagman directed Harry Langdon comedies, first shorts, then features like *Long Pants* (1927). He became famous for a series of 1930s comedies: *Lady for a Day* (1933), *It Happened One Night* (1934), *Mr Deeds Goes to Town* (1936), etc. Less tough than *Hawks, C. was admired for his gentle satire, the goodness of his sentiments, and unobtrusive technical skill. His recent work, like *Pocketful of Miracles* (1961), a remake of *Lady for a Day*, has shown a lack of style.

capriccio (Italian, 'caprice'). Musical term applied (1) in the 17th c. to a piece in fugato style; (2) from the early 18th c. on to a piece in free form as for example Tchaikovsky's *Capriccio Italien*; (3) from the 19th c. also to brilliant short exercises on themes from other composers. The term is also used in the visual arts of fantasy pictures, the most remarkable examples being *Los Caprichos* of Goya.

Captain Brassbound's Conversion (1899). Play by G. B. Shaw.

Captain's Daughter, The (1836). Novel by *Pushkin.

Caracciolo. *Annunciation*

Capuana Luigi (1839–1915). Italian poet, playwright, novelist and critic. His works include the realistic novel *Giacinta* (1879), *C'era una volta* (1882; *Once Upon a Time Fairy-tales*, 1892), and *La reginotta* (1883).

Caracciolo Giovanni Battista called 'Battistello' (1570–1637). Neapolitan painter whose Caravaggesque style strongly influenced 17th-c. Neapolitan painting.

Carafa (di Colobrano) Michele Enrico (1787–1872). Italian opera composer who settled in Paris (1827), becoming professor of composition at the Conservatoire (1840).

Caragiale Ion Luca (1894–1912). Rumanian playwright and short-story writer. His works satirize bourgeois society.

carat (Arabic *quirat*, 'a weight of 4 grains'). (1) A measure for weighing precious stones; the exact weight of the c. varies in different places, but is usually 3·163 troy grains. (2) A measure for determining the fineness of gold; pure gold is said to be '24 c.', thus '12 c.' gold is an alloy with 50 per cent gold and 50 per cent base metal.

Caravaggio. The name taken from his birthplace by Michelangelo Merisi or Amerighi (1573–1610), an Italian painter. He was trained in Milan by an undistinguished mannerist. By 1593 he was in Rome working for other painters, very poor and already appearing in police records as a bravado. In about 1596 his fortunes changed dramatically. Some of his paintings were bought by the influential Cardinal del Monte and he was commissioned to paint a series of large religious paintings for the Contarelli chapel, S. Luigi de' Francesi. Previous to this C. had painted some of the 1st true still-lifes, notably *The Basket of Fruit* (Ambrosiana, Milan), a series of paintings of a model as 'Bacchus' (Uffizi; and Gal. Borghese, Rome), *The Musical Party* (Met. Mus.) and a masterly double half-portrait of a man and woman entitled *The Fortune Teller* (Louvre), which obviously owes something to Giorgione in subject and composition, though the lighting and feeling reveal a quite new and original talent. For the Contarelli chapel C. painted an altarpiece, *St Matthew and an Angel*, and 2 large canvases for the side walls, *The Calling of St Matthew* and *The Martyrdom of St Matthew*. These pictures caused a sensation. The 'St Matthew' (original destroyed 1945) of the altarpiece was considered vulgar and sacrilegious by the clergy and C. painted the 2nd version, still in the church. Other major works of the period are *The Conversion of St Paul*, *The Martyrdom of St Paul* for S. Maria del Popolo, *The Supper at Emmaus* (N.G., London), *The Death of the Virgin* (Louvre) and *The Deposition of Christ* (Vatican). At the height of his success C. killed a companion in a brawl and had to flee Rome. The last years of his life consisted of short periods of asylum, spent painting, at Naples, in Malta and Sicily. Each period ended in a brawl and renewed flight. Wounded in Palermo he reached Porto Ercole where he died. Although recent scholarship has modified C.'s reputation as a revolutionary, he remains one of the true innovators. He declared early in his career that he had rejected the Renaissance search for the ideal and would study no teacher but nature. His method of painting directly from the model and his choice of models from low life, presented just as they were even in his large religious works, were both complete breaks with tradition. However, to consider him a realist before his time is to

Caravaggio. *The Supper at Emmaus*. See also colour plate 54

Caravaggio. *Bacchus*

miss his other innovation, a heightening of dramatic effect by the use of lighting that was always contrived and often highly artificial. Attacked by many, his works were protected by powerful patrons during his life and after his death. The imitation of his work inspired a school of painting in Spain and led to the art of Velazquez. In N. Europe he had even more followers; the most directly affected were G. de la Tour in France and G. Honthorst in Holland, and Rembrandt learned much from him.

carbuncle (from Latin *carbunculus*, 'a small coal'). In jewellery, applied to precious stones of a red or fiery hue. Formerly: rubies, spinels, sapphires. Nowadays usually applied to garnets cut en *cabochon.

carcan or carcanet. A short necklace of elaborate links, often jewelled, worn by women in the 16th c., often forming part of a *parure.

Carco Francis. Pseud. of François Carcopino-Tusoli (1886–1958), French poet and novelist of Bohemian life in Montmartre. His best-known novel is *La Bohème et mon cœur* (1912) and his numerous vols of poetry include *Chansons aigre-douces* (1913) and *L'Homme traqué* (1922).

Cardarelli Vincenzo (1887–1959). Italian poet and prose writer. In his youth he collaborated on various literary reviews such as *La Voce* and *Lirica* before taking part in the founding of *La Ronda*, which advocated a return to neo-classicism in literature and strict formalism in poetry. His verse is strictly disciplined and eloquent with more than a hint of Leopardi's influence.

Cardew Cornelius (1936–). English composer, son of Michael C., a follower of J. *Cage.

Cardew Michael (1901–). English artist potter. After 3 years (1923–6) with Bernard *Leach, C. took over a large disused pottery at Winchcombe, Gloucestershire and exhibited at the 1938 London Exhibition; from 1942 he worked in W. Africa and in 1950 organized a government pottery in Nigeria. Deriving formal inspiration from English medieval pottery and slipware C. aims to produce reasonably priced useful ware but he has also produced some of the finest pieces of 20th-c. art pottery.

Card Players, The (1890–2). Paintings by *Cézanne.

Carducci (Carducho) Bartolommeo (Bartolomé) (1560–1610). Italian painter of religious subjects who settled in Spain and was one of the first to work in a baroque style there.

Carducci Giosue' (1835–1907). Italian poet, and the 1st Italian Nobel literature prize-winner (1906). He was brought up in a liberal and patriotic background by his father who was a doctor. C. studied philosophy and letters and became a teacher and later a professor of Italian literature at the univ. of Bologna. Politically C. began as a fierce republican, but in later years he was able to accept the idea of monarchy and in 1890 became a senator of the new kingdom of Italy. He loved the quiet of his native Maremma and always had a deep feeling for the beauties of nature, but the real inspiration of his poetry is his patriotic love for Italy. C.'s classic style and his personal dignity of spirit as the poet of the national unification of Italy represented a refreshing break from the flowery exaggeration of Italian romanticism. His influence on Italian thought and letters, throughout his 40 years of teaching, was profound.

Carducci (Carducho) Vincenzo (Vincente) (1568–1638). Italian baroque painter, chiefly of religious subjects, who accompanied his brother Bartolommeo to Spain and settled there. In 1633 he publ. *Diálogos de . . . la Pintura . . .* which gives an account of contemporary Spanish and Italian painters and illustrates the tensions which existed between mannerist and baroque aims.

Caresme (Jacques-)Philippe (1734–96). French painter of scenes from classical mythology; pupil of C.-A. Coypel.

Carestini Giovanni (1705–60). Italian castrato singer (alto) who sang in Handel's London opera (1733–5) as the rival of *Farinelli at the opera of the nobility.

Caretaker, The (1960). Play by Harold *Pinter on which a film (1963) directed by Clive *Donner was based.

Carew Thomas (*c.* 1595–*c.* 1640). English poet and courtier, one of the 1st Cavalier lyricists. His work was influenced by Jonson and Donne

Thomas Carew

Giosue' Carducci

V. Carducci. *The Dream of St Hugh of Grenoble*

Caravaggio. *The Basket of Fruit*

Dish by Michael Cardew

Carlevaris. *Reception in Venice of the Earl of Manchester as British Ambassador*

Carjat. Portrait of Puvis de Chavannes. Also *Baudelaire

Caricature: Hogarth, *The Old Baby*

Caricature: Goya, *Correction*

Caricature: Daumier, *The Growler* (detail)

Caricature: Grosz, *Waving the Flag* (1947–8)

but lacked the powerful emotion of the latter, even in his best poem, *The Rapture*, which is sensual and passionate.

Carey Henry (d. 1743). English poet and composer. His farce *The Contrivances* (1715), for which he composed music (1729), was popular throughout the 18th c. He also wrote the words of 'Sally in our Alley' (his original tune is not now used), many other songs, cantatas and stage works. His son GEORGE SAVILLE C. (1743–1807), writer and actor, claimed, wrongly, that his father wrote the tune of the national anthem.

Cariani Giovanni Busi, called (*fl.* early 16th c.). Italian painter of the Venetian school. He was a pupil of Giovanni Bellini but had a varied style chiefly derived from Palma Vecchio, Giorgione and Titian. He retained an individual boldness of style in his portraiture.

caricature. The representation of a person's characteristic features or attitudes in an exaggerated manner so as to produce a ludicrous effect; in frequent use as an instrument of social and political criticism. The grotesque figures found in medieval sculpture and the physiognomical studies of Leonardo da Vinci are among the predecessors of the c., which was developed as we know it by the Carracci; the word 'c.' first appears in Italian writings of the 17th c. Apart from its use in the Press of the 19th (e.g. Gillray) and 20th cs, its exponents have included Hogarth, Goya, Daumier and Grosz.

carillon. A musical instrument of bells, hung 'fixed' (usually in a church tower), and played by clappers controlled from a keyboard and pedal-board. The c. is chromatic through a range of three to four 8ves, and is capable of music in 3 or more parts and of dynamic expression; it is particularly common in Belgium and the Netherlands.

Carissimi Giacomo (1605–74). Italian composer important in the early development of oratorio. In 1630 he became musical director at the Jesuit church of S. Apollinare in Rome, remaining there till his death. C.'s music showed a strongly developed sense of tonality and harmonic direction and a control of formal organization. He was a master of declamatory recitative after the style of Monteverdi, of expressive harmony and melodic line, and had a strong dramatic sense. His pupils included A. Scarlatti. Like such contemporaries as L. Rossi, C. secularized church music, developing the cantata as well as the oratorio; his 16 surviving oratorios include his masterpiece, *Jephte*; *Jonah, Historia di Abramo e Isacco* and *Oratorio del Crocefisso.* Many of his works were lost in the disposal of 'rubbish' from S. Apollinare at the suppression of the Jesuits in the 18th c.

Carjat Étienne (1828–1906). French portrait photographer much of whose work showed exceptional insight into character. He was also a caricaturist and ed. of *Le Boulevard.*

Carleton William (1794–1869). Irish storyteller, novelist and journalist whose best work is to be found in *Traits and Stories of the Irish Peasantry* (1830–3). W. B. Yeats introduced a selected *Stories from Carleton* (1889).

Carlevaris Luca (1665–1731). Italian painter and etcher who lived in Venice from 1679 and painted scenes of the city for foreign visitors. In this he was a precursor of Canaletto and Guardi, though he maintained a greater interest in figure groups.

Carlsund Otto Gustaf (1897–1948). Swedish painter who pioneered *avant-garde* painting in Sweden. After attendance at Dresden and Oslo academies he went to Paris (1924) to work under Léger. Through contact with Mondrian he was converted to neo-plasticism. In 1930 he joined Van Doesburg's Art Concret group. Between 1931 and 1944 he gave up painting and turned to art criticism.

Carlyle Thomas (1795–1881). Scottish historian, literary critic and publicist. C.'s idiosyncratic prose style is uneven and sometimes over-involved, but at its best it is passionate and vital, and combines wit with rhetoric. His historical writing was popular because of its emphasis on individual action in history, its drama and vivid characterization. He expounded his view of great men as the motivating forces of history in *On Heroes, Hero-Worship . . .* (1841). Important historical works were *The French Revolution* (1837), *Oliver Cromwell's Letters and Speeches* (1845) and *The History . . . Frederick the Great* (1858–65). *Sartor Resartus* (1836), on moral philosophy, recounted his spiritual revival. C. was an important interpreter of German literature; his

Carlyle: photograph by J. M. Cameron

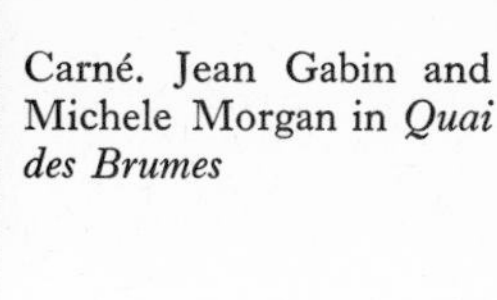

Carné. Jean Gabin and Michele Morgan in *Quai des Brumes*

critical works include *The Life of Schiller* (1825), *German Romance* (1827). C.'s writings influenced his great friend Emerson.

Carman (William) Bliss (1861–1929). Canadian-born poet, living mainly in the U.S. His verse is vigorous and carefree and includes *Low Tide on Grand Pre* (1893) and *Pipes of Pan* (1905). In collaboration with Richard Hovey he wrote the famous *Songs from Vagabondia* (1894–1901). In 1928 he was appointed Canadian poet laureate.

Carmen. Opera by *Bizet, libretto by H. Meilhac and L. Halévy after Mérimée; 1st performance in Paris in 1875.

Carmen Jones (1954). Film directed by O. *Preminger.

Carmichael Franklin (1890–1945). Canadian painter, one of the *Group of Seven.

Carmina Burana. Late 13th-c. coll. of German and Latin songs called after the Benediktbeuren monastery in Bavaria where the ms. was found. There are 4 main groups, moral and satirical verses, love-songs, drinking-songs and spiritual verses; some by students and goliards, others tentatively ascribed to churchmen and poets. C. Orff set some of the verses in his 'scenic cantata' *Carmina Burana.*

Carnaval (French, 'Carnival'). A set of 21 piano pieces by *Schumann.

Carnaval, Le. 1-act ballet with choreography by Fokine, music from Schumann and décor by Bakst; 1st performance 1910.

Carnaval des animaux, Le. A fantasy in 14 movements by Saint-Saëns for 2 pianos and orchestra (English title *The Carnival of Animals*); it includes the famous 'The Swan' (no. 13).

Carnaval romain, Le. Overture (English title *Roman Carnival*) by Berlioz, based on his opera *Benvenuto Cellini.*

Carné Marcel (1909–). French film director. C. was a journalist and assistant to Clair and Feyder before making a documentary, *Nogent, Eldorado du Dimanche* (1930). Apart from a crazy comedy, *Drôle de Drame* (1937), C.'s famous 1930s films were brilliantly acted pessimistic melodramas. The fatalism of *Quai des Brumes* (1938) and *Le Jour se lève* (1939) typified much of the French cinema of the 1930s. Both this and the quality of the latter film owe a great deal to the poet Jacques Prévert, who also collaborated on the 2 period films *Les Visiteurs du soir* (1942) and *Les Enfants du Paradis* (1945), a complex and ambitious exercise in romantic fatalism. Thereafter C.'s work declined, although *Thérèse Raquin* (1953) was a good adaptation of Zola and *Les Tricheurs* (1958) had great commercial success.

Carnet de Bal, Un (1937). Film directed by J. *Duvivier.

Carnival (1891). Overture by Dvořák, the second of 3 overtures originally collectively entitled *Nature, Life and Love. Carneval*, the German for the Czech 'Karneval', is sometimes used in English.

carol. A medieval lyric musical form consisting of uniform stanzas (the text having the characteristic rhyming pattern *aaab*) preceded and interspersed with a burden, or refrain. C.s were didactic, processional, occasional (e.g. the Agincourt song) and religious; in modern usage the name is given to hymns sung at Christmas-time.

Caroline verse: *Cavalier verse

Carolingian renaissance. Name given to the revival of scholarship and the arts under the Frankish emperor, Charlemagne (d. 814). The revival of education, promoted by the founding of schools throughout the empire, sprang from the return to Latin literature and scholarship directed at Charlemagne's court at Aachen by the Anglo-Saxon scholar, *Alcuin. A major achievement of the C. r. was the copying of classical mss and the development of the strongly-formed and clear minuscule script. In architecture the C. r. marked the return, in Europe, to large-scale building; works such as the cathedral at *Aachen led to the development of the *Romanesque style.

Caron Leslie (1931–). French dancer who studied at the Paris Conservatoire and joined the Ballets des Champs-Elysées in 1948. In the same year she danced in the original production of Lichine's *La Création*, an experimental ballet without music or décor. She left ballet for films in 1956, starring in, e.g., *Gigi* (1958).

Carolingian renaissance. The Gospels of St Médard de Soissons, early 9th c.

Carolingian renaissance. Corvey, W. front. Also *Aachen

Carpaccio. *Two Venetian Ladies*

Carpaccio. *The Dream of St Ursula*

Carrickmacross lace

Carrá. *My Son*

Carpeaux. *The Dance*

Carossa Hans (1878–1956). German doctor, writer and lyric poet whose compassion and concern for the individual are evident in his works, e.g. autobiography *Eine Kindheit* (1922; *A Childhood*, 1930); *Das Jahr der schönen Täuschungen* (1941; *The Year of Sweet Illusions*, 1951); the novel *Der Arzt Gion* (1931; *Doctor Gion*, 1933).

Carpaccio Vittore (*c.* 1460–*c.* 1525). Italian painter of the Venetian school, trained in the style of the Vivarini and the Bellini. C.'s best-known work is the cycle of paintings *The Legend of St Ursula* (Accademia, Venice). A story-teller of great imagination, C. related the incidents of the legend against the background of an idealized version of the Venice he knew. Thus the enchanting *Dream of St Ursula* shows the bedroom of a Venetian noblewoman. Similarly in *The Vision of St Augustine* (Scuola di San Giorgio, Venice) the artist depicts the grandiose study of some Renaissance scholar-churchman. C. has always been a popular painter and there has been considerable critical interest in his work in recent years. His range of subjects and feeling is shown by such works as *Two Venetian Ladies* (Correr Mus., Venice), the *St George* cycle of paintings) Scuola di San Giorgio), *Preparations for the Entombment of Christ* (Berlin), *The Presentation of Christ in the Temple* (Accademia, Venice), *Meditation on the Passion of Christ* (Met. Mus.).

Carpeaux Jean-Baptiste (1827–75). French sculptor who adopted an individual, painterly technique to express his realistic approach in opposition to pseudo-classicism. His best work is found in the model for a monument to Watteau (*c.* 1863; Ny Calsberg Glyptotek, Copenhagen) and the group *The Dance* for the Paris Opéra (1869; Louvre).

carpe diem (Latin, 'pluck the day'). Expression from Horace (*Odes*, I. xi. 8) applied to love-poems, e.g. Ronsard's *Mignonne, allons voir si la rose* and Herrick's *Gather ye rosebuds*, advising that youth's pleasures be enjoyed while they last.

Carpenter John Alden (1876–1951). U.S. composer. He used his fluent, melodic invention, colourful orchestration, and formal mastery to write music sometimes witty, sometimes whimsical. His works include the ballets *Krazy Kat* (1922) and *Skyscrapers* (1926; commissioned by Diaghilev); the orchestral suite *Adventures in a Perambulator* (1915); *Song of Faith* (1932) for chorus and orchestra and a violin concerto (1937).

Carr Emily (1871–1945). Canadian painter, notably of Indian villages and of stylized totemic figures. She was also a writer.

Carrà Carlo (1881–). Leading Italian futurist painter who signed the *Manifesto of Futurist Painters* (1910). After World War I he followed *Chirico's 'metaphysical 'style. From 1921 he produced peaceful, more naturalistic work influenced by Giotto.

Carracci. 3 Italian artists from Bologna: Lodovico and his cousins, the brothers Agostino and Annibale, who was the major artist of the 3. In 1585 the C. founded an academy in Bologna to teach painting and to revive the canons of classical art as it was then understood. All 3 of the C. painted in Bologna. In 1595 ANNIBALE (1560–1609) was summoned to Rome to paint the decorations of the Palazzo Farnese. His most accomplished work is the Galleria Farnese of the Palace. This ambitious fresco cycle of subjects taken from classical mythology, such as *The Triumph of Bacchus and Ariadne*, at once established Annibale's fame. The frescoes were compared with those of Raphael and Michelangelo in the Vatican. In the Galleria Farnese, and in smaller works such as the delightful *Flight into Egypt* (Gal. Doria, Rome), Annibale created the ideal classical landscape, chosen by many later artists, including N. Poussin. Other important paintings by Annibale are *Domine Quo Vadis?* (N.G., London) and the unusual composition *Butcher's Shop* (Christ Church, Oxford). AGOSTINO (1557–1602) assisted his brother at the Palazzo Farnese. His chief work is *The Last Communion of St Jerome* (Pina., Bologna). He was an important art theorist and a notable engraver. LODOVICO (1555–1619) continued the Academy when his cousins left for Rome. His own paintings are chiefly large altarpieces, e.g. *The Madonna of the Bargellini* (Pina., Bologna). Domenichino and Guido Reni were among the many pupils of the C.

Carreño de Miranda Juan (1614–85). Spanish painter who worked in the style of Rubens and Velazquez. He painted frescoes in the cathedral of Toledo, mythological subjects and portraits. In 1669 he became court painter to Charles II.

Annibale Carracci. *Flight into Egypt*

Cartier-Bresson. *Sunday on the Marne*

Carrickmacross lace. From the town of that name in Ireland; a popular 19th-c. lace, worked in floral patterns. In one type appliqué is applied to machine-made net; in the 'guipure' type a thread is run round a design on fine lawn or muslin. The thread is then overcast, much of the background trimmed away, the centres of the flowers filled with open stitches and the background spaces connected with bars.

Carriera Rosalba (1675–1757). Venetian pastellist, sister-in-law of G. A. Pellegrini; one of the first to work in pastel. She achieved European popularity as a portraitist. In Paris during 1720–1 she introduced pastel technique, revealed its possibilities to M.-Q. de Latour and kept an interesting journal of her visit, *Diario* . . . (1865).

Carrière Eugène (1849–1906). French painter of romantic portraits and pictures of motherhood in which the figures emerge mysteriously from a vaporous grey-brown obscurity.

Carrillo Julián (1875–). Mexican composer, a pioneer and developer of microtonic music. He has written choral works, symphonies and chamber music employing the micro intervals, quarter-, eighth- and sixteenth-tones (often employed simultaneously) and has developed the theory called 'Sonido 13'.

Carroll Lewis. The pseud. of Charles Lutwidge Dodgson (1832–98). English writer of children's books and a lecturer in mathematics at Oxford. *Alice's Adventures in Wonderland* (1865) and *Through the Looking-Glass* (1872) relate a little girl's adventures with the Cheshire Cat, the Mad Hatter, the Queen of Hearts and other creatures who talk nonsense and behave absurdly with great seriousness and show of reason. C. catches the accent of adult argument so skilfully that the books have become classics for readers of all ages. His works include the nonsense poem *The Hunting of the Snark* (1876).

Carroll Paul Vincent (1900–). Irish dramatist. C. gives universality to life in a small village; his plays include *The Things That are Caesar's* (1932), *Shadow and Substance* (1937) and *The White Steed* (1939).

Carrosse d'Or, Le (1952). Film directed by J. *Renoir.

Carrucci Jacopo: Jacopo *Pontormo

Carstens Asmus Jakob (1754–98). German painter and sculptor who settled in Rome and modelled his style on the works of classical antiquity and Michelangelo. Few of his completed paintings survive; it is chiefly cartoons for large-scale unexecuted mythological murals which remain. He made very limited use of colour, and the strength of his work lies in its power of draughtsmanship and intensity of feeling. The Schlossmus., Weimar has the chief coll. of his work.

cartellino (Italian 'label'). Scroll or piece of paper painted either on the background of a picture or on a ledge in the foreground. It is used for the artist's signature or sometimes for a motto or inscription. Examples occur in the paintings of Giovanni Bellini and Antonello da Messina.

Carter Elizabeth (1717–1806). English poet and classical scholar. She was one of the *blue stocking group and a friend of Richardson and Dr Johnson, who included some of her essays in *The Rambler*.

Carter Elliot (Cook) (1908–). U.S. composer. C. has written music in many styles, but with his 1st string quartet (1951) finally consolidated a new technique whereby one rhythm or tempo can be derived from another by cumulative superimposition ('rhythmic modulation'); hence the idea of recurrent rhythms and tempi performing a similar function in atonal music to that of key in tonal music (*tonality).

Cartier-Bresson Henri (1908–). French photographer who, with R. Capa and D. Seymour, pioneered the medium of photo-reportage with the 35 mm. camera. C.-B.'s theory of photography holds that the photographer must become as inconspicuous as possible in order to capture the subject unawares in a series of 'decisive moments'. The camera is an 'extension of the eye' used to evoke a 'truth'. In 1947 C.-B. helped to found the photo agency *Magnum. His numerous books, including *The Decisive Moment* (1952) and *The Europeans* (1955), have become an indispensable part of every photographic library.

cartoon. The term has 2 well-defined meanings. Originally it was used of a full-scale and detailed preparatory drawing or painting for a tapestry, painting or fresco; famous examples

Cartellino: detail from Giovanni Bellini's *Lady at her toilet*

Carriera. *The Dancer Barbarina Campani*

Lewis Carroll

Lewis Carroll: illustration by Sir John Tenniel for *Alice's Adventures in Wonderland*

Cartoon. Leonardo's *Madonna and Child with St Anne*

Joyce Cary: photograph by Eisenstadt

Casanova

Caruso as Des Grieux in Massenet's *Manon*

are the c.s by Raphael (7 in the V. and A., London) for tapestries originally intended for the Sistine Chapel and now in the Vatican, and c.s by Leonardo da Vinci on the *Madonna and Child with St Anne*, 1 now in the N.G., London. The term c. is now generally used, in a 2nd meaning, of a satirical drawing with a specific point, usually political.

cartoon film: *animated film

cartouche. Originally a form of ornamentation in the shape of a scroll, such as a volute of an Ionic capital, it was later adapted in engraving and sculpture as a ground for titles and armorial bearings, and in this form is usually oval with a scrolled frame.

Cartouche (1632)

Cartwright William (1611–43). English poet and playwright. He wrote lyrics and plays including a comedy *The Ordinary* (*c.* 1634–5) and the tragi-comedy *The Royall Slave* (1636). He was the friend of Ben Jonson, Henry Vaughan and Izaak Walton.

Caruso Enrico (1873–1921). Italian tenor; the most famous of this c. To phenomenal breath control C. added an unmatched power and vocal range. He was one of the 1st performers whose reputation was helped by the gramophone.

Carver Robert (1487?–after 1546). 16th-c. Scottish composer; his work shows affinities to G. Dufay. 5 masses (one on *L'*homme armé*), and the motets *O bone Jesu* for 19 voices and *Gaude flore virginali*, for 5 voices, have survived.

Cary Joyce (1888–1957). English novelist. After studying art in Edinburgh and Paris, C. joined the Nigerian political service in 1913 and remained in Africa until 1920, serving in the Nigeria Regiment during World War I. He draws on this African background in his novels *The African Witch* (1936) and *Mister Johnson* (1939). His 1st novel, *Aissa Saved*, appeared in 1932, and he wrote 9 more, of which the best known is *The Horse's Mouth*, which traces the force of creative individuality in the career of Gully Jimson, an artist-become-tramp. In addition C. publ. political studies and 2 vols of poetry.

Caryatid from the Erechtheum

caryatid. The term refers to a pillar or pilaster in the form of a draped female figure as found in the portico of the Erechtheum in Athens. It is also applied to supports in the shape of a female figure on furniture and in interior decoration.

Casablanca (1943). Film directed by M. *Curtiz.

Casadesus Robert (Marcel) (1899–). French pianist and composer of piano concertos and symphonies.

Casals Pablo or Pau (1876–). Spanish cellist, conductor, composer and also pianist; living in France from 1940 because of his hatred for the Franco dictatorship. C. is recognized as the greatest cellist of the 1st half of the 20th c., and above all as the master exponent of J. S. Bach's solo sonatas. He has organized an annual festival at Prades, his home, since 1950.

Casanova di Seingalt Giacomo (1725–98). An Italian, born in Venice, whose career of amorous intrigue and adventure in most European countries is recorded in his *Mémoires. . .* (1826–38; *Memoirs. . . ,* 1863), written in French. They are a valuable and entertaining account of 18th-c. European society. C.'s name has become synonymous with 'the great lover'.

Casella Alfredo (1883–1947). Italian composer; studied under Fauré. C. sought for a valid idiom for a resuscitated Italian school after the period of *verismo and, after rejecting folk-music and an excursion into atonalism, formulated in the 1920s a programme of anti-romantic ideals, clarity of tonality and contrapuntal structure, and a classical form, e.g. the *Partita* for piano and orchestra (1925). Other works included the ballet *La Giara* (1924), after a Pirandello novel; the oratorio *Il Deserto Tentato*; symphonies; *Concerto romano* (1926) for organ and chamber orchestra; chamber and piano music.

Cask of Amontillado, The (1846). Story by Edgar Allan *Poe.

Caslon William (1692–1766). English typecutter and typefounder, whose distinctive 'old style' roman types enabled English printers to become independent of continental printers, above all the Dutch. He cut his 1st founts in the early 1720s, and although his 1st specimen sheet appeared in 1734, it is believed that his roman letter had already come into use before that date.

Casque d'Or (1952). Film directed by J. *Becker.

cassation (derivation unclear). An 18th-c. musical form, orchestral or chamber, divided into several movements, the first of which was usually a march. It has similarities to the *divertimento and *serenade.

Cassatt Mary (1845–1926). U.S.-born painter of the French impressionist school. She studied in Paris, where she settled and became a disciple of Degas. Her finest paintings were studies of mother and child, scrupulously firm and unsentimental, e.g. *The Bath* (A. Inst. of Chicago), *Mother and Child* (Wichita Art Mus., Kansas), and her studies of everyday life in dry point and aquatint have recently received recognition. *Young Woman Sewing* (Louvre) is a fine example of her work in oil. She made an exquisite series of colour prints under Japanese influence.

Cassavetes John (1929–). U.S. film actor and director. *Shadows* (1960) was a low-budget production shot on 16 mm. It was largely improvised and its direct emotional appeal was enhanced by a rough-and-ready technique; it was reasonably successful commercially. C.'s films in Hollywood, *Too Late Blues* (1961) and *A Child is Waiting* (1963), appeared merely inept, although the latter was mutilated by its producer Stanley Kramer.

Casson Sir Hugh (1910–). British architect; director of architecture for the *Festival of Britain, 1951. He has been professor of interior design at the Royal College of Art since 1952. He has designed univ. buildings, including the Sidgwick Site at Cambridge. Recently he has worked on the new building for the Royal College of Art and the Elephant House at London Zoo. His activities also extend to town development plans and opera sets for Glyndebourne and Covent Garden.

Casson Sir Lewis (1875–). English actor and producer who has directed many of the greatest successes of his wife Dame Sybil Thorndike. Together they have toured the world as a man and wife partnership.

cassone. A richly decorated type of large rectangular wooden chest peculiar to Italy from the 14th to 16th c. *Cassoni da nozze* or 'marriage chests' form an important class. Decoration could take the form of applied leather, tooled and painted; of inlay; of relief carving; or of ornament impressed with a stamp on damp stucco and then painted in polychrome or gilded. The most spectacular *cassoni* are, however, those adorned with narrative panels painted in tempera on gesso, a type that prevailed, especially in Tuscany, from the 15th c. The Bible, classical myth, Italian literature and contemporary history provided the subjects, which were executed in such exalted workshops as those of Uccello, Pesellino, Gozzoli and Ghirlandaio.

Cassou Jean (1897–). French writer and critic, born in Spain. His critical essays include *Éloge de la folie* (1925), *Harmonies viennoises* (1926) and *Pour la poésie* (1935). Among his novels are *De l'Étoile au Jardin des Plantes* (1935) and *Massacres de Paris* (1936). C. was imprisoned during the Occupation; he wrote *Trente-trois sonnets composé en secret* (1944), which appeared under the pseud. 'Jean Noir'.

Castagno Andrea del (*c.* 1423–*c.* 57). Florentine painter whose style shows clearly the influence of Masaccio, but which borrows sculptural qualities from Donatello, with whom C. had a close emotional affinity. He is first heard of as the painter of a cautionary or propaganda picture showing the bodies of rebels hung in chains. This work gave C. the reputation of pursuing realism to the point of violence. Few of his paintings survive, but the *Assumption of the Virgin* in Berlin is a fine work. C.'s masterpiece is undoubtedly his *Last Supper* (Castagno Museum, Florence), a fresco of great intellectual and emotional intensity. By keeping alive and vital the harsh preoccupation with figure drawing and tactile values of the early painters and sculptors of Florence, C.'s work was of great importance to the later Florentines, Signorelli, Leonardo da Vinci and, above all, Michelangelo.

castanets (from the Spanish *castaneta*, 'chestnut wood'). Percussion instruments typical of Spanish gipsy music. A pair of c., small shell-shaped wooden 'clappers', are held in the flexed hand and vibrated by the fingers. A modified type in which c. are attached to a handle and shaken is sometimes used in the orchestra.

Cassatt. *The Loge*. Also *impressionism

Cassavetes. *Shadows*

The Nerli Cassone

Casson. The Royal College of Art

Castagno. *Last Supper*. Also *Boccaccio

Giovanni Castiglione. *The Angel appearing to the Shepherds*

Castleford teapot

Baldassare Castiglione: painting by Raphael

Castelar Emilio (1832–99). Spanish statesman and writer. In 1864 C. founded the republican journal *La Democracia.* His novels include *La hermana de caridad* (1857) and *El suspiro del moro* (1870). Among his historical works are *Tragedias de la historia* (1881) and *La revolución religiosa* (1880–3).

Castel Durante. Italian town, in the duchy of Urbino, the centre of production, during the early 16th c., of some of the finest maiolica. Much of the outstanding C. D. painted pottery was the work of Nicola Pellipario.

Castellani Renato (1913–). Italian film director. C. was one of the pioneers of neo-realism, and with the exception of his *Romeo and Juliet* (1954), he has remained close to that tradition, although lately with little success. He achieved fame in Italy with *Un colpo di pistola* (1942) and abroad with *E'primavera* (1950) and *Due soldi di speranza* (1952).

Castello Branco Camillo (1825–90). Portuguese novelist who had a romantic and scandalous career including a period in prison after an elopement. His literary output was prolific and varied; it was somewhat sentimental, but his gift for narrative and fine style won him lasting popularity. His best works are perhaps the novels of regional life, e.g. the series *Novellas do Minho* (1875–7).

Castelnuovo-Tedesco Mario (1895–). Italian composer; he was a pupil of I. Pizzetti; he has lived in the U.S. since 1939. C.-T. has been called 'the Italian Brahms'; his works include: the operas *La Mandragola* (1926), after Machiavelli, and *The Merchant of Venice* (1959), after Shakespeare; overtures to Shakespeare's plays and settings of his songs; the violin concerto *The Prophets* (1933); the *Sacred Service* . . . (1943), and film music.

Castiglione Baldassarre (1478–1529). Italian writer, courtier, diplomat and soldier. C.'s book *Il Libro del Cortegiano* (1528; *The Courtyer*, 1561) gave Europe a new code of social refinement. It is a discussion of the manners, duties and qualities essential to the courtier; the debate takes place in the ducal palace at Urbino and the book reveals a vivid picture of Italian court life. C. was a lifelong friend of Raphael; the latter's portrait of him is now in the Louvre.

Castiglione Giovanni Benedetto called 'Il Grechetto' (*c.* 1610–65). Genoese painter of genre and monumental religious and mythological subjects in baroque style and usually including animals; from 1648 court painter at Mantua. Also an etcher, he followed the Netherlandish school, particularly Rembrandt. He is the 1st artist known to have used *monotype. He evolved a lively sketching technique in oil paint on paper.

Castiglioni Niccoló (1932–). Italian composer. C. has written symphonies (on Brecht) and other serial music, recently developing a simple decorative style. *Eine Kleine Weihnachtmusik* for chamber orchestra, and *Décors* for full orchestra, exhibit a sensuous feeling for delicate sonorous textures.

Castillon (de Saint-Victor), Alexis (vicomte) de (1838–73). French composer, and one of Franck's leading pupils. To his contemporaries he was an outlandish modernist, but his songs anticipated the work of H. Duparc and E. Chausson, and his chamber music was important in French musical history.

Castle, The (1926). Novel by Franz *Kafka.

Castleford. Cream-coloured earthenware produced at the factory at Castleford in Yorkshire founded *c.* 1790 by David Dunderdale, an apprentice of the Leeds pottery. An illustrated catalogue written in several languages was issued. The best known of C. wares are the white teapots of squarish shape with panels of relief decoration.

Castle of Otranto, a Gothic Story, The (1764). Novel by Horace *Walpole.

Castle Rackrent (1800). Novel by Maria Edgeworth.

castrato. A male eunuch singer castrated before puberty to give a contralto or, more usually, soprano range (also *falsetto); first used in the 17th c. in Italian church choirs but in the 18th c. in Italian opera also. Although the c. had a boy's voice in pitch he had a man's lung capacity and power, nor was his training interrupted by the breaking of the voice. Because of their unique tone, unimaginable virtuosity and legendary feats, the castrati were more highly regarded than natural male voices.

Catena. *Virgin and Child with Kneeling Warrior*

Angelica Catalani

Castro Américo (1885–). Spanish scholar, critic and essayist. His best-known works are his *Vida de Lope de Vega* (1919); *El pensamiento de Cervantes* (1925) and his historical interpretation of Spain, *La realidad histórica de España* (1948).

Castro Eugénio de (1869–1944). Portuguese symbolist poet whose works include *Cristalizações da morte* (1884), *Oaristos* (1890), a play, *O Anel de Policrates* (1907) and *Ultimos versos* (1938). His poetry at its best has a jewelled artificiality, original in imagery and colour yet formally exquisite.

Castro Guillén de (1569–1631). Spanish playwright and man of letters. He was friendly with Lope de Vega, who dedicated a play to him. C.'s own most famous play is *Las Mocedades del Cid*, in which he celebrated the youthful exploits of the Cid, Spain's national hero, in fervent, vigorous poetical language. The work inspired Corneille's play *Le Cid.*

Castro José M. Ferreira de (1898–). Portuguese novelist. His 1st real success came with *Emigrantes* (1928) and its sequel *A selva* (1930), novels set in and around the forests of the Amazon and showing acute observation of the people and their life–the result of C.'s 10-year stay in Brazil.

Castro Rosalía (1837–85). Spanish poet and after G. A. Bécquer the most original of the late 19th c. When she first publ. she was living in Madrid with an unsympathetic husband. The illegitimate daughter of a lady of family, she felt accursed from the start. She wrote, principally in the Galician dialect, delicately rhythmed poems of nostalgia for her native province; some of them are so close to the popular style that they have been confused with folk-songs. Her later poems became increasingly literary, and her final vol., which appeared just before her death from cancer, was in Castilian. Her complete works, *Obras completas,* were publ. in 4 vols in 1909–11.

catacomb. Subterranean burial-ground. The most famous c.s are those at Rome used by the early Christians. They contain wall paintings and carved sarcophagi, and provide the earliest examples of Christian art, dating from the 3rd c. A.D.

Catalini Angelica (1780–1849). Italian soprano. She was employed at the Lisbon Opera (1804), virtually took over the King's Theatre, London (great successes with 'God Save the King' and 'Rule Britannia') and directed the Italian opera in Paris.

catch (possibly derived from Italian *caccia*). An unaccompanied part song common in 17th- and 18th-c. England, similar to the *round and *glee. At the height of their popularity (under Charles II) c.s were written so that mispronunciation of the words and/or interweaving of the parts would throw up absurd or obscene by-meanings. Early c. colls were T. Ravenscroft's *Pammelia . . .* (1609), *Deuteromelia . . .* (1609). Members of the London CATCH CLUB (founded 1761) included the Prince Regent.

Catcher in the Rye (1951). Novel by J. D. *Salinger.

Catena Vincenzo di Biagio called (*c.* 1475–1531). Italian painter of the Venetian school, his early work, e.g. *Virgin and Child* (Walker Gal., Liverpool), closely resembling that of Giovanni Bellini and Cima. Later he was more strongly influenced by Giorgione, Titian and Palma Vecchio. An inscription on the back of Giorgione's *Laura* (K. Mus., Vienna) refers to C. as a 'colleague' of his; *Virgin and Child with Kneeling Warrior* (N.G., London), once believed by Giorgione, is now attributed to C. Also by C. is the portrait of Doge Andrea Gritti (N.G., London) previously attributed to Titian.

catharsis: *Aristotle

Cather Willa (Sibert) (1876–1947). U.S. novelist, poet, short-story writer, newspaperwoman; her novels of immigrant and pioneer life in Nebraska include *O Pioneers!* (1913), *The Song of the Lark* (1915), *My Antonia* (1918). She is concerned with traditional moral and spiritual standards threatened by modern life, and devotes her great craftsmanship to perfection of form in the novel, e.g. *A Lost Lady* (1923), *The Professor's House* (1925) and *My Mortal Enemy* (1926). *Death Comes for the Archbishop* (1927) and *Shadows on the Rock* (1931) have explicitly Catholic themes. Her short stories are also outstanding. *Not Under Forty* (1936), essays, reveals her interest in the aesthetics of fiction.

Rosalía Castro

Catacombs of St Sebastian, Rome: vault of M. Clodius Hermes

Cavalcanti. *Coalface*

Constantine Cavafy

Catherine of Siena St (1347–80). Italian ascetic and author of one of the few genuinely mystical works in Italian literature; her 'book of the Divine Doctrine' she claimed to have heard dictated by God. The letters she wrote in Tuscan to kings, nobles and high dignitaries of the Church all over Europe are of outstanding literary and historical interest and reveal her as a great stylist.

Cat on a Hot Tin Roof (1955). Play by Tennessee *Williams, the basis of a film (1958) directed by R. *Brooks.

Cat's fugue. Nickname for a keyboard piece by D. Scarlatti.

Catullus Gaius Valerius (87?–54? B.C.). Latin poet born at Verona and, it has been suggested, of partly Celtic stock. His father left C. well enough endowed to participate in the extravagant life of Rome, where he fell in love with the notorious Clodia. His verses addressed to her as 'Lesbia' range from the tenderly lyrical to the obscenely recriminatory. In 57 B.C. he travelled to Bithynia as an official in the entourage of C. Memmius, the governor. Several travel pieces resulted, and invectives against Memmius. He visited his brother's tomb in the Troad and composed for it one of his finest elegies. In Rome again, he inveighed against Caesar in some of his bitterest epigrams. C. belonged to a coterie of deliberate and scholarly poets who aimed to domesticate the forms and themes of Alexandrian verse at Rome. Vigour and craftsmanship mark his poetry–particularly his skill in handling the rhetorical tricks of his school to achieve a casual, almost conversational tone. Of the Roman poets C. makes the most direct appeal to modern sensibilities. Apart from the lyrics, in metres imitated from Sappho and the Alexandrians, and the epigrams and elegies, C. also wrote a handful of longer pieces: a startling version of the Attis legend, in a uniquely difficult metre; an epyllion, or short epic, dealing with the marriage of Peleus and Thetis; and 2 epithalamia. All these, though modelled on Hellenistic examples, show the vigorous command of language and metre characteristic of C.

Caucasian Chalk Circle, The (1948). Play by B. *Brecht.

caudle-cup. A 2-handled cup of silver related to the porringer and posset-cup. The distinction between them is at best a tenuous one. C. was a warm drink of thin gruel and wine; c.-cups are usually of gourd shape and are also lavishly embossed. Like porringers they have scrolled handles and domed covers.

Caudle-cup and cover; London, 1668

Caulfield Pat (1936–). English painter; studied at the R.C.A. (1959–62). His work is very much influenced by the art and architecture of the 1930s; a sophisticated banality marks subject-matter and treatment.

Causeries du Lundi (1851–62). Series of critical articles by *Sainte-Beuve.

Causley Charles (1917–). English poet. *Union Street* (1957) and *Johnny Alleluia* (1961) use traditional metres, folk-song and narrative which, combined with a dramatic imagination, produce poetry of spareness and integrity.

Cavafy Constantine P. (Konstantinos P. Kabaphes) (1863–1933). One of the greatest modern Greek poets; he spent most of his life in Alexandria, Egypt. Greek history (classical, Hellenistic, Greco-Roman and Byzantine) and homosexual love provide the subjects of much of his poetry. Intrigued by human contradictions and conflicts, C. used historical figures to express the essential and universal in life. C. completely freed himself from traditional forms and diction and opened a new field for poetic expression: the colloquial language of educated Alexandrian Greeks. His poetry is realistic and dramatic, not lyrical, and its power lies in restrained emotion and simplicity.

Cavalca Domenico (*c.* 1270–1342). Italian Dominican whose trs from Latin and *Lives of the Saints* are important early examples of Italian prose.

Cavalcanti Alberto (1897–). Brazilian film director. C.'s association with the French *avant-garde* of the 1920s started when he worked as designer for L'Herbier, and continued with his own films like *Rien que les heures* (1926), which already had the documentary approach that was to take him to Britain as director of the GPO film unit which made *Nightmail* and for which he directed *Coalface* (1936). From 1943 he produced and directed features at Ealing. From 1949 to 1954 in Brazil he ran the state-sponsored film co. which made L. *Barreto's *O Cangaceiro*. Since then he has directed in Italy, Austria and Britain.

Cavalcanti Guido (*c.* 1255–1300). Italian poet, Dante's 'first friend'. C.'s influence can be found in many of the younger Florentine poets, and is evident in Dante's earlier poems, especially those for Beatrice. The theme of C.'s poetry is love, usually its sadder aspects. Most of it was written for a woman named Giovanna whom C. calls 'Primavera'. About 50 poems can be attributed to him–2 *canzoni*, including the celebrated *Donna mi prega*, and the rest *ballate* and sonnets. In the political disputes of 1300 Dante voted that the leaders of the Guelph faction be exiled; C. was among them and died in exile.

Cavalier also called **Caroline verse.** Terms used of a body of lyrical English verse written during the reign of Charles I. The leading poets were R. Herrick, T. Carew, Sir J. Suckling and R. Lovelace. The Caroline period had also a characteristic drama in which complicated plots were decorated with florid dialogue.

Cavalieri Emilio de' (*c.* 1550–1602). Italian composer, a member of the *camerata although none of his own works are considered true operas. His works include *La rappresentatione di anima e di corpo*, in effect a mystery play with music but seen also as an early form of oratorio.

Cavalleria Rusticana. Opera by P. *Mascagni; libretto by G. Targioni-Tozzetti and G. Menasci after *Verga; 1st performance in Rome in 1890.

Cavalli Pietro Francesco (1602–76). Venetian opera composer; the pupil and great successor of Monteverdi. C. was successively organist and music director at St Mark's, Venice; he visited Paris where he produced for the wedding of Louis XIV his *L'Ercole Amante* (1662). C. consolidated and developed a Venetian opera style dominated by a highly rhythmic recitative and with few choruses. He produced at least 12 operas, of which *Didone* (1641) and *Il Giasone* (1649) are among the best surviving.

Cavallini Pietro (*fl.* 1273–1308). Italian painter who worked in Rome and, at about the same time as Cimabue, began to move away from stereotyped Byzantine forms towards naturalism. There are mosaics (1291) by him in S. Maria in Trastevere, Rome, and fragments of a fresco, *The Last Judgement*, in S. Cecilia, Rome.

Cavallino Bernardo (1616–56). Neapolitan painter of religious subjects who worked in an individual style which was graceful and sophisticated. His figures were slightly elongated, his colour combinations unusual and his background landscapes approached the romanticism of Salvator Rosa.

Cavalotti Felice Carlo Emanuele (1842–98). Italian writer and politician who fought under Garibaldi. His many verses, patriotic, satirical and polemical, include *Anticaglie* (1879), in which he attacks the kind of 'truthfulness' in literature which is an excuse for ostentation and eroticism. His plays include *I pezzenti* (1871), *Guido* (1872) and *Alcibiade* (1873).

cavatina. Musical term for (1) an operatic song in 1 section, as opposed to the 3-section aria; (2) a short slow instrumental piece such as J. J. Raff's famous c. for violin and piano.

Cavazzola Paolo Morando called (1486–1522). Veronese painter of portraits and religious subjects. He was a pupil of D. Morone but became increasingly influenced by Raphael.

cave art of the upper palaeolithic era was discovered in 1879 in the Spanish cavern of Altamira, where the roof is painted with polychrome bison. Archaeologists accepted these as prehistoric only after the discovery in 1894 of engravings and paintings in the previously sealed cave of La Mouthe, in the Dordogne. Discoveries have multiplied ever since in limestone areas N. and S. of the Pyrenees. In contrast to upper palaeolithic sculpture on limestone overhangs, the pictorial art is in caverns away from daylight. Beasts of the chase are depicted naturalistically (oxen, horses, reindeer, bison, etc., less commonly mammoth) in various techniques, engraving, drawing in black or coloured outline, and painting (chiefly reds and ochres). Engraving and pigment are frequently combined, and images were often suggested by the shape of the rock. Crude composition occurs, though images are mostly superimposed. This c. a. was ritual, beyond which its purposes are disputed, recent opinion holding that myths were frequently depicted. The artists were *homo sapiens* whose migrations into a sub-glacial Europe began *c.* 30,000 B.C. The art spans about 18,000 years, the developed polychrome naturalism belonging to the millennia before 12,000 B.C. when the retreat of the glaciers brought the hunting cultures to an end.

Cavallini. Detail, showing angels, from *The Last Judgement*

Cavallino. *St Cecilia*

Cave art. Painting from *Lascaux

Cave art. Engraved deer from *Altamira

Caxton presenting the *Recuyell* to the duchess of Burgundy

Caxton's imprint

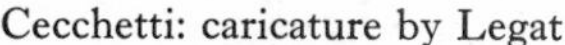

Cecchetti: caricature by Legat

Celadon ware; Sung dynasty

Caves du Vatican, Les (1914). Novel by A. *Gide.

Cavos Catterino (1776–1840). Italian composer who in 1798 settled in St Petersburg. He later became director of the French, Russian and Italian operas there, writing works to libretti in all 3 languages.

Caw John (1723–1807). English architect. His numerous works, mostly in a competent Palladian style, include Kirby Hall, Yorkshire; Harewood House, Yorkshire; Newark town hall; and The Crescent, Buxton.

Caxton William (1422?–91). The 1st English printer. C. learned the craft in Germany (probably Cologne) in 1471–2. He publ. his trs. *Recuyell of the Histories of Troy* in *c.* 1475 on the Continent and set up a press in England (1476), printing as his 1st book *Dictes or Sayengis of the Philosophres* (1477).
C.'s use of the London E. Midland dialect helped to establish it as the basis of standard English. He made numerous trs, which are important in the history of English prose in their deliberate attempt at style.
74 of his 90 books were in English and included Chaucer's *Canterbury Tales* (1478), Gower's *Confessio Amantis* (1483) and Malory's *Morte d'Arthur* (1485).

Cayatte André (1909–). French film director famous for a series of social melodramas centred on ideas of justice and punishment: *Avant le Déluge* (1953), *Justice est faite* (1951), *Nous sommes tous des Assassins* (1952) and *Oeil pour Oeil* (1956).

Caylus Marie-Marguerite, marquise de (1673–1729). Cousin of Mme de Maintenon. Her *Souvenirs*, dictated shortly before her death, and 1st publ. in 1770 with preface and notes by Voltaire (trs. as *Memoirs of the Court of Lewis XIV*, 1770), contain anecdotes of the court of Louis XIV and portraits of celebrated contemporaries, particularly of Mme de Maintenon and Mme de Montespan.

Cecchetti Enrico (1850–1927). Italian ballet master. He was a teacher and dancer in St Petersburg, creating the roles of Fairy Carabosse and Bluebird in *The Sleeping Beauty*, director of the Imperial Ballet School in Warsaw, and taught, among others, Pavlova, Nijinsky, Massine and Serge Lifar. He was ballet master and teacher with Diaghilev's ballet co. from 1909 to 1918, when he opened a school in London, bringing the tradition of classical Russian training to English ballet. The C. method gives perfect placing of the body and purity of line, its arm exercises being particularly effective. It is now the standard training method used for teaching classical Russian ballet.

Cecchetti Society, The. Formed (London, 1922) by C. Beaumont to continue the tradition of Cecchetti and to maintain high standards of ballet throughout the Commonwealth. It is now incorporated with the Imperial Society of Teachers of Dancing.

Cecchi Emilio (1884–). Italian journalist, essayist and critic. C.'s best-known work is in his *Pesci Rossi* (1921), containing essays on G. K. Chesterton and various English themes. He has done much to spread the understanding of U.S. literature in Italy.

Cecilia St (2nd c.). From the late middle ages the patron saint of music (and the blind) and traditionally inventor of the organ; but her connection with music seems arbitrary.

Cecilian movement. A movement for the reform of Roman Catholic church music originating in Germany in the mid 19th c. It advocated a return to plainsong and 16th-c. polyphony.

celadon. A pale willow-green; used specifically to denote porcelain wares of this colour first produced in the kilns of Chekiang province in China of the Sung dynasty (960–1279), where they developed from the Yüeh wares of the *T'ang dynasty. The most widely appreciated c.s (they were exported all over Asia) are the Sung Lung-ch'üan wares (which continued manufacture into the Ming dynasty, 1368–1644) with their light grey bodies and green or bluish green glazes, often crackled, sometimes with floral designs delicately incised or moulded in relief. Their chief beauty lies not in the decoration but in refinement and simplicity of form. Another Sung c. centre was at Ju Chou; the well-known northern c.s, with incised decorations and an olive-green glaze, were manufactured there, as was the rare light blue Ju ware made entirely for the use of the Chinese imperial court.

Blaise Cendrars

Cellini. *Perseus holding the head of Medusa.* See also colour plate 56

Céleste Céline (1811–82). French dancer and actress who danced with the Paris Opéra. She introduced *La *Sylphide* to the U.S. in 1835.

Celestina, La. The common name, derived from one of the characters, of the Spanish novel *Tragicomedia de Calisto y Melibea* (1499–1502; *Celestina. . .*, 1631). It is in 21 acts and the probable author of all except the first was the Jewish writer Fernando de Rojas (d. 1541). L. C. herself, based on Juan *Ruiz's Trotaconventos, is a scheming old procuress and the influence of the novel is seen in the number of similar 'go-betweens' in 16th- and 17th-c. Spanish literature.

Célibataires, Les (1934). Novel by Henri de *Montherlant.

Céline Louis-Ferdinand. Pseud. of L.-F. Destouches (1894–1961). French novelist whose *Voyage au bout de la nuit* (1932; *Journey to the End of Night*, 1934) was a *succès de scandale*. This fictional autobiography is a slangy, savage, disgusted and obscene account of C.'s experiences during and after World War I, one of the most misanthropic of all novels. He also wrote *Mort à crédit* (1936; *Death on the Instalment Plan*, 1938).

Celliers Jan F. E. (1865–1940). S. African poet and playwright, writing in Afrikaans. His verse includes *Unie Kantate* (1910; *Union Cantata*, 1910).

Cellini Benvenuto (1500–71). Florentine goldsmith, sculptor, medallist and adventurer whose boastful and entertaining autobiography (written 1558–62; publ. 1728; trs. 1771) is an invaluable record of life in Renaissance Italy. Commissioned by emperors, kings, popes and princes, he was renowned throughout Italy. His famous gold salt-cellar for Francis I (K. Mus., Vienna) is a typically florid piece, superbly executed. His work in coins, medals and medallions includes the famous gold *Leda and the Swan*. His large bronze sculpture of *Perseus holding the head of Medusa* is an intense early mannerist work. Among lost bronzes are a pair of doorways and a huge statue of Mars.

Celtes (Celtis) Konrad (1459–1508). German humanist and outstanding poet of Latin verse; crowned as Germany's foremost poet by the Emperor Frederick III (1487). C. discovered the imitations of Terence by the nun Hrotsvitha of Gandersheim.

Celtic Twilight, The (1893). Vol. of stories by W. B. Yeats; the title is sometimes used (pejoratively) to indicate the mystical side of the *Irish literary renaissance or CELTIC REVIVAL.

cembalo. Italian word for dulcimer and in the 18th c. considered as an abbreviation for clavicembalo ('keyed dulcimer'). Hence c. was used to mean harpsichord and, by transference, keyboard in a general sense, or the continuo usually played on a harpsichord.

Cenci, The (publ. 1819). Poetic drama by *Shelley.

Cendrars Blaise. Pseud. of Frédéric Sauser (1887–1961). French novelist and poet, whose powerful, colourful work is semi-autobiographical and combines startling invention with lyricism. He has influenced many writers including Jacob, Cocteau and Salmon. He agreed with surrealist aims and was a friend of Apollinaire. Works include: *Anthologie nègre* (1921; *The African Saga*, 1927), *L'Or* (1925; *Sutter's Gold*, 1926), *Poésies complètes* (1944).

Cennini Cennino (late 14th–early 15th c.). Italian painter, none of whose works are known, and author of the artist's handbook *Libro dell' Arte* (*c.* 1390), important for its information about the techniques of the school of Giotto, which C. derived through A. Gaddi, a pupil of T. Gaddi who was a pupil of Giotto.

Cent nouvelles nouvelles, Les (15th c.). A coll. of 100 anonymous prose tales, closely modelled on Boccaccio's *Decameron*, purporting to be told by members of the Burgundian court; sometimes attributed to a courtier, A. de la Salle.

cento. A medley of lines of verse taken from existing works and put together to make new verses.

central-plan. Architectural term for a symmetrical or nearly symmetrical plan of a building.

centre-piece. A large object, often fanciful in design, used to decorate the centre of a dining-table, normally, in England, of a municipal, collegiate or regimental establishment. Usually made of silver or silver-gilt, it replaced the

Centre-piece; Augsburg silver, 1775

Centula: engraving by Petau

Cerrito, Taglioni, Grisi and Grahn in the *Pas de Quatre*

ceremonial salt which went out of fashion in the 17th c. C.-p.s often supported candle-branches as well as dishes for sweetmeats, and in this way performed a similar function to that of the *epergne. Examples of the rococo period were particularly large and elaborate.

Centula (or St Riquier) France. Carolingian monastery, one of the most ambitious buildings of the 8th c. It had double transepts and high towers. Apart from excavations, the only evidence for its appearance is a 17th-c. engraving of a 12th-c. drawing.

Centuries of Meditation. Mystical book by Thomas Traherne.

Cephisodotus. Name of 2 Greek sculptors (1) (*fl.* early 4th c. B.C.) probably the father of Praxiteles. A copy of his *Irene bearing the infant Plutus* is in the Glyptothek Museum, Munich and one of Dionysus in the B.M., London; (2) (*fl.* late 4th c.) the son of Praxiteles. No complete work of his survives but among the work he is known to have executed was a statue of Menander in the Theatre at Athens.

Cerano, Il: Giovanni Battista *Crespi

Cernuda Luis (1904–). Spanish poet whose melancholy style is tinged with surrealism. His poetry includes *Perfil del aire* (1927) and *Donde habita el olvido* (1934). Among his prose works is *Variaciónes sobre un tema Mexicano* (1952).

Cerrito Fanny (1817–1909). Italian dancer who was a pupil of *Blasis and made her début in Naples in 1832. Between 1836 and 1856 she danced throughout Europe, helping to spread *Blasis's influence. She danced with Taglioni, Grisi and Grahn in the famous *Pas de Quatre* (1845).

Certosa ('Charterhouse', i.e. a Carthusian monastery). The most famous is that near Pavia, Italy, begun in 1396 as a memorial to the Visconti family. The late 15th-c. façade, by a variety of architects, employs Renaissance motifs in a profuse, undisciplined style typical of Lombardy, and was the most important single influence on early Renaissance architecture in France.

Cervantes Saavedra, Miguel de (1547–1616). Spanish novelist and writer. Although born in Castile, C. was of a Cordovan family, his father being a doctor, but he seems to have had little formal education. He was an avid reader of contemporary Spanish and Italian literature, and those romances of chivalry which were to inspire his great creation *Don Quixote.* In 1569 C. went to Italy as a gentleman-in-waiting to Cardinal Acquaviva at Rome, and then took up a soldier's career. He took part in several campaigns against the Turks and Moors and played a gallant part in the battle of Lepanto in 1571. While returning to Spain (1575) his ship was captured by corsairs. During 5 years of captivity C. displayed great energy, courage and resourcefulness, winning the respect of his captors and even the viceroy of Algiers. He was finally ransomed.

On his return to Madrid (1580) C. was beset by financial troubles which were to remain with him for the rest of his life, and he turned to literature. *La Galatea* (1585; trs. 1867), a 'pastoral' novel, was an artistic but not financial success and, after failure as a dramatist, C. was obliged to go into business, becoming a naval purchasing agent (1587) and assembling stores for the Armada. He had endless quarrels with merchants, officials and creditors, and was imprisoned more than once for debt. He began *Don Quixote* during one of these prison sentences and publ. part 1 in 1605. It was an instantaneous success, and within a few weeks 3 pirated eds had been printed at Lisbon. Despite European acclaim C. had to fight against unauthorized reprints and was involved in further financial troubles and a series of family scandals. He continued to write, producing *Novelas ejemplares* (1613; *Exemplarie novells* (selected trs.), 1638), a series of tales, *Viaje del Parnaso* (1614) a burlesque poem, and a series of comedies and dramatic interludes. Before C.'s promised sequel to *Don Quixote* was completed, a false 2nd part, by one 'Alonso Fernández de Avellaneda' was publ. at Tarragona in 1614. Nevertheless, C.'s own version (1615) proved better even than the 1st part, showing a maturer and subtler style and humour. C.'s fame was assured but in 1615 he was described as 'old, a soldier, a gentleman, and poor'. His last work was *Los Trabajos de Persiles y Sigismunda* (posth. 1617; *The Travels of Persiles and Sigismunda*, 1619).

Although some of C.'s finest writing is to be found in his *Exemplary Novels*, nothing else he wrote is even remotely comparable with *Don Quixote* (i.e. *El ingenioso hidalgo Don Quixote de la Mancha*, 1605, 1615; Eng. trs. 1612,

Certosa di Pavia

Miguel de Cervantes

1620). In describing the adventures of this honourable yet eccentric scholar turned knight errant, travelling 16th-c. Spain with his 'esquire' the burly peasant Sancho Panza, and living by a wildly idealistic and 'quixotic' code of chivalry, C. did far more than merely parody the artificial romances of chivalry: he created an immortal character and a wonderfully rich story in which breadth of humanity and compassion, acute psychological perception, charm, style and wit are all combined with a magnificent portrait of the whole of Spanish society in the 16th c. In its way *Don Quixote* is much more of a real romance of chivalry than all the tedious and affected sagas that C. burlesqued. Don Quixote's noble ideals and his insistence on practising them in defiance of logic and everyday realities make him into a noble and even a tragic figure. The character of Sancho Panza reinforces the dualism implicit in the book: between man at his highest and his most commonplace.

César Birotteau, Histoire de la grandeur et de la décadence de (1837). Novel by Balzac.

Céspedes Pablo de (1538–1608). Spanish mannerist painter, sculptor, architect, poet and priest who spent over 15 years in Italy. He became a friend and pupil of the Zuccaro brothers and was strongly influenced by Raphael and Michelangelo; the latter is celebrated in C.'s didactic poem *Poema de la pintura*. His altarpiece *The Last Supper* in Cordova cathedral is a good example of his work.

Cesti Pietro Antonio (also called Marc' Antonio) (1623–69). With P. F. Cavalli the leading composer of Italian opera in the mid 17th c. C.'s stage music was influenced by Cavalli and the Venetian school, his church music by G. Carissimi (his teacher) and the Roman school. His operas were remarkable for their magnificent arias and arioso passages, and the integration of arias, chorus and instrumental interludes into dramatic entities. C.'s finest opera was *Il pomo d'oro* (1667).

Cetina Gutierre de (?1520–?57). Spanish poet, much influenced in theme and metre by Italian poetry. His surviving work, including madrigals, sonnets, odes and *epistolas*, was publ. in 1895.

Cézanne Paul (1839–1906). French painter born in Aix-en-Provence the son of a well-to-do banker. He studied in the same school as Zola, and formed a close friendship, which had a decisive effect on the course of C.'s life. Destined by his father to study law he was eventually, at the age of 22, allowed to devote himself entirely to painting; a yearly allowance from his father enabled him to work without distraction for the next 23 years until his father's death, when he became a man of means. His 1st visit to Paris proved disappointing and he returned to Aix as a clerk in his father's office, but in 1862 C. was in Paris again for a decisive stay. He worked hard, and with Zola became involved in the revolutionary creative ferment directed against the bourgeoisie and academism. Yet he submitted work for the Salon and applied for admission to the École des Beaux-Arts. He failed in both. For the rest of his life he regularly sent paintings to the Salon. In 1882 he succeeded in having a portrait accepted as the result of friendly intervention. He exhibited in the Salon des Refusés of 1863. In 1886 he married his mistress; they had had a son in 1872. About this time C. worked with his friend Camille Pissarro, taking part in the 1st impressionist exhibition of 1874. Choquet, a collector, became his friend and patron. Again he showed with the impressionists in 1877, then refused to take part in any more exhibitions and retired to the south. His friendship with Zola was broken off in 1886 and later he also broke with Choquet. He withdrew more and more, but his fame was growing and he was becoming an almost legendary figure. In 1895 the dealer Vollard gave him a 1-man show consisting of 150 canvases, and in the same year 2 of his paintings entered the Luxembourg Mus. as part of the Caillebotte bequest. He was invited to show in Brussels and with the Vienna and Berlin Sezession. In 1901 Maurice Denis exhibited his painting *Homage to Cézanne* and the 1904 Salon d'Automne showed his paintings in a separate room. A large retrospective Cézanne exhibition was organized in the 1906 Salon d'Automne.
C.'s development divides into a number of phases. From 1862 to 1870 was a time of fervent research, study devoted to the museums absorbing influences of Courbet, Zurbarán, Poussin, Manet and the sculptor Puget. C. was striving for a realism, searching for exactitude in revolt against the banality of the bourgeois Salons and the official Academy. His paintings tended to be clumsy, coarse in texture, painted

Cézanne. *Self-portrait*

Cesti. *Il pomo d'oro*; contemporary engraving

Céspedes. *The Last Supper*

Cézanne. *Maison du Pendu*

Cézanne. *Still-life with black clock.* See also colour plate 72

Cézanne. *Card Players*

with a palette-knife, turbulent almost brutal: greys, browns, earth colour and heavy black shadows with occasional flashes of brilliant colour. Characteristic of this period is a portrait, painted in 1866, of his father reading a newspaper and the *Still-life with black clock.* Both are monumental, showing an interest in architectural composition and a sense of plasticity.

C. retired to l'Estaque during the 1870 Paris Commune and here, in close contact with the landscape, his sensibility developed. When he joined Pissarro at Pontoise in 1872 a radical change was inevitable. The former heaviness slowly gave way to a more controlled and subtle surface, his palette lightened with the increased use of primary colours, their division and related tones. C. acknowledged Pissarro as his master, but he also influenced Pissarro, though to a lesser extent. Both painters preserved their identity.

The *Maison du Pendu* (Louvre, Paris) shown at the 1st impressionist exhibition (1874) typified this new palette. The realization of this change was of necessity slow and painful as increasingly colour and a colour-tone hierarchy became his dominant sensation and means of expression. A false note meant a fresh start–hence the deliberate brush-stroke, the incessant work in front of the model requiring countless sittings, immense effort, patience and genius to maintain and nourish the intensity of emotion. From 1880 onwards this research is intensified in his portraits, self-portraits, still-lifes, landscapes and in compositions as the *Card Players* (1890–2; Courtauld Gal., London and Louvre) where the subject is interpreted in the classical tradition of Poussin. C. used watercolour for its heightened purity and brilliance, especially during his last years when his strong feeling for nature was surest. He was now an heir to the great colourists of the past, from the Venetians to Delacroix and he expressed volume and light in his own way by a system of superimposed glazes of pure colour and tone relations, where each colour temperature corresponded to a mood both of the physical world and of the world of painting. Thus he achieved a synthesis of reality and abstraction as in his *Bathers* (1900–6; Merion Barnes Foundation, U.S.) and showed the way to the new developments of the 20th c., first fully expressed by the painters of cubism.

Chaadayev Pyotr Yakovlevich (*c.* 1793–1856). Russian writer and philosopher, the first of whose philosophical letters in French (publ. 1836) severely criticized Russian isolation from the West, regarding Russia's culture as inferior. As a result he was officially declared insane but was later allowed freedom on condition that he publ. no more.

Chabrier (Alexis) Emmanuel (1841–94). French composer associated with the early impressionist painters and musical followers of C. *Franck, and ardently pro-Wagner. Increasing nervous excitement, verging on madness, killed him. His works include the orchestral rhapsody *España* (1883) and the operas *Le roi malgré lui* (1887) and *Gwendoline* (1886).

Chabrol Claude (1930–). French film director; his *Le Beau Serge* (1957) was the 1st feature

Chabrol. Bernadette Laffont in *Les Bonnes Femmes*

Emmanuel Chabrier

of the *nouvelle vague. He began by taking thematic inspiration from Hitchcock, both in *Serge* and *Les Cousins* (1958), but the Hitchcock influence became increasingly stylistic rather than thematic in a mystery film, *À Double Tour* (1959) and *Les Bonnes Femmes* (1960), his best film, about 4 Paris shop-girls. His fascination with the grotesque ran riot in *Les Godelureaux* (1961). In *Landru* (1963), from a script by the novelist F. Sagan, the grotesque clashes with the delicate and tragedy with comedy in a story of multiple murder.

chaconne. Originally, like the passacaglia, a dance in slow triple time and composed on a *ground bass. From the 17th c. on, it was an instrumental form; the ground may occur in upper parts or may disappear altogether as a theme, only its harmonic structure persisting, as in Bach's mighty c. in the Partita no. 2 in D min. for solo violin. The other famous c. is Purcell's CHACONY (17th-c. English form of the word) in G min. for strings.

Chadwick George Whitefield (1854–1931). U.S. composer, one of the 'Boston classicists', and successor to J. K. *Paine. His music showed technical mastery, melodic invention and wit, and he was important in establishing an American style. Works include a comic opera, 3 symphonies and chamber music.

Chadwick Lynn (1914–). British sculptor. He started making mobiles in 1945, and in the early 1950s emerged as one of the leading figures of a group of young English artists whose linear constructions were in direct contrast to Moore's monumental style. In these early works, e.g. *Inner Eye* (1962; M.M.A., New York), and in later works like *Encounter VI* (1957; British Council Coll.) in which the linear structure was covered with a skin of angular planes, C. creates images which have a close resemblance to reality but whose inorganic forms add a disturbing surreal significance.

Chagall Marc (1889–). Russian artist of a devout Jewish family, born in Vitebsk. He went to St Petersburg in 1907 where he entered a minor art school, at the same time working as a sign painter; throughout his work a foundation of Russian art and the sign painters' technique has remained. He went (1910) to Paris where he came in contact with the cubists; his work began to show cubist influence but subjects remain of life in Vitebsk. In 1914 he returned home and contributed to Larionov's exhibitions and the Knave of Diamonds group. After the Revolution, in 1918, C. was appointed director of the Vitebsk art school, which became a centre of *avant-garde* ideas, but was soon ousted by Malevich and left for Moscow. From 1919 to 1922 he worked as theatrical designer for the Jewish State Theatre, executing murals there. In 1922 he went to Berlin, executing *Mein Leben* etchings for Vollard who then invited him to Paris (illustrations for *Dead Souls*). In 1925–6 he completed a set of illustrations for an ed. of La Fontaine's *Fables* and held a 1-man show in New York. In 1930 his autobiography, *Ma Vie*, was publ., and C. began illustrations for the Bible, travelling to the Middle East. He went to the U.S. in 1941, producing the décor for Massine's ballet *Aleko* (1942) and Bolm's *Firebird* (1945) both for the Ballet Theater. He returned to France after the war. Of recent work, his designs for stained-glass windows should be mentioned, and his paintings for the ceiling of the Paris Opéra.

chainés or déboulés. In classical ballet, a series of fast turns in which the weight is rapidly transferred from one foot to the other, the feet remaining close to the ground; executed in a straight line or a circle as the dancer moves across the stage.

Chaliapin(e) or **Shaliapin** Fyodor Ivanovich (1873–1938). Russian bass singer outstanding as well for his acting as his voice. His 1st success came (1896) in the 'Private Opera' of the Russian patron, S. J. Mamontov, and his reputation rapidly became world wide. One of his greatest roles was Boris Godunov in Mussorgsky's opera.

chalice. The wine-cup used in the celebration of the Eucharist. In the later 16th c. there was a sharp distinction between the Roman Catholic chalice and the Protestant communion-cup.

chalumeau. Early single-reed musical instrument of the clarinet type; the term is also used to designate the lower register of the clarinet.

Chamberlain Houston Stewart (1855–1927). English writer, who became Wagner's son-in-law and settled in Germany. His *Die Grundlagen des neunzehnten Jahrhunderts* (1899; *The Foundations of the Nineteenth Century*, 1911) propounded race theories which anticipated (and influenced) Nazism.

Chamberlain, Powell and Bon. London firm of architects. Their Bousfield School in The Boltons, Kensington (1955) is light and elegant, but their later work has departed from this to more heavy, complex forms. Their Barbican scheme, commenced in 1963 on the adjoining site, is the most important piece of urban redevelopment in England.

Chamberlain's Men, The. Theatrical co. in which Shakespeare acted and for which he wrote most of his plays. In 1599 the co. had to leave J. Burbage's Theatre in Shoreditch, which was to be demolished, and transferred to The *Globe Theatre, which members of the co. owned and maintained on a profit-sharing basis. When James I became their patron they were thereafter known as 'The King's Men'. The original co. disbanded soon after the death of Shakespeare in 1616.

chamber music. Music for a small group of performers, usually instrumentalists, each part being given to 1 performer only; by convention works for only 1 or 2 performers are not regarded as c. m. The most common combination is the string quartet. In form it is a *symphony for 2 violins, viola, and cello and has been the medium of some of the very greatest music since the work of Haydn who established the form. Other common combinations are the string quintet, with 2 violas or 2 cellos; the string trio, upper strings and cello, and piano trio, i.e. piano, violin and cello (note that clarinet quintet signifies 1 clarinet

The Tassilo Chalice; Carolingian, *c.* 780

Chadwick. *Encounter VI*

Chagall. *Self-portrait with seven fingers*

Chagall. Stained-glass window for a Jerusalem synagogue

Chambord

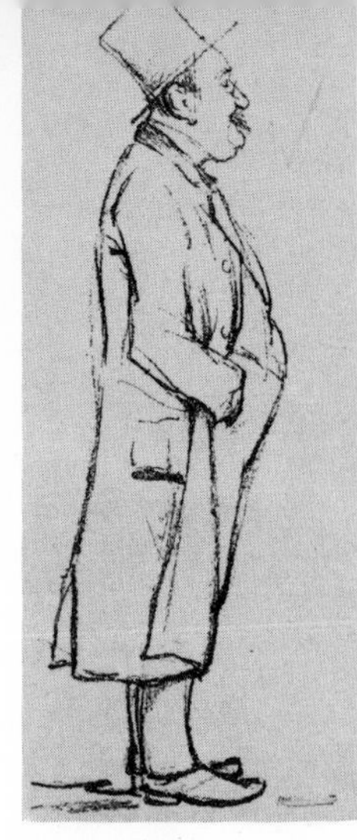

Cartoon of Champfleury

with 4 string instruments). A chamber orchestra is simply a small orchestra, not one with 1 instrument only to each part.

Chamber Music (1907). Coll. of poems by James Joyce.

Chambers Robert (1802–71). Scottish publ. and writer who, with his brother William, formed a publ. firm which produced the 1st ed. of *Chambers's Encyclopaedia* (1859–68). He was joint ed. of *Chambers's Edinburgh Journal* (started 1832).

Chambers Sir William (1723–96). English architect. Born and brought up in Sweden, he began architecture only after 9 years as an agent of the Swedish East India Co., spent 5 years in Italy and settled in England in 1755. He first gained attention by designing the ornamental buildings (Pagoda, temples, etc.) at Kew, publ. in one of his several books of designs. In 1782 he became Surveyor-General, in which capacity he carried out a wide variety of commissions–town halls, streets, prisons, country-houses, etc. His most famous work is Somerset House, London (central portion only, 1776), an elegant neo-classical composition but lacking in grandeur. He also designed the royal state coach, still used at coronations.

Sir William Chambers. Original design for the Pagoda at Kew

Chambonnières Jacques Champion de (*c.* 1602–*c.* 72). French composer and harpsichord virtuoso and teacher, the most famous of his period. His pupils included R. Cambert, L., F. and C. Couperin, N. Le Bèque and G. Nivers; abroad his style affected J. J. Froberger. C.'s compositions were important in the history of French keyboard music.

Chambord France. The most spectacular of the show-palaces of Francis I. Though based on the traditional French castle (square-plan, massive circular towers, curtain walls, etc.) the details, such as windows, balustrades and chimneys, are full of N. Italian Renaissance motifs. It dates mainly from 1519 to 1537.

Chamfort Sébastien-Roch Nicolas de (1741–94). French writer and author of the penetrating *Maximes, caractères et anecdotes* (1795).

Chaminade Cécile (1857–1944). French composer for whom, as a child, Bizet prophesied greatness. She wrote a comic opera, ballets and orchestral pieces and elegant short piano works being herself a concert pianist.

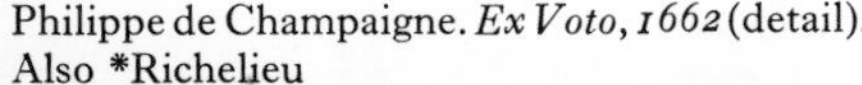

Philippe de Champaigne. *Ex Voto, 1662* (detail). Also *Richelieu

Chamisso Adelbert von (pseud. of Louis-Charles Adelaide Chamisso de Boncourt) (1781–1838). Poet and novelist of French origin who settled in Germany and wrote in German. He produced sentimental romantic lyrics of great freshness and simplicity, ballads and narrative poems. His story, *Peter Schlemihls wundersame Geschichte* (1814; *The Wonderful History of Peter Schlemihl*, 1843) is an allegory of his life and the history of Germany.

Champaigne Jean-Baptiste de (1631–81). Painter, nephew of P. de C. and his assistant. He was born in Brussels, moved to Paris in 1643 and took French nationality in 1655.

Champaigne Philippe de (1602–74). Painter of portraits and religious subjects, born in Brussels and trained as a landscapist there. In 1621 he moved to Paris and with N. Poussin assisted on decorations for the Luxembourg Palace. In 1628 he was appointed painter to Marie de' Medici and was patronized by Louis XIII and Cardinal Richelieu. For the latter he painted frescoes in the dome of the Sorbonne church, a full-length portrait (1635; N.G., London) and a triple portrait (N.G., London) as a model for Bernini's bust. During this period his portraits, though more sculptural, resembled Van Dyck's and his religious paintings, e.g. *Adoration of the Shepherds* (*c.* 1630; Wallace Coll., London), showed the influence of Rubens's baroque, though much restrained. His most original work was produced after *c.* 1647 when he began to associate with the Jansenists of Port-Royal. Under the influence of the harsh, puritanical doctrines of this Catholic sect his tendency to coldness and restraint was accentuated and all baroque contrapposto eliminated, his work achieving a beauty new in French art founded on extreme simplicity and austerity. Outstanding examples of this period are his half-length *Portrait of an Unknown Man* (1650; Louvre) and the picture *Ex Voto, 1662* (Louvre) painted in thanks for the wonderful healing of his daughter, a nun at Port-Royal.

Champfleury. The pseud. of Jules Husson or Fleury (1821–89). French writer and art historian. His critical study, *Le Réalisme* (1857), was one of the 1st studies of the movement. He wrote many books on ceramics, caricature and popular art, including *Histoire de la caricature antique* (1865–90). His novels include

Champneys. Newnham College

Chandelier; made in the 1770s

Souffrances de professeur Delteil (1853; *Naughty Boys, or the Sufferings of Mr Delteil*, 1855).

champlevé. A kind of enamel where the troughs or cells are cut on the metal surface, leaving a raised line between them which forms the outline of the design. After the enamel has been fired, it is filed and polished smooth.

Champneys Basil (1842–1935). English architect, one of the last of the neo-Gothic school. His chief works are Girton and Newnham colleges, Cambridge.

Chamson André (1900–). French Protestant novelist, born at Nîmes. His best-known works, studies of life in the Cevennes, include *Roux le Bandit* (1925; *Roux the Bandit*, 1929), *Les Hommes de la route* (1927; *The Road. . .* , 1929) and *Le Crime des justes* (1928).

chancel. The part of a church, including the altar and choir, reserved for the clergy; it is sometimes separated from the nave by a CHANCEL-SCREEN.

chandelier. Originally a candle-stand pendant from the ceiling, made of metal, wood, crystal, china, or more usually glass. Used as early as the 14th c., it later became the excuse for the most elaborate decoration, achieving a sumptuous effect by the use of many reflecting facets.

Chandler Raymond (1888–1959). U.S. writer of detective fiction in the 'hard-boiled' style of Dashiell Hammett. His works include *The Big Sleep* (1939), *Farewell My Lovely* (1940), *The Little Sister* (1949), *The Long Good-bye* (1954).

Changeling, The (1623?). Tragedy by *Middleton and *Rowley.

changement. In classical ballet a step of elevation where a jump, great or small, is made from the 5th *position, the legs fully stretched and the toes pointed. The positions of the feet are reversed in the air and the dancer lands again in the 5th position.

change ringing: *bell

chanson. Part song written by French composers during the late medieval/early Renaissance periods. Of music in the early part of this period, the term can be used generically of *virelais*, ballades and *rondeaux*, etc.; of 16th-c. music the term is best restricted to a French part song, more formal in structure than the Italian madrigal.

chansons de geste. 12th- and 13th-c. French epics of chivalry and valour in war, dealing largely with wars between Christian and Saracen and battles between feudal lords. The most famous is the *Chanson de *Roland.*

Chantrey Sir Francis (Legatt) (1781–1841). English neo-classic portrait sculptor and, in his youth, painter, renowned for his tender portrayal of children. He left his fortune to the R.A. mainly for the purchase of 'works of Fine Art . . . executed in Great Britain' to be known as the CHANTREY BEQUEST (purchases now in the Tate).

chant royal. Medieval French verse form used for allegorical subjects; it had 5 stanzas of 11 lines rhyming *ababccddede*, and an *envoi* of 5 lines rhyming *ddede* which explained the allegory. The last line of the 1st stanza is repeated as the last line of succeeding stanzas and of the *envoi.*

Chapayev (1934). Film directed by S. and G. *Vassiliev.

chapbook. A pamphlet or booklet of popular stories or ballads formerly sold by 'chapmen' up to the early 19th c.

Chapeau de Paille, Le. Portrait by *Rubens.

Chapelain Jean (1595–1674). French writer, an *habitué* of the Hôtel de *Rambouillet. As a critic C. advocated the *unities in drama. He was a member of the original Académie, and drafted its censure of Corneille's *Le Cid.*

Chapel Royal. The corporate body of musicians serving at the English court; its earliest records date from the 12th c. Very many English musicians, among them Tallis, Byrd and Purcell, were employed either as choirboys or choirmen or organists.

Chaplet Ernest (1835–1909). One of the most important of French 19th-c. artist potters. After an apprenticeship at Sèvres he worked independently, endeavouring to achieve glazes comparable to the Chinese.

Chantrey. The poet George Crabbe

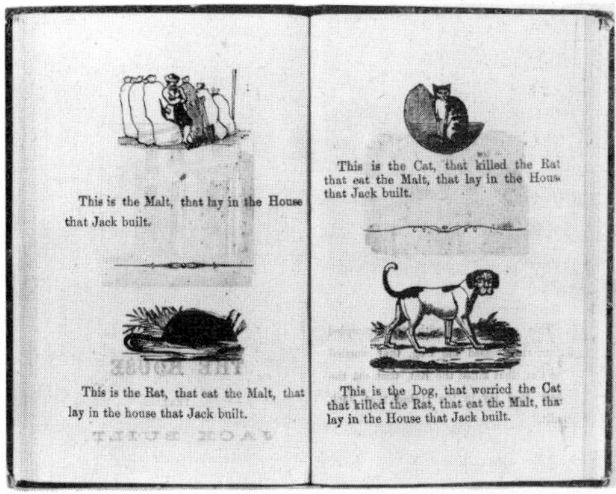

This is the Malt, that lay in the House that Jack built.

This is the Cat, that killed the Rat that eat the Malt, that lay in the House that Jack built.

This is the Rat, that eat the Malt, that lay in the house that Jack built.

This is the Dog, that worried the Cat that killed the Rat, that eat the Malt, that lay in the House that Jack built.

Chapbook. *The House that Jack Built* (1850)

Chaplin in *City Lights*

Charcoal. Käthe Kollwitz, *Self-portrait* (1938)

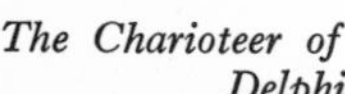

The Charioteer of Delphi

Chaplin Charles (1889–). British-born film actor and director. Touring the U.S. with Fred Karno's music-hall troupe, C. joined Sennett's Keystone films in 1913. At Keystone he played in many costumes, but from 1915 at Essanay and later elsewhere, he was able to direct and to develop the famous tramp figure in such films as *The Bank* (1915), *Easy Street* (1917), *The Immigrant* (1917) and *Shoulder Arms* (1918). In the 1920s he made features instead of shorts, but still retaining the tramp figure: *The Kid* (1921), *The Pilgrim* (1923), *The Gold Rush* (1925). *A Woman of Paris* (1923) was a non-slapstick comedy starring not C. but his leading lady since 1915, Edna Purviance. *City Lights* (1931) and *Modern Times* (1936), respectively his 1st sound and talking pictures retained 'the little fellow' although they were now far from being simple comedies with a touch of pathos, but aimed to use comedy as a means to overt statements. This tendency went even further in *The Great Dictator* (1940), in which he abandoned his character and played a dictator modelled on Hitler, and a Jewish barber. *Monsieur Verdoux* (1947), perhaps his most remarkable film, was a satirical version of the Bluebeard story. 2 later films, made in Britain, were a straight tragedy, *Limelight* (1952), and a comedy, *A King in New York* (1957).

Chapman George (1559?–1634). English dramatist and poet, a member of the *school of night, whose creed is presented in his *Shadow of Night* (1594). C.'s finest work was his masterly, individualistic trs. of Homer, for which he claimed to have had a special inspiration. Characteristic of his tragedies are the larger-than-life protagonist and a grandeur which can rise to passionate poetry or degenerate into bombast. C. continued Marlowe's *Hero and Leander* (1598) and collaborated with Jonson and J. Marston in *Eastward Hoe* (1605). Works include the tragedies *Bussy D'Ambois* (1607), *The Revenge of Bussy D'Ambois* (1613) and the tragi-comedy *The Gentleman Usher* (1606).

Chappell William (1908–). British ballet dancer and designer. Trained by Marie Rambert, he joined the Sadler's Wells in 1934 where he designed the décor for Ashton's *Les Patineurs* (1937) and other ballets. He has also written books on ballet and produced revues.

chapter-house. Room in a monastery or cathedral where the governing body meet.

Char René (1907–). French poet. He left the surrealist movement in 1937 and, working in his Provençal milieu, created a brooding, aphoristic yet lyrical verse. He made his reputation with the poems of *Fureur et Mystère* (1948).

character dancers and actors. Dancers or actors who specialize in the portrayal of a limited number of character types as opposed to 'straight' dancers or actors, who perform roles calling for a more subtle psychological interpretation.

charcoal. Sticks of charred wood, usually willow. There is literary evidence that c. was used as a drawing medium by the Greeks, but extant drawings date only from *c.* 1500. It is very soft and needs to be 'fixed' if used on paper. In general it is unsuitable for detailed work but lends itself to the bold statement; it is widely used for compositional sketches because it is so easily rubbed off that corrections can be made indefinitely. It is often used in conjunction with white chalk on toned paper.

Chardin Jean-Baptiste-Siméon (1699–1779). French painter, master of still-life and genre. The son of a court craftsman, he was trained in the rococo tradition of P.-J. Cazes and Noël-Nicolas Coypel and worked as a restorer of the Vanloo decorations at Fontainebleau. Despite this, his early work was mistaken by contemporaries for that of the Dutch masters of still-life. His modest nature, individual style and choice of subjects from everyday middle-class life retarded his success in the age of Boucher and Fragonard, but he was elected a member of the French Academy in 1728, while his genre subjects were made popular by engravers. When the court art of the 18th c. went out of favour the reputation of C. rose. The simplicity of his composition, his single figures of kitchen-maids at work and children absorbed in their games, had an influence upon the painters of everyday life in the 19th c. Manet was greatly influenced by the unstressed brilliance of C.'s still-life painting, as Courbet had been before him. The chief coll. of his works, including the dramatic still-life with fish and cat, *La Raie*, is in the Louvre.

Charioteer of Delphi, The. Classical Greek sculpture in bronze, a single figure with outstretched arms (to hold reins); it was originally part of a life-size group including a chariot with 4 horses.

Chardin. *Self-portrait*; pastel

Chardin. *La Raie.* Also *genre

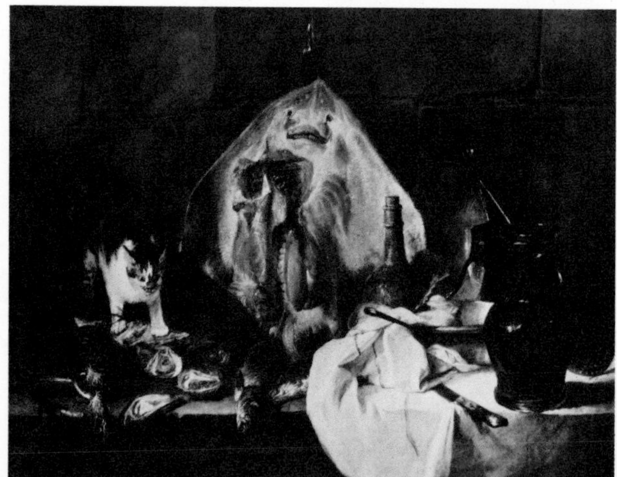

Charlet. *French Dragoon with Flag*

Charlemagne: head on a silver denier

Charisse Cyd (1923–). U.S. film star. A song and dance performer, C.'s big break came in *Words and Music* (1948). She became the musical draw of the 1950s: her films include *Singin' in the Rain* (1951), *Band Wagon* (1953).

Charivari. French/Latin word of medieval origin. A serenade of 'rough music', extemporized with household utensils, used to express popular disapproval. Also the name of a magazine founded (1832) by C. *Philipon.

Charlemagne (742–814). Frankish king and 1st of the medieval emperors. His great military and political achievement throughout Europe brought him legendary status, e.g. *Chanson de *Roland*, and his patronage caused a brief revival in the arts (*Carolingian renaissance).

Charles d'Orléans (1391–1465). French poet and important patron of poets, duke of the royal house and father of Louis XII. C. d'O. was prominent in the internal strife in France, was captured at the battle of Agincourt (1415) and spent 25 years in captivity in England (he was ransomed in 1440). The majority of his poems are short, rondels or ballades on love or the seasons in the courtly convention, employing allegory and designed not to express personal emotion but to exploit the verse forms with brilliance and effect.

Charles IV (1316–78). Holy Roman emperor and king of Bohemia; under him Prague enjoyed its golden age in the arts. C.'s autobiography is one of the earliest.

Charlet Nicolas-Toussaint (1792–1845). French graphic artist and painter, a pupil of A.-J. Gros and friend of Géricault. His paintings depicted romanticized episodes of the Napoleonic era; more successful were his lithographs and woodcuts illustrating informal incidents of life in Napoleon's army.

Charonton Enguerrand: *Quarton

Charpentier Gustave (1860–1956). French composer whose 'musical romance' *Louise* (1900) had great and immediate success. C. also wrote *Impressions d'Italie* (1892) which made his name, *Vie d'un poète* (1892) a 'symphony drama' and the lyric drama *Julien* (1913) based on this.

Charpentier Marc-Antoine (1636?–1704). French composer associated with the Théâtre-Français (1672–85) and musical director of the Sainte-Chapelle (from 1698). He studied under G. Carissimi and his work is characterized by a mastery of counterpoint and bold modulations and use of dissonance; his stage music shows the influence of Lully. Compositions included music for plays by Molière and others, several operas and pastorals, and many outstanding oratorios and church cantatas.

Charrat Janine (1924–). French dancer and choreographer who appeared in the film *La Mort du Cygne* (1936). Although taught in the Russian classical tradition she developed mainly in the modern idiom and was co-founder of les Ballets des Champs-Élysées. Her works as a choreographer include *Jeu de Cartes* (1945), *Concerto* (1951) and *Les Algues* (1953). *Répétition de Phaedre* (1964) marked her return as a choreographer after several years inactivity following a near-fatal accident.

Charrière Mme Isabelle de, known as 'Belle de Zuylen' (1740–1805). French writer of Dutch origin. Her novels, shrewd analyses of the passions, include *Les Lettres de Mistress Henley* (1784) which is obviously autobiographical and tells of a woman made miserable by a virtuous, dull husband. Her friendship with the novelist Benjamin Constant lasted until her death.

Charterhouse of Parma, The (1839). Novel by *Stendhal.

Chartier Alain (*c.* 1385–1435). French writer, author of the poem *La belle dame sans mercy* (1424; trs. *La Bele Dame Sauns Mercy*, 1526?, once attributed to Chaucer). He was greatly admired as a writer, but grotesquely ugly. Margaret of Scotland, wife of the Dauphin, once kissed his lips while he slept because they spoke so many beautiful words. In his *Livre de quatre dames* 4 ladies lament the loss of their lovers at Agincourt. C.'s best-known prose work is *Le Quadrilogue invectif* (1422), a cry for French unity against the enemy.

Chartier Émile August: *Alain

Chartres cathedral. One of the key buildings in the history of Gothic architecture, sculpture and stained glass. (1) Architecture. Begun in 1195 and finished *c.* 1230, C. comes in the middle of the development of Île de France Gothic 3-storey elevation, plate-tracery of a very late kind, and quadripartite vault. (2) Sculpture.

Chartres cathedral

Chartres. Sculptures on the porch

Chateaubriand

Belongs to 2 periods: the W. front is a survival from the previous cathedral of *c.* 1145: its free-standing figures, though still stylized and partly assimilated to the shape of the shafts against which they stood, are beginning to show a Gothic freedom and naturalism. The sculpture (1220–50) on the porches of the N. and S. transepts is mature Gothic and forms an iconographical scheme of extreme elaboration. (3) Stained glass. C. is unique in possessing all its mid-13th-c. stained glass; colours are rich and jewel-like, the designs still hieratic, making full use of the medium but not seeking to go beyond it in the direction of naturalism.

Chartreuse de Parme, La (1839). Novel by *Stendhal.

William Merritt Chase. *Hide and Seek*

chase. In silversmithing, a technique of decoration in low relief; the punch merely indents the surface in a line without cutting any metal away. It should be distinguished from punching in which a pattern effect is sought with each single stroke, rather than a continuous line or lines.

Chase William Merritt (1849–1916). U.S. portrait, landscape, genre and still-life painter. He went to Munich in 1872 and worked under F. Wagner and K. von Piloty; after returning to the U.S. he gained a great reputation as a teacher.

Chasins Abram (1903–). Russian-born U.S. composer and pianist, also musical director of the New York State Radio.

Chasles (Victor Euphémion) Philarète (1798–1873). French writer who did much to spread a knowledge of foreign literatures into France. He was given the Chair of Modern European Languages at the Collège de France. His works include: *Le Dixhuitième siècle en Angleterre* (1846); *Études sur l'antiquité . . .* (1847) and *Mémoires*, 2 vols (1876–7).

Chassériau Théodore (1819–56). French historical and portrait painter and engraver. C. was born in the French West Indies; he studied in Paris and Rome, chiefly under Ingres, but was later influenced by Delacroix and the romantics, particularly in his use of colour and his choice of subjects. In the *Chaste Susanna* (Louvre) this combination of firm drawing with romantic feeling can be seen. C. painted murals for a number of churches and in the Palais D'Orsay and fashionably romanticized versions of African life; he engraved several sets of illustrations to Shakespeare.

Chassériau. *Chaste Susanna*

Chasse Spirituelle, La. Lost work by Rimbaud. A very successful hoax was perpetrated in 1949 when a poem bearing this title was publ. in France.

Chastellain (or Chastelain) Georges (*c.* 1405 or *c.* 1415–75). Flemish author of a *Chronique des choses de ce temps* (i.e. 1419–75). This chronicle, which was continued by J. Molinet, is preserved in fragmentary form. C. was also a poet and author of various moral and political pieces including *Les Princes*, a poem describing 24 types of bad ruler.

Chateaubriand François-René, vicomte de (1768–1848). French writer, important in the development of French romanticism. He travelled to America (1791) and returned to join the Armée des Émigres: was exiled in England (1793–1800): served Napoleon, but was disgraced (1807) for comparing Napoleon with Nero and retired to Aubray until 1814; he served (1814–16) under Louis XVIII, and was French foreign minister from 1823 to 1824. He became the grand old man of French literature and was buried at his own request on an island off Saint-Malo.

Atala (1801), a brief tale set in Louisiana with its rhapsodic descriptions of nature, made his reputation, and *Le Génie du Christianisme* (1802), a lyrical and eloquent apologia, incorporating *Atala* confirmed it. *René* (1805), a 2nd fictional excerpt from *Le Génie*, epitomizes the characteristic sensibility of romanticism. *Les Natchez* (1826), a Red Indian prose epic which completes *Le Génie*, was actually composed first, in England. His most celebrated work is the autobiography *Mémoires d'outre-tombe* (posth. 1849–50), it contains inspired evocations of the author's childhood and youth, the period of the Revolution. Other works include: *La Vie de Rancé* (1844), a biography of a celebrated Trappist monk, and a trs. of *Paradise Lost* (1836).

Chatelain (Chatelin, Chatelaine) Jean-Baptiste-Claude (1710–71). English draughtsman and engraver of French Huguenot origin. He specialized in landscapes and was one of the first to exploit the Lake District; his drawings have sometimes been attributed to Gainsborough. He executed engravings after Rembrandt, Claude, G. Poussin, S. Ricci and others.

Chatelaine and watch, late 18th c.

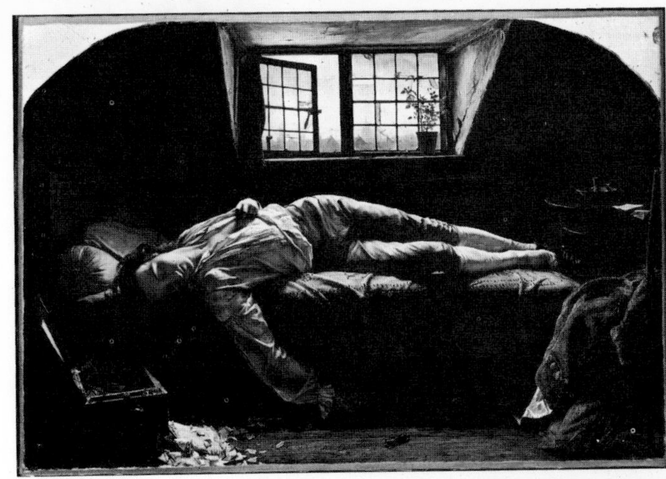

The Death of Chatterton by Wallis

chatelaine. A brooch or clasp fastened at the waist, from which keys, scissors, trinkets and similar objects could be hung by short chains. The word derives from *châtelaine*, meaning a 'mistress of a castle' who would carry the castle keys hanging from her girdle. Gold, silver, enamel and *pinchbeck chatelaines were especially fashionable in the 18th and 19th cs.

Chatterton Thomas (1752–70). English poet, who produced poems and documents which he claimed to be authentic antique mss, mostly by a fictitious 15th-c. monk, Thomas Rowley; he temporarily convinced H. Walpole. Depressed by his extreme poverty he took arsenic. In mood and its Gothicized language C.'s work prefigured the romantics and had a measurable influence on Blake and Wordsworth. The works include remarkable poems, e.g. *Bristowe Tragedie*, *Mynstrelles Songe* (in *Songe to Aella*) and *Excelente Balade of Charitie*. His suicide was the subject of a Pre-Raphaelite painting (in the Tate) by J. Wallis, for which George Meredith was the model.

Chaucer Geoffrey (*c.* 1340–1400). English poet. A Londoner of prosperous bourgeois family, C. spent his life in the royal service, beginning as a page in the duke of Clarence's household in 1357. He went to France with the army, and as an esquire of the royal household, spent 10 years in various diplomatic missions to France and Italy, where he came under the influence of continental literature. He held official positions in London (1374–89) but then shared in the decline of the fortunes of his patron, John of Gaunt. He died soon after his rehabilitation under the new king, Henry IV. C. wrote for a sophisticated court audience, enjoying a high reputation in his own time, which has never seriously declined since. His literary influence in the 15th c. was enormous, though, as illustrated in the work of poets like Lydgate and Hoccleve, not always beneficial. But the Scots poets *Dunbar and *Henryson, working in a more independent cultural environment, were able to make better use of his example. The next great English poet, Edmund Spenser, was C.'s avowed pupil. C. began writing under French influence, and early attempted a trs. of *Le *Roman de la Rose*, some of which survives. *The Book of the Duchess* (1369–70), in the manner of Machaut and Froissart, a formal dream-allegory, is slight and conventional but a poem of great charm and accomplishment. *The Hous of Fame* (*c.* 1380) gives a much clearer indication of C.'s potential, though it too uses the conventional form, and though his inspiration ran out half-way. The influence of the Italians, notably Dante, begins to be apparent; the vicissitudes of Fame replace Love as the subject, and C.'s genius for comedy is displayed in the figures of the Dreamer and his guide, the Eagle. The next period (1380–6) shows his complete assimilation of a variety of influences, amongst which that of Boccaccio is predominant. The delightful *Parliament of Fowls* (1381) treats a traditional subject again, the birds in council over a love-dispute, but though it is sometimes prized for its comic treatment of the lower orders of birds, it deals with a serious problem, the relationship of earthly love to universals, which is the dominant theme of C.'s greatest finished work, *Troilus and Criseyde* (*c.* 1380). The source for this is Boccaccio's *Filostrato*, but C. transforms it, both by observing the conventions of courtly and epic poetry, and by treating it in depth. He develops dialogue and psychological analysis, especially in his treatment of Troilus, Criseyde and Pandarus, making this one of the richest of all medieval poems. Also within this period come his trs. of *Boethius, and *The Legend of Good Women*, in which the dream convention is used to frame a coll. of stories of 'martyrs of love'. It contains some magnificent passages, and reveals C.'s narrative skill, not least in the liberties he takes with his classical sources; but the subject seems to bore him, and the poem is unfinished. Soon after this he began work on the great story coll. *The Canterbury Tales*, which occupied him until the end of his life. It is set in the framework of a pilgrimage to the Shrine of Thomas à Becket at Canterbury; each pilgrim is to tell 4 tales and the best raconteur to have dinner at the others' expense when the party returns to the Tabard Inn, Southwark. The plan (not completed) is agreed between the pilgrims and they are introduced in the brilliant and famous *Prologue*. The convention is similar to Boccaccio's in *The Decameron* but handled more imaginatively, and in the 'prologues' to the various tales the pilgrims emerge as full-blooded characters. The tales range from a romance of chivalry to sheer bawdy, and the perfect adaptation of style over such a wide scale is a measure of C.'s versatility and his true pre-eminence in medieval English literature.

Chausson Ernest (1855–99). French composer. His music shows the influence of Franck, his

Chaucer: from an early 15th-c. ms. of Hoccleve

Chatelain. *View on a River*

Chelsea. *Four Seasons* (1753–5)

Chelsea. Candlestick with birds (*c.* 1765)

Anton Chekhov: drawing by his nephew

Yvette Chauviré with Jean Babilée

teacher, and has been called a link between Franck and Debussy; it includes stage works, choral works, the symphony in B♭, the *Poème* for violin and orchestra (1896) and songs in the tradition of Duparc.

Chauviré Yvette (1917–). French dancer. Launched by Lifar at the Paris Opéra in his ballet *Istar* (1941), she danced in many of his ballets, but is primarily a classical dancer, her finest role being that of Giselle.

Chávez Carlos (1899–). Mexican composer and conductor, director of the National Conservatory (1928–52). Early visits to Europe and the U.S. produced futurist and abstract works, e.g. the ballet *H.P.* (i.e. 'horse-power'), *Polígonos* for piano and *Energía* for 9 instruments. Later he concentrated on a Mexican national idiom, e.g. *Sinfonía India* and *Xochipili-Macuilxochitl* for Mexican instruments. Other works include an opera (1956), 4 symphonies, 3 string quartets, *Soli* for 4 wind instruments, and the book *Toward a New Music* (1937).

Checkmate. 1-act ballet with choreography by *de Valois, music by Bliss and décor by McKnight Kauffer; 1st performance 1937.

Chekhov Anton Pavlovich (1860–1904). Russian writer of short stories and plays, the son of an unsuccessful shopkeeper. C. studied medicine at Moscow Univ. (1879–84) and took a degree, though he never practised. At the same time he was supporting himself and his family by writing humorous sketches–mainly hack-work which, with farces like *The Bear* and *The Proposal*, long remained his most popular work in Russia. The success of *Motley Stories* (1886) enabled C. to produce more serious work. His play *Ivanov* was performed in 1887, but after the failure of *The Wood Demon* (1889) he returned to the short story for some years. He wrote a book of reportage, *Sakhalin Island* (1891), after visiting the notorious prison there; and the resulting publicity helped to bring about reforms. From 1897 C. was forced to live at resorts (notably Yalta) by the tuberculosis which killed him.

C.'s most typical work skilfully creates atmosphere and exploits basic situations; there is virtually no plot and little orthodox character-drawing. The tone is lyrical and melancholy, the themes are boredom, futility, triviality, isolation. C. has been widely imitated, and influenced such dissimilar writers as Gorky (in his plays) and Katherine Mansfield. C.'s stories are charged with a painful humour ('laughter through tears'); in, e.g., *Misery* (1886), an old cabman fails to interest anybody in his son's death and at last tells the story to his horse. In the plays too, communication is impossible: each character pursues his thoughts without listening to or being heard by others. C. returned to the theatre with *The Seagull* (1898; 1912), which turns on the fate of Nina, the 'seagull' whose life is destroyed by the writer Trigorin 'just to pass the time'. *Uncle Vanya* (1899; 1923) describes the disrupting effect of the beautiful Yeliena on the routine existence of a provincial group. Here, as in C.'s other plays, work is the only escape from suffering and happiness possible only for future generations. The sisters in *Three Sisters* (1900; 1916) believe they can be happy–in Moscow; but they never succeed in leaving their provincial home. In *The Cherry Orchard* (1904; 1912) the economic and spiritual decline of the landowning classes is symbolized by the sale and destruction of the orchard. These plays have established C.'s European fame. Each describes a period in the lives of a provincial group–a crucial period for some of them; but (a dramatic innovation) all the characters receive the same attention, and personal tragedies are set in the context of the trivialities and frustrations of ordinary life. Stories by C. include *Sleepy* (1888), *The Duel* (1892), *My Life* (1895), *The Lady with the Dog* (1898) and *Betrothed* (1903).

Chelsea. From the C. factory come the earliest dated specimens of English porcelain manufacture; some 'goat and bee' jugs carry the date 1745. The manufacture was a soft-paste *porcelain of French type, and this earliest period (1745–9) is known as 'triangle-marked'; its products are perhaps the most beautiful, being glassy and translucent. About 1750 the mark changed to a relief or raised anchor; the ware became richer and smoother. From 1753 the mark was a red anchor, from 1758 a gold anchor. From 1770 the factory (having passed under the control of the owners of the Derby factory) produced in *Derby rather than C. styles, and its products are called 'C.-Derby'.

Chênedollé Charles-Julien de (1769–1833). French poet, author of didactic poems in the 18th-c. manner, e.g. *Le Génie de l'Homme* (1807), but also of poetry celebrating nature which anticipates romanticism in France.

Chénier André-Marie de (1762–94). French poet, an active Revolutionary whose opposition to the Jacobins led to arrest and execution. His poetry was classical in subject and inspiration, but anticipated the romantics in its unusual technical freedom. Only 2 poems were publ. in his lifetime, but the 1st ed. of his collected works, publ. in 1819, made a great impression on the young romantics.

Cherbuliez Victor (1829–99). French novelist who wrote polished, rather improbable stories, often with a historical setting. His work was influenced by George Sand and includes *Le Comte Kostia* (1863), *Un Cheval de Phidias* (1864; *A Phidian Horse*, 1893) and *Le Roman d'une honnête femme* (1866).

Chéri (1920) and **The Last of Chéri** (1926). Novels by *Colette.

Cherkasov Nikolai (1903–). Russian actor and a member of the Communist party of the U.S.S.R. He is principally known outside Russia for his performances in the films of Eisenstein, notably in *Ivan the Terrible*.

Cherry Orchard, The (1904). Play by *Chekhov.

Cherubini Maria Luigi (1760–1842). Italian composer. In 1784 he went to London and in 1788 settled in Paris, becoming one of the inspectors of the new Conservatoire (1795), director of the Chapel Royal (1816) and of the Conservatoire (1822–41). C.'s music, highly regarded by Beethoven, reveals him as one of the great masters of counterpoint, is harmonically rich and has striking modulations. His mature opera style begins with *Lodiska* (1791), influential for its expressive orchestration, and reaches a climax with *Medée* (1797), with its restrained passion, dry melody and severe style, and *Les Deux Journées* (1801), less severe in mood and influential on Beethoven's *Fidelio*. C.'s mature church music includes the requiem in C min. and the mass in C maj.

Chesterfield Philip Dormer Stanhope, Lord (1694–1773). English statesman, diplomatist and writer chiefly remembered for the lucid and elegant letters (publ. posth. 1774) he wrote to his illegitimate son. They are full of a worldly good advice on matters of diction, deportment and conversation. C. was the recipient of a famous rebuke from Dr Johnson, who rejected the patronage C. offered only after Johnson was successful.

Chester Plays, The. Cycle of 14th-c. English *miracle plays.

Chesterton Gilbert Keith (1874–1936). English novelist, essayist, critic and poet. His novels were fantasies expressing a hatred of pretension and a support of orthodoxy; they include *The Napoleon of Notting Hill* (1904) and *The Innocence of Father Brown* (1911), the first in a series featuring a detective priest. His best verse is humorous–e.g. *Wine, Water and Song* (1915)–or satirical; he also wrote criticism. C. became a Catholic in 1922, and he and his great friend Belloc engaged in many disputes with the socialist writers G. B. Shaw and H. G. Wells.

Chestnutt Charles Waddell (1858–1932). U.S. Negro author, teacher, journalist and lawyer, whose works deal with racial prejudice. Works include his best-known book, *The Conjure Woman* (1899), containing stories of slave life, *The Wife of His Youth . . .* (1899), *The House behind the Cedars* (1900), and *The Colonel's Dream* (1905).

chest voice. Musical term for the lower register of any singer's range as contrasted with upper register called the head voice; often to the listener the c. seems to have a fuller more vibrant quality.

Chettle Henry (*c.* 1560–1607). English playwright; author of the *revenge tragedy *Hoffman* (*c.* 1602).

Chevalier Albert (1862–1923). English music-hall singer famous for such songs as 'My Old Dutch'.

Chevalier Maurice (1888–). French singer and actor who starred at the Eden Music Hall in Paris in 1904 and has ever since been a world star famous for his boater, twinkling eyes and the song 'Louise'. C. appeared with *Mistinguett in 1909 and played his 1st London season in 1918. He made an international reputation as a film star in such Lubitsch comedies as *The Love Parade* (1929). Other films are Wilder's *Love in the Afternoon* (1957) and *Gigi* (1958).

Chevallier Gabriel (1895–). French novelist, best known for his comic novel, *Clochemerle*

Cherubini

Lord Chesterfield: painting by Benjamin Wilson

Maurice Chevalier in *Gigi*

G. K. Chesterton: cartoon by James Pryde

(1934; *Clochemerle*, 1936), to which *Clochemerle-Babylone* (1954; *Clochemerle-Babylon*, 1955) and *Clochemerle-les-bains* (1963) are sequels.

Chevreul (Michel-) Eugène (1786–1889). French chemist whose writings on optics and the composition of light influenced Seurat (*divisionism) and later R. Delaunay.

Chevy Chase, The Ballad of (15th c.). One of the oldest surviving English *ballads. Deals with the rivalry between the two border families, Percy and Douglas, and the larger quarrel between England and Scotland. It is included in T. *Percy's *Reliques*, and was one of the ballads most valued by the 18th-c. pre-romantics. *Addison wrote 2 essays on it.

chiaroscuro (Italian, 'light-dark'). In painting this refers to the use of strong contrasts of light and shade for dramatic impact, as in the paintings of Caravaggio and Rembrandt.

Chicago school. In the 1880s and early 1890s the Chicago Loop was the scene of much building activity in the form of framed buildings. William Le Baron Jenney built the Home Insurance Building (1885), the 1st major steel-framed urban building, and this was followed by a series of steel-framed buildings by Adler and Sullivan, Burnham and Root, Holabird and Roche and others. After the Chicago Columbian Exhibition of 1893, the revivalist architecture of *McKim, Mead and White gained the ascendancy. The work of Mies van der Rohe is often called the 2nd Chicago school.

Chichester Festival Theatre. Sussex theatre (the idea of L. E. Martin, Mayor of Chichester, inspired by the theatre at Stratford, Ontario) built in the arena style and designed by Sean Kenny. It opened in 1962 under the direction of Sir Laurence Olivier. It is now used as a summer theatre by the National Theatre Co.

Chien Andalou, Un (1929). Short film directed by L. *Buñuel.

Chienne, La (1931). Film directed by J. *Renoir.

Chiesa Francesco (1871–). Italian-Swiss poet and novelist. His most representative and best work is the novel *Tempo di Marzo* (1925), nostalgically evoking his childhood and adolescence. Other works include the vols of verse, *Preludio* (1897) and *La stellata* (1933).

Chikamatsu Monogatari (1954). Film directed by K. *Mizoguchi.

Chikamatsu Monzaemon. Pseud. of Sugimori Nobumori (1653–1725), Japan's most famous dramatist. C. wrote *kabuki* plays, but his best work was in his *jōruri* plays (for puppets), which fell largely into 2 groups: historical, fantastic dramas, e.g. the heroic *Kokusenya kassen* (1715; *The Battles of Coxinga*, 1951), and contemporary domestic tragedies.

Child Francis James (1825–96). U.S. philologist and folk-lorist. He was professor of English Literature at Harvard Univ. (1876–96) and built there the most important folk-lore coll. in the U.S. His *English and Scottish Popular Ballads* (1882–98) contains 305 ballads.

Child William (1606?–97). English composer and organist to both Charles I and Charles II. His large output of church music included 25 services; he also wrote instrumental music, catches and ayres.

Childe Harold's Pilgrimage (1812–18). Poem by *Byron.

Childe Roland. A Scottish ballad in which the sister of C. R., son of King Arthur, is carried away by the fairies to the castle of the king of Elfland. Helped by Merlin, the wizard, C. R. finds the castle and rescues his sister. *Childe Roland to the Dark Tower Came* (1855), a dramatic poem by Browning, is based on the original ballad; the title comes from a speech by the 'mad' Edgar in Shakespeare's *King Lear*.

Childhood (1852). Novel by Tolstoy.

Childhood of Christ, The (1854). English title of *L'Enfance du Christ*, an oratorio by Berlioz, who also wrote the text.

China. The revelation of Chinese civilization to the West has been slow and vitiated by misunderstanding. The reasons for this lie in the unique nature of Chinese civilization and the physical remoteness of C. itself. It was not until the Mongol, Jenghiz Khan, conquered North C. in 1215 that the 1st real period of Sino-European contact began. Administrative stability stretched across the whole Eurasian heart-land, supplying physical security for travellers from Europe to C. Merchants saw the possibilities of lucrative trade. Christians, enflamed by the fable of Prester John, the Christian monarch of a kingdom somewhere west of C., sent ecclesiastics along the trade routes, firstly to find him and then–when they did not–to convert the Great Khan. These men approached C. in fear and wonder, and imagination embroidered their accounts of what they saw. Their narratives were plundered by Sir John *Mandeville, that prince of literary impostors, for his *Travels* which, with the *Description of the World* of Marco *Polo, who visited China in the middle of the 13th c., stimulated the 1st real European interest in C. Both works appealed primarily to the imagination, conjuring up a fantasy world of riches, luxury and wisdom.
The fall of the Mongol dynasty in 1368 again severed C. from the West. The Portuguese explorers of the 16th c. were followed by the Jesuits, seeking to convert the Chinese emperors to Christianity. Their publs were to stimulate theologians and philosophers, and to create in Europe a literature of calculated adulation. The works of the Jesuits presented C. as a strong, self-sufficient state ruled by a benevolent despot with the assistance of a civil service of philosophers, according to a set of moral and political maxims laid down by *Confucius. At a time when Europe was sick of doctrinal disputes and religious wars, and her thinkers were on the lookout for more rational systems based upon 'natural religion', the thought of a nation ruled by philosophers had a strong appeal to European philosophers anxious to be rulers. A host of writers took up and publicized what they believed to be Chinese ideas and what they thought to be the Chinese way of life: unfortunately their ideas were based on faulty trs. Voltaire's *Essaie sur les Mœurs* and *Orphelin de la Chine*, and Oliver Goldsmith's *The Citizen of the World* are examples of this literary and philosophical chinoiserie. The French Revolution put an end to the idea of benevolent despotism and replaced it with that of democratic liberalism. From that time onwards, Chinese civilization was despised as morally corrupt and reactionary, and only in the present day has the West looked once again to C., this time drawing upon the quietist philosophy of the *Tao te ching* (ascribed to Lao Tze) and Ch'an (Zen) Buddhism (*Japan).

Chichester Festival Theatre

Chicago school. Jenney's Home Insurance Building

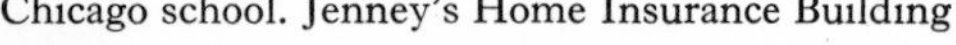

Chicago school. Burnham and Root's Reliance Building (1890–4)

The great writers and thinkers who in the 19th and 20th cs have drawn upon Chinese ideas are few in number. Tolstoy wrote on Chinese philosophy; Carl Jung upon *The Secret of the Golden Flower*; the playwright Bertolt Brecht admired the 'alienation-effects' in the Chinese theatre and used a Chinese source for *The Good Woman of Setzuan*, as did Ezra Pound in his *Cantos*. But it is perhaps to Arthur Waley that most people owe their acquaintance with Chinese philosophy and literature, through his incomparable trs.

The real influence of C. upon European fine art has been minor. In the 18th c. the vogue for *chinoiserie was all-pervading. Porcelain, furniture, wallpaper and 'Chinese' gardens fascinated European taste. Some art critics have seen a close resemblance to Chinese forms in the clouds painted by Watteau in such works as *The Embarkation for Cythera* as well as in the work of the English painter John Cozens. But the cult of chinoiserie in art survived no longer than the cult of chinoiserie in literature and philosophy. Chinese elements were, however, fundamental to the emergence of the *rococo style.

China-clay: *kaolin

Chinese Lowestoft. Name previously given in error to Chinese export porcelain which resembled some Lowestoft wares.

Chinese wood block (also called 'Chinese or Korean temple block'). A percussion instrument, used in the dance band and sometimes in the orchestra, consisting of a hollow wood block struck by a stick. Different sizes are used giving different pitches but not true notes.

Ch'ing. The name for the Manchu dynasty of rulers of China (1644–1912). The reigns of the emperors K'ang Hsi (1662–1722) and Ch'ien Lung (1736–95) were remarkable for the high technical achievement and the last decadent flourish of traditional Chinese porcelain, lacquer furniture and the minor arts, including a revived use of jade for highly ornamented and intricately carved cups, brush-pots, snuff-bottles and the like. This was the dynasty during which China exported pottery wares and furniture to flood the European markets and was therefore the most well known.

chinoiserie. European imitation of Chinese, or sometimes nondescript oriental forms and designs. It was popular throughout Europe from about 1670, but is associated especially with the rococo movement. The motifs were applied to architecture, room decoration, both pictorial and sculptural, porcelain (itself a direct imitation of the Chinese), silver and furniture.

Chippendale Thomas (1718–79). One of the most famous English cabinet makers. The son of a joiner, he was born in Otley, Yorkshire. By 1750 he had established himself in London; he became senior partner in the firm of Chippendale, Haig and Co. in 1771. Much of his fame rested upon the 1st comprehensive catalogue of furniture ever publ. – *The Gentleman and Cabinet-Maker's Director* (3 eds, 1754–62). Although issued by C., most of the designs in these catalogues were by other craftsmen at the factory. Much of his finest work was in the neo-classical style and consisted of marquetry and inlaid pieces, possibly after designs by Robert Adam.

Chirico Giorgio de (1888–). Italian painter associated with the school of Paris. Böcklin and Klinger influenced him during studies in Munich, and 15th-c. painting during a stay in Italy. C. worked in Paris (1911–15) and came into close contact with the *avant-garde* movement and the poet Apollinaire. He was then painting, in what he later called his 'metaphysical' style, pictures of strange pseudo-classical buildings, shown in exaggerated perspective framing empty squares and dreamy sculpture. This dream-like quality was increased by the juxtaposition of unexpected objects in an incongruous setting painted with calm objectivity. His 2nd 'surrealist' phase was characterized by mannequins, mechanical drawing instruments and strange haunted interiors. From 1929 his work degenerated into a mannered naturalism, and after 1933 he openly repudiated the modern movement.

Chisholm Erik (1904–). Scottish composer, pianist and conductor and professor at Cape Town Univ. from 1946. He has written operas, symphonies, piano concertos and chamber music, and some works show the influence of his travels in the Far East.

chittarone. A musical instrument developed from the *lute.

Chinoiserie interior by Chippendale

Chippendale: typical chair style

Ch'ing armorial ware for export. Also *blanc-de-chine

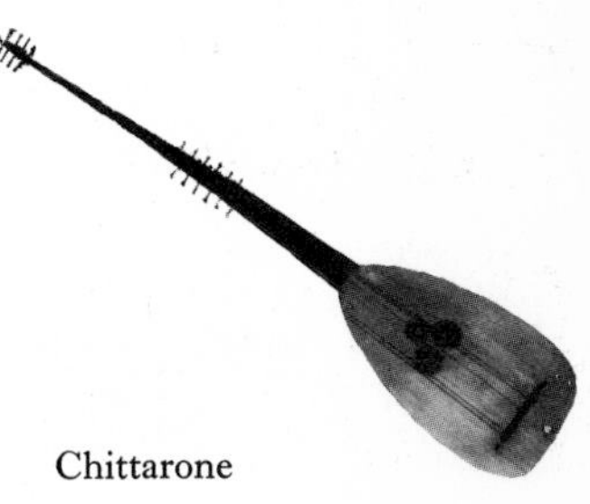

Chittarone

De Chirico. *Soothsayer's Recompense* (1913)

Chopin: painting by Delacroix

Chodowiecki. *The Emotional Responses of the Four Temperaments*

Chocano José Santos (1875–1934). Peruvian poet and revolutionary who, exiled from Peru for murder, was finally assassinated in Chile. C.'s poetry brought a nationalist spirit to *modernismo* poetry, voicing his dislike of the U.S. and his admiration for Indian and Spanish traditions. He was much influenced by R. Darío. Works include *Alma America* (1906), *Iras Santas* (1895) and *Fiat Lux!* (1908).

Chodowiecki Daniel Nicolas (1726–1801). Polish painter, engraver, illustrator and miniaturist who worked in Germany from 1743. For his valuable pictures of German middle-class life and manners he was known as the 'German Hogarth' but disclaimed the title.

Choephori, The. 2nd part of Aeschylus' dramatic trilogy the **Oresteia.*

choir. (1) In music: (*a*) the group of singers in a church which sings alone, or leads the singing; also sometimes used of the chorus in a large sacred work; (*b*) an abbreviation of CHOIR ORGAN, one of the 3 main sections of an organ, usually having soft stops suitable for accompaniment. This is sometimes called 'chair organ' since its pipes were sometimes encased behind the organist's chair or stool. (2) In architecture that part of a church where the choir sits, often loosely used of the *chancel. In medieval churches the c. was usually in the E. part of the chancel but sometimes under the crossing or farther W. Diagram *basilica.

choir tone. A musical term; the literal, and incorrect, English for the German *Chorton*, 'CHOIR *PITCH'. It is about a semitone above modern concert pitch and survives on the famous *Schnitger organ at Cappel, Germany.

Chopin Frédéric (1810–49). Polish composer and virtuoso pianist, born at Zelazowa Wola of a French father and Polish mother. He gave his 1st concert when aged 8, and received private lessons at the Warsaw Conservatoire from J. Elsner before entering the Conservatoire. In 1830 he left Poland, going to Vienna and then Paris, where he began his career as a fashionable teacher, and gave concerts with Liszt and Berlioz. In 1838 the novelist George *Sand became his mistress, and they lived together in Majorca for a year. The famous romance finally broke up after the publ. of Sand's novel *Lucrezia Floriani* (1846), in which C. was unfairly misrepresented as a weak romantic. In 1848 C. visited England giving concerts in aid of Polish refugees; he died of consumption in London. C.'s reputation as a pianist became legendary. He exploited improvements in piano manufacture and from an astounding, apparently effortless technique facilitated by unconventional finger work, he developed a cantabile style, continued by Liszt, combining with it unique range of touch, tone and dynamics and a characteristic, finely controlled rubato. His compositions are marked by elaborate ornamentation, cascading scales and arpeggios and cantabile writing. In essence this was an inspired extension of the work of J.-N. Hummel and J. Field, but C.'s great inventiveness and later harmonic audacities established the new style.
C.'s great corpus of piano music includes mazurkas and polonaises, overt evidence of his devotion to the Polish national idiom; studies, of which the 12 'Grand Studies' (1829–32) include the famous 'Revolutionary Study' and the 'Black Keys Study'; *24 Preludes* (1836–9) reflecting study of J. S. Bach's *Well Tempered Clavier*; waltzes; ballades; *nocturnes and impromptus, the *Fantasy* in F min. (1841) and the great *Barcarolle* in F♯ maj. (1846). His 2 piano concertos reveal C.'s weakness in the development of ideas on a large scale.

Chopsticks. Waltz tune played on the piano by 2 players (usually children) one providing a dominant tonic *vamp bass, the other 'chopping' out the tune with the side of the hands. In 1880 a set of 24 variations on it was publ. jointly by Borodin, Cui, Liadof, Rimsky-Korsakov and Liszt.

chorale. In music, the English term for those congregational hymns of the German Evangelical Church which were composed, or 'corrected' from the Catholic plainsong melodies, and set to German words by Luther and his contemporaries. These c.s were used in *passions and *cantatas, etc. and re-harmonized by subsequent composers, above all J. S. Bach, and were the basis for the *chorale prelude. In German the term *Choral* originally, and still strictly, refers to the plainsong.

chorale prelude. A musical form developed by the German organ school of the 17th and early 18th c., beginning with S. Scheidt (d. 1654) and culminating with Bach (d. 1750) and used by later composers such as Brahms. It is based on a *chorale melody used (1) as a *cantus firmus; (2) for a series of variations forming a programmatic commentary on the verses of the chorale (often called a chorale partita); (3) as a theme for elaboration – in this case the opening phrase only of the chorale is used.

Choral Symphony, The. Nickname of Beethoven's symphony no. 9 in D min. (1824) the last movement of which is a setting of Schiller's *Ode to Joy* employing chorus and 4 soloists. The term 'choral symphony' is also used of similar works by other composers, e.g. Mahler's symphony no. 8, and sometimes of symphonic works for unaccompanied voices.

chord. Musical term describing merely a group of notes simultaneously sounded; it has none of the harmonic connotations of *concord.

chording. Musical term used (1) of the intonation of chords by a group of performers; (2) of the spacing of the intervals of a chord (by the composer); (3) in the U.S. of the adding of chords, usually on a guitar, as an accompaniment to a melody.

choreography. The 18th-c. term for *dance notation, now used to mean the actual creation of a ballet, i.e. the choice and grouping of the various movements and steps.

Choromański Michał (1904–). Polish novelist and playwright, author of *Zazdrość i medycyna* (1933; *Jealousy and Medicine*, 1946), a psychological novel making skilful use of a disrupted time sequence.

chorus. In the theatre, *Greek drama.

chorus in music. (1) Synonymous with *choir. (2) Equivalent to the refrain in a folk-song, etc., in which everyone joins in with a recurring passage. (3) In jazz, the solo or improvisation on the sequence used in the particular piece (e.g. 3 choruses means the soloist has run through the sequence 3 times). (4) A choral passage in an oratorio, opera, etc.

Chouans, Les (1829). Novel by Balzac.

Chrétien Henri: *Cinemascope

Chrétien de Troyes (d. 1195/8). French poet. All that survives of his earlier work is the poem *Philomena* (based on Ovid) but he is important as the author of some of the earliest Arthurian

Christine de Pisan. Title-page of *La Cité des Dames*

Boris Christoff as Boris Godunov

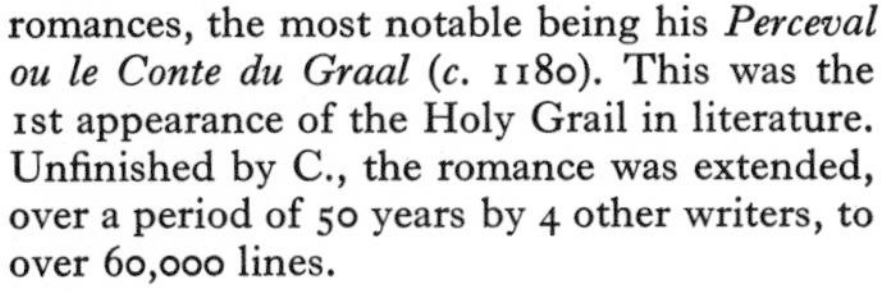

romances, the most notable being his *Perceval ou le Conte du Graal* (*c.* 1180). This was the 1st appearance of the Holy Grail in literature. Unfinished by C., the romance was extended, over a period of 50 years by 4 other writers, to over 60,000 lines.

Christabel (1816). Poem by *Coleridge.

Christie Agatha (Mary Clarissa) (1891–). English writer of detective fiction, creator of the detective Hercule Poirot. Many of her novels have been dramatized.

Christine de Pisan (*c.* 1364–*c.* 1430). French writer born in Venice and brought up in Paris. She was widowed at 25 and ended her life in a convent. In 1400 she wrote *Dit de la Rose*, ardently defending women against Jean de Meung's criticisms in *Le Roman de la Rose*. Her other prose works include *La Cité des Dames* (trs. 1521), largely a trs. of the *De claris mulieribus* of Boccaccio, and *Le Livre des Trois Vertus*, a treatise on women's education. She composed several ballades and long love-poems, and a eulogy of Joan of Arc.

Christ in the House of His Parents (1850). Painting by *Millais.

Christmas Carol, A (1843). Book by *Dickens.

Christoff Boris (1918–). Bulgarian bass, now living in Italy. He is known for the dramatic power of his performances, especially as Boris Godunov and as King Philip in Verdi's *Don Carlos*.

Petrus Christus. *St Eligius and the Lovers*

Christus Petrus (*c.* 1400–72?). Early Netherlands painter. He was made a master at Bruges in 1444. He may have been a pupil or assistant of Jan van Eyck, and all his pictures have been confused with the greater master's at some time. It is still not clear whether C. visited Italy and was thus responsible for transmitting the style and technical achievements of the best northern painting to Antonello da Messina and other Italian painters. The delightful *Portrait of a Lady* (W. Berlin) by C. is a major work of the Netherlands school.

chromatic. In music this term is used of notes not belonging to the key in which the piece is written; thus in the key of C maj. C♯ is a c. note. A c. scale is one in which all the semitones appear consecutively. A piece of music

Petrus Christus. *Portrait of a Lady*

Sir Winston Churchill

Caius Gabriel Cibber. *Raving Madness*

Colley Cibber: coloured plaster bust by Roubiliac

Alberto Churriguera. S. Sebastian

José Benito Churriguera. Altarpiece of S. Sebastian, Salamanca

is characterized as c. when it makes use of c. notes and usually, of portions of the c. scale (e.g. *Chromatic fantasia and fugue* by J. S. Bach).

Chronicles. (3rd c. B.C.). One of the books of the *Bible (Old Testament), in Christian eds divided into 2 books; a history of the Israelites from Adam to the end of their Babylonian captivity, using much of the materials in *Samuel and *Kings.

Chrysander Friedrich (1826–1901). German music scholar, biographer of Handel and ed. of his works (not complete). He thought all post-Handelian music modern and offensive.

Chukrai Grigory (1922–). Soviet film director. C.'s 1st film, *The Forty-First* (1956) was hailed as a liberalization in the Soviet cinema–the heroine falls in love with a White Russian. The chief qualities of *Ballad of a Soldier* (1959) and *Clear Sky* (1961) are a direct emotional appeal and a strong, if sometimes naïve story line.

Church Frederick Edwin (1826–1900). U.S. landscape painter in the romantic tradition of the Hudson River school; a pupil of T. Cole.

Churchill Winston (1871–1947). U.S. writer of historical novels, e.g. *Richard Carvell* (1899) about the U.S. Revolution, and *The Crisis* (1901) about the Civil War, and sociological novels, e.g. *The Inside of the Cup* (1913).

Churchill Rt Hon. Sir Winston (Leonard Spencer) (1874–1965). English statesman, orator, historian and amateur painter. In 1953 he received the Nobel prize for literature. Works include *The World Crisis* (1923–9), an account of World War I; the *Life of Marlborough* (1933–8) and *A History of the English-speaking Peoples* (1956–8).

Churchyard Thomas (1520?–1604). English poet and writer of pamphlets and broadsides; he wrote the poem *Shore's Wife* (in 1563 ed. of *Mirror for Magistrates*) and *The Worthiness of Wales* (1587), an antiquarian survey.

Churriguera. Family of Spanish architects and sculptors, originally from Catalonia but settling in Madrid *c.* 1670. Its earliest members were stucco artists and makers of altarpieces. José Benito (1665–1725) was the first to turn to architecture. He built the town, palace and church of Nuevo Baztán, and many altarpieces, one of them over 90 ft high. His brother Joaquín (1674–1724) did an extravagant design for the dome of Salamanca cathedral, with barley-sugar columns and shell-niches (it was dismantled in 1755). The 3rd, most talented, brother, Alberto (1676–1750), laid out the Plaza Mayor at Salamanca, designed S. Sebastian, Salamanca, and parts of other churches, including the cathedral. The family continued to be important in the next generation and gave its name–'Churrigueresque'–to the whole middle phase of Spanish baroque (*c.* 1700–60). This is characterized by the fantastically lavish use of relief ornament, stucco, gilding and sculpture. The style lasted longest, and was taken to its greatest extremes, in Spanish Mexico.

Chute, La (1956). Novel by *Camus.

CIAM, i.e. '*Congrès Internationaux d'Architecture Moderne*' (1928–59). The leading organization of modern architecture during its heroic phase. It instituted organizations committed to modern architecture in many countries (as the MARS group in England), and most important of all, acted as a meeting-place for architects and students from many countries to meet and discuss their activities.

CIAM held 10 major meetings, the most important was CIAM IV which produced the 'Athens Charter', a document which laid down, possibly too rigidly, the fundamentals of future cities.

Cibber Caius Gabriel (1630–1700). Danish sculptor who settled in England; father of Colley C. He worked in a smoothly modelled, tentatively baroque style, e.g. his relief for The Monument, London (1674) and the Sackville tomb, Withyham church, Sussex (1677). His most famous and vigorous sculptures were the figures *Melancholy* and *Raving Madness* (*c.* 1680) for the Bethlehem Hospital (now in Guildhall Mus.).

Cibber Colley (1671–1757). English comic actor and playwright, son of Caius C. In 1730 he became poet laureate, probably for his Whig loyalties. This aroused repeated attacks from Dr Johnson, Fielding and Pope. His works include *The Careless Husband* (1705) and *The Non-Juror* (1717), an adaptation of Molière's *Tartuffe*. His *Apology for the Life of*

Cicéri. Décor for Meyerbeer's *Robert le Diable*

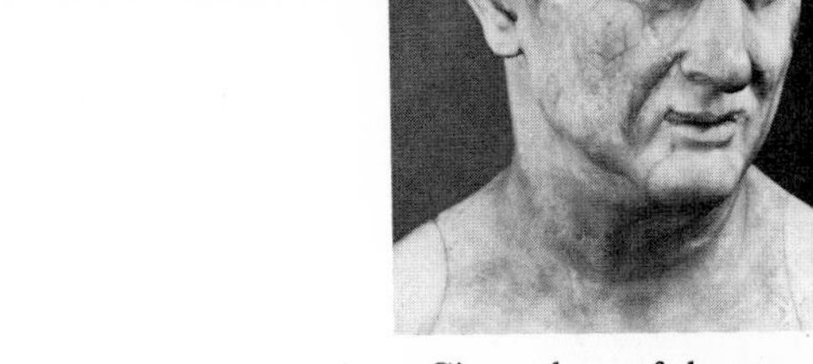

Cicero: bust of the 1st c. A.D.

Mr Colley Cibber Comedian . . . (1740), satirized by Fielding in *Tom Thumb the Great*, contains interesting accounts of contemporary actors. C.'s version of Shakespeare's *Richard III* was preferred to the original on the stage until well into the 19th c.

Cicéri Pierre-Luc-Charles (1782–1868). French decorative painter and chief designer of sets and costumes at the Paris Opéra. His extravagant romanticism set an example which influenced theatrical design in France until the end of the Second Empire. He introduced gas lighting to the Opéra in 1822. His son EUGÈNE (1813–90) was a romantic landscape painter and lithographer.

Cicero Marcus Tullius (106–43 B.C.). Roman orator, philosopher and statesman. Born at Arpinum and educated at Rome, he became consul in 63 and successfully suppressed Catiline's revolutionary conspiracy. In the civil war between Caesar and Pompey he joined Pompey but subsequently submitted to Caesar. He discreetly applauded Caesar's assassination, however (March 44), and in September vituperatively attacked Mark Antony, Caesar's would-be successor and was therefore proscribed at Antony's instance and assassinated (December 43). Apart from more than 100 forensic and political orations (58 survive), C. wrote innumerable letters (931 extant), 2 rather bad poems and many good verse trs from the Greek, critical works on rhetoric–*de Oratore* (55), *Brutus* and *Orator* (46)–and in the last 2 years of his life a series of works which provided Latin and the Romance languages with a vocabulary and medium of philosophic thought: the *Academica* deal with epistemology, *de Finibus* ('on ends') and the *de Officiis* ('on duties') with ethics, *de Natura Deorum* ('on the nature of the Gods') with religion, and the *Tusculan Disputations* with pleasure and pain. C.'s rhetorical style is full and rich, musical and meticulous, and very versatile. It is, uniquely perhaps in any language, a norm to which all other Latin prose may be referred.

Cicognani Bruno (1879–). Italian writer whose 1st success was his novel *La Velia* (1923), a story of decadence of a bourgeois family. His other novels include *Villa Beatrice* (1931), but his best writing is autobiographical, as in *L'età favolosa* (1941) and *Viaggio nella vita* (1952).

Cid, El i.e. Rodrigo Díaz de Vivar (1040?–99). Spanish soldier of fortune and hero of the first and best of the Spanish *chansons de geste*, the *Poema de Mío Cid* (*c.* 1140) of which the early parts follow his history though the later are legendary. The language of this anonymous epic is terse and bare of adjectives; it derives from the French epic. Its incidents are treated afresh in many romances which have the same terseness. The C. remained a popular hero and was the subject of plays by Guillén de *Castro and *Corneille.

Cignani Carlo (1628–1719). Late baroque painter of the Bolognese school; pupil of F. Albani. In his active atelier he upheld the academic traditions established by the Carracci Academy.

Cileà Francesco (1866–1950). Italian composer and teacher. As an opera composer he belongs to the group including Puccini, Mascagni and Leoncavallo, his best-known opera being *Adriana Lecouvreur* (1902).

Cimabue (*c.* 1240–1302?). Florentine painter. C.'s reputation as the 1st artist of the Italian Renaissance rests upon his mention by Dante in a famous passage, which, literally trs., states that 'C. believed he held the field in painting, but now the cry goes out for Giotto so that the fame of the former is obscured.' Tradition may be right in calling C. the teacher of Giotto. He was also believed by Vasari and others to be the painter of the *Rucellai Madonna* (Uffizi) now given by most authorities to Duccio. However, in spite of difficulties of attribution which may never be resolved, it seems certain that C., or another Tuscan artist, was responsible for the all-important break with the rigid conventions of painting in Byzantine art, giving greater scope to the natural, as opposed to the conventional and stylized form, and in choosing from a far wider range of subjects.

C. is known to have been in Rome in 1272 and is documented to have been working on the mosaic figure of St John in the apse of Pisa cathedral in 1302. No attributions except for the *St John* are certain, but C. was probably the painter of the very damaged frescoes in the choir of the upper church and of the *Madonna Enthroned with four angels and St Francis* in the lower church at Assisi. The superb *Crucifix* (S. Domenico, Arezzo), a second *Crucifix* (S. Croce, Florence), the large *Madonna and Child Enthroned* (Uffizi) and a few other works in

Cignani. *Apollo and Daphne*

Cimabue. *Madonna and Child Enthroned*

Cimarosa

Cinderella. Ashton and Helpmann as the Ugly Sisters in the 1948 production

Cire perdue. Head of an Akkadian king; 3rd c. B.C.

Cire perdue. Pierino da Vinci's *Samson and the Philistines*

Florence, Paris, Washington and elsewhere are given to C. on the grounds of style and the authority of tradition which dates back almost to his own lifetime.

Cima da Conegliano Giovanni Battista (1459/60–1517/18). Venetian painter strongly influenced by Giovanni Bellini. His many works include a *Virgin and Child* in the N.G., London.

Cimarosa Domenico (1749–1801). Italian opera composer. He was the son of poor parents but by the 1780s was the rival of *Paisiello; he held posts at the courts of St Petersburg and Vienna but in 1799 was imprisoned at Naples for his too enthusiastic reaction to the entry of the French Revolutionary army. C.'s orchestration sometimes shows an almost Mozartian delicacy but his real mastery is in the voice parts where his rich invention and wit have full play. C. excelled at *opera buffa* and his most famous was *Il matrimonio segreto* (1792; based on *The Clandestine Marriage* (1766) by G. Colman and D. Garrick), others including *Le astuzie femminili* (1794; revived by Diaghilev, 1920).

cimbal or **cimbalom.** The Hungarian *dulcimer, used by Kodály in his *Háry János* suite.

Cinderella. Ballet based on Perrault's fairytale. Its 1st production was in 1822; the 3-act version with choreography by Petipa, Ivanov and Cecchetti, produced in St Petersburg in 1893, established it as a favourite. Prokofiev composed music for the Bolshoi production of 1945, this music was again used in Ashton's presentation for Sadler's Wells (1948) and in Alfred Rodrigues's version for La Scala, Milan.

Cinemascope. Widescreen film process in which the image is 'squeezed' horizontally by an anamorphic lens to fit a standard 35 mm. film frame. A compensating lens on the projector expands the picture to its original width. Invented *c.* 1925 by French physicist Dr Henri Chrétien (1879–1956), it was first used commercially by 20th Century Fox in *The Robe* (1953).

cinéma-vérité: *film techniques

Cinerama. Ultra-widescreen film process. The image is registered by 3 lenses on 3 strips of film, projected side by side in exact alignment on a curving screen designed to correspond to the audience's circle of vision. Invented by Fred Waller (1886–1954) *c.* 1938; first used in *This is Cinerama* (1952). Kramer's *It's a Mad, Mad, Mad, Mad World* (1963) introduced a simplified single-film version of C.

Cino da Pistoia (*c.* 1270–*c.* 1336). Italian poet, highly praised by both Dante–who considered him the greatest love-poet of his time–and by Petrarch, who wrote a famous sonnet on learning of C.'s death.

Cinq auteurs, Les. 5 French playwrights who wrote under the direction of Richelieu. They included *Corneille and *Rotrou.

Cione Andrea di: Andrea *Orcagna

Cipriani Giovanni Battista (1727–85). Italian painter and draughtsman, the 1st exponent in England of an elegant, superficial neo-classicism. Meeting Sir W. Chambers and J. Wilton in Rome, he returned (1755) with them to England, settled there and became the leading history and decorative painter; as a decorator he was an early exponent of the Adam style (Robert *Adam).

Circus. Roman race-course where the chariot-races were held. The largest was the Circus Maximus in Rome, which held 255,000 spectators and had a circuit of about half a mile. Its early history is lost, but it was in use until the fall of Rome and even later.

cire perdu (French, 'lost wax'). A very ancient technique of casting in bronze. The sculptor first makes a plaster core, roughly the shape of the finished work and pierced with iron rods; on this he models, in wax, the details of the sculpture. Next the wax surface is coated with a liquid clay which is left to harden. There is now an outer mould (pierced with vents) and an inner core, held together by rods and 'sandwiching' the thin wax 'outline' of the projected work. The wax is melted and molten bronze poured in in its place. Mould and core are removed. The method was used in ancient Greece and Rome and revived in the Renaissance; it was also used by the *Benin sculptors.

Cities of the Plain (1921–2). Novel by *Proust.

Clair. *The Italian Straw Hat*

John Clare

Citizen Kane (1941). Film directed by O. *Welles.

Citizen of the World, The (coll. 1762). Book by *Goldsmith.

cittern. Fretted stringed musical instrument dating from the middle ages but enjoying its greatest popularity in the 16th and 17th cs. It is a treble plucked instrument with steel strings (2 to each note). The size varies greatly and the number of *courses also (from 4 to 12); bass (ARCHCITTERN) and descant instruments were built. Also *bandora.

City Lights (1931). Film directed by C. *Chaplin.

City of Dreadful Night, The (1874). Poem by James *Thomson.

Čiurlionis Mikalojus (1875–1911). Lithuanian composer and later painter of quasi-abstract works given musical titles, e.g. *Sonata of the Stars*. From 1906 until his death he worked in St Petersburg where he exhibited with the *World of Art group. The magazine *Apollon* No. 3 in 1914 was devoted to work of this artist who, in his interest in the analogies between music and painting, can be compared with Kandinsky.

cladding. In architecture, the use of surface material to decorate or protect the structure.

Claesz Pieter (1597/8–1661). Dutch still-life painter. From a few commonplace objects standing on part of a sideboard or table he created an uncommon, almost mystical harmony between each of these objects and a plain background. He used brownish tones occasionally enlivened by a brighter colour.

Clair René (1898–). French film director. After the semi-surrealist *Paris Qui Dort* (1923) and the *dada *Entr'acte* (1924) C.'s elegant, witty and precise style found full expression in *The Italian Straw Hat* (1927), from *Labiche, a masterpiece of silent comedy. C.'s visual inventiveness was matched, at the start of the talkies, by an equally free, often non-realistic use of sound and music, and with *Sous les Toits de Paris* (1930) and *Le Million* (1931) he became the most famous and successful French comedy director of the time. The alternation of controlled and charming sentiment (*14 Juillet*, 1933) or wry comedy (*À Nous la Liberté*, 1932) is characteristic of his work. Following the commercial disappointment of *Le Dernier Milliardaire* (1934), he worked in England (*The Ghost Goes West*, 1936) and America (most notably, *I Married a Witch*, 1942). Returning to France after the war, he made *Le Silence est d'Or* (1947) a nostalgic evocation of the silent film studios, with Maurice Chevalier, and a version of the Faust legend, *La Beauté du Diable* (1950). *Les Belles de Nuit* (1952), *Porte des Lilas* (1957) and *Tout l'Or du Monde* (1961) are in familiar, if slightly disenchanted vein, but *Les Grandes Manœuvres* (1955), a classical comedy of manners in a period setting, allies perfection of form with an unusual depth of feeling.

Clairon Claire (1723–1803). French actress who triumphed in her 1st performance at the Comédie-Française in Racine's *Phèdre* (1743). Later she acted privately in Voltaire's theatre and at the age of 50 wrote *Mémoires et Réflexions sur l'Art Dramatique* and lived on the proceeds until her death.

Clare John (1793–1864). English poet. He was born in the poverty of a Northamptonshire peasant's cottage, learnt to read and write in the village school and was much affected by an early reading of Thomson's *Seasons*. His *Poems Descriptive of Rural Life and Scenery* (1820) brought brief celebrity and he became a contributor to *The London Magazine*, with De Quincey, Lamb, Hazlitt and others. He suffered a 1st attack of madness in 1836; from 1841 to his death he was an inmate of the Northampton asylum. The many poems of his 1st phase C. found in the external nature he knew best. As his life grew blacker, his vision deepened, under the influence of the ideas of Coleridge and Wordsworth; and in the early years at Northampton he wrote his finest lyrics, in which he felt that he had passed beyond love of women and nature into a sun-illumined eternity of freedom. His later poems include *Love lives beyond the Tomb*, *It is the Evening Hour*, *I Am*, *A Vision*, and *First Love*; they are remarkable for their purity of English, their rhythms and tragic serenity, and set him high among English poets.

Clarendon Edward Hyde, Earl of (1609–74). English statesman, 1st minister of Charles II from 1660 to 1667, and author of *The History of the Rebellion . . .* (1702–4) on the Civil War,

Cittern

Claesz. *Still-life*

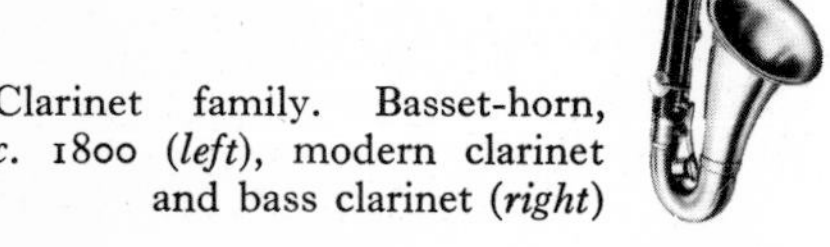

Clarinet family. Basset-horn, *c.* 1800 (*left*), modern clarinet and bass clarinet (*right*)

Classical ballet. *Hercule à Thèbes*, 1661

Classicism. *Adam interior showing the principles of c. as applied in the neo-classical period

Claude. *Classical Landscape*, another interpretation of the ideals of classicism (for Claude also *coulisse)

written in the grand style and notable for its character drawing. From profits on *The History* (presented to the Univ. by his heirs) the Clarendon printing-house was built for Oxford Univ. Press.

clarinet. Single-reed, woodwind musical instrument of cylindrical bore, developed in the late 17th c. The c. is a *transposing instrument and the most common of the family is the B♭ with a range from the D below middle C upwards for over three 8ves. Also common is the A c. a semitone lower than the B♭, and other members of the family include the BASS c., an 8ve below the standard B♭, the very rare DOUBLE BASS or PEDAL c. another 8ve lower, and the now rarely used BASSET-HORN, in effect a tenor c. The c. appeared in the orchestra from the mid 18th c. but Mozart first fully exploited its potentialities, both orchestral and solo.

clarino. Musical term, formerly used in Italian to mean trumpet, of the 17th and 18th cs for a high-lying and florid trumpet part. Such parts were extremely difficult and were played by specialists (usually on a natural trumpet in D) whose art is now lost. The so-called 'Bach' trumpets are hybrid instruments, invented since the 19th c., to assist modern players in c. parts.

Clarissa Harlowe (1747–8). Novel by Samuel *Richardson.

Clarke Jeremiah (*c.* 1670–1707). English composer, from 1704 joint organist of the Chapel Royal. He left church, stage and instrumental music, and also contributed to *A Collection of Ayres for Harpsichord* (1700) a piece *The Prince of Denmark's March*, identical to the tune commonly called *Purcell's Trumpet Voluntary*.

Clarke Marcus (1846–81). English-born writer, a school-friend of G. M. Hopkins. C. went to Australia at 16. Self-styled Bohemian, worked as journalist, publ. his best-known work *For the Term of His Natural Life* in 1874; this novel of the Australian convict era, of loneliness and brutality, becomes a tragedy despite tawdry literary conventions.

Clarke Shirley. U.S. film director. After being a dancer with Martha Graham and a choreographer she made a series of shorts from 1952, mainly on ballet. Her features made in New York are *The Connection* (1960) and *The Cool World* (1963). Stylistically very ambitious, neither of these films, dealing with beatnik life, has lived up to its pretensions.

classical ballet. A dance form with its roots in the royal courts of 16th-c. Italy and France and, later, Russia. Courtiers performed dances for amusement, and eventually ballet received the accolade with the foundation by Louis XIV of the National Academy of Music and Dance in 1661; in St Petersburg the Empress Anne founded the Imperial Academy in 1738. The classical style followed a set technique using 5 basic *positions, and only with the Diaghilev revolution of 1911 did this style give way to freer forms.

Classical Symphony. *Prokofiev's 1st symphony.

classicism. (1) Term describing the qualities of the art of classical antiquity (ancient Greece and Rome) and of works directly inspired by classical art (*Renaissance, neo-classicism), i.e. simplicity, elegance, restraint, harmonious form, and, in painting and sculpture, naturalistic depiction of the human figure at its most beautiful and powerful. (2) C. is also frequently used in a general sense, usually as the opposite of *romanticism. On this view, c. and romanticism are permanent and conflicting tendencies in the history of art. C. is held to be objective and social in content where romanticism is subjective; simple and lucid in treatment where romanticism is cloudy and turgid; and formally well proportioned where romanticism is formless. Further difficulties are sometimes caused by the application of these terms to only one element in a work–e.g. its form–or by such formulas as 'classical in form, romantic in spirit'.

Claude Lorraine originally named Claude Gelée (1600–82). French landscape painter and draughtsman. Little is known about his personal life. He went to Rome as a youth, and is thought to have earned his living as a pastry-cook before returning to Paris in 1625. He lived in Rome from 1627, devoted to his work and famous for his picturesque landscape compositions. To prevent forgeries he recorded his paintings in a portfolio of drawings the *Liber Veritatis* in the coll. of the duke of Devonshire since *c.* 1770, publ. in mezzotint in 1777. C. was a passionate observer of light and atmospheric changes, and he made numerous

Paul Claudel: photograph by Karsh

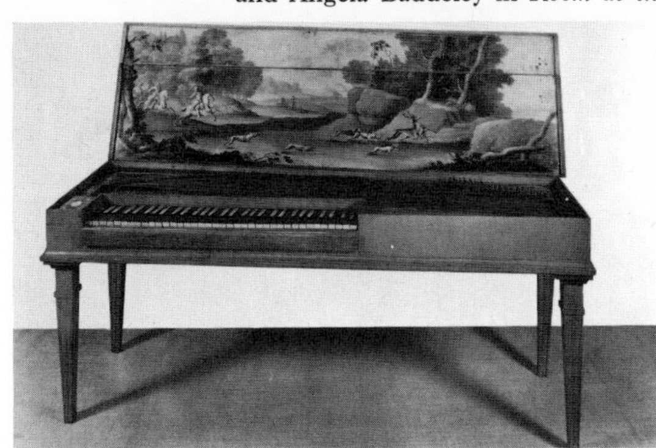

Clavichord; Brunswick, 1751

Clayton. Simone Signoret (foreground) and Angela Baddeley in *Room at the Top*

line and brush drawings of dawn and dusk, working out of doors. Many of these studies are now in the Print Room of the B.M., London. Compared with the landscapes of Nicolas Poussin, his contemporary, C.'s work is more sensual and atmospheric and his drawings retain the spontaneity of an impression. He painted many large compositions–Biblical, mythological, religious and pastoral subjects, views of Rome and sea views which have made him famous and influential. C. was a stimulus and inspiration to the great landscape painters of the 17th–19th c., Hubert Robert, Watteau, Wilson and Turner, who painted his *Dido Building Carthage* in emulation of C.

Claudel Paul (Louis-Charles-Marie) (1868–1955). French poet and dramatist and the foremost French Catholic writer of his day. He composed his works in the leisure hours of his long career as a diplomat, which took him all over the world. He invented his own form of free verse, at once Biblical and colloquial in flavour, which he used both in his poetic dramas, such as *L'Otage* (1911; *The Hostage*, 1917), *L'Annonce faite à Marie* (1912; *The Tidings Brought to Mary*, 1916) and *Le Soulier de Satin* (1930; *The Satin Slipper*, 1931), and in his celebratory poems, *Cinq Grandes Odes* (1910) and *Corona benignitatis Anni Dei* (1915). A robust, dogmatic Christian, he was fond of showing how human passions bend to the will of God. *Le Soulier de Satin*, a long, theatrical pageant set in the late 16th c. and representing the sacrifice of human love to the Divine purpose, is his most characteristic work.

Claudian (*c.* 400 A.D.). Latin poet, probably born at Alexandria. He became court poet (395–404) to the Western emperor Honorius and his regent Stilicho. His invectives and panegyrics illuminate the history of Honorius' reign. They are pagan in conception, but vigorous in execution and classical in form and diction, often echoing *golden age poets like Virgil.

Claudin: Claude or Claudin de *Sermisy

Claudius Matthias (1740–1815). German poet and writer, closely connected with the poets of the Göttingen circle. Under the pseud. 'Asmus' he ed. the review *Der Wandsbecker Bothe* (1771–5). His simple verse includes patriotic songs popular even today, e.g. *Rheinweinlied* and *Abendlied*.

Claussen Sophus Niels Christen (1865–1931). Danish poet. One of the symbolists who reacted against the rise of prose realism in Denmark and preached a worship of beauty. C. interprets all nature symbolically. His poetry is sensual, sophisticated and involved. Works include *Naturbørn* (1887), *Pilefløjter* (1899), *Heroica* (1925) and *Hvededynger* (1930).

clausula. In 13th-c. music, a short usually 2-part section, often an instrumental interlude, in the organum where the tenor moves at the same speed as the other part. Early motets were often merely a c. with words added to the top part.

clavecin. The French word for 'harpsichord'; a *claveciniste* meant a performer or composer for the harpsichord (especially applied to the late 17th–early 18th-c. schools of *clavecinistes*, e.g. Couperin).

clavicembalo: *cembalo

clavichord. Stringed keyboard instrument originating in the middle ages, falling out of general use in the late 18th c. and now revived. The key operates a metal 'tangent' which sets the string (damped by felt at one end) vibrating in its free length. As there is no escapement the tangent, until the key is released, remains on the string which vibrates between the *bridge and tangent. Thus one string can serve 2 tangents arranged to produce 2 notes (like a violinist's fingers on the string); a c. using this principle is FRETTED. Vibrato and also sustained notes are possible by movements of the tangent on the string. Although very quiet, the c. is capable of dynamic gradations.

Clavier (now Klavier). A German musical term, taken from the French *clavier*–'keyboard', originally applied to mean merely the keyboard, then as a generic term for stringed keyboard instruments (18th c.), finally (19th c.) to mean piano.

Clavierübung (German, 'Keyboard Exercise'). Comprehensive title given by Bach to 4 vols of works (1731, 35, 39, 42) for harpsichord and organ. It includes the *Italian concerto* and the Goldberg variations.

Clayden Pauline (1922–). British dancer who joined the then Sadler's Wells Ballet in 1942 and danced many different roles, the most memorable of which were Ophelia in Helpmann's *Hamlet* and the Suicide in his *Miracle in the Gorbals*. She retired in 1956.

Clayhanger (1910). Novel by Arnold *Bennett.

Clayton Jack (1921–). British film director. His 1st feature was *Room at the Top* (1958), from the novel by John *Braine. Its working-class hero, social preoccupations and northern setting introduced a new trend into British cinema. *The Innocents* (1961), from Henry *James's *The Turn of the Screw*, and Penelope Mortimer's *The Pumpkin Eater* (1964), although very different in subject-matter, are equally careful, stylish and literary.

Clea (1960). Novel by Lawrence *Durrell.

clef. In musical notation, a sign which fixes the pitch of one note (and thus all the others); the c.s are stylizations of decorative versions of the letters 'G', 'F' and 'C'. The G or TREBLE c. fixes the 2nd line up on the staff as the G above middle C; the F or BASS c. or the 2nd line down as the F below middle C; the movable C c. fixes middle C: thus the ALTO c. or and the TENOR c. on the 2nd line down.

Cleland John (1709?–89). English miscellaneous writer, author of *The Memoirs of a Woman of Pleasure* (*c.* 1750) an erotic novel describing the career of the prostitute Fanny Hill which was (and remains) notorious: the Privy Council gave C. a pension on the understanding that he would write no more books of the sort; works include *The Memoirs of a Coxcomb* (1751).

Clemens Samuel Langhorne: Mark *Twain

Clemens non Papa. Nickname, of obscure origin, for Jacques Clement or Jacob Clements (*c.* 1510–*c.* 58), Flemish composer and one of the leading successors of Josquin des Prés. His simple style is marked by its wealth of fine melodies but sometimes spoiled by excessive imitation. He wrote 15 masses, 230 motets, and psalms in Flemish on popular melodies.

Clement. Maria Schell in *Gervaise*

Clodion. *Satyr crowning a Bacchante*

Cliché verre. Corot's *Horseman in a Wood*

Cloisonné. Ostrogothic brooch showing metal dividers but robbed of its precious stones

Cloisonné. Chinese Ming censer

Clement René (1913–). French film director. C. made a short (with *Tati) and documentaries before making his 1st feature, *La Bataille du rail* (1946), about the collective resistance efforts of French railway workers, and collaborating with *Cocteau on *La Belle et la Bête* (1946). The powerful *Les Jeux Interdits* (1952), showing the effect of war on 2 children, made C.'s reputation, and was followed by a comedy, *The Knave of Hearts* or *Monsieur Ripois* (1954), on a Frenchman in London. *Gervaise* (1956) was a painstaking adaptation from Zola. The commercially unsuccessful *The Sea Wall* (1958) from M. *Duras, and *Plein Soleil* (1960), a characterless mystery film, did little to advance his reputation.

Clementi Muzio (1752–1832). Italian virtuoso pianist, composer, teacher and music publ. In 1766 he was brought to England; from 1773 he was in London where his success was immediate and overwhelming. In 1781, at Vienna, he engaged in a piano-playing competition with Mozart; from 1782 he made extensive European tours but lived mainly in England. C. was a major figure in the shaping of piano technique; his pupils included J. B. Cramer and J. Field, and his compositions the vastly influential 100 studies *Gradus ad Parnassum* (1817), and excellent piano sonatas; these, with Mozart's, completed the formulation of the sonata form and were highly admired by Beethoven.

Clemo Jack (1916–). English poet. *Map of Clay* (1961), his coll. poems, displays the dramatic quality of his poetry and its spiritual searchings. He has also written a novel, *Wilding Graft* and 2 parts of his autobiography, *Confession of a Rebel* and *The Invading Gospel.*

Clérambault Louis-Nicolas (1676–1749). French composer and organist. Appointed by Louis XIV as director of music in the household of Mme de Maintenon; he also held several organist posts. His music, refined and formally faultless, includes masterly secular cantatas, motets and many keyboard compositions.

clerestory. Architectural term for the storey of a medieval church above the arcade and triforium, i.e. the window-range (hence 'clear storey') rising above the roofs of the aisles and lighting the nave of the church. *Basilica.

Clerihew: Edmund Clerihew *Bentley

Cleve Joos van: *Joos van Cleve

cliché verre. Type of print invented by Corot, combining photographic and graphic techniques. A design was scratched on a sheet of glass which had been covered with black paint or albumen and made opaque through exposure to the sun; this was then used as a negative and printed on sensitized paper. The technique was also used by Delacroix, Daubigny, Rosseau and Millet.

Clift Montgomery (1920–). U.S. method actor often described as Hollywood's most sensitive actor; he often portrays characters groping in insecurity. He has starred in *Red River* (1947), *From Here To Eternity* (1953), Dmytryk's *The Young Lions* (1957), and Huston's *The Misfits* (1961).

Cline Eddie (1892–). U.S. film director. C. started work in films for M. *Sennett. He was the favourite director of W. C. *Fields, for whom he directed, among others, *Million Dollar Legs* (1932), *The Bank Dick* (1940) and *Never Give a Sucker an Even Break* (1941).

Clochemerle (1934). Comic novel by Gabriel *Chevallier.

Clodion Claude Michel called (1738–1814). French sculptor, in Rome (1762–71). He produced many statuettes of pastoral figures but his sensual manner fell out of favour in the period following the Revolution; he then turned to monumental sculpture.

cloisonné enamel. The melting of coloured glass fragments into cells made by thin metal wire attached to the metal form of plates, boxes, bowls, mirrors, amulets, sword-guards, etc., the wires making either the outlines of coloured forms or linear designs in themselves. The technique of enamelling in cells, to begin with a substitute for precious stones and metal inlays, was first developed in Mycenaean Greece; but the 1st full flowering of cloisonné proper was Byzantine in the 10th and 11th c. Byzantine and Islamic pieces appeared in China under the Mongol empire and the technique was then learned and flourished in the Ming and Ch'ing dynasties. It was also taken up in Japan, where the finest examples

Clouzot. Yves Montand (top) in *The Wages of Fear*

are of the 18th and 19th c. An off-shoot of the technique in China was in ceramics, where the design is made of clay threads separating different coloured enamel glazes.

cloisonnism (derived from *cloisonné*). Technique used by the French symbolist painters, notably Gauguin. It is characterized by flat colour areas and heavy outlines. Émile Bernard claimed to have been its originator, though this was denied by Gauguin.

cloister. A covered walk or arcade, usually surrounding a square court, a feature of monasteries and colleges.

Cloister and the Hearth, The (1861). Novel by Charles *Reade.

close. In music an alternative term for *cadence, a full c. being a perfect cadence, a half c. an imperfect cadence.

closet drama. Term for plays written to be read rather than acted. The tragedies of *Seneca were probably intended to be read aloud and works such as Byron's *Manfred* and Shelley's *Prometheus Unbound* are clear examples of c. d.

Clouard Henri (1885–). French writer and critic, best known for his *Histoire de la littérature française du symbolisme à nos jours* (1947–9), an analytical study of the literary scene in France from 1885 to 1940.

Cloud of Unknowing, The. 14th-c. English mystical treatise.

Clouds, The (423 B.C.). Comedy by *Aristophanes.

Clouet François (*c.* 1510–72). French court portrait painter, miniaturist and draughtsman, son of Jean C. His work, e.g. portrait of the apothecary Pierre Quthe (1562; Louvre), shows Florentine influence. His drawings were more meticulous and his paintings more brilliant and more elaborate than his father's and he acquired a great contemporary reputation.

Clouet Jean (*c.* 1485–1540/1). Flemish portrait painter, miniaturist and draughtsman; father of François C. He worked at the court of Francis I of France. His paintings show earlier Flemish influence but his drawings in black or red chalk have the solid modelling of form typical of the Italian Renaissance.

Clough Arthur Hugh (1819–61). English poet, the subject of M. *Arnold's *Thyrsis.* Most of C.'s verse, free from the worst faults of Victorian poetic diction, reflects his spiritual conflicts. His poems include his famous piece of irony *The Latest Decalogue* and 'Say not the struggle nought availeth'.

Clouzot Henri-Georges (1907–). French film director. After *Le Corbeau* (1943), an unsympathetic account of hysteria induced in a provincial French town by poison-pen letters, C. was accused of Collaboration and banned from working. He made a triumphant return in what is considered his best film *Quai des Orfèvres* (1947), a murder melodrama. Apart from *Le Mystère Picasso* (1955), an inventive study of the artist at work, he has concentrated on mysteries and thrillers, such as *The Wages of Fear* (1953) and *Les Diaboliques* (1954) which brutally play on the audience's nerves. *La Vérité* (1960) with Brigitte Bardot, was not up to the same standard.

clown. Originating in the antics of the village idiot the c. developed through the comic types of the **commedia dell'arte* and the improvised slapstick of comic actors, e.g. William *Kempe in Shakespeare's plays. The c. gained the status of a professional entertainer with Joseph ('Joey') *Grimaldi. He set the white-face tradition, established the traditional attribute of the c., the sadness and failure behind his comic mask, and became the forerunner of the circus c. 'Auguste'. The greatest c. of all, *Grock, transferred Auguste from the circus to the music-hall.

Cluny France. One of the greatest monasteries of medieval Europe, and an influential centre of architecture and art. The church was rebuilt for the 3rd time (and so is known as Cluny III) between 1088 and 1120. It had a long nave (411 ft) with double aisles and a tunnel-vault, an elaborate E. end with 2 pairs of transepts, and towers at the W. end, over the main transepts and over the crossing. The capitals of the chancel columns (*c.* 1095) are among the finest examples of Romanesque sculpture. The abbey was almost totally destroyed in the French Revolution.

François Clouet. *Portrait of Pierre Quthe*

Jean Clouet. *Mme de Lautrec*; drawing

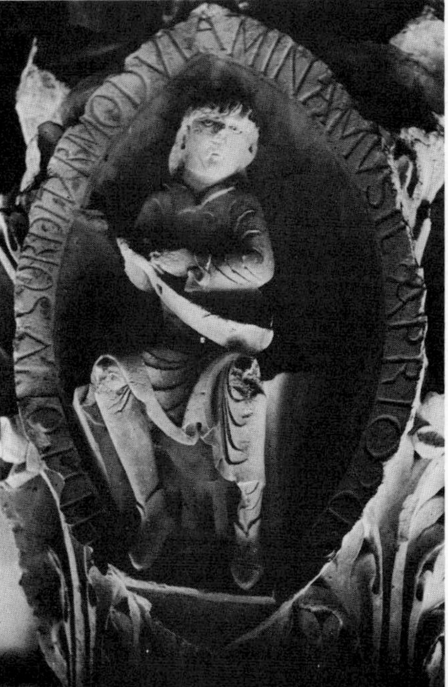
Cluny. Carved capital from the chancel

William Cobbett

Clurman Harold (1901–). U.S. director who founded the *Group Theater (1931) and has directed many of the great modern plays in the U.S.

Clutsam George Howard (1866–1951). Australian-born composer settled in England, 1889; the Schubert pastiche *Lilac Time* is a fair sample (1923) of his many stage works.

Coade stone. An artificial (cast) stone resembling terracotta manufactured by Coade and Seeley of London and used mainly for *dressings in the late 18th and early 19th c.

Coalport or **Coalbrookdale.** A porcelain factory in Shropshire, England, founded in 1796 and lasting into the 20th c. Its 19th-c. work was largely imitative of Sèvres, Dresden and Chelsea styles but achieved for a period remarkably translucent quality.

Coade stone dressings in Bedford Square

Coates Albert (1882–1953). Anglo-Russian conductor and composer. He studied under A. Nikisch, was a principal conductor (1914–19) at St Petersburg, meeting Scriabin there, conducted the British National Opera Co., toured Europe and the U.S. and finally settled in S. Africa. His compositions include the opera *Samuel Pepys* (1929).

Coates Eric (1886–1957). English violist and composer of popular and colourful orchestral suites, piano music and song cycles.

Coates Wells (1893–1958). A leading British architect of the 1930s, and an enthusiastic member of CIAM. His Isokon flats in Lawn Road, Hampstead were the 1st large modern building in London; his greatest commission, for the new town of Iroquois on the St Lawrence Seaway, was not built according to his designs.

Cobbett William (pseud. 'Peter Porcupine') (1762–1835). English journalist, ed. of the popular newspaper *Cobbett's Weekly Political Register*, and reforming political agitator. His famous *Rural Rides* (1830) gives a vivid and detailed picture of the English countryside, declining because of the Napoleonic Wars, encroaching industrialism and the growing cities like the 'Great Wen', London. His prose is direct, vigorous and unadorned.

Cobden-Sanderson T. J. (1840–1922). Printer and bookbinder, who formed the private *Doves Press (1900–17), with Emery Walker as adviser. C.-S.'s revival of *Jenson's type was extremely successful, and he was noted also for the bindings of his eds. His major work was a 5-vol. Bible and an ed. of *Hamlet* (1909).

Cobra. Corneille's *Souvenir of Amsterdam*

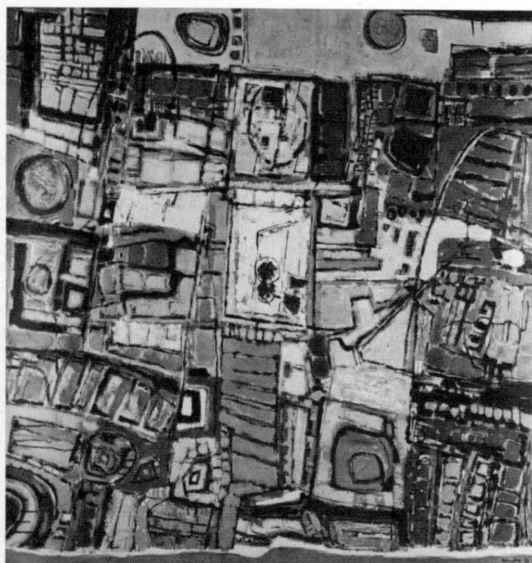

Cobra. An international art group (1948–51) named from the 1st letters of the cities Copenhagen, Brussels and Amsterdam. The best-known participants are Asger Jorn, Alechinsky and Corneille. The group held an exhibition at the Stedelijk Museum, Amsterdam in 1949; animals and insect life treated in a free abstract style showed the artists' admiration for prehistoric, primitive and unsophisticated art.

Cochin. Family of French artists. They included NICOLAS (1610–86), an engraver in the style of J. Callot, his brother NOËL (1622–95), a painter and engraver who settled in Venice, CHARLES-NICOLAS the Elder (1688–1754), an engraver after contemporary French masters such as Watteau, Chardin and Lancret, and his son and pupil CHARLES-NICOLAS the Younger (1715–90), famous as an engraver of vignettes, frontispieces and scenes of court festivities executed from his own drawings. He visited Italy in 1749 and in 1755 publ. *Supplication aux orfèvres* which initiated the reaction against rococo ornamentation.

Cochran Sir Charles Blake (1872–1951). Leading impresario of his time, best known for promoting *revues of a particularly lavish nature.

Cockerell Charles Robert (1788–1863). Leading English architect, and like his friend Byron an admirer of things Greek. His Westminster Fire Office in the Strand (1832) uses Greek Doric columns and shows his bigness of scale and boldness of conception. Other works include: the Ashmolean and Taylorian Institute, Oxford (1845) and the Bank Chambers, Liverpool (1849).

Cocktail Party, The (1949). Verse play by T. S. Eliot.

Cocteau Jean (1889–1963). French writer who was one of the most versatile figures on the Parisian scene–poet, novelist, dramatist, essayist, artist and film producer. C. first became famous in the heyday of his friend Diaghilev, after World War I, and belonged to various *avant-garde* movements until his death. One

C.-N. Cochin. *Pleasure Boat*

Cole. *In the Catskills.* Also *Hudson River school

Jean Cocteau (right) in *Le Testament d'Orphée*

of his last activities was the redecoration of churches with wall paintings. His poetry has proved less memorable than some of his celebrated aphorisms about life and art, the best of which are contained in *Le Rappel à l'ordre* (1926; *A Call to Order*, 1926). In the theatre he exploited ancient and medieval legend, e.g. *La Machine Infernale* (1934; *The Infernal Machine*, 1936), a reworking of the *Oedipus story, and *Les Chevaliers de la Table Ronde* (1937; *The Knights of the Round Table*, 1954), as well as modern subjects, as in *Les Parents Terribles* (1938; *Intimate Relations*, 1956). Perhaps the most profound of his writings is the short novel, *Les Enfants Terribles* (1929–30), about a brother and sister who live a secluded life in a room which they have transformed into a womb-like nest. His films, *L'Éternel retour* (1943), *La Belle et la Bête* (1945), *Orphée* (1950), and *Le Testament d'Orphée* (1960), were a notable part of the French cinematographic revival. In addition to being an active, if sometimes superficial, creator, C. also distinguished himself as a discoverer and encourager of talent, his 2 most celebrated protégés being the writer Raymond Radiguet and the actor Jean Marais.

coda (Italian, 'tail'). A concluding passage to a musical composition or section of it, e.g. 1st movement sonata form may have a c. added to the exposition (*codetta) and another to the end of the movement. Before Mozart this c. was merely a short tail-piece but he, and even more Beethoven, developed it into an important and extended section.

Codde Pieter (1599–1678). Dutch genre painter of small but spirited drinking scenes and conversation pieces. He completed *The Marksmen* by Hals.

codetta. Musical term used as the diminutive of *coda, but also sometimes applied specifically to the coda after the exposition in 1st movement sonata form. In fugue the episode between the 2nd and 3rd entries is called a c.

Codex argenteus: *Wulfila

Coello Alonso Sánchez (1531/2–88). Spanish court portrait painter, pupil of A. Mor. His figures are stiff and melancholy but elaborate details of dress are given meticulous care, e.g. *Portrait of a Young Man* (N.G., Dublin).

Coello Claudio (1642–93). Late baroque Spanish painter, influenced by J. de Carreño and the last important representative of the Madrid school. Of his huge decorative works his masterpiece is *La Sagrada Forma* (1685–90; Sacristy, Escorial), a religious and historical picture with portraits of Charles II and his court, composed to give the illusion of being a continuation of the sacristy.

Coerne Louis Adolphe (1870–1922). U.S. composer, conductor and teacher. He studied under J. K. Paine and, in Germany, under Rheinberger. His works included the opera *Zenobia* (1905), the symphonic poem *Hiawatha*, many instrumental works, a mass in D min. and songs. He publ. the thesis *The Evolution of Modern Orchestration* in 1908.

Coffee Cantata (*c.* 1723). Nickname for Bach's secular cantata *Schweiget stille, plaudert nicht* (German, 'Be quiet, don't chatter'), a humourous comment on the craze for coffee and coffee-houses.

coffering. Architectural term for the placing of sunken panels (coffers) in a ceiling.

Cohen Bernard (1933–). Leading English pop artist; studied at the St Martin's School of Art and the Slade, London.

Coiners, The (1926). Novel by *Gide.

coin glass. In the late 17th c. English glasses often had large, well-rounded knops. These were frequently hollow and contemporary coins were sometimes placed inside them. The fashion continued until the 19th c. with much earlier coins often incorporated in later glasses.

Colbert Claudette (1905–). French-born film and stage actress, chic and charming; she enjoyed success in such films as De Mille's *The Sign of the Cross* (1932) and *Cleopatra* (1934), and especially Capra's *It Happened One Night* (1934).

Cold Comfort Farm (1932). Humorous novel by Stella *Gibbons.

Cole Thomas (1801–48). English-born U.S. landscape painter, a founder of the Hudson River school. C. considered his allegorical and

Coello. *Prince Alexander Farnese*

Coffering in the Palazzo Farnese, Rome

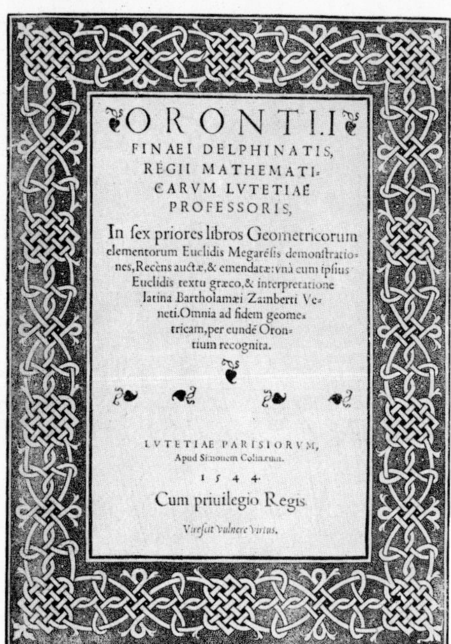

ORONTII
FINAEI DELPHINATIS,
REGII MATHEMATI-
CARVM LVTETIAE
PROFESSORIS,
In ſex priores libros Geometricorum
elementorum Euclidis Megarēſis demonſtratio-
nes, Recēns auctæ, & emendatæ: vnà cum ipſius
Euclidis textu græco, & interpretatione
latina Bartholamæi Zamberti Ve-
neti. Omnia ad fidem geome-
tricam, per eundē Oron-
tium recognita.

LVTETIAE PARISIORVM,
Apud Simonem Colinæum.
1544.
Cum priuilegio Regis.
Vireſcit vulnere virtus.

Colines. Title-page of his ed. of Euclid

Samuel Taylor Coleridge.
Also *Allston

religious pictures his best work but these have been far less influential or lastingly popular than his romantic landscapes of the Hudson Valley.

Coleridge Hartley (1796–1849). English poet and literary journalist, eldest son of S.T.C. His best poems are sonnets, often reflecting the desolation of his life.

Coleridge Samuel Taylor (1772–1834). English poet and critic, the son of a Devonshire parson. C. was educated at Christ's Hospital and Cambridge, which he left briefly to serve in the Dragoons. Moved by the ideals of the French Revolution, he and Southey proposed to found a 'Pantisocracy' or utopian colony in America. After lecturing on politics in Bristol, he founded a short-lived newspaper, *The Watchman* (1796), and publ. a vol. of poems. He saw Wordsworth, with whom he formed a deep friendship, almost every day in 1797–8 (the most fruitful period of C.'s life) and accompanied Wordsworth and his sister to Germany in 1798–9. His health broke down–partly the result of taking opium–and he spent 1804–6 in Malta and Italy. Later he lectured, wrote fitfully, ran a periodical, *The Friend*, and was universally admired for his brilliant conversation.

Although C.'s output was small, he wrote some of the most haunting and powerful poems in English, including the richly textured *Kubla Khan* (1816; composed in 1797), a fragment inspired by a dream, and *The Rime of the Ancient Mariner*. The latter, C.'s masterpiece, is a symbolic tale of sin and redemption (in the apparently simple form and diction of the ballad) which inspires dread and creates suspense. It appeared in *Lyrical Ballads* (1798), a coll. of poems by C. and Wordsworth. At the same time C. wrote the first of the 2 parts of *Christabel* (1816), a Gothic poem of the supernatural; it employs a metre based on counting stresses instead of syllables. *Biographia Literaria* (1817) contains fragments of autobiography, and philosophical argument derived from Schelling and Kant; but its importance lies in C.'s statements about the nature and purpose of poetry, and his generous and penetrating criticism of Wordsworth. His works include the ode *Dejection*, which records his sense of waning powers; plays, including *The Fall of Robespierre* (in collaboration with Southey); a trs. of 2 parts of Schiller's *Wallenstein*; and colls of his *Table Talk*.

Collage by Braque: *The Clarinet* (1913)

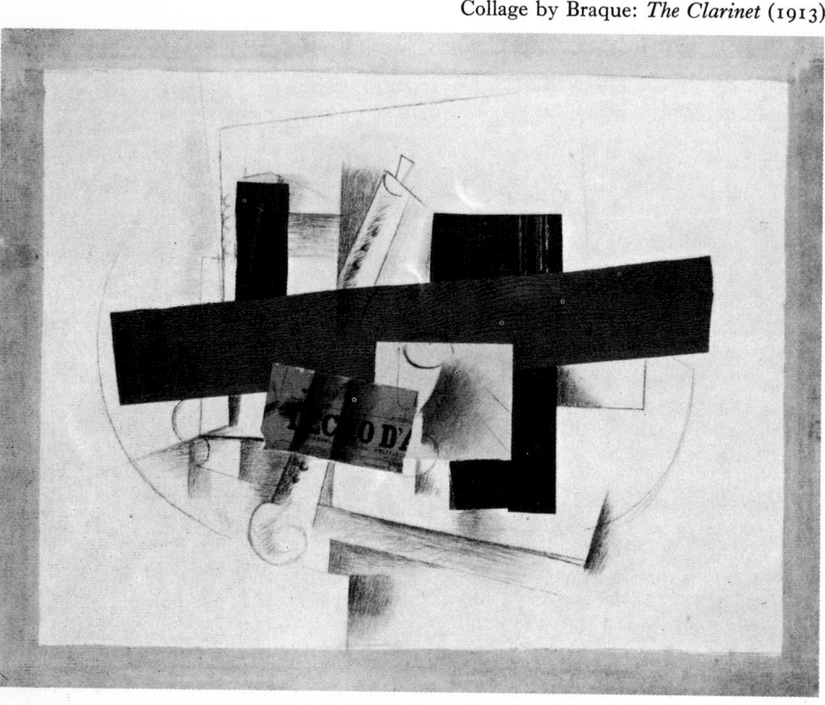

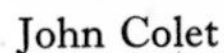
John Colet

Colette

R. G. Collingwood

Wilkie Collins

Coleridge-Taylor Samuel (1875–1912). British composer, son of a Sierra Leone doctor and an Englishwoman. His style shows affinities to Dvořák and Mendelssohn but suffers from over-sentimentality. Besides his famous *Hiawatha's Wedding Feast* (1898) he wrote choral, orchestral and chamber music.

Colet John (1467?–1519). Dean of St Paul's, the leading English humanist of his time and a close friend of Erasmus. He founded St Paul's School, London for which, with W. Lily, he composed a Latin grammar, later revised by Erasmus and a standard work into the 18th c. He encouraged trs of liturgy and Bible into the vernacular.

Colette Sidonie Gabrielle (1873–1954). French writer. She was brought to Paris by her 1st husband, 'Willy', who put his signature to the *Claudine* series (1900–3). She wrote out of her experience of country life and the literary, artistic and theatrical Bohemia of Paris. She applies her amoral peasant sagacity and exceptional powers of lyrical description to the sensual and psychological complexities of *demi-mondaines*, adolescents, homosexuals, frustrated wives and questing husbands in *Le Blé en herbe* (1923; *The Ripening Corn*, 1931), *La Chatte* (1933; *Saha the Cat*, 1936) and *Mes apprentissages* (1936; *My Apprenticeships*, 1957). *Chéri* (1920; *Chéri*, 1930) and *La Fin de Chéri* (1926; *The Last of Chéri*, 1933) are more ambitious in that they turn the unhappy gigolo into a tragic hero.

Colin Clout's Come Home Again (1595). Satirical poem by Spenser.

Colines Simon de (d. 1546). French printer and type-cutter, who took over the business of Henri *Estienne in 1520, on marrying his widow. Along with Estienne's son Robert, he was the 1st of the French Renaissance printers. He designed Greek and Italic founts, and the roman St Augustin Sylvius (1531), the ancestor of all types designed by Claude Garamond.

collage. Composition made up of various materials – cardboard, string, fabric, etc. – pasted to a canvas or board and sometimes combined with painting or drawing. It was a technique used by the cubists and much favoured by members of the dada movement.

Collé Charles (1709–83). French dramatist. His comedy of contemporary manners, *La Vérité dans le Vin*, was prohibited because of its coarseness. The comedies *Dupuis et Desronais* (1763) and *La Partie de chasse de Henri IV* (1774) were extremely successful.

college cup. A bulbous silver cup with 2 heavy ring handles at the neck, so called because it is chiefly found among the college plate at Oxford and Cambridge. Also called 'ox-eye cups' and 'silver pots with ears', they were usually presentation cups or souvenirs.

Collier Jeremy (1650–1726). English clergyman whose *A Short View of the Immorality and Profaneness of the English Stage* (1698) provoked a pamphlet war between C. and Dryden, Vanbrugh and Congreve. The authorities were stung into brief activity against the stage, Congreve and T. D'Urfey being prosecuted, Betterton and Mrs Bracegirdle fined.

Collin d'Harleville Jean-François (1755–1806). French playwright, author of several successful comedies, notably *Le Vieux Célibataire* (1792). Others include *L'Inconstant* (1786), *L'Optimiste* (1788), *Malice pour malice* (1803) and a farce, *M. de Crac dans son petit castel* (1791), whose hero became the type of the boastful Gascon.

Collingwood Lawrence (1887–). English opera conductor and composer. He was assistant to A. Coates at St Petersburg, and principal conductor of the Sadler's Wells Opera (1931–47); his operas *Macbeth* (1934) and *The Death of Tintagiles* (1950) were performed there.

Collingwood Robin George (1889–1943). English philosopher and historian. C.'s aesthetic theories were strongly influenced by *Croce. *The Principles of Art* (1938) emphasizes the communicative function of art, which generates the emotions necessary to a healthy social life. C. also wrote a study of the development of his thought, *An Autobiography* (1939).

Collins Charles Allston (1828–73). English painter and author, brother of Wilkie C. He was strongly influenced by Pre-Raphaelite ideals.

Collins (William) Wilkie (1824–89). English novelist and master of suspense fiction; son of William C. Famous thrillers are *The Woman in White* (1860) and *The Moonstone* (1868), an English forerunner of the detective novel. He was a friend of Dickens with whom he collaborated in *Household Words* and *All the Year Round*.

Collins William (1721–59). English poet, an important influence on the Lake Poets. Insanity cut short his work, and he publ. only *Persian Eclogues* (1742) and *Odes* (1747), on which his reputation rests. *Ode on the Popular Superstitions of the Highlands* appeared posth.

Collins William (1788–1847). British painter of landscapes and anecdotal pictures. C. was a follower and friend of Sir D. Wilkie and father of C.A.C. and the writer W.W.C. His paintings were mediocre but such works as *The Sale of the Pet Lamb* (1812) achieved huge popularity.

Collinson James (1825?–81). English painter, an original member of the Pre-Raphaelite Brotherhood; he painted *An Incident in the Life of St Elizabeth of Hungary* (1851; Johannesburg A. Gal.) according to their ideals. The breaking of his engagement to Christina Rossetti was the occasion of many of her saddest and most exquisite poems.

Collodi Carlo. Pseud. used by Carlo Lorenzini (1826–90). Italian journalist and writer, and author of the world-famous children's book *Pinocchio* (1883; *The Story of a Puppet*, 1892). C. also wrote uninspired plays and novels, and a number of didactic works for children.

collodion negative. Photographic process invented by F. S. Archer in 1851; it rapidly displaced the *calotype because of its greater speed and better definition. The plates had to be made, exposed and developed within 15 minutes still wet. This process became obsolete by 1880 with the invention of gelatine dry plates.

Colman George the Elder (1732–94). English playwright and theatre manager, whose successful comedies ridicule the sentimentality of the period. They include *Polly Honeycombe* (1760), *The Jealous Wife* (1761), an adaptation of Fielding's *Tom Jones*, and *The Clandestine Marriage* (1766), written in collaboration with his friend Garrick.

Cologne cathedral from the east

Cologne cathedral: the nave

Colquhoun. *Seated Woman with Cat* (1946)

The Colossi of Memnon

The Colosseum: part of the façade. See also colour plate 14

Colman George the Younger (1762–1836). English dramatist and theatre manager. His plays include the romantic comedy *Inkle and Yarico* (1787), *The Heir at Law* (1797), featuring Dr Pangloss the pedant, and *John Bull or The Englishman's Fireside* (1805).

Colman Ronald (1891–1958) British-born film star, debonair, adventurous and romantic, of U.S. films, e.g. *Under Two Flags* (1936).

Cologne cathedral Germany. Begun in 1248, C. is firmly in the French Île de France style, and owes little to any previous German architecture. It is the largest church in N. Europe (91,000 square ft) with double aisles and 150-ft-high vault: the vertical emphasis is also expressed in the exterior by high openwork towers and spires covered in filigree tracery. The church stood unfinished all through the middle ages (only the E. end and part of one W. tower were built) being finally completed between 1824 and 1880; the 19th-c. nave was largely destroyed in World War II and later rebuilt.

Colonna Francesco (1433–1527). Dominican monk, living in Venice, author of the strange prose romance, **Hypnerotomachia Poliphili*.

Colonna Vittoria (1490–1547). Italian poet whose chief fame rests on her lasting platonic friendship with Michelangelo. Her book of love-lyrics, *Rima della divina Vittoria Colonna* (1538) ran to many eds during her lifetime.

colophon. The inscription or device which used to be placed at the end of books, containing the title and details of the printing.

coloratura (Italian 'coloured'). Musical term applied to an elaborate soprano part, usually high lying and always with rapid runs, etc., requiring virtuoso technique.

Colosseum Rome. Amphitheatre for games and spectacles, built A.D. 70–82 (top storey added in the 3rd c.). The tiers of seats are supported on rings of arches. The C. is remarkable for its size, for its dependence on brick and concrete (only the ornamental parts were of stone) and for its use of 'superimposed orders' (Doric, Ionic and Corinthian half-columns) on the exterior. This last feature became one of the most constant motifs of the Renaissance.

Comédie-Française: performance by Molière and his co.

Commedia dell'arte figures; Venice, *c.* 1770

Colossi of Memnon Thebes (*c.* 1400 B.C.). 2 colossal seated statues of Amenophis III believed by classical historians to represent the mythical king, Memnon. Carved from quartz and originally *c.* 68 ft high, the figures flanked the gateway of the Pharaoh's mortuary temple. Before restoration, that on the north emitted a musical note at sunrise and was consequently known as the 'singing Memnon'.

Colossus of Maroussi, The (1941). Book by Henry *Miller.

Colossus of Rhodes. Bronze statue (105 ft high) of Helios, the sun god, by Chares of Lindos, erected by the harbour at Rhodes *c.* 280 B.C., and one of the 7 wonders of the ancient world. It was overthrown by an earthquake in 225 B.C. The remains were not removed until A.D. 656.

Colpi Henri (1921–). French film director and critic. As an ed. C. worked for Chaplin, Clouzot and *Resnais, the influence of whose *Hiroshima mon amour*, and even more so that of M. *Duras who wrote the script, was apparent in C.'s 1st feature, *Une Aussi Longue Absence* (1960). C. has since made in Rumania a careful literary adaptation, *Codine* (1962).

Colquhoun Robert (1914–63). Scottish painter; his work, influenced by J. *Adler and also Picasso, is similar to that of his friend R. MacBryde.

Coltrane John (1929–). U.S. *jazz tenor saxophonist.

Colum Padraic (1881–). Irish writer important in the *Irish literary renaissance and a founder of *The Irish Review*. In work of quiet simplicity he brings a new approach to old traditions. He wrote 3 plays for the Abbey Theatre. Works include: the plays *The Land* (1905) and *The Fiddler's House* (1907); the verse *Wild Earth* (1907) and *The Story of Lowry Maen* (1937); and many books for children.

Columbine (Italian, 'Columbina'). Character in the Italian **commedia dell'arte*.

columnar and trabeate. In architecture, using column and beam; i.e. as opposed to using arches.

Colville Alex (1920–). Canadian painter. After World War II (in which he served as war artist) he developed a characteristic style formally well organized and extremely realistic in subject and treatment.

Comédie-Française, La. The National Theatre of France and so called to distinguish it from La Comédie-Italienne, was founded in 1680 by the amalgamation of several cos including that of Molière and thus was also known as '*La Maison de Molière*'. In 1689 the co. moved to a new theatre in St-Germain-des-Prés where it stayed until 1770. After the Revolution the co. was re-formed in the theatre in the Palais-Royal where it still is. It is a co-operative society in which each actor holds a share and, after a certain number of years' service, receives a pension. It has created a strong tradition but, by its very nature, tends to discourage experiment.

Comédie humaine, La (1842–8). Generic title under which *Balzac publ. a coll. ed. of his novels.

Comédie-Italienne, La. 17th-c. Parisian theatre co. deriving from the *commedia dell'arte* cos which played in Paris in the 16th c., and whose mode of acting the C.-I. still practised, though performing entirely in French by 1697, when the co. was expelled from France. After its return (1716) it gradually lost its Italian character. In the 2nd half of the 18th c. it turned to *opera buffa*, finally (1801) amalgamating with the Théâtre Feydeau to become the Opéra-Comique.

comédie larmoyante or 'comedy through tears'. A type of sentimental comedy, the term being first associated with La Chaussée and other 18th-c. French dramatists. The plays of Chekhov and Gogol, in which the sadness of the situations is allowed to colour the humour in them, are also so described.

comedy. Term used in the theatre since the Athenian *Old Comedy. In general it is less concerned with the deepest human emotions than is tragedy, usually has humour as an important element, may deal with social rather than personal themes but, more loosely, may simply be any play with a 'happy ending'.

Comedy of Errors, The (1594; publ. 1623). Comedy by *Shakespeare, written *c.* 1593, and performed at court in 1604. Its sources were Plautus' *Menaechmi* and Gower's *Confessio Amantis*, and perhaps the *Amphitruo* of Plautus.

comedy of manners. A play dealing with the foibles and fashions of the contemporary society and presenting type figures rather than psychologically subtle characters. The Restoration drama in England offers many examples.

Comfort Alex(ander) (1920–). English novelist, poet, sociologist and doctor, whose works include: the novels *The Power House* (1944) and *On this Side Nothing* (1949); and *Authority and Delinquency in the Modern State* (1950).

Com(m)ines Philippe de (1447–1511). Flemish chronicler and historian, confidential counsellor to Louis XI and Charles VIII. His *Cronique et hystoire par Phelippe de Commines* and *Croniques du Roy Charles* (1524 and 1528, known as his *Mémoires*) are vital and accurate historical sources for the 2 reigns and inspired Scott's *Quentin Durward*, in which C. himself figures.

commedia dell'arte. Form of Italian popular drama based on mime and improvisation, in which the actors wore characteristic masks. It reached the height of its popularity in the 16th c., often mocking the tragedies of the poets. From Italy it spread over S. Europe and to a lesser extent to N. Europe. Towards the end of the 17th c. it began to be eclipsed by Molière, who had learned much from it and later by the Italian C. Goldoni, who abolished the masks. Although they were subject to change within any one troupe and from one performance to another, the following main characters formed the basis of the drama: The Doctor (eternal chatterbox); The Captain (under different names but usually a swashbuckling hero); Columbine (usually a saucy and ingenuous lady's maid); Harlequin (the scheming and cunning servant in the distinctive chequered costume); Pulcinella (a forerunner of Punch with a hooked nose, hunch back and spindly legs); Pantalone (the old man, usually a Venetian, and always someone's dupe); Scaramouche (the 'little skirmisher', similar to the Captain, but interested only in minor skirmishes and also wine and women). Also *Punch and Judy, *Harlequinade and *pantomime. The characters of the c. d.'a. provided a favourite theme for 18th-c. porcelain artists.

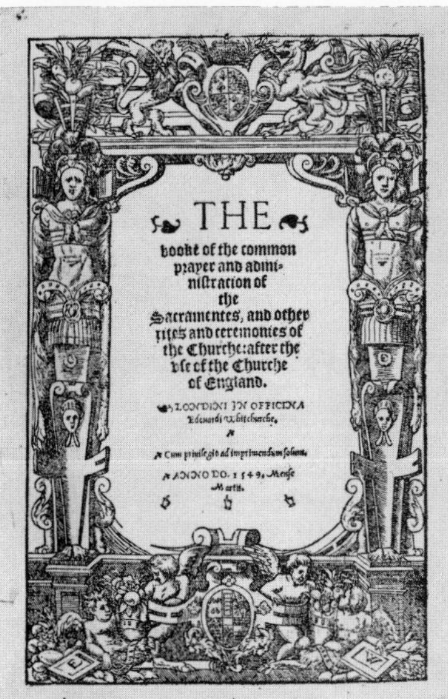

The Book of Common Prayer: title-page of the 1549 ed.

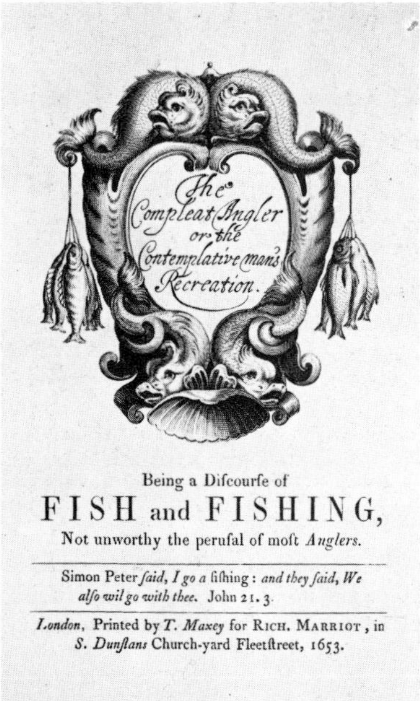

The Compleat Angler: title-page of the 1st ed.

commode. A chest of drawers generally of 2 deep drawers, but the form varies greatly; the term is used in describing continental furniture only. At first its purpose was practical, but later it graduated to the *salon* from the bedroom and was used for display, being decorated with marquetry, ormulu and marble tops.

Common Prayer, The Book of. The service book of the Church of England. First drawn up in 1549 under the direction of Archbishop Cranmer, taken almost entirely from medieval liturgical books and trs. from Latin into English. After revisions by Cranmer in 1552 and others in 1559, the final text was publ. in 1662. Cranmer may have been assisted by his chaplain, Nicholas Ridley.

compass. In music, the usable range of (1) a voice as defined by the lowest and highest attainable notes of acceptable quality or (2) an instrument, defined by its lowest note and the highest note of acceptable quality. Certain instruments such as the *trombone do not have a full chromatic c., i.e. a complete chromatic *scale cannot be played from the lowest to highest note.

complaint. A poem, particularly medieval, complaining of disappointment in love. In his humorous *Compleynt to His Purs* Chaucer apostrophizes his purse as a light, fickle lady.

Complaint, The, or Night Thoughts on Life, Death and Immortality (1742–5). Poem by Edward *Young.

Compleat Angler, or the Contemplative Man's Recreation, The (1653). Book by Izaak *Walton.

composition. The formal arrangement of a painting or work of graphic art; also a piece of music or writing, or the act of writing or composing.

composition piston or **pedal.** On an organ a hand- or foot-operated device which makes available a pre-selected combination of stops.

Compton-Burnett Ivy (1892–). English novelist. Her novels consist of witty and stylized dialogue which often conceals an undercurrent of malignance and horror. Works include: *A House and Its Head* (1935), *Elders and Betters* (1944), *Mother and Son* (1955) and *A Heritage and its History* (1959).

Comte (Isidore) Auguste (1798–1857). French philosopher, founder of positivism, a philosophy expounded in his *Cours de philosophie positive* (1830–42; *The Positive Philosophy of Auguste Comte*, 1853), which recognizes only proven facts of sense experience and observable phenomena, excluding metaphysical speculation. C.'s influence was profound in the years of transition from romanticism to realism in literature, and his scientific thought had a parallel in the aesthetic theories of Zola.

Comus. A masque by *Milton with music by H. Lawes. 2-scene ballet, based on the story of the masque with choreography by Helpmann, music from Purcell and décor by Messel; 1st performance 1942.

Conca Sebastiano (1680–1764). Italian decorative painter in baroque style who studied in Naples under F. Solimena. From 1706 he was in Rome, his work there including the ceiling fresco *Crowning of St Cecilia* (1725). In 1751 he returned to Naples.

conceit. Literary term applied to elaborate and far-fetched similes and metaphors, and usually appealing to the mind rather than the imagination. Its use is particularly associated with the *metaphysical poets.

concertante (Italian, 'in the nature of a concerto'). A musical term usually implying an orchestral piece with a small group of solo instruments; thus a SINFONIA c. or simply c. used as a noun. The solo instruments in such a case are sometimes called the c. instruments.

concertina. Musical instrument of the reed organ family invented in the 1820s and consisting of a hexagonal bellows with finger-studs in the end-pieces, controlling notes and chord combinations. There are German and English types; the latter, much the more versatile, was highly popular in the 19th c., Tchaikovsky even including 4 in his 2nd orchestral suite.

concert master. The U.S. term for the *leader of an orchestra; like many U.S. musical terms it results from a literal trs. of a German term, in this case *Konzertmeister*.

concerto. A musical composition for solo instrument or instruments and orchestra. The classical c. was established in the later 18th c. by J. C. Bach and others; having 3 movements,

Auguste Comte

Commode, 18th-c. Venetian

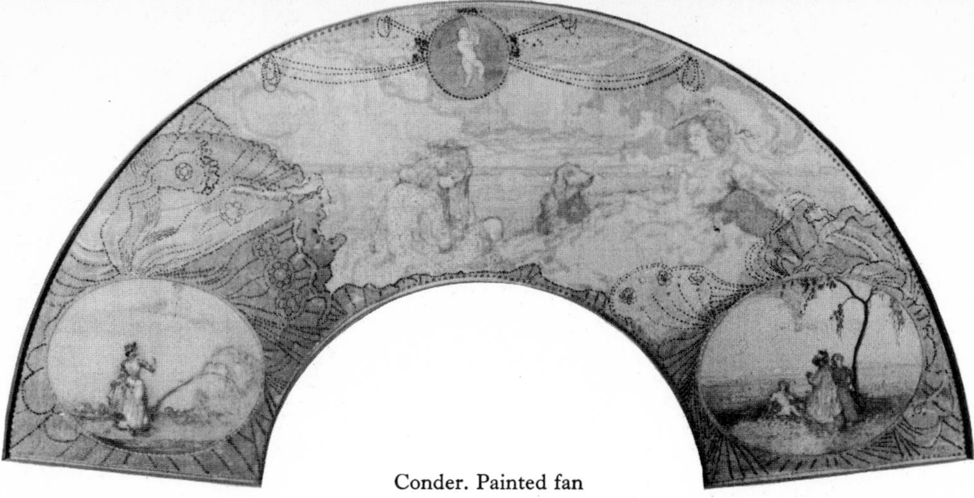

Conder. Painted fan

of which the 1st is in sonata form. In the 17th c. the term was used for various types of music, instrumental and vocal, but by the end of the c. the *concerto grosso had emerged and in the early 18th c. the solo concerto developed. A characteristic of the c. is a strong element of contrast, between the solo instrument(s) and the orchestra; this element of contrast, between many instruments, is present in *Bartók's *Concerto for Orchestra*.

Concerto Barocco. Ballet in 3 movements with choreography by Balanchine, music by J. S. Bach (concerto for 2 violins in D min.) and décor by Berman; 1st performance 1941.

concerto grosso. Musical form evolved in the late 17th c. It is a sequence of movements (no fixed number) usually for a group of solo instruments ('the concertino') and orchestra ('the ripieno'); virtuoso writing in the solo parts is not mandatory: the essence of the form is contrast and dialogue between the larger and smaller ensembles. One of the earliest publ. colls (1700) was T. Albinoni's, admired by Bach, and the c. g. was fully developed by A. *Corelli, *12 Concerti Grossi*; *Bach's Brandenburg concertos and *Handel's *12 Concerti Grossi* are later examples. Modern examples include E. Bloch's c. g. for strings.

concord. In music, a chord which seems to require no harmonic resolution and to be harmonically at rest; a discord on the other hand seems inconclusive and to need resolution on to another chord.

concrete art (German, *konkrete Kunst*; French, *art concret*). Artistic term introduced by van *Doesburg in 1930 in preference to 'abstract art'. According to M. Bill, its greatest propagandist, it 'refers to those works that have developed through their own, innate means and laws' and are therefore autonomous, i.e. not dependent on a process of abstraction.

Condamné a Mort s'est Échappé, Un (1956). Film directed by R. *Bresson.

Condell Henry: John *Heming

Conder Charles (1868–1909). English painter and lithographer. After government work in Australia he studied art in Paris. He produced delicate, elusive pastoral designs, influenced by Watteau and oriental art, sometimes executed on white silk and often for fans. In 1901 he settled in London.

Condition Humaine, La (1933). Novel by André *Malraux.

Condorcet Marie-Jean (1743–94). One of the French **philosophes*.

conductor. The man who directs the body of players or singers in a musical performance. His original function was to give the *tactus*, i.e. beat time either by gestures of the hand, or quite literally beating out the time with a stick on desk or floor. Up to the early 19th c. instrumental works were usually directed by the c. (often the composer) from a keyboard instrument on which he played the continuo, in conjunction with the leading violin, still called the 'leader'. During the 19th c. the c.'s baton, encountered as early as the 15th c., was universally adopted.

conductus. In medieval music, a homophonic piece consisting of a secular or composed (never sacred) *cantus firmus with 2 lower parts vocalizing on a vowel.

Confessio Amantis, The (1386–90). Allegory by J. *Gower.

Confessions, Les (posth. publ. 1781–8). Autobiography of J.-J. *Rousseau.

Confessions of an English Opium Eater (1822). Autobiographical book by *De Quincey.

Confessions of Zeno, The (1923). Novel by Italo *Svevo.

Confidence-Man, The: His Masquerade (1857). Novel by Herman *Melville.

Confidential Clerk, The (1954). Play by T. S. Eliot.

Confucius. The European name for K'ung fu-tzu (*c.* 551–*c.* 479 B.C.) the great Chinese sage and philosopher to whom have been attributed many writings; his sayings surviving in various colls have been trs. into English as the *Analects of C.* His work was first trs. into a European language by Jesuit missionaries in *Sapientia Sinica* (1662). Also *China.

Congreve William (1670–1729). Restoration playwright. Educated in Ireland and trained in

Congreve: mezzotint after Kneller

Confucius

the law, C. brought to the Restoration stage a more powerful intellect and a more cultivated mind than any other playwright except Dryden. His best comedies, *Love for Love* (1695) and *The Way of the World* (1700), are remarkable chiefly for the beauty, wit and elegance of their language. His plots are no less licentious than those of Wycherley, but the indecencies are less coarsely dwelt on, and in his finest play, *The Way of the World*, there is a touch of genial gaiety which saves the minor characters from becoming mere contemptible caricatures and gives the central relationship of Mirabell and Millamant a quality of disguised and flirting tenderness. Works also include *The Double Dealer* (1694).

Coningsby, or The New Generation (1844). Novel by *Disraeli.

Coninxloo Gillis van (1544–1607). Flemish landscape painter and engraver who settled in Amsterdam in 1595. His work marks a transition in landscape painting from the stylization of the early work of P. Bril and J. de Momper to the realism of the 17th-c. Dutch landscapists. J. Bruegel and Rubens were among those he influenced.

Connecticut Wits, The: *Hartford Wits

Connecticut Yankee in King Arthur's Court, A (1889). Novel by Mark Twain.

Connell, Ward and Lucas. London architectural practice from 1927 to 1939, members of MARS group and builders of the first reinforced concrete houses in England. Their work is almost all domestic, and they were among the best English practitioners of the international style.

Connolly Cyril (Vernon) (1903–). Anglo-Irish writer, journalist and critic. With S. Spender and P. Watson he publ. the critical review *Horizon* (1939–50). Works include *The Unquiet Grave* (1944), under the pseud. 'Palinurus', a representative book of his generation; his novel *Rock Pool* (1936); and the autobiographical *Enemies of Promise*, a criticism of contemporary literature (1938).

Conques France, abbey of St Foi. Romanesque church on the route *Santiago de Compostela. It was built *c.* 1940–50, smaller than the other 'pilgrimage' churches but conforming to the same type. It has a notable *Last Judgement* tympanum.

Conquest Robert (1917–). English poet. As ed. of the *New Lines* anthology (1955) he introduced many new poets, e.g. Gunn, Wain and Elizabeth Jennings to a wider audience. His *Poems* (1956), influenced by Graves and Auden, attempt to integrate intellect and feeling.

Conrad Joseph (1857–1924). Polish-born English novelist. C. visited England for the 1st time in 1878, after 4 years at sea, and became a British citizen in 1886. His 1st novel, *Almayer's Folly*, begun during a voyage to the Congo, was publ. in 1895, a year after he left the merchant service.
Ostensibly adventure stories in an exotic setting which extol the simple virtues of loyalty and devotion to duty, many of C.'s novels are in fact of profound moral complexity. The finely realized and described settings are used to express the nature of evil in the protagonists – the secretive jungle in the short story *The Heart of Darkness* (1902), the squalor of Victorian London in the novel *The Secret Agent* (1907). A common theme is the moral collapse of inadequate or ambiguous personalities – *Lord Jim* (1900) or Decoud in *Nostromo* – when corrupted by some lie or inward fanaticism; their failure is viewed with an ironic detachment which forbids both pity and contempt. At the heart of C.'s work is a profound pessimism and a sense of the mystery of human destiny, which cannot be baulked or eluded. In *Under Western Eyes* (1911), a novel which depends for its haunting atmosphere on C.'s memories of Russian Poland, Razunov is involved against his will with the Revolutionary student Haldin; from this events develop with a sense of a trap closing. In the face of this inscrutable fate man can oppose only integrity and stoicism; it is to the simple-hearted men of action that C. accords his full respect.
Under Western Eyes is C.'s most perfect novel. *Nostromo* (1904), although it has some of his deepest insights and most spare and haunting writing, is a flawed masterpiece, betrayed by a touch of false romanticism in the drawing of the titular hero and by C.'s peculiar ineptitude in portraying relationships between men and women. In the grandeur of its conception and the actuality with which it creates the geography and politics of an entire community it is, however, unique among 20th-c. novels.

Conradi Hermann (1862–90). German realist poet and novelist, was joint ed. of the lyrical anthology *Moderne Dichtercharaktere* (1885) setting out the aims of realism. C.'s work was rebellious and idealistic, but his early death prevented the realization of his great potentialities. His works include lyrics and fiction (influenced by Zola), e.g. *Adam Mensch* (1889).

Conscience Hendrik (1812–83). Flemish romantic novelist and chief contributor to the 19th-c. Flemish literary revival. Among his many historical novels, in the style of Sir W. Scott, is the splendid *De Leeuw van Vlaanderen* (1838; *The Lion of Flanders*, 1855).

consecutives. A musical term applied when 2 parts separated by a given interval maintain that interval between them during a phase of their movement. Thus if parts on D and F (i.e. separated by a 3rd) move up to E and G respectively we have consecutive 3rds and the parts move by parallel *motion. From the 15th to late 19th cs consecutive 5ths were, in theory, unacceptable as were consecutive 8ves, and both are still prohibited in academic contrapuntal training. A basic movement of parts by 5ths or 8ves obscured by ornamentation is termed HIDDEN or CONCEALED 5ths and 8ves.

Consolatione Philosophiae, De. Philosophical dialogue by *Boethius.

console. In music, describes that part of an organ from which the player controls the pipes, i.e. the keyboard manuals, the pedal-board; the stops and pistons.

console table. A table of bracket construction often used in conjunction with a mirror. Originally called a 'clap table' it dates from the early 18th c. Rococo examples are elaborately decorated, the most popular supports being eagles with outstretched wings, and intertwined dolphins.

consonantal rhyme. Term sometimes used to describe the 'rhyme' (words with the same consonants, e.g. 'like' and 'lake') introduced by Wilfred Owen.

consort. English Renaissance musical term for a group of instruments playing together, i.e. IN C. A group all of the same family of instruments was a WHOLE C., a mixed group, e.g. woodwind and strings, a BROKEN C.

Conques.
Detail from the tympanum

Joseph Conrad

Conspiracy of Catiline. History by *Sallust.

Constable Henry (1562–1613). English poet. His poems, e.g. the sonnet coll. *Diana*, betray French and Italian influence, and in some cases were almost literal trs of Desportes.

Constable John (1776–1837). English landscape painter. Born at East Bergholt, Suffolk, the son of a miller, C. worked for a time in his father's windmills, which he said later taught him to study 'the natural history of the skies'. He was encouraged in drawing by a village amateur and copied from Girtin and Claude. In 1795 he came to London determined to be a painter, and in 1799 entered the R.A. as a student. He grew impatient of the Italianate landscape painting of the time, which was still under the spell of Wilson, and in 1802 he returned to Suffolk, writing the famous letter in which he says: 'there is room enough for a natural painture [*sic*]'. Apart from discouraging periods in London painting portraits C. now gave his time wholly to teaching himself how to reproduce every effect of changing light and weather in the skies and the river meadows of the Stour. The work of these years was little known or appreciated until 1888 when over 300 drawings and paintings were given to the nation by C.'s daughter. This superb coll., now at the V. and A., contains sketches for many of his major paintings in oil, as well as cloud studies, flower pieces and large watercolours such as the *Study of a Tree*. 'Lights–dews–breezes–blooms–and freshness' could be used to sum up the impression they give. But if the results were lyrical, the study behind them was hard, slow and not materially rewarding. Gradually C. evolved an infinitely subtle modulation of greens and a strict, though hidden, sense of composition. Recognition of his genius was almost equally slow. Although he continued to exhibit large paintings at the R.A. almost every year, it was 1819 before he became an Associate and 1829 before he was an Academician. In contrast to this, his exhibition of the *Hay Wain* (N.G., London) at the Paris Salon in 1824 won him a gold medal and caused great excitement among French painters. Delacroix, it is said, repainted his *Massacre of Chios* on seeing it. C.'s influence on the French *Barbizon school of landscape painters is undisputed and his paintings of ships and harbours, such as the brilliant sketch in oil, *Brighton Beach, Colliers* (V. and A., London) or the large work, *Marine Parade and Chain*

Constable. *Hay Wain*

Constable. *Brighton Beach, Colliers*

Console table; mahogany with veined marble top, *c.* 1740

Coninxloo. *Midas in a Landscape*

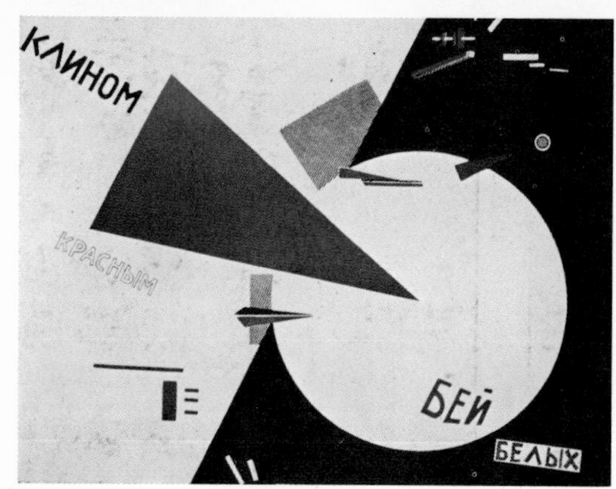

Constructivism. Bolshevik poster during the civil war; by Lissitzky

James Fenimore Cooper

Constructivism. Tatlin, model for the *Monument to the 3rd International*

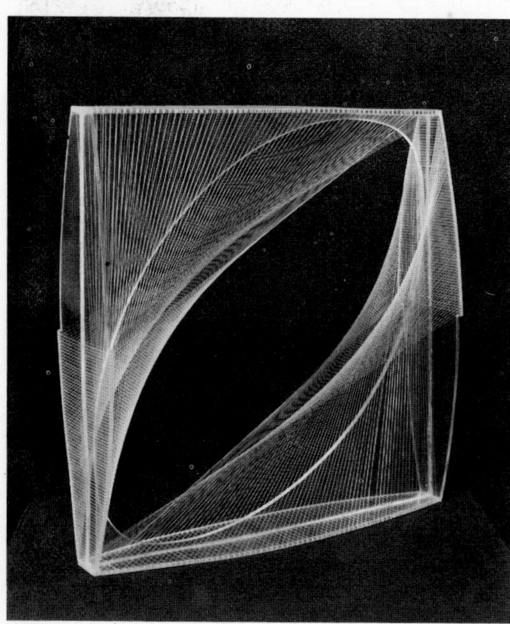

Constructivism. Naum Gabo, *Linear Construction*

Pier, Brighton was obviously a formative influence on Boudin.
In England, despite continuing French enthusiasm, C. suffered from comparison with Turner and from the unfavourable opinion of Ruskin. C.'s art seemed, curiously enough, too easy and too ordinary when contrasted with that of the Pre-Raphaelites and Turner.

Constant Couple, The, or a Trip to the Jubilee (1699). Play by *Farquhar.

Constant de Rebecque Benjamin (1767–1830). French writer, politician and journalist. He publ. an attack on Napoleon in 1813, but served him in the more liberal régime of the 100 Days and remained an important figure in French politics. His long liaison with Mme de Staël is reflected in the autobiographical novel *Adolphe* (1816; 1816), the story of a weak but sensitive young man involved with an older woman. Its perceptiveness and economy of style make it an outstanding example of the novel of psychological analysis. A complete ed. of C.'s *Journaux intimes* was publ. in 1952.

constructivism. An aesthetic which arose in Russia based on the futurist cult of the machine and first expressed in the 'Relief Constructions' of 1913–17 by V. Tatlin. Its ideas became crystallized and assumed the importance of a movement in 1921/2 when there was a split between Muscovite abstract painters, some opting for the principle of 'pure' art and others for utilitarian and propaganda work. The latter group became known as 'constructivists' or 'artist-engineers'. In their attempt to overcome the isolation of the artist from society, they entered the fields of industrial design (Tatlin, Rodchenko, Popova, Lissitzky), the theatre and film (Meyerhold, Eisenstein), and architecture (Melnikov, Ginzburg, Golossov, the 3 Vesnin brothers). Apart from Tatlin's unrealized *Monument to the 3rd International* of 1919/20, constructivist buildings include Lenin's mausoleum by Shchusev and the *Izvestia* Building by Barkhin, both in Moscow. Constructivist principles produced the 1st examples of the 'new typography' (*Lissitzky) and pioneer work in poster and exhibition design (Soviet Pavilion of the International Press Exhibition, Cologne, 1930 designed by Lissitzky). Through Kandinsky, Gabo and Moholy-Nagy constructivist ideas had a basic influence on the creation of the 'international functionalist style' of architecture and industrial design in W. Europe in the 1920s, chiefly propagated by the Bauhaus.

Consuelo (1842). Novel by George Sand.

Conti princes of. A cadet branch of the House of Bourbon-Condé. Notable members were Armand (1629–68), who patronized Molière, though he later wrote a *Traité de la comédie et des spectacles* (1666) condemning the theatre; and Louis-François (1717–76), who befriended J.-J. Rousseau and Beaumarchais.

continuity: *film techniques

continuo (this Italian term is more common than the English, 'thorough bass' or 'through bass'). From about 1600 a convention developed of writing a separate part, the basso c., which consisted simply of the lowest notes throughout the composition. This reinforcement of the lower parts became more important as polyphony gave way to *harmonic writing, the c. becoming the foundation of the harmonic structure. This bass line, played on a keyboard instrument and a string instrument, often, though not always, had numbers to denote the harmonies required (*harmony) and given this FIGURED BASS the keyboard performer could provide the basic chords, embellished tastefully, or not.

continuous representation. A painting which represents on the same canvas various consecutive elements in a story; the type was sometimes used by medieval and early Renaissance artists.

contour. In a painting or drawing, the line defining a shape. A line in this sense can suggest, by modulation in thickness and intensity, spatial relationships and textures, and thus is not simply an outline.

contralto. The lowest pitched female voice with the approximate compass of an 8ve and a 6th up from the G below middle C. Also *alto.

contrapposto. Italian term used also in English to describe a posture of the human body, in a painting or sculpture, in which the upper torso is twisted on the same axis as the legs but in a different plane.

Contrat Social, Du (1762). A treatise on political philosophy by J.-J. *Rousseau.

Conversation piece. Zoffany's *Queen Charlotte and her two sons*

Continuous representation. Giovanni di Paolo's *St John the Baptist*

contredanse: *country dance

conversation piece. A type of group portrait, common in the 18th c., often of a family depicted in the setting of their library or garden. The sitters are normally engaged in some everyday occupation. There are a few 20th-c. examples such as Orpen's *Homage to Manet.* To use the term of an object so unusual as to be likely to provoke conversation is a recent and unconnected idea.

Converse Frederick Shepherd (1871–1940). U.S. composer and up to 1907 teacher at the New England Conservatory and Harvard. His own teachers included J. K. Paine and J. Rheinberger and his music has close affinities to the Boston classicists. Works include *The Pipe of Desire* (1906), the 1st U.S. opera performed by the New York Metropolitan Opera, the fantasy for orchestra *Flivver Ten Million* (1927), on the 10 millionth Ford car, 4 symphonies, choral works and chamber music.

Conway Jack (1887–1952). U.S. film director. C. specialized in adventure films during the 1920s. In the 1930s his work included 2 Jean Harlow films as well as the most famous version of *A Tale of Two Cities* (1935) in which the action sequences were directed by Val Lewton and Jacques Tourneur, their 1st collaboration.

Cooke Arnold (Atkinson) (1906–). English composer at first heavily influenced by Hindemith, his teacher, but later gaining independence and showing affinities to Brahmsian classicism. C. has written the opera *Mary Barton*, a symphony, a piano concerto, and chamber music.

Cooper Alexander (*fl.* 1630–60). English painter and brother of S.C. He was trained by his uncle J. Hoskins and worked mainly on the Continent.

Cooper Gary (1901–61). U.S. film actor. Rugged and laconic hero of dozens of westerns and war films, C. was already starring during the 1920s in comedies and action films. His pictures include: *The Virginian* (1929), *Morocco* (1931), *Mr Deeds Goes to Town* (1936), *Sergeant York* (1941), which won an Oscar, *High Noon* (1952), another Oscar.

Cooper James Fenimore (1789–1851). U.S. novelist. Imitating European fashion, he began as a self-conscious recreator of Scott's manner in America but concluded with a career which laid the foundations for U.S. fiction and mythology. Admired by Hugo and other 19th-c. romantics, he was influential in Europe as in his native country. C.'s achievement rests firmly on the Leatherstocking Saga: *The Pioneers* (1823), *The Last of the Mohicans* (1826), *The Prairie* (1827), *The Pathfinder* (1840) and *The Deerslayer* (1841). His theme is the confrontation of Western civilization and indigenous American life at the frontier. His scene is American nature. His heroes are Natty Bumppo, the naturally pious skilled white hunter refusing urban life, and Chingachgook, the American natural gentleman in the form of the Noble Savage, the Red Indian.

Cooper Merian C. (1893–). U.S. film director and producer. After collaborating with *Shoedsack, C. became a producer.

Cooper Samuel (1609–73). English miniaturist whose portraits have a high place, both as historical records and as works of art. He was trained by his uncle, J. Hoskins, miniaturist at the court of Charles I. According to Horace Walpole, C. 'first gave the strength and freedom of oil to the miniature'. His skill appears to have been limited to painting the face of his subjects. Some of his best work is at the V. and A., London, but there is a fine, unfinished portrait from life of Oliver Cromwell in the coll. of the Duke of Buccleuch.

Cooper William. Pseud. of Harry Summerfield Hoff (1910–). English novelist whose works, e.g. *Scenes from Provincial Life* (1950) and *Scenes from Married Life* (1961), often satirize class and sexual taboos.

Coornhert Dirck Volkertsz (1522–90). Dutch theologian, engraver, poet and playwright. C. was the 1st Dutch poet to produce morality plays which departed from the traditions of *rederijker verse.

Copeau Jacques (1879–1949). French actor and producer who has had great influence in Europe and America. In 1913 he opened his own theatre, the Vieux-Colombier in Paris; opposed to modern realism, he produced much Molière and Shakespeare, trs. many of the latter's plays into French.

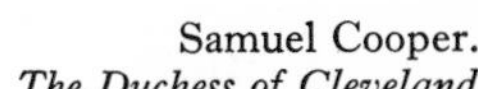

Samuel Cooper.
The Duchess of Cleveland

Contrapposto.
Michelangelo's *Victory*

Corbels

Aaron Copland

Cor anglais

Coperario or Coprario (originally 'Cooper') John or Giovanni (1575?–1626). English composer who Italianized his name and style during a visit to Italy. His most important work was in the development of the viol fantasy and particularly his suites and fantasies for viols with organ continuo.

Copland Aaron (1900–). American composer taught by Goldmark and Boulanger; he has also written and lectured on music and championed U.S. music, e.g. organizing with R. Sessions a series of concerts (1928–31). C. made a conscious attempt at a specifically American idiom using jazz elements, e.g. *Dance Symphony* (1925), and N. American folk-tunes and Latin American themes. His earlier work was rhythmically complex and harmonically austere but from the mid 1930s he aimed to simplify his style. His works include the opera *The Tender Land* (1954), the ballets *Rodeo* (1942) and *Appalachian Spring* (1944), 3 symphonies, a piano concerto, the orchestral suite *El salón México* (1936), chamber music and film music, e.g. for *Of Mice and Men* (1939) and *Our Town* (1940). C.'s books include *Our New Music* (1941).

Copley John Singleton (1737–1815). U.S. painter. From 1774 he lived first in Italy, then in England, where he was greatly influenced by Reynolds and Benjamin West. Having won a reputation as a portrait painter, he embarked on large historical paintings, e.g. *Death of Major Pierson* (1783; Tate) in which C. paints himself as a child fleeing with his family from the battle. This expansion of a small incident to the proportions of a panorama was copied in both French and English 19th-c. painting.

Coppée François (1842–1908). French poet and author of several successful comedies. Called '*poète des humbles*' because he wrote about ordinary people. His 1st poems were Parnassian in style, but in such works as *Les humbles* (1872) he developed a more intimate manner.

Coppélia. Ballet with music by L. Delibes, choreographed by A. Saint-Léon, 1st performed in Paris in 1870. Frantz, the hero, falls in love with a life-size doll, C., in the window of the village toy maker, old Dr Coppélius, who tries to bring C. to life. Swanilda, Frantz's fiancée, takes the doll's place and convinces Coppélius of his success. The doll is broken, the old man repaid for its loss and Frantz and Swanilda happily married. The original version, with choreography based closely on Hungarian folk-dances, and with a girl playing Frantz, is still performed by the Paris Opéra, the Royal Ballet using the version by L. Ivanov and E. Cecchetti.

Coppo di Marcovaldo (1225–74). Florentine painter in the Byzantine style.

Coq d'Or, Le. 3-act opera-ballet with choreography by Fokine, music by Rimsky-Korsakov and décor by Goncharova, 1st performance 1914; Fokine shortened it to a 1-act ballet in 1937.

Coques Gonzales (1614–84). Flemish portrait and genre painter known as the 'little Van Dyck' because he adapted Van Dyck's stately manner to small-size pictures, often conversation pieces.

Coquillart Guillaume (*c.* 1450–1510). French poet. His *La plaidoié d'entre la Simple et la Rusée*, *L'Enqueste . . .* and *Droits Nouveaux* are *causes grasses*, i.e. farcical versions of legal proceedings usually performed by associations of lawyers' clerks.

cor anglais. A tenor musical instrument of the *oboe family. A literal trs. of the name is 'English horn' but the instrument has no connection with the horn, except that it was once slightly curved in shape, and no special connections with England.

Corbeau, Le (1943). Film directed by H.-G. *Clouzot.

corbel. Architectural term for a block of stone projecting from a wall and acting as a bracket; a CORBEL-TABLE is a stone parapet round the tops of a wall (in effect a cornice) supported by corbels. A CORBELLED ARCH OF VAULT is constructed of blocks of stone, each block slightly overlapping the one below to the point where the 2 sides can be spanned by a slab.

Corbière Édouard-Joachim, called Tristan (1845–75). French poet, little known until noticed by Verlaine and included in his *Les *Poètes maudits* (1884). The only vol. to appear during his lifetime was *Les Amours jaunes* (1873; selection trs. 1954).

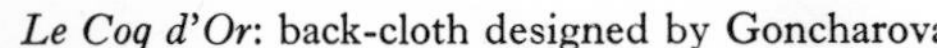

Le Coq d'Or: back-cloth designed by Goncharova

Copley. *Death of Major Pierson*

Corinth. *Walchensee Panorama* (1924)

Corelli Arcangelo (1653–1713). Italian composer and violin virtuoso and teacher. He studied the violin at Bologna Academy (1670) but settled at Rome from about 1675. Here he met Queen Christina of Sweden, dedicating to her his op. 1, twelve 3-part church sonatas, and became friend and music director to Cardinal P. Ottoboni, nephew of Pope Alexander VIII. C.'s music, all of it instrumental, is restrainedly classical in style, and his writing for the violin, though not technically advanced, has a sensitivity and fitness for the instrument not previously equalled; for this C. is considered the founder of violin style. His works include the famous *12 Concerti Grossi* (the first of which was performed in 1682) which established the form of the *concerto grosso; his music influenced Couperin 'Le Grand', Bach and Handel's early work besides the succeeding Italian generation, e.g. G. Tartini. His violin school at Rome included F. Geminiani and P. Locatelli among its pupils.

Corelli Marie. Pseud. of Mary Mackay (1855–1924). English novelist. Among her once very popular melodramatic novels are *Barabbas* (1893), *The Sorrows of Satan* (1895) and *Boy* (1900).

Corinth Lovis (1858–1925). German painter. G. studied at Königsberg Academy (1876–80) and the Académie Julian, Paris (1884–5). He became one of the leaders of German impressionism, joining the Munich *Sezession; but his late style–e.g. his paintings of the Walchensee–comes close to expressionism, developing from his interest in dramatic scenes and facial expression using *impasto, and very free brushwork.

Corinthian: *Orders

Coriolan or 'Coriolanus' (1807). Overture by Beethoven to a play by H. von Collin.

Coriolanus (publ. 1623). Tragedy by *Shakespeare, written *c.* 1607. Its sources were Sir Thomas *North's trs. of Plutarch and possibly Camden's *Remaines.*

Corman Roger (1926–). U.S. film director. From his 1st films in the mid 1950s C. has specialized in B features, of which he has directed about 40 and produced 20 more. With *The Fall of the House of Usher* (1960), he launched a series of more elaborate adaptations from *Poe, which were commercially very successful. His one personal film, *The Intruder* or *The Stranger* (1961), about an *agent-provocateur* in the Deep South, is among the most intelligent screen treatments of the colour bar.

Corneille Pierre (1606–84). French playwright, the founder of classical drama in France. A lawyer by profession, he belonged to the provincial bourgeoisie, and rarely frequented the literary world of the Parisian *salons.* Yet the even tenor of his life contrasted strongly with his dramatic works. Here he explored the psychology of the human will, stripping the action of external events and concentrating it within the limits of the *unities of time, place and action. C.'s boldness and simplicity of language, combined with logical precision, and an acute sense of the rhythm of classical French, constitute a style eminently suited to a drama of intellectual conflict, where the passions are consciously subdued by reason, and heroism is the affirmation of will. His greatest tragedies *Le Cid* (1637; 1637), *Horace* (1640; 1671), *Cinna* (1640; 1713), *Polyeucte* (1641; 1655), *Rodogune* (1644; 1765) and *Nicomède* (1651; 1671) present a study of psychological crisis of permanent universal significance. But they also reflect the manners of the age. Although he drew most of his characters from classical history, C. made little attempt to reconstruct their real personalities. Instead he presented an idealized portrait of powerful intellect and driving ambition, typical of contemporary political leaders such as the Cardinal de Retz. However, the main literary influences in his work are those of Latin writers, Seneca and Livy for instance, and of 16th-c. Spanish dramatists. *Le Menteur* (1643) is the best known of C.'s comedies. The tragedies he wrote after 1659–*Oedipe, Sertorius, Sophonisbe, Othon, Agésilas, Attila, Tite et Bérénice, Suréna*–were too complicated and obscure for public taste and were overshadowed by those of his younger contemporary Racine.

Corneille Thomas also known as 'Corneille de l'Isle' (1625–1709). French playwright, brother of Pierre C., whom he replaced in the Académie (1685). C. was a skilful and prolific, but not particularly original writer. He wrote *Timocrate* (1656) and *Ariane* (1672), and the comedies *Le Festin de pierre* (1677), a verse adaptation of Molière's *Don Juan*, and *Le Geôlier de soi-même* (1655).

Arcangelo Corelli

Pierre Corneille

French theatre in the time of Corneille

Corot. *View of the Roman Forum*

Corot. *Woman with a Pearl.* Also *cliché verre

Corneille de Lyon (attributed). *The Earl of Hertford*

Coromandel lacquer screen; Chinese, reign of K'ang Hsi (1662–1722)

Corneille de Lyon (*fl.* 1534–74). Dutch portrait painter who worked at Lyons. Although his contemporary reputation was considerable no authenticated work by him exists. Usually attributed to him are a number of small portraits in some respects resembling F. Clouet's work.

Cornelisz Cornelis (Cornelis van Haarlem) (1562–1638). Dutch mannerist painter of portraits and Biblical and mythological subjects; a pupil of P. Aertsen.

Cornelisz Jakob (Jakob van Oostsanen) (d. before 1533). Dutch painter who worked in Amsterdam and is sometimes known as 'C. van Amsterdam'. He was an early representative of the Dutch school; to a hard style reminiscent of late Gothic he added ornamental features.

Cornelisz Lucas (1495–1552). Dutch portrait painter and court painter to Henry VIII of England.

Cornelius Peter (1824–74). German composer. In 1852 he became associated with *Liszt and a publicist for the New German school, writing for the *Neuen Zeitschrift für Musik.* His famous work, the comic opera *Der Barbier von Bagdad*, failed at its 1st performance in Weimar, 1858. His grand operas *Der Cid* (1865) and the uncompleted *Gunlöd* show Wagner's influence.

Cornelius Peter von (1783–1867). German painter, for a time a member of the *Nazarene group before settling in Munich, where he did much work, notably large-scale frescoes.

Cornet

cornet. Valved brass instrument in B♭ or A, similar to the trumpet in range but with a wider bore and deeper mouthpiece and consequently a less brilliant tone. It was developed in the 1820s and displaced the trumpet in many 19th-c. European orchestras. Parts specifically for c., i.e. not trumpet parts played on it, sometimes occur, e.g. Bizet's opera *Carmen* and Stravinsky's ballet *Petrushka.* It is now chiefly found in traditional jazz bands, brass and military bands.

Cornett

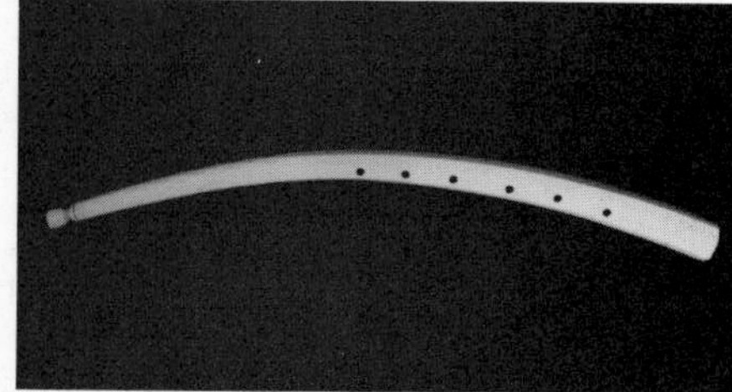

cornett. Musical wind instrument of soprano compass important from the 16th to early 18th c. It was made of wood bound in leather, or of ivory, with finger-holes like those of a recorder but played with a mouthpiece comparable to a trumpet's. It formed the natural soprano to the trombones and usually played parts of virtuoso brilliancy In the MUTE C. the mouthpiece was not detachable but hollowed out of the tube itself (also *serpent).

Cornfield Hubert (1929–). U.S. film director. After making 3 good low-budget thrillers like *Plunder Road* (1958) he made a more ambitious picture in *The Third Voice* (1959), the story of a perfect crime. His only completed film since then, *Pressure Point* (1962), was re-ed by its producer, Stanley *Kramer.

Cornhill Magazine, The. English monthly magazine founded in 1860. Thackeray was its 1st ed. (1860–2).

cornice. Architectural term for the top, projecting section of an entablature; also applied in non-classical architecture to any similar horizontal, projecting feature on a building, or inside a room where wall and ceiling meet. Diagram *Orders.

Cornyshe William (*c.* 1468–1523). English composer and court musician to Henry VIII in charge of the masques and court entertainment; he wrote church music and instrumental fantasies but above all songs of great poignancy and beauty.

Coromandel screen. Oriental folding screens of painted lacquerware or incised Coromandel ware, were much imported into Europe in the 17th c. mainly through the Dutch trading station of Bantam in the Malay Peninsula (also known as 'Bantam-work').

Coronach. A lamentation sung in Scotland and Ireland in the 16th c. at the funeral of a clan leader. During the chanting, it was customary for the women to set up a great wailing.

Coronation concerto. Nickname for *Mozart's piano concerto in D (K.537; 1788).

Coronation Mass. Nickname (1) for Mozart's mass in C (K.317; 1779); (2) an alternative name for Haydn's *Nelson Mass.*

Corot (Jean-Baptiste) Camille (1796–1875). French painter of landscape and portraits. Trained in the classical tradition of French landscape, founded chiefly on Poussin, C. went to Italy in 1825 and returned there many times. There are 3 distinct styles in his painting. His early classical landscapes, painted in rich panels of colour, often in the full glare of an Italian noon, e.g. *View of the Colosseum* (Louvre), influenced Cézanne and other post-impressionists in their composition by tonal contrasts instead of strict drawing. In the 2nd style are the soft and silvery woodland scenes painted from the 1850s to his death, e.g. *Ville d'Avray* (Met. Mus.). Finally he painted a few portraits and studies of women, e.g. *Woman with a Pearl* (Louvre). The last are of a very high quality and have recently won recognition.

corps de ballet. A group of dancers, performing together as one body, who form the 'chorus' of a ballet, commenting in movement on the main action of the solo dancers.

Correggio born Antonio Allegri (*c.* 1494–1534). Italian painter called after his birthplace in Emilia. C. worked all his life in the district around Parma, yet he seems to have been aware to a remarkable degree of the innovations in painting in Rome, Florence and Venice. He was probably the pupil of F. Bianchi Ferrari, but an early visit to Mantua brought him under the influence of L. Costa and Mantegna. Soon, however, the revolutionary style of Leonardo had softened C.'s painting. He combined this softness, a sort of 'golden haze', which is characteristic of all his major work, with a strong sense of modelling and a delight in rendering flesh tones. Unlike most N. Italian painters of the time, he did not simply surrender himself to the style of Leonardo: instead of Leonardo's creation of an unearthly beauty, C.'s subjects, however idealized, are sensual and very much of this earth. There is no evidence that C. was ever in Rome, but he was certainly informed of Michelangelo's frescoes in the Sistine Chapel and those of Raphael in the Vatican Stanze. Qualities of all 3 of the leading painters of the high Renaissance are reflected in C.'s madonnas. Equally popular were his mythological subjects, e.g. *Mercury Instructing Cupid Before Venus* (N.G., London). Today, he is chiefly considered important for the boldness of his imagination. C. was one of the 1st major artists to experiment with the dramatic effects of artificial lighting, e.g. *Agony in the Garden* (Wellington Mus., London), in which the figure of Christ alone lights the dark garden, and in *Holy Night* (G. Gal., Dresden), in which the light comes from the Christ-child in the crib. C. is also seen as the vital link between the early experiments in illusionist painting of Mantegna at Mantua and the baroque painters of ceilings. In *Ganymede* (K. Mus., Vienna) C. successfully depicts the figure of the shepherd carried into space by the bird of Jove. In his frescoes in the Camera di S. Paolo, Parma, or in the cupola of S. Giovanni Evangelista, Parma, figures flying freely in space are seen from below, and in the *Assumption* (Cathedral, Parma) a vision of a mass ascent into Heaven is rendered for the spectator in visually convincing terms.

Del Cossa. *April*

Corsair, The (1814). Narrative poem by Byron.

Corsaire, Le (1831). An overture by Berlioz based on Fenimore Cooper's novel *The Red Rover*.

Corso Gregory (1930–). U.S. poet, one of the *beats. C.'s poems show surrealist influence, proceeding by word- or image-association. His colls include *The Vestal Lady of Brattle* (1955), *Gasoline* (1958) and *The Happy Birthday of Death* (1960).

Cortegiano, Il Libro del (1528). Book by *Castiglione.

Cortona Pietro da: *Pietro da Cortona

Corvo Baron: Frederick *Rolfe

Così fan tutte (1790). *Opera buffa* by *Mozart, text by L. da Ponte.

Cosimo Piero di: *Piero di Cosimo

Cossa Francesco del (*c.* 1435–*c.* 77). Ferrarese painter, possibly a pupil of C. Tura but influenced by Mantegna and Squarcione; some of his work, e.g. *Autumn* (Berlin) follows Piero della Francesca. His masterly frescoes *The Months* (*c.* 1470) for the Palazzo di Schifanoia, Ferrara, depict, in a detailed style, fanciful scenes of court activities.

Costa Joaquín (1844–1911). Spanish historian and literary critic. He wrote on the reasons for Spain's decadence as a great nation, and the need for a national revival. He was also the author of several valuable studies on early Spanish poetry.

Correggio. Angel musicians; detail from the *Assumption*

Correggio. *Holy Night*

Cosway. *Mrs Fitzherbert*

Cotán. *Quince, Cabbage, Melon and Cucumber*

Lorenzo Costa. *A Concert*

Cotes. *Paul Sandby*

Lucio Costa, Niemeyer, and others. Ministry of Education and Health (1937–43)

Costa Lorenzo (1459/60–1535). Italian painter of the school of *Ferrara. With F. Francia he worked for the Bentivoglio family in Bologna painting portraits and religious subjects. In 1507 he succeeded Mantegna as court painter at Mantua.

Costa Lucio (1902–). The patriarch of modern architecture in Brazil. Both as teacher and architect he is responsible for the high standard of the best Brazilian buildings. He was responsible for inviting Le Corbusier to design the Ministry of Health Building in Rio, a building which led to the adoption of a lyrical, luxurious architecture in Brazil based on the work of Le Corbusier. His 1956 town plan for Brasilia, the new capital, is now being executed.

Costa Sir Michael (Andrew Agnus) (1808–84). Naturalized English composer and conductor, Italian by birth. His stage music and operas were highly successful but above all, as a conductor, he set a new high standard for English orchestral playing.

costruzione legittima. An early form of *perspective used in the 1st half of the 15th c.; it used only 1 vanishing point and produced a certain amount of distortion.

costumbristas. School of 19th-c. Spanish novelists who dealt with the life of their native cities and provinces. Descriptions of local types and customs and the locality itself were emphasized rather than plot or the writer's views or feelings. The leading c. were Fernán Caballero, Larra, Mesonero Romanos and Estébanez Calderón.

Cosway Richard (1740–1821). Fashionable English miniaturist, portrait painter, picture dealer and eccentric, a friend of the Prince Regent. He revived the art of portrait miniatures and extended the use of ivory as a ground. His delicate, elegant, superbly executed work forms a complement to the artificiality of his age. One of his finest portraits is that of Mrs Fitzherbert (Wallace Coll., London). His wife MARIA (*fl.* 1820) was an etcher and book illustrator.

Cotán Juan Sánchez· (1561–1627). Spanish still-life painter whose compositions created an esoteric relationship between a few simple objects painted with great naturalism and 3-dimensional solidity. C.'s work, like that of his contemporary F. de Zurbarán, was influenced by the still-life of Caravaggio.

Cotes Francis (1726–70). English portrait painter and pastellist; a founder-member of the R.A. His early oils were influenced by pastel technique but in the late 1750s he imitated Reynolds's style. His oil portrait of the artist Paul Sandby (1759; Tate) is one of the best examples of his work. His brother SAMUEL (1734–1818) was a miniaturist.

cotière. A long chain with pendant jewel worn by great ladies in the 16th c. It was often elaborately wrought and set with jewels and was frequently worn square, bordering the low square neckline.

Cotman John Sell (1782–1842). English painter and engraver of the *Norwich school and 1st professor of drawing at King's College, London. His austere early watercolours, landscapes often painted in broad washes of a minimum number of colours: yellows, greens, browns and blues, are now highly prized. A number of them, including *Chirk Aqueduct*, are at the V. and A., London. C. visited Normandy in 1817–18 and 1820. He made many engravings of buildings there and in England illustrated books on antiquities.

Cottafavi Vittorio (1914–). Italian film and television director. Given his first chance to direct by de *Sica with *I nostri sogni* (1942) from U. Betti, his 1st films were neo-realist works, but from the early 1950s his work has been in melodramas and period spectaculars, a limited genre which he has handled with unique brilliance. In particular, *Hercules Conquers Atlantis* (1961) is remarkable for its handling of action and setting.

Cotten Joseph (1905–). U.S. actor. As a member of Orson Welles's theatre co., C. made his début in *Citizen Kane* (1941), continuing with *The Magnificent Ambersons* (1942) and other films. The best of his other films were *Duel in the Sun* (1948) and *The Third Man* (1949).

Cottin Madame Sophie (1770–1807). French novelist, author of 5 sentimental novels of adventure which achieved considerable popularity. They include *Mathilde* (1805; *Matilda and Malek Adhel, the Saracen*, 1833) and *Élisabeth, ou les Exilés de Sibérie* (1806; 1809).

Cotman. *Chirk Aqueduct*

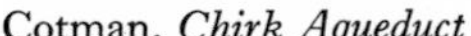

Cotman. *Mountain pass in the Tyrol*

Cotton Charles (1630–87). English poet and trs. He wrote a 2nd part to the 5th ed. of *Walton's *Compleat Angler,* and trs. (1685) the essays of Montaigne. Outstanding among his poems are *The Retirement, Epistle to John Bradshaw,* once among the series of *Quatrains,* the fantastic *Winter Quatrains* and the *Evening Quatrains* (which figure in Britten's *Serenade* for tenor, horn and strings).

couching. An embroidery stitch in which threads laid on the surface of the fabric are held down with a 2nd thread, i.e. the c. thread. This travels at the back of the fabric, emerging only occasionally to make a small stitch encompassing the main thread or threads. Many elaborations of the stitch occur, of which the most important is underside c. In this widely used medieval stitch the c. thread encompasses the main thread, then passes back through the same hole in the fabric and is drawn down to the back of the work.

cou-de-pied. French term used in ballet to describe the lower part of the leg between calf and ankle. Sur le c.-d.-p. is a position from which many ballet steps are begun, with one foot resting against that part of the supporting leg.

Coughtry Graham (1931–). Canadian painter. His most recent works are of anonymous figures in impasto, conveying a feeling of uneasiness, sometimes of horror.

coulisse. The French term for the *wings of a theatre, used in English as an art term to describe buildings, trees, etc., which may flank a landscape scene and thus conduct the eye to the horizon; Claude often used the device.

Counterfeiters, The (1926). Novel by *Gide.

counterpoint (probably derived from the Latin *punctus contra punctum,* i.e. 'point against point' or 'note against note'). The art of composing independent lines of music so that they shall form a coherent whole when played simultaneously. In contrapuntal music the primary interest is the 'horizontal' movement of the independent parts; in *harmonic music the primary effects come from the sequence of vertical structures formed by the notes sounding at any given time, i.e. the chords. During the ascendancy of the major-minor harmonic system (from the mid 17th c. to the 20th c.) the chords and harmonic progressions of contrapuntal music (e.g. Bach's) conformed to this system, and such music is therefore sometimes called HARMONIC C. Before the 17th c. (*polyphony) and in much 20th-c. music such harmonic considerations are not paramount and such writing is therefore sometimes called LINEAR C. The rules of academic or STRICT C. were derived from the methods of the polyphonic composers. In actual composition these rules are naturally bent or broken, producing FREE C. When the upper and lower parts of a composition can be interchanged without producing a bad musical effect we have INVERTIBLE C.

Count of Monte Cristo, The (1845). Novel by A. *Dumas *père.*

country dance. English type of round dance which became popular at court. In England the village peasant dance became popular at court in the 16th c.; and in the 17th c., partly following John *Playford's compilation of c. d.s *The English Dancing Master* (1650), became popular abroad, e.g. the French term *contredanse,* which derived from the English.

Country Wife, The (1675). Comedy by W. *Wycherley.

coup de théâtre. A surprising and theatrically effective event in the action of a play; it is not simply an unexpected turn of events but some shocking or sudden thing which seizes the spectator and leaves him breathless.

Couperin. Family of French musicians stemming from Chaumes-en-Brie whose most important members are listed alphabetically below.

Couperin Armand-Louis (1725–89). Son of Nicolas C. and his successor as organist at St-Gervais and organist at other churches including Notre-Dame. He was one of the most renowned organists of his time. His compositions were elegant but slight.

Couperin Céleste-Thérèse (1793–1860). Granddaughter of Armand-Louis and last of the family.

Couperin Charles (1638–78/9). Youngest brother of L.C. and his successor as organist of St-Gervais. He was father of François C. 'Le Grand'.

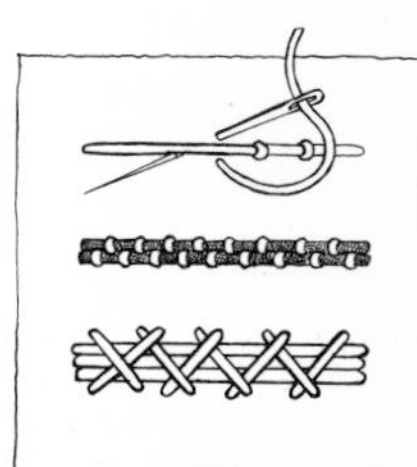

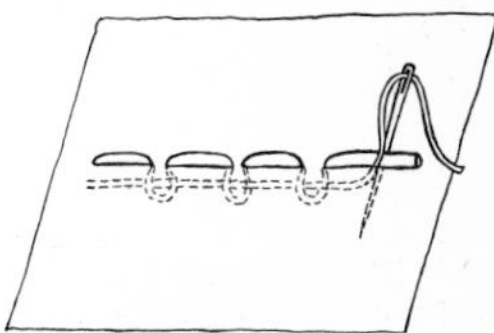

Couching

Coulisse. Turner's *Rome, from the Vatican*

Coulisse. Claude's *Seaport Embarkment of the Queen of Sheba*

François Couperin 'Le Grand'

Couperin François (*c.* 1630–1701). Younger brother of L.C., a pupil of Chambonnières.

Couperin François called 'Le Grand' (1668–1733). French composer, organist and harpsichordist; son of Charles C. In 1693 he joined the Chapel Royal and rapidly rose as music teacher in court circles. In 1730 he retired from his posts as organist and royal harpsichordist and died virtually forgotten, his music having become unfashionable. His eclipse, especially in France, lasted for over a c.
C. disliked effect for its own sake–'I prefer what touches me to what surprises me' he said. As a young man he was influenced by Corelli, particularly the trio sonatas, himself introducing this form to France; he later reacted against the Italian style, and then in 1724 wrote his famous series of pieces *Les Goûts Réunis* to reconcile the contemporary conflict between the French and Italian styles. C.'s music is often intensely lyrical; its prevailing style is of restrained classicism but there are moments when the mood appears almost romantic. His church music includes 2 early organ masses and the 3 surviving sections of *Les Leçons des Ténèbres*, his great setting of the *tenebrae* written for solo soprano voices and continuo; the bold harmonies, variations of rhythm and tonality and the exactly contrived ornamentation make this one of the great works of religious music. Among C.'s chamber works are the 4-part sonata *La Sultane*, the trio sonatas *L'Impériale*, *Apothéose de Lulli* (1725) and *L'Apothéose de Corelli* (1724) and suites for 2 viols (1728). His *Ordres* or suites for harpsichord consist of several short pieces with such titles as *The Voluptuary* or *The Butterflies*. In his treatise on harpsichord technique *L'Art de toucher le clavecin* (1716), used by J. S. Bach, C. emphasized that ornamentation was an integral part of the music and should be played as directed by the composer.

Courbet. *L'Atelier du peintre* (detail)

Couperin Louis (1626–61). French musician. About 1650 C. and his younger brothers, François and Charles were introduced to Paris by J. Chambonnières, royal harpsichordist, who had been impressed by a birthday aubade they had performed for him. C. was a pupil of Chambonnières and became organist of St-Gervais. His audacious harmonies, bold chromaticism and vigour combined with elegance make him one of the greatest French composers of his time.

Couperin Marguerite-Louise (*c.* 1676–1728). Soprano singer, daughter of François C. the Elder and famous interpreter of works by her cousin François C. 'Le Grand'.

Couperin Nicolas (1680–1748). Son of François the Elder and successor of his cousin François 'Le Grand' as organist at St-Gervais.

Couperus Louis (1863–1923). Dutch novelist, whose work reflects his view of man as a helpless victim of heredity and environment. Works include *Eline Vere* (1889; 1892), *De boeken der kleine zielen* (1901–3; *The Books of the Small Souls*, 1914–18) and his charming *Van en over myzelf en anderen* (1910–17).

Courbet (Jean-Désiré-)Gustave (1819–77). The leading French realist painter of his time, C. was controversial both as an artist and as a public figure. Born at Ornans, Franche-Comté, he studied at Besançon and Paris, but was scornful of tuition and largely self-taught. He first took his subjects from life in the artists' studios in Paris and from the countryside around Ornans. In 1850 C.'s *Burial at Ornans* (Louvre) caused a sensation at the Salon. This enormous painting, containing over 30 life-size figures, was attacked on the alleged grounds that it presented the clergy as cynical and the peasants as brutalized. C. had intended it as a sincere, but not conventionally idealized, group portrait of the villagers with whom he had grown up. Seascapes, landscapes, flower paintings, studies of animals, nudes and a few large-scale genre paintings followed. All were savagely criticized. C. responded with an arrogant and angry wit which became celebrated. Many of the nudes are splendidly coloured–perhaps only Titian could have equalled the contrasts C. achieves between the tones of a fur or of a girl's hair against the tones of her flesh. The winter landscapes, e.g. *Rocks at Ornans* (Phillips Coll., Washington), have a rough and earthy texture which makes them at the same time realistic and evocative.
In 1855 and 1867 C. withdrew from the Salon and held his own exhibition in the grounds, an action which was to set a precedent followed by the impressionists. In 1871 he sided with the Commune, was made director of Museums and organized the destruction of the Napoleonic column in the Place Vendôme. For these activities he was later imprisoned and heavily fined. He died in exile in Switzerland.

Courbet. *Rocks at Ornans*

Courbet. *Woman with a Parrot*

By rejecting the ideals of both the classical and the romantic schools and by choosing such subjects as the everyday life of the poor, C. prepared the way for artists as diverse as Millet and Degas. The independence of his behaviour and scorn of academic training had a lasting influence on the artists of Paris.

course. In plucked musical instruments such as the lute and guitar, 2 strings often serve 1 note, thus increasing the volume; these 2 strings tuned in unison or at the 8ve are called a course.

Courteline Georges. Pseud. of G. Moinaux (1858–1929). French humorous writer. His works include the stories *Les Gaîtés de l'Escadron* (1886) and *Boubouroche* (1893), and the novel *Lidoire et la biscotte* (1892).

Courtier, The (1528). Book by *Castiglione.

courtly love: *Provençal culture

Courtois (Cortese) Guillaume (Guglielmo) (1628–79) called 'Il Borgognone'. French baroque painter. He went to Italy with his brother J.C. and studied in Rome under Pietro da Cortona. *Martyrdom of St Andrew*, over the high altar of S. Andrea al Quirinale, is an example of his work in Roman churches.

Courtois (Cortese) Jacques (Giacomo) (1621–75) called 'Il Borgognone'. French painter who worked in Italy, specializing in battle scenes which rivalled those of Salvator Rosa. Towards the end of his life he became a Jesuit and painted religious subjects for the churches of the order.

Court Theatre London: *Royal Court Theatre

Cousin Jean the Elder (*c.* 1490–1560/1). French painter and designer. Working in Sens he designed the stained-glass window of St Eutropius (1536) for the cathedral and painted (probably) there the 1st great French nude, *Eva prima Pandora* (Louvre). He designed the tapestries of the life of St Mammès (begun 1543) for Langres cathedral.

Cousin Jean the Younger (*c.* 1522–*c.* 94). French painter, influenced by mannerism and best known for *The Last Judgement* (Louvre). He was also a miniaturist, engraver, goldsmith, book illustrator and designer for stained glass.

Cousine Bette, La (1846). Novel by Balzac.

Cousin Pons, Le (1846–7). Novel by Balzac.

Cousins, Les (1958). Film directed by C. *Chabrol.

Coustou Guillaume (1677–1746). French sculptor, nephew and pupil of A. Coysevox and brother of the baroque sculptor NICOLAS C. (1658–1733). The baroque style exercised slight influence on Guillaume's work, which had a classic restraint. He is best known for his *Horses* made for the park at Marly and now at the entrance to the Champs-Élysées, Paris. His son GUILLAUME (1716–77) was also a sculptor whose work included statues of Mars and Venus for the Sans Souci Palace at Potsdam.

Couture Thomas (1815–79). French portrait, historical and genre painter. His small *commedia dell'arte* paintings are still popular, while the paintings on classical themes, such as the celebrated *Romans of the Decadence* (1847; Louvre) and *A Roman Feast* (Wallace Coll., London) have lost their appeal. Manet was C.'s pupil for 6 years and undoubtedly learnt much from his strong, free brushwork and bold contrasts, shown especially in the sketches and a few fine landscapes.

Covent Garden The Royal Opera House, London. First built in 1732 by John Rich and burned down in 1808; rebuilt 1809 and burned down again in 1856. The present theatre was opened in 1858. The cos now in residence are the Covent Garden Opera Co. and the Royal Ballet.

Coventry carol. An English lullaby carol preserved with music as sung in 1591 and words recorded in 1534. It is the song of the women of Bethlehem to their children about to be killed by Herod's soldiers, and was originally part of the Coventry Christmas mystery play.

Coventry Plays, The. Cycle of 14th-c. English *miracle plays.

Coverdale Miles (1488–1568). English Protestant reformer, trs. and bishop, who made the 1st English trs. of the entire Bible (1535). He worked from Latin and German versions, assisted by Tyndale's New Testament. The trs. of the Psalms from C.'s Bible is still printed in *The Book of Common Prayer*, and has had the profoundest influence on English prose.

Jean Cousin the Younger. *The Last Judgement* (detail)

Guillaume Coustou. One of the *Horses* at the entrance to the Champs-Élysées

Jean Cousin the Elder. *Eva prima Pandora*

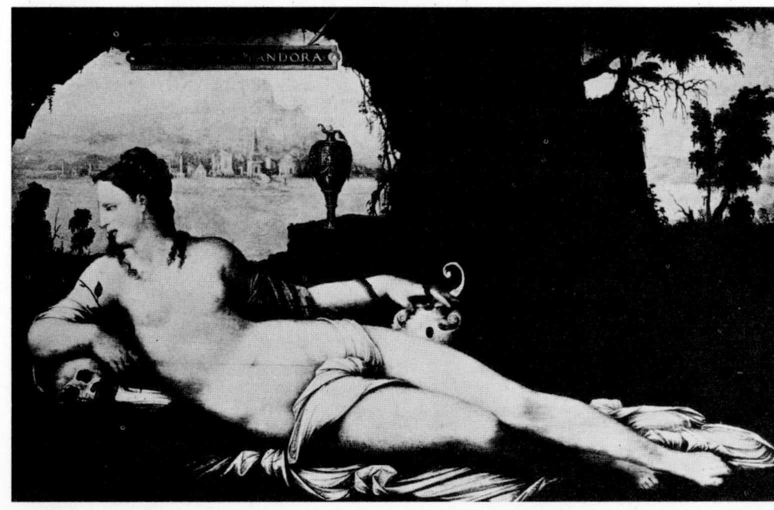

Couture. *A Roman Feast*

Cox. *Rhyl Sands*

J. R. Cozens. *The Lake of Nemi*

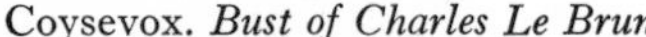

Coysevox. *Bust of Charles Le Brun*

Cowper: painting by Romney

Covered Wagon, The (1923). Film directed by J. *Cruze.

Coward Noël (Pierce) (1899–). English actor, dramatist, composer and entertainer. His plays include *Hay Fever* (1925), *Private Lives* (1930; film 1931), *This Happy Breed* (1943; film 1944) and *Blithe Spirit* (1941; film 1945). He has also written revues and operettas, including *Bitter Sweet* (1929; film 1945) and also the film script **Brief Encounter* (1945).

Cowboy (1957). Film directed by D. *Daves.

Cowell Henry (Dixon) (1897–). U.S. composer and pianist and active publicist and supporter of U.S. composers. He invented the piano *tone cluster and the 'Rhythmicon', an electronic device producing a variety of different rhythms simultaneously. His compositions include the ballets *The Building of Bánba* (1922) and *Atlantis* (1926), 4 symphonies, a piano concerto (1929), and *Reel* (1933) and *Tales of our Countryside* (1941) for orchestra.

Cowen Sir Frederic Hymen (1852–1935). English composer and conductor. He was a precocious child pianist and composer; his 1st symphony (1869) brought him recognition and his 3rd symphony *The Scandinavian* (1880) a European reputation. He also wrote stage works and oratorios.

Cowley Abraham (1618–67). English poet, essayist and botanist. Friend of R. Crashaw, and Royalist exile in Paris. Though much of his verse is full of complex conceits, he could be master of an attractive straightforwardness (*The Wish, Of Solitude, On the Death of Mr William Hervey*), which also informs his essays. His *Proposition for the Advancement of Experimental Philosophy* (1661) was a step to the foundation of the Royal Society, of which C. was a Fellow.

Cowper William (1731–1800). English poet. An extremely shy and sensitive man, Cowper suffered from attacks of depressive insanity which prevented his following a career or leading a fully independent life. His happiest years were spent in Huntingdon and Olney with the Unwin family, and it was there that most of his poetry and letters were written. His poems, mainly generalized essays of a religious or moral character of which *The Task*, also containing fine descriptions of nature, is the best, or shorter pieces on small incidents of his daily life, reveal a personality of singular humour and sweetness. Only in occasional poems can the terrible pessimism which haunted and finally overcame him be glimpsed.

Cox David (1783–1859). English painter in watercolours and oils. His *A Treatise on Landscape Painting and Effect in Water-colours* (1814) and other writings had an influence on artists throughout the 19th c. His own work became very free and broad in style and some of the effects he achieved look forward to the French impressionists, e.g. *By-road with Gipsy Tent* (V. and A., London).

Coxcie (Coxie) Michiel van (1499–1592). Flemish painter and engraver of religious subjects in the Raphaelesque style adopted after he visted Italy with his master B. van Orley. For Philip II of Spain he copied the van Eycks' altarpiece *The Adoration of the Lamb.*

Coypel Antoine (1661–1722). French painter and designer for Gobelins tapestries; son of N.C. He produced 2 of the most unequivocally baroque decorations of his age in France, the ceiling of the great gallery, Palais-Royal, Paris (1702) and the ceiling of the chapel at Versailles (1708/9), the latter based on Baciccia's ceiling for the church of the Gesù, Rome. His son CHARLES-ANTOINE (1694–1752) was also a painter.

Coypel Noël (1628–1707). French decorative painter, strongly influenced by Poussin, designer for Gobelins tapestries and for several years director of the French Academy at Rome. His son NOËL-NICOLAS (1690–1734), a mediocre but popular painter of religious and mythological subjects, was a teacher of Chardin.

Coysevox Antoine (1640–1720). French baroque sculptor at the court of Louis XIV, famous for his expressive portrait busts and his decorations at Versailles for the Galerie des Glaces, Salon de la Guerre and Escalier des Ambassadeurs. C.'s statues there, in Girardon's classical manner in which he was trained, are uninspired.

Cozens Alexander (*c.* 1717–86). One of the earliest English landscapists in watercolours; he was born in Russia and settled in England in 1746. He wrote several books; best known is

Craig set and costumes for the Moscow Art Theatre performance of *Hamlet* (1909–10)

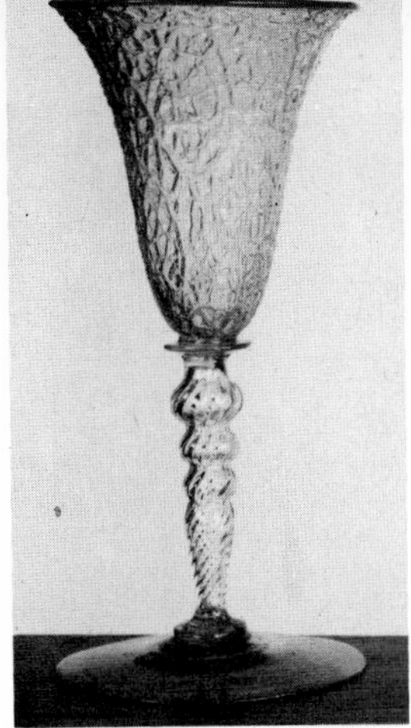

Crackle-glass, 16th-c. Venetian

Cranach. *Madonna and Child*

A New Method of Assisting the Invention in Drawing Original Compositions of Landscape (1785) describing his method of composing landscapes out of accidental ink blots (*blot drawing).

Cozens John Robert (1752–99). English landscapist in watercolours, pupil of his father Alexander. Constable described him as 'the greatest genius that ever touched landscape'. C. visited Italy via Switzerland in 1776 and again in 1782. The muted tones and generalized handling of his subjects show them to be expressions of poetic feeling rather than topographical records, and as such they influenced Turner, Girtin and other English landscape painters.

Crabbe George (1754–1832). English poet whose work draws upon the memories of his boyhood in Aldeburgh, Suffolk for its clearly observed and unsentimentalized scenes of rural life. After taking orders C. publ. *The Village* (1783) and *The Newspaper* (1785). A silence of 22 years followed during which he wrote copiously but burned most of his manuscripts. *The Parish Register* (1807) was followed by *The Borough* (1810), which contains the tragedy of Peter Grimes, a fisherman falsely accused of murder by his village. Never a polished writer, C. used Pope's rhymed decasyllabic couplet without his flexibility and brilliance. The chief beauty of his poems lies in their austere pathos and realism.

crackle-glass more properly called 'ice-glass'. The hot glass, while being blown, is momentarily plunged into water so that it is cracked and fissured into a fine network of lines often resembling frozen snow. The glass is then reheated and finished. A similar effect is said to have been achieved by rolling the heated glass in a bed of small particles of broken glass. The technique was discovered in 16th-c. Venice.

Craig Sir (Edward) Gordon (1872–). English actor, producer, son of Ellen Terry. C. regarded the theatre as comprehending all the arts; his original views had influence in America and Europe and are expressed in his works *The Art of the Theatre* (1905), *The Marionette* (1918), etc. C. believed that the director should control all aspects of a production including the set design. He himself designed and was also a woodcut artist.

Cramer Johann Baptist (1771–1858). German pianist, teacher and composer and music publ. In 1772 his father, the violinist Wilhelm C. (1745–99), moved to London; C.'s teachers included M. Clementi. C. made frequent continental tours and taught in Paris and Munich before retiring to London; he had a great reputation as a teacher and Beethoven admired his playing. His great '84 studies for piano', part of *Grosse Praktische Pianoforte Schule* (1815) are fundamental in piano literature.

Cranach. *Henry of Saxony*

Cranach Lucas, the Elder (1472–1553). German painter, engraver and book illustrator named after his birthplace. One of the most important of German artists, his training is obscure but his father was probably a painter. He travelled about the German states as an itinerant painter. In 1505 he was at Wittenberg and by 1508 he had become court painter to the Electors of Saxony, a position he held under 3 successive Electors. He was ennobled, served as burgomaster and ran a large workshop which combined a studio, an apothecary shop and a printing and bookselling establishment. He became a personal friend of Luther and many of his woodcuts were designed to promote the Protestant cause. C.'s sons, Hans (d. 1537) and Lucas the Younger (1515–86), continued his workshop and his work is thus often hard to identify. Religious paintings, particularly madonnas depicted in landscapes, often with birds and animals in the foreground, survive to show the same love of detail as those of the *Danube school, e.g. *Madonna and Child* (Alte Pina., Munich). His portraits, e.g. those of Luther, Duke Henry of Saxony and his Duchess (Dresden) are important documents of the time and some are among the 1st full-length portraits. C.'s rather awkward and self-conscious nudes are well known. One of the most natural and graceful of them is the Eve in *Adam and Eve* (Dahlem, W. Berlin). Another painting which shows C.'s very individual, almost whimsical talent is the *Judgement of Paris* (Louvre) in which Paris, shown as an elderly warrior in full armour, presents the apple to one of a group of C.'s nudes.

Crane Harold Hart (1899–1932). U.S. poet. He worked briefly in his father's candy business, as a munitions worker, a labourer and advertising man. Alcohol and homosexuality dominated his private life. He committed suicide. His initial book of poems, *White Buildings* (1926), contains some of his best shorter works.

Cranach. *Charity*. Also *Luther and colour plate 52

Cream-coloured earthenware: Wedgwood tureen, stand and cover, 1774

Lorenzo di Credi. *Madonna and two Saints*

Stephen Crane

Thomas Cranmer

The Bridge (1930) uses American myths, e.g. Brooklyn Bridge, Columbus, Pocahontas, Rip Van Winkle, Whitman, Poe and the New York subway. It was intended as an optimistic reply to *The Waste Land*, but such strength as it has lies in concentrated symbolist images, influential in post-1946 American poetry. *Collected Poems* (1933) includes the previously unpubl. and remarkable West Indian poems.

Crane Stephen (1871–1900). U.S. novelist, short-story writer, poet and war correspondent. His works, like those of his close friend Conrad, were concerned with the moral aspect of conduct. Though vigorous and realistic, his stories were written in poetic symbolic language. Works include the novels *Maggie . . .* (1893); *The Red Badge of Courage* (1895), a young soldier's 1st experience of war; *The Open Boat . . .* (1898); the short stories *The Monster . . .* (1899); and free verse *The Black Riders . . .* (1895), inspired by Emily Dickinson.

Cranes are Flying, The (1957). Film directed by M. *Kalatozov.

Cranford (1851–3). Novel by Mrs *Gaskell.

Cranko John (1927–). South African choreographer who joined Sadler's Wells in 1946. His 1950s ballets showed a great variety of composition, from the high-spirited *Pineapple Poll* (1951) to the symbolic life-cycle *Harlequin in April* in the same year. As ballet director at Stuttgart (1961), he has remounted the classics, including *Swan Lake* (1964) and brought the co. a considerable reputation.

Cranmer Thomas (1489–1556). Archbishop of Canterbury, supporting Henry VIII's claim as supreme head of the Church in England and nullifying his marriage to Catherine of Aragon. Under Queen Mary, he was martyred as a heretic. He was responsible for the First (1549) and the Second (1552) Books of *Common Prayer which he compiled with the assistance of 12 other divines.

craquelure. The fine cracks on an old painting produced by movement and shrinkage in the paint surface, the ground and the varnish. Different grounds and paint surfaces give characteristic patterns, slightly varied according to the age of the painting and the skill of the painter.

Crashaw Richard (1612/13–49). English devotional poet and priest. C. reacted from a Puritan upbringing to the High Church party, was a friend of N. Ferrar (and A. Cowley), and finally became a Roman Catholic, removing first to Paris, then to Rome. His finest religious verse (*Hymn to St Teresa*, *The Flaming Heart*, *In the Holy Nativity of our Lord God*) abandons Protestant restraint for a baroque sensuousness, multi-coloured, soaring and on fire. Besides *Steps to the Temple . . .* (1646), publ. with his secular *Delights of the Muses*, C. wrote devotional epigrams in Latin.

Crawford Francis Marion (1854–1909). U.S. writer whose wide travels provided settings for his many novels. His romantic, historical narrative was once very popular. Works include the novels *Mr Isaacs* (1882), *Saracinesca* (1887), *The White Sister* (posth. 1909), and the play *Francesca da Rimini* (1902).

Crawford Joan (1908–). U.S. film star. She is the doyen of the emotional 'woman's picture'. Not a great actress, she has adeptly tailored her personality to fashion. Among her films have been *Mildred Pierce* (1945) and *Whatever Happened to Baby Jane?* (1962).

cream-coloured earthenware. High-quality earthenware body perfected by *Wedgwood under the name of 'Queensware' and used by many Staffordshire potters from the mid 18th c.

Creation, The. English title for Haydn's oratorio *Die Schöpfung* (1798); the text was a German trs. of an English adaptation of parts of Genesis and Milton's *Paradise Lost.*

Creation Mass. Haydn's mass in B♭ (1801) so called because in the *Qui tollis* occurs a theme the composer used in his oratorio *The Creation.*

Crébillon Prosper Jolyot de (1674–1762). French dramatist. His tragedies, which include *Rhadamiste et Zénobie* (1711), are melodramatic and romantic. After a long eclipse he made a triumphant return to the theatre with *Catilina* (1748). His son Claude-Prosper, usually called CREBILLON FILS (1707–77), wrote witty novels and stories of contemporary manners.

Credi Lorenzo di (*c.* 1459–1537). Italian painter of the Florentine school and a fellow

Crenellation. The walls of Ávila

pupil of Leonardo da Vinci under Verrocchio. His style, which changed little, was formed by both these masters; his work shows the best professional manner of Florentine painting at the period. The *Noli me Tangere* (Uffizi) is a typical work.

Cremona. Italian town, home of the greatest violin-making families, the *Amati, the *Guarneri and the *Stradivari. The C. violin is distinguished not only in tone and workmanship but also by its rich red-brown varnish.

crenellation. Architectural term for an indented battlement; c.s were originally made to provide gaps (embrasures) to shoot through, though they later became purely decorative.

Cre(c)quillon Thomas (d. 1557). One of the leading Flemish composers between Josquin and Lasso. His music is characterized by its grandeur and rich harmonies, but he made no technical innovations, exploiting existing techniques, e.g. systematic imitation and the parody mass. His greatest works are his 16 masses and numerous motets, but he also composed about 200 *chansons*.

Crescentini Girolamo (1762–1846). Italian soprano, one of the last great castrati. In 1806 he was called to Paris by Napoleon, remaining there 6 years.

Cresilas (5th c. B.C.). Cretan sculptor who with Phidias and Polycleitus took part in a competition to produce figures of Amazons for the Temple of Artemis at Ephesus. Various copies of C.'s *Wounded Amazon* exist. There are also copies of his idealized portrait of Pericles.

Crespi Giovanni Battista called 'Il Cerano' (*c.* 1557–1633). Italian painter, sculptor and architect of the *Lombard school. He was head of the Milanese Academy from 1620; Guercino was his pupil.

Crespi Giuseppe Maria (1665–1747). Bolognese painter of religious subjects, portraits and genre who broke from the academic affectations of the Bolognese school. In deep tones and with heavy chiaroscuro he treated his subjects in naturalistic, even prosaic, terms, e.g. his pictures *The Seven Sacraments* (G. Gal., Dresden). His son LUIGI (1709–79) was a painter and the continuator of C. C. Malvasia's lives of the Bolognese painters.

cresting. A term derived from medieval architecture and frequently applied to silver-work. It is a foliate form of decoration, regularly and horizontally repeated, often along the top of the object. It was a common device on elaborate medieval pieces.

Crèvecoeur Michel-Guillaume Jean de, known as 'J. Hector St John de' (1735–1813). French emigrant to Canada whose extensive travels in America are described in *Voyage dans la Haute Pennsylvanie et dans L'état de New York* (1801). His best-known book is *Letters from an American Farmer* (1782), which shows Rousseau's influence and a naïve idealization of nature and primitive society. It was acclaimed by many of the English romantic poets.

crewel-work. An embroidered design, generally on linen or heavy cotton worked in colours in thin worsted. A stout needle with a large eye is used.

Crichton Charles (1910–). British film director. One of the chief directors at M. *Balcon's Ealing Studios. He achieved a reputation equal to *Hamer and *Mackendrick with a series of comedies like *Hue and Cry* (1946) and *The Lavender Hill Mob* (1951).

Crime and Punishment (1866). Novel by *Dostoyevsky.

Crime de Sylvestre Bonnard, Le (1881). Novel by Anatole France.

criselling. Until modern times the proportioning of the ingredients for glass making was in no way exact and this sometimes resulted in faulty glass which was unstable in composition, often because of an excess of alkali. Such glass occasionally develops a cloudy interior with a network of fine cracks and eventually disintegrates. This process is known as 'c.'

Cristofori Bartolommeo (1655–1731). Paduan instrument maker and maker of the 1st efficient piano (1709). He had moved to Florence in the 1690s and held various posts under Ferdinand de' Medici and his son Cosimo III.

Critic, The, or A Tragedy Rehearsed (1779). Comedy by R. B. *Sheridan.

Crito. Dialogue by *Plato.

Cresting. Silver-gilt steeple cup; London, 1608

Cresilas. *Pericles* (copy)

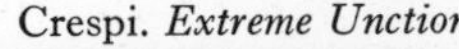

Crespi. *Extreme Unction*

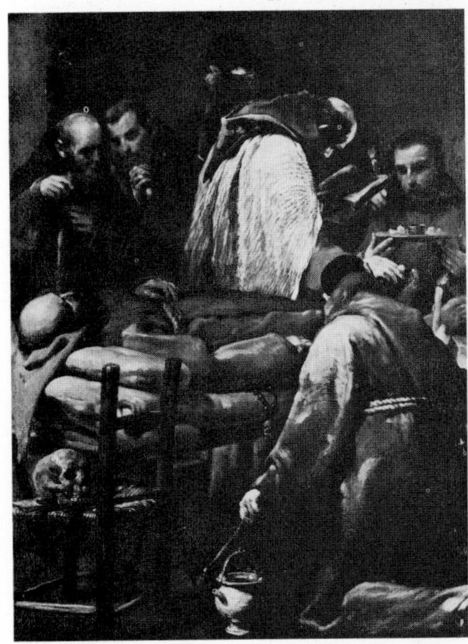

Benedetto Croce

John Crome. *Mousehold Heath near Norwich*

Crivelli. *The Annunciation*

Cronaca. Strozzi Palace, begun by Benedetto da Maiano; the cornice is the most notable part of Il Cronaca's continuation

Crivelli Carlo (*c.* 1430–95). Italian painter of the Venetian school. Although trained, probably by the Vivarini in Venice, C. worked all his life outside the developing Venetian tradition, living in Ancona, Ascoli and other towns of the Marches where altarpieces painted by C., his relatives and pupils are still to be found. His style shows many diverse influences. In his use of swags of fruit and other classical motifs he follows the Paduan painters, but his decorative handling of gold and the stiffly posed figures belongs to the conventions of the international Gothic style which was already out of fashion. C. was a highly original artist who combined such different elements within a hard, flowing, highly decorative style of draughtsmanship, matched only perhaps by Botticelli. 2 small *Madonna and Child* panels (V. and A., London and N.G., Washington) combine this mastery of decoration with a simple and direct piety. On a grander scale the *Demidoff Altarpiece* (N.G., London) and the *Madonna and Child* (Brera Gal., Milan) retain the same grace and feeling with a greater impression of power. *The Annunciation* (1486; N.G., London) is a rare and outstanding work in which all the unusual talents of this artist reach their culmination.

Croce Benedetto (1866–1952). Italian critic and philosopher of aesthetics and politician; he became minister of education in 1920 but retired from public office to oppose the Fascist régime. In the restored democratic system he was leader of the Liberal party until 1947. In 1903 he founded *La Critica* a bi-monthly review of literature, history and philosophy contributing to it until his death. C.'s aesthetic, propounded in *L'Estetica* (1902; 1909; vol. i of *La Filosofia dello spirito*), regards art as an intuition revealed by the artist with the tools of ink, stone, paint, etc. The work of art is the image which exists in the artist's mind before its mechanical reproduction. C. considered his aesthetic theory to cover expression of all kinds; his thinking greatly influenced the English philosopher R. G. Collingwood.

Croft William (1678–1727). English organist and composer of church and harpsichord music and the hymn tune *St Anne*.

croisé. French term usually used in reference to the 4th *position in ballet when the dancer is facing a corner of the stage; it derives from the crossed position of the feet. Bras c., describes a position of the arms when they are held parallel, with one crossing in front of the dancer's body.

Croker John Wilson (1780–1857). English politician and critic notable for his violent attack on Keats's *Endymion*. He was probably the original for Rigby, the jobbing politician in Disraeli's *Coningsby*.

Crome John, called 'Old Crome' (1768–1821). English painter of landscape in oil and watercolour. C. was born in *Norwich and was a founder of the Norwich Society of Artists. The influence of Dutch landscape painters (M. Hobbema and Ruisdael in particular) is obvious; so is his close study of Gainsborough and R. Wilson when he was a copyist, but a powerful imagination informs his richly coloured, formally composed yet romantically emotional compositions, e.g. *Moonrise on the Yare* (N.G., London), *Mousehold Heath near Norwich* (Tate). His son John Bernay C. (1794–1842) was also a landscape painter of the Norwich school.

Crome Yellow (1921). Novel by Aldous Huxley.

Cromwell John (1888–). U.S. film director. Maker of a long series of melodramas starting in 1929, many with David O. *Selznick, including a version of Somerset Maugham's *Of Human Bondage* (1934). He was renowned for his handling of many of Hollywood's more remarkable female stars. *The Goddess* (1958) is an excellent treatment of a Paddy Chayefsky script about a neurotic film star.

Cronaca Il (1454–1508). Italian architect. He completed the Palazzo Strozzi, Florence, one of the greatest of early Renaissance palaces; the whole exterior is heavily rusticated and there is a huge cornice.

Cronin A(rchibald) J(oseph) (1896–). Scottish novelist, a physician. His books, written in a conventional narrative style, are popular because of their human interest. Works include: *Hatter's Castle* (1931; film 1942), *The Citadel* (1937; film 1938), *The Keys of the Kingdom* (1942; film 1944), *The Spanish Gardener* (1950; film 1956).

crook. A musical term for an extra length of tubing which had to be added to *brass instruments (e.g. the natural horn) to alter their

Cruikshank. *Oliver introduced to the Respectable Old Gentleman*

pitch, before the development of efficient valve or piston instruments in the early 19th c.

Crosby Bing (1904–). U.S. singer and film star. C. made his début in *The King of Jazz* (1930); by 1932 he was a household name. Songs rather than titles are remembered of some 60 other films, except for *The Bells of St Mary's* and the *Road* series with Bob Hope and Dorothy Lamour during the 1940s. He gained an Oscar for *Going My Way* (1944).

Cross Henri-Edmond (1856–1910). French painter, an exponent of divisionism which he used with greater freedom than Signac or Seurat. His brilliant colours influenced the fauves.

Crossfire (1947). Film directed by E. *Dmytryk.

crossing. In a cruciform church, the central area where chancel, nave and transepts meet.

cross relation: *false relation

cross stitch. An embroidery stitch commonly worked on canvas or on an even thread fabric. The stitch is frequently used to cover the ground completely, and many variants are known. Also *tent stitch and *gros point.

Crotch William (1775–1847). English composer and a child prodigy as organist and composer giving daily organ recitals in London at the age of 4; 1st principal of the R.A.M. (1822). His compositions in later life did not fulfil his early promise.

crotchet. In music a note with time-value a quarter that of the semibreve and in U.S. terminology called the 'quarter note'. It is notated thus, ♩ and its rest thus, 𝄽 or ɼ.

Crouch Frederick Nicholls (1808–96). English conductor and composer who emigrated (1849) to the U.S., fighting in the Confederate army. His many songs include the famous 'Kathleen Mavourneen' (1839–40).

Crowd, The (1928). Film directed by K. *Vidor.

Crucible, The (1953). Play by Arthur *Miller.

Cruickshank George (1792–1878). English comic artist whose individual style showed traces of Gillray's influence. He first became widely known with his caricatures of the leading figures in the scandal of Queen Caroline's trial. His later satirical drawings attacked, among other things, the savage criminal code of his time, the slave trade, patronage and the evils of drink. His illustrations to Dickens (*Sketches by Boz, Oliver Twist*) are well known, but perhaps the works which best matched his own flair for the grotesque were the trs of fairy-tales by the Grimm brothers.

Cruz Ramón de la (1731–94). Spanish playwright. He produced more than 300 plays of all kinds, but his most successful were his *sainetes*, a kind of farcical interlude which was very popular in the Spanish theatre, and which combined delightful comedy with sharp observation of popular life in Madrid.

Cruze James (1884–1942). U.S. film director, originally an actor in serials (1911–14). His most famous film was *The Covered Wagon* (1923), the 1st large-scale western and one of the most profitable, shot on location in Nevada instead of on the studio back-lot. His diverse later work includes the comedy *Ruggles of Red Gap* (1923), the epic *Old Ironsides* (1926) and the drama *I Cover the Waterfront* (1933).

crwth. Ancient string instrument associated with Britain and particularly Wales. It consisted of strings, over a finger-board, on a rectangular frame, the bottom half of which was filled in by a sound-box. The c. was bowed or plucked.

crypt. An underground chamber under the E. end of a church.

crystal-glass. Glass makers have always tried to achieve the clarity and brilliance of rock-crystal in their work. Basically the technique employed involves decolourizing the glass with manganese. The secret was known to the Romans, lost in the middle ages and rediscovered by the Venetians, perhaps before the 15th c. It was known then as *cristallo* and its adoption was a reason for the supremacy of Venetian glass during the Renaissance. By 1680 the Germans had perfected a formula including potash and chalk which attained approximately the effect of crystal, while *Ravenscroft in England had discovered 'a new sort of

Cruze. *The Covered Wagon*

Crystal-glass. 16th-c. Venetian goblet

Crwth

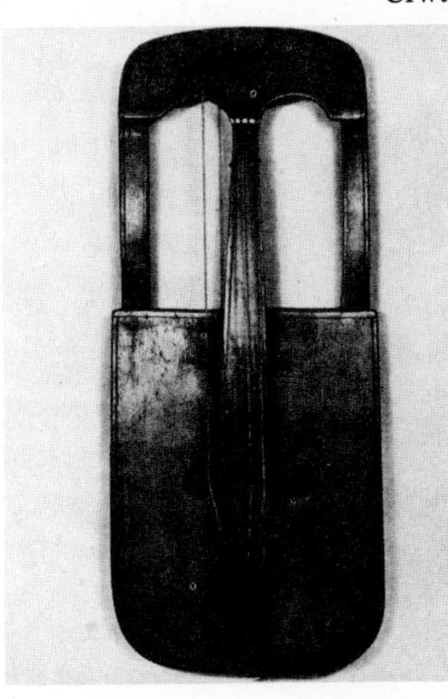

Cubism. Picasso's *Nude in the Forest* (1908)

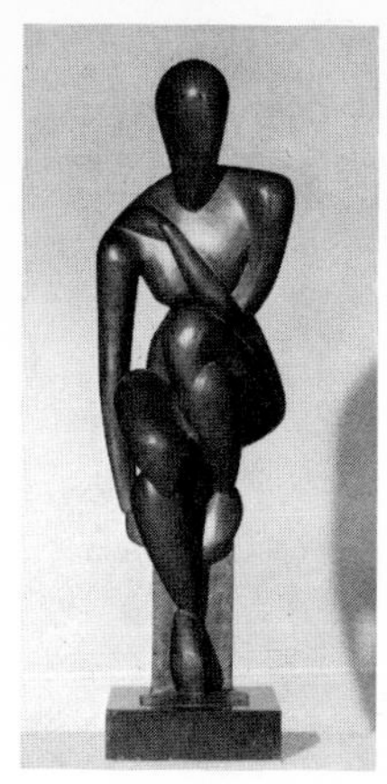

Cubism. Duchamp-Villon's *Seated Woman* (1914)

Cubism. Juan Gris's *The Watch* (*The Sherry Bottle*) (1912)

Cubism. Braque's *The Portuguese* (1911)

Cubism. Picasso's *Woman with a Guitar* (1912)

Cubism. Archipenko's *Boxing* (1913)

crystalline glass'. Holland and France followed in evolving crystal-glass of their own.

Crystal Palace, The (1851). Architect, Joseph *Paxton.

Cry, The Beloved Country (1948). Novel by Alan *Paton.

csardas. A Hungarian national dance dating back to the 10th c. and introduced into formal ballet in *Coppélia* (1870).

Csontváry Tivadar Mihály Kosztka called (1853–1919). Hungarian painter of imaginative works inspired by landscape and religious themes. A pantheistic mystic, he painted strange, symbolic canvases with an intensity of colour and often a naïve realism of style which increase the fantastic quality of his vision.

Cuba Si! (1961). Film directed by C. *Marker.

cubism. The 1st abstract art style of the 20th c. named by the art critic Louis Vauxcelles, who took up a remark of Matisse's about Braque's little cubes. The major period of the style is from 1907 to 1914, and the originators were Picasso and Braque, who worked closely together. Various divisions of c. into periods have been suggested: the names 'analytic', 'hermetic' and 'synthetic' are in general use: but the term 'analytic' does not adequately describe the earliest cubist works, which are influenced by Iberian and African art as in the *Demoiselles d'Avignon* by Picasso (1907), so that some critics have suggested 'pre-cubist' or 'proto-cubist' for this phase.
If such works are seen as the prelude to c., the 1st truly cubist works are those in which objects, landscapes and people are represented as many-sided (or many-faceted) solids. Cézanne's later work was a catalyst for this painting, and was known to cubists from the important showing of his work after his death in 1905; his advice to Émile Bernard 'deal with nature by means of the cylinder, the sphere and the cone' was taken as a justification of cubist experiments. *Woman with a Guitar* by Picasso is a clear example of this phase of c. Braque and Picasso then turned to a flatter type of abstraction, in which the allover pattern becomes more important, and the objects represented are largely or wholly indecipherable (hermetic c.). At this period colour was almost wholly absent from their work, which is mainly monochromatic, grey, blue or brown and white. Colour reappeared in the final phase of c., called 'synthetic', from its combination of abstraction with real materials. Many other artists worked in the cubist style, which replaced fauvism as the leading artistic movement in Paris from about 1909. The most significant contributions were made by Juan Gris and Fernand Léger, but there were many others including Gleizes and Metzinger (who publ. a book on c.), Derain, Friesz, de la Fresnaye and Marcoussis. Cubist sculptors included Archipenko and Henri Laurens. C. was represented in the Salon d'Automne, and a group was formed called the Section d'Or: in this the Villon brothers, Jacques Villon, Raymond Duchamp-Villon and Marcel Duchamp are the major figures. This activity in Paris had far-reaching effects, stimulating the futurist movement in Italy, the vorticists in Britain, and having some effect on expressionist art in Germany: it was also an important precedent for other movements with abstract aims such as those in Russia (constructivism, suprematism) and the Netherlands (de stijl). C. developed in Paris in 2 main ways, towards a decorative style, in which the subjects are treated geometrically but remain clearly recognizable, or towards a greater degree of abstraction as in Delaunay's rhythmic paintings of coloured segments and circles (orphism).
C. has continued to have an important influence on 20th-c. art. An attempt was made by Ozenfant and the architect Le Corbusier to return to a simpler purified c., but by 1920 c. was already too much a part of the general artistic vocabulary to be restricted to this purism. Cubist ideas and techniques continue to be used up to the present, particularly *collage invented in the synthetic period.

Cubist Painters, The (1913). Prose work by *Apollinaire.

cubist-realism (also known as 'precisionism'). Style of U.S. painting of the 1920s and 1930s which effected a compromise between cubism and straight representational painting. Its chief exponents were Demuth and Sheeler. While their subject-matter–urban or industrial architecture–remained recognizable it was schematized into a formal geometricized design executed with hard-edged precision.

Cubitt Lewis (1799–date of death not known). English architect who designed King's Cross

Station (1851), one of the most lucid and advanced buildings of its time. In partnership with his brothers Thomas and Joseph, C. had a hand in designing several streets in London, including Bloomsbury and Belgravia.

cubo-futurism: *futurism

Cueva Juan de la (*c.* 1543–1610). Spanish poet and playwright. He wrote a treatise on poetical theory, *Ejemplar poético* (written 1606), and 14 plays, including *El Infamador* (1581), which somewhat anticipated Tirso de Molina's *Don Juan.* He produced allegorical, mythological and epic poems, the latter often inspired by Spanish history.

Cui César Antonovich (1835–1918). Russian musician, self-taught and one of the *Mighty Handful. His father was an immigrant French officer and C. entered the army, becoming a professor of military engineering at St Petersburg. C.'s delicate and refined music shows little originality. His works include 11 operas, among them *William Ratcliff* (1869), his operatic masterpiece, and *Angelo* (1876), and orchestral and choral pieces; but his lyrical gifts are best displayed in his songs and chamber music.

Cuijpers P. J. H. (1827–1921). Dutch neo-Gothic architect who built the Maria Magdelenakerk, the Rijksmuseum and the Central Station, all at Amsterdam. He also restored medieval churches and earned the nickname of 'the Dutch *Viollet-le-Duc'.

Cukor George (1899–). U.S. film director. C. started working in the theatre *c.* 1918, had his 1st big directorial success on Broadway with *The Great Gatsby* in 1926 and started in the cinema as dialogue director for *All Quiet on the Western Front.* He built up a formidable reputation as a director of actresses like Katharine Hepburn (*Little Women*, 1933) and Garbo (*Camille*, 1936). Although he directed M.G.M.'s prestige adaptations of *David Copperfield* (1934) and *Romeo and Juliet* (1936), the reputation of his comedies like *The Women* (1939) and *The Philadelphia Story* (1940) has survived, just as his post-war fame rested mainly on his series of comedies with Garson Kanin, like *Adam's Rib* (1949), *Born Yesterday* (1950) and *Pat and Mike* (1952). In 1954 he moved from these small-scale, if starry, movies into melodramas like *A Star is Born* (1954) and *Bhowani Junction* (1955). The musicals, *Les Girls* (1957) and *Let's Make Love* (1960), showed a remarkable choreographic use of the camera, while in *Heller in Pink Tights* (1960) and *The Chapman Report* (1962) he and his consultant, George Hoyningen-Huene, used colour to great effect. *My Fair Lady* (1964) is the largest film of his career.

Culture and Anarchy (1869). Book by Matthew *Arnold.

cummings e(dward) e(stlin) (1894–1962). U.S. poet and novelist who came to prominence in the experimental surge of the 1920s. *The Enormous Room* (1922) is a remarkable novel based on his experiences in a French prison camp during World War I, in which he served as a volunteer ambulance driver. His reputation as a lyric poet grew throughout the 1920s with the publication of several vols, including *Tulips and Chimneys* (1923), *XLI Poems* (1925) and *Is 5* (1926). His typographical devices and playfulness of presentation obscure the fact that he is a very simple direct poet in the tradition of Whitman or, to make a closer analogy, of D. H. Lawrence. His work shows 2 main tones–one lyric-erotic, often highly simplified though capable of great subtlety of feeling, one satirical, wryly parodying American life and engaging the reader with a biting toughness. It is possible to argue that his experimental façade allowed him an extreme simplicity of spirit, and unlike many of his contemporaries he does not develop greatly. His prolific production continued to his death with *ViVa* (1931), *Fifty Poems* (1940), *95 Poems* (1958), etc.; and colls appeared in *Collected Poems* (1938), *Poems 1923–1954* (1954) and *Poems 1923–58* (1960).

Cunning Little Vixen. Opera by *Janáček, libretto by R. Těsnohlidek; 1st performance in Brno, 1924.

Cupid and Psyche: *Apuleius

cupola. Architectural term virtually synonymous with dome; most usually applied to onion-shaped domes.

Curé de Tours, Le (1832). Novel by Balzac.

Curel François de (1854–1928). French playwright. His works–typical 'problem plays'–include *L'Envers d'une sainte* (1892), *Les*

e.e. cummings

César Cui

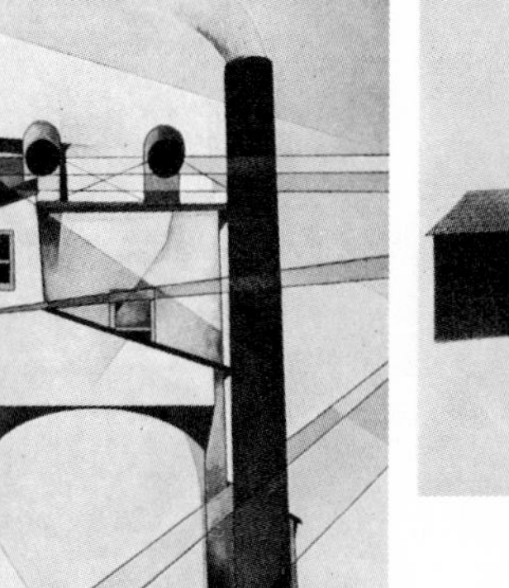

Cubist-realism. Sheeler's *Bucks County Barn*

Cubist-realism. Demuth's *My Egypt* (1927)

Cukor. Robert Taylor and Greta Garbo (together, left) in *Camille*

Currier and Ives. *Burning of the 'Lexington'*

Curtain wall: Aigues-Mortes, France

Curtain wall (modern): Equitable Savings Bank, Portland, Oregon

Fossiles (1892; *The Fossils*, 1915), *L'Invitée* (1893) and *La Nouvelle Idole* (1899).

Currier and Ives prints. Series of hand-coloured lithographs publ. in New York depicting all aspects of the American scene in the 2nd half of the 19th c. NATHANIEL C. (1813–88) began the series in 1835 and took J(AMES) MERRITT I. (1824–95) into partnership in 1857.

Curros Enriquez Manuel (1851–1908). Spanish poet (in the Galician dialect) and journalist. His lyrics are distinguished by their deep feeling and descriptive qualities. He steadfastly campaigned on behalf of the poverty-stricken Galician peasantry and fiercely attacked the Church, eventually being prosecuted for blasphemy.

Curry John Steuart (1897–1946). U.S. regionalist painter who depicted in narrative style scenes of Kansas life.

curtain wall. (1) Architectural term for a wall which is not structurally important, the building being supported by concrete pillars, etc.; (2) in medieval castles, the length of wall between 2 towers or bastions.

Curtis Tony (1925–). U.S. actor, principally in adventure films, e.g. *Houdini* (1953). *The Sweet Smell of Success* (1957), *The Defiant Ones* (1958) and *Some Like It Hot* (1959) revealed his dramatic and comic potential.

Curtiz Michael (1888–1962). Hungarian-born film director. A stage actor and director in Budapest, C. started films in Sweden under Sjöström and Stiller as actor and then director. He worked in Hungary and Germany before World War I and afterwards in France, Italy, Britain and Denmark. He was taken to the U.S. by Warners to make *Noah's Ark* (1929), and made at least 3 films each year until 1953. His steadily competent and varied output includes a spectacular thriller *Casablanca* (1943), and *Mildred Pierce* (1945), the high-power melodrama which firmly re-established Joan Crawford as a top star.

cut and engraved glass. Glass has been cut since Roman times, when gem cutter's techniques were used. Cutting is done with revolving wheels or grind-stones of various sizes, made out of stone, iron or copper. These are fed with sand or emery acting as abrasive and cooled with water. Finer wheels are used for wheel-engraving of designs, while a diamond point is needed for minute and delicate decoration.

cut board figures. Fretted wooden figures popular as decorations in the late 17th and early 18th cs painted on 1 side to resemble a man or a woman. Usually well under life-size, they were placed in a corner of a room.

cutting: *film techniques

cut-work. A method of working embroidery in which shaped areas of the foundation material are cut away after the outlines have been secured with buttonhole stitch. A rich effect is gained by the construction of bars running across the cut spaces. Elaborate kinds are Renaissance, Richelieu and Italian c.-w., the last having small open squares crossed with bars of buttonhole stitch arranged in geometric patterns.

Cuvilliès François (1695–1768). Flemish architect; he trained in Paris and worked chiefly in Munich. His Amalienburg, a small pleasure-house in the grounds of the Nymphenburg Palace, and his theatre in the Residenz are masterpieces of exquisite secular rococo.

Cuvilliès. Amalienburg.
See also colour plate 66

Cuyp. *Herdsman with five Cows by a River*

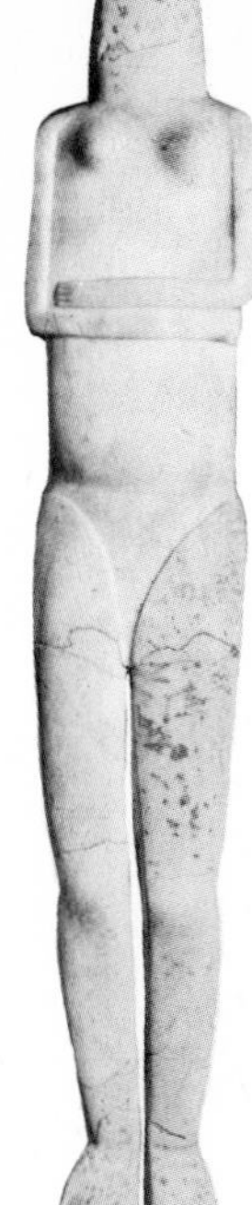

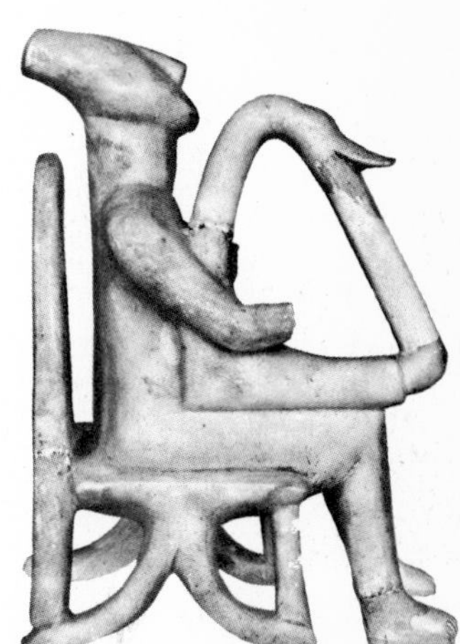

Cycladic life-size figure, possibly of the Mother-goddess (left); and smaller figure of harp player

Cuyp Aelbert (1620–91). Dutch painter influenced by earlier Dutch landscape painters, in particular van Goyen. There is a strong element in his work of Italianate Dutch painters, such as Jan Both, especially in his handling of light. He painted portraits, still-lifes, seascapes, landscapes and town scenes, but is best known for studies of animals in the mellow light of a summer evening. There are a number of fine examples in the N.G., London including *Landscape, Cattle and Figures, Evening*. C.'s work was greatly admired by English collectors and by English landscape painters of the early 19th c.

cycladic. Term applied to vases and (notably) the marble idols found in the Cyclades, a group of islands in the Aegean, and evidence for what appears to have been a flourishing culture between 2600 and 1100 B.C.

cyclic form. A musical term. (1) It may mean simply a form consisting of several movements, e.g. a suite. (2) A piece may be described as in c. f. when 1 or more themes recur as an element of continuity in 2 or more movements. C. Franck extensively employed this system.

cyclopean masonry. Architectural term for building which uses huge and irregular blocks of stone without mortar.

cyclorama. Device used in the theatre; it consists of a curved, smooth surface upon which light can be projected in order to obtain scenic effects, e.g. a changing sky.

Cygne, Le. Solo dance devised for Pavlova (1905) by Fokine to music by Saint-Saëns.

cyma. An architectural moulding of double curvature, concave and convex. When the upper part is concave it is 'c. recta'; when the upper part is convex it is 'c. reversa'. The moulding is used in interior decoration, furniture and silver.

cymbals. Untuned *percussion instruments known in Europe since the middle ages but first used in orchestral music in the later 18th c. They are convex discs, made from a special metal alloy, held by a leather thong; the player usually has a pair which he strikes together. Various effects are possible. Also a single suspended c. can be played with drumsticks. CHOKE c.s are 2 c.s mounted face to face and struck with a drumstick or operated by a pedal.

Cymbeline (1611; publ. 1623). Play by *Shakespeare, written *c.* 1609. Its main source was a story by Boccaccio, and *Holinshed.

Cynewulf (*fl.* 8th c.). Anglo-Saxon poet, whose name appears in runic characters in the epilogues of 4 poems in *The Exeter Book*, and the probable author of *The Dream of the Rood* (an illustration of the current cult of the Cross).

Cynthia's Revels (1600). Play by Ben *Jonson.

Cyrano de Bergerac Savinien de (1619–55). French writer celebrated for his long nose. His most important works are the *Histoire comique des états et empires de la Lune* (posth. 1657) and *Histoire . . . du Soleil* (posth. 1662), joint Eng-lish trs. *The Comical History of . . . the Moon and Sun* (1687), in which the fantastic setting allows much political and social satire, the comedy *Le Pédant joué* (publ. 1654); and the tragedy *La Mort d'Agrippine* (1653). He was the prototype of Rostand's play *Cyrano de Bergerac*, where he becomes a Gascon knight whose noble heart is hidden beneath a comical exterior.

Czechowicz Józef (1903–39). Polish poet, linked with the Awangarda movement, who combined modern technique with the lyricism of Polish folk-lore. In his poems, which are deeply musical and full of striking imagery, he captured the fairy-tale atmosphere of the Polish country town.

Czerny Carl (1791–1857). Austrian pianist, composer and teacher. He was a pupil of Beethoven, and himself taught Liszt. His very numerous works include a famous series of piano studies but more interesting is his ed. of Bach's *Well Tempered Clavier* which claims to give Beethoven's interpretations of the preludes and fugues.

Czyżewski Tytus (1880–1945). Polish poet and painter, one of the founders of the formist movement. C. conducted interesting poetic experiments by mixing modernistic themes with primitive folk-lore.

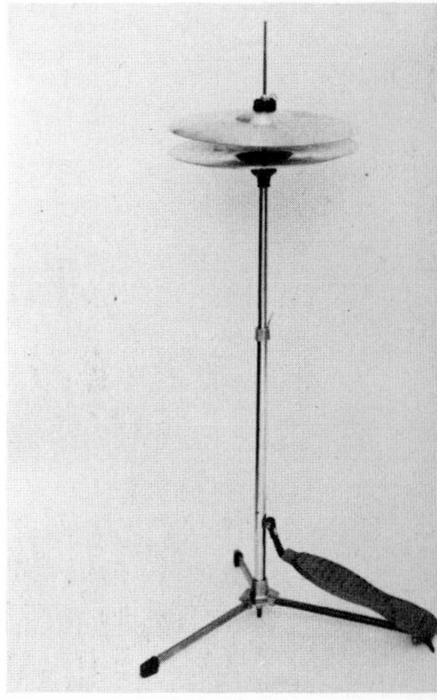

Choke cymbals

Carl Czerny

D

Daddi. *The Martyrdom of St Stephen*

Cartoon of Daguerre

The earliest surviving daguerreotype (1837)

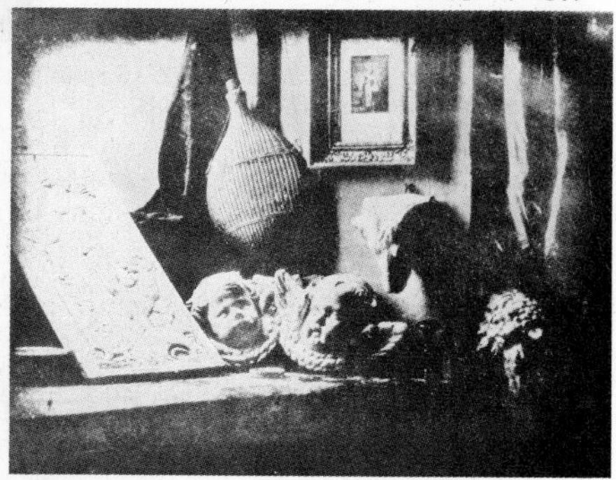

Dahl. *Self-portrait*

Dabit Eugène (1898–1936). French novelist, author of *L'Hôtel du Nord* (1930), set in a small hotel in a poor district of Paris, and other novels of Parisian life.

Dąbrowska Maria (1889–). Polish novelist and playwright. She made her reputation with a vol. of short stories *Ludzie stamtąd* (1925) dealing with the hardships of the Polish peasantry. Her acknowledged masterpiece *Noce i dnie* (1932–4) is a vivid chronicle novel of life in Poland in the 2nd half of the 19th c.

da capo (Italian, 'from the beginning'). In music a direction (often abbreviated as D.C.) placed at the end of a piece, if the composer wishes the 1st section played again as a conclusion; thus a DA CAPO ARIA is one in 3 parts, the last being a repeat of the 1st, the 2nd a contrasting section.

Dach Simon (1605–59). German poet, professor at Königsberg Univ. and the leading member of the Königsberg circle. His verse, most of which was occasional, reveals a true lyric gift; he respected the theories of *Opitz, but they contributed little to his poetry.

Da Costa Isaac (1798–1860). Dutch poet, at first a pupil of Bilderdijk. Da C. was the first Dutch poet to show strong romantic tendencies, trs. Byron and writing much exotic verse as well as such patriotic poems as *De Verlossing van Nederland* (1814).

dactyl: *metre in verse

dada (French, 'hobby-horse'). Movement begun in Zürich in 1916 by a group of writers and painters (Tristan Tzara, André Breton, Hans Arp, etc.) opposed to all established institutions and ideas, deeply interested in the irrational unconscious mind and deliberately shocking and irreverent in behaviour (e.g. Duchamp's picture of the *Mona Lisa*–bewhiskered). In the 1920s *surrealism developed from dadaism.

Daddi Bernardo (*c.* 1290–*c.* 1349). Italian painter and leading artist in the generation which followed Giotto in Florence. His much-damaged frescoes, *The Martyrdom of St Laurence* and *The Martyrdom of St Stephen* (Sta Croce, Florence), are very close to Giotto in style. Later D. was greatly influenced by Sienese painting, particularly by that of the Lorenzetti brothers, and by French and Italian sculpture. These influences can be traced in a major work, the polyptych altarpiece of S. Pancrazio (Uffizi). Other important works are *The Virgin and Child with Eight Angels* (Or San Michele, Florence), *St Paul and worshippers* (N.G., Washington) and the portable altar (Fogg Mus., Cambridge, Mass.).

dado. The lower part of a wall when marked off as a separate surface by the decoration.

Daguerre Louis-Jacques-Mandé (1787–1851). French photographer. In 1838, using knowledge obtained from N. *Niepce, D. perfected the 1st commercially feasible process for obtaining photographs on metal plates. D.'s method, published by the French government in 1839, was responsible for the spread of photography throughout the Western world. In the DAGUERREOTYPE, highly polished silvered copper plates were sensitized by exposure to iodine fumes. The latent image was developed by exposing the plate to fumes of heated mercury, yielding a delicate silvery image that could not be reproduced. The process was rendered obsolete by 1860 due to the invention of the wet-plate (*collodion) process, making possible any number of prints.

Dahl Michael (1656/9–1743). Swedish portrait painter who settled in London in 1688, becoming painter to Queen Anne and the rival of Sir G. Kneller. His work is less pretentious than Kneller's and his colours softer; it is marred by uneasy poses and lack of psychological insight.

Daisy Miller (1879). Short story by Henry *James.

Dalayrac (originally d'Alayrac) Nicolas-Marie (1753–1809). French composer, very popular in continental Europe during the 1st half of the 19th c. His many *opéras-comiques* include *L'Éclipse Totale* (1782), *Nina* (1786) and *Maison à vendre* (1800), revived in the 20th c. He also produced a set of 6 string quartets.

Dalem Cornelis van (*c.* 1535–75). Flemish landscape painter; Bartholomeus Spranger was his pupil. Little of his work has survived; it includes the melancholy *Landscape with Farm* (1564; Munich).

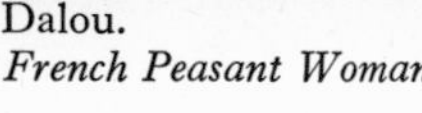

Dalou. *French Peasant Woman*

Dalmau. *Virgin and Councillors* (detail)

Damascening: 16th-c. bucket of engraved brass damascened with silver; by a Saracenic craftsman settled in Venice

Dali Salvador (1904–). Spanish painter, designer of jewellery, etc. and for the stage, book illustrator and writer, notorious for his extravagant and eccentric statements about himself. He joined the surrealist movement in Paris in 1929 making the surrealist films *Le Chien Andalou* (1929) and *L'Âge d'Or* (1931) with L. Buñuel and painting such works as *The Persistence of Memory* (1931; M.M.A., New York) and *Premonition of Civil War* (1936; M. of A., Philadelphia). His paintings, which he has called 'hand-painted dream photographs', are characterized by minute detail, virtuoso technique, ingenuity and showmanship together with elements of Freudian dream symbolism. In more recent years he has devoted himself to dramatic religious works, e.g. *Christ of St John of the Cross* (1951; Gal. and Mus., Glasgow).

Dalin Olaf von (1708–63). Swedish writer and historian, ed. of the weekly *Then Swänska Argus* (1732–4), modelled on *The Spectator*. His many works, notably his plays, introduced the style and subjects of French classical writing to Sweden.

Dallapiccola Luigi (1904–). Italian 12-note composer and pianist. His 1st significant work, the *Partita* for orchestra and soprano (1933), neo-classical in idiom, showed D.'s emotive use of instrumental tone colour and was distinguished by his exploitation of, and his interest in, the combination of voice and instruments. From the *Divertimento* for voice and 5 instruments (1934) he gradually explored 12-note technique, increasingly introducing serial elements but blending them with tonal elements, e.g. using series with tonal thematic potentialities. D.'s important works are: the operas *Volo di notte* (1940), based on Saint-Exupéry's *Vol de nuit*, and the masterpiece *Il prigioniero* (1949) a poignant manifesto for liberty, a theme inspiring D.'s greatest works; the ballet *Marsia* (1943); *Job, sacra rappresentazione* (1950); *Sei cori di Michelangelo Buonarotti il Giovane* (1936) for chorus and orchestra; *Tre Laudi* (1937) for chorus; *Canti di prigionia* (1941) for chorus, piano, harp and percussion; 3 sets of Greek lyrics for voice and chamber orchestra; the *Canti di Liberazione* for chorus and orchestra using unadulterated 12-note technique; and *Musica per 3 pianoforti* (1935).

Dalmau Luis (d. 1460). Spanish painter who worked at the court of Aragon and helped to extend the influence of Flemish painting in Spain. In 1431 D. was sent on a mission to Bruges and probably there learnt to follow van Eyck's style, evident in his great work *Virgin and Councillors* (1445; Barcelona Mus.).

Dalou Jules (1838–1902). French sculptor. Such works as *French Peasant Woman* (1873; Tate) showed a realism similar to that of Courbet's paintings. For his monumental *Triumph of the Republic* (Place de la Nation, Paris) D. adopted a style approaching the baroque. He worked (1871–80) in England.

damascening. The art of inlaying gold, silver or copper wire on the surface of iron, steel or bronze, which has been undercut, the furrows holding the hammered thread in place. Originally the technique came from Damascus and was much used for armour, especially during the Renaissance. It is still widely employed in the Orient.

damask. A silk or linen fabric with a raised pattern woven into it, used extensively in upholstery and curtaining.

Dame aux camélias, La (1848). Novel by Alexandre *Dumas *fils*, which he dramatized (1852).

Dames du Bois de Boulogne, Les (1945). Film directed by R. *Bresson.

Damiani Damiano (1922–). Italian film director; an associate of *Zavattini, who collaborated with him on the scripts of *Il Rossetto* (1960) and *L'Isola di Arturo* (1962). He has now moved on to larger films with *La Noia* (*The Empty Canvas*, 1963) based on Moravia's novel.

Damnation of Faust, The (1846). Operatic work by *Berlioz; called a dramatic legend and 1st performed as a concert piece.

Damrosch Leopold (1832–85). German conductor and violinist. At Weimar he met Liszt and also Taussig, and as a conductor at Breslau (1858–71) promoted the music of Berlioz, Liszt and Wagner. From 1871 he worked in New York, founding the Oratorio Society and the Symphony Society and giving the 1st German opera season (1884–5). His son FRANK HEINO D. (1859–1937) was a choral conductor.

Damrosch Walter Johannes (1862–1950). U.S. conductor, composer and music educationist, son of Leopold D. whom he assisted at

Dali. *The Persistence of Memory*

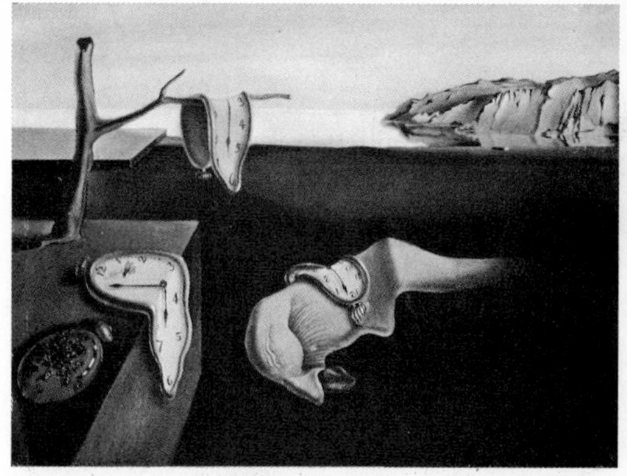

Dali. *Premonition of Civil War*

The Dance of Death; French wall painting, *c.* 1465

Danby. *Liensford Lake, Norway*

George Dance Jr. Newgate Prison (woodcut)

George Dance Sr. The Mansion House

the Metropolitan Opera's German season and succeeded as conductor of the New York Oratorio and Symphony Societies in New York. He toured with his DAMROSCH OPERA Co. (1894–9). D. was musical adviser to the National Broadcasting Co. (1927–47).

Dana Richard Henry Jr (1815–82). U.S. writer whose narrative *Two Years Before the Mast* (1840), about his experiences as a common sailor, exposed barbarous shipboard conditions and precipitated a number of maritime reforms. The book was admired by Melville.

Danby Francis (1793–1861). Irish painter who worked in England and Geneva. His early work, small landscapes, e.g. *Blaise Castle Woods* (*c.* 1822; Bristol Art Gal.), has a charming verity but Turner's influence encouraged him to an aerial romanticism of sunsets and seascapes. For a while he painted dramatic apocalyptic subjects, e.g. *The Opening of the Sixth Seal* (1826; N.G., Dublin).

Dance George Sr (d. 1768). English architect. In 1735 he became clerk of the City Works, London, and carried out many official commissions, notably the Mansion House; St Leonard's, Shoreditch; and St Botolph's, Aldgate. He also rebuilt London Bridge (demolished 1832). His style (English Palladian) shows originality without much finesse.

Dance George Jr (1741–1825). English architect, son of the above. He studied in Italy and succeeded his father as clerk of the City Works in 1768. He designed the S. front of the Guildhall and the fine church of All Hallows, London Wall. His masterpiece was Newgate Prison, a grim building influenced by Palladio, Guilio Romano and the engravings of Piranesi, whom D. knew.

dance notation. The recording of dance movement by means of written symbols. Since R. Feuillet's *Chorégraphie ou l'Art de Décrire la Danse* (1700) many different systems of notation have been devised. However, the best known and the most widely used are: (1) Labanotation, based on work by R. von Laban, using abstract symbols and therefore being easily adapted to record any human movement and (2) the Benesh system, a simple method in which the symbols indicating the dancers' movement are drawn on to a music stave, invented in 1955 by J. and R. Benesh.

Dance of Death (French, *danse macabre*; German, *Totentanz*). A mimed dance, particularly performed in the 15th c., which gave dramatic form to the concept of Death as the ubiquitous leveller. The earliest painting of the dance, with dialogue subscribed, a processional in which all, from page and emperor to servant and child have a place and are led by their own skeletons to the grave, was in Les Innocents church, Paris (1424; destroyed 1669). A fine woodcut series was engraved (1538) by Hans Lützelburger from the drawings of the *Totentanz* by Hans Holbein the Younger.

Dancourt Florent Carton (1661–1725). French actor and playwright. His comedies of manners include: *Le Chevalier à la mode* (1687), *Le Notaire obligeant* (1685) and *Les Bourgeoises à la mode* (1692), which Vanbrugh adapted in *The Confederacy*.

dandyism. Name given to a 19th-c. cult of personal elegance and distinction in dress originated in England by Beau Brummel. Such ideas were taken up by French artists and writers, e.g. Baudelaire, *Barbey d'Aurevilly and Delacroix, and modified to fit in with their own views on the separateness of the artist in a bourgeois society; the English gentleman was their model of hauteur and aloofness, his clothes their badge of distinction.

Danican: *Philidor

Daniel. One of the books of the *Bible (Old Testament; partly in Aramaic) about the life of the Israelite D. at the Persian court, including his interpreting the writing on the wall at Belshazzar's feast and his escape from the lions' den.

Daniel or **Danyel** John (*c.* 1565–1630). English lutenist and composer, and a brother of Samuel D. He publ. a set of 20 lute songs (1606) and an ed. of his brother's poetical works (1623).

Daniel Samuel (1562–1619). English poet, critic and dramatist. D.'s smooth technique and elegant language anticipated the Augustans. He defended the use of English as a poetic language in a prose work, *A Defence of Ryme* (1603), replying to the criticism of T. *Campion. His verse includes the sonnets *Delia* (1592); *The Complaint of Rosamond* (1592); and the epic *Civile Wares* (1594–1609); and he wrote

Dance of Death. Holbein's *Death Comes to the Monk*

Danilova with Anton Dolin in *Le Bal*

the tragedies *Cleopatra* (1594) and the *Tragedie of Philotas* (1604).

Daniell William (1769–1837). English landscape painter and engraver. With his uncle THOMAS (1749–1840), also a landscape painter, he travelled to India (1784) and together they produced *Oriental Scenery* (1808), 6 vols of aquatints. William D.'s most remarkable plates illustrate *A Voyage around Great Britain* (1814–25)–text by Richard Ayton–a monumental coll. of romantic landscape themes.

Danilov Kirsha (1722–90). Russian writer who put together the 1st coll. of Russian folk-tales (publ. posth. 1804, 1818).

Danilova Alexandra (1904–). Russian-born dancer; she studied at the Imperial Ballet School, St Petersburg. In 1924 D. joined a small group of dancers led by Balanchine and subsequently joined Diaghilev's Ballets Russes, with which she stayed until it was disbanded in 1929. In 1938 she became leading dancer in Col. de Basil's co. and in 1953 formed her own co.

Danilova Marie (1793–1810). Russian dancer of the Imperial Ballet, St Petersburg. While still a pupil she triumphed in *The Loves of Venus and Adonis* (1808), but died of consumption before she reached full maturity as a dancer.

Danish Ballet, The Royal. Resident co. at the Royal Theatre, Copenhagen. It is unique among state ballets in preserving its past repertoire intact, having Galleotti's *Les Caprices de Cupidon* (1786), the oldest ballet still performed anywhere in the world. The ballets performed under A. Bournonville during 1829–79 are the foundation of the repertoire–*Napoli, Kermesse in Bruges*, traditional ballets with very little dancing 'on points' and a great deal of mime. Although the Russian influence began to be felt when Vera Volkova took charge of the School in 1951, the traditional style of dancing is still very closely adhered to.

Dan(c)kerts or **Dankers** Hendrik (1630?–1680?). Dutch landscape painter and portrait engraver; he visited Italy (1653) and lived in England from 1668 to 1679. He painted views of famous places for Charles II and some large classical landscapes in the style of Claude Lorrain. His brother JOHN (*fl.* 1660) was an historical painter who also worked in England.

D'Annunzio Gabriele (1863–1938). Italian poet, novelist and playwright whose career shows affinities with both the *decadence and Fascism: his thirst for action culminated in his leading an unofficial force to annex Fiume (Trieste), disputed between Italy and Yugoslavia, which he controlled for a year (1919). His 1st poems, *Primo vere* (1878), while largely imitative of Carducci, already showed those characteristics which were to mark his later poetry–linguistic and metrical fluency, a search for sensations, a cruel sensuality and a taste for violence. His 1st vol. to bring recognition was the brilliant and colourful *Canto novo* (1882). His novels included *Il Piacere* (1889; *The Child of Pleasure*, 1898), *Trionfo della morte* (1894; *The Triumph of Death*, 1898) and *Il Fuoco* (1900; *The Flame of Life*, 1900), the story of his love-affair with the great actress Duse. His dramatic works, including *Francesca da Rimini* (1901), a recasting of the Dante and Beatrice story, became famous largely through magnificent interpretations by Duse.

danse macabre: *Dance of Death

danseur noble. In ballet, term applied to a principal male classical dancer.

Dante Alighieri (1265–1325). Italian poet born in Florence of a noble but impoverished Guelph family. When still a child he saw, walking on the Ponte Vecchio, Beatrice Portinari, the woman whom he worshipped all his life. In about 1285, however, he married Gemma Donati who bore him 3 sons and 2 daughters. In 1289 D. fought in the battle of Campaldino. He took an active part in the political life of Florence, siding with the moderate White Guelphs against the Black party. D. became a member of the Council of the People (1295) and of the Council of One Hundred (1296), the body responsible for the most vital decisions of the city. In 1300 he was appointed one of the *priori* and as such banished from Florence the leaders of the Whites and Blacks. In 1301 the Blacks seized power and reprisals began. D. was banished from Tuscany for 2 years. He hoped to be able to return to Florence by force of arms, but soon became

Daniell. *Carlingford Castle*

Gabriele D'Annunzio

Dante: 15th-c. bronze

Danti. *The Decollation of St John the Baptist*

Danube school. Altdorfer's *Landscape near Regensburg in the Danube Valley*

Lorenzo da Ponte

disillusioned by the self-seeking stupidity and intrigues of the other exiles and gave up hope of ever returning. His 1st refuge was Verona and later Ravenna where, much revered as a poet and scholar, he died.

D. was the 1st major poet of the European vernacular literatures and it was his choice of the Tuscan dialect which established it as the literary language of Italy. His work is coloured by the restlessness of the exile but reveals a profound yet simple intellect. The diction of his greatest work, *The Divine Comedy*, reflects this simplicity of intention, being purposely framed to the modes of everyday speech, rejecting rhetoric and achieving immediate, direct statement. *The Divine Comedy* was probably begun about 1310 but not completed until D.'s last years. It is the history of the poet's spiritual development and presents, in larger terms, the gradual progress of the human soul to the restoration of its lost dignity. It is in 3 parts and describes the poet's journey through Hell (*Inferno*), Purgatory and Paradise. The poet's companion and guide on the 1st part of his journey is Virgil, symbol of human reason; in Paradise, he is escorted by Beatrice, symbol of revelation. Each part has 33 cantos and an introductory one, and the verse form is the *terza rima, invented by D., a stanza of 3 hendecasyllabic lines with the rhyming pattern *aba*, *bcb*, *cdc*. An interesting feature of the work is D.'s comments on near-contemporaries and historical figures, whom he meets during the journey.

D.'s other works include: the *Rime*, about 100 lyrics mainly on love and allegorical subjects, the earlier ones in the tradition of the *dolce stil nuovo but others showing a strong *Provençal influence; *Vita nuova* (*c.* 1293), 31 poems celebrating D.'s love for Beatrice, interspersed with prose commentaries; *De Vulgari Eloquentia* (1303–4), on Italian dialects and contemporary poets; *Convivio* (1304–7), a work in poetry and prose treating in Italian subjects hitherto discussed only in Latin, e.g. philosophy, astronomy, metaphysics and the nature of imperial authority; and *De Monarchia* (completed in 1313), prompted by the hope that the Emperor Henry VII would effectively restore imperial authority in Italy. This treatise is important in the developing medieval theory of the empire and particularly the contention (supported by D.) that the emperor derives his temporal power direct from God; after D.'s death Pope John XXII had it publicly burnt.

Dante Symphony (1867). Programmatic symphony for female chorus and orchestra by Liszt. It is based on Dante's *Divine Comedy* and was dedicated to Wagner.

Danti Vincenzo (1530–76). Perugian sculptor strongly influenced by Michelangelo. He executed a statue of Pope Julius III (1555) in the cathedral, Perugia, but later worked in the Baptistery, Florence, where he completed Sansovino's *Baptism of Christ* and produced his greatest work, *The Decollation of St John the Baptist*.

Dantons Tod (1835). Historical tragedy by *Büchner.

Danube school. Name used to describe the developments in landscape painting which took place in the Danube region in the early 16th c. The artists working there, who included Altdorfer, Huber and Lucas Cranach (as a young man), introduced a romantic awareness of landscape as an expressive adjunct to human action. They also produced a large number of pure landscape drawings.

Daphnis and Chloe (2nd or 3rd c. A.D.). Greek pastoral novel attributed to Longus (of whom nothing is known) and typical of the genre, about a boy and girl brought up as shepherds, their love, separations, discovery that they have wealthy parents and final union.

Daphnis and Chloe. 3-scene ballet with choreography by Fokine, music by Ravel and décor by Bakst, 1st performance 1912; a later version (1951) was arranged by Ashton with décor by Craxton.

Da Ponte Lorenzo (1749–1838). Italian poet and Mozart's librettist for the operas *The Marriage of Figaro*, *Don Giovanni* and *Così fan tutti*. Da P. was dismissed from a professorship of rhetoric in 1776 for spreading Rousseauistic doctrines, was banished from Venice in 1779 and became (1782) official poet to the imperial theatres in Vienna, where he met Mozart. In 1804 he went to the U.S.

Daquin (d'Aquin) Louis-Claude (1694–1772). French keyboard virtuoso and composer, a pupil of L. Marchand. D. held several organ posts, among them that of the Chapel Royal. His compositions for organ and harpsichord include *Le Coucou*.

Dassin. *Naked City*

Daret. *Nativity with the Annunciation to the Shepherds*

D'Arblay Madame Frances: Fanny *Burney

Daret Jacques (*c.* 1403–*c.* 68). Early Netherlands painter trained by the *Master of Flémalle. Rogier van der Weyden was probably a fellow-pupil. 2 parts of an altarpiece, the *Nativity with the Annunciation to the Shepherds* (Thyssen-Bornemisza Coll., Lugano) and the *Adoration of the Kings* (Berlin), are fine and typical examples of his work.

Dargomizshky Alexander Sergeyevich (1813–69). Russian composer, a lifelong friend of Glinka. After the success of his opera *Russalka* (1857) D. toured Europe during 1864/5. His early music, e.g. the operas *Esmeralda* (1847) and *The Triumph of Bacchus* (written 1845) and songs, showed little originality but he developed a style compounded of national idiom, vigorous anti-romantic realism and a strict regard for words, e.g. *The Stone Guest* (produced posth. 1872) orchestrated by Rimsky-Korsakov. His later songs virtually originated the Russian art song.

Daring Young Man on the Flying Trapeze, The (1934). Story by William Saroyan.

Darío Rubén. Pseud. of Félix Rubén García Sarmiento (1867–1916). Nicaraguan poet, the prime originator of the *modernista* style, which affected all the Spanish-speaking countries. His new rhythms and imagery were partly derived from the French Parnassians and symbolists, partly founded on medieval forms, and partly his own. D.–the Swinburne of Spanish poetry–was copiously inventive but prone to drop into rhetorical repetition. *Prosas profanas* (1896; 1922), his most revolutionary coll., treated with original verbal music themes historical, exotic and cosmopolitan. Aristocratic and religious themes followed in a succession of vols written in freer verse forms which culminated in the ecstatic *Canto a la Argentino* (1914). D. travelled widely in the Spanish-speaking world, and his flamboyant personality reinforced his poetic fame. Latterly his work has been praised less for itself than for its innovating influences. Nevertheless, a number of his poems, particularly those with a tropical setting, are masterpieces of pictorial evocation.

Darke Harold Edwin (1888–). English composer and organist. His works include *A Hymn of Heavenly Beauty* (1935) and *A Song for David* (1956) for chorus and orchestra, a symphony and other instrumental music.

Darkness at Noon (1940). Novel by Arthur *Koestler.

Darrieux Danielle (1917–). French film actress, a stylishly sophisticated and romantic comedienne. Her films include *Mayerling* (1935), *Occupe toi d'Amélie* (1949), *La Ronde* (1950) and *Le Rouge et le Noir* (1954).

Dart (Robert) Thurston (1921–). English musicologist, harpsichordist and conductor; professor at Cambridge and, from 1964, London univs.

Darwin Charles (Robert). (1809-82). English biologist, author of *On the Origin of Species ...* (1859), which propounded a theory of the evolution of life based on natural selection. It encountered fierce opposition (especially from the religious) but has long been accepted as essentially correct.

Darwin Erasmus (1731–1802). English doctor, scientist and poet, grandfather of Charles D. His poetry, successful in his day, was didactic and artificial. *The Botanic Garden* contained 2 parts, *The Economy of Vegetation* (1791) and *The Loves of the Plants* (1789).

Dass Petter (1647–1708). Norwegian clergyman and poet. His chief work, *Nordlands Trompet* (posth. 1739), was full of intense national fervour, and began the revival of Norwegian nationalism and Norwegian poetry.

Dassin Jules (1912–). U.S. film director. D. became known for the documentary-style thrillers *Brute Force* (1947) and *Naked City* (1948), made for Mark *Hellinger, and followed with the similar *Thieves Highway* (1949) and *Night and the City* (1950). Black-listed in Hollywood for political reasons, he has since worked in France on *Du Rififi chez les Hommes* (1955) and in Greece on the comedy *Never on Sunday* (1960).

date letter. The stamped letter of the alphabet, denoting the year, marked on English gold and silver objects at the assay office. Each cycle, from A to Z, has a different script. The d. l. seems to have originated in the late 15th c.

Rubén Darío

Charles Darwin

Erasmus Darwin: painting by Joseph Wright of Derby

Daumier. *The Painter before his Easel*

Alphonse Daudet

Dauberval (Jean Bercher) (1742–1806). French dancer and choreographer, a pupil of Noverre. Although he had been part of the establishment at the Paris Opéra (1770–83) he rebelled against the neo-classicism of the day by producing the 1st comedy ballet, *La Fille Mal Gardée* (1786), a story of village love.

Daubigny Charles-François (1817–78). French landscape painter associated with the Barbizon school. D. painted chiefly in the Île-de-France, but travelled in Italy, Spain, England and Holland. Typical of his work are *The Lock at Optevoz* (Louvre) and *River Scene with Ducks* (N.G., London).

Daudet Alphonse (1840–97). French novelist. D.'s career was spent in the Parisian literary world, where he was a friend of the Goncourt brothers and wrote mainly *naturalistic novels about contemporary life. The most notable are *Le Nabab* (1877; *The Nabob*, 1878) and *Sapho* (1884; 1886). Better remembered are his poetic and humorous sketches of southern life in *Lettres de mon moulin* (1866 in *Le Figaro*; *Letters from my Mill*, 1880) and the boastful, lovable southern type, Tartarin, in a series of novels beginning with *Tartarin de Tarascon* (1872; *The New Don Quixote. . .*, 1875). D. was also the author of the play *L'Arlésienne* (1872), for which Bizet wrote the music.

Daumier. Don Quixote charges a platoon of sheep

Daumier Honoré (-Victorin) (1808–79). French painter, caricaturist, graphic artist and sculptor. Trained in Paris and attracted to lithography, D. made his living from 1830 with cartoons in the satirical journals *La Caricature* and *Le Charivari*. He lampooned the government (being imprisoned in 1832 for his attack on King Louis-Philippe), the bourgeoisie in the *Robert Macaire* series, and the legal profession. From about 1848 D. attempted to establish himself as a serious painter in oils, but he was hampered by his fame as a left-wing cartoonist, his dependence on his fellow-painters for most of his subjects and his refusal to give his works the finish then considered necessary. A brief period of success under the Third Republic was followed by neglect, poverty and near-blindness. Since his death he has been recognized as a pioneer, chiefly of expressionism, e.g. *The Painter before his Easel* (Phillips Coll., Washington), a master draughtsman, e.g. *We want Barabbas!* (Mus. Folkwang, Essen), a major graphic artist and a sculptor of vigour and expressiveness. In his sketches and oil paintings of Don Quixote and Sancho Panza D. created a great modern reinterpretation of Cervantes's characters, e.g. *Don Quixote* and *Sancho Panza* (Courtauld Gal., London).

Daumier. *For the Defence*. Also *caricature

D'Avenant Sir William (1606–68). English poet and dramatist; poet laureate (1638). D'A. was rumoured to be Shakespeare's natural son. As a theatre manager, he was one of the first to use women actors; and his *Siege of Rhodes* (1656) was the 1st English 'opera'. Works include: *Gondibert* (1651), a romantic epic in 4-line stanzas; and the plays *The Tragedy of Albovine . . .* (1627–9) and *The Wits* (licensed 1634).

Daves Delmer (1904–). U.S. film director. D. was a script writer (e.g. on *McCarey's *Love Affair*) until he started directing in 1943; since then he has usually written, and lately produced, his films. He gained a reputation for 'serious' westerns like *3.10 to Yuma* (1957) and *Cowboy* (1957). However, after the great success of *A Summer Place* (1959) he has continued with similar lush teenage novelettes.

David. Sculpture by *Michelangelo.

David Félicien-César (1810–76). French composer. He travelled in the Middle East and after his return had great success with the programmatic 'ode-symphony' *Le Désert* (1844). His music is unequal, but Berlioz recognized his skill as a melodist and orchestrator. Oriental elements frequently occur in his operas. He also wrote chamber music and songs.

David Ferdinand (1810–73). German violinist, from 1835 leader of the Gewandhaus Orchestra, Leipzig, and from 1843 violin professor at the Conservatory there; his pupils included Joachim. D.'s violin studies, *Violinschule* (1863), are a classic; he advised Mendelssohn on his violin concerto and gave the 1st performance.

David Gerard (*c.* 1460–1523). Netherlands painter who succeeded Memlinc as the most important painter of the school. Born in Oudewater, D. was admitted to the painters' guild in Bruges in 1484. He was influenced by earlier Netherlands masters, in particular van Eyck and van der Goes, but his work shows close relationship with the painting of Geertgen tot Sint Jans and the miniaturists of Bruges. He was commissioned by the town of Bruges to paint a number of works, including 2 pictures to warn officials of the stern retribution for corruption and injustice–*The Judgement of Cambyses* and *The Flaying of Sisamnes* (both in the City Mus., Bruges)–a *Last Judgement* (lost) and *Virgin with Child and Angels* (Rouen Mus.). Other important works are *The Baptism of Christ* (City Mus., Bruges), *The Marriage at Cana* (Louvre), 2 landscapes (Mauritshuis, The Hague), and *The Virgin and Child with Saints and Donor* (N.G., London), the most serene and successful **sacra conversazione* painted in N. Europe.

David Jacques-Louis (1748–1825). French painter, the leading figure of neo-classical painting. Trained in the rococo tradition of Boucher by J.-M. Vien, D. repudiated this training with his *Oath of the Horatii* (Louvre), shown in Rome and Paris in 1784 and immediately recognized as a landmark in painting. Its colouring was lucid and cool, its drawing strong, simple and severe. In its theme it advocated a return from the diversions of a pleasure-loving aristocracy to the traditionally austere virtues of the early Roman republic. D. became virtual dictator of the arts in France from the outbreak of the Revolution to the fall of Napoleon; few men have exercised such power over the art and taste of their period. His subjects–allegory, history and mythology–and his search for an ideal beauty based on the supposed canons of classical sculpture were to become the hall-marks of academic art in the 19th c. D. celebrated the victories and extolled the martyrs of the Revolution, e.g. *The Death of Marat* (M. R. des B.-A., Brussels); in *Return of the Sons of Brutus* (Louvre) the theme of republican virtue recurs. D. was himself a deputy and was briefly imprisoned after the fall of Robespierre (1794); from his cell he painted the *View of the Luxembourg Gardens* (Louvre), a small masterpiece of landscape painting, wholly romantic and warmly evocative in feeling. His portraits too, are far from austere, e.g. of M. Seriziat and Mme Seriziat (both Louvre), and of the famous beauty and conversationalist Mme Récamier (1800; Louvre). Later he became the painter-advocate of Napoleon, e.g. *The Coronation of Napoleon* (Louvre) and his work was fundamental in the creation of the Empire style.

David Pierre-Jean, known as 'David d'Angers' (1788–1856). Neo-classic sculptor who was born at Angers and studied in Paris and Rome. He executed the monument to Condé at Versailles and the Gutenberg monument, Strassburg. More forceful are his portrait busts and medallions.

David and Lisa (1962). Film directed by F. *Perry.

David Copperfield (1849–50). Novel by *Dickens.

Davidson John (1857–1909). Scottish poet, novelist and playwright. D. committed suicide by drowning. His poetry, best in his lyrics, was generally uneven; but D.'s mastery of a colloquial idiom in verse influenced T. S. Eliot, particularly the poem *Thirty Bob a Week* in *Ballads and Songs* (1894).

Davie Alan (1920–). Scottish artist who studied at Edinburgh School of Art. His abstract paintings, e.g. *Seascape Erotic* (1955), often have a tortured, expressionistic quality.

Davie Donald (1922–). English poet and critic. His increasingly strict discipline of diction and metre, e.g. *Bridges of Reason* (1955) and *Events and Wisdoms* (1964), intensifies the impact of the nuances of flat everyday speech.

Davies Arthur Bowen (1862–1928). U.S. painter of romanticized landscapes with whimsical, elongated figures, e.g. *Crescendo* (1910; Whitney Mus., New York). He was a member of The *Eight. He supported new trends and artistic independence and took a leading part in organizing the *Armory Show. After it he worked for a time in a modified cubist style.

Davies Sir Henry Walford (1869–1941). English composer, organist (at the Temple church, 1898–1923), broadcaster and Master of the King's Music from 1934. D.'s greatest achievement was his series of broadcasts on music, to schools (1923–34) and 'Music and the Ordinary Listener' (1926–9). His compositions include choral works, e.g. the cantata *Everyman* (1904), songs and part songs.

Davies John (1565?–1618?). English poet whose chief work was *Microcosmos* (1603), based on the trs. of Du *Bartas by J. Sylvester. D.'s epigrams, contained in *The Scourge of Folly* (1611?), give interesting information about such contemporary poets as Jonson and Fletcher.

Gerard David. *The Baptism of Christ*

J.-L. David. *Oath of the Horatii.* Also *The *Death of Marat*, **Récamier*

A. B. Davies. *Crescendo*

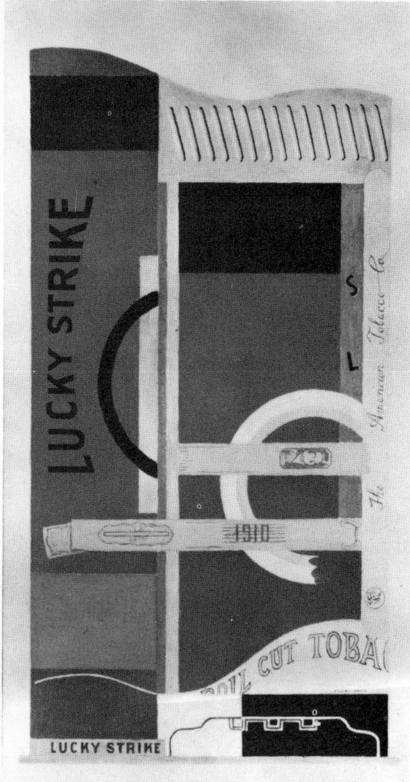

Stuart Davis. *Lucky Strike*

Lawrence Daws. *The Simgazer II* (1961)

Miles Davis

Dearden. *Sapphire*

Davies Sir John (1569–1626). English lawyer and poet. The strong clear quatrains of his masterpiece, *Nosce teipsum* (1599), are akin to the soliloquizing of Hamlet. He also wrote admirable verse in *Orchestra* (1596) and *Hymnes of Astraea* (1599).

Davies Peter Maxwell (1934–). English composer; one of the group taught by Richard Hall at the Royal Manchester College of Music. Study of Indian and medieval music clearly affected his compositions, which often employ plainsong or other similar themes in conjunction with serial methods. At Cirencester Grammar School (1958–60) D. taught his pupils to compose in an advanced idiom. His works include: *Alma Redemptoris Mater* for wind sextet; *Prolation for Orchestra*; *O magnum mysterium* for children's voices, orchestra and organ, and *Ricercar* and *Doubles* for chamber ensemble.

Davies Robertson (1913–). Canadian journalist, critic, dramatist and novelist. His controlled satire and refreshingly sharp wit are best developed in his novel *A Mixture of Frailties* (1958).

Davies William Henry (1871–1940). Welsh poet. D. began writing verse at the age of 34; most of his work is traditional in themes and techniques, though some poems contain sharp social criticism. His early life as a tramp and pedlar is recorded in *The Autobiography of a Super-tramp* (1908).

Davis Bette (1908–). U.S. actress who, without glamour, reached the top in 3 years from her début in 1932. Her films have seldom been equal to her powerful personality and considerable talent. She won Oscars in 1935 and 1938; notable performances include *The Petrified Forest* (1936), *The Little Foxes* (1941), *All About Eve* (1950) and *Whatever Happened to Baby Jane?* (1963).

Davis Miles (1926–). U.S. trumpeter. The concentrated intensity of his style, abandoned and poignant in turn, has made him one of the leading influences in modern jazz. After early experience with groups led by Charlie *Parker, he led a short-lived 9-piece band (1949) that had a revolutionary influence on jazz orchestration. Since then he has led small groups and collaborated with arranger Gil Evans.

Davis Richard Harding (1864–1916). U.S. writer and war correspondent whose active world-wide career as a journalist is reflected in his books; these include *Gallegher and Other Stories* (1891), *Van Bibber and Others* (1892) and *Soldiers of Fortune* (1897).

Davis Stuart (1894–). U.S. painter and graphic artist. His early work was in the realist tradition of Robert Henri, under whom he studied in New York, but he subsequently submitted to cubist influences, in particular that of Léger. The turning-point in his career came in 1927, when he began to experiment with still-life abstractions in his *Eggbeater* series. The strident colour, bold pattern and calligraphic features of his later work reflect the contemporary U.S. city scene.

Davydov Denis Vasilyevich (1784–1839). Russian poet, and an officer who served in the 1812 campaign against Napoleon. Much of his work celebrates military virtues and pleasures.

Daws Lawrence (1927–). Australian painter. His work, characterized by rich glowing colours, has the Australian landscape as its inspiration; the style is semi-abstract, the treatment increasingly metaphysical.

Day Doris (1924–). U.S. film actress endowed with a charming voice and personality. D.'s early films were indifferent musicals, *Calamity Jane* (1954) and *The Pajama Game* (1957) being exceptions; she has since turned more to drama and comedy.

Day John (1522–84). One of the earliest to print music in England; in 1560 he publ. a 4-part setting of choral items in the Anglican prayer book.

Day John (*c.* 1574–*c.* 1640). English dramatist, author of the allegorical masque *The Parliament of Bees* (1608–16).

Day of Wrath (1943). Film directed by C. *Dreyer.

Dead Souls (1841). Novel by *Gogol.

Dean James (1931–55). U.S. film actor; D.'s broodingly violent film character made him an adolescent hero; his early death in a car crash, after only 3 films, caused a wave of worshipping hysteria. The films he appeared in were:

East of Eden (1954), *Rebel without a Cause* (1955) and *Giant* (1956).

Dearden Basil (1911–). British film director. Starting with co-direction credits on Will Hay comedies, D. went to Ealing, working from 1948 with Michael Relph as producer and/or co-director. Their most recent period has been characterized by attempts to popularize social themes by grafting them on to mystery/thriller plots, e.g. the colour problem with *Sapphire* (1959), homosexuality with *Victim* (1961).

Death and the Maiden. Nickname for Schubert's string quartet in D min. (written 1826), so called because the 2nd movement uses part of his song of the same name as a theme for variations.

Death and Transfiguration. The English version of *Tod und Verklärung* (1890), a symphonic poem by R. *Strauss.

Death Comes for the Archbishop (1927). Novel by Willa *Cather.

Death in the Afternoon (1932). Book by *Hemingway.

Death in Venice (1913). Long short story by Thomas *Mann.

Death of a Salesman (1949). Play by Arthur *Miller.

Death of Ivan Illyich, The (1886). Short novel by Tolstoy.

Death of Marat, The. Painting by J.-L. *David.

déboulés: *chaînés

Debucourt Philibert-Louis (1755–1832). French painter and graphic artist, caricaturist of manners.

Deburau Jean-Gaspard (1796–1846). French actor, the creator of the melancholy yet eagerly hopeful love-lorn Pierrot typified in Jean-Louis Barrault's performance in the film *Les Enfants du Paradis*.

Debussy Achille-Claude (1862–1918). French composer born at St-Germain-en-Laye, near Paris. He entered the Conservatoire as a piano student in 1873; in 1880 he met Tchaikovsky's patroness Nadezhda von Meck and travelled in Europe in her entourage for a year; in 1884 D. won the Rome prize with his cantata *L'enfant prodigue*. An important year was 1888, when D. made his 1st visit to Bayreuth; the following year, at the Exposition Universelle, D. heard and was much impressed by examples of Javanese music. In 1899 he had left his mistress Gabrielle Dupont to marry Rosalie Texier, and in 1904 he abandoned her for the rich Mme Emma Bardac, whom he married in 1905. In 1908–9, on a visit to London, he suffered the 1st attack of the cancer which was to kill him. Apart from the composer Erik Satie, a lifelong friend, D. numbered among his acquaintances the poets Mallarmé and Maeterlinck, whose works he set, *Nijinsky with whom he collaborated in *Jeux*, the sculptor Rodin and many others.
D.'s interests in the other arts, in the paintings of Turner and Hokusai, in the poetry of Swinburne and the new aesthetic of art nouveau were fully in line with his desire to bring music, literature and painting into a single communicating world of art.
His works include early compositions showing a debt to German and French composers of the mid 19th c., e.g. the songs *Cinq Poèmes de Baudelaire* (1888) and *Ariettes oubliées* (1890), the *Fantaisie* for piano and orchestra (composed 1889) and the *Suite bergamasque* (1890). By the 1890s, influenced by contemporary developments in painting and poetry, D. had evolved that 'impressionistic' style of elusive melodic line and shifting harmonies usually regarded as characteristic of him. Works in this brilliantly sensitive and evocative idiom include the opera *Pelléas et Mélisande* (1902), from Maeterlinck, a masterpiece to be compared with Wagner's music-dramas; *Prélude à l'Après-midi d'un faune* (1894), a re-evocation in musical terms of the allusive symbolism of Mallarmé's poem; *3 Nocturnes* for orchestra (1899), the string quartet (1893), the songs *Fêtes galantes* (1892) and *Pour le piano* (1896), *Estampes* (1903) and *Images I* (1905).
In the early 1900s D.'s style became harder, more precise and more descriptive. The masterpieces of his last period include: *La Mer* (1903–5), *Gigues*, *Ibéria*, and *Rondes de Printemps* (1906–12); *Le Martyre de saint Sebastien* (1911), incidental music to a mystery play by d'Annunzio; and the ballet *Jeux* (1912) commissioned by Diaghilev, thought by some to foreshadow the polytonalities of Stravinsky's *Rite of Spring*. Other works include *Children's Corner* (1906–8), *Préludes* (book I 1910; book II 1910–13), *Études* (1915), all for piano.

decadence. A term applied to any period of artistic or moral decline. It has also a specific and not necessarily pejorative meaning in connection with the late 19th-c. movement originating in France and characterized by emphasis on the isolated role of the artist, hostility to bourgeois society, a taste for the morbid and perverse, and a belief in the superiority of the artificial to the natural. This was a development of some of the attitudes of *romanticism, first exemplified by Baudelaire's *Les Fleurs du Mal*. It reached its full development in the last 2 decades of the 19th c., reacting against *naturalism; Huysmans's *À Rebours* became the virtual textbook of the movement and a magazine, *Le Décadent*, was publ. briefly (1886). In England d. was at its height in the 1890s; representative figures were Oscar Wilde and Aubrey Beardsley.

Decameron, The. Book by *Boccaccio.

Decamps Alexandre (Gabriel) (1803–60). French painter who exploited Near Eastern subject-matter in the belated romanticism of the French school, visiting Constantinople and Asia Minor before Delacroix went to Morocco, and winning contemporary acclaim for his exotic scenes. He also painted landscapes and historical subjects and was draughtsman, lithographer, caricaturist and book illustrator.

Decembrio Pier Candido (1399–1477). Italian humanist and apostolic secretary to Nicholas V; author of biographies of Francesco Sforza and Visconti. D. completed the Latin trs. of Plato's *Republic* begun by his father and dedicated it to Duke Humphrey of Gloucester.

Decline and Fall (1928). Novel by Evelyn *Waugh.

Decline and Fall of the Roman Empire, The History of the (1776–88). History by Edward *Gibbon.

Decline of the West, The (1918–23). Historical work by Oswald *Spengler.

Decoeur Émile (1876–). The leading French artist potter of the early 20th c.; he is a master of colour and glaze techniques but his work has been criticized for weakness in form.

Claude Debussy

The Death of Marat

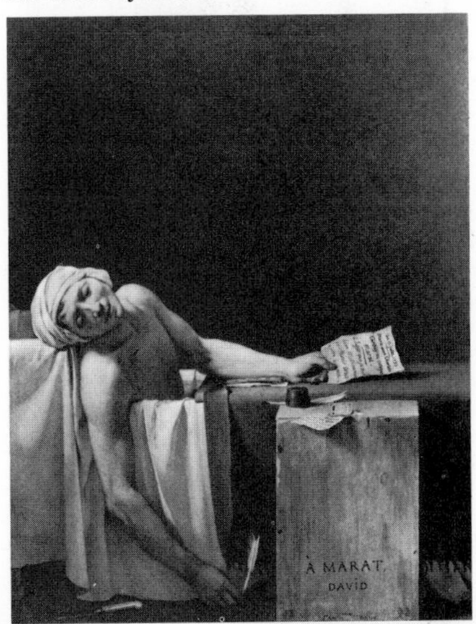

Decamps. *The Bell Ringers*

Decorated. Stained-glass window (called 'The Bishop's Eye') at Lincoln cathedral

Decorated. Detail from the Lady chapel, Ely cathedral

Daniel Defoe

Thomas Dekker

décor. Comprehensive term for scenery and costumes used in theatrical productions, i.e. ballet, drama and opera.

decorated style. A term used of the prevalent style in English *Gothic architecture of the late 13th c. and the 14th c. The simple lancet windows of *Early English gave place to large windows with increasingly complicated curvilinear tracery, elaborate rib-vaulting came to replace the more robust earlier style, and such decorative features as naturalistically carved foliage were introduced.

Dedekind Friedrich (d. 1598). German author of the Latin satire *Grobianus* (1549; German trs. 1551). In the tradition of S. Brant's *Narrenschiff* it attacked contemporary grossness and viciousness.

Deeping (George) Warwick (1877–1950). English author of somewhat sentimental, conventional novels; his best known is *Sorrell and Son* (1925).

Deering Richard: *Dering

Deerslayer, The (1841). Novel by James Fenimore Cooper.

Defence of Poetry, A (1821). Essay by *Shelley.

Deffand Marie, marquise du (1697–1780). French society woman whose *salon* was frequented by d'Alembert and other *philosophes*. She conducted a correspondence with Horace Walpole.

Defoe Daniel (1661?–1731). English writer. Intended for the Dissenting ministry, D. went into business instead, but was bankrupted in 1692, probably as a result of political distractions–he supported first Monmouth and afterwards William III, whom he served as a polemicist, e.g. the satirical poem *The True-born Englishman* (1701). From 1700 onwards D. was involved in controversy between the High Church party and the Dissenters; this led to his imprisonment in 1703 for libelling the Church in his pamphlet *The Shortest Way with the Dissenters*; his technique here as elsewhere was to give ironic approval to a logical but ridiculous extension of his opponents' policies. In prison he began to publ. *The Review*, a periodical which appeared from 1704 to 1713 and generally attempted a temporizing line: it became the model for 18th-c. periodicals. From his release in 1704 D. became more and more involved in dubious political activities: in 1715 he attempted to explain his position in the *Appeal to Honour and Justice* which is the chief authority for his life.
D. was a phenomenally prolific polemical writer both in prose and verse, but is now remembered chiefly for his prose narratives, *Robinson Crusoe* (1719), *Moll Flanders* (1722), and also *A Journal of the Plague Year* (1722). Famous in his lifetime as a 'mystifier', he gave documentary weight and conviction to his fictions by the accumulation of significant detail. *A Journal of the Plague Year* traces the events of the Great Plague of 1665 and the reactions of Londoners from early apprehensions, through frantic despair, to final numb indifference to death and horror with such authenticity that it has been taken for a contemporary document. D.'s vivid circumstantial imagination can be seen also in *Robinson Crusoe*, where he embellished accounts of the contemporary Alexander Selkirk's shipwreck not only with plausible detail, but also with an acute sense of the probable emotions of a man in that situation. This famous book had a great European vogue, being particularly important in German literary history (J. G. *Schnabel). D.'s style, consistently grave, lucid and explanatory, heightens the effect of sober truth. *Moll Flanders* can stand as an example of D.'s other stories: a good-humoured first-person account of a harlot's progress to married respectability; its morality, though paraded, is perfunctory. The novel *Roxana, or the Fortunate Mistress* (1724) tells of a deserted wife turned woman of fortune.

De Forest John William (1826–1906). U.S. writer chiefly remembered for *Miss Ravenel's Conversion from Secession to Loyalty* (1867), a realistic novel of the Civil War, based on his own experiences. D.'s other novels include a satire on political life, *Honest John Vane* (1875).

dégagé. French term used in ballet to describe the disengaging of the working leg, usually in preparation for a step.

Degas (Hilaire Germain) Edgar (1834–1917). French painter, draughtsman, sculptor and graphic artist, the son of a rich banker and a Creole mother. After a typical bourgeois education he studied law, but in 1855 went to the École des Beaux-Arts in Paris, then to Naples and Rome. In 1861 he was back in Paris, where he painted portraits and compositions in a severely classical style, later turning to the painting of dancers, the races, town life and portraits in an environment, which established his reputation. Though not in agreement with impressionist theory he allied himself with the movement from its beginning in protest against sterile academic theory and practice, and exhibited with the impressionist painters until 1886. His life was marred by hypochondria increasing with old age, and with his eyesight failing towards the end of his life, he shunned all society.
D. discovered and appropriated the new environment of 19th-c. industrial man–the townscape, the street, the interiors of the places of entertainment and work of all social classes. He observed the behaviour of the female and male human animal against this setting with analytical detachment, biting wit and an unfailing eye for the typical. For this purpose he made use of photography, the store of knowledge accumulated in museums, the technical knowledge of craftsmen and the visual discoveries of the impressionist painters. He strove after perfection in every possible way, for he believed that given sensibility the mastery of the technical means was decisive. He experimented therefore with graphic media, perfected the art of pastel, made monotypes and etchings and modelled in clay and wax in order to understand better the movements of his dancers and racehorses. These studies, which were never intended for exhibition, were cast in bronze after his death and thus

preserved. He never painted on the spot, but composed only after much observation, many studies and a most intimate knowledge of the subject, relying on a prodigious visual memory. The vision of eternal truth in fleeting reality was D.'s characteristic contribution. There is a gradual development from the early classical composition of the *Young Spartans* (1860; Tate) with its cool colours, to the new science of colour and movement in the *Washerwomen* (1879; private coll., New York), the *Miss Lola* (Tate), and the series of ballet dancers, drawings, paintings and pastels of women at their toilette, washing themselves and dressing.

Degas. *Young Spartans*

degenerate art (German, *Entartete Kunst*). The term of official denigration in Nazi Germany for the work of *avant-garde* artists such as Klee, Dix, Nolde, Marc, Kandinsky, Kokoschka, Beckmann, Grosz, Feininger, Modersohn-Becker, Corinth and Chagall. Their works were held up for public contempt in an exhibition which opened in Munich, and public galleries were stripped of all 'degenerate' exhibits.

De Haviland Olivia (1916–). U.S. film actress, a stately dark beauty who acts with a controlled intensity; she has had important roles in *Gone with the Wind* (1939), *The Heiress* (1949) and *My Cousin Rachel* (1953).

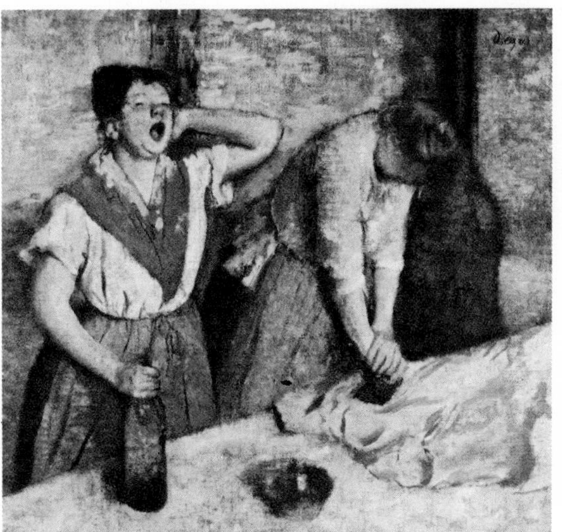

Degas. *The Laundresses* (Louvre)

Degas. *Four Dancers*; pastel

Dehmel Richard (1863–1920). German lyric poet and playwright, one of a generation strongly influenced by *naturalism.

Deineka Alexander (1899–). One of the 1st generation of Soviet painters. He was trained in Kharkov art school and then the Moscow *Vkhutemas, chiefly by *constructivists. His early work of a monumental character can be compared to Eisenstein's film methods in its use of photomontage techniques. Since 1928 D. has taught in Moscow; he is one of the most influential painters in the U.S.S.R.

Deinocrates (4th c. B.C.). Greek or Macedonian architect, favoured by Alexander the Great. He is said to have suggested carving Mt Athos into a colossal statue; the 2nd Temple of Artemis at Ephesus and the town plan of Alexandria are attributed to him by ancient writers.

Déjeuner sur l'Herbe, Le (1861–3). Painting by *Manet.

Dekker Thomas (1572?–1632). English dramatist, pamphleteer and poet, playwright for The Admiral's Men. He collaborated in works with Middleton, Webster, Massinger, Rowley and Ford, etc. D. was ridiculed by Jonson in *The Poetaster* as Demetrius Fanius, and retaliated with the satirical play *Satiro-mastix* (1601). Among his many plays are the lively comedy *The Shoemaker's Holiday* (1599) and *The Honest Whore* (*c.* 1604) (part I with Middleton), excellent portrayals of contemporary London life and manners. D.'s prose pamphlets have the same realism and vitality, pathos and humour, e.g. *The Wonderfull Yeare* (1603), a moving account of the plague, and *The Guls Horne-booke* (1609), satirizing Elizabethan fops.

De Kooning Willem (1904–). Dutch painter who moved to the U.S. (1926) where he worked as a decorator. He worked on the W.P.A. art

Degas. *The Little Dancer aged 14*; bronze. Also *impressionism

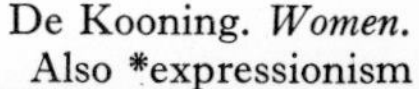

De Kooning. *Women*. Also *expressionism

Delacroix. *Dante and Virgil in the Inferno*

Delacroix. *Massacre of Chios* (detail)

Delacroix. *Liberty leading the People*

Delacroix. *Women of Algiers*. Also *Chopin and colour plate 69

project (1935) and joined the New York Group of abstract painters, of which he is still a leading member. His painting has its roots in Gorky's surrealism and he often uses open allusions to reality which may be the starting-point or may accidentally occur during the painting's execution. His best-known series, the *Women* (1952; M.M.A., New York) was the first sign of the 'new figuration' in New York painting.

Delacroix (Ferdinand Victor) Eugène (1798–1863). Leading French romantic painter, draughtsman, lithographer, writer and art critic. It is possible that he was a natural son of Talleyrand. After studies with Guérin, a follower of David, he worked at the École des Beaux-Arts for a while. In 1821, when D. was in financial difficulties, he was helped by his friend Géricault, whose work he greatly admired. D. became known from 1822 with his painting *Dante and Virgil in the Inferno*, shown in the Salon. During a visit to England in 1825 D. met Lawrence and Wilkie. In 1831 he was awarded the Légion d'Honneur and during the following year visited Morocco and Spain, a journey which proved to be crucial for the further development of his work. In 1833 a commission to decorate a *salon* in the Palais Bourbon was the beginning of a period of very intense work and a number of public commissions on a large scale, which established D. State honours followed and in 1857, after 7 rejections, he was at last elected a member of the French Institute. He was frequently ill now, but his monumental work increased and he employed about 30 assistants. His last great work, paintings for the church of St-Sulpice, occupied him until 1861.

D. used the works of his contemporaries Géricault, Gros, Constable, and of the past masters, Michelangelo, Poussin, Rubens and others, as sources from which he took what he needed. He applied the same approach to his study of nature and to reality as a whole. He made use of literature for his subjects, of science in his studies of colour relationships, of photography in his study of form, and of lithography in his graphic work. He saw painting as a bridge between painter and spectator, and colour as its most important element. He was original in the realization of related as against local colour, and in the use of complementaries and of simultaneous contrast, but it is wrong to see D. as a colourist only. His concern for form and composition increased, and towards the end he achieved a synthesis of these elements. His use of broken colour and the freedom of his brushwork was decisive in the formation of the later realist and impressionist painting. D. is best known today for his *Massacre of Chios* (1824) and the *Death of Sardanapalus* (1827), both in the Louvre, and also for the *Liberty Leading the People* (1830). He is also celebrated for his paintings of Morocco in the Louvre, such as the *Women of Algiers* (1834), his compositions of animal subjects and many watercolours. His religious paintings, e.g. the *Pietà* (1848; M. of Fine A., Boston), are less known; so are his mural paintings, mainly because of lack of access. His journals and critical writings are valuable as historical documents and as works in their own right.

Delaherche Auguste (1857–1940). One of the French artist potters whose work was an inspiration to the English artist potter movement of the early 20th c.

De l'Allemagne (1810). Book by Mme de *Staël.

De La Mare Walter (1873–1956). English poet and miscellaneous writer. His best poems, from 1902 (when he was a London businessman) into old age, are obsessions of the mind losing its everyday security. His weakness, in territory pioneered by historical romanticism, was romantic cliché (which damages his novels and tales), his strength an exceptional delicacy and individuality of cadence. Colls include *The Listeners . . .* (1912) and *Memory . . .* (1938).

Deland Margaret(ta Wade Campbell) (1857–1945). U.S. novelist whose *John Ward, Preacher* (1888), based on the marriage of a Calvinist to a free-thinking woman, was considered somewhat outspoken in its day; *The Awakening of Helena Richie* (1906) is a sequel.

Delannoy Jean (1908–). French film director. D. directed with Jean *Cocteau the latter's wartime version of the Tristan and Yseult legend, *L'Éternel Retour*. His post-war films are usually of literary successes like *La Symphonie Pastorale* (1946) from Gide, and the *Maigret* series from Simenon, with Gabin.

Delannoy Marcel-François-Georges (1898–). French composer, largely self-taught. The great success of his *opéra-comique, Poirier de Misère* (1927), effectively started his musical career. His music is bold in inspiration and technique, and makes use of 'folk' or 'popular' elements. His works include: operas, *Ginevra* (1942) after Boccaccio, *Puck* (1946) after Shakespeare; ballets, *Les Noces fantastiques* (1943); vocal works, the cycles *Trois chansons* and *Deux chansons de Clarin*; 2 symphonies and chamber music.

Delany Shelagh (1938–). English playwright born in Salford, Lancashire, which is the setting of her work; it includes the very successful *A Taste of Honey* (1958) and *Lion in Love* (1960).

de la Roche Mazo (1885–1961). Canadian novelist whose popular chronicles of the Whiteoaks family have been compared with Galsworthy's. The genre encourages the comparison, but her family is significantly matriarchal and country life is idealized throughout.

Delaroche Paul (properly Hippolyte) (1797–1856). French painter of historical subjects of romantic or sentimental interest derived from works by Sir Walter Scott, Shakespeare and others. Pictures painted with extreme naturalism such as *Children of Edward* (the Princes in the Tower) (1830; Louvre) were popular and widely used in history textbooks.

Delaunay Robert (1885–1941). French painter and the originator of orphism, which extended the cubist practice of fragmentation into the field of colour. He started painting *c.* 1904. His works of 1905–7 are painted in a brilliantly coloured divisionist technique. In 1907, under the influence of Cézanne, his palette was temporarily subdued, and during his military service (1908) he began his study of optics. He met Léger in 1909, and their sombre-coloured paintings pursued a parallel search for structural organization. In the *Saint-Severin* and *The Eiffel Tower* series (1909–10) he returned to his highly coloured palette and by 1912, in the *Fenêtre Simultané* paintings (M.M.A., Paris), he had isolated pure colour areas from the motif. In orphist paintings, D. writes, 'the breaking up of form by light creates coloured planes; these are the structure of the picture and nature is no longer a subject for description but a pretext'. He saw orphism as a logical development of impressionism and neo-impressionism, but his transition to pure abstraction was probably inspired by Kupka (*c.* 1911–12). D. was visited in 1912 by Marc, Macke and Klee, who later trs. his essay *On Light*. His influence upon the Blaue Reiter group was considerable and by 1914 he was probably the most influential artist in Paris. His later work, like Léger's, attempted to reconcile his innovations with more traditional forms.

Delaunay.
The Eiffel Tower

Delaunay-Terk Sonia (née Terk) (1885–). Russian painter who settled in Paris (1905), married R. Delaunay (1910) and with him was a pioneer of abstract painting (*orphism). After World War I she concentrated on textile and fashion design but returned to painting in the late 1930s.

Delaunay-Terk.
Portuguese Market

Delavigne Jean-François-Casimir (1793–1843). French dramatist and poet, author of much popular verse on national themes, and of comedies, notably *L'École des vieillards* (1823).

Delft. Early in the 17th c. this small Dutch town became renowned for fine tin-glazed earthenwares. The painters' guild controlled the pottery industry also, and demanded the highest standards of manufacture and decoration. At first the wares were close imitations of the Chinese blue-and-white porcelains and the Chinese and Japanese polychrome porcelains; these styles and colourings were used for scenes of Dutch origin.
By the mid 18th c. D.'s industry was declining before greater imports of genuine porcelain into Europe and competition from *Meissen.

Delft. Milk-pan

delftware. Name used in England to describe both Dutch and English fine tin-glazed earthenwares; many of the English ware antedate the rise of *Delft. A buff clay body of low-fired earthenware is covered with a lead glaze made opaque by the addition of oxides of tin. This low-fired glaze makes a good ground for decoration. Delftwares in England were manufactured at London (Lambeth), Bristol and Liverpool, etc.

Delftware tiles: picture of St Mary's Redcliffe, Bristol

Delibes (Clément-Philibert) Léo (1836–91). French composer of outstanding ballet music and a pupil of A. Adam. He wrote the music to *Coppélia* (1870) and *Sylvia* (1876) and also wrote operas, e.g. *Lakmé* (1883), church music and songs.

Delius Anthony (1916–). South African poet, younger than Roy Campbell from whom,

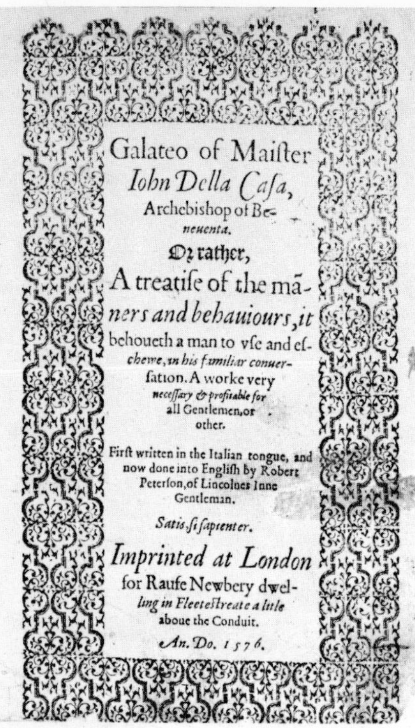
Galateo of Maiſter
Iohn Della Caſa,
Archebishop of Be-
neuenta.
Or rather,
A treatiſe of the mã-
ners and behauiours, it
behoueth a man to vſe and eſ-
chewe, in his familiar conuer-
ſation. A worke very
neceſſary & profitable for
all Gentlemen, or
other.
Firſt written in the Italian tongue, and
now done into Engliſh by Robert
Peterſon, of Lincolnes Inne
Gentleman.
Satis ſi ſapienter.
Imprinted at London
for Raufe Newbery dwel-
ling in Fleeteſtreate a litle
aboue the Conduit.
An. Do. 1576.

Della Casa. Title-page of 1st English trs. of *Galateo*

Delluc. *La Femme de nulle part*

stylistically, he appears to have learnt much. In *Unknown Border* (1954) and the political satire *The Last Division* (1959) he displays a fine seriousness of purpose in facing problems of being a poet writing in English in South Africa.

Delius Frederick (1862–1934). Composer of German extraction born at Bradford, England. In his early 20s D. was an orange planter in Florida; returning to Europe he studied at the Leipzig Conservatory (1886–8) and then moved to Paris, finally settling (1899) in the French village of Grez-sur-Loing. From about 1924 he gradually went blind and became paralysed; nevertheless he dictated 7 further works to his secretary E. *Fenby. His work, always popular in Germany, was established in England largely by the work of Sir Thomas Beecham, whose performances were fully approved by D. as definitive. The music is late romantic in mood, impressionistic in its sensuous tonalities, and shows occasional similarities to the work of D.'s friend, Grieg. D. wrote: the operas *Koanga* (1904), *A Village Romeo and Juliet* (1907), based on G. Keller's story *Romeo und Julia auf dem Dorfe*; the choral works *Appalachia* variations (1902), *Sea Drift* (1903), words from Walt Whitman, *A Mass of Life* on Nietzsche's *Also sprach Zarathustra* (1905), *A Song of the High Hills* (1912); the orchestral works *On Hearing the First Cuckoo in Spring* (1912), *Paris . . . a nocturne* (1899), *Brigg Fair: an English Rhapsody* (1907) and *In a Summer Garden* (1908), a fantasy.

Dell Floyd (1887–). U.S. novelist, author of *Moon Calf* (1920), *The Briary Bush* (1921) and *Janet March* (1923), novels of the Bohemian life in Greenwich Village. His *An Unmarried Father* (1927) was successfully staged as *Little Accident* (1928). He has also written *Love in the Machine Age* (1930) and an autobiography, *Homecoming* (1933).

Della Casa Giovanni (1503–56). Italian writer and ecclesiastic (later an archbishop). His famous book the *Galateo* (posth. 1558; 1576) was a treatise on the etiquette of civilized society; its title derived from Galeazzo Florimonte, a renowned churchman who suggested the subject. Della C. also wrote youthful licentious poems, leading a reaction in poetry against the sterile imitation of Petrarchan models, and works in Latin including a tract against heresy.

Della Casa Lisa (1919–). Soprano operatic and recital singer of Swiss origin. She is particularly noted in roles by Mozart and R. Strauss.

della Crusca, Accademia. Italian society founded in 1582. It aimed to purify the language and regarded Tuscan as its model. The DELLA CRUSCANS were a group of English poets who first met in Florence *c.* 1785 and took their title from the Accademia, of which one of the circle, R. Merry, was a member. The banality of their work was exposed by W. *Gifford.

Deller Alfred (George) (1912–). English singer who, through his unique tone quality and musicianship, revived the *counter-tenor as a solo voice.

Dello Joio Norman (1913–). U.S. composer, professor of composition at Mannes College, New York, and composer to the Columbia Broadcasting System. D. studied composition under Hindemith, whose influence was strong in his early work; D.'s mature style is lyrical and with impressionistic traits. Works include the opera *The Trial at Rouen* (1956), the ballets *On Stage* (1947) and *Air Power* (1957), orchestral and chamber music.

Delluc Louis (1890–1924). French film director; a key figure in the rise of the French cinema after World War I and leader of an *avant-garde* group including *Dulac, L'Herbier, *Gance and Jean *Epstein. D. looked to realistic U.S. and Swedish models, rather than the stagey French cinema. He wrote and directed 4 films, including *Fièvre* (1921) and *La Femme de nulle part* (1922).

Deloney Thomas (1543?–1607?). English writer, by trade a silk weaver. D. wrote early genre prose novels, substituting stories from the craftsman's world for the customary romance themes; his realistic description may have influenced Defoe, but he also skilfully introduced elements of romance into his plots. He wrote *Thomas of Reading*, *The Historie of Jacke of Newberie* and *The Gentle Craft*, which last Dekker used for his *The Shoemaker's Holiday*. D. also wrote ballads, often on current problems, e.g. *Ballad on the Want of Corn*, and pamphlets.

De L'Orme Philibert (*c.* 1510–70). French architect, patronized by Henry II and Catherine

De l'Orme. Château Anet, the entrance

de Médicis. He wrote 2 books and invented the so-called 'French order'. Although he visited Rome, his architecture is basically French in style, with Renaissance elements borrowed from Serlio. His chief works are: St-Maur-les-Fossés (1540), a château with corner pavilions and a big entrance porch; Anet (1552), of which only fragments remain, including the 'Frontispiece', the Tower of the Orders and the Chapel; and the beginning of the Tuileries (1564).

Delphi Greece. One of the religious centres of ancient Greece, sacred to Apollo. It occupies a steeply sloping site on Mt Olympus, and is centred upon a temple to Apollo, originally dating from the 6th c. B.C. Here the Pythian oracle, which was treated as absolutely authoritative, was delivered. There was also a theatre, a stadium for games, and numerous 'treasures' where the offerings from the various Greek states were kept (that of Athens has been restored).

Delvaux Laurent (1695–1778). Flemish baroque sculptor whose style showed leanings towards classicism. He worked in England and Italy before settling in the Low Countries, where he was sculptor to the Emperor Charles VI and later to Charles, Duke of Lorraine. The pulpit (1745) in Ghent cathedral is one of the best examples of his work.

Delvaux Paul (1897–). Belgian painter associated with surrealism. He studied first architecture, then painting at the Brussels Académie Royale des Beaux-Arts, and in his early work followed the expressionists Permeke and de Smet. In the 1930s he came under the influence of de Chirico and the surrealists, though never wholeheartedly adhering to their programme. In characteristic works such as *Venus Asleep* (1944; Tate) and *The Hands* (1941; Coll. Claude Spaak, Choisel) he places female nudes, juxtaposed with clothed figures, in incongruous architectural settings, imbuing the whole with the mysterious, disquieting inconsequentiality of a dream, reminiscent of de Chirico's 'metaphysical' painting.

Delvincourt Claude (1888–1954). French composer, winner of the Rome prize in 1913. He was badly wounded in World War I and active in the Resistance in World War II. His works include the dance-poem *L'Offrande à Siva* (1926), remarkable for its orchestration, and the lyric drama *Lucifer* (1948).

De Maistre Roy (1894–). Australian-born painter of French descent who settled in London in 1936. His best-known paintings–religious subjects such as the *Pietà* (1950; Tate)–are in a heavily formalized naturalistic style, deeply indebted to cubism.

demi-caractère danse. French ballet term for stylized character dancing, retaining the character idiom but transposed into the classical technique.

demi-contretemps. In ballet a step of elevation; during the leap one leg describes an arabesque before being brought forward to take the dancer's weight.

De Mille Agnes (1911–). U.S. dancer and choreographer who was an innovator in bringing American folk-tales to the ballet stage. Her *Rodeo* (1942) takes place on a ranch and *Fall River Legend* (1948) retells the story of Lizzie Borden. In her choreography for *Oklahoma!* and other shows of the 1940s she revitalized dancing in musical comedy.

De Mille Cecil B. (1881–1959). U.S. film director. His film *The Squaw Man* (1913) was one of the first made in Hollywood. The part-Biblical, part-modern *The Ten Commandments* (1923) combined sex with moralizing; *The King of Kings* (1927) was a spectacular on the life of Christ. His vast commercial success and popular reputation rested on these and their few successors, e.g. *Samson and Delilah* (1949) and *The Ten Commandments* (1956); but his main output included famous westerns, e.g. *The Plainsman* (1936), sex comedies, etc.

demi-pointe. Ballet term for the 'tiptoe' position of a dancer when taking the weight on the ball of the foot, half-way between full pointe and à terre.

demi-position. Ballet term which describes the position of the foot usually when half-way between en l'air and à terre.

Democratic Vistas (1871). Book by Walt Whitman.

Demoiselles d'Avignon, Les (1907). Painting by *Picasso.

De Morgan William Frend (1839–1917). English potter. His lead-glazed earthenware

Delphi. The Round Temple

Paul Delvaux. *Hands* (1941)

Laurent Delvaux. Pulpit of St Bavon cathedral, Ghent (detail)

De Mille. *The Ten Commandments* (1923)

Demuth. *'Lancaster'*. Also *cubist-realism

Denis. *Homage to Cézanne*

De Morgan tile

Denby spirit flasks

shows the influence of Persian, Syrian and Turkish pottery in technique, particularly the methods of applying lustre, the brilliant colours (peacock-blue, turquoise, green, pink, mulberry) of his vases, bowls and dishes, and their designs. Much of his work was in sympathy with the arts and crafts movement, and his beautiful tiles often figured in William Morris's schemes of decoration. De M. also wrote novels.

Demosthenes (384–322 B.C.). By ancient and modern consent the greatest of the Athenian orators: even Cicero took him for a model. He gained forensic experience in prosecuting his guardians for malversation, and though he won his suit, the costs of the case so impoverished him that he became a professional speech writer. About a dozen private speeches survive; the other 20 or so surviving speeches that are certainly genuine deal with public issues. Many of them, including the longest and most celebrated, *On the Crown*, were composed for political lawsuits in which D. or his friends were involved, but the great series of 'philippics' were delivered in the Athenian assembly. From his entry into political life at the age of 30, D. spoke against the growing power of Philip II, King of Macedon. After Philip's victory over the Greeks at Chaeronea in 338, D. acquiesced in the Macedonian supremacy until Alexander's death in 323, when he raised a revolt. Alexander's successors hounded him, and he took poison to evade capture. Though his opposition to Macedon was politically unrealistic, D. has been revered as the authentic voice of freedom, for the fire and sincerity of his words, the 'force' that Cicero especially admired. By studying Thucydides, Isocrates and Plato he acquired a mastery of expression, from the simplest narrative to the most complex period or the sharp bark of contempt, each of which he subordinates to his purpose.

Demuth Charles (1883–1935). U.S. painter, with Sheeler the most important exponent of cubist-realism (or precisionism), and illustrator. His preferred subject-matter was colonial and industrial architecture, which he treated with exceptional clarity and delicacy of line and colour. His early paintings, many in watercolour, included vaudeville subjects and flower pieces.

Demy Jacques (1931–). French film director. D.'s 1st feature, *Lola* (1960), was shot entirely on location, as were his later films, and his strength lies in his romantic treatment of seemingly banal, everyday events. *Les Parapluies de Cherbourg* (1963) has entirely sung dialogue, and takes up part of the plot from *Lola*.

Denby. English pottery near Derby founded early in the 19th c.; most of its wares are stonewares for domestic use. Notable decorative wares have included excellent brown salt-glaze 'Reform Spirit' flasks and hunting-jugs with relief decoration.

Denham Sir John (1615–69). English courtier, dramatist and poet. His finest works are his tragedy *The Sophy* (1641) and the contemplative, descriptive poem *Cooper's Hill* (1642), which established an English genre of moralistic topographical poems, particularly about world, life and time surveyed from hill-tops.

Denis Maurice (1870–1943). French painter who followed various styles. He was a leader of the *nabis and made the famous statement 'A picture–before being a horse, a nude or an anecdotal subject–is essentially a flat surface covered with colours arranged in a certain order.' His picture *Homage to Cézanne* (1900; M.M.A., Paris) shows members of the nabis admiring a still-life by Cézanne. He painted decorative murals and Biblical subjects in modern settings.

Dennis John (1657–1734). English writer and perceptive critic who angered Addison, Steele and Pope with his criticism of their work; Pope satirized D.'s play *Appius and Virginia* (1709) in *The Essay on Criticism* and ridiculed him in *The Dunciad*.

Dennis Nigel (Forbes) (1912–). English novelist and playwright with an idiosyncratic approach: he castigates with biting wit the egalitarianism and loss of individuality in British society, developing his theme via situations mixing farce and fantasy. Works include the novel *Cards of Identity* (1955) and the plays *The Making of Moo* (1958) and *August for the People* (1960).

dénouement (French, 'unknotting'). The part of a play, following the climax, in which the complexities and mysteries of the plot are resolved and unravelled. It may be a short scene or part of a scene, in which affairs are put straight, or the greater part of an act, in

Derain. *The Pool of London*

which the tensions of the climax are gradually worked out.

Dent Edward Joseph (1876–1957). English writer on music, professor of music at Cambridge Univ. (1926–41) and composer. Besides books on music, particularly opera, of all periods he trs. opera libretti, notably Mozart's.

Denza Luigi (1846–1922). Italian opera composer and teacher who settled in London in 1879. 'Funiculi, funicula' (1880) is one of his very numerous songs.

De Profundis (1905). Letter by Oscar *Wilde.

De Quincey Thomas (1785–1859). A leading critic and imaginative prose writer of the English romantic movement. From early childhood sensitive, independent and intellectually precocious, he ran away from Manchester Grammar School, wandered about England and Wales, then led a Bohemian life in London. He left Worcester College, Oxford, abruptly, and although married in 1816, continued to live an unsettled existence engaged in miscellaneous journalism, struggling against debt and addiction to opium. D.'s prose is sometimes contrived, but at its best, flexible, eloquent and rhythmic, as in the book which made him famous *Confessions of an English Opium Eater* (publ. in *The London Magazine* 1821; in book form 1822), a compelling account of his earlier life and his experiences with opium. Much distinguished literary criticism appears among his voluminous writings, notably his essays on the Lake Poets and *On the Knocking at the Gate in Macbeth* (1823). His essays include the splendidly ironic *On Murder considered as one of the Fine Arts* (1827), *Suspira de Profundis* and *The English Mail Coach* (1849).

Derain André (1880–1954). French painter, who studied at the Académie Carrière. D. was one of the most original of the *fauve painters, working at first with Vlaminck at Chatou and then at Collioure with Matisse. *The Pool of London* (1906; Tate) shows him using a neo-impressionist technique with a freedom inspired by Matisse. Between 1906 and 1909 he was working along parallel lines to Braque and Picasso, whom he had met, and even preceded them in his fusion of African and Cézannesque forms, e.g. *Baigneuses* (1906; private coll.); but he never wholly responded to cubism and after about 1919 withdrew from the *avant-garde*.

Derby Day (1858). Painting by *Frith.

Derby porcelain. Factory founded in 1750; pieces produced were modelled on *Chelsea or *Meissen styles, D. claiming to be a 'Second Dresden'. The work was generally less fine than the originals, but some pieces are distinguished by the work of 2 painters, one decorating the wares with flowers of Meissen style but with fine thread-like stalks, the other having moths as a favourite motif. Characteristic of this period are the 'patches' of discoloration found on the base of the wares. The *'Chelsea-D.' period also produced figure groups; the last fine work was produced during the Crown Derby period (up to 1811). The Royal Crown Derby Porcelain Co. was founded in 1876.

De Rerum Natura. Poem by *Lucretius.

De Reszke Jean (1850–1925). Polish tenor. He and his brother ÉDOUARD (1853–1917), a bass, were leading operatic performers in Paris, London and New York at the turn of the century.

Dering Richard (*c.* 1580–1630). English composer and organist to an order of English nuns in Brussels and later to Charles I's queen, Henrietta Maria. D.'s instrumental music shows affinities to Gibbons and Weelkes, but his vocal works, especially the *Cantiones sacrae* with continuo (1617), show Italian and Flemish influences. His motets were very popular in 17th-c. England.

Derkovits Gyula (1894–1934). An important and progressive artist in Hungary between the World Wars. Cubist and expressionist influences are apparent in his early paintings, but in the 1930s he evolved a sensitive personal style of marked sincerity and restraint. A major part of his work, e.g. his famous woodcut series on the life of György Dózsa, leader of the Hungarian peasants' revolt of 1514, was devoted to social themes determined by his political adherence to Communism.

Dernier Milliardaire, Le (1934). Film directed by R. *Clair.

Derome. Family of 14 French bookbinders of whom NICOLAS-DENIS 'Le Jeune' (1731–*c.* 1788) was the greatest. He was famed for his lace-like gold ornamentation, but he mercilessly trimmed the books he bound.

Thomas De Quincey

Derby porcelain group

Derome binding

Desiderio da Settignano. Marsuppini tomb

Desiderio da Settignano. *Bust of a Woman*

Tibor Déry

Déry Tibor (1894–). Hungarian novelist and playwright. A leading Communist writer, D. was imprisoned for 5 years for his activity in the 1956 Revolution. His earlier novels presented sharp social criticism of pre-war Hungarian society, while his *Niki* (1956; 1958) and his short stories in *Vidám temetés* (1960) described the years of Stalinism in Hungary with forceful realism. His latest novel *G.B. úr X.-ben* (1964) is a strong protest against totalitarian dictatorships.

De Sanctis Francesco (1817–83). Italian critic and teacher, also politically active in the early history of the Italian state. His lectures as professor of comparative literature at Naples Univ. (1871–7) clearly show the influence of Hegel's aesthetic; his major work, a history of Italian literature (1870–1), established him as the greatest of 19th-c. Italian literary critics and has affected all his successors.

Des Barreaux Jacques Vallée, sieur (1602–73). French poet. His sonnet, *Recours du pécheur à la bonté de Dieu* confesses and deplores past licentiousness and irreligion.

descant. A musical term. 'English d.' was a medieval form for 3 voices moving homophonically in simple chords, the melody usually in the lowest voice. The term d. is now used of a decorative top line above a harmonized melody; a 3rd usage, as in 'd. recorder', derives from an earlier use of the term to mean a high (treble) part.

René Descartes

Descartes René (1596–1650). French philosopher. D. is considered to be the 1st great modern philosopher for his use of extreme scepticism as a starting-point in philosophical inquiry. His celebrated dictum '*cogito ergo sum*' ('I think; therefore I am') reflects his view that, doubting all else, he could not doubt that he was a thinking being, which provided a basic criterion of certainty upon which to build. The method and rules of procedure to be employed are set out in his *Discours de la méthode* (1637; an essay also notable for being the 1st major philosophical discourse written in French), and the resulting philosophical position in the *Meditationes* (1641, in Latin), where he uses the '*cogito*' to establish the equally famous notion of Cartesian dualism, the relationship of union which obtains between the separate substances of mind and body. D. also made important contributions in mathematics and the natural sciences.

'Monsù' Desiderio. *An Explosion in a Church*

Descaves Lucien (1861–1949). French novelist, who early rejected Zola and naturalism. His novels include *Sous-offs* (1889), a critical account of army life, and *Les Emmurés* (1894) and *La Colonne* (1901), studies of *petit-bourgeois* families.

Deschamps (Deschamps de Saint-Amand) Émile (1791–1871). French romantic poet, a founder of *La *Muse française*. His brother ANTONY (1800–69) was also a poet.

Deschamps Eustache (*c.* 1346–*c.* 1406). French poet. D. was educated by Guillaume de *Machaut, and became his disciple.

Deserted Village, The (1770). Poem by *Goldsmith.

Desfontaines Pierre-François Guyot, abbé (1685–1745). French writer; he wrote scathingly of contemporary authors and had several skirmishes with Voltaire. D. publ. an early French trs. of *Gulliver's Travels* (1727).

Deshoulières Antoinette du Ligier de la Garde (1638–94). French poet and hostess. Her *salon* was frequented by Corneille.

Desiderio 'Monsù' (*fl.* early 17th c.). 'Painter' of architectural fantasies, recently discovered to be in fact 2 painters from Lorraine, Didier Barra and Francesco de Nome, who worked in the same studio. Paintings by D. include *An Explosion in a Church* (Fitzwilliam Mus.) and *St Augustine* (N.G., London).

Desiderio da Settignano (*c.* 1430–*c.* 1464). Florentine sculptor. Born in a family of stone-masons and carvers, D. was greatly influenced by Donatello, of whom he may have been a pupil. Many of D.'s studies of the Madonna and Child and busts of Florentine women and children have an unsentimental grace and great beauty, e.g. *Bust of a Woman* (Bargello, Florence). His 2 major works are the tomb of the humanist scholar Carlo Marsuppini (Sta Croce, Florence) and the *Tabernacle of the Sacrament* (S. Lorenzo, Florence).

Desire Under the Elms (1924). Play by Eugene *O'Neill.

Desmarées Georg (1697–1776). Swedish portrait painter, a pupil of G. B. Piazetta in Venice. He worked chiefly in Munich in a rococo style.

Despiau. *Antoinette Schulte*; bronze (1934)

Desnoyer. *Escales* (1940)

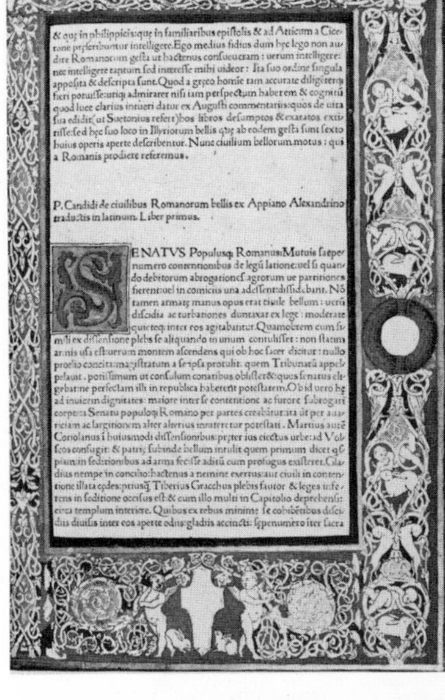

& quę in philippicis: quę in familiaribus epistolis & ad Atticum a Cicerone prę[s]eribuntur intelligere. Ego medius fidius dum hęc lego non audire Romanorum gesta ut hactenus consueueram: uerum intelligere: nec intelligere tantum sed interesse mihi uideor: Ita suo ordine singula apposita & descripta sunt. Quod a gręco homie tam accurate diligēterq; fieri potuisse: utiq; admirarer nisi iam perspectum haberem & cognitū quod luce clarius intueri datur ex Augusti commentariis: quos de uita sua edidit (ut Suetonius refert) hos libros desumptos & exaratos extitisse: sed hęc suo loco in Illyriorum bellis quę ab eodem gesta sunt sexto huius operis aperte describentur. Nunc ciuilium bellorum motus: qui a Romanis prodiere referemus.

P. Candidi de ciuilibus Romanorum bellis ex Appiano Alexandrino traductis in latinum. Liber primus.

SENATVS Populusq; Romanus: Mutuis saepenumero contentionibus de legū latione: uel si quando debitorum abrogationes: agrorum ue partitiones fierent: uel in comiciis una adessent: dissidebant. Nō tamen armatę manus opus erat ciuile bellum: uerū discidia ac turbationes duntaxat ex lege: moderate quieteq; inter eos agitabantur. Quamobrem cum simili ex dissensione plebs se aliquando in unum contulisset: non statim armis usa est: uerum montem ascendens qui ob hoc sacer dicitur: nullo proelio concitata: magistratum a se ipsa protulit: quem Tribunatū appellarunt. potissimum ut consulum conatibus obsisteret: quos senatus eligebat: ne perfectam illi in republica haberent potestatem. Ob id uero hę ad inuicem dignitates: maiore inter se contentione ac furore subrogati corporis Senatu populoq; Romano per partes creabantur: ita ut per auariciam ac largitionem alter alterius inuaderetur potestati. Martius autē Coriolanus i huiusmodi dissensionibus: pręter ius eiectus urbe: ad Volscos confugit: & patrię subinde bellum intulit quem primum dicet q[illegible]piam: in seditionibus ad arma fecisse aditū cum profugus existeret. Gladius nempe in concilio: hactenus a nemine exertus: aut ciuili in contentione illata cędes: priusq̄ Tiberius Gracchus plebis fautor & leges inferens in seditione occisus est: & cum illo multi in Capitolio deprehensi: circa templum interiere. Quibus ex rebus minime se cohibētibus discidiis diuisis inter eos aperte odiis: gladiis accincti: sępenumero iter sacra

De Speir. Page from an ed. of Appian

Desmarets de Saint-Sorlin Jean (1596–1676). French poet, a founder-member of the Académie Française. His choice of a Christian rather than a classical theme in the epic poem *Clovis ou la France Chrestienne* (1657) was one of the starting-points of the *Ancients and Moderns Controversy.

Desnoyer François (1894–). French landscape and figure painter whose style is an attempt to combine the structural qualities of cubism with a fauvist approach to colour. Decorative murals and designs for tapestries are among his most important works.

Desnoyers Auguste Gaspard Louis Boucher (1779–1857). French engraver. D. made a famous engraving of Raphael's *Belle Jardinière*; he worked for Napoleon.

Desorgues Joseph-Théodore (1763–1808). French writer of Revolutionary songs, the best known being 'Hymne à l'Être Suprême'.

De Speir Johann (d. 1470) and Wendelin (d. 1478). Printer-publs from the Rhenish Palatinate who opened the 1st press in Venice in 1467. Their 1st work, Cicero's *Epistolae ad familiares*, was publ. the following year. Other works include the *Canzoniere* (1470), one of the 1st books publ. in Italian, a trs. into Italian of the Bible (1471) and Appian's *Civil Wars* (1472).

Des Périers Bonaventure (*c.* 1500–*c.* 1544). French writer. His anti-Christian *Cymbalum Mundi* (1538; trs. 1712), 4 satirical dialogues in the style of Lucian, was suppressed; only 1 copy survives. *Les Nouvelles récréations et joyeux devis* (1558), a coll. of short humorous tales is attributed to him.

Despiau Charles (1874–1946). French sculptor who worked as Rodin's assistant and for a time followed his style. D.'s characteristic work was more weighty and controlled, and closer to that of A. Maillol.

Desportes Alexandre-François (1661–1743). French painter renowned for his hunting scenes and tapestry designs. He also painted portraits.

Desportes Philippe (1546–1606). French poet, a disciple of Ronsard. D. wrote many delicate love-poems and a verse trs. of the Psalms. He had a great influence on contemporary English poets.

Despréaux Jean (1748–1820). French ballet dancer whose book *Mes Passe-Temps* (1806) includes historically valuable information in the notes to a long poem on ballet.

dessous. A French term used in ballet when the working foot passes behind the supporting one.

dessus. Ballet term for the position of the working foot when it passes in front of the supporting one.

de stijl. A group of artists, among them the Dutch abstract painter Piet *Mondrian, who took the name from a magazine ed. by Theo van Doesburg, painter and theoretician, from 1917. De s. advocated the use in art of basic forms, particularly cubes, verticals and horizontals: in an essay entitled *Neo-Plasticism* (1920), Mondrian suggested that such an abstract art best expresses spiritual values. Architects such as Rietveld and J. J. Oud were connected with the group, which became international with the adherence of artists like Hans Richter, El Lissitzky and Brancusi. De s. ideas influenced the Bauhaus (where van Doesburg lectured) and geometric abstract art of the 1930s. The group had split up by van Doesburg's death in 1931.

De stijl. Sideboard designed by *Rietveld

Destouches Philippe Néricault, known as (1680–1754). French dramatist. His somewhat conventional comedies include *Le curieux impertinent* (1706), *Le Philosophe marié* (1727; *The Married Philosopher*, 1732) and *Le Glorieux* (1732).

détourné. Ballet term to describe a turn in which the dancer, both feet close together, twists himself round on the balls of his feet.

deus ex machina (Latin, 'god out of the machine'). Greek stage machinery included a contraption for the simulation of flight; playwrights, particularly Euripides, often had complex plots resolved by a god introduced on this machine. The phrase now describes any convenient, yet improbable or artificial device for the resolution of difficulties.

Deuteronomy. The 5th book of the *Bible (Pentateuch) giving the final words and death of Moses.

De stijl. *Mondrian, *Composition*. See also colour plate 76

De Valois.
The Rake's Progress

Dame Ninette de Valois

Deutsche blumen. Meissen bowl, cover and stand, 1745–50

Devis. *The Love Song*

Deutsch: Niklaus *Manuel

deutsche blumen. A style of painted floral decoration used first on Vienna and then Meissen porcelain from *c.* 1740. It was a revival of an earlier style of faïence decoration based upon accurate botanical drawings and at first somewhat formal. Later examples show a less rigid and meticulous representation. The style became popular throughout Europe.

Deutscher Werkbund. German organization founded in 1907 to promote progressive ideas and better quality design in architecture and in industry. It was instrumental in Behrens becoming designer to AEG and its exhibitions gave modern architects their rare chances to build. The 1914 Werkbund Exhibition in Cologne gave major buildings to Gropius, Hoffman, Bruno Taut, van de Velde and Behrens, and the 1927 Weissenhof Housing Exhibition in Stuttgart employed most of the leading modernists.

De Valois Dame Ninette (born Edris Stannus) (1898–). Irish dancer and choreographer who began her career in pantomime but after her success with the Diaghilev co. (1923–6) opened a ballet school in London. With these pupils she presented dances for Lilian Baylis's Old Vic productions and in 1931 was the prime mover in the foundation of the Vic-Wells Ballet, grandparent of the Royal Ballet Co., of which she was director until her retirement in 1964. Her works include *The Rake's Progress* (1935), *Checkmate* (1937), *The Prospect Before Us* (1940), and it is primarily due to de V. that there is a British ballet tradition.

development. A musical term meaning the exploitation of the salient rhythmic or melodic features of a theme or motif by the composer, so as to display its latent possibilities. In *sonata form the d. section (sometimes called the 'working out') follows the exposition.

developpé. An exercise in ballet in which the dancer stands on one leg and draws the working foot up the calf of the supporting leg until the working thigh is at a right angle to the body and the leg is then straightened to a horizontal position. The movement is sometimes used in choreography.

devil in music: *intervals

Devil is a Woman, The (1935). Film directed by J. von *Sternberg.

Deville Michel (1931–). French film director. D.'s 4 films, *Ce soir ou jamais* (1960), *Adorable menteuse* (1961), *À cause, à cause d'une femme* (1963) and *Appartement des filles* (1963), are comedies in the French style, precise and sharp, which find their antecedents in Marivaux.

Devil on Two Sticks, The (1707). Novel by Le Sage.

Devils, The (1873). Novel by *Dostoyevsky.

Devil's Disciple, The (1897). Play by G. B. *Shaw.

Devine George (1910–66). English actor and producer; from 1955 to 1965 he was artistic director of the English Stage Co. which has fostered many of the best new writers and actors of recent years.

Devis Arthur (1711–87). English painter of small portraits and conversation pieces of the provincial gentry; he flourished until the 1760s when he was ousted by J. Zoffany. His style was essentially primitive and the naïvety, stylization and tranquillity of his work gave it great charm. D. was 'discovered' in the 1930s along with his son ARTHUR WILLIAM (1763–1822) and his brother ANTHONY (1729–1816).

De Voto Bernard (Augustine) (1897–1955). U.S. literary critic and social historian who decried contemporary writers for ignoring American themes. Works include studies of Mark Twain and (historical writing) *Across the Wide Missouri* (1947).

Dewasne Jean (1921–). French abstract painter (since 1943) and teacher. Director, with E. Pillet, of the Academy of Abstract Art, Paris (1950–2). His brilliant flat colours and bold shapes make his work most suited to murals.

Dewey John (1859–1952). U.S. philosopher and writer. D.'s 'instrumentalist' philosophy (a form of pragmatism) and his progressive theory of education are outlined in *Reconstruction in Philosophy* (1920) and *Democracy and Education* (1916).

De Wint Peter (1784–1849). English landscape painter in oil and watercolour, influenced by

Deutscher Werkbund. Gropius and Meyer, model factory at the Werkbund Exhibition (1914)

Deutscher Werkbund poster by F. H. Ehmcke

Serge Diaghilev

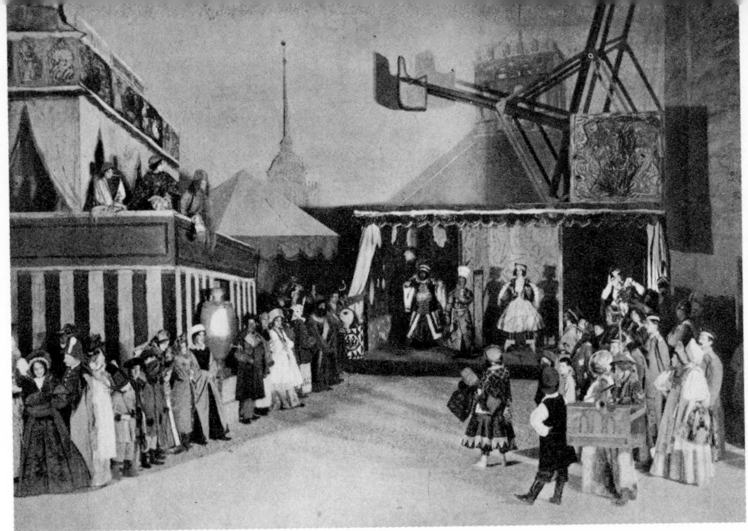
Diaghilev. *Petrushka* (décor by Benois)

Girtin and Varley. De W. used a technique of broad washes, enlivening his blocks of sober colour with subtle variations of light. A good example of his work is *Landscape near Gloucester in 1840* (V. and A., London).

De Worde Wynkyn (d .1535). Alsatian-born printer, assistant to Caxton, taking over the business on Caxton's death. He brought the 1st italic face into England in 1528. He was probably the 1st publ. to make school-books the mainstay of his business and inaugurated what is now known as 'house style' (i.e. a set of rules adopted by a publ. to ensure uniformity). His best works include an English trs. of *The Golden Legend* (1493), and 2 reissues of *The Canterbury Tales*.

Dexter John (1925–). English director who has worked often for the English Stage Co., for whom he has directed most of the works of Arnold Wesker. He is now an associate director of the National Theatre where among other plays he directed *Othello* during the 1st season.

Deyrolle Jean (1911–). French painter who turned to abstraction in the mid 1940s under the influence of Domela. He has travelled widely.

Diabelli Anton (1781–1858). Austrian composer, mainly for piano, and music publ. As a publ. venture, D. invited 50 composers to write one variation each on a waltz by him. Although not invited, Beethoven produced his great 33 DIABELLI VARIATIONS on this theme.

Diable au Corps, Le (1947). Film directed by C. *Autant-Lara.

Diable boiteaux, Le (1707). Novel by Le Sage.

Diaboliques, Les (1954). Film directed by H.-G. Clouzot.

diabolus in musica: *intervals

Diaghilev Serge (1872–1929). Russian opera and ballet impresario and chief propagandist of the ideas of the *World of Art group. His Ballets Russes, which first performed in Paris in a joint opera and ballet programme in 1909, introduced the dancers Pavlova, Nijinsky, Karsarvina and Massine, the composers Stravinsky and Prokofiev, and the artists Benois and Bakst to Western Europe, with profound effect there; modern Western ballet is immediately descended from it. With the war in 1914, D. was cut off from Russia, but continued to produce new ballets each year, drawing on W. European artists such as Picasso, Matisse, Poulenc and Ravel. The ballets were short, 1 act, often storyless, on contemporary themes, creating a complete break with the classical tradition; not only did D. thus revolutionize ballet, but brought together all that was most alive in the fields of art.

Dial, The. Name of 4 U.S. literary magazines. Emerson was a co-founder of the first (1840–4), a platform for such transcendentalist writers as Thoreau. The eds of the third (1880–1929) included R. H. Stoddard, Conrad Aiken, Padraic Colum and Van Wyck Brooks; under Scofield Theyer (ed. 1919–25) this *Dial* publ. works by leading world writers. The 4th *Dial* was founded in 1959.

dialogue (Greek, 'through speech'). The words spoken between the characters of a play, novel, etc. In literature a d. is also a prose form in which 2, or sometimes more, interlocutors expound a topic by discussion; famous examples are the d.s of Plato.

Diamante Fra (1430–*c.* 98). Italian painter, pupil of Fra Filippo Lippi and his assistant on the frescoes in Prato and Spoleto cathedrals. Filippo's son Filippino was left in his care.

Diamond David (1915–). U.S. composer. He studied under N. Boulanger in Paris. D.'s music usually has a strong rhythmic element, is predominantly contrapuntal in texture and tends to use modal formulae. His works include: 6 symphonies; a violin concerto; *Psalm for Orchestra* (1936) dedicated to Gide; the ballet *Tom* (1936), book by e.e. cummings. D. also used e.e. cummings's texts in other works; he gained an international reputation with *Rounds for Strings* (1944).

Diana Benedetto (*c.* 1460–1525). Venetian painter in the manner of Giorgione.

diapason. A musical term meaning the basic tone of the *organ. D. pipes may be 'open' or 'stopped'.

Diaper William (1685–1717). English poet, rediscovered in 1952, when his poems were

Deyrolle. *Sydney 1955*

De Worde. The Squire in Chaucer's *Canterbury Tales*

Diaper-work. Choir screen, Lincoln cathedral

Charles Dickens

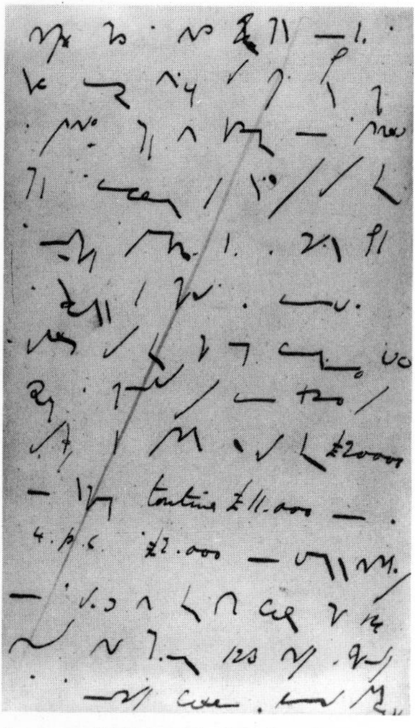

A page of Dickens's shorthand

Emily Dickinson

first collected. Befriended by Swift, ridiculed unfairly by Pope (*The Dunciad*), D., who died young, wrote charmingly fresh eclogues and country pieces and a witty trs. of 2 books of Oppian's *Halieutica* (on the nature of fishes).

diaper-work. A simple pattern based on small geometric or floral forms repeated uniformly over a surface. It is found in textiles, manuscripts, murals and panel painting, metalwork, sculpture and architectural detail, especially in the middle ages.

Diary of a Chambermaid. Films directed by J. Renoir (1946) and L. Buñuel (1964).

Diary of a Madman (1835). Story by *Gogol.

Diary of a Nobody (1892). Book by George *Grossmith.

Diary of Antoine Roquentin (1938). Novel by *Sartre.

diatonic: *scale

Diaz (de la Peña) Narcisse Virgile (1808–76). French painter of Spanish descent. As a landscape painter he was taught by T. Rousseau and belonged to the *Barbizon school. He also painted mythological figure groups which conceal weak draughtsmanship by theatrical effects.

Dibdin Charles (1745–1814). English composer and writer. He was the author of many famous songs of the sea such as 'Tom Bowling'; many were written for the 'table entertainments' which D. composed and performed himself.

Dibdin Thomas Frognall (1776–1847). English writer and bibliophile remembered for his *Bibliomania* (1809).

Dichterliebe (1840; German, 'Poet's Love'). Song cycle by Schumann, a setting of 16 poems by Heine.

Dickens Charles (John Huffam) (1812–70). English novelist, the son of a dockyard clerk. After a sickly, bookish childhood in Portsmouth, Chatham and London, he worked briefly in a blacking factory (1824) while his improvident father was in prison for debt. D. went to school until 1827, when he became first a lawyer's clerk, then a reporter. His articles in *The Monthly Magazine* and *Evening Chronicle* were coll. and publ. as *Sketches by Boz* (1836) with illustrations by Cruikshank. *Pickwick Papers* (1836–7), publ. serially like all his novels, made him famous; and to the end of his life his works were immensely popular. In addition to writing novels D. was an active journalist, founding *Household Words, All the Year Round* and the less successful *Daily News*. He toured Britain and the U.S., giving readings from his works–an effort which hastened his death from overwork. His marriage (1836) was unhappy; the couple separated in 1858.
The fame and popularity of D.'s novels rests on their complex and melodramatic plots, liberal use of humour and pathos, and variety of memorable characters like the Wellers, Fagin, Micawber and Barkis. D. was a master of powerful description used to evoke atmosphere–especially, as in *Bleak House* (1852–3), the claustrophobic atmosphere of evil. Throughout his life he wrote (usually with hindsight) as a reformer–from *Oliver Twist* (1837–9) and *Nicholas Nickleby* (1838–9), which criticize workhouses and private schools, to the descriptions of the debtors' prison in *Little Dorrit* (1856–7). D.'s works contain a strong autobiographical element, clearest in *David Copperfield* (1849–50). In spite of this, the books, though authentic and self-contained creations, are not realistic studies: their characters, though brilliantly drawn, are stock figures or grotesques; and the turns of their plots are dictated by sensationalism or sentimentality. *Hard Times* (1854) is, however, unusual in its simplicity and economy of construction and realistic treatment of human relations. Works include *The Old Curiosity Shop* (1840–1); *Barnaby Rudge* (1841), set at the time of the Gordon Riots; *American Notes* (1842) and *Martin Chuzzlewit* (1843), fruits of D.'s visit to the U.S.; *A Christmas Carol* (1843), the first and most popular of 5 such books; *Dombey and Son* (1846); *A Tale of Two Cities* (1859), inspired by Carlyle's *The French Revolution*; *Great Expectations* (1864–5); and the unfinished *Mystery of Edwin Drood* (1870).

Dickerson Robert (1924–). Australian painter. He was labourer, factory hand and professional boxer, taking up serious painting in 1950. His theme is contemporary life.

Dickinson Emily (Elizabeth) (1830–86). U.S. poet. She lived all her life in a small area of

Diderot: bust by Houdon

Diebenkorn. *Berkeley No. 2*

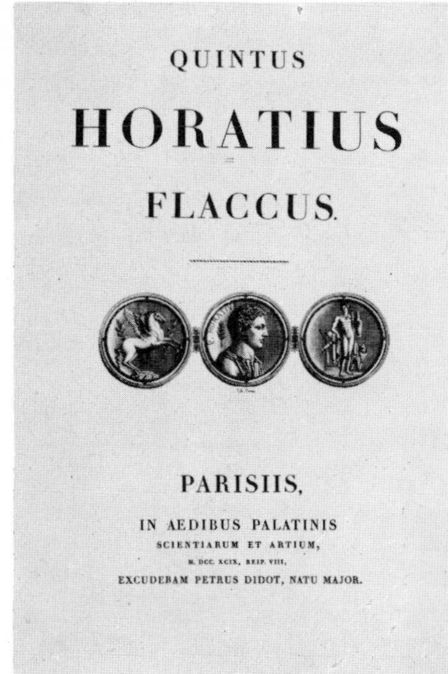
QUINTUS
HORATIUS
FLACCUS.

PARISIIS,
IN AEDIBUS PALATINIS
SCIENTIARUM ET ARTIUM,
M. DCC. XCIX, REIP. VIII,
EXCUDEBAM PETRUS DIDOT, NATU MAJOR.

Didot. Ed. of Horace, 1799

Massachusetts. But from her intense interior life, passionate and intelligent, she wrote a few truly great lyrics. Her verse dramatizes late 19th-c. philosophical conflicts concerning the relationships between nature, God, organized religion, death and private, sensuous passion. She publ. little, and her monotonous metres and occasionally eccentric language betray the lack of a critical audience. But her best work has the concentrated power of 17th-c. metaphysical poetry and an unusually direct honesty of utterance.

Dickinson Goldsworthy Lowes (1862–1932). English humanist and writer. His biography was written in 1934 by his friend E. M. Forster. Among his philosophical and sociological works are *The Greek View of Life* (1896) and *Letters from John Chinaman* (1901).

Dickinson Thorold (1906–). British film director. He has a predilection for elaborate décor and camerawork, as in *Gaslight* (1940) and *The Queen of Spades* (1948), from Pushkin. *Hill 24 Doesn't Answer* (1954), made in Israel, and *Next of Kin* (1942), a Forces training film, show his ability to deal successfully with action.

Dickinson William (*c.* 1671–1725). English architect. He worked in Wren's office, assisting him with the City churches. He specialized in Gothic, and may have had a hand in St Michael, Cornhill, and the restorations of Westminster Abbey.

diction. Term used in literature for a writer's choice and arrangement of words to achieve different effects. In another sense the word is used of the enunciation of a speaker, singer or actor, etc.

didactic literature. Literary works of this genre aim to instruct, whether in the techniques of agriculture as in Hesiod's *Works and Days*, the techniques of literature as in Horace's *Art of Poetry*, or in the disciplines of Christian living as in Bunyan's *The Pilgrim's Progress*. The term is also loosely used of any work 'with a message' aimed to teach or proselytize.

Didelot Charles-Louis (1767–1836). French dancer from the Paris Opéra who went to St Petersburg in 1801. His teaching at the Imperial School and his work as choreographer were at a time when Russian ballet was growing, and its tradition was greatly enriched by his academic influence.

Diderot Denis (1713–84). French savant. His *Pensées philosophiques* (1746) are a sceptic's answer to Pascal: his *Lettre sur les Aveugles* (1749), a sceptical examination of the evidence of the senses. *L'*Encyclopédie* (1751–72), of which he was ed. and bore the chief share, enshrines the rationalistic, democratic and scientific spirit of the **philosophes*. His *salon* reviews, contributed to Grimm's newsletters (1759–81), influenced Goethe and Lessing as well as French taste. D. also wrote the novel *Le Neveu de Rameau* which by dialogue portrays as a depraved and idle character the nephew of the composer Rameau. The book, unpubl. in the 18th c., was first widely known in a German trs. by Goethe (1805).

Dido and Aeneas (*c.* 1689). Opera by *Purcell, with libretto by N. Tate.

Didot. Firm of French printers founded (1713) by FRANÇOIS D. (1689–1757). His son FRANÇOIS-AMBROSE (1730–1804) completed the development of the system of standard type measure (now called after him) originated by S.-P. Fournier. His younger son FIRMIN (1764–1836), one of the great type-cutters, was responsible for the introduction of the 'modern' type-face with its distinctive strictness and regularity of line; he also devised the 1st completely successful stereotype process (*c.* 1795). With his brother PIERRE (1761–1853) he produced many fine books.

Diebenkorn Richard (1922–). U.S. painter. He studied (1946) and taught (1947–50) at the California School of Fine Arts. He achieved recognition as an abstract painter but in 1955 turned to a figurative style.

Dientzenhofer. Family of Bavarian architects who flourished in the late 17th and early 18th c. There were 5 brothers–Georg, Christoph, Leonhard, Johann and Wolfgang–and the son of Christoph, Kilian Ignaz. They were largely responsible for germanizing the style of Guarini and forming the distinctive S. German baroque. Among their chief works are the churches of Waldassen, Kappel, Fulda and Banz (all in Germany) and St Niklas, Prague.

Diepenbrock Alphons (1862–1921). Dutch composer. Self-taught, he evolved a personal

Dientzenhofer. Waldassen church

Dijon. Capital from St Bénigne

Directoire

Marlene Dietrich in *The Blue Angel*

style owing much to his study of 16th-c. Netherlands polyphonic composers, to the chromaticism of Wagner and later to Debussy. His works include the monumental and influential *Missa in die Festo* (1894) for tenor, double male chorus and organ; the *Te Deum* (1902) for 4 soloists, double chorus and orchestra; 6 solo songs for voice and orchestra, e.g. Novalis's *Hymnen an die Nacht*; and incidental music, e.g. to Sophocles' *Electra*.

Dierdre of the Sorrows (1910). Play by J. M. Synge.

Dieren Bernard van (1884–1936). Dutch composer who settled (1909) in London. He was self-taught, being influenced by the work of his friends Busoni and Delius. His densely contrapuntal and technically difficult music includes a symphony for voices and orchestra, with text from Chinese poets, and a comic opera, *The Tailor*; he also wrote the musical essays *Down among the Dead Men* (1935).

Dierx Léon (1838–1912). French Creole poet, born in Reunion Island, one of the *Parnassians and an intimate friend of Leconte de Lisle. His colls include *Les Aspirations* (1858) and *Les Lévres closes* (1867).

dies irae (Latin 'day of wrath'). The metrical sequence of the requiem mass with words by Thomas of Celano (13th c.). The plainsong for it is quoted with tremendous effect in the *Symphonie Fantastique* of Berlioz. Other composers have also quoted it.

Dieterle William (1893–). German-born film director; one of Hollywood's best directors, with the ambitious series of biographies *The Story of Louis Pasteur* (1936), *The Life of Émile Zola* (1937), *Juarez* (1939), all starring Paul Muni. D. is equally at home with less serious themes, as in the satire *All That Money Can Buy* (1941) or the thriller *The Turning Point* (1952).

Dietrich Marlene (1904–). German-born film star and entertainer; she now lives in the U.S. A presence rather than an actress, a sensuous *diseuse* rather than a singer, Marlene the legend dates from her most famous film, *The Blue Angel* (1930). She gained a further reputation as a cabaret entertainer and worked for the Allied troops during the war. Among her pictures are: *The Devil is a Woman* (1935), *Destry Rides Again* (1939), *Rancho Notorious* (1952) and *Touch of Evil* (1958).

Dijon, Church of St Bénigne. One of the formative designs of early Romanesque architecture (1000–1020). All that remains is the crypt of the E. rotunda, a large circular space with ambulatory, modelled on the Holy Sepulchre, Jerusalem. St Bénigne was copied at St Augustine's abbey, Canterbury and elsewhere.

Dillon George (1906–). U.S. poet and ed. of the magazine *Poetry*; he has publ. the vols of lyrical verse *Boy in the Wind* (1927) and *The Flowering Stone* (1931), and a trs. of *Les Fleurs du Mal* (1936).

diminution: *augmentation

Dinis King of Portugal (1261–1325). His many fine love-poems are written in the Galician-Portuguese lyric style, and were also influenced by Provençal poetry; they are simple in form and content and conventional in inspiration.

Diocletian's Palace Split, Yugoslavia. The best preserved and one of the most elaborate of Roman palaces (built *c.* A.D. 300). It has the same form as a Roman military camp–a fortified rectangle with 4 gates and arcaded streets crossing each other at the centre. The S. side had a long arcaded gallery facing the sea; behind it were the emperor's apartments and farther back his octagonal Mausoleum (now the cathedral). Part of the present town is built inside the ruins.

diptych. 2 pictures (often a portrait facing the portrayal of a saint) hinged together and thus a free-standing unit when opened out. Several survive from the late middle ages.

Directoire. A term sometimes applied to the style in the applied arts in France (*c.* 1790 to *c.* 1800). It is essentially a continuation of Louis XVI but has a much greater simplicity of line and far less ornament; the detailing tends to be somewhat coarser than in the earlier period.

dirge. A lyrical poem or song of lament for the dead.

Dirty Hands (1948). Play by Sartre.

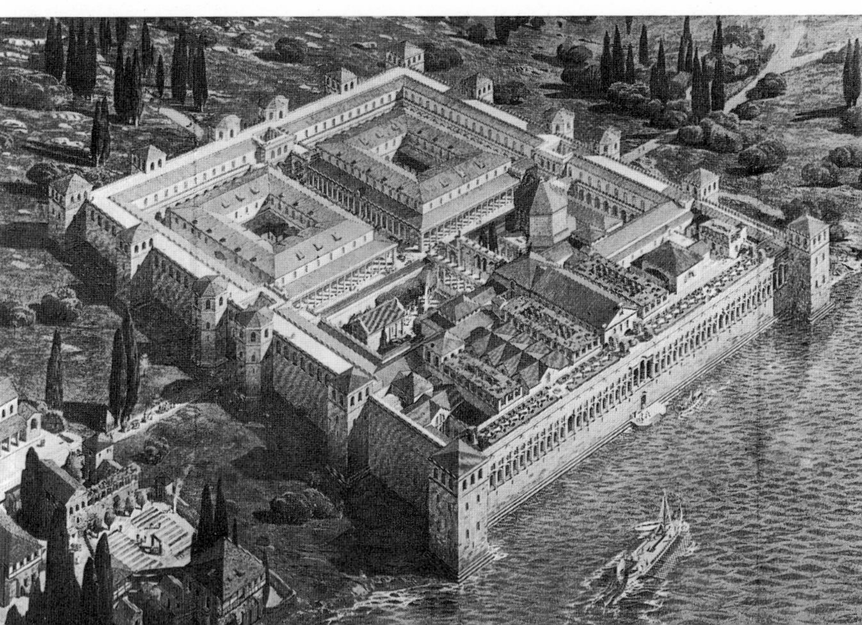
Diocletian's Palace (reconstruction)

Disputà del Santissimo Sacramento

The Disasters of War: *Fuerte Cosa es!*

Disasters of War, The (*Los Desastres de la Guerra*). Series of 80 aquatint engravings by Goya.

discord: *concord

Discours de la méthode (1637). Philosophical treatise by *Déscartes.

Disderi Adolphe-Eugène (1819–90). French photographer. D. perfected a technique of putting 8 to 12 different exposures on 1 plate which yielded small photographs called '*cartes de visite*' and which eventually swept across Europe and the U.S. as the major popular form of photography during the mid 19th c.

Disney Walt (1901–). U.S. film producer and director. After directing a number of silent and sound cartoon films, D. became a producer. The inventiveness and witty drawing of his cartoons, tinged with macabre grotesquerie as in *Skeleton Dance* (1930), and a gallery of such characters as Mickey Mouse, Donald Duck and Pluto, made them world famous. D. was the first to use the improved 3-strip Technicolor process, for one of his 'Silly Symphonies', *Flowers and Trees* (1932), and achieved tremendous success with the colour cartoon *Three Little Pigs* (1933), with its anti-Depression hit song 'Who's afraid of the Big Bad Wolf?'. He developed synchronization of picture, music and effects to such a degree that any close matching of visuals and sound became known as 'mickey-mousing'; the fanciful use of colour was also exploited, notably in the abstract sequence set to Bach in *Fantasia* (1940). D.'s 1st full-length cartoon was *Snow White and the Seven Dwarfs* (1938), a perennial success, followed by *Pinocchio* (1940), *Dumbo* (1941) and *Bambi* (1942). Although far in advance of other cartoons, these began to exploit 'realism' too obviously, with excessively slick 'chocolate-box' drawing: a trend seen clearly in *The Three Caballeros* (1945) where Donald Duck was combined with live South American cuties. D. now appears to have abandoned this style for an exceptional delicacy of drawing, especially in *101 Dalmations* (1961). His 'True Life Adventures', brilliantly photographed wild-life documentaries, are spoiled by sentimental commentaries and artificial synchronization of live action and music. His production is now mainly live-action fiction films, deliberately aimed at a family audience.

Disputà del Santissimo Sacramento. Fresco by *Raphael.

Disraeli Benjamin, 1st Earl of Beaconsfield (1804–81). English political statesman and novelist, prime minister in 1868 and from 1874 to 1880. D.'s colourful and witty romances are a strange amalgam; they reflect his 'new Tory' politics and faithfully portray the English social situation, yet also reveal his intense (racial, not religious) consciousness of his Jewishness and frequently include exotic Eastern elements. Most important are *Coningsby* (1844) and *Sybil* (1845).

dissolve: *film techniques

distemper. A painting medium of powder colours mixed in water used since classical times for interior decoration. It is impermanent but was occasionally used by Renaissance artists for cartoons.

distich. A literary term for 2 lines of metrical verse making a self-contained significant statement.

distyle. In classical architecture, a *portico supported by 2 columns.

Dittersdorf Karl Ditters von (originally Karl Ditters, ennobled in 1773) (1739–99). Austrian composer and violin virtuoso. He was a friend of Gluck, Haydn and Mozart. His music was stylistically elegant, witty and rich in melody, and his operettas were fantastically successful, *Doktor und Apotheker* (still occasionally performed) eclipsing even Mozart's *Figaro* on its 1st performance (1788). But of over 40 stage works few are remembered; more important is his instrumental music, particularly the string quartets and symphonies similar in style to Haydn's.

divertimento (Italian, 'amusement'). A musical entertainment, usually for a small group of instruments, in several movements; similar to the *suite.

divertissement (French, 'an amusement'). In ballet, a suite of dances without any connecting plot. In music it is usually a set of pieces based on familiar or popular tunes, or a musical interlude between the acts of a play or opera, i.e. an entr'acte.

Divine Comedy, The. Epic poem by *Dante.

Disney. Scene from *Pinocchio*

Benjamin Disraeli

Disderi. *Carte de visite* of Ingres

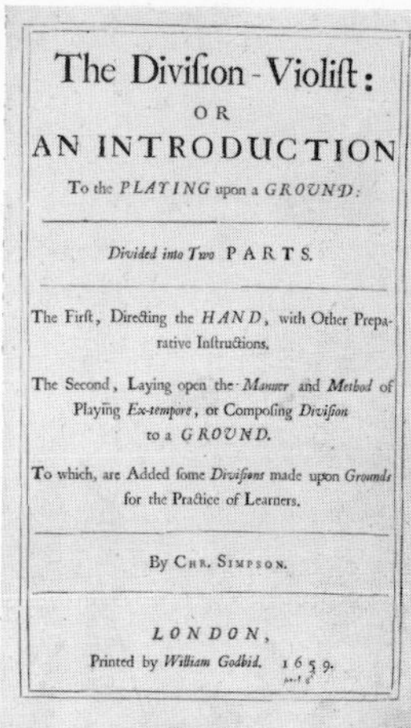
The Diviſion-Violiſt:
OR
AN INTRODUCTION
To the PLAYING upon a GROUND:

Divided into Two PARTS.

The Firſt, Directing the HAND, with Other Preparative Inſtructions.

The Second, Laying open the Manner and Method of Playing Ex-tempore, or Compoſing Diviſion to a GROUND.

To which, are Added ſome Diviſions made upon Grounds for the Practice of Learners.

By CHR. SIMPSON.

LONDON,
Printed by William Godbid. 1659.

Division. Title-page and illustration from Simpson's manual

Dix. *The Artist's Parents*

Dix. *Self-portrait as a Soldier* (1917)

Dobson. *Endymion Porter* (detail)

Divinity School Address, The (1838). Lecture by *Emerson.

divisionism. An alternative term for the techniques of *neo-impressionism.

divisions. A musical term used of the 17th- and 18th-c. practice of decorating a melodic line with florid runs and embellishments which 'divide' it into many notes. Singers and instrumentalists would improvise such *ornamentation and C. Simpson's *The Division Violist* (1659) was a popular guide to the art. Composers often wrote d. (i.e. variations) on a ground.

Dix Otto (1891–). German painter and graphic artist best known for his paintings and etchings of protest based on his experience of World War I. He became famous with a portfolio of etchings publ. in 1917. His early paintings resemble the primitive style of the Douanier Rousseau, but he later adopted the principles of the *new objectivity and like George Grosz exposed the corruption of post-war Germany with biting satire; the Hitler era brought persecution to D. Since the war he has painted mainly religious subjects.

Dixieland. A form of classical *jazz.

Dixon Richard Watson (1833–1900). English poet, clergyman and historian. D. was a member of the *Pre-Raphaelite 'Birmingham group' and a friend of G. M. Hopkins and R. Bridges, who contributed a memoir to D.'s *Poems . . . A Selection* (1909). He wrote an ambitious narrative poem, *Mano* (1883), but never surpassed a few of his short nature lyrics.

Dmytryk Edward (1908–). Canadian-born U.S. film director. After working as an ed. and directing B features, D. worked his way up to direct for Dore *Schary *Crossfire* (1947), a social-conscience picture about anti-Semitism which resulted in his black-listing in 1949. After clearing himself in 1951 he graduated via films like *The Sniper* (1952) for Stanley *Kramer to a series of prestige pictures like *The Young Lions* (1958).

Dobell Sydney Thompson (1824–74). English poet of the *Spasmodic school. His poems include *The Roman* (1850) and *Balder* (1853).

Dobell William (1899–). Australian painter, among the earliest to achieve wide recognition. D. is not as openly nationalistic as many of his younger contemporaries; he lived in London from 1929 to 1939, and his cruel realistic portraits owe as much to Hogarth and Rembrandt as to contemporary national or international movements.

Döblin Alfred (1878–1957). German expressionist writer; he lived in exile from 1933 to 1945. *Berlin Alexanderplatz* (1929), a major expressionist novel, deals with an unsuccessful attempt at social rehabilitation by a released prisoner; later works include *Der unsterbliche Mensch* (1946).

Dobroven Issay Alexandrovitch (1894–1953). Russian conductor and composer who championed Russian music in Europe and the U.S. His music, influenced by Brahms, includes an opera and a piano concerto.

Dobson William (1611–46). English painter, best known for his portraits of Royalist officers. D.'s robust style is quite unlike that of Van Dyck, his great contemporary. The full-length portrait *James Compton, 3rd Earl of Northampton* (Coll. Duchess of Northampton) has been called 'the best thing of its kind painted by an Englishman before Hogarth'. Another fine example is *Endymion Porter* (Tate).

doccia. A type of porcelain made at Doccia, near Florence, since 1735. Notable in the early production were small versions of famous statues and commissioned designs by leading baroque sculptors, besides the more usual ware often painted with miniature scenes. The early paste is grey and rough-looking; colour schemes tend to be vivid red, violet, emerald-green, black, gold.

Dr Jekyll and Mr Hyde, The Strange Case of (1886). Novel by R. L. *Stevenson.

Doctor Mabuse, the Gambler (1922), **The Testament of–** (1932), **The Thousand Eyes of–** (1960). Films directed by F. *Lang.

Doctor's Dilemma, The (1906). Play by G. B. Shaw.

Dr Zhivago (1957). Novel by Boris *Pasternak.

documentary. A film which uses actual settings and usually non-professional actors to present a response to actual conditions or any subject of interest; there is usually a didactic

William Dobell. *The Charlady* (1936)

Doccia. Figure of Diana copied from a bronze by Giovanni da Bologna

element present or the intention to instruct or inform. Some of the outstanding makers of d. films are R. *Flaherty, G. *Franju, J. *Grierson, C. *Marker and P. *Rotha.

Dodds the brothers Johnny (1892–1940), clarinettist, and Baby (1898–1959), drummer. Famous U.S. jazz musicians in the New Orleans style.

dodecaphonic music or techniques (from Greek *dodeka*, '12'): *twelve-note music

Dodgson Charles Lutwidge: Lewis *Carroll

Dodsley Robert (1703–64). English publ. and poet. His most notable publs were *A Collection of Poems. By Several Hands* (1748), an anthology of contemporary verse, many times enlarged in subsequent eds, and *A Select Collection of Old Plays* (1744), early drama up to the death of Charles I.

Dodsworth (1929). Novel by Sinclair Lewis.

Doesburg Theo van (real name C. E. M Küpper) (1883–1931). Dutch painter, writer on art, poet; leader of the movement *de stijl and founder of its journal. In 1916 he began to collaborate with the architects J. P. Oud and J. Wils and in 1923 with C. van Eesteren in applying the principles of de stijl to building and interior decoration; in 1922 he taught at the Bauhaus, Weimar. In the same year he publicized dadaism in the Netherlands and under the pseud. 'I. K. Bonset' ed. the dada periodical *Mecano*. In 1930 he ed. a pamphlet entitled *Art Concret* introducing this term as an alternative to 'abstract art'.

Doge's Palace i.e. Palazzo Ducale, Venice, next to St Mark's. The main external façade facing the water belongs to 1309–40, that facing the Piazzetta to 1423–38. The ground storey consists of an open arcade or loggia with wide arches on ornate figure-capitals; the next stage has a row of delicate ogee arches surmounted by quatrefoils in circles and the top (main) storey is in plain pinkish brick with a diaper pattern and has large traceried windows. The inner *cortile* belongs to Renaissance architecture, with elevations by Pietro Lombardo and Scarpagnino; it includes the Scala dei Giganti with Sansovino's *Mars and Neptune*. The interior of the palace contains large pictures by Titian, Tintoretto and others. The Bridge of Sighs (1595) connecting the palace with the prison next door is a high covered bridge with elliptical arch and rusticated pilasters; it was much copied.

doggerel. Roughly written verse, usually humorous. Its crudities result either from a technically incompetent poet doing his best or from a good poet aiming at an effect.

dog-tooth ornament. Architectural term for a carving zigzag design, a characteristic decoration in Norman architecture in England.

Dohnányi (Ernö) Ernst von (1877–1960). Hungarian composer, pianist and conductor, also (1931) musical director of the Hungarian Broadcasting Service; in 1949 he settled in the U.S. D. pioneered modern music in Hungary, particularly Bartók's and Kodály's, although his own music used classical forms in a Brahmsian idiom. He wrote the *Variations on a Nursery Tune* (1913) for piano and orchestra; other works included 3 operas, a ballet, 3 symphonies, a festival overture for the jubilee concert, which he conducted, of the union of Buda and Pest (1923), the suite *Ruralia Hungarica* (1926) with Lisztian 'folk' elements, the *American Rhapsody* (1954) and chamber music.

Doisneau Robert (1912–). French photographer best known for his intimate and humorous vision of French life.

dolce stil nuovo. (Italian, 'new sweet style'). The words were used by Dante to signify the new style of 13th-c. Tuscan poetry which sprang from emotion inspired by the spiritual love of a fair lady. Guinizelli and Cavalcanti were the principal exponents of the school.

Dolce Vita, La (1960). Film directed by F. *Fellini.

Dolci Carlo (Carlino) (1616–86). Florentine painter whose work exemplifies one aspect of the decline of baroque painting. The tenderness and piety affected by his languorous, softly modelled half-length madonnas and female saints were popular with his contemporaries but have since appeared sentimental.

Dolet Étienne (1509–46). French humanist writer and printer. D. established a press at Lyons in 1538 which produced a variety of works. He was burned at the stake as an atheist.

Doesburg. *Composition* (1917)

Dog-tooth ornament

The Doge's Palace; also showing St Mark's (left)

Dolin partners Markova in *The Nutcracker Suite*. Also *Danilova

Domenico Veneziano. *St Francis Receiving the Stigmata*

Domenichino. *Martyrdom of St Cecilia*

Dolin Anton. Pseud. of Patrick Healey-Kay (1904–). Irish dancer trained under Astafieva in London. D. joined Diaghilev in 1921 and was with the Vic-Wells Ballet from 1931 to 1935, when he and Alicia Markova founded the Markova/Dolin Co. In 1939 he went to the U.S. where, as chief dancer in the Ballet Theater, New York, he established his reputation as a great classical dancer and one of the finest partners in contemporary ballet. In 1950 he and Markova founded London's *Festival Ballet.

Doll's House, The (1879). Play by *Ibsen.

Dolmetsch Arnold (1858–1940). Musician, musicologist and instrument maker of French-Swiss origin. He pioneered the view that early music should not be played with modern instruments and techniques though his theories on these techniques have since been questioned. He built clavichords, harpsichords, viols and recorders, rediscovered the English viol music of the 17th c. and instituted the Haslemere festivals of early music (1925). CARL (1911–), the recorder virtuoso, is his son.

dome. The 1st important example of this architectural feature is the d. of the *Pantheon in Rome; another major example is the flat saucer d. of *S. Sophia. A d. is usually erected over a square area such as the crossing of a church, and the engineering problems of erecting a circular roof on a square base have been variously solved. In Western architecture the d. is most commonly supported on a drum, i.e. a circular wall; this in turn rests on a circular base formed by the apexes of the 4 arches of the crossing and pendentives (curved triangular surfaces filling in the space between adjoining main arches) or squinch arches (another means of filling in the spaces between the main arches).

Domela (Nieuwenhuis) Cesar (1900–). Dutch painter in the constructivist tradition. D. first exhibited non-figurative work with the November group, Berlin in 1923; in 1925 he joined the de stijl group after contact with Mondrian and van Doesburg in Paris. He subsequently began making coloured relief constructions composed of various contrasting materials.

Domenichino Domenico Zampieri called (1581–1641). Bolognese painter, pupil and assistant of the Carracci. He worked in Rome, becoming the leading exponent of the Bolognese school there; in 1630 he moved to Naples. His frescoes in Rome included *Scourging of St Andrew* (1608; S. Gregorio Magno) and *Scenes from the life of St Cecilia* (1615–17; S. Luigi de' Francesi); the latter marked the peak of classicism in his painting. A tendency towards the baroque in his work in S. Andrea della Valle, Rome (1624–8), was further developed in his frescoes (1630–41) in Naples cathedral.

Domenico di Bartolo (Domenico Ghezzi) (*c.* 1400–*c.* 1445). Sienese painter, pupil of Taddeo di Bartolo.

Domenico Veneziano (d. 1461). Italian painter of the Florentine school (although he was probably born in Venice: his work shows a stronger sense of colour than that of most of his Florentine contemporaries). He is known to have been in Perugia in 1438 and in Florence between 1439 and 1445. The story in Vasari of D.V.'s murder by Castagno is disproved by the fact that he died after Castagno. D.V.'s work has recently been critically revalued and his influence traced in the painting of Piero della Francesca. D.V.'s surviving masterpiece is the signed *St Lucy Altarpiece*, consisting of the central panel, *Madonna and Child with Four Saints* (Uffizi), 2 very fine predella panels, *The Miracle of St Zenobius* and *Annunciation* (Fitz. Mus., Cambridge), and the panels *St John in the Wilderness* and *St Francis Receiving the Stigmata* (N.G., Washington) and *The Martyrdom of St Lucy* (Berlin).

dominant. In music, the 5th degree of the *scale. The chord of the DOMINANT SEVENTH (G, B, D, F in the key of C) is common in music; it is harmonically speaking a discord and is usually resolved on to the chord of the tonic. Also *harmony.

Donatello (*c.* 1386–1466). Italian sculptor of the Florentine school. Probably no artist so shaped the whole artistic expression of the Italian Renaissance. In himself he found the whole range of that expression, from the lyrical joy of the dancing cherubs, or *putti*, to the high tragedy and the extremes of religious passion given daring expression in works such as the *Magdalen* (Baptistery, Florence). At the same time, in the bronze *David* (Bargello, Florence), *St George* (Bargello) and the *Gattamelata*

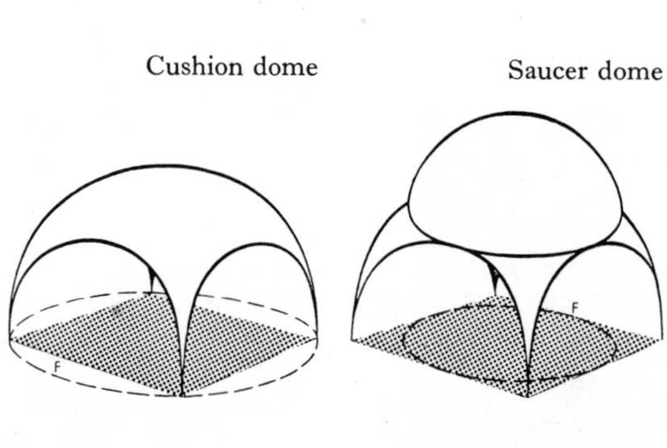

Donatello. *David*; bronze

(Padua), D. demonstrates that enormous confidence in himself and his destiny which marks the man of the Renaissance.

Little is known about D.'s life. He was trained as a goldsmith and in other crafts, entered the workshop of L. Ghiberti at 17 and was probably taught to carve marble by Nanni di Banco, with whom he collaborated on figures for Or San Michele. His earliest work is probably the marble *David* (Bargello, Florence). D. is first mentioned in records of artists working on Florence cathedral in 1406 and he executed commissions for the cathedral throughout his life. In this early period he became a friend of Brunelleschi. Critics now believe the traditional account of a trip to Rome taken by D. and Brunelleschi together, but differ on the date. Classical motifs and conceptions become important in the work of both artists from the 1420s. Other of D.'s major works include: the figures for Or San Michele, Florence, which include *St George* (now in Bargello) and the plaque *St George slaying the Dragon* (Or San Michele), important because it creates a scene in depth for the 1st time and the illusion of perspective in carved relief; the figures for the cathedral; the wall tombs executed with Michelozzo, such as the tomb of the Antipope John XXIII (Baptistery, Florence); the *Crucifix* (S. Croce, Florence); the carvings on the Siena font, including the scene *Herod's Feast* (Siena Baptistery); *Judith and Holofernes* (Piazza Signoria, Florence); the important panel in low relief, *Ascension* (V. and A. Mus., London); the bronze *David* (Bargello), the singing gallery or *Cantoria* of Florence cathedral (Museo dell'Opera del Duomo); and in Padua, the equestrian statue *Gattamelata* and the high altar of the Santo; finally the influential and enormously powerful carving in wood, the *Magdalen* (Baptistery, Florence).

D.'s influence is traceable in the work of every Florentine artist, notably the painters Masaccio and Castagna, Botticelli to some extent, and, to the greatest degree of all, Michelangelo. The Paduan artists under Mantegna and even the Venetians drew upon the enormous technical and spiritual wealth inherent in his work. Almost all later schools have made use of some aspects of D.'s work, e.g. the *putti* in the rococo period, the 'rediscovery' of D.'s values in sculpture by Rodin and the way in which emotional tension is reproduced in much contemporary sculpture.

Donati Enrico (1909–). Italian painter. In the 1930s he lived in Paris where he was associated with Breton and other surrealists. He settled in the U.S. in 1940 and developed an abstract expressionist style. Heavy, textured blocks of colour of irregular shape characterize his austere, impressive compositions.

Don Carlos. A play by *Schiller (1787), and opera (1867) by *Verdi with a French libretto by F.-J. Méry and C. du Locle, based on the play.

Donen Stanley (1924–). U.S. film director. His 1st film, *On the Town* (1949), was co-directed by Gene Kelly. This, reacting against the Busby *Berkeley massed choreography, developed the choreographic relationship between camera and one or a few dancers. Other films include: *Singin' in the Rain* (1952), also with Kelly; *Seven Brides for Seven Brothers* (1954); *Funny Face* (1956); *Indiscreet* (1958); and *Charade* (1963), a comedy-thriller shot in Paris.

Dongen Kees van (1877–). Dutch painter who settled in Paris in 1897. He joined the fauves in 1905 and became an important member of the group; he also exhibited with Die Brücke. After World War I he was successful as a society portraitist of wit and sophistication.

Don Giovanni (1787). Opera by Mozart with libretto by L. da Ponte, originally entitled *Il Dissoluto Punito, o sia il Don Giovanni*, i.e. 'The Reprobate Punished or Don Giovanni'. It is based on the story of *Don Juan.

Doniol-Valcroze Jacques (1920–). French film director and critic. An ed. of *Cahiers du Cinéma*, script writer for P. *Kast and actor. His 1st film, *L'Eau à la Bouche* (1959), was a *divertimento* which combined charm and worldliness. He has since made *Le Cœur battant* (1960) and *La Dénonciation* 1962), an off-beat thriller.

Donizetti Gaetano (1797–1848). Italian opera composer. From 1830 to 1838 he worked and taught in Naples, later moving to Paris; from 1845 he suffered increasingly from melancholia verging on madness. D. composed at astonishing speed, with complete technical mastery and an instinctive dramatic sense but uneven musical inspiration; of over 70 operas the following are still performed: *L'elisir d'amore* (1832), a village comedy about a shy young man who buys a love-potion from a quack; *Lucrezia*

Donen. *Singin' in the Rain*

Dongen. *Woman with Hat* (1908)

Donatello. *The Condottiere Gattamelata*

Donatello. *Putti* from the *Cantoria* for Florence cathedral

Borgia (1833); *Lucia di Lammermoor* (1835), set in 17th-c. Scotland and based on Scott's novel *The Bride of Lammermoor*; *La figlia del reggimento* (1840), *La favorita* (1840), *Linda di Chamounix* (1842) and *Don Pasquale* (1843), a comedy about a rich old man manipulated by his nephew.

Don Juan. The archetypal figure of the great seducer created by *Tirso de Molina in his *El burlador de Sevilla . . .* (publ. 1630). The character, variously interpreted, is the theme of Molière's play *Dom Juan. . .*, Mozart's opera *Don Giovanni*, *Byron's poem *Don Juan*, a story in Hoffmann's *Fantasiestücke . . .* and appears in Shaw's play *Man and Superman*.

John Donne: anon. contemporary painting

Donne John (1572–1631). English poet and churchman. In 1596 he went on Essex's Cadiz expedition, on his return becoming secretary to Sir Thomas Egerton. Elopement with his employer's niece, Anne More, destroyed his hopes of a secular career and in 1615 he was ordained, becoming dean of St Paul's in 1621. A new tenderness appears in his poetry after his marriage, reflecting his love for his wife. The 'Divine Poems' belong to a prolonged period of moral crisis culminating in his ordination and followed 2 years later by his wife's death. As dean of St Paul's he preached the series of sermons which are his greatest prose achievement.

Essentially there is little division between the passionate 'metaphysical' poet, using conventional Elizabethan themes–the parting, the cruel mistress–with an urgency and individuality apparent even in his earliest works, and the magnificent popular preacher. Sometimes careless of metre and euphony, D.'s poetry is the vehicle of his thought: profound and often tortuous ideas are traced through a web of imagery which calls upon both scholasticism and the new world of scientific and geographical discovery. Similar preoccupations and images can be traced in the sermons, which like the mature love-poetry and the 'Divine Poems' are private exercises in self-examination as well as works of art. Despite their intellectual sub-structure, the poems have frequently a direct colloquial, almost dramatic vigour and this quality too is echoed in the sermons. Few love-poets have such range of mood as D., from lust or playfulness to a meditation upon the nature of love such as *The Ecstasie* or the noble elegy for a friendship of the *Nocturnal upon St Lucies Day*. The 'Divine Poems', which frequently use carnal imagery to express the longing for union with God, share the same sombre passion.

D.'s work fell into neglect during the 18th and 19th cs, but his influence on modern writers has been considerable.

Hilda Doolittle

Donner Clive (1926–). British film director. His success as a director started with *Some People* (1962), an 'anti-romantic' musical about Bristol teenagers. *The Caretaker* (1963) is a good and faithful adaptation of *Pinter's play; *Nothing But the Best* (1964) is a social comedy.

Don Pasquale (1843). Comic opera by *Donizetti.

Don Quixote de la Mancha (1605–15). Novel by *Cervantes; also the basis for a series of sketches and oil paintings by Daumier.

Donskoi Marc (1897–). Soviet film director. D.'s fame rests almost entirely on his Maxim Gorky trilogy of 3 films from Gorky's autobiography: *My Childhood* (1938), *My Apprenticeship* (1939), *My Universities* (1940). These are personal, lyrical films of a very different kind from the romantic rhetoric of the big Russian films of the 1930s. His more recent films include 2 more from Gorky, *Mother* (1956), previously filmed by *Pudovkin, and *Foma Gordayev* (1959).

Doolittle Hilda (1886–1961). U.S. poet and one of the first and most significant of American imagists; she signed her verses 'H.D.'. Her early years in Philadelphia and her 1911 journey to Europe, where she met Ezra Pound, were the formative facts of her life. Her work appeared in Pound's *Des imagistes* in 1914. After her marriage to Richard Aldington, she lived for a period in England, where her 1st vol., *Sea Garden*, appeared in 1916. *Hymen* (1921) and *Heliodora and Other Poems* (1924) prepared for her *Collected Poems* (1925). Her later vols include *The Walls Do Not Fall* (1944), *Tribute to the Angel* (1945) and *The Flowering of the Rod* (1946), a trilogy in verse about World War II. *Helen in Egypt* (1961), a 300-page lyrical poem, is one of her last works and probably her finest.

Doon de Mayence Cycle. Group of 12th- and 13th-c. **chansons de geste* about rebels against authority (particularly Charlemagne's), including one called *D. de M.* The most famous is probably **Renaud de Montauban*.

Donner. *Some People*

Donskoi. *The Childhood of Maxim Gorky*

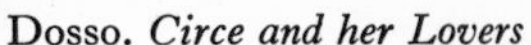

Dosso. *Circe and her Lovers*

Doré. Illustration for Dante's *Inferno*

John Dos Passos

Dostoyevsky: painting by Serov. Also *Konenkov

Dorati Antal (1906–). Hungarian-born U.S. conductor and also composer. From 1935 to 1945 he conducted Colonel de Basil's ballet co., from 1945 the Dallas, from 1949 the Minneapolis Symphony Orchestra. He has arranged music by J. Strauss the Younger as a ballet, *Graduation Ball.*

Doré Gustave (1832–83). French graphic artist, painter and sculptor. He visited London for a period, and for a time there was a Doré Gallery there exhibiting his ambitious but now thought unsuccessful oil paintings. D.'s best work results from the unrestrained outpouring of his fantastic imagination and gift for the grotesque; it includes illustrations for Dante's *Divine Comedy* and Cervantes's *Don Quixote* and plates in *London*, publ. by Blanchard Jerrold.

Doric: *order

Doshi Balkrishna Vithaldas (1927–). Indian architect trained by Le Corbusier. He heads a practice in Ahmedabad which became known for designs in the late manner of Le Corbusier–rough concrete and heavy structure. His most recent work shows relaxation of the Corbusian approach, and a growing influence from Louis Kahn.

Dos Passos John (Roderigo) (1896–). U.S. novelist. His 1st important work, *Manhattan Transfer* (1925), a grim vision of modern city agony, is ambitiously successful both linguistically and in plot structure. It forms a preparation for his greatest work, the trilogy *U.S.A.*, consisting of *The 42nd Parallel* (1930), *1919* (1932) and *The Big Money* (1936), about social classes and conflicts within American capitalist society. This has been imitated by writers as different as Norman Mailer and Jean-Paul Sartre. Dos P. describes characters as types and his selection of types is fitted into a vision of meaningless, destructive competition. This is diversified by employing a number of prose styles which constitute a pattern of brief biographies of the famous, newsreels, stream-of-consciousness lyricism and straight narrative.

Dosso Dossi. The name used by Giovanni di Lutero (d. 1542), Italian painter of Ferrara, greatly influenced by Giorgione, Titian and Raphael, but a strongly individual painter. He borrows the theme of Giorgione's pastoral in his best-known picture, *Circe and her lovers in a landscape* (Borghese Gal., Rome), but replaces the poetic evocation with a sense of drama and worldly splendour. There is a second, very fine version in the N.G., Washington, in which the lovers have been turned into animals by the enchantress. Both D. and his brother Battista (d. *c.* 1548) were employed as painters, designers and craftsmen at the Ferrarese court. D. painted a number of warriors in armour at this time: variations exist in Liverpool, Florence, Modena and the British Royal Colls.

Dostoyevsky Fyodor Mikhailovich (1821–81). Russian novelist, the son of a doctor. D. entered the Military Engineers' School at St Petersburg in 1837, received a commission (1841), but resigned in 1844. The publ. of *Poor Folk* (1846), a novel of letters, was greeted enthusiastically by the radical critics Belinsky and Nekrasov. D.'s membership of the socialist Petrashevsky circle led to his arrest (1849); he was sentenced to 4 years' penal servitude at Omsk (1850–4) and an indefinite period of service as a private soldier. He was amnestied in 1859. From this time his epileptic attacks were violent and frequent. During his imprisonment he returned to Orthodox Christianity and rejected Western materialism. He married–unhappily–in 1857. Between 1861 and 1864 he ed. the reviews *The Time* and *The Epoch*; when the latter closed, he was bankrupt and his wife and beloved brother Mikhail were dead. To this period belong his passion for Apollinaria Suslova and the beginning of his craze for roulette; both are reflected in *The Gambler* (1866), which he dictated to a secretary, Anna Grigorievna, who became his wife in 1867. They left Russia to avoid D.'s creditors, returning in 1873 after years of hardship, during which his greatest conceptions matured. D.'s reputation steadily increased, and his Address on the unveiling of the Pushkin Memorial, delivered shortly before his death, received unprecedented acclaim.

The early novels, *Poor Folk* and *The Double* (1846), were strongly influenced by Gogol; but although the characters are ridiculous, even grotesque, their sufferings are described with compassion. D.'s humour–a painful humour derived from his obsession with humiliation–is displayed in *A Friend of the Family* (1859) and the story *A Nasty Predicament* (1862). *The Insulted and Injured* (1861) and *The House of the Dead* (1861), an account of his prison

Dou. *The Young Mother*. Also *genre

Dou. *Man with a pipe*

experiences, optimistically preach the saving virtue of compassion. *Notes from Underground* (1864), however, anticipates the complex and ambiguous sympathies of the 4 great novels which followed. On the surface these are sensational stories of mystery and suspense–indebted to Dickens, Balzac and Eugène Sue–which proceed by successive revelations; every trick of melodrama is used to thicken the atmosphere. There are extended dialogues, and characters reveal themselves by the most sublime, grotesque or disgusting actions. But they also embody ideas–indeed, their ideological roles enhance their vitality. The major theme of the novels is the struggle between religious and atheistic values. D.'s reactionary political ideas and racial prejudices are obsolete; but his conception of Christianity has had great influence. It emphasizes charity and compassion rather than purity of morals, and holds that sin and suffering are necessary for salvation. He insists that 'if there is no God, then everything is allowed'. In *Crime and Punishment* (1866; 1886), Raskolnikov kills an evil old woman, a usurer, after convincing himself that the murder will demonstrate his freedom and benefit everybody. But his convictions are gradually destroyed by remorse: he confesses, repents, and is purified by suffering. *The Devils* (1873; 1914) are a group of nihilists whose beliefs lead them to suicide, murder and arson. *The Idiot* (1868; 1887) depicts a Christ-figure in the Russia of D.'s time; his simplicity and goodness are taken for cretinism. *The Brothers Karamazov* (1880; 1912) are Dmitry, passionate and self-willed; Ivan, an atheist intellectual; and the gentle Alyosha, a monastic novice. The action concerns the murder of their father, Fyodor, and its consequences. Dmitry is suspected and eventually condemned. The murderer, however, is his half-brother, Smerdyakov, an idiot who has taken literally Ivan's doctrines of ruthless action. Ivan realizes his own responsibility and tries unsuccessfully to save Dmitry. The famous set-pieces in the book are the story of the Grand Inquisitor, Father Zozima's death, and Ivan's dialogue with the Devil. D.'s other works include the novels *The Eternal Husband* (1870), *A Raw Youth* (1875), and *Netotchka Nezvanova* (left unfinished in 1849); *Winter Notes on Summer Impressions* (1863), a critical account of his visits to Paris and London; and *A Writer's Diary*.

dotted note. In musical notation a dot placed after a note extends its duration by half again; thus ♩. = ♩♪ In late 17th- and early 18th-c. music the performer was free to interpret ♩. ♪ as ♩♪♪ or ♩♪♬ according to the context or his own taste. L. Mozart introduced the double dot for the 2nd meaning. Also *staccato.

Dou Gerard or Gerrit (1613–75). Dutch painter of portraits and genre, and the founder of the fijnschilders ('fine-painters'). D. was first apprenticed to his father, an engraver on glass, then became a pupil or companion of the young Rembrandt. After Rembrandt left Leyden, *c.* 1631, D. became the city's leading painter. Close to Rembrandt's style is *A Hermit* (Wallace Coll., London). D.'s highly finished scenes, often of dramatically lit interiors with figures, e.g. *The Young Mother* (Mauritshuis), were very popular and had a lasting influence even outside Holland. Among D.'s pupils were F. van Mieris the Elder, G. Metsu and G. Schalcken.

double. In music this word is used adjectively (1) to mean of low pitch, thus 'double bassoon'; (2) in 'd. concerto', i.e. one with 2 solo instruments or 2 orchestras; (3) in 'd.-handed', meaning a performer competent on 2 instruments of different families; (4) in 'd. 8ves' or 'd. 3rds', meaning 8ves or 3rds played simultaneously in both hands on the keyboard. The verb is used to mean (1) the simultaneous performance of a melody by 2 or more performers, thus 'the chorus parts are doubled by trombones'; (2) the use by one player of 2 different instruments during the course of one work; thus 'the 3rd oboist may d. on cor anglais'.

double bar. In musical notation a sign which marks the end of a section or the whole piece, thus 𝄁

Double Dealer, The (1694). Play by Congreve.

Double Indemnity (1944). Film directed by B. *Wilder.

Doughty Charles Montagu (1843–1926). English traveller, writer and poet. His *Travels in Arabia Deserta* (1888) was admired for its insight into Arab society and character and for its style, which curiously blends Elizabethan, Chaucerian and Arabic elements; it strongly influenced T. E. Lawrence.

Doughty Thomas (1793–1856). U.S. romantic landscapist of the Hudson River school. Carefully observed sky effects and silvery grey tones characterize his paintings.

Douglas Lord Alfred (Bruce) (1870–1945). English poet, intimate friend of Oscar *Wilde. His poetry includes the sonnets *A Triad of the Moon* and *To Olive*. His *Autobiography* was publ. in 1929.

Lord Alfred Douglas

Thomas Doughty. *River Landscape*

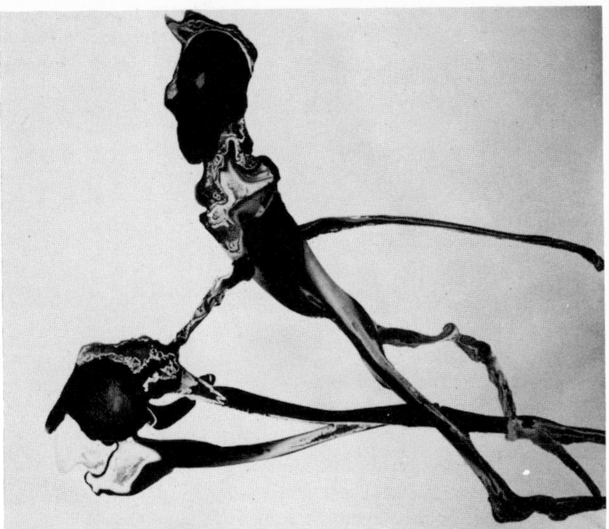

Dova. *Painting, 1952*

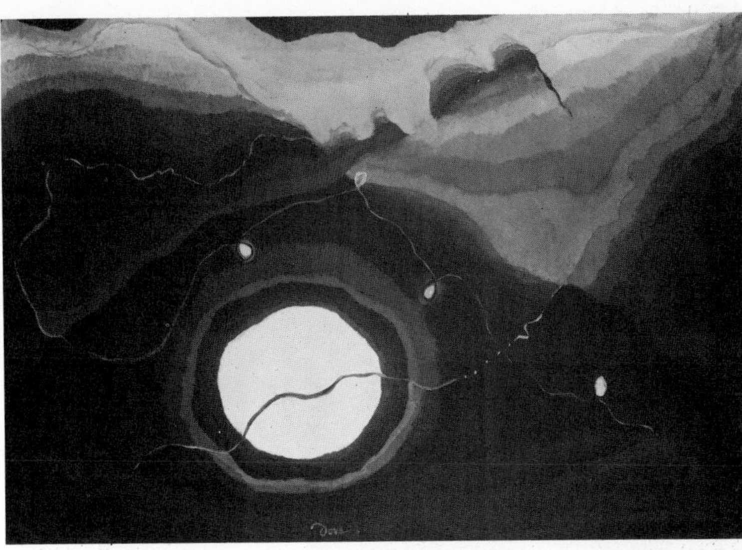

Dove. *Rise of the Full Moon* (1937)

Douglas Gawin or Gavin (1475?–1522). Scottish bishop and poet whose *The xiii Bukes of Eneados* (1533) was the first direct trs. of Virgil's *Aeneid* into English. D.'s 'Chaucerian' verse includes the allegories, *The Palis of Honoure* (1553?) and *King Hart*.

Douglas Gordon (1909–). U.S. film director. D. was an actor for Hal *Roach and directed 30 *Our Gang* shorts before making his 1st feature in 1939. His best work is technically excellent but rather impersonal: *Them!* (1954), *The Fiend Who Walked the West* (1958), *The Sins of Rachel Cade* (1961), and *Follow That Dream* (1962) with Elvis Presley.

Douglas Kirk (1916–). U.S. film actor who made his screen début in 1946. Many of his roles have been of tough and honest individualists with physical strength used for the common good. Among his best films are: *Lust for Life* (1956), *Paths of Glory* (1957) and *Spartacus* (1959–60).

Douglas Lloyd C[assel] (1877–1951). U.S. religious novelist. His books include the best-sellers *Magnificent Obsession* (1929; films 1936 and 1954), *The Robe* (1942; film 1953) and *The Big Fisherman* (1948; film 1959).

Doulton. Stoneware pottery established at Lambeth early in the 19th c. The earliest manufacture was of salt-glazed stoneware with relief decorations (including bottles, Toby jugs, etc.). The firm prospered and commercial wares were produced in response to the demands of expanding industry. After 1856 due to the co-operation of Henry D. with the newly founded school of art at Lambeth, wares designed and executed by artists and craftsmen were added to the production.
In 1877 works were acquired also at Burslem and here bone china and earthenware tablewares are manufactured.

Dova Gianni (1925–). Italian painter using an exact, highly finished technique; he creates grotesque, autonomous animal, bird and plant forms.

Dove Arthur G[arfield] (1880–1946). U.S. painter and, in his youth, commercial illustrator. He began experiments in abstraction after a visit to Paris (1907/8) and was a pioneer of abstract painting in the U.S. His paintings as exemplified in *Rise of the Full Moon* (1937; Phillips Coll., Washington) recognizably relate to natural forms.

Doves Press. One of the great English private presses which led the revival of European typography. It was founded by T. J. Cobden-Sanderson and Emery *Walker who designed the D. type. The press operated from 1900 to 1916, a 5-vol. Bible (1903) being considered its masterpiece.

Dovzhenko Alexander (1894–1956). Soviet film director. D.'s films, like those of *Pudovkin, personalize their themes by building stories round a central person who remains a symbol rather than being developed as a character. Although often concerned with social progress, e.g. dam-building in *Ivan* (1932), they are often pastoral in inspiration, celebrating the landscape and the peasant population. His most famous films are *Zvenigora* (1928), *Arsenal* (1929), *Earth* (1930), *Aerograd* (1935) and *Shors* (1939).

Dowland John (1562–1626). English composer and lutenist. He enjoyed an international reputation and worked in Paris, Germany and Italy, studying under Marenzio in Florence; he was lutenist to Christian IV of Denmark, before finally returning to England in 1606, receiving at last a court appointment in 1612. D.'s reputation as a master has never been disputed and his beautiful, often melancholy, lute songs are a major landmark in the development of the art song. Besides 3 books of songs he publ. *A Pilgrims Solace* (1612), works for lute and viols, lute solos and the magnificent and famous *Lachrymae* (1604), a set of '7 passionate pavannes', for viols and lute.

Dowland Robert (1588–1641). English musician, son of the above and court lutenist to Charles I. He publ. *A Varietie of Lute Lessons* (1610) and *A Musicall Banquet* (1610), both containing works by many other composers.

Doulton stoneware jug; early 19th c.

IN THE BEGINNING GOD CREATED THE HEAVEN AND THE EARTH. ¶ AND THE EARTH WAS WITHOUT FORM, AND VOID; AND DARKNESS WAS UPON THE FACE OF THE DEEP, & THE SPIRIT OF GOD MOVED UPON THE FACE OF THE WATERS. ¶ And God said, Let there be light: & there was light. And God saw the light, that it was good: & God divided the light from the darkness. And God called the light Day, and the darkness he called Night. And the evening and the morning were the first day. ¶ And God said, Let there be a firmament in the midst of the waters, & let it divide the waters from the waters. And God made the firmament, and divided the waters which were under the firmament from the waters which were above the firmament: & it was so. And God called the firmament Heaven. And the evening & the morning were the second day. ¶ And God said, Let the waters under the heaven be gathered together unto one place, and let the dry land appear: and it was so. And God called the dry land Earth: and the gathering together of the waters called he Seas: and God saw that it was good. And God said, Let the earth bring forth grass, the herb yielding seed, and the fruit tree yielding fruit after his kind, whose seed is in itself, upon the earth: & it was so. And the earth brought forth grass, & herb yielding seed after his kind, & the tree yielding fruit, whose seed was in itself, after his kind: and God saw that it was good. And the evening & the morning were the third day. ¶ And God said, Let there be lights in the firmament of the heaven to divide the day from the night; and let them be for signs, and for seasons, and for days, & years: and let them be for lights in the firmament of the heaven to give light upon the earth: & it was so. And God made two great lights; the greater light to rule the day, and the lesser light to rule the night: he made the stars also. And God set them in the firmament of the heaven to give light upon the earth, and to rule over the day and over the night, & to divide the light from the darkness: and God saw that it was good. And the evening and the morning were the fourth day. ¶ And God said, Let the waters bring forth abundantly the moving creature that hath life, and fowl that may fly above the earth in the open firmament of heaven. And God created great whales, & every living creature that moveth, which the waters brought forth abundantly, after their kind, & every winged fowl after his kind: & God saw that it was good. And God blessed them, saying, Be fruitful, & multiply, and fill the waters in the seas, and let fowl multiply in the earth. And the evening & the morning were the fifth day. ¶ And God said, Let the earth bring forth the living creature after his kind, cattle, and creeping thing, and beast of the earth after his kind: and it was so. And God made the beast of the earth after his kind, and cattle after their kind, and every thing that creepeth upon the

27

Doves Press Bible

Dovzhenko. *Earth*

Richard Doyle. Front cover for *Punch*

Conan Doyle

Drapery. Study by Leonardo

Drapery. *Madonna and Child* by Sluter

Down and Out in Paris and London (1933). Book by George Orwell.

Downman John (d. 1824). English painter, notably of small-scale portraits in crayon tinted with watercolour; pupil of Benjamin West.

Dowson Ernest (Christopher) (1867–1900). English poet of the aesthetic movement, a friend of W. B. Yeats and L. Johnson. His famous poem *Non sum qualis eram. . .* , with the refrain 'I have been faithful to thee, Cynara! in my fashion' appeared in *Verses* (1896). The Latin title is from Horace.

Doyle Sir Arthur Conan (1859–1930). English doctor and writer, the creator of the detective Sherlock Holmes and his chronicler and assistant Dr Watson. Among the *Holmes* novels were *A Study in Scarlet* (1887), *The Sign of Four* (1890) and *The Hound of the Baskervilles* (1902), but some of D.'s best work appeared in the numerous *Holmes* short stories. D.'s historical romances include *The White Company* (1891).

Doyle Richard (1824–83). English draughtsman and illustrator. His vigorous gift for grotesque comedy appears in the famous cover for *Punch*, drawn for the first issue (1841), his illustrations for Ruskin and Dickens and his comic social histories, *Ye Manners and Customs of Ye Englishe, drawn from ye Quick* and *The Foreign Tour of Brown, Jones and Robinson*, for which he was admired by the Pre-Raphaelites.

D'Oyly Carte Richard (1844–1901). English theatrical impresario who formed and encouraged the partnership of W. S. *Gilbert and Sir Arthur Sullivan: he founded the D'Oyly Carte Opera Co. for the production of their operas in 1875 and in 1881 opened the Savoy Theatre, London, with *Patience*. This theatre became the home of the Gilbert and Sullivan operas.

Drachmann Holger Henrik Herholdt (1846–1908). Danish poet, novelist and playwright. Although his sympathy with G. Brandes's radicalism is evident in his earlier work, in the 1880s he took up a nationalistic position in politics and literature. His semi-autobiographical novel, *Forskrevet* (1890), reveals a complex character.

Dracula (1897). Novel by Bram *Stoker; made into a film (1931) directed by T. *Browning.

Dragonetti Domenico (1763–1846). Italian double-bass virtuoso (establishing the use of the concave violin type of bow as opposed to the convex curved bow) and composer. He toured England, where he met Haydn and began his 50-year partnership with the cellist R. Lindley; he was a close friend of Beethoven.

dramatic monologue. A long poem in which the poet analyses a personality, either real or imaginary, through the means of reminiscences and reflections. Browning originated the form.

Draper Ruth (1889–1956). U.S. entertainer who composed and performed unique one-woman shows such as *Three Generations*, *The Italian Lesson*, *Opening a Bazaar* and *Vive La France*. With an acute observation of character and situation, D. combined an extraordinary range of voices and dialects and a fantastic ability to 'people' the stage with characters.

drapery. In sculpture, painting and drawing the representation of the folds in a garment. Artists have used d. as an important expressive medium and different schools and periods render it in a characteristic style. Hence it is a valuable guide to the art historian in identifying and classifying a work of art. Leonardo da Vinci, Dürer and Grünewald are among the artists to have made fine studies of d.

Drapier's Letters, The (1724). Series of pamphlets by Swift.

drawing. In the Western tradition the instruments used for d. have normally been pen, charcoal, chalk or pencil (however, watercolours are sometimes classified as drawing); d.s can be merely preparatory studies for a painting or work of sculpture, or independent works entire in themselves. The importance of d. in the visual arts has been much debated since the 16th c. and contrasted with the importance of colour. Florentine art, Poussin and Ingres are ranged against the Venetians, Rubens and Delacroix. In Chinese and Japanese art there is no distinction between painting and drawing, as the only instrument used is a brush, normally with ink.

drawn-fabric work. A type of embroidery in which the threads of the material are pulled or drawn into groups. No threads are cut or withdrawn. During the 17th and 18th cs the

Drawn-thread work; English, 17th c.

Michael Drayton: anon. contemporary painting

Theodore Dreiser

technique was developed into a form close to needle-point lace.

drawn-thread work. A type of embroidery in which chosen weft and warp threads of the material are cut and withdrawn to give an open lace-like texture. Decorative stitches are worked in the resultant spaces and on surrounding areas. Commonly white materials are used.

Drayton Michael (1563–1631). English poet of great energy, versatility and professionalism, at home in sonnet, ode, pastoral, elegy, historical poem. He was playwright for R. Henslowe and collaborated in dramatic writing with Chettle, Dekker and Munday. Though naturally influenced by Sidney and his friend Spenser, his idiom and particular sparkle of style are highly personal. Notable poems are the sonnet *Since ther's no helpe*, *To the Virginian Voyage*, *The Ballad of Agincourt*, *To . . . Henery Reynolds Esquire* and *The Poly-olbion* (1613, 1622), D.'s vast, infinitely entertaining survey of England and Wales and their rivers.

dream allegory. A frequently recurring convention in medieval allegories is that the allegory or some part of it is a dream (thus liberating the poet from the demands of probability), e.g. the whole action of *Le Roman de la Rose* is said to be the poet's dream.

Dream of Gerontius, The (1866). Poem by J. H. *Newman; set as an oratorio (1900) by *Elgar.

Dream of John Ball, A (1886). Book by William Morris.

Dream of the Rood, The. Religious poem in Old English, variously attributed to *Caedmon or *Cynewulf.

Dreigroschenoper, Die (1929). Work by *Brecht and *Weill.

Dreiser Theodore (Herman Albert) (1871–1945). U.S. novelist, the child of a poor Indiana family. D.'s naturalistic novels helped to enlarge the scope of U.S. literature by their use of social analysis and frank presentation of sexual relationships; and though D.'s style and construction are clumsy, his vitality and largeness of vision remain impressive. His 1st novel, *Sister Carrie* (1900), describes how an innocent Wisconsin girl becomes a kept woman and at last a successful but lonely actress. *An American Tragedy* (1925), the story of the downward path of Clyde Griffith from unskilled worker to murderer, indicts hypocrisy, Puritanism and the callousness of the industrial system. Novels include *Jennie Gerhardt* (1911); *The 'Genius'* (1915); and the trilogy *The Financier* (1912), *The Titan* (1914) and *The Stoic* (posth. 1947).

Dresden Germany, capital of Saxony. During the 17th and 18th cs D. became the cultural centre of Protestant Germany under the Electors Frederick and Augustus. Famous as the perfect baroque city of N. Europe (*Pöppelmann and *Bähr), it was almost completely destroyed by British bombing in March 1945 but is now being carefully reconstructed.
A faïence factory was started in D. in 1708 by J. F. Böttger, a little before his discovery of a method for porcelain manufacture and the subsequent establishment of a factory for its production at Meissen. D. has been a common English misnomer for *Meissen ware since the 18th c. The D. factory produced at first tiles in the Dutch manner worked by Dutch potters, but soon turned to faïence wares of good quality mostly in an oriental style, imitating Chinese blue-and-white wares; it ceased production in 1784.

Dresden. Detail of a painting by Bellotto

Dresden Sem (1881–1957). Dutch composer and chorus master. He studied composition under H. Pfitzner, founded (1914) the great *a capella* choir, the Madrigaalvereeniging, was director of the Amsterdam Conservatory (1924–37) and the Royal Conservatory, The Hague (1937–49). His music, early influenced by French impressionism, includes the 1-act opera *François Villon*; the oratorio *Saint Antoine* (1955); *Chorus tragicus* and *Chorus symphonicus* for voices and orchestra; the operetta *Toto* (1945); *a capella* choral music, *Vocalises for Soprano and Seven instruments* (1937); *Dansflitsen* for orchestra, violin and oboe; piano concertos and much chamber music.

dressings. Architectural term for smooth stone blocks used e.g. on a brick building as *quoins or round doors and windows.

Dreyer Carl Theodor (1889–). Danish film director. D. wrote his 1st script in 1912 and directed his 1st film in 1920. He worked in Scandinavia and Germany before making in France *The Passion of Joan of Arc* (1928), a

Dreyer. Renée Falconetti in *The Passion of Joan of Arc*

Military tenor drums
(from Burgkmair's *Triumphs of Maximilian*)

Orchestral bass drum

Snare drum

Drouais. *The Young Marie-Antoinette*

Drury Lane: section through the auditorium; engraving (1825)

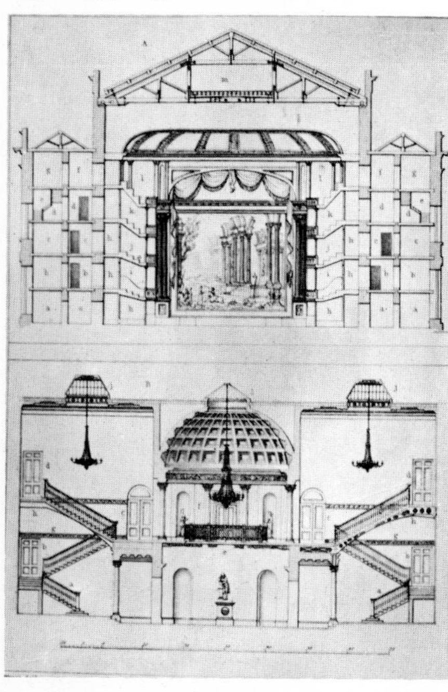

film made almost entirely in big close-ups to remove any aspects of pageantry and to force the audience to participate in the action. One of the very few films he has made since is *Vampyr* (1930), a ghost-story from Sheridan le Fanu. His next feature, *Day of Wrath* (1943), resumed his spiritual investigations from *Joan* in its story of a parson's wife accused of witchcraft in Puritan 17th-c. Denmark. *Ordet* (1955) was about a farmer who believes he is Christ. *Gertrud* (1964) combines D.'s visual mastery with an intimate, domestic theme.

Drieu La Rochelle Pierre-Eugène (1893–1945). French novelist and extreme right-wing political essayist; novels include *Fond de cantine* (1920), *L'homme couvert des femmes* (1925) and *Gilles* (1939). He was director of the *Nouvelle Revue Française* during the German occupation of France, committing suicide when it ended.

Drifters (1929). Film directed by J. *Grierson.

Drigo Riccardo (1846–1930). Italian composer and director of the St Petersburg opera. He wrote ballets, e.g. *Il talismano* and *Millions d'Arlequin*, a serenade from which became very popular.

Drinkwater John (1882–1937). English playwright and poet. His historical plays include *Abraham Lincoln* (1918).

Droeshout Martin (*fl.* 1620–51). English portrait engraver of Flemish parentage. His copper-plate engraving of Shakespeare prefixed to the 1st folio (1623) and commissioned by Shakespeare's friends and eds, Heminge and Condell, is one of the 2 authenticated portraits of the poet. It was probably taken from a portrait now lost.

Drouais François-Hubert (1727–75). French portrait painter, especially of women and children in a graceful, if over-facile, rococo style. He was a favourite with Mme de Pompadour and Mme Du Barry.

Drouais Germain-Jean (1763–88). French neo-classic painter, son of the above and pupil of J.-L. David, by whom he was strongly influenced. From 1785 he worked in Rome.

drum. Percussion instruments of this family are usually untuned, i.e. give an indefinite note. The BASS D. in dance, jazz and brass bands is about 2 ft in diameter with a 'head', i.e. the stretched vellum or skin, on both sides of the cylindrical frame; the bass d. used in a symphony orchestra is usually 4 or 5 ft in diameter with a head on only one side; both types are played in a vertical position. The SIDE D. is about 15 ins in diameter and is about 6 ins deep; it is played in a horizontal position; a SNARE D. is a side drum with wires stretched across the lower head so as to rattle when the upper d. head is struck. The TENOR D. has about the same diameter as a side d. but is about 2 ft deep and gives a deeper sound when struck. Other kinds of untuned d. are the *tabor and the *naker. The *timpani or kettledrums give a definite note and are sometimes machine or pedal tuned.

drum. In architecture, the cylindrical wall holding a dome.

Drum Mass. Nickname of Haydn's mass in C (1796); the kettledrums are extensively used.

Drummond of Hawthornden William (1585–1649). Scottish poet who has been called 'the Scottish Petrarch' for his accomplished but rather sweet sonnets, influenced by Sidney and the Italian poets. He corresponded with M. Drayton and was a friend of Jonson, on whom he reflected somewhat unfortunately in *Conversations of Ben Jonson*. Works include: *Teares on the Death of Meliades* (1613); *Poems* (1616), mainly inspired by love for his dead mistress; *Flowres of Sion* (1623); and the very fine prose meditations after illness *The Cypresse Grove* (1623).

Drumont Édouard (Adolphe) (1844–1917). French writer, author of the anti-Semitic *La France juive* (1886) and a prominent anti-Dreyfusard.

Drum-Roll Symphony. Nickname of Haydn's symphony no. 103 in E♭ (1795) given because of the drum-roll which opens the slow introduction to the 1st movement.

Drum-Taps (1865). Coll. of poems by Walt *Whitman.

Drury Lane The Theatre Royal. London theatre, the oldest still in use. The first, built by T. *Killigrew and opened in 1663, burned down in 1672. The second building, also erected by Killigrew, was designed by Sir C. Wren; it was replaced in 1794 by a much larger one, burned down in 1809. The present theatre (1812) was designed by B. Wyatt. Since the production of *Oklahoma!* just after World War II, it has become the home of lavish musicals.

Dryden John (1631–1700). English poet. Before becoming poet laureate in 1668 D. worked as a dramatist and adapter of plays. *Absalom and Achitophel*, a satire upon the Shaftesbury conspiracy, was publ. in 1681; *Mac Flecknoe*, which satirized the Whig author Shadwell and became the model for Pope's *Dunciad*, in 1682. At the same time D. was writing *Religio Laici*, a verse defence of the Anglican faith. Although at the height of his powers, D. earned little; the threat of poverty enforced his dependence upon the reigning monarch and may have dictated his conversion to Roman Catholicism shortly after the accession of James II. The allegorical poem *The Hind and the Panther* (1687) does, however, show evidence of genuine religious feeling, and D. adhered to his faith after the 1688 Revolution. In the last decade of his life he publ. a trs. of Virgil; the *Fables*–versions of the classics, Chaucer and Boccaccio–and some lyrics.

D. was the first great master of the plain, strong, direct style; his forthrightness and vigour were ill-adapted to the comic stage of his time, which maintained a delicate balance between grossness of content and refinement of style. His tragedies were more successful and the best of them, *All for Love*, is the noblest tragedy of the period. It has inevitably suffered by comparison with Shakespeare's *Antony and Cleopatra*, dealing as it does with the same theme, but succeeds within its own conception of classical decorum; and D.'s grave verse gives it an austere dignity. His most characteristic works are the rhymed satires and trs; with a gift for vigorous argument in verse and an earthy solidity of imagery he can create emblems of anger or disgust which transcend the immediate polemical purpose. Works include *Annus Mirabilis* (1667), celebrating English naval victories of the year 1665–6; and *Mac Flecknoe*, a satire directed against the poet Thomas Shadwell.

dry point: *engraving

Drysdale Russell (1912–). English-born painter who emigrated to Australia as a child. He was among the earliest painters to apply new semi-abstract techniques to depict the rugged mountains and deserts of Australia and their poor inhabitants, among whom he has lived since childhood.

Dubliners (1914). Coll. of short stories by James *Joyce.

Dubois (François-Clément) Théodore (1837–1924). French composer and organist; winner of the Rome prize and from 1896 to 1905 director of the Paris Conservatoire. He had to resign following public outcry against the Conservatoire's refusal to permit *Ravel to sit for the Rome prize.

Dubuffet Jean (1901–). French painter who took up painting seriously only in 1942. Strongly influenced by *l'art brut* (primitive, psychotic and child art), he creates an irrational, primitive world and through varied textural surfaces produced by experimenting with sand, cement, tar, lacquer, etc., gives to his work a supra-pictorial existence. In 1954 he exhibited sculptures which he called *Little Statues of Precarious Life*, made from ephemeral and cast-off materials such as newspaper, worn-out sponge and string.

Duccio di Buoninsegna (*c.* 1260–*c.* 1319). Italian painter, the creator of the Sienese school as Giotto was that of the Florentine school. D.'s break with the conventions of Byzantine painting was far less revolutionary than Giotto's, and the great success with which he filled many of the old forms with the new spirit, combined with his superlative colour sense, his feeling for composition, and the dramatic rendering of familiar religious scenes, meant that those Sienese painters who followed him were often content to remain detached from the search for more natural forms of representation which was being pursued in Florence and elsewhere.

The documents of D.'s life tell of his frequent clashes with the government of his city. Despite this he was trusted with important commissions and rose to a position of power, wealth and influence. It may have been during a period of exile from Siena that he executed the earliest picture attributed to him. Most critics now agree that the famous *Rucellai Madonna* (Uffizi) is the painting D. was commissioned to paint for the Chapter of Sta Maria

Dryden: painting by Kneller

Drysdale. *Emus in a Landscape* (1950)

Dubuffet. *Vache la belle allegre*

Duccio. *Maestà*

Duccio. *The Rucellai Madonna*

Duchamp. *Nude Descending a Staircase No. 2*

Duchamp. *Ready-made*

Duchamp-Villon. *Horse*. Also *cubism

Novella in 1285. While the figure of the Madonna remains a type of Byzantine art, the graceful angels and the Child are alive with the new spirit.

The work which displays every quality of D.'s greatness is unquestionably the *Maestà* (Cathedral Mus., Siena) which D. was commissioned to paint in 1308 and which, according to tradition, was carried to the cathedral with rejoicing in 1311. Apart from the *Maestà* itself, there are some 44 panels on the front and back of the altarpiece representing scenes from the Bible and the lives of the saints; 10 of these panels are now separated. Among these are the outstanding *Calling of the Apostles Peter and Andrew* (N.G., Washington) and *Annunciation* (N.G., London).

Du Cerceau Jacques Androuet the Elder (*c.* 1520–84). French architect. Du C. went to Rome in the 1540s and later publ. books of engravings of great French houses, on which his fame mainly rests. His 2 rather fantastic châteaux, Verneuil (1565) and Charleval (1573), have been demolished. His sons Baptiste and Jacques Androuet the Younger, and grandson Jean were also architects.

Duchamp Marcel (1887–). French painter, brother of Jacques Villon and Raymond Duchamp-Villon. He studied part-time at the Académie Julian, Paris, while working as a librarian at the Bibliothèque Ste-Geneviève. He abandoned painting in the 1920s but contributed to surrealist exhibitions in 1938 and 1947. The influence of his now legendary small œuvre is difficult to assess, but his name is treated with an almost mystical respect by artists of subsequent generations. His first paintings (1911–12), deeply influenced by the cubists, analysed the movement of form in space. *Nude Descending a Staircase No. 1* (1911) and *No. 2* (1912) (both in Philadelphia), inspired like contemporary futurist painting by chronophotography, attempted to create an autonomous equivalent to the moving figure, and he originally intended that the construction *The Bride Stripped Bare by her Bachelors Even* should actually move. The 2nd version of the *Nude Descending* was rejected from a 1912 cubist exhibit and became the most notorious exhibit at the famous *Armory Show. The public exhibition of his 'ready-mades', e.g. *Bottle Rack* (1914), *Comb* (1916), *Fountain* (1917), etc., foreshadowed the polemical 'anti-art' character of dada.

Duchamp-Villon Raymond (1876–1918). French sculptor, brother of Gaston (known as Jacques Villon) and Marcel Duchamp. He took up sculpture in 1898 after studying medicine and was first influenced by Rodin. In 1910 he joined the cubists. Cubist sculpture reached its apogee in his *Horse* (1914; M.M.A., Paris), a masterly synthesis of organic and mechanical elements.

Duchess of Malfi, The (publ. 1623). Tragedy by *Webster.

Duck Soup (1932). Film directed by L. *McCarey and featuring the *Marx Brothers.

Duclos, Charles Pinot or Pineau (1704–72). French writer, linked with the **philosophes*. His chief works are memoirs and studies in contemporary society manners.

Ducos du Hauron Louis (1837–1920). French photographer and inventor who produced the 1st successful photographs in colour. His process, called 'trichromie', involved the exposure of 3 separate negatives, 1 for each of the primary colours. The developed negatives were superimposed to produce a single image in natural colour.

Dudintsev Vladimir Dmitrievich (1918–). Soviet author of a novel, *Not by Bread Alone* (1956; 1957), which attacks Soviet bureaucratic materialism, protests that man lives 'not by bread alone' and argues that true Communism is based on ethical values, fraternity and truth; though D. was severely criticized, the fact of publ. indicated some relaxation of state control of literature. D.'s other work includes *A New Year's Tale* (1960).

Dudok Willem (1884–1959). Dutch architect on the fringes of the modern movement. His work, as at the town hall at Hilversum (1930), is carefully built of brick, often in large blocks like a cubist painting, and the detailing is strongly influenced by Frank Lloyd Wright.

Dudow Slatan (1903–). Bulgarian-born film director. After making documentaries, D. directed *Kuhle Wampe* (1932), with a *Brecht script and music by Hanns Eisler, the strongest exposition of the Communist viewpoint in the German cinema of the 1930s. His post-war work in E. Germany includes *Der Hauptmann von Köln* (1956).

Du Cerceau. Château Verneuil

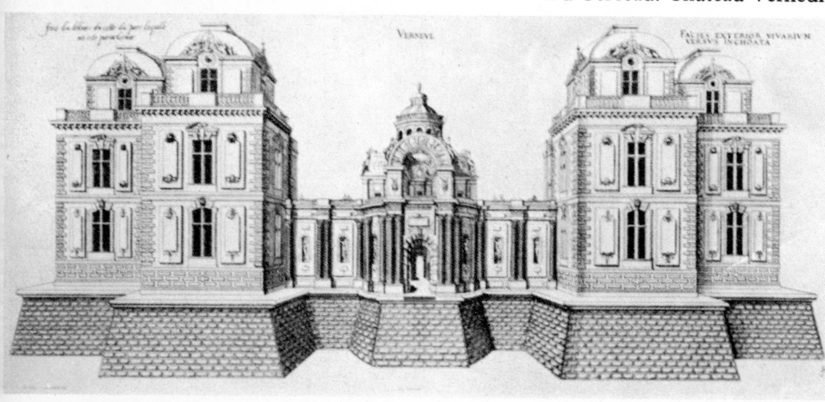

Dudok. Hilversum town hall

Dufay: from a 15th-c. ms. Martin Le Franc's *Champion des Dames*

Dufy. *Les Trois Baigneuses*

Duel in the Sun (1947). Film directed by K. *Vidor.

Duenna, The (1775). Comic opera by Sheridan.

Due Soldi di Speranza (1952). Film directed by R. *Castellani.

Dufay Guillaume (*c.* 1400–74). Flemish composer. After training as a choirboy at Cambrai he worked for a period, during the 1420s and 1430s, in Italy. From *c.* 1437 he travelled widely in Europe, working in Cambrai, Savoy and Mons and holding an honorary position as a chaplain to the duke of Burgundy. The clarity and elegance of D.'s style shows the influence of his period in Italy. His early work follows the dissonantal idiom of the 14th-c. *ars nova but it develops towards a greater euphony, partly influenced by the English school headed by John *Dunstable. D. also adapted from the English the cyclic tenor *mass, increasing its unifying effect by the addition of 'mottos' which recur at the beginning of the movements. His clear part writing and harmonic procedures foreshadow 16th-c. polyphony. The major part of D.'s output was church music, and his greatest work is in his masses, e.g. *L'Homme armé*, *Ecce ancilla domini*, *Ave Regina Coellorum* and the *missa sine nomine.*

Dufresne Charles (1876–1938). French painter and designer who combined the stylistic influences of fauvism and cubism with romantic subject-matter. A visit to Algeria (1910–12) stimulated his interest in exotic subjects–*Patio à Alger* (1913; M.M.A., Paris). Among his last works were murals for the Palais de Chaillot (1937) and the École de Pharmacie (1938), Paris.

Dufresne Jacques (1922–). French sculptor, son of the above and pupil of H. Laurens; he works in a variety of materials, producing severe figures full of tension.

Dufresny Charles Rivière (1648–1724). French writer. His *Amusements sérieux et comiques d'un Siamois* (1699), an imaginary record of the impressions of a Siamese in Paris, anticipate Montesquieu's *Lettres Persanes*. He also wrote *Le Chevalier joueur* (1697), about a gambler, and a number of comedies.

Dufy Raoul (1877–1953). French painter, born in Le Havre, where he met Braque and Friesz. He studied at the École des Beaux-Arts. Under Matisse's influence he produced fauve paintings around 1905 with strong colour areas and an intermittent heavy black contour–e.g. *La Plage de Ste-Adresse* (1904). Cubism and the influence of Cézanne prompted a monumental sense of form as in *Les Trois Baigneuses* (1919; M.M.A., Paris), but after 1920 D.'s paintings of racecourses, regattas and casinos were conceived, like his textiles, as a tapestry of clear colours. His brother Jean (1888–) is also a painter, mainly in watercolour.

Dughet Gaspard: Gaspard *Poussin

Duhamel Georges (1884–). French poet, novelist, dramatist and essayist, one of the *Abbaye Group and later associated with the *unanimists. He made his name as a poet with *Selon ma loi* (1910) and *Compagnons* (1912) and wrote 2 story colls about World War I, *Vie des Martyrs* (1917; *The New Book of Martyrs*, 1919) and *Civilisation* (1918; 1919). But he is best known for 2 *romans-fleuves*, the 5 vols of *Vie et aventures de Salavin* (1920–32; *Salavin*, 1936) and the *Chronique des Pasquier* (1933–45, 10 vols; *The Pasquier Chronicle*, from 1937).

Duineser Elegien (1923). Cycle of poems by *Rilke.

Dujardin Karel (1622–78). Dutch painter of Italianate landscapes with animals or figures, genre pieces and portraits. He was a pupil of N. Berchem and twice visited Italy.

Dukas Paul (1865–1935). French composer, and professor of the orchestral class at the Paris Conservatoire (1910–13) and of composition there and at the École Normale de Musique (1913–35). His pupils included Messiaen. D.'s music shows complete and individual mastery of post-Wagnerian methods, and above all imaginative orchestration. Besides the symphonic poem *The Sorcerer's Apprentice* (1897), he wrote the opera *Ariane et Barbe-Bleue* (1907), the dance poem *La Péri* (1912), *Variations, interlude and finale* (1907) on a theme by J. Rameau, and a piano sonata (1901) said to be the first by a major French composer..

Dukelsky Vladimir (1903–). Russian-born U.S. composer, influenced by G. Gershwin,

Dufresne. *Tropical Forest* (1919)

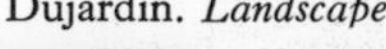
Dujardin. *Landscape*

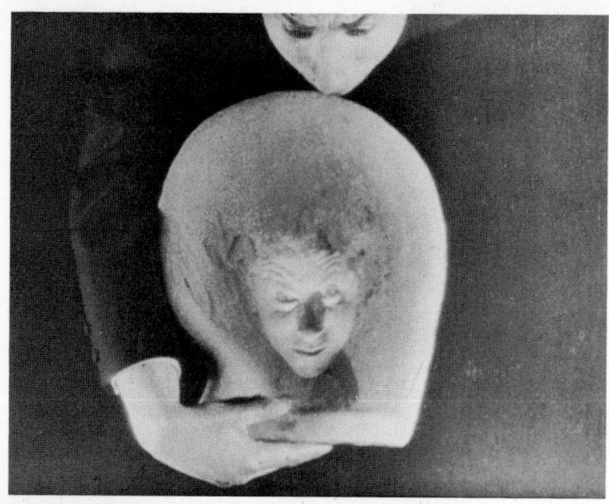

Germaine Dulac. *La Coquille et le Clergyman*

Alexandre Dumas *père*

A dulcimer in a medieval Paradise Garden (detail)

Du Maurier. Svengali and Trilby

Dumitresco. *The Forest* (1958)

particularly in his film music written under the pseud. 'Vernon Duke'. His other compositions include ballets, e.g. *Zéphyre et Flore*, commissioned by Diaghilev, 3 symphonies, concertos and chamber music.

Dulac Edmund (1882–1953). French-born British illustrator, watercolour painter, portraitist and designer. Some of the best known of his fantastic, intricate illustrations are the watercolours for *The Arabian Nights*, *The Rubá'iyát of Omar Khayyám*, *Sinbad the Sailor*, *The Tempest* and many books of fairy-tales.

Dulac Germaine (1882–1942). French film director. Her best-known films are *La Fête Espagnole* (1919), written by Delluc, *La Souriante Madame Beudet* (1923, from an André Obey play), and the surrealist *La Coquille et le Clergyman*, written by Antonin Artaud. D. also directed a newsreel, *France Actualités* (*c.* 1930–40).

dulcimer. Ancient musical instrument. It has a range of about three 8ves from the C below middle C and consists of strings stretched over a sound-board between a trapeze-shaped frame about 3 ft wide at its greatest width. The strings are vibrated by striking with small hammers held in the player's hands.

Dullin Charles (1885–1947). French actor and director, founder of an important experimental theatre. He was trained at the Vieux Colombier, and at his own Théâtre de l'Atelier introduced many foreign plays, all his productions being in an individual, vigorous yet intimate style.

Dumas Alexandre (*pére*) (1802–70). French dramatist and novelist, a quadroon (his grandmother was a Negress) and the son of an aristocrat who became a Revolutionary general. D. leapt to fame in 1829 with his romantic drama *Henri III et sa cour* and was to remain a popular historical dramatist during his lifetime, although his works are now never performed. His world-wide celebrity is based on the historical novels of adventure he produced in collaboration with a number of hacks, e.g. *Les Trois Mousquetaires* (1844; *The Three Musketeers*, 1846), *Vingt Ans Après* (1845), *Le Vicomte de Bragelonne* (1848–50), *Le Collier de la Reine* (1849–50). Whatever help he may have had, D. put into the novels his boundless energy and zest for life, with the result that he has imposed his vision of French history on countless readers, in spite of his frequent inaccuracies and lack of psychological depth. Because of his child-like flamboyance and his unbelievably prolific output in all subjects from animals to cookery, D. is sometimes underestimated. In *Les Trois Mousquetaires* he created a permanent image of youthful comradeship and in *Le Comte de Monte-Cristo* (1844–5; *The Count of Monte Cristo*, 1846), the story of the revenge of the wrongly imprisoned Edmond Dantès, a classic adventure story.

Dumas Alexandre (*fils*) (1824–95). French novelist and dramatist, the illegitimate son of the above. His novel *La Dame aux camélias* (1848; *The Lady with the Camellias*, 1856), founded partly on the story of a real-life courtesan, Marie Duplessis, was turned into a play in 1852 and has remained one of the great vehicles for tragic actresses, in spite of the feebleness of its construction and the sentimentality of its plot. It also provided the libretto for *Verdi's *La Traviata*. D. wrote many other moralizing plays now forgotten, which made him the foremost serious dramatist of the Second Empire.

Du Maurier Daphne (Lady Browning) (1907–). English novelist, daughter of actor Gerald Du M. and granddaughter of George. Du M.'s romantic, often melodramatic novels, many of which have been filmed, include *Rebecca* (1938), *Frenchman's Creek* (1941), *My Cousin Rachel* (1951).

Du Maurier George (Louis Palmella Busson) (1834–96). Anglo-French novelist and draughtsman who drew for *Punch*. His novel *Trilby* (1894) deals with artists' life in the Parisian Latin Quarter; by the hypnotic power of Svengali the heroine, Trilby, becomes a *prima donna*.

Dumitresco Natalia (1915–). Rumanian painter of the school of Paris; wife of Istrati. She paints abstract compositions of subtle and unusual colour.

dumka plural *dumky* (Ukranian, 'lament, complaint'). Dvořák gave this name to movements in some of his chamber works, e.g. the piano trio (op. 90) is called 'Dumky'.

Dumoustier (Dumonstier). Large family of French artists working in the 16th–17th c.

Paul Dunbar

Isadora Duncan

dump (uncertain derivation). English 16th- and early 17th-c. musical term describing a piece in duple time for solo instrument and in the nature of a lament. Beethoven arranged an Irish d. (with words by Joanna Baillie) taken from an 18th-c. coll. of Irish dance tunes.

Dunbar Paul Laurence (1872–1906). U.S. Negro writer. Although he used the 'massa and de darkies' genre, his later work is a bitter portrayal of Negro life in America, and predicts trouble. He wrote poetry, e.g. *Majors and Minors* (1895) and *Lyrics of Lowly Life* (1896), and novels, e.g. *The Uncalled* (1898) and *The Sport of the Gods* (1902).

Dunbar William (*c.* 1460–1521?). Scottish poet, one of the 'Scottish Chaucerians'. Little is known of his life but he was apparently a courtier and seems to have travelled on diplomatic missions for James IV. D. was master of a variety of poetic forms and poetic diction ranging from elaborate Latinate language to a fantastic vernacular; he excels in satire, against the court and Church and society, e.g. *The Tretis of the Twa Mariit Weman and the Wedo*, but achieved a sombre grandeur in his great *Lament for the Makaris* with its famous refrain 'Timor mortis conturbat me'.

Duncan David (1916–). U.S. war photographer who travelled with the Marines during both World War II and the Korean conflict. His intimate portraits of fighting men in action create a unique and subtle indictment of war.

Duncan Isadora (1878–1927). U.S. dancer who rejected conventional ballet dress, dancing barefoot and in flowing draperies. Her performance in Russia in 1905 provided the stimulus for Diaghilev, Fokine and Benois, who were already dissatisfied with contemporary Russian ballet.

Dunciad, The (1728). Poem by *Pope.

Dunham Katherine (1914–). U.S. anthropologist and dancer whose research in the Caribbean (1937–8) inspired her to form her own co. of West Indian dancers. D. produced ballets for this group, incorporating native style and legend, and has toured in Europe and the U.S., proving her own exceptional talent as a dancer and mime.

Dunlap William (1766–1839). One of the 1st great figures in American theatre. Many of his plays were trs and adaptations of French and German writers, especially A. von Kotzebue, but D.'s *André* (1798), with the War of Independence as its background, was the 1st U.S. tragedy on a native theme. He wrote *A History of the Rise and Progress of the Arts of Design in the United States* (1834) and *History of the American Theatre* (1832), important sourcebooks. He was also a portrait painter.

Dunne Philip (1908–). U.S. film director and writer, always for 20th Century-Fox. D. was an excellent script writer (*Pinky*, *Way of a Gaucho*, which he also produced). In 1955 he became a director and has known critical (*Ten North Frederick*, 1958) and commercial (*Blue Denim*, 1959) success.

Dunsany Baron (Edward John Moreton Drax Plunkett) (1878–1957). Irish dramatist, poet and story writer of fanciful tales. D.'s many plays for the Abbey Theatre, Dublin, began with *The Glittering Gate*, produced by W. B. Yeats in 1909.

Dunstable John (1380/90?–1453). English composer. He was in the service of John, Duke of Bedford, English regent in France; most of his compositions survive in continental mss and his continental reputation was vast. The Flemish theorist Tinctoris observed that 'the English with D. at their head' brought a new art to the Continent. These English techniques introduced by D. and *Leonel Power were a euphonius harmonic structure and the cyclic tenor *mass. D.'s individual and revolutionary innovation was to abandon the dissonances of continental *ars nova for a style of almost consistent euphony with the rare dissonances 'prepared'. Other new and important elements of D.'s style were his faithful adherence to the rhythm of the words in the declamatory motets, such as the great *Quam. pulchra es*, and his fluent melody. Although D.'s most famous work is the beautiful song 'O rosa bella', most of his 60 or so surviving compositions are ecclesiastical.

Duparc (Marie-Eugène) Henri (Fouques) (1848–1933). French composer, a pupil of Franck. In 1885 he suffered a mental breakdown, stopped composing and lost all interest in his life and his friends. He was highly self-critical and destroyed many works; but

THE
DUNCIAD,
VARIORVM.
WITH THE
PROLEGOMENA of SCRIBLERUS.

LONDON.
Printed for A. DOD. 1729.

The Dunciad. The 2nd ed. (1729) gave the names (instead of the initials) of those attacked

Dunlap. *The artist showing his picture of a scene from Hamlet to his parents*

Dürer. *Self-portrait*, 1500

Dürer.
Nemesis (*the 'Great Fortune'*)

Dupré. *Over the Bridge*

Durand. *Kindred Spirits*

Duquesnoy.
St Andrew

14 songs, classical in style but intense in mood, survive and have been highly influential on French song composition.

Dupont E. A. (1891–1956). German film director. His *Vaudeville* or *Variety* (1925) flamboyantly extended the use of the moving camera originated by *Murnau in *The Last Laugh* and resulted in his going to Hollywood for *Love Me and the World is Mine* (1927) and Britain for *Atlantic* (1929).

Dupré Jules (1811–89). French landscape painter, one of the leading members of the *Barbizon school. He visited England in 1831 and was greatly impressed by Constable, though his own work gave a more romanticized and introspective interpretation of nature.

Dupré Marcel (1886–). French organist (a pupil of Widor), composer, improviser and teacher. His music, basically tonal, includes organ compositions, church music and a symphony for organ and orchestra.

Duquesnoy François (1594–1643) called 'Il Fiammingo'. Flemish sculptor who settled in Rome. His major works are the marble statues *St Andrew* (St Peter's) and *St Susanna* (Sta Maria di Loreto). In his own time he was renowned for his **putti*. He represented the classical tradition in the age of Bernini's baroque.

Durán Agustín (1793–1862). Spanish scholar and man of letters. He publ. an important essay on the traditional Spanish theatre and *Romancero general* (from 1828), a comprehensive anthology of ancient ballads and folksongs.

Durand Asher Brown (1796–1886). U.S. landscape painter, founder, with T. Cole, of the *Hudson River school. He abandoned a successful career as an engraver to become a painter, first of portraits and Biblical and anecdotal subjects, later of quiet, romantic landscapes.

Durante Francesco (1684–1755). Italian composer and teacher of composition. Despite a high contemporary reputation, his work shows little originality, following the style of Scarlatti. He wrote no operas but produced his best music for the church. His pupils included Jomelli, Paisiello and Pergolesi.

Duras Claire de Kersaint, duchesse de (1772–1828). French author of the very popular sentimental novels, *Ourika* (1823; 1824) and *Édouard* (1825; *Edward*, 1826). During the Restoration she presided over a highly successful literary *salon*.

Duras Marguerite (1914–). French novelist. D. has written realistic novels, e.g. *Un Barrage contre le Pacifique* (1950; *A Sea of Troubles*, 1953), as well as more imaginative and symbolic works like *Les Petits Chevaux de Tarquinia* (1953; *The Little Horses of Tarquinia*, 1960) and *Le Square* (1955; *The Square*, 1959). She also wrote the scenarios of **Hiroshima mon amour* (1959) and *Une Aussi Longue Absence* (1961).

Dürer Albrecht (1471–1528). German painter, engraver, designer of woodcuts and major art theorist. D. was born in Nuremburg and trained first under his father, a goldsmith. He was apprenticed (1486–90) to M. Wolgemut, in whose workshop he became familiar with the best work of contemporary German artists and with the recent technical advances in engraving and drawing for woodcuts. D. was soon providing illustrations himself for his godfather, the printer A. Koberger. In 1490 he went on the first of the journeys that were so to affect his art, visiting Colmar, Basle and Strassburg. He was in Nuremburg for his marriage in 1496, but left in the autumn of that year for Italy. In this visit and during the longer stay of 1505–7, D. made a profound study of Italian painting at the very moment when it was being changed by the revolutionary ideas of Leonardo da Vinci and others. He also studied the whole intellectual background of the Italian Renaissance, the writings of the humanists and, in particular, Mantegna's attempts to re-create in engravings and paintings the classical canon of art. D. was thus able to make his own personal synthesis of the arts of the north and south, a synthesis which was to have immense importance to European art. From 1495, when D. established his workshop in Nuremburg, his success and reputation increased rapidly. Until 1499 he was engaged chiefly on engravings and designs for his books of woodcuts. Comparatively easy to reproduce in large numbers and to transport, this work made him more widely known than any but the almost legendary Italians. He was encouraged by an enthusiastic patron, the Elector of Saxony, and he became the friend of many

Dürer. *The Four Horsemen of the Apocalypse*

Dürer. *Melancholia*

Dürer. *The large tuft of grass.* Also *bagpipes, *engravings, *fine manner and colour plate 51

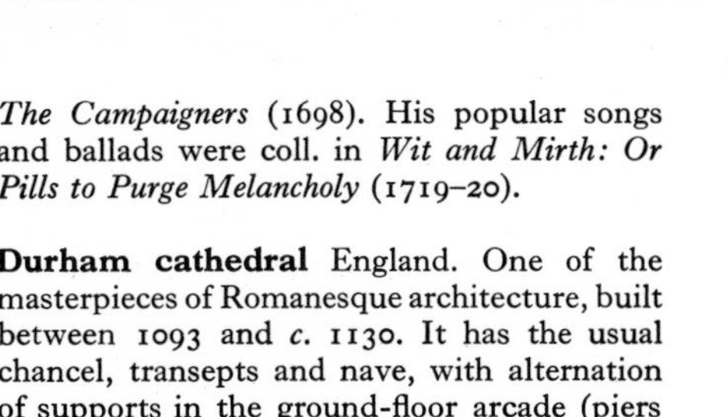

of the chief figures of the Reformation. Though he never broke with Catholicism, D. was deeply involved in the religious controversy until his death. In 1512 he was made court painter to the Emperor Maximilian. This honour was confirmed by Charles V, and when D. visited the Netherlands in 1520 he was widely fêted. In his last years he planned and partly composed a thesis on the theoretical basis of the arts.

To mention only his greatest works: *The Madonna of the Rose Garlands* (N.G., Prague) and *The Adoration of the Trinity* (K., Vienna) were painted almost in competition with the Italians. His portraits are of great interest, particularly the series of self-portraits: that of 1493 (Louvre), of 1498 (Prado), of 1500 (Alte Pina., Munich) and of 1522 (K.-halle, Bremen). Probably his major work in oils is the late *Four Apostles* (Alte Pina., Munich). However, D.'s greatest single achievement and one which establishes him as supreme among graphic artists is his book of woodcuts, *The Apocalypse* (1498). Other series of woodcuts are: *The Great Passion, The Life of the Virgin* and *The Lesser Passion.* Single woodcuts of outstanding quality are: *The Last Supper* and *The Men's Bath House.* Of his engravings the series *The Engraved Passion*, and the single plates: *Adam and Eve, Melancholia, Knight, Death and the Devil, The Prodigal Son, St Jerome in his Study* and *St Eustace* are the finest in quality. D.'s smallest sketches are often masterpieces of draughtsmanship and feeling, e.g. *Crowned Death on a Thin Horse*, charcoal (B.M., London). His watercolours of places (often scenes done on his travels), people, animals and plants are evidence of his desire to record the world around him with the greatest precision, yet with no surrender of the passion of an artist before the objectivity of the scientist.

Durey Louis (1888–). French composer, one of The *Six, ed. of old music and music critic. Stravinsky, Schoenberg, Satie and Ravel have influenced him, but he uses classical or modern techniques as the music requires; from 1945 his music followed Communist ideals of a popular art. His works include several songs, choral music and chamber music.

D'Urfey Thomas (1653–1723). English writer of French Huguenot extraction, one of those attacked by J. *Collier and prosecuted as a result. He replied in the preface to his comedy *The Campaigners* (1698). His popular songs and ballads were coll. in *Wit and Mirth: Or Pills to Purge Melancholy* (1719–20).

Durham cathedral England. One of the masterpieces of Romanesque architecture, built between 1093 and *c.* 1130. It has the usual chancel, transepts and nave, with alternation of supports in the ground-floor arcade (piers alternating with thick circular pillars carved with incised patterns). The quadripartite ribbed vaults (chancel 1107, nave 1130) are certainly the earliest in France and England and possibly in Europe: diagonal arches are round, transverse pointed (a device to make them the same height) –a striking anticipation of Gothic. There is lavish late Norman decoration (chevron, billet, lozenge, etc.); towers and E. chapels were added later.

Durrell Lawrence (George) (1912–). English novelist and poet who has spent most of his life in the Mediterranean area. Known as a poet and writer of books about Corfu, Rhodes and Cyprus (*Bitter Lemons*, 1957), D. became famous with 'The Alexandrian Quartet', a cycle of 4 novels–*Justine* (1957), *Balthazar* (1958), *Mountolive* (1958) and *Clea* (1960)– which evoke the presence of the ancient city in a richly poetic prose. Each vol. tells the same story but interprets the actors' motives differently; human beings, it is implied, must necessarily have a partial view of reality. D.'s works include the early novel *The Black Book* (Paris, 1938).

Dürrenmatt Friedrich (1921–). Swiss dramatist and novelist. D. is a highly inventive writer of sombre, suspenseful, stageworthy 'comedies' characterized by a mingling of satire, parody and farce with moral earnestness and the macabre. Much of D.'s work–which abounds in implied meaning–concerns themes relating to justice and mercy. His works include the play *Die Physiker* (1962; *The Physicists*, 1963), radio plays and novels.

Durtain Luc. Pseud. of André Nepveu (1881–). French novelist and poet. D. was associated with the *Abbaye and *unanimist groups. His novels, under the general title of *Les Conquêtes du monde* (in fact concerned with self-discovery), include *Douze cent mille* (1922), *La source rouge* (1924) and *La femme en sandales* (1937).

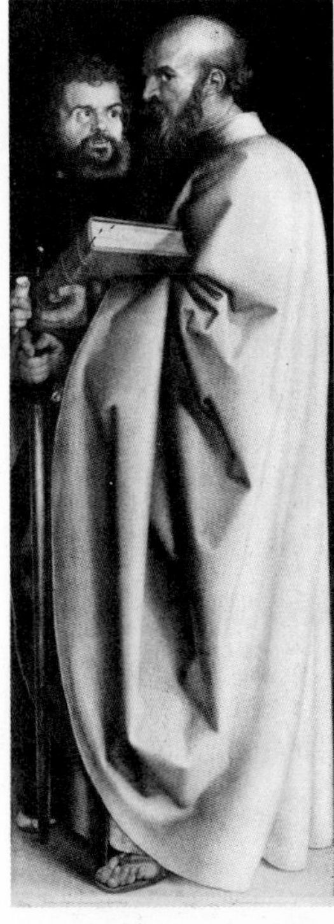

Dürer. St Paul and St Mark, one of 2 panels of the *Four Apostles*

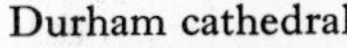

Durham cathedral

Eleonora Duse

Dyce. *Pegwell Bay*

Dvořák

Duvivier. Françoise Rosay (left) in *Un Carnet de Bal*

Dusart Cornelis (1660–1704). Dutch genre painter and engraver, pupil and close friend of A. van Ostade, whose style he followed. On van Ostade's death D. inherited his pictures and completed a number of them.

Duse Eleonora (1859–1924). Italian actress, a famous tragedienne. D. was the great rival of Sarah Bernhardt, her subtlety and restraint matching Bernhardt's more emotional playing. Her appearances in the plays of her lover *D'Annunzio made them famous.

Dussek or **Dusik** Johann Ladislaus (1760–1812). Czech musician famous throughout Europe for the new 'singing' tone he achieved on the piano, and as a virtuoso on the glass harp. D.'s piano music frequently has rich, sometimes advanced, harmonies and was among the earliest to prescribe exactly for the sustaining pedal.

Dutt Toru (1856–77). Indian writer, younger sister of the equally talented Aru D. (d. 1874). Both sisters died young, having produced *A Sheaf Gleaned in French Fields* (1876), English trs from French. D.'s posth. *Ancient Ballads and Legends of Hindustan* (1882) displays the same mellifluousness as her occasional poetry.

Duun Olav (1876–1939). Norwegian writer, the most distinguished novelist in the Nynorsk language (*Aasen). His works include a series of 6 novels (1918–23), *Junikfolke*, the story of 4 generations of 19th-c. peasant landowners.

Duvernay Pauline (1813–94). French dancer who studied under Vestris and made her début at the Paris Opéra in 1831, becoming popular on both sides of the English Channel. D. often performed dances created by Elssler; although extremely successful, she retired at the age of 24.

Duvivier Julien (1896–). French film director. D. started making films in 1920 but did not become famous until the 1930s with *Poil de Carotte* (1932), made 'subjectively' from the point of view of its boy hero. He also made *La Bandera* (1935), *La Belle Équipe* and *Pepe-le-Moko* (1937), all with Jean Gabin; *Un Carnet de Bal* (1937); *The Great Waltz* (in the U.S., 1938); and *Anna Karenina* (in Britain, 1948).

Duyster Willem Cornelisz (1598/9–1635). Dutch genre painter who specialized in social gatherings of officers, etc., e.g. *Players at Tric-Trac* and *Soldiers Quarrelling* (both N.G., London).

Dvořák Antonín (1841–1904). Czech composer. D. went to Prague in 1857, studying music at the Organ school there and from 1859 working as a freelance violinist and teacher. Success as a composer began only with the choral work *Hymnus* in 1873, but in the following year D. met Brahms, whose sponsorship was responsible for the publ. (1877) of D.'s *Moravian duets* and *Slavonic Dances* for piano duet, in Germany. In the 1880s D. made tours of Europe, conducting his own works with great success, above all in England. He subsequently became professor of composition at the Prague Conservatory and director (1901), having directed the National Conservatory of Music at New York from 1892 to 1895. Like Smetana D. had a strong nationalistic impulse but unlike Smetana's, his music is not 'heroic' in its nationalism. D. had a close knowledge of folk-poetry and Czech history; he drew on Czech folk-music and was a keen pan-Slavist (*dumka). D.'s obvious indebtedness to folk-music and the German romantics does not obscure a gift for spontaneous melody similar to Schubert's, masterly instrumentation and purity of style in chamber music. His major works are: the operas *Russalka* (1901) and *Armida* (1904); the cantata *The Spectre's Bride* (1884); 9 symphonies (2 unpubl., one publ. posth.–hence some confusion in the numbering), among them no. 5 or 9 *From the New World* (1893), written during his stay in the U.S.; *Slavonic Dances* (originally for piano duet) and *Slavonic Rhapsodies* for orchestra; a piano concerto; violin concerto; cello-concerto; 14 string quartets (among them the 'American'), a piano quintet and 4 piano trios. He also wrote piano music, songs and part songs.

Van Dyck. *Self-portrait*

Van Dyck. Drawing of Sir Kenelm Digby

Dwan Alan (1885–). Canadian-born U.S. film director. He directed such films as *Robin Hood* (1922) with Douglas Fairbanks. His vast output since then achieved no great fame until *Sands of Iwo Jima* (1949). His 1950s films were mainly westerns and war and adventure films remarkable for their terse and economical style, and their use of the action itself to be expressive.

Dwight Timothy (1752–1817). American writer and poet, a member of the *Hartford Wits. Besides the long Biblical allegory *The Conquest of Canaan* (1785) he wrote *Greenfield Hill* (1794) describing Connecticut scenery, history and social conditions.

Dyce William (1806–64). Scottish painter. Early sympathy with the *Nazarenes encountered by him in Rome (1827) made him welcome the Pre-Raphaelites. Though his frescoes in the House of Lords and elsewhere lack inspiration, his *Pegwell Bay* (Tate) is an admirable piece of mid-19th-c. realism.

Dyck Sir Anthony Van (1599–1641). Flemish painter chiefly famous for portraits of the English aristocracy, though he also painted a number of large religious, allegorical and mythological subjects. D. was trained in Antwerp by H. van Balen and became the chief assistant of Rubens. He was in England for some months in 1620–1, then embarked on a prolonged tour of Italy, where he spent periods at Venice, Genoa and Rome, executing portraits and commissions for churches. He painted for a further period in Antwerp before he settled in England in 1631 as court painter. Typical of his rich but refined and elegant portrait style, which flattered almost all his sitters with a look of distinction and intelligence, are *Philippe le Roy* (Wallace Coll.), *Frans Snyders* (Frick Coll., New York), *Charles I* (N.G., London) and the more ambitious *Charles I in Hunting Dress* (Louvre). This style set a pattern, especially for English portrait painters, for at least 200 years. Larger works include *The Crucifixion of St Peter* (M.R. des B.-A., Brussels), *Samson and Delilah* (Dulwich Gal., London), *Rinaldo and Armida* (M. of A., Baltimore), and *Amarillis and Mirtille* (A. Mus., Gottenberg).

Dyer Sir Edward (d. 1607). English courtier, musician and lyric poet; he was a friend of Sidney. Byrd wrote a musical setting for D.'s famous poem *My minde to me a Kyngdom is.*

Dyer John (1700?–58). Anglo-Welsh painter and poet. His finest poem is *Grongar Hill* (1725–6), a moral-topographical contemplation simply expressed and free of stilted convention. *The Ruins of Rome* (1740) and *The Fleece* (1757) have good passages.

Dying Swan, The: Le *Cygne

Dykes John Bacchus (1823–76). English composer of church music and cleric. His hymn tunes include 'Nearer, my God to thee' and 'Jesu, lover of my soul'.

dynamics. Musical term for the degree of loudness and softness in a piece.

Dynasts, The (1904, 1906, 1908). Long poem by Thomas *Hardy.

Dyson Sir George (1883–). English composer, teacher and writer on music and director of the R.C.M. (1938–52). His music, in the tradition of Parry and Stanford, includes the cantatas *The Canterbury Pilgrims* (1931) and *St Paul's Voyage to Melita* (1933) and a symphony; his books *The New Music* (1924), on European developments, and *The Progress of Music* (1932).

Dziga-Vertov (1896–1954). Soviet film maker, born Denis Kaufman; his youngest brother was Boris *Kaufman. D.-V. was responsible for a series of newsreels and documentaries (*Kino-Pravda*, 1922–5). His montage of documentary material became enormously complicated, e.g. in *The Man with the Movie Camera* (1928). As a theorist he influenced other documentarists, e.g. *Ruttmann. *Three Songs about Lenin* (1934) was equally experimental, though without great success, in its use of sound.

Van Dyck. *Charles I in Hunting Dress*

Dziga-Vertov. *The Man with the Movie Camera*

Eames. Dining chair (manufactured by Herman Miller); mid-1950s

Eakins. *Max Schmidt in Simple Scull*

Eakins Thomas (1844–1916). U.S. painter and photographer. Trained as a painter in Paris and influenced by Manet, E. became one of the major American realists, e.g. his studies of surgeons operating. His paintings include brilliantly composed sculling pictures, e.g. *The Biglen Brothers Turning the Stake* (M. of A., Cleveland). E. revolutionized U.S. art teaching, insisting on drawing from the nude and sound anatomical knowledge. As a photographer he continued Muybridge's experiments in the photography of motion, improving on them by using 1 camera to produce a series of images on a single plate rather than a number of cameras producing single images. E.'s composite plates inspired Duchamp's famous painting *Nude Descending a Staircase.*

George Eastman: anon. photographer. Printed by E. on his new paper, 1884

Ealing comedies. A number of extremely successful post-war British film comedies were made at Ealing Studios, notably *Mackendrick's *The Man in the White Suit* (1951), *Hamer's *Kind Hearts and Coronets* (1948) and *Crichton's *The Lavender Hill Mob* (1951).

Eames Charles (1907–). U.S. designer best known for the chairs he has designed for Herman Miller. In these designs, which have been very widely copied, he uses industrial materials and techniques. He built himself a house in Los Angeles in 1949, entirely from industrial components ordered out of a catalogue. He is also known as a film maker and as a designer of toys.

Earle John (1601?–65). English bishop and writer, whose principal work was *Microcosmographie . . .* (1628), witty and satirical character sketches modelled on Theophrastus.

Earle Ralph (1751–1801). Self-taught, itinerant U.S. portraitist and, for his battle scenes of Lexington and Concord (1775), believed to be the earliest historical painter in America. He worked for a time in London, replacing the attractive untutored stiffness of his early pictures with the smoother style of fashionable English portraiture.

Early English. The 1st style in English Gothic architecture of the late 12th c. and the 13th c. It marks a lightening of the heavy Norman style, using lancet windows, which gradually give way to windows with geometrical tracery, and simple rib-vaults. Salisbury and Worcester cathedrals provide fine examples.

Early English. Window at Salisbury cathedral

Earth (1930). Film directed by A. *Dovzhenko.

earth colours. Pigments such as yellow and red ochres, raw sienna, raw umber and *terre verte* which are found in their natural state in the earth. Ochres in particular were used in prehistoric cave painting. They are among the most permanent and least expensive colours.

earthenware. Baked clay, or objects made from baked clay.

Easdale Brian (1909–). English composer, with Britten musical director of the Group Theatre (1937–9). E. has written the operas *The Corn King* (1935; performed 1950), *The Sleeping Children* (1951), a ballet, incidental and orchestral music, and has worked much in films.

East Michael (*c.* 1580–*c.* 1648). English composer, probably son of Thomas E.; one of his madrigals appears in *The Triumphs of Oriana.*

East Thomas (d. *c.* 1608). English music printer and publ. of works by Byrd, Morley, Wilbye, Weelkes and Dowland, etc. In 1592 E. publ. 4-part settings of the Psalms, having employed such composers as Dowland and Farnaby for the harmonizations.

Easter Island: *Oceanic art

Eastlake Sir Charles Lock (1793–1865). English painter, writer on art and administrator. As keeper (1843–7) and 1st director (1855–65) of the N.G., London, he devoted energy, scholarship and taste to building up one of the greatest colls of Italian art, particularly the work of the so-called 'primitives'. E.'s early landscapes deserve attention.

Eastman George (1854–1932). U.S. photographic manufacturer who developed a system for large-scale manufacture and processing of a simple portable box camera and flexible strip film (1888–9). E.'s technological innovations were responsible for spreading the practice of photography to the great mass of people, and the continued researches of his co. were important in the eventual development of motion pictures.

Eastman Max (Forrester) (1883–). U.S. critic, poet and trs.; his aesthetic work *The Enjoyment of Poetry* (1913) remains his most

Earle. *Chief Justice Ellsworth and his Wife*

Eastlake. *Lord Byron's Dream*

popular. Converted to Marxism, E. became a founder and ed. of *The Masses* (1913–17) and trs. Trotsky's *History of the Russian Revolution*. *Artists in Uniform* (1934) revealed E.'s disillusionment with Soviet Communism.

East of Eden (1954). Film directed by E. *Kazan, based on the novel (1952) by *Steinbeck.

Eastward Hoe (1605). Comedy by *Jonson, Marston and Chapman.

Easy Street (1917). Short film directed by C. *Chaplin.

ébéniste. A French cabinet maker, distinct from the *menuisier*, who specialized in carved furniture (mainly chairs). From *c.* 1660 almost all furniture in Paris made by the é.s had a veneer of either *Boulle-work or marquetry. Other workmen's guilds were responsible for such ormulu fittings, painting, or marble-work as were added. Each piece had to be passed and stamped by a committee of the guild or '*juré des menuisiers-é.s*' with the letters 'J.M.E.'. Many pieces are not so marked as certain parts of Paris were outside the guild's jurisdiction and the king could grant special immunity to workers for the crown.

Ebers Georg (1819–90). German Egyptologist whose sentimental novels set in ancient Egypt include *Eine ägyptische Königstochter* (1864) and *Homo Sum* (1878).

Ebert Johann Arnold (1723–95). German writer and trs. whose version (1751) of Young's *Night Thoughts* had an important influence on his contemporaries.

Ebner-Eschenbach Maria (Freifrau) von (1830–1916). Austrian writer of long short stories, notably those set in Moravia where she grew up. Her novels include *Das Gemeindekind* (1887; *The Child of the Parish*, 1893).

Eccard Johannes (1553–1611). German composer, pupil of Lasso. E. was of importance in the development of the Lutheran hymn and chorale, producing over 250 sacred and secular part songs and motets. His great work was the 51 five-part settings of songs in the *Geistlicher Lieder* (1597).

Eccles Henry (d. 1742). English violinist and composer. In 1710 he moved to Paris, becoming a member of Louis XIV's band and publ. 2 books of violin sonatas, the first being largely adaptations from G. Valentini. His son JOHN (d. 1735) collaborated with Purcell on incidental music for *Don Quixote*.

Eccles Solomon (1618–83). English violinist and composer who became a Quaker *c.* 1660 and for some years abandoned music.

Ecclesiastes. (*c.* 3rd c. B.C.). Greek title (meaning 'The Preacher') for a book of the *Bible (Old Testament); the admonition 'Vanity of vanities saith the Preacher; all is vanity' opens and concludes the book.

Ecclesiasticall Politie, Of the lawes of (1594). Theological work by *Hooker.

Ecclesiasticus (2nd c. B.C.). A book of the *Apocrypha; it includes the passage beginning 'Let us now praise famous men'.

échappé. A step in ballet, in which the feet commence in any of the 'closed' *positions and 'escape' in a sharp movement to demi- or full-*pointe in an open position.

Echegaray José (1832–1916). Spanish playwright, mathematician and statesman, Nobel prizewinner in 1904. He wrote a great number of once very successful plays, the best known being *El Gran Galeoto* (1881). He was a slick and competent master of theatrical technique.

Eckermann Johann Peter (1792–1854). German writer and Goethe's secretary and biographer. He recorded conversations with Goethe in his famous *Gespräche mit Goethe* (1836–48; 1925).

Eckhart (*c.* 1260–1327). German Dominican mystic properly called 'Meister Eckhart'. His vernacular sermons, in which he presented his revolutionary, sometimes 'heretical' philosophy of paradox, are the 1st examples of mature German prose.

eclecticism. Loosely definable as the drawing on many styles by an artist, more specifically the practice of selecting the best from various styles in an attempt to create a style of greater perfection. The term used to be applied to the work of the Carracci who were believed (wrongly) to have deliberately formulated such a programme.

Johann Peter Eckermann

Ébéniste. Top of a writing-table by A.-C. Boulle

Blake Edwards. Bing Crosby (dressed as a woman) in *High Time*

Maria Edgeworth

eclogue. A short poem, bucolic or pastoral, like the *Eclogues* of Virgil; it may also be simply a verse dialogue on a pastoral theme, or, in more recent examples, on any theme.

École des femmes, L' (1662). Play by Molière.

École des maris, L' (1661). Play by Molière.

école du bon sens. 19th-c. French movement in the theatre which reacted against the extravagances of the romantic drama, adopting a more 'common-sense' view of man and society. Members included *Augier and *Ponsard.

écossaise. A form of *contredanse, probably 18th-c. French in origin, related to the German *Schottische*, both representing ideas of a 'Scottish' dance. The é. was originally in a quick duple time but Beethoven, Schubert and Chopin wrote é.s in triple time.

Edda. Name given to a coll. of ancient alliterative poems (also called the *Elder E.*) about the Scandinavian heroes and gods, discovered by 17th-c. Icelandic scholars. It probably stems from the oral tradition of the 8th c. (or even earlier) and is the earliest literature of Norway and Iceland; the majority of the poems were written down in the 10th and 11th cs. *Snorri Sturluson wrote a *Younger* or *Prose E.* in the 13th c., using some of the material in the *Elder E.*

Edelstein, Der. Coll. of fables by Ulrich *Boner.

Eden Emily (1797–1869). English writer, author of 2 books about India (where she lived for some years with her brother, the governor-general) and of 2 novels of graceful social comedy, *The Semi-Detached House* (1859) and *The Semi-Attached Couple* (1860).

Edgeworth Maria (1767–1849). Irish novelist, daughter of RICHARD LOVELL E. (1744–1817), who greatly influenced her work and with whom she wrote *Practical Education* (1798), showing traces of Rousseau's thought. Both Turgenev and her friend Scott claimed indebtedness to her realistic stories of Irish life, e.g. *Castle Rackrent* (1800) and *Ormond* (1817).

Edinburgh Festival. Festival of music and drama, founded in 1948, which takes place in August and September. It is important internationally and many musical works and plays have been given their world première there. In recent years many univ. and other amateur groups have presented interesting and often new plays on the fringe of the festival, i.e. unofficially.

Edinburgh Review, The (1802–1929). Scottish periodical which improved the standard of English literary criticism, though now best remembered for its attacks on the *Lake Poets.

editing: *film techniques

Education of Henry Adams, The (1907). Book by Henry *Adams.

Éducation sentimentale, L' (1869). Novel by *Flaubert.

Edward II (1593). Play by *Marlowe.

Edwards Blake (1922–). U.S. film director. E. acted in the cinema and wrote for theatre, radio, television and cinema (for R. *Quine). He first directed in 1955. *Mister Cory* (1956) skilfully combined a coll. of standard movie scenes and situations into a satirical comedy of success. Of his subsequent series of 5 comedies, *Operation Petticoat* (1959) was hugely successful and gave him the freedom to make *Breakfast at Tiffany's* (1961), a *haute couture* adaptation of Capote's *nouvelle.* In a sharp change of tone, he made *Experiment in Terror* (1962), an unnerving thriller, and *Days of Wine and Roses* (1963), about alcoholism.

Edwards Richard (d. 1566). English poet and composer, master of the children of the Chapel Royal (1561). He wrote the 2 early 'masques' *Damon and Pithias* and *Palamon and Arcite* and the words and probably the music to the madrigals 'In going to my naked bed' and 'When griping griefs'.

Eeckhout Gerbrand van den (1621–74). Dutch painter of portraits, religious subjects and genre, a favourite pupil of Rembrandt and a close imitator of his style, e.g. *Officers of the Amsterdam Coopers' Guild* (N.G., London). About 1665 he began to paint genre scenes in the style of G. Ter Borch.

Egg Augustus Leopold (1816–63). English painter of anecdotal subjects whose popularity revived in the mid-20th-c. vogue for Victoriana. He was a friend of Dickens and travelled with him to Italy.

Eeckhout. *Officers of the Amsterdam Coopers' Guild*

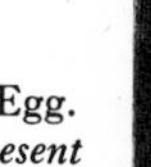

Egg. *Past and Present*

Egyptian Black

Egyptian Black: Wedgwood teapot

Egyptian style. Louis XVI candelabra

Eggeling Viking (1880–1925). Swedish painter and pioneer of *avant-garde* films. In 1915 he met Hans Arp in Paris, moved to Switzerland and joined the *dada movement. In Germany he and H. Richter experimented with abstract picture strips which formed the basis for *Symphonie diagonale* (1921), an early abstract film.

Eggleston Edward (1837–1902). U.S. clergyman, novelist, reformer, author of readable novels of regional (Indiana) life, e.g. *The Hoosier Schoolmaster* (1871), *The End of the World* (1872), *Roxy* (1878), and *The Hoosier Schoolboy* (1883).

egg-shell porcelain. The original production of the so-called e.-s. p. was perfected in Japan; the name derives from its extreme thinness.

Egk Werner (1901–). German composer, largely self-taught. His music, in a basically tonal idiom, is distinguished by brilliant orchestration and a strong dramatic sense. E. has written the operas *Die Zaubergeige* (1935) using folk-tunes and very popular, *Peer Gynt* (1938), and *The Government Inspector* (1957) after Gogol; the dramatic ballets *Joan von Zarissa* (1940) and *Abraxas* (1948); radio music, including the opera *Columbus* (1933); and an oratorio.

Egmont (1791). Play by Goethe written between 1775 and 1787. *Beethoven's famous overture was part of his incidental music for a revival of the play at Vienna in 1810.

Egoist, The (1879). Novel by *Meredith.

Egyptian Black. A black unglazed stoneware, descending from Roman and medieval types, evolved in the Burslem district of Staffordshire by potters in the 1st half of the 18th c. and refined by Josiah *Wedgwood, who renamed it basaltes. His predecessors used it to imitate antique objects, particularly the matt black paint of Greek vases and Egyptian objects in black stone such as granite. However, its poor colour and texture made it an unsatisfactory medium for this.

Egyptian style. Decorative motifs drawn from Egyptian sources became popular during the Regency period in England and the First Empire in France. Sphinxes, lions and lotuses were particularly popular during an eclectic period when decorative motifs were drawn from every possible source.

Ehrenburg Ilya Grigorievich (1891–). Soviet novelist of middle-class Jewish origin. From 1909 E. mixed in artistic circles in Paris, where Picasso became his close friend; he has recently written his recollections of the period (part of several vols of memoirs). He at first supported the Whites in the Civil War, but accepted the Bolshevik victory. He spent most of his time until 1941 working in the West as a Soviet journalist, and made a considerable reputation as a war correspondent.
E. has written prolifically and fluently, but although his intelligence is subtle and alert his themes are rarely executed with complete success, and his characterization is shallow. His best work is perhaps *The Extraordinary Adventures of Julio Jurenito . . .* (1921; 1930), a biting satire on the follies of civilization which attacks the Bolsheviks as well as the West, and interprets World War I as the beginning of an iron age of increasing regimentation. His works generally reflect changes in official attitudes; *The Thaw* (1954; 1955), for example, was a symptom of the more liberal atmosphere after the death of Stalin. E.'s novels include *The Love of Jeanne Ney* (1924; 1929) and *The Fall of Paris* (1941; 1942), an analysis of the degeneration of French society before World War II.

Ilya Ehrenburg

Ehrenstahl David Klo(c)ker von (1629–98). German portrait painter known as the 'father of Swedish painting'. He was in Italy (1654–8) but worked mainly at the Swedish court, introducing a style of portrait with allegorical figures and **putti*.

Ehrke Hans (1898–). Low German playwright and poet. His plays include the successful *Füer* (1927) and the historical *Hans Brüggemann* (1930).

Eichendorff Joseph (Freiherr) von (1788–1857). German writer, a Prussian civil servant. Mistakenly regarded as typically romantic, his work also anticipates Biedermeier and realism: his heroes are romantic but their fates are not. The short novel *Aus dem Leben eines Taugenichts*

Joseph von Eichendorff

Eiffel. Truyère Bridge, Garabit, France

Eiermann. Handkerchief Mill, Blumberg

Eijck. Municipal Orphanage, Amsterdam

(1826; *Memoirs of a Good-for-Nothing*, 1866), relates the adventures of a happy-go-lucky idler preserved by God's care and ultimately absorbed by bourgeois society. Other stories include *Das Marmorbild* (1819; *The Marble Statue*, 1927) and *Das Schloss Dürande* (1837). At its rare best his lyric poetry is unsurpassed, especially in capturing nocturnal moods (*Die Mondnacht*, *Sehnsucht*, *Nachts*) and supernatural seduction (*Waldgespräch*, *Das kalte Liebchen*).

Eichheim Henry (1870–1942). U.S. violinist, conductor and composer; he was strongly influenced by oriental music, sometimes including its instruments in his scores.

Eichner Ernst (1740–77). German bassoonist and one of the best young *Mannheim composers. His numerous works include symphonies, keyboard concertos and chamber music.

Eiermann Egon (1904–). The best known of the post-war German architects. His best work owes much to Mies van der Rohe, with structure clearly and regularly expressed and immaculate detailing. His mill at Blumberg (1951) was the 1st post-war German building to receive international publicity, and his German Pavilion at Expo 58, Brussels, was the most admired at the fair. His ecclesiastical architecture includes the rebuilding of the Memorial Church, Berlin (1961).

Eiffel Gustave (1832–1923). French engineer and designer of numerous bridges as well as the famous tower, built for the Paris International Exhibition (1889). He evolved lattice construction as the logical way to use rolled steel, a new material at the time, and the resulting forms were to have a powerful influence on later painters and architects, both for their exhilarating sense of space and for their structural clarity.

Eight, The. Group of 8 U.S. painters–Henri, Luks, Sloan, Glackens, Shinn (previously the Philadelphia Realists), joined by Prendergast, Lawson, Davies–formed in 1907 as a gesture of protest against the National Academy. Stylistically the members differed considerably and they exhibited together only once (New York, 1908); they were, however, united in seeking independence of the Academy and supporting progressive trends in art; and they played a vital role in organizing the *Armory Show and in founding the Society of Independent Artists (1917).

8½ (1963). Film directed by F. *Fellini.

Eijck Aldo Van (1918–). Dutch architect known for his Municipal Orphanage, Amsterdam, a concrete structure; its plan wanders as function dictates, but on a module. The influence of Kahn is evident: each structural bay has its own domed roof, to make a recognizable space within which the children can feel they belong.

Einem Gottfried von (1918–). Swiss-born Austrian composer, pupil of B. Blacher. His orchestration shows R. Strauss's influence and his formal organization Stravinsky's. He has written the operas *Dantons Tod* (1947), after Büchner, and *Der Prozess* (1953), after Kafka, the ballets *Turandot* (1944) and *Rondo vom goldenen Kalb* (1952), orchestral and piano music and songs.

Einhard (*c.* 775–840). German churchman, educated at the monastery of Fulda and biographer of Charlemagne. His *Vita Caroli Magni*, the 1st secular medieval biography, was modelled on the style of Suetonius.

Einstein Albert (1879–1955). German physicist whose theories of relativity, first expounded in papers in 1905 (the special theory) and 1916 (the general theory) have dominated 20th-c. speculation in physics and influenced thought in all fields.

Einstein Alfred (1880–1952). German-born U.S. musicologist, cousin of the above. Important books by him include *Zur deutschen Literatur für Viola da Gamba* (1905), *Heinrich Schütz* (1928), *The Italian Madrigal* (1949), *Music in the Romantic Era* (1947), and a revised ed. of Köchel's Mozart catalogue (1937).

Eisenstadt Alfred (1898–). German-born U.S. photographer. His reputation was established with the appearance of his photo-essay on Ethiopia in 1935. In the same year he began working for the newly founded *Life* magazine. To date he has completed more than 1,300 *Life* assignments and the sum of his work has been called 'a true encyclopedia of the world in all its domains'.

Albert Einstein

Eisenstein. *Battleship Potemkin*

Eisenstein. *Alexander Nevsky*

Eisenstein Sergei Mikhailovich (1898–1948). Soviet film director. E. came to the cinema in 1923 by interpolating a film in a play by Ostrovsky which he directed, by editing the Russian version of **Doctor Mabuse, the Gambler*, and with an article on the 'montage of attraction'. His 1st full-length film was *Strike* (1924) which already used the technique of cutting into sequences shots embodying visual similes. *Battleship Potemkin* (1925), like E.'s other silent films, represents mass rather than individual actions, the mutiny of sailors in the abortive 1905 Revolution. Here he experimented with the expansion of time at climactic moments (as in the 'Odessa Steps' sequence) by shots which in reality would have a temporal overlap. In 2 more films, *October* (1928) and *The General Line* (1929), he further elaborated his editing technique, which found theoretical inspiration in Japanese ideograms, where the juxtaposition of word pictures produces a new idea (eye+water=crying). However shaky his justification for his type of montage, the technique (in diluted form) had profound effects on film editing for the next 20 years. In Hollywood (1930) all E.'s projects were abortive, while his Mexican film **Que Viva Mexico!* (1931–2), and one in Russia, *Bezhin Meadow* (1932), were not finished because of disagreements with respectively his backer, the novelist Upton Sinclair, and the Soviet government. *Alexander Nevsky* (1938) was historical and had a central heroic figure, as in a more complex way did *Ivan the Terrible* (1944–6), conceived in 3 parts, of which (due to ideological troubles) only 2 were shot; the 2nd was not shown until 1958, and then only outside Russia.

Eisler Hanns (1898–1962). German composer. He wrote film music in Hollywood from 1942 to 1948 from which year he lived in E. Berlin. An unusually creative Marxist thinker on music, he wrote revolutionary workers' choruses but also deployed (especially in film music) any techniques suitable to the effects he desired–even the 12-note methods of his teacher Schoenberg.

Eisteddfod (Welsh, 'a gathering'). A Welsh competitive festival of music, poetry and dance with origins in the early middle ages but with no continuous tradition since that time. Apart from the National E., an annual event since the mid 19th c. devoted specifically to maintaining Welsh language and culture, there are regional E.s, and, since 1947, an International Musical E. at Llangollen with the emphasis on singing and folk-dancing.

Either/Or (1843). Book by Kierkegaard.

Ekk Nicolai (1902–). Soviet film director. E. achieved fame with the 1st Soviet sound film, *The Road to Life* (1931), a rather naïve attempt at a naturalistic study of child delinquency, which was also his 1st feature film after working in the theatre, studying under Kuleshov, Eisenstein and Pudovkin, and making documentaries.

Electra (413 B.C.). Play by *Sophocles based on *The Choephori* in Aeschylus' **Oresteia* (or the common mythical source) but focusing on E., Orestes' sister. She is also the subject of plays by Euripides, Pérez Galdós, Giraudoux and Hofmannsthal (whose play was the basis of the opera by Richard Strauss).

electronic music. Its materials are sounds produced, under laboratory conditions, by electronic oscillators and its method of composition is the combining of these sounds on recording tape. The pioneer work was done in Germany in the 1950s but there are now studios in Holland, Milan, Tokyo, Cologne, Stockholm, Vienna, Darmstadt and Columbia Univ., New York.

electroplate. Silver plating deposited on a base metal by electrolysis. The base is now an alloy, but in the mid 19th c. copper was used. The process was discovered in 1840 in Birmingham by John Wright and was taken up by the firm of Elkington who for long had the monopoly.

elegy. A verse form. Originally, in Greek and Roman literature, any poem using the elegiac couplet of dactylic hexameters (*metre), but from the 16th c., a reflective poem, often on death or the death of a person, sometimes in the pastoral convention (e.g. Milton's *Lycidas*). Thomas *Gray's *Elegy in a Country Churchyard* (1750), is the best-known example in English.

E(h)lers the brothers David (1656–1742) and John Philip (1664–1738). Potters, German-Dutch in origin. They set up a factory in London (*c.* 1690). In 1693 they and others were cited by John Dwight as having infringed his patented rights to the manufacture of red

Scene from the myth of Electra: late 6th-c. Greek vase

Elers red china

George Eliot

Elgar: portrait by Sir William Rothenstein

T. S. Eliot: painting by Wyndham Lewis

stoneware. They moved to N. Staffordshire and were thus responsible for the introduction of the so-called *red china to that county.

elevation. In ballet a term used of a dancer's grace, control and command of height in steps involving a jump or the dancer being lifted by a partner.

Elgar Sir Edward (William) (1857–1934). English composer. He was largely self-taught, but was born into a musical Worcester family and was early involved in the Three Choirs Festival. He began his career in a solicitor's office, but succeeded his father as organist at St George's Catholic church and after his marriage (1889) devoted himself to music. From 1891 to 1904 he lived and worked in Malvern, then moved to London and finally returned to Hereford.
E. was unusual among early 20th-c. English composers in that his music showed no influence of folk-music or the Tudor composers. The flavour of his music is typically English and his attitude was nationalistic; but his individual musical idiom derived in the first instance from the German late romantics and Wagner. His major works include: the oratorios *The Dream of Gerontius* (1900), acclaimed by R. Strauss at its Düsseldorf performance, and the *The Kingdom* (1906); the symphonies, no. 1 in A♭ (1908) and no. 2 in E♭ (1910); the symphonic study *Falstaff* (1913); the overtures *Froissart* (1890) and *Cockaigne* (1901); the 'Enigma Variations' (*Variations on an Original Theme, for orchestra*, 1899), each variation portraying one of Elgar's friends, indicated by initials or a similar clue; the orchestral suites *The Wand of Youth* (1907, 1908); a violin (1910) and a cello (1919) concerto; *Introduction and Allegro for strings* (1905); and the orchestral marches *Pomp and Circumstance*, no. 5 (1930) being the best known.

Elgin Marbles: *Parthenon

Elgström Per (1781–1810). Swedish poet and pamphleteer who was of considerable importance in the establishment of romanticism in Sweden.

Elia, Essays of (1823). Book of essays by *Lamb.

Elijah. An oratorio by Mendelssohn to a text taken from the Old Testament; first produced at the Birmingham Festival (1846).

Eliot George. Pseud. of Mary Ann Evans (1819–80). English novelist brought up in rural Warwickshire, the setting of her early fiction. A serious girl, E. read omnivorously, particularly on religious subjects. She trs. Strauss's controversial and unorthodox *Life of Jesus* (1846); became assistant ed. of *The Westminster Review* (1851–3); and trs. Feuerbach's *Essence of Christianity* (1854). About this time she met George Henry Lewes, with whom she lived until his death in 1878. He encouraged her to finish and publ. *Scenes of Clerical Life* (1858), a book of 3 stories which gained instant recognition. In 1880 she married John Walter Cross.
E.'s best novels are realistic descriptions of Midlands society–rural in *Adam Bede* (1859), *Mill on the Floss* (1860) and *Silas Marner* (1861), urban in *Middlemarch* (1871–2). But they also contain studies of conflict and interaction between character and environment: her understanding of social and spiritual transgressions–and the situations which provoke them–creates sympathy without renouncing judgement. Increasing delicacy of treatment appears as the misfortunes of a Hetty Sorrel (*Adam Bede*) or Maggie Tulliver (*Mill on the Floss*) give way to the subtler errors of Dorothea Brooke and Dr Lydgate in E.'s masterpiece, *Middlemarch*. Her works have considerable humour and, in the garrulous Mrs Poyser, one immortal comic figure. The historical novel *Romola* (1863); *Felix Holt, the Radical* (1866), and *Daniel Deronda* (1876), are less successful. E.'s best-known poem is *The Spanish Gypsy*.

Eliot T(homas) S(tearns) (1888–1965). U.S.-born British poet; he studied at Harvard and the Sorbonne before coming to Oxford in 1914. He worked for a time as a master at Highgate School and subsequently in Lloyds Bank, becoming a British subject in 1927.
E's. poetry represents an extended and profoundly serious search for meaning, in the process of which he produced a vibrant metaphysical poetry not only larger in scale but also more truly heroic than that of any of his contemporaries with the possible exception of Yeats. In 1915 he publ. *The Love-Song of J. Alfred Prufrock*, a monologue of a timid, middle-aged man who reviews the missed emotional opportunities of his life. Its direct and 'ordinary' language, and its deliberate use of 'un-poetic' images, marked a vivid break with the staleness of the existing conventions.

Duke Ellington

Elizabeth I: anon. painting, *c.* 1575

With the publ. of *The Waste Land* in 1922 this break was recognized as revolutionary. *The Waste Land* is a complex and difficult poem on the futility of life without convictions. Its imagery is widely derived, from the rush-hour of modern London to the symbolism of the Tarot and the Hindu religion. Technically it introduces the device of quotation from other poets in such a way as to give the original a new and often ironic resonance. It was partly this device and partly the extreme complexity of the sequence of thought that led to numerous charges of obscurity. In the same period E. was writing *The Sacred Wood* (1920), critical essays so influential that their premises have almost become the axioms of modern criticism. The sense of futility expressed in *The Waste Land* reached its nadir with the *Hollow Men* (1925); his confirmation into the Church of England (1927) points the path towards salvation. With *Ash Wednesday* (1930) and *Four Quartets* (1935–44) E. established himself as the major religious poet of our time. *Four Quartets*, one of his greatest works, is constructed on an elaborate system of parallelisms in both music and imagery; in it he discusses the nature of redemption largely in terms of the philosophical question of time and eternity.

In 1932 a long obsession with poetic drama began with *Sweeney Agonistes* and *The Rock* (1934). *Murder in the Cathedral*, on the murder of Thomas à Becket, E.'s most successful attempt in this line, followed in 1935. Subsequent plays, *The Family Reunion* (1939), *The Cocktail Party* (1949), *The Confidential Clerk* (1954) and *The Elder Statesman* (1959) were attempts to forge a type of verse low-toned, flexible and colloquial enough to be acceptable in the modern theatre. In 1939 a book of verse for children, *Old Possum's Book of Practical Cats*, showed the immense power of his poetry attractively turned to lighter purposes.

elision. The omission of a vowel either in colloquial speech (e.g. 'it's' for 'it is') or in a line of verse, so that the line shall conform to the metrical pattern.

Elizabeth I (1533–1603). English queen (1558–1603), the subject of many contemporary poets' verses. She is the 'Gloriana' of Spenser's *Faerie Queen*, possibly the 'Oriana' of the important coll. of madrigals *The Triumphs of Oriana* (1601) and Raleigh's 'Cynthia, the lady of the sea'. E. was herself a considerable linguist and scholar, and on occasion a powerful orator.

Elizabethan stage. Most Elizabethan theatres were roughly circular in shape. The acting area consisted of 3 stages. The apron stage, the most used, jutted out into the arena; behind this, and between the 2 doors which led from the actors' tiring-house or dressing-room, was the inner stage, across which a curtain could be drawn; above this was the upper stage, part of the gallery which ran all round the theatre, used to represent battlements, balconies, etc. In the rest of the gallery, overlooking the stage, sat the richer patrons, but most of the audience ('groundlings'), sat or stood on the ground, around the apron. Apart from these public theatres, there were later private ones such as the Blackfriars, which were more elaborate roofed buildings in which all the audience were properly seated. In these theatres more scenery was used and special effects could be created.

Elizabethan style. Conventionally held to be the style predominating in the reign of Elizabeth I (1558–1603); in fact there is no break between the last decades of the 16th c. and the first decades of the 17th c. In interior decoration and the applied arts, notably silver and furniture, it involved the absorption of Italian Renaissance forms and motifs, usually by way of Germany and the Netherlands, with the use of strap-work, grotesques and mythological subjects where appropriate. At first these were applied without understanding, but by *c.* 1570 the new ideas had been integrated to form a coherent style. For architecture *Tudor style.

Ellington Edward Kennedy 'Duke' (1899–). U.S. composer and arranger. The foremost jazz composer, and an important influence on 20th-c. music generally. His unique compositions and orchestral effects, specifically conceived for the individual members of his own band, represent an unforced, organic development of the idiomatic and tonal resources of jazz. His band, in existence for nearly 40 years with comparatively few changes in personnel, has been an essential part of his success as a composer. His greatest works include *Mood Indigo*; *Harlem Airshaft*; *Black, Brown and Beige*; and *Concerto for Cootie*.

Ellis (Henry) Havelock (1859–1939). English critic and scientific writer whose *Studies in the Psychology of Sex* (1897–1928) pioneered a more honest approach towards sexual problems.

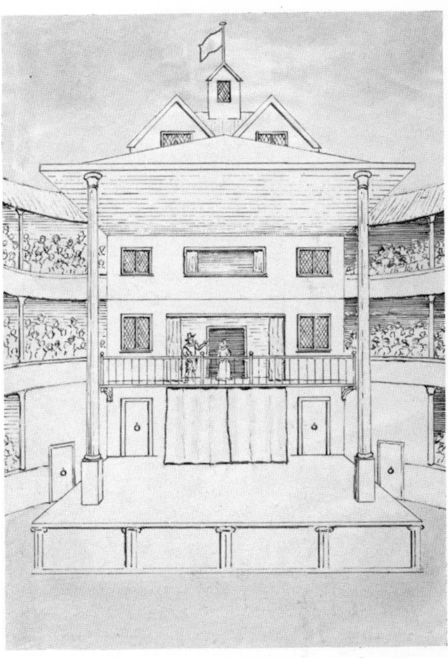

Elizabethan stage, a modern reconstruction. Also *apron stage

Elizabethan style. Bed, 2nd half of the 16th c.

Elsheimer. *Flight into Egypt*

Violetta Elvin as Odette in *Swan Lake*

Ely cathedral. Also *decorated

Ellison Ralph (Waldo) (1914–). U.S. writer and lecturer on Negro culture. His 1st novel, *Invisible Man* (1952), concerning the Negro in America, was widely acclaimed.

Elmer Gantry (1927). Novel by Sinclair *Lewis; also made into a film (1960), directed by R. *Brooks.

Elmes Harvey Lonsdale (1814–47). English architect of St George's Hall, Liverpool, a combination of large concert hall and assize courts; it is in a Greek style.

Elsheimer Adam (1578–1610). German painter, trained chiefly in Italy. He specialized in small highly finished works, often painted on copper. The landscape is given great importance and E. experiments with effects of lighting. In one example of a scene he painted many times, *Flight into Egypt* (Alte Pina., Munich), half the picture is lit by moonlight, half by the light from a bonfire.

Elssler Fanny (1810–84). Austrian dancer who studied under Marie Taglioni's father in Vienna. She made her début there in 1822 and later toured the world, often dancing with her sister Therese, *en travesti, as partner. She was a contemporary and rival of Taglioni, and they both acquired considerable partisan followings. She introduced national dancing into ballet and her Spanish cachucha in Coralli's *Diable Boiteux* (1836) became her most popular performance.

Elton Sir Arthur (1906–). British film producer. E. directed *Housing Problems* (1935) with E. *Anstey. Since then he has held several important appointments, e.g. producing documentaries for the British government and (1957–60) for Shell.

Éluard Paul. Pseud. of Eugène Grindel (1895–1952). French poet who took a prominent part both in the surrealist movement and in the Resistance and who reached the peak of his fame in the years after World War II when his poem on liberty was widely quoted for a time. Like his contemporary, Aragon, he deals with both public and private themes, and celebrates monogamous love. His form is simple, too simple perhaps for some tastes, and it is uncertain how much will survive from the selections he himself made: *Poésie et Vérité, 1942* (1942; *Poetry and Truth, 1942*, 1944), *Choix de poèmes* (1941) and *Le Livre ouvert* (1947).

Elvin Violetta (Prokhorova) (1924–). Russian ballet dancer who received her early training with the Bolshoi. She married an English diplomat and brought the 1st glimpse of post-war Russian style to England in 1945. She danced many leading classical and modern roles with the then Sadler's Wells Ballet Co. and retired to Italy in 1956.

Ely cathedral England. English cathedral, originally built in the *Norman style (1181–*c.* 1200); in 1322 the crossing tower collapsed and was replaced by the wooden octagon, an outstanding example of *decorated. It expands the crossing space into the aisles (taking an extra bay in each direction), uses diagonal lighting for the 1st time, and evolves a new conception of the vault as a half-cone. Features such as the nodding ogee, the shaft running *through* another motif and emerging the other side, windows with an odd number of lights, etc., also characterize the Lady chapel, built at the same time.

Elyot Sir Thomas (1490?–1546). English scholar; his treatise *The Boke named the Governour* (1531), considers the education of rulers. It was influenced by contemporary Italian as well as classical authors. R. Ascham (*The Scholemaster*) and J. Locke (*Some Thoughts Concerning Education*) both developed themes from it. E.'s readable trs helped to popularize the classics.

Elzevir family. Dutch printers at Leyden and Amsterdam (from 1638) who in the c. following 1580 publ. more than 1,500 works. Their many famous publs include the 1st ed. of Grotius's *Mare Liberum* (1609) and works by other contemporary authors such as Bacon, Pascal, Molière, Milton and Hobbes.

Émaux et Camées (1852). Coll. of poems by *Gautier.

emblems. Books of e.s were not uncommon in the 17th c. They consisted of short poems, etc., based on passages of Scripture and with quotations from the Fathers of the Church and were decorated with engravings. A well-known example was publ. by Francis Quarles.

embossed work. Raised decoration made to stand out in relief from a flat surface, either pressed out with engraved dies or hammered out. It applies to metal, leather, textiles, paper

Elzevir title-page

Reſpublica,
ſive
STATVS REGNI
SCOTIÆ ET HIBER
NIÆ.
Diverſorum
Autorum.

LVGD. BAT.
Ex officina
Elzeuiriana
A° cIↄ Iↄ cxxvII.
Cum priuilegio.

Emblems

I.

1. A Ship at Sea, that comes full Sail into Port. *Spes Proxima.* Her Deſire is nigh accompliſh'd.

2. A Man in a Chariot drawn by two Lions. *Etiam ferociſſimos domari.* A Wiſe Man may tame the moſt furious and ungovernable.

3. An Elephant. *In me mea ſpes omnis.* My Hope is in myſelf.

4. A Warrior and the Picture of Juſtice. *Unum nihil, duos plurimum poſſe.* One can do nothing of himſelf, but both together may do any thing.

5. A Lion attack'd by ſeveral little Animals. *Temeritas.* It repreſents Raſhneſs.

6. *Hercules* ſitting with his uſual Arms, and attack'd by a Child with a Sword. *Temeritas.* 'Tis a raſh Inſult.

7. A Sun-Flower beholding the Sun. *Non inferiora ſequutus.* I ſeek not after things beneath me.

8. An old Man laid down and looking at the Stars. *Deſidia.* Sloth.

9. An Elephant. *Par viribus virtus.* I have Courage equal to my Strength.

10. A lean Woman with Thorn about her Head, and Snakes in her Hand. *Invidia.* Envy.

11. A Goat ſuck'd by a young Wolf. *Sibi damna parat.* She nouriſhes her own Ruin.

12. *Narciſſus* admiring himſelf in a Fountain. *Philautia.* Self-Love.

13. Several Birds flying to a Cherry-Tree loaded with Fruit. *Paraſiti.* They are Paraſites.

14. A Satyr ſitting at the ſide of a Wood. *Luxuria.* Luſt.

15. A Wolf that would devour a Colt, but quits him to go for a Sheep, which he miſſes. *Oblivio paupertatis parens.* To forget one's Buſineſs is the Way to be Poor.

B

P. H. Emerson. *Gathering Water-lilies* (1885)

and similar substances. Extensively used in 17th-c. silverware, where a richly worked effect was required.

Emerson Peter Henry (1856–1936). English photographer, a practitioner of natural photography, under natural light conditions, at a time when artificial studio photography was at the peak of its popularity. In 1886 E. publ. *Life and Landscape of the Norfolk Broads*, 40 prints of the life of the marsh-dwellers, and in 1889 a statement of his credo, *Naturalistic Photography*. He believed that since the eye does not see everything in its field of vision clearly, the camera should not focus sharply on the entire scene, but abandoned this theory after 1890.

Emerson Ralph Waldo (1803–82). U.S. writer born in Boston. E. was a Unitarian minister until 1832, when he resigned. He visited Europe, where he met Carlyle, Coleridge and Wordsworth. On his return he began a series of lectures which are the basis of his reputation, crystallizing in *Nature* (1836), which combines the elements he acquired from Unitarian deism, optimistic nationalism, Platonism and romanticism. Cultural nationalism is the subject of *The American Scholar* (1837), and his *Divinity School Address* (1838) attacks formal religion in the name of personal experience and transcendental intuition of the World Soul. His lectures found permanent form in the books of *Essays* (1841 and 1844) on such themes as Self-Reliance, the Over-Soul, Love, Manners, and Politics, essays all concerned with the optimistic religion of the self which is also the subject of his poetry. There followed *Representative Men* (1850), lectures on England in *English Traits* (1856), and *The Conduct of Life* (1860) in which, reflecting developing tensions in America, his optimism is mingled with bewilderment. His *Journals* afford a shrewd and moving record of his inner conflicts.

Émile (1762). Treatise by J.-J. *Rousseau.

Eminent Victorians (1918). Book by Lytton *Strachey.

Eminescu Mihail. Pseud of Mihail Eminovici (1850–89). Rumanian romantic poet; a number of his 60 poems and some of his short stories have been trs. into English and other W. European languages.

Emma (1814). Novel by Jane *Austen.

Émmanuel Pierre (1916–). French poet whose many colls include *Elégies* (1940), *Le poète fou* (1944) and *Cantos* (1943). Among his other works are the epic poem *Babel* (1951) and the prose work *Qui est cet homme?* (1947).

Emmer Luciano (1918–). Italian film director. E. and Enrico Gras made a series of famous documentaries on art. His 1st feature, *Domenica d'agosto* (1949), which he has not since equalled, is a 'slice of life' in the mainstream of neo-realism. *Isole della laguna* (1948) is a beautiful and lyrical exploration of the islands in the lagoon of Venice.

Emmett Daniel Decatur (1815–1904). U.S. composer of 'Dixie' and connected with one of the earliest 'Negro Minstrels' groups.

Emperor Concerto. The English nickname (possibly given by J. B. Cramer) of Beethoven's piano concerto no. 5 in E maj. (1809) dedicated to the Archduke Rudolf.

Emperor Jones (1920). Play by Eugene *O'Neill.

Emperor Quartet. Nickname of Haydn's string quartet in C maj., op. 76, no. 3, the slow movement being variations on his *Emperor's Hymn*.

Emperor's Hymn, The. Tune by Haydn written (1797) to patriotic verses by L. L. Haschka. The tune is the German national anthem and is known in England as the hymn tune *Austria*.

Empire. A development of the neo-classic Louis XVI and Directoire styles in the French decorative arts, roughly corresponding to the Regency period in England. Although named after the First Empire it dates from *c.* 1800–20. It is characterized by an eclectic use of motifs, chiefly derived from classical, Egyptian and Etruscan sources. Although affecting all the decorative arts, it particularly applies to furniture.

Empire Ballets. Ballets performed at the Empire Theatre, London (1884–1914), which presented many of the classical ballets to London audiences. Cecchetti, Adeline Genée and C. Wilhelm were some of the celebrities associated with the theatre.

Ralph Waldo Emerson

Empire. Napoleon I candelabra

Empire. Napoleon I chair

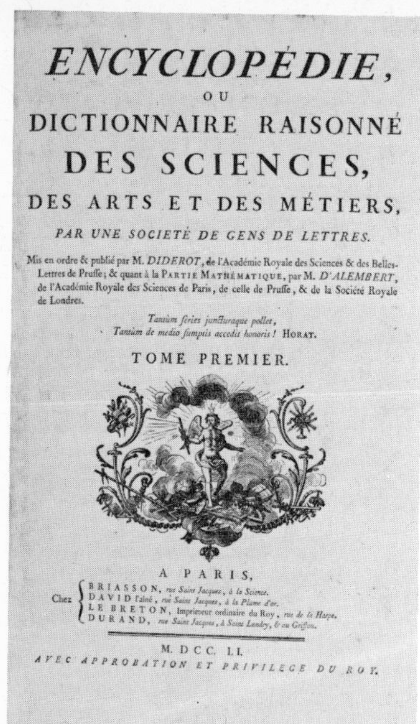

ENCYCLOPÉDIE,
OU
DICTIONNAIRE RAISONNÉ
DES SCIENCES,
DES ARTS ET DES MÉTIERS,
PAR UNE SOCIETÉ DE GENS DE LETTRES.

Mis en ordre & publié par M. *DIDEROT*, de l'Académie Royale des Sciences & des Belles-Lettres de Prusse; & quant à la PARTIE MATHÉMATIQUE, par M. *D'ALEMBERT*, de l'Académie Royale des Sciences de Paris, de celle de Prusse, & de la Société Royale de Londres.

Tantùm series juncturaque pollet,
Tantùm de medio sumptis accedit honoris! HORAT.

TOME PREMIER.

A PARIS,
Chez BRIASSON, *rue Saint Jacques, à la Science.*
DAVID l'aîné, *rue Saint Jacques, à la Plume d'or.*
LE BRETON, Imprimeur ordinaire du Roy, *rue de la Harpe.*
DURAND, *rue Saint Jacques, à Saint Landry, & au Griffon.*

M. DCC. LI.
AVEC APPROBATION ET PRIVILEGE DU ROY.

Encyclopédie. Title-page of vol. 1 of the 1st ed.

Encaustic wax. Roman-Egyptian mummy portrait, 2nd c. A.D.

Empson William (1906–). English poet and critic. E.'s verse, influenced by 17th-c. metaphysical poetry, is intellectual and compressed, playing on the meanings of words. His *Collected Poems* (1955), and criticism in *Seven Types of Ambiguity* (1930) and *Some Versions of Pastoral* (1935), contains seminal work on the verbal and structural analysis of poetry.

enamel. A decorative medium in which a compound of silica, minium and potash stained with metallic oxides is fused with the surface of a metal–gold, silver or copper. The process of enamelling, either on clay or metal, was known to ancient Egypt, Assyria, Greece and Rome. Mosan and *Limoges are the best-known medieval centres and Jean Pénicaud and Leonard Limousin are the 1st outstanding artists in the medium. The finest productions in England in the 18th c. came from Battersea and S. Staffordshire. Here the colours were painted on, and all kinds of articles, both useful and decorative, and all of the highest quality, were produced, the style being close to porcelain.

enamelled glass. Enamels may be fused on to glass by firing in a *muffle kiln, or be powdered and painted on in an oily medium. The technique was extensively used by Islamic, Venetian, German and Bohemian glass makers from the 15th c. onwards, but it was first practised in England at Newcastle and Bristol in the 18th c. (*Beilby).

encaustic wax. A technique of painting in which the *medium for the powdered colour was hot wax; the method was used in classical antiquity but not since.

enchaînement. A sequence of steps in ballet put together to form a group.

Encina Juan del (1468–1529). Spanish playwright, poet and musician, often considered to be the founder of the great Spanish theatre of the 16th century, although the importance of his plays is mainly historical, marking the transition from sacred to secular drama. He also wrote a treatise on Castilian poetry, and a number of fervently pious lyrics (*Canciones*, 1496).

encore (French, 'again'). In English-speaking countries the word used by a concert audience calling for the repeat of an item or simply for more music from the performer or performers. Thus an 'e.' is often an extra piece not on the programme.

Encyclopédie ou Dictionnaire raisonné, L' (1751–80). Summary of all then existing knowledge, ed. by Diderot and d'Alembert. Voltaire, Rousseau, Turgot and Montesquieu contributed articles. Inspired by current rationalistic ideas, the *E.* attacked religious belief and political injustice; it enjoyed enormous success, and was the subject of numerous attempts at suppression.

en dedans. (French, 'inwards'). Describes the action of the working leg in ballet. It can be an anti-clockwise rotation of the working leg or the bringing of it in towards the supporting leg from an extended position.

en dehors. (French, 'outwards'). Describes the action of the working leg in ballet when used in a clockwise rotation, mostly in a pirouette, fouetté and a ronde de jambe.

Endgame (1957). Play by Samuel *Beckett.

End of St Petersburg, The (1927). Film directed by V. I. *Pudovkin.

End of the Affair, The (1951). Novel by Graham Greene.

end-stopping: *enjambment

Endymion (1818). Poem by *Keats.

Enemy of the People, An (1882). Play by *Ibsen.

Enesco Georges. Name adopted by George Enescu (1881–1955), Rumanian violinist and composer living, from 1895, mainly in Paris. His compositions include the opera *Oedipe* (1936), 3 symphonies, *Rumanian Rhapsodies* for orchestra, and chamber music. Y. Menuhin studied under him.

Enfance du Christ, L' (1854). Musical work by *Berlioz.

Enfants du Paradis, Les (1945). Film directed by M. *Carné.

Enfants Terribles, Les (1929). Novel by Jean *Cocteau; made into a film (1949) directed by J.-P. Melville.

Enamel. Limoges crucifix. See also colour plate 19

Enamelled glass; German (Franconia), 1671

Line engraving.
Dürer, *Prodigal Son*

Dry point.
Rodin's *Cupids guiding the World*

Etching and dry point.
Rembrandt's *The Omval*

English Bards and Scotch Reviewers (1809). Verse satire by *Byron.

English horn: *cor anglais

English Opera Group. Founded (1947) by B. Britten, J. Piper and E. Crozier to perform 'chamber' operas. At first its repertory was exclusively works by Britten, *Albert Herring* being composed for it; it appears regularly at the *Aldeburgh Festival.

English Stage Co. English group formed in 1956, closely associated with the Royal Court Theatre, where John Osborne's *Look Back in Anger* was presented during the 1st season. Under G. *Devine, its 1st director, the co. has supported such modern writers as Osborne, Arden and Wesker. It has also championed Brecht.

English suites. 6 suites for harpsichord by Bach (written *c.* 1725, publ. posth.). The title may have been given because of their long preludes, considered a characteristic of the English suite form, or they may have been written for an English patron.

engraving. The term covers many techniques for multiplying prints, either of a picture designed by the engraver himself for the medium, or of a reproduction of a work in another medium by another artist. Correctly e. refers only to *intaglio techniques. All these involve a metal plate, usually copper, on which the ink is held in furrows and crevices cut or bitten by acid into its surface: a print is obtained by rolling the plate, covered by a sheet of dampened paper, through a press; so that the paper is forced into the engraved markings, thus picking up the ink.

LINE ENGRAVING. A copper plate is polished and often covered with chalk. The main contours of the picture are marked in the chalk and the lines cut in the copper with a graver or burin; graduated tones can be obtained by hatching. Line e. achieved its greatest expressiveness in the N. schools, especially in the work of Dürer. Later it was used mainly for making reproductions.

DRY POINT. A steel stylus is used on a copper plate; but whereas in line e. the burr of copper is polished away, in dry point it is left. In printing, the ink caught in this burr gives a characteristic 'bloom' to the line. This technique is often used with etching, notably in Rembrandt's work.

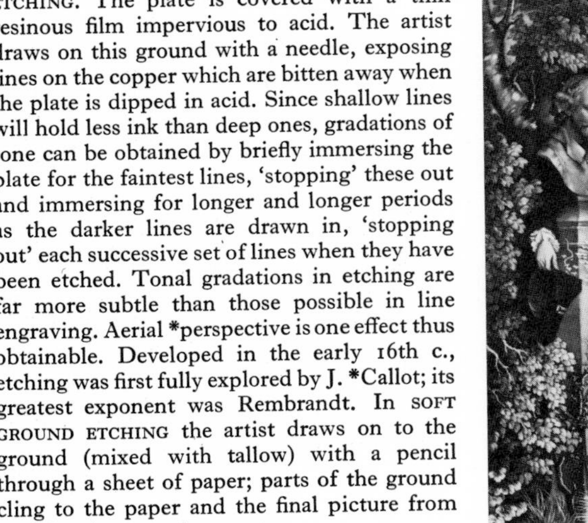

ETCHING. The plate is covered with a thin resinous film impervious to acid. The artist draws on this ground with a needle, exposing lines on the copper which are bitten away when the plate is dipped in acid. Since shallow lines will hold less ink than deep ones, gradations of tone can be obtained by briefly immersing the plate for the faintest lines, 'stopping' these out and immersing for longer and longer periods as the darker lines are drawn in, 'stopping out' each successive set of lines when they have been etched. Tonal gradations in etching are far more subtle than those possible in line engraving. Aerial *perspective is one effect thus obtainable. Developed in the early 16th c., etching was first fully explored by J. *Callot; its greatest exponent was Rembrandt. In SOFT GROUND ETCHING the artist draws on to the ground (mixed with tallow) with a pencil through a sheet of paper; parts of the ground cling to the paper and the final picture from the plate has a grainy texture.

MEZZOTINT. Unlike line e. or etching, mezzotint (invented in the mid 17th c.) works with tones rather than lines; it was thus suitable, and in the 18th c. widely used, to reproduce paintings. A curved file or 'rocker' is rocked over the plate to give a uniformly burred surface like sandpaper. This, when inked, would print as a solid black. By scraping off the burr to a greater or lesser extent or by burnishing it away entirely, the amount of ink carried by different areas can be controlled and gradations of tone or highlights (the burnished areas will carry no ink) obtained.

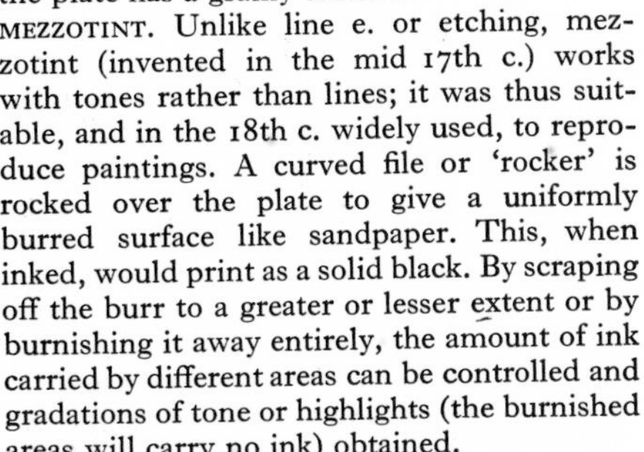

AQUATINT. A tone process (invented by J.-B. Leprince) which uses acid as in etching. The plate is covered with a porous ground which allows the acid to bite away a fine mesh of tiny dots. The artist first stops out the white areas of the picture, immerses the plate briefly for the next lightest tone, stops out these areas in turn and repeats the process for the successively darker tones. Unlike the mezzotint, the aquatint is incapable of fine modulations of tone, each tone being uniform and bounded by an abrupt contour.

SUGAR AQUATINT is a linear technique combined with aquatint tone. The design is brushed on to the copper with a black ink or gouache dissolved in sugar-water, and the plate is covered with a ground and dipped in warm water. The sugar mixture dissolves, leaving the plate exposed where the drawing was. A second ground is laid and the plate bitten as for an ordinary aquatint.

Mezzotint. Portrait of David Garrick; after Gainsborough

Etching and aquatint from Goya's *Los Caprichos*

Sugar aquatint. Picasso's *Head of a Goat* (1952)

Ensor. *The Rower*

Ensor. *Death and Masks*

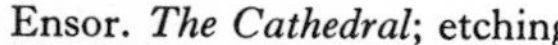

Ensor. *The Cathedral*; etching

enharmonic. A musical term used of such intervals as B♯ to C♮ or B♭ to A♯. Acoustically there is fractional difference in pitch between these; but on instruments with fixed notes, such as the piano (*temperament), 1 note serves for both and the distinction is in notation only. An ENHARMONIC MODULATION exploits the smallness of such intervals, treating the 2 notes as one common factor between 2 chords.

Enigma Variations (1899). The familiar name for *Elgar's *Variations on an Original Theme, for orchestra.*

enjambment. In verse, running the sense of a line (or couplet, etc.) on to the next line–as opposed to end-stopping, where there is a break in the sense which coincides with the end of the line.

en l'air. A term in ballet applied to steps which the dancer performs in the air. These steps put the dancer's elevation to the test.

Enlightenment, The. English term for the German *Aufklärung*, used of the movement in European literature and philosophy during the last years of the 17th c. and the greater part of the 18th c.; in England the period is often called 'The Age of Reason'. It is the age of classicism and rationalism in literature, and of deism in religion. In Germany it was also connected with paternalism in politics, and during the period such courts as those of Weimar and Mannheim became centres of brilliant and intense artistic activity.

Ennius (239–169 B.C.). The 'father of Latin poetry' (Cicero) was born at Rudiae in S. Italy, so that he was familiar with Greek as well as Latin. His patron Q. Fulvius Nobilior procured him Roman citizenship in 184. His *Annals*, a history of Rome from the earliest legends down to his own times, was the 1st Roman epic to employ the Greek hexameter metre, which thereafter became the standard metre for Latin verse. He also adapted tragedies from the Greek, including many of Euripides', and wrote a didactic poem on theology as well as satires and humorous pieces. Both Lucretius and Virgil admired and imitated his work; only fragments of it have survived.

Enoch Arden (1864). Poem by Tennyson.

Enormous Room, The (1922). Book by e.e. *cummings.

Ensor. *Portrait of the Artist in a flowered hat* (detail)

Enright D(enis) J(oseph) (1920–). English poet, for a time teaching at Singapore Univ. His verse, mainly satirical, includes *The Laughing Hyena* (1953), *Bread Rather Than Blossoms* (1956) and *Some Men Are Brothers* (1960).

Enríquez Gómez Antonio (*c.* 1600–*c.* 60). Spanish poet, novelist and playwright. In his plays he was influenced by Calderón. His most important and personal work is his combination of satire and picaresque novel, *El Siglo pitagórico y vida de Don Gregorio Guadaña* (1644), which has affinities with Quevedo's satires.

ensemble (French, 'together'). Used in English to describe the degree of coherence or teamwork in a musical performance. An e. in opera or in ballet is an item for a group of soloists. Also the word may simply mean a group of performers.

Ensor James (1860–1949). Belgian painter and engraver, born in Ostend of an English father and a Flemish mother. E. studied at the Brussels Academy, but otherwise seldom left Ostend. Neglected by all but a few writers like Verhaeren and Maeterlinck, E. was awarded later recognition in the 1920s and created a baron in 1930. Today he is considered a major pioneer of both expressionism and abstract expressionism. E. began by painting sombre interiors, portraits, landscapes and seascapes (*The Rower*, M. R. des B.A., Antwerp) as well as a few superb still-life studies. About 1883 his palette changed to lighter, brilliantly contrasted colours. This very Flemish choice of colour can first be seen in a variation in a self-portrait by Rubens, *Portrait of the Artist in a flowered hat* (Ensor Mus., Ostend). Of E.'s engravings of this period, one of the greatest is *The Cathedral* (1886). The macabre carnival paintings of fighting skeletons and masked revellers, with the echoes of the Dance of Death, Bosch, Bruegel the Elder, Callot, Magnasco and Goya, now made their appearance. The most celebrated of these, *Christ's Entry into Brussels* (M. R. des B.A.), was rejected in 1889 after a scandal by Les XX, an *avant-garde* group which E. had helped to found. E. continued to paint until 1939; his later work is less fierce in character, e.g. *Coup de Lumière* (1935; Tate).

entablature. In classical architecture, the 3 horizontal sections (architrave, frieze, cornice)

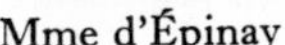

Mme d'Épinay

Épergne, *c.* 1778

above the capitals of the supporting columns. Diagram *orders.

entasis. In Greek architecture, a convex swelling on a pillar. Exaggerated in the early period, it was gradually refined and was perfected in the Parthenon (an e. of $\frac{3}{4}$ in. in a height of 34 ft); here the object was probably to correct the optical illusion which makes the middle of a straight, upright pillar seem too thin.

Entertainer, The (1957). Play by John *Osborne; also a film (1959) directed by Tony Richardson.

Entführung aus dem Serail, Die (1782). Opera by *Mozart.

entr'acte (French). Interval between 2 acts of a play, opera, etc.; music performed during the interval.

en travesti. In 19th-c. ballet it was common for the male lead to be taken by a woman dressed e. t., i.e. as a man.

entrechat. A step in ballet which involves springing from the floor with feet in 5th *position, toes pointed, and neatly exchanging the position of the feet.

Eothen (1844). Travel book by *Kinglake.

Eötvös József (1813–71). Hungarian novelist, poet and essayist; a liberal philosopher and statesman. His novels were aimed at social reform: in *A'falu jegyzöge* (1845; *The Village Notary*, 1850) he ruthlessly exposed the faults of the semi-feudal administration.

epaulé (French). A position in ballet when the body–noticeably the shoulders–is facing either corner downstage and the leg and arm nearer the audience are the working ones.

épaulement (French). The deportment of the shoulders in ballet. The placing of the shoulders is an important ingredient in the effect the dancer creates.

épergne. An elaborate silver centre-piece for the table, dating from the 18th c., with dishes for fruit, condiments or sweetmeats. The most common design is that of a large central dish surrounded by 4 others. It provided opportunity for the most lavish and fantastic decoration by rococo silversmiths.

Ephesus, Temple of Artemis. One of the 7 wonders of the ancient world. The archaic temple, an early example of the Ionic order (*c.* 550 B.C.) had double rows of 8 columns across the front and 20 along each side; it was over 60 ft high. The bases had sculptured reliefs. This temple was burned down in 356 by Eratostratus in order to render his name immortal. It was replaced by a Hellenistic building, also Ionic, on a similar scale.

epic. A long poem on some heroic or great theme. The *Iliad* is the 1st great example; other great e.s of antiquity include the *Aeneid* of Virgil. Essentially the e. is an artistic composition and though long strings of lays or sagas such as the Finnish *Kalevala* may loosely be called 'national e.s', they lack the coherence and unity of a true e. The Renaissance saw a revival of the form, e.g. *Camoen's *Lusiadas* and later John Milton's *Paradise Lost.*

Epicurus (342–270 B.C.). Athenian philosopher who tried to free men from fear of the gods and held that happiness was the only good, being best achieved by avoiding pain; his philosophy is not therefore 'epicurean' in the modern sense of 'pleasure-loving'. Lucretius adopted and expanded E.'s philosophy and probably developed his atomic theory from E.'s teachings.

epigram. In classical Greece an inscription, usually in verse and often on a tomb, or by way of commemoration. *Simonides was famous for his witty, pithy and brief e.s; and the term is now applied to any statement with these qualities.

Épinay Louise-Florence, Mme d' (1726–83). French intellectual, a friend of Diderot and protector of J.-J. Rousseau until F.-M. de Grimm took the latter's place in her affections. Her *Mémoires* (1818) throw valuable light on Rousseau's career.

Epipsychidion (1821). Poem by *Shelley.

episode. A section of a piece of music in which secondary or new thematic material is developed; particularly in *fugue, where it describes the sections between the expositions of the subject.

epistolary novel. Novel taking the form of a series of letters. *Richardson's *Pamela* was a highly influential example both in England and

Ephesus. Marble replica (discovered in 1956) of the cult image of Artemis in the Temple

Ephesus. Base of a column from the later Temple of Artemis

Entasis on a Doric column

Epstein. *Ecce Homo*

Epstein. *Adam*

Epstein. *St Michael and the Devil*

Erbslöh. *Bavarian mountain landscape*

Erasmus

The Erechtheum. Also *Acropolis

on the Continent. The convention persisted into the late 18th c.

epithalamium. Nuptial song or poem, e.g. Spenser's *E.* Originally sung before the bridal chamber.

epode. Term used by Horace of certain of his lyric poems; more generally one of the sections of a lyric ode.

Epstein Sir Jacob (1880–1959). American-born portrait and monumental sculptor who settled in London in 1905. His fame and notoriety were established with the 18 figures in semi-relief carved for the British Medical Association Building in the Strand. Many sculptures of his early and middle period were rejected by the general public as ugly and attacked by the critics either for the deliberate distortion of the human figure or on formal grounds: the *Risen Christ* (1919) showed Christ as a Jew, and the influence of primitive art is apparent in the *Ecce Homo* (1934–5) and the alabaster *Adam* (1938–9), a barbaric and energy-charged figure. The 3 major religious commissions of E.'s last years, the *Madonna and Child* (Cavendish Square, 1951–2), the *Christ in Majesty* (Llandaff cathedral, 1953–7) and the *St Michael and the Devil* (Coventry cathedral, 1955–7) were more traditional compositions. His bronze portrait heads of children and of great contemporaries are masterpieces.

Epstein Jean (1899–1953). French film director and critic. E. was one of the group around L. *Delluc. His early films and particularly the most famous, *Cœur Fidèle* (1923), were realist works, which he followed with some *avant-garde* films including a version of *The Fall of the House of Usher* (1928). *Finis Terrae* (1929) and *Morvran* (1930) were documentaries.

equale (plural 'equali'). A musical term for a piece for 4 trombones, elegiac in mood and used at funerals and solemn ceremonies. Beethoven wrote 3 famous equali which were performed at his funeral.

Erasmus Desiderius, of Rotterdam (1496–1536). Dutch humanist. He was the illegitimate son of a priest but received a good education and became an Augustinian monk. In 1499 he went to England where he became the friend of Grocyn, More and Colet, studying Greek at Oxford; he travelled widely in Europe, taught for some years at Cambridge Univ., and lived much at Basle, where he collaborated with the printer Froben. E., the greatest scholar of his age, was universally revered and, a man of tolerance in an age of intolerance, was appealed to by Pope and Reformers alike. His brilliant and versatile intellect and pervading wit are revealed in his correspondence with all the major figures of his time. E.'s important ed. of the New Testament and trs. of it into Latin (1515) undermined the authority of the Vulgate, and his attacks on abuses undoubtedly lowered the prestige of the Catholic Church. He took no part in the Reformation, however, and ultimately engaged in controversy with Luther. Of his works the best remembered is the *Encomium moriae* (*Praise of Folly*; written 1509); his other 2 main works are the *Adagia*, a coll. of proverbs from classical authors, and the *Colloquies*, containing incisive comments on contemporary life.

Erbslöh Adolf (1881–1947). German expressionist painter, a member of the New Artists' Federation (Neue Künstlervereinigung, 1909) led by Kandinsky. He disapproved of the increasing tendency towards abstraction in Kandinsky's work and was partly responsible for bringing about his resignation from the Federation in 1911.

Ercilla y Zúñiga Alonso de (1533–94). Spanish warrior-poet. After fighting in Chile against the Araucanians he returned to Spain to continue his fine epic poem based on his experiences, *La Araucana.* Written in rhyming octaves, publ. in 3 parts, but never completed, it is distinguished by its narrative and descriptive power.

Erckmann-Chatrian. Pseud. jointly adopted by the Alsatian writers Émile Erckmann (1822–99) and Pierre-Alexandre Chatrian (1826–90). Their historical novels of the Revolution and the First Empire included *L'Illustre Docteur Mathéus* (1859), *L'Ami Fritz* (1864) and *Waterloo* (1865).

Erechtheum. Ionic (*order) temple on the Acropolis, Athens, named after Erechtheus, the legendary founder of Athens. Designed by Mnesicles, it was built between 420 and 393 B.C. and never completed. Unlike nearly every other Greek temple, the E. is irregular in plan, with no exterior colonnade and 3 different floor and roof levels. The porch on the

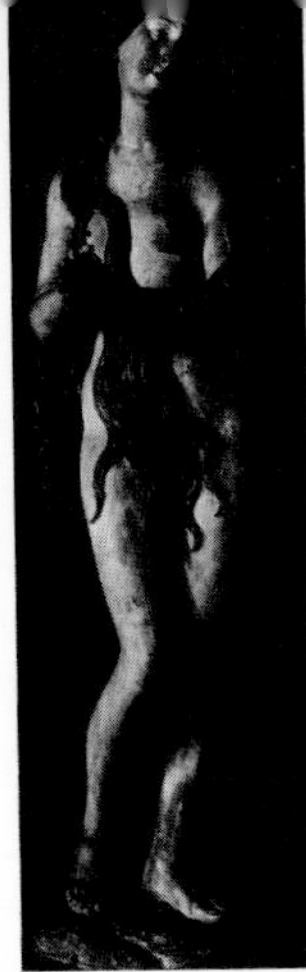
Erhart. *La Belle Allemande*

Max Ernst. *Moon Mad* (1914)

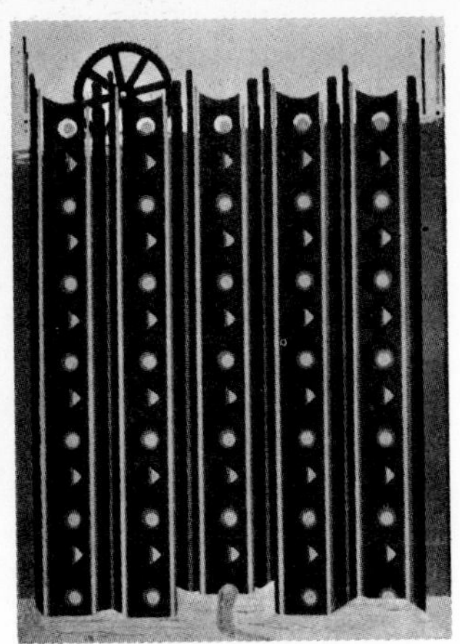
Max Ernst. *The Little Tear Gland that says Tic Tac*

S. side contains the famous caryatids, columns in the form of draped female figures supporting an architrave; this feature is copied in the parish church, St Pancras, London.

Erewhon (1872). Book by Samuel *Butler.

Erhart Gregor (d. 1540). German sculptor in wood and stone, trained in late Gothic style but subsequently influenced by the Renaissance. Most famous are his painted figures on the high altar of the Klosterkirche, Blaubeuren; other works include the *Frauenstein Madonna* (Wallfahrtskirche, Frauenstein) and *La Belle Allemande* (Louvre), a figure of Mary Magdalene.

Erlanger Frédéric, Baron d' (1868–1943). French-born composer, English by naturalization. His music is lucid in form and English in idiom, and includes the opera *Tess* (1906), after T. Hardy; a requiem (1931); orchestral works, and a violin concerto.

Ermler Frederick (1898–). Soviet film director. E. directed one of the most famous Soviet silent films, *Fragment of an Empire* (1929), which aimed much more at psychological content than the works of Eisenstein and Pudovkin, with its narrative about an NCO who loses his memory.

Ernst Jimmy (1920–). German-born abstract expressionist painter who settled in the U.S. in 1938; son of Max E. His paintings combine imagery of the surrealist type with formal features of geometric severity.

Ernst Max (1891–). German painter who first studied philosophy at Bonn (1909–14). Untrained as an artist, he visited Paris in 1913 and met Macke, Delaunay and–more significantly –Apollinaire and Arp. After the war he founded the Cologne dada group in 1919. By this time he had seen the work of Picasso, Klee, de Chirico, and the Zürich dadaists, and his paintings combined found objects (pieces of wood, wallpaper, etc.) with painted objects into a fantasy imagery whose disturbing ambiguity was emphasized by the titles–*The Little Tear Gland that says Tic Tac* (1920; M.M.A., New York). His one-man exhibition in Paris in 1920 was acclaimed by the surrealists. His invention of 'frottage' paralleled the automatic writing of Breton and Éluard in eliminating the conscious creative role of the artist, e.g. *Histoire Naturelle* (publ. Paris 1926). The painting and sculpture which has made him one of the major influential figures of international surrealism since then depends either on the irrational juxtaposition of unrelated elements, e.g. *Of this Men shall know Nothing* (1923; Tate) or on a more imaginative nightmare improvisation of organic forms (*The Horde*, 1927; Stedelijk Mus., Amsterdam). E. spent the war years in the U.S., later settling in France.

Eroica. The title of Beethoven's symphony no. 3 in E♭ (1805). On learning that Napoleon, 'the great liberator', had become emperor, he changed the original title *Sinfonia grande Bonaparte* to *Sinfonia eroica, per festeggiare il souvenire d'un grand' uomo*–'Heroic symphony to celebrate the memory of a great man.'

Erri Agnolo and Bartolomeo (*fl.* after 1450). Italian painters who worked in Modena.

Erskine Ralph (1914–). British architect practising in Sweden; he now ranks among the best architects of that country. His early work was a series of houses, showing great concern for the local climate, continued in his designs for settlements at Lulea and Kiruna, in N. Sweden, where whole streets are roofed over.

Erziehungsroman. Interchangeable with **Bildungsroman.*

Escorial Madrid: Juan de *Herrera

Esdras. Name of 2 books in the *Apocrypha.

Esenin Sergey Alexandrovich (1895–1925). Russian peasant poet. Blok recognized his gifts of melody and imagery and encouraged him to make a literary career. E.'s best poems are inspired by rural life, and he called himself 'the last of the village poets'. He welcomed the Revolution, which he interpreted in *Inonia* as a resurgence of peasant Russia. In 1919 he joined the imaginists, an offshoot of the symbolists and futurists. Their lives, like their writings, ignored convention; E.'s poems *Confession of a Hooligan* and *Tavern Moscow* depict this phase. His marriage (1922) to the dancer Isadora Duncan was short-lived. E. tried without success to adjust to the new régime and committed suicide.

Espinel Vicente (1550–1624). Spanish poet and novelist, author of the *picaresque novel

Max Ernst. *L'Éléphant 'Célèbes* (1921)

Jimmy Ernst. *A Time for Fear* (1949)

Sergey Esenin

José de Espronceda

Estève. *Tacet* (1956)

Marcos de Obregón (1618) which was to suggest to Le Sage many incidents in his *Gil Blas*. E.'s *Varias Rimas* (1591) are lively and technically accomplished and he also introduced a stanza of 10 octosyllabic lines, known as the *espinela*, into Spanish poetry.

Espinosa Pedro (1578–1650). Spanish poet and prose writer. He wrote beautiful sonnets, *canciones*, and narrative poems under *Góngora's influence, in a highly coloured and elaborate style full of descriptive passages, e.g. *Fábula del Genil*, and in 1605 publ. an excellent anthology of the best poets of his age.

Esplá Oscar (1886–). Spanish composer; in voluntary exile in Belgium from the Civil War to 1951. The landscape and music of his native district of Alicante has impinged on E.'s work, which includes the symphonic poem *Don Quijote velando las armas* (1924), a choral symphony (1950), and chamber and piano music.

Espoir, L' (1937). Novel by *Malraux, the basis of the film (1939) which he directed.

Ésprit des lois, De l' (1748). Book by *Montesquieu.

Espronceda José de (1808–42). The outstanding Spanish romantic poet. In politics he was a revolutionary liberal; but both in politics and love he was disappointed. His principal work, *El diablo mundo* (1840/1), remains unfinished. It is uneven; the finest part, the *Canto a Teresa*, addressed to a woman he had loved, is unconnected with the rest. The central figure recalles Faust and Byron's Don Juan; he is the man who lives in accordance with nature, and is persecuted by society. E.'s best poem, *El estudiante de Salamanca* (in *Poesías*. . . , 1840), is the story of a libertine who dies after being shown a vision of his own funeral. He also wrote several much-anthologized romantic lyrics.

essay. Montaigne wrote the 1st book of e.s; the earliest example in English is the *Essays* of Francis Bacon. The term is often loosely applied to any non-imaginative prose work of moderate length, and even, occasionally, to a poem, e.g. Pope's *Essay on Man.*

Essex James (1722–84). English architect. He designed many college buildings at Cambridge, was one of the pioneers of neo-*Gothic (he worked for Walpole at Strawberry Hill) and did some careful restoration of medieval cathedrals.

estampie or **estampida.** A medieval musical instrumental form probably deriving from the vocal form of the *sequence; the earliest known e. is the troubadour *Kalenda maya* (*c.* 1200). Basically the e. is a series of melodic units in the pattern a,a,b,b.

Estense Baldassare (d. 1504). Ferrarese painter, the illegitimate son of Niccolo d'Este III, Duke of Ferrara. The only signed work by him disappeared in the 19th c., but a number of other pictures in a severe, intellectual style are believed to be his, e.g. *Family Group* (Alte Pina., Munich).

Estève Maurice (1904–). French painter of the school of Paris. After surrealist and cubist-influenced representational work he turned slowly towards abstraction, developing his distinctive style *c.* 1950. His compositions are constructed with bold, loosely interpenetrating forms in vibrant expressive colours.

Esther (*c.* 150 B.C.). One of the books of the *Bible (Old Testament), though an entirely secular story in which the Jewess Esther marries the Persian King Ahasuerus and, with the assistance of her uncle Mordecai, saves the Jews from being massacred.

Esther Waters (1894). Novel by George *Moore.

Estienne Robert (1503–59). The most eminent scholar-printer of the 16th c., largely responsible for making the reign of Francis I the golden age of French typography. He took control of the family business (founded by Henri E. *c.* 1502) in 1525 and was subsequently assisted by his son HENRI (1528–98). E. employed Garamond as type-designer and adviser; his famous books included *Thesaurus linguae latinae* (1531) and many classical works. In 1550 E. founded a press in Geneva which was continued by his son and grandson; the line ended in 1674 with the death of Antoine E. in Paris.

etching: *engraving

Ethan Brand (1851). Story by *Hawthorne.

Estienne title-page, 1535

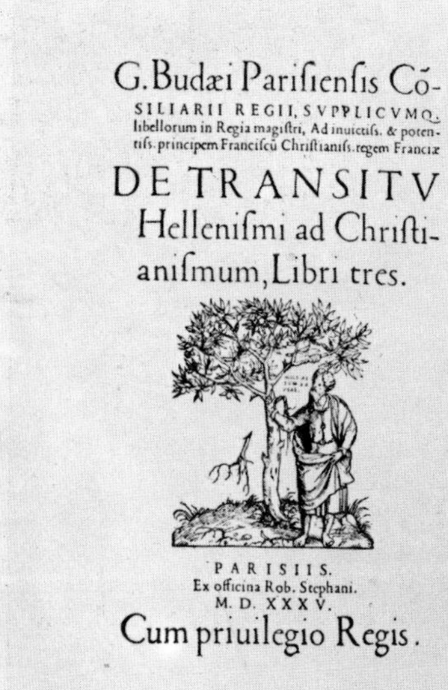

G.Budæi Parisiensis Cõ-
SILIARII REGII, SVPPLICVMQ.
libellorum in Regia magistri, Ad inuictiss. & potentiss. principem Franciscũ Christianiss. regem Franciæ
DE TRANSITV
Hellenismi ad Christianismum, Libri tres.

PARISIIS.
Ex officina Rob. Stephani.
M. D. XXXV.
Cum priuilegio Regis.

Etherege (or Etheredge) Sir George (1634?–91). English playwright whose works had some influence on the development of comedy, being mainly written in prose, and employing heroic couplets for serious scenes. E.'s comedies are: *The Comical Revenge, or Love in a Tub* (1664), *She wou'd if she cou'd* (1668), and *The Man of Mode, or Sir Fopling Flutter* (1676).

Étienne Charles-Guillaume (1777–1845). French playwright and journalist, ed. of the *Journal de l'Empire* (**Journal des Débats*) and a founder of the journal *La Minerve Française*. His comedies included one on the King Lear theme, *Les Deux Gendres* (1810).

étoile. A title given to the leading dancers at the Paris Opéra, denoting their seniority in the co. The classification is given by appointment and the lower grades are filled by annual examinations, being: premiers danseurs, grands sujets, petits sujets, coryphées, premiers quadrilles, deuxièmes quadrilles (and their female equivalents) and the young students, élèves, known as 'les rats'.

Eton MS. Late 15th- to early 16th-c. English music ms. originally containing 93 works, of which 39 motets and 4 magnificats survive complete and another 21 pieces in part. The composers represented include Cornyshe and Fayrfax; among the lost works was a 5-part motet by J. Dunstable, the only work in 5 parts known to have been written by him.

Etruria. Factory opened by Josiah *Wedgwood.

Ettrick Shepherd, The. Pseud. of James *Hogg.

Etty William (1787–1849). English painter best remembered for his studies of the nude, e.g. *The Bather* (Tate).

étude. The term often retained for *studies by Chopin, Liszt and other composers.

étui. A small tapering box or pendant case designed to hold an 'equipage' of, for example, sewing or drawing implements. Such objects were popular in the 18th c. and later, and examples are often found in gold, silver, enamel or *pinchbeck and could be suspended from matching chatelaines.

Eugene Onegin. Poem by *Pushkin. Tchaikovsky based his opera (1879) on it, collaborating with K. S. Shilovsky for the libretto.

Eugénie Grandet (1833). Novel by *Balzac.

Eugenius II bishop of Toledo (7th c.). The greatest of the Spanish Visigothic poets in Latin; most of his poems are extremely beautiful melancholy lamentations on the brevity of life and the inevitability of death and decay. He also wrote an exquisite poem on a nightingale.

Eumenides, The. Third part of Aeschylus' dramatic trilogy, the **Oresteia*.

euphonium. Valved brass musical instrument of wide conical bore and played with a cup mouthpiece; it has a range of over 3 octaves from the B♭ below the bass staff. Also *tuba.

Euphronios (6th–5th c. B.C.). Greek potter and vase painter in the *red-figured style whose drawing showed a new interest in anatomical structure.

Euphues (1578–80). Prose romance by *Lyly.

eurhythmics. A system of expressing musical rhythms in movements of the body, designed to stimulate awareness of and response to rhythm, and claimed to increase general mental alertness. It was invented by E. *Jaques-Dalcroze.

Euripides (484–406 B.C.). Greek tragedian. Little is known of his life: the anonymous ancient biography proves to be a farrago of nonsensical anecdotes drawn from the comic theatre – he lived alone in a cave at Salamis; his mother was a greengrocer; he quarrelled unhappily with both his wives. But one reliable ancient source states that E. was well-born; among his friends is named Socrates, who would go to the theatre only to see E.'s plays. He won only 5 dramatic victories, but at Syracuse in 413 Athenian captives might save themselves from slavery by reciting E.'s choruses. Aristophanes quotes and parodies him constantly for his unconventional views, but after his death his popularity and influence eclipsed that of Aeschylus and Sophocles. He first produced in 455 and won his 1st victory in 441. He shared Aristophanes' antipathy to the great Peloponnesian War and towards the end

Etty. *The Bather*

Étui; grey striated agate with gold mounts; 18th c.

Euphonium

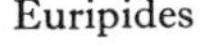

Euripides

Euphronios. *Rider*, *c.* 510 B.C.

Edith Evans as Millamant in *The Way of the World*

Euston Road school. Claude Rogers, *Cottage Bedroom*

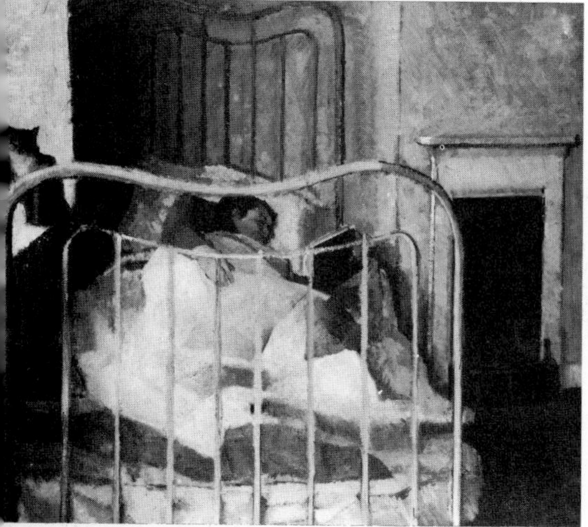

of his life left Athens for Macedon, where he died. That year Sophocles presented his chorus at the Dionysia in mourning, and the following year Aristophanes paid the last tribute of ridicule with *The Frogs*. Inheriting a tradition of myth, E. realized it in modern terms: the earliest play, **Alcestis* (438), shows his gift for naturalistic character drawing to conform with the deeds predicated of his actors by the legend. Many of the myths include acts of barbarous violence–matricide, parricide, infanticide, incest, adultery and perversion: E. shocked his contemporaries by portraying characters who might credibly appear capable of such acts, and since many of them are women he was mocked as being a misogynist. So his Hecuba, victim of war and bereavement, becomes a termagant; his Medea, who murdered her host as well as her own children, is savagely jealous; Electra, the matricide, is neurotic to the point of paranoia. At the same time he implicitly criticizes many of the legends for the picture they present of divinity: Apollo in the *Ion* is shown as a ruthless philanderer, Athene and Poseidon in *The Trojan Women* a pair of callous bargain-hunters, and Dionysus in *The Bacchae* a dangerous fanatic. But his scepticism does not extend to the fact of religion: in **Hippolytus* Artemis (chastity) and Aphrodite (love), though all but personified abstractions, represent real forces in the world, and in *The Bacchae* E. pleads the power of enthusiasm very strongly indeed: King Pentheus, who persecutes the votaries of Dionysus, himself suffers the ritual fate of the god–to be torn to pieces. E.'s aversion to war inspires several of the plays, notably *Hecuba* and *The Trojan Women*, which describes the fall of Troy and its consequences–murder and enslavement–from the point of view of the leading women of the city. E. seems to have chafed at the conventions of the Attic theatre: several of his most beautiful lyrics are inorganic, and the chorus seldom participates in the action. In this, and in his invention of the romantic tragedy with a happy ending, he foreshadowed the new comedy of the late 4th c. 17 tragedies out of more than 70 survive: *Alcestis* (438), **Medea* (331), *Hippolytus* (428), *Hecuba*, **Andromache*, *Herakleidae*, *The Suppliants*, *Hercules*, *The Trojan Women* (415), *Ion*, **Electra* (413?), *Helen* (412?), **Iphigenia in Tauris*, *Phoenissae*, **Orestes* (408), *The Bacchae*, **Iphigenia in Aulis* (unfinished): also the satyr play, *Cyclops*, and many hundreds of quotations.

Europeans, The (1878). Novel by Henry *James.

Euston Road school. A group of British artists, led by William Coldstream, Lawrence Gowing, Claude Rogers and Victor Pasmore who conducted a school (1938–9) of painting and drawing in London in which artists worked alongside their students. Realistic townscapes, landscapes and interiors were painted in opposition to the abstract and surrealist painting current in Britain.

Eutychides (4th–3rd c. B.C.). Greek sculptor, pupil of Lysippus and famous for his statue of Tyche (Fortune), tutelary goddess of Antioch in Syria, showing her seated on a cliff with the river god Orontes at her feet. There is a Roman copy in the Vatican.

Evans Sir Arthur John (1851–1941). English archaeologist whose discoveries of a pre-Phoenician script in Crete and the Late Bronze Age Palace of Minos at Knossos revealed a previously unknown civilization called by E. 'Minoan'. In books, and by actual reconstructions of the sites, he proposed interpretations later hotly disputed.

Evans Dame Edith (1888–). English actress who made her first appearance as an amateur in 1912. After this she toured with Ellen Terry, and in 1924 firmly made her reputation as Millamant in Congreve's *Way of the World*. Versatile, she has distinguished herself in parts such as Cleopatra, Portia, Lady Bracknell, Mrs Malaprop and Volumnia.

Evans Gil (1912–). Canadian/American *jazz arranger.

Evans Walker (1903–). U.S. photographer who worked with the Farm Security Administration under Roy *Stryker and did photographic essays illustrating such works as Hart Crane's *The Bridge* and James Agee's *Let Us Now Praise Famous Men*. E.'s work has been an important influence in shaping modern documentary photography.

Eve Nicolas. 16th-c. French bookbinder to Henry III, credited with some very handsome vols magnificently decorated with fleurs-de-lis in gold.

Evelina (1778). Novel by Fanny *Burney.

Walker Evans. *Graveyard in Easton*, Pennsylvania (1936)

Eutychides. Statue of Tyche and Orontes

Evelyn John (1620–1706). English writer, active Royalist, and founder-member of the Royal Society. Like his close friend Pepys, E. was a conscientious civil servant (many of his lesser works are on civic topics) and kept an important *Diary* (publ. posth. 1818, complete 1955). E.'s diary is less intimate than Pepys's, but covers a far longer period and contains accounts of court life. Works include *Sculptura* (on the art of engraving; 1662), *Architecure . . . Architects* . . . (trs. from French, 1664), and *Sylva* . . . (1664), recommending afforestation.

Everdingen Allart van (1621–75). Dutch landscape painter who visited Scandinavia (1640–4). His pictures of rough, romantic mountain scenery were the first of their kind in Holland and affected the later work of J. van Ruisdael.

Everdingen Cesar Boetius van (d. 1678). Dutch painter of portraits and mythological subjects in a highly finished Caravaggesque manner. He was the brother of Allart van E.

Everyman. 15th-c. English *morality play, probably of Dutch origin (*Elckerlyjk*). E. is called by Death; he finds that of his friends (Fellowship, Knowledge, Beauty, etc.) only Good Deeds will accompany him.

Every Man in his Humour (1598) and **Every Man out of his Humour** (1599). Comedies by Ben *Jonson.

Ewald Johannes (1743–81). Danish poet. After bitter disappointment in love as a young man, E. became increasingly embittered and dissipated, and his last years were passed as an invalid and in neglect and suffering. E., Denmark's greatest lyric poet, had a great influence; he returned to the sagas and mythology of Scandinavian folk-lore; and in his poetry he introduced a new freshness and vitality into Danish verse and like the pre-romantics in other countries, turned to nature for inspiration. His works include: the lyrical drama *Fiskerne* (1779), his greatest work and containing the words of the Danish national anthem; lyrical poems; and an important autobiography, *Levned og Meninger* (publ. 1804–8).

ewer. A jug used from early times with a basin for the washing of hands at table. Usually made of silver or pottery, they were large and elaborately decorated, and also performed an ornamental function. Common shapes were the baluster and the helmet.

Eworth Hans, or Jan Euworts, Flemish painter who worked chiefly in England (*c.* 1545–74). He painted portraits or flattered his patrons by including them in elaborate allegories close in style to the school of Fontainebleau, e.g. *Queen Elizabeth puts the Goddess to Flight* (Royal Colls). A mysterious and evocative work is *Sir John Luttrell Saved from Drowning* (Courtauld Gal., London).

Excursion, The (1814). Poem by *Wordsworth.

Exekias (6th c. B.C.). Greek potter and famous vase painter in the *black-figured style whose masterpiece is an amphora now in the Vatican showing Achilles and Ajax playing a game, possibly draughts. See also colour plate 1.

Exemplary Novels (1613). Coll. of stories by *Cervantes.

Exeter Book, The (10th c.). Coll. of Old English poems in Exeter cathedral.

Exeter cathedral England. Apart from the towers over the transepts, a church entirely in the *decorated style (1275–1350). The principle of bay-division gives way to that of clustered shafts from which the ribs fan out at the top like palm leaves; 11 tierceron ribs radiate from each pier but there are as yet no liernes.

Exiles (written 1914). Play by James Joyce.

existentialism. Modern philosophical and religious tendency or set of attitudes rather than a doctrine or school; but of great influence on 20th-c. art, especially on literature. Existentialist attitudes stem above all from *Kierkegaard, but owe something to Dostoyevsky and Nietzsche. The characteristic of existentialist thought is its religious approach to life (this in spite of the atheism of Sartre and Camus): it employs such concepts as choice, responsibility, anguish, commitment. E. represents a reaction against determinism, against preoccupation with the abstract and universal, stressing the individual's responsibility to make choices–and, in effect, moral judgements–in concrete and particular (and therefore complex and difficult) situations. Of modern writers and philosophers only Sartre

John Evelyn: engraving after Kneller

Everdingen. *Rocky Landscape with Saw-mill*

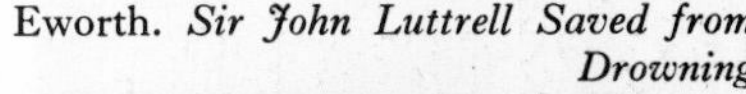

Eworth. *Sir John Luttrell Saved from Drowning*

Exekias. *Achilles and Ajax*

Ewer. London, 1765

Exeter cathedral

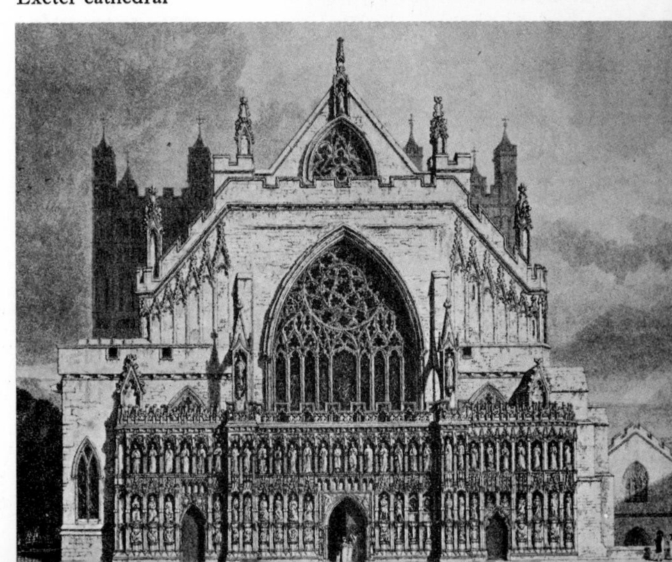

Expressionism. Van Gogh, *Grove of Cypresses*

Expressionism. Munch, *Dance of Life*

Expressionism. Rouault, *Three Clowns*

Expressionism. Soutine, *Femme de Profil*

Expressionism. Permeke, *Les Fiancés*

Expressionism. Zadkine, *Van Gogh drawing*

Expressionism. De Kooning, *Gotham News*

calls himself an existentialist; but the term is applied with some justice to, e.g., the German philosophers Jaspers and Heidegger, and Camus and Gabriel Marcel.

Exodus. Sometimes called the 2nd book of Moses. 2nd book of the *Bible (Old Testament) containing the epic account of the Jewish liberation from slavery in Egypt and their wanderings in search of 'the promised land'.

exposition. Musical term for (1) the 1st section in *sonata form in which the main subjects are proclaimed; (2) those sections of a *fugue in which the subject is successively given in the various voices.

expressionism. Term used to describe works of art in which reality is distorted in order to express the artists' emotions or inner vision, e.g. in painting, emotional impact is heightened by deliberate use of strong colours, distortion of form, etc. In this sense, the paintings of El Greco and Grünewald are sometimes called expressionist, though the term is usually restricted to artists of the last 100 years. Thus Van Gogh in painting and Strindberg in drama are regarded as the forerunners of modern e.
An overtly expressionist movement developed in the German theatre after World War I (Kaiser, Toller) and there are expressionist elements in the work of, e.g., O'Neill, O'Casey and Brecht; in other branches of literature there has been no avowed expressionist movement, though similar effects have frequently been sought (e.g. by Kafka).
The most conscious expressionist movements, however, have been in the visual arts, notably Die *Brücke and *Blaue Reiter groups in Germany. Munch's influence was strong in Germany; his work had been shown in exhibitions and admired since the 1890s.
Other important expressionist painters are Oskar Kokoschka, Chaim Soutine, Georges Rouault and Max Beckmann (his later allegorical works). Ossip Zadkine and Ernst Barlach are important expressionist sculptors. A group of expressionist painters formed round Constant Permeke at Laethem-Saint-Martin in the Netherlands, including Gustave de Smet, Fritz van der Berghe and Franz Masereel. In France the work of Édouard Georg, François Gruber, Gromaire and Bernard Buffet is also described as expressionist.
The term e. is sometimes used of architecture, e.g. of the work of Peter Behrens and Eric Mendelsohn (the Einstein Tower at Potsdam, 1920), and of the picturesque Goetheanum built by Rudolf Steiner. There was much contact between architects and other artists after

Jan van Eyck.
Man in a Red Turban (detail)

World War I, especially in the *November group.

ABSTRACT EXPRESSIONISM describes the free abstract painting of Jackson Pollock, Willem de Kooning, Clyfford Still, Mark Rothko and others. Much of this painting excludes any sort of representation, but not all: there are human figures in some of de Kooning's work. The term usually refers to painting from the U.S., but it has also been extended to precursors (especially Kandinsky) and European artists such as Appel.

In music the work of certain 20th-c. composers, notably Schoenberg, is sometimes described as expressionistic. Characteristic features of such music are free rhythm, marked contrasts in instrumentation, extremes of pitch, and rapid changes in melodic direction. In a general sense e. in music can be considered as the final stage in the emphasis on subjective emotion introduced by the romantic composers.

Exter Alexandra (1884–1949). Russian futurist and abstract painter; she emigrated to Paris in 1924. She is important chiefly as a theatrical designer for Tairov, director of the Kamerny Theatre in Moscow; famous productions were for *Salome* (1917) and *Romeo and Juliet* (1921).

extravaganza. A stage entertainment, of an extravagent kind, with music; similar to a burlesque. Thus Gilbert and Sullivan's *Trial by Jury* is subtitled 'an Extravaganza'. A purely musical e. is simply a fanciful light-hearted work in free form.

Eyck Jan van (*c.* 1390–1441) and Hubert or Hubrecht (d. 1426). Early Netherlands painters. The great altarpiece of the cathedral of St Bavon, Ghent (*The Adoration of the Lamb*) bears an inscription stating that the work was begun by Hubert van Eyck and completed by Jan. This inscription has been a stumbling-block to scholars ever since. A number of attempts have been made to separate the work of the 2 brothers, but none has been universally accepted. Hubert's name appears only on the Ghent altarpiece, while signed and dated works by Jan are numerous.

Despite these difficulties of attribution, Jan emerges as unquestionably the greatest artist of the early Netherlands school. He was probably born at Maaseyck near Maastricht. From 1422 to 1424 he was in the service of John of Bavaria, Count of Holland. On the count's death he joined the court of Duke Philip the Good of Burgundy at Lille, acting as his envoy on missions to Spain (1426) and to Portugal (1428). From 1430 he lived at Bruges. Thereafter there is evidence of his increasing wealth and importance as a court painter, diplomat and city official of Bruges.

The earliest works attributed to Jan are the miniatures identified in 1902 as the *Turin-Milan Book of Hours*, some pages of which are in the M. Civ., Turin.

The Eycks' clarity and realism were revered and sometimes imitated, but they proved too difficult for most painters to follow and there was an inevitable reaction against such work. Although the tradition that one or other of the brothers was the inventor of oil paint has been disproved, their mastery of the technique and the improvements they introduced undoubtedly changed the whole nature of the medium. Jan's pupil, Petrus Christus, may have been responsible for teaching the secrets of the technique to Antonello da Messina and the Italians.

Jan executed a number of large commissions for donors who presented them to churches. Among these are *The Virgin of Chancellor Rolin* (Louvre), *Virgin and Child and the Canon van der Paele* (M. Com., Bruges), *Virgin and Child with Saints and a Carthusian* (Frick Coll., New York). Similar subjects are *The Virgin and Child in a Church* (Dahlem, Berlin), *The Annunciation* (N.G., Washington, Mellon Coll.) and the *Virgin and Child*, a triptych (Dresden Gal.). Among his portraits are the early *Tymotheos* (N.G., London), *The Painter's wife, Margaret* (M. Com., Bruges), *Man in a Red Turban* (N.G., London) and *Cardinal Niccolo Albergati* (K. Mus., Vienna). Perhaps the best known of his paintings is the *Arnolfini Marriage Group* (N.G., London), which is at the same time, a double-portrait of great psychological insight, a meticulously rendered interior and one of the 1st genre paintings. The greatest aspect of Jan's genius was in depicting such a scene with the utmost clarity and naturalism and yet creating from apparently mundane subjects a mystery so rich that it has eluded all analysis.

Eyeless in Gaza (1936). Novel by Aldous *Huxley.

Ezekiel. One of the books of the *Bible (Old Testament), 3rd of the books of the 'Major Prophets'; it contains the life of the priest E. (6th c. B.C.) and his prophecies of the fall and ultimate restoration of Jerusalem.

Ezra and **Nehemiah** (3rd c. B.C.). One of the books of the *Bible (Old Testament), probably a continuation of *Chronicles, usually divided into 2 books in Christian editions. It contains accounts of the return of the Israelites from their Babylonian captivity and the rebuilding of the walls of Jerusalem by Nehemiah.

Jan van Eyck. Ghent altarpiece, showing the 2 outer wings. Also *The *Adoration of the Lamb*, *grisaille and colour plate 38

Jan van Eyck. *The Virgin of Chancellor Rolin*

Faïence tulipière; French

F

Fabritius. *Self-portrait*

Fabri. *Professor Hannibal*

fable. A story about animals behaving like human beings, and having a moral. The 1st great coll. of European tradition is that of *Aesop; La Fontaine is the greatest fabulist of modern times but many other writers have used the form.

Fable, A (1954). Novel by William Faulkner.

Fables choisies, mises en vers (1668–94). Book of fables by *La Fontaine.

fabliaux. Name given to verse short stories written in 12th- and 13th-c. France. They are humorous and usually have sex as the theme.

Fabre Ferdinand (1827–98). French writer. His novels, e.g. *L'Abbé Tigrane* (1873) and *L'Abbé Roitelet* (1890), are set in rural Provence and are penetrating in their treatment of the country priest.

Fabre d'Olivet Antoine (1767–1825). French writer whose *Le Troubadour, poésies occitaniques* (1803) was a mixture of genuine and forged texts and trs of medieval verse in *Provençal and *langue d'oc* dialects.

Fabri Zoltán (1917–). Hungarian film director. His reputation outside Hungary is based on *Merry-go-Round* (1955), influenced by *Welles, and particularly *Professor Hannibal* (1957), about the persecution of a schoolmaster with unorthodox historical ideas. This latter is perhaps the best post-war Hungarian movie to have reached the West.

Fabritius Carel. Name used by Carel Pietersz (1622–54), Dutch painter, killed in the explosion of the powder-magazine at Delft, which probably also destroyed many of his paintings. The few surviving pictures show him to have been technically very accomplished. He was the pupil of Rembrandt and the master of Vermeer. One of his most interesting paintings is the small *View of Delft* (N.G., London) in which the unique planned perspective shows F.'s interest in creating optical illusions. Other works are: *Man in a Fur Cap* (N.G., London), the strong *Self-portrait* (Boymans-Van Beuningen Mus., Rotterdam) and the popular *Goldfinch* (Mauritshuis).

faburdon: *fauxbourdon

façade. In architecture, the main face of a building.

Façade. A group of poems by Edith Sitwell using words for sound effects rather than meaning. A selection, recited in strict rhythm against music for a chamber ensemble by Sir W. Walton, was given as an entertainment privately at the Sitwells' house (1922), publicly in 1923. Walton arranged 2 orchestral suites from the music and F. Ashton choreographed a ballet (1931).

Face, The (1958). Film directed by I. *Bergman.

Face in the Crowd, A (1957). Film directed by E. *Kazan.

faceting. Grinding a piece of glass so as to give it a number of flat surfaces, often producing diamond shapes. This technique does not appear on English glasses until the 1st half of the 18th c. but by then it was already highly developed in Germany. It appears on Middle Eastern glass as early as the 8th c. In England it was generally used on the bowl or the stem; English 18th-c. lead-glass was particularly suited to the technique as it brought out its brilliance and clarity.

facing. Architectural term for a covering of material on the face of a wall, concealing a core of inferior material, e.g. a marble f. over a brick core.

fade: *film techniques

Fadeyev Alexander Alexandrovich (1901–56). Soviet novelist. F.'s *The Nineteen* (1927; 1929), a description of the Civil War, influenced many later Soviet writers.

Faerie Queen, The (1589, 1596). Poem by *Spenser.

fagott, fagotto. German and Italian names for *bassoon.

Faguet Émile (1847–1916). French literary critic. His works include: *Les Grands Maîtres du XVII Siècle* (1885), *Le XIX Siècle* (1887) and *Notes sur le Théâtre contemporain* (1889–91). He also wrote monographs on Voltaire, Flaubert and Zola.

faïence. Pottery term, derived from Faenza, an important centre of *maiolica, but adopted in several European countries to describe

Douglas Fairbanks Sr in *The Thief of Bagdad*

Falconet. *Peter the Great*

Falk. *The Journalist Refalov*

De Falla: drawing by Picasso (1920)

painted tin-glazed earthenware in general; in England it is increasingly used to describe wares produced from the middle of the 17th c. and outside the maiolica tradition–either original or in Delft-Chinese style. In an archaeological context f. denotes the glazed quartz frit-ware of the ancient Egyptians.

failli. A ballet step in which the dancer jumps from the 4th or 5th *position, makes a quarter-turn and lands on one foot with the other extended behind, then swishes the working leg through to the front.

Fairbanks Douglas Sr (1883–1939). U.S. film star; the all-American, athletic optimist–star of swashbuckling romance, thrilling adventure and daredevil stunting. His films include: *Mark of Zorro* (1920), *Robin Hood* (1922), *The Thief of Bagdad* (1924) and *The Black Pirate* (1926). His son DOUGLAS F. Jr (1909–) played the same kind of roles.

Fairburn A(rthur) R(ex) D(ugard) (1904–58). New Zealand poet. *The Disadvantages of Being Dead* (1958) embodies most fully the engaging qualities evident in his poetry written during the 1930s. The same incisive wit exists beneath a new maturity, while the earlier stridency has disappeared.

Fairweather Ian (1890–). Scottish-born painter. A life of adventurous wandering took him to China and the East Indies, where he did much painting. He visited Australia in 1933 and settled there after World War II, becoming the leading abstract painter working there.

Fairy Queen, The (1692). An anon. adaptation, possibly by E. Settle, of *A Midsummer Night's Dream* by Shakespeare; Purcell wrote the incidental music.

Faithful Shepheardesse, The. Play by John *Fletcher.

Falconer William (1732–69). Scottish poet, author of *The Shipwreck* (1762), vividly describing a shipwreck of which F. was a survivor.

Falconet Étienne-Maurice (1716–91). French sculptor. He was a pupil of J.-B. Lemoyne and director of sculpture at Sèvres (1757–66). For Sèvres biscuitware he produced many graceful rococo models. His masterpiece was a monumental equestrian statue of Peter the Great (St Petersburg) in the baroque tradition.

Falconetti Renée (1893–1946). French actress; a distinguished stage performer, but also famous for a single appearance in films–as Joan in Dreyer's *The Passion of Joan of Arc* (1928).

Falk Robert (1886–1958). Russian painter and a founder of the Muscovite *Knave of Diamonds group. Cézanne was the most important influence on F., although during the 1920s he gradually evolved a more personal vision and technique. Still-life, portrait and landscape subjects predominate. As a teacher in Moscow he was important to less academic young artists.

Falkner John Meade (1858–1932). English novelist, poet and armaments manufacturer. *Moonfleet* (1898), his classic adventure story, was followed by *The Nebuly Coat* (1903), a murder story partly satirizing Sir G. Scott the Victorian architect.

Fall, The (1956). Novel by *Camus.

Falla Manuel de (1876–1946). Spanish composer. After 2 years under F. Pedrell, F. lived in Paris (1907–14) meeting there Debussy, Dukas and Ravel; from 1940 he lived in Argentina. F.'s music derives its most powerful inspiration from Spanish folk-music, life and landscape. His works include: the ballet *The Three Cornered Hat* with choreography by Massine, produced by Diaghilev in 1919; the rhapsodic *Nights in the Gardens of Spain* for piano and orchestra (1916); and the ambitious and unfinished *La Atlantida* (performed posth. 1961) for chorus, soloists and orchestra, completed by E. *Halffter.

Fall of the House of Usher, The (1839). Short story by Edgar Allan *Poe; also made into films directed by J. *Epstein (1928) and R. *Corman (1960).

false relation. In music the term describes the effect when a note and its sharpened or flattened unison or 8ve occur simultaneously or in immediate succession in different parts. For example f. r. would occur if $C\natural$ were followed by $C\sharp$ or if middle C were followed by $C\flat$ the 8ve above. The U.S. term is 'cross-relation'.

Famille verte; K'ang Hsi period. Confucian literati entertaining themselves

Famille noire; early K'ang Hsi period

Fantin-Latour. *Homage to Manet. Standing:* Schoederer, Renoir, Zola, Maître, Bazille, Monet. *Seated:* Manet, Astruc

falsetto. A high register of a man's voice, the 'fossil' as it were of his boy's voice. The register can be developed as a true singing voice to give the counter-tenor or male alto and, exceptionally, a male soprano. In the 16th c., Spanish falsettists were famous in Europe, singing the soprano parts in the Papal choir; on their decline *castrati took their place.

Falstaff. Opera by *Verdi, libretto by A. Boito; 1st performance in Milan in 1893.

famille noire, rose, and verte. Enamelled porcelain wares of the Chinese *Ch'ing dynasty and especially of its K'ang Hsi period (1662–1722), in which 5-colour decoration painted in enamel colours, and usually of flowers, dragons, sometimes landscapes, appears over the glaze on a background of black, rose or green. Also used of European porcelain in which the same technique is used.

Family Chronicle (1856). Novel by *Aksakov.

Family Reunion, The (1939). Play by T. S. Eliot.

Fanck Dr Arnold (1889–). German director of a notable series of mountaineering films, e.g. *The White Hell of Pitz Palu* (1929).

fancy. In music, alternative term for *fantasy.

Fancy Free. 1-act ballet with choreography by *Robbins, music by Leonard Bernstein, scenery by Oliver Smith and costumes by Kermit Love; 1st performance 1944.

fandango. Lively Spanish dance in triple time; the music is usually a song accompanied by guitar, castanets (or drum) and bagpipes (or shawm).

fanfare. A call or flourish for trumpets for military or ceremonial purposes. Composers have used the f. in opera and are occasionally asked to write elaborate f.s for coronations, etc.

Fanny Hill. Heroine of John *Cleland's erotic novel *Memoirs of a Woman of Pleasure* (*c.*1750).

fantasia: *fantasy

Fantasia (1940). Animated film produced by Walt *Disney.

Fantastic Symphony. English title for *Berlioz's *Symphonie fantastique: épisode de la vie d'un artiste* (1830).

Fantin-Latour Ignace-Henri-Jean-Théodore (1836–1904). French painter, especially of flowers and a few large group portraits. F.-L. studied under his father and under Courbet. In his *Homage to Manet* (1869) and *Homage to Delacroix* (1864) (both Louvre) he included many of the leading artists of his day and he repeated this formula for group portraits of writers and musicians. A fine single portrait of Manet is in the A. Inst., Chicago. F.-L. was friendly with a number of the most advanced contemporary artists. Of his many studies of flowers *Bouquet of Dahlias* (Birmingham A. Gal.) is typical.

Fantomas (1913–14). Film serial directed by L. *Feuillade.

farandole (derivation uncertain). Provençal dance in a rhythmically accentuated 6:8 measure. A chain of dancers, holding hands, weaves through the town; the best-known f. is that of the festival of the Tarasque at Tarascon. A f. appears in Bizet's *L'Arlésienne.*

farce. A form of comedy involving highly improbable situations, mistaken identity, disguise, concealment, slapstick, etc. It flourished in France in the 17th c. under Molière and has been popular ever since. Most farce nowadays has small literary merit but high entertainment value.

Farewell Symphony (1772). Nickname of Haydn's symphony no. 45 in F♯ min.

Farewell to Arms (1929). Novel by *Hemingway.

Fargue Léon-Paul (1878–1947). French poet and a founder-member of the *Nouvelle Revue Française.* Poems of his symbolist period, influenced by Verlaine, include the coll. *Tancrède* (in book form 1911); those of his cubist period the colls *Espaces* and *Sous la Lampe* (1929). His reminiscences of Paris literary life are contained in *Le Piéton de Paris* (1939).

Farinelli. The name used by Carlo Broschi (1705–82), an Italian castrato male soprano singer; legendary for his power, breath control, imaginative and virtuoso ornamentation and expressive singing. He was a pupil of Porpora, singing in his Italian opera in London (1734–6). From 1737 to 1759 F. was at Madrid serving Philip V (whose depressive melancholia he relieved by his singing) and Ferdinand VI. Besides founding an Italian opera in Madrid F. gained considerable political influence.

Farington Joseph (1747–1821). English landscape and topographical draughtsman. He became an influential member of the R.A. (elected 1785) and his *Diary* (publ. 1922–8) provides one of the chief sources for our knowledge of English painting and the R.A. in the late 18th–early 19th cs.

Farleigh Richard of. 14th-c. English architect who designed the tower and spire of Salisbury cathedral, one of the masterpieces of the decorated style. He is also known to have worked at Exeter cathedral.

Farmer John. English organist and composer of the late 16th–early 17th c. F. contributed to T. *East's *Whole Booke of Psalmes* and to T. Morley's *The Triumphs of Oriana*. He also publ. a set of madrigals.

Farnaby Giles (*c.* 1560–1640?). English composer. He contributed to T. *East's *Whole Booke of Psalmes* and T. Ravenscroft's *Psalter*; apart from this only 20 canzonets for 4 voices (1598) and 52 pieces in the **Fitzwilliam Virgnali Book* survive. His music frequently has bold chromatic harmonies, e.g. the canzonet 'Construe my meaning', and his advanced and florid keyboard style is second only to Byrd's.

Farnese Palace Rome: Antonio da *Sangallo the Younger

Farquhar George (1678?–1707). Irish dramatist and actor. F.'s spirited comedies were extremely successful, satisfying the new public taste for more vigour, good-nature and sentiment than Restoration comedy had provided. F.'s most important works are *The Constant Couple . . .* (1699), *The Recruiting Officer* (1706), inspired by his experiences as an officer in the army, and *The Beaux' Stratagem* (1707).

Farrant Richard (d. *c.* 1580). English composer and gentleman of the Chapel Royal. His few surviving works include a service, 3 anthems and a secular song, apparently the only remnant of the incidental music he wrote for the annual plays produced before Elizabeth I.

Farrebique (1946). Film directed by G. *Rouquier.

Farrell James T(homas) (1904–). U.S. novelist. His subject is usually downtown city life, his treatment frank and ruthlessly naturalistic, his techniques of character presentation frequently *stream-of-consciousness. His best-known work is the *Studs Lonigan* trilogy (1932–5).

Farren William (1725–95). Head of a distinguished English theatrical family; he played in the 1st performances of *The School for Scandal* and *The Critic*. His 2 sons, PERCIVAL (1784–1843) and, in particular, WILLIAM (1786–1861) also made their impact in the theatre and William's granddaughter was ELLEN F. (1848–1904), renowned for her playing of boys' parts.

Farron Julia (1922–). British dancer who joined the Sadler's Wells Ballet in 1936. She developed as a classical and demi-caractère soloist, dancing many roles ranging from the Red Queen in *Checkmate* to the Prostitute in *Miracle in the Gorbals*.

Farrow John (1904–63). Australian-born U.S. film director. His best work is found in a group of westerns including *Hondo* (1954). He received an Academy Award (with 2 others) for the script of *Around the World in 80 Days* and directed the 1st Bronston spectacular, *John Paul Jones* (1959).

Farwell Arthur (1872–1952). U.S. composer and teacher; his teachers included Humperdinck and Guilmant. He studied American-Indian music and founded the Wa-Wan Press to publ. American music, particularly that showing Indian influences. These are often apparent in his work, e.g. *Dawn* for chamber orchestra and piano pieces. He also wrote stage works and *Symbolist Studies* for orchestra.

Fast Howard (1914–). U.S. novelist of leftist convictions and associated with Communism up to the 1950s. His novels, many historical, express his libertarian convictions. They include *The Last Frontier* (1941) and *Spartacus* (1958).

Father, The (1887). Play by *Strindberg.

Father Brown, The Innocence of (1911). Coll. of stories by G. K. *Chesterton.

Farinelli (centre) with Metastasio (left) and Amigoni, who painted the picture

James T. Farrell

Farington. *Worcester Cathedral and the Canons' Houses*

Farleigh. Salisbury cathedral

William Faulkner

Fautrier. *La Mare aux Grenouilles* (1957)

Gabriel Fauré

Faulkner William (Harrison) (1897–1962). U.S. novelist, short-story writer, Nobel prize-winner (1949). His fiction, which in recent years has been acclaimed in America and throughout the world, deals chiefly with the American South, where he was born, lived and died. He turned the South into a mythical, universal land painfully suffering the turmoil, conflict and corruption of 20th-c. humanity. In many novels he gave historical treatment to his fictional Yoknapatawpha County, with its county seat, Jefferson, and its famous families (Sartorises, Compsons, McCaslins, Snopeses, etc.). Some are comic and show an inventiveness of incident and character creation recalling the lighter Dickens, but it is the dark, symbolic Dickens who is recalled by the major works, with their melodrama, symbolism, and profound revelation. F.'s South is at once the promised land and a land cursed by slavery, a land of great resources for full humanity and also for extreme corruption and violence. Agrarian richness raped by industrialization is a recurrent theme, worked out in relation to a dense social structure, and with an interpretative tone that owes much to the Bible. His complex method of presentation, his use of the extended sentence, the interior monologue and of moments of stasis in the action can repel the reader, but it is usually his most technically ambitious books that are the most successful. His 3rd novel, *Sartoris* (1929), begins his maturity. Thereafter came *The Sound and the Fury* (1929), *As I Lay Dying* (1930), *Light in August* (1932), *Absalom, Absalom!* (1936), *The Unvanquished* (1938) and *The Hamlet* (1940), forming the body of his best work. *Sanctuary* (1931), written as a potboiler, is his most sensational novel, *A Fable* (1954) his chief failure. *These Thirteen* (1931) and *Doctor Martino* (1934) contain some of his most remarkable short stories.

Fauré Gabriel (Urbain) (1845–1924). French composer and organist. He studied at the École Niedermeyer, Paris (1854–65), meeting Saint-Saëns there. F. himself joined the staff (1872) and became professor of composition at the Conservatoire (1896) and director in 1905. Despite his encroaching deafness, he retired only in 1920. F.'s pupils included Ravel and Enesco. At first showing clear romantic influences and a melodically and harmonically elegant style, his music increasingly used modulation and his last works verged towards the atonal. His refined esoteric music is at its best in the poetically intense song cycles *La Bonne Chanson* (1892–3) and *La Chanson d'Eve* (1906–10). Other works are the *Requiem* (1887), the 2nd violin sonata (1917) and 2 piano quintets. He also wrote incidental music (1898) to Maeterlinck's *Pelléas et Mélisande*, piano music, many songs and the operatic work *Penelope* (1913).

Faust. In European legend a magician who sells his soul to the Devil in return for a period of years of liberty and luxury. Legends on this theme crystallized round the historical figure of the German Dr Johannes Faust (d. *c.* 1540); the *Faustbuch*, publ. in German (1587) and soon followed by an English trs., was the basis of *Marlowe's and *Goethe's tragedies. Goethe's play was the basis for an opera, *Faust* (1859), by Gounod with libretto by J.-P. Barbier and M. Carré, and a dramatic legend, *The Damnation of Faust* (1846), by Berlioz. The legend also inspired Thomas *Mann's novel *Doktor Faustus* (1949) and a film (1925) directed by F. W. *Murnau.

Fautrier Jean (1898–1961). French painter whose informal abstracts of the late 1920s anticipated by some years the similar works of Tobey and Pollock. During World War II he secretly painted a series of *Hostages*, abstract symbols of protest against German occupation of France; in these, and the later series of *Nudes and Objects*, pictorial image and surface texture become unified in amorphous impasto shapes.

fauvism. A style of painting in which colours are the all-important theme of the work. The art critic Louis Vauxcelles described a room at the 1905 Salon d'Automne in which a sculpture in a classical style by Albert Marquet was surrounded by paintings of Matisse and others as '*Donatello parmi les fauves*' (i.e. 'Donatello among the beasts'). A divisionist style gave way to flat patterns and free, bold handling of colour (influenced by the work of Van Gogh). The most important members of the group were Matisse (the leader), Marquet, Derain, Vlaminck, Friesz, Dufy, Kees van Dongen and for a short time Braque; Rouault, friendly with the group, worked in a markedly different style. F. gave way to cubism after a few years.

fauxbourdon. In 15th-c. music, a system of composition in 3 parts. The top 2 parts (the top one giving the *cantus firmus) move in parallel 4ths.

Fauvism. Vlaminck, *The Painter's House*

Fauvism. Marquet, *André Rouveyre*

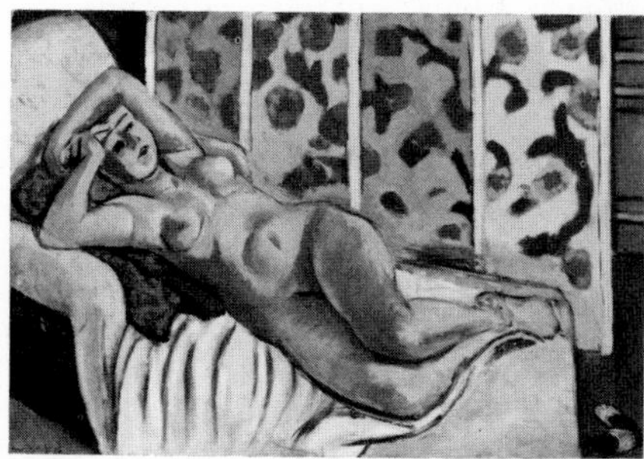

Fauvism. Matisse, *Nu au Canapé Jaune*

Faux-Monnayeurs, Les (1926). Novel by *Gide.

Favart Charles-Simon (1710–92). French playwright, an important figure in the development of the *opéra-comique*. Works include *La Chercheuse d'esprit* (1741) and *Les Trois Sultanes* (1761).

Fay the brothers Frank (1870–1931) and William George (1872–1947). Irish actors prominent in the Irish National Theatre Society; they were mainly responsible for the style of acting associated with the *Abbey Theatre.

Fayrfax Robert (1464?–1521). English composer. He was a member of the Chapel Royal and from 1502 organist at St Albans abbey. F.'s greatest music is in the masses and motets –passages of 3-part polyphony contrast with 5-part sections forming climaxes; the harmony is austere, the rhythm frequently intricate and the counterpoint conceived in long phrases using imitation sparingly. Some secular part songs survive, and two 5-part magnificats.

Fear and Trembling (1843). Book by Kierkegaard.

Fearing Kenneth (1902–61). U.S. poet and novelist; a major theme was the mechanical nature of urban society. Apart from verse he wrote the well-known thriller, *The Big Clock* (1946).

Federal Theater. U.S. theatre (1935–9), part of the Works Progress Administration (*W.P.A.) established to give work to actors and to establish theatres in areas where there were none. Its great artistic success included the 'Living Newspaper', i.e. short dramatic commentaries on contemporary themes; performances of the classics and great modern plays; and the formation of a Negro theatre. Its popular success was equally great but it was closed by Congress on political grounds.

Fedorovich Sophie (1893–1953). Russian artist who in 1920 came to Britain where she created décor for many ballets. She became artistic adviser to the Sadler's Wells Ballet and among ballets she worked on were *Dante Sonata* (1940) and *Symphonic Variations* (1946). Her designs were always recognizable for their simplicity and complete reflection of the ballet's mood.

Fedotov Pavel Andreyevich (1815–53). Russian satirical genre painter who depicted the manners of the urban bourgeoisie and the army. His satire now appears harmless and so discreet as to be hardly noticeable, but it nevertheless received official censure. His choice of commonplace subjects broke with contemporary idealist theories.

Feher Imre (1926–). Hungarian film director. His most famous film, *A Sunday Romance* (1957), was one of the small group of films which received wide distribution during the short period of the Hungarian cinema's international fame–after the 1956 Revolution. Its story is a bitter-sweet period romance with political implications.

Fehrs Johann Hinrich (1838–1916). Low German short-story writer and novelist; most of his work describes village life in Holstein.

Feinberg Samuel Evgenyevich (1890–). Russian composer and pianist. His work, a continuation of that of Scriabin and Miaskovsky, includes 2 piano concertos, works for piano and songs.

Feininger Andreas (1906–). German-born U.S. photographer, trained at the Bauhaus. F., one of the master technicians of this c., has concerned himself with exploring the physical limits of the medium, doing unusual and experimental work in all aspects of the field, from micro-photography and infra-red photography to extreme wide-angle and telephoto work. He has written several books of advanced technical information. He has worked for a long time with *Time* magazine.

Feininger Lyonel (1871–1956). Painter, born in New York of German-American parents. All the early influences upon him were subsequently reflected in the subjects of his paintings: music, toy making, Manhattan skyscrapers, trains, bridges and ships. F. studied music in Berlin, then became a cartoonist, first for German, later for French and American journals. In Paris he came into contact with the work of R. Delaunay and the cubists. From 1913 he made Germany his home, associating himself with the Blaue Reiter group under Franz Marc, and later teaching at the Bauhaus in Weimar and Dessau. In 1924, F. joined W. Kandinsky, P. Klee and A. von Jawlensky in Die *Blaue Vier ('The Blue Four'). Named among the 'degenerate' artists by Hitler's

Fedotov. *The Major's Matchmaking*

Andreas Feininger. *Oil Derricks, Signal Hill, California*

Lyonel Feininger. *Bicycle Riders*

Fedorovich. *Dante Sonata*

Lyonel Feininger. *Grützturm*

Feke. *The Reverend Thomas Hiscox*

Fénelon

government, F. returned to the U.S., where his teaching, writings and last watercolours were influential in the birth of abstract expressionist painting. F.'s art altered from the early works of child-like fantasy to 'dynamic orchestrations', in which the forms of buildings, the masts and sails of ships, the rays of the sun, etc. appear to radiate like the spokes of a wheel, or to mass like the pipes of a giant organ, e.g. *Grützturm in Treptow* (Landesmus., Darmstadt), *Gilmeroda VIII, 1921* (Whitney M. of A., New York).

Feke Robert (*fl.* 1741–50). Colonial American portrait painter who worked mainly in Philadelphia and Boston and was possibly taught by the English painter Smibert. Strong characterization and an emphasis on elaborate dress give distinction to his rather stereotyped poses.

Félibrige, Le. Movement to revive the use of the Provençal language; it began (1854) with a meeting between 7 poets, including F. *Mistral and J. *Roumanille.

Felix Krull, The Confessions of (1954). Comic novel by Thomas *Mann; he publ. an early version of the novel in 1922.

Fell Dr John (1625–86). Dean of Christ Church, Oxford, later bishop of Oxford. As patron of the Univ. Press he introduced a coll. of types from the Netherlands. F. was responsible for the rebuilding of Christ Church Tower. His name was made familiar by the epigram of Tom *Brown:

I do not love thee, Dr Fell,
The Reason why I cannot tell.

Fellini Federico (1920–). Italian film director. He wrote scripts for *Rossellini, e.g. *Roma Città Aperta*, before collaborating with *Lattuada on the direction of *Luci del Varietà* (1950). In his own films F. presents direct, simple, emotionally rather than intellectually conceived studies of people in a complex environment or situation. He directed *Lo Sciecco Bianco* (1952), and established a style and reputation with *I Vitelloni* (1953), a partly autobiographical study of young men in a provincial town. *La Strada* (1954), *Il Bidone* (1955) and *Le Notti di Cabiria* (1957) showed a full-blown emotionalism that threatened to become facile. *La Dolce Vita* (1959) is more like *I Vitelloni*, though now the central figure is older, lost in the grotesque corruption of modern Rome. *8½* (1963), showed this man's confusion to be also F.'s, elaborately portrayed in terms of a mingling of reality and dream, past and present. A similar technique is used in *Giulietta degli Spiriti* (1965), F's 1st colour feature.

Fellowes The Rev. Edmund Horace (1870–1951). English music scholar responsible for the 1st comprehensive eds of English Elizabethan and Jacobean music though his ed. methods are in some points now rejected. He produced the *English Madrigal School* (36 vols 1913–24), the *English School of Lutenist Song Writers* (32 vols 1920–32) and a complete ed. of W. Byrd's works (20 vols 1937–50).

Feltre Vittorino da: *Vittorino da Feltre

feminine ending. In English verse, the term for a line with an extra, unstressed syllable at the end. It occurs very frequently, e.g. in the basically iambic pentameters (*metre) of Keats's *Endymion*:

A thing of beauty is a joy for ever.

Femme de Nulle Part, La (1922). Film directed by L. *Delluc.

Femmes savantes, Les (1672). Play by Molière.

Fenby Eric (1906–). English composer. He became secretary to the paralysed F. Delius and took down 7 works at his dictation.

Fénelon François de Salignac (or Salagnac) de la Mothe (1651–1715). French theologian and writer whose *Traité de l'éducation des filles* (1687) gained the attention of Bossuet and Mme de Maintenon; but the quietism and political criticism in his later works led to his exile to his diocese of Cambrai. F. wrote a natural yet harmonious prose; his many works include the *Explication des maximes des Saints* (1697), the *Dialogues des Morts* (1700–18) and *Télémaque* (1699).

Fenton Roger (1819–69). British photographer who undertook the world's 1st photographic reportage of war in the Crimea, 1855.

Ferber Edna (1887–). U.S. novelist. Her books include novels on 20th-c. U.S. society; *Show Boat* (1926), the basis of the musical by Kern and Hammerstein, and *Giant* (1952), made into a film.

Fenton. Crimean War, *cantinière* and wounded man, 1855

Fellini. *La Dolce Vita*

Ferrari. *Crucifixion*

W. G. Ferguson. *Dead Game*

Ferguson Howard (1908–). Irish composer. His music, basically diatonic with affinities to Brahmsian classicism, includes *Partita* for orchestra, *Overture for an occasion* (Coronation, 1953), an octet and 2 violin sonatas.

Ferguson Sir Samuel (1810–86). Irish poet and antiquarian, influential in the Irish literary renaissance. He wrote several lyrics of rhythmic originality and charm, especially versions of Irish originals. His works include *Lays of the Western Gael . . .* (1865), *Congal* (1872) and *Poems* (1880).

Ferguson William Gouw (1632/3–90?). Scottish still-life painter who worked in the Netherlands and England; his paintings have sometimes been confused with those of Jan Weenix and other Dutch artists.

Ferlinghetti Lawrence (1919–). U.S. poet, one of the *beats. F. uses free verse, often with repetitions or variations of one line, suitable for declamation. Much of it, however, is witty or light in tone, owing something to Prévert. F.'s colls include *Pictures of the Gone World* (1955) and *A Coney Island of the Mind* (1958).

Fernández (Hernández) Gregorio (1576–1636). Leading Spanish baroque sculptor of religious subjects in painted wood; he worked in Valladolid. Many of his most expressive sculptures, e.g. *Pietà* (1617) and *St Veronica* (both Valladolid Mus.), are life-size figures (*pasos*) designed to be carried in Holy Week processions. He also carved the high altar of Plasencia cathedral (1624–34).

Fernández de Moratín Leandro (1760–1828). Spanish playwright. He adapted comedies by Molière, who strongly influenced him, and wrote 5 original comedies, culminating in the very successful *El sí de las niñas* (1806). He forfeited his popularity by accepting a position under Joseph Bonaparte, and the last years of his life were spent in exile in France.

Fernández de Moratín Nicolás (1737–80). Spanish playwright, father of Leandro F. de M. He wrote indifferent comedies in the French style, of which he was an ardent champion, and a poem on bull-fighting (*Fiesta de toros en Madrid*) which has become a classic anthology piece.

Ferrabosco Alfonso (1543–88). Italian madrigal composer who from 1562 to 1578 served Elizabeth I of England both as musician and member of her secret service. F.'s music was unoriginal, but he was important in England as the 1st madrigalist there. He wrote some church and lute music.

Ferrabosco Alfonso (*c.* 1575–1628). English composer of Italian parentage, son of the above. F.'s music shows great polyphonic skill, his most important compositions being viol fantasies and pavans, e.g. the *Four-note Pavan* and the *Dovehouse Pavan*, and In nomines. He also wrote music for masques by Ben Jonson and was one of the first to write for the lyra viol.

Ferrara, school of. School of Italian painting which flourished in the 2nd half of the 15th c. and is represented by Tura, Cossa, Ercole de' Roberti and Costa. Its marked austerity of style derived from the influence of Piero della Francesca and Mantegna.

Ferrari Gaudenzio (d. 1546). Italian painter of the Lombard school. His major works, dramatic and overcrowded with figures, are frescoes in several chapels on the Sacro Monte, Varallo; a screen depicting scenes from the life of Christ (Madonna delle Grazie, Varallo); an altarpiece and frescoes in S. Cristoforo, Vercelli; and the *Choir of Angels* in the dome of S. Maria dei Miracoli, Saronno.

Ferrari Paolo (1822–89). Italian playwright. He made his début with popular light comedies and historical plays, but later turned to contemporary social and psychological problems.

Ferreira Antonio (1528–69). Portuguese poet and playwright, a great upholder of the classical tradition. His poetical works, coll. in the *Poemas Lusitanos*, are written in an extremely latinized form of Portuguese. His play *Iñes de Castro* (written *c.* 1557), is his most important work and the 1st great tragedy in Portuguese literature.

Ferreri Marco (1928–). Italian film director. After working with *Zavattini, F. moved to Spain where he made 3 black comedies, the best known of which is *El Cochecito* (1960). He has since returned to Italy.

Ferri Ciro (1634–89). Roman baroque painter. He was the principal follower of Pietro da

Ferri. Ceiling, Sala di Saturno

Fernández. *St Veronica*

Kathleen Ferrier in Gluck's *Orfeo*

Cortona and on the death of the latter completed his frescoes in the Pitti Palace, Florence. F.'s own work includes an altarpiece for S. Ambrogio, Rome, Biblical frescoes in S. Maria Maggiore, Bergamo and frescoes of the seasons in the Villa Falconieri, Frascati.

Ferrier Kathleen (1912–53). English contralto singer who died of cancer at the height of a brilliant career. The part of Lucretia in Britten's opera *The Rape of Lucretia* was written for her and she achieved great success in the title-role of Gluck's *Orfeo.*

Fête champêtre. Giorgione's *Concert Champêtre*

Festing Michael Christian (*c.* 1680–1752). English violinist and composer, mainly for the violin. He was a pupil of F. Geminiani and was a director of the Italian opera in London.

Festival Ballet, London's. Co. created in 1950. The leading dancers and founders of the co., Markova and Dolin, concentrated on ballets of the Fokine era, and guest artists in the early days of the co.'s existence included many names from the Ballets Russes, such as Toumanova, Riabouchinska and Danilova. Although Markova and Dolin have now left, the co. takes an important place in ballet today, and when not touring in Britain or abroad its London home is the Royal Festival Hall.

Festival of Britain 1951. To mark the centenary of the Great Exhibition in the Crystal Palace, the British government sponsored a series of exhibitions, the most important being on the South Bank of the Thames. Under the direction of Hugh Casson, a group of architects produced a number of exhibition buildings in a characteristically sensitive, relaxed, often fanciful style. The Festival Hall is among Britain's most distinguished post-war buildings.

Fête galante by Nicolas Lancret (detail)

Festival of Britain. The Festival Hall; behind it is the Skylon

festoon. Originally a festal garland or wreath. In the decorative arts f. applies to a conventional arrangement of flowers, fruit or foliage hanging from ribbons which in turn can hang from lions' mouths, bulls' heads or decorative knobs. F.s were often used in classical and Renaissance architecture. They are frequently called swags.

Festus (1839). Long poem by P. J. *Bailey.

Fet Afanasy Afanasyevich (1820–92). Russian poet, unusual among his contemporaries

Feti. *The Good Samaritan*

Feuerbach. *Nanna*

Feuillade. *Fantômas*

(politically and socially engaged poets like Nekrassov) since he wrote concise, finely wrought lyrics, usually about love and nature.

fête champêtre. French term used to describe a type of painting in which a group of townspeople is depicted relaxing in rural surroundings. Giorgione's *Concert Champêtre* (Louvre) is an example.

fête galante. French term used to describe a French 18th-c. genre of painting in which members of the court amuse themselves in love making, dancing and music in a park, garden or rural setting. It is a particular form of the *fête champêtre and was practised most notably by Watteau but also by J.-B.-J. Pater, Lancret and others. The term was first used in 1717 when Watteau was admitted to the French Academy and described as a painter of f.s g.s.

Fet(t)i Domenico (1589–1623). Italian painter, trained in Rome. He was court painter at Mantua (1613–21) but settled in Venice in 1622. Characteristic works such as *The Good Samaritan* (Met. Mus.) are richly coloured, broadly executed cabinet pictures of Biblical subjects as genre. In these he was influenced by A. Elsheimer, Rubens and the Venetian school.

Fétis François-Joseph (1784–1871). Belgian music scholar, composer, teacher and critic. He was a teacher of composition at the Paris Conservatoire and produced in Paris the influential critical *Revue Musicale*. From 1833 he was director of the newly founded Brussels Conservatoire. His books include an unfinished history of music.

Feuerbach Anselm (1829–80). German painter of classical subjects and portraits whose painting marked the end of German academic classicism. He was influenced by T. Couture in Paris and spent many years in Italy. His best work, e.g. the portrait *Nanna* (1861; Landeskunstsammlungen, Stuttgart) and *Orpheus and Eurydice* (1869; K. Mus., Vienna) is majestic and controlled, his inferior work sombre and artificial.

Feuillade Louis (1874–1925). French film director. An ex-journalist who wrote scripts and started directing about 1906. His current critical fame rests on his serials, enormously complicated and fantastic thrillers. There were 5 series: *Fantômas* (1913–14), *Les Vampires* (1915), 2 series of *Judex* (1916–17), and *Tih Minh* (1918). These precise and beautiful films were the most influential produced in France at the time, admired for their swiftness and grace and imagery.

Feuillère Edwige (1907–). French actress, one of the greatest tragediennes of the c. Her most famous performances have been in *La Dame aux camélias*, *L'Aigle à deux têtes* and especially *Phèdre*.

Feuillet Octave (1821–90). Popular French novelist and dramatist, author of such sentimental novels as *Roman d'un jeune homme pauvre* (1858) and *Julia de Trécœur* (1872).

feuilleton. Newspaper supplement, usually detachable, including criticism, humour, etc.; it originated in France in the early 19th c. The *roman-f.* (novel serialized in a f.) began in the 1830s; its writers included Eugène Sue, Dumas *père* and Balzac. Dickens's novels were issued by the same method, one which encouraged suspenseful, complex and melodramatic plots.

Féval Paul (1817–87). Prolific French writer of mystery and adventure novels, including *Les Mystères de Londres* (1844), *Les Amours de Paris* (1845) and *Le Bossu* (1858).

Feydeau Ernest-Aimé (1821–73). French novelist, a friend of Flaubert and Gautier, whose fame rests on the realistic novel *Fanny* (1858); its *succès de scandale* temporarily surpassed that of Flaubert's *Madame Bovary* (1857).

Feydeau Georges (1862–1921). French dramatist, son of Ernest F., whose successful farces include *Occupe-toi d'Amélie* (1908), the basis of Noël Coward's *Look after Lulu* (1959), *La Dame de chez Maxim's* (1899), *Tailleur pour dames* (1886).

Feyder Jacques (1888–1948). French film director. After acting, F. started directing in 1915, but his 1st famous film was the spectacular *L'Atlantide* (1921). After the modernized version of an Anatole France tragicomedy of Paris life, *Crainquebille* (1922), he made in Germany a remarkable version of Zola's *Thérèse Raquin* (1928). His satirical *Les Nouveaux Messieurs* (1928), on French politics, ran into censor trouble and F. departed for 4 years and 6 films at M.G.M. (including *The Kiss*, 1929, with Garbo, the last important silent film made in Hollywood). His remaining films (until 1942) except for the British *Knight Without Armour* (1937) with Marlene Dietrich starred his wife, Françoise Rosay. They include *Le Grand Jeu* (1933), a harsh and atmospheric story of the Foreign Legion in Morocco, and *La Kermesse Héroïque* (1935), probably his best-remembered film–a warm comedy, set in 17th-c. Flanders.

Fiammetta. Prose romance by *Boccaccio.

Fibich Zdeněk (1850–1900). Czech composer. He studied at Leipzig under Moschelles and Richter, and in Paris; from 1871 he worked in Prague. F. was twice married but had a romantic passion for the poet A. Schulzová. After Smetana and Dvořák F. was the 3rd great figure in 19th-c. Czech music; his work was subjective, less concerned with national and folk idioms, and much influenced by the German romantics, particularly Schumann. His music includes 7 operas, among them *Hédy* (1896) and *Šarka* (1897), librettos by Schulzová; a great trilogy of *melodramas, *Hippodamia* (1890–1); and 3 symphonies.

Fichte Johann Gottlieb (1762–1814). German idealist philosopher, a disciple of Kant; also important for his addresses *Reden an die deutsche Nation* (1807–8) which stimulated Prussian resistance to Napoleon. Works include *Grundlage der gesammten Wissenschaftslehre* (1794).

Ficino Marsilio (1433–99). Italian humanist. He was patronized by Cosimo de' Medici for whom he trs. a body of Hermetic literature (*Hermes Trismegistos) which he entitled *Pimander* (1464). F. also publ. trs of Plato and commentaries, but his speculations in natural magic are a main theme of his work.

fidel. Ancient musical instrument, probably Eastern in origin but widely used in medieval Europe.

Fidelio. Opera by *Beethoven, libretto by J. von Sonnleithner; 1st performance in Vienna in 1805.

Field John (1782–1837). Irish-born pianist and composer, a pupil and employee of Clementi. In the early 1800s he settled in Russia but enjoyed a European reputation for

Feyder. Françoise Rosay in *La Kermesse Héroïque*

Ficino; medal

Fidel: from a medieval illuminated ms.

John Field

W. C. Fields in *The Bank Dick*

Elaine Fifield in *Pineapple Poll*

his piano concerto and other piano works. His *Nocturnes were Chopin's models, and Liszt and Schumann praised F.'s music.

Fielding Henry (1707–54). English novelist. From about 1728 onwards F. led a financially precarious life in London, mainly as a dramatist and adapter of plays. He was known as a wit and was popular with women. In 1734 he married Charlotte Cradock, the original Sophia Western, the heroine of *Tom Jones*. He read and qualified for the Bar (1737–40) but his health deteriorated and he was forced to return to writing. His 2nd marriage in 1747 was followed the next year by his appointment as Justice of the Peace for Westminster, an office to which he brought knowledge, humanity and integrity rare in his time. His health remained poor, and in 1754 he sailed on medical advice to Lisbon, where he died. His *Journal of a Voyage to Lisbon* was publ. posth.

F.'s novels present a detailed portrait of an age which touched extremes of refinement and grossness, where poverty and misery were the foundation for a superficial structure of elegance and cultivation that was itself often corrupt and degraded. His long novels are constructed with skilful craftsmanship, especially in *Tom Jones*, where the complex ramifications of the plot are controlled with consummate ingenuity. F. abandoned Richardson's letter convention and brought the English novel at a stride to an amazing technical maturity and assurance.

Joseph Andrews (1742) was conceived solely as a parody of the narrow and calculating morality of Richardson's *Pamela*. But F.'s humour and creative sympathy were too great for so limited a task, and the book developed an independent life of its own, so that Joseph's manly efforts to resist seduction are often forgotten while F. creates rounded and idiosyncratic characters such as Parson Adams. In *Jonathan Wild* (1743), a satire upon greatness, reverently describing the career of a 'great' criminal, the same exuberant invention is at work. With *Tom Jones* (1749) F. reached the height of his powers. Basically it is the story of a young man's moral education: Tom is lusty, frank and sweet-natured, plotted against and misrepresented by his hypocritical relation Blifil; his moral perceptions are sharpened and his sense of responsibility deepened by each of the hilarious adventures which alternately lead him towards and away from his sweetheart, the virtuous and charming Sophia. *Amelia* (1751) is less successful; it is mainly devoted to exposing social abuses.

Fielding: engraving after Hogarth

Fields W. C. (1879–1946). U.S. actor. F. entered films in 1924 and rapidly became the arch comic reprobate–hating children and dogs and consuming his time in cheap bars. He suffered indignities in such films as *Million Dollar Legs* (1932), *David Copperfield* (1934) as Mr Micawber, *The Bank Dick* (1940) and *Never Give a Sucker an Even Break* (1941).

Fiesta (1926). Title used in Britain for Hemingway's novel *The Sun Also Rises*.

fife. Small, high-pitched, transverse *flute primarily associated with military music since the 15th c.

Fifield Elaine (1930–). Australian dancer who came to Britain in 1945, becoming a principal dancer of the Sadler's Wells Theatre Ballet 2 years later. Until her retirement (1958) she danced classical and soubrette roles, her finest being Poll in *Pineapple Poll*.

fifteenth. An organ stop; if the player depresses the note middle C and is using only this stop the C two 8ves (i.e. 15 notes) higher will sound. The stop is used in combination with others to add brilliance to the tone.

fifth. The musical *interval between one note and the 5th note above it in the diatonic scale. Also *consecutives.

Figaro. Character created by *Beaumarchais and the hero of operas by Mozart and Rossini.

Fighting Téméraire, The (1838). Painting by *Turner.

figurative art. A relatively new term; it of course applies to all representational paintings, but can also be used of some abstract paintings, for example early cubist work, in which the basic motif is recognizably a human figure.

figured bass: *continuo

Filarete Antonio (1400–69). Italian architect, sculptor and writer living in Milan. F. drew up vast schemes for palaces and ideal cities to be laid out according to elaborate astrological rules. His *Trattato d'Architettura* (1460–4) was called by Vasari 'perhaps the most stupid

Filarete. Temple design

Filigree. Etruscan ear-rings

book that was ever written'. He did, however, design the Ospedale Maggiore, Milan (1457)–intended as a mere fragment of an enormous edifice, never built–which shows a mixture of Gothic and Renaissance motifs, and his writings had an influence on the centrally-planned church.

filigree. Delicate wire-work, usually of gold or silver, used in jewellery. Fine threads of metal are plaited and then soldered. Beads of the same metal are often set at the joins or at spaced intervals to set the wire-work off. It is a very ancient method most effectively used by the Etruscan and the early Irish jewellers.

Fille Mal Gardée, La. 2-act ballet, first produced in 1786 by *Dauberval and perennially popular. A recent version for the Royal Ballet has choreography by Ashton (1960).

fillet. The word is usually applied to a flat band separating mouldings from each other or ending a suite of mouldings. Originally applied to classical architecture, it also applies to the decorative arts, and in particular silver.

film technique. F. t. can be conveniently divided into 3 phases–camerawork, editing and optical effects. A director may have control over all 3, or, as in many studio productions, part only.

CAMERAWORK: apart from the use of *camera angles* and different lenses for subjective effects (*wide-angle* lens to encompass a greater view than normal, with exaggeration of perspective and sharpness in both foreground and background, sometimes known as *deep-focus*; and *telephoto* lens to bring distant objects apparently close, with flattened perspective) a director can predetermine the style of a film by certain camera movements. *Tracking:* moving the camera bodily to follow a character or explore a set. *Panning:* swinging the camera round horizontally (*Tilt:* vertical movement). *Crane shot:* the camera is mounted on a crane, allowing movement in any direction. *Zoom:* visually similar to tracking, but produced by a special lens able to change smoothly from wide-angle to telephoto. Also important is the choice of different types of film and the use of fast and slow motion. In recent years cameras have become more mobile and can be hand-held: this has produced the free style of cinéma-vérité.

EDITING: the assembly of lengths of film into their final sequence. *Cutting* determines the duration of an action and the point at which it starts. *Cross-cutting:* interweaving 2 or more separate sequences, so that they appear to take place simultaneously. *Jump-cut:* a sharp break produced by omitting a connecting link between 2 parts of a sequence, or showing only the beginning and end of an action without altering the camera position.

OPTICAL EFFECTS: apart from the *cut*, in which the screen image instantaneously changes, it is possible to introduce other visual effects when the film is printed. *Fade:* gradual darkening of the screen (a *fade-in* is the reverse). *Dissolve:* the gradual replacement of one scene by another, in which both scenes are for a time mixed. *Superimposition:* simultaneous showing of more than 1 image. *Wipe:* gradual replacement of one scene by another by altering their respective composite areas. *Montage:* commonly used to describe a rapid assemblage of images, often in quick dissolves; the term originally indicated the aesthetic use of cutting for emotive purposes. Other optical effects are *masking* (altering the shape of the projected picture) and *freezing* of a single frame, in which 1 image is printed repeatedly to give a 'still'. *Process work*, mainly used for trick effects, is also carried out during printing; it is basically a method of combining images from separate lengths of film into one, with no visible joins or overlapping. Thus backgrounds can be printed on to actors filmed in a studio, the relative scale of objects can be altered, live action combined with animation.

Filonov Pavel (1883–1941). Russian painter and graphic artist with a very individual style and vision in some ways reminiscent of Klee and the surrealists. He was associated with the Russian futurist movement from the outset and designed the scenery for Mayakovsky's 1st play; F. also illustrated a number of booklets of futurist poetry. In 1925 he founded a school of 'analytical painting' in Leningrad, dissolved in 1928, like all such private institutions in the U.S.S.R.

Filostrato, Il. Epic poem by *Boccaccio.

final. A musical term for the defining note of a *mode.

Financier, The (1912). Novel by Dreiser.

Filigree. The Dowgate Hill brooch; Anglo-Saxon, 9th–10th c.

Filonov. *Man and Woman*

Fine manner. Maso Finiquerra, *The Planet Venus*

Broad manner. *Aristotle and Phyllis*; late 15th c.

Ronald Firbank

Firebird, 1910; Karsavina and Bolm

fin de siècle (French, 'end of century'). Used adjectivally of works, styles, etc. (particularly those of the late 19th-c. *decadence) having some or all of the supposed characteristics of 'the end of an era'–elaborateness, artificiality, weariness, perversity.

Fine Irving (1914–). U.S. composer, conductor and univ. teacher; his teachers included W. Piston and N. Boulanger. His early work was influenced by Hindemith and Stravinsky; some later works show the impact of 12-note methods.

fine manner. One of 2 classifications used by scholars of Florentine engravings of the 2nd half of the 15th c.; the engravings are classified according to whether the line is generally fine (f. m.) or bold (broad manner).

Fingal (1762). An epic poem by J. *Macpherson, one of his *Poems of Ossian*. FINGAL'S CAVE is an alternative name for *Mendelssohn's *Hebrides Overture*.

Finger Gottfried (*c.* 1660–after 1723). Moravian composer and keyboard virtuoso. During a stay in England he wrote much for the stage, often in conjunction with English composers, e.g. J. Eccles; he also produced operas and instrumental music.

Finger variation. Name given to the Golden Vine Fairy's variation in the prologue of the Royal Ballet's version of *The Sleeping Beauty*, so called because of the pointed finger movements of the dancer.

Finlandia (1900). Orchestral work by *Sibelius.

Finnegan's Wake (1939). Book by James *Joyce.

Finney Albert (1936–). English actor. In his 1st season at the Birmingham Repertory Theatre he played Macbeth and Henry V, and in 1959 had a season at Stratford. London successes included *The Party* (1958), *Billy Liar* (1960) and *Luther* (1961). He has become a world star with the films *Saturday Night and Sunday Morning* and *Tom Jones*.

Finson or Finsonius, Ludovicus (Louis) (d. 1617). Netherlands painter of portraits and religious subjects. He visited Italy, where he worked under Caravaggio, and later painted a number of altarpieces in Provence. His style combined elements from Caravaggio with mannerism, and influenced Provençal artists.

Finzi Gerald (1901–56). English composer influenced by Vaughan Williams. His best music is in song cycles, especially 3 on Thomas Hardy but he also wrote choral music, the cantata *Die Natalis* for voice and orchestra, and instrumental works.

fioriture (from Italian *fiore*, 'flower'). Musical *ornamentation often improvised by the performer, usually a singer, and at its height in the 18th c.

fipple flutes (also called 'whistle flutes'). A class of musical instruments including the *recorder and penny whistle. A block or 'fipple' at the mouthpiece leaves only a narrow aperture; through this the air is led to a 'lip', lower on the instrument, which vibrates.

Firbank (Arthur Annesley) Ronald (1886–1926). English novelist. He began writing seriously with *Vainglory* (1915); before that he led a frivolous and hedonistic life in Café Royal society at Oxford and abroad. Out of this varied experience he was able to create the nuances and accents of society in the years before World War I in such novels as *Inclinations* (1916), *Valmouth* (1918) and *Concerning the Eccentricities of Cardinal Pirelli* (1926); a concern for a kind of decorative religion is a staple of his stories. The world of his novels, with its aestheticism, its ennui, and its omnipresent hints of perverse wickedness, has the fragile intensity of a dream. His chief merits lie in his subtly inconsequential dialogue–the very flavour of the small-talk of highly intelligent but purposeless minds–his ironic insight into the petty concerns of society women, and the marvellous flippant descriptive phrases, suddenly illuminating their object from an unexpected angle, in which his work abounds.

Firebird. 1-act ballet with choreography by Fokine, music by Stravinsky and décor by Golovine (Firebird's costume by Bakst); 1st performance 1910. It has had several important revivals: in 1926 with new décor by Goncharova; in 1945 with new choreography by Bolm and décor by Chagall; in 1949 with new choreography by Balanchine; in 1954 with new choreography by Lifar; and in the same year

Finson. *Decollation of the Baptist*

the Royal Ballet revived the original by Fokine with the Goncharova sets.

Fires were Started (1943). Film directed by H. *Jennings.

Fireworks Music. Music composed by Handel for the display of fireworks intended for the celebrations of the Peace of Aix-la-Chapelle (1749).

Firmin: *Didot

Fischart Johann (1546–89/90). The greatest German satirist of his period. He was a Protestant and his main target the Jesuit order in such books as *Das Jesuiterhütlein* (1580). The most important of F.'s works is *Die Geschichtklitterung* (1575; 2nd ed. 1582), a germanized version of Rabelais. F. extends and modifies the French original but the result is a richly detailed panorama of contemporary Germany.

Fischer Johann Michael (1692–1766). S. German baroque architect. He was successful and prolific; many of the most splendid Bavarian churches are his work: Diessen, Berg-am-Laim and Ottobeuren are among the most noteworthy. At his best he is a master of spatial organization, often basing his plans on octagons or intersecting ovals.

Fischer-Dieskau Dietrich (1925–). German baritone. His expressive, perfectly controlled voice is at its best in *Lieder*, especially those of Schubert and Hugo Wolff, but he also sings in opera.

Fischer von Erlach Johann Bernhard (1656–1723). Austrian architect. He trained in Rome under Carlo Fontana, studied Borromini's work, travelled in Germany and Holland and settled in Vienna. In 1685 he became court architect, working in a more sober and classical style than most of his contemporaries. He also did sculpture and wrote *A Plan of Civil and Historical Architecture* (1721). His palaces in and around Vienna reflect the influences of Palladio (possibly by way of English architecture) and Louis XIV's France. The Batthyany-Schönborn Palace is the most delicate, the royal Schönbrunn Palace the largest–another attempt to rival Versailles. F. also designed some notable churches at Salzburg: the Dreifaltigskeitkirche with façade modelled on Borromini's S. Agnese; the Kollegienkirche, the Univ. church, with a convex W. front, 2 towers and central dome; the Ursulinenkirche; and the Karlskirche, Vienna (1716)–an eclectic design chiefly using elements from ancient Rome (the Pantheon plus Trajan's Column doubled).

Fisher John (1469–1535). Bishop of Rochester. Although he ardently advocated humanism he opposed Henry VIII by supporting Papal supremacy, and was executed. He was canonized in 1935. F. produced distinguished rhetorical prose, writing in both English and Latin.

Fisher Vardis (1895–). U.S. novelist, author of a group of autobiographical works and also *Children of God* (1939), about the early Mormons.

Fiske Minnie Maddern (1865–1932). American actress who first appeared at the age of 3 as Little Minni Maddern. Later she established herself as the leading lady of America, playing a wide variety of parts, such as Mrs Alving in *Ghosts* and Mrs Malaprop in *The Rivals*, and often starring in musical comedy.

Fitch (William) Clyde (1865–1909). U.S. playwright. His works include the study of jealousy *The Girl with the Green Eyes* (1902).

Fitzgerald Edward (1809–83). English poet and trs. of *The *Rubá'iyát of Omar Khayyám* (1859, anon.; extensively revised in subsequent eds). F. transformed the Persian original, creating a magnificent English poem in quatrains; it has the unusual rhyme scheme *aaba*. He made others trs from Persian, Spanish and Greek; his sparse original work comprises a prose dialogue *Euphranor . . .* (1851) and delightful letters.

Fitzgerald F(rancis) Scott (Key) (1896–1940). U.S. novelist. F. studied at Princeton during the early years of World War I, joined the army but, to his regret, never served abroad. His 1st novel *This Side of Paradise* (1920) made him famous, and he became a legend as playboy and best-selling novelist, chronicler and idol of the Jazz age (a term F. himself coined). Then his beautiful wife Zelda had a mental breakdown, F. became an alcoholic and experienced the physical and spiritual collapse so memorably described in *The Crack-Up* (posth. 1945). His novels were ignored in the more socially conscious 1930s and F. produced much

Scott Fitzgerald

Dietrich Fischer-Dieskau

J. M. Fischer. Benedictine abbey church, Ottobeuren

Fischer von Erlach. Karlskirche, Vienna (completed by his son). Also *baroque.

Flamboyant style. Façade of Trinity church, Vendôme

Flashing. Roman glass amphora

Thomas Flatman. *Charles Beale the Elder*

Flaherty. *Louisiana Story*

hack-work (including film scripts). He was working on *The Last Tycoon* (posth. 1941), his 1st novel for 6 years, when he died.
In recent years there has been renewed appreciation of F.'s graceful, nervous prose and his descriptions of the gaiety and irresponsibility of the 1920s. He was fascinated by the life of the rich, but all his works ultimately condemn it. *The Beautiful and the Damned* (1922) and *Tender is the Night* (1934) are studies of the enervation produced by the life F. himself was leading. *The Great Gatsby* (1925), his most famous novel, describes the destruction of Gatsby, a dreamer and idealist in spite of his career as a gangster, by the selfishness of Daisy, the rich, well-born, spoiled object of his love. F. also wrote some outstanding short stories, including *The Diamond as Big as the Ritz*.

Fitzgerald R(obert) D(avid) (1902–). Australian poet exploring philosophical concepts. His celebrated *Essay on Memory* (1938) and the long *Between Two Tides* (1952) are more obviously speculative than the terser, more colloquial poems in *This Night's Orbit* (1953), the condensed nature of which has led to charges of obscurity.

Fitzwilliam Virginal Book. 17th-c. music ms. now in the Fitzwilliam Mus., Cambridge, containing over 400 keyboard pieces mostly by English composers from about 1560 to 1620. The book's history before the early 18th c. is unknown but some evidence suggests that it was written in the Netherlands (*c.* 1620) for a family of English Roman Catholic refugees.

Five Fingers (1952). Film directed by J. L. *Mankiewicz.

flageolet. Musical instrument, similar to the recorder but with 2 thumb-holes and only 4 finger-holes.

Flagstad Kirsten (1895–1962). Norwegian soprano opera singer, also noted in oratorio. She excelled in Wagnerian roles and was distinguished by the dramatic force of her interpretations, the power and control of her voice and a strong feeling for style.

Flaherty Robert J. (1884–1951). U.S. film director. F. was an explorer who started making amateur movies around 1913. On most of his features, he photographed as well as writing and directing. The first, *Nanook of the North* (1922), about an Eskimo, started a form of documentary drama where events that are commonplace parts of a way of life are acted or re-enacted by those who would naturally be involved. Such, too, were *Moana* (1926), set in Polynesia, and *Man of Aran* (1934), set in Ireland. Sporadic efforts to use F. to make exotic but conventional fictional dramas failed, e.g. *White Shadows of the South Seas* (1928), finished by W. S. Van Dyke. *Tabu* (1931) co-directed by F. and *Murnau, again in Polynesia, was in result a Murnau film. In 1931 he went to Britain and was associated with Grierson, who ed. his *Industrial Britain* (1932). Back in the U.S., he made *The Land* (1941) with the Pare Lorentz unit for the Department of Agriculture. His last film, *Louisiana Story* (1948), photographed by R. Leacock, returned to documentary drama.

flamboyant style. Term applied to 14th- and 15th-c. French architecture, the final period of French *Gothic; it derives from the elaborate, flowing, 'flame-like' *tracery on f. windows.

Flamenca (mid 13th c.). Provençal courtly romance of some 9,000 lines; a description of the growth of love between a married woman and a young nobleman.

flamenco: *cante hondo

flashing. The superimposition of a layer of coloured glass on clear glass, by dipping a lump of clear glass attached to a blowing-tube into molten coloured glass. All medieval ruby window-glass was made by this means. The 'f.' or 'casing' on glasses could be cut through to make a pattern on the clear glass beneath. This technique was practised by the Romans (cameo glass) and was particularly popular in 19th-c. Bohemian and English glass.

flat. A musical sign (♭) which indicates that the note before which it is placed is to be lowered a semitone. F.s in the key signature affect the notes they refer to whenever these notes occur, unless the f.s are cancelled. A note 'a bit flat' is a shade under the required pitch and the performer is out of tune.

Flatman Thomas (1637–88). English poet and gifted painter of miniatures, the best being that of Charles II and 2 self-portraits. F.'s poetry was esteemed by his contemporaries;

Gustave Flaubert

Flegel. *Still-life with Candle*

Flaxman. Memorial to Lord Mansfield. Also* neo-classicism

his *A Thought of Death* influencing Pope's *The Dying Christian to his Soul.*

flats. Pieces of theatrical scenery, usually wooden frames with painted canvas stretched over them.

Flaubert Gustave (1821–80). One of the 3 greatest French novelists of the 19th c. The son of a surgeon, he spent most of his life in or near Rouen. In his early manhood he was afflicted with an obscure nervous disease, but fortunately his modest wealth allowed him to devote himself entirely to literature. He never married; for many years he was in love with an older woman, and he had a tempestuous love-affair with the writer, Louise Colet, which is well documented. His temperament was unrestrainedly romantic, as can be seen from his early works, unpubl. in his lifetime, and from his *Correspondence* (definitive ed. 9 vols 1926–33; *Letters. Selected* . . . 1950). His stylistic ideal of *le mot juste* and his desire for perfectly controlled construction curbed his natural exuberance, and made him a literary martyr who would labour for days on a single page, reading each phrase out aloud to test its sonority.
His works deal partly with contemporary life–*Madame Bovary* (1857; *Madame Bovary*, 1886), *L'Éducation sentimentale* (1869; *Sentimental Education*, 1898), *Un Cœur simple* (in *Trois Contes*, 1877) and *Bouvard et Pécuchet* (1881, *Bouvard and Pécuchet*, 1896)–and partly with sumptuous oriental themes–*Salammbô* (1863; 1886), *La Tentation de saint Antoine* (1874; *The Temptation of Saint Anthony*, 1895) and *La Légende de saint Julien l'hospitalier* (in *Trois Contes*, 1877; trs. in *Gustave Flaubert*, 1903)–and they all express unremitting pessimism. Emma Bovary, the dissatisfied wife of a country doctor, yearns for romantic adventure, but her love-affairs bring her nothing but sorrow and she kills herself. In *L'Éducation sentimentale*, Frédéric Moreau, a young man with some resemblance to F. himself, begins his career with high artistic and sentimental ambitions, but none of his dreams come true and his life is a gradual process of disillusionment. 2 serious-minded petty-bourgeois (*Bouvard et Pécuchet*) set out to conquer all fields of knowledge in turn, and their efforts add up to an encyclopaedia of failure. The oriental books drive home the same lesson in an exotic setting. Yet even readers who find this gloom oppressive are fascinated by F.'s sense of poetic form and his unique literary professionalism.

Flaxman John (1755–1826). English neo-classical sculptor and draughtsman who began his career as a designer of cameos and classical friezes for Josiah Wedgwood. Working in Rome (1787–94) he won a European reputation with his famous line drawings illustrating Homer, Dante and the tragedies of Aeschylus. F.'s largest sculptural commission was the memorial to Lord Mansfield (Westminster Abbey), but he did many other portrait busts, bas-reliefs and monumental groups of great technical accomplishment. F. was a friend of *Blake.

Flecker James Elroy (1884–1915). English poet, dramatist and consular official in the Near East. His poems, influenced by the French *Parnassians, have a rhythmical and formal skill which distinguish them from the *Georgian verse of his time. F.'s romantic verse drama *Hassan* (posth. 1923; produced with incidental music by Delius) has considerable felicities and deservedly held the stage.

Flecknoe Richard (d. 1678?). Roman Catholic priest, poet and playwright, probably English though portrayed by Dryden as Irish. He was lampooned by Marvell in *Fleckno, an English Priest at Rome* which suggested him to Dryden as Shadwell's predecessor as king of nonsense in *Mac Flecknoe*.

Fledermaus, Die (German, 'The Bat'). Light opera by J. *Strauss the Younger, libretto by C. Haffner and R. Genée; 1st performance in Vienna in 1874.

Flegel Georg (1563–1638). German painter, first of landscapes, later of prosaic still-life subjects in subdued tones. He was influenced by Flemish painting.

Fleischer Richard (1916–). U.S. film director. His work is characterized by outdoor shooting, massive compositions and adventurer heroes: *Bandido* (1956), *These Thousand Hills* (1959). His qualities as a technician are further revealed in a thriller, *Violent Saturday* (1955), the comic-strip history of *The Vikings* (1958) and *Barabbas* (1962). He also has a more intimate style which appeared in *Girl in the Red Velvet Swing* (1955).

Fleischmann Adolf Richard (1902–). German abstract painter. He was first interested in expressionism and cubism but in the late 1930s

Fleischer. Anthony Quinn and Vittorio Gassmann in *Barabbas*

Fleischmann. *Op. No. 24* (1954)

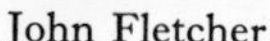

John Fletcher

Flinck. Portrait of Rembrandt

Flitcroft. Woburn Abbey, centre of W. elevation

Florence cathedral

turned to pure abstraction as alone valid in the 20th c., eventually adopting the rigid horizontal-vertical framework of *neo-plasticism. In 1952 he settled in the U.S.

Fleming Paul (1609–40). German poet, a disciple of *Opitz von Boberfeld; he worked as a physician and also visited Russia and Persia (1633–9). F.'s verse developed from rather conventional exercises in Latin and German, introducing unmistakably personal emotions–religious and amatory–into his lyrics.

Fleming Victor (1883–1949). U.S. film director whose films are excellent examples of Hollywood craftsmanship. The most famous are one of the 1st western talkies, *The Virginian* (1929); *Red Dust* (1932), starring the highly successful comedy team of Jean Harlow and Clark Gable; *Captains Courageous* (1937), which firmly type-cast Spencer Tracy as a father-figure with his role as a Portuguese fisherman, and *The Wizard of Oz* (1939). This fantasy musical made Judy Garland's reputation. F. also directed **Gone with the Wind.*

Fleshly School: R. W. *Buchanan

Fletcher Sir Banister Flyte (1866–1953). English author of *History of Architecture on the Comparative Method* (1896; 17th ed. 1964). The book has been much criticized for being no more than a catalogue of styles and buildings, but it remains the most complete textbook of architectural history.

Fletcher Giles the Elder (1549?–1611). English poet in the style of Spenser, father of Giles F. the Younger and Phineas, and uncle of John F. the dramatist. The sonnets *Licia . . .* (1593) are his finest work.

Fletcher Giles the Younger (1588?–1623). English clergyman and poet, son of the above and brother of Phineas F. His most notable work was the mellifluous *Christ's Victorie and Triumph . . .* (1610).

Fletcher John (1579–1625). English playwright, nephew of Giles F. the Elder and educated at Cambridge. F. is mainly known as a dramatist in conjunction with Francis Beaumont (1584–1616), though he also worked with Massinger, Rowley and possibly with Shakespeare on *The Two Noble Kinsmen* and *Henry VIII.* With Beaumont, he wrote (among others) the romantic comedy *Philaster, The Maide's Tragedy, A King and no King*; *The Knight of the Burning Pestle,* however, is sometimes attributed to *Beaumont alone. F. is credited with *The Faithful Shepheardesse,* a pastoral drama containing numerous lyrics.

Fletcher Phineas (1582–1650). Son of Giles F. the Elder. English clergyman and poet who closely imitated Spenser. His *The Purple Island or the Isle of Man* (1633) is an elaborate allegory of the human mind and body, resembling the 'House of Alma' in Spenser's *The Faerie Queene.* He and his brother G.F. the Younger, in their rendering of Spenserian forms and subjects, strongly affected Milton's conception of Spenser.

flic flac. A step in ballet in which the dancer quickly whips out the working foot from behind the calf of the supporting leg, to brush the ground, and returns it to the front of the supporting leg.

Flies, The (1943). Play by Sartre.

Flinck Govert (1615–60). German portrait and subject painter who settled in Amsterdam. He was a pupil of Rembrandt and until the early 1640s a close imitator of his master; later he followed the more fashionable style of B. van der Helst. A portrait of Rembrandt (1639) by F. is in the N.G., London.

Flint Sir William Russel (1880–). English society watercolourist, known for his Spanish gipsy subjects.

flint-glass. Developed by George *Ravenscroft and probably so called because calcined and ground English flints were substituted for Venetian pebbles to supply the silica needed in the glass. Before long sand replaced flint, but the name persists.

Flitcroft Henry (1697–1769). English Palladian architect. Beginning as a carpenter, F. was taken up as a draughtsman by Lord Burlington and was soon successfully designing churches and country-houses for the nobility. He did business as a building contractor as well as as an architect. His chief works are St Giles-in-the-Fields, London (the spire modelled on a design by Gibbs) and Woburn Abbey, Beds.

Florence, school of. The history of modern European painting is dated from the work of the Florentine artist Giotto (d. 1337) but the great period of Florence as a centre of the arts was the 15th and 16th cs. In the work of such painters as Fra Angelico, Leonardo da Vinci, Michelangelo, Botticelli and Raphael the school reached its apogee. The Florentine preoccupation with form and line may be contrasted with the later Venetian emphasis on colour.

Florence cathedral i.e. S. Maria del Fiore. Italian Gothic church, begun in 1296 to designs by Arnolfo di Cambio. Building went on, with interruptions, until the early 15th c. under Giotto, F. Talenti and Andrea Pisano. In 1421 the crossing was covered by Brunelleschi's octagonal dome–a triumph of engineering which is still basically Gothic but already contains Renaissance features. The octagonal Baptistery in front of the cathedral is Tuscan Romanesque, consecrated in 1059 (though altered later by Arnolfo di Cambio). It shows pronounced classical influence: demi-columns, fluted pilasters, window pediments alternately triangular and segmental, etc. The famous bronze doors are by Ghiberti and Andrea Pisano. The separate Campanile ('Bell-tower'), an unusual square tower with marble facing, was begun in 1334 to Giotto's designs and continued by Andrea Pisano and Talenti.

Florentine stitch, also called flame stitch, cushion stitch, or Irish stitch. Name for an embroidery motif consisting of a zigzag pattern of short stitches. Hungarian stitch is similar.

Florey Robert (1900–). French-born U.S. film director. F. made experimental movies in the U.S. around 1928. He returned to France to direct in the early 1930s but went back to Hollywood and made a number of *Tarzan* films. He has also directed a famous horror film, *The Beast with Five Fingers* (1947). He assisted Chaplin with the direction of *Monsieur Verdoux* (1947).

Florian Jean-Pierre Claris de (1755–94). French writer, author of comedies of bourgeois life (*Le Bon Ménage, Le Bon Père,* etc.); romances, including *Galatée* (1783) and *Estelle* (1787); and *Fables* (1792).

Florio John (or Giovanni) (1553?–1625). English trs. and lexicographer, son of an Italian Protestant refugee. He is famed for his

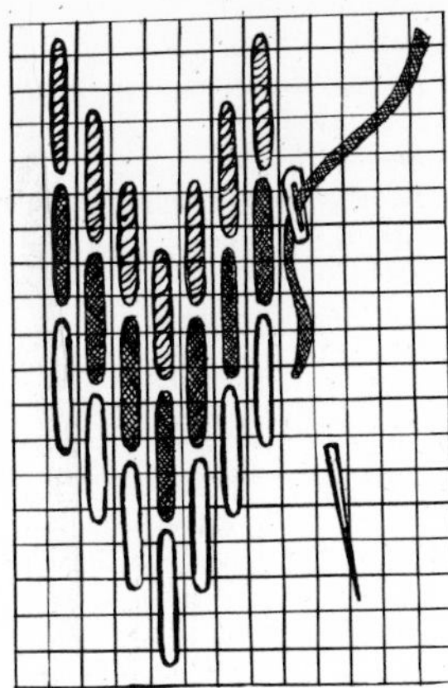

Florentine stitch

Floris. Antwerp town hall

Fluting from the Erechtheum

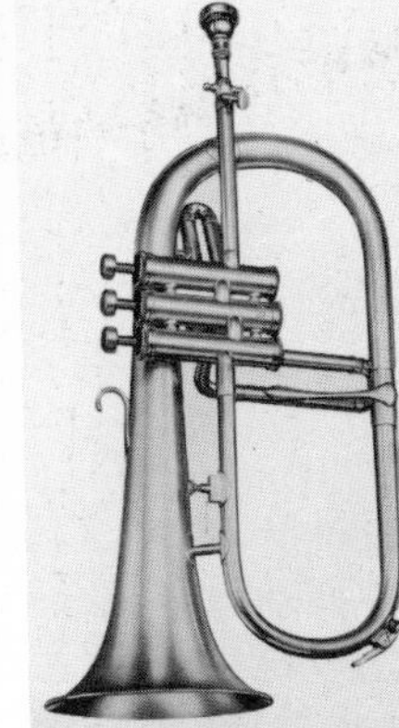

Flugelhorn

ebullient rendering of Montaigne's *Essays* which he freely trs. (1603).

Floris Cornelis (Cornelis de Vriendt) (1514–75). Flemish architect and sculptor who exercised an important influence on the development of Renaissance architecture in the Netherlands. After travelling in Italy he publ. an influential book of engravings of florid adaptations of Roman grotesque ornamentation. His masterpiece, Antwerp town hall (begun 1561), combined Flemish gable and Italian Renaissance palace façade, and set a new style of public building.

Floris Frans (Frans de Vriendt) (1516–70). Flemish painter, the brother of C.F.; he worked in Antwerp. He visited Italy (*c.* 1542–6) and was an influential exponent of Italian mannerism in the Netherlands.

Flotow Friedrich von (1812–83). German composer whose best-known work, the romantic comic opera *Martha* (1847) contains the famous 'Last Rose of Summer', derived from a folk-song. F. also wrote an opera on the legends surrounding A. *Stradella.

flue stops. One of the 2 major classes of *organ stops, the other being reed stops. In f. s. the air column in the pipe is made to vibrate by an aperture with lip cut out of the pipe, somewhat like a recorder.

flugelhorn. Musical brass wind instrument. It has a wide conical bore and cup mouthpiece, like the cornet, but its tone is more mellow. In England it is an important brass-band instrument.

flute. Name specifically applied to a *woodwind instrument (now often made of metal) with a range of about three 8ves from middle C. The f. is a tube about 2 ft long, held sideways projecting beyond the player's right shoulder; the air column is activated by blowing across a hole at the mouthpiece (in the same way as one can get a note from a bottle by blowing across its top). This type of f. was improved by T. *Boehm (d. 1881). The piccolo is in effect a treble f. pitched an 8ve higher; there is also an alto or bass f. pitched a 4th or a 5th lower (a transposing instrument). The term f. is also loosely used of other instruments, such as the *recorder ('English f.'); sometimes, to avoid confusion in early music, the f. described above is called a 'transverse f.'.

fluting. Half-round furrows parallel with each other, first used as decoration on classical pillars. Later adapted in many of the decorative arts in a vertical curved or diagonal pattern. Frequently used with alternate gadrooning as an embossed edging to silver plate.

flying buttress: *buttress

Flying Dutchman, The. English title for *Wagner's opera *Der Fliegende Holländer*; 1st performance in Dresden in 1843

Flynn Errol (1909–59). Irish actor, *the* adventure hero of the 1940s. F. starred in very many films half-remembered chiefly for their colourful brio.

Fogazzaro Antonio (1842–1911). Italian novelist and poet. His main poetical works were the romances *Miranda* (1874) and *Valsolda* (1876). His novels became very popular after being taken up by French literary critics, and his 2 finest are the *Piccolo mondo antico* (1895), dealing with the Risorgimento, and *Il Santo* (1905), the latter involving him in a violent Catholic controversy and being condemned by the Vatican.

Fokine Michael (1880–1942). Russian dancer who became one of the most prolific choreographers of all time. Although trained in the Imperial School tradition, he broke away from the classicism that was Petipa's legacy. Teaming up with Diaghilev's co. in Paris (1909), F. created such ballets as *Schéhérezade*, *Firebird* and *Carnaval* (all in 1910) and *Petrushka* in the following year. These works rebelled against the classical pattern of long mime passages and used each bar of music to set the atmosphere or relate the story in dance. *Les Sylphides* (1909) and *Le Spectre de la Rose* (1911) were in a romantic style and *Le Cygne* (1905), a solo for Pavlova, was a simple tale rather than a vehicle for a virtuoso.

Folengo Teofilo (Girolamo) (1491–1544). Italian *macaronic poet. His famous *Baldus*, which was to inspire Rabelais, is full of the coarse humour combined with high-flown and pedantic language typical of the macaronic genre. After the 1st ed., publ. in 1517 under the pseud. 'Merlin Cocai', F. publ. 3 expanded and revised versions (4th ed. 1552).

Folia. (1) An old Portuguese dance comparable to the early English Morris and, like that, noisy,

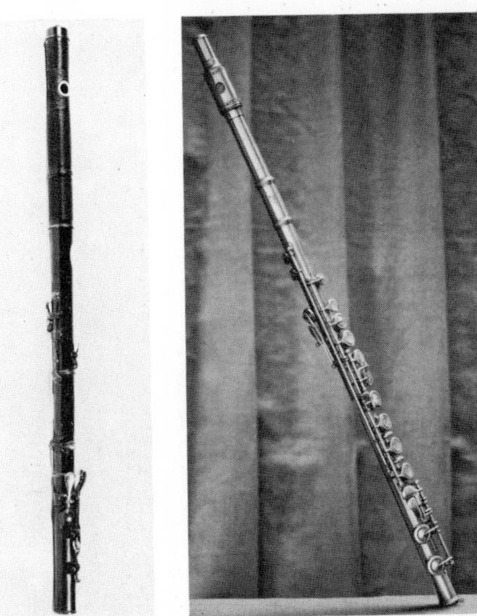

Early 19th-c. flute (*left*); *right:* orchestral flute showing the complicated key mechanism which followed Boehm's improvements

Fokine in *Schéhérazade*

Theodor Fontane

School of Fontainebleau. *Gabrielle d'Estrées and her sister in the bath*

Fontainbleau. The Salle du Council

vigorous and abandoned, hence the name. (2) A piece of music associated with the dance. The F. is closely associated with the type **passamezzo antico* and **romanesca* and it was used by innumerable composers from Juan del Encina (d. 1529) to J. S. Bach (d. 1750).

Folies Bergère. Parisian cabaret theatre opened in 1869; probably the world's most famous theatre.

folio. Printer's term for a sheet of paper folded once, and hence for a book printed on such paper. The term FIRST F. refers to the 1st coll. ed. of Shakespeare's plays (1623), containing 36 of the 38 plays attributed to him.

folly. In architecture the term for a 'ruin' or other such caprice built merely to improve the view or at the whim of a patron.

Fonda Henry (1905–). U.S. actor with a screen reputation as a lone and laconic outsider–often seeking justice; he is often thought of as a 'western' star. His pictures include: *The Grapes of Wrath* (1940), *The Oxbow Incident* (1943), *Fort Apache* (1947), his own production *Twelve Angry Men* (1957) and *The Tin Star* (1957).

font. Receptacle (usually of stone) for baptismal water, placed in the W. end of a church unless there is a separate baptistery. Late Gothic f.s sometimes have roughly conical, elaborately carved wooden covers.

Fontainebleau France. A royal palace of Francis I begun in 1528 and added to for the next 200 years. The Cour du Cheval Blanc and Cour d'Honneur (including the Porte Dorée) are by G. *Lebreton. The Galerie François I (1533–40) introduces the so-called 'F. style' of interior decoration, a combination of sculpture, metalwork, stucco, woodwork and painting. It was evolved by the Italian artists Rosso, Primaticcio and Niccolò dell' Abbate, who worked for Francis I from *c.* 1530 to *c.* 1560. This 1st SCHOOL OF FONTAINBLEAU introduced mannerism to France. A decorative revival under Henry IV, known as the '2nd school of F.', was less important.

Fontana Carlo (1634–1714). Italian baroque architect, pupil and chief assistant of Bernini whom he succeeded as Papal architect. He was responsible for the trend towards classicism in the late baroque period, exemplified in his ordered use of baroque motifs on his façade for S. Marcello al Corso, Rome (1682–3). By 1700 he had attained a position of immense importance in Rome, working on almost every significant project for architectural or public works. He was assisted by his son FRANCESCO (1668–1708) and his nephew GIROLAMO (1697–1700).

Fontana Domenico (1543–1607). Italian architect who worked in Rome from 1563 and became chief architect to Pope Sixtus V. He built the Lateran Palace (1587–8) and additions to the Vatican. Contemporaries praised his engineering feat of erecting the huge Egyptian obelisk (brought to Rome by Caligula) on its present site before St Peter's, after moving it from the Vatican Circus. His brother GIOVANNI (1540–1614) was his assistant and succeeded him as Papal architect. D.'s son GIULIO CESARE built the Palazzo Reale, Naples.

Fontana Lavinia (1522–1614). Bolognese painter of portraits and, less successfully, of religious subjects; daughter of the mannerist painter PROSPERO F. (1512–97), a pupil of Vasari. She settled in Rome, where her portraiture became fashionable among the leading families.

Fontane Theodor (1819–98). German novelist, the most important in the 19th c. and the most European. A journalist and freelance writer, F. began by writing historical ballads, then surveyed the antiquities of his homeland in *Wanderungen durch die Mark Brandenburg* (1862–82). His 1st (late) novel *Vor dem Sturm* (1878) draws on this historical material. His fame, however, rests on the novels set in contemporary Brandenburg, especially Berlin: *L'Adultera* (1880), *Irrungen, Wirrungen* (1887; *Trials and Tribulations*, 1917), *Unwiederbringlich* (1891; *Beyond Recall*, 1964), *Effi Briest* (1894; 1962), *Der Stechlin* (1897). Often tragic, these deal with the clash between individual inclination and social pressures, especially in situations of adultery and *mésalliance*. The narration is veiled and non-committal, the narrator an ironic and resigned observer. Irony, too, characterizes his comic masterpiece *Frau Jenny Treibel* (1892).

Fontenelle Bernard Le Bovier de (1657–1757). French writer, nephew of Corneille and author of many learned, rational, sceptical

Folly; French, 1770s

Carlo Fontana. S. Marcello al Corso

Johnston Forbes-Robertson as Caesar

Fonteyn and Nureyev in *Swan Lake*

Aleksander Ford. *Knights of the Teutonic Order*

books popularizing science and unobtrusively questioning religious doctrines; in many respects they anticipate the attitudes of the **philosophes*. F. took the side of the Moderns in the *Ancients and Moderns Controversy. Works include *Dialogues des Morts* (1683), *Entretiens sur la pluralité des mondes* (1686) and the *Histoire des oracles* (1687).

Fonteyn Dame Margot (married name de Arias) (1919–). English dancer; she studied under Astafieva and within a year of joining the Sadler's Wells (1934) took over most of the major parts left vacant by Markova's resignation from the co.; she became leading dancer and has shown great versatility by dancing roles of all types with equal success, but has emerged primarily as a classical dancer. Her popular partnership with *Helpmann lasted until he left the co. (1950). Michael Somes was her partner up to 1962. She has danced with *Nureyev and they have become the most celebrated team in the West.

fool. In medieval and Elizabethan times, the royal jester or court fool, often a dwarf and usually dressed in the traditional garb of cap, bells and parti-coloured costume; he carried a stick with either a fool's head or a pig's bladder on the end of it. In drama he can be traced back to the character of the Vice in medieval plays. In the plays of Shakespeare he sometimes takes an important, no longer purely comic part.

Foolish Wives (1921). Film directed by E. von *Stroheim.

foot. In English verse a metrical unit, usually of 2 or 3 syllables (*metre in verse).

Foote Samuel (1720–77). English dramatist and actor who specialized in mimicry, producing topical farces and libellous impersonations at his unlicensed theatre in the Haymarket. His pungent wit influenced Sheridan's *The Critic* and Garrick.

Foppa Vincenzo (*c.* 1427–1515/16). Italian painter, the leading artist of the Milanese school before Leonardo da Vinci visited Milan. He was probably trained by the Paduans and was influenced both by Mantegna and the Bellini. Among his works are *The Adoration of the Kings* (N.G., London), *St Francis Receiving the Stigmata* (Brera, Milan) and a *Madonna and Child* of great beauty in the Berenson Coll., Settignano.

Forain Jean-Louis (1852–1931). French painter and graphic artist. F. contributed illustrations of Parisian life to journals for many years. He chose similar subjects to Degas and Toulouse-Lautrec, but his wit is more sardonic and often at the expense of his models. Later he concentrated on oil painting, e.g. *The Court of Justice* (Tate).

Forains, Les. 1-act ballet with choreography by *Petit, music by Sauguet and décor by Bérard; 1st performance 1945.

Forbes-Robertson Sir Johnston (1853–1937). English actor, extremely successful from his début in 1874; as manager of the Lyceum Theatre (from 1895) a major figure in the English theatre; Shaw wrote the part of Caesar (in *Caesar and Cleopatra*) for him. The F.-R. family has produced a number of actors of distinction.

Ford Aleksander (1908–). Polish film director. F. started making films in 1930 but made his name after the war. A founder of Film Polski, a state organization, he was the 1st Polish director to achieve international fame with *The Young Chopin* (1952) and *Five Boys from Barska Street* (1954). He has since made *The Eighth Day of the Week* (1958) and the spectacular *Knights of the Teutonic Order* (1960).

Ford Ford Madox, originally Hueffer (1873–1939). English novelist and critic, founder and ed. of *The English Review* (1908), which publ. the first short stories of D. H. Lawrence, and later of *The Transatlantic Review* in Paris. F.'s studies and reminiscences of his grandfather Ford Madox Brown, Henry James, Conrad (with whom he collaborated on *The Inheritors* and *Romance*), Swinburne and others, are fascinating but unreliable. Novels include: *The Good Soldier* (1915), an intense, economically written domestic tragedy; an historical trilogy beginning with *The Fifth Queen* (1906); and *Some Do Not* (1924) and its 3 successors, the anti-war novels around the character of Christopher Tietjens.

Ford Glenn (1916–). U.S. film actor, versatile and authentic, e.g. *The Sheepman* (1957), *The Blackboard Jungle* (1954).

Ford John (*c.* 1586–after 1639). English playwright. He collaborated with Dekker and Rowley on the fine 'crime play', *The Witch of Edmonton*. His own plays include the

Forain. *The Court of Justice*

Foppa. *The Adoration of the Kings*

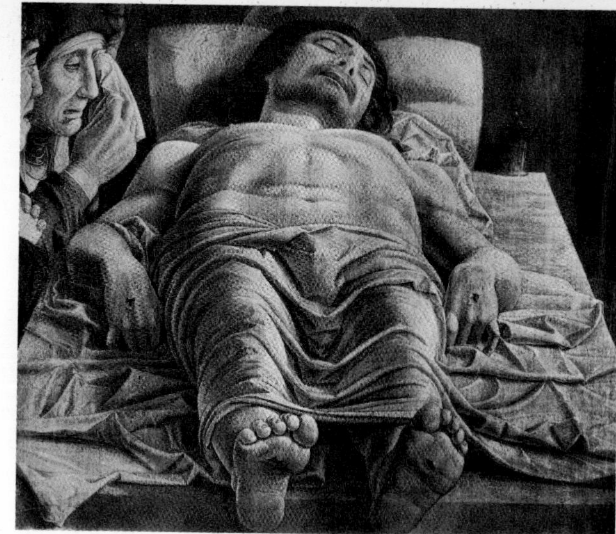

Foreshortening. Mantegna's *Dead Christ*

John Ford. Victor McLaglen in *The Informer*

sensational *Tis Pitty Shees a Whore* (publ. 1633), a lurid tragedy of incestuous love, set in Italy; *The Broken Heart*, and the historical chronicle, *Perkin Warbeck*. Though very unequal, they still have power to move the emotions, chiefly by the force of several scenes of intense passion, and some fine pathos. The frequently prevailing mood was perhaps inspired by Burton's *Anatomy of Melancholy*.

Cia Fornaroli

Ford John (1895–). U.S. film director. F. started directing westerns with Harry Carey in 1917. Thereafter, until 1959, he rarely made less than 2 films a year. He is renowned for his sureness of working which results in very economical shooting, whether on the cheap silent westerns, the Cinerama of *How the West Was Won* (1962) or the 70 mm. of *Cheyenne Autumn* (1964). F.'s favourite form is the western, although he has achieved fame for films of social or religious content: *The Informer* (1935); *The Grapes of Wrath* (1940); *The Fugitive* (1947). In his westerns, his viewpoint is conservative and nostalgic, sympathetic to pioneer and Indian rather than to homesteaders and legislators. From his 1st big success, *The Iron Horse* (1924), he has made a series of westerns rivalled in both quality and quantity only by those of Walsh: *Stagecoach* (1939), *My Darling Clementine* (1946), *She Wore A Yellow Ribbon* (1949), *Wagonmaster* (1950), *Rio Grande* (1950), *The Searchers* (1956). In his latest films, like *Two Rode Together* (1961), he has eliminated the pictorialism of his 1930s movies in favour of a more terse style, nowhere more evident than in *The Man Who Shot Liberty Valance* (1962), with *Cheyenne Autumn* his definitive treatment of the destructive efforts of progress. F.'s Irish origins have deeply affected his work notably in *The Informer* and *The Quiet Man* (1952).

Foreign Correspondent (1940). Film directed by A. *Hitchcock.

E. M. Forster

Foreman Carl (1923–). U.S. film writer, producer, director. F. was S. *Kramer's chief script writer in the period 1948–52 (e.g. *High Noon, The Men*). He was black-listed and left Hollywood to write anonymously the script of *The Bridge on the River Kwai*. He produced a number of films in Britain including *The Guns of Navarone* (1961) and directed a war drama *The Victors* (1963) a disappointingly shallow example of the socio-political content for which his work has been admired.

foreshortening. In painting and drawing perspective applied to single objects or figures to create the illusion of projection and depth. F. is first found in Greek vase painting (*c.* 500 B.C.) but was not developed until the Renaissance, e.g. *Dead Christ* (Brera Gal., Milan) by Mantegna; it was fully exploited during the baroque period, e.g. *sotto in sù* illusionism.

For Esmé–with Love and Squalor (1953). Coll. of stories by J. D. Salinger.

forestage. Stage acting area in front of the proscenium arch and front curtain, which originated in the Elizabethan *apron stage.

form. Term used in the arts for (1) an accepted framework of expression, e.g. the sonnet f. in literature and sonata f. in music; and (2) the structural qualities of a work, e.g. the harmonious proportioning of the various parts and their arrangement in order to create tensions and bring about climaxes.

Fornaroli Cia (1888–1954). Italian dancer who studied under Cecchetti and became leading dancer at the Metropolitan Opera, New York (1910). She returned to Italy to dance at La Scala and in 1929 was appointed director of the Ballet Academy, but left Italy for political reasons and settled in the U.S., teaching in New York.

Forster E(dward) M(organ) (1879–). English novelist who has been extremely influential despite his small œuvre. After he left Cambridge, F. lived for a time in Italy, the background of *Where Angels Fear to Tread* (1905) and *A Room with a View* (1908). His work is filled with a conviction of the necessity of understanding and communication between men, but rarely underestimates the difficulties: the relationship between the Englishman Fielding and the Indian Aziz in *A Passage to India* (1924) is a subtle and complex analysis of the problem. *Howards End* (1910) describes the destinies of 2 families, and through them the conflict of cultures and values in early 20th-c. English society. Works include the novel *The Longest Journey* (1907) and a study, *Aspects of the Novel* (1927).

Forster John (1812–76). English historian, biographer and critic, ed. of *The Examiner*. He wrote important lives of his friends Dickens (1872–4) and W. S. Landor. The Forster

Fortuny y Carbo. *The Spanish Marriage*

bequest (Dyce and Forster Coll., V. and A., London) includes most of Dickens's original mss.

Forsyte Saga, The (1906–21). Series of novels by *Galsworthy.

Fort Paul (1872–1960). French poet and playwright, best known for his many vols (written over more than 50 years) of *Ballades françaises et chroniques de France*, in various metres but printed as if prose. F. was also the founder of the Théâtre d'Art (1890), formed to promote symbolist drama.

fortepiano: *piano

For the Fallen (1914). Poem by Laurence *Binyon.

Fortner Wolfgang (1907–). German composer, conductor and teacher at the Institute for Evangelical church music at Heidelberg. His music, dry in character and developing from a dissonant idiom to 12-note methods in the early 1950s, includes a fine violin concerto (1945); the cantata *An die Nachgeborenen* (1948) on texts from Brecht; a symphony; the ballet *The White Rose* (1950) after Oscar Wilde; and the oratorio scene *The Sacrifice of Isaac* (1952).

Fortunatus Venantius Honorius Clementianus. 6th-c. bishop of Poitiers and poet. Among his longer works are a poem on the life of St Martin and the *De excidio Thoringiae*. However, he is most famous for his hymns, 'Vexilla regis prodeunt' and 'Pange, lingua, gloriosi proelium certanimis', composed for the reception of the relic of the Cross sent by the Emperor Justin II to France.

Fortuny y Carbo Mariano (1838–74). Spanish painter of history and genre. F. first attracted notice with his paintings of the Moroccan campaigns of General Prim, e.g. *Battle of Wad-ras* (M.M.A., Madrid). Later he worked in Rome on large canvases, rich in incident and detail, which sold for record prices, e.g. *The Spanish Marriage* (M.M.A., Barcelona).

42nd Parallel, The (1930). Novel by *Dos Passos.

Forty-Second Street (1933). Film directed by L. *Bacon.

Forty-Seven Workshop. Theatre workshop started by G. P. *Baker.

For Whom the Bell Tolls (1940). Novel by *Hemingway.

Forza del destino, La (Italian, 'The Force of Destiny'). Opera by *Verdi, libretto by F. M. Piave; 1st performance in St Petersburg in 1862.

Foscolo Ugo (1778–1827). Italian poet and patriot. He fought against the Austrians as a volunteer under Napoleon, held for a time the chair of rhetoric at Pavia and eventually settled in England (1816). He wrote the novel *Le ultime lettere di Jacopo Ortis* (finished 1802), the story of an anguished patriot who commits suicide, and poetic works full of haunting, sonorous language and poignant emotion, e.g. his ode, *I Sepolcri* (1807; *The Sepulchres*, c. 1820) summoning Italy's dead heroes to rise and fight for freedom.

Ugo Foscolo

Foss Lukas (1922–). German-born U.S. composer, pianist, conductor and, from 1950, Stravinsky's successor as professor of composition at the Univ. of California. His music includes the opera *The Jumping Frog of Calaveras County* (1950), which uses American folk elements; the cantatas *The Prairie* (1942), also adapted for orchestra, and *Song of Songs* (1946); *Psalms* (1957) for voices and orchestra; a symphony (1944) and 2 piano concertos (1943, 1952).

Foster Myles Birket (1825–99). English painter and book illustrator, e.g. of Longfellow. He produced a very large number of extremely popular drawings and watercolours (and, for a period, oil paintings), almost always of rustic life.

Foster Stephen (Collins) (1826–64). U.S. composer of many songs, most famous of which are 'Old Folks at Home' and 'My Old Kentucky Home'.

Foulis Andrew (1712–75) and Robert (1707–76). Printers to the Univ. of Glasgow. Their tradition of sound typographical principles, especially in their treatment of title-pages, bore fruit in the 19th c. Robert publ. an ed. of Horace (1744), and both a fine ed. of Homer (1756–8) and *Paradise Lost* (1770).

found object: **objet trouvé*

ΤΗΣ ΤΟΥ

ΟΜΗΡΟΥ

ΟΔΥΣΣΕΙΑΣ

Ο ΤΟΜΟΣ ΠΡΟΤΕΡΟΣ.

RURSUS, QUID VIRTUS, ET QUID SAPIENTIA POSSIT,
UTILE PROPOSUIT NOBIS EXEMPLAR ULYSSEM.

GLASGUAE;
IN AEDIBUS ACADEMICIS,
EXCUDEBANT ROBERTUS ET ANDREAS FOULIS
ACADEMIAE TYPOGRAPHI,
MDCCLVIII.

Foulis. Ed. of the *Odyssey*

Fouquet. *Charles VII*

Fragonard. *The Swing*

Fouquet. Miniature from *Antiquités Judaïques*

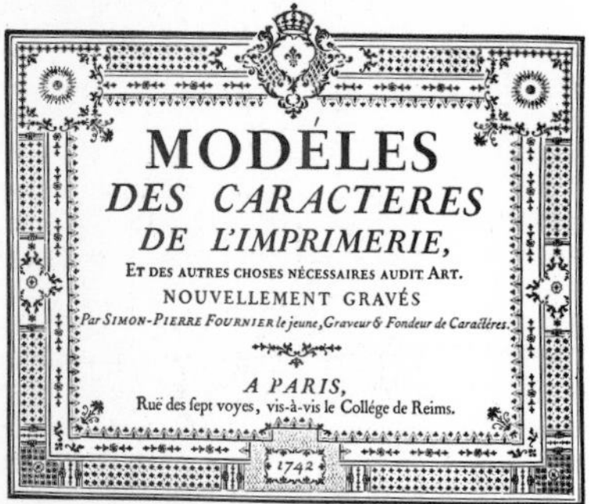

MODÈLES
DES CARACTERES
DE L'IMPRIMERIE,
ET DES AUTRES CHOSES NÉCESSAIRES AUDIT ART.
NOUVELLEMENT GRAVÉS
Par SIMON-PIERRE FOURNIER le jeune, Graveur & Fondeur de Caractères.
A PARIS,
Rue des sept voyes, vis-à-vis le Collége de Reims.
1742

Pierre-Simon Fournier. *Modèles des Caractères de l'Imprimerie*

Anatole France

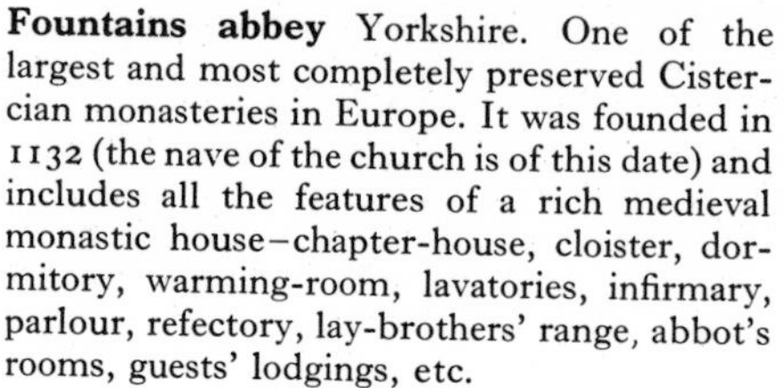

Fountains abbey Yorkshire. One of the largest and most completely preserved Cistercian monasteries in Europe. It was founded in 1132 (the nave of the church is of this date) and includes all the features of a rich medieval monastic house–chapter-house, cloister, dormitory, warming-room, lavatories, infirmary, parlour, refectory, lay-brothers' range, abbot's rooms, guests' lodgings, etc.

Fouqué Friedrich de La Motte (1777–1843). German novelist. F.'s romances, based on medieval traditions and Nordic sagas, were very popular. He wrote the fairy-tale *Undine*, which Giraudoux used for his play *Ondine*.

Fouquet Jean (*c.* 1425–*c.* 80). French painter. F. was born in Tours and probably trained in Paris. He travelled in Italy and brought many of the achievements of Italian painting back to France on his return to Tours in 1448. F. was painter to the French kings and probably the major French artist of the 15th c. Only the miniatures in a copy of the *Antiquités Judaïques* (Bib. N., Paris) are documented, but other attributed works include: the *Melun Diptych* (panels are in the M. R. des B.-A., Antwerp and Berlin), the portraits *Charles VII* and *Jouvenel des Ursins* (both Louvre) and the monumental *Pietà* (Parish church, Nouans, France).

Four Chimneys (1953). Film directed by H. *Gosho.

Four Feathers, The (1902). Adventure novel by A. E. W. Mason.

Four Horsemen of the Apocalypse, The. Film (1921) directed by R. *Ingram. Film (1961) directed by V. *Minnelli. Both derived from the novel (1916) of *Blasco Ibañez.

Fourier François-Marie Charles (1772–1837). French social philosopher whose socialistic theories (Fourierism), expounded in *Théorie des Quatre Mouvements* (1808) and subsequent books, had considerable influence in the 19th c. (e.g. the establishment of communities in the U.S.).

Fournier Henri-Alban: *Alain-Fournier

Fournier Pierre (1906–). French cellist, among the greatest in the world; like Casals he is distinguished for his interpretations of Bach's unaccompanied sonatas.

Fournier Pierre-Simon (1712–68). French type-founder who cut a beautiful adaptation of the *romain du roi*, which was to be transitional between the 'old style' and the 'modern' typeface. It was shown in his *Modèles des Caractères de l'Imprimerie* (1742). F. was the first to cut his types in 'families', i.e. an ordinary roman, with matching bold, condensed and lighter faces. F. also originated the 'point' system, standardizing the measurement of type (1737), which he later expounded in his *Manuel Typographique* (1764); the system was to be perfected by F.-A. *Didot. F. also created ornamental initials, shaded capitals and type flower designs which are notable for their delicacy of treatment.

Four Quartets (1943). Cycle of 4 poems by T. S. *Eliot.

fourth: musical *interval

Fox George (1624–91). English religious reformer and founder of the Quakers. His *Journal* was publ. in 1694.

Foxe John (1516–87). English Protestant martyrologist; his *Actes and Monuments* (1563, Latin ed. 1559), better known as 'Foxe's Book of Martyrs', acquired almost Biblical authority among Protestants. Though no stylist, he wrote with virulence and passion, particularly in the descriptions of the Marian persecutions.

Fragonard Jean-Honoré (1732–1806). French rococo painter who studied under Chardin, Boucher and Van Loo, then in Italy. There he was influenced by the painting of Tiepolo and Murillo. A large historical painting won him immediate fame, but he abandoned the grand manner to paint the familiar lovers in gardens, e.g. *The Swing* (Wallace Coll.), and the incidents of clandestine love-affairs, e.g. *The Stolen Kiss* (Hermitage, Leningrad). Some of his finest works are the rapid drawings he made with pencil, sepia and bistre wash, or red chalk. 2 examples of these are *The Bed* (Besançon Mus.) and *Villa d'Este* (Albertina, Vienna).

Framley Parsonage (1861). Novel by Trollope.

France Anatole. Pseud. of Jacques Anatole-François Thibault (1844–1924). French novelist and man of letters. In his earlier years he worked for a publ. but at the age of 32 was made assistant librarian of the Senate, a post which he combined with writing and journalism.

Fountains abbey

Franciabigio. *Knight of Rhodes*

Frans Francken. *The Jews Having Crossed the Red Sea*

Francesco di Giorgio Martini. *Deposition*

For the last 20 years of his life, he dominated the French literary scene. His famous association with Mme Caillavet provided him with a *salon* and encouraged him to produce, while his championship of Dreyfus in the famous crisis which shook the Third Republic, gave him a world-wide reputation as a liberal-minded Socialist. He was awarded the Nobel prize for literature in 1921. After his death, a former secretary publ. an intimate account, *Anatole France en pantoufles* (1924), which revealed him to have been an inveterate amorist and set a fashion in scandalous revelation.
His works, written in a mellifluous, allusive style, with frequent flashes of naughtiness, express humorous scepticism and a kindly understanding of human weaknesses. They are perhaps best described as Montaigne-like essays, presented in novel form. *Thaïs* (1890; 1902), *Le Lys Rouge* (1894; *The Red Lily*, 1937), *L'Île des Pingouins* (1908; *Penguin Island*, 1931), *Les Dieux ont soif* (1912; *The Gods are athirst . . .*, 1951) and *La Révolte des Anges* (1914; *The Revolt of the Angels*, 1933) are amongst his best productions. In the 4 vols of *L'Histoire contemporaine* (1896–1901), he created Monsieur Bergeret who is an endearing caricature of himself.

Francesco di Giorgio Martini (1439–1501/2). Sienese painter, sculptor, architect and engineer. There are a few paintings by F. but after 1477 he devoted himself to other work. This included a great chain of fortifications for the duke of Urbino, the church of S. Maria delle Grazie al Calcinaio at Cortona, a series of bronze reliefs, most famous of which is the *Deposition* in S. Maria del Carmine, Venice, and 4 bronze *Angels* for Siena cathedral. He also wrote a technical treatise on architecture, *Trattato d'architettura* (publ. 1841).

Francia Francesco (Francesco Raibolini) (*c.* 1450–1517/18). Bolognese goldsmith and from 1486 painter in an eclectic style derived mainly from Perugino and L. Costa; until 1507 he worked in partnership with the latter. An altarpiece (N.G., London) *The Virgin with St Anne* with a *Pietà* in the lunette is probably his best-known painting.

Franciabigio Francesco di Cristofano called (*c.* 1482–1525). Florentine painter influenced by Andrea del Sarto, with whom he collaborated on frescoes in the church of the Annunziata, Florence, and elsewhere, and by Raphael, to whom his *Madonna del Pozzo* (Uffizi) was once attributed. F.'s portraits, e.g. *Knight of Rhodes* (N.G., London), are his most distinctive works.

Francis Sir Philip (1740–1818). English administrator and, during his service in India, a bitter opponent of Warren Hastings. There is very strong evidence that he wrote *The Letters of *Junius*.

Francis Sam (1923–). U.S. tachiste painter who settled in Paris in 1950. His interest in painting began when he was in hospital, wounded in World War II; he produced his 1st abstract work in 1947. His work includes murals for the K.-halle, Basle (1956–8) and the Sofu School of Flower Arrangement, Tokyo (1957).

Francis of Assisi St (1182–1226). Italian mystic and poet, canonized in 1228. He was the son of a prosperous merchant but abandoned the comfortable life in early youth to embrace evangelic poverty and preach brotherhood and humility; he founded the Franciscan order.
The beautiful and mystical hymn, *Canticle of the Sun*, proclaiming the brotherhood of all creatures in the eyes of God, was probably written in 1224 and is the 1st surviving poetic composition in Italian. The *Fioretti* (*Little Flowers*) is a coll. of fragments by F. dictated to his disciples, and conveys the same mystical spirit.

Franck César (1822–90). Belgian-born composer and organist working in Paris from the early 1840s. He worked as a church organist, was appointed organ professor at the Paris Conservatoire in 1872 and received true recognition as a composer later still. His pupils include d'Indy, and Debussy admired his work. F.'s music has strong affinities with the contemporary German romantic composers; it includes: symphony in D min. (1889) in which F. employs *cyclic form; the symphonic poems *The Djinns* and *Le Chasseur maudit*, based on Burger; *Symphonic Variations* for piano and orchestra, a string quartet and other chamber music and organ music. His music is romantic, academic and mystical, making great use of pedal-points and using very rich meandering modulations, a style no doubt influenced by hours at the organ-loft.

Francken (Franck) a family of Flemish painters extending from Nicolas F. (*c.* 1525–96) to Constantinus F. (1661–1717). Probably the most talented was FRANS F. the Younger

Sam Francis. *Summer No. 1* (1957)

César Franck

Benjamin Franklin: painting by Charles Willson Peale

Franju. *Les Yeux sans Visage*

S. Maria Gloriosa dei Frari

Frankenthal group

Frankenthal Chinese tea-house (detail)

(1581–1642) who painted altarpieces and small, somewhat crowded scenes with a mannerist emphasis on lighting and eccentric detail, e.g. *The Jews Having Crossed the Red Sea* (K.-halle, Hamburg).

François de Sales St (1567–1622). Savoyard bishop, an outstanding figure in the Counter-Reformation, and notable also for his sermons, correspondence and writing. F.'s *Introduction à la vie dévote* (1609) was a model for Jeremy Taylor's *Holy Living*.

Franju Georges (1912–). French film director. Co-founder of the Cinémathèque Française; his late début as a feature director (1958) was preceded by a series of 13 shorts (1949–58). As he has no great facility for handling narrative, his shorts and features are very similar in their virtues. His style is marked by the 'poetic' expression of complex implications with a single image. His intense lyricism is not limited to his more gentle work, *Le Grand Méliès* (1952) or *La Première Nuit* (1958), but extends over the horrifying images of the slaughterhouse (*Le Sang des Bêtes*, 1949), the asylum (*La Tête contre les Murs*, 1958) and the operating-table (*Les Yeux sans Visage*, 1959). Among his other works are the documentaries *Le Théâtre National Populaire* (1956) and *Notre-Dame, cathédrale de Paris* (1957). His most recent feature is *Judex* (1963), an act of homage to *Feuillade.

Frankel Benjamin (1906–). English composer. His works include a violin concerto, sub-titled *For the Six Million* (i.e. the Jews killed by the Nazis), *Youth Music* for strings, original title *Music for Young Comrades*, and much film music.

Frankenheimer John (1930–). U.S. film director. F. has become the favourite director of the more domineering actor/producers: Douglas, Sinatra and particularly Lancaster, who has appeared in 4 of his films. After his 1st film, *The Younger Stranger* (1957), his films have become more elaborate stylistically. Recently he has been exploring a line of political fantasy in *The Manchurian Candidate* (1962) and *Seven Days in May* (1963), exceptionally well-made thrillers.

Frankenstein or the Modern Prometheus (1818). Novel by Mary *Shelley; also made into a film (1931), directed by J. *Whale.

Frankenthal. German (hard-paste) *porcelain factory (1755–99) opened by Paul-Antoine Hannong, owner of the *Strassburg faïence factory, which set the style for early F. productions; later work showed the influence of Sèvres. Important modellers working at F. include Johann Wilhelm Lanz (*fl.* 1745–60), at first working at Strassburg, and the sculptor Konrad Linck (1732–93). The best work was produced between 1755 and *c.* 1775.

Franklin Benjamin (1706–90). U.S. statesman prominent in the struggle for independence from Britain, a writer who helped to draft *The Declaration of Independence*. F. was a printer by trade; he wrote and publ. the *Pennsylvania Gazette* (1729–66). His many works are written in plain style and exemplify 18th-c. faith in reason and humanity, common sense, science and deism. His yearly *Poor Richard's Almanack* (1732–57) contained his downright philosophizing and many of his quasi-proverbial sayings.

Franny and Zooey (1961). Book of 2 long linked stories by J. D. Salinger.

Franz Robert (1815–92). German song composer. His 1st set of 12 songs (1843) were acclaimed by R. Schumann. For many years F. directed the singing academy at Halle, but had to resign because of deafness (1867). He wrote over 350 songs, of consistently fine workmanship, but restrained in sentiment, style and scope.

Franzén Franz Michael (1772–1847). Swedish poet and churchman; an important figure in the Swedish romantic movement.

Frari. S. Maria Gloriosa dei Frari, Venice; one of the 2 great friars' churches of Venice. Built *c.* 1250–1350, it is typical of Italian Gothic–wide, spacious and totally lacking in vertical emphases. The nave arcade is of tall cylindrical piers held together both longitudinally and laterally across the nave by wooden tie-beams (unthinkable in the Gothic of France or England) which perform the function of buttresses. The vault, of brick, is quadripartite. The church contains numerous works of art including Titian's *Assumption*.

Frauenlob. The name commonly given to the German poet Heinrich von Meissen (*c.* 1250–1318), after a lay of his in praise of the Virgin

Mary. He wrote 2 other lays and numerous lyrics and is believed to have founded the 1st *mastersinger school.

Frazer Sir James George (1854–1941). Scottish anthropologist and writer, author of *The Golden Bough* (2 vols 1890, 12 vols 1907–15), an anthropological work of immense importance, which, though since disputed, did much to establish anthropology as a subject worthy of serious study. This and F.'s trs of Pausanias (1898) also rate high as works of literature.

Freaks (1932). Film directed by T. *Browning.

Fréchette Louis-Honoré (1839–1908). French-Canadian poet who became known throughout the French-speaking world, and a Revolutionary politician who spent some years in exile in the U.S. His colls include *Les Oiseaux de Neige* (1879) and *Les Fleurs Boréales* (1881).

Freda Riccardo (1909–). Italian film director. One of the few talented directors who makes Italian spectaculars.

Frederick II 'the Great', King of Prussia (1712–86). F. patronized Voltaire for a time, and himself wrote extensively in French, including an *Anti-Machiavel* (1740) and *De la litérature allemande* (1780). He also composed and prided himself on his flute playing.

Fredro Aleksander (1793–1876). Polish poet and dramatist who served under Napoleon as a young man. His comedies, written in the style of Molière and Goldoni, have become classics of the Polish stage; they include *Maż i żona* (1826), *Śluby panieńskie* (1830; *Maidens' Vows*, 1940), *Pan Jowialski* (1834), *Zemsta* (1838) and *Dożywocie* (1838).

Freeman Mary Eleanor, née Wilkins (1852–1930). U.S. regional novelist and short-story writer; her subject is New England.

free verse. Verse which follows no regular metrical or rhyming scheme. Although anticipated e.g. by Klopstock and Matthew Arnold (*The Strayed Reveller*), f. v. was in effect an innovation of Laforgue and the symbolists; Walt Whitman and T. S. Eliot introduced it into English.

Fregonese Hugo (1908–). Argentinian film director. Between his emergence from the Argentinian cinema to direct his 1st Hollywood film, *One Way Street* (1949), and his disappearance into the jungle of Italian cinema with *Marco Polo* (1961), F.'s work was marked by an unusually rigorous directorial style, which applied in a series of westerns culminating in *Blowing Wild* (1953) and a violent thriller, *Black Tuesday* (1954). His best work was the British thriller *Harry Black* (1958).

Freie Bühne, Die. German theatre group founded in 1889, corresponding to the *Théâtre Libre in Paris, to produce the realistic plays of Ibsen and those influenced by him.

Freischütz, Der (German, 'The Hunter'). Opera by *Weber, libretto by F. Kind; 1st performance in Berlin in 1821.

Fréminet Martin (1567–1619). French painter of the 2nd school of *Fontainebleau who spent about 15 years in Italy and was strongly affected by the mannerism of the Chevalier d'Arpino. In 1603 Henry IV recalled him to France, where his works included decorations for the Trinité chapel, Fontainebleau (begun 1608).

French Leonard (1908–). Australian painter. His work often has religious themes and uses abstract shapes.

French Revolution, The (1837). History by T. *Carlyle.

French suites. Nickname of a set of 6 keyboard suites in the French style by J. S. *Bach.

French Without Tears (1936). Play by Terence Rattigan.

Freneau Philip (Morin) (1752–1832). American poet, journalist and Revolutionary of Huguenot ancestry. He participated actively in the War of Independence and also wrote bitter satires against the British. His most popular works were the post-war light satirical poems on American subjects, but he also wrote such full-length poems as *The Power of Fancy* (1770).

Frenzy (1944). Film directed by A. *Sjöberg.

Frere John Hookham (1769–1846). English writer of light verse, mock-heroics and parodies; he made excellent trs of Aristophanes.

Fréron Élie-Catherine (1718–76). Celebrated French critic. F. ed. 2 of the earliest literary

Frederick II with his orchestra

Fregonese. Ruth Roman and Gary Cooper in *Blowing Wild*

Fréminet. Trinité chapel

Fresco. Details of Renaissance frescoes, showing characteristic effects. See also colour plate 36

Sigmund Freud

Frescobaldi

Fretting. Chippendale design

Freundlich. *Composition* (1933)

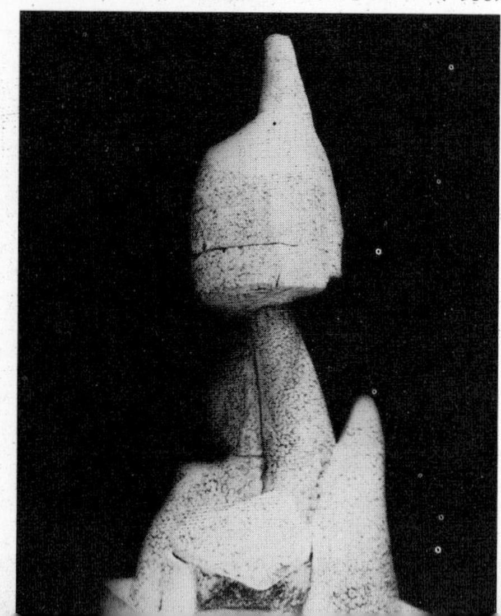

periodicals, notably the *Année littéraire*, through which he attacked Voltaire and the **philosophes*.

fresco. Properly, the technique of wall painting on unset plaster. In true or *buon f.* layers of lime-plaster are applied; while the final layer (*intonaco*) is still wet the painter applies his colours so that they become integrated with the wall. This technique, perfected in Renaissance Italy, produces very durable works in suitable climatic conditions; the most famous example is the ceiling of the Sistine Chapel by Michelangelo. In *f. secco*, painted on lime-plaster which has set, flaking tends to occur and the range of colours is restricted; but it produces light colours and delicate tones which made it a popular technique in the rococo period.

Frescobaldi Girolamo (1583–1643). Italian composer and organist. He studied under L. Luzzaschi and spent a few months in the Netherlands. He was organist at St Peter's, Rome from 1608 to 1628 and from 1634 onwards, serving at Florence in the interim. J. J. *Froberger was his pupil. F.'s organ music, among it the famous coll. *Fiori musicali* (1635), shows a transition from the formalism and fantasy of Renaissance music to the architectonic compositions of the baroque; in its chromaticism, use of popular songs as themes for partitas and even its use of rubato, it was the great culmination of a long tradition. He also wrote *canzoni* for instruments, madrigals and arias, but much vocal music has been lost.

Freshman, The (1925). Film with H. *Lloyd.

Freson Robert (1926?–). Belgian-born U.S. photographer known for his carefully controlled colour work and the utilization of long exposures whenever possible. A long-time student and disciple of Irving Penn.

fret. In certain musical stringed instruments, among them the guitar, lute and viol, the finger-board is crossed by bars of wood or metal or by pieces of gut; these are the f.s. When the player's finger presses the string down on to the finger-board the string length is shortened thus giving a higher note. The f.s are so placed that stopping the string successively at each raises the pitch by semitones. The tone quality is affected by how far the finger is placed behind the f. Also *clavichord.

fretting. Decoration by cutting all the way through and removing areas of a material, creating a kind of patterned grating. The term fret has a particular meaning with reference to the cut-out geometrical designs used in 'Chinese' furniture in mid-18th-c. England (also *key pattern).

Freud Lucien (1902–). German-born British painter. He paints with a hard, linear realism, mostly portraits, but also paintings showing a mysterious relationship between plants and human beings which are almost surrealistic in character. He has lived and worked in Paris and Greece.

Freud Sigmund (1856–1939). Austrian psychologist and writer. F.'s work as a clinical neurologist led him to study neurotic illnesses and evolve theories which have become fundamental in psychology. Some of these have directly affected the arts; F.'s description of the unconscious mind and psychoanalysis, his method of investigating it by free association, was used by the surrealists (e.g. their experiments with automatic writing) and action painters. Generalized–and not always accurate–ideas of psychoanalytical theory have become all-pervasive, and all art since the 1920s has in some respects been influenced by them. Also important have been F.'s emphasis on infant sexuality and the sublimation of the sex drive in other activities–including artistic activity, e.g. *Eine Kindheitserinnerung des Leonardo da Vinci* (1910; *Leonardo da Vinci*, 1916). F.'s works include *Die Traumdeutung* (1900; *The Interpretation of Dreams*, 1913) and *Zur Psychopathologie des Alltagslebens* (1904; *The Psychopathology of Everyday Life*, 1914).

Freundlich Otto (1878–1943). German painter, sculptor and graphic artist. Living in Paris from 1909 he took part in abstractionist experiments. He exhibited with the cubists and the November group in Berlin and was a member of the Cercle et Carré and Abstraction-Création groups. His work was classified as 'degenerate' by the Nazis. F., a Jew, died in the concentration camp at Lublin, Poland.

Freyssinet Eugène (1879–1962). French engineer and a pioneer in the use of reinforced concrete, and later patentee (1928) of pre-stressed concrete. Most of his work has been bridges, but his fame among architects rests on his airship hangars at Orly (built 1916–24, destroyed in 1944), where a powerful architectural form was created by a bold engineering solution.

Freytag Gustav (1816–95). German playwright, novelist and journalist. His works include: the comedy *Die Journalisten* (1852), the novel *Soll und Haben* (1855; *Debit and Credit*, 1857), a saga of 19th-c. commercialism, and *Bilder aus der deutschen Vergangenheit*, a series of historical studies which formed the basis for a 'national epic' cycle of novels.

Fricker Peter Racine (1920–). English composer whose teachers included M. Seiber. Dense and complex linear counterpoint, dissonance and latterly 12-note methods are main characteristics of his music. His works include: the choral work *The Vision of Judgement* (1956); 2 symphonies; *Litany for Double String Orchestra* (1955); piano and violin concertos; and chamber music, including a wind quintet and 2 string quintets.

Friedrich Caspar David (1774–1840). Leading German romantic landscape painter and engraver who studied in Copenhagen (1794–8) and settled in Dresden. His characteristic subjects, depicted in a sharply delineated style, were Gothic ruins, stark contorted trees, bleak seascapes and mountain crags often seen under mysterious lighting effects and peopled with lonely figures, insignificant before nature. Well-known examples are *Abbey Graveyard under Snow* (Berlin), *Capuchin Friar by the Sea*, *Man and Woman Contemplating the Moon* (both Berlin) and *Wreck of the 'Hope'* (K.-halle, Hamburg).

Friesz Othon (1879–1949). French post-impressionist painter and designer, friend of Raoul Dufy and Matisse and for a time a member of the fauves.

frieze. Architectural term for (1) the middle section of an entablature, between architrave and cornice; f.s of the Doric order consist of *triglyphs and *metopes; (2) a band of relief carving round the top of a building or room; and (3) the space between a picture-rail (or the top of panelling) and the ceiling or cornice.

Frisch Max (1911–). German-Swiss novelist e.g. *Stiller* (1954; *I'm not Stiller*, 1958) and *Homo Faber* (1957) and dramatist. Preoccupied with problems of love, marriage (responsibility, commitment), success and failure, and, above all, identity. What one is conflicts with what one was–or is thought to be. Preconceptions, 'images' destroy. Of his plays *Andorra* (1961; 1963), a harrowing study in prejudice (anti-Semitism), exposes–*inter alia*–the smallness and complacency of a small country; *Biedermann* (1953; *The Fire Raisers*, 1958) denounces the ostrich-like pusillanimity of an unprincipled, 'respectable' bourgeois businessman in the face of overt and destructive extremism.

frit. In the manufacture of glass some of the ingredients were occasionally melted together before use. Materials so used included the alkali and some of the sand. These were fused in a furnace and when cool were known as f. This was then ground and added to the final mixture which went into the crucible to be melted into glass ready for blowing. A similar f. is also used in porcelain manufacture.

Frith William Powell (1819–1909). English painter of anecdotal subjects, so popular when first exhibited at the R.A. that they required special railings for protection; best known is *Derby Day* (1858; Tate). Although possessed of formidable technical skill he sacrificed the overall effect of his pictures to various independent incidents and human 'types'.

Froben Johann (1460–1527). German printer and publ. who as the successor to J. Amerbach (d. 1513) at the Amerbach Press, Basle, played a major part in German humanism. His books were fine works of art and, in conjunction with Erasmus, editorial adviser to the firm, important contributions to the new scholarship. F.'s publs included an ed. of St Jerome and Erasmus's ed. of the Greek New Testament (1516).

Froberger Johann Jacob (1616–67). German composer and organist, for 4 years a pupil of G. *Frescobaldi. He integrated Italian and French techniques of keyboard composition into his own work to found the German style inherited by J. S. Bach. F.'s compositions show the virtuosity characteristic of German performers; he also developed the French suite, shaping its classical form, took over and expanded Frescobaldi's use of rubato and developed fugal writing, exploring and stabilizing the use of the subject/counter-subject motif.

Fröding Gustav (1860–1911). Swedish journalist and poet. From about 1894 his persistent mental instability became madness but before and in lucid periods thereafter, he developed

Friedrich. *Wreck of the 'Hope'*

Frith. *Derby Day* (detail)

Freyssinet. Airship hangar, Orly

Frieze. Detail from the Great Frieze of the Altar, Pergamon

Froment. *Burning Bush*

Robert Frost

a mature poetic style which established him as one of the very greatest Swedish lyric poets. His major work is the cycle *Gralstank* (1898).

Frogs, The (405 B.C.). Comedy by *Aristophanes.

Froissart Jean (*c.* 1337–*c.* 1405). The greatest historical chronicler of the 14th c., as well as an able poet. His chronicles of the 100 Years War, written (in French) for the English royal family, are vivid and masterly re-creations of experience rather than scholarly analysis, and flattered F.'s aristocratic audiences by portraying their exploits in the language of chivalry.

Froment Nicolas (15th c.). Provençal painter who worked in Italy and at the court of René of Anjou. There are 2 documented works, both triptychs but stylistically far apart–the awkwardly realistic *Raising of Lazarus* (1461; Uffizi) and the symbolical and more accomplished *Burning Bush* (1475/6; cathedral, Aix-en-Provence).

Fromentin Eugène (1820–76). French 'oriental' painter who followed P. Marilhat and Delacroix. He is, however, remembered for his discerning criticism of Dutch and Flemish painting, *Les Maîtres d'autrefois* (1876; *The Masters of Past Time*, 1913). He also wrote a nostalgic autobiographical novel, *Dominique* (1862; 1932), and 2 books describing N. Africa.

From Here to Eternity (1953). Film directed by F. *Zinnemann; from the novel (1951) by James *Jones.

From the New World. Name given by *Dvořák to his symphony in E. min.

fronte nuovo delle arti. Movement in Italian art founded after World War II by painters and sculptors who recognized the need for Italian artists to free themselves from tradition and come to terms with modern movements elsewhere in Europe. The group (originally the Nuova Secessione Artistica) broke up after exhibiting in Milan (1947) and at the Venice Biennale (1948) because of the disparate opinions of its members, who included both realists and abstractionists.

Frost Robert (Lee) (1874–1963). U.S. poet born in San Francisco. F. attended Dartmouth College and Harvard. He took many jobs, publ. only a handful of poems until his stay in England (1912–15) where his 1st colls, *A Boy's Will* (1913) and *North of Boston* (1914), appeared. He returned to America a recognized poet, and settled down on his New Hampshire farm. By the time of *Mountain Interval* (1916) F. had found a voice, a poetic character, a characteristic rhythm and personal themes which never changed fundamentally; this book contains such typical pieces as *The Road Not Taken*, *Birches*, *Out*, *Out-* and *The Sound of Trees*. F. made himself the New England farmer-poet, writing deeply personal poems which seem to stem from this particular landscape. He never experimented with poetic form and rhythm; he perfected a personal stance: the wry countryman, the common-sense Yankee farmer, the anti-political *laissez-faire* sceptic. His finest lyrics concern the relationship between poet and nature, but are speculative rather than romantically assertive. He also wrote many longer dramatic poems in the form of monologues or dialogues. F. was a unique regional poet in a time of international poetic experiment and urban influences. Works include the colls *New Hampshire* (1923) and *In the Clearing* (1962), and 2 blank-verse plays, *The Masque of Reason* (1945) and *The Masque of Mercy* (1947).

Frost Terry (1915–). English painter working mainly in oils and watercolours; he started painting in a German prisoner-of-war camp. He studied in St Ives and London, where his work received lasting influences from his contact with Victor Pasmore.

frosted silver. A silver alloy from the immediate surface of which the copper or other base metal has been chemically abstracted, so as to leave a very thin and brilliantly white layer of silver. The metal is heated in air until a thin film of copper oxide forms; this is removed by dipping the metal in hot dilute sulphuric acid. Exactly the same process is used for obtaining a thin gold surface on 'coloured gold'.

frottage. Transferring a relief design on to paper by placing the paper over the design and rubbing the paper with charcoal or crayon, etc. Brass rubbings are taken in this way, but the technique received its French name when it was introduced into painting by Max Ernst.

frottola. Late 15th- early 16th-c. musical and poetic form developed in Italy; a forerunner of the madrigal.

Froissart's chronicle. *The Abdication of Richard II*; from a 15th-c. illuminated ms.

Frueauf the Elder, Rueland (1440/50–1507). German painter of altarpieces in a severe Gothic style. He worked in Salzburg and Passau. His son Rueland the Younger was also a painter, of the *Danube school.

Fruits of the Earth (1897). Book by André *Gide.

Fry Christopher (1907–). English verse dramatist. F.'s plays display considerable verbal dexterity and wit; they include religious plays, e.g. *A Sleep of Prisoners* (1951); comedies, e.g. *The Lady's Not for Burning* (1948), *Ring Round The Moon* (1950) a trs. and adaptation of Anouilh's *L'Invitation au Château*, and *A Phoenix too Frequent* (1947); also *Venus Observed* (1950), *The Dark is Light Enough* (1954) and *Curtmantle* (1962).

Fry E. Maxwell (1899–). Pioneer of modern English architecture in the 1930s, and partner of Walter Gropius (1934–6). His houses, particularly those at Kingston and in Frognal Way, Hampstead are among the best British examples of the international style. He now heads a large practice with his wife Jane Drew, with work in India and Africa as well as England.

Fry Roger Eliot (1866–1934). English painter and critic, originally an expert on the masters of the Italian Renaissance but after seeing work by Cézanne in 1906 a powerful propagandist for art of the period and organizer (1910) of the 1st exhibition of post-impressionist paintings in England. In insisting that this revolutionary art be assessed on colour and form alone he followed in the tradition of late 19th-c. aestheticism. His articles and lectures were collected in *Vision and Design* (1920) and *Transformations* (1926). *Omega Workshops.

Frye Northrop (1912–). Leading Canadian critic, whose views, particularly of Blake in *Fearful Symmetry* (1947), appear to have influenced such Canadian poets as James Reaney, Jay Macpherson and Douglas Le Pan.

Füger Friedrich Heinrich (1751–1818). German portrait painter, often in miniature. From 1776 to 1783 he lived in Italy, then settled in Vienna. His style was influenced by late baroque and English portraiture given subtlety by the use of *sfumato* effects.

Fugitive, The (1922–5). Little magazine publ. at Nashville, Tennessee, an important factor in the development of Southern regionalism in literature. Contributors included Ransom, Laura Riding, Tate and Robert Penn Warren.

fugue. A type of musical composition deriving from *canon. It was developed during the 17th c. and perfected by J. S. Bach. A simple f. is in 2 or more *parts or 'voices'; it revolves round a brief musical phrase called the 'subject'. One of the voices announces the subject and then takes up another phrase called the 'counter-subject'; in turn each voice gives subject and counter-subject and then moves into a new line: such a passage, in which each voice in turn enters with the subject, is called an 'exposition'. During the f. there may be many expositions, separated by passages where the subject is absent ('episodes'), and other passages where the subject occurs in 1 voice only. However, a f. has no fixed form, it does not need a counter-subject, does not need episodes, does not require that all the voices appear in the 1st exposition. The only essential feature is the subject, announced by each voice at its 1st entry and recurring fairly frequently during the f. The subject can be modified by *augmentation, diminution or *inversion; it can also be announced by succeeding voices in 'stretto' which occurs when a 2nd voice enters with the subject before the 1st voice has completed it. In classical f. the 1st and 3rd entries of the subject are in the tonic key and the 2nd and 4th, called the 'answers', in the dominant key; if the subject is exactly repeated in the answer, we have a 'real' answer, if the subject has to be modified for harmonic reasons we have a 'tonal' answer.
More complex f.s have 2, 3 or 4 subjects, separately developed and then gradually combined; these are sometimes called 'double, triple or quadruple f.s'. A 'mirror f.' is one in which the various parts can be interchanged and inverted, e.g. the treble line inverted may be transposed into the bass.

Fuldà Hesse. German (hard-paste) *porcelain factory (1765–90) founded by the prince-bishop of F. and producing (now rare) finely modelled and painted ware.

Fulham. A pottery factory was founded at Fulham, Middlesex, by John Dwight, who took out his 1st patent in 1671 for the manufacture of 'transparent earthware' and 'stoneware', never before made in England. In the greyish ware produced he manufactured mostly

Frueuf the Elder. *Ascension of the Virgin*

Christopher Fry

Roger Fry

Fulda figure

Fulham. Salt-glazed stoneware figure

E. Maxwell Fry. Co-operative Bank offices, Accra, Ghana

Isaac Fuller. *Self-portrait*

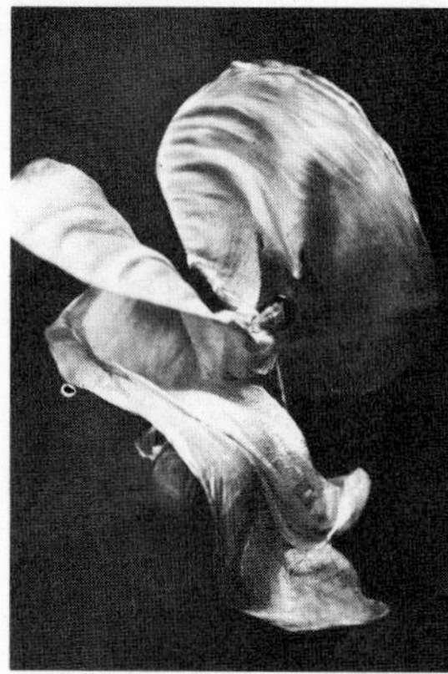

Loie Fuller

Buckminster Fuller. Geodesic dome

Furniss. Caricature of Beerbohm Tree

Furtwängler conducts

vessels for domestic and even commercial use. Also attributed to Dwight are the rare figures and busts in salt-glazed stoneware, finely modelled by an unidentified artist, possibly Grinling Gibbons. A fine red stoneware sometimes called 'red porcelain', was also produced at Fulham *c.* 1693. The factory continued into the 19th c., but its productions were unremarkable.

Fuller Henry B(lake) (1857–1929). U.S. novelist whose *The Cliff Dwellers* (1893), on Chicago and modern city life, is an early example of naturalism in U.S. literature.

Fuller Isaac (d. 1672). English painter of murals and portraits. He studied under F. Perrier in France and worked in Oxford and London, leading an increasingly dissolute life. His decorative works are now lost but his portraits, particularly the raffish *Self-portrait* (1670) in the Bodleian Library, Oxford, have great dash and bravura.

Fuller Loie (1862–1928). U.S. dancer of the Isadora Duncan school whose speciality was the *Serpentine Dance*, using yards of veils and unusual lighting effects. An acquaintance of Debussy, she used music from his *Nocturnes* for her *Nuages* and *Sirènes*. She toured widely in Europe and America with her co.

Fuller Richard Buckminster (1895–). U.S. 'comprehensive designer' (his own phrase); his designs range from cars to map making to a project for a dome over Manhattan. His aim 'maximum gain of advantage from minimal energy input' leads to building forms, usually domes, related to efficient structure, not to efficient function. His domes are built of alloy, plywood, plastics or cardboard, his biggest is a railroad repair shop of 385 ft diameter. F. is a great propagandist and tours the world lecturing at schools of architecture. He lives in a plywood dome of his own design on the campus of the Univ. of Southern Illinois. His publs include *No More Second Hand God* (1963).

Fuller Roy (1912–). English poet and novelist who began writing in the 1930s and, unusually, has constantly improved. His dry manner and use of traditional forms does not conceal his shrewdness and vigour. Colls include *Brutus's Orchard* (1957).

Fuller Samuel (1911–). U.S. film director, writer and producer. Crime reporter, pulp novelist, script writer and war correspondent before he started directing in 1948, his origins show in his predilection for crime and war subjects and in his terse 'tabloid' style, evident in *The Steel Helmet* (1951) and refined through to *Underworld U.S.A.* (1960).

Fuller Sarah Margaret (1810–50). U.S. transcendentalist writer and critic. She was admired for her scholarship and intellect and was with Emerson a co-founder of *The *Dial* magazine. Her books include *Woman in the Nineteenth Century* and influential trs of Goethe.

Fuller Thomas (1608–61). English writer and preacher, a chaplain to Charles II. *The Worthies of England* (publ. posth. 1662), on English counties, with biographies of notable local figures, is typical in its imaginative wit and imagery.

Funambules, Théâtre des. Paris theatre (1816–62) famous for its acrobats and performances of pantomime. It was elaborately equipped for scenic transformations and spectacular effects.

functionalism. A major principle of modern architecture and of much modern thinking about design is that the form of a building, tool or piece of equipment should follow from its purpose or function; it is also important that materials should not be forced into decoration. The theory was clearly expressed in the practice of the *Bauhaus, and the ideas of *Le Corbusier have also been influential. In the 1930s architectural designs frequently stressed the structure of the building, for example using glass *curtain walls. Functionalist theories derived inspiration from 19th-c. engineering and utilitarian building such as warehouses.

fundamental note. In music the 1st note of a *harmonic series.

Funny Face (1956). Film directed by S. *Donen.

Furetière Antoine (1619–88). French author; he wrote *Le Roman bourgeois* (1666; *City Romance*, 1671), a novel describing middle-class Parisian life with unusual realism. F. was expelled from the Académie Française in 1685 for publ. his own dictionary before that of the Académie was completed.

Furini Francesco (*c.* 1600–46). Florentine painter of Biblical and mythological subjects heavy with female nudes, and of single half-length nudes in oppressive bluish tones with strong *sfumato*. In the 1630s he became a priest and devoted himself to religious works in the manner of G. Reni.

Furniss Harry (1854–1925). Anglo-Irish caricaturist, illustrator and writer. He settled in London (1873) and drew for various illustrated magazines. He illustrated complete eds of Dickens (1910) and Thackeray (1911) and in 1887 held an exhibition parodying works shown at the R.A.

Furphy Joseph (1843–1912). Australian novelist, who, under the pseud. 'Tom Collins', publ. what he described as his 'offensively Australian' *Such Is Life* (1903), occasionally thought to have unusual literary merit. Self-conscious as well as self-confident, it represents an aspect of Australian literature whose importance is now mainly historical.

Furtwängler Wilhelm (1886–1958). German conductor, son of the archaeologist ADOLF F. (1853–1907). F. was conductor of the Berlin Philharmonic from 1922, of the New York Philharmonic (1925–7 and 1937–8). He resigned his German appointments in 1934 on the prohibition of Hindemith's music, but returned to the Berlin Philharmonic in 1935.

Fury (1936). Film directed by F. *Lang.

Fuseli Henry (1741–1825). Swiss-born painter, engraver, draughtsman of great power and penetrating art critic, associated with the English school. After studying art in Berlin and Rome, where he copied Michelangelo, F. settled in London. *The Nightmare*, based on a painting by Reynolds won him early fame and his eccentric style, combining Italian mannerism with German elements, had both a vogue and an influence in England; as professor of painting at the R.A. he taught many leading early 19th-c. English artists. He made the celebrated remark that his friend Blake was 'good to steal from'.

Fust Johann (d. 1466). German printer who took over *Gutenberg's press (1455) following a foreclosure suit in his favour. Along with Peter Schoeffer F. was the first to use *fere humanistica* (miniscule hands containing elements of both Gothic and Roman style) in print, and also the first to make experiments in the printing of ornamental letters in colour. Publs include a magnificent 48-line Bible (1462), *Psalterium Moguntinum* (1457 and 1459) and *De Officiis* (1465).

Fustel de Coulanges Numa-Denis (1830–89). French historian, author of *La Cité antique* (1864; *The Ancient City*, 1874), analysing the evolution of religion in antiquity, and works on the Germanic invasions of Gaul.

futurism. Italian literary and artistic movement. The 1st futurist manifesto was publ. in *Le Figaro*, in 1909 by the poet and dramatist Marinetti. In 1910 3 manifestoes were publ., including the painters' 'Technical Manifesto'. F. celebrated the machine (proclaiming the racing-car more beautiful than the *Victory of Samothrace*), rejected the art of the past and advocated the destruction of museums. F. paintings represented figures and objects in motion; poetry employed 'industrial' imagery and a grammar and vocabulary deliberately distorted in the interests of onomatopoeia. Artists concerned included Boccioni, Carlo Carrà, Russolo and Giacomo Balla; writers, Soffici and Papini; architects, Sant'Elia. After World War I f. became associated with Fascism. It had several off-shoots, e.g. Robert Delaunay's simultanéisme, which was also related to cubism. More specifically a marriage of these 2 movements was Russian cubo-futurism, represented in e.g. Malevich's painting and the poems of Khlebnikov, Mayakovsky and Pasternak. It also influenced such painters as Fernand Léger and Marcel Duchamp.

Fux Johann Joseph (1660–1741). Austrian composer, organist and music theorist, author of *Gradus ad Parnassum* (1725) which dominated the teaching of counterpoint for over a c. and was used by Mozart and Haydn. F.'s own compositions were in the tradition of Corelli and included: 50 masses, among them the *Missa Canonica*, demonstrating all the devices of counterpoint; 19 operas, e.g. *Constanza e Fortezza* (1723); 11 oratorios and over 30 trio sonatas.

Fyt Jan (1611–61). Flemish painter of still-life, especially trophies of the hunt, and a few outstanding flower paintings. Trained by Frans Snyders, he probably painted some of the animals in paintings by Jordaens and Rubens. Typical of his rich colour and technical brilliance is *Still-life with Pageboy and Parrot* (Wallace Coll., London).

Fuseli. *The Death of Oedipus*

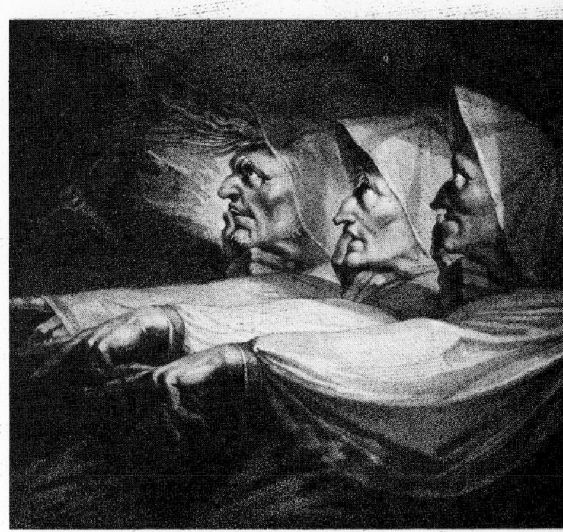

Fuseli. The 3 Witches, from *Macbeth*

Cubo-futurism. Malevich, *Head of a Peasant Girl* (1912–13)

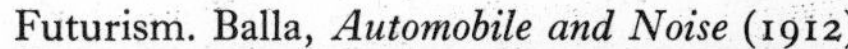

Futurism. Balla, *Automobile and Noise* (1912)

Fyt. *Still-life with Pageboy and Parrot*

Gadrooning. Cover of a spice-box by David Willaume

G

Jacques-Ange Gabriel. The Petit Trianon

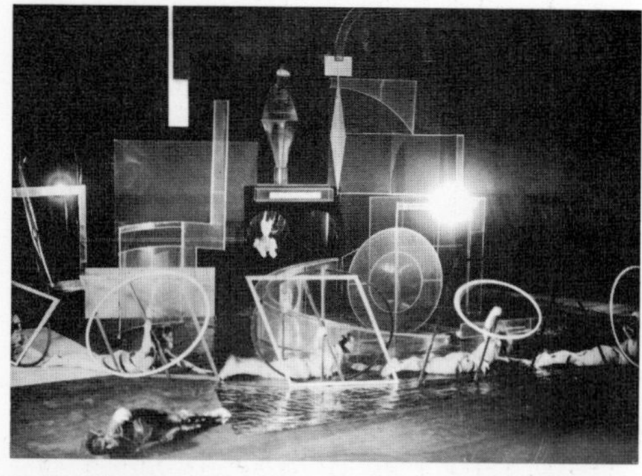
Gabo. Set for the ballet *La Chatte* (1927). Also *constructivism

Agnolo Gaddi. Detail from *The True Cross* cycle

G. A group named after the magazine *G* (*Gestaltung*, German, 'construction') founded by El Lissitzky. It rejected the fine-art tradition for a constructivist aesthetic; the architect Mies van der Rohe was a member.

Gabin Jean (1904–). French film actor; he reached his peak under Renoir in his masterpiece against war – *La Grande Illusion* (1936) and under *Carné in *Quai des Brumes* (1938) and *Le Jour se Lève* (1939). Still the typical Frenchman, he returned to films after the war.

gable. Architectural term for the triangular end of a roof with 2 sloping sides (i.e. a GABLE-ROOF).

Gable Clark (1901–60). U.S. film actor. Endowed with aggressive appeal for women, brutal rather than romantic, confident, masterful and imperious, G. was the undisputed king of Hollywood for nearly 30 years. Classics amongst his films are *Mutiny on the Bounty* (1935), Van Dyke's *San Francisco* (1936) and Fleming's *Gone with the Wind* (1939).

Gabo Naum (né Pevsner) (1890–). Painter of Russian origin trained as an engineer in Munich before turning to the creation of abstract constructions. The first of these was *Bust* (1915), a cubist-influenced work executed in planes of wood. In 1917 he returned to Russia with his elder brother, the painter Antoine Pevsner, and settled in Moscow, becoming associated with the local *avant-garde* led by Malevich and Tatlin. In 1920 the Pevsners issued their 'Realist Manifesto' which declared against the functionalism of Tatlin and Rodchenko's constructivism; a year later they left Russia, finding the artistic climate unsympathetic, for Berlin. G. continued to develop his ideas in constructions made of glass, plastics and metals, after Berlin, in Paris, then England and, since 1939, in the U.S.

Gaboriau Émile (1832–73). French novelist, author of the 1st French detective novels and creator of Monsieur Lecoq, a forerunner of Sherlock Holmes. His many novels include *Le Dossier No. 113* (1867; *Warrant No. 113*, 1884), *Monsieur Lecoq* (1869; 1887), and *La Corde au cou* (1873; *In Deadly Peril*, 1888).

Gabriel. Family of French architects. Jacques I (*c.* 1630–86), his son Jacques II (1667–1742) and grandson Jacques-Ange (*c.* 1710–82) were all employed by the French crown. Jacques-Ange worked at Versailles for Louis XV, his chief contributions being the theatre and the Petit Trianon, a separate villa in pure classical style.

Gabrieli Andrea (*c.* 1510–86). Venetian composer and organist, uncle and teacher of G.G. He studied under A. Willaert at St Mark's, Venice and through his German pupils, e.g. H. L. Hassler, propagated the Italian style in Germany. He was 2nd organist at St Mark's to C. Merulo, whom he succeeded in 1585. Developing *Willaert's experiments with antiphonal treatment of polyphonic settings of the Psalms, G. evolved a type of composition in which 2 or 3 choirs of instruments and voices were used for effects of strong contrast. G. also wrote secular and sacred choral music.

Gabrieli Giovanni (*c.* 1555–1612). Venetian composer, pupil of O. Lasso at Munich, and of his uncle A.G., whom he succeeded as principal organist of St Mark's, Venice. G.'s own influence, especially in northern Europe, was great and his greatest pupil was H. Schütz. By developing the antiphonal use of choirs of voices and instruments, evolved by his uncle, G. established this new form, and the elaborate ornamentation of some of his solo instrumental parts prefigures the instrumental concerto. G.'s works include the *Sacrae Symphoniae* (1597), among them the *Sonata pian e forte* for violin, cornett and 6 trombones. This is one of the earliest written specifications of instruments.

Gabriel y Galán José Maria (1870–1905). Spanish poet whose poem *El Ama* (1901) suddenly made him famous. His poetry is strong and vigorous, and is mainly inspired by the traditions and life of his native Castile.

Gaddi. A family of Italian artists who sustained the style of Giotto for 2 generations in Florence. Taddeo G. (d. 1366) was probably an assistant to Giotto. His own best-known work is the fresco cycle *Life of the Virgin* (S. Croce, Florence). His sons, Agnolo and Giovanni, were working in the Vatican in 1369. Agnolo painted the fresco cycles *The True Cross* (S. Croce, Florence) and *Life of the Virgin* (Prato cathedral) as well as a number of panels, e.g. *Coronation of the Virgin* (N.G., Washington).

Gainsborough. *Cornard Wood*

Gainsborough. *Mr and Mrs Andrews*

Gade Niels Vilhelm (1817–90). Danish romantic composer. In 1840 his overture *Echoes from Ossian* won a prize and in 1843 Mendelssohn conducted G.'s symphony no. 1 in C at Leipzig, where G. became Mendelssohn's assistant (1844–7). G. became conductor of the Copenhagen Music Society and a director of the new Copenhagen Conservatory (1866).
The spontaneity and nationalist inspiration of G.'s early work, e.g. the piano sonata in E min. (1840, revised 1854) and the choral work *Elverskad* (1853), gradually faded. Later works include: 8 further symphonies, 4 large cantatas and the 1st and 3rd acts of A. Bournonville's ballet *Et Folkesagn* (1853).

gadrooning. Decoration with semicircular ridges; often used as a decorative border to silver plate of the 17th and 18th cs.

Gafori Franchino, also called 'Franchinus Gaffurius' (1451–1522). Italian composer, music theorist and teacher, musical director of Milan cathedral. His music shows the prevailing Flemish influence; his major didactic work was *Practica Musicae.*

Gagliano. Family of Italian violin makers whose finest work was done in the 18th c. The most important members were ALESSANDRO (d. *c.* 1730) and his sons NICOLA and GENNARO who worked in the tradition of Stradivarius.

Gagliano Marco da (*c.* 1575–1642). Italian composer, working at Florence, associated with the *camerata. His opera *Dafne* (1608), admired by J. Peri, has a preface in which G. complains of the excessive embellishments added by singers to their parts; it requires clear enunciation of the words and also gives performing instructions for the instrumentalists. His brother GIOVANNI BATTISTA was also a composer.

Gagnebin Henri (1886–). Swiss composer, organist and director of the Geneva Conservatory (1925–57). He has composed oratorios, symphonies and string quartets.

Gaiety Theatre. London theatre (1868–1939) famous for its musical shows and its chorus of Gaiety girls. The Gaiety Theatre, Manchester, founded by Annie *Horniman, was important in the history of the repertory movement.

Gaimar Geoffroi. 12th-c. Anglo-Norman poet who composed *Estoire des Engleis,* a verse chronicle of England; it includes a version of the legend of Havelok the Dane.

Gainsborough Thomas (1727–88). English painter of landscape and portraits. Born at Sudbury, Suffolk, G. was trained in London. His early style was formed by a study of the figures in Watteau and other French rococo painters while working for the engraver Gravelot, combined with the influence of the Dutch masters of landscape, especially J. van Ruisdael and J. Wynants.
G. returned to Suffolk and between *c.* 1750 and 1759 painted some of his finest work, including the combination of a double portrait and a landscape, *Mr and Mrs Andrews* (N.G., London) and the large landscape *Cornard Wood* (or *Gainsborough's Forest*) (N.G., London). In 1759 G. was astute enough to move to Bath, where he soon came to the notice of the fashionable world. When his reputation spread to London he moved there in 1774. In a few years he disputed with Reynolds the enormous profit and prestige of being the leading portrait painter in England and even in Europe. Though a founder-member of the R.A., G. later withdrew and exhibited his paintings in his own home, Schomberg House, Pall Mall. His success continued to his death and his rival, Reynolds, did much to confirm his fame. In his later portraits G. borrowed from Van Dyck, e.g. *The Blue Boy* (San Marino, California). He was most successful in painting women of obvious spirit and animation, e.g. *Countess Howe* (Kenwood, London), such sympathetic studies as the newly married couple in *The Morning Walk* (N.G., London), and the delightfully informal sketches of his 2 daughters (paintings in V. and A., Dulwich Gal. and N.G.–all London).
G. preferred to paint idealized landscapes and what Reynolds called his 'fancy pictures'. His strange lighting was his own, but Rubens was an influence on his later work. The feathery brushwork, lyrical style and rich sense of colour can be seen in many galleries. A masterpiece is *The Harvest Wagon* (Barber Inst., Birmingham; version N.G., Ottawa). *Two Shepherd Boys with Dogs Fighting* (Kenwood) is a good example of the 'fancy pictures' and shows the late influence of Murillo. Many of G.'s oil sketches and drawings are of an unusually high quality: *Housemaid* (Tate), and *Mrs Gainsborough Going to Church* (Ashmolean, Oxford).

Gainsborough. *Self-portrait*

Gainsborough. *The Blue Boy.* Also *engraving and colour plate 67

Galileo. Title-page of the *Dialogo* . . .

Galileo Galilei

G. had a lasting influence on English painting, but his only direct follower was his nephew, GAINSBOROUGH DUPONT (*c.* 1754–97), who worked in his studio, completed many of his late portraits and was a skilful imitator of his style.

galante style. Term used of music of certain composers of the rococo period, among them J. C. Bach. The style is marked by elegant melodic line and is an harmonic rather than contrapuntal idiom.

Galgario. *Self-portrait*

Galateo (1559). Book on etiquette by *Della Casa.

Galczyński Konstanty Ildefons (1905–33). Polish lyrical poet, one of the most original talents of the mid 20th c. His poetry presents a curious mixture of sentiment, humour, mockery and genuinely inspired poetic fantasy.

Galdós Benito Pérez: *Pérez Galdós

Gale Zona (1874–1938). U.S. novelist. Her books include *Miss Lulu Bett* (1920), about a downtrodden spinster in a Middle West family; for her dramatization of this she won the 1921 Pulitzer prize.

Galgario Fra Vittore del (Giuseppe Ghislandi) (1655–1743). One of the most important Italian portrait painters of the late baroque period. After studying in Venice under S. Bombelli he worked mainly in Bergamo. His paintings combine the richness of Venetian colouring with a directness derived from G. Moroni.

Galileo Galilei (1564–1642). Italian scientist and astronomer, born in Pisa. Professor of mathematics at Padua, he attracted pupils from all over Europe. G. made fundamental contributions to many branches of science, especially in his *Dialogo sopra i due massimi sistemi* (1632; *The Systeme of the World*, 1661) which established the probability of the heliocentric theory of the solar system. His impact was the greater because he wrote in the vernacular, not Latin; indeed all G.'s writings are distinguished by an elegant and forceful Italian prose style. G.'s trial and confinement by the Inquisition on account of this book made him, for subsequent generations, a martyr.

Galileo Galilei, Das Leben des (1947). Play by Bertolt *Brecht.

Fernando Gallego. *Christ in Majesty*

Gallego Fernando (*fl.* 1466–1507). Spanish painter who worked in and around Salamanca. His style, especially reminiscent of R. van der Weyden, and his use of oils, show him to have been under the Flemish influence strong in Spanish art at the time. There are altarpieces by G. in Zamora cathedral and the Prado.

Gallego Francisco (*fl.* late 15th c.). Spanish painter under Flemish influence, possibly father of Fernando G. The latter's work and his own are not easily distinguishable.

galliard. A vigorous court dance, in 3/4 time, popular in the 16th c. It was usually danced after the stately pavan; pavan and g. were contrasted in mood and were considered a natural combination.

Gallone Carmine (1886–). Italian film director; a veteran director who has made over 100 films since his first in 1914. The most famous is *Scipione l'Africano* (1937), a bloated spectacular sponsored by the Fascist government. He has also made a number of opera films, e.g. *Madame Butterfly* (1955) with Sophia Loren.

Galpin Canon Francis William (1859–1945). English archaeologist and musicologist. He assembled a major coll. of musical instruments, donated in 1917 to the Museum of Fine Arts, Boston (Mass.). The G. Society for the study of musical instruments was founded in 1947.

Galsworthy John (1867–1933). English novelist and playwright. G.'s satires on the moneyed class and social injustices–notably the series of novels *The Forsyte Saga* (1906–21)–are marred by sentimentality over the bourgeois life he questions. His problem plays, e.g. *Strife* (1909), about a miners' strike, and *Justice* (1910), are more vigorous.

Galt John (1779–1839). Scottish novelist whose excellent portrayals of Scottish rural life and manners include *The Ayrshire Legatees* (1821), *Annals of the Parish* (1821), *The Entail* (1823) and *The Provost* (1822).

Galuppi Baldassare (1706–85); also nicknamed 'Il Buranello' from his birthplace, the island of Burano, near Venice. He was an Italian composer of many comic operas. G.'s music was very popular in England, where he lived for a time; from 1748 he was a musical director

Gance. *Napoleon*

of St Mark's, Venice. He wrote numerous serious operas, oratorios, and instrumental and keyboard music.

gamba, viola da (Italian, 'leg viol'). The name formerly used to distinguish the *viols, all of which are rested on or between the legs when played, from members of the violin family (*viola da braccia*, or 'arm viol'), some of which were rested on the arm. The abbreviation, 'gamba' is sometimes affected in English to describe the bass viol.

Game at Chesse, A (1624). Play by Thomas *Middleton.

gamelan. The Indonesian name for the orchestras of Bali and Java. There are various types, but in all of them percussion instruments, especially metal ones, predominate. A g. performed at the Paris Exhibition of 1889, greatly impressing Debussy, and the g.'s highly characteristic instrumental effects have influenced more recent composers such as P. Boulez.

Gammer Gurton's Needle (publ. 1575). Rhymed doggerel play; it and *Ralph Roister Doister* were the earliest English comedies.

gamut. Originally a musical term for the G at the bottom of the bass staff, this being the lowest note in the system of *hexachords. By extension the term was used of the scale above the note and is now used, largely metaphorically, to mean compass or range.

Gance Abel (1889–). French film director; self-taught philosopher and poet, flamboyantly romantic. His early films, despite cinematic skill and critical success, were grandiloquent in style and content, and startlingly naïve. Starting with melodramas like *Mater Dolorosa* (1917) and *La Dixième Symphonie* (1918), he achieved fame with the anti-war film *J'accuse* (1919). After this he was able to raise money for 2 years' shooting on *La Roue* (1922), about railway workers. His most famous film, *Napoleon* (1927), was filmed on a huge budget with sequences using a triptych screen and 3 projectors. *La Fin du Monde* (1931), in which G. played the lead and for which *Ruttmann edited the climatic scenes of the destruction of Paris, was released unfinished and G. was reduced to less ambitious projects. *La Tour de Nesle* (1955), *Austerlitz* (1960), and *Cyrano contre d'Artagnan* (1963) are swash-buckling period adventures.

Gandhi Mohandas Karamchand called Mahatma (1869–1948). Indian mystic and political leader. His simplicity of life is reflected in his prose style, the best available example being his autobiography, a work essential to understanding G. or India.

Ganivet Angel (1865–98). Spanish novelist, essayist and critic and one of the main fore-runners of the *generation of '98. Although his novels show his talent for epic description, his most famous work is his philosophical essay *Idearium español* (1897) which attempts an analysis and interpretation of Spanish history.

Garamond Claude (1480–1561). The major 16th-c. French type-cutter and designer, also the first to devote himself solely to the production of types for trade use. His types freed France from the Gothic letter features, and his models of both roman (cut from 1531 onwards), and Greek (based on the Greek types of Aldus Manutius) typography were in vogue for 2 cs. He cut the famous *grecs du roi* for the printing of Greek mss in the Royal Library.

Garbo Greta (1905–). Swedish actress who went to Hollywood in 1926. She soon 'struck' for better parts; against all expectations, she won. Her beauty and increasingly tragic personality are seen in: *Flesh and the Devil* (1927), *Anna Christie* (1930), *Queen Christina* (1933), and the comedy *Ninotchka* (1939). She retired in 1942.

Garborg Arne (1851–1924). Norwegian writer in Nynorsk (*Aasen). The works of his maturity, such as the novel *Fred* (1892; *Peace*, 1930) and poetry and plays, deal with peasant life and folk-lore.

García de la Huerta Vicente (1734–87). Spanish playwright. He squandered talent on literary and political polemics but his powerful *Raquel* (1778) is the only worth-while 18th-c. Spanish tragedy; neo-classical but within the great Spanish tradition with its powerful style and strong characterization.

García Gutiérrez Antonio (1813–84). Leading Spanish romantic playwright; his 1st successful play *El Trovador* (1836) became the

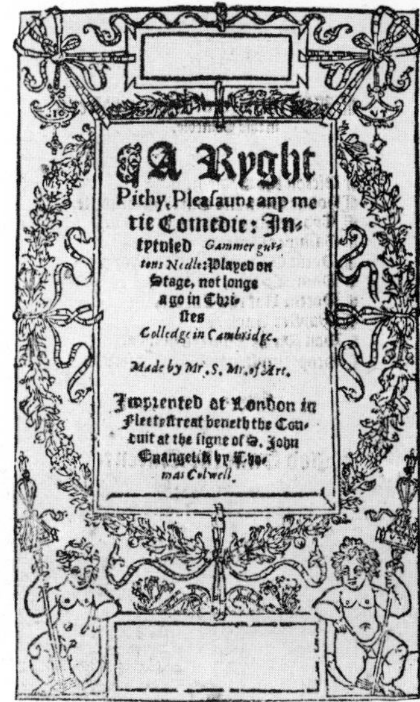

A Ryght
Pithy, Pleasaunt and merie Comedie: Intytuled Gammer gurtons Nedle: Played on Stage, not longe ago in Christes Colledge in Cambridge.
Made by Mr. S. Mr. of Art.
Imprented at London in Fleetestreat beneth the Conduit at the signe of S. John Evangelist by Thomas Colwell.

Gammer Gurton's Needle; title-page of the 1st ed.

¶ Quis credidit Auditui noſtro: & uelatum eſt, Et aſcendit ſicut virgultum radix de terra deſerti: Non erat forma ei,
Petit Canon de Garamond.
Aſpeximus autem eum, & non erat aſpectus, & No ctus fuit & Reiectus inter viros vir dolorum, & expert faciei Ab eo, deſpectus inquam, & non putauimus eu & dolores noſtros portauit, nos Autem reputauimus Deo & HVMILIATVM. W

Garamond. Roman types, 1592

Gamelan orchestra, Bali

Judy Garland in *Meet Me in St Louis*

Gargoyle, Notre-Dame, Paris

Gardella. Block of flats, Alessandria (1952)

Gardener. Abraham Lincoln and General McClellan on the battle-field of Antietam (1862)

basis for Verdi's opera *Il Trovatore*, and another play was used for Verdi's *Simone Boccanegra*.

Garcilaso de la Vega (1503–36). The 1st great poet of the Spanish Renaissance, the 'Prince of Castilian poets'. He was courtier and soldier, led a turbulent life involving exile, and was killed in a military skirmish in S. France. G., who spent his later years in Naples, was steeped in the culture of the Italian Renaissance and his poems are based on Italian and Latin models; their style, however, is highly original and greatly influenced succeeding poets. His finest poems, usually on the theme of unrequited love, are distinguished by their sonorous melancholy and mastery of rhythm; they include sonnets, eclogues and odes in which he adapted Italian metres with assured fluency (*Boscán).

Gardella Ignazio (1905–). Italian architect whose Tuberculosis sanatorium at Alessandria (1937) was one of the most famous Italian buildings of the 1930s. Since the war he has developed a free manner of designing, in contrast to his disciplined 'rationalist' buildings before the war. This freedom sometimes takes him to the verge of historical revivalism, as in a house by him on the Grand Canal, Venice.

garden carpets. A large class of Persian carpet, recorded from the 16th c., in which a garden is represented in schematic or map-like form, often divided into rectangular flower beds and showing flowing water.

Gardener Alexander (1821–82). U.S. photographer, assistant to Mathew *Brady; he was Photographer to the Army of the Potomac during the American Civil War.

Garden of Delights, The. Painting by *Bosch.

Garden Party, The (1922). Short story (and title of a vol.) by Katherine *Mansfield.

Gardner Ava (1922–). U.S. film star. In her early career a statuesque but passionate brunette, G. obtained her 1st important dramatic part in *The Killers* (1946). Among her films since then have been *Barefoot Contessa* (1954) with Humphrey Bogart, *Bhowani Junction* (1956) and Ray's *55 Days at Peking* (1962).

Gargantua. Character created by *Rabelais.

gargoyle (from Old French *gargouille*, 'a throat'). Architectural term for the stone spouts which in medieval buildings were outlets for water collected in the parapet gutter. The term is also applied to the grotesque often carved on the end of the spout; these, like misericords, provided opportunities for the medieval craftsman to exercise his powers of fantasy and satire.

Garland (Hannibal) Hamlin (1860–1940). U.S. novelist and short-story writer. He began his career, encouraged by W. D. Howells, with realist stories about Middle Western life, urging social reform; the novel *Rose of Dutcher's Coolly* (1895) continues the theme but G. followed this with a popular series on the Far West. His best work is in the series on pioneer life which begins with *A Son of the Middle Border* (1917).

Garland Judy (1924–). U.S. singer and actress who made her most famous film in 1939 (*The Wizard of Oz*), and a series of hit musicals including *Meet Me in St Louis* (1944), *Easter Parade* (1948) and the re-make of *A Star is Born* (1954).

Garnett David (1892–). English novelist. His *Lady into Fox* (1922) was an imaginative and entertaining novel of human metamorphosis into animal. His autobiography *The Golden Echo* (1953) illuminates the *Bloomsbury Group. Edward G. was his father.

Garnett Edward (1868–1937). English critic and playwright who encouraged Conrad (G. read and praised *Almayer's Folly* when he was a publ.'s reader) and D. H. Lawrence.

Garnett Tay (1898–). U.S. film director. G. entered films in 1920 and wrote scripts (1926–8) before starting to direct. He has directed a wide variety of subjects: comedies like *Stand-in* (1937), dramas like *One Way Passage* (1932), *The Postmen Always Rings Twice* (1946). His last two films, *A Terrible Beauty* (1960) and *Guns of Wyoming* (1963) show a remarkable terseness of style.

Garnier Robert (*c.* 1545–90). French dramatist, foremost among 16th-c. tragedians.

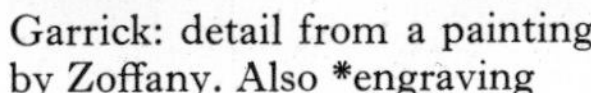

Garrick: detail from a painting by Zoffany. Also *engraving

Mrs Gaskell

Garofalo, Il. Name used of Benvenuto Tisi (1481–1559), Ferrarese painter of religious and mythological subjects, the last representative of the school of Ferrara. In Ferrara he studied under B. Boccaccino and worked with Dosso Dossi; in Rome he met Raphael. The successive influence of these artists is apparent in his work, much of which is in Ferrara.

Garrick David (1717–79). English comic and tragic actor, a member of Johnson's literary circle and once his pupil. G. became manager of Drury Lane Theatre and wrote comedies, tragedies, musicals and farces; *The Clandestine Marriage* (1766) was written in collaboration with G. Colman the Elder. G. was responsible for restoring to the stage much of the original text of Shakespeare's plays, though on occasion he took great liberties with the text He was the 1st actor to be buried in Westminster Abbey.

Garson Greer (1906–). British-born U.S. film star, mainly in romantic or light roles, e.g. *Mrs Miniver* (1942).

Garth Sir Samuel (1661–1719). English poet and physician. G. proposed dispensaries for the poor to save them from exploitation by grasping apothecaries, whom he ridiculed in his mock-heroic poem *The Dispensary* (1699).

Gärtner Friedrich von (1792–1847). German architect who revived Italian Renaissance styles. He studied at the Munich Academy where he was later professor of architecture and director. His principal buildings are the Ludwigskirche (1829–44) and the Staatsbibliothek (1831–42), both in Munich.

Gary Romain. Pseud of R. Kassef (1914–). French novelist; his works include *Les Racines du ciel* (1957; *The Roots of Heaven*, 1958), a novel with metaphysical undertones, of one man's desperate struggle to prevent the extinction of the African elephant.

Gascoigne George (1525?–77). English poet, playwright and writer. G. produced early examples in English of: prose comedy, *Supposes* (1566) from Ariosto; verse satire, *The Steel Glass* (1576); the critical essay *Certayne Notes . . . of Verse . . .* (1575) and the blank-verse tragedy *Jocasta* (1566), from Euripides.

Gascoygne David (1916–). English poet. G. publ. a book of poems and a novel before he was 18 and had a considerable amount of work behind him when he publ. *Poems 1937–42* (1943), perhaps his best coll. Others are *A Vagrant* (1950) and *Night Thoughts* (1956).

Gaskell Mrs (Elizabeth Cleghorn) (née Stevenson) (1810–65). English novelist intensely concerned with moral and social questions. *Mary Barton . . .* (1848), dealing with industrial problems, aroused the interest of Dickens and she began contributing to his *Household Words* and *All the Year Round*. In the former first appeared her *Cranford* (publ. in book form 1853), a sympathetic portrayal of life in a small village. Other works include *Ruth* (1853), *Wives and Daughters* (in book form 1866) and the biography of her friend, *The Life of Charlotte Brontë* (1857).

Gaspard de la nuit (1908). A group of piano pieces by *Ravel; inspired by the coll. of prose poems (1842) by Louis *Bertrand.

Gassman Vittorio (1922–). Italian actor and director who has had his own co. since 1951. He appears in films as well as plays and has often won awards as the best Italian actor. He created the touring Teatro Popolare Italiano.

Gastein. Austrian spa where Schubert stayed in 1825; the so-called 'G.' symphony is now lost, but it has been suggested that the 'Grand Duo' for piano duet, op. 140, is a version of it.

Gates of Paradise, The (1430–47). Doors for the Florentine Baptistery carved by *Ghiberti.

Gate Theatre. Dublin theatre, founded in 1928 by Hilton Edwards and M. *Mac Liammóir. Unlike the Abbey Theatre in Dublin which concentrated on Irish plays, the Gate has always presented a wide variety of world drama and has achieved a European reputation.

Gatti Armand (1924–). Monégasque-French writer and film director. Reporter and writer of plays, novels and poems, G. shared the political views and globe-trotting habits of C. *Marker, on 2 of whose documentaries (on Peking and Siberia) he worked. His 1st film, *L'Enclos* (1961), was a prison-camp drama. His second, *El oltro Cristobal* (1962–3), made in Cuba, was an unsuccessful attempt at *avant-garde* political musical.

Garofalo. *Madonna*

Gärtner. Ludwigskirche, Munich

Gauguin. *Jacob Wrestling with the Angel*

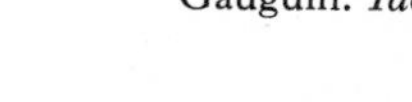

Gauguin. *Idol*

Gauguin. *Nevermore*

Gaudí. Casa Batlló

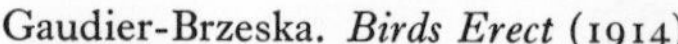

Gaudier-Brzeska. *Birds Erect* (1914)

gaucho poetry. Sophisticated poetry on cowboy themes which flourished in the river Plate estuary in the mid 19th c. The originator, Bartolomé Hidalgo (1775–1823), wrote patriotic songs and political dialogues for guitar accompaniment. Hilario Ascásubi (1807–75) wrote political ballads against the dictator Rosas and an epic on an 18th-c. g. hero. The outstanding poems in the g. manner, however, are *Fausto* by Estanislao del Campo (1834–80), the story of Gounod's opera as told by a cowboy to his friend on the ranch; and *Martín Fierro* by José Hernández (1834–86), a poem typical of the oral tradition, full of murders, violence and maimings, which immortalizes the old lawless barbarism of the cattle-ranches. The language of these poems is modelled on that of the *payadores* or popular balladists.

Gaudí Antoni (1852–1926). Catalan architect working in Barcelona; he produced buildings which were irregular and often fantastic, but he had a keen sense of structure, and there is often a logical structural reason behind his seemingly wild forms.
His most famous work is the church of the Sagrada Familia, begun 1883 and still unfinished. It has Gothic overtones, but the details are extravagantly original. Apartment buildings like the Casa Batlló (1907) and the Casa Milà (1910) show him applying his free sense of form to urban buildings, partly lit by beautifully handled light-wells. His Park Güell (1914) is a charming folly, with large areas covered with broken plates set in concrete, giving an effect of great richness.

Gaudier-Brzeska Henri (1891–1915). Sculptor and draughtsman; born in France but associated with the English school. Although only 23 when killed in action, G.-B. had already achieved an astonishing maturity as an artist. From 1911 he lived in England, working by day as a clerk, encouraged by his companion Sophia Brzeska (whose name he adopted), and a few sympathetic patrons. In 1913 he identified himself briefly with the vorticists. Such works as *The Dancer* (Schiff Coll., London), *Horace Brodzsky* (Tate) and *Birds Erect* (M.M.A., New York) explore the potentialities of modern sculpture, representational, cubist and abstract; while G.-B.'s drawings, especially the superb outline drawings of nudes, birds and animals, are now highly valued.

Gauguin Paul (1848–1903). French painter, sculptor and graphic artist. With Van Gogh

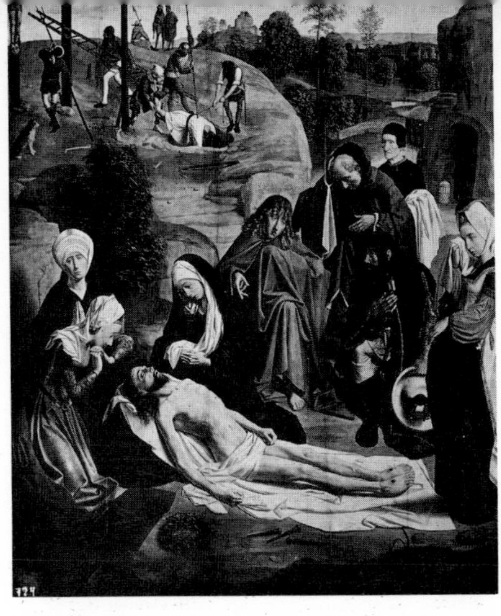

Théophile Gautier

Geertgen tot Sint Jans. *Lamentation Over the Dead Christ*

Gavarni. *A Private Room at Pétron's.* Also *Goncourt

and É. Bernard, G. was the creator of a new conception of painting, and his work was a formative influence on 20th-c. art. Like Van Gogh's, his life has become almost a modern legend. Born in Paris but brought up chiefly in Peru, he served first in the French merchant marine, then became a successful stockbroker in Paris, painting in his spare time. He exhibited with the impressionists (1880–6), and the 1st evidence of great original talent was *Study of the Nude* (1880; Ny Carlsberg Glyptothek, Copenhagen). In 1883 he gave up his job to paint full-time with disastrous financial consequences. After an attempt to support his family in Denmark, he left them, dividing his time between painting in Brittany and a number of jobs, such as bill-sticking in Paris and working as a navvy on the Panama Canal. At Pont-Aven, Brittany, in 1888 he met Bernard with whom he evolved a much-simplified, non-naturalistic style of painting with emphasis on decorative line and the use of flat bright colour. Based on many models (illustrations in children's books and Japanese colour prints among them), the new style was called 'synthetism'. A masterpiece of the period is *Jacob Wrestling with the Angel* (N.G., Edinburgh). Late in 1888 came the disastrous visit to Van *Gogh at Arles. In 1889–90 he was painting at Pont-Aven and Le Pouldu, Brittany. In 1891 he left Europe for Tahiti. The remainder of his life was spent in the South Seas, except for an unsuccessful attempt to sell his paintings in France (1893–5). When G. died in poverty at Atuana, Marquesas Islands, he left behind not only many paintings, including *The White Horse* (Louvre), *Mango Blossoms* (Met. Mus., New York), *Where Do We Come From . . .* (M. of Fine A., Boston) and *Nevermore* (Courtauld Gal., London), but carvings, woodcuts, watercolours, lithographs and ceramics; while his writings, chiefly journals and letters, are also of interest. The most important of these are *Noa-Noa* and *Avant et Après*.

Gaulli Giovanni Battista: *Baciccia

Gautier Théophile (1811–72). French poet, novelist and journalist, who came originally from S. France but spent his life in Paris. He began as an art student, but was at once involved in the literary 'battle of romanticism', since it was he, wearing a red waistcoat, who led the romantic forces at the 1st night of Victor Hugo's *Hernani* (1830). From then on he became a writer, specializing in the more grotesque and ambiguous subjects, e.g. *Mademoiselle de Maupin* (1835; 1887) with its sexual peculiarities, and *La Morte Amoureuse* (1836; *The Dead Leman*, 1889), a vampire story. At the same time he evolved the theory of 'art for art's sake' and invented the still current *avant-garde* catch-phrase: *'épater le bourgeois'*. After 1835 he was primarily a successful journalist and Parisian man-about-town, who often complained about not having time to write works of literature. He did, however, produce 2 further novels: *Le Roman de la momie* (1858; *The Romance of a Mummy*, 1886) and *Le Capitaine Fracasse* (1863; *Captain Fracasse*, 1902) as well as his most famous vol. of poems, *Émaux et Camées* (1852), which inspired Baudelaire and the Parnassians. His insistence on formal perfection and picturesque beauty encouraged the movement towards aesthetic discipline; indeed G.'s importance as a literary figure outweighs his importance as a writer.

Gavarni Paul. Pseud. of Sulpice-Guillaume Chevalier (1804–66). One of the leading French graphic artists of the 19th c., satirist, illustrator, wood engraver and lithographer. His contributions to *Le Charivari* and other papers illustrated the absurdity of the human comedy with elegance and good humour. His visits to London (1847, 1849–52) opened his eyes to vice and poverty, and an increasing bitterness and disillusionment appeared in his work. *Masques et Visages* (1852), which includes the series *Les Propos de Thomas Vireloque*, is typical of this period. His own apt captions give additional point to his drawings.

gavotte. French dance of folk origin, popular at court in the 17th c. and part of the classical dance suite of the 18th c. It is in moderately quick common time and begins on the 3rd crotchet in the bar.

Gawain and the Green Knight, Sir (14th c.). Alliterative poem; its hero is one of King Arthur's knights (*alliterative verse).

Gay John (1685–1732). English poet and dramatist, a master of burlesque, as in *The Shepherd's Week* (1714), a pastoral parody, and *Trivia . . .* (1716). G.'s most enduring work was his *The Beggar's Opera* (1728), a 'Newgate pastoral' about the adventures of Captain Macheath the highwayman and incidentally a political satire and parody of Italian opera. It remained popular throughout the 18th c., was revived in the 19th and 20th, and was the basis for Brecht's and Weill's *Dreigroschenoper*. Its sequel, *Polly* (publ. 1729), was banned from the stage. G. wrote the libretto to Handel's *Acis and Galatea*.

Gaynor Janet (1906–). U.S. film star. Sweet and wholesome, her career encompassed *Sunrise* (1927) and *A Star is Born* (1937).

Gebrauchsmusik. Literally 'utility music'; term coined by *Hindemith.

gedackt or **gedact** (archaic form of German *gedeckt*, 'covered'). A type of stopped pipe in an *organ.

Geddes Andrew (1783–1844). Scottish portrait painter and etcher, friend of David Wilkie. His best-known painting, which shows the strong influence of Rembrandt on his work, is his portrait of his mother (N.G., Edinburgh), of which he also made an etching.

G(h)eeraerts the Elder, Marcus (1510?–90?). Flemish painter of historical and religious subjects who came to England with his son in 1568.

G(h)eeraerts the Younger, Marcus (1561–1635). Flemish portrait painter who settled in England; son of the above. Paintings in a variety of styles are attributed to him; probably he collaborated with the other Flemish artists in England, J. de Critz and I. Oliver, in producing the costume portraits of the late Elizabethan and Jacobean periods.

Geertgen tot Sint Jans (*c.* 1465–*c.* 95). Early Netherlandish painter. Born in Leyden and a pupil of A. van *Ouwater, G. is poorly documented. 2 works, *Lamentation Over the Dead Christ* and *Julian the Apostate Orders the Bones of St John the Baptist to be Burnt* (both K. Mus., Vienna) are almost certainly his and his curiously effective, if naïve, style and smooth egg-shaped heads (probably influenced by wood carving) have been traced in a number of works including the harrowing *Man of Sorrows* (Archiepiscopal Mus., Utrecht) and the *Nativity* (N.G., London), a small, brilliantly lit night scene of mystical intensity.

Geibel Emanuel (1815–94). German poet. His lyrical verse in the romantic tradition is

Gelder. *Christ taken captive in the Garden* (detail)

distinguished by technical excellence rather than originality.

Geijer Erik Gustaf (1783–1847). Swedish romantic poet and historian; in both roles he described and evoked the Gothic past of Sweden.

Gelder Aert de (1645–1727). Dutch painter of Biblical subjects and portraits, a pupil of S. van Hoogstraten and in the 1660s of Rembrandt, whose style he followed closely. His work was unfashionable during his lifetime but was later sought after when thought to be by Rembrandt.

Gelée Claude: *Claude Lorrain

Gellert Christian Fürchtegott (1715–69). German writer; a member of the Bremer Beiträger group of less rigidly rationalistic representatives of the Enlightenment. Student and (1751) professor at Leipzig: the 'teacher of Germany', preaching moral restraint; he wrote didactic and sentimental *Fabeln und Erzählungen* (1746–8), *Geistliche Oden und Lieder* (1757), and plays (*Die Betschwester*, 1745, a **comédie larmoyante*). His novel *Das Leben der schwedischen Gräfin von G**** (1748) has epistolary sections and links Richardson with Goethe's *Werther*.

Geminiani Francesco Saverio (1679/80–1762). Italian violinist, one of A. Corelli's pupils, and composer. From the 1710s he worked mainly in England, making extended visits to Ireland and Paris. His influential *The Art of Playing the Violin* (publ. anon. 1731) spread the principles of Corelli's technique in England; *The Art of Accompaniament* [*sic*] (1755) is historically valuable.

gemshorn. (German, 'chamois horn' or 'goat horn'.) An organ stop, usually of metal pipes of 8 ft pitch or higher. The pipes taper towards the top and produce a light tone.

Adeline Genée

Genée Dame Adeline (Isitt) (1878–). Danish dancer who in her teens danced leading roles in many European centres and for 10 years remained the lead at the Empire Theatre, London (1897–1907), her most celebrated role being Swanilda in *Coppélia*. G. contributed greatly to the activities of the Royal Academy of Dancing, becoming its 1st president (1920–54), and was also co-founder of the Camargo Society (1930).

General, The (1926). Film directed by B. *Keaton.

Generalbass. German term for *continuo.

Generale Della Rovere, Il (1959). Film directed by R. *Rossellini.

General Motors Technical Center Warren, Michigan (1955). Architect Eero *Saarinen.

Generation, A (1954). Film directed by A. *Wajda.

generation of '98. A group of Spanish writers whose declared purpose, prompted by the loss of Cuba in 1898, was to analyse the reasons for Spain's 'decadence', to revitalize Spanish culture and institutions and to bring Spain into the mainstream of European culture. Leading figures in the movement were Unamuno, Angel Ganivet, Pío Baroja, the Machado brothers, Azorín and Jiménez and the great biologist Ramón y Cajal.

Genesis. Sometimes called the 1st book of Moses. Greek title for the 1st book of the Bible, containing the 2 versions of the Hebrew creation myth and the story of Abraham's covenant with God.

Genet Jean (1910–). French novelist and playwright who has had the distinction of being subjected to lengthy existentialist analysis by Jean-Paul Sartre in *Saint Genet, comédien et martyr* (1952). An illegitimate child who never knew his parents, he has been imprisoned for the crimes he describes in his books; himself a delinquent he aims to give his inverted universe the dignity of noble literary expression. The rhapsodic novels contained in the 2 vols of his *Oeuvres complètes* (1951, 1953), as well as the separate short book, *Journal du voleur* (1949), all deal with the psychology of homosexual criminals, who have their own code of beauty and morals. Although very loosely constructed, these works contain passages of unique and striking quality. The same types are presented dramatically in the play *Haute Surveillance* (1949; *Death Watch*, publ. 1961). *Les Bonnes* (1947; *The Maids*, 1955), *Le Balcon* (in France 1960; *The Balcony*, 1957) and *Les Nègres* (1958; *The Blacks*, 1960) use

Jean Genet

Genre. Dou, *Poulterer's Shop*

different characters but, in fact, project the dilemma of the delinquent invert on to a wider background.

Genga Girolamo (*c.* 1476–*c.* 1551). Italian painter and architect who worked mainly for the court at Urbino. He studied under Signorelli and assisted him on the frescoes in Orvieto cathedral. He softened his style under the influence of Perugino and Raphael and later came close to mannerism. He designed the church of S. Giovanni Battista, Pesaro (1543).

Génie du Christianisme, Le (1802). Book by *Chateaubriand.

'Genius', The (1915). Novel by Dreiser.

Genlis Stéphanie-Félicité Ducrest, Mme de (1746–1830). French writer who enjoyed great popularity in Parisian society. Author of numerous popular romances, including *Mademoiselle de Clermont* (1802) and *La Duchesse de la Vallière* (1804), and *Mémoires* (1825).

genre (French 'type', 'kind'). The painting of the life of ordinary people, first found as an independent subject of paintings in Dutch 17th-c. art. Religious art and paintings of ceremonial occasions are not g. although details in such paintings may be so called. G. paintings are more common in N. European art than in Italy; they were frequent in the 19th c. but the term is not used for pictures telling a story or with identifiable persons represented.

Gentile da Fabriano (*c.* 1370–1427). Italian painter working in Florence; there his refined decorative sense acted as a counterbalance to the pursuit of representation. G.'s 2 great paintings are *Adoration of the Magi*, a masterpiece of the international Gothic school, and the exquisite *Flight into Egypt* (both Uffizi); other works include the early *Madonna and Child* (Berlin).

Gentileschi Artemisia (1597–1651). Italian painter, daughter of O.G. She worked mainly in Naples in a strongly Caravaggesque style.

Gentileschi Orazio (1563–1647?). Italian Caravaggesque painter; from 1576 in Rome and from 1626 court painter to Charles I of England. His painting was emotionally gentler and his palette eventually lighter than Caravaggio's, though the latter's naturalism remained the major influence on G.'s work. In England there are paintings at Marlborough House and Hampton Court.

Gentle Art of Making Enemies, The (1890). Book by the painter *Whistler.

Gentleman Francis (1728–84). Irish actor, critic and playwright, author of *The Modish Wife* (1761).

Gentlemen Prefer Blondes (1925). Novel by Anita *Loos; the basis of a film (1953) directed by H. *Hawks.

Geoffrey of Monmouth (1100?–1154?). English chronicler and bishop of St Asaph, from whose account of early British kings, *Historia Regum Britanniae* (*c.* 1135), stems the classic medieval version of the Arthurian legend (King *Arthur).

Geoffrin Marie-Thérèse Rodet (1699–1777). French society woman. G.'s *salon* was attended by artists (e.g. Boucher) and writers (e.g. Fontenelle and Marivaux).

George Stefan (1868–1933). German poet. He studied and travelled abroad (1888–90), was active as a trs. (Baudelaire, 1901; *Zeitgenössische Dichter*, 1905; Shakespeare, *Sonnette*, 1909), and was strongly influenced by the symbolists, as also by Nietzsche. A leader of the neo-romantic 'art for art's sake' movement, in opposition to the naturalism of the 1890s, G. founded a periodical, *Blätter für die Kunst*, and built up a circle of disciples (Georgekreis). His poetry (trs. 1949) is esoteric, using symbolic scenes and figures; it is formally highly worked, with set stanzas, onomatopoeia, rare rhymes and rich vocabulary, and an idiosyncratic typography, capitalization and unconventional punctuation which he called 'barbed wire against the non-elect!'. In the early vols, e.g. *Hymnen* (1890), *Pilgerfahrten* (1891), *Algabal* (1892), *Die Bücher der Hirten- und Preisgedichte . . .* (1895), *Das Jahr der Seele* (1897), aestheticism is dominant; later, *Der Teppich des Lebens . . .* (1900), *Der siebente Ring* (1907), *Der Stern des Bundes* (1914), *Das neue Reich* (1928), ethical considerations of the poet's role in society take over.

George Dandin (1668). Play by Molière.

Orazio Gentileschi. *Lutenist*

Stefan George

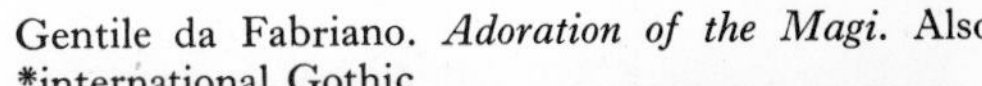

Gentile da Fabriano. *Adoration of the Magi.* Also *international Gothic

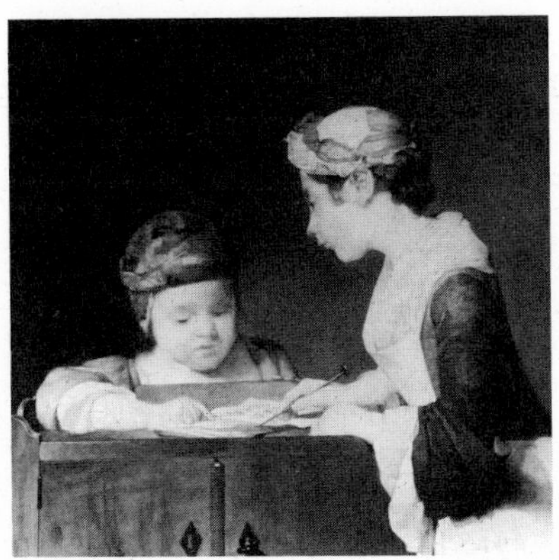

Genre. Chardin, *The Young Schoolmistress*

Gérard. *Madame Récamier*

Géricault. *The Raft of the 'Medusa'*

Géricault. *The Madwoman*

Georgian poetry. Term applied to English verse of the 2nd decade of the 20th c., particularly to the work of most of the poets who contributed to Edward Marsh's 5 anthologies *Georgian Poetry* (1912–22). Its keynote – war poetry aside – was the quiet celebration of English ways and the English countryside. Contributors included Rupert Brooke, Wilfred Owen, Edward Thomas, Robert Graves and Edmund Blunden.

Georgian style. A term used loosely to cover the arts from *c.* 1725 to *c.* 1800 although several styles can be distinguished within this period. In architecture and room decoration it is roughly equivalent to the Palladian style and the styles of Kent, Chippendale and the Adam brothers. In the other decorative arts it is so vague and imprecise as to have no helpful meaning.

Georgics (*c.* 2 B.C.). Poem on husbandry by *Virgil.

Gerald McBoing Boing (1951). Cartoon film directed by R. *Cannon.

Gérard François, baron (1770–1837). French neo-classical painter of portraits and historical subjects, painter to both Napoleon and Louis XVIII. He was a pupil of J.-L. David but softened and sweetened his master's style so that he stands closer to J.-B. Regnault. Portraits such as *Jean-Baptiste Isabey and his Daughter* and *Madame Récamier* (both Louvre) are superficial but charming.

Gerdt Paul (1844–1917). Russian dancer of outstanding talent who created the leading male roles in such ballets as *The Sleeping Beauty* (1890), *Nutcracker* (1892) and *Cinderella* (1893) at the Maryinsky Theatre, St Petersburg. Although he continued to appear on the stage for most of his life he later taught at the Imperial School and Pavlova, Nijinsky and Fokine were among those he helped to shape.

Gerhaert Nicolaus (d. 1473). German Gothic sculptor in a markedly naturalistic style. He worked in Trier, Strassburg, Constance, Baden-Baden, Vienna and Wiener-Neustadt. Works attributed to him include the tomb of Archbishop Jacob von Sierck (Liebfrauenkirche, Trier), *Crucifixion* (Alter Friedhof, Baden-Baden) and the tomb of the Emperor Frederick III (St Stephen's cathedral, Vienna).

Gerhaert. *Self-portrait* (?); sandstone

Gerhard Roberto (1896–). Spanish-born composer living in England since 1938. He studied under F. Pedrell and Schoenberg. His early music was affected by old Spanish music and French impressionism but from the 1930s he adopted 12-note techniques, though not consistently. He is mainly known for his odd instrumentation and harsh dry sound effects and is one of the very few important composers of electronic music in England. His works include: the opera *The Duenna* (1951); the ballet, *Don Quixote* (1947); 2 symphonies, a violin concerto, a concerto for piano, strings and percussion (1956); and a wind quintet, octet and nonet.

Gerhardt Paul (1607–76). Lutheran pastor and one of the greatest of German hymn writers. Among his simple powerful lyrics is his version of the Latin hymn 'Salve caput Cruentatum' ('O Sacred Head sore wounded'), famous as the 'Passion Chorale' in J. S. Bach's *St Matthew Passion.*

Géricault Théodore (1791–1824). French painter, graphic artist and sculptor of great promise and originality who strongly influenced his close friend Delacroix and French 19th-c. painting as a whole. G. was the pupil of the fashionable painters Vernet and Guérin; he studied at the Louvre, visited Italy and later England, but the example of Le Gros, painter of contemporary subject-matter, decided the course of his development. His restlessness, excitement and disappointments found expression in his turbulent paintings and often morbid subject-matter. His most famous composition *The Raft of the 'Medusa'* (1819; Louvre) was based on the experiences of survivors from an actual shipwreck and is painted with a compelling realism based on the study of corpses and sickness. The painting was intended to shock, and to protest; inevitably it caused a scandal. G. became a leader of French romantic painting. His interest in racing and riding is obvious from his paintings and lithographs of horses, where animal life achieves a symbolic significance as an expression of ferocious power. In these paintings he was influenced by the popular English sporting print and by the English painter J. Ward. His portraits of the insane, e.g. *The Madwoman* (Lyons; *c.* 1822), are extraordinary documents revealing G.'s psychology and insight.

Germ, The. The magazine of the *Pre-Raphaelites.

George Gershwin

Gérôme. *The Cock Fight*

Gerolamo dai Libri. *Madonna and Child with St Anne*

German Sir Edward (1862–1936). English composer of incidental music and operettas, notably *Merrie England* (1902); he also wrote 2 symphonies and other orchestral works.

German Requiem, A. Sometimes used in English as the title of *Brahms's work, *Ein deutsches Requiem* (1868).

Germi Pietro (1914–). Italian film director and actor. G.'s roots lie in neo-realism, the spirit of which informs his earlier films, including *Il cammino della speranza* (1950) and *La città si difende* (1952). He achieved international fame with a pair of comedies about Sicilian morals, *Divorzio all'italiana* (1961) and *Sedotta e abbandonata* (1964).

Germigny des Prés France. A rare survival of Carolingian architecture, the oratory of Bishop Theodulph, built *c.* 806. It is square in plan, divided inside into 9 compartments, the central one surmounted by a tower. Apses project E., N. and S.

Germinal (1885). Novel by *Zola.

Germinie Lacerteux (1864). Novel by the *Goncourt brothers.

Gerolamo dai Libri (*c.* 1474–1555). Veronese painter. The development of his style owed most to Mantegna but also something to Moroni and other Veronese painters. His works include *Madonna and Child with St Anne* (N.G., London) and *St Anne with Virgin and Saints* (S. Paolo, Verona).

Gérôme Jean-Léon (1824–1904). Facile French academic painter and sculptor, pupil of David and an exponent of a prettified Davidian classicism. In some of his work he followed the vogue for oriental subjects.

Gerona cathedral Spain. The most impressive example of Spanish late Gothic. The E. end is 14th c., with a high vaulted chancel and ambulatory. But in 1416 it was decided not to continue with a conventional nave arcade the same width as the chancel, but to expand the whole nave into one huge room as wide as chancel and ambulatory combined. It has a span of 73 ft (quadripartite vault) and is 100 ft high. The architect was Guillermo Boffiy.

Gershwin George (1898–1937). U.S. composer who began his career writing popular songs and also produced several famous musical comedies, e.g. *Lady be Good* and *Funny Face*. In 1924, commissioned by Paul Whiteman, he wrote *Rhapsody in Blue*, a symphonic jazz work for piano and orchestra. He subsequently produced a piano concerto, the symphonic poem *An American in Paris* (1928) and the Negro opera *Porgy and Bess* (1935).

Gerstenberg Heinrich Wilhelm von (1737–1823). German writer. Poems such as *Gedicht eines Skalden* (1766), inspired by Ossian, and the critical work *Briefe über Merkwürdigkeiten der Literatur* (1766–7) with its discussion of the nature of genius, presage the storm and stress period. His best-remembered work is the horrific tragedy *Ugolino* (1768) based on Dante.

Gessner Salomon (1730–88). German-Swiss writer whose pastoral prose *Idyllen* (1756, 72) gained him the name of the Swiss Theocritus.

gesso. A form of plaster used as a ground for modelling or painting; it has a brilliantly white, smooth-textured surface. Frequently used on furniture in low relief, and gilded.

Gesualdo Don Carlo, Prince of Venosa (*c.* 1560–1613). Italian composer, notorious to posterity for ordering the murder of his 1st wife and her lover (1590). His madrigals harp on death and their insistent, audacious and intensely emotive chromatic harmony is the richest example of the style of the Italian madrigal in its decadence. About 150 madrigals for 5 or 6 voices survive, many with words by Tasso. G. also wrote sacred songs and some instrumental music.

Gevaert François-Auguste (1828–1908). Belgian composer, teacher and music historian. In the late 1860s he was director of the Paris Opéra. In 1871 he succeeded F. Fétis as director of the Brussels Conservatoire; as a teacher he emphasized the importance of a characteristically national idiom.

Gezelle Guido (1830–99). Flemish poet, important in the Flemish cultural revival of the 19th c., a fine romantic lyric poet.

Ghedini Giorgio Federico (1892–). Italian composer and ed. of Italian music of the 16th and 17th cs; his early compositions were neoclassical. Works include: the operas *Maria*

Germigny des Prés; Theodulph's oratory

Gerona cathedral

Ghiberti. *Baptism of Christ,* detail from the font in the Baptistery of St John, Siena

Ghiberti. Self-portrait on *The Gates of Paradise.* See also colour plate 41

Ghirlandaio. *Old Man and his Grandson*

Ghirlandaio. *Adoration of the Shepherds* in the Trinità

Detail from rug using the Ghiordes knot

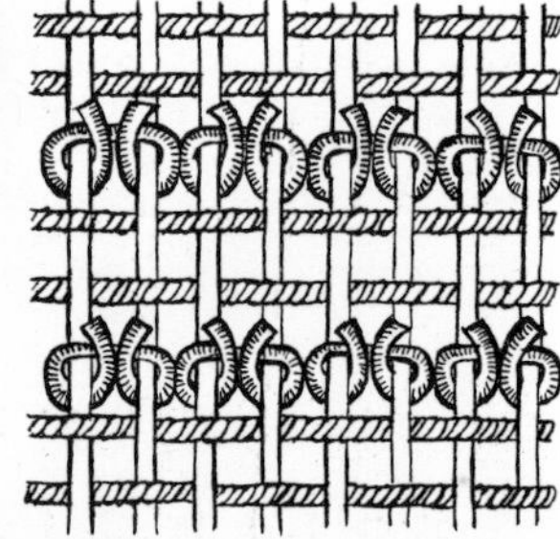

Diagrams showing method of weaving the Ghiordes knots (*right*)

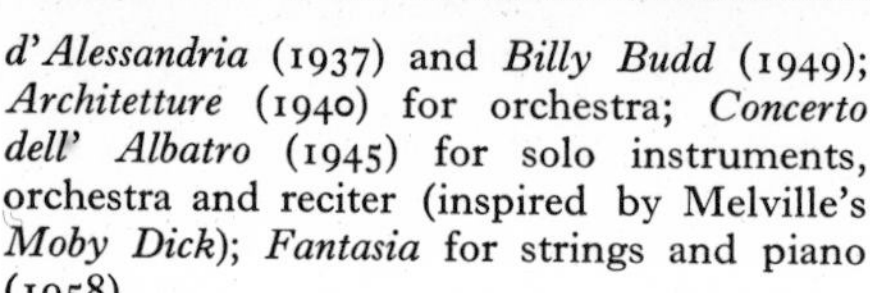

d'Alessandria (1937) and *Billy Budd* (1949); *Architetture* (1940) for orchestra; *Concerto dell' Albatro* (1945) for solo instruments, orchestra and reciter (inspired by Melville's *Moby Dick*); *Fantasia* for strings and piano (1958).

Ghent altarpiece. Painted by the van *Eyck brothers.

Ghiberti Lorenzo (*c.* 1378–1455). Italian sculptor, goldsmith, architect and writer on art of the Florentine school. Trained as a goldsmith, G. won the competition for the making of a pair of bronze doors for the Baptistery, Florence, in 1402, when he was about 20. His winning panel, *Sacrifice of Isaac*, can be compared with that of his older competitor, Brunelleschi, at the Bargello, Florence. Most of G.'s life was spent making the 28 panels for these doors (1404–24) and those of the even more celebrated *Gates of Paradise*, a 2nd pair also for the Baptistery (1430–47). His 3 large bronze figures for Or San Michele, Florence, *St John the Baptist*, *St Matthew* and *St Stephen*, were technically and artistically more ambitious than anything attempted before and won G. a wide reputation. To the famous baptismal font in Siena he contributed 2 panels in relief, *The Baptist before Herod* and *Baptism of Christ*. His large workshop was the training school of a whole generation of Florentine artists: Donatello, Uccello and Michelozzo were among his pupils. Despite this, every commission undertaken bears the unmistakable mark of his own very individual talent. Furthermore, G. was a leading citizen of Florence. He was also a humanist and scholar, the friend of such men as Leonardo Bruni. His own work shows study of the international Gothic style, the masters of Sienese painting and classical bas-reliefs. His learning and taste are reflected again in his writings on art, the 3 books of his *Commentarii*. Traditionally, it was *Michelangelo who said that the 2nd pair of G.'s Baptistery doors were worthy to stand as the Gates of Paradise.

Ghil René (1862–1925). French symbolist poet, a disciple of Mallarmé. G. believed that the laws of acoustics could be applied to poetry; his important critical essays are *Le Traité du verbe* (1886) and *De la poésie scientifique* (1909). His verse includes *Légende d'âmes et de sangs* (1885) and *Les dates et les œuvres* (1923).

Ghiordes knot. Or Gördes, a town in Turkey. The commonest of the knots used in handmade pile carpet weaving, found in all Caucasian and English, nearly all Turkish and many Persian carpets. Successive rows of G. knots are generally separated by a line of weft. Also called the Turkish knot.

Ghirlandaio Domenico (1449–94). Italian painter of the Florentine school. Trained as a goldsmith by his father, G. later won a reputation chiefly as a fresco painter, creating a serene style which reflects the full development of Florentine painting before Leonardo da Vinci. His earliest known works are the frescoes above the Vespucci altar, Ognissanti, Florence. Later, for the same church, he painted *St Jerome* and a *Last Supper* warm with the mellow light of a Tuscan evening. In 1481–2 G. was in Rome painting 2 frescoes for the Sistine Chapel, the survivor of which, *The Calling of the Apostles Peter and Andrew*, shows G.'s habit of including portraits of people he knew among the witnesses to a religious scene. Again, in the frescoes of the Sassetti chapel (S. Trinità, Florence) he includes portraits of members of the Medici, Sassetti and Spini families.

Other works by G. are *Visitation* (Louvre), *Birth of the Virgin* and other frescoes (S. Maria Novella, Florence), and *Madonna and Saints* (Uffizi). G.'s workshop assistants included his brother Davide (1452–1525). His son Ridolfo (1483–1561) was a minor Florentine painter. More important, Michelangelo was a pupil and learned from G. the technique of fresco painting.

Ghislandi Giuseppe: Fra Vittore del *Galgario

Ghosts (1881). Play by *Ibsen.

Ghost trio. Nickname for Beethoven's piano trio in D, op. 70 no. 1 (1808); the slow movement suggested the name.

Giacometti Alberto (1901–66). Swiss sculptor; his father GIOVANNI (d. 1883) and 2nd cousin AUGUSTO (1877–1947) were painters. G. studied at the Geneva School of Arts and Crafts (1919) and under Bourdelle in Paris (1922–5) where (apart from the war years) he thereafter lived. G.'s early works, e.g. *Two Figures* (1926), have an elemental, primitive force; later, more surrealist constructions like *The Palace at 4 a.m.* (1933; M.M.A., New

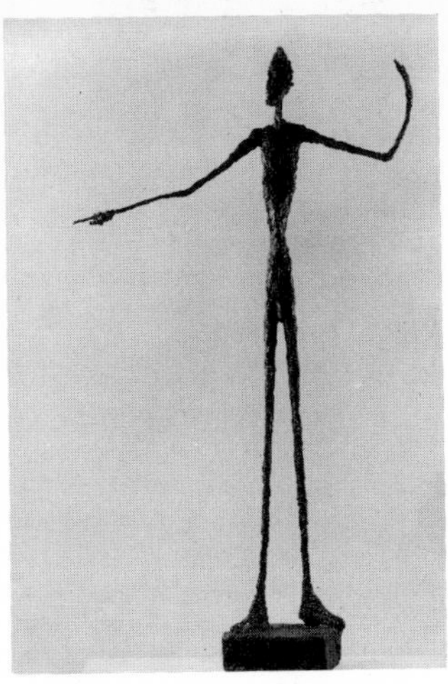

Giacometti. *Woman with her throat cut*

Giacometti. *Man Pointing* (1947)

Giambono. *Madonna*

York) already have the attenuation which increasingly became the feature of the human figures he produced from *c.* 1940. The frailty of these strange, desolate matchstick-men (e.g. the group *City Square*, 1949) is emphasized by the heavy bases on which they are usually placed; the spatial relationships created, quite different from the monumental quality of traditional sculpture, have had great influence on contemporary work. G. also painted, e.g. his *Portrait of Jean Genet* (1955).

Giacosa Giuseppe (1847–1906). Italian writer. His plays, at first heavily romantic, later became naturalistic dramas of bourgeois society. He collaborated with Illica on the librettos of Puccini's operas *La Bohème*, *Tosca*, and *Madam Butterfly*.

Giambologna: Giovanni da *Bologna

Giambono Michele Giovanni Bono called (*fl.* 1420–62). Venetian painter influenced by the international Gothic style of Gentile de Fabriano and Pisanello. His best-known authenticated work is his *Madonna* in the Palazzo Venezia, Rome.

Giannini Vittorio (1903–). U.S. composer; his teachers included R. Goldmark. G. studied in Europe and the influence of European 19th-c. music is apparent in his work. His opera *The Scarlet Letter* (1938) was first performed at Hamburg, G.'s sister, the soprano DUSOLINA G. (1902–), taking the main role.

Giant (1956). Film directed by G. *Stevens; based on the novel (1952) by Edna Ferber.

Giardini Felice de (1716–96). Italian violinist and composer. He worked for many years in London, producing operas there, teaching and performing; he died in Moscow during a tour.

Gibberd Frederick (1908–). English architect whose best-known and most important work is the London Airport Building (1950).

Gibbon Edward (1737–94). English historian. A temporary convert to Roman Catholicism at Oxford, he had an undistinguished career in Parliament (1774–82), briefly holding minor office. On a visit to Rome G. conceived the idea of his *The History of the Decline and Fall of the Roman Empire* (6 vols 1776–88). Its urbane, balanced periods, perfect construction and sound scholarship gained it immediate recognition though G., a sceptic, was obliged to publ. a vindication of his account of ecclesiastical history. *The Memoirs of My Life and Writings* (1796), sometimes called his *Autobiography* but in fact a coll. of 6 unfinished sketches, was publ. by his friend the earl of Sheffield.

Gibbons Christopher (1615–76). English musician, 2nd son of Orlando G.; organist at the Chapel Royal under Charles II, collaborated with M. Locke on the masque *Cupid and Psyche* and wrote string fantasies.

Gibbons Grinling (1648–1721). English wood carver. He enjoyed royal patronage under Charles II and George I and also worked under Wren. G.'s ornamental carving was of exquisite finesse and delicacy; his preferred subjects were fruit, flowers, lace motifs, etc. Examples of his work are at Windsor, St Paul's, London, and many country-houses, most notably Petworth, where there is a magnificent room by him.

Gibbons Orlando (1583–1625). The major English composer between Byrd and Purcell. He studied under his brother EDWARD (1568–*c.* 1650), and his father WILLIAM (*c.* 1540–95) was also a musician. G. was organist at the Chapel Royal and at Westminster Abbey. He wrote many church anthems with soloists and string accompaniments, as opposed to the unaccompanied polyphony of his predecessors, and established the form of the verse anthem; in 1612 he publ. 20 madrigals and motets of 5 parts 'apt for viols and voices' containing the famous madrigals 'The Silver Swan' and 'What is our Life'. His viol fantasies and In nomines are of great beauty and complexity; like some of his contemporaries he also wrote fantasies on the street cries of London, and his keyboard music is masterly.

Gibbons Stella (1902–). English novelist. Her most famous book, *Cold Comfort Farm* (1932), is a hilarious parody of the earthy-passion-and-doom type of novel.

Gibbs Cecil Armstrong (1889–). English composer. His earliest works included the comic opera *The Blue Peter* (1924), book by A. P. Herbert.

Gibbs James (1682–1754). British architect; the most successful of his time. He tended to keep apart from the prevailing Palladianism and is more in the tradition of Wren,

Orlando Gibbons

Edward Gibbon

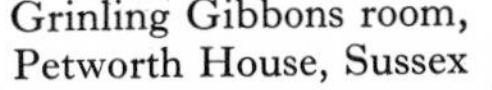

Grinling Gibbons room, Petworth House, Sussex

Gibbs. St Martin-in-the-Fields

Gibbs. The Senate House, Cambridge

owing something also to Hawksmoor. His chief works are: the Derby parish church, now the cathedral (1723); at Oxford the Radcliffe Camera, a striking and attractive domed library with certain mannerist features (1737); at Cambridge the Senate House, a noble classical front with giant columns (1722); and in London the 2 churches of St Mary-le-Strand (1714) and St Martin-in-the-Fields (1722); the former the more interesting (it shows his Italian training most clearly), the latter the more influential–it seems to have begun the fashion of placing a steeple over a classical portico. G. publ. 3 large vols of designs, executed and unexecuted, and these were widely used as source-books in England and, even more, in America.

André Gide

Gibson John (1790–1866). English neo-classical sculptor who went to Rome in 1817 and settled there, only returning to England in 1844 and 1850 to execute royal commissions. He worked under A. Canova and B. Thorwaldsen and ranked next to them in importance. In later works he revived the Greek practice of tinting marble, as in his *Tinted Venus*.

John Gielgud and Pamela Brown in *The Lady's Not For Burning*

Gide André (1869–1951). One of the most famous French men of letters of the 1st half of the 20th c. He belonged to the cultured, leisured middle class, and devoted himself entirely to literature. His 1st work was a lyrical, introspective diary, *Les Cahiers d'André Walter* (1891) and the whole output of his long life can be considered as analytical self-revelation, whether publ. as such in his *Journal*, covering the years 1889–1949 (*The Journals of André Gide*, 1947–9), or written as autobiography in *Si le grain ne meurt* (1926; *If it die*, 1950), or transposed into poetically phrased treatises, such as *Les Nourritures terrestres* (1897; in *Fruits of the Earth*, 1949), or novels: *L'Immoraliste* (1902; *The Immoralist*, 1930), *La Porte étroite* (1909; *Strait is the Gate*, 1924), *Les Caves du Vatican* (1914; *Lafcadio's Adventures*, 1928; *The Vatican Cellars*, 1952), *La Symphonie pastorale* (1919; in *Two Symphonies*, 1931) and *Les Faux-Monnayeurs* (1926, *The Counterfeiters*, 1928). His subject is self-realization, the throwing off of religious and social taboos and the achievement of freedom and happiness. An important factor was the urge to justify his homosexuality. His works are perhaps less significant as individual creations than as part of his immense self-portrait. His influence on the literature and atmosphere of his time was enormous. His works often anticipated later attitudes. The impulsive, unmotivated murder committed by Lafcadio in *Les Caves du Vatican* has frequently been interpreted as an existentialist gesture to establish the freedom of the will. G. helped to found the great literary review *Nouvelle Revue Française* and he was awarded the Nobel prize in 1947.

Gibson. *Tinted Venus*

Giedion Siegfried (1893–). Swiss writer and historian on social and artistic subjects. His influential *Space, Time and Architecture* (1941) is based on the proposition that the modern observer is a moving one, as opposed to the Renaissance concept of a static viewer seeing objects in perspective.

Gielgud Sir John (1904–). English actor and director, the great-nephew of Ellen Terry. His 1st appearance was at the Old Vic in 1921, and at that theatre in 1929 he played Romeo, Richard II, Macbeth and Hamlet. With his exquisite voice and fine face he is at his best in Shakespeare but he has also had success in *The Importance of Being Earnest* and as Mendip in Fry's *The Lady's Not For Burning*. His film performances have been few but include Cassius in *Julius Caesar* (1952).

Gieseking Walter (1895–1956). German pianist, born in France and particularly noted for interpretations of French works.

Gifford William (1756–1826). English critic and satirical poet, ed. of *The Anti-Jacobin* and *The Quarterly Review*. He was a fierce critic of contemporary literature, attacking the *Della Cruscans, and probably the author of the onslaught (in *The Anti-Jacobin*, 1819) on Keats's *Endymion*.

Gift of the Magi, The (1906). Story by O. Henry.

Gigli Beniamino (1890–1957). Italian lyric tenor of world renown. He made his début in 1914, and toured the world in 1920 (he performed in 12 successive seasons at the Metropolitan Opera House and was on its staff until 1932), but returned to Italy for the duration of World War II, resuming his tours in 1955.

Gilbert Sir John (1817–97). English draughtsman, illustrator and painter known as 'the Scott of painting' because of his choice and romantic treatment of historical and chivalric themes. He worked for *The Illustrated London News* (1842–72) and illustrated an ed. of Shakespeare (1856–60).

Gilbert John (1895–1936). U.S. film actor, the great romantic lead of the late 1920s silent cinema; his best sound film was *Queen Christina* (1933).

Gilbert Sir William Schwenck (1836–1911). English comic poet and librettist. The immense popularity of the Gilbert and Sullivan operas (produced by *D'Oyly Carte), including *H.M.S. Pinafore* (1878), *The Pirates of Penzance* (1879), *Patience* (1881) his satire on aestheticism, *Iolanthe* (1882), *The Mikado* (1885), *The Yeomen of the Guard* (1888), and *The Gondoliers* (1889), owed as much to Gilbert's librettos as to Sir A. *Sullivan's music. Apart from the operas, G.'s best comic verse was coll. in *The Bab Ballads* (1869).

Gil Blas de Santillane, The Adventures of (1715, 1724, 1735). Novel by *Le Sage.

Gildas (or Gildus) (d. *c.* 570). British historian, author of the *De Excidio et Conquestu Britanniae*, an interesting but not always reliable source for early British history.

gilding. The process by which another metal is covered with a thin layer of gold. Traditionally silver was the most common metal to be gilded, but base metals are also used extensively. The old method of g. was by a mercury distillation process, but in the 19th c. electrolysis provided a safer, cheaper though less efficient method.

Gilgamesh, The Epic of. A Sumerian myth. G. and his companion Enkidu maddened the goddess Ishtar with their insolence and strength and their death is decreed. G. then made a protracted and arduous journey in search of immortality but failed and returned home to await his destiny.

Gill Eric (Rowland) (1882–1940). English sculptor, wood engraver and typographer. G. was deeply religious (he became a Catholic in 1913) and held views of the artist-craftsman and the social place of the arts similar to those of William Morris. G.'s simple yet strong line was best adapted to bas-relief, e.g. the *Stations of the Cross* in Westminster cathedral (1913–18), and its grandest and perhaps most lasting expression is in the chiselled elegance of his Perpetua and Gill Sans-serif type-faces. His writings include: *Christianity and Art* (1927) and *Work and Property* (1937).

Gillespie (John Birks) 'Dizzy' (1917–). U.S. trumpeter and band-leader. With Charlie Parker the co-founder of modern jazz, and one of the greatest living jazz musicians. His advanced harmonic and technical command at first concealed a stylistic debt to Roy Eldridge, the leading trumpeter of the 1930s. His big band of the 1940s was the first to present modern jazz to a wide audience.

Gillot Claude (1673–1722). French decorative and genre painter and draughtsman of the rococo period. He was director of costumes and decoration at the Paris Opéra and the 1st French painter to produce *commedia dell'arte* scenes. Both Watteau and Lancret were his pupils.

Gillray James (1757–1815). English engraver and caricaturist, best known for his cartoons of the Napoleonic Wars period. He exploited the same vein of satire as Hogarth, but was far more personal in his attack. Even at their most scurrilous, his drawings are composed with skill and wit, e.g. *A Voluptuary*, lampooning the greed of the Prince Regent.

Gilly Friedrich (1771–1800). German architect, a pioneer of 'romantic classicism'. He died young and few of his ideas were realized, but he had a powerful influence on later architects such as Klenze and Schinkel. His project for a monument to Frederick the Great (a huge Doric temple on a masonry sub-structure) is the protype of Klenze's Walhalla.

Gilman Harold (1876–1919). English painter of portraits, interiors and landscapes, member of the Camden Town Group and 1st president of the *London Group. He was originally associated with Sickert but later fell under the influence of the post-impressionists. His masterpiece is his portrait of his landlady, *Mrs Mounter* (Walker Art Gal., Liverpool; small version, Tate), a sculpturesque work built up in broad planes of brilliant colour.

Gilpin John (1930–). British dancer, trained by the Ballet Rambert, who joined the Festival Ballet (1950) and remains the co.'s principal male dancer. His lyrical style is admirably

Gilly. Design for a theatre in Berlin

Gilman. *Mrs Mounter*

Gillray. *Dido in Despair!* (cartoon of Lady Hamilton)

Gilgamesh. Babylonian cylinder seal: G. and Enkidu fight a sacred bull and lion

Gill. *Stations of the Cross*, No. 1

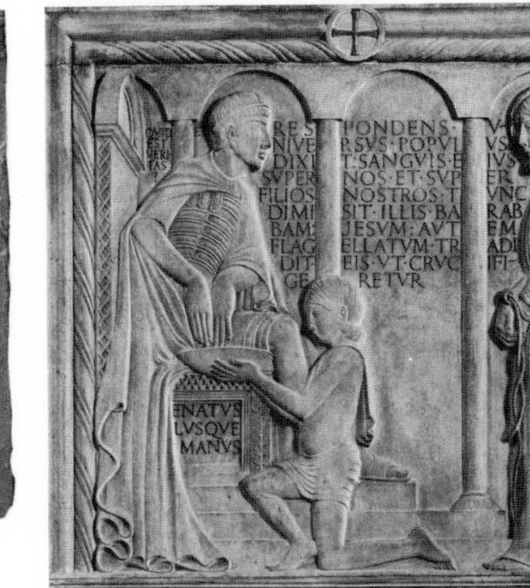

Gilpin. *Horses in a Thunderstorm*

Luca Giordano. Ballroom ceiling, Palazzo Riccardi

Allen Ginsberg

Giorgione. *Castelfranco Madonna*. Also *fête champêtre and colour plate 45

suited to the classical ballets produced by this co. and he is readily adaptable to the Diaghilev revivals in the repertoire.

Gilpin Sawrey (1733–1807). English painter of animals, particularly horses, sporting scenes and (less successfully) historical subjects. He was a considerable draughtsman and his horse paintings were ancestral to French romantic painting.

Gilson Paul (1865–1942). Belgian composer and teacher. He himself studied under F.-A. Gevaert and drew inspiration from the 19th-c. Russian composers, whose work he popularized in Belgium. His compositions include the cantata *Sinai* and the symphonic poem *La Mer* (1890), the latter showing G.'s mastery of orchestral technique and harmony.

Gil y Carrasco Enrique (1815–46). Spanish poet, novelist and journalist. His poetry has great delicacy and lyrical beauty but his most famous work was his historical novel *El Señor de Bembibre* (1844), dealing with the Knights Templar in medieval Spain, the 1st great Spanish romantic novel.

gimel. Style of medieval part singing, particularly associated with England, using consecutive 3rds and 6ths.

Ginsberg Allen (1926–). U.S. poet, one of the leading *beats. G.'s use of long lines, strong rhythms and a rhetorical style give him affinities with Whitman. His poems include *Howl* (1955), a violent lament for the self-destruction of many of his contemporaries, and *Kaddish* (1961), a more restrained description of his mother's life and death.

Gioconda, La. Alternative title for *Leonardo's *Mona Lisa.*

Giocondo Fra (1435–1515). Italian Renaissance architect. He designed the Palazzo del Consiglio, Verona, with a loggia modelled on Brunelleschi's. During the last 2 years of his life he was one of 3 architects in charge of the building of St Peter's.

Giono Jean (1895–). French novelist whose philosophy, based on a love of solitude, pacifism and individualism, is expressed in novels describing the peasant life of his native Provence–*Colline* (1929; *Hill of Destiny*, 1929), *Un des Baumugnes* (1929; *Lovers are never Losers*, 1932), *Regain* (1930; *Harvest*, 1939), *Le Hussard sur le toit* (1951; *Hussar on the Roof*, 1954).

Giordani Giuseppe (called 'Giordaniello') (1753–98). Italian opera composer frequently confused with Tommaso G., but no relation to him.

Giordani Tommaso (*c.* 1730–1806). Italian composer who worked most of his life in London and Dublin. He composed over 50 operas and instrumental music in the *galante style of J. C. Bach.

Giordano Luca (1632–1705). Neapolitan painter, pupil of Ribera and Pietro da Cortona and remarkable for his facility and eclecticism. He helped to change the character of Neapolitan art, previously dominated by Ribera, by introducing a baroque style and lighter treatment. His prodigious output included the ballroom ceiling, Palazzo Riccardi, Florence (1682) and ceilings in the Escorial, Madrid (1692).

Giordano Umberto (1867–1948). Italian opera composer of the *verismo tradition whose early work, e.g. *Mala Vita* (1892), shows the influence of Mascagni. He also wrote *Andrea Chenier* (1896) and *Siberia* (1903).

Giorgione, born Giogio, or Zorzi, da Castelfranco (*c.* 1477–1510), Italian painter of the Venetian school. Despite his great influence on painting and a reputation which has lasted without fluctuating for 400 years, little is known of his life and few paintings are certainly by him. His master was Giovanni Bellini. In 1508 he was a colleague of Catena, in 1507–8 he was painting at the Doge's Palace, Venice. In 1508 there was a dispute over the frescoes he was painting on the outside of the Fondaco dei Tedeschi, Venice. Titian was also engaged on this commission. Most authorities are agreed that G. was the more original genius of the 2 and that Titian bore G.'s influence for the rest of his life, but this cannot be proved on evidence–almost nothing remains of the frescoes.

Although G. painted commissions for churches such as the *Castelfranco Madonna* (S. Liberale, Castelfranco), it was the small paintings in oil he painted for private collectors which are G.'s great innovation in art. These are neither

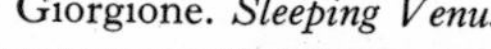

Giorgione. *Sleeping Venus*

portraits, nor recognizable subjects from myth or history. Indeed, it is almost impossible to determine what is happening in *The Tempest* (Accademia, Venice), though a profoundly evocative mood is created and, instead of resenting the fact that there is no obvious subject, the imagination is gratified by being freed. However quietly accomplished by G., this was a revolutionary new conception of what a painting should be. Such paintings found patrons; they were highly prized before G.'s early death (probably of plague), and works left unfinished in his studio were completed by other artists: *Sleeping Venus* (G.-Gal., Dresden) by Titian and *Three Philosophers* (K. Mus., Vienna) by Sebastiano del Piombo. Other major works attributed include: *Adoration of the Magi* (N.G., Washington), *Judith* (Hermitage), *Laura* (K. Mus., Vienna), *Shepherd with Pipe* (R. Coll., Hampton Court) and *Fête Champêtre* (Louvre).

Giotteschi. Name given to the followers of Giotto. They included Bernardo Daddi, Giottino, Maso di Banco and Taddeo Gaddi but many works in Giotto's style are anon.

Giottino. Florentine painter of the mid 14th c. A somewhat shadowy figure, probably a pupil of Giotto, perhaps identical with a Giotto di Maestro Stefano. The work generally attributed to him is the *S. Remigio Deposition* (Uffizi).

Giotto di Bordone (*c.* 1266–1337). Italian painter and architect. The significance of G.'s original vision of the natural world and his genius in communicating it were proclaimed by Dante, Petrarch and Boccaccio in the 14th c. and G. has been celebrated ever since as the true founder of Florentine painting and an initiator of Western art. The outline of his life can only be put forward tentatively. By tradition he was the pupil of Cimabue, working with his master both in Florence and Rome. Then or later he was undoubtedly in contact with the work of the Roman painter P. Cavallini and the sculptor Arnolfo di Cambio, which paralleled the break Cimabue had made with the conventions of Byzantine art in Italy. G.'s earliest work may have been connected with the mosaics of the Baptistery, Florence. He was almost certainly painting at Assisi by about 1290. In 1300 he was probably employed in Rome and soon after in Florence. The famous frescoes of the Arena, or Scrovegni chapel, Padua, occupied him during the 1st decade of the 14th c. Either in 1300, or, more likely, in about 1313, G. designed the *Navicella*, 'Ship of the Church', mosaic in St Peter's, Rome. During the 2nd decade of the 14th c. he painted the Cappella di S. Maddalena at Assisi, the frescoes of S. Antonio and the Palazzo della Ragione, Padua, and works in Rimini. In the 3rd decade much of his time was spent in Florence, where among other undertakings he painted the frescoes of S. Croce. Subsequently he painted in both Naples and Milan, but in 1334 he was present to be nominated architect of Florence cathedral and the city fortifications. Later that year he began the Campanile, which still bears his name, but which was considerably altered from his plan.

G. consolidated the break others had made with Byzantine art, but his real achievements were those of a narrator of genius and a master draughtsman. The last enabled him to create the illusion of texture, weight, expression and, above all, depth in his paintings. Thus his scenes are visually convincing. What is more, he was able to give expression to complex human emotions in a way that is both subtle and tellingly simple. G.'s influence, paramount for a generation after he died, later surrendered to others, only to be revived by artists, chiefly Florentine, who were interested in draughtsmanship as a means of expressing reality. Michelangelo admired and made copies of his work.

Of G.'s works, the frescoes attributed to him in the upper and lower churches, Assisi, have been frequently challenged. The *St Francis* cycle in the upper church is almost certainly his, though the later frescoes were probably painted to his design by assistants. *Crucifixion*, *Lamentation* and *Joachim's Dream* are among the most outstanding scenes depicted in the Scrovegni chapel, Padua. Among his panel pictures the most important is unquestionably the *Ognissanti Madonna* (Uffizi); while other works generally attributed to him are *Crucifix* (S. Maria Novella, Florence) and *Dormition of the Virgin*.

Giovanni da Bologna: *Bologna

Giovanni da Milano (*fl.* mid 14th c.). Italian painter, follower of Taddeo Gaddi. He worked in Florence and Rome. There are frescoes by him in the Rinuccini chapel, S. Croce, Florence.

Giotto. *Ognissanti Madonna*

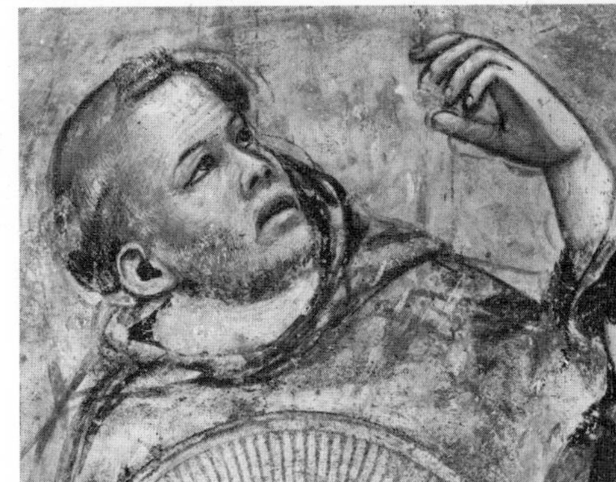

Giotto. Detail from *The Funeral of St Francis*. See also colour plate 36

Giorgione. *Laura*

Giotto. *St Francis receiving the stigmata*

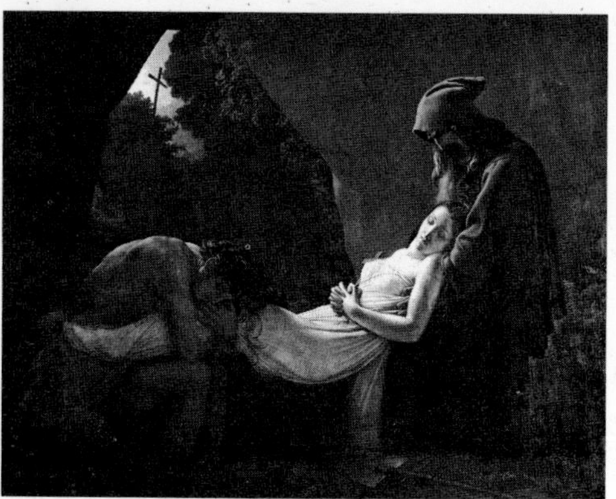

Girodet. *The Burial of Atala*

Girtin. *Kirkstall Abbey*

Gischia. *Maternité* (1958)

Girandole; French, 1750

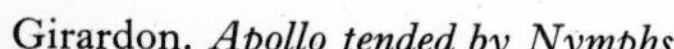

Girardon. *Apollo tended by Nymphs*

Giovanni di Paolo or Giovanni dal Poggio (*c.* 1403–82/3). Italian painter of the Sienese school. G.'s paintings must have appeared old fashioned even in his own day, but his strong narrative sense makes strangely effective such imaginative and brightly coloured works as *A Paradise* (Met. Mus.) and versions of scenes from the life of St John the Baptist (N.G., London; Provinzial Mus., Münster and A. Inst., Chicago).

Giraldi Giambattista (1504–73). Italian playwright who took Seneca as his model in the gory tragedy *Orbecche* (1541).

Giraldus Cambrensis (Giraldus de Barri) (1146?–1220?). Norman-Welsh historian whose chief work is the topographical *Itinerarium Cambriae* on his travels in Wales. Other writings include *Expugnatio Hibernica* and *Topographia Hibernica.*

girandole. (1) A large type of branched candlestick or a type of bracket chandelier. (2) An ear-ring brooch or pendant consisting of a flat down-curved or bow-shaped top piece, with 3 pendant drops of which the central is the lowest.

Girardon François (1628–1715). French sculptor, famous exponent of classicism who worked for Louis XIV at Versailles. His most famous sculptures there are *Apollo tended by Nymphs* (begun 1666; original grouping altered) in the grotto of Thetis, and *Rape of Persephone* (begun 1677) in the gardens. His other work includes the monument to Richelieu (1675–7) in the Sorbonne, Paris.

Giraudoux Jean (1882–1944). French novelist and playwright, diplomat and, eventually, minister of propaganda. He first distinguished himself with whimsical novels, full of elaborate conceits and reflecting the intelligent, humane mischievousness of a certain type of French academic mind: e.g. *Suzanne et le Pacifique* (1921) and *Siegfried et le Limousin* (1922). With his plays, which are in the same vein of sceptical poetic fancy, he reached a much wider public. The best known, *La Guerre de Troie n'aura pas lieu* (1935; *Tiger at the Gates*, publ. 1955) helped to set the fashion in adapting ancient legend for the modern stage. **Amphitryon 38* (1929) and *Électre* (1937) rework classical myths. *Judith* (1931), *Intermezzo* (1933; *The Enchanted*, publ. 1950) and *Ondine* (1939; *Ondine*, publ. 1956) have also been recently revived.

Girl of the Golden West, The. Opera by *Puccini, libretto by G. Civinini and C. Zangarini; 1st performance in New York in 1910.

Girodet de Roucy-Trioson, Anne-Louis (1767–1824). French painter, illustrator and poet; pupil of David. His painting *The Burial of Atala* (1808; Louvre), based on a novel by Chateaubriand, is a notable early expression of French romanticism in theme and presentation although it retains the balanced composition and smooth technique of the classical school.

Girtin Thomas (1775–1802). English painter. Together with Turner, G. revolutionized watercolour technique, chiefly by abandoning the use of underpainting for a much freer style in which colours were applied directly on to semi-absorbent paper. G. travelled all over the British Isles painting and on a visit to Paris painted street scenes, etc. which show the variety and richness of the effects that could be achieved in the new technique. G. did much to raise English landscape painting in watercolour from topographical drawing to a fine art. Among his best paintings are *Kirkstall Abbey* (B.M., London) and *The White House* (Tate).

Gischia Léon (1903–). French painter, theatrical designer and writer on art. He studied under Friesz and Léger, whose influence is apparent in his early figurative work. In 1927 he stopped painting and went to the U.S. In 1937 he worked with Ozenfant and Le Corbusier on the decoration of the Les Temps Nouveaux Pavilion at the Universal Exhibition, Paris. Since World War II he has painted mostly in an abstract idiom.

Giselle. A 2-act ballet based on a story by Gautier and St-Georges, with music by Adolph Adam and choreography by Perrot and Coralli. First presented in 1841, it revived the interest in romantic ballet that had been awakened 9 years before by Taglioni's *La Sylphide*, and has endured as the greatest ballet of that era. It is still in the repertoire of most of the leading cos, and although it has been restaged with added choreography from time to time, most productions follow closely the original version. The role of G. requires both technical perfection and dramatic talent.

Glarner. *Relational Painting* (1947–8)

Gislebertus. *Eve*

Gish Lillian (1899–). U.S. film star. G. has been acting since 1912, when D. W. *Griffith first starred her sweet fragility, in classics like *Broken Blossoms* (1919) and *Way Down East* (1920). Her later parts include those in *The Scarlet Letter* (1926), *Duel in the Sun* (1946) and *Winds Across the Everglades* (1957). She also appeared on the stage and in 1936 played Ophelia to the Hamlet of John Gielgud in New York.

Gislebertus. French sculptor who signed his name under the tympanum of Autun cathedral, Burgundy (1120–30), and was presumably the master in charge of the whole sculptural programme. The tympanum shows the Last Judgement, the capitals inside the church episodes from the life of Christ, allegories and parables. They are among the masterpieces of Romanesque art, ranging from horrific images of damnation and terror to the sensuous charm of the well-known *Eve*, now in Autun Mus.

Gissing George (Robert) (1857–1903). English novelist influenced by French realism and Dickens. His novels of squalor and despair, e.g. *The Nether World* (1889), *New Grub Street* (1891), *Born in Exile* (1892) and his short stories, *Human Odds and Ends* (1898) and *The House of Cobwebs* (1906), stem from his own London experience of extreme poverty and unhappy marriage. His autobiographical *The Private Papers of Henry Ryecroft* (1903) wears less well than his fiction.

Giulio Romano (Giulio Pippi) (1492 or 9–1546). Italian mannerist painter and architect, a pupil of Raphael, whom he assisted in the Vatican Stanze and Loggie. He continued Raphael's later style, but with harsher colours, greater distortions and more violent composition; he also did a famous series of pornographic engravings. In 1524 he went to Mantua in the service of the duke and turned mainly to architecture. There he built the Palazzo del Tè (1526–34), his masterpiece and the prime example of mannerist architecture: orthodox classical motifs are wilfully misused, rhythms are irregular, keystones dropped, columns left rough as if from the quarry, etc. The impression of instability is epitomized in the Sala dei Giganti (also painted by G.R.), where the architecture of the room appears to be on the point of collapsing; the illusionistic frescoes *The Fall of the Titans* covering the whole room from floor to ceiling, showed a melodramatic exaggeration of Raphael's style. His own house (1544) shows the same architectural qualities – entablature but no columns, sill-course violently pushed up to form a pediment, etc. He made additions to the ducal palace, including the fantastic tilting-yard, and built Mantua cathedral. This last is in the purest Roman classical style without a trace of eccentricity.

Giusti Giuseppe (1809–50). Italian writer and poet, considered by many of his contemporaries as the finest writer of Tuscan prose of his age. His poems also were extremely popular during his lifetime although they are of uneven quality.

Gjellerup Karl Adolph (1857–1919). Danish novelist who settled in Germany. He was for a period a disciple of G. *Brandes but later attacked him violently. In 1917 G., with H. Pontoppidan, received the Nobel prize for literature.

Glackens William James (1870–1938). U.S. painter (in an impressionist style influenced by Renoir) and illustrator; member of The *Eight.

Gladstone William Ewart (1809–98). English Liberal statesman and outstanding orator, 4 times prime minister. His publs included works on literature, e.g. *Studies on Homer and the Homeric Age* (1858).

Glanvill Joseph (1636–80). English writer and divine whose sceptical *The Vanity of Dogmatizing* (1661, republ. as *Scepsis Scientifica*) rates nature a more reliable textbook than philosophy. This work contains the legend of the Scholar Gipsy (on which M. Arnold based his poem) and also a prophecy of the electric telegraph.

Glarner Fritz (1899–). Swiss painter, the leading exponent of neo-plasticism in the U.S. where he settled in 1936; in New York he became a friend and disciple of Mondrian. After Mondrian's death G. modified the basic rectilinear form of pure neo-plasticism by introducing oblique lines into his compositions, all entitled *Relational Painting*.

Glasgow Ellen (1874–1945). One of the best U.S. regional novelists. Her subject is her native South but she treats it dispassionately and is unaffected by the myths surrounding Southern society. Her books include *Barren Ground* (1925).

Ellen Glasgow

Giulio Romano. Palazzo del Tè

Glinka

Gleizes. *Harvesters*

Glazunov

Glasgow School of Art

Glasgow School of Art (1907–9). Architect, C. R. *Mackintosh.

Glaspell Susan (1882–1948). U.S. playwright and novelist, one of the organizers of the *Provincetown Players. Her plays include *Alison's House* (1930), suggested by the life of Emily Dickinson, which deals with the problems created by the discovery of a dead woman's love-letters.

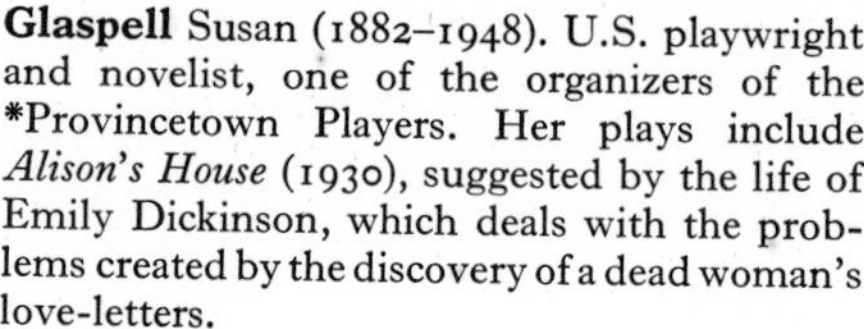

Glass Menagerie, The (1945). Play by Tennessee *Williams.

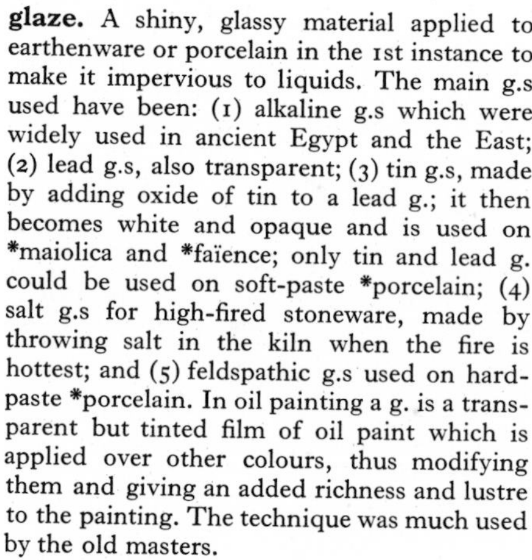

glaze. A shiny, glassy material applied to earthenware or porcelain in the 1st instance to make it impervious to liquids. The main g.s used have been: (1) alkaline g.s which were widely used in ancient Egypt and the East; (2) lead g.s, also transparent; (3) tin g.s, made by adding oxide of tin to a lead g.; it then becomes white and opaque and is used on *maiolica and *faïence; only tin and lead g. could be used on soft-paste *porcelain; (4) salt g.s for high-fired stoneware, made by throwing salt in the kiln when the fire is hottest; and (5) feldspathic g.s used on hard-paste *porcelain. In oil painting a g. is a transparent but tinted film of oil paint which is applied over other colours, thus modifying them and giving an added richness and lustre to the painting. The technique was much used by the old masters.

Glazunov Alexander Konstantinovich (1865–1936). Russian composer. He was encouraged by M. Balakirev and Rimsky-Korsakov, and studied privately with the latter. His works were soon performed abroad. He taught at the St Petersburg Conservatory, becoming its director in 1906, composing little subsequently. He settled in Paris in 1928. Initially G. associated himself with the Russian nationalist composers, but most of his work belongs to the mainstream of European music. He wrote some programme music, e.g. the symphonic poems *Stenka Razin* (1885), *The Kremlin* (1890), but he preferred classical forms. His works include 8 symphonies, concertos for piano, for violin and for saxophone, chamber music, incidental music and ballets.

glee. (From the Old English *gliw*, 'musical entertainment'.) An unaccompanied part song for 3 or more voices (often male), developed in England during the 18th c. and remaining popular into the 19th. It used an harmonic idiom, achieving characteristic effects by contrasted tempi. The Glee Club (London) met from 1783 to 1857.

Gleim Johann Wilhelm Ludwig (1719–1803). German poet whose *Preussische Kriegslieder . . .* (1758), in the metre of the English ballad *Chevy Chase*, became famous. G. was a friend of leading writers encouraging E. C. von Kleist to become a poet.

Gleizes Albert (1881–1953). French painter; deeply impressed by a painting by Le Fauconnier, he abandoned his early impressionist manner in 1910 and came in contact with other cubist painters. He was influenced by Léger and later by Gris, but paintings like *Harvesters* (1912; Guggenheim Mus., New York) reveal a limited conservative understanding of cubism. He exhibited with the main cubist group in 1911 and 1912 and his attempt to revive the group after the war suggests a need to belong to a corporate movement. *Du Cubisme* (1912) by G. and Metzinger was an attempt to clarify its history and principles.

Gleyre (Marc) Gabriel-Charles (1808–74). Swiss history and genre painter who settled in Paris, took over the studio of Delaroche and is remembered for having taught there Monet, Renoir, Whistler, Sisley and Bazille among others. Though strictly academic himself he acknowledged the talents of these younger artists.

Glière Reinhold Moritzovich (1875–1956). Russian composer. He was a pupil of M. Ippolitov-Ivanov and S. Tanaief and a professor at the Moscow Conservatory from 1920. His works include: operas, e.g. *Shah Senem* (1934), based on Azerbaijan melodies; ballets, e.g. *The Red Poppy* (1927); symphonies, patriotic overtures, chamber music, incidental music, and songs. In his later work he employs folk-melodies from E. Russia.

Glinka Fyodor Nikolayevich (1786–1880). Russian poet, a cousin of the composer M. Glinka. He wrote mystical poetry and several songs (e.g. 'Troika') which have remained popular.

Glinka Mikhail Ivanovich (1804–57). Russian composer, called 'the father of Russian music'.

He studied music in Milan, and in Berlin with S. W. Dehn, before producing his 2 operas in St Petersburg. In 1844 he travelled again staying in Paris, Spain, Warsaw and Berlin, where he died. The opera, *A Life for the Czar* (1836), now called *Ivan Sussanin*, is still Italian in style, but already shows folk influence and is national in subject-matter. In his 2nd opera *Ruslan and Ludmilla* (1842) G. created a characteristically Russian style, also originating the 'oriental' vein in Russian composition. His other works include orchestral and chamber music, piano pieces and songs, and often employ folk material.

glissando (Italianized form of French *glisser*, 'to slide'). A musical effect achieved by rapidly dragging the finger over the keys or strings of a piano or harp, or along the string of a bowed instrument, so as to sound the intervening notes between 2 notes of the scale. It is a well-known effect on the jazz trombone and can also be achieved on machine drums. Also *portamento.

Globe Theatre, The. Elizabethan theatre built in 1598 or 1599. Shakespeare was a shareholder and several of his plays were originally performed there. The G. T. was a circular building of wood and had a thatched roof which was the cause of its being burned down in 1613. It was rebuilt and finally demolished 1644. A modern London theatre bears the name.

glockenspiel (German, 'play of bells'). Musical percussion instrument. It consists of tuned metal plates played either with hammers held in the hands, or from a keyboard.

Gloria: *mass

Gloucester cathedral. Norman cathedral (begun 1089) of which most of the structure remains: chancel with radiating chapels, crossing, transepts and nave with high circular piers and narrow triforium and clerestory. In 1332–77 the S. transept and chancel were refaced in the *perpendicular style, of which G. c. is the earliest surviving example and one of the grandest (e.g. the E. window and crossing tower). The cloisters (*c.* 1350) contain the earliest fan-*vaulting.

Gluck Christoph Willibald (1714–87). German composer born at Eresbach, the son of a chief forester. Little is known of his early life; he was at Prague, probably at the univ., in 1731 and then, under the patronage of Prince Melzi, went to Milan, where he studied under Sammartini. He made his début in 1741 with *Artaserse* to a libretto by Metastasio. In 1741 he visited Paris and then London, where he met Handel, giving a concert with him, and after concerts in other parts of Europe, sometimes appearing as a virtuoso on the glass harmonica, he settled in Vienna in 1752, composing operas and also French comic operas for the court. In 1762 G.'s *Orpheus and Eurydice*, the first of his 'reform' operas was produced.
G. is generally considered the 1st composer of opera in the modern sense, revolting against what he considered the sterile conventions of Italian and Neapolitan opera. He abandoned the set pattern of recitative and aria for a more fluent, simple and dramatically coherent form. He proclaimed his principles in the historic preface to *Alceste* (1767): music in opera should have the secondary functions of supporting and heightening the emotional impact of the poetry and the dramatic situation, it should not obtrude with elaborate ornamentation; the dramatic development of the plot should take precedence over any formal arrangement of recitatives, etc.; the overture should be an integral part of the opera, an introduction to the drama to come rather than a florid preliminary; the chorus should, as in Greek drama, be an essential part of the action. These ideals, which his librettist Calzabigi brilliantly furthered, were violently contested by the supporters of the Italian school when G. produced his new operas in Paris in the 1770s; the rival school proposed the Italian composer Piccinni as its champion. The controversy was essentially conducted by the intelligentsia and aristocracy, the 2 composers taking little part. G. wrote numerous 'Italian' operas; the important so-called 'reform' operas are *Orpheus and Eurydice* (Vienna, 1762), *Alceste* (1767), Italian librettos by Calzabigi, and *Iphigenia in Aulis* (Paris, 1774), French libretto by F.-L.-L. du Roullet after Racine, all 3 on classical themes; *Armida* (Paris, 1777), French libretto of P. Quinault after Tasso; *Iphigenia in Tauris* (Paris, 1779), French libretto by N.-F. Guillard on the Greek legend.

Glyn Elinor (1864–1943). English writer of extravagant romantic novels such as *The Visits of Elizabeth* (1900) and *Three Weeks* (1907).

Gluck

The 2nd Globe Theatre

Gloucester cathedral: the nave. See also colour plate 33

Gloucester cathedral:
entrance to the N. transept

Jean-Luc Godard. Jean-Paul Belmondo in *À Bout de Souffle*

Cartoon of William Godwin

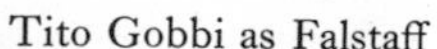

Tito Gobbi as Falstaff

Glyndebourne Festival Theatre. An opera house opened on his Sussex estates in 1934 by J. Christie. It holds a short but brilliant international summer season, and since 1954 has been owned by G. Arts Trust Ltd.

glyptic. Term meaning 'carved', used in sculpture to describe the method of working in which the form is carved directly from wood, stone, etc. instead of being built up in wax or clay prior to casting.

Gnessin Mikhail Fabianovich (1883–1957). Russian-Jewish composer, a pupil of Rimsky-Korsakov and A. K. Liadov. He also studied folk and ancient Hebrew music in Palestine. His works include: the operas, *The Youth of Abraham* and *The Maccabees*; a symphonic prelude, chamber music and arrangements of Jewish folk-songs.

Gobbi Tito (1915–). Italian baritone, outstanding both for his singing and acting. He is the leading interpreter of Verdi and Puccini baritone roles (Iago, Falstaff, etc.).

Gobelins. A firm of Paris tapestry weavers, transformed by Louis XIV and Colbert in 1662 into the Manufacture Royale des Meubles de la Couronne with the twofold aim of supplying the royal palaces with furnishings and building up a state manufacture of luxury articles to prevent the need for foreign imports. The presiding genius was Charles Le Brun the painter, who provided designs for all kinds of furnishings and controlled the factory in the greatest detail to ensure the highest standards of workmanship. Not only tapestries were produced, but also furniture, sculpture, works in gold and silver, carriages and architectural details, even door-locks.

Gobineau Joseph-Arthur, comte de (1816–82). French diplomat, author of the *Essai sur l'inégalité des races humaines* (1853–5; *The Inequality of Human Races*, 1915); its theories had some influence on the racial theories of Nazism.

Goblin Market (1862). Poem by Christina *Rossetti.

Godard Benjamin-Louis (1849–95). French composer of great facility, large output and little originality. Apart from the dramatic symphony with chorus *La Tasse* (1878) he produced 6 operas, 5 symphonies and many *salon* pieces for piano.

Godard Jean-Luc (1930–). French film director who made his 1st feature, *À Bout de Souffle* (1959), with the support of *Truffaut and *Chabrol. The daring charm of its young amoral characters, its nihilism, the deliberate tributes to American gangster B pictures, made it the most 'new wave' of all new-wave pictures. Technically it was very adventurous. Editing was no longer designed for smoothness and coherence–the omission of connecting shots, the air of improvisation, was an assault on the French cinema's idea of the well-made film. The film was a great commercial success and G. has worked continuously since. His style ranges from the hand-held camera and grubby monochrome of *Le Petit Soldat* (1960) to the stately wide-screen and colour of *Le Mépris* (1963); from the rigorous discipline of *Les Carabiniers* (1962) and the formal divisions of *Vivre sa vie* (1962) to the apparent but calculated chaos of *Bande à Part* (1964). Seriously comic or ludicrously tragic, G.'s films present a world of paradox, in which he is master of the cinematic aphorism.

Goddard Paulette (1911–). U.S. film actress who made her screen début in **Modern Times* (1936) as a typical Chaplin waif, a role she repeated in his *The Great Dictator* (1940). Her best roles were in Cukor's *The Women* (1939); Renoir's *The Diary of a Chambermaid* (1946) and Korda's *An Ideal Husband* (1948).

Godfrey Sir Daniel (Eyers) (1868–1939). The founder conductor of the Bournemouth Municipal Orchestra (1893–1934). He came of a long line of musicians, most of whom were military bandmasters.

Godowsky Leopold (1870–1938). Polish pianist and composer who settled in the U.S. in 1914; his compositions and piano transcriptions reflect his great virtuosity as a pianist.

Gods are Thirsty, The (1912). Novel by Anatole France.

Godwin William (1756–1836). English writer and radical political philosopher, who greatly influenced Shelley (who eloped with his daughter), Coleridge and Wordsworth. G., who held that man's reason is the only necessary guide to behaviour, pursued his theories in *An Enquiry Concerning the Principles of Political Justice . . .* (1793) and the propagandist novel *The Adventures of Caleb Williams* (1794), the

Gobelins. *Louis XIV Visiting the Gobelins Factory*; from a cartoon by Le Brun

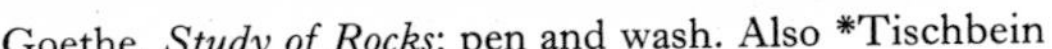

Goethe. *Study of Rocks*; pen and wash. Also *Tischbein

Goethe in 1817

story of the persecution of one man by another. In 1798 he wrote a biography of his wife, Mary Wollstonecraft, 'vindicator of women's rights'.

Goehr Walter (1903–60). German-born conductor and composer; he lived in Britain from 1933.

Goeneutte Norbert (1854–94). French painter, engraver and lithographer; friend of Manet and Renoir. He specialized in Paris street scenes, and was admired by his contemporaries for his remarkable and subtle draughtsmanship, his keen observation and satirical humour. His *Le Boulevard de Clichy* is in the Tate.

Goes Hugo van der (*c.* 1440–82). Early Netherlands painter and, after van Eyck, the most gifted artist of the school; probably born in Ghent. He entered the artists' guild there in 1467 and was dean in 1474. Shortly afterwards he became a lay brother at the monastery of Roode Clooster near Brussels and from this time he was subject to increasing attacks of depression and mental instability. He continued to paint until about 1481. His greatest work is unquestionably the large triptych commissioned by the Florentine merchant Portinari in 1475. Taken to Florence (now Uffizi) this masterpiece had a considerable influence on Florentine painting, e.g. in the later work of Ghirlandaio. Among other important works are *Adoration of the Shepherds* and *Adoration of the Kings* (Berlin), *Fall of Adam* and *Lamentation* (both K. Mus., Vienna), *Virgin and St Anne* (M.R. des B.-A., Brussels), the 2 large organ shutters at Holyrood Palace, Edinburgh, *Crucifixion* (Correr Mus., Venice) and the almost mystically intense *Death of the Virgin* (M. Com., Bruges). G.'s only true follower was the *Master of Moulins.

Goethe Johann Wolfgang von (1749–1832). German writer and polymath; born in Frankfurt-am-Main of a well-to-do family. He was a law student at Leipzig (1765–8), then at Strassburg (1770–1) where he met Herder and fell in love with Friederike Brion, who inspired a group of lyrics. In 1772 G. returned to Frankfurt and in 1775 settled in Weimar, where (1776) began his friendship with Charlotte Stein; G. became a government minister in 1780 and was ennobled in 1782. G.'s very many love-affairs often influenced his work; e.g. the epistolary novel *Die Leiden des jungen Werthers* (1774; 1779) was written in the intense depression following an unhappy love for Charlotte Buff. It gained immediate European fame, causing the 1st wave of romantic morbidity. Just as with this and the play *Götz von Berlichingen* (1773; 1799) G. dominated the *storm and stress movement, so in *Iphigenie auf Tauris* (1787; 1793) he established 'Weimar classicism', a restrained romanticism using classical forms; in the novel *Wilhelm Meisters Lehrjahre* (1795–6; 1824) he created the model for subsequent German *Bildungsromane*; and with the verse drama *Faust* produced the acknowledged German masterpiece in this field. His development spans a c. of German literary history from rococo (in the early poems) to romanticism, with anticipations of symbolic realism in *Novelle* (1827; 1832). In **Faust* he modifies the legend, e.g. developing the character of Gretchen, the innocent girl seduced by Faust, and granting the hero, symbolic of man the restless inquirer, ultimate salvation. The final work, after the original version, the *Urfaust* (1774), is in 2 parts, of which part I (1808; 1823) is frequently performed, part II (publ. posth. 1832; 1838) being more a mystical-philosophical dramatic poem. Like his creation Faust, G. believed in that human development through experience which he so strikingly exemplifies. His creative writing mirrors this experience; his poetry moves from a direct expression of it to a symbolic mode. The poems are at once sensuous (visual and tactile) and intellectual. Form is organically related to content; there is a great range of subjects (love and nature, science and philosophy, and ballad themes) and of metres, and an unobtrusive mastery of sound effects. The poems often consist of units whose relationship is expressive: before 1775 of the antithesis of opposing values, from 1775 of antitheses and synthesis. This pattern, which G. formulated as 'polarity and advancement' in connection with his studies of plant morphology and colour, represents a principle he saw at work on all sides; it reappears in his drama and fiction. *Götz* and *Werther* show only polarity: the claims of the individual 'daemon' (psyche) are in fatal conflict with those of organized society. In *Egmont* (1788, trs. 1837) and *Tasso*, however, the clash leads to resolution in a different sphere, in Egmont's vision, and in Tasso's recognition of his poetic gift; in *Iphigenie* the conflict itself is resolved; while *Wilhelm Meister* shows the education of the sensitive, gifted individual for and by the community. This development is accompanied

Hugo van der Goes. *Fall of Adam*

Hugo van der Goes.
Right wing of the Portinari triptych

Van Gogh. *The Potato Eaters*

Van Gogh. *Sunflowers*

Van Gogh. *Self-Portrait with ear cut off*

Van Gogh. *Cypresses by Moonlight.* Also *expressionism and colour plate 71

by formal changes: from the sprawling structure, vast cast and slangy prose of *Götz* to the concision and verse elegance of *Tasso* and *Iphigenie*; from the 1st person outpourings of *Werther* to the deliberate narration of *Wilhelm Meister*. G.'s late works emphasize now the polarity, as in the poignant conflict in *Die Wahlverwandtschaften*, now the harmony, as in the elevated close of *Novelle*. The blank clash in the *Urfaust* between Faust's longing for growth and Gretchen's need of permanence becomes in the final version part of a chain of polarities by which both finally attain salvation.

Goff Bruce (1904–). U.S. architect practising in Oklahoma, an admirer of Frank Lloyd Wright. He produced wild, fantastic buildings, often based on circles and spirals, and constructed of industrial waste products–silos, old oil derricks, etc. His buildings seem crazy, but close examination reveals a highly personal sense of logic and a sure sense of form.

Gofman Victor Victorovich: V. V. *Hofman

Gogh Vincent van (1853–90). An artist whose work is one of the formative influences of 20th-c. art and whose life has become almost a legend. The son of a Dutch parson, he was employed by a firm of art dealers in The Hague, London and Paris. Afterwards he became in turn a schoolmaster in England, a missionary to the miners in the Borinage, Belgium, and finally, in 1880, an artist. Van G. was virtually self-taught, though he received some technical advice in oil and watercolour painting from a cousin, the artist A. Mauve. In 1886 he left Holland for Paris, where he lived with his brother Theo, one of the few art dealers encouraging such artists as Gauguin, Seurat, Degas, Toulouse-Lautrec and É. Bernard. Impressed by the work and personalities of these painters, Van G. conceived the idea of founding a 'Studio of the South' at Arles as a working community for progressive artists. He himself went to Arles early in 1888, but the only other painter he persuaded to join him was Gauguin, who visited him at the end of 1888. A violent quarrel between the 2 precipitated the first of Van G.'s periodic attacks of madness in which he cut off part of his ear. 2 years later, at Auvers-sur-Oise, he shot himself. He had sold 1 picture during his lifetime.
Early work of Van G.'s Dutch period is heavy, rich but subdued in colour, with a few fine effects. *The Potato Eaters* (Coll. V. W. Van Gogh, Laren) is typical. After his contact with other painters in Paris, with Japanese prints and the work of such original colourists as Delacroix and A. Monticelli, Van G.'s style changed radically to the brilliant colour and frenzied, thick brushwork of his Arles period. Among hundreds of paintings of the last two and a half years are: *Cornfield and Cypress Trees* (Tate), *Starry Night* (M.M.A., New York), *La Mousmé* (N.G., Washington), *Sunflowers* (Neue Staatsgal., Munich) and *Self-portrait* (Courtauld Gal., London). His watercolours (e.g. *Fishing Boats at Santeo Maries*, B. Koehler Coll., Berlin) and drawings are of equal intensity and value, while the letters he wrote to his brother Theo are important literary and human documents in their own right.

Gogol Nikolay Vasilyevich (1809–52). Russian novelist and playwright. The son of a small squire, G. attended a provincial grammar school until 1828, when he moved to St Petersburg. After publ. a bad poem which was derided, he joined the civil service. In 1831 he became a history teacher. Appointed assistant professor of history at the Univ. at St Petersburg (1834), he was clearly incompetent, and resigned in 1835. The 6 vols of stories and miscellaneous prose which he publ. between 1831 and 1835 established his reputation. They included *Taras Bulba* (1835), a novel about a 17th-c. Cossack leader. G. lived abroad, mainly at Rome, from 1836 to 1848, when he made a pilgrimage to Palestine. He suffered increasingly from religious melancholia and, terrified of the possibility of damnation and weakened by ascetic practices, died virtually insane at Rome, after destroying the 2nd part of his novel *Dead Souls*.
G.'s effects are achieved by verbal wizardry, the contrivance of hilarious situations and caricature. His artistic and political intentions were misinterpreted: his introduction of vulgar, humdrum and grotesque elements widened the scope of Russian literature and led contemporaries to hail him a great realist. The novel *Dead Souls* (1842; 1886) was regarded as a protest against serfdom because the hero, Chichikov, plans to buy serfs – the 'souls' – who have died since the last census and are therefore officially alive, 'settle' them on his land and then pawn them. *The Inspector-General* (1836; 1890, also called *The Government Inspector*) is a comedy of types which satirizes provincial bureaucracy. In both cases G.'s satire is moral, not political in intention – directed against individual vices, not the social system. Hence the disillusion of Belinsky and the radicals when G. publ. his *Selected Passages from a Correspondence with Friends* (1847) which revealed his religious preoccupations and reactionary politics. His stories include *Memoirs of a Madman* (1835) and *The Greatcoat* (1842), which concern the sufferings of poor clerks who are at once pathetic and ludicrous; their influence on Dostoyevsky (especially in *The Double*) is evident.

Göhler Karl Georg (1874–1954). German conductor and a great champion of Mahler's music. G.'s own compositions employ orthodox tonality.

Going My Way (1944). Film directed by L. *McCarey.

gold. From early times g. has been highly prized, not only for its colour (ranging from white to red) but also for its malleable and ductile qualities which allow it to be most elaborately worked with great variation of texture and decoration. Its rarity and consequent value as well as the considerable amount used in the past as coinage, make it more commonly employed in jewellery, which can be displayed, than in domestic use, although this has not prevented the employment of g. in household wares, in times of great prosperity, to emphasize luxury and wealth.

Goldberg Johann Gottlieb (1727–56). German harpsichordist to Count von Keyserlingk. He was the pupil for a time of J. S. Bach, who wrote for him, on the commission of the count, the great set of 30 variations for 2-manual harpsichord which are called after G.

Golden Age. Term used of Latin literature, and especially prose, of the 1st c. B.C., covering such great names as Cicero, Caesar and Virgil. It was used by the Greeks from Hesiod on to refer to a mythical age of perfect peace, happiness and prosperity. It is also used by extension of the great periods of other literatures.

Golden Ass, The. Book by *Apuleius (2nd c. A.D.) containing the well-known story *Cupid and Psyche*.

Golden Bough, The (1890–1915). Pioneer work of anthropology by Sir J. G. *Frazer.

Golden Bowl, The (1904). Novel by Henry *James.

Golden Boy (1937). Play by Clifford *Odets.

Golden Fleece, The. A monthly magazine, printed in Moscow, running from 1906 to 1909, ed and publ. by the wealthy painter Nikolai Ryabushinsky. Chiefly an art magazine, profusely illustrated, it also publ. poetry and literature of the late symbolist school. It sponsored 2 historic Franco-Russian art exhibitions in Moscow in 1908 and 1909 which introduced the French fauves and first brought together the Moscow and Paris *avant-garde* painters.

Golden Legend. (1) A medieval handbook of devotional writings, including lives of the saints, homilies and commentaries on religious rites. It was one of the most popular books printed by Caxton. (2) A poem (1852) by Longfellow retelling a 12th-c. German legend.

golden section, golden mean. The name given in art to the mathematical relationship between 3 points in a straight line (see diagram) in which the ratio AC : BC equals the ratio BC : AB.

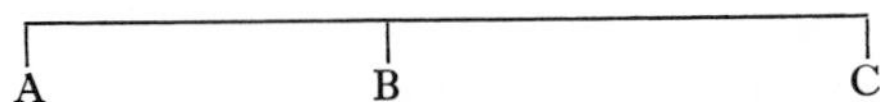

This relationship was invested with an almost mystical significance by some Renaissance theorists and used extensively by certain painters, above all Piero della Francesca.

Golden Treasury of Songs and Lyrics, The (1861). Anthology by F. T. *Palgrave.

Goldfaden Abraham (1840–1908). Ukrainian-Jewish playwright and regarded as the founder of the Yiddish theatre. He toured Europe and the U.S. and he settled in New York in 1903.

Goldfinger Erno (1902–). Hungarian-born architect. After study in Paris, he settled in England in 1934 where he was a pioneer of modern architecture. His own house in Hampstead (1938), is one of the most famous of the modern houses of the 1930s. His practice grew in the late 1950s, culminating in the Headquarters Building of the Ministry of Health, Elephant and Castle, London (1960–2).

Golding Arthur (1536?–1605?). English trs. His fine trs. of Ovid's *Metamorphoses* (1565–7)

Gogol

The Golden Fleece. Illustration by Vasily Miliuti

Golden Legend, printed by Wynkyn de Worde (1498)

influenced Shakespeare and, in the 20th c., Ezra Pound; also notable is G.'s rendering of Caesar's *Gallic War* (1565).

Golding William (1911–). English novelist. G.'s 1st novel, *Lord of the Flies* (1954; film 1962), is a horrifying exposition of man's savagery illustrated by the degeneration of a group of public schoolboys stranded away from the adult world by an air crash. All G.'s novels are reinterpretations of religious themes. They include *The Inheritors* (1955), *Pincher Martin* (1956), *Free Fall* (1959) and *The Spire* (1964).

Goldoni: painting by Alessandro Longhi

Goldmark (Karoly) Karl (1830–1915). Hungarian composer, the son of a Jewish cantor. Besides Hungarian folk and Jewish church traditions, his music shows such diverse influences as Mendelssohn and Wagner. He wrote 6 operas, *The Queen of Sheba* (1875) demonstrating his control of orchestral effect; orchestral works, e.g. the overture *Sakuntala* (1865) and the symphonic poem *Country Wedding* (1876).

Goldmark Rubin (1872–1936). U.S. composer and teacher of composition at the Julliard School of Music, New York; nephew of the above. His pupils included A. Copland and V. Giannini. His music, orthodox in tonality, includes *A Negro Rhapsody* (1922) for orchestra.

Goldoni Carlo (1707–93). Venetian playwright, in the early 1760s he settled in France. The best of C.'s many comedies use Venetian themes and dialect, e.g. *I Rusteghi* (1760) and *Le Baruffe chiozzotte* (1762); he introduced the character comedy of Molière into Italian, displacing the *commedia dell'arte*. Other works include *La Locandiera* (1753) and his memoirs, publ. in French in 1787.

Goldsmith: painting by Reynolds

Gold Rush, The (1925). Film directed by C. *Chaplin.

Goldschmidt Berthold (1903–). German-born composer and conductor who emigrated to England in 1935 (naturalized British). He conducted the Glyndebourne Opera at the Edinburgh Festival of 1947, and has been the director of the Jooss Ballet. His music has affinities to Stravinsky and P. Hindemith in its tonality, and uses jazz rhythms.

Goldschmidt Meïr Aron (1819–87). Danish-Jewish novelist and journalist, founder of the radical journal *Corsarea* ('The Corsair') he was involved in a long dispute with Kirkegaard in connection with the paper.

Goldsmith Oliver (1728–74). Irish writer, a friend of Dr Johnson and his circle. G. came to London in 1756, set up briefly as a physician (his qualifications were dubious) and thereafter supported himself by prolific and skilful hack-writing. He made at least one important contribution to each branch of English literature. He wrote *The Citizen of the World* (coll. 1762), the 'letters' of an imaginary Chinaman living in London, which makes gentle fun of English manners; the novel *The Vicar of Wakefield* (1766), a charming social comedy which contains the famous lyric *When lovely woman stoops to folly*; and the poem *The Deserted Village* (1770), a moving description of rural depopulation. But G.'s greatest work was the sturdy comedy *She Stoops to Conquer, or The Mistakes of a Night* (1773), in which the hero mistakes a private residence for an inn and the daughter of the house for a servant–with admirable results, since he is too shy to make love to a woman of quality. G.'s works include the poem *The Traveller* (1764) and the comedy *The Good-natur'd Man* (1768).

Goldwyn Samuel (1884–). Film producer. G. worked as a glove salesman in New York (1913). He produced the 2nd version of C. B. *De Mille's *The Squaw Man* and helped found the co. which became Famous Players Lasky Corporation. His Goldwyn Picture Corporation was sold to Metro Productions to form part of Metro-Goldwyn-Mayer in 1924. Thereafter he worked as an independent producer, and was from 1927 to 1940 one of the owners of United Artists. His best achievement as a producer is the series of films directed by W. *Wyler from *Dodsworth* (1936) to *The Best Years of our Lives* (1946).

Golestan Stan (1875–). Rumanian composer who studied in Paris under d'Indy and Roussel and Dukas; he has worked largely in Paris. His works, which make frequent use of folk-melodies, include: *Rhapsodie roumaine*, a 'Rumanian' concerto for violin, a 'Moldavian' concerto for cello and 2 string quartets.

Gollins, Melvin, Ward and Partners. Firm of London architects. Their best-known works

Gollins, Melvin, Ward and Partners. Library of the University of Sheffield

Goncharov (far left) with other contributors to the magazine *The Contemporary*. Seated: Turgenev, Druzhinin, Ostrovsky. Standing: Leo Tolstoy and Grigorovich

are Castrol House, Marylebone Road, London (1958), and Sheffield Univ. Library (1958) and Students Union (1963).

Golovlyov Family, The (1876–80). Novel by *Saltykov.

Goltzius Hendrick (1558–1617). Dutch engraver and, from 1600, painter influenced by Italian mannerism. He worked in Haarlem and was the 1st engraver to exploit all the tonal possibilities of line engraving. Although his work lost some of the characteristics of the medium it achieved something of the subtle gradations of oil painting and exercised great influence on the growth of reproduction engraving.

Gombaud Jean Ogier de (*c.* 1570–1666). French poet, an original member of the Académie Française. G.'s works include a verse drama, *Amaranthe* (printed 1631), and a prose romance *Endymion* (1624; *Endymion*, 1639).

Gombert Nicolas (*c.* 1500–*c.* 56). Flemish composer, one of the greatest of the school of Josquin. Regarded as an innovator by contemporaries, he aimed to write music fitting his text and wrote in a style of subtle and fully worked out imitation; frequently voices imitate each other in pairs and the melodic line is simple and flowing.

Gomberville Marin Le Roy de (1600–74). French writer, author of *La Carithée* (1621), *Polexandre* (1637) and *La Cythérée* (1642), romances with pseudo-historical backgrounds.

Gombrowicz Witold (1905–). Polish novelist and playwright, one of the most original and talented of contemporary Polish authors. His satirical novel *Ferdydurke* (1937; 1961) exerted a great influence on younger writers. In the novel *Transatlantyk* (1953) G. ridicules the excesses of patriotism.

Gomes (Antonio) Carlos (1836–96). Brazilian composer whose opera *Joanna de Flandre* (1863) won him a scholarship to study in Milan; he worked much in Italy and was heavily influenced by Verdi. In 1870 his opera *Il Guarany* received a triumphant première at La Scala.

Gómez de la Serna Ramón (1888–). Spanish writer, anticipating surrealism. He had a talent for inventing humorous and extravagant metaphors known as '*greguerías*' and his more imaginative works tend to give life to inanimate objects and to express the subconscious in striking verbal images. His writings include poems, novels, books on art and articles.

Gonçalves Nuno (*c.* 1438–81). Portuguese painter rediscovered in the 20th c. and regarded as the founder of the Portuguese school. He is known to have been active as court painter to Alfonso V *c.* 1450–72; the only work attributed to him with certainty is the polyptych for the convent of St Vincent, Lisbon (*c.* 1465–7), 6 panels which depict the whole of Portuguese society crowded about King Alfonso and Henry the Navigator as they pray to St Vincent. G. was a master of colour and of composition. The modelling of his figures is sculpturesque and their heads are painted with a sharp insight which anticipates the psychological portrait.

Gonçalves. Detail from the St Vincent polyptych

Goncharov Ivan Alexandrovich (1812–91). Russian novelist of merchant stock. G.'s life as a civil servant was uneventful, apart from the visit to Japan he described in *The Frigate 'Pallada'* (1856); he seems to have been as inactive as some of his characters. The novel *A Common Story* (1847) compares unfavourably the dreamy idealist with the practical man. In G.'s most important work, *Oblomov* (1859; 1915), the hero spends most of his time in bed. Oblomov has generous sentiments and clever ideas, but degenerates steadily through lack of self-discipline and effort. The public immediately recognized him as a symbol of the Russian gentry and intelligentsia. Stolz, the practical man, is–significantly–half-German. The outwardly staid G. revealed psychopathic tendencies in *An Uncommon Story* (posth. publ.), a document accusing Turgenev and Flaubert of plagiarizing *The Precipice* (1869), his last, and unsuccessful, novel.

Goncharova Natalia (1881–1962). Russian painter and theatrical designer who studied under the sculptor Trubetskoy in Moscow where she met Larionov, the major influence in her work as well as a life-long companion. A preoccupation with icon painting and national folk-art characterizes her best-known work such as designs for Diaghilev's *Le Coq d'Or*, *Les Noces* and *Firebird*. Before leaving Moscow for Paris in 1915, she was well known in Russia as a futurist and rayonnist painter.

Goncharova. Two of *The Evangelists*. Also *Le *Coq d'Or*

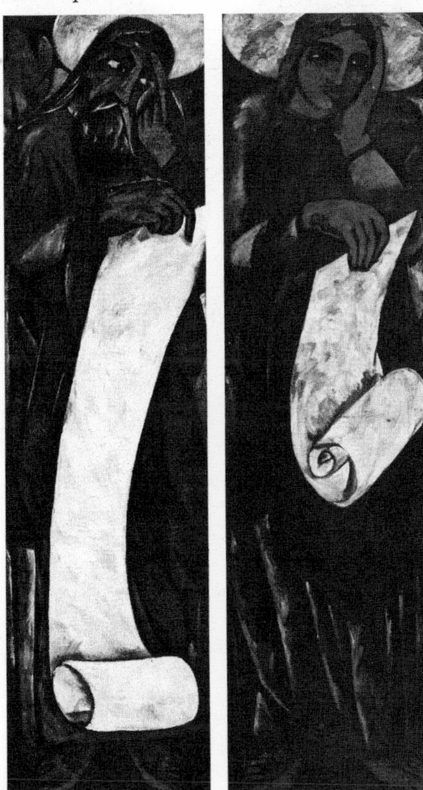

Eva Gonzalès: painting by Manet

Góngora y Argote

The Goncourt brothers: lithograph by Gavarni

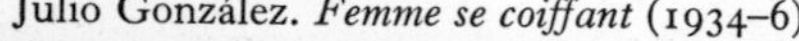

Julio González. *Femme se coiffant* (1934–6)

Goncourt the brothers Edmond de (1822–96) and Jules de (1830–70). French writers who worked in collaboration until the younger died of syphilis. Edmond cherished the memory of Jules, continued the diary they had begun in collaboration and left money for the founding of the Académie G. and the Prix G., by which they were to be jointly commemorated. Well-to-do, self-absorbed bourgeois, they looked upon themselves as exceptional, sensitive creatures with a literary and artistic mission. They helped to create a fashion in 18th-c. French furniture and paintings and in Japanese art. Their extremely detailed books on the social and artistic life of the 18th c. are still read. They applied the same technique of close documentation and mannered writing, which they called *'l'écriture artiste'*, to the lurid contemporary social subjects they dealt with in their novels, and so were pioneers of realism and naturalism: *Germinie Lacerteux* (1864, *Germinie Lacerteux*, 1887) and *Madame Gervaisais* (1869). Now their chief claim to fame is the *Journal des Goncourt* (complete text, 22 vols 1956–8; *The Journal of the De Goncourts* (extracts) 1915). Its accounts of the conversation of Flaubert, Turgenev, Sainte-Beuve, Gautier, Zola, Daudet, etc. are absorbing though often malicious.

Gondoliers, The *or The King of Barataria* (1889). Operetta by Sir A. Sullivan and W. S. Gilbert, their last successful collaboration.

Gone With the Wind (1936). Novel by Margaret *Mitchell; made into a film (1939) directed by V. *Fleming, G. *Cukor and S. *Wood.

Góngora y Argote Luis de (1561–1627). Spanish poet, the master of an elaborate style which is called by his name, GONGORISM. Its characteristics are an exaggerated Latinism both of vocabulary and syntax, a use of often obscure mythology, and a trick of periphrasis by which an object is defined not by name but by colour. G.'s early poetry was Italianate, and much of it, although he had taken deacon's orders, was love-poetry. In the early 1600s he elaborated his style and turned to satire, compliment and polemic. At 50 he retired to write his masterpieces, *Fábula de Polifemo y Galatea* (1612) and the unfinished *Soledades* (1627). Afterwards he went to court and sought in vain for preferment or a pension. He had many enemies, including Lope de Vega and Quevedo, who scorned his poetry and attacked him. Others defended him vigorously and many younger poets adopted his style (e.g. Pedrosato de Rojas), among them some of his critics.
In the 18th c. G.'s poetry fell into disrepute and the term Gongorism became one of abuse. His reputation was revived in the 1920s and his influence was for a while strong again among Spanish poets.

Gonzalès Eva (1849–83). French impressionist painter, pupil and close follower of Manet. There is a famous portrait of her by Manet in the Tate.

Gonzáles Martínez Enrique (1871–1952). Mexican poet; by profession a doctor, later a diplomat. In the 1910s he rejected the ideals of the *modernismo, despite the early influence of Darío on his verse, and gave the new rebellious generation a catch-phrase, 'Wring the swan's neck'—the 'swan' being a formal perfection without inner truth. G.M.'s verse is an austere record of spiritual experience.

González Julio (1876–1942). Spanish sculptor, who lived in Paris from 1900. He began his career as a painter but found his métier as a sculptor in iron, making use of new industrial processes, and inspired by a desire to create forms based on the natural limitations of the material. In his abstract and realistic work alike, observed nature was the source of his ideas.

Goodbye to All That (1929). Autobiography by Robert *Graves.

Goodbye to Berlin (1939). Book by Christopher *Isherwood.

Good Companions, The (1929). Novel by J. B. *Priestley.

Goodman Benny (1909–). U.S. *jazz clarinettist and band-leader.

Good Soldier Schweik, The (1920–3). Comic novel by Jaroslav *Hašek, the basis of a play by Bertolt Brecht.

Good Soldier, The (1915). Novel by Ford Madox *Ford.

THE
TRAGEDIE OF GORBODVC,
where of three Actes were wrytten by
Thomas Nortone, and the two laste by
Thomas Sackuyle.
Sett forthe as the same was shewed before the
QVENES most excellent Maiestie, in her highnes
Court of Whitehall, the .xviij. day of January,
Anno Domini. 1561. By the Gentlemen
of Thynner Temple in London.

IMPRYNTED AT LONDON
in Fletestrete, at the Signe of the
Faucon by William Griffith: And are
to be sold at his Shop in Sainete
Dunstones Churchyarde in
the West of London.
Anno. 1565. Septemb. 22.

Gore. *North London Girl*

Gorboduc; title-page of 1565 ed.

Arshile Gorky. *The Betrothal* (1947)

Good Woman of Setzuan, The (1943). Play by Bertolt *Brecht.

Goossens Sir Eugene (1893–1962). British composer of Belgian descent. From 1923 he conducted in the U.S. and from 1947 to 1955 in Sydney, also directing the New South Wales Conservatorium. French impressionism was an important early influence on G.'s delicate music; the idiom is predominantly chromatic, later works tend towards classicism. His brother LEON (1896–) is an outstanding oboe virtuoso.

Gopal Ram (1920–). Indian dancer who has contributed greatly towards establishing Indian dancing as a theatre form. With his co. he has toured in the West and brought with him the taste for this style of dance.

Gorboduc, or Ferrex and Porrex (1561). Tragedy by Thomas *Sackville and Thomas Norton.

Gordimer Nadine (1922–). South African woman novelist whose *These Living Days* (1953) and *Six Feet of Country* (1956) have intellectual vigour matching their emotive power. She uncompromisingly attacks racist attitudes.

Gordon Adam Lindsay (1833–70). Australian poet born in the Azores and educated at Oxford; he went to Australia (1853) as a remittance-man. He became wealthy, but committed suicide. Only a few of his poems–e.g. *The Sick Stockrider*–are Australian in inspiration.

Gordon Michael (1909–). U.S. film director. G. made a film on euthanasia, *The Right to Kill* (1948), followed by a number of other films including *I Can Get It For You Wholesale* (1949), written by *Polonsky, and *Cyrano de Bergerac* (1950), written by *Foreman and produced by *Kramer. In 1951 he fell victim to the McCarthy black-list and made no more films until 1959. Since then he has specialized in comedies of which the first, *Pillow Talk* (1959), was the best and most successful.

Gore Frederick Spencer (1878–1914). English painter of landscapes, ballet and music-hall scenes and interiors, closely associated with Gilman and 1st president of the Camden Town Group. He first worked in France and was strongly influenced by impressionist painting through his friendship with Lucien Pissarro; he later followed the post-impressionists.

Gore Walter (1910–). British dancer who was a pioneer of British ballet during its emergence in the early 1930s. He danced with the newly formed Ballet Rambert and the Vic-Wells but later turned to choreography; some of his productions are *Valse Finale* (1938), *Mr Punch* (1946) and *Night of Silence* (1958).

Goring Marius (1912–). English actor whose 1st appearance was at the Old Vic in 1929. He led the co. at the Stratford Memorial Theatre in 1953, playing with equal success Richard III, Octavius in *Antony and Cleopatra*, Petruchio in *The Taming of the Shrew* and the Fool in *King Lear*.

Gorky Arshile (1904–48). Armenian-born U.S. painter in the surrealist tradition. Influenced by Miró, later by Matta, Breton and other emigrant surrealists, he evolved (early 1940s) a complex and fanciful style, a fusion of symbolic imagery and free-form abstraction which affected and enlivened the development of abstract expressionism in the U.S. He committed suicide after a series of personal tragedies.

Gorky Maxim. Pseud., meaning 'bitter', of Alexey Maximovich Peshkov (1868–1936). Russian novelist and playwright of proletarian origin. G. earned his own living from the age of 8, taking many jobs and wandering all over Russia. Following the publ. of 2 vols of his stories (1898) he became the most famous Russian author after Tolstoy. His Bolshevik sympathies caused him occasional difficulties; and after the failure of the 1905 Revolution he lived in Capri (until 1913). When the Bolsheviks came to power he preserved his independence, using his prestige to help many writers. Between 1921 and 1929 he lived abroad, nominally for the sake of his health, but thereafter supported Stalin. His death was supposedly the result of a 'Trotskyite' plot.
G.'s early works employ realistic methods, but treat their characters–often vagabonds and criminals–in a romantic spirit. *Twenty-six Men and a Girl* (1899) ends this phase. He then wrote a series of ambitious though unsatisfactory social-philosophical novels, including *Foma Gordeyev* (1900; 1901) and *The Mother* (1907; 1907). During this period his play *The Lower Depths* (1902; 1912), set in a flop-house,

Michael Gordon. Lloyd Nolan and Lana Turner in *Portrait in Black*

Maxim Gork

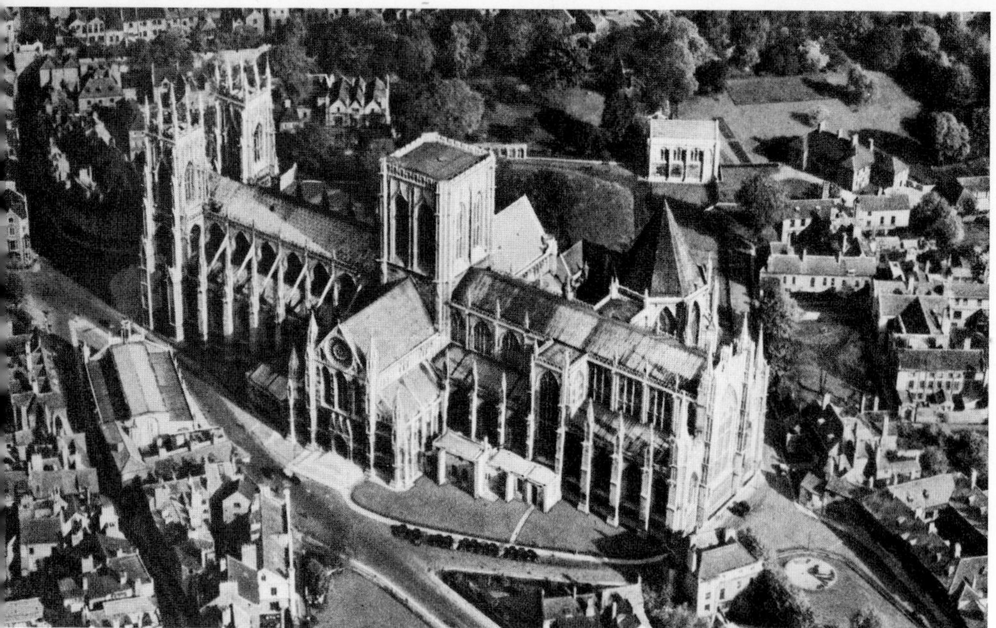

Gothic. York Minster

Gothic. Amiens cathedral. See also colour plates 30, 32 and 35

Gothic. León cathedral

The 'Gothick'. Strawberry Hill

Sir Edmund Gosse

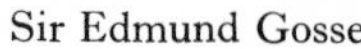

caused a sensation. G.'s humanity and power of observation were better employed in the autobiographical series (later a film trilogy directed by Mark *Donskoi) *Childhood* (1914; 1915), *In the World* (1916; 1917) and *My Universities* (1923; 1924); in *Reminiscences of Tolstoy, Chekhov and Andreyev* (1924–31), and in *Notes for a Diary* (1924; 1924). They are probably his best works. He returned to naturalistic studies with *The Artamanovs* (1925; 1927), a novel about the decay of a merchant family; *Yegor, Bulychov and Others* and *Dostigaev and Others*, an unfinished dramatic trilogy; and 4 completed novels of the cycle *The Life of Klim Samgin*.

Görres Johann Joseph von (1776–1848). German writer and political figure. He is important for *Die teutschen Volksbücher* (1807) and other works reviving medieval German tradition. He also conducted the nationalist journal *Rheinische Merkur* (1814–16).

Gorsky Alexander (1871–1924). Russian dancer of the Imperial School; he became premier danseur in 1900. He transferred as régisseur to the Bolshoi Theatre, Moscow and there rebelled against his former teacher, Petipa, by remaking some of his ballets (and Saint-Léon's), adding dances and altering their interpretation.

Gosho Heinosuke (1902–). Japanese film director. He is best known for a sombre domestic drama, *Four Chimneys* (1953). His later work has become more lush, e.g. *When a Woman Loves* (1959).

Gospels: *Bible

Gossaert (Gossart), Jan: *Mabuse

Gosse Sir Edmund (1849–1928). English critic and poet and librarian of the House of Lords. He is remembered for *Father and Son* (1907), his classic portrayal of bigotry and of the Victorian conflict between science and belief. As a critic G. furthered English acquaintance with the works of Ibsen and Donne.

Gossec François-Joseph (1734–1829). Hainault-born composer who worked in Paris. He studied under J.-P. Rameau and was influenced as a young man by the Mannheim school. He became an inspector of the Conservatoire and official composer to the French Republic. His music achieved dramatic orchestral effects comparable to Berlioz, and included several operas, e.g. *Thésée* (1782), influenced by Gluck; the ballet *Mirza* (1779); a requiem (1760); over 30 symphonies and many Revolutionary hymns, e.g. 'L'Hymne à l'Être suprême'.

Gothic. General term applied to the style in the arts of the high middle ages; it was coined contemptuously in the 17th c., the Goths being among the barbarian ancestors of medieval Europe. In architecture it is applied to the style developed in the Île de France in the 12th c. (*Suger) characterized by the pointed arch, soaring piers, elaborate vaults, extensive use of glass and increasingly intricate tracery.

Rib-vaults and pointed arches are found in Romanesque, but their fusion, with the added element of the flying buttress, produced G., a new style in architecture. The emphasis was on dynamic line rather than on weight and mass, as in Romanesque, and the more elegant working out of engineering problems combined with the new spirit of religious mysticism and aspiration produced an ever stronger emphasis on vertical and height, evidenced in spires and flèches. Extensive use was made of sculpture and stained glass as decorative features. The style spread to England, where it developed the 3 periods of *Early English, *decorated and *perpendicular, and somewhat later to Germany. Spanish G. was deeply influenced by French, though a distinct national style evolved in the 15th and 16th cs. Italy remained outside the mainstream (e.g. *Siena cathedral; *Frari, Venice). In England the gradual 18th-c. renewal of interest in all things *'Gothick' led eventually to the GOTHIC REVIVAL of the 19th c. and the NEO-GOTHIC style in architecture. *International G. is a term used in painting.

'Gothick', The. 18th-c. British fashion for the pseudo-medieval–for irregular beauty, for the mysterious and the gloomy; one of the factors in the development of *romanticism, manifesting itself, e.g., in *Gothick novels, in such poetry as Edward *Young's *Night Thoughts*, in *Walpole's Strawberry Hill, *Beckford's Fonthill, the folly, the sham ruin, etc. Architecturally the 'G.' led to the 19th-c. Gothic revival.

Gothick novels. 18th-c. novels of mystery and terror, usually including supernatural events and set in pseudo-medieval backgrounds; part of the cult of the *'Gothick'. Walpole's *Castle of Otranto* (1764) started the fashion; other writers in the genre were Mrs Anne Radcliffe, whom Jane Austen satirized in *Northanger Abbey*, and 'Monk' *Lewis.

Götterdämmerung (German, 'Twilight of the Gods'). Opera by *Wagner; 1st performance at Bayreuth in 1876.

Gottfried of Strassburg. German poet, author of the German court epic version (*c.* 1210) of the legend of the lovers Tristan and Isolde. His style, a development of that of Hartmann von Aue, is sensitive, refined and technically masterful in its control of rhyme, rhythm and language; characteristic is a delight in antithesis and repetition, and the use of allegory. G.'s range and subtlety as a poet are outstandingly revealed in his handling of the love element in his story.

Gotthelf Jeremias. Pseud. of Albert Bitzius (1797–1854). Swiss novelist and clergyman. His realistic, unsentimental narratives of the peasants of his rural parish are often written in dialect. His cautionary tales advocate natural life and simple morality based on Christian and, increasingly, conservative principles. The best-known novel is . . . *Uli, der Knecht* (1841; *Ulric the Farm Servant*, 1886–8). His short stories include a spine-thrilling mythic account of the visitation of evil, *Die schwarze Spinne* (1842; *The Black Spider*, 1958).

Gottlieb Adolph (1903–). U.S. abstract expressionist painter, with Rothko and others a founder of the Ten Group, New York (1935). Early in the 1940s, under the influence of primitive art, he invented the 'pictograph', the compartmental arrangement of symbolic calligraphic motifs. More recently he has concentrated on exploring the relationship between 2 contrasted shapes. His decorative works include murals for the Post Office, Yerington, Nevada (1939) and tapestries for the Synagogue, Millburn, New Jersey (1951).

Gottsched Johann Christoph (1700–66). German critic who introduced French standards of good taste and correctness into Germany, expounding them in *Versuch einer Critischen Dichtkunst* . . . (1730) and *Grundlegung einer deutschen Sprachkunst* (1748). He also helped to restore the connection between literature and the theatre; and his tragedy *Der sterbende Cato* (1731) was popular. In the last 20 years of G.'s life his influence waned.

Götz Hermann Gustav (1840–76). German composer whose comic opera on Shakespeare's *The Taming of the Shrew* (1874) is similar in style to O. Nicolai's work. G.'s other music such as the choral work *Nanie* (1874) and his piano, chamber and symphonic music shows affinities to that of Brahms and Mendelssohn.

Götz Karl Otto (1914–). German abstract expressionist painter, member of a group in Frankfurt known as 'neo-expressionists'. He also exhibited with the Cobra group. His later work is flowing and dynamic.

Götz von Berlichingen mit der eisernen Hand: ein Schauspiel (1773). Play by *Goethe.

gouache. Watercolour paint made opaque by the addition of white. Effects similar to those of oil paint can be obtained with g. but it has the defects of lightening in colour as it dries and cracking if used thickly. It was used by the medieval ms. illuminators and later by many continental artists. In England it was less popular than transparent watercolour but was used by Sandby. It has been revived by 20th-c. painters and designers. In less good quality it is known as poster colour.

Goudimel Claude (*c.* 1514–72). French Huguenot composer, killed in the St Bartholomew massacres. Before his conversion he wrote masses and motets; more important are 2 complete harmonizations of the Psalter and 8 settings of Psalms in 4, 5 and 6 parts for the Protestant service. G. also wrote *chansons*.

Goujon Jean (*fl.* 1540–62). The greatest French sculptor of the mid 16th c. who worked first in Rouen, then in Paris. He was influenced by the mannerism of Parmigianino, G. B. Rosso and Cellini but gave the style a personal interpretation derived from classical sculpture. He executed relief decoration for the rood-screen of St Germain l'Auxerrois, Paris, and the Fontaine des Innocents, Paris (both Louvre), and decorative work for the Louvre (spoilt by 19th-c. restoration).

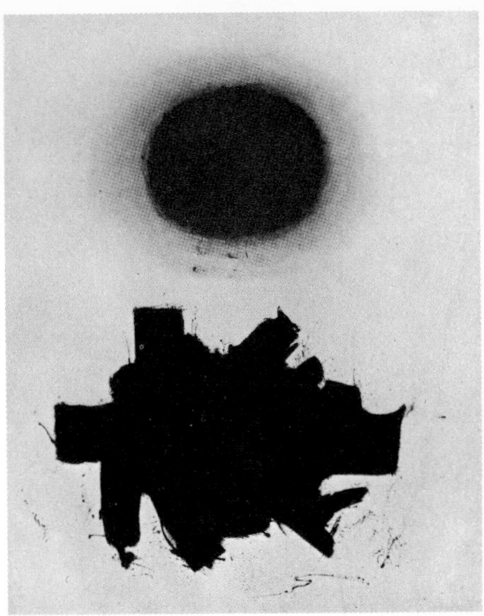

Gottlieb. *Cool blast* (1960)

Karl Otto Götz. *AGDE* (1957)

Gouache. Nolde, *Die Nackte*

Goujon. Nymph from the Fontaine des Innocents

Goya. *Self-portrait*

Goya. *Maja Clothed*

Goya. *Los Caprichos*, No. 2: *They say yes . . .*

Goya. *Maja Unclothed*

Goya. *Charles IV and Family*

Goya. *The Third of May* (*Executions*). Also *Bayeu, *caricature, **Disasters of War*, *engraving

Gould John (1804–81). English ornithologist whose works on British and foreign birds were beautifully illustrated with coloured lithographs, produced with the help of his wife and others; these introduced new standards of accuracy and artistry into bird illustration.

Gounod Charles (François) (1818–93). French composer and organist, a pupil of Halévy; he won the 1st Rome prize. G.'s work was praised by many French composers and above all by Fauré. His music, sentimental and charming, is often effective and his opera *Faust* (1859) based on Goethe, his masterpiece, has remained in the repertory. His other works include: other operas including *Romeo and Juliet*, much church music including an oratorio, and an 'Ave Maria' using the 1st Prelude of book I of J. S. Bach's *Well Tempered Clavier*.

Goupi Mains Rouges (1943). Film directed by J. *Becker.

Gourmont Remy de (1858–1915). French writer, the leading symbolist critic and one of the founders of the *Mercure de France* (1889). G.'s imaginative works include the novel *Sixtine: roman de la vie cérébrale* (1890). His writing was graceful, witty and aphoristic in studies, sketches and criticism. Among these are *Le Livre des masques* (1896), *La Culture des idées* (1901), *Le Problème du style* (1902) and *Promenades littéraires* (1904–27).

Gournay Marie de Jars, demoiselle de (1565–1645). French writer, adopted daughter of Montaigne. After his death she issued an ed. of his *Essais* (1595). She wrote many pamphlets and treatises including *Défense de la poésie et du langage des poètes* (1634).

Government Inspector, The (1836). Satirical comedy by *Gogol.

Gower John (*c.* 1330–1408). English poet, a friend of Chaucer, and an important poet in 3 languages, G. enjoyed a high reputation in his own lifetime and afterwards. In him, and in Chaucer, French literary culture has become fully assimilated into English. All his works have a moral and didactic purpose: the *Mirour de l'Omme* (1376–9), the Latin *Vox Clamantis* (*c.* 1382), and the most famous, the English *Confessio Amantis* (1390–2), a well-constructed allegory combining the themes of courtly love and Christianity. Using the Seven Deadly Sins as a framework, the poet confesses the sins he has committed against Venus; in the stories which illustrate these themes, C. shows himself a sound stylist and a good narrator, with a talent for creating romantic atmosphere.

Goya y Lucientes, Francisco José de (1746–1828). Spanish painter and graphic artist. Born at Fuendetodos, by 1760 G. was apprenticed in Saragossa to José Luzán, an artist who studied under Neapolitan masters. Francisco Bayeu, a former pupil of Luzán, had won fame in Madrid as assistant to the royal painter A. R. Mengs, and G. followed Bayeu, became his pupil and married his sister in 1773.

Meanwhile, in 1771, G. had made a visit (which is rich in legend if not in facts) to Italy and he painted commissions for churches in the vicinity of Saragossa at the end of the same year. He settled in Madrid in 1775 and in 1776 was commissioned to paint cartoons for the royal tapestry works. At first G. followed conventional subjects, the court pastorals that relied on French and German rococo models and the painting of Tiepolo and the Neapolitans. Soon, however, his own painting became noticeably freer and he introduced scenes observed from Spanish life, e.g. *Stilt Walkers, Blind Guitarist* (both Prado). In the course of his work he was admitted to the Royal Colls where he engraved copies of Velazquez. Stimulated by Velazquez and by mezzotints after Gainsborough and Reynolds, he began to paint portraits.

The 1780s record his increasing fame and an amazing variety of activity. In 1782 he portrayed the powerful minister Floridablanca (Urquiro Bank, Madrid); in 1786 he painted *Charles III Hunting* (Prado). He had many commissions from the Church including the 2 *St Francis Borgia* scenes for Valencia cathedral. Among small works he did for his own pleasure is the remarkable view of Madrid, *Fiesta of San Isidero* (Prado). In 1780 he had submitted his *Crucifixion* (Prado) to the academy of San Fernando, being elected a member unanimously and appointed deputy director in 1785. At the court he was progressively *pintor del rey* (1786), *pinto de cámara* (1789), and *primer pintor de cámara* (1799). A change in his style is noticeable after his illness in 1792, which left him deaf. The portraits show greater insight, e.g. *Dr Peral* (N.G., London) and almost cruel objectivity in the famous *Charles IV and Family* (Prado). G.'s attachment to the duchess of Alba is celebrated in 2 fine portraits (Coll. Duke of Alba, Madrid, and Hispanic Society, New York). He castigated the follies of the court, superstition and the vanity of women in *Los Caprichos*, his engravings of 1796–8. In the same period he painted the *Maja Clothed* and *Maja Unclothed* (both Prado). His religious paintings are revolutionarily free in technique, but obviously profoundly felt, e.g. *Betrayal of Christ* (Toledo cathedral) and the frescoes of S. Antonio de la Florida, Madrid. Subsequently G. chronicled the horrors of Napoleonic occupation in *The Second of May* (*Uprising*) and *The Third of May* (*Executions*) (both Prado) as well as in the engravings *Disasters of War* and his drawings. After the restoration of the reactionary Ferdinand VII, G. retired to the outskirts of Madrid. The decorations in his own house, called during his lifetime the *House of the Deaf Man*, now removed to the Prado, remain among the strangest and most original paintings ever painted both in subject and technique. They include *Witches' Sabbath, Saturn Devouring his Child* and *Fantastic Vision*. In a self-chosen exile in France G. continued to paint, engrave and practise lithography with undiminished vigour until his death. *Milkmaid of Bordeaux*, one of his last works, has a frenzied brushwork which looks forward to the effects of the post-impressionists. G. was the favourite of French writers such as Baudelaire. Artists of almost every major school have been influenced by his work in painting and the graphic arts from Delacroix and Géricault, Manet and Daumier to Käthe Kollwitz and Picasso.

Goyen Jan van (1596–1659). Dutch painter and father-in-law and teacher of Jan Steen. With Pieter de Molijn and S. van Ruysdael G. established the early school of Dutch naturalistic landscape painting. He executed a great number of paintings. Those of the middle period are often so austere in colour as to be almost monochrome, and they were once thought to have faded. His best-known works are views of the towns of Holland, of which *View of Dordrecht* (Rijksmus., Amsterdam) is a good example with its wide sky and low horizon, the bustle of human life confined to the bottom quarter of the painting.

Van Goyen. *Scene on the Ice by a Drinking Booth*

Gozlan Léon (1803–66). French dramatist, friend of Balzac. Besides several dramas and comedies, he wrote the novel *Le Notaire de Chantilly* (1836), 1-act sketches, including *Le Lion empaillé* (1848), and reminiscences of Balzac, *Balzac en pantoufles* (1856).

Gozzi Carlo (1720–1806). Italian poet, playwright and literary polemicist. Opposed to the more realistic drama as represented by Goldoni, he tried to revive the *commedia dell'arte* in his series of plays based on oriental and popular tales, *Fiabe* (1761–5). He wrote tragi-comedies and an autobiography of some interest.

Gozzoli Benozzo. Name adopted by Benozzo di Lese (*c.* 1421–97), Florentine painter. Best known for the *Procession of the Magi* frescoes in the Medici-Riccardi Palace, Florence, G. was an assistant to both L. Ghiberti and Fra Angelico before painting frescoes and altarpieces in a number of towns, including Rome, San Gimignano and Pisa. A typical altarpiece is *The Virgin with Saints* (N.G., Ottawa).

Gozzoli. *Procession of the Magi*

Grabbe Christian Dietrich (1801–36). German playwright whose wild 'romantic' career was punctuated by such grandiose projects as *Don Juan and Faust* (1829) and 4 historical dramas, among them *Napoleon . . .* (1831), influenced by Shakespeare. His later work developed towards realism.

Grace Abounding to the Worst of Sinners (1666). Religious work by John *Bunyan.

Gracián y Morales Baltasar (1601–58). Spanish Jesuit writer and moralist; he finally rebelled against his order's insistence on absolute obedience, was forbidden to publ. his books, and died in prison after attempting to leave the order. His main works include a treatise on style, *Agudez y arte de ingenio* (1642), and his most famous work, *El Criticón* (1651–7), an allegorical novel, written in a terse, deliberate style, expounding his rather gloomy philosophy of life and his recipe for living. It was largely forgotten, together with his other works, after his death until rediscovered and highly praised by Schopenhauer. The coll. of aphorisms *Oráculo manual y Arte de prudencia* (1647; *The Courtiers Manual Oracle*, 1685) was drawn on by later writers.

gradual. A section of the plainsong of the proper of the mass.

Gradus ad Parnassum (Latin, 'Steps towards Parnassus'). The title of a musical

Graf. *The Soldier's Farewell*

Granacci. *Madonna and Four Saints*

Martha Graham in *Herodiade*

dans l'Isle de Saint-Amand, & Doüay. Aprés quoy il se camp terreur dans tout le Pays, qu'il f Enfin il marcha vers Condé, 8 cauld, il fit faire un logement mesme, 25 d'Aoust, le Gouvern Comte demeura aux environs

Grandjean, *romain du roi*

treatise by *Fux and of a coll. of piano pieces by *Clementi (also *Debussy).

Graf Urs (*c.* 1485–1527/8). Swiss draughtsman, engraver, painter, goldsmith and mercenary soldier. From 1509 he worked in Basle and is famous for his drawings, influenced by Baldung Grien and Dürer, often depicting military genre scenes. Only 1 painting, *War* (*c.* 1515; Basle), can definitely be ascribed to him.

Graff Anton (1736–1813). Swiss portrait painter who worked in Dresden. He abandoned the idealized portraiture of the rococo period and specialized in half-length portraits with naturalistic poses and subdued tones, e.g. his picture of the painter Daniel Chodowiecki (*c.* 1800; Alte. Pina., Munich).

Graham Harry (1874–1936). English author of **Ruthless Rhymes for Heartless Homes* (1909); besides *Verse and Worse* (1905) and *More Ruthless Rhymes . . .* (1930), he wrote plays and novels.

Graham Martha (1893–). U.S. dancer, one of the greatest personalities of 20th-c. ballet by her projection of the modern dance method. This employs natural movement and often enacts psychological situations rather than the story-telling found in more conventional dancing. Among her works are *Appalachian Spring* (1944), music by Copland, and *Cave of the Heart* (1946).

Graham W. S. (1918–). Scots poet, author of *Cage Without Grievance* (1942), *The Seven Journeys* (1943), *Second Poems* (1945), *The White Threshold* (1949) and *The Nightfishing* (1955).

Grahame Kenneth (1859–1932). Scottish writer, secretary of the Bank of England. His story *The Wind in the Willows* (1908; stage version by A. A. Milne, *Toad of Toad Hall*, 1930) vitalized that kind of modern whimsical tale for children in which animals are endowed with human speech and personality.

Grahn Lucile (1819–1907). Danish dancer and disciple of Bournonville. A contemporary of Taglioni, G. danced Taglioni's role in *La Sylphide* (Copenhagen, 1836) and was one of the ballerinas in the famous *Pas de Quatre* (1845).

Grainger Percy Aldridge (1882–1961). Australian composer and pianist. He studied in Europe; became Grieg's close friend, performing his piano concerto all over Europe. In 1914 he settled in the U.S. where he had a long career as teacher, conductor and pianist. G. is best known for his fresh and vigorous works in English folk idiom but constantly experimented as a composer and at the end of his life developed an electronic instrument.

Granacci Francesco (1477–1543). Florentine painter. Although most heavily influenced by his master Ghirlandaio, he sometimes modified his style towards Michelangelo, sometimes towards Lorenzo di Credi or Fra Bartolommeo. This changeability has made his paintings difficult to identify.

Granada Fray Luis de (1504–88). Spanish writer on religious subjects; his oratorical style is the finest example of its type in 16th-c. Spanish literature.

Granados Enrique (1867–1916). Spanish composer, a pupil of Pedrell. G. worked with Falla and Albéniz to free 19th-c. Spanish music from the dominating influence of Italy. His nationalist idiom derives from Spanish folk-music although it also exhibits the influences of Chopin, Liszt and Grieg. His most famous work is the *Goyescas* (inspired by Goya) composed for piano (1911) and arranged as an opera (1916).

Grande Illusion, La (1937). Film directed by J. *Renoir.

Grande Jatte, Une Dimanche d'Eté à la (1884–6). Painting by *Seurat.

Grandes Manœuvres, Les (1955). Film directed by R. *Clair.

Grand Gorky Theatre. Leningrad theatre founded in 1919. Gorky himself took a great interest in its work and all his plays were given their 1st performances in this theatre. After a period of *constructivism during which foreign plays were produced, it presented the work of Soviet writers.

Grandi Ercole di Giulio Cesare: Ercole d'Antonio de *Roberti

Les singularitez des seize
premiers Livres de Pline,
historien naturel.

Pline naturel historien
fut nay souz l'Empereur Tyberien, et mourut souz l'Empereur Tite, qui destruit Hierusalem apres la passion de nostre Seigneur, auquel il attribua ses œuvres.

Au premier Livre qui est bref il fait seulement ses preambules.

Au second il traite du monde, & des autres choses. Il descrit que le monde est seul et rond, immobile naturellement, combien qu'il y ayt aucunes parties mobiles, et qui se peuvent mouvoir, par concavitez de la terre, pleines de vent. Il y ha quatre Elements, la terre, l'air, l'eau, et le feu en hault, par dessus l'air prochain au premier Ciel, qui est feu naturel, parquoy n'y fault point de bois pour le continuer. Au dessouz de la terre, sont les planettes (que l'on dit erran-

A ij

Granjon's *civilité*

Grandville. *Je n'y suis pour personne*; from *Les Métamorphoses du jour*

Grandjean Philippe (1666–1714). Eminent French type-cutter whose *romain du roi*, cast on order of Louis XIV in 1692, began the evolution of the 'modern' face letter with its marked contrast between the thicks and thins of the face. G. also introduced the finishing of a letter by a flat, unbuttressed serif. His types were used mainly for administrative documents.

Grand Meaulnes, Le (1913). Novel by *Alain-Fournier.

Grand Testament, Le (written 1461–2). Poem by François *Villon.

Grandville Jean-Ignace-Isidore Gérard called (1803–47). French graphic artist whose fantastic imagination and satirical humour make him an important figure in 19th-c. graphic art. Besides political cartoons he produced *Les Métamorphoses du jour* (1828), *Une Autre Monde* (1844) and illustrations to *Robinson Crusoe* and La Fontaine's *Fables*.

Granjon Robert (*fl.* 1540–80). Paris printer, publ., type-cutter and type-founder who was the first after *Garamond to supply types for commercial use on an international scale. He designed a beautiful italic, known as the '*lettre de civilité*'; of irregular slope, modelled on the fashionable handwriting of the time. G. was also responsible for a set of Arabic founts designed for the Stamperia Vaticana Press Arabic ed. of the Gospels (1590). His experiments (from 1560 onwards) in the building up of printers' flowers into headpieces and borders of arabesques were extremely successful, and enjoyed much popularity. His influence on 16th-c. typography was probably as great as that of *Garamond. G. spent the final years of his life working on oriental types for the Vatican Press in Rome.

Grant Alexander (1925–). New Zealand dancer who joined Sadler's Wells School in 1946 and has developed as one of the leading character dancers of the Royal Ballet Co. His best original creation was the Barber in *Mam'zelle Angot* (1947) but he is successful as the Miller in *Le Tricorne* as well as in *La Fille Mal Gardée*.

Grant Cary (1904–). British-born film actor who has played 'with amiable assurance' in his 70 or so films, mostly light comedy, e.g. *She Done Him Wrong* (1933), *Bringing Up Baby* (1937), *Philadelphia Story* (1940) and *Charade* (1964).

Grant Duncan (1885–). English landscape, portrait and decorative painter and designer, member of the *Bloomsbury Group and the *London Group and closely associated with R. Fry and the *Omega Workshops. He was among the 1st British artists to be influenced by the post-impressionists.

Grant James (1822–87). Scottish novelist who wrote historical novels and books based on his military experiences. They include *The Romance of War* (1846–7) and *The Adventures of an Aide-de-Camp* (1848).

Grantchester (1912). Poem by Rupert *Brooke.

Granville-Barker Harley (1877–1946). English actor-manager, dramatist, producer and critic whose work helped to revitalize the English theatre. From 1904 to 1907 he co-managed with Vedrenne at the *Royal Court Theatre; His Shakespeare season at the Savoy Theatre (1912–14) set new standards in Shakespearean production. He wrote his *Prefaces to Shakespeare* between 1927 and 1948. His plays include *The Marrying of Ann Leete* (1901) and *The Voysey Inheritance* (1905).

Grapes of Wrath, The (1939). Novel by John *Steinbeck, made into a film (1940) directed by J. *Ford.

graphic arts. The collective term for the pictorial arts outside painting, e.g. engraving, lithography, silk screen, etc.

Grass (1925). Film directed by E. *Schoedsack and M. C. Cooper.

Grass Günter (1927–). German novelist. His best-known work, *Die Blechtrommel* (1959; *The Tin Drum*, 1963) is the critico-satirical, highly digressive, colourful, at times repellent autobiography of a freakishly endowed 30-year-old dwarf. Set largely in Danzig and–from 1945–Düsseldorf, it spans the years 1899 to 1954.

Grassi Anton (1755–1807). Viennese sculptor. He did much work at the palace of Schönbrunn, Vienna, but his finest pieces were porcelain figures in a rococo and later a more classical style.

Harley Granville-Barker

Duncan Grant. *Flowers* (*c.* 1956)

Grassi. *The Portrait Painter*. Viennese porcelain

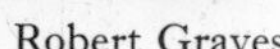
Robert Graves

Thomas Gray

Morris Graves. *Guardian* (1952)

Gravelot. *The Absent-minded Man*

Graun Carl Heinrich (*c.* 1703–59). German composer. He wrote operas for the newly founded Berlin opera, instrumental music and also church music, e.g. the Passion cantata *Der Tod Jesu* (1755), which was performed almost annually down to the 1880s.

Gravelot Hubert (François) (born H.-F. Bourguignon) (1699–1773). French draughtsman, book illustrator and engraver who brought the style of Watteau to England. He worked for several years in London, where Gainsborough studied under him. His work was light and delicate and often on a very small scale.

graver: *burin

Graves Morris (1910–). U.S. painter, a mystic and visionary whose use of symbolism links his work with surrealism. He is an isolated and introspective painter who has evolved a very personal imagery derived from nature and wild life, and a calligraphic style influenced by Tobey's 'white writing' technique; he imbues his paintings with poetry and wit. Series of paintings on the same theme, e.g. the notable *Inner Eye* series (1941), are typical of his method of working.

Graves Richard (1715–1804). English poet and novelist whose novels include *The Spiritual Quixote* (1773).

Graves Robert (Ranke) (1895–). English poet and outstanding historical novelist, e.g. his *I, Claudius* (1934) and *Claudius the God* (1934), the 'autobiographies' of the Roman emperor. G. has joined no poetic school and generally avoids displaying his intellect and scholarship in verse. He uses traditional forms and a deceptively simple diction; his verse can convey deep pain, yet its precision of expression frequently creates elegant and witty effects. *The White Goddess* (1948) examines the role of the mother-goddess in pre-classical mythologies and argues that she was and is the muse who inspires all true poetry. He has also written a famous autobiography, *Goodbye to All That* (1929), describing his education at Charterhouse and experiences in World War I.

graveyard school. Name given to 18th-c. English poets whose verse imitated the mood of Edward *Young's *Night Thoughts* and Robert *Blair's *The Grave*.

Gray Henry Peters (1819–77). U.S. academic painter who made several visits to Italy and was influenced by the Venetian school. From 1869 to 1871 he was president of the National Academy, New York.

Gray John (1866–1934). English poet and Roman Catholic priest. Rejecting his early *fin de siècle* verse, G. wrote *The Flying Fish* (in *The Long Road*, 1926), a poem of bizarre originality; also a utopian novel *Park . . .* (1932), depicting an England ruled by philosophic Negroes. G. was probably the original of Dorian Gray in the novel by Oscar *Wilde.

Gray Thomas (1716–71). English poet. After visiting France and Italy with Horace Walpole G. returned to Cambridge to study and to perfect his poetic talent. The *Ode on a Distant Prospect of Eton College* appeared in 1747 and was followed in 1751 by his most enduring poem, the *Elegy in a Country Churchyard*, which showed G.'s consummate mastery of rhythm and euphony. The *Pindaric Odes* (1757) were less successful but are an interesting attempt to break away from 18th-c. decorum of diction and strictness of form. His interest in Icelandic and Celtic poetry, his choice of subjects and above all the intensity of his idealized vision of nature revealed in his famous letters, mark G. as a forerunner of the romantics.

Grazzini Anton Francesco (1503–84). Italian poet and playwright. He took an active part in Florentine academic and literary controversies, and wrote an interesting and original coll. of stories (*Le Cene*) in the Florentine idiom.

Great Dictator, The (1940). Film directed by *Chaplin.

Great Expectations (1860–1). Novel by *Dickens.

Great Gatsby, The (1925). Novel by F. Scott *Fitzgerald.

Great God Brown, The (1926). Play by Eugene *O'Neill.

Great McGinty, The (1940). Film directed by P. *Sturges.

Great Train Robbery, The (1903). Film directed by E. S. *Porter.

Great Wall of China, The (1931). Short story by Kafka.

Greaves Walter (1846–1930). English painter. Originally a Thames boatman but taught to paint by Whistler in return for rowing him on the river. G. chose his subjects from the Thames and often followed Whistler's style though *Hammersmith Bridge on Boat Race Day* (*c.* 1862; Tate), one of the best English pictures of its period, has a directness and precision unlike anything of Whistler's.

Grecian revival. Term for an architectural style prevalent in England *c.* 1810 to *c.* 1825. Whereas neo-classicism took inspiration from classical models, the buildings of the G. r. actually copied them; e.g. St Pancras parish church, London.

Greco, El i.e. 'The Greek'. Domenikos Theotokopoulos (1541–1614), Spanish painter born in Crete. G. was trained as a painter of icons in the Byzantine tradition. About 1560 he went to Venice (Crete was a Venetian colony) and became a pupil of Titian, then to Rome with an introduction to Cardinal Farnese from Giulio Clovio, of whom he painted a portrait. He attracted some attention and had pupils but *c.* 1570 moved to Toledo, where he lived until his death.

There are 3 main phases in his development. The pictures from the 1st phase (1570–80) show Venetian influence and especially Titian's: line drawing disappears, the use of colour is unlimited and the purely pictorial dominates (compare Titian's *Golgotha* with G.'s). G.'s dramatic use of light and shade and his portrait style indicate Tintoretto's influence as well as that of Veronese, Bassano and perhaps Correggio. *The Holy Trinity* (1577–8; Prado) belongs to this period.

The 2nd phase (1580–1604) combines some Byzantine features (especially plastic forms) with a growing sense of rhythm and movement; it includes *The Martyrdom of St Maurice* (1580; Escorial, near Madrid), commissioned by Philip II in 1580 but not accepted, and *Golgotha* (1590; Prado). *The Burial of Count Orgaz* (1586; Church of San Tomé, Toledo), a legendary theme, shows St Augustine and St Stephen lowering the body into the grave. The canvas is filled with figures, some of them portraits, and contrasts yet unifies the human and heavenly worlds, the austerity and solemnity of the lower part of the painting and the

Greaves. *Hammersmith Bridge on Boat Race Day*

Emilio Greco. *Seated Figure*

El Greco. *The Burial of Count Orgaz*

radiance of the Holy Ghost in the upper. The eye is led upwards to the figure of Christ, who is beseeched by John the Baptist to receive the count's soul. This spiritual exaltation is typical of G.; another example is *The Despoiling of Christ* (1583; Cathedral, Toledo). The best of the portraits painted in this period is the *Cardinal Don Fernando Niño de Guevara* (1598; Met. Mus).

From about 1590 G. concentrated increasingly on portraying inner beauty and in the last phase achieved complete inward expression. From 1604 the rhythm and the simplicity of form and colour increase. The combination of Byzantine influence with rhythm, movement, intensity of expression obtained through elongation and distortion of form, use of light and unusual colour (the blues and lemons), convey the exaltation and radiance of the Holy Ghost. The later paintings include the *Vision of St John the Divine* (1610–14; Met. Mus.) and the *View of Toledo* (1608; Met. Mus.). The latter is no mere landscape: it is a vision in which nature has overcome man.

Works include: *St Martin and the Beggar* (1597–9; N.G., Washington); *Resurrection of Christ* (1597–1604; Prado); *Assumption of the Virgin Mary* (1608–13; Mus. de San Vicente, Toledo); and *Adoration of the Shepherds* (1612–14; Prado).

Greco Emilio (1913–). Italian sculptor trained in the workshop of a marble mason; he studied at the academy in Palermo while in the army, coming to the fore only after the war. He creates sensual, rounded figures in the classical tradition, e.g. *Seated Figure* (1951).

Greed (1924). Film directed by E. von *Stroheim.

Greek drama. G. d. grew out of choric dances performed in honour of the god Dionysus. The *orchestra* (the circular dancing-floor in front of the stage) was the centre of the theatre and was generally sited in a hollow at the foot of a hill. Permanent seating and the *skene* (building used as the background of the stage) were added much later. The festivals at Athens–the Dionysia in March and the Lenaea in January –included dramatic contests, the poets competing in tragedy from *c.* 534 B.C., comedy from 486. Each competitor had to present 3 tragedies and a satyr play, i.e. a burlesque treatment of a heroic theme, in which the chorus usually represented satyrs, the horse-tailed attendants

El Greco. *View of Toledo*

El Greco. *Cardinal Don Fernando Niño de Guevara*. Also *mannerism and colour plate 53

Grecian revival. St Pancras parish church

Greek drama. Theatre of Dionysus, Athens

Greek drama. Costumed actor holding a mask (krater fragment, late 4th c. B.C.)

Greek drama. Clytemnestra killing Cassandra; red-figured bowl, *c.* 430 B.C.

Greek drama. Men dressed as horses; vase painting, 6th c. B.C. See also colour plates 5 and 6

of Dionysus. The state appointed a 'choregus' to bear the expenses of each poet's production, and the poet directed and often acted in his own plays. The chorus which commented on the action in word, song and dance, remained an integral part of both tragedy and comedy until the end of the 5th c. but thereafter it provided little more than entr'actes. The actors, of whom there were eventually 3 (*Aeschylus and *Sophocles), doubled their parts by changing their *masks, conventional representations of character types. (Also *Euripides and *Aristophanes.)

Green Henry (1905–). English novelist whose social comedies describe many classes, professions and types. G. chose to work as a labourer for some time after leaving Oxford; the result was *Living* (1929). Works include *Caught* (1943), *Loving* (1945), *Back* (1946) and *Concluding* (1948).

Green John Richard (1837–83). English historian and author of the classic *A Short History of the English People* (1874; enlarged in *History of the English People*, 1877–80), for many years the standard popular history.

Green Julien (1900–). French novelist and playwright. His parents were American, and the U.S. South has provided the setting for some of his work, notably the novel *Mont-Cinère* (1926; *Avarice House*, 1927) and a play, *Sud* (1953; *South*, 1956). His works are melodramatic, full of violence, and preoccupied with ideas of evil, heredity and predestination; they include the novels *Adrienne Mesurat* (1927; *The Closed Garden*, 1928), *Moira* (1950; 1951) and *Chaque Homme dans sa nuit* (1960; *Each in his Darkness*, 1961).

Green Matthew (1696–1737). English poet whose witty poem in octosyllabic couplets, *The Spleen, an Epistle inscribed to . . . Mr Cuthbert Jackson* (1737), earned the praise of Pope and Gray. It was included in R. Dodsley's coll.

Greenaway Kate (1846–1901). English artist and writer and close friend of Ruskin, famous as an illustrator of children's books, chiefly her own works. Her characters, oddly costumed in early 19th-c. style, started a fashion in children's clothes.

TO MYSTERY LAND.

OH, dear, how will it end ?
Peggy and Susie how naughty you are.
You little know where you are,
Going so far, and so high,
Nearly up to the sky.
Perhaps it's a Giant who lives there,
And perhaps it's a lovely Princess.
But you very well know
You've no business to go ;
You'll get yourselves into a mess.

Oh, dear, I'm sure it is true ;
Whatever on earth can it matter to you?
For you know it—oh, fie—
That it's naughty to pry
Into other's affairs—
Into other folks houses to go,
Where you know
You're not asked.
So you'd better come back
While there's time, it is plain.
Go home—and be never
So naughty again.

Greenaway. *To Mystery Land*; from *Marigold Garden*

Greene Balcomb (1904–). U.S. painter and teacher. He was a geometric abstractionist, e.g. murals for the New York World Fair (1939), until the early 1940s when he began to react against pure abstraction. He turned to semi-abstract studies of landscape and the human figure in which form is made vague and ambiguous by the interpenetration of light.

Greene (Henry) Graham (1904–). English novelist. G. was converted to Roman Catholicism in 1927 and his work deals with questions of salvation in the manner of Mauriac, often finding the sinner nearer to God–because his spirit is alive–than mediocre people incapable of excess of good or evil. *The Power and the Glory* (1940) describes the struggle between faith and materialism in Mexico and how a bad priest none the less fulfils God's purpose. G.'s novels have strong, dramatic qualities; he excels in creating the charged tedium of tropical outposts where violence is just beneath the surface, e.g. *The Heart of the Matter* (1948) and *A Burnt-Out Case* (1961), and in evoking the politically sinister, e.g. *The Quiet American* (1955). Works include *Brighton Rock* (1938); *The End of the Affair* (1951); many 'entertainments'–G.'s name for his less serious adventure novels like *Our Man in Havana* (1958); the novel-cum-film-script *The Third Man* (1950); and plays.

Greene Maurice (*c.* 1695–1755). English organist and composer in the style of Handel whose friend he was for a period. His best work was in church anthems and he also wrote a number of operas.

Greene Robert (1560?–92). English dramatist, writer and poet. Influenced by Lyly's *Euphues* . . . , G. produced a number of prose romances e.g. *Pandosto* . . . (1588) (the basis of Shakespeare's *The Winter's Tale*) and *Menaphon* (1589), which contain exquisite lyrics such as *Weepe not my wanton*. He was possibly co-author of the original *Henry VI* plays on which Shakespeare based his own, and his romantic comedies, e.g. *The Honorable Historie of Frier Bacon and Frier Bongay* (1594), considerably influenced those of Shakespeare. Works of contrasting realism are G.'s pamphlets, topical or autobiographical, humorous, occasionally pathetic. They include *Greene's groats-worth of Witte* . . . (1589/92), in which he attacks Shakespeare, and the *Conny-catching* tracts exposing the London underworld. G. was defended by his friend Nashe against the vituperation of G. *Harvey.

Robert Greene. *Notable Discovery of Cozenage*

Now daily practised by sundry lewd persons, called Connie-catchers, and Crosse-byters.

Plainely laying open those pernitious sleights that hath brought many ignorant men to confusion.

Written for the generall benefit of all Gentlemen, Citizens, Aprentises, Countrey Farmers and yeomen, that may hap to fall into the company of such coosening companions.

With a delightfull discourse of the coosnage of Colliers.

Nascimur pro patria. By R. Greene, Maister of Arts.

LONDON
Printed by Thomas Scarlet for Thomas Nelson.
1592.

Green Henry (1854–5). Novel by Gottfried *Keller.

Greenhill John (*c.* 1644–76). English portrait painter, pupil of Sir P. Lely. In his late work G. began to break from Lely's influence and paintings such as *Naval Officer* (Greenwich) have a solidity and reserve which anticipates the next generation of English painters.

Green Mansions (1904). Novel by W. H. *Hudson.

Greenmantle (1916). Novel by John *Buchan.

Greenough Horatio (1805–52). U.S. neo-classic sculptor whose working life was spent in Italy. His seated half-nude of Washington as Zeus (1833–43; Smithsonian Inst., Washington) is the 1st important example of U.S. monumental sculpture. His writings, which expound an early functionalist theory of beauty, include *Aesthetics in Washington* (1851).

Greensleeves. This famous English song is first recorded in the 16th c. and seems to have been of N. English origin. Vaughan Williams wrote a suite on it.

Green Table, The. 8-scene ballet with choreography by *Jooss, music by Fritz Cohen and décor by Heckroth; 1st performance 1932.

Greenway Francis Howard (1777–1837). English architect. He was a pupil of Nash and designed important parts of Clifton, a fashionable suburb of Bristol. In 1812 he was convicted of forgery and transported to Australia. Here he restored his fortunes, was appointed government architect and designed St James's church, the court house, Macquerie Tower and many other public buildings in Sydney.

Gregoretti Ugo (1930–). Italian film director. G.'s 1st film, *I Nuovi Angeli* (1961), was an anecdotal, mainly comic treatment of morality in modern Italy with its complex of technology, capitalism and backwardness. His other films show a predilection for social comedy.

Gregorian chant: *plainsong

Gregory Lady Isabella Augusta (1852–1932). Irish writer of prime importance in the Irish literary renaissance. She wrote mostly character comedies, e.g. *The Pot of Broth*, capturing in her plays the character of Irish peasant life. She played a major part in the birth of the *Abbey Theatre and was a close friend of Yeats.

Gregory of Tours (*c.* 538–*c.* 94). Frankish bishop and author of the important Latin *History of the Franks*.

Gremillon Jean (1902–59). French film director. His best work is found in 3 films directed during the war, *Remorques* (1939–41) and *Lumière d'Été* (1942), both partly written by J. Prévert, and *Le Ciel est à Vous* (1943), partly written by Charles Spaak. After the war G. mainly made documentaries on art (*Kast). *Pattes Blanches* (1949) was an oppressive, forceful study of an isolated farming community, written by Anouilh.

Gresset Jean-Baptiste-Louis (1709–1777). French poet and dramatist remembered for his humorous poem *Vert-Vert* (1733; *Vert-Vert or the Nunnery Parrot,* 1759).

Grétry André-Ernest-Modeste (1741–1813). Belgian composer working in France; he was one of the inspectors of the Conservatoire on its foundation in 1795. G. was the leading composer of *opéras comiques* of the 18th c.; his music is slightly influenced by Gluck but unmistakably in the French tradition, remarkable particularly for its lightness, spontaneity and wit. G. was called 'the Molière of music'. An aria from one of his numerous operas is quoted in Tchaikovsky's opera *The Queen of Spades*, for period effect.

Greuze Jean-Baptiste (1725–1805). French painter who became famous with the appearance of his *Father of the family reading the Bible* at the Paris Salon of 1755. Praised by Diderot and other moral philosophers, his large-scale genre subjects usually had a moral lesson to tell, as in *Return from the Wineshop* (A. Gal., Portland, Oregon). They were made famous from England to Russia through engravings. However, it is his portraits, particularly of children (*Boy with Lesson Book*, N.G., Edinburgh), which are preferred today. His art had declined even before the outbreak of the Revolution, which ruined him.

Greville Charles Cavendish Fulke (1794–1865). English diarist whose authoritative

Greenough. *Washington*

Greenhill. *Naval Officer*

Graham Greene

André Grétry

Greuze. *Boy with Lesson Book*

Charles Cavendish Fulke Greville

Greville Memoirs (8 vols 1874–87), record 40 years' acute observation of contemporary English society, politics and politicians, many of whom, such as Wellington and Palmerston, he knew intimately.

Greville Fulke, Lord Brooke (1554–1628). English poet and statesman, Elizabethan courtier and friend of Sidney, whose life he wrote (publ. 1652). His lyrical verse in *Caelica* (publ. in *Workes*, 1633) is dry and remote, seldom rising to the excellence of the sonnet to Cupid, *Farewell sweet boy, complain not of my truth.*

Grévin Jacques (1538–70). French dramatist and well-loved disciple of Ronsard until his conversion to Protestantism (1560). Author of *La Trésorière* (1559), a satirical comedy against women and high finance, and *La Mort de César* (1561), a tragedy in Senecan style.

Beryl Grey in *Swan Lake*

Grey Beryl (1927–). English dancer who, by the time she was 15, was dancing such parts as Odette/Odile in *Swan Lake*, with the Sadler's Wells Co. Very tall for a dancer, she has used her height to enhance her lyrical style; she was the 1st British ballerina to appear in Russia (at the Bolshoi Theatre, 1958).

Grey Sir George (1812–98). New Zealand administrator, etc., important in literature for his work on Maori traditional poetry.

Griboyedov Alexander Sergeyevich (1795–1829). Russian playwright whose *Woe from Wit*, written in rhymed verse, satirizes the pettiness and provincialism of Russian society. Hampered by official disapproval and obstruction it nevertheless circulated widely from 1825 onwards and became popular; many of its lines became proverbial.

Edvard Grieg

Grieg Edvard Hagerup (1843–1907). Norwegian composer. He studied at Leipzig, at Copenhagen under Gade, and for a time at Rome. G.'s music, based on Norwegian folk-tunes and springing from the composer's passionate, almost fanatical love for his country, is the most undiluted manifestation of national romanticism. His most important works are the *Peer Gynt* suites (1876) using music composed for Ibsen's play at Ibsen's request; *The Holberg Suite* for strings written in honour of the 18th-c. Norwegian playwright L. Holberg; a piano concerto and *Lyric pieces* for piano.

Grien: *Baldung Grien

Grierson Sir Herbert John Clifford (1866–1961). Scottish scholar. His notable ed. of the poems of John Donne (1912) and his anthology *Metaphysical Lyrics and Poems of the Seventeenth Century . . .* (1921) influenced modern English poets in their rejection of Victorian idealism and Georgianism.

Grierson John (1898–). British film maker. G. directed only 1 film, a long documentary, *Drifters* (1929), influenced by the work of *Eisenstein, *Pudovkin and *Flaherty. He was the formative force behind the British documentary movement, both through his writings and as a producer. He founded and ran the Empire Marketing Board Film Unit which produced the movement's 1st films by B. *Wright, H. *Watt, etc.

Griffes Charles Tomlinson (1884–1920). U.S. composer who, until his early death, was regarded as one of the most promising of young U.S. composers. G.'s style was thick and sensuous, reminiscent of Scriabin; it is probable that the present U.S. film-music style owes something to him. His works include *The Pleasure Dome of Kubla Khan* and *The White Peacock* for orchestra.

Griffith D(avid) W(ark) (1875–1948). U.S. film director. Coming from a Southern family ruined by the Civil War, G. was an unsuccessful actor who drifted into films, for which he wrote and acted before starting to direct in 1908. For the next 5 years in 1- and 2-reel films numbering some hundreds, he introduced a series of innovations: closer shots of actors (breaking the one scene/one shot tradition), close-ups of faces, and cutaways to simultaneous actions – all breaking the fixed audience viewpoint and temporal/spatial unity of the theatre. Other improvements were the use of lighting to supplement and replace daylight, more realistic acting (aided by a nucleus of exceptionally talented players), and cross-cutting between protagonists at climaxes. The competition of the more spectacular Italian product of *Pastrone, etc. led G. to make the first American 4-reeler (lasting an hour), *Judith of Bethulia* (1913), which had 4 counter-pointed themes, like the later *Intolerance. The Birth of a Nation* (1914), running over 3 hours, was not merely the most expensive film so far made but also the most remarkable, being the

D. W. Griffith. *The Birth of a Nation*

D. W. Griffith. Lillian Gish in *Broken Blossoms*

Dmitri Grigorovich. Also *Goncharov

fulfilment of all G.'s technical researches. Following 2 families, one Southern and one Northern, through the Civil War period, it was attacked for taking the part of the South (unsurprisingly in view of G.'s antecedents). A film of unprecedented sensitivity and beauty, it gained from its technical refinements a new power of expression. The camerawork of Billy Bitzer is particularly notable. The even larger and technically more daring *Intolerance* (1916) was in part an answer to the critics of *The Birth of a Nation* in the obvious liberalism of theme embodied in its 4 interwoven plots. G.'s career after *Intolerance* is often dismissed as a running down because of the smaller scale of the projects and their sentimentality: *Broken Blossoms* (1919), *Way Down East* (1920). The decline is illusory except in one respect–he became commercially unsuccessful. His last films were made in the early sound period–*Abraham Lincoln* (1930) and *The Struggle* (1931)–although he may have worked thereafter on films not signed by him.

Griffo Francesco (d. 1518). Italian type-cutter and designer who cut the 1st italic and 'old style' type-faces, which along with the types of *Garamond and *Jenson formed the source of all subsequent roman and italic types. His italic, which was based on the cursive humanist script, in turn derived from the script of the Papal Chancery, was used primarily for a series of classics publ. by Aldus *Manutius. G.'s roman was based on the inscriptional lettering of imperial Rome, and used in *De Aetna* (1495) and *Hypnerotomachia Poliphili* (1499). He also designed the 1st Greek types, again for Manutius.

Grignion (Grignon) the Elder, Charles (1717–1810). English engraver of French parentage; uncle of C. G. the Younger. He studied under H. Gravelot and in Paris under J.-P. Le Bas. He engraved the plates for various publications including H. Walpole's *Anecdotes of Painting in England* and was employed by Hogarth.

Grignion the Younger, Charles (1754–1804). English history and portrait painter, nephew of C. G. the Elder. He studied under G. B. Cipriani and at the R.A. In 1782 he settled in Rome.

Grigorovich Dmitri Vasilyevich (1822–99). Russian writer of novels and short stories whose tales *The Village* (1846) and *Anton Goremyka* (1847) were the first to describe peasant life sympathetically. They were not, however, of great literary value, being quickly eclipsed by Turgenev's *Sportsman's Sketches*. G. helped to make Dostoyevsky and Chekhov known.

Grigoryev Apollon Alexandrovich (1822–64). Russian critic and poet who became a friend of Dostoyevsky. His belief that literature should be national and organic–a 'product of the soil'–was in opposition to that of the dominant radical and utilitarian school of criticism led by Belinsky. G.'s poetry was forgotten until Blok revived his gipsy pieces (including the famous *Two Guitars*).

Grigson Geoffrey (1905–). English poet and critic; as ed. of *New Verse* (1939) and *Poetry of the Present* (1949) he helped to introduce much of the best verse of 2 decades.

Grillparzer Franz (1791–1872). Austrian dramatist employed as tutor, librarian and treasury official. His plays show features of many movements–baroque 'morality' themes, classical structure and subjects, romantic motifs, quietism, symbolic realist visual correlatives–while retaining a Viennese delicacy and humour. His main theme is the clash between inclination (love or ambition) and vocation (poetry, priesthood or kingship): the individual recognizes too late which he should follow. The interest lies in G.'s subtle psychological insight into the varied weighting of these 2 forces: initially favouring variety of experience, he increasingly advocates cautious concentration–explicitly in the dream-play *Der Traum, ein Leben* (1834; *A Dream is Life*, 1946). His works include plays on classical Greek subjects–*Sappho* (1818; 1820); *Das goldene Vliess* (trilogy, 1821; *The Golden Fleece*, 1879; 1942); *Des Meeres und der Liebe Wellen* (1831; *Hero and Leander*, 1938); on Austrian or Czech history–*König Ottokars Glück und Ende* (1825; *King Ottocar, his rise and fall*, 1907), *Ein Bruderzwist in Habsburg* (publ. 1872; 1940), *Libussa* (1872; 1941); a comedy, *Weh dem, der lügt* (1838; *Thou Shalt not lie. . .*, 1939); short stories, e.g. *Der arme Spielmann* (1848); poems; and essays.

Grimaldi Joseph (1779–1837). English clown of Italian parentage who came to fame at Covent Garden in 1806 in the pantomime

Franz Grillparzer

relato mirabondo,&
reſtai ignaro,& dilla it
uo. Non era auſo perc
iore in queſto loco tetr
ume. Niente di manc
nte porta ſtimulante,
e altro. Dique ſencia a
odo dapo la contempla
rnare, Et piu tranquill
gli humani ingegni,

Griffo's roman: from his ed. of *Hypnerotomachia Poliphili*

Mr Grimaldi, as Clown

Harlequin and Mother Goose. It was he who made famous the character Joey the Clown.

Grimm Friedrich Melchior, Baron von (1723–1807). German writer (in French), the lover of Mme d'Épinay and friend (until they quarrelled) of J.-J. Rousseau. He was the Paris correspondent of a number of German rulers, and his newsletters were circulated among the courts of Europe.

Jakob and Wilhelm Grimm

Grimm the brothers Jakob (Ludwig Karl) (1785–1863) and Wilhelm Karl (1786–1859). German philologists and folk-lorists. Their *Kinder- und Hausmärchen* (1812–15) and *Deutsche Sagen* (1816–18) – *Grimms' Fairy Tales* – known throughout the Western world, are among the great achievements of the romantic movement in literature and, in the G.s' scientific approach, introduced a method of rigid scholarship new in the study of folk tradition. Jakob GRIMM'S LAW (1822), which enunciated a principle of consonantal shift in the Indo-European languages from Sanskrit, Latin and Greek to the Germanic languages, is a basic tenet of scientific philology. Jakob's other important scholarly works include *Deutsche Mythologie* (1835), and together the brothers launched the great German dictionary *Deutsches Wörterbuch* (1852–1961 – *sic*).

Grimmelshausen. *Die . . . Landstörtzerin Courasche*

Grimmelshausen Hans Jakob Christoffel von (*c.* 1622–76). German novelist. Orphaned by the 30 Years War, G. became a soldier, later factor to his former commanding officer, innkeeper, and (in 1667, on his conversion to Roman Catholicism) mayor of Renchen (Baden). These experiences inform his great novel *Der abenteuerliche Simplicissimus* (1669; *The Adventurous Simplicissimus. . .* , 1912), a 1st-person narrative by a hero initially naïve, of his wartime and other adventures. Drawing on the satirical vigour of the Spanish picaresque novel, G. yet displays a native metaphysical temper, juxtaposing earthily realistic incidents with development towards spiritual wisdom. Other novels – including *Trutz-Simplex oder . . . Landstörtzerin Courasche* (1669), Brecht's source for *Mutter Courage* – do not reach quite the same level.

Grimod de la Reynière Balthazar (1758–1838). French gastronome, and author of the *Almanach des Gourmands* (1803–12), the *Manuel des Amphitryons* (1808), and the *Journal des gourmands et des belles* (1806–7). There are many anecdotes about his strange life, lavish entertaining and eccentric behaviour.

Gringore Pierre (*c.* 1475–1538). Norman poet and playwright, primarily of mystery plays and farces. His best-known satirical work, the *Jeu du Prince des Sots* (1512) written under the patronage of Louis XII, criticizes the Papacy and defends the king's foreign policy. G.'s allegorical poems include *Château de labour* (1499) and *Château d'amour* (1500). He appears as Gringoire in Hugo's *Notre-Dame de Paris*.

Gris Juan (originally José Gonzalez) (1887–1927). Spanish painter, sculptor and draughtsman. G. studied in Madrid and settled in 1906 in Paris, where he became Picasso's friend and one of the *avant-garde*. His development was slow. He earned his living as an illustrator but continued to paint, and exhibited from 1912. His work was noticed by the art dealer Kahnweiler, who placed him under contract. G. as a result was able to devote himself entirely to painting and became a leading cubist. He remained faithful to the cubist aesthetic; his work developed from simplified, precise forms based on the world of objects to the monumental compositions of 1916–19, a flat coloured architecture. From this time he experimented with polychrome sculpture, inspired by the sculptor Lipchitz. His last period expressed his increasing preoccupation with colour. G. regarded himself as a classical painter; for him a painting was a self-contained creation and within its context he used objects to express ideas.

Juan Gris. *L'Arlequin* (1917); also *abstract art, *cubism, *Jacob

grisaille. Monochrome painting in greys sometimes used as an underpainting or to imitate sculptural features as in the paintings of early Netherlandish artists such as Dirk Bouts or Jan van Eyck. Also a type of stained-glass painting of which the most famous example is the 'Five Sisters' window in York Minster.

Grisi Carlotta (1819–99). Italian dancer who was the inspiration for Gautier's ballet *Giselle* which he created for her (1841). She danced all over Europe and was one of the most popular ballerinas of her era. She was one of the dancers in the celebrated *Pas de Quatre* (1845).

Grock (1880–1959). Swiss-born clown who spent most of his working life in Great Britain.

Gris. *Still-life with newspaper* (1914)

Grisaille. Van Eyck, *Saint Barbara*

Gropius and Meyer. Fagus factory, Alfeld an der Leine; for Gropius also *Bauhaus and *Deutscher Werkbund

Grolier. Paris binding in brown morocco and gold tooling; G. commissioned only 4 such architectural patterns

His real name was Adrien Wettach but he adopted his now famous name in 1903. He trained in the circus and achieved fame when he was engaged for the Palace Theatre, London by Sir Charles Cochran (1911).

Grocyn William (1446–1519). Oxford humanist important as an early Greek scholar; he was a friend of Erasmus.

Grofé Ferde (1892–). U.S. composer of popular symphonic music; he orchestrated Gershwin's *Rhapsody in Blue*, and his own works include the *Grand Canyon Suite*.

groin. Architectural term for the point at which 2 vaults intersect.

Grolier Jean, Grolier de Servier, Vicomte d'Aguisy (1479–1565). Treasurer-General of France, renowned for his taste and discernment in collecting books and in supervising their binding and decoration, principally the work of French craftsmen. He had the books stamped in gold with the legend IO GROLIERII ET AMICORUM, for he lent them freely. He was a generous patron of Aldus Manutius. The GROLIER CLUB was founded (1884) in New York to promote 'the arts entering into the production of books'.

Gromaire Marcel (1892–). French painter in a heavy expressionist style which he developed after World War I and applied to his special subjects, the massive figures of labourers on the land and in industry; he has also painted the female nude and views of Paris and New York. He made his reputation with *La Guerre* (1925; Petit Palais, Paris). He has produced notable engravings and with Lurçat played an important part in reviving the art of tapestry in France.

Gröndal Benedikt Sveinbjarnarson (1826–1907). Icelandic writer chiefly remembered for his prose satires.

Gropius Walter (1883–). German architect. One of the most distinguished of modern architects, and creator of the *Bauhaus. After World War I, G. combined the Weimar Art School and the Weimar Arts and Crafts School into 1 organization called the Bauhaus, where art and technology were to be regarded as one, and all the arts relating to building were taught. The Bauhaus emphasis on machine production led to an admiration for teamwork and cooperation which has been a strong feature in G.'s career. G. resigned as director of the Bauhaus in 1928 to devote all his time to his practice, and the Bauhaus was closed when the Nazis came to power.

From 1937 to 1952 G. was professor of architecture in the Graduate School of Design at Harvard, and trained many of the most brilliant of America's young architects; and he has held their respect although many of them have rejected his functionalism for a more formally-conscious architecture.

G. is an essentially modest man, and his belief in group-work has led him to associate with other architects for almost all his buildings.

As an architect he began practice in 1910, and in 1911 he and Adolf Meyer designed the Fagus shoe-last factory; the workshop block design was very advanced, with curtain walling and glazed corners. In 1914 they designed the Deutscher Werkbund Pavilion in Cologne, with adventurous use of glass. G.'s Bauhaus Building of 1926 is the 1st large masterpiece of modern architecture, and G.'s most convincing bnilding; where his earlier buildings had contained pieces of traditional design mixed with the new, the Bauhaus is modern throughout; its concept is 3 wings–workshops, studios and classrooms, each expressing the activity within, yet linked to form an architectural whole.

G. had to flee from the Nazis and he was in partnership with Maxwell Fry in London (1934–7). They designed some houses and a school at Impington, Cambridgeshire, which has had great influence on post-war British schools.

In 1937 he went to the U.S., at first in partnership with Breuer, then with a group of young architects called 'The Architects Collaborative'. The houses of the Collaborative are pleasant and relaxed, but the larger buildings have been less successful, and in the case of the Pan-Am Building in New York, have been severely criticized.

Gros Antoine-Jean (1771–1835). French painter whose earlier work exerted a powerful influence on the development of romanticism in France. His training by J.-L. David and intellectual assent to classicism eventually stifled his temperamental bias towards romanticism, and after David's death (1825) he took over the leadership of the outmoded classical school, produced unsatisfactory paintings and committed suicide. Among his important works

Marcel Gromaire. *La Guerre*

Antoine Jean, Baron Gros. Detail of *Napoleon at Arcoli*

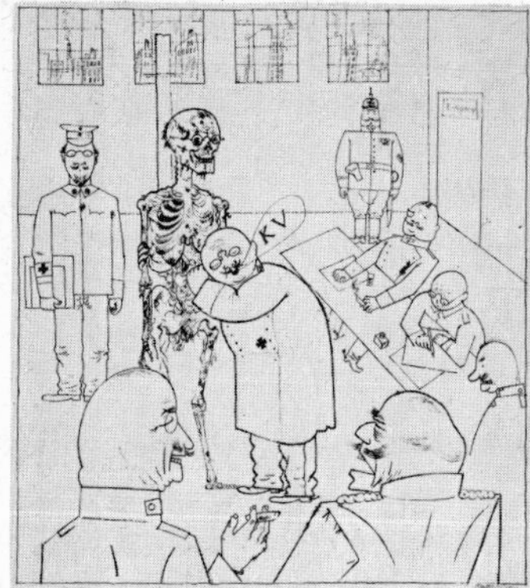

Grosz. *Fit for Active Service* (1918)

Group portrait by Rembrandt, *Syndics of the Drapers' Guild*

Grosz. *Man and Wife* (1930).
Also *caricature, *new objectivity

Grotesque. From the Raphael Loggia in the Vatican

are *Napoleon Visiting the Plague-stricken at Jaffa* (1804) and *The Battle of Aboukir* (1806) (both Louvre).

gros point: *petit point

Grossmith George (1847–1912). English writer and comedian for the D'Oyly Carte Opera Co., who with his brother, contributed to *Punch The Diary of a Nobody* (in book form 1892), a telling and very funny satire of the English *petit-bourgeois*; illustrated by his brother WALTER WEEDON G. (1854–1919).

Grosz George (1893–1959). German expressionist painter and graphic artist best known for his pen and ink drawings satirizing the German nation during and after World War I; in 1933 he settled in the U.S. His own experiences of the war in the German army, as a civilian in Berlin (1916–17) and in a military asylum, made a searing impression. Stylistically influenced by the *new objectivity movement he exposed with merciless and horrifying precision the officials and profiteers who lived off the war and, after it, the vice, the political chaos and the complacency of the bourgeoisie. His work lost something of its bite after he went to the U.S. His paintings during World War II were symbolical and, in contrast with the particularity of his earlier work, generalized expressions of hatred of the bestiality of war.

grotesque. Originally derived from the mural decoration of excavated classical grottoes. These consisted of panels where fantastic shapes of human beings, animals, etc. were joined together by flowers, garlands and arabesques into a symmetrical design covering the wall or ceiling. Very popular in the 16th c. The term came to be applied to distorted exaggerations, humorous or horrifying, in various art forms, especially sculpture.

Groth Klaus (1819–99). The major lyric poet of 19th-c. Low German literature. Best known is his coll. of poems on peasant life in Dithmarschen, *Quickborn* (1852). Brahms and other composers set some of his poems.

Grotius Hugo de Groot called (1583–1645). Dutch writer remembered as the author of *De Jure Belli ac Pacis* (1625), the 1st thorough exposition of international law.

ground. Term used in (1) painting, of the foundation surface of white oil paint or gesso laid down on the canvas or panel to receive the painting; (2) music, for a repeated figure played in the bass and serving as a support for variations above it; (3) embroidery, of the basic overall background over which the pattern is worked.

groundlings: *Elizabethan stage

Group of Seven. Group of Canadian landscape painters influential and controversial in the 1920s and 1930s; they stressed design and colour, and aimed to produce decorative but specifically Canadian landscapes. The group was founded in 1919 by Lawren Harris, F. H. Varley, Arthur Lismer, Franz Johnston, A. Y. Jackson, J. E. H. MacDonald and F. Carmichael, though deriving from the Algonquin school before World War I.

group portrait. Term applied to the painting of a family or other group of real people, as opposed to mythological, historical, religious and other paintings in which a number of people appear. Such portraits were often commissioned and were a great challenge to the artist, who had to give each sitter equal importance while producing a work of art. The genre flourished in 17th-c. Holland; its famous exponents include Rembrandt and Hals.

Group Theater. New York theatre established as an independent body in 1931. The principles of group acting practised in this theatre are based on those of Stanislavsky and the Moscow Arts Theatre. The G. T. encouraged new playwrights and discovered Clifford Odets.

Grove F. P. (1872–1948). Canadian novelist. Sombre, tragic feeling invest such novels of the Canadian West as *Over Prairie Trails* (1922), *A Search for America* (1927), and *To the Master of the Mill* (1944) with seriousness of purpose that was new and is still rare in Canadian literature; some of the reasons are suggested in G.'s *Search for Myself* (1946).

Grove Sir George (1820–1900). English engineer, writer on music and the first director of the R.C.M. (1883–94). His *Dictionary of Music and Musicians* (1879–89) was the most exhaustive work of its kind in English and has gone through several eds.

Gruber Francis (1912–48). French realist painter whose work has affinities with expressionism. He studied at the Académie Scandinave, Paris where his teachers included Dufresne and Friesz, but his development owed more to the influence of Dürer, Grünewald and Callot than to any contemporary artist. Emaciated figures and ravaged landscape recur in his stark, uncompromising compositions. Before his death he painted a number of portraits of his wife.

Gruen Victor (1903–). U.S. architect, the pioneer of the out-of-town shopping centre, e.g. Northlands, Detroit (1952) and Southdale, Minneapolis. In city planning, as in his plan for Fort Worth, Texas, his technique is to ring the city centre with a freeway and garages, and allow no cars within.

Gruenberg Louis (1884–1964). Russian-born U.S. composer and concert pianist. Early in his career as a composer he developed the interest in jazz and Negro music generally that was to colour much of his music, e.g. *Daniel Jazz* (1923), *The Creation*, both for voice and chamber ensemble, and his best-known work, the opera *Emperor Jones* (1933), after Eugene O'Neill. His other works include symphonies and a violin concerto.

Grumbold Robert (1639–1720). English mason and architect. He worked for Wren on the Library of Trinity College, Cambridge, and later did other work there in his own rather coarse style.

Grün Anastasius. Pseud. of Anton Alexander von Auersperg (1806–76). Austrian poet. His works, including *Spaziergänge eines Wiener Poeten* (1831), expressed G.'s distaste as a liberal for the reactionary policies of Metternich, anticipating the attitudes of *Young Germany.

Gründgens Gustaf (1899–1963). German actor and producer who was director-general of the Berlin state theatres (1937–45). He had directed in most main German cities and from 1955 worked at Hamburg. As an actor his most famous roles were Hamlet, and Mephistopheles in Goethe's *Faust*.

Grundtvig Nicolai Frederik Severin (1783–1872). Very influential Danish scholar, poet and churchman (he became a bishop in 1861) who wrote many enduringly popular songs and hymns.

grüne Heinrich, Der (1854–5). Novel by Gottfried *Keller.

Grünewald Mathias or Mathis Gothart Nithart called (*c.* 1475–1528). German painter, born in Würzburg, Bavaria. G. was trained in Alsace in the style of Schongauer, and travelled through Germany, living in Isenheim, Seligenstadt, Aschaffenburg and Mainz, where he was court painter to the Elector. He died in Halle, where he painted a series of pictures in the cathedral for the Elector of Mainz.

G.'s masterpiece is the set of 10 paintings for the Isenheim altar (finished *c.* 1515; now at the Mus. Unterlinden, Colmar). They were intended to be seen in 3 groups which changed as panels were opened and shut: 2 scenes from the life of St Anthony flanking the carved centre-piece (*c.* 1505, by Backoffen) of St Anthony enthroned with SS Augustine and Jerome; the *Annunciation*, *Concert of Angels*, *Virgin and Child* and *Resurrection*; and the *Crucifixion*, *St Anthony* and *St Sebastian* (supposedly a self-portrait). Below these was the *Pietà* which disclosed the carved Christ and Apostles of the predella (also by Backoffen).

The spirit of the Renaissance is remote from G.'s work, but he imbued the medieval German art to which he adhered with an entirely original personal vision expressed in the distorted, tortured forms and strange colouring of the *Crucifixions* (Basle, Karlsruhe, Isenheim). His range is enormous, encompassing the horrifying *Crucifixion* and serene *Virgin and Child* of the Isenheim altar. The Karlsruhe *Crucifixion*–the greenish, blood-spattered body of Christ, its deformed limbs, where even the nails pinning the claw-like hands, the crown of thorns and the draperies are painted in the same tortured manner–is utterly different from the *Madonna* (Stuppach) who stands in a beautiful garden, fresh and tender. *The Mocking of Christ* (Alte Pina., Munich) is filled with large figures caught in frenzied movement. Christ, his eyes covered, is gripped by the hair by his assailant, whose fist is poised ready to strike; another, holding Christ's bonds, is about to lash him with the knotted end of a rope. The figure of Christ in this painting, abused and defiled, directly contrasts with that in the *Resurrection*, in which Christ ascends

Grünewald. *The Resurrection* from the *Isenheim altar

Grünewald. *The Mocking of Christ*

Grünewald. *The Crucifixion*, Karlsruhe

Guercino. *Aurora*

Guarini. Cupola in the church of S. Lorenzo, Turin; also *baroque

Guardi. *Ascent in a Balloon*

suffused with a golden celestial light. G. also painted *The Meeting of St Erasmus and St Maurice* (Munich) which formed part of the Halle commission.

Gryphius Andreas (1616–64). German playwright and poet whose work is marked by intense religious feeling and a sense of the tragic. His prolific output includes poems, *Son- undt Feyrtags- Sonnete* (1639); tragedies, *Ermordete Majestät, oder Carolus Stuardus, König von Gross-Britannien* (publ. 1657), about the execution of Charles I of England, written in the year it happened (1649); and comedies, *Die gelibte Dornrose* (1660).

Guardi Francesco (1712–93). Venetian landscape painter and draughtsman, brother-in-law of Giambattista Tiepolo and son of a painter. His son Giacomo (1764–1835) carried on his workshop. G.'s development was slow and his early paintings lacked originality since he was mainly concerned with satisfying the popular demand for small religious and genre paintings. He absorbed the influence of his contemporaries Canaletto and Longhi but evolved a new type of landscape painting, which became very popular. He can be ranked with Constable, Turner and the painters of Barbizon as a pioneer of a new approach to landscape for his subjective use of light and atmosphere expressed with a nervous, calligraphic touch. In his maturity he portrayed Venetian social life brilliantly and accurately. He recorded the excitement of the *Ascent in a Balloon* (Berlin) and the ceremonial of the *Doge embarking on the Bucintoro* (N.G., London).

Guareschi Giovanni (1908–). Italian writer and journalist, best known outside Italy for his series of humorous novels dealing with the perpetual feud between a country priest, Don Camillo, and the Communist mayor of the parish. The series began with *Il Mondo Piccolo Don Camillo* (1948; *The Little World of Don Camillo*, 1951).

Guarini Giovanni Battista (1538–1612). Italian poet, Tasso's successor as court poet in Ferrara. His reputation is mainly founded on his *Pastor Fido* (1590; *The Faithfull Shepheard*, 1647), a pastoral romantic verse drama which was widely popular in Europe and which, together with Tasso's *Aminta*, was the finest example of the genre.

Guarini Guarino (1624–83). Italian architect. From 1639 to 1647 he lived in Rome and studied the churches of Borromini, which were then in course of construction; Borromini remained the most powerful influence on him. After periods at Modena, Messina and Paris, G. settled (1666) at Turin, the capital of Piedmont. Here within 2 years he designed 2 startlingly original buildings – the Capella delle Sta Sindone, attached to the cathedral, and the church of S. Lorenzo. Both show extreme geometrical complexity, especially in the domes: that of S. Lorenzo is an 8-pointed star of free-standing arches; that of the Capella della Sta Sindone a diminishing series of small segmental arches standing on top of one another. He also built the Palazzo Carignano, Turin (1679) with an undulating concave-convex façade in brick. G. stands at the end of the baroque tradition in Italy, but had a profound influence on the architects of the next c. in S. Germany and Austria.

Guarneri. 17th–18th-c. family of Cremonese violin makers.

Guarnieri Camargo (1907–). Brazilian composer who studied in São Paulo and (1938) under Koechlin in Paris; returning to the Americas he conducted concerts of his own works in the U.S. and has won numerous major composition prizes. His music derives something from folk tradition but transcends it to achieve a more general validity. G.'s works include: *Danca Brasileira* (1928) for piano; the comic opera *Malazarte* (1932), symphonies, etc.

Guercino, Il ('the squint eyed') Giovanni Francesco Barbieri called (1591–1666). Italian painter. He was born at Cento near Ferrara and worked there for much of his life; he also worked in Rome (1621–3) and Bologna (from 1642). The Carracci, Caravaggio and the Venetian school were important influences on his development. Between 1616 and 1621 in a number of notable altarpieces he evolved a colouristic, painterly style which culminated in *Aurora*. This fine illusionistic painting was the model for many later baroque ceiling paintings and makes an interesting comparison with Reni's more restrained treatment of the same subject (1613) in the Palazzo Rospigliosi, Rome. In *Burial and Reception into Heaven of St Petronilla* (Capitoline Mus., Rome), also painted in Rome, G. abandoned the vigorous treatment of *Aurora* in favour of Annibale Carracci's type of classicism. The power and originality of his work steadily declined as he became involved in the Counter-Reformation under the influence of which he painted uninspired pietistic altarpieces, many of them in the manner of his rival Reni. On the death of Reni, G. took over his workshop in Bologna. The Royal Library, Windsor has the best coll. of G.'s very fine drawings.

guéridon. A tall stand, usually on tripod feet, which serves to support a lamp or a candelabrum. Later additions of shelves and a cupboard made it into an occasional table. The name is derived from a famous Moorish slave and originally a g. was in the form of a Negro holding a tray.

Guérin (Georges) Maurice de (1810–39). French writer. His older sister EUGÉNIE DE G. (1805–48) dominated his life with a possessive love, and none of his works were publ. during his lifetime. They include the prose poems *Le Centaure* (1840; 1899) and *La Bacchante* (1862; 1899), and a *Journal intime* or *Cahier vert* (1861; *Journal of M. de G.*, 1867). Eugénie also wrote a *Journal intime* (1862; 1865) for her brother.

Guérin Pierre-Narcisse (1774–1833). French painter, pupil of J.-B. Regnault. As an exponent of classicism he alternated between the styles of J.-L. David and Regnault but in either case produced work of extreme banality. Géricault and Delacroix studied under him.

Guernica (1937). Painting by *Picasso; also the title of a short film (1950), directed by Alain *Resnais and using paintings by Picasso.

Guerra Antonio (1810–46). Italian dancer and one-time partner of Taglioni and Elssler. He danced in many European centres and turned to choreography; among works he produced was *Le Lac des Fées* (1840).

Guerra Nicola (1862–1942). Italian dancer who became chief dancer at La Scala (1878). After gaining an international reputation by his appearances in the U.S. and Europe, he turned to choreography. One of his works was *Artemis Troublée* (1922) for which Bakst designed the set and costumes.

Guevara Fray Antonio de (1480?–1545). Spanish Franciscan writer whose works had a decisive influence on the evolution of 16th-c. Castilian prose. His most famous work was the *Relox de Principes* (1529; *The Golden boke of Marcus Aurelius*, 1539), a moralistic work which had a great success. His elaborate literary style was greatly admired and imitated.

Guicciardini Francesco (1483–1540). Italian historian and political theorist; his *L'historia d'Italia* (1561; 1579) is one of the earliest examples of modern historiography.

Guido d'Arezzo (*c.* 995–*c.* 1050). Italian monk whose system of sight singing (*hexachord) lasted well into the Renaissance; the GUIDONIAN HAND was a further aid—a mnemonic, equating notes with joints of the fingers.

Guido da Siena (13th c.). Italian painter, the founder of the Sienese school. A signed *Madonna in Majesty* (Palazzo Pubblico, Siena) is dated 1221 but there is controversy among art historians as to whether in fact it does not come from the 1260s or 1270s like other works in a similar style.

Guildford John of (13th c.). Possible author of *The *Owl and the Nightingale*, though a Nicholas de Guildford, mentioned in the poem, is an alternative suggestion.

Guillaume d'Aquitaine (1071–1127). 9th duke and the earliest known Provençal troubadour. Of his few surviving *chansons*, a number are direct and sensual; others display what were to become characteristic features of courtly love.

Guillaume de Loris. 13th-c. French poet, author of *Le *Roman de la Rose*.

Guillaumin Armand (1841–1927). French impressionist painter. He was a friend of C. Pissarro and Cézanne and exhibited at the 1st (1874), and most subsequent, impressionist exhibitions. Pale violet and orange predominate in his landscapes.

Guillén Jorge (1893–). One of the leading modern Spanish poets; he has lived in the U.S. since 1938. Most of his verse celebrates the joy of living, revelling in the immediacy of sensation. G. is a refined craftsman: his mode of expression is simple, his language austere. His coll. *Cantico* contains all his work, having been constantly enlarged from 1928 to 1950.

Guilmant Alexandre (1837–1911). French organ virtuoso of European fame, a composer

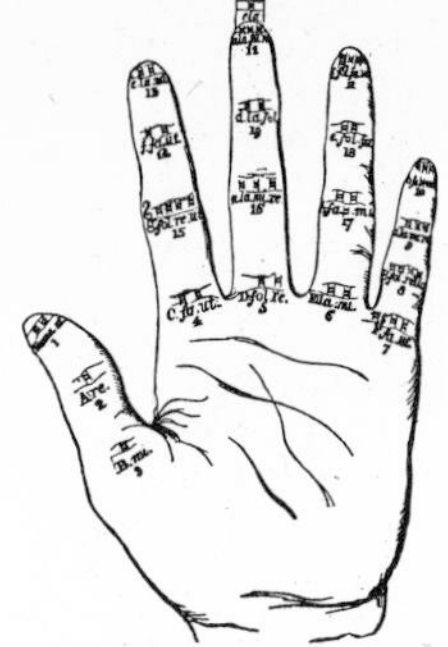

Guidonian hand; from a medieval treatise

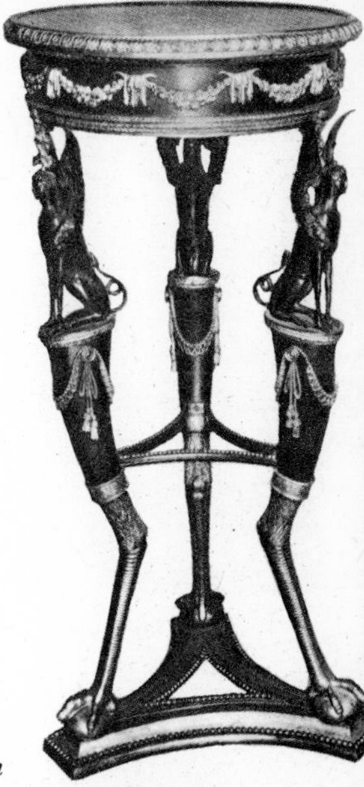

Empire style *guéridon*

Guido da Siena. *Madonna in Majesty*, Siena

Guernica

Alec Guinness in *The Lavender Hill Mob*

Spanish guitar Electric guitar

and teacher; with d'Indy a co-founder (1894) of the Schola Cantorum, Paris.

Guinizelli Guido (*c.* 1230–76). Italian poet of the *dolce stil nuovo; he influenced Dante. A few of G.'s poems, e.g. *A cor gentil ripara sempre amore*, display a new idea of love, as exalted as the courtly ideal but in which nobility resides in the soul rather than the lineage.

Guinness Sir Alec (1914–). English stage and film actor. He played Hamlet in modern dress at the Old Vic in 1938 and was again with the Old Vic Co. at the New Theatre (1946–8) when he played in *Richard II* and J. B. Priestley's *An Inspector Calls*. More recently he distinguished himself as T. E. Lawrence in Rattigan's *Ross*. G.'s film career has been equally successful and his characterizations equally varied – in *Great Expectations*, *Oliver Twist*, *Kind Hearts and Coronets*, *The Man in the White Suit*, *The Lavender Hill Mob*, *The Bridge on the River Kwai*, etc.

guitar. Stringed musical instrument. The g. has a flat back, frets on the finger-board and strings which are sounded by being plucked by the fingers or by a plectrum; it usually has 6 metal strings with a range of about three 8ves from the E below the bass stave. The instrument is Spanish in origin, being a traditional folk instrument there, but its vogue as a drawing-room instrument, especially in the 19th c., and recent virtuosi such as Segovia, Julian Bream and Williams, have resulted in a sizeable literature. The ELECTRIC G., i.e. one equipped with an amplifying system, is now a staple instrument of 'pop' music; modern 'folk' and 'blues' singers use the unmodified g.

Guitry Lucien (1860–1925). French actor who first appeared as Armand in *La Dame aux camélias* in 1878. He acted with Sarah Bernhardt and for several years was manager of the Théâtre Renaissance in Paris.

Guitry Sacha (1885–1957). French writer, actor and director in the theatre and cinema, son of the above. G. wrote over a 100 plays, the best known being *Nono* and *Castles in Spain*. His films, mostly made in the last 20 years of his life, are almost unknown outside France, where they have a critical following. The most famous was *Le Roman d'un Tricheur* (1936).

Guittone d'Arezzo (*c.* 1225–*c.* 94). Italian poet. G. wrote love-poetry in his youth, was converted to the religious life and thereafter wrote didactic verse on political and moral subjects to some effect.

Gulliver's Travels (1726). Satire by *Swift.

gum bichromate print. Paper used in photography; it is made sensitive to light with a chemical coating that hardens on exposure. Development consists of washing away the unexposed areas with water. This system produces a very soft misty image but permits great control in the development process and allows the print to be re-sensitized many times. It was used from 1895 to 1915, and much of *Steichen's early work was in this technique.

Günderode Karoline von (1780–1806). German poet, a friend of Bettina von Arnim, who publ. a biography of her. G. committed suicide from despair in love.

Gunn Tom (1929–). English poet whose travels find a reflection in the slightly frenetic, self-assertive quality of many poems in *Fighting Terms* (1954), *The Sense of Movement* (1957) and *My Sad Captains* (1961). Gesture, pose and a search for the heroic often mar the results of what is clearly a wide sensibility.

Günther Franz Ignaz (1725–75). Bavarian sculptor whose painted wood sculptures of religious subjects are among the greatest works of the rococo period. Best known of these are *The Annunciation* (1764; Rosenkranzbrüderschaft, Weyarn) and his last surviving work, the *Pietà* (1774) in the Friedhofkapelle, Nenningen (Württemberg) which has great depth of feeling.

Günther Johann Christian (1695–1723). German poet whose early death followed a dissipated and frustrated life. From his tragic life sprang poetry, above all love-lyrics, of great feeling and power; his style owed something to the simplicity of the German folk-song.

Sacha Guitry

Franz Ignaz Günther. *Pietà*. See also colour plate 65

Gurrelieder. Choral work by *Schoenberg.

Guston Philip (1913–). Canadian painter who lives in the U.S. and is a leading exponent of action painting. His early abstract paintings of the late 1940s were called 'abstract impressionist' as reminiscent of Monet's late work. He began to develop his characteristic style in the early 1950s.

Gutenberg Johann Gensfleisch zum (*c.* 1395–1468). German printer, generally regarded as the inventor of printing. A goldsmith by profession he began experimenting with printing work *c.* 1440. His experience as a goldsmith in the cutting of dies and working in relief would have given him much of the technical knowledge which he was later to apply to the cutting of matrices. Besides inventing the system of printing with movable types, he devised the mould system for casting these types, developed an ink suitable for use with metal types, and a printing press with which his work was carried out. By 1450 he was able to commence production. He reached a state of technical efficiency not radically improved upon until the 19th c.
Following a foreclosure suit in 1456, G. lost most of his equipment to a partner, Johann *Fust, and an employee, Peter *Schoeffer, who continued the business successfully. He set up again almost immediately with what little he had salvaged, but retired in 1460, and was made a gentleman of the Mainz court in 1465. G.'s works include the famed 42-line Bible (1452–5) and a 36-line Bible which may have preceded it. Also the *Donatus* (1451?), some 'Letters of Indulgence' (1454 or 5 and 1460), a *Catholicon* (1460) and several pamphlets and calendars.

Guthrie Sir Tyrone (1900–). English director; since 1953 director of the Shakespeare Festival Theatre, Stratford, Ontario. G.'s 1st London production was of James Bridie's *The Anatomist* (1931). He is famous for his Shakespeare productions, often in modern or unconventional dress, e.g. *Coriolanus* at the new Nottingham Playhouse (1963). He has produced operas ranging from those of Britten to Gilbert and Sullivan.

Gutiérrez Antonio García: *García Gutiérrez.

Guttuso Renato (1912–). Italian painter and member of the Communist party, the leading exponent of socialist realism in the West.

Gutzkow Karl Ferdinand (1811–78). German playwright, novelist and radical journalist of the *Young Germany movement. His major novel was *Die Ritter vom Geist* (1850–1) but G. was more important as a pioneer theorist of the German social novel. His plays include: *Zopf und Schwert* (1843), *Uriel Acosta* (1846), *Der Königsleutenant* (1852).

Guy Mannering (1815). Historical novel by Sir Walter Scott.

Guy of Warwick. 14th-c. English verse romance. The hero is the son of the earl of Warwick's steward; to win the earl's daughter he performs amazing feats of valour against Saracens, giants and monsters; later he becomes a hermit.

Guys Constantin (1802–92). French draughtsman and illustrator famous for his vivacious sketches of English and French society—manners and changing fashions, carriages and military occasions, courtesans and dandies. This 'modernity' was commended by Baudelaire in his appreciation of G.'s work, *Peintre de la Vie Moderne* (*Le Figaro*, 1863; *The Painter of Victorian Life*, 1930). G. was reporter-illustrator for *The Illustrated London News* during the Crimean War.

Guys and Dolls (1932). Vol. of short stories by Damon *Runyon, the basis of a famous musical comedy (1952).

Guzman Martin Luis (1887–). Mexican novelist, author of *Le águila y la serpiente* (Spain, 1928; *The Eagle and the Serpent*, 1930) about the Revolutionary period.

Gyrowetz Adalbert (1763–1850). Bohemian composer, follower of Haydn. He wrote stage works, symphonies, etc. which enjoyed great popularity at the time.

Guston. *Zone*

Guttuso. *The Beach* (1946)

Guys. *La Promenade*, watercolour and pen

Guys. *Street in Constantinople*, watercolour and pen

Gutenberg; page from the 36-line Bible

Rider Haggard

H

Haanstra Bert (1916–). Dutch film director. H. is the maker of an excellent and widely admired short, *Glass* (1958), which contrasts the visual rhythms obtainable from a bottle-making machine with the process of glass-blowing. He also directed an intelligent art film, *Rembrandt, Painter of Man* (1957) and other shorts before making a feature, *Fanfare* (1958), a comedy.

Haas Joseph (1879–). German composer, a pupil of Reger, and important as a teacher at Munich. In such works as the oratorio *Die Heilige Elisabeth* (1931) and the 'people's opera' *Tobias Wunderlich* (1937) he offered a religious solution to contemporary social tensions. He also wrote the comic opera *Die Hochzeit des Jobs* (1943) and the 'folk oratorio' *Das Jahr im Lied* (1952).

Hadrian's Villa

Hába Alois (1893–). Czech composer, a pupil of Novak and Schreker. He draws inspiration from Czech and Moravian folk-music but developed an athematic style of composition (one that does not rely on thematic repetition as a unifying element) and is the major pioneer of *microtone composition using both quarter tones, e.g. the opera *The Mother* (1930), and sixth tones, e.g. the suite for solo cello and violin (1955). His brother Karel (1898–), a violinist and violist, is also a composer.

Habakkuk. One of the minor prophetic books of the *Bible (Old Testament).

Habeneck François-Antoine (1781–1849). French conductor of German descent. He introduced Beethoven's symphonies to Paris (1828–31) and founded (1828) the Société des Concerts du Conservatoire.

Haberl Franz Xaver (1840–1910). German priest and musicologist, and founder of the School of Ecclesiastical Music at Regensburg, a major body in the reform of Roman Catholic church music. H. also ed. the works of Palestrina and founded a Palestrina Society.

Habington William (1605–64). English Catholic poet whose best work is *Castara* (1634), a coll. of religious poems and love-sonnets to his future wife.

Hadewijch. 13th-c. Dutch mystic. Her poems, prose, letters and 'visions' written in the vernacular are a peak of Dutch medieval literature.

Hadow Sir William Henry (1859–1937). English writer on music and educationalist who was vice-chancellor of Sheffield Univ. (1919–30), and also composer. His books include *Studies in Modern Music* (1892–3).

Hadrian's Villa. Palace and gardens laid out at Tivoli, near Rome by the Emperor Hadrian in about A.D. 120. It had several picturesque features in imitation of places the emperor had visited–the Lyceum, the Vale of Tempe, the Canopus, etc. It is described by the historian Spartian, but not all its features are identifiable with certainty. The Canopus (a valley in Egypt) has been restored.

Haffner. A Salzburg family. Mozart's 'H. serenade' (K. 250 in D. 1776) was composed for the marriage of one of the daughters; his 'H. symphony' (K 385 in D, 1782) was, in its original form, probably performed at the ennoblement of a son of the family.

Hafiz Shams-ud-din Muhammad called (*c.* 1300–88). Persian poet. His principal work is the *Divan* (or *Diwan*), a coll. of short lyrics praising the joys and pleasures of life and castigating the hypocrisies of the puritanical sufis. A trs. prompted Goethe to write the *West-östlicher Diwan.*

Hagedorn Friedrich von (1708–54). German lyric poet who for a time lived in England. He is classed as an anacreontic but Horace was an important model and his most popular work was *Fabeln und Erzählungen* (1738).

Hagenau. German faïence factory, *Strassburg.

Haggai. A minor prophetic book of the *Bible (Old Testament).

Haggard (Sir Henry) Rider (1856–1925). English writer of adventure stories, the most successful of which, including *King Solomon's Mines* (1885), *She* (1887), *Allan Quatermain* (1887) and *Ayesha: The Return of She* (1905), are set in an Africa, then unfamiliar and forbidding. They have often been filmed.

Hagiographa: *Bible

Thomas Haliburton

Pottery by Sam Haile

Egyptian half-columns with papyrus flower capitals

hagioscope. Alternative term for the *squint in a church wall.

Hahn Reynaldo (1875–1947). Venezuelan-born composer and conductor who lived in France from infancy; at the Paris Conservatoire his teachers included J. Massenet. H. wrote mainly for the stage. His songs include 'If only my songs had wings'. He became director of the Paris Opéra in 1945.

haiku. Japanese epigrammatic verse of 17 syllables. 20th-c. Western poets have given the name to poems of their own.

Haile (Thomas) Sam(uel) (1909–48). English artist potter. He studied at the R.C.A. under W. S. Murray, held various teaching posts; moved to the U.S. after his marriage (1938) to Marianne de Trey, and after considerable successes returned (1945) to England. As a painter H. exhibited with the English surrealists; his pottery, drawing on Minoan, Cycladic, Pueblo Indian and medieval English forms, has powerful primitive shapes and highly imaginative idiosyncratic decoration.

Hairy Ape, The (1922). Play by Eugene *O'Neill.

Hakluyt Richard (1552?–1616). English geographer, archdeacon of Westminster and ed. of *The Principall navigations . . . of the English nation* (1589). It was intended as a patriotic eulogy of English exploits at sea but is also a coll. of hard, strong and vividly descriptive prose. It consists of authentic records and includes moving descriptions of voyages of Hawkins, Drake and Frobisher. The Hakluyt Society for publ. works on early discoveries was founded in 1846.

Hale Edward Everett (1822–1909). U.S. writer, a clergyman. He wrote short stories and books of autobiography, but is now remembered as author of the famous story *The Man Without a Country* (1863); the protagonist, Philip Nolan, curses the U.S. and is exiled at sea, where he learns that love of country is ingrained in him. Walter Damrosch composed an opera on the subject.

Halévy Jacques-François Fromental, originally named Elias Levy (1799–1862). French-Jewish opera composer. He entered the Conservatoire in 1809, studying under Cherubini, and won the Rome prize in 1819. His reputation was established by *La Juive* and the comic opera *L'Éclair* (both performed 1835); his many other works included the comic operas *La Dilettante d'Avignon* (1829) and *Le Val d'Andorre* (1848). H. taught at the Conservatoire, his pupils including Bizet and Gounod.

Halévy Ludovic (1834–1908). French novelist and librettist; with Henri Meilhac responsible for the librettos of some of *Offenbach's operettas, e.g. *La Vie Parisienne*. H. also publ. novels, among them the sentimental *Abbé Constantin* (1882).

half-column. Architectural term for half of a column (vertically divided) which is attached to a wall; it is usually, but not always, ornamental.

Halffter Ernesto (1905–). Spanish-German composer, resident in Portugal, and brother of R. H. He studied under M. de *Falla, who strongly influenced his work. H. has written the ballet *Sonatina* (1928); *Sinfonietta D* (1923–7) for orchestra; and piano and film music.

Halffter Rodolfo (1900–). Spanish-German composer; a Republican, he settled in Mexico in 1939. He studied under Falla; has used polytonality and later, as in *3 pieces for string orchestra* (1957), 12-note techniques. Other works include: the ballet *Elena la Traicionera* (1945); an overture concertante for piano and orchestra (1932), and piano music.

half note. U.S. term for a *minim.

half-timbered. Architectural term describing a building with a substantial timber skeleton; the timbers are narrowly spaced and the interstices are filled with brick, plaster, or other materials. H.-t. houses were common in S. and parts of W. England (because of the scarcity of stone) from the 15th to the mid 17th c.

Haliburton Thomas (1795–1865). Early Canadian author of sketches on Sam Slick, Yankee clock-peddler, whose exploits appeared in book form in 1836. H., through his caricature, manages to satirize both natives and immigrants, the old world and new.

Halifax George Savile, 1st Marquess of: *Savile

Half-timbering. Old Hall Farm, Woodford, Cheshire (*c.* 1540)

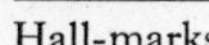
Hall-marks

Hallstatt bronze bucket

Dirck Hals. *A Party of Young Men and Women at Table*

Sir Charles Hallé

Hall (Halle) Edward (d. 1547). English writer. His 'history' *The Union of the Two Noble and Illustre Famelies of Lancastre and Yorke*, eulogizing the Tudors' ancestors, the House of Lancaster, was used by Shakespeare in his history plays.

Hall Joseph (1574–1656). English bishop, a writer and notable preacher. H. was the first to imitate Juvenal in English; his verse satire *Virgidemiarum* (1597–8) attacked contemporary institutions and personages, including Spenser. H.'s prose sketches *Characters of Vertues and Vices* (1608) are based on Theophrastus.

Hall Peter (1930–). English director and manager who as director of the Arts Theatre (1955–6) was responsible for the 1st production in England of Beckett's *Waiting for Godot*. His 1st production at Stratford was *Love's Labour's Lost* (1956) and in 1960 he was appointed director of The Shakespeare Memorial Co. Under his management the co. also acquired control of the Aldwych Theatre, London.

Hallam family. Lewis H. (1714–56) was an English actor who went to Virginia in 1752 and later built the 1st theatre in New York. His son Lewis (1740–1808) led The American Co. and distinguished himself by playing Romeo to his mother's Juliet in New York in 1759.

hall-church (from German *Hallenkirche*). A Gothic church whose aisle vaults spring from the same height as those of the nave; unusual in France and England but common in Germany.

Hallé Sir Charles (1819–95). German-born conductor and pianist originally named Karl Halle. As a young man he moved to Paris where he met Chopin, Liszt, Berlioz and Wagner. In 1848 he settled in England, founding the H. Orchestra in Manchester in 1857.

Hallelujah. The Hebrew for 'praise Jehovah'. Several composers wrote H. choruses but *the* H. chorus is that in Handel's *Messiah*. Handel's H. concerto for organ frequently echoes the opening phrase of the chorus.

Hallelujah! (1929). Film directed by K. *Vidor.

Haller Albrecht von (1708–77). German poet who was also a great anatomist and physiologist, establishing the European reputation of his univ., Göttingen. *Versuch schweizerischer Gedichte* (1732–34) contained the nature poem *Die Alpen* and the didactic poem *Über den Ursprung des Übels.*

hall-marks. Most pieces of English gold and silver have stamped on them: the mark of the Goldsmiths' Co., usually the lion passant, denoting the correct fineness of silver or gold; the town mark; the date letter denoting the year of manufacture; and finally the maker's mark, usually composed of his initials. The monarch's head was also stamped on gold and silver objects as a duty mark from 1784 to 1890. English h.-m.s date back to the 14th c., and are so called because Goldsmiths' Hall was the 1st place where gold and silver objects could be assayed. Foreign marks often vary from town to town.

Hallstatt. Site in Austria which has given its name to the 1st W. European Iron Age culture; the H. period produced a geometrical art less interesting than that of the subsequent *La Tène period.

Hals Dirck or Dirk (1591–1656). Dutch painter. His painting is close in style to that of his brother, the more famous F. H. His best-known works are convivial gatherings such as *A Party of Young Men and Women at Table* (N.G., London).

Hals Frans (1580 or 85–1666). Dutch portrait painter. H. lived all his life in Haarlem. He probably studied under K. van Mander and may have visited Rubens in Antwerp (1616). He must have won a considerable reputation as a portrait painter prior to 1616, when he was commissioned to paint *The Banquet of the Haarlem Civic Guard, Archers of St George* (Frans Hals Mus., Haarlem). In this work H. confidently solves the enormous problems of composition involved in a group portrait where no figure can be subordinate. Other militia portraits were commissioned for the same mess in 1627, 1633 and 1639, while H.'s fame had spread to Amsterdam, whose Civic Guard he was invited to paint in 1633, a picture he left unfinished. Married, with numerous children, one an imbecile, another a delinquent, H. was in continuous financial difficulty. He gave lessons and among his pupils were probably Brouwer, Molenaer, Leyster and Wouwerman. In 1641 H. painted *The Governors of St Elizabeth Hospital* (Frans Hals Mus., Haarlem). In

Frans Hals. *Women Governors of the Haarlem Almshouse*

Frans Hals. *Banquet of the Civic Guard of St Adrian.* Also **Laughing Cavalier*

Frans Hals. *Hille Bobbe*

Vase by Hamada

Hamer. Alec Guinness (centre) and Dennis Price in *Kind Hearts and Coronets*

1644 the entrance fee of the Haarlem Guild was waived to allow H. to become a member. In 1664, in return for a small grant of money and fuel from the city, H. painted 2 of his most masterful and technically bold group portraits, *Men . . .* and *Women Governors of the Haarlem Almshouse* (Frans Hals Mus., Haarlem). Of his single portraits, perhaps the best known is the one called *The Laughing Cavalier* (Wallace Coll., London). Among others which show the brilliance of his brushwork and which capture the spontaneity of gesture he was famous for, are *Gipsy Girl* (Louvre), *Elderly Woman* (N.G., Washington), *Hille Bobbe,* or *The Witch of Haarlem* (Berlin) and *Young Couple in a Landscape* (Rijksmus., Amsterdam). H. was an important influence on the style of Manet.

Halvorsen Johan (1864–1935). Norwegian composer, violinist and orchestral leader. His music is in the tradition of Grieg and uses Norwegian folk-music elements.

Hamada Shoji (1892–). Japanese potter. After a period at the Kyoto Institute of Pottery, he came to England with Bernard Leach (1920–3), exerting some influence on other English potters. Returning to Japan, he worked in the small potting village of Mashiko, hiring himself out as a worker, despite his great reputation, and establishing his own kiln only in 1931. He continued to send selected pieces to England and in 1952 had a 1-man exhibition in London. His stoneware, rooted in Japanese peasant traditions, has great formal vigour combined with decorative brushwork of great sensitivity.

Hamann Johann Georg (1730–88). German critic, a cultural philosopher opposed to the exclusive trust in reason of the Enlightenment. He believed in an intuitive approach to life and learning and was regarded as a prophet by the storm and stress movement. H. greatly influenced Herder, introducing him to Ossian and Shakespeare and, in such aphorisms as 'Poetry is mankind's mother tongue', hinted at ideas important in Herder's system.

Hamburger Michael (1924–). English poet and trs. born in Germany. Colls include *Poems 1950–1* (1952) and *Weather and Season* (1963).

Hamer Robert (1911–63). English film director. H. started as an editor, and began directing after the war, his 1st notable film being a realist drama, *It Always Rains on Sunday* (1947). His great success was *Kind Hearts and Coronets* (1948), an acidly comic period piece. Afterwards he made a thriller, *The Long Memory* (1953) and an adaptation of G. K. Chesterton's *Father Brown* (1954). His last important film, *The Scapegoat* (1958), possibly his best, was drastically cut by its producers.

Hamilton Gavin (1723–98). Scottish neo-classical history and portrait painter and antiquary. After studying in Rome he worked as a portrait painter in Britain (*c.* 1752–4), then settled in Rome. There he became an important member of the neo-classical school centred round A. R. Mengs and J. J. Winckelmann.

Hamilton Gordon (1918–59). Australian dancer who took leading roles with the Sadler's Wells during the 1940s. He excelled in character roles as he was a particularly good mime. He was appointed ballet master at the Vienna State Opera (1954).

Hamilton Thomas (1784–1858). Scottish architect who designed the High School, the purest and most influential of many Greek revival buildings in Edinburgh.

Hamlet, Prince of Denmark (1602; publ. 1603). Tragedy by *Shakespeare, written *c.* 1600. Its sources were *Saxo Grammaticus's *Gesta Danorum*, and a play, *Hamlet* (1589?), possibly by Kyd. It has often been filmed, notably in 1948, directed by *Olivier.

hammer-beam. Architectural term for a short beam projecting at right angles from the top of a wall (i.e. like a bracket) and carrying struts, etc.; it was used in place of a tie-beam in order to increase the height (and therefore the impressiveness) of the interior. The h.-b. roof is peculiar to 15th- and 16th-c. England.

Hammerklavier. Nickname for *Beethoven's piano sonata op. 106 in B♭, although he entitled both this and 3 other sonatas '*für das Hammerklavier*'.

Hammett Dashiell (1894–1961). U.S. writer, and the 1st important one, of 'hard-boiled' fiction. His best crime novels have tremendous pace as well as punchy laconic dialogue; they

Gordon Hamilton in *Promenade*

Hammer-beam roof, Wymondham abbey, Norfolk. In this type (angel roof) the hammer-beams are continued in the form of angels

are *Red Harvest* (1929), *The Maltese Falcon* (1930) and *The Thin Man* (1932).

Knut Hamsun

Hamsun Knut (1859–1952). Norwegian writer and Nobel prizewinner (1920). As a young man he went to the U.S. for 2 years and he made 2 subsequent visits to the U.S. before a life of literary activity in Norway. Besides verse, plays and above all novels, he produced important critical work representing a reaction against the social preoccupations of the 19th c. in favour of concern with the individual. His major novels are: *Sult* (1890; *Hunger*, 1899) describing the effect of starvation on a sensitive intelligence; *Pan* (1894; 1920), in which H.'s lyrical descriptions of nature soften the human tragedy he portrays; *Victoria* (1898; 1929); and *Markens Grøde* (1917; *The Growth of the Soil*, 1920).

Handel

Handel Georg Friderick (1685–1759). German composer, also a keyboard virtuoso, working in England from 1712, being naturalized in 1726. He turned musician against his father's will, but completed his legal studies. In 1703 he gained a post as harpsichordist at the Hamburg opera, where his 1st opera was performed (1705). In Italy (1706–9) he met D. *Scarlatti and Corelli; in 1710 became Kapellmeister to the Elector of Hanover but in the same year went to London, where he produced the opera *Rinaldo* (1711) and returned. In 1712 he left again, and overstayed his leave, thereby incurring the electoral displeasure. Nevertheless, a reconciliation was achieved after the Elector's accession as George I of England. From 1718 H. was musician to the duke of Chandos, but in 1720 took charge of the new Royal Academy of Music, supported by the king, for the production of operas at the King's Theatre, London; it closed down in 1728, damaged by the rivalry of the composers (H. and Bononcini) and singers and the success of Gay's **Beggar's Opera*. From 1729 to 1737 H., now independent, continued his struggle as an opera producer, at first in competition with the 'Opera of the Nobility' (sponsored by the Prince of Wales). During these years he also produced the oratorios *Esther* (1732) and *Deborah* (1733). H.'s last, unsuccessful attempt to revive opera was in 1740/1. In 1742 he visited Dublin, where his *Messiah* (written 1741) gained an immediate success, not however repeated on its performance in London in 1743. Nevertheless, the Handelian oratorio was increasingly taken up as a fashion by the London bourgeoisie. In 1752, after an unsuccessful operation for cataract by the same surgeon as had treated J. S. Bach, H. went totally blind.

H.'s style, which derived in part from Italian sources and the music of Purcell, was admired by his English contemporaries for its simplicity, grandeur and masculine nobility. He had an intuitive gift for melody of classic beauty, an ability to write music of stately grandeur, as in the *12 Concerti Grossi* (1739), and above all was inspired to write choruses of apocalyptic power, of which the 'Hallelujah' chorus from *Messiah* is the greatest example. Behind all his work lay H.'s deep religious faith. His music became part of English musical life and the regular performances of *Messiah* built up a tradition of choral singing which inspired Haydn and impressed Berlioz. Of H.'s Italian operas, the following are among the best: *Giulio Cesare* (1724); *Admeto* (1727); *Sosarme* (1732); *Berenice* (1737); *Serse* or *Xerxes* (1738), one of the arias having become famous as 'Handel's Largo' (actually a satirical ode to a vegetable marked 'larghetto'!), and *Imenco* (1740). Secular choral works include: *Acis and Galatea* (1719–20), *Alexander's Feast* (1736) and *Ode for St Cecilia's Day* (1739), both with words by Dryden, and *Semele* (1744) with words by Congreve. In his English Biblical oratorios, a form he virtually invented, H. took over the recitatives, arias and dramatic scenes from Italian operas but gave the chorus a far more important role. The most important of these works are *Saul* (1739); *Israel in Egypt* (1739); *Samson* (1743), based on Milton; *Judas Maccabaeus* (1747), composed with the *Occasional Oratorio* (1746) to celebrate the defeat of the Young Pretender, and *Jephtha* (1752). H.'s other works include church music: the Utrecht *Te Deum* (1713); the *Chandos Anthems* (*c.* 1717–20); 4 Coronation anthems including *Zadok the Priest* (1727), a regular part of the Coronation Service ever since; and the Dettingen *Te Deum* (1743); instrumental music such as concertos, notably those for organ; suites, fugues and sonatas for keyboard, and the orchestral suites *The Water Music* (1715) and *Music for the Royal Fireworks* (1749).

Handel. Ms. of 'I know that my Redeemer liveth' (*Messiah*)

Handl (Hándl) Jacobus (1550–91). Slovene composer also known as 'Petelin' or as 'Gallus'. He worked in the Viennese court chapel and from 1585 at Prague. His polyphonic church music frequently uses chromaticism, exploits the multiple chorus (A. *Gabrieli), and is

Thomas Hardy

designed to support the meaning of the words. H. wrote many parody masses, over 350 motets and over 50 madrigals.

Hangmen also Die (1943). Film directed by F. *Lang.

Hansel and Gretel. One of the *Grimms' fairy-tales; the theme was used in an opera by *Humperdinck; 1st performance at Weimar in 1893.

Hansen Christian Fredrik (1756–1845). Danish neo-classical architect. His masterpiece is the Vor Frue Kirke, Copenhagen (1808). The interior has a wide coffered tunnel-vault, rows of Doric columns along the sides on an arcaded sub-structure, and an apse with semi-dome at the E. end. Along the nave stand the *Christ* and *12 Apostles* by Thorwaldsen.

Hanslick Eduard (1825–1904). Prague-born aesthetician and music critic who worked in Vienna and taught at the univ. His book *Vom musikalisch-Schönen* (1854) argues that music has no ulterior purpose. H. was the apostle of Brahms and attacked Wagner (who savaged him as Beckmesser in *The Mastersingers*) and the New German school inspired by Wagner and Liszt.

Hans von Tübingen (d. 1462). Austrian painter trained in France and Burgundy and active from 1433 in Wiener-Neustadt.

hard-paste: *porcelain

Hard Times (1854). Novel by *Dickens.

Hardwick Philip (1792–1870). English architect. He did work of all kinds–terraces of houses, churches, railway stations (Euston Arch, 1836: demolished 1963) and public buildings (Goldsmiths' Hall, London, 1829). His 'Greek' style was his best.

Hardwicke Sir Cedric (1893–1964). English actor. He played Caesar in Shaw's *Caesar and Cleopatra* and appeared often at the Malvern Festival. From 1939 he lived in the U.S., working in Hollywood; he had a season at the Old Vic in 1948.

Hardy Alexandre (*c.* 1570–1632). French playwright. His work attained unusual dramatic effectiveness by concentrating on action, omitting the chorus and employing relatively short monologues.

Hardy Thomas (1840–1928). English poet and novelist. H. became an architect and came to London in 1862. His poems were unrecognized and H. turned to writing novels. The greatest of them are notable for their evocation of S.W. England (which H. christened 'Wessex') and ironic yet compassionate description of men struggling to attain their ideals, thwarted by the mandates of Necessity in an indifferent or even hostile universe. This, combined with the sympathetic treatment of a 'fallen woman' in *Tess of the D'Urbervilles* (1891), and of a married man's adultery in *Jude the Obscure* (1895), finally made H. so unpopular that he returned to poetry. His other novels include *Far From the Madding Crowd* (publ. anon. 1874), *The Return of the Native* (1878), with its compelling descriptions of Egdon Heath, *The Mayor of Casterbridge* (1886) and the gentler lyrical *The Woodlanders* (1887). H.'s 2nd wife publ. a biography of him (1928–30) much of which he may in fact have written.

H.'s rugged and sinewy verse breaks with the Victorian tradition in its natural, conversational style, as in its tragic outlook. He wrote lyrics of an extraordinary variety throughout his life, including the moving poems about his 1st wife, Emma, in *A Procession of Dead Days* (1922). His most ambitious work was a poetic drama of epic length about the Napoleonic Wars, *The Dynasts* (1903–8), which is impressive if not entirely successful.

Häring Hugo (1882–1958). German architect widely respected, late in life, for his theory of 'organic' architecture, that a building's form should grow out of its function. Since he tackled each new problem without preconceived ideas his buildings have little overall unity, but a good sense of workability; his farm at Garkau, near Lübeck, is the best-known example.

Harington Sir John (1561–1612). English writer, Queen Elizabeth's godson. His best-known work is the trs. of Ariosto's *Orlando Furioso* (1591) containing a preface *Briefe Apologie for Poetrie*. He also wrote *The Metamorphosis of Ajax* (1596), on the water-closet (Ajax, i.e. 'a jakes'), a type of which he invented.

Harlequin, harlequinade. A name deriving from the 16th c. which describes scenes played

Sir John Harington

Häring. Garkau farm

Hardwick. Entrance portico, Euston Station

Hansen. Vor Frue Kirke

Harp. French instrument (*c.* 1779) with pedal action

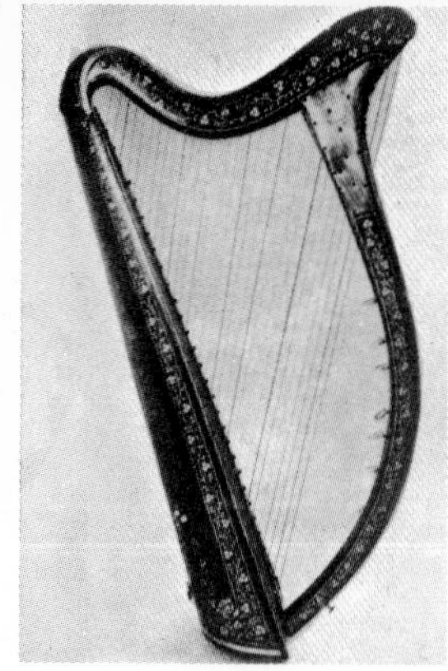

Irish harp (*c.* 1820)

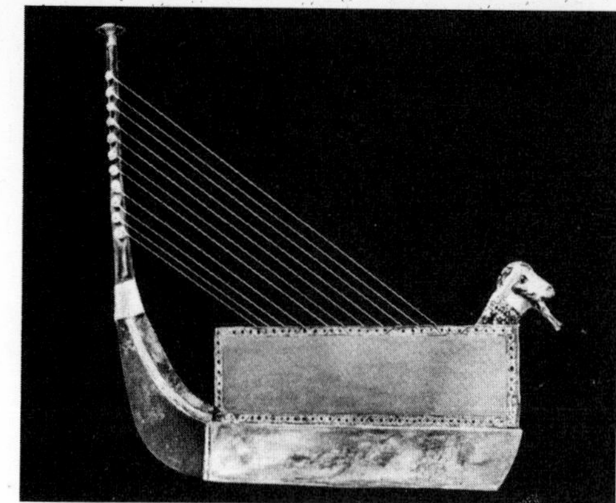

Harp from Ur. Like the Egyptian instrument (*right*) this is a bow harp, i.e. without a full frame

between the *commedia dell'arte* characters of Harlequin and Columbine. In the 17th c. Harlequin was a dancer who never spoke; by the 19th c. he had practically disappeared in pantomime, his character being overshadowed by the slapstick of the clown.

Harlow Jean (1911–37). U.S. film star. Blonde bombshell of the 1930s, turbulent and sentimental; her 1st big part was in *Hell's Angels* (1930). She also had some talent for sophisticated comedy.

harmonica. Musical instrument of the *reed organ family, also called the mouth-organ.

harmonic series. The notes derived from a single musical resonator. When, for example, a column of air (say an organ pipe) vibrates in its full length, it gives a single, clearly heard note (called the '1st harmonic' or 'fundamental') and a number of faint notes above this, called the 'upper harmonics' or 'upper partials'.
The interval between the fundamental and the 2nd harmonic is an 8ve; between the 2nd and 3rd harmonics a perfect 5th; between the 3rd and 4th a perfect 4th; between the 4th and 5th harmonics a 3rd; and so on, the intervals becoming progressively smaller. Thus a natural *horn in C (i.e. a brass tube 8 ft long) would have the following notes:

The characteristic tone colours of various instruments derive from the degree to which different harmonics predominate.

harmonic writing. A term descriptive of music in which 1 line, usually the top, is melodically predominant, being supported harmonically by a bass line, the other lines providing the harmonies thus dictated. This style of music gained ground in the 17th c. and finally supplanted contrapuntal music (*counterpoint) as the prevailing idiom in the early 18th c. Whereas in h. w. the parts, even if not of equal importance (*polyphony), can move independently, in homophony (Greek, 'same-sounding') the parts move together, in block chords, e.g. as in a hymn tune.

harmonium. Keyboard instrument of the *reed organ family. It has a range of about four 8ves from the C below the bass stave, is usually found as an accompanying instrument in small churches or chapels but has been occasionally used by composers, e.g. Webern in his *Pieces for Orchestra.*

harmony. In Western music, the art of combining sounds in a pleasing or meaningful way within a framework using keys or some system of tonality. Fundamental to 'classical' harmony in the system of major and minor *keys are the opposite concepts of *concord (sounds in equilibrium) and discord (sounds in tension), their conflicts and resolutions. 2 or more notes sounded together are called a chord; basic in Western music from the 17th to the 19th cs was the triad, formed by a note sounded together with 2 superimposed 3rds (*interval), e.g. ; this is the major triad of the key of C maj. in its 'root' position; there are 2 other ways (called 'inversions') of arranging the order of the notes e.g. the 1st inversion, and the 2nd inversion. New chords are formed by adding more 3rds. In a min. key the middle note of the triad (i.e. the 3rd above the root note) is flattened a semitone. The notes immediately available to the composer are those of the diatonic *scale of the key he is writing in (i.e. all the notes of this scale of C maj. in the key of C maj.) but he can modulate (i.e. move), according to certain rules, from key to key and can give heightened colour to his music by introducing notes not belonging to the diatonic scale (i.e. chromatic notes). Too extensive a use of such chromatic effects naturally weakens the sense of clearly defined keys, and increasing use of chromaticisms led in the 19th c. to the gradual break-up of the harmonic system of the maj. and min. keys and its replacement in the 20th c. by other systems, either non-harmonic (e.g. *12-note music) or based on other chords than the triad (e.g. chords built of superimposed 4ths), different scales or the use of more than 1 key simultaneously.

Harnett William Michael (1848–92). Irish-born U.S. still-life painter, a virtuoso exponent of *trompe l'œil* illusionism. Interest in his work was revived by the surrealists.

Harold in Italy. 'Symphony' by *Berlioz, for viola and orchestra, based on Byron's *Childe Harold.*

Harold in Italy. Ms. of the Theme, signed by Berlioz

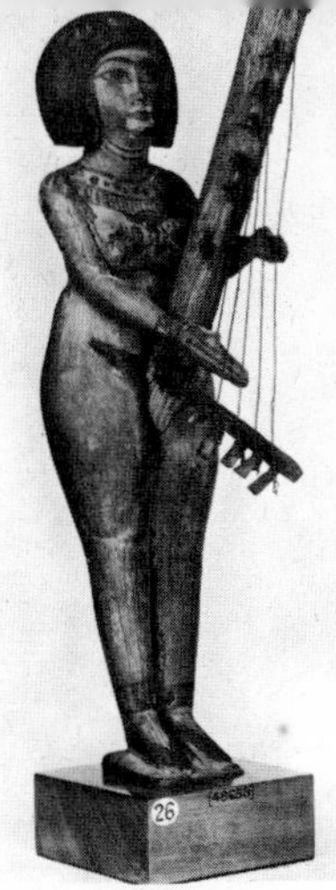

Egyptian bow harp

Harpsichord by Baffo of Venice, in embellished case (1574)

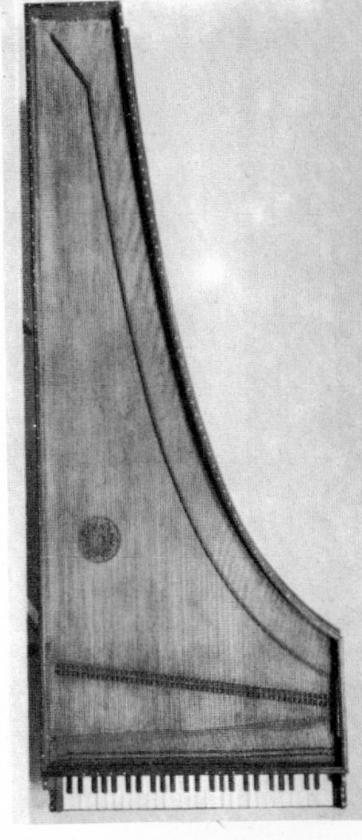

The same harpsichord, removed from its case, showing sound-board pierced by the row of jacks which carry the quills

harp. An ancient musical instrument, consisting basically of a frame on which are stretched strings of varying length and thickness, and thus of different pitches; these are sounded by being plucked with the fingers of one or both hands. The modern orchestral 'double action' h. has a range of about seven 8ves; the strings are tuned to the diatonic *scale of B maj. and a pedal action of 7 pedals allows each degree of the scale to be raised by either a semitone or a tone. By this means the diatonic scale is possible in all keys but the instrument is virtually incapable of a chromatic scale, i.e. one with all the semitones.

Harper's Magazine founded as *Harper's New Monthly Magazine* in 1850. In its 1st years it serialized the works of the popular English novelists such as Dickens, Thackeray and George Eliot. Later these were displaced by American writers such as W. D. Howells, Mark Twain and Booth Tarkington.

Harpignies Henri-Joseph (1819–1916). French landscape painter, a follower of Corot.

harpsichord. With the organ, the major keyboard instrument from the Renaissance to the late 18th c. The strings are plucked (not struck, as on the *piano) by a short quill forced up by pressure on the key. Modulated variations of dynamics cannot be obtained by striking the key harder or lighter (*piano) but, to make possible various tone qualities, each note may have 3 or 4 different types of string made available by adjusting hand stops; larger instruments usually had 2 manuals (i.e. keyboards) each with its own sets of strings, thus increasing the possibilities of variety. The h. has been revived in the 20th c. primarily for early music, but modern composers write for it.

Harris Frank (1856–1931). Irish-born writer; he became a prominent literary personality in London, editing *The Fortnightly Review* and *Saturday Review*. He wrote an autobiography about his literary and sexual adventures, *My Life and Loves* (1923–7; unexpurgated 1964).

Harris Joel Chandler (1848–1908). U.S. journalist, humorous writer and novelist, famous as the author of *Uncle Remus, His Songs and His Sayings* (1880) and many more colls of stories in dialect which are supposedly told by the old Negro Uncle Remus and concern Brer Rabbit, Brer Fox and other animals.

Harris Lawren (Stewart) (1885–). Canadian painter, one of the *Group of Seven; he also wrote verse.

Harris Roy Ellsworth (1898–). U.S. composer who studied under Farwell and Nadia Boulanger. His music, which is often avowedly patriotic, includes: *Symphony for voices* (1935) using texts from Walt Whitman, *A Folksong Symphony* (1939), *Johnny Comes Marching Home* for orchestra (1934); violin and piano concertos; choral works; a piano quintet (1936) and other chamber music.

Harrison Julius Alan Greenway (1885–). English composer and conductor. His work, which includes the mass in C (1948), draws on English folk-songs and shows similarities to Vaughan Williams.

Harsanyi Tibor (1898–1954). Hungarian-born composer who studied under Kodály, but, resident in Paris from the 1920s, was influenced by Debussy. He wrote *Illusion* (1949) and 1 other opera; 3 ballets; the symphony in C (1951); divertimento no. 2 for trumpet and strings (1943); chamber works and much piano music.

Harsdörffer Georg Philipp (1607–58). German poet, member of the literary society the Fruchtbringende Gesellschaft and a founder of the society of the Pegnitz Shepherds. His handbook on poetry, *Der Nürnberger Trichter* (1647–53), extends the theories of Opitz.

Hart. The German critics, the brothers HEINRICH (1855–1906) and JULIUS (1859–1930), by attacking such contemporary novelists as Spielhagen pioneered the way to a greater realism. Jointly they ed. such magazines as *Kritische Waffengänge* (1882).

Hart William S. (1876–1946). U.S. film actor who became a tough realistic hero of western films directed by Thomas H. Ince.

Harte (Francis) Bret(t) (1836–1902). U.S. short-story writer, poet and journalist who capitalized on his experiences in the West, using local colour and dialect in the creation of the melodramatic, picturesque, sentimental, and enormously popular world depicted in such short-story colls as *The Luck of Roaring Camp and Other Sketches* (1870). H.'s abilities

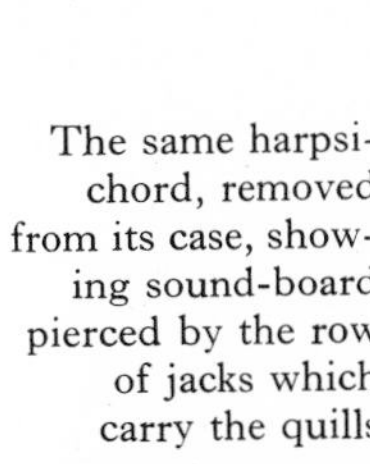

Bret Harte

Frank Harris

Harpignies. *Summer*

Marsden Hartley. *The Old Bars, Dogtown* (1936)

Hartigan. *Grand Street Brides*

Hartung. *Painting T54–16*

as a parodist are shown in the coll. *Condensed Novels and Other Papers* (1870) and the comic poem *Plain Language from Truthful James* (1870).

Hartford Wits, The known also as 'The Connecticut Wits'. A group of American Federalist writers of the late 18th and early 19th c., producing political satire. The chief members were J. *Trumbull, T. *Dwight, R. *Alsop, D. *Humphreys and J. *Barlow, all of Yale College.

Hart House Theatre. Small experimental theatre founded in 1918 in the Univ. of Toronto. For a time it was used as a professional theatre, Raymond Massey acting and directing there, but it is now exclusively used by undergraduates.

Hartigan Grace (1922–). U.S. abstract expressionist painter influenced by de Kooning. She made her 1st abstract paintings in 1948; after a period of figurative work (1952–5) in which she painted *Grand Street Brides* (1954; Whitney Mus., New York) she returned to abstraction but her compositions almost always relate indirectly to her environment.

Hartley L(eslie) P(oles) (1895–). English novelist. H.'s *The Go-Between* (1953) is a study of a boy's involvement in adult conflicts and its effect on his personality. H.'s novels include *The Shrimp and the Anemone* (1944), *A Perfect Woman* (1955) and *Facial Justice* (1960).

Hartley Marsden (1877–1943). U.S. painter and poet, best remembered for his paintings of his native state, Maine, e.g. *Camden Hills From Baker's Island, Penobscot Bay* (Univ. of Minnesota), though his extensive travels in Mexico, the West Indies, France and Germany also inspired many works, e.g. *Portrait of a German Officer*, or *Painting No. 5 1914* (Met. Mus.).

Hartmann Karl Amadeus (1905–) German composer; a pupil of Webern but not a strict serialist. His works include the opera *Des Simplicius Simplicissimus Jugend* (1949, written 1934; new version 1955); symphonies, concertos for violin, for piano and for viola and piano, and 2 string quartets. In 1945 he founded Musica Viva for the performance of modern music.

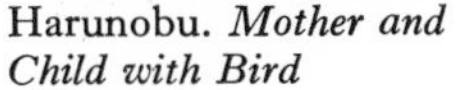
Harunobu. *Mother and Child with Bird*

Hassam. *Washington Arch, Spring*

Jaroslav Hašek

Hathaway. James Stewart and Carroll Baker in *How the West was Won*

Hartmann Moritz (1821–72). Austrian writer and journalist of radical political views; after exile in Paris he worked (from 1868) for *Neue Freie Presse*. His literary output includes short stories and political verse, e.g. *Kelch und Schwert* (1845), and *Reimchronik des Pfaffen Mauritius* (1849).

Hartmann von Aue (*c.* 1170–*c.* 1215). German poet. He took part in the 3rd Crusade but little else is known of his life. He was admired by Gottfried von Strassburg for the clarity and purity of his style as the greatest German poet of his time and his influence on Gottfried is noticeable. H.'s works include the Arthurian epics *Erec* and *Iwein*, derived from Chrétien de Troyes, and the lyric narrative *Der arme Heinrich*.

Hartung Hans (1904–). German-born painter of the school of *Paris. He was painting abstract watercolours in 1922. He later travelled in Italy, Holland and France and in 1935 settled in Paris. Although the elements of his paintings are simple–a network of swift but calculated lines on a contrasting background–he achieves great variety within these limits.

Harty Sir Herbert Hamilton (1879–1941). English composer, and conductor from 1920 to 1933 of the Hallé Orchestra. His works include the cantata *The Mystic Trumpeter* (1913) on a text from Walt Whitman.

Hartzenbusch Juan Eugenio (1806–80). Spanish poet and playwright (son of a German father), and a student of classical Spanish literature. His highly romantic drama *Los Amantes de Teruel* (1837) was a huge success, and his later plays, e.g. *Doña Mencía* (1838), are equally distinguished for their passionate sense of drama and strong, powerful language.

Harunobu Suzuki (*c.* 1725–70). The great 18th-c. master of the Japanese colour print. His main themes were girlhood and scenes from everyday life, and he endowed these commonplace subjects with a grace and beauty far excelling anything in the Japanese tradition before or after his time.

Harvey Gabriel (1550?–1631?). English writer, friend of Spenser, over whom he exerted some influence with his predilection for classical metres; he claimed to be the originator of the English hexameter. His attacks on Nashe and, in *Foure Letters . . .* (1592), on Greene (publ. after Greene's death), started an interchange of pamphlet invective between him and Nashe.

Harvey Sir John Martin- (1863–1944). English actor-manager who at one time managed the Lyceum Theatre. He was a romantic actor but also achieved great success in the title-role of *Oedipus Rex*, produced by Max Reinhardt in 1912.

Háry János. Opera and orchestral suite by *Kodály.

Has Wojciech (1925–). Polish film director. H. is one of the most interesting of post-war Polish directors. His romanticism found its most satisfactory expression on the screen in the delicate *Farewells* (1958).

Hašek Jaroslav (1883–1923). Czech novelist. After an erratic career as a bohemian humorous journalist, practical joker, soldier, prisoner-of-war and Bolshevik commissar, H. returned to Czechoslovakia and wrote the unfinished *Osudy dobrého vojáka Švejka* (1920–4; *The Good Soldier Schweik*, 1930), certainly the funniest book about World War I. The hero is Schweik, a subnormal dog-stealer drafted into the Imperial Austrian army; he gets into a series of scrapes with his bungling superiors, but his disarming mixture of candour and cunning always enable him to escape.

Haskell Arnold (1903–). English critic and writer on ballet, and a prime mover in the establishment of the Sadler's Wells School (1947). He has written many books on ballet, *Balletomania* (1934), *Ballet* (1938), etc.

Haskin Byron (1899–). U.S. film director. He has specialized in westerns and adventure films, e.g. *Treasure Island* (1949). He also made science-fiction films, including H. G.*Wells's *War of the Worlds* (1953) for effects expert George Pal, who also produced H.'s best picture, *The Naked Jungle* (1953).

Hassam Childe (1859–1935). U.S. painter and graphic artist. After studying in Boston he went to Paris, where he was strongly influenced by the technique and high colour range of the impressionists. He was one of the 1st U.S. artists to adopt impressionism and also to paint the New York scene.

Hassan (1922). Play by James Elroy *Flecker.

Hasse Johann Adolf (1699–1783). German opera composer, called in Italy the 'divine Saxon'. He studied with Porpora and A. Scarlatti at Naples; married the famous soprano singer Faustina Bordoni; was director of the Dresden court opera (1734–73) and retired to Venice. His music was praised by both J. S. Bach and Berlioz; it includes over 50 Italian operas, largely to librettos by Metastasio; oratorios, chamber and keyboard music.

Hassler Hans Leo (1564–1612). German composer who studied with A. Gabrieli in Venice; H. was the 1st important German composer to study in Italy. He held organist appointments in Augsburg, Nuremberg, Ulm, Prague and Dresden. H. wrote much church music, e.g. the motets *Cantiones sacrae* (1591, 97, 1607) and madrigals and canzonets, but most important is his work as a melodist in the coll. of songs *Lustgarten neuer teutscher Gesäng* (1601, 05, 10).

hatching. To create the effect of tone or shadow by a series of parallel lines or, in the case of CROSS-HATCHING, of parallel lines crossed by others.

Hathaway Henry (1898–). U.S. film director. Specializing in adventure films, he quickly became successful with *Lives of a Bengal Lancer* (1935), *Peter Ibbetson* (1935), and *The Trail of Lonesome Pine* (1936), the first Technicolor film shot on location. He has a reputation for his 1940s documentary-style thrillers, e.g. *The House on 92nd Street* (1945) and *Call Northside 777* (1948). As a top contract director at Fox he was responsible for such diverse works as *Kiss of Death* (1947), which launched Richard Widmark as a psychopath, and *Niagara* (1952) which launched Marilyn Monroe as a vamp. His best films are *Prince Valiant* (1954), from an Arthurian strip cartoon, *Legend of the Lost* (1957), where the characters (like those of *Garden of Evil*, 1954) are exposed to the elemental truths of nature, *North to Alaska* (1960), a burlesque 'western' set in the Far North and his three-fifths of *How the West was Won*.

Hauch Johannes Carsten (1790–1872). Danish poet and novelist. His early work was inspired by Oehlenschlaeger and H. became a leading figure of Danish romantic literature. He wrote historical novels modelled on those of Sir Walter Scott.

Hauer Joseph Matthias (1883–). Austrian composer whose theories on atonal composition are now recognized as antedating Schoenberg's 12-note system and the note row. H. developed his ideas by analogy from Goethe's colour theory of light. Romanticism underlies H.'s compositions, e.g. the cantata *Der Menschen Weg* (1934; revised 1952) is based, like other of his works, on texts from Hölderlin.

Gerhart Hauptmann

Hauptmann Gerhart (Johann Robert) (1862–1946). German dramatist. A Silesian, he studied agriculture and art in Breslau, sculpted in Rome, and became in Berlin the leading naturalist writer, associated with the *Frele Bühne (1889). A prolific and varied author, his reputation is now uncertain: perhaps his centre of interest lies in the psychology of human failure. His success sprang from contemporary problem plays influenced by the Ibsen of *Ghosts*. They use the 'slice-of-life' technique (inconclusive structure, broken syntax, dialect), with the slice always from the seamy side; lengthy stage-directions are designed to establish precisely the milieu, which is all-important; the viewpoint is deterministic, pessimistic. Best known are *Vor Sonnenaufgang* (1889; *Before Dawn*, 1909) and *Einsame Menschen* (1891; *Lonely Lives*, 1898), but more rewarding are *Fuhrmann Henschel* (1898) and *Rose Bernd* (1903). A similar technique was applied to historical material in *Die Weber* (1893; *The Weavers*, 1899) and, very successfully, to comedy in *Der Biberpelz* (1893). A romantic, even symbolist tendency, latent in earlier work, became explicit in *Hannele* (1893; 1894), reappearing in *Die versunkene Glocke* (1897; *The Sunken Bell*, 1899); henceforth naturalism and romantic idealism co-exist in H.'s work, e.g. in the intriguing, enigmatic novel *Der Narr in Christo Emanuel Quint* (1910; *The Fool in Christ: Emanuel Quint*, 1911). Later, H.'s writings became disorientated, attempting sometimes to revive naturalism (*Vor Sonnenuntergang*, 1932), and sometimes to modernize classical myths.

Sir John Hawkins

Haussman Georges-Eugène (1809–91). French town planner who, as prefect of the Seine department under Napoleon III, drove the boulevards through Paris to make its buildings 'more pleasing to the eye, afford easier access on days of celebration and simplify defence on days of riot'. The characteristic quality of the boulevards is due to his tree planting and to his use of standardized façades, very restrained by 19th-c. standards.

hautboy or **hoboy.** Anglicized form of the French for 'high (i.e. loud) wood', and an old name for *oboe.

Havelock the Dane, The Lay of. 14th-c. English poem.

Haviland George (1792–1852). English architect who emigrated to the U.S. in 1816. He specialized in prison architecture, e.g. the Eastern State Penitentiary, Philadelphia, an advanced building for its time. His Miners' Bank, Pottsville, Pa., is an early use of cast-iron in architecture.

Hawker Robert Stephen (1803–75). English poet and clergyman, vicar of Morwenstow in 'Arthurian' Cornwall, which suggested more than one of his poems. Best known for his *The Song of the Western Men*, and for the eccentricity of his life.

Hawkins Coleman (1904–). U.S. tenor saxophonist; the 1st jazz musician to adapt successfully the tenor saxophone to jazz. His majestic and full-toned style made him the most influential musician on this instrument until the advent of Lester Young. His recording of *Body and Soul* (1939) was a landmark in jazz history, and he remains a prolific improviser.

Hawkins Jack (1910–). English film star whose solid integrity has been seen in many roles–spectacular, e.g. *The Bridge on the River Kwai* (1957), and small scale, e.g. *The Prisoner* (1955).

Hawkins Sir John (1719–89). Author of *General History of the Science and Practice of Music* (5 vols 1776). It is unsystematic, but contains valuable information on 18th-c. musical life, much old music not previously printed, and many references useful to, among others, C. *Burney. H. also publ. (1787–9) a biography of his friend Dr Johnson and an ed. of his works.

Hawks Howard W. (1896–). U.S. film director. His 1st important film was *A Girl in*

Haussman. Boulevard Richard-Lenoir

Every Port (1928). H. is one of the most consistent and professional of Hollywood directors, with a strong personal style and approach. He has made adventure films: *Only Angels Have Wings* (1939), *The Dawn Patrol* (1930); thrillers: *Scarface* (1932), *To Have and Have Not* (1944), *The Big Sleep* (1946); westerns: *Red River* (1948), *Rio Bravo* (1959); personal films: *Sergeant York* (1941). In all of them appears the elemental H. hero, a man of whom courage is demanded by his job, which he carries through because he is a professional, with no sense of heroic display. Reversing this theme, H. makes many of his comedies hinge on the destruction of male self-respect, usually by a woman: *Twentieth Century* (1934), *Bringing Up Baby* (1938), *His Girl Friday* (1941), *I Was a Male War Bride* (1949), *Monkey Business* (1952). H. also made the musical *Gentlemen Prefer Blondes* (1953), from the Anita *Loos novel.

Hawksmoor Nicholas (1661–1736). English baroque architect. He began as a pupil and assistant of Wren, later holding several posts in the Office of Works and also acting as assistant to Sir John *Vanbrugh at Castle Howard and Blenheim. Of his secular buildings the most important are: the Clarendon Building, Oxford; All Saints College, Oxford (in Gothic, to harmonize with the chapel); and the Mausoleum of Castle Howard (a lonely circular building surrounded by a huge colonnade). In London he designed 6 churches of outstanding quality which show him to be in many ways the most original English architect since the middle ages: St Alphege, Greenwich; St Anne's, Limehouse; St George's-in-the-East, Wapping (gutted in 1941); St Mary Woolnoth, City; St George's, Bloomsbury; and Christchurch, Spitalfields (badly damaged). All are extremely personal, even eccentric buildings, freely using towers, steeples, columns, cornices, niches, porticoes, etc., for the sake of exciting and dramatic effects. In this respect he is close to Italian baroque (which he never saw) but he retains a dignity and massiveness that derive from his study of ancient Roman architecture. H. also built the 2 W. towers of Westminster Abbey and the steeple of St Michael's, Cornhill, London; but he was not at his best in Gothic.

Hawthorne Nathaniel (1804–64). U.S. novelist. Most of his life was spent uneventfully at Salem and Concord, apart from a brief stay (1841) in the utopian, communistic community at Brook Farm, Massachussetts (recounted in *The Blithedale Romance*, 1852) and 7 years (1853–9) in the consular service in England and Italy.

H.'s themes of guilt, intellectual pride, and secret sensuousness, reach their greatest form in his novel *The Scarlet Letter* (1850), set in 17th-c. Salem. Hester Prynne is publicly condemned as an adulteress and must wear the scarlet letter 'A'; Arthur Dimmesdale, the minister, the father of her child, eventually confesses; but the real sinner is the revengeful Roger Chillingworth, Hester's husband, who tries to control Dimmesdale. To H. the 'unpardonable sin' was the violation of the human soul, a theme present in *The House of the Seven Gables* (1851), a novel with a contemporary setting, about a family curse, and in the Faustian myth *Ethan Brand*, one of the stories in *The Snow Image and Other Twice-Told Tales* (1851). *The Marble Faun* (1860), in which H.'s themes and characters are transported to Rome, anticipates Henry James in its treatment of Americans in Europe. Works include the story colls *Twice-Told Tales* (1837) and *Mosses from an Old Manse* (1846), and *Tanglewood Tales* (1853), a children's book retelling some of the Greek myths.

Hayden Henri (1883–). Polish-born painter who settled in Paris in 1907. His interest in Cézanne and a meeting with Gris and Delaunay in 1916 led him to work as a cubist, but in 1922 he turned to a more traditional style.

Haydn Franz Joseph (1732–1809). Austrian composer; his fine soprano voice enabled him to go to Vienna (1740) as a singer at St Stephen's; later he was an accompanist at Porpora's singing academy, receiving lessons in return. In 1760 he contracted his unfortunate marriage with an insensitive and ill-tempered wife; in 1761 he joined the service of the Esterházy family, becoming director of music in 1766; in 1769 the court moved from Eisenstadt to Esterháza. In 1790 the musical establishment was disbanded but H. retained the title of Kapellmeister and a large pension; his comparative freedom enabled him to leave Austria for the 1st time and in the years 1791–2 and 1794–5 he visited London at the instance of the violinist Salomon. H. was fêted, received an honorary degree at Oxford (1792) when the 'Oxford' symphony was first performed, and also made 24,000 gulden. He died in

Hawks. Marilyn Monroe in *Gentlemen Prefer Blondes*

Nathaniel Hawthorne

Haydn

Hawksmoor. St. George's, Bloomsbury

Hawksmoor. Castle Howard Mausoleum

Hayman. *May Day*

Haydon. *Chairing the Member*

Haymarket Theatre when newly built (1821), showing the position of the previous theatre before its demolition

Hayter. *Etching* (1924). Also *Atelier 17

Haydn. Ms. from *The Creation*, signed by H.

Vienna a few days after Napoleon captured the city.

H. was for a time the teacher of Beethoven and from 1782 he and Mozart came to know each other well. Both his great younger contemporaries were indebted to H. and his friendship with Mozart inspired H. himself in his last great period. His music has a unique vigour and strength, passages of the sweetest lyricism, touches of wit and the occasional telling use of folk-tunes; all this within an impeccable formal framework. At its full maturity H.'s music is the embodiment of the classical style of the late 18th c. Historically his long career as a composer spans the period from the late baroque to the beginnings of romanticism. By the 1770s he had become master of the emerging forms of the symphony, piano sonata and string quartet, all of which he moulded into their accepted classical forms. In the early 1780s he produced a number of operas and other stage works and the orchestral *Seven Last Words* (1785) for church use during Lent; he went on to compose the great series of 'London' symphonies. After 1795 a new burst of creative energy resulted in the 6 great masses and the oratorios *The Creation* (1798), on passages from Genesis and Milton's *Paradise Lost*, and *The Seasons* (1801), with words from J. *Thomson's poem.

His works include: 18 operatic works; church music including the 'Drum' mass in C (1796), the *Heiligmesse* in B♭ maj. (1796), the 'Nelson' mass in D min., also called 'Imperial' or 'Coronation' (1798), the *Theresien Mass* in B♭ maj. (1799), the *Creation Mass* (1801) in B♭ maj. and the *Harmoniemesse* in B♭ maj. (1802). The symphonies: no. 6 in D *Le Matin*, no. 7 in C *Le Midi*, no. 8 in G *Le Soir* (all *c.* 1761); no. 22 in E♭ *The Philosopher* (1764); no. 26 in D *Lamentation*; no. 43 in E♭ *Merkur* (*c.* 1771); no. 44 in E *Trauer* (*c.* 1771); no. 45 in F♯ min. the 'Farewell' (1772) in which in the last movement the music dwindles and the players leave their seats one by one, a hint to the prince that the musicians wished to return to Vienna; no. 48 in C *Maria Theresia* (1772/3); no. 55 in E♭ *The Schoolmaster*; no. 73 in D *La Chasse* ('The Hunt') (1781); the 6 'Paris' symphonies (1786), among them *L'Ours*, *La Poule* and *La Reine*; no. 92 in G the 'Oxford' (written *c.* 1788); the 'London' or 'Salomon' symphonies, including no. 94 in G the *Surprise* (1791); no. 96 in D the 'Miracle' (1791; at its 1st performance a falling chandelier miraculously hurt no one); no. 100 in G the 'Military' (1794), using *Janissary music; no. 103 in E♭ the 'Drum-Roll' (1795), and no. 104 in D the 'London' (1795). His other works include: 84 quartets, piano concertos, violin concertos, a concerto for the keyed trumpet (1796), over 100 works for baryton and more than 50 piano sonatas.

Haydon Benjamin Robert (1786–1846). English historical painter and writer, a friend of Wordsworth and Keats. His attempts to paint in the grand manner were not successful and he committed suicide after imprisonment for debt. *Chairing the Member* (Tate) is an example of his style. In his clear-eyed and vivid *Autobiography and Memoirs* H. discusses art patronage and chronicles the art world of his time.

Hayman Francis (1708–76). English painter and book illustrator, founder-member of the R.A. He was best known for his decorative paintings at Vauxhall Gardens, London (2 of these are in the V. and A.). He also painted portraits and small portrait groups which influenced the young Gainsborough. H.'s work shows French influence, possibly through contact with H. Gravelot.

Haymarket Theatre. The 2nd oldest theatre in London, founded in 1720. The original building was demolished in 1820 and the present one opened in 1821. Among the famous actor-managers who have controlled the theatre have been Cibber and Beerbohm Tree.

Hayter Stanley (William) (1901–). English graphic artist responsible for giving a new impetus to engraving techniques, widely extending their field of reference by his imaginative use of mixed techniques. In Paris he founded (1927) the very influential experimental workshop *Atelier 17.

Hay Wain, The. Painting by *Constable based on a scene near Flatford Mill in Suffolk. Also the name for one of *Bosch's major paintings.

Hayworth Rita (1919–). U.S. film star, a top sultry sex symbol until the middle 1940s, reaching a peak with *Gilda* (1946).

Hazlitt William (1778–1830). English essayist. In 1798 he met Coleridge, and this experience inspired him to write, though without much success until 1805. In 1812 he became a journalist, pioneering independent dramatic criticism. His writing displays pungent good

William Hazlitt. Also *Lamb

sense, and his pure style is flexible and eloquent. Other essayists achieve finer moments but none are more consistently stimulating. *The Spirit of the Age* (1825) contains the best of much perceptive, if sometimes bad-tempered literary criticism. He attacked Wordsworth and Coleridge for abandoning their radical beliefs, but continued to admire much of their work. His best essays are in *Table-Talk* (1821–2), *The Plain Speaker* (1826), and *Winterslow* (1850) but he also gave popular lectures, which were publ. in such vols as *The English Comic Writers* (1819).

headvoice: *chest voice

Hearn (Patricio) Lafcadio (Tessima Carlos) (1850–1904). U.S. novelist and travel writer, of Anglo-Greek parentage and brought up in Dublin. H. emigrated to the U.S. in 1869. He was strongly influenced by French writers, especially Gautier, whom he trs. His style was delicate and precise, his subjects exotic: e.g. the novels *Chita: A Memory of Last Island* (1889) and *Youma* (1890), are set in the West Indies; and from 1890 H. lived in Japan, about which he wrote many books.

Heartbreak House (1917). Play by G. B. *Shaw.

Heart is a Lonely Hunter, The (1940). Novel by Carson *McCullers.

Heart of Midlothian (1818). Historical novel by *Scott.

Heart of the Matter, The (1948). Novel by Graham *Greene.

Heath-Stubbs John (1918–). English poet and critic. His verse, neo-romantic in tone, has a stringent diction and felicitous rhythms. Colls include *Wounded Thammuz* (1942) and *The Triumph of the Muse* (1958).

Heaton Anne (1930–). British dancer who became a soloist with the Sadler's Wells Theatre Ballet (1945). She developed primarily as a classical dancer and with the senior co. danced Giselle (1954); a sensitive dancer, she interpreted the role with a new simplicity. She has now left the co. and makes occasional appearances in musicals.

Heaven and Hell, The Marriage of (1790–3). Prose work by William Blake.

Hebbel (Christian) Friedrich (1813–63). German playwright, and an important lyric poet. His parents were very poor and he had a precarious existence in his early years, though supported by Elise Lensing, by whom he had 2 sons; however, he deserted her and married (1846) the rich and influential actress Christine Enghaus, an act which he justified as being demanded by the necessities of his poetic talent.

H.'s great contribution to the development of the drama was his psychological perception and grasp of motive; hence he was able to reinterpret fruitfully the Biblical story (*Judith*, 1840) and medieval legend (*Genoveva*, 1843), as well as creating the 'tragedy of common life' *Maria Magdalena* (1844). In H.'s later tragedies there is still psychological observation, but it is overshadowed by larger themes (the claims of the individual and of the state, etc.); they include *Agnes Bernauer* (1852) and the verse tragedies *Herodes and Mariamne* (1849; 1938), *Gyges und sein Ring* (1856) and the trilogy *Die Nibelungen* (1855–6; 1921). H. also wrote comedies, and a revealing diary, *Tagebücher* (1885–7).

Hecht Ben (1892–1964). U.S. writer and film director. An ex-journalist who wrote the script for *Underworld* and became a leading Hollywood writer until his death, e.g. for **Scarface*, *Nothing Sacred* and Hathaway's *Legend of the Lost* (1957). Many of the plays he wrote with Charles McArthur in the 1930s were filmed, including *Twentieth Century*. They also directed with cameraman Lee Garmes *The Scoundrel* (1935) and others. H. also directed with Garmes and alone (*Actors and Sin*, 1952).

Heckel. German firm of woodwind instrument makers which perfected the modern German bassoon and, following a suggestion by Wagner for an instrument an 8ve lower than the oboe and with a tone quality similar to the alphorn, produced the HECKELPHONE. This double-reed instrument is conical in bore and about $4\frac{1}{2}$ ft long. It was first used by R. Strauss in *Salome* (1905).

Heckel Erich (1883–). German expressionist painter and graphic artist, with Kirchner and Schmidt-Rottluf founder of Die Brücke. The brooding introspection of his work up to 1920 gradually diminished and he turned away from expressionism, developing a more decorative

Anne Heaton

Friedrich Hebbel

Heckel. *Day of Glass* (1913)

Cornelis de Heem. *Still-life with fruit and oysters*

Heifitz. *The Lady with a Little Dog*

Heemskerck. *Self-portrait with the Colosseum*

Hegel

style and a lyrical sensitivity to landscape. He produced important woodcuts such as *The Crouching One* (1914) which conveys his tragic sense of man's isolation.

Heda Willem Claesz (1594–1682). Dutch still-life painter who worked in Haarlem in the manner of P. Claesz. H.'s son GERRIT WILLEMSZ worked in the same style.

Hedda Gabler (1890). Play by *Ibsen.

Heem Jan Davidsz de (1606–83/4). Dutch still-life painter, as was his father, DAVID DE H. (1570–1632). He worked mainly in Antwerp but also in Leyden and Utrecht. He specialized in elaborate flower pieces influenced by those of D. Seghers but used a lighter range of colours. He had many pupils and imitators including his son CORNELIS (1631–95).

Heemskerck Maerten Jacobsz van (1498–1574). Dutch painter of portraits and religious subjects, pupil of J. van Scorel, from whom he learned an Italianate style which he further established in Rome (1532–5). There he made sketches which give important information about the appearance of classical monuments in the 16th c. His *Self-portrait with the Colosseum* is in the Fitzwilliam Mus., Cambridge.

Hegel Georg Wilhelm Friedrich (1770–1831). German philosopher of great influence in spite of his tortuous style. H.'s major contribution to philosophy was to establish the importance of the history of philosophy, especially in his *Phänomenologie des Geistes* (1807; *Phenomenology of Mind*, 1910); philosophies are regarded not as rivals but as stages in the development of the human spirit, a more mature outlook often emerging from 2 extremes. This system of dialectic–thesis and antithesis producing a new synthesis–was adapted by Karl Marx. Works include *Philosophie des Rechts* (1821; *Philosophy of Right*, 1855) and *Logik* (1812; *The Subjective Logic of Hegel*, 1855).

Heiberg Johan Ludvig (1791–1860). Danish man of letters. For a time he was professor of Danish at Kiel Univ., returning to Copenhagen in 1825. He was director of the Danish National Theatre from 1847 to 1854. He wrote a number of comedies modelled on the French vaudeville, much important literary criticism and articles criticizing the excesses of romanticism. Among his more important plays are the comedy *En Sjael efter Døden* (1841) and the romantic play on national themes, *Elverhoi* (1828).

Heidegger Martin (1889–). German philosopher. In spite of his protests H. is invariably held to be the father of modern existentialism. His most important work, *Sein und Zeit* (1927), has strongly influenced philosophers and writers in France, Germany and Belgium.

Heidenstam Verner von (1859–1940). Swedish writer and Nobel prizewinner (1916). His poems, mostly written before 1900, are among the finest lyrics in Swedish; as a prose writer he produced a number of increasingly nationalistic historical studies.

Heifetz Jascha (1901–). Russian-born U.S. Jewish violinist. He rapidly gained an international reputation both by a technique distinguished by unfailing intonation and singing purity of tone and by his musicianship. He commissioned concertos from L. Gruenberg and W. Walton.

Heifitz Joseph (1905–). Soviet film director. H. made with Alexander Zharki one of the most famous Soviet films of the 1930s, *Baltic Deputy* (1937). He started directing alone in 1954 and in 1960 made *The Lady with a Little Dog* from Chekhov, a film widely admired for its atmospheric evocation of a period.

Heimskringla (12th c.). Norse history by *Snorri Sturluson.

Heine Heinrich (1797–1856). German poet; born in Düsseldorf, the child of a Jewish merchant. He entered his uncle's bank, studied (1819–25) in Bonn, Göttingen and Berlin, adopted Christianity in 1825 and in 1831 emigrated to Paris. One of the few lyric poets whose work has been a commercial success, H. attracted attention at home and abroad. His work was admired, not always for aesthetic reasons but for its witty gibes at the political and religious establishment; its confessional element; its reflection of contemporary *Weltschmerz*; and its shrewd mixture of sentiment and irony: characteristic is the emotional build-up followed by the last-line pin-prick, often an outrageous rhyme. He is linked with romanticism by his cult of emotion, his feeling for nature and the supernatural, and his breaks

Heinrich Heine

Hélion. *Painting* (1935)

of mood (romantic irony); with the *Young Germany movement by anti-authoritarian views, which led to the suppression of his works in 1835. H. exports well because his attraction depends on relatively conscious linguistic fireworks and on a warm if quirky humanity. The bitter-sweet flavour is well caught by Schumann in the *Dichterliebe* cycle, from *Buch der Lieder* (1827; *The Book of Songs*, 1856); it reappears in his travel books, especially *Die Harzreise* (1826; *Tour in the Harz*, 1846). Later poems–*Romanzero* (1851; *Romancero*, 1892–1905)–reveal a somewhat more objective projection of personality, sometimes through the ballad, and a more sombre outlook, intensified in the poems (publ. posth.) written during his last years when he was confined to his bed with a spinal disease.

Heinrich von Veldecke. 12th-c. poet born near Maastricht. He was admired by Gottfried von Strassburg. H.'s *Eneit* (*c.* 1190), based on a French courtly version of Virgil's *Aeneid*, was the 1st German court epic. He also produced a trs. of the legend of St Servatius (*c.* 1170).

Heinse Johann Jakob Wilhelm (1746–1803). German novelist whose passionate *Ardinghello . . .* (1787), publ. on his return from a stay in Rome, deals with an artist who founds a utopia; it is in effect the 1st **Kunstlerroman* and has considerable importance in the European romantic movement.

Heinsius Daniel (1580–1655). Dutch scholar and poet. His work is important in that it transmitted the Renaissance forms learnt from du Bartas into Dutch literature.

Heisler Stuart (1894–). U.S. film director. Although he has tackled most genres, including the musical (*Blue Skies*, 1946) and the problem picture (*Storm Warning*, 1950), his staple work has been action films.

Heldenleben, Ein. Symphonic poem by R. *Strauss.

Heliand. 9th-c. Saxon poem in the form and using the techniques of the medieval epic; its subject however is the Christian Gospel and its aim evangelical.

Hélion Jean (1904–). French painter. He collaborated with van Doesburg on the pamphlet *Art Concret* and was a member of the Abstraction-Création group. He spent several years in the U.S. After working under the influence of the cubists and Mondrian he reverted to representational painting.

Helladic. Term applied to the early architecture of mainland Greece, and including that of the Mycenaean period; the H. period ends with the Dorian invasions, *c.* 1100 B.C.

Heller Joseph (1923–). U.S. novelist, author of the anti-war novel *Catch-22* (1961), a farcical, fantastic, satirical and macabre account of the U.S. Air Force in Italy during World War II.

Heller Stephen (1813–88). Hungarian-born pianist and romantic composer, living in Paris from the 1830s. His piano music, mostly short pieces with programmatic titles, avoided virtuosity for its own sake; it includes a well-known tarantella.

Hellinger Mark (1903–47). U.S. film producer. H. worked on Broadway with Ziegfeld before becoming a script writer and then producer. With L. de *Rochemont he pioneered the journalistic documentary look for thrillers in the late 1940s with *The Killers, The Naked City*, etc.

Hellman Lillian (1905–). U.S. playwright. Her works include *The Children's Hour* (1934), *The Little Foxes* (1939) and *Toys in the Attic* (1960).

Hell's Angels (1930). Film directed by H. *Hughes.

helm roof. Architectural term for a pointed roof with 4 diamond-shaped sides; each face of such a building therefore has a gable.

Héloïse (d. 1163). Mistress, later wife of Peter *Abelard; she wrote 3 famous letters to him. Pope wrote the poem *Eloisa to Abelard* (1717) and G. Moore the novel *Héloïse and Abélard* (1921).

Helpmann Robert (1909–). Australian dancer, choreographer, actor and producer, who joined the Vic-Wells Ballet in London in 1932. Within a year he was premier danseur, partnering Fonteyn until he left the co. in 1950; their popularity was an important contribution to the growth of British ballet. He interpreted

Helm roof, Sompting, Sussex

Robert Helpmann as Satan in *Job* (*left*), and as Dr Coppélius in *Coppélia*. Also **Cinderella*

Helst. *Banquet of the Civic Guard, 1648*

Ernest Hemingway

his many roles in a powerfully dramatic way. His works include *Comus* (1942), *Hamlet* (1942), *Miracle in the Gorbals* (1944), etc. H. has appeared in several films and has helped to re-mount classical ballets, e.g. *The Sleeping Beauty* (Paris, 1960) and *Swan Lake* (London, 1963).

Helst Bartholomeus van der (1613–70). Dutch portrait painter who worked in Amsterdam and replaced Rembrandt in popular estimation. Although not in the class of Rembrandt or Hals, both of whom influenced his work, H. produced well-composed portrait groups, e.g. *Banquet of the Civil Guard, 1648* (Rijksmus., Amsterdam), delighting in the ostentatious display of finery.

Heltai Jenö (1871–1957). Hungarian writer; influenced by French authors of the *fin de siècle*. H. depicted the Budapest *demi-monde*. His style is simple, almost colloquial, his attitude somewhat cynical; some novels and the neo-romantic play *A néma levente* (1936; *The Silent Knight*, 1937) have been trs. into English.

Helvétius Claude-Adrien (1715–71). French philosopher, one of the *philosophes*, most of whom frequented his wife's *salon*.

Hely-Hutchinson Christian Victor (1901–47). English composer born in South Africa. He wrote settings of nursery rhymes, a 'Carol Symphony' and the operetta *Hearts are Trumps*.

Heming(es) John (d. 1630). H. and Henry Condell (d. 1627) were actors in the same co. as Shakespeare, and eds of the 1st folio of his plays (1623).

Hemingway Ernest (Miller) (1899–1961). U.S. novelist, short-story writer and Nobel prizewinner. He began his career as a journalist and as an ambulance driver in World War I was severely wounded. After further newspaper work he spent several years in Paris as an expatriate writer. Influenced by Gertrude Stein, *Huckleberry Finn* and the discipline of journalism, he developed a distinctive fictional manner, terse, vernacular, unabstract, concerned with 'the real thing, the sequence of motion and fact which made the emotion'. His fictional world is typically a cruel, violent, disordered one, in which men lose all they possess; his heroes are tortured sleepless men overcoming their situation with stoicism, or men with skills which make them precise and controlled – the bull-fighter, fisherman, soldier or game-hunter. His novels concern individual searches for the pure, spare life in a world where social obligations and even emotional attachments become a trap. Distantly behind it lies a glimpse of a paradisial agrarian world of romantic simplicity and innocence. *The Sun Also Rises* (1926; in England *Fiesta*, 1927), *A Farewell to Arms* (1929), *To Have and Have Not* (1937), *For Whom the Bell Tolls* (1940), *Across the River and into the Trees* (1950) and *The Old Man and the Sea* (1952) are his novels, and there are several vols of short stories, some of them (e.g. *The Snows of Kilimanjaro*, 1936) among his finest work. Other works include *Death in the Afternoon* (1932), about bull-fighting, and *Green Hills of Africa* (1935).

Hémon Louis (1880–1913). French novelist whose *Maria Chapdelaine* (posth. 1914; 1927), a story of rural life among the French-Canadians of Quebec, was a stimulus to French-Canadian literature.

Henderson Fletcher (1898–1952). U.S. jazz band-leader, pianist and arranger. His use of saxophone and brass sections in conjunction and against each other, though primitive from the point of view of orchestration, represented an effective streamlining of the jazz orchestra in the interests of rhythmic precision, and formed the basic big-band style of the 1930s.

Hennebique.
Spinning Factory at Tourcoing

Hennebique François (1842–1921). French architect, one of the pioneers of the modern style. In the late 19th c. he was an innovator in the use of exposed iron and concrete, introducing and patenting the plate-girder. The Spinning Factory at Tourcoing, France, is his most influential work.

Hennique Léon (1851–1935). French novelist and dramatist, a contributor to *Les *Soirées de Médan*.

Henri Robert (1865–1929). U.S. realist painter who studied at Pennsylvania Academy of Fine Arts and in Paris, and in the 1890s founded the group called 'Philadelphia Realists', later The Eight; an organizer of the Armory Show. He was an important and stimulating teacher, encouraging his pupils to seek inspiration in the contemporary scene. Some of his essays and classroom notes were publ. as *The Art Spirit* (1923).

Robert Henri. *Summer Evening–North River*

Hans Werner Henze

Henri Brulard, La Vie de. Autobiographical book by *Stendhal.

Henry, O. Pseud. of William Sidney Porter (1862–1910). U.S. short-story writer who turned to writing during his 3 years in prison for embezzlement. His 1st book of tales, *Cabbages and Kings*, appeared in 1904, and subsequent colls poured out until his death and even beyond (in at least 4 vols). His humour, irony, ingenious plotting of coincidence, and above all his surprise 'twist' endings were much imitated. His best-known stories are probably *The Gift of the Magi*, *The Furnished Room*, *The Ransom of Red Chief* and *A Municipal Report*.

Henry IV parts 1 (before 1600; publ. 1598) and 2 (before 1600; publ. 1600). Plays by *Shakespeare, written *c.* 1597. Their sources were *Holinshed and an anon. play, *The Famous Victories of Henry the Fifth* (registered 1594).

Henry IV (1922). Play by *Pirandello.

Henry V (before 1600; publ. 1600). Historical play by *Shakespeare, written *c.* 1598 and performed at court in 1605. Its sources were *Holinshed and an anon. play, *The Famous Victories of Henry the Fifth.* It was made into a film (1944), directed by *Olivier.

Henry VI parts 1 (1592?; publ. 1623), 2 (publ. 1594) and 3 (before September 1592; publ. 1595). Dramatic trilogy by *Shakespeare–probably in collaboration–written between 1589 and 1591. Its main sources were Holinshed and Hall.

Henry VIII (1613; publ. 1623). Historical play by *Shakespeare, perhaps in collaboration with Fletcher; written *c.* 1612. Its main sources were *Holinshed and Foxe's *Book of Martyrs.*

Henry Esmond, Esquire, The History of (1852). Historical novel by *Thackeray.

Henryson Robert (*c.* 1425–*c.* 1506). Scottish poet, and next to Dunbar the greatest of the 'Scottish Chaucerians'. H. is not adequately accounted for by that label, though his greatest work, the *Testament of Cresseid*, was directly inspired by Chaucer's *Troilus and Criseyde*. H.'s tone is characteristically sober, and sometimes stern, and he lacks the stylistic exuberance and versatility of Dunbar though his versions of Æsop's *Fables* are full of humorous observation. But the *Testament* is a formal triumph, the severity of style matching the sobriety of mood, and there are numerous accomplished lyrics.

Henschel Sir George (Isidor Georg) (1850–1934). German-born baritone singer, composer and conductor. He worked in Europe and the U.S. (conductor of the Boston Symphony Orchestra, 1881–4) settling in Britain in the 1880s. He wrote 3 operas, choral and orchestral works and songs.

Henslowe Philip (d. 1616). Elizabethan theatre owner who at various times had control of the Rose, Fortune and Hope Theatres. His stepdaughter married the actor Alleyn. His *Diary* gives useful information about conditions in the contemporary theatre. He was the only known theatre manager of the time who was not also an actor.

Henty George Alfred (1832–1902). English writer of stories of historical adventure for boys, e.g. *With Clive in India* (1884) and *The Young Carthaginian* (1887).

Henze Hans Werner (1926–). German composer; his teachers included Fortner and Leibowitz. H. was artistic director of the State Theatre Ballet in Wiesbaden for a period but since the early 1950s has lived by composition. Since 1953 he has lived in Italy. H. has an astonishing facility in composition. He has written examples of all the main genres, displaying enthusiasm for a variety of styles, from the tonal to 12-note. His works include: the operas *Boulevard Solitude* (1951), *King Stag* (1955), *The Prince of Homburg* (1960) after Kleist; ballets, including *Jack Pudding* (1949), *Ondine* (for Covent Garden) (1956); 3 symphonies; a violin concerto (1947); *Ode to the West Wind* (1953) for cello and orchestra; *Sonata per archi* (1958) and *3 Dithyrambs* (1958) for chamber orchestra.

Hepburn Audrey (1929–). Belgian-born film actress who came to London as a refugee. She has played in England and Italy, but mainly America. As a 'gamine' sophisticate, she got her lucky break in *Roman Holiday* (1953). The film version of Tolstoy's *War and Peace* (1956) brought her notices as a dramatic actress.

Hepburn Katharine (1909–). U.S. film actress. A fascinating, feminine harum-scarum,

O. Henry

Katharine Hepburn in *Suddenly Last Summer*

Audrey Hepburn in *War and Peace*

Hepworth. *Two Figures*

Hepworth. Model for *Meridian*

with a dynamic and dramatic personality; her forte is in comedy. *A Bill of Divorcement* (1932), her 1st film, was an instant success; she took an Oscar the following year in *Morning Glory* (1933). Other films include: *Philadelphia Story* (1940), *The African Queen* (1951) and *Long Day's Journey Into Night* (1963).

Hepplewhite George (d. 1786). English cabinet maker, usually associated with the neo-classic movement in English furniture. He followed rather than set the fashion, and *The Cabinetmaker and Upholsterer's Guide*, the book of furniture designs for which he is best known, was publ. only in 1788, when the influence of Adam and neo-classicism was already widespread. H.'s reputation is largely posth. and, because of the difficulty of attributing any particular piece to him, his name is used to describe a style rather than individual works.

Heptaméron, L'. Coll. of stories by *Marguerite d'Angoulême.

Hepworth Dame Barbara (1903–). English sculptor. Born at Wakefield, Yorkshire, H. was taught modelling at Leeds Art School and carving, chiefly in Italy. Early works such as *Doves* (stone, 1929; City A. Gal., Manchester), already give an impression of monumental power in repose, close in spirit to Egyptian art. Her work became more abstract and is allied to that of Henry Moore and the painting of her 2nd husband, Ben Nicholson (marriage dissolved). In 1933 she joined the Abstraction-Création group, Paris, and met Mondrian. She was a member of the Circle Group, London (1935), and joined in the group publ. *Circle* (1937). Her work won far wider recognition after World War II. She was awarded the C.B.E. in 1958 and foreign awards include the International grand prix, São Paulo Biennale, 1959. Her drawings include those of surgeons and operating theatres (exhibited in 1947). She has also designed sets and costumes, notably for Tippett's opera, *The Midsummer Marriage* (1955). Recent sculpture shows experiments in new substances, including sheet-metal, wire and bronze. There has been a gain in power without loss of the early nobility, subtlety or flawless rendering of surfaces. Among recent works are *Icon*, in mahogany (British Council) and *Meridian*, a 14-ft work in bronze (State House, Holborn, London).

Hepworth Cecil (1874–1953). British film director. H. was the best-known British pioneer film maker. His most famous film is *Rescued by Rover* (1905), a story film about a stolen baby rescued by a dog. He continued directing into the 1920s with such films as *Alf's Button* (1920) and *Tansy* (1921).

Herbert Sir Alan Patrick (1890–). English author, notably of light verse. As M.P. he secured, in 1937, revision of the English divorce laws; he had attacked them in *Holy Deadlock* (1934). Works include verse, *Laughing Ann . . .* (1925), novel *The Water Gipsies* (1930), essays and comic operas.

Herbert Edward (1st Baron Herbert of Cherbury) (1583–1648). English poet, philosopher and historian, elder brother of George H. His verse is scholarly and obscure, and less dramatic than that of his model, Donne. His chief philosophical work, *De Religione Gentilium . . .* (1645), lays the foundations of deism. Other works include his autobiography, publ. in 1764.

Herbert George (1593–1633). English religious poet. In 1630 he was ordained and presented to the living of Bemerton in Wiltshire where he remained until his death. Untroubled by intellectual doubts, H.'s submission to God's will was nevertheless not achieved without a struggle. Naturally ambitious, he chafed under a sense of frustration exacerbated by frequent illness. His poetry which, unlike that of his master, Donne, has never fallen into neglect, is among the most purely devotional in the English language, speaking simply of God's love and of obedience to Him. His finest lyrics, e.g. *The Collar*, display a subtle mastery of cadence, a flair for apt and telling images and a colloquial and direct English.

Herbert Zbigniew (1924–). Polish poet. His philosophical poetry has a strong sense of the physical world. His *Barbarzynca w orgrodzie* (1962), a coll. of essays inspired by a visit to France and Italy, shows how deeply H. is involved in the Western cultural tradition.

Herbin Auguste (1882–1960). French painter in a formal abstract style. He settled in Paris in 1901 and came under cubist influence before turning to abstraction. He was co-ed. with

Hepplewhite. Master's chair (*extreme left*) and senior warden's chair, both in mahogany

George Herbert

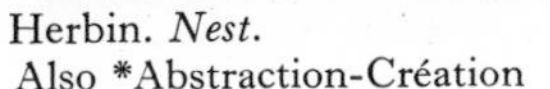

Herbin. *Nest.*
Also *Abstraction-Création

Herder

Vantongerloo of the magazine *Abstraction-Création.* He invented a pictorial alphabet on which he based his compositions, e.g. *Composition on the Word 'Rose'* (1947; Guggenheim Mus., New York) and by means of which he invested forms and colours with verbal symbolism. He explained his alphabet and his colour theories, in part derived from Goethe's, in *L'art non-figuratif, non-objectif* (1949).

Herculaneum. Ancient Roman town near to Pompeii in S. Italy. The rediscovery of the splendidly preserved ruins of these 2 towns in the mid 18th c. was an important factor in the neo-classical revival.

Herder Johann Gottfried von (1744–1803). German critic and thinker, by profession a clergyman. His meeting with Goethe in Strassburg (1770) established the *storm and stress movement. H.'s critical works–including *Fragmente . . .* (1767–8), essays on Ossian and Shakespeare in *Von deutscher Art und Kunst* (1773)–conceive literature as evolving, determined by time and place; consequently, he stresses naturalness and originality. In the *Abhandlung über den Ursprung der Sprache* (1772; *Treatise upon the origin of Language*, 1827) H. denies the divine origin of language and sees it historically, as the expanding record of man's experience; while the *Ideen . . .* (1784–91; *Outlines of a philosophy of the history of man*, 1800) and *Briefe zur Beförderung der Humanität* (1793–7) see in history as a whole a progress towards true humanity. His wide-ranging coll. of *Volkslieder* (1778–9) encouraged simplicity in lyric poetry.

Heredia José-Maria de (1842–1905). Cuban-born French *Parnassian poet. All his work was coll. in *Les Trophées* (1893; *Sonnets. . .*, 1897); it contains 118 sonnets which are masterpieces of compression, rhythm and colour, constructed with faultless technique.

'Heriger': Spruch

Hering Loy (15th–16th c.). German sculptor of the Renaissance whose major work is the over-life-size seated figure of St Willibald in Eichstätt cathedral.

Herland Hugh (*fl.* 1360–1405). English carpenter who built the timber roof of Westminster Hall, London (1394); it has a span of nearly 70 ft. It is the earliest dated example of the hammer-beam roof, a distinctive feature of the perpendicular style.

Her Majesty's. London theatre built by Beerbohm Tree in 1897 and originally managed by him. In 1916 the musical *Chu-Chin-Chow* ran there for 2,238 performances, a record only recently broken. The theatre becomes 'His Majesty's' when there is a king on the throne.

Hermes Trismegistos. During the Renaissance, works erroneously believed to be by an Egyptian seer (predating Plato and called H. T.) were brought from Byzantium. The HERMETIC writings were in part trs. by M. Ficino and they became widely popular, influencing many scholars. Chiefly works of the occult sciences and somewhat degraded philosophy, they were, in fact, probably the works of Greek writers in the 2nd and 3rd cs A.D.

Hernandez Miguel (1910–42). Spanish poet of peasant origin; much of his finest poetry was inspired by the agony of the Civil War, in which he fought for the Republic. His poetry combines rich imagery and burning passion with sober classical forms, e.g. *Vienta del pueblo* (1937).

Hernani (1830). Poetic drama by Victor *Hugo.

Hero and Leander (1598). Narrative poem by *Marlowe.

Herodotus (*c.* 490–*c.* 425 B.C.). Greek historian, called the 'father of history', who was born at Halicarnassus. He left home in his thirties and visited Egypt and much of the Levant before settling for a time at Athens, where he became a friend of Sophocles and perhaps of Pericles, received the citizenship and then joined the new Athenian colony at Thurii (443). His *Histories* were perhaps largely inspired by his sojourn at Athens. He coll. material from previous authors by travelling and by interrogating eyewitnesses or picking up hearsay. His aim, he says, is to show the reasons for the great war between Greeks and Persians and this entails 6 books of preliminary study devoted to the *mores* and previous history of the combatants. The campaigns of Xerxes occupy only the last 3 books. His method is cumulative and he borrows the epic licence of digression to include incidental material. He employs the tragic concepts of

Herculaneum. See also colour plate 16

Herland. Westminster Hall

Herrera the Elder. *St Basil dictating his Rule*

Juan de Herrara. The Escorial

Robert Herrick

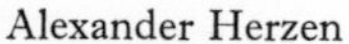

Alexander Herzen

hybris and *nemesis* to explain events, but this deliberate artifice does not compromise his responsibility as an historian, nor does the ironic scepticism he shares with the Ionian philosophers inhibit his recording of a good story just because he does not believe it: but statements for which he vouches are generally accepted as accurate. Deliberately unrhetorical, his style is the simplest of all Greek prose.

heroic couplet. In English verse, 2 rhyming lines of 10 syllables.

Hérold Louis-Joseph-Ferdinand (1791–1833). French composer. His teachers included Méhul. He won the 1st Rome prize in 1812; he is remembered for the opera *Zampa* (1831) about a pirate dragged into death by the marble statue of his fiancée.

Hero of Our Time, A (1840). Novel by *Lermontov.

Herrera Fernando (1534–97). Spanish poet, and leading humanist scholar in the literary circles of his native Seville. He wrote patriotic poems, Italianate love-lyrics, an important commentary on Garcilaso de la Vega and a life of Thomas More, and invented his own system of spelling and punctuation.

Herrera Francisco the Elder (d. 1656). Spanish painter of religious and genre subjects treated with coarse realism. He worked in Seville and Madrid and from 1611 to 1612 was master of Velazquez. The vigour and free brushwork of his style at its best is seen in *St Basil Dictating his Rule* (1639; Louvre).

Herrera Francisco the Younger (1622–85). Spanish painter, son of F. H. the Elder and from 1672 court painter and architect at Madrid. He went to Rome to escape his father's brutal treatment and there became famous for still-life paintings. On returning to Spain in 1656 he turned to portraits and religious subjects, imitating contemporary Italian styles.

Herrera Juan de (*c.* 1530–97). Spanish architect, famous for building the Escorial, near Madrid, though the original plans were not by him. It was laid out by Juan Bautista de Toledo; in 1567, when he died, the S. façade was already built. H. did not take over until 1572. The Escorial was intended by Philip II to combine monastery, palace, cathedral and mausoleum. It is one of the largest buildings in the world–675 by 685 ft, a simple rectangle with the church near the centre. The exterior is plain and austere. H.'s main contributions are the pavilion-towers at the corners and the church itself, centrally-planned and domed. He also built the Exchange, Seville and designed Valladolid cathedral (only partially executed but very influential).

Herrara y Reissig Julio (1875–1910). Uruguayan poet, part of the *modernismo movement, of which he represents the more extravagant side in his obscurity, neologisms and bizarre imagery.

Herrick Robert (1591–1674). English lyric poet. Apart from a period between 1647 and 1662 when he was deprived of his living because of his Royalist sympathies and enabled to return to London, most of his life was spent as vicar of a remote Devonshire parish.

H. celebrated in his poetry country life and the pleasures of youth and beauty. His theme is the pagan one of **carpe diem*, and the only sorrow to cloud his verse is the transience of earthly joy. The slightness and grace of his lyrics conceal the poet's art. He had considerable formal and rhythmical skills. Much of his best work appeared in the coll. *Hesperides* (1648).

Herries Chronicle, The (1930–3). Series of 3 novels by Hugh Walpole.

Herrman Bernard (1911–). U.S. composer, conductor and radio musical director. His works include the cantata *Moby Dick* (1940) and music for Welles's film *Citizen Kane.*

Hertfordshire County Council Architects Department. Under C. H. Aslin (1893–1959) it became well known for its post-war schools policy, developing a standardized steel and concrete 'kit of parts' which could be assembled on an 8 ft 3 in. module to suit the needs of any school. The department gained a European reputation.

Herz Henriette (1764–1847). German society woman whose Berlin *salon* was frequented by many of the leading romantics.

Herzen Alexander Ivanovich (1812–70). Russian writer and Revolutionary. H. spent the last 18 years of his life in England, where he ed. *The Bell*, a periodical in Russian which was smuggled into the country and circulated widely. His literary reputation rests on the political essays in *From the Other Shore* (1850; 1956), and the autobiography *My Past and Thoughts* (1855; 1855).

Hesdin Jacquemart de (d. *c.* 1410). French miniaturist of Flemish origin. He worked for John, Duke of Berry, decorating several Books of Hours, the most famous being the *Belles Heures* (Bibliothèque Royale, Brussels). Subtlety of colour and use of borders with birds and foliage characterize his work. His representation of architecture suggests Sienese influence.

Heseltine Philip: Peter *Warlock

Hesiod (8th c. B.C.?). Greek poet, son of a poor farmer of Boeotia. He denounced his brother Perses for devouring his inheritance, in the *Works and Days*, the 1st Greek autobiographical poem. This closely imitates the epic metre and dialect of Homer and retells old legends such as the story of Pandora and the declension of mankind from the Golden Age. Its practical instruction in the art of husbandry had a long literary influence culminating in the *Georgics* of Virgil. The *Theogony*, of doubtful authorship, is the 1st attempted rationalization of Greek mythology.

Hesperides (1648). Coll. of poems by Herrick.

Hess Dame Myra (1890–1965). English pianist, also author of *Jesu, joy of man's desiring*, a piano transcription of a chorale from one of Bach's cantatas.

Hesse Hermann (1877–1962). German writer best known for his novels, which embody an often autobiographical search for life's meaning, following the explicit rejection of middle-class values. *Peter Camenzind* (1904) abandons civilization for nature; *Demian* (1919; 1923) introduces a more mystical neo-romanticism, developed in *Siddharta* . . . (1922; 1954), which deals with the antithesis between soul and senses, in an Indian setting. This polarity is also explored in *Der Steppenwof* (1927; 1929) and in his last, most-admired utopian novel *Des Glasperlenspiel* (1943; *Magister Ludi*, 1950). His poems echo romantic forms, language and motifs.

Heston Charlton (1924–). U.S. actor, known principally for his 'heroic' roles in spectacular 'blockbuster' productions, which require a strong physical presence as well as acting talent. H. has starred in *The Ten Commandments* (1957/8), *Ben Hur* (1959) and *El Cid* (1961).

hexachord (Greek, 'six sounds'). A group of 6 consecutive notes in the diatonic scale with the interval of a semitone in the middle, devised in the 11th c. by Guido d'Arezzo, to help singers learning to sight read. He imposed a system of h.s upon a 2-octave range, beginning the first on the lowest G on the bass staff, the second on the C above the 3rd on the F above and so on. Within each group of 6 notes the notes were named: 'ut, re, mi, fa, sol, la', with mi-fa the semitone interval. Relating his line of music to this rigid and familiar framework of intervals helped the singer to pitch the intervals before him.

Hexameron. A work for piano consisting of variations on the march from Bellini's opera *I Puritani*; 6 composers contributed variations, among them Czerny, Chopin and Liszt, who also wrote the introduction, linking passages and conclusion.

hexameter. A *metre in verse.

Heyden Jan van der (1637–1712). Dutch painter and engineer, 1 of the earliest townscape painters in Holland and the first in Amsterdam. He also worked in Cologne. Though very detailed, his views cannot be considered topographically accurate.

Heywood John (1497?–1580?). English playwright and poet. His interludes, using comic debate between human characters, were important as departures from the didacticism and personifications of the morality play. They include . . . *the Four P.'s* (between 1520–2) and *The Play of the Wether* (publ. 1533).

Heywood Thomas (1574?–1641). English poet and dramatist. He, like Dekker, treated middle-class subjects. His domestic dramas include the tragedy *A Woman Kilde With Kindnesse* (1603) and the comedy *The Fair Maid of the West* (publ. 1631). He also produced numerous historical and legendary plays. Other works include *The Hierarchie of the Blessed Angells* (1635), chiefly verse, and *An Apology for Actors* (1612) in defence of the theatre.

Hesdin. *Très Belles Heures du Duc de Berri*; the duke with SS. Andrew and John the Baptist

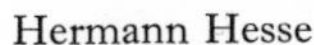

Hermann Hesse

Van der Heyden. *Mastelaarsgracht, Amsterdam*; also *Keyser

Highmore. *Pamela is married*

The Rev. Edward Hicks. *The Peaceable Kingdom*

Hill. *The Bird Cage*

Hiawatha, The Song of (1855). Poem by *Longfellow.

Hicks Edward (1780–1849). The greatest of the itinerant, self-taught American folk artists or 'primitives', famous for his versions of *The Peaceable Kingdom* illustrating Isaiah 11, with W. Penn signing his treaty with the Indians shown in the background.

Hicks Sir (Edward) Seymour (1871–1949). Leading English actor-manager; also a playwright. H. often played opposite his wife, Ellaline Terriss; his most successful role was in his play *Sleeping Partners*.

Higden (or Higdon) Ranulf (d. 1364). English chronicler, who wrote the *Polychronicon*, a book of history and legend from Creation to his own day. He has also been suggested as author of the *Chester Cycle of mystery plays.

Higgins Frederick Robert (1896–1941). Irish lyric poet and dramatist, associated with W. B. Yeats. H. was director of the Abbey Theatre, Dublin, where his own *Deuce of Jacks* was produced. His verse includes: *Salt Air* (1923), *Island Blood* (1925) and *Arable Holdings* (1933).

highboy: *lowboy

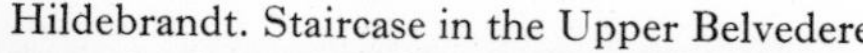

Hildebrandt. Staircase in the Upper Belvedere

Highmore Joseph (1692–1780). English painter of portraits and conversation pieces but more famous for his lively paintings (Tate and elsewhere) illustrating Richardson's *Pamela*, which compare superficially with Hogarth's *Marriage à la Mode* series. H.'s work, however, lacks the moral and social implications of Hogarth's and has a greater daintiness of execution through French influence.

High Noon (1952). Film directed by F. *Zinnemann.

High Wind in Jamaica, A (1929). Novel by Richard Hughes.

Hilanderas, Las (*c.* 1657). Painting of the interior of a tapestry workshop by *Velazquez.

Hildebrand: Nicolaas *Beets

Hildebrand Adolf von (1847–1921). German sculptor who, like his friend H. von Marees, aimed at a timeless classical purity of form. He publ. his theories on art in *Das Problem der Form . . .* (1893; *The Problem of Form. . .*, 1907) which influenced Heinrich Wölfflin and the development of art criticism. The Wittelsbach and Hubertus fountains in Munich are among his best works.

Hildebrandslied. Lay, surviving in fragments in a Low German alliterative version of the early 9th c.; it tells of a combat between warrior father and son. The original was probably Langobardic.

Hildebrandt Johann Lukas von (1668–1745). Austrian architect. His father was in the Genoese army and his mother was Italian. He spent his early life in Italy, studying architecture and military engineering. In 1699 he built St Lawrence at Gabel, Bohemia, to a design closely influenced by Guarini–overlapping squares and ovals in the plan; concave and convex walls; diagonal, tilting arches. His great work is the Upper Belvedere, Vienna (1721). The exterior has octagonal corner-pavilions, shallow domes and twisty gables; the interior is famous for the staircase and the garden-room with its straining giant figures. H. also built the Peterskirche and the Piaristenkirche, Vienna. At Warzburg he co-operated with Neumann on the Residenz.

Hildesheim Germany, St Michael's. Early Romanesque church (*c.* 1000–33). It has 6 towers, 2 transepts (at E. and W. ends), 2 apses and alternation of supports in the nave. It houses the famous bronze doors and column, 2 of the greatest masterpieces of early Romanesque sculpture, made for Archbishop Bernward in 1015–20.

Hilferding Van Wewen Franz (1710–68). Austrian dancer and teacher who taught in Stuttgart and Vienna and was appointed by the Empress Elisabeth to teach in St Petersburg (1765). He was responsible for raising the standard of dancing there and importing fresh ideas from other European centres into Russian development.

Hill David Octavius (1802–70). Scots painter and photographer who collaborated with Robert *Adamson in early photographic work, using the paper negative process called *calotype. The 2 men enjoyed wide success and by the 1850s their calotyped portraits and views were being favourably compared with Rembrandt etchings.

Hilliard. *Man against a background of flames*; also *miniature

Hilliard. *Man leaning against a tree with rose-bushes*

Paul Hindemith

Hiller Ferdinand (1811–85). German-Jewish composer, conductor, teacher and music journalist; in Paris as a pianist (1828–35). His friends included Schumann, Wagner, Liszt and Mendelssohn; he later became a conductor at Leipzig. He wrote operas, oratorios, symphonies and chamber music, and an important book on theory.

Hiller Johann Adam (1728–1804). German composer and conductor. His 13 *Singspiele*, e.g. *Die Jagd* (1770), were among the earliest examples of the form; he founded the *Wöchentliche Nachrichten* (1766–70), the 1st modern music magazine, and was (1781–5) the 1st conductor of the Leipzig Gewandhaus Orchestra.

Hilliard Nicholas (*c.* 1547–1619). The 1st native-born artist of the English school whose work and life are reliably documented. The son of an Exeter goldsmith, H. held a warrant as a goldsmith from Queen Elizabeth. His best-known works, however, are miniature portraits of very high quality, invaluable also as lively historical records, e.g. *Queen Elizabeth* (N.P.G., London). His style is close to French court art and he visited France in 1577–8. Among his best portraits are *Alice Hilliard, Man leaning against a tree with rose-bushes* and *Man against a background of flames* (all V. and A., London). The last 2 closely parallel in visual terms the symbolism of the love-poetry of H.'s friend Sir Philip Sidney. H. also wrote a treatise on miniature painting entitled *The Arte of Limning*; I. Oliver was his pupil.

Hilton James (1900–54). English novelist. His books include: *Goodbye Mr Chips* (1934, film 1939), *Lost Horizon* (1933, film 1937), in which appears the fabulous country Shangri-la, and *Random Harvest* (1941, film 1942).

Hilton (or Hylton) Walter (d. 1396). Augustinian canon and author of the mystical prose work *The Scale of Perfection* (or *Ladder of Perfection*).

Hind and the Panther, The (1687). Allegorical poem by *Dryden.

Hindemith Paul (1895–1963). German composer. After a varied early career in cinema and dance orchestras H. entered the Frankfurt Conservatory to study composition. By 1915 he had already progressed from viola player to conductor of the Frankfurt opera. In 1921 he helped to found the Amar Quartet, with whom he soon became internationally known as a performer and a composer. After Hitler's advent he had to leave Germany, like so many of the best European composers. And like them, having tried unsuccessfully to gain employment in England, he emigrated to America in 1939, where he eventually became head of music at Yale Univ. He was always a thoroughly practical musician. As a young man he reacted very strongly against the current view of music, which he regarded as 'beating the audiences into submission'. As an exponent of *Gebrauchmusick* ('functional music') he collaborated with Brecht on 2 *Lehrstücke* ('plays of instruction') one of which was broadcast without the choruses to schools, the pupils had to sing. In the other, film was used and the audience had to take part. H. asserted that music could not be renewed from above. It should be used, not merely heard. He wrote much radio, film and educational music. He was also associated with *Gemeinschaftmusik*–'music for amateurs'–and wrote a great deal of music for this purpose including sonatas for almost every instrument in existence. At the same time he used the traditional forms, symphony, opera, etc. Later these tended to predominate, but his tendency to bold gesture and clear texture and construction remained. He was a master in traditional harmony and counterpoint. Some critics have noted a certain pedantry in his music. He sought to restore music as a craft and wrote various books on the subject, which propose a new theory of harmony, etc. H.'s stage works include: the operas *Cardillac* (1926), set in 17th-c. France and *Mathis der Maler* (1938; also symphony 1934), based on the 16th-c. German painter Grünewald and his Isenheim altar; the ballet *Nobilissima Visione* (*St Francis*; 1938) with choreography by Massine, on the life of Francis of Assisi, and works with Brecht and Weill. His other principal works include: *Concert music for strings and brass* (1931); *Die Harmonie der Welt* (opera 1957; symphony 1951); *Trauer musik* (1936) both for viola and orchestra; *Das Marienleben* (1924) for voice and piano; *Ludus Tonalis* (1943), a prelude and fugues and interludes for piano, didactic in intent. Among H.'s important theoretical writings are: *The Craft of Musical Composition* (1937) and *Traditional Harmony* (1943).

Hippolytus (428 B.C.). Play by *Euripides. Phaedra, wife of King Theseus of Athens, falls

Hildesheim.
The 11th-c. bronze Christ column

St Michael's, Hildesheim

Hiroshige. *Sunset at Seta*

Hitchens. *Damp Autumn*

Hispano-Moresque ware. Drug jar with design in iridescent glaze (*left*) and dish painted in lustre and blue

Hitchcock in his *The Birds*

in love with his illegitimate son, H. When H. –a votary of Diana, goddess of chastity– repulses her, Phaedra accuses him before Theseus of making love to her. H. is dragged to death by his horses; Phaedra hangs herself. Seneca and Racine wrote tragedies about Phaedra.

Hiroshige Ando Tokitaro called (1797–1858). Japanese artist of the Ukiyo-e school, one of the great masters of the coloured woodcut. He adapted block printing to landscape subjects being best known for his poetical prints of the Yedo (Tokyo) district and the old high road to Kyoto. His work exerted a powerful influence on the impressionists and other 19th-c. European artists.

Hiroshima mon amour (1959). Film directed by A. *Resnais.

Hispano-Moresque. Describes the tin-glazed lustred earthenware made by Moorish potters in Spain, produced in the 14th c. in Malaga and in the 15th in the region of Manises near Valencia. After being fired with the tin glaze, sometimes with a pattern picked out in cobalt-blue, it was painted with a lustre of copper and silver and refired. The lustre varied in effect from pale or bright yellow-gold to reddish brown-gold. More or less debased Islamic patterns eventually gave way to a successful combination of Christian and Islamic motifs. 15th-c. examples from Manises (large dishes, bowls, plates, etc.) are often decorated with all-over plant designs, such as vine leaves and grapes, together with heraldic devices.

history painting. Alberti, in the 15th c., used the word *istoria* to describe any subject picture with more than 1 figure. In the 17th c., h. p. had come to mean pictures with subjects taken from the histories, that is poetry, history (especially of antiquity) and religion; it was held to be the highest form of art. In the 18th c. Reynolds stated 'a history painter paints man in general: a portrait painter, a particular man, and consequently a defective model'. Scenes of contemporary history in modern dress were only slowly accepted at the beginning of the 19th c.

Hitchcock Alfred (1899–). British-born film director. H. started as a sub-title artist (1920), working up to direct his 1st film, *The Pleasure Garden*, in 1925. His 1st famous film was a version of Mrs Belloc Lowndes's *The Lodger* (1926), perhaps the most personal of his British films. Although his British films–e.g. the comedy thrillers: *Blackmail* (Britain's 1st sound film, 1929), *The 39 Steps* (1935), *Young and Innocent* (1937), *The Lady Vanishes* (1938)–contained remarkable sequences, they were made within the technical and artistic limits of the British cinema of the time and in general were lightweight works. In 1939 he left to make *Rebecca* (1940) for Selznick in Hollywood, where he has been based ever since. H. has moved farther and farther away from the plot-bound formula of the mystery thriller. He uses shock-tactics in construction and editing and creates suspense not only from the audience's growing awareness of the situation but also from positive identification with a character–sharing his feelings or desires–a method made explicit in *Rear Window* (1954). H. portrays a world of uncertainty in which life can be disrupted at any moment by chance disaster, and in *I Confess* (1952), *The Wrong Man* (1956) and *Vertigo* (1958), the coincidences may even appear to have the function of divine retribution for sins. The strong element of humour that appears in many of his films finds full expression in *The Trouble with Harry* (1955). His most important films include *Foreign Correspondent* (1940), *Shadow of Doubt* (1943), *Spellbound* (1945), *Rope* (1948), *Strangers on a Train* (1951), *I Confess* (1953), *North by Northwest* (1959), *Psycho* (1960) and *The Birds* (1963).

Hitchens Ivon (1893–). English painter. Studied at the St John's Wood School of Art and at the R.A. schools. He belonged to the London Group and the now defunct Seven and Five Group. He has lived most of his life in the heart of the Sussex countryside, and his paintings are concerned with communicating the poetic beauty of his environment. His main influence is obviously Matisse, and whilst his work borders on abstraction, he never divorces himself completely from natural forms. His work seems to embody those aspects of painting which transcend the rapid changes in fashion and style by which many of the younger generation are judged.

Hoban James (*c.* 1762–1831). Irish architect who emigrated to America about 1785 and designed the original White House, Washington.

Hobbema. *The Avenue, Middelharnis*

Hodgkins. *Seated Woman* (1924–30; drawing)

Thomas Hobbes

Hobbema Meindert (1638–1709). Dutch painter of landscape. A period of activity while he was the pupil and friend of Jacob van Ruisdael ended when H. became an excise officer in 1668. He painted few works after this, but *The Avenue, Middelharnis* (N.G., London), one of the most popular of all Dutch naturalistic landscapes, is an exception, and is now dated 1689. Neglected and poorly paid in his lifetime, H. was the favourite of English landscape painters and collectors of the 18th and early 19th cs. His quiet scenes lack the dramatic qualities of Ruisdael's. All detail is subordinated to the overall effect. The contrast in colour between the red of a tile roof and grey-green foliage is very typical. Of the many variations of the same subject, *The Mill* (Louvre) is a fine example.

Hobbes Thomas (1588–1679). English philosopher. In his *Leviathan* (1651) H. attempted to provide a rational justification for the authority of the state. Assuming that man is by nature aggressively self-interested, he argued that the only protection against the anarchy of the state of nature, in which life is 'solitary, poor, nasty, brutish and short', is a powerful government, justified not by any divine ordination but by its utility.

hoboy: *hautboy

Hoby Sir Thomas (1530–66). English diplomat and trs. of Castiglione's *Il Libro del Cortegiano* (*The Courtyer*, 1561); its portrayal of the courtly ideal had great influence on Elizabethan literature and education.

Hoccleve Thomas (1370?–1450?). English poet and government clerk. He was a disciple of Chaucer, whom he eulogizes in his long moral poem *The Regement of Princes*. He used an artificial and pedantic diction, and his dull fluency is relieved only by some flashes of autobiography in his minor poems, notably *La Male Règle*.

Hochhuth Rolf (1931–). German playwright. His play *Der Stellvertreter* (1964; *The Representative*, 1964), on the Papal attitude to the Nazi extermination of the Jews, caused a furore in Catholic countries.

hocket. Term in medieval music for a passage in which short, strongly rhythmic phrases pass from one part to another.

Hockney David (1937–). English painter; he studied at the R.C.A. (1959–62). Of special significance is an early etching entitled *My Three Heroes*, his heroes being Walt Whitman, Ghandi and himself. His pictures are often autobiographical, his composition more akin to the graphic designer, and his manner suggests the influence of U.S. painters, particularly Larry Rivers and de Kooning.

Hoddinott Alun (1929–). One of the leading young Welsh composers; his music was at first influenced by Stravinsky and Hindemith.

Hodgkins Frances (1870–1947). New Zealand painter whose best work was done in water-colour. From 1900 she lived in England and France. Her early work was impressionist but after World War I she evolved a poetic personal style of landscape and still-life painting which grew increasingly closer to abstraction.

Hodler Ferdinand (1853–1918). Swiss painter, a precursor of *expressionism. Deliberately rejecting impressionism, he developed a precise and expressive linear style which relates to the German Jugendstil movement. He painted landscapes, portraits and large-scale historical and mythological subjects, but his fame rests on his symbolical works such as *Night* and *Disillusioned Souls* (both Kunstmus., Berne), and *Towards the Infinite* (Kunsthaus, Zürich). The combination of realism and mysticism in these paintings gives him a solitary place among the artists of his time.

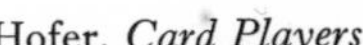

Hofer Karl (1878–1955). German expressionist painter. He spent several years in Paris and Rome before World War I. His work was condemned as 'degenerate' by the Nazis and he was forced to give up teaching; he was later president of the Berlin Academy (1945–55). H. started as a follower of von Marees and Cézanne, whose influence is still apparent in his mature landscape and figure compositions of the early 1920s. His work, which developed as the expression of his forebodings about political events in Germany and his bitter disillusionment, is characterized by a restraint which sets it apart from the mainstream of German expressionism.

Hoffmann Ernst Theodor Amadeus (*recte* Wilhelm) (1776–1822). German novelist and composer (opera *Undine*, 1816). Without the

Hodler. *Eurythmie*

Hofer. *Card Players*

Josef Hoffmann. Palais Stoclet, Brussels (1905)

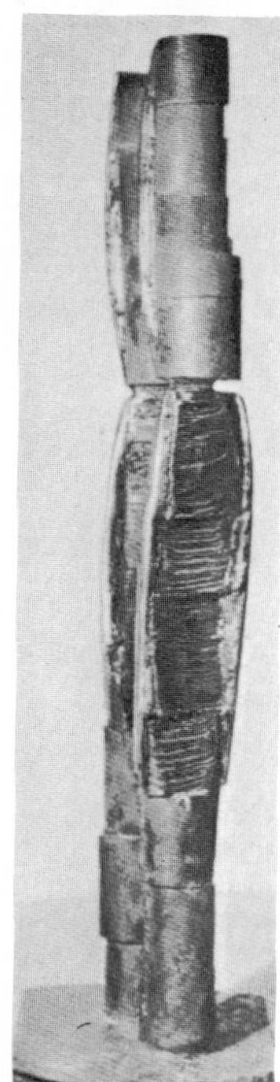

Hoflehner. *Doric Figure* (1958)

Hugo von Hofmannsthal and Richard Strauss in 1911

metaphysical intensity of earlier romantics, he is an absorbing master of the weird, grotesque and macabre, its effect intensified by its plastic presentation and the detailed realism of the world it invades. The artist is seen as daemonically possessed. H. influenced foreign writers such as Hugo and Poe, and his stories inspired works by *Schumann, *Delibes, *Offenbach and *Hindemith among others. His works include the story colls *Fantasiestücke in Callots Manier . . .* (1814–15, including *Kreisleriana* and *Der goldene Topf*), *Nachtstücke* (1817, including *Der Sandmann*), *Die Serapions-Brüder* (1819–21, including *Die Bergwerke zu Falun* and *Das Fräulein von Scudéri*); and the novels *Die Elixiere des Teufels* (1815–16) and *Lebensansichten des Katers Murr . . .* (1820–22).

Hoffmann Heinrich (1809–74). German doctor and author of the children's classic *Struwwelpeter* (1847; *The English Struwwelpeter*, 1848).

Hoffmann Josef (1870–1956). A pupil of Otto Wagner, H. was an early pioneer of modern architecture in Vienna. He founded the Wiener Werkstätte, craft workshops, and was later involved in the Wiener Sezession, an art nouveau movement. His buildings were among the earliest of the white cubes of the international style, but they carried a great deal of elegant ornament, and his influence was eclipsed by the Spartan work of his contemporary, A. Loos.

Hoffmann von Fallersleben August Heinrich (1798–1874). German writer of nationalistic verse and songs among them the famous *Deutschland Lied* (1841), now the W. German national anthem.

Hoflehner Rudolph (1916–). Austrian sculptor, trained first at a college of machine engineering. His preferred medium is welded sheet-iron, and his style, influenced by a visit to Greece in 1954, has changed from pure abstraction to monumental figure sculptures.

Hofman Victor Victorovich (1884–1911). Russian poet and short-story writer, author of lyrics expressing a sophisticate's nostalgia for the simple life of the country.

Hofmann Hans (1880–1966). German painter and teacher who settled in the U.S. in 1931. He was a friend of Matisse, Delaunay, Braque and Picasso in Paris before World War I. In 1915 he opened an art school in Munich and in 1933 another in New York which powerfully influenced the development of contemporary U.S. painting. His work was representational in the expressionist tradition until the early 1940s when he began to develop an exuberant abstract style.

Hofmannsthal Hugo von (1874–1929). Austrian writer; associated with Stefan George until 1905, though closer in spirit to Rilke. His sparse early poems convey subtle sensations in musically expressive language, often with a *fin de siècle* emphasis on transience; impressionism also characterizes his early verse playlets, e.g. *Der Tod des Tizian* (1892; 1913), *Der Tor und der Tod* (1893; *The Fool and Death*, 1913)–which, while warning of the dangers of aestheticism, show an aesthete's distaste for naturalism or entertainment in art–and his atmospheric stories, e.g. *Reitergeschichte* (1899), *Das Erlebnis des Marschalls von Bassompierre* (1900). The problem of communication, implicit in the playlets and the sonnet *Die Beiden*, becomes critical in the fictional *Brief des Lord Chandos* (1901), where H. expresses his fear of the failure of words. There follows a period of 'festival' drama, traditional moralities, e.g. *Jedermann* (1911; *The Play of Everyman*, 1917) and *Das Salzburger grosse Welttheater* (1922), and of librettos for Richard *Strauss: attempts, perhaps, to summon other powers–music, spectacle, tradition–to the aid of language. In his last 10 years H. was occupied with prose dramas which explore the individual's social role. In the comedy *Der Schwierige* (1921), written in the dialect of the Austrian aristocracy, hero and heroine finally communicate through silence. *Der Turm* (1927) was much revised, and its interpretation is still controversial.

Hofman von Hofmannswaldau Christian (1617–79). German poet in his time called 'the German Ovid'. His *Heldenbriefe* (1680) is a coll. of love-letters, in verse and prose.

Hogarth William (1697–1764). English painter, engraver and caricaturist whose innovations in art and genius in depicting the English national character give him an importance even beyond his great talent as an artist. H. was trained as an engraver on plate. He studied painting at the rudimentary academies then open in London but undoubtedly profited more from his study of European paintings from engravings and his incredible visual memory. Later he apprenticed himself to Sir James Thornhill, marrying Thornhill's daughter in 1729 and inheriting from him the academy which was to be a forerunner of the R.A. H. won an early reputation for small groups and conversation pieces (*Assembly at Wanstead House*, M. of A., Philadelphia) and for brilliantly captured dramatic scenes, such as the many versions of *The Beggar's Opera* (Tate and elsewhere). In 1731 he won a far wider fame with the first of his story-series of paintings, *The Harlot's Progress*. This form was quite new, certainly to secular painting. The series combined the appeal of the street ballad with that of a play, having a strong plot, allusions to contemporaries and a moral none could miss. So popular were the engravings made from this series that H. was forced to defend himself by promoting a Copyright Act before issuing the later series: *The Rake's Progress* (original paintings Soane Mus., London), *Marriage à la Mode* (original paintings N.G., London) and *The Industrious and Idle Apprentice*. Similar in style are the 4 electioneering paintings (Soane Mus., London) and the famous *O the Roast Beef of Old England* (Tate). H. campaigned vigorously in his engravings against cruelty, drinking crude spirit and the domination of English taste by foreign artists. He undoubtedly suffered as a painter from the prejudice against native-born artists and from his own popularity as a propagandist and caricaturist. In 1753 H. publ. *The Analysis of Beauty*. This was in part a polemic against uncritical appreciation in the arts and in part a serious contribution to aesthetics, describing a 'line of beauty' supposed to be present in all works of visual art. His history paintings, *Pool of Bethesda* and *The Good Samaritan* (both in St Bartholomew's Hospital, London) were ignored, his *Sigismunda* (Tate) was abused; even the originals of his famous engravings often remained unsold or were sold for very little. More important, H.'s unusual talent as a portrait painter went unrewarded. Fine examples are *Captain Coram* (Foundling Hospital, London), *Graham Children* (N.G., London), *William Jones* (A. Gal., Worcester, U.S.), *Self-portrait with Pug* (Tate), *The Artist's Servants*, a masterly study of contrasting character, and the vigorous, charming and technically fascinating *Shrimp Girl* (both N.G., London).

Hogg James ('The Ettrick Shepherd') (1770–1835). Scottish poet and novelist inspired and encouraged by Scott (also Christopher *North). His lyric and narrative poems have not worn well, but H. wrote a masterpiece, his novel *The . . . Confessions of a Justified Sinner* (1824), an exploration of the darker terrors of the Calvinist mind, much admired by Gide.

Hokusai Katsushika (Nakajima Tet-Sujiro) (1760–1849). Extraordinarily prolific Japanese painter and graphic artist, to Europeans the most famous exponent of the colour print, which had great influence on Western painting (*Japan). *The Wave* is the best-known print by H.

Holbach Paul Thiry, baron d' (1723–89). French philosopher, a rich man whose houses were meeting-places of the *philosophes*.

Holbein Hans the Younger (1497/8–1543). German artist. H.'s father, Hans H. the Elder, had a large workshop in Augsburg. When this was disbanded, H. and his brother Ambrosius apprenticed themselves to a painter in Basle. H. soon won a wide reputation for his work undertaken for the Basle book printers. Besides designs for wood blocks, he was already painting portraits and commissions for churches. In his larger works a certain awkwardness and overcrowding is noticeable. In 1517 H. visited Lucerne and may have entered N. Italy. Returning to Basle, he married and quickly became a citizen of importance. At this period his fame was spread throughout Europe by the illustrations to the Luther Bible and the woodcuts of the famous *Alphabet of Death* and *Dance of Death*. Despite this success, H. was driven by doubts of his financial future during the disturbed conditions of the Reformation to seek work in England. During his 1st visit in 1526 he was patronized by the circle of Sir Thomas More. He went back to Basle for a period, but was in England once more in 1532. His patrons of the 1st visit were disgraced or dead. H. first painted the German merchants of the Steelyard and was then introduced to the king. Until his death H. was employed by Henry VIII in a wide assortment of tasks, ranging from designing court costumes, silverware, jewellery and triumphal arches to painting the actual and prospective brides of the monarch. Outstanding among H.'s portraits are the superb *Christina of Denmark* (N.G., London), *George Gisze* (Berlin), *The*

Hogarth. Scene 3 from *The Harlot's Progress*

Hogarth. *The Artist's Servants*

Hogarth. Scene 4 from *Marriage à la Mode* (detail). Also *Beggar's Opera*, *caricature, *Fielding

Hokusai. *The Wave*

Holbein. *Self-portrait, aged 45*

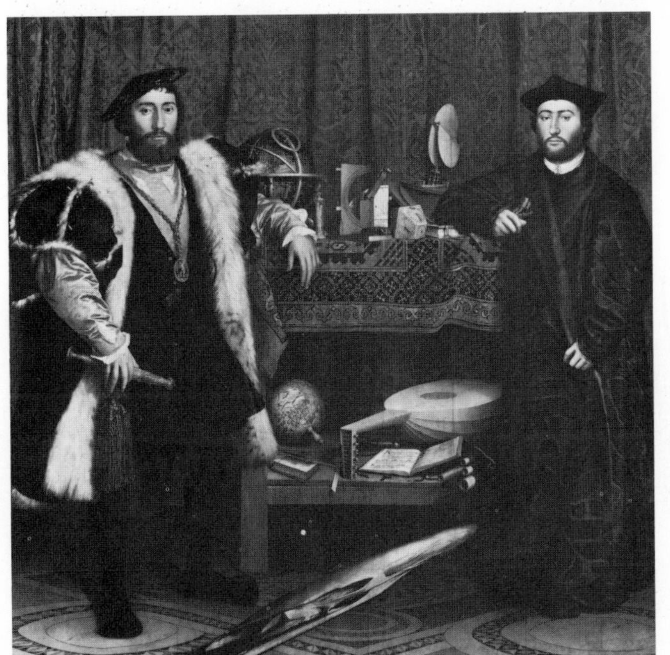

Holbein. *The Ambassadors*

Holbein. *Anne Boleyn*

Friedrich Hölderlin

Artist's Wife and 2 Children (K. Mus., Basle), *Anne of Cleves* (Louvre) and his 'showpiece' the double portrait, *The Ambassadors* (N.G., London). H. made many drawings for portraits and those of the court ladies (R. Coll., Windsor Castle) are among the masterpieces of portrait drawing. Of H.'s other work, his miniature painting is important for itself, e.g. *Mrs Pemberton* (V. and A., London), and for its influence on English miniature painting. H.'s outstanding early works for churches are the *Dead Christ* (K. Mus., Basle) and the *Madonnas* of Solothurn and Darmstadt.

Holberg Ludvig Holberg, Baron (1684–1754). Norwegian-born Danish writer. He studied at Copenhagen Univ. and after extensive travels in Europe settled there. In 1721 H. became director of the 1st Danish theatre, but despite the numerous fine plays he wrote for it the theatre had to be closed in 1727; however, in 1747 the theatre was reopened and H. again became its director for a period. H. was the founder of Danish literature (until his time all serious writing was in Latin, French or German) but also a figure of European stature displaying a versatility comparable to Voltaire's. His works include the long satirical poem *Peder Paars* (1719); a series of masterly comedies inspired by many models, notably Molière, and including *Henrik og Pernille* (1724); essays; and a number of important historical works including a history of Denmark. He also wrote the satirical Latin work *Nicolai Klimii iter subterraneum* (1741; *A Journey to the World Under-Ground*, 1742).

Holberg suite. Work by *Grieg in honour of the above.

Charles Holden.
Southgate Underground Station

Holborne Anthony (d. 1602). English composer of *Pavans, Galliards, Almains and other short Aers* for 5 instruments (1599); with his brother William he publ. a *cittern tutor containing many pieces for that instrument.

Holbrook David (1923–). English poet whose publs include *Iron, Money and Gold, Lights in the Sky* and *Llaraggub Revisited. Imaginings* (1961) and *Against the Cruel Frost* (1963), still working with everyday experience –of country domesticity–show a greater dramatic power arising from an unusual willingness to assert values while appreciating the subtlety of forces that threaten them.

Holcroft Thomas (1745–1809). English writer who shared the radical opinions of *Godwin and Tom *Paine. His theories are presented cautiously in the novel *The Adventures of Hugh Trevor* (1794) (modelled on Godwin's *Caleb Williams*) and the play *The Road to Ruin* (1792). His *Memoirs. . .*, completed by W. Hazlitt, were publ. in 1816.

Holden Charles (1874–1960). British architect; notable for his designs for London Underground stations (1906–26), and for collaborating with sculptors, including Epstein, Gill and Moore, in urban architecture. Towards the end of his career he was engaged in town planning, including a controversial City plan, in association with Sir William Holford.

Holden William (1918–). U.S. film actor. His films include: *Sunset Boulevard* (1950), *Sabrina Fair* (1954), *The Bridge on the River Kwai* (1957), and *The World of Suzie Wong* (1960).

Hölderlin (Johann Christian) Friedrich (1770–1843). German poet. He held (1796–8) the post of tutor in the Frankfurt-am-Main household of the banker Gontard, whose wife Susette ('Diotima') became his inspiration. After a disturbed period, he finally went mad in 1806 and henceforth was in the care of a Tübingen carpenter. H.'s poetry was of philosophic rather than lyric cast: linked to Weimar classicism by his restraint and harmony of form and his use of Greek metre and material, and to romanticism–especially Novalis–by his longing for a golden age and his view of history. Neglected in the 19th c., H. was rediscovered, especially after Hellingrath's ed. (1913–): modern poets in Germany and abroad have been deeply influenced by him. His poems appeared in periodicals and were first coll. by Uhland and G. Schwab (*Gedichte*, 1826): odes, hymns and elegies in Greek stanzas, especially alcaics, in the line of Klopstock, Hölty and Schiller, which praise nature, God and Greece; lament both the passing of integration and harmony and the task of the poet in unpropitious times; and anticipate a 'new Greece' in Germany. Outstanding among the major hymns are *Der Archipelagus* (1800), *Brot und Wien* (1801), *Patmos* (1802?). The same themes inform his rhapsodical novel in modern Greek dress, *Hyperion* (1797/9)–part *Bildungsroman*,

Elias Holl. Augsburg town hall

Henry Holland. Brooks's Club, interior

part autobiography–and his unfinished play *Empedokles* (versions 1797 and 1800).

Holford Sir William (1907–). English architect and planner, became famous as planning consultant in various controversial cases, as at Piccadilly Circus and St Paul's precinct. He was an assessor in the competition for the city of Brasilia. He is less well known as an architect but is in charge of the projected Univ. of Canterbury.

Holiday Billie (1915–59). U.S. jazz singer. She first achieved fame in the 1930s with a series of recordings with Teddy Wilson's orchestra featuring supporting musicians such as Lester Young. Her laconic and deeply personal interpretations of the commercial songs of the 1930s remain unrivalled, and her influence on other vocalists is comparable with that of Louis Armstrong and Charlie Parker on other instrumentalists.

Holinshed (or Hollingshead) Raphael (d. 1580?). English chronicler who compiled the ... *Chronicles of England, Scotland and Ireland* (1577); contributors included E. Campion and R. Hooker, and their sources H. *Boece, J. Major and *Giraldus Cambrensis. H.'s *Chronicles* provided material for many contemporary dramatists; Shakespeare used it for *Macbeth*, the history plays, part of *Cymbeline*, and possibly *King Lear*.

Holl Elias (1573–1646). German architect. He visited Venice, later helping to introduce the Renaissance style into Germany. His chief work is Augsburg town hall.

Holland Henry (1745–1806). English architect. In 1771 he went into partnership with 'Capability' Brown (later marrying his daughter Bridget) and carried out the architectural parts of Brown's commissions. As a speculative builder he laid out over 100 acres of Chelsea, including Sloane Street. His style was close to the Adam brothers'. Buildings designed by him include Brooks's Club, St James's.

Holland Philemon (1552–1637). English trs. who produced ornate versions of Plutarch, Livy, Pliny the Elder and Xenophon. In 1610 he trs. W. *Camden's *Britannia*. . . .

Hollar Wenceslaus (1607–77). Draughtsman and engraver born in Prague; worked in England from 1636. His output was enormous and covered a wide range of subjects. His topographical views of London before the Great Fire of 1666 and his works on costume, *Ornatus Muliebris Anglicanus* (1640) and *Theatrum Mulierum* (1643), are of considerable historical interest.

Hollow Men, The (1925). Poem by T. S. *Eliot.

Holmes John Clellon (1926–). U.S. novelist, author of *Go* (1952; also called *The Beat Boys*), an early description of the *beats, and *The Horn* (1958), a study of jazz musicians modelled on famous originals.

Holmes Oliver Wendell (1809–94). U.S. writer, professor of anatomy at Harvard and reformer in the field of medical hygiene. H. was a famous conversationalist and found a vehicle for his wit and erudition in the dialogues of *The Autocrat of the Breakfast Table* (1858; it also contained his best-known poem, *The Chambered Nautilus*); *The Professor at the Breakfast Table* (1860); *The Poet at the Breakfast Table* (1872) and *Over the Teacups* (1891). H. also wrote novels, including *Elsie Venner: A Romance of Destiny* (1861).

Holst Gustav (Theodor) (1874–1934). English composer and teacher at Morley College, London and at the R.C.M. H. began his musical career as a trombonist. His music is essentially romantic but uneven time measures, such as 5 in a bar, a strong rhythmic interest, a distinguished melodic gift and the vein of mysticism as seen in settings of the *Rig Veda* all add up to a highly personal style. His works include: the opera *The Perfect Fool* (1921) to his own libretto; the orchestral suites *St Paul's* (1913), *The Planets* (1917) and *Egdon Heath* (1927); the choral works *The Hymn of Jesus* (1917) and the *Mystic Trumpeter* for soprano and orchestra (1904).

Holst Imogen (1907–). English musician, daughter of the above. H. was connected with Dartington music school; she has written several books about her father and an educational book, *Tune*.

Holt Seth (1923–). British film director. H. was an ed. at Ealing, where he also became, from 1954 to 1956, an associate producer. His 1st film, *Nowhere to Go* (1958), was an ambitious

Oliver Wendell Holmes

Gustav Holst

The Historie of Scotlande. 243

Holinshed's *Historie of Scotland*; Macbeth and Banquo meet the witches

Holt. *Nowhere to Go*

Hollar. *The Tower of London*; etching

Winslow Homer. *Gloucester Farm*

Homeric vase by Josiah Wedgwood

Arthur Honegger

thriller. After the badly written *Taste of Fear* (1961), he managed to turn the novelettish *Station Six Sahara* (1963) into a personal statement.

Holy Children, The Song of the Three. One of the books of the *Apocrypha, about the 3 men cast into the fiery furnace on the order of Nebuchadnezzar and delivered by an angel; the *Benedicite* canticle is taken from this book.

Holy Living, The Rule and Exercise of (1650) and . . . **Holy Dying** (1651). Prose works by Jeremy *Taylor.

Holy Sinner, The (1951). Novel by Thomas Mann.

Holz Arno (1863–1929). Major German theorist of realism in literature, expounding his views in *Die Kunst, ihr Wesen und ihre Gesetze* (1890) and *Revolution der Lyrik* (1899). His works include the play *Familie Selicke* (1891).

Homage to Delacroix (1864; Louvre). Portrait group by *Fantin-Latour.

Homage to Sextus Propertius (1919). Poem by Ezra *Pound.

Homer. The reputed author of the **Iliad* and the **Odyssey*. The Greeks revered him as the greatest of their poets, had much of the great epics off by heart, and would appeal to them as to an historical authority, but knew nothing of the poet's life. Ancient estimates of his date range over 500 years; several cities claimed his birth; he was generally believed to have been blind. Other poems were attributed to him but only the 2 epics were generally accepted and in the 3rd–2nd c. B.C. Alexandrian scholars purged the text of even these by marking lines and episodes that they deemed spurious. A few Hellenistic scholars doubted whether both poems were by the same author, or even if either were the work of a single poet, attributing their compilation to a redactor working at Athens in the 6th c. B.C. 19th-c. German scholars doubted the poet's existence; Samuel Butler eccentrically argued that the *Odyssey* was written by a woman. The poet of the *Iliad* most probably lived during the 8th c. B.C. on the island of Chios. The *Odyssey* is perhaps by a younger contemporary. Both poems belong to a tradition of oral poetry extending back over perhaps 500 years or more, even to a period before the probable date of the Trojan War itself. H.'s language therefore includes many archaic and obsolete elements preserved in the traditional formulae which attach themselves inseparably to the names of the heroes, and in the many phrases, half-lines and clauses which recur. These repetitive elements are a mark of the epic style which distinguish it from the deliberately literary manner of Virgil or Milton. So in his historical reporting H. preserves the tradition he has inherited of a quasi-feudal aristocratic Bronze Age society fighting with weapons and tactics proper to that period, but occasionally later elements creep into the picture anachronistically; iron is mentioned once or twice and modern methods of warfare and modern customs. H.'s innovation may have been the elaboration of similes, which are such a marked feature of the *Iliad* and the idea of constructing an epic on such a vast scale. Although many scholars still question the relevance of some episodes and demonstrate the occasional incoherence of one section with another, both *Iliad* and *Odyssey* are plainly conceived in terms of a single plot; the wrath of Achilles in the one case and the return of Odysseus in the other. The character-drawing in both poems is consistent and acute. The *Iliad*, besides preserving a substratum of historical truth, however exiguous, embodies the reflection of a compassionate man on the misery and tragedy of warfare. His view of the gods is mocking and sophisticated and heralds the rise of Ionian scepticism. The *Odyssey* preserves much more of folk-lore; both the wanderings and the vengeance, including several conflicting accounts of the return, have been applied to the 'historical' figure of Odysseus, but the poet is more concerned with social ironies.

Homer Winslow (1836–1910). U.S. painter, pictorial journalist and illustrator. He covered the Civil War for *Harper's Weekly* and achieved recognition as a painter with *Prisoners from the Front* (1866; Met. Mus.). Between 1867 and 1880 his subjects were broadly treated rural genre scenes, e.g. *Gloucester Farm* (1874; M. of A., Philadelphia) but after a visit to England (1881–2) he returned to violent realistic paintings connected with the sea, e.g. *The Life Line* (1884; M. of A., Philadelphia). Later he adopted an impressionistic watercolour technique.

Homeric Hymns. Hymns attributed to Homer, though inferior in quality to the *Iliad* and *Odyssey*. They were invocations to the gods intended to be sung or recited before the recitation of an epic, but seem themselves to have developed into epic proportions. 34 examples survive.

Homeric vase. Made in jasperware by the potter Josiah *Wedgwood from an original design by the sculptor Flaxman (*c.* 1776). The vase was made in a blue and black version with the figure subject *The Apotheosis of Homer* applied in white. A companion-piece, *The Apotheosis of Virgil*, was also designed. Many examples of the Homeric vase were made, of which the first was presented to the British Mus.

Homme armé, L' (French, 'The Armed Man'). Old French melody used in many cyclic masses of the 15th c. and as late as the 17th c.

Homme révolté, L' (1952). Book by *Camus.

homophony: *harmonic writing

Hondecoeter Melchior d' (1636–95). Dutch painter notable for his pictures of birds. He studied under his father GIJSBERT GILLISZ (1604–53), an animal painter, and his uncle J. B. Weenix, and worked at The Hague and Amsterdam.

Hone Nathaniel (1718–84). Irish-born portrait miniaturist in enamel and watercolour who worked in England; founder-member of the R.A. From 1750 to 1752 he studied in Italy and subsequently painted some large-scale portraits in oils. He satirized Reynolds in a painting entitled *The Conjurer* (rejected R.A., 1775).

Honegger Arthur (1892–1955). French-Swiss composer, a member of The *Six. After studying at Zürich he went to Paris, where he finally settled in 1920 as a composer and conductor. Despite such diverse influences as Bach, Stravinsky and Strauss, polyphonic, polytonal and jazz elements, H. achieves a powerful and highly individual style, somewhat heavier than others of The Six. His most famous works are the Biblical oratorio *King David* (1921); the symphonic movement *Pacific 231* (1923), a throbbing evocation of a journey on an express train, and *Joan of Arc at the stake* (1938), music to a play by Claudel. H.'s other works

Hone. *The Piping Boy*

Melchior d'Hondecoeter. *A Cock and other Birds*

Pieter de Hoogh. *Courtyard in Delft*

include the opera *Antigone* (1927), with libretto by Cocteau; 4 other oratorios; ballets; operettas; the 'mimed symphony' *Horace victorieux* (1921); 5 symphonies, film music and choral works.

Honiton lace. Honiton in Devon was a centre of bobbin *lace making from the 16th c. The term H. l. generally denotes a lace (latterly machine-made) in which bobbin-made sprigs and flowers are sewn or appliquèd to net. In the 17th and 18th cs imitations of Brussels lace were developed.

Honthorst Gerard or Gerrit van (1590–1656). Dutch painter, trained in Utrecht, but in Rome by about 1610. H. was very popular in Italy, where he was known as 'Gherardo delle Notti' because of his dramatically lit night scenes after Caravaggio (*Christ before the High Priest*, N.G., London). H. was largely responsible for bringing the innovations of Caravaggio to Holland on his return there in 1620. Enjoying an international reputation, he was invited to the English court in 1628 (*Charles I and Henrietta Maria with the Liberal Arts*, R. Colls, England) and to the Danish court in 1635. As Dutch court painter he painted the baroque decorations at Huis-ten-Bosch.

Hood Thomas (1799–1845). English poet and journalist. H. was a master of outrageous punning in his humorous verse, but he also wrote poems of social protest, e.g. *The Song of the Shirt* and *The Bridge of Sighs*, and such morbidly powerful long poems as *The Haunted House* and *The Last Man.*

Hooft Pieter Cornelisz (1581–1647). Poet, playwright and historian; an outstanding figure in Dutch literature. His 1st tragedy, *Achilles ende Polyxena*, was performed in 1598, after which he travelled abroad (1598–1601), visiting Italy and studying Italian literature (especially Tasso) which profoundly influenced him. After his return he produced a quantity of lyrical poetry and more plays, including the pastoral *Granida* (1615), *Ware-nar* (1617) and *Baeto oft Oorsprong der Hollanderen* (1626). In 1618 he turned to history, producing a masterly Dutch history (1642, 1654).

Hoogh or **Hooch** Pieter de (1629–after 1684). Dutch painter, the contemporary of N. Maes and Vermeer of Delft and, like them, a recorder of scenes of middle-class life. H. is first recorded as 'painter and footman' in the household of a rich merchant. After 1654 he lived in Delft and his art declined when he moved to Amsterdam, *c.* 1663, and tried to portray a higher stratum of society. Like Vermeer, he was interested in optics and the fall of light. His colour harmonies are simple and very effective. Among his best works are: *Courtyard in Delft* (N.G., London), *Woman Peeling Apples* (Wallace Coll., London), *The Pantry* and *The Linen Cupboard* (Rijksmus., Amsterdam).

Hoogstraten Samuel van (1627–78). Dutch painter of portraits, genre and religious subjects and architectural fantasies. He studied under Rembrandt in Amsterdam. He was famous for his experiments with *trompe-l'œil* and perspective illusionism, e.g. his peep-show box in the N.G., London.

Hook James (1746–1827). English composer; organist and composer to Vauxhall Gardens (1774–1820). His huge output of ballad operas, keyboard concertos and songs includes the song 'The Lass of Richmond Hill'.

Hooker Richard (1554?–1600). English priest and writer, author of the prose masterpiece *Of the lawes of ecclesiasticall politie* (1594, 1597; books 6–8 posth. 1648), an Anglican reply to Puritan attacks. It is outstanding for its calm reasoning, eloquence and clarity.

Hope A(lec) D(erwent) (1907–). Australian poet. His satire, technically accomplished and controlled, is incisive and wide ranging, e.g. *The Wandering Islands* (1955); lack of control sometimes vitiates his criticism.

Hope Anthony (1863–1933). Pseud. of Anthony Hope Hawkins, English writer of the adventure novel *The Prisoner of Zenda* (1894) and its sequel *Rupert of Hentzau* (1898), both set in 'Ruritania' (the name was invented by H.).

Hope Bob (1903–). British-born wisecracking U.S. vaudeville artist. His speciality is the cowardly but endearing amorous braggart who finds himself constantly in situations of intrigue and peril; as such he starred in all the *Road* films with *Crosby and also *Paleface* (1948) with Jane *Russell.

Hope Thomas (1770?–1831). Anglo-Dutch furniture designer and collector of ancient and

Honthorst. *Christ before the High Priest*

Thomas Hope. Library table

Gerard Manley Hopkins

Hoppner. *Princess Mary*

Hopper. *Early Sunday Morning*

neo-classical sculpture, who settled in England after extensive travel. His book *Household Furniture and Interior Decoration* (1807), containing careful studies of classical and ancient Egyptian furniture, created a vogue for imitation of the styles of these periods based on archaeological research. He also wrote *Anastasius* (1819), a novel originally attributed to Byron.

Hopkins Anthony (1921–). English composer of much incidental and film music and also operas and chamber operas. He is a frequent broadcaster on music.

Hopkins Gerard Manley (1844–89). English poet and Jesuit. H. wrote his major poem, *The Wreck of the Deutschland*, in 1876. His poetry, which served and came second to his vocation, embraces an almost mystical sense of God's immanence and a terrible spiritual isolation and sterility. Both his occasional obscurity and his finest poetry, such as *God's Grandeur* and *The Windhover*, stem from his attempt to convey the 'inscape' of things–their essential and individual beauty; to this end he experimented freely with language and rhythm, creating new compound words and a more flexible metre which he called 'sprung rhythm'. This was an adaptation of the accentual rhythm of Old English alliterative verse and was based on the normal stresses of speech. The stressed syllables form the pattern, the number of unstressed syllables being immaterial.
The poems, first ed. by R. Bridges in 1918, attracted little attention until 1930. Publ. of the notebooks, letters and journal followed in 1935–8.

Hopkinson Francis (1737–91). American statesman and poet and also the earliest known composer of N. America; he wrote several songs.

Hopper Edward (1882–). U.S. realist painter of urban and architectural subjects in which severity of composition and harsh lighting contribute to create an atmosphere of hostility and withdrawal.

Hoppner John (1758–1810). Portrait painter born in England of German parentage. He gained sufficient contemporary popularity to rank as Lawrence's chief rival, although his style was based almost entirely on borrowings from other artists including Reynolds, Romney and later Lawrence.

Horace (65–8 B.C.). Quintus Horatius Flaccus, Roman poet born at Venusia in Apulia, the son of a poor freedman. His father took him to Rome to be educated, daily escorted him to school and perhaps shared his lessons. His father's comments on their joint experiences of snobbish Roman society formed H.'s mind and he several times acknowledges his debt to his father's good sense. At 21 H. was reading philosophy at Athens when Brutus arrived to raise forces for the Republican war against Caesar's heirs, Antony and Octavian (later Emperor Augustus). H. became a military tribune under Brutus but, by his own account, did not distinguish himself. Returning to Rome in 42 he found his father dead and his property confiscated, but obtained a job in the treasury office and took to scribbling to fend off penury. About 38 B.C. his work, which had already brought him the friendship of Virgil and Varius, won him, through their good offices, the friendship and patronage of Maecenas, who 5 years later gave him the Sabine farm he often mentions, and to whom most of his books are dedicated. His earliest work, coll. and publ. in 30 B.C., were the *Epodes*–satiric, often vituperative, sketches of contemporary manners in the manner of the 7th-c. Greek poet, Archilochus. At the same time H. had been composing the first of his *Discourses* or *Satires*, conversational, reflective, humorous pieces which contain a good deal of autobiography and social comment. The 1st book was publ. in 35, the second in 30 B.C. The next 7 years H. spent polishing the *Odes*, publ. in 3 books in 23, which he regarded as his most important work. Technically they are unique: no other Roman poet attempted the range of metres handled so easily by H. The prevailing tone is personal and Epicurean, the theme the impermanence and the vanity of life and the language taut, allusive and compressed. In 20 B.C. he publ. a book of epistles intended as his last book. These are in the same manner as the *Discourses*, but more gentle, mature and refined. Under pressure from Augustus he wrote a 4th book of lyrics, publ. in 13 B.C. and 3 long epistles, including that known as the *Ars Poetica*, dealing with literary criticism.

Horace (1640). Tragedy by Corneille.

horn. *Brass musical instrument played with a conical mouthpiece. The modern orchestral h. in F (fitted with valves) has a range of about 3 and a half 8ves from the B below the bass staff. It is basically a coiled tube about 11 ft long, conical in shape gradually widening in diameter from about a quarter of an in. to about 1 in. and terminating in a flared bell about 18 ins across. It has developed from an ancient instrument used in war and on the hunting-field, gradually introduced to art music from the late 17th c. The 'natural' (i.e. valveless) h. had available the notes of the *harmonic series but early in the 18th c. it was discovered that the player could modify the pitch of the harmonics by squeezing his hand into the bell of the instrument; these hand notes made possible a more complete range. For this instrument Mozart wrote his h. concertos. Early in the 19th c. a system of valves was developed to give a fully chromatic compass. The 2 types of modern orchestral h. are the narrow-bore French instrument and the wide-bore German h.; the latter has a heavier tone and is easier to play than the former.

Horn Charles Edward (1786–1849). British light composer and conductor working much in the U.S. His numerous compositions include the song 'Cherry Ripe'. His father KARL FRIEDRICH H. (1762–1830) was also a composer, from Germany who settled in London in the 1780s.

Horne Richard Henry (or Hengist) (1803–84). English playwright and poet, author of the allegorical poem *Orion* (1843), and poetic dramas *Cosmo de' Medici* (publ. 1837) and *The Death of Marlowe* (publ. 1837).

Horniman Annie Elizabeth (1860–1937). English theatre manager who was a pioneer of the repertory movement. She founded the Abbey Theatre, Dublin (1904) and later bought the Gaiety Theatre, Manchester, which she ran as a repertory theatre (1908–21).

hornpipe. Vigorous English dance, dating at least from the 17th c.; now associated with sailors.

Horse Feathers (1931). Film with the *Marx Brothers.

Horse's Mouth, The (1944). Novel by Joyce *Cary.

Horta Victor (1861–1947). Leading architect of the Belgian art nouveau. At the turn of the c. he designed a series of houses in Brussels which carried art nouveau to its extreme. The planning is seriously and rationally thought out, but walls sway and curve like waves and decorative elements like hand-rails and glazing bars run riot in curvilinear ironwork. He built several large structures; the most important is the Maison du Peuple, Brussels (1899), with the whole façade curved, built of glass and iron, foreshadowing curtain walls.

hortensia. A step in ballet in which the dancer with one foot behind the other reverses their position by a 'shunting' jump and this is usually repeated in quick succession.

Hosea. One of the minor prophetic books of the *Bible (Old Testament).

Hosiasson Philippe (1898–). Russian-born painter of the school of Paris; also an illustrator and theatrical designer.

Hostage, The (1958). Play by Brendan *Behan.

Hôtel de Bourgogne, Théâtre de l'. The 1st theatre in Paris (1548). In 1673 its actors merged with others to form the *Comédie-Française, but the theatre itself was in use until 1783.

Hôtel des Invalides (1952). Film directed by G. *Franju.

Houbracken Arnold (1660–1719). Dutch painter remembered as the author of *De groote Schouburgh . . .* (1718–21), an important source of information about 17th-c. Dutch and Flemish painters despite its inaccuracies. His son JACOBUS (1698–1780) was a portrait engraver.

Houckgeest Gerard (*c.* 1600–61). Dutch painter who worked in Delft. He specialized in church interiors.

Houdar de la Motte Antoine (1672–1731). French poet and playwright who took the side of the moderns in the *Ancients and Moderns Controversy, writing a new version of the *Iliad.*

Houdon Jean-Antoine (1741–1828). French sculptor who studied under J.-B. Pigalle and J.-B. Lemoyne and worked in Rome from 1764 to 1768; there he came under the influence of J. J. Winckelmann and his circle. For some time he followed the style of late baroque sculpture but gradually adopted the colder manner of classicism. His best and most numerous works are portraits, which include busts of Diderot, Rousseau, Voltaire and George Washington.

Hound of Heaven, The (1891). Religious poem by Francis *Thompson.

Hours, Book of. These were bound colls of the prayers prescribed for each of the 'hours' of the liturgical day. Wealthy clerics and laymen frequently commissioned elaborately illuminated books of hours; among the most famous is *Les Très Riches Heures du Duc de Berry.*

House of Seven Gables, The (1851). Novel by *Hawthorne.

House of the Dead, The (1861). Book by *Dostoyevsky.

Housing Problems (1935). Film directed by A. *Elton and E. *Anstey.

Housman A(lfred) E(dward) (1859–1936). English poet, a distinguished classical scholar. H.'s oeuvre is small; his 1st coll., *A Shropshire Lad* (1896), made him famous, but he publ. nothing until *Last Poems* (1922). His short, simple, economical lyrics treat general themes –above all that of the brevity of life and the death of the young; the tone is nostalgic, disillusioned, occasionally rising to anger. He also publ. *More Poems* (1936).

Housman Laurence (1865–1959). English novelist, playwright and poet; brother of the above. Among his plays are *Prunella* (with H. Granville-Baker, publ. 1906), the cycle *Little Plays of St Francis* (publ. 1922), and the series about Queen Victoria, *Victoria Regina* (publ. 1934) and *Happy and Glorious* (publ. 1945).

Hous of Fame, The. Poem by *Chaucer.

Howard Andrée (1910–). British choreographer who began her career as a dancer with Rambert. H. produced her 1st significant ballet, *Death and the Maiden*, in 1937 and since then has become one of the most prolific British choreographers. Other ballets she has created

Bedford Book of Hours; The Creation

A. E. Housman

Houdon. Full-length sculpture of George Washington; Capitol, Richmond, Virginia. Also *Diderot

Horta. Maison du Peuple, interior of auditorium. Also *art nouveau

Thomas Howard, Earl of Arundel, in his gallery, by Mytens

Huber. *The Danube Valley*; pen drawing

William Dean Howells

include *Lady into Fox* (1939) and *Assembly Ball* (1946).

Howard Charles (1899–). U.S. painter whose work combines surrealism and abstraction. He lived in London before World War II and was associated with the surrealist group. During the war he left England for the U.S., but returned in 1946. He exhibited symbolic abstractions at the Whitechapel Gal., London, in 1956.

Howard Ebenezer (1850–1928). English father of the garden city. His book *Tomorrow: A Peaceful Path to Reform* (1898) outlines the advantages of small self-sufficient towns, and led to the founding of Letchworth (1903) and Welwyn Garden City.

Howard Henry: *Surrey

Howard Leslie (1893–1943). Leading romantic star of British and U.S. films, e.g. *The Scarlet Pimpernel* (1935), *Gone With the Wind* (1939), until his death in a plane crash.

Howard Sidney (Coe) (1891–1939). U.S. playwright, whose works include *They Knew What They Wanted* (1924).

Howard Thomas, 2nd Earl of Arundel (1585–1646). English collector and patron of the arts; he acquired pictures, books, jewels, statuary, and most important, the 'Arundel Marbles'; these include the famous 'Parian Chronicle', a marble slab on which are recorded events in Greek history and myth.

Howard Trevor (1916–). English actor, originally on the stage; he made his film début in 1944 with *The Way Ahead.* His corncrake voice and engaging ugliness are most often exploited in roles as repulsive-but-fascinating villain; but he has a far wider range of abilities, e.g. his parts in *Brief Encounter* (1945), *Sons and Lovers* (1960) and *Mutiny on the Bounty* (1962).

Howards End (1910). Novel by E. M. *Forster.

Howe Edgar Watson (1853–1937). U.S. journalist and novelist known for his trenchant, pessimistic aphorisms. His novel *The Story of a Country Town* (1883) is of historical importance, marking a stage in the development of U.S. realism.

Howells Herbert (1892–). English composer and teacher at the R.C.M. and Morley College, London. His music includes the choral works *Sine nomine* and *A Kent Yeoman's Wooing Song*; orchestral, chamber and organ music.

Howells William Dean (1837–1920). U.S. novelist, a leading journalist and critic who was self-educated. He became a literary force as ed. of *The Atlantic Monthly* and to the end of his life encouraged rising young writers. H. wrote many novels, generally about the conflict between family breeding and business and consequent middle-class marriage problems; their realistic treatment is best seen in *The Rise of Silas Lapham* (1885), set among the newly rich in Boston, and *Hazard of new Fortunes* (1890), in New York. H.'s work quickly seemed old fashioned but he prepared the way for later naturalistic novels.

How the West Was Won (1962). Film directed by H. *Hathaway, J. *Ford and G. *Marshall.

How to Write Short Stories (1924). Coll. of short stories by Ring Lardner.

Hrotsvitha (*c.* 935–*c.* 75). German nun of Gandersheim who wrote in Latin a number of plays which, she hoped, would replace the works of the pagan Terence in monasteries. They probably did since H., an advocate of chastity, outlined in some detail the temptations attendant on it.

Huber Hans (1852–1921). Between 1870 and 1910 the leading Swiss composer and teacher. His music was influenced by Schumann and Brahms and includes: 5 operas; much church music; 8 programme symphonies; concertos and many piano and chamber works.

Huber Wolf (*c.* 1490–1553). German painter, draughtsman and woodcut artist who, after Altdorfer, was the most important member of the *Danube school. He worked in Regensburg and Passau. Few paintings by him are known and it is in his woodcuts and drawings that his lyrical approach to landscape can best be seen.

Thomas Hudson. *Gentleman*

Hudson River school. Cole, *View of the White Mountains*

Hubley John (1914–). U.S. animated-film maker who worked for Disney, then UPA. Unlike the other U.S. cartoonists except *Pintoff, H. now works as an independent. His fluid style depends on brush-strokes with the use of line restricted to details, particularly faces. His work has an increasing message content from *Adventures of a* * (1957), on the appreciation of modern art, to the pacifism of *The Hole* (1963).

Hucbald (d. 930). Netherlands monk regarded, until the late 19th c., as a major music theorist; the *De harmonica institutione*, of minor importance, is now the only treatise ascribed to him. He also wrote several lives of saints.

Huckleberry Finn (1884). Comic novel by Mark *Twain.

Hudibras (1663–78). Verse satire by S. *Butler.

Hudson Rock (1924–). U.S. actor. He made a dramatic impression in *Giant* (1956); his appearances in *Something of Value* (1957) and *A Farewell to Arms* (1958) extended his dramatic range, and he has also played in comedy.

Hudson Thomas (1701–79). English portrait painter, son-in-law and pupil of J. Richardson the Elder and master of Reynolds. His sound, conventional work was popular before the rise of Reynolds.

Hudson W(illiam) H(enry) (1841–1922). Novelist and naturalist of U.S. parentage; he lived in Britain from 1869 and was naturalized in 1900. His most famous work is *Green Mansions* (1904), a romance set in the forests of S. America, where he was born.

Hudson River school. Name loosely applied to a number of 19th-c. U.S. romantic landscape painters who worked mainly, though not exclusively, in the vicinity of the Catskill Mountains and the Hudson River. They were never an organized group but shared a sense of wonderment at the grandeur of the newly discovered American landscape. Painstaking attention to detail is a common feature of their style. T. Cole, T. Doughty and A. Bierstadt are among the many representatives of the school.

Huet Jean-Baptiste (1745–1811). French painter (of animal and pastoral subjects) and engraver, pupil of J.-B. Leprince. He designed for Gobelins and Beauvais tapestries, following the style of Boucher.

Huet Paul (1803–69). French romantic landscape painter and engraver, influenced by Delacroix and the English painters Constable and Bonington.

Hughes Dom Anselm (1889–). English pioneer in the study of medieval music.

Hughes Arthur (1832–1915). English painter of the later phase of Pre-Raphaelitism. The Tate has several of his paintings including *April Love* and *The Eve of St Agnes* (both 1856).

Hughes Howard (1904–). U.S. film producer and director. An enigmatic figure who presided over the dying years of R.K.O. He was a highly speculative promoter whose work in the cinema is marked by passion for flying–*Hell's Angels* (1930), which he directed, and *Jet Pilot*–and devotion to sex-appeal–Harlow in *Hell's Angels*, Russell in *The Outlaw* (1943), which he also directed, and which was held up by the censor for its (then) considerable daring.

Hughes Richard (Arthur Warren) (1900–). English novelist, playwright and poet. His novels include the striking fantasy *A High Wind in Jamaica* (1929) (American title *The Innocent Voyage*), *In Hazard* (1938) and *Fox in the Attic* (1962); his verse, *Gipsy-Night* (1922); and his plays, *The Sisters' Tragedy* (publ. 1922).

Hughes Ted (1930–). English poet. He has given his theme as 'the war between vitality and death', and by his use of animal images and references to the physical world he adds to the sinewy quality in his varied rhythms. The colls *The Hawk in the Rain* (1957) and *Lupercal* (1960) are outstanding.

Hughes Thomas (1822–96). English novelist whose *Tom Brown's Schooldays* (1857), about Rugby under the headmastership of Dr Arnold, is the classic description of 19th-c. English public-school life.

Hugh Selwyn Mauberley (1920). Poem by Ezra *Pound.

Hugo Victor-Marie (1802–85). The most celebrated and prolific French poet of the 19th c.,

Huet. *View of Avignon*; etching

Arthur Hughes. *April Love*

Howard Hughes. Jean Harlow and Ben Lyon in *Hell's Angels*

Huguenots.
Ewer by David Willaume

Huguet. *St George* (detail)

Victor Hugo in 1872

Hugo. Contemporary representation of 'the battle of Hernani'

considered by some critics to be the greatest of all French poets. The son of a Napoleonic general, he spent part of his childhood in Spain, which helps to explain his choice of Spanish subjects for his early dramas; he was always sensitive to the grandeur of the Napoleonic epic although he later became a Royalist, then a Republican. His genius was precocious and in his early twenties he was already the ringleader of the romantics. After the *coup d'état* of Napoleon III in 1852, he went into exile, finally settling in Guernsey at Hauteville House, where his situation as a renowned sea-girt refugee had a great effect on his writings. After the French defeat at Sedan (1870), he returned to Paris as the grand old man of French literature, and his funeral in 1885 was a national event. His private life was eventful, since his sensuality was demanding and led him into many adventures, even when he was an old man. His early infidelities encouraged his wife to have her famous affair with Sainte-Beuve. His liaison with the actress Juliette Drouet became almost a second marriage. A neurotic strain in the family is indicated by the fact that one of his brothers and his daughter went mad.

As the leading romantic, he produced epoch-making dramas–e.g. *Cromwell* (publ. 1827), *Hernani* (1830; 1830), the occasion of violent demonstrations and counter-demonstrations by the romantics and their opponents, and *Ruy Blas* (1838; 1850)–which destroyed the old neo-classical conventions; also several vols of verse distinguished by their technical innovations, exotic colouring and linguistic brio: *Odes et Ballades* (1826), *Les Orientales* (1829; *Les Orientales: or Eastern Lyrics*, 1879), and *Les Chants du Crépuscule* (1835; *Songs of Twilight*, 1836). His greatest poetry, however, was written later when he embarked on the vast historical panorama entitled *La Légende des Siècles* (1859–83; *The Satyr*, adaptation 1889), a cycle of short epic poems. The subject is the long struggle of mankind towards the establishment of freedom and love.

He displays a similar poetic, if factually inaccurate sense of historical development in his novels, which breathe confidence in the destiny of man at the same time as they show the tragedy of life: *Notre-Dame de Paris* (1831; *Notre-Dame, a tale of the 'Ancient Régime'*, 1833), *Les Misérables* (1862; *Les Misérables*, 1862), *Quatre-Vingt-treize* (1873; *Ninety-three*, 1874).

H.'s genius is undeniable, and much of his work has become part of the French national consciousness, but it is generally recognized that he has the romantic weaknesses of grandiloquence and exaggeration. He is undoubtedly the greatest poetic rhetorician in the language.

Huguenots. Name for French Protestants. When Louis XIV began to persecute them in 1685 many came to England, including skilled goldsmiths. Their style, with its characteristic strap-work, cast decoration and classical motifs became popular, and caused a reaction against the heavy Dutch baroque style previously in vogue. The most famous 1st-generation Huguenots were Simon Pantin, Pierre Platel, David Willaume, Philip Rollos and Pierre Harache.

Huguet Jaime (*fl.* 1448–87). Spanish painter of the Catalan school who worked in Barcelona. Not only were his paintings influential in Spain but, through exporting altarpieces to Sardinia, he was responsible for the development of a Catalan school there. His figures are elongated and sumptuously clothed with rather similar lean sad features. Extensive use of gold paint also characterizes his work.

Huit Clos (1944). Play by *Sartre.

Hullah John Pyke (1812–84). English music teacher and composer. His school of singing and sight reading for working men was immensely popular and successful, but his methods, based on those of G. Wilhem, were superseded by the introduction of tonic solfa, which H. strongly opposed.

Hulme T(homas) E(rnest) (1883–1917). English philosopher and poet killed in World War I, the 'founder' of *imagism, which began among the members of the Poets' Club H. founded in London. His 5 short poems were publ. by Ezra Pound in 1912. *Speculations* (posth. 1924) is a coll. of H.'s essays and fragments; it includes interesting theories about the difference between the classical and romantic spirit.

Human Condition, The (1933). Novel by André *Malraux.

humanism. The *Renaissance intellectual movement away from medieval theological preoccupations and the prescribed scholastic authors, e.g. Aquinas; the scholar-writers of

David Hume:
painting by Allan Ramsay

the period–the HUMANISTS–turned to the study of the thought of classical antiquity. Since the 19th c. the term h. has been loosely applied to movements or systems which assign the most important role to human (as opposed to supernatural) activities.

Hume David (1711–76). Scottish philosopher; the mainstream of British philosophy has been in the Humean empiricist tradition and he decisively influenced Kant and Rousseau. H. demonstrated in *A Treatise of Human Nature* (1739–40) and *Inquiry Concerning the Human Understanding* (1748), works noted for their pellucid style, that human knowledge is ultimately derived from experience, via the senses, and that reason has only the role of organizing such knowledge. He held that no amount of reasoning could demonstrate any 'necessary connection' as the theory of causation was commonly held to have; only a study of human nature would reveal the relationships between objects of thought and experience. H. also wrote an important *History of England* (5 vols 1754–62).

Humfrey Pelham (1647–74). English composer and Master of the Children in the Chapel Royal, teacher of Purcell. H. travelled in France and Italy, and Italian influence is apparent in his anthems and other church music.

Hummel Johann Nepomuk (1778–1837). Hungarian pianist and composer. He studied with Mozart, M. Clementi, J. G. Albrechtsberger and A. Salieri. He made extensive concert tours and in his *Pianoforte School* described improved fingering methods. He wrote 7 piano concertos and other piano music, also operas, chamber music and choral music.

Humperdinck Engelbert (1854–1921). German composer who studied under F. Hiller, Lachner and Rheinberger. He met Wagner in Italy in 1879 and assisted him in Bayreuth (1880/1). He is said to have written some bars for the transformation scene in *Parsifal*, which was too short for scenic requirements. He was music critic for the *Frankfurter Zeitung*. His works include: incidental music; songs; *Moorish Rhapsody* for orchestra (1898); and 6 operas, *Hänsel und Gretel* (1893), based on folk-lore, being outstandingly popular. It illustrates his ability in writing felicitous melodies despite the almost incompatible Wagnerian instrumental and dramatic design.

Humphreys David (1752–1818). U.S. poet remembered as the probable originator and co-author of the satirical and parodic *The Anarchiad: A Poem on the Restoration of Chaos and Substantial Night* (1786–7) produced by the *Hartford Wits.

Humphry Clinker, The Expedition of (1771). Novel by *Smollett.

Hunchback of Notre-Dame, The (1831). Historical novel by Victor *Hugo.

Hundertwasser Fritz (1928–). Austrian painter whose 'spiral' paintings on cosmic and mythic themes give him a leading position among younger Austrian painters. He was a surrealist before turning to abstraction.

Hungarian Rhapsody. *Liszt gave a number of piano pieces (some later orchestrated) this name.

Hunt, The (French *La Chasse*). Nickname given to Haydn's symphony no 73 in D (1781), from the last movement; his string quartet no. 1 in B flat, from its opening phrase, and Mozart's string quartet, K.458, also from its opening subject.

Hunt (James Henry) Leigh (1784–1859). English writer. H. found his true métier as journalist on various radical periodicals which he ed. with his brother. He was an acute critic and ed., playing an important part in gaining popular recognition for the romantic poets, especially Keats and Shelley, although he later attacked Byron as a poseur. The diction of his uneven narrative poem *The Story of Rimini* (1816) influenced Keats, but most of H.'s poetry has worn badly; 2 short pieces, *Abou Ben Adhem* and *Jenny kissed me*, remained very popular. His importance lies in his most sustained work, the delightful *Autobiography* (1850), and in his light miscellaneous essays.

Hunt William Holman (1827–1910). English painter who, with D. G. Rossetti and J. E. Millais, founded the *Pre-Raphaelite Brotherhood and alone remained faithful to its principles. He visited Palestine to obtain the correct settings for *The Scapegoat* (1856; Lady Lever A. Gall., Port Sunlight). H. painted the famous *The Light of the World* (1854; Keble Coll., Oxford). His unpretentious portraits and

Hundertwasser. *Cette fleur aura raison des hommes* (1957)

Leigh Hunt

Holman Hunt. *The Scapegoat*

Hunting carpet, 17th c.

John Huston. Thelma Ritter, Clark Gable and Marilyn Monroe in *The Misfits*. Also *Bogart

Aldous Huxley

small landscapes have considerable realistic force.

hunting carpets. A well-known class of Persian carpet, sometimes called animal carpets. They present a hunt of wild animals in the traditional Persian fashion, that is by driving the game into an enclosure where horsemen and trained hunting cheetahs slaughter indiscriminately.

Hunting of the Snark, The (1876). Nonsense poem by Lewis *Carroll.

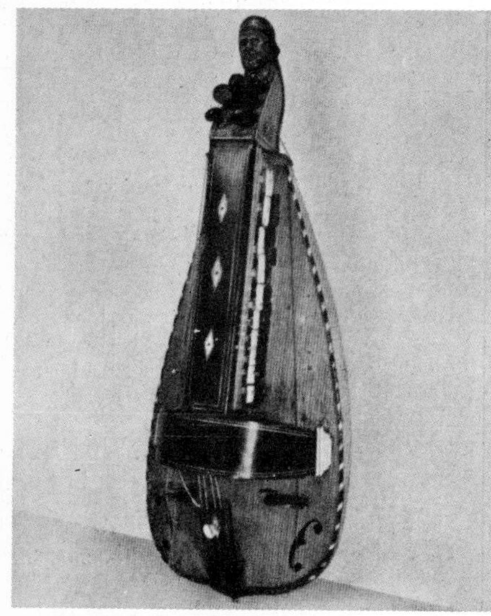

Hurdy-gurdy; French, *c.* 1700

hurdy-gurdy. Stringed musical instrument of ancient origins. The strings are stopped, not by the fingers as on a violin, but by finger-keys, and the bow of the violin is replaced by a wheel which, when turned, rubs against the strings; 2 supplementary strings provide a drone. In the late 18th c. this peasant instrument was popular in high society, Haydn composing for it for noble patrons.

Hurok Sol(omon) (1888–). Russian impresario who became a U.S. citizen in 1914. He began his career by managing weekly concerts in New York (1915) and since then has been responsible for introducing international artists, such as Pavlova, Chaliapin, Jean-Louis Barrault and Fonteyn to the American public.

Hurry Leslie (1909–). English painter and designer whose set and costumes for the ballet *Hamlet* (1942) were a perfect example of atmosphere on the stage. H. has also designed for opera, e.g. *The Force of Destiny* (Edinburgh, 1951) and many Shakespearean plays for the Old Vic.

Hurtado de Mendoza Diego (1503–75). Spanish writer and poet, scholar and diplomat, once thought to have written the *picaresque novel *Lazarillo de Tormes*. He wrote a magnificent history of the rebellion of the *moriscos* of Granada in 1568, a number of elegant poems, and a series of fables in traditional Spanish metre.

Jan Hus

Hus Jan (1369?–1415). Czech religious reformer and writer. In theology his inspiration was the teaching of John Wycliffe, and H.'s heresy caused his death by burning at the Council of Constance. He wrote important scholarly works and sermons and hymns in Latin and Czech and made an important reform of Czech orthography.

Huston John (1906–). U.S. film director. Briefly boxer, Mexican soldier, and actor before entering the cinema as a writer. His first directorial work was the thriller *The Maltese Falcon* (1941) from Dashiell Hammett. H.'s aims resemble in many ways those of *Hawks and *Walsh, whose *Sergeant York* and *High Sierra* he scripted. He differs from them in his intellectual pretensions, which have led him to literary adaptations like *The Red Badge of Courage* (from Stephen Crane, 1950), *The African Queen* (C. S. Forester, 1951) and *Moby Dick* (Herman Melville, 1955). His best films are his most good-humoured–*The African Queen* and *Beat the Devil* (1953)–but his critical reputation rests less on these than on *The Treasure of Sierra Madre* (1947) and *The Asphalt Jungle* (1950). His reputation began to slump in the mid 1950s but he had a big success with *Night of the Iguana* (1964) from Tennessee Williams.

Huston Walter (1884–1950). U.S. film actor, father of John H., in whose *The Treasure of Sierra Madre* he gave a typically incisive performance.

Hutten Ulrich von (1488–1523). German Protestant Reformer and patriot. He wrote theology in Latin and German poems and songs, including the popular 'Ich hab's gewart' (1521).

Hüttenbrenner Anselm (1794–1868). Austrian composer of several hundred songs and male voice quartets; he also wrote symphonies, chamber and church music. He was a friend of Beethoven and Schubert, his notes on the latter's life being very important; H. withheld the score of Schubert's 'Unfinished' symphony until 1865.

Huxley Aldous (Leonard) (1894–1963). English novelist, grandson of T. H. H. An eye infection which troubled him for much of his life prevented H. from becoming a doctor. In 1937 he settled in California. During the 1920s and 1930s he publ. a series of harshly satirical novels, the best of which are *Point Counter Point* (1928), *Eyeless in Gaza* (1936), and the futuristic *Brave New World* (1932) describing a scientifically controlled utopia of contentment in which personality is an antisocial force, as well as several vols of essays and literary criticism. Later he became interested in the varieties of spiritual perception; *The Perennial*

Philosophy (1945) is a study of mystical experience, and *The Doors of Perception* (1954) and *Heaven and Hell* (1956) describe his experiments with the drug mescalin. Other novels include *Antic Hay* (1923), *Those Barren Leaves* (1925) and *Crome Yellow* (1921).

Huxley T(homas) H(enry) (1825–95). English biologist. In the controversy over the correctness of the theory of evolution H. was Darwin's chief supporter. He coined the word 'agnosticism'.

Huygens Constantijn (1596–1637). Dutch poet, musician and statesman, one of the most brilliant figures in Dutch literature. He frequently visited England, being knighted by James I. He wrote in Latin, French and Italian as well as Dutch. His word-play bears some resemblance to the works of John Donne, which he greatly admired, but above all he achieved a flexibility of language not approached by earlier Dutch poets.

Huysmans J(oris)-K(arl) (1848–1907). French novelist, a civil servant. H. was a prominent naturalist, contributing to *Les *Soirées de Médan*. In the 1880s he moved away from naturalism: *À Rebours* (1884; *Against the Grain*, 1922), the story of the wealthy, neurasthenic Des Esseintes, who retires from society and cultivates refined, exquisite and artificial satisfactions, was a representative book of the 'decadent' spirit and widely imitated (e.g. by Oscar Wilde in *The Picture of Dorian Gray*). A later series of novels, beginning with *Là-bas* (1891), relates the search for faith and ultimate conversion to Catholicism which H. himself, like so many of the decadents, underwent.

Huysum Jan van (1682–1749). Dutch flower painter who imitated nature with unequalled virtuosity; he worked in Amsterdam. He used a higher range of tones in his elaborate compositions than any Dutch flower painter before him and was responsible for introducing light backgrounds. He had many imitators, above all his brother Jacob (1687–1740) who, working in England from *c.* 1721, marketed Jan's work as his own. Their father Justus (1659–1716) was also a flower painter.

hydraulis or water organ. The oldest known form of organ, dating from the 3rd c. B.C. Wind pressure to the pipes was kept stable by water pressure on the wind reservoir.

Hydrotaphia, Urne-Buriall (1658). Treatise by Sir Thomas *Browne.

Hymn of Jesus, The. Choral work by *Holst.

Hyperion (1820). Poem by *Keats and an epistolary novel (1797–9) by *Hölderlin.

Hypnerotomachia Poliphili. One of the world's most remarkable books; written (1467) by F. Colonna. The 1st ed., using F. Griffo's 3rd roman fount, was printed in 1499 by Aldus Manutius in Venice, with 200 woodcuts by an unknown artist, and is in itself the most famous illustrated incunabulum. It is an obscure allegorical narrative, written in a mixture of languages including Italian, Greek, Latin and Hebrew, and telling of a dream journey through the realms of Art and Free Will. The numerous detailed architectural descriptions are partly fantasy and partly derived from a knowledge of classical architecture. Colonna particularly delighted in the descriptions of ruins and decay, symbols of the impermanence of human life. These imaginary monuments were an endless source of themes to Renaissance painters, sculptors and engravers.

hypostyle. Architectural term describing a large hall whose whole roof rests on columns (i.e. the columns are not just along the sides of the hall).

Jan van Huysum. *Flowerpiece*

Hypnerotomachia Poliphili

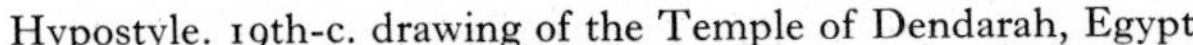

Hypostyle. 19th-c. drawing of the Temple of Dendarah, Egypt

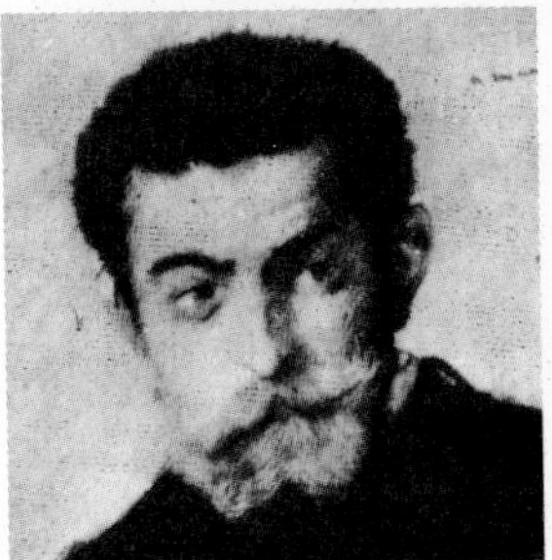

J.-K. Huysmans

Henrik Ibsen

I

Icon. *The Virgin of Vladimir*; 13th-c. Byzantine

Icon. *SS Boris and Gleb*; 16th-c. Russian

I am a Fugitive from a Chain Gang (1932). Film directed by M. *Le Roy.

iamb: *metre in verse

Ibañez Vincente Blasco: *Blasco Ibañez

Iberia. The name for (1) sets of piano pieces by Albéniz, (2) an orchestral work by Debussy.

Ibert Jacques (François-Antoine) (1890–1962). French composer; teachers included Fauré. In 1919 he won the Rome prize; he was for a period director of the French Academy in Rome and headed the administration of the Opéra (1955–6). His works include: a suite from incidental music to *The Italian Straw Hat* which became the popular burlesque, *Divertissement* for orchestra (1930), the orchestral suite *Escales*, the comic opera *Le Roi d'Yvetot*, a concerto for saxophone, and *3 pièces brèves* for wind quintet.

Ibsen Henrik (Johan) (1828–1906). Norwegian playwright and poet, the son of a merchant whose bankruptcy (1832) reduced the family to penury. I. was apprenticed to an apothecary when he was 15, began to write poetry, and had his 1st play produced in 1850. He became writer-manager-director at Bergen (1851–7), then manager of the Norske Theatre until its failure (1862); his plays during this period were mainly on national themes suggested by the sagas. In 1863, embittered by failure, I. went to Italy, where he wrote the 2 verse dramas which first made him famous. *Brand* (1866; 1891), an austere study of a pastor whose religion allows no compromise with the needs of ordinary life, won I. a pension and relative security; in contrast are the rich comedy and fantastic adventures of *Peer Gynt* (1867; 1892). I. lived abroad until 1891.

His plays were seen as a breakthrough in theatrical realism, treating frankly such personal and social problems as the subjection of women in *Et Dukkehjem* (1879; *The Doll's House*, 1883), and the effects of syphilis in *Gengangere* (1881; *Ghosts*, 1888). Attention was thus concentrated on the plays of the period 1869–82; these, including *Samfundets Støtter* (1877; *The Pillars of Society*, 1888), and *En Folkefiende* (1882; *An Enemy of the People*, 1900–1), attack majority tyranny, social lies and the sacrifice of individuality, truth and happiness to respectability. But although I. had adopted prose in the 1870s, he retained a poet's vision; and from *Vildanden* (1884; *The Wild Duck*, 1905), a demonstration that truth destroys those not strong enough to bear it, his work grows increasingly charged with symbols; dream-like sequences appear, yet the settings and characters are firmly rooted in reality. The result is complex and sometimes elusive. In *Hedda Gabler* (1890; 1891), the assertive, destructive and sterile Hedda is frustrated by a narrow society and her limited role as a woman; but she is also a victim of her lack of courage. These plays hint at I.'s personal preoccupations, e.g. the problem of the education of children in *Lille Eyolf* (1894; *Little Eyolf*, 1895) and the conflict between the generations in *Bygmester Solness* (1892; *The Master Builder*, 1893); and I. himself is perhaps *John Gabriel Borkman* (1896; 1897), the fallen Titan who has become a 'corpse' by sacrificing life's riches to his ambition; but this material is transformed into interior dramas haunted by symbols of an unattainable freedom and power. Works include *Kejser og Galilaeer* (1873; *Emperor and Galilean*, 1876); *Rosmersholm* (1886; 1889); *Fruen fra Havet* (1888; *The Lady from the Sea*, 1890); and *Naar vi døde vaagne* (1899; *When We Dead Awaken*, 1900).

Iceman Cometh, The (1946). Play by Eugene *O'Neill.

Ichikawa Kon (1915–). Japanese film director. I. became famous in the West with *The Burmese Harp* (1955) for its (albeit inadequately expressed) pacificist sentiments. His later films have often had strange or repellent subjects: voyeurism in *Odd Obsessions* (1959) and some cannibalism in *Fires on the Plain* (1959).

icon (Greek, 'image'). Religious picture used as an object of worship and often portraying the Virgin and Child. The term is particularly used of pictures of the Byzantine school and later of the Russian school. Russian i.s show clear derivation from Byzantine art and maintained a stylized convention of composition and posture. The works of such artists as *Rublev and his school, to which is ascribed the *Old Testament Trinity* (Tretyakov Mus., Moscow), show the range of emotional and artistic expression possible in this form. In later Russian i.s the painted figure was often surrounded by a halo of precious metals and stones.

An ICONOSTASIS in a Greek Orthodox church is a screen covered with i.s, usually between the congregation and the altar.

Ictinus (*fl.* mid 5th c. B.C.). One of the architects of the *Parthenon, Athens.

Ideal Husband, An (1895). Play by Oscar Wilde.

idée fixe (French, 'fixed idea'). In many of Berlioz's compositions the various movements are linked by a single recurring theme, or i. f., modified according to the mood or programme of the music.

Idiot, The (1868). Novel by *Dostoyevsky.

Idomeneo. Opera by *Mozart; 1st performance at Munich in 1781.

idyll. Term used to describe any work or part of a work of art which conveys or describes uninterrupted and uncomplicated happiness; originally a poem or part of a poem describing an idealized rural life.

Idylls of the King, The (1842–59). Series of poems by *Tennyson.

Idzikowski Stanislas (1894–). Polish dancer, a pupil of Cecchetti. I. joined Diaghilev in 1914 and proved to be one of the finest dancers of his generation (which included Nijinsky, Fokine and Massine). Ashton created for I. the brilliant leading male role in *Les Rendezvous* (1933).

Ife. A town in W. Nigeria, traditionally the spiritual centre of the Yoruba people, where a number of very beautiful terracotta heads and remarkable brass heads have been discovered since the beginning of the 20th c. These have been tentatively dated to the 12th to 14th cs. I. art is naturalistic and reveals an extremely high standard of accomplishment. It has therefore been compared with Greek statuary, but there is no evidence that it was not completely indigenous. The art of brass-casting was probably passed on to the people of *Benin in the 14th c.

Iffland August Wilhelm (1759–1814). German actor, dramatist and essayist and a close friend of Schiller. He favoured a natural style of acting in reaction to the declamatory Weimar school, and wrote a number of articles on dramatic theory including: *Neue Beiträge . . .* (1809–12). Of his plays, *Die Advokaten . . .* (1796; *The Lawyers*, 1799), and *Die Jäger . . .* (1785; *The Foresters. . . ,* 1799), are the best known.

If it Die (1924). Autobiographical book by André Gide.

Île des pingouins, L' (1908). Satirical novel by Anatole France.

Ilf Ilya. The pseud. of Ilya Arnoldovich Fainzilberg (1897–1937). Soviet humorous novelist whose best work was done in collaboration with Yevgeny Petrovich PETROV, pseud. of Y. P. Katayev (1903–42). Their work includes *Twelve Chairs* (1928;1930; also called *Diamonds to Sit On*) and *The Little Golden Calf* (1931; 1932).

Iliad, The. Greek epic poem by *Homer. It deals with an episode in the last year of the siege of Troy. Achilles, slighted by Agamemnon the king, withdraws to his tent. Despite Agamemnon's apology, Achilles sulks and the Greeks are driven back upon their ships. Patroclus borrows his friend Achilles' armour to impress the Trojans, but Hector kills him. Achilles returns to the fight with new armour fresh-forged by Hephaestus, kills and savages Hector and holds funeral games for Patroclus. At the instance of the gods he accedes to Priam's request for the return of the body of Hector, whose exequies conclude the poem.

illumination. The decoration of mss, one of the most common forms of medieval visual art; because of its monastic origins, usually of religious texts. The practice extends from heavy decorations of initial letters and interwoven margin patterns (as in Celtic examples) to miniatures and full-page illustrations, often of a formal and grandiose kind (as in Byzantine mss). Rich colours are a common feature, in particular a luxurious use of gold and silver. I. survived the advent of printing for some time and only died out with the rise of printed illustration in the 16th c. Well-known examples are: *The Book of *Kells, The *Lindisfarne Gospels, The *Luttrell Psalter* and *Les *Très Riches Heures du Duc de Berry.*

Illuminations, Les (1886). (1) Poetic work by *Rimbaud; (2) A song cycle based on the poem

Illumination. The mid-12th-c. Flemish *Floreffe Bible*

Illumination. Portrait of Hippocrates from a Byzantine ms. (*c.* 1342)

Illumination from *The Luttrell Psalter*. See also colour plate 26

Ife. Head of a King; bronze, probably late 14th c.

Iconostasis from Polotsk cathedral, Russia, 18th c.

Illusionism. The Villa Imperiale, Pesaro, Italy. Also *Guercino and colour plate 49

Imago pietatis by Giovanni Bellini

Ince. *Civilisation*

(for tenor and strings) by *Britten, which has been adapted as (3) a 1-act ballet with choreography by *Ashton and costumes by Beaton; 1st performance 1950.

illusionism. Term used in painting of a style which exploits all the technical procedures of perspective, etc., not merely to represent 3-dimensional space in 2 dimensions but rather to give the impression that the pictorial space is an extension of the real space; sculptured 3-dimensional figures are often integrated into paintings to heighten the fusion of real and artistic space. The term is especially used of baroque art.

Illusions perdues (1837–43). Novel by Balzac.

Illyés Gyula (1902–). Hungarian poet, populist writer and playwright. I. derives his main inspiration from his peasant origin. His probings into the dark recesses of a servile existence place him among the writers of great confessions as revealed in *Puszták népe* (1936; *People of the Puszta*, 1965).

Images. Name given by *Debussy to a group of piano works and a group of orchestral works.

imagism. Anglo-U.S. poetic movement *c.* 1910–18 led by T. E. Hulme and Ezra Pound. It was distinguished by its insistence on precise images, avoidance of stock poetic diction and advocacy of free verse.

imago pietatis (Latin, 'image of piety'). Representation, especially in the late middle ages, of the dead Christ standing in his grave, sometimes supported by other figures. Emblems of the Passion are often included to stress the redemptive significance of his sufferings.

Imai Tadashi (1912–). Japanese film director. I. started directing during the war and became one of the more important directors in post-war Japan. His films are typically realist works with present-day subjects and social or political comment.

imitation. Musical term describing the use in one voice of a motif shortly before stated in another voice. This form of repetition of ideas is found in most Western music but strict i., when voices copy one another over long periods, was the staple technique of late 15th-c. and 16th-c. polyphonic music.

Imitation of Christ, The. Mystical work by *Thomas à Kempis.

Immermann Karl Leberecht (1796–1840). German romantic playwright and novelist. His plays include *Merlin, eine Mythe* (1832); more important however are the novels *Die Epigonen* (1836), which reflects the conflict between the commercial and aristocratic classes, and *Münchhausen* (1838), containing the classic short story of peasant life, *Der Oberhof* (trs. 1879).

Immoralist, The (1902). Novel by André Gide.

impasto. In oil painting, thick heavy application of paint. Where the strokes of the brush or palette-knife are very pronounced, causing the paint to stand up in relief, the term LOADED I. is used.

Importance of Being Earnest, The (1895). Play by Oscar *Wilde.

impost. Architectural term for the (usually) moulded masonry on which the ends of an arch rest; the top of the i. is on the springing-line. Diagram *arch.

impressionism. A major movement in 19th-c. art. The name comes from a painting exhibited by Claude Monet in 1874, catalogued as *Impression Sunrise.* The word was used as a label for the whole group of artists who exhibited as the 'Society of Painters, Etchers and Engravers'. It has been said that i. was not a style but a moment in time. Nevertheless, the term is applied most frequently to paintings where the artist has aimed to capture the visual impression made by a scene, usually of a landscape, and not make a 'factual' report on it; impressionist painters are characteristically absorbed by the play of light on a scene. In a sense an impressionist picture is the sketch as opposed to the finished picture, a painting catching atmosphere, in Monet's own words 'a spontaneous work rather than a calculated one'.
The 1st impressionist exhibition was in 1874, but impressionist works had been seen in the Salon des Refusés in 1863. The 1860s were the formative years in which the possibilities of working in the open air, using a light palette, and close analysis of the actual colours in landscape were explored. Monet, Renoir and Sisley were students together and form the most close-knit group. In the 1870s the group experienced much opposition, and their exhibitions were generally unsuccessful. The impressionist painters were divided as to who should exhibit, Degas arguing that work by conventional painters would make the exhibitions more accessible to the general public. Manet never exhibited with the impressionists although his work strongly influenced them. Their interest in the effects of light on landscape was not at first acceptable, nor was the time of day they chose to paint–clear sunny afternoons, as opposed to scenes of twilight or early morning. In the 1880s these subjects had become more general, and the movement achieved slow recognition and success. But i. became less coherent and less of a common style: Monet continued to analyse his visual perceptions with extreme care, and Sisley continued to paint landscapes: but Renoir turned to a style which stressed line, became accepted as a portraitist, and began to paint many important figure paintings, especially nudes. Camille Pissarro came under the influence of Seurat's divisionist theory, and exhibited works in this style from 1886, the year of the last impressionist exhibition, at which Seurat and Signac also showed work. Other impressionists include Jean-Frédéric Bazille, Gustave Caillebotte, Mary Cassatt and Berthe Morisot.
I. became widely accepted as an artistic style

from the late 1890s, spreading through Europe. No sculptor was directly associated with the movement, but both Degas and Renoir did sculpture (Renoir at the end of his life working through an assistant). Rodin has been called impressionist because of the interest he took in the effects of light on his sculpture, and Medardo Rosso's evocative technique has caused his work to be so called. The 2 composers whose music is sometimes cited as impressionist are Debussy and Ravel.

impromptu. A musical composition, usually for keyboard, designed to sound like improvisation; Schubert, Chopin and Schumann wrote the best-known examples.

improvisation. The performance of music not previously composed but conceived at the instrument and immediately performed; not usually written down. Frequently the performer improvises on a given theme, and this form of i. has been an important aspect of European music, above all folk-music, since the middle ages; i. reached its highest point at the hands of the 18th-c. keyboard virtuosi such as J. S. Bach who improvised, as a matter of course, complex fugues from a given theme.
In art music, the i. of decorations was also an important part of the opera singer's art, a feature of instrumental concertos (e.g. in the cadenzas) and even early orchestral playing; in the 20th c. it is being reinstated by such composers as Stockhausen.
I. is fundamental to the *jazz musician as a means of self-expression and is likely to remain so in spite of the increasing importance of the arranger/composer.

In Camera (1944). Play by *Sartre.

Ince Thomas (1882–1924). U.S. film director and producer, an actor who started directing 1-reel films in 1911. His speciality was westerns and Civil War films, and he discovered the most famous early western star, William S. Hart. From 1914 he made larger films and abandoned direction, except in *Civilisation* (1916), supervising the work of other directors, particularly Reginald Barker, who co-directed *Civilisation*.

incidental music. Term for music written to accompany a play; not used of music written for a film.

incunabula (Latin, 'swaddling clothes'). Term used of books printed before 1501, i.e. during the 1st half c. of printing, when the art was still in its infancy. In fact the greatest masterpieces of printing were produced during the period so that i. are valuable not only for their antiquity but also for their beauty.

India. Indian philosophical ideas were known with some accuracy to the world of Greece and Rome, and there are parallels between Greek and Indian thought which cannot adequately be explained away by coincidence. Later, in the 2nd c. A.D., when gnostic ideas were being developed in Alexandria (a city to which merchants from I. came), it is possible to trace Buddhist elements in the gnostic philosophers' attempt to fuse classical, Platonic and oriental ideas into a new syncretism. The pessimism of

Impressionism. Monet, *Impression Sunrise*

Impressionism. Pissarro, *View from Louveciennes*

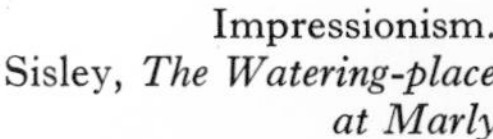

Impressionism. Sisley, *The Watering-place at Marly*

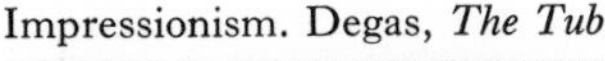

Impressionism. Degas, *The Tub*

Impressionism. Renoir, *Luncheon of the Boating Party*

Impressionism. Cassatt, *Lady at the Tea-Table*. See also colour plate 70

Paul Vincent d'Indy

Inlay. Copper basin inlaid with silver; Mameluk, 14th c.

Inlay. Side table inlaid with seaweed marquetry; 18th-c. English

Ingram. Rudolph Valentino in *The Four Horsemen of the Apocalypse*

the Buddha, who saw sorrow and suffering as implicit in human activity, is echoed by the gnostic writers who also accepted the essentially oriental belief in the transmigration of souls.
On a less rarefied level, many Eastern fables found their way into European literature. Most of these reached Europe through the medium of the Arabic language. The story of the Ebony Horse from *The Arabian Nights' Entertainments* is of Hindu origin and appears in Chaucer's *Squire's Tale*. Another coll. of tales known in Europe as *The Fables of Pilpay* (or *Bidpai*) was one of the most popular books of the middle ages. Some of these fables were later used by La Fontaine. In 1498, with the arrival of the Portuguese explorer Vasco da Gama at Calicut on the W. coast of I., a new and fruitful period of direct intercourse between I. and the Western world began. Da Gama was followed by the Dutch, the English and the French and the 17th c. saw the publ. of a vast quantity of travellers' tales. From these John Milton drew his metaphors for the description of Satan in *Paradise Lost*, and exotic Asian names pepper the poem. Dryden, too, portrayed the brilliant if fantastic state of the Great Mogul, Emperor of I. in his play *Aurengzebe*. But Europe had to wait until the very end of the 18th c. for the astonishing revelation of Sanskrit literature and Hindu religious texts.
The proximate cause of this revelation was the growing power of the British in I. During the administration of Warren Hastings (1774–85) the study of Sanskrit was encouraged in order to assist in the compilation of a code of law for Hindus now subject to British rule. A marginal effect of this research appeared in 1785 with the publ. of Charles Wilkins's trs. of the *Bhagavad-gita*, a long discourse in 18 cantos in which the god Krishna, in the guise of a charioteer, lectures the hero Arjun before a battle upon life and death, the nature of self-less duty, and the necessity for absolute devotion to the supreme divinity. A few years later, Sir William Jones–an eminent judge who had trs. the *Laws of Manu*–was introduced by an Indian friend to the treasury of Sanskrit drama. In 1789 the European literary world was astonished to read his trs. of Kalidasa's masterpiece *Sakuntala* (4th–5th c. A.D.). Jones's trs. and the work of the German poet Schlegel, *On the Language and the Wisdom of the Indians* (1808), revealed an unknown world of metaphysical ideas and lyric poetry. Its effect upon the writers and philosophers of the German romantic movement was profound. The philosopher Schopenhauer claimed that Schlegel's book 'has been the solace of my life, it will be the solace of my death'. Kant's phenomenology owes much to Hindu ideas; Heine, in *Die Lotusblume* and other poems, gives expression to the Hindu spirit; Goethe modelled the prologue to *Faust* on the Sanskrit dramatic convention as used by Kalidasa. In English literature the effect of Hindu ideas is more difficult to trace, but critics have found it in the pantheism of Shelley and in the romanticism of Wordsworth. The American transcendentalists and, in particular, Ralph Waldo Emerson, owed a considerable debt to Hindu ideas. In 1875 *Sacred Books of the East*, under the editorship of Max-Müller, made available a vast body of hitherto unknown Sanskrit literature. In a like manner, the publs of the Pali Text Society drew Europe's attention to the literature of Buddhism.
In the 20th c. Hindu religion has influenced modern artists, particularly writers (Yeats and Auden, each of whom collaborated in trs, Aldous Huxley and Christopher Isherwood); Buddhism has been most influential in the Japanese form of Zen (*Japan). The great achievements of Indian painting and sculpture have had virtually no influence on Western art despite Western admiration for the Taj Mahal and the Ajanta Caves. Classical Indian music rests on a system of *ragas*, similar to Western *modes, and *talas*, or rhythmic modes; the notes of the *ragas* are associated with human qualities and states of mind and the *ragas* themselves are considered suitable for specific times of the day or year. *Messiaen has been influenced by certain of these concepts, but otherwise his work has little in common with Indian music which, for example, makes greater use of improvisation than Western art music.

In Dubious Battle (1936). Novel by John *Steinbeck.

Indy Paul-Marie-Théodore Vincent d' (1851–1931). French composer. He studied harmony with Lavignac and the piano with Diémer and Marmontel. From 1872 he studied with César Franck whose tradition he continued as teacher and composer. His work reflects also the influence of Liszt and Wagner and I.'s interest in plainsong and folk-song. In 1894 he founded the Schola Cantorum with Charles Bordes and Guilmant, and taught there until his death. His works include: *Fervaal* (1897) and 5 other operas; symphonies; the tone poems *Wallenstein* (1882), *Jour d'été à la montagne* (1905), *Symphonie sur un chant montagnard français*, (1886) for orchestra and piano; chamber music, piano music and songs. He also publ. a *Cours de la Composition Musicale* (1897–1933).

Infernal Machine, The (1936). Play by Jean *Cocteau.

Inferno. 1st part of *Dante's *Divine Comedy*.

Informer, The (1935). Film directed by J. *Ford.

Inge William (1913–). U.S. playwright, author of *Come Back Little Sheba* (1950) and other successful dramas, frequently filmed.

Ingemann Bernhard Severin (1789–1862). Danish romantic poet, playwright and author of such very popular historical novels about medieval Denmark as *Erik Menveds Barndom* (1828; *The Childhood of King Erik Menved*, 1846).

Inglesby Mona (1918–). British ballet dancer who in 1940 formed her own co., the International Ballet, and became leading dancer. The co. contributed greatly to the increased demand for ballet and presented many Diaghilev ballets as well as the full-length classics. I. retired in 1953 and the co. broke up in the same year.

Ingoldsby Legends (1840–7). Book of verse by R. H. *Barham.

Ingram Rex (1892–1950). U.S. film director. His *The Four Horsemen of the Apocalypse* (1921) was the film in which Valentino made his name. It launched I. on a series of swashbuckling romances like *The Prisoner of Zenda* (1922) and *Scaramouche* (1923), both with Ramon Novarro. He directed only one talkie, *Baroud* (1932).

Ingres Jean-Auguste-Dominique (1780–1867). French painter and draughtsman. After the Academy of Toulouse he entered the studio of David in 1797, and later the École des Beaux-Arts, Paris. In the Salon of 1806 his portrait of *Napoleon I on the Imperial Throne* created a stir and received adverse criticism which he had to suffer from critics most of his life. During a difficult period after the downfall of his patrons, the Bonaparte family, portrait drawings became his main source of income and he lived in Italy for a time. He returned to Paris, was elected to the Academy (1825) and was able to open a successful atelier; by the 1840s he was a celebrated public figure and eventually became a Senator. I. was the painter of an ideal reality. He sought to reconcile a searching truth (expressed in the silhouette, relief-like modelling, purity of line and perfection in craftsmanship, strongly influenced by the Italian schools and David), with the romanticism of his time, from which he could not escape. His most famous paintings are *La Grande Baigneuse* (1808), *La Grande Odalisque* (1819) and *Le Bain turc* (1864). Though he had many pupils he had no significant followers until Degas reinterpreted his classical draughtsmanship.

inlay. A method of ornamenting the surface of one substance by inserting into it a different substance. Extensively used in the manufacture of furniture and artistic objects of wood, shell and stones. Enamelling is a form of i., as is niello, where the surface of the metal, usually gold or silver, is incised with an engraved design and filled with a black metallic substance. *Damascening is another form of inlaying.

In Memoriam A.H.H. (1850). Poem by *Tennyson.

Innes James Dickson (1887–1914). Welsh landscape painter, pupil of Wilson Steer at the Slade School, London, and friend of Augustus John; exhibitor at the N.E.A.C. From 1910 when he painted *The Waterfall* (Tate) his work began to show a post-impressionistic sense of design and intensity of colour.

Inness George (1825–94). U.S. landscape painter who made several visits to Europe where he studied the paintings of Corot and the Barbizon school. His work showed a gradual loosening of his early attachment to the Hudson River school in favour of these European influences.

Innisfree, The Lake Isle of (1893). Poem by W. B. Yeats.

Innocents Abroad or The New Pilgrim's Progress, The (1869). Book by Mark *Twain.

Ingres. *Self-portrait*

Ingres. *Le Bain turc*. Also *Disderi and colour plate 68

Inness. *The Lackawanna Valley*

Innes. *Canigou in Snow*

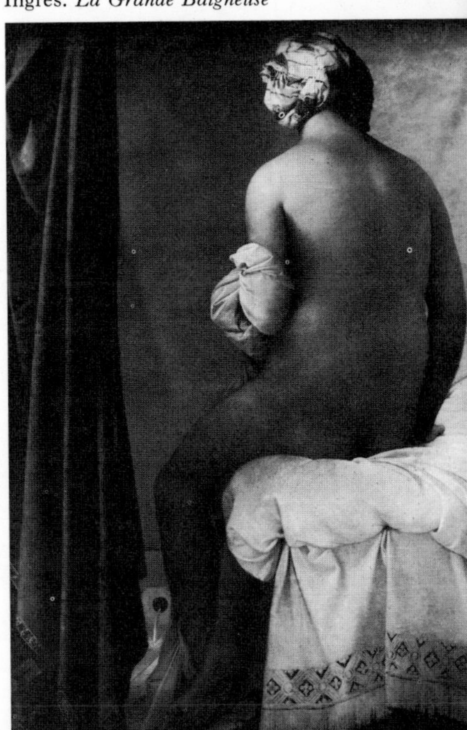

Ingres. *La Grande Baigneuse*

International Gothic. Gentile da Fabriano, *Madonna* from the Quaratesi altarpiece (1425)

International Gothic. Limbourg brothers; from *Les Très Riches Heures du Duc de Berry*

Intaglio. Greek gem, late 5th c. B.C. See also colour plate 17

Intermezzo at Versailles (1664)

In nomine. A piece of instrumental music found only in the works of English 16th- and 17th-c. composers but there in great profusion. The I. n. is a piece based on the *cantus firmus beginning with the words 'In nomine domini' used first in the mass by J. Taverner, *Gloria Tibi Trinitas.*

Insect Play, The (1921). Play by Karel and Josef *Čapek.

Inspector General, The (1836). Satirical comedy by *Gogol.

instrumentation. Term used in music when discussing a composer's sense for instrumental technique when writing score. It concerns such things as the range of the instrument, knowledge of its best *registers, understanding of which fingerings, etc. are easy or awkward, and so forth. Orchestration is related but refers to the blend of instrumental tone colours.

intaglio. The incised carving on a gem or hardstone, the converse of *cameo, in which the design is in relief.

intarsia: *marquetry

intercolumniation. Architectural term for the spaces between columns; also for spacing according to classical rules of proportion.

interlude. Short dramatic scene, acted during a banquet or similar celebration, or between the acts of a long play. The i.s arising in the late middle ages–short farcical plays on secular subjects–marked an important advance in the development of drama in its departure from the moralities (John *Heywood).

intermezzo. Originally a piece of music performed in some operas during breaks in the action, the stage being empty. The term is also used of comic operas, written in the 18th c., to supply entertainment during the intervals of a serious opera (also R. *Strauss).

International Ballet du Marquis de Cuévas. The South American-born Marquis founded the Ballet International in the U.S. in 1944, and 3 years later took over the Nouveau Ballet de Monte Carlo; the marriage of the 2 formed the Grand Ballet du Marquis de Cuévas (its former name). Although many U.S. dancers figure prominently in the co., it has its headquarters in Paris and tours mostly in Europe. The co. aims at keeping alive the Diaghilev tradition.

international Gothic. Sophisticated late Gothic style of painting which spread through Europe in the late 14th and 15th c. It is a decorative linear style with its origins in French Gothic art, particularly ms. illumination, and is characterized by refined and elegant figures, graceful curves of drapery, jewel-like colour and naturalistic detail. Examples include Melchior Broederlam's Dijon altarpiece, which owes a good deal to the Sienese influence of Simone Martini, who worked at Avignon; also from Burgundy is the ms. *Très Riches Heures* by the *Limbourg brothers. In Italy i. G., which was highly developed in the work of Gentile da Fabriano and Pisanello, existed simultaneously with Masaccio's new realism. The style also flourished in Germany, Bohemia and Spain. A variant on i. G. found in German painting and sculpture is known as the SOFT STYLE, characterized by softly flowing drapery and a sweetness of sentiment which found particular expression in the representation of the Madonna and Child (*Schöne Madonnen*).

International Style, The (1932). A book by Hitchcock and Johnson, and the name now widely used to describe the European-based architectural style of white walls and flat roofs predominant in the 1920s and 1930s.

interval. The difference in pitch between 2 notes, described by convention in terms of the scale; thus notes at the same distance as the 1st and 4th degrees of the scale are said to be at the i. of a 4th. The i.s of the 4th, 5th and 8ve are termed 'perfect' for reasons of musical theory and also because they seem, to the musical ear, stable in a way which other i.s are not; all these others may be major or minor, the latter being 1 semitone smaller than the former. The term compound interval is sometimes given to i.s greater than an 8ve. From the earliest period 1 interval, the tritone, i.e. the i. containing 3 whole tones, was considered peculiarly ugly and was nicknamed '*diabolus in musica*' ('the devil in music'). Determination to avoid this i. as part writing became increasingly complex was a contributory factor in the break-up of the medieval system of modes. The smallest i. used in Western music is conventionally the semitone (e.g. C to C♯, C to D being a tone) but in the 20th c. *microtones have been used.

Inwood. St Pancras parish church. Also *Grecian revival

Intimations of Immortality. Ode by *Wordsworth.

intimism. Term invented to describe the type of painting of domestic interiors executed by Bonnard and Vuillard.

Intolerance (1916). Film directed by D. W. *Griffith.

intonation. In music, (1) the term used when speaking of the pitching of his notes by a singer or instrumentalist. Good i. is accurate pitching; the notes are 'in tune'. (2) In plainsong the opening of a passage is sung by the precentor to give the choir the starting note; this phrase is the i.

invention. Name given by J. S. Bach to a group of simple keyboard pieces in 2 parts; later the name was applied to other similar works by Bach, and other composers have used it.

inversion. Term in music for (1) the reversal of a melodic line so that all the upward leaps become downward leaps and vice versa (*counterpoint); and for (2) the arrangement of notes in a chord in other than the root position (*harmony).

Invitation, The. 1-act ballet with choreography by *Macmillan, music by Seiber and décor by N. Giorgiadis; 1st performance 1960.

Invitation to a Beheading (in Russian, 1938; 1959). Novel by Nabokov.

Invitation to the Dance. Work for piano by *Weber.

Inwood William (*c.* 1771–1843). English architect. His St Pancras church, London (1819) with its classical portico, steeple modelled on the Tower of the Winds, Athens, and caryatid porches copied from the *Erechtheum, is an outstanding work of the Greek revival in England. He was assisted on it by his eldest son, Henry William I.

Iolanthe. Light opera by W. S. Gilbert and Sir Arthur Sullivan; 1st performance in London and New York in 1882.

Ionesco Eugène (1912–). French playwright; his father was Rumanian. I. came to the fore only in the 1950s. His most typical plays move from wild fantasy to the pessimistic and macabre, from laughter-provoking incongruities of situation, and banalities exposed and given often sinister connotations by stating, distorting, reversing or shuffling them, to an apprehension of the obsessive elements beneath the surface of life. I.'s plays include *La Cantatrice chauve* (1950; *The Bald Prima Donna*, 1958), *La Leçon* (1951; *The Lesson*, 1958), *Les Chaises* (1951; *The Chairs*, 1958), *Victimes de la devoir* (1952; *Victims of Duty*, 1958) and the simpler allegory *Le Rhinocéros* (1960; 1960), in which more and more people change into rhinoceroses–a change which becomes fashionable and ultimately mandatory.

Eugène Ionesco

Ionic order: *order

Iphigenia in Aulis. Play by Euripides based on legend; it was unfinished at his death. It describes how Agamemnon, about to lead the Greeks against Troy, sacrifices his daughter, I., in order to appease Artemis and sail without hindrance. The legend is also treated in a play by Racine and an opera by Gluck.
In Euripides' *Iphigenia in Tauris* (*c.* 414 B.C.), the girl has escaped the sacrifice (a phantom took her place) and has been carried away to Tauris. She has become a priestess and it is her duty to sacrifice all strangers who arrive in the land; when her brother Orestes and his devoted friend Pylades arrive, I. tricks the King of the Taurians and the three escape. The story is the subject of a play by Goethe and of another opera by Gluck.

Ippolitov-Ivanov Mikhail Mikhailovich (1859–1935). Russian composer and conductor. He studied with Rimsky-Korsakov. In 1905 he became director of the Moscow Conservatory. His interest in folk-music, especially Georgian, is reflected in his work, e.g. in the orchestral *Caucasian Sketches* (1894). His compositions include operas, tone poems, orchestral suites, chamber music, cantatas and songs.

Ireland John (Nicholson) (1879–). English composer. He was influenced by Brahms, the French impressionist composers, and Stravinsky; his compositions are frequently inspired by landscape. His works include: *The Forgotten Rite* (1913) for orchestra; the symphonic rhapsody *Mai-Dun* (1920–1); *A London Overture* (1936); *These Things Shall Be* (1937) for

John Ireland

Irish glass

Washington Irving

Isenbrant. *Our Lady of Seven Sorrows*

Sir Henry Irving as Lear. Also *Beerbohm

L.-G.-E. Isabey. *Return to Port*; lithograph

chorus and orchestra; song cycles, e.g. *Marigold* (1917); many songs, including 'Sea Fever' (1915), and piano works.

Ireland William Henry (1777–1835). English forger of Shakespearean mss and signatures, which succeeded in convincing a number of scholars. The fraud was admitted after the unsuccessful production of one of these forgeries, the blank-verse play *Vortigern . . .* (1796).

Irish glass. Glass making proper began in Ireland in the 18th c. A Waterford glass house was established in 1783 and others at Cork and Dublin in 1783 and 1785. Connections with English manufacturers were numerous, many of them working in Ireland, and this is one of the reasons why it is impossible to attribute much glass, other than vessels marked with the place of manufacture, to Irish glass houses; it has been proved that there are no grounds for associating blue-tinted glass with Waterford.

Irish literary renaissance. Term for the movement comprising such writers as Yeats, Synge, A.E., Augusta Gregory, etc., who incorporated dialect phrases and rhythms, and Irish–often peasant–subjects into their writings (in English). Its roots were in the 1890s, but it flourished from *c.* 1904 (when the *Abbey Theatre, with which it was particularly associated, was founded) to *c.* 1920.

Iron Heel, The (1907). Novel by Jack *London.

Irving Sir Henry (1838–1905). English actor-manager, the most famous actor of the day and instrumental in winning respectability for that profession; he was knighted in 1895. I. was a tall, handsome man with angular, ascetic face and compelling eyes; his acting was intense and considered to be highly realistic. As a director he was also a stickler for realism and in *Becket* had trees on the set, each separate leaf being wired to the wings and operated by stage-hands to produce the effect of wind blowing. He achieved fame as an actor playing Mathias in the melodrama *The Bells* (1871) at the Lyceum Theatre, of which he became manager in 1878. His best performances were as Shylock, and as Becket in the play by Tennyson (1893). He often played opposite Ellen Terry.

Irving Washington (1783–1859). U.S. writer. Most of his work was satirical, including *The Letters of Jonathan Oldstyle, Gent.* (1802–3), *Salmagundi* (1807–8, with his brother and James Paulding) and *A History of New York* (1809). I.'s style is polished and witty, based on 18th-c. English writing; his later works are often rather lifeless. But *The Sketch-Book of Geoffrey Crayon, Gent.* (1819–20) contained 2 stories, based on European folk-tales, which have become classics–*The Legend of Sleepy Hollow*, about the 'headless horseman' and Ichabod Crane the schoolmaster, and *Rip Van Winkle*, the story of a man who slept for 20 years.

Isaac Henricus (*c.* 1450–1517). Flemish composer. He worked in Florence under Lorenzo de' Medici, setting many of his songs, and as court composer to the Emperor Maximilian I, returning to Florence at the end of his life. L. Senfl was his pupil. I. was a prolific and versatile master, composing with equal ease and excellence Italian *frottole*, German *Lieder*, French *chansons* and in the Flemish imitative style. His 'Innsbruck ich muss dich lassen', soon gained the status of a folk-song but the rest of his great output, both secular and sacred, is still much underrated. His *Choralis Constantius* consists of 58 four-part settings of the proper of the *mass, for the whole ecclesiastical year.

Isaacs Edith Juliet (1878–). U.S. critic who was ed. (1919–45) of the influential magazine *Theater Arts.*

Isabella, or the Pot of Basil (1820). Poem by *Keats.

Isabey Jean-Baptiste (1767–1855). French portrait painter and miniaturist; pupil of David. His son LOUIS-GABRIEL-EUGÈNE I. (1803–86) was a painter and engraver whose romantic landscapes and seascapes connect him with the Barbizon school.

Isaiah. One of the books of the *Bible (Old Testament), the first of the books of the 'Major Prophets', attributed to I. (late 8th c. B.C.) but probably a coll. of at least 3 sets of prophetic writings from different periods. Some of the prophecies are said to refer to the advent of Christ.

Isenbran(d)t Adriaen (d. 1551). Painter of the early Netherlandish school who worked at Bruges; follower of G. David. The altarpiece *Our Lady of Seven Sorrows* (Notre-Dame,

Christopher Isherwood

Isenheim altar: *The Crucifixion*

Bruges) is the chief work attributed to him but he is better known for small panels such as *The Rest on the Flight* (Alte Pina., Munich) and *The Magdalen in a Landscape* (N.G., London).

Isenheim altar. Altarpiece with paintings by *Grünewald.

Isherwood Christopher (1904–). English writer. From 1933 to 1937 I. taught English in Berlin and subsequently travelled in Europe: his experiences provided the material for his best-known books *Goodbye to Berlin* (1939) and *Mr. Norris Changes Trains* (1936) which catches with dispassionate clarity the atmosphere of Berlin in the years immediately before the war. A journey to China with W. H. Auden in 1938 produced the travel book *Journey to a War*; he also collaborated with Auden in 3 plays using expressionistic technique of which *The Ascent of F.6* is the most successful. He has also publ. travel books and books on Eastern religion, and the novel *Down There on a Visit* (1962).

Isidore of Seville St (*c.* 560–636). Scholar and didactic writer. His main work was his encyclopaedic *Etymologiae*, a vast compilation of scientific, historical and literary information, a main source-book for writers during the middle ages (*bestiary). His numerous works include a history of the Visigoths.

Isidorus of Miletus (*fl.* 1st half of 6th c. A.D.). One of the architects of *S. Sophia, Constantinople.

Isla José Francisco de (1703–81). Spanish Jesuit writer, theologian, outstanding satirist. His novel *Fray Gerundio* (1758–70; 1772) was a devastating attack on the pompous, over-elaborate clerical oratory of his day, and was banned by the Inquisition in 1760. He trs. *Le Sage's *Gil Blas* into Spanish.

Islam. Founded by Muhammad in the early 7th c. A.D., incorporating Judeo-Christian elements. I. was the last great cultural force to emerge from late Hellenistic civilization. The true legacy of I. to medieval Europe was the legacy of Greek culture preserved and continued by the Arabs, whose empire extended from Persia to Spain; they became heirs to a tradition of Hellenism unbroken in the Middle East but lost to Europe with the fall of Rome in the 5th c. A.D. Many philosophical attempts were made to synthesize Muhammad's teachings with Aristotelianism and Platonism, as in the works of 'Abd al-Masih al-Kindi (A.D. 796–873) and his pupils, and those of the mystic al-Farabi (A.D. 872–941), whose works attempting to correct Plato by using Aristotle, as well as a treatise pertinent for the classification of the sciences into 5 branches, were to be of great importance for Western scholasticism.

The major Arab contribution to the West was in the realm of science. Greek scientific speculation was combined with Eastern innovations such as the Chinese discovery of the magnetic compass, gunpowder and paper, and the Hindu numerical system using the zero; Arab mathematicians made fundamental contributions to arithmetic, astronomy, optics and perspective, and developed algebra. But the impact of I. on the West was felt in many other spheres. Already under Ummayyad rule in Spain and 10th-c. Sicily, Arab science and medicine, as well as aspects of the arts and literature were disseminated farther north. However, the vast cultural impact which I. was to have in the Christian world came as a result of trs undertaken by Christians primarily in the 12th and 13th cs, particularly during the reign of Alphonse the Wise in Spain and Frederick II in Sicily. Part of the interest in I. arose from the view held, e.g. in the Byzantine empire, that I. was a Christian heresy. Early sources of information concerning Islamic theology were the *Koran* (trs. by Robertus Anglicus) and al-Kindi's *Resalah* ('Apology') (a 12th-c. trs. sponsored by Peter the Venerable). An effort to place values of the faith on a rational foundation undertaken *c.* 1000 by Ibn Sina (Avicenna) in Persia ('God is the fulfilment of rational man's quest for happiness, the highest good'), crystallized under Ibn Rushd (Averroes) in Spain and had enormous influence in Western thought, indeed Muslim Cordoba of the 11th c. was the major intellectual centre in Europe. Whereas Platonic ideas had been nurtured in the West throughout the middle ages, the revival of Aristotelianism made possible through Ibn Batriq (*Secretum Secretorum*), Avicenna and Averroes, was to be exemplified by works of Albertus Magnus, Thomas Aquinas, Roger Bacon, Grosseteste and Ramón Lull.

The Islamic concept of Paradise, Hell and the afterlife, gaining popularity in the West through trs. of the *Liber Scalae Machometi* (Mi'raj-nama) and the transmission of eschatological legends through the allegorical writings of Ibn Arabi of Murcia, *Futūhat*, was exploited by such Western writers as Dante. Connections have been made between Platonic love literature in Persia of the 9th and 10th cs, the works of Ibn Hazn of Cordoba in the 11th c., and the arts and music of the courtly love of the troubadours. Popular works, as the *Tacuinum Sanitatis* (a household manual) and *Kalila and Dimna* stories, were also read and often illustrated in the West. The Arabic tales, the *maqanah*–in which various morals are pointed through the adventures of a hero–were the undoubted source of the Spanish picaresque novel.

The arts of Ummayyad Spain have been thought to be reflected in the masonry of certain Ottonian and Romanesque buildings and some sculptural motifs on Romanesque monuments. In the realm of ceramics various glaze wares, especially lustre, developed originally in Egypt or Mesopotamia, were diffused throughout Europe, particularly through Hispano-Moresque and Sicilian workshops of the 14th and 15th cs. Islamic textiles, sometimes found in the tombs of saints in the north (e.g. St Cuthbert's tomb), gained greater prominence from the mid 12th c., through the famous *tiraz* workshops, especially noted for works of silk and gold. In a later phase, Venetian manufacturers made sumptuous adaptations. Church vestments are sometimes found bearing in Arabic script–apparently because of its decorative quality–the name of Allah. Islamic influence can also be seen in the use of enamelling and damascening in metal ware.

In the late 18th and early 19th cs, as Europe began to discover the Middle East and North Africa, there emerged what can only be described, on the analogy of chinoiserie, as 'arabesque', a romantic evocation of the Arab world seen through the rose-tinted glasses of European romantic writers and artists. Examples of this can be found in such works as William Beckford's *Vathek*, the tales of Théophile Gautier, and the lush canvases of Delacroix.

isorhythmic motet. A musical form of the 14th and 15th c. Its basis was a piece of plainsong, usually given in the tenor, divided into a number of sections, rhythmically identical (Greek *isos*, 'equal'). This 'isorhythmic tenor' was repeated throughout the piece, other parts weaving about it.

Israëls. *A Son of the Chosen People*

Ivory chessmen found on the Isle of Lewis; 12th-c. English or Scandinavian

Ivory. Throne of Archbishop Maximian; 1st half of the 6th c.

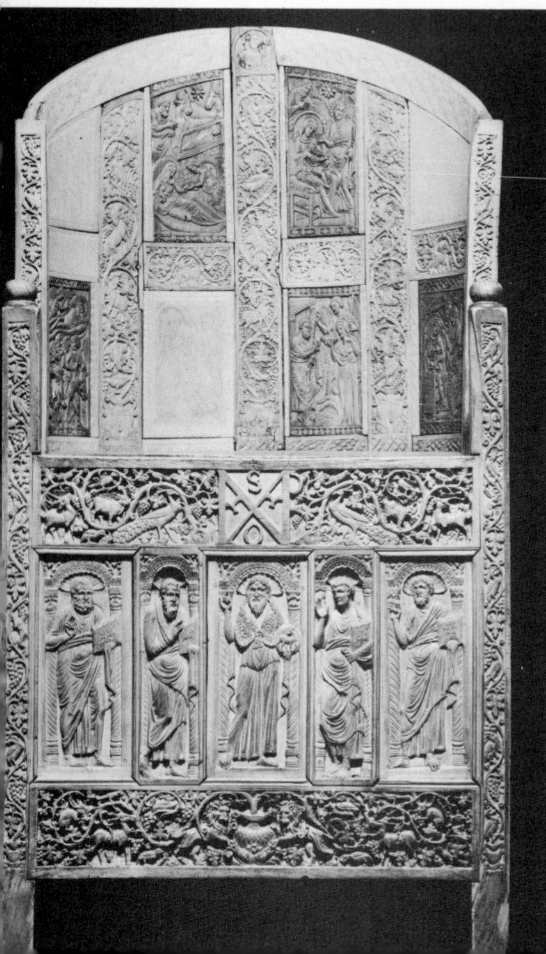

Israëls Jozef (1824–1911). Dutch painter of Jewish parentage who worked at The Hague and was known as 'the Dutch Millet'. He painted the poverty-stricken peasantry, particularly fishermen, with compassionate realism.

Istrati Alexandre (1915–). Rumanian painter of the school of *Paris.

Italian Painters of the Renaissance. Coll. of essays by Bernard *Berenson.

Italian Straw Hat, The (1927). Film directed by R. *Clair.

Italian symphony. Common name for *Mendelssohn's 4th symphony.

italic script: Francesco *Griffo

It Happened One Night (1934). Film directed by F. *Capra.

Iturbi José (1895–). Spanish pianist and conductor working largely in the U.S.

Ivan (1932). Film directed by A. *Dovzhenko.

Ivanhoe (1819). Historical novel by *Scott.

Ivanov (1887). Play by Chekhov.

Ivanov Lev (1834–1901). Russian choreographer who began his career in St Petersburg (1852) and became 2nd ballet master there in 1885. Although he contributed much of the choreography of the classics – *Nutcracker* (1892) and *Swan Lake* (1895), he was not always recognized as he worked under Petipa.

Ivanov Vsevolod Vyacheslavich (1895–). Soviet novelist and short-story writer, author of the novel *Armoured Train 14–69* (1922; 1933), a tale of the Civil War between Reds and Whites, which achieved great success when it was dramatized (1927). I.'s style was rich and ornate, his theme the futility of war. His later work, including *The Taking of Berlin* (1945), has been conventional.

Ivanov Vyacheslav Ivanovich (1866–1949). Russian poet, for a time one of the leaders of the *symbolist movement. He left the Soviet Union in 1924.

Ivan The Terrible (1944–6, shown part 1 1945, part 2 1958). Film directed by S. M. *Eisenstein.

Ivens Joris (1898–). Dutch film director. A specialist in documentary, who made the experimental film *Rain* (1929), and a film on the reclamation of land, *Zuydersee* (1933). He filmed, from a Communist viewpoint, wars in Spain (*Spanish Earth*, 1937) and China (*The 400,000,000*, 1938). Thereafter he worked in the U.S. and elsewhere. In 1956 he co-directed with G. *Philipe a fiction film, *Til Eulenspiegel*.

Ives Charles (Edward) (1874–1954). U.S. composer. He held various posts as organist but earned his living in business, composing in his spare time. From the beginning of his career as a composer I. was a pioneer in experimenting in new harmonic and rhythmic techniques, but his work became only slowly recognized as the 1st and among the most original of modern U.S. music. His works include 4 symphonies (1896–1916), choral works, piano music and many songs.

Ives J(ames) Merritt: *Currier and Ives prints

ivory. The elephant or walrus tusk has been used for carving since palaeolithic times. It is one of the most durable of all materials and lends itself to a variety of techniques, relief, entire carvings and to the most subtle and intricate interweaving of shapes. It has been employed equally for ornamentation and use at all times, and there exist combs, brooches, pendants, chessmen, boxes as well as statuettes, altarpieces, etc. Although most naturally lending itself to miniature work i. has been used as a decoration for large objects, notably e.g. the throne of Archbishop Maximian at Ravenna.
Ivories were the predominant form of Byzantine sculpture and the dispersion of Byzantine ivories in W. Europe was an important vehicle of cultural influence; Carolingian and Romanesque work produced further outstanding examples in the medium. The high period of medieval European i. carving was during the 9th–11th cs; superb pieces from other cultures include the carvings from African centres such as *Benin and *Ife.

Ivory panel of St Gregory and scribes; Trier (?), 9th–10th c.

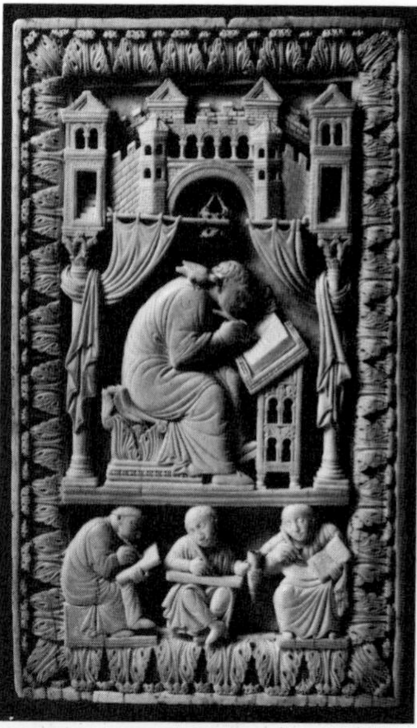

Ivory casket from Córdoba (964). See also colour plate 20

THE ARTS OF THE WEST form a connected historical sequence, reflecting in their changing styles and subjects the social as well as the artistic environment that gave them birth. In the section of colour plates which follows, certain key works have been selected to represent the achievements of each epoch, while a brief commentary shows how these works depend upon yet modify the tradition leading to them.

VASE PAINTINGS are almost all that survives of Greek painting, but from them we are able to trace a clear development from early geometric styles of decoration through stylized animal and human forms to the lithe drawing of this black-figured amphora of Exekias. Achilles (left) is playing a game with Ajax; both are identifiable by the names written above them. Of the many details of dress and armour shown, the elaborate decoration of the cloaks is especially interesting.

1 Black-figured amphora by Exekias: Achilles and Ajax playing a game (*c.* 540–530 B.C.)

2 Girl in a sleeved chiton from the Acropolis (archaic period; 6th c. B.C.)

3 Aphrodite rising from the waves; from the Ludovisi throne (*c.* 460 B.C.)

GREEK SCULPTURE, like vase painting, developed from a rigid formalism to the stiff but slightly animated poses of the archaic period (see plate 2). Increasingly the light drapery of the chiton was used to give life to the surface. The figure of the young girl, like many Greek sculptures from its period, shows traces of painted decoration.

The 5th c. B.C. is generally regarded as the high point of classical achievement in Greek sculpture. The increasing liberation of form is combined perfectly with discipline of composition to produce an idealized expression of the human figure. The greatest masterpieces of this style are found at Athens, above all in the sculptures of the *Parthenon, the so-called 'Elgin Marbles', yet during this period sculptors in all parts of the Greek world achieved similar triumphs. The relief of Aphrodite rising from the waves, here illustrated in detail, comes from Sicily or Southern Italy (*c.* 460). The goddess is being raised from the water by two attendants, and her wet gown clings to her body; the drapery of the gown is used for the familiar purpose of lending life to the composition, but a change has occurred. The drapery is less fussy than the little folds of the chiton, and the rhythms more sweeping; this effect, gained here by the device of a wet clinging garment, is common to most sculpture of the classical period, in which the light chiton of the figures of the archaic period is replaced by the heavier, more stately gown, the 'peplos'. In effect 5th-c. sculptors used greater freedom in disposing the limbs to achieve movement and more dramatic compositions, but in their return to restraint in the handling of drapery avoided mere liveliness and kept the balance between the freedom and dignity of form.

4 Temple of Hephaestos, Athens (*c.* 450–440 B.C.)

5 Theatre at Epidaurus (late 4th c. B.C.)

6 Temple of Athena Nike, Athens (*c.* 425 B.C.)

7 Fragment of a krater from Taranto: stage scenery and figures (mid 4th c. B.C.)

IN ARCHITECTURE, as in painting and sculpture, the Greek preoccupation is with form. The high point of Greek architecture is reached in the 5th c.; the Temple of Hephaestos below the *Acropolis is among the best preserved and finest examples. It demonstrates the perfection of proportions in the mature Doric temple (*orders). The decorative *triglyphs alternating with metopes represent the sawn beams of an earlier age of wood building. The somewhat later Temple of Athena Nike flanking the Propylaea (the entrance gate to the Acropolis) exhibits the more slender proportions of the Ionic order.

The Theatre at Epidaurus demonstrates the typical features of the *Greek theatre, utilizing a natural hollow in the hills to provide the raked auditorium round the central dancing-floor (*orchestra*); behind this can be seen the remains of the *skena*. The 4th-c. vase painting gives a good idea of the way in which the architectural *skena* was utilized.

THE MOMENT OF BALANCE in Greek sculpture passed (see commentary to plates 2 and 3) and poses became more supple, more expressive, less idealized. The new style achieved works of great beauty such as this 4th-c. youth in bronze from Olympia, and the contemporary *Praxiteles displays a virtuoso mastery of fluid line. Later still, sculp-

8 Bronze statue of a youth (4th c. B.C.)

ture was to move further along this path towards sentimentality and melodrama. The loosening of the style made it, however, a perfect vehicle for the informality of everyday subjects such as the group opposite. The gold diadem illustrates the superb craftsmanship exhibited by the Magna Graecia jewellery.

9 Gold diadem from Canosa di Puglia (4th c. B.C.)

10 Terracotta group of two women gossiping, from Myrina (*c.* 300 B.C.)

11 Detail from the Alexander sarcophagus (late 4th c. B.C.)

GREEK SETTLEMENTS had from an early period spread throughout the eastern Mediterranean area. The islands of the Aegean, the cities of Ionia (the littoral of Asia Minor) and Southern Italy and Sicily, and even far-flung outposts on the Black Sea coast, were members of that Greek world unified by language, religious ideas and a common veneration for the Homeric canon, which transmitted the inheritance of earlier civilizations to a new culture which has shaped and influenced the West. In the second half of the 4th c. the scattered, fiercely independent city-states were momentarily unified by the rule of *Alexander the Great, King of Macedon. His quicksilver conquests carried the spirit of Hellenism even to the boundaries of India, but his ideal of Hellenizing the world died with him. This detail from the relief decoration of his sarcophagus shows the way in which the controlled movement of the Parthenon sculptures developed towards more dramatic, more frenzied action.

The ambition of world empire which escaped Alexander was nearly achieved in the centuries after his death by the Italian city-state of Rome. Yet, ironically, this favoured the spread of Hellenization more effectively than the work of Alexander himself, for Rome took over the Greek tradition almost unchanged. This mosaic scene of Plato's Academy, possibly copied from a late Greek work, can be taken to symbolize the impact of Greek philosophy as well as literature and art on Roman civilization. Yet although Roman art was in many ways derivative from Greek, it made important contributions to technique and style. The very material used here, stone mosaic, became a standard feature of interior decoration and provided a medium for major art later to reach its apogee in the modified technique, glass mosaic, of the Byzantines. The poses and expressions of the philosophers, depicted as real men rather than as the idealized figures of classical Greek sculpture, show the trend towards greater personalization taken by late Hellenistic art; emphasis on portraiture was to be the great distinguishing feature of Roman sculpture and painting.

12 Mosaic of Plato's Academy, from a villa near Pompeii (before A.D. 79)

OMINVM IN SANCTIS EIVS
LAVS EI

13 Interior of the Pantheon, Rome (A.D. 120–4). Detail from a painting by G. P. Pannini

14 The Colosseum, Rome (late 1st c. A.D.)

15 The Temple of Vesta, Tivoli (*c.* A.D. 125–38)

ARCHITECTURE AND ENGINEERING were the greatest achievement of Rome in the arts. Of course, certain elements were taken over from Greece, most obviously the system of the orders, Roman architects favouring above all the Corinthian (plates 13 and 15) and developing the superimposition of Corinthian upon Ionic upon Doric (plate 14). Yet Rome's was the first architecture in the West to perfect the principles of the arch and the dome thus making a decisive break with the trabeated architecture of Greece. The very use of multiple orders, typified in the Colosseum, was an important new technique which bore its full fruit with the Renaissance, when the buildings of Rome, above all the Colosseum itself, provided the first models.

16 Wall painting of theatrical architecture, from Herculaneum (before A.D. 79)

ROME'S GRANDEUR was manifested in the vast civic buildings throughout the empire, the greatest among them being the Colosseum and the Baths of Caracalla and Diocletian in the imperial capital itself. Belief in a mission to world empire and pride in its achievement and maintenance were two potent inspirations in the heyday of empire, well expressed in this cameo. It shows the goddess Roma seated with the Emperor Augustus, who is being crowned by Victory. To the left, the Emperor's stepson and successor, the leader of his armies, Tiberius, is descending from a triumphal chariot, his charioteer a winged genius of victory. Below, prisoners sit disconsolately while soldiers erect a trophy. The gem carved in onyx, besides being a masterpiece of the cutter's art, is a perfect combination of a political expression in art, ideals of grandeur and a realistic commentary on everyday life.

17 The Gemma Augustea (*c.* A.D. 10)

A sizeable corpus of Roman wall painting survives, and often gives the spectator an unexpected feeling of familiarity. The detail illustrated, for example, uses illusionistic perspective and the broken pediment which is reminiscent of mannerism in architecture. The elaborate type of *skena* used in the Roman theatre, as shown here, was very unlike the simple Greek structure illustrated by plate 7. The stage area in Roman theatres was roofed in; drapes are just discernible at the top of the picture. The illustration not only shows the sort of rich wall painting which might decorate the villas of the wealthy, but also the way in which paint-work, stucco and gold-leaf ornament were used to embellish architecture itself.

18 Wall painting of The Aldobrandini Wedding, from Rome (1st c. B.C.)

THESE PICTURES SHOW TWO WORKS in the same medium from the same city; and although separated by three centuries, both were painted during the period when the tradition of Roman world empire was meaningful. Yet in every other respect–in mood, in subject-matter, in style, even in locality–they are worlds apart. The one, in the urbane and polished style of a fashionable art, is believed to represent the preparation of a bride for a society wedding. She sits on the couch, awaiting the arrival of the groom; her companion is possibly the goddess Venus. The other two main figures seem to be completing preparations for the ceremony. The scene was part of the decorations of a great town-house. The other picture, from the catacombs beneath the city, is probably the work of an artist from an oppressed, outlawed minority–the Christians. The subject of mother and child may be an early representation of the Virgin and Child; the simple treatment gives a vigour lacking in the suave, finished work of the fashionable artist.

19 Wall painting of the late 3rd c. Catacomb of Priscilla, Rome

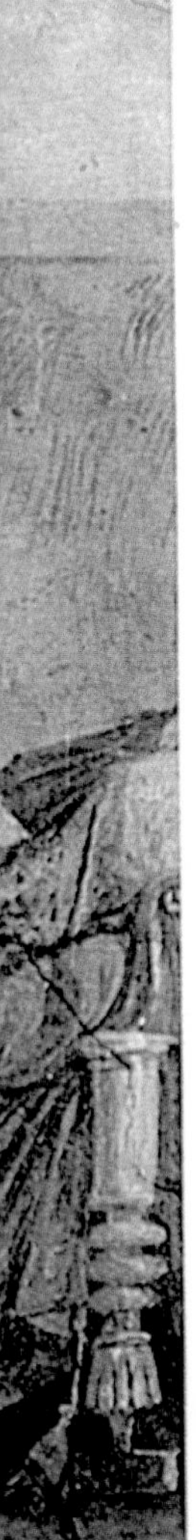

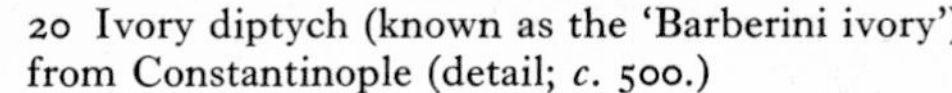

20 Ivory diptych (known as the 'Barberini ivory') from Constantinople (detail; *c.* 500.)

UNDER THE EMPEROR CONSTANTINE paganism gave place to Christianity as the official imperial religion. His foundation of Constantinople in 330 was regarded by later generations as the inspired inauguration of the new era of the Christian Roman empire. The influence of Rome faded gradually, yet even as late as the 6th c. the style of late Roman sculpture persisted in this detail from an ivory thought to represent the Emperor Anastasius. Further, the dress of the emperor is Roman and the allegory of the winged victory saluting him and mother earth supporting him clearly harks back to pagan imagery.

Ivory carving was the most characteristic expression of Byzantine glyptic art, of which plate 20 is a magnificent example; yet it was glass mosaic that became the medium of the greatest achievements of Byzantine art.

THE MOSAIC opposite comes from the Baptistery of the Orthodox at Ravenna, erected in the mid 5th c. The brilliant-coloured glinting mosaics on walls and domes provided a dramatized commentary on the faith. Despite the clinging symbolism of Pagan Rome–the personified river god Jordan, the floral arabesques, the pictured architecture–this dome provides a fine example of such a commentary. The artist has disciplined all his resources to present the structure of the 'true religion'. On the columns supporting the dome (not in the picture) are portrayed the Old Testament Prophets of Christ and parallels between the Old and New Testaments; at the base of the dome the classical niches contain the open books of the four Gospels (the Scriptural foundation of the faith) and the Throne of the Apocalypse. Above this are the Apostles, the missionaries of the faith, and at the apex is the scene of Christ's baptism, showing the descent of the Holy Spirit into Christ himself.

21 Cupola of the Baptistery of the Orthodox, Ravenna (430–78)

22 Presbyterium of S. Apollinare in Classe, Ravenna (*c.* 549)

IN THIS SECOND MOSAIC from Ravenna, the artist presents the relationship of the faithful on earth to Christ. The patron saint of the city, St Apollinaris, believed to have been the first bishop of Ravenna, stands among his flock with hands upraised. Above the saint the Transfiguration of Christ is represented by the Cross flanked by Moses and Elias and witnessed by the apostles Peter, James and John, portrayed as sheep. Above the arch is Christ in Glory surrounded by the creatures symbolic of the Four Evangelists. In the centre stands the miracle of God-become-man ascending to glory; at his feet, represented as sheep, are the Twelve Apostles. The link between sinful man and God is complete; at every stage men, Christ's flock, are able to partake of the glory.

BARBARIAN ARTISTS often sought to emulate the works of the Roman-Byzantine world they had entered, but their native idiom was very different. Typical was the animal style, found in various forms in all the arts of the Northern Barbarian peoples and illustrated here by two Visigothic brooches.

The art of the jeweller achieved a peak in the kingdoms which grew up in Europe after the collapse of the empire in the West. This late 10th-c. reliquary, made to hold the sandal of St Andrew, comes from the court of the Ottonian emperors at Trier; the heavy incrustation with gold and precious stones is typical of the period. The remains of saints and holy men were venerated throughout the Christian world, and richly worked reliquaries were a natural medium for the jeweller's art.

23 Visigothic eagle brooches from Estamadura (early 6th c.)

24 Reliquary of the sandal of St Andrew, Trier (late 10th c.)

THE LAST ROMAN EMPEROR in the West was deposed in 476, but after the coronation of Charlemagne in 800 the title 'emperor' was assumed by the Frankish kings. Plate 26, an illustration from a Gospel book (*c.* 998) depicts the young emperor Otto III, who of all the emperors since Charlemagne felt himself most fully the heir of the Caesars. The composition shows classical influence, but the exaggerated size of the emperor (indicating his status as a ruler) and the faces in the capitals are medieval traits in the work.

25 Detail of the Bayeux Tapestry (late 11th c.)

THE BAYEUX TAPESTRY is unusual among surviving medieval works of art in its secular theme, Duke William's conquest of England, and in the lively narrative technique employed. This scene may be based on the tradition that during the battle of Hastings a rumour spread that the duke had been killed; in order to rally his troops he raised his helmet so that he might be easily recognized. The Latin commentary reads 'here is William the Duke'.

26 Otto III enthroned; from the *Gospel Book of Otto III* (*c.* 998)

27 Interior of the abbey church of La Madeleine, Vézelay, looking east

28 Martinus Presbyter. *Virgin and Child* (1199)

IN CLASSICAL ANTIQUITY art had treated religious subjects, but many of its greatest triumphs were, as we have seen, secular; for more than a millennium after the establishment of Christianity, however, the greatest creative talents of the Christian world were directed towards religion. This orientation was fixed in the early history of Byzantium, and began to waver only during the Renaissance.

The religious impulse found its greatest realization in the cathedrals of medieval Europe. The nave of Vézelay, here illustrated, employs the rounded arch, massive piers and uncomplicated groin-vault characteristic of Romanesque. When stone began to be used for massive cathedrals in the 11th c., the medieval architect drew guidance and inspiration from the surviving Roman buildings and engineering works. The very size of the new cathedrals indicates the growing wealth and stability of Christian Europe, while the carving on the capitals, no longer conforming to the classical orders, is the first hint of the exuberant decoration which was to be a feature of the subsequent Gothic style. The chancel was built about a century after the nave, and we can see how the rounded arch, though echoed in the new section, has given pride of place to the Gothic pointed arch, and how the groined vaulting has been disregarded for the new principle of ribbed vaulting. In the applied arts enamel was admirably suited to the medieval taste for rich decoration; the book-cover illustrated (plate 29) is a fine example of *Limoges, and the theme, Christ in Glory, a favourite one of the period.

29 Book-cover of Limoges enamel showing Christ in Glory (late 12th century)

30 Interior of Amiens cathedral, looking east (1st half of the 13th c.)

GOTHIC WAS BORN in the mid 12th c. at a time when medieval culture was exhibiting a remarkable dynamism and adventurousness. The ambitiousness and aspirations of this new style in architecture accorded well with the new spirit of inquiry and audacious questioning epitomized in the work of Peter Abelard. The interior of Amiens cathedral (plate 30) is Gothic in its maturity. The verticals leading the eye up, the pointed arch, the simple, elegant rib-vaulting and bar-tracery of the windows are the hall-marks of the style, but there is no exaggeration, no excessive ornamentation. Plates 32 and 33 illustrate the changes brought by a century and more of development. The rose-window became a frequent feature of large churches; the rich stained glass and elaborate tracery provided a star-burst of colour above the great West door. As Gothic developed, greater mastery of vaulting and tracery enabled the architect to fill the area between structural verticals with glass set in delicate stone branches and filigree. The trend was towards increasingly ornate tracery, as is seen at Strassburg. The rose-window itself was built *c.* 1360 and the tracery web in front of it added about 25 years later.

In England the logical development towards the flamboyant excesses of continental work was deflected by the popularity of the perpendicular style. Gloucester provides the earliest example. The fan-vaulting (plate 33) does not attempt to express function in the lines of its ribs, and the decoration is rich. Yet it is in repeating units which do not break their boundaries. These units were probably carved at the quarry and assembled on site, which would have reduced the cost of building; the style was used in the great parish churches built during the 14th and 15th c. from the pious donations of wealthy wool merchants. Medieval sculpture followed a development parallel to that seen already in the Greek; from the static pose to one of greater movement. The figures at Chartres do not break out from the simple vertical column, but within it the movement of line becomes more sinuous and expressive, and drapery is used to break up and vary the surface of the stone. The growing liberation of form can be seen in the figures at Strassburg.

31 Statue of St John the Baptist on the north transept of Chartres cathedral (*c.* 1220)

32 Rose-window on the West front of Strassburg cathedral (*c.* 1360)

33 Walk in the cloister of Gloucester cathedral (*c.* 1350)

34 A sower: detail of a stained-glass window in Canterbury cathedral (early 13th c.)

STAINED GLASS was most significant among the arts employed in the embellishment of the great churches. This was the characteristic expression of medieval Christendom; the wide areas of glass were not designed to flood the church with light but rather to surround the sanctuary and the worshipping faithful with a brilliant procession of saints and tableaux of the faith (plate 34).

35 Façade of Orvieto cathedral (begun in 1309)

IN ITALY THE GOTHIC, an essentially Northern style, never developed as fully or elaborately as it did in France, Germany or England. The façade of Orvieto cathedral, (plate 35) modelled on that of Siena shows an amalgam of Gothic and Romanesque elements, e.g. the combination of the rounded arch and the pointed, the latter being used primarily as a decorative motif, rather than as a structural unit. The overall geometric composition seems out of tune with developments north of the Alps. At about the same time, the painter Giotto at Florence was producing work as radically different from the style prevalent in Italy–until then much inspired by Byzantine models–as from the art of the North. The near-naturalistic proportions and postures of the figures are in contrast with the work of such of his contemporaries as Simone Martini of Siena, whose *Annunciation* is illustrated overleaf. In Giotto the figures seem to breathe life; those in Martini's picture sit in unnaturalistic and formalized postures, inhabiting a spiritual world of their own, magical and remote.

36 Giotto. *Lamentation over the Dead Christ* (*c.* 1306). Fresco in the Scrovegni chapel, Padua

38 Jan van Eyck. *The Arnolfini Marriage Group* (1434)

37 Simone Martini. *The Annunciation* (early 14th c.)

40 Rogier van der Weyden. *Portrait of a Lady* (mid 15th c.)

39 Master of Flémalle. *St Barbara* (1438)

WHEREAS IN ITALY during the middle ages, the basic political unit was the city and its surrounding *contàdo*, north of the Alps territorial units evolved gradually from dynastic estates. Most remarkable of the dynastic rulers were the dukes of Burgundy, a cadet branch of the French Royal House. A consistent marriage policy raised their House to a position from which they might have succeeded in founding a new European monarchy. Their wealth was based on the growing industries of the Low Countries, and their subjects numbered some of the greatest musicians and artists in Europe. Of the painters here illustrated, Jan van Eyck was in the service of Philip the Good of Burgundy and Rogier van der Weyden worked for members of the court.

Plate 38, entitled *The Arnolfini Marriage Group*, is thought to have been painted for an Italian merchant, Giovanni Arnolfino, who settled in Flanders. The movements of trade and commerce are paralleled by those of artistic influences, and the new style of oil painting, developed in the Low Countries and used here by van Eyck, was taken up by the Italian Renaissance painters. The picture is rich in symbolism (for example the dog, symbol of faithfulness), and exhibits two characteristics of Flemish painting in its meticulous detail and interest in the domestic interior. Particularly interesting is the convex mirror, beneath which is an inscription which translated means 'Jan van Eyck was here'. Just discernible is the reflection of a third figure (the painter himself, it has been suggested); the mirror together with the open window typify a device frequent in Flemish interior scenes, the use of the long perspective penetrating the enclosed space of the room.

The device is more obvious in the Master of Flémalle's *St Barbara*. This, like many Flemish masterpieces, has such an atmosphere of innocence and repose that the commonplace room seems almost sanctified by the saint's presence; the open window seems like a door between this sanctum and the mundane world beyond. The furnishings and utensils shown provide an interesting study in the style of the applied arts of the period:

The atmosphere of calmness and poise, which pervades so much 15th-c. Flemish art, is personified by van der Weyden's *Portrait of a Lady*. Her fashionable rings, plucked forehead and gauze veil do not detract from her almost otherworldly serenity.

THE CITY-STATES OF ITALY varied greatly in wealth and size but at their best shared the same high culture. The pictures here represent works executed for one of the greatest, Florence, and one of the smaller states, Urbino. In the 15th c. Florence based her great prosperity upon the wealth of her merchant-bankers, above all the Medici; this wealth was used to beautify the city and such patronage was an important contributory factor in the growth of the Renaissance.

In 1402 Ghiberti won the competition for a pair of doors for the Florence Baptistery which should match those already erected by Andrea Pisano. In 1425 he was commissioned to design a third pair of doors and plate 41 shows a panel from this later pair. Ghiberti regarded himself as a humanist and the design is based on the principles of perspective investigated and formalized by others such as his older contemporary Brunelleschi. The relief modelling as illustrated shows these principles at work and the effect of depth is heightened by the more incised moulding of the foreground figures and the low-relief treatment of the background. Yet despite this humanist apparatus the style of the work, notably the architectural background, shows the way in which Gothic ideas lingered in Ghiberti's work.

This picture of Duke Federigo da Montefeltro in triumph is the back of one wing of a diptych painted for the duke by Piero della Francesca. The duke on his triumphal chariot is being crowned by Victory and is accompanied by the four cardinal virtues, Justice, Prudence, Temperance and Fortitude. The other side of the diptych shows his wife the duchess in similar triumph driving to meet him. The landscape, which extends over both panels, is an important feature of the work and shows the increased importance of landscape as a genre during the 15th c.; Piero's presentation of the Umbrian countryside is remarkable for its success in conveying atmospheric effects. On the front of the two panels are profile portraits of the duke and duchess. Duke Federigo during a long and prosperous reign built his small duchy into a considerable power on the proceeds not of trading but of warfare. Yet despite his prowess as a soldier his reputation was for enlightened government and munificent patronage.

42 Piero della Francesca. *The Triumph of Federigo da Montefeltro* (1465–6)

FROM ITS BEGINNINGS FLORENTINE painting followed the tradition set by Giotto of clarity in colour applied in flat areas. To this style Botticelli brought an individual sinuosity and line which inspires and characterizes all of his greatest works. The figures and draperies all assist this supple linear composition and the humanism of his pictures is also suffused by a deeply religious inspiration. As in so many works of this period the sacred scene is backed by a vista of the unidealized landscape of Italy. In this case linked with the interior by the continuing lines of the pavement. The linear elegances of Botticelli's work was in marked contrast to the work of his great contemporary Leonardo da Vinci, who was concerned with colour as used to model the figures in the painting rather than as decorative applied areas. Leonardo's importance in the history of painting in part derives from his theory of *sfumato* seen in its practical application in plate 44. Pursuing his ideal of realistic representation, Leonardo endeavoured to soften the artificial contours of painting so that they should more nearly represent the merging of planes in the physical world and to achieve this he suffused his paintings with an overall 'haze' which connected the receding planes. The unusual background of the religious scene emphasizes the artist's scientific interest and particularly his interest in geological rock formations; the postures of the figures are in accordance with his theories of 'decorum', that is, that the treatment of a subject should be fitting to its nature, theories which were later to hold an important place in 16th-c. Italian religious art.

43 Botticelli. *The Annunciation* (1489–90)

44 Leonardo da Vinci.
The Virgin of the Rocks
(*c.* 1483)

THE TECHNIQUES by which Giorgione achieves an all-pervading atmosphere and softening of contours in *The Tempest* may be compared with the *sfumato* developed by Leonardo. Giorgione too was one of the great innovators of painting. The richness of his colour, and his warm sensuous use of paint to convey the texture of physical things and the quality of light, helped to form the style of his contemporary Titian (who outlived him by the length of a normal man's lifetime) and with it the whole tradition of Venetian art.

The mood of this picture, that of the sweltering heat before a thunderstorm, contrasts with the seeming indifference of the two figures and the apparently haphazard architectural elements of the foreground. It may be that this puzzle (to the modern spectator) would be easily explicable to contemporaries in terms of a symbolism whose meaning is now lost; still, the mystery concerning the work is increased by the discovery, through X-ray photography, that Giorgione changed the composition considerably while painting the picture.

45 Giorgione. *The Tempest* (1505–8)

46 Michelangelo. *The Holy Family* (1504)

THE RELIGIOUS THEME OF MICHELANGELO'S Holy Family is unmistakable and avowed yet the Holy Family is here used for the artist's exercise in composition rather than presented as an object for reverence and adoration. Both in the background figures and in the central group it is clear the artist's interest is primarily sculptural–an interest further shown in the simple compositional use of colour in the garments of the foreground figures. The sculpture tondo by Michelangelo in the Royal Academy, London, shows strong parallels in its treatment of this subject and the tondo itself was a very popular form with artists of the period.

MICHELANGELO'S DESIGN FOR THE CAPITOL at Rome was a grandiose conception of town planning which has remained virtually unchanged to this day. The buildings are grouped round the Roman statue of the Emperor Marcus Aurelius, and the pavement surrounding it is part of the Renaissance architect's overall plan. Michelangelo regarded architecture as a grand and monumental art and plate 47 well illustrates the giant Corinthian order (seen on the pilasters stretching from ground to cornice) which he invented, and which was much used by his successors. His influence on all Italian art in painting, in sculpture and in architecture was immeasurable and determined the development of the mannerist style. In architecture this style culminated in an almost wilful manipulation of and disregard for the classical principles of architecture rediscovered by the Renaissance theorists. Small indications of this trend are already present in the magnificent façade and are summed up by the large first-floor window. Here Michelangelo uses two pediments, one triangular, one segmental and introduces the broken pediment.

THE RESTRAINED MANNER OF PALLADIO was a contrast to mannerism. It was to impress later English visitors to Italy and gave rise to the Palladian style in England. Like Michelangelo, Palladio decorated his work freely with sculpture, indeed the figures over the pediments would seem to be derived from Michelangelo's Medici tombs. But Palladio employed the orders in a more orthodox Roman manner. The superimposition of Ionic upon Doric follows the Roman pattern and his Doric order is the Roman unfluted style with a base. It is interesting to note that this careful classicism gives rise to a direct quotation from Greek architecture in the alternating metopes and triglyphs round the frieze above the ground-floor colonnade of pillars.

48 Palladio. Palazzo Chiericati, Vicenza (1550–7)

47 Michelangelo. The Palazzo dei Conservatori, on the Capitol, Rome (begun in 1546)

49 Intarsia panelling in the private study of Federigo da Montefeltro; in the Ducal Palace, Gubbio (1479–82)

THE INTERIORS of rich Renaissance palaces were frequently decorated with marquetry and the technical excellence of this work is well illustrated by the intarsia panelling for the private study of Duke Federigo da Montefeltro by Francesco di Giorgio Martini and B. Pontelli. The work shows the developed repertory in style and subject of the medium – the delight in *trompe l'œil* effects and the themes of learning and music and measuring instruments of time and extension. The books are especially fitting as the duke, whose reputation for enlightenment we have already noticed, was particularly famed for his magnificent library of manuscript books (he disdained to include printed works in his collection).

50 *The Garden of Love*; tapestry from Touraine (*c.* 1503)

EUROPE NORTH OF THE ALPS was slow to relinquish its traditional medieval style, by now so widespread and uniform that it is known as 'international Gothic'. This style, somewhat lacking in strength, was of extreme elegance and charm, full of the beauties of nature, jewel-like colours, graceful figures and courtly sentiments; a style well suited to the art of tapestry–the most characteristic form of wall decoration in France and Flanders. The example shown portrays a favourite theme of medieval literature, The Garden of Love. As in all art of this period, the work is full of allegorical meanings, the fountain, the animals and the figures all having a distinctive significance. Of particular interest are the musical instruments shown–the lady playing a positive organ, the young boy playing the lute and the girl in the right foreground playing a fidel. A point of stylistic significance is the way in which the subordinate figures of the huntsman (left background) and the two young ladies in the foreground are shown in a reduced size, not for any reason of perspective, but simply to indicate their subordinate station.

1498

51 Dürer. *Self-portrait* (1498)

52 Cranach. *Venus and Cupid stung by a bee* (1531)

DURING THE 15TH C., developments in Italy had an increasing impact on Northern artists. Albrecht Dürer was the first great German artist to come to Italy and the man who did most to bring the Renaissance to the North. His work shows an interesting combination of his national tradition and his acquired Italianate manner. This self-portrait has the assured pose of the 'Renaissance man', and the use of flamboyant costume is typically Venetian. But there is still much that is Northern in the meticulously detailed features and the strange soulfulness of his self-scrutiny. Much of Dürer's greatest work was done in the medium of woodcut and wood engraving, techniques fully mastered and typical of German artists.

The same union of influence, though producing a startlingly different effect, is seen in this painting by Lucas Cranach. The finish of the work clearly owes much to Italian styles and the subject, a nude Venus, is obviously one inspired by Renaissance symbolism. Yet the posture of the figure and the whole mood of the work is unmistakably in the Northern tradition, and the traces of Italian influence are only a secondary element in the impact of the painting as a whole. The ancestors of this Cranach Venus were not Zeus and the Aegean but guilty Eve, Vanity looking in her glass and the timid risen souls of a Gothic Last Judgement.

53 El Greco.
St Martin and the Beggar (1597–9)

54 Caravaggio.
The Musical Party (1594–5)

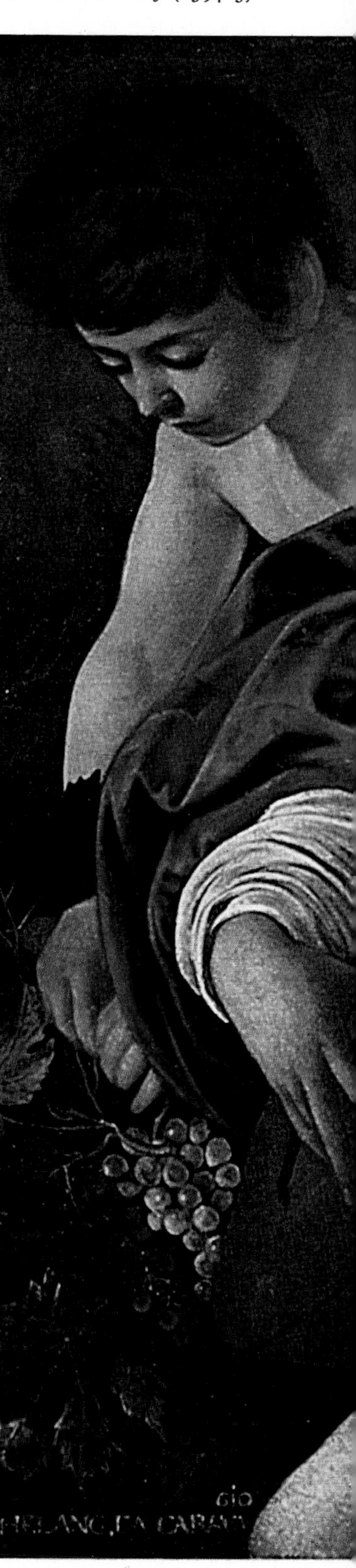

THE PRINCIPLES OF RENAISSANCE Italian painting, outside Italy, were variously influential and interpreted in different ways. As painting and the arts developed in Italy itself, the original impulse underwent equally striking modifications. Most notable was the mannerist style, which took its source from the work of Michelangelo. His increasingly free disposition of the limbs of the human body and increasingly ambitious and uneasy poses led artists of the generation after his death to outright distortion of form and contrivance of composition. This style found many exponents in Italy, but perhaps the most remarkable of the mannerist painters was El Greco, a Cretan and a pupil of Titian, who worked for most of his life in Spain. The distorted elongation of his figures is a familiar aspect of his work. It is not surprising that mannerism should have produced such a style, but it must also be remembered that El Greco's training in his earliest years was affected by the traditions of Byzantine art, which despite modifications in its later period was concerned less with realistic, than with dramatic compositional effects.

That drama and realism were not incompatible was shown in the work of that stormy petrel of Italian painting, Caravaggio. His work was the subject of heated controversy during his lifetime: it was often rejected by the official bodies which had commissioned it (for example on the grounds that his treatment of religious subjects lacked the decorum required) yet was eagerly bought by private patrons and collectors. Besides a bold approach to his subject-matter, Caravaggio used the technique of chiaroscuro to give dramatic life to his painting.

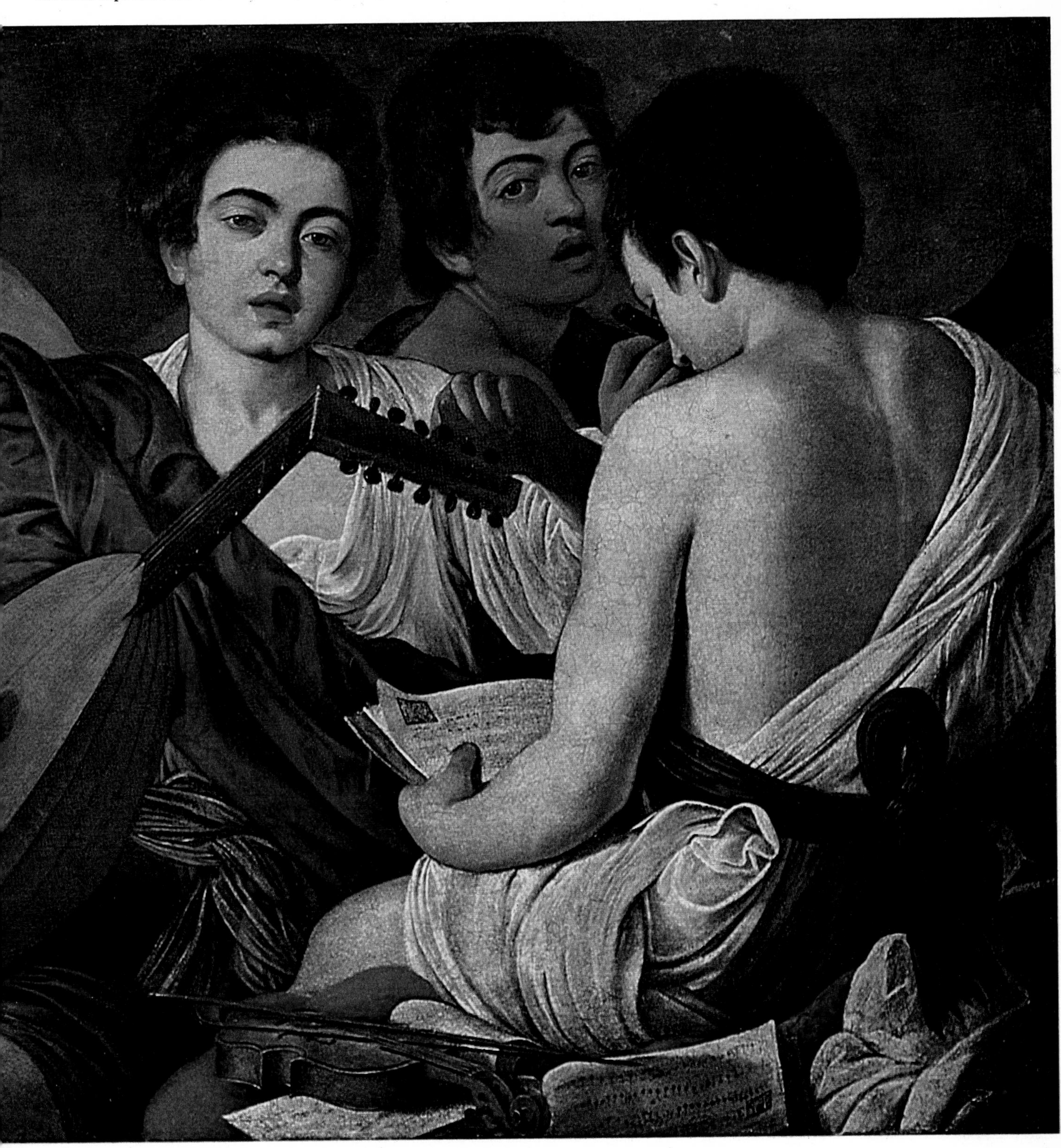

THE SUPERB EXAMPLES of the craftsman's work shown here, are examples of the way in which the styles of high art influenced and infiltrated the applied arts which flourished richly during the Renaissance. The uneasy poses of Neptune and his consort on the *Cellini salt-cellar remind us of mannerist painting and sculpture; the arabesque decorations on the *maiolica wine-cooler are modelled on the *grotesques of Raphael, which he in turn derived from rediscovered Roman wall paintings.

One of the most brilliant courts of Europe was that of the Habsburg emperor Rudolf II at Prague. Besides artists the emperor patronized philosophers and scientists: both Kepler and Tycho Brahe held positions at the court. The terrestrial and celestial globes illustrated, were commissioned for the scientific studies at Prague, from Europe's greatest centre of metalworking, Augsburg.

55 Celestial and terrestrial globe made for Rudolf II; Augsburg (1588)

56 Cellini. Gold salt-cellar (1570)

57 Wine-cooler made for the duke of Urbino in the studio of Fontana (1565–71)

58 Poussin. *Bacchanalian Revel before a Term of Pan* (*c.* 1635)

IN FRANCE the fashionable style of art in the early 16th c. was shaped by the work of such Italian mannerist artists as Primaticcio, summoned by Francis I to decorate the Royal Palace at Fontainebleau. The later development towards the baroque in Italian painting was highly influential in the 17th c. through the work of the court painter Vouet. Nicolas Poussin was also deeply influenced by his studies in Italy, where he spent much of his life; but he came to reject the fashionable and to him superficial elegance of Vouet and the increasing luxuriance of the developing baroque style. More and more Poussin became concerned with classical composition using forms and areas of unmodelled local colour as compositional elements. Even this *Bacchanal*, despite its apparent abandon, is carefully disciplined within a formal framework and quite drained of sensuality.

No stronger contrast can be imagined than that between Poussin and Rubens, and these two men gave their names to the conflicting schools of 17th-c. French artists. The dispute was over the place of colour in painting, the Poussinistes regarding it as secondary to composition and design, the Rubénistes emphasizing its primacy in the representation of nature. The most obvious point of contrast between the two pictures on these pages is in the rendering of the flesh tints; but the sensuality of Rubens's paint also extends into the rich vibrancy of the fur and background.

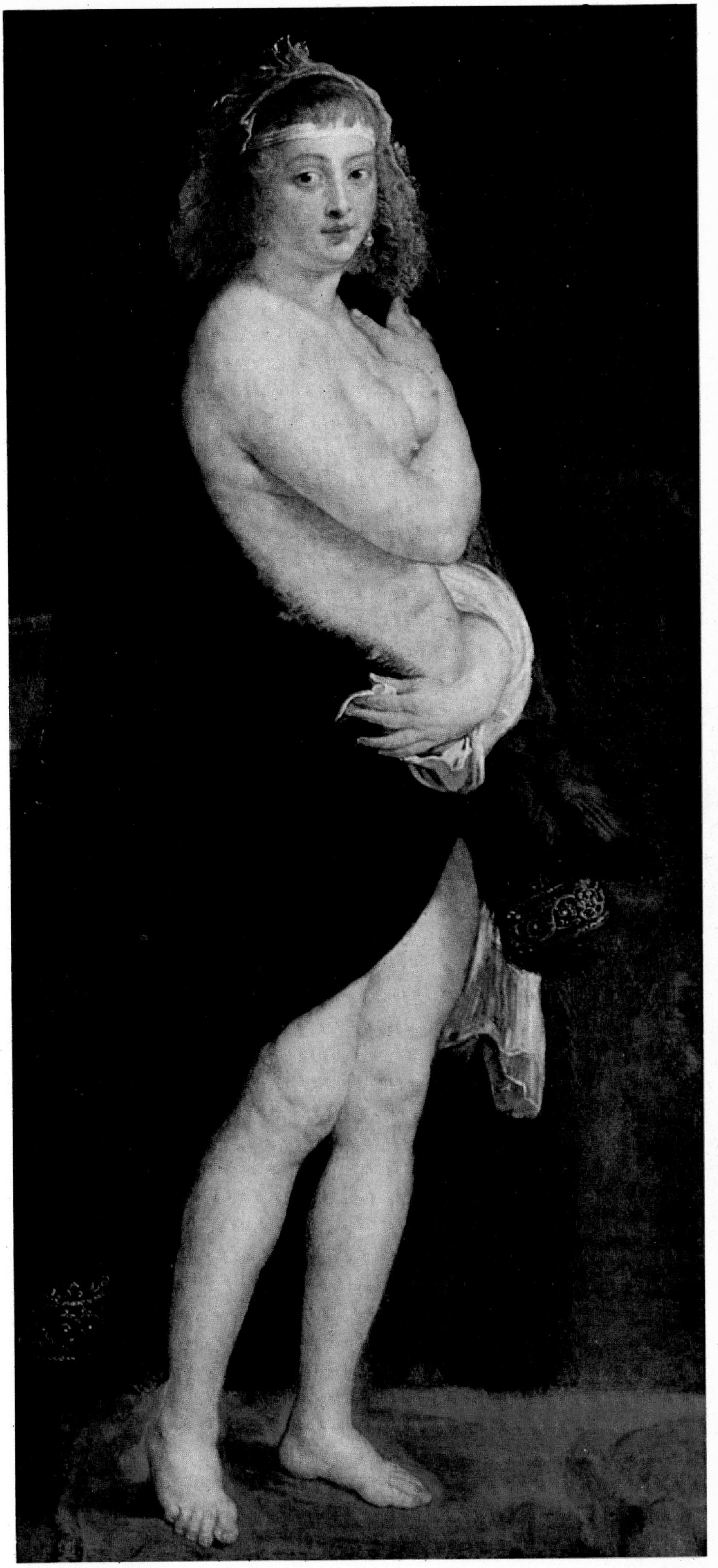

59 Rubens. *Hélène Fourment in a Fur Coat* (after 1630)

60 Rembrandt. *Titus Reading* (*c.* 1656)

REMBRANDT, RUBENS AND POUSSIN rather than any Italian painters were the colossi of European painting during the 17th c. Vermeer was a master of almost equal stature, although his influence made its full impact only in the 20th c. He and his famous contemporary Rembrandt had in common an inspired appreciation and mastery of lighting. In the portrait of his son Titus, Rembrandt exploits the boy's natural position for reading, with sunlight falling over one shoulder, to perfect pictorial effect; and Vermeer uses the natural daylight lighting of his studio as suffused atmosphere which affects and transmutes the everyday objects of a painter's workshop.

Unlike Vermeer, however, Rembrandt uses paint as an expressive medium: the swirls and strokes of the brush are in themselves pictorial elements. His virtuoso mastery of oils, the so-called painterly or *malerisch element in his work, has ensured Rembrandt's stature in the eyes of subsequent generations of artists.

61 Vermeer. *The Artist's Studio* (1665–70)

62 Heda. *Still-life* (1637)

IN THE HOLLAND of Rembrandt and Vermeer one of the most popular and demanded genres of painting was the unpretentious still-life picture. At its best the Dutch still-life, using commonplace objects of everyday life, combined them into elegant almost abstract formal compositions; and when minor masters such as Heda worked in the genre, they almost always displayed an astonishing facility in the representation of material textures. The objects have an interest in themselves as examples of mid-17th-c. styles in silver and glass; notice particularly the Venetian type of drinking-glass to the left.

63 *Salon* in the Château de Champs (18th c.)

THE ORNATE THEATRICAL manner of the *baroque spread throughout Europe, developing during the first half of the 18th c. into the less heavy though still decorative style of rococo. This Louis XV interior shows the elegance and lightness of the new style as it evolved in France. The flat decorative wall painting, the delicate chair coverings and the shapely cabriole legs of the tables, all suggest the new mood. The large wall-mirrors are an increasingly frequent element in the style; unlike illusionistic baroque paintings they do not intrude on the real space yet introduce a new spaciousness by breaking the barriers of the walls.

64 Zimmermann. Pilgrimage church '*In der Wies*' (Wieskirche) (1746–54)

65 Franz Ignaz Günther. *The Guardian Angel* (1763)

OUTSIDE FRANCE the main centre of rococo was southern Germany, where the style acquires a unique character through contact with Italian baroque. In this church by Zimmermann the brilliance of the colouring lightens the whole interior; but the restless movement between real and illusionistic space is truly baroque. The apparent profusion is disciplined by a strict theological scheme into which the frescoes and statues, and even the symbolic colours of the imitation-marble columns are integrated. Nothing can be added or taken away without damaging the total effect. Of special interest is the way in which the once structural elements such as columns and vaulting are now employed simply for decorative effect and manipulated so as to conceal the structural articulation of the building in the interest of the created space of the interior. The spectator can hardly decide where the wall ends and the ceiling begins.

Such architecture enlisted all the arts for an overall effect, the sculptured figures of the saints playing their part in the drama. The magnificent piece shown in plate 65, would originally have been designed as a part of such an interior as the Wieskirche. The convention of using paint for heightened effect persisted far longer in wood sculpture than in stone.

THE ELEGANT ROCOCO style for interiors, which originated in the private apartments of the court of Louis XV, was adapted during the century to a variety of purposes and is typified in its southern German development by this theatre auditorium from Munich. It was in such theatres as this that the formal Italian opera in vogue would have been performed, and where the operas of Mozart would have received their premières. But concurrently with the formalism and elegance of this court art a new passion for nature and dislike of artificiality was developing. This culminated in the romantic movement.

66 François de Cuvilliès. The Old Residence Theatre, Munich (1751–3

67 Gainsborough. *The Morning Walk* (*c.* 1785)

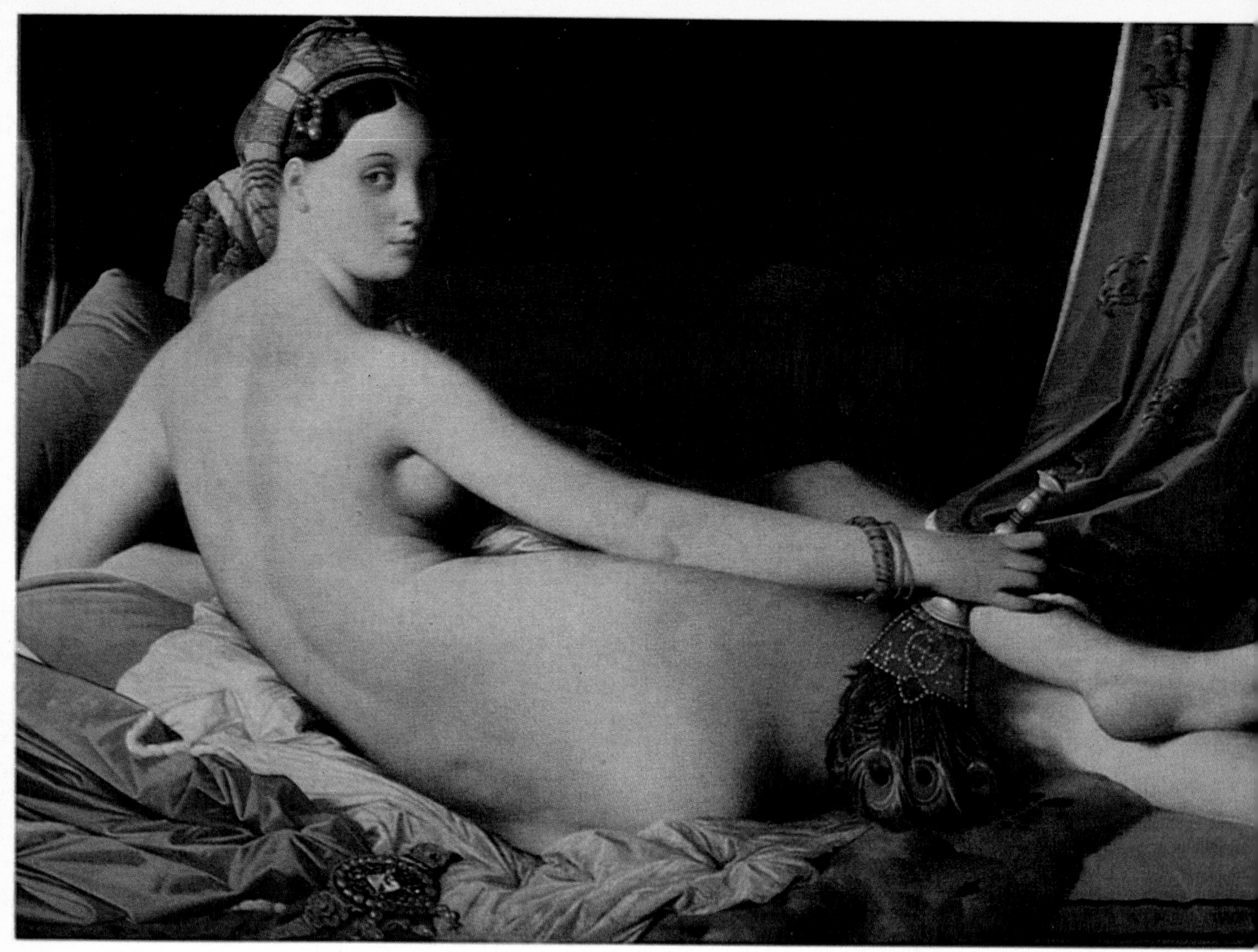

68 Ingres. *La Grande Odalisque* (1819)

69 Delacroix. *Arab on Horseback attacked by a Lion* (detail; 1849)

THE IDEA THAT THE NATURAL WORLD is in itself a legitimate subject for the artist rather than simply the quarry for his imagination, was not new in the 18th c. but it was to acquire increasing importance, notably in the work of English nature poets such as James Thomson. This new emphasis in literature is paralleled in the arts in the work of the English landscape gardeners who, in theory at least, endeavoured not to discipline nature into formal geometrical appearance but to re-create in an ordered manner 'natural' landscape effects. The painting by Gainsborough (plate 67) shows a typical English couple of the upper classes taking a walk in just such a natural landscape. To the modern spectator there is a contrast between the formal, artificial dress of 18th-c. society and the free undisciplined trees blown in the wind. The technique of the painting itself, whatever the artist's attitude towards nature, is not in this case one of a naturalistic realism; the surface of the canvas is overlaid by the repeated stylistic mannerism of Gainsborough's feathery brushwork. In other works Gainsborough showed a marked realistic appreciation of nature, and this element in English painting was to reach its high point in the work of John Constable.

THE GROWING MOVEMENT IN LITERATURE known as Romanticism made its full impact in the visual arts in the early 19th c.; in England the movement is represented in the work of Turner. In many of his techniques the French painter Delacroix, like all artists, rested heavily on the tradition in which he was born; but there is a new mood of the exotic and passionate to be found in his work. In his departure from the austere principles of French academic art Delacroix reflected the prevailing attitudes of Romanticism, and French painting was for a time dominated by the conflict between Delacroix and his arch-opponent, Ingres.

Ingres was regarded as the great exponent of classical purity of line and draughtsmanship. The posture of such figures as the odalisque illustrated here is often influenced by considerations of 'mannerist' distortion, yet there is a repose and calm about his work rarely found in that of the Romantic school. The conflict of style is apparent in the brushwork of the two paintings illustrated.

70 Monet. *Field of Poppies* (1873)

FRENCH PAINTERS from about the 1860s, without denying the traditions of the great masters of the past, made contributions to painting which seemed to contemporaries to deny the true nature of painting itself and to posterity to open new fields of visual awareness. The first great experimental school which was to give Paris its hegemony for the next fifty years was that of the impressionists. The aim, a true representation of man's vision of nature, was not new; indeed it had exercised Renaissance theorists such as Leonardo. But the means employed to achieve this aim produced a new style. Believing that the apparent contours of the physical world were never fully registered by the human eye, the impressionist painters endeavoured to present on their canvases the optical impressions of a scene as it is received by an eye innocent of visual convention. Their means towards this were painting from life, that is to say in the open air rather than from prepared sketches in the studio, and the full deployment of paint in an endeavour to capture light and movement. This work by Monet is a fine example of their style.

The impressionists were concerned above all with visual sensations. After them the vision begins to turn inwards, in the work of expressionist painters whose aim was to present not so much the appearance of reality as the painter's interpretation of the mood of the landscape or of the human actor. The direction of this new style was already clear in the work of Vincent van Gogh, whose early impressionistic works gave place to canvases in which the tortured brush-strokes provide a visual sensation, certainly, but whose overall impact is one of drama and atmosphere. Later, in the works of Edvard Munch, expressionism turned to the regeneration of human emotions in paint.

71 Van Gogh. *Road with Cypresses* (detail; 1889)

72 Cézanne. *Mont-Ste-Victoire* (detail; 1904–6)

THE FERTILITY OF THE IMPRESSIONIST movement is shown by the way in which its original members travelled along quite different roads. We have seen how Van Gogh gave birth to a new aesthetic of expressionism. In the work of Cézanne a more austere, almost classical mind takes control and produces paintings in which neither expression nor impression are the aim but rather an understanding and presentation of the structure of the world. His late landscapes of Mont-Ste-Victoire are a painterly composition of form and colour derived from his understanding of the structure of the landscape, and the colour of his thought is illustrated by his famous observation that the painter should aim to portray nature through the geometrical shapes of the cylinder, sphere and cone.

THE *CUBISM of Picasso and Braque launched in the 1910s was inspired by Cézanne but moulded his ideas into new shapes to produce new methods of expression. An historic work in the history of 20th-c. art is Picasso's painting *Les Demoiselles d'Avignon*, which contains elements which were to dominate cubism and much of subsequent painting. The geometricity of the forms was to be the basis of the cubist aesthetic, yet in the two figures to the right of the painting we see the first significant impact of primitive sculpture on Western art. The five figures indeed present contrasting inspirations. That on the left would seem to derive clearly from Egyptian models, the two figures in the centre to be inspired by classical poses, and, as mentioned, the two figures to the right to derive from the sculpture of alien and primitive cultures. In this revolutionary work we nevertheless observe the way in which the tradition of Western art, which we have traced from the Greeks, has not entirely been lost sight of.

73 Picasso. *Les Demoiselles d'Avignon* (1907)

74 Kokoschka. *Windsbraut* (1914)

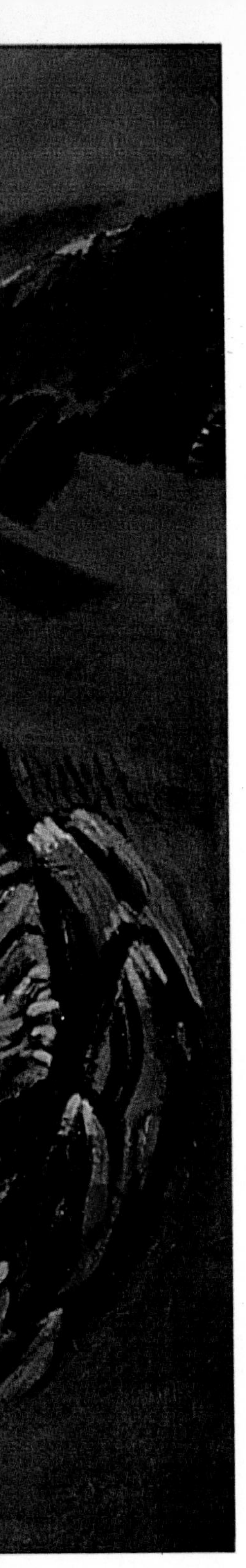

THE WORK OF OSCAR KOKOSCHKA is generally associated with the German school of expressionism. The free use of paint and the powerful mood of paintings such as the one illustrated both lend colour to this identification. But his work as a whole is far too individual to be confined within this convenient category. Indeed, one might prefer to use by extension the term baroque when speaking of such a picture as the one illustrated. The swirling sense of movement and the drama of the composition both bring to mind those qualities most characteristic of the baroque.

IN THE WORK OF JACKSON POLLOCK we are confronted with another typically individual 20th-c. pioneer. In the abstract composition below there is in common with some art of all epochs a sense of dynamic movement and a continuity of line. Yet Pollock's work, which gave rise to a school known as abstract expressionism, differs fundamentally from earlier traditions in that it derives from the manipulation of accidental effects and depends on the painter's successful liberation of his activity as a painter from the conscious direction of his mind. The possibilities of accidental effects producing stimulating ideas had already been observed as far back as Leonardo da Vinci, and by the English painter Alexander *Cozens; but Pollock and his successors in action painting were the first to use this mode of expression consistently in order to produce serious art.

75 Jackson Pollock. *Painting* (1948)

76 Mondrian. *Rhythm of Straight Lines* (*c.* 1936

77 Eero Saarinen. T.W.A. Building, Kennedy Airport, New
York (1956–61)

78 Mies van der Rohe. Seagram Building, New York (1958)

THE EARLY DECADES OF THE 20TH C. were marked by experimentation of an almost frenetic nature, and the art world of this period was perennially disturbed by new techniques, new insights, new discoveries. The variety of these discoveries is well illustrated by the contrast between the work of Kokoschka (see plate 74) and the geometrical, seemingly rigid compositions of the Dutch painter Piet Mondrian. To the uninitiated spectator these austere paintings seem to be the final, most abstract of the classical ideals of formal structure, yet we must beware of being misled by appearances since the artist himself was inspired by a mystical philosophy derived ultimately from the neo-Platonists of the first centuries of the Christian era.

It is tempting to see an influence from the painting of Mondrian in the cellular architecture of Mies van der Rohe, and it is legitimate to draw attention to the similarities apparent in the work of these two artists. But although such works may appear to be inspired by similar principles, we have already seen that Mondrian's inspiration was deeper and less calculating than the nature of his work suggests. On the other hand, the repetitive character of Mies van der Rohe's buildings developed from and is perfectly suited to the massive skyscraper buildings appearing first in America and now forming the characteristic expression of 20th-c. urban building.

The airport lounge of Eero Saarinen illustrates the way in which the 20th-c. architect handles the relaxed atmosphere of an informal interior.

79 Henry Moore. *Seated Figure* (1962)

TWO THEMES were present in Western art at its origins in ancient Greece; the abstract and the figurative. The earliest style of vase painting was one of geometrical pattern, and sculptural forms in the early archaic period were formal abstractions of the organic world; as Greek art developed, it aimed at a more and more realistic expression of natural forms. We have seen how after the Greeks, the elements of form, that is abstractions of line and mass, and the requirements of symbolism or realistic representation, presented conflicting tensions whose resolution in acceptable balance was a major task of the artist. The British sculptor Henry Moore is one of the greatest of living artists who can be regarded as continuing the search for this balance. Taking his inspiration from the world of organic form, he uses it to produce works unmistakably figurative yet with a character dictated by his materials and his own view of the underlying structure of that world. Although other great artists in the 20th c. have been concerned primarily with the nature of their materials, the social import of their work or its purely visual impact, the two great themes of the abstract and the figurative continue to be fertile in inspiration.

Max Jacob: drawing by Juan Gris

J

J'accuse. Famous article by *Zola.

Jackson A(lexander) Y(oung) (1882–). Canadian painter, one of the *Group of Seven.

Jackson Sir Barry (1879–1961). English theatrical manager, author, adapter and trs. Founder and director of the *Birmingham Repertory Theatre (1913). In 1935 he gave the theatre to the public as the Sir Barry Jackson Trust, remaining himself as governing director. He was also founder and director of the Malvern Festival (1929–37) and director of the Stratford Memorial Theatre (1945–8).

Jackson Helen (Maria Fiske) Hunt (1830–85). U.S. novelist and poet. J. drew on her intimate knowledge of the life of the poet Emily Dickinson for the novel *Mercy Philbrick's Choice* (1876). *A Century of Dishonour* (1881), a tract, and the novel *Ramona* (1884) attack government injustice to the American Indian.

Jacob Gordon (Percival Septimus) (1895–). English composer, conductor and teacher, working as professor of composition and instrumentation at the R.C.M. (1926–54). J.'s compositions, distinguished by their imaginative orchestration, include: 2 ballets; *Donald Caird* for chorus and orchestra (1930); 2 symphonies; concertos and 3 orchestral suites.

Jacob Max (1876–1944). French poet and artist, a friend of Apollinaire and Picasso in the early days of cubism. Although a Jew, he was converted to Catholicism through seeing a vision, and for the last 30 years of his life was a fervent worshipper. He died in the concentration camp at Drancy. He was perhaps more interesting as an attractive, eccentric personality than as a writer or painter. His prose poems–e.g. *Le Cornet à dés I* and *II* (1922 and 1955)–have the whimsical charm of slight unbalance.

Jacobi Frederick (1891–1952). U.S. conductor and composer; his teachers included R. Goldmark and E. Bloch. From 1936 to 1950 J. taught composition at the Juillard School, New York and was active in advocating and promoting modern music. J.'s music includes: the opera, *The Prodigal Son* (written 1943/4); *Ave Rota*, 3 pieces for piano and orchestra (1939); 2 symphonies; *Indian Dances* (1928) and chamber music.

Jacobi Johann Georg (1740–1814). German poet whose lyrics anticipate Goethe's work in this genre. His brother FRIEDRICH HEINRICH (1743–1819) was also a writer and a friend of Goethe, to whom he introduced the work of Spinoza.

Jacobite glasses. Produced, many probably at Newcastle, in the mid 18th c.; these glasses carried mottoes and emblems showing Jacobite sympathies.

Jacobite glasses

Jacobsen Arne (1902–). Danish architect. J.'s work has followed most of the trends since 1930, but is always intelligent and sensitive. In the 1930s he was the best-known practitioner of the international style in Denmark. After the war he designed very elegant, original, brick houses, and in the 1950s beautifully proportioned curtain wall office blocks, as the SAS Building in Copenhagen (1959), and elegant villas, followed by a building in immaculately finished concrete for St Catherine's College, Oxford (1964).

Jacobsen. St Catherine's College, Oxford

Jacobsen Jens Peter (1847–85). Danish writer and naturalist, the trs. of Darwin's *Origin of Species*. J. is among Denmark's greatest prose stylists, writing in an intense and highly polished style which is however sometimes over precise. His works are: the historical novel *Fru Marie Grubbe* (1876; 1914), the novel *Niels Lyhne* (1880; 1919), the short stories *Mogens* (1882; 1921) and a verse coll.

Jacobson Maurice (1896–). English-born composer, pianist and music administrator. His works include the ballet *David* (1936), which shows the influence of synagogue music; the cantata *The Hound of Heaven* (1953) after Francis Thompson, and incidental music to many Shakespearean plays.

Jacob's Room (1922). Novel by Virginia Woolf.

Jacopo da Lentino. 13th-c. poet of the school centred upon the Sicilian court of the Emperor Frederick II. He was a master of the *canzone* and seems to have anticipated the sonnet form.

Jacopone da Todi (1230–1306). Italian religious and mystical poet and Franciscan friar. He wrote mainly in the Umbrian dialect and his *Laude spirituali* are among the finest and

Maya jade carved in low relief

White jade tiger; Chinese, Ch'ing

Henry James: painting by Sargent

William James: self-portrait

most ecstatic mystical poems of the middle ages. He is also credited with the authorship of the famous Latin hymn, the 'Stabat mater'.

Jacquemart de Hesdin: *Hesdin

jade. Properly the term refers only to nephrite, a silicate of lime and magnesia, but it is more often extended to include jadeite, a silicate of sodium and aluminium, and further to any stone that resembles nephrite in its hardness, translucency and colouring (light green, bluish, white, and even ochre). It is a stone laboriously difficult to work, but its tactile and visual beauty have recommended it since prehistory to the Chinese, Maori and pre-Columbian American cultures; the archaic Chinese products–ritual implements, emblems of rank, ornaments and small figures in the round–are the best known. The Chinese *Ch'ing dynasty produced fine examples.

Jaenisch Hans (1907–). German painter and sculptor. He represents animal and human figures in an archaic-symbolic style in which there is a quality of sly humour.

James Henry (1843–1916). U.S. novelist and writer of *nouvelles* and short stories. J. was the brother of William J. and son of a wealthy writer on Swedenborgian theology. He was educated at a succession of schools in the U.S. and Europe, briefly attended Harvard Law School (1862) and began publ. stories and travel sketches. In 1869 he made his 1st independent visit to Europe and was overwhelmed by the beauty of Italy. He visited Europe again (1872–4) and left the U.S. for good in 1875; he stayed in Paris where he met Flaubert, Turgenev (an important influence) and their circle and finally settled in England, enjoying great social success. He was naturalized in 1915.
J. brought to the novel an artistic consciousness which expressed itself in preoccupation with form and a sense of verbal nuances matching his apprehension of the complexities and tensions developing in social encounters, and of fine social distinctions. His canvas is limited to the scenes and problems of 19th-c. respectable society, but his exploration is extensive and the manners described provide a setting for elaborate and subtle treatment of moral problems. In the 1870s the 'international situation'–the impact of the sophisticated, sometimes corrupt culture of Europe on Americans–is J.'s main theme, appearing in such *nouvelles* as the extremely popular *Daisy Miller* (1879), in which an emancipated American girl comes to grief by ignoring the European proprieties; in J.'s 1st important novel, *Roderick Hudson* (1876); and in *The Europeans* (1878), where the 'Europeans' are expatriates attempting to readjust to an unsophisticated U.S. society. J.'s 1st undeniable masterpiece, however, is *The Portrait of a Lady* (1881), in which Isobel Archer, a young heiress, marries a fortune-hunter, but rises above her unhappiness by caring for his daughter Pansy. Other novels of the period–*Washington Square* (1880), *The Bostonians* (1886) and *The Princess Casamassima* (1886)–do not reach quite the same level. J. wrote for the theatre without much success in the 1890s, giving up after the failure of *Guy Domville* (1895). The increasing elaborateness of his style, already noticeable in the 2 studies of moral growth *What Maisie Knew* (1897)–a *tour de force* in which the action is seen through the eyes of a child–and the *Awkward Age* (1899), reaches its limit in *The Wings of the Dove* (1902), *The Ambassadors* (1903) and *The Golden Bowl* (1904), 3 novels in which J. returns to the 'international situation'; they have by some been considered unreadable; others have called them his masterpieces. Other works include the novels *The Tragic Muse* (1890) and *The Spoils of Poynton* (1897); the *nouvelles The Last of the Valerii* (1875), *The Aspern Papers* (1888) and *The Turn of the Screw* (1898); *The Art of the Novel* (coll. 1934), extremely valuable prefaces to an ed. of his novels; and important critical works.

James John (*c.* 1672–1746). English architect who designed St George's church, Hanover Square, London.

James William (1842–1910). U.S. psychologist and philosopher, brother of Henry J. Most of J.'s works employ a functionalist approach, regarding what a thing *does* as a more fruitful piece of information than what it *is*, e.g. *The Principles of Psychology* (1890). So, in his *Pragmatism* (1907), J. stated that beliefs are to be judged by their effectiveness in attaining human ends. He also wrote an important study of the psychology of mystical phenomena, *The Varieties of Religious Experience* (1902).

James I (1394–1437). King of Scotland; held in captivity by the English from 1406? to 1423; murdered at Perth. J. is credited with authorship of the dream-allegory *The Kingis Quair*,

Jaenisch. *Miniature Garden*

John James.
St George's church

James I: probably painted by John de Critz (1610)

Ewer by Jamnitzer

a poem in the Chaucerian tradition, on J.'s imprisonment and winning of Jane Beaufort.

James I of England (and VI of Scotland) (1566–1625). Himself a writer, J. appointed a committee to revise the English Bible; the result was the Authorized Version. His works include *Basilicon Doron* (1599) on government, *A Counterblaste to Tobacco* (1604), and *Daemonologie* (1597) for the suppression of witchcraft.

Jamesone George (d. 1644). Scottish portrait painter, by tradition supposed to have studied under Rubens. He worked in Edinburgh in a style similar to that of C. Johnson in England.

Jammes Francis (1868–1938). French poet and novelist. J.'s verse is mainly about nature or religion. His novels include *Le Roman du lièvre* (1903).

Jamnitzer Wenzel (1508–85). German goldsmith, the only one outside Italy comparable with Cellini. He worked mainly for the Habsburg court and helped to found the Prague school of goldsmiths under Rudolf II. His work is renowned for its extreme elaboration and technical ingenuity; in it the imagination is allowed to run riot.

Janáček Leoš (1854–1928). Czech composer. He studied at Prague Organ School, Leipzig and Vienna. In 1881 he was a founder of the Organ School at Brno and remained its director until 1919, when he became a professor of composition at the newly founded Prague Conservatory with residence at Brno. He was little known outside Brno until the performance of his opera *Jenufa* at Prague, but thereafter rapidly gained a world reputation.
J.'s music shows, in the early works, reminiscences of Smetana, and throughout his oeuvre the atmosphere of folk-music recurs; but the style is unique. He uses a shifting tonality but ignores modulation; the rhythms are varied and strong; characteristic is the brief pregnant phrase and rich, stark and contrasting orchestration. Above all J. took as a basis for his style, speech inflexions and rhythms and natural sounds.
His most important work is in the operas, which include: *The Beginning of a Romance* (1894); *Jenufa* (German title of *Její pastorkyna*, 'Her Foster-Daughter', 1904), a complex story of tragedy and love with libretto by J.; the expressionist tragedy *Katya Kabanova* (1921), based on Ostrovsky's *The Storm*; the impressionistic *The Cunning Little Vixen* (1924), a comedy of animals and humans; *The Makropulos Affair* (1926), based on Čapek; and *From the House of the Dead* (posth. 1930), after Dostoyevsky. Other important works are the *Glagolithic Mass* (1926), the orchestral rhapsody *Taras Bulba* (1918), a piano concertino (1925), *Sinfonietta* for large orchestra including 12 trumpets (1926), a string quartet inspired by Tolstoy's *Kreutzer Sonata* (1923), and a 2nd string quartet, 'Intimate Letters' (1928).

Janco Marcel (1895–). Rumanian painter, member of the Zürich dada group and propagandist of contemporary art in Rumania in the 1920s and 1930s. He settled in Israel and was founder of the artists' village Ein Hod.

Jane Eyre (1847). Novel by Charlotte *Brontë.

Janin Jules-Gabriel (1804–74). French critic and novelist. J.'s *Histoire de la littérature dramatique* (1858), containing a selection of the articles he wrote as dramatic critic of the *Journal des Débats*, is of historical interest.

Janissary music. The music of the Janissary regiments of the Turkish army enjoyed a wide vogue in 18th-c. Europe. Its characteristic instruments were the Turkish crescent of bells, the bass drum, the side drum, cymbals and triangle; the last 4 being gradually introduced into serious music by Gluck, Mozart and Haydn among others. Mozart wrote his famous 'Turkish rondo' in imitation of J. music.

Jannequin Clement (*c.* 1475–1560). French composer who enjoyed a great contemporary reputation for his *chansons*. More than 280 survive, some of them being programmatic, e.g. the famous 'La Guerre' on the battle of Marignano, 'La Chasse' and 'Le Rossignol'.

Jannings Emil (1884–1950). Swiss-born film actor. In his 3 greatest films *The Last Laugh* (1924), *Variety* (1926), and–most famous of all–*The Blue Angel* (1930), he plays a character humbled by circumstance, the tragedy being heightened by J.'s considerable dramatic presence.

Jannon Jean. 17th-c. French type-cutter and designer who cut the *caractères de l'univ.* (1620) later used in the Royal Printing House founded by Cardinal Richelieu in 1640. These types

Janáček

Emil Jannings in *The Last Laugh*

Japan. Chest in green lacquer

Japan. Lacquer table-top

Japan. *Standing courtesan*; wood-block print (*c.* 1710) by Kaigetsudo Dohan

Japan. *Warrior* (*c.* 1660); wood-block

were formerly ascribed to Garamond, whose fame has eclipsed J.

Janssen Werner (1899–). U.S. composer and conductor; taught by F. Converse and Respighi. He has toured widely in Europe and founded the J. Symphony of Los Angeles and conducted other U.S. orchestras. His compositions include: *New Year's Eve in New York*, *Louisiana Suite*, *Foster Suite*, and *Kaleidoscope* for string instruments.

Janssens van Nuyssen Abraham (d. 1632). Antwerp painter of religious, mythological and allegorical subjects in an Italianate style close to Bolognese classicism, e.g. *Scaldis and Antwerpia* (1609; M.R. des B.-A., Antwerp). His later work was influenced by Rubens.

Japan. First European contacts with J. followed the arrival of the Portuguese there in 1542; Jesuit missions were established and much of Europe's early knowledge of J. came from the publs of the missionaries. Following an edict of 1614 the missions were closed down and J. was virtually isolated from the West until the expedition of the American, Commodore Perry in 1853. There followed a cult of 'japaneserie' both in Europe and America, which reached its height in the last 2 decades of the 19th c. and lasted until 1914. Much of the taste was created by the Japanese colour print and the works of such writers as Pierre Loti in *Madame Chrysanthème* (1887) and Lafcadio Hearn, an American who became a Japanese national and who wrote a number of explanatory books, the best of which was *In Ghostly Japan* (1899). Examples of musical works in the 'Japanese taste' are the operetta *The Mikado* by Gilbert and Sullivan (1885) and Puccini's opera *Madame Butterfly* (1904). Japanese influences had their most creative effect on French painting of the late 19th c. Ironically, it was the art of the colour print, held in low repute by the Japanese, which was to excite the minds of European painters; many of the 1st prints that reached the West did so not as works of art, but as wrappings round Japanese goods. In Japan the colour print was a popular art which had grown up in the 1st half of the 17th c. A school of painting known as 'Ukiyo-yé' ('passing-world picture') had developed to satisfy popular demand. It is possible that the 1st Japanese prints were an imitation and development of European woodcuts introduced to J. by the Jesuits and later by the Dutch. The subjects chosen were of popular appeal, studies of actors and geisha and, later, of landscapes, all portraying a real world and often, inside the formal design, expressing a deep emotion.

When the colour prints first arrived in France is not known, but small numbers were available in Paris in the 1860s. The works of such Japanese artists as Hiroshige, Hokusai and Utamaro were eagerly discussed by non-academic painters and admired for their fresh view of nature. The use of flat areas of colour and of high and low angles of view seemed daring stylistic innovations. Degas used such angles in his studies of ballet dancers. The technique of viewing from odd and unusual angles was used by such different artists as Berthe Morisot and Toulouse-Lautrec, Manet and Van Gogh. Toulouse-Lautrec, with his posters, used certain of these stylistic devices, disregarding academic rules of design. Japanese influences can also be seen in such works as Renoir's *Les Parapluies*; in the placing of trees and branches in Cézanne's *Mont-St-Victoire*; and later, in the position of the figures and the use of bold masses of colour in the portraits of Bonnard and Vuillard.

In the 20th c., through the trs of Arthur Waley, Donald Keene, and others, Japanese literature has become widely known in the West. The drama of the *Nō, an essentially symbolic theatre where the text and the gestures of the actors are intended to suggest unspoken and indefinable realities, has had considerable effect upon such European playwrights as Eugène Ionesco. Japanese motion pictures, with their stylized conventions based upon the theatre of Nō and *Kabuki, have introduced the works of such dramatists as the writer of puppet plays, *Chikamatsu (1653–1725), to a very wide audience in the West. The Japanese adaptation of Ch'an Buddhism, taken from China and renamed Zen, has had considerable vogue since World War II. The essence of Zen is the 'sudden enlightenment'. The disciple, after meditating meaningless paradoxes and being subjected to nonsensical questions, baffling answers, sudden blows and shouts, may reach a state of such nervous tension that a well-chosen word or sound from the master may break the last barriers of the intellect and submerge the disciple in the state of 'no-mind', in which Enlightenment is experienced. In modern Western literature, the most startling effect of Zen ideas can be seen in the American novelist Jack Kerouac's *The Dharma Bums* (1960).

Japan. Used indiscriminately for all kinds of lacquer in the 18th c., when the process was called 'Japanning'. The term strictly used refers to Japanese lacquer, which reached its highest standard in the 17th c. and is generally regarded as unrivalled for boldness and variety of design. Black, gold and red were the usual colours.

Jaques-Dalcroze Émile (1865–1950). Swiss teacher and composer and inventor of *eurhythmics. After a period as director of a theatre in Algiers, he taught harmony at Geneva Conservatory. In 1910 he founded a school devoted to his system; through his pupils, notably Marie *Rambert, it had great influence on ballet. J.-D.'s best compositions are operas.

Jardin aux Lilas. 1-act ballet by *Tudor with music by Chausson and décor by H. Stevenson; 1st performance 1936.

Jarnach Philipp (1892–). Composer, of a Spanish father and French mother. He was educated largely in France but has held various teaching posts in Germany. In Paris he met Debussy and Ravel, but his friendship from 1915 with Busoni was the decisive influence. His music includes: *Sinfonia Brevis* (1925), Concertino in E min. (1935) for string orchestra, and piano works.

Jarry Alfred (1873–1907). French writer, an alcoholic eccentric not taken very seriously in his lifetime but influential on later writers. In the play *Ubu Roi* (1896; *Ubu roi*, 1951), the 1st performance of which was a public scandal, he created the character of *le père* Ubu, a grotesque, foul-mouthed, neo-Rabelaisian creature, almost an embodiment of the Id. J. himself behaved in real life in Ubu-fashion and his vigorous anti-rationalism was one of the sources of surrealism. He also created a 2nd character, the anti-scientist Dr Faustroll, whose nonsense-subject was '*la pataphysique*'. An association of admirers of J., the Collège de Pataphysique, includes several eminent contemporary writers.

Jaspers Karl (1883–). German philosopher, with Heidegger the leading exponent of *existentialism in Germany. J. dismisses all systems and admonishes his reader to concern himself with his own existence, thus discovering the limits of reason. His major work is *Philosophie* (1932).

jasperware: Josiah *Wedgwood

Jawlensky Alexei von (1864–1941). Russian painter, trained at a military school in Moscow; he studied at St Petersburg Academy (1889) and then in Munich (1896) under Azbe as a fellow-student of Kandinsky. While in France during 1905 he was deeply impressed by Matisse's free use of colour. In 1909 he joined Kandinsky's New Artists' Association in Munich. His early work (1911–14) reveals a Kandinsky-inspired interest in the expression of feeling through brilliant colour and violent execution, but in his mature work, e.g. *Head* (1935; Redfern Gal., London), forms are controlled with a cubist sense of structure, and the image has a deeper icon-like mysticism. He exhibited with Klee, Kandinsky and Feininger (Der Blaue Vier in 1924), but mostly worked in isolation at Wiesbaden, where he died.

jazz. A style of music, in which improvisation is a fundamental means of expression, which emerged from the folk-music of the American Negro in the 19th–early 20th c.; most of the major j. musicians have been Negroes. The basis of j. melody is the 'blues' scale. It differs from the European maj. scale in that the 3rd and 7th degrees are flattened to a greater or lesser extent. The concept of 'correct' intonation is foreign to j.–slurs, glissandi, vibrato, note 'bending' and variation in texture of sound are integral parts of the melodic style, reflecting j.'s origins in vocal folk-music. J. harmony is for the most part an adaptation of 19th-c. European harmony, and that of French impressionist composers such as Debussy and Ravel. The combination of these borrowed harmonies with the blues scale provides j. harmony with its individual flavour. A traditional small j. group consists of a 'front line', i.e. trumpet, clarinet, and trombone, and a 'rhythm section', i.e. drums, piano and the double bass. The typical modern small group consists of trumpet, saxophone and rhythm section. The typical 'big band', playing arranged or composed j., has a reed section of 4 or 5 saxophones, a brass section of 4 trumpets and 3 or 4 trombones and a rhythm section.
The simplest kind of improvised small-group j. performance takes the form of a theme statement by the group ('chorus'), followed by solo improvisations on the theme or its harmonic structure, followed by a group restatement of the theme. The themes most commonly used

Jawlensky. *Still-life* (1909)

Jawlensky. *White Feather* (1909)

Jazz. Art Blakey

Jazz. Dizzie Gillespie

Renée Jeanmaire in *Carmen*

Jean Paul

as a basis for improvisation are the 12-bar blues, and the 32-bar popular song

The 'New Orleans' style of j., developed by about 1900, represented the adaptation of the instrumentation and repertoire of the military brass band to the purposes of the Negro. The front line of trumpet, clarinet and trombone proved to be the best suited to a simple, collectively improvised, polyphonic style, combining elements of folk blues, march tunes and French dance tunes. A parallel style to evolve during this early period was rag-time piano music, which was a formative influence on the classic 'stride' style of j. piano playing.

The 1920s saw the supersession of the collective improvisation of the traditional New Orleans style by 2 developments, that of the improvised solo and of the large ensemble. By far the most important figure in the development of the improvised solo was the trumpeter Louis *Armstrong.

The 1930s were the classic era of the big bands. The ensemble style pioneered by Fletcher *Henderson was brought to a peak of rhythmic precision by such 'swing' bands as those of Duke Ellington, Count Basie and Bennie Goodman. In the early 1940s, there developed a radically new style of j., at first known as 'bebop' (or 'bop'), of unprecedented melodic and rhythmic flexibility. The leading figures were the saxophonist Charlie Parker and the trumpeter Dizzy Gillespie; the middle and late 1940s were occupied with assimilating their innovations into the mainstream of j. and translating them into big band terms by such arrangers and composers as Tadd Dameron and Gil Fuller. But already in the late 1940s a new, 'cool' style was emerging (*West coast), which rejected the angularities of bop. During the 1950s, drummer Art Blakey was the leading figure in the style know as 'hard bop', characterized by an insistent rhythmic drive and directness of emotional expression. The Modern Jazz Quartet, led by pianist-composer John Lewis, blended modern j. improvisation with the formal devices of classical chamber music. The 1960s have seen the appearance of a school of 'abstract' or 'free' improvisers, headed by alto saxophonist Ornette Coleman, in which the use of harmony and tonality as a basis for improvisation has been discarded.

Jazz Singer, The (first shown 6 October 1927). The 1st feature-length film with talking sequences, starring Al Jolson.

Jean Barois (1913). Novel by Roger *Martin du Gard.

Jean Christophe (1904–12). Cycle of 10 novels by Romain Rolland.

Jeanmaire Renée (Zizi) (1924–). French ballet dancer trained at the Paris Opéra; she was an original member of the Ballets des Champs-Élysées. Her leading role in *Carmen* (1949), with choreography by her husband, Roland Petit, brought her instant fame. She has turned with equal success to singing, cabaret and films, and opened in 1964 in the New York revue *Zizi* staged by her husband.

Jean Paul. Pseud. of Johann Paul Friedrich Richter (1763–1825). German writer of romances. His works were enormously popular, appealing to the prevalent cult of sentiment, though they now seem diffuse and unreal. Works include *Hesperus, oder 45 Hundsposttage* (1795; 1865), *Leben des Quintus Fixlein* (1796; 1827); *Siebenkäs* (1797); *Flower, Fruit and Thorn Pieces* (1845); *Titan* (1803; 1862), its hero Albano, a romantic hero and idealist, and the unfinished *Flegeljahre* (1805).

Jefferies (John) Richard (1848–87). English writer of books describing countrymen and the countryside. His work includes *Wild Life in a Southern County* (1879), *Hodge and his Master* (1880); 2 children's books of charm, *Wood Magic* (1881) and *Bevis* (1882), and an essay in spiritual autobiography, *The Story of My Heart* (1883).

Jeffers Robinson (1887–1962). U.S. poet whose residence in the barbaric, isolated Carmel-Point Sur region of California is strongly reflected in his work. J.'s poems fall into 3 main groups: Californian narratives, elegies and conversation pieces, and dramatic poems with Greek themes and 20th-c. philosophies, all full-blooded and powerfully emotional. His 1st (unoriginal) vol. appeared in 1912 but he only decided to be a poet after the reception of *Californians* in 1916. Some of his most important work is: *Tamar* (1924), a Biblical verse narrative on the curse of heredity, set in California; *Roan Stallion* (1925), on the lust of a woman who identifies an elemental god with a horse; *Cawder* (1928), an American version of the Hippolytus story; and *Give Your Heart to the Hawks* (1933), an heroic tale of a passionate, neurotic woman. His last book was *The Beginning of the End* (1963).

Jazz. The Woody Herman band

Jazz. The Modern Jazz Quartet

Humphrey Jennings. *Fires Were Started*

Thomas Jefferson. Villa at Monticello

Jefferson Joseph (1829–1905). The most famous of a prolific theatrical family, English in origin and one of the foremost actors of the U.S. stage, remembered for his creation of Rip Van Winkle. His great-grandfather, THOMAS J. (1732–97), was the first of the family to gain fame as an actor, and his eldest son, JOSEPH (1774–1832), established in the U.S. a family reputation which was to continue through 4 successive generations.

Jefferson Thomas (1743–1826). A founding statesman of the U.S. and 3rd president. *The Declaration of Independence* reflects his deeply felt attitudes and literary style. His ideas have affected U.S. politics, arts and ideology, and may be found chiefly in *Notes on Virginia* (1784), his *First Inaugural Address* (1801), *Thoughts on Government* (1776) and his many and excellent letters. He was also a very gifted designer of buildings, e.g. his own Palladian villa at Monticello. His Univ. of Virginia campus at Charlottesville (1819–25) is a beautiful classical composition of great charm.

Jelinek Hanns (1901–). Austrian 12-note composer, largely self-taught despite contacts with Berg and Schoenberg. He was a bar pianist, wrote music for films and believes light music can be a serious vehicle. Besides the operetta *Bubi Caligula* (1947) he has written a book on 12-note composition (1952) and composed the didactic *Zwölftonwerk* (1947–50) for piano, woodwind and strings, and *Zwölftonfibel* (1953–4) for piano.

Jemnitz Sándor (1890–). Hungarian composer and conductor who studied under Reger and Schoenberg. His complex music, never entirely atonal, is ornamental in line and subtle in instrumentation; it includes the ballet *Divertimento* (1947), *Seven miniatures for orchestra* (1948), and chamber and piano music.

Jena symphony. Discovered in Jena in the early 1900s and inscribed as by Louis van Beethoven; it is attributed by some to Beethoven, by others to his grandfather.

Jenkins John (1592–1678). English viol player, lutenist and composer at the courts of Charles I and Charles II. J.'s viol fantasies continue, with those of H. Lawes and M. Locke, the tradition of Byrd and Gibbons; but his *12 Sonatas for 2 Viols and a Base* (1660) follow Italian models.

Jennie Gerhardt (1911). Novel by Dreiser.

Jennings Elizabeth (1926–). English Catholic poet. Colls are *Poems* (1953), *A Way of Looking* (1955), *A Sense of the World* (1958) and *Songs for a Birth or a Death* (1961). Her poems evince muted nostalgia for childhood.

Jennings Humphrey (1907–50). British film director. A documentarist who did his most famous work during the war. He attempted to approach his audience on a more friendly, personal level than *Wright, *Watt and others did during the 1930s. With wartime Britain as his subject he made *Listen to Britain* (1941), the feature-length *Fires Were Started* (1943) and *A Diary for Timothy* (1945).

Jensen Adolf (1837–79). German song composer, like Franz a gifted follower of Schumann, although his work also shows affinities to Chopin and Liszt. Besides such song cycles as *Dolorosa* and *Gaudeamus*, he wrote a group of piano pieces, *Wanderbilder*.

Jensen Johannes Vilhelm (1873–1950). Danish writer and Nobel prizewinner (1944). His stories, *Himmerland Historier* (1916), are distinguished examples of regional literature, and he also produced novels and lyrical verse of fine quality.

Jenson Nicholas. 15th-c. French printer and type-founder in Venice whose roman type-face found its perfection in Cicero's *Epistolae ad Brutum* (1470). J. started as a die cutter and probably learnt printing in Mainz, where he had been sent on order of Charles VII to investigate the possibilities of printing. He was probably the 1st non-German printer and excelled all his contemporaries and predecessors as a type-founder.

Jenufa. An opera by *Janáček with libretto by the composer based on a play by Gabriela Preissová; 1st performance at Brno in 1904.

Jeremiah. One of the books of the *Bible (Old Testament), the 2nd of the books of the 'Major Prophets'. The prophecies of J. (*c.* 628–*c.* 586 B.C.) relate to the conquest of the Israelites by the Assyrians.

Jeremiáš Otakar (1892–). Czech composer and conductor; director of the National Theatre, Prague (1945–51). He was a pupil of

Thomas Jefferson, 3rd U.S. president

TSI NON Dubitabam quin hanc epiſ
nūcii fama deīq; eſſ& ipſa ſua celeritate ſu
tuq; āte ab aliis auditurus eſſes annū tertii
deſiderio noſtro & labori tuo: tamen exiſti
quoq; tibi huius moleſtiæ nūcium perferr
Nam ſuperioribus litteris: non unis: ſed p

Jenson type: *Ciceronis Epistolae*

Douglas Jerrold

St Jerome: from a 14th-c. English copy of St Jerome's Latin Bible

V. Novák and his music is typically Czech in idiom, showing the influence of Smetana and J. B. Foerster. His works include the opera *The Brothers Karamazov* (1928) and 2 cantatas. J.'s father Bohuslav (1859–1918) was a composer and teacher, and his brother Jaroslav (1889–1919) a pianist, conductor and gifted composer, e.g. the oratorio *Jan Hus*.

Jeremy, The Epistle of. One of the books of the *Apocrypha.

Jerome St (*c.* 348–420). Scholar and a Doctor of the Church born in Dalmatia and educated in Rome; as a young man he lived for 4 years as an ascetic in the desert; he settled in Jerusalem in 385, conducting a large and interesting correspondence. His great work is the Vulgate, the trs. of the Scriptures into Latin, then the vulgar (i.e. common) tongue.

Jerome Jerome K(lapka) (1859–1927). English novelist and playwright, author of the humorous novel *Three Men in a Boat* (1889). Chief of his plays is *The Passing of the Third Floor Back* (1908). He was ed. of *The Idler* and *Today*.

Jerrold Douglas William (1803–57). English humorous writer (a contributor to *Punch*), one of a well-known theatrical family. He wrote many popular plays, including *Black-Eyed Susan or All in the Downs* (1825).

Jerusalem Church of the Holy Sepulchre. Founded by Constantine, rebuilt and repaired many times, especially by the Crusaders. It has a complex (largely accidental) plan consisting of a large cloister, apsidal W. end, short nave of 2 unequal bays, transepts and circular choir where the Holy Sepulchre stands. The choir was the model for many round churches throughout the middle ages, and for the churches of the Templars.

Jerusalem Delivered (1575). Poem by *Tasso.

Jerusalem, The Emanation of the Giant Albion (1804). Prophetic poem by Blake.

Jesse window. Stained-glass window with a (real) tree representing the genealogical tree of Jesus, i.e. the House of David, whose father was Jesse. There is a fine example at Dorchester, Oxfordshire.

Jesuit ballet. A form of dance drama performed by Jesuits on religious themes and in the 17th c. put on for important events in the scholastic calendar; particularly spectacular were those at the Paris College of Louis-le-Grand.

Jesuit drama. Plays performed in Jesuit schools and colleges, the 1st known one dating from 1551. The plays were didactic in character, taking their stories from Biblical and historical themes. There were tragedies and comedies both usually performed in Latin. The plays flourished in Europe until the Jesuit order was (temporarily) suppressed in 1773.

jeté (French, 'thrown'). A step in ballet in which the working leg is thrown in a straight position either sideways, backwards or forwards while the dancer is springing from one foot to another. 'Grand j. en tournant' means that the dancer's body makes a complete turn in the air while the step is being performed.

Jeune France: *Young France

Jeune Homme et la Mort, Le. 1-act ballet with choreography by *Petit and Cocteau, to music by J. S. Bach and décor by G. Wakhevich; 1st performance 1946.

Jeux Interdits, Les (1952). Film directed by R. *Clement.

Jewett Sarah Orne (1849–1909). U.S. short-story writer, novelist and poet. J. drew the subjects and backgrounds of her stories from Maine, where she was born and spent her life. Her works include *The Country of the Pointed Firs* (1896), a series of linked stories, and several colls of stories, including *A White Heron* (1886).

Jewish War, The. History by *Josephus.

Jew of Malta, The (*c.* 1592). Play by *Marlowe.

Jew's harp (also Jew's trump; possible derivation from Dutch *Jeugd tromp*, 'child's trumpet'). Musical instrument of ancient Asiatic origin. The stirrup-shaped end is placed in the player's mouth and the metal tongue twanged; altering the size of the mouth cavity reinforces different *harmonics of the vibrator. In the 1st half of the 19th c. the instrument had a number of virtuosi.

Church of the Holy Sepulchre, Jerusalem

Jesse tree; Canterbury cathedral, 13th c.

Joachim and Clara Schumann: pastel portrait by Adolf Menzel

Juan Ramón Jiménez

jig. (1) A lively English country dance. (2) A stage entertainment comprising song and dance and much stage 'business', developed in late 16th-c. England by Tarleton, Kempe and others. It was popularized on the Continent by English strolling players and was a forerunner of the **Singspiel.*

Jiménez Juan Ramón (1881–1958). One of the most important and representative Spanish poets of modern times. When he began his career foreign influences–notably the French symbolists–dominated Spanish poetry. J. soon reacted against the prevailing taste for over-stylization and emphasis on outward form, striving rather for simplicity. His early poems used lyrical descriptions of landscapes to express sentiments and were sometimes highly elaborate, e.g. *Baladas de primavera* (1910). After 1916, when he wrote *Diario de un poeta recién casado* ('Diary of a newly-married poet') (1917), he sought to create pure poetry in which he used free verse, composing many very short but highly charged verses to express the essence of an emotion in the simplest language. Many of his poems are characterized by their tone of gentle sadness and great delicacy, e.g. *Arias tristes, Poemas májicos y dolientes.* He won wide and lasting popularity with a poetic prose work *Platero y Yo* (1917; *Platero and I,* 1950), which related his wanderings through Andalusia with his beloved donkey.

Jirák Karel Boleslav (1891–). Czech composer, a pupil of V. Novák, conductor and teacher. He was director of the Brno opera and the Prague Philharmonic, and professor of composition at Prague Conservatory. In 1947 J. emigrated to the U.S. His master works show the influence of Smetana and Fibich; they include 5 symphonies, chamber music, songs and a requiem.

Joachim Joseph (1831–1907). Hungarian violinist and composer. He worked with Mendelssohn at Leipzig (1843–50), was briefly at Weimar with Liszt, later dissociating himself from the Liszt-Wagner school, then music director at Hanover (1853–66); from 1868 he taught at Berlin. He gave frequent concerts in London. Despite unequalled virtuosity J. avoided merely virtuoso works and was a strict interpreter of the classics. His own compositions, which include violin concertos and cadenzas, are stylistically similar to Schumann. He formed the J. QUARTET in 1869.

Job (between the 5th and 3rd cs B.C.). One of the books of the *Bible (Old Testament), mainly in verse dialogue, in which the worth of the righteous man J. is tried by a series of afflictions sent by God.

Job, a Masque for Dancing in 8 scenes. Choreography by Ninette de Valois, music by Vaughan Williams and décor by Raverat; 1st performance 1931.

Joconde, La. Alternative name for *Leonardo's *Mona Lisa.*

Jode the Elder, Pieter de (*c.* 1570–1634). Flemish engraver, pupil of H. Goltzius. His son PIETER the Younger (1606–after 1674), also an engraver, worked in England reproducing paintings by Rubens and Van Dyck.

Joel. One of the minor prophetic books of the *Bible (Old Testament).

Johann von Tepl (or Saaz) (*c.* 1350–1414). German writer and author of the poem *Ackermann aus Böhmen* (written *c.* 1400; *Death and the Ploughman,* 1917), in which a peasant reproaches Death for having robbed him of his wife. It is remarkable for its logical yet compassionate argument and the sustained power and effectiveness of the writing.

John Augustus Edwin (1878–1961). English painter and draughtsman. J.'s brilliant gifts as a draughtsman attracted attention when he was a student; he also corresponded to the popular idea of the artist as a Bohemian; in his youth he lived with gipsies and led an unconventional life. He owed much to the study of the old masters and to 19th-c. French painters, but established a style of his own, striking and spontaneous if not deep. Paintings of his wife Dorelia, the *Madame Suggia* (*c.* 1923; Tate) and the portrait of Bernard Shaw (*c.* 1914; R. Coll.) assure him a place amongst British portrait painters.

John Gwen (1876–1939). English painter. She studied at the Slade School, where she was influenced by Ambrose McEvoy, then in Paris, where she settled from 1898, working in Whistler's studio and later in close friendship with Rodin and the poet Rilke. She became a Catholic, and associate of Jacques Maritain. J. developed in almost complete isolation a sheltered and refined art. *Self-portrait* (*c.* 1900)

Augustus John. *Madame Suggia.* Also *Lawrence

Gwen John. *Self-portrait*

and the later *Portrait of a Nun* (both Tate) are sensitive to an extreme in their response to character and their subtle tonal relationships.

John, The Gospel according to St (*c.* A.D. 100). One of the books of the *Bible, the 4th book of the New Testament; its account and interpretation of the life of Jesus differs in several respects from that of the other 3 (synoptic) Gospels. Whether the author can be identified with the disciple 'whom Jesus loved' is still in dispute.

Eastman Johnson. *Not at Home*

John Brown's Body (1928). Epic poem by Stephen Vincent Benét.

John Bull's Other Island (1904). Play by G. B. Shaw.

John Gabriel Borkman (1896). Play by *Ibsen.

John Gilpin, The Diverting History of (1785). Poem by William *Cowper.

John Inglesant (1880). Novel by J. H. *Shorthouse.

John of Salisbury. 12th-c. English scholar whose *Policraticus* contains interesting and amusing satire on court life.

John of the Cross, St (1542–91). Spanish mystic and poet. A Carmelite monk, he led a life of strict asceticism and self-mortification after meeting St *Teresa of Avila. During an 8-month imprisonment by unreformed friars of his own order he wrote most of his few poems. They are among the most beautiful of their kind and possess an extraordinarily intense lyrical fervour expressed in simple language. He expresses the passionate outpouring of his love for God in the terms of a woman searching for her lover, and uses the language of carnal love to express the heights of mystical-religious ecstasy.

Cornelius Johnson. *Englishwoman*

Johns Jasper (1930–). U.S. 'pop' painter who specializes in extremely realistic representation of actual objects, e.g. the U.S. flag (*Flag*, 1958), a can of beer, etc.

Johnson or Janssens Cornelius (1593–1661). Portrait painter of Flemish parentage born in London, where he worked until 1643, when he left for Holland. His popularity waned after Van Dyck's arrival in England in 1632 and his style, previously very similar to that of D. Mytens, increasingly showed the influence of Van Dyck. In Holland his work deteriorated.

Johnson (Jonathan) Eastman (1824–1906). U.S. genre and portrait painter. He studied in Düsseldorf and worked for some years in Holland before returning to the U.S. in 1855. He was a successful portraitist but is best known for his American genre scenes, e.g. *Corn Husking in Nantucket* (Met. Mus.). He painted Indian and Frontier life in Wisconsin and Negro life in the Southern states.

Johnson Lionel (Pigot) (1867–1902). Irish poet, author of polished lyrics reflecting his Catholicism and love of Ireland. His best-known poems are *By the Statue of King Charles at Charing Cross* and *Dark Angel.*

Johnson Nunnally (1897–). U.S. film writer, producer and director. J. was a remarkable script writer who worked for *Hawks, *Lang, and *Ford (*The Grapes of Wrath*) and in 1954 became a producer/director. 2 of his 8 films, *The Man in the Grey Flannel Suit* (1956) and *The Three Faces of Eve* (1957) made some impression, but on the whole he did not succeed as a director and has returned to script writing, e.g. on Siegel's *Flaming Star* (1960).

Johnson Philip (1906–). U.S. architectural historian who became so fascinated by modern architecture that he entered Harvard to study it under Gropius. In the 1950s his work was very influenced by Mies van der Rohe. His own glass house at New Canaan, Connecticut established his international reputation, and from it he developed a series of houses for wealthy New Englanders. His relationship with Mies culminated in their collaboration on the Seagram Building, New York. His later work has abandoned the Miesian direction for various neo-historical styles.

Johnson Richard (1573–*c.* 1659). English prose writer. His romance *The Most famous History of the Seaven Champions of Christendome* (1596–7) recounts the legends of famous national saints of Europe, and had a long life as a children's book.

Johnson Dr Samuel (1709–84). English man of letters whose personality dominated literary

Dr Johnson

Philip Johnson. Johnson House, New Canaan (1949)

Al Jolson

Mór Jókai

London. J. came to London in 1737 and began reporting parliamentary debates for *The Gentlemen's Magazine*. *London*, a verse satire in imitation of Juvenal, was publ. anon. in 1738 and was followed in 1744 by a life of the poet Savage, which reveals J.'s warmth of sympathy and indignation with indifference and cruelty. A 2nd long poem, *The Vanity of Human Wishes*, appeared in 1749; then J. became ed. of a periodical, *The Rambler* (1750–2); the style of J.'s essays in it is rotund and elaborate, using to magnificent effect the rolling Latinate period and cadence. In 1755 his *Dictionary of the English Language* set a new standard in English lexicography. *The Idler*, a rather lighter journal, replaced *The Rambler* in 1758; his novel *Rasselas, Prince of Abissinia* (1759) was written in a week to defray his mother's funeral expenses. He was granted a £300 pension in 1762, and in 1763 he met James Boswell, who preserved his pungent and sensible conversation in his *Life of Johnson*. An ed. of Shakespeare (1765) was followed in 1775 by the *Journey to the Western Isles of Scotland*, an account of an expedition made with Boswell. From 1779 to 1781 he publ. the *Lives of the English Poets* (originally prefaces; coll. 1781), some of them deformed by prejudice, others models of sympathetic and well-judged criticism.

Johnson Uwe (1934–). German novelist. His *Mutmassungen über Jakob* (1959; *Speculations about Jakob*, 1963) are fragmentary thoughts, reports and conjectures relating to the seemingly accidental death in 1956 of a young East German railwayman. *Das dritte Buch über Achim* (1961) is a similarly disjointed account of the vain attempt by a W. German journalist to reconstruct the true life story of a celebrated E. German cyclist.

Johnson Wax. Familiar name for the administrative building of S. C. Johnson and Son, Racine, Wis.; architect (1936–9) Frank Lloyd *Wright.

Johnston Edward (1872–1944). English calligrapher who designed initials for the *Doves Press, among others; J. was largely responsible for the revival of calligraphy in England.

Johnston Franz (i.e. Francis Hans) (1883–1949). Canadian painter, one of the *Group of Seven.

John Street Theatre. The 1st permanent playhouse in New York; it opened in 1767, with *The Beaux' Stratagem*, and closed in 1798.

Joinville Jean, sire de (1224–1317). French chronicler and seneschal of Champagne who took part in the 1st Crusade of Louis IX and came to know the king well. J.'s *Histoire de saint Louis* is the 1st–and a surprisingly vivid and human–prose biography in French.

Jókai Mór (1825–1904). The most widely read Hungarian novelist both in his native country and abroad; over 20 of his novels appeared in England in numerous eds. J. loved the exotic, his novels were set in all parts of the world: his characters belong to many nations. In descriptive power he has few rivals but his plots and characterizations are unreal. His best novels present Hungarian society of the Reform era, e.g. *Egy magyar nábob* (1853; *An Hungarian Nabob*, 1898).

Jolivet André (1905–). French composer, a pupil of Le Flem and Varèse. He was a member of the group La Jeune France, and music director of the Comédie-Française (1945–63). J. believes that music should express psychic forces exploited in primitive religions. His works include: a symphonic poem *Psyché* (1946); *Five Ritual dances* (1939) and *Suite transocéane* (1955) for orchestra; *Trois complaintes du soldat* (1940) for baritone and orchestra; 'Five incantations' for solo flute (1936) and *Mana*, 6 pieces for piano (1935). J. has also written for electronic instruments (*Martenot).

Jolson Al, originally Asa Yoelson (1886–1950). American singing star famous for a series of sentimental songs such as 'Mammy' and as star of the *The Jazz Singer* (1927).

Jommelli Niccolò (1714–74). Italian opera composer, pupil of Leo and Durante. J. developed the accompanied recitative and made full use of chorus and arioso passages, harnessing all musical resources to heighten the dramatic moment. As composer at the court of Stuttgart he developed a German style of orchestral expression and harmonic fluency. Over 50 operas survive; his church music includes a fine *Miserere* for 2 voices.

Jonah. One of the books of the *Bible (Old Testament); it relates the life of the prophet

Joinville. Medieval ms. of the *Histoire de saint Louis* showing the battle of Damietta

gaudere autem
quod nomina
vestra scripta

Edward Johnston's 'Foundational Hand', based on an Old English script

Johnson Wax

Inigo Jones. Design for Jonson's masque *Chloridia*; pen and ink drawing

Ben Jonson: anon. contemporary painting

Inigo Jones. Design for a masquer in *The Masque of Blackness*

Inigo Jones. The Queen's House, Greenwich

Inigo Jones. The Banqueting House, Whitehall

Jonah, who is shipwrecked and swallowed by a sea-monster (popularly thought of as a whale) when he tries to escape from his destiny.

Jonathan Wild the Great, The Life of (1743). Satirical novel by Henry *Fielding.

Jones Daniel (1912–). Welsh composer known for his work with complex and compound rhythmical patterns. He has written: 5 symphonies; tone poems; 8 string quartets and a sonata for 3 kettledrums.

Jones Henry Arthur (1851–1929). English dramatist. He chose subjects of moral and social significance, but above all in his critical writings supported the new theatre of his contemporaries such as Shaw.

Jones Inigo (1573–1652). English architect. He visited Italy in 1601, learned to draw and took a scholarly interest in the ancient and modern buildings. During the next 10 years he was greatly in demand as a designer of scenery and costumes for court masques (by e.g. Ben Jonson), often with fantastic architecture. He went abroad (1611–12) with the earl of Arundel, sight-seeing and note-taking. He studied Palladio and Serlio and referred to their publ. designs for the rest of his life–almost every detail in his buildings can be traced to one of them. In 1615 he was appointed surveyor of works to the king, and his subsequent commissions were mostly official. Chief works: (1) the Queen's House, Greenwich (1617), a cool, austere but attractive house, the main hall a perfect cube; (2) The Banqueting House, Whitehall (1619), a lucid design with columns accentuating the middle 3 bays and pilasters on either side; (3) Chapel of St James (1623); (4) additions to Old St Paul's, notably a west-front with huge columns and scrolls, destroyed in the Great Fire; (5) Covent Garden church and 'piazza' (1630), the 1st London square, imitated from the Place Royale, Paris; (6) Wilton House (1635 and 1649), altered later. J. also made grandiose plans for a new Whitehall Palace. The outbreak of the Civil War put a stop to this and to his career. J.'s work marks a decisive break in the history of English architecture. He was the 1st Englishman to use the developed style of the Italian Renaissance with confidence and understanding, and all the architects of the late 17th c., up to and including Wren, regarded themselves as his followers.

Joos van Cleve. *Death of the Virgin*

Jones James (1921–). U.S. novelist, author of the massive and best-selling *From Here to Eternity* (1951), a powerful naturalistic novel of army life in Hawaii.

Jones Jennifer (1917–). U.S. actress; in 1943 she won an Oscar for her part in *The *Song of Bernadette*. Her aggressive femininity and considerable talent are seen in, e.g. *Duel in the Sun* (1947), *Carrie* (1951) and *Beat the Devil* (1953).

Jones Margot (1913–55). U.S. stage producer and director, the founder of an important experimental theatre in Dallas, Texas.

Jones Sir William (1746–94). Welsh oriental scholar and jurist who trs. *Sakuntala* (1789) from Sanskrit. His trs had great influence on Goethe and the romantics. Also *India.

Jongen Joseph (1873–1953). Director of the Brussels Conservatory (1925–39) and composer whose best work is in his chamber music.

Jongen Léon (1884–). Belgian composer and pianist, director of the Brussels Conservatory (1939–49); brother of the above.

Jongkind Johan Barthold (1819–91). Dutch land- and seascape painter and engraver who worked mainly in France and was a leading pioneer of impressionism and *plein air* painting. He was interested in capturing the transitory effects of light and preceded Monet in depicting the same scene under different atmospheric conditions.

jongleur. Name given to wandering public entertainers of all kinds in the middle ages, including reciters of poetry, play-actors and musicians. The '*j.s de gestes*' arranged and recited the cycles of *chansons de geste*.

Jonson Ben(jamin) (1572–1637). English playwright. He fought against the Spaniards in the Low Countries and returned to England in about 1592 to become an actor and playwright. He became a Roman Catholic in 1598 (he abjured in 1610) and his 1st great play *Every Man in His Humour* was produced in the same year. It was followed in 1599 by *Every Man Out of His Humour* which satirized the city tradesmen; satires upon the court (*Cynthia's Revels*) and poets (*The Poetaster*) followed in 1600 and 1601. His tragedy *Sejanus* (1603) was not very successful and he reverted to satire in *Eastward Ho* written in collaboration with Marston and Chapman. Some expressions in this play offended James I and the authors were imprisoned for a while. J. received a court pension in 1616. In 1623 his books and manuscripts were destroyed by fire.
During the 18th c. J. was generally considered a greater writer than Shakespeare because of his 'correctness'; his plays observe the classical unities and display considerable scholarship. However, the people of J.'s plays are 1-dimensional 'humours', not the rounded and subtle characters of Shakespeare; but they are vividly drawn and Jonson distils a savage satire from the interplay of types. Such plays as *Bartholomew Fair* (1614) present a gallery of generalized contemporary portraits. J.'s other great gift as a dramatist was the manipulation of plot; this is best seen in *The Alchemist*, in which the different lines of intrigue converge to a perfect climax and solution. Although he did not achieve Shakespeare's masterly fusion of poetry and drama, J. produced some passages of great richness and beauty, and his poems and masques show an original lyrical gift. J.'s great plays are *Volpone or The Fox* (1606) in which a wealthy Venetian, aided by his parasite Mosca, pretends to be dying and extracts rich presents from various gulls; *Epicoene or The Silent Woman* (1609); and *The Alchemist* (1610) in which Face, manservant to a gentleman temporarily out of London, uses the house, with his associates Subtle, the Alchemist, and Dol Common, as a base for a practice in profitable 'alchemy'.

Jongkind. *Dutch Scene*; etching

Jooss Kurt (1901–). German dancer of the modern school who learned from Von Laban theories on *modern dance. He put these into practice with his Essen Folkwang Schule (founded 1927) and later with the Essen opera co. where he became ballet master in 1931. His satirical *Green Table* won the 1st prize at an international competition in Paris in 1932 and the fame that this brought J. enabled him to advance the popularity of modern dance throughout Europe. J. left Germany to found a school at Dartington Hall, England (1934) and some 15 years later returned to Essen where he is now director of the Folkwangballet, continuing to teach his method of free movement.

Jooss. *Green Table*

Joos van Cleve (Joose van der Beke) (*c.* 1480–1540). Flemish painter identified with the Master of the Death of the Virgin. He worked in Antwerp and for Francis I in France, painting

Joos van Gent. *Crucifixion* triptych

portraits and religious subjects. The dispassionate realism of his portraits owes something to the influence of Quentin Massys, but wide stylistic differences are apparent in his work as a whole. The 2 altarpieces *The Death of the Virgin* are in Cologne and Munich.

Joos van Gent (Joose van Wassenhove) called 'Justus of Ghent' (*fl.* 1460–80). Flemish painter influenced by Bouts and van der Weyden, and active in Antwerp and Ghent before going to work at the court at Urbino. His works include *Adoration of the Magi* (Met. Mus.), *Crucifixion* (Ghent cathedral) and *Last Supper* (Ducal Palace, Urbino).

Jordaens. *Man and his Wife*

Jordaens Jacob (1593–1678). Flemish painter working in Antwerp. He collaborated with Rubens on at least 2 pictures and was greatly influenced by him. His paint is thicker, however, and his robust sense of *joie de vivre* often becomes outright vulgarity, e.g. *The Wife of Candaules* (N.G., Stockholm). His portrait style at its best is seen in *Man and his Wife* (N.G., London).

Jordan Dorothea or Dorothy (1762–1816). English actress, best as a comedienne. J. was admired by Hazlitt, Lamb, Leigh Hunt and Byron, who thought her greatest in 'tom-boy' roles. She was mistress to the Duke of Clarence (William IV) and bore him 10 children.

Jordan Wilhelm (1819–1904). German poet in a revived medieval style, producing such works as the patriotic *Nibelungen* (1868–74) which is written in alliterative verse.

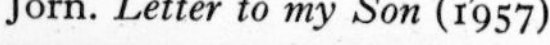

Jorn. *Letter to my Son* (1957)

Jorn Asger (1914–). Danish painter and writer, a forerunner of action painting in Europe, a founder of the Cobra group and a contributor to the Exhibition of Experimental Art, Amsterdam (1949). Between 1957 and 1961 J. was an important member of the international situationist movement. In the production of his richly impasted, feverishly expressionistic canvases he relies on the practice of automatism, which often results in the appearance of child-like images.

Jorrocks' Jaunts and Jollities (1838). Novel by Robert *Surtees.

Jōruri. A form of Japanese Ningō-shibai puppet drama in which the story is chanted by a chorus. J. began purely as a recital of tales. Dolls were introduced about the 16th c. This poetic drama was highly stylized and melodramatic, and deliberately avoided realism, eventually bringing the puppeteers into view of the audience. Plays were generally historical and heroic, or sentimental love-tragedies. J. reached its height in the time of *Chikamatsu (d. 1725).

Joseph and his Brothers (1933–43). Novel tetralogy by Thomas Mann.

Joseph Andrews and his friend Mr Abraham Adams . . . (1742). Comic novel by Henry *Fielding.

Josephus Flavius (d. *c.* A.D. 100). Jewish writer and a leader in the Jewish Rising of 66. He was captured but gained favour with the Emperor Vespasian, becoming a Roman citizen. His account of the *Jewish War* and Jewish history, written in Greek, survived in Latin trs. throughout the middle ages and is still read.

Joshua (*c.* 400 B.C.). One of the books of the *Bible (Old Testament), describing the conquest of Palestine by the Israelites.

Josquin des Prés (*c.* 1450–1521). Flemish composer; the greatest European master of his time. Little is known of his life: he may have been a pupil of Ockeghem's; he went at an early age to Italy, where he worked in Milan and at the Sforzas' court, was in the Papal choir from 1486 to 1494, worked for a time at the court of Ferrara, and was at the end of his life a prebendary at Condé. J.'s music was the wonder and model of his contemporaries. His technical brilliance as a contrapuntist was equalled by his ability to set music for all moods; his style varied from complexity to intense simplicity, and behind all his work was a fervent, sometimes mystical religiosity. His diverse treatment of the *cantus firmus in some aspects foreshadowed the parody *mass and his extended and masterly use of imitation set the pattern for a generation of composers. Yet despite this virtuosity J. rarely fell into the then common fault of obscuring the words of a text through over-elaborate music. His music, mostly for the church, includes: 20 4-part masses, among them *Pange lingua*; 90 motets; and over 50 masterly *chansons*.

Josten Werner (1885–). German-born U.S. composer and conductor who produced 1st

Josquin des Prés

James Joyce

Attila József

performances of Monteverdi and Handel operas in America. His music includes: *Ode for St Cecilia's Day* (1925); the African ballet *Batouala* (1931); *Jungle* for orchestra (1929) inspired by the art of H. Rousseau; *Concerto Sacro* for strings and piano based on the *Isenheim altarpiece, and *Canzona seria* (1957) for woodwind and piano.

jota. Peasant dance from N. Spain in 3:4 time adapted to ballet by Massine in his *Three Cornered Hat* (1919) and often included in programmes presented by Spanish dancing cos.

Jouhandeau Marcel. Pseud. of M. Provence (1888–). French novelist, a Christian writer with a strong sense of evil; his books are set in 'Chaminadour', in fact his native town of Guéret, and chronicle the lives of its inhabitants.

Jour de Fête (1949). Film directed by J. *Tati.

Journal des Débats, Le (1789–1939). Distinguished French newspaper; many leading authors (e.g. Chateaubriand), musicians (e.g. Berlioz), etc. wrote for it.

Journal des Savants, Le. French literary and scientific periodical publ. from 1665; it was the 1st periodical proper in Europe.

Journal d'un Curé de Campagne, Le (1950). Film directed by R. *Bresson; from the novel (1936) by Bernanos.

Journal du Voleur (1949). Autobiographical book by Jean *Genet.

Journal of the Plague Year (1722). Book by *Defoe.

Journal to Stella. Book by *Swift.

Journey's End (1928). Play by R. C. *Sherriff.

Journey to the End of Night (1932). Novel by L.-F. *Céline.

Jour se lève, Le (1939). Film directed by M. *Carné.

Jouve Pierre-Jean (1887–). French poet briefly associated with the *Abbaye Group. Most of J.'s verse reveals his preoccupation with metaphysical and religious problems; it includes the colls *Les Noces* (1928), *Sueur de sang* (1935), *La Vierge de Paris* (1945) and *Diadème* (1949). He has also written novels.

Jouvenet Jean-Baptiste (1644–1717). French decorative painter, pupil of Lebrun. He decorated the Hall of Mars at Versailles.

Jouvet Louis (1887–1951). French actor and producer, notably of Giraudoux, on whom he had great influence. J. was actor-manager at the Théâtre de l'Athénée from 1934 to 1951.

Jovellanos Gaspar Melchor de (1744–1811). Spanish statesman and writer. He wrote plays, essays, satires, but his finest writings, in exquisitely lucid prose, are those on politics and economics and his candid *Diary*.

Joyce James (1882–1941). Irish writer. Brought up in Dublin, J. knew the city minutely and was intensely involved with his Irish background. Feeling the absolute artistic necessity of breaking with a religious tradition in which he no longer believed and a stifling literary climate, he left Ireland for the Continent in 1904. In 1907, while teaching, he publ. *Chamber Music*, a collection of poems; in 1914 came *Dubliners*, short stories remarkable for their realism, subtlety and beauty of writing. The semi-autobiographical novel *Portrait of the Artist as a Young Man* followed in 1916, and *Ulysses*, publ. in Paris because of censorship restrictions, in 1922. For the next 17 years, during which he became almost blind, he worked on *Finnegans Wake*; single chapters were separately publ. under the titles of *Anna Livia Plurabelle* (1928) and *Haveth Childers Everywhere* (1930).
The Stephen Dedalus of *Portrait of the Artist* is J. himself. The book gives a vivid account of Dublin at the turn of the c., ruled by its priests and overshadowed by the memory of Parnell; it is also an affectionate and humorous record of the author's family and an account and justification of the mental struggle which ended in his leaving Ireland. In addition it relates moments of heightened perception and intense joy, which J. called his 'epiphanies', but they are human, not mystic, experiences, triggered off by trivial incidents and indicating the holiness of life itself.
Ulysses is a novel on many planes. On one level it is a burlesque *Odyssey*, in which the Ulysses, an Irish Jew named Leopold Bloom, is eventually united with his Telemachus, Stephen Dedalus; the incidents of Ulysses' wanderings are parodied and the women who cross Bloom's lecherous path represent Nausicaa and Circe, with his wife Molly as an unfaithful Penelope. On another level Bloom represents *l'homme moyen sensuel*, Stephen the artist and intellectual, with their perpetual interdependence. The action of the novel covers 24 hours and a cross-section of Dubliners, using a *stream-of-consciousness technique similar to that of Virginia Woolf to convey the specific quality of their thoughts and fantasies. Unlike Woolf's work, however, the novel is firmly rooted in the actuality of Dublin, its topography, sights and scents, all of which J. recreates with astonishingly precise and minute recollection. Intoxicated with language, J. creates his characters with a wide variety of parody and wit, and with a subtle ear for the cadences of speech and the inconsequentialities of thought. His most famous achievement of this kind is the long rambling monologue of Molly Bloom which ends the book, establishing in its earthiness, its child-like romanticism, and its nostalgic yearnings the very texture of her mind and character.
Finnegans Wake, planned as a novel of similar type recording the dreams of a single night, pushed the expressionistic use of words which he began to explore in *Ulysses* to the point where it became practically a private language, and the book has remained fairly inaccessible to the ordinary reader. If in *Ulysses* J. created a new kind of novel, it is probable that *Finnegans Wake* explored its possibilities to the limit. Works include an early draft of *Portrait of the Artist*, more conventional in narrative method, publ. in 1944 as *Stephen Hero*; the play *Exiles* (written 1914), showing Ibsen's influence; and *Pomes Penyeach* (1927).

Joyless Street, The (1925). Film directed by G. W. *Pabst.

József Attila (1905–37). One of the greatest Hungarian poets. In his poetry he protested against the grinding poverty of the proletariat from which he sprang. He joined the Communist party and was hounded from its ranks by narrow-minded doctrinaires. Years of misery, nervous breakdowns and isolation combined with the ghastly realities of Fascism to drive him to suicide. He was a poet of the slums, the hungry villages, of his own vulnerable and irreconcilable spirit and frustrated love.

C. G. Jung

Ernst Jünger

Juan de Flandes. *Raising of Lazarus*

Juniper. *Still-life 1959*

Jullien at Navarino; from *Punch*

Juan de Flandes (active 1496–*c.* 1519). Artist of the Spanish school and painter to Queen Isabella of Castile, though probably born in the Netherlands. J.'s sensitive style is close to that of H. van der Goes and the Burgundian miniaturists, e.g. *Pietà* and *Portrait of Joanna the Mad* (both Thyssen-Bornemisza Coll., Lugano).

Juan Manuel Infante Don (1282–1349?). Castilian nobleman and a most important and prolific prose writer of the Spanish middle ages. Many of his works, including poems and treatises, have disappeared, but among the most important of his surviving works are a coll. of short stories, *El Conde Lucanor*, and some didactic treatises.

Jude the Obscure (1895). Novel by Thomas *Hardy.

Judex. Film serial (1961) directed by L. *Feuillade; film (1964) directed by G. *Franju.

Judges (5th c. B.C.). One of the books of the *Bible (Old Testament), a history of the Israelites from the death of Joshua to the time of Samuel.

Judith. One of the books of the *Apocrypha, the story of the Jewish heroine J., who kills the Assyrian general Holofernes.

Jugendstil. German term for *art nouveau.

Jugurthine War, The. History by *Sallust.

Juliana of Norwich (*c.* 1343–1415). English anchoress, author of the devotional *Revelations of Divine Love* in Middle English prose.

Julius Caesar (1599?; publ. 1623). Tragedy by *Shakespeare, written *c.* 1599. Its source was Sir Thomas *North's trs. of Plutarch. It has been made into a film several times; the most recent production was in 1952.

Jullien Louis-Antoine (1812–60). French conductor and impresario who, to avoid creditors, came to London in 1838. His concerts combined popular with serious music but he also organized 'monster' concerts and composed and produced show-pieces, e.g. *Destruction of Pompeii.* He toured the U.S. (1853) with Barnum, was arrested for debt in Paris (1859) and died in a mad-house.

Jung Carl Gustav (1875–1963). Swiss psychologist, for a time Freud's leading disciple. J.'s most striking postulate was that there is, besides the individual unconscious, a collective human unconscious containing archetypal figures which emerge, e.g., in mythology.

Jünger Ernst (1895–). German expressionist writer. His theme is the erosion of human values by the advance of the machine age and the dangers to civilization itself. His works include: *In Stahlgewittern* (1921; *Storm of Steel*, 1929), one of the famous books on World War I; *Strahlungen* (1949), diaries of World War II, and the novel *Auf den Marmorklippen* (1941; *On the Marble Cliffs*, 1947) against Nazism.

Jungfrau von Orleans, Die (1801). Play by *Schiller.

Jungle, The (1906). Novel by Upton *Sinclair.

Jungle Book, The (1894) and *The Second Jungle Book* (1895). Children's books by Rudyard *Kipling.

Jung-Stilling Heinrich (1740–1817). German physician and writer, a fellow-student of Goethe. His autobiography reveals a pietistic personality but is comparable in method to Rousseau's *Confessions*; it was publ. in parts, the first (1777) being *Heinrich Stillings Jugend* (*Heinrich Stilling: His childhood, youthful years and wanderings*, 1835).

Juniper Robert (1929–). Australian painter living in England from 1936 to 1949; he works in an elegantly abstract style.

Junius, The Letters of (1769–71). Series of letters in *The Public Advertiser* attacking the governments of the day. The identity of J. is unknown, but much evidence–including computer results–suggests that the author was Sir Philip *Francis.

Juno and the Paycock (1924). Play by Sean *O'Casey.

Juon Paul (1872–1940). German-Swiss composer, a teacher in the Berlin Music Academy. His music, Russian and Nordic folk motifs handled in a German manner, includes a symphony in A maj.; 3 violin concertos, a triple concerto for violin, cello and piano; much chamber music and several books on music theory.

Jupiter. Nickname for *Mozart's symphony no. 41 in C.

Jurgens Curt (1912–). German-born international film actor, whose skill, e.g. the remake of *The Blue Angel* (1959), is often wasted on inferior roles.

Justine (1957). Novel by Lawrence *Durrell.

Justine ou les malheurs de la vertu (1791). Novel by the Marquis de *Sade.

Just So Stories (1902). Children's book by Rudyard *Kipling.

Juvarra Filippo (1678–1736). Italian architect, trained under Carlo Fontano, and in his early years working in stage design, coats of arms, book illustration, etc. His best work was done in the service of the duke of Savoy (from 1714). He was an extremely prolific architect, working with equal virtuosity in a dynamic baroque style and a chaste, dignified neoclassical. Although reflecting influence from Michelangelo, Bernini, Borromini and even German Gothic buildings, his works always have a strong personal flavour. His most notable works are: the Palazzo Madama, Turin; the Stupinigi, a huge country palace with a domed centre and 4 wings; the Superga, a domed church and monastery on the hill overlooking Turin; and the church of the Carmine, Turin.

Juvenal (A.D. 50/60–*c.* 130). Decius Iunius Iuvenalis, Roman satirist, a friend of Martial and probably a victim of Domitian's persecution. He wrote 16 satires, publ. in 5 books, between 100 and 130, in which he attacks the vices of the age: sodomy, luxury, extravagance, violence and arrogance. They are the savagest works in Latin literature, vigorous, epigrammatic and terse. They provide a vivid picture of the seamy side of Roman life from the point of view of a brilliant wit driven by poverty to toady to the mean, the debauched, the despicable rich. Adaptations by Dryden, particularly of the 'Sixth Satire', contain some of the most brilliantly hard English verse.

Just So Stories. Old Man Kangaroo, illustration by Kipling

Juvarra. The State Staircase, Palazzo Madama

Juvarra. The Superga

Juvenile Kabuki actors: colour print by Shuntei (1801)

Franz Kafka

Kahn. Richards Medical Research Building, University of Pennsylvania

K

K.: L. A. F. Ritter von *Köchel

Kabalevsky Dmitry (1904–). Soviet composer. He was a pupil of Miaskovsky, and produced symphonies, etc. which showed his teacher's influence, but more importantly operas, e.g. one based on R. Rolland's novel *Colas Breugnon*, produced in 1937, and *The Taras Family* (1944; revised 1949).

Kabuki. Japanese popular lyric drama which developed in the late 16th c. and was a freer, rather debased form of *Nō drama. Although K. retained strict conventions in actions and make-up, it allowed the actor somewhat greater scope; and 'flower-ways' through the audience, forming entrances to the stage, brought close contact with the spectators.

Kafka Franz (1883–1924). Czech novelist writing in German. Of Jewish family, he studied law in Prague and Munich and worked in an insurance office, developed tuberculosis in 1917, and died after a brief period of happiness in Berlin. His work, suppressed by the Nazis, was long undervalued in Germany. Abroad, his reputation is immense: he is the archetypal 20th-c. writer, depicting man's isolation and consequent anxiety in a world which, for all his science, he cannot understand. Influenced by Kierkegaard and by Freud, K. displays affinities with expressionism in Germany, and with surrealism and existentialism in Europe, creating in a lucid style a dream-world in which physical reality and mental life are not separated. He himself publ. only short stories including *Das Urteil* (1913), *Die Verwandlung* (1915; *Metamorphosis*, 1937), *In der Strafkolonie* (1919; selections, 1933, 1949, 1954), many reflecting a sense of guilt, especially Oedipal guilt. His 3 great unfinished novels, publ. posth. and against his wishes by his friend Max Brod, *Amerika* (1927; 1938), *Der Prozess* (1925; *The Trial*, 1937), *Das Schloss* (1926; *The Castle*, 1930) present allegorically the individual's search for meaning in a hostile world: they are fairy-tales in reverse. Their interpretation, like that of the stories, is controversial, in the novels because of uncertainties about the text itself, in novels and stories because of the idiosyncratic symbols used and the unusually uncommitted manner of narration, often a 1st-person narrative without the perspective provided by an author-narrator's comments.

Kahn Gustave (1859–1936). French poet, critic and novelist, a leader of the symbolist movement and one of the 1st poets to use free verse.

Kahn Louis (1901–). U.S. architect, almost unknown until the mid 1950s, but by 1960 the most discussed, and one of the most influential architects in the world. Since 1955 he has been professor at the Univ. of Pennsylvania. His Yale Art Gallery (1954) was a tough design often compared with English brutalism; the Trenton Bath House (1956) demonstrated his thesis of an architecture made by structure defining spaces which 'serve' and spaces which are 'being served'; this was developed in the Richards Laboratories, Philadelphia, where the spaces which serve (ducts, staircases, etc.) are expressed as great towers. He has also been influential in the field of city planning, and has prepared plans for Philadelphia.

Kailyard school. Late 19th-c. literary movement in Scotland, which nostalgically idealized the life of the village and the poor; it is usually associated with the works of J. M. Barrie, Ian Maclaren and S. R. Crockett.

Kaiser Georg (1878–1945). The leading German expressionist playwright; in 1933 his work was banned from the stage. In his plays the dramatic conflict is that of ideas, and the 'characters' are mouthpieces without personality. K. wrote over 60 plays, 3 of great importance: the anti-war *Die Bürger von Calais* (written 1914, very successful première 1917); *Von Morgen bis Mitternachts* (1917; *From Morn to Midnight*, 1920), in which a bank clerk tries to escape his routine existence and *Gas I* (1918; 1924) on a regenerate social order.

Kalatozov Mikhail (1903–). Soviet film director. A cameraman and then, from 1941, a director. He became suddenly famous with *The Cranes are Flying* (1957) notable for a new actress Tatiana Samoilova and for its attempt at a grandly romantic style.

Kalevala. Finnish national folk-epic which survived in oral form into the 19th c.; it was coll. by Lönnrot and publ. as a coherent text only in 1849; Forsman publ. the fullest text (1887). It contains an account of the creation of the universe and a unique folk-mythology. Sibelius drew extensively on the *K.* and Longfellow modelled *Hiawatha* on it.

Kalf. *Still-life*

Kandinsky.
Woodcut for the *Klänge* series (1913)

Kalf Willem (1622–93). Dutch still-life painter who worked mainly in Amsterdam. His faïence bowls and vases, glasses, gold and silver vessels, fruit and shells are painted with taste and economy in warm, luminous colours which shine out from a dark background.

Kalkbrenner Friedrich (1785–1849). German virtuoso pianist also important as a teacher; he worked in London from 1814 and Paris from 1823.

Kálmán Emmerich (germanized form of Imre) (1882–1953). Hungarian light opera composer who settled in Vienna and worked for a time (1940–9) in the U.S., taking U.S. citizenship. His *Tatárjárás*, performed in Budapest in 1908, had instant success throughout Europe and in the U.S. (*The Gay Hussars*, 1909).

Kama-Sutra. The earliest surviving Indian textbook of the science and art of sex and love, written about the 3rd c. A.D. by Vatsyayana, a religious student. Regarded as the most authoritative discussion in Sanskrit literature of '*Kama*', or the life of the senses, it was 1st trs. into English (1885) by Sir R. Burton and F. F. Arbuthnot.

Kameradschaft (1931). Film directed by G. W. *Pabst.

Kaminski Heinrich (1886–1946). German composer and teacher, his pupils including Orff. K.'s music, late romantic in idiom, was directed by his mystical view of life and art; it includes: the operas *Jürg Jenatsch* (1929) and *King Aphelius* (1951); *Concerto grosso* (1922) for double orchestra; and *Magnificat* (1925) for choir and orchestra.

Kanal (1957). Film directed by A. *Wajda.

Kandinsky Vassily (1866–1944). Russian painter, born in Moscow, generally considered the pioneer of abstract painting. His 1st work to be so described was a watercolour of 1910; however, all representational elements disappeared from his work only in the 1920s. K. was trained as a lawyer and took up painting when he was 30, studying the art first in Munich. His early work was related to the Russian symbolists and the Sezession groups. In 1906 he went to Paris for a year and exhibited at the current Salons. On his return to Munich his work began to reflect the ideas of the French *nabis and *fauves and became related to the Die Brücke group; from the beginning the city of Moscow, Russian icon painting and folk-art strongly influenced him, providing a link with the Moscow *avant-garde.* By 1909 K. was painting landscapes called *Improvisations* which reflect a growing detachment from nature. In 1910 he painted his 1st abstract works, making contact with the Muscovite *avant-garde,* who invited him to exhibit at the 1st Knave of Diamonds Exhibition. His *On the Spiritual in Art* was publ. in 1912. In 1911 he was a co-founder of the *Blaue Reiter. In 1912 K. had his 1st one-man show at the Berlin Sturm Gallery and publ. 2 plays, *Yellow Tone* and *Violet*, which reflect his interest in relations between colour and music; he also became interested in the German romantic philosophers, Rudolf Steiner and occultism. With the Bolshevik Revolution he was drawn into administrative work in the art field. In 1920 he drew up a programme for a new teaching system in art schools, but its symbolist philosophy was rejected by the constructivists and was put into practice only after he had left Russia and joined the Bauhaus school in Weimar (1922). In 1920 K. began to paint again, introducing geometrical forms which became strictly abstract, reminiscent of suprematist and constructivist work; such forms remained typical throughout his Bauhaus period up to 1933, when he moved to France and came under the influence of Miró, his forms becoming more fluid and surrealist. While at the Bauhaus he wrote *Point and Line to Surface* (1926), which deals with the nature of form.

Kangaroo (1923). Novel by D. H. *Lawrence.

Kanin Garson (1912–). U.S. writer. K. was a playwright who directed a number of films between 1938 and 1945, when he made with C. Reed *The True Glory*, a documentary on the Allied campaign in Europe. His *My Favourite Wife* (1940) is a comedy in the Capra/McCarey tradition. After the war he wrote and Cukor directed a notable series of comedies: *Adam's Rib, Born Yesterday*, etc.

Kant Immanuel (1724–1804). German philosopher, chiefly influenced by Leibniz and Hume. The central concept of K.'s theory of knowledge is the 'synthetic *a priori* statement' (i.e. a statement *about* the world whose truth is known independently of experience of the

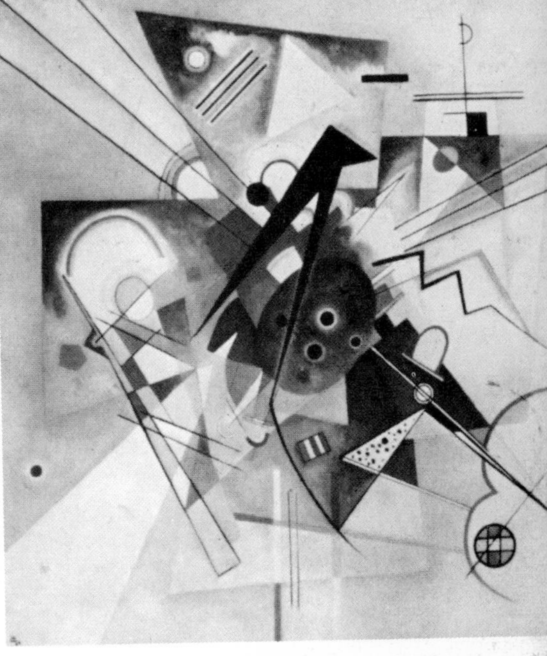

Kandinsky. *Yellow Accompaniment*

Kandinsky. *Battle.*
Also *abstract art, *Blaue Reiter, *Munter

Immanuel Kant

Karajan conducts

Karsavina and Nijinsky in *Le Spectre de la Rose*. Also **Firebird*

Karnak. Hypostyle hall, Temple of Amon

world) set out in his famous *Kritik der reinen Vernunft* (1781; *Critique of Pure Reason*, 1838). The *Kritik der praktischen Vernunft* (1788; *Critique of Practical Reason*, 1895) and *Grundlegung zur Metaphysic der Sitten* (1785; *Groundwork for a Metaphysic of Morals*, 1938) propound the concept of the categorical imperative: it asserts that an action is moral if the actor is prepared to see everybody behave in the same way. K.'s style and language make his work difficult to read. His influence has been felt throughout Western philosophy, giving rise to German idealism and supporting ethical intuitionism.

Kantemir Prince Antioch Dmitrievich (1708–44). Russian poet and diplomatist whose satires (written 1729–39; publ. 1762) were early works in the 'classical' tradition that dominated 18th-c. Russian literature.

kaolin. The purest kind of clay, burning white when fired; it is essential to porcelain and English bone china. The word comes from a Chinese hill famous for its deposits of k.

Kapellmeister. German term for musical director. A *Kapelle* was the body of musicians maintained by a secular or ecclesiastical prince or by a church.

Kapital, Das (1867, 1885, 1895). Book by Karl *Marx.

Karajan Herbert von (1908–). Austrian conductor, one of the most brilliant of this c. He combines precision and great attention to detail with fire and sensibility. He has held positions with the Berlin Philharmonic, the Vienna State Opera, La Scala, Milan and the Salzburg Festival.

Karamzin Nikolay Mikhaylovich (1766–1826). Russian writer who continued the work of M. Lomonosov in reforming the language. He rejected hundreds of Slavonic words and introduced many Gallicisms, creating the language used by Pushkin. K. displayed and popularized a sensibility derived from J.-J. Rousseau in his *Letters of a Russian Traveller* (1792; 1803) and tales like *Poor Liza* (1792; 1803). His political views became increasingly conservative with age, and his *History of the Russian State* (12 vols, publ. 1818–26) emphasized the creative role of the autocracy.

Karel Rudolf (1880–1945). Czech composer whose teachers included Dvořák. He was professor of composition at Prague Conservatory (1923–41). In 1943 he was arrested by the Gestapo but continued to compose; he died in a concentration camp. He wrote 3 operas, the symphonic poem *Demon*, symphonies and chamber music.

Karelia Suite. Orchestral work by *Sibelius.

Karg-Elert Sigfrid (1877–1933). German composer, organist and pianist. Encouraged by Grieg he composed a symphony, string quartet and much vocal and instrumental music. He is, however, especially known for his organ music, notably the *Passacaglia in E minor*, *66 Chorale Improvisations* (1908–10), *20 Choral Preludes and Postludes* (1912) and impressionistic pieces. These works are often elaborate and are characterized by florid chromaticism.

Karinthy Frigyes (1887–1938). Hungarian author of excellent literary caricatures and parodies. His account of his brain operation is unique in literature, *Utazás a koponyám körül* (1937; *A Journey Round My Skull*, 1939).

Karlfeldt Erik Axel (1864–1931). Swedish lyric poet, awarded the Nobel prize posth. (1931), having refused it earlier.

Karloff Boris (1887–). British-born actor who went into films in 1916; K. made his name as a horror specialist and all-round 'heavy'. His most famous role was as the monster in *Frankenstein* (1931).

Karlson Phil (1908–). U.S. film director. K.'s most successful work has been in crime pictures, often of remarkable violence like *The Phenix City Story* (1955).

Karnak. Village near *Luxor, Egypt, and the site of some of the ruins of the ancient capital, Thebes. Most remarkable of the surviving monuments is the Great Hall of the Temple of Amon; the space is filled with 134 huge columns, 70 ft in height and standing in 16 rows.

Karsavina Tamara (1885–). Russian dancer trained at the Imperial School, St Petersburg by Gerdt and Cecchetti. K. joined Diaghilev's co. as leading ballerina (1909) and Fokine created many ballets for her. One of the most outstanding dancers of her generation, she continued active in ballet after settling in London; she was co-founder of the *Camargo Society (1930) and has collaborated on Royal Ballet productions.

Karsh Yusuf (1908–). Turkish-born Canadian photographer known for his revealing portraits of the leading artists and statesmen of the 20th c. A superb technician, K. has discarded the standard back-drops of portrait photography in favour of careful use of light to create atmosphere and reveal character.

Kasprowicz Jan (1860–1926). Polish poet of peasant origin, linked with the neo-romantic Young Poland movement. His early poetry was concerned with social injustice; later he grappled with the problem of evil and waged war against God (*Ginacemu światu*, 1902). The vol. *Ballada o słoneczniku* (1908) marks the end of K.'s period of revolt and looks forward to the peace and reconciliation found in his last works, e.g. *Księga ubogich* (1916). He was also a prolific and inspired translator.

Kast Pierre (1920–). French film director. A critic who progressed to directing by working as an assistant and making shorts of which the most famous are *Les Charmes de L'Existence* (1949), co-directed by Gremillon, on 19th-c. art, and *Les Désastres de la guerre* (1951) from Goya etchings. Starting with *Le Bel Âge* (1959), he made a series of very talkative films on modern sexual relationships.

Kastalsky Alexander Dmitrievich (1856–1926). Russian composer, a pupil of Tchaikovsky among others. He was active in the organization of musical life after the Revolution and produced a number of nationalistic works and also church music.

Kästner Erich (1899–). German author, e.g. of the children's story *Emil und die Detektive* (1929; *Emil and the Detectives*, 1930); he also ed. the children's magazine *Pinguin*.

Katayev Valentin Petrovich (1897–). Soviet novelist and playwright. His works include *The Embezzlers* (1926; 1929), a comic novel about the adventures of 2 rogues in the years after the Revolution, and the play *Squaring the Circle* (1928; 1934).

Katona József (1791–1830). Hungarian playwright; his one masterpiece, *Bánk bán* (publ. 1821; performed 1833), is a national classic. The exceptional psychological and theatrical qualities of the play outweigh the clumsiness of diction and uncertain versification.

Kauffmann Angelica (1741–1807). Swiss rococo decorative and portrait painter. She worked in England from 1766 to 1781, becoming the friend of Joshua Reynolds and a founder-member of the R.A.; she worked in conjunction with R. Adam on many interiors. Her work became widely known through engravings by Bartolozzi and was also a favourite source of motifs for porcelain factories.

Kaufman Boris. Polish-born, Russian educated cameraman, brother of *Dziga-Vertov. K. left Russia for Poland and then France where around 1928 he met *Vigo shooting many of his films. Since 1942 he has lived in the U.S., working in New York. His American work includes *On the Waterfront*, *Baby Doll*, *Twelve Angry Men* and *Splendour in the Grass*.

Kaufman George S(imon) (1889–1961). U.S. playwright. K.'s witty, satirical plays were almost always written with collaborators, who included Edna Ferber, Ring Lardner and Nunnally Johnson. With Moss Hart he wrote *You Can't Take It With You* (1936), *The Man Who Came to Dinner* (1939) and *George Washington Slept Here* (1940); with Morrie Ryskind and George Gershwin, *Of Thee I Sing* (1932).

Kaun Hugo (1863–1932). German composer and choral conductor; he worked in the U.S. (1887–1902). His music, influenced by the late romantics, includes many male choruses; he also wrote operas, symphonies, concertos, etc.

Kautner Helmut (1908–). W. German film director whose delicate *Romanze in Moll* (1943) was adapted from a Maupassant short story. He followed this in a very different style with *Die Grosse Freiheit Nr. 7* (*La Paloma*) (1944) an interesting blend of naturalism and exaggeration. Both *The Last Bridge* (1951) and *The Devil's General* (1955) were war films. Since then his work has included satire, *The Captain from Kopenick* (1956) and a modern version of *Hamlet, Der Rest ist Schweigen* (1959).

Kaverin Veniamin. The pseud. of Veniamin Alexandrovich Zilberg (1902–). Soviet

Angelica Kauffmann. *Roundel*

George S. Kaufman

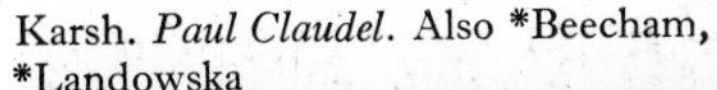

Karsh. *Paul Claudel*. Also *Beecham, *Landowska

Erich Kästner. Emil and his detectives; illustration by Walter Trier

Nikos Kazantzakis

Edmund Kean

Nora Kaye in *The Cage*

novelist. K.'s *The Unknown Artist* (1931; 1947) stresses the creative role of the individualistic artist. His later work employs a more conventional socialist realism.

Kawalerowicz Jerzy (1922–). Polish film director. K. started directing in 1951. His most famous work is *Mother Joan of the Angels* (1961), a version of the story also told by Aldous Huxley in *The Devils of Loudun.*

Kaye Danny (1913–). American actor. A tongue-twisting, singing, satiric comedian of super-dynamic vitality, who dances too. His films, which since 1950 have been aimed more and more at children, include Mcleod's *The Secret Life of Walter Mitty* (1947) from a story by James Thurber, and *Hans Christian Andersen* (1952).

Kaye Nora (1920–). U.S. dancer who joined the corps de ballet of Ballet Theater on its formation (1940). Within 2 years Tudor created *Pillar of Fire* for her; she met with instant success and this has remained her finest role. Although she has danced romantic and classical parts her style is best suited to dance drama.

Kazan. James Dean and Julie Harris in *East of Eden*

Kazan Elia (1909–). Constantinople-born U.S. director. K. was an actor at the Group Theater (1933–9) and in a couple of films (1940–1) before starting to direct on Broadway, which he has continued to do ever since (notably plays by *Miller and *Williams). In 1947, he was co-founder of the Actors' Studio, many of whose graduates he has launched on their cinematic careers (Marlon Brando, Eva Marie Saint, James Dean). His 1st film came from a play he had directed on Broadway–*A Tree Grows in Brooklyn* (1944). Some of his early films had 'social' subjects–*Boomerang* (1946), *Gentleman's Agreement* (1947)–and caused trouble with the McCarthy committee. K. is a director whose overt defence of progressive social order, whether it is threatened by the corrupt trade unionists of *On the Waterfront* (1954) or the conservatives and racialists of *Wild River* (1960), always overlies his subconscious identification with the violently anti-social. This tension is evident in all his most interesting films–*A Streetcar Named Desire* (1950), *Viva Zapata!* (1951), *East of Eden* (1954), *Baby Doll* (1956). This series reached its peak with *Wild River,* which also showed at its greatest his prowess in handling the relationship between camera, characters and environment, particularly in his use of the subjective shot. His latest films are *Splendour in the Grass* (1961), from Inge, and *America, America* (1964), from his own script about the migration of his Armenian forebears.

Kazantzakis Nikos (1885–1957). Greek poet and novelist. All K.'s works reflect his spiritual perplexities and endless search for a meaningful and creative way of life. *The Odyssey, A Modern Sequel* (1938; 1958) is a vast epic in which Odysseus, the man who loves life, embraces many creeds and passes through countless adventures and visions. Works include *Zorba the Greek* (1946; 1952) and a retelling of the story of Christ, set in Turkish-occupied Greece, *Christ Recrucified* (1954; 1954).

Kazinczy Ferenc (1759–1831). Hungarian author. The literary dictator of his age, K. was largely responsible for the reform of the Hungarian language and the birth of modern Hungarian literature.

Kean Edmund (1787–1833). English tragic actor, whose wild nature made him best in fiery and passionate parts such as Richard III, Iago and Shylock. He was not made to play noble characters but with his wide range of facial expression made a compelling villain.

Buster Keaton in *The General*

Keaton Buster (1896–1966). U.S. film actor and director. K. started in vaudeville with his parents and from 1917 made shorts with Fatty Arbuckle, then from 1919 made shorts alone. His 1st feature, *The Three Ages* (1923), had 3 plots of different eras in parody of **Intolerance.* After this followed a series of features until the end of the silent period–*The Navigator* (1924), *Seven Chances* (1925), *The General* (1926), *Steamboat Bill Junior* (1928) and *The Cameraman* (1928). K. was the cinema's greatest exponent of physical, rather than facial, mime. His comedy was much more pure than Chaplin's, and much less sentimental. His success ended with the coming of sound, although he made a few more films, and played small parts in *Sunset Boulevard, Limelight,* etc.

Keats John (1795–1821). English poet. K. was the eldest son of a livery-stable manager in London and was introduced to poetry by the son of his schoolmaster. He became an apothecary's assistant in 1811, then studied at Guy's and St Thomas's hospitals, becoming a

John Keats

staying a short time with Mrs
Brawne who lives in the House
which was Mrs Dilke's. I am excessively nervous: a person I am
not quite used to entering the
room half chokes me. 'Tis not
yet Consumption I believe, but
it would be were I to remain
in this climate all the Winter:
so I am thinking of either voyag-
ing or travelling to Italy. Yesterday I received an invitation
from Mr Shelley, a Gentleman
residing at Pisa, to spend the
Winter with him: if I go I must
be away in a Month or even
less. I am glad you like the Poems
you must hope with me that
time and health will produce
you some more. This is the first
morning I have been able to
sit to the paper and have many Letters to write if I can
manage them. God bless you
my dear Sister.
Your affectionate Brother
John.

Keats. Ms. of a letter to his sister, written during his last illness

qualified surgeon in 1816. In that year he met Leigh Hunt, who encouraged him and publ. his sonnet *O Solitude*, and later *On first looking into Chapman's Homer*, in *The Examiner*. Hunt introduced him to his circle of artistic and literary friends, to whom K. wrote many of the vivid letters concerned with self-discovery and poetic theory which form a pendant to his poetry. He met (1818) and became engaged to Fanny Brawne. In an unsuccessful attempt to arrest his rapidly developing tuberculosis K. went to Italy (1820), where he died.
The wonderful music, colour and movement of his poetry is perfectly disciplined in the great odes and the austere *La Belle Dame Sans Merci*. *Endymion* (1818) revealed K.'s weakness: the account of Endymion's love for Cynthia the moon goddess is blended with other imaginative and symbolic themes, but some of the effect of passages of great beauty is dissipated by their uncontrolled profusion. The unfinished *Hyperion* attempts the epic style of Milton with uneven success. But the coll. of 1820, in which it appeared, revealed K.'s full stature, containing the long narrative poems *Isabella* (written 1818), *The Eve of St Agnes* (1819) and *Lamia* (1819); the odes *to a Nightingale, on a Grecian Urn, to Psyche, to Autumn* and *to Melancholy*; and *The Mermaid Tavern*. *The Eve of St Agnes* is the most successful of the narratives, a precise and controlled evocation of sensual beauty in which the rapture of the lovers is contrasted with the silent, numb winter setting, and their passion with the hostility between their families. K.'s works include the unfinished *Fall of Hyperion*, in which K. identifies himself with the fallen Titan, seeking beauty and immortality through suffering; the early *Poems* (1817); the sonnets *When I have Fears*, *To Sleep* and *Bright Star!*; the dramas *Otho the Great* and *Stephen*; and *Cap and Bells*.

Keble John (1792–1866). English cleric and poet, fellow of Oriel College, Oxford, where Newman and Pusey were his contemporaries. K. launched the Anglo-Catholic Oxford Movement with a sermon on 'National Apostasy', and wrote several of the Movement's *Tracts for the Times*. His poetry includes *The Christian Year* (1827).

Keene Charles Samuel (1823–91). English draughtsman, etcher, painter and engraver. K. is one of the most fascinating draughtsmen of the 19th-c. English school and is mentioned admiringly in Pissarro's letters; as a painter he produced a masterly self-portrait (Tate).

Keighley William (1889–). U.S. film director. K. was a director whose varied output included Marc Connelly's *Green Pastures* (1936), and a Mark Twain adaptation, *The Prince and the Pauper* (1937), but his best films were tough crime pictures such as *G-Men* (1935) and others with James Cagney, and *Street With No Name* (1948) with Richard Widmark.

Keirincx Alexander (1600–52). Flemish landscape painter and engraver who settled in Amsterdam and specialized in forest scenes. From 1640 to 1641 he worked in England where he was known as 'Carings'.

Keiser Reinhard (1674–1739). German composer working mainly at Hamburg where he was director and manager of, and composer to the opera during its most brilliant period. His elegant and expressive style, his melodic gift and imaginative instrumentation gained his German operas contemporary adulation. His church music, theatrical in idiom, includes dramatic oratorios and a *St Mark's Passion*.

Keller Gottfried (1819–90). Swiss novelist. Feuerbach, whom he heard in Heidelberg in 1848, intensified K.'s this-worldly, humorously physical outlook. His novel *Der grüne Heinrich* (1854–5; *Green Henry*, 1960), an autobiographical **Bildungsroman*, describes the ultimate failure of a would-be painter: the settings are realistic and vividly conveyed. A disappointing late novel, *Martin Salander* (1886) shows its hero's inability to face his materialistic age. More uniformly successful are K.'s short stories, especially the 2 vols of *Die Leute von Seldwyla* (1856, 74), a series of cautionary tales, dealing with eccentrics and told with loving humour, centred on the imaginary town of Seldwyla: exceptional among them is the tragic masterpiece *Romeo und Julia auf dem Dorfe*, the basis of Delius's opera. K. uses not provincial landscapes like his fellow poetic realists Stifter and Storm, but houses, personal possessions, clothes and physical appearance to mirror and symbolize character and fate: he is a genre painter. The *Züricher Novellen* (1877) are set at various periods of the city's history; other cycles are the *Sieben Legenden* (1872; *Seven Legends*, 1911), dealing with the interplay of saintly and sensual, and *Das*

Gottfried Keller

Keene. *Portrait of the Artist*

Page from *The Book of Kells*

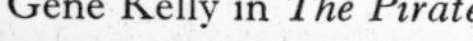

Gene Kelly in *The Pirate*

John Philip Kemble

Kenny. Set for *Maggie May*

Kemps nine daies vvonder.
Performed in a daunce from London to Norwich.
Containing the pleasure, paines and kinde entertainment of William Kemp betweene London and that City in his late Morrice.
Wherein is somewhat set downe worth note; to reproove the slaunders spred of him: many things merry, nothing hurtfull.
Written by himselfe to satisfie his friends.

LONDON
Printed by E. A. for Nicholas Ling, and are to be solde at his shop at the west doore of Saint Paules Church. 1600.

William Kempe's account of his morris-dance to Norwich

Kelmscott Press ed. of Chaucer

Sinngedicht (1881), dealing with that of love and modesty.

Kelley Edgar Stillman (1857–1944). U.S. composer, organist, conductor and teacher. His works include the *New England* symphony and various books on music.

Kellgren Johann Henric (1751–95). Swedish poet, a leading neo-classicist and literary adviser to Gustav III. He wrote fine lyrics, odes and satires, in his later verse anticipating romantic attitudes.

Kells Book of (*c.* 800; Trinity College, Dublin). Elaborately illuminated copy of the Gospels written in Latin, long one of the treasures of the Columban monastery of Kells in Ireland. The work of monks from Iona, it is the masterpiece of the Celtic school of illumination.

Kelly Gene (1912–). U.S. dancer and choreographer working mainly in films. He has an easy, fluid style; his films include *Anchors Aweigh* (1945) and *Invitation to the Dance* (1954), and 2 which he co-directed with *Donen, *On the Town* (1949) and *Singin' in the Rain* (1952).

Kelmscott Press. Founded by William Morris in 1891 at Hammersmith, London. Morris modelled his types on type-faces of the 15th and 16th cs and his work was marked by a meticulous attention to every element in book production. The K. P. was the first of a number of experimental private presses which eventually transformed the standards of commercial typography. Morris designed 3 types, the Golden, the Troy and the Chaucer; the last was used for the K. P. ed. of *The Works of Geoffrey Chaucer* (1896), reckoned its masterpiece. The printer Emery *Walker contributed essentially to the achievements of the Press.

Kemble John Philip (1757–1823). English actor of great dignity who was best in heavy dramatic parts and rarely attempted comedy. Thus his best roles were Hamlet, Wolsey in *Henry VIII* and especially Coriolanus.

Kempe Margerie (*c.* 1373–after 1438). English mystic, author of the vivid *Book of Margerie Kempe*, the 1st prose autobiography in English. Dictated to a priest (K. was illiterate), it records her spiritual life and extensive pilgrimages.

Kempe William (*fl.* 1600). Elizabethan clown who first played Dogberry in *Much Ado About Nothing*. He played in Holland in 1586 with the Earl of Leicester's Co. In 1600 he morris-danced from London to Norwich.

Kenilworth (1821). Historical novel by Sir Walter *Scott.

Kennedy-Fraser Marjorie (1857–1930). Scottish singer and collector of Hebridean songs: *Songs of the Hebrides* (3 vols 1909–21). She wrote the libretto for G. Bantock's opera *The Seal Woman* which employs Hebridean melodies.

kenning. Metaphor or standard phrases in Scandinavian, Anglo-Saxon and other Germanic verse, e.g. 'ice of battle' for a gleaming sword and 'whale-road' for the sea. It is most elaborate in *skaldic verse.

Kenny Sean (1927–). Irish architect and stage designer who with his intricate sets using much stage machinery has established himself as a leading young British designer. He has designed nearly all the musicals of Lionel Bart, and has also done considerable work at Stratford and the National Theatre.

Kensett John Frederick (1816–72). U.S. landscape painter of the *Hudson River school.

Kent William (*c.* 1685–1748). English architect. One of Lord Burlington's protégés, K. began as a painter and did no serious architecture until he was over 40. His works form the epitome of Lord Burlington's Palladian style, though in interior decoration and small-scale buildings he shows a much freer fancy. He designed the Horse Guards, London; Holkham Hall, Norfolk (the most consistent and grandest of English Palladian houses) and Stowe, Bucks, with some of its fascinating ornamental buildings. He was also a pioneer of English landscape gardening, leading that revolt against formal Dutch and French styles which created 'K.'s school' and was completed by L. ('Capability') *Brown.

Kentuckian, The (1955). Film directed by B. *Lancaster.

Kermesse Héroique, La (1936). Film directed by J. *Feyder.

Kern Jerome (David) (1885–1945). U.S. composer of the musical *Show Boat* (1927) containing the song 'Ol' Man River'. K.'s style influenced Gershwin and Rodgers.

Kerner Andreas Justinus Christian (1786–1862). German writer, physician and fellow-student of Uhland. He wrote lyric poetry, romantic in mood, ballads and songs, but he is remembered as the author of *Die Seherin von Prevorst* . . . (1829; *The Seeress of Prevorst*, 1845). This describes a local peasant woman who came to K. for treatment of a mental disorder.

Kerouac Jack (1922–). U.S. novelist and poet, one of the leading *beats. K.'s work draws directly on his life: he writes in the 1st person and many of the characters can be identified. He employs a markedly idiomatic 'spontaneous prose' with long unpunctuated sentences. At its best it creates an impression of breathlessness and exuberance–effective, e.g., in *On the Road* (1957), the novel which made K. famous. This successfully conveys the intoxication induced by fast travel over the spaces of America. K.'s work includes the novels *The Subterraneans* (1958), *Doctor Sax* (1959) and *The Dharma Bums* (1959); and the verse coll. *Mexico City Blues* (1959).

Kerr Deborah (1921–). British-born romantic but not sentimental film actress, of strong presence and psychological perception. Her films include: *Major Barbara* (1941), *The King and I* (1956), *Tea and Sympathy* (1957) and *The Innocents* (1962).

Kershner Irvin (1923–). U.S. film director. A documentary and television director who made a critical reputation with the off-beat treatment of his 1st low-budget feature, *Stakeout on Dope Street* (1959).

Kessel Jan van (1626–79). Flemish still-life painter famous for his minutely detailed miniatures of butterflies and insects. He worked in Antwerp.

Kessel Johan van (1641/2–80). Dutch landscape painter, pupil and follower of J. van Ruisdael. He painted mountain scenes with rushing water and panoramic views.

Ketel Cornelis (1548–1616). Dutch painter, mainly of portraits but also of historical and allegorical subjects. He worked in Gouda and Amsterdam and for a time in England. His style of portraiture was close to that of H. Eworth with slightly stronger characterization.

kettledrum: *timpani

key. The ambience in which a piece of music may be written. If a piece of music is written, for example, in the k. of C maj., it uses, primarily, the notes belonging to the scale of C maj.; other notes are *chromatic and are said to be foreign to the k. Some scales have several notes in common with C maj.; they are said to be 'related k.s'. Other scales, e.g. C maj., have few notes in common; they are 'remote k.s'. In so far as all k.s use the same scales they are all scientifically the same; nevertheless, many musicians associate particular k.s with particular moods. D maj., for instance, is almost universally a key of glory and joy. The k. provides a framework of reference, every note in the piece holding some relationship to the key-note, and this hierarchy of relationships within a k. (i.e. tonality) dominated European music during the greater part of the 17th to the end of the 19th c.
The k. of a passage of music is indicated by a KEY SIGNATURE. Thus 𝄞♭♭♭ prescribes that all the 'Bs', 'Es' and 'As' are to be flattened and thus indicates the keys of E♭ maj. or C min.

key. The predominant tone and colour values in a painting if light are said to be in a 'high k.' if dark in a 'low k.'.

Key Adriaen Thomasz (*c.* 1544–*c.* 1590). Flemish portrait painter, nephew and pupil of WILLEM K. (d. 1568), a portrait and history painter, pupil of Lambert Lombard.

Key Francis Scott (1779–1843). U.S. poet, author of *The Star Spangled Banner* (1814).

keyboard instruments. Those musical instruments in which a set of keys (the keyboard) operate a mechanism which acts on strings as in the *piano or *harpsichord or on columns of air as in the *organ. The term 'keyboard music' covers works written for any one of these instruments.

keyed bugle. Now obsolete musical instrument; in range and function it was comparable with the cornet but had keys like a saxophone, not valves; it was related to the *ophicleide (also *trumpet).

Kent. Holkham Hall

Adriaen Thomasz Key. *William the Silent*

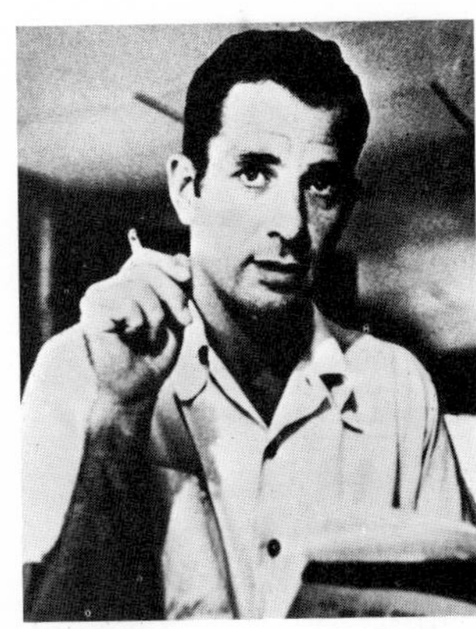

Jack Kerouac

Johan van Kessel. *Torrent in a Mountainous Landscape*

Key pattern. Round mouth of an 8th-c. B.C. Attic jug

Thomas de Keyser. *Constantijn Huygens and his Clerk*

Hendrick de Keyser. The Westerkerk: painting by Jan van der Heyden

Keyes Sidney (1922–42). English poet, a neo-romantic who was regarded by many as the most promising of the war poets. Colls include *The Iron Laurel* (1942) and *The Cruel Solstice* (posth. 1944).

key pattern. A repetitive frieze pattern derived from classical Greek decoration. It is used as a motif in furniture, fabrics and metalwork as well as in architecture during the neoclassical period.

Keyser Hendrick de (1565–1621). Dutch sculptor and architect to the city of Amsterdam. There his work includes the Zuiderkerk and the Westerkerk and the Erasmus monument. He also executed the tomb of William the Silent at Delft. His sons PIETER (1595–1676), WILLEM (1603–after 1674) and HENDRICK (1613–65) were sculptors.

Keyser Thomas de (1596/7–1667). Dutch portrait painter, son of H. de K. He worked in Amsterdam and based his style on that of N. Eliasz and later of Rembrandt. He painted small-size group and equestrian portraits, e.g. *Pieter Schout on Horseback* (Rijksmus., Amsterdam).

keystone: *arch

Khatchaturian Aram (1903–). Armenian composer and conductor. He studied in Moscow under Gnessin and Miaskovsky. He is among the topmost figures of the musical hierarchy in Soviet Russia, having received numerous distinctions and held such posts as secretary of the Union of Composers. During the Zhdanov period he was criticized for 'formalism' and modernism (1948) but in 1951 became professor of composition at Moscow Conservatory.
K.'s brilliant music derives inspiration from Armenian folk-music and may be seen as the continuation of the work of the 19th-c. national composers in Russia. Most famous of all his music is the *Sabre Dance* from the ballet *Gayane* (1942); also well known are the piano concerto (1937), violin concerto (1940) and cello concerto (1946), and the ballet *Spartacus* (1956).

Khlebnikov Velemir, originally Victor Vladimirovich (1885–1922). Russian poet, the founder of cubo-*futurism, the leading poetic movement in the years before the Revolution. K. was the most original and probably the most fruitful writer of 'trans-sense' poetry–at worst nonsense attempting to subsist on the sound values of language alone, but in much of K.'s work (based on sound etymological knowledge) extremely rich and suggestive.

Khomyakov Alexey Stepanovich (1804–60). Russian poet, philosopher and theologian. K. was one of the most important of the Slavophils (who held that Russia should not imitate the Western society and institutions but follow her own path), influencing Dostoyevsky's thought. His poetry is largely concerned with his Messianic conception of Russia's mission.

Kid, The (1921). Film directed by *Chaplin.

Kidd Michael (1919–). U.S. dancer and choreographer who joined Ballet Theater in 1942. His 1st significant work, *On Stage* (1945), was a 'behind the scenes' tale of pathos and the role he danced himself earned him considerable praise. K. has since directed films and musicals.

Kidnapped (1886). Historical novel by R. L. *Stevenson.

Kiel Friedrich (1821–85). German composer and teacher in Berlin, latterly at the Music Academy there. His prolific output includes the oratorio *Christus* and numerous instrumental compositions, but his most important work was pedagogic.

Kielland Alexander Lange (1849–1906). Norwegian novelist and playwright, a realist whose works aimed to expose social injustices. Novels include *Garman og Worse* (1880; 1885) and *Skipper Worse* (1882; 1885).

Kienzl Wilhelm (1857–1941). Austrian pianist, conductor, composer and writer on music; he held posts in Graz and at the Hamburg and Munich operas. His music, despite a strong Wagnerian influence, shows many folk elements and is best in his songs and operas, e.g. *Der Evangelimann* (1895).

Kierkegaard Søren Aabye (1813–55). Danish philosopher and theologian regarded as the precursor of existentialism. He reacted against the Hegelian theologians in Denmark, denouncing organized religion–'Christianity is not yet a reality' and held that the act of choice by the individual was all-important. Using

Aram Khatchaturian

Søren Kierkegaard: from a drawing (*c.* 1840) by his cousin

Ukrainian Kilim

the notions of dread, choice, duty, freedom and change, K. laid emphasis on the peculiar problems of existence which face each individual; during the course of the argument the distinction is drawn between objective and subjective (or existential) thinking, the latter being concerned with the individual's dilemmas. K.'s works include *Enten–Eller* (1843; *Either/Or*, 1944); *Frygt og Bæven* (1843; *Fear and Trembling*, 1939); *Begrebet Angst* (1844; *The Concept of Dread*, 1944); *Afsluttende uvidenskabelig Efterskrift* (1846; *Concluding Unscientific Postscript*, 1941) and *Sygdommen til Døden* (1848; *The Sickness Unto Death*, 1941).

Kilhwch and Olwen. One of the earliest (10th c.) Arthurian tales, included in the *Mabinogion*.

Kilim or Kelim (Gilim). A tapestry-woven carpet with no pile. Each line of weft thread passes over and under alternate warp threads, successive lines reversing the course. The weft is beaten down to hide the warp completely, producing a smooth surface.

Killigrew Thomas (1612–83). English courtier and dramatist, a favourite of Charles II. At the Restoration K. erected the original Theatre Royal, *Drury Lane for his co., the official King's Players (*D'Avenant). He wrote a bawdy comedy *The Parson's Wedding* and tragi-comedies, *Claracilla* and *The Prisoners*.

Killigrew Sir William (1606?–95). English courtier and dramatist, brother of T. K. He wrote the comedy *Pandora* (publ. 1664) and the tragi-comedy *The Siege of Urbin* (1666?).

Kilpinen Yrjö (Henrik) (1892–). Finnish composer, virtually self-taught. He excels as a song writer working in the tradition of Hugo Wolf and setting the works of Finnish, Swedish and German poets and the Finnish folk-poetry, *Kanteletar*. K. has an intuitive feeling for a text well shown in his cycle *Tunturilauluja* about the mountains of N. Finland.

Kim (1901). Novel by *Kipling.

Kindertotenlieder. Work by *Mahler.

Kind Hearts and Coronets (1948). Film directed by Robert *Hamer.

King Henry (1592–1669). English metaphysical poet, bishop of Chichester and intimate of Jonson and Donne, both of whom influenced his verse. His poems include *The Exequy*, a moving, powerful elegy to his dead wife, with the celebrated lines on his pulse beating his approach to death and to his wife 'like a soft drum'.

King Henry (1888–). U.S. film director. Entered films in 1912 and first directed (a serial) in 1916. He has since made over 100 films, half of them silent, including *Tol'able David* (1921). His métier in the sound cinema was the lush romance, e.g. *The Song of Bernadette* (1943). He occasionally broke out from his formula–with an interesting western, *The Gunfighter* (1950), and a war film, *Twelve O'Clock High* (1949).

King William (1663–1712). English writer and poet, author of *The Art of Cookery . . .* (1708), a travesty of Horace's *Art of Poetry*. K. joined the dispute between Sir W. *Temple and R. Bentley with a prose satire attacking the latter, *Dialogues of the Dead* (1699).

King Alisaundre. 13th-c. English verse romance based on legendary stories about Alexander the Great.

Kingis Quair, The. Poem by *James I of Scotland.

King John (publ. 1623). Historical play by *Shakespeare, perhaps written *c.* 1596. Its source was an anonymous play, *The Troublesome Raigne of John, King of England*, publ. in 1591.

King Kong (1933). Film produced by E. *Schoedsack and M. C. Cooper.

Kinglake Alexander William (1809–91). English writer, author of the highly successful travel book *Eothen* (1844), describing journeys in the Middle East. His *The Invasion of the Crimea* (1863–87), is based on Lord Raglan's papers.

King Lear (publ. 1608). Tragedy by *Shakespeare, written *c.* 1605 and performed at court in 1606. Its sources included *King Leir*, an anonymous play (registered 1594, publ. 1605) and Sidney's *Arcadia*.

Thomas Killigrew

Kinglake

Kirchner. *Five Women in the Street* (1913); woodcut

Kirchner. *Amselfluh* (1923). Also *Brücke

Rudyard Kipling. Also **Just-So Stories*

Charles Kingsley

King's pattern knife and fork

king-post. Architectural term for a vertical beam in a roof; it connects the tie-beam with the ridge-beam, i.e. if the roof is viewed in section as a triangle, the k.-p. divides the roof into 2 right-angled triangles.

Kings. One of the books of the *Bible (Old Testament); in Christian versions *Samuel is usually incorporated as the 1st 2 books of K., the Hebrew K. being treated as the 3rd and 4th. The historical narrative of Samuel is continued through the reign of Solomon, the building of the Temple, the lives of Elijah and Elisha, and the division of Israel into 2 kingdoms (Israel and Judah), to the destruction of Jerusalem (586 B.C.).

Kingsley Charles (1819–75). English writer, a cleric whose Christian Socialist beliefs colour all his works, including the historical novels *Westward Ho!* (1855), set in the Elizabethan period, and *Hereward the Wake* (1866). K.'s *The Water Babies* (1863) is a fairy-tale about a little sweep who falls into a river and becomes a water baby. K.'s criticism of Newman prompted the latter's *Apologia.*

Kingsley Henry (1830–76). English novelist, younger brother of C. K.; his novels of adventure include *The Recollections of Geoffrey Hamlyn* (1859) and *Ravenshoe* (1861).

king's pattern. The shaping of the handle of silver flat ware (i.e. spoons and forks) dating from the Regency period. The basic shape is that of a fiddle with scrolled edges, anthemion and scrolls in relief, which give it a more massive appearance than the similar queen's pattern.

Kinoshita Keisuke (1912–). Japanese film director. He is unusually catholic in his sources, using the vignetting technique of old photographs for the flashbacks of *She Was Like a Daisy* (1956) and the most complete cinematic exploitation of the techniques of *Kabuki in *The Legend of Narayama* (1958).

Kinsky Georg Ludwig (1882–1951). German musicologist, a co-ed. of *Geschichte der Musik in Bildern* (1929; *History of Music in Pictures,* 1930).

Kinugasa Teinosuke (1896–). Japanese film director. From 1917, K. was an actor specializing in female parts. (There were no actresses in the Japanese cinema at the time.) He started directing in 1922; *Crossways* (1928) is the most famous Japanese silent film. *Gate of Hell* (1954) was particularly admired for its use of colour.

Kipling (Joseph) Rudyard (1865–1936). English poet and short-story writer, originally a journalist in India, his birthplace. He won fame in the 1890s, when his patriotic sentiments and interest in army, sea and empire found favour during an upsurge of popular imperialism. His reputation has declined with the imperialist ideal, but his work is more subtle and sensitive, and less facile than is generally supposed, and many of his stories are masterpieces of atmosphere and economy. *Plain Tales from the Hills* (1888) was succeeded by *Barrack-Room Ballads* (1892), where his use of vigorous rhythmic stanzas and the Cockney idiom gained an immense triumph. His *Jungle Books* (1894–5) and the coll. of fables *Just-So Stories* (1902) are children's classics and *Kim* (1901) a classic boys' adventure story in a vividly described Indian setting. His works also include the story coll. *Soldiers Three* (1888) and the boys' book *Stalky & Co.* (1899).

Kipps (1905). Novel by H. G. *Wells.

Kirbye George (*c.* 1565?–1634). English madrigal composer whose notebooks of contemporary Italian compositions (e.g. by de Monte and Marenzio) enabled these to become more widely known in England.

Kirchner Ernst Ludwig (1880–1938). German expressionist painter. He studied architecture at Dresden (1901–5) where he met Heckel and Schmidt-Rottluff, co-founders in 1905 of Die Brücke. Led by K. and inspired by Gauguin, Van Gogh, Munch and above all by primitive art, Die Brücke was the first manifestation of German expressionism–superficially similar to Parisian fauvism, but deliberately more violently and directly expressive of human emotions. The intensity of their art and philosophy, deeply rooted in Nietzsche, is a parallel to the Italian futurists' fervent belief in a new world.
The Artist and his Model (1907; Hamburg) is a typical example of K.'s deployment of pure colour–brilliant oranges and pinks juxtaposed –producing a jarring visual sensation. In his woodcuts the same effect is achieved by the crudeness of his harsh outlines, partly inspired by his admiration of German primitive art but

with exaggerated distortions. He moved to Berlin in 1911, joined Nolde's Neue Sezession and was associated with Der Sturm circles. His work became more aggressively angular and sombre coloured: the *Five Women in the Street* (1913; Cologne) are stark, primitive images of the modern city.
He suffered a nervous breakdown during the war and convalesced (1917) at Davos, where he continued to live. His late landscapes are more serene, profound formalizations at their purest (1921–5) and then becoming abstract in 1928. His art was suppressed as 'degenerate' by the Nazis (1937) and he committed suicide in 1938.

Kirchner Theodor (1823–1903). German composer of short piano pieces in the tradition of Schumann.

Kirkman Jacob (1710–92). Swiss-born harpsichord maker (original name Kirchman) who settled in London in the 1730s, taking British nationality; Shudi (*Broadwood) was his chief rival. The firm of K. remained independent until 1896.

Kirkpatrick Ralph (1911–). U.S. harpsichord and clavichord virtuoso who studied under W. Landowska, N. Boulanger and A. Dolmetsch. His book on D. Scarlatti (1953) is the major authority and K.'s numbering of his works is replacing Longho's.

Kirkup James (1918–). English poet. His colls include *The Prodigal Son* (1959) and *A Correct Compassion* (1952); in the fine title-poem of the latter, dealing with a surgical operation, K.'s ability to record is heightened by the occasion.

Kirnberger Johann Philipp (1721–83). Composer, violinist and leading German musical theorist of his time; a pupil of J. S. Bach. He composed fugues of exemplary strictness.

Kirov State Theatre of Opera and Ballet Leningrad; originally called the Maryinsky Theatre. The Imperial ballet theatre of St Petersburg opened in 1860, producing through its school most of the great names in Russian ballet history. The theatre's name was changed to the State Academy of Opera and Ballet (1920) and again in 1935 in honour of the Soviet politician Kirov, whose assassination triggered off the great purges.

Kirsanov Dimitri (1899–1957). Estonian-born French film director. One of the French *avant-garde* of the 1920s. His most famous film is *Ménilmontant* (1924). He continued working into the sound era, e.g. *Rapt* (1933).

Kisling Moïse (1891–1953). Polish-born painter of the school of Paris. He settled in Paris in 1910 and joined the Bateau-Lavoir group, then the circle round Modigliani; he was in the U.S. during World War II. In the 1920s he developed and never substantially altered a personal expressionist style which owed something to Derain and Modigliani. He painted female nudes and portraits touched with melancholy and lasciviousness.

Kiss, The (*Le Baiser*; 1886). Sculpture by *Rodin.

kit. A small violin, called in French '*pochette*', used by dancing masters of the 18th c.; it could be put in the pocket while the master demonstrated a step. K.s were often elaborately decorated and are now collectors' pieces.

kitchen sink. Term applied to the work of the English playwrights of the *Angry Young Men school and other such recent works, and the paintings of the English social realist painters.

Kjerulf Halfdan (1815–68). Norwegian composer, teacher and conductor. He wrote songs, many to words by B. Björnson, and piano music which antedates Grieg in its use of Norwegian folk-music elements.

Klangfarbenmelodie: *Webern

Klee Paul (1879–1940). Painter born near Berne, Switzerland. He studied in Munich (1898–1900) under Knirr and Stuck, visited Italy (1901) and then returned to Berne (1902–6). Most of his early work was in black and white graphic media: the precision of his draughtsmanship and the recurrent expressionist fantasy element (e.g. *Inventions* etchings, 1903–5) link him with the N. European tradition.
K. settled in Munich in 1906 and in 1911 made contact with the Blaue Reiter artists (Kandinsky, Marc, Macke) and contributed to their exhibition in 1912. In 1912 also he visited Paris, met *Delaunay and trs. his essay *Sur La Lumière*. The accumulation of his contacts with the colouristic paintings of the Blaue Reiter,

Kirkman harpsichord

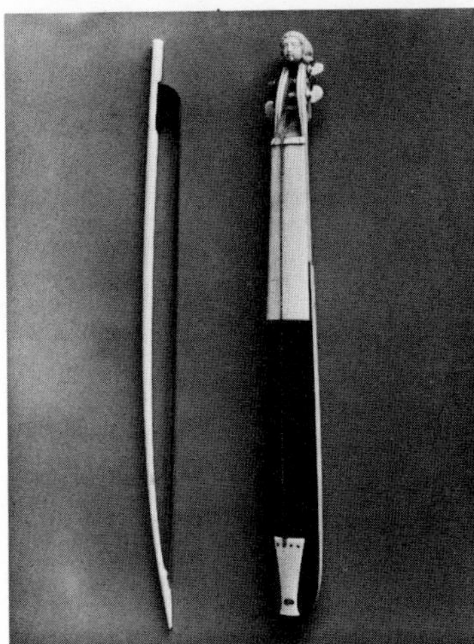

Kit; French, late 18th c.

Kisling.
Woman in a Polish Shawl

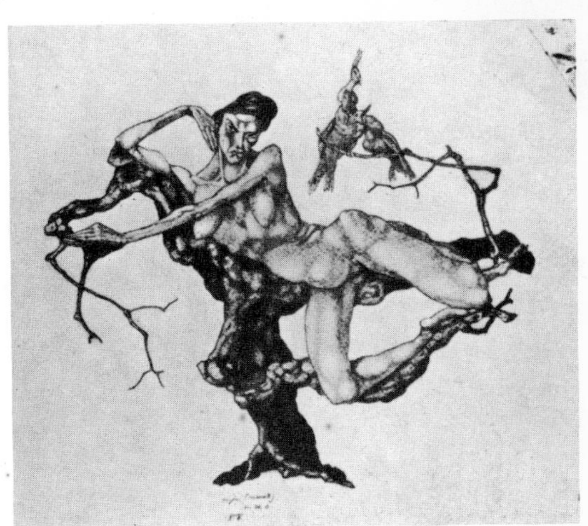

Klee.
Virgin in a Tree (1903)

Klee. *A Young Lady's Adventure*

Klee. *Kinderspiel* (1939)

and with Delaunay's orphism, and finally his experience of Tunis, which he visited with Macke in 1914, resulted in K.'s release from his early monochromatic discipline. He now felt ready to paint and his watercolours of 1914–16 are subtle arrangements of glowing translucent colour areas. During the war he served in the army (1916–18) and was deeply distressed by the deaths of Macke (1914) and Marc (1916).

From 1920 to 1931 he taught at the Bauhaus, Weimar and Dessau. His *Pedagogical Sketchbook* was publ. in 1925 as a Bauhausbuch. The principle of his art and his influential teaching is best expressed in his own metaphor of the tree whose trunk is the artist. The pattern of growth of the roots is the pattern of nature (the artist's source of forms and ideas); this pattern is reflected in the growth of the branches and blossoms, but in this final flowering (which is the work of art) nature has been transformed by the richness of the artist's imaginative instincts. Improvisation plays an important part: the work of art is allowed, like a doodle, to follow its own evolution, subconsciously guided by the artist rather than consciously controlled. These ideas, disciplined by a rare self-knowledge and humility, which lie behind so many later developments, have made him a very influential thinker in art; the persistent quality of his prolific and varied oeuvre, exquisitely sensitive in line, colour and texture and often laced with fantasy and humour, has made him one of the c.'s most original artists. *A Young Lady's Adventure* (1922; Tate) shows his subtle colour, fluid line and uninhibited wit, but it is difficult to appreciate the character of his art without experiencing its full range.

He left the Bauhaus (*c.* 1931) and held a professorship at Düsseldorf until 1933, when he was expelled by the Nazis.

Kleiber Erich (1890–1956). Austrian-born conductor. General musical director of the Berlin State Opera from 1923, he left Germany in 1935 in protest against Nazism and worked mainly in S. America during World War II. Apart from exemplary performances of the classics he gave premières of modern works, e.g. A. Berg's *Wozzeck* (1925).

Klein Abraham Moses (1909–). Canadian writer. His earliest work owes much to Jewish background, that of the 1930s to Revolutionary fervour; his protest continued in the war, the object more clearly defined. His best work is in *The Rocking Chair* (1948), and the novel *The Second Scroll* (1951), and particularly in the poem *Portrait of the Poet as Landscape*.

Kleine Nachtmusik, Eine. Suite of music for strings by Mozart; the literal trs. is 'A Small Night Music' (i.e. serenade).

Kleist Ewald Christian von (1715–59). German poet and an officer in the Prussian army; he died on active service. Of all his poetry *Der Frühling* (1749; *Kleist's Vernal Season*, 1818), inspired by a trs. of Thomson's *Seasons*, is the finest and best known. K.'s love of nature and his natural melancholy pervade the poem, yet his sensitive descriptions evoke the robust freshness of spring.

Kleist (Bernd) Heinrich (Wilhelm) von (1777–1811). German writer. Born in Frankfurt-an-der-Oder, of a military family, he became an officer, but left the army in 1799 to study, only to experience the so-called 'Kant crisis': a pessimistically slanted reading of Kant (or Fichte?) led to shattering mistrust of human reasoning. A restless life followed, ending in suicide.

In his emphasis on feeling K. is close to the romantics, but his dramatic vigour recalls the *storm and stress, his psychological probing anticipates Büchner and the modern 'pathological' drama. His pervading theme of the vanity of human intelligence in a hostile world has appealed to the troubled 20th c., especially the existentialists. His analysis of human thought- and speech-processes is reflected in his apparently unwieldy syntax, while in *Über das Marionettentheater* (1810) he stresses man's need to recapture the intuitive grace of puppets, beasts and gods. His early plays *Amphitryon* (publ. 1807), *Penthesilea* (publ. 1808; 1959), are tragedies of human error; later, error is precariously avoided, in the dramas *Das Käthchen von Heilbronn* (1810) and *Prinz Friedrich von Homburg* (1821; 1956; the basis of Henze's opera) by child-like faith and mature intuition respectively, in the earthy comedy *Der zerbrochene Krug* (1808) by the intervention of a wise inspector. Misunderstanding and its consequences also form the mainspring of his powerful stories (*Erzählungen*, 1810–11, various separate trs); again there is a development from pessimism (*Michael Kohlhaas*) towards modified optimism (*Der Zweikampf*). K. employs here some degree of historical realism, and a chronicle-style narration that is rapid, deadpan, and inexorable.

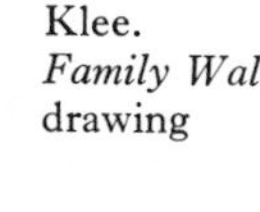

Klee. *Family Walk*; drawing

Klee. *Death and Fire* (1940)

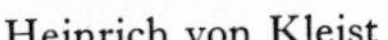
Heinrich von Kleist

Friedrich Gottlieb Klopstock

Kleitias. Detail of the François vase

Kleitias (early 6th c. B.C.). Greek vase painter. Only 5 works signed by him have survived but these are in a lively style, showing marked originality despite traces of Corinthian influence.

Klemperer Otto (1885–). German conductor, director of the Cologne opera (1917–24) and the Kroll Opera, Berlin (1927–31); in 1933 he migrated to the U.S., after the war working again in Europe. In several seasons since 1957 he has conducted the 9 symphonies of Beethoven. K.'s compositions include *Missa sacra* and *Psalm 42*.

Klenau Paul (1883–1946). Danish conductor and composer. His music was influenced by German composers, especially R. Strauss, and includes the opera *Gudrun auf Island.*

Klengel August Stephan Alexander (1783–1852). German composer, a pupil of Clementi. His *Canons and Fugues* for piano are clearly influenced by study of J. S. Bach.

Klengel Julius (1859–1933). German cello virtuoso, 1st cellist of the Leipzig Gewandhaus Orchestra (1881–1924) and composer for his instrument. K. was a friend of Brahms, Joachim and Reger. His brother PAUL (1854–1935) was a violinist, pianist, composer (especially of songs), conductor (e.g. of the Deutscher Liederkranz, New York, 1898–1903) and teacher.

Klenze Leo von (1784–1864). German architect, leader of Greek and Italian Renaissance revivals in Munich where he was court architect from 1816. His buildings include the Glyptothek, the Alte Pina., the Propylaea, the Odeon and the Königsbau, an imitation of the Pitti Palace, Florence. Outside Munich he built the Walhalla, a replica of the Parthenon, near Regensburg and also the Hermitage Mus., Leningrad.

Kletzki Paul (1900–). Polish conductor and composer (originally named Pawel Klecki), chief conductor of the Liverpool Philharmonic Orchestra (1954–). His compositions include symphonies, concertos and songs; as a conductor he excels in modern works.

Klimt Gustav (1862–1918). Austrian painter and designer associated with the symbolist and Jugendstil movements and a leading member of the Vienna Sezession. He devoted much of his time to architectural decoration (e.g. *The Kiss*, mosaic for Palais Stoclet, Brussels built by Josef Hoffmann) and considerably influenced the decorative arts in Austria.

Klindworth Karl (1830–1916). German pianist and a close friend of Wagner with whose authority K. publ. his famous piano transcription of *The Ring*. K. also produced major critical eds of Chopin's works, of Beethoven's sonatas and J. S. Bach's *Well Tempered Clavier.*

Kline Franz (1911–62). U.S. abstract expressionist painter whose stark black and white compositions on a huge scale made him one of the most powerful exponents of the calligraphic approach to abstract expressionism. He reintroduced colour into his late works.

Klinger Friedrich Maximilian von (1752–1831). German dramatist and novelist whose play *Der Wirrwarr oder *Sturm und Drang* (1775), set in the American War of Independence, gave the name to the next 20 years of German literature. Another work in the same passionate spirit was *Die Zwillinge* (1774), a story of fratricide and jealousy. From 1780 K. served in the Russian army. From the 1790s he publ. a series of novels and other prose works in a more philosophical classical mood than his early plays.

Kloos Willem (Johannes Theodoorus) (1859–1938). Dutch poet, one of the leaders of the literary revival of the 1880s. His sensual, musical verse was very influential.

Klopstock Friedrich Gottlieb (1724–1803). German poet. His religious epic on Christ's salvation of man, *Messias* (12 cantos 1748–73), was planned while he was at school, under the influence of Homer and Milton. The publ. of the 1st 3 cantos in 1748 (English trs. *The Messiah*, 1763) was the major literary event in 18th-c. German poetry up to that year; K.'s real talent, his enthusiasm and powerful descriptive passages ensured his success but inspiration faded in the later parts and the work now seems tedious. His coll. of *Odes* (1771; 1848) contains some fine poetry.

Knapton George (1698–1778). English portrait painter and pastellist, pupil of J. Richardson the Elder. He was a founder-member of the

Otto Klemperer

Klimt.
Mme Fritsa Riedler (1906)

Kline. Untitled drawing in ink and oil (1955). Also *calligraphy

Knossos: the Palace of Minos

Knobelsdorff. Sans-souci

Kneller. *The Chinese Convert.* Also *Addison, *Congreve, *Dryden, *Locke, *Newton, *Prior

Knop. 18th-c. glass with knopped stem

Society of Dilettanti and as official painter to the Society executed portraits of the members. F. Cotes was his pupil.

Knaths Karl (1891–). U.S. expressionist painter in a post-cubist idiom.

Knave of Diamonds. Group of young Russian Paris-orientated artists who rebelled against the Moscow Art School in 1909. Headed by Larionov, they organized their 1st exhibition of the newest Franco-Russian art in 1910; exhibitions continued to be held in Moscow under this name up to 1922 though after the first, Larionov left the group, which then became synonymous with painters of the Russian Paris school such as Falk, Mashkov, Lentulov and Konchalovsky.

Kneller Sir Godfrey (1646 or 49–1723). Painter, born (Kniller) in Lübeck, but usually associated with the English school. He studied in Amsterdam under F. Bol, and, possibly, Rembrandt and was influenced by C. Maratta and other Italian portrait painters during a period in Italy. In 1674 he settled in England, where he rapidly became the leading portrait painter. K. was knighted in 1692 and was the 1st painter to become an English baronet (in 1715). He founded the 1st English Academy of Painting in 1711. K.'s success made it necessary for him to establish a workshop; the standard of his painting declined and he often fell back on the conventional poses of Lely. Among his best works are the 42 portraits known as the *Kit Cat series* (all N.P.G., London), while an unusually fine example is *The Chinese Convert* (R. Coll., Kensington Palace).

Knight Dame Laura (1887–). English painter of circus and ballet subjects.

Knight Richard Payne (1750–1824). English writer and connoisseur. He popularized the rustic cottage, the castellated mansion and the Italian villa, and built himself a combination of all 3 at Downton Castle, Herefordshire. He opposed the theories of L. ('Capability') *Brown, giving his own views of the *'picturesque' in gardening in the poem *The Landscape* (1794); K. left an important coll. of classical antiquities, mainly bronzes, to the British Mus.

Knight of the Burning Pestle, The (publ. 1613). Comedy by *Beaumont and Fletcher.

Richard Payne Knight. Downtown Castle

Knights, The (424 B.C.). Comedy by *Aristophanes.

Knipper Lev (1898–). Soviet composer; his teachers included Glière. K.'s work aims at a fusion of folk-song (particularly oriental) and the orchestral idiom, as in his fine symphonic suite *Vantch* (1932); other works include 14 symphonies.

Knobelsdorff Georg Wenzel von (1699–1753). German architect to Frederick the Great of Prussia, famous as the designer of the Sans-souci Palace and gardens at Potsdam. His other work includes the Opera, Berlin and the E. wing of the Palace at Charlottenburg. His style combines a formal classicism with rich rococo decoration. He was also a landscape and portrait painter.

knop. A slightly flattened swelling in the stem of a glass which joins the foot to the bowl. It is a decorative feature that allows of almost endless variation although a number recur sufficiently often to acquire names. The 'annular' k. is ring-shaped; the 'acorn' is in the shape of an inverted acorn; there are also 'ball', 'cylinder', 'egg', 'dumb-bell' and 'mushroom' shaped k.s.

Knossos Crete. Centre of the Minoan civilization (3rd–2nd millennium B.C.). The Palace of Minos covered over 5 acres and contained numerous halls, ceremonial rooms and staircases, all grouped round a large central courtyard. Frescoes, pottery and clay tablets (inscribed in the Linear A and Linear B scripts) have been among the most important finds. It was excavated from 1900 onwards by Sir Arthur Evans, who also reconstructed it.

Knox John (1505–72). Scottish Protestant religious reformer and virulent preacher. He became the leader of the Scottish Reformation and the first and greatest prose writer in the Scottish vernacular. His fiery prose includes a history of the Scottish Reformation (publ. posth.) and the *First Blast of the Trumpet against the Monstrous Regiment of Women* (1558).

Knyazhnin Yakov Borisovich (1742–91). Russian playwright, mainly notable for his daring treatment of political subjects, e.g. *Vadim of Novgorod.*

Kobayashi Masaki (1916–). Japanese film director. His trilogy of three-hour war films, *The Human Condition* (1958–60), about the fortunes of an unwilling conscript to the Japanese army, achieved fame for going further than any predecessors in depicting the degradation of war.

Kochanowski Jan (1530–84). Polish poet and playwright, the most important writer in early Polish literature. K. travelled in France and Italy and was a courtier, for a time secretary to the king. He wrote poems in Latin and Polish; the latter include lyrical poems, epigrams, *Treny* (1580; *Laments*, 1920) for his dead daughter, Ursula, and a verse rendering of the Psalms.

Köchel Ludwig Alois Ferdinand Ritter von (1800–77). German musicologist (also a botanist and mineralogist) who in 1862 publ. his monumental chronological-thematic catalogue of Mozart's publ. and unpubl. works. When identifying a work by Mozart the Köchel (K.) number is always given.

Kock (Charles) Paul de (1794–1871). French popular novelist who wrote a large number of crude, but comic and exciting stories of Parisian life.

Koczwara (also Kotzwara) Frantisek (*c.* 1750–91). Czech composer of *The Battle Song of Prague*, long a favourite in London and comparable to Beethoven's 'Battle Symphony'.

Kodály Zoltán (1882–). Hungarian composer. He studied at the Budapest Conservatory, taught composition there from 1907 and lectured at Budapest Univ. from 1930. He collaborated with Bartók in collecting and systematizing the folk-music of Hungary, which became the chief influence in his composition, the influence of Brahms being apparent in his earlier works, and also that of Debussy, as in *Nine Pieces for the Piano* (1909–10). K.'s music is not revolutionary but he has used established methods with originality and passion. He shows a preference for vocal and choral music, which includes *Háry János* (1926) and other operas, *Psalmus Hungaricus* (1936) and songs; other works include *Dances of Marosszek* (1930) and *Dances of Galanta* (1933) for orchestra, and chamber music including a sonata for unaccompanied cello (1915).

Koestler Arthur (1905–). Hungarian-born Jewish writer who fled from the Horthy régime to Germany, finally settled in Britain, and has written in the 3 languages. In his equally sudden conversion to and rupture with Communism, and his changing interests – in Zionism, science, mysticism, etc. – K.'s life and work epitomize the 20th-c. European intellectual. Best known of his books is the novel *Darkness at Noon* (1940), an interpretation of the psychology of victims of the Stalinist purges. *The Sleepwalkers* (1964) aims to give an account of the scientific mind at work.

Koffler Józef (1896–1943/4). Polish composer who introduced 12-note composition to his country.

Kokoschka Oskar (1886–). Austrian painter who studied (1905–8) in Vienna, a vital centre of new intellectual currents: Freud, Schoenberg, Kraus, Max Dvořák and Adolph Loos were there and the last three became his friends and patrons. In 1910 he went to Berlin to work on Herwarth Walden's magazine *Der Sturm*. His early graphic work was intensely personal, using a Klimt-like curvilinear calligraphy as an expressionist vehicle, but the majority of his early paintings were the portraits which constitute his major achievement. *Auguste Forel* (1910; Mannheim) is typical in its concentration on head and hands, taut draughtsmanship and in the tattoo-like incisions in the painted surface. The tone of his early work is depressed and cynical and his disgust with reality was heightened by the war. He was injured in 1915. He taught at Dresden Academy (1919–24) and then travelled in Europe, Africa and the Near East. He became a British subject in 1947 and a C.B.E. in 1959.
The intense wiry complexity of his style disappeared into the solid impasto of *Woman in Blue* (1919; Stuttgart), but his real release from reality came with the landscapes: the same panoramic world landscapes that Altdorfer, Bruegel and Turner painted (e.g. *Polperro, Cornwall*, 1939/40; Tate). They have a baroque sense of infinite space and elemental force that is also present in the *Prometheus* triptych (1950; Count Seilern Coll., London).

Kolbe Georg (1877–1947). German sculptor influenced by Rodin. In the best of his figures, e.g. *Dancer* (1912; Berlin), he achieved a remarkable rhythmic beauty lost in the 1930s when he produced 'heroic' works conforming to Nazi ideals.

Arthur Koestler

Zoltán Kodály

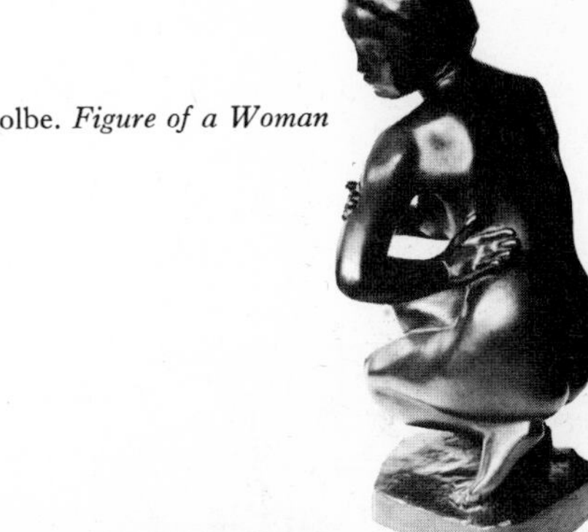

Kolbe. *Figure of a Woman*

Kokoschka. *Herwarth Walden* (1910)

Kokoschka. *Woman in Blue*. See also colour plate 74

Kokoschka. *Thames Landscape* (1956)

Kollwitz. *The Weavers*

Kollwitz. *Killed in Action*; crayon and pencil. Also *charcoal

Konenkov. *Dostoyevsky* (1933)

Kölcsey Ferenc (1790–1838). Hungarian poet and critic. An ardent supporter of Kazinczy's language reform. His *Hymnus* (1823) has been adopted as the Hungarian national anthem; K. also made the first conscious adaptations of folk-poetry.

Kollwitz Käthe (1867–1945) .German graphic artist, sculptor and draughtsman. Her experiences as a doctor's wife in a poor district of Berlin during and after World War I resulted in her best-known work–drawings, lithographs and engravings, chiefly of the sufferings of women and children. Examples of her engraving include: 6 subjects from Gerhart Hauptmann's play *The Weavers* (exhibited 1898), *Peasants War* cycle (1902–8), and *Run Over* (1910); the posters–*Never Again War!*, *Bread*, *Children Starving* (all 1924); the woodcuts–*War* cycle (1922–3); the lithographs–*Death* cycle (finished 1936); and the sculptures–*Father* and *Mother* (1931), Roggevelde Cemetery, Flanders.

Koltsov Alexey Vasilyevich (1809–42). Russian poet. Many of his poems in the style of folk-songs enjoyed long and wide popularity among the people.

Komarov Matvey (18th c.). Russian author of adventure stories widely circulated as chapbooks.

Konenkov Sergey (1874–). One of the best-known Russian sculptors; he spent many years in the U.S. before returning again to Moscow after World War II. Many of his best-known works are executed in wood or plaster such as his bust of Paganini in the Tretyakov Gal. Of the generation of Vrubel and the symbolists, K. later came to work in a more classical tradition.

Koninck Philips (1619–88). Dutch painter, probably a pupil of Rembrandt. His portraits and genre subjects in the manner of Brouwer are undistinguished but he is justly famous for his panoramic views of low-lying country under an expanse of sky, e.g. *Landscape in Gelderland* (N.G., London). His drawings have been confused with those of Rembrandt, as have those of Salomon K. (1609–56), a distant relative, painter of genre and Biblical subjects in a Rembrandtesque style.

Konrad von Regensburg. German poet whose *Rolandslied*, based on the French *Chanson de Roland*, was written about 1170.

Konrad von Soest (late 14th–15th c.). German painter in the soft style active in Dortmund from 1394. A signed polyptych in Niederwildungen parish church is his major work.

Konrad von Würzburg (d. 1287). The last important writer of Middle High German literature. His best work is in the shorter romances, *Das Herzemaere* and *Engelhard*, but he also wrote a number of religious poems such as *Die goldene Schmiede*, in honour of the Virgin Mary, and the vast and formless epic *Der Trojanerkrieg*.

Kops Bernard (1926–). English playwright; his works include *The Hamlet of Stepney Green* (1958) and *The Dream of Peter Mann* (1960).

Korda Sir Alexander (1893–1956). Hungarian-born film producer and director. After working in Hollywood and Europe, K. became famous with *The Private Life of Henry VIII* (1933), with Charles Laughton. It was the 1st big British success in the American market, and set the British film industry on its 1st disastrous cycle of prestige pictures. After the war, K.'s British Lion Corporation was involved in a 2nd similar disaster. This was wound up and taken out of his hands in 1954.

Körner Theodor (1791–1813). German poet and dramatist, son of Schiller's close friend, Judge Christian Gottfried K. He died fighting in the German wars of liberation and his patriotic songs and poems, publ. posth. by his father as *Leyer und Schwert* (1814; *The Lyre and the Sword*, 1834), enjoyed a great occasional reputation.

Korngold Erich Wolfgang (1897–1957). Austrian composer who became a U.S. citizen in 1943. The pantomime *Der Schneeman* was performed in 1910 but K.'s gifts declined although the opera *Die tote Stadt* (1920) had wide success; he wrote much film music.

Korolenko Vladimir Galatikonovich (1853–1921). Russian writer of Polish origin, a life-long Socialist who endured arrest and exile. Most of his energies were devoted to progressive journalism, but in stories like *Makar's*

Koninck. *Extensive Landscape with Hawking Party*

Konrad von Soest. Detail from the Niederwildungen polyptych

Sergei Koussevitzky

Dream (1885; 1891) his message is that poverty and injustice are responsible for the crimes of men, who are fundamentally good. *The History of my Contemporary* (1906–22) is an autobiography of historical interest.

Kósa György (1897–). Hungarian composer and pianist; his teachers included Bartók and Dohnányi. K.'s music has been affected by Schoenberg's expressionism and 12-note technique and influenced by Bartók. His works include: 6 operas; 6 symphonies and 6 pieces for orchestra; church and chamber music and many expressive songs.

Koster Henry (1905–). German-born U.S. film director. K. worked as a script writer and director in Europe before moving to Hollywood as a director in 1936. He specialized in comedies and musicals, but in 1953 directed *The Robe*, the 1st film in Cinemascope. Thereafter K. mainly made turgid dramas until the success of *Mr Hobbs takes a Vacation* (1962) set him on a new series of comedies.

Kosztoiányi Dezsö (1885–1936). Hungarian writer of the *Nyugat* (*Ady) generation. His sensitive poetry reveals a restless spirit baffled by life. His novels include *A véres költö* (1921; *Nero, the Bloody poet,* 1927) and the psychologically perceptive story of a servant girl *Édes Anna* (1926; *Wonder Maid,* 1947).

Kotzebue August von (1761–1819). German dramatist of mediocre talent, prolific output and vast European reputation; 88 of his plays were produced at Weimar under *Goethe's management. Travels in Russia and the Czar's favour led to K. becoming a paid Russian agent; his assassination by the student Revolutionary Karl Sand precipitated Metternich's Carlsbad Decrees.

Koundouros Nikos (1926–). Greek film director. Less famous than Cacoyannis, K. is perhaps the most interesting director working in Greece, even on the strength of *Young Aphrodites* (1963), his latest and, apparently, least good film. His best-known film is *The Ogre of Athens* (1956).

Koussevitzky Sergei Alexandrovich (1874–1951). Russian conductor, initially a double-bass virtuoso. In 1904 he founded an orchestra which toured Russia. He conducted a series of concerts in Paris in 1921 and became conductor of the Boston Symphony Orchestra in 1924. He conducted many première performances of works by Ravel, Stravinsky, Prokofiev and others He founded the K. Music Foundation to finance commissions of works from contemporary composers.

Kozeluch Leopold Anton (1752–1818). Czech composer and pianist of European fame. K.'s works, predominantly *galante in style, are influenced by Mozart but also contain premonitions of Schubertian romanticism. His large output includes: about 30 symphonies; 13 piano concertos; 57 piano trios and much church music. His uncle JOHANN ANTON K. (1738–1814) was also a composer and Leopold's teacher.

Kozintzev Grigori (1905–). Russian film director. With *Yutkevitch and *Trauberg, founded in 1922 FEKS, a group whose sources were circus, music-hall and *avant-garde* theatre. K. and Trauberg made 4 films at FEKS: *The New Babylon* (1929) was an historical film on the Paris Commune. They also made the *Maxim* trilogy (1935–9), like the later *Donskoi trilogy, about Gorky. In 1957 K alone made a *Don Quixote.*

Krafft Adam (d. 1509). German late Gothic sculptor in stone. Almost all his work is in Nuremberg including his masterpiece, the 62-ft-high tabernacle in the church of St Lawrence, and the Schreyer monument, St Sebald's church.

Kraft Anton (1749–1820). German cellist for whom Haydn wrote his cello concerto and Beethoven the cello part in his triple concerto. K. also composed; he was formerly credited with Haydn's concerto. K.'s son NIKOLAUS (1778–1853) was also a virtuoso cellist and composer.

Krak des Chevaliers Syria. The best-preserved and one of the largest of medieval castles. It was built in the mid 12th c. by the Knights Hospitallers as a frontier defence against the Saracens, and consists of a double ring of massive walls and towers. This concentric system (derived from the walls of Constantinople) was introduced into Europe by the Crusaders and from the 13th c. to the introduction of artillery was the standard method of fortification. K. was taken by the Saracens in 1271.

Krafft. *Self-portrait*; supporting figure, St Sebald's

Krak des Chevaliers

Fritz Kreisler

The Kremlin: view of the S. wall, showing defence towers and cathedrals

Kramer. Marlene Dietrich and Spencer Tracy in *Judgement at Nuremberg*

Krater (Italian, *c.* 440–430 B.C.), showing a procession in honour of Apollo

Kramer Stanley (1913–). U.S. film producer and director. After working for M.G.M. and for Columbia as a producer, K. has become an independent. As producer of *High Noon* and *The Wild One*, etc., he was associated with some black-listed artists like *Foreman and *Dymtryk, but saved himself quickly and set up in 1955 as producer/director of a number of earnest films like *The Defiant Ones* (1958). In 1962, he also resumed as a producer, and for *Cassavetes and *Cornfield a very repressive producer. In 1963 he directed an indefatigable comedy *It's a Mad, Mad, Mad, Mad World* in Cinerama.

Krapp's Last Tape (1959). Play by Samuel *Beckett.

Krasicki Ignacy (1735–1801). Polish writer who became archbishop of Gniezno, a typical 18th-c. figure, combining rationalism and moderate scepticism with humour, irony and kindliness. He wrote fables, satires and mock-heroic poems in an elegant, highly polished style modelled on classical and French authors. His *Mikołaja Doświadczyńskiego przypadki* (1776) is in effect the 1st Polish novel.

Krasiński Zygmunt (1812–59). Polish romantic poet, playwright and novelist. At the age of 23 he publ. his masterpiece, the prose drama *Nieboska komedja* (1835; *The Undivine Comedy*, 1924); written in short concentrated scenes, it envisaged the class conflict of the future. His next play, *Irydion* (1836; *Iridion*, 1927), set in 3rd-c. Rome, argues the futility of vengeance. After *c.* 1840 K. devoted all his creative energies to an ideology which attributed to Poland a Messianic role.

Kraszewski Józef Ignacy (1812–87). Polish novelist, poet, critic, playwright, historian and journalist; one of the most prolific of Polish writers. He played a vital role in the development of the Polish novel, writing on Polish peasant life, the landed gentry, historical themes and on the individual and society.

krater. A large bowl from 12 to 18 ins high with a wide mouth and 2 small handles, used in ancient Greece for mixing wine. Besides their use at table, these bowls were also used in funeral and marriage ceremonial. The shape varied considerably and k.s were normally decorated. They were produced between the 9th and 4th cs B.C., narrowing in shape during this period.

Krauss Clemens (1893–1954). Austrian conductor; director of the Vienna State Opera (1929–34), of the Berlin State Opera (1935), intendant of the Bavarian opera (1937–44), and reorganizer of the Salzburg Mozarteum.

Krebs Johann Ludwig (1713–80). German organist and composer; pupil of his father Johann Tobias K. (1690–1762) and for 9 years of J. S. Bach who gave him a dazzling testimonial. His organ compositions sometimes approach the grandeur of his master's.

Kreisler Fritz (1875–1962). Austrian violinist, renowned for the brilliance and elegance of his playing, and composer. He studied in Vienna and Paris and settled in America in 1940. His compositions include: operettas, a string quartet, and violin pieces, some of which he publ. under the names of 17th- and 18th-c. composers.

Kremlin Moscow. The original 'Acropolis' of Moscow, now a large triangular area surrounded by high walls. No extant building in it is earlier than the 15th c. Ivan III (1462–1505) had his new fortress laid out by Italian architects, who took the Castello Sforzesco, Milan, as their model, with high battlements and monumental gate-towers; inside he built the churches of the Dormition and the Archangel Michael–also by Italians but in a Byzantine style and decorated by native artists–and the Annunciation, by a Russian. The Faceted Palace (1635) is by Ruffo and Solario. Later Czars introduced the classical style (Catherine II's Senate House by Kazakov) and the neo-Russian-Byzantine (Nicholas I's Great Palace by the German architect K. Thon).

Krenek (Křenek) Ernst (1900–). Austrian composer who settled in the U.S. (1938) and took U.S. citizenship (1945). As assistant to P. Bekker at Kassel opera K. wrote stage music of all kinds and the success of his 'jazz opera' *Johnny Spielt auf* (1927) enabled him to devote himself to studying musical theory. Contacts with Berg and Webern strengthened K.'s development towards 12-note techniques. K.'s compositions include: the operas *Leben des Orest* (1930), the 12-note *Karl V* (1938), *Dark Waters* (1950); 5 symphonies and symphonic music for 9 solo instruments.

Kreutzer Rodolphe. (1766–1831). German composer and violinist to whom Beethoven dedicated his violin sonata op. 47; inspired by this, *Tolstoy wrote his story *The Kreutzer Sonata*, which in turn inspired Janáček to write his string quintet of that name.

Kreutzer Sonata, The (1889). Novel by Tolstoy.

Kreymborg Alfred (1883–). U.S. poet and ed., one of the founders of the modern little magazine movement. K. started *The Glebe* (1913), which publ. the work of Pound, William Carlos Williams, Joyce and others; *Others* (1914–19); and *Broom* (1921–4). K.'s poems include the coll. *Mushrooms* (1916); he has also written novels and verse plays.

Krieger Adam (1634–66). German composer, poet and organist at Leipzig and, from 1657, at the court of Dresden; he was a pupil of S. Scheidt. His colls of *Lieder* with instrumental ritornelli, *Arien* (1657) and *Neuen Arien* (posth. 1667 and 1676), evince a fresh and varied melodic gift and establish K. as the master of the baroque *Lied*.

Krieger Johann (1652–1735). Brother of J. P. K.; considered by Handel 'one of the best writers of his time for the organ'. The fugues in K.'s *Anmuthige Clavier-Übung* (1698) contain elements foreshadowing J. S. Bach's methods, and his *Sechs Musicalische Partien* (1697) expand the *Froberger suite by an additional dance group. K. wrote numerous arias and cantatas.

Krieger Johann Philipp (1649–1725). German composer. Early in his career he made a 2-year visit to Italy but thereafter worked at German courts. A major German composer of his time, K. introduced French and Italian techniques into his instrumental music, e.g. the trio sonata of Corelli. He also wrote German operas and church music.

Krieghoff Cornelius (*c.* 1812–72). German- or Dutch-born Canadian painter; from the 1840s he painted colourful landscapes and anecdotal scenes, mainly of French-Canadian life in Quebec.

Kriemhild's Revenge–Die Nibelungen part 2 (1924). Film directed by F. *Lang.

Krimpen Jan van (1892–1958). Dutch typographical adviser and type-designer to one of the finest firms of typefounder-printers of this c., Enschedé and Zonen, Holland, for whom he designed an extremely graceful roman, Lutetia (1923–4), and accompanying italic and swash letters. K. also designed some fine Greek types and 2 other roman types, Romulus (1931), for bookwork, and Spectrum (1941–3), which was specially commissioned for a Bible.

Kruchonykh Alexey Yeliseyevich (1886–). Russian poet, a cubo-futurist who, like *Khlebnikov, wrote 'trans-sense' poems.

krumhorn. Old musical woodwind instrument; it is a tube about 20 ins long curved at the end and having finger-holes. Like the oboe it is played with a double reed but this is blown through a reed cap and does not enter the player's mouth.

Krylov Ivan Andreyevich (1769–1844). Russian fabulist whose chequered career ended peacefully when he was given a sinecure at the St Petersburg public library–a reward for his *Fables* (1st ed. 1809; trs. 1869), which are the Russian classics in this genre. Some are trs of Aesop and La Fontaine, but most are original and completely Russian in spirit. Written in more colloquial language than was then usual, they were immediately popular, and many lines became proverbs.

Kschessinskaya Mathilde (Princess Krassinska) (1872–). Russian dancer and teacher who studied at the Imperial School, St Petersburg and was made prima ballerina assoluta at the Maryinsky (1895), a title bestowed only twice in the theatre's history. She was the 1st Russian to perform the 32 fouettés and to challenge the technically brilliant Italian ballerinas.

Kubelik Jan (1880–1940). Czech-born violinist and composer whose works include violin concertos and an *American Symphony* (1937). His son RAPHAEL (1914–) is a distinguished conductor; since 1950 he has worked much in England and the U.S., since 1955 at the Covent Garden Royal Opera House.

Kubin Alfred (1877–1959). Austrian painter and graphic artist associated with the Blaue Reiter group. His choice of subject-matter particularly in his graphic work of the early 1900s

Rodolphe Kreutzer

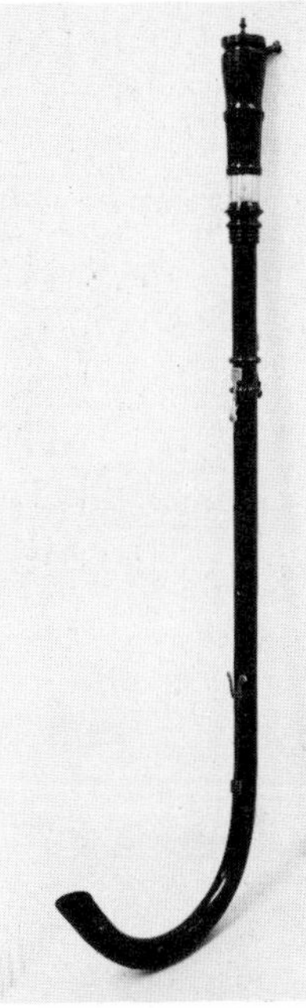

Modern German bass krumhorn, based on early models

Krylov (left) with the writers Pushkin, Zhukovsky and Gnedich; painting (1832) by Chernetsov

Kubin. *Kriegsruf* (1922)

Kubrick. Sterling Hayden and Peter Sellers in *Dr Strangelove*

Kuhnau. *Neue Clavier–Übung*: frontispiece with the composer's portrait

was grotesque, even repulsive. He wrote and illustrated a surrealistic novel *Die andere Seite* (1909) which led him to concentrate on book illustration, e.g. works by Poe, Nerval, d'Aurevilly and Dostoyevsky.

Kubla Khan (1816). Poem by S. T. *Coleridge.

Kubrick Stanley (1928–). U.S. film director. A journalist who had made amateur movies on 16 mm, he acted as producer, writer, photographer, editor as well as director on his first films, *Fear and Desire* (1953) and a remarkable thriller, *Killer's Kiss* (1955). His critical reputation springs from an elaborately constructed crime movie, *The Killing* (1956), and from *Paths of Glory* (1958) about a particularly inglorious military incident in World War I. After a spectacular, *Spartacus*, on which he finished work begun by Anthony *Mann, he moved to Britain for an adaptation of *Nabokov's *Lolita*. *Dr Strangelove* (1963) is a comedy which carries the grotesque elements in *Lolita* over into sick farce.

Kulmbach. *Martyrdom of St Catherine*

Küchelbecker Wilhelm Karlovich (1797–1846). Russian poet, a school-fellow and friend of Pushkin. He spent 20 years in prison and Siberian exile for his part in the Decembrist Conspiracy of 1825. Apart from an elegy on the death of Pushkin, K.'s poetry is spoiled by its overblown romanticism.

Kuhlau Friedrich Daniel Rudolph (1786–1832). German-born composer who settled in Copenhagen writing largely for the stage, e.g. the music to J. L. Heiberg's play *Elverhøj* (1828), but also chamber music. On a visit to Vienna (1825) he swapped champagne and canons with Beethoven. K. is remembered mainly for his sonatas for piano, used universally for beginners.

Kuhnau Johann (1660–1722). German composer and scholar and J. S. Bach's predecessor at St Thomas's, Leipzig. His keyboard music, e.g. *Neue Clavier–Übung* (1689, 92) and *Frischer Clavier Früchter* (1696), adapts the Italian trio sonata to the keyboard producing a sonata of movements as opposed to a suite. His Biblical sonatas were among the first solo keyboard sonatas in the modern sense; they were programmatic in intent, each one describing a different Biblical story, and each movement a different scene.

Kuleshov Lev (1899–). Russian film director. K. started making films in 1917. In 1922 he founded an *avant-garde* group called Experimental Workshop, where Barnett and Pudovkin studied with him, and put to the test his theories concerning the emotional potential of montage.

Kulmbach Hans Süss von (*c.* 1480–1522). German painter, pupil of Jacopo de' Barbari and follower of Dürer. He worked in Nuremberg and probably for a time in Cracow, Poland. His works include the Tucher altarpiece designed by Dürer in St Sebald's church, Nuremberg, altarpieces in churches in Cracow, *Adoration of the Magi* (Dahlem Mus., Berlin) and portraits.

Kuniyoshi Yasuo (1893–1953). Japanese-born U.S. painter. His early work combines fantasy with covert humour in a way which recalls Chagall. In the 1930s he turned to figure studies, chiefly of languorous women sensitively drawn and coloured, showing the

Kuniyoshi. *Fishermen* (1924)

Kupka. *Architecture philosophique* (1913)

Kusnetsov. *Holiday* (*c.* 1906). Also *Blue Rose group

influence of Pascin, whom he met in Paris. His late work has an imaginative and colouristic intensity closer in spirit to his earlier period.

Künstlerroman (German, 'artist novel'). Novel describing the life and development of a writer, painter, etc.

Kupetzky Johann (1667–1740). Portrait painter of Czech origin who lived for many years in Italy, then worked as court painter at Vienna and finally settled in Nuremberg.

Kupka Frantisek (1871–1957). Czech painter who arrived in Paris (1894) via the academies of Prague and Vienna. He is historically important for the paintings he made *c.* 1910. These reveal the emancipation of pure colour areas from any descriptive role and are among the first abstract paintings in Paris, probably preceding and inspiring the similar developments in Delaunay's painting. From 1931 he was connected with the Abstraction-Création group in Paris.

Kurosawa Akira (1910–). Japanese film director. K. is best known in the West for his period action films: in 1951 his *Rashomon* was the 1st Japanese film to win a grand prix at the Venice Film Festival. He has been strongly influenced by American westerns, especially in *The Seven Samurai* (1954). *Living* (1952) is a present-day study of an old man dying of cancer, told with dignity. K. is ambitious in his sources: *The Idiot* (1951) from Dostoyevsky, *The Lower Depths* (1958) from Gorky. *Throne of Blood* (1956) is an interpretation of *Macbeth* in a Japanese setting.

Kurz Hermann (1813–73). German writer and trs., a friend of Mörike. He wrote the 2 outstanding historical novels, *Schillers Heimatjahre* (1843) and *Der Sonnenwirt* (1854), poetry and trs from Shakespeare, Byron and Ariosto.

Kusnetsov Pavel (1878–). Soviet painter, a founder-member of the Blue Rose group and with Saryan its most distinguished artist. His most characteristic works depict the Kirghiz people and countryside such as *Mirage in the Steppes* (1912) painted in a symbolist blue-green palette; in later years his colours have become brilliant and his subjects less exotic. He lives in Moscow.

Kuzmin Mikhail Alexeyevich (1875–1936). Russian symbolist poet. K.'s works include the poems *Songs of Alexandria* (1906) and *Seasons of Love* (1907) and the novel *Wings* (1907).

Kyasht Lydia (1885–1959). Russian dancer and pupil of Gerdt at the Imperial School, St Petersburg, who graduated in 1902. She came to England and founded her own co. in 1939, Ballet de la Jeunesse Anglaise, whose aim was to provide a platform for new talent and ballets. The co. disbanded in 1946.

Kyd (or Kid) Thomas (1558–94). English dramatist. K. provided the prototype of Elizabethan revenge tragedy with his notoriously successful play *The Spanish Tragedy* (*c.* 1585). It exceeds its model Seneca in lurid sensationalism, yet made important advances in construction and psychological approach to character. K. may have written the earlier *Hamlet*, no longer extant, which was the basis of Shakespeare's play.

Kyrie: *mass

Kurosawa. *Rashomon*

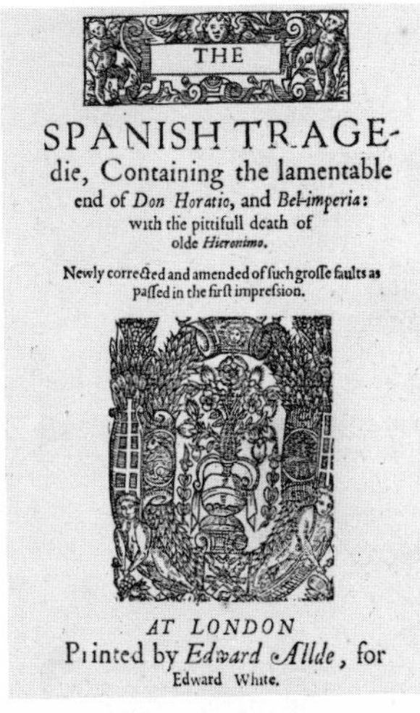

THE

SPANISH TRAGE-
die, Containing the lamentable
end of *Don Horatio*, and *Bel-imperia*:
with the pittifull death of
olde *Hieronimo*.

Newly corrected and amended of such grosse faults as
passed in the first impression.

AT LONDON
Printed by *Edward Allde*, for
Edward White.

Kyd. 1st extant ed. of *The Spanish Tragedy* (1592?)

Bobbin lace, showing the '*réseau*'; English, mid 19th c.

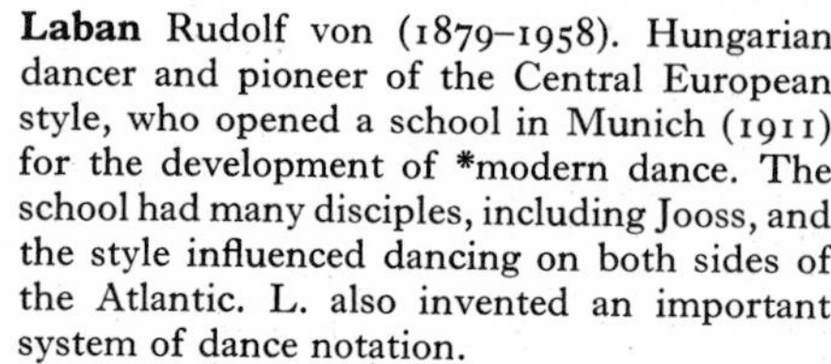

La Bruyère

English needlepoint lace of the early 17th c.

Brussels bobbin lace, mid 19th c.

Lace. Venetian *gros point*; mid 17th c.

A Bruges lace worker

Laban Rudolf von (1879–1958). Hungarian dancer and pioneer of the Central European style, who opened a school in Munich (1911) for the development of *modern dance. The school had many disciples, including Jooss, and the style influenced dancing on both sides of the Atlantic. L. also invented an important system of dance notation.

Là-bas (1891). Novel by J.-K. *Huysmans.

Labé Louise (*c.* 1525–65). French poet, '*la belle cordière*', who wrote lyrical poems about unfulfilled love. According to tradition, when she was still a girl she dressed as a soldier and went to the wars.

Labiche Eugène-Marin (1815–88). Prolific and popular French writer of farces, usually in collaboration, including *Un Chapeau de paille d'Italie* (1851; *An Italian Straw Hat*, 1956), the basis for R. *Clair's film; *La Grammaire* (1867; *Cabbages and Culture*, 1957) and *29° a' l'ombre* (1873; *90° in the Shade*, 1962).

La Boétie Étienne de (1530–63). French writer. L.'s treatise *Contr'un* or *Discours de la servitude volontaire* (posth. 1576; 1735) attacks tyranny. He was the close friend of Montaigne, who often refers in his essays to their intimacy.

Labroca Mario (1896–). Italian composer and music critic; pupil of Respighi and Malipiero. His music is influenced both by the neo-classicism of Casella and folk-music.

La Bruyère Jean de (1645–96). French writer, trained as a lawyer, who entered the household of the prince de Condé as a tutor; he evidently became embittered by his lack of advancement. His *Caractères de Théophraste traduits du grec* (1688; *The Characters, or the Manners of the Age*..., 1699) contained a trs. of *Theophrastus with some of B.'s essays appended. These were enlarged in subsequent eds, and the final version (1694) is a sizeable book of portraits of contemporary types, essays and aphorisms. L. wrote a terse, direct and ironic prose; he satirizes institutions as well as individual vices, and takes the part of the writers of antiquity in the *Ancients and Moderns Controversy.

La Calprenède Gauthier de Costes de (1610–63). French novelist and playwright. His long historical romances were much admired and many were trs. into English within a few years. L.'s plays include *Ieanne, reyne d'Angleterre* (publ. 1638), about Lady Jane Grey, and *Le Comte Dessex* (publ. 1639), the story of Elizabeth I and Essex.

La Cava Gregory (1892–1949). U.S. film director. Although L. directed films from 1924 to 1947, and made non-comic movies, he is remembered as a director of 1930s comedies, with all the talent for directing actors that this implies. His most famous films were *My Man Godfrey* (1936) and *Stage Door* (1937).

lace. A fabric used principally for decorative purposes on female and previously also male dress. In one form it consists of a fine mesh background, called the '*réseau*' on which are worked, or to which are attached, decorative motifs. The mesh, before the introduction of machine-made net in the early 19th c., was made with bobbins, the lace maker working on a pillow. In the manufacture of BOBBIN LACE the pillow is stuck with rows of pins, and threads attached to bobbins are woven round these pins to form the fine mesh and sometimes form motifs.

In NEEDLEPOINT LACE the individual decorative motifs are worked with needle and thread over a design, drawn on paper, attached to the pillow: a type of open looped stitch is employed. The motif is next detached from the cushion to which it has been fixed for ease of working by loose anchoring threads. Motifs are joined together, either in the hand, or more usually on the cushion over the design with a series of elaborated buttonholed bars or 'brides'. Traditionally needlepoint was first practised in Italy, then in Spain, whence it spread to Flanders. The richest type is the padded rose point, or raised Venice point ('*gros point de Venise*') of the 16th and 17th cs.

Lach Robert (1874–1958). Austrian composer and musicologist. His music is late romantic in idiom, his major book is *Studien zur Entwicklungsgeschichte der ornamentalen Melopoie* (1913), a 'biology' of music.

Lachaise Gaston (1882–1935). French sculptor who emigrated to the U.S. in 1906. He is known chiefly for his imposing female nudes of exaggerated but balanced proportions. Famous examples are his versions of *Standing Woman* (1912–27, Whitney Mus.; 1932, M.M.A.; both New York).

La Chaussée Pierre-Claude Nivelle de (1692–1754). French playwright, the creator of the *comédie larmoyante*, in which pathos is mingled with comedy. L.'s plays include *Mélanide* (1741) and *Paméla* (1743), an adaptation from Richardson.

Lachner Franz (1803–90). South German composer in the tradition of Schubertian romanticism. His vast output includes: 8 symphonies, operas, oratorios, chamber music, etc. His brothers IGNAZ (1807–95) and VINCENZ (1811–93) were also composers.

Laclos Pierre Choderlos de (1741–1803). French novelist; an artillery officer, ultimately a Revolutionary general. His only work, *Les Liaisons dangereuses* (1782; 1784), an epistolary novel, gives an account of 2 cold-blooded seducers, the Vicomte de Valmont and Mme de Merteuil, who are indifferent to the suffering they inflict, and whose real pleasure lies in the manipulation of difficulties. L. is completely detached; hence, in spite of the perfunctory punishment of the seducers, the novel created a scandal. The development of the story and the analysis of character under stress (especially the gradual collapse of the besieged women's defences) are masterly.

lacquer. Properly refers only to the resin of the lac tree, nowadays found only in S. China, Vietnam, Korea and Japan, but can refer to any resin which hardens on application and has high resistance to heat, water and acids. It can be used as paint or, on a base of wood or textile, to form solid vessels and even furniture; it is a kind of natural plastic. Mixed with dye, coloured l. paints are used on vessels of l. or other materials. The Chinese of the 3rd c. B.C. to 3rd c. A.D. first excelled in the production of l. with painted designs, but most popular are *Ming Chinese furniture and vessels with carved relief in floral or pictorial designs in red, or layered with strata of variously coloured l. By the 15th c. the Japanese had learned and excelled Chinese craftsmen in the art of l. application and carving. The technique came to Europe in the mid 17th c. and quantities of the material were long imported from the East, either made up as boxes or screens, or as panels for furniture. Spa in Belgium and Usk and Pontypool in Wales were centres of production.

Lacretelle Jacques de (1888–). French novelist. His books include *Silbermann* (1922; 1923), the 4-part *Les Haut-Ponts* (1932–5) and *Le Pour et le contre* (1946).

Ladd Alan (1913–1964). U.S. film actor. His 1st real success was in *This Gun for Hire* (1942); most of his subsequent films were unremarkable, except *Shane* (1952), but he remained a reliable, 'tough' box-office star until his early death.

Ladder of Perfection, The. Mystical work by Walter Hilton.

Ladmirault Paul-Émile (1877–1944). Breton composer whose sensitive music, praised by Debussy, evokes the atmosphere of his native province.

Lady and the Fool, The. 1-act ballet with choreography by Cranko, music from Verdi, arranged by Mackerras, and décor by Beer; 1st performance 1954.

Lady and the Unicorn (Cluny Mus. Paris). Set of 6 tapestries showing a lady with a lion and a unicorn, which bear the arms of the Le Viste family. 5 of the tapestries are believed to represent the 5 senses, the 6th is entitled *À mon Seul désir*; the tapestries were possibly made for the marriage of Claude Le Viste and Jean de Chabannes in 1513 though the date and place of manufacture are unknown.

Lady chapel. In a cathedral or large church, a chapel dedicated to the Virgin Mary, either E. of the chancel or, in a smaller church, at the E. end of an aisle.

Lady Chatterley's Lover (1928). Novel by D. H. *Lawrence.

Lady from the Sea, The (1888). Play by *Ibsen.

Lady in the Lake, The (1946). Film directed by R. *Montgomery.

Lady into Fox. 3-scene ballet with choreography by A. Howard, music by Honegger and décor by Nadia Benois; 1st performance 1939. From the novel (1922) by David *Garnett.

Lady of Shalott, The (1882). Poem by Tennyson.

Lady's Not for Burning, The (1948). Verse play by Christopher Fry.

Cup and stand in red lacquer; Chinese, Ming Dynasty

Imperial throne in red lacquer; Ming

The Lady and the Unicorn: *À mon Seul désir*

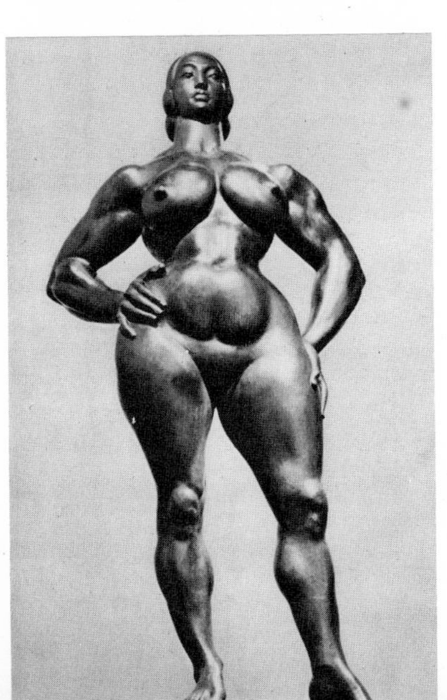

Lachaise.
Standing Woman (1932)

Mme de La Fayette

Laer.
Outside the inn

Lady Vanishes, The (1938). Film directed by A. *Hitchcock.

Lady Windermere's Fan (1892). Play by Oscar Wilde.

Lady with a Little Dog, The (1960). Film directed by J. *Heifitz, based on the short story by Chekhov.

Laer Pieter van (nicknamed 'Bamboccio', Italian 'bonny baby') (d. 1642). Dutch painter who spent most of his working life in Rome specializing in the scenes of low life which influenced many Dutch artists. *bambocciata.

Laethem-Saint-Martin. Belgian village with which 2 groups of 20th-c. artists have been associated. The first was a symbolist group led by Valerius de Saedeleer (1867–1947) and Gustaaf van de Woestijne (1881–1947) the second and more important an expressionist group represented by van den *Berghe, *Permeke and Gustave de *Smet.

La Farge John (1835–1910). U.S. painter, designer and writer on art; of French parentage. He studied in Paris under T. Couture and visited England, coming under the influence of the Pre-Raphaelites. Back in the U.S. he concentrated on mural decoration and stained-glass work.

La Farge. *Aurora*; stained-glass window

La Fayette Marie-Madeleine, comtesse de (1634–93). French novelist who separated from her husband and settled in Paris (1659) where she moved in the best society. She lived with La *Rochefoucauld from 1665; his share in her work is uncertain.
L.'s novels (publ. anon.) are short, lucidly and economically written studies of character under stress, the first of their type in French and a complete departure from the diffuse and exaggerated romances then prevalent. In *La Princesse de Clèves* (1678; 1688) the heroine never yields to her love for the Duc de Nemours, although her firmness brings her no happiness. L. also wrote *La Princesse de Montpensier* (1662; 1666); *La Comtesse de Tende* (1724); and a coll. of stories, *Zaÿde* (1670; 1678).

La Fontaine

La Fontaine Jean de (1621–95). French writer. Enjoying the constant generosity of such patrons as Fouquet and Madame de la Sablière, he matured late then spent a leisurely 30 years producing his *Contes* (1665–74), and the 12 books of the *Fables*, which were publ. in 3 instalments: 1668, 1678–9, 1694 (trs. 1734). Like his contemporaries, La F. acknowledged two masters, nature and antiquity; thus his ideas were sometimes commonplace, and his subjects were traditional, being drawn from Aesop, Phaedrus, Pilpay, Marot, Rabelais and others. Yet the choice of the fable, a form little exploited and therefore still flexible, as a vehicle for poetry, indicated not only originality but also versatility.
The *Fables* present both the human comedy and a picture of contemporary life, brilliantly disguised as the animal world of the French countryside, in a series of dramatic sketches, where tragedy, comedy, realism, lyricism, elegy and anecdote are intermingled. La F.'s epicurean concern for pleasure was well served by his sure taste and acute observation; while his delicate irony and discreet sensibility combined to produce a lyricism quite exceptional in this 'age of reason'. His poetry is also characterized by an unusually rich vocabulary, full of archaisms and regional terms.
The moral doctrines of the *Fables* are practical and secular, closely resembling those of the playwright Molière.

Laforgue Jules (1860–87). French poet. Born at Montevideo, educated at Tarbes in the Pyrenees, came to Paris in 1876 but worked in Berlin from 1881. He returned to Paris on his marriage (1886) but died within a year. The tone of L.'s verse is one of calculated irony: he is important because his experiments in free verse considerably influenced the succeeding generation of French poets and also T. S. Eliot in England. *Les Complaintes* (1885), *L'Imitation de Notre-Dame de la Lune* (1886), *Le Concile féerique* (1886) were his principal colls of verse.

La Fresnaye Roger de (1885–1925). French painter, studied in Paris at the Académie Julian (1903), the École des Beaux-Arts and the Académie Ranson (1908), where he met Denis and Sérusier. Their influence was succeeded by Cézanne's, which prepared him for cubism. He exhibited with the other cubist painters in 1911 and at the Section d'Or of 1912, without ever really subscribing to cubist principles. In paintings such as *La Conquête de l'Air* (1913; M.M.A., New York) he adopted the superficial manner of cubism–particularly its structural clarity–to suit traditional requirements.

La Fresnaye.
La Conquête de l'Air

Laguerre. Wall paintings on the staircase at Petworth, Sussex

A very accomplished painter, he was the 1st 'academic' in the new idiom.

Lagerkvist Pär (1891–). One of the most versatile and prolific of Swedish writers and Nobel prizewinner (1951). His best-known work is the novel *Barabbas* (1950; 1952) but he has also written the autobiographical *Gäst hos verkligheten* (1925; *Guest of Reality*, 1936), poems and short stories.

Lagerlöf Selma (Ottiliana Louisa) (1858–1940). Swedish novelist and Nobel prizewinner (1909). Her books on historical, Biblical and mythical themes include: *Gösta Berlings Saga* (1891; 1898) set in the Napoleonic Wars, and *Jerusalem* (1902; 1915), dealing with a group of Swedish peasants who settled in Palestine in the 1890s.

Laguerre Louis (1663–1721). French painter who worked under C. Lebrun before settling in England as assistant to A. Verrio. He executed decorative work at several of England's greatest houses.

La Hire (Hyre) Laurent de (1606–56). French painter of religious subjects and landscape. The Caravaggesque style of his work up to 1640 probably derived from Vouet as he did not himself visit Italy; in his later work he followed Poussin.

lai. A medieval French verse form, being a short narrative or lyric poem, in lines of 8 syllables.

Laing Hugh (1911–). British dancer who studied under Rambert and Preobrajenska and danced many leading roles for Marie Rambert's Ballet Club, as well as designing the décor for their *Judgement of Paris* (1938). He settled in the U.S., joining Ballet Theater on its foundation (1940).

Lajtha László (1892–). Hungarian composer, conductor, folk-song coll. (he worked with Bartók and Kodály) and professor of folk-music research at Budapest Music Academy. At first influenced most strongly by Bartók and Hungarian folk-music forms, L.'s work later showed harmonic similarities to Ravel, Dukas and late Debussy. He has written: 3 ballets, including *Lysistrata* (1937); 7 symphonies; much chamber music, including 8 string quartets; and piano music.

Lake Poets. The collective name for the English poets Wordsworth, Coleridge and Southey who lived and worked in the Lake District for a period during the 1790s and early 1800s.

La Lande Michel-Richard de (1657–1726). French composer. He superseded Lully at court when old age and Mme de Maintenon began to direct Louis XIV's attention towards religion. La L. wrote ballets and instrumental music but his greatest work is in his church music, e.g. his 42 motets, *Leçons de ténèbres* and *Miserere*. In these works, it is claimed, he anticipated and influenced Bach and Handel.

Lallans revival. A 20th-c. literary movement in Scotland. It attempted to revitalize the Scots vocabulary, especially 'Lallans' (Lowland Scots dialects), *vis-à-vis* the modern world, and to purge Scottish literature of the homely sentimentality of the *Kailyard school. It is particularly associated with the poetic works of Hugh MacDiarmid, S. G. Smith, Douglas Young and William Soutar.

Lalo Édouard (1823–92). French composer. Although a minor talent, he had a notable strength of expression and was in some ways a forerunner of the new school in French music represented by Fauré, Debussy and Ravel. His works include: the opera *Le roi d'Ys* (1888), a violin concerto, and the well-known *Symphonie espagnole* (1873; actually for cello and orchestra).

Lam Wilfredo (1902–). Cuban painter influenced by Picasso and surrealism. His work evokes the savage world of the jungle and the primitive mythology of Cuba. He makes recurrent use of the theme of metamorphosis as in *The Jungle* (1943; M.M.A., New York).

La Marche Olivier de (*c.* 1425–1502). Burgundian chronicler and poet who served the dukes of Burgundy. He wrote *Mémoires* and the allegorical poems *Le Parement et triumphe des dames* and *Le Chevalier délibéré*.

Lamartine Alphonse-Marie-Louis de Prat de (1790–1869). French romantic poet, the son of a landowner. A diplomat (1820–8) and an ardent Republican who was for some years an influential orator, L. became a member of the Revolutionary government (1848) but was crushingly defeated by Louis-Napoleon when he stood for the presidency. His 1st coll., *Les*

Lam. *The Jungle*

Alphonse de Lamartine

Charles Lamb: painting by his friend, the writer William Hazlitt

Lamerie. Silver-gilt sideboard ewer (*left*) and tea-caddy

Méditations poétiques (1820), containing the famous poem *Le Lac*, was a landmark in the development of French romanticism, achieving great popularity by the gentle melancholy of its lyrical evocations of love and nature, and its undercurrent of sentimental religious feeling. Works include the coll. *Les Harmonies poétiques et religieuses* (1830) and the narrative poems *Jocelyn* (1836) and *La Chute d'un ange* (1838).

Lamb Charles (1775–1834). English essayist and critic. He spent 23 years in irksome service as a clerk in the East India Company; his home life was burdened by his decision to look after his sister Mary, who had killed their mother in a fit of insanity. Nevertheless, he made his home a centre for literary London. His *Tales from Shakespear* [*sic*] (1807, with his sister), *Specimens of the English Dramatic Poets* (1808), and his brilliant if limited literary criticism, made his reputation; but his finest work appears in *Elia* (1823) and *Last Essays of Elia* (1833), coll. pieces from *The London Magazine*. Here, by means of archaisms and a delicately mannered style, he infuses his subject with a highly individual charm.

Lambeth dish (1635)

Lambert Constant (1905–51). English composer, conductor and writer. His music includes: the ballets *Romeo and Juliet* (1926), commissioned by Diaghilev, *Horoscope* (1938) and *Tiresias* (1951), and *Les Patineurs*, arranged from Meyerbeer; *Music for Orchestra* (1927) and *The Rio Grande* (1927–9) for piano, chorus and orchestra. L. wrote *Music Ho!: a Study of Music in Decline* (1934).

Lambeth ware. A number of earthenware factories in Lambeth, Vauxhall, Aldgate, Southwark and perhaps other London boroughs manufactured delftware and other tin-glazed earthenware from the late 16th c. (with a certain amount of assistance from Dutch immigrants) to the 18th c. Most of the products were articles for domestic use, decorated with crude, vivid colours in Dutch, Italian or Chinese styles.

Lamentations of Jeremiah. One of the books of the *Bible (Old Testament), acrostic poems lamenting the fall of Jerusalem. In the Roman Catholic Church year, the service of Matins (also called Tenebrae) on the Thursday, Friday and Saturday of Holy Week takes its 1st lesson from this book. Of the many polyphonic settings, those of Vittoria, Tallis and R. White must be mentioned, and the 1- and 2-part settings *Leçons de Ténèbre* by Couperin 'Le Grand'.

Giuseppe di Lampedusa

Lamerie Paul de (1688–1751). The greatest English goldsmith of the 18th c. and one of the most prolific. Of Huguenot descent, L. entered his mark at Goldsmiths' Hall in 1712. His early work is in the restrained Huguenot style but by the 1720s he was working in a freer and more exuberant idiom. This culminated in his superb rococo pieces, where his extravagant sense of design, superb modelling and fine execution made him the most gifted exponent of the style. Even in his small domestic articles his design and craftsmanship are of a very high order.

Lamia (1820). Narrative poem by Keats.

Lamming George (1927–). West Indian novelist from Barbados, which forms the background to the autobiographical *In the Castle of My Skin* (1954). *The Emigrants* (1955), pursues problems of West Indians living in England. Both books are notable for their sensitivity; the second also for its skilful handling of situation.

La Motte Fouqué Friedrich Baron de: Friedrich Baron de la Motte *Fouqué

Lamour Dorothy (1914–). U.S. film star. Typed as a sarong-wearing siren, L. appeared notably in the *Road* series with Bob *Hope and Bing *Crosby.

Lamoureux Charles (1834–99). French violinist and conductor who not only organized performances of *Messiah* and Bach's *St Matthew Passion* but also performed contemporary composers' works and championed Wagner.

Lampedusa Giuseppe Tomasi, Prince of (1896–1957). Italian novelist who publ. none of his work. The protagonist in *Il Gattopardo* (posth. 1958; *The Leopard*, 1960) is the prince of Salina, a character modelled on T.'s great-grandfather. Each chapter is set in a different period of his life, beginning with the overthrow of the Bourbon régime in Sicily; each describes only a few hours, but effectively contrasts the change and death of men and societies with the unchangeable spirit of Sicily. T. also wrote *Racconti* (1961; *Two Stories and a Memory*, 1962).

Lancret. *L'Adolescence.* Also *fête galante

Landini. Late 15th-c. ms. showing the composer playing the organetto

La Muse française (1823–4). Early French romantic magazine. Victor Hugo was a contributor.

Lancaster Burt (1913–). U.S. film actor, producer and director. L. is an ex-acrobat who made his début as a film actor in the leading part in *The Killers*. He mixed acrobatic parts (Tourneur's *The Flame and the Arrow*, 1950) with his undoubted talent for serious acting (*Come Back Little Sheba*). As producers, he and his partner Harold Hecht have been ambitious and intelligent. His only film as a director, *The Kentuckian* (1955), was a remarkable combination of extreme violence and tenderness.

lancet. Architectural term for the tall narrow window characteristic of Early English.

Lancret Nicolas (1690–1743). French painter of fêtes galantes and *commedia dell'arte* scenes, an imitator of Watteau, with whom he studied under Gillot. He is well represented in the Louvre and the Wallace Coll.

Lander Harald (1905–). Danish dancer and choreographer who studied at the Royal Danish Ballet School, being only one generation removed from Bournonville. Further training in Russia and America (1926–7) influenced his style when he was appointed ballet master at the Opera House, Copenhagen (1932–51). He restored the declining co. and created many ballets. He married Margot Gerhardt in 1931 and Toni Petersen in 1950.

Lander Margot (née Gerhardt) (1910–). Danish dancer; leading ballerina in 1942. She achieved great personal success in classical, romantic and demi-caractère roles before retiring in 1948. She married Harald Lander in 1931.

Lander Toni (née Petersen) (1931–). Danish dancer of the Royal Ballet School, Copenhagen who graduated as a solo dancer in 1950. In the same year she married the ballet master, Harald L. and in 1955 danced the leading role in his ballet *Études* (a new version of his *Étude*, 1948) for the Festival Ballet in London.

Landini (Landino) Francesco (*c.* 1335–97). Florentine virtuoso on the portative organ, composer of the ars nova period, and poet. He wrote madrigals and *caccie* but above all polyphonic *ballate*, excelling all his contemporaries in wedding the polyphonic idiom to the lyrical freedom of this traditionally monodic form. L. was also a master of melismatic composition.

Ländler. Folk-dance common to the S. German-speaking peoples. It is in the nature of a heavy waltz; Mozart, Haydn, Beethoven and Schubert wrote many pieces of this type.

Landor Walter Savage (1775–1864). English poet and prose writer, is remembered chiefly for his epigrams, among the best in the English language, and his *Imaginary Conversations . . . of Literary Men and Statesmen* (1824, 28, 29), *. . . of Greeks and Romans* (1853) in which his prose is often eloquent, forceful and penetrating. Unlike other English romantic authors he governed his writing by neo-classical principles of precision and clarity, preferring the Greek to the Gothic. Politically and in spirit the forces which moved him were an early Jacobinism.

Landowska Wanda (1879–1959). Polish harpsichord virtuoso, teacher and musicologist. She lived in France up to 1941, then in the U.S. From her 1st public harpsichord recital in 1903 she worked for the most authentic interpretation of early music, founding École de Musique Ancienne (1925). The revival of the harpsichord was largely her work.

Landré Guillaume Louis Frédéric (1905–). Dutch composer, pupil of his father, the composer and critic WILLEM L. (1874–1948), and W. Pijper–the latter's influence being noticeable in L.'s early work. His work includes: the light opera *De Snoek* (1934); 4 symphonies; and suite for string orchestra and piano (1936).

landscape architecture. The organization of natural horticultural elements to achieve an aesthetic effect. The art is very ancient, having been cultivated in ancient Egypt and Mesopotamia, and has had many sources of inspiration. Underlying principles have ranged from the symbolic use of plants, water, rocks, etc. in Chinese and Japanese garden architecture to the formal geometrical patterns of the French garden architecture of the 17th c. In England in the early 18th c. a school of landscape gardeners developed whose avowed aim was to create an artificial landscape apparently natural but in fact often highly contrived. The

Wanda Landowska; photograph by Karsh

Landscape architecture. The 16th-c. Villa Medici, Rome

Landscape architecture. Palladian bridge at Wilton, Wiltshire

Landseer.
The Monarch of the Glen

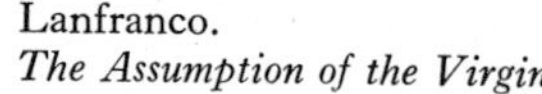

Lanfranco.
The Assumption of the Virgin

great French masters aimed at a coherent plan of garden and building orientated on a main axis.

Landseer Sir Edwin (1802–73). English artist, immensely popular in the 19th c. and early 20th c. He invented, or at any rate popularized, the animal, heroic or domestic, embodying popular virtues, e.g. the dog of *The Old Shepherd's Chief Mourner* (V. and A., London), the stag of *The Monarch of the Glen* (Coll. Dewar and Sons Ltd). L. modelled the lions for Nelson's Column in Trafalgar Square.

landsmål: Ivar *Aasen

Lane Edward William (1801–76). English Arabic scholar who produced an expurgated trs. of *The Arabian Nights' Entertainments* (*The Thousand and One Nights*, 3 vols 1839–41) and a valuable *Arabic-English Lexicon* (1863–74).

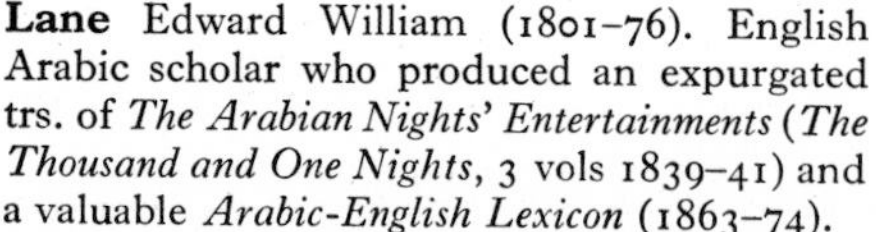

Lanfranco Giovanni (1582–1647). Italian baroque painter, pupil of Agostino Carracci and influenced by the ceiling paintings of Correggio. He worked in Rome and Naples and decorated the domes and apses of many churches with illusionistic paintings, a famous example being the dome of S. Andrea del Valle, Rome (1625–8).

Fritz Lang. *The Testament of Doctor Mabuse*

Lang Andrew (1844–1912). Scottish scholar and writer. As an anthropologist he produced colls of fairy-tales and controversial works in comparative religion and mythology. His verse includes sonnets such as *The Odyssey*, the narrative poem *Helen of Troy* (1822), Scottish ballads and imitations *of* medieval French metres; his prose, the essays *Letters to Dead Authors* . . . (1886).

Lang Fritz (1890–). Austrian film director. *Die Spinnen* (1919), a complex thriller, had scientific trappings like *Feuillade's serials; but L.'s underworld organizations exist to do evil as much as to make profit, and the idea of organized evil has persisted 40 years in the **Doctor Mabuse* series, which have also retained the scientific equipment. Science is also important to his 2 films set in the future, *Metropolis* (1926) and *Das Frau Im Mond* (1928) but these have as their theme the idea of destiny, which recurs throughout his films, particularly in *Der Mude Tod* (*Destiny*, 1921) and the 2 parts of *Die Nibelungen* (1924), his version of the German legends of Siegfried and Kriemhild. In all these silent films, the expressionist style of acting and towering architectural sets, negated any attempt at character drawing, but the naturalistic techniques of the sound film, aided by an extraordinary performance by Peter *Lorre, enabled L. to combine social purpose and insight with some expressionist elements in his masterpiece: *M* (1931). A child sex-murderer (Lorre) is hunted down by the criminal underworld. To escape the Nazi régime, L. moved first to France, then to Hollywood, where his first pictures had a social character, e.g. *Fury* (1936). Though exceptionally well made, L.'s U.S. films lack the imaginative stretch of earlier work; they include westerns: *Rancho Notorious* (1952); crime stories: *The Big Heat* (1953) and *Beyond a Reasonable Doubt* (1956; his last U.S. picture); an anti-Nazi movie, *Hangmen Also Die* (1943; part written by *Brecht) and even a period movie, *Moonfleet* (1955). 2 of his American films remade subjects used by J. *Renoir, *Scarlet Street* (1945) and *Human Desire* (1954) from *La Chienne* and *La Bête Humaine*. He returned to Germany to make *Das Indische Grabmal* (1960).

Lang Paul Henry (1901–). Hungarian-born U.S. naturalized (1933) musicologist, music critic and ed. of *Columbia Univ. Studies in Musicology*. His major book is *Music in Western Civilization* (1941).

Langdon Harry (1884–1944). U.S. film comedian who created the character of a round-eyed, white-faced childish innocent, combining pathos with slapstick. When he insisted on directing himself, his career disintegrated almost within the year. Best of his pictures were *Tramp, Tramp, Tramp* (1926) and *Long Pants* (1927).

Lange Dorothea (1895–). U.S. photographer best known for her stark portraits of migrant workers made under the auspices of the Farm Security Administration during the great depression.

Langhorne John (1735–79). English trs. and poet whose rendering of Plutarch's *Lives* (1770) (written in collaboration with his brother William) was once the standard version.

Langland William (*c.* 1332–1400?). Name traditionally given to the English author of the long allegorical poem *The Vision of William concerning Piers the Plowman* (*c.* 1377 in the

Harry Langdon in *Long Pants*

Lanyon.
Coast Wind (1957)

Laocoön

Lantern of the Baptistery, Florence

fullest version). From the account in the poem, L.–who calls himself 'long Will'–was born near Malvern, Hertfordshire, took minor orders and moved to London with his wife and daughter, writing his poem and living by singing Psalms and working as a copyist. L. may also have written the poem *Richard the Redeless*. *Piers Plowman* was in effect part of the mid-14th-c. W. Midland efflorescence of alliterative verse (elsewhere giving way to rhyming verse with metres on classical models). It is a religious allegory operating on many levels–Piers is variously plowman, St Peter and Christ himself–and incidentally a vivid portrait of 14th-c. life, an exposition of social problems, and a ferocious and bitter attack on a corrupt clergy. The range and vitality of the poem, the vigorous and detailed treatment which brings to life its allegorical figures, and the fervour of the poet's visions, make *Piers Plowman* the greatest religious poem of its period.

Langley Batty (1696–1751). Pioneer of English landscape gardening. In 1740 he started a school of architectural drawing, undertaking to design 'Grottos, Cascades, Caves, Temples, Pavillions and other Rural Buildings of Pleasure'. He produced over 20 books of engravings and instructions on building and landscaping which had widespread influence on taste. He helped to popularize Gothic architecture as an exotic style, though his attempt to classify it in 5 'orders' was a failure.

langue d'oc and **langue d'oïl.** The French languages spoken in S. and N. France respectively during the middle ages (*Provençal culture).

Lanier Nicholas (1588–1666). English musician and painter of French descent, Charles I's agent in Italy for the purchase of paintings. He composed music for masques by Ben Jonson, singing the masque *Lovers made Men* (1617) in Italian recitative style and designing the set. He also left numerous songs and a self-portrait.

Lanier Sidney (1842–81). U.S. poet and critic. L. emphasized the importance of poetic technique (rather than statement or imagery) in securing effects, likening poetry to music. His theory, described in *The Science of English Verse* (1880), produced many fine poems, including *The Symphony* (1875), in which each part reproduces the pitch and tone of a given musical instrument.

Lanner Josef (1801–43). Austrian violinist and dance composer, the rival of J. Strauss the Elder. He wrote *Ländler* as well as waltzes.

Lanner Katti (1831–1908). Austrian dancer, daughter of composer Josef Lanner, who made her début in Vienna in 1845. She opened one of the earliest ballet schools in London (*c.* 1877) and later, during her 10 years as ballet mistress at the Empire Theatre, she was responsible for introducing many foreign dancers to London, notably Adeline Genée.

Lanskoy André (1902–). Russian-born painter of the school of Paris. His early works were influenced by Van Gogh and Matisse but he began to turn to abstraction just before World War II later developing his own intensely lyrical abstract style.

lantern. Architectural term for a small turret or tower on a dome, roof, etc., with windows admitting light into the interior of the building.

Lanyon Peter (1918–64). English painter. He studied at the Penzance and Euston Road art schools and held his 1st one-man exhibition at the Lefevre Gal., London in 1949. He was one of the artists who worked at St Ives, Cornwall. His abstract compositions relate to land- and seascape.

Laocoön (*c.* 50 B.C.; Vatican Colls). Highly naturalistic and emotional late Hellenistic marble group of the Rhodian school. The Trojan priest L. was killed with his sons for offending the gods. Found in Nero's palace on the Esquiline in 1506, the statue profoundly influenced Michelangelo. *Laokoon* is the title of a treatise on art by *Lessing.

Laon and Cynthia. Original title of *Shelley's *Revolt of Islam.*

Laon cathedral France. Early Gothic cathedral (*c.* 1170–1225) built on a spectacular hilltop position and containing several unusual features–a square E. end, a combination of round and pointed arches and 6 towers with open-work niches from which life-size figures of oxen gaze down. The interior elevation is 4 storeyed and the vault sexpartite.

Lao-Tze or **Lao-tzu.** Chinese philosopher said to have lived in the 6th c. B.C. and proposed as the author of the quietistic philosophical

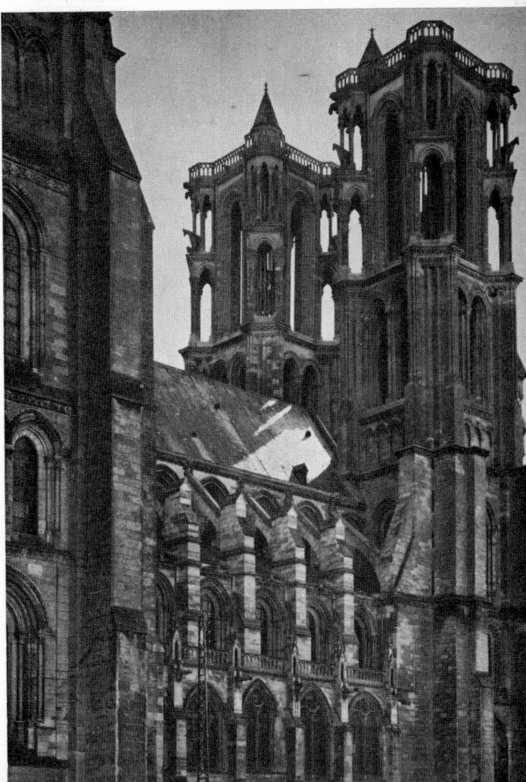

Laon cathedral

Larionov.
Soldier at the hairdresser

Larionov.
Spring (1912)

Ring Lardner

La Rochefoucauld

Largillière. *Elisabeth de Beauharnais*

system Taoism, and of its fundamental document, the *Tao te ching*.

Laparra Raoul (1876–1943). French composer; his teachers included Gédalge and Fauré. His music, which reflects his interest in Spanish music, includes the opera *La Habanera* (1908).

Lapicque Charles (1898–). French painter. In his early work in the 1920s and 1930s he alternated between abstract and representational styles but has since combined these elements in his vivacious compositions. After a series of paintings in the 1940s relating to the sea he turned to race-course and regatta themes in the early 1950s.

lapis lazuli. Deep blue, opaque semi-precious stone used since earliest times in jewellery and inlay work. The richest source of the material is located in Afghanistan. The jewellers of Assyria and Egypt exploited its rich decorative qualities; it was later extensively used in Italy during the Renaissance.

Laplace Pierre-Antoine de (1707–93). French writer whose *Théâtre Anglais* (1745–8) contained the 1st important trs. of Shakespeare.

Larbaud Valéry (Nicolas) (1881–1957). French novelist and critic; his best-known novel was *A. O. Barnabooth* (1913; 1924), about a S. American multi-millionaire. L. was also important as an interpreter of English literature to the French.

Lardner Ring(gold Wilmer) (1885–1933). U.S. short-story writer and newspaperman. L. worked for several Middle Western dailies, by 1919 he had established a reputation for sports writing and was publ. syndicated articles. L.'s short stories, bitter descriptions of the emptiness and vulgarity of U.S. life, revealed that he was a great satirist. They include *You Know Me, Al: A Busher's Letters* (1916; revised 1925), purportedly written by an illiterate baseball player, and the colls *How to Write Short Stories* (1924) and *The Love Nest* (1926).

Largillière (Largillierre) Nicolas de (1656–1746). French rococo portrait painter. He studied in Antwerp, then worked in London as assistant to P. Lely. In 1682 he went to Paris, where he became the favourite painter of the wealthy bourgeoisie. He brought a new freedom and fluency to French portraiture.

largo (Italian, 'broad'). In music the term used to indicate that the piece should be played in a stately manner. The piece universally known as 'Handel's Largo' is an arrangement of one of the arias from his opera *Serse*.

Larionov Mikhail (1881–1964). Russian painter trained in Moscow where he met Goncharova. He was a prolific worker and a highly energetic personality who soon attracted a nucleus of Muscovite painters round him with whom he organized exhibitions such as the Golden Fleece, the 1st *Knave of Diamonds show, and in 1913 publ. his *Rayonnist Manifesto* which laid the foundations of abstract art in Russia. L. is important in Russian art history for his creative absorption of contemporary (1905–8) French ideas in painting; for his subsequent synthesis of these ideas with national folk-arts, e.g. in his *Soldier* series (1908–11); and for his rayonnist work (1910–14), much of it abstract and among the first of such modern work, although not basically a system of non-representational composition. After 1914 he left Russia to work as a designer for Diaghilev's Ballets Russes, and from then lived in Paris.

Larkin Philip (1922–). English poet and author of 2 novels. His 1st coll., *The North Ship*, appeared in 1945, but his mature achievement is seen in the 1955 coll., *The Less Deceived* and subsequent poems. Perhaps influenced by Hardy, whom he admires, L.'s poetry is technically assured and has an appealing humanity, the result of wide sympathies and of ironic, unpretentious fortitude.

La Rochefoucauld François, duc de (1613–80). French writer, successively a rebel against Royal authority and *habitué* of the literary *salons*. Here the favourite pastime was the invention of maxims, or short, penetrating observations on human character and behaviour; a form depending on abstraction and generalization, in which Cartesian method and fashionable taste met.
La R.'s *Maximes* (1665; 1685) present a psychological analysis in which the primacy of self-interest is emphasized; and their effect is sharpened by a clear, concise, antithetical style. His taste for paradox undoubtedly led to over-simplification and almost unvarying pessimism, but the *Maximes* were nevertheless an honest assessment of his contemporaries and an antidote to the idealism of creative

literature. La R. lived with Mme de *La Fayette from 1665 and helped her to write *La Princesse de Clèves*.

Laroon the Elder, Marcellus (1653–1702). Dutch painter and engraver who settled in England and worked as assistant to Kneller.

Laroon the Younger, Marcellus (1679–1774). English painter and mezzotint engraver, actor and soldier, a pupil of Kneller. He is best known for his conversation pieces similar in type to those of his friend Hogarth but painted in an unusual agitated style. There is an element of caricature in much of his work.

Larra Mariano José de (1809–37). Spanish journalist whose newspaper articles satirized Spanish manners and characters, and dealt with art, politics and literature in a forceful, witty style; he was the most gifted Spanish prose writer of his time. He also wrote a verse drama and a novel.

Larsen Gerd (1921–). Norwegian dancer who settled in England in the 1930s and joined the Sadler's Wells Ballet in 1944. L. developed as a classical soloist but now specializes in character parts excelling as a brilliant mime; she also teaches at the Royal Ballet.

Larsson Lars Erik (1908–). Swedish composer. He has been called the last of the national romantics, but Hindemith as well as Nielsen and Sibelius has influenced his work, which is generally light and unprofound.

Lartigue Henri (1896–). French photographer. Between the ages of 6(!) and 20, starting with a box camera given him as a gift, L. captured the flavour of pre-World War I Europe in photographs that reveal an acute sense of the bizarre, and which freeze people in motion in a fashion much in advance of the time.

La Rue Pierre de (*c.* 1460–1518). Flemish composer; perhaps the only one of his contemporaries whose work was comparable to that of the great Josquin. He served at the court of Brussels (1492–1516), visiting Spain in the entourage of Philip the Fair. He wrote 36 masses, 38 motets, and *chansons*; his work making characteristically intensive use of canon.

Laroon the Younger.
Interior with figures

La Sal(l)e Antoine de (1388–after 1469). French writer of romances, including *Petit Jehan de Saintré* (*c.* 1455) and *Réconfort de Madame du Fresne* (1458). The **Cent nouvelles nouvelles* has sometimes been attributed to him.

Lascaux. Cave in the Dordogne discovered only in 1940 and containing paintings of bulls, horses, deer, etc. executed by Cro-Magnon men in the Aurignacian period of the upper paleolithic era (*c.* 20,000 B.C.). The growth of a fungus which endangered the paintings–evidently caused by increased humidity–led to the sealing off of the cave. Also *cave art.

Lasdun Denys (1914–). English architect. He was a member of the Tecton Group in the 1930s and 1940s, then of Fry, Drew, Drake and Lasdun until 1958, when he opened his own office; tower blocks at Bethnal Green (1960) for the council and flats in St James's Place (1961) overlooking Green Park show his versatility. These were followed by the College of Physicians, Regent's Park (1964) and the National Theatre.

Lasky Jesse L. (1880–1958). Film producer. L. was with De Mille and Goldwyn founder of the Jesse L. Lasky Feature Play Co. which became Famous Players-Lasky. In 1932 he became an independent producer, and his most notable production was *Sergeant York*.

Lasso Orlando di (*c.* 1532–94). Flemish composer, called also 'Orlandus, Orlande or Roland Lassus'. He was a choirboy at Mons, then at the chapel of Ferdinand Gonzaga, with whom he visited Sicily and Milan. He was director of the Vatican choir and worked in Antwerp, before settling in the employ (1556) of Albert V of Bavaria. His work there made the fame of the 'divine Orlando', this 'prince of music', European wide; his pupils included G. Gabrieli. L. and Palestrina are reckoned the 2 greatest continental composers of the late 16th c. L.'s work is noted not only for its prodigious extent (over 2,000 works) but also for its versatile mastery. He shows equal facility in ecclesiastical or secular forms, in Italian madrigals, or *morescas*, in German *Lieder* or French *chansons*. The style of his church music abandons the *through-imitation of the school of Josquin and replaces long melodic *melismas with short, rhythmic phrases which often produce dramatic, declamatory effects. L.'s

The Bavarian court chapel under Orlando di Lasso; a contemporary illuminated ms.

Lasdun. Cluster block in Bethnal Green

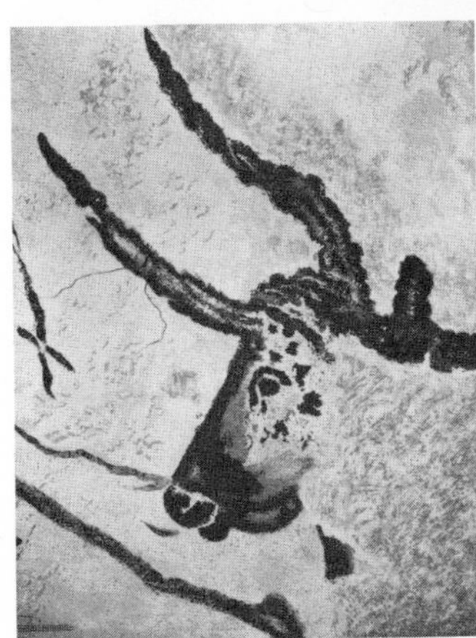

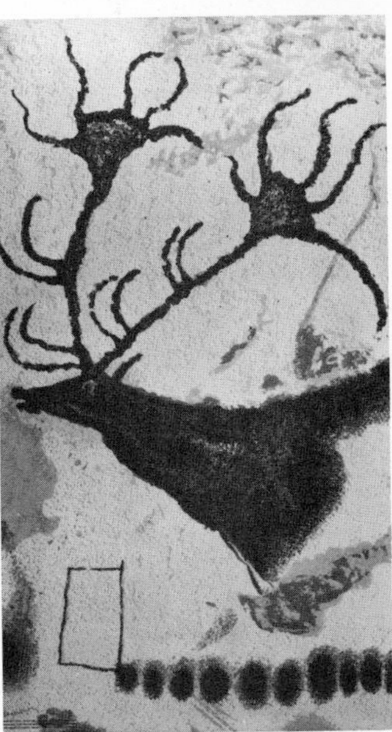

Lascaux. Head of a bull (*above*) and of a stag

Lastman. *Susanna at the Bath*

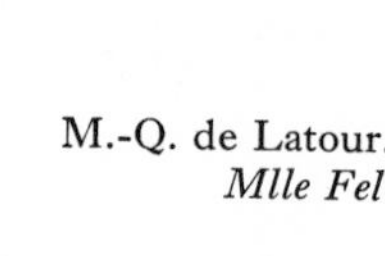

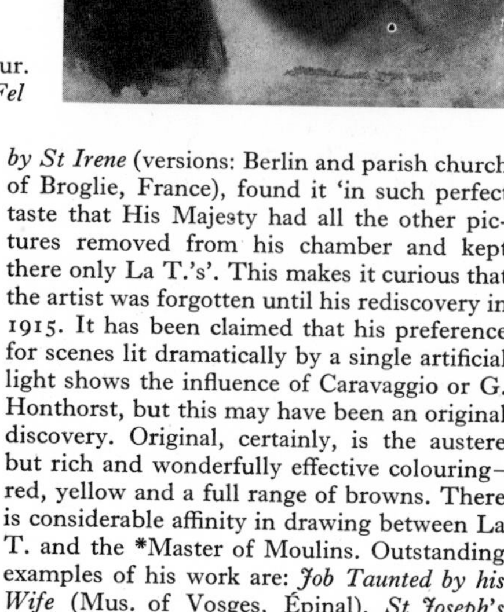
M.-Q. de Latour. *Mlle Fel*

greatest work is in his 1,200 motets; they have an immense range and depth of expression and, through his pupils L. Lechner and Eccard, influenced the development of the German motet. L.'s other important church music includes his masses and his setting of the penitential Psalms (composed *c.* 1565).

Last Days of Pompeii, The (1834). Novel by *Bulwer-Lytton.

Lastman Pieter Pietersz (1583–1633). Dutch painter of religious, mythological and historical subjects, and engraver who worked in Amsterdam. He visited Italy, where he was influenced by Caravaggio's use of chiaroscuro. Rembrandt and Jan Lievens were his pupils.

Last of the Mohicans, The (1826). Novel by James Fenimore *Cooper.

Last Supper, The (1495–7). Wall painting by *Leonardo.

Last Tycoon, The (1941). Unfinished novel by F. Scott *Fitzgerald.

La Suze comtesse de (1618–73). French writer whose *salon* was connected with the Hôtel de *Rambouillet.

La Tène torc with an iron core and a thick coating of silver

La Taille Jean de (*c.* 1535–*c.* 1608). French playwright whose *De l'art de la tragédie*, insisting on the observation of the unities, was important in the development of the French theatre. L.'s plays included *Les Corrivaux*, the 1st French comedy in prose, and 2 Biblical tragedies, *Saül le furieux* and *La Famine, ou les Gabaonites.*

La Tène. A site in E. Switzerland which has given its name to a style of Celtic art and a culture centred upon it and expanding throughout Central Europe and into Britain; it flourished in the last 5 cs B.C. Its characteristic motifs are stylized and sinuous animal and plant forms; the style became increasingly abstract, especially in the art of Celtic Britain.

La Tour Georges de (1593–1652). French artist born at Vic in Lorraine. La T. lived all his life in the province, working at Lunéville from 1620. Despite this isolation, he won recognition and rewards. In 1623 the duke of Lorraine became his patron. In 1638 King Louis XIII, accepting his *St Sebastian tended by St Irene* (versions: Berlin and parish church of Broglie, France), found it 'in such perfect taste that His Majesty had all the other pictures removed from his chamber and kept there only La T.'s'. This makes it curious that the artist was forgotten until his rediscovery in 1915. It has been claimed that his preference for scenes lit dramatically by a single artificial light shows the influence of Caravaggio or G. Honthorst, but this may have been an original discovery. Original, certainly, is the austere but rich and wonderfully effective colouring – red, yellow and a full range of browns. There is considerable affinity in drawing between La T. and the *Master of Moulins. Outstanding examples of his work are: *Job Taunted by his Wife* (Mus. of Vosges, Épinal), *St Joseph's Dream* (Mus. des B.-A., Nantes), *The Newborn* (Mus. des B.-A., Rennes) and *Magdalene with the Lamp* (Louvre).

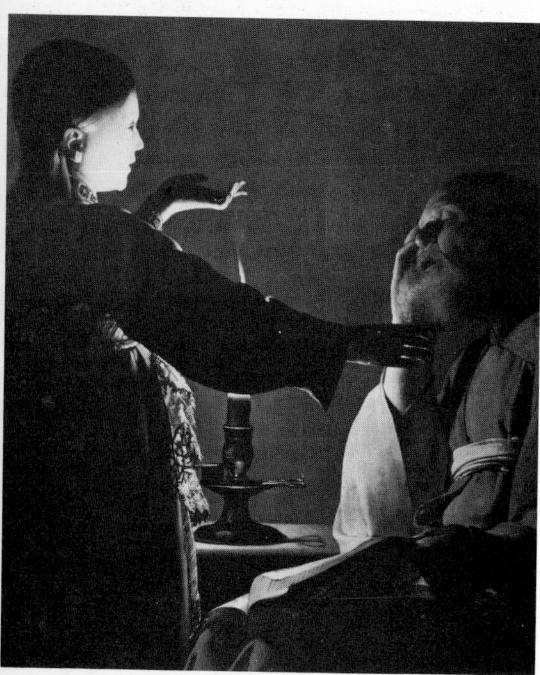
Georges de La Tour. *St Joseph's Dream*

Latour Maurice-Quentin de (1704–88). French portraitist in pastel, one of the great masters of that medium, appointed painter to Louis XV in 1750. His work shows a degree of individual characterization outstanding in the portraiture of the rococo period.

La Tour du Pin Patrice de (1911–). French poet whose works include *Une Somme de Poésie* (1946) and *La Contemplation errante* (1948).

Latrobe Benjamin Henry (1764–1820). English architect who emigrated to Virginia in 1796. His chief work is Baltimore cathedral (1804 onwards), an aisled rectangle with a big shallow dome in the middle, owing something to Soane's Bank of England. L. also built the Bank of Philadelphia (destroyed) and part of the Capitol, Washington.

latten. A form of *brass.

Lattuada Alberto (1914–). Italian film director. L., after the neo-realist *Senza pietà* (1948) and *Il Mulino del Po* (1949), co-directed *Fellini's 1st film, *Luci del varietà* (1950). Since then he has broadened his range in an elegant spectacular, *Tempest* (1958), from Pushkin, and a most unpleasant suspense film, *L'Imprévu* (1961).

Lauder Sir Harry (1870–1950). Scottish music-hall artist who became world famous as the singer of 'I Love a Lassie' and 'Roamin' In the

Charles Laughton rehearsing *Galileo*

Laurel and Hardy in *Putting Pants on Phillip*

The Laughing Cavalier

Gloamin''. He was knighted in 1919 for his services in entertaining troops during World War I.

Laude spirituale. Devotional songs particularly popular in Counter-Reformation Italy and one of the elements in the birth of the *oratorio in the early 17th c.

Laughing Cavalier, The (1624; Wallace Coll., London). Popular title of a portrait of a smiling young gentleman by Hals. The sitter's identity is not known.

Laughton Charles (1899–1962). English actor. L. started acting in films in 1933 and had a great success in Korda's *The Private Life of Henry VIII* and in *The Hunchback of Notre-Dame.* Apart from his career as a film star, which continued successfully right up to *Advise and Consent*, his stage work included acting in and adapting (with Brecht) the first production in English of Brecht's *Galileo*, directed by Losey in Hollywood (1947). He directed one film, *Night of the Hunter* (1955), a remarkable amalgam of folk-art and expressionist or Wellesian influences.

Laurel Stanley (1890–1965), **Hardy** Oliver (1892–1957). Film comedians. British-born L. and American H. made some 200 films, working as a team for over 20 years. Their style was developed by L. although he neither produced nor directed: he was responsible for the replacement of traditional high-speed slapstick by slow-paced comedy created by the situation rather than the gags. L.'s short thin simplicity and H.'s tall fat dignity endeared their knockabout 'comedy of anticipation' to the public, e.g. in *Leave 'em Laughing* (1927), *The Music Box* (1932) and *Way Out West* (1937).

Laurencin Marie (1885–1956). French painter, designer and illustrator. Although she was a friend of *avant-garde* painters and poets in Paris her work was unaffected by modern movements. The grace and sensitivity of her paintings of young girls derive in part from her study of Persian miniatures and rococo art.

Laurens Henri (1885–1954). French sculptor and graphic artist, one of the leading cubist sculptors. His work at that time dealt with the structural correlation of geometric forms and his use of contrasting materials provided a sculptural parallel to collage. His polychrome sculptures in sheet-iron of 1914 anticipated constructivist ideas. From 1930 he concentrated on the female figure as a basis for his work but remained preoccupied with the interplay of forms, organic instead of geometric. In much of his sculpture and graphic work he reinterpreted themes from Greek mythology.

Lautréamont comte de. Pseud. of Isidore Ducasse (1846–70). French writer born in Montevideo (he came to France in 1860). L.'s unfinished *Les Chants de Maldoror* (1868; *Maldoror*, 1944) is a prose work full of startling, grotesque imagery and sudden, nightmarish turns, which profoundly influenced the surrealists.

Lavengro, the Scholar–the Gypsy–the Priest (1851). Novel by George *Borrow.

La Vigne André or Andrieu de (*c.* 1457–1515). French writer, the author of the companion stage pieces the *Mystère du glorieux Saint Martin* (1496) and the *Moralité de l'Aveugle et le Boiteaux* (1496).

Law William (1686–1761). English divine and mystic who combated in lucid and often fervent and beautiful prose the deism of the 18th c. His *Serious Call to a Devout and Holy Life* (1728) influenced Wesley; and in later writings he transmitted the nature mysticism of Boehme to English readers, helping to shape the concept of imagination in Blake, Coleridge and Wordsworth.

Lawes Henry (1596–1662). English composer, a pupil of Coperario. The finest song writer of his day, he developed the declamatory air perfected by Purcell. He wrote music to the masques *Comus* by Milton and *Coelum Britannicum* by T. Carew (both performed 1634) and set poems by T. Herrick and R. Lovelace among others.

Lawes William (1602–45). English composer, brother of H. Lawes and a pupil of Coperario. He composed instrumental music of all kinds, including excellent and bold viol fantasies, and also wrote for the voice; his setting of R. Herrick's *Gather ye rosebuds while ye may* being immensely popular.

Lawler Ray (1922–). Australian dramatist whose *The Summer of the Seventeenth Doll* (1957) was acclaimed in Europe and Australia

Laurencin. *Rehearsal*

Laurens. *Siren*

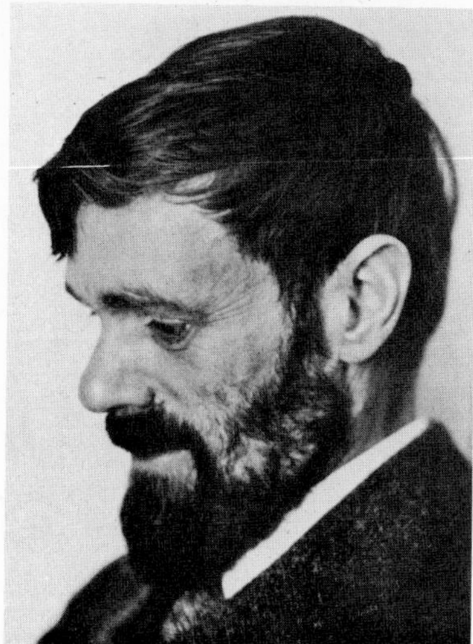
D. H. Lawrence

T. E. Lawrence: painting by Augustus John

Sir Thomas Lawrence. *Miss Farren*. Also *Blessington

as the beginning of Australian drama. It is important in Australian literature generally for its recognition of the country's urbanization, a fact few writers have acknowledged. *The Piccadilly Bushman* (1959) has the first play's rhetorical faults, without its dramatic strengths.

Lawrence D(avid) H(erbert) (1885–1930). English novelist, short-story writer, son of a Nottinghamshire coal-miner and a school-teacher. L. studied at Nottingham Univ. College, then worked as a school-teacher (1908–11) before publ. his 1st novel, *The White Peacock* (1911). In 1912 he eloped with Frieda von Richthofen, a German aristocrat married to an English professor. They lived in Italy (1912–14), married (1914), and spent the war years in England, under constant suspicion because of Frieda's nationality. They left England in disgust and travelled in Italy, Australia and Mexico. L. died of tuberculosis.
His work was not ignored during these years, but it was widely misunderstood and officially persecuted. His novel *The Rainbow* (1915) was suppressed as obscene; an exhibition of his paintings was closed (1928); and *Lady Chatterley's Lover* (Italy; 1928) was publ. unexpurgated in England only in 1960–and was then the subject of a famous trial.
L. conceived his mission to be the restoration of a body-consciousness destroyed by Puritanism and industrialism; he attacked the primacy of will and intellect in the name of trust in life and harmony with nature. In sexual terms this meant replacing the sentimental–yet fundamentally grasping–attempt to 'understand' and dominate with a sexual tenderness which recognizes the separateness of the love-object. Much of L.'s work has strong autobiographical interest: the novel *Sons and Lovers* (1913) describes his youth, dominated by a too-loving mother; *Women in Love* (1920) analyses his love for Frieda and attempt to form a mystical *blutbruderschaft* with J. Middleton Murry; the cycle of poems *Look! We have come through!* (1917) celebrates his achievement of a fruitful relationship with Frieda. L. had an extraordinary gift for conveying mental states, and for evoking the atmosphere of a landscape, e.g. the description of the stark, uncanny Australian bush in *Kangaroo* (1923). His poems, mainly in free verse, describe encounters with almost all existing beasts, with flowers and trees, and his intense and stormy life with Frieda. Works include the novels *The Trespasser* (1912), *Aaron's Rod* (1922) and *The Plumed Serpent* (1926); and many fine short stories and short novels, including *The Escaped Cock*, later called *The Man Who Died* (1929).

Lawrence Gertrude (1898–1952). English musical comedy actress who played in many Noël Coward successes, e.g. *Private Lives*. She also appeared in the film *The Glass Menagerie*.

Lawrence Sir Thomas (1769–1830). English painter. At 22 his *Miss Farren* (Met. Mus.) made him the rival of Reynolds, whose portrait style he followed, adding a bravura of his own. An unfinished portrait, *Wilberforce* (N.P.G., London), shows the quality beneath the glittering surface. *Sarah Moulton Barrett* (Huntington Gal., San Marino, Calif.) is one of the most vivacious of his popular studies of children. Among the many men of the day he painted, his portraits *The Duke of Wellington* (Wellington Mus., London) and *George IV as Prince Regent* (Vatican Gal.) are outstanding examples.

Lawrence T(homas) E(dward) (1888–1935). English writer and adventurer, 'L. of Arabia', famous in World War I for his part in the Arab revolt against the Turks; the story of the revolt is told in *The Seven Pillars of Wisdom*, publ. in a limited ed. in 1926 (the abridged ed., 1927, was called *Revolt in the Desert*). After the war he joined the R.A.F. under an assumed name; his account of this experience, *The Mint*, was publ. after his death in a motor-cycle accident. L.'s fame owes more to the glamour of his legend and the fascination of his withdrawn and ambiguous personality than to his mannered and self-conscious writings: these, however, show fine descriptive powers.

Lawson Ernest (1873–1939). U.S. painter of rural and urban landscapes in an impressionistic style. He was a member of The *Eight and one of the sponsors of the Armory Show (1913).

Lawson Henry (1867–1922). Australian writer, highly considered today for his short stories, though during the 1890s his verse was more widely acclaimed. The stories deal sympathetically and ironically with characters and conditions in the outback, though sentimentality ruins some.

Laxness Halldór (Gudjonsson) Kiljan (1902–). Icelandic novelist and playwright whose

Ernest Lawson. *High Bridge*

work is notable for its scathing social criticism. Works include *Sjalfstætt folk* (1934–5; *Independent People,* 1945). L. was awarded the Nobel prize in 1955.

Layamon. Author of *Brut* (*c.* 1200), the 1st important work in Middle English. It is a history of England from the legend of Brutus to the 7th c., written in alliterative verse; it contains the 1st mention in English of Arthur, Lear and Cymbeline.

lay figure. Wooden figure with jointed limbs, and often life-size, used to establish a pose or carry drapery. It is said to have been invented by Fra Bartolommeo.

Lays of Ancient Rome (1842). Book of poems by *Macaulay.

Layton Irving (1912–). Canadian writer; his Jewish origins have provided much of his richness. With Raymond Souster and Louis Dudek, L. produced in *Cerberus* (1952) poetry whose passion was in its rebellion against prevailing emphases on technique and mythopoeic quality in Canadian poetry. *Red Carpet for the Sun* (1959) is less self-conscious and more successful.

Leach Bernard (1887–). English artist potter. Born in Hong Kong, L. was educated in England and studied at the Slade School before going to Japan (1909). Here he began his career as a potter (1911), studying with the last representative of a dynasty of Japanese potters. L. won a large reputation in Japan. In 1920, together with Shoji *Hamada, L. returned to England; they established the L. Pottery at St Ives, Cornwall. This was organized as a community studio, in which glaze recipes, etc. were shared, and rapidly became the most important centre of English studio pottery; L.'s many students included M. *Cardew. L. rediscovered certain techniques of the English tradition and his work shows English as well as Japanese influences. L. toured the U.S. in 1950 and 1960, and spent a further 2 years in Japan (1952–4). His important publs include: the highly influential *A Potter's Book* (1940), *A Potter's Portfolio* (1950), *A Potter in Japan* (1960). L.'s son DAVID (1911–) worked at St Ives until 1955, when he established an independent pottery at Bovey Tracey, Devon.

Leacock Richard (1921–). British-born film maker. His short documentary *Toby* (1954) was noticed by Robert Drew, with whom L. formed Drew Associates. Their 1st documentary, *Primary* (1960), was shot with a portable tape-recorder and a noiseless 16-mm camera (developed by L.) during the Kennedy-Humphrey Presidential Primary. Unlike Rouch, they used the camera to record and not as a catalyst: their best films were made in situations so intense that the presence of the camera had little effect, e.g. *Football* (1961), *Eddie* (1961) about a racing driver's attempts to win at Indianapolis, *Jane* (1962) about Jane Fonda's starring début on Broadway and *The Chair* (1962) about the legal fight to obtain a reprieve for a condemned man. L. made his best film alone in a low-intensity situation, *Quint City U.S.A.* (1963), about the birth of quintuplets in a small town.

Leacock Stephen (Butler) (1869–1944). Professor of economics who became Canada's best-known humorist. Writing at a time of national expansion, in his *Sunshine Sketches of a Little Town* (1912) and *Arcadian Adventures with the Idle Rich* (1914), he satirized the idea of 'hustling', or living for size and speed. What he lacks in wit, he has in comicality.

leader. The senior 1st violin of an orchestra is in England called the l., in the U.S. the 'concert master'. He takes solo violin passages, may conduct rehearsals and can determine the orchestra's morale and 'attack' in performance.

leading note. The 7th degree of the major *scale, so called because it gives the ear the impression of leading on to the *tonic.

Lean David (1908–). English film director. L. was an ed. before co-directing with Noël Coward a war film, *In Which We Serve* (1942). L. then directed 3 more films written by Coward, *This Happy Breed* (1943), *Blithe Spirit* (1944) and *Brief Encounter* (1945), and 2 Dickens adaptations, *Great Expectations* (1946) and *Oliver Twist* (1947). His last 2 films, *The Bridge on the River Kwai* (1957) and *Lawrence of Arabia* (1962) were lengthy and expensive. The star performances, and forceful stories made them outstanding commercial successes. L. is an expert craftsman whose feeling for the medium breathes cinematic life into his literary sources.

Stephen Leacock

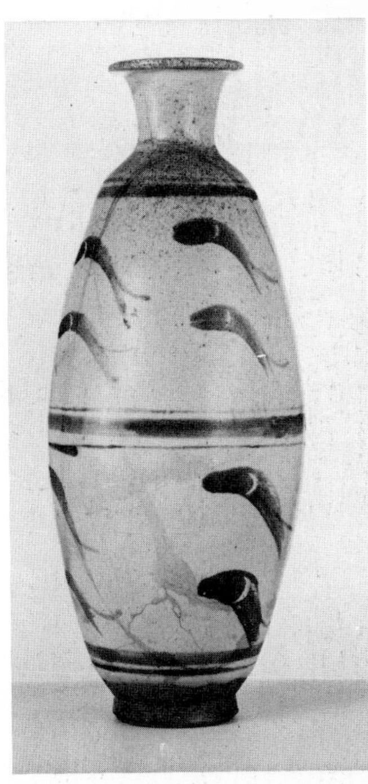

Vases by Bernard Leach (*above and below*)

Lean. Alec Guinness and Arthur Kennedy in *Lawrence of Arabia*

Lear. *Rocella*

Lear. *Foss, Passant*

Lebreton. Galerie François I

Lear Edward (1812–88). English poet and artist. His smoothly efficient Mediterranean and Aegean landscapes explain why he was once drawing master to Queen Victoria. In his nonsense drawings and poems (*Book of Nonsense*, 1846; *Nonsense Songs*, 1871; *More Nonsense*, 1872; *Laughable Lyrics*, 1877; *Nonsense Songs and Stories*, 1895) he found relief from the mannered idealism of his age in line and verse at once timelessly direct and a parody of Victorianism.

Leaves of Grass (1885). Book of poems by Walt *Whitman.

Leavis F(rank) R(aymond) (1895–). English literary critic, founder of *Scrutiny* magazine, where he first formulated many of his critical judgements (1932–53). His criterion is the author's 'awareness of the possibilities of life', as, e.g., in *The Great Tradition* (1948). L. emphasizes textual analysis but practises it slightly; in *New Bearings in English Poetry* (1932), *The Common Pursuit* (1952) and *D. H. Lawrence, Novelist* (1955), he vehemently insists on the moral significance of literature.

Le Bas Jacques-Philippe (1707–83). French rococo designer and engraver.

Leblond Alexandre-Jean-Baptiste (*c.* 1680–1719). French architect. He went to Russia in 1716 and designed the Peterhoff, Leningrad, for Peter the Great.

Lebreton Gilles (d. 1552). French architect. From 1528 until 1550 he worked at Fontainebleau, building among other parts the Porte Dorée, the Galerie François I, the Cour du Cheval Blanc and the Tour du Peristyle. He was among the first to introduce Italian Renaissance motifs into French architecture, though his basic structure is traditional.

Le Brocquey Louis (1916–). Irish painter, self-taught; a teacher of textile design. Most of his paintings are of symbolic figure groups, e.g. *The Family* (1951).

Lebrun Charles (1619–90). French painter, a student under Vouet and also in Rome, where he was influenced by Poussin. L.'s elegant and decorative classicism is thin-blooded, but as chief painter to the king (from 1662) and director of the Gobelins Factory (from 1663), under the patronage of Colbert, he controlled the arts in France into the 1680s. He was also a founder and later director of the Royal Academy of Painting and Sculpture. His works include much of the decorations at Versailles.

Lebrun Marie Vigée: *Vigée-Lebrun

Lechner Leonhard (*c.* 1553–1606). Austrian Protestant composer. He produced his important corpus of secular *Lieder* for the town music circle at Nuremberg, and later, at Stuttgart, church music, which included fine motets.

Lechoń Jan. Pseud. of Leszek Serafinowicz (1899–1956), Polish poet, one of the founders of the Skamander group. He wrote, in impeccable classical metres, poems celebrating the Polish nation and its literary tradition.

Leck Bart van der (1876–). Dutch painter and designer strongly influenced by Mondrian and associated with van Doesburg in the 1st issue of *De Stijl*.

Leclair Jean-Marie, the Elder (1697–1764). French composer and violinist. L.'s 49 violin sonatas on a basso continuo follow French and Italian models but show remarkable harmonic similarities to Bach and Handel; they are among the foundation works of violin literature. His style is a remarkable amalgam of baroque and galante, serious and light. L. also wrote violin concertos and an opera.

Lecocq Alexandre-Charles (1832–1918). French operetta composer. His works, rich in gay melodies, have remained popular; they include: *Le Docteur Miracle* (1857), *La Fille de Mme Augot* (1872) and *Giroflé-Girofla* (1874).

Leconte de Lisle Charles-Marie-René (1818–94). French poet, born and brought up on Reunion Island. As a young man he moved to Paris, where he eventually became the leader of the movement known as 'Le Parnasse' (*Parnassians), so called because its members contributed to the anthology entitled *Le Parnasse contemporain* (1866). His early political idealism quickly gave way to comic despair, which did not exclude a sense of exotic or classical beauty. He turned away from contemporary subjects to produce stoical, formally perfect, descriptions of ancient or legendary episodes in *Poèmes antiques* (1852) and *Poèmes barbares* (1862). His nihilism is still more clearly expressed in *Poèmes tragiques* (1884) and *Derniers poèmes* (1895).

Le Corbusier. *Still-life* (1920)

Lebrun. *Chancellor Séguier*. Also *Gobelins

Le Corbusier

Le Corbusier. Maison Suisse, Paris

Le Corbusier. Notre-Dame-de-Haut, Ronchamp

Le Corbusier originally named Charles-Édouard Jeanneret (1887–1965). One of the greatest modern architects. He was born in Switzerland, but his practice was always based on Paris. Other masters of modern architecture have emigrated to the U.S., but Le C. was very much a European in the urban, Mediterranean tradition, and would not have been at ease with the advanced technology of American building.

In addition to being an architect, Le C. was a propagandist for architecture, a founder of CIAM and author of many books, the most influential being *Vers une Architecture* (1923). He was also a painter of some note, and in 1917 founded the movement purism with Ozenfant; purist paintings were within the cubist tradition, with a preference for transparent, machine-made forms like glasses: they publ. an influential magazine called *L'Esprit Nouveau.*

In the 1920s he went into practice with his cousin Pierre Jeanneret, and they designed a series of houses, culminating in the superb examples at Garches and Poissy. The interiors were original, with double height living-rooms derived from painters' studios. The exteriors, smooth, white and geometric, were not only seen as buildings in their own right, but also as prototype dwellings for a new kind of city, for, parallel with their practice, they produced a series of designs for new cities, which were publ. in *L'Esprit Nouveau.*

In 1928 they entered a competition for the League of Nations Building at Geneva; their project was not built, but was widely publ. Soon after this they built a series of large buildings–the Ministry of Light Industry in Moscow, a Salvation Army Building, a Swiss students' hostel (Maison Suisse) and a block of flats, all in Paris.

The slump brought an end to building and Le C. broke up the partnership with his cousin; henceforth he worked alone. There was time to think, if little to build, and Le C. produced a series of designs for buildings and cities. The buildings of this period were rugged masonry and rough timber; the polished perfection of his earlier buildings disappeared, the machine aesthetic was changed for an earthy, almost peasant, imagery. After the war he built his Unité d'Habitation at Marseille, a vertical garden city for 1,600 people, an elephantine building of rough concrete and brilliant colour, supported on pilotis but containing all the elements of a small town in 1 building; it was crammed with new ideas, was followed by 3 other Unités, and was the masterpiece of Le C.'s 2nd creative phase, as the houses at Garches and Poissy had been of the first. Its influence was very great, particularly in Japan and on the London County Council. Of his more recent buildings, the church at Ronchamp has been widely publ., the Jaoul houses (1955) have had great influence on domestic architecture in England, and his work in Chandigarh and Ahmedabad in India has developed his rough concrete (*'le béton brut'*) aesthetic, with powerful forms, very surely handled, combined with crude construction and slapdash workmanship. Before his death he designed a new Museum of Modern Art for Paris.

ledger (leger) lines (derivation uncertain). In music the term used to describe the extra line drawn above and below the stave to carry notes which are too high or too low for it; e.g.

Ledoux Claude-Nicolas (1736–1806). French architect. Appointed architect to the king in 1773. His chief works are the Besançon Theatre, some Paris toll-houses and the building for the Chaux salt-works. L. was an architect of extraordinary originality: some of his ideas seem to point forward to the 20th c., others to verge on fantasy. His earlier designs are in a simplified Greek idiom, with emphasis on geometrical forms–cubes, hemispheres and cylinders. His plans for the 'Ideal City' of Chaux (only partly realized) go much further–one house is a free-standing sphere, another a horizontal cylinder with a river running through it. He publ. his theories and projects in 1804 in a book that has had a powerful though sporadic influence ever since.

Lee Laurie (1914–). English poet whose autobiography, *Cider With Rosie* (1959), was a best-seller.

Lee Nathaniel (1653–92). English dramatist, collaborator with Dryden, celebrated for verse plays of rant and thunder, e.g. *The Rival Queens* (1677), about the wives of Alexander the Great–extravagant but not always ridiculous in language and trope. He was confined in Bedlam for some time.

Leeds. The Old Pottery (*c.* 1760–1878) flourished until 1820; its most distinctive product was a delicately pierced cream-coloured

Le Corbusier. Palace of the Assembly, Chandigarh. Also *brise soleil, *Unité d'Habitation, *modulor

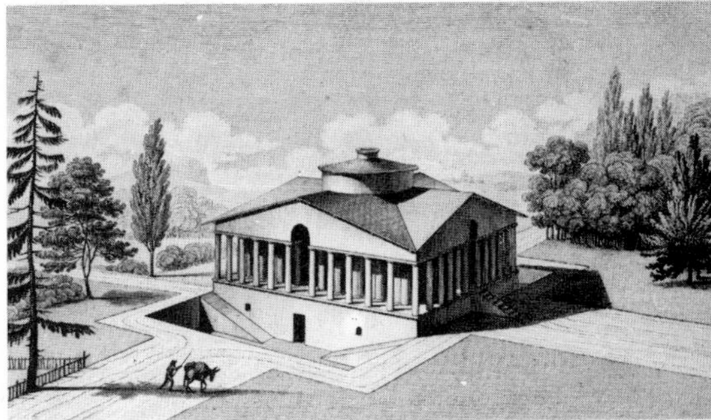

Ledoux. Project for woodcutter's house

Leeds teapot

Leenhardt. Lilli Palmer in *Les Rendez-vous de Minuit*

Legnani in *Le Corsaire*

Léger. *Nus dans un Paysage*

earthenware with a glaze having a greenish tone. A rival firm in L. was the Hunslett Hall Pottery (*c.* 1792–*c.* 1880).

Leenhardt Roger (1903–). French film critic, director and producer. L. anticipated the critical admiration for U.S. cinema which became so influential on the French nouvelle vague. He directed and produced numerous shorts including *The Birth of the Cinema* (1947) as well as two features, *Les Derniers Vacances* (1948) and *Les Rendez-vous de Minuit* (1962).

Leeuw Ton de (1924–). Dutch composer, a pupil of Badings and Messiaen. He has written experimental works such as the 'radiophonic' oratorio *Job* and *Electronic Suite*, and works in 12-note technique, e.g. *String quartet* (1958).

Le Fanu Joseph Sheridan (1814–73). Irish novelist, dramatist and poet chiefly remembered for his chilling tales of suspense, such as *The House by the Church Yard* (1863) and *Uncle Silas* (1864).

Le Gascon. The name of an early 17th-c. French bookbinder, possibly Jean Gillede. Some handsome, richly decorated morocco bindings are attributed to him and he is thought to have bound for Cardinal Mazarin.

Legat Nicholas (1869–1937). Russian dancer and teacher at the Maryinsky Theatre, St Petersburg. He greatly influenced his pupils, Fokine, Nijinsky, Pavlova, etc. In 1929 he opened a school in London and passed on to his English students (Markova, Brae, Shearer, etc.) some of his 1st-hand knowledge of *Petipa and some of the Danish tradition which his teacher Johanssen had learned from Bournonville.

Legend of Good Women, The. Poem by *Chaucer.

Legend of St Ursula, The. Series of paintings by *Carpaccio; *Memlinc also painted 6 small panels on the theme.

Legend of Sleepy Hollow, The (1820). Story by Washington *Irving.

Léger Fernand (1881–1955). French painter, trained initially as an architectural designer. He studied in various Paris studios between 1903 and 1907 when, like many others, he discovered Cézanne. For the next 7 years, reacting against the diffuseness of his early neo-impressionist manner, he worked towards a concentrated structural strength in his painting. His early cubist paintings (nicknamed 'tubist') differed from the mainstream in their volumetric solidity, in their deep space and in a futurist 'tendency towards the dynamic'. With his friend Delaunay he was one of the most influential cubist painters: Mondrian greatly admired him and the transitional works (*c.* 1911–12) of Malevich seem to derive directly from paintings like *Nus dans un Paysage* (1909–11; Kröller-Müller Mus., Otterlo). By 1912 (*La Femme en Bleu*, K. Mus., Basle) he was nearing abstraction.
He attributed his post-war abandonment of this path to his wartime discoveries first of the working man and secondly of the beauty of machinery. His major works are of contemporary subjects, simple in their black contours and bold colour areas and endowing the ordinary man with a 19th-c. monumentality, e.g. *Les Loisins* (1948–9; M.M.A., Paris). His contact with de stijl circles in the 1930s did not diminish his deep respect for the figurative tradition. He also collaborated on a film, *Le Ballet Méchanique* (1923–4), and designed for stained glass, mosaics, ceramics and the stage.

legitimate drama. A term dating from the 18th c. to differentiate plays from other kinds of stage entertainment.

Legnani Pierina (1863–1923). Italian dancer who was the first to perform 32 fouettés (London, 1892). She stayed in St Petersburg (1893–1901), dancing Odette/Odile in the first successful production of *Swan Lake* (1895). L. was the only foreign dancer to be honoured with the title prima ballerina assoluta at the Maryinsky Theatre, St Petersburg.

Legrand Marc-Antoine (1673–1728). French actor and author who joined the Comédie-Française as an actor but later wrote very successful plays on topical contemporary themes.

Léger. *The City* (1919)

Léger. *Divers on a Yellow Background* (1941)

Legros. *The Ex-Voto*

Lehmbruck. *Kneeling Woman*

Legrenzi Giovanni (1626–90). Italian composer, organist and music director of St Mark's, Venice. His 17 operas were the logical development of Monteverdi's and Cavalli's work towards the 18th-c. show opera; he wrote also instrumental trio sonatas, important forerunners of Corelli, and church music, including solo cantatas.

Legros Alphonse (1837–1911). French painter and etcher. He was associated with the early impressionists and was a friend of Whistler, who persuaded him to come to England, where he settled. He was Slade Professor at Univ. College, London (1876–92).

Lehár Franz (1870–1948). Hungarian composer who studied at Prague Conservatory and became a military bandmaster for a time. In 1902 he settled in Vienna, becoming famous as a composer of operettas, notably *The Merry Widow* (1905). Others include *The Count of Luxembourg* (1909), *Gypsy Love* (1910) and *Frederica* (1928). He also wrote marches, waltzes, etc.

Lehmann Lotte (1885–). German operatic soprano, a naturalized U.S. citizen. After her début in 1910 she sang in the 1st production of Strauss's *Ariadne auf Naxos* (1916) and *Die Frau ohne Schatten* (1919). She is also a novelist and autobiographer.

Lehmann Rosamond Nina (1903–). English novelist who draws significance from her characters' fragmentary impressions of people and places. Works include: *Dusty Answer* (1927), *Invitation to the Waltz* (1932), *The Ballad and the Source* (1944).

Lehmbruck Wilhelm (1881–1919). German sculptor. After living in Paris (1910–14) he returned to Germany at the beginning of World War I; shocked by his experiences as a nurse in a military hospital he committed suicide. His early work was influenced by A. Maillol. In 1911 with *Kneeling Woman* (M.M.A., New York) he began to create the slender, melancholy, expressionistic type of figure characteristic of his maturity.

Leibl Wilhelm (1844–1900). German portrait, genre and subject painter, the most important representative of 19th-c. German realism. He was a painter of intensity and power, frequently taking peasant life as his subject, e.g. *Three Women in Church* (K. halle, Hamburg).

Leibniz Gottfried Wilhelm (1646–1716). German philosopher who attempted to provide a rational basis for Christian belief. His thought culminated in the metaphysical doctrine of monads (simple non-spatio-temporal substances), transmitters of energy. The world of appearance and diversity is the manifestation of the systems of monads; God is explained as a completely active monad. L. has been greatly admired by 20th-c. philosophers for his original (and only lately discovered) work in logic.

Leibowitz René (1913–). Polish-born French conductor and composer, a pupil of Schoenberg and Webern. His compositions particularly explore Schoenberg's notion of 'serial complexes'. His works include: *L'Explication des métaphores* for speaker, 2 pianos, harp and percussion (1950); a chamber symphony; a sonata for piano and flute; a piano concerto and the book . . . *Schoenberg et son école* (1946).

Leigh Vivien (1913–). English actress; of great distinction, but best known for performances as kittenish but dangerous women – e.g. as Scarlett O'Hara in the film of Margaret *Mitchell's *Gone With the Wind.* Her Blanche du Bois in Tennessee Williams's *Streetcar Named Desire* (play and film) was also acclaimed.

Leighton Frederic, Lord (1830–96). English painter and sculptor, the leading exponent of the sentimental classicism and idealism of the late Victorian era. He was brought up and studied on the Continent but settled in London in 1860. He was the 1st painter to receive a peerage (1896).

Leighton Kenneth (1929–). English composer, lecturer in music in Edinburgh Univ. (1956–); his teachers included G. Petrassi. His music, influenced by Hindemith and Bartók and serial techniques, includes: concertos for violin, cello and viola-harp-timpani, and a sinfonia sacra, *The Light Invisible* for tenor, chorus and orchestra (1958).

Leitmotiv (German, 'leading motif'). In music the name for a device of composition, exploited and developed by Wagner. It is a brief theme, figure or harmonic progression by which situations, characters or ideas in a drama or opera are represented and with which they are identified. The *L.* undergoes a metamorphosis as the character or idea develops.

Lekain Henri-Louis (1729–78). French actor who started as an amateur (1748) but was then seen by Voltaire. They became lifelong friends

Leibl. *Three Women in Church*

Leibniz

Lord Leighton. *The Garden of the Hesperides*

Sir Peter Lely. *Painter and Family*

Jean-Baptiste Lemoyne. *Mlle Dangeville as Thalia*

Jacques Lemercier. Church of the Sorbonne

Le Moal. *Feast of St John, Midsummer Day*

and he joined Voltaire's co., later achieving great popularity at the Comédie-Française.

Lekeu Guillaume (1870–94). Belgian composer of the school of Franck. D'Indy admired his work and completed L.'s cello sonata, piano quartet and string quartet; his other works include *Fantaisie sur deux airs angevins* for orchestra.

Lélian Pauvre: Paul *Verlaine

Lely Sir Peter, born Pieter van der Faes (1618–80). Portrait painter, probably born and certainly trained in Holland, but chiefly associated with the English school. L. arrived in England about 1641 where, in spite of early hesitation in style, some competition from native-born painters and the Civil War, he became the chief portrait painter after Van Dyck's death. *The Children of Charles I* (1647; Petworth House, Sussex) is close in style to Van Dyck. *Oliver Cromwell* (1651; Pitti, Florence) is more confident. At the Restoration L. was appointed principal painter to Charles II. Numerous commissions necessitated setting up a workshop. This grew larger and L.'s control diminished, as did the standard of paintings bearing his name. Of high quality: *The Capel Sisters* (Met. Mus., New York), *Painter and Family* (Courtauld Gal., London), *Lady Byron* (R. Coll., England) and the famous *Admirals* (N. Maritime Mus., Greenwich). Already showing the decline of L.'s art are the equally famous *Beauties* (R. Coll., Hampton Court).

Lemaire des Belges Jean (*c.* 1473–*c.* 1524). French poet, one of the *rhétoriqueurs. L. worked as secretary or chronicler at several courts. He visited Italy 3 times and introduced the terza rima into France. His works include the prose *Illustrations de Gaule et Singularités de Troie*, which recounts the supposed Trojan origins of the French, and an allegory, *La Concorde des deux langages* (1511), advocating harmony between French and Italian.

Le Maistre Mattheus (*c.* 1505–77). Franco-Flemish composer who worked largely at Dresden. His most important compositions are his spiritual and secular *Lieder*, in the tradition of L. Senfl, e.g. *Geistliche und Weltliche Teutsche Geseng* (1566).

Lemaître Frédérick (1800–76). French actor of great versatility, equally good in tragedy and burlesque, who achieved both popular and critical acclaim.

Lemaître Jules (1853–1914). French theatre critic and playwright; his criticism is coll. in *Les Contemporains* (1885–6, 1918; *Literary Impressions*, 1921) and *Impressions de Théâtre* (1888–1920; *Theatrical Impressions*, 1924).

Le Maître de Saci Louis-Isaac (1613–84). French priest, director of the abbey of *Port-Royal, which was the centre of the austere Jansenist movement within Catholicism. L. trs. the Old Testament and collaborated in a trs. of the New Testament.

Lemercier Jacques (1585–1654). French architect. He designed the domed church of the Sorbonne, Paris (begun 1635), under strong influence from Roman baroque; the château and town-plan of Richelieu; and part of the Louvre (Pavilion de l'Horloge, 1644).

Lemercier (Louis-Jean) Népomucène (1771–1840). French playwright whose *Pinto ou la Journée d'une conspiration* (1800), written in prose, was the 1st French historical comedy.

Lemieux Jean-Paul (1904–). French-Canadian painter, for a long time of Quebec landscape and folk-lore; since the 1950s he has worked in a primitive and symbolic style.

Lemmon Jack (1925–). U.S. film actor and leading comedian/farceur. His innocence contrasted with B. Wilder's directorial cynicism has brought him particular success in *Some Like It Hot* (1959), *The Apartment* (1960) and *Irma La Douce* (1963).

Le Moal Jean (1909–). French painter and designer who studied under Bissière at the Académie Ranson, Paris (1934–8). In the early 1940s he began to develop his characteristic abstract style of vibrating colours within a loose linear framework. He has designed tapestries and stained glass, notably a window (1956) for the church of Notre-Dame at Rennes.

Lemon Mark (1809–70). English humorist and writer, joint-founder and ed. of *Punch* (1841). He contributed to various periodicals including *Household Words*, and produced novels, plays and operas.

Le Moyne (Lemoyne) François (1688–1737). French decorative painter. He was an admirer of the work of Pietro da Cortona and one of the last French artists to follow the baroque decorative tradition. He was employed at Versailles, where he painted his masterpiece, the ceiling of the Salon d'Hercule.

Lemoyne Jean-Baptiste (1704–78). French sculptor to Louis XV, pupil of his father Jean-Louis L. and R. Le Lorrain. His finest monumental works for the king were destroyed during the Revolution and his reputation rests on his portrait busts. E.-M. Falconet, J.-B. Pigalle, A. Pajou and J.-A. Houdon were his pupils.

Le Nain the brothers Antoine (1588–1648), Louis (1593–1648) and Mathieu (1607–77). French painters, rediscovered in the 19th c. Details of their lives are still obscure, but it is known that in 1648 they were members of the Academy. It is difficult to differentiate between them. Recent research has sought to establish Louis as the most significant; his pictures of peasants in their surroundings are painted with realism and formal strength, and show the influence of Velazquez. The *Family Portrait* (N.G., London) is a good example. Antoine worked mainly on a small scale and Mathieu produced more polished and pleasing paintings of cavaliers and genre.

Lenbach Franz von (1836–1904). German portrait painter.

Lenclos Anne de, known as Ninon de (1620–1705). French society woman whose *salon* was frequented by Boileau, La Fontaine, Molière, Racine and others.

Lendvai Erwin (1882–1949). Hungarian-born composer, conductor and teacher; a pupil of H. Koessler and Puccini. He composed an opera, and symphonic and chamber music, but most important are his works for chorus.

L'Enfant Pierre-Charles (1754–1825). French architect who emigrated to the U.S. He prepared the plans from which Washington was built.

Leni Paul (1885–1929). German film director, a pupil of M. *Reinhardt who became a set designer then director (1918). He made one of the most famous German silent films, *Waxworks* (1924). He made 4 films in Hollywood (1927–9) before his death there.

Lenica Jan (1928–). Polish graphic designer and animated-film maker. L. made in collaboration with *Borowczyk 2 animated films; the comic *Once Upon A Time* (1957) with paper cut-outs, and the threatening but impenetrable *Dom* (1957), using 3-dimensional objects. L. moved to France and made a cartoon, *Monsieur Tête* (1959), from an Ionesco script. *Labyrinth* (Poland; 1962) uses tinted cut-outs from steel engravings to tell its story of destruction.

Lenin Vladimir Ilyich. Pseud. of V. I. Ulyanov (1870–1924). Russian revolutionary, chief architect of the Bolshevik October Revolution of 1917 and 1st leader of the Soviet state (1917–24); he also wrote voluminously, and his works –with those of Karl *Marx, whose theories L. expanded, added to and adapted–provide the doctrinal rationale (Marxist-Leninism) of the Soviet state and its policies.

Lennep Jacob van (1802–68). Dutch novelist and poet chiefly remembered for his historical novels, especially *De lotgvallen von Ferdinand Huyck* (1840; *The Count of Talavera*, 1880).

Lenngren Anna Maria (1754–1817). Swedish poet. Most of her verse is satirical and didactic, usually directed against the extravagances of the aristocracy.

Leno Dan (1860–1904). English music-hall comedian who began his career as a clog-dancer in London public-houses. He often played the 'Dame' in pantomimes at Drury Lane.

Lenormand Henri-René (1882–1951). French playwright strongly influenced by Freud. L.'s plays include *Le Mangeur de rêves* (1922; *Dream Doctor*, 1928) and *Le Lâche* (1925; *The Coward*, 1928).

Le Notre André (1613–1700). French garden designer who established the French garden as the reigning style in Europe in succession to the Italian, until the ascendancy of the English garden in the 18th c. He succeeded his father, Jean Le N., as royal gardener in the Tuileries, Paris in 1637. He studied painting under Vouet and the garden work of the Mollets and of J. Boyceau, whom he outdistanced in the grandeur

Lenin: drawing by Leonid Pasternak, father of writer Boris Pasternak

Le Notre. Vaux-le-Vicomte

Le Notre. Park of the château of Versailles

Louis Le Nain. *Family Portrait*

Leonardo. *Virgin of the Rocks* (Louvre)

of his classic designs. Parterres, avenues, artificial lakes, terraces, flower and fruit gardens, fountains, basins were ordered in geometric schemes which were fitting complements to the architectural style of the great French châteaux such as Vaux-le-Vicomte, Chantilly and Dampierre, and of royal palaces such as the Tuileries, Choisy, Marly, Versailles and Trianon. Formalism was the keynote of his work.

Lenz Jacob Michael Reinhold (1751–92). German poet and dramatist. He developed an obsessive admiration for Goethe, endeavouring to excel him and aping his life in every respect; L.'s eccentricities ended in a period of insanity. He was a fine lyric poet but wrote more for the theatre on the Shakespearean principles expressed in his theoretical work *Anmerkungen übers Theater* (1774). L. rejects the *unities and in the dramas *Der Hofmeister* (1774) and *Die Soldaten* (1776) achieves a realistic presentation of character and attempts, unsuccessfully, to combine comedy and tragedy.

Leo Leonardo (1694–1744). Italian composer and teacher working at Naples; his pupils included N. Jommelli and N. Piccinni. L.'s best work is in his comic operas and church music.

León Luis de (1527–91). Spanish Augustinian theologian and poet, author of a small number of lyrical and mystical poems (publ. posth.) which are among the finest in Spanish literature. He also wrote theological and mystical works in prose.

Leonardo. *Last Supper*

Leonardo da Vinci (1459–1519). Florentine painter, sculptor and draughtsman, a universal genius who was architect, town planner, inventor, scientist, writer and musician. L. was the natural son of the notary at Vinci, then under Florentine rule. His extraordinary gifts were soon apparent and he was apprenticed (*c.* 1470) to Andrea Verrocchio, leading Florentine artist. His fellow-apprentices were Lorenzo di Credi and Botticelli. Little is known about this period except that L. came under the patronage of Lorenzo de' Medici and in 1472 became a master, a member of the Guild of St Luke. In 1482 he entered the service of Lodovico Sforza, Duke of Milan, where he was active as court painter, sculptor, architect and military engineer until the fall of Sforza in 1499, when the French armies occupied Milan. L. fled to Mantua, then to Venice, where he was employed as a military engineer. In 1500 he went to Florence, 2 years later joined Cesare Borgia in his campaigns, but on Borgia's defeat returned to Florence, where he remained until 1508. The *Mona Lisa* was painted in Florence between 1503 and 1506. In 1508 L. was recalled to Milan by the French governor of the city, Charles d'Amboise, and for 5 years was occupied with scientific studies and plans for the construction of a canal. With his pupil and assistant, Francesco Melzi, he travelled to the Vatican in 1513 to seek the favour of the Medici Pope Leo X, but left disappointed in 1517 to join the court of the French king, Francis I. In Rome L. was surrounded by intrigue; in France, however, he was greatly appreciated and admired. He lived at the royal château de Cloux, near Amboise, until his death.

Leonardo. *Head of an old man*; drawing

Leonardo. Drawings of projected military machines

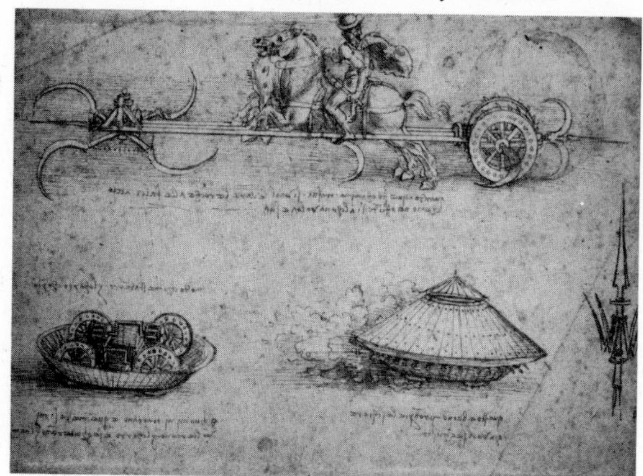

L. left few authentic paintings. The Angel kneeling at the extreme left in Verrocchio's *Baptism of Christ* is believed to be his work. He assisted Verrocchio on a number of paintings, and this has led to a great deal of controversy over their authorship. The *Annunciation* (*c.* 1474; Uffizi) is attributed to L. on account of the mysterious landscape and the scientific rendering of depth; 2 *Madonnas*, in Munich and Leningrad, now much restored, are also attributed to this period. In 1481 L. undertook a painting the *Adoration* (Uffizi) for the monks of San Donato at Scopeto, but left it unfinished. The composition was significant for its grouping of figures, their expressive gestures and its chiaroscuro effect (also a characteristic of the unfinished *St Jerome* in the Vatican). During 1483 L. worked on the painting the *Virgin of the Rocks*, possibly the version at the N.G., London. The version at the Louvre is considered to be earlier and of greater artistic value. He painted a number of portraits of court ladies during his stay in Milan; the *Lady with the Ermine* (Cracow) was probably the duke's mistress. It is a masterly rendering of form and a profound psychological study. The *Last Supper*, painted 1495–8 for the refectory of the monastery of S. Maria delle Grazie, Milan has, though recently carefully restored, been much damaged and overpainted; moreover, because of L.'s experiment in this picture with oil paint, the wall surface was already affected by 1517. The spectator is drawn to participate in the action: Christ and the Apostles are sitting at a table which seems to stand in an extension of the refectory. In the *Mona Lisa* (1503; Louvre) L. expressed with consummate skill his feeling for the mystery of existence. The forms are precise yet melting, fused into each other with subtle tonal transitions, the **sfumato* perfected by L. and exploited by his followers. The cartoon of the *Battle of Anghiari*, painted at the same time in Florence, is now lost; several copies, including one by Rubens, have survived. When L. moved to France, he took with him the *Mona Lisa*, *John the Baptist*, and the *Virgin and Child with St Anne* (Louvre). No authentic sculpture by L. is known. In Milan he made a model of an equestrian monument but it was destroyed by French soldiers before it could be cast in bronze. Numerous landscape drawings and studies of heads and nude figures survive; many form part of his notes and scientific studies. L.'s draughtsmanship has never been equalled. His notebooks, written backwards and unknown to his contemporaries, contained profound scientific observations on proportion, perspective, optics, anatomy, geology and such inventions as cannons, tanks, a diving-suit and flying machines. His celebrated *Treatise on Painting*, which has survived in a fairly accurate copy by another hand, circulated widely in the 16th c. L. greatly influenced his contemporaries, del Sarto, Raphael, Correggio and Giorgione, with his compositions and use of light. He influenced Rubens and foreshadowed the chiaroscuro of Rembrandt.

Leoncavallo Ruggiere (1858–1919). Italian *verismo composer and poet of the 2-act opera *Pagliacci* (1892) ('The Players'); a story of love and jealousy in which the stage lives and real lives of the actors in a village pageant are tragically juxtaposed. Amongst L.'s other operas are *La Bohème* (1897) and *Zaza* (1900).

Leonel Power (d. 1445). After Dunstable, with whose works L.'s have been confused, the foremost English composer of his time. L.'s style changes from dissonantal late ars nova to the suaver consonantal style of Dunstable. His 50 surviving compositions are in the Old Hall and continental mss. L. also wrote a theoretical treatise.

Leoni Giacomo (*c.* 1686–1746). Venetian architect who worked in Germany and England. He supervised and prepared the engravings for the English editions of Palladio (1715–16) and L. B. Alberti (1726). He designed or added to several English country-houses.

Leoni Leone (*c.* 1560–1627). Italian composer working in Vicenza; his style is Venetian, showing mastery of the double chorus.

Leoninus (Léonin). 12th-c. French composer of the school of Notre-Dame of Paris, a predecessor of Pérotin. A book of his organa survives (*organum).

Leonora overtures. 3 overtures written by *Beethoven for his opera *Fidelio*; its heroine is called 'Leonora'.

Leonov Leonid Maximovich (1899–). Soviet novelist and playwright. L.'s early novels, especially *The Badgers* (1924; 1947) and *The Thief* (1927; 1931) give a fairly objective account of the difficulties of the period after the Revolution. *Soviet River* (1930; 1931) was the 1st important work describing Soviet industrialization.

Leopard, The (1958). Novel by Guiseppe di *Lampedusa; also made into a film (1963), directed by L. *Visconti.

Leopardi Count Giacomo (1798–1837). One of the greatest Italian lyric poets. His father's reactionary politics and literary tastes were a stifling atmosphere for the young L., but the family's library fired an ambition to excel in philology. Intense study affected a delicate constitution and left him in ill-health for life. Throughout L.'s work runs a pessimism amounting at times to nihilism. L. views sentience itself as suffering, man's insignificance in the universe overpowers him, life is merely a slow dying, a purposeless misery, and human unhappiness a law of nature. Besides his masterpiece, the lyric coll. *Canti* (1831), L. wrote a coll. of prose dialogues, *Operette Morali*, and the *Zibaldone*, a prose miscellany written with a depth and purity of style which place him among the greatest of Italian prose writers.

Leopold Carl Gustaf af (1756–1829). Swedish poet and playwright in the neo-classical manner, which he ardently defended against the romantics.

Leopold Jan Hendrik (1865–1925). Dutch poet whose sensitive, tragic verse reflects his loneliness and despair (caused in part by deafness).

Leonardo. *Adoration of the Magi*

Leonardo. *Virgin and Child with St Anne.* Also *cartoon, *drapery, **Mona Lisa* and colour plate 44

Leopardi

Lépine. *Rue de Norvins, Montmartre*

Mikhail Lermontov

Nikolay Leskov

Lépine Stanislas-Victor-Edmond (Édouard) (1835–92). French painter who with L.-E. Boudin and J. B. Jongkind was a forerunner of impressionism. He was a pupil of J.-B. Corot.

Leprince Jean-Baptiste (1734–81). French painter and engraver, inventor of the aquatint process of *engraving.

Lermontov Mikhail Yurievich (1814–41). Russian novelist and poet. After a brief attendance at Moscow Univ. (1830), he enrolled in the St Petersburg School of Ensigns, being commissioned in the Hussars of the Guard in 1834. With aristocratic connections, he mixed freely in society until 1837, when the circulation of *Death of a Poet*, a poem which blamed the government for Pushkin's death, led to his transfer to a regiment of the line in the Caucasus (which provides the setting for much of his work). He was killed in a duel during a 2nd period of service in the Caucasus.
L.'s personality and work owed much to Lord Byron and Pushkin. In *A Hero of Our Times* (1840; 1854), a novel of 5 linked stories, the central figure is Pechorin, a noble, a society man who despises society, admiring the intensity and generosity of primitive feeling; without capacity or opportunity for it, he can only act – usually maliciously – in order to relieve his boredom. The simplicity and restraint of its style put this among the best Russian novels. L. realized the immaturity of his early poetry (*The Angel*, written in 1832, is an exception) and publ. nothing until 1835. Later poems like *Hajj Abrek, The Demon, Mtsyri* and *New Year's Night* still exploit the romantic themes of revenge, the exotic, doomed love, and disenchantment. But *Borodino, The Testament* and *Valerik* are increasingly realistic; and pieces like *The Song of the Merchant Kalashnikov*, which are still romantic in outlook, have a conciseness and clarity which promised complete mastery. L. wrote when the age of romantic poetry was giving way to that of prose realism; and his influence on writers was limited until the advent of Blok and the symbolists.

Lerner Irving (1909–). U.S. film director. L. was cameraman for *Flaherty on *The Land* (1941). After making shorts (e.g. *Muscle Beach*, 1947–8), his 1st feature was *Man Crazy* (1953), followed by 2 ambitious low-budget thrillers, *Murder by Contract* and *City of Fear* (both 1958), and a literary adaptation, *Studs Lonigan* (1960).

Leroux Gaspard. Late 18th-c. French composer of harpsichord music and church music in the tradition of Charpentier and Lalande. J. S. Bach knew L.'s work, adapting a phrase of his in a gigue.

Le Roy Mervyn (1900–). U.S. film director and producer. Since he started directing in 1927, L. has made every type of film with efficiency. In the 1930s he was famous for a gangster thriller, *Little Caesar* (1930), and 2 effective social protest movies, *I am a Fugitive from a Chain Gang* (1932) and *They Won't Forget* (1937). He also made broad comedies like *Tugboat Annie* (1933) and musicals like *Gold Diggers of 1933*. He produced *The Wizard of Oz* (1939). His later work is at its best when he can make use of his inherent vulgarity: *Little Women* (1949), the spectacular *Quo Vadis?* (1951) and especially the musical *Gypsy* (1962).

Le Sage Alain-René (1668–1747). French novelist and dramatist. He trs. much from the Spanish including Calderón and Lope de Vega, After a number of plays his reputation was consolidated by *Gil Blas* (1715–35), a picaresque novel owing much to Spanish models and widely admired for its dramatic narrative and its detached fidelity to human nature. He composed more than 100 pieces for the fairground as well as other romances, including *Le Diable boiteaux* (1707; *The Devil upon Two Sticks*, 1708).

Lescot Pierre (d. 1578). French architect, one of the pioneers of the Renaissance in France, though he never went to Italy and relied entirely on books. His fame rests on his part in the rebuilding of the Louvre (1546 onwards), half of one side of the Cour du Vieux Louvre, the oldest part now extant. His design combines French elements (the division into pavilions, arches over windows, high roof) with Italian (classical pilasters and relief sculpture with Renaissance motifs).

Leskov Nikolay Semyonovich (1831–95). Russian novelist and short-story writer. L. had relatively little formal education and worked at a variety of jobs, acquiring a knowledge of Russian life and speech which, together with a great narrative gift, made him a master of *skaz*, humorous or satirical stories told by a fictitious narrator – usually one of the lower classes – in his own idiom. Famous examples are *The Hare Park* (posth. publ. 1917) and *A*

Alain-René Le Sage

Le Roy. Rosalind Russell and Natalie Wood in *Gypsy*

Lescot. Cour du Vieux Louvre

Gotthold Ephraim Lessing

Lady Macbeth of Minsk (1865; 1922), on which Shostakovich's opera is based. Outside Russia L. is best known for *Cathedral Folk* (1872; 1924), a novel of clerical life in a cathedral town.

Leslie Charles Robert (1794–1859). English painter of U.S. parentage who specialized in small paintings illustrating scenes from literature. He is remembered as author of *Memoirs of John Constable, R.A.* (2nd ed. 1845), an important biography largely composed of extracts from Constable's correspondence.

Leśmian Bolesław. Pseud. of B. Lesman (1878–1937), the chief representative of symbolist poetry in Poland. Essentially a poets' poet, he combined fantasy with a deeply sensuous and concrete approach to reality. He trs. into Polish some of Poe's tales. His poetic output was not large, but he exerted a great influence on younger poets.

Lespinasse Julie-Jeanne-Éléonore de (1732–76). French intellectual. L. became the companion of Mme du Deffand (1754) but later set up her own *salon*, which became a meeting-place for d'Alembert, Turgot and other *philosophes*. She appears in Diderot's *La Rêve de d'Alembert*.

Lessing Doris (May) (1919–). English writer born in Africa. Her works, particularly the short stories, e.g. *Five* (1953), have been acclaimed for their psychological perception and technical finish; they also include the novel *The Habit of Loving* (1957) and the plays *Each His Own Wilderness* (1959) and *Play with a Tiger* (1962).

Lessing Gotthold Ephraim (1729–81). German writer, thinker and influential critic. The literary leader of the later Enlightenment (replacing Gottsched's excogitated rules by principles based on experience).

L. studied in Leipzig and became (1748) a free-lance in Berlin, resident adviser at the new Hamburg Theatre (1767), and librarian in Wolfenbüttel (1770). No. 17 of *Briefe die neueste Litteratur betreffend* (1759–65) attacks Gottsched's francophilia and recommends English models, including Shakespeare. *Die Hamburgische Dramaturgie* (1767–9; 1879) re-interprets Aristotle, whom French theorists had misunderstood. *Laokoon* (1766; 1767), starting from a remark by Winckelmann, distinguishes –too sharply–the spheres of literature (action in time) and plastic art (stasis in space). L.'s early plays include *Miss Sara Sampson* (1755; 1789), which although sentimental in language and naïve in characterization initiated German middle-class tragedy. *Minna von Barnhelm* (1767; *The Disbanded Officer*, 1786), the 1st great German comedy, shows the shrewd heroine regaining her stiff-necked lover, Tellheim, by affection and guile. The characters are rounded and individual; the setting is contemporary and realistic (ex-servicemen's problems). *Emilia Galotti* (1772; 1794) established middle-class tragedy in prose, influencing Goethe and Schiller. The sensual prince is foiled by the virtuous if susceptible heroine, a commoner, who manipulates her father into killing her; psychologically shrewd but over-conscious. *Nathan der Weise* (1779; 1781), the 1st notable German play in blank verse, explores the clash between religious faith and toleration. All 3 plays have a linguistic texture like a Socratic dialogue, exploring analytically the implication of concepts; in *Minna*, 'honour'; in *Emilia*, 'aims and media'; in *Nathan*, 'humanity'. L.'s essay *Die Erziehung des Menschengeschlechts* (1780; *The Education of the Human Race*, 1858) proposes a humanitarian ethic.

Le Sueur Eustache (1616–55). French painter of religious and mythological subjects, pupil of S. Vouet, who strongly influenced his early work. He subsequently followed Poussin's classicism, evident in his 22 paintings *The Life of St Bruno* (1645–8; Louvre) for the Charterhouse, Paris. In his late work he became a dull imitator of Raphael.

Le Sueur Hubert. French sculptor of the early 17th c., from 1629 in England, where he did much mediocre work for Charles I.

Le Sueur Jean-François (1760–1837). French composer, who as musical director of Notre-Dame of Paris (1786–7) aimed to make the services dramatic and descriptive. He was an inspector (1795) of the Conservatoire, musical director to Napoleon and professor of composition at the Conservatoire, his pupils including Berlioz and Gounod. His compositions include operas, e.g. *Ossian, ou les Bardes* (1804), oratorios and masses.

Lesur Daniel-Jean-Yves (1908–). French organist, composer and teacher, a co-founder of the group *Jeune France. L.'s music, 'modal' in character, elegant and poetic, includes: an

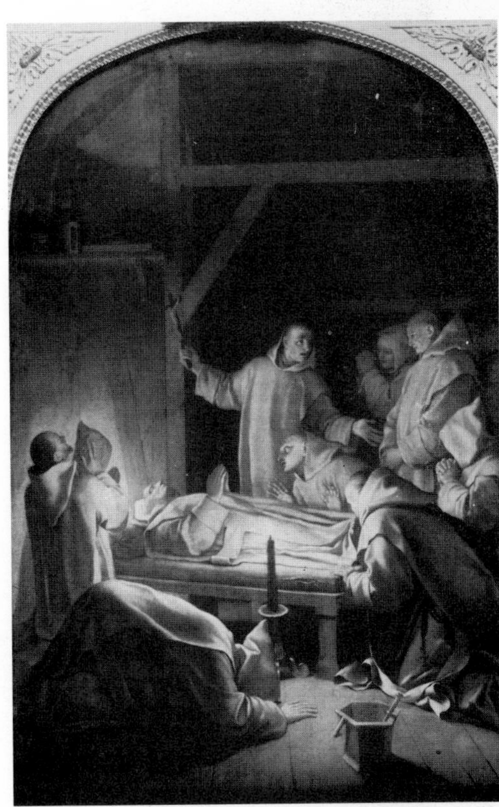
Eustache Le Sueur. *The Death of St Bruno*

Le Vau. Vaux-le-Vicomte

Lever House

orchestral overture to A. de Musset's play *Andrea del Sarto*; *Chansons Cambodgiennes*; and *Symphonie de Danse*.

Letter from an Unknown Woman (1948). Film directed by M. *Ophuls, based on a story by Stefan Zweig.

Lettres persanes (1721). Book by *Montesquieu.

Lettres philosophiques (1734). Series of letters by *Voltaire.

Le Vau Louis (1612–70). French architect. His patrons were predominantly the new bourgeois class, not the court. Chiefly known for the château of Vaux-le-Vicomte, a huge showy building with a bulging façade and domed hall, and the Collège des Quatre Nations, Paris (now the Institut de France), a large complex of courts with Italianate decoration. He also built part of the old Versailles, including the Escalier des Ambassadeurs (demolished).

Lever House New York (1952). Architects *Skidmore, Owings and Merrill.

Leviathan, The (1651). Political treatise by *Hobbes.

Levine Jack (1915–). U.S. expressionist painter whose work is devoted to social themes. The savage satire of *The Feast of Pure Reason* (1937; M.M.A., New York) has been moderated in his more recent paintings by a more tolerant attitude towards humanity.

Levinson André (1890–1933). Russian ballet critic of great influence. He moved to Paris in 1918 and was only gradually won over to the new style of Fokine.

Levitan Isaac (1860–1900). Among the earliest painters of Russian landscape. A member of the *Abramtsevo Colony, he contributed designs for some of the earliest productions of Mamontov's 'Private Opera'. At the Moscow College he was an influential professor among the future *avant-garde*, e.g. Kusnetsov, Larionov, Tatlin and Falk.

Leviticus. The 3rd book of the *Bible (Pentateuch) containing many of the laws given to the Hebrews by Moses.

Lewin Albert (1902–). U.S. film director. L. was a producer at M.G.M. and Paramount (1931–41) and thereafter was artistic supervisor at M.G.M. The films which he has written and directed, mostly from literary sources, are characterized by their elaborateness. They include *The Moon and Sixpence* (1942), *The Picture of Dorian Gray* (1945), *The Private Affairs of Bel Ami* (1947), *Pandora and the Flying Dutchman* (1951).

Lewis Alun (1915–44). Welsh poet; he died in India. Robert Graves has written highly of L.'s achievement and potential; certainly his work achieves a robust maturity. Colls are *Raiders Dawn* (1942) and *Ha! Ha! among the Trumpets* (posth. 1944).

Lewis C(ecil) Day (1904–). Irish poet. He worked as a schoolmaster until 1935 and was in the Ministry of Information during World War II. With Auden and Spender he formed in the 1930s part of a group which aimed to use poetry to express the social discontents of the time. His later poetry has become more direct, more sensuous and more personal; childhood, the loss of innocence, love and the passing of youth are his themes. In addition to his poetry he has trs. Virgil and has publ. a number of detective stories under the pseud. 'Nicholas Blake'.

Lewis C(live) S(taples) (1898–1963). English writer and critic. His important *The Allegory of Love* (1936) examines the literary tradition of courtly love from Chrétien de Troyes to Spenser. L.'s Christian apologetics include the humorous and satirical fantasy *The Screwtape Letters* (1942), Screwtape being an elderly devil, and science-fiction works.

Lewis Frederick Christian (1779–1856). English engraver and landscape painter. His brother George Robert L. (1782–1871) was a portrait and landscape painter, e.g. *View in Herefordshire: Harvest* (Tate).

Lewis Jerry (1926–). U.S. film comedian and director. L. made a series of films (1949–59) with his partner Dean Martin, who acted as feed man and singer. The basic L. character is a more desperate development of the Stan *Laurel simpleton. In 1960 L. directed *The Bellboy* which he followed, notably, with *The Ladies' Man* (1961) and *The Nutty Professor* (1963).

Levine. *The Feast of Pure Reason*

Levitan. *Above Eternal Peace*

C. Day Lewis

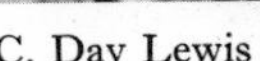

Sinclair Lewis

Lewis John Frederick (1805–76). English painter of oriental subjects, son of F. C. L. The brilliant colour and minute detail of his paintings attracted the admiration of Ruskin and anticipated the Pre-Raphaelites.

Lewis Matthew Gregory ('Monk') (1775–1818). English novelist, author of the sensational and horrific *Gothick novel *The Monk* (1795), which had a tremendous vogue. Byron was his friend and admirer.

Lewis (Harry) Sinclair (1885–1951). U.S. novelist and Nobel prizewinner. He was born in Sauk Center, Minnesota; his most famous novels deal satirically with bourgeois small-town and small-city life. His early fiction was sentimental, but satirical mockery gave him the method of his best books, which work through a mixture of caricature and realistic, panoramic description of large social subjects. His most famous novels are: *Main Street* (1920), a blistering attack on small-town mores and values, and *Babbitt* (1922) in which George F. Babbitt, a high-powered real-estate man senses, at 46, the emptiness of his life and tries, unsuccessfully, to rebel. Babbitt gave his name to the American type of go-getter. L.'s works include *Arrowsmith* (1925), *Elmer Gantry* (1927) and *Dodsworth* (1929).

Lewis (Percy) Wyndham (1884–1957). English writer and painter. After that period of his art called *vorticism, the 2 violently polemical numbers of the magazine *BLAST* (1914, 15) and war service, L. emerged as the most powerful and one of the most imaginative figures in English art, revered by some artists, increasingly rejected by cultural and social orthodoxy. L.'s novels and critical writings were radical and ruthless attacks on contemporary art and society. He despised the 'average' intellect, and in art held to the 'great ideals of structure and formal significance'; impressionism, in his view, marked the decay of realism and neither cubism, futurism nor abstract art were the true way out of the impasse of 20th-c. art. Art, he believed, was the science of the outside of things, and his own paintings and his drawings have a precise, tense, controlled line and a steely angularity of form and surface. His writings include: the novels *Tarr* (1918); *The Apes of God* (1930), on the superficialities and pretensions of 1920s society; *Revenge for Love* (1937), and *The Human Age*, a trilogy–*The Childermass* (1928), *Monstre Gai* (1955) and *Malign Fiesta*; the critical work *Time and Western Man* (1927) and the autobiographical *Blasting and Bombardiering* (1937). His paintings include: famous portraits of T. S. Eliot (1938 and 1949), Ezra Pound (1938) and Edith Sitwell (1923–35); *Surrender of Barcelona* (1936); and *Mud Clinic* (1937). He also produced numerous outstanding graphic works.

Lewton Val (1904–51). Film producer. After working as story ed. for Selznick and co-directing action sequences for a Selznick production (with J. Tourneur), he became a producer at R.K.O. He is famous for a series of intelligently made low-budget horror films, which began with *The Cat People.*

Leyden Lucas van: *Lucas van Leyden

Leyster Judith (1609–60). Dutch genre and portrait painter, wife of the painter Jan Molenaer.

L'Herbier Marcel (1890–). French film director, one of a group of *avant-garde* film makers led by *Delluc. His most famous film *Eldorado* (1921) was impressionist in style. He then became influenced by German expressionism. After the failure of the 'ultra-modern' *L'Inhumaine* (1923) his films decrease in interest. In 1954 he left the cinema to work for television.

Lhote André (1885–). French painter and influential teacher and writer on art. His admiration for the work of Cézanne led him to join the cubists, and in 1912 he exhibited with the Section d'Or group. His later work in a modified cubist style became somewhat academic.

Liadov Anatol Konstantinovich (1855–1914). Russian composer, teacher and conductor. He coll. and studied Russian folk-songs together with Balakirev and Liapunov. He composed little. He is best known for his fine piano pieces *Birulki* (1876) and *Tabatière à musique* (1893) and for his orchestral tone poems *Babe Yaga* (1904) and *Kikimore* (1909). His compositions are frequently inspired by folk-lore and they include *8 Russian Folk-songs* for orchestra (1906) and many arrangements of Russian folk-songs for voice and piano.

Liaisons dangereuses, Les (1782). Epistolary novel by *Laclos.

Wyndham Lewis. *Surrender of Barcelona.* Also *Eliot, *Sitwell, *vorticism

Leyster. *Boy playing the Flute*

Lhote. *Rugby* (1917)

Liberal arts. Gregor Reisch, *Margarita philosophica: Grammar*

Lichine and Rostova in *Cotillon* (1932)

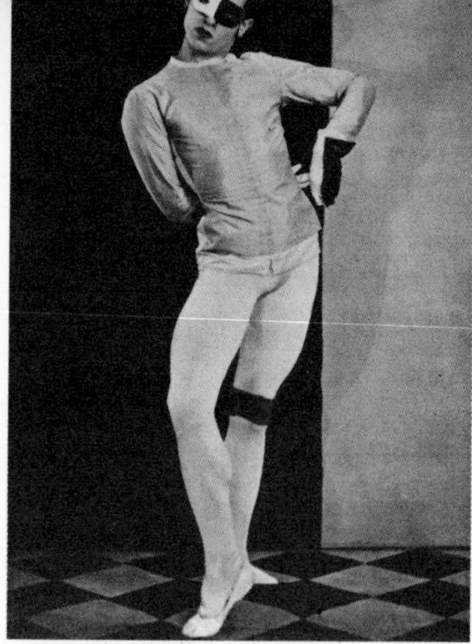

Lifar in *Romeo and Juliet*. Also *Ballets Russes

Liapunov Sergei Mikhailovich (1859–1924). Russian composer of the nationalist school whose work was influenced by his friend *Balakirev.

Libanius (314–*c.* 393). Greek sophist who taught at Constantinople and Nicomedia. A pagan, he was imperial secretary under Julian the Apostate. A large number of his letters and orations survive.

Max Liebermann. *Self-portrait* (1934)

liberal arts. The 7 subjects taught in medieval schools and universities: grammar, logic and rhetoric (called 'the Trivium') and arithmetic, geometry, music and astronomy ('the Quadrivium').

Liber Studiorum (1807–19). Series of landscape etchings and mezzotints by *Turner.

Liber Veritatis (*c.* 1675–80; British Museum). Coll. of 200 pen and bistre drawings by *Claude Lorrain.

libretto (Italian, 'little book'). In music the term used for the words of an opera; these were originally printed separately for sale to the audience. Among the greatest of librettists were the 18th-c. P. Metastasio and L. da Ponte.

Lichine David (1910–). Russian dancer who studied in Paris (from 1926) under Nijinska, becoming a soloist in Ballet Russe de Monte Carlo (1932–41). He turned to choreography and his most successful ballet, *Graduation Ball* (1940), has gone into the repertory of several cos. L.'s *La Création* (1948) was an experimental ballet without music or scenery.

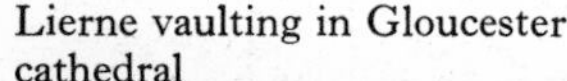

Lierne vaulting in Gloucester cathedral

Lichtenberg Georg Christoph (1742–99). German scholar and writer distinguished for brilliant if lightweight satire. Visits to England produced a series of 'Letters' and a commentary on Hogarth's engravings.

Lichtenstein Roy (1923–). U.S. painter; he studied and taught for a time at Ohio State Univ. Like many of his contemporaries he takes the impedimenta of modern American culture for subject and glorifies their supreme ordinariness. Typical paintings are a very large picture of a hamburger; a blown-up section from a comic strip; a painting of a plastic waste-bin.

Lie Jonas Lauritz Idemil (1833–1908). Norwegian novelist. His most frequent subject was middle-class family life, e.g. *Familjen paa Gilje* (1883; *The Family at Gilje*, 1920) and *Kommandørens Døtre* (1886; *The Commodore's Daughters*, 1892).

Liebelei (1932). Film directed by M. *Ophuls.

Liebermann Max (1847–1935). German painter and etcher. L. studied in Amsterdam, where he was influenced by the realism of Jozef Israëls, and in Paris, where he came into contact with Munkácsy, Courbet and the painters of the Barbizon school. In 1873 he worked in Barbizon, then from 1884 in Berlin as an accomplished master of naturalism, opposed to the theatrical school of Böcklin. His paintings of this period were dark and heavy, but from the 1890s the influence of Manet and the French impressionists increased; he was elected president of the Berlin Sezession in 1898. Famous and highly productive, L. became the most important German impressionist.

Liebermann Rolf (1910–). Swiss composer and director of the Hamburg opera (1959–). He follows, but not consistently, 12-note methods of composition; his works include the operas *Leonore 40/45* (1952) and *School for Wives* (1955), and *Concerto for Jazz-band and Symphony Orchestra*.

Lied (plural *Lieder*). The German word for song, used in English with particular reference to German 19th-c. song (from *Schubert to *Wolf); romantic poetry is used, and the accompaniment is regarded as of major importance in interpreting the words.

Lied von der Erde (German, 'Song of the Earth'). Setting by G. *Mahler of 6 Chinese poems, for voice and orchestra.

lierne. Architectural term for a subordinate rib (ornamental) between *tiercerons.

Lievensz (Lievens) Jan (1607–74). Dutch painter of portraits and religious, allegorical and genre subjects, pupil of Lastman. He worked for a time in Leyden with Rembrandt and in a very similar style. By 1635 he had moved to Antwerp, where his portraiture was influenced by Van Dyck and his other work to a lesser extent by Rubens and Brouwer.

Raising of Lazarus (Brighton Art Gal.) is a fine example of his work. His son JAN ANDREA (1644–80) was a portrait painter.

Lifar Serge (1905–). Russian dancer and choreographer who studied under Nijinska and Cecchetti. L. joined Diaghilev in 1923 and after a great success with the co. took over the *Paris Opéra as premier danseur and ballet master (1932), introducing the Russian style of dancing there. His 1st work was *Renard* (1929) and he has been a director of the Institut Choréographique since 1958.

Life on the Mississippi (1883). Book by Mark *Twain.

lift. In classical ballet, the male dancer simply lifts his partner by the waist during a movement of a few steps; but the l. has increasingly been used for new effects, the 2 dancers being posed in tableaux of great complexity.

ligature. In music, a line over 2 or more notes indicating that they are to be phrased as a group. The name is also given to the metal tie which holds the reed of the clarinet or saxophone in place.

Light in August (1932). Novel by William Faulkner.

Light of the World, The (1854). Painting by Holman *Hunt.

Liliencron Detlev von (1844–1909). German poet whose verse takes its subject-matter from L.'s career as a Prussian officer and his impressions of Holstein, his home state. His best work is in his lyric poetry, where his fresh and vivid observation of nature, his humour and lack of pretentiousness show him a fine minor poet. His verse colls include *Adjutantenritte* (1883); he also wrote a series of war novels including *Unter flatternden Fahnen* (1888) and a long verse satire.

Lilliburlero. A popular tune dating from the late 17th c. and once attributed to Purcell. It has had various words, most of them strongly Protestant in tone. The Orangemen of Ulster used the tune for the song 'The Protestant Boys'.

Lillie Beatrice (1898–). Canadian-born British cabaret performer. She is well known on both sides of the Atlantic for her hilarious one-woman shows. In London (1958) she played the title-role in *Auntie Mame.*

Lillo George (1693–1739). English dramatist whose play *The London Merchant, or the History of George Barnwell* (1731) was the 1st domestic tragedy in prose, substituting an apprentice for the usual noble tragic hero. Its influence on the Continent is evident in Diderot's *Le Fils Naturel* (1771) and Lessing's *Miss Sara Sampson* (1755).

Limb(o)urg de, the brothers Paul (Pol), Jean (Hennequin) and Herman (Hermant). Artists born in Flanders, probably the nephews of the painter J. Malouel. The brothers first entered the service of the dukes of Burgundy. From 1411 they worked for the duke of Berry, succeeding J. de Hesdin. Paul, the greatest, was chiefly responsible for *Les Très Riches Heures du Duc de Berry* (Mus. Condé, Chantilly). This illuminated book of hours, one of the masterpieces of the *international Gothic style, is a superb evocation of the age of chivalry and courtly love painted in its last years. The landscape backgrounds, especially of the calendar, are justly famous. All 3 artists were dead by 1416.

limerick. A 5-line verse, self-contained and making some witty, amusing or improbable point, usually about a person (fictional or actual). The form, dating from the early 19th c., is associated above all with Edward Lear, though he did not invent it.

limning. An obsolete word meaning the painting of miniature portraits.

Limoges. A town in France, home of a school of enamel working. The *champlevé produced at L. from the 12th c. was displaced in the late 15th c. by a new technique in which copper was painted in fused enamel colours in a manner approximating to miniature painting. Devotional subjects in the late Gothic style gave way (mid 16th c.) to classical, Old Testament and portrait subjects, influenced by, when not actually taken from, engravings of the school of Raphael, executed in grisaille on a black background. The L. school declined in the late 16th c.

Lincoln Abraham (1809–65). U.S. president during the Civil War; he opposed the extension of slavery and eventually (1863) emancipated

Limburg. *The Month of May*; from *Les *Très Riches Heures.* Also *international Gothic

Limoges enamel. Grave plate of Geoffrey Plantagenet (*c.* 1150)

Jan Lievensz. *Self-portrait*

Abraham Lincoln in 1860. Also *Gardener

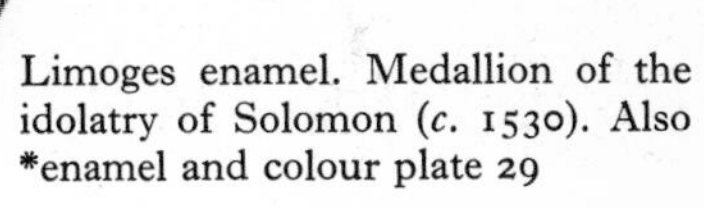

Limoges enamel. Medallion of the idolatry of Solomon (*c.* 1530). Also *enamel and colour plate 29

Lincoln cathedral

Vachel Lindsay

Linenfold. Tudor chair

the slaves. As a member of the new Republican party he took part in a famous series of debates with Stephen Douglas in the 1858 senatorial campaign and 2 years later was elected president. He was assassinated by the fanatic John Wilkes Booth on 14 April 1865. His public speeches are models of political rhetoric and popular expressive feeling (the Gettysburg Address, 1863; the Second Inaugural Address, 1865; the Reconstruction Speech, 1865). L.'s style is Middle Western, pungent, colloquial, direct and formal in various lively combinations and ranges from the simple to the high rhetorical.

Lincoln cathedral England. A key example of the Early English style. Begun in 1192, it follows *Canterbury, but adopts the English rather than French features of Gothic–use of Purbeck marble, separate shafts to piers, rather low proportions, etc. There are sexpartite vaults in the transepts, a unique asymmetrical design (known as the 'crazy vault') in the choir and an evolved tierceron vault (7 ribs to each pier) destined to be the pattern in England for the next 100 years, in the nave. The Angel Choir (begun 1256) is influenced by *Westminster Abbey and introduces bar-tracery.

Lincoln's Inn Fields Theatre. London theatre, opened by Sir William Davenant in 1661, believed to have been the first theatre with a proscenium arch. In its final season as a theatre (1733–4) it housed *Porpora's Italian opera, formed in rivalry with Handel's.

Lind Jenny (1820–87). Swedish operatic soprano, known as the 'Swedish Nightingale'. After world success in opera she settled in England, singing in oratorio and teaching at the R.C.M.

Linder Max (1883–1925). French film director, writer and actor. L. was a music-hall actor who started appearing in films in 1905. In 1908 he made a long series of slapstick comedies (some from 1917 in the U.S.) until his suicide. Although he lacked any real screen personality, he was most skilful, elegant and often witty. Chaplin has acknowledged L. as his master.

Lindisfarne Gospels (*c.* 700; B. Mus.). Copy of the Vulgate written, and probably illuminated, by Eadfrith, Bishop of Lindisfarne. The illuminations are a masterpiece of the Celtic style with the exception of 4 full-page miniatures of the Evangelists based on early Christian models. An interlinear Anglo-Saxon gloss was added about 950. It is also known as the *Book of St Cuthbert* or the *Durham Book*.

Lindsay or Lyndsay, Sir David (1490–1555). Scottish poet, playwright and courtier. M.'s works, satires on court and church, include the morality play *Ane Pleasant Satyre of the Thre Estaitis* (1540).

Lindsay Norman (1879–). Australian artist, known mainly for his illustrations of Rabelais, Petronius and Villon, and also the poetry of Kenneth Mackenzie; which introduced to Australian readers an element of gusty sensuality that most found distasteful or bogus.

Lindsay (Nicholas) Vachel (1879–1931). U.S. poet. L. zealously tried to spread love of poetry. His verse draws on the most diverse popular sources, e.g. Salvation Army chants in *General William Booth Enters into Heaven* (1913) and rag-time in *The Congo* (1914). It became popular for its folk quality and rhythmic cadences, and its praise of democracy and the values of agricultural life. Among L.'s best-known poems are: *Abraham Lincoln Walks at Midnight* (1914), *The Santa Fe Trail: A Humouresque* (1914) and *The Chinese Nightingale* (1917).

linenfold. A form of decorative pattern of Flemish origin, used in wooden furniture and panelling. It was introduced into England in the latter half of the 15th c. but was beginning to die out at the beginning of the Elizabethan period.

Linklater Eric (Robert Russell) (1899–). Scottish writer. His wide travels, e.g. in India and the U.S., colour his work, which includes the novels *Poet's Pub* (1929) and *Private Angelo* (1946).

Linley Thomas (1733–95). English composer and singing teacher. He became manager of the oratorios at the Drury Lane Theatre in 1774, subsequently becoming its part-owner and music director. He composed numerous stage and vocal works. All his children were musicians, and his son THOMAS (1756–78) was a brilliant violinist and the close friend of Mozart while studying in Florence.

Lindisfarne Gospels. Illuminated initial

Lipchitz. *Chant des Voyelles*

Linnell John (1792–1882). English artist, friend and benefactor of Blake and father-in-law of Palmer. He painted portraits, miniatures on ivory, landscapes and religious subjects. His best works are the early portraits and landscapes, e.g. *Kensington Sand Quarry* (Tate).

linocut. Form of relief printing similar in technique to the woodcut. Lino, invented in the mid 19th c., is easier to work than wood and is therefore often used when the durability of the block is not an important consideration. It is suited to bold, simplified rather than naturalistic effects.

lintel. Architectural term for a horizontal piece of wood, stone, etc. above a doorway or window, supporting the walling above.

Linz symphony. Nickname of Mozart's symphony in C, K.425 composed at L. in 1783.

Liotard Jean-Étienne (1702–89). Swiss pastellist and miniaturist who specialized in society and genre portraits, a fine example of the latter being *Chocolate Girl* (Dresden Gal.). He spent 5 years in Constantinople and on his return continued to wear Turkish dress and a beard, which earned him the nickname 'The Turk' and brought him publicity and patronage all over Europe. He painted several portraits of himself thus attired (Uffizi, Florence; Dresden Gal.; Geneva Mus.); also famous is his portrait of himself as an old man (1773; Geneva).

Lipchitz Jacques (1891–). Lithuanian-born sculptor who first studied architecture; he settled in Paris (1909), studying at the École des Beaux-Arts and then at the Académie Julian. He has lived in New York since 1941. His first one-man show was in 1920. In Paris he met Picasso, Gris and Archipenko, and his work from 1915 to about 1925 is cubist in character. Figures and heads are reduced to a simple block-like structure, whose flat planes are sometimes coloured (*Man with Guitar*, 1947; Yale Univ. A. Gal., New Haven). In the late 1920s his work underwent a change in form and content. The structural angularity gave way to a looser spatial play and the disciplined formal analysis was abandoned for a free use of evocative natural forms. The idol-like *Figure* (1926–30; M.M.A., New York) shows his affinity to the Parisian surrealism of the 1930s, while *Chant des Voyelles* (1931; K. haus, Zürich) or the *Prometheus* made for the International Exhibition (Paris, 1937) illustrate the concern of his mature style to appeal to the spectator through direct association with natural forms and emotions. He has executed several important commissions in New York and had a retrospective exhibition at the M.M.A. in 1954.

Lippi Filippino (*c.* 1457–1504). Florentine painter, the son of Fra Filippo L. and almost certainly the pupil of Botticelli. His finest work is *The Vision of St Bernard* (Badia, Florence). *Madonna and Child with St Dominic and St Jerome* (N.G., London) and *Portrait of a Young Man* (N.G., Washington) are also representative of the graceful style of Florentine painting before the revolution of Leonardo da Vinci. Early frescoes by L. are found beside those of Masaccio and Masolino in the Brancacci chapel, Carmine church, Florence. More important, and showing L.'s interest in classical art, are the cycle in the Strozzi chapel, S. Maria Novella, Florence. In his last years he worked in Rome, where he painted many panel pictures and the frescoes of the Caraffa chapel, S. Maria sopra Minerva.

Lippi Fra Filippo (*c.* 1406–69). Florentine painter. L. was received into a religious order as a child. He was certainly influenced by Masaccio, who painted his frescoes in the Carmine at the time when L. was growing up there. His 1st important work is the *Tarquinia Madonna* (N.G., Rome). His *Barbadori altarpiece* (Louvre) shows an almost complete movement away from Masaccio. Its composition is complicated and makes much of decorative elements, and the whole spirit is one of grace and refinement. At Prato L. painted his most important cycle of frescoes. Of special interest are the 2 scenes *St Stephen's Funeral* and *The Feast of Herod* (Duomo, Prato). In Prato he eloped with a nun; their son was the painter Filippino Lippi. Among many later paintings in which L.'s special grace is best seen are *Madonna and Child* (Uffizi) and *Madonna Adoring the Child in a Wood* (Berlin). The fresco cycle at Spoleto cathedral was unfinished at his death and was completed by others.

lira da braccio. Musical bowed string instrument widely used in high Renaissance Italy. About the size of a modern violin, it had 5 strings played on the finger-board and sometimes 2 additional bass strings. The LIRA DA

Filippino Lippi. *Madonna and Child with St Dominic and St Jerome*

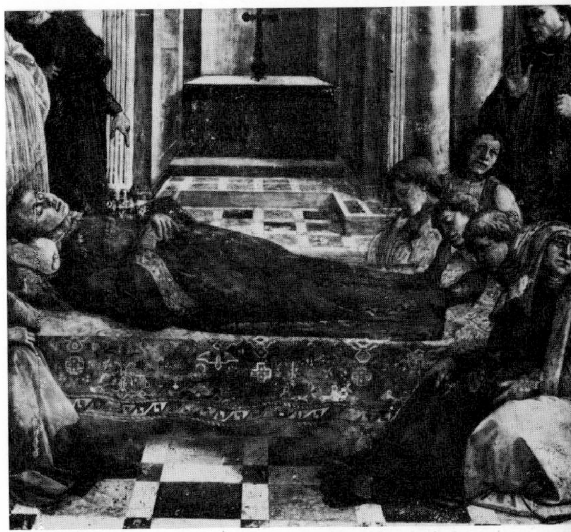

Fra Filippo Lippi. *St Stephen's Funeral* (detail)

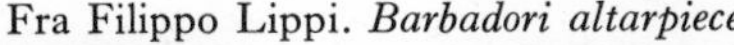

Fra Filippo Lippi. *Barbadori altarpiece*

Lipchitz. *Figure* (1926–30)

Liotard. *Self-portrait*

Lissitzky. *Proun 99*. Also *constructivism

Liss. *The Inspiration of St Jerome*

Franz Liszt

GAMBA, the size of a small cello, had as many as 15 strings.

Lismer Arthur (1885–). English-born Canadian painter (arriving in 1911) and an influential teacher; one of the *Group of Seven.

Liss (Lys) Johann (Jan) (d. 1629) nicknamed 'Pan'. German painter of genre, Biblical and mythological subjects who went to Italy (*c.* 1619) after being trained in the Netherlands. He settled in Venice and with Feti brought new vigour to Venetian painting of the early 17th c.

Lissitzky El (Eleazar) (1890–1941). Russian pioneer of modern design in the fields of typography and exhibition design in the 1920s; he also transmitted Russian ideas to W. Europe. In 1919 he met Malevich in Vitebsk; painting his 1st abstract paintings which he called *Prouns*. His *Story of Two Squares* (1920) is considered the 1st example of modern typographical design; in 1921 he helped to organize and design the Russian exhibition in Berlin. Group G which he founded in Berlin in 1920, fusing suprematist and constructivist ideas, made contact with de stijl, leading architects and, through the other founder-member Moholy-Nagy, with the Bauhaus.

Lithography. Poster (1892) by Toulouse-Lautrec for the Divan Japonais

Liszt Franz (Hungarian form Ferencz) (1811–86). Hungarian composer and pianist. His precocious talents were fostered by his father and after lessons in Vienna from Czerny (piano) and Salieri (composition) L. was taken to Paris where he gave a public concert in 1824. After studying in Paris he spent several years as a concert pianist; during this period he lived with Countess Marie d'Agoult; they had 3 daughters of whom Cosima married von Bülow and then Wagner. L. lived with Princess von Sayn-Wittgenstein from 1848 to 1861.

L.'s years as music director at Weimar (1842–61) saw many of his greatest compositions (e.g. tone poems and a great deal of piano music), and the beginnings of the controversy between the New German school (L., his friend Wagner and his pupils, e.g. von Bülow) and the school of Schumann, Mendelssohn and Brahms. L. made Weimar a centre of the new in music, performing e.g. Berlioz; he was the greatest pianist of his, possibly any, generation and through his numerous pupils revolutionized piano technique; as a composer he, with Berlioz, made programme music the most important 19th-c. genre. L. originated the one-movement symphonic poem and innovated in harmony, his work anticipating later developments, e.g. atonality. He wrote: 13 symphonic poems, among them *Tasso: Lament and Triumph* (1849), *Orpheus* (1854), *Mazeppa* (1851) also in a piano version, and *Les Préludes* (1854); the programme symphonies, *Faust* (1854) and *Dante's Divina Commedia* (1857; also a piano version); *Two Episodes from Lenan's Faust* (1861) including the first *Mephisto Waltz* for orchestra; *Malediction* for piano and orchestra (written 1827) and 2 piano concertos. His piano works include the great sonata in B min. (1853); *20 Hungarian Rhapsodies*, transcriptions of works by other composers, and many volumes of virtuoso piano pieces; also stark and simple experimental pieces, written in his last years, which reach the ultimate bounds of tonality and even develop a crude serial technique.

Literaturbriefe (1759–65). Name of a German literary journal in which some of *Lessing's most important criticism appeared.

lithography. A surface printing technique, invented (1798) by A. Senefelder, which depends on the fact that grease and water do not mix. The design is drawn with a greasy chalk on the 'stone' (originally a porous limestone, now always zinc plate), which is then wetted. The water runs off the chalked areas and the greasy ink will take on these areas but not on the damp stone. At first used simply for reproductions, l. developed into an independent art and was used by many 19th-c. artists notably H. *Daumier. Colour l. was developed early but was pioneered as an art form by *Toulouse-Lautrec.

Litolff Henri-Charles (1818–91). French musician, a pupil of Moschelles and one of the most brilliant pianists of the Chopin-Liszt era. He also composed, being a gifted orchestrator, especially in his symphonic concertos. In 1851 he married the widow of G. M. Meyer the music publ.; the firm's name was changed to L. Under his adopted son THEODOR (1839–1912) the firm produced the famous *Collection L.* of cheap scores of classical works.

Little Caesar (1930). Film directed by M. *Le Roy.

Little Demon, The (1907). Novel by Fyodor *Sologub.

Little Dorrit (1857–8). Novel by Dickens.

Little Eyolf (1894). Play by *Ibsen.

Little Flowers of St Francis: *Francis of Assisi

Little Foxes, The (1941). Film directed by W. *Wyler.

Little Lord Fauntleroy (1886). Novel by F. E. H. *Burnett.

Little Women (1868). Girls' book by Louisa M. *Alcott; also made into films directed by G. *Cukor (1933) and M. *Le Roy (1949).

Littlewood Joan. English director who began her career with the Manchester Repertory Theatre, worked for the B.B.C. and in 1945 founded *Theatre Workshop. L. has fostered much modern acting and writing talent. She has been the champion of young authors and in recent years has directed many plays to eventual success, e.g. *Behan's *Quare Fellow* (1956) and *The Hostage* (1958); Shelagh *Delaney's *A Taste of Honey* (1958); the entertainment *Oh What A Lovely War* (1963) and F. Norman's and L. Bart's *Fings Aint Wot They Used to be* (1959).

Liverpool. An important English centre of delftware (i.e. tin-glazed earthenware), usually painted with the popular Chinese subjects, from *c.* 1710 to *c.* 1750. Cream-coloured earthenware was also produced in quantity. Transfer printing on earthenware was introduced, perhaps even invented at Liverpool *c.* 1750, and reproductions of book illustrations, paintings, etc. were popular, printed decoration being executed for other manufacturers who sent their wares to Liverpool.

Liverpool Playhouse. The oldest existing repertory theatre in Britain; it opened in 1911. The 1st producer was Basil Dean, and another distinguished director and producer was William Armstrong (1922–44). Many distinguished actors have begun there, notably Michael Redgrave.

Lives of the English Poets, The (1779–81). Major critical work by Dr *Johnson.

Living (1952). Film directed by A. *Kurosawa.

living newspaper: *Federal Theater

Livy (59 B.C.–A.D. 17). Titus Livius, Roman historian. Born at Padua, he was received at Rome into the literary circle surrounding the Emperor Augustus. His history ('*ab urbe condita*': 'from the city's founding'), begun when he was 30 and continued for 40 years, filled 142 books: 35 survive. L. summarized earlier annalists, and modern critics have excoriated his inconsistencies and inaccuracies and particularly his incompetent handling of military matters. But L.'s power of vivid visualization of persons and events, his shrewd understanding of psychology and his rich and varied style, suitably elevated to achieve his aim of providing a Roman history worthy of Rome's heritage, have guaranteed his popularity.

Lloyd Harold (1896–). U.S. film actor and producer, a music-hall comedian who made his 1st films in 1911. From 1915 he had his own series as 'Lonesome Luke'. In 1918 he assumed his famous screen personality, the ordinary, insignificant man in horn-rimmed spectacles and straw boater. His particular invention is the 'thrill' comedy like *Safety Last* (1923), where physical danger became a source of laughs. He made occasional films in the 1930s and had the lead in P. *Sturges's *Mad Wednesday* (1947).

Lloyd Marie (1870–1922). English music-hall artist, world famous but especially associated with Drury Lane Theatre where she often appeared in pantomime.

loa. Name given to the *prologue in the early Spanish theatre, often written by a different author from that of the main play.

local colour. Term used in painting of the actual colour of an object in natural diffused light. Shadows or strong neighbouring colours may modify local colour.

Locandiera, La (1753). Comedy by Goldoni.

Locatelli Pietro Antonio (1695–1764). Italian violin virtuoso, a pupil of A. Corelli, and composer. His works, largely publ. by L. himself in Amsterdam, include: concerti grossi, sonatas for unaccompanied violin, and also 'capriccios' for violin–embarrassing exhibitions of technique.

Harold Lloyd in *Safety Last*

Marie Lloyd

Liverpool: porcelain chinoiserie wall vases (*c.* 1765)

Lochner. *Madonna with Two Kneeling Kings* (detail); from the altarpiece in Cologne cathedral

Mikhail Lomonosov

Lochner Stefan. 15th-c. German painter mainly active in Cologne. He acted as a link between later Gothic and early Renaissance painting. He assimilated the tradition of the harsh S. German and the courtly, lyrical Cologne schools. *The Virgin of the Rose Garden* (W.-R. Mus., Cologne) combines charm with geometry; and his most famous work, the altarpiece in Cologne cathedral, combines the decorative with a monumental realism, influenced by Flemish art.

Locke David Ross: Petroleum Vesuvius *Nasby

Locke John (1632–1704). English philosopher, an influential contributor to the British empiricist school. In his *Two Treatises of Government* (1690) L. argues that a sovereign's rights are limited by the law of nature and that a social contract exists between ruler and ruled; if the ruler breaks the contract he can be removed. L.'s *Essay Concerning Human Understanding* (1690) sets out his theory of knowledge; it rejects the concept of innate ideas, positing that all knowledge derives from experience.

John Locke: painting by Kneller

Locke Matthew (*c.* 1630–77). English composer of stage and church music; an influential predecessor of Purcell. He wrote the masque *Cupid and Death* (1653) with C. Gibbons and incidental music to a version of Shakespeare's *Macbeth* and *The Tempest.*

Lockhart John Gibson (1794–1854). Scottish biographer, novelist, and ruthless critic. A major contributor to *Blackwood's Edinburgh Magazine* and ed. of *The Quarterly Review.* L.'s most noteworthy work was a biography of his father-in-law, Sir Walter Scott (1837–8).

Lockwood Margaret (1916–). English film actress; *The Wicked Lady* (1945) typed her as a romantic adventuress.

Lodge Thomas (1558?–1625). English poet, pamphleteer and writer of romances, notably *Rosalynde, Euphues Golden Legacie* (1590), the source of Shakespeare's *As You Like It.* His verse includes the sonnet sequence *Phillis.*

Lodger, The (1926). Film directed by *Hitchcock.

Loeillet Jean-Baptiste (1680–1730). Belgian composer working mostly in London, where he was celebrated as a virtuoso flautist, oboist, and recorder player. As a composer L. still has a following among chamber-music players for his trio sonatas, recorder pieces, etc.

Loewe Johann Carl Gottfried (1796–1869). German composer who gave a musical form to the literary form of the ballad as created by Uhland. His music shows melodic facility; the piano accompaniments range from a simple underlay for the voice to colourful scene painting. Besides his numerous ballads, e.g. his setting of Goethe's *Erlkönig* (1824), L. composed operas and choral and instrumental works.

Logan Joshua (1908–). U.S. film director, and a very successful stage director, mainly of musicals. His career as a director really dates from *Picnic* (1955) and *Bus Stop* (1956), both from William Inge. Apart from a small and charming comedy, *Tall Story* (1960), his work has consisted of expensive, romantic pictures: *Sayonara* (1957), *South Pacific* (1958) and a remake of *Pagnol's *Fanny* (1960).

loggia. Architectural term for a roofed area open on at least one side.

Logroscino Nicola (1698–*c.* 1765). Italian composer whose dialect parody operas are important in the development of the *opera buffa*; L. also was one of the first to terminate acts with a vocal ensemble finale.

Lohengrin. Opera by *Wagner; 1st performance at Weimar in 1850.

Lohenstein Daniel Casper von (1635–83). German baroque writer. His plays, e.g. *Agrippina* (1665) and *Ibrahim Sultan* (1673), have frequent scenes of horror and their style is overrhetorical, but his novel *Grossmüthiger Feldherr Arminius* (publ. posth. 1689), on the Saxon hero who fought the Romans, has a number of fine passages.

Lola (1960). Film directed by J. *Demy.

Lola Montes (1955). Film directed by M. *Ophuls.

Lolita (1955). Novel by Vladimir *Nabokov.

Lollobrigida Gina (1927–). Italian film actress who after some years in 'peasant beauty' roles in France and Italy, notably *Bread, Love*

Logan.
Marilyn Monroe in *Bus Stop*

and Dreams (1953), was 'discovered' by Hollywood and prominently featured in *The Hunchback of Notre-Dame* (1956) and K. *Vidor's *Solomon and Sheba* (1958).

Lombard Carole (1908–1942). U.S. film star who specialized in exquisite interpretations of sophisticated comedy in the later 1930s. She scored a hit opposite John Barrymore in *20th Century* (1934). Later films included *Nothing Sacred* (1937) and Lubitsch's *To Be or Not To Be* (1942). She was killed in an air crash.

Lombard Lambert (1506–66). Flemish painter and architect who went to Rome in 1537 and on his return was influential as a Romanist. His pupils included Frans Floris and Goltzius.

Lomonosov Mikhail Vasilyevich (1711–65). Russian poet, literary theorist and scientist who was the real founder of modern Russian literature. Although the son of a fisherman, he acquired a fine education by his own efforts, becoming assistant professor at the Academy of Science in 1741, and its effective head in 1758. His *Rhetoric* and *Russian Grammar* created a literary language by fusing Slavonic and Russian elements (a process comparable to the fusion of the Latin and vernacular tongues in W. Europe). He reformed poetic metre and, perhaps less happily, introduced a word order based on Latin and German. His poetry glorifies Russia, the Enlightenment and a benevolent Deity; it includes 2 *Meditations on the Divine Poetry* and an *Ode, selected from Job.*

London Jack (1876–1916). U.S. novelist, the first of America's 'tough' writers. L. was self-educated, and in his youth was sailor, tramp, and miner in the Klondike gold rush. He was a passionate Socialist: *The Iron Heel* (1907) describes the development of class conflict into bourgeois tyranny and proletarian revolution according to Marx's formula. L. also admired Nietzsche; many of his novels feature heroes of extraordinary strength and will, though in *The Sea-Wolf* (1904) these qualities are found insufficient. L.'s novels include the famous dog stories *The Call of the Wild* (1903) and *White Fang* (1906).

London Ballet. Formed by the choreographer Antony Tudor in 1938, several of the co. having been with him at the Ballet Rambert. The L. B. merged back into the Ballet Rambert in 1940, a year after Tudor had settled in the U.S.

London County Council. In the late 1940s the architectural direction of the L.C.C. under Robert Matthew changed from dreary neo-Georgian to an enterprising outlook which produced the Royal Festival Hall and many good schools and flats, particularly at Roehampton. When Matthew left in 1953 this direction was continued by Leslie Martin and later by Hubert Bennett.

London Group. An exhibiting society founded in 1913 in opposition to the New English Art Club, which was held to have become conventional and academic. Harold Gilman was the 1st president, and both the *Camden Town painters and the *vorticists exhibited. Between the wars Roger Fry, Duncan Grant, Vanessa Bell and Paul Nash were among the exhibitors; in the post-war period such figurative painters as David Bomberg and Cliff Holden.

London symphony. Nickname for *Haydn's symphony no. 104 in D.

long. A time value in medieval musical *notation.

Long Day's Journey into Night (1956). Play by Eugene *O'Neill; also a film directed by S. *Lumet (1961).

Longest Journey, The (1907). Novel by E. M. Forster.

Longfellow Henry Wadsworth (1807–82). U.S. poet. He was at Bowdoin College with Hawthorne; later becoming professor there (1829–35). In 1836 he began teaching at Harvard but travelled widely before finally settling in Cambridge, Mass. In 1854 he resigned his professorship to write more poetry. He was an extremely popular best-selling poet but has little depth or originality of language. Popular favourites include *Hymn to the Night* and *A Psalm of Life*, and in his *Ballads* (1841), *The Village Blacksmith*, *The Wreck of the Hesperus* and *Excelsior*. *Hiawatha*, on Red Indian themes, appeared in 1855.

Longford Edward Arthur Henry Pakenham, Earl of (1902–61). Irish manager and author, a director of the Dublin Gate Theatre from 1931 to 1936; also the proprietor of a co., Longford Productions. He did much to foster the theatre in Ireland.

Longhena Baldassare (1598–1682). Italian architect. His most famous work is the church of S. Maria della Salute (begun 1632) which dominates the entrance to the Grand Canal, Venice. It is octagonal in plan, surmounted by a huge dome surrounded by scroll buttresses. He also designed the Palazzo Pesaro and Ca' Rezzonico, Venice, and was the leading exponent of baroque there.

Longhi. A family of Italian architects: (1) MARTINO the Elder (d. 1591) built the church of S. Girolamo degli Schiavoni, Rome (1588). (2) ONORIO (*c.* 1569–1619), son of Martino, also worked in Rome. (3) MARTINO the Younger (1602–57), son of Onorio, is famous for the façade of SS Vincenzo ed Anastasio (1650), one of the most dramatic compositions of the whole baroque period in Rome.

Longhi Alessandro (1733–1813). Italian portrait painter and engraver, son of Pietro L., best known for his *Compendio delle Vite de' Pittori Veneziani . . .* (1762), an account of the lives of contemporary Venetian painters and an important source-book for the period.

Longhi Pietro Falca called (1702–85). Venetian painter of the rococo period famous for his delicate, slightly ironical paintings and sketches of Venetian life and manners. He was a pupil of G. M. Crespi at Bologna. The N.G., London, has several of his paintings including *Exhibition of a Rhinoceros at Venice* and *A Fortune-teller at Venice.*

'Longinus': *On the Sublime

Henry Wadsworth Longfellow

Longhena. Palazzo Pesaro

Pietro Longhi.
Exhibition of a Rhinoceros at Venice. Also *Goldoni

Longton Hall. *Shepherd* (*c.* 1755)

Adolf Loos. Steiner House, Vienna (1910)

Lope de Vega

Lydia Lopokova in *La Boutique Fantasque*

Longo Alessandro (1864–1945). Italian pianist and composer whose critical ed. of the keyboard sonatas of D. Scarlatti is of major importance. Scarlatti sonatas are often identified by 'L.', or Longo, numbers.

Longton Hall Staffordshire. English (soft-paste) *porcelain factory (1750–60); its products frequently have a rich blue glaze and include some finely modelled figures, and also dishes and vessels formed as leaves or with leaf motifs.

Longus: *Daphnis and Chloe

Look Back in Anger (1956). Play by John *Osborne; also a film (1959) directed by Tony Richardson.

Look Homeward, Angel: A Story of the Buried Life (1929). Novel by Thomas *Wolfe.

Loos Adolf (1870–1933). Austrian architect, pupil of Otto Wagner in Vienna. L. was architect of very pure, severe buildings, white, with flat roofs, forerunners of the international style; and all beautifully worked out and planned. His influential book *Ornament and Crime* (1908) equates ornament, e.g. of the type common in art nouveau, with crime, not only in buildings, but also clothes.

Loos Anita (1893–). Versatile U.S. writer (she has, e.g., written much for films), widely known for *Gentlemen Prefer Blondes* (1925), the entertaining and period-flavoured 'diary' of a naïve-but-smart-too gold-digger.

Lopatnikov Nikolay (1903–). Estonian-born composer and pianist; working in Germany then London and since 1939 in the U.S., latterly as a teacher. He is a declared enemy of 'theories' of music. Works include 2 symphonies and chamber music.

Lope de Vega more correctly Lope Félix de Vega Carpio (1562–1635). One of the greatest and most prolific of the Spanish poets and playwrights, as celebrated for his extraordinary rate of production as for the endless scandals of his private life. His youth was turbulent and in 1588 he was banished from Madrid and Castile for circulating criminal libels against his mistress Elena Osorio, soon afterwards defying the ban by returning to Madrid to elope with another woman. After marrying her by proxy he joined the Armada against England, but returned unscathed. His wife died young, he was again embroiled with the law, involved in many scandals and married again (1598) having acquired a new mistress shortly before. When his 2nd wife died in 1613 Lope took priest's orders and settled down in Madrid to begin a period of feverish literary activity, turning out poems, short lyrics, pastorals, sonnets and innumerable plays. His power and influence grew until he was treated almost as an equal by the Spanish nobility. His last years were tragic, for his son Lope died early, and his daughter Antonia eloped against his wishes. Heartbroken, he gave himself up to fits of pious frenzy and self-mortification. His vast public funeral was attended by every section of society. Upwards of 400 plays survive together with a roughly equal number of non-dramatic writings, which include some exquisite sonnets. Nearly all the plays show signs of haste, few are faultless masterpieces but equally few are without passages of great charm and beauty. His ability to create well-rounded characters only showed itself intermittently, although some of his heroines rank among the most charming in the whole of Spanish literature. The main types of play he wrote were the '*comedias historicas*' dealing with national heroes and events; '*comedias de capa y espada*' ('cloak and dagger'), sensational, romantic dramas with intricate plots, revolving round love and honour; comedies of character and satire; allegorical plays for religious festivities; and '*comedias mitologicas*' based on classic myths. In his *Arte Nuevo de hacer comedias en este tiempo* (1609) L. expounded his ideas on drama. He also wrote an outstanding novel, *La Dorotea* (1632), which imitates *La *Celestina*.

Lopes Fernão (*c.* 1380–1460). Portuguese chronicler of literary skill and advanced historical method.

Lopez Pilar (1912–). Spanish dancer and choreographer of superb style who has been influenced strongly by her sister, La Argentinita. L. formed Ballet Español in 1946, a co. which tours with many ballets created by the 2 sisters, including *Bolero* and *Goyescas*, incorporating flamenco and court dancing.

López de Ayala Pero (1332–1407). Spanish nobleman, chancellor of Castile and writer. His chronicles of the reigns he lived through are perceptive and psychologically acute, and are written in a fine prose style. L. also produced trs from the Latin classics and the long poem *Rimado de Palacio*, a series of verse dissertations on various topics, religious, political and social.

López de Mendoza: *Santillana

Lopez Velarde Ramón (1888–1921). Mexican poet whose work represents the transition between modernismo and ultraism in South American verse. His work is distinguished by its taste for the macabre and the use of religious terms in connection with sensual experiences. His best-known coll. is *Zozobra* (1919).

Lopokov Fedor (1886–). Russian dancer, brother of Lopokova, who trained at the Imperial School, St Petersburg. He was one of the 1st Russian dancers in America, touring with Pavlova's co. in 1911; but he became chief choreographer at the Maryinsky Theatre (1922) where his work included *The Ice Maiden* (1931) and *Taras Bulba* (1940).

Lopokova Lydia (1892–). Russian dancer who studied at the Imperial School, St Petersburg, but her career with the Diaghilev co. proved to have been her heyday when she created several roles in Massine ballets, e.g. *La Boutique Fantasque* (1919), *Good Humoured Ladies* (1917). She married Lord Keynes (1925) and since her retirement has remained an active patron of the arts.

Lorca Federico García (1899–1936). One of the best known of 20th-c. Spanish poets and playwrights. He was born on his father's farm in Andalusia near Granada and his life-long attachment to his native region was a major influence in his work. As a youth he studied music, and then law. His 1st coll. of poems, *Libro de poemas*, was publ. in 1921. His book of 'gipsy ballads', the *Primer Romancero Gitano* (1928) was a great popular success in Spain and Latin America, and in it Lorca upheld the passionate individuality of the Andalusian gipsies against the soulless materialism of the modern world. He was on close terms with Salvador Dali and some of the surrealists, whose influence he showed in his *Poeta en Nueva York* (written 1929; publ. 1940) a strident cry of protest arising out of a short stay in the U.S. On his return to Spain he became increasingly interested in the theatre and directed La Barraca, an itinerant gipsy theatre co., and wrote his gipsy plays *Bodas de sangre* (1933; *Blood Wedding*, 1947) and *Yerma* (1934; 1947). He was brutally murdered by Fascists.
L.'s poems have won wide popularity abroad for their colourful and striking imagery, and their emphasis on gipsy themes and bull-fighting. Their primitive, fierce passion and melancholy, and their preoccupation with blood and death are exemplified in his famous elegy for the death of his friend, the bull-fighter Sanchez Mejias.

Federico García Lorca

Lord Jim (1900). Novel by *Conrad.

Lord of the Flies (1954). Novel by William *Golding; made into a film (1962) directed by Peter Brook.

Lord Randal. An English ballad which tells in dialogue form how a young hero is poisoned while visiting his sweetheart. The song is well known throughout Europe and North America; one Negro version calls the hero Boss Randal.

Lorelei. A cliff on the W. bank of the Rhine below Coblenz; *Heine's poem *Die L.* is based on the legend of a river sprite who, by her singing, lured sailors to their deaths on the rock.

Sophia Loren

Lorentz. *The River*

Loren Sophia (1934–). Italian film star who became another casualty in Hollywood's search for Latin glamour. After S. Kramer's *The Pride and the Passion* (1957) and *Desire Under the Elms* (1958), she returned to Italy for her most exacting part, in de Sica's *Two Women* (1960). She now decorates *El Cid* (1961) and other spectaculars, where her cool beauty and considerable talent are wasted.

Lorentz Pare (1905–). U.S. film maker. L. was the director of a number of remarkable propagandist documentaries made for U.S. government agencies: *The Plow that Broke the Plains* (1936) for Resettlement Administration on the Dust Bowl, and *The River* (1937) on the Tennessee Valley Authority. Transformed into the U.S. Film Service, L.'s unit produced films by *Ivens, *Flaherty (*The Land*, 1941) and L.'s feature-length *Fight for Life* (1941) before it was disbanded by an anti-New Deal Congress.

Lorenzetti the brothers Ambrogio and Pietro. 14th-c. Sienese painters, probably pupils of Duccio; both almost certainly died in the plague of 1348. Both were greatly influenced by Giotto, their works leaning towards narrative

Pietro Lorenzetti. *Madonna and Child* (detail)

Ambrogio Lorenzetti.
Good Government in the City (detail)

Lorsch. The gatehouse

Losey. Dirk Bogarde in *The Servant*

Lotto. *Andrea Odoni*

rather than decorative qualities. Important paintings by Pietro include the altarpiece of the Carmine church (1329; Pina., Siena) and *The Birth of the Virgin* (Duomo Mus., Siena). Of his frescoes in the lower church of St Francis, Assisi, the 2 outstanding subjects are *Madonna and Child* and *Descent from the Cross*. In both frescoes everything else is subordinated to the creation of emotional intensity; in the *Descent* pain has distorted the figure of Christ but has not robbed it of grandeur. Ambrogio's best-known works are the frescoes on the theme *Good and Bad Government* in the town hall, Siena. Here he displays an imaginative genius for ordering the elements of a townscape or a landscape. Other important panel paintings by Ambrogio are: 4 scenes from the Legend of S. Nicholas of Bari (Uffizi), *Presentation in the Temple* (Uffizi), a polyptych altarpiece (Pina., Siena) and *St Catherine of Alexandria* (M. of A., Cleveland).

Lorenzo di Credi: Lorenzo di *Credi

Lorenzo Monaco: *Monaco

Lorna Doone (1869). Historical novel by R. D. *Blackmore.

Lorrain Jean. Pseud. of Paul-Alexandre-Martin Duval (1856–1906). French novelist and poet. L.'s novel *Monsieur de Phocas* (1899) is a typical symbolist production.

Lorre Peter (1904–64). Hungarian-born actor, discovered in the *avant-garde* theatre of Berlin by *Lang, for whom he made his greatest film, **M* (1931). This led to Hollywood and similar parts suited to his boyish face and silkily menacing voice–but his aim was comedy. At best he combined the two, in the *Mr Moto* series and as Joel Cairo in *The Maltese Falcon* (1941). His later parts were ill-chosen and squandered his talents on self-parody.

Lorris Guillaume de: *Le *Roman de la Rose*

Lorsch Germany. Site of a great Carolingian monastery. Only the gatehouse survives, but this provides a unique example of early 9th-c. decoration–on the ground storey 3 arches inside a row of demi-columns with entablature (i.e. the normal Roman system, as at the Colosseum); above this, patterned brickwork and a row of fluted pilasters carrying triangular arches.

Los Angeles Victoria de. Stage-name of Victoria López (1923–). Spanish soprano; she made her début in 1945, and is particularly known for her interpretations of Spanish songs.

Losey Joseph (1909–). U.S. film director. L. first worked in the theatre–he directed the world première (1947) of Brecht's *Galileo Galilei* with Charles Laughton in Hollywood, where he then made films with subjects reflecting his beliefs: a pacificist fantasy (*The Boy With Green Hair*, 1948); a film about race prejudice (*The Lawless* or *The Dividing Line*, 1949); a remake of a *Lang film (*M*, 1951). The starting-point of *The Prowler* (1951) is the temptation which capitalism places in the way of a policeman. While making *Stranger on the Prowl* (1952) in Italy, political black-listing made it impossible for him to return to Hollywood. Direction of this and 2 films made in Britain was not credited to him, but he resumed working under his own name with a period movie, *The Gypsy and the Gentleman* (1957), and 3 thrillers in which he managed to embody his concern with the foundations of capitalist society and with its ideas, e.g. of punishment: *Time Without Pity* (1957), *Blind Date* (1959) and *The Criminal* (1960). His science-fiction story *The Damned* (1961) showed the discovery of preparations for the survival of the human race after inevitable nuclear war. His next films were made in conditions of complete freedom, although *Eve* (1962) was mutilated by its producers. *The Servant* (1963) uses its inversion of the master-servant relationship as a peg for shrewd observation of British social patterns. *King and Country* (1964) shows the trial and execution of a World War I soldier technically guilty but morally innocent of desertion.

Lost Weekend, The (1945). Film directed by *Wilder.

Loti Pierre. Pseud. of Louis-Marie-Julien Viaud (1850–1923). French novelist and author of travel books. L.'s large oeuvre was produced in the course of his career as a naval officer. His exotic novels of romance, e.g. *Aziyadé* (1879) and *Fontôme d'Orient* (1892; *A Phantom from the East*, 1892) made L. famous; but his novels about the life of Breton fishermen are now preferred. They are *Mon Frère Yves* (1883), *Pêcheur d'Islande* (1886; *An Iceland Fisherman*, 1888) and *Matelot* (1893).

Lotos-Eaters, The (1833). Poem by Tennyson.

Lotti Antonio (1667–1740). Italian composer and organist and later musical director of St Mark's, Venice. He was a pupil of G. Legrenzi, his own pupils numbering D. Alberti and Galuppi. L.'s operas show the influences of the Venetian school of Monteverdi, Cavalli and Cesti, and also of A. Scarlatti; his expressive church music, e.g. the *Miserere* still performed at St Mark's on Maundy Thursday, makes use of dramatic chromaticism.

Lotto Lorenzo (*c.* 1480–1556). Venetian painter. L. trained probably under A. Vivarini in Venice, though most of his working life was spent in towns outside Venice–Treviso, Recanati, Rome (*c.* 1508), Bergamo (1513–28), Ancona and Loreto, where he died as a lay brother in a religious order. Although influenced at different periods by Giovanni Bellini, Titian and Palma Vecchio, L. remained a strongly individual painter. His frescoes in and near Bergamo and his altarpieces in towns where he worked are often marred by stylistic idiosyncrasies. However, his own unusual personality often gives him a rare insight into the personalities of his sitters when he turns to portraits, e.g. *Man on a Terrace* (M. of A., Cleveland), the superbly alive *Youth Before a White Damask Curtain* (K. Mus., Vienna), and *Andrea Odoni* (R. Coll., Hampton Court). The *St Jerome in the Wilderness* (Louvre) and *St Nicholas of Bari in Glory* (Carmine, Venice) are outstanding for their landscape backgrounds, while the *intarsias of S. Maria Maggiore, Bergamo, are notable for their rare decorative sense and draughtsmanship, e.g. *Vision of Elijah*. Paintings such as *The Annunciation* (S. Maria Sopra Mercanti, Recanati) and *Christ taking leave of His Mother* (Berlin) are close in style to mannerism.

Louis XIV (1643–1715). The exaltation of the French monarchy from 1660 involved the elaboration of court life and ceremonial, and called for a suitable palace–hence Versailles–and the means of furnishing it–hence the *Gobelins. L. took a close interest in the arts and regulated them through the academies, down to the smallest detail. The style going under the name 'LOUIS QUATORZE' is associated with ponderous grandeur and the greatest emphasis on costly magnificence and show, reflecting the glories of the king and France under his rule. It was essentially a court style and was going out of fashion before 1715.

Louis XIV armchair

Louis XIV day-bed

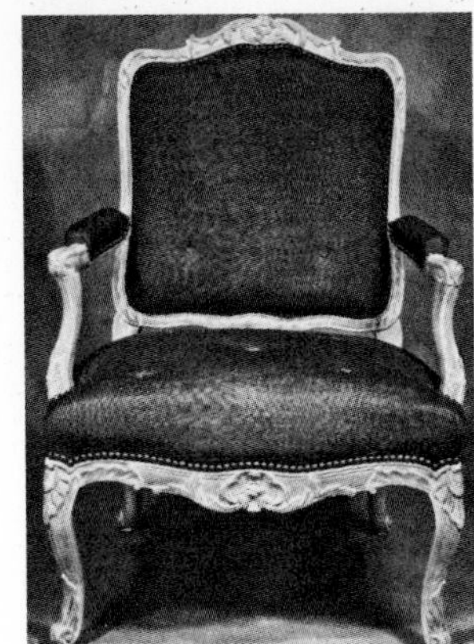
Louis XV chair

Louis XV (1715–74). The personal taste of this monarch encouraged a greater intimacy, in reaction to the parade of public life, expressed in the nest of comfortable and discreet apartments built at Versailles after 1738; they are regarded as the official recognition of the new *rococo movement. This greater informality was to be found both at court and in Paris from about 1720, and often goes under the name of 'régence', after the regent, Orléans. Mme de Pompadour, the king's mistress (1745–64), patronized most of the rococo artists (she also patronized writers such as Voltaire) and guided the royal tastes. Lightness, grace and a touch of the frivolous, exotic and amorous are the quintessence of 'LOUIS QUINZE'.

Louis XV commode

Louis XVI chair. Also *banding, *Egyptian style

Louis XVI (1774–93). This reign is often equated with the neo-classical movement in France, but this was well under way 10 years before L.'s accession. The king was less concerned about the arts than his 2 predecessors although the crown continued to be an active patron through the furnishing of the royal palaces.

Louisiana Story (1948). Film directed by R. *Flaherty.

Louis Lambert (1832). Novel by Balzac.

Louvre Paris. The Cour du Vieux Louvre, which replaced the medieval royal castle, dates from 1546 to 1664 and contains work by *Lescot, *Lemercier and *Le Vau. The E. front (1667–74), a subject of keen competition (even Bernini submitted designs), is a compromise between *Perrault, Lebrun and Le Vau. During the 19th c. the L. was greatly enlarged in a neo-17th-c. style which has influenced French civic architecture ever since. It houses the major mus. and art gal. of France.

The Louvre: colonnade

The Louvre: the Cour Carrée

Louÿs Pierre. Pseud of Pierre Louis (1870–1925). French novelist and poet, one of the founders of the reviews *La Conque* (1891) and *Le Centaure* (1896). His novels include *Aphrodite: mœurs antiques* (1896; *Aphrodite. A novel of ancient manners*, 1906), an elegant, voluptuous story of ancient Alexandria, and *La Femme et le Pantin* (1898; *Woman and Puppet*, 1908). L.'s *Chansons de Bilitis* (1894; *The Songs of Bilitis*, 1928), purporting to be trs. from a woman poet contemporary with Sappho, was a very successful literary hoax.

Tankard decorated by Löwenfinck

Lowestoft porcelain group

Robert Lowell

Love for Love (1695). Play by Congreve.

Lovelace Richard (1618–58). English Cavalier lyricist; an active supporter of Charles I, he was twice imprisoned under the Commonwealth. His poems include the celebrated *Going to the Warres* from *Lucasta* (1649), a coll. of lyrics named after his mistress.

Love of Three Oranges. Opera by *Prokofiev; 1st performance at Chicago in 1921.

Love Parade, The (1929). Film directed by E. *Lubitsch.

Lover Samuel (1797–1868). Irish novelist, author of *Rory O'More* (1837) and *Handy Andy* (1842), a humorous tale of an incompetent servant.

Lover's Complaint, A. Poem attributed to Shakespeare and publ. (1609) with his sonnets.

Love's Labour's Lost (1597?). Comedy by *Shakespeare, written *c.* 1594, the first to be publ. with his name (1598). It was performed at court in 1605.

Love's Labour's Won. Comedy by *Shakespeare which is lost or, perhaps in a revised version, known by another title. Suggestions include *The Taming of the Shrew, All's Well that Ends Well* and *Troilus and Cressida.*

L. S. Lowry. *River Scene* (*c.* 1942)

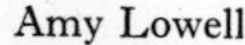

Amy Lowell

lowboy. A small table fitted with 1 or 2 rows of drawers, popular in the 18th c. It was normally used as a dressing-table or side-table. A 'tallboy' (or 'highboy') by contrast, was a double chest of drawers popular at the same period.

Lowell Amy (Lawrence) (1874–1925). U.S. poet and critic, one of the famous Boston L.s. Her poems, which include the coll. *Sword Blades and Poppy Seeds* (1914), were influenced by the imagists, of whom she became a leading member. She also wrote *A Critical Fable* (1922), a book of essays modelled on James Russell L.'s *A Fable for Critics*, and the biography *John Keats* (1925).

Lowell James Russell (1819–91). U.S. poet, essayist and diplomat, one of the famous Boston L.s. He was the 1st ed. of *The Atlantic Monthly* (1857) and joint ed. of *The North American Review* (1864). His works include the verse satires *A Fable for Critics* (1848) and the *Biglow Papers* (1848), the poem *The Vision of Sir Launfal* (1848) and miscellaneous essays and criticisms in colls like *My Study Windows* (1871).

Lowell Robert (1917–). U.S. poet. One of the Boston L.s, he is considered one of the foremost poets of his generation. L.'s distaste for Puritan values led him to Catholicism (which he has since rejected). During World War II he was imprisoned as a conscientious objector. His best verse is well-knit, rhythmic, often witty, and packed with hard, vivid images. Among his important verse colls are: *Lord Weary's Castle* (1946), *The Mills of the Kavanaughs* (1951) and *Life Studies* (1959).

Löwenfinck Adam Friedrich von (1714–54). German ceramic painter apprenticed at Meissen; he was founder and director (1746–9) of the faïence factory at Höchst. L. painted many of the best chinoiseries, and as director of Hagenau (1750–4) greatly influenced *Strassburg styles and may have had a part in the introduction of enamel-painted faïence.

Lower Depths, The (1902). Play by Maxim *Gorky.

Lowestoft. Factory manufacturing soft-paste *porcelain (1757–1802) by methods similar to (and according to tradition imitated from) those of the Bow factory. The chief L. productions were table-wares and small objects intended as souvenirs, toys, etc.; hence they were frequently painted with local views. Oriental designs were common and much L. ware imitates Chinese export porcelain. In the last years of the factory sprig decorations occur.

Lowry L(awrence) S(tephen) (1887–). English painter. His characteristic subject is industrial N. England. The paintings, with strangely expressive matchstick figures, are in a *faux-naïf* 2-dimensional style. They present forcibly the dehumanizing and depressing atmosphere of an environment produced by haphazard industrialization; but underlying this there is a deep humanitarian feeling.

Lowry (Charles) Malcolm (1909–57). English novelist who spent long periods in Mexico and Canada. *Under the Volcano* (1947) has many autobiographical elements, describing with extended flashbacks the last days in the life of

Lubarda. *Mediterranean* (1952)

Lubitsch. Herbert Marshall, Kay Francis and C. Aubrey Smith in *Trouble in Paradise*

an alcoholic English consul in a Mexican town. Works include *Ultramarine* (1933) and the short-story coll. *Hear Us O Lord from Heaven Thy Dwelling Place* (1961).

Loyola St Ignatius of (1491–1556). Spanish founder of the Society of Jesus and religious writer. His *Ejercicios espirituales* (written 1522, printed 1548; *Spiritual Exercises*, 1915) had an enormous influence on subsequent religious and mystical literature both inside and outside Spain. The book's main object was to apply the precepts of the Gospel to the individual soul, and to convince the reader of the reality of sin, divine justice and eventual judgement.

Lubarda Petar (1907–). Yugoslav painter who worked partly in Paris before World War II and has been responsible for making known to younger Yugoslav painters the ideas of the school of Paris. He combines abstract and figurative elements in an expressionist style.

Lübeck Vincent (1654/6–1740). German composer and organist at St Nicholas's, Hamburg. Surviving organ works show striking similarities to J. S. Bach's style.

Lubitsch Ernest (1892–1947). German-born film director, a stage actor with M. *Reinhardt before starting to act in and direct comedy shorts during World War I. The reputation which caused his importation to Hollywood (to direct Mary Pickford in *Rosita*, 1923) came from spectacular dramas like *Anne Boleyn* (1920). Once there, he specialized in sophisticated (i.e. sexy) comedy, apart from a last unfortunate attempt at 'serious' drama in *The Man I Killed* (1932). The famous 'L. touch' was a graceful wit which enabled him to suggest what the Hayes Code of censorship forbade to be mentioned. Films like *The Love Parade* (1929–L. was one of the first Hollywood directors to do important work in talkies) and *Trouble in Paradise* (1932) showed that L. was unrivalled as a maker of comedies of manners. In the world of his characters manners stood duty as morals. The linking of gaiety and sadness is strongest in his most famous film, *Ninotchka* (1939), with Garbo. Later films include *That Uncertain Feeling* (1941), *To Be or Not To Be* (1942) and *Cluny Brown* (1946). The last film to bear his signature, *That Lady in Ermine* (1948) was completed by Preminger after L.'s death.

lubok. 17th-c. Russian woodcut similar to the English chapbooks; at first religious, then political in subject, or often simply a means of circulating songs and dances among the peasants. The l. had a considerable influence in forming Larionov and Goncharova's 'primitivist' style (1908–12) so noticeable, e.g., in Goncharova's designs for *Firebird*.

Lucan (A.D. 39–65). Marcus Annaeus Lucanus, Roman poet, born at Cordoba, Spain, nephew of Seneca, educated at Rome and Athens; he achieved a great reputation as a rhetorician but was obliged to commit suicide for his part in a conspiracy against Nero. His *Pharsalia* deals with the wars between Pompey and Caesar. In accordance with the then fashionable Stoic view, L. backs the Republican side represented by Pompey and Cato and much of his finest oratory is devoted to the theme of freedom (hence Shelley's admiration for him). The style is epigrammatic and rhetorical, unfashionable at the moment, but one of the best examples of its kind.

Lucas Edward Verral (1868–1938). English writer and assistant ed. of *Punch*. L. was an authority on Lamb, wrote travel books and compiled anthologies, notably *The Open Road*.

Lucasta (1649). Coll. of poems by Richard *Lovelace.

Lucas van Leyden (*c.* 1494–1533). Early Netherlandish painter and engraver. Taught by his father and C. Engelbrechtsz, L. was a celebrated engraver by the age of 15. Among his engravings, often valued second only to those of Dürer, are *Ecce Homo* and *Mohammed and the Monk*. He met Dürer in the Netherlands in 1521 and travelled in the Netherlands with Mabuse in 1527. Like Dürer, L. was very interested in bold technical experiments, perspective, detailed studies from nature, and character, if not oddity, in human beings. His colour is bright, his composition is restless, while serene and lovingly painted landscapes provide relief in such paintings as *Last Judgement* (Lakenkal Mus., Leyden), *The Adoration of the Kings* (A. Inst., Chicago), *Healing of the Blind Man* (Hermitage) and *The Worship of the Golden Calf* (Rijksmus., Amsterdam).

Lucia di Lammermoor. Opera by *Donizetti; 1st performance at Naples in 1835.

Lubok of Krylov's fable *The Industrious Bear*

Lucas van Leyden. *Last Judgement* (above) and *Conversion of St Paul* (engraving, below; detail)

Ludwigsburg porcelain group

Lu Hsün

Lucian (A.D. *c.* 120–*c.* 190?). Greek satirist. Born at Samosata in northern Syria on the Euphrates, he became an accomplished Greek stylist in the fashionably archaic manner modelled on ancient Athenian usage and composed about 80 essays and dialogues satirizing, more or less philosophically, contemporary manners and ideas. He drew largely and eclectically on previous literature, particularly the satires of Menippus (the 3rd-c. cynic philosopher of Gadara, who figures in several of his pieces), the dialogues of Plato and the old comedy of Athens. His ideas are scarcely profound but his eye for the pretentious and ridiculous is shrewd and he illustrates contemporary life acutely.

Lucky Jim (1954). Comic novel by Kingsley *Amis.

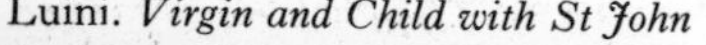

Luini. *Virgin and Child with St John*

Lucretius Titus Carus (94?–55? B.C.). Roman poet. Nothing is known of his life apart from St Jerome's fantastic story that he was driven mad by a love-potion, wrote his poem in his intervals of lucidity and died by his own hand. Cicero is said to have ed. L.'s poem *De Rerum Natura* ('Concerning the Nature of Things'). The poem belongs to the genre of didactic poetry which had long been fashionable among the scholar-poets of Alexandria. L. sets out to present in verse the physical and ethical system of his master, the Greek philosopher *Epicurus. Although the subject demands a great deal of detailed 'scientific' exposition, L.'s almost religious zeal for it–Epicurus, he believed, had delivered him from the terrors of superstition–and his power of vivid visualization transmute it into the most golden and passionate verse in Latin. Language and metre are deliberately archaic: he follows the rugged example of Ennius and the older poets rather than the fashionably smooth manner of the Alexandrians whom his contemporaries imitated. Alliteration and simplicity of expression make for vigour and power. Although the poem is unfinished, presumably owing to the poet's early death, it gained and retained the admiration of later poets, especially Virgil.

Ludus Tonalis. Work for piano by *Hindemith.

Ludwig Otto (1813–65). German novelist and dramatist. His masterpiece, the novel *Zwischen Himmel und Erde* (1856), set in his native province of Thuringia, is outstanding in its construction and the eloquence of its prose. L.'s play *Der Erbförster* (1850), meticulous in its detail, is a pioneer work of realism but his creativity was hampered by intense self-criticism and a critical activity devoted mainly to Shakespeare.

Ludwigsburg. German (hard-paste) *porcelain factory (1756–1824) at Württemburg; one of the 7 leading German factories. The factory's best work was in its modelled figures and figure groups.

Lugné-Poë Aurélien-Marie (1869–1940). French actor and director, particularly important in promoting symbolist drama in the 1890s and early 1900s at his Théâtre de l'Oeuvre.

Lugones Leopoldo (1874–1938). Argentinian poet, author of much popular, patriotic verse, often in narrative form.

Lu Hsün. Pseud of Chu Shao-yin (1881–1936), Chinese essayist, trs. and short-story writer. His life and writing were devoted to showing the inadequacy of traditional Chinese values and to promoting their renewal in the modern revolution. While he was the foremost promoter of literary realism and the use of colloquial Chinese, he was also a conscientiously slow writer and punctilious stylist. He regarded himself as the Gogol of China. The most complete coll. of his stories in English is vol. I of *Selected Works of Lu Hsün* (Peking, 1956).

Luini Bernardino (*c.* 1481–1532). Italian painter of the Milanese school, one of the most popular. His personal idiom was fresh and lighthearted but after a series of frescoes in this style he turned to imitating Leonardo. This brought him success but deadened a delightful artistic talent.

Lukács György (1885–). Hungarian Marxist philosopher and literary critic. His conversion to Marxism–shortly after World War I–took the traditional leap from 'left Hegelianism' to the philosophy of the young Marx. His works include: *A történelmi regény* (1947); *The Historical Novel* (1962) and *Goethe und seine Zeit* (1947); *Studies in European Realism* (1950).

Luke, The Gospel according to St (late 1st c.). One of the books of the *Bible, the 3rd book of the New Testament. It is longer than

Jean-Baptiste Lully

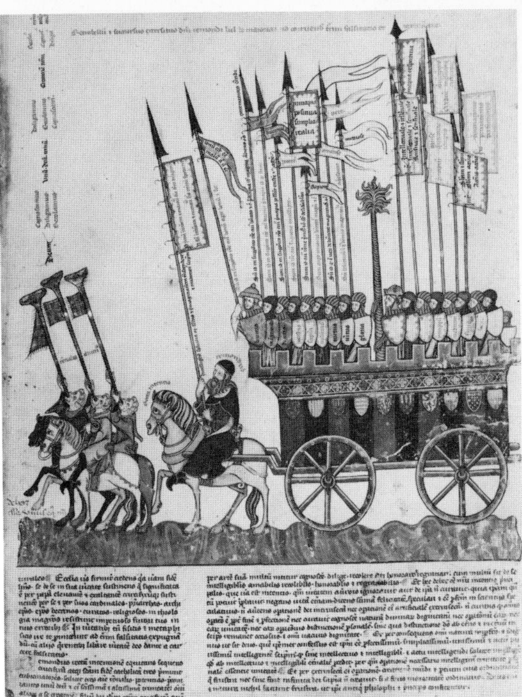

Ramón Lull leading the army of Truth: from a contemporary life of Lull

the Gospels of St Matthew or St Mark, and its version of the life and teaching of Jesus is a more deliberately literary composition. The traditional author, St Luke, was a physician, a friend of St Paul and St Mark.

Luks George (1867–1933). U.S. painter of low urban life, member of The Eight.

Lull Ramón (*c.* 1235–1315). Catalan writer, missionary, scholar and philosopher. He wrote both in Catalan and Latin and his vast output includes lyric poems, a utopian romance *Blanquerna*, an encyclopaedic compilation, a bestiary, a work on alchemy, and two fine autobiographical poems, besides several mystical and philosophical treatises.

Lully Jean-Baptiste (1632–87). Italian-born French composer (original name Lulli), naturalized in 1661. L. came to France as a boy and already in 1652 was at the court of the then 14-year-old Louis XIV. L.'s expertise as a dancer and as a courtier brought him the immediate and lasting favour of the young king; by 1662 he was Master of the Music of the Royal Family and in 1672 successful intrigue and a law suit brought him the monopoly of musical stage productions, indeed, his most important achievements were for the theatre. Despite his Italian extraction L. established a French style of opera and gave the French *overture its characteristic form. 2 fruitful and important collaborations span his stage career: with Molière from 1662 to 1673, including *Le Bourgeois Gentilhomme* (1664), during which the foundations of the French opera style were laid; and from 1673 with P. Quinault, a masterly adapter of classical tragedies and mythology. Apart from numerous operas, ballets and pastorals L. also wrote some church music.

Lulu (1937). Opera by *Berg with his own libretto.

Lumet Sidney (1924–). U.S. film director; theatre director and big-time TV director before filming a television play, *Twelve Angry Men* (1957), produced by the star, Henry Fonda. Apart from the excellent *That Kind of Woman* (1958), he has specialized in adapting prestige theatrical works: *The Fugitive Kind* (1960) from Tennessee Williams's *Orpheus Descending*, Arthur Miller's *A View from the Bridge* (1961), O'Neill's *Long Day's Journey into Night* (1962), doing best by the first, minimizing the defects of the second and at least respecting the text of the third. Capable at bringing out what is in a script rather than adding to it, he has turned from plays to novels with *The Pawnbroker* (1963) and *Fail Safe* 1964).

Lumière Louis (1864–1948) and Auguste (1862–1954). French inventors and industrialists, inventors of a form of camera and projector, the Cinématographe Lumière, which had its 1st show in 1895 (the Edison version, the Vitascope, was not shown until the following year). During 1895 Louis shot over 40 little films for their shows, particularly of places (their 1st film, *La Sortie des Usines Lumière*) and events (*Arrivée d'un Train*) and a few simple comic anecdotes (*Repas de Bébé*, *Arroseur arrosé*). The L. tradition referred to by some French critics is the mainstream of that cinema which exploits its potential as a recording mechanism (as opposed to the Méliès tradition of using the trickery that is possible on film).

Lumière d'Été (1942). Film directed by J. *Gremillon.

Lundis. *Sainte-Beuve's *Causeries du Lundi* (1851–62), series of critical articles.

lunette. Architectural term for a semicircular window or opening.

Lunt Alfred (1893–). U.S. actor. He and his wife Lynne Fontanne (1887–) formed a famous partnership in such plays as *The Taming of the Shrew*, *The Seagull* and more recently *The Visit* (London, 1960). There is a theatre bearing their name in New York.

Lupino. English family of actors, dancers and acrobats, of Italian descent of whom Henry George (1892–1959) became famous as Lupino Lane and created and performed the dance *The Lambeth Walk*.

Lupino Ida (1917–). British-born U.S. film actress and director. She starred in *Dwan's *Her First Affair* (1932). From 1934 in Hollywood she played leading parts for over 20 years. She also became a song writer, producer for TV and films, director and script writer.

lur. Ancient Scandinavian musical instrument, a long bronze trumpet.

Lumière programme (1895)

Lumet. Anna Magnani and Marlon Brando in *The Fugitive Kind*

Lurçat tapestry

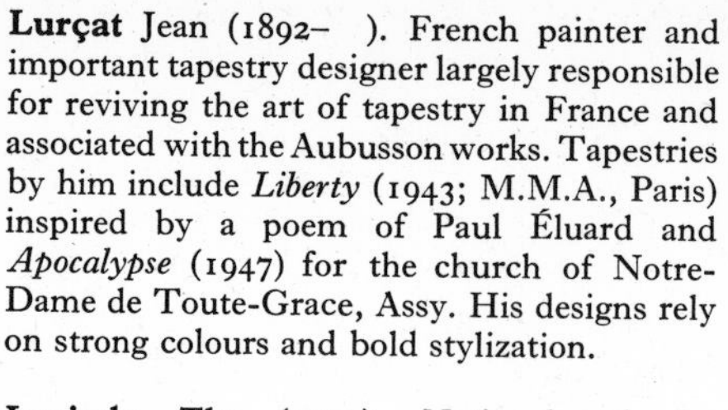

Lurçat Jean (1892–). French painter and important tapestry designer largely responsible for reviving the art of tapestry in France and associated with the Aubusson works. Tapestries by him include *Liberty* (1943; M.M.A., Paris) inspired by a poem of Paul Éluard and *Apocalypse* (1947) for the church of Notre-Dame de Toute-Grace, Assy. His designs rely on strong colours and bold stylization.

Lusiads, The (1572). National epic by *Camoens.

Lustra (1916). Coll. of poems by Ezra Pound.

lustre. On glass, a shimmering iridescence, often silvery in colour, produced by similar methods to those used for making lustreware pottery. Metallic compounds, usually silver, copper or gold and, in modern times, platinum or bismuth, are painted on to the glass. They are then reduced to their metallic state with the aid of carbon, in a furnace which is deliberately made smoky.

Lute. This modern instrument was built from notes by a 15th-c. maker

lute (Arabic *al ud*). Stringed musical instrument of ancient origins; it was imported into Europe in the middle ages, was a major instrument there until the 17th c., is still common in Arab countries and has been revived in Europe for the performance of early music. In Europe it is fretted (*fret) and plucked with the fingers, has 5 or more pairs (i.e. 'courses') of strings, each pair being tuned in unison or 8ves, and generated a family of variants, the most important being the 'theorbo' and the 'chitarrone' which were, in effect, l.s with additional, unstopped bass strings strung from the bridge to a very long extra 'neck'. Its music is notated in *tablature.

Martin Luther: painting by Cranach

Luther Martin (1483–1546). German religious reformer, initiator of the European Reformation. L. was successively an Augustinian friar, a priest and a member of the univ. staff at Wittenberg. His growing anger with unregenerate practices in the Church exploded in the 95 theses against Indulgences which he nailed to the door of the castle-church, Wittenberg. In 1517 there followed revolutionary doctrines: the secular ruler's competence in religious matters was asserted; the authority of the Bible invoked against that of the Pope; the individual Christian conscience against the mediating priesthood. Following his excommunication and refusal to recant at the Diet of Worms (both 1521) L. devoted his energy to establishing the Reformed religion. His trs. of the Bible (1522: 1534) in a forceful colloquial style in the Saxon dialect was not only a great literary achievement but also by its popularity throughout Germany established an accepted national language above the regional dialects. Apart from his theological works, L.'s 2nd main contribution to German literature and religious life was the coll. of hymns *Geistliche Lieder* (1524). Reworked from the Psalms and other religious texts, they reveal L.'s considerable poetic talent and, in some cases where he composed the tunes, his gifts as a musician. In these hymns were the origins of the German *chorale.

Luttrell Psalter (*c.* 1340; B.M., London). Illuminated Psalter executed for Sir Geoffrey Luttrell of Irnham, Lincolnshire, who is portrayed in one of its miniatures with his wife and daughter-in-law. Though artistically it represents the East Anglian school in its decadence, its tinted marginal illustrations, which include scenes of contemporary life and labour, are of great value to the historian.

Lutyens Sir Edwin Landseer (1869–1944). British architect. He gained a reputation at the beginning of the c. with large-scale domestic architecture. He also designed the Cenotaph and other memorials, and the British Embassy in Washington; but his greatest work, with Sir Herbert Baker, was the building of New Delhi (1913–30), the final flowering of aristocratic imperialist architecture. His grand designs for Liverpool Catholic cathedral shows the romanticism of his inspiration.

Lutyens Elisabeth (1906–). English composer, daughter of Sir E. L.; her teachers include H. Darke and G. Caussade. In the late 1930s L. adopted 12-note techniques, her music showing affinities to Webern and also French music, and traditional film-music style where suitable. She has withdrawn most of her early compositions. Her works include 6 chamber concertos; the London overture *Proud City* (1945); 6 string quartets; *Aptote* for solo violin (1948); *The Pit*, a 'dramatic scene' for voices and orchestra (1947); *6 tempi for 10 instruments* (1958), and film and radio music.

Luxor. Town in Upper Egypt. It is on the right bank of the Nile and was in ancient times the site of the capital, Thebes. The grandest of

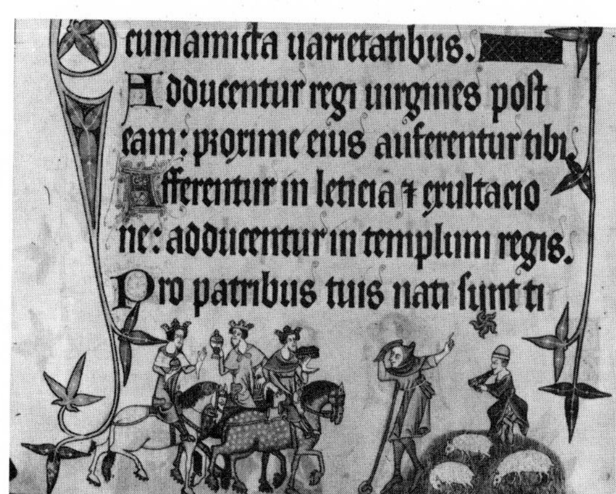

Luttrell Psalter. Sir Geoffrey Luttrell with his wife and daughter-in-law (far left) and a marginal painting of the journey of the Magi. Also *illumination

:dwin Landseer Lutyens. Deanery Garden, ıing, Berks. (1900–1)

Temple of Luxor

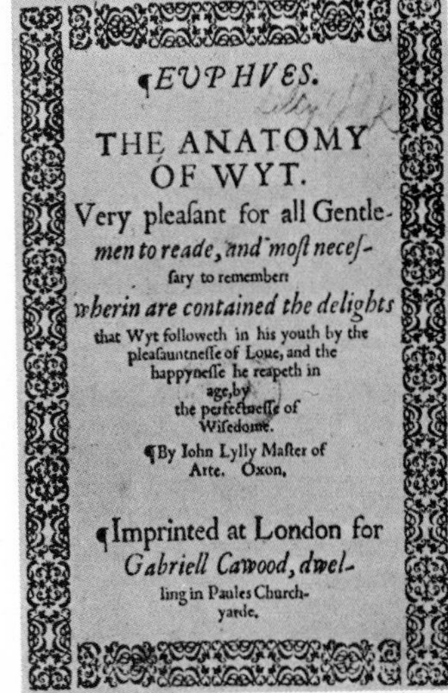
¶EVPHVES.

THE ANATOMY OF WYT.

Very pleaſant for all Gentlemen to reade, and moſt neceſſary to remember:

wherin are contained the delights that Wyt followeth in his youth by the pleaſauntneſſe of Loue, and the happyneſſe he reapeth in age, by the perfectneſſe of Wiſedome.

¶By Iohn Lylly Maſter of Arte. Oxon.

¶Imprinted at London for Gabriell Cawood, dwelling in Paules Churchyarde.

Lyly. 1st ed. of *Euphues: The Anatomy of Wit*

the surviving ruins are those of the Temple of L. built by Amenophis III (1413–1377 B.C.); the great colonnade is remarkable for its vast proportions and interesting in that the columns are in the form of a papyrus stem and the capitals of a papyrus bud.

Luzán Ignacio de (1702–54). Spanish literary critic and poet. His treatise *La Poética* (1737) is a precise, brilliantly written exposition of his basically neo-classical views of poetry and drama.

Lvov Alexey Fedorovich (1799–1870). Russian violinist and composer. He studied with his father, the director of the imperial Court Chapel. In 1833 he wrote 'God save the Czar' which remained the official national anthem until the Revolution. In composition he followed the Italian school. His works include a violin concerto which he played in Leipzig in 1840, and the operas *Bianca* (1844), *Ondine* (1847) and *Starosta Boris* (1854).

Lyceum Theatre. The premises were built in 1765 but were first used as a theatre in 1809 (in 1802 Mme Tussaud's waxworks had been given their English première at the L.). Destroyed by fire it was rebuilt in 1830 and after several vicissitudes became famous under Irving. It closed as a theatre in 1939 and is now a dance hall.

Lycidas (1638). Poem by *Milton.

Lydgate John (*c.* 1370–*c.* 1450). English poet, a prolific versifier, usually trs. and expanding, as in *The Troy Book* (from Italian) and *The Story of Thebes* (from French). For a long time he was thought Chaucer's equal.

Lyly John (1554?–1606). English writer, one of the *University Wits. He was educated at Oxford, an M.P., and contributed a pamphlet to the Marprelate Controversy. His fame rests on his plays, and 2 moralistic romances: *Euphues: The Anatomy of Wit* (1579) and *Euphues and his England* (1580), which spread the fashion for 'euphuism', the elaborate, artificial style of deliberately balanced antitheses, with a wealth of imagery drawn from the classics and the properties of natural phenomena. L.'s plays are mostly delicate comedies of aristocratic love, steeped in the atmosphere of classical mythology, the best known being *Campaspe* (1584) and *Endimion* (1591). He also wrote lyric poetry.

Lyons Eric (1912–). British architect and industrial designer. Working before 1939 for Gropius and Fry, he became particularly interested in the architecture of private dwellings, and began building flats immediately after the war. He has designed complete estates, avoiding traditional street layout and retaining variety in enclosed 'courtyard' spaces.

lyra viol. A small-sized bass *viol used for a style of playing particularly popular in England, in which plucking as opposed to bowing predominated. The music of the l. v. was written in *tablature.

lyre. Ancient Greek stringed musical instrument, played with a plectrum; the illustration shows the characteristic shape of the l.

Boy with a lyre: detail from a 5th-c. B.C. Greek relief

Lyrical Ballads (1798). Vol. of poems by *Wordsworth and *Coleridge.

Lyric Opera House Hammersmith. W. London theatre which was opened in 1890 and first flourished as a home of melodrama. Nigel Playfair took over its management (1918–32) and under him the theatre prospered. Since then it has had a chequered history and apart from a period when John Gielgud's co. acted there, it has in recent years lost its popularity.

lyric poetry. Name for short poems in which the poet fully exploits the musical qualities of words and deals with some single idea, emotion or subject. Originally the term may have been restricted to poems intended to be sung (to the lyre accompaniment).

Lysippus (*fl.* late 4th c.). Greek sculptor of the early Hellenistic period, official sculptor to Alexander the Great. His works combined idealization with movement and pathos.

Lysippus. Head of Alexander

Lysistrata. Comedy by *Aristophanes.

Lytton Edward Bulwer: *Bulwer-Lytton

Mabuse. *The Adoration of the Kings*

Rose Macaulay

Lord Macaulay

M

M (1931). Film directed by F. *Lang.

Mabinogion. A coll. of heroic Welsh tales gathered and trs. by Lady Caroline Guest (1838–49). Except for *Taliesin*, where the ms. is 16th c., the legends exist in 14th-c. ms. The stories include pre-Christian legends and versions of Arthurian and Irish myths.

Mabuse also called Jan Gossaert (1470/80–*c.* 1533). Early Netherlands artist, born probably at Maubeuge, Hainault and a master of the Antwerp Guild in 1503. In 1508 he visited Rome and from this date Italian elements appear in his work, which had been close to that of G. David before this. *Neptune and Amphitrite* (Berlin) shows M.'s humanist interest in antique sculpture, the nude and classical architecture following the journey. It also shows a close study of Dürer's *Adam and Eve.* All M.'s work has a fine and carefully calculated finish. In the outstanding early work *The Adoration of the Kings* (N.G., London) this has been described as 'an enamel-like purity'. Among other paintings are: *Adam and Eve* and *Portrait of the Children of Christian II of Denmark* (both Royal Colls, England), and *Danaë* (Alte Pina., Munich).

macaronic verse. Burlesque type of verse in which 2 or more languages are mixed and constructions and endings transposed; used especially of Latin and a vernacular.

Macaulay Rose (1881–1958). English novelist. The main theme of M.'s novels is the problem of belief in an age of uncertainty, described with wit and exuberance; they include *Potterism* (1920), *And No Man's Wit* (1940) and *The Towers of Trebizond* (1956).

Macaulay Thomas Babington, Lord (1800–59). English essayist, historian and statesman; he won instant fame in 1825 by his essay on Milton in *The Edinburgh Review*, to which he contributed 35 other articles, still reprinted. The success of the 1st two vols (1849) of his *History of England* from 1688 broke all publ. records, but he did not live to carry it beyond 1704. The work displayed M.'s mastery not only as a historian but as a writer of English prose. He also wrote poems, notably the popular coll. *Lays of Ancient Rome* (1842). He combined a life-long devotion to literature with energetic political service as an M.P., and his power as an orator is seen in his selection of *Speeches* (1854).

Macbeth (1611; publ. 1623). Tragedy by *Shakespeare, probably written *c.* 1605. Its source was *Holinshed. It was filmed in 1915 (featuring Beerbohm Tree); in 1948, directed by Orson *Welles; and in a Japanese version (*Throne of Blood*, 1956) directed by *Kurosawa.

Maccabees. 2 books of the *Apocrypha relating the struggle of the Jews under the family of the M. (or Hasmoneans) against Syrian rule.

MacCaig Norman (1910–). Scottish poet. *The Inward Eye* (1946) reflects his early involvement with neo-romanticism but *A Common Grace* (1960) shows his development into a fine writer of 'cerebral' verse.

McCarey Leo (1898–). U.S. film director. M. started in movies in 1918 and progressed to be an assistant director, then director and writer of 2-reel comedies (notably of Laurel and Hardy). He started to direct features in 1929, and became a top comedy director in the 1930s with *Duck Soup* (Marx Brothers; 1933), *Belle of the 'Nineties* (Mae West; 1934) and in a more sophisticated vein, *The Awful Truth* (Cary Grant; 1937). The most famous of his pre-war films is *Love Affair* (1939; remade by him as *An Affair to Remember*, 1957). Jean Renoir remarked that M. understood people, and in the absence of any visual style, his greatness lies in his handling of characters so that they reveal themselves through their comic actions–M.'s gags are his essential means of expression. His 2 exceptionally successful films with Bing Crosby, *Going My Way* (1944) and *The Bells of St Mary's* (1945), made him the highest paid U.S. movie personality in those years, but since the war he has made only 5 films, of which the best was a comedy, *Good Sam* (1948), as was *Rally Round the Flag Boys* (1958). *My Son John* (1952) is one of the violently anti-Communist films made in post-McCarthy Hollywood, and the sentiments are repeated in a comedy drama about priests in Korea, *Satan Never Sleeps* (1962).

MacCarthy Sir Desmond (1878–1952). Distinguished English critic; books include studies of Leslie Stephen (1937) and G. B. Shaw (1951).

McCarthy Mary (1912–). U.S. novelist and critic, one of the shrewdest contemporary observers. M.'s writing is analytical, witty and polished, frequently taking as its subject the

McCarey. Clifton Webb and William Holden in *Satan Never Sleeps*

fumbling attempts of the intellectual to come to grips with modern society. Her works include the autobiography *Memories of a Catholic Girlhood* (1957), and the novels *The Company She Keeps* (1942), *The Groves of Academe* (1952) and *The Group* (1963).

McClure Michael (1932–). U.S. poet. Although one of the *beats, his verse has unusual discipline. Colls include *Dark Brown* (1961).

McCrae Hugh (1876–1958). Australian poet. *Satyrs and Sunlight* (1911), his best-known vol., and *Forests of Pan* (1944), indicate his connection with Norman Lindsay. Superficially, his poetry often appears 'poetic' and outmoded in its conventions. Closer study reveals an adventurous imagination to which later Australian poetry is indebted.

McCullers Carson (1917–). U.S. novelist, born in Georgia. M.'s works transmute the violence of Southern life into Gothic fantasy; her theme is human isolation, revealed in the situations of those who are (or believe they are) excluded from the group–of the adolescent, the sick, the mute, the hunchback. M.'s works include *The Heart is a Lonely Hunter* (1940), *Reflections in a Golden Eye* (1941), *The Member of the Wedding* (1946; dramatized 1950), *The Ballad of the Sad Café* (1951) and *Clock Without Hands* (1961).

MacCunn Hamish (1868–1916). Scottish composer and conductor. His music is much influenced by the German late romantics and includes the opera *Jeannie Deans* (1894) and the overture *The Land of the Mountain and the Flood* (1887).

MacDiarmid Hugh. Pseud. of Christopher Murray Grieve (1892–), Scottish nationalist, Communist and poet; considered by the Scots to lead their literary renaissance, and by Englishmen to be it. Some of his best poetry, based on *Lallans, appeared in *Penny Wheep* (1926) and particularly in *A Drunken Man Looks at a Thistle* (1926); in the 1930s, through the influence of Marxism, M. became fascinated by social realism and the need for change; it led him to a more general English in *First* and *Second Hymn to Lenin* (1932, 35), invested still with fervent generosity of heart. Other works include *Scots Unbound* (1932) and *Lucky Poet* (1943).

Macdonald Alexander (*c.* 1700–*c.* 70). Scottish poet who took part in the 1745 Jacobite Rebellion. His *Ais-eiridh na Sean Chánoin Albannaich* (1751) was the 1st book of secular poetry publ. in Gaelic.

Macdonald George (1824–1905). Scottish novelist–author of such tales of Scottish rural life as *Alec Forbes* (1865) and *Robert Falconer* (1868)–and a poet writing in dialect.

MacDonald J(ames) E(dward) J(arvey) (1873–1932). English-born Canadian painter (arriving in 1887); one of the *Group of Seven.

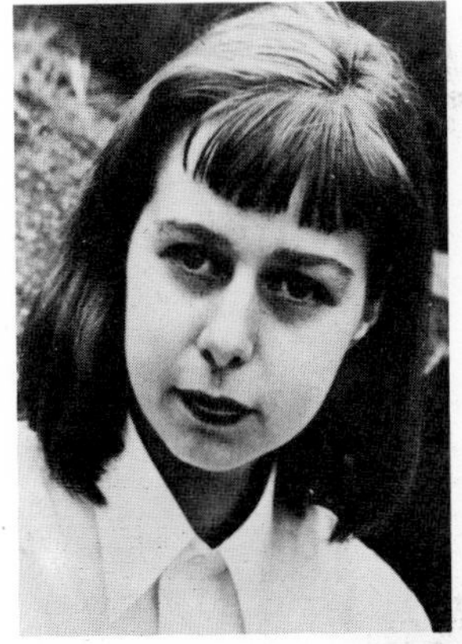
Carson McCullers

Macdowell Edward Alexander (1861–1908). U.S. composer, pianist and teacher. He studied composition in Frankfurt with J. Raff, whose friendship and influence is apparent in his work especially in his 1st suite for orchestra (1891). His compositions are frequently programmatic and generally romantic in their poetical expression. They include the symphonic poems *Hamlet and Ophelia* (1885), *Lancelot and Elaine* (1886), *Lamia* (1908) and *Indian Suite* for orchestra (1896) in which he employs American Indian melodies; *Woodland Sketches* (1896); 4 piano sonatas, 2 piano concertos and songs.

Hugh MacDiarmid

Mace Thomas. 17th-c. English musician and author of *Music's Monument* (1676). It deals with methods of vocal performance and the building and playing of the lute among other topics, and ranks with the work of *Morley and *Simpson as a major source for English 17th-c. music.

McEwen Sir John (1868–1948). Scottish composer and teacher and later director of the R.A.M., London. His numerous works include: the 'Solway' symphony in C♯ min. and *14 poems for inflected voice and orchestra* (1943) which introduced the *Sprechgesang* to Britain.

Mcfee William (Morley Punshon) (1881–). English-born novelist who settled in the U.S. (1911). M.'s seafaring experiences provided much of the material for such novels as *Aliens* (1914), *Captain Macedoine's Daughter* (1920) and *Command* (1922).

Mac Flecknoe, or a Satyr upon the True-Blew-Protestant Poet, T. S. (1682). Satirical poem by *Dryden.

Edward Macdowell

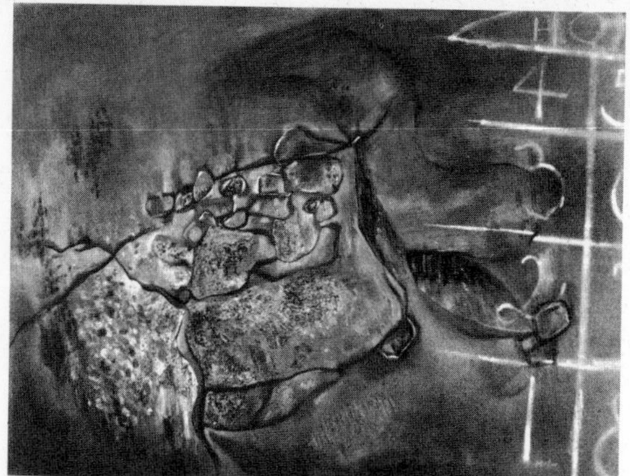
MacIver. *Hopscotch* (1940)

Macke. *Kairouan I* (1914)

Niccolò Machiavelli

Antonio Machado y Ruiz

McGinley Phyllis (1905–). U.S. writer of light verse and children's books. Her agile and skilful verse wittily describes the absurdities of sophisticated urban life. Among her colls of verse are: *A Pocketful of Wry* (1940); *Love Letters of Phyllis McGinley* (1954) and *Times Three: Selected Verse from Three Decades* (1960).

Mácha Karel Hynek (1810–36). The greatest Czech poet, whose work fused the impulses of romanticism and national and linguistic revival. His greatest work is the Byronic epic, *Máj* (1836; 1932).

Machado de Assis Joaquim Maria (1839–1908). Brazilian novelist and poet, author of naturalistic novels, and verse influenced by the *Parnassians.

His considerable reputation rests on such novels as *Quincas Borba* (1891; *Philosopher or Dog?*, 1954) and *Dom Casmurro* (1900; 1953), which show his concern for social justice.

Machado y Ruiz Antonio (1875–1939). Spanish poet whose rugged economy of image and line, in strong contrast with the rhetoric of Darío, has strongly influenced the generations since the Civil War. Politically a pessimistic radical, M. took the Republican side and died in the last days of the War (having tramped over the Pyrenees into France). Though of Andalusian birth, he describes the bare landscape of Castile, in whose cities he taught. The crucial event of his life was the death of his young wife, which drove him into even deeper retirement than before; many of his finest poems, e.g. in *Galerías* (1907), are explorations of the galleries of his own mind, for which he finds images in the countryside. But he also writes of the Spanish character and its backward-looking hopelessness and, in metaphysical mood, examines the implications of nihilism. He was the best Spanish poet of the early 20th c., with the terseness of Hardy, and the same folk-like simplicity.

Machado y Ruiz Manuel (1874–1947). Spanish poet, brother of the above; his verse, however, shows the influence of Darío and celebrates Andalusian life. Works include *Cante hondo* (1912).

Machau(l)t Guillaume de (*c.* 1300–77). French composer, poet and cleric. He was in the service of King John of Bohemia, after whose death (1346) M. went into the service of the French royal house. His music is in the *ars nova style; the great 4-part mass observes the principles of isorhythmy in all movements but the Gloria and Credo. M. also wrote *isorhythmic motets in French and Latin, and much secular music, e.g. *ballades*, *rondeux* and *virelais*. As a poet M., famous abroad and admired by Chaucer, standardized the ballade and rondeau form. He wrote in the convention of courtly love, though with a new personal note.

Machiavelli Niccolo (1469–1527). Florentine statesman and writer. While holding an important office of state he came into contact with Cesare Borgia, whose ruthless methods he had in mind when writing *Il Principe* (1532; *Nicholas Machiavel's Prince*, 1640), which gives advice on most objects of policy, arguing that a ruler must be guided only by the end to be achieved, regardless of morality. It quickly became notorious and is, e.g., often referred to in Elizabethan drama. In his *Discourses on Livy* (publ. 1531; trs. 1636) he shows unexpected sympathy with republican institutions. M. also wrote prose comedies, including *Mandragola* (1520), the most famous Italian Renaissance play, and *Clizia* (1525).

MacInnes Colin (1914–). English writer, author of many careful studies of the contemporary English scene, including the novels *City of Spades* (1957), about West Indians and Africans, and *Absolute Beginners* (1959), a sympathetic description of teenage life.

McIntire Samuel (1757–1811). U.S. architect. His later houses show the influence of Bulfinch.

Macintyre Duncan (1724–1812). Scottish poet writing in Gaelic, mainly on rural or Highland themes.

MacIver Loren (1909–). U.S. painter, virtually untrained, who has produced a feminine, refined and unusual art. Besides figurative, abstract and symbolic works, she has painted a number of sympathetic portraits of friends; she moves freely and with a constant sense of poetry from precise realism to a sophisticated abstraction.

Mackaye Percy (Wallace) (1875–1956). U.S. playwright and poet. M.'s plays, often suggested by literary classics, include *The Canterbury Pilgrims* (1903); *Caliban, by the Yellow*

Macke. *Grande Vitrine Brillante* (1912)

Mackendrick. Edward G. Robinson in *Sammy Going South*

Charles Macklin as Shylock

Sands (1916), a community masque; and *The Mystery of Hamlet King of Denmark: or What we will* (1949), a tetralogy of verse plays which relate the histories of the major characters up to the time Shakespeare's tragedy begins.

Macke Auguste (1887–1914). German painter. He studied at Düsseldorf Academy (1904–6) and under Corinth in Berlin (1907–8). He visited Paris, admiring Seurat and Matisse for their free use of colour. He was a founder-member in 1911 of the *Blaue Reiter group, Munich, with Kandinsky and Marc. His visit to Delaunay in Paris (1912) with Marc, and his trip to Tunis (1914) with Klee were the conclusive factors in the emergence of his personal colouristic style. *Landscape with Cows and Camel* (1914; Zürich) is characteristic in its radiant crystalline colour areas. Like Marc, he was nearing abstraction, but his early brilliance remained unfulfilled: he was killed in action in September 1914.

Mackendrick Alexander (1912–). U.S.-born British film director. M. made shorts and documentaries before joining Ealing Studios as a writer. He directed many of the best Ealing comedies, including his 1st film, *Whisky Galore* (1950), and later *The Man in the White Suit* (1951), *The Maggie* (1954) and *The Ladykillers* (1954). He had made one non-comic film, *Mandy* (1952), before going to the U.S. and dealing astonishingly with megalomania in the brilliant *The Sweet Smell of Success* (1957). After illness and starting films that were finished by others, he made *Sammy Going South* (1963) and *A High Wind in Jamaica* (1965) from the novel by Richard Hughes.

Mackenzie Sir Alexander Campbell (1847–1935). Scottish composer and principal of the R.A.M., London; he knew both H. von Bülow and Liszt, and enjoyed a European reputation. His works include: 7 operas and operettas, the oratorio *The Rose of Sharon* (1884) and a 'Burns' *Scottish Rhapsody* (1881).

Mackenzie Sir (Edward Montaigne) Compton (1883–). English novelist, author of *Sinister Street* (1913–14) and *Whisky Galore* (1947).

Mackenzie Henry (1745–1831). Scottish writer, author of the popular novel *The Man of Feeling* (1771), a series of episodes describing the mistakes of a well-intentioned innocent; it is significant in literature and history as being a book of feeling and sentiment during the 'age of reason'.

McKim, Mead and White. New York firm of architects founded in 1879. Their early work was influenced by Richardson and Norman Shaw, but they soon rejected this for an extremely formal Italianate manner, e.g. Boston Public Library (1892); this influence was so great that more indigenous American styles, such as the Chicago school and the shingle style, withered away.

Mackintosh Charles Rennie (1868–1928). Scottish art nouveau architect, noted for his country-houses, as that for Dr Blackie, Helensborough (1902), where he designed all the furniture, cutlery, etc., and for the Glasgow School of Art (1898–1909). It is one of the finest art nouveau buildings, and for a while M.'s career is parallel with his contemporary, Frank Lloyd Wright. But while Wright continued to develop, M.'s architectural career was brief, and he devoted most of the rest of his life to furniture, fabrics and watercolours.

Macklin Charles (*c.* 1700–97). Irish actor who established (1741) the now accepted interpretation of Shylock as a serious part; before M.'s sympathetic performance it had generally been played by a comedian. M. also wrote plays, notably *Love à La Mode* (1759) and *The Man of the World* (1781).

McKnight-Kauffer Edward (1890–1954). U.S. graphic artist and designer; he produced the 1st advertisement in a cubist style but also worked as a designer for the stage, e.g. the ballet *Checkmate*.

McLaglen Victor (1886–1959). English-born U.S. film actor. *The Informer* gave him a notable chance to deploy his tough looks and sympathetic character in a taxing dramatic role.

Maclaine Shirley (1934–). U.S. film dancer and comedienne of great charm and style who co-starred in her 1st film, *The Trouble with Harry* (1954); she often plays a girl with a good heart and doubtful morals. Her best performances include starring roles in Minelli's *Some Came Running* (1958) and Wilder's *The Apartment* (1960).

McKim, Mead and White. Boston Public Library

Mackintosh. Project for a concert hall (1898)

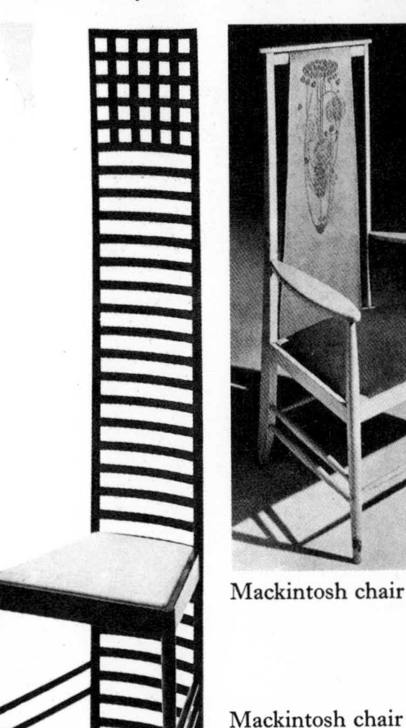
Mackintosh chair (1902)

Mackintosh chair (*c.* 1902)

MacLaren. *Le Merle*

Louis Macneice

Micheál Mac Liammóir

Maclise. Drawing of Charles Dickens with his wife and Mary Hogarth

MacLaren Norman (1914–). English-born animated-film director, working in Canada. M. has experimented not only with drawing images directly on to the film, but also drawing the synchronized sound track. His works include: *Blinkity Blank* (1954); *Rythmetic* (1956); *Chants Populaires* (1944–5).

Macleish Archibald (1892–). U.S. poet. His long public life has included a legal practice, the Congress librarianship, a professorship at Harvard and the chairmanship of UNESCO. His 1st poems appeared in 1917. *Conquistador* gained a Pulitzer prize in 1932 and *Collected Poems 1917–1952* received 3 national awards. His characteristic styles are extremely eclectic, his tone nostalgic, elegiac and apprehensive, presenting the uneasiness of his time. His finest work is in *Ars Poetica* (1926), *Frescoes for Mr Rockefeller's City* (1933) and the radio play *The Fall of the City* (1937).

Maclennan Hugh (1907–). Canadian novelist whose 5 novels since World War II have been acclaimed. His *Two Solitudes* (1945) is an intelligent exploration of identity and antagonism between French and English Canadians, *The Watch That Ends the Night* (1959) a highly imaginative evocation of contemporary experience, meaningful beyond Canada.

McLeod Norman (1898–1964). One of Hollywood's most adroit directors of comedy (and comedians), e.g. the Marx Brothers in *Monkey Business* (1931) and *Horse Feathers* (1932); 2 *Topper* films (1937, 38); Bing Crosby in *Pennies from Heaven* (1936); Danny Kaye in *The Secret Life of Walter Mitty* (1947); and Bob Hope in *The Paleface* (1948).

Mac Liammóir Micheál (1899–). Irish actor, director and designer who in 1928, together with Hilton Edwards, established the *Gate Theatre, Dublin where he has played Romeo, Othello, Antony and Faust. In 1950 he played Iago in Orson Welles's film of *Othello* and more recently has achieved world fame for his performance as Oscar Wilde in a one-man entertainment he devised, *The Importance of Being Oscar*.

Maclise Daniel (1806–70). Irish-born artist who became one of the leading Victorian painters of grandiose historical subjects. 2 frescoes, *The Death of Nelson* and *The Meeting of Blücher and Wellington*, are in the House of Lords. M. was also noted for portraits of famous contemporaries which appeared in *Fraser's Magazine*.

Macmillan Kenneth (1930–). Scottish dancer and resident choreographer with the Royal Ballet. He is one of the most prolific and talented contemporary choreographers; his works usually deal with human emotions and include *The Burrows* (1958), *The Invitation* (1960), and his version of *The Rite of Spring* (1962) which compared well with Nijinsky's original. This was followed by his inventive *Images of Love* (1964), part of the quatercentenary homage to Shakespeare.

MacMurray Fred (1908–). U.S. film actor, equally adept at comedy, e.g. *The Absent Minded Professor* (1961), or drama, e.g. *Double Indemnity* (1944).

Macneice Louis (1907–63). English poet. He collaborated with W. H. Auden in the verse miscellany *Letter from Iceland* (1937), which he followed with one of his own, *I Crossed the Minch* (1938). From 1929 he publ. at intervals books of ironic and questioning poems, often concealing harsh pain or disgust beneath their off-hand colloquial realism. He is a lyric poet delighting in surfaces, acid colours, quirks, the unusual aspects of the usual. His last book, *The Burning Perch*, foreshadowed his death, and *Memoranda to Horace* sums up the preoccupations and attitudes of his writing.

Maconchy Elizabeth (1907–). English composer whose teachers included Vaughan Williams, influential on her early style, and K. Jirák in Prague. Her best work is in her chamber music, especially her 7 string quartets, but she has also written 2 operas, a piano concerto (1930), a symphony (1950), *Impromptu* for piano (1939), and *A Winter's Tale* for soprano and string quartet.

McPhee Colin (1901–). Canadian composer whose teachers included Le Flem and Varèse. Impressed by Indonesian gamelan music, M. lived on the island of Bali for some years. His orchestral *Tabuh-Tabuhan* (1936) is directly influenced by Indonesian methods and he has written articles and books, e.g. *A Home in Bali* (1946).

Macpherson Charles (1870–1927). Scottish organist and composer, largely of church music, e.g. his setting of Psalm 137 for chorus and orchestra.

Macpherson James (1736–96). Scottish poet, author of *Fragments of Ancient Poetry . . . translated from the Gaelic . . .* (1760) and 'Ossian'–a name assigned to Oisin, son of Finn and a Gaelic warrior-bard of legendary prowess. It was from Oisin's works that M. claimed to have his epic poems, *Fingal* (1762) and *Temora* (1763). Though Goethe and others admired the works and they were important in the development of European romanticism, their publ. resulted in much speculation, Dr Johnson being among those who doubted their authenticity. It now seems clear that M. inserted genuine versions of Gaelic work into his own pastiches of their style.

Macready William Charles (1793–1873). English tragic actor, as a young man the rival of Kean and outstanding in his interpretations of Hamlet, Lear and Macbeth. He did great service to Shakespearean theatre by reverting to the original texts and abandoning the 'revisions' of the 17th and 18th cs.

McTeague (1899). Novel by Frank *Norris.

McWilliam F. E. (1909–). Irish sculptor; he studied at the Slade School (1928–31) and in Paris (1931–2) and has exhibited widely. M. is eclectic and prolific, working in a variety of materials and in more than one style. Most notable perhaps are his human figures (e.g. *Princess Macha*, 1957), which have become increasingly stylized.

Madách Imre (1823–64). Hungarian author of the philosophic drama *Az ember tragédiája* (1861; *The Tragedy of Man*, 1933). The Dante-like wealth of M.'s sombre ideas reveals a profound thinker.

Madame Bovary (1857). Novel by *Flaubert.

Madame Butterfly (Italian *Madama Butterfly*). Opera by G. *Puccini, based on a story by J. L. Long; 1st performed at La Scala, Milan and then in a revised, successful version at Brescia (both 1904).

Madame Récamier (1800). Portrait by J.-L. *David; Gérard also painted Mme *Récamier's portrait.

Madariaga Salvador de (1886–). Spanish writer who has written extensively in English and French. He is known for brilliant expositions of Spanish history and culture.

Mademoiselle de Maupin (1835). Novel by *Gautier.

Maderna Bruno (1920–). Italian composer and conductor. With *Berio he is director of the studio for electronic music in Milan. As a conductor M. has become known for his clear and sympathetic performances of both *avant-garde* and classical music. As a composer of *serial music (electronic and instrumental) he is likewise notable for his lyricism, clarity and directness. Among his works are: *Composizione in 3 tempi* (1951) for orchestra, and *Continuo* (1957) for electronic devices.

Maderno Carlo (1556–1629). Italian architect, nephew and pupil of Domenico Fontana. His church of S. Susanna (1603) in Rome is usually regarded as the beginning of baroque architecture. The façade has some basic features of mannerist design (e.g. Il Gesù)–columns, half-columns, scroll buttresses, etc. –but is now fused into a dynamic whole with a thrusting upward rhythm. M. is here the direct forerunner of Bernini, Cortona and Borromini. He had a large though not clearly defined part in the design of the Palazzo Barberini. His most famous work is the completion of St Peter's–the eastern bays of the nave and the main façade–with huge columns and heavy uninspired details, though it suffers by the 2 corner-towers remaining unbuilt. The date is 1607–15, but the style looks back (probably deliberately) to the high Renaissance of 80 years earlier.

Madonna of the Rocks: **Virgin of the Rocks*

madrigal. In music, a type of part song originating in 14th-c. Italy and reaching its climax in the 2nd half of the 16th c. Characteristics of the m. are that the music and form are more subservient to the emotions expressed in the words than was the case in the formally elaborate forms such as the rondeau, and that the texture is generally polyphonic. The immense range of emotional expression, from delicate wit to intense searching passion, is seen in the work of such men as Arcadelt, Palestrina, Orlando di Lasso, Marenzio,

William Charles Macready

McWilliam. *Baal* (1960)

Maderno. S. Susanna

Maderno and Michelangelo. Interior of St Peter's

Maes. *Woman scraping parsnips*

Magnasco. *Landscape with St Anthony*

Anna Magnani (left) in *Nella Città L'Inferno*

Magnelli. *Tranquillité sidérale*

Gesualdo and Monteverdi. The Italian m. popularized in England in the late 16th c. by M. *Yonge gave rise to a native school represented by such composers as Byrd, Pilkington, Weelkes and Gibbons.

Maekawa Kunio (1905–). Tange and M. are the leaders of the new movement in Japanese architecture. In contrast with the lightness and elegance of traditional work, the new is often of heavy, rough shuttered concrete, influenced by the late work of Le Corbusier. M.'s Harumi Apartments, Tokyo, are a brutalist version of a Corbusier Unité on the outside, but internally are sympathetic to traditional Japanese living.

Maerlant Jacob van (*fl. c.* 1260). Netherlands poet who stopped writing chivalric romances and turned to didactic works in rhyme, including a history of the world, *Spieghel Historiel*; he had many followers.

Maerten van Veen. Name by which M. J. van *Heemskerck is sometimes known.

Maes (Maas) Nicolaes (1632–93). Dutch portrait and genre painter who studied under Rembrandt; best known for his intimate domestic scenes. A visit to Antwerp in 1670 led to a change in style and the production of fashionable and suave portraits in the Flemish manner.

maestà (Italian, 'majesty'). Short name given to paintings of the Madonna and Child enthroned in majesty with saints and angels in adoration.

Maeterlinck Maurice (Polydore-Marie-Bernard) (1862–1949). Belgian symbolist writer. M.'s mystical ideas are apparent in his plays, e.g. *L'Oiseau bleu* (1909; *The Blue Bird*, 1909), allegories outside time and space which hint at a world beyond that of the everyday. M. also wrote the play *Pelléas et Mélisande* (1892; 1894), adapted by Debussy as an opera and used by Schoenberg for a symphonic poem, and the book *La Vie des abeilles* (1901; *The Life of the Bee*, 1901). He was awarded the Nobel prize in 1911.

Maffei Francesco Scipione (1675–1755). Italian scholar and playwright. He wrote a valuable history of Verona; his plays, e.g. his verse drama *Merope* (1713), trs. into French by Voltaire (1743), are important in the history of 18th-c. Italian theatre.

Maggie: A Girl of the Streets (1892). Short novel by Stephen Crane.

Magic Flute, The (German *Die Zauberflöte*). Opera in 2 acts by *Mozart with libretto by E. Schikaneder; 1st performance at the Theater an der Wien, Vienna, 1791.

Magic Mountain, The (1924). Novel by Thomas *Mann.

Magnani Anna (1910–). Italian actress. One of the last great emotional players, M. waited 11 years before making a notable film–*Roma, Città Aperta* (1945). Her later pictures include *Bellissima* (1951) and *The Rose Tattoo* (1955), which was specially written for her by Tennessee Williams.

Magnard Albérich (1865–1914). French composer, a pupil of d'Indy. His music, influenced by Wagner, includes the operas *Yolande*, *Guercœur* and *Bérénice*, and orchestral and chamber works. He died defending his property against invading German troops and most of his music was destroyed when his home was burnt down.

Magnasco Alessandro (1667 or 81–1749). Italian painter in the manner of Salvator Rosa, of monks, gipsies, etc. in wild stormy landscapes.

Magnelli Alberto (1888–). Italian non-figurative painter working in Paris. His 1st works in this idiom appeared before World War I. Joined by Kandinsky in 1932, he became one of the chief abstract painters in Paris in the 1930s.

Magnificat. 'The Song of the Blessed Virgin Mary' as recorded in Luke i. 46–55, beginning 'My soul doth magnify the Lord'. It is used in the office of Vespers in the Roman Catholic and Anglican liturgies and has plainsong and innumerable polyphonic settings.

Magnificent Ambersons, The (1942). Film directed by *Welles, from the novel (1918) by Booth *Tarkington.

Magnum. Photo agency founded by Cartier-Bresson, Robert Capa and David Seymour in Paris, to free creative photographers from the exploitation of agents. It has maintained a dominant position in the field of photo-reportage ever since.

Magritte. *La Grande Guerre* (1964)

Gustav Mahler

Norman Mailer

Magritte René (1898–). Belgian surrealist painter who studied at Brussels; he then moved to Paris where, by 1930, he was a leading surrealist painter and follower of Breton. M. returned to Brussels (1931) and founded the Belgian surrealist movement with P. Delvaux.

Mahagonny, The Rise and Fall of the City of (1927). Opera by Kurt *Weill and Bertolt *Brecht.

Mahler Gustav (1860–1911). Austrian composer and conductor. After studying at Vienna, where he greatly admired Bruckner's teaching, he deputized for Nikisch at Leipzig for 6 months (1886). Thereafter he directed the Hamburg opera from 1891 to 1897, becoming a Roman Catholic in this year; in 1907 he became director of the court opera; in 1909 he took over the directorship of the Metropolitan Opera, New York, but ill-health forced his return to Germany. M.'s music is the link between the Viennese school of Beethoven, Schubert and Bruckner and, in its intense chromaticism, the new Viennese school of Schoenberg. M.'s style ranged from the epic Brucknerian grandeur to a polyphonic texture, a new approach to harmonic structure, and ensembles of chamber dimensions. M.'s important works include: the symphonies, no. 1 in D maj. (1888); no. 2 in C min. (1894) *Death and Resurrection*, for soprano, alto and chorus, text from Klopstock and *Arnim and Brentano's *Wunderhorn*; no. 3 in D min. (1896) for alto and chorus, text from Nietzsche and *Wunderhorn*; no. 4 in G (1900) with soprano, text from *Wunderhorn*; no. 5 in C min. (1902); no. 6 in A min. (1904), no. 7 in E min. (1905); no. 8 in E♭ (1907), the *Symphony of a Thousand* for 8 soloists, double chorus, children's chorus and organ; no. 9 in D min. (1909); no. 10, unfinished, versions completed by E. Krenek and Deryck Cooke (1964). Among his other works are *Lieder eines fahrenden Gesellen* (1884) for voice and orchestra, words by M.; *5 Kindertotenlieder* (1902) for voice and orchestra or piano, to a text by F. Ruckert; *Das Lied von der Erde* (1908; 1st performance 1911) for mezzo-soprano, tenor and orchestra, text taken from Chinese poems.

Maid's Tragedy, The (publ. 1619). Tragedy by Beaumont and Fletcher.

Mailer Norman (1923–). U.S. novelist of Jewish origin, author of the best-selling novel about World War II *The Naked and the Dead* (1948). Works include *Barbary Shore* (1951), *The Deer Park* (1955), the coll. of stories and essays and fragments *Advertisements for Myself* (1959), and the novel *An American Dream* (1965).

Maillart Robert (1872–1940). Swiss engineer whose works, particularly his concrete bridges, were advanced statically and superb as objects in a landscape. By using all elements, including the roadway, to produce a structural unity, he created light and elegant designs.

Maillart. Bridge over the river Thur at Felsegg (1933)

Maillol Aristide (1861–1944). French sculptor. He studied painting and sculpture at the École des Beaux-Arts, Paris (1882–6). He was associated with the nabis as a painter and tapestry designer and did not concentrate solely on sculpture until *c.* 1897, when his sight was failing. His early works (wood carvings and terracotta statuettes) provided the basis of his later sculpture, most of which was cast in bronze.
He was influenced at first by Rodin (the 2 men shared a mutual respect), but his mature treatment of the figure, strengthened by a visit to Greece in 1906, has a sensuality which is closer to classical art than to Rodin's expressive and sometimes erotic romanticism. M.'s whole oeuvre is built round the female nude. His most original work (*c.* 1898–1910) is important for its renewed respect for mass after the fluid surface richness of Rodin and the impressionist sculpture of artists like M. Rosso. *Torso* (1906; Tate) is typical in its massive simplicity of closed form with a strong sense of a contained dynamic energy. After 1910 his work was relatively uninventive and ranges from the prosaic stylization of his *Memorial to Cézanne* (1912–25; Tuileries, Paris) to the rather theatrical quality of symbolic figures like *Air* and *River* (1939–43; M.M.A., Paris).

Maillol. *Air* (1939–43)

Maimonides Moses (1135–1204). Spanish-born Jewish philosopher and theologian; most of his working life was spent in Egypt. M.'s *Guide for the Perplexed* (finished in 1190; written in Arabic) attempted to reconcile Hebrew theology with Aristotelian philosophy; it was extremely influential on subsequent Hebrew, Islamic and Christian thought.

Mainardi Sebastiano di Bartolo (*c.* 1460–1513). Italian painter, follower and assistant of Domenico Ghirlandaio, who worked chiefly on altarpieces and frescoes. His 1st dated work is

Maillol. *Torso* (1906)

Maiolica plate; Urbino, 1533. See also colour plate 57

Bernard Malamud

Mainz cathedral

The Maison Carrée

at the Collegiata, San Gimignano; but he later worked mainly in Florence. The early influence of Verrocchio was later superseded by that of Filippino Lippi.

Maine Louise de Bourbon, duchesse du (1676–1753). French society woman whose *salon* at Sceaux was frequented by Voltaire and Fontenelle.

Mains sales, Les (1948). Play by Sartre.

Main Street (1920). Novel by Sinclair *Lewis.

Mainz cathedral. One of the 3 important Rhineland Romanesque cathedrals. It is a mixture of styles: the W. towers are 11th c.; the nave (alternation of supports, grim block-capitals), octagonal crossing tower, and chancel (on a trefoil plan with 2 towers) are 12th c.; rib-vault 13th c.; the top of the crossing tower is baroque.

maiolica. Tin-glazed earthenware made in Spain and Italy from the 14th c.; typical 15th- and 16th-c. m. wares were large dishes, basins, jars and drug-pots decorated with an opaque white or bluish white tin-glaze ground on which were painted Renaissance motifs in a range of colours that included blue, green, reddish brown, yellow and aubergine, with blue predominating for the lines of the design. Heraldic, allegorical and historical subjects were common, the drawing often being reminiscent of contemporary engravings. The term m. is applied by extension to all tin-glazed ware in the Italian tradition, as opposed to *faïence and *delftware.

Mairet Jean (1604–86). French playwright who advocated obedience to the *unities; his *Sophonisbe* (1634) was the 1st French play to follow the rules of tragedy. M. was for a time one of the *cinq auteurs who wrote plays under the direction of Cardinal Richelieu.

Maison Carrée Nîmes. A typical Roman temple and the best preserved. It dates from 16 B.C., stands on a high podium approached by steps at one end only, and has a portico of Corinthian columns with half-columns continuing all round the sides and back.

Maison Tellier, La (1881). Short story by *Maupassant.

maître de ballet. Formerly the man responsible for all aspects of balletic productions at court or palace, now the ballet master in a co.; he keeps the dancers in practice and rehearses them for performances.

Maja, The Naked and **The Clothed Maja.** Portraits by *Goya.

majolica. 19th-c. name for earthenware decorated with coloured glazes; also commonly but wrongly used as an alternative for *maiolica.

major. Musical term, *key, *harmony and *scale.

Major Barbara (1905). Play by G. B. *Shaw.

make-up in the theatre. Now used to restore to an actor's face the colour which would otherwise be obliterated by strong stage lighting. In medieval dramatic presentations paint was often used to disguise, and paint and chalk were similarly used in Elizabethan theatre; only with Garrick, however, was make-up used much as it is now. Greasepaint was introduced towards the end of the 18th c.

Maklakiewicz Jan Adam (1899–1954). Polish composer. He studied at the Warsaw Conservatory (where he subsequently taught harmony) and under Dukas in Paris. Influenced by French modernism, he wrote a number of works in an advanced style, notably *Four Japanese Songs* (1931), in which he employs quarter tones. Other works include the ballet *Cagliostro in Warsaw* (1946), the symphonic poem *Grünewald* (1945), *The Prague Overture* (1947), cello and violin concertos, some chamber music, and settings to Polish folk-songs.

Malachi. One of the minor prophetic books of the *Bible (Old Testament).

Malade imaginaire, Le (1673). Comedy by *Molière.

Malamud Bernard (1914–). U.S. novelist and short-story writer. M.'s work is compassionate and deeply concerned with moral issues, though it displays considerable humour and a strong vein of fantasy. He frequently describes the sufferings of poor Jews, finding human brotherhood–and therefore a meaning to life–in the worst situations. His books include: *The Natural* (1952); *The Assistant*

(1957); *The Magic Barrel* (1958), a coll. of stories; and *A New Life* (1961).

Malbone Edward Greene (1777–1807). U.S. portrait painter especially noted as a miniaturist. He studied under Samuel King in Boston, and worked in Boston, New York, Philadelphia and Charleston.

Malcolm George (1917–). English harpsichordist, pianist and conductor.

Malcuzynski Witold (1914–). Polish pianist, a pupil of Paderewski and distinguished for his performances of Chopin. He worked much outside Poland, especially in the U.S.

Malczewski Antoni (1793–1826). Polish poet, author of *Marja*, a Byronic tale in verse which ranks among the finest works of Polish romantic poetry.

Maldon, The Battle of (late 10th c.). Old English narrative poem in epic style, one of the finest embodiments of the Anglo-Saxon heroic spirit and code of loyalty. Its subject is the Viking defeat of the Saxons at Maldon, Essex, in 991. The hero is the ealdorman Byrhtnoth, leader of the English, who scornfully refuses to buy off the Vikings; in the ensuing battle he is finally killed. The end of the poem is lost.

malerisch (German, 'painterly'). The art historian Heinrich Wölfflin gave a particular meaning to this term by using it to characterize the type of painting which expresses form in terms of colour and tone (e.g. Rembrandt and Titian) as opposed to line (e.g. Botticelli).

Malevich Kasimir (1878–1935). Russian painter born in Kiev, coming to Moscow about 1905 and working for the next few years in a private studio run by Roerich. From 1908 to 1910 M.'s work underwent rapid development under the impact of French post-impressionism (*Golden Fleece) and came to the notice of *Larionov, who invited him to contribute to the 1st Knave of Diamonds Exhibition. For the next 2 years he associated closely with Larionov and Goncharova, sharing their interest in national folk-art as well as continuing his enthusiasm for the work of Matisse, Picasso, Cézanne and Van Gogh. Intimate with Russian futurist poets, e.g. Mayakovsky and Khlebnikov, M. designed scenery and costumes for *Victory over the Sun*, produced in St Petersburg (1913), one of the back-cloths being an abstract black and white square. According to M., this production launched suprematism. During the next 2 years he painted a series of surrealist and 'non-sense realist' works, e.g. *An Englishman in Moscow*. In 1915 he exhibited 36 abstract canvases, including the famous *Black Square*. In this later period of suprematism (1917–18), e.g. *Sensation of the Space of the Universe*, soft amorphous forms combined with geometric; 2 series dominated, those using a cross form and a *White on White* series such as the painting of a white square on a white ground of 1918 (M.M.A., New York). After this M. ceased to paint except as illustration to theories expounded in a series of pamphlets and small books. His 1st idealized architectural drawings (1915–16) developed into 3-dimensional plaster sculptures, *Architectonicas*; during the 1920s M. was influential as a teacher in Vitebsk and Moscow and from 1922 in Leningrad.

Malherbe François de (1555–1628). French poet and critic who aimed to purify the decadent facility of the *Pléiade. His ideals were concision, clarity, sobriety, purity of language, grammatical regularity and precision, and versification according to strict metrical rules. Many of his lyrics deal with political subjects: he also paraphrased the Psalms and trs. parts of Livy and Seneca.

Malipiero Gian Francesco (1882–). Italian composer, musicologist and teacher; director of the Marcello Conservatory, Venice (1939–53). M. produced a complete ed. of Monteverdi's works (1926–42) and studied the work of other 17th- and 18th-c. Italian composers; his music shows strongly the impact of these studies. A stay in Paris brought him into contact with the work of Debussy, Ravel and Casella. M.'s most important work is in his numerous operas.

Malipiero Riccardo (1914–). Italian composer, nephew of the above. His early teachers included his uncle but after 1945 he turned to 12-note techniques. His work includes: 2 operas; 3 symphonies; *Sinfonia Cantata* (1956); and chamber music, including *Sei poesi di Dylan Thomas* (1957).

Mallarmé Stéphane (1842–98). French poet who earned his living, unhappily, as a teacher of English in various secondary schools, mainly in Paris. In him, the cleavage between bread-winning and the pursuit of the literary ideal

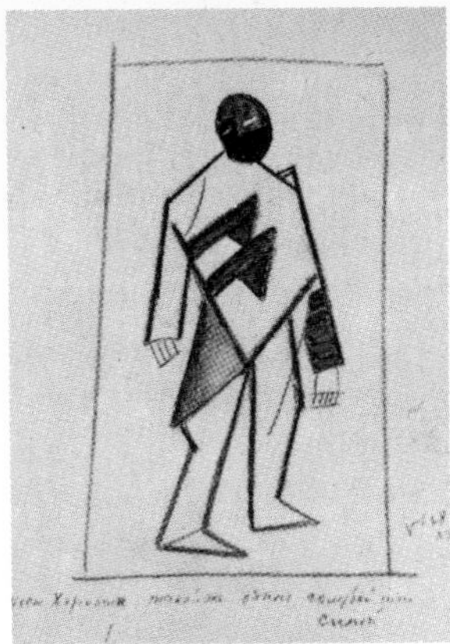

Malevich. Costume for *Victory over the Sun*

Malevich. *Black Square*

Malevich. *White on White* (1918)

Mallarmé: lithograph (1893) by Whistler

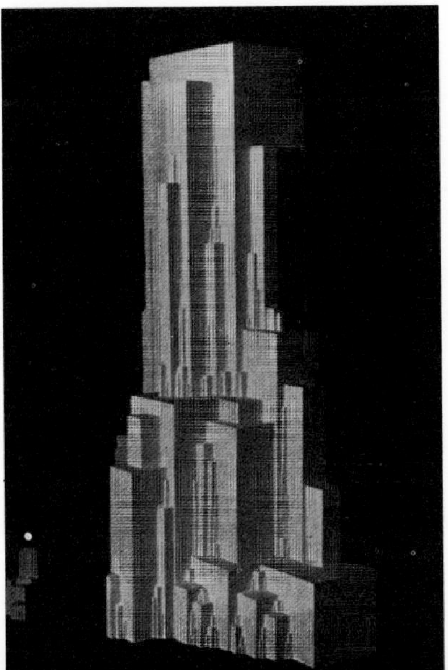

Malevich. *Architectonica*. Also *futurism, *suprematism

Malle. Jeanne Moreau and Jean-Marc Bory in *Les Amants*

Malouel. *The Dead Christ with God the Father, the Virgin Mary, St John and Angels*

was complete. All his spare time was devoted to the production of a small number of elaborately worked poems publ. in *Poésies* (1887) and *Vers et Prose* (1893), or to the composition of equally elaborate prose fragments coll. in *Divagations* (1897). He had a mystic conviction that the world existed to be translated into perfect literary expression, and even went so far as to envisage the writing of a book, *le Livre*, which would be the centre of a religious, literary cult. He exerted a wide influence, not only through his writings but also through the Tuesday evening meetings at his flat in the Rue de Rome. He was, even more than Baudelaire, a 'poets' poet', whose dictum 'to purify the language of the tribe' and use of allusion and symbols were an inspiration to such widely divergent younger men as Claudel and Valéry. His eclogue, *L'Après-midi d'un faune* (1876; trs. 1956) prompted Debussy's *Prélude*. A few of M.'s works have a unique force and beauty. Others are tortured and impenetrable, especially his last poem, *Un coup de dés* (1914; trs. 1956) in which his mysticism seems to lead him over the borders of literary sanity.

Malle Louis (1932–). French film director. M. directed 2 shorts and co-directed Jacques-Yves Cousteau's *Le Monde du silence* before making his 1st feature, *Ascenseur pour l'échafaud* (1957), an intermittently brilliant but sentimental piece on doomed love. The sentimentality took over in *Les Amants* (1958). In *Zazie dans le métro* (1960) he tried to replace Queneau's literary style with camera tricks. After *Vie Privée* (1961), which was memorable for its colour and its use of the Bardot myth, he finally succeeded in harnessing his great technical expertise in *Le Feu Follet* (1964).

Malleson Miles (1888–). English character actor, dramatist and the trs. into English of many of the plays of Molière, notably *The Miser*, *Sganarelle* and *The Imaginary Invalid*. He has starred in many parts of his own trs.

Mallet David, originally called D. Malloch (1705?–65). Scottish poet, author with James Thomson of the masque *Alfred*, containing the song 'Rule Britannia'–which was, however, probably by Thomson.

Malley Ern. The name 2 Australian poets, James Macauley and Harold Stewart, gave to the supposed author of poems that hoaxed practitioners of esoteric verse in Adelaide in

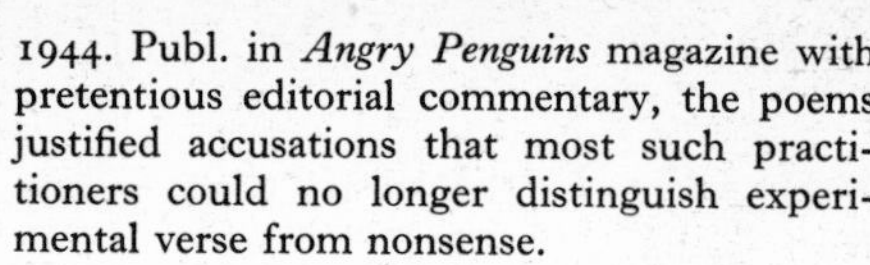

1944. Publ. in *Angry Penguins* magazine with pretentious editorial commentary, the poems justified accusations that most such practitioners could no longer distinguish experimental verse from nonsense.

Malone Edmond (1741–1812). Irish scholar and critic who attempted to date Shakespeare's plays. M. helped Boswell to revise his *Life of Johnson*.

Malone Dies (1951). Novel by Samuel *Beckett.

Malory Sir Thomas (d. 1471). English writer. M.'s turbulent career (during the period of the Wars of the Roses) included several terms in prison, where he may have written *Le Morte Darthur* (1469/70), the 1st important imaginative work in English prose. The central stories in it are of the dissolution of the Round Table and the quest for the Holy Grail; M. seems to have selected and blended elements from various forms of the Arthurian legend. It was printed by Caxton in 1485.

Malouel Jean (d. 1419?). Flemish artist and court painter (from 1397) to Philip the Bold and John the Fearless, dukes of Burgundy. He was commissioned to paint 5 altarpieces for the Chartreuse of Champmol in 1398 and was one of the earliest panel painters of N. Europe.

Malraux André (1901–). French novelist, art critic, film director and Minister of Culture. He began his career as an archaeologist in the Far East, then took part in Communist activities in China. Later he fought on the Republican side in the Spanish Civil War. Since 1940 he has been a Gaullist. His best-known novel is *La Condition humaine* (1933; *Storm in Shanghai . . .* , 1934, better known as *The Human Condition* or *Man's Fate*), about the tragedy of political activity in Shanghai. *L'Espoir* (1937; *Days of Hope*, 1938) deals with the Spanish Civil War and was the basis of M.'s only film, the semi-documentary *L'Espoir* (1939), which he directed in Barcelona during the last months of the Spanish Republic; in its treatment of a popular movement it has antecedents in the epics of the Soviet cinema. After the publ. of his unfinished novel, *Les Noyers de L'Altenburg* (1943; *The Walnut Trees of Altenburg*, 1952), M. devoted himself to a vast panorama of world art, *Essais de la psychologie de l'art*.

André Malraux

Mandolin by Antonio Vinaccia (2nd half of the 18th c.)

Manessier. *Crown of Thorns*

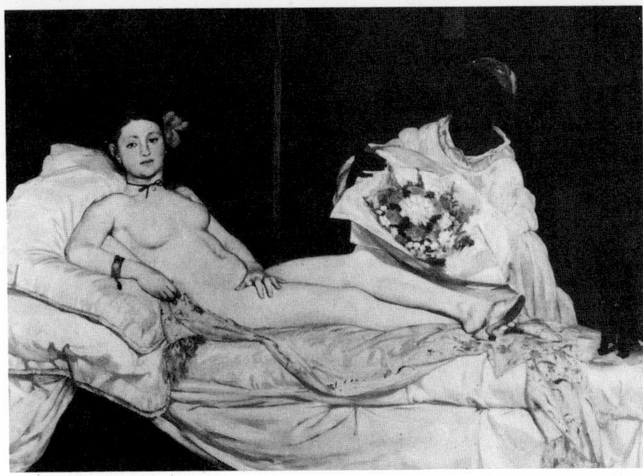

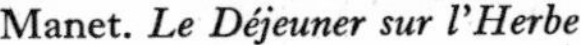

Manet. *Le Déjeuner sur l'Herbe*

Manet. *Olympia*

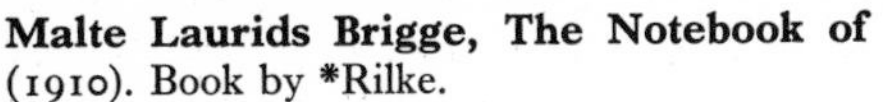

Malte Laurids Brigge, The Notebook of (1910). Book by *Rilke.

Maltese Falcon, The (1930). Detective novel by Dashiell *Hammett; also made into a film (1941) directed by J. *Huston.

Malthus Thomas Robert (1766–1834). English pioneer in the scientific study of population. His famous *Essay on the Principles of Population* (1798) argued that population would always tend to outrun resources, and that improvement in the conditions of the mass of the people would be destroyed by the increased birth-rate it encouraged.

Malvern Festival. English summer festival founded by Sir B. V. *Jackson in 1929, and dedicated to the presentation of English plays, especially those of G. B. Shaw; the inaugural season was devoted to his work. Abandoned because of the war, it was revived in 1949.

Mälzel Johann Nepomuk (1772–1838). German inventor, perfector of the metronome. His many other devices included the panharmonicon, a mechanical orchestra for which Beethoven wrote his 'Battle Symphony', and a metrical 'chronometer' which inspired Beethoven's canon 'ta, ta, ta . . . lieber, lieber Mälzel', transformed into the theme of the 2nd movement of his 8th symphony. M. died on tour in the U.S.

Mameli Goffredo (1827–49). Italian poet and patriot, author of the patriotic song 'Fratelli d'Italia' which later became the Italian national anthem.

Mamontov S. I. Muscovite merchant and railway tycoon who during the 1870s and 1880s gathered round himself on his estate at *Abramtsevo the most prominent painters of the Wanderers group. In 1883 he opened his 'Private Opera' in Moscow where he introduced the music of Rimsky-Korsakov, Borodin and Mussorgsky to the Russian public and where Chaliapin made his début. These productions were also revolutionary in their use of painters as stage designers, a tradition continued directly by Diaghilev. *Stanislavsky was a cousin of M.

Mamoulian Rouben (1898–). Russian-born U.S. film director. M. studied law in Paris and Moscow as well as studying theatre under *Stanislavsky. He became one of the most important directors on Broadway, where his work has included the 1st productions of *Porgy and Bess* and *Oklahoma!*. His 1st film, *Applause* (1929), was made at a time when Hollywood was coping with the arrival of sound by wholesale importation from the stage. M. gained a reputation as an innovator for helping to restore the mobility of the camera with *Applause* and *City Streets* (1932). His version of *Dr Jekyll and Mr Hyde* (1932) is remembered for the technical achievement of its transformation scenes. It was hardly surprising that M. was chosen to direct the 1st feature film in full Technicolor, *Becky Sharp* (1935). M. has made only 2 films since the war, both musicals, *Summer Holiday* (1948) and *Silk Stockings* (1957), although he has left a number of films including *Porgy and Bess* (finished by Preminger) and *Cleopatra*.

Man and Superman (1903). Play by G. B. *Shaw.

Manasses, The Prayer of. One of the books of the *Apocrypha.

Manchurian Candidate, The (1962). Film directed by J. *Frankenheimer.

Mandarins, Les (1954). Novel by Simone de *Beauvoir.

Mandelstam Osip Emilievich (1892–1942?). Soviet writer. M.'s essentially private, often difficult verse made no attempts to meet the requirements of socialist realism. He was sent to a labour camp in the 1930s.

Mander Karel van (1548–1606). Dutch painter, poet and art historian, in Rome from 1574 to 1577. His early work is a mixture of Flemish and Italian mannerist styles, but he later tended to greater realism. He founded the Academy of Painting at Haarlem. His history of art, *Het Schilderboeck* (1604), was modelled on Vasari's work, and also contained an introduction on the techniques of painting.

Mandeville Bernard de (1670–1730). Dutch-born writer of poems and essays in English, author of a verse satire, *The Grumbling Hive, or Knaves turned Honest* (1705), later called *The Fable of the Bees*. . . .

Mandeville Sir John. Ostensible author of a 14th-c. book of travels; the author may have been a certain Jean d'Outremeuse. The book contains accounts of the East–often fabulous –compiled from previous writers; it is written in French and was trs. in the 15th c. It was tremendously popular, and for several cs influenced the European conception of the East.

mandolin. Stringed musical instrument similar to the lute but smaller and with a more convex back. It has 4 or 5 courses of strings, the lowest being the G below middle C, and is played with a plectrum.

Mandragola, La. (1520). Play by *Machiavelli.

Manessier Alfred (1911–). Painter and decorative artist of the French school; in the 1930s he studied in Paris, where he was influenced by cubism and expressionism. His works include a tapestry for the Dominican convent at Saulchoir. He has also designed stained glass; he won a prize at the Venice Biennale in 1962.

Manet Édouard (1832–83). French painter born in Paris. He studied at the École des Beaux-Arts (1850–6) under Couture. His *Spanish Guitar Player* (1860; Met. Mus.) was awarded an honourable mention at the 1861 Salon, his only real public success. He continued to cherish official recognition, believing the Salon to be the 'real field of battle' and was reluctant to link his name with younger revolutionaries. In the 1860s, however, he was himself the main object of controversy and ridicule. The barrage of hostility which greeted *Le Déjeuner sur l'Herbe* (1861–3; Louvre) at the famous Salon des Refusés of 1863 was followed in 1865 by the scandalized outcry against *Olympia* (1863–5; Louvre). From the start M. had followed the advice of Baudelaire and Courbet to paint modern life. The main public objection was that reality was not adequately disguised: the unabashed nakedness of the female figures was offensive to a public that could approve open eroticism in the right classical garb. In fact M. was little concerned with subject-matter: he used highly respectable traditional compositions taken from Giorgione, Raphael and Titian on which to base his scenes of modern life: his primary interest was in the organization of the picture surface.

Manet. *Le Fifre.* Also *Fantin-Latour, *Gonzales

Manet. *Le Bar aux Folies-Bergères*

Mankiewicz. Ann Baxter and Marilyn Monroe (bottom of the stairs) in *All About Eve*

Anthony Mann. Arthur Kennedy and Julia Adams in *Bend of the River*

Olympia is flooded with a strong frontal light producing simple tonal contrasts and flattening form and space.

The chief formative influence on M.'s style was that of Spanish art; already fervently Hispanophile, he visited Spain in 1865 and declared Velazquez 'the painter of painters'. The figure of M.'s *Le Fifre* (1866; Louvre) is isolated against a nondescript grey ground, and his early ideas crystallized in the maturity of *Le Balcon* (1868; Louvre) and *Le Déjeuner à l'Atelier* (1868; Munich), with a fluid directness of execution and a cool grey/green palette that owe much to Velazquez. He admired the same painterly facility in Frans Hals while visiting Holland in 1872.

During the 1870s at Argenteuil he came under the influence of the impressionists. Although often linked with them by his contemporaries (he was congratulated for 2 Monet seascapes in 1865, much to his dismay), he is really important with Courbet as their predecessor: in the steadfast integrity of his stand against official disapproval, in his lack of concern for subject-matter in painting and in the establishment of the artist's complete freedom in handling colours and tone. He never exhibited with the impressionists and during the 1870s continued to paint highly composed studio pictures (*In the Conservatory*; 1879, Berlin). His last important work, *Le Bar aux Folies-Bergères* (1882; Courtauld, London), returned to his ideas of the 1860s.

He was appointed Chevalier de la Légion d'Honneur in 1882, but he died bitter and cynical about this late recognition. A large memorial exhibition was held at the École des Beaux-Arts, bastion of officialdom, in 1884.

Manfred. Verse drama by *Byron; it inspired an overture by *Schumann and a symphony by *Tchaikovsky.

Manfredi Bartolommeo (*c.* 1580–*c.* 1620). Italian painter, born near Mantua, who worked in Rome (1610–19). His paintings were influenced by, and are sometimes mistaken for, those of Caravaggio. M. influenced the Utrecht school. He later adopted mannerism and painted religious subjects in a genre idiom.

Mangan James Clarence (1803–49). Irish poet, author of many trs and pretended trs from Irish, German and oriental languages. His poems include *The Nameless One.*

Manhattan Transfer (1925). Novel by John *Dos Passos.

Man in the White Suit, The (1951). Film directed by A. *Mackendrick.

Mankiewicz Joseph L. (1909–). U.S. film writer, producer and director. Until 1935 he wrote scripts, including *Million Dollar Legs* (1932) for W. C. Fields. In 1936 at M.G.M. he graduated from writer to producer and was responsible for *Fury*, *The Philadelphia Story*, etc. He started directing in 1946 with *Dragonwyck*, written by him for production by Lubitsch, who fell ill and assigned direction to him. After 2 charming period comedies from scripts by P. Dunne, he gained increasing freedom from the success of 2 comedies, *Letter to Three Wives* (1949) and *All About Eve* (1950), as well as a thriller, *Five Fingers* (1952). For M. directing is an extension of writing: the virtues of his films start with the words, which he has usually written (though unlike Welles's *Othello*, his *Julius Caesar* (1953) is faithful to Shakespeare). Where spectacle is required, M. usually fails, as with *Guys and Dolls* (1955) and *Cleopatra* (1963), where his filming cannot match the richness of the pageantry presented. He is at his best in the Dunne movies, particularly *The Ghost and Mrs Muir* (1947); a film about racialism, *No Way Out* (1950); and a melodrama, *The Barefoot Contessa* (1954).

Mann Anthony (1907–). U.S. film director. After a period in the theatre he started film directing in 1942 with a series of B features, some of which like *T-Men* (1947) and particularly *Reign of Terror* (1949), a low-budget film about the French Revolution, gave scope for his gritty talents. His great opportunity came when he took over direction of *Winchester '73* (1950) from Fritz Lang. Its success started him on his great series of westerns, including *Bend of the River* (1952), *The Naked Spur* (1953), *The Far Country* (1955), *The Man from Laramie* (1955), *The Last Frontier* (1956) and *Man of the West* (1958). Unlike Ford's, M.'s westerns are not nostalgic. More than any other major director of westerns, he deals in purely moral terms of duty, of good and evil; the physical harshness of the life is a catalyst for men's weakness or evil. *Man of the West* is one of the bleakest of westerns: the hero's only honourable course involves shooting the relations who brought him up. Outside the westerns his best films are *Men in War* (1957) and *God's Little Acre* (1958). His 2 *Bronston spectaculars *El Cid* (1961) and *The Fall of the Roman Empire* (1964) are less satisfactory.

Mann Daniel (1912–). U.S. film director. M. was a stage director who worked with Kazan. His 1st film was the screen version of Inge's play *Come Back Little Sheba* (1952). Thereafter he was typed as a director of emotional dramas and/or stage adaptations, e.g. *The Rose Tattoo* (1955). After a war picture, *The Mountain Road* (1959), and a melodrama, *Butterfield 8* (1960), he has turned to comedies.

Mann Delbert (1920–). U.S. film director. M. was a successful television director who gained a considerable reputation from his 1st film, *Marty* (1955). This was written by Paddy Chayefsky, who also scripted *The Bachelor Party* (1957) and *Middle of the Night* (1959). After some adaptations (from O'Neill, Rattigan and Inge), he moved into the safer field of Doris Day comedies.

Mann Heinrich (1871–1950). German writer, brother of T. M., whose novel *Professor Unrat* (1905; *The Blue Angel*, 1931) describing a professor's self-destructive infatuation for a night-club singer, has been frequently filmed; like other of his novels it bitterly satirized pre-1914 German society. M. also wrote the short novel *Die Kleine Stadt* (1909; *The Little Town*, 1930).

Mann Thomas (1875–1955). German novelist. Child of a patrician Lübeck family, he lived in Munich from 1893 as ed. and writer, emigrating to Switzerland (1933) and the U.S. (1939). He returned to Zürich at the end of his life.
In M. many intellectual currents met: German music (Wagner), philosophy (the pessimism of Schopenhauer and Nietzsche) and literature (Goethe, Fontane), and the English and Russian novelists. What these and others meant to him is expressed in his essays. His earliest works, especially the novel *Buddenbrooks* (1901; 1924, subtitle: *The Decay of a Family*), and the story *Tonio Kröger* (1902; 1913–15) follow Fontane in combining the German regional novel and the European social novel, and in their ironic narration, while their evocative use of the *Leitmotiv* is modelled on Wagner. In the localized yet cosmopolitan background, largely autobiographical, of a Hanseatic city, M. adumbrates his perennial theme of the clash of burgher and artist, healthy philistine and over-sensitive aesthete (sensitivity is associated with decadence as well as with percipience). In his later works he often goes farther afield for his settings: to the south, Venice in *Der Tod in Venedig* (1913; *Death in Venice*, 1925), Davos in *Der Zauberberg* (1924; *The Magic Mountain*, 1927), and to figures from the past, e.g. *Joseph und seine Brüder* (1933–43; *Joseph and his Brothers*, 1934–45); the medieval Gregorius in *Der Erwählte* (1951; *The Holy Sinner*, 1952); Goethe in *Lotte in Weimar* (1939; 1940). Other novels have modern settings, but echo traditional figures, e.g. in *Doktor Faustus* (1947; 1949), and the picaresque hero in . . . *Felix Krull* (1954; 1955). All these works deal in some way with the gifted individual's position in workaday life; discuss, directly or otherwise, a range of contemporary psycho-social problems; and use irony and even parody, shifts in linguistic level and in narrative angle, in short a command of style unequalled in his age, to attain their effects. M. is one of the few novelists to combine tradition with modernity, particularity with universality, breadth with profundity, and so to appeal alike to popular and highbrow taste.

mannerism. Any affectation of style, but used more specifically of Italian painting, sculpture and architecture of the period between the high Renaissance and the baroque period. Architecturally it differs from Renaissance in its deliberate contradiction of classical rules (e.g. regarding the use of orders), aiming at discord instead of harmony and strain instead of repose; and from baroque in not fusing all its elements into unified, dynamic patterns, but producing effects of ambiguity and discomfort rather than energy and confidence. It is first fully realized in Michelangelo's Vestibule of the Laurentian Library (1523) and characterizes most of the works of Giulio Romano, Ammanati, Ligorio, Buontalenti, and Vignola. Similar qualities appear in French and English architecture slightly later. M. painting is also characterized by a search for novelty and excitement leading to capriciously elongated figures on complicated *contrapposto, asymmetrical composition with huge discrepancies in scale, and harsh colour. Michelangelo (in his late work), Tintoretto and El Greco are the great creative exponents of m., but the style is best exemplified in the paintings of such neurotic artists as Parmigianino,

Delbert Mann. Betsy Blair and Ernest Borgnine in *Marty*

Thomas Mann

Mannerism. El Greco, *Laocoön*

Mannerism. Vestibule of the Laurentian Library

Mannerism. Rosso Fiorentino, *Descent from the Cross*

François Mansart. Château de Maisons

Jules-Hardouin Mansart. The Invalides

Rosso and Pontormo; other mannerist painters and sculptors include Daniele da Volterra, Niccolò dell'Abbate, Bronzino, Cellini and Giovanni da Bologna.

Mannheim gold. An alloy developed by Edward Pinchbeck in the early 18th c. consisting of an alloy of copper, zinc and tin.

Mannheim school. The name of the group of composers and virtuoso instrumentalists patronized by the Elector Palatine, Karl Theodor, resident at Mannheim from 1743 to 1778. The orchestra, called by Burney 'an army of generals', was the finest in Europe; the leading members of the school were J. Stamitz and his sons Karl and Anton, F. R. Richter, E. Eichner, C. Cannabich and J. Cramer. The school innovated in performance and composition techniques, introducing many new instrumental textures, such as gradual crescendi, which led to the classical symphonic style.

Man of Aran (1934). Film directed by R. *Flaherty.

Manon Lescaut, Histoire du chevalier des Grieux et de (1731). Novel by the Abbé *Prévost; also the subject of operas by Massenet, Auber and Puccini.

Manrique Gómez (*c.* 1415–90?). Spanish poet and playwright. He wrote unoriginal lyrics and didactic poems, but also a simple but moving nativity play and *Lamentations for Holy Week.*

Manrique Jorge (1440?–79). Spanish poet and nephew of Gómez M. His poems and love-lyrics are mediocre but his magnificent elegy on the death of his father, *Coplas por la muerte de su padre*, has become one of the great classics of Spanish poetry.

mansard roof Architectural term for a roof with 2 slopes on each face, the higher of low pitch, the lower very steep.

Mansart François (1598–1666). French architect, trained under a colleague of S. de Brosse. M. stands at the beginning of French neo-classicism, though he remained rooted in French tradition and never visited Italy. He built the churches of Feuillants (1623), W. front only, based on de Brosse's St Gervais, but less orthodox; St Marie de la Visitation, Paris (1632); and the Val-de-Grâce, Paris (1645), completed by Lemercier. All were very influential. His châteaux include Berny (1624), of which only 1 wing survives; Balleroy (1626); the Orléans wing at Blois (1635) with a charming open staircase; and Maisons (1642), a break with tradition in not being built round a courtyard. M. also built town hôtels and submitted a project for finishing the Louvre. His designs are complex and subtle; he was well known for fastidious attention to detail.

Mansart Jules-Hardouin (1646–1708). French architect, a great-nephew of François M. His work at Versailles, begun in 1678 and lasting most of his life, made him the most important single influence on French neo-classical architecture, which was itself widely imitated all over Europe. M.'s part at Versailles, including the chapel and the Galérie des Glaces, puts the emphasis on horizontality, symmetry and pure classical detail. His other notable work is the chapel of the Invalides, Paris (now Napoleon's mausoleum) with a dome recalling the Sorbonne.

Man's Fate (1933). Novel by André *Malraux.

Mansfield Katherine. Pseud. of Kathleen Mansfield Beauchamp (1888–1923). New Zealand short-story writer who left for Europe to find not merely fame but a freer intellectual atmosphere. Her work, however, as she herself acknowledged, owed much to her homeland, and at its best is impressive by any standards in its sensitivity and evocation of mood. Her stories are some of the most accomplished in English; the 1st coll. was dedicated to her husband J. Middleton Murry, the critic. There followed *The Garden Party* (1922) and other colls.

Mansfield Park (1814). Novel by Jane *Austen.

Mantegna Andrea (*c.* 1431–1506). Northern Italian painter and engraver. M. appears to have been both the apprentice and the adopted son of the antiquarian and painter F. Squarcione, for 6 years in Padua, before freeing himself in a lawsuit. Squarcione's studies of antiquity, the humanistic influences of Padua Univ. and the masterpieces resulting from Donatello's 10-year stay in the city were each important in the formation of M.'s art. He

Mantegna. *The Martyrdom of St James*

painted *The Assumption*, *4 Scenes from the Life of St James* and *The Martyrdom of St Christopher* in the Ovetari chapel, Eremitani church, Padua (1448–59). Unfortunately all but the last of these important frescoes were destroyed during World War II. In them, and in such paintings as the *St Zeno Altarpiece* (St Zeno, Verona) and *St Sebastian* (K. Mus., Vienna), M.'s debt to Donatello is obvious: not only are the monumental qualities of sculpture reproduced but even the surface often appears to be made of metal or stone. Classical motifs are actually distracting in the *St Sebastian*, and M. attempts to reproduce the effect of a Roman bas-relief in paint on canvas in such monochrome works as *Judith with the Head of Holofernes* (N.G., Dublin). In predella panels, e.g. the superb *Crucifixion* (Louvre), the figures are less sculptural, though the landscape is ordered with the same rigour. M. married the daughter of Jacopo Bellini in 1453, and the strengthening of his connection with the Venetians is illustrated by *The Agony in the Garden* (N.G., London), a painting based on a drawing by Bellini. In 1460 M. became court painter to the Gonzaga family, and in their palace at Mantua painted frescoes of incidents in the lives of his patrons. Most important is the ceiling of the Camera degli Sposi. An illusion of an opened roof above the spectator's head is created, with a blue sky and a circle of figures gazing down into the room. This is the first use of such effects and it was to lead directly to Correggio and the baroque masters' exploitation of illusionistic perspective.

At the Gonzaga court M. formed a coll. of classical works of art which was the envy of the Pope. He also executed the fine engravings on classical subjects, such as *Battle of the Sea Gods* and *Death of Orpheus*, which was to influence Dürer and other graphic artists. For the Gonzagas he painted *The Triumphs of Caesar* (Royal Coll., Hampton Court). One of his last works was the magnificent *Dead Christ* (Brera, Milan).

manual (from Latin *manus*, 'hand'). In music the term is used to distinguish the organ keyboard for the hands from the pedal-board, i.e. the keyboard for the feet.

Manuel Niklaus (1484–1530). Swiss painter and poet and statesman; formerly sometimes wrongly called N. M. Deutsch on the basis of his monogram N.M.D.: the 'D' is now thought to stand for the surname 'Degen'. As a member of the Inner Council of Berne, M. had an important influence on the debates on religious reform, having already made a name with plays attacking ecclesiastical abuses. As a painter M. was obviously affected by the work of Dürer and Baldung Grien; but his richly coloured pictures of Biblical and mythological subjects frequently have dramatic effects of lighting and mood of landscape peculiar to him. His paintings include: *The Execution of John the Baptist* (Berne) and the *Judgement of Paris* (Basle).

Manutius Aldus (1450–1515). Italian scholar/printer working in Venice from *c.* 1495, the greatest printer of the 16th c. M. employed the type-designer *Griffo and initiated the publ. of a series of classical authors in a handy, inexpensive format which was extremely popular and extremely beautiful, and for which Griffo's italics were specially designed. His 1st work was the *Grammatica Graeca* of Constantine Lascaris (1493), followed by his celebrated work, P. Bembo's *De Aetna* (1495) (which employed Griffo's earliest, and probably one of his finest romans), an ed. of Aristotle (1495–8), the famous **Hypnerotomachia Poliphili* (1499), and many classical, religious and educational works.

Man who was Thursday, The (1908). Novel by G. K. Chesterton.

Man Without Qualities, The (1930–43). Novel by Robert *Musil.

Manzoni Alessandro (1785–1873). Italian novelist and playwright, a grandson of the political writer Beccaria. In early youth M. was a rationalist and anti-clerical, but he soon returned to Catholicism and all his work has religious and moral purpose.

M.'s famous novel *I promessi sposi* (1827, revised 1840; *The Betrothed Lovers*, 1828) is set in 17th-c. Milan. Despite its huge canvas, every character comes to life and the clear yet rich style is still accepted as a model of Italian prose. A quiet good humour pervades the whole work. M. also wrote 2 historical tragedies in which he broke with the neo-classical patterns and rejected mythological themes: *Il conte di Carmagnola* (1820), on a 15th-c. *condottiere*, and *Adelchi* (1821), dealing with Lombard Italy. Other works include *Il Cinque Maggio* (1821), an ode on Napoleon's death, and 5 hymns.

Manuel. *Judgement of Paris*

cum religioso tripudio plaudendo & iubilando, Quale erano le Nym
phe Amadryade, & agli redolenti fiori le Hymenide, riuirente, salienc
iocunde dinanti & da qualũq; lato del floreo Vertunno stricto nella fr
te de purpurante & meline rose, cum el gremio pieno de odoriferi & sp
ctatissimi fiori, amanti la stagione del lanoso Ariete, Sedendo ouante s
pra una uetertima Veha, da quatro cornigeri Fauni tirata, Inuinculati
strophie de nouelle fronde, Cum la sua amata & bellissima moglie P
mona coronata de fructi cum ornato defluo degli biõdissimi capigli,
re a ello sedéte, & a gli pedi dellaquale una coctilia Clepsydria iaceua,
le mane tenente una stipata copia de fiori & maturati fructi cum imix
fogliatura. Præcedéte la Veha agli trahenti Fauni propinq; due form
Nymphe añsignane, Vna cũ uno hastile Trophæo gerula, de Ligoni
denti. sarculi. & falcionetti, cũ una ꝑpendéte tabella abaca cũ tale titu

INTEGERRIMAM CORPOR. VALITVDINEM, E
STABILE ROBVR, CASTASQVE MEMSAR. DE
TIAS, ET BEATAM ANIMI SECVRITA
TEM CVLTORIB. M. OFFERO.

m iiii

Manutius. *Hypnerotomachia Poliphili*

Mantegna. *Battle of the Sea Gods*. Also *foreshortening, **sotto in sù*

Mantegna. *The Agony in the Garden*

Marc. *Blue Horses* (*c.* 1911)

Marc. *Fighting Forms*

Manzù. *The Cardinal* (1948)

Maquettes by Henry Moore for his *Madonna and Child* (1942)

Marcel Marceau

Manzù Giacomo (1908–). Leading Italian sculptor. Much of his work is religious, e.g. the doors for St Peter's, Rome and for Salzburg cathedral, and the work of Donatello is recalled by M.'s use of low relief and his handling of religious imagery. M. obviously owes a debt also to Rodin, and some of his free-standing sculptures have affinities with Marini.

Map or Mapes, Walter (d. *c.* 1208). English writer, author of the witty miscellany *De nugis curialium*; many works, including Arthurian romances, have been attributed to him, but none with certainty.

maquette. In sculpture a small preliminary model in wax or clay.

maraca. A rhythm instrument; in effect a rattle. It consists of a dried gourd partly filled with dried beans, or it may have a close-fitting net of beads round the outside. A pair of m.s is frequent in Latin American dance bands.

Maragall Juan (1860–1911). Catalan poet, trs. and member of the Catalan separatist movement. His work is full of philosophical themes, mainly drawn from Goethe and Novalis, and a great feeling for nature.

Marais Jean (1913–). French actor, of powerful, brooding presence, e.g. *La Belle et la Bête*, *Orphée*, and other Cocteau films.

Marais Marin (1656–1728). French bass viol virtuoso and composer in the tradition of Lully. He produced pieces for 1 and 2 viols, trios for flute, violin and viol, and pieces for violin, viol and harpsichord.

Maratta or **Maratti** Carlo (1625–1713). Italian baroque decorative artist and portrait painter who studied in Rome. His work was influenced by that of Correggio and Guido Reni. Examples of his fresco work are in S. Giovanni in Fonte and S. Giuseppe dei Falegnani, Rome.

marbled wares. Pottery made to resemble marble or agate; it was especially popular during the 18th c. and was made by (1) mixing clays of different colours, e.g. Staffordshire 'solid agate' ware; (2) using metallic oxides on the fluid lead-glaze so that the colours run into each other and produce a mottled appearance; and (3) the use of coloured clay 'slips' worked over with comb and sponge (e.g. Staffordshire and other slipware from the late 17th c.).

Marble Faun, The (1860). Novel by *Hawthorne.

Marc Franz (1880–1916). German expressionist painter born in Munich; he studied philosophy and theology at the University and then painting at the Academy. He was one of the founders of the *Blaue Reiter group in Munich in 1911. He was killed at Verdun.
Working in close association with Kandinsky, M. explored the expressive values of colour. This preoccupation with colour was partly inspired by the orphist paintings of Delaunay, whom he visited in Paris with Macke in 1912, and probably also by Goethe's *Farbenlehre*. Although he remained a painter of animals, paintings like *Tiger* (1912; Köhler Coll., Berlin) are primarily expressive through their simple planes of colour; and in *Fighting Forms* (1914; Munich) he was nearing a point of abstract expressionism.

Marcantonio Raimondi (1480–1534). Italian engraver; his most important works are engravings reproducing paintings by Raphael and his school, an art which he was the first to practise.

marcasite. A faceted crystal of iron pyrites, popular in early 19th-c. jewellery. Often extended to include modern cut-metal imitations.

Marceau Marcel (1923–). French actor, the outstanding contemporary European mime. His main creation is the character of BIP, a modern *Pierrot at odds with present-day life, who figures in many of M.'s pantomimes. In 1947 he founded a co. to reawaken interest in the art of mime; its subject-matter has included *The Overcoat* by Gogol, which was also one of the films–mostly short features–in which the co. has appeared. They have toured extensively and made numerous television appearances.

Marcel Gabriel (1889–). French philosopher and playwright, a leading Christian existentialist. M. is said to have been the 1st French writer to use the term 'existentialism'.

Marcello Benedetto (1686–1739). Italian composer and violinist, pupil of A. Lotti and F.

Gasparini; he worked in Venice. His masterpiece was *Estro poetico-armonico*, settings for 1, 2, 3 and 4 voices of the first 50 Psalms, trs. into Italian and paraphrased by his friend G. A. Giustiniani. His brother ALESSANDRO M. (1684–1750) also composed.

march. A drum-beat pattern or piece of music used in army manœuvres; or simply a musical form. In the 17th c. national march rhythms were a subject of patriotism and many European regiments still have traditional or specially composed marches.

March Auzias (*c.* 1395–1460?). One of the greatest Catalan poets. Most of his poems are concerned with his tortured love for a lady named Teresa; when his works were trs. into Castilian, his use of Italian and Provençal metres had great influence on such 16th-c. Spanish poets as Garcilaso de la Vega.

March Fredric (1897–). American film actor whose fine voice and handsome sulkiness, not unlike *Brando's, shot him into romantic leads. Dramatically established by R. Mamoulian's *Dr Jekyll and Mr Hyde* (1932), he also played Count Vronsky in *Anna Karenina* (1935), and in *A Star is Born* (1937), *The Best Years of Our Lives* (1946) and J. Frankenheimer's *Seven Days in May* (1963).

Marchand Colette (1925–). French dancer trained at the Paris Opéra; as principal dancer with the Ballets de Paris of Roland *Petit (1948) she achieved great personal success, particularly in her vaudeville dance in *Oeuf à la Coque* (1949), which led to a career in musical comedy and films.

Marchand Louis (1669–1732). French organ virtuoso, composer and roué. Touring Germany during temporary banishment from the French court he became involved in an organ-playing contest with Bach; M.'s failure to attend the fixture has been variously interpreted.

Märchen. A German word, loosely used by folk-lorists, meaning 'fairy-tale': it should more precisely be applied to fictional stories, as distinct from sagas which give accounts believed by the teller to be of real events.

Marchi Emilio de (1851–1901). Italian novelist and poet. He was a prolific and varied writer who was at his best in describing the *petit-bourgeois* Milanese society of his time; his novels also show his talent for psychological analysis.

March of Time (1935–50). Series of topical documentary films which were financed by *Time* magazine.

Marcks Gerhard (1889–). German sculptor; his work has been almost exclusively on the theme of the nude figure with little departure from natural appearances. The pathetic element in his work links him with the tradition of Barlach and Lehmbruck. His work was suppressed by the Nazis in 1937. He has spent much of his life teaching: in Berlin (1918–20); at the Bauhaus (1920–5), where he ran the pottery studio; at Halle (1925–33) and Hamburg (1946–50). Since 1950 he has lived in Cologne.

Marcoussis Louis (Markous) (1883–1941). Polish painter who came to Paris in 1903 and was associated with the cubists from 1907. He made no original contribution to cubism, but of the group which exhibited together in 1911 and 1912, he seems to have most fully understood Picasso and Braque, e.g. *Nature Morte au Damier* (1912; M.M.A., Paris).

Marcus Aurelius Antoninus (121–80). Roman emperor and philosopher, whose *Meditations* (written in Greek) propound a stoicism which urges the need for men to find their place, by using reason, in the divinely inspired rational order of the universe.

Marées Hans von (1837–87). German painter who studied in Berlin but later worked in Munich and, after 1865, in Rome. He specialized in frescoes and large landscapes, and his work influenced that of A. Böcklin and M. Beckmann.

Marenzio Luca (1553–99). Italian composer. He worked for various aristocratic houses in Rome and was for a time in Florence (1588–9) where Caccini and Peri worked under him. M. was one of the great masters of the madrigal; he used all means to present the text vividly–strongly chromatic harmonies, elegant contrapuntal writing and free formal invention. His work was especially influential on the English madrigalists (through N. *Yonge's *Musica Transalpina*).

Marcks. *Albertus Magnus*

Marcoussis. *Nature Morte au Damier*

Marcus Aurelius

Marées. *Self-portrait*

Marguerite d'Angoulême

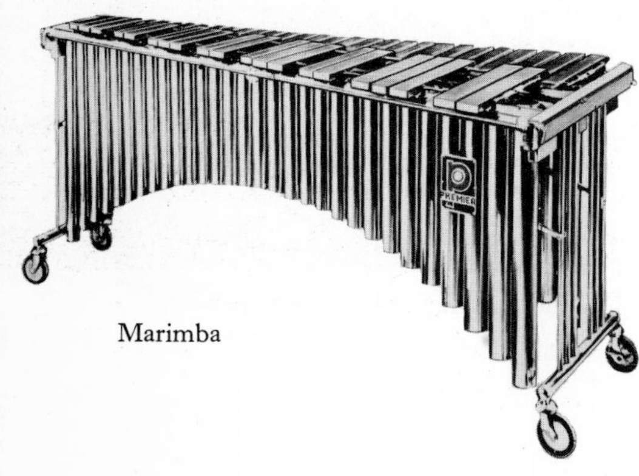
Marimba

Marin. *Street Crossing, New York*

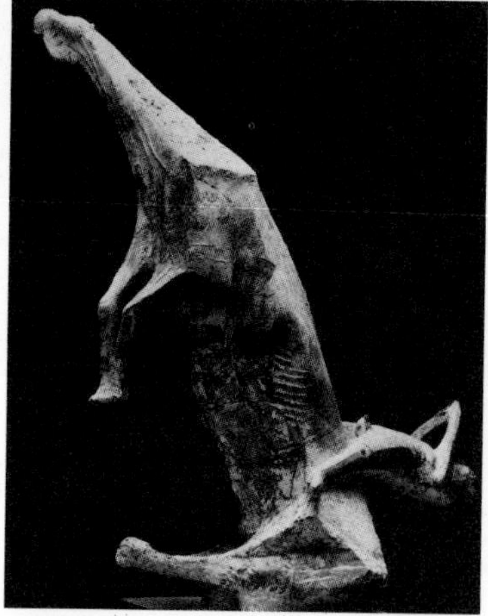
Marini. *The Miracle*

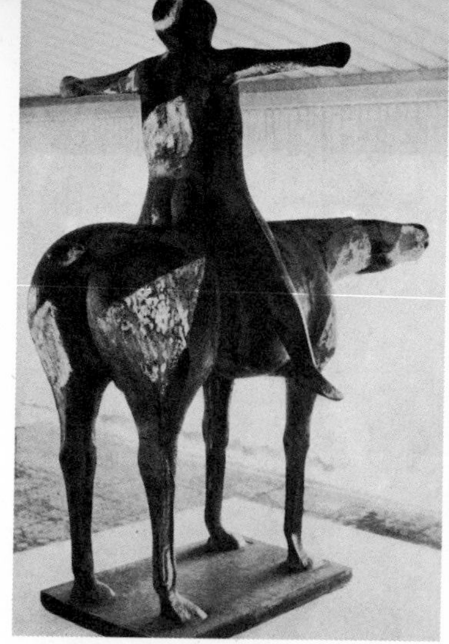
Marini. *Horse and Rider* (1949)

Margarito of Arezzo. Italian painter sometimes identified with Margaritone of Magnano. According to Vasari he lived from 1236 to 1316. He painted in a rigid, linear 'Romanesque' style, producing many paintings of St Francis.

Marguerite d'Angoulême duchesse (1492–1549). French writer, poet and patron of writers. Her unfinished *L'Heptaméron* (posth. 1558), is modelled on Boccaccio's *Decameron*: the stories are told by a group of travellers isolated by floods–but, by contrast, love is treated as an elevated and difficult passion.

Marianne, La Vie de (1731–41). Novel by *Marivaux.

Maria Stuart (1800). Poetic drama by *Schiller.

Maria Theresa symphony. Nickname of Haydn's symphony no. 48 in C (1773) written for a visit of the empress to Esterház.

Marie de France. 12th-c. French poet who spent most of her life in England; she wrote a number of *lais*, short narrative poems containing love-stories and marvellous adventures.

marimba. Percussion instrument of African origin and used sometimes in the symphony orchestra; common in Mexico. It consists of wooden resonators, each with an individual sound-box; the tone is given a characteristic 'buzzing' quality by a small skin head attached to the end of each resonator.

Marin John (1870–1953). U.S. painter and engraver. M.'s watercolours and engravings of buildings in Europe (1905–9, 1910–11) and the skyscrapers of New York were made known in America by Alfred Stieglitz. Later, scenes of Maine, e.g. *Maine Islands* (1922; Phillips Coll., Washington), and New Mexico made M. the leading U.S. watercolour painter. He worked in a free style reminiscent of Kandinsky, but with a strong and usually obvious element of construction–probably a legacy of his early training as an architect. In his last years he painted many of the same landscapes in oil.

marine trumpet: *tromba marina

Marinetti Filippo Tommaso (1876–1944). Italian poet (writing in French and Italian) and novelist, remembered as the founder of *futurism: he publ. its 1st manifesto in 1909.

Marini Marino (1901–). Widely recognized as the leading Italian sculptor since Boccioni and Rosso. He studied painting and sculpture at the Florence Academy and then sculpture in Paris (1928). His oeuvre includes paintings and prints in several media, and some of his sculpture is itself painted. Since 1940 he has been professor of sculpture at the Brera Academy, Milan.

His principal theme has been that of the horse and rider. The first, in 1936, was related to his current interest in acrobats and performers, but as the theme developed it became more subjective and assumed a deeper symbolic significance. M. has said: 'My equestrian figures are symbols of the anguish I feel when I survey contemporary events.' The evolution of this symbol can be seen by comparing such works as *Horseman* (1947; Tate), *The Miracle* (1954; K. halle, Mannheim) and *Equestrian Monument* (1959; The Hague). There is a stark simplicity in early examples, but the horse-rider relationship becomes increasingly unstable and uncontrolled. In the latest versions the helpless doomed figures lose not only their poise but also their characteristic forms.

Marino Giambattista (1569–1625). Italian poet, author of the long, lavish poem *Adone* (1623) about Venus and Adonis.

Marinus van Reymerswaele (*c.* 1493–after 1567). Flemish painter influenced by contemporary German styles and that of Quinten Massys; he painted portraits of bankers, businessmen and grasping excisemen; his work was known in Italy and Spain.

Marinuzzi Gino (1882–1945). Italian composer and conductor, finally at La Scala, Milan; his son GINO (1920–) is also a conductor and composer.

marionette: *puppet

Maritain Jacques (1882–). French Catholic apologist and neo-Thomist philosopher. His writings on aesthetics include *Art et scholastique* (1920; *The Philosophy of Art*, 1923; also called *Art and Scholasticism*) which takes medieval scholasticism as its starting-point.

Marius (1929). Play by Marcel *Pagnol, who supervised the film (1932), which was the 1st

Marinus van Reymerswaele. *Moneychanger and his wife*

Marker. *Cuba Si!*

Marivaux

of the *M.* trilogy (completed with *Fanny* and *César*).

Marius the Epicurean (1885). Novel by Walter *Pater.

Marivaux Pierre Carlet de Chamblain de (1688–1763). French dramatist and novelist. His plays, dealing with the psychological niceties and refined analysis of the passion of love, enjoyed a vogue for a time which gave rise to the term MARIVAUDAGE to describe the subtleties of his style and treatment. M. is best known as the author of the novel *La Vie de Marianne* (1731–41) which sensitively traces the career of a virtuous orphan girl; M. also publ. a 2nd novel *Le Paysan parvenu* (1735/6). Imitating Addison he publ. (1722–3) *Le Spectateur français.*

Mark, The Gospel according to St (2nd half of the 1st c.). One of the books of the *Bible, the 2nd book of the New Testament. It is the shortest of the 4 Gospels describing the life and teaching of Jesus, but is the most important source for those of St Matthew and St Luke.

Markelius Sven (1889–). Swedish architect and town planner of Stockholm. M. was a pioneer of modern architecture in Sweden, with his *international style concert hall at Hälsingborg (1932). After the war he developed in the rather provincial way of Swedish design, as in his own house at Kevinge. As town planner of Stockholm he was responsible for the policy of satellite towns at Vällingby and Farsta.

Marker Chris (1921–). French writer, photographer and film maker. Author of one novel, a book on Giraudoux and a photo-essay, *Coréennes*, M. is the cinema's one essayist. A left-wing intellectual; his films have typically been lively, idiosyncratic essays based on his travels, *Dimanche à Pekin* (1956), *Lettre de Sibérie* (1958), *Description d'un Combat* (1960), on Israel, and *Cuba Si!* (1961). A development of these was *Le Joli Mai* (1962) which used the cinéma-vérité equipment of *Cuba Si!* and a more quirky version of the *Rouch interview technique in a study of Paris during May 1962. M.'s 1st film was *Les Statues meurent aussi* (1948–52), co-directed by Resnais and long banned for its anti-colonialism. He also made an animated film, *Les Astronautes* (1959), with *Borowczyk, and a short science-fiction story, *La Jetée* (1963), told in stills.

Markevich Igor (1912–). Russian-born Italian composer and conductor. In Paris he studied under N. Boulanger and was encouraged by Diaghilev; his reputation as a composer came with a cantata with text by Cocteau (1930) and an oratorio on *Paradise Lost* (1935).

Markham Gervase (1568–1637). English writer. Most of his books are treatises on horsemanship, husbandry and country pursuits.

Markova Alicia. Stage-name of Alice Marks (1910–), English dancer who trained under Astafieva, Legat and Cecchetti and was one of the 1st members of the Diaghilev co. from Britain (1925). By the time the co. broke up (1929) she had achieved ballerina status and later joined the Vic-Wells Co. She was noted for her lightness, and her Giselle has been compared with the great Taglioni's. Her long partnership with Anton Dolin, which lasted from the early 1930s until 1952, played a tremendous part in the development of English ballet, and their co., the *Festival Ballet (1950), still performs many of the Diaghilev works with which she was closely associated. She is now director of ballet at the Metropolitan Opera House, New York.

Marlowe Christopher (1564–93). English poet. M.'s short life is wrapped in mystery. It is probable that between 1581 and 1587, while a student at Corpus Christi, Cambridge, he began to be employed upon espionage for the government. After taking his M.A. degree, he went to London where he became well known in the literary and theatrical world. He was a violent man; his name figures in police records for brawling and, more dangerously, on suspicion of blasphemy: he was about to be arrested for the latter when stabbed to death in a quarrel.
While at Cambridge M. trs. Ovid's *Amores* and wrote his 1st tragedy, *Tamburlaine the Great*, produced in 1587. A sprawling processional play in 2 parts, it was the first to use blank verse supply and vigorously for dramatic purposes. His 2nd tragedy, *The tragical history of Doctor Faustus*, followed in 1588; its construction is poor and it sags disappointingly in the middle, but its finest scenes achieve a fusion of poetry and drama which no previous English playwright had attained. *The Jew of Malta* (*c.* 1592), more black farce than tragedy, flags

Markelius. Concert hall at Hälsingborg

Markova in *Le Chant du Rossignol* (1925). Also *Dolin

Marquetry top of a Louis XV writing-table

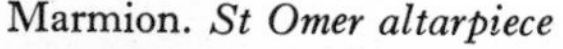

Marquet. *Matisse painting in Manguin's Studio* (1905). Also *fauvism

after a fine beginning, and only in *Edward II* (1593) did M. begin to master dramatic construction. The first 2 sestiads of the narrative poem *Hero and Leander*, all that M. lived to finish, were publ. in 1593: the sensuous theme is handled with a tact and lightness of touch which keep it from cloying, and the poem shows a playfulness and humour absent from the plays. The theme of the plays is man's aspiration to a God-like domination – Tamburlaine through conquest, Barabbas through wealth, Faust through knowledge. The theme is present in the political rise and fall of Mortimer in *Edward II*. For all, death is the final invincible adversary, but all except Faust meet it with defiance or scorn. The peculiar horror of Faust's situation is that by the nature of his rebellion he alone fully realizes the extent of his damnation. Most naturally a lyric poet, M. was only beginning, in *Edward II*, to overcome the problems of dramatic writing; in that play the dramatic impetus is maintained and lyrical monologue is kept in check, while the characterization is more profound and mature. In Edward's death scene and in the tremendous final scene of *Faustus* M. wrote poetic drama of a power and depth surpassed only by Shakespeare, who built upon the foundation of M.'s blank verse.

Marlowe Society. Cambridge Univ. amateur dramatic group, founded in 1908. Its productions have often been directed by George Rylands; distinguished alumni include Miles Malleson, Michael Redgrave and Peter Hall.

Marmion Shackerley (1602–39). English poet and playwright, author of the allegorical poem *Cupid and Psyche* (1637).

Marmion Simon (d. 1489). Franco-Flemish illuminator and panel painter who worked in Amiens, Valenciennes and Tournai, and for Philip the Good, Duke of Burgundy. His principal work was a 22-panel altarpiece for St Omer abbey.

Marmontel Jean-François (1723–99). French novelist and playwright, a disciple and friend of Voltaire. Most of M.'s work is didactic in intention; he wrote most of the articles on literature in the **Encyclopédie* (coll. as *Éléments de littérature*, 1787) and became ed. of the *Mercure de France*. His plays include *La Bergère des Alpes* (1763; *The Shepherdess of the Alps*, 1780).

Marot Clément (1496–1544). An important transitional figure in French verse, M. began as a skilled technician in the medieval modes, but as a court poet, he found tastes changing, and began to imitate the manner of the Italian Renaissance. He was one of the first to write sonnets in French, and made some trs of Petrarch. His interests were also scholarly and religious: he ed. Villon and *Le Roman de la Rose*. Though he is a charming and assured secular poet, M.'s metrical trs. of the Psalms is perhaps his most impressive work; as a Calvinist he frequently found himself in trouble with the religious authorities.

Marpurg Friedrich Wilhelm (1718–95). German music theorist of the *Enlightenment, a friend of Winckelmann and Lessing. Marpurg's major works include *Abhandlung von der Fuge*; others popularized Rameau's harmonic theories in Germany.

Marquand John P(hillips) (1893–1960). U.S. novelist. M. drew directly from his own experiences, describing the manners of exclusive Boston society. His novels include *The Late George Apley* (1937), *H. M. Pulham, Esq.* (1941) and *Point of No Return* (1949).

Marquet Albert (1875–1947). French painter who studied under Gustave Moreau. He subsequently became a fauve and a friend of Matisse, with whom he went to Morocco in 1913. M. later frequently returned there to paint.

marquetry. An inlay of ornamental woods or other decorative materials applied in a veneer to furniture or panelling, in a variety of patterns and designs. The distinction between marquetry, figurative and floral designs, and parquetry, where there are geometrical patterns only, is no longer made.
In Italy, inlaid panelling known as 'intarsia' was used in the middle ages and Renaissance in choir stalls, sacristies, private apartments (especially the study), and in furniture. The geometrical or pictorial inlay was often of extreme elaboration.

Marquina Eduardo (1879–1946). Spanish poet, playwright and novelist. He began writing poetry under the influence of Rubén Darío but later gave expression to his highly coloured vigorous imagination in poems on patriotic and traditional themes, e.g. *Las Vendimias* (1901) and *Canciones del momento* (1910).

Marmion. *St Omer altarpiece*

Marriage à la Mode: Shortly after the Marriage

The Marriage of Figaro; playbill for the Burgtheater

Marseille faïence pot (*c.* 1750)

Marquis Don(ald Robert Perry) (1878–1937). U.S. writer; after working as assistant to Joel Chandler Harris on *Uncle Remus's Magazine* M. became a leading New York journalist. Of his many works the best remembered is *archy and mehitabel* (coll. from M.'s column, 1927) and its sequels–free-verse poems 'written' by archy, a poet who has been reincarnated as a cockroach, about him and mehitabel, a disreputable lady cat who claims to be Cleopatra. The poems contain no capital letters since the cockroach cannot manage the shift-key of the typewriter.

Marriage à la Mode (1743–45). Title of a story series of 6 paintings by *Hogarth.

Marriage at Cana, The (1562–3). Huge painting by *Veronese.

Marriage of Figaro, The (Italian *Le Nozze di Figaro*). An *opera buffa* by *Mozart, libretto by L. da Ponte based on *Beaumarchais's play; 1st performance at the Burgtheater, Vienna in 1786.

Marryat Captain Frederick (1792–1848). English novelist, author of tales of life at sea, including *Mr Midshipman Easy* (1836) and *Masterman Ready* (1841–2), and the children's classic *The Children of the New Forest* (1847).

Marschner Heinrich August (1795–1861). German composer. He worked at the Dresden opera with Weber, at Leipzig, and at Hanover (1831–59). As a composer for the stage M. occupies a position midway between Weber and Wagner. He left 13 operas, of which *Hans Heiling* (1833) brought him an immense reputation, and 2 *Singspiele.*

Marseillaise, La. The French national anthem, written (1792), both words and music, by Captain Rouget de Lisle, as a patriotic song for volunteers for the Revolutionary army.

Marseille faïence. From the 16th c. faïence was manufactured at Marseille, but it is the enamel-painted wares of the 18th c. (*c.* 1750–75) which are now most prized. The characteristic motifs of flowers, fishes, etc. are disposed in attractive asymmetrical rhythmic patterns.

Marsh Sir Edward (Howard) (1872–1953). English anthologist, a civil servant. With Rupert Brooke he conceived the idea of popularizing contemporary (*Georgian) poetry by publ. anthologies–the 5 influential vols *Georgian Poetry* (1911–22).

Marsh Reginald (1898–1954). U.S. painter of city scenes who worked on newspapers and studied under K. H. Miller. His etchings of New York life verge on caricature.

Marshall Benjamin (1767–1835). English painter of sporting subjects, above all horse-racing.

Marshall George (1891–). U.S. film director. A veteran who has been in films for 50 years and has been directing for 30, with an output of about 2 films per year. Although he has tried all genres, he has done best with comedies and/or westerns (especially the delightful *Destry Rides Again* (1939), which revitalized Dietrich's career), e.g. *Destry* (1954) and *The Sheepman* (1957). He also directed a western-musical in stylized décors, *Red Garters* (1953).

Marston John (1575?–1634). English playwright, author of the tragedy *The History of Antonio and Mellida* (publ. 1602) and the comedy *The Dutch Courtezan* (publ. 1605). In 1605, M., Jonson and Chapman were imprisoned for writing the comedy *Eastward Ho.* M. stopped writing after taking orders (*c.* 1607).

Martello Pier Jacopo (1665–1727). Italian poet and man of letters who wrote a series of tragedies inspired by the French theatre in an attempt to renew Italian drama. He wrote a literary treatise proposing the adoption of rhyming couplets of 14 syllables as the Italian equivalent of the French alexandrine.

Martenot Maurice (1898–). French musician and inventor of the electronic instrument 'ondes musicales' (1928) now called 'ondes Martenot'. He has taught the instrument at the Conservatoire since 1947 and numerous composers, e.g. Honegger, Messiaen and Jolivet have written for it. He is devising another instrument.

Martial (A.D. *c.* 40–*c.* 104). Marcus Valerius Martialis, Roman poet born in Spain. He arrived in Rome about 64 to make a living out of literature by flattering any patron he could persuade to support him. His 14 books of

Marsh. *Why Not Use the 'L'?*

George Marshall. James Stewart and Marlene Dietrich in *Destry Rides Again*

John Martin. *Sadak in search of the Waters of Oblivion*

Sir Leslie Martin and C. St John Wilson. Library group, Oxford

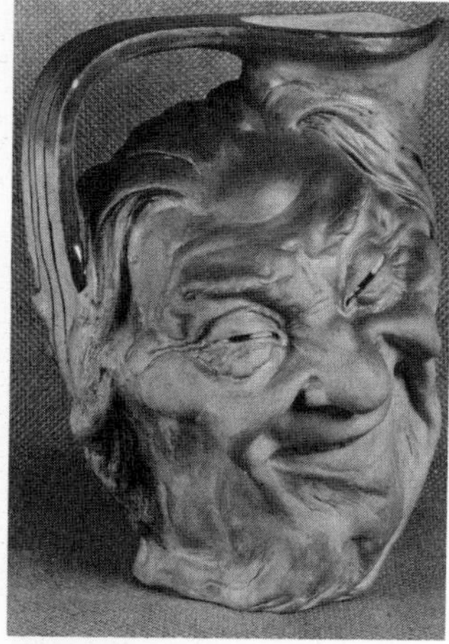

Grotesque by the Martin brothers

Frank Martin

epigrams deal with every aspect of his society, high life and low life. To his friends Juvenal, Quintilian and Pliny he seems to have been genuinely devoted, but he flattered the Emperor Domitian ceaselessly and profitably and abused his many other reluctant patrons. M. is witty, terse, compact. He uses puns (a rare phenomenon in Latin literature since Plautus), obscenities and conceits to make his points.

Martin. The 3 brothers of this name, Robert Wallace (1843–1923), Walter (1859–1912) and Edwin (1860–1915), working together from 1873 were an important factor in the English artist potter movement. Their best-known, though not their best works, are the grotesque face and bird jugs and vases mainly by Wallace. They made long and arduous experiments with high-temperature firing.

Martin Dean (1917–). U.S. film star and singer. 'Straight' partner for Jerry Lewis until 1956. His relaxed style is seen in comedy and drama, e.g. *Rio Bravo*.

Martin Frank (1890–). Swiss composer. In Geneva he was a teacher (1928–38) at the Institute of Jaques-Dalcroze, whose theories on rhythm were of great importance to the young M. Subsequently he worked much in Holland and also in Germany. His early work was influenced by the French impressionist composers but from the 1930s he began to use 12-note methods in conjunction with a highly individual harmonic idiom, making characteristic use of major-minor triad combinations. His music also reveals a great interest in instrumental texture. M.'s important works include: the opera *Der Sturm* (1956) after Shakespeare's *The Tempest* and containing the *Five Ariel Songs* (1950; for *a capella* choir); the oratorios *Le Vin herbé* (1941) on the Tristan and Isolde legend, and the moving and dramatic *Golgotha* (1948); the popular *Symphonie concertante* for harpischord, harp, piano and strings (1945) and harpsichord concerto (1952); *Der Cornet* (1943), texts from Rilke, for alto and chamber orchestra; and *Six Monologues from Everyman* (1943), after Hofmannstahl, for voice and orchestra.

Martin Homer Dodge (1836–97). U.S. landscape painter who was largely self-taught. He came under the influence of impressionism, partly through W. Hart, and this led to a break with the literal manner of the Hudson River school. Travels in France (1881–6) confirmed this stylistic preference.

Martin John (1789–1854). English romantic painter of landscape and other subjects; he also painted heroic or Old Testament subjects, with hundreds of figures often in fantastic architectural settings.

Martin Sir Leslie (1908–). English architect, professor of architecture at Cambridge Univ., chief architect to the *London County Council in the early 1950s and chief designer of the Royal Festival Hall. His department produced housing and schools of a high standard. He left to open a practice with Colin St John Wilson and they are best known for their work for Gonville and Caius College, Cambridge (1961).

Martin Chuzzlewit, The Life and Adventures of (1843–4). Novel by *Dickens.

Martin du Gard Roger (1881–). French novelist, awarded the Nobel prize (1937). Most of his work deals with the reactions of youth to the conventions and pressures of bourgeois society; e.g. the 2 brothers–one bourgeois, the other a pacificist Socialist–in M. du G.'s major work, the **roman-fleuve*, *Les Thibault* (1922–40; 1933–40). The novel *Jean Barois* (1913) is on similar themes.

Martineau Harriet (1802–76). English writer who wrote popular stories, e.g. in *Poor Law and Paupers Illustrated* (1833), designed to spread political and economic knowledge and aid reform.

Martineau Robert Braithwaite (1826–69). English genre and portrait painter, pupil of Holman Hunt. His *Last Day in the Old Home* is in the Tate.

Martinet Jean-Louis (1912–). French composer, a pupil of Messiaen. Besides Messiaen's influence, that of Stravinsky and Bartók has affected M. and he also occasionally uses 12-note techniques. He has written *Variations* for string quartet (1946), *6 songs for choir and orchestra* (1948) to texts by Char and *6 symphonic movements* (1953–8).

Martínez de la Rosa Francisco (1787–1862). Spanish dramatic poet whose poems and plays

Padre Martini

Bohuslav Martinů

Simone Martini. *Guidoriccio da Fogliano* (detail)

are interesting as examples of the transition from Spanish neo-classicism to romanticism.

Martínez Sierra Gregoria (1881–1948). Spanish novelist and playwright who obtained great success with his cleverly constructed and delicately written plays, including *El reino de Dios* (1916; *The Kingdom of God*, 1927). He was also a distinguished impresario and theatre director who brought many important foreign plays into Spain, and wrote ballet scenarios such as *El Amor Brujo*.

Martini Padre Giovanni Battista (1706–84). Italian composer, scholar and priest who worked in his native town of Bologna; he corresponded with the leading musicians of Europe and gave lessons to N. Jommelli, J. C. Bach, and Mozart. His music, largely for the church, was strictly contrapuntal; more important was his vast music library (still at Bologna) and his work as a scholar.

Martini Simone (*c.* 1284–1344). Sienese painter, the pupil of Duccio. M. drew upon Duccio's colour harmonies while pursuing his own experiments in using line for decorative purposes, so that his later works become almost abstract compositions. By 1315 he was sufficiently well thought of to be commissioned to paint a *Maestà* for the town hall of Siena. This work makes obvious M.'s debt to Duccio, but it also shows his knowledge of the sculpture of the Pisani and of the use of line in Sienese art. He was brought in direct contact with the court art and literature of France when he was summoned to the French kingdom of Naples by Robert of Anjou in 1317 to paint *St Louis of Toulouse Crowning the King* (N. Gal., Naples). In 1320 he was painting in Pisa and Orvieto. By 1328 he was in Siena to paint the famous portrait of Guidoriccio da Fogliano reviewing his battle-lines on horseback, and other frescoes in the town hall. He was in Florence in 1333, working with his brother-in-law Lippo *Memmi. Both artists signed the *Annunciation* (Uffizi), which is one of the masterpieces of Sienese painting. In 1339 M. was at the court of the Papacy at Avignon. Here he became the close friend of Petrarch; he is known to have painted Petrarch's Laura, but this portrait has been lost. 'Surely my friend Simone was once in paradise', Petrarch said, and it was M.'s conception of the earthly paradise as the scene of courtly love that was to influence the artists of the *international Gothic style throughout Europe.

Martinů Bohuslav (1890–1959). Czech composer; his teachers included Suk and Roussel. He worked in Paris (1924–40) then the U.S., was composition professor at Prague Conservatory (1946–8) but returned to the U.S. His early works are strongly nationalistic; there followed a period of neo-classicism and then a return to a modified nationalism, in a very personal, strongly expressive but precise, modern idiom. His very numerous works include: 12 operas, among them *Comedy on the Bridge* (1937); 11 ballets; a concerto for string quartet and orchestra; some extremely fine chamber music, *La Revue de cuisine* (1927), using light music and jazz idioms; and a famous double concerto for 2 string orchestras and piano and timpani (1938).

Martín y Soler Vicente (1754–1806). Spanish *opera buffa* composer who, often in conjunction with L. da Ponte, made a reputation in Italy. He continued his success in London, again with da Ponte, and in St Petersburg. His *Una cosa rara* (1786), from which Mozart quotes in *Don Giovanni*, briefly eclipsed Mozart's *Marriage of Figaro*, and contains a waltz which helped to popularize that dance.

Marton Andrew (1904–). Hungarian-born U.S. film director. M. worked as an editor in Vienna (1922) and went to Hollywood with Lubitsch (1923). He directed his 1st films in Europe. From 1938 he worked in Hollywood, was co-director of *King Solomon's Mines* (1950) and *The Longest Day* (1962) and directed *The Thin Red Line* (1964), etc. He is the most sought after second unit director in Hollywood, and worked on *The Red Badge of Courage* and *Cleopatra*.

Martorell Joanot. 15th-c. Catalan writer; author of *Tirant lo Blanch* (1490), a tale of knight-errantry distinguished by its realistic detail and vivid style.

Marty (1955). Film directed by Delbert *Mann.

Marvell Andrew (1621–78). English poet. Friend of Milton, and assistant under the Commonwealth in Milton's secretaryship of state. His small output (*Miscellaneous Poems*, 1681; *Works*, 1726) includes markedly individual love-poems, satires, poems of occasion and a series (*The Garden*; *Upon Appleton House*, etc.) written when tutor in the country household of Lord Fairfax, in which wit manipulates

Simone Martini. *Maestà* (detail). See also colour plate 37

Andrew Marvell

Karl Marx

The Marx Brothers in *Horse Feathers*

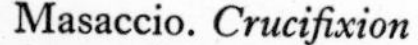

Masaccio. *Crucifixion*

a sensuous apprehension of environment. He was a master of the *conceit (*Definition of Love*; *To His Coy Mistress*) and of direct nobility of statement, e.g. *On Mr Milton's Paradise Lost* and *An Horatian Ode upon Cromwell's Return from Ireland* (1650).

Marx Karl (Heinrich) (1818–83). German philosopher, economist, historian and political agitator, the 1st systematic Socialist thinker; his works form the ideological basis of modern Communism. He spent most of his life in exile (after 1849 in England).
M. accepted *Hegel's dialectic, but interpreted it in material terms. He held that it is the mode of production that determines social relations, and therefore the nature of man, his religion, philosophy and art. (Elaborated and applied to modern conditions by 20th-c. Marxists, this became in art *socialist realism.) M.'s great work *Das Kapital* (1867, 85, 95; *Capital*, 1887) analysed contemporary (bourgeois) capitalism, which he believed would succumb to revolution by the proletariat, who would set up a Socialist, ultimately a Communist society. M. worked closely with his friend Friedrich Engels (1820–95) with whom he wrote *Das Manifest des Kommunisten* (1848; *The Communist Manifesto*, 1850).

Marx Karl (1897–). German composer and teacher, himself an early pupil of his friend Carl Orff.

Marx Brothers, The. Groucho (1895–), Harpo (1893–1964) and Chico (1891–1961), U.S. stage comedians who took advantage of the introduction of sound to transfer their fast wise-cracking to films. A 4th brother, Zeppo, dropped out after the early pictures. Groucho, with cigar, painted moustache and bouncing eyebrows; dumb Harpo, the enraptured harpist in a curly blonde wig, and Chico the Italianate pianist, made 12 zany comedy classics including *Animal Crackers* (1930), *Duck Soup* (1934), *A Night at the Opera* (1935) and *A Night in Casablanca* (1946).

Mary Barton, A Tale of Manchester Life (1848). Novel by Mrs Gaskell.

Maryinsky Theatre: *Kirov State Theatre

Masaccio. The nickname of Tommaso di Giovanni (1401–28?). Florentine painter, one of the great innovators of European art: the revolution he brought about in painting was recognized by his contemporaries even within the short span of his own lifetime. Little is known of his early years and his nickname, variously interpreted as 'naughty Tom', 'clumsy Tom', or 'hulking Tom' gives little clue. Vasari simply maintains that he was impractical in everyday affairs. M. became a member of the Florentine Guild in 1422, which leaves a period of some 6 years in which he was to accomplish his revolution, before setting out for Rome never to be heard of again. *Masolino is said to have taught him, but if this is so, the roles of master and pupil were to be reversed almost at once. What is certain is that M. was profoundly influenced by those elements of Giotto's art that had been retained and exploited better by the sculptor Donatello and the architect Brunelleschi, than by any contemporary Florentine painter. M. took up Giotto's search for a way of expressing the more exalted human emotions through figures in action in terms of painting. Where the painters of the *international Gothic style allowed line to flow, to proliferate, to become pure decoration, M. tightened it almost to breaking-point. His style is austere. His drawing of the human figure achieves an incredible degree of realism, the illusion of weight and modelling, with the sparest of means. Yet from reality he chooses only what human presence or the Divine Spirit can make noble. The Pisan polyptych altarpiece, one of his earliest works, has been divided and scattered – the central panel *Madonna and Child* (N.G., London), *Crucifixion* (Pina., Naples), *Adoration of the Magi* and *Beheading of the Baptist* (both Berlin). A similar early work on panel is the *Madonna and Child with St Anne and Five Angels* (Uffizi). The fresco *The Trinity* (S. Maria Novella, Florence) is undoubtedly the most successful and moving rendering of this subject. But M.'s fame, both as an artist and as the teacher of a whole c. of Florentine painters, rests with the frescoes of the Brancacci chapel, S. Maria del Carmine, Florence. Masolino and, later, Filippino *Lippi also painted subjects in this chapel; a third of the scheme was destroyed by fire, and some difficulty of attribution remains. Generally

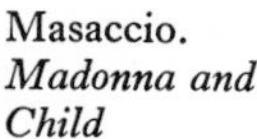

Masaccio. *Madonna and Child*

Masaccio. *Madonna and Child with St Anne and Five Angels*

Maso di Banco. *St Sylvester restores two clerks to life*

accepted as being by M. are: *The Tribute Money, Expulsion from Paradise, St Peter and St John healing the Sick by letting their Shadows fall on them, St Peter and St John distributing Alms, The Raising of the King's Son* (most) and *St Paul visiting St Peter in Prison* (part).

Mascagni Pietro (1863–1945). Italian opera composer known abroad for the 1-act *Cavalleria Rusticana* (1890) but in Italy next to only Verdi and Puccini in popularity. Other operas by M. are *L'Amico Fritz* (1891) and *Iris* (1898), a forerunner in theme of Puccini's *Madame Butterfly* and musically a worthy forerunner.

Masefield John (1878–). English poet, novelist and playwright, the poet laureate since 1930. M. ran away to sea as a boy, and the experience is reflected in, e.g., the coll. *Salt-Water Ballads* (1902), containing the famous 'I must go down to the sea again,' and the narrative poem *Dauber* (1913). His best verse is marked by its energy and use of strong rhythms, as in the narrative poems *Reynard the Fox, or The Ghost Heath Run* (1910) and *The Everlasting Mercy* (1911), which had immediate and remarkable success on publ. in *The English Review*. Works include the novels *Sad Harker* (1924) and *The Bird of Dawning* (1933).

Masereel Frans (1889–). Belgian painter who studied in Ghent, London and Paris, where he finally settled, illustrating books and painting Parisian street scenes and shore scenes at Boulogne. He is known in particular for his expressionist cartoon stories in woodcut.

Masina Giulietta (1921–). Italian film actress, wife of the director Fellini. Her waif-like charm, pathos and humour, are seen in many of his films, e.g. *Cabiria*.

Masip or **Macip** Juan Vicente (*c.* 1490–1550). Spanish painter working in Valencia, painting in the style of Raphael. His son (*c.* 1523–79) and pupil (of the same name) studied Raphael, Michelangelo and Leonardo and later painted passionate religious pictures in a dramatic mannerist style.

mask. Cover or disguise for the face, originating in the Greek *satyr plays. M.s were made in a stylized form, a little larger than life, to represent a character or character-type. The Greek actor Thespis (6th c. B.C.) introduced the idea of using m.s to enable actors to play more than one part. The Romans continued the use of m.s.

Maso di Banco (*fl.* mid 14th c.). Italian painter and one of the greatest of Giotto's followers; he is sometimes confused with Giottino. The only works which can be ascribed to him with certainty are the fresco cycle *St Sylvester and the Emperor Constantine* in S. Croce, Florence.

Masolino (*c.* 1383–*c.* 1432). Florentine painter trained in the *international Gothic style, perhaps by Ghiberti, e.g. *Madonna* (K. halle, Bremen). He was influenced by Masaccio, a much younger man, when working with him on frescoes in the Brancacci chapel, Carmine church, Florence. He was in Hungary (1425–7) and later worked in Eripoli, Todi and Rome.

Mason A(lfred) E(dward) W(ooley) (1865–1948). English novelist, author of the adventure novel *The Four Feathers* (1902).

Mason Daniel Gregory (1873–1953). U.S. composer and teacher, grandson of Lowell M.; his teachers included Paine and d'Indy, who strongly influenced him. M.'s music, of the Boston classicist school, shows also his admiration for Brahms and includes *A Lincoln Symphony* and 2 others, and much chamber music. He also wrote many books on music.

Mason James (1909–). English film actor who made his name in *Hatter's Castle* (1941) and *Odd Man Out* (1946), after which he filmed mainly in the U.S. He was apparently typed as a smooth villain, but his emotional intensity and intelligence broke through in J. Mankiewicz's *Julius Caesar* (1953) and *Lolita* (1962). He has played in many different genres, always with distinction.

Mason Lowell (1792–1872). U.S. composer and teacher whose coll. of Psalm tunes and hymns publ. as *The Boston Handel and Haydn Society's Collection of Church Music* (1822) was an immediate success. He founded the Boston Academy of Music (1833), and publ. many other such colls, as well as glees and part songs. His son WILLIAM (1829–1908) was a pianist; he studied for 4 years at Leipzig and at Weimar under Liszt. This period is described in his book *Memories of a Musical Life* (1901).

Mason R(onald) A(lison) K(ells) (1905–). New Zealand poet, most of whose best work was done in the 1930s. His vol. *Dominion* (1938) fully exemplifies the tough and honest brevity that he and his admirers most value in poetry. Later poems are equally tough and brief but display a political rigidity that appears cramping.

Masolino. *Madonna*

Masks. Hellenistic masks, comic (above; terracotta) and tragic (below; bronze)

Massine in
La Boutique Fantasque

Masson. *Il n'y a pas de monde achevé*; drawing (1938)

masque. A form of entertainment at its height in the 17th c. in England. It combined music, poetry and scenery, but unlike a play there was little or no plot. Its origins are obscure, but from the 14th c. it was customary for friends to visit a house and dance before the host, bringing with them musicians and wearing masks and carrying torches. M.s were very popular in Elizabethan times, when the performers, often aristocrats, disguised themselves to mime an allegorical story; but it was in the reign of James I that the m. reached its peak; poets like Ben Jonson wrote examples and Inigo Jones designed sets.

mass. The Roman Catholic service for the celebration of the Eucharist. The liturgy is divided into the 'proper', i.e. those parts which change according to the church calendar each feast day, having responses, etc. proper to it, and the 'ordinary', those parts of the liturgy which are sung throughout the church year. The proper is sung by the priest and his assistant to traditional plainsong settings, the ordinary in choral settings has been the medium of some of the world's greatest compositions. It consists of 5 main parts: the Kyrie, the Gloria, the Credo, the Sanctus and Benedictus, and the Agnus Dei. *Missa Brevis* may mean simply a short mass setting or a setting of only the Kyrie and Gloria used in Lutheran liturgy, examples being written by Bach. *Missa Solennis* is used of especially grand settings, as Beethoven's in D. During the polyphonic period (i.e. the 15th and 16th cs) the dominant types of m. were the cyclic tenor m., in which a fixed melody recurs throughout the sections as a unifying element; and the parody m. in which the composer uses material either from his own works or from other composers.

Massacre of Chios, The (1824). Painting by *Delacroix.

Massenet Jules (1842–1912). French opera composer. From 1878 he was professor of composition at the Conservatoire, where G. Charpentier was a pupil. His masterpiece is *Manon* (1884), based on the story by the Abbé Prévost.

Massine Leonide (1896–). Russian dancer who trained at the Bolshoi Theatre and joined the Diaghilev co. in 1914. He took over from Fokine as choreographer for that co. and his 1st significant ballet was *The Good Humoured Ladies* (1917). M. was greatly influenced by his stay in Spain during World War I, and the *Three Cornered Hat* (1919) was a result. M. was a revolutionary choreographer, doing away with the corps de ballet and taking Fokine's dogma further in making all the music 'work'. Other works include *La Boutique Fantasque* (1919) and *Mam'zelle Angot* (1943).

Massinger Philip (1583–1640). English playwright occasionally collaborating with Fletcher and Dekker. M.'s tragedies rarely attain the highest level, but he was a fluent comic dramatist: his most popular work, *A New Way to Pay Old Debts* (1633), contains the vigorous portrait of the extortioner Sir Giles Overreach; and *The City Madam* (1632) is also a notable comedy of manners. M.'s other plays include the tragedy *The Roman Actor*; a somewhat overwrought drama of Renaissance intrigue, *The Duke of Milan*; and *The Maid of Honour*.

Mass of Bolsena, The (1511–14). Fresco by *Raphael.

Masson André (1896–). French painter who joined the surrealist movement in 1924. He later quarrelled with André Breton and developed a form of surrealism which influenced the abstract expressionist movement in the U.S.

Massys Quinten (1465/6–1530), also spelt 'Quentin' and 'Matsys' or 'Metsys'. Early Netherlandish painter born in Louvain but made a master of the Antwerp Guild in 1519. M.'s style carries the Netherlands search for refinement and spiritual sensitivity to an extreme in his religious work and his portraits; his painting had a considerable influence, especially among the Italianate painters of the Netherlands. His range of subjects is large. An outstanding early painting is the central panel of the *St Anne altarpiece* (M. R. des B.-A., Brussels). Portraits of scholars at their work such as *Erasmus* (Palazzo Barberini, Rome) anticipate a favourite subject of Holbein. In his *Virgin and Child* (M. R. des B.-A., Brussels), *Rest on the Flight into Egypt* (A. M., Worcester, Mass.) and other studies of the Holy Family there is a profound melancholy. The caricature drawings and the faces of the crowd in *Ecce Homo* (Prado) provide the reverse side of the refinement. Genre paintings such as *Money-changer and his Wife* (Louvre) are in the tradition of van Eyck and Petrus Christus. Late, highly finished panels like *The Temptation of St Anthony* (Prado) were often the result of a collaboration with J. *Patenier. Finally, the exceptional painting in tempera on linen, *The Virgin and Child with St Barbara* (?) *and St Catherine* (N.G., London) gives evidence of Italian influences, particularly of Raphael and Leonardo da Vinci.

mastaba. Egyptian stone tomb with a flat top and sloping sides; the pyramids developed from m.s.

Master Bertram. German artist working at Hamburg from 1367 to 1410. His workshop produced an altarpiece for St Peter's, Hamburg, now in the Kunsthalle.

Master Builder The (1892). Play by *Ibsen.

Master Francke (d. after 1424). Painter who worked in Hamburg; information about his activities is slight. Owing to the influence of French illuminated mss evident in his work he is believed to have been in Paris. His painting shows an advance on that of the slightly older Hamburg artist Master Bertram, in its composition, brilliance of colour, observation of life and expressiveness coupled with restraint. Most famous are his *St Thomas Altar* (1424; K. halle, Hamburg), on Thomas à Becket, including the gentle *Nativity* panel, and 2 versions of the *Man of Sorrows* (Hamburg and Leipzig).

Master of Ballantrae (1889). Novel by R. L. *Stevenson.

Master of Flémalle. Early Netherlandish painter, now generally accepted to have been the same artist as both the Master of Mérode and Robert Campin (*c.* 1380–1444). Campin worked in Tournai, becoming a citizen in 1423. Despite being 'mildly persecuted' for political activity and 'living in concubinage' his reputation remained high. J. Daret and Rogier van der Weyden were his pupils. No major works were known before the association of his name with works attributed to the Master of Flémalle, which include: *Nativity* (M. des B.-A., Dijon), *The Werl altarpiece* and *Miracle of the Rod and Betrothal of the Virgin* (both Prado), *Portrait of a Man* and *Virgin and Child before a Fire-screen* (both N.G., London), *Madonna in Glory* (M., Aix-en-Provence) and works at

Massys. *St Anne altarpiece*

Master Francke. *St Thomas altarpiece*

the Städelsches K. inst., Frankfurt. Attributed to the Master of Mérode is the important and delightful triptych now in the Metropolitan Museum. As controversial as the artist's identity is the question of his precedence in relation to Jan van Eyck. His naturalism of style shows a quite different feeling to van Eyck's but is hardly less revolutionary. He was probably the inventor of the painted statues in grisaille on the backs of the wing panels of altarpieces and of distant views of townscapes seen through windows.

Master of Moulins (active *c.* 1483–*c.* 1500) also known as the 'Master of the Bourbons', or 'Maître aux Anges'. French painter, influenced by Netherlandish artists, especially H. van der Goes, but with a very individual and graceful style which can be seen at its best in the altarpiece, Moulins cathedral. Works include: *Nativity* (Mus., Autun), *St Mary Magdalene and Female Donor* (Louvre), *The Annunciation* (A. Inst., Chicago), and *Charlemagne and the Meeting at the Gopdeu Gate* (N.G., London). Formerly, wrongly, identified with J. *Perreal.

Master of St Giles. French or Netherlandish artist who worked for the French court in Lyons, Paris and the Loire Valley in the last years of the 15th c. He is named after 2 panels, *St Giles and the Hind* and *The Mass of St Giles* (both N.G., London). 2 panels with incidents from the life of St Remi (N.G., Washington) are also attributed.

Master of the Aix Annunciation. The painter of an altarpiece, *Annunciation*, for Église des Prêcheurs, Aix-en-Provence, *c.* 1445 (main panel in church; other parts: M. R. des B.-A., Brussels; Boymans Mus., Rotterdam and on loan to the Louvre from the Rijksmus.). The artist was probably French, though influenced by van Eyck's *Adoration of the Lamb* and the Master of Flémalle. The Rijksmus. panel, an outstanding still-life study of books and papers, may also show the link in style between Netherlands and Neapolitan painters.

Master of the Death of the Virgin. A painter of the early 16th c. usually identified with *Joos van Cleve.

Master of the Duke of Bedford. French artist, working in Paris during the English occupation, who executed a breviary for the English Regent (Bib. Nat., Paris) and *The Bedford Hours* (1423; B.M., London).

Master of Flémalle. *Annunciation with Donors and St Joseph* (*St Mérode altarpiece*)

Master of Moulins. *Madonna and Child with Angels and Donors*

Master of St Giles. *The Mass of St Giles*

Master of the Aix Annunciation. Main panel of the *Annunciation*

Master of the Housebook. *Lovers*

Master of the Virgo inter Virgines. *Madonna and Child Surrounded by Four Holy Women*

Master of Třěbŏn. *Christ on the Mount of Olives*

Master of the Rohan Book of Hours. *God the Father judging a dying man*

Master of the St Lucy Legend. *The Virgin of the Rose Garden*

Master of the Female Half-Lengths. Early Netherlandish artist active about 1530 in Antwerp, who often painted young girls playing musical instruments or reading. His graceful, rather mannered style is close to that of Massys, e.g. *Three Girls Playing Instruments* (Gal. Harrach, Vienna.)

Master of the Housebook. Late 15th-c. German or Dutch artist called after the *Hausbuch* at Schloss Wolfegg. This contains many drawings depicting contemporary life; and the numerous engravings attributed to this master, important early examples of the technique, have similar subjects.

Master of the Legend of the Magdalen. Early Netherlandish painter active at the beginning of the 16th c. at Brussels. He followed Rogier van der Weyden and others. Works include the *Annunciation* triptych (M. R. des B.-A., Brussels) and *St Mary Magdalen Preaching* (Johnson Coll., Philadelphia).

Master of the Life of the Virgin. German painter active in Cologne *c.* 1463–80. His serene style, showing Netherlands influences, is seen best in the beautiful *Annunciation* from the altarpiece which gave him his name (Alte Pina., Munich). Other important works: *The Presentation in the Temple* (N.G., London) and a triptych including *The Crucifixion* (W.-R. Mus., Cologne).

Master of the Rohan Book of Hours. French artist active *c.* 1420, named for *Les Grandes Heures du Duc de Rohan* (Bib. Nat., Paris). M. had a predilection for Last Judgement themes, suffering, violence and death, often rendered in almost expressionist terms.

Master of the St Lucy Legend. Early Netherlandish painter, active in Bruges *c.* 1480–90, named after *Scenes from the Life of St Lucy* (St Jacques church, Bruges). Other attributed works include *St Catherine* (M. of A., Philadelphia) and *Madonna with Magdalen and Virgins* (M. R. des B.-A., Brussels). Gérard David and others were influenced by the master's quality of elegance in painting the female saints, the richness of their costume and brilliance of landscape detail.

Master of the St Ursula Legend. Early Netherlandish artist working at Bruges at the end of the 15th c., a close follower in style of Rogier van der Weyden and Memlinc, who painted the *4 Scenes from The St Ursula Legend* (Convent of the Black Sisters, Bruges).

Master of the Virgo inter Virgines. Early Netherlandish artist, probably working in Delft at the end of the 15th c., who painted the *Madonna and Child Surrounded by Four Holy Women* (Rijksmus).

Master of Třěbŏn or **Wittingau.** Bohemian Gothic painter whose masterpiece is *The Resurrection*, a panel from the parts of an altarpiece painted *c.* 1380 for a church in Třěbŏn, or Wittingau, now in Czechoslovakia (N.G., Prague).

Masters Edgar Lee (1868–1950). U.S. writer, author of *Spoon River Anthology* (1915), a coll. of free-verse epitaphs spoken by the buried inhabitants of a small Middle Western town. The whole was a biting commentary on small-town life, and influenced the tone and subject-matter of U.S. literature for a generation, being the 1st important example of a book dealing analytically with U.S. provincial life.

mastersingers. German poets who belonged to the elaborately regulated guilds and schools which developed from the *Minnesingers in 15th-c. towns. To become a member of the highest class (*Meister*) the poet had to compose a new melody to his original verses. The m. reached the peak of their achievement in the 16th c.; Hans *Sachs was the greatest of them. The singing contest, a prime feature of *Meistergesang*, is depicted in Wagner's *Mastersingers of Nuremberg*.

Mastroianni Marcello (1923–). Italian film actor whose 1st international film of any importance was *Le Notte Bianche* (1957). He was selected by Fellini to star in *La Dolce Vita* (1959); his smouldering aristocratic elegance made him enormously popular, but he has a wide range from comedy, e.g. P. Germi's *Divorzio all'Italiana* (1961), to psychological drama, as in E. Petri's *L'Assassino* (1961).

Mataré Ewald (1887–). German sculptor who started his career as a painter, studying under Lovis Corinth; a frequent subject is animal shapes reduced to their simplest formal elements. A major commission was the new doors for Cologne cathedral.

Mate Rudolph (1898–). Polish-born U.S. film director. Perhaps M. will be remembered mainly as the cameraman of Carl Dreyer films like *Le Passion de Jeanne d'Arc* and *Vampyr*, but his work as a director, mainly of action films, is worthy of note. He has made thrillers like *D.O.A.* (1949), *Union Station* (1950), and *Second Chance* (1953), as well as westerns (*The Far Horizons*, 1955) and spoof historical movies (*The Black Shield of Falworth*, 1954), all with considerable panache.

Mather Cotton (1663–1728). American clergyman and writer, apologist of the Salem witchcraft trials. He wrote many theological and literary works, as did his father, INCREASE M. (1639–1723).

Mathieu Georges (1921–). French painter in a lyrical abstract idiom. His first non-figurative work appeared in 1944. He has strong affinities with U.S. painters, for whom he organized an exhibition in Paris in 1950.

Mathilde Princesse (1820–1904). French society woman, niece of Napoleon I and cousin of Napoleon III. Flaubert, Gautier, Sainte-Beuve and Edmond de Goncourt regularly visited her *salon*.

Mathis der Mahler (German, 'Mathis the Painter'). Opera by *Hindemith with libretto by the composer; 1st performance at Zürich in 1938.

Matin, Le (French, 'The Morning'). The name of a symphony, no. 6 in D, by Haydn; it forms a group with *Le Midi* ('The Midday') no. 7 in C and *Le Soir et la tempête* ('The Evening and The Tempest'), no. 8 in G. They were composed *c.* 1761.

Matisse Henri (1869–1954). French painter. Until the advent of cubism, he was the most influential painter in Paris, if not in Europe, and he remains one of the most important artists of the c. His emancipation of colour has an historical importance comparable to cubism's role in releasing form from representation, and his *Notes d'un Peintre* (1908) stated clearly for the 1st time several principles that lie behind later developments in 20th-c. painting. He first studied law in Paris and worked as a lawyer's clerk at St-Quentin. He started to draw and paint *c.* 1890 and in 1892 studied in Paris, first under Bouguereau at the Académie Julian and then (1893–8) in Moreau's studio at the École des Beaux-Arts, where Marquet became his close friend and he met Rouault, Manguin and other future fauves. His early independent works painted in Brittany (1896–8) were restrained objective interiors and still-lifes, reflecting his admiration for Chardin. In the late 1890s, under the influence of impressionism and neo-impressionism, he began to paint in heightened colour, but dissatisfied with divisionism, he turned to Cézanne. Although poor at the time, he purchased from Vollard in 1899 the small Cézanne *Bathers* which later 'sustained me spiritually in the critical moments of my career as an artist'. Working at the Académie Carrière (*c.* 1899–1900) where he met Derain, and later in a studio at Quai St-Michel, M. concentrated until 1904 on structural strength in his painting. *Académie Bleu* (*c.* 1900; Tate) shows the transition from brilliant colour to crudely simple draughtsmanship and solidly modelled form. Significantly he made his 1st sculpture at this time: sculpture continued throughout his career to be an extension of his painting.
The experimental phase ended when in 1904, working at St-Tropez, the renewed contact with the brilliant neo-impressionist palette proved the springboard to *fauvism. M.'s leadership was recognized and in his major works of the period, *Luxe, Calme et Volupté* (1905; Paris Coll.) and *Joie de Vivre* (1905–6; Barnes Foundation, Philadelphia) the fundamental character of his whole oeuvre was emerging.
M. was concerned with an expressive art, with a seriousness of purpose comparable to the German expressionists (whom he influenced) but totally different from them in mood and technique. In his art primitive forms are assimilated without their disturbing violence, e.g. *Portrait of Madame Matisse* (1913; Leningrad), and his treatment of colour and line never loses sight of their artistic, pictorial values.
The difference is fully apparent in his belief that 'only one who is able to order his emotions systematically is an artist'. He wrote in his *Notes d'un Peintre* (1908): 'What I dream of is an art of balance, purity and serenity, devoid of troubling or depressing subject-matter . . . which might be . . . like an appeasing influence, a mental soother, something like a good armchair in which to rest from physical fatigue.'
He worked in brilliant colour at Collioure (1905) with Derain; their portraits of each

Matisse. *Luxe, Calme et Volupté*

Matisse. *Joie de Vivre*

Matisse. *Portrait of Madame Matisse*

Matisse. *Seated Nude* (1925)

Matisse. *Self-portrait*

Matisse. *Painter and his Model.* Also *fauvism, *neo-impressionism, *odalisque, *Prokofiev

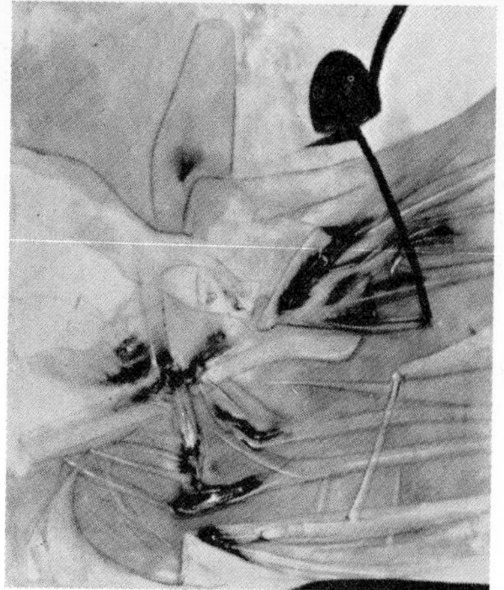

Matta. *Yo-U* (1950)

Matting. Silver-gilt bell salt (1600)

Sir Robert Matthew. New Zealand House

other are in the Tate. Although his palette was somewhat subdued during the 1910s, e.g. *Pond at Trivaux* (*c.* 1916; Tate) or *Painter and his Model* (1916; M.M.A., Paris), he was as little touched by cubism as Picasso was by fauvism. He was deeply impressed by an exhibition of Near Eastern art in Munich (1910) and visited Morocco. His love of oriental fabrics and ceramics is reflected in the exotic decorative details and character of the great *Odalisques* of 1920–5.
From 1917 he lived at Nice, with a visit to America and Tahiti in 1930–1. He worked on the chapel at Venice (1949–51) and his other late works include the collages of cut-out, gouache-coloured paper shapes arranged in terms of expressive abstract rhythms, e.g. *l'Escargot* (1953; Tate).

Matsys Quinten: *Massys

Matta Echaurren (1912–). Chilean-born painter who studied architecture under Le Corbusier from 1934 but joined the surrealists in 1937 and began painting, contributing his own brand of demonic fantasy.

Mattei Stanislao (1750–1825). Italian composer and professor of counterpoint at Bologna. He was a pupil and friend of Padre Martini, and his own pupils included Rossini and Donizetti.

Matteis Nicola. 17th-c. Italian violinist and composer who settled in London in 1672, writing an ode for the St Cecilia Day celebration of 1696. In his *Diary* John Evelyn refers (1674) to him as 'that stupendous violin'.

Matteo di Giovanni (active *c.* 1435–95). Sienese artist who worked in association with Giovanni di Pietro at Siena and Piero della Francesca at Borgo San Sepolcro. M. was influenced by Vecchietta and, later, by the Pollaiuolo brothers. Among many works, *The Assumption of the Virgin* (N.G., London) is notable for the great beauty of the painting of the Virgin herself.

Mattheson Johann (1681–1764). German composer, singer, keyboard performer and writer. At the Hamburg opera (1696–1705) he was a colleague of Handel although a question of precedence at the harpsichord provoked a duel between them. The most important of his numerous works were *Der Vollkommene Capellmeister* . . . (1739), an encyclopaedia of contemporary musical practice, and *Ehren-Pforte* (1740), containing numerous musical biographies.

Matthew Sir Robert (1906–). Architect to the *London County Council from 1946 to 1953; under his direction it changed from a neo-Georgian outlook to one of the best offices in the country, producing the Royal Festival Hall and the Roehampton Flats. Since 1957 he has developed a large practice with Stirrat Johnson Marshall; work includes New Zealand House, Haymarket (1962) and the Commonwealth Institute, Holland Park (1963).

Matthew, The Gospel according to St (2nd half of the 1st c.). One of the books of the *Bible, the 1st book of the New Testament but derived in part from St *Mark. It describes the life and teaching of Jesus, and was evidently addressed to Jewish Christians, being at pains to prove that Jesus was the Messiah prophesied in the Old Testament. It is doubtful whether the author is M. the disciple of Jesus.

matting. In metalwork and woodwork, the effect produced with a pattern of tiny impressed dots punched with a matt tool; e.g. small circles can be punched closely together (in silverware) to give a broken surface texture to contrast with a polished one.

Mattson Arne (1919–). Swedish film director. His *One Summer of Happiness* (1951) perhaps owes its great fame less to its undoubted qualities as a pastoral romance than to a single nude scene.

Maturin Charles Robert (1782–1824). English writer, author of the *Gothick novel *Melmoth the Wanderer* (1820), the story of a man who sells his soul to the devil.

Matveev Alexandr (1878–). Russian sculptor of Saratov, like his close friend and hero Borissov-Mussatov; one of M.'s best-known works is his memorial (1910) to this artist. He began as an architect but soon took to sculpture. He worked in *Mamontov's ceramic factory for some years. After a visit to Paris in 1906 he became the only sculptor in the Blue Rose group. For many years he was an influential teacher both in Leningrad and in Moscow. Many of his portraits are of young girls and

Guy de Maupassant

François Mauriac

Somerset Maugham: painting by Graham Sutherland

Maulbertsch. *Ascension of the Virgin*

boys, executed in a mood and technique little changed since his first mature works of the Blue Rose period.

Maud (1855). Poem by *Tennyson.

Maude Cyril (1862–1951). English actor-manager who in 1896 took over the Haymarket Theatre, where he presented many successful seasons with his wife Winifred Emery as leading lady.

Mauduit Jacques (1557–1627). French composer and lutenist, a member of J.-A. de Baïf's academy of music and poesy. M. set 23 4-part *Chansonettes mesurées* (1586) to texts by Baïf, exemplifying the latter's theories on music in the service of poetry. M. is said to have introduced the Venetian double chorus (A. *Gabrielli) into France.

Maugham William Somerset (1874–1965). English novelist, short-story writer and playwright, one of the most prolific and popular writers of the 20th c. The comparative lack of success of his early novels, apart from *Liza of Lambeth* (1897), led him to write plays, usually extremely successful comedies of manners (now rather dated). He returned to the novel with *Of Human Bondage* (1915), a semi-autobiographical novel relating the lame Philip Carey's education in life. M.'s appeal lies in his ability to tell a story, his straightforward style and the ironic detachment with which he records the victory of passion over principles and affections. Works include the novels *Mrs Craddock* (1902); *The Moon and Sixpence* (1919), based on the life of Gauguin; *Cakes and Ale* (1930), an acid description of typical contemporary writers; *The Razor's Edge* (1944); and the famous short story *Rain.*

Maulbertsch Franz Anton (1724–96). The most important of the Austrian baroque decorative painters. He worked in Vienna, throughout Austria, Hungary and Czechoslovakia, and also at the Residenz in Dresden.

Maupassant Guy de (1850–93). The greatest French exponent of the short story. A Norman by birth and breeding, he was treated almost as a spiritual son by his fellow-countryman, Flaubert, whose stylistic lessons he absorbed. He was a minor civil servant to the age of 32 and then lived by his writings; he was one of the few French authors of the 19th c. to make a fortune, and he spent it in riotous living, partly on the Côte d'Azur. During the last 3 years of his life he was reduced to insanity by syphilis.
A member of the *naturalist group, founded by Zola and his disciples, he shared their interest in violent passion and sordid episodes, although his stories are also often illuminated by humour and physical poetry. Whether he is dealing with Norman peasants, the civil service world or high society, he has the short-story writer's indispensable sense of construction and an admirably direct style. A number of his stories rank as permanent classics, e.g. *Boule-de-suif* (1880; *Boule de Suif,* 1899) and *La Maison Tellier* (1881; *Madame Tellier's Girls,* 1897), an account of a country outing by the ladies of a brothel. His novels–*Une Vie* (1883; *A Woman's Life,* 1887), *Bel-Ami* (1885; *Bel-Ami,* 1923), *Pierre et Jean* (1888; *Pierre and Jean,* 1902) and *Fort comme la mort* (1889; *Strong as Death,* 1900)–express the same bitter view of life.

Mauriac François (1885–). French novelist, dramatist and journalist. Although he lives in Paris, he belongs to the Bordeaux area, and is often classed as a regional novelist, since he uses the sombre landscapes and sultry climate of his native setting to emphasize the psychological tension in his novels. He was awarded the Nobel prize in 1952. He has become a prominent supporter of de Gaulle. His subject-matter is sensual passion in conflict with a middle-class convention and religious scruples, and he excels in the description of claustrophobic middle-class family atmospheres. His most characteristic novels are *Le Baiser au lépreux . . .* (1922; *The Kiss to the Leper. . . ,* 1923), *Génetrix* (1923; *Genetrix,* 1950), *Le Désert de l'amour* (1925; *The Desert of Love,* 1949), *Thérèse Desqueyroux* (1927; *Thérèse,* 1928), *Le Nœud de vipères* (1932; *Vipers' Tangle . . . ,* 1933), *Les Chemins de la mer* (1939; *The Unknown Sea,* 1948).

Maurois André. Pseud. of Emile Herzog (1885–). French writer. During World War I he was a liaison officer with the British army, an experience which produced *Les silences du colonel Bramble* (1918; *The Silence of Colonel Bramble,* 1919). Afterwards he wrote a series of fictionalized biographies of Shelley, Lord Byron, Disraeli and Edward VII. Novels about his French background include *Bernard Quesnay* (1926; *Bernard Quesnay,* 1927),

The Mausoleum (reconstruction)

Vladimir Mayakovsky

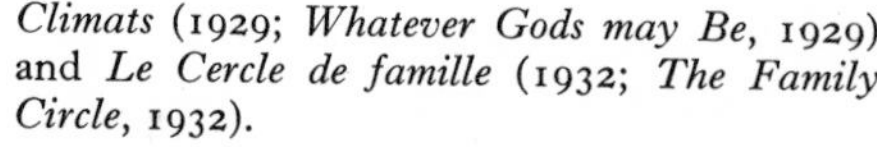

Climats (1929; *Whatever Gods may Be*, 1929) and *Le Cercle de famille* (1932; *The Family Circle*, 1932).

Maurras Charles (1868–1952). French poet, essayist and journalist. He was one of the founders of the école romane, a group of poets who, reacting against symbolism, sought to revive Graeco-Latin influence on French poetry. M. became a monarchist after the Dreyfus case, helped to found the Action Française group and became ed. of its newspaper. After World War II he was imprisoned for having collaborated.

Mausoleum. The original M. was the tomb of King Mausolus at Halicarnassus, Asia Minor, erected by his wife in 355 B.C.–an elaborate example of Hellenistic monumental architecture. It consisted of a high square podium, a peristyle of Ionic columns, a pyramidal roof and a huge statue of Mausolus in a chariot, but the details of the design are no longer known. Scopas was among the sculptors. Fragments of the frieze and the statue of Mausolus are preserved in the British Museum.

Marble statue of Mausolus from the Mausoleum

Mauve Anton (1838–88). Dutch painter in oil and watercolour. The muted colours and atmospheric effects in his landscape subjects show affinities with Millet, Corot and Daubigny. He was an important member of the Dutch 'Barbizon' school.

Maxim Gorky Trilogy (1938–40). Films directed by M. *Donskoi.

Maximova Ekatrina (1940–). Russian dancer of the Bolshoi co. since 1958. Her soft, lyrical style and strong technique have helped to make Giselle and Cinderella her finest roles She is married to Vladimir Vasiliev.

May Hugh (1622–84). English architect, one of the leading figures in the sparse period between Jones and Wren. He went to Holland with Charles II and picked up Dutch Palladianism. His chief surviving work is Eltham Lodge, Kent, in brick and with classical details, but keeping the old Jacobean-style staircase.

Hugh May. Eltham Lodge

May Joe (1880–1954). Pioneer German film director, principally of serials similar to those of *Feuillade; the most famous is *Die geheimnissvolle Villa* (1913). *Das indische Grabmal* (1921) was remade by M.'s erstwhile scenarist, F. *Lang. M. later directed in France (1931–2) and the U.S. (from 1934).

May Pamela (1917–). British dancer; one of the 1st ballerinas produced by the Sadler's Wells School; she developed mainly as a classical dancer, creating one of the roles in *Symphonic Variations* (1946). A great mime, she is also associated with 'queen mother' roles and now teaches at the Royal Ballet School.

Maya art: *Pre-Columbian art

Mayakovsky Vladimir Vladimirovich (1893–1930). Soviet poet and playwright. M. joined the Bolsheviks when he was 14, was arrested several times and spent some months in prison. He studied painting and in 1912 joined the cubo-futurists. M.'s early poetry is negative, attacking established conventions and institutions; but after the October Revolution he worked devotedly for the Bolsheviks, designing and writing the texts of thousands of posters, writing poems and film-scripts and making speeches for Red victory in the Civil War. At this time he was virtually the official poet of Communism, a position he began to lose as futurism became less acceptable to the régime, but regained after his suicide.
M.'s verse gives an impression of great power, vigour and enthusiasm; its pounding rhythms, deliberately loud, harsh, coarse and rhetorical tone, ingenious rhymes and verbal innovations admirably convey M.'s sense of being a new kind of man in a new age. His poems are intended to be declaimed; hence their (then) unorthodox typography and use of lines in which only the number of stressed syllables is regular. Elements of the fantastic and grotesque appear, notably in the poems *The Cloud in Trousers* (1915; 1945) and *150,000,000* (1920), and the verse play *Mystery-Bouffe* (1921; 1933). Other notable poems are *At the Top of My Voice* (1930; 1942) and *Vladimir Ilyich Lenin* (1924; trs. in part 1942). The plays *The Bedbug* (1929; 1963) and *The Bath-house* (1930; 1963) satirize Soviet bureaucracy.

Maybeck Bernard (1862–1957). U.S. architect who built in California in a variety of styles, the most influential being redwood siding and low sloping roofs, which developed into the Bay Region style.

Mayer Carl (1894–1944). Austrian-born German film writer. M. was one of the key figures

The Temple Newsam Mazer; England, *c.* 1611

Binding by Samuel Mearne

in the German cinema of the 1920s. He wrote *The Cabinet of Dr Caligari* and led the development of a more intimate style of acting and camera movement in German cinema. He wrote scripts for Murnau, including *The Last Laugh* (1925), *Tartuffe* (1926) and *Sunrise* (1927). Influenced by seeing Eisenstein's *Battleship Potemkin*, he provided the original idea for Ruttmann's *Berlin*.

Mayer Louis B. (1885–1957). Head of Metro-Goldwyn-Mayer film studios from the co.'s foundation in 1924 until 1951. Starting with a single small cinema, he became co-owner of a cinema circuit and then formed his own production co., which became part of M.G.M. M. was at M.G.M. the most powerful producer in Hollywood, and can claim to be the creator of the star system. He 'discovered' Garbo, Joan Crawford, Valentino and Clark Gable.

Mayor of Casterbridge, The (1886). Novel by Thomas *Hardy.

Maywood Augusta (1825–76?). U.S. dancer who, as a child prodigy, acted and sang as well as danced. She was the 1st U.S. ballerina in Europe, where she stayed until her retirement (1862), dancing in Paris, Milan and Vienna.

Mazeppa Ivan (1644–1709). Polish nobleman (who became a Cossack leader), subject of a poem by Byron (1819) and a play by Pushkin, *Poltava*. The latter was the basis for Tchaikovsky's opera *M.*, 1st performance at Moscow in 1884. Liszt named a symphonic poem after M.

mazer. The most common medieval drinking-bowl, without stem or foot, made of hardwood, often maple. Frequently decorated with silver or gilt mounts round the lip, and inside the bowl on the boss. The silver lip-band is often decorated with ornamental engraving, sometimes with an inscription.

Mazo Juan Batista del (*c.* 1612–67). Spanish painter, pupil and son-in-law of Velazquez, whose portraits strongly influenced him. His copy of Velazquez's *Infanta* is in Vienna, together with the original.

mazurka. A Polish folk-dance from the province of Mazovia, with the 2nd or 3rd beat often strongly accentuated. It was used extensively in composition by Glinka, Tchaikovsky and other Russian composers, but especially by Chopin, who wrote at least 50 m.s.

Mazzini Giuseppe (1805–72). Italian Revolutionist and political theorist; in exile from 1831, apart from a period of power in the brief Roman Republic (1849). M. exercised enormous influence on the movement for Italian liberation and unification–though ultimately disappointed by the way it was achieved–through his Revolutionary activities and practical and theoretical writings, e.g. *Doveri dell' uomo* (1860; *The Duties of Man*, 1862).

meander. Alternative term for *fret.

Mearne Samuel (d. 1683). English bookbinder, the creator of a new, elegant yet simple style. He worked for Charles II after the Restoration.

measure. In music, the U.S. term for *bar.

Measure for Measure (1623). Play by *Shakespeare, written *c.* 1603 and performed at court in 1604. Its sources were George Whetstone's *Promos and Cassandra* (1578), based on a story in Giraldi Cinthio's *Hecatommithi* (1565).

Meaulnes, Le Grand (1913). Novel by *Alain-Fournier.

Mechlin (or **Malines) lace.** From the town of that name in Flanders, but also used to describe nearly all Flemish lace before the mid 17th c. Made all in one piece on a pillow with bobbins. Like *Valenciennes, of floral type with an open net background, but comparatively a less fine lace.

Medea (331 B.C.). Play by *Euripides based on myth, the story of M., the princess of Colchis who helped Jason to steal the Golden Fleece. While they are living in exile Jason deserts M. and marries the daughter of the king of Corinth. M. kills her children by Jason and his new bride, and magically disappears. There are plays on the subject by Seneca, Corneille and Anouilh.

Médecin malgré lui, Le (1666). Play by *Molière.

mediant. Musical term for the 3rd degree of the scale.

Medici Lorenzo de' ('The Magnificent') (1449–92). Ruler of Florence, politician and poet and one of the greatest art patrons of the Italian

Mechlin bobbin lace

Medea. The renewing of Jason's youth: Greek hydria showing Medea sprinkling medicaments on a ram in an urn

Lorenzo de' Medici

Meissen mug with chinoiserie decoration (*c.* 1725)

Meissen figurines of *commedia dell'arte* characters modelled by Kaendler. Scaramouche and Columbine (left; *c.* 1741) and the Harlequin family (*c.* 1740). Also *deutsche blumen

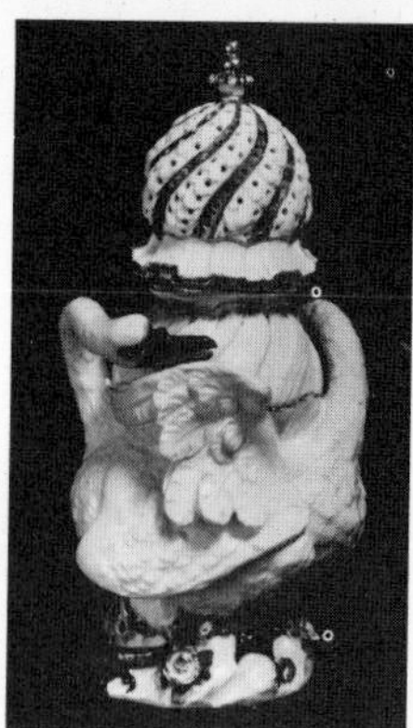

Meissen. *Swan* service by Kaendler (1737)

Medina. *Portrait of an artist* (self-portrait)

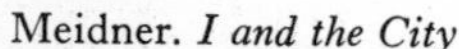

Meidner. *I and the City*

Renaissance. His lively and elegant poems deal mainly with platonic and sensual love and nature (*Trionfi e canti carnascialeschi*, *Selve d'amore*). He was influenced by the *dolce stil nuovo, Petrarch and the neo-Platonists. He also wrote a religious drama, and a number of parodies and satires. Other members of the M. family, notably Lorenzo's father, COSIMO (1389–1464), and his son Giuliano (1479–1516), who became Pope LEO X, were important art patrons.

Medici porcelain. The 1st European soft-paste *porcelain was produced in Florence during the last quarter of the 16th c. under the patronage of Francesco Maria de' Medici.

Medina Sir John (1655/60–1711). Portrait painter of Spanish origin who settled and worked in Scotland after 1688. He also illustrated Milton's *Paradise Lost*.

medium. (1) The liquid or vehicle (linseed oil, gum arabic, etc.) used to bind powdered pigments to render them usable as paint. (2) The liquid or vehicle (water, turps, etc.) used to thin prepared paint to render it more workable. The word is also used (3) in the more general sense of the technical means by which a work is executed (pastel, charcoal, pen and ink, fresco, etc.).

Medtner Nikolay Karlovich (Nicholas) (1880–1951). Russian composer of German extraction. He was a professor at the Moscow Conservatory but in 1921 left Russia, settling in Berlin; in the 1920s he toured France, England and the U.S. as a pianist and from 1935 lived in London. His music, sometimes reminiscent of Rachmaninov, is in a classical-romantic idiom; M. wrote almost exclusively for the piano, e.g. his delicate miniatures *Fairy Tales* (1905–29).

Meegeren Henricus Anthonius van, called Han (1889–1947). Dutch painter and renowned forger of Vermeers and de Hooghs, notably the magnificent *Christ at Emmaus* (1937) supposedly by Vermeer. He successfully deceived art experts and was only caught on his own confession in 1945 when he was arrested as an enemy collaborator for being involved in the sale of an old master–in fact one of his own forgeries–to Goering.

Meet Me in Saint Louis (1944). Film directed by V. *Minnelli.

Méhul Étienne (1763–1817). French composer. From 1778 he studied and taught in Paris. Gluck encouraged him and he became a successful composer. He wrote many operas, notably *Uthal* (1806) and *Joseph* (1807). His works are distinguished for dramatic effect and novel orchestration, and include cantatas, ballets and songs.

Meidner Ludwig (1884–). German lithographer and painter. M. was initially influenced by impressionism but turned to an extreme expressionism which contained a strong vein of social criticism. In the late 1920s he was occupied with writing. He lived in Britain between 1939 and 1953, when he returned to Germany.

Meiland Jakob (1542–77). German composer reckoned by his contemporaries the equal of Lasso and Clemens non Papa, in his motets. He introduced the Italian villanella style into his *Lieder* and was the first to write free-form crowd scenes in his German Passions.

Meiningen Players. Theatre co. founded by George, Duke of Saxe-Meiningen and his wife in 1874; it had a profound effect on European theatre through the example of its thorough and integrated productions.

Meissen. Town in Germany near Dresden. The porcelain factory founded here by Augustus the Strong of Saxony in 1710 produced the 1st European hard-paste *porcelain; the process was discovered by J. F. Böttger. M. remained the leading European porcelain factory until the occupation of Dresden by Frederick the Great of Prussia; later the leadership passed to Sèvres. The artistic supremacy of M. was largely created by Johann Gregor Höroldt–who was in charge of the painting shop until 1765, improved the porcelain recipe and introduced new enamels and styles, notably *chinoiseries–and by Johann Joachim* Kaendler, chief modeller from 1731. From 1740 the influence of *rococo was predominant; French painting (especially that of Boucher) was influential and Kaendler's famous *Swan* service introduced a new style of highly modelled tableware with moulded ornament on the surface of the plates and little painted decoration. At this time, too, the formalized oriental flower decorations gave way to *deutsche blumen. From 1763 M. tried to adjust to the now prevalent *neo-classical style, producing rather stiff work in imitation of Sèvres. 19th-c. M. ware, quasi-rococo and often over-elaborate, was particularly popular in England and the U.S. In England M. porcelain is called 'Dresden'. The factory is still in production.

Meissonier Jean-Louis-Ernest (1815–91). French artist, pupil of L. Cogniet, whose large historical canvases of the Napoleonic Wars were very popular at the time.

Meistermann Georg (1911–). German painter who studied under Heusser at the Düsseldorf Academy (1929–33), and also under Nauen and Mataré. Works after 1937 include glass for church windows. He has been a professor at the Düsseldorf Academy since 1955.

meistersinger: *mastersingers

Melba Dame Nellie (1859–1931). Australian operatic soprano. She came to Paris in 1886, making her début in 1887 in Brussels. She became a great lyric and coloratura singer. The name-part of Saint-Saëns's *Hélène* (1904) was written for her.

Melchior Lauritz (1890–). Danish-born U.S. tenor, originally a baritone; distinguished in Wagnerian roles.

Meleager of Gadara (*fl.* 60 B.C.). Greek epigrammatist; his *Garland* is an anthology which contains pieces by M. and many other poets.

Meléndez Luis Eugenio (1716–80). Spanish painter, son and pupil of Francisco M. (1682–*c.* 1752). His work included portraits and still-lifes. Some paintings are in the Escorial and there is a self-portrait in the Louvre.

Meléndez Valdés Juan (1754–1817). Spanish poet. M. V. took the French side in the Napoleonic Wars and ended his life in exile in France. His lyrical verse, although it now seems somewhat vapid and monotonous, served to renovate and introduce a new sensibility into exhausted forms.

Méliès Georges (1861–1938). French film director. M. directed a Paris theatre where he performed as a magician. In 1896, only a year after the 1st *Lumière show, he started filming his tricks and by 1898 was beginning to use manipulation of film in the camera as part of his technique. His trick films developed into story films which also involved trick effects, and he built a studio for making elaborate films like *Le Voyage dans la lune* (1902) and *Le Voyage à travers l'Impossible* (1904). The stories included not only fantasies but potted history (*Cléopâtre*, 1899), literature (*Hamlet*, 1908) and religion (*Le Christ marchant sur les eaux*, 1899). He even shot newsreels of events reconstructed in his studio, e.g. the coronation of Edward VII (1902). He made films until 1913, turning out a total of 430.

melisma (plural, melismata). Musical term for a phrase of many notes set to one vowel, common in plainsong and medieval vocal music, as well as in arias and songs of later times.

Melissus Paul, originally Paul Schede (1539–1602). German humanist scholar, poet (in Latin) and writer of German Psalms.

Melo Francisco Manuel de (1608–66). Portuguese poet and prose writer, soldier and diplomat; imprisoned (1644–55) and exiled to Brazil (1655–9) as the result of an intrigue. He wrote in Spanish and (with more originality) Portuguese, poems, histories, over 500 letters, and the comedy *O Fidalgo Aprendiz.*

melodrama. Originally a stage form in which the actors spoke their words against, or in alternation with, a musical accompaniment. Rousseau's *Pygmalion* (1762) was a precursor and G. Benda's *Ariadne* (1775) the 1st true example. In the 19th c. it came to mean dramas which aimed to create a horrific atmosphere and often dealt with crime, e.g. *Maria Marten or Murder in the Red Barn* (1830), *Sweeney Todd; the Demon Barber* (1847) and *The Bells* (1871), in which Irving used to freeze his audience.

Melozzo da Forli (1438–94). Italian painter who worked in Rome from 1476. Work includes frescoes and commissions for the Papacy; much other work is dubiously attributed to him.

Melville Herman (1819–91). U.S. novelist, born in New York City. After 2 years as a clerk he signed on as seaman to a Liverpool-bound vessel; from 1839 to 1841 he was a

Melozzo da Forli. *Platina appointed Vatican Librarian*

Meissonier. *The Barricade*

Georges Méliès. The shooting of *Le Voyage dans la lune*

Dame Nellie Melba

Herman Melville

J.-P. Melville. Jean-Paul Belmondo in *Le Doulos*

teacher but then again went to sea, this time on the whaler *Acushnet* to the South Seas. In 1842 he deserted, living with the cannibal Taipis for a time before returning to the U.S. in 1844. *Typee* (1846) is partly autobiographical, partly worked up from travel books and partly a profound excursion into his inner life; *Omoo*, roughly a sequel, appeared in 1847, the year he married and settled in New York. The following years are a story of failure to find work, until in 1866 he was appointed district inspector of customs in New York, and the production of a major body of literature. After travel in Europe in 1850 he lived in Pittsfield, not far from Hawthorne; their intimacy, recorded in articles and letters, is an important turning-point in U.S. literature. M. toured Europe and Palestine in 1856–7 and then sailed in his brother's ship to San Francisco in 1860. Lecturing afforded him a small livelihood and he died almost unnoted and remained so until the 1930s.

M.'s masterpiece is *Moby Dick* (1851). This densely packed narrative recounts the *Pequod*'s whaling voyage from Nantucket to the Pacific in search of whales for money, and the white whale, Moby Dick, to satisfy Captain Ahab's heroic obsession. This great book illustrates to the full M.'s power for organization of recurring symbols; it operates at levels of realistic documentation, tragedy and parable. M.'s works include: *Redburn* (1849) and *White-jacket* (1850), voyage novels showing his growing interest in the ship as a community containing important disciplinary and personal relations between leaders and led; *Pierre* (1852), an extraordinary fable of a young man torn by emotional involvements which drive him to suicide. *Israel Potter* (1855), an historical burlesque, and the *Piazza Tales* (1856), which include the 2 stories *Bartleby* and *Benito Cereno*, were followed by *The Confidence Man* (1857), a brilliant satire on American optimism. *Billy Budd*, his last fiction, a study of leadership, innocence and evil during the British naval mutinies of 1797, did not appear until 1924.

Memlinc. *Madonna and the two SS John*

Melville Jean-Pierre (1917–). French film writer-director-producer. M.'s work antecedes the French *nouvelle vague. The flexible methods of shooting adopted in *Le Silence de la Mer* (1947–8) and its cameraman (Henri Decaë) were adopted 10 years later by *Chabrol and *Truffaut. Its narrative style influenced *Bresson. If his Cocteau adaptation *Les Enfants Terribles* (1949) was more Cocteau than M., he made 2 very personal films in *Bob le Flambeur* (1956) and *Deux hommes dans Manhattan* (1959).

Melzi Francesco (1493–*c.* 1570). Italian painter, pupil and friend of Leonardo da Vinci, working with him in Rome, Bologna and, in 1515, in France. His style is very close to that of his master, e.g. *Portrait of a Young Woman* (Hermitage).

Member of the Wedding, The (1946). Novel by Carson *McCullers.

Memlinc or **Memling** Hans (*c.* 1433–94). Painter, born at Seligenstadt near Frankfurt-am-Main but trained in the early Netherlands tradition, probably by Rogier van der Weyden. M. worked in Bruges, where he became a leading citizen. His talent, unoriginal but otherwise of a high order, is contrasted unfavourably at present with that of D. Bouts and Rogier van der Weyden, from whom he frequently borrows. This may be in retribution for his over-valuation in the 19th c. M.'s painting shows little development and he repeats himself, e.g. in the composition of *The Mystical Marriage of St Catherine* (Hôpital St Jean, Bruges) and the triptych painted for Sir John Donne of Kidwelly (N.G., London). His portraits combine extreme sensibility with a serene self-confidence, e.g. *Tommaso Portinari* and *Maria, Wife of Tommaso Portinari* (both Met. Mus.). Other important examples of his paintings are: *The Passion of Christ* (Sabauda Gal., Turin), *The 7 Joys of the Virgin* (Alte Pina., Munich), the panels of *The Shrine of St Ursula* (Hôpital St Jean, Bruges) depicting the St Ursula legend, *Adoration of the Magi* (Prado) and the diptych *Descent from the Cross* and *Holy Women and St John* (Capilla Real, Granada).

Memmi Lippo (documented 1317–47). Sienese painter, the pupil and brother-in-law of Simone *Martini. His signature appears with Simone's on the *Annunciation* (Uffizi) and the Saints on each side are attributed to him. He painted frescoes at S. Gimignano and designed the graceful bell-tower of the Torre del Mangia, Siena. One of his finest pictures is *Madonna and Child* (Pina., Siena).

Mémoires d'outre-tombe (1849–50). Autobiography of *Chateaubriand.

Memlinc. *The Shrine of St Ursula*

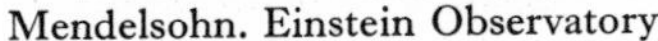

Mendelsohn. Einstein Observatory

Mendelsohn. De la Warr Pavilion, Bexhill

Memoirs of a Fox-Hunting Man (1928) and **Memoirs of an Infantry Officer** (1930). Autobiographical books by Siegfried *Sassoon.

Mena Juan de (1411–56). Spanish poet. His most famous work is a long allegorical poem, *El laberinto de Fortuna*, also known as *Las tres cientas* on account of its 300 stanzas. An imitation of Dante, it contains episodes inspired by Ovid, Virgil and Lucan, and is written in latinized and rather pedantic language.

Menander (342–291 B.C.). The most distinguished practitioner of the *new comedy at Athens. He wrote more than 100 plays, the earliest in 324, and enjoyed a long posth. popularity. He is one of the most quoted of ancient authors (e.g. 'Evil communications corrupt good manners' 1 Cor. xv. 33, one of only 2 pagan quotations in St Paul) and provided most of the plots for the Roman theatre. Until the papyrus finds in Egypt at the turn of this c. his work was unknown apart from quotations and Latin adaptations; but 4 plays were recovered in a sufficient state of completeness to allow reconstruction of their plots. In 1958 a complete play, the *Duskolos*, was discovered and publ. M.'s plays are the earliest examples of social comedy: his plots owe much to the romantic tragedies of Euripides (recognition scenes are a common feature) and the characters, more or less stereotyped, are drawn from contemporary life. A very few of the farcical elements of the *old comedy persist.

Ménard Louis (1822–1901). French poet, one of the *Parnassians. M.'s pagan outlook, derived from classical antiquity, e.g. *Rêveries d'un paiën mystique* (1876), influenced Leconte de Lisle and Barrès.

Mencken H(enry) L(ouis) (1880–1956). U.S. newspaperman, ed., commentator. After newspaper experience in Baltimore he worked on *The Smart Set*, then ed. *The American Mercury* (1924–33), which attacked American Puritan culture with vigorous comic polemic. His ideas, influenced by Shaw and Nietzsche, had a strong aristocratic element which gradually lost him his many followers. His writings were coll. in many vols, including *A Book of Burlesques* (1916), *Damn! a Book of Calumny* (1918) and the 6 series of *Prejudices* (1919–27). In 1919 appeared his most substantial work, *The American Language*, a scholarly and infinitely entertaining examination of American English, enlivened by his attacks on English language-proprietors and American schoolmarms.

Mendelsohn Erich (1887–1953). German architect influenced by the expressionist movement; his Einstein Observatory, Potsdam (1920) is the most famous expressionist building; he also designed office buildings and some magnificent department stores for Schocken. He came to England in 1933 and practised with S. Chermayeff; their work includes the De le Warr Pavilion at Bexhill and a house in Old Church Street, Chelsea. In the late 1930s he practised in Palestine before settling in San Francisco, where he built the Maimonides Hospital and designed several synagogues for other U.S. cities.

Mendelssohn (-Bartholdy) Felix (Jakob Ludwig) (1809–47). German composer, the grandson of Moses M. and the son of a wealthy banker who had taken the additional name of Bartholdy on adopting Lutheran Christianity; M. showed precocious talents for composition and conducting. As the pupil of C. F. Zelter M. gained acquaintance with J. S. Bach's music and also met Goethe and Weber. A dazzling career began with a public performance of his works in 1822; in 1829 he conducted the 1st performance of *Bach's *St Matthew Passion* since the master's death; in 1829 also he made his 1st visit to England and toured Scotland. In 1835 he became director of the Gewandhaus concerts at Leipzig, which he made a major centre and where, in 1843, he founded the Conservatory. M.'s music is conveniently classed as classical-romantic, classical in form, romantic in mood; he excels in melodic invention, as in the famous E min. violin concerto and can achieve brilliant as well as delicate orchestral effects. His works include: the oratorios *St Paul* (1836) and *Elijah* (1846) and the symphony-cantata *Hymn of Praise* (1840); the symphonies, no. 3 in A min. the *Scottish* (1842), no. 4 in A the *Italian* (1833), no. 5 in D, the *Reformation* (1830; later revised); the overtures *A Midsummer Night's Dream* (1826), the *Hebrides* also called *Fingal's Cave* (1830; revised 1832) and *Ruy Blas*; piano concertos in G min. (1831) and D min. (1837); violin concertos in E min. (1844) and D min. (1822); much excellent chamber music and piano music, e.g. *Lieder ohne Worte*, i.e. *Songs Without Words* (1829–45).

Felix Mendelssohn

H. L. Mencken

Mengs. *Self-portrait*

Mengs. *Jupiter and Ganymede*

Mendelssohn Moses (1729–86). German writer and philosopher of the Enlightenment, close friend of *Lessing and founder contributor to his *Literaturbriefe*. His most important works were the Platonic dialogue *Phädon* (1767; *Phaedon*, 1789), on the immortality of the soul, and *Jerusalem* (1783; 1838) for the emancipation of German Jews. M. was grandfather of the composer Felix M.

Mendès Catulle (1841–1909). French poet, playwright, novelist and critic, one of the *Parnassians and founder of the *Revue fantaisiste* (1861).

Menéndez Pidal Ramón (1869–). Spanish literary historian and philologist famous for his critical ed. of *El Cid* and other medieval epic texts, and for his research into early Spanish lyric poetry.

Menéndez y Pelayo Marcelino (1856–1912). Spanish scholar, literary critic and historian. In a series of essays, *Ciencia española* (1876), M. upheld Spanish traditions against the onslaughts of reformers. His histories of Spanish literature established him as a leading Spanish scholar and outstanding prose writer.

ménestrel: *minstrel

Mengelberg Willem (1871–1951). Dutch conductor of the Concertgebouw Orchestra of Amsterdam (1895–1945) and responsible for its world reputation. He advocated the music of such composers as Diepenbrock, Wagenaar and Dopper but was renowned as a Strauss and Mahler interpreter.

Mengs Anton Raphael (1728–79). German painter and writer on art. Most of his life M. worked in Rome or as court painter in Spain. First influenced by Correggio, he belonged to the neo-classicist circle of Winckelmann and became the most famous of the early neo-classical painters. M. was much sought after as a painter of religious and historical compositions and as a portrait painter. A characteristic example of his later, dry and colourless manner is the ceiling painting the *Parnassus*, for the Villa Albani, Rome.

Meninas, Las (1656). Intimate portrait group by Velazquez; the picture was the subject of a series of 44 variations painted (1957) by Picasso.

Menjou Adolphe (1890–1963). U.S. film actor. Although typed in suave man-of-the-world roles, his talent was considerable, e.g. *A Woman of Paris*, *Paths of Glory*.

Men of Good Will (1932–47). A series of 27 novels by Jules *Romains.

Menotti Gian Carlo (1911–). Italian opera composer, librettist and stage director, working in the U.S. from 1928. M. writes his own librettos, and his stagecraft is outstanding; his opera music, modern in setting yet reminiscent of Verdi and Puccini, has several brief yet pregnant melodies which characterize the mood of the scene. His operas include: *The Medium* (1946; film 1951), *The Telephone* (1947), *The Consul* (1950), *The Saint of Bleecker Street* (1954). He has also written instrumental music, including 4 pieces for string quartet, and a symphonic poem, *Apocalypse* (1951).

Menschen am Sonntag (1929). Film directed by R. *Siodmak.

Menteur, Le (1643). Comedy by Corneille.

Menuhin Hephzibah (1920–). American pianist. She married in 1938, retiring for a time from the concert platform. She has given concerts since, chiefly accompanying her brother Yehudi at music festivals.

Menuhin Yehudi (1916–). American violinist. An infant prodigy, he made his début at the age of 7 and has since gained world-wide renown. He has instituted music festivals at Bath and Gstaad (Switzerland) and has founded a school for gifted child musicians in London. He has introduced Schumann's 'lost' concerto, Mendelssohn's D minor and Mozart's 'Adelaide' concertos to the concert repertory.

Menzel Adolf von (1815–1905). German painter of historical and military subjects, chiefly known for paintings of scenes in the life of Frederick the Great, in particular the military campaigns. M. also glorified the achievements of Bismarck and William I.

Mephisto (i.e. Mephistopheles) **Waltzes.** The name given by Liszt to 3 works; nos 1 and 2 for orchestra or piano, and no. 3 for piano.

Merbecke (Marbeck) John (1510?–*c.* 1585). English composer and scholar whose musical

Las Meninas

Menzel. *Day of Judgement*. Also *Joachim

Yehudi Menuhin

settings *Booke of Common Praier Noted* (1550) met the need created by the establishment of the English liturgy by the Act of Uniformity of 1549. M. also publ. in 1550 the 1st English concordance of the Bible.

Mercadante Giuseppe Saverio Raffaele (1795–1870). Italian opera composer and director of the Naples Conservatory. In his operas subsequent to *Il Giuramento* (1837) M. consciously attempted to purge Italian opera of triviality and bombast. Liszt praised M. for his serious music and Verdi was influenced by him. Other operas include: *I Briganti* (1836) and *La Vestale* (1840).

Mercantini Luigi (1821–72). Italian poet who composed songs for the volunteers of the Risorgimento. The most famous is his hymn to Garibaldi.

Merchant of Venice, The (before 1600; publ. 1600). Play by *Shakespeare, written *c.* 1596. Its sources may have included the lost plays *The Jew* and *The Jew of Venice* (attributed to Dekker), and Marlowe's *Jew of Malta.*

Mercier Louis-Sébastien (1740–1814). French playwright and critic whose *Nouvelle Essai sur l'art dramatique* (1773) and *De la littérature et les littérateurs* (1778) attacked classical drama and the *unities. His play *Jeunesse* (1768) was based on *Lillo's *History of George Barnwell.*

Mercury Theatre London. Converted from a church hall, the 1st permanent home of ballet in England. It was used for Marie *Rambert's Ballet Club (1931) and remained until 1955 the headquarters of the Ballet Club's successor, the Ballet Rambert.

Meredith George (1828–1909). English novelist and poet, a leading Victorian writer and, after the publ. of *Diana of the Crossways* (1885), dealing with the difficult position of a woman separated from her husband, very popular; but he is now not much read, partly because of his involved and mannered style. M.'s best-known novel, *The Egoist* (1879), is a comedy detailing the marital misfortunes of the proud and selfish Sir Willoughby Patterne. *The Ordeal of Richard Feverel* (1859) describes the unfortunate effects of a father's determination to bring up his son under rigid control. M.'s verse includes the long sequence of poems *Modern Love* (1862).

Meres Francis (1565–1647). English writer, author of *Palladis Tamia, Wits Treasury* (1598), a book of reflections. One chapter is especially valuable for its account of Marlowe's death and a list of 12 plays by Shakespeare.

Merezhkovsky Dmitry Sergeyevich (1865–1941). Russian writer, one of the leaders of the symbolist movement. M. was exiled from Czarist Russia (1906–12) and the Soviet Union (from 1919). His interpretation of history as alternating manifestations of flesh and spirit destined at last to synthesize, was embodied in a trilogy of novels, *Julian the Apostate . . .* (1896; 1901), *Leonardo da Vinci . . .* (1901; 1902) and *Peter and Alexis* (1905; 1905); they had considerable influence on the symbolist poets. M. encouraged and publ. Blok and Bely.

Mérimée Prosper (1803–70). French writer and also, for the major part of his career, Inspector-General of Historical Monuments. A friend of Stendhal and Turgenev, he was a man of wide culture, acquainted with several literatures. He began, with characteristic dry humour, by publ. pseudo-trs, e.g. *Le Théâtre de Clara Gazul* (1825), purporting to be from the Spanish, and *La Guzla* (1827), a supposed coll. of Illyrian songs. *Chronique du règne de Charles IX* (1829; *A Chronicle of the Reign of Charles IX,* 1853) was a typical romantic historical novel. His major contributions to literature were long short stories of which he publ. 4 colls: *Mosaïque* (1823), *Colomba* (1841; *A Story of Corsica,* 1854), *Nouvelles* (1852) and *Dernières nouvelles* (1873). The best-known story, *Carmen,* inspired Bizet's opera. M. was something of a post-romantic dandy, interested in violent, exotic passion, but keeping it well under control.

Mermaid Theatre. London theatre opened in 1959 at Puddle Dock, partly over the river Thames; the culmination of earlier experiments and efforts by the founder, Bernard Miles. It is an open-stage theatre without proscenium arch, footlights or orchestra pit, combining elements from Greek and Elizabethan drama.

Merriman Henry Seton. Pseud of Hugh Stowell Scott (1862–1903). English historical adventure writer, author of *The Slave of the Lamp* (1892), *In Kedar's Tents* (1897) and *Barlasch of the Guard* (1903).

Merry Devill of Edmonton, The (16th c.; publ. 1608). Comedy sometimes attributed to Shakespeare.

Merry Widow, The. Comic opera by Lehár; 1st performance at Vienna in 1905.

Merry Widow, The (1925). Film directed by E. von *Stroheim.

Merry Wives of Windsor, The (before 1602; publ. 1602). Comedy by *Shakespeare, probably written *c.* 1598 and performed at court in 1604. It is said that he wrote this, a new play about Falstaff, at the command of Queen Elizabeth. Otto *Nicolai's opera on the play was first performed at Berlin in 1849. Verdi's opera **Falstaff* is derived from the play.

Merula Tarquinio (d. after 1652). Italian composer important in the development of the trio sonata.

Merulo Claudio (1533–1604). Italian composer; senior organist at St Mark's, Venice (1566–84) and at Parma. He wrote parody masses and madrigals, but more important are his organ works, e.g. *Ricercari da cantare* (1574). His toccatas helped to establish that form and with their ricercar passages presage the prelude and fugue. M.'s *La Tragedia* (1574), to words by C. Frangipane, was a forerunner of opera.

Mesdag Hendrik Wilhelm (1831–1915). Dutch marine painter. At first M. was a banker, but turned to painting in 1866, studying under Alma Tadema in Brussels. He soon became very popular, more for his subject-matter than for his questionable technical standards.

Mesonero Romanos Ramón de (1803–82). One of the leading writers of the Spanish *costumbrista school, producing sketches and articles and short stories dealing with typical scenes and characters in Madrid. He wrote interesting memoirs and influenced Pérez Galdós.

Messager André (1853–1929). French operetta composer, conductor and director of the Paris Opéra and Opéra-Comique where he gave the 1st performance of Debussy's *Pelléas et Mélisande* (1902). M.'s own works,

George Meredith: painting by G. F. Watts

Prosper Mérimée

André Messager

The Mermaid Theatre

Messel. *The Sleeping Beauty*

Mestrovič. *Bust of Bishop Njegoš*

Metaphysical painting. De Chirico, *Melancholy and Mystery of a Street*

Pietro Metastasio. Also *Farinelli

praised by Fauré for their exquisite simplicity and freshness, include *La Basoche* (1890) and *Véronique* (1898).

Messel Oliver (1904–). British theatrical designer; mainly for opera and ballet but also for the legitimate theatre and films. In such productions as *The Sleeping Beauty* (Covent Garden, 1946) he demonstrated a fine choice of colours and taste for the rococo. He has held exhibitions in London and New York.

Messerer Asaf (1912–). Russian dancer of the Leningrad School who graduated to become one of the most brilliant male dancers in Russia. He now teaches at the Bolshoi School, Moscow and his pupils have numbered Ulanova, Struchkova and his niece, Plisetskaya.

Messiaen Olivier (1908–). French composer, and an organist. At the Conservatoire his teachers included Dukas for composition and Dupré for organ; in 1931 M. became a co-founder of the *Young France group and in 1942 he was appointed a professor at the Conservatoire. M.'s early music followed from the work of Debussy and also showed the influence of the Russian school, and of Dukas (*La Péri*), and Scriabin and Franck. M.'s exotic mysticism exceeded even theirs, but there is a naïvety in his music and a sensitivity to every detail which marks his works as among the most outstanding of this c. His later work is based on tonal and rhythmic modes inspired by Indian music and bird music. His pupils number the major figures of the *avant-garde* in Europe, among them Pierre Boulez. M.'s major works include: *Sept Visions de l'Amen* for 2 pianos (1943); the *Turangalîla Symphonie* (1948) using electronic instruments; *Oiseaux exotiques* for piano and orchestra (1956); and *Chronochromie* (1960) for orchestra. His books on music include *Technique de mon langage musical* (1944) and *Traité du Rythme* (1954).

Messiah. Oratorio by *Handel; to words adapted from the Bible by C. Jennens; 1st performance at Dublin, for charity, in 1742. The original version of *M.* was written in just over 3 weeks.

Messias, Der (1748–83). Epic poem by *Klopstock.

Mestrovič Ivan (1883–1961). Yugoslav sculptor. He studied at the Vienna Academy, became a friend of Rodin in Paris (1907–8) and during World War I visited Rome, Geneva and London, rapidly earning a considerable European reputation. Back in Yugoslavia between the wars he worked on several public commissions and taught at Zagreb Academy. From 1947 until his death he lived in the U.S. and held a professorship at Syracuse Univ. Most of his work is carved in stone or wood, apart from the bronze portrait busts, e.g. *Sir Thomas Beecham* (1915; Tate), and remained untouched by the major 20th-c. developments. It is related to A. Maillol in its massive simplicity, e.g. *Torso* (1908; Tate), although always more highly finished, and has a deep affinity with Rodin in its intensely expressive naturalism.

Metamorphoses. Poetic work by *Ovid.

metamorphosis. In music this term is sometimes used to denote a variation form in which the basic material is used to create new themes: well-known examples are Hindemith's *Symphonic Metamorphoses on themes of Weber* (1943) and R. Strauss's *Metamorphosen* for 24 solo strings.

Metamorphosis (1915). Short story by Kafka.

metaphysical painting (Italian *pittura metafisica*). Term used of the work of the Italian painters de *Chirico and *Carrà between about 1910 and 1920. Their use of dream imagery in architectural fantasies and the juxtaposition of incongruous elements foreshadowed certain aspects of surrealism.

metaphysical poetry. Term applied to much English verse of the 17th c., notably that produced by Donne, George Herbert, Vaughan, Carew, Cowley and Marvell; its characteristics are compression; an intellectuality of approach (even in love-poems) which includes frequent use of *conceits; and colloquial language.

Metastasio Pietro (1698–1782). Italian poet and librettist. M. became poet laureate at the Imperial court of Vienna in 1730 and won great popularity with his lyrical and pastoral verse (*canzonette*). His style as a librettist dominated 18th-c. opera and his librettos were set by the leading composers such as Hasse and Scarlatti. Although his compositions depend on music

Olivier Messiaen

Metsu. *The Sick Child*

for their full effect, they reveal M.'s considerable dramatic gifts. He also wrote a number of important critical and theoretical essays on poetry and dramatic art.

Method, The. One of the most misunderstood terms in modern theatre. Its principles are based on the teaching of Stanislavsky and are especially practised in the New York *Actors' Studio; but every good modern actor, consciously or not, works to the Method. It means simply: naturalism achieved by close study of the text, relaxation and improvisation. It arose in reaction against the stylized acting of the 19th c.

metope. Architectural term for the plain (later sculptured) square space between 2 triglyphs on a frieze of the Doric *order.

metre in verse. Metre (from Greek, 'measure') describes the rhythm of a poem according to the number and character of the feet in a line (*foot). Greek and Latin feet are determined by quantity-patterns of syllables with long (–) and short (◡) sounds; English verse is accentual, stressed syllables replacing long syllables, unstressed syllables replacing the short. Important types of feet are:

Iamb ◡ –	Amphibrach ◡ – ◡
Trochee – ◡	Tribrach ◡◡◡
Spondee – –	Molossus – – –
Pyrrhic ◡◡	Amphimacer – ◡ –
Dactyl – ◡◡	Bacchic ◡ – –
Anapaest ◡◡ –	Anti-bacchius – – ◡

Dimeter (2), trimeter (3), tetrameter (4), hexameter (6), etc. refer to the number of feet in the line; the iambic pentameter, i.e. 5 iambs, is the most common in English verse:

◡ – / ◡ – / ◡ – / ◡ – / ◡ –
The curfew tolls the knell of parting day

but (to avoid monotony) the pattern is rarely uniform throughout a poem. Many modern poets, following G. M. *Hopkins, have written verse in which only the number and pattern of stressed syllables is important, or have turned to free verse, which depends mainly on use of rhythm.

metronome. A machine used by composers to establish the speed of their compositions, e.g. M.M.𝅗𝅥 = 60 demands a speed of 60 minims per minute. It consists of a steel beam about 7 ins long, weighted by a lead bob and by an adjustable brass weight. The beam is kept swinging by a clockwork and escapement; the length, and hence speed, of its swing is determined by the placing of the adjustable weight (*line drawing). The m. was invented by D. M. Winkel of Amsterdam but patented by J. N. Mälzel; hence the initials 'M.M.' for '**Mälzel's M.**'.

Metropolis (1926). Film directed by F. *Lang.

Metropolitan Opera House New York. Built in 1883 by an architect, J. Cleaveland Cady, whose boast was that he had never entered a playhouse. Part of the building was gutted by fire in 1892 but it was restored and completed by 1903. The 'Met.', which has a capacity of 4,000, has resident opera and ballet cos.

Metsu Gabriel (1629–67). Dutch painter, probably the pupil of G. Dou, though later influenced by Rembrandt. He worked in Leyden and Amsterdam. His genre studies of middle-class life are painted with great care and unusually genuine feeling for the subject, e.g. *The Sick Child* (Rijksmus., Amsterdam).

Metzinger Jean (1883–1956). French painter of the school of Paris. Born in Nantes, he studied in Paris where he was influenced by neo-impressionism and then by cubism. M. publ. *Du Cubisme* with A. Gleizes in 1912. His contribution to cubism was to use bright colours in flat, 2-dimensional compositions.

Meulen Adam Franz van der (1632–90). Flemish painter of genre and landscape pictures. He was related to Charles Lebrun by marriage and became court painter to Louis XIV.

Meung Jean de: *Le *Roman de la Rose*

Meunier Constantin (1831–1905). Belgian painter and sculptor. After a period of religious then impressionistic paintings, he turned to sculpture, carving figures of labourers in a 'heroic' manner. There is a Meunier Mus. in Brussels.

Meyer Conrad Ferdinand (1825–98). Swiss writer born in Zürich, but educated in Lausanne and influenced by French culture: the return to German was completed by the

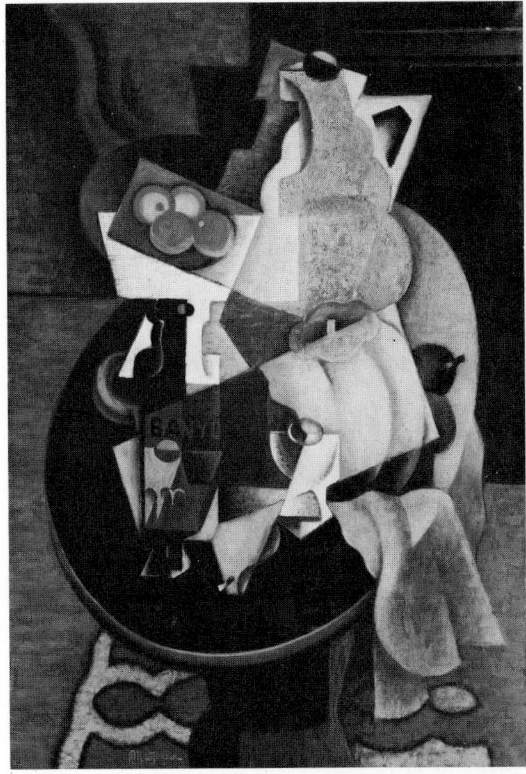

Metzinger. *Still-life*

Meunier. *The Docker*

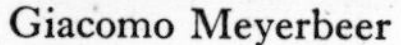

Giacomo Meyerbeer

Vsevolod Meyerhold

Michelangelo. *Creation of Adam* (detail; Sistine Chapel)

Franco-Prussian War. He had mental breakdowns in 1852 and 1892. A poetic (i.e. symbolic) realist who finds his material in historical, not geographical regions: the past, especially the Renaissance, masks his own feelings in the novel *Jürg Jenatsch* (1874) and a series of successful *Novellen*, including *Der Schuss von der Kanzel* (1877); *Der Heilige* (1879; 1885), the story of Thomas à Becket; *Die Hochzeit des Mönchs* (1884; 1887); and *Die Versuchung des Pescara* (1887; *The Tempting of Pescara*, 1890). Nowadays, however, many prefer his poems, e.g. *Zwanzig Balladen* (1864); *Romanzen und Bilder* (1870); *Gedichte* (1882). Most are 'object-poems' (*Rilke): things or scenes are observed from nature, expressing M.'s preoccupations, e.g. with transience and death, in a symbolic mode, and using repeatedly certain fixed motifs.

Meyer Felix (1653–1713). Swiss painter and engraver noted for his rapidity of execution, mainly of Swiss landscapes and pastoral scenes.

Meyer Jean (1914–). French actor and director who has worked both in theatre and cinema and has also devoted much of his time to the teaching of his art.

Meyer-Amden Otto (1885–1933). Swiss painter and lithographer who studied under Hoelzel in Stuttgart from 1909 to 1912. He formed a circle of artists, some of whom (Baumeister and Pellegrini) were of more importance than himself.

Meyerbeer Giacomo, properly Jakob Liebmann Beer (1794–1864). German pianist and composer. He started his career as a pianist, making his début at the age of 7. He subsequently studied theory and composition under C. F. Zelter, A. Weber and Abbé Vogler, giving concerts intermittently. His first 2 operas, *Jepthas Gelübde* (1812) and *Wirth und Gast* (1813), later known as *Alimelek*, were failures. Acting on Salieri's advice, M. went in 1815 to study in Venice and subsequently produced Italian operas with great success. In 1826 *Il Crociato* was performed in Paris, where M. settled. From 1842 he spent a good deal of time in Berlin as general music director to the king of Prussia, chiefly conducting and producing operas. He is best known for his sensationally successful operas *Robert le Diable* (Paris, 1831), produced in collaboration with the librettist Scribe and notable for its grand romantic manner and theatrical effectiveness, and *Les Huguenots* (Paris, 1836), remarkable for its vigour and dramatic force. He is noted for his eclecticism in relinquishing the German idiom while employing the Italian and French conventions. His other works include the operas *Le Prophète* (1849) and *L'Africaine* (1865), choral works, songs, instrumental music.

Meyerhold Vsevolod (1874–1942). Soviet actor and director and instigator of the method of production known as *bio-mechanics. He worked at the Moscow Art Theatre, then on his own in a variety of theatres, putting his theories into practice. As his work grew more experimental and revolutionary, almost denying the human element in any art, he fell into disfavour and in 1938 his own state-subsidized theatre was disbanded, leaving M. unable to continue his experiments.

mezzanine. Architectural term for a low storey between 2 higher ones.

mezzotint. A form of *engraving.

Miaskovsky Nikolay Yakovlevich (1881–1950). Soviet composer. After military service (1914–21) M. taught at Moscow Conservatory where his pupils included Khachaturian. M.'s major work is in his 27 symphonies (1908–49); these reveal the development of a style deriving from Tchaikovsky and Rimsky-Korsakov into a personal idiom drawing on folk-song. M.'s formal clarity, individual and imaginative use of tonality, sensitivity of expression, often nostalgic, have made him highly regarded in Russia. Prokofiev, in particular, acknowledges a deep debt to him.

Micah. One of the minor prophetic books of the *Bible (Old Testament).

Michaux Henri (1899–). Belgian poet and prose writer; also a painter and graphic artist producing strange and frightening forms (he often works under the influence of drugs). M.'s writing is vigorous and colloquial, full of sonorous neologisms, sometimes lyrical or humorous but characteristically Kafkaesque in intensity and vision (e.g. the stories about 'Plume', always attempting to adapt yet always accused). Works include *Un Barbare en Asie* (1922; *A Barbarian in Asia*, 1949).

Michel Georges (1763–1843). French landscape painter, the pupil of Taunay; he became known as 'the Ruisdael of Montmartre' and most of his subjects were scenes in and around Paris. M. was a forerunner of the Barbizon school.

Michelangelo Buonarroti (1475–1546). Florentine sculptor, painter, poet and architect. M. was born at Caprese where his father was the chief Florentine official. He was trained in Florence, first in the technique of fresco painting by D. Ghirlandaio; then under the patronage of Lorenzo the Magnificent, in the Medici School. Here he became a sculptor. Here too, his mind was formed by the companionship of the neo-Platonic philosophers, artists, poets and men of letters Lorenzo had drawn to his household. M.'s own genius was recognized and encouraged from the beginning. After the death of his patron he went to Bologna and then to Rome, where, at 23, he began the *Pietà* of St Peter's. On his return to Florence M. carved the large marble *David* (Accademia, Florence) for the city. Among other works of this period are the *Bruges Madonna* (Notre-Dame cathedral, Bruges), the painting *Holy Family*, or *Doni Tondo* (Uffizi) and the large cartoon or design for a fresco, *The Battle of Cascina*, done in competition with Leonardo da Vinci. This important work was destroyed, but not before the studies of the nude in violent action had influenced many artists in a way that led ultimately to *mannerism. In 1505 M. was recalled to Rome by Pope Julius II and ordered to design and execute the tomb which would glorify the Pope after death. Only 1 of the 40 large figures originally envisaged was ever completed, *Moses* (S. Pietro in Vincoli, Rome). 2 unfinished but wonderfully realized figures of captives or slaves are in the Louvre. M. quarrelled with the Pope and fled from Rome; he was later reconciled with him and returned in 1508, not to complete the tomb, but to decorate the whole of the ceiling of the Sistine Chapel in the Vatican with frescoes. This enormous undertaking took him over 4 years, working virtually single-handed. His attempt to return to sculpture and the Julian Tomb was again frustrated by the successor of Julius II, the Medici pope Leo X, who ordered him to provide a façade for the unfinished church of S. Lorenzo, Florence. Although this project was abandoned in 1520, M. remained in Florence working for the Medici, chiefly on

Michelangelo. Drawing for Adam

the chapel which was to contain the family tombs, the Medici chapel, and the Laurentian library, both attached to S. Lorenzo. The city rose against the Medici in 1527 and M. was divided between his loyalty to his patrons and his Republican sympathies. He took an active part in the defence of Florence as engineer in charge of fortifications, but when the Medici recaptured the town, M. was forgiven. He returned to his work in the Medici chapel, completing the tombs of Giuliano and Lorenzo de' Medici, with the symbolic figures *Day* and *Night*, *Dawn* and *Evening*, before he was again recalled to Rome in 1534 to paint his 2nd great fresco, the *Last Judgement*, which covers the whole area of the altar wall of the Sistine Chapel. In Rome, where he stayed until his death, he met Vittoria Colonna, a chief influence on his later years. 2 further frescoes, *Conversion of St Paul* and *Crucifixion of St Peter* (Cappella Paolina, Vatican) were painted (1542–50). The tomb of Julius II, much reduced in scale, was completed at S. Pietro in Vincoli (1545). In 1546 M. was appointed architect-in-chief of St. Peter's and architect for the new plan and building of the Roman Capitol. Despite all this, designing the dome of St Peter's, supervising the actual building of the church and work on other architectural projects, M. executed 3 of his most profoundly imagined sculptures at this time, *Pietà* (Duomo, Florence), the *Palestrina Pietà* (Accademia, Florence) and the *Rondanini Pietà* (Castello, Milan). Many of his finest sonnets were also written in these last years.

Probably no artist has ever exerted a greater influence than M. To his contemporaries he was 'The Divine M.', and though the greatness of the man was apparent and recognized, the creative power within him inspired an awe in wordly popes, scholars and soldiers, so that they spoke of his '*terribilità*'. His friend *Vasari made the achievement of M. the culmination of that gathering splendour in the arts that had begun with Giotto. For over 300 years the frescoes of the Sistine Chapel have been studied by painters, their patrons and all who judged the art of their own times. ('Until you have seen the Sistine Chapel, you can have no adequate conception of what man is capable of accomplishing', Goethe wrote). M.'s influence as a poet might have been equally great if his sonnets had not had to wait until 1863 before they were publ. in their original form. The mutilated and bowdlerized version publ. in 1623 by M.'s great-nephew

Michelangelo. *Last Judgement* (detail). Also *Maderno, *mannerism and colour plates 46, 47

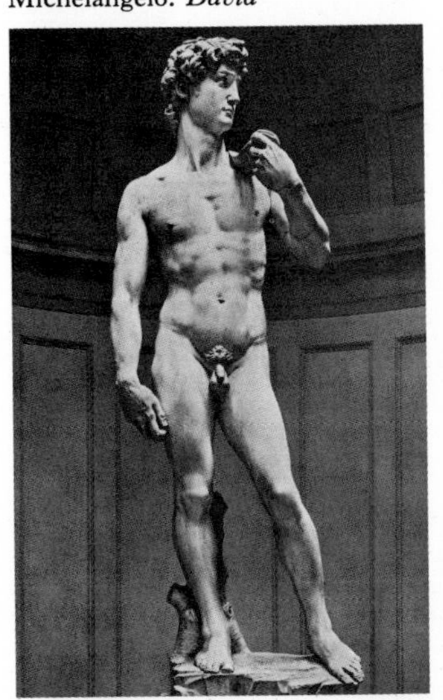

Michelangelo. *David*

Michelangelo. *Moses*

Michelangelo. *Pietà* of St Peter's

Michelangelo. The Medici Tomb: the figures *Day* and *Night* below the statue of Giuliano de' Medici

Adam Mickiewicz

Miereveld.
Old Lady with a Ruff

Michelozzo.
Palazzo Medici-Riccardi

had little value and aroused interest chiefly as a curiosity. It is often difficult to grasp the total meaning of the sonnets but M.'s genius is as clear in such sonnets as *Giunto è già 'l corso della vita mia* (title given by J. A. Symonds, *On the Brink of Death*) as it is in those last *Pietàs* in which the struggle in search of meaning almost destroys meaning.

Michelet Jules (1798–1874). French historian whose books, romantic narratives of considerable literary stature, include *L'Histoire de France* (1833–67; trs. from 1844) and *La Révolution Française* (1847–53; trs. from 1847).

Michelozzo Michelozzo (1396–1472). Italian architect who worked in Florence; one of the 1st generation of Renaissance architects. His chief work is the Palazzo Medici-Riccardi (1430); it is basically traditionally medieval (big rusticated blocks, no columns or pilasters) but has a cornice instead of machicolation, and some classical details.

Mickiewicz Adam (1798–1855). Polish romantic poet and dramatist, and ardent nationalist; he was born in Lithuanian Poland. He was educated at the Univ. of Vilna, but in October 1824 was exiled to Russia. There he enjoyed brilliant social and literary successes and met Pushkin and the Decembrists. He left Russia in 1829 and after an unsuccessful attempt to join the Polish Revolutionary movement of 1831, lived in exile. M.'s series of lyrical ballads, *Ballady i romanse* (1822), ushered in the Polish romantic period. In his epic tales in verse, *Grazyna* (1823; 1851) and *Konrad Wallenrod* (1828; 1841), he portrayed the struggle of the medieval Lithuanians with the Teutonic knights. His poetical drama *Dziady* mingles in parts II and IV (1823) folklore and passionate love motifs; part III (1832; *Forefathers Eve*, 1926) portrays with cruel realism the sufferings of the Polish nation. His cycle *Sonety krymskie* (1826) contains the finest sonnets in Polish and is a bold exercise in exotic vocabulary. In his *Ksiegi narodu polskiego i pielgrzymstwa polskiego* (1832; *The . . . Polish Nation and . . . Pilgrimage*, 1925) he gave a Messianic interpretation of Polish history. His masterpiece, the epic poem *Pan Tadeusz* (1834; 1917), describes the traditional life of the Polish gentry at the beginning of the 19th c.

microtones. The division of the 8ve into 12 semitone intervals has been an accepted convention in W. European music but certain 20th-c. European composers, e.g. A. Hába and J. Carrillo, have written compositions using m.s, i.e. quarter-tone, sixth- or eighth-tone intervals.

Middlemarch (1871–2). Novel by George *Eliot.

Middleton Thomas (1580–1627). English playwright, frequently associated with various collaborators, including Dekker, Rowley and Munday. He is notable for his frequent delicacy, his shrewd perception of human weaknesses and his skilful dramatic development of moral conflicts. M. is best known for 2 powerful tragedies of intrigue, *The Changeling* (1622; with Rowley), and *Women beware Women* (1621?), but he also wrote the realistic comedies of city life, *A Trick to catch the Old-One* (1606?), *A Mad World, my Masters* (1604?), *The Roaring Girle* (1610?) and *A Chast Mayd in Cheape-side* (1613). In 1624 his political satire, *A Game at Chesse*, was banned from the stage and M. summoned before the Privy Council.

Midsummer Night's Dream, A (before 1600; publ. 1600). Comedy by *Shakespeare, written *c.* 1595. *Mendelssohn wrote a famous overture for the play. It has been filmed several times, notably in 1935, directed by M. *Reinhardt.

Miereveld Michiel van (1567–1641). Dutch portrait painter working in Delft and The Hague, and portrait painter to the House of Orange. Charles I tried to attract him to England in 1625. His portraits are frequently small and restrained in style.

Mieris the Elder, Franz van (1635–81). Dutch portrait painter and engraver, born at Leyden, notable for his handling of colour and for his treatment of silks, satins and jewellery. He was reputed to have painted on a gold base.

Mies van der Rohe Ludwig (1886–). German-born architect, one of the great masters of modern architecture. He worked largely in Germany until 1937 when he emigrated to the U.S. to escape Nazism.
He had no architectural training, but gained understanding of construction as a stonemason's apprentice, and later as assistant to Behrens he learnt the potential of industry and the formal language of the Schinkel school architects. An early commission took him to Holland, where he encountered Berlage's work, and from him learnt that structure is the mainspring of architectural form.
After World War I, M. produced projects for skyscrapers which postulated 'skin-and-bones' architecture, and were entirely clad in glass. As vice-president of the Deutscher Werkbund (1926–7) he directed the Weissenhof Housing Exhibition in Stuttgart where all the leaders of modern architecture collaborated.
His Barcelona Pavilion (1929) and Tugendhat House (1930) reveal his full mastery. In their open plans all is luxurious perfection, with superb materials and workmanship and the most beautiful 20th-c. furniture. His last significant European work was a series of designs for 'court houses', single-storey houses with rooms facing on to internal gardens; the concept did not catch on until the 1960s, and none have yet been built with the verve of his designs.
In 1938 he was made head of the architecture school at Illinois Institute of Technology (I.I.T.) in Chicago, and architect for its new campus. American technology and the Chicago school were absorbed, and by the end of the war the first I.I.T. buildings were finished and the direction of the American M. was established–clear regular structure of steel painted black, infill of brick and glass, fine proportions and the utmost simplicity–the phrase 'less is more' is attributed to him. He has tried in his American work to make function universal, for the use of a building is always changing; so to give architectural expression to rooms or functions is meaningless: only the structure and the quality of the architecture last the life of the building. M. divides buildings into 2 main types–those which are one 'great space' and those which are 'repeated units'.
Of the 'great-space' buildings, the Farnsworth House at Plano, Illinois (1950) is a pavilion of steel and glass, the most elegant building ever built in America. The architecture school at I.I.T. (1952) is a single room; the great beams which roof this 120 ft × 220 ft room are revealed externally, an exemplar to the students within of M.'s strong, almost religious belief in structure. Later designs for 'great-space' buildings include the museum of 20th-c. art to be built in Berlin, a single vast room, entirely glazed, the roof supported by 8 great columns.

Mignard.
Marquise de Seignelay as Thetis

M.'s 'repeated-unit' buildings have been skyscrapers for speculators, and all except Seagram were built to low budgets–repetition, logical use of materials and the sense of quality produced buildings which are successful in a tough competitive market. 860 Lakeshore Drive, Chicago (1957) is the most powerful visually, and it popularized the idea of the mass-produced curtain wall; most curtain walls look slick, but at 860 there is a strong expression of structure, and the mullions are so deep that façades seen obliquely look solid. M. and Johnson's Seagram Building, New York (1958) is a refined version in bronze, but as in all the later M. towers, service ducts force the structure back from the surface of the building and the structural clarity is lost.

Mighty Handful, The. The group of Russian musicians, also known as 'The Five', formed by M. L. Balakirev, including Mussorgsky, Borodin, Rimsky-Korsakov and Cui, who, by letters to newspapers, articles, etc., organized a campaign to create a nationalist school of music, employing folk-music and using specifically Russian subject-matter. *Glinka had already made a beginning in that direction.

Mignard Pierre (1612–95). French painter. He studied under Boucher and then went to Rome where he became popular, producing Madonnas, called 'Mignardes'. He returned to France and from 1658 onwards began painting court portraits, including that of Cardinal Mazarin. After long and uneasy rivalry he succeeded Lebrun as first court painter in 1690.

Mignone Francisco (1897–). Brazilian composer and conductor; his music, although influenced by study in Italy (1920–9), is based on Brazilian material and includes operas, e.g. *O Contratador dos Diamantes* (1924); *Fantasias Brasileiras* for piano and orchestra, and 7 *Quadros Amazónicos* for chamber orchestra (1949).

Migot Georges (1891–). French composer whose highly original style owes less to modern masters than to the inspiration of the *polyphonic era. Apart from the orchestral work *La Paravent de laque aux cinq images*, his best music is in chamber works and vocal works such as the oratorios *Le Sermon sur la montagne* (1936), *La Passion* (1942) and *St Germain d'Huxesse* (1947).

Mies van der Rohe.
Project for a glass skyscraper (1920–1)

Mies van der Rohe. German Pavilion at the International Exhibition (Barcelona, 1929)

Ludwig Mies van der Rohe

Mies van der Rohe. Farnsworth House

Mies van der Rohe. 860 Lakeshore Drive. Also *Bauhaus and colour plate 78

Darius Milhaud

John Stuart Mill

Milestone. Lew Ayres (foreground) in *All Quiet on the Western Front*

Milan cathedral

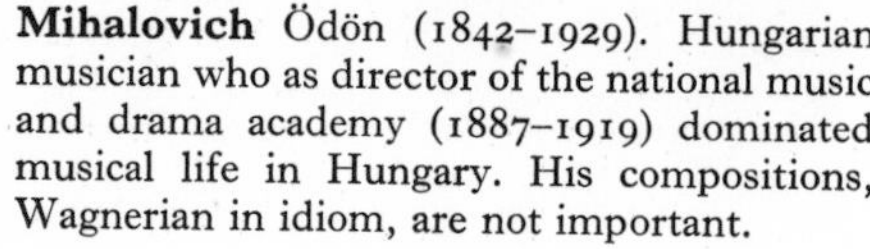

Mihalovich Ödön (1842–1929). Hungarian musician who as director of the national music and drama academy (1887–1919) dominated musical life in Hungary. His compositions, Wagnerian in idiom, are not important.

Mihalovici Marcel (1898–). Rumanian-born French composer, a pupil of d'Indy and a member of the school of Paris. His essentially lyrical style has developed through chromaticism to 12-note techniques.

Mikado, The. Operetta by W. S. Gilbert and Sullivan; 1st performance at London in 1885.

Mikszáth Kálmán (1847–1910). Hungarian novelist and short-story writer. A shrewd observer with a strong satirical bent; his humour and charm, his gusto and love of simple people were the outstanding features of his stories, e.g. *A jó palócok* (1882; *The Good People of Palócz*, 1893). His novels include *Szent Péter esernyöje* (1895; *St Peter's Umbrella*, 1900).

Milán Luis (*c.* 1500–after 1561). Spanish courtier, poet, composer and vihuelista. His *vihuela tutor, *El Maestro* (1535), contains Spanish, Portuguese and Italian songs and fantasies, tientos and pavanes, but also valuable information on expression and performance. M. also publ. *El Cortesano* (1561), similar to B. *Castiglione's *Cortegiano*.

Milan, school of. 15th–16th-c. school of Italian painting brought into prominence by Vincenzo Foppa but subsequently dominated by Leonardo (in Milan 1483–99) and his followers, e.g. Boltraffio and Bernardino Luini.

Milan cathedral Italy. Late Gothic cathedral (begun 1386) the result of years of compromise between architects of different nationalities. (Nearly 50 architects either contributed designs or were consulted: they came from Germany, France, Italy, Bohemia and Poland.) The cathedral, the 2nd largest in Europe, has double aisles and is built entirely of white marble (even the roof), the exterior being covered in a dense forest of pinnacles and statues. Window-tracery is especially flamboyant but the proportions of the whole are squat and do not emphasize verticality. There are only small clerestory windows, so that the interior has the character of a *hall-church and the lighting is dim. The octagonal lantern over the crossing was built in 1500, the open-work spire in 1750 and the W. front not finished until *c.* 1810.

Milestone Lewis (1895–). Ukrainian-born U.S. film director. M. started directing in 1925, and had a great financial and critical success with *All Quiet on the Western Front* (1930). Throughout his career he has often returned to similarly pacificist films: *North Star* (1943), *A Walk in the Sun* (1945), *Halls of Montezuma* (1950) and *Pork Chop Hill* (1959). He has also been praised for a *Hecht/MacArthur comedy, *The Front Page* (1931), a musical, *Hallelujah, I'm a Bum* (1933), and *Of Mice and Men* (1939.)

Milford Robin Humphrey (1903–59). English composer, a pupil of Holst and Vaughan Williams and influenced also by Finzi and English folk-music. His work includes *The Darkling Thrush* for violin and orchestra (1928), the oratorio *A Prophet in the Land* (performed 1931), and much other choral music.

Milhaud Darius (1892–). French composer, a member of The *Six and a teacher at the Conservatoire. M. is an extremely prolific composer; his music, using a polytonal idiom, is best in the small forms; here his subtly varied orchestration and rhythms, his clearly articulated sense of form and varied melodic facility are well used. Indeed, he wrote a series of 5-minute symphonies, and operas. He has an astonishing facility, in particular for complex counterpoint (e.g. 2 string quartets that can be played separately or together) and for word setting (he has set to music a farm-implements catalogue, etc.). His most important works include: the opera *Christophe Colombe* (1930) with libretto by Claudel; the jazz-influenced ballet *La Création du monde* (1923) with book by B. Cendrars and sets by F. Léger; *Suite Provençale* (1936); the dance suite *Saudades de Brasil* (1921) and many chamber, symphonic and choral works.

Military symphony. Nickname for Haydn's symphony no. 100 in G (1794). It is so called because it uses *Janissary music.

Mill John Stuart (1806–73). English economist and political thinker, author of the essays *Utilitarianism* (1863) and *On Liberty* (1859).

Millais Sir John Everett (1829–96). Leading Victorian artist and a founder of the

Edna St Vincent Millay

Arthur Miller

Henry Miller

*Pre-Raphaelite Brotherhood in 1848. His friendship with Ruskin ended with M.'s marriage to Ruskin's former wife. Growing away from Ruskin's ideas and those of the Pre-Raphaelite Brotherhood, he became the greatest academic painter of his day, and was president of the R.A. His youthful work *Christ in the House of His Parents* (1850) caused a scandal by its realistic treatment of the Holy Family.

Milland Ray (1905–). Welsh-born U.S. film actor and director. M. acted in films from 1931 and received an Oscar for his performance in *The Lost Weekend.* He also appeared in *Dial M for Murder* and *The Girl in the Red Velvet Swing*. He started directing with *A Man Alone* (1955) and continued with thrillers like the strange *Lisbon* (1956) and *The Safecracker* (1957). His *Panic in the Year Zero* (1962) is about the psychological effects of nuclear war.

Millay Edna St Vincent (1892–1950). U.S. poet who early made her reputation, and remained very popular for her simple style and use of traditional forms. She is best known for the 52 sonnets of *Fatal Interview* (1931).

millefiori glass (from Italian, 'a thousand flowers'). A decorative technique producing the effect of simplified flowers embedded in plain glass. Thin rods or canes of coloured glass are fused together in small bundles, either vertically or with a spiral twist. These are then cut through at right angles or slantwise to the direction of the rods. The result can resemble the veining of agate or variegated stars and rosettes. A variation of this technique was practised by the Romans, who fused together pieces of glass mosaic. The Venetians used the same method in the 16th c. but it is most commonly found in English or French Clichy or Baccarat paper-weights of the 19th c.

Miller Arthur (1915–). U.S. playwright whose socially orientated plays express his conviction that tragedy is possible in the modern theatre but that its hero is correctly 'the small man'. *All My Sons* (1947) dramatizes the conflict between the related ethics of patriotism and profit. *Death of a Salesman* (1949), M.'s most famous play, analyses the self-deception which the success myth imposes on the failure: the silk-stocking salesman Willie Loman cannot shake free of the myth even in his suicide. In *A View from the Bridge* (1955), Eddie Carbone, a New York longshoreman, is forced to the bewildered acknowledgement of his passion for his step-daughter and violation thereby of traditional codes of morality. With *The Crucible* (1953) M. turned to 17th-c. New England witch trials in order to comment on the McCarthyite hysteria of the 1950s. *After the Fall* (1964) includes a role allegedly suggested by M.'s wife Marilyn Monroe, the film star; he scripted *The Misfits*, in which she appeared. He has produced a novel, *Focus* (1945), on anti-Semitism.

Miller David (1909–). U.S. film director. M. started as an ed. and graduated to directing features via shorts at M.G.M. His talents, which have always lain in the direction of melodrama, were most exercised in *The Story of Esther Costello* (1957). His *Lonely Are the Brave* (1962) was admired for its apparent concern with the disappearance of the traditional values embodied in the old West.

Miller Henry (Valentine) (1891–). U.S. writer. He has lived in Paris, Greece and California but always individualistically detached from the environment; his books ignore organized society, treating human existence as a sensuous, sexual, and metaphysical whole. His frank, often grotesque physicalities caused most of his books to be banned in England and America until the 1960s; but his rampaging exuberant prose often achieves magnificence. In *Tropic of Cancer* (1934) he cleared himself of expatriate poverty-stricken experiences in Paris. *Black Spring* (1936) is a series of episodes dramatizing the conflict between private vitality and social convention and inertia. *Tropic of Capricorn* (1939) is partly a hilarious account of his early days in New York and partly the story of his engulfment in sexual love. *The Colossus of Maroussi* (1941) describes the reviving impact of Greece on his disillusion, and *The Air-Conditioned Nightmare* (1945) his search for genius and warmth throughout America. M. has written a number of books of philosophical, critical essays, and innumerable occasional pieces and stories, which may be found in, for example, *The Cosmological Eye* (1939) and *Big Sur and the Oranges of Hieronymus Bosch* (1955).

Miller Joaquin, originally Cincinnatus Hiner M. (1839–1913). U.S. poet, journalist, pioneer, prospector, and in Western pose, celebrity in London, where he publ. *Pacific Poems* (1870;

Ray Milland in *The Lost Weekend*

Millefiori glass casket; Alexandria, 1st c. A.D.

Millais. *Christ in the House of His Parents.* Also *Pre-Raphaelites, *Ruskin

Milles. *Europa and the Bull* (bronze; 1924)

John Milton

in the U.S. *Songs of the Sierras*). M.'s galloping rhythms and racy narrative style are shown to effect in the famous *Kit Carson's Ride*.

Miller Patricia (1927–). S. African dancer, one of the young, talented dancers who launched the Sadler's Wells Theatre Ballet. This co. provided the opportunity for untried choreographers such as John *Cranko to mount new and progressive ballets; *Harlequin in April* (1951) being one in which M. created the leading role.

Millet. *The Winnower*. Also *The *Angelus*

Miller Sanderson (1717–80). English architect. He was not a professional, but a rich amateur with a taste for romantic effects. As early as 1744 he was building thatched cottages and castellated ruins. His chief works are Hagley Park, Worcestershire; the Shire Hall, Warwick, and parts of Lacock Abbey, Wilts. He was influential in fostering the *Gothic revival.

Milles Carl (1875–1955). Swedish sculptor. He studied in Paris (1897) and was subsequently very much influenced by the work of Rodin. His work is well represented in fountains and on public buildings in Stockholm, and also in the U.S., where he had a considerable reputation.

Millet Jean-François (1814–75). French painter, etcher and draughtsman. He studied in great poverty in Paris, absorbing the lessons of Flemish painting and of French classicism, above all Poussin. He created his most significant work at *Barbizon after 1848. His best-known work, *The Angelus* (1858–9; Louvre), expresses his sympathy for the peasant's simplicity and devotion in the face of nature. M. reconciled classicism with realism in direct impressions from nature; his work inspired Van Gogh and contemporary social realists.

Robert Mills. Church at Camden, S. Carolina

Million, Le (1931). Film directed by R. *Clair.

Million Dollar Legs (1932). Film directed by E. *Cline.

Millöcker Karl (1842–99). German composer of the operetta *Der Bettelstudent* (*The Beggar Student*, 1882) and about 20 others.

Mill on the Floss (1860). Novel by George *Eliot.

Mills Peter (*c.* 1600–70). English architect. His terrace houses in Great Queen Street are among the earliest to use a formula that was to become standard for 200 years – semi-basement, entrance up steps, main rooms on 1st floor, etc.

Mills Robert (1781–1855). U.S. architect, pupil of Latrobe. He built churches in Philadelphia, Richmond (the interesting octagonal Monumental Church) and Baltimore, and then began to receive important official commissions: the Insane Asylum, Columbia (another octagonal plan); the Washington Memorial, Baltimore (a huge Doric column); and the Treasury, Patent Office and old Post Office Department, Washington – all dignified public buildings with Grecian porticoes.

Milne A(lan) A(lexander) (1882–1956). English writer, author of a series of children's classics including *Winnie-the-Pooh* (1926) and *The House at Pooh Corner* (1928), about the boy Christopher Robin and his bear, Pooh.

Milne David (Bruce) (1882–1953). Canadian painter of landscapes, notably of Ontario, working in an impressionistic style.

Miłosz Czesław (1911–). Polish poet and prose writer. After an early connection with the Awangarda movement, M. has increasingly used traditional verse forms. In 1953 he won the Prix Littéraire Européen for his political novel *Zdobycie władzy* (*The Usurpers*, 1955).

Milton (1804). Prophetic poem by Blake.

Milton John (1563–1647). English composer of madrigals, string fantasies and anthems, by profession a scrivener; father of the poet.

Milton John (1608–74). English poet and prose writer, the son of a prosperous Puritan scrivener. M. was born in London and brought up in an atmosphere of piety and culture. He was educated at home by a tutor, then at St Paul's School and Christ's College, Cambridge; he showed a precocious love of learning, and the poem *At a Vacation Exercise*, written when he was 19, reveals his lofty literary aims. M. abandoned his intention of taking holy orders because he disliked Laud's church policy; instead he continued his education at home in Horton, Buckinghamshire (1632–8). He travelled in Italy (1638–9), where he visited Galileo. On his return he became the tutor of

Blue Mosque and minarets, Istanbul

Spiral minaret by the Great Mosque at Samarra, Iraq

his nephews. In 1641 he was drawn into the pamphlet war, writing in support of the Parliamentary cause, and for 20 years devoted himself to public affairs. He wrote numerous pamphlets attacking the evils of the Established Church, especially prelacy: *The Doctrine and Discipline of Divorce* (1643), in part suggested by his marital difficulties; *Areopagitica* (1644), a defence of freedom of the Press, addressed to the Long Parliament and opposing a recent ordinance passed by it; *The Tenure of Kings and Magistrates* (1649), defending the execution of Charles I; and *The Readie and Easie Way to establish a Free Commonwealth* (1660). M.'s tone ranges from bland reasonableness to virulent abuse, his argumentative method from ruthless logic to rhetorical splendour. He advocated a wide measure of personal liberty and invoked the autonomy of the individual conscience against oppression by custom and traditional authority. In 1649 M. became Secretary for Foreign Tongues to the Council of State; his sight gradually failed but, although he was blind by 1654, he continued to work with assistance (including that of the poet Marvell). On the Restoration he was arrested and fined. The rest of his life was spent in retirement writing his later masterpieces.

M.'s earlier poetry revealed great lyrical gifts and complete technical mastery. In 1629 he composed the great ode *On The Morning of Christ's Nativity*. *L'Allegro* and *Il Penseroso* (1632) are urbane companion portraits of the cheerful and the reflective temperaments; but the masque *Comus*, written for performance at Ludlow Castle (1634), in some respects anticipates the high themes of his later work. The Lady's successful resistance to the god of licence symbolizes the Puritan struggle against temptation and the triumph of virtuous moderation over 'sensual folly' and excess. *Lycidas* (1637) is a pastoral lament for Edward King, a college acquaintance drowned in the Irish Sea, in which M. also reflects on his own destiny. Until the Restoration he wrote sonnets which increasingly employ the sombre music of his later work, e.g. *Avenge O Lord thy slaughtered Saints*. *Paradise Lost* (1667) is an epic poem recounting in 10 (later 12) books of sublime power and magnificence the events leading up to the temptation of Eve by Satan, and the Fall of Man. The outstanding parts of the poem include the majestic portrayal of the fallen Satan in books I and II, and the idealized description of the beauties of Eden in book IV. Milton's theology, his latinized diction and syntax, his amplitude and sonority, his deliberate remoteness from everyday life, have been endlessly debated by critics, but the poem remains one of the most unanimously acclaimed works of English literature. *Paradise Regained* (1671), a sequel, tells of Christ successfully withstanding the temptations in the wilderness, thus expiating Adam's original transgression. *Samson Agonistes*, a dramatic poem publ. at the same time, is modelled on Greek tragedy; it traces Samson's recovery of faith after captivity and blindness have made him despair of God's favour, and closes with the news that he has died destroying the Philistines.

mime. (1) Under the Roman empire and into the Dark Ages, a form of dramatic entertainment using words and action and usually performed by strolling players; it was invariably vulgar and obscene, presenting every possible kind of vice. (2) A type of entertainment developed from the *commedia dell'arte* and relying entirely on the ability of the actor to tell a story by using gesture and facial expression alone. It is a difficult and beautiful art, especially popular and brilliantly performed in France by such actors as M. *Marceau and J.-L. *Barrault. (3) The vocabulary of formalized gestures used in romantic ballet as a substitute for words.

minaret. A tower, close to or part of a mosque; it has a gallery from which the muezzin (priest) calls Muslims to prayer.

Ming. The Chinese dynasty (1368–1644) during which Chinese culture, having been under Mongol occupation, was restored, compiled in enormous encyclopaedias, and traditionalized. During its course Chinese painting became stereotyped and sculpture declined. It was a period for the minor arts, except perhaps jade and bronze, of which M. examples are rare. The use of cobalt in pottery glazing, first discovered in the previous dynasty, was taken up and fully developed in the famous *blue-and-white wares; *porcelain was refined to a purity and hardness never since achieved, and, based on the factories of Ching-te-chen (*kaolin), its manufacture became a major industry. The export trade in porcelain was developed from the 16th c. through Portuguese, Spanish and Dutch merchant-adventurers. Decorative glaze and underglaze painted porcelain was a specifically M.

Ming temple-vase with elephant-head handles (1351)

Ming porcelain dish (*c.* 1430)

Ming blue-and-white ewer of the period 1522–66

Ming bowl (1557); the earliest Chinese bowl with an inscription in a European language (Portuguese)

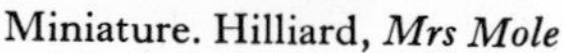

Miniature. Hilliard, *Mrs Mole*

Miniature. Cosway, *Georgiana, Duchess of Devonshire*

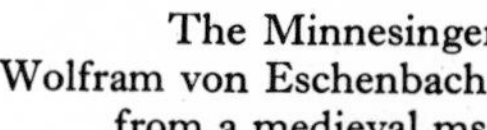

The Minnesinger Wolfram von Eschenbach; from a medieval ms.

Minnelli. Cyd Charisse and Kirk Douglas in *Two Weeks in Another Town*

Mino da Fiesole. *Niccolò Strozzi*

technique. This and all M. porcelain, and the blanc-de-chine ceramic figures especially from the Wan-li period (1573–1616), became the wonder of Europe and were to stimulate the growth of such now famous wares as Meissen and Wedgwood. Blue was only one of the many new M. glaze colours, used either in monochrome or polychrome; perhaps the most well known are the polychrome enamel wares. The use of enamel in Chinese ceramics was probably borrowed from Chinese *cloisonné metalwork. M. is also famous for its carved red and layered *lacquer vessels and furniture.

miniature. Term originally applied to the art of ms. *illumination but later used of paintings, usually portraits, executed on a very small scale. The earliest miniaturists or limners (16th c.) continued to use the materials of the illuminators, painting in gouache on vellum or card. In the 18th c. it became usual to paint in transparent watercolour on ivory, though some mss were painted in oils on metal. In the mid 19th c. the art began to decline. Famous miniaturists include Hilliard, Isaac Oliver, Cooper, Cosway (in England), J. and F. Clouet, Petitot and Jean-Baptiste Isabey (in France), Fuger (in Germany).

minim. The English name for the sign 𝅗𝅥 in musical *notation. Its time value is half the *semibreve; hence the German '*Halbenote*' and the American 'half note'.

Minnelli Vincente (1913–). U.S. film director. He worked as a set and costume designer before directing musicals and ballets on Broadway. He started working for Paramount in 1937 but moved to M.G.M. (1940) where he made his 1st film, a Negro musical, *Cabin in the Sky* (1942). Working for Arthur Freed, producer of the great post-war M.G.M. musicals, he made some of the best in *Meet Me in St Louis* (1944), *Yolanda and the Thief* (1945), *The Pirate* (1948), and *The Band Wagon* (1953), and has made occasional musicals since, e.g. *Gigi* (1958). His background and colour sense are ideal equipment for directing musicals. His non-musicals employ physical action to reveal the meaning of each incident for the characters. Among the best are *The Clock* (1944), *The Bad and the Beautiful* (1952), *The Cobweb* (1954), *Home from the Hill* (1960) and *The Courtship of Eddie's Father* (1962).

Minnesingers. German poets of the 12th to early 14th c. whose theme was courtly love ('*Minne*') and the service of their lady ('*Frauendienst*'). They followed in the tradition of *Provençal literature and among the greatest was Walther von der Vogelweide.

Mino da Fiesole (1430/1–84). A leading Florentine sculptor of his period. His work shows an interest in classical models but also imagination and technical mastery, notably in in his fine portrait bust of Niccolò Strozzi (Berlin).

minor. Musical term, *key, *harmony and *scale.

minstrel. Originally *ménestrel*, a medieval musician and general entertainer, in effect a *jongleur but one permanently employed in a noble household; the term later replaced 'jongleur' as a description of an itinerant entertainer.

minuet. A dance form popular in Europe from the late 17th to the end of the 18th c.; it was taken up by composers, usually in conjunction with another m. called a trio (perhaps because this 2nd m. was originally written in 3 parts), becoming an optional movement in the *suite and a movement in the *symphony. The m. is in a steady 3 beats in a bar and in *ternary form.

minuscule Carolingian. Script introduced in the 8th c., one of the achievements of the *Carolingian renaissance, mainly created by the abbeys of Corvey and St Martin of Tours (*Alcuin); it was modelled on the classical script, was imitated at the Renaissance and is the basis of modern printed letters.

Minute Waltz. Nickname for Chopin's piano valse, op. 64 no. 1 in D♭, so called because of the time it is supposed to last.

Miracle in the Gorbals. 1-act ballet with choreography by Helpmann, music by Bliss and décor by Burra; 1st performance 1944.

miracle plays (also called 'mystery plays'). Medieval religious drama which probably developed from the dramatization of the liturgy and reached its climax in huge colls, or cycles, aiming to cover the entire Biblical story and sometimes non-Biblical themes such as saints' lives. There are 4 great English cycles: those of Coventry, Wakefield ('Towneley plays'), Chester and York. Although the cycles are by diverse authors, individual writers of talent are discernible, e.g. the 'York Realist', largely responsible for the powerful Passion scenes, and the 'Wakefield Master', author of such humorous episodes as the 2nd Shepherd's play. The performance, the responsibility of the trade guilds, took place on wagons in the open air on important feast days such as Corpus Christi. Guilds usually chose a story which was suited to their occupation or 'mystery'; thus the story of Noah was often acted by the Water Carriers and the Fall of Lucifer by the Tanners.

Miracle symphony. Nickname for *Haydn's symphony no. 96 in D (1791). At its 1st performance, in London, a chandelier fell into the audience but, 'miraculously', hurt no one.

Miranda Francisco de Sá de (1481–1558). Portuguese poet and playwright. S. introduced Italian verse forms into Portugal, wrote *Os Estrangeiros*, the 1st prose comedy, and *Cleopatra*, the 1st tragedy in Portuguese.

Miró Gabriel (1879–1930). Spanish novelist. Using a slow, rather discursive but glowing style he aimed at creating the warm, sensual atmosphere of the Latin world in novels impregnated by his ardent, optimistic Catholic faith. Among the best and the most individual of his books are *Nuestro Padre San Daniel* (1921; . . . *Scenes of Clerical Life*, 1930) and *Figuras de la Pasion del Señor* (1916; *Figures of the Passion of Our Lord*, 1924).

Miró Joan (1893–). Spanish painter who trained (1907–15) in Barcelona at the School of Fine Art and the Academy Cali. As a student he had a great admiration for Catalan art, popular arts and the extreme art nouveau forms of Gaudí's architecture. His early painting passed through Cézannesque and fauve phases. He was in Portugal with Delaunay during World War I and in 1920 settled in Paris, where he met and was influenced by his compatriots Picasso and Gris.
During the 1920s he became closely associated with the surrealists and contributed to all their important exhibitions. His freely invented calligraphy of highly coloured forms earned from Breton the description 'the most surrealist of us all'; the decorative complexity of *Harlequinade* (1924–5; Albright Gal., Buffalo) gave way in the 1930s to a simpler use of expressive colours and symbols which influenced Kandinsky and probably Picasso.
Back in Barcelona since 1940, he has continued to paint highly personal subjective images, e.g. *Women, Bird by Moonlight* (1949; Tate) but has nevertheless remained a very influential figure, particularly for U.S. artists like Gorky and Calder. His public commissions include the 2 ceramic-tile walls, *The Sun* and *The Moon* (1955–8; UNESCO, Paris) which won the 1958 Guggenheim International Award.

Mirror for Magistrates, A. Coll. of verse stories on the theme of the fall of great men, popular in Elizabethan England; there were several eds between 1559 and 1610.

Misanthrope, Le (1666). Comedy by *Molière.

mise-en-scène. In a play, all the items seen on stage during the performance, i.e. costumes, scenery, properties.

Misérables, Les (1862). Novel by Victor *Hugo.

miserere. The Psalm beginning '*Miserere mei Deus*'; 'Have mercy upon me, O God' and numbered 50 in the Hebrew and Anglican canon and 51 in the Vulgate, concludes the office of *Tenebrae. Since the early 16th c. composers have written special settings (G. *Allegri).

misericord. A small bracket underneath the seats (which tip up) in the choir of a church which gives support in a position between sitting and standing. It was used during the singing of Psalms and dates from the middle ages. The underside of the bracket is often decorated with carved scenes from contemporary life, proverbs or with a formalized motif.

missa: *mass

Miss Julie (1889). Play by *Strindberg, made into a film (1951), directed by A. Sjöberg.

Mr Deeds Goes to Town (1936). Film directed by F. *Capra.

Mr Midshipman Easy (1836). Novel by Captain *Marryat.

Misericord of Richard III; from Christchurch priory, Hampshire

Miró. *Dutch Interior* (1928)

Miró. *Harlequinade*

Miró. *Woman in black granite* (1950)

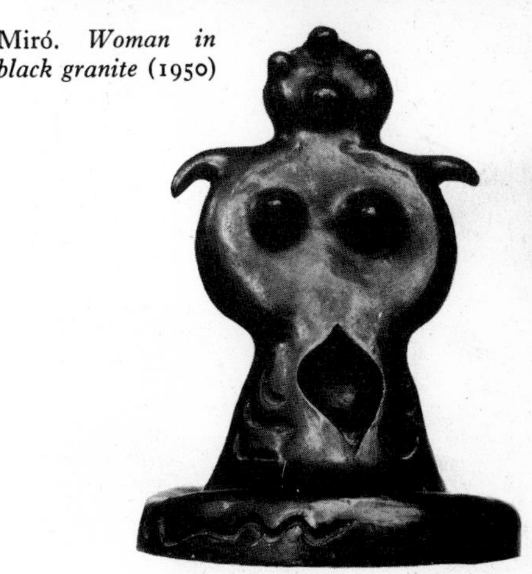

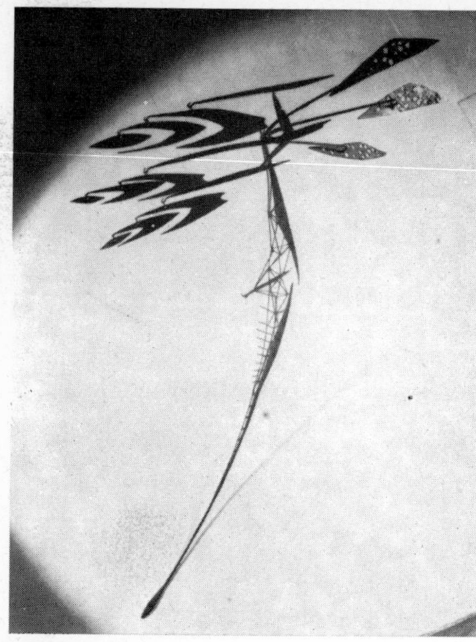

Mobile. Chadwick, *Dragonfly*

Mizoguchi. *Ugetsu Monogatari*

Mistinguett in the 1920s

Mr Norris Changes Trains (1935). Novel by Christopher *Isherwood.

Mr Polly, The History of (1910). Novel by H. G. *Wells.

Mistinguett (born Jeanne Bourgeois) (1875–1956). French cabaret star, famous for her beautiful and highly insured legs, who began in music-hall and later became part-proprietor of the Moulin-Rouge, where she also performed. She partnered Maurice *Chevalier at the Folies-Bergères and Casino de Paris.

Mistral Frédéric (1830–1914). French poet who, with Joseph Roumanille, attempted to revive the Provençal language. M. wrote only in Provençal; his works include the poems *Mirèio* (1858; 1867) and *Calendau* (1867), and a Provençal dictionary. He received the Nobel prize in 1904.

Mistral Gabriela. Pseud. of Lucila Godoy Alcayaga (1889–1957). Chilean poet, awarded the Nobel prize in 1945. Her lyrics are conventional in form and romantic in inspiration.

Mitchell Margaret (1900–49). U.S. novelist, author of 1 book, the best-selling *Gone with the Wind* (1936; filmed in 1939), an epic of the U.S. South during the Civil War and Reconstruction periods, describing the career of Scarlett O'Hara, at first a spoilt girl, later an ambitious, selfish but indomitable woman.

Mitchell S(ilas) Weir (1829–1914). U.S. novelist, an outstanding neurologist. M.'s novels are psychological studies, often set in the War of Independence or the Civil War; they include *Roland Blake* (1886), *Hugh Wynne: Free Quaker* (1897) and *The Red City* (1907).

Mitchum Robert (1917–). U.S. film actor often in war films, e.g. *The Story of G.I. Joe* (1945), and in criminal parts.

Mitford Nancy (1904–). English novelist, author of *The Pursuit of Love* (1945), *Love in a Cold Climate* (1949) and other amusing and sophisticated novels.

Mitropoulos Dimitri (1896–1960). Greek conductor and pianist who as conductor of the Minneapolis Symphony (from 1937) and the New York Philharmonic orchestras (from 1949 to 1958) introduced and strongly advocated works of such composers as Schoenberg. He took U.S. citizenship in 1946.

Mix Tom (1880–1940). Leading U.S. silent and sound film star, noted for romanticized cowboy roles, e.g. *Lonesome Trail* (1931).

mixture stop. Organ stop with a number of pipes to each note, tuned to produce and thus reinforce certain of the upper harmonics of the note sounded (*harmonic series).

Mizoguchi Kenji (1898–1956). Japanese film director. M. started directing in 1922, shooting rather occidental subjects including adaptations of *Arsène Lupin* (1922) and of O'Neill's *Anna Christie* (1924). Apart from an adaptation of *Boule-de-Suif* (1935) and one co-production set in China (*Yang Kwei Fei*, 1955), his films have found their inspiration in Japanese tradition, whether artistic (*Utamaro and his five women*, 1946) or heroic–*The Loyal 47 Ronin of the Genroku Era* (1941), with all 47 committing hara-kiri (offscreen) at the end, and *Shin heike monogatari* (1955). He was particularly fascinated by the predicament of women in Japanese society, often in relation to the clash between traditional customs and modern life (*Sisters of Gion*, 1935; remade as *Gion Music*, 1953). However, M.'s films are not mere social or historical documents, for he is one of the few very great directors whose works are remarkable on every possible plane. Perhaps the best of his work is the series of period films which he made in the last 5 years of his life: *Ugetsu Monogatari* (1953), *Chikamatsu Monogatari* and *Sansho Dayu* (1954) and his 2 films in colour, *Yang Kwei Fei* and *Shin heike monogatari.*

Mnesicles (*fl.* 2nd half of 5th c. B.C.). Greek architect who designed the *Erechtheum and *Propylaea, Athens.

Moana (1926). Film directed by R. *Flaherty.

mobile. A form of sculpture invented in the early 1930s by A. *Calder; m.s consist of a number of objects of various shapes suspended on wire rods in such a way that they move in continuously changing relationships when placed in a current of air. By creating movement in space m.s get away from the traditionally static nature of sculpture.

Mochi. *St Veronica*

Moby Dick or The White Whale (1851). Novel by Herman *Melville.

Mochalov Pavel (1800–48). Russian tragic actor greatly admired by V. Belinsky whose greatest roles were Hamlet, Lear and in plays of Schiller. He was an 'intuitive' actor, relying on inspiration and emotion and his performances were erratic and often unrealistic.

Mochi Francesco (1580–1654). Italian sculptor, strongly influenced by Florentine styles, who worked in Florence, Rome and Piacenza. Among numerous equestrian statues is that of Alessandro Farnese at Piacenza. His religious works include the *Annunciation* group in Orvieto cathedral and *St Veronica* in St Peter's, Rome.

mode. A type of scale used in Western music from the time of St Ambrose (d. 397) up to the 16th c. Each m. in the system had 5 intervals of a tone and 2 intervals of a semitone but the semitones occurred in different positions for each m. and thus the 'feel' of each m. was different. The modern major scale descends from the 'Ionian' m. rejected by the medieval church but used much in medieval secular music. Each m. had a keynote, called the '*finalis*' because it was the note on which a melody in the m. ended, and a '*tenor*' (or 'dominant', normally a 5th above the *finalis*) which was the note 'held' during passages of recitation. Ambrose established 4 m.s for the classification of church melodies and these, named after ancient Greek m.s as Dorian, Phrygian, Lydian and Mixolydian, were known as 'authentic'. Pope Gregory I (d. 604) introduced 4 new forms of these m.s, known as the 'plagel' m.s and designated by the prefix '*hypo-*' (i.e. 'below'). Thus the Hypodorian kept the *finalis* of the Dorian but the m. was extended down below this *finalis* for 4 notes.

modelling. (1) In sculpture to build up form in clay or other plastic material; the opposite of carving. (2) In painting to give an appearance of 3-dimensional solidity on a 2-dimensional surface, used particularly with reference to the human figure. (3) Posing as a subject for an artist.

modello. Small version of a large painting executed by the artist for his patron's approval. Unlike a sketch, a m. is often highly finished.

modern dance. A system of art dance radically differing from classical ballet technique. It started in Munich with Von *Laban and was also known as Central European dance. 2 of Von Laban's pupils, Mary Wigman and Kurt Jooss spread the movement in the U.S. and Germany respectively and in America such dancers as Isadora Duncan and Martha Graham developed the method. The essence of m. d. is that it does not have a stylized technique but uses free movements stemming from a relaxed state of mind. Many contemporary choreographers have produced work combining classical ballet and m. d. techniques.

modern face. In typography a style of face in which there is a strong contrast between the thick verticals and the thin horizontals and in which the serifs are simple and unbracketed. Apart from the work of *Diderot and *Fournier, *Bodoni was the 1st important printer to use such a face; R. *Austin introduced it to England.

modernismo. Late 19th-c. Spanish poetic movement originating in Spanish America and associated above all with Rubén *Darío; it absorbed the techniques of the French symbolists and Parnassians, and abandoned romantic topics for introspection.

Modern Jazz Quartet. American chamber group, *jazz.

Modern Painters (1843–60). Book by John *Ruskin.

Modern Times (1936). Film directed by *Chaplin.

Modersohn-Becker Paula (1876–1907). German painter, and a friend of the poet Rilke. Her painting is expressionist in the sense that she was primarily concerned with the expression of personal feeling; but the mood of her work is predominantly a gentle poetic romanticism without strident colour or harsh distortion. Her *Self-portrait* (1907; Folkwang Mus., Essen), the best known of several, shows simple form and restrained colour used to create a feminine tenderness of expression.

Modest Proposal. . . , A (1729). Satirical pamphlet by Swift.

Modello (*left*) and large painting (*below*) by Tiepolo: *St Thecla delivering the City of Este from the Plague*

et designat oculis ad cædem unumquemque nostrum. Nos autem, viri fortes, satisfacere reipub-

A B C D E F G H I J K L M N O P Q R S T U V

A B C D E F G H I J K L M N O P Q R S T U V W X Y Z

£ 0 1 2 3 4 5 6 7 8 9

Pica Italic, No. 3.

Quousque tandem abutere, Catilina, patientia nostra? quamdiu nos etiam furor iste tuus eludet? quem ad finem sese effrenata jactabit audacia? nihilne te nocturnum præsidium palatii, nihil urbis

Modern face

Modersohn-Becker. *Self-portrait with Camelia*

Modigliani. *Bride and Groom*

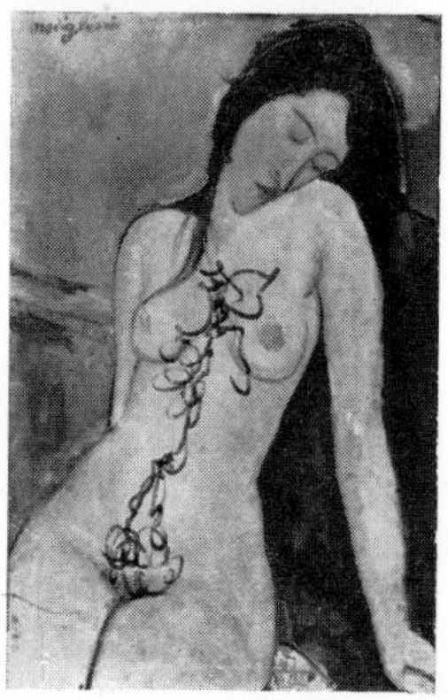

Modigliani. *Nude*

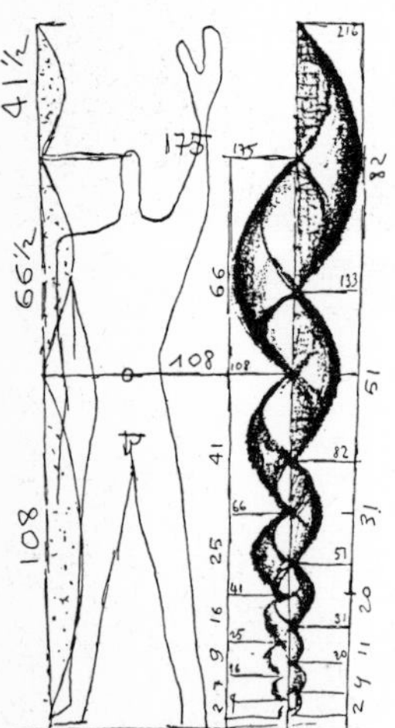

Le Corbusier modulor

Modigliani Amedeo (1884–1920). Italian painter, sculptor and draughtsman; born in Leghorn, of Jewish descent. M. studied in Venice and Florence and arrived in Paris in 1906. Without associating himself with any particular group or movement, M. took what he wanted from the paintings of Toulouse-Lautrec, Cézanne, Negro sculpture, the fauves, cubism and other experimental work of Picasso and Braque. More decisive was his meeting with Brancusi; and between 1910 and 1913 it was sculpture that absorbed him. Forced to give this up because the dust thrown off by the chisel damaged his lungs, already weakened by disease, M. applied many sculptural effects in his portraits and nudes, particularly the characteristic elongation of the head, the long raised ridge of the nose and the long neck. His superb drawings show a strange affinity with the draughtsmanship of Botticelli, while his colours are far closer to those of early Sienese masters than to any painter of the school of Paris. The legend of his life as a Montparnasse eccentric–handsome, poor, proud, amorous and drugged or drunk–was cultivated by his literary friends, especially after his genuinely tragic and dramatic death at 35. The legend ignores his intense concentration on his painting in his last years. Outstanding examples of his paintings are: *Jacques Lipchitz and his Wife* (A. Inst., Chicago), *Nude on a Cushion* (Coll. Mattioli, Milan), *Bride and Groom* (M.M.A., New York), *The Little Peasant* (Tate).

modulation. Musical term used to describe the movement from one key (or more properly 'key region') to another. The basic principle is to surprise the original key by the introduction of a chord belonging to the 2nd key, and then to justify the shock by sinking into the new key.

module. In building, a unit of measurement repeated throughout the building; thus a moduler building is one in which a preferred dimension is continually repeated. Brickwork naturally gives a small m., but with industrialized building techniques the m. becomes larger and more significant architecturally.

modulor. Contraction of '*Module du Section d'Or*' ('Module of the Golden Section'); it is a scale of proportions used by Le Corbusier. It is claimed that by relating the proportions of man and the mathematics of the golden section, buildings can be designed which have human quality and ideal proportions.

Moeran Ernest John (1894–1950). English romantic composer. His music, rooted in folk-songs and inspired by the English countryside, includes: a symphony (1937), influenced by Sibelius; 2 orchestral rhapsodies and *Sinfonietta* (1944). His best work is in his songs, e.g. *6 Norfolk Folksongs* (1923), *7 Poems of James Joyce* (1929), and choral works.

Moeschinger Albert (1897–). Swiss composer. In his highly individual music he aims to reinterpret the forms of the past. This never produces pastiche and later works have experimented with 12-note techniques. Besides much chamber music he has written 3 symphonies and many choral works.

Moffat James (1870–1944). Scottish-born U.S. clergyman who made a trs. of the Bible (New Testament, 1901; Old Testament, 1924) into contemporary English.

Moholy-Nagy László (1895–1946). Hungarian sculptor, painter, designer and photographer. He trained in law but by 1920 was working in Berlin with El Lissitzky; his originality was soon recognized by Gropius, who appointed him to run the metalwork-shop at the *Bauhaus. He was again in Berlin (1928–32), a member of the Abstraction-Création group in Paris (1932–6); in London (1935–7) and finally Chicago, where he directed a New Bauhaus (1938–46). His transparent *Space Modulators* (one in the M.M.A., New York) are influenced by N. Gabo. Like him, M.-N. was concerned with the dynamic relationships of forms in space. His teaching at the Bauhaus (1922–8) also concentrated upon the use in art of 20th-c. materials and techniques (including photography–in which he experimented with the technical possibilities to produce the montage, double exposure and photogram–and the cinema and telephone). These are the themes of his *Von Material zu Architektur* (1929, as a Bauhausbuch; *The New Vision*, 1930).

Molenaer Jan Miense (*c.* 1610–68). Dutch painter of genre and historical subjects. Both he and his wife, Judith Leyster (married 1636) were probably pupils of Hals, whose work theirs resembled closely in subject and style. M. had a particular fondness for genre pieces involving musical scenes.

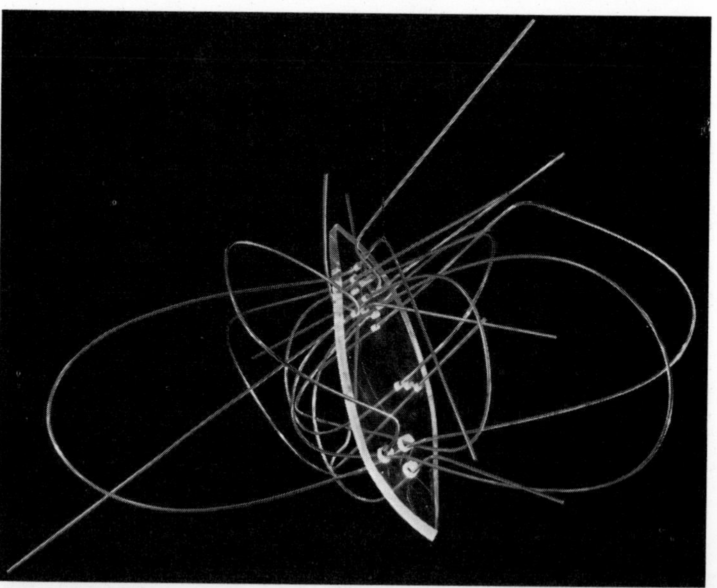

Moholy-Nagy. *Wire curve* (1946)

Molière. Pseud. of Jean-Baptiste Poquelin (1622–73), the creator of French classical comedy and one of the greatest men of the theatre in European culture. After a classical education in Paris M. joined a troupe of strolling players and for 12 years toured the provinces, working his apprenticeship as an actor-manager. The success in 1659 of his farce *Les Précieuses ridicules* brought him royal approbation.

Each of M.'s works combines elements of traditional farce with comedy of manners and the satire of general human vices, especially hypocrisy and pretentiousness. In his greatest comedies M. aimed to exploit the comic potentialities of each individual as a complete person, creating characters capable of arousing sympathy as well as mirth, and not simply comic types. This kind of pure comedy had little need of elaborate intrigue. Dramatic structure in the plays, especially in the farces, is sound, but in general M. made no attempt to avoid artificiality. His dialogue draws on the richness of everyday speech and always reflects the idiosyncrasies of his characters. As a performer M. was responsible for a renewal of the art of mime in the French theatre.

His main works are *L'École des maris* (1661); *L'École des femmes* (1662); *Dom Juan* (1665); *Le Misanthrope* (1666; 1677), a portrait of a man unable to tolerate the deceptions and hypocrisies of society (even, e.g., to praise a courtier's bad verse); *L'Amour médecin* (1665; 1705), *Le Médecin malgré lui* (1666; 1672) and *Le Malade imaginaire* (1673; 1769) which ridicule hypochondria and the pretensions of the medical profession; *Amphitryon* (1668; 1690, by Dryden); *George Dandin* (1668; 1706); *L'Avare* (1668; 1672), which relates the humiliation of the miser Harpagon; *Le Tartuffe* (1664; revised 1667; trs. 1670), which censures hypocritical piety; *Monsieur de Pourceaugnac* (1669; 1673); *Le Bourgeois gentilhomme* (1670; 1672), satirizing the social ambitions of the *nouveau riche* Monsieur Jourdain; *Les Fourberies de Scapin* (1671; 1677); *La Comtesse d'Escarbagnas* (1671); and *Les Femmes savantes* (1672; 1693).

Møller Poul Martin (1794–1838). Danish novelist and poet, author of the short novel of student life, *En dansk Students Eventyr* (written 1824), the 1st Danish novel to deal with contemporary subjects.

Moll Flanders (1722). Novel by *Defoe.

Molloy (1951). Novel by Samuel *Beckett.

Molnár Ferenc (1878–1952). Hungarian playwright. He emigrated to the U.S. His *carpe diem philosophy, brilliant technique and rapid and sophisticated dialogue gained him an international reputation. His best-known plays are: *Liliom* (1909; 1921), *A hattyú* (1920; *The Swan*, 1929), *Játék a kastélyban* (1926; *The Play's the Thing*, 1926).

molossus: *metre in verse

Molvig Jon (1923–). Australian painter. His work, notably the series *Ballad of the Dead Stockman*, holds a central position in contemporary Australian art.

Moment musical. This French term was used by Schubert and others to describe short pieces for piano.

Mommsen Theodor (1817–1903). One of the great generation of 19th-c. German 'scientific' historians, author of the monumental *Römische Geschichte* (1854–85; *The History of Rome*, 1862–75).

Momper Joos de (1564–1635). Flemish painter. He painted Alpine landscapes (he travelled in Italy and Switzerland) and also scenes around Antwerp. *The Miraculous Deliverance of the Emperor Maximilian* is at Antwerp.

Mompou Federico (1893–). Catalan composer for the piano, a follower of Debussy but master of a subtle, individual style. M. describes his work as 'music in the pure state reacting against the cerebralism of our time ...'.

Monaco Lorenzo, i.e. 'Lorenzo the Monk', Piero di Giovanni called (*c.* 1370/2–*c.* 1425). Italian painter and illuminator of the Florentine school. He moved from Siena to Florence, where he entered the monastery of S. Maria degli Angeli, a famous centre of ms. illumination. His style of painting as seen in *Coronation of the Virgin* (versions Uffizi, Florence; N.G., London) derived from the tradition of Giotto and the Sienese school; however, a late painting, *Adoration of the Magi* (Uffizi), is one of the earliest examples of the international Gothic style in Florence.

Monaco Mario del (1915–). Italian tenor of exceptional power and dramatic force, e.g. in Verdi roles.

Molière in theatrical costume

Lorenzo Monaco. *Coronation of the Virgin* (*above*; detail) and *Adoration of the Magi* (*below*)

Molenaer. *The Painter's Workshop*

Mona Lisa

Mondrian. *Still-life with Ginger-pot*

Mondrian. *Composition in Brown and Grey*

Mondrian. *Composition with Red, Yellow and Blue* (1921). Also *abstract art, *de stijl and colour plate 76

Mona Lisa (1503–6). Portrait by *Leonardo, probably the most famous picture ever painted.

Monamy Peter (1669–1749). Self-taught British marine painter, influenced by the work of Willem van der Velde. The historical piece *The Embarkation of Charles II at Scheveningen, 1660* is in Dublin.

Monarchia, De. Treatise by *Dante.

Monckton Lionel (1861–1924). English composer of the operetta *The Quaker Girl* (1910).

Mondrian Piet (1872–1944). Dutch painter; he studied at the Amsterdam Academy. His earliest works, sombre-coloured landscapes, are patently in the Dutch tradition. During the years 1907–10 the landscape became more heavily stylized and expressively brilliant in colour, with echoes of Munch as well as Matisse, e.g. the series of *Church Tower* paintings (*c.* 1909).

In 1909 he moved to Paris and the experience of cubism was the turning-point in his evolution. His colouristic expressionist tendencies were suppressed and he submitted his formalizations to a rigorous linear discipline. In a series such as the *Still-life with Ginger-pot* paintings (1912) the motif is analysed in terms of linear and planear relationships which became, progressively, more important than the motif itself. The debt to cubism is emphasized by the shallow space illusion and by the familiar blue/grey or ochre monochromatic palette.

He returned to Holland in 1914 and by 1917 realized that the perfect expressive harmony that he sought was hindered by starting from a given motif–'The emotion of beauty is always obstructed by the appearance of the "object"; therefore the object must be eliminated from the picture.' His *Compositions* (1914–17) comprise simple flat rectangles of colour, their austerity heightened (*c.* 1916) by the use of primary colours only. The final evolution of his mature style was in eliminating the depth-suggesting spaces between the rectangles: from *c.* 1917 on the coloured shapes are divided by a flat grid of black lines. His mature oeuvre using only the primary colours and non-colours (black, white and sometimes grey), consists of a series of refined variations on this simple theme.

M.'s importance lies in his development of 'pure' abstraction–he called his art neo-plasticism–in which the shapes, lines and colours have their own absolute, autonomous values and relationships, divorced from any associative role whatsoever. He was a member of the Dutch Theosophical Society from 1909 and it is clear from his writings in the **De Stijl* journal (founded in 1917 with van der Leck and van Doesburg) and in his pamphlet *Néo-Plasticisme* (1920), that M., inspired by the Dutch philosopher Schoenmaekers, saw his art as an expression of a perfect universal harmony, to whose creation he was contributing.

It is impossible to study M.'s art in England: the most representative colls are in Holland (Gemeente Mus., The Hague, and Kröller-Müller Mus., Otterloo).

Monet Claude (1840–1926). French painter. He was born in Paris but educated at Le Havre where, in 1858, he met Boudin who encouraged him to paint nature on the spot. At the Atelier Suisse in Paris in 1860 he met Pissarro and Cézanne and after military service in Algiers (1861) returned to Paris to study under Gleyre. A fellow-student of Renoir, Sisley and Bazille (1862–4), he painted with them at Chailly, near Fontainebleau. He was the least satisfied with Gleyre's teaching and learnt more from Jongkind and Boudin; and working with them at Honfleur (1864), he began to paint the landscape in terms of its atmospheric appearance. His paintings of the Seine estuary –very well received at the 1865 Salon–already revealed the extraordinarily acute judgement of tonal values that prompted Cézanne to call him 'only an eye, but my God what an eye'.

Around 1865/6 he tried to rework the theme of Manet's *Déjeuner sur l'Herbe* without its studio artificiality. The projected large painting was probably never completed; but the study, dated 1866 in Moscow, is a remarkably complete attempt to represent figures in a glade with the sunlight filtering on to them through the leaves. This was to become a recurrent impressionist theme.

In the late 1860s M. and Renoir worked in a partnership of mutual advantage and produced the 1st pure impressionist paintings. In *La Grenouillère* (1869; Met. Mus., New York) he began to break up local colour into strokes of pure colour and in *The Magpie* (*c.* 1870; Société Guerlain, Paris)–an evenly toned snowscape–the pale blue of the shadow vibrantly complements the touches of yellow flecked across the snow's surface. *Impression Sunrise* (1872; Mus.

Marmottan, Paris) which earned the group their derisive name suggests a debt to Constable's empirical directness and to Turner's atmospheric generalizations (M. was in London in 1871). He contributed to 5 of the 8 impressionist exhibitions and suffered as much as Pissarro and Sisley from hostility and lack of patronage.

Working mainly at Argenteuil with Renoir, Sisley, Manet and Morisot during the 1870s, M. remained dedicated to the study of light and its changing effect on nature. In 1876 he began the first of his series of paintings on a single subject–the *Gare St Lazare* (1876–7) was followed by the *Haystacks* (1890–2), *Poplars* (1890–2), and *Rouen Cathedral* (1892–4). Their object was to observe the transformation of the motif under changing light and atmosphere, but they almost incidentally led to the surface richness of colour and paint of his late style which has earned comparison with abstract expressionism.

The 1880s were prolific years, but years of continued poverty and depression until in 1889 he had his 1st big public success at an exhibition shared with Rodin. In 1890 he bought the house at Giverny where–apart from visits to London (1891, 1899, 1903) and Venice (1908–9)–he spent the rest of his life. The late *Water-lily* paintings painted in the water gardens ('outdoor studios') which he built there, were still responses to his eye, but–increasingly subjective–they embody a larger, cosmic sense of nature closer to late Turner than to impressionism. He presented the vast canvases in the Orangerie, Paris, to the state in 1921. The only impressionist to achieve full public recognition in his lifetime, he died totally blind.

Monicelli Mario (1915–). Italian film director. M. wrote scripts (e.g. *Bitter Rice*), and directed comic films. He had a great success with a burlesque crime story, *I Soliti Ignoti* (1958), which he followed with a large-scale serious war film, *La Grande Guerra* (1959).

Moniuszko Stanisław (1819–72). Polish composer regarded as the founder of a national style. His works include operas, e.g. *Halka* (1848), based on folk-tales, and choral works and church music.

Monk Thelonious (1920–). U.S. pianist and composer. A key figure in the foundation of modern jazz, his individual style has nevertheless set him apart from its mainstream. His improvisations are based on harmonic and rhythmic paraphrase, generally of his own compositions. His unorthodox technique, based on strange distortions of Hollywood harmonies, 'wrong' notes and whole tones, gives a haunting quality to his themes which makes them ideally suited to this approach. *Round About Midnight*, *Off Minor*, and *Ruby My Dear* are some of his best-known compositions.

Monk, The (1796). Novel by M. G. *Lewis.

Monkey. Novel by Wu Ch'eng-en (*c.* 1505–80); partially trs. by Arthur Waley (1942). *M.*, properly *Hsi Yu Chi* ('Pilgrimage to the West'), is compounded of legends and facts surrounding the pilgrimage of the 7th-c. Buddhist Hsüan Tsang to bring sutras to China from India.

Monkey Business. Film (1931) with the *Marx Brothers. Film (1952) directed by H. *Hawks.

Monnoyer Jean-Baptiste (1636–99). The outstanding Flemish flower painter of the age; he worked mainly in France, at the Trianon and at Marly. In England in 1685 he painted decorative flower pieces for Montagu House, Hampton Court, Windsor Castle and Kew Palace.

monochord. An ancient plucked musical instrument consisting of a single string (hence the name) stretched across a sound-box over a movable bridge. This bridge was shifted to obtain varying vibrating string lengths. The m. was used by theorists, from ancient Greece onwards, analysing the ratios of musical intervals.

monody (Greek, 'singing alone'). The style, developed in the late 16th c. by the *camerata, thought to approximate to Greek music and intended to give the clearest possible musical setting of a poetic text. A solo vocal line, melodically limited, free of violent declamation and closely following the syllabic and line structure of the verse was sung to a simple, harmonically restricted, instrumental accompaniment.

Mon Oncle (1958). Film directed by J. *Tati.

Monnoyer. *Still-life*

Monet. *Water-lilies* (1906)

Monet. *Poplars on the Epte*

Monet. *Rouen Cathedral* (1894). Also *Fantin-Latour, *impressionism and colour plate 70

Montagna. *Madonna and four Saints*

Silver monstrance: woodcut by Cranach

Michel de Montaigne

Monreale cathedral. The main apse

Monreale cathedral. Detail of the bronze door by Bonanno

monophony (Greek, 'single voice'). Strictly this musical term is applied to a piece for a single part or voice but sometimes also to a piece for single part with simple accompaniment.

monothematic. Term applied to a musical composition, in 1 or several movements, in which only 1 main *theme is developed.

monotype. In art, the painting of a picture in oils on a metal plate from which a print is taken. Both Castiglione and Degas experimented with the medium, which produces characteristic textures.

Monreale cathedral Sicily. Romanesque basilican church (begun 1174) showing a combination of European, Byzantine and Islamic styles. It is remarkable for the preservation of its furniture and decoration, which are almost entirely 12th c.–marble veneer and screens, mosaic covering the whole interior above the arcade, a cloister with inlaid colonnettes and figured capitals, and 2 extremely fine bronze doors with reliefs.

Monro Thomas (1759–1833). English amateur painter in watercolour, but known mainly as the enlightened patron of Turner, Girtin, Cotman, de Wint and Cozens. His London home became a meeting-place and unofficial academy for watercolour painters.

Monroe Harriet (1860–1936). U.S. founder and ed. of *Poetry: A Magazine of Verse* (1912), which became a force in the literary world and inspired many little magazines. M. publ. in it much experimental and unconventional work, including poems by T. S. Eliot, D. H. Lawrence, Vachel Lindsay and Ezra Pound. Her anthology *The New Poetry* (1917) included much free verse.

Monroe Marilyn (1926–1962). U.S. film actress who moved from calendar nude to dumb blonde star in *Niagara* (1953). Possessing a sparkling yet appealingly innocent personality, she tried in vain to escape her status as sexual merchandise worth $200m.; she committed suicide. An excellent comedienne–*Gentlemen Prefer Blondes* (1953) and *Some Like It Hot* (1958)–she had considerable emotional power, best seen in *The Misfits* (1963), written by her husband, the playwright Arthur Miller.

Monsieur Beaucaire (1900). Short novel by Booth Tarkington.

Monsieur Hulot's Holiday (1953). Film directed by J. *Tati.

Monsieur Verdoux (1947). Film directed by *Chaplin.

Monsigny Pierre-Alexandre (1729–1817). French composer of the *opéras-comiques*, *Les Aveux indiscrets* (1759), *Le Roi et le fermier* (1762), *Le Déserteur* (1769) and *Félixe, ou l'Enfant trouvé* (1777). His training in harmony and instrumentation was sketchy but his melodic gift was considerable.

monstrance. A vessel of metal and glass in which, during the Roman Catholic mass, the Host is displayed at Benediction or is carried in procession, especially at Corpus Christi. A circular glass disc is surrounded by golden rays and is supported on a stand. Usually of silver, a m. is often encrusted with gems.

Montagna Bartolommeo (*c.* 1450–1523). Italian painter of frescoes and religious subjects, e.g. the frescoes in the oratory of S. Biagio, Verona (1493–6). His work is mainly confined to N. Italy. He was assisted by his son Benedetto.

Montagu Lady Mary Wortley (1689–1762). English traveller and writer; the wife of Edward Wortley M., ambassador to Turkey from 1716. M.'s letters from Turkey were admired by such men as Gibbon and Voltaire. In 1739 M. settled on the Continent, publ. *Town Eclogues*. Her reputation as a vicious eccentric derives largely from the attacks of her one-time friend, Alexander Pope.

Montaigne Michel Eyquem de (1533–92). French essayist. He was educated experimentally in Latin by word of mouth before learning his native French, and later at the Collège de Guienne at Bordeaux. He became a counsellor in the Parlement (1555–6) and later visited Paris and the court; in 1571 he settled at Montaigne as a recluse to study. His trs. of Raymund de Sabunde's *Theologia Naturalis*, composed for his father, was publ. in 1569 and he ed. the work of his dead friend Étienne de la Boétie, but from 1572 he seems to have worked at the *Essais*. He was mayor of Bordeaux from 1580 to 1586. The 3rd book of

Essais (1588) included a revised ed. of the 2 previous books (1580) and M. continued to annotate until his death. 2 friends, Marie de Jars de Gournay, affectionately styled *'fille d'alliance'* by M., and Pierre de Black, a poet of Bordeaux, collated 2 independently annotated copies of the 1588 ed., to produce the ed. of 1595, generally accepted as standard. Inconsequent and discursive, written in an easy flexible style, with vigorous, racy language, sometimes quaint and picturesque, the *Essais* apparently form a new literary genre, owing little to classical exemplars, though they are stuffed with quotations from ancient authors, but widely admired, imitated and plundered. Bacon, Cowley, Temple, Dryden, Burton and Browne all owe them something: Shakespeare apparently quotes from Florio's trs. (1603) in *The Tempest* and a copy of it in the B.M. bears a signature said to be his. M.'s humorous scepticism and apparently unstudied self-revelation spring from his purpose of leaving for his friends a mental portrait of himself. Philosophically he was a sceptic but outwardly he lived and died a pious Catholic, and his book was not put on the Index till 1676.

Montale Eugenio (1896–). Italian poet and critic. M. has worked in publishing, as a librarian, and as literary ed. of the *Corriere della sera* of Milan. His verse is remarkably concentrated, though it rarely sacrifices lucidity; it describes the poet's inner life–his moments of joy, his alienation from society, his sense of the mysterious natural forces driving mankind–using striking, rapidly changing imagery. M.'s colls include *Ossi di seppia* (1925), *Le occasioni* (1940), *La bufera* (1956) and *Farfalla di Dinard* (1956).

Montanez Juan Martínez (1568–1649). Spanish sculptor whose work is best represented in Seville. His sculptures are chiefly religious works ,and include crucifixes, statuary and altarpieces.

Montansier Marguerite (1730–1820). French actress-manageress whose wit and beauty made her a favourite of Marie-Antoinette. She gave her name to a theatre she managed at the Palais-Royal.

Montchrétien Antoine de (*c.* 1575–1621). French playwright and writer on political economy who wrote for the Hôtel de Bourgogne, the birthplace of French professional drama. All his 6 tragedies are literary rather than dramatic products, and he shows to best advantage in his lyrical passages and long declamatory speeches. He wrote 2 plays on Biblical subjects, but his best-known work is *L'Éscossaise* (1601), based on the life of Mary, Queen of Scots.

Monte Philippe de (1521–1603). Flemish composer; in England (1555) under Mary, later (from 1568) imperial Kapellmeister initiating the dominance of the Italian style at Vienna and Prague. He was one of the very finest composers of polyphonic church music and also produced many madrigals, including some settings of Ronsard.

Monte Carlo. A major centre of ballet since Diaghilev made it his headquarters in 1912. The performances are given in the Salle Garnier, part of the Casino opened in 1897.

monteith. A punch-bowl with a scalloped rim, often detachable, for glasses to hang there by the foot, named after a Scot who wore his cloak notched in the same way. They are almost always of silver and date from the late 17th c.

Montemayor Jorge de (*c.* 1520–61). Spanish poet and novelist of Portuguese origin. His pastoral prose romance *La Diana* (1559; 1598) was the earliest in Spain and inspired numerous imitations. It was trs. in France and Germany and constantly re-publ. until the late 17th c.

Montereau Pierre de (d. 1267). French medieval architect. He tended to eliminate solid wall in favour of glass. In his masterpiece, the Sainte-Chapelle, Paris (1245–8), the upper storey consists simply of huge stained-glass windows and a stone vault. M. also rebuilt the nave of St Denis, glazing all the levels including triforium; the S. transept of Notre-Dame, Paris, with a huge rose-window; and the Lady chapel of St Germain-des-Près, Paris (demolished).

Montesquieu Charles de Secondat, baron de (1689–1755). French philosopher whose *De l'Esprit des lois* (1748; *The Spirit of Laws*, 1750) was the 1st comparative study of political and social institutions; it contributed to the unpopularity of absolutism in France and influenced the provisions of the U.S. constitution

Monteith; London, 1695

Montereau. The Sainte-Chapelle

Montesquieu

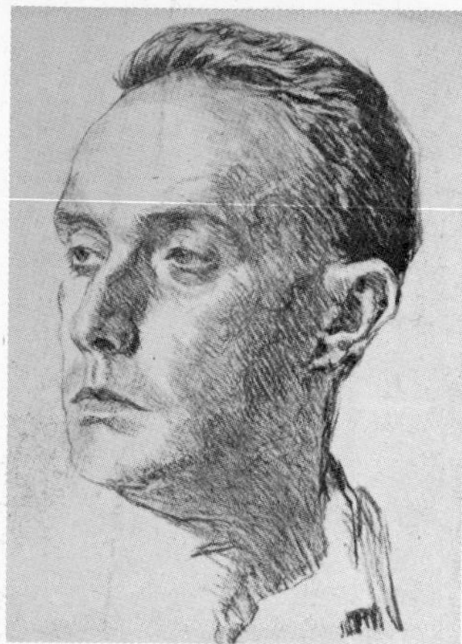
Henry de Montherlant

Claudio Monteverdi

Robert de Montesquiou

and of the French constitutions after the Revolution. In *Lettres persanes* (1721; *Persian Letters*, 1730) M. satirizes French society through the imaginary letters of 2 Persians.

Montesquiou comte Robert de (1855–1921). French poet, an eccentric aristocrat who was probably the model for characters created by Huysmans (Des Esseintes in *À Rebours*) and Proust (the Baron de Charlus).

Monteux Pierre (1875–1964). French conductor. With Diaghilev's Ballet co. M. conducted the 1st performance of Stravinsky's *Rite of Spring* (1913) and Debussy's *Jeux* (1913). From 1916 to 1924 M. worked in the U.S. and again from 1936 to 1952. In 1963 he became conductor of the London Symphony Orchestra.

Monteverdi Claudio (Zuan) (1567–1643). Italian composer. In his native Cremona M. studied with Ingegneri and had already publ. 2 books of madrigals when he entered the service of the duke of Mantua as a viol player (soon after 1590). He accompanied the duke to Hungary (1595) and Belgium (1599), where he encountered French music and musicians. Only in 1602 was he appointed master of music to the duke, whereupon he was granted citizenship of Mantua. In his introduction to his 5th book of madrigals (1605) he wrote of the impossibility up to that time of expressing anything but tranquil moods, and answered Artusi's criticisms of modern composers' use of unprepared dissonances, etc., by claiming that the 'new music' was to be based on truth to nature. With *Orfeo* (1607) and still more with *Ariana* and *Il ballo dell'Ingrate* (1608), which according to contemporary accounts reduced an audience of thousands to tears, he established a formidable European reputation. His patron died in 1612, and M. quarrelled with his successor; after a year's unemployment he was made master of music in Venice. He stayed there for the rest of his life, producing a great quantity of work; he took orders during the plague. He was visited by Schütz and others, and e.g. Praetorius and Tomkins were deeply affected by his music.
M.'s music was responsive to the slightest sway of mood. On this rests the whole of his technique; to this end the simplest means are employed for the maximum effect. His recitatives are given shape by emerging and subsiding melody. Many bars based on one chord might yield to a new one; sudden change might disrupt the whole direction of harmony or pages of austere recitative melt almost imperceptibly into a duet. In *Orfeo* M. became the 1st composer to specify exact instrumentation throughout and to use accompanied recitative at points of dramatic tension. *Il Combatimento di Tancredi e Clorinda* (1624) contains the 1st use of pizzicato and repeated chord effects (to portray a battle). With his last opera, *Incoronazione di Poppea*, M. at 74 showed a facility unprecedented before or since in portraying all kinds of people in all kinds of situations; the human drama, unfettered by any attempts to moralize, fully expresses itself through music. This work also begins to differentiate aria from recitative. Other surviving theatrical works (most have been lost) are: *Tirsi e Clori* (1615) and *Il Ritorno di Ullisse in Patria* (1641). Other works (publ. dates): 14 masses for voices and basso continuo (1610); 15 masses and Psalms (1650) mostly with instruments; *Selva Morale e Spirituale*, a coll. of religious music in 'modern' style; *21 Canzonettas* (1584); madrigals in 9 vols (1587–1651): vol. 5 first uses instruments and vol. 7 basso continuo, and vol. 8 is entitled *Madrigals of Love and War*; and 2 books of *Scherzi Musicale* ('Musical Games').

Montez Lola (1818–61). Irish dancer, born Eliza Gilbert, who launched herself on London (1843) as a Spanish dancer, aiming to exploit the popularity given to this form of dancing by Elssler a few years earlier. M. was involved in many scandals, from a bigamy case to becoming the mistress of King Ludwig I of Bavaria (1847).

Montgomery Robert (1904–). U.S. film actor and director. M. started acting in the 1920s in Cukor's theatrical company. In films from 1929, he appeared in *Mr and Mrs Smith* (Hitchcock; 1941), *Night Must Fall* (1939) and John Ford's *They Were Expendable* (1945), which was completed by him. Of his 5 films as director, the most famous is the first, *Lady in the Lake* (1946), for its use of the camera as one of the characters.

Montherlant Henry (Millon) de (1896–). French novelist and playwright. M has joined no school; his style is sinewy, pure and economical, his manner objective. His sympathies are ultimately with aristocratic pride, a self-discipline which despises the softness of women, and the pursuit of sensual pleasure; and he praises athletics, bull-fighting and war. His work, however, encompasses a wider range of types, e.g. the portrait of 2 seedy aristocrats in *Les Célibataires* (1934; *Lament for the Death of an Upper Class*, 1935; also called *Perish in their Pride* and *The Bachelors*). Works include the novels *Le Songe* (1922; *The Dream*, 1962) and *Les Bestiaires* (1926; *The Bullfighters*, 1927; also called *The Matador*); and the plays *La Reine morte* (1942; *Queen After Death*, 1951) and *Le Maître de Santiago* (1947; *The Master of Santiago*, 1959). In *Chaos et la nuit* (1963; *Chaos and Night*, 1964), M.'s 1st novel for many years, the central figure is a seedy Spanish anarchist and the theme the dissolvent effect of approaching death on his ideas.

Month in the Country, A (1872). Play by *Turgenev.

Monti Vincenzo (1754–1828). Italian poet and playwright. M. wrote poems indiscriminately celebrating the powerful–the Papacy, Napoleon, finally Austria; nevertheless, he had great dexterity with words and produced much fine, lucid verse, a long-admired trs. of the *Iliad* and 3 tragedies, including *Caio Gracco* (1788).

Monticelli Adolphe (1824–86). French painter of figures, portraits and still-lifes. Popular and patronized by Napoleon III, he moved to Marseille on the fall of the Second Empire in 1871. His style changed and he continued to work in Marseille and shunned the life of a fashionable painter.

Moon and Sixpence, The (1919). Novel by W. Somerset *Maugham.

Moon and the Bonfire, The (1950). Novel by Cesare *Pavese.

Moonlight sonata. Nickname of Beethoven's piano sonata in C♯ min. op. 27 no. 2, described by the composer as '*Sonata quasi una fantasia.*'

Moonstone, The (1868). Novel by Wilkie *Collins.

Moore Albert Joseph (1841–92). English painter, son of William Moore, mural and decorative painter. M. exhibited at the R.A. but was never an Academician.

Moore Douglas Stuart (1893–). U.S. composer; his teachers were d'Indy, Bloch and N. Boulanger. Since 1926 M. has taught at Columbia Univ. and has been honoured with the presidencies of national cultural organizations and prizes. His music, conservative in style, includes operas, e.g. *Giants in the Earth*, orchestral and chamber works.

Moore George (Edward) (1852–1933). Irish man of letters acquainted with most of the leading literary and artistic personalities in Paris and London in the late 19th c. His works include the novel *Esther Waters* (1894), marking a new concept of social realism, and the historical novels *The Brook Kerith* (1916) and *Héloïse and Abélard* (1921). M.'s knowledge of the human heart did not match his originality and his long novels now seem prosy and over-involved. His autobiographical writings are important, e.g. *Confessions of a Young Man* (1888), *Memoirs of My Dead Life* (1906) and *Hail and Farewell* (1911–14).

Moore Gerald (1899–). English pianist, outstanding as an accompanist to the world's leading singers and instrumentalists. His books include *The Unashamed Accompanist* (1943).

Moore Henry (1898–). English sculptor. M. studied at Leeds College of Art (1919–21) and at the Royal College of Art, London (1921–5), where he was a fellow-student of Barbara Hepworth.
The 1st major British sculptor of international standing, M. has exerted a considerable influence on succeeding generations, although this was to some extent superseded by the rise of British constructivism in the 1950s.
3 main influences dominated his work from the beginning: first primitive and archaic arts (encouraged by reading Roger Fry's *Vision and Design*, and by the precedent of Epstein, who admired and encouraged his early work); secondly the contemporary work of Brancusi and Picasso (M. made several visits to Paris from 1923); and thirdly his visit to Italy (1925) on a scholarship, where he discovered Giotto and Masaccio but was little interested in the 'perfection' of Renaissance art.
In 1928 M. had his 1st one-man exhibition and his 1st public commission – the *North Wind* relief on the London Transport Executive Building, St James's. Around 1927–9 he made his first reclining figure, the theme which was to be central to his whole oeuvre. In

Henry Moore. *Helmet Head No. 2*

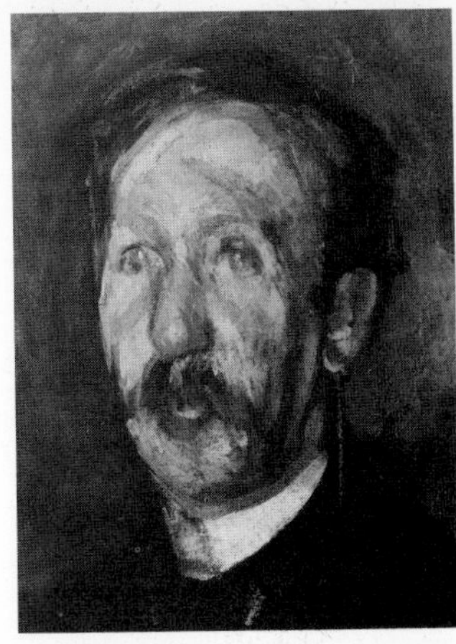

George Moore: painting by Sickert

Henry Moore. *Reclining Figure* (1930)

Henry Moore. *Reclining Mother and Child* (1960–1)

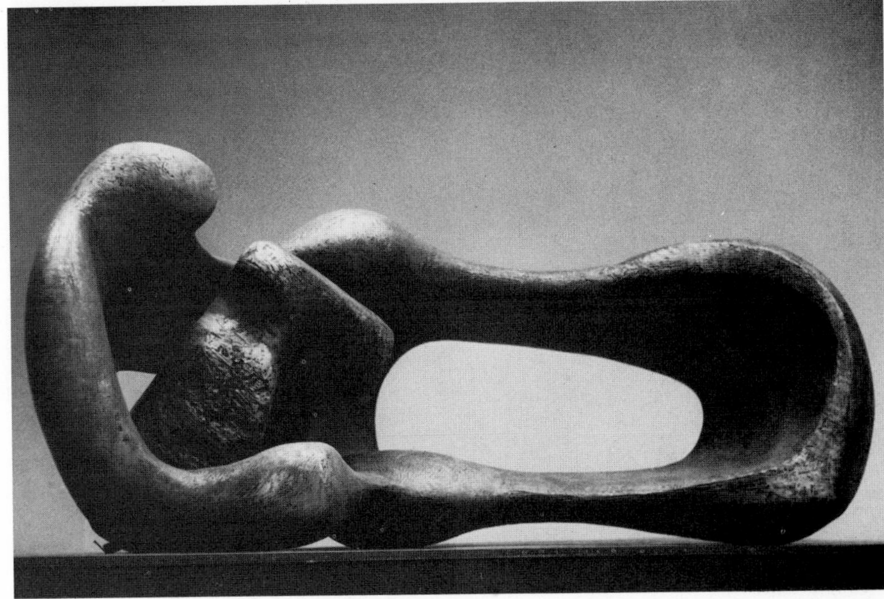

Henry Moore.
King and Queen. Also *maquette and colour plate 79

Henry Moore. *Madonna and Child* (St Matthew's)

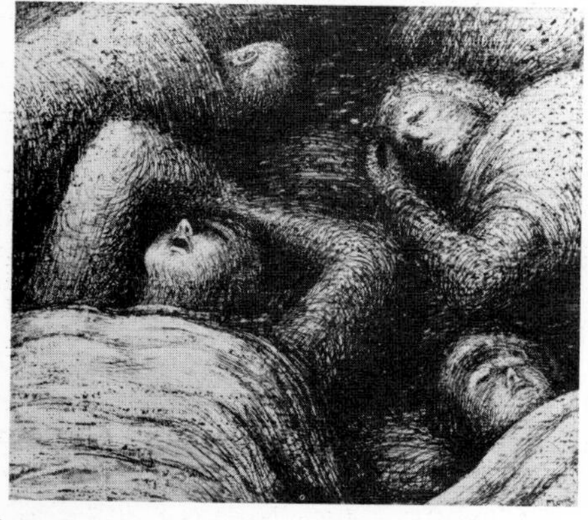

Henry Moore. *Platform Scene* in the Underground (*c.* 1941)

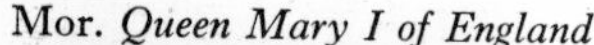

Mor. *Queen Mary I of England*

treating the figure he was never concerned with its superficial appearance, but with creating an elemental living image. The hollows in *Reclining Figure 1930* (N.G., Ottawa), for example, reveal space contained within a volume and are at the same time womb-like fertility symbols. There are also subconscious analogies to landscape–hillsides, caverns, etc.–in many of his figures. Brancusi, he said, made him 'shape-conscious', but M.'s shapes at their most abstract retain a vital sense of organic growth, often in an ambiguous part-animal, part-vegetable metamorphosis. All of his pre-war work is characterized by his truth to the nature of his materials (carving allowed him this closeness of contact), full three-dimensionality and an unidealized urgent sense of energy and vitality.

In 1933 M. was a founder-member of Unit One with Nash, Hepworth and Nicholson. His work in the 1930s ranged from strange surrealist metamorphoses influenced by Tanguy and Picasso, to his most abstract works–the *String Figures* of 1937–40, inspired by Gabo and Nicholson; the *Helmet Head* (1939–40; British Council Coll.) was the first of his ideas on a theme of forms-within-forms. The *Shelter* drawings of the London Underground which he made as a war artist (1940–3) pursue this interest with the small figures enclosed within the throat of the tunnel. There is also an expressive element of pathos in these wartime drawings, which in general abandon surrealism for a naturalism full of feeling for humanity.

Since the war he has continued to work on the reclining figure theme (e.g. UNESCO Building, Paris, 1957–8)–the figure often divided into 2 or 3 monumental pieces. The general development of his post-war sculpture, most of it in bronze, is towards an overpowering dominance of mood and a massive sense of scale. The domesticity of his *Madonna and Child* (1943–4; St Matthew's, Northampton) has given way to the primeval cult character of the *King and Queen* (1952–3; Tate) and the early surrealist organisms to the pantheistic, totem-like *Glenkiln Cross* (1955–6; Marlborough Fine Art, London).

Moore Marianne (Craig) (1887–). U.S. poet. M. was acting ed. of *The Dial* (1925–9) which she made an outstanding magazine. Her poems are witty and intellectual, often obscure (drawing on a wide knowledge revealed in footnotes), and employ unconventional metres. Her colls include *Poems* (1921); *The Pangolin and Other Verse* (1936); *What Are Years?* (1941) and *Nevertheless* (1944).

Moore Thomas (1779–1852). Irish poet; author of *Irish Melodies* (1808–34), once highly popular (some are still sung), and the long poem *Lalla Rookh* (1817). The latter, a series of oriental tales based on Indian models was one of the most famous poems of contemporary Europe. M. was a friend and biographer of Byron (whose memoirs, bequeathed to him, he destroyed) and himself wrote a famous diary.

Moosbrugger. Family of Swiss-Austrian architects, flourishing in the late 17th and early 18th cs. The leading member was CASPAR (1656–1725), architect (among others) of the church of Weingarten and of the abbey of Einsiedeln, Switzerland, of which he was a lay brother.

Mor Antonio (*c.* 1519–*c.* 1575). Netherlandish portrait painter, also called 'Moro or Anthonis Mor van Dashorst'; trained by Jan van Scorel in Utrecht and later court painter to Philip II of Spain, with whom he may have come to England in 1554. M. combines great skill in painting costume with a sharp if diplomatic eye for character in his sitter, e.g. *Sir Thomas Gresham* (Rijksmus., Amsterdam) and the very fine *Queen Mary I of England* (Prado, Madrid).

Móra Ferenc (1879–1934). Hungarian regional novelist and short-story writer. M. successfully reconciled romanticism with realism, elegance of style with the simplicity of anecdotes. His *Ének a búzamezőről* (1927) appeared in English as *Song of the Wheatfields* (1932).

Moraes Dom (1938–). Indian poet whose 1st book, *A Beginning*, written while he was an Oxford undergraduate, won the Hawthornden prize in 1957. His poetry explores traditional Indian attitudes, particularly towards time in its relation to man.

Moraes Francisco de (*c.* 1500–72). Portuguese novelist, author of *Palmerín de Inglaterra* (1547; 1602), a romance of chivalry in the strain of *Amadis de Gaula* which became enormously popular and was praised even by Cervantes. It was far more readable than the imitations it inspired, having a clear plot, well-defined characters and an attractive, forceful style.

Morales Cristobal (*c.* 1500–53). Spanish composer; he worked in the Papal chapel from 1535 to 1545 and then, returning to Spain, was musical director at Toledo cathedral for a time. The 1st Spanish composer of European reputation, he adapted the tradition of Josquin in a highly individual and yet very Spanish manner; his work, above all in the motets, is distinguished by its simplicity of means and dramatic effects; his polyphony is the natural precursor of Victoria's. M.'s church music includes: 21 masses; 16 magnificats; 91 motets and a superb setting of the **Tenebrae*.

Morales Luis de (*c.* 1509–86). Spanish painter, devoted almost exclusively to religious subjects, especially of the head of Christ crowned with thorns. His style was based on a fusion of those of Leonardo da Vinci and Michelangelo. M. often painted on wood and copper.

morality play. Late medieval form of allegorical drama which probably developed from the miracle play. The characters are personifications of qualities, vices and virtues; the subject is usually the conflict between good and evil. These plays were important in the development of a professional secular drama: they were popular and inexpensive to perform, and companies in the early Tudor period in England still had m. p.s in their stock. Examples are **Everyman*, Skelton's *Magnyfycence* and Sir David Lindsay's *Satyre of the Thre Estaitis.*

Morand Paul (1888–). French novelist. M.'s works include the 3 stories of *Tendres Stocks* (1921; *Green Shoots*, 1923) with a preface by Proust.

Morandi Giorgio (1890–1964). Italian painter in whose work the early influence of Cézanne has lingered. In 1918 he joined the metaphysical school of painters and then subsequently the Novecento group. He was one of the prizewinners in the Venice Biennale in 1948.

Moravia Alberto. The pseud. of Alberto Pincherle (1907–). Italian novelist. M. is one of the most widely known modern Italian writers. Most of his novels and short stories deal with the sexual relationship and are distinguished by their rather dry, objective style and somewhat pessimistic view of human nature. They include *Gli Indifferenti* (1929; *The Indifferent Ones*, 1932); *La Romana* (1947; *The Woman of Rome*, 1949); *L'Amore Coniugale* (1949; *Conjugal Love*, 1951); and *La Ciociara* (1957; *Two Women*, 1958).

mordent. A musical ornament (*ornamentation).

More Hannah (1745–1833). English writer and philanthropist, one of Dr Johnson's circle. Her works include the tragedy *Percy* (1777).

More Sir Thomas (1478–1535). English statesman executed for his opposition to Henry VIII's marriage to Anne Boleyn and repudiation of Papal authority; M. was canonized in 1935. He was a friend of Colet and Erasmus and patron of the arts (Holbein is said to have worked for him). M.'s writings include *Utopia* (1516, in Latin; English trs. 1551), a scathing attack on English conditions, which are contrasted with the benevolent, communistic society of the island of Utopia (a word coined by M.).

Moréas Jean. Pseud. of Iannis Pappadiamantopoulos (1856–1910). French poet, born in Athens. M. abandoned his early symbolism and in 1891 founded the école romane (*Maurras).

Moreau Gustave (1826–98). French painter who studied under F.-E. Picot. A painter in the academic tradition, he favoured large, involved Biblical or classical subjects, painted in great detail. Most celebrated of M.'s works is the *Salomé* described by Huysmans in his novel *À Rebours*; it was admired by the novelist for its *'decadence' of mood. M.'s views on the use of colour and his valuable teaching at the École des Beaux-Arts had some influence on surrealism, and stimulated his outstanding pupils, Matisse and Rouault, and several of the lesser fauve painters.

Moreau Jean-Baptiste (1656–1733). French composer of stage music. He was highly praised by Racine and wrote incidental music to his *Esther* (1689).

Moreau Jeanne (1928–). Leading French actress of the 1960s, sensitive and intelligent, forceful yet always chicly feminine. She is at

Luis de Morales. *Pietà*

Gustave Moreau. *Salomé*

Morandi. *Still-life* (1946)

Sir Thomas More

Alberto Moravia

Louis Moreau. *View of Vincennes from Montreuil*

Christian Morgenstern

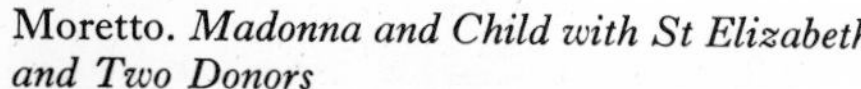

Moretto. *Madonna and Child with St Elizabeth and Two Donors*

her best with psychological scripts like *Les Amants* (1958), her 1st film success, or *La Notte* (1961); she happily combined this with comedy in *Jules et Jim* (1962).

Moreau Louis (1740–1806). French painter of landscapes in the Île de France, in water-colour and oil. His work combines precise observation with a certain spontaneous freshness. His work found great official favour under the governments of the Revolution and Empire.

Morellet the abbé André (1727–1819). French writer closely connected with the **philosophes* and a contributor to the **Encyclopédie*. His *Mélanges de littérature et de philosophie au XVIIIe siècle* (1818) contains selections from his works.

Moreno Villa José (1887–1955). Spanish poet, painter and critic. His poetry is extremely original, rather introspective and written in very simple language; M. often uses the form of *villancicos* or popular dance-songs.

moresque. Decoration found on silver, wall panelling and ceilings, closely allied to Moresque (Moorish) designs, especially on pottery and tiles. Conventional flowers and leaves are intertwined into a scroll-like pattern. It was popular in the 16th c.

Moreto y Cavaña Agustín (1618–69). Spanish playwright and poet. M. was notorious as a plagiarist and adapter, but although his plots lack originality his most famous plays show a brilliant theatrical sense and great skill in the depiction of human weaknesses and eccentricities They include *El lindo Don Diego* and *El Desdén con el Desdén.*

Moretto Alessandro Bonvicino ('Moretto of Brescia') (*c.* 1498–1554). Italian painter and pupil of Ferramola, with whom Moretto decorated the choir of Brescia cathedral (1518). Influenced by Titian and Raphael, he was one of the chief Renaissance painters of N. Italy, and is noted for his preference for silvery or yellowy greys. Moroni was his pupil. He is credited with introducing the full-length portrait into Italy.

Morgan Charles Langbridge (1894–1958). English novelist and playwright. His works include the novels *The Fountain* (1932) and *Sparkenbroke* (1936), and the play *The Burning Glass* (1953).

Morgan Michele (1920–). French film actress, graceful, mysterious, beautiful, who consolidated her reputation with *Quai des Brumes* (1938). She then filmed in Italy, the U.S. and Britain without success, before returning to rebuild her reputation in France; Clair's *Les Grandes Manœuvres* (1955) is her finest picture.

Morgenstern Christian Otto Josef Wolfgang (1871–1914). German poet, an Edward Lear or Lewis Carroll. The poems are loosely grouped round Gallows Hill and the figures of Korf and Palmström; the humour is sometimes typographical, e.g. *Fisches Nachtgesang*, more often linguistic, as in *Der Werwolf*; sometimes satirical (*Die Behörde*), more often surrealist (*Das Nasobem*). Beneath the linguistic playfulness, this nonsense verse conveys a protest against the 20th-c. domination of materialist causality and political conformism; a selection was trs., with surprising success, in 1963. His serious verse, now neglected, is mystical, in late life anthroposophical. His poems include: *Galgenlieder* (1905), *Palmström* (1910), *Palma Kunkel* (1916) and *Der Gingganz* (1919).

Morhange Charles Henri Valentin: C. H. V. *Alkan

Moriae Economium (written 1509). Satire by *Erasmus.

Móricz Zsigmond (1879–1942). Hungarian writer of the *Nyugat* (*Ady) generation. In his stories and novels of peasant life M. shattered the idyllic picture previously presented. His works include *A fáklya* (1917; *The Torch*, 1931) and, in a different genre, the children's classic *Légy jó mindhalálig* (1920; *Be Faithful unto Death*, 1962).

Mörike Eduard (1804–75). German writer, a Swabian; born in Ludwigsburg, educated in Tübingen, vicar in various villages, from 1851 lecturer in literature at a Stuttgart girls' school. As a lyric poet (*Gedichte*, 1838), he is second only to Goethe; after subjective early poetry inspired by the irrational and daemonic, e.g. *Peregrina*, he adopted more reticent modes: the poem with fictional, often folk speaker, e.g. *Das verlassene Mägdlein*, and the object-poem (*Dinggedicht*), e.g. *Auf eine Lampe*. He thus

Eduard Mörike

Morland. *Inside of a Stable*

develops from romanticism through Biedermeier to symbolic realism, while retaining his own unemphatic but not unimpressive individuality. His themes are love, often unhappy; the supernatural, especially in ballads; and the beauty of nature and art, linked with a cult of the small-scale. His characteristic vision is ambivalent, a simultaneous awareness of the joyous and sorrowful (ultimately, the vital and mortal aspects) of phenomena, expressed through symbols as in *Zitronenfalter im April* or directly, e.g. *Verborgenheit*. Early morning, Janus-faced, often points the ambivalence. Sometimes his attitude is quietist, almost escapist (e.g. *Gebet*), sometimes there is a courageous acceptance of dichotomy (*Denk es, o Steele*). He also wrote puckishly humorous poems, e.g. *Elfenlied, An Philomele*. M. is a master of many stanza forms (classical, Romance, Germanic) and metres: metrical variation often parallels polarity of content (e.g. *Um Mitternacht*) as well as of plastic yet symbolic imagery. Hugo Wolf's settings of the poems are famous.

His early novel *Maler Nolten* (1832), a *Bildungsroman* descended from Goethe, Novalis and Tieck, personifies the clash between daemonic and Biedermeier in the figures of Elsbeth and Agnes, while his late **Novelle Mozart auf der Reise nach Prag* (1855; *Mozart on the Way to Prague*, 1934) explores the personality of the creative artist in a vividly realized episode from the composer's life, suggesting an inescapable link between the bright surface world of inspiration and the daemonic underworld of corporeality.

Morison Stanley (1889–). English typographer whose influence has done much to invigorate modern typography. M. was typographical adviser to the Cambridge Univ. Press, the Oxford Univ. Press and *The Times*, for whom he designed the extremely successful newsprint type-face, Times New Roman (1932).

Morisot Berthe (1841–95). French painter who studied at the École des Beaux-Arts (1856–9) and then from 1860 under Corot. She exhibited in 7 of the 8 impressionist exhibitions and her sensitive *impressionism influenced Manet, her brother-in-law, during the 1870s. *The Cradle* (1873; Louvre) was shown in the 1st impressionist exhibition (1874).

Moritz Karl Philipp (1727–93). German novelist, a friend of Goethe and author of *Anton Reiser* (1785–90; 1926), the late *storm and stress novel. This describes with great insight a young man's struggle through hard experience to maturity. M.'s other works include a travel book on England, *Reisen eines Deutschen in England* (1782; *Travels through various parts of England in 1782*, 1798).

Morland George (1763–1804). English painter who rose quickly to fame, but was soon encumbered with debts and died in squalor. His rustic scenes, usually depicting idealized village life, were popularized by a Morland Gallery and by engravings; they created a new public for such pictures. His popular legacy was divided between those who took up his genre subjects, such as Sir D. Wilkie, and the generations of English sporting and animal painters who followed such works as *Shooting Sea Fowl* (Birmingham City Mus. and Art Gal.) and *Inside of a Stable* (Tate).

Morley Christopher (Darlington) (1890–1957). U.S. novelist, poet and literary columnist, a learned, witty writer with a good ear for the stylistic possibilities of language. His novels include *Kitty Foyle* (1939); *Parnassus on Wheels* (1917); *The Haunted Bookshop* (1919) and *Thunder on the Left* (1925).

Morley Thomas (1557–1603). English composer, a pupil of Byrd. His *A Plaine and Easie Introduction to Practical Musicke . . .* (1597) was a first-rate textbook and his delightfully fresh compositions include excellent canzonets (especially those for 2 and 3 voices) and madrigals and airs. He ed. the madrigal coll. *The Triumphs of Oriana* and composed the song 'It was a lover and his lass' for the 1st performance of *As You Like It*.

Morocco (1930). Film directed by J. von *Sternberg.

Morone Francesco (1471–1529). Italian fresco painter. He painted religious works and frescoes for the churches of Verona and also an altarpiece for S. Maria dell'Organa.

Moroni Giovanni Battista (*c.* 1525–78). Italian painter, pupil of Moretto and much influenced by Lotto. Apart from a number of uninteresting religious pictures, he painted astonishing portraits of ordinary people, combining German and Dutch realism with the technical skill of the Venetian school. In his

Morisot. *The Cradle*

Moroni. *Portrait of a Tailor*

Morris.
La Belle Iseult

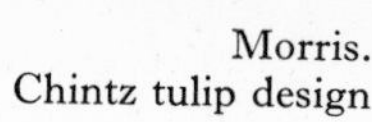

Morris.
Chintz tulip design

Morris. *King Arthur and Sir Lancelot*; cartoon for stained glass. Also *Kelmscott Press

day he was the rival of Titian in reputation. His *Portrait of a Tailor* is in the N.G., London.

Morosov Ivan. One of the great Muscovite merchant patrons (who had an influence on the development of modern art in Russia) and among the first to buy post-impressionist French painting in Russia. His coll. of 135 works (acquired 1905–14) is now divided between the Pushkin Mus., Moscow and the Leningrad Hermitage. Cézanne, Monet, Gauguin and Renoir predominate with specially commissioned panels by Bonnard, Vuillard and Maurice Denis.

Morrice James W(ilson) (1864–1924). Canadian painter. Most of M.'s life was spent in France, though on visits he painted Quebec landscapes. He was primarily a colourist and was heavily influenced by Matisse.

Morris Reginald Owen (1886–1948). English composer and teacher. From 1920 he was professor of counterpoint at the R.C.M., London and exerted a notable influence on English composers, with his books on form and on 16th-c. musical techniques.

Morris William (1834–96). English writer, designer, craftsman and Socialist. At Oxford (1853–5) he met Burne-Jones; in 1859 M. married and commissioned the Red House from P. *Webb. From 1876 M. became increasingly involved in political activities, although he continued to publ. poetry, lecture on politics, and take up and master new crafts until his death.

M., like Ruskin, who strongly influenced his ideas, was appalled by the deadening effect of industrialism; he believed that art derived from the workman's pleasure in his 'daily necessary work' and that decoration, the beginning of art, was the expression of this pleasure; the 1st move towards a rebirth of art must be to raise the condition of the workers. Thus M.'s political and artistic convictions were closely interwoven. This craft theory of art, which was coupled with an admiration for the middle ages, together with his contempt for 19th-c. English art, led M. to the founding of 'The Firm' to design and manufacture wallpapers and furniture for the Red House; besides M. the designers were Burne-Jones, Rossetti, Ford Madox Brown and Webb. Originally a private venture, 'The Firm' continued in production for the commercial market. The *arts and crafts movement was the development of M.'s work. His concern that the artist-designer should understand craft processes and 'honour' his material, is reflected in the principles of the *Bauhaus. The rich but always lucid, vigorous and living patterns of M.'s great fabric designs are unsurpassed, but work at his *Kelmscott Press (opened 1891) as a book designer, was even more influential, leading to a revolution in typography. M.'s important political writings include: *To the Workingmen of England* (1877), *A Dream of John Ball* (1886) and *News from Nowhere* (1890). His poetry, highly coloured by romantic medievalism, includes *The Defence of Guenevere* (1858), *The Earthly Paradise* (1868–70) and *Poems by the Way* (1891).

Morris-dance (possibly from *Moresca*, 'Moorish'). English (and French) folk-dance using such traditional characters as the May Queen, the Fool, etc.; later, characters from the Robin Hood myths appeared. Sticks, handkerchiefs, etc. were often used, and bells worn round the ankles. The M.-d. was banned by the Puritans and never recovered its general popularity.

Morrow George (1869–1955). Irish caricaturist and illustrator who was one of the principal humorists in *Punch* between the World Wars.

Morse Samuel (1791–1872). U.S. inventor of the telegraph and M. code though by profession a painter and sculptor.

Morsztyn Jan Andrzej (*c.* 1613–93). Polish baroque poet, a courtier and diplomat; he was charged with high treason in 1683 and sought refuge in France. His 2 colls of poems, *Kanikuła albo psia gwiazdo* (1647) and *Lutnia* (1661), betray the strong influence of the Italian poet Marino. M. trs. into Polish Corneille's *Le Cid* and Tasso's *Aminta*.

Morte Arthur, Le. An English late 14th-c. stanzaic poem on the last days of Arthur, also describing Lancelot's affair with Queen Guinevere. There is another 14th-c. alliterative poem MORTE ARTHURE which makes passing references to contemporary history.

Morte Darthur, Le. Sir Thomas *Malory's famous work on Arthur.

Morte d'Arthur, The (1842). A poem by Tennyson later incorporated in *The Idylls of the King*.

Mortensen Richard (1910–). Danish abstract painter living in Paris from 1947. His work, which frequently uses vividly contrasting colours, is marked by its elegance and refinement.

Mortimer John Hamilton (1741–79). English painter of portraits, religious and historical subjects, and pupil of Reynolds. For an 18th-c. painter his choice of historical subjects, e.g. *King John granting Magna Carta*, was unusual.

Mortimer John (Clifford) (1923–). English playwright and novelist. M. has written plays for stage, radio and television, encompassing comedy/fantasy (*The Dock Brief*, 1958) and realism (*The Wrong Side of the Park*, 1960). His wife PENELOPE (RUTH) is also a novelist (*The Pumpkin Eater*, 1962).

Morton 'Jelly Roll'. Ferdinand la Menthe (1885–1941). U.S. pianist, composer and bandleader, who brought the traditional New Orleans style of jazz to a peak of sophistication and formal elegance with his compositions for his Red Hot Peppers group in the 1920s. His compositions include *King Porter Stomp*, *Milenburg Joys*, *Wolverine Blues*, *The Pearls*, and *Wild Man Blues*.

mosaic. A design composed of coloured squares of glass, marble or clay embedded in walls, floors or ceilings, either inset in small squares or covering a large area. Both pictorial and abstract designs are found. The Romans were the most extensive users of mosaic and the early Christians continued the tradition, which survived into the early middle ages, and under the Byzantine empire was raised to an unsurpassed level.

Moscheles Ignaz (1794–1870). German pianist, composer and conductor. Resident in London from 1826, he was a director of the Philharmonic Society, but in 1846 he accepted Mendelssohn's invitation to become piano professor at Leipzig Conservatory. His music includes the piano concerto *Pathétique* in C.

Moscherosch Johann Michael (1601–69). German writer. His satirical novel *Gesichte Philanders von Sittewald* (1642), modelled on the *Sueños* of F. de *Quevedo, attacks among other things German subservience to foreign fashions (*À la mode Kehraus*) and the freebooting soldiery of the Thirty Years War (*Soldaten Leben*).

Moschus (2nd c. B.C.). Greek poet from Syracuse; the chief poem with which he is credited is the *Lament for Bion.*

Moscow Art Theatre (founded 1898). This theatre established its reputation with the production methods of *Stanislavsky and its production of Chekhov. It still plays Chekhov but has a large repertoire of other classical and modern plays. The co., which regularly tours outside Russia, is one of the greatest in the world.

Moser Lucas. German 15th-c. painter whose only known work is the *Magdalen Altar* (1431) at Tiefenbronn, near Pforzheim, in Swabia. Stylistically, this altarpiece is a German counterpart to the work of van Eyck or Campin.

Moser Rudolf (1892–1960). Swiss composer and conductor; his music is independent of modern movements and aims to infuse new life into old forms, occasionally using the church modes.

Moses. Sculpture by *Michelangelo.

Moses Grandma (Anna Mary Robertson) (1860–1961). U.S. primitive painter. She took to painting in her old age and rapidly gained widespread attention in the U.S. An exhibition of her work was held in Paris in 1951.

Moses and Aaron. Opera by *Schoenberg, libretto by the composer; 1st stage performance at Zürich in 1938.

Moss Marlow (1890–). English abstract painter and sculptor. She was a member of the Abstraction-Création group in Paris and was a close follower of Mondrian in the 1920s.

Mossolov Alexander Vassilievich (1900–). Soviet composer who won a brief reputation in the late 1920s with an orchestral work, *The Iron Foundry*.

Mostaert Jan (*c.* 1475–*c.*1555). Dutch painter from Haarlem probably identifiable with the Master of Oultremont; he probably worked for the Regent of the Netherlands. He travelled in Italy and painted court portraits and religious subjects. A large number of works by other hands have been attributed to him.

Lucas Moser. *Magdalen Altar*

Mostaert. *Portrait of a Man*

Christian mosaic pavement from Aquileia, Italy (4th c.). See also colour plates 12, 21 and 22

Roman hunting mosaic from Lillebonne

Byzantine mosaic. *St Theodore*; Chios, Greece (*c.* 1050)

Motherwell. *Personage with Yellow Ochre and White* (1947)

Mouldings on a Hellenic column

Mouldings on an arch in the nave of Hereford cathedral

Mount Mellick embroidery

Moulin Rouge: lithograph poster by Toulouse-Lautrec

Moszkowski Moritz (1854–1925). Polish pianist, teacher and composer. He studied in Dresden and in Berlin where he lived as teacher and performer untll 1897, when he settled in Paris. His *Spanish Dances* (1907) are most widely known amongst his numerous piano compositions. His works are light and elegant and include the opera *Boabdil der Maurenkönig* (1892) and the ballet *Laurin* (1896).

motet. A piece of church music composed originally in 3 parts: '*tenor*' (giving the plainsong), the '*motetus*' (from French *mot*, giving the sacred words), and the '*triplum*' (the 3rd voice, often giving the words of a secular song). This was the main form of church composition up to the mid 15th c. when masses came to be composed in increasing numbers; an elaborate form was the *isorhythmic motet. The term came to be loosely applied to any choral composition for the church service to words not in the liturgy; by extension modern composers have called serious secular choral works m.s.

Mother (1907). Novel by Maxim *Gorky, the basis of films directed by I. *Pudovkin (1925) and M. *Donskoi (1956).

Mother Courage (1945). Play by Bertolt *Brecht.

mother-of-pearl. The hard and iridescent internal layer of certain shells, in particular an oyster. Frequently used in inlay-work, particularly during the 19th c.

Motherwell Robert (1915–). U.S. abstract *expressionist painter and a leading art theorist and ed. of the *Documents of Modern Art*. He studied philosophy, then turned to painting, originally attracted to surrealism and the theory of automatism; he is largely self-taught as a painter. Characteristic of his work is the series *Elegies to the Spanish Republic*.

motion. In music a part is said to have: CONJUNCT m. when the intervals between succeeding notes do not exceed a tone, e.g.

DISJUNCT m. when these intervals do exceed a tone, e.g.

The m. of 2 contrapuntal parts relative to one another is described as: CONTRARY when they move in opposite directions, e.g.

OBLIQUE when one part holds a note and the other moves, e.g.

SIMILAR when both parts move in the same direction, e.g.

PARALLEL when both parts move at a fixed interval, e.g.

Motley John Lothrop (1814–77). U.S. historian, diplomat and novelist, author of the classic *The Rise of the Dutch Republic* (1856).

moto perpetuo (Italian, 'perpetual motion'). In music the term sometimes applied to a piece in which a solo line of rapid notes of equal value is maintained unbroken throughout. The Latin '*perpetuum mobile*' is an alternative term.

Mouches, Les (1943). Play by Sartre.

moulding. Term for the decorative outline (projecting or incised) worked on an architectural member or other objects; where a continuous pattern is carved on the member, its m. is said to be 'enriched'. Various styles and periods have had their distinctive m.s.

Moulin Rouge. Parisian dance-hall and cabaret which was opened in 1889 and was the scene of the first performance of the Can-Can. Its atmosphere has been well recorded in the paintings of Toulouse-Lautrec, whose life is the subject of the film *M. R.* (1952) directed by John *Huston.

Mount William Sidney (1807–68). U.S. genre and still-life painter. His work is represented in the museums of Brooklyn and Philadelphia.

Mount Mellick embroidery. Originally a peasant work practised in 19th-c. Ireland, particularly at Mountmellick in Leinster. Realistic designs of flowers and fruit are embroidered in bold relief in coarse white cotton on closely woven white materials.

Mountolive (1958). Novel by Lawrence *Durrell.

Mourning Becomes Electra (1931). Play by Eugene *O'Neill.

Moustiers. Important centre of French *faïence production; its best (notably blue-and-white) wares were produced by or under the influence of the factory of the Clerissy family, between *c.* 1690 and *c.* 1740.

mouthpiece. Removable part of a wind instrument with which the lips come into contact. Its size and shape, etc. are of decisive importance on the tonal characteristics of *brass and woodwind musical instruments.

movement. Musical term for a section, usually independent, of a work such as a suite, sonata and symphony. A m. is formally coherent and self-contained and contrasted with other m.s in the same work in mood, and above all, speed.

Mozarabic. Term applied to the Christian communities and the mixed style produced by Christian artists working under and for the Moorish rulers of Spain (8th–15th cs).

Mozart Leopold (1719–87). German composer and violinist, father and teacher of W. A. M. and Kapellmeister at Salzburg. From 1762 to 1778 his time was devoted to educating and touring with his children, Maria Anna and Wolfgang. M. enjoyed a high contemporary reputation as a composer (some of his works have been confused with his son's) but more important was his violin tutor (1756).

Mozart Maria Anna (1751–1829). German pianist, sister of W. A. M. She was a child prodigy and toured Europe with her father Leopold M. and brother.

Mozart Wolfgang Amadeus (1756–91). Austrian composer. His genius was evident from childhood and was cultivated by his father, Leopold M. M.'s sister Anna was also brilliantly gifted as a pianist and the family made frequent tours throughout Europe, the children performing on the piano and on the violin. The 1st tour was in 1762, to Munich and Vienna; the following year they went through Germany to Paris and Versailles; in 1764, when Wolfgang's earliest piano and violin sonatas were printed, they visited London, where he met J. C. Bach. In 1767 he was again in Vienna, receiving his 1st opera commission; 2 years later, with his father, M. visited Italy and from 1769 to 1771 he toured Italy, meeting Martini at Bologna; Jommelli at Naples; Piccinni and Paisiello. His 3rd Italian visit ended in 1773; it was the 1st brilliant epoch of his career. In the previous year the man who was to overshadow M.'s future career, Hieronymous, Count Colloredo, became archbishop of Salzburg. In 1777 M. and his mother visited Mannheim, where *Cannabich directed the famous orchestra, and then moved on to Paris; his mother's death here struck him fearfully. In 1779 he resumed his activities at the Salzburg court but left 2 years later, exasperated by the archbishop's contemptuous treatment of him. From this period, in a hectic struggle for existence, he lived by teaching, concert performances, his piano concertos being written for his own use, and composition. He lived mainly in Vienna, married Constance Weber in 1782, became a Freemason in 1784 and enjoyed an immense success with *The Marriage of Figaro*. He made a last tour, visiting Berlin and, *en route*, Leipzig where he heard a motet of J. S. Bach's performed. He died of a blood disease and was given a pauper's funeral.
M. drew on the full musical resources of his age in the formation of his style: the baroque traditions of Vienna and Salzburg and of N. Italy, the work of J. S. Bach and Handel, and the work of his great friend Haydn. His astonishing gift of assimilation was the result of fiercely hard work as well as natural brilliance, and his own burning genius welded the

Leopold Mozart

W. A. Mozart's 1st composition

Leopold Mozart with Wolfgang (at the piano) and Maria Anna in Paris (1763)

9th-c. Mozarabic illuminated ms.

Mozarabic architecture. St Miguel de Escalada, Leon (10th c.)

Wolfgang Amadeus Mozart

Mulligan. *To Kill a Mockingbird*

various elements into an unmistakable personal style. His music is perfect in form and technique, it is strong yet elegant, vivacious and delightful, lighthearted and witty; yet it can move us to sadness and fear and religious wonder. There follows a list of M.'s main works. The operas: *Bastien and Bastienne* (1768) for Anton Mesmer; *Il re Pastore* (1775), libretto by Metastasio; *Idomeneo* (1781), libretto by G. B. Varesco–Idomeneo, King of Crete is delayed on his return from Troy but all ends happily; *Die Entführung aus dem Serail* (1782; *The Abduction from the Seraglio*), a *Singspiel* with libretto by G. Stephanie; *The Marriage of Figaro* (1786), with libretto by Lorenzo da Ponte after *Beaumarchais; *Don Giovanni* (1787), libretto by da Ponte on the legend of *Don Juan; *Così fan tutte* (1790), libretto by da Ponte on the theme of the flightiness of women; *Die Zauberflöte* (1791; *The Magic Flute*), with libretto by Emmanuel Schikaneder, an opera set in mythological times and thick with symbolism connected with Freemasonry and a kind of humanistic philosophy; the flute is a talisman of enlightenment. His last opera, *The Clemency of Titus* (1791), was written for the coronation of Leopold II as king of Bohemia. His church music includes: 17 masses, among them the 'Coronation' mass in C maj., K.317 (1779), the uncompleted mass in C min. K.319 (1771/2) and the great unfinished *Requiem in D min.* Of M.'s symphonies the best known are: no. 29 in A; no. 35 in D (1782), called the 'Haffner'; no. 36 in C (1783), the 'Linz'; no. 38 in D. (1797), the 'Prague'; and the 3 great last symphonies all composed in the summer of 1788, no. 39 in E♭, no. 40 in G min. and no. 41 in C, called the 'Jupiter'. M. wrote 21 piano concertos; violin concertos; concertos for various wind instruments, e.g. the famous horn concertos, and a sinfonia concertante for violin and viola. Some of his greatest music is found in chamber works, which include 27 string quartets, among them the *Adagio and Fugue* in C min. (1788); 6 string quintets, a horn quintet (1782) and a clarinet quintet (1789). His other works number piano sonatas, rondos and variations, violin sonatas, and divertimentos and serenades for various combinations of instruments.

Mrożek Sławomir (1930–). Polish humorist and playwright, author of *Policja* (1958), a comedy dealing with the problems of an ideal police state. In his plays M. uses the techniques of the theatre of the absurd for satirical purposes.

Mrs Dalloway (1925). Novel by Virginia Woolf.

Mrs Miniver (1942). Film directed by W. *Wyler.

Mrs Warren's Profession (written 1893–4). Play by G. B. *Shaw.

Much Ado About Nothing (before 1600; publ. 1600). Comedy by *Shakespeare, written *c.* 1598. It was twice performed at court in 1612–13.

Mudarra Alonso (d. 1580). Spanish vihuelista (*vihuela) whose *Tres libros de música para vihuela* (1546) contains, besides several works by M., fragments of works by Josquin, who greatly influenced him.

Mueller Otto (1874–1930). German painter and graphic artist, one of the members of Die *Brücke from 1907 to 1913, and from 1919 a teacher at the Breslau Academy. He painted subjects mainly of women bathing or grazing horses; expressionist in manner, he was influenced by Gauguin.

muffle kiln. Used for fixing the colour of the decoration of a ceramic article. The 'muffle' is the box in which the objects are placed to protect them from smoke and flames.

Muir Edwin (1887–1959). Scottish poet, critic and 1st trs. of Kafka. His verse is dense, often obscure; the most successful examples of his self-explorations are perhaps the poems couched in parable form in *Poems 1921–58* (1960).

Müller Friedrich (1749–1825). German writer and painter. He wrote prose 'idylls' in the style of Gessner, a dramatized version of the Faust legend and the powerful *Golo und Genoveva* (1775–81; publ. 1811), indebted to Goethe's *Götz von Berlichingen.*

Müller Wilhelm (1794–1827). German poet whose cycle of love-poems *Die schöne Müllerin* and travel poems *Reiselieder* were set by Schubert as *Müllerlieder* and *Winterreise* respectively.

Muller William James (1812–45). English watercolour painter noted for his fresh and direct style of work. M. travelled in Italy, Greece and the Near East. His subject-matter was mainly landscapes or architecture. He was influenced by Constable and David Cox.

Mulligan Robert (1925–). U.S. film director. A very successful TV director when he made his 1st film, *Fear Strikes Out* (1957). Like Frankenheimer, he became a favourite director of big stars: Tony Curtis–*The Rat Race* and *The Great Impostor* (both 1960); Rock Hudson–*Come September* (1961) and *The Spiral Road* (1962); and Gregory Peck–*To Kill a Mockingbird* (1962). Although the Curtis films are by far the most interesting, *Mockingbird* was M.'s big success and has given him much freedom for future productions.

Mulliner Book. 16th-c. ms. coll. of English music (over 130 pieces, mostly for organ) by such composers as Farrant, Shepherd, Tallis, Taverner, Tye, Whyte and Thomas Mulliner himself, organist at St Paul's and Corpus Christi College, Oxford.

mullion. Architectural term for a vertical bar (or one of several such bars) dividing a window; the areas created are called 'lights'.

Müllner (Amand Gottfried) Adolf (1774–1829). German playwright whose *Der 29. Februar* (1812) was one of the earliest of the spate of 'fate tragedies' modelled on Werner's *Der 24. Februar*. Better known is M.'s fate tragedy *Die Schuld* (1816; *Guilt*, 1819).

Mulready William (1786–1863). Irish-born landscape and genre painter; with Morland he was the leading genre painter in England in the early 19th c., following the popular manner and subject-matter of Wilkie.

Multscher Hans (*c.* 1400–before 1467). German sculptor and painter working mainly in Ulm, where he produced a number of carvings. The *Wurzach Altar* (1437; Berlin), the only picture known to be by him, exhibits a realism nearer to contemporary Flemish than German painting.

Mumford Lewis (1895–). U.S. writer and social theorist; his *Technics and Civilization* (1934), *The Culture of Cities* (1938), *The Condition of Man* (1944) and *The City* (1963), have

Mueller.
Three women; lithograph

been influential on the international debate on urban life in their plea for social planning and communal land ownership.

mumming play. Amateur entertainment common in England from the 17th to the 19th c. at such festivals as Christmas; a few still survive, but origins are obscure. The m. p. recounted the battle between St George and a Turkish knight and this traditional plot was embellished by such stock figures as Father Christmas.

Munch Edvard (1863–1944). Norwegian painter. He studied at Oslo (1880–2). His early work is influenced by the social realism of his friend Christian Krohg. His work became widely known through periodicals in Paris and Berlin (1895–1905, his most creative period) and was one of the main artistic sources of German *expressionism. He returned to Norway (1909) after a nervous breakdown and painted the mural decorations for Oslo Univ. (1909–10), several portraits, and reworked some earlier themes. He was condemned as 'degenerate' by the Nazis. *The Sick Child* (1885–6; N.G., Oslo)–a later version is in the Tate–was inspired by his sister's death from tuberculosis and shows the neurotic expressionism with which he intensified images from reality.
His mature paintings and prints were concerned with the expression of his feelings in face of reality rather than representing the appearance of reality. In Paris (1889–92) he gained confidence in his developing ideas from Van Gogh's art and from the current symbolist movement (Gauguin, Mallarmé, Moreau, Redon) and was impressed by the brilliant colours of neo-impressionism. In his most characteristic work, *The Cry* (1893; N.G., Oslo), he builds up rhythms of colour and swirling lines–as Van Gogh had done in his self-portraits–to a pitch of hysterical intensity.

Munchausen Baron. Character created by Rudolph Erich *Raspe.

Munday Anthony (1553–1633). English playwright. M.'s works include *The Downfall of Robert, Earl of Huntingdon*, about Robin Hood, and a trs. of the romance **Amadis de Gaule*.

Mundy John (d. 1630). English organist and composer, son and pupil of William (*c.* 1529–*c.* 91). M. contributed a 5-part madrigal to

Muller.
Bristol Cathedral

Mulready. *A Cottage at St Albans*

Multscher. *Christ bearing the Cross*

Munch.
The Sick Child

Munch. *Self-portrait with Cigarette*

Munch. *The Cry*.
Also *expressionism

Munter. *Portrait of Kandinsky*; woodcut (1907)

Paul Muni in *Scarface*

Murillo. *Beggar boys throwing dice*

Murillo. *Madonna* (Corsini Gal.)

Morley's *Triumphs of Oriana* and has a few keyboard pieces in the *Fitzwilliam Book.*

Muni Paul (1897–). Austrian-born actor. A gangster role on Broadway led to similar parts in Hollywood, particularly in *Scarface* (1932). M. then starred immediately in another classic, of social content, *I am a Fugitive from a Chain Gang* (1932). His Oscar-winning *The Story of Louis Pasteur* (1936) and other biographical roles kept him a top box-office star of the 1930s.

Munk Andrzej (1921–61). Polish film director. M. made documentaries before making his 1st feature in 1955. *Man on the Tracks* (1956), a story about an ageing railway worker, showed M.'s concern with humanist values, as did both *Eroica* (1957) and *Passenger.* (1961; uncompleted but ed. by his colleagues, 1963) which used depiction of life in German prison camps as a particular framework for a generalized statement about attitudes of mind and ways of living.

Munk Kaj (1898–1944). Danish playwright, a cleric; he was murdered by the Nazis. His plays, mainly on religious themes, include *En Idealist* (1928) and *Ordet* (1932).

Munkácsy Mihály von (1844–1909). Hungarian subject and portrait painter, strongly influenced by Courbet. In 1872 he settled in Paris, where he enjoyed a formidable reputation in his lifetime. His paintings include *The Last Day in the Life of a Condemned Prisoner* (versions Mus. of Fine Arts, Budapest and Wilstach Coll., Philadelphia).

Munnings Sir Alfred (1878–1959). English painter of horses and country life and president of the R.A. (1944). M. was noted for his facile handling of paint and dexterity in painting horses, and also for his virulent attacks on most forms of modern art not in the academic tradition.

Munro H(ector) H(ugh) (1870–1916). English writer. Author, under the pseud. 'Saki', of many short stories which blended fantasy with sometimes sharp savage irony, and the novel *The Unbearable Bassington* (1912). He was killed in World War I.

Munter Gabriele (1877–). German painter and engraver, at one time married to Wassily Kandinsky. Her style was initially influenced by the impressionists, but after 1908 by the *expressionists, and she contributed to the Blaue Reiter and Storm groups in their Munich exhibitions.

Munthe Axel (1857–1946). Swedish doctor and novelist, author of the best-seller *The Story of San Michele* (1929). This semi-mystical, sentimental and episodic autobiography describes M.'s fantastic success as a society physician, his wide travels and the building of his house, San Michele, on Capri. It was written in English.

mural painting. Painting on a wall, either directly on to the surface, as a fresco, or on a panel which is mounted in a permanent position; a type of architectural decoration which can either exploit the flat character of a wall or create the effect of a new area of space.

Murano: *Venetian glass

Murder in the Cathedral (1935). Verse play by T. S. *Eliot.

Murders in the Rue Morgue, The (1841). Story by Edgar Allan *Poe.

Murdoch Iris (1919–). English philosopher and novelist. Such novels as *The Bell* (1958) and *A Severed Head* (1961) comment wittily and shrewdly on the difference between human nature and the sophisticated attitudes people pretend to.

Murger Henry (1822–61). French novelist whose *Scènes de la vie de Bohème* (1848; *The Bohemians of the Latin Quarter*, 1887) is a romantic account of poor artists in Paris which has deeply influenced the popular conception of their lives and characters; it was the basis for *Puccini's opera *La Bohème.*

Murillo Bartolomé Estéban (1618–82). Spanish painter. Highly esteemed in his own time, M. was the 1st president of the Seville Academy (1660). A lesser artist than his contemporary Velazquez, he perfected popular genre paintings and sentimental Biblical themes painted in the prevailing bombastic and polished mode of the Spanish Counter-Reformation; his beggar boys, fruit-sellers, Madonnas and saints are presented with

Murnau. *Nosferatu*

shallow feeling. The *Beggar boys throwing dice* (Alte Pina., Munich) and the *Madonna* (Corsini Gal., Rome) are among his best and most sincere paintings.

Murnau Friedrich W. (1889–1931). German film director. M. started directing films in 1919. Among his early films is a vampire story, *Nosferatu* (1922). The film which made his name was *The Last Laugh* (1924), which is famous for the very mobile camera style evolved for the film by M. with his script writer Carl *Mayer and his cinematographer Karl Freund. Although camera movement had been used before, it had never played a predominant part in cinematic expression. In a less publicized way the film had an influence comparable to that of the work of Eisenstein and Pudovkin. It was followed by other German movies like Dupont's *Variety* (also photographed by Freund) and spread to the U.S. with the migration of M., Dupont and Freund. Before his departure, M. made versions of *Tartuffe* (1925) and *Faust* (1926). His 1st Hollywood film was *Sunrise* (1927) from a script by Mayer, with no expense spared to equal and even better German achievements. The result on this occasion justified the expense. After 2 more films, *Four Devils* (1928) and *City Girl* (1930), M. co-produced *Tabu* (1931) with R. *Flaherty; and while the South Seas setting and native performers are characteristic of the latter, the story and direction obviously owe much more to M. He was killed in a motor accident.

Murner Thomas (1475–1537). German monk whose satire on society and clerical, particularly monastic, abuses is in the tradition of *Brant but coarser, more brutal and deadlier than the model. M.'s works include: *Die Narrenbeschwörung* (1512) and *Die Schelmenzunft* (1512); in *Von dem grossen Lutherischen Narren* (1522) M. lashed the Reformers in the bitterest of all his works.

Murphy (1938). Novel by Samuel *Beckett.

Murray Sir (George) Gilbert (Aimé) (1866–1957). Australian-born English writer and scholar known for his very popular verse trs of classical Greek dramatists, especially Euripides; they were above all important in being actable and therefore beginning the 20th-c. revival of staging the classical dramatists.

Murray Sir James Augustus (1837–1915). English writer, principal ed. of *The Oxford English Dictionary*.

Murray William Staite (1881–). English artist potter; he also exhibited paintings with Ben Nicholson and others. M. taught pottery at the R.C.A. (1925–39), his pupils including S. T. Haile, and from the 1920s held regular London exhibitions. A meeting with Shoji *Hamada at St Ives in the early 1920s was important but M.'s native talent was great. His attitude and work helped to establish pottery as a vehicle of pure art. From a lyrical oriental decorative idiom M. achieved a mature original style, of bold, robust, free forms.

Murrill Herbert (Henry John) (1909–52). English composer, professor at the R.A.M. and Music Programme Organizer at the B.B.C. His works include: 2 cello concertos, *Suite Française* for keyboard, sonata for recorder and keyboard and a string quartet.

Murry John Middleton (1889–1957). English critic, married for a time to the short-story writer Katherine Mansfield, and an intimate friend of D. H. Lawrence, about whom he publ. important books. He ed. *The Athenaeum* and *The Adelphi*, and produced much important criticism as well as books on social and mystical subjects.

musette. A piece of music in 6:8, 3:4 or 2:4 time, pastoral and gentle, usually with a bass *pedal. It derives its name from an elegantly modified version of the bagpipe popular among the aristocracy of late 17th- and 18th-c. France.

Music Antoine (1909–). Italian painter deeply influenced by the Venetian landscape (e.g. *Barques de Pallestrina*, 1956) and Byzantine art. His works have become increasingly abstract in feeling, though a reference to landscape remains in his use of large fields of luminous colour in which float darker toned irregular shapes like lilies on a pond.

musica ficta. As modal music (*modes) became increasingly harmonic it was necessary to flatten or sharpen certain degrees of the scale to avoid discordant clashes; these flats or sharps were not always written in, since within a modal structure they were, theoretically, impossible–musicians flattened or sharpened the notes in performance for necessity or beauty.

Murner. Luther (as fool) humiliated; from the 1st ed. of *Von dem grossen Lutherischen Narren*

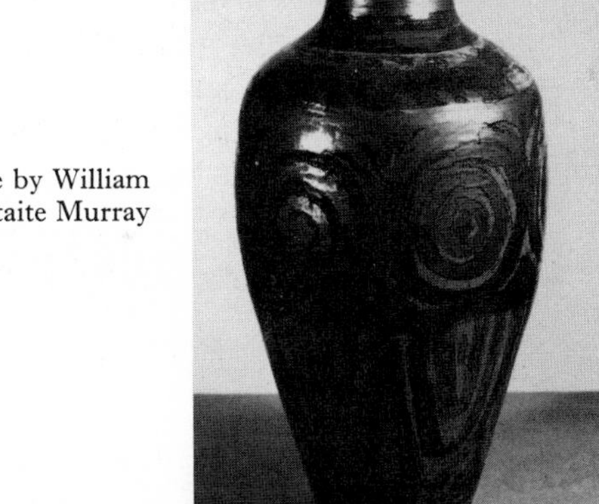
Vase by William Staite Murray

Musette: from a French engraving (1672)

Muybridge. Wet-plate photographs of the racehorse Sallie Gardner (1878)

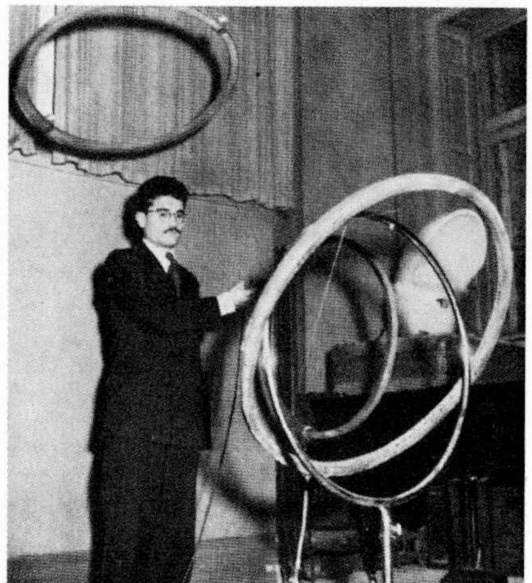

Musique concrète. Pierre Henry at the controls of a musique concrète appliance

Robert Musil

Alfred de Musset

Modest Mussorgsky: painting by Repin. Also *Boris Godunov*

musical comedy. An entertainment originally a combination of burlesque and light opera, having little story and with essentially tuneful songs. The first of this kind was *In Town* (1892) and 2 other famous musical comedies were the American *Belle of New York* (1898) and the British *Floradora* (1899). These, together with later shows such as *The Desert Song* (1927) and *Showboat* (1928), were the forerunners of the modern 'musical' such as *Oklahoma!* (1945) and *My Fair Lady* (1956). Examples of the genre have acquired an increasingly stronger story line and more spectacular set pieces.

musica reservata. A term current between 1550 and 1625. Its meaning is now unclear but it may have been applied to music which by its refinement or complexity was most suited to connoisseurs.

Music Box, The (1932). Short film with *Laurel and Hardy.

music-hall. An entertainment peculiar to England; under the auspices of a 'master of ceremonies', singers, comedians, acrobats and dancers provide a programme of variety numbers. Originating in public-houses in the 18th c., m.-h. reached its height in the 19th c. when special theatres were built. Since the coming of the cinema it has almost disappeared but strangely enough is having a small revival in the 1960s, especially in public-houses.

Musil Robert von (1880–1942). Austrian novelist. He had a varied life as lecturer, librarian, soldier, civil servant and writer; was little known during his lifetime but influential since 1945. Wrote stories (*Drei Frauen*, 1924), but his important work is his fascinating portmanteau novel *Der Mann ohne Eigenschaften* (three vols 1930, 33, 43, incomplete; fuller text 1952; *The Man Without Qualities*, 1953–60). Begun in 1901–related material appeared in *Die Verwirrungen des Zöglings Torless* (1906; *Young Torless*, 1955)–and with many psychological, philosophical and other disquisitions, it presents ironically, in the setting of a disintegrating culture–the Habsburg empire–its semi-autobiographical hero Ulrich's search for a sphere of activity.

musique concrète (English, 'concrete music'). The name given by Pierre Schaeffer to a form evolved by him in experiments in the research studio of Radiofusion-Télévision Française, Paris, in 1948. He used as his materials recorded sound of every description from street noises to performances of musical works; these fragments, subjected to distortions in speed, dynamics, etc. were organized into a composition on a tape. Composers such as Boulez, Messiaen, and in England Roberto Gerhard, experimented in this form of composition which apart from antecedents in work by Hindemith and Toch in the late 1920s is a new and now established mode of artistic expression, though there is now greater interest in the wider possibilities of *electronic music.

Musset Alfred de (1810–57). French poet, one of the major romantics, and a precocious, Byronesque dandy. The major external event of his life was his tempestuous liaison with George Sand between 1833 and 1835. His character was unstable; it is now believed that he was a cyclothymic who wilfully destroyed himself with drink in his periods of depression. His poetry is mainly a harmonious, if self-pitying, expression of the suffering romantic ego and '*le mal du siècle*', e.g. *Rolla* (1833), *Poésies complètes* (1840) and *Premières poésies* and *Poésies nouvelles* (1852). There was also a witty, astringent, though still poetic, side to his nature, which found an outlet in prose tales and *proverbes dramatiques, e.g. *On ne badine pas avec l'amour* (publ. 1834; 1947).

Mussorgsky Modest Petrovich (1839–81). Russian composer. He was a friend of Balakirev, who helped in his music studies, and a member of the *Mighty Handful. M. served for a time in the army and later in the civil service; he became increasingly subject to the alcoholism which killed him.
M. is the most original of the group of Russian nationalist composers; his music shows an uncanny gift for capturing the intonations of Russian speech and the nuances of a character or situation; his failure to observe academic conventions resulted in his works being 'improved' and 'corrected' by Rimsky-Korsakov; even M.'s greatest work, *Boris Godunov* (1874), was not left untouched. This great opera, with libretto by M. after Pushkin, deals with the life of the Czar, Boris (d. 1605); it displays M.'s sympathy with the suffering of the Russian peasantry. M. left unfinished 2 other operas *The Khovansky Affair*, completed by Rimsky-Korsakov, and *Sorochintsy Fair*. M. made no concessions to sentimentality or false individualism; characteristically his music

goes straight to the dramatic point, not letting up for development or repeats, etc. In this he has been influential on 20th-c. composers, e.g. Janáček and Prokofiev.
His other works include: the orchestral work *St John's Night on the Bare Mountain* usually performed in a revised version of Rimsky-Korsakov; the piano work *Pictures at an Exhibition* (1874) orchestrated by Ravel (and others) and a cycle of 4 songs, *Songs and Dances of Death* (1875–7), as well as many other songs, dramatic, lyrical, satirical, etc.

mute. Device for dampening the volume of a musical instrument. On stringed instruments of the violin family a pronged clip is fixed over the bridge thus reducing its vibrations; on *brass instruments a specially designed stopper is thrust into the bell. M.s can be used for special effects–brilliant, harsh or mysterious.

mutation stop. An organ stop whose pipes sound one of the upper harmonics of the note played; e.g. a m. s. called 'the twelfth' sounds the 3rd harmonic, a note a 12th above the note played (*harmonic series).

Muthesius Hermann (1861–1927). German architect and author of *Das englische Haus* (1904–5). This spread knowledge of the new domestic style of architects such as Webb and Voysey to the Continent.

Muybridge Edweard James (1830–1904). British-born U.S. photographer also known as 'Edward Muggeridge'. E.'s early experiments (using 12 or more cameras to produce related series of photographs of animals and people in motion) revolutionized many of the artistic and scientific concepts of his day. His zoogyroscope, which allowed a series of still photographs to be projected rapidly on a screen, was a direct forerunner of the motion picture.

My Antonia (1918). Novel by Willa *Cather.

Mycenae. A fortified hill in N.E. Peloponnese, Greece, excavated by Schliemann in 1876. It proved to be the centre of the 1st high civilization of the Greek mainland, dating from the mid 2nd millennium B.C. (probably destroyed *c.* 1200 B.C.). The chief remains are the wall, including the Lion Gate, 2 'grave circles' containing burials with gold death-masks and jewellery, and the 'Treasury of Atreus', a beehive tomb with circular corbel-vaulting.

My Darling Clementine (1946). Film directed by J. *Ford.

My Fair Lady (1964). Film directed by G. *Cukor; from the famous musical comedy (1956) by Alan Jay Lerner and Frederick Loewe, which was in turn based on G. B. *Shaw's comedy *Pygmalion.*

Myron (*fl.* 480–440 B.C.). Greek sculptor, a pupil of Hageladas of Argos. Working in the Athens of Pericles, he was noted for the exact proportions and the sense of movement in his figures, mainly of athletes and wrestlers. Among his works was the *Discobolos.* Many spurious works were subsequently attributed to him.

Mysteries of Udolpho, The (1794). Novel by Mrs Anne *Radcliffe.

mystery plays: *miracle plays

Mytens Daniel (*c.* 1590–before 1648). Dutch portrait painter, probably a pupil of Miereveld, who became court painter to James I of England (1614) and subsequently to Charles I. One of the best portrait painters of the time, he lost in rivalry to Van Dyck and returned to The Hague in 1635. His style was influenced by Rubens, then by Van Dyck.

Myth of Sisyphus, The (1942). Book by *Camus.

Mytens. *The First Duke of Hamilton.* Also *Howard

Mycenae. The Lion Gate

Mycenae. The 'Treasury of Atreus'

Myron. The *Discobolos*; Roman marble copy after the bronze original

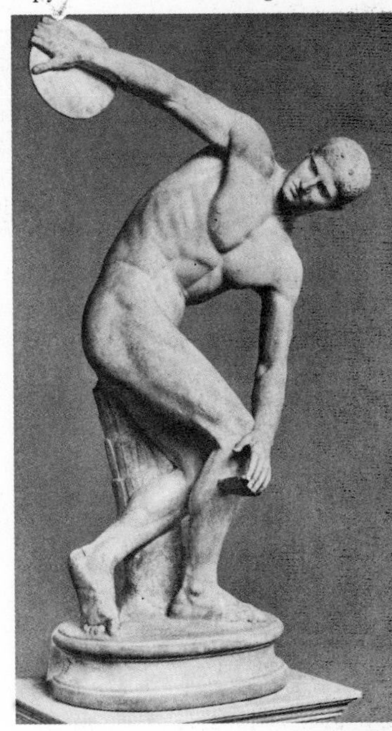

Nadar elevating photography to the status of Art; cartoon by Daumier. Also *Sand

N

Nabis. Denis, *Les attitudes sont faciles et chastes* (*top*) and Vuillard, *The Game of Draughts*

Vladimir Nabokov

nabis, the (Hebrew, 'the prophets'). A group of artists who exhibited together from 1891 to 1900, of whom the best known are Édouard Vuillard and Pierre Bonnard; Ranson, K.-X. Roussel and Maillol were other members. The style they had in common was partly derived from Gauguin's flat pattern compositions done in Brittany; Maurice *Denis wrote several articles which outlined n. ideas. Lithography was especially congenial as a medium and well used in book illustration, posters and theatre decoration.

Nabokov Nicolas (1903–). Russian-born composer; he left the U.S.S.R. in 1919 and has lived in Paris and Berlin. His works include the opera *The Holy Devil* (1958), libretto by Stephen Spender, on Rasputin, and the ballet *Ode . . .* (1928).

Nabokov Vladimir (1899–). U.S. novelist born in Russia, which he left after the Bolshevik Revolution. N. has written a number of novels in Russian including *The Defence* (1930; 1964), but began to publ. works in English with *The Real Life of Sebastian Knight* (1941). They are notable for their virtuoso handling of words and vein of grotesque humour; Gogol, of whom N. wrote a study (1944), has obviously influenced him. *Lolita* (Paris, 1955), the story of a middle-aged man's passion for a 12-year-old girl, made N. famous. Works include *Bend Sinister* (1947), *Pnin* (1957), *Invitation to a Beheading* (in Russian 1938; 1959) and an autobiography, *Speak, Memory* (1951). *Pale Fire* (1962), a pastiche in verse and prose, displays N.'s considerable gifts as a poet. In 1965 he publ. a brilliant trs. of Pushkin's *Eugene Onegin*.

Nabucco. Opera by *Verdi, libretto by T. Solera; 1st performance at Milan in 1842.

Nadar (1820–1910). French photographer, born Gaspard Félix Tournachon. N. took the first aerial photographs from a balloon in 1856–8. His studio was a meeting-place of the artists and writers of the day, whose portraits by N. are now to be found in the Bibliothèque Nationale, Paris.

Nadezhdin Nikolay Ivanovich (1804–56). Russian journalist and critic whose ideas anticipated those of V. Belinsky. His journal *The Telescope* was supressed for publ. P. Chaadeyev's philosophical letters.

Nahum. One of the minor prophetic books of the *Bible (Old Testament).

Naidu Sarojini (1879–1949). Indian poet whose *The Golden Threshold* (1905), *The Bird of Time* (1912) and *The Broken Wing* (1917), and especially *The Temple*, influenced 'Indo-Anglian' (i.e. written in English by Indians) literature. She devoted her later life to political activity. She makes use of traditional Indian philosophy, which, because of its concern with the senses, strengthens the appearance of lyrical spontaneity in her poetry.

nail violin. A musical curiosity invented in the 1740s by the German violinist J. Wilde. 'Nails' of varying sizes set in a wooden sounding-board are vibrated with a bow.

Naipaul V(idiadhar) S(urajprasad) (1932–). Trinidadian (Indian) writer. His subtle and imaginative *A House for Mr Biswas* (1961) is a remarkable novel of exuberance, tenderness and compassion. Other works include: *The Mystic Masseur* (1958), a bitter, satirical novel; *Miguel Street* (1959); and *Mrs Stone and the Knights Companion* (1963).

Nairne Carolina Oliphant, Baroness (1766–1845). Scottish poet, author of the Jacobite songs 'Will ye no come back again?' and 'Charlie is my Darling'.

Naked and the Dead, The (1958). Film directed by R. *Walsh, from the novel (1948) by Norman *Mailer.

Naked City, The (1948). Film directed by J. *Dassin.

Naked Lunch, The (1959). Novel by William *Burroughs.

naker (Arabic *naqqara*). Medieval percussion instrument, like a small kettledrum.

Nałkowska Zofia (1885–1954). Polish novelist and playwright. She wrote realistic fiction in a clear, concise style of deceptive simplicity. Her novel *Granica* (1935) is a penetrating study of Polish society between the World Wars.

Nana (1880). Novel by *Zola; made into a film (1926), directed by J. *Renoir.

Nanni di Banco (d. 1421). Florentine sculptor who like Donatello returned to classical models.

He and Donatello executed companion figures, very similar in style, of *Prophets* in Florence cathedral. N.'s other work includes the statues *Quattro Santi Coronati* for Or San Michele and *Assumption of the Virgin* above the Porta della Mandorla, Florence cathedral.

Nanook of the North (1922). Film directed by R. *Flaherty.

Nanteuil Robert (1623–78). One of the most important of French portrait engravers. His engravings, which show remarkable powers of characterization and masterly linear modelling, were based on his own drawings from life, mainly in pastel. He also engraved portraits by Champaigne. His influence gained engravers the privileges accorded by the government to artists as opposed to craftsmen.

Naogeorgus. Latin name used by Thomas Kirchmair (1511–63). Protestant German playwright; he wrote the anti-Papal play *Pammachius* (1538; *The Popish Kingdom*, 1570).

Naples. The soft-paste *porcelain production here was founded by the Bourbon King Charles in 1743 at the Palace of Capo di Monte. The great period ended when Charles became king of Spain (*Buen Retiro). Work produced included a porcelain room for a royal palace and a series of admired porcelain figures; in the late 18th c. neo-classical patterns were derived from the finds at Herculaneum and Pompeii. Neapolitan maiolica followed the style of near-by CASTELLI. Here Carlo Antonio Grue (1655–1723), one of a famous family, evolved a characteristic style of hand-painted pottery, elaborate baroque border friezes enclosing vividly realistic scenes.

Naples, school of. 17th-c. Italo-Spanish school of painting characterized by pictures of torture and martyrdom in a *tenebrist style derived from Caravaggio, exemplified in the work of Ribera.

Napoleon (1926). Film directed by A. *Gance.

Napoleon of Notting Hill, The (1904.) Novel by G. K. Chesterton.

Napravnik Eduard Franzevich (1839–1916). Czech-born composer and conductor working in Russia. As an opera conductor he raised the standards at the Maryinsky Theatre, St Petersburg to the very highest level.

Narayan R. K. (1906–). Indian novelist who, while analysing the attitudes of the Indian middle class, does so in an enviably pure English that can accommodate everything from high seriousness to uproarious comedy. *The Financial Expert* (1952), *Waiting for the Mahatma* (1955), and *The Man-Eater of Malgudi* (1961) reveal his imaginative range.

Nardini Pietro (1722–93). Italian violinist and composer, the most important pupil of Tartini. He worked at Stuttgart and other German courts and from 1770 at Florence. Both in performance and composition he avoided mere virtuosity and his purity of style was praised by L. Mozart.

narrative painting. Type of painting which flourished in the 19th c.; it relies on anecdotal subject-matter to create interest. The title is an important part of the whole: *Last Day in the Old Home* by Martineau and '*When did you last see your father?*' by William Frederick Yeames are examples.

Narrenschiff, Das (1494). Poem by Sebastian *Brant.

narthex. Vestibule or room across the main (i.e. W.) entrance to early Christian and a few later churches.

Nasby Petroleum Vesuvius. Pseud. of David Ross Locke (1833–88). U.S. humorous journalist whose *Letters of P. V. N.*, satirizing Southern attitudes towards Negroes, were thought by some contemporaries to have contributed to the Northern victory in the Civil War.

Nash John (1752–1835). English architect, one of the leading figures of the *'picturesque' movement. In 1791 he set up in partnership with Repton. In 1798 he married a woman who had useful connections with the Prince of Wales, and became highly successful. In 1806 he began work on the most extensive exercise in town planning ever carried out in London: Regent's Park (with impressive terraces round it and–as planned–villas and a palace in the middle) linked to Carlton House Terrace by Portland Place (including the church of All Souls, Langham Place), Regent Street, with its Quadrant (demolished) and Lower Regent Street. Other works include the Haymarket Theatre; the Royal Pavilion, Brighton, in a gay 'oriental' style; and Buckingham Palace,

Nanni di Banco. *Isaiah*

Narrative painting. Martineau, *Last Day in the Old Home*

Naples porcelain

John Nash. Carlton House Terrace (*below*) and the Royal Pavilion, Brighton (*right*)

Ogden Nash

Nast. *The Tammany Boys Whipped out of their Boots*

London (much altered later, including the façade). His taste for the romantic also produced some interesting neo-*Gothic castles and Blaise Hamlet, Bristol, an early 'garden suburb' of thatched cottages.

Nash Ogden (1902–). U.S. poet who has produced a quantity of light humorous verse, extravagantly unconventional in metre, diction and rhymes; much of it has appeared in *The New Yorker*.

Paul Nash. *Pillar and Moon* (1932–42)

Paul Nash. *Northern Adventure* (1929)

Nash Paul (1889–1946). English painter, mainly of landscapes, in oils and watercolour. He studied at the Slade School (1910–11); his early works were influenced by Rossetti, but his reputation was made as an official war artist (1917–18). N. then continued to paint landscapes in a formalized, decorative manner, striving to express the *genius loci*. In the 1930s he fell under the influence of surrealism and in 1933 was one of the founders of the Unit One group. During World War II he was again an official war artist, painting aircraft, reverting to landscapes and symbolic pictures of an intense and mystical quality in the years before his death. An incomplete autobiography, *Outline*, was publ. in 1949. His brother, JOHN (1893–), also a painter of landscapes, shows affinities of style, but his formalized shapes remain closer to naturalistic forms and he has specialized more in botanical subjects.

Nashe Thomas (1567–after 1601). English writer, one of the *University Wits, educated at Cambridge. N. was a versatile prose writer, a master of the ingenious employment and invention of words and a formidable controversialist. His chief targets were fellow-authors (*The Anatomie of Absurditie*, 1589) and the Puritans (he contributed to the Martin Marprelate debate of 1589–90 under the name 'Pasquil'). He waged a bitter feud with Gabriel *Harvey. *Pierce Pennilesse* (1592) is a cruelly funny description of fashionable vices. The racy adventure story, *The Unfortunate Traveller* (1594), marks an important stage in the development of the English novel. N.'s play *Summer's Last Will and Testament* (1592) contains some fine poems, including *In Plague Time*. He also collaborated with Jonson in writing the suppressed comedy *The Isle of Dogs* (1597).

Nasmyth Peter (1787–1831). English landscape painter, known as 'the English Hobbema'. He was one of the founders of the Society of British Artists (1824).

Nast Thomas (1840–1902). German-born painter who lived in the U.S. from 1846. He began his career by illustrated work in newspapers and, after fighting in the Civil War, specialized in political cartoons, becoming the father of American caricature and cartoon work.

Natchez, Les (1826). Prose epic by *Chateaubriand.

Nathan George Jean (1882–1958). U.S. dramatic critic. Iconoclastic, sardonic, erudite, N. was a notable contributor to *The New Yorker*, ed. *The Smart Set* and later *The American Mercury* with H. L. Mencken, and started his own periodical, *The American Spectator*. His works include *The Autobiography of an Attitude* (1925); *The World of George Jean Nathan* (1952) and *The Theatre in the Fifties* (1953).

Nathan Isaac (1792–1864). British composer, singer and conductor of Polish origin. He was a close friend of Lord Byron, who supplied the words to N.'s *Hebrew Melodies* (1815–22). In 1841 he settled in Sydney; there he gave the 1st performances in Australia of several of the classics.

National Theatre. A state-endowed theatre intended as a centre of and standard for the drama of a nation. Well established in most civilized countries, a N. T. has been the subject of debate in Great Britain for over a c.; finally in 1949 a Parliamentary bill was passed. In 1951 a foundation-stone was laid on the South Bank, by the Queen Mother, in 1962 Sir Laurence Olivier became director of the N. T. Co. which opened its 1st season at the Old Vic in 1963. Denys Lasdun is to be architect of the building.

Natsume Sōseki. Pseud. of Natsume Kinnosuke (1867–1916). Japanese novelist. His early work is witty, almost satirical in tone; the style is easy, the pace slow. Later novels show a developing philosophy of the denial of the ego, quite contrary to N.'s original thesis. His novels include: *I am a Cat* (1905–6; 1906–9) and *Kokoro* (1914; 1941).

Nattier Jean-Marc (1685–1766). French painter of historical subjects, noted particularly

Nattier. *Manon Balletti*

Nay. *Alpha* (1957)

Nay. *Stars* (1963)

for his delicate portraits of young ladies and for starting the vogue for classical and mythological trappings in portraiture. As a fashionable portraitist he painted members of the Russian and French Royal Houses. His pictures were delicate and fragile in feeling, with a fondness for bluish colouring.

natural. In musical notation the sign which, placed before a note, indicates that any previous sharpening or flattening of the note is cancelled (*sharp and *flat).

naturalism. Late 19th-c. French literary movement led by *Zola, a development of *realism which stressed the importance of documentation, using the novel and drama to work out the fate of characters whose course is determined by their heredity and environment. N. became notorious for its use of sordid backgrounds and emphasis on sex and violence, but it was also notable for portraying men at work; this, and the naturalist stress on the importance of social conditions, led many writers towards *socialist realism. N. ended as a movement by 1900, but naturalistic works are still written, and n. has had a great influence on the 20th-c. U.S. novel.
In painting the term signifies only fidelity to nature (irrespective of the subject or period treated).

Naumann Johann Gottlieb (1741–1801). German composer, the most important figure at Dresden between Hasse and Weber. On visits to Stockholm and Copenhagen he organized the reform of the opera there. His operas included *Cora* (1782) for Stockholm, but he also wrote church and chamber music and songs. He is essentially a forerunner of the romantics.

Nausea, The (1938). Novel by *Sartre.

Navagero Andrea (1483–1529). Italian humanist and philologist. While in Spain as Venetian ambassador, he met Boscán and encouraged him to introduce Italian poetical forms into Spanish.

nave. The body of a church W. of the crossing or (where there are no transepts) of the chancel; it is flanked by the aisles.

Navigator, The (1924). Film directed by *Keaton.

Nay Ernst Wilhelm (1902–). German painter and graphic artist who studied in Berlin under Karl Hofer from 1925 to 1927. Since World War II he has evolved a personal form of abstract expressionism.

nazarenes. A group of German artists who formed a brotherhood of painters, the Lucasband, in Vienna in 1809. The following year Overbeck and Pforr were joined by Cornelius at the monastery of Isodoro outside Rome. The intention of these artists was to revive German religious art after the examples of Dürer, Michelangelo, Perugino and the young Raphael.

Nazarin (1958). Film directed by L. *Buñuel, based on the novel by Pérez Galdós.

N.E.A.C.: *New English Art Club

Neal John (1793–1876). U.S. novelist. N. spent several years in England, served as Jeremy Bentham's secretary and contributed to *Blackwood's Magazine* (until then biased against U.S. writers). His works include *Keep Cool: A Novel Written in Hot Weather by Somebody* (1817) and *Rachel Dyer* (1828).

Nebrija (Elio) Antonio de (1441–1522). Leading Spanish humanist; besides works of classical scholarship he produced the 1st Spanish grammar (1492), which was also the 1st important grammar of a European vernacular.

nécessaire. A small box of silver or gold embellished with mother-of-pearl, enamel or gems, containing sewing equipment, scent-bottles, ivory tablets, a snuff-spoon, etc.

Neefe Christian Gottlob (1748–98). German composer, for 2 years a pupil of J. A. Hiller. As Bonn court organist from 1782 he was Beethoven's teacher and mentor, introducing him to Bach's *Well Tempered Clavier* and strongly influencing his early development. N. composed numerous operas, operettas and *Singspiele*, and instrumental music.

Neefs (Neeffs or Nefs) Peter (*c.* 1578–1656/61). Flemish painter of architectural subjects, probably the pupil of van Steenwyck. He painted many pictures of Antwerp churches and added the architectural detail to the paintings of other contemporary artists. His son,

Nazarenes. Cornelius, *Wise and Foolish Virgins*

Nazarenes. Overbeck, *Wise and Foolish Virgins*; pencil and colour wash

Christian Gottlob Neefe

Aert van der Neer. *A River by Moonlight*

Neo-classicism. The *Homeric vase made by Wedgwood from Flaxman's design

Neo-classicism. Thorwaldsen, *Shepherd-Boy*

PIETER (1620–after 1675), painted the same subjects in the same idiom, which has led to confusion in attribution.

Neel (Louis) Boyd (1905–). English conductor and founder (1932) of the Boyd Neel String Orchestra.

Neer Aert van der (1603/4–77). Dutch landscape painter, influenced by the works of Camphuysens and Avercamp. He became a painter late in life; his later work was mainly of landscapes under snow, under strong atmospheric conditions or with dramatic lighting.

Neer Eglon Hendrik van der (d. 1703). Dutch painter chiefly of genre subjects, son of A. van der N. His work is similar to that of G. Metsu and J. Ochtervelt.

Nefertiti (*c.* 1360 B.C.; Dahlem, W. Berlin). Brightly coloured limestone portrait bust of Queen Nefertiti, the wife of the Egyptian king Akhenaton. It was found in the workshop of the sculptor Thutmose in Akhenaton's new royal city of Tel-el-Amarna by the German expedition of 1912–14, and is in the naturalistic Tel-el-*Amarna style.

Negri Pola (1894–). Leading romantic female star of German and U.S. silent films, e.g. *Forbidden Paradise* (1924).

Negulesco Jean (1900–). Rumanian-born U.S. film director. N. started directing in Hollywood in 1934. His post-war work has centred on the woman's picture with great box-office success. His best-known films are *Johnny Belinda* (1948) and *Three Coins in the Fountain* (1954).

Nehemiah. One of the books of the Bible, *Ezra.

Nehru Jawaharlal (1889–1964). English-educated Indian statesman. As India's 1st prime minister he was more practical than his master, Gandhi. His books include: *Autobiography* (1936), *India and the World* (1936), *Before and After Independence* (1950).

Neidhart von Reuenthal (*c.* 1180–*c.* 1250). German lyric poet of the 1st half of the 13th c. For a courtly audience he described rural scenes and rustic escapades, often with himself as the Don Juan. His poems, which use dance rhythms, usually open with a description of the season.

Neilson John Shaw (1872–1942). Australia's finest lyric poet. Many of his poems remain uncollected, even undeciphered, because N.'s bad eyesight led to poems being taken down by illiterate comrades, with whom he worked as a labourer. Such widely anthologized poems as *The Orange Tree*, *May*, and *Love's Coming* are admired for their spontaneity.

Nekrasov Nikolay Alexeyevich (1821–78). Russian poet, and publ. of radical opinions. His journal *The Contemporary* (1846–66) publ. the early work of Tolstoy and Turgenev; later he owned *Fatherland Notes*. His most successful poetry is written in folk style, and includes the famous *Who is Happy in Russia?* and *Frost the Red-Nosed*; its main subject is the people's suffering under Czarist autocracy.

Nelson mass. Nickname of Haydn's mass in D min. (1798). News of the battle of Aboukir is said to have reached Haydn while he was composing the mass; also it is said to have been performed on Nelson's visit to Eisenstadt in 1800. It is also called the 'Imperial' mass.

Németh László (1901–). Hungarian novelist, playwright and essayist. A versatile populist writer, N. created outstanding female characters in such novels as *Iszony* (1947) and *Egetö Eszter* (1956). His historical dramas deal with the conflicts of honest men seeking reform (Galileo, Pope Gregory VII).

Nemirovich-Danchenko Vladimir Ivanovich (1859–1943). Russian producer who had a long and distinguished career. He was co-founder with Stanislavsky of the *Moscow Art Theatre, and mainly responsible for its choice of plays (notably of Chekhov's *The Seagull*).

Nennius. Late 8th-c. British writer, reputed author of the *Historia Britonum*, which includes the story of a British general, Arthur (the 'King Arthur' of legend), who defended the country against the Saxon invaders.

neo-classicism. In painting the name given to the late 18th- and early 19th-c. revival of classical motifs, subjects and decorations. Its inspiration came from the excavations at Herculaneum and Pompeii (begun 1748) and

Neo-classicism. Vanvitelli's Palazzo Reale, Caserta

the publ. writing of the German archaeologist Winckelmann. In Britain the sculptor Flaxman, Wedgwood's Etrurian ware, and the Adam style of interior decoration were all inspired by the revival; in Rome the sculptors Canova and Thorwaldsen were the great exponents of n.-c.; and in France, where it became associated with the Revolution, the painter Jacques-Louis David. In architecture n.-c. developed in the 17th c. in Italy and spread to France, England and Russia (18th c.). Its characteristic features are the use of the *orders (columns or pilasters), pediments, entablatures, friezes and classical ornamental motifs. Architects include Juvarra, Vanvitelli, Mansart, Gibbs and Nash. Also *Grecian revival.

neo-impressionism. A late 19th-c. style of painting also known as pointillism or divisionism, associated above all with Seurat but also practised by Camille Pissarro, Signac, Cross and, in some of their works, Van Gogh, Toulouse-Lautrec, and even Matisse. Instead of mixing pigments on the palette the artist applied pure colours, in small dots or dashes (hence pointillism); seen at the right distance the fragmented areas of vivid colour dots produced the effect of colour areas more subtle and rich than could be achieved by conventional techniques.

neo-plasticism. Term coined by the 20th-c. Dutch painter *Mondrian.

neo-realism in the cinema. Movement originating in the early 1940s in the work of such Italian directors as de Sica, Rossellini and Visconti. They took the camera out of the studio, using for their subject-matter events of everyday life.

Neri Filippo (1515–95). Italian priest whose classes of devotion and confession ('*esercizi dell'oratoria*') developed into the religious order of the Oratorians (1575); N. was canonized in 1622. Such men as Palestrina, Animuccia and G. and F. Anerio wrote music for the Roman oratory (*oratorio).

Nerina Nadia (1927–) (Nadine Judd). South African dancer who joined the Sadler's Wells Theatre Ballet (1946) and since then has become a ballerina with the Royal Ballet. She is one of the most important dancers in Britain today and dances all the classical roles. She gained great personal success as a guest artist in Moscow (1960).

Neroccio di Bartolomeo Landi (1447–1500). Italian painter and sculptor of the Sienese school, the pupil of Vecchietta. He worked for a time with his brother-in-law, Francesco di Giorgio. His paintings are religious or devotional, in the tradition of Simone Martini.

Neruda Pablo. Pseud. of Neftalí Ricardo Reyes (1904–). Chilean poet and for some years a diplomat. His early work, e.g. *Viente poemas de amor y una cancíon desperada* (1924), explored his private world; later, as in *Residencia en la tierra* (1933; *Residence on Earth*, 1946), he absorbed surrealist techniques and attitudes. The turning-point in his development was the Spanish Civil War, which drove him to Marxist political commitment and led him to evolve a new approach, rhetorical and epic, seen in his great American epic *Canto general* (1950).

Nerval Gérard de. Pseud. of Gérard Labuinie (1808–55). French author. He turned vagabond, and after a mental breakdown (1841) finally became insane and hanged himself. N.'s wandering life and mental instability produced his greatest work, *Aurélia*, contained in *Le Rêve et la vie* (1855). It is a record of his hallucinations remarkable for the disparity between the measured rationalism of the style and the illusions of an unbalanced mind which it portrays. N. also wrote a trs. of Goethe's *Faust* (1828) praised by Goethe himself; *La Main enchantée*, a horror story, and *Sylvie* (1854), his finest story, a tale of young love; he publ. various prose and verse colls.

Nervi Pier Luigi (1891–). Italian engineer and contractor who has used the drama of great structures to produce results of great architectural impact. His belief is that the 'Ideal Architecture of Truth' is based on structural calculations, producing buildings which 'because of their perfect adherence to the laws of structural equilibrium, represent the goal of perfect technology'.
His Communal Stadium at Florence (1932) and hangars at Orvieto (1936) established him as one of the great creators of modern architecture. After the war, exhibition halls at Turin (1949), a sports stadium in Rome (1957), the Palace of Labour at Turin (1961), and a bus terminal in New York (1963) showed continued mastery of the same theme. He also

Neo-impressionism.
Seurat, *Entrée du port du Honfleur*

Neo-impressionism.
Matisse, *Luxe, Calme et Volupté*

Pablo Neruda

Gérard de Nerval

Nervi. Communal Stadium, Florence

Nervi. Palazzo del Sport, Rome

Nevers bottle (second half of the 17th c.) and dish (mid 17th c.)

Neutra. Kaufmann Desert House, Palm Springs, California (1946–7)

Neumann. Vierzehnheiligen pilgrimage church

Nevinson. *Star Shell*

works in collaboration with architects, as in the Pirelli Building, Milan and UNESCO, Paris.

Nervo Amado (1870–1919). Mexican poet, among the most important of Latin American *modernism. He was a founder of the review *Revista Moderna*; his best work, influenced by French symbolism, includes *Perlas Negras* (1898). Later works lack the inspiration of his youth; they include novels, stories and essays.

Nesfield William Andrews (1793–1881). English landscape painter and landscape gardener who worked on the layout of St James's Park, London, and Kew Gardens, Surrey.

Nest of Gentlefolk, A (1858). Novel by Turgenev.

Nestroy Johann Nepomuk (1802–62). Austrian writer of comedies and farces, e.g. *Lumpazivagabundus* (1833) in the style of *Raimund's fairy drama, and *Das Mädl aus der Vorstadt* (1841).

Netscher Caspar (1639–84). Dutch genre and portrait painter, pupil of G. Terborch. He made a trip to France (1659) before settling at The Hague, where he joined the painters' guild and taught. His portraits of women are somewhat French in mood and feeling.

Neue Sachlichkeit, Die: *new objectivity

Neue Sezession: *Sezession

neum(e): musical *notation

Neumann Balthasar (1687–1753). German architect. In early life he studied mathematics and military engineering. He visited Paris and Vienna, but the main influences on him were probably Italian (Borromini, Guarini). Like them N. thought first in terms of geometry, not (like the Asam brothers and Zimmermann) in terms of decoration. Of his churches the chief are St Paulinus at Trier; the Hofkirche, Würzburg; Vierzehnheiligen pilgrimage church; and the abbey church of Neresheim (completed after his death). These are among the most splendid baroque churches in Germany, combining spatial excitement with linear elegance and bold theatrical effects–unexpected vistas, rhythmical curves and concealed lighting. In secular architecture N. was responsible for the palaces of Würzburg, Bruchsal and Bruhl. Their most distinctive features were the staircases; rising in contrasting levels, dividing and reuniting with fascinating cross-views, they made walking upstairs a major aesthetic experience.

Neutra Richard (1892–). Vienna-born architect who, after working with leading European architects and with Frank Lloyd Wright, settled in Los Angeles (1926). His Lovell House of 1928 is one of the pioneer houses of the *international style, and superior to anything else being done in the U.S. at that time. This was followed by many other houses, culminating in an extraordinary burst of creative activity in the late 1940s, resulting in some beautiful, luxurious, expensive houses, finely executed and superbly landscaped. Since then he has received larger commissions, but they have not been architecturally significant.

Neveau de Rameau, Le. Posth. publ. novel in dialogue by *Diderot.

Never Give a Sucker an Even Break (1941). Film directed by E. *Cline.

Nevers. In the 16th and 17th cs a factory here produced the 1st French *faïence to approach the tradition of Italian *maiolica. Italian inspiration is clear but the style is bold and recognizably French, and the finest examples are masterpieces in their own right; the most important of the styles peculiar to N. is the 'blue Persian'.

Neveux Georges (1900–). French playwright and poet born in Russia, notable for his surrealistic treatment of dreams, especially in *Juliette, ou la clé des songes* (1930).

Nevinson Christopher Richard Wynne (1889–1946). English painter, largely responsible for introducing futurist ideas into England, and thereby drawn into the Wyndham Lewis orbit. His pictures as an official war artist in World War I reduced the men in the trenches to the level of mechanical automata, as did his subsequent pictures of factory workers.

New Atlantis, The (1626). Book by Francis *Bacon.

New Babylon, The (1929). Film directed by G. *Kozintzev and L. *Trauberg.

Newbolt Sir Henry (John) (1862–1938). English writer, author of the widely anthologized poem *Drake's Drum.*

Newcastle glass. Newcastle upon Tyne was an important glass-making centre from the late 17th c. For long a principal centre of window-glass making, it attracted glass makers from Lorraine and Italy. Newcastle became well known for the fine quality of its lead glass, which was often used for engraving elsewhere because it was particularly suited to this type of decoration (also *Beilby).

new comedy. Dramatic form which emerged in Greece in the late 4th c. B.C. *Menander was its leading exponent. The n. c. dealt with real types and situations (largely excluding farce, mythology and fantasy) and usually centred on the complications of love, mistaken identity, etc.

Newcomes, The (1853-5). Novel by *Thackeray.

new criticism. Name given to a 20th-c. school of criticism which seeks to explain how a poem achieves its effects by detailed examination of its technique and imagery (as opposed to relating it to the rest of the author's work, his life or the works of other writers).

New English Art Club. Exhibiting society founded in 1886 as a protest against the Royal Academy. Whistler, Sickert and Steer were original members. The club's position as the leading progressive art exhibition was lost to the *London Group, founded in 1913.

New Grub Street (1891). Novel by George Gissing.

New Hall Staffordshire. English factory producing hard-paste *porcelain (1782–*c.* 1825); the patent for the manufacture was bought (1781) from the Bristol factory of Champion by several Staffordshire master-potters.

new humanism. U.S. literary movement which originated in the early 1900s, led by Irving Babbitt and P. E. More. It attacked contemporary *naturalism and what it regarded as the decadence of modern life, advocating a moral conservatism, a return to classical models and the creation of literature showing the strength and excellences of man. In the 1930s it was in turn attacked by a new generation of critics including Marxist and socially orientated writers, and the exponents of the *new criticism.

Newman Ernest. Pseud. of William Roberts (1868–1959). English music critic and writer whose work on Wagner, culminating in *The Life of R. Wagner* (1933–46) first exposed the 'inconsistencies' in Wagner's autobiography.

Newman John Henry, Cardinal (1801–90). English theologian and writer, one of the leaders of the Anglo-Catholic Oxford Movement. *Apologia pro Vita sua* (1864) is an account of N.'s spiritual life until his conversion to Roman Catholicism (1854) and defends the integrity of his conduct against an attack by Charles Kingsley. His works include the poem *The Dream of Gerontius* (1866), used by Elgar, and the hymn 'Lead Kindly Light'.

Newman Joseph M. (1909–). U.S. film director. N. started directing in 1942. He has tackled a wide range of subjects with a rather anonymous talent. His best work is characterized by considerable toughness, even behind its humour, particularly in his later crime films like *The Lawbreakers* (1960) and *The Big Bankroll* (1961), and a western, *A Thunder of Drums* (1961). His other work has included a version of *The Outcasts of Poker Flats* (1952) and a good science-fiction film, *This Island Earth* (1955).

Newman Paul (1924–). U.S. *method actor of brooding good looks who made a great impact with his psychological study of Billy the Kid in *The Left-Handed Gun* (1958); he also gave notable performances as a gambler in *The Hustler* (1961) and in another 'western', *Hud* (1963).

new objectivity (German *Neue Sachlichkeit*). A term used of the paintings of Max Beckman, George Grosz and Otto Dix. Clear, detailed satirical paintings and drawings are characteristic of these artists, who reacted against the violent distortion of other expressionists. An exhibition was held in 1925.

New Orleans: *jazz

new realism. Name sometimes applied to the work of *social realist painters.

Newcastle glass beaker (*c.* 1762) with enamelled decoration by the Beilby family (*left*); and tankard by Tyzack (late 18th c.)

Cardinal Newman

Joseph M. Newman. *A Thunder of Drums*

New objectivity. Dix, *The War* (1924)

New objectivity. Grosz, *Evening Party* (1925)

Sir Isaac Newton: engraving after Kneller

New York City Ballet. *Age of Anxiety*

Ben Nicholson. *Still-life* (1930–42)

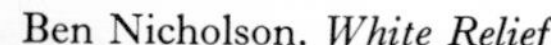

Ben Nicholson. *White Relief*

News from Nowhere (1890). Book by William Morris.

New Testament: *Bible

Newton Sir Isaac (1642–1727). English mathematician and physicist whose theory of gravitation marked an epoch in the history of science; his famous work propounding this theory is *Philosophiae Naturalis Principia Mathematica*, read to the Royal Society in 1686. N.'s other major work was on optics. His English is a beautiful vehicle of exposition.

New Verse (1939). Influential little magazine ed. by Geoffrey *Grigson.

new wave: *nouvelle vague

New Way to Pay Old Debts, A (publ. *c.* 1625). Comedy by *Massinger.

New York City Ballet. Co. formed in 1948; its home theatre was the New York City Center. Under the guidance of the co-founders, George Balanchine and Lincoln Kirstein, the N.Y.C.B. has taken its place among the leading ballet cos of the world. Balanchine is chief choreographer, and the co. has put on a number of his works and revived many of the classics. The New York State Theater was built for the co. in 1964.

Nibelungen, Die (1923–4). 2 films directed by F. *Lang.

Nibelungenlied (*c.* 1200). One of the most important medieval German heroic epics; written by an unknown (probably Austrian) poet. Part history, part myth, the *N.* is based on heroic legend of the 4th–5th cs, common to other Germanic literature including the Icelandic prose *Volsunga Saga* (13th c.) and much earlier Eddic lays (**Edda*).
In the *N.* version Siegfried marries Princess Kriemhild, but his deception of the warrior-maiden Brunhild leads to his murder by a henchman of Kriemhild's brothers; Kriemhild becomes Etzel's (Attila's) queen and avenges herself. The *N.*, and elements from less chivalric Icelandic versions, inspired Richard *Wagner's *The Ring of the Nibelungs.*

Niblo Fred (1874–1948). U.S. film director. One of a group of directors trained by *Ince, N. made the silent version of *Ben Hur* (1926).

Niccolini Giovan Battista (1728–1861). Italian playwright. His early works, classical in idiom, include *Nabucco* (1815), against tyranny; but his best play, *Arnaldo du Brescia* (printed 1843 in France), presenting the case of Italian nationalism, reflects his reading of Shakespeare and the romantics.

Niccolò di Liberatore (Niccolò da Foligno) (*c.* 1425/30–1502). Minor Italian painter of the Umbrian school. His work was influenced by Benozzo Gozzoli and later by Carlo Crivelli and the Vivarini.

niche. In architecture, a recess in a wall, usually containing a statue or other ornament.

Nicholas Nickleby (1838–9). Novel by *Dickens.

Nichols Dudley (1895–1960). U.S. film writer and director. N. started writing films in 1930 and began working for John Ford on *Pilgrimage* (1933). This collaboration continued until *The Long Voyage Home* (1940) and included, notably, *The Informer* (for which he won an Oscar) and *Stagecoach.* He also worked for Renoir and Clair in their American periods, Hawks (*Bringing up Baby*), Hathaway, Kazan, etc. He produced and directed *Sister Kenny* (1946) and *Mourning Becomes Electra* (1947) from O'Neill.

Nicholson Ben (1894–). English painter, son of Sir William N. He spent one term at the Slade (1911) and then travelled (1911–18) in France, Italy, Spain and America. In the 1920s he began to paint seriously in an experimental manner reflecting *cubism (he first saw a Picasso in 1921), Christopher Wood, and the Cornish primitive Alfred Wallis (whom he discovered with Wood in 1928). A naïve pictorial freedom of scale is fused with great textural sensitivity in the grained and scratched paint surface (e.g. *Bistro II,* 1932; City A. Gal., Nottingham).
He married Barbara Hepworth in 1930, was a founder-member of Unit One (with Nash, Moore, and Hepworth) in 1933 and edited *Circle* with Gabo in 1937. During the 1930s he emerged as the major pioneer in British abstract painting. Through his objective analysis of the still-life he evolved an art of pure formal and colour relationships. In his *Notes on Abstract Art* (1941) he compares these relationships with musical harmonies and states

his aim to create from them an equivalent to reality. Whether his 'equivalents' were figurative or abstract was irrelevant. His revelatory meeting with Mondrian (Paris, 1934) probably inspired the confident austerity of his first abstract reliefs–e.g. *White Relief* (1935; Tate). Since then he has produced a refined series of harmonic variations on freely abstracted still-life themes. N. lived in St Ives from 1940 to 1956 and since 1958 has been resident in Switzerland. He won the first Guggenheim International Award (1956) and, with Moore, contributed largely to the post-war international status of British art. His historical significance lies in his unyielding and solitary championship of abstract art in Britain.

Nicholson Sir William (1872–1949). English painter of portraits, landscapes and particularly of still-lifes. He studied in Paris at the Académie Julian. With his brother-in-law James Pryde, he revolutionized poster design, under the pseud. 'The Beggarstaff Brothers'. He was also noted for woodcuts of well-known late Victorian characters.

Nicias (Nikias) (*fl.* 348–308 B.C.). Athenian painter, the pupil of Antidotus. His work was praised by Praxiteles.

Nicolai Otto (Carl Ehrenfried) (1810–49). German composer of the comic opera *The Merry Wives of Windsor* (1849), based on Shakespeare, a delightfully fresh work rich in melodies. While director of the court music at Vienna, N. launched the Vienna Philharmonic Orchestra.

Nicomède (1651). Tragedy by Corneille.

Niderviller. Town in Lorraine, an important 18th-c. centre for the manufacture of *faïence; N. faïence figures are of especial delicacy of moulding and glazing.

Niedermeyer (Abraham) Louis (1802–61). Swiss-born composer working most of his life in Paris directing the École Niedermeyer for church music. N.'s finest compositions are for the church and his songs were important forerunners of the work of Duparc.

niello: *inlay

Nielsen Asta (1881–). Danish silent-film actress, with an economical, powerful style, as in *Hamlet* (1920), which revealed that Hamlet was a woman.

Nielsen Carl (August) (1865–1931). Danish composer. He studied under Gade, was a violinist, then director of the court music; later he became a teacher, then director of the Copenhagen Conservatory. N. is one of the finest Scandinavian composers; his music is in a distinctive contrapuntal polytonal idiom. His works include 6 symphonies, e.g. the well-known no. 2, the *Four Temperaments* (1902) and no. 4 *The Unquenchable*: the tonality of movements often 'progresses', i.e. starts in one key and ends in another; also instrumental concertos and much chamber music.

Nielsen Riccardo (1908–). Italian composer and since 1954 director of the Frescobaldi Liceo at Ferrara. His style was at first neo-classical but since the early 1940s he has written in a 12-note idiom.

Niemcewicz Julian Ursyn (1757–1841). Polish writer and statesman. Although a mediocre poet, he assimilated various foreign genres into Polish literature, introducing the ballad form and writing the 1st Polish historical novel. His trs from English contributed to the development of the romantic movement in Poland.

Niemeyer Oscar (1907–). The best-known architect in Brazil. N. worked with Le Corbusier and on the Ministry of Health Building in Rio, and ever since, with an incredibly busy practice, he has been freely developing the Le Corbusier vocabulary. But while the later buildings of Le Corbusier became more chunky and rough, the work of N. became more elegant, lyrical and smooth. His buildings at Pampulha (1942–3) showed sub-tropical luxury to a world that had practically stopped building, and his public buildings in Brasilia (1962) are among architecture's most startling forms, clear geometry set down on a flat site.

Niepce Joseph Nicéphore (1765–1833). French scientist considered the inventor of photography. His experiments with light-sensitive bitumen dissolved in animal oil were successful in 1822 in producing the first permanent photographic image. In 1829 he formed a co. with Daguerre, who developed N.'s discoveries into a commercially practicable system.

Sir William Nicholson. *Gurnards* (*c.* 1931). Also *Pryde

Niderviller teapot (*c.* 1770)

Niderviller dish (late 18th c.)

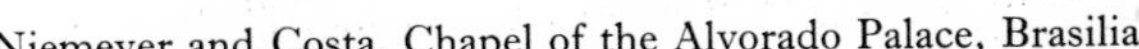

Niemeyer and Costa. Chapel of the Alvorado Palace, Brasilia

Joseph Nicéphore Niepce

Nijinska
in *Le Dieu Bleu*

Friedrich Nietzsche

Nijinsky in *Jeux*

Nijinsky in *Le Dieu Bleu.* Also *L' *Après-Midi d'un Faune*, *Benois, *Karsavina

Nietzsche Friedrich Wilhelm (1844–1900). German philosopher, the son of a pastor; professor of philology at Basle Univ. until forced to retire by ill-health (1879), thereafter suffering almost constantly and becoming insane in 1889. As a young man a follower of Schopenhauer and friend of Wagner, the mature N. rejected the one and conducted a pamphlet war against the other.
N. has been widely misinterpreted, and courted misinterpretation–by his style, lucid, elegant and witty but delighting in pun and paradox; by his intellectual ruthlessness in dissecting moral assumptions; and by his admiration of the self-respecting, morally self-determined (e.g. Renaissance) man–and consequent loathing of Christianity, the bourgeoisie and the masses. Among writers and artists, however, his influence has been great, less for his positive theories–the Will to Power, the Superman (*Übermensch*) and Eternal Recurrence–than for his important attempt to formulate a philosophy for an age in which 'God is dead'. Works include *Die Geburt der Tragödie* (1872; *The Birth of Tragedy*, 1909), which challenges *Winckelmann's view of classical antiquity, distinguishing between its 'Dionysian' and 'Apollonian' elements; *Also sprach Zarathustra* (1883–4, 92; *Thus Spake Zarathustra*, 1896), a symbolic prose poem and therefore the most difficult of N.'s works; and *Jenseits von Gut und Böse* (1886; *Beyond Good and Evil*, 1909).

Nievo Ippolito (1831–61). Italian novelist and poet who fought in Sicily with Garibaldi and recorded his experiences in *Amori garibaldini*. His autobiographical novel *Le confessioni di un Ottuagenario* (posth. 1867; 1957) covers the whole period of the Risorgimento.

Night at the Opera, A (1935). Film with the *Marx Brothers.

Night Flight (1931). Novel by *Saint-Exupéry.

Night Mail (1936). Short film directed by H. *Watt and B. *Wright.

Nightmare Abbey (1818). Novel by *Peacock.

Night on the Bare Mountain. An orchestral work, being the revision by Rimsky-Korsakov of an earlier work by *Mussorgsky.

Nights in the Gardens of Spain. Work for piano and orchestra by *Falla.

Night Thoughts on Life, Death and Immortality (1742–5). Sub-title (and familiar title) of Edward *Young's *The Complaint*.

Night Watch, The (1642). Revolutionary group portrait by *Rembrandt.

Nijinska Bronislava (1891–). Tartar dancer of the Imperial School, St Petersburg and sister of Nijinsky. They left Russia together in 1911 to join Diaghilev, and she was chief choreographer to the co. for 4 years. Since 1938 she has lived and taught in both the Americas and in 1964 she remounted *Les Biches* for the Royal Ballet–a work she first produced for Diaghilev in 1924.

Nijinsky Vaslav (1890–1950). Tartar dancer trained at the Imperial School, St Petersburg and brother of Nijinska. N.'s batterie and elevation were supreme and his dancing is a legend. Diaghilev admired N. enormously and presented many ballets as vehicles for his superb dancing, e.g. *Le Spectre de la Rose* (1911). N. himself was a choreographer, his works including *L'Après-Midi d'un Faune* (1912), *Rite of Spring* and *Jeux* (both 1913). N. married in 1913, broke with Diaghilev and in 1916 suffered a mental breakdown from which he never fully recovered; during it he kept a diary (1918–19; publ. 1936), a strange mixture of spiritual insight and hallucination.

Nikisch Arthur (1855–1922). Austro-Hungarian conductor. He conducted at the Leipzig opera, the Boston Symphony, the Berlin Symphony and the Leipzig Gewandhaus orchestras, and taught conducting at the Leipzig Conservatory.

Nilsson Birgit (1918–). Swedish soprano, most famous in Wagnerian roles but also distinguished in *Turandot* and other Italian operas.

1984 (1949). Novel by George *Orwell.

1919 (1932). Novel by *Dos Passos.

Ninotchka (1939). Film directed by E. *Lubitsch.

ninth. A musical *interval.

Nin y Castellanos Joaquín (1883–1949). Spanish-born composer, writer on music and

Modern performance of a Nō play

Nolan. *Burke and Camel*

pianist, particularly known as an interpreter of old music. He settled in Cuba. His son JOAQUÍN is also a composer.

Niven David (1909–). Scottish film actor. N. has starred in dozens of films since 1935. Suave, charming, by turns heroic and amorous, stiff upper-lipped and comic, he has had parts in *Raffles* (1939), *The Way Ahead* (1944), *The Moon is Blue* (1953) and *55 Days at Peking* (1962).

Njáls Saga: *saga

Nō. The classical Japanese drama, traditionally the preserve of the court and still the theatre of the sophisticated; more popular are the *Kabuki and *Jōruri. The N. plays are lyrical dramas which date from the end of the 14th c. and originate from the ritual dances of the temples. The presentation is highly stylized, using only 2 main actors, no scenery but lavish costumes; there is a chorus of singers and a dignified dance set piece. An evening of N. comprises several plays on different themes, interspersed with short farces called '*kyogen*'.

Noailles comtesse Anna de (1876–1933). French poet and novelist, of Greek and Rumanian ancestry. Her verse expresses intensely personal emotions in strict forms. Colls include *Le Cœur innombrable* (1901).

Nobel prizes. 5 prizes, each worth about £17,000, have been given annually since 1901 from a fund established by the will of Alfred Bernhard Nobel (1833–96), the Swedish inventor of dynamite. They are awarded to individuals of any nationality for outstanding achievement in physics, chemistry, physiology or medicine, peace and literature; the literary prizewinner is nominated by the Swedish Academy of Literature and the French and Spanish Academies.

Nobre Antonio (1867–1900). Portuguese poet. As a student in Paris he was influenced by the symbolist movement. His own poetry, *Só* (1892–8), highly influential in Portugal, is eclectic: he assimilates into an essentially neo-romantic idiom elements of symbolism and also of folk-lore.

Noces, Les (French, 'The Wedding'). 4-scene ballet with choreography by *Nijinska, music and chorus by Stravinsky and décor by Goncharova; 1st performance 1923.

nocturne. This French word, derived from the Italian word for 'night', was used by J. Field for a set of piano pieces and adopted by Chopin. Whistler used it as a title for paintings and Swinburne for poems. *Debussy wrote *3 Nocturnes* for orchestra, *Nuages*, *Fêtes* and *Sirènes*.

Nodier (Jean-Emmanuel) Charles (1780–1844). Novelist and poet, one of the precursors of French romanticism, whose *salon* became a famous centre of the movement. His novels include *Le Peintre de Salzbourg, journal des émotions d'un cœur souffrant* (1803) and *Smarra ou les Démons de la nuit* (1821).

No Exit (1944). Play by *Sartre.

Nolan Sidney (1917–). Australian painter. N. started painting in 1937. His early experimental art reveals a knowledge of European artists like Klee and Moholy-Nagy; it was later enriched by his admiration for Australian aboriginal art. N. spent his army service (from 1942) in remote parts of Australia. In 1950 he came to Europe, where his outback mythologies and folk-histories (*Ned Kelly*, 1945–7; *Burke and Wills*, 1948) were well received. He created for the European a lasting image of the untamed Australian landscape (e.g. *Glenrowan*, 1956–7; Tate). He has continued to work on Australian themes–*Kelly* (1954–5), *Mrs Fraser* (1957)–as well as others (e.g. *Leda*, 1960) which retain the same strange mood.

Nolde Emil (1867–1956). German expressionist painter. N. studied at Flensburg (1884–8), Karlsruhe (1889), and with Hoelzel at Dachau (1889). He moved to Munich *c.* 1900 and was an invited member of the *Brücke group (1906–8). In Berlin (1910) he founded the revolutionary Neue *Sezession and was associated with the *Blaue Reiter, but remained a solitary individual in his work.

His art had a strong folk-art background: he was only able to give all his time to painting through the financial success of his coloured postcards (painted *c.* 1896–8) of peasant mythologies (mountain spirits, trolls, goblins, etc.); and this element of primitive imagery remained the basis of his work. His early admiration for Rembrandt, Goya and Daumier was replaced *c.* 1905 by the influence of Van Gogh, Munch and Ensor (whom he met in 1911). His major religious paintings (*c.* 1909–15) were interspersed with paintings like the

Nolde. *The Legend of Maria Aegiptiaca* (1912)

Nolde. *Gnome* (*c.* 1925)

Nollekens. *Lord Mansfield*

Nolde. *Young Woman with Men*. Also *gouache

Luigi Nono

Lillian Nordica as Elsa in *Lohengrin*

Candle Dancers (1912; Seebüll) which in their emotional violence of colour and paint typify the sensual anti-intellectual character of expressionism in its purest form.
He visited the South Seas and the Far East (1913–14). After the war he divided his time between Berlin and Seebüll. Condemned as 'degenerate' in 1933 and in 1941 forbidden to paint by the Nazis, he produced his *Ungemalte Bilder* ('Pictures I did not paint'), a cycle of several hundred watercolour studies–subjective primitive images, many of which became paintings after the war.

Nollekens Joseph (1737–1823). The greatest English sculptor of the later 18th c. He studied and worked in Rome from 1759 to 1770. Returning to England, he became a R.A. (1772) and, under George III's patronage, rapidly became renowned for portrait busts.

nonet. A musical composition for 9 instruments.

non-figurative. Abstract art in which no figures or recognizable motifs appear. It is a moot point whether geometric figures (triangles, circles) are figurative: the term usually refers to paintings in which not even these appear.

Nono Luigi (1924–). Italian serial composer, Schoenberg's son-in-law, who extended the latent pointillism of *Webern's *Klangfarbenmelodie* and applied the principle to choruses and large orchestras by the use of blocks of sound, each singer or player rarely having more than one note or syllable successively, but one performer following on from the last, often overlapping, so that a texture is created whereby melody, harmony and orchestration become inextricable. The clarity of his use of such procedures is characteristic of N., whose social commitment has meant that he has always been concerned with the ordinary listening public. His compositions include: *Polifonia-monodia-ritmica* (1951) for wind and percussion, *Incontri* (1955), *Il Canto Sospeso* (1956) for soloists, chorus and large orchestra, to texts on letters from victims of Nazism, *Coro di Didone* (1958) for female chorus and percussion, the opera, *Intolleranza* (1960), an attack on all restrictions of freedom and *Sul Ponte di Hiroshima* for chorus and orchestra, on the 1st atomic-bomb explosion.

Nonsense Songs . . . (1871). Book by Edward Lear.

Noon Wine (1939). Short novel by Katherine Anne Porter.

Noort Adam van (1572–1641). Flemish painter of portraits and historical subjects. Dull and conservative in style, he was unimportant except as the teacher of Rubens, Jordaens and van Balen.

Noot Jan van der (1539–1595). The major Dutch poet of the 16th c. and the 1st Dutch Renaissance poet. Little is known of his career (in London for a period he was a friend of Spenser) and his reputation faded soon after his death. After a youthful period influenced by the *rederijker tradition N. studied and imitated the work of Ronsard although his work often reflects the spacious Flemish landscape and the Flemish love of detail. His works include the verse coll. *Het Bosken* (London, 1570 or 71) and the unfinished long allegorical poem *Olympias* stylistically derived from the **Hypnerotomachia Poliphili*.

Nordenflycht Fru Hedvig Charlotta (1718–63). Swedish poet, a leading member of the literary society Tankebyggarorden. Her 1st poems sprang from the emotional experience of her husband's death and her later work continued to reflect her personal experience and also the increasing influence of Rousseau.

Nordica Lillian (1857–1914). U.S. operatic soprano (originally named Norton). For her great versatility and outstanding performances in Wagnerian roles she is considered one of the greatest of American sopranos. She sang at the Metropolitan Opera, Covent Garden and Bayreuth.

Nordoff Paul (1909–). U.S. pianist and composer. His teachers included Goldmark; he has produced ballets, operas and incidental music.

Nordraak Rikard (1842–66). Norwegian classical-romantic composer. He was a cousin of B. Bjørnson, setting many of his poems, of which 'Ja, vi elsker dette landet' is the Norwegian national anthem.

Nordström Ludvig Anshelm (1882–1942). Swedish novelist and short-story writer; his work is pervaded by a utopianism similar to

Northcote. *Richard II and Bolingbroke entering London*

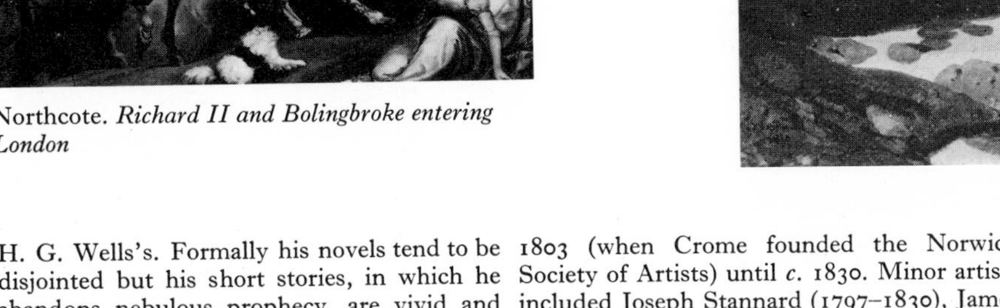

Norwich school. Cotman, *Greta Bridge*

H. G. Wells's. Formally his novels tend to be disjointed but his short stories, in which he abandons nebulous prophecy, are vivid and amusing pictures of rural life.

Norma. Opera by V. Bellini, libretto by F. Romani. 1st performance at Milan in 1831. It is set in Roman-occupied Gaul; N. is a Druid priestess.

Norman. Architectural term for English *Romanesque.

Norris (Benjamin) Frank(lin) (1870–1902). U.S. novelist. *McTeague* (1899), *Vandover and the Brute* (1914) and *The Octopus* (1901) are naturalistic novels, the first in U.S. literature; their plots are sensational in the manner of Zola. They were important in breaking with current sentimental writing and preparing the way for subsequent realistic fiction.

North Christopher. Pseud. of John Wilson (1785–1854), Scottish poet and critic, when he contributed 41 of the 71 sketches comprising *Noctes Ambrosianae*, which appeared in *Blackwood's Magazine* (1822–35). The *Noctes* were a series of discursive tavern conversations between 'the Ettrick Shepherd' (James Hogg), 'Christopher North' and others.

North Sir Thomas (1535?–1601?). English writer famous for his trs, especially of Plutarch's *Lives* (1579; from the French of Jacques Amyot); Shakespeare used it as his chief source for the classical histories, often closely following its phraseology. N.'s strong style influenced the development of Elizabethan prose.

Northanger Abbey (1818). Novel by Jane *Austen.

North by Northwest (1959). Film directed by *Hitchcock.

Northcote James (1746–1831). English painter, art critic and poet. He was the pupil of Reynolds, whose biography he wrote in 1813. N.'s output in portraits was prodigious; he also painted scenes from Shakespeare for John Boydell.

Norwich school. English regional school of landscape painting, the only local school in English art history which is comparable with the earlier Italian schools. Its leaders were Old *Crome and *Cotman, and it flourished from 1803 (when Crome founded the Norwich Society of Artists) until *c.* 1830. Minor artists included Joseph Stannard (1797–1830), James Stark (1794–1859), John Berney Crome (1794–1842) and George Vincent (1796–1831).

Norwid Cyprian Kamil (1821–83). Polish romantic poet, painter and dramatist. N. became a voluntary exile and spent most of his life in extreme poverty in Paris. He wrote philosophical lyrics, expressing religious and patriotic feelings, examining the nature and significance of art, and paying tribute to past and present great men. His poetic language is condensed and exact; his metric experiments led him to free verse, and in the verse dialogue *Promethidion* (1852) he created a new type of poetry, based on colloquial speech. He also wrote important dramas and prose tales.

Nostradamus Michel de Nostre-Dame, called (1503–66). French astrologer and physician, author of the *Prophéties* (1555), called the *Centuries* a book of remarkable prophecies written in quatrains; they were widely read and variously interpreted.

Nostromo (1904). Novel by *Conrad.

notation, musical. A system of presenting sounds as visual information. The most common system, 'staff' n., shows the duration of each note and its pitch relative to the others. The 1st requirement is met by varying the symbol – e.g. the long semibreve is represented thus: 𝅝; the minim, half the semibreve, is represented thus: 𝅗𝅥; the crochet a quarter the length of the semibreve, thus: ♩. The 2nd requirement is met by the use of a stave of 5 lines and 4 spaces; the pitch of one line is indicated by a *clef and the pitch of the other notes follows from this. This system developed from the medieval system of 'neums', signs originally denoting merely the outlines of a plainsong melody, but increasingly used in conjunction with a stave and eventually differentiated into the *longus* and the *brevis*, the 'long' and the 'breve' or 'short' (also *tablature and *tonic sol-fa). The 'semibreve' was in origin half the time value of the breve.

Not by Bread Alone (1956). Novel by Vladimir *Dudintsev.

note. In musical terminology a musical sound of specific pitch and duration. By transference

Norwich school. Crome, *Silver Birches*

Cyprian Norwid

Nostradamus

the term has come to be used of the written symbol which represents the n. in a written out score, and, on keyboard instruments, the actual keys which when struck produce the ns.

note cluster: *tone cluster

note row: *twelve-note music

Notes from Underground (1864). Fictional work by Dostoyevsky.

Notre-Dame du Port, Clermont-Ferrand

Nothing Sacred (1937). Film directed by W. *Wellmann.

Notker Balbalus (840–912). Monk of St Gallen, important as a composer of *sequences.

Notre-Dame Paris. The cathedral of Paris, rebuilt as one of the series of Île de France Gothic churches from 1163 onwards. It has a 4-storey elevation, short transepts not projecting beyond the aisle buttresses, double aisles, sexpartite vaulting and a 'chevet' (ambulatory with radiating chapels). During the 19th c. it was drastically restored by Viollet-le-Duc.

Notre-Dame de Paris (1831). Historical novel by Victor *Hugo.

Notre-Dame du Port Clermont-Ferrand, France. Romanesque church (*c.* 1100) typical of the Auvergne style–2-storey elevation, tunnel-vault and bays N. and S. of the crossing raised as an abutment against the tower. The important 12th-c. churches of Issoire, St Nectaire, Orcival and St Saturnin are similar.

Notte di Cabiria, Le (1957). Film directed by F. *Fellini.

Nottingham. English town notable in the 18th c. for its fine salt-glazed stoneware and lead-glazed brown earthenware; it succumbed to the rivalry of such centres as Denby and Swinton.

Nottingham Playhouse. Leading English provincial theatre which was rebuilt in 1963. This exciting new building, which can be adapted to various stage forms, houses an excellent repertory company under the direction of the actor John Neville. Peter Ustinov was also an artistic director in its 1st season.

Nourrit Adolphe (1802–39). French operatic tenor whose style was formative in the history of French opera. He also wrote the scenario of the ballet *La Sylphide* and introduced Schubert's songs to French audiences.

Nourritures terrestres, Les (1897). Book by André *Gide.

nouvelle. French literary term for a piece of prose fiction dealing with a single incident or personality or situation, and (as now used) about the length of a short novel. The German term is *Novelle.*

Nouvelle Héloïse, La Julie ou la (1761). Novel by Jean-Jacques *Rousseau.

Nouvelle Revue Française (1909–43). Extremely influential French periodical, founded by Gide, Copeau, Schlumberger and others; it (or its associated publishing firm) made known many of the most important 20th-c. French writers. Since 1953 there has been a *Nouvelle N.R.F.*

nouvelle vague (French, 'new wave'). Term loosely applied to a group of younger French film directors who came into prominence about 1959, connected with the *avant-garde* critical magazine *Cahiers du Cinéma.* The first n. v. film was *Chabrol's *Le Beau Serge.* Their films were based on visual style and atmosphere rather than content, distinguished by a free technical approach and an admiration of U.S. 'commercial' directors, especially Hitchcock, Preminger, Minelli, and of the western. Associated are 2 cameramen whose technical bravura has contributed largely to the visual novelty, Raoul Coutard and Henri Decal. N. v. is, however, only a convenient generalization when applied to such dissimilar directors as Truffaut, Resnais and Godard.

Novak Kim (1933–). U.S. film actress, e.g. O. Preminger's *The Man With the Golden Arm* (1956).

Novák Vitězslav (1870–1949). Czech composer and professor of composition at the Prague Conservatory (1909–39), where his pupils included Hába, O. Jeremiáš and the German, Kleiber. In N.'s musical development the early influences of Brahms, Liszt and Grieg were followed by that of folk-music and then French impressionism. His works include: 3

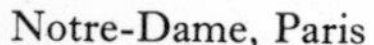

Notre-Dame, Paris

Nottingham stoneware mug (1771)

Novalis

Vincent Novello

operas; 2 ballets; the cantatas *The Storm* (1910) and *The Spectre's Bride* (1913); symphonic poems, e.g. *In the Tatra* (1902), *Slovakian Suite* (1903) and *De Profundis* (1941) for orchestra; and the monothematic 5-movement tone poem *Pan* (1910) for piano.

Novalis. Pseud. of Friedrich (Leopold) von Hardenberg (1772–1801). German writer and thinker, the profoundest of the German romantics and one of the most influential. N., the son of an aristocratic, pietistic family, became a mining administrator. In 1794 he fell in love with the 12-year-old Sophie von Kühn; her death in 1797 released the poetic spring within him. The mystical *Hymnen an die Nacht* (1797–1800; *Hymns to the Night*, 1841) interweave this personal experience with the Crucifixion and with a cyclic myth of history: Night, Sleep, Death, Sophie, Christ all mediate the higher light and life beyond this world. Religious mysticism expressed in the imagery of love characterizes the *Geistliche Lieder* (1799; *The Spiritual Songs of Novalis*, 1876). In the semi-allegorical novel *Heinrich von Ofterdingen* (part I only, 1799; publ. 1802; *Henry of Ofterdingen*, 1842), inspired by, yet thematically in revolt against, Goethe's *Wilhelm Meister*, and expanding motifs from the fragmentary *Die Lehrlinge zu Sais* (1797; *The Disciples at Sais*, 1903), N. shows a young man's education for his poetic mission through experience of life, poetry and love. N.'s backward-looking view of history is set out discursively in *Die Christenheit oder Europa* (1799; *Christianity in Europe*, 1844); he also wrote many *Fragmente*–aperçus and epigrams –unsystematic, but full of penetrating illuminations.

Novarro Ramon (1905–). Athletic and handsome major star of U.S. silent films, e.g. *Ben Hur* (1926), who successfully adapted to sound.

novel. A very loose literary category; the term can be applied to most long pieces of prose fiction and has even been attached to some verse narratives, e.g. Pushkin's *Eugene Onegin*. It generally displays some kind of unity–if only that of a central character who takes part in a series of episodes (as in the *picaresque n.) –or development in *plot or character. There are many kinds of n.–the moral and social satire (e.g. Swift and Voltaire); the epistolary novel, in which the action is seen through letters written by one or more characters (e.g. Richardson's *Pamela*); the n. of social analysis (e.g. Balzac and novelists connected with *realism and *naturalism); the psychological n. (e.g. Tolstoy and Proust); and the n. describing individual development (the autobiographical n., **Bildungsroman* and **Künstlerroman*). The 20th c. has witnessed many innovations, notably the *stream-of-consciousness technique used by James Joyce and Virginia Woolf.

Novelle: *nouvelle

Novellette. Term used by Schumann for short, romantic piano pieces.

Novello Clara (1818–1908). English soprano, daughter of Vincent N.; she sang at Leipzig under Mendelssohn and made her opera début at Padua.

Novello Ivor (1893–1951). English composer and writer, originally called I. N. Davies. His many songs include 'Keep the Home Fires Burning'. He wrote plays and very successful romantic musical comedies, e.g. *Glamorous Nights* (1935), *The Dancing Years* (1935), *Perchance to Dream* (1945).

Novello Vincent (1781–1861). English organist, pianist, composer and music publ., son of an Italian father and English mother. In 1811 he launched his 1st publ.; important early publs were colls of Mozart and Haydn masses and *Purcell's Sacred Music* (1828–32). N.'s wide circle of acquaintances included Keats, Shelley, Charles Lamb, Liszt and Mendelssohn. N.'s son JOSEPH ALFRED (1810–96) expanded the publ. firm, issuing the earliest cheap eds of many standard works.

Novembergruppe. A movement, formed in Berlin in 1918, of expressionist artists, writers, and architects, the leaders being Max Pechstein and César Klein. The aim was for the unity of the arts, architecture, and city planning in the Socialist state. It sponsored publications, composers, radio broadcasts, and abstract film experiments (1920 and 1921 by Viking Eggeling and Hans Richter).

Noventa Giacomo (1898–1960). Italian poet and essayist. His verse in Venetian dialect (coll. 1956) is the work of a sophisticated and cultured intellect.

Novembergruppe. Feininger, *Cathedral of Socialism* (1919) and Pechstein, *Our Daily Bread* (1921; *bottom*)

Jean-Georges Noverre

Nureyev as Siegfried in *Swan Lake*

Noyon cathedral

Noverre Jean-Georges (1727–1810). French dancer who broke away from the tradition of court dancing in favour of the ballet d'action. In his *Lettres sur la danse et les ballets* (1760) N. proposed many changes along lines which have in fact been followed in 20th-c. ballets. N. was a fluent choreographer, producing about 150 ballets, and worked mainly in Paris, Vienna and Stuttgart, but came to London during the French Revolution.

Novikov Nikolay Ivanovich (1744–1818). Russian journalist and publisher. He ed. the satirical journals *The Drone* (1769–70) and *The Painter* (1772–3). After they were suppressed, largely as a result of N.'s attacks on serfdom, he started a publ. business which made an incalculable contribution to Russian culture. It was suppressed in 1791 and N. was imprisoned for a time.

Novodvorsky Andrey Osipovich (1853–82). Russian short-story writer who used the pseud. 'A. Osipovich'. N.'s ironic stories usually concern the failure of the intellectual Populists (a radical Socialist party which idealized the peasants) to understand the people.

Novum Organum (1620). Latin treatise by Francis *Bacon.

Noyes Alfred (1880–1958). English poet; he wrote much traditional (especially narrative) verse, ignoring modern developments. Works include the epic *Drake* (1908).

Noyes Eliot (1910–). U.S. architect and designer. He directed the Museum of Modern Art furniture competition which made Saarinen and Eames famous. His most famous architectural work is a house for his own use at New Canaan, Connecticut. As industrial designer he is product stylist for I.B.M.

Noyon cathedral France. One of the group of cathedrals in the Île de France through which the French Gothic style was evolved. Begun in 1157, N. has pointed arches, ribbed vaults (sexpartite) and the earliest dated example of plate-tracery.

Nude Descending a Staircase No. 1. (1911) and No. 2 (1912). Paintings by *Duchamp.

Nuit et Brouillard (1956). Short film directed by A. *Resnais.

Numbers. The 4th book of the *Bible (Pentateuch), describing the further wanderings (*Exodus) of the Israelites in search of the 'promised land'.

Núñez de Arce Gaspar (1834–1903). Spanish poet and politician. His work suffers from excessive rhetoric and a lack of new ideas. Best known is the coll. *Gritos del combate* (1875).

Nureyev Rudolf (1938–). Tartar dancer of the Kirov school who, when the co. was appearing in Paris (1961) defected to the West bringing with him the style and tradition of his training. He has become the most famous dancer this side of the Iron Curtain; remarkable for his elevation and batterie, he excels as a virtuoso and as a danseur noble. His partnership with *Fonteyn has been tremendously popular and he has advised on and contributed choreography to the remounting of several classics in the Royal Ballet's repertoire.

nut. On string instruments, a small piece of ebony at the end of the finger-board over which the strings pass; the n. keeps the strings clear of the finger-board when they are not depressed by the player's fingers. The name is also given to part of the *bow of a string instrument.

Nutcracker. French title *Casse Noisette*. 2-act ballet with choreography by L. I. Ivanov, music by Tchaikovsky and décor by Botcharov and K. M. Ivanov; 1st performance 1892.

Nymphenburg. Ducal palace at Munich, Bavaria, and the site of a porcelain factory founded in 1753. Under Max III Joseph (d. 1777) N. produced some of the very finest European porcelain; the factory, in private hands since 1862, still exists.

Nynorsk: Ivar *Aasen

Nystroem Gösta (1890–). Swedish composer and music critic; in Paris (1919–31) his teachers included d'Indy. One of Sweden's best contemporary composers, N. has written: the opera *Herr Arnes penningar* (1959), *Sinfonia breve* (1931), *Sinfonia espressiva* (1935) and *Sinfonia del mare* (1948). He has also exhibited paintings.

Nymphenburg figure (1754–5)

Nymphenburg. *Love among the Ruins* (*c.* 1754)

Objets trouvés assistés. Méret Oppenheim, *Fur-Covered Cup, Saucer and Spoon* (1936)

Oath of the Horatii, The (1785; Louvre). Painting by J.-L. *David.

Obadiah. One of the minor prophetic books of the *Bible (Old Testament).

obbligato (Italian, 'obligatory'). A musical term written originally over an instrumental part which must not be left out. From this it came to be used generally in the special sense of an instrumental solo accompanying and decorating a voice part (e.g. aria for soprano with flute o.).

obelisk. (1) Egyptian monument consisting of a tapering stone shaft, square or rectangular in section and pyramidal at the apex; Cleopatra's Needle (Thames Embankment) and its twin in Central Park, New York are 68 ft high, but some o.s reach 100 ft. (2) A mark–a horizontal line, sometimes with a dot above or below it–used in ancient mss to indicate a doubtful or spurious word or passage. (3) The sword-shaped printer's mark (†) indicating a footnote.

Obermann (1804). Epistolary novel by *Senancourt.

Oberon Merle (1919–). Actress in British and U.S. films, noted for dramatic and romantic roles, e.g. *Wuthering Heights*.

Oberon or the Elf King's Oath. Opera by *Weber with libretto by J. R. Planché after Wiegland; 1st performance at London in 1826.

Obey André (1892–). French playwright; his works include *Le Viol de Lucrèce* (1931; *Lucrece*, 1933) and *Noë* (1931; *Noah*, 1935).

objet trouvé (French, 'found object'). The surrealists held that any object could become a work of art if chosen by an artist. Marcel Duchamp exhibited a bottle-rack as a sculptural object, but o. t.s are more commonly natural forms such as shells, tree roots and pebbles, altered or added to by the artist ('objets trouvés assistés').

Oblomov (1859). Novel by *Goncharov.

oboe (a corruption of the French *hautbois*, 'high wood'). A woodwind musical instrument played with a double reed and having a conical bore; the range is approximately two and a half 8ves from middle C. The early o.s (16th c. and 17th c.) had a far coarser and louder tone than the modern instrument and probably, like the horn, came into the orchestra from the hunting-field. Hence the term '*o. da caccia*' found in early 18th-c. scores to distinguish it from the '*o. d'amore*', somewhat lower in pitch and slightly mellower in tone owing to its globular, rather than flaring, bell. The cor anglais (derivation of the name not known) is pitched a 5th lower than the o. and has a globular bell. The *heckelphone is of baritone pitch and the bass of the o. group is the *bassoon.

Obrecht Jacob (*c.* 1452–1505). Flemish composer working mainly in the Low Countries, although he visited Italy, dying in Ferrara. His music was greatly esteemed by contemporaries; it has resemblances to that of *Josquin des Prés.

O'Brien Flann. The pseud. of Brian Nolan (1911–). Irish novelist, author of the exuberant *At Swim-two-birds* (1939), a mixture of fantasy and knockabout humour.

obsidian. An opaque natural glass, generally black, produced by the cooling of volcanic lava, a form of rhyolite. It was much used for weapons, tools and ornaments in ancient civilizations, e.g. by the Egyptians from Predynastic times, in the Aegean Bronze Age civilization, and by the Mayas of Central America.

ocarina. A musical instrument. It is a small hollow vessel shaped like a bulging cigar and having finger-holes and a pipe mouthpiece.

O'Casey Sean (1884–1964). Irish playwright, born in Dublin; after 1928 self-exiled in Devon. O. read early and omnivorously and began writing in his thirties, moulding his experiences of Dublin tenements and Civil War into tragi-comedies. His best work was written for the *Abbey Theatre. When *Juno and the Paycock* was produced in 1924, O. was, with Shaw, already the most distinguished living playwright writing in England. The play, set in the immediate past of Irish Revolutionary activity, is a tragi-comedy about the inadequacies of ordinary people in a great and tragic situation. Later his plays became more didactic, the result of Socialist political sympathies and a readiness to experiment. Other plays include: *The Shadow of a Gunman* (1925), *The Plough and the Stars* (1926), *Within*

Sean O'Casey

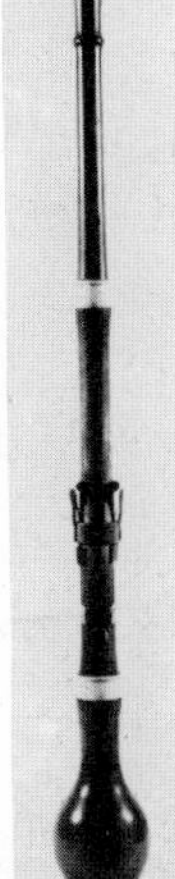

Early 19th-c. oboe

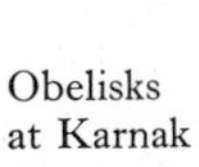

Obelisks at Karnak

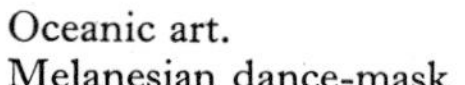

Oceanic art. Melanesian dance-mask

Reclining Odalisque; drawing (1931) by Matisse. See also colour plate 68

the Gates (1934) and *The Star Turns Red* (1949). Complementary to the plays is his long autobiography, *Mirror in My House*, the 6 sections of which appeared between 1939 and 1954.

Occleve Thomas: *Hoccleve

Oceanic art. Polynesian ancestor figure (*left*) and stone statue from Easter Island

Ochtervelt. *A Woman Standing at a Harpsichord*

Oceanic art. The term refers to the *primitive art of the island populations of the Pacific. 3 main areas are distinguished: Melanesia (New Guinea and surrounding islands), Micronesia (islands to the N. of Melanesia), and Polynesia (the triangle formed by the Hawaii Islands, New Zealand and Easter Island).
The art objects include ancestor figures, canoe-prow ornaments, ceremonial shields and clubs, masks, decorated human skulls, stone carvings, carved stools and other cult objects and artifacts. Besides wood and stone, the materials used include shells, wicker, feathers, cane, fibre, bamboo, rattan and bark cloth. As distinct from *African art, various materials are often used in combination, and may be painted in bright pigments, the surfaces with stylized designs of the human face or figure. The range of styles among such widely scattered peoples is enormous, though many groups reveal related art motifs. Among the most famous examples of O. a. are the giant stone ancestor-cult figures of Easter Island, the convoluted designs of Maori wood carvings and the vast production of carved drums, masks, stools and shields of the Sepik river area on the N. coast of New Guinea.

Ochtervelt Jacob (1634/5–1708/9). Dutch genre and portrait painter, the pupil of Berchem. He was influenced by Metsu and Terborch, and above all by Pieter de Hooch, and therefore by Vermeer. He worked in Rotterdam but spent his later years in Amsterdam. *A Woman Standing at a Harpsichord* and *A Woman Playing a Virginal* are in the N.G., London.

Ockeghem Jean or Johannes (*c.* 1430–*c.* 95). Flemish composer. He was a choirboy at Antwerp, possibly studied under Binchois and in the early 1450s was appointed chief musician at the French court, a position he held until his death. O. was considered one of the greatest composers of the day and was also a renowned and important teacher. His music is technically brilliant and immensely varied in style; his greatest work is in his masses, e.g. the *Missa caput*.

O'Connor James (1792–1841). Irish landscape painter who moved to London in 1813 and later settled there. Trained as an engraver, he tried, unsuccessfully, to make a living as a landscape painter. His style is modelled largely on that of R. Wilson.

octave: musical *interval

octet. A group of 8 musical instruments or a piece for such a group.

octobass. A freak musical instrument invented by the Frenchman J.-B. Vuillaume *c.* 1850; it was a double bass 10 ft high, the strings being stopped mechanically. Berlioz much admired the instrument.

October (1928). Film directed by S. M. *Eisenstein.

Odalisque, La Grande (1819). Painting of a nude by Ingres; an 'odalisque' is an Eastern slave or concubine. Matisse painted a series of *Odalisques* (1920–5).

Odd Man Out (1947). Film directed by C. *Reed.

ode. A lyric intended to be sung, e.g. the choral o.s in Greek tragedy and the o.s of Pindar. In modern usage, a serious and dignified poem usually addressed to a person or thing. Famous English examples are Gray's *The Bard*, Wordsworth's *On the Intimations of Immortality*, Shelley's *Ode to the West Wind* and Keats's *Ode to a Nightingale* and *Ode on a Grecian Urn*. The HORATIAN or SAPPHIC o. is one in which all the stanzas have a common metrical pattern.

Odéon, Théâtre Royal de l'. Paris theatre built in 1816 and now the home of the co. run by J.-L. *Barrault and his wife Madeleine Renaud.

Odets Clifford (1906–63). U.S. playwright; he also directed and wrote for films. O. worked as an actor with the Theater Guild and the Group Theater, whose production of his play *Waiting for Lefty* (1935) made O. famous; in the same year *Awake and Sing!*, *Till the Day I Die* and *Paradise Lost* were produced. He had established himself as America's finest social and political dramatist, the major product of the *Group Theater. *Golden Boy* (1937)

Clifford Odets

Offenbach: caricature by André Gill

Offenbach. Title-page of *Orpheus in the Underworld*

extended his theme of human deterioration in urban, competitive society to the boxing racket. O.'s plays include *Night Music* (1940); *Rocket to the Moon* (1938); *The Big Knife* (1949); *Clash by Night* (1941); *The Country Girl* (1950) and *The Flowering Peach* (1954).

Odyssey. Greek epic poem (*Homer). 10 years after the fall of Troy, Telemachus, son of Odysseus, King of Ithaca, searches for his father, who has not yet returned. Odysseus (Ulysses), driven off-course by Poseidon, and then detained by Calypso's passion, has been released by Zeus' command to complete his homeward journey. Shipwrecked at Phaeacia, he tells Alcinous, his host, about his adventures – of the Lotus-eaters, the Cyclops, and Circe; the descent into Hades; the Sirens; and Scylla and Charybdis. Reaching Ithaca, he meets Telemachus, who has also returned, and revenges himself on the insolent suitors who have been wasting his wealth and pestering his wife Penelope.

Oedipus Tyrannus (*c.* 428 B.C.). Tragedy by *Sophocles based on myth. Oedipus is fated to commit a terrible crime – to kill his father Laius, King of Thebes, and after solving the riddle of the Sphinx, become king by marrying Jocasta, his mother; he knows the prophecy but must – unwittingly – fulfil it. Years later he seeks to discover the hidden crime which has caused a plague in Thebes; ironically, it is Oedipus' remorseless investigation which reveals his incest and parricide – and that he is therefore the undiscovered criminal. Jocasta hangs herself; Oedipus puts out his eyes and, supported by his daughters *Antigone and Ismene, leaves Thebes. His death is related in *Oedipus at Colonus*. Oedipus is also the subject of plays by Seneca, Corneille, Voltaire, Hofmannsthal and Cocteau; and of an opera-oratorio by Stravinsky.

Oehlenschlæger Adam Gottlob (1779–1850). Danish poet and playwright, founder of the romantic school in Denmark, which might be dated from O.'s poem *Guldhornene* (1802; *The Gold Horns*, 1913). In the next 5 years he was prolific and at the peak of his poetic inspiration, producing lyrics, ballads and epic poems. Of his later poetry, only the cycle *Helge* (1814) reaches the same level. O.'s plays include *Aladdin eller den forunderlige Lampe* (1820; 1857) and *Hakon Jarl* (1848; 1857).

O'Faoláin Séan (1900–). Irish writer. His novels include *A Nest of Simple Folk* (1933), *Bird Alone* (1936), *A Purse of Coppers* (1937) and *Come Back to Erin* (1940). He has written travel books and biographies of de Valera (1933), Constance Markievicz (1934) and Daniel O'Connell (1938).

Offenbach Jacques (1819–80). French composer of German origin. After studying at the Paris Conservatoire, O. worked as a cellist in various orchestras and then enjoyed a career as a virtuoso cellist. From 1850 he worked as composer and director of music in Parisian theatres. He composed over 100 operas, averaging 5 or 6 a year, and gained a huge reputation for his brilliant, witty and delightfully piquant operettas, e.g. *Orpheus in the Underworld* (1858; expanded 1874), *La Belle Hélène* (1864) and *La Vie Parisienne* (1866). His last stage work, the opera *The Tales of Hoffmann* (unfinished), based on the life and work of E. T. A. *Hoffmann, was produced posth. (1881).

offertorium. The music which accompanies the offertory during the Roman Catholic mass.

Of Human Bondage (1915). Novel by W. Somerset *Maugham.

O'Flaherty Liam (1897–). Irish novelist. O.'s best-known works, including *The Informer* (1926) and *The Assassin* (1928), deal with Irish Revolutionaries in the 20th-c. struggle against British rule.

Of Mice and Men (1937). Long short story by John *Steinbeck; made into a film (1939) directed by Lewis Milestone.

Ogaryov Nikolay Platonovich (1813–77). Russian Revolutionary journalist and poet. O. lived in exile for many years, helping *Herzen ed. the Russian journal produced in England, *The Bell*.

ogee. In section, an S-shaped moulding made up of a concave curve above and a convex curve below. Used widely in furniture and metalwork.

Ognyov N. Pseud. of Mikhail Grigorievich Rozanov (1888–1938). Russian writer, author of *The Diary of a Communist Schoolboy* (1927;

Ogee arch at St John the Evangelist, Shobdon, Herefordshire

Isaac Oliver. *Unknown Man*

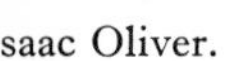

Isaac Oliver.

Peter Oliver.
Self-portrait

O'Keefe. *The White Flower* (1931)

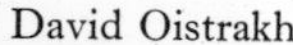

David Oistrakh

1928), which describes school life in the early years of the Soviet régime.

O'Hara John (Henry) (1905–). U.S. novelist. O.'s tough, realistic works, almost all of them filmed, include the novels *Appointment in Samarra* (1934); *Butterfield 8* (1935); *A Rage to Live* (1949); *Ten North Frederick* (1955), and *From the Terrace* (1958); and the short-story coll. *Pal Joey* (1940).

Oil! (1927). Novel by Upton *Sinclair.

oil painting. An increasingly important technique in European painting since the late 15th c. Powdered colours, mixed with a fine oil (usually linseed) until the resulting paint is sufficiently viscous, are applied to a prepared ground–usually stretched canvas with an overall coating in a neutral pigment. The technique at its most elaborate, as in the work of the old masters, involved a careful application of colours building up from dark to lighter tones and relying on extensive technical knowledge of the interaction between the various pigments–the various chemicals involved can act on one another and, if not carefully applied, can over a period of time damage the layers of paint above and next to them. Colours can be laid down with the intention that they should show through upper layers to a certain extent, while coloured transparent glazes can be applied for further gradations of tone. Apart from the immense tonal subtlety of the medium, surface texture can also be varied by *impasto and *brushwork.
O. p. in one form or another had been known since antiquity for coarse work such as house painting, but the technique was immensely refined in early 15th-c. Flanders, the improved medium being gradually taken up by Italian painters.

Oistrakh David Fyodorovich (1908–). Soviet violinist, teacher at the Moscow Conservatory since 1934. O. represents the ultimate point in that style of violin playing which seeks to hide the physical activity involved. His extraordinary fluency and warm overall vibrato are immediate distinguishing-marks. Most of the celebrated Soviet composers have written works for him, but his repertoire is all-inclusive. His son IGOR (1931–) has established as great a reputation now as his father.

Ojetti Ugo (1871–1946). Italian writer who turned from writing novels to literary and art criticism. O.'s finest novel was *Mio figlio ferroviere* (1922), a sharply observed study of social tensions.

O'Keefe Georgia (1887–). U.S. painter and wife of Alfred *Steiglitz; she was one of the prominent figures in the 1920s American reaction against *avant-garde* European ideas and movement towards a romantic, naturalistic art. Her own painting, however–'magical realism'–has surrealist undertones. The exotic colour and form of plants and flowers is heightened by taking them out of their natural context.

Okhlopkov Nikolay Pavlovich (1900–). Soviet stage director and actor; he studied under Meyerhold. He was artistic director (1932–8) of the *Realistic Theatre.

old comedy. Dramatic form in 5th-c. B.C. Greece; *Aristophanes is the only playwright whose works survive. The o. c. originated in the '*Komos*', a bawdy ritual in honour of Dionysus; as a form it retains elements of fertility ritual (e.g. wearing of phalluses) as well as mixing fantasy, slapstick, wit, poetical comment and caricature of famous people.

Old Curiosity Shop, The (1840–1). Novel by *Dickens.

Old Hall MS. A medieval music ms. containing compositions of the 14th and 15th c.; it was discovered at Old Hall in Herts.

Oldham John (1653–83). English satirist, author of *Satires against the Jesuits*, marked by indecorous vigour. His early death was mourned in a famous poem by Dryden.

Old Man and the Sea, The (1952). Long short story by *Hemingway.

Old Mortality (1816). Novel by Sir Walter Scott.

Old St Paul's (1871). Historical novel by Harrison Ainsworth.

Old Testament: *Bible

Old Vic. London theatre. When it was built (1818) it was called The Coburg, but after a visit by the future Queen was renamed The Victoria (1833); the nickname 'O. V.' later

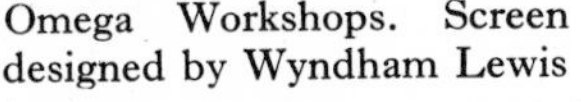
Omega Workshops. Screen designed by Wyndham Lewis

Olmi. *Il Posto*

Sir Laurence Olivier as Othello

acquired official status. In 1898 Lilian *Baylis became manageress and as a result of her work the O. V. established a tradition of regular and craftsmanlike performances of Shakespeare. In 1963 the National Theatre Co. took possession to use the theatre until the building of its own premises.

Old Wives' Tale, The (1908). Novel by Arnold *Bennett.

Olesha Yury Karlovich (1899–1960). Soviet novelist. O.'s 1st book, *Envy* (1927; 1936), was an ambiguous tale of 2 men unable to adapt to Soviet life; they are portrayed as despicable, yet in many respects of deeper insight than the energetic Communists with their simple scheme of values. O. became steadily more unpopular as the implications of his work were realized, and he publ. little.

Oliphant Margaret (1828–97). Scottish novelist, prolific writer chiefly remembered for a series of novels, the *Chronicles of Carlingford*.

Oliver Isaac (d. 1617). English miniaturist of French Huguenot parentage. He studied under Hilliard and became his master's principal rival, developing a style of portraiture less linear than Hilliard's. He painted Elizabeth I and Mary, Queen of Scots, and worked at the court of James I. A visit to Venice in 1596 stimulated him to paint religious and classical subjects. His son PETER (*c.* 1594–1647) was also a miniaturist.

Oliver (Joseph) 'King' (1885–1938). U.S. jazz cornetist (in the New Orleans style) and band-leader; his was one of the 1st Negro groups to make records. O. encouraged and employed (1922) Louis Armstrong.

Oliver Twist (1837–8). Novel by *Dickens.

Olivier Sir Laurence (Kerr) (1907–). English stage and film actor and director. He was co-director at the Old Vic (1944–5) and also acted under his own management at the St James's Theatre. O. is the leading English actor, amazingly versatile, and distinguishing himself in all the main Shakespearian parts and in modern plays (e.g. Osborne's *The Entertainer*). In 1962 he became director of the *Chichester Festival Theatre, in 1963 of the British *National Theatre. On the screen his best performances were for Hitchcock (*Rebecca*) and Wyler (*Wuthering Heights*). He starred with Elisabeth Bergner in *As You Like It* (1937) and has directed and acted in 3 other Shakespearian adaptations, *Henry V* (1944), *Hamlet* (1948) and *Richard III* (1955); although they at times sacrifice words to image or image to words, they are to date the most successful attempts to film Shakespeare.

Olmedo José Joaquín (1780–1847). Ecuadorian poet and politician. In 1845 he led a successful revolt in Ecuador, but although he became a candidate for the presidency he was not elected. His poetry, among the earliest Latin-American literature, is romantic in mood; it includes a famous ode to Bolivar (1825) and a trs. of Pope's *Essay on Man*.

Olmi Ermanno (1930–). Italian film director. After directing in the theatre, he made about 30 shorts (1953–9). To date he has made 3 features, *Time Stood Still* (1959), *Il Posto* (1961) and *I Fidanzati* (1963). They are characterized by their detailed observation of working-class life, noted with care and affection and aesthetic perceptiveness.

Olvidados, Los (1951). Film directed by L. *Buñuel.

Olympia (1863–5). Painting by *Manet derived from Titian's *Venus of Urbino*.

Olympische Spiele (1937). Film directed by L. *Riefenstahl.

Omar Khayyám, The Rubá'iyát of: Edward *Fitzgerald

Omega Workshops. Founded by Roger Fry in 1913; several painters including Duncan Grant, Vanessa Bell and Wyndham Lewis took part. Furniture, fabrics and pottery were designed and decorated in the workshops following current fashions in painting (e.g. *vorticism) and issued anonymously with the Greek letter *omega* as sole mark; the actual construction, weaving, etc. of their products was done by craftsmen.

Omoo: A Narrative of Adventures in the South Seas (1847). Novel by Herman *Melville.

O'Neill Eugene (Gladstone) (1888–1953). U.S. playwright, the son of a touring actor. O. attended several schools, entered Princeton for a year, and after a series of unsatisfactory jobs became a seaman, a career which afforded him subject-matter all his life. Against commercial odds and critical uninterest O. created a large corpus of plays unmistakably American in theme, mood and treatment. No U.S. playwright experimented so courageously, none took his vocation so seriously. O. received the Nobel prize in 1936. After studying at G. P. Baker's 47 Workshop, he joined the Provincetown Players, who first produced one of his plays, *Bound East for Cardiff* (1916). His earlier plays of frustration tend to be staged expressionistically, with a number of technical innovations and special, stylized language conventions, as in *The Emperor Jones* (1920), *The Hairy Ape* (1922), and *Desire under the Elms* (1924). *The Fountain* (1925) and *The Great God Brown* (1926) contain a more psychological approach to social themes while retaining the expressionist manner, a combination found in *Strange Interlude* (1928), the beginning of his large dramatic schemes, the most famous of which is *Mourning Becomes *Electra* (1931), a trilogy which sets the Greek family themes in post-Civil War New England. Between 1935 and 1943 he planned and began to execute a series of one-act plays called *By Way of Orbit* and a cycle of full-length plays, *A Tale of Possessors Dispossessed*, about the development of interrelated families; of these he finished only *A Touch of the Poet* (1958) and *More Stately Mansions* (publ. 1964). *The Iceman Cometh* (1946) largely sheds earlier technical and philosophical ambitions and deals simply and movingly with illusions and disillusions in a New York bar. *Long Day's Journey into Night* (1956) is the most famous of his family plays, closely modelled on autobiographical experience; so is his other late masterpiece, *A Moon for the Misbegotten* (1957).

On Hearing the First Cuckoo in Spring (1912). Orchestral work by Delius.

Only Angels Have Wings (1939). Film directed by H. *Hawks.

On ne badine pas avec l'amour (publ. 1834). Play (properly, a *proverbe dramatique) by Alfred de Musset.

Onofri Arturo (1885–1928). Italian poet. O.'s large poetic output consisted at first of lyrics

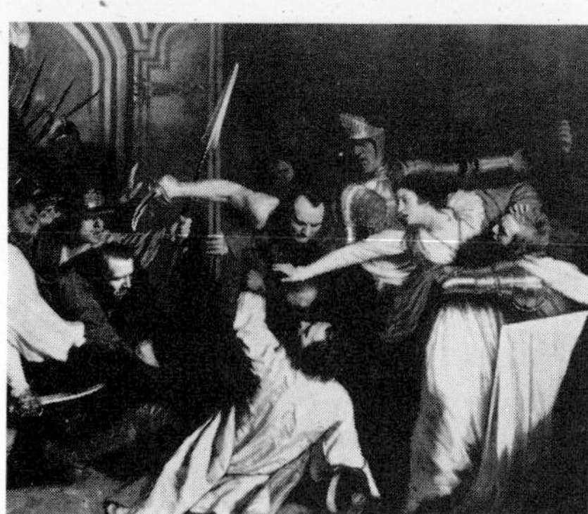

Opie. *The Murder of Rizzio*

Opsomer. *Professor Muls* (1942)

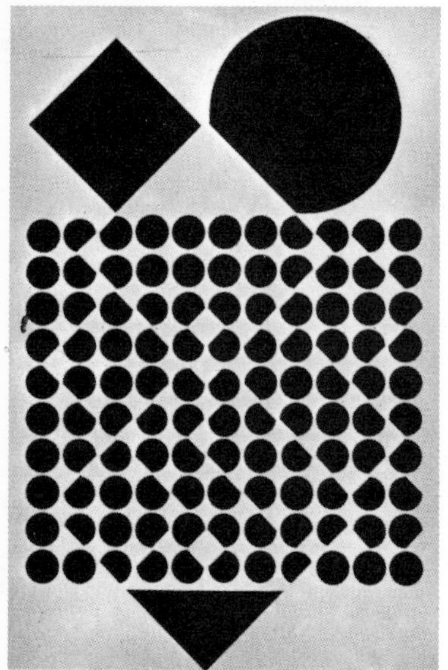

Op art. Vasarely, *Cassiopee* (1957)

Op art. Vasarely, *Markab* (1958)

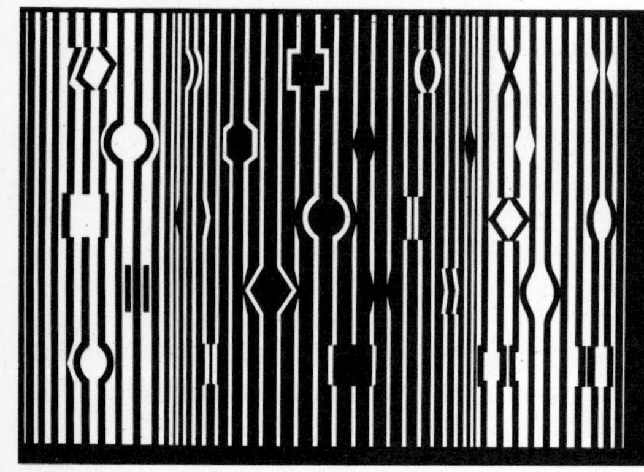

Ophuls. Anton Walbrook and Simone Signoret in *La Ronde*

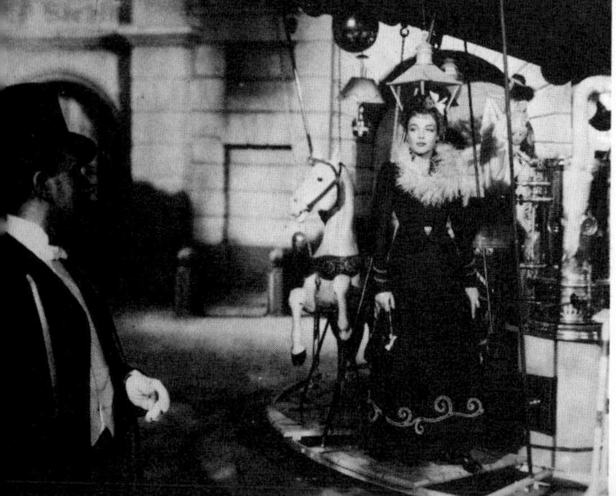

written under the influence of the *symbolists in an attempt to produce 'pure', intuitive poetry, but with the publ. of *Le trombe d'argento* (1924) his tone became increasingly mystical and pantheistic, with a strong vein of moral and humanitarian feeling which often weakened its lyrical quality.

Onslow André-Georges-Louis (1784–1852). French composer, related to the 1st Lord Onslow and studying for a time in London. His music, particularly his chamber music, once enjoyed immense success.

On the Bowery (1956). Film directed by L. *Rogosin.

On the Eve (1860). Novel by Turgenev.

On the Sublime. Greek treatise on style once attributed to a 3rd-c. 'Longinus', now thought to be by an unknown 1st-c. author. Literary excellence is said to arise from grandeur of thought as well as stylistic features, and the extinction of democratic liberties under Imperial Rome and contemporary moral decline are held responsible for the death of exalted writing. It rapidly became known in Europe after the 1st ed. in 1554, especially influencing writers such as Boileau, Fénelon, Addison, Hume, Pope, Gibbon and Burke.

On the Town (1950). Film directed by S. *Donen and G. *Kelly.

On the Waterfront (1954). Film directed by E. *Kazan.

op(tical) art. Term which gained currency in the 1960s for a fashion in painting deriving from the work of such painters as Victor Vasarely. O. a. concerns itself with purely visual sensations, relying for its effects upon optical illusions; often canvases are a mass of small shapes, lines or vivid colours constantly shifting under the eye.

open-work. Architectural term, the same as *fretting.

opera. A dramatic text set throughout to music. Its origins are in the 16th-c. pastoral play with musical interludes and the experiments of the Florentine *camerata with *monody; the earliest o.s (*c.* 1600) were passages of monody interspersed with musical interludes. *Monteverdi's *Incoronazione di Poppea* (1642) is the 1st opera with discernible *arias and *recitatives and by the mid 17th c. the Italian o. was established with its grand spectacle, set arias and recitatives, florid and emotive vocal parts increasingly for the *castrato voice. 18th-c. 'Neapolitan' OPERA SERIA, dealing with classical themes and consisting of arias alternating with recitatives, degenerated into a vehicle of mere vocal virtuosity until *Gluck broke with convention, making the dramatic development again of central importance; *Wagner's integrated 'music drama' was the last major operatic development.

opera-ballet. *La Liberazione di Ruggerio dall Isola d'Aleina* (Venice, 1625) was the first recorded o.-b. and introduced dancing into opera; but for many years the dancing remained in entre'act form. *Noverre in the late 18th c. raised the value of dancing to integrate it into the action, and the fashion for ballets in opera has developed from there.

opera buffa. A form of Italian opera generally on a comedy theme. It developed in the 18th c., had spoken dialogue and concluded acts with an ensemble piece for several soloists, a feature taken up by *opera seria* (i.e. 'serious opera'). The French term was *opéra bouffe*.

opéra comique. French term meaning literally 'comic opera' but used of any opera with passages of spoken dialogue.

Opera Comique. London theatre (1871–99) used for a brief spell by the D'Oyly Carte Co.

operetta. A light, slight opera; often using spoken dialogue.

ophicleide. Obsolete early 19th-c. brass musical instrument superseded by the tuba. It had keys like a saxophone.

Ophuls Max (1902–57). Saar-born German film director. O. was a theatrical director in Breslau and Berlin before directing his 1st film in 1930. At the least, O. was the cinema's leading exponent of bitter-sweetness. But even at their sweetest–often very sweet–his films were built on the threat of tragedy. His 1st famous film, *Liebelei* (1932), ends with a suicide, as does *La Signora di tutti* (1934). Although he worked in various parts of Europe during the

1930s, then in the U.S., where he made 3 films (1947–9) before returning to France in 1950, O. was in spirit Viennese–2 of his best films, *Liebelei* and *La Ronde* (1950), are adaptations from Arthur Schnitzler, and one, *Letter from an Unknown Woman* (1948), is from Stefan Zweig. His style is characterized by much camera movement, which he used to follow his actors around in a way that gave his films a particularly lyrical flow. His films always have an immaculate visual surface: in *La Ronde* and *Le Plaisir* (1951) he used décors often of elaborate elegance; but in his last film, *Lola Montes* (1955), which was his first in colour and Cinemascope, he used décors of unbelievable richness. A financial disaster, it was a film of megalomaniac genius.

Opie John (1761–1807). English painter. In 1781 he was introduced to London as the self-taught 'Cornish Wonder' by J. Wolcot (Peter *Pindar). He excelled in portraits and in genre scenes in which he made notable use of chiaroscuro effects. The quality of his work declined as he became increasingly fashionable. His wife AMELIA (1769–1853) was author of numerous popular, moralizing domestic novels.

O Pioneers! (1913). Novel by Willa *Cather.

Opitz von Boberfeld Martin (1597–1639). German writer, a Silesian; he studied in Heidelberg and travelled in Holland and Denmark before returning as a court poet. Caught up in the Thirty Years War, he died in Danzig of the plague. O. set up rules and models which the next baroque generation, more inspired, outgrew. His *Buch von der deutschen Poeterey* (1624), a neo-classical manual for writers, stresses learning and a mastery of technique (set structure, purified German decoratively used, natural verse in which metrical and speech stresses coincide). His poems (*Teutsche Poemata*, 1624; *Weltliche Poemata*, 1644; *Geistliche Poemata*, 1638) exemplify these principles: preference for sonnets, epigrams; elegant wit, not individual feeling. He trs. approved models (an opera libretto, plays by Seneca and Sophocles, novels by Sidney and Barclay) or provided them (. . . *Hercinie*, a pastoral, 1630; *Judith*, a tragedy, 1635).

Opsomer Isidore (1878–). Belgian painter, pupil of A. de Vriendt. His main work was in portraiture and scenes in Antwerp. His studio at the Institut Supérieur des Beaux-Arts was one of the leading influences in Belgian art.

optical work: *film techniques

opus. Latin word for 'work'; its abbreviation, 'op.', with a number, is sometimes used by composers in enumerating their works; op. numbers ideally run in chronological sequence but often do not. An op. may be a set of short works which are differentiated by further numbers, thus op. 137 no. 2.

Opus Anglicanum. Latin term used of English ecclesiastical embroidery of the period from the Norman Conquest to the Reformation, although Anglo-Saxon embroideries were already famous before the Conquest and the art declined during the 15th c. Great copes surviving at Melk, Pienza, Bologna and Toledo, and also 13th- and 14th-c. inventories of church vestments, especially the Vatican Inventory of 1295 listing a great number of pieces, are indicative of the degree to which O. A. was sought after by great princely and spiritual rulers on the Continent. The embroideries comprise sacred scenes and figures of saints in architectural settings, frequently with gold backgrounds. The stitches most commonly used in the best period are underside *couching of gold thread, and *split stitch in coloured silks for the figures.

oratorio. A religious work for voices and instruments, dramatic in nature though not acted. It originated in the meetings in the late 16th c. at the Oratory of St Philip *Neri in Rome, where a major part of the service was the singing of *laude spirituale*. These, linked with dialogue and expanded by choruses, produced the o. Early examples were written by *Carissimi; among the best known are those of Handel. Since Handel, and especially in the 20th c., composers have given the name to secular compositions similar in form and serious in mood.

Orcagna Andrea (Andrea di Cione) (*c.* 1308–68). Florentine painter, sculptor and architect in a traditional Gothic idiom. His only certain painting, the *Strozzi altarpiece* in S. Maria Novella, Florence, rejects many of Giotto's innovations (definition of space, solidity, etc.), returning to a more hieratic, less humanist religious idiom. His tabernacle in Or San Michele, Florence, is a riot of crockets, gables

Opitz von Boberfeld

Opus Anglicanum. Christ carrying the cross; on an orphrey

Orcagna.
Detail of the tabernacle in Or San Michele

Orcagna. *Christ, the Virgin and Saints*

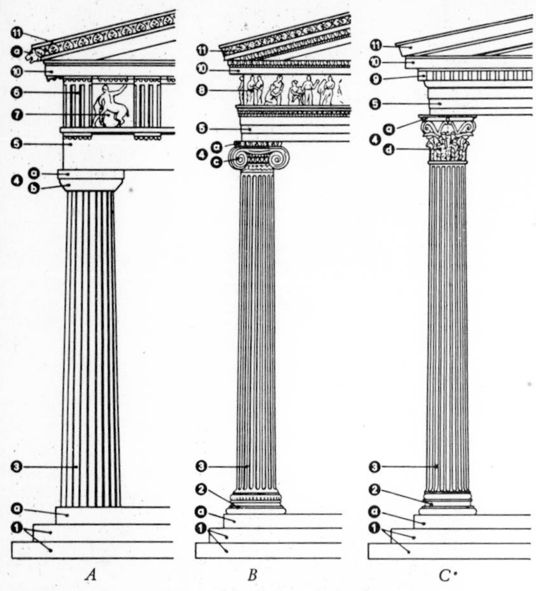

Greek orders: A Doric, B Ionic, C Corinthian
1 Base
1a Stylobate
2 Attic base
3 Shaft
4 Capital
4a Abacus
4b Echinus
4c Ionic volute
4d Corinthian volute with acanthus leaves
5 Epistyle
6 Triglyph
7 Metope
8 Frieze
9 Dentils
10 Facia
11 Pediment moulding
11a Waterspout

Carl Orff

and finials. As an architect he was also traditional: the Loggia dei Lanzi, Florence (attributed to him on Vasari's authority) is still wholly Italian Gothic in spite of its round arches. His brothers NARDO (*fl.* 1343–65) and JACOPO (*fl.* 1365–98) were both painters.

Orchardson Sir William Quiller (1832–1910). Scottish subject and portrait painter known principally for his picture *Napoleon on Board the 'Bellerophon'* (Tate).

orchestra. In the theatre, *Greek drama.

orchestra. A large group of musical instruments, from 15 to 100 or more, of different tone colours. The modern o. consists of a large body of strings (violins, violas, cellos, double basses); a woodwind section (flutes, oboes, clarinets, and bassoons); a brass section (horns, trumpets, trombones, and a tuba); and a percussion section (timpani and numerous tuned and untuned percussion instruments); piano and harp, sometimes. The o. has changed its constituents from the Renaissance onwards; the classical 18th-c. o. contained the above instruments except for the trombones, tuba and extra percussion instruments. Composers naturally use such instruments as they require, but the above is a frequently used combination.

orchestration. Musical term for the way in which the instruments are combined and their different tone colours exploited in a piece of music.

Ordeal of Richard Feverel, The (1859). Novel by George *Meredith.

orders. Architectural term applied to the various distinctive ways of moulding, decorating and proportioning Greek and Roman columns and their entablatures; only the most important of the differences in detail can be indicated. There were 3 Greek o.s. The DORIC, the most widely used (e.g. for the Parthenon) had a sturdy column with no base, a capital with a plain moulding below the flat abacus, and a frieze with triglyphs and metopes. The IONIC (e.g. the Erechtheum) has volutes beneath the abacus. The CORINTHIAN, the most ornate (e.g. the Maison Carrée, Nîmes) came into use after the others; it has acanthus leaves and other foliage on the capital and an abacus with concave edges and chamfered corners. The Romans adapted all the Greek o.s, using a form of Doric (with a base) called the TUSCAN, but showed particular preference for the Corinthian and developed the even more ornate COMPOSITE, which combines the Ionic volutes with Corinthian foliation.

Ordet (1955). Film directed by C. T. *Dreyer.

Oresteia (458 B.C.). Dramatic trilogy by *Aeschylus based on myth. In *The Agamemnon*, the protagonist is king of Argos, to which he returns after the Trojan War (*Iliad*); there he is murdered by his wife Clytemnestra and her lover Aegisthus. This is partly a result of the curse on his House (the House of Atreus), partly of his own sins and impieties, especially the sacrifice of his daughter *Iphigenia. *The Cheophori* relates the arrival of Orestes, the son of Agamemnon and Clytemnestra, his reunion with his sister *Electra, and slaying (on Apollo's command) of Aegisthus and Clytemnestra. At once the Furies, grisly shapes he alone can see, begin to pursue the matricide. In *The Eumenides* Orestes argues his case before the Areopagus, the highest Athenian court, and is saved from the Furies by the casting vote of the goddess Athene. The Furies agree to become kind spirits (Eumenides). There are plays about Orestes by Euripides, Alfieri and Sartre.

Orfeo, La Favola d'. Opera by *Monteverdi; 1st performance at Mantua in 1607.

Orff Carl (1895–). German composer and teacher. In 1924 he founded a school for 'gymnastics, dance and music' at Munich. Since 1950 he has taught composition at the Munich Academy of Music. O. is also a conductor and he has made many adaptations of early music. As a composer O. writes mainly for the stage, aiming at a new synthesis of dramatic and musical elements. His music is popular in style and uses very basic melody and rhythm (often employing a large percussion section, mainly of instruments designed by himself, originally for teaching purposes); repetition is the most common feature, and the structure is immediately apparent. As an educator he has devised methods whereby children learn by playing and improvising. His works include the popular 'scenic cantata' **Carmina Burana* (1937), *Catulli Carmina*, (1934), *Trionfo di Afrodite* (1953) and the opera *Antigone* (1949).

Positive organ; from the Ghent altarpiece by the van Eycks

The 'Bruckner organ' (built 1770–83) at the monastery of St Florian, Austria

Ormolu. Bracket-clock with tortoiseshell and ormolu case

Ormolu. Commode with ormolu decoration

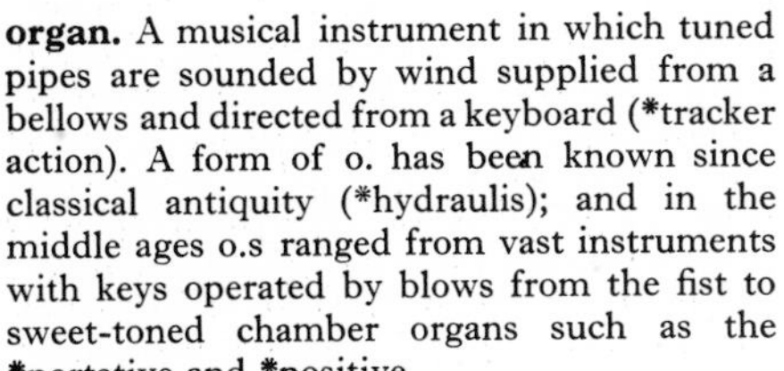

organ. A musical instrument in which tuned pipes are sounded by wind supplied from a bellows and directed from a keyboard (*tracker action). A form of o. has been known since classical antiquity (*hydraulis); and in the middle ages o.s ranged from vast instruments with keys operated by blows from the fist to sweet-toned chamber organs such as the *portative and *positive.

The pipes of a modern o. may range in length from 1 in. to 64 ft (the length of pipe of course determining its pitch) and can be designed in an almost limitless range of tone qualities. Such differences in tonal qualities depend on the material of the pipe (wood or metal), the shape of the pipe and the wind pressure applied to blow it, etc. There are 2 basic families of o. pipe–the flue pipes, which use the same principle as the *fipple flutes; and the reed pipes, which use basically the principle of the *clarinet. Flue pipes can be sealed at the top, which not only alters their tone, but also lowers their pitch an 8ve; such pipes are said to be 'stopped'.

These pipes themselves are grouped into sections controlled from the *console by separate manuals or keyboards. Thus the 'great' o. has predominantly full-sounding *diapason toned flue pipes; the 'swell' o. has predominantly more strident or rough reed pipes; the 'choir' o. has soft-toned pipes suitable for accompanying the choir (hence possibly the name). In addition to these sections or 'manuals' (found on most o.s) there is the 'pedal' o. and there may be other manuals such as the 'echo' (very soft pipes) or 'solo' (a selection of solo pipes). With this wealth of different styles of pipe and the possibility of many combinations of the resources of the different manuals, the o. is capable of a vast variety of tone and volume. Its versatility is increased by the *mixture and *mutation stops and the swell-box–the swell o. is enclosed in shutters or louvres (operated by a foot-pedal) which can be gradually opened thus creating a swell of sound volume.

organistrum. Latinized name for *hurdy-gurdy.

organum. The earliest form of part music, dating from the 9th c. The plainsong melody was accompanied by other parts at fixed intervals.

Oriana: *Elizabeth I

Oriani Alfredo (1852–1909). Italian novelist. O.'s mediocre novels were revived under Mussolini because of his advocacy of a ruthless imperialism.

oriel window. Architectural term describing a *bay-window on an upper floor and supported by brackets or corbels.

Original Ballet Russe. The name given in 1939 to the company previously called the *Ballets Russes de Monte Carlo.

Origin of Species, On the (1859). Book by Charles *Darwin.

Orlando (1928). Novel by Virginia *Woolf.

Orlando Furioso (1532). Poem by *Ariosto.

Orlando Innamorato (1483). Poem by *Boiardo.

Orléans Charles d': *Charles d'Orléans

Orley Bernard (Bernaert) van (*c.* 1492–1541). Flemish painter of altarpieces and portraits and designer of tapestries and stained glass. Influenced by Raphael, whose Vatican tapestry cartoons (V. and A.) were for several years in Brussels, he became one of the principal *Romanists. He designed the famous *Hunts of Maximilian* tapestries in the Louvre.

Orly hangars (1916–24). Architect E. *Freyssinet.

Ormandy Eugene (1899–). U.S. conductor, Hungarian-born and originally named Blau; conductor of the Philadelphia Orchestra since 1936.

ormolu. Cast and chased bronze which has been dipped in acid and gilded to give it a highly polished surface. The best examples are from 18th-c. France where the art was carried to the highest perfection, especially by Pierre Gouthière (1732–1813/14). O. is found either by itself in candlesticks, wall lights and clocks, or as an addition to furniture. Originally this was to protect the corners from knocking, but the decorative qualities were soon realized and o. became an integral part of furniture, spreading over the whole surface. It was also used to mount oriental and European porcelain in that juxtaposition of the exotic so dear to the 18th c.

Orley. *The Job Altar*

Oriel window in Prague

Ortega y Gasset

Orpen. *Homage to Manet*

Orphism. Delaunay, *Simultaneous Disc* (1912)

Orozco. *Zapata* (1930)

ornaments in music. A musical ornament may be simply described as any embellishment to the main melodic line. There are a number of such decorations in traditional use. The commonest of them are: the acciaccatura: which sounds approximately the appoggiatura: which sounds approximately, the mordent which sounds approximately, the inverted mordent, which sounds approximately, the turn which sounds approximately (or sounds), and the trill (shake) which sounds approximately

Interpretation, however, of these signs varies from place to place and epoch to epoch.

Ornstein Leo (1895–). Russian-born U.S. composer, conductor and teacher at the Philadelphia Music Academy and at the Ornstein School of Music, Philadelphia. In the 1920s and 1930s his advanced idiom made him the centre of discussion and controversy.

Orosius Paulus (*fl. c.* 400). Author of a famous *History against the Pagans*, widely read in the middle ages.

Orozco José Clemente (1883–1949). Mexican painter, trained as an architect, but who turned to painting in 1909. At first working in water-colours, he later became a leading fresco painter, much in demand for decorating public buildings in Mexico and the U.S. His subject-matter tended to social realism, but it was treated in a decorative, formalized and rhythmic manner. In this sense O. gave a new aspect to the Revolutionary epic style initiated by Rivera.

Orpen Sir William Newenham Montague (1878–1931). Irish painter, a founder of and exhibitor at the *New English Art Club. He painted portraits of great technical virtuosity, interiors and conversation pieces of historical interest, including the famous *Homage to Manet* (1909; Manchester City A. Gal.) with Sickert, Wilson Steer, George Moore and others grouped in front of Manet's portrait of Eva Gonzalès.

Orphée (1950). Film directed by J. *Cocteau.

Orpheus. 3-scene ballet with choreography by Balanchine, music by Stravinsky and décor by the Japanese sculptor, Noguchi; 1st performance 1948.

Orpheus and Eurydice. Opera by Gluck, with libretto by Calzabigi; 1st performance at Vienna in 1762.

Orpheus in the Underworld. English title of *Orphée aux Enfers*, an operetta by *Offenbach with libretto by Crémieux and Halévy; 1st performance at Paris in 1858.

orphism. In 1913 Apollinaire called the cubist painting of *Delaunay 'orphic', linking it with that of Léger, Picabia, Marcel Duchamp and some works of Picasso. The name has only stayed with the painting of Delaunay and his wife Sonia Terk Delaunay, who experimented with colour circles, segments and rhythms in a style called 'simultaneity'. 2 U.S. painters, MacDonald-Wright and Morgan Russell, stressed colour in a similar way (synchronism).

Ortega y Gasset José (1883–1955). Spanish philosopher and writer. He founded (1923) the very influential review, *Revista de Occidente*; he was a Republican, was exiled from Spain in the Civil War but returned in 1945. In *La rebelión de las masas* (1930; *The Revolt of the Masses*, 1932) he attributed Western 'decadence' to the emergence of the mass man in conflict with the select creative minorities of the past.

Orvieto cathedral Italy. Italian Gothic church, the façade (begun 1309) closely modelled on that of *Siena, with the addition of marble relief, at ground-level, probably by Lorenzo Maitani. A chapel contains famous frescoes by *Signorelli.

Orwell George. Pseud. of Eric Arthur Blair (1903–50). English essayist and novelist. After Eton, he served in Burma with the Indian police, lived a vagrant life in England and Europe, and fought for the Republicans in the Spanish Civil War. These experiences, described in *Burmese Days* (1934), *Down and Out in Paris and London* (1933), *Homage to Catalonia* (1938), etc., confirmed him in deeply Socialist ideals, expressed in works like *The Road to Wigan Pier* (1937). O.'s trenchant essays drew attention to modern political and cultural problems, such as 'mass media', and the loss of power and expressiveness in English prose. In 1945 came *Animal Farm*, a political fable satirizing the Communist régime in Russia, followed by *1984* (1949), a grim prophecy of totalitarianism.

Ory 'Kid' (Edward) (1886–). U.S. jazz trombonist in the New Orleans style.

Orzeszkowa Eliza (1842–1910). Polish novelist who wrote realistic prose fiction dealing with contemporary social problems. Her novels include *Meir Ezofowicz* (1878; 1898), describing the conflict of a young progressive Jew with the reactionary elements in the ghetto, and *Nad Niemnem* (1889), a novel about the Polish-Lithuanian gentry.

Osborne John (James) (1929–). English playwright, one of the *Angry Young Men, originally an actor. *Look Back in Anger* (1956), a funny, blistering attack on the emotional debility and caste-snobbery of the English, made O. famous. There is a similar theme in *The Entertainer* (1957), a portrait of a third-rate variety comedian. Works include *Luther* (1961) and a number of film scripts for O.'s own film co., including that of *Tom Jones*.

Oshima Nagisa. Japanese film director. O. uses many of the techniques of the French *nouvelle vague in his films. His first 2, *Naked Youth* (1960) and *The Sun's Burial* (1960), have teenage-sex-and-violence stories, but provide (apart from considerable visual beauty) a view of modern Japan, both physical and social, that is quite new.

Ossessione (1942). Film directed by L. *Visconti.

Ossian: James *Macpherson

Ostade Adriaen van (1610–85). Dutch painter working in Haarlem, perhaps the pupil of Frans Hals or of Salomon van Ruysdael. His genre pictures of peasant, country and tavern life were highly popular. He was closely associated in his work with A. Brouwer. O. later in life produced watercolours, etchings and religious paintings.

Ostberg Ragnar (1866–1945). Swedish architect who designed Stockholm town hall (begun 1909), an original building for its date, though containing elements from many past styles (including medieval civic buildings). Its setting on the water's edge adds to its effect.

ostinato. This Italian word for obstinate is used in music of any persistently repeated figure or rhythm; sometimes such a figure occurs in the bass, in which case it may be termed 'basso ostinato'.

Ostricil Otakar (1879–1935). Czech composer and conductor. He championed the works of such composers as Mahler and Schoenberg, but his own music is influenced by Fibich and Czech folk-music as well as Mahler. His 5 operas contain much fine music. •

Ostrovsky Alexander Nikolayevich (1823–86). Russian playwright, the son of a civil service clerk. O. provided the Russian theatre with a corpus of plays of high quality–some 40 in prose and 8 in verse, comedies and tragedies–and has always been immensely popular. His works are little known in the West, perhaps because they have an intensely Russian flavour and subordinate social and ethical discussion to dramatic necessity: they are dramas of situation, often loosely constructed, but with plots that are theatrically very effective and a wealth of convincing realistic detail. Characters speak in

Ostberg. Stockholm town hall

Orvieto cathedral. See also colour plate 35

George Orwell

Alexander Ostrovsky. Also *Goncharov

Ostade. *Peasants playing shuffle-board at an inn*

Thomas Otway

Oudry. Illustration for La Fontaine's *Fables*

Peter O'Toole as Hamlet (1963)

O'Sullivan. *Panama–Limon Bay at High Tide* (1870)

Oud. Workers' housing estate, Hook of Holland (1924)

the idiom of their class, but represent particular vices or virtues rather than social types or complex individuals. O.'s most famous play is *The Storm* (1859; 1899), the study of a woman stifled by the narrowness of life in a merchant family (a background frequently used by O.) and at last driven to suicide. Works include *Poverty is no Crime* (1854; 1917), *The Forest* (1871; 1926); *Easy Money* (1870; 1944); and *Even a Wise Man Stumbles* (1868; 1944).

Ostrovsky Nikolay Alexeyevich (1904–37). Soviet novelist whose best-selling autobiographical novel *The Making of a Hero* (1936; 1937) describes a crippled boy's life during and after the Revolution.

O'Sullivan Timothy H. (1840–82). U.S. photographer, a student of *Brady. He worked under A. Gardener photographing the Civil War, and later documented exploratory and survey expeditions into the U.S. West. He made the earliest mine photographs underground using magnesium flash.

Oswald Gerd (1916–). German-born film director, son of a German director who went to work in the U.S. He was an assistant in Europe in the 1930s and in the U.S. (1940–52), and was a producer at 20th Century-Fox, where he directed his 1st film, *A Kiss Before Dying* (1956), an off-beat thriller. Off-beatness has since been characteristic of him.

Oswald von Wolkenstein (1377–1445). Tyrolese poet. Gifted and versatile, he left drinking- and love-songs and work in the tradition of the **Minnesang* and the *Meistergesang* (*Mastersingers).

Othello, The Moor of Venice (publ. 1622). Tragedy by *Shakespeare, written *c.* 1602 and performed at court in 1604. It follows a story in Giraldi Cinthio's *Hecatommithi* (1565). It is the subject of an opera by *Verdi, and has been filmed several times, notably in 1951, directed by Orson *Welles.

Oton, Sire de Granson (d. 1397). French poet much admired by Chaucer, who also trs. some of his works.

O'Toole Peter. English actor whose first performances were at the Bristol Old Vic (1955–8). He was at Stratford in 1960 and played Shylock, Petruchio in *The Taming of the Shrew* and Thersites in *Troilus and Cressida*, and has since become a world star for his performance in the title-role of the film *Lawrence of Arabia*. He played Hamlet in Bristol (1958) and in the 1st production of the National Theatre (1963).

ottava rima. Italian stanza of 8 11-syllable lines rhyming *abababcc*; it originated in the 14th c. and was employed by Ariosto and Tasso. It was adapted to English (with 10-syllable lines), was used by Chaucer, and became a favourite form with Byron.

Otto e Mezzo (1963). Film directed by F. *Fellini.

Otway Thomas (1652–85). English playwright, an unsuccessful actor and, briefly, a soldier. His best works are well-constructed tragedies with sensational plots; they include *Don Carlos* (1676), *The Orphan* (1680) and *Venice Preserved* (1682), which concerns a conspiracy against the Venetian state.

Oud Jacobus Johannes Pieter (1890–1963). Pioneer Dutch architect associated with the *de stijl movement; unlike other modern architects in the 1920s he was given plenty of work, and his practicality led to a quarrel with the theoretical van Doesburg. His early terrace housing is among the best housing of its period.

Oudry Jean-Baptiste (1686–1755). French painter, illustrator and tapestry designer, and director of the Beauvais tapestry works. He began as a still-life and portrait painter but after being commissioned to paint Louis XV's pack of hounds turned to painting animals, hunting scenes and landscapes. He illustrated La Fontaine's *Fables*.

O.U.D.S. i.e. the Oxford Univ. Dramatic Society, founded in 1885. Its productions, given in the Oxford Playhouse or in college gardens, have tended to be of the established dramatic classics. Distinguished alumni of O.U.D.S. include Emlyn Williams, Richard Burton, George Devine and Tony Richardson.

Ouida. Pseud. of Marie-Louise de la Ramée (1839–1908). English novelist, author of popular, well-told but conventional narratives, including *Under Two Flags* (1867).

Our Lady of the Flowers (1944). Novel by Jean *Genet.

Oudry. *The Dead Wolf*

Our Town (1938). Play by Thornton *Wilder.

Out of the Cradle Endlessly Rocking (1859). Poem by Walt Whitman.

Outsider, The (1942). Novel by Albert *Camus.

Outsider, The (1956). Book by Colin *Wilson.

Ouwater Albert van (mid 15th c.). Dutch painter who worked at Haarlem. Very little is known about him and his reputation rests on the one painting definitely attributable to him, *The Raising of Lazarus* (Berlin). Geertgen tot Sint Jans was his pupil.

Overbeck Johann Friedrich (1789–1869). German painter. After studying in Vienna, he went to Rome (1810) and became well known after an exhibition of work there in 1819. He founded, in Rome, the German *nazarene movement with Cornelius. His subjects were mainly historical and religious.

Overbury Sir Thomas (1581–1613). English courtier poisoned to silence him during a famous court scandal. He is remembered for his *Characters* (1614), modelled on Theophrastus.

Overlanders, The (1946). Film directed by H. *Watt.

overtone. Alternative term in music for upper harmonics (*harmonic series).

overture. A piece of music serving as an introduction to a larger work, especially an opera or oratorio, or a piece composed specifically for concert performance. In the late 17th c. and 18th c. there were 2 main styles of overture: the French, opened with a slow movement followed by a fast movement, and the Italian, basically a sequence of 3 movements, fast-slow-fast. The *symphony developed from the latter, above all the Italian o.s of A. Scarlatti.

Ovid (43 B.C.–A.D. 17/18). Publius Ovidius Naso, Roman poet; born at Sulmona in the Abruzzi, and educated in law and rhetoric at Rome and Athens. Refusing to undertake a senatorial career, he settled at Rome as a socialite given to writing verses. In A.D. 8 he was banished to Tomis on the Black Sea for his verses and for some error apparently connected with Augustus' infamous granddaughter Julia, in one of whose intrigues Ovid was inculpated by association. It is doubtful whether he was her lover: he was too shrewd to tangle with anyone so important and notorious; and his verses were presumably dragged into the accusation against him as a blind. From his banishment he wrote the *Tristia* and *Epistulae ex Ponto*, elegiac letters to his friends lamenting his misfortune, pleading for pardon and vividly describing his manner of life. He died in exile. His earliest works–*Amores, Heroides, Medicamina Faciei Femineae, Ars Amatoria, Remedia Amoris*–are designedly trivial: smart, cynical pieces untroubled by passion. The *Amores* (*c.* 16 B.C.) are conventional love-elegies addressed to a probably fictitious mistress, Corinna. The *Heroides*, letters of heroines of legend to their absent lovers, belong to the rhetorical type, the '*suasoria*' or 'speech of appeal'. O.'s easy command of rhetorical convention and his deft touch redeem these pieces, in which the feeling is factitious and the supposed occasion artificial or melodramatic, from their inherent absurdity. The *Medicamina*, only fragmentary, is a mock-didactic poem on cosmetics. The *Ars* and the *Remedia* (*c.* 1 B.C.), O.'s most brilliant and justly famous works, are a flippant parody of the didactic genre, professing to teach the art of 'love' as a science–how to find, maintain and delicately discard a mistress or a lover. As O. points out in the *Remedia* and in the *Epistulae ex Ponto*, his teaching is not immoral since he deals with the world of the professional courtesan only, and does not recommend promiscuous behaviour with free-born Romans.

His biggest work, the *Metamorphoses*, 15 books in hexameters, is a collection of legends, each dealing with some kind of transformation. The construction of the book follows an Alexandrian pattern: short and allusive episodes, strung loosely together by some more or less trivial association between one and the next. Its elegant, pointed language, which is always easy to read, and its sharp imagery, heightened by rhetorical conceits, have made it perennially popular. Medieval and Renaissance writers, including Shakespeare, drew their knowledge of classical mythology from it. O. never publ. a final version and the work survives only in copies privately circulated. The *Fasti*, of which only the first 6 of a projected 12 books in elegiac couplets were finished, is a versified

Ouwater. *The Raising of Lazarus*

Overbeck. *Madonna and Child.* Also *nazarenes

Wilfred Owen

Oystershell-veneered writing-cabinet (*c.* 1679)

calendar of the Roman religious year, containing the legendary and antiquarian lore appropriate to each season. O. finished and publ. it in exile.

ovolo. A rounded moulding deriving from classical architecture and consisting, in section, of simply a quarter-circle or quarter-ellipse.

Owen Daniel (1836–95). Leading 19th-c. novelist writing in Welsh.

Owen Goronwy (1723–69). Welsh poet, important for his production during a period when Welsh was generally ignored as a literary language.

Owen Robert (1771–1858). English industrialist, an early Socialist thinker and social reformer; he set up a mill in New Lanark run by the workers themselves. His writings include *A New View of Society* (1813) and an autobiography (1857–8).

Owen Wilfred (1893–1918). English poet. The outbreak of World War I found O. in France: in 1916 he returned there on active service, and was killed in action in 1918. Tension between twin convictions, of the war's evil and of his duty to bear a part in it, provided the motive power of his poetry. Its greatness lies in its objectivity and in the intense power of sensuous realization, similar to that of Keats, which he brought to the horrors of the Front. His chief technical innovation was the use of *consonantal rhyme, which increases the atmosphere of brooding uneasiness in many of his poems. Most famous is *Strange Meeting*, one of the O. poems set by Britten in his *War Requiem*.

Owl and the Nightingale, The (13th c.). Poem in octosyllabic couplets, in the form of a debate between the 2 birds.

Ox-Bow Incident (1943). Film directed by W. *Wellman.

Oxenstierna Johan Gabriel (1750–1818). Swedish poet whose mystical, melancholy feeling for nature anticipated one side of romanticism. Works include *Skördarna* (1796).

Oxford. The oldest univ. in England and architecturally notable for its college buildings. New College (founded 1379 by William of *Wykeham) set the pattern for all later colleges. Oxford cathedral, now part of Christ Church, is Norman with a late perpendicular pendant-vault. Several other colleges (Merton, Magdalen) contain medieval parts. For later architecture at Oxford see *Wren, *Hawksmoor, *Gibbs, *Butterfield and *Jacobsen.

Oxford symphony. Nickname for *Haydn's symphony no. 92 in G. maj.

oystershell. A form of veneer introduced in Holland in the late 17th c. which became popular in England. Branches of walnut, laburnum and other trees were cut transversely and laid together to produce a variegated decorative effect.

Ozenfant Amédée (1886–1966). French painter and one of the theorists of the school of Paris. He was a pupil of Dunoyer de Segonzac, and then travelled in Europe. He was a leading exponent of purism, collaborating in writings with the architect *Le Corbusier. He founded the Académie Ozenfant (1930) in Paris, but subsequently went to live in New York.

Ozu Yasujiro (1903–64). Japanese film director. O.'s work shows an extraordinary constancy of subject (domestic dramas), technique (a complete absence of any camera movement) and actors. Within his chosen and uniquely restricted range he shows an admirable sensitivity in his handling of complex interlocking groups of relationships, e.g. among his later works, *The Tokyo Story* (1953) and *An Autumn Afternoon* (1962). *Early Autumn* (1961) shows his mastery of decorative colour.

Ozenfant. *Still-life* (1920)

Oxford

P

Pabst. *The Threepenny Opera*

Pacheco. *Man*

Paalen Wolfgang (1905–59). Viennese-born painter of the surrealist school. He studied in Paris, but later lived and worked in Mexico.

Pabst Georg Wilhelm (1885–). Bohemian-born film director whose 1st famous film was the anti-romantic *The Joyless Street* (1925), with Garbo. His psychological probing, expressed symbolically, was taken even further in *Secrets of a Soul* (1926), supervised by 2 disciples of Freud. A taste for symbols survived into the more naturalistic *The Loves of Jeanne Ney* (1927) and *Pandora's Box* (1929), the latter adapted from 2 Wedekind plays. *Westfront 1918* (1930) and *Kameradschaft* (1931) were as naturalistic in style as they were pacificist in feeling. Between them he filmed *Weill and *Brecht's *Threepenny Opera* (1931). After a triple-language version of *Don Quixote* (1933), an unimportant film in Hollywood and 3 in France, he returned to Germany in 1939, and made *Paracelsus* (1943). His most famous post-war films are both anti-Nazi: *Der Letzte Akt* (1954) and *The Jackboot Mutiny* (1955). P. has received considerable acclaim for his sureness of touch, technical excellence, and insight into character.

Pacchierotti Gasparo (1740–1821). Soprano singer, one of the last great Italian castrati.

Pacheco Francisco (1564–1654). Spanish painter, writer and poet. Studied painting under Luis Fernandez and became a leading painter in Seville. He painted for several religious establishments and among his pupils was Velazquez. From 1623 to 1625 he lived in Madrid but then returned to Seville and abandoned painting for literature.

Pachelbel Johann (1653–1706). German organist and composer important for integrating the middle and S. German organ styles. After studying in Nuremberg he worked in Vienna, Eisenach, where he knew J. S. Bach's father, and other cities. His finest work was in forms based on chorales and in variations, his style being characterized by cantabile part writing and harmonic simplicity.

Pacher Michael (*c.* 1435–98). Tyrolese painter and sculptor. P. was a highly original painter who, under the influence of Mantegna, achieved a new spatial clarity in his essentially German style; his work, however, remained for long unknown outside the Tyrol. P.'s best-known work is the *St Wolfgang altarpiece* in the Salzkammergut. The carved and painted central panel and the frame are by his hand and are proof of his remarkable mastery of form. The frame, still Gothic in style, is part of painted compositions which in themselves are in the Renaissance spirit of scientific perspective and objective observation.

Pachmann Vladimir von (1848–1933). Russian pianist of Austrian parentage, distinguished as a Chopin interpreter. As he grew older he enlivened his recitals by comments on his playing addressed to himself or his audience.

Pacini Giovanni (1796–1867). Italian opera composer, called 'master of the *cabaleta', whose European success lasted from the last years of Rossini's ascendancy to the beginning of Verdi's. His outstanding success was *Saffo* (1840).

Pacuvius Marcus (220–*c.* 130 B.C.). Roman tragedian, said also to have been a painter of note. Of his 12 tragedies only fragments quoted by other authors survive.

Padeloup. A 17th- and 18th-c. French family of bookbinders. ANTOINE-MICHEL (1685–1758), among the first binders to sign his work with a ticket, is renowned for the excellence and beauty of his work and for his pleasing innovation of dentelle borders. He was a binder to Louis XV.

Paderewski Ignacy Jan (1860–1941). Polish pianist and composer. He won an international reputation as a performer and became prime minister and foreign minister of independent Poland (1919–20). His compositions include an opera and symphony as well as piano music.

Padovanino, Il (1590–1650). Italian painter in the style of Titian.

Padua, school of. School of Italian painting which became important in the 15th c. under Squarcione and through his pupils Mantegna, Tura and Crivelli powerfully influenced the Ferrarese and Venetian schools.

Paër Ferdinando (1771–1839). Italian opera composer who worked at Vienna, Dresden, as Napoleon's musical director and, with Rossini, at the Théâtre Italien in Paris. His works, often with similarities to Beethoven's, include

Pacher. *Expulsion of the Money-changers from the Temple*; detail from *St Wolfgang*

Padeloup binding (*c.* 1725)

Paestum: Temple of Neptune. Also *pediment

Paganini

Pagnol. *Marius*

Great Wild Goose Pagoda, Ch'ang-an (*c.*701–5; *left*) and brick pagoda near Ch'ang-an (*c.* 828)

Camilla . . . (1799), *Leonora* . . . (1804) and *Le Maître de Chapelle* (1821).

Paestum. Greek colony, later a Roman town, S. of Naples. It is important for its 3 well-preserved Doric temples – the so-called 'basilica' (mid 6th c. B.C.), the Temple of Neptune (*c.* 450 B.C.) and the Temple of Ceres (*c.* 530 B.C.). The real dedications are probably to Hera and Athena.

Paganini Niccolò (1782–1840). The most famous of violin virtuosos; his wandering life, passionate nature, fantastic virtuosity and numerous love-affairs gave rise to legends such as that he was in league with the Devil, and that he murdered one of his mistresses. He was also a virtuoso guitarist and viola player, commissioning Berlioz's *Harold in Italy*. P.'s own compositions, not mere show pieces, included concertos, capriccios and the variations *The Carnival of Venice*.

Page William (1811–85). U.S. painter of portraits, landscapes, historical and genre subjects. The pupil of Herring and Morse, P. lived in Italy (1849–60). His works include portraits of J. G. Adams (Boston Mus.); John Quincy (Boston Mus.); and General Winfield Scott (N.G., Washington).

pageant. Originally the cart on which medieval miracle plays were performed. The meaning has been extended to denote many entertainments, usually in the open air and in the form of a procession or series of spectacles.

Pagliacci. Short opera by *Leoncavallo, libretto by the composer; 1st performance at Milan in 1892.

Pagnol Marcel (Paul) (1895–). French playwright and film director. His plays include the famous stories of life in Marseille *Marius* (1929) and *Fanny* (1931). He scripted and supervised the filming of these (*Marius* directed by Korda, *Fanny* by Allegret) and himself directed *César*, which completed the film trilogy (1932–6). He set up his own studio near Marseille and continued to write and direct similar films (peasant comedies), e.g. *La Femme du Boulanger* (1939), *La Rosier de Madame Husson* (1950) and *Lettres de mon Moulin* (1954). His writings include *Souvenirs d'enfance* (1957–8; *The Days were too Short*, 1960).

pagoda. A tall tower of rectangular or multiangular plan, in masonry or wood, divided into horizontal partitions marked on the outside either by pent-roofs and balconies or by simple cornices; of Chinese origin. In China it is the product of 2 types of tower, the watch-towers and pleasure-towers of Chou (1122–249 B.C.) and Han dynasty (206 B.C.–A.D. 220) nobility, and Indian Buddhist towers and stupas. Pagodas were at first (early 5th c.) an essential part of Buddhist temple precincts in China, replacing the stupa of Indian temples. By the 10th c. they were no longer built on the main axis of temple plans and finally were dissociated from Buddhism altogether. They became part of Chinese landscape art, built at strategic points in the country expressly to enhance the aesthetic and metaphysical influences of nature. As such, via the descriptions of William Chambers and others, they were taken up in Europe as *chinoiserie and part of the Anglo-Chinese landscape garden. A confusingly similar word, PAGOD, signifies the figures of chinoiserie deities erected in 18th-c. gardens and featured in chinoiserie landscape painting.

Pailleron Édouard (1834–99). French playwright. His *Le Monde où l'on s'ennuie* (1881; *The Upper Ten*, 1891) satirized the intrigues and pretentiousness of academic life.

Paine James (1725–89). English architect who, with Sir Robert Taylor, dominated the English scene between Kent and Robert Adam. He designed country-houses in the Midlands and N. of England, e.g. Nostell Priory and Kedleston (both completed by Adam), Worksop Manor and the stables and bridge at Chatsworth. P. was influenced by Inigo Jones and Palladianism; his later work was modified by the Adam style.

Paine (Thomas) Tom (1737–1809). English political writer and radical politician, holding posts under the U.S. government and a member of the French Revolutionary Convention. He expressed his views in clear forthright prose in *The Rights of Man* (1791, 2) and *The Age of Reason* (1794).

Painlevé Jean (1902–). French scientific-film maker. P. made his 1st biological film in 1928 after studying medicine. He is the only specialist in scientific films whose work has gained critical acceptance as cinema. The most

Paine. Kedleston Hall

famous, *The Sea-Horse* (1934), had music by Milhaud. P. wrote the commentary for *Le Sang des Bêtes*.

painterly: *malerisch

Paisa (1946). Film directed by R. *Rossellini.

Paisiello (Paesiello) Giovanni (1740–1816). Italian opera composer; he worked largely at Naples but spent 8 years at St Petersburg and was honoured by Napoleon. Changing dynasties and modes of government affected P.'s income from patronage. His operas include: *La serva padrona* (1781), *Il barbiere di Siviglia* (1782), a hugely popular predecessor of Rossini's opera, and *Nina* (1789).

Pajou Augustin (1730–1809). French sculptor, and pupil of Lemoyne. He spent some years working in Rome and was a regular exhibitor at the Paris Salon until 1802. Greatly favoured by the French court, he decorated the church of St Louis (Versailles) and the chapel of the Palais-Bourbon.

Palace of Pleasure (1566–7). Coll. of English trs of Boccaccio and others made by William Painter. Elizabethan dramatists took many of their plots from it.

Palacio Valdés Armando (1853–1938). Spanish novelist whose many skilful, amusing and very popular comedies of manners include *La hermana San Sulpicio* (1889; *Sister Saint Sulpice*, 1890).

Palau Boix Manuel (1893–). Spanish composer, folk-song coll. and conductor; director of the Valencia Conservatory. His music, influenced by impressionism and folk-music, includes *Concierto levantino* for guitar and orchestra.

Palazuelo Pablo (1916–). Spanish-born painter who studied and works in Paris. He exhibited with the group known as 'Les mains éblouies' in the 1950s.

Palazzo Barberini Rome. Baroque palace built for the family of Urban VIII; designed by several architects, it reflects the development of the baroque style from 1626 onwards –the lower part of the main façade is by Maderno, the upper storey by Bernini and parts of the garden front by Borromini.

Palazzo Pubblico Siena. The best surviving example of medieval civic architecture in the republics of Central Italy. It dates from the 13th c. The façade is in 3 storeys with large pointed windows, topped by battlements. At one side is a tall square tower (*Memmi) typical of the period (e.g. Palazzo Vecchio, Florence). Inside are frescoes by Simone Martini and Lorenzetti.

Palazzo Vecchio Florence, Italy. Palace dating from *c.* 1300 onwards and designed (mainly by Arnolfo di Cambio) as the seat of the Florentine Signoria. It is built of rusticated stone blocks, with entrance and tall machicolated tower (308 ft high) placed asymmetrically. There are later additions by Michelozzo, Buontalenti and Vasari.

Pale Fire (1962). Novel (prose and verse) by *Nabokov.

Palestrina Giovanni Pierluigi da (*c.* 1525–94). Italian composer born in the village of Palestrina. After an organist's post in his home town (1544–51) he went to Rome and in 1555 held an appointment in the Sistine Chapel for a few months; after this he worked at S. John Lateran, S. Maria Maggiore, the Jesuit Collegium Romanum, for Cardinal Ippolito d'Este and from 1571 at St Peter's; in 1593 he was planning to resume his post in his home town. Other positions he held included his work for the Oratory of St Philip Neri. P. is generally considered the greatest master of the polyphonic era and his style was officially recognized as the model for Catholic composers after the reforming Council of Trent, which laid down that liturgical music should not be of such intrinsic interest as to divert attention from the service. P.'s music is distinguished, then, for its fluency, ease and evenness; discords are rare and, when they do appear, are unobtrusively prepared and resolved, any quickening of the pace is gradual and short-lived, each phrase in each voice part slowly rises and falls; all the techniques employed remain carefully hidden. His output includes: 2 books of masses for 4, 5, 6 and 8 parts, (among them the famous 6-part *Missa Papae Marcelli*, written probably to the memory of Pope Marcellus II, d. 1555), 202 motets and several settings of the *Lamentations.

palette. Flat thin board on which a painter lays and mixes his colours. By derivation used

Pajou. *J.-B. Lemoyne*

Palestrina

Palazzo Barberini

Palazzo Pubblico

Palazzo Vecchio

Palladio. Villa Rotunda, Vicenza

Palladio. S. Giorgio Maggiore. See also colour plate 48

Palladian bridge by Flitcroft, Wilton House, Wiltshire. Also *Burlington, *Kent

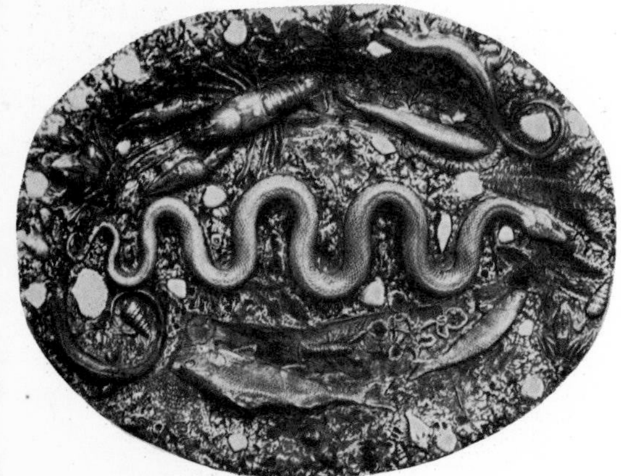

Palissy ware

Palma. *Venice crowned by Victory*

of an artist's choice of particular colours as a characteristic of his style.

Palgrave Francis Turner (1824–97). English poet, critic and anthologist, the compiler of *The Golden Treasury of Songs and Lyrics* (1861). He was professor of poetry at Oxford for 10 years, late in life.

palinode. Poem in which the author retracts a previous statement or belief.

Palissot de Montenoy Charles (1730–1814). French playwright who satirized Rousseau and the *philosophes* in *Les Originaux* (1755) and *Les Philosophes* (1760).

Palissy. The ware made, near Saintes in W. France after 1540, by the French potter BERNARD P. (*c.* 1510–90) and his school. Known as 'rustic pottery', plates, dishes, etc. were decorated with modelled ornament in the form of plants, fish, reptiles, snails and the like executed with startling verisimilitude; subtle polychrome glazes enhanced the naturalistic effect. Other examples had figure subjects, sometimes in high relief against backgrounds of architecture and landscape in which effects of perspective were achieved.

Palladianism. Style of 18th-c. English architecture born of Lord *Burlington's admiration for *Palladio. Lord Burlington's own villa at Chiswick and Colin Campbell's Mereworth Castle are straight copies of Palladio's Villa Rotunda. Also *Kent.

Palladio Andrea (real name Andrea di Pietro) (1518–80). Italian architect, born in Padua but spent nearly all his life at Vicenza. He was the son of a miller, and was 'discovered', patronized and even given the name by which he is known by the Vicenzan humanist Trissino. His works, apart from his Venetian churches, are all at Vicenza or in the surrounding countryside. His style has been analysed into 3 elements: (1) the antique: P. made a close study of Roman remains and of Vitruvius, though he never clearly differentiated between temples and domestic buildings–hence his use of porticoes, etc. for private houses; (2) the architects of the high Renaissance, especially Michelangelo: P. by-passed mannerism, sustaining the purity and enthusiasm of the earlier generation; (3) his system of proportion: P. adopted L. B. Alberti's analogies with musical harmonies, and the various dimensions of his designs all stand in simple ratios to one another (ratios which he was always careful to include in his printed plans). P.'s influence, the result as much of the designs publ. in *I Quattro Libri dell'Architettura* as of his actual buildings, was far reaching. It was mainly due to him that classical porticoes (columns plus pediment) are so universal a part of our civic architecture. Among his villas near Vicenza are the Villa Rotunda, with 4 identical porticoes and a dome over the middle; the Villa Malcontenta; the Villa Trissino, a grandiose plan with curved wings; and the villa for the Mocenigo family (never built), the grandest design of all, with 4 curved quadrant colonnades. His buildings at Vicenza include the Basilica, a recasing of the medieval town hall, with influences from Bramante and Sansovino; the Palazzo Chiericati; the Palazzo Thiene; the Palazzo Valmarana; and the Loggia del Capitano. In these he experimented with giant orders, rustication, cornices, etc. mostly in stucco on brick, not stone. The Teatro Olimpico is a re-creation of a Roman theatre, complete with scenery. P.'s 2 Venetian churches are S. Giorgio Maggiore and Il Redentore, both with carefully calculated façades based on triangles, and coolly classical interiors.

Pallavicini Carlo (1630–88). Italian opera composer who worked at Dresden and Venice. His works, characteristic of the middle and late Venetian school, include *La Gerusalemme liberata* (1687).

Pallavicini Stefano Benedetto (1672–1742). Italian librettist, son of C. P., and already Dresden court poet in 1688. He later worked at Düsseldorf. P. gained fame by his German trs of Horace; his librettos were used by Handel and Hasse among others.

Pallavicino Benedetto (d. 1601). Italian madrigal composer.

Palma Jacopo (called 'Il Giovane') (1544–1628). Italian painter of the Venetian school, concerned mainly with historical subjects. Rising rapidly in reputation, he became a great rival to Tintoretto; in later years his work declined in quality. He worked in the Doge's Palace and in the churches of Venice and also under the patronage of the duke of Urbino.

Palma Vecchio (Jacopo) (*c.* 1480–1528). Italian painter of the Venetian school, a native of Serimalta, near Bergamo. P. V. may have studied with Titian and Giorgione under Giovanni Bellini. His reputation was estab- by 1520, when he painted the altarpiece for the church of S. Antonio. This painting and an *Adoration of the Magi* of 1525 are his only datable works. Although his contemporary reputation was great, he does not appear to have been commissioned to paint in the public buildings of Venice to any extent. P. V. was noted for his ample modelling and figures, especially for a female type of generous proportions and blonde beauty (probably copied by Titian). He also painted the *Sacre Conversazioni*. P. V. was influenced by Giorgione and Titian and in turn influenced many painters, including Moretto and Romanino.

Palmer Humphrey. 18th-c. English potter, an imitator of Wedgwood working at Hanley from *c.* 1760 onwards. P. imitated first the black basaltes of Wedgwood, then agates, red wares and many other types of Wedgwood ware. The quality of the production was, however, excellent, and was always stamped with the maker's name.

Palmer Samuel (1805–81). English painter. Very precocious, he exhibited at the R.A. from 1820 onwards. He became friendly with John Linnell (his future father-in-law) who introduced P. to John Varley and, in 1824, to William Blake. This meeting was decisive; P. was overwhelmed by Blake's illustrations to *Job*. Between 1824 or 1825 and about 1835 P. produced his greatest work, a series of sketchbooks, small ink and wash landscapes and a few oil paintings, in which Blake's influence, Christian mysticism, pastoral idealism and the landscapes in the Shoreham Valley, Kent, were combined in a powerful manner. P. lived in Shoreham from 1826 to 1835, living simply and surrounded by such friends as John Linnell and George Richmond; the group called themselves 'The Ancients'. In 1835 P. returned to London; his visionary intensity of observation and statement was declining. A subsequent visit to Italy and a growing reputation as an academic painter altered his style completely. His early work was rediscovered in the 1930s and 1940s and influenced a generation of painters in England. Many of the Shoreham period paintings are in the Ashmolean Museum, Oxford.

Palmer Vance (1885–1959). Australian writer. The short stories mark a shift in emphasis from narrative to evocation; novels, *The Passage* (1930), *The Swayne Family* (1936) and *Golconda* (1948) trace the aimlessness of much Australian rural life; *The Legend of the Nineties* (1954) perceptively analyses the decade's importance in Australian literary development.

Palmerin of England (Palmeirim de Inglaterra). 16th-c. chivalric romance attributed to the Portuguese Francisco de Moraes or to the Spaniard Luis Hurtado.

palmette. A classical palm-leaf motif used in metalwork and furniture decoration, and resembling an opened fan in appearance.

Palmgren Selim (1878–1951). Finnish composer and pianist. His lyrical and impressionistic music was highly popular during his lifetime; he wrote mostly for piano, including 5 concertos, but also a number of beautiful songs and choral works.

Paludan (Stig Henning) Jacob (Puggaard) (1896–). Danish novelist. Much of P.'s work attacks the growth of materialistic values in Danish life. Works include *Fugle omkring Fyret* (1925; *Birds around the Light*, 1928) and the cycle *Jørgen Stein* (1932–3).

Paludan-Müller Frederik (1809–76). Danish poet. In his important verse P.-M. is a strict moralist, preaching asceticism. His chief work is the satirical epic *Adam Homo* (1841–8).

Pamela, or Virtue Rewarded (1740). Novel by Samuel *Richardson.

Pamphilos (*fl.* 390–350 B.C.). Greek painter. He was the pupil of Eupompus, and possibly the master of Apelles, Melantheus and Pousias. His contemporary reputation was extremely high.

pampille (from French *pampe*, a 'blade of corn'). A small, dripping cascade of diamonds used as part of an elaborately designed naturalistic corn- or flower-bouquet brooch. Popular about 1840–55.

Pan (1894). Novel by Knut *Hamsun.

Panama Norman (1914–) **and Frank** Melvin (date not known). U.S. film writers, producers and directors. This collaboration

Palma Vecchio. *A Blonde Woman*

Palmette from an Ionic treasury at Delphi

Samuel Palmer. *Cornfield by Moonlight with the Evening Star* (watercolour, gouache and pen)

Samuel Palmer. *Ruth* (1824; chalk and wash)

The Pantheon: engraving by Piranesi. See also colour plate 13

Panini. *View of the Forum.* See also colour plate 13

Pan pipes. Carving on Chartres cathedral

Pantoja de la Cruz. *Margarita of Austria*

extended to co-directing their earlier films. Now either directs and the other produces. They made 2 Danny Kaye comedies, *Knock on Wood* (1954) and *The Court Jester* (1955), a version of the stage musical *Li'l Abner* (1959) and *The Baited Trap* (1958), directed by P., a good thriller.

pandora. Musical instrument, same as *bandora.

Pandora and the Flying Dutchman (1951). Film directed by A. *Lewin.

Pandora's Box (1929). Film directed by G. W. *Pabst.

Pandosto, or Dorastus and Fawnia (1588). Prose romance by R. *Greene, the basis of Shakespeare's *The Winter's Tale.*

pange lingua. Hymns by Venantius Fortunatus (6th c.) and by St Thomas Aquinas (written in 1263) open with these words. The plainsong for the latter is used as a cantus firmus in a famous mass by Josquin des Prés and by other composers.

panharmonicon: J. N. *Mälzel

Pan(n)ini Giovanni (1691/2–1765). Italian landscape painter noted particularly for his picturesque portrayal of ruins, and an admirer of the work of Salvator Rosa. His very large output included historical scenes in architectural settings and capriccios. Many of his large works were lost or destroyed.

Panizzi Sir Anthony (1797–1879). Italian writer, an exile who became assistant librarian of the British Mus. (1831) and ultimately head librarian (1856–66). P. was largely responsible for the vast acquisitions which made the library one of the greatest in the world; he designed the famous dome of the Reading Room and ed. a complete catalogue.

panning: *film techniques

Panormo George Lewis (1774–1842). English guitar maker of Italian ancestry; his 18th-c. forebears specialized in violins.

pan pipes. Musical instrument consisting of a number of end-blown pipes giving a scale and fastened together side by side; the instrument dates from antiquity.

Pan Tadeusz (1834). Epic poem by *Mickiewicz.

Pantagruel. Book by *Rabelais.

Pantalone (English, Pantaloon). Character in the Italian **commedia dell'arte.*

Pantheon Rome. Roman temple, probably so called because dedicated to 'all the Gods'. It consists of a huge octostyle Corinthian portico (period of Augustus) leading into a circular domed space (the Rotunda, period of Hadrian, A.D. 120–4) whose proportions are built to simple geometrical ratios: height from floor to apex of dome equals the diameter, and the height of the dome itself equals that of the circular wall supporting it. The dome is practically solid and exerts no lateral thrust. The only lighting comes through the circular opening at the top. On the ground storey there are 7 great niches (plus the entrance), alternately semicircular and rectangular in plan, crossed by Corinthian columns. Much of the marble veneer and the bronze plating of the coffered vault has disappeared, but the original bronze doors remain. The P. is uniquely well preserved and few buildings have had so potent an influence, both during and after the Renaissance.

Pantoja de la Cruz Juan (1551–1608). Spanish painter of animals, historical subjects and portraits. He was a favourite painter of Philip II and painted many royal subjects, including Philip III. He also painted the retable for the monastery church of St Augustine, Valladolid.

pantomime. A term with meanings ranging from mimed plays in Greece and Rome to 18th-c. ballets; now almost exclusively used to describe British Christmas entertainments. These derive from *commedia dell'arte* and Harlequinade and the first was reputedly *Harlequin Executed* (1717) by John Rich. During the 19th c. the modern stories, e.g. *Cinderella* and *Aladdin*, were introduced at Drury Lane. These aimed to combine female beauty, scenic spectacle and broad comedy, the last usually being provided by the principal comedian as Dame, and the beauty by the *principal boy.

pantomimus. Actor in ancient Rome who presented his story entirely by means of stylized gesture in a performance of dignity and beauty.

pantoum. Verse form consisting of quatrains rhyming *abab*, *bcbc*, *cdcd*, etc., the 2nd and 4th lines of one quatrain forming the 1st and 3rd of the next.

Paolozzi Eduardo (1924–). Edinburgh-born sculptor; he studied at the Slade School, London (1943–7) and then worked (1947–50) in Paris. His 1st one-man show was in London 1947. After early phases of cage-like and, later, heavily modelled solid images, P. has worked in a highly imaginative manner that is closer to Dubuffet's art brut than to any of his British contemporaries. His *Jason* (1956; M.M.A., New York) or *Large Frog* (1958; British Council) are the product of a metamorphosis of unrelated ordinary objects–often fragments of abandoned machinery–into a new being with its own tragic identity.

papiermâché. Paper pulp moulded when wet and often japanned and polished when dry to resemble varnished or lacquered wood. It was introduced into Europe from the East and came to England via France in the 17th c. Small articles of furniture were made from it (often inlaid with mother-of-pearl) in the late 18th and 19th cs.

papiers collés (French, 'glued paper'). Term which refers to the technique of incorporating various types of paper–newspaper, wallpaper, bus-tickets, etc.–into a composition. It was first used by Braque, then by other cubist painters such as Picasso and Gris.

Papini Giovanni (1881–1956). Italian critic and futurist writer. P.'s best work is his autobiography, *Un uomo finito* (1912; *A Man–Finished*, 1924).

Papworth John Buonarotti (1775–1847). English painter, architect and landscape gardener. He designed a palace for the king of Württemburg, and also painted a number of watercolour views of London.

Paracelsus (1835). Dramatic poem by Robert Browning.

Paradise Lost (1667) and **Paradise Regained** (1671). Epic poems by *Milton.

Paradiso. 3rd part of *Dante's *Divine Comedy*.

Parapluies de Cherbourg, Les (1964). Film directed by J. *Demy.

Pardo Bazán Emilia (1851–1921). Spanish novelist and critic who wrote many novels and stories of Galician life somewhat in the *costumbrista style, with a strong dramatic flavour and a realism perhaps inspired by Zola. Her best novel is generally considered to be *Los pazos de Ulloa* (1886; *The Son of the Bondwoman*, 1908).

Pareja Juan de (*c.* 1610–70). Spanish painter, known as 'the slave of Velazquez'. He worked under Velazquez and remained in his house even after Philip IV had made him a freeman on seeing one of his paintings. He was primarily a genre painter, but a religious painting, *The Calling of St Matthew*, is in the Prado, Madrid.

Parents Terribles, Les (1948). Film directed by Jean *Cocteau, from his own play (1938).

Parini Giuseppe (1729–99). Italian poet. His main work was a series of *Odi* (written 1756–95), odes in the manner of Horace. Many of his poems have social and moral themes and in *Il Giorno* P. satirized the effete aristocracy and upheld the dignity of the honest working man.

Paris Matthew (d. 1259). English historical chronicler, writing in Latin; he is also recorded to have been a painter.

Paris, school of. The name given to 20th-c. art in Paris, whether by French or foreign artists; the school includes the greatest names in modern painting.

Paris Opéra Ballet. The oldest continuous ballet co. (founded 1669). Tradition had tended to arrest progress until Serge *Lifar took control (1932–58); he enriched it with a Diaghilev vitality and new choreography. The co. has a rigid system of promotion (*étoile).

Paris Psalter (10th c.; Bibliothèque Nationale, Paris). Byzantine codex of the golden age of Byzantine illumination when artists returned to classical paintings for their illustrations. The text is in Greek minuscules and it contains 14 full-page miniatures including one of David with his harp. Derived from a Graeco-Roman picture of Orpheus taming the beasts, it became very popular and was much copied.

Paolozzi. *Large Frog*

Pareja. *The Flight into Egypt*

Paris Psalter

Ms. of Matthew Paris: *Virgin and Child*

Papiermâché chair

Parmigianino. *Madonna of S. Zachary*

Parmigianino. *Madonna and Child with St John the Baptist and St Jerome*

Charlie Parker: painting by Barry Fantoni

Parrish. Jean Seberg and Stanley Baker in *In the French Style*

Parker Charlie (1920–55). U.S. alto saxophonist, with Dizzy *Gillespie the co-founder of modern jazz; his position as the most outstanding jazz improviser has not yet been seriously challenged. His astonishing melodic, rhythmic and harmonic originality and emotional profundity have made him the dominant influence on jazz since the mid 1940s.

Parkman Francis (1823–93). U.S. historian whose works include *La Salle and the Discovery of the Great West* (1879). P. spent some time with the Sioux, as recorded in the journal *The California and Oregon Trail* (1847). He also left the recently discovered *Journals of Francis Parkman* (1947).

Park Theater, New York. The 1st major U.S. theatre, known as 'Old Drury of America' (1798–1848), had great success presenting English and continental stars. Rebuilt (1821) after a fire, it was again destroyed by fire (1848) and not rebuilt.

Parlement of Foules, The, or **The Parlement of Briddes.** Poem by *Chaucer.

Parliament of Bees, The (1608–16). Allegorical masque by John Day.

Parma, school of. School of Italian painting which flourished in the 15th and 16th cs under the patronage of the Farnese family. Correggio and his pupil Parmigianino were its most influential members.

Parmigianino Il, born Girolamo Francesco Maria Mazzola (1503–40). Italian mannerist painter and engraver named after his birthplace, Parma. He fled Parma *c.* 1521, was taken prisoner at the Sack of Rome (1527), sought asylum in Bologna, returned to Parma (1531), only to die in Casalmaggiore, again a refugee. Frescoes can be found in the churches of most of these cities, notably in S. Maria delle Steccata, Parma. P.'s art, influenced by Correggio, Raphael and Michelangelo, is characterized by the elongation of the figures, and influenced in its turn the school of *Fontainebleau. Typical of his altarpieces is the *Madonna and Child with St John the Baptist and St Jerome* (N.G., London), while among the warmest of mannerist portraits, reserved yet somehow intimate, is the masterly *Portrait of a Woman* (Gal. N., Naples), probably portraying P.'s mistress, Antea 'la Bella'.

Parnassians. A group of French poets who, rejecting the weakness and excesses of late romanticism, wrote with formal and verbal precision and maintained a strict impersonality; nature was a frequent subject but it was described with static detachment. The group, led by Leconte de Lisle, produced 3 vols of work, *Le Parnasse contemporain* (1866, 71, 76), hence the name of the group.

Parnell Thomas (1679–1718). Irish poet and churchman, a friend of Pope.

parquetry: *marquetry

Parratt Sir Walter (1841–1924). English organist, teacher and composer, an important figure in the 20th-c. renaissance of English music. His choice of music for St George's chapel (1882–1924), ranging from Tallis to S. S. Wesley, set a new norm for English churches.

Parrhasios (*fl. c.* 400 B.C.). Classical Greek painter who was born at Ephesus. He was the pupil of Euphranor and the rival of Xeuxis. He was noted for his vanity, as well as for his ability as a figure painter; he styled himself 'the prince of painters'.

Parrish Robert (1916–). U.S. film director. He worked on J. Ford's army film unit during the war and helped to ed. film evidence for the Nuremberg trials. As an ed., he won an Oscar for *Body and Soul* before starting to direct. His best work includes a war film, *The Purple Plain* (1955), and a western, *The Wonderful Country* (1959).

Parrott Ian (1916–). English composer, from 1950 professor of music at Aberystwyth; he has increasingly identified himself with the Welsh national school. His works include: the opera *The Black Ram* (1957), symphonic poem *Luxor* (1947) and a concerto for cor anglais (1958).

Parry Sir Charles Hub[illegible]48–1918). English composer, teacher [illegible] writer on music; director of the R.C.M. from 1894. His best-known works include th[illegible]*lest Pair of Sirens* and the 6 'motets' [illegible]*arewell.*

Parsifal. Opera by *W[illegible]his last). 1st performance at Bayreuth in 1882. Also *Perceval and *Parzival.

The Parthenon. Also *Acropolis

Metope from the Parthenon (from the Elgin Marbles)

part books. Much music of the polyphonic era survives only in p. b.s. These were either in several vols, 1 to each part, or were in 1 vol., the PARTS being so arranged on the double page as to be easily legible to the various singers.

parterre. Level part of a garden used for flower-beds.

Parthenon. Doric temple on the Acropolis, Athens, built 447–432 B.C. and dedicated to Athena the Virgin ('*parthenos*'). The architects were Ictinus and Callicrates, and the master sculptor Phidias. It has 8 columns across the shorter ends, 17 columns along the sides. The subtleties and refinements of Greek proportion are here carried to their greatest perfection (e.g. *entasis). The sculpture (of which the largest coll., known as the 'Elgin Marbles', is in the British Mus.) consisted of (1) large free-standing figures in the pediments representing Athena, Poseidon and other gods; (2) the high reliefs of the *metopes, alternating with triglyphs, showing the fight between the Lapiths and Centaurs; and (3) the continuous low-relief frieze round the top of the outside *cella* wall, showing the Panathenaic procession of youths and maidens bringing the sacred 'cloak' ('*peplos*') to the goddess. Inside the *cella* was the huge ivory and gold statue of Athena by Phidias. The P. survived almost intact until 1687 when it was blown up during a war between the Venetians and the Turks. Lord Elgin removed most of the sculpture in 1801, but some remain *in situ*. There are also portions of the frieze in the Louvre.

partial: *harmonic series

Partie de Campagne, Une (1937). Film directed by J. *Renoir.

Partisan Review. U.S. magazine founded in 1934; at first politically radical. It has been influential in disseminating the work of the *avant-garde* and intelligentsia.

parure (French, 'adornment'). A set of matching jewellery. The fashion developed for men in the early 16th c., probably at the court of the Emperor Maximilian. Women imitated the fashion a little later. A p. must always include a grand necklace; other items are clasps or brooches, head ornaments, ear-rings, and bracelets. A 'demi-p.' consisted usually only of a necklace and ear-rings or head ornament.

Parzival (13th c.). Epic by *Wolfram von Eschenbach. Also *Perceval and *Parsifal.

Pascal Blaise (1623–62). French writer and scientist. In his youth P. achieved fame as a mathematician and physicist, being the 1st French scientist to replace rational deduction by empirical methods. He was always attracted to religion and was finally converted to a religious life after a mystical experience (1654). P. felt that he had discovered the limitations of scientific reason and exchanged it for the certainty of faith; this sensation of human inadequacy distinguishes him clearly from his contemporaries, and reveals the deep influence of Montaigne.

The *Lettres provinciales* (1656–7), a series of pamphlets defending Jansenism against Jesuit attacks, are written in a style which derives its strength from absolute simplicity and objectivity. They constitute the 1st prose masterpiece of the classical era of French literature. Fragments of an uncompleted work, the *Apologie de la religion chrétienne*, were coll. and publ. as the *Pensées* (1670; *Monsieur Pascal's Thoughts*, 1688); the mystical insights and penetrating analyses of human character which it contains has given the book a European influence.

Blaise Pascal

Pascin Jules (1885–1930). Bulgarian-born U.S. painter and decorative artist. He made an early reputation as a cartoonist in Germany and also illustrated the works of Heine. He then turned to serious painting, working in France and the U.S. (becoming a citizen in 1925); his subject-matter was primarily the female nude.

Pascoli Giovanni (1855–1912). Italian poet. His verse is sensitive, melancholy and mystical, employing an extremely rich vocabulary.

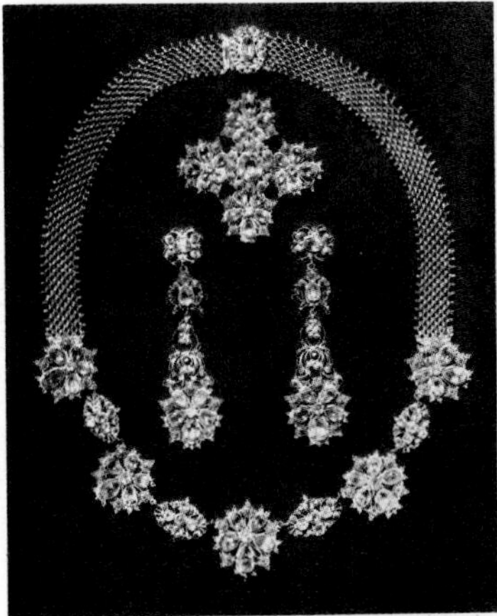
Parure of topazes; French, *c.* 1830

pas de chat. Literally 'step of a cat' in which the ballet dancer travels from left to right or vice versa. Standing in 5th position, the dancer draws the working foot up the supporting calf in a pointed position, then, tracing a small arc in the air with the working toe, springs and lands with feet together in 5th position.

pas de deux. A dance for 2, usually the climax of an act or complete ballet in which the hero and heroine of the action dance together; it is sometimes an extraneous show-piece dance introduced into a larger work or performed separately.

Pascin. *Cinderella*

Pasolini. *Accattone*

Pasek Jan Chryzostom (1630–1701). Polish nobleman, soldier and author of famous memoirs. The *Pamiętniki*, written in a vivid, colloquial style, give an unconsciously frank picture of life in 17th-c. Poland.

Pasmore Victor (1908–). English painter and a founder of the *Euston Road School (1937) and from 1954 to 1962 a teacher at Durham Univ. By 1945 he had earned a reputation with paintings like *The Studio of Ingres* (1945–6; Coll. Sir Kenneth Clark): interiors painted with a strong sense of organization and great technical accomplishment. By 1952, possibly encouraged by a period of collaboration with Nicholson, he made a total break with representation. P.'s conversion to abstraction was an important development in post-war British painting. His influence has originated in part from his championship of autonomous abstraction, from his exploitation of 3 dimensions in collages, reliefs and constructions and from his use of contemporary materials such as aluminium and laminated plastics. His abstract paintings, e.g. *Abstract in White, Black, Indian Red and Lilac* (1957; Tate) have been succeeded by constructions like *Projective Painting in White, Black and Ochre* (1963; Coll. the artist).

Pasmore. *The Thames at Chiswick*

Pasmore. *Relief Construction in White, Black, Red and Maroon* (1956–7)

Pasolini Pier Paolo (1922–). Italian film director. P. was famous for his novels of Rome's lower depths before directing his 1st film, *Accattone* (1961). Both this and *Mamma Roma* (1962) were set among Rome's thieves, pimps and prostitutes.

Pasquier Étienne (1529–1615). French writer and jurist; his chief work is the literary-historical miscellany *Recherches de la France* (1560–1621).

Pasquier Chronicles, The (1933–41). Series of novels by Georges Duhamel.

passacaglia. Equivalent to *chaconne.

Passage to India, A (1924). Novel by E. M. *Forster.

passamezzo (derivation uncertain). Italian dance, similar to the pavan, popular in the late 16th and early 17th c. It was composed to a harmonic ground, i.e. an unchanging chord pattern; the most common of these grounds, all of 8 measures, were the 'p. antico' (English, 'passing measures pavan') and the 'p. moderno' (English, 'quadran pavan').

Passavanti Jacopo (*c.* 1302–57). Italian writer, a Dominican friar. P.'s *Lo Specchio della vera penitenza* (*Mirror of True Repentance*) contains a number of moralistic short stories, early examples of the genre in Italian, as well as visions of Heaven and horrific descriptions of Hell.

passepied. A French provincial dance in triple time which became fashionable at the court of Louis XIV. The dancers glided in quick minuet-like steps.

passing-note. A musical term for a note which although discordant in the harmonic context carries the melody between two notes both of which are concordant in that context.

Passion. In music the name reserved for extended choral settings of the story of Christ's sufferings and death as told in the Gospels; particularly those by German composers of the 17th and 18th c., e.g. Schütz and Bach. The P. grew out of the liturgy, surrounding the Gospel account, for Holy Week. In its fully developed German form it consisted of a narrative given by a solo voice; choruses commenting on the story; solo voices taking the parts of the leading dramatis personae in the story and *chorales in which the congregation participate.

Passionate Pilgrim, The (1599). Coll. of 21 poems attributed to Shakespeare. Only 5 are certainly his, and the publ. later removed Shakespeare's name from unsold copies.

Passion de Jeanne d'Arc, Le (1928). Film directed by C. T. *Dreyer.

Passion play. A form of play which told the Good Friday story, the most famous being that which has been performed every 10 years since 1633 at Oberammergau in Bavaria, in thanksgiving for deliverance from the plague. The medieval tradition of P. p.s died out in the 15th c. in most parts of Europe.

paste jewellery. Imitation gems, prepared from strass (specially prepared glass) which is very transparent and refractive. If uncoloured it is used for imitation diamonds and the addition of metallic oxides gives coloured pastes. P. j. (not used till the 18th c.) is often of high technical and artistic quality.

pastel. Drawing material consisting of artificial chalks made of ground white chalk and powder colour. A form of p. was used in the 15th c., but it was fully developed only in the 18th c., a period which found sympathetic its subtlety, charm and ability to portray light. Degas revived it and his work in the medium influenced the impressionists.

Pasternak Boris Leonidovich (1890–1960). Soviet poet and novelist. P. began to attract attention during World War I as a futurist poet, especially with the widely circulated and influential coll. *My Sister, Life* (written 1917). After the Revolution he was frequently criticized for the non-political outlook of his poems and turned to trs. (notably of English and German poets). The publ. in Italy of his novel *Dr Zhivago* (1957; 1958; still unpubl. in the U.S.S.R.) gave P. an international reputation; it also caused him political difficulties (he was threatened with deportation) exacerbated by the award of a Nobel prize (1958) which he renounced. P.'s verse has influenced poets (e.g. Mandelstam and Tsvetayeva), but although formally correct and extremely musical has never been popular: meaning is implied in brief, fragmentary images which make it inaccessible to a public conditioned to the explicitness of socialist realism. P. was not a political poet, but his verse reveals that he was conscious–even glad–that he lived in a cataclysmic period. *Doctor Zhivago* is an episodic but intensely poetic description of the Revolution and its aftermath. Its protagonist, Zhivago, is presented as having too much intelligence and sensibility to join a faction, and he therefore remains ineffective; yet his epoch does not allow him the private life which, as a poet, he strives to protect. P.'s prose works include the autobiographical *Safe Conduct* (1931; 1945); *The Last Summer* and *The Childhood of Luvers*.

pastiche, pasticio. In its general sense the term is used of a work of art (often a musical work) made up from several styles; specifically the term 'pastiche' is applied to a piece of writing or a picture done in the style of one other artist.

Pastoral. The name given by Beethoven to his 6th symphony; its movements programmatically illustrate the events of a day in the country. Beethoven's piano sonata in D maj. (op. 28) was also given the name, by its publ.

pastorale or **pastoral.** A stage piece (with or without music) on a pastoral or legendary theme. The genre originated in Renaissance Italy, inspired by the *Eclogues* of Virgil and the idylls of Theocritus; but it was particularly popular in 17th- and 18th-c. France, where p.s with music gave wide opportunity for ballets.

pastoral literature. A literary genre either in verse or prose or in dramatic form, concerned with the loves, sorrows and daily lives of idealized shepherds in an idealized countryside. Earliest examples are the poems of *Theocritus and the *Eclogues* of Virgil; from then the theme has been a recurring one in European literature (*Arcadia).

pastourelle. Medieval French lyric poem recounting the meeting and wooing of knight and shepherdess.

Pastrone Giovanni (1882–1959). Italian film director of *Cabiria* (1913), the most famous early Italian spectacular, with a script by the Italian poet D'Annunzio.

patchbox. A small box of gold, silver, porcelain or enamel of various shapes and forms which was used in the 18th c. to carry patches (pieces of black court plaster cut into circles, crescents and so on, and applied to the face as an ornament). They usually have a mirror on the inside of the lid.

Patenier (Patinir or Patinier) Joachim (*c.* 1485–1524). Landscape painter active at Antwerp. Influenced by, and possibly the pupil of, Gérard David, he was a collaborator of Quinten Massys and a friend of Dürer. His rocky landscapes with a wide sweeping vista and figures reduced to mere compositional elements had a lasting influence on Flemish religious painting. Technical perfection, smooth finish, naïve vision combined with a rich and controlled imagination, are characteristic of his work. The 3 signed paintings *Flight into Egypt*, *Baptism of Christ* and *St Jerome* are certainly his; there are numerous others in his style.

Pater Jean-Baptiste François (1695–1736). French painter, pupil and follower of Watteau. He worked with incredible industry, burning himself out at the age of 40. P. had great talent, but lacked individuality and often repeated

Boris Pasternak

Pastel. Degas, *Le Bain*

Pastrone. *Cabiria*

Jean-Baptiste Pater. *Soldiers Revelling*

Patenier. *St Jerome*

Walter Pater

Coventry Patmore: painting by Sargent

Cesare Pavese

Adelina Patti

Napoleon I study chair decorated with patera

himself to satisfy the demands of patrons. The *Toilette* (Louvre) illustrates his brilliant gifts as a decorator, but lacks the sensitivity and psychological penetration which marked Watteau's work.

Pater Walter Horatio (1839–94). English writer and aesthete. From 1864 to 1885 he was a fellow of Brasenose College, Oxford. He became famous on the publ. of *Studies of the History of the Renaissance* (1873), which presented the Renaissance as an impulse moving men to seek the beautiful in art, radiating from Italy throughout Europe. Here as elsewhere P. seeks not to evaluate, but to evoke, in controlled, rhythmical prose, the beauty of his subject. The closing essay contains his famous plea that men should 'burn with a hard gem-like flame', at the highest pitch of sensuous consciousness. In *Marius the Epicurean* (1885) he recounts the philosophic quest of a young Roman in Antonine times for truth and inner peace. Other important works are *Imaginary Portraits* (1887), *Appreciations* (including studies of Wordsworth, Shakespeare and Lamb) (1889) and the autobiographical *The Child in the House* (1894).

patera. A circular or oval disc, adapted from the shallow saucer of the same name used in sacrificial libations, applied or carved as an ornamental motif in neo-classical furniture and also used in plate during the same period.

Pather Panchali (1956). Film directed by S. *Ray.

Pathetic symphony. Name accepted in its French form of *Symphonie pathétique* by Tchaikovsky as the title for his symphony no. 6 in B min. (1893).

Pathfinder, The (1840). Novel by James Fenimore Cooper.

Paths of Glory (1957). Film directed by S. *Kubrick.

patina. A thin coating, often of a carbonate of copper, green in colour, which forms on bronze sculptures, etc., after prolonged exposure to the air, or burial, or is induced artificially. The term is also used to describe the oxide that forms on the surface of other metals, and by extension to describe the surface, achieved by age, handling and polishing over the years, of furniture, silver, etc.

Patmore Coventry (Kersey Dighton) (1823–96). English poet, an associate of the Pre-Raphaelites. His works include *The Angel in the House* (1854–62), 4 poems in praise of marriage; and *The Unknown Eros* (1877).

Paton Alan (1903–). South African novelist, short-story writer and poet. In *Cry, the Beloved Country* (1948) and *Too Late the Phalarope* he investigates with great delicacy South African race relations. Artistic tolerance strengthens his moral protest; latterly his efforts have been in active politics.

Patrick Spens, Sir. Early Scottish ballad included in *Percy's *Reliques*.

Patti Adelina (1843–1919). Italian coloratura soprano singer; her career began in the U.S. but a London début in 1861 established her world reputation. Her voice was not powerful but her virtuosity was immense.

Pattison Mark (1813–84). English scholar; his interesting and revealing memoirs were publ. in 1885.

Paul Bruno (1874–). German painter, architect and art critic. He studied at the School of Fine Art in Dresden (1886–94) and then in Munich (1894–1907). In 1907 he became director of the School of Decorative Arts in Berlin and did cartoons for the magazine *Simplicissimus*.

Paulding James Kirke (1778–1860). U.S. novelist. P. and Washington Irving publ. a humorous periodical, *Salmagundi*. P.'s works, far more realistic than most writing by his contemporaries, include several anti-British satires and the novels *Koningsmarke, The Long Finne . . .* (1823); *The Dutchman's Fireside* (1831) and *The Puritan and His Daughter* (1849).

Paul et Virginie (1787). Novel by *Bernardin de Saint-Pierre.

Paumann Konrad (*c.* 1415–73). German composer and organist working mainly at Munich but with a European reputation; he is regarded as the forebear of the German organ school.

Pausanias. Greek writer of the 2nd c. A.D. whose survey of Greece the *Periegesis* contains descriptions of many of the masterpieces of

Greek architecture and sculpture in their pristine state.

pause. In music a sign 𝄐 over a note indicating that it is to be held longer than its strict time value. The length of the p. is generally at the performer's discretion. A 'general pause' affects all performers and is basically decided by the conductor or leader.

pavan. Courtly dance of 16th-c. Italy (possibly deriving its name from Padua colloquially called 'Pava'), popular throughout Europe. It was a slow-moving, stately dance in 4:4 time and was usually followed by a faster moving one such as the galliard.

Pavese Cesare (1908–50). Italian novelist. He was born on a farm; his father died when he was still a child and he soon learnt the meaning of hardship. He managed, however, to take a degree in literature with a thesis on Walt Whitman. He became a schoolmaster and trs. from Defoe, Dickens, Joyce, Melville and Faulkner. In 1935 he was arrested for anti-Fascism and sentenced to preventive detention in a village in Calabria; this produced the book *Il carcere* (1949; *The Political Prisoner*, 1955). He was always obsessed with the idea of suicide and in 1950 he took his life. His work is increasingly pervaded by a sense of melancholy but a powerful and poetic style combined with a mastery of formal device and subtlety of perception and expression have made him one of the most admired of recent Italian novelists. In his *La luna e i falò* (1950; *The Moon and the Bonfire*, 1952) the past is recalled and its missed opportunities for living regretted.

pavilion (from French *pavillon*, 'a tent'). Term originally applied to a marquee; it now describes an ornamental summer-house in a garden or park, or similar buildings (e.g. a sports p.).

Pavlova Anna (1882–1931). Russian dancer who achieved fame and acclamation as the greatest ballerina of her age. Trained at the Imperial School, St Petersburg, she became leading dancer in 1906. Although enormously popular in Russia, she joined Diaghilev in 1909 and toured, both with him and later with her own co. The role most closely associated with P. was *The Dying Swan* (1905) which fully revealed her talent for dancing with her entire body and exercising her tremendous stage personality rather than depending on an extravagant technique.

Pavlova Karolina Karlovna (1807–93). Russian poet, the wife of Nikolay Pavlov, a novelist. P. had a popular Moscow *salon*. Her poems, technically of very high standard, reflect the melancholy and frustration of her life.

Pawlikowska Maria (1895–1945). Polish poet and playwright, renowned for her epigrammatic lyrics.

Pawnshop, The (1916). Short film directed by *Chaplin.

Paxinou Katina (1904–). Greek actress rightly acclaimed as the first lady of the Greek stage. She has played all the Greek classical roles, Shakespeare and Ibsen, both in her own country and England and America. Recently she has enhanced her reputation by brilliant performances in films like *Rocco And His Brothers*.

Paxton Sir Joseph (1803–65). English architect, designer of the Crystal Palace to house the Great Exhibition of 1851. As gardener to the duke of Devonshire P. became familiar with greenhouse construction and built the Great Conservatory at Chatsworth (1840) on an ingenious prefabrication system; his Crystal Palace was a magnificent example of the prefabrication principle with means of erection, construction and drainage all integrated into one system. P.'s confident handling of iron and glass in this vast building (it covered an area of 700,000 sq. ft) made it a precursor of the modern movement in architecture.

Payne John Howard (1791–1852). U.S. actor and playwright. P.'s greatest success, *Clari, The Maid of Milan* (1823), contained the song 'Home, Sweet Home'.

Payne Roger (d. 1797). The most famous English bookbinder. P. was one of the earliest to use Russia leather, and his richly decorated vols display his fine craftsmanship and excellent taste.

Peace (421 B.C.). Comedy by *Aristophanes.

Peacham Henry (*c.* 1576–*c.* 1642). English author of the treatise *The Compleat Gentleman* (1622).

Anna Pavlova

Katina Paxinou

Roger Payne binding; red morocco, gold tooled with floral border

Paxton. Crystal Palace in 1851

Pearce.
Sir Christopher Wren

Peale. *Self-portrait with a Mastodon Bone.* Also *Franklin

Pechstein. *Red Girl at Table* (1910). Also *Novembergruppe

Thomas Love Peacock

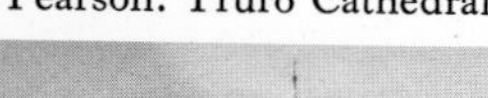

Pearson. Truro Cathedral

Peacock Thomas Love (1785–1866). English novelist, the friend of several writers of the romantic period. P.'s own fame rests on his 7 short satirical novels, among them *Headlong Hall* (1816), *Nightmare Abbey* (1818) *Crochet Castle* (1831) and *Gryll Grange* (1860). P.'s most characteristic device is to assemble a group of figures, representing actual persons or embodying human foibles, at a lively country-house party where they argue their idiosyncratic points of view. P.'s main targets are the excesses of romanticism, 'the march of mind', cranks of all kinds, pretentiousness and hypocrisy. He also wrote *The Four Ages of Poetry* (1820), which led his friend Shelley to write *The Defence of Poetry*.

Peale Charles Willson (1741–1827). U.S. portrait painter and miniaturist. He studied under B. West in London, then had a successful career as a portraitist in Philadelphia. His ability to get a likeness made him popular in spite of a certain rigidity in his style. His brother JAMES P. (1749–1831) was a miniaturist. Of his sons, all named after the old masters, RAPHAEL(LE) (1774–1825) was a miniaturist and REMBRANDT (1778–1860) a painter of portraits and historical subjects.

Pearce (Pierce) Edward (d. 1695). English sculptor and wood carver; he did much work for Wren and also carved a portrait bust of him.

Pears Peter (1910–). English tenor singer, known above all for his interpretations of works by Britten. Since 1938 he and Britten (at the piano) have gained a world reputation as recitalists.

Pearsall Robert Lucas (de) (1795–1856). English composer. Although he lived mainly in Germany he wrote excellent madrigals in the style of the English 16th- and 17th-c. madrigal school. His ballads and glees in 19th-c. idiom were less successful.

Pearson John Loughborough (1817–97). English architect, a leading figure of high Victorian Gothic. His chief works are Truro cathedral, Cornwall; St Augustine's, Kilburn, London; and Brisbane cathedral, Australia. The elements of his style are entirely derivative (and he took pains to copy correctly) but his handling of them shows originality and a keen sense of mass and space.

Peau de chagrin, Le (1830–1). Novel by Balzac.

Pechstein Max (1881–1955). German painter. In Dresden he met Heckel and Kirchner and became a member of Die *Brücke (1906). His style at the time shows a complete if more decorative assimilation of their ideas, both in his taste for the raw and unsophisticated and in his expressive use of colour and paint–*Under the Trees* (1911; Detroit Inst.). In 1910 he joined Nolde's Neue Sezession. His later work, like Müller's, involved a more obviously sophisticated, decorative form of primitivism. He taught at the Berlin Academy from 1923 to 1933, when he was dismissed by the Nazis, and again from 1945.

Peck Gregory (1916–). U.S. film actor. P. brings a romantic aura into action films; handsome and relaxed, he has distinguished many unremarkable pictures. Among his best are *Duel in the Sun* (1947), *Captain Hornblower, R.N.* (1951), *Roman Holiday* (1953) and C. Foreman's *The Guns of Navarone* (1960).

Pecock Reginald (1395?–1460?). His great work *The Repressor of Overmuch Blaming of the Clergy* (1455), an argument against the Lollards, was suppressed for showing too much tolerance towards them, and P. was deprived of his bishopric of Chichester. It is important in the history of English prose, being the earliest academic treatise in English.

pedal. (1) Various musical instruments have pedal-operated mechanisms which affect their pitch (e.g. the *harp or machine *timpani) or tone (e.g. the *harpsichord). (2) On the *organ the PEDAL-BOARD is a *keyboard operated by the feet. (3) In harmony a p., or 'p. point' is a long note held, generally in the bass, over several bars. The device, frequent in organ compositions (hence perhaps the name) builds up climax–the upper parts weaving changing harmonies against the insistent p. note. (4) In *brass instruments, particularly the trombone, the lowest notes are called 'p. notes'.

pedestal. Architectural term for the base of a column, statue, etc.

pediment. Term used in classical architecture for the triangular end of a sloping roof; the shape has frequently been used purely decoratively.

Pedrell Felipe (1841–1922). Spanish composer, folk-lorist, scholar and teacher at Madrid and Barcelona. By his eds of the great Spanish masters such as Victoria, by his pioneer research on Spanish folk-song and by his music journalism, P. launched the modern school of Spanish composers; his pupils included Albéniz, Granados and de Falla.

Peele George (*c.* 1558–*c.* 97). English poet and playwright, one of the *University Wits. Among P.'s plays are *The Arraignment of Paris* (1584), *David and Bethsabe* (*c.* 1594) and *The Old Wives' Tale* (1591); his best works are the lyrics in them. He also wrote pageants.

peep-show. A box with an eye-piece at one end and scenes (either historical or dramatic) which are viewed in perspective inside it. P.-s.s date from the 15th c. and were still to be seen in the 19th c.

Peer Gynt (1867). Poetic drama by *Ibsen; the title of 2 suites by *Grieg.

Peerson Martin (1572–1650). English composer of verse anthems, motets and viol fantasies, and a well-known virginals piece, *The Fall of the Leafe.*

Peeters Bonaventura I. (1614–52). Flemish landscape and marine painter and satirical poet, who lived and worked in Antwerp. He was the brother of the painters JAN (1624–72), CATHARINA (1615–after 1676) and GILLIS (1612–53). In 1639 he painted a picture of the Siege of Calloo (with his brother Gillis) for the municipal authorities at Antwerp.

Péguy Charles-Pierre (1873–1914). French poet. P. ran a bookshop which became a meeting-place for intellectuals and founded a periodical, the *Cahiers de la quinzaine* (1900–14), in which most of his work appeared. It reflected his development from anti-clerical Socialist to Catholic mystic (although he never formally joined the Church). P.'s work includes 3 dramatic poems, together called *Les Mystères de Jeanne d'Arc* (1910–12), and the colls of verse *La Tapisserie de Sainte Geneviève et de Jeanne d'Arc* (1912) and *La Tapisserie de Notre-Dame* (1913).

Peintres cubistes, Les (1913). Prose work by *Apollinaire.

Peiper Tadeusz (1891–). Polish poet, critic and playwright. His vol. of theoretical writings *Tedy* (1930) became the bible of the Awangarda movement.

Peletier du Mans Jacques (1517–82). French poet, one of the *Pléiade; he first suggested poetic reform to Ronsard and du Bellay. His opinions are found in a preface to his trs. (1545) of Horace's *Ars Poetica* and in his own *L'Art poétique* (1555).

Pelin Elin. Pseud. of Dimitar Ivanov (1878–1949), the leading Bulgarian writer of the generation after I. Vázov. His reputation rests on his short stories.

Pellan Alfred (1906–). French-Canadian surrealist painter. He worked in Paris from 1926 to 1940, and after his return to Canada exercised an invigorating influence. His paintings are energetic, with elements of the gay and the macabre, complex in design and boldly coloured.

Pelléas and Mélisande. Play by *Maeterlinck which inspired works by *Debussy and *Schoenberg, among other composers.

Pellegrini Giovanni Antonio (1675–1741). Italian painter and decorative artist who studied under Ricci and Pagani. He worked very rapidly and painted much in an idiom similar to Tiepolo's. His works, all over Europe, covered Biblical, historical and classical subjects.

Pellicer Carlos (1899–). Mexican poet of considerable verbal dexterity and aural appeal; colls include *Piedra de Sacrificios* (1924).

Pellico Silvio (1789–1854). Italian poet and playwright best known for his moving account of his imprisonment by the Austrians for political activities, *Le mie prigione* (1832), which strongly influenced the Risorgimento. Besides poems, he wrote a number of undistinguished romantic tragedies, the best known being *Francesca da Rimini* (1814; 1851).

Peloponnesian War, The. History by *Thucydides.

Penal Colony, The (1919). Short story by Kafka.

Pendennis, The History of (1848–50). Novel by *Thackeray.

Pellan. *Underground*

Pellegrini. *The Education of Cupid by Painting and Drawing*

Charles Péguy

Pediment. Temple of Neptune, Paestum

Ramón Pérez de Ayala

Benito Pérez Galdós

Pepys: painting by Kneller

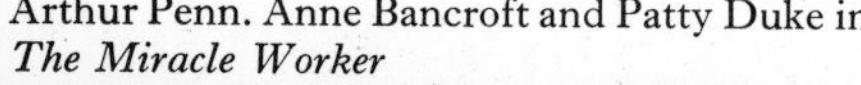
Arthur Penn. Anne Bancroft and Patty Duke in *The Miracle Worker*

pendentif or **pendentive.** Architectural term, *dome.

Penguin Island (1908). Satirical novel by Anatole France.

penillion. An elaborate style of improvised song practised by the Welsh bards; the voice singing one melody, the harp playing another, the whole being performed according to certain traditional conventions.

Penn Arthur (1922–). U.S. film director. P. worked in TV and directed a play on Broadway before making his 1st film, *The Left-Handed Gun* (1958), which examines the subject and origins of myths about Billy the Kid. *The Miracle Worker* (1961), about the childhood of Helen Keller, he directed for TV and theatre before filming. *Mickey One* (1964) is a comedy.

Penn Irving (1917–). U.S. photographer famed for his mastery of colour photography. P.'s early fashion work for the Condé Nast publs and his highly original style of reportage have influenced a whole generation of younger photographers.

Pensées (1670). Book by Blaise *Pascal.

Penseroso, Il (1632). Poem by *Milton.

pentameter: *metre in verse

Pentateuch: *Bible

pentatonic: *scale

pentimento. Term sometimes used in painting of figures, etc. which the artist painted over but which, through the course of time, have become visible through the superimposed layers of paint.

Pepe-le-Moko (1937). Film directed by J. *Duvivier.

Pepusch John Christopher (Johann Christoph) (1667–1752). German-born composer who settled in England in 1700. He arranged and composed the music to J. Gay's *Beggar's Opera* (1728); he also composed cantatas, while organist to the duke of Chandos, and instrumental music. His interest in early music influenced the work of W. *Boyce.

Pepys Samuel (1633–1703). English diarist and an outstanding naval administrator. P.'s famous *Diary*, written in cipher, was only decoded and publ. in 1825 as *Memoirs*. . . . It records P.'s life between 1660 and 1669, and is a splendid portrait of his robust character and the age in which he lived.

Perceval ou le Conte du Graal (*c.* 1180). Poem by *Chrétien de Troyes. Also *Parzival and *Parsifal.

percussion instruments. The family of musical instruments which 'speak' when struck; it is divided into the vast group of untuned and the relatively small group of tuned instruments. The latter includes the timpani and xylophone but not the *piano (although strictly speaking its strings are set in vibration by percussive means and it is sometimes used for percussive effects in the orchestra). The PERCUSSION BAND used in schools, to introduce children to simple rhythmic patterns, usually comprises a bass drum, cymbals, triangles and tambourines.

Percy Thomas (1729–1811). English antiquarian and bishop of Dromore. His *Reliques of Ancient English Poetry* (1765) quickened the study of national ballad literatures throughout Europe and thus exerted a considerable influence on the development of the romantic movement. The material for this coll. of ballads and romances included the 17th-c. PERCY FOLIO. P. also publ. *Fives Pieces of Runic Poetry* (1763), trs. from the Icelandic.

Pereda José María de (1833–1906). Spanish regional novelist from the district round Santander. Aggressive reactionary views in politics and religion spoil some of his novels, but others, e.g. *Sotileza* (1885), on a fishing village, and *Peñas Arriba* (1894), on mountain peasant life, reveal a talent for descriptive writing.

Père Goriot, Le (1834). Novel by *Balzac.

Peregrine Pickle, The Adventures of (1751). Picaresque novel by *Smollett.

Peretz I(saak) L(oeb) (1852–1915). Polish-Jewish writer. He studied widely and trained as a lawyer. He took to writing while young, for the most part in Yiddish in order to reach the poor Jewish populations, whose jokes, myths and conversations inspired the stories.

His stories, pathetic, satirical, sentimental, visionary or humorous, vividly describe simple downtrodden characters, their scarcely more successful oppressors, their desires, fantasies, etc.

Pérez de Ayala Ramón (1880–). Spanish novelist. P. established his reputation with the novel *Tinieblas en las cumbres* (1907). The most important of his later works are *A.M.D.G.* (1910), a bitter attack on his Jesuit education, the picaresque *Troteras y danzaderas* (1913), *Belarmino y Apolonio* (1921) and *Tigre Juan* (1926; *Tiger Juan*, 1933), all distinguished by a beautiful if elaborate style, superb sense of humour and satire, and profound sympathy with his characters.

Pérez de Guzmán Fernán (1376–1460). Spanish poet and chronicler, the finest Castilian prose writer of his time. His works include lyrical and didactic verse, and the biographical sketches *Mar de historias*.

Pérez de Hita Ginés (1544?–1619?). Spanish historian and prose writer. His experience as a soldier in the campaigns against the rebellious Moriscos inspired his most famous work, the vividly written *Guerras civiles de Granada* (2 parts 1595, 1619) which was both a historical novel and an eye-witness account of the war.

Pérez Galdós Benito (1843–1920). Spanish novelist. He had great gifts as a story-teller and a creator of characters, a characteristic dryly humorous style and an eye for telling detail, and has been compared to Balzac and Dickens. He aimed at writing a kind of national prose epic beginning with *Trafalgar* (1873; 1884) and eventually completing some 46 vols in various series under the general title of *Episodios nacionales* (1873–1912). He also wrote several other novels dealing with social life, manners and foibles of Spanish society of his time, as well as treating certain moral and religious problems. The best known of his novels include *Doña Perfecta* (1876; *Lady Perfecta*, 1894), *Fortunata y Jacinta* (perhaps his masterpiece) (1887), *Angel Guerra* (1891), and *Nazarín* (1895), the last being recently adapted as a film by L. Buñuel.

pergola. An arbour or walk bordered by trellis-work covered with climbing plants.

Pergolesi Giovanni Battista (1710–36). Italian composer. His *opera buffa*, *La serva padrona* (1733) held the stage to the early 19th c.; its 2nd Paris performance (1752) sparked off the '*querelles des Bouffons*' between the supporters of French and Italian opera. P.'s other music includes 30 trio sonatas and a very beautiful *Stabat Mater* for soprano, alto, strings and organ. *Stravinsky used themes from P. in *Pulcinella*.

Peri Jacopo (1561–1633). Italian composer and singer working at the ducal court of Florence where he was one of the *camerata. His 'pastoral fable' *Dafne* (1597) with words by Rinuccini is generally considered the 1st opera but his *Euridice* (1600; publ. 1601) is the 1st opera whose music has survived; the words are again by Rinuccini and some of the music by G. *Caccini. P.'s other works include *Le varie musiche . . .* (1609) a coll. of settings of strophic poems which with *Caccini's *Le Nuove musiche* (1601) determined the development of solo song.

Pericles, Prince of Tyre (*c.* 1608; publ. 1609). Play by *Shakespeare. Its main source was Gower's *Confessio Amantis*.

Peries Lester. Sinhalese film director. Films for Ceylon are generally made in India and highly artificial; P.'s feature *Rekava* (1957), shot outdoors in Ceylon, broke completely away from these. In spite of total lack of resources, it is very successful, particularly in the musical numbers.

Perino del Vaga (1500–46). Also known as 'Pierino del Vaga' and 'Pietro Buonaccorsi'. An Italian painter of the Roman school. He studied under Raphael and was employed on the decoration of the Vatican where, after 1520, he took over much of Raphael's work. He also worked in Florence (1523–5) and Genoa, decorating the Palazzo Doria. He was, with Giulio Romano, the greatest successor to Raphael's Academy.

peristyle. Architectural term for a row of columns round a building or courtyard.

Perk Jacques (1859–81). Dutch poet, a friend of Kloos and forerunner of the literary revival of the 1880s. His best work is his love-poetry, notably the sonnet cycle *Mathilde*.

Perkins Anthony (1932–). U.S. film star, combining lean dark looks with a nervous, mannered intensity, e.g. in *Psycho*.

Pergolesi

Pergola

Peristyle of the Temple of Horus, Edfu

Permeke. *The Sow*. Also *expressionism

Perréal. *Portrait of Louis XII*

Permoser. *Apotheosis of Prince Eugene*

Perpendicular. W. window of St George's chapel, Windsor, with Tudor stained glass

Perrault. Louvre, E. façade

Perret. Apartment block, Rue Franklin

Permeke Constant (1886–1952). Belgian painter, one of the major 20th-c. realists. He studied at the academies of Bruges and Ghent, then moved to Ostend (1912–14). Wounded during World War I, he convalesced in England where he painted his 1st independent works; he returned to Belgium in 1918. Most of his paintings are of peasants, fishermen and rural landscape, with an expressionist involvement in human feelings and a monumental simplicity of form, e.g. *The Harvest* (1927; Tate). His sculpture–e.g. the early bronze *Marie Lou* (1936; Brussels Mus.)–is in the same vein.

Permoser Balthasar (1651–1732). German baroque sculptor. He created sculptural decoration for *Pöppelmann's Zwinger at Dresden.

Perosi Lorenzo (1872–1956). Italian composer and music director of the Sistine Chapel from 1898. P.'s church music, which includes 13 oratorios, attempts to unite polyphonic writing in the voice parts with Wagnerian orchestration.

Perotinus (French Pérotin). 13th-c. composer of the school of Notre-Dame. He wrote organa (*organum) in 2, 3 and 4 parts.

perpendicular or **rectilinear.** Architectural term for the last phase of English *Gothic, a reaction against the previous *decorated style; it probably began in London, but the earliest example is at Gloucester (*c.* 1330) and, with modifications, lasted into the 16th c. The main characteristics of p. are the use of straight tracery, depressed (4-centred) arches and fan-vaulting. The treatment of p. buildings is more standardized than that of decorated; their most impressive features are external, notably their towers.

Perrault Charles (1628–1703). French writer and critic, a member of the Académie. In his poem *Siècle de Louis le Grand* (1687), P. proclaimed himself on the side of the Moderns in the *Ancients and Moderns Controversy, and he later publ. other works attacking Boileau's views. P. is remembered above all for the prose fairy-story coll. *Histoires et contes du temps passé* (1697; 1729) publ. under the name of his young son.

Perrault Claude (1613–88). French architect, brother of Charles P. He was a doctor and an amateur in architecture, whose only notable work is the main (E.) front of the Louvre (1665); his design (coupled columns and central pediment) closely follows an earlier project by Le Vau.

Perréal Jean, or Jean de Paris (*c.* 1455–*c.* 1530). French artist, famous in his own time for portraits and designs for festivals and tombs. P. worked in Lyon from 1483, but visited Italy (*c.* 1500) and England (1514). Few works survive, but *Portrait of Louis XII* (R. Colls, Windsor) is almost certainly his. P. was formerly confused with the Master of Moulins.

Perret Auguste (1874–1954). French architect and builder, the 1st master of reinforced concrete as a building material; he studied at the

École des Beaux-Arts. His flats in the Rue Franklin (1903) had great influence because the framed structure was clearly expressed and was used to free the ground-floor plan; his later work, such as the rebuilding of Le Havre after World War II, shows less structural clarity and a dull neo-classic discipline.

Perrin Pierre: Robert *Cambert

Perronneau Jean-Baptiste (*c.* 1715–1783). French painter who studied engraving but later turned to pastel and became known for his portraits in that medium. He was very prolific, but the successful rivalry of Latour drove him from Paris.

Perrot Jules (1810–92). French dancer, pupil of Vestris and sometime partner of Taglioni; as ballet master at Her Majesty's, London (1842–8) and St Petersburg (1849–58), P. became a leading figure in the romantic movement with his choreography for many ballets, particularly his revised production of *Giselle* (1849), which is the version used by most ballet cos today.

Perry Frank (1930–). U.S. film director. P. was a theatre producer with the Actors' Studio who had not worked in the cinema before he directed *David and Lisa* (1962), written by his wife, Eleanor, a playwright. The unexpected success of this romantic story of 2 mentally-subnormal adolescents allowed him to direct *Ladybug, Ladybug* (1963), about schoolchildren in a nuclear alert.

Perse Saint-John (1887–). French poet who, under his real name of Alexis Léger, worked in the French diplomatic service until 1940. He was born in Guadeloupe and has long been domiciled in America. These factors may account for the global nature of his poetry with its vast exotic landscapes and seascapes, and its epic rhythms. His *Anabase* (1924) found an enthusiastic reader in T. S. Eliot, who trs. it into English (1930). His later verse, coll. in *Oeuvre poétique* (1953), is in the same strain of grandiose rhetoric. P. was awarded the Nobel prize in 1960.

Personae (1909). Coll. of poems by Ezra Pound.

perspective. In art a system for representing the 3-dimensional space of actuality on the 2-dimensional space of the picture plane. The basic observations behind systems of perspective are that objects in the distance appear smaller than objects close to the spectator and that parallel lines appear to meet in the far distance. Working from such premises and the earlier system of *costruzione legittima, 15th-c. Florentine artists, Brunelleschi, Uccello, Piero della Francesca and above all L. B. Alberti, evolved the principles of linear p., dependent upon, among other things, the correct use of vanishing points (i.e. the points where parallel lines appear to converge). AERIAL PERSPECTIVE achieves effects of distance by exploiting the changes in colour and tonal values as objects recede from the observer; the apparent blue of distant mountains is an obvious effect which can be used in aerial p.

perspective tables. Italian tables inlaid with coloured marbles and semi-precious stones where the lines of the design, receding in a mathematically calculated perspective, give an illusion of depth. They are associated particularly with Florence and were produced in large quantities in the 16th and 17th c.

Persuasion (1818). Novel by Jane *Austen.

Perugino (Pietro Vannucci) (*c.* 1445–1523). Italian painter of the Umbrian school; his work was influenced by his master Verrocchio, Signorelli and the Flemish painters among others. He used the novel technique of oil painting with great mastery and painted the luminous quality of the Umbrian landscape: green-brown foreground and middle distance, bluish far distance are typical of his colour scheme; his figures are gracefully elongated, with clearly articulated joints, sculpturesque draperies and dreamy expressions. P. was called to Rome by Pope Sixtus IV in 1481 to decorate the Sistine Chapel with a fresco series. Of these *Christ giving the Keys to St Peter* is the most important. A severely symmetrical composition, it shows P.'s mastery of perspective and disposition of figures in a monumental geometry. The fresco *The Crucifixion* painted in Siena in 1496 is a masterpiece. The frescoes painted in the Cambio, Perugia (1498–1500) show his style in decline. Lack of originality results in stereotypes and genuine feeling is replaced by sentiment. These frescoes had a profound influence on the development of Italian art, as they shaped the youthful work of P.'s pupil and assistant Raphael.

Peruzzi Baldassare (1481–1536). Italian architect and painter. He was born near Siena but came to Rome in 1503 and designed the Farnesina – a simple façade with pilasters, the attic-storey made into a sculptured frieze with oval windows; inside P. painted *trompe l'œil* frescoes (the ground-floor was decorated by Raphael). He was in charge of St Peter's from 1520 onwards, but his contribution has been entirely obliterated. He kept Bramante's centralized plan. In 1535 he designed the Palazzo Massimi, Rome, important as marking the development of high Renaissance into mannerism; significant features are the curved façade, columns on the ground-floor, rusticated stonework above (instead of vice versa) and the complicated shape of the window-frames of the 1st floor.

Pervigilium Veneris. Anon. Latin poem about love, probably A.D. 2nd c.

Pesellino Francesco (1422–57). Florentine painter who studied under his father Stefano di Francesco and inherited his studio workshop. His style combined elements from Fra Filippo Lippi, Masaccio and Fra Angelico. He appears to have worked with Lippi, who completed the altarpiece *The Holy Trinity* (N.G., London) after P.'s death. P. worked with Ucello on battle scenes for the Medici Palace, Florence and also painted panels for *cassone* ('bridal chests').

Peshkov Alexey Maximovich: Maxim *Gorky

Pesne Antoine (1683–1757). French painter of portraits and historical subjects at the court

Jules Perrot in *La Filleule des Fées*

Perronneau. *A Girl with a Kitten*

Perugino. *Christ giving the Keys to St Peter* (detail)

Pesellino. *The Holy Trinity*

Peruzzi. The Palazzo Massimi

Marius Petipa

Lucien Petipa and Carlotta Grisi in *Giselle*

Marie Petipa in *Le Marché des Innocents* (1861)

Petrarch: 14th-c. miniature

Peterborough cathedral

of Prussia, contributing to the French influences at the court of Frederick II. He also painted portraits at many other francophile German courts.

Pessoa Fernando (1888–1935). Portuguese poet. He spent his youth in South Africa learning English, in which he wrote a number of poems. His Portuguese works are of great subtlety and strongly introspective. Yet P.'s was an objective self-analysis, and this detachment is exteriorized by his use of pseuds; these were not merely *noms de plume* but each of the 3, 'Alberto Casiro', 'Ricardo Reis' and 'Alvaro de Campos', were to project specific aspects of his complex personality. Most of P.'s poems were publ. (1945–51) after his death.

Peterborough cathedral England. One of the most notable examples of Norman architecture, begun in 1118. The chancel, crossing, transepts and nave were finished by 1190. It is a very long church with arcade, gallery, clerestory and wooden roof. The W. front (1190–1210) is Early English and of unique design, having 3 huge niches or porches with no relation to the structure behind.

Peter Grimes. Opera by *Britten with libretto by M. Slater; 1st performance at London in 1945. The story is taken from Crabbe's poem *The Borough*.

Peter Pan or the Boy who wouldn't grow up (1904). Play for children by J. M. *Barrie.

Petipa Lucien (1815–98). French dancer and brother of Marius Petipa. Although a fine soloist he also excelled at partnering at a time when it was not unusual for women to dance en travesti. He created Albrecht in *Giselle* (1841) and often danced with Grisi and Elssler before becoming ballet master at the Paris Opéra (1860–8).

Petipa Marie M. (1857–1930). Russian dancer of the Imperial School, St Petersburg and daughter of Marius and Marie S. P. A lyrical dancer, she created the role of the Lilac Fairy in her father's ballet *The Sleeping Beauty* (1890).

Petipa Marie S. (1836–82). Russian dancer of the Imperial School, St Petersburg, the wife of Marius P. and the mother of Marie M. P. She acquired a great personal following throughout Europe, particularly for her character dancing; her husband created several dances for her, e.g. *The Little Moujik*.

Petipa Marius (1819–1910). French choreographer and dancer and brother of Lucien P. He achieved great popularity in Europe and America before going to the Maryinsky Theatre, St Petersburg as premier danseur (1847). In 1862 he took over as ballet master and became the most prolific choreographer of all time, producing, with his assistant *Ivanov, over 50 new ballets apart from divertissements for operas, until his retirement in 1903. His finest works were *The Sleeping Beauty* (1890) and *Swan Lake* (1895). During his 'reign' Russia saw the invasion of visiting Italian ballerinas and P. incorporated their pyrotechnics into his choreography.

Petit Roland (1924–). French dancer, choreographer and husband of Renée Jeanmaire. P. is a major personality in modern French ballet. He helped to found Les *Ballets des Champs-Elysées and created modern ballets often using classical technique but always a highly dramatic theme. His works include *Le Jeune Homme et La Mort* (1947), *Les Demoiselles de la Nuit* (1948), and more recent works for film and television.

petit point. A term used to describe certain stitches used in the embroidery of canvas, or fabric or even weave, taken over a single thread of the material. 'Gros point' describes those stitches which are worked over 2 or more adjacent threads, e.g. *Florentine stitch.

Petofi Sándor (1823–49). Hungarian poet and patriot; he died as a soldier in the Revolutionary army. His meteoric genius created a new world of poetry; abandoning the restrained classicism of his predecessors, he achieved a synthesis with the language of folk-poetry and in his epic poem *János vitéz* (1844) penetrated the 'collective unconscious' of the Hungarian peasants. He had many imitators in Hungary and English trs of his work appeared in 1866, 1881 and 1948.

Petrarch (Italian Petrarca) Francesco (1304–74). Italian poet and humanist. He was born at Arezzo where his father, a notary, had taken refuge after having been banished from Florence. Later the family went to live at Avignon, where on Easter Friday 1327, in the church of St Claire, P. first saw Laura, the woman who

Roland Petit and Margot Fonteyn in *Les Demoiselles de la Nuit*. Also *Ballet des Champs-Élysées

inspired his most sensitive poems and whom he loved from afar until her death. He took minor orders (1330) and entered the service of Cardinal Colonna, was crowned (1341) on the Capitol in Rome with a laurel wreath as Italy's greatest living poet, and lived in Italy, the much-sought guest of princely patrons. He died at Arquà, nursed by his natural daughter Francesca.

The most beautiful of P.'s poems are written in Italian in the form of canzoni, sonnets, ballades and madrigals. The recurrent theme is the poet's love for Laura and his feelings. In his striving to articulate and present his own personality P. is the first to exhibit a sensibility typical of European thought since his time. Several canzoni are of political or religious inspiration, some are concerned with moral problems. P. himself coll. his Italian poems (nearly 400 of them) in a work commonly called *Canzoniere*.

But most of his writing is in Latin, by him considered the true literary language of Italy. It includes the verses *Epistolae metricae*, a vast number of letters to friends, kings, popes, cardinals and relatives on personal or political matters; *De viris illustribus*, a series of biographies of great men, from Romulus and ending with Julius Caesar, and *Secretum*, a dialogue between St Augustine and P. which is a violent argument on religious ideals and spiritual happiness.

Petrassi Goffredo (1904–). Italian composer and teacher–since 1939 at the St Cecilia Conservatory, Rome. Up to the 1940s his work was neo-classical: the *Partita* (1932) for orchestra was influenced by Casella and Hindemith, as well as by early Italian composers, the large choral work *Psalm IX* (1936) reminiscent of Palestrina. *Coro di Morti* (1940–1) begins a development towards atonality and dodecaphony confirmed in the cantata *Noche oscura* (1951). He has also written 2 operas and 2 ballets including *Portrait of Don Quixote*, etc.

Petri Elio (1929–). Italian film director. P. worked as a critic and a script writer as well as making shorts for more than 10 years before attempting his 1st feature, *L'Assassino* (1961) about a man accused of murder. His 2nd and more successful film, *I Giorni Contati* (1962) was about an old man about to die.

Petri Olaus (*c.* 1493–1552). Swedish churchman and statesman. He was an important figure in the Reformation and in Swedish literature, trs. the New Testament and wrote a history of Sweden.

Petronius (d. A.D. 66). Roman dandy, Nero's 'arbiter of elegance' in Tacitus' phrase, who was driven to suicide by false charges of treason. He was probably the P. who wrote the picaresque novel the *Satyricon*, of which only a fragmentary part survives. It satirizes contemporary behaviour, parodies fashionable forms and styles in literature (both prose and verse) and is our richest source of vulgar Latin of the imperial period. It has much in common with Joyce's *Ulysses*, with which it may share a structural foundation in the *Odyssey*; what survives details the peregrinations and misfortunes, literary, gustatory and obscene, of a homosexual scholar-tramp doomed to impotence by the wrath of Priapus.

Petrov-Vodkin Kuzma (1878–1930). Russian painter and an influential teacher. After studying in Moscow under Levitan and Serov he went to Africa, whose art and peculiar light and colour influenced his later work, as did the work of Matisse. He was a member of the Blue Rose group but later adopted a neo-classical style; *Playing Boys* of 1911 is a typical work.

Petrov-Vodkin. *Playing Boys*

Petrucci Ottaviano dei (1466–1539). Italian music publ. working at Venice (1490–1511) and Fossombrone (1511–23). P. invented the 1st method of printing music with movable type and his productions were the earliest and are still the most beautiful. Among his important publs. (1501 onwards) are masses by Josquin, Pierre de la Rue and A. Agricola.

Petrushka. 4-scene ballet with choreography by Fokine, music by Stravinsky and décor by Benois; 1st performance 1911.

Pevsner Antoine (Noton or Anton) (1886–1962). Russian painter and sculptor. In 1911 he went to study in Paris, drawn by the new French painting shown in the colls of Morosov and Shchukin and the Golden Fleece exhibitions in Moscow. There he made friends with Modigliani and Archipenko. In 1913 P. began to paint in cubist style; Byzantine art was also fundamental to the development of his later construction-sculpture. On his return to Russia in 1917, P. was appointed professor in Moscow *Vkhutemas. With his brother

Pevsner. *Abstract Forms* (1913)

Pevsner. *Portrait of Marcel Duchamp* (1926)

Phidias. *Dionysus*; from the pediment of the Parthenon

Naum *Gabo he took a stand against functionalist constructivism in 1920, a year later leaving Russia for Berlin where he made his 1st construction, not yet abstract, in celluloid. With Gabo he designed *La Chatte* in 1927 for Diaghilev. P. settled in Paris, working on progressively more abstract sculpture in bronze and other metals.

pewter. An alloy consisting of tin and lead. In the early middle ages it was found in the richest houses only, but it became eventually a cheap substitute for silver and closely followed the forms of silverware. The softness of the metal makes it easily workable and its dull surface is appreciated by connoisseurs. The proportion of lead varies, but is usually about 16 per cent.; Roman pewter had as much as 25 per cent.

Pfitzner Hans (1869–1949). German composer and teacher. His music is a highly personal extension of the classical-romantic tradition and P. vigorously opposed modern developments in music in articles and books. He wrote operas, among them his masterpiece *Palestrina* (1917), choral works, 3 symphonies and chamber music.

Phaedo. Dialogue by *Plato.

Phaedrus. Roman fabulist of the early 1st c. A.D. His verse fables often draw on Aesop and were widely read in medieval Europe in a prose version; P.'s name was forgotten, but in the 16th c. a restored ed. was publ. under his name. He was one of La Fontaine's models.

The Pharos: coin of Antoninus Pius

Pharos. Famous lighthouse (a tower with a fire burning constantly) on a peninsula at Alexandria; it was completed *c.* 280 B.C. and reckoned one of the 7 wonders of the ancient world. It was destroyed by an earthquake in the 14th c. and its dimensions are not known.

Pharsalia. Title usually given to *Lucan's *Bellum Civile.*

Samuel Phelps

Phelps Samuel (1804–78). English actor-manager. P. established Sadler's Wells Theatre as a centre for fine Shakespearean productions at a time when dramatic standards were very low, reviving *Antony and Cleopatra* for the 1st time in 100 years. Later he appeared in dramatizations of Walter Scott's novels in the provinces.

Phidias (*c.* 500–*c.* 432 B.C.). Greek sculptor and painter, pupil of the sculptors Hegias and Ageladas of Argos (who influenced him in the direction of Doric realism). He is reputed to have painted Pericles as Jupiter but his most important work was in sculpture for the Acropolis, including a statue of Athena and the Athena Chryselephantine for the interior of the Parthenon, and much of the subsidiary sculpture. P. also carved the statue of Zeus at Olympus, whither he may have moved after being accused in Athens of embezzling the precious metals he used for his major works.

Philadelphia Story, The (1940). Film directed by G. *Cukor.

Philaster, or Love lies a-bleeding (1611). Play by *Beaumont and *Fletcher.

Philidor. A 17th–18th-c. French family of musicians originally called 'Danican'. The most important member was FRANÇOIS-ANDRÉ DANICAN P. (1726–95), also the greatest chess player of his time. His many very successful comic operas included *Tom Jones* (1765), from Fielding's novel.

Philipe Gérard (1922–59). French film and stage actor whose good looks and magnetic warmth were coupled with a graceful talent. He was a leading member of the Théâtre National Populaire. Such films as *L'Idiot* (1946), *La Ronde* (1950) and *Les Grandes Manœuvres* (1955) are typical, but he could be swashbuckling–in *Fanfan la Tulipe* (1951) –or suggest decadence, if not evil, as in R. Vadim's *Les Liaisons Dangereuses* (1959).

Philipon Charles (1800–62). French journalist and caricaturist who founded and ed. the satirical journals *La Caricature* (1830) and *Le Charivari* (1832), for which Daumier worked.

Philippe Charles-Louis (1874–1909). French novelist. P.'s books, mainly studies of poverty, include *Marie Donadieu* (1904; 1949).

Philippics. Speeches by *Demosthenes against Philip II of Macedon, also applied by Cicero to his speeches and writings against Mark Antony.

Philips Ambrose (1675–1749). English pastoral poet remembered for a literary quarrel with Pope.

Philips John (1676–1709). English poet, author of a burlesque poem in Miltonic verse, *The Splendid Shilling* (1701), and the didactic *Cyder* (1708).

Philips Katherine (1631–64). English poet called 'the matchless Orinda'. Her early verses appeared with Henry Vaughan's *Poems* (1651), and were much admired by other poets.

Philips Peter (1560/1–1628). English composer who, because of his Catholicism, emigrated to the Continent. He worked in Rome (1585–90), toured France, Spain and the Netherlands, where he met J. P. Sweelinck, and settled in Brussels in 1597. Of his virginals compositions, e.g. 19 pieces in the *Fitzwilliam Virginal Book*, the pavans and galliards are English in manner while other pieces show the influence of Sweelinck and C. Merulo; his madrigals are stylistically similar to those of L. Marenzio and F. Anerio.

Phillips David Graham (1867–1911). U.S. novelist. P.'s journalistic problem stories include *Susan Lenox: Her Fall and Rise* (1917), about the career of a prostitute.

Phillips Edward (1630–*c.* 96). English writer, author of a philological dictionary, the *New World of English Words* (1658). P. was a nephew of Milton.

Phillips John (1631–1706). English writer, nephew of Milton and brother of Edward P. He wrote the anti-Puritan *Satyr against Hypocrites* (1655).

Phillips Peter (1934–). English painter; studied at the R.C.A. (1959–61). He tries to achieve the synthesis of 'art' and environment by painting such subjects as American cars, pin-up girls and pop stars.

Philoctetes (409 B.C.). Play by *Sophocles.

philosophes. Term loosely used to describe those 18th-c. French writers, philosophers and scientists who were rational and sceptical in outlook and critical of established institutions. They included Montesquieu, Voltaire, Diderot, d'Alembert, Rousseau, Turgot, Buffon, d'Holbach and Helvétius. Many of them contributed to the **Encyclopédie*.

Philoxenos (*fl.* early 4th c. B.C.). Greek painter known for his painting of the battle of Issus, of which the *Alexander mosaic may be a copy.

Phoenix and the Turtle, The. Title generally given to *Let the bird of loudest lay*, a poem attributed to *Shakespeare which appears in the coll. *Loves Martyr: Or, Rosalins Complaint* (1601).

phrase. In music the term is used of fragments of the melodic line which give the feeling of being in some way a unit or a distinct section. An important part of a performer's art consists in his ability to make his PHRASING clearly articulated yet fluent and true to the music.

Piaf Edith (1915–63). French singer, actress and cabaret artist. She combined the earthy enthusiasm of the Parisian street singer with complete professionalism and enjoyed a worldwide reputation.

piano. The Italian word 'soft' used in music in the abbreviation '*p*' to indicate quiet passages; *pianissimo* abbreviated '*pp*' means 'very soft' and *pianississimo* or '*ppp*' means 'as softly as possible'.

piano. A keyboard musical instrument made with strings stretching either horizontally, a 'grand' p., or vertically, an 'upright' p. Pressure on the finger-key causes a felt hammer to strike the string, an escapement allowing it to fall back again; the string continues to vibrate until the key is released when a felt 'damper' moves against the string, deadening it. The sustaining pedal enables the player to hold back the dampers at will; the soft pedal makes the hammer strike less hard or on fewer strings. Volume modulation from soft to loud (hence the Italian *piano forte*, 'soft-loud') varies with the power with which the key is struck; this facility for modulation was not new (*clavichord) but the p.'s volume range was greater. The piano evolved *c.* 1700, improvements (e.g. to the escapement) made it the major keyboard instrument in the 19th c. Developments such as the iron frame, allowing greater string tensions, increased the instrument's power and the modern grand p. differs from that of Liszt as much as his p. differed from Mozart's.

pianola. A piano with a mechanical device which reproduces a performance. A pneumatic

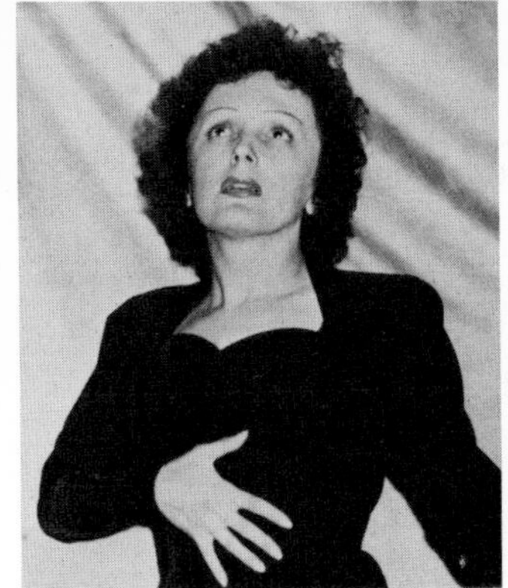

Edith Piaf

Square piano (Broadwood and Sons)

Forte piano

Pianoforte

system for operating the piano mechanism is controlled by a punched roll of paper which represents the 'recorded' performance by a virtuoso. The p. player can control dynamics and tempi to a certain extent. Some composers, including Stravinsky, Malipiero and Hindemith, have written direct for such instruments.

Piazzetta. *Beach Idyll*

Pianta Francesco. 17th-c. Italian sculptor in wood whose most notable work was in carving the stalls in the Scuola di San Rocco in Venice.

Piatigorsky Gregor (1903–). Russian-born U.S. cellist; besides his career as a virtuoso performer he has held various teaching posts.

Piatti Alfredo (1822–1901). Italian cellist and composer for his instrument. His virtuosity and musicianship won him a European reputation but he was particularly associated with England, appearing there regularly from 1859.

Piaubert Jean (1900–). French painter. His earlier works were mainly landscapes; he then joined the Abstraction-Création group and exhibited at the Salon des Réalité Nouvelles. Thereafter he moved into the field of severely organized and clearly defined non-figurative painting.

Piazzetta Giovanni Battista (1682–1754). Venetian painter, the pupil of Antonio Molinari; he came under the influence of Guercino when working in Bologna. P. returned to Venice as director of the Venetian Academy in 1750. His work formed a link between that of Caliari and Tiepolo and can be seen in the churches of SS Giovanni e Paolo and at the Santo in Padua.

Pibrac Guy du Faur de (1529–84). French poet. His *Cinquante Quatrains* (1574, later enlarged; the *Quatrains of Guy de Faur, Lord of Pibrac*, 1605), 4-line poems embodying a maxim of wisdom or behaviour, enjoyed long popularity.

Picabia. *Edtaonisl* (1913)

Picabia Francis (1878–1953). Paris-born painter. After an early post-impressionist phase, he became involved successively with cubism, orphism and futurism, but is most significant as a pioneer of dada in Paris. Working with Marcel Duchamp, whom he met in 1910, he was also responsible for the passage of dada to New York, where he ed. the dada magazines *291* and *391*. He joined the Zürich dadaists in 1918 and from 1920, in contact with André Breton, was active as a surrealist. His best early works are in the cubist idiom, e.g. *Undine* (1913; M.M.A., Paris). Many of his dada collages and constructions parody machinery, e.g. *Parade Amoureuse* (1917; Janis Gal., New York).

picaresque novel (from Spanish *pícaro*, 'ragamuffin'). The most typical and frequent form of the Spanish realistic novel of the 16th and 17th cs, it deals with low life and the adventures of a wandering and roguish hero who serves under various masters and whose life is a long series of escapades and cunning deceits. The tone is usually free from moralizing, rather cynical, satirical, hard, observant and psychologically acute; the structure is extremely loose, with little or no logical connection between the various incidents. The earliest example of the genre was the anon. *La vida de Lazarillo de Tormes* (1554; *The Pleasant Historie of Lazarillo. . .* , 1586) another famous one being Alemán's *Guzmán de Alfarache* (1599, 1604); the term is now loosely used of episodic tales of strange escapades.

Picasso Pablo (1881–). Spanish painter, born in Malaga. He studied principally in Barcelona where he lived from 1895 to 1904. He showed prodigious artistic ability from his youth; his earliest works like *Portrait of Coquiot* (1901; M.M.A., Paris) reflect the influences of art nouveau and post-impressionist painting which he knew through periodicals in Barcelona and from his visits to Paris of 1900, 1901 (when he had a 1-man exhibition there) and 1902–3. His paintings of 1901–4 (his 'blue period') are mainly of poor and suffering people, e.g. the *Old Guitarist* (1903; A. Inst., Chicago). The restricted colour and simplified forms combine to create an intense melancholy and pathos.

Settling in Paris–his home until 1945–in 1904, he began to meet artists and writers including Apollinaire, Jacob, Jarry and Van Dongen and his early patrons, the Steins, Uhde and Shchukin. The pessimism of his earlier work gave way to the so-called 'rose period', e.g. *Boy with Horse* (1905; Tate), lighter in mood and palette. All of his early work exemplifies his extraordinary power to assimilate very varied influences and his uninhibited will to experiment in order to arrive at a more satisfactory mode of expression. Although untouched by fauvism, the experimental nature of his work intensified around 1906/7. Inspired on the one hand by primitive forms (ancient Iberian sculpture at first and later African masks and carvings) and on the other by Cézanne's empirical reorganization of his motifs, P. achieved a major revolution. The epoch-making *Les Demoiselles d'Avignon* (1907; M.M.A., New York) was a conscious attempt to complete his researches and although these were obviously still evolving during its execution, this painting seen in retrospect was the vital step in freeing the artist from his traditional obligation to natural appearances. The Negro art which P. first saw *c.* 1906/7 was not inhibited by a representational tradition and its strange forms (both distorted and invented) were a precedent of paramount importance. Cubism was evolved by Picasso and Braque through tempering this freedom with Cézanne's sense of structural discipline.

In early ('analytical') cubist paintings like the *Portrait of Vollard* (1909–10; Pushkin Mus., Moscow) the motif is still clearly recognizable although freely dissected and reconstructed in terms of a complex arrangement of overlapping translucent planes in which the figure and its shallow spatial setting are wholly integrated. Later the rearrangement itself becomes more obviously self-sufficient. In 'synthetic' cubism –e.g. *The Violin* (1913; Philadelphia Mus.)– the use of real objects (newspaper, etc.) on the picture surface firstly placed an outspoken emphasis on that surface and secondly declared in a revolutionary manner that painting creates its own reality rather than imitates the reality of nature. The impact of cubism on the history of European painting and sculpture, both figurative and abstract, has been indefinably extensive and various.

P.'s works since 1914, when his partnership with Braque was broken by the outbreak of war, can all be seen to derive in some way from cubism. Until 1921 he continued to work with a synthetic cubist idiom culminating in the monumental *Three Musicians* (1921; M.M.A., New York). Between 1917 and 1924 he worked on designs for several of Diaghilev's ballets (e.g. drop-curtain for *Parade*, 1917; M.M.A., Paris) and visited Rome, Naples, Florence and Barcelona with the company. His visits to Italy possibly encouraged the strong classical flavour of his figure compositions of 1919 to 1925. The static and monumental figures become grotesque and violently active and lead on to the disturbing fantasy of the period *c.* 1925–40. This includes the frenzied *Three Dancers* (1925; now in the Tate), the freely inventive anatomies of the 1930s with their ambiguous organic forms and *Guernica* (1937; M.M.A., New York on loan) and reveals the latent expressive force of P.'s art, suppressed during cubism.

He exhibited in the 1st surrealist exhibition (Paris, 1925) and contributed etchings and writings to official surrealist literature. He did not sign their manifesto, but he was, like them, becoming increasingly personally involved with the current political unrest in Europe. He associated himself with the Spanish Republican cause with works like the *Dream and Lie of Franco* (etchings 1937; M.M.A., New York) and *Guernica. Guernica*, a protest against the bombing of a Basque town by pro-Franco German bombers, combines a violent surrealist distortion with restrained subtlety of colour in a complex symbolic allegory. It was shown at the International Exhibition at Paris in 1937.

P.'s most original sculpture includes cubist bronzes (*c.* 1909), collage constructions (1912–16), the wrought-iron constructions made with González (1931–4), and several witty 'ready-mades', e.g. *Bull* (1943).

Leaving Paris in 1946, he has since lived in Antibes, Vallauris (1948–58), and Vauvenargues. His post-war work includes family portraits and several variations on works by other artists (Poussin, Delacroix, Velazquez) as well as a prodigious volume of graphic work and ceramics. Still prolifically productive, he remains one of the most versatile and influential artists of the c. After cubism, his major contribution to modern art has been the empirical freedom which characterizes every aspect of his work.

Piccinni Niccolò (1728–1800). Italian opera composer. After successes in Rome, such as *Alessandro nell' Indie* and the *opera buffa La cecchina. . .* , based on S. Richardson's novel *Pamela*, he settled (1776) in Paris. There he was unwillingly made the figurehead of the anti-Gluck party, his *Iphigénie en Tauride* (1781) being purposely commissioned to compete with Gluck's. P.'s best French opera was *Didon* (1783).

Piccolomini Aeneas Silvius (1405–64). Italian humanist writer, later Pope Pius II. His early literary production included some famous Latin love-lyrics, a comedy (*Chrysis*) and a charming romantic novel, *Euryalus and Lucrezia.* Later he wrote brilliant *Commentaries* on the history and personalities of his time.

Picasso. *Old Guitarist*

Picasso. *Portrait of Vollard*

Picasso. Two panels from *Dream and Lie of Franco*

Picasso. *Baboon and Young* (1951)

Picasso. *Three Musicians.* Also *Apollinaire, *cubism, *Falla, *engraving, **Guernica*, **profil perdu*, *Satie, *Stein, *Stravinsky, **Three-Cornered Hat*, *Vollard, and colour plate 73

Mary Pickford in *Pollyanna*

Pico della Mirandola

Pickford Mary (1893–). Film actress, 'America's Sweetheart'. Acting an orphaned golden-haired waif, P. was at her peak between 1915 and 1920. Her films include *Heart of the Hills* (1919) and *Pollyanna* (1920); in 1929 she made *The Taming of the Shrew*, a talkie, with her husband, Douglas Fairbanks. In 1933 she retired and became an executive.

Pickwick Papers, The (*The Posthumous Papers of the Pickwick Club*) (1836–7). Comic novel by *Dickens.

Pico della Mirandola Giovanni, Count (1463–94). Italian humanist. In his 900 theses (1486) P. attempted to synthesize religion and philosophy; he was deeply influenced by Cabalism and Hermetic studies (*Hermes Trismegistos) and was for a time condemned by the Pope. His oration *On the Dignity of Man* (in fact publ. 1487) was influential on subsequent Renaissance thought.

Picture of Dorian Gray, The (1891). Novel by Oscar *Wilde.

'picturesque, the'. Term used in late 18th-c. England to describe the qualities of ruggedness and irregularity–particularly of rocks, ruins, etc.–felt to enhance the aesthetic appeal of landscapes, e.g. those of Salvator Rosa and Claude Lorrain. 'The p.' was thus an element in the growth of romanticism; theorists and controversialists about its nature include Richard Payne *Knight, Sir Uvedale *Price and Edmund Burke.

Pidgeon Walter (1897–). U.S. actor who was a musical star before entering films in 1925. Always handsome, he has matured from romantic leads in films like *Saratoga* (1937) to the *bon viveur* of *The Last Time I saw Paris* (1954) and the elder statesman of *Advise and Consent* (1962).

piecrust. A decorative edging, scalloped and similar to the outer edge of a piecrust. Frequently found on 18th-c. tea-tables and china tables.

Pied Piper of Hamelin, A Child's Story, The (1845). Poem by *Browning, based on an old German legend.

pier. In architecture, the free-standing vertical support of an arch, etc.; it is usually thicker but is functionally the same as a column.

Pierce Pennilesse, His Supplication to the Divill (1592). Prose satire by T. *Nashe.

Piero della Francesca (1410/20–92). Italian painter and mathematician. For relatively short periods he worked in Florence, Urbino, Ferrara and Rome but most of his life he lived in Arezzo and Borgo San Sepolcro, his birthplace, where he was a town councillor in 1442. He led an uneventful provincial life and died relatively unknown.

A number of influences are fused in his work. Domenico Veneziano was his master and the intellectual ferment of Masaccio, Alberti, Uccello and the mathematicians of his time helped to form his style, which intimately joined science and art. His love and mastery of mathematics is fully expressed in his paintings, constructed within a rigid framework of geometry

Piero della Francesca. *Madonna and Child with Angels*

Piero della Francesca. *Madonna of Mercy*

Piero della Francesca. *Flagellation*. See also colour plate 42

but controlled by a sensibility and genius for colour, pattern, scale and proportion. P. was overshadowed by his more fashionable contemporaries but he was hailed by the cubists and is also seen as a central figure of the Renaissance his influence extending through his pupils Perugino and Signorelli to the main Italian schools.

The *Madonna of Mercy*, a polyptych, is P.'s 1st known commissioned work. The 2 centre pieces only, the *Madonna* and the *Crucifixion*, are by P., painted against a gold background as stipulated in the contract; his awareness of abstract, solid and clearly defined forms is in conflict with the decorative treatment required of him. This conflict he was able to resolve with mastery. Masaccio's influence is clearly seen in the *Crucifixion*, but the drama is heightened by a lower viewpoint and more agitated stark silhouettes. The *Baptism of Christ* (N.G., London) although an early work is already typical of his vision. The action takes place against a hilly landscape and blue sky, patterned by horizontal clouds and establishing a strong horizontal–vertical rhythm with the figures and tree of the foreground. P.'s powers of observation are clearly shown in one of the background figures. The composition is filled with a light and brightness of unearthly quality.

His monumental commission for San Francesco in Rimini brought him into contact with the architect and theoretician Alberti in 1451. P.'s monumental style is here at its purest, intimately connected with the architecture it serves. The figures are placed in a clearly defined space which is broken by columns serving to offset or obscure the characters of the action. The sense of order pervades all.

In the *Flagellation* at Urbino, believed to have been painted somewhat later than the *Baptism*, the figures, set like chessmen on a floor of chequered tiles, are contained by an architectural framework, constructed along the principles of Renaissance architectural theory, which produces a pattern of cubes within the picture space.

The frescoes the *Story of the True Cross*, painted in the choir of San Francesco, Arezzo between 1452 and 1466, were based on a story popular at that time. The subject is represented with more emphasis on pictorial than literary values; chronological sequence is abandoned in the interest of compositional symmetry. Thus the 2 battle pieces are placed along the lowest sections of 2 opposite walls, and above them the courtly scenes are contrasted. Each scene has been conceived with complete clarity and mastery of form and is related to the unified concept of the wall and entire spatial distribution of the choir. The effect of light and colour is at its most dramatic in *The Dream of Constantine*.

The *Resurrection*, a further illustration of P.'s great spirituality, poetry and clarity, may have been painted at the end of this period.

The double portraits of Battista Sforza and his wife are assumed to date after 1472. Both are placed in strict profile against an ideal landscape suggesting infinity.

The unfinished *Nativity* (N.G., London) and the *Madonna and Child with Angels* (Brera, Milan) are late works. The former shows some Flemish influence in conception and treatment, the latter that growing passion for mathematics which induced him to devote the remainder of his life to the study of mathematics and the publ. of works on harmony and perspective.

Piero di Cosimo (*c.* 1462–*c.* 1521). Italian painter. Although trained in the Florentine tradition by a long apprenticeship to Cosimo Rosselli, which probably included working with Rosselli in Florence and Rome (Sistine Chapel), and also influenced by painters such as Signorelli and Leonardo da Vinci, nevertheless P. showed a strikingly individual imagination. He lived for many years as a recluse with a reputation as an eccentric, painting scenes from allegories and classical myths difficult to decipher. Typical of his work is the mythological subject, e.g. the *Death of Procris*, a hauntingly evocative work; serene in comparison with the strange and violent *Fight Between the Lapiths and the Centaurs* (both N.G., London). P.'s imagination found an outlet in designs for festivals, masques and processions, including the celebrated *Triumph of Death* of 1511.

Pierre, or The Ambiguities (1852). Novel by Herman *Melville.

Pierrot. A stage and mime character whose origins lie in the **commedia dell'arte*; he started life as a simple sturdy servant but through a series of transformations, most importantly that by J.-G. *Deburau, became a lovelorn whimsical figure.

Piers Plowman, The Vision of William concerning (14th c.). Poem by *Langland.

pietà (Italian 'pity'). Painting or sculpture of the Virgin nursing the dead Christ. The idea, developed in Germany in the 14th c., is similar to that of the imago pietatis but lays greater emphasis on the human and less on the symbolical aspects of Christ's suffering. One of the most famous of all p.s is that from Avignon (*c.* 1460) now in the Louvre.

Pietà of Villeneuve, The or **The Avignon Pietà** (Louvre). Painted *c.* 1460, by an anonymous artist. The austere colouring, abstract gold background and almost carved figures are used to convey a feeling of religious devotion of the highest intensity. This masterpiece has been claimed for many schools, including the Catalan and Portuguese, but it seems almost certain that the painter was French.

pietre dure. Semi-precious stones such as onyx, malachite and lapis lazuli used in room or church decoration or on table-tops; produced in Florence (and other parts of Italy) during the 16th–18th cs. The stones are cut to fit into a geometric or floral pattern or pictorial design, and then polished.

Pietro (Berettini) **da Cortona** (1596–1669). Italian painter and architect active in Rome from 1613, a devoted follower of Raphael and of classical antiquity. P. was influenced by Bernini and collaborated with him on a number of buildings. His patrons were the Pope, and the Pope's family, the Barberini. He thus worked in St Peter's and painted the huge ceiling of the Great Salon of the Barberini Palace, Rome (1633–9). This ceiling was an allegorical fresco painting *Divine Providence*

Early 14th-c. German pietà (wood)

Pietre dure (lapis lazuli and cornelian). 17th-c. Florentine table

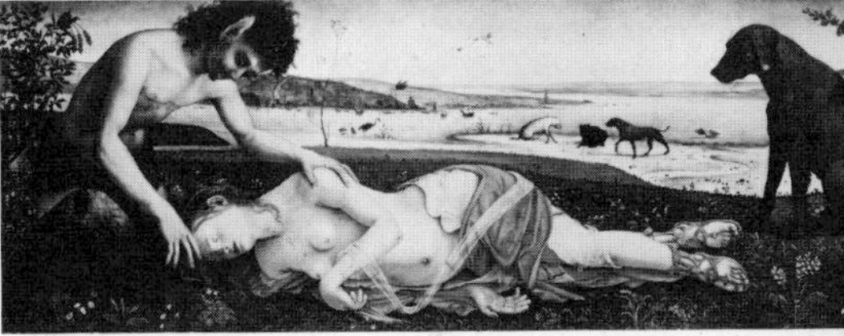

Piero di Cosimo. *Death of Procris*

Pietro da Cortona. Ceiling of the Great Salon of the Barberini Palace. Also *stucco

Pignon. *Paysage* (1957)

Pimenov. *Give to Heavy Industry*

exuberant and bold in conception, ingenious in its symbolism. His easel painting *Alexander's defeat of Darius* (Capitol Gal., Rome) was influential as the first of its kind, showing a battle in violent, theatrical, but ordered confusion.

Pigalle Jean-Baptiste (1714–85). French sculptor and pupil of Le Lorrain and Lemoyne. He became a popular sculptor in court circles, producing work for Louis XV and Madame de Pompadour, and statues of Voltaire and of the Mareschal de Saxe (for the latter's mausoleum).

Pignon Édouard (1905–). French painter and important member of the school of Paris since 1945. He became a full-time painter in 1943 and formed a group with Estève, Fougeron and Le Moal. Ostend harbour was a favourite subject and also mining and miners. He has been a regular exhibitor at the Salon de Mai.

Pijper Willem (1894–1947). Dutch composer. He studied under J. Wagenaar and himself taught many of Holland's leading contemporary composers. After a succession of influences, e.g. Mahler, Debussy and Stravinsky, he evolved a personal 'peri-tonal' style using special scales and brief melodic kernels 4 or 5 notes long but affording wide possibilities for development. His works include: 2 operas, orchestral music, e.g. *6 Epigrammes*, and much chamber music.

pilaster. Architectural term for a flattened column attached to or (usually) built into a wall from which it projects slightly; in classical architecture it became purely decorative.

Pilgrim, The (1923). Film directed by *Chaplin.

Pilgrim's Progress from this World to that which is to come, The (1678). Allegorical book by John *Bunyan.

Pilkington Francis (*c.* 1565–1638). English madrigal composer, working at Chester cathedral. He publ. 2 sets of *Madrigals and Pastorals* (1613, 1624) and a *Book of Songs or Ayres in 4 Parts* (1605).

pillar carpet. A small Chinese carpet in which the design is only seen complete when the 2 long sides are brought together. Designed for temple pillars; a typical design would be of a dragon appearing to encircle the pillar.

Pillar of Fire. 2-scene ballet with choreography by Tudor, music by Schoenberg and décor by Mielziner; 1st performance 1942.

Pillars of Society, The (1877). Play by *Ibsen.

Pilnyak Boris. The pseud. of Boris Andreyevich Vogau (1894–1937?). Soviet novelist. P. was in constant difficulties with the authorities, dying in prison. His most interesting works, including *The Naked Year* (1922; 1929), portray the Revolution as a merciless upsurge of peasant Russia; he is, however, better known for the more conventional Five-Year Plan novel, *The Volga Flows into the Caspian Sea* (1930; 1931) which was a revision of *Mahogany* (Berlin, 1929), denounced as anti-Soviet.

Pilo Carl Gustav (1712–92). Swedish portrait painter and sculptor, and pupil of O. P. Earning his living at first in Vienna and the German courts, he became painter to the Danish court (1748) and director of the Danish Academy (1771) and later returned to direct the Stockholm Academy.

Pil(l)on Germain (*c.* 1535–90). French sculptor. Early mannerist influences on his work were displaced by a greater realism. He carved Francis I's tomb (1558–9) and Henry II's tomb (1564–83) at St-Denis, and sculptures for Fontainebleau and the Louvre and at the château d'Anet (for Diane de Poitiers).

pilotis. Free-standing concrete columns, supporting a building above ground-level so that the ground-floor level is open. The device is a characteristic of the architectural idiom of *Le Corbusier.

Piloty Karl von (1826–86). German history painter, a leading exponent of the realist school; professor at the Munich Academy, later director.

Pimenov Yury (1903–). Soviet painter, like Deineka typical of the 1st post-Revolution generation of Soviet painters in his revolt against the constructivists' tenet that easel painting was dead. His work, however, is on a monumental scale more related to wall painting than the easel; in mood it much resembles

Pigalle. Monument of d'Harcourt

Pilon. *The Three Graces bearing an urn containing the heart of Henry II* (Louvre)

Pineapple Poll

Pinchbeck metal bracket-clock (*c.* 1775)

Pinter. From the film of *The Caretaker*, with Donald Pleasance and Robert Shaw

Eisenstein's early films, in technique principles of photo-montage are characteristic. *Give to Heavy Industry* (1927) is a typical work.

Pimmer William (1816–79). English-born U.S. sculptor, painter and anatomist, author of *Art Anatomy* (1877). He established his reputation as a sculptor with the nude figure *Falling Gladiator* (1861; Met. Mus.). His important commission for a draped figure of Alexander Hamilton for Commonwealth Avenue, Boston, was not successful.

Pinchbeck Christopher (1670?–1732). A London clock maker; he invented in 1732 an alloy close to brass which simulated gold; the metal was extensively used for small articles such as fobs, watch-cases and personal jewellery.

Pindar (518–438? B.C.). Greek lyric poet, born at Thebes and educated at Athens, who travelled over much of the Greek world to fulfil commissions for various patrons. He claimed noble birth, and the aristocratic principle is among his commonest themes, ironically, because most of his clients were of doubtful pedigree; however, P. believed that wealth conferred glory on a worthy possessor. His complete works filled 17 books, but only 4 survive: the epinician odes written for victors in the games at Argos, Corinth, Delphi and Olympia, and some fragments. The odes, composed to be sung by a chorus of dancers, are written in the conventional literary Doric dialect, but the language of P. is unique–compressed, extravagant, obscure and rich with metaphors and epithets. P. frequently includes a myth, apparently a traditional component of the choral ode, and interprets it with a pious moral drawn in conclusion. His conventional piety occasionally yields to the philosophic scepticism of the age so far as to modify a legend in the interests of propriety, but he was jealous for the honour of the gods, particularly his master and patron Apollo, and may even have shared the Orphics' view of the after-life. After Homer he was the poet most revered in antiquity.

Pindar Peter. Pseud. of John Wolcot (1738–1819), English verse satirist and physician best known for his attacks on George III. His works include *The Lousiad* (1785), *Bozzy and Piozzi* (1786) and *Ode upon Ode* (1787). He was responsible for establishing the painter J. Opie in London.

Pineapple Poll. 3-scene ballet with choreography by Cranko, music from Sir A. Sullivan and décor by Osbert Lancaster; 1st performance 1951.

Pinero Sir Arthur Wing (1855–1934). English playwright. P.'s *The Second Mrs Tanqueray* (1893) became famous as a problem play in a period dominated by melodrama, though it has dated. He also wrote *The Notorious Mrs Ebbsmith* (1895) and *Trelawny of the 'Wells'* (1898).

Pinky (1949). Film directed by E. *Kazan.

pinnacle. Architectural term for a small pointed or tapering turret used ornamentally, and sometimes structurally, e.g. to resist the outward thrust of a vault.

Pinocchio (1883). Children's book by C. *Collodi.

Pinter Harold (1930–). English playwright and actor. P. has a startling ability to create an atmosphere of menace from ordinary and often very funny dialogue and situations. His plays include *The Caretaker* (1960), *The Birthday Party* (1960), *A Slight Ache* (1961), and (for television) *The Tea Party* (1965).

Pintoff Ernest (1931–). U.S. film maker. After being a painter P. went to U.P.A. where he worked with R. Cannon, whose influence is detectable in his work. The sources of P.'s style are to be found in graphics and Press cartoons. The fable form of his 1st film, *Flebus* (1957), persisted in *The Violinist* (1959) and *The Old Man and the Flower* (1962) but was abandoned for the more adventurous forms of *The Interview* (1960) and *The Critic* (1963). He has also made 2 live-action films, *The Shoes* (1961) and *Harvey Middleman, Fireman* (1964).

Pinturicchio (Bernardino di Betto) (*c.* 1454–1513). Umbrian painter. An assistant to Perugino in the Sistine Chapel and a fertile and facile painter of Renaissance court life. Many of his compositions are based on his master's work. The lavish use of gold, brilliant colour and pattern is characteristic of his frescoes. He decorated the Borgia apartments of the Vatican (1493–4) for Alexander VI. His most important work is the fresco cycle dealing with the life of Pope Pius II, the former Aeneas Silvius *Piccolomini.

Pinnacle from Rheims

Pinero: caricature by Spy (1891)

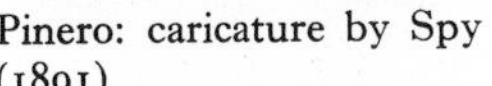

Pinturicchio. *Aeneas Silvius Piccolomini at the court of Scotland*

Luigi Pirandello

Piranesi. *The Basilica of St Maxentius.* Also *Pantheon, *Rainaldi

Pirosmanishvili. *A Family Picnic* (1907)

Pisanello. *Vision of St Eustace*

John Piper. Somerset Place, Bath

Pisa cathedral and campanile

pipe and tabor. A musical combination dating from the middle ages used to accompany dancing. The pipe, a small fipple flute, is played with one hand while the other beats out a rhythm on the tabor, a small drum.

Piper John (1903–). English painter. He worked in his father's solicitor's office until 1928, then studied at the R.C.A. and the Slade until 1930. During the 1930s P. responded to the main body of European art, coming into contact with Braque, Léger, Brancusi and Nicholson and Hepworth. Both as painter and designer he tried to integrate successfully cubism and later movements into the English tradition of romanticism. He was a war artist of considerable distinction, his watercolours of bombed churches being particularly fine; he designed the windows for Coventry cathedral.

Pippa Passes (1841). Dramatic poem by Browning.

Pirandello Luigi (1867–1936). Italian writer who gained international recognition only when, in middle age, he wrote plays (for which he received the Nobel prize in 1934). The most famous, *Sei personaggi in cerca d'autore* (1921; *Six Characters in Search of an Author*, 1923) and *Enrico IV* (1922; *Henry IV*, 1923), are technical *tours de force* which operate on several levels; in them P. questions accepted distinctions between reality and illusion, sanity and madness, concluding that only habit and convention mask the instability of the personality. His plays include *Così è (se vi pare)* (1918; *Right you Are–If You Think You Are*, 1923); *L'uomo dal fiore in bocca* (1923; *The Man with the Flower in His Mouth*, 1928), and *Vestire gli ignudi* (1922; *The Naked*, 1925). He also wrote poems, novels and short stories.

Piranesi Giovanni Battista (*c.* 1720–78). Italian engraver and architect, famous for his views of the ruins of Rome and fantastic compositions of building interiors. His profound knowledge of archaeology found full expression in imaginary studies of prisons, ruins, vaults and arcades full of highly contrasting light and dark shadows. Influenced by the landscape painting of Claude Lorrain, his own work helped to establish the pattern of the Italian romantic landscape. Of his great output of etchings and engravings the *Imaginary Prisons*, a series of plates issued in 1750, is justly the most famous. His son FRANCESCO (*c.* 1758–1810) completed and reissued a number of his plates.

Pirelli Building Milan (1958). Architects Gio *Ponti and Pier Nervi.

Piron Alexis (1689–1773). French poet and playwright, author of *La Métromanie* (1738), a verse comedy satirizing poets and hitting at Voltaire.

Pirosmanishvili Niko (1863–1919). Russian painter. By training an artisan sign painter, he was taken up by Larionov and invited to contribute to his exhibitions. A primitive in style, P. showed talent comparable to the Douanier Rousseau's and his painting enjoyed in Russia a cult similar to Rousseau's in Paris.

pirouette. A step in ballet in which the dancer stands on one foot, on full pointe or demi-pointe, and revolves like a spinning top.

Pisa cathedral Italy. One of the largest and finest of Tuscan Romanesque churches. Begun in 1063, it is built of polychrome marble and has a nave with double aisles, long transepts and an oval dome over the crossing. The W. front has rows of dwarf-galleries. The round Campanile (the 'LEANING TOWER') dates from 1174 and consists of 6 tiers of dwarf-galleries. The belfry was added in 1350 in an attempt to counteract the tilt (now 13 ft 10 ins). The foundations have been strengthened with concrete. The separate Baptistery (1153–1278) is a circular building with ambulatory and gallery above, its roof a cone partly covered by an outer hemispherical dome. The whole group is completed by the Campo Santo, a walled cemetery with frescoes by Traini and Gozzoli, mostly destroyed in World War II.

Pisanello Antonio Pisano, called (1395–1450). Italian court painter and medallist, the most celebrated of his time. His work is characterized by a minute and accurate observation of reality and his naturalism, though within the decorative convention of his time, stands out in marked contrast to the more idyllic and linear expression of his great contemporary Gentile da Fabriano. He was a draughtsman of genius and his drawings became examples for the artists of the Renaissance. As a medallist he carried the craft to its highest peak. The early *Vision of St Eustace*, perhaps his greatest and most imaginative painting, is an excellent

Giovanni Pisano. *Nativity*; detail from the pulpit, Pisa cathedral

Nicola Pisano. *Nativity*; detail from the pulpit, Pisa cathedral

illustration of his naturalism, his rendering of the splendour of knighthood and his joy in nature both animate and inanimate. His frescoes in Rome, Venice, Pavia and Mantua have been lost; only 2 frescoes in Verona have survived.

Pisano Andrea (*c.* 1270–1348). Italian goldsmith, sculptor and architect. In 1330 he was commissioned to execute the 1st pair of bronze doors of the Baptistery at Florence. Completed in 1336, the doors show scenes from the life of St John the Baptist and allegoric themes of the Cardinal and Christian Virtues. P.'s style is distinguished by the clear disposition of detached and grouped figures against a simple background. His association with the Duomo at Florence continued for the rest of his life, as he was appointed in 1337 to complete Giotto's Campanile with the addition of 2 storeys and reliefs. Influenced by Giotto and Giovanni Pisano, he himself exercised a profound influence on some of the most important Florentine sculptors, e.g. Ghiberti, Donatello and Luca della Robbia. His son NINO (*c.* 1315–1368?) was also a sculptor.

Pisano Giovanni (*c.* 1252–*c.* 1314). Italian sculptor and architect, son of Nicola P. The dramatic quality of his sculpture influenced Giotto, but its form is more French and more Gothic than his father's; the forms are sinuous, the draperies graceful. P. also designed the façade of Siena cathedral.

Pisano Nicola (*c.* 1215–*c.* 77). Italian sculptor who with his son Giovanni carved the pulpits in the Pisa Baptistery, in Pisa cathedral, in Siena cathedral and at Pistoia. The first 2 are mainly by Nicola, the last 2 mainly by Giovanni; but their exact shares are in dispute. Possibly trained in Southern Italy which, under the Emperor Frederick II, witnessed a Roman revival in the mid 13th c., P. copied Roman reliefs, evolving a plastic style with horizontal composition in depth, new in medieval art and anticipating Renaissance methods. Other works executed jointly with his son include the reliefs on the Fontana Maggiore, Perugia (1278).

Piscator Erwin (1893–). German theatre director, an important innovator in the 1920s by his use of mechanical devices, films, etc. on the stage, and by his didactic treatment of socio-political questions. Both profoundly influenced *Brecht, who occasionally worked with P.

piscina. In Christian churches, a stone basin for washing sacred vessels, generally attached to the wall S. of the altar.

Pisemsky Alexey Feofilaktovich (1820–81). Russian novelist and playwright, author of such radical realistic works of country life as the novel *A Thousand Souls* (1858; 1959) and the play *A Bitter Fate* (1860; 1933).

Pissarro Camille (1830–1903). French impressionist painter, born in St Thomas, Dutch East Indies, but educated in Paris. He worked under Corot and at the Académie Suisse where he met Manet, Monet and probably Courbet and Cézanne. Corot advised him to paint small sketches before nature and above all to 'study light and tonal values: execution and colour simply add charm to the picture'. Early landscapes like *The Marne at Chennevières* (1864–5; N.G., Edinburgh) were highly praised by Zola, Castagnary and other critics but received little public recognition; P. earned his living painting decorative blinds and fans. From the late 1860s he was a major figure of the impressionist circle: he alone exhibited at all 8 exhibitions (1874–86) which he largely organized. Despite great poverty and hardship he refused to 'weaken' and seek Salon recognition.

Influential as a teacher–for Cézanne and for Gauguin (*c.* 1879–83)–he was himself open to changing influences. In the 1880s, dissatisfied with his own technique, he imitated Seurat's divisionist manner and his series of paintings of the single motifs under changing conditions were directly inspired by Monet. Despite this, his work is remarkable for its consistency.

He was in London from 1870 to 1872 (*Penge Station*, 1871; Courtauld Gal., London) where he admired Constable, Turner and Dutch painting, but lived principally at Pontoise until 1884 when he settled at Eragny. His paintings differ from those of the other impressionists in 2 major respects. Firstly the Pontoise paintings particularly, e.g. *Côte du Jallais* (1867; Met. Mus.) are more carefully composed with a high horizon, controlled recession and dense colour areas. These are the paintings that influenced Cézanne, who worked with P. at Pontoise at intervals (1872–7). Secondly his landscape, as well as being a direct observation of certain conditions, was always inhabited. He admired Millet and Daumier and shared their respect for the working man. There are often strong Socialist undertones in his letters.

Andrea Pisano. *Naming of the Baptist*; detail from the doors of the Baptistery, Florence.

Pissarro. *Rouen* (1896)

Pissarro. *Penge Station*. Also *impressionism

Lucien Pissarro. *Snow Scene* (1917)

Pittoni. *Nero and the Corpse of Seneca*

The Place des Vosges

Pissarro Lucien (1863–1944). French painter, the son of Camille P. He first exhibited with the impressionists in 1886 and at the Salon des Indépendents from 1886 to 1894. From 1893 he lived and worked in England and was later associated with the New English Art Club. His style and subject-matter was much influenced by that of his famous father.

Piston Walter (1894–). U.S. composer and teacher; at Harvard from 1926, becoming professor of composition there in 1944. His works are in a predominantly neo-classical style, showing a virtuoso command of technique, and include the ballet *The Incredible Flutist* (1938), 6 symphonies, orchestral suites and chamber music. He also wrote authoritative textbooks on orchestration, counterpoint, etc.

Pit and the Pendulum, The. Short story by Edgar Allan *Poe.

pitch. The p. of a musical note is determined by the frequency of the vibrations causing it; the more rapid the vibrations the higher the p. There is now an international standard for concert p. which fixes the A above middle C as 440 vibrations per second. There have been many conventions regarding p. and, for a reason not fully clear, the accepted standard has fluctuated over the cs. There are still different standards, brass-band music being written for instruments a fraction of a tone higher in p. than concert instruments. *Absolute p.

Pitti Palace Florence. Built for Luca Pitti, 1440 onwards. The central section is probably by Brunelleschi, using very heavy rustication; the garden façade by Ammanati (1568) goes even further, with rusticated demi-columns and pilasters.

Pittoni Giovanni Battista (the Younger) (1687–1767). Venetian painter and the pupil of his uncle F. P. Most of his religious pictures are small in size, but he also painted classical subjects. His works include *The Sacrifice of Polyxenes* (Louvre) and *Crassus Despoiling the Temple at Jerusalem* (Accademia, Venice).

Pixerécourt René-Charles Guilbert de (1773–1844). Prolific French playwright who popularized melodrama.

Pizzetti Ildebrando (1880–). Italian composer and teacher. His style is essentially harmonic. His career began as a composer for the theatre, providing music for plays by G. D'Annunzio, basing his 1st opera *Fedra* (1905) on one; other operas are *Debora e Juele* (1921) and *La Figlia di Iorio* (1954), also based on D'Annunzio; he has also written orchestral, chamber and film music and choral music.

pizzicato. The Italian word for 'pinched', used in music as a direction (abbreviated to '*pizz*'.) to performers on bowed stringed instruments that the notes so marked are to be plucked, not bowed.

Place des Vosges Paris (formerly Place Royale). The 1st 'square' in the world and the beginning of modern town planning. It was built in 1605 as part of Henry IV's Paris 'improvements', on land reclaimed from a marsh. Though partly classical in design (arcade over the pavement) the buildings are still basically French (dormer-windows, central pavilions, etc.) with some Flemish influence.

Plague, The (1948). Novel by Albert *Camus.

Plain Dealer, The (1677). Play by *Wycherley.

plainsong. A style of unison liturgical music. The term originates from the Latin *cantus planus* as opposed to *cantus mensurabilis* and *cantus figuratus*; in other words undecorated music in free or irregular rhythm. Some decoration for soloists and at cadences did exist, but for the most part prose texts were chanted by whole congregations, thus making regular rhythm and ornamentation equally unsuitable. In accordance with the form of the texts, binary form was common. 4 modes were advocated by the authorities at the time of Bishop Ambrose of Milan (late 4th c.); and 8 by Pope Gregory (late 6th c.); and it is from this that the terms Ambrosian and Gregorian chant derive. Gregorian chant predominated in Rome and Western Europe. The recitation was centred round the dominant of the mode which was led up to by a short *intonation*, often interrupted by a *mediation* and ended by a fall (*cadence*) on to the tonic. Another convention was, at some moments in the service, the use of *antiphon*, dramatic echoings and re-echoings between soloists and congregation.

Plain Tales from the Hills (1888). Coll. of stories by Kipling.

The Pitti Palace

Plateresque. Upper part of the portal, S. Gregorio, Valladolid

Plantin. Polyglot Bible

Plato: marble head of the 1st c. B.C. from a 4th-c. B.C. bronze original

Planché James Robinson (1796–1880). English dramatist, writer of 'fairy-plays', extravaganzas and burlesques. He wrote the standard *History of British Costumes* (1834) and helped to reform the theatrical copyright laws.

Planchon Roger (1931–). French director and founder of the Théâtre de la Comédie in Lyon. A leading figure in the French theatre, he is now director of the Théâtre de la Cité in Villeurbanne.

Planets, The. Orchestral suite by Holst. The music was used for a 1-act ballet with choreography by Tudor and décor by Stevenson; 1st performance 1934.

planish. To smooth or polish a metal by hammering, normally with a polished broad-faced hammer upon an anvil.

Plantin Christophe (1514–89). French-born master printer working in Antwerp (1555–89). P. used many of the roman types of *Garamond and the italic, Greek and '*civilités*' of *Granjon, employed the best woodcutters and engravers in Holland, revived the illustrated book in the Netherlands, and by 1575 was the arbiter of book styles in Europe. P. publ. a specimen of his types, *Index characterum* (1957); his famous Polyglot Bible (1573) in Hebrew, Greek, Latin, Chaldaic and Syriac; *Theatrum orbis terrarum* by Abraham Ortelius; and a book about Holland (1582); also many liturgical works. A modern type-face is called after him.

plasticity. This word is sometimes used in art criticism when discussing paintings in which the 2-dimensional figures give a strong impression of solidity.

plate (from the Spanish *plata*, 'silver'). The older meaning of the word up to the 19th c. refers only to silver; since then, with the introduction of Sheffield plate, the word is often used to describe silver-plated ware.

Platen (-Hallermünde) August Graf von (1796–1835). German poet. P. was a pederast (cf. Mann, *Der Tod in Venedig*). His verse, romantic in theme, shows mastery of strict form and aspired to a statuesque, objective quality: *Ghaselen* (1821), oriental strophes; *Sonette aus Venedig* (1825); best known is his ballad *Das Grab im Busento* (1820). His comedies satirize romantic excesses, e.g. fate tragedy in *Die verhängnisvolle Gabel* (1826).

plateresque (Spanish *plateria*, 'silverwork'). Term applied to the delicate and intricate decorative style (incorporating Renaissance elements) which predominated in late 15th- and early 16th-c. Spanish architecture.

Plath Sylvia (1932–63). U.S. poet who lived in England, the wife of the poet Ted Hughes. *The Colossus* (1960) and the poems written shortly before her death display a refined but vigorous sensibility.

platinotype. Photographic process invented by W. Willis. Paper made sensitive with salts of platinum is used; the advantages of this system are wide tonal scale and greater permanence. It became obsolete about 1930.

Plato (*c.* 427–347 B.C.). Greek philosopher and founder of the *Academy in Athens. Most of P.'s life was spent teaching and studying there, apart from unsuccessful periods (367 and 361) in Syracuse as tutor and adviser of its ruler, Dionysius.
P. was the father of Western philosophy, the first whose writings (all those publ. have survived) state most of the central philosophic problems and attempt rigorous definitions and close argument. The theories and method of *Socrates are preserved only in these works, in which Socrates is generally the protagonist; his contributions and those of P. cannot be clearly distinguished. P. is also the greatest Greek prose stylist and the creator of the dialogue (used in all his works but the *Apology*, an account of Socrates' defence at his trial) as a literary form. His search for universal standards led him to postulate the existence of a world of 'forms' or 'ideas', the pure and eternal qualities (truth, beauty, etc.) found only in imperfect form in the visible world. The *Republic*, probably P.'s masterpiece, describes the ideal city-state of Callipolis, in which the ruling élite would receive a long education which would make them philosophers exercising their power reluctantly; there would be communal property and marriage. The *Laws*, P.'s last dialogue, is more practical but also more authoritarian in political outlook. The *Apology*, *Crito* and *Phaedo* deal with the trial and the last days of Socrates; the *Symposium* describes a banquet in which Socrates discourses upon the nature of love to an audience including Aristophanes and Alcibiades. Other dialogues include the *Timaeus*, on the origin of the world; *Protagoras*, on crime and punishment; *Meno*, on innate knowledge; *Gorgias* and *Phaedrus*, on rhetoric; and *Critias* and *Parmenides*.

Plautus Titus Maccius (before 250–184 B.C.). Roman comic dramatist, born at Sarsina in Umbria. He seems to have made his living out of writing. Like Shakespeare he collaborated with other authors and more than 100 plays were attributed to him in antiquity. 21 survive, probably the only genuine ones. Plautus derived his plots from *Menander and other writers of the Attic new comedy, but the wealth of puns and topical allusions show that he adapted rather than translated. His language is racy and vigorous and his metres, though formally scanned after the Greek quantitative pattern, are all but accentual, reinforced with alliteration. His verbal exuberance, including new coinages and etymological tricks as well as puns, is unparalleled in Latin. His characters are the stock types of Greek comedy, but borrow the vigour of their author so that the plays enjoyed a long popularity at Rome and have influenced modern authors such as Shakespeare (*The Comedy of Errors* from the *Menaechmi*), Molière (a version of P.'s **Amphitryon* and *L'Avare* from the *Aulularia*) and Brecht (*Die Dreigroschenoper* from the *Trinummus*).

Playboy of the Western World, The (1907). Play by J. M. *Synge.

player-piano. Mechanical piano (*pianola).

Playfair Sir Nigel (1874–1934). English actor, director and extremely successful manager of the Lyric Opera House, Hammersmith between 1918 and 1932

Playfair William Henry (1789–1857). Scottish neo-classical architect who designed many public buildings in Edinburgh, including the Royal Scottish Institution and the National Gallery of Scotland.

Playford John (1623–86). English music publ. and writer on music. P.'s many important publs include *The English Dancing Master* (dated 1651; issued 1650), a coll. of country-dance tunes (*contredanse), J. Hilton's *Catch that Catch can* (1652; revised as *The Musical Companion*, 1667) and his own book *Briefe Introduction to the Skill of Music* (1654).

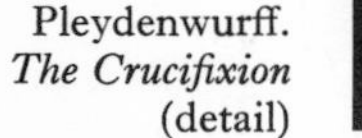
Pleydenwurff. *The Crucifixion* (detail)

Maya Plisetskaya

William Plomer

plectrum. In music, a small piece of wood, leather, metal or plastic used by players of plucked instruments such as the guitar or banjo for striking the strings. In a harpsichord the key mechanism operates plectra which pluck the strings.

Pléiade, La. Group of 7 French writers of the 16th c. who took their name from 7 great Greek poets of the 3rd c. B.C. named after the constellation of the Pleiades. The chief members of the French P. were Ronsard, du Bellay and Baïf; they remodelled French poetry on classical and Italian lines, enriched the language from Greek and Latin and by new French formations, and established rules for French prosody.

plein air (French, 'open-air'). Term used of paintings which convey an open-air feeling, and particularly of those actually painted out-of-doors. Hence it is most frequently used of the work of the impressionists.

Pleydenwurff Hans (d. 1477). German painter who was working in Nuremberg between 1450 and 1472. Little is known of this primitive painter of religious subjects. 2 works, *The Crucifixion* and *The Mystical Marriage of St Catherine*, are in Munich.

Pleyel Ignaz Joseph (1757–1831). Austrian composer, a pupil of Haydn for 5 years; he settled in Paris in 1795, founding there a piano factory. He wrote symphonies, chamber music, etc. and also a piano tutor.

plié. A basic exercise in ballet, used for 'loosening up'. The dancer goes through each of the 5 positions in turn, bending the knees and keeping the body erect.

plinth. Architectural term for the projecting block at the base of a statue, column, wall, etc.

Pliny the Elder (A.D. 23–79). Gaius Plinius Secundus, Roman encyclopaedist. P. served with the cavalry in Germany, then became governor of provinces successively in Gaul, Africa and Spain. In the intervals of his official duties, at meals, at the baths, while travelling, he would have a book read to him, and excerpt it. Of all his erudition one work survives, the *Natural History* in 37 books, a digest of miscellaneous information collected from nearly 500 different authorities. It deals with the physical universe, geography, ethnology, anthropology, physiology, zoology, botany, pharmacology, mineralogy and metallurgy and preserves a great deal of fascinating and sometimes erroneous information, because P. considered it his task to hand on whatever he received from his reading, without criticizing his authorities. The middle ages treated the work with the respect due to antique authority and perpetuated many of its quaint tales.

Pliny the Younger (A.D. 61–*c.* 113). Roman letter writer. Nephew of the preceding, by whom he was adopted. He was a lawyer, held the various magistracies up to the consulate and in 111 became governor of Bithynia. His letters (intended for publ.) are a pale and deliberate shadow of Cicero's correspondence. His correspondents include Tacitus, Suetonius and Martial, and the Emperor Trajan. The letters give a clear picture of contemporary life and events: he describes his own villa at length, records the eruption of Vesuvius in which his uncle lost his life and in the correspondence with Trajan asks for instructions on the treatment of the Christians, one of the earliest pagan references to the sect.

plique à jour. A process of cloisonné enamelling where most of the metal ground is removed leaving strips of metal to keep the enamel, which is translucent, in place. Often used as an additional ornament on silver.

Plisetskaya Maya (1928–). Soviet dancer of the Bolshoi Ballet, Moscow and niece and pupil of Asaf Messerer. P. is one of the most talented ballerinas in Russia today, with attack and a grand manner style. Apart from creating parts as the *Bird-maiden in Shurale* (1955) and *Laurencia* (1956) she has recently taken over many of the classical roles associated with Ulanova.

Plomer William (Charles Franklyn) (1903–). South African-born English poet. P. has written lyrics—notably some of his 'African' poems—but is best known as a satirist, e.g. *Father and Son: 1939* and *Mews Flat Mona: A Memory of the 'Twenties*, which castigate the irresponsible, 'gay' life of the smart set, and exercises in the comic-macabre like *The Dorking Thigh.*

plot. The sequence of events in a novel, play, book, etc., especially when they are linked causally, i.e. distinct from the story, which may be a sequence of unconnected episodes.

Plotinus (205–70). The last great Hellenic philosopher. His mystical philosophy of a transcendent first principle was developed by a school now called the neo-Platonists. In his system of aesthetics P. systematizes aesthetic problems raised by Plato and boldly identifies the realm of Beauty with the realm of Ideas. Plato depreciated art as merely creating images and as limited by ordinary perception; P. enunciates a doctrine of the symbolic relation between art and reality. His writings were arranged by his disciple Porphyry in 6 books, called *Enneads.*

Plough and the Stars, The (1926). Play by Sean O'Casey.

Plow that Broke the Plains, The (1936). Short film directed by P. *Lorentz.

Plumed Serpent, The (1926). Novel by D. H. Lawrence.

Plutarch (*c.* A.D. 46–*c.* 120). Greek essayist and biographer, born at Chaeronea in Boeotia of good family, lived and lectured in Rome for a time but retired to his home town, where he held an hereditary priesthood of Apollo, to write and study literature. In old age he enjoyed the confidence and respect of the Emperor Trajan. His *Moralia* or essays cover historical, philosophical, educational, religious, ethical and scientific questions. They include all sorts of out-of-the-way information, some valuable, some of doubtful authenticity, the fruit of a lifetime's wide, inquisitive and attentive reading. The great series of Greek and Roman biographies (the *Lives*) which he wrote in retirement, belongs to the same genre. He admits that he has no intention of writing history. Like Herodotus he has a gift for a good story and for the presentation of character: he includes whatever material will throw a strong light on the personality of his subject. The lives are arranged in pairs, one Greek and one Roman whose careers show parallel development, and in spite of their unreliability as historical sources they have enjoyed an immense and deserved popularity for their readability. Shakespeare is only one of Plutarch's admirers and imitators.

Plymouth. The 1st English hard-paste *porcelain factory opened (1768) by William Cookworthy, who had been attempting for at least 20 years to find the secret of making

Plymouth mug

Poelzig. Grosses Schauspielhaus, Berlin

porcelain. In 1770 the factory moved to Bristol where much of the best work was done, often in Derby styles; in 1781 the patent was sold to a co. which opened a factory in New Hall, Staffordshire.

Pnin (1957). Novel by Nabokov.

Poccetti Bernardino Barbatelli (*c.* 1542–1612). Florentine painter. During a period in Rome P. saw pictures by Raphael which influenced his style; he reacted against Florentine mannerism, painting with great realism, and became the chief representative of late Florentine 16th-c. academic style. He did many frescoes.

pochette: *kit

podium. Architectural term for the platform beneath classical temples and similar buildings; also the lowest part of a column-pedestal.

Poe Edgar Allan (1809–49). U.S. short story writer and poet. His mother and father died in 1810 and the boy was brought up, though not adopted, by John Allan, a Scottish tobacco merchant. P. was schooled for a time in England (1815–20), then at Richmond, Virginia and the Univ. of Virginia (1826). In 1827, under an assumed name and age, P. entered the army and in 1830, with Mrs Allan's help, entered West Point, being dismissed, however, a year later. In 1835 he became a newspaper ed., but was dismissed for alcoholism in 1836, the year of his marriage to his 13-year-old cousin. After her death in 1847 his alcoholism increased and he died in Baltimore after being robbed and beaten while drunk.
P.'s influence has been widespread, stemming in Europe from Baudelaire, who trs. and wrote much about him. P. took horror and mystery as his subject and his powerful and morbid imagination gave it a new seriousness. In both stories and poems he aimed to create a single, predetermined effect (see his critical essay *The Philosophy of Composition*, 1846), using the suggestive and onomatopoeic qualities of words to the full. Typical stories are *The Cask of Amontillado* (1846), a tale of revenge; *The Fall of the House of Usher* (1839), an uncanny story with undertones of incest and vampirism; *The Premature Burial* (1844); and *The Tell-Tale Heart* (1843), in which a murderer believes that he can hear the heart of his victim–buried under the floorboards–still beating; *The Gold Bug* (1843); and *The Murders in the Rue Morgue* (1841), which effectually established the detective story as a form. In the allegorical *William Wilson* (1839), an evil man is constantly rebuked and thwarted by a double whom he finally kills; Stevenson derived *Dr Jekyll and Mr Hyde* from the story. P. considered the death of a beautiful woman the most poetical subject, and used it in *To Helen* (1831), *The Raven* (1845), *Ulalume* (1847), and *Annabel Lee* (1849). Other notable poems are *Al Aaraaf* (1829), *Israfel* (1831) and *The Bells* (1849).

Poelzig Hans (1869–1936). One of the forerunners of modern architecture in Germany, P. designed some highly original industrial structures before World War I. He then moved through an expressionist phase, e.g. the water tower at Posen, and a phase of pure fantasy, as his Grosses Schauspielhaus, Berlin (1919). His later work does not have the dynamism of the earlier and is of less interest.

Poetaster, The (1601). Play by Ben *Jonson.

Poètes maudits, Les (1884). A critical work by *Verlaine.

Poet Laureate. Title for the English court poet, i.e. a poet who receives a pension from the crown and who usually composes odes and verses on official occasions. Ben Jonson held the post in all but name; since Dryden, the 1st P. L., the position has been held by (among others) Wordsworth and Tennyson.

Poil de Carotte (1894). Novel by Jules *Renard; made into a film (1932) directed by J. *Duvivier.

Point Counter Point (1928). Novel by Aldous *Huxley.

Pointe Courte, La (1955). Film directed by A. *Varda.

pointillism: *neo-impressionism

Polack Hans (Johann) (d. 1510). German painter of frescoes and panels; he was an important master of the late Gothic style in Bavaria where he mainly worked. Altar panels by P. are in the National Museum in Munich. *The Disputation of St Stephen* and *The Entrusting of the Rule by St Benedict* are in the Museum of German Art, Munich.

Poelzig. Water tower, Posen

Edgar Allan Poe

Poliakoff. *Composition 1959*

Marco and Niccolò Polo received by Kublai Khan; from the 15th-c. *Livre des Merveilles*

Pollaiuolo. *Martyrdom of St Sebastian*

Pollaiuolo. *Apollo and Daphne*

Pollock. *She Wolf*

Pollock. *Number Twenty-Eight* (1950). Also *action painting and colour plate 75

Polaert Joseph (1817–79). Belgian architect who designed the immense Palais de Justice in Brussels (1866–83). The elements are basically classical, but the proportions massive, heavy and depressing.

Polanski Roman (1933–). Polish film director. P.'s film school exercise, *Two Men and a Wardrobe* (1957), a fable, gained him an immediate reputation. His feature film *Knife in the Water* (1962) upheld this with its sexual tension and self-assured technique, as did *Repulsion* (1965).

Polenov Vassily (1844–1927). Russian painter chiefly of landscape and religious subjects, a member of the Wanderers group of artists and also a leading spirit in the formation of the *Abramtsevo Colony. As a teacher in the Moscow Art School in the 1880s and 1890s he was influential on a whole generation of Russian artists such as Levitan and Konstantin Korovin (the theatrical designer to Mamontov and later Diaghilev).

Poliakoff Serge (1906–). Russian painter; he went to Paris in 1923. After his introduction to painting (1930), his early pictures were almost exclusively academic nudes and landscapes. A visit to London in 1935 found him formulating a personal style, tending to abstraction. Encouraged by his friendship with Kandinsky and influenced by visits to the studio of Delaunay, he turned to painting abstracts of contrasting and interlocking colour shapes. P.'s work is also clearly influenced by iconography.

Polidoro da Caravaggio (1495–1543). Italian painter, pupil of Raphael and assistant on decorative works in the Vatican. After the Sack of Rome (1527) he worked in Naples and Messina. He painted monochrome imitation antique frescoes on Roman house façades and was among the earliest classical landscapists; he was admired by Poussin and Claude.

Poliziano Angelo ('Politian') (1454–94). Italian poet and humanist. While still very young, P. showed great talent as a classical student and attracted Lorenzo de' Medici's attention; like many others, including Botticelli, he worked at court, and the atmosphere of his poetry has often been compared with that of the painting *Primavera*. In 1480 he became professor of Greek and Latin literature in the Univ. of

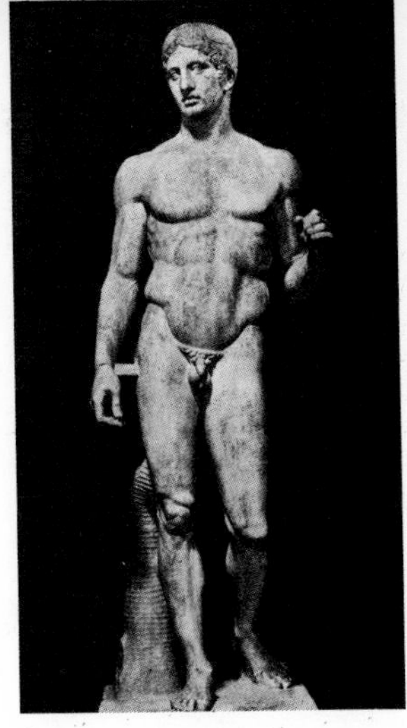

Polycleitus. The *Doryphorus* (copy)

Pompeii. Interior of a wine shop

Florence. He wrote many short poems in the form of epigrams in Latin and Greek, and Latin elegies and odes. In Italian P. wrote many light and witty lyrics in the form of '*strambotti*' and about 30 dance songs called '*ballata*'. He also wrote a secular play, pagan in spirit, the *Farvola di Orfeo*. P. dedicated the last years of his life to lecturing on philological studies, becoming famous as a humanist in Italy and abroad.

polka. A lively dance in duple time which emerged from folk origins in Bohemia *c.* 1830 and which, in a stylized form, swept European and U.S. society by 1850.

Pollaiuolo Antonio (*c.* 1432–98). Italian painter, sculptor, engraver and goldsmith believed to have been the pupil of Andrea del Castagno; he worked closely with his brother PIERO (1443–96). Their work is strongly influenced by antiquity. Early scientist-artists of the Florentine Renaissance, according to Vasari they practised dissection in order to understand the human body. Their undoubted masterpiece is the *Martyrdom of St Sebastian* (N.G., London); this innovates in showing figures with a clearly defined muscular structure, showing variations of the same movement from every side and many angles. In the engraving *Battle of the Nude Men*, influenced by Mantegna, the action is even more violent and the display of muscular structure complete. *Apollo and Daphne* (N.G., London) and *Hercules and Nessus* set their subject in a lyrical landscape closely observed but transcending mere topographical observation. The brothers spent their last years working on the bronze tombs of Sixtus IV and Innocent VIII in Rome. The gesture of the Pope and the arrangement of figures on the tomb of Innocent was copied on later funeral monuments.

Pollock Jackson (1912–56). U.S. painter. He studied at Los Angeles art school (1925), and under Benton in New York in 1929; he worked for the W.P.A. Art Project (1938). His early work is characteristic of the American romantic realism of the 1930s but by 1936 he was influenced by surrealism–particularly by Picasso and by Masson. He became the central figure of American abstract *expressionism, and made a deep impact on British painting in the 1950s. His achievement was an important contribution to the rise of modern American painting and his early death in a road accident (1956) has added a romantic legendary character to his reputation. He contributed to the International Surrealist Exhibition, New York (1942) and became associated with other New York surrealists. *She Wolf* (1943; M.M.A., New York) shows the closeness to Masson at this point, but he developed the automatic techniques to a more instinctive, personal form, relying more fully on chance and accident. He painted his 1st 'drip painting' (in which the paint was allowed to fall from the brush or vessel on to a canvas laid on the floor) in 1947 and this led to *action painting. The form of his very large images was not preconceived and only emerged during the act of execution. ('The painting has a life of its own. I try to let it come through.') His late works–*Blue Poles* (1953)–although violently executed, result in a lacework of coloured and silver lines of extraordinary delicacy.

Polly (publ. 1729). Ballad opera by John *Gay.

Polo Marco (1254–1324). Venetian explorer and author of one of the world's great travel books, the account of his voyages throughout Central Asia and to China and India; it was familiarly known as *Il Milione*. 85 mss of the work are still in existence.

polonaise. A Polish court dance in a grave 3 in a bar time; it dates from the Renaissance. *Chopin wrote 13 p.s for piano.

Polonsky Abraham (dates not available). U.S. film writer and director. P. wrote a few film scripts including *Body and Soul* and M. Gordon's *I Can Get It For You Wholesale* before directing *Force of Evil* (1948), the most remarkable of the late 1940s socially slanted thrillers. A victim of the Hollywood blacklist, during the period of McCarthyism, he has not made any other films.

Polovtsian Dances. From Borodin's opera *Prince Igor*; they are performed as a concert piece.

Polycleitus. Among the greatest Greek sculptors of the 5th c. B.C. His figures were described by ancient writers as conforming to an almost unvaried formal pattern; the few surviving copies show that P. introduced a new sense of rhythm into sculptural form.

Polyeucte (1641). Tragedy by Corneille.

Polygnotus (*fl.* 480–450 B.C.). Greek painter, considered as among the 1st great masters by classical writers; his work marked an advance in figure composition and expressiveness. He was established in Athens *c.* 463 B.C., decorating one of the city gates with scenes from the Trojan War.

polymodality. Term used of some 20th-c. musical compositions which are thought to employ several *modes at once.

Poly-olbion, The (1613, 1622). Poem by *Drayton.

polyphony (Greek, 'many-voices'). This term applicable to all music in more than one part is used in particular of music of the late 15th, 16th and early 17th cs. During this period writing in several independent parts of equal melodic validity was a major idiom.

polyptych (Greek, 'with many folds'). Several painted panels, usually of wood, grouped as a single screen, the outer panels often being hinged so that they can fold upon the centre ones. Altarpieces were frequently in the form of p.s.

polytonality: *tonality

Pomes Penyeach (1927). Coll. of poems by James Joyce.

pommer. Obsolete musical instrument of the *shawm family.

Pommer Erich (1889–). German film producer, head of the U.F.A. company in its inter-war heyday. The charming, stylish musical *Congress Dances* (1931) is among his many famous productions.

Pompadour Antoinette Poisson, marquise de (1721–64): *Louis XV

Pomp and Circumstance. Name of 5 marches by *Elgar.

Pompeii. Roman town S. of Naples overwhelmed by an eruption of Vesuvius in A.D. 79 and undisturbed from then until the 18th c. Large areas of it are intact up to 2nd-storey level and it thus provides the most valuable of all sources of knowledge for Roman painting, domestic architecture, town planning and daily life.

Pontormo.
The Deposition

Pope: bust by Roubiliac

Pondal Eduardo (1835–1917). Spanish poet in the Galician dialect. His works are full of nostalgic, melancholy love for his province. His main poems are in the 2 colls, *Rumores de los Pinos* and *Queixumes d'os Pinos*.

Ponge Francis (1899–). French poet, or as he prefers to be known, 'poet'. He attempts in his work the perfect definition, expression, metamorphosis, of the object into words. His works include the coll. *Le Parti pris des choses* (1942) and the long poem *Le Soleil placé en Abîme* (1954).

Pons Lily (1904–). French-born U.S. soprano singer; she has made a number of films, e.g. *I Dream Too Much.*

Pont du Gard

Ponsard François (1814–67). French playwright, leader of the école du bon sens, which reacted against the excesses of romanticism. His works include the verse plays *Lucrèce* (1843; *Lucretia*, 1848), a tragedy, and the historical comedy *Le Lion amoureux* (1866).

Pontano Giovanni (1426?–1503), also called 'Jovianus Pontanus'. Italian humorist and poet. P.'s Latin verse is remarkably easy and natural, and successfully communicates his personal feelings.

Pont du Gard S. France. Roman aqueduct built about A.D. 14; it is 882 ft long and 155 ft high, it has 3 levels, the arches diminishing in size as they go up, the masonry of the 2 lower levels of arches being laid dry without mortar.

Ponte Jacopo da, and family: *Bassano

Ponti. The Pirelli Building

Ponti Gio (1891–). Internationally known Italian architect, designer of straightforward modern buildings, e.g. his Montecatini blocks in Milan. His best-known work is the Pirelli Building, Milan (1958), the most famous European skyscraper, which he and Nervi designed, with form and structure logically designed to meet the wind loading of a high building.

Pontoppidan Henrik (1857–1943). Danish novelist and, in 1917, co-winner of the Nobel prize. His earlier works attacked social conditions in Denmark, above all the depressed state of the peasantry; 3 great novel cycles gave a clear-sighted if not always favourable analysis of the Danish character.

Pontormo Jacopo da, born J. Carrucci (1494–1556/7). Among the earliest and most influential of the Italian mannerist painters, P. was named after his birthplace, a village near Empoli, but was trained in the Florentine school–certainly by Andrea del Sarto, and possibly by Leonardo da Vinci and Piero di Cosimo. In 1521 he won his reputation with his lyrical decorations for the Medici villa, Poggio a Caiano, near Florence. Another cycle of frescoes, scenes from the Passion (Certosa di Galluzzo, near Florence), was painted in 1523. P.'s angular style of draughtsmanship – showing the influences of Michelangelo and Dürer's engravings, yet highly original in feeling–and his unusual colour sense are probably best seen in his masterpiece, *The Deposition* (S. Felicità, Florence), while a fine example of his mannerist portraiture is *Lady with a Lapdog* (Städelsches K. Inst., Frankfurt). Rosso Fiorentino was his rival and Bronzino his pupil and follower.

Poole Ernest (1880–1950). U.S. novelist who collaborated with Upton Sinclair for a time. His works include the socialistic *The Harbor* (1915) and *His Family* (1917).

Poor Folk (1846). Novel by *Dostoyevsky.

Pope Alexander (1688–1744). English Augustan poet. Deformed by a childhood illness and excluded by his Roman Catholicism from a public career, P. began writing early. His *Essay on Criticism* was publ. in 1711; *Windsor Forest* (1713) brought him the friendship of Swift, Gay, Arbuthnot and Congreve, and with the mock-heroic poem *The Rape of the Lock* (1712) he had already achieved artistic maturity. The publ. of a trs. of the *Iliad* gave him financial independence for life and enabled him to settle at Twickenham; later he produced a trs. of the *Odyssey* with the help of collaborators.

P.'s 1st important work was a poetic essay which dealt with the canons of taste and judgement in writing and in criticism. Although the *Essay on Criticism* sometimes strays into epigrammatic statements that have little validity, the confidence shown in the choice of subject was not misplaced. In their meticulous craftsmanship, their precise elegance, and their firm control both of sense and metre, P.'s poems epitomize the 18th-c. literary ideal. His sensitive and resentful temperament led him to squander his satiric powers upon objects too small for it, and much of the interest of *The*

Pordenone. *Christ nailed to the Cross* (fresco; Cremona)

Dunciad (1728), a satire on hack-writers, consequently perished although passages are genuinely comic. P.'s satire is most effective in the polished and playful ironies of *The Rape of the Lock* and in the deeply felt portraits of Atticus and Sporus in the *Epistle to Dr Arbuthnot* (1734–5): the first is an acute character study etched in the strongest acid, the second an accumulation of images of disgust which shows P.'s enormous power of sensual response and evocation. Used in the *Epistle* for the poetry of hatred, it creates elsewhere passages and lines of a beauty and immediacy the more telling for the strict control with which they are used.

P. used the decasyllabic rhymed couplet with amazing flexibility and verve, whether in the speculation of the philosophical poem *Essay on Man* (1734) or the more easy autobiographical vein of the *Epistle*, among his finest and most original performances, in which the strict form is used to achieve a natural, almost conversational tone.

Popov Alexei (1892–). Soviet director who in 1936 took control of the Central Theatre Of The Red Army in Moscow. In 1944 he directed the controversial play *Stalingrad*. Russia's foremost director, he has always encouraged new writers.

Popova Liubov (1889–1924). Russian painter, the most distinguished painter among Malevich's suprematist followers, after the Revolution also a constructivist abandoning painting to work as a textile designer in a factory. She also worked for Meyerhold designing sets and costumes. P. studied in Paris under Metzinger and Le Fauconnier in 1912; on her return to Moscow she began contributing cubist works such as *Seated Figure* (1915) to the Knave of Diamonds exhibitions. Her 1st abstract works date from 1916; after 1917 many, entitled *Architectonic Compositions*, show the influence of Malevich and Tatlin. *Architectonic Painting* (1917; M.M.A., New York) is the only work in a Western public coll.

Pöppelmann Matthaus Damel (1662–1736). German architect. He was sent by Augustus the Strong of Saxony to study in Vienna and Rome, and then (1711–22) built the Zwinger, Dresden, a huge ornamental courtyard for pageants. Gay, exuberant, full of curving lines and broken rhythms, it is the epitome of 18th-c. German rococo.

porcelain. True or 'hard-paste' p. is the high-fired ceramic ware containing felspar, *kaolin and flint. At about 1400° centigrade the felspar and flint form a melt and their silica content and that of the kaolin fuses. When this fusion cools it hardens into a white and completely non-porous translucent body, which gives a clear note when struck. P. was first developed by the Chinese out of the stonewares of the 7th or 8th cs. European attempts to emulate the Chinese p. produced at *Meissen in the early 18th c. a hard-paste true equivalent of p.; English soft-paste p., composed of clay and powdered glass or frit fired at a comparatively low temperature and then lead glazed and fired again to achieve a porcelainous effect; and English *bone china. The term p. is now generically used to cover the 3 above variants.

Pordenone Giovanni Antonio (1483–1576). Italian painter of historical subjects, much influenced by Giorgione. Favoured by the Emperor Charles V, he was a strong, if only temporary, rival of Titian. P. painted frescoes in the cathedral at Cremona and in S. Maria di Campagna at Piacenza.

Porpora Nicola Antonio (1686–1768). Italian composer and singing teacher working in Naples, Venice, London, where he was director and composer to the anti-Handel 'Opera of the Nobility', and Vienna. His pupils included the singers Cafarelli and Farinelli, the librettist Metastasio and, for a time, the composers J. A. Hasse and Haydn.

porringer. A 2-handled cup and cover, often with a separate salver, dating from the 1670s. The tub-shaped bowl is usually supported on a shallow foot, and the domed cover often has a turned or cast finial. The name derives from 'potager' (a container for soup), but its function seems to have been that of a ceremonial drinking-cup.

Porson Richard (1759–1808). English classical scholar who effected a great advance in textual criticism in his eds of Euripides.

Porta Giacomo della (*c.* 1540–1602). Italian architect working at Rome. He was engaged on the completion of the dome of St Peter's to the designs of Michelangelo but did very much original work, including the façade of Il Gesù, much of the Chigi Palace and the Villa Aldobrandini at Frascati.

Popova. *Italian Still-life* (1914)

Porringer; London, 1676

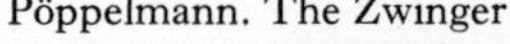

Pöppelmann. The Zwinger

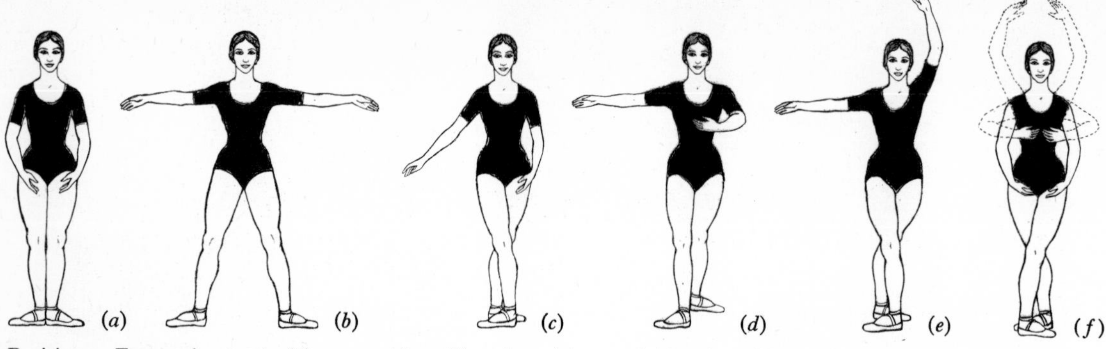

Positions. Feet and arms in (a) 1st position, (b) 2nd position, and (c) 3rd position; (d) 4th position, with feet open and arms en avant; (e) 4th position, with legs crossed and arms en haut; (f) 5th position, with arms en bas and (dotted lines) en avant and en haut

Portative organ (detail from a painting by Memlinc)

Edwin S. Porter. *The Great Train Robbery*

Katherine Anne Porter

Posset-pot; Staffordshire, early 18th c.

Porta Joseph (Salviati the Younger) (1520–70). Venetian painter (having followed his master, Francesco Salviati to Venice from Rome). He decorated the façade of the Palazzo Loredano and provided religious works for Venetian churches. Summoned to Rome by Pope Pius IV, he competed (unsuccessfully) with Taddeo Zuccaro to provide ceiling frescoes for the Papal chamber.

portative organ. A small pipe organ, often used in processions, which lost its vogue in the 16th c. The performer's right hand operated the keyboard (range about two 8ves), his left the 'book bellows' behind the instrument (*ill.).

port de bras. In ballet the carriage of the arms, used in ballet practice as well as often being an integral part of the choreography.

porte-cochère. Architectural term for a porch large enough to cover a coach, so that people alighting from the coach are sheltered.

Porte étroite, La (1909). Novel by André Gide.

Porter Cole (1893–1964). U.S. light composer. After studying law at Harvard he went to Paris to study composition. During the 1930s and 1940s he became widely known as a song writer ('Don't Fence me in', 'I get a kick out of You', 'What is this thing called Love?', etc) and all jazz players have used his themes. He wrote a great many musicals of which the best known is probably *Kiss me Kate* (1946), loosely based on Shakespeare's *The Taming of the Shrew*.

Porter Edwin S. (1869–1941). Pioneer U.S. film maker, who directed *The Great Train Robbery* (1903), one of the 1st story films which, ahead of its time, used outdoor shooting, montage and intercutting of parallel actions. It has a claim to be the 1st western.

Porter Katherine Anne (1894–). U.S. short-story writer and novelist. Much of P.'s work is centred on the American South and investigates the impact on individual lives of the real and mythical Southern past. Her works include the coll. of stories *Flowering Judas* (1930); *Pale Horse, Pale Rider* (1939), containing 3 short novels, *Noon Wine, Old Mortality* and the title-story; and the novel *Ship of Fools* (1959).

portico. Architectural term for a colonnaded roofed area.

Portinari Candido (1903–62). Brazilian painter; his reputation rests primarily on his large-scale murals. P.'s work, essentially a stylized realism, is usually drawn from life in the hinterland of Rio de Janeiro.

Portland Vase. Hellenistic vase now in the British Museum, one of the finest examples known of *cameo glass. It is a work of the 1st c. B.C., probably made by Greeks in Alexandria. The figures are in white glass on a dark blue ground: their interpretation is still obscure. The vase was sold by the Barberini family to Sir William Hamilton who sold it to the duchess of Portland (1785). Many copies have been made, notably by Josiah Wedgwood in jasperware and by John Northwood in cameo glass. In 1845 the vase was smashed deliberately by a maniac; it was not successfully repaired until 1948.

Portrait of a Lady (1881). Novel by Henry *James.

Portrait of the Artist as a Young Man (1916). Novel by James *Joyce.

position. (1) The technique of instruments of the violin family requires that the left hand be at certain 'p.s' on the finger-board to reach high notes or simplify the fingering in certain passages. (2) The *trombone slide is said to have 7 'p.s' of extension.

positions. All classical ballet technique is based on 5 positions for the feet and arms (see diagram).

positive organ (from Latin *positus*, 'placed'). Medieval term for a small, stationary as opposed to *portative organ; the term came to mean a chamber organ or a manual on a large organ.

Possessed, The (1873). Novel by *Dostoyevsky.

posset-pot. A low cylindrical vessel with 2 loop handles and a curving spout springing from the base; posset, which often contained sack, was frequently taken by invalids. Some early examples of the 17th c. bear the raven's head mark associated with Ravenscroft. The type persisted into the 18th c.

Post (Poost) Frans (*c.* 1612–80). Dutch landscape painter who lived in Brazil (1637–44), painting scenes there. On his return he became a member of the Haarlem Guild of Painters (1646), and painted landscapes of the Netherlands. In the Amsterdam Mus. are several Brazilian landscapes, unusual and rare documents of life in South America at that time.

poster. Form of graphic art with antecedents in antiquity, in signboards, handbills, playbills, woodcuts, etc., but assuming its modern form and requirements (simple design, bold colours, etc.) with the invention of colour *lithography. Since *Toulouse-Lautrec's famous p.s, many artists (e.g. Picasso, Matisse, Chagall) have designed and executed them, and some (e.g. McKnight-Kauffer) have specialized in them. The p. is the only form in which the general public have without difficulty accepted such 20th-c. artistic developments as expressionism, cubism and abstraction.

post horn. Small natural horn roughly the same pitch as a trumpet, originally used by the guards of stage-coaches. The famous *P. H. Gallop* was written by the 19th-c. cornet virtuoso Koenig.

post-impressionism. Term coined in England to describe the artists exhibiting in an exhibition in the Grafton Galleries in 1910; they included Cézanne, Manet, Gauguin, Van Gogh, Seurat, Matisse, Derain, Rouault and Picasso. The term does not imply any similarity of style, although it is true that all these artists reacted against the impressionist preoccupation with visual appearances.

Posto, Il (1961). Film directed by E. *Olmi.

Poston Elizabeth (1905–). English ed. of 17th- and 18th-c. music, and composer much influenced by Peter Warlock and Elizabethan composers. Her works include: *The Nativity* for voices and strings (1951), sonata for violin and piano (1928) and *Sonatina* for wind instruments and piano (1952).

post-romantic. Term used of some music of such late 19th-c. composers as Mahler. In p.-r. works the orchestral resources are vast and the harmonic idiom follows from Wagner.

Pot Heindrick Gerritsz (*c.* 1585–1657). Dutch painter of portraits, genre and historical subjects, and possibly the pupil of Carel van Mander, although his work was much influenced by that of Frans Hals. He painted members of the Royal Family while visiting London (1631–3) and was director of the Haarlem Guild of Painters (1626–35). There is a portrait of King Charles I in the Louvre.

Potgieter Everhardus Johannes (1808–75). Dutch poet and prose writer, an ed. of the romantic journals *De Muzen* and *De Gids*; his works stress the importance of national consciousness and constantly invoke 17th-c. Dutch greatness as an ideal.

Potocki Wacław (1625–96). Polish poet and moralist, author of the long epic poem *Wojna Chocimska* describing an episode during the Polish wars against the Turks. He also wrote 2 large colls of satiric anecdotes and sketches in verse.

Potter Frank Huddlestone (1845–87). English genre and landscape painter. Among his works is *The Music Lesson* (Walker A. Gal., Liverpool).

Potter Paulus (1625–54). Dutch landscape painter noted particularly for his realism, as in showing the famous urinating cow in *The Farm* (Hermitage). He studied under his father Pieter P. and then under Camphuysen and Jacob de Weth of Haarlem, and himself worked mainly in Amsterdam and at The Hague.

pottery. In the widest sense, any objects made from clay hardened by fire, and therefore including stoneware, china and porcelain; but as now used, the term excludes these vitrified or translucent products, applying only to opaque fired earthenware (faïence, maiolica, etc.).

Poulenc Francis (1899–1963). French composer, member of The *Six, meeting Satie in 1918; he was also a pianist and made several concert tours with the baritone Pierre Bernac. His music, neo-classical, sometimes witty, always graceful and well written, includes: the operas, *Les Dialogues des Carmelites* (1957) and the comic opera *Les Mamelles de Tiresias* (1944); the ballet *Les Biches* (1923; English, *The House Party*); orchestral music including an organ concerto; chamber music, often for wind instruments, and songs.

pounce. (1) Powdered cuttlefish or resin used to dry ink; later the term was transferred to black sand used for the same purpose–hence

The Portland Vase

Paulus Potter. *The Young Bull*

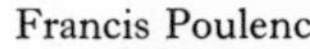

Francis Poulenc

Poster by McKnight-Kauffer for the ballet *Checkmate*

Poster by Toulouse-Lautrec; colour lithograph

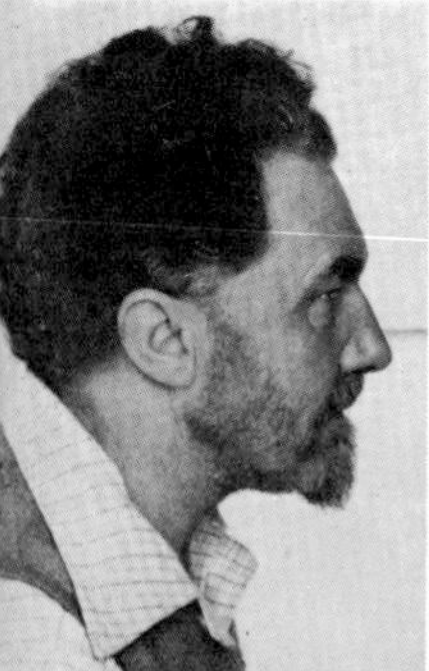

Ezra Pound

Pieter Pourbus. *J. van der Gheenste, Échevin of Bruges*

Gaspard Poussin. *Elias*

Nicolas Poussin. *Annunciation*

Nicolas Poussin. *The Inspiration of the Poet*

Nicolas Poussin. *Landscape with Polyphemus.* Also *Arcadia and colour plate 58

pounce-box in an inkstand. (2) A means of decorating silver by punching a design from the back or underpart of the surface.

Pound Ezra (1885–). U.S. poet. After wrongful dismissal from an academic post he settled in Europe, publ. his 1st book *A Lume Spento* (1908) in Venice. His literary activity in England, France and Italy was intense; the important writers he influenced and whose writings he indefatigably promoted included Eliot, Yeats and Hemingway. Meanwhile, he himself produced, in profusion, poetry, literary and social criticism, letters and trs. He visited the U.S. in 1939 to receive a D.Litt. at Hamilton College. In 1940 he began the series of Rome radio broadcasts which led to his indictment for treason, arrest and solitary military confinement in an open steel cage near Pisa, and remand in St Elizabeth's Hospital for the criminally insane (1946). He continued to write there at that time and after his release in 1958, when he returned to Italy. P.'s poetry is distinguished above all by its integration of the poetic forms, attitudes, quotations and trs from the poetry of past and alien cultures. His concept of ideograms attempts to use the principle of the Chinese ideogram, which often has several related meanings, with the phonetic Latin alphabet; fragments of lines are arranged in ideogrammatic shapes; the impact of the whole page is designed to convey the poetic idea. His major life work is the *Cantos*, constantly added to and including *Section: Rock Drill* (1956), *Thrones* (1959) and *Pisan Cantos* (1946). His important works also include the colls *Personae* (1909), *Cathay* (1915) and *Lustra* (1916), the trs.-cum-adaptation *Homage to Sextus Propertius* (1919) and the major long poem *Hugh Selwyn Mauberley* (1920), an extended attack on philistia which strongly influenced T. S. Eliot's *Waste Land*.

Pourbus Pieter (1510–84). Flemish painter of portraits (in an austere, naturalistic style) and religious subjects. He worked in Bruges. His son FRANS P. the Elder (1545–81) painted mainly portraits and religious subjects and studied under his father and F. Floris. His son, FRANS P. the Younger (1569–1622), was court painter at Mantua and painter to Marie de Médicis in Paris.

Poussin (Dughet) Gaspard (1615–75). French painter, born in Rome where in later life he settled. He was the brother-in-law and pupil of N. P., to whose influence he later added the warmth of Claude Lorrain. He became a leading landscape artist of the classical idiom, using figures and architectural features in carefully balanced settings.

Poussin Nicolas (1594–1665). The most important French painter of the 17th c. He settled in Rome after 1624 having lived in Paris in great poverty, returned in 1640 at the command of the king and Cardinal Richelieu as superintendent of the Academy but in 1642 left again for Rome. He led the life of an artist-philosopher, painting and meditating amongst the Roman ruins and hills. His work became the embodiment of French classicism. Held in great esteem by his contemporaries, when asked about his method, he once remarked in a letter 'I am forced by my nature towards the orderly.'

The greatness of P. lies in his relentless search after perfection, the seeking of solutions to problems of his own making and shunning easy success. His historical 'machines' constructed with great deliberation and after much experimentation with models, became the prototypes of the academic history picture. P. absorbed many influences in his work. In composition and the sculpturesque treatment of his figures Mantegna and Raphael were his masters, but even mythological subjects such as the Dresden *Flora* were seen and treated as part of life, seen with the eyes of modern man. A slow and gradual evolution can be traced in his work. The *Massacre of the Innocents* is one of the earliest still baroque compositions of the Roman period. From 1630 onwards his preoccupation with mythological subjects became marked and he became increasingly concerned with the study of nudes, as in the Louvre *Bacchanales*. The discovery of Titian and the study of antique cameos had a decisive influence on these paintings.
From 1638 P. entered a highly creative and inspired phase. The classical influence is paramount and can be seen in the *Bacchanal* (N.G., London) and the *Triumph of Pan* (Louvre). Here the unity of an ideal art and the fullness of life are completely realized. After 1648 Biblical subjects became the theme of a series of great history paintings. Landscape gains increasingly in importance and his brush drawings and pen and wash studies of sunsets and morning in the Campagna are some of his greatest and most lasting achievements. The feeling of stillness of poetry lifts the subject of *Landscape with a snake* (N.G., London) into the world of dreams constructed by a philosopher of vision. P.'s influence on most French painters from David to Cézanne has been immense.

Poussinisme: *Rubénisme

Powell Anthony (Dymoke) (1905–). English novelist. P.'s novels are social comedies; they include *A Question of Upbringing* (1951) and other titles of the series *The Music of Time.*

Powell Michael (1905–). British film director. His most famous early film is *49th Parallel* (1941). In 1943 he teamed up with Emeric Pressburger and made *The Life and Death of Colonel Blimp.* Following *A Matter of Life and Death* (1946), with its elaborate fantasy sequences and notable experiments with colour, they made *The Red Shoes* (1948), containing an interesting attempt at filmed ballet. This trend culminated in *The Tales of Hoffman* (1950), from Offenbach's opera—heavily ornate, over-heated, and using every device of trick photography. P.'s quality as a director is clearly seen in the brilliantly repulsive *Peeping Tom* (1959), a decadent shocker.

Powell and Moya. Leading firm of British architects; their work is always careful and often outstanding. The practice was formed on winning the Pimlico housing scheme in 1946 (main scheme completed 1962). Their most distinguished work includes hospitals for Swindon and Wythenshawe, residential accommodation for Brasenose College, Oxford and the Festival Theatre, Chichester.

Power Tyrone (1795–1841). Irish actor who gained popularity in Irish parts and also wrote some light comedies and farces. He made 2 visits to the U.S. His grandson TYRONE (1869–1931) also enjoyed great success there; and his son TYRONE (1913–58) was a well-known U.S. film star (*Lloyd's of London*, 1936; *The Eddy Duchin Story*, 1956).

Power and the Glory, The (1940). Novel by Graham *Greene.

Power of Darkness, The (1888). Play by Tolstoy.

Powys John Cowper (1872–1964). English novelist, critic and poet. His works, marked by extreme romanticism, include the novels *Wolf Solent* (1929) and *A Glastonbury Romance* (1933).

Powys Theodore Francis (1875–1953). English novelist. His books have highly fanciful themes but are religious in inspiration. The cultivatedly naïve style is derived from the Authorized Version, Bunyan and country dialects. The strange world of such books as *Mr Weston's Good Wine* (1927) is reminiscent of Stanley Spencer's paintings.

Poynter Sir Edward (1836–1919). English painter of historical and genre subjects in oil and watercolour. He studied under Gleyre in Paris, exhibited at the R.A. from 1859, became an R. A. in 1876, and succeeded Millais as president in 1896.

Pozzo Fra Andrea (1642–1709). Italian painter, art historian and architect; after becoming a Jesuit he produced much decorative religious work in Genoa which inspired Rubens. P.'s accomplished *trompe l'œil* effects can be seen in churches in Turin, Arezzo and Modena. He also built Laibach cathedral (1708) and the Univ. church in Vienna. His treatise *Perspectiva Pictorum* (1693–8) was extremely influential throughout Europe.

Pradon Nicolas (1632–98). French playwright. P.'s tragedy *Phèdre et Hippolyte* (1677) was written on the instructions of Racine's enemies and produced 2 days after his *Phèdre*, which it was intended to outshine.

Praed Winthrop Mackworth (1802–39). English humorous poet. His works include *The County Ball, Goodnight to the Season* and *The Red Fisherman.*

Praetorius Michael (1571–1621). German composer and music theorist. His very numerous compositions include major contributions to the music of the Evangelical Church, e.g. *Musae Sionae* (1605–10), but outside Germany he is remembered for his monumental treatise *Syntagma musicum* (1615–20). This deals with music from the earliest times but above all gives detailed information on contemporary performing methods and an exhaustive catalogue of contemporary instruments.

Pragmatism (1907). Book by William *James.

Pozzo. Ceiling of S. Ignace, Rome

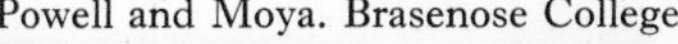

Powell and Moya. Brasenose College

School of Prague. *Annunciation* from the *Hohenfurth altarpiece*

Prandtauer. Melk

School of Prague. *Christ on the Mount of Olives*; from the *Wittingau altarpiece*

Prampolini. *Lines of Force in Space* (1914)

Prassinos. *Moon and Tree* (1957)

Prague, school of. Bohemian school of painting which flourished in the 2nd half of the 14th c. at the court of the Emperor Charles IV of Prague. He encouraged artists from Germany, France and Italy to work for him and a realistic style of painting was developed influenced by both the *soft style and the work of Giotto. Chief representatives of the school were Theodoric of Prague and the Masters of Hohenfurth and Wittingau.

Prague symphony. Nickname for Mozart's symphony in D, K.504; performed in Prague in 1787.

Praise of Folly, The (written 1509). Satire by *Erasmus.

Prampolini Enrico (1895–). Italian painter, sculptor and architect. He exhibited in Rome in 1918 at a showing of 'independent' art and became a principal painter in the futurist movement. Favoured by Mussolini, he held several official positions in connection with the arts.

Prandtauer Jakob (1660–1726). Austrian architect who built the monastery and church of Melk (1702–14) on a spectacular site overlooking the Danube.

Prassinos Mario (1916–). Turkish-born painter and illustrative artist of the French school. Influenced by the surrealists in the 1930s, he produced hallucinatory paintings after World War II. Later his colour became less strident, and more abstract and constructional in manner. He has illustrated *Contes Fantastiques* by Nodier, *Hérésiarque et Cie* by Apollinaire and *Mur* by Sartre.

Prati Giovanni (1814–84). Italian romantic poet and patriot. His very large output includes sonnets, lyrics, patriotic verse (*Canti Politici*, 1852); he was influenced by Byron, Carducci and Lamartine.

Pratolini Vasco (1913–). Italian novelist, the son of a waiter; P. is self-educated. His novels which describe poetically, yet truthfully the poor quarters of Florence, include *Il quartiere* (1945; *A Tale of Santa Croce*, 1952; also trs. as *The Naked Street*) and *Cronaca di poveri amanti* (1947; *A Tale of Poor Lovers*, 1949).

Pratt E(dwin) J(ohn) (1883–1964). Canadian poet whose work, e.g. the moving *Brebeuf and*

Pre-Columbian art. Maya ball-court marker

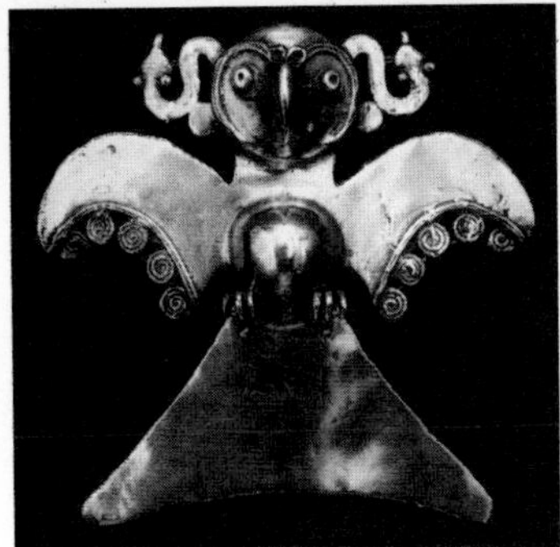

Pre-Columbian art. Gold pendant bird from Panama; cire-perdue

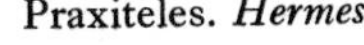

Praxiteles. *Hermes*

His Brethren (1940), written in traditional forms, has a robustness in its attitude to man and to the Canadian scene which was new in Canadian poetry.

Pratt Sir Roger (1620–84). English architect who designed Coleshill, Warwickshire (1650), one of the earliest English houses in the classical style (burnt down in 1952).

Praxiteles. Greek sculptor of the mid 4th c. B.C. Copies of his figures of young gods and goddesses survive, notably those of the famous Cnidian Aphrodite (at Munich and in the Vatican). P.'s style has soft contours and supple, almost languorous treatment of the human figure; he was a forerunner of Hellenistic art. He was also an innovator in portraying Aphrodite and other divine figures in the nude.

Précieuses ridicules, Les (1659). Play by Molière.

precisionism: *cubist-realism

Pre-Columbian art. The term refers to all forms of art (architecture, sculpture, pottery, metalwork, weaving, etc.) of all the successive Indian civilizations of Central America up to the time of the Spanish Conquest at the beginning of the 16th c., which completely destroyed them. Archaeological rediscovery of these cultures began in the 19th c. At the time of the Conquest the main civilizations were the Aztec, centred on the Valley of Mexico, the Maya in the Yucatan Peninsular, and the Inca, who held sway from the Andean Highlands down to the Peruvian coast. But the Aztec and Inca civilizations were late developments in the area compared to the antiquity of the Mayan. The Maya were remarkable for their advanced knowledge of astronomy and their invention of a method of recording dates and the names of gods, as well as for their remarkable stone temples built on top of high pyramids. Among the earliest monuments are the enormous pyramid temples of Teotihuacán in Central Mexico. Large stone statues and stelae abound throughout the entire area. Quantities of *cire-perdue gold ornaments survive, particularly in Colombia and the Andean Highlands. The range of pottery is vast; among the most famous is that of Mochica and Nasca found in Peru. The many examples of weaving from Paracas on the Peruvian coast are the finest in the world.

predella. The long narrow platform often less than 1 ft high which forms the base of an altarpiece. Also the paintings or reliefs executed on it. These are usually scenes from the lives of the saints depicted on the main panels of the altarpiece.

Predis (Predo) Ambrogio (1450/60–*c.* 1515). Milanese painter. Most of his datable works come from the years 1494–1502. A portrait of the Emperor Maximilian was painted in 1499. He probably painted the side panels of the altar for S. Francesco, Milan, of which Leonardo's *Madonna of the Rocks* formed the centre-piece.

Predis Cristoforo di (d. 1486). Milanese miniature painter, and probably the father of Ambrogio de Predis. A portrait of Galeazzo Maria Sforza is in the Wallace Coll.

Prejudices (1919–27). Coll. of essays (6 series) by H. L. Mencken.

prelude. A piece of music usually introductory to another, as for example the p.s J. S. Bach wrote to his fugues. The term indicates no special form (except in the *chorale prelude) and was applied by Wagner to the overture of his operas *Tristan* and *The Mastersingers* and by Chopin to short independent piano pieces. The term originated in the improvisatory pieces that soloists would play in order to 'warm up' or to make sure the instrument was in tune.

Prelude, The (1850). Poem by *Wordsworth.

Prélude à l'Après-Midi d'un Faune. Poem by *Mallarmé which inspired *Debussy to write his symphonic work of the same name.

Préludes, Les. Symphonic poem by *Liszt.

Première Nuit, La (1958). Short film directed by G. *Franju.

Preminger Otto (1906–). Austrian-born U.S. film director. P. worked as an actor for Max Reinhardt and took over from him as director of the Josefstadt Theatre. He started making films in Vienna in 1931 and in Hollywood in 1936, but his 1st important film was *Laura* (1944). Since then, and especially since he started as an independent producer/director with *The Moon is Blue* (1953;

Pre-Columbian art. Colossal statue of the Aztec earth goddess Coatlicue

Pre-Columbian art. Maya feathered serpent column

Pre-Columbian art. Inca stirrup-spout jar

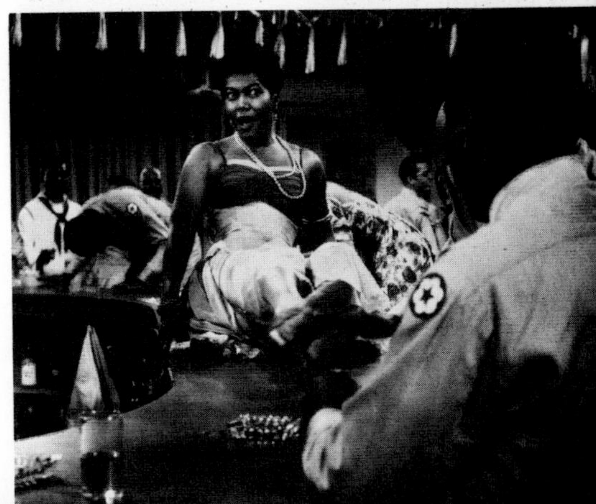

Preminger. Pearl Bailey in *Carmen Jones*

Jacques Prévert

The abbé Prévost

Prendergast. *Notre-Dame, Paris* (*c.* 1910)

Pre-Raphaelites. D. G. Rossetti, woodcut on title-page of his sister's *Goblin Market*

Pre-Raphaelites. Millais, *Lorenzo and Isabella*

from F. Hugh Herbert's play), his subjects have characteristically been taken from best-selling novels or hit plays, e.g. *Forever Amber* (1947; novel by Kathleen Windsor), *The Fan* (1949; from Oscar Wilde), *The Man With the Golden Arm* (1956; novel by Nelson Algren). P.'s technique is to present characters and actions rather than show his own feelings about them. His films place the onus of judgement upon the audience, from which he demands a high level of alertness, particularly in his most recent films like *Exodus* (1960; novel by Leon Uris), a 4-hour film composed of a number of interlocking narratives of the Israeli struggle against British and Arabs, and *Advise and Consent* (1962; novel by Allen Drury), a complex narrative about U.S. politics with at least a dozen main characters. P.'s films include: *Daisy Kenyon* (1947), *River of No Return* (1954), *Carmen Jones* (1954; a modernized Negro version of Bizet's *Carmen*, lyrics by Hammerstein), *Bonjour Tristesse* (1957; novel by Françoise Sagan), *St Joan* (1957; from G. B. Shaw), *Anatomy of a Murder* (1959; novel by Robert Traver) and *In Harm's Way* (1965).

Prendergast Maurice Brazil (1859–1924). U.S. painter, the leading pioneer of post-impressionism in America. He was a member of The *Eight and an exhibitor at the Armory Show. He studied in Paris where he was influenced by impressionism, from which he developed a semi-abstract style consisting of touches of colour interwoven with decorative tapestry-like effects.

Preobrajenska Olga (1871–1962). Russian dancer of the Imperial School, St Petersburg and pupil of Ivanov. After the Revolution she established a school in Paris, an important centre of teaching in the Russian tradition in Western Europe. Her pupils included the *baby ballerinas.

Pre-Raphaelites. A group of 7 young English painters and sculptors, D. G. Rossetti, John Everett Millais, Holman Hunt, Thomas Woolner, W. M. Rossetti, J. Collinson and F. G. Stephens. They wished to revive in British painting the purity of art before Raphael and hoped to achieve their aim by clarity of colour and line, and simple not grandiose subjects. Their realistic treatment of Biblical subjects provoked indignation, but they were defended by John Ruskin. They remained as a group from 1848 to the early 1850s, sometimes signing their work with the initials P.R.B. (Pre-Raphaelite Brotherhood) but despite its short life (their periodical *The Germ* went to only 4 numbers), the movement affected several succeeding painters, e.g. Ford Madox Brown.

presbytery. E. part of the chancel, reserved for the clergy; or a priest's house.

presto. The Italian word for 'fast', used as a musical direction; the superlative PRESTISSIMO indicates that the passage is to be performed as fast as possible.

Preti Mattia (also called 'Il Calabrese') (1613–99). Italian painter and pupil of Guercino. He gained a reputation as a decorative artist, painting religious scenes in several churches in Rome in 1657, then in the Carthusian chapel in Naples, and also frescoes for the cathedral at Valletta, Malta.

Prévert Jacques (1900–). French poet, author of *Paroles* (1946; *Selections from Paroles*, 1958) and other colls of verse which owe something to surrealism, treating metaphysical themes with gaiety and wit. He wrote many notable film scripts, e.g. for *Carné.

Previtali Andrea (*c.* 1470–1528). Italian painter and pupil of Giovanni Bellini, whose style he followed closely. His fine colouring and good landscape compositions led to attribution of his work to Giorgione (including the works *Christ Ascending from Hell* and *The Crossing of the Red Sea*). His chef d'oeuvre was the altar-piece at S. Spirito, Bergamo.

Prévost (Antoine-François) the abbé (1697–1763). French novelist. P. was a soldier, became a Benedictine, fled (1728) to Holland and later to England, was reconciled with the Church and (apart from another short period of exile) spent the rest of his life writing. His prolific production includes histories and trs (notably of Samuel Richardson's *Pamela*, 1742) as well as fiction; but he is remembered for the one book, *L'Histoire du chevalier des Grieux et de Manon Lescaut* (1731), which appeared as part of his *Mémoires d'un homme de qualité* (1728–31). When publ. separately in 1733 *Manon Lescaut* was an immediate success. It is the story of des Grieux's disastrous passion for Manon, for whom he defies his parents and sacrifices his rank, for a time even practising as a card-sharper; though Manon loves him, she

J. B. Priestley

Primitives. Rousseau, *Peasant Marriage*

is led into infidelities by her need for luxury and distraction. After many adventures des Grieux is parted from Manon only by her death.

Prévost Marcel (1862–1941). French novelist, author of *Les Demi-vierges* (1894) and other psychological novels.

Price Sir Uvedale (1750–1824). English writer and coll. of bronzes and coins. In *An Essay on the Picturesque, as compared with the Sublime and the Beautiful* (1794) P. sought to define and describe the *'picturesque', which he regarded as a distinct category of aesthetics.

Pride and Prejudice (1813). Novel by Jane *Austen.

Priestley J(ohn) B(oynton) (1894–). Popular English novelist and playwright. His best-known works are the novels *The Good Companions* (1929), the story of a theatrical troupe, and *Angel Pavement* (1930). He has written a number of successful plays, including *Laburnam Grove* (1933), and, in recent years, much social criticism.

prima donna. This Italian term meaning 'first lady' is used of the leading female singer (usually a soprano) in an opera.

Primary (1960). Film directed by R. *Leacock and others.

Primaticcio Francesco (1504–70). Italian artist from Bologna, often called 'Il Bologna', or, in France, 'Le Primatice', P. was the leader of the 1st school of Fontainebleau after the death of *Rosso Fiorentino. He worked on the Palazzo del Tè, Mantua, under Giulio Romano and developed a mannerist style influenced above all by Parmigianino. He was invited to Fontainebleau by Francis I in 1532 and assisted Rosso on the decorations of the Galerie François I. His greatest work, executed with Niccolò dell' *Abbate, the decorations of the Galerie d'Ulysse, was destroyed, as were most of his large decorative schemes at Fontainebleau. An exception is the Chambre de la Duchesse d'Étampes (1541–44). Here the flamboyant decorative style of the 1st school of *Fontainebleau is found in its fullest phase. P.'s talent as a draughtsman can be seen in the drawings for the decorations preserved in the Louvre. *Ulysses and Penelope* (Coll. Wildenstein, New York) is a good example of his mannerist style in painting. P. was also a sculptor and architect, but little of this work remains.

Primavera (*c.* 1478). Highly complex compound allegory of Spring and of the Virtues painted by *Botticelli.

primitive art. The term refers to the art of primitive peoples, i.e. peoples with a comparatively low standard of technological development, and should be carefully distinguished from the art of the *primitives. In the early 20th c., p. a., particularly from *Africa and *Oceania, began to have a profound influence on Western painting and sculpture (*cubism, *Picasso) which still continues today (*Lipchitz, *Moore).

primitives. Name given to certain artists, usually self-taught, whose technique is by academic standards gauche, and whose work is sometimes naïve in approach and vision. Despite these 'shortcomings' the work of such great p.s as 'Le Douanier' Rousseau often has great power and inventiveness.

Prince Igor. Opera by *Borodin with libretto by the composer and others; 1st performance at St Petersburg in 1890. Dances from it were used for a ballet with choreography by Fokine and décor by Roerich; 1st performance 1909.

principal. Formerly the name (Italian *principale*) for a low-lying trumpet part, now the name for an organ stop.

principal boy. The chief character in pantomime, e.g. Aladdin and Prince Charming, traditionally played by an attractive girl. This particular tradition was established in the Drury Lane pantomimes of the 1880s but transvestism has been known in theatricals since the Roman Saturnalia.

Principia Mathematica (1686–7). Usual title of *Newton's *Philosophiae Naturalis Principia Mathematica.*

Pringle Thomas (1789–1834). Scottish pioneer and poet in South Africa; his *Afar in the Desert* (1824) and *Ephemerides* (1828), the earliest English South African literature, uses his experiences in the bush.

Primaticcio. Ceiling of the Galerie d'Ulysse; engraving by du Cerceau

Primaticcio. Stucco decoration with figures (Fontainebleau)

Matthew Prior: painting by Kneller

Profile perdu.
Picasso, *Study* (1906)

Prokofiev: drawing by Matisse

Playbill for the Promenade Concerts, 1905

Prinz Friedrich von Homburg (publ. 1821). Play by Heinrich *Kleist.

Prior Matthew (1664–1721). English poet, a diplomatist popularly thought to be responsible for the Treaty of Utrecht (1713). P.'s best verses are short occasional pieces.

Prishvin Mikhail Mikhailovich (1873–1954). Soviet writer, author of many stories and sketches which display his love of nature, including *Nature's Calendar* (1925; 1951) and *Jen Sheng: the Root of Life* (1932; 1936). He has also written an autobiographical novel, *Kashchey's Chain* (1926–9).

Prisoner of Chillon, The (1816). Poem by Byron.

Prisoner of Zenda, The (1894). Novel of adventure by Anthony *Hope.

Private Lives (1930). Play by Noël Coward.

Prix de Rome: *Rome prize

Procaccini Ercole (the Elder) (1515–95). Italian painter who worked extensively in the churches of Bologna. He moved to Milan and founded an academy of painting which had a high reputation. His son Giulio Cesare P. (*c.* 1570–1625) was a notable sculptor and decorative painter, and another son, Camillo P. (1546/51–1629), painted frescoes in Milan cathedral and also in other churches in that city.

process work: *film techniques

producer. In the theatre the term was used until recent years to describe the person responsible for the artistic interpretation of a play, conducting rehearsals and directing the actors. He is now called the director; the p., as in films, presents the work or provides the money to back it.

profil perdu (French, 'lost profile'). Term used to describe the head when turned so far from the spectator that the profile of the face is lost and only the outline of the cheek is seen.

programme music. This is music designed to represent some extra-musical theme, such as a landscape, a hunting scene or a dramatically developing human situation. Music of this kind has been known at least since the medieval caccia but in the 19th c. it became a major musical genre. Beethoven's *Pastoral symphony*, describing a day in the country, is an obvious example but with Berlioz's music the programme became more complex, e.g. the *Symphonie Fantastique* which describes the emotions of a love-affair.

Prokofiev Serge (1891–1953). Russian composer. Born into a cultured family, P. began composing very early with a fertility and a precociousness that never left him. After studying with Glière he entered the St Petersburg Conservatory in 1904; his teachers there were Liadov and Rimsky-Korsakov. Very soon he was giving sensational public piano recitals of audacious grotesqueries. In 1918 he left Russia for a series of concert tours in the U.S. and elsewhere. In 1920 he settled in France, working for a time with Diaghilev and becoming known as music's '*enfant terrible*'. He returned to the U.S.S.R. in 1932 and continued writing for the stage and also for films (collaborating with S. M. Eisenstein). Illness plagued him from 1945 until his death in 1953. P. was obsessed with originality. He could not stand routine, though he was very meticulous. His themes undergo little 'development' and are rarely repeated exactly; sequences are rare. He was inspired by movement (most of his large-scale orchestral music consists of reworkings of material from opera, ballet or film scenes). He was generally aware of expressing some concrete experience. He conveyed the greatest variety of passions by a jagged tunefulness. His most vivid forms often approximated to those of tableaux. He once characterized his musical style as having the following elements: the classical (or neoclassical); innovation (firstly in harmony and later in orchestration and stage technique); the toccata or motor element (the least important) and the lyrical (underrated). The grotesque element or what he preferred to call 'scherzoness' he graded into 'jest', 'laughter' and 'mockery'. Influences which he acknowledged include Beethoven, Schumann, Glinka, Borodin, Mussorgsky and Rimsky-Korsakov. His principal works include: the operas *The Love for Three Oranges* (1921) the *Flaming Angel* (1928), *The Duenna* (1946), after Sheridan, and *War and Peace* (1946); the ballets *Pas d'Acier* (1927), *The Prodigal Son* (1929), *Cinderella* (1945), *Romeo and Juliet* (1940) and *The Stone Flower* (1954); the well-known *Classical symphony* (1918) and 6 others; 2 violin concertos; 5 piano concertos and 9 piano sonatas; the cantata *Seven They are Seven* (1924); *Overture on Hebrew themes*; and the film music *Lieutenant Kije* (1933), *Alexander Nevsky* (1938) and *Ivan the Terrible* (1942–5).

Prolecult. Soviet administrative body concerned with the arts, founded in 1906 by pre-Revolutionaries and made effective in 1917 with the Bolshevik Revolution. In its early years P. was associated with the experimentalism of Russian *avant-garde*–above all, the attempts to unite art and industry. In 1932, in common with all other artistic bodies, P. was incorporated into the Union of Artists.

prologue. Introductory monologue or short dramatic piece, related to and preceding the play.

Promenade Concerts. A summer season of concerts in the Royal Albert Hall, London, sponsored by the B.B.C.; the 'promenade' is the area of cheap standing room. Forerunners include the popular concerts given by *Jullien at Drury Lane but the modern 'Proms' began under Sir H. *Wood at the Queen's Hall, London, in 1895, being continued by the B.B.C. from 1927.

Promessi Sposi, I (1827). Historical novel by Alessandro *Manzoni.

Prometheus Bound. Play by *Aeschylus.

Prometheus Unbound (1820). Verse drama by *Shelley.

Propertius (Sextus) (*c.* 50–*c.* 16 B.C.). Roman elegist. Born at Assisi of middle-class parents, he came young to Rome for his education, took up with the courtesan Hostia and for her, under the name of 'Cynthia', wrote most of his verses. His manner is abstruse and recondite after the model of mythological erudition set by his master, the Alexandrian Callimachus, but many critics from antiquity to the present have considered him the best of the Roman elegists for the strength of his verse and compressed brilliance of his style. After the publ. of his 1st book *c.* 30 B.C. he was patronized by Maecenas and reluctantly handled a number of public themes. 4 books, somewhat mangled, survive.

The Propylaea.
Also *Acropolis

Marcel Proust

Propylaea Athens. The monumental entrance to the Acropolis, built by Mnesicles (437–432 B.C.). It consists of a front and rear portico (Doric) and a colonnaded passageway between (Ionic).

proscenium arch. In the theatre, the arch at the front of the stage which divides the stage from the audience. It forms the '4th wall' of the stage and a frame for the action. The name proscenium was in the Elizabethan theatre applied to the fore-stage, and the p., as now understood, is of course absent from *theatre-in-the-round.

prosody. The science of the technical structure of poems, i.e. of the use and effects of metre, rhyme, alliteration, etc.

Proudhon Pierre-Joseph (1809–65). French political writer, an early Socialist; his most famous statement was 'property is theft'.

Proust Marcel (1871–1922). The foremost French novelist of the 20th c. Half-Jewish (on his mother's side), he belonged to the prosperous, professional Parisian middle class. He was delicate and asthmatic from childhood, and at first led the life of a dilettante and diner-out, frequenting aristocratic circles. He did not settle down to write his major work until he was well over 30, but it was to occupy him ceaselessly until his death. He was slow in starting, perhaps because he was afraid of his own originality and needed the example of Ruskin's style (he trs. 2 of his books: *La Bible d'Amiens*, 1904, from *Our Fathers have told us* and *Sésame et les lys*, 1906; *Sesame and Lilies*) to encourage him to believe in the justifiability of his long sentences, and also perhaps because he could not reveal his homosexuality until after the death of his mother, to whom he was devoted. The last part of his life was spent, under the care of a faithful servant, mainly in bed in a cork-lined room, where he seems to have subsisted largely on coffee made with milk. This strange existence made him a legend in the literary circles of his day, but the full extent of his achievement was not realized until after his death.

His early works, *Les Plaisirs et les jours* (1896; *Pleasures and Regrets*..., 1950) and *Pastiches et mélanges* (publ. in book form in 1919) display an interesting minor talent, and are revealing when seen in the light of what was to come later. Publ. posth. were an unfinished novel, *Jean Santeuil* (1952; *Jean Santeuil*. . . , 1955) and a remarkable collection of critical articles and sketches called *Contre Sainte-Beuve* . . . (1954; *By Way of Sainte-Beuve*, 1958). They show him moving towards the conception of *À la recherche du temps perdu*, the long novel cycle in 7 sections–*Du Côté de chez Swann* (*Swann's Way*, 1922), *A l'ombre des jeunes filles en fleurs* (*Within a Budding Grove*, 1924), *Le Côté de Guermantes* (*The Guermantes Way*, 1925), *Sodome et Gomorrhe* (*Cities of the Plain*, 1929), *La Prisonnière* (*The Captive*, 1929), *Albertine disparue* (*The Sweet Cheat Gone*, 1930), *Le Temps retrouvé* (*Time Regained*, 1931)–first publ. between 1913 and 1927. This immensely complicated work is, basically, an account of the narrator Marcel's discovery of his artistic vocation. At first, he thinks he has no literary gift and that time is bearing all his experiences away unused but then, through a series of acts of involuntary memory connected with sensation, he realizes he can recapture the past and enshrine it in language. In so doing, he produces a wonderful gallery of characters, drawn from all levels of society and analysed with a minuteness, a humour and a poetry that no novelist has surpassed. The main personage is, of course, the narrator himself, who represents perhaps the most complete picture of a modern consciousness to be found in literature. P. has his limitations; his obsession with homosexuality tends to invade all the latter part of the work and, being himself a neurotic contemplative, he has little to say about the everyday world of action. Yet these shortcomings are brilliantly offset by the sheer force of his genius.

Prout Ebenezer (1835–1909). English composer and musical theorist who wrote standard works on instrumentation, harmony, counterpoint and fugue, stressing that fugal analysis should begin with the works of Bach rather than a preconceived academic framework. His theories have in turn been criticized for their academicism.

Prouvé Jean (1901–). French builder using pressed metal techniques. One of the leaders in the field of prefabrication, he has produced a series of buildings and components which have given form to his chosen material. The cladding of the Maison du Peuple at Clichy (1939) was an early example of true curtain walls.

Jean and Henri Prouvé, and André Sive. Experimental houses, Meudon (1954)

Prouvé. Refreshment room, Evian (completed in 1957)

Psaltery: from a painting by Memlinc

Psalter from Canterbury (mid 8th c.)

Prud'hon. *The Empress Josephine*

Provençal culture. From the 10th c. a flourishing culture developed in S. France. *Guillaume d'Acquitaine was the first of a long line of poets–the troubadours–who wrote in the *langue d'oc* dialect of the region, producing the earliest French lyric poetry–short, elaborately-wrought pieces on the themes of '*amour courtois*' ('courtly love'). This was a concept of love which profoundly influenced the literature and life of Europe. Woman was idealized; the lover (who could not be her husband, according to the courts of love) was her devoted servant, promised his ultimate reward but first to be subjected to long and arduous trials which would prove his worth. P. c. was in effect destroyed by the Albigensian Crusades (early 13th c.) but its traditions were continued, e.g. by the *trouvères and *mastersingers and are strongly reflected in Chaucer's works. For the Provençal revival of the 19th c. *Félibrige.

proverbes dramatiques. Dramatic sketches illustrating some proverbial saying, written for private–occasionally public–performance; they originated in the French *salons* of the 17th c. Alfred de Musset wrote many famous p. d.

Proverbs. One of the books of the *Bible (Old Testament) containing colls of maxims and sayings traditionally ascribed to Solomon but probably from several sources and periods.

Provincetown Players (1915–29). Important U.S. experimental theatre group in Provincetown, Mass., later in New York; founded by the writer George Cram Cook (1873–1924) and his wife Susan *Glaspell. It performed the works of many native writers, notably the 1st plays of Eugene *O'Neill.

Provincial Letters (1656–7). Pamphlets by *Pascal.

Provo(o)st Jan (*c.* 1465–1529). Flemish painter of religious subjects, pupil of S. Marmion. He worked in Antwerp and Bruges. David and Massys were the chief influences on his style until 1521, when he met Dürer.

Prudentius Aurelius Clemens (348–*c.* 410). The finest early Christian Latin poet. His works include the political-religious work *Contra Symmachum* and the *Psychomachia,* on the conflict between Christianity and paganism.

Pryde and Nicholson ('Beggarstaff Brothers'). Poster for *Harper's Magazine.* Also *Chesterton

Prud'hon Pierre-Paul (1758–1823). French painter and designer. He admired the works of Correggio in Rome (1781–7) and, in the age of David, developed a softly modelled, emotionally romantic style. His portraits of the Empress Josephine and those of his pupil Mlle Constance Mayer, to whom he was deeply attached, are among his most charming works. He also executed large decorative compositions, e.g. *Crime Pursued by Vengeance and Justice* (Louvre). In a neo-classical idiom he designed the furniture and décor for the bridal suite of the Empress Marie-Louise.

Prufrock, The Love-Song of J. Alfred (1915). Poem by T. S. Eliot.

Prus Bolesław. Pseud. of Aleksander Głowacki (1847–1912), Polish novelist and short-story writer who wrote simple, clear and expressive prose. *Placówka* (1886; *The Outpost,* 1921) deals with the Polish peasant's love for his land; *Lalka* (1890) gives a vivid picture of middle-class Warsaw; *Emancypantki* (1894) discusses the position of women in society; *Faraon* (1896; *The Pharaoh and the Priest,* 1902) is a political novel set in ancient Egypt.

Pryde James (1866–1941). Scottish painter, with William Nicholson responsible for the posters of the 'Beggarstaff Brothers'. He painted romantic architectural compositions enveloped in an aura of mystery and drama with disproportionately small figures and in many cases a large bed as the central feature.

Przybós Julian (1901–). Polish poet and critic, one of the leaders of the Awangarda movement. Writes short, powerful lyrics, highly charged with metaphor, celebrating the modern city and technical progress.

Przybyszewski Stanisław (1868–1927). Polish playwright, novelist and critic, one of the pioneers of the neo-romantic Young Poland movement. He came under the influence of Strindberg and the German 'modernists'. He propagated 'art for art's sake' and laid a great emphasis on the erotic. Considered a precursor of Polish expressionism, he is more important as an influence than as an original writer.

Psalms, Book of. The great coll. of sacred songs in the Old Testament; many are ascribed to King David. They contain some of the most magnificent Hebrew verse, have a fundamental part in Christian liturgies and have been set innumerable times by Christian composers.

Psalter. The Book of Psalms bound as a separate vol. In the middle ages copies of the P. were often given the most lavish illumination.

psaltery. Now obsolete plucked stringed instrument, similar to the *zither family.

Psycho (1960). Film directed by *Hitchcock.

Ptushko Alexander (1900–). Russian animated-film director. P. made a number of films, both sound and silent. *The New Gulliver* (1935), ingeniously combined puppets and an actor. *The Stone Flower* (1946) was a version in colour of a Russian legend. Both this and *Sadko* (1952) showed inventiveness of setting and realistic animation.

Public Enemy (1931). Film directed by W. *Wellman.

Puccini Giacomo (1858–1924). Italian opera composer of the *verismo who enjoyed a popularity unequalled either before or since. He combined a powerful melodic gift with an intuitive dramatic sense for a good libretto. P.'s art lay in holding back the melody, allowing fragments to appear and disappear, juxtaposed in unexpected keys, like an enormous development section, creating great dramatic tension which could only be relieved by the tune finally bursting out. His 1st great success was *Manon Lescaut* (1893) after the Abbé *Prévost with libretto by several collaborators. There followed his masterpiece *La Bohème* (1896) with libretto by G. Giacosa and L. Illica, after *Murger; sensitive liaison between librettists and composer produced a poignant tragedy of student life. P.'s other main works are: *Madame Butterfly* (1904) libretto by Giacosa and Illica after *Belasco; *Tosca* (1900) libretto by Giacosa and Illica after Sardou; *The Girl of the Golden West* (1910) libretto by G. Civinini and C. Zangarini after *Belasco; and the unfinished *Turandot* (1926), libretto by G. Adami and R. Simoni, set in ancient imperial China.

Pudd'nhead Wilson, The Tragedy of (1894). Novel by Mark *Twain.

Pudovkin Vsevolod I. (1893–1953). Russian film director. P. was from 1922 a script writer and actor at *Kuleshov's Experimental Laboratory. His famous books on film technique and acting are partly reports of Kuleshov's work, but include P.'s ideas on editing, acting and the portrayal of character and emotion. P.'s theories had a wider effect than those of *Eisenstein; even Hitchcock acknowledges that his editing technique is indebted to P. P.'s 1st film, *Mechanics of the Brain* (1925), presented the discoveries of Pavlov. His 1st long fiction film was *Mother* (1926) from Gorky, in which he used visual metaphors parallel to the action–the final riot led by the heroine to allow her son to escape from prison is intercut with shots of ice on a river breaking up. Unlike the silent films of Eisenstein, P.'s use an individual hero to represent the proletariat rather than using the masses themselves as a corporate hero. P.'s most famous films after *Mother* are *The End of St Petersburg* (1927), *Storm Over Asia* (1928) or *Descendant of Genghis Khan*, the title under which P.'s sound version was released after the war, and *Deserter* (1933). He continued making films until his death and acted in *Ivan the Terrible* (part I).

Puget Pierre (1620–94). French sculptor. His essentially baroque style, its vigour and movement, made him unacceptable at court, where more restrained and classical work was admired.

Pugh Clifton (1924–). Australian painter. He is a fine portraitist in the 'new humanist' style but an awareness of violence is frequently revealed in this aspect of his work as well as in his paintings of Australian fauna.

Pugin Auguste-Charles (1762–1832). French architect who fled to England in the French Revolution and worked as a draughtsman for Nash. He was one of the 1st men in England to study Gothic architecture seriously and assisted Nash when he was commissioned to do work in that style.

Pugin Augustus Welby Northmore (1812–52). English architect, the son of Auguste-Charles P. P. was converted to Roman Catholicism and in 1836 publ. *Contrasts*, advocating Gothic as the only truly Christian style. More than anyone else, he provided the serious ethical-religious justification for the Gothic revival. Ruskin and Morris both owed much to him. He designed many churches himself but they

Giacomo Puccini

Pugin. Interior of St Giles's church, Cheedle

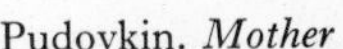

Pudovkin. *Mother*

Puget. *Caryatids*

Pulcinella: Meissen figure

Punch and Judy show

String puppet

Rod puppet

Purbeck marble; from Salisbury cathedral

are all somewhat disappointing. His profoundest influence was exerted through his books, designs for furniture, stained glass, etc., and his interior decoration. P. collaborated with C. Barry on the Houses of Parliament, designing much of the elevation and being responsible for the detailing and the decoration.

Pugnani Giulio Gaetano (1731–98). Italian composer in the galante style and virtuoso violinist, important as the teacher of *Viotti.

Pulci Luigi (1432–84). Florentine poet and author of one of the masterpieces of Italian humorous literature, *Morgante Maggiore* (1483; 'Morgan the Giant'), a semi-burlesque version of the epic of Charlemagne, in 28 cantos. P. also wrote a number of fine letters to his patron, Lorenzo de' Medici.

Pulcinella. Character in the Italian **commedia dell'arte*, from which *Stravinsky derived the title for his ballet.

Pulitzer Joseph (1847–1911). U.S. newspaper-owner, a Hungarian emigrant who endowed Columbia Univ., New York with $2,000,000 to set up a school of journalism and award Pulitzer prizes for outstanding U.S. literary works; they have become the most important U.S. award.

Punch and Judy. A glove-puppet entertainment dating from about 1800 in which the character of Punch, hunch-backed and hook-nosed, probably derives from Pulcinella of the *commedia dell'arte*. Other characters in the traditional story are Judy, the Baby, Vice or Clown, and the Beadle who has become a policeman in recent times. Very popular in the 19th c., shows are now comparatively rare.

puppet. The most intricate p., the 'marionette', has all its limbs articulated and is operated from above by strings. The 'rod p.' is similar to this but is operated from below. In the 'glove p.', as used in *Punch and Judy shows, the hand goes inside the puppet, the thumb, index and middle fingers operating its arms and head. Other kinds of puppet are found in the *Shadow Theatre and *Toy Theatre.

Purbeck marble. A kind of very dark limestone resembling marble, found at Purbeck, Dorset; it was widely used for decoration in *Early English architecture, e.g. Salisbury cathedral, since the colour contrast between P. m. and the lighter stone of the body of the building made possible the achievement of delicate linear effects.

Purcell Daniel (*c.* 1660–1717). English composer, brother of H. P.; he composed much stage music.

Purcell Henry (1659–95). English composer. P. was a child in the Chapel Royal (a pupil there of H. Cooke and Pelham Humphrey, also receiving lessons from Blow); keeper of the royal musical instruments and a copyist at Westminster Abbey; court composer (1677) for the violins; organist at the Chapel Royal (1682). P.'s music has an unsurpassed strength of expression; a command of the hearer's passions, extorting and persuading exaltation or sadness, bringing delight and admiration and enlivening the spirit. He is master of the grand, pompous, ceremonial mood, the poet of meditation of a delicate and moving expressiveness. From an early mastery of the English viol fantasy he went on to an exploration of the Italian instrumental techniques and a set of pieces in the still young form of the trio sonata, stating it as his intention to introduce the Italian style to England. All P.'s work is stamped by his rhythmic inventiveness, his unparalleled gift for the setting of English words to music and his bold chromatic harmonies. His influence on Handel is clear.

P. was a composer to the occasion. His works include: the opera *Dido and Aeneas* (1689), composed for a Chelsea girls' school, with libretto by Nahum Tate dealing with Aeneas' abandonment of Dido, Queen of Carthage–it contains the exquisite 'Dido's lament', P.'s masterpiece in a genre of which he was a master, composition on a *ground; music to the play-operas *Dioclesian* (1690), the text based on Beaumont and Fletcher; *King Arthur* (1691), text by Dryden; *The Fairy Queen* (1692), an anon. adaptation of Shakespeare's *A Midsummer Night's Dream*; *The Tempest* (1695) by Shadwell after Shakespeare; *The Indian Queen* (1695) by Dryden and R. Howard. Some of his finest music occurs in the 6 *Birthday Odes* for Queen Mary (1689–94), the *Odes for St Cecilia's Day*, and his numerous church anthems. P.'s instrumental music includes the great viol fantasies, and *Sonatas* in 3 and 4 parts for violins (1683 and 1697 respectively), a 4-part chaconne and a sonata for violin and harpsichord.

Purgatorio. 2nd part of *Dante's *Divine Comedy*.

Purim plays. 1-act plays performed on the Jewish festival of P. down to the 19th c., when they were absorbed by the revived Yiddish theatre. Their subjects were taken from the Bible, but they drew on European carnivals and the **commedia dell'arte*. Much of the dialogue was at first extemporized and was interspersed with songs, dances and poetry; gradually a traditional costume and style of acting evolved. Comic, occasionally bawdy types developed and were at times the main feature of P. p., which in some areas attracted large Christian audiences.

purism: *Le Corbusier

Puritani, I. Opera by *Bellini with libretto by C. Pepoli; 1st performance at Paris in 1835.

Puritan spoon. A spoon, dating from the Commonwealth period, with a spade-shaped bowl, a long flat stem and a square end often with 2 notches right at the top. The square end was erroneously supposed to be the result of Cromwellian soldiers cutting off the images of Apostles from Apostle spoons. Sometimes called a 'stump-top'.

purlin. Architectural term for a horizontal beam some way up the slope of a roof and running parallel with the ridge-beam.

Pushkin Alexander Sergeyevich (1799–1837). The greatest Russian poet, and a novelist and playwright of distinction. P. was educated at Tsarskoe Selo, a new school of high standard. There he began to write verse in Russian (he may have made earlier attempts in French) and joined the Arzamas, a circle of enthusiasts for *Karamzin's reforms, where he met and was influenced by Zhukovsky and Batyushkov. His 1st poems appeared in 1814. In 1817 he obtained the sinecure in the civil service customary for young aristocrats. The circulation of his political poems and epigrams led to his exile from St Petersburg and transfer to S. Russia. Arrested for complicity in the Decembrist Conspiracy of 1825, P. was pardoned by Nicholas I and retained at court–a mark of favour which did not preclude close supervision of his person and censorship of his work. His requests to be allowed to travel abroad were refused; and his debts made him increasingly dependent on royal favour. After 1830 public taste turned from poetry, and although P. attempted to regain popularity by writing prose, he was revered rather than read or imitated. In 1836 he was allowed to found a literary journal, *The Contemporary*, but it was unsuccessful. His marriage (1831) was unhappy, and a quarrel over his wife led to his death in a duel.

P.'s style was based on the elegant language created by Karamzin, although he used it more vigorously. His early poetic models were Voltaire and André Chenier; and although technically brilliant, this work lacks warmth. But from 1820 he was strongly influenced by Byron, and showed a predilection for the flexible Byronic form of narrative poem. *The Prisoner of the Caucasus* (1822), *The Fountain of Bakhisaray* (1824), *The Gipsies* (1827) and *Poltava* (1829) show this influence in form and (exotic) content. So does *Eugene Onegin* (1831; 1881), the novel in verse which is his most famous work. Onegin, his sensitivity smothered by boredom and lack of purpose, is the prototype of the heroes of Lermontov, Turgenev's 'superfluous men' and other characters in Russian literature. The heroine, Tatyana, is noble and strong. Onegin at first despises her love; by the time he realizes his mistake, she is married and, still in love with him, firm enough to dismiss him. P. was always a conscientious craftsman in the classical manner, using a few images; but *Onegin* also looks beyond Byron in content–in its treatment of character and problems. This is even clearer in the so-called *Little Tragedies* of 1830 (*Mozart and Salieri, The Stone Guest, The Covetous Knight* and *The Feast during the Plague*) and *The Bronze Horseman* (publ. posth. in 1841; 1955). The latter, perhaps his masterpiece, examines the conflicting interests of society and the individual. St Petersburg was built as Russia's 'window on the West' by order of Peter the Great, in a flood area. The sweetheart of Yevgenyi, a poor clerk, is drowned in the inundation of 1824; he goes mad and imagines that the equestrian statue of Peter is chasing him.

P.'s prose is easy, bare and economical, modelled on that of Voltaire. His only complete novel, *The Captain's Daughter* (1836; 1859), treats the Pugachev Rebellion (1773–4) as sympathetically as the censorship allowed. He also wrote a *History of the Pugachev Rebellion* (1834). Other prose works are the unfinished novel about Hannibal, his great-grandfather, an Ethiopian who was *The Negro of Peter the*

Henry Purcell

Purcell. Ms. of the 'Golden Sonata'

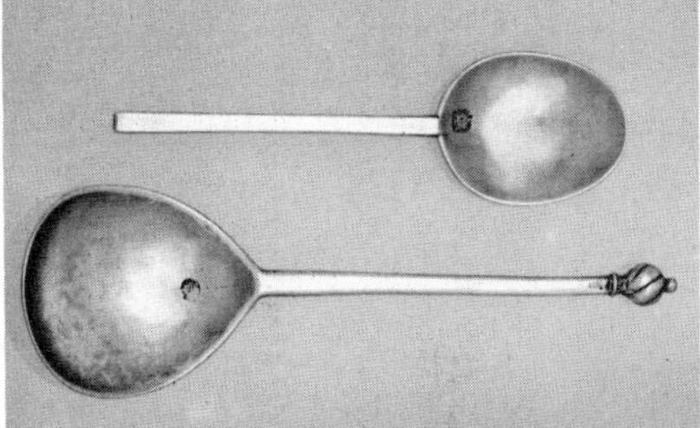
Puritan spoons

Alexander Pushkin: painting by Tropinin. Also *Krylov

Puvis de Chavannes. *Ste Geneviève watching over Paris.* Also *Carjat

The Pyramids at Gizeh

ASSERTIO SEPTEM SA=
cramentorum aduersus Martin.
Lutherũ, ædita ab inuictis=
simo Angliæ et Fran=
ciæ rege, et do. Hy=
berniæ Henri=
co eius no
minis
oc=
ctauo.

Pynson. *Assertio septem sacramentorum . . .*

Great; *Dubrovsky*, also unfinished; the 5 *Tales of Belkin*; and the famous short story *The Queen of Spades.*
His verse includes *Boris Godunov*, an unsuccessful attempt at a 'Shakespearian' chronicle-play; the tales of country life, *Count Nulin* and *The House at Kolmna*; fairy-tales, including *Ruslan and Lyudmila*, his first major work (1820); *The Garriliada*, a blasphemous mock-epic; *Songs of the Western Slavs*; *Angelo*; and a quantity of lyrical poetry.

Put Out More Flags (1942). Novel by Evelyn Waugh.

Putto from the Palazzo Ducale, Urbino

Puttenham. The anon. *Arte of English Poesie* (1589) was attributed by a contemporary to a P., probably one of the brothers Richard and George.

putto (Italian, 'little boy'). The word is usually found in the plural *putti*, plump naked little boys as found in Renaissance and baroque painting and sculpture.

Puvis de Chavannes Pierre-Cécile (1824–98). French mural painter who studied in Italy and with Couture and Delacroix. Essentially a monumental painter, he was bitterly attacked by contemporary critics but was supported by his friends and admirers the poets Baudelaire and Gautier. P., though contemporary with the impressionists, went his own way, basing his style on early Italian frescoes, Poussin, Ingres and Chassériau. He gave new vigour to 19th-c. mural painting and his flat, decorative style was decisive for the development of Gauguin and the nabis.

15th-c. English puzzle-jug

puzzle-jugs. Vessels made in the form of a jug or pitcher from which it is impossible to drink in the usual manner because the cylindrical neck is of a pierced or open-work design; they can only be drained without spilling if the liquid is sucked through a small hole, usually placed unobtrusively under the handle or in the spout. Such vessels made in earthenware have been known since the middle ages; they were most popular in the 17th and 18th cs, being made then in faïence and pottery, notably at Liverpool.

Pygmalion (1912). Play by G. B. *Shaw.

Pylos. One of the 3 notable Mycenaean sites, the others being Mycenae and Tiryns.

Ivory pyx from a village near Trier (*c.* 400)

Pynacker Adam (1622–73). Dutch landscape painter; a fashionable exponent in Delft of lighthearted landscapes of Italian scenes; he studied in Italy.

Pynas Jan (1583/4–1631). Dutch painter of Biblical and historical subjects. He travelled in Italy after 1605. Among his works are *The Raising of Lazarus* and *The Entombment* (both Louvre).

Pynson Richard (d. 1530). English printer whose 400 books include the best, typographically and technically, in English incunabula. He publ. *The Canterbury Tales* (1492), Lydgate's trs. of Boccaccio's *De Casibus Vivorum Illustrium* (1494), one of his finest works, a *Horae* (1495) and 3 Missals, *The Castell of Labour* and Henry VIII's *Assertio septem sacramentorum adversus Martinum Lutherum* (1521).

pyramids. Ancient Egyptian tomb structures made of stone; a p. has a square base and sides sloping to meet at a point. It evolved from the *mastaba, and held the body of a pharaoh or member of the Egyptian royal family. The most important examples were built in the 4th and 5th cs B.C., containing all necessary provision for the dead man's after-life and a complex of corridors, barriers and chambers designed to prevent the looting of the tomb. The most famous p.s are the 3 at Gizeh, notably the Great P. of Cheops. (*c.* 4700 B.C.).

pyrrhic: *metre in verse

Pythagoras. 6th-c. B.C. Greek philosopher, born on the island of Samos. No works survive, so that it is difficult to distinguish between P.'s thought and that of his school in S. Italy. He is credited with a belief in the transmigration of souls; the discovery of the geometrical 'theorem of P.'; and of the proportional relationships within the musical scale. The school of P. held that the laws of number governed the universe.

pyx. (1) In liturgical usage it is the round metal box in which the Host is reserved, either for veneration in church, or for carrying in procession, especially to administer the sacrament to the sick. (2) Also a chest into which specimens from the new coinage are put for testing in the 'trial of the mint p.' at the mint.

Q

Q: *Quiller-Couch

quadrille. Early 19th-c. dance for groups of couples; it developed from the movement of the '*scuadra*' ('squadrons') of show-parade horsemen in 17th-c. Italy. The q. proper is in 5 sections, derived from *contredanses; 'The Lancers' is derived from the '*q. des lanciers*' of 1856.

quadrivium. The part of the medieval univ. curriculum containing arithmetic, geometry, music and astronomy, 4 of the 7 *liberal arts.

quadruplet. In music, a group of 4 notes to be played in the time of 3, in a place where the rhythmic units are multiples of 3, e.g.

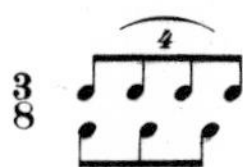

Quai des Brumes (1938). Film directed by M. *Carné.

Quai des Orfèvres (1947). Film directed by H.-G. *Clouzot.

Quantz Johann Joachim (1697–1773). German composer, theorist and flautist, court composer (from 1741) to Frederick II of Prussia. His *Versuch einer Anweisung die Flute traversiere zu spielen* (1752) was a model for subsequent instrument tutors and, in its remarks on all aspects of performance and musical taste, a valuable guide on contemporary practice. His compositions include 300 flute concertos.

Quare Fellow, The (1956). Play by Brendan *Behan.

Quarles Francis (1592–1644). English poet, author of **Emblems* (1635), a book of religious poems.

Quarterly Review, The. Scottish periodical, founded in 1809, with the support of Sir Walter Scott, as a Tory rival to the Whig *Edinburgh *Review*. An article by J. W. *Croker attacking *Endymion* was supposed to have killed or helped to kill Keats.

quarter note. U.S. musical term for *crotchet.

quarter tone: *microtones

quartet. A piece for 4 instrumentalists or the group itself; some of the greatest *chamber music has been written for string quartet, which consists of 2 violins, 1 viola and 1 cello.

quarto. Printers' term for a sheet of paper folded twice, and hence for a book of such sheets, each of which provides 4 leaves. The Shakespearean 'q.s' are the 1st printings (in q.) of his individual plays made during his lifetime and for some years after his death.

Quarton or Charonton, Enguerrand (*c.* 1410–*c.* 61). French painter, born at Laon in the north, but working at Avignon from 1447 to 1461. 2 paintings are documented: *Virgin of Mercy* (Condé Mus., Chantilly) and the large-scale altarpiece *Coronation of the Virgin* (Hospice, Villeneuve-lès-Avignon). The imaginative conception and detail of the latter show evidence of great talent.

Quasimodo Salvatore (1901–). Italian poet; he was awarded the Nobel prize in 1959. His early work was deeply influenced by Ungaretti. Later colls like *Giorno dopo giorno* (1947), *La vita non e sogno* (1949) and *Il falso e vero verde* (1956) are more accessible, showing Q.'s response to 20th-c. suffering and conflict.

Quatre Cents Coups, Les (1958). Film directed by F. *Truffaut.

Quatre Fils Aymon, Les: *Renaud de Montauban

quaver. In music, a note with a time value an eighth that of a *semibreve; hence the German, '*Achtelnote*' and the U.S. 'eighth note'. The q. is notated ♪ or 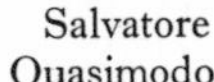 etc. when in groups; its rest is notated 𝄾 .

Quayle Anthony (1913–). English actor and director. Director of the Shakespeare Memorial Theatre, Stratford (1948–56), where he also played parts such as Iago, Coriolanus, Othello and Falstaff. He played Tamburlaine in New York (1956) and has also appeared in many films.

Queen Anne style. Term applied to those English domestic buildings which since the 17th c. have been built in brick with stone

Quarton. *Coronation of the Virgin*

Francis Quarles

Salvatore Quasimodo

Anthony Quayle as Falstaff

Queen Anne style. 66 Lincoln's Inn Fields, London

Queen Mary's Psalter: St Edmund

Queen's ware.
Wedgwood sauce-tureen (1798)

corners and window surrounds, usually rectangular in plan and with a pediment over the façade. The popularity of the style continued into the 19th c.; it was revived by Norman *Shaw and is still in favour in the suburbs.

Queen Kelly (1928). Film directed by E. von *Stroheim.

Queen Mab (1813). Poem by *Shelley.

Queen Mary's Psalter (*c.* 1330; B.M., London). Masterpiece of the East Anglian school of illumination; it was presented to Queen Mary in 1553. It contains 200 exquisite tinted drawings of scenes from Old Testament history, a calendar showing the signs of the zodiac and the monthly occupations, and a series of tinted marginal drawings of sports, pastimes and animal lore.

Queen of Spades, The. Opera by Tchaikovsky, libretto by his brother Modest after Pushkin; 1st performance at St Petersburg in 1890.

queen-posts. Architectural term for 2 vertical beams in a roof which stand on the tie-beam, supporting a rafter and/or purlins.

Queen's Theatre. Opened in 1705 in the Haymarket, London, now the site of Her Majesty's Theatre. Sir John Vanbrugh designed the theatre and he and Congreve were the directors. The venture was unsuccessful and the theatre eventually became the home of opera until it was destroyed by fire in 1876. Since 1907 there has been a Q. T. in Shaftesbury Avenue.

Queen's ware. *Wedgwood pottery type.

Queirós José Maria de Eça de (1845–1900). Portuguese novelist. Q. held a number of posts in the consular service, serving in England from 1874 to 1888. His *O Crime do padre Amaro, Cenas da vida devota* (1876; *The Crime of Father Amaro*, 1962) introduced the naturalist novel into Portugal. Works include *O Primo Basilio* (1878), *A Relíquia* (1887; *The Relic*, 1925) and *Os Maias* (1888).

Queneau Raymond (1903–). French novelist and poet whose works, including the fantasy novel *Zazie dans le métro* (1959; *Zazie*, 1960), made into a film by L. *Malle, show the influence of surrealism.

Quental Anthero Tarquínio de (1842–91). Portuguese poet, a leader of the generation which revolted against romanticism, and for some years an active Socialist. A disease of the spine drove him to suicide. Most of Q.'s verse is in the sonnet form, in which he records his inner conflicts and search for a satisfactory philosophy of life.

Quentin Durward (1823). Historical novel by *Scott.

Quercia Jacopo della (*c.* 1374–1438). Sienese sculptor, one of the most notable early 15th-c. Italian sculptors; his work uniquely combines classical and non-classical elements. He entered the competition for the 1st bronze doors for the Florence Baptistery (won by Ghiberti) but his entry has not survived. Other early works include the tomb of Ilaria del Carretto, Lucca cathedral (*c.* 1406) and the Fonte Gaia, Palazzo Pubblico, Siena. He worked with Ghiberti and Donatello on reliefs for Siena Baptistery (1417–31) and from 1425 executed reliefs illustrating scenes from Genesis for the doorway of S. Petronio, Bologna and figures in the lunette. He had a strong feeling for linear design and his style evidences familiarity with N. Italian sculpture and probably with that of Claus Sluter at Dijon.

Querelle des Anciens et des Modernes: *Ancients and Moderns Controversy

Quevedo y Villegas Francisco Gómez de (1580–1645). Spanish poet, satirist and novelist. Q. was unfortunate in his political patrons. He was banished after working in Italy and towards the end of his life suffered 4 years' imprisonment, the reason for which is unknown. Unhappy love-affairs were followed by a disastrous marriage. His harsh and disillusioned love-poetry is written in a style rich in conceits, which have been called '*conceptions*'. His satire sometimes, as in the *Epistola satirica y censoria*, addressed to the count of Olivares, has classical austerity. But more often it is angry, and full of disgust for sex, court life and indeed for humanity in general. His burlesques are ribald, and often funny. His best poems, however, show a stoical resignation in face of his country's decay and his own misfortunes. His prose works include a picaresque novel in an elaborate style, *Historia de la Vida del Buscón* (1626; . . . *Buscon the Witty Spaniard*, 1657) and a series of visions of Hell and its inhabitants entitled

Quercia. *The Creation of Man* (S. Petronio) and *Madonna* (*far right*) from the *Trenta altar*, S. Frediano, Lucca

Quevedo y Villegas

James Quin: painting by Hogarth

Y Discursos de Verdades (1627; *Visions, or Hell's Kingdome*. . ., 1640), also some treatises on politics and religion.

Que Viva Mexico! (1931–2). Uncompleted film directed by S. M. *Eisenstein. Footage later used for films by Sol Lesser (*Thunder Over Mexico*) and Marie Seton (*Time in the Sun*).

Quidor John (1801–81). U.S. painter of portraits and humorous scenes from the books *A History of New York* and *The Sketch-book of Geoffrey Crayon, Gent.* by Washington Irving.

Quiet Flows the Don, And (1928–40). Novel by *Sholokhov.

Quiet Man, The (1952). Film directed by J. *Ford.

Quiller-Couch Sir Arthur Thomas (1863–1944). English writer, usually under the pseud. 'Q'. He wrote a number of novels and stories, often using his native Cornwall as a background. His work as an anthologist includes *The Oxford Book of English Verse 1250–1900* (1900).

Quilter Roger (1877–1953). English composer. His output was largely of choral works but he is best remembered for the orchestral *A Children's Overture.*

Quin James (1693–1766). English actor noted especially in Shakespearian roles, including Othello, Macbeth and, most notably, Falstaff. His style was in the tradition of declamation, and after Garrick's début in 1741 the 2 actors were in constant rivalry.

Quinault Philippe (1635–88). French playwright. His works include the tragedy *Astrate, roi de Tyr* (1664) and the comedy *La Mère coquette ou Les Amans brouillez* (1665). In his later years Q. turned to opera and became *Lully's librettist.

Quine Richard (1920–). U.S. film director. He is known for comedies: *Operation Mad Ball* (1957) and *Bell, Book and Candle* (1958), but has made thrillers, *Drive a Crooked Road* and *Pushover* (both 1954), and a musical (*My Sister Eileen*, 1955).

Quinet Edgar (1803–75). French historian and philosopher. His democratic views were also embodied in imaginative writing, notably a dramatic epic, *Ahasuérus* (1833).

Quinn Anthony (1915–). U.S. film actor, Mexican-Irish by descent; has a full-voiced theatricality and considerable emotional perception; among his best films are *The Ox-Bow Incident* (1943), *Viva Zapata!* (1952), *La Strada* (1954), *Lust for Life* and *Lawrence of Arabia* (1962).

quint. In music the term (1) for an organ stop (*acoustic bass); (2) in the 16th c. for a deep tenor voice part (also called 'quintus').

Quintana Manuel José (1772–1857). Spanish liberal statesman, encyclopaedist and poet. He was a staunch upholder of the 18th-c. neoclassical style and was once regarded as the greatest poet of his time. His verse is now recognized as being greatly inferior to his interesting biographical studies, *Vidas de Españoles célebres.*

quintet. A group of 5 instrumentalists or a piece of chamber music for such a group. A wind q. consists of flute, oboe, clarinet, horn and bassoon; a string q. consists of 2 violins, 2 violas and a cello (sometimes 1 viola and 2 cellos). A piano quintet consists of a piano and string *quartet.

Quintillian (*c.* A.D. 35–*c.* 100). Marcus Fabius Quintillianus, Roman rhetorician, a distinguished teacher given the title of consul by Domitian. His *De Institutione Oratoria* describes the wide and liberal education necessary to produce a good public speaker.

quintuplet. Musical term to describe 5 notes played in the time of 4.

quod libet (Latin, 'what you please'). A piece of music whether composed or extemporized in which many tunes, usually popular, are combined against one another. It was a favourite pastime in 17th-c. Germany indulged by J. S. Bach's family; he concludes his Goldberg variations with a q. l.

quoin. Architectural term for the large cornerstones at the external angle of a building, or for the angle itself.

Quo Vadis? (1895–6). Historical novel by Henryk *Sienckiewicz; also made into films directed by Enrico Guazzoni (*c.* 1912); Ambrosio, D'Annunzio and Jacoby (1924); and M. *Le Roy (1951).

Quoins (Hampton Court)

François Rabelais

R

Pantagruel.

M. D XXXVII.

Rabelais. Title-page of *Pantagruel* (1537)

Sergey Rachmaninov

Rachel as Phèdre

Raabe Wilhelm (1831–1910). German novelist. A poetic realist, R. portrayed, in historical and contemporary settings, the lives and fortunes of people 'of no importance'–the estimable yet unobtrusive, the underprivileged, the eccentric–exposed to a predominantly shallow, inimical, materialistic world. His pessimism is tempered–particularly in later works–by whimsical humour, irony, compassion, and a wry but determined acceptance. Digressive, allusive, structurally complex, his tales reflect the influence of 18th- and 19th-c. English novelists. Among his books are: *Die Chronik der Sperlingsgasse* (1857), *Der Hungerpastor* (1864; 1885), *Abu Telfan* (1868; 1881), *Der Schüdderump* (1870), *Unruhige Gäste* (1886), and *Der Stopfkuchen* (1891).

Rabelais François (*c.* 1490–1553). French writer, born of wealthy parents, who became a Franciscan in 1520. His desire to learn Greek alarmed his superiors, and he left the order, eventually being ordained as a secular priest *c.* 1530. He then took a medical degree, and was in practice at Lyon in 1532, when his literary career began. On the model of the anon. popular chapbook, *Grandes et inestimables croniques du grant et énorme jéant Gargantua* (*The Great Chronicles of Gargantua*) he publ. *Les Horribles et esponentables faietz et provisses du très renommé Pantagruel* (1533) (*The Terrible Deeds and Acts of Prowess of Pantagruel*) which was condemned by the Sorbonne for its attacks on the clergy, but proved immensely popular. Though R. was attacked throughout his life by the religious authorities, he had powerful patrons, like the bishop of Paris, later Cardinal du Bellay, and even the king himself. In 1537 he revised *Pantagruel*, first publ. 1534, and followed it with his own version of *Gargantua*, *La vie inestimable du grand Gargantua, père de Pantagruel*, adding a 3rd vol. in 1546, which was again condemned by the theologians. When his 4th vol. (1548) of *Pantagruel* appeared, R. found himself in trouble. His last years were spent in obscurity–he may even have gone to prison–and the final vol. *L'Isle Sonnante* (*The Ringing Island*) did not appear until 1564, 11 years after his death. The 1st English trs. (17th c.) was by Sir Thomas Urquhart, completed by Peter Motteux.
The adjective which he has given to the world does not really define R.'s achievement, for though his books abound in gross and scatological humour, this is only the most obvious manifestation of his appetite for experience in all its forms. He is, above all, a writer who is drunk with learning and words, and his brutality does not stem from physical disgust, but from enjoyment of the possibilities of the medium: indeed, his favourite method of satire is parody. There are obvious ways in which R. is a man of the Renaissance–his respect for thinkers like Erasmus and More, the central theme of the discovery of a new world, the triumphant celebration of earthly life in all its forms. But he probably satirizes More in the picture of the English philosopher, Thaumaste; and though he creates a world of giants and of voyages of discovery, he seems to do so in order to present realistic scenes from ordinary life. And it is the preaching style of his old teachers and enemies, the Franciscans, with its grotesque mixture of sententiousness and graphic observation which is the model of his style, just as he shows his complete familiarity with all forms of scholastic learning. But he puts the techniques to a new use–not the presentation of an ordered Christian universe, but a world of phenomena piled up in apparent confusion and limited only by the imaginative grasp of the writer's mind.

Rachel. The pseud. of Élisa Félix (1820–58). Great French actress who did much to foster the revival of classical tragedy in the 19th c. She was at her best in the plays of Corneille and Racine, her greatest part being Phèdre.

Rachmaninov Sergey (1873–1943). Russian late romantic composer and virtuoso pianist. He studied first at St Petersburg, then (1885–8) at Moscow, where his teachers included Scriabin. At the Revolution he left Russia, settling finally in the U.S. His music, inspired by Tchaikovsky, is emotional, dramatic, sensitive to detail but, on his own admission, not always coherent. Apart from the famous *Prelude* in C♯ min. and the 2nd piano concerto, he wrote: 3 other piano concertos; 3 operas; 3 symphonies and *Rhapsody on a Theme by Paganini* for piano and orchestra, and vols of preludes for piano, etc.

Racine Jean (1639–99). French playwright in whose work the aesthetic ideal of French classicism found its most perfect expression. His family was connected with the Jansenist community of Port-Royal des Champs, where he grew up and was educated. To it he owed not only a deep feeling for Greek literature,

Jean Racine

but also an austere conception of human nature. While studying philosophy in Paris he was drawn into literary society, made the acquaintance of La Fontaine, Boileau and Molière, and decided to become a dramatist. After 11 years, however, he renewed his association with the community, married, and, renouncing the theatre, accepted the office of royal historiographer.
Accepting the general outlines which Corneille had established for the tragedy, R. intensified the unity of action by replacing complex plots dependent upon external events for their development with simple situations created by the violent conflicting passions of the characters themselves. Interest was now transferred from the interplay of personalities to the psychological crises which men and women, deprived of grace and consequently dominated by irresistible passions, must inevitably suffer. The tyranny of love is strongest and cruellest; R. excelled in painting its ravages in women, where extreme weakness engenders extreme violence.
R.'s sensitive and passionate nature is reflected in his work. Although his style is simple and impersonal, his verse derives its great beauty from this clarity and precision joined with vivid imagery and an acute sense of verbal harmony. Most of his themes are classical, his most important tragedies being: *Andromaque* (1667; 1675), *Britannicus* (1669; 1803), *Bérénice* (1670; 1803), *Bajazet* (1672; 1717), *Mithridate* (1673), *Iphigénie* (1674; *Achilles*, 1700), *Phèdre* (1677; 1776), *Esther* (1689; 1848), *Athalie* (1691; 1726). He wrote 1 comedy, *Les Plaideurs* (1668; 1715). *Athalie*, a Biblical work written after he had left the theatre, was perhaps his masterpiece.

Racine Louis (1692–1763). French poet, son of Jean Racine, of whom he wrote the unreliable *Mémoires sur la vie de Jean Racine* (1747).

rackett. Obsolete bass musical instrument; it was played with a double reed like the bassoon but the tube was so doubled back on itself as to make the r. only a few ins tall.

Radcliffe Mrs Ann (1764–1823). English novelist, author of the *Gothick novel *The Mysteries of Udolpho* (1794). Her work is satirized in Jane Austen's *Northanger Abbey*.

Radiguet Raymond (1903–23). French novelist and poet who strongly influenced Cocteau. His novels, remarkable for their mature, clear and precise style, are *Le Diable au Corps* (1923; *The Devil in the Flesh*, 1949), a study of the maturity of an adolescent in wartime, and *Le Bal du comte d'Orgel* (posth. 1924; *Count d'Orgel opens the Ball*, 1952).

Raeburn Sir Henry (1756–1823). Scottish portrait painter. At first a miniaturist, he turned to oil portraits about 1776. A good marriage (1778) made him financially independent. R. visited Sir Joshua Reynolds in London (1785), then visited Italy, returning to Edinburgh in 1787. He exibited at the R.A. (London) from 1792 and became an Academician in 1815. R. was particularly successful in obtaining patrons and produced about 1,000 portraits.

Raeburn. *Colonel Alastair Macdonnell of Glengarry*

Raff Joseph Joachim (1822–82). German-Swiss composer, encouraged by Mendelssohn, Liszt and von Bülow. His output included operas, symphonies and chamber music and 'Raff's celebrated Cavatina' for violin.

Raffaellino del Garbo (d. *c.* 1527). Florentine painter, probably the pupil of Filippino Lippi.

Raffet Auguste (1804–60). French graphic artist, pupil of Gros and Charlet and famous for his romanticized presentation of the Napoleonic era. He was among the earliest illustrators to make extensive use of lithography.

Raffet. *La grande revue nocturne*; lithograph

Raft George (1895–). U.S. film actor, identified with gangster roles, e.g. *Scarface*.

Raft of the 'Medusa', The (1819). Huge painting by *Géricault.

Raimondi Marcantonio (*c.* 1480–after 1527). Italian engraver, the first to specialize in the reproduction of original paintings, etc. After studying under F. Francia at Bologna he went to Venice where he copied Dürer's engravings. In 1510 he moved to Rome and made engravings of works by Raphael. It is for these that he is remembered.

Raimondi. *Elymas struck blind*; engraving after Raphael

Raimondi Pietro (1786–1853). Italian composer whose vast output included a trilogy of oratorios, *Potifar*, *Joseph* and *Jacob*, designed to be and actually performed (1852) separately and simultaneously.

Raimund originally Raymann, Ferdinand (1790–1836). Austrian dramatist, actor and

Sir Walter Raleigh: anon. painting (*c.* 1588)

Rainaldi. Piazza del Popolo: etching by Piranesi

Dame Marie Rambert

Raised work

The Rake's Progress: The Levée

director. With a popular appeal that springs from the Viennese theatrical tradition, his plays, e.g. *Der Alpenkönig und der Menschenfeind* (1828), juxtapose a romantic fairy-world with a homely Biedermeier milieu, the whole lightened by R.'s elegance and humour, yet with a tragic undertone; he himself committed suicide.

Rainaldi Carlo (1611–90). Italian architect, working in Rome. Among much else he designed S. Maria in Campitelli, finished S. Andrea della Valle (begun by Maderno) and drastically modified Borromini's S. Agnese. He also conceived the 2 symmetrical churches that form the focal point of the Piazza del Popolo. R. epitomizes the grandiose, restless spirit of the great age of Roman baroque.

Rainbow, The (1915). Novel by D. H. *Lawrence.

Raine Kathleen (1908–). English poet whose 1st contributions were to *New Verse* in the 1930s. Her best lyrics, avowedly indebted to Blake, combine intense religious feeling with poetic discipline.

Rains Claude (1889–). English film actor. R. made his début playing in *The Invisible Man* (1933). Considering the variety of his roles, he can best be classed as one of the great character actors, seldom top billed except in *Caesar and Cleopatra* (1945).

Rain, Steam and Speed (1844). Impressionistic late work by *Turner inspired by the railway.

raised work. A type of picture embroidery popular in the mid 17th c. and often inaccurately called 'stump-work'. Silk embroideries consisting mainly of closely knit rows of detached buttonhole stitches are built up into fabrics over padding or stuffing.

Rake's Progress, The (1733). 8 paintings by Hogarth, engraved by the artist in 1735. Also the title of a ballet by Ninette de Valois and an opera (1951) by Stravinsky (libretto by W. H. Auden and C. Kallman).

Raleigh Sir Walter (1552–1618). English poet, courtier and explorer, a favourite of Queen Elizabeth and organizer of the colonization of Virginia. He was imprisoned (1603–16) by James I, released to search for gold in Guiana and, after the failure of the expedition, executed. R.'s poems, which circulated in manuscript and appeared in his lifetime only in miscellanies are direct, compressed and elliptical, exhibiting his awareness of mortality and the inconstancy of fortune, e.g. *The Passionate Mans Pilgrimage* and *The Lie*. This is also found in his *History of the World* (written in prison), a work of noble lucidity and one of the great achievements of English prose.

Ralph Roister Doister (*c.* 1552). The earliest English stage comedy, by Nicholas *Udall.

Rambert Marie, originally Miriam Ramberg (1888–). Polish-born British dancer. She studied Jaques-Dalcroze *eurythmics in Switzerland (1910), joined Diaghilev's co. in 1912; and later came to London where in 1930 she founded the Ballet Club and at the *Mercury Theatre (opened by her husband Ashley Dukes) provided English ballet with its 1st permanent home. The Ballet Club, now the Ballet Rambert, is the oldest English ballet co. R.'s vision and encouragement to young dancers, choreographers, designers and musicians were a tremendous contribution to the growth of British ballet. With limited resources she was able to foster the talent she recognized in Ashton, Turner, Tudor, Howard, etc.

Rambler, The (1750–2). Periodical issued and largely written by Dr Johnson.

Rambouillet, Hôtel de. *Salon* of the marquise de Rambouillet (1588–1665) which softened manners, influenced the course of French literature and was the model for subsequent *salons*. R. was frequented by Malherbe, Gombauld, Saint-Evremond, Bossuet, Corneille, La Rochefoucauld and many others. It created the fashion for clear, simple, precise and delicate language.

Rameau Jean-Philippe (1683–1764). French composer. After studying in Italy he succeeded his father as organist in his home town of Dijon (1709) and finally settled in Paris in 1723. There he opened a school for composition; became house musician to the patron La Poupelinière, meeting Voltaire, and began his career as an opera composer (1733). His music set off a controversy between his supporters and those of the style of Lully, but by 1750 R. was supreme in France; with the '*Querelles des Bouffons*' he became the rallying-point for

Jean-Philippe Rameau

Ramsay. *The Artist's Wife*. Also *Hume

French music against the Italian *opera buffa* style. As an opera composer R. showed great melodic gifts and a rich harmonic sense, and also unparalleled imagination in the use of instruments (e.g. his use of woodwind). He wrote picturesque and dramatic harpischord suites (colls of character pieces). His style is variously sparse, decorative, awkward, graceful, dramatic and humorous, and always serious. His *Traité de l'Harmonie* . . . (1722) is the 1st theoretical explanation of harmony as such, and the source of all modern theories. It was R. who summed up the musical potentialities of his age by the remark 'melody is born of harmony'.

Ramsay Allan (1685–1758). Scottish poet and playwright. R.'s colls of old Scottish poetry helped to renew interest in Scots vernacular. He wrote a pastoral comedy, *The Gentle Shepherd* (1725).

Ramsay Allan (1713–84). Scottish portrait painter; son of the above. After studying in Italy he settled in London and became painter to George III. His most notable portraits are of women; in them he could give free expression to the grace and delicacy characteristic of his style, e.g. his painting of his 2nd wife, Margaret (N.G., Edinburgh). An important male portrait is that of the philosopher Rousseau (N.G., Edinburgh). In the 1760s he delegated most of his work to assistants and joined the literary group round Dr Samuel Johnson.

Ramuz Charles-Ferdinand (1878–1947). Swiss novelist and poet. R.'s work describes peasant life in his native canton of Vaud. He wrote the libretto for Stravinsky's *L'Histoire du Soldat*.

Rancho Notorious (1952). Film directed by F. *Lang.

Randolphe Thomas (1605–35). English playwright. His works include *The Muses' Looking-Glasse* (publ. 1638) and *Hey for Honesty* (publ. 1651), a version of Aristophanes' *Plutus*.

rank. A set of *organ pipes designed for a given tonal effect over the whole range of the keyboard and controlled by a *stop. Sometimes as in *mixture stops more than 1 rank of pipes is made available by drawing the stop.

Rank J. Arthur (Lord) (1888–). English film producer, one of a rich flour-milling family who wished to make religious films in the 1930s. However, by the end of World War II he had become owner of the Gaumont and Odeon circuits of cinemas, of 2 studios and the largest distributor of British films. In the late 1940s R.'s strenuous efforts to make the best possible British films failed through the inadequacy of native directors and the unprofitability of their products, and his co. thereafter took up a flatly commercial attitude.

Ranke Leopold von (1795–1886). Master of the great German 'scientific' historians; he had a great influence outside Germany. His greatest works were *Die römischen Päpste* (1834–6; *The . . . history of the Popes. . .*, 1842) which occasioned one of Macaulay's finest essays, and *Deutsche Geschichte . . . der Reformation* (1839–47; *History of the Reformation in Germany*, 1845–7).

Ransom John Crowe (1888–). U.S. poet, a leading member of the Southern regionalists and the originator of the term *new criticism. R. contributed to *The Fugitive* and in 1939 founded *The Kenyon Review*. His poetic output is small, but has been very influential. R.'s manner is ironic, witty, disillusioned, but his meaning is wholly serious. His colls include *Poems about God* (1919), *Chills and Fever* (1924), *Grace After Meat* (1924) and *Two Gentlemen in Bonds* (1927).

Raoul de Houdenc. French poet (early 13th c.) who wrote an Arthurian romance, *Méraugis de Portlesguez*, and 2 allegories, the *Roman des ailes de la courtoisie*, a description of chivalric ideals, and the religious *Songe d'Enfer*.

Rape of Lucrece, The (1594). Narrative poem by *Shakespeare, dedicated to the earl of Southampton, his patron.

Rape of the Lock, The (1712). Poem by Alexander *Pope.

Raphael (1483–1520). Raffaelo Sanzio, Italian painter, with Michelangelo and Leonardo da Vinci one of the three masters of the high Renaissance. Born at Urbino, already a flourishing centre of the arts, and the son of a painter, R. was brought into contact with the highest artistic achievements from childhood. He was trained by Perugino, who was then at the height of his own career. R.'s precocious talent was recognized long before he was 20 and his early

John Crowe Ransom

Raphael. *Vision of a Knight*

Raphael. *Betrothal of the Virgin*

Raphael. *La Belle Jardinière*

Raphael.
The School of Athe
Also *Castiglione,
**Disputà*, *grotesq
*The *Sistine Mado*

Vision of a Knight (N.G., London) shows an astonishing maturity. R. was astute enough to realize that the art of Leonardo da Vinci and Michelangelo was transforming the whole conception of painting and in 1504 he went to Florence to study it. *Betrothal of the Virgin* (1504; Brera) shows the transition between the teaching of Perugino and the assertion of the new influences. R.'s colour and the emotional qualities of his work always remained within the tradition of Central Italian painting, while his sense of composition and the dynamic power of his draughtsmanship were learned from the Florentines. Early portraits too, show how much he owed to Leonardo da Vinci's *Mona Lisa*, e.g. *Maddalena Doni* (Pitti). In his Madonnas, e.g. the famous *La Belle Jardinière* (*c.* 1520), the influence of Fra Bartolommeo is combined with that of Leonardo's drawings of St Anne with the Madonna and Child, e.g. *Madonna with the Goldfinch* (Uffizi) and *Madonna del Granduca* (Pitti). By 1508 R. was receiving offers from both the French court and the Pope; late in that year he went to Rome to take part in the grandiose decorative schemes of Pope Julius II for the new Papal apartments in the Vatican. R.'s response to the enormous artistic challenge his part of the scheme presented, is also one of those astonishing 'leaps forward' in art history and is matched, perhaps, only by Masaccio's painting of the frescoes in the Carmine church, Florence, 100 years earlier, and the exactly contemporary (1508–12) frescoes of Michelangelo in the Sistine Chapel. When he found himself the peer and the rival of Michelangelo R. was 26. Considered for their composition alone, *The School of Athens*, *Parnassus* and *Disputà* (*Disputation concerning the Holy Sacrament*) (all Stanza della Segnatura, Vatican) are probably supreme in art. They were immediately studied by every artist in Rome and remained an 'art school in themselves'. At the same time R. was painting portraits such as the celebrated *Young Cardinal* (Prado). The next 8 years were, indeed, a record of astonishing achievement: R. and his assistants continued the Vatican frescoes–in the Stanza d'Eliodoro there is a richer use of colour, especially in *The Mass of Bolsena*; while in the Stanza dell' Incendio del Borgo the almost forced dramatic quality shows his study of the Michelangelo frescoes. In 1514 R. was preferred to Michelangelo by the new Pope, Leo X, as successor to Bramante, architect-in-charge of St Peter's. In 1518 he was to be made, with A. da Sangallo, 'Superintendent of the Streets of Rome', which made him responsible for town planning as well as for the day-to-day upkeep of the entire city. Before this, he had decorated the Farnesina Villa (1514). The famous *Galatea* (Farnesina, Rome) is, with Botticelli's *Venus* and *Primavera*, the supreme Renaissance evocation of the classical 'Golden Age'; it is also unmatched in its interpretation of spontaneous and graceful female action. The classical themes remind one too, that R. was also responsible for the Papal colls of antiquities. In 1515–16, R. drew the cartoons for the tapestries which, woven in Flanders, were hung in the Sistine Chapel. 7 of the cartoons are preserved (V. & A., London). Yet he also found time to paint altarpieces, e.g. *The Sistine Madonna* (G. Gal., Dresden) and *The Transfiguration* (Pina., Vatican), a painting left unfinished when he died of fever. It was completed by *Giulio Romano, one of the founders of the mannerist school which borrowed so much from R.

Rashomon (1951). Film directed by A. *Kurosawa.

Raspe Rudolph Erich (1737–94). German writer working in England for a period as a mining engineer in Cornwall. He knew Herder and introduced him to *Percy's *Reliques*. R.'s *Baron Munchausen's Narrative* (publ. first in England 1785, in German trs. 1786) is a coll. of wildly fantastic tales based on the adventures claimed to himself by Baron Karl von Münchausen (1720–97), a cavalry officer.

Rasselas, Prince of Abissinia, The History of (1759). Didactic novel by Samuel *Johnson.

Rastrelli Bartolommeo Francesco (1700–71). Italian architect who was brought to St Petersburg by his father as a youth and stayed there, apart from trips to W. Europe to study architecture, for the rest of his life. He designed many large palaces and public buildings (some, now destroyed, in wood) and is largely responsible for the classical appearance of Leningrad today. His chief works are the Winter Palace and the Smolny church, St Petersburg, and the palace of Tsarskoe Selo. The style is a graceful and attractive rococo.

Ratdolt Erhard (1447–1527/8). German printer working in Venice from 1474 to 1486. Beflourished initials on black backgrounds,

Rastrelli. Tsarskoe Selo

Shield-top spoons with rat-tails

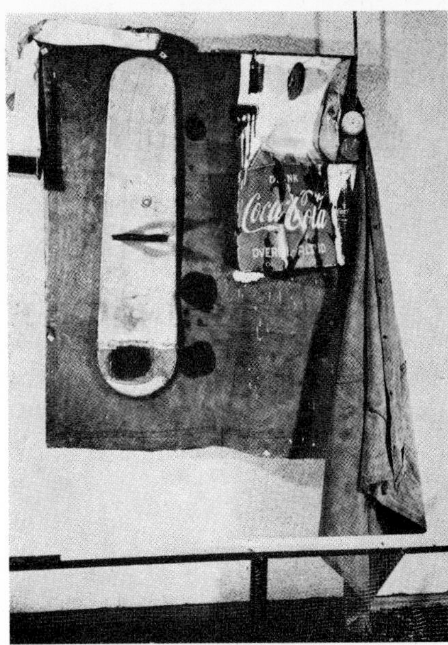

Rauschenberg. *Dylaby II* (1962)

'rotunda' and roman types all reflect Venetian influence. R. is notable for having publ. the earliest known type specimen sheet (1486), and the 1st real title-page (1476). He also publ. magnificent liturgical works, adorned by coloured woodcuts, Euclid's *Elementa geometriae* (1482) and *Lehenrechtbuch* (1493).

Rathaus Karol (1895–1954). Polish-born composer who settled (1938) in New York, teaching at the Queens College there. R.'s numerous works, which include the *Vision dramatique* (1945), are tonal in idiom and late romantic in mood. The K. R. Memorial Association was founded for students of music.

rat-tail. The tongue running half-way down the back, or occasionally the front, of the bowl of *trifid spoons and the slightly later shield-top or waved-end spoons. The Hanoverian rat-tail, however, runs half-way down the stem from the curled over end as a sharp ridge.

Rattigan Terence Mervyn (1911–). Prolific and popular English playwright whose successes include *French Without Tears* (1936), *Love in Idleness* (1944), *The Winslow Boy* (1946), *The Browning Version* (1948), *The Deep Blue Sea* (1952), *Separate Tables* (1954), and *Ross* (1961), on the life of T. E. *Lawrence.

Räuber, Die (1782). Play by *Schiller.

Rauch Christian (1777–1857). German sculptor of monumental works and portrait busts. In Rome (1804–11) he was strongly influenced by B. Thorwaldsen. His chief works include the tomb of Louise, Queen of Prussia, at Charlottenburg and the equestrian monument to Frederick the Great in Berlin.

Rauschenberg Robert (1925–). U.S. painter. He studied in the U.S. and Paris before finally settling in New York, where he has worked with the Merce Cunningham Ballet. R. was the 1st prizewinner at the Venice Biennale of 1964. He is a leading exponent of *pop art, employing such ready-made objects as stuffed goats' heads and chimney-cowls in his work. Recently he has used silk screen and photographic processes.

Ravel Maurice (1875–1937). French composer. His teachers at the Paris Conservatoire included Fauré; he was known also as a pianist and conductor, made concert tours but lived otherwise a retired life devoted to composition. R. is the most important French composer of the generation following Debussy and his work shows the impact of the older master. But R.'s incisive way of thinking owes little to Debussy's 'otherworldliness'; far from wishing to break with the external world of music, R. adopted existing material to distort it to his own purposes; e.g. Spanish music in *Rhapsodie Espagnole* (1907), the 1-act opera *L'Heure Espagnole* (1907), and the famous *Bolero* (1928), Viennese music in *La Valse* (1920), 18th-c. French music in *Le tombeau de Couperin* (1917), and jazz in the piano concerto (1931). Other works include the ballet *Daphnis and Chloe* for Diaghilev (1912), the opera *L'Enfant et les Sortilèges* (1925) and *Mother Goose Suite* (1908; orchestrated 1912), which contain some of his most endearing music. Many of these works are brilliant orchestrations of piano pieces, etc. Piano works include: *Gaspard de la nuit* (1908), and *Pavane pour une Infante Défunte* (1899). He also wrote a good deal of chamber music.

Terence Rattigan

Raven, The (1845). Poem by Edgar Allan *Poe.

Ravenscroft George (1618–81). English glass maker employed (1673) by the Glass-Sellers' Co. to research into methods and materials which would make English glass making independent of Europe. R. appears to have introduced ground flints such as silica and potash as alkali. His early efforts led to *criselling in the glass and to counteract this effect he introduced the use of oxide of lead. This was a major improvement and was the great English contribution to glass chemistry. In 1676 R. was allowed to apply a personal seal of a raven's head to glasses made by the co.

Maurice Ravel

Rawsthorne Alan (1905–). English composer; largely self-taught, Hindemith being an early influence. R.'s individual harmonic idiom stamps his works, which include: 3 symphonies; *Symphonic Studies* (1938); 2 piano concertos; *Concerto for String orchestra* (1949); *Street Corner* overture, and an important vocal work *A Canticle of Man* (1952).

Ray Man (1890–). U.S. painter, photographer, film maker; one of the founders of the New York dada movement and long associated with surrealism, though by temperament an eclectic. In the 1920s and 1930s he worked in Paris, mainly as a photographer: he and Moholy-Nagy explored the principles of space

Man Ray. *Solarized Portrait* (1931)

Satyajit Ray. *Pather Panchali*

Nicholas Ray. Farley Granger and Howard da Silva in *They Live By Night*

Sir Herbert Read

Raymond. Reader's Digest Building, Tokyo

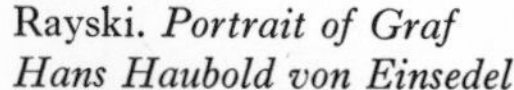

Rayski. *Portrait of Graf Hans Haubold von Einsedel*

and motion in a type of photography that bypassed the camera and concerned itself with forms produced directly on the photographic printing paper. He has written an autobiography, *Self Portrait* (1963).

Ray Nicholas (1911–). U.S. film director. R. studied architecture with Frank Lloyd Wright, but became an actor, eventually on Broadway. He was Kazan's assistant on his 1st film, *A Tree Grows in Brooklyn*, and directed on Broadway before making his own 1st film, *They Live By Night* (1947). R. places great value on the meaning of composition. His sensitivity to the structure of images and particularly to the horizontal line has made him use Cinemascope to particular effect, e.g. in *Party Girl* (1958). His use of symbolism is very direct, often from nature: fire and water in the Biblical *King of Kings* (1961). Often he deals in extremes of symbolism, composition and situation: Cortisone-induced megalomania in *Bigger than Life* (1956). Violence and directness are linked through R.'s interest in folksong, which informs the spirit of *The True Story of Jesse James* (1956) and *Johnny Guitar* (1953). His heroes are typically insecure or at odds with society, although they are seeking to come to terms with it, like the Eskimo hero of *The Savage Innocents* (1960) or the James Dean character in *Rebel Without a Cause* (1955). Other notable films are *In a Lonely Place* (1949) and *The Lusty Men* (1952).

Ray Satyajit (1921–). Indian film director, aristocratic, intellectual, refined: his work is India's most important contribution to world cinema. The trilogy *Pather Panchali* (1955), *Aparajito* (1957), and *The World of Apu* (1958), in which the hero progresses from village childhood to adult city life, combines brilliant evocations of time and place with the most delicate observations of human relationships. R.'s integrity, humour and unforced naturalism are his own, though he has some affinities with Renoir and de Sica; like theirs, his technique is always subservient to what he is saying. In *Jalsaghar* (1958; also known as *The Music Room*), a study of an ageing nobleman's obsession with music, and *Two Daughters* (1961), from stories by *Tagore, R. further extends his range without losing his personal qualities.

Raymond Antonin (1890–). Czech architect. R. worked for Frank Lloyd Wright in Wisconsin and then settled in Japan to become the leading modern architect there in the 1920s and 1930s. His Reader's Digest Building, Tokyo (1949) was the 1st important post-war Japanese building but his fame is eclipsed by the brilliant young Japanese architects, many, including Mackaira, trained in his office.

Raynal Paul (1885–). French playwright, author of *Le Tombeau sous l'Arc de Triomphe* (1924; *The Unknown Soldier*, 1928).

Rayski Ferdinand von (1806–90). German painter. Under the influence of the French romantics, Gros, Delacroix and Géricault, he painted military subjects and sketches on the theme of the murder of Thomas à Becket, with an extraordinary freedom and vigour, contrasting favourably with his other work, chiefly portraiture. His late paintings show the influence of Courbet; he gave up painting in the 1870s.

Razor's Edge, The (1944). Novel by W. Somerset Maugham.

Read Sir Herbert (1893–). English writer. R. is an important poet in the romantic tradition, has written fiction (the 'romance' *The Green Child*, 1947) and autobiography (coll. as *The Contrary Experiences*); but he is most widely known as an influential critic, historian and philosopher of art (*The Meaning of Art*, 1931; *Art Now*, 1933; *Education Through Art*, 1943; histories of modern painting, 1959, and sculpture, 1964), and particularly of modern art, helping to gain recognition for the outstanding 20th-c. British artists (e.g. *Unit One).

Reade Charles (1814–84). English novelist. Much of his work aimed to expose social abuses, but he is chiefly remembered for *The Cloister and The Hearth* (1861), a historical novel suggested by the mystery surrounding Erasmus's birth; the main characters are the humanist's parents.

realism. Term often used in a general sense, meaning fidelity to life (as opposed to idealization, caricature, etc.), but more usefully confined to the 19th-c. movement in painting and literature. This was a reaction against the subjectivity and cloudiness of romanticism, insisting on the portrayal of ordinary contemporary life and current manners and problems, and in fact (as part of its anti-romanticism) tending to emphasize the baser human motives and more squalid activities. In literature the novel became the predominant form: Balzac, Stendhal and Dickens contain realistic elements, but Flaubert and Tolstoy are considered the great masters of r. *Naturalism was an extension of the principles of r. Courbet was the 1st major realist painter. *Impressionism may be regarded as an offshoot of r., and a 20th-c. version was *social realism.

Realistic Theatre Moscow. Russian theatre which originated in 1918 when a splinter group broke away from the Moscow Art. In 1932 Nikolai Okhlopkov became its artistic director and under him the group tried to break away from conventional play production, using different stages all over the auditorium. The theatre closed in 1938.

realize. In music this word is used in a technical sense. Much music of the 17th and 18th cs was not written out in full by the composer but consisted of a bass line (*continuo) and a melodic line which, with certain indications, were sufficient for contemporary musicians familiar with the conventions. These conventions are not now known by all performers and the music needs 'realization', that is writing out in full, by a skilled ed.

Rear Window (1954). Film directed by *Hitchcock.

rebec. Musical stringed instrument played with a bow, known first in Spain in the 13th c. and probably derived from the Arabic rebáb.

Rebel, The (1952). Book by *Camus.

Rebel Without a Cause (1955). Film directed by N. *Ray.

Rebikov Vladimir Ivanovich (1866–1920). Russian composer who wrote in a style reminiscent of Tchaikovsky until about 1900 but thereafter experimented with the whole tone *scale, etc.

Rebora Clemente (1885–1957). Italian poet. R.'s work gradually moved from romantic to religious themes, and in 1931 he entered a monastery and gave up writing for a long period. His works include a verse autobiography *Curriculum vitae* (1955).

Récamier Jeanne-Françoise, Mme (1777–1849). French society woman, a famous beauty; David painted the well-known portrait of her. Her *salon* attracted the leading literary and political figures of the Napoleonic and Restoration periods; its chief figure was her lover, Chateaubriand.

recapitulation: *reprise

recitative. In opera, etc., a declamatory passage for a solo voice, to be sung with great freedom of rhythm (and sometimes of pitch) and in which melody is, to a degree, sacrificed for a telling 'recitation' of the words. It is used e.g. in dialogue or for a soliloquy preceding an aria. In ACCOMPANIED R. the orchestra provides a background of chords agitated, broken or sustained to suit the mood; RECITATIVO SECCO is unaccompanied but is usually punctuated with chords, e.g. from the keyboard.

recorder. Musical woodwind instrument. Sound production is on the principle of the *fipple flute. The r. was common from the Renaissance to the 18th c. and has been revived for the performance of old music. The modern revival is based on the 18th-c. instrument; the Renaissance r. (models of this are becoming available) has a stronger, more incisive tone. From soprano to tenor the r.s are blow directly but the bass instrument, about 4 ft long, is blown through a side pipe; the range of the family is about four 8ves from the F below middle C.

Recruiting Officer, The (1706). Play by *Farquhar.

Red and the Black, The (1831). Novel by *Stendhal.

Red Badge of Courage, The (1895). Novel by Stephen *Crane, made into a film (1951) directed by J. *Huston.

red china. Name sometimes given to the fine red stoneware manufactured for the 1st time in Staffordshire by the immigrant Elers brothers *c.* 1693. In the manufacture of their unglazed red teapots, often decorated with relief ornamentation in oriental style, the Elers used local Staffordshire clay which produced a ware dense, hard and fine in texture; the pieces were made light and thin by turning on a lathe after throwing.

Recorders

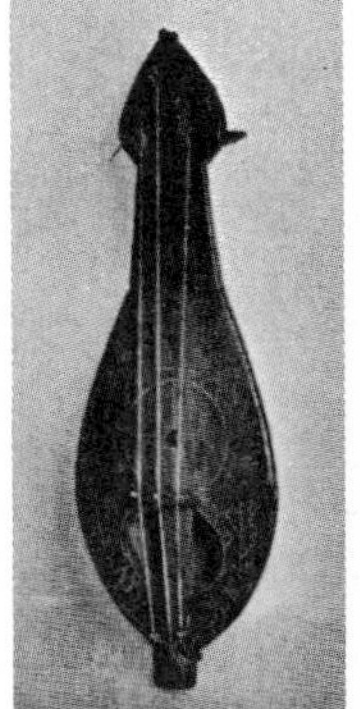
Rebec

Madame Récamier: painting by David. Also *Gérard

Red-figured stamnos (*c.* 430 B.C.) by the Kleophon painter

Sir Michael Redgrave as Uncle Vanya

Reeding from S. Sabina, Rome

rederijkers. Members of the chambers of rhetoric, societies of burghers formed in the Netherlands late in the 14th c. to study, compose and recite verse and perform plays. They were an offshoot of the French *rhétoriqueurs. *Elckerlyjk*, the probable original of **Everyman*, is a creation of the r.

red-figured style. Style of Greek vase painting where the figures are painted in red on a black ground; supposedly invented by the Andokides painter (*fl.* 530–520 B.C.), it continued until the mid-4th c. B.C.

Redford John (d. 1547). English organist whose compositions (many surviving in the *Mulliner Book*) were influential and much admired.

Redgauntlet (1824). Historical novel by Sir Walter Scott.

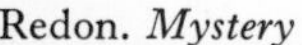

Redon. *Mystery*

Redgrave Sir Michael (1908–). English actor, of classical roles including most of the important Shakespearian parts. He played Claudius in *Hamlet*, in the opening production (1963) of the National Theatre, where he also played the title-roles in *Uncle Vanya* and *Hobson's Choice*. He has made many films including *Dead of Night* and *The Browning Version*, and has written plays and excellent books on acting.

Redgrave Peter (1932–). English poet who has publ. 3 books of poetry. His descriptions of the elements, the struggle between them and against them, achieve considerable dramatic force. Colls are *The Collector* (1959), *The Nature of Cold Weather* (1961) and *At the White Monument* (1963).

Red House, The. Bexleyheath, Kent (1859). Architect, Philip *Webb.

Redi Francesco (1626–98). Italian poet and scientist who wrote a long, amusing poem in praise of the wines of Tuscany, *Bacco in Toscana* (1685).

Redon Odilon (1840–1916). French painter, draughtsman, graphic artist and writer. Until about 1878 he painted landscapes in oil and pastel under the influence of Courbet and Corot; later he turned to charcoal drawing and lithography. R. was concerned with the realities of the imagination, in opposition to the visual emphasis of impressionism. His middle period, lasting till the turn of the c., was an expression of mysticism and the symbolism of his friends Huysmans and Mallarmé; then he became associated with the *nabis and painted portraits and flower pieces, with rare intuition.

Red River (1948). Film directed by H. *Hawks.

Reed Carol (1906–). English film director. R. made his 1st film as director in 1936. He made his reputation with *The Stars Look Down* (1939), about coal-miners. He was also admired for 2 war films, *The Way Ahead* (1944) and *The True Glory* (a documentary by R. and Kanin, 1945), but his great successes were dramas. *Odd Man Out* (1947) dealt with an I.R.A. man on the run; *The Fallen Idol* (1948) was from a story by Graham Greene, who wrote the script of *The Third Man* (1949), about crime in stricken post-war Vienna. *Our Man in Havana* (1959) is a good adaptation of Greene's novel.

Reed John (1887–1920). U.S. writer. R. won fame as a journalist reporting the Mexican Revolution and World War I. He became an ardent supporter of the Bolsheviks and wrote an eyewitness account of the Russian Revolution, *Ten Days That Shook the World* (1919). He founded the U.S. Communist party (1919).

reeding. The carving of wood–or the featuring of metalwork–in convex parallel shafts simulating reeds in relief. This is the reverse of the effect created in *fluting.

reed instruments. Musical wind instruments most of which are *woodwind instruments; the *saxophones, however, although reed instruments, are made of brass.

reed organ. A type of musical instrument in which the sound is produced by reeds vibrated by a pulse of air and not, as in the organ proper, by vibrating columns of air in pipes; the harmonium, accordion and harmonica are examples, as was the *regal.

Reeves James (1909–). English poet, whose best work from 4 previous books is in *Collected Poems* (1960). His 1st vol., *The Natural Need* (1936), was publ. by Laura Riding and Robert Graves. Graves's technical ease and Norman Cameron's unpretentious honesty appear to have had a lasting effect on R.'s poetry, which is unspectacular, rooted in the particular and the immediate.

Reflections on the Revolution in France (1790). Political treatise by Edmund *Burke.

Reformation symphony. *Mendelssohn's 5th symphony.

Refusés: *Salon des Refusés

regal. A small *reed organ in use from the 15th to 17th cs; Bible regals could be folded up like a Bible for ease of carrying.

régence (French, 'regency'). Term used to describe styles in architecture and interior design prevalent in France in the late part of the reign of Louis XIV (d. 1715) and the early reign of Louis XV. It was the precursor of rococo.

Regency. Used to designate the prevalent style in England from *c.* 1800 to 1825, although in fact the Regency lasted from 1811 to 1820. It is an adaptation to middle-class domestic architecture, furniture and interior decoration of the style set by the *Adam brothers, *Chippendale, etc. in the late 18th c. Predominantly neo-classical, it also admitted exotic elements from Greek, Egyptian, Gothic, Chinese and Indian art. In silver the maximum effect of grandeur was achieved, often at the expense of taste, using great quantities of metal.

Reger Max (1873–1916). German composer, organist of precocious gifts, and teacher. R. taught at Munich and at Leipzig, held conducting posts and was a concert organist. His many pupils included J. Haas. R. took Brahms as a model in his concern with absolute music, but his own work has typically post-Wagnerian chromatic harmonies and complex contrapuntal writing. He composed much in all genres, a major part of his output being for organ.

register. In music the term applied to: (1) the pipes controlled by an organ stop when decribing their tone quality, hence REGISTRATION, the combining of various stops to achieve different tone colours and effects; (2) different areas of the compass of a voice or musical instrument with characteristic tone qualities, thus the rich 'chalumeau r.' at the bottom of the clarinet compass.

Règle du Jeu, La (1939). Film directed by J. *Renoir.

Regnard Jean-François (1655–1709). French playwright who wrote comedies for Les Italiens and the Comédie-Française. They include *Le Légataire universel* (1708; *Wit's Last Stake; a farce*, 1769) and *Le Retour Imprévu* (1700; *The Intriguing Chambermaid*, 1734, trs. by Henry Fielding).

Regnault Henri (1843–71). French painter best known for *Automédon and the Horses of Achilles* (1868; M. of Fine A., Boston). His violent, romantic treatment of this subject clearly shows the influence of Delacroix. He was killed in the Franco-Prussian War before he produced any mature work.

Regnault Jean-Baptiste (1754–1829). French neo-classical painter. He followed only the superficial features of neo-classicism, e.g. *The Three Graces* (1799; Louvre).

Regnier Henri de (1864–1936). French poet and novelist. R.'s verse, from *Lendemains* (1885) to *Vestigia flammae* (1921), absorbed several influences (notably symbolism) but returned to classical forms and subjects. His novels remained under symbolist influence; the best known is *La Double Maîtresse* (1900).

Regnier Mathurin (1573–1613). French poet. *Les Satyres du Sieur Regnier* (1609), notable for their descriptions of characters and professions, foreshadow Molière.

Regnier Paule (1888–1950). French novelist. Her *Journal* (1951) describes the loneliness and spiritual problems which at last led her to suicide.

Rehearsal, The (1961). Play by Jean *Anouilh.

Reicha Antonin (1770–1836). French-naturalized composer of Czech parentage. He was a fellow-musician with Beethoven in the orchestra at Bonn (1788–94) and was a friend of Haydn. His numerous works reveal a style independent of the French, German and Czech traditions he drew upon. His theoretical works had a European currency.

Reidy Affonso Eduardo (1909–64). A leading Brazilian architect who worked with Le

Regency. Rosewood commode (*c.* 1820)

Régence. Silver wall-light

Regency. Interior of the Pavilion, Brighton

Reidy. Pedregulho estate, Rio de Janeiro

Johann Adam Reincken

Max Reinhardt. *Oedipus Rex* (Covent Garden, 1912)

8th-c. French reliquary of gold, decorated with pearls, garnets and coloured pastes. See also colour plate 24

Rejlander. *The Two Ways of Life* (detail)

Corbusier on the Ministry of Health Building in Rio; his subsequent numerous commissions, as the Pedregulho estate, Rio (1950), have a relaxed, lyrical quality that is typically Brazilian.

Reincken (Reinken) Johann Adam (1623–1722). German organist and composer who received his musical education in Deventer, Holland. From 1663 he was at Hamburg, where J. S. Bach visited him for lessons, thus establishing a direct contact with the school of J. P. *Sweelinck.

Reinhardt (Jean-Baptiste) 'Django' (1910–53). Belgian guitarist, one of the few European jazz musicians to achieve a status comparable to that of their U.S. counterparts. His unique style, using a technique developed to overcome the loss of 2 fingers and the partial paralysis of his left hand, combined jazz influences with his native gipsy music, and has been an important influence on jazz guitarists.

Reinhardt Max (1873–1943). Austrian actor and director who began directing in Berlin in 1903, quickly establishing himself as an important influence in world theatre. He took advantage of the mechanical improvements in stage technique, making great use of lighting effects, much stylized scenery and an arena stage, thereby mounting very spectacular productions, lavish and highly elaborate. In 1912 he directed *Oedipus Rex* at Covent Garden with J. Martin-Harvey. He was the founder of the Salzburg Festival (1920) but when Hitler came to power (1933) he left Germany and went to the U.S., where he lived until his death. His film career there (*A Midsummer Night's Dream*, 1935, directed in conjunction with William Dieterle) was unsuccessful.

Reiniger Lotte (1899–). German animated-film director. R. uses cut-paper silhouettes, often very elaborate, to tell her charmingly naïve stories. The delicacy and grace of her work is seen in *Adventures of Prince Achmed* (1925), *Carmen* (1933) with music by Bizet, and *Papageno* (1935) with music by Mozart.

Reinmar von Hagenau. Early 13th-c. Alsatian-born poet working at the court of Vienna, an early *Minnesinger. Much of his verse laments unrequited love.

Reinmar von Zweter (*c.* 1200–*c.* 1260). Rhenish-born poet working in Austria and Bohemia; he frequently wrote didactic and satirical verse on political and religious subjects.

Reisz Karel (1926–). Czech-born British film director. He worked as a critic and wrote a standard work on editing before making a short with T. Richardson, *Momma Don't Allow* (1956). After another documentary, *We Are the Lambeth Boys* (1958), and the success of Richardson's 1st Woodfall films, he made *Saturday Night and Sunday Morning* (1960). He produced *This Sporting Life* (1962) for his critical colleague Anderson, and directed *Night Must Fall* (1963), from an Emlyn Williams melodrama.

Reizenstein Franz (1911–). German-born pianist and composer working in England from 1934. He was a pupil of Hindemith (he dedicated *Twelve Preludes and Fugues* for piano to him) and of Vaughan Williams. His other works, all in a tonal idiom, include the cantata *Voices of the Night* (1952), violin, piano and cello concertos and chamber music. R. at present teaches at the R.A.M.

Rej Mikolaj (1505–69). Polish prose writer and poet, one of the most respected champions of the Reformation in Poland and the 1st Polish author to write consistently in the vernacular. His prose works include the *Postilla* (1557), a coll. of sermons, and the *Żywot człowieka poczciwego* (1568), a moral treatise; and his poetry includes *Kro'tha rocprawa.*

Rejlander Oscar G. (1813–75). Swedish photographer. R. popularized in England his allegorical daguerreotypes, which were prints made from a series of negatives placed to form 1 composite photograph, usually duplicating a theme from the Bible or traditional academic paintings. He was also a pioneer of candid rapid photography with a series of photographs showing fleeting facial expressions for Darwin's *Expression of the Emotions* (1872).

relief. Sculpture executed on a surface so that the figures project but are not free-standing; the projection may be considerable (high relief) or slight (low relief or bas-relief).

Religio Medici (1642). Book by Sir Thomas *Browne.

reliquary. A glass and metal container for the preservation and display of holy relics to be venerated on or under an altar. The metal is silver, silver-gilt or copper-gilt, often richly adorned with jewels.

Remarque Erich Maria. Pseud. of Erich Paul Remark (1898–). German novelist, author of many realistic works, including novels about both World Wars; but his outstanding success was *Im Westen nichts Neues* (1929; *All Quiet on the Western Front*, 1929), the most popular of all books describing the horrors of World War I and a famous film (1930) banned by the Nazis.

Rembrandt (Harmensz Van Rijn) (1606–69). Dutch painter, draughtsman and etcher, the son of a miller, born at Leyden. R. was sent to Leyden Univ. at the age of 14, but soon became a painter's apprentice. After 3 years he moved to Amsterdam, where he worked under Pieter Lastman, who transmitted Italian chiaroscuro to him. In 1625 he returned to Leyden and set up as an independent artist. He became popular as a portrait painter and as a result moved to Amsterdam (1631), where he lived until his death. R. quickly established his fame with a group portrait of surgeons, the *Anatomy Lesson of Professor Nicolaes Tulp* (Mauritshuis). The following year he married Saskia van Uylenburgh and in 1641 she bore him a son, Titus. At that time his life seemed prosperous and happy; he had numerous pupils and from 1636 his output of drawings and etchings increased; like his paintings they reflect the richness and exuberance of his life. His wife died in 1642 (the year he painted *The Night Watch*) and thereafter his affairs grew increasingly desperate until his bankruptcy in 1656. From 1660, when he moved into a smaller house near the Jewish quarter, R. became a prey to his creditors; to protect him his mistress, Hendrickje Stoffels, and his son, Titus, acted as agents, looking after the financial side of the sale of his works. In 1654 R.'s 2nd child Cornelia was born. Hendrickje died in 1662; Titus 6 years later. Though he died a pauper, contemporary references to his work show that R. remained famous and received important commissions, such as the group portrait *The Syndics* in 1662. His fame, though eclipsed for a few years after his death, soon grew again, and his work became a prize possession of collectors everywhere. It has been established with reasonable accuracy that R. left about 600 oil paintings, 1,500 drawings and 350 etchings. His works can be most conveniently grouped under their subject-matter as individual, group and self-portraits, Biblical, historical and mythological subjects, genre, studies and landscapes.

R. was the first to establish that the handling of paint, light and colour can equal subject-matter in importance. Therefore he could extend subject-matter to embrace the full range of human experience, and could portray old age without sentiment or revulsion. This attitude enabled him to penetrate into the essence of the subject, to lay bare its structure and find the visual equivalent. It enabled him to break the rules of composition and create new ones based on his wide sensibilities. Paint became a tool with which to express feeling, and the tonal range extended from velvety brown to black to sparkling white. R.'s immediate followers were Bols, Maes and Fabritius. He influenced all the great realists, including Courbet; Van Gogh freely copied some of his paintings. The drawings and etchings of R. created new genres, and raised them to an importance previously accorded only to oil painting. No other artist was able to give such a full expression to his personal life. R. had the power to transform a humble domestic scene into a Biblical event, as in *The Holy Family* (1631; Alte Pina., Munich), and comment on the most profound aspects of human nature in over 100 self-portraits. The *Self-portrait* of 1629 (Munich Bavarian State Coll.), one of the earliest, displays complete mastery of the use of light, richness of texture and profound interest in the depth of psychological content. There are also many paintings, drawings and etchings of R.'s family and closest friends, often in fantastic or picturesque clothes, or mythological and religious settings. At the height of his success, he painted *Saskia as Flora* (1635; N.G., London), as a glorification of life, an offering of colour and light. The portraits of his son Titus are in the most varied moods, e.g. the *Titus Reading* at Vienna. He painted a number of portraits of old women. Of these, *Portrait of an 83-year-old woman* (1634; N.G., London) is one of the most moving. R.'s group portraits were revolutionary in raising the genre from a documentary to a high artistic level. In the early *Anatomy Lesson* psychological relationships already override formal interest. This is carried still further in the *Sortie of the Shooting Company of Captain Frans Banning Cocq*, better known as *The Night Watch* (1642; Rijksmus., Amsterdam), once believed to be a night scene as a

Rembrandt. *Self-portrait as a young man*

Rembrandt. *Saskia as Flora*

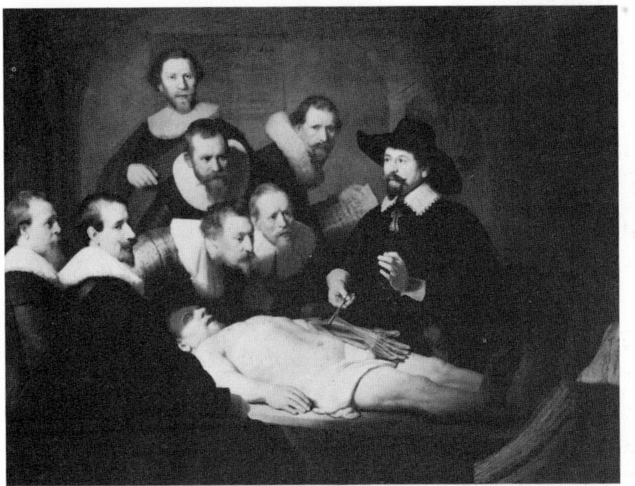

Rembrandt. *The Anatomy Lesson of Professor Nicolaes Tulp*

Rembrandt. *Françoise von Wassenhove*

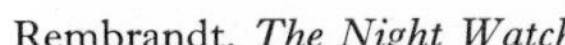

Rembrandt. *The Night Watch*

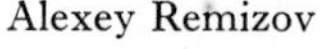
Alexey Remizov

Ernest Renan

Rembrandt. *Woman Bathing.* Also *engraving, *Flinck, *group portrait, *The *Syndics* and colour plate 60

Rembrandt. *Flayed Ox* (Louvre)

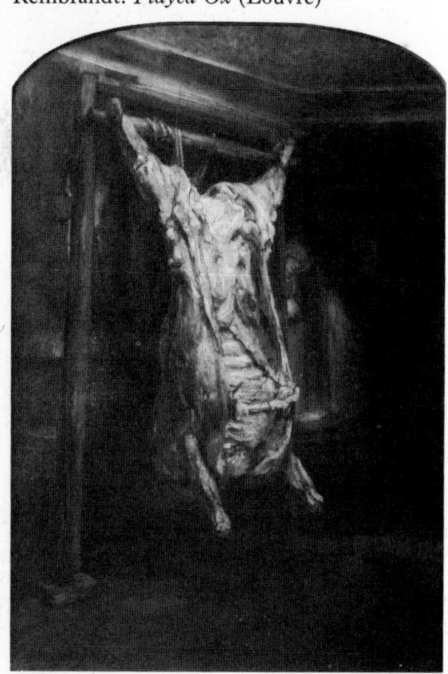

result of revarnishing and the accumulation of dirt; it was properly cleaned only in 1947. In 1715 its size was cut down; as a result 2 figures on the left are lost and the balance of the composition has been upset. The picture is outstanding for its brilliant use of colour and extreme chiaroscuro. In *The Syndics* (1662; Rijksmus., Amsterdam), the group is graver, almost menacing, seemingly about to judge the onlooker. The studies and landscapes such as the *Woman Bathing* (1655; N.G., London), the *Flayed Ox* studies (Cassel and Louvre) and the *Winter Landscape* (1646) are experiments, and in their freedom in handling paint, impasto and glazing broke new ground for the realist painters.

Remembrance of Things Past (1913–27). Novel by *Proust.

Remizov Alexey Mikhailovich (1877–1957). Russian émigré novelist and short-story writer, a master-juggler with words and fabricator of dreams and hallucinations; he often wrote *skaz* stories like *Leskov's. Only a few works have been trs., e.g. *The Clock* (1904; 1924) and *On a Field Azure* (1922; 1946).

Renaissance. The cultural and artistic revolution which originated in the N. Italian city-states of the 14th c. It manifested a new confidence in the power and dignity of man and was inspired by an increasingly intensive study of the artists and thinkers of classical antiquity. The growing importance of the secular order in European culture was reflected in the very large part played by lay aristocratic patronage in the R.; nobles such as Lorenzo de' *Medici were, moreover, themselves artistically gifted. Nevertheless, the Church continued as a great patron and the sponsorship of such great artists as Michelangelo by popes Alexander VI, Julius II and Leo X not only changed the face of Rome but also the development of European art. As well as changes in the pattern of patronage, the R. brought a radical change in the position of the artist: hitherto regarded as a skilled, if respected, craftsman, he began to be admired, sometimes with awe, as a superior kind of man, an inspired creator. Besides admiring great artistic inspiration, R. society also held the ideal of 'universal' or 'many-sided' man–skilled in every art, well read in the classics and an able scientist, engineer, courtier, soldier, etc. The work of the greater and lesser humanist scholars of the R. changed the character of European literary culture. The scholar-writer, the humanist Petrarch being perhaps the first, prided himself on knowledge of the classics rather than the metaphysical edifices of St Thomas Aquinas and the schoolmen. Good Latin and Greek grammars and pedagogical imitative prose laid the essential foundations of an elegant and formed style, Cicero being the admired model. The work of men like *Erasmus provided critical eds of classical texts and the Bible, and the rediscovery of much of Plato's work gave a new impulse to thought. The revolutionary invention of printing was welcomed by the most enlightened humanists who collaborated, as literary advisers, with such printers as *Froben and *Amerbach in producing scholarly texts; the printer's art too, in the work of such men, achieved standards of beauty not surpassed since. In the arts of painting and sculpture such masters as *Giotto, *Masaccio, *Donatello, Claus *Sluter, *Leonardo da Vinci and *Michelangelo originated and perfected a new visual language in which, as in classical art, the human figure and countenance became the most important vehicle of the artist's intention. Growing attention to anatomy and the formulation of the laws of perspective produced figures expressive in movement and gesture and with a bodily weighty 'presence', moving in a well-modulated and coherent picture space or standing freely and confidently in actual space. In architecture the work of L. B. *Alberti and *Brunelleschi returned to Greek and Roman buildings with their austere proportions, *orders and simple line, and the very ground-plan of the central-plan church placed the observer at the focus of the building rather than the altar, as in the basilican-planned church. In literature and the visual arts the R. can be said to have 'begun' in the 14th c. and to have been gradually submerged in the styles of mannerism from the 1520s. In music, however, it is the work of such 15th-c. composers as *Dunstable, *Dufay and *Josquin which introduced and established the harmonic principles of euphony, the formal principles of the cyclic mass and the parody mass, etc. and the imitative polyphony, which radically affected composition in succeeding cs. The great polyphonists of the 16th c. such as Lassus and Palestrina represent the late R. in music; and the new form of *opera is, in its conscious attempt to recreate Greek theatre, the last great manifestation of an epoch motivated by an admiration for classical antiquity.

Renan Ernest (1823–92). French writer. He was originally intended for the priesthood but his philological studies of the Bible led to a loss of faith. Although he was the outstanding French critic of Christianity in the 19th c. his writings–e.g. *Histoire des Origines du Christianisme* (1863–83; *The History of the Origins of Christianity*, 1889, 90) and especially vol. I, *La Vie de Jésus* (*The Life of Jesus*, 1864) –are composed in a suave, unctuous, almost mystical style, which won him many readers.

Renard Jules (1864–1910). French writer who, despite his association with the symbolists, was closer in feeling to the bitter naturalists such as Maupassant. His best-known work, *Poil de Carotte* (1894; *Carrots*, 1946), the partly autobiographical story of an unhappy childhood, helps to explain his resentful attitude to life and his constant tendency to look on the sordid side. He wrote other short novels and plays, and his *Journal* (publ. posth. 1925–7), covering the years 1887–1910, is both a document about the literary life of his times and a further revelation of his character.

Renart Jean. 13th-c. French poet whose romances of love and adventure are remarkable for their realistic descriptions of contemporary life and manners.

Renaud Madeleine (1903–). French actress. She is married to J.-L. Barrault and with him is co-director of their own co., which has played at the Odéon, Paris, since 1947. Her film appearances include B. Lévy's *La Maternelle* (1933) and Max Ophuls's *Le Plaisir* (1951).

Renaud de Montauban or **Les Quatre Fils Aymon** (*c.* 1300). A **chanson de geste*, one of the *Doon de Mayence Cycle*, relating the struggle of Renaud and his 3 brothers, sons of Aymon de Dordogne, against Charlemagne; their successful resistance is in part a result of the powers of Renaud's marvellous horse Bayard.

René (1802). Story by *Chateaubriand.

René d'Anjou (1408–80). Duke of Anjou, count of Provence and titular king of Naples, known as 'Good King René'. Patron of poets and musicians. His own poems include *Regnault et Jehanneton* and, in prose and verse, the *Livre du cueur d'amour espris*.

Reni Guido (1575–1642). Bolognese painter, pupil of L. Carracci. A refined colourist and sensitive draughtsman, he perfected an eclectic classicism. His melodramatic images of such diverse subjects as Christ, Lucretia and Cleopatra were much sought after, and he became the idol of the fashionable circles of Rome and Bologna. *The Massacre of the Innocents* at Bologna is his most dramatic and celebrated work. The composition, of great dramatic power, owes much to Raphael and the study of the antique. *Aurora*, a fresco painted for the Casino Rospigliosi in Rome in 1610, is perhaps his best-known work. Other work includes *St John the Baptist preaching* (Dulwich Gal., London).

Renn Ludwig (1889–). German novelist; his most famous work is *Krieg* (1929; *War*, 1929), a semi-autobiographical account of life in the trenches in World War I.

Renoir (Pierre) Auguste (1841–1919). French painter born in Limoges, moved to Paris in 1845. He trained and worked with great facility as a porcelain painter (1856–9). With his earnings he entered the École des Beaux-Arts (1862–4) and became a pupil of Gleyre with Monet, Bazille and Sisley. Working with them in Paris and during summers at Fontainebleau, he emerged as one of the most naturally gifted of the future impressionists. He exhibited in 4 of the 8 impressionist exhibitions.

The character of impressionism emerged from the paintings of Monet and R. between 1867 and 1870. Mutually inspired, they painted directly from the subject (poppy-fields, figures under trees, riverscapes) and to retain the momentariness of nature's changing appearance developed a technique of broadly painted broken brush-strokes. The living immediacy of their landscapes was further emphasized by their empirical use of complementary colour in shadows, clear scintillating colour in Monet, more sensitive subtle relationships in R., e.g. *Lise* (1867; Folkwang Mus., Essen). The difference between them is evident in their paintings of *La Grenouillère* (Met. Mus; and Nat. Mus., Stockholm) painted side by side in 1869, Monet's in aggressive clean strokes of fresh blue and ochre, R.'s in soft feathery areas of muted green, pink and violet. The climax of R.'s important contribution to impressionism is in works like *The Swing* and *Moulin de la Galette* (both 1876; Louvre) in

Madeleine Renaud

René d'Anjou: medal by Pietro da Milano

Reni. *Aurora* (detail). Also *Bologna

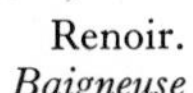

Renoir. *Baigneuse*

Renoir. *Lise*

Renoir. *Moulin de la Galette*

Auguste Renoir.
Diana

Auguste Renoir. *Les Parapluies*

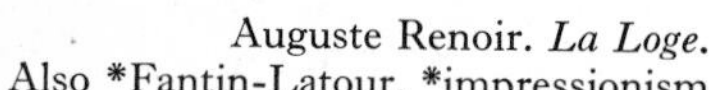

Auguste Renoir. *La Loge*.
Also *Fantin-Latour, *impressionism

Jean Renoir.
Le Déjeuner sur l'herbe

which gay Paris life flickers under a patchwork of mottled light.

Right through his career, R.'s work never reveals the introspective seriousness of Monet or Cézanne (he shocked Gleyre by saying 'if painting were not a pleasure to me I should certainly not do it') and unlike Courbet, Pissarro or Zola (of whom R. said 'he thinks he has portrayed the people by saying that they stink') never dwelt on any but the pleasing aspects of life. His lack of intellectual seriousness led to a disturbing fluctuation in his early work from the pure impressionism (1869–76), to Salon-conscious academicism, e.g. *Diana* (1867; N.G., Washington) and a literary anecdotal element present in *La Loge* (1871; Courtauld Gal., London). The constants in his work are his superb touch and his unfailing colour sense.

In the late 1870s he scored a great Salon success with works like the sweet and charming *Mme Charpentier and Daughters* (1878; Met. Mus.), but with the end of his impressionist phase he felt uncertain. Paintings like *Dance at Bougival* (1883; Boston) and *Les Parapluies* (*c.* 1883; N.G., London) show him attempting to organize his forms with a more sculptural strength. The major work of this '*manière aigre*' was the large *Baigneuses* (1884–7; Tyson Coll., Philadelphia): the figures very tightly drawn and modelled against the softness of the landscape. The classical character of this period reflects his visit to Italy in 1881 and his current admiration for Raphael, Ingres and French Renaissance sculpture.

His later works are at once more freely painted and strongly coloured (oppressively hot reds and oranges), but retain this sense of monumentality, e.g. *Seated Bather* (1914; A. Inst., Chicago). The transition to sculpture in his last years was almost predictable. The bronze *Venus Victrix* (1914; Tate) is a typical example.

Renoir Jean (1894–). French film director. The son of Auguste R., R. started directing in 1924 with *La Fille de L'Eau*, and his 2nd film, *Nana* (1926) from *Zola, was already a work of great accomplishment. His comedy of Service life, *Tire-au Flanc* (1929), was 30 years ahead of its time in making extensive use of the hand-held camera. After big failures with *Le Tournoi* and *Le Bled* (both 1929), his 1st sound film was a brilliant adaptation of a Feydeau comedy, *On Purge Bébé* (1931), written in a week, and shot in less. This obtained for him the chance to make *La Chienne* (1931) in which are evident the ideas central to R.'s cinema: that freedom is not the absence of external restrictions but an individual matter of choice of action in the face of them, and that 'everyone has his reasons'. These 2 principles are expounded through the decisions of the tramp who has been fished out of the Seine and made respectable in *Boudu sauvé des eaux* (1932), to return to tramping, or of the aristocratic officer in *La Grande Illusion* (1937) to sacrifice his life flamboyantly to allow a workman and a Jewish banker to escape from the prison camp. Although R. has handled with great success the sophisticated tragi-comedy of *La Règle du Jeu* (1939), literary adaptations like *Les Bas-Fonds* (1936) and *La Bête Humaine* (1938), and directed a bleak forerunner of neo-realism in *Toni* (1935), perhaps his most characteristic films are his warmest and least pretentious in which all the interest comes from R.'s handling of the people: *Boudu, Chotard et Cie* (1933), *Une Partie de Campagne* (shot 1936, left uncompleted and shown in 1946), *The Diary of a Chambermaid* (one of his 5 films in the U.S., 1946), *The Golden Coach* (1952), *Le Déjeuner sur l'herbe* (1959). His *Le Caporal Épinglé* (1962), is set, like *La Grande Illusion*, in a prisoner-of-war camp.

Renwick James (1818–95). U.S. architect, representative of the 'picturesque' movement in America. He designed St Patrick's cathedral, New York, and the Smithsonian Institution, Washington, both neo-Gothic in style.

repertory. A movement which largely owed its inception to Miss A. *Hornimann, who in 1903 rebuilt the *Abbey Theatre, Dublin and in 1908 established the Gaiety Theatre, Manchester as the 1st repertory theatre in Britain. A co. had several plays in its season's repertoire, performed a different play every night; this system is now being revived in some theatres but most repertory cos give each play in their repertoire a run of from 1 to 3 weeks.

répétiteur. French term now used in English for the man who coaches opera singers in their parts in preliminary rehearsals.

Repin Ilya (1844–1930). Russian painter, the best known and probably the most brilliant of the *Wanderers group. His work is considered a model for the *socialist realist school in Russia. *The Volga Boatmen* (1870–3), one of his most famous works, is typical in having the poorest and most miserable Russian peasants as subject. Apart from social themes, R. was a talented portraitist and landscape painter.

replica. An exact copy of a painting either by the painter of the original or under his direction. The word is frequently used to describe identical works when it is not known which was produced first.

Representative Men (1850). Coll. lectures by Emerson.

reprise. Term used in music for: (1) the repeat of the 1st themes after the development section, in *sonata form, equivalent to recapitulation; (2) the repeat of a song in a musical comedy.

reproduction. Copy of a painting or drawing made by some means which renders it capable of being printed in large numbers for the purpose of popularization. From the 17th to the late 19th c. engraving was the means of r., mezzotint being the most widely used technique; this has been superseded by photographic processes.

Repton Humphry (1752–1818). British landscape gardener. At first he followed the methods of L. 'Capability' Brown but later modified his style reintroducing flower-beds round houses with attention to the 'picturesque' saying: 'A garden is not a landscape but a work of art using the materials of nature.' 200 or more of the *Red Books* of watercolour sketches for his clients testify to his great success, which laid the foundations of English 19th-c. gardening for J. C. Loudon. R. publ. several works: *Sketches and Hints on Landscape Gardening* (1795) and *Observations on . . . Landscape Gardening* (1803) with his own novel illustrations of estates before and after his improvements.

Republic, The: Dialogue by *Plato.

requiem. A mass for the dead. In addition to the sections of the *mass, the r. has an introit, opening with the words '*requiem aeternam dona eis, Domine*'; the gradual and tract; the famous sequence *Dies irae*; the offertory and the communion *Lux aeterna*. Among the great r.s are those by Palestrina, Victoria, Mozart, Berlioz, Verdi and *Brahms's *Ein deutsches Requiem.*

Requiem for a Nun (1951). Novel by William *Faulkner.

reredos. An ornamental screen covering the wall behind and above the altar.

réseau: *lace

resin or **rosin.** Dried refined gum of turpentine which is applied to the bows of stringed instruments to improve their 'grip' on the strings.

resist. One method of pottery decoration involves screening the pattern areas and then covering the object with coloured matter, usually a metallic solution. The screening material or r.–which can be water-resistant fluid or wax painted on, or paper cut to the pattern–is burnt off in the kiln. The pattern is left in the natural colour of the ware or foundation colour against a bright background.

Resnais Alain (1922–). French film director. R. began with personal 16-mm. *avant-garde* films which he followed with shorts on painters. *Guernica* (1951) uses the Picasso painting, sculptures and a poem by Éluard to recall an event in the Spanish Civil War. Of the 1st characteristic shorts, *Les Statues Meurent Aussi* (with Marker, 1952) uses museum specimens to describe the effects of colonialism, and *Nuit et Brouillard* (1955), about concentration camps, intercuts coloured present with monochrome past, and makes extensive use of tracking shots. *Toute la Mémoire du Monde* (1956), about the Bibliothèque Nationale in Paris, and *Le Chant du Styrène*, about the industrial synthesis of Polystyrene, exploit the otherworldliness of their settings. His 1st feature, *Hiroshima mon amour* (1959), script by Marguerite Duras, takes memory as the starting-point for a series of juxtapositions of past and present, linked by intercut tracking shots which can be traced to R.'s admiration for Hitchcock. In *L'Année Dernière à Marienbad* (1961) past and present, real and imaginary are mixed in a way so abstractly complicated that the film demands to be approached as a puzzle. *Muriel* (1963) reintroduces character, which had been so notably absent from *Marienbad*, and an elaborate observation of quotidian life as a background for R.'s intellectual preoccupations.

Renwick. The Smithsonian Institution

Repton. Pavilion from *Observations*

Repin. *They did not expect him.* Also *Mussorgsky

Resnais. *Hiroshima mon amour*

Reticella. Part of a handkerchief (late 16th or early 17th c.)

Retable (alabaster) at Huerta cathedral

Revell. Toronto city hall

Respighi Ottorino (1879–1936). Italian composer. His colourful music shows the influence of his teacher Rimsky-Korsakov, and affinities to the work of R. Strauss and the French impressionists. It includes: the symphonic poems, *The Fountains of Rome* (1917) and *The Pines of Rome* (1924), and the orchestral suite *The Birds* (1927), based on themes by Rameau, Pasquini, etc.; he also arranged, from Rossini, the music for the ballet *La Boutique Fantasque* (1919).

respond. Architectural term for a half-pillar (or *pilaster, *corbel, etc.) joined to a wall and supporting the side of the last arch of an arcade at the point where it meets the wall.

Restif de la Bretonne Nicolas-Edme (1734–1806). French novelist who produced over 250 vols of realistic stories, mainly about the lower classes. They include *Le Paysan perverti* (1775), which describes how a young peasant is corrupted by Parisian life, and his memoirs, *Monsieur Nicolas . . .* (1796–7; 1930–1).

Restoration comedy. Term applied to the witty, bawdy comedies of manners produced in England from the restoration of Charles II (1660) until *c.* 1710. The main authors indicated are *Wycherley, *Congreve, *Farquhar and *Vanbrugh; some of Dryden's comedies are of this type.

resultant note. An acoustic effect resulting from the loud sounding of 2 notes fairly close in pitch. It may be possible to hear another note above them – called the 'summational note' (the sum of the 2 frequencies); or another note below them – the 'differential tone' (the difference between the 2 frequencies).

retable. Carved or painted screen raised behind the altar of a church. R.s were widely used until the early 15th c. when their place was taken by the winged altarpiece. They were particularly highly developed in Spain where they continued in use until well into the 16th c.

Reth Alfred (1886–). Hungarian-born painter of the school of Paris. He settled in Paris in 1905 and became a cubist; he was later a member of the Abstraction-Création group. Much of his time has been devoted to experiments with new materials and techniques.

Rethel Alfred (1816–59). German painter and graphic artist chiefly remembered for his powerful series of woodcuts (1848) on the *Dance of Death* theme in the manner of Dürer and Holbein the Younger. Idealized historical paintings formed the major part of his work, e.g. frescoes illustrating the life of Charlemagne, in the town hall, Aachen.

reticella (Italian, 'small net'). A simple form of needlepoint lace; made from the late 15th c. onwards.

Retté Adolphe (1863–1930). French poet and critic, ed. of 2 early symbolist reviews, *La Vogue* and *L'Ermitage*.

Return of the Native, The (1878). Novel by Thomas *Hardy.

Retz (Jean-François) Paul de Gondi, Cardinal de (1613–79). French archbishop who played an important part in the Fronde; his *Mémoires* (1717; *Memoirs*, 1723) give a vivid, if unreliable picture of the period.

Reubke Julius (1834–58). German composer and pianist whose dramatic work for organ the *94th Psalm* shows the obvious influence of his teacher Liszt.

Reuchlin Johann (1455–1522). German humanist, the leading Hebrew scholar of his time and the fount of Hebrew and Greek teaching in Germany. He was the centre of a famous controversy which produced the anon. *Epistolae Obscurorum Virorum* (1518), a humanist satire (ridiculing scholasticism) which had a European success.

Reuter Christian (1665–*c.* 1712). German writer, author of a series of books about 'Frau Schlampampe' and 'Schelmuffsky', parodying contemporary novels.

Reuter Fritz (1810–74). German writer in Low German dialect; after the verse coll. *Läuschen un Rimels* (1853) followed novels and autobiographical works which made his name known beyond his native province.

Revell Viljo (1910–). A leading Finnish architect. R. worked for a time in Aalto's office and built up an extensive practice in the 1950s by designing rational, well-detailed buildings. Many important young Finnish architects went through his office. In 1958 he won the competition for Toronto city hall with a structure of 2 blocks, wilfully curved in an attempt to give it a special character as the city hall.

revenge tragedy. In Elizabethan and Jacobean drama revenge was a frequent and popular theme, and one which gave an opportunity for a great deal of bloodshed on stage. Kyd's *The Spanish Tragedy* started the vogue of the r. t. (which derived from the tragedies of Seneca) and Shakespeare's *Hamlet* contains many of its typical features.

Revolt in the Desert (1927). Book by T. E. *Lawrence.

Revolt of Islam, The (1818). Poem by *Shelley.

Revolutionary Study. Nickname of *Chopin's study, op. 10 no. 12 (1831).

revue. Name derived from the French; it means a collection of sketches, monologues and musical items mainly satirizing topical events. In the 1890s the English r.s were mainly spectacular displays of costume, music and dancing, a style continued in the U.S. by Florenz *Ziegfeld. In England, Sir Charles *Cochran was responsible for many r.s which were witty rather than spectacular and this trend continued until World War II. In recent years the satirical aspect has predominated.

Reyer (originally Ray) Louis-Étienne-Ernest (1823–1909). French composer and journalist (pro Wagner and Berlioz). His works include the operas, *La Statue* (1861), *Erostate* (1862) and *Sigurd* (1884). His symphonic ode *Le Selam*, based on F. *David's *Le Désert*, with words by T. Gautier, and his opera *Maître Wolfram* won the praise of Berlioz.

Reymerswaele Marinus van: *Marinus van Reymerswaele

Reymont Władysław Stanisław (1867–1925). Polish novelist and short-story writer. In his 1st novel, *Komediantka* (1896; *The Commedienne*, 1921) he describes the life of itinerant actors. In the 4-vol. novel *Chłopi* (1904; *The Peasants*, 1925–6), for which he was awarded the Nobel prize in 1924, he gave one of the best pictures of peasant life in world literature.

Reynard: **Roman de Renart*

Reth. *Corner of the Studio* (1913)

Rethel. *Dance of Death*

Reynolds. *Self-portrait aged about 25*

Reynolds Sir Joshua (1723–92). English painter of portraits and genre allegorical subjects, founder-member and 1st president of the R.A. (1768). R. studied with Thomas Hudson, and, under Admiral Keppel's patronage, visited Europe (1749–52). His portrait of Keppel (1753–4; Greenwich) led to many other portrait commissions, great affluence and influence, and he painted portraits of George III and Queen Charlotte (1779). R. himself became an art collector and also founded the R.A. Schools. Friendly with and accepted in aristocratic circles, he was also friendly with Dr Johnson, Sheridan and theatrical and literary circles in London. R. also painted somewhat sentimental pictures of children, and, especially in his later years, mythological and allegorical paintings. Among his works are: *Mrs Siddons as the Tragic Muse* (Huntington Foundation, San Marino, California), *The Infant Samuel* and *The Age of Innocence* (N.G., London). R.'s views on art and paintings were publ. as *Discourses Delivered to the Students of the Royal Academy by Sir Joshua Reynolds.*

Reynolds. *The Triumph of Truth*

Reynolds. *Lady Smith and her Children.* Also *Goldsmith, *Siddons

Rheims cathedral France. The royal cathedral of France, and one of the great series of churches built in the Île de France during the late 12th and early 13th c. It was begun in 1211 with a compact plan, 3-storey elevation (including the 1st use of bar-tracery) and a high quadripartite vault. The 2-tower W. front (2nd half of 13th c.) marks the climax of a development in which the separate levels are merged into one another (contrast Notre-Dame, Paris); the area of glazing and open-work tracery is expanded to cover almost all the surface, while the sculpture (which again marks the high point of Gothic naturalism and drama) grows out of the architecture in a single ectstatic movement.

Rheinberger Joseph Gabriel (1839–1901). German organist-composer, who enjoyed a European reputation as a teacher of organ and composition.

Rhenish stoneware. During the 16th and early 17th cs production in the potteries of Cologne, Frechen and Raeren, as well as other Rhenish towns, reached very great heights of artistic excellence; the style was distinguished by powerful relief designs and fine proportion. Well-known types of ware include *Bellarmine jugs.

Rheims cathedral: detail of the right portal

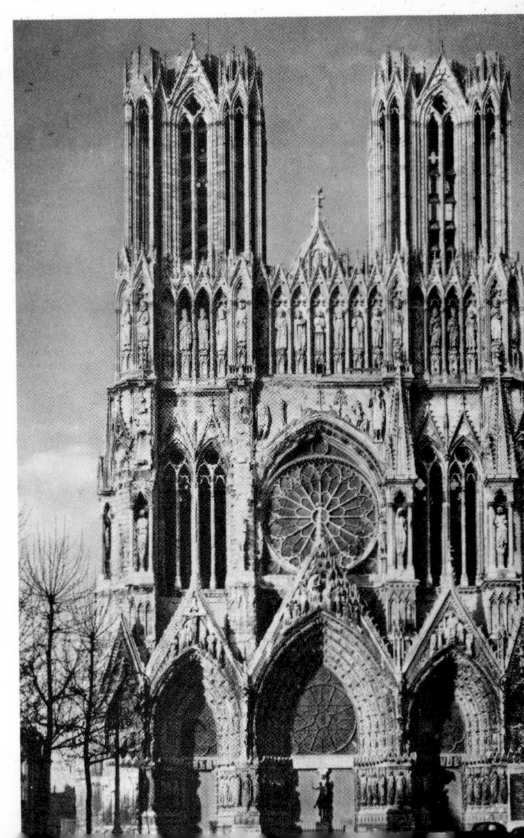
Rheims cathedral. Also *Apocalypse

Ribalta.
The Vision of Father Simon

Tatania
Riabouchinska

Jusepe Ribera. *St Peter Repentant*

rhetoric. The art of speaking effectively was first seriously studied and taught by the Greek sophists from about the 5th c. B.C. Aristotle's *Rhetoric* treated the subject as an offshoot of logic, and it thereafter contained 2 not always compatible and variously stressed elements, the study of persuasive and of logical speech. In Roman times r. was a popular art and study (*Cicero and *Quintillian); it was one of the 7 *liberal arts in the middle ages and became a key to advancement during the Renaissance. It declined as a study during the 18th c. The modern meaning (often used pejoratively) expresses only its persuasive and emotional connotations.

rhétoriqueurs. Term applied to a number of 15th-c. French poets, including *Chastellain, *La Marche, Jean *Marot, *Gringore and *Lemaire de Belges, whose verse was very artificial; they did, however, considerably expand poetic technique.

Rhine Gold, The (German *Das Rheingold*). The 1st part of *Wagner's opera cycle *The Ring of the Nibelung.*

Rhinoceros (1960). Play by Eugène *Ionesco.

rhyme. In single or MASCULINE r.s the final syllables of the rhyming words have similar sounds, e.g. day/away, in double or FEMININE r.s. the last 2 syllables, e.g. measure/treasure. Triple and even quadruple r.s occur, usually in comic verse.

rhyme royal. Decasyllabic stanza of 7 lines, rhyming *ababbcc*. Chaucer first used it in English; it is the scheme of Shakespeare's *Rape of Lucrece.*

rhythm. In music and language the pattern of accented notes or syllables. The rhythmic framework of a piece of music, for example, is determined by the number of beats in the bar; this gives a rigid system of accented beats (the metre) which the music may adhere to or more commonly may surround with conflicting systems. The more complex this conflict of patterns, the more complex the rhythm of the piece. Other aspects of rhythm are the lengths of phrases and motifs and the speed at which the harmony changes. In English verse, regular patterns of accented and unaccented syllables form the various metres (*metre in verse).

Jusepe Ribera.
Boy with a club foot

Riabouchinska Tatania (1917–). Russian dancer taught by Preobrajenska. As a *baby ballerina with Col. de Basil's co. she enjoyed great personal success; her talent was not merely precocious and she developed style; she created roles in several ballets by her husband, Lichine, e.g. *Graduation Ball* (1940).

Riba Carles (1893–). Catalan poet and trs. His finest poetical work, *Estances*, is written in a highly intellectual and precise style. He has trs. both Greek and Roman classics and works by Grimm, Poe and other 19th-c. authors into Catalan.

Ribalta Francisco (1565–1628). One of the 1st Spanish painters to use tenebrist effects in scenes of intense religious fervour. He was trained in Madrid, probably under Navarrete, then settled in Valencia. His paintings include *The Vision of Father Simon* (1612; N.G., London) and *The Vision of St Francis* (*c.* 1620; Prado). His son JUAN (*c.* 1597–1628) was his pupil and collaborator.

Ribeiro Bernardim (1482–1552). Portuguese writer. Little is known of his life beyond what is implied in his romance *Menina e Moça* (1554), a semi-autobiographical pastoral novel of passionate love and grief, which also contains many fine poems.

Ribeiro Tomás (1831–1901). Portuguese poet, author of the long patriotic poem *Dom Jaime.*

Ribemont-Dessaignes Georges (1884–). French painter and writer, member of the Paris dada group.

Ribera Jusepe (*c.* 1590–1652). Spanish painter and etcher. In 1616 he settled in Italy; his life was full of dramatic incidents and this is reflected in the violent subject-matter of his paintings, the contrasted modelling of his figures and the theatrical lighting of his compositions. He was strongly influenced by Caravaggio and Correggio and his own powerful style we associate today with the Spanish baroque. His uncompromising realism is demonstrated in the *Boy with a club foot.* In his last paintings he achieved a mastery of light similar to Velazquez's.

Ribera Pedro (*c.* 1683–1742). Spanish architect. He developed Spanish baroque, being influenced by Italian architects like Borromini.

Pedro Ribera.
Entrance to
the Madrid Museum

Ricchino. Palazzo Brera

Marco Ricci. *Landscape*

His works include the Virgin del Puerto, Madrid (a centralized church with pretty dome) and the Hospicio de San Fernando, Madrid, where all the ornament is concentrated on an immensely lavish doorway.

Ricard Louis-Xavier (1843–1911). French poet, one of the original *Parnassians; they met in his mother's *salon.*

Ricchino Francesco Maria (1583–1658). Italian baroque architect. Born in Milan, he went to Rome as a young man and probably saw Maderno's S. Susanna in course of building. He returned to Milan in 1603. In 1607 he designed S. Giuseppe, which initiates the true baroque style in N. Italy. The plan is an octagon plus a square, the façade (not completed until 1630) a rich but unified composition using scrolls, half-columns, and a variety of pediment shapes. R.'s Collegio Elvetico, Milan (1627) has perhaps the earliest curved façade of the baroque. He built many other buildings in Milan including the Palazzo Brera (now the art gal.).

Ricci the brothers Luigi (1805–59) and Federico (1809–77). Prolific and successful Italian opera composers best known for their joint effort, the comic opera *Crispino e la comare* (1850).

Ricci Marco (1676–1729). Venetian landscape painter, nephew and collaborator of Sebastiano R. He was often employed to paint landscape backgrounds in his uncle's religious works. He was the originator of romantic landscape painting in 18th-c. Venice and N. Italy.

Ricci Sebastiano (1659–1734). Venetian painter active in Vienna, Paris and London. He painted the *Resurrection* in Chelsea Hospital chapel and left decorations in Burlington House unfinished. He was chiefly influenced by Veronese but had a looser lighter style which in turn influenced G. B. Tiepolo.

Riccio Andrea Briosco called (1470–1532). Paduan sculptor influenced by Donatello's work; most of his sculpture is in bronze. A heavily ornamented Paschal candlestick for the Santo, Padua is his most celebrated achievement. His many statuettes include *Warrior on Horseback* (V. and A.).

Rice Elmer (1892–). U.S. playwright. R.'s play *The Adding Machine* (1923) uses expressionist techniques to satirize the machine-like human beings produced by industrialism. His plays include *Street Scene* (1929), *Counsellor-at-Law* (1931) and *Dream Girl* (1945).

ricercare (Italian, 'search'). The name, in the 16th c., for a polyphonic piece for instruments using *imitation; later the term was applied to especially elaborate fugues, e.g. the 6-part ricercar in Bach's *Musical Offering.*

Rich Barnabe (*c.* 1540–1617). English writer of romances and pamphlets. His reminiscences, *Riche his Farewell to Militarie Profession* (1581), contains a story *Apolonius and Silla* from which Shakespeare created *Twelfth Night.*

Richard I (1157–99). King of England (1189–99), called 'the Lionheart', the author of 2 lyric poems in French, one written in captivity. Returning from the 3rd Crusade, R. was captured by Leopold of Austria (*Blondel).

Richard II (1595; publ. 1597). Tragedy by *Shakespeare, written 1595. Its source was *Holinshed. The deposition scene appears to have been cut during Elizabeth's reign, except for a performance paid for by the earl of Essex's supporters on the day before his Rebellion (1601).

Richard III (1593?; publ. 1597). Historical drama by *Shakespeare, written *c.* 1592. Its sources were *Holinshed and perhaps Sir Thomas More's *History of Richard III.* It has been filmed several times, notably in 1955, directed by Olivier.

Richards Ceri (1903–). Welsh painter trained at Swansea and the R.C.A., London. In the early 1930s, influenced by Picasso and Ernst, he was one of the 1st British artists to experiment with relief and collage constructions. After a surrealist phase he turned to informal abstraction of ebullient lyricism. Music has been the inspiration for some of his finest work, e.g. the important *La Cathédrale Engloutie* series of paintings and constructions based on Debussy. He has also used themes from Dylan Thomas's poems.

Richards I(vor) A(rmstrong) (1893–). English critic, an authority on romanticism; with C. K. Ogden he wrote *The Meaning of Meaning* (1923) and created Basic English. His

M. and S. Ricci. *Adoration of the Magi*

Riccio. *Christ in Limbo*: Paschal candlestick for the Santo

Riccio. *Warrior on Horseback*

Ceri Richards. *La Cathédrale Engloutie*

Jonathan Richardson the Younger. *Self-portrait*

Jonathan Richardson. *George Vertue*

H. H. Richardson. Marshall Field Wholesale Store. Also *Chicago school

Sir Ralph Richardson as Peer Gynt

Samuel Richardson: painting by Joseph Highmore

very influential critical works include *Principles of Literary Criticism* (1924).

Richardson Sir Albert (1880–1964). British architect. Enthusiasm for the 18th c. led him to live a theatrical existence on a Georgian stage set and to vituperate frequently while president of the R.A. (1954–6) against modern architecture. His work includes academic buildings, e.g. the Battle of Britain chapel in Westminster Abbey.

Richardson Dorothy (1882–). English novelist, the 1st to use the *stream-of-consciousness technique. Her main work is *Pilgrimage* (1915–38), a cycle of 12 novels.

Richardson Henry Handel (1870–1946). Pseud. of Mrs Ethel Florence Lindsay Robertson, Australian novelist who spent most of her life in Europe. The novel *Maurice Guest* (1908) displays an intellectuality rare in Australian novels, while her trilogy *The Fortunes of Richard Mahony* (1917) probes the immigrant mind with a skill and sympathy even rarer.

Richardson Henry Hobson (1838–86). U.S. architect and pioneer of modern large-scale commercial buildings. He worked for a time in Paris, acquiring a lavish Second Empire-cum-Gothic manner (various public buildings and churches). He broke with this traditional style when he built a department store at Hartford, Conn. (1875), and his mature masterpieces are the Allegheny County Jail, Pittsburgh, and the Marshall Field Wholesale Store, Chicago (demolished). These works are austere and massive, relying on straight lines, flat surfaces and exposed masonry (though often iron-frame in construction). His chief influence was on *Sullivan and the Chicago school.

Richardson Jonathan (1665–1745). English portrait painter and writer, pupil of J. Riley. Though he succeeded Kneller as leading portraitist in England his writings are of more interest than his stereotyped paintings. He publ. essays on the theory of painting, art criticism and connoisseurship and with his son JONATHAN (1694–1771) produced the 1st English guide-book to the art treasures of Italy, *An Account of some of the Statues and Bas-Reliefs, Drawings and Pictures in Italy* (1722).

Richardson Sir Ralph (1902–). English actor equally good in Shakespearian and modern parts. His best performances have been in *Peer Gynt*, in J. B. Priestley's *An Inspector Calls* and as Falstaff, all at the Old Vic (1944–7) and more recently he had great success as the Father in Pirandello's *Six Characters in Search of an Author* (1963).

Richardson Samuel (1689–1761). English novelist. A printer by trade, R. began his 1st novel, *Pamela,* as a set of patterns for letter-writing, but the tale of a virtuous servant-girl's resistance to her master's attempts to seduce her grew into a romance and became, on its publ. in 1740, an enormous success. It was followed by *Clarissa Harlowe* (1747–8) and *Sir Charles Grandison* (1753–4), novels which the author designed to set forth the patterns, respectively, of a good woman and a good man. The novels were quickly trs. into several European languages and had a wide influence particularly in France, where Rousseau modelled *La Nouvelle Héloïse* upon them.

For his contemporaries, and particularly for the women of the age, R.'s novels combined the emotional delights of a romance with the moral irreproachability of a tract. To modern readers their sentiment seems lachrymose and over-strained and their morality founded more upon bourgeois prudence than upon principle. Pamela's marriage to her master makes her resistance seem more calculation than chastity. Their length and leisurely pace, too, make them tedious. Nevertheless, R. was a careful observer and reliable recorder of life as he saw it; his characters do not degenerate into dolls or caricatures, but remain human beings of some complexity of motive.

He lacked Fielding's breadth of experience and knowledge of the world, but within his limitations he provides an equally good picture of the society of his time, particularly the 'below-stairs' society of servants and small tradesmen. With Sterne, whose work he loathed, R. founded the cult of 'sentimentalism' which replaced the balance and reticence of the Augustans and paved the way for 'Gothick' literature and the romantics. *Pamela*, the 1st epistolary novel, besides providing the bait which tempted a greater writer, *Fielding, to the novel form, was the 1st novel of introspection; the device of using the characters' intimate letters and journals permitted their inward thoughts and attitudes to be fully recorded.

Richardson Tony (1930–). British stage and film director. Most of his stage work has been for the *English Stage Co. He has directed all John Osborne's plays, including *Look Back in Anger*; he also directed the film (1959) for Woodfall, partly owned by Osborne, after making one short with *Reisz. Apart from *Sanctuary* (1960) for Fox in Hollywood, all his films have been for Woodfall and are fashionable adaptations of British modern plays and novels, e.g. *The Entertainer* (1959), except for *Tom Jones* (1963), from Fielding.

Richelieu Armand-Jean du Plessis de, Cardinal (1585–1642). French statesman who broke the semi-independent power of the French Protestants, strengthened the monarchy and prepared the successful French entry into the Thirty Years War. R. founded the Académie Française (1635), which he encouraged to criticize Corneille's *Le Cid.* He had literary ambitions and employed the *cinq auteurs.

Richepin Jean (1849–1926). French poet, novelist and playwright. *Les Chansons des Gueux* (1876), a coll. of poems describing the life of tramps with unusual realism and using their slang, made R. famous (he was imprisoned for publ. them).

Richler Mordecai (1931–). Canadian novelist whose work depends for much of its prolific richness on his Jewish background. 4 untidy but vehement early novels made his reputation as an *enfant terrible*; e.g. *The Apprenticeship of Duddy Kravitz* (1959).

Richter Adrian Ludwig (1803–84). German book illustrator and landscape painter, a representative of late romanticism. He was a prolific illustrator of German folk-tales and fairy-tales. His autobiography *Lebenserinnerungen eines deutschen Malers . . .* was popular.

Richter Ernst Friedrich Edward (1808–79). German composer and music theorist, author of a famous work on harmony.

Richter Franz Xaver (1709–89). German-Moravian composer, violinist and singer, a leading member of the *Mannheim school.

Richter Hans (1843–1916). German conductor. He worked for a year as copyist to Wagner, became a leading exponent of Wagner and shared with that master the direction of the London Wagner concerts in 1877. He conducted the famous Orchestral Festival Concerts (1879–97) in London and was conductor of the Hallé Orchestra (1897–1911).

Richter Hans (1888–). German painter and pioneer of the *avant-garde* film. He joined the dada group in Zürich (1916) and in 1917 painted his first abstracts. In 1918 he began to develop abstract themes on rolls of paper and in 1921 produced his 1st abstract film, *Rhythm 21.* He was connected with the surrealist cinema in the late 1920s. In 1941 he settled in the U.S. His films include *Dreams That Money Can Buy* (1947).

Richter Karl (1926–). German organist and conductor resident at Munich but touring widely in Europe and the U.S.

Richter Sviatoslav (1914–). Soviet pianist of outstanding technical virtuosity and of great musicianship. He has toured in the West making a particular impression as an interpreter of Beethoven.

Rickman Thomas (1776–1841). English architect and writer. He was a pioneer of the Gothic revival, designing a very large number of churches in that style, as well as the new court of St John's College, Cambridge, and other domestic buildings. But he is chiefly famous for the 1st reliable book on Gothic architecture in England (publ. 1817), in which R. coined the names, followed by all later writers, 'Norman', 'Early English', 'Decorated', and 'Perpendicular'.

Rideau Cramoisi, Le (1952). Short film directed by A. *Astruc.

Riders to the Sea (1904). 1-act play by J. M. Synge.

ridge-beam. Architectural term for the horizontal beam running along the top of a pitched roof, i.e. along the line where the 2 slopes meets.

Riding Laura (1901–). U.S. poet, long an expatriate in Europe. The stature of her elliptical and experimental verse is still unclear. Among her works are: *A Survey of Modernist Poetry* (with Robert Graves, 1927) and a novel, *A Trojan Ending* (1937). Her religious preoccupations have led her to renounce poetry.

Tony Richardson. Albert Finney and Joan Greenwood in *Tom Jones*

Richelieu: painting by Philippe de Champaigne

Adrian Ludwig Richter. *Italian Landscape near Castelgandolfo*; drawing

Hans Richter

Hans Richter. Frames from the film *Rhythmus* (1921)

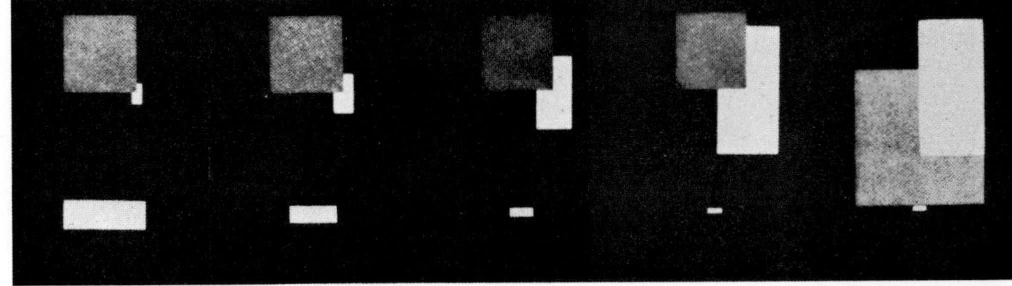

Riley. *Bridget Holmes, Housemaid*

Rigaud. *Louis XIV in Robes of State.* Also *Bossuet

Riefenstahl. *Triumph of the Will*

Rietveld chair. Also *de stijl

Riemenschneider. *Ascension of the Virgin*

Riefenstahl Leni (1902–). German film director. R. studied painting and ballet and became a dancer. She started in films acting in 2 mountaineering films of Arnold Fanck, one of which was *The White Hell of Pitz Palü* (1929). She directed *The Blue Lamp* (1932) and acted in it. She is famous for her 2 long documentaries, *Triumph of the Will* (1934), about the Nuremberg Rally, and *Olympiade* or *Olympische Spiele* (1936), both events designed to be filmed from camera positions planned in advance. Both are intensely propagandist works, and *Triumph of the Will*, with its infectious scenes of mass enthusiasm and adulation, is a unique example of art completely, blatantly and yet successfully serving a political idea.

Riegl Alois (1858–1905). Austrian art historian notable for his reassessment of late Roman art. He saw in it not a decline in technical competence and inspiration, but rather a change in artistic intention.

Riehl Wilhelm Heinrich von (1823–97). German short-story writer, usually on historical and didactic subjects. Colls include *Kulturgeschichtliche Novellen* (1856).

Riemann Hugo (1849–1919). German music scholar and theorist, author of the great *Musiklexikon* (1882), a 12th ed. of which appeared (1959–61), and a still important general history of musical theory (1898).

Riemenschneider Till (Tilman) (*c.* 1460–1531). German late Gothic sculptor active in Würzburg and famed for his work in wood; it includes the *Ascension of the Virgin* on the altar in the church of Our Lord, Creglingen. In stone he executed the tombs of bishops Scherenberg and Bibra in Würzburg cathedral and the memorial sarcophagus in Bamberg cathedral of its 11th-c. founder, the Emperor Henry II, and his wife.

Rienzi (originally subtitled 'The Last of the Tribunes'). Opera by Wagner, based on a novel by Bulwer-Lytton; 1st production at Dresden in 1842.

Riesener Jean-Henri (1734–1806). Generally considered the greatest *ébéniste of the 18th c., he was of German origin but worked in Paris where he was apprenticed to Oeben (second only to R. himself). Most of his furniture was made for the crown and is predominantly in the neo-classical style, of the highest technical and artistic finish.

Rietveld Gerrit Thomas (1888–1964). One of the leading modern Dutch architects. A cabinet maker by training, R. became a member of the de stijl group, designing much de stijl furniture, particularly the 'Red-Blue' chair of 1918. His Schröder House, Utrecht (1924) is the building on which his fame rests, and is the only major architectural realization of de stijl.

Rififi chez les Hommes, Du (1955). Film directed by J. *Dassin.

Rigaud Hyacinthe (1659–1743). French portrait painter to Louis XIV and Louis XV. He reflected the temper of the age, excelling in formal portraiture where sumptuous robes and decorations took priority over characterization, e.g. *Louis XIV in Robes of State* (1701; Louvre). His poses were often based on those of Van Dyck. He also painted more intimate unofficial portraits which bridge the gap between baroque court portraiture and the naturalistic portraits of the 18th c.

Rights of Man, The (1791–2). Book by Tom *Paine.

Rigoletto. Opera by Verdi, with libretto by Piave based on *Le roi s'amuse* by Hugo; 1st performance at Venice in 1851.

Riis Jacob A. (1849–1914). Danish-born U.S. social reformer who used his revolutionary photographs of slum conditions in Lower Manhattan to campaign for civic action. His graphic representation of the city and its poor anticipated the work of Stieglitz and the later social realists.

riksmål: Ivar *Aasen

Riley James Whitcomb (1849–1916). U.S. poet. R.'s verse in Hoosier (Indiana) dialect, including *Little Orphant Annie*, was extremely popular.

Riley (Ryley) John (1646–91). English portrait painter, pupil of G. Soest. With Kneller he was appointed chief painter to William and Mary although some of his best portraits are of less exalted people, e.g. *Bridget Holmes, Housemaid* (1686; R. Coll.).

Rainer Maria Rilke

Rilke Rainer Maria (1875–1926). German poet, the greatest in the last hundred years. Born in Prague, he studied there and in Munich and Berlin, and travelled widely in Europe. Influential were his visits to Russia with Lou Andreas-Salomé in 1899 and 1900; a period in Paris from 1902, part of it as Rodin's secretary; and his stay at Duino Castle (Adriatic) from 1911. His early poems are neo-romantic effusions of feeling, like the lyrical story *Die Weise von Liebe und Tod des Cornets Christoph Rilke* (1899; *The Lay of Love and Death of Cornet Christopher Rilke*, 1932), which brought him acclaim. He is best approached, however, through 3 books of poems from his middle period (several trs of selections): *Das Stundenbuch* (1905), *Das Buch der Bilder* (1902; revised ed. 1906), and *Neue Gedichte* (1907–8). Here while retaining his mastery of tonal values, he acquires a new ability to bend and stretch the materials of language (word forms, syntax, imagery); verse structure and metre–though not phrasing–are of lesser importance, the sonnet being a favourite form. Subjective feeling gives way to the sensuous re-creation of things ('*Dinge*'), often as symbols: these are called 'object poems'. The novel *Die Aufzeichnungen des Malte Laurids Brigge* (1910; *The Notebook of Malte Laurids Brigge*, 1930) says farewell to youthful subjectivity; the hero is a less robust persona of R. After a gap, 2 cycles of difficult late poems, using semi-private symbols (e.g. '*die Engel*') appeared: *Duineser Elegien* (1923; *Elegies from the Castle of Duino*, 1930), and *Die Sonette an Orpheus*, (1923; *Sonnets to Orpheus*, 1936). Here, as in single late poems coll. posth. (trs. 1957), the emphasis moves from the appearance of things to their essence, and to the role of the poet (Orpheus) as praiser and preserver.

Rimbaud (Jean-Nicolas) Arthur (1854–91). French writer, and probably the most precocious genius in literature. He was born in Charleville near the Belgian frontier, and began writing while still at school. He ran away several times, and finally came to Paris in 1871, where he began a friendship, later a homosexual liaison, with *Verlaine. They travelled together in Belgium and England and their association ended in a drunken brawl in Brussels, during which Verlaine fired on R. The latter came back to England, where he taught French for some months. Then he set off on travels which took him across Europe and to the Far East, until he finally settled as a trader in Harar, now part of Abyssinia. 11 years later, he was brought back to Marseille with a tumour on the knee and his leg had to be amputated; he survived the operation only a few months. R. lost all interest in literature from the age of 21, for reasons which have never been explained. R. was the 1st great exponent of poetry as frenzied, fragmentary expression of the subconscious and as such has had an incalculable influence on the whole of modern literature. The interpretation of his works is a subject of great controversy. They include: the brilliant descriptive verse he wrote at school, *Le Bâteau ivre* (1884; *The Drunken Boat*, 1942), an astonishing allegory, and two poetic cycles, *Une Saison en enfer* (1873; *A Season in Hell*, 1932) and *Les Illuminations* (1886; *Prose Poems from Les Illuminations*, 1932).

Rimbaud (right) and Verlaine: from a painting by Fantin-Latour

Rimsky-Korsakov Nikolay Andreyevich (1844–1908). Russian composer, conductor and important teacher. He began his career in the navy but friendship with Balakirev (1861), membership of the *Mighty Handful of nationalist composers and increasing musical commitments (he taught at the St Petersburg Conservatory from 1871) led him to leave the force and make a thorough study of musical theory. His pupils included Glazunov, Respighi, Stravinsky and Prokofiev. R.-K.'s nationalistic music is marked by his outstanding feeling for orchestral colour; he reorchestrated and academically and officiously rearranged (sometimes unnecessarily) the work of *Mussorgsky, *Borodin and others. His own works include: the operas *The Snow Maiden* (1882), libretto by R.-K. after Ostrovsky; *Sadko* (1898), libretto by R.-K. and V. I. Bielsky, a minstrel's fantastic adventures; *Mozart and Salieri* (1898), a setting of Pushkin's dramatic poem on the legend that Salieri poisoned Mozart; *The Golden Cockerel* (1909), libretto by V. I. Bielsky after Pushkin, banned by the authorities (it portrays a foolish and lazy tyrant). His other works are the symphonic suite *Schéhérazade (1888) from *The Arabian Nights' Entertainments*; *Capriccio Espagnol* for orchestra (1887); 3 symphonies; and chamber music.

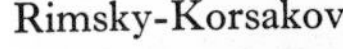

Rimsky-Korsakov

Ring and the Book, The (1868–9). Poem by *Browning.

Ring of the Nibelungs, The (German *Der Ring des Nibelungen*). Opera cycle by *Wagner; 1st production as a whole at Bayreuth in 1876.

Rivera. *The Making of a Fresco* (1931)

Rivers. *Africa* (1963)

Riopelle. *Purple Track*

Rite of Spring: 1913 performance

Rivette. *Paris nous appartient*

Rinuccini Gino (*c.* 1350–1417). Italian poet in the style of Petrarch.

Rinuccini Ottavio (1562–1621). Italian poet, a member of the *camerata and as such the 1st opera librettist. He wrote *Favola di Dafne* set by J. Peri (1597), the *Euridice* set by Peri and Caccini (1600), and *Arianna*, his most important work, set by Monteverdi (1608).

Rioja Francisco (1583–1659). Spanish poet; a disciple of Herrera, influenced by the latter's fondness for adjectives and for words expressing colours. R.'s poems are filled with a gentle melancholy and are often concerned with flowers, whose wilting suggests melancholy reflections on the passing of time.

Riopelle Jean-Paul (1923–). French-Canadian painter; he has lived in Paris since 1948. He was early associated with surrealism, later turning to action painting; he has passed through several phases in technique and style – in recent years from kaleidoscopic mosaic-like works (early 1950s) to freer, more dramatic, and sometimes frightening compositions. He has also sculpted.

ripieno (Italian, 'full'). In music a term used of the full body of instruments, in a concerted piece, when distinguishing them from the solo instruments.

Rippl-Ronai József (1861–1927). Hungarian painter who went to Paris in 1887 and worked for 2 years under Munkácsy but subsequently joined the nabis group. He developed a flat cloisonniste style and produced some notable paintings predominantly in black and grey. On his return to Hungary (1900) he adopted a light gay palette and specialized in interiors which have similarities with those of his friend Vuillard. Many of his late works, particularly portraits, were in pastel.

Rip Van Winkle (1820). Short story by Washington *Irving.

Rise of Silas Lapham, The (1885). Novel by William Dean *Howells.

Risi Dino (1916–). Italian film director. He made a number of documentaries followed by neo-realist comedies like *Il segno di Venere* (1955), a formula which boomed financially in *Poveri ma belli* (1956), and its successors. He has lately acquired a critical reputation with *Il sorpasso* (1962), a study in selfishness and its consequences.

Rist Johann (1607–67). German poet and hymn writer, founder of the Elbschwan Orden group of poets. His hymns are still used in the Lutheran Church.

Rite of Spring. 2-scene ballet with choreography by Nijinsky, music by Stravinsky and décor by Roerich; 1st performance 1913. In 1962 the Royal Ballet presented a new version with choreography by Macmillan.

ritornello (from Italian, 'return'). Those recurring passages in a musical work for soloist or soloists and ensemble in which the ensemble instruments perform an 'interlude', the solo part being silent. The technique is common in 17th- and 18th-c. music.

Ritt Martin (1920–). U.S. film director. His 1st film, *A Man Is Ten Feet Tall* (1956), set among the dockers of New York, gained him critical recognition. After some well-acted literary adaptations for Wald, he made *Hud* (1963) for Paul Newman, an intellectual western also exceptionally well acted.

Ritter Alexander (1833–96). German composer, important as a friend and adviser of R. Strauss: it was R. who persuaded Strauss to write his tone poems, in the tradition of Liszt.

Rivals, The (1775). Comedy by *Sheridan.

Rivarol Antoine de (1753–1801). French writer, a celebrated wit who wrote pamphlets and satires. R.'s works include the *Discours sur l'universalité de la langue française* (1784).

Rivera Diego (1886–1957). Mexican painter. He came under cubist influence while working in Paris (1911–20) and on a visit to Italy (1920–1) was deeply impressed by Renaissance frescoes. He returned to Mexico in 1921 and painted several monumental mural decorations for the new Socialist government's public buildings. In America (1930–3), he decorated the California Stock Exchange and Detroit Institute of Arts. His social realism was responsible for the modern revival of Mexican art and an important influence, through artists like Shahn, on the realist development in U.S. art in the 1920s and 1930s. His *Portrait of Helen Wills Moody* (1930) is in the Tate.

Rivers Larry (1923–). U.S. artist of the New York school; he was a jazz saxophonist and began painting only in 1944. Much of his work is in an idiom close to pop art, on the development of which his *George Washington crossing the Delaware* (1955) was an important influence. *Parts of the Face* (1961) is in the Tate.

Rivette Jacques (1928–). French film critic and director, a leading contributor to the influential magazine *Cahiers du Cinéma* with Chabrol, Truffaut and Godard. After making a witty short, *Le Coup du berger* (1956), he directed a metaphysical mystery thriller, *Paris nous appartient* (1960).

rivière. A very long diamond necklace, particularly common in the 19th c.

Rivière Jacques (1886–1925). French critic and essayist. R. became secretary, later director of *La Nouvelle Revue Française.* R. was at the centre of French literary life: he knew Gide well and corresponded with Alain-Fournier (1905–14), Claudel (1902–4) and Proust (1911–22). His works include *De la sincérité envers soi-même* (1925) and a novel, *Aimée* (1922).

Roach Hal (1892–). U.S. film producer, notably of Laurel and Hardy comedies, including *Way Out West* (1937), *A Chump at Oxford* (1940). Other films include the fantasy comedies of the *Topper* series (1937, 1938, 1941) and the deeply moving *Of Mice and Men*, directed by Lewis Milestone.

Road to Wigan Pier, The (1937). Book by George Orwell.

Robbe-Grillet Alain (1922–). French novelist. His works break sharply with the traditional novel, especially in their extended descriptions of objects; R.-G. has said that he describes the surfaces of things in order to free man from the tragic sense by demonstrating that the material world is indifferent to him. Works include the novels *La Jalousie* (1957; *Jealousy*, 1959) and *Le Voyeur* (1955; *The Voyeur*, 1959); and film scripts, notably *L'Année Dernière à Marienbad.*

Robbers, The (1782). Play by *Schiller.

Robbery Under Arms (1888). Novel by Rolf *Boldrewood.

Robbia Luca della (1400–82). Florentine sculptor regarded by his contemporaries as the equal of Ghiberti and Donatello. An important figure of the early Renaissance, he made use of classical Greek and Roman models but his work reflects a warm personality and lacks dramatic grandeur. Among his works are the Cantoria and the Sacristy doors for Florence cathedral. R. evolved a technique for applying pottery glazes, in various colours, to terracotta figures and established a factory continued by his nephew ANDREA (1435–1525) and GIOVANNI (1469–after 1529) and GIROLAMO (1488–1566) the sons of Andrea.

Robbins Jerome (1919–). U.S. dancer and choreographer in the jazz idiom; associate artistic director of the New York City Ballet from 1949, he formed his own co., Ballets U.S.A., in 1958. His 1st work, *Fancy Free* (1944) put the jitterbug into ballet and his dance arrangements for the Broadway musical *West Side Story* (1957), when made into a film (1961), won him the 1st ever American Motion Picture Award for choreography.

Robe, The (1942). Historical novel by Lloyd C. Douglas; also made into a film (1953), directed by H. *Koster.

Robert Hubert (1733–1808). French painter called 'Robert des Ruines'. He went to Rome (1754) where the example of Pannini led him to devote himself to painting ruins. He also became a close friend of Fragonard with whom he visited Paestum and Naples. On his return to Paris (1765) he painted imaginary landscapes with 18th-c. figures in settings of classical ruins. He was imprisoned during the Revolution but saved by the fall of Robespierre.

Robert de Bor(r)on (late 12th or early 13th c.). French poet, author of a poetic trilogy on the subject of the Holy Grail.

Roberti Ercole d'Antonio de' (d. 1496). Ferrarese painter. He was probably assistant to Cossa in Ferrara and later in Bologna before he displaced Tura as painter to the Este court in Ferrara in 1486. His major works are an altarpiece (1480; Brera Gal., Milan) and *Pietà* (Walker A. Gal., Liverpool). Until 1933 some of his paintings were attributed to Ercole de' Grandi, said to have been a painter who worked in Bologna and died in 1531. There is no evidence for this.

Luca della Robbia. *Trumpeters*; from the Cantoria

Giovanni della Robbia. *Bust of Christ*

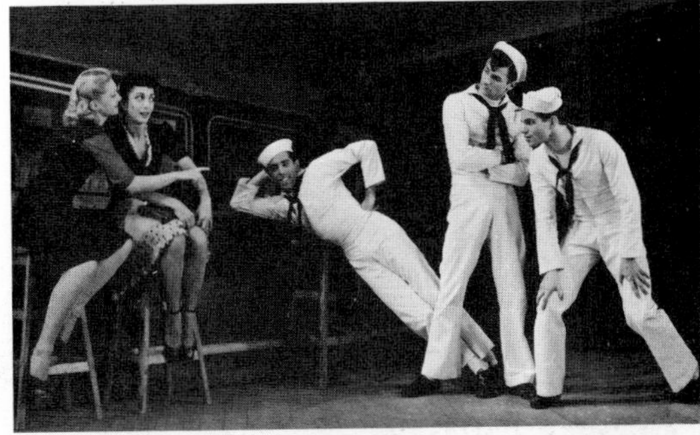

Jerome Robbins (far right). *Fancy Free*

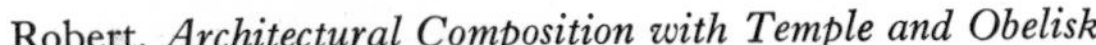

Robert. *Architectural Composition with Temple and Obelisk*

Roberti. *Pietà*

Alain Robbe-Grillet

William Roberts. *The Game of Chess*

Robie House

Henry Peach Robinson. *When the Day's Work is Done* (1877)

Paul Robeson as Emperor Jones: photograph by Steichen

Edwin Arlington Robinson

Roberts Elizabeth Madox (1886–1941). U.S. novelist and poet. R. used her Kentucky background in most of her work, including the novels *The Time of Man* (1926) and *The Great Meadow* (1930).

Roberts Goodridge (1904–). Canadian painter, mainly of sombre rugged landscapes; in recent years with increasing use of impasto.

Roberts Kenneth (Lewis) (1885–1957). U.S. historical novelist. R.'s books are vigorous, readable and accurate; they include *Arundel* (1930); *Rabble in Arms* (1933); *Northwest Passage* (1937) and *Lydia Bailey* (1947).

Roberts William (1895–). English painter in a cubist idiom applied to scenes of working-class life; associated with the vorticist movement, member of the London Group and an official war artist in World Wars I and II.

Robertson Thomas William (1829–71). English playwright. His works, including *Caste* (1867), brought a greater realism and more natural dialogue to the 19th-c. English stage.

Robeson Paul (1898–). U.S. Negro bass singer and actor who has done much to develop the popularity of Negro folk-music, which he sings to piano accompaniment in the style of *Lieder*. He has also acted with distinction in the plays of O'Neill, especially *Emperor Jones* and *All God's Chillun*, and has played Othello many times in England and the U.S.

Robey George (1869–1954). Music-hall comedian nicknamed 'The Prime Minister of Mirth'. He played in pantomime, revue, farce; sang, and once played Falstaff in *Henry IV*, part I. His distinguishing characteristics were his bowler hat and bushy black eyebrows.

Robie House Chicago (1909). Architect Frank Lloyd *Wright.

Robins Elizabeth (1865–). U.S. actress who was responsible for introducing many Ibsen plays to the English stage. She also wrote some novels and theatrical reminiscences.

Robinson Edward G. (1893–). U.S. film actor. After a start in gangster roles, e.g. *Little Caesar*, he has matured and deepened his characterizations, e.g. *Scarlet Street*.

Robinson Edwin Arlington (1869–1935). U.S. poet. R.'s psychological development was influenced by a neurotic and diseased family background and a mastoidal operation he underwent as a young man. He always saw himself as a pathetically buffeted figure and his philosophy derived from his state of mind. He printed his 1st poems privately in 1896 (*The Torrent and the Night Before*) and lived thereafter destitute in New York until success came with a verse novel, *Captain Craig* (1902), about an eccentric but indomitable vagabond and poet. R.'s works include the colls *The Children of Night* (1897) and *The Man Against the Sky* (1916); and *Tristram* (1927), a verse novel which was a best-seller.

Robinson Henry Crabb (1775–1867). English journalist, foreign ed. of *The Times*, whose *Diary, Reminiscences and Correspondence . . .* (posth. 1869) contains valuable portraits of Wordsworth, Coleridge and other writers.

Robinson Henry Peach (1830–1901). British photographer, an exponent of the belief that photography could only achieve the status of an art by duplicating the themes and compositional treatment of academic paintings. He publ. *Pictorial Effect in Photography* (1869), a manual encouraging and advocating the use of artificial studio-produced effects.

Robinson Lennox (1886–). Irish director and author of many plays, most of which have been performed at the Abbey Theatre, Dublin. He is general manager of the Irish National Theatre Society.

Robinson Crusoe, The Life and strange surprising Adventures of (1719). Novel by *Defoe; also made into a film (1953), directed by L. *Buñuel.

Rob Roy (1817). Historical novel by *Scott.

Robson Dame Flora (1902–). English actress who has made her name in serious and intense parts, notably Alicia Christie in *Black Chiffon* (1949) and Miss Tina in *The Aspern Papers* (1959). She has played Lady Macbeth in New York and was also in several Hollywood films in the 1930s.

Robson Mark (1913–). U.S. film director. R. was an ed. at R.K.O. where he worked on **Citizen Kane* and first directed in 1943, for *Lewton, whose *Isle of the Dead* (1945) he also directed. After a serious period which included *Champion* and *Home of the Brave* (1949) his work became more diverse. With a good script, he managed some very proficient work: a comedy, *Phffft* (1954), and two exposés, *Trial* (1955) and *The Harder They Fall* (1956).

Rocco and his brothers (1960). Film directed by L. *Visconti.

Rochefort Henri de (1830–1913). French writer, a political journalist who founded the weekly *La Lanterne* (1868) and wrote an account of his turbulent life, *Les Aventures de ma vie* (1896–8).

Rochemont Louis de (1899–). Film producer. R. worked on newsreels before founding the *March of Time* series (1935–50). As a producer of feature films, he carried over a documentary look to thrillers including *Boomerang*. Later worked for Cinerama and produced the similar, but abortive Cinemiracle.

Rochester John Wilmot, Earl of (1647–80). English poet, a Restoration wit, debauchee and courtier. R. wrote a number of excellent lyrics, but his finest works were satirical, notably *A Satyr against Mankind* (1675?).

rocker. Tool used in mezzotint (*engraving).

Rockingham. English earthenware and porcelain manufactory at *Swinton.

rococo (from French *rocaille*, 'shell-work'). 18th-c. style, essentially French, a reaction against the ponderous and formal atmosphere of Louis XIV's court, and therefore adapted to the decoration of intimate interiors, using soft colours and delicate curves to produce gay, elegant and charming effects. The painting of the period (Watteau, Boucher, Fragonard) has the same qualities. In the 2nd half of the 18th c. r. gave way to *neo-classicism. The other main centre (notably of r. churches, e.g. of Dominikus Zimmermann), was S. Germany and Austria; elsewhere r. produced important individual works (e.g. by Tiepolo, Goya) but was never the dominant movement.

Rod Édouard (1857–1910). Swiss novelist. His psychological novels include *La Vie privée de Michel Teissier* (1893).

Rodchenko Alexander (1891–1956). Russian painter and designer who, coming to Moscow in 1914, came under the influence of *Tatlin and *suprematism. In 1915 he began doing abstract compositions with a ruler and compass. In 1918 he exhibited his *Black on Black* series of paintings in answer to *Malevich's *White on White* and from this period R. became leader of a group of 'non-objectivist' artists who in 1922 decided to leave easel painting and 'speculative activity' for industrial design, calling themselves 'constructivists'. R. began working as a typographer, photographer and furniture designer, applying his principles of abstract design to create a modern system of design, since become universal.

Rode Helge (1870–1937). Danish poet and playwright, a religious mystic and aesthete who attacked contemporary scientific thought.

Roderick Random, The Adventures of (1748). Picaresque novel by *Smollett.

Rodgers Richard (1902–). U.S. composer of the musical comedies *Pal Joey* (1940) with Lorenz Hart (1895–1943) and *Oklahoma!* (1943), *Carousel* (1945), *South Pacific* (1949), *The King and I* (1951) and *The Sound of Music* (1959) all with Oscar Hammerstein II (1895–1960).

Rodin Auguste (1840–1917). French sculptor who until 1882 worked as a craftsman in porcelain factories and workshops. His 1st sculptures, bronze portrait busts which he made in the evenings, were rejected from the Salon. Working in Brussels (1871–7), he paid his 1st visit to Italy (1874–5) and was overwhelmed by Michelangelo's spiritual intensity and his vigorous modelling of the figure. R.'s 1st Salon success, *Age of Bronze* (1875–7; Tate), reflects this rippling life-like vitality and was such a sensational contrast to academic conventions that he was accused of using life-casts. He made *St John the Baptist* (1878–80; Tate) larger than life to disprove this.
His mature work, either in bronze or marble (often deliberately left in a Michelangelesque half-finished state), developed an intense emotional expressiveness and the tragic *Burghers of Calais* (1884–95) illustrates his identification of composition with psychological content. The *Gate of Hell*, a doorway commissioned for the Musée des Arts Décoratifs, Paris (1880–1905) was unfinished, but

Rodchenko.
Compass and ruler drawing (1915)

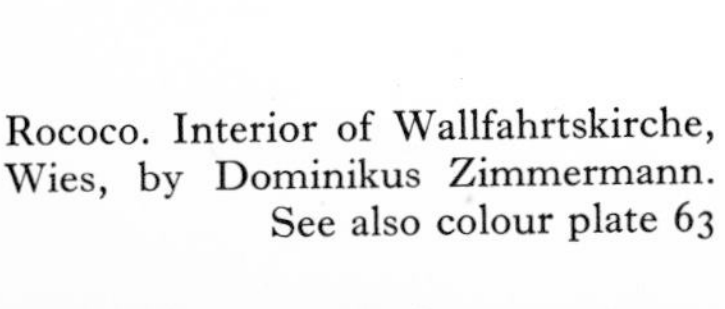

Rococo. Interior of Wallfahrtskirche, Wies, by Dominikus Zimmermann.
See also colour plate 63

Rodin.
Age of Bronze

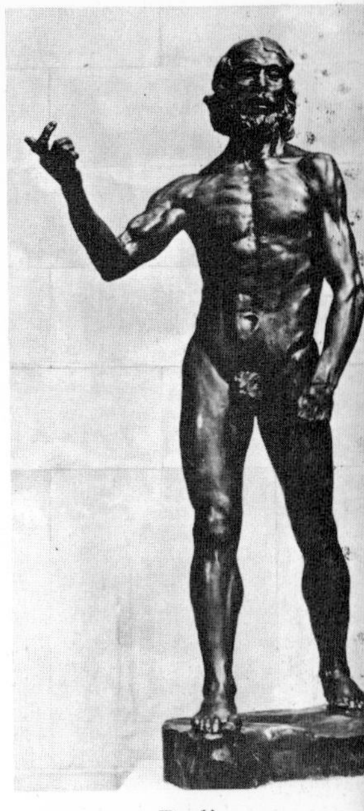

Rodin.
St John the Baptist

Rodin. *The Gates of Hell* (detail)

Rodin. *The Burghers of Calais*.
Also *Le *Baiser*, *engraving, *The *Thinker*

Roelas. *The Martyrdom of St Andrew*

David Roentgen. Writing-table (*c.* 1775)

Roerich.
Set for *Prince Igor*

several motifs from it – *The Thinker* (1894), *The Kiss* (1886; Tate), etc. – were developed separately. *Balzac* (1893–4; Boulevard Raspail, Paris) was his outstanding portrait.
R.'s great influence lay in his fusion of the realist and symbolist streams of the late 19th c. and in works like *Le Jongleur* (1909; Mus. R., Paris) he foreshadowed the 20th-c. preoccupation with space.

Rodogune (1644). Tragedy by Corneille.

Rodrigo Joaquín (1902–). Spanish composer who after studying in France and Germany settled in Madrid, later teaching at the univ. there. His music, influenced by de Falla, includes *Concierto de Aranjuez* (1939) and *Concierto de Estío* for violin and orchestra (1943).

Rodrigues Lobo Francisco (*c.* 1580–1622). Portuguese writer noted for his prose style, as in his masterpiece *Côrte na aldeia e Noites de Inverno* (1619), a dialogue modelled on *Castiglione's *Courtier*. His other works, some in Spanish, include pastorals in prose and verse.

Roelas Juan de (1588/90–1625). Spanish painter of religious subjects, master of Zurbarán. His style is close to that of Veronese and he may have studied in Italy. He worked in Seville where almost all his paintings are to be found.

Roentgen David (1743–1807). German cabinet maker to the French and other European courts, son of the cabinet maker ABRAHAM R. (1711–93) whose workshop at Neuweid he took over in 1772. He specialized in furniture veneered with pictorial marquetry and fitted with mechanical devices such as secret drawers.

Roerich Nikolay (1874–1947). Russian landscape painter, archaeologist and stage designer, an important member of the St Petersburg World of Art group. His archaeological excavations influenced both his painting and his sets for Diaghilev's Paris production of *Prince Igor* (1909). In 1918 he left Russia for India.

Roethke Theodore (1908–63). U.S. poet. R. worked in several styles, most successfully perhaps when displaying his wit and ingenuity, and in formally looser poems evoking his childhood. Colls include *Words for the Wind* (1958).

Rogers Bruce (1870–1957). Eminent American typographer, much influenced by William Morris, and notable for his fine taste and delicacy in the treatment of book decoration and layout. R. was adviser to both the Cambridge and Oxford Univ. Presses. He was responsible for the rediscovery of *Baskerville's types in 1917, and the redesigning of *Jenson's roman for machine composition (1915).

Rogers Ginger (1911–). U.S. film actress and dancer, famous as Fred Astaire's partner in legendary musicals like *Top Hat* (1935).

Rogers Samuel (1763–1855). English poet, R. declined the laureateship in 1850. His best work is perhaps *The Pleasures of Memory* (1792).

Rogers Will (William Penn Adair) (1879–1935). U.S. comedian, once a cowboy, whose wise-cracking patter made him a star of Broadway in the Ziegfeld Follies and later in Hollywood films.

Rogosin Lionel (1924–). U.S. film director. *On the Bowery* (1954) is an apparently impromptu dramatized documentary. Using a similar technique, *Come Back Africa* (1958) was set in South Africa.

Rohlfs Christian (1849–1938). German painter and graphic artist chiefly associated with expressionism. He turned from realism to impressionism in the early 1890s, to post-impressionism in the early 1900s and was an expressionist by 1912, influenced by Nolde. His late work verged on abstraction. He produced some very fine hand-coloured woodcuts.

Rojas Fernando de (*c.* 1465–1541). Spanish novelist and author of a large part if not all of the celebrated *La *Celestina* (*Comedia de Calisto y Melibea*), a novel in dialogue form publ. anon. in 1499.

Rojas Zorrilla Francisco de (1607–48). Spanish playwright, a follower of Calderón. R.'s production was equally varied and prolific, but often more natural and spontaneous in spirit. His best-known play is *García del Castañar*, a

Rohlfs. *Two Dancers*

Will Rogers

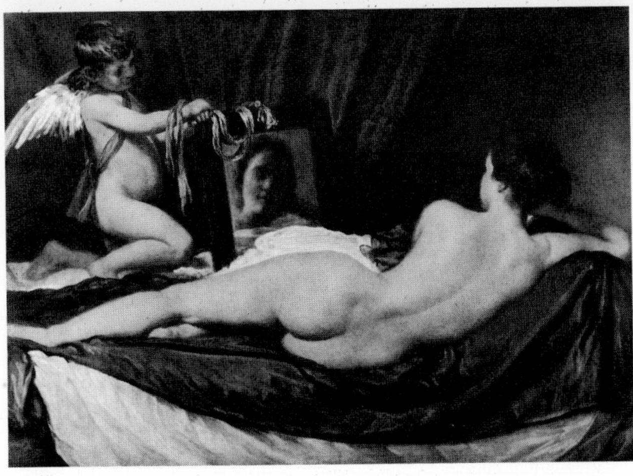

The Rokeby Venus

drama on the theme of honour. He also wrote some excellent comedies.

Rokeby Venus, The (1658). A painting by *Velazquez of a female nude.

Roland, La Chanson de (*c.* 1100). **Chanson de geste* which tells the story of a desperate rear-guard action by Roland and Oliver against the Saracens at Roncevaux in S. France and of Charlemagne's subsequent rout of the Moors.

Roland Holst Adriaan (1888–). Dutch poet avowedly influenced by Yeats; although he took part in the Dutch resistance to the Nazis, as a poet R. H. is preoccupied with a distant past which he regards as the only source of beauty and greatness.

Roland Holst Henriette (1869–1952). Dutch lyrical poet whose ardent Socialism, based on a gospel of love, pervades her work.

Rolfe Frederick William (1860–1913). English novelist, self-titled 'Baron Corvo' or 'Fr Rolfe'. R. studied for the priesthood, was expelled from the Scots College in Rome, and led an unstable, paranoic existence in England and Italy, dying in Venice. R.'s masterpiece, *Hadrian the Seventh* (1904), is a remarkable work of wish-fulfilment, revealing his obsessions and fantasies, the story of an Englishman long slighted and wronged who becomes a great reforming pope. R.'s novels include *The Desire and Pursuit of the Whole* (1934) and *Nicholas Crabbe, or The One and the Many* (1958).

Rolland Romain (Edmé-Paul-Émile) (1868–1944). French writer. During World War I he remained in Switzerland and, after the publ. of *Au-dessus de la mêlée* (1915, *Above the Battle*, 1916), became world famous as a champion of pacificism; he was awarded the Nobel prize for literature in 1916. R. is a powerful and noble writer, whose style tends to become overheated. The best known of his writings are his life of Beethoven (1903; *Beethoven* ... 1907) and *Jean-Christophe* (1904–12; *John Christopher*, 1910–13), a novel in several vols about a musical genius with some resemblance to Beethoven.

Rolle of Hampole Richard (*c.* 1300–49). English mystic. R. wrote many meditations and commentaries; those in English are important contributions to the development of the language. Among his Latin works *Incendium Amoris* (*The Fire of Love*) is best known.

Rolli Paolo (1687–1765). Italian poet, author of a great deal of elegant Arcadian verse in the style of Anacreon and Catullus. He trs. Milton's *Paradise Lost* into Italian and encouraged a taste for Italian opera in London, where he spent much of his life.

Rollins Sonny (1929–). U.S. *jazz tenor saxophonist.

Rölvaag Ole Edvart (1876–1931). Norwegian-born U.S. novelist; he emigrated in 1896. His novels include *I de dage* (Norway, 1924–5; *Giants of the Earth: A Saga of the Prairie*, 1927), the story of an immigrant family in 19th-c. S. Dakota.

Roma Città Aperta (1945). Film directed by R. *Rossellini.

Romains Jules (1885–). Pseud. of Louis Farigoule. French writer, originally a poet and founder of *unanimism. At first a teacher, he soon abandoned teaching for literature. He played a much-publicized but ineffectual part in Franco-German relations in the 1930s. He spent the war years in America. R.'s vast panorama of modern France in 27 vols, *Les Hommes de bonne volonté* (1932–47; *Men of Good Will*, from 1933), breaks down into a coll. of individual stories or episodes, often brilliantly narrated. It is likely to remain as a permanent document, in spite of the doubtful literary merit of some parts.

Roman Johan Helmich (1694–1758). Called the father of Swedish music for his compositions, his theoretical works and his activity in linking the Swedish musical world with Europe. His English contacts included Handel who heavily influenced R.'s style.

romances. Spanish ballads, the earliest dating from the 2nd half of the 14th c.; they can be regarded either as in 8-syllable lines or 16-syllable lines with a strong caesura; vowel assonance runs through the even lines. The earliest treat incidents in the wars between the Spanish kingdoms. Then follow r. of Moorish wars, heroic ballads of the past, and others on the Arthurian and Carolingian cycles and the tales of chivalry. The language is condensed, but contains many stock repetitions. A few have lyrical feeling and a few are magical, but none achieve the imaginative quality of the best Border ballads. The r. became popular among the gentry in the 15th c., and were revived in an artificial form in the 17th. They spread to

Frederick William Rolfe

Romain Rolland

Jules Romains

Le Roman de la Rose ms.

Romanesque. Christ enthroned in Glory (after 1096; St Sernin). See also colour plates 27, 28

Romanesque. The monastery church of St Austremoine, Issoire (beginning of the 12th c.)

Portugal, Catalonia and throughout the Spanish-speaking world.

Roman d'Alexandre, Le. 12th-c. French verse romance based on the legends about Alexander the Great derived from the Greek compilation, the *Pseudo-Callisthenes* (late 2nd c. A.D.). The romance was reworked by many poets, ultimately in a 12-syllable line which therefore came to be called an 'alexandrine'.

Roman de la Rose, Le. After the Bible and Boethius this great allegory was, despite ecclesiastical condemnation, the most influential book of the middle ages. The original poem was by GUILLAUME DE LORRIS (*c.* 1212–37). In this courtly allegory of love Idleness strays into a garden where he sees a beautiful rose–his attempts to pluck it are thwarted or encouraged by personified qualities. Guillaume made use of Ovid, and of *Chrétien de Troyes, but his originality is revealed best in his delicate use of allegory for psychological purposes. Matter and form are conventional, yet the allegory is a precise exploration of real emotional experience. The narrative is fluid; the description bright and clear. Guillaume's unfinished poem was continued by JEAN DE MEUNG (*c.* 1240–1305), but in a spirit quite alien to the original. He used the framework of the love-allegory to carry an encyclopaedic discussion of the thought of the age. His poem is no psychological exploration of Love, but a rational analysis of it as a natural force. He is a great comic poet, and a great realistic one; his weakness is one of organization, for his inherited allegory cannot comprehend all he wants to say.

Roman de Renart, Le. Coll. of French verse tales produced between the late 12th and early 14th cs, satirizing human society by depicting the adventures of Renard the fox and other animals. The earliest tales, mostly the work of unknown authors, are the most famous and best.

romanesca bass. In music of the late medieval and Renaissance periods, a *ground bass similar to the *Folia.

Romanesque. In W. European architecture, sculpture, painting and the minor arts the style which evolved in the mid 10th c. following Charlemagne's revival of the arts and lasted until the late 12th c. Its architectural characteristics are: round arches, thick columns or composite piers, thick walls, heavy proportions, small windows and tunnel-vaults. There are great regional variations within R. Italy remained close to classical models; France was divided into different schools, e.g. Aquitaine favoured domes, Provence low single-storey naves (Avignon), Auvergne a heightening of the transepts next to the crossing (Issoire), etc.; England followed Normandy with very long basilican churches, mostly with square E. ends and 2-tower W. fronts (Durham); Germany went on developing R. after other countries had turned to Gothic. In the late 12th c. (beginning in the Île de France) the development of vaulting techniques and the desire for more light led to the evolution of Gothic. Relief sculpture was used extensively in R. churches, especially on the capitals of the interior columns and the tympana; free-standing sculpture appeared only at the end of the period. Many mural paintings have survived in churches in France, Italy and Spain. As in architecture there is great stylistic variety within R. painting and sculpture which combines elements from the early Christian-Byzantine tradition and, particularly in N. Europe, barbarian art. Common features are distorted elongated figures, stylized vegetation, geometric and interlaced patterning and strong rhythmic movement. Similar characteristics appear in the jewellery, metalwork and ms. illumination which flourished during the period.

roman-feuilleton: *feuilleton

roman-fleuve. A series of novels (each of which may be complete in itself) describing the development of a person, family or group, e.g. Zola's *Les Rougon-Macquart*.

Romanino Girolamo Romani called (1484/7–after 1562). Italian painter influenced by the Venetian school. He lived in Brescia, near Milan, but travelled extensively in N. Italy. He painted mainly religious subjects which include a *Pietà* (1510; Accad., Venice), his earliest dated work, and a polyptych *Nativity with Saints* in the N.G., London.

romanist. Name used to describe Northern artists of the early 16th c. whose style was influenced by Italian Renaissance painting, usually as a result of a visit to Italy. Mabuse, B. van Orley, M. van Heemskerk, Q. Massys and M. van Reymerswaele are important r.s.

Romano Giulio: *Giulio Romano

Romanesque. Christ enthroned (*c.* 1125); S. Clemente, Tahull

Romanesque carving (Oloron-Sainte-Marie)

Romanticism. Friedrich, *Abbey under Oak Trees*

Romanticism. Lord Byron: painting attributed to Géricault

Romanticism. Delacroix, *Abduction of Rebecca*. See also colour plate 69

romans bretons. 12th- and 13th-c. French narrative poems (by e.g. *Chrétien de Troyes) about King Arthur and his knights, a subject which enabled the poet to combine the heroic themes of the **chansons de geste* with the *Provençal conception of courtly love. The name derives from the setting of these poems, a 'Brittany' (not the French province) which included Wales, Cornwall and Ireland.

romanticism. A profound revolution in the human spirit gathering momentum in the 18th c. and in full flood in the 19th. The movement in the arts was at its height during the 50 years *c.* 1790–*c.* 1840. The most important elements in r. were: feeling for nature (foreshadowed by the *'picturesque'); emphasis on subjective and individual (as opposed to typical and general) emotion; and interest in the past, the mysterious and the exotic. The last led to the vogue of the oriental tale, the historical novel as created by Sir W. Scott and of the 'medieval' (with its roots in the *'Gothick' and nostalgia for 'the age of chivalry'), and all the elements combined to produce the typical romantic rejection of society and later of industrialized society in particular.

In literature r. developed first in Britain through Thomson's *The Seasons*, the ballad coll. of T. Percy, J. Macpherson's Ossianic poems and E. Young's *Night Thoughts*. Their influence in Europe was immense. Effectually, however, Rousseau in France, Herder and the *storm and stress movement in Germany, and Karamzin in Russia ushered in continental r. The movement culminated in, e.g., Wordsworth, Coleridge, Shelley, Byron (the most significant personality in European r.), Scott, Keats, Chateaubriand, Hugo, Dumas, Goethe, Schiller, Manzoni, Leopardi, Pushkin, Lermontov. The repercussions of r. continued throughout the 19th c., certain of its elements (e.g. in Poe, Baudelaire) early developing in the direction of the *decadence.

R. in painting began in England in the works of Constable and Turner, which show a new awareness of landscape; later the paintings of Samuel Palmer (a disciple of William Blake) reveal an essential romantic genius. In Germany, the medieval townscapes of Shinkel and Moritz von Schwind and the mysterious landscapes of Caspar David Friedrich are typical manifestations of r. whereas the genius of Goya in Spain, although unquestionably an expression of r., far transcends its confines.

Beethoven's music contained all the seeds of r.: the expression of the composer's subjective emotion, or such themes as fate and freedom in music; the use of an enlarged orchestra, of violent dynamic contrasts and the forging of a new harmonic language. Tonality tended to become unstable (Berlioz), ambivalent (Schubert's last quartet) or suspended (Liszt, Wagner, etc.). The form, as a consequence, became freer or simpler, and in either case tended to affect the details less than hitherto, for the interest was more in the sensuous moment than in the structure; orchestration became more colourful and textures more exotic. The connection which was to come between r. and nationalism is foreshadowed in Chopin's work and explicit in Dvořák's; Berlioz made *programme music a major genre, Liszt developing it in the new form, the symphonic poem. Certain 20th-c. composers such as Elgar and R. Strauss are considered romantics.

Romantic symphony. Nickname of *Bruckner's symphony no. 4 in E♭.

Romany Rye, The (1857). Novel by George Borrow.

Romaunt of the Rose (14th c.). Poem of which parts may have been written by Chaucer; it is a paraphrase of *Le *Roman de la Rose.*

Romberg. Family of German musicians of whom the violinist and composer ANDREAS JACOB (1767–1821) was a friend of Beethoven and Haydn.

Romberg Sigmund (1887–1951). Hungarian-born U.S. composer of light operettas, among the most popular being *The Student Prince* (1924) and *The Desert Song* (1926).

Rombouts Theodor (1597–1637). Antwerp painter. He studied under A. Janssens, then spent several years in Rome where he came under the influence of Caravaggio's followers. His work is of 2 kinds: Caravaggesque genre scenes and religious subjects after the manner of Rubens.

Rome, school of. School of Italian painting of importance from the mid 15th to the late 19th c. Both Michelangelo and Raphael worked in Rome, making it the centre of the high Renaissance; in the 17th c. it was the centre of the baroque movement represented by Bernini

Romanticism. Turner, *Passage of St Gothard*

Rombouts. *The Musicians*

Romney. *Emma, Lady Hamilton*

Romney. *Mrs Wilbraham Bootle.* Also *Cowper

Pierre de Ronsard

and Pietro da Cortona. From the 17th c. the presence of classical remains drew artists from all over Europe including Poussin, Claude, Piranesi, Pannini and Mengs.

Romeo and Juliet (before 1597; publ. 1597). Tragedy by *Shakespeare, written *c.* 1595. The sources were Arthur Brooke's poem *The Tragicall Historye of Romeus and Iuliet* (1562), a story in *The *Palace of Pleasure* and perhaps a lost play. It has often been filmed; notably in 1954, directed by Renato Castellani.
The play was the inspiration for orchestral works by Berlioz and Tchaikovsky.
A ballet version of the play was first performed in Copenhagen in 1811 and has since been produced by different choreographers to music by many composers. The 3-act Soviet version, with choreography by Lavrovsky and music by Prokofiev (1940), and the K. Macmillan production to the same music (1965) are by far the most interesting.

Rome prize. A competitive award made annually at the Paris Conservatoire to enable young composers to study at Rome. Similar awards are made by the Brussels Conservatoire and the New York.

römer. A glass for white wine developed by 15th-c. German glass makers. Its name may be derived from the Lower Rhenish '*roemen*' ('to boast'), not from 'Roman'. The foot of a typical early r. was made of a thread of glass wound on to a conical core. Later the foot was blown and a glass thread applied as surface decoration. Another feature of the r. was the use of small drops of glass attached to the vessel which were drawn out to form decorative loops.

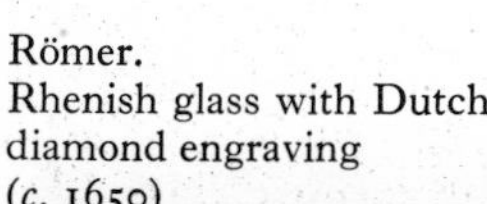
Römer.
Rhenish glass with Dutch diamond engraving
(*c.* 1650)

Romm Mikhael (1901–). Soviet film director. R. started as a director with a silent version of *Maupassant's *Boule-de-suif* (1934). He made 2 films on Lenin, *Lenin in October* (1937) and *Lenin in 1918* (1938), which presented the official Soviet view of history. His latest film is *Nine Days of One Year* (1962).

Romney George (1734–1802). English painter of portraits and historical subjects. Beginning as a portrait painter in Westmorland, he moved to London in 1762, where his *Death of Wolfe* (1763) attracted attention, but led to a quarrel with Reynolds, whose style, together with that of Gainsborough, influenced R. R. became a fashionable portrait painter. A visit to Italy (1773–5) and the study of Raphael, Titian and Correggio, brought new maturity to his art. He greatly admired Emma, Lady Hamilton and painted over 50 works in which she appeared, usually in a historical role. His clientele declined in the 1790s, and in 1798 he retired to Kendal, where he died.

rond de jambe. A ballet exercise in which the dancer stands on one leg and describes a circle with the other foot either à terre, with the entire leg, from the hip down, working, or en l'air when the thigh is horizontal and the leg moves from the knee.

Ronde, La (1950). Film directed by M. *Ophuls.

rondeau. Verse form originating in medieval France, originally meant to be sung. Its typical form has 3 stanzas comprising 13 lines with 2 rhymes (*a* and *b*) plus a refrain (*c*); thus: *aabba*; *aabc*; *aabbac*. The similar RONDEL has 14 lines and rhymes *abbaababab baab*; lines 7 and 8, and the last 2 lines repeat the 1st couplet. These forms were revived in 19th-c. English poetry, notably by Swinburne.

rondo. Classical musical form (probably derived from the medieval lyric form, rondeau) in which a theme recurs interrupted by subsidiary themes. There is no exact formula (e.g. Beethoven's are usually simpler than Mozart's), but basically the principle described above applies, making, e.g. ABACADBA, etc.

Ronsard Pierre de (1524–85). French poet. R. became a page at the French court, visited Scotland and travelled in Germany and the Netherlands. Partial deafness caused him to retire from the court and devote himself to literature. His poems brought him fame, wealth and, in the 1560s, great influence at court; later he was neglected and returned to his studies.
R. was the leader of the *Pléiade and consequently of the French poetic renaissance, decisively influencing du *Bellay and establishing the importance of the alexandrine and the sonnet; the most enduring influences on his poetry were Horace and Anacreon. R.'s work lost its popularity after his death and its significance was only fully realized in the 19th c. His works include the *Odes* (1550, 52); *Amours* (1552), a coll. of sonnets addressed to Cassandre Salviati, and 2 more colls of *Amours*

(1555, 56) to an unknown 'Marie'; *Sonnets pour Hélène* (1578), to the maid of honour Hélène de Surgères; political poems, e.g. the *Discours des misères de ces temps*; a treatise, *L'Abrégé de l'art poétique français* (1565); and an epic of the French monarchy, *La Franciade* (1572).

rood. Crucifix, used especially of a crucifix suspended between the nave and the chancel in a church, supported by a gallery, the 'r.-loft', or standing on the 'r.-screen'. This screen, often richly carved, in medieval and some later churches separates the nave from the chancel, i.e. the part of the church used by the congregation from that used by the clergy.

Rooker Michael called 'Michael Angelo' (1743–1801). English landscape painter and engraver remembered for his watercolours of architectural ruins made on a series of tours of English counties. He was a pupil of P. Sandby.

Room Abram (1894–). Soviet film director. R.'s work in his most famous film, *Bed and Sofa* (1926), was the opposite of Revolutionary subjects tackled by *Eisenstein and *Pudovkin. His film is intimate and relies on acting rather than montage to show personal not political situations. He also made *The Ghost That Never Returns* (1929), a political drama.

Room with a View, A (1908). Novel by E. M. *Forster.

Rooney Mickey (1922–). U.S. film actor. Known as a juvenile star of the *Andy Hardy* series (*c.* 1940), he is now seen mainly in comedy.

Root George Frederick (1820–95). U.S. composer of the 'Battlecry of Freedom' and other popular Civil War songs.

Rope (1948). Film directed by A. *Hitchcock.

Rops Félicien (1833–98). Belgian graphic artist, a master of etching techniques. He settled in Paris in the mid 1870s and acquired a reputation for satanism and decadence.

Rore Cyprian (Cipriano) de (1516–65). Flemish composer, a pupil of Willaert in Venice. R. worked in several Italian towns, notably Parma, and on his master's death held, for a year, the music directorship of St Mark's, Venice. R.'s finest work is in his madrigals, usually set to outstanding texts such as Petrarch.

Rorke Kate (1866–1945). English actress; leading lady to many famous actor-managers and in her later years a famous teacher of dramatic art.

Rosa Salvator(e) (1615–73). Italian painter, engraver, poet, musician and actor, noted chiefly for a flamboyant and dramatic style of landscape painting in opposition to the classicism of Claude and Poussin. He was probably a pupil of Jusepe da Ribera. Apart from turbulent battle scenes, R.'s fame lies mainly in his somewhat theatrical landscapes, peopled by saints and banditti. The subjects, the dramatic lighting and the wild natural settings of these works started a vogue in the 18th c. for 'sublime' and 'picturesque' landscape.

Rosalynde, Euphues Golden Legacie (1590). Romance by Thomas *Lodge.

Rosario. Spanish dancer, *Antonio.

Rosay Françoise (1891–). French film actress of considerable power and range, often seen in films by her husband, J. *Feyder, e.g. *Le Grand Jeu*, *La Kermesse Héroïque*.

Rosenberg Isaac (1890–1918). English poet. R., the child of Russian Jews, was brought up in the East End of London. He was killed in World War I. *Trench Poems* brought him posth. fame; they include *Break of Day in the Trenches*.

Rosenkavalier, Der ('The Rose Cavalier'). Opera by R. Strauss, with libretto by H. von Hofmannsthal; 1st performance at Dresden in 1911.

Rosenmüller Johann (*c.* 1619–84). German composer. His instrumental music, which includes an early *sonata da camera (1667), blends Italian and German elements.

Rosenplüt Hans, known also as 'Hans Schnepperer' (*fl.* 1430–60). German poet, and brass worker, from Nuremberg. He became a *mastersinger and wrote many political songs and didactic verses.

Rose Tattoo, The (1950). Play by Tennessee *Williams; made into a film (1955) directed by D. Mann.

Rops. *The Hanged Man*; etching

Root. *Just before the Battle, Mother*

Rosa. *St John in the Wilderness*

Kate Rorke

ood-screen from Stoke-by-Hartland, Devonshire

13th-c. rood at Rolagsbro, Sweden

Late 13th-c. rose-window, Chalons-sur-Marne cathedral. See also colour plate 32

Rosi. *Salvatore Giuliano*

Roslin. *The Artist's Wife with a Fan*

rosette. Architectural term for any stylized flower motif.

rose-window. In Gothic architecture, a circular window with *tracery radiating like spokes (or, later, like the veins of a leaf) from the centre.

Rosi Francesco (1922–). Italian film director. R.'s 1st solo directorial effort was a thriller with social implications, *La Sfida* (1958). His 3rd film, *Salvatore Giuliano* (1962), inquired into the murder of the Mafia leader, employing an extraordinarily complicated method which used some of the narrative conventions of the American exposé film of 10 years before to leave the events mysterious but the forces surrounding them clear. In *Le Mani sulla città* (1963) his starting-point was the collapse of old houses undermined by new building works in Naples, and the film investigated the workings of the political set-up in the city council.

rosin: *resin

Roslin Alexander (1718–93). Swedish rococo portrait painter in the style of J.-M. Nattier. R. worked mainly in Paris but visited St Petersburg, Warsaw and Vienna.

Rosmersholm (1886). Play by *Ibsen.

Rosselli Cosimo (1439–1507). Florentine painter who had an important share in the decoration of the Sistine Chapel for Sixtus IV. In Florence his paintings include frescoes in S. Annunziata and S. Ambrogio. He worked in a severe static manner. Fra Bartolommeo and Piero di Cosimo were his pupils.

Rossellini Roberto (1906–). Italian film director. He became famous with *Roma Città Aperta* (1945), and *Paisa* (1946), episodic treatments of life in German-occupied Italy. These were the films for which the term neo-realism was coined. Shot in natural settings with minimal resources (for economic reasons), they achieved a spontaneity and passion which was never equalled by the later neo-realist works of de Sica or Visconti. He has occasionally returned to this area of reconstructed actuality: *Germania Anno Zero* (1948), *India* (1958). R.'s Catholicism is reflected in *Francesco, giullare di Dio* (1950), a coll. of simple and often humorous anecdotes about St Francis of Assisi, and in *Jeanne au Bucher* (1956) from the Claudel/*Honegger work. But *Stromboli* (1950) and *Viaggio in Italia* (1954), although secular stories of personal relationships, are no less Catholic films. He is deeply concerned with freedom, which for him lies in the recognition of the nature of one's own imprisonment. R. displays his intense patriotism in films like *Vanina Vanini* (1961) and *Viva l'Italia* (1960), concerned with the building of Italy, and *Il Generale della Rovere* (1959) and *Era Notte a Roma* (1960) with its salvation from the Nazis.

Rossellino the brothers Bernardo (1409–64) and Antonio (1427–79). Florentine sculptors. Bernardo, the more gifted also worked as an architect for the Vatican, which he proposed to rebuild in imitation of classical architecture. His most important buildings are in Pienza, near Montepulciano. In 1444 Bernardo completed the funeral monument for the humanist Leonardo Bruni, erected in the church of S. Croce, Florence. The figure lies prostrate on a bier over a sarcophagus and is flanked by ornamented pilasters; this became the prototype of the Renaissance monument. Antonio R. was mainly active as a funeral sculptor; one of his best-known works, the tomb of the cardinal of Portugal (1459; S. Miniato, Florence), shows realism and some originality in composition.

Rossen Robert (1908–). U.S. film writer and director. R. was a playwright who became (1937) a Hollywood script writer and started directing in 1947. His second film, *Body and Soul* (1947), about boxing, may owe much to the distinguished collaborators, Polonsky, Parrish, etc. After his 4th film, *The Brave Bulls* (1951), he was black-listed and his next films (from 1955) were made outside the U.S. His work recovered from increasing stodginess with *The Hustler* (1961).

Rossetti Christina Georgina (1830–94). English poet, daughter of Gabriele R. and sister of Dante Gabriel R. She lived a sheltered life, devoted to her Anglican faith and the care of her mother; she twice rejected offers of marriage. She was closely associated with the Pre-Raphaelite Brotherhood. The bulk of R.'s poetry is at once religious, expressing deeply felt convictions in lucid lines of extreme simplicity, and intensely personal, as in the sonnet sequences *Monna Innominata* and *Later Life*, which deal with the rival claims of divine and

Rosselli. *Procession of the Relics* (S. Ambrogio)

Antonio Rossellino. *Matteo Palmieri*

Bernardo Rossellino. Monument to Beata Villana

Rossellini. *Il Generale della Rovere*

Christina Rossetti: pencil drawing by her brother

D. G. Rossetti. *Beata Beatrix*

D. G. Rossetti. *Wedding of St George and the Princess.* Also *Pre-Raphaelites

human love – a theme which perhaps reflected the crisis of her relations with William *Scott. *Goblin Market* (1862), a fantasy, condemns worldly pleasure. Her works include *The Convent Threshold* and an allegory, *The Prince's Progress.*

Rossetti Dante Gabriel (1828–82). English poet and painter, son of Gabriele R. With Millais and Holman Hunt he was a founder of the *Pre-Raphaelite Brotherhood and his mystical poem *The Blessed Damozel* appeared in its periodical *The Germ* (1850). R.'s poetry shows variously the influence of the medieval ballad, the sensuous aspects of romanticism, and Italian poets, especially Dante. His poems are occasionally over-wrought and derivative but at their best reveal a natural gift and fine independence. Typical examples are *My Sister's Sleep,* the ballad *Sister Helen* and the sonnet sequence *The House of Life.* As a painter R.'s romantic imagination was out of sympathy with the realism and moral earnestness of Millais and Holman Hunt and their early association was brief. The most famous painting of his early period is *Ecce Ancilla Domini* (1850; Tate). Between 1850 and 1860 R. worked chiefly in watercolour; also important are his drawings of his wife Elizabeth Siddal and the idealized portrait of her, *Beata Beatrix* (Tate). She and Mrs William Morris provided R. with an ideal of feminine beauty which is recurrent in his work. His late paintings were chiefly on Arthurian and Dantesque themes.

Rossetti Gabriele (1783–1854). Italian poet, an exile in London after the failure of the Neapolitan Revolution of 1821. He produced much religious and patriotic verse.

Rossi Franco (1919–). Italian film director. He became famous for his 4th film, *Friends For Life* (1955), about a friendship between 2 schoolboys. His *Morte di un amico* (1960) was made from a Pasolini script about the Roman underworld. *Calypso* (1958) and *Odissea nuda* (1961) were semi-documentary travel stories, and *Smog* (1962) was about Italians in America.

Rossi Karl Ivanovich (born Carlo) (1775–1849). Italian architect working in Russia. He planned much of the Leningrad schemes. His chief individual works are: building for the General Staff (crescent shaped with a huge arch in the middle); the Alexandra Theatre; and the Senate and Synod (two palaces joined together by another big arch). R.'s style is a cooler, more neo-classical version of *Rastrelli, but with some bold perspective effects.

Rossi Luigi (1598–1653). Italian composer whose *Orfeo* (1647) was the 1st opera designed expressly for performance in Paris though not the 1st opera performed in France. As important as his operas are the cantatas, e.g. that on the death of Gustavus Adolphus of Sweden (1632), and arias.

Rossi Michel Angelo (*c.* 1600–*c.* 74). Italian composer, pupil of Frescobaldi. He extended still further Frescobaldi's dissonant style in his organ toccatas, etc. and developed a form almost equivalent to the later overture forms in its variety of tempi and textures.

Rossini Gioacchino Antonio (1792–1868). Italian opera composer. He studied at Bologna and from 1810 enjoyed a rapidly growing reputation confirmed with *The Barber of Seville* (1816) after Beaumarchais; this was at first ignored by the public for R.'s presumption in setting the libretto of an immensely admired opera (1782) by Paisiello. After visits to Vienna and London R. divided his time from 1825 between Paris and Bologna. After the opera *William Tell* (1829) R. abandoned opera; his other music includes a *Stabat Mater* (1831–41). R.'s reputation suffers on 2 counts: most of his 38 operas are set to bad librettos, all are written for an age of virtuosity now dead. He has been dismissed as superficial, but incontestable is the superb vigour of his music, its overflowing melodic invention, its vital rhythmic pulse and R.'s subtle and evocative orchestration.

Rosso Medardo (1858–1928). Italian sculptor, patronized by Zola and a friend of Degas and Rodin. The spontaneous appearance of R.'s work has led to comparisons with the paintings of the impressionists. Works include *Conversazione in Giardino.*

Rosso Fiorentino born Giovanni Battista di Jacopo di Gasparre (1494–1540). Florentine artist, one of the founders of the school of Fontainebleau and a leading *mannerist painter. R. was trained, briefly, under Andrea del Sarto and was influenced by Michelangelo and Dürer's engravings. He painted in Florence and Rome and in 1530 he was invited to the French court by Francis I. R.'s major surviving work is the cycle of pagan subjects,

Karl Ivanovich Rossi. Theatre Street, Leningrad

Rosso. *Conversazione in Giardino*

Rosso Fiorentino. Galerie François I

Rouault. From the *Guerre et Miserere* series

Rouault. *Head of a Clown.* Also *expressionism

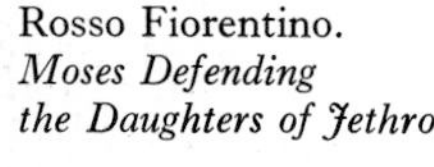

Rosso Fiorentino. *Moses Defending the Daughters of Jethro*

Mstislav Rostropovich

Rothko. *Red Light over Black*

representing an elaborate allegory on the character of the French king, painted in the Galerie François I, Fontainebleau. One of the most original and ambitious decorative schemes of the age, this involved stucco-work, woodcarving, frescoes and mosaics. It required many assistants to execute, the chief being *Primaticcio, R.'s successor at Fontainebleau. R.'s daring effects and contrived visual illusions did much to prepare French artists and patrons for the arrival of the baroque. Other important works are: *Descent from the Cross* (Pina., Volterra), *Moses Defending the Daughters of Jethro* (Uffizi) and *Marriage of the Virgin* (S. Lorenzo, Florence).

Rostand Edmond (Eugène-Alexis) (1868–1918). French playwright, author of the famous *Cyrano de Bergerac* (1897; 1898), a romance about the 17th-c. writer, and *L'Aiglon* (1900; 1900), about Napoleon's son.

Rostropovich Mstislav (1927–) Soviet cellist, one of the greatest of his generation. Since 1957 he has been professor of his instrument at Moscow Conservatory, and he has toured widely in Europe and the U.S. since 1950. Many composers, e.g. Prokofiev, Shostakovich and Britten, have written works specially for him.

Rotha Paul (1907–). English film critic and director. His book, *The Film Till Now* (1930) was accepted as a standard history of the cinema. He made a series of documentaries (1932–50) and, since then, 3 feature films and 2 documentaries.

Rothko Mark (1903–). Russian-born U.S. painter; one of the leading figures of the post-war New York school. He studied painting under Weber in New York, worked on the *W.P.A. Art Project (1936–7) and founded an art school (1948) with Newman, Motherwell and Baziotes in New York where he still lives. He was initially inspired by the freedom of expression of Miró, Ernst and American surrealists but his mature work–e.g. *Number 10* (1950; M.M.A., New York)–has a meditative quality in its arrangement of 2 large coloured shapes.

Rotrou Jean de (1609–50). French playwright, a professional who worked for the co. at the Hôtel de Bourgogne and was one of Richelieu's *cinq auteurs. R.'s works, from which many writers, notably Molière, borrowed, include the tragedies *Le Véritable Saint Genest* (1645) and *Venceslas* (1647), and the comedies *Les Sosies* (1636) and *La Sœur* (1645).

Rottenhammer Hans (1564–1625). German painter of religious mythological subjects who spent many years in Venice and Rome. He was strongly influenced by Venetian painting.

rotunda. Architectural term for a circular building, especially (though not necessarily) one with a dome.

Rouart Henri Stanislas (1833–1912). French amateur painter who exhibited with the impressionists and was an early collector of impressionist paintings.

Rouault Georges (1871–1958). French painter, born in Paris (traditionally to the accompaniment of the Prussian bombardment); apprenticed as a craftsman in stained glass. He studied painting in the studio of Gustave Moreau (1892–8) and on Moreau's death (1898) became curator of the Mus. Moreau, a post he held until his own death. His early religious paintings reflect both the jewel-like character of Moreau's art and his own taste for medieval art. His intense religiosity was heightened by his contacts with Huysmans who nearly talked R. into a monastery, and with Léon Bloy whose passionate Catholic novels of sordid Parisian life prompted the *Prostitute* series of 1903–7–e.g. *At the Mirror* (1906; M.M.A., Paris). Superficially close to Lautrec in subject and technique, these were the crudely painted images that linked R.'s name with the fauves at the 1905 Salon d'Automne. But in fact these pictures were conceived as moralities of sin and redemption foreshadowing the intensely religious character of his mature style. This had in common with contemporary German painting a Gothic sense of inner necessity for expression.
He concentrated on graphic work (1916–29), and these prints–particularly the *Guerre et Miserere* etchings–are his most expressionist works. His paintings, laboriously painted and with a heavy black outline reminiscent of the lead in stained glass, are the more profound hieratic images which made him the major religious artist of the c. He designed for Diaghilev's *Prodigal Son* (1929) and made stained-glass windows for a church at Assy (1948).

Roubiliac. *Handel.*
Also *Cibber, *Pope

Rouch. *Chronique d'un Été*

Le Douanier Rousseau. *The Dream*

Roubil(l)iac Louis-François (1705–62). French sculptor, one of the most important sculptors working in England in the 18th c. He was pupil of the baroque sculptor Permoser, then of Nicolas Coustou. He settled in England (*c.* 1732) and made his reputation with a statue of Handel for Vauxhall Gardens. His many works include the statue of Sir Isaac Newton at Trinity College, Cambridge, the Argyll monument in Westminster Abbey and a statue (B.M., London) and the 'Davenant' bust (Garrick Club) of Shakespeare.

Rouch Jean (1917–). French anthropologist and film maker. Shorts taken during his anthropological researches in Africa were made into a feature, *Les fils de l'eau* (1948–51; released 1955). Another short, *Les Maîtres-Fous* (1955), showed the absorption of British colonial customs into tribal ritual. In *Moi, un Noir* (1958) some of the inhabitants of an African town, Treichville, act their lives for the camera, and one of them improvises a commentary to the images. From here, via *La Pyramide Humaine* (1960), in which the presence of the camera in recently desegregated lycées in Abidjan help the progress of integration, it was no great step to the '*psychodrame*' *Chronique d'un Été* (co-directed by Edgar Morin, 1961) in which the camera's presence is a catalyst for the confession of the people who then watch and comment on the film.

Roucher Jean-Antoine (1745–94). French poet whose *Les Mois* (1779) was modelled on Thomson's *The Seasons.*

Rouen. Important French centre of pottery production. In the 16th c. it produced some of the earliest French *maiolica, in the 17th c. the 1st French 'soft-paste' *porcelain; but its great achievement was the *faïence produced from *c.* 1690 to *c.* 1770. The impressive dishes and tureens of the period up to *c.* 1730 are usually in blue, and are decorated with elaborate scroll-work, but with severity and heaviness characteristic of the Louis XIV period. Later, in competition with Delft, many beautiful *rococo pieces were produced in polychrome, richly decorated with Chinese motifs.

Rouge et le Noir, Le (1831). Novel by *Stendhal.

Rouget de Lisle Claude-Joseph (1760–1836). French soldier who, as a captain in the Revolutionary army, wrote 'La *Marseillaise'.

Roughing It (1871). Book by Mark *Twain.

Rougon-Macquart, Les (1871–93). Series of 20 novels by *Zola.

Roumanille Joseph (1818–91). French poet, with F. *Mistral the founder of the movement to revive the Provençal language (*Félibrige).

round. A part song, in fact a simple species of perpetual *canon. It differs, however, from canon in that the voices can follow one another only at the unison or 8ve and that the theme is a short simple tune which is sung ad lib. by the various parts, e.g. the well-known 'London's Burning'. The earliest known r. is the famous 13th-c. 'rota' 'Sumer is icumen in'.

Rouquier Georges (1909–). French film director. A specialist in documentaries whose first, *Vendanges*, was made in 1929. Apart from shorts, e.g. *Le Tonnelier* (1942), *Arthur Honegger* (1954), he has made 2 long documentaries, *Lourdes et ses Miracles* (1955) and *Farrebique* (1946) which sets the story of a peasant family against the cycles of days and seasons; and fiction films.

Rousseau Henri called 'Le Douanier' (1844–1910). French primitive painter. He served in the army (1870–1) and then as a minor customs official in Paris. He began to paint *c.* 1880 and when he retired in 1885, painted full time, becoming the greatest of the self-taught 'primitives'. His only tuition was the advice of Canabel and the copies he made in the Louvre. The naïve directness of his work ranged from the simplicity and hieratic scale of his *Self-portrait* (1890; Prague) to the intense visionary quality of *War* (1894; Louvre). He was acclaimed by Jarry, Apollinaire, Delaunay and Picasso, all of whom he met *c.* 1906. The child-like simplicity of form and the uninhibited imaginativeness of subject in works like *The Sleeping Gypsy* (1897; M.M.A., New York) came as a revelation to artists seeking new means of expression. Contact with such people fostered the more conscious, exotic sophistication of late works like *The Snake Charmer* (1907; Louvre). The legendary banquet in his honour was organized in 1907 by Apollinaire and Picasso, whom he told: 'You and I are the greatest painters of the day.'

Rousseau Jean-Jacques (1712–78). French-Swiss writer born at Geneva. He left home at

Le Douanier Rousseau. *The Sleeping Gypsy.*
Also *primitives

Rouen cup and wafer-box (late 17th c.)

Jean-Jacques Rousseau

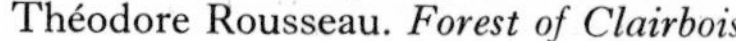

Théodore Rousseau. *Forest of Clairbois*

Albert Roussel

The Rout of San Romano (detail)

Rowlandson. *Vauxhall Gardens*

Rowlandson. *Dr Syntax at Cards*

the age of 16 and after various adventures with a series of patrons and a liaison with the much older Mme de Warens, came to Paris in 1742. An opera of his was presented at court in 1752, and he would probably have received a pension had he not been too shy to present himself. In 1756 Mme d'Épinay gave him the use of L'Ermitage, a house N. of Paris, but he quarrelled with her and moved to a cottage. Driven into exile for his unorthodox opinions, he settled for a while in Switzerland (1762), found a brief refuge in England (1766) where he received a pension, and after further wanderings returned to Paris. R. suffered from a persecution mania, hence his frequent quarrels with his friends.

He is viewed as one of the formative precursors of romanticism for his theory of the 'noble savage' and the theory that society tended to be corrupt and distort men's essential nature. His advocacy of the simple life and his revolutionary views on the existence of fundamental rights and liberties of man were among the ideas that made 'Rousseauism' a potent influence on later writers and thinkers. His most important works are: the discourses *Si le rétablissement des sciences et des arts a contribué à épurer les mœurs* (1750) and *L'origine . . . de l'inégalité . . .* (1754); the *Lettre à d'Alembert . . .* (1758) on the theatre; the novel *Julie, ou la Nouvelle Héloïse* (1761; 1761) on morality of marriage; *Émile* (1762; 1763), a partly fictional treatise on education; *Du Contrat Social* (1762; 1764) R.'s study of political institutions and their legitimacy, and the *Confessions*, written from 1764 to 1770 and publ. posth., which explore his personality in intimate detail and were supplemented by *Rousseau juge de Jean-Jacques* and *Rêveries du promeneur solitaire.* R. also wrote music entries for the *Encyclopédie* and a *Dictionnaire de Musique* (1767).

Rousseau (Pierre-Étienne) Théodore (1812-67). French landscape painter, leader of the *Barbizon school. He was strongly influenced by Constable and the 17th-c. Dutch landscapists. He stayed several times at Barbizon before settling there in 1848 after continued refusals in the Salon. His work combines objective observation of nature with melancholy romanticism.

Roussel Albert (1869–1937). French composer. He abandoned a naval career for music (1894), studying under d'Indy from 1898 to 1902. He joined no school but after the success of his ballet *Le Festin de l'Arraignée* (1912) gained an increasing reputation and his importance in French music has been compared with Ravel's. His music, romantic in mood, is stamped by a strong and idiosyncratic rhythmic sense; a complex texture, an equally complex but unsensational use of tonality and classical tonal forms, and frequent dramatic effects of orchestration. His works include: the opera-ballet, *Padmâvati* (1914–18; performed 1923) showing the influences of an Indian visit; 4 symphonies and 2 orchestral suites.

Roussel Ker-Xavier (1867–1944). French painter, one of the *nabis but unusual in his frequent choice of mythological subjects. With his brother-in-law É. Vuillard he executed decorative paintings and stage designs.

Rout of San Romano, The (1454–7). Title of 3 decorative panels by *Uccello.

Rovani Guiseppe (1818–74). Italian novelist and playwright; his novel *I Cento anni* (1859–64) is an encyclopaedic study of the period 1750–1850.

Rovetta Gerolamo (1851–1910). Italian novelist and playwright who became famous with his novel *Mater Dolorosa* (1882). His most famous work is his play *Romanticismo* (1901), dealing with the anti-Austrian resistance in Italy during the struggle for Italian unity.

Rowe Nicholas (1674–1718). English playwright. R. became poet laureate in 1715. His plays include *Tamerlane* (1702), in which the hero is meant to be William III; *The Fair Penitent* (1703); and *Jane Shore* (1714).

Rowlands Samuel (*c.* 1570–*c.* 1630). English satirical writer. Many of his works are studies of criminals, in the manner of Greene and Nashe; they include *Greene's Ghost haunting Conie-catchers* (1602) and *Martin Mark-all* (1610).

Rowlandson Thomas (1756–1827). English painter and social caricaturist, working mainly in ink and watercolour wash. He studied at the R.A. Schools and in Paris. His exuberant, robust, exaggerated and sometimes savage caricatures of English life show consummate draughtsmanship. R.'s success began with his Academy picture *Vauxhall Gardens* (1784);

besides caricatures he painted watercolour landscapes and illustrated a series of books: *Tour of Dr Syntax in Search of the Picturesque* (1812), *Dr Syntax in Search of Consolation* (1820), *Dance of Death* (1814–16), and the works of Smollett, Sterne and Goldsmith.

Rowley William (*c.* 1585–1642). English playwright and actor. His best work, above all *The Changeling* (1621), was written in collaboration with *Middleton.

Roxana, or the Fortunate Mistress (1724). Novel by *Defoe.

Roy Bimal (1909–). Indian film director. R. made *Two Acres of Land* (1954) which was the 1st Indian film to attract international critical attention (before S. *Ray). Although like most Indian films it has musical numbers, R. was clearly influenced by de Sica.

Royal Ballet. The national ballet co. of Great Britain with its home at Covent Garden. It was founded by Ninette *de Valois as the Vic-Wells Ballet (1931) and became known as the Sadler's Wells Ballet because of its regular seasons at that theatre. It was granted a Royal Charter in 1958.

Royal Court Theatre London. Opened as the New Chelsea in 1870; it became the R. C. in 1871. In 1904 J. E. Vedrenne and H. Granville-Barker became its managers and for 3 years presented new plays and revivals which profoundly influenced the English theatre–plays by Maeterlinck, Hauptmann, Galsworthy, and above all Bernard Shaw, whom their productions finally established as a major dramatist. The R. C. was bombed in 1941, reopened in 1952 and since 1956 has been leased to the *English Stage Co.

Różewicz Tadeusz (1921–). Polish lyrical poet, one of the few young writers who survived the German Occupation. In a terse, laconic style R. seeks positive values in a world rendered meaningless by war.

Rozier Jacques (1926–). French film director. R. made 2 shorts, *Rentrée des classes* (1955) and *Blue Jeans* (1958), which in their spirit and technique heralded all that was youthful and offbeat in the French nouvelle vague. His only feature, *Adieu Philippine* (1960–2), integrated spontaneity with neo-realist ambitions.

rubáiyát. A Persian poetic form in which each quatrain is an independent unit, the whole assembled alphabetically. An English version of the famous r., linked with the 12th-c. Persian poet and astronomer, Omar Khayyám, was made by E. *Fitzgerald.

rubato or **tempo rubato** (Italian, 'robbed time'). Musical term used to describe the fractional retardation or acceleration of tempo used by performers, usually pianists, as a means of expression. Also used freely for any temporary change in tempo.

Rubbra Edmund (1901–). English composer, a pupil of Holst and heavily influenced by English 16th- and 17th-c. music. His work includes 7 symphonies, 2 masses and chamber music.

Rubénisme. Late 17th-c. movement in French painting opposed in the French Academy by Poussinism. The Rubénistes, admirers of Titian and Rubens, whose great cycle *Life of Marie de Médicis* was in Paris, claimed that colour was the most important element in painting because it enabled the artist to achieve a more perfect semblance of reality. Led by Lebrun, the Poussinists, followers of the Carracci and Poussin, maintained that colour was only of decorative value and was of less significance than the more formal elements of drawing and design which gave intellectual instead of sensual satisfaction. By the end of the 17th c. the Rubénistes had won, opening the way for Watteau and *rococo.

Rubens Peter Paul (1577–1640). Flemish painter, draughtsman, etcher and diplomat. R. had a classical education. He studied under the Dutch mannerist, Otto van Veen, in Antwerp, where he became a member of the Guild of St Luke (1598). His journey to Italy in 1600 greatly influenced his future development; it gave him an opportunity to study Titian, and later the Carracci and Caravaggio in Rome. In 1603 he undertook his first diplomatic mission to the court of Spain, sent by his patron Duke Vincenzo Gonzaga of Mantua. Here he came into further contact with the paintings of Titian. R. returned to Rome in 1605, where he studied Graeco-Roman antiquity and met the painter Elsheimer, who taught him the art of etching. On his mother's death in 1608 R. returned to Antwerp and became the favourite of the Spanish governor, Albert, and his wife, Isabella. He married and settled in Antwerp,

Rozier. *Adieu Philippine*

Rubens. 2 drawings after the Roman statue *Spinario*. Also *sketch

Rubénisme.
Coronation of Marie de Médicis

Rubens. *Rubens and Isabella Brant*

Rubens. *Le Chapeau de Paille*

Rubens. *War and Peace.*
See also colour plate 59

Rudé. *La Marseillaise*

Rublev. *The Old Testament Trinity*

where he won increasing admiration from his patrons and fellow-artists. The famous double portrait with Isabella Brant, his wife (*c.* 1609; Alte Pina., Munich) dates from this period. R. established himself in a sumptuous palace, where his paintings were displayed and sold to the nobility and crowned heads of Europe. Artists eager to learn the secrets of his art flocked to his studio, which produced many copies and variations; R. often retouched and sold them as originals. The most important paintings of this period are religious and mythological compositions and hunting scenes, including *The Last Judgement*, *The Battle of the Amazons*, and *The Lionhunt* (1616–17; Alte Pina., Munich). The pressure of work increased and R. employed Anthony Van Dyck as his chief assistant. In 1621 he worked for Charles I of England and in the following year was ordered to Paris by Marie de Médicis to plan large-scale decorations for the Luxembourg Palace. These were completed within 3 years and comprised 22 large canvases and a number of portraits. In 1625 further diplomatic missions took him to Spain, where he met Velazquez, and to England. He was knighted by Charles I, who commissioned decorations for the Whitehall Palace. In 1630 he married Hélène Fourment, who was the subject of many of his later works; the famous portrait *Le Chapeau de Paille* (*The Straw Hat*–not in fact of straw), once thought to be of Hélène, is now believed to be of her elder sister Susanna. He retired to the château de Steen where, though beset by illness, he painted a number of splendid landscapes and compositions of rustic life.

The work of R. shows continuous development and can be divided roughly into periods. The first covers his formative years, his stay in Italy and early, eclectic work in Antwerp. Colours were laid on broadly, the paintings were strong in contrast with harsh modelling of the figures and academic drawing. The influence of Tintoretto, Veronese and Titian is very evident. From about 1612 a gradual change took place. The paint became more luminous, though still opaque, and the chiaroscuro less violent. Fluency and facility combined and formed an exuberant style suitable to workshop practice and the mass production of paintings. This was the beginning of the Antwerp school. During the last phase from about 1625 he achieved complete mastery with his vital, free and expressive brushwork, the brilliance and luminosity of colour and an exuberantly sensual feeling for the tactile–human flesh and materials–which has not been paralleled since. Contemporary taste and criticism finds this aspect of R.'s least acceptable, but it was in fact his greatest achievement. His influence on Flemish, French and English painting has been enormous. Both Watteau and Delacroix learnt a great deal from the subtle colour relationship of his paintings and the portrait painters of the 18th-c. English school, Reynolds, Gainsborough and later Ward and Constable, owed their freedom in the handling of paint to him. Other famous paintings by R. are *The Three Graces* (Prado) and *War and Peace* (N.G., London).

Rubinstein Anton Grigorievich (1829–94). Russian pianist, composer and conductor. As a pianist he had a technique and power of expression comparable to Liszt's and was fêted throughout Europe. His services to Russian music as organizer and as 1st director of the St Petersburg Conservatory (1862–7) are unquestionable. His music, influenced by Mendelssohn, is now forgotten but he wrote the 1st Russian symphony and the 1st Russian piano concerto; it is largely owing to him that music in Russia became a serious profession.

Rubinstein Artur (1886–). Polish pianist; he settled in the U.S. in 1940 and was naturalized in 1946. He has a wide repertoire but is particularly famous for his interpretations of Chopin.

Rubinstein Ida (1885–1960). Russian dancer, protégée of Fokine, who joined the Diaghilev co. in 1909, creating the leading role in *Schéhérazade* (1911). Forming her own co. (1928), R. was able with her own considerable private fortune to commission leading choreographers, composers and artists, including Fokine, Massine, Stravinsky, Ravel, Bakst and Benois and her co. continued until 1935.

Rublev Andrey (1370?–*c.* 1430). The greatest Russian religious painter, a monk working at Andronnikov where he painted 3 icons for the cathedral of the Annunciation, Moscow, murals in the cathedral of the Assumption, Vladmir (with his friend Daniel Chorny), and icons for the church of the Savvino-Storozhevsk monastery; he also worked at Zagorsk, where he decorated the walls of the cathedral of the Trinity and painted his most famous work, the icon *The Old Testament Trinity*. His painting is pervaded by tranquil devotion, and characterized by delicacy of line and full, subdued and harmonious colours.

Ruby Gentry (1952). Film directed by K. *Vidor.

Rucellai Giovanni (1475–1525). Italian humanist poet best remembered for his short poem *Le Api*, based on Virgil's 4th Georgic. He also wrote *Rosmunda*, a lifeless tragedy on Greek models.

Ruckers. Family of Flemish harpsichord makers (active 1575–1667). Their renowned instruments, of which 88 survive, were in use up to the late 18th c. and, by reason of magnificent sounding-boards, retained their reputation for a delicate silvery tone.

Rückert Friedrich (1788–1866). German romantic poet, author e.g. of *Deutsche Gedichte* (1814), verses inspired by the struggle against Napoleon, but most important for his skilful trs of such oriental works as the Chinese *Schi-King* (1833) and the Persian *Rostem und Suhrab* (1838).

Rudé François (1784–1855). French sculptor who abandoned neo-classicism for a more naturalistic and romantic approach. The statue of Marshal Ney in the Place de l'Observation, Paris and the striking relief *La Marseillaise* on the Arc de Triomphe are his finest works.

Rudin (1856). Novel by *Turgenev.

Rudolf von Ems (*fl.* 1220–54). German poet, an erudite, didactic follower of *Gottfried von Strassburg, though less inspired. Works include *Der Gute Gerhard*, *Barlaam und Josaphat*; and 2 unfinished works, . . . *Alexanders des Grossen* and the widely imitated *Weltchronik*.

Rudolph Paul (1918–). U.S. architect, trained by Gropius at Harvard. He achieved great success designing small houses in Florida in partnership with R. S. Twitchell in the late 1940s. He is now chairman of Yale Univ. department of architecture, and mainly designs buildings for education in an elegant version of the late works of Le Corbusier.

Rueda Lope de (*c.* 1510–65). Spanish playwright, one of the founders of the Spanish theatre. He established a theatre co. which toured the main towns in Spain and wrote mostly comedies for it in a flowing idiomatic style.

Ruffini Giovanni (1807–81). Italian novelist who wrote most of his work in English while he was in exile. His best-known novel (*Lorenzo Benoni, or passages in the life of an Italian*, 1853), is mostly based on his experiences as a follower of Mazzini. He also wrote the libretto for Donizetti's opera *Don Pasquale* (1843).

Ruffo Vincenzo (*c.* 1510–87). Italian composer. His 260 madrigals hold an important place between the generations of Willaert and G. Gabrieli; he also wrote much church music, later compositions being often inscribed as composed on the principles adopted by the Council of Trent.

Ruisdael Jacob Isaac(k)z van (1628/9–82). Dutch landscape painter, born in Haarlem; also a practising physician. R. was probably the pupil of his father and uncle (Salomon van Ruysdael). His painting reinvigorated the realistic landscape and was a major influence on later painting in the genre; his predilection was for melancholy scenes, usually with some elements suggesting decay–heavy and oppressive, as in *The Great Forest* (K. Mus., Vienna), or tranquil, as in *The Water-Mill* (Rijksmus.). Hobbema was his pupil.

Ruiz Juan (*c.* 1280–*c.* 1350). The greatest Spanish medieval poet; as archpriest of Hita, near Madrid, he wrote verses for singing and recitation. His famous series of narrative poems, *Libro de Buen Amor*, consists of a mixture of pious praises of the Virgin, short lyrics, bawdy tales of profane love, fables and burlesque incidents in many of which the archpriest himself claims to have been involved. The work introduces the figure of the traditional Spanish go-between or procuress, in the character of Trotaconventos, which was to inspire Rojas's *Celestina.

Ruiz de Alarcón Juan (d. 1639). Mexican-born Spanish playwright whose comedies, especially *El tejedor de Segovia*, are considered classics. His *La verdad sospechosa* was adapted by Corneille as *Le Menteur*.

rummer. A drinking-glass with a wide mouth and a deep, pointed bowl with a short or almost non-existent stem. These glasses were popular from the late 18th c. well on into the 19th c. when they frequently had domed and square feet. They are found cut and engraved and occasionally moulded.

Ruckers. The rose on the sounding-board, showing the maker's monogram

Ida Rubinstein in *Schéhérazade*

Ruisdael. *The Water-Mill*

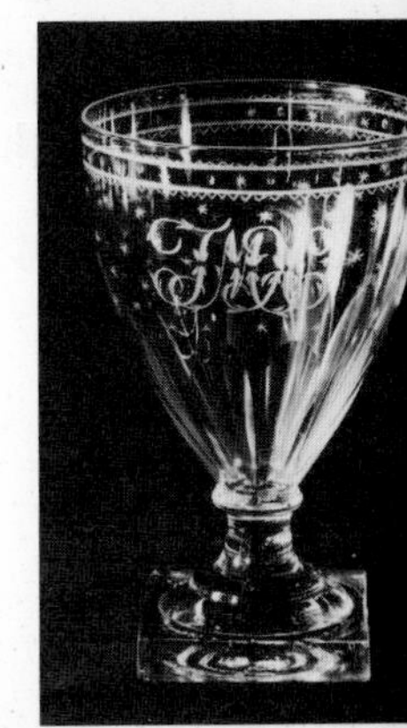

Rummer (late 18th c.)

Rudolph. Cultural Center, Wellesley College, Massachusetts (1955–9)

Ruskin: painting by Millais

Ruskin. *End of the Façade of the Doge's Palace*

Runge. *The Hülsenbeck Children*

Morgan Russell. *Four Part Synchromy, Number 7* (1914)

Damon Runyon

Bertrand Russell

Rundell, Bridge and Rundell. The largest and most important firm of English Regency silversmiths, at one time employing over 1,000 hands. They were responsible for the Prince Regent's massive dinner service of 2,000 pieces and other important commissions. Much of the plate commissioned through them was executed by other silversmiths like Storr, Scott and Digby, as they received more orders than they could fulfil.

Runeberg Johan Ludvig (1804–77). Finnish poet and playwright writing in Swedish, an important figure in the literatures of both countries. Much of his verse is patriotic, e.g. on the Swedish victories against Russia (1808). Works include *Kung Fjalar* (1844; *King Fjalar*, 1904) and *Fänrik Ståls Sägner* (1849; *The Songs of Ensign Stål*, 1925).

Runge Philipp Otto (1777–1810). German painter, etcher and writer, with Caspar David Friedrich the leading artist of the German romantic school. He was mainly active in Hamburg, famous for his portraits painted with a melancholy symbolism. He went to study in Denmark, attracted by the then prevalent interest in the legendary epics and mythology of Scandinavia. The mystical spirit of R.'s historical, Biblical and mural compositions foreshadowed Wagner and the Pre-Raphaelites.

Runyon (Alfred) Damon (1884–1946). U.S. short-story writer and journalist. R.'s humorous stories about gamblers, gangsters and their like are set on Broadway and employ its slang; their effect is heightened by the use of the present tense throughout. R.'s colls include *Guys and Dolls* (1932); *Blue Plate Special* (1934); *My Old Man* (1939) and *Runyon à la Carte* (1944).

R.U.R. (1921). Play by Karel *Čapek.

Rural Rides (1830). Travel diary by William *Cobbett.

Rush William (1756–1833). An early American-born sculptor famous for his ship-figureheads; all examples are now lost. Among his surviving works are a life-size statue of Washington (Independence Hall, Philadelphia); *Nymph with Bittern* (Fairmount Park, Philadelphia) and a self-portrait (Pennsylvania Academy).

Ruskin John (1819–1900). English writer on art, economics and social reform; with Carlyle, and others, one of the 'prophets' of the Victorian age. The work of Turner, which he began to collect when young, triggered his meditations on art, eloquently paraded in *Modern Painters* (1843–60), *Seven Lamps of Architecture* (1849), and *The Stones of Venice* (1851–3), valuable less for judgements *ad hoc* than for his recognition that 'the whole function of the artist . . . is to be a seeing and feeling creature' (*Stones of Venice*), and that the excellence of art, though reached through nature is independent of representation. At its best his prose (favourite reading with Proust) is of unsurpassed magnificence, though in earlier work sometimes losing relevance, especially in his descriptions of nature. In his social and economic writings, of world-wide influence, e.g. *Unto This Last* (1862), the essays of which Thackeray refused to continue printing in *The Cornhill*; *Fors Clavigera* (1871–84); *Munera Pulveris* (1872), he stated the case against capitalism and for the values of living with a seldom-matched beauty and power of denunciation. He left a classic autobiography in *Praeterita* (1886–9).

Russell Bertrand Arthur William, 3rd Earl (1872–). English philosopher. R.'s most famous work *Principia Mathematica* (1927; in collaboration with A. N. Whitehead) was a major contribution in the development of symbolic logic. He has led a vigorous political life and has often been a controversial public figure. His many works include a popular *History of Western Philosophy* (1945).

Russell George William: *A.E.

Russell Jane (1921–). U.S. film actress who was launched as 'The Bust' in H. *Hughes's *The Outlaw* (1943), issued only after heavy cuts in 1946; her best performances have been in comedy.

Russell Morgan (1886–1953). U.S. painter, with S. MacDonald-Wright founder of 'synchromism'. He studied under Henri in New York, then went to Paris, where he began to paint 'synchromies' in 1912–*Four Part Synchromy, Number 7* (1914; Whitney Mus., New York). After World War I he returned to representational painting.

Russell Rosalind (1911–). U.S. stage and film actress who usually plays sophisticates; her films include *His Girl Friday* (1941).

Russo Ferdinando (1868–1927). Italian poet notable for his narrative vigour and realism.

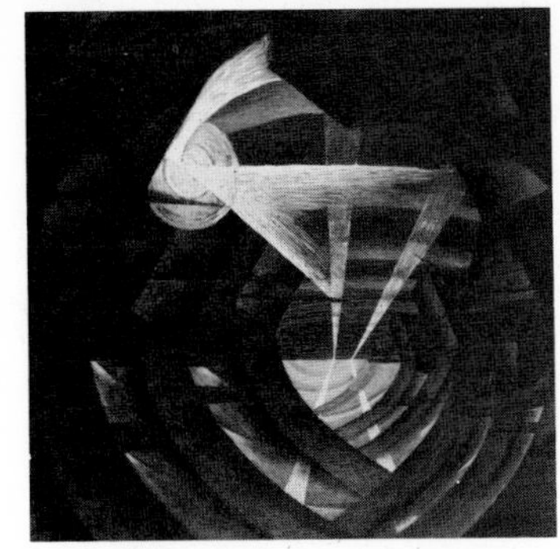

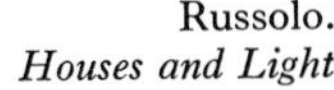

Russolo. *Houses and Light*

Ryder. *Death on a Pale Horse*

Much of his verse was inspired by his native city of Naples. R.'s most ambitious and imaginative work was his long poem *'N Paraviso* (1891), a bizarre vision of Heaven, full of striking imagery and considerable humour.

Russolo Luigi (1885–1947). Italian painter and composer, a signatory of the futurist manifesto (1910). His paintings were not outstanding but his music (bruitism) and his noise-making instruments (*'intonarumori'*) made a significant contribution to the futurist movement. He expounded his principles in *L'Arte dei rumori* (1916).

rustication. In architecture, giving a rough surface to the external face of stone building-blocks; the object was to obtain a strong, rugged appearance. For this reason, too, the edge of each block was often chiselled away, producing a groove where any 2 blocks met and thus emphasizing the role of each; this procedure is (even when applied to smooth blocks) often called r.

Rutebeuf. 13th-c. French poet and jongleur. R. had a lyric gift and considerable technical skill. He wrote satires, fabliaux and *Le Miracle de Théophile*, a religious drama.

Ruth. One of the books of the *Bible (Old Testament), the story of the Moabite Ruth–said to be an ancestor of King David–and of her devotion to her Jewish mother-in-law Naomi.

Rutherford Margaret (1892–). English character actress, e.g. as the eccentric Mme Arcati in Noël Coward's *Blithe Spirit*, as Miss Prism in *The Importance of Being Earnest*, and in many comedy films.

Rutherford Mark. Pseud of William Hale White (1831–1913). English novelist. His works are spiritual self-explorations; they include *The Autobiography of Mark Rutherford* (1881), *Mark Rutherford's Deliverance* (1885) and *The Revolution in Tanner's Lane* (1887).

Ruttmann Walter (1887–1941). German film maker. His *Berlin, the Symphony of a Great City* (1927) from an idea by C. Mayer, is a film of enormously complex montage. *Melodie der Welt* (1930) also used a montage technique for its sound-track–an idea then boldly original. He ed. the climax of Gance's *La Fin du Monde* (1931), collaborated on *Olympische Spiele* and made a documentary *Deutsche Panzer* (1940) before his death from wounds received on the Russian Front.

Ruysbroeck common English version of Ruusbroec, Jan van (1293–1381). Dutch mystical writer. He was ordained as a priest in 1317 and in 1343 became prior of an abbey at Groenendaal. His greatest and most famous work is *Die chierheit der gheesteleker brulocht* called in English *The Adornment of the Spiritual Marriage* or *The Spiritual Espousals.*

Ruysch Rachel (1664–1750). Dutch still-life and flower painter, pupil of W. van Aelst. In 1708 she was appointed painter to the Elector Palatine.

Ruysdael Salomon van (*c.* 1602–70). Dutch landscape painter who worked in Haarlem; uncle of J. van Ruisdael. His early work resembles the work of J. van Goyen. He was later influenced by the Italianate landscapes of J. Both.

Rydberg Abraham Viktor (1828–95). Swedish novelist and poet, and a writer on theology who introduced modern Biblical criticism into Sweden. His early novels express his political radicalism, in historical form in *Den siste Atenaren* (1859; *The Last Athenian*, 1869); later he turned increasingly to poetry, displaying an idealism tempered by doubts about the future of man.

Ryder Albert Pinkham (1847–1917). U.S. painter of visionary and poetic imagination. Living a solitary life in a New York attic he painted small romantic landscapes and scenes of the sea by night as well as symbolic and literary subjects. *Death on a Pale Horse* (M. of A., Cleveland) is a famous and characteristic work. His paintings have deteriorated as a result of his constant repainting.

Rysbrack John Michael (1694–1770). Antwerp sculptor who settled in England and was chief rival to L.-F. Roubiliac. His work, in a more restrained style than that of most of his contemporaries, includes the Marlborough family tomb at Blenheim, the equestrian statue of William III at Bristol and fine portrait busts.

Rzewuski Henryk (1791–1866). Polish novelist. His *Pamiątki J. Pana Seweryna Soplicy* (1839) gives a vivid picture of the life of 18th-c. Polish gentry; with it he created a new genre: the *'gawęda'*. This is a loose, informal narrative, told by a fictitious speaker and accompanied by his comments and reflections.

Rysbrack. *Sir Robert Walpole*

Ruttmann. *Berlin*

Rustication (Radcliffe Camera, Oxford)

S

Sackbuts: from Sandford's *Coronation of James II* (1688)

Hans Sachs: from a 16th-c. Nuremberg handbill

Sacchi. *Vision of St Romuald*

Saarinen Eero (1910–61). U.S. architect, son of Eliel S. S. made his international reputation with General Motors Technical Center (1950–5), a vast complex of buildings in Detroit, shining, metallic, disciplined and technically a great advance for the building industry. His approach was not to develop in a given direction, as Mies and Corbusier have done, but to follow different directions for different commissions, so that such buildings as the U.S. Embassy in London, the T.W.A. Building at Kennedy Airport and Morse College at Yale are based on different sets of values.

Saarinen Eliel (1873–1950). Finnish architect, designer of Helsinki Station (1914). His entry for the Chicago Tribune Tower (1922) was placed 2nd, and was so widely acclaimed that S. moved to the U.S.; none of the skyscrapers he designed were built, but their influence was tremendous. S. designed the Cranbrook campus near Detroit in the 1930s and went into partnership with his son Eero in 1937.

Saavedra Fajardo Diego de (1584–1648). Spanish diplomat, author of *Idea de un príncipe político-cristiano representada en cien empresas* (1640), intended as a counter to Machiavelli, which portrays an able Christian ruler.

Saavedra y Ramírez Duque de Rivas (1791–1865). Spanish statesman, poet and playwright. He began writing poems and tragedies in the neo-classical style, then was converted to romanticism. His romantic drama *Don Álvaro* (1835) caused as much furore in Madrid as did Hugo's *Hernani* in Paris and later inspired Verdi's opera *The Force of Destiny*.

Saaz Johann von: Johann von *Tepl

Saba Umberto. The pseud. of U. Poli (1883–1957). Italian poet brought up in poverty by his Jewish mother (his father deserted the family shortly after S.'s birth). His poetry is largely private and lyrical, and melancholy in tone; it has been little affected by more extreme poetic theories. Colls include *Poesie* (1911) and *Mediterranee* (1947).

Sablé Madeleine, marquise de (*c.* 1599–1678). French society woman. La Rochefoucauld and Mme de La Fayette frequented her *salon*, and her influence on their work was considerable.

Sacchetti Franco (*c.* 1332–1400). Italian poet and short-story writer. Many of S.'s *canzoni* and madrigals were set to music. He wrote an interesting and lively coll. of short stories, the *Trecentonovelle*, in idiomatic Florentine prose.

Sacchi Andrea (1599–1661). Roman painter, a leading representative of the classical tradition of Poussin and Algardi during the high baroque period. He was a pupil of Albani and influenced by the Carracci. His paintings include *Divine Wisdom* (Barberini Palace, Rome) and *Vision of St Romuald* (Vatican). Maratta was his pupil.

Sacchini Antonio Maria Casparo (1730–86). Italian opera composer of European reputation working in Italy, London (1772–82) and finally Paris, where he was in rivalry with Piccinni. His masterpiece, *Oedipe à Colone* (1786), like other later compositions shows the impact of Gluck's work.

Sacconi Giuseppe (1854–1905). Italian architect who designed the Vittore Emmanuele Monument, Rome. It consists of a huge staircase crowned by a colonnade, all in white marble, and has been called 'the most pretentious of all 19th-c. monuments'. It was begun in 1884 and finished after S.'s death in 1911.

Sachs Hans (1494–1576). German writer, master-cobbler and *mastersinger of Nuremberg who wrote some 7,000 Shrovetide farces, tragedies, master-songs, epigrams and fables. His work has vitality rather than polish or depth and S. is a genial exponent of bourgeois life and morality. His drama uses classical, medieval and Renaissance material, stock figures and racy, humorous doggerel; his lyrics are strangled by fixed strophes, or are overtly didactic. His *Die Wittembergisch Nachtigall* (1523) supported the Lutheran Reformation.

Sachs Maurice (1906–45). French writer. S.'s autobiography, *Le Sabbat* (1946; *Witches' Sabbath*, 1965), contains a frank record of his homosexuality and a number of cruel portraits of famous writers he knew well.

sackbut. The English name for *trombone up to the 18th c.; the s. was different from the modern trombone in having a narrower bore and a less flared bell; these features gave it a less heavy tone.

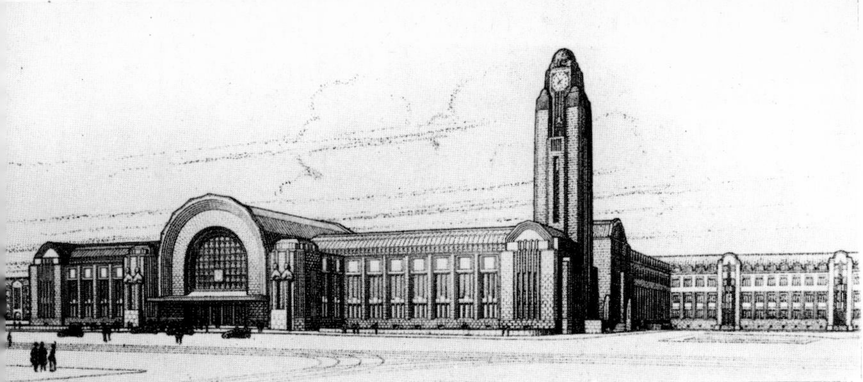

Eliel Saarinen. Project for Helsinki Station

Eero Saarinen. General Motors Technical Center. See also colour plate 77

Sackville Charles, 6th Earl of Dorset (1638–1706). English poet and patron (Dryden was one of his dependants). He wrote satires and some pleasant lyrics.

Sackville Thomas, 1st Earl of Dorset (1536–1608). English poet and playwright. S. contributed 2 poems to the coll. *Mirror for Magistrates* and collaborated with Thomas Norton (1532–84) in *The Tragedy of Gorboduc, or Ferrex and Porrex* (1561), the 1st English tragedy and the 1st English play to be written in blank verse.

sacra conversazione (Italian, 'holy conversation'). Painting of the Madonna and Child with Saints in which the figures are together on a single panel and are involved with one another. Developed in the 15th c. in the work of Fra Angelico, Fra Filippo Lippi and Domenico Veneziano, this type of representation replaced that of the Gothic polyptych in which the Madonna and Child group occupied the central panel and each of the Saints a separate side panel.

Sacred Wood, The (1920). Critical work by T. S. *Eliot.

Sade (Donatien-Alphonse-François) the marquis de (1740–1814). French novelist long famous for the sexual excesses and cruelty portrayed in his works (hence 'sadism'). He was imprisoned (1777–89, mainly in the Bastille) for poisoning a group of prostitutes (in fact an accident) until the Revolution, became an active revolutionary, later offended Napoleon and was confined in Charenton asylum (1803–14), where he produced plays acted by the other inmates. S.'s reputation has fluctuated violently; he undoubtedly influenced subsequent writers by his peculiar atheism (which elevates evil into a universal principle), his advocacy of complete liberty of the instincts, and his obsession with the corrupt and cruel. In the mid-20th c. he has been admired as the 1st philosopher of absolute revolt. Works include *Justine ou les malheurs de la vertu* (1791), *Juliette ou les prospérités du vice* (1792), and *Les 120 Journées de Sodome* (1904).

Sadler's Wells. N. London theatre. In 1683 a Mr Sadler discovered a medicinal well; near it he built a 'Musick House' for the entertainment of visitors. In 1765 a theatre was built there. In the 19th c. it was controlled by Samuel *Phelps who achieved great success with his Shakespearian seasons (1844–62). In the early 20th c. the theatre became derelict, but in 1931 Lilian *Bayliss took over the management and ran it on similar lines to the Old Vic. It has since become the home of the Sadler's Wells Opera Co.

Saenredam Pieter (1597–1665). Dutch painter of church interiors and architectural draughtsman, working at Haarlem. He made many elaborate and accurate drawings and punctiliously recorded any details in which his paintings differed from reality for artistic reasons. Bare walls and hatchments often form a large part of his austere, geometric compositions. The N.G., London, has *Interior of the Buurkerk at Utrecht* and *Interior of the Grotekerk at Haarlem*, both fine examples of his work.

Safety Last (1923). Film with Harold *Lloyd.

Saftleven (Sachtleven) Cornelis (1607–81). Dutch painter best known for his peasant genre scenes in the manner of Brouwer. He also painted interiors, landscapes and historical subjects.

Saftleven Herman (1609–85). Dutch painter of landscapes and religious subjects, pupil of J. van Goyen and brother of Cornelis S. In the early 1640s his work was influenced by the Italianate manner of J. Both and later by the detailed style of Jan Bruegel the Elder.

saga (Icelandic, 'something said'). Term applied to the prose accounts of the lives of kings, heroes, bishops, etc. written in Iceland (and sometimes Norway) between the 12th and 14th cs; the *First Saga of St Olaf* is the oldest s. known. The 3 main types of s. are the 'history s.' (e.g. *Snorri Sturluson's *Heimskringla*), the 'family s.' (e.g. the late 13th-c. *Saga of Burnt Njall*), and the 'mythical s.' (*The Volsunga Saga*, also 13th c.).

Sagan Françoise. Pseud of Françoise Quoirez (1935–). French novelist and playwright. The novel *Bonjour Tristesse* (1954; 1955) made her internationally famous when she was 19. Works include the novel *Un Certain Sourire* (1956; *A Certain Smile*, 1956) and the play *Un Château en Suède* (1960).

Sagan Leontine (1889–). German film director. Her most famous work is *Mädchen in*

Sacra Conversazione. Domenico Veneziano, *St Lucy altarpiece*

Saenredam. *Interior of the Buurkerk at Utrecht*

St Basil: after the *Chronicle* of Adam Olearius

Uniform (1931), a study of emotional pressures in a girls' school.

Saint-Amant Marc-Antoine de Gérard de (1594–1661). French poet, courtier, diplomat and soldier, author of many fresh, extravagant, often burlesque poems, frequently suggested by tavern life.

S. Ambrogio Milan. One of the outstanding Romanesque churches of N. Italy. Parts belong to the 9th c., but it is mostly early 12th. The interior elevation has an arcade (pronounced alternation of supports–pier and pillar) and gallery but no clerestory. The rib-vaulting (quadripartite) is probably *c.* 1120, among the earliest in Europe.

S. Antonio Padua. Italian church dedicated to St Anthony in his home town, begun in 1232 and showing an unusual combination of Romanesque, Byzantine and Gothic elements. The chancel has an apse and 9 radiating chapels (French Gothic influence); the crossing, transepts and nave are roofed by domes (Byzantine via St Mark's, Venice), while the W. front has an arcaded gallery running across the whole width (as in Tuscan or Lombard Romanesque).

S. Croce: the nave

St Basil Moscow. The cathedral of Moscow, built (1555–60) by 2 Russian architects, Postnik and Barma. Like most Russian churches, it is small and cramped, consisting of an octagon only about 30 ft wide, surrounded by an ambulatory which is in turn surrounded by 8 domed chapels. From outside it is a cluster of small towers topped by onion-domes, against the high octagonal centre. Decoration displays a wild variety of colours, scale and pattern.

St-Cloud. The 1st important French (soft-paste) *porcelain factory, founded *c.* 1675. Works following the fashions for chinoiseries and Japanese Kakiemon styles were produced; characteristic are smoothness of texture, heaviness of form and a yellow tone.

S. Croce Florence. Italian Gothic church, begun in 1295. At the E. end it opens into a transept with chancel and 10 chapels. It is notable both for the number of famous Florentines buried in it (including Michelangelo and Machiavelli) and for the frescoes in the E. chapels by Giotto and his school. In the cloister is the Pazzi chapel by Brunelleschi.

Saint-Denis Michel (1897–). French theatre director and teacher. He founded La Compagnie des Quinze in France (1930), was co-founder of the Old Vic School in London and director of it (1946–52), ran a theatre school in Strassburg (1952–7) and has also done advisory work in Canada. He was also head of the B.B.C. French section (1940–4) and since 1962 has been an artistic director of the Royal Shakespeare Co.

St Denis Abbey near Paris, France. A building of key importance in the history of architecture, since it is usually held to be the 1st example of the Gothic style. Abbot *Suger's work consisted of a new W. front (1135–40) which used the pointed arch and the rib-vault, and an E. end (1140–4) where the new style is even more vividly expressed: it has an ambulatory with radiating chapels, the walls between which are omitted, forming another outer ambulatory. The chancel itself was much altered during the early 13th c. and the nave (which had not been touched by Suger) later rebuilt by Pierre de *Montereau.

Sainte-Beuve Charles-Augustin (1804–69). The most celebrated French critic and a prominent figure in the romantic movement. He was trained initially as a medical student, but soon went into journalism. He became a friend of Victor Hugo and later the lover of Mme Hugo. His early liberalism was soon dimmed by sceptical doubts, but he showed some political courage during the repressive period of the Second Empire. He never married and, during most of his life, suffered from melancholy and frustration. The romantically pathetic aspect of his nature is expressed in his creative writings, especially in *Vie, Poésies et Pensées de Joseph Delorme* (1829) and the novel, *Volupté* (1834). His criticism, on the other hand, is the first vigorous attempt to explore literature with a combination of scientific thoroughness and aesthetic appreciation. His major work is generally held to be *Port-Royal* (1840–61), a study of the 17th c. from the point of view of the Jansenist movement; of his numerous critical articles the most famous is the series *Causeries du Lundi* (1851–62; complete trs. *Causeries du Lundi* 1909–11). He has been accused of not appreciating his contemporaries, particularly Baudelaire, and of being interested in character and anecdote rather than in literary achievement. Although there is truth in both accusations, his position remains unchallenged.

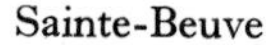
Sainte-Beuve

St Denis: the choir

Sainte-Chapelle Paris: Pierre de *Montereau

Saint-Évremond Charles de Saint-Denis de (1613–1703). French man of letters. After his *Lettre sur le Traité des Pyrénées* (1661) he was forced to leave France and thereafter lived mainly at the English court. He wrote elegant essays on many subjects; some of them were trs. into English (1685), and a coll. of 1692 carries a description of S.-E. by Dryden.

Saint-Exupéry Antoine de (1900–44). French writer of aristocratic birth who found an ideal of service in flying. A pioneer of civil aviation, he became a leading figure in the Free French movement during the war and was lost during a reconnaissance mission. His earlier works–*Courrier Sud* (1928), *Vol de nuit* (1931; *Night Flight*, 1932) and *Terre des hommes* (1939; *Wind, Sand and Stars*, 1939)–are lyrical meditations on his experiences as an airman, which he made the basis of a warm-hearted, if not altogether logical philosophy. The unfinished parable *La Citadelle* (1948; *The Wisdom of the Sands*, 1952), written in Biblical prose and strongly coloured by his fascination with North Africa, was to be a *summa* of his thoughts about life and service. He also wrote a highly successful children's tale, *Le Petit Prince* (1943; *The Little Prince*, 1944).

S. Francesco Assisi Italy. The mother church of the Franciscans and burial-place of St Francis. It was built (in opposition to his wishes) soon after his death (1253) and consists of an upper and lower church–the lower like an extended crypt. Though contemporary with the Île de France cathedrals, it shows no influence from them but follows the style of Angers, W. France–thick walls, no aisles, very wide quadripartite vault. It is especially notable for the frescoes by Giotto, Cimabue, Lorenzetti and Simone Martini.

St Front Périgueux, France. Romanesque church, built (*c.* 1120) in imitation of St Mark's, Venice, and the only centrally-planned church of its date in France. It has the same 5 domes as St Mark's but the absence of marble veneer and mosaic makes it seem bare.

St Gall Switzerland. Benedictine monastery (18th-c. baroque); in its library is preserved a ms. plan of unique value in the history of architecture. Drawn in Cologne *c.* 830 as a guide for the builders of St G., it shows a long basilican church with an apse at both ends and 2 towers, together with all the conventual buildings, the school, infirmary, farm, guests' lodgings and the cemetery–all in minute detail even to the furniture.

Saint Gaudens Augustus (1848–1907). Irish-born U.S. sculptor who, after study in France and Italy, became the leading sculptor in N. America. His work is clearly influenced by Renaissance and neo-classical ideals but has an individual vigour and plasticity marred occasionally by sentimentality. His works include: the Farragut Monument (Madison Square, New York) and the General Sherman Monument.

Saint-Gelais Mellin de (1487–1558). French poet, nephew of Octovien S. His light verse introduced the sonnet and other Italian verse forms into France. He wrote a tragedy, *Sophonisbe* (1559), taken from the Italian of Trissino.

Saint-Gelais Octovien de (1468–1502). French poet who became bishop of Angoulême (1495), one of the *rhétoriqueurs. His works include the allegory *Le Séjour d'honneur*, the erotic *Histoire de Eurialus et Lucresse*, and trs from Homer, Virgil and Ovid.

S. Gimignano Italy. Medieval town, almost unchanged since the 15th c. and especially notable for the number of house-towers which have survived; they were built for security and defence and were once common in every Italian town.

S. Irene Constantinople (*c.* 740). Byzantine church with the same basic features as S. Sophia, though inferior in size and design, but notable as containing the 1st known use of a drum with windows underneath the dome.

St Joan (1923). Play by G. B. *Shaw, made into a film (1957) directed by Otto Preminger.

St John Lateran Rome. The cathedral of Rome (as distinct from the Vatican) and for long periods in the middle ages the home of the popes. The church was built *c.* 330 as a normal basilica, but was repaired frequently and in the 17th c. drastically altered by *Borromini, who filled in every alternate pair of columns with stucco decoration. The Baptistery (*c.* 430–40) is octagonal, in 2 storeys with antique

St Front

St John Lateran: interior of the Baptistery

S. Gimignano

St Mark's

S. Miniato al Monte

porphyry columns. The Palace, adjoining the church, is now a museum.

Saint-Lambert Jean-François, marquis de (1716–1803). French poet, author of *Les Saisons* (1769), an imitation of Thomson's *The Seasons*.

Saint-Léon Arthur (1821–70). French dancer and choreographer; the most famous of his ballets is *Coppélia* (1870), and he wrote a book, *La Sténochorégraphie* (1852), on the method of dance notation which he devised to record his ballets.

S. Maria de Naranco Spain. Church, originally the royal hall of King Ramiro I of Asturias (842–50)–a unique survival of a 9th-c. secular building. It has a tunnel-vault, transverse arches, and an open loggia at each end.

S. Maria Maggiore Rome. Early Christian basilica, built *c.* 432. It has colonnades of Ionic columns carrying straight entablature, and fine mosaics in the clerestory and chancel arch.

St Mark's Venice. The finest example of Byzantine architecture in W. Europe. It was begun in 1063, the plan (based on a now destroyed church in Constantinople) being a Greek cross with domes over the 4 arms and the crossing. The interior is divided up by marble pillars (some of them antique); the walls are faced with coloured marble, and the upper parts and domes covered in mosaic (of all dates, from the 12th to the 17th cs). The W. end and sides of the nave are surrounded by a narthex, also domed and decorated with fine mosaics. The W. front, originally plain round arches on clustered columns, was embellished with Gothic ogee arches and lavish stone ornament in the 14th c. St M. is outstanding for the richness of its materials, warm colours, subtle effects of lighting and the complex relations of its interior spaces.
The separate brick Campanile, in the square to the W. of the cathedral, was begun in the 14th c. and finished in the 16th. It is the tallest building in Venice, collapsed in 1902 but was exactly restored.

St Martin Cologne (begun 1185). The largest of the great series of Romanesque churches at Cologne, distinguished by its big, thick tower with low spire–a feature of Cologne's skyline until the war. St M. was destroyed by bombing but is being rebuilt.

S. Miniato al Monte near Florence, Italy (late 11th c.). The best example of the Tuscan Romanesque style, which preserved so many classical features and exerted so strong an influence on *Brunelleschi that it is often known as the 'Proto-Renaissance'. The façade (which is patterned with polychrome marble) and the interior have arcades of round arches resting on Corinthian capitals. The interior arcade is subdivided in an unusual way, with 3 arches per large bay, the bays being divided by a diaphragm arch resting on Corinthian half-columns at right angles to the arcade, which gives it an even more classical appearance.

S. Paolo fuori le Mura Rome. The largest of the early Christian basilicas, built *c.* A.D. 380. It has double aisles (the colonnades carrying arches) and a 'Triumphal Arch' E. end. It was destroyed by fire in 1823 but carefully restored.

St Peter's Rome. (1) Old St Peter's was founded by Constantine over the reputed tomb of St Peter. It had a large atrium, a narthex extending the whole width of the front, a long basilican nave with double aisles, and transepts. This church was pulled down by Pope Julius II in 1506 to make room for (2) New St Peter's. The original design–a centralized plan–was by *Bramante, later modified by Sangallo, Peruzzi, Raphael and *Michelangelo, who finished the E. end and dome. Nave and façade were added by *Maderno and the Baldacchino and Piazza by *Bernini.

Saint-Pierre Jacques-Henri Bernardin de: *Bernardin de Saint-Pierre

St-Porchaire. French town, the site of the potteries which produced (*c.* 1525–*c.* 60) the Henri II style of pottery. St-P. wares are unique in the history of pottery for their technique of decoration by the inlay of coloured clays.

San Rocco, Scuola di Venice. Guildhall containing a cycle of paintings of the Life of Jesus by *Tintoretto.

Saint-Saëns Charles-Camille (1835–1921). French composer and professor of organ. He was also known as a keyboard player and conductor of his own works. The elegance and eclecticism of his style marked him off from the current Wagnerian and impressionist vogues. He would make use of clichés taken

S. Maria de Naranco

New St Peter's: etching by Piranesi. Also *Bramante and, for Old St Peter's, *basilica

from 18th-c. music or sentimental ballads, and incorporate them stylishly into a part-grandiose, part-academic texture: his 3rd symphony uses a huge orchestra including 2 pianos and organ; and his opera *Samson and Delilah* (1877) was banned in England for a generation and had great success in France for its sensational sensuousness. His *Le Carnaval des animaux* was a parody of all that was holy at the Conservatoire where he taught, and S.-S. would not allow it to be performed in public until after his death. Other works include piano concertos (which Ravel considered on a plane with Mozart's), 5 symphonies, 11 further operas, the symphonic poems *Omphale's Spinning Wheel* (1869) and *La danse macabre* (*Dance of Death), and many other works of all kinds.

St Sernin Toulouse (1080–96). One of the largest and best preserved of the Romanesque pilgrimage churches; all show the same basic features–long nave with arcade, gallery (no clerestory) and tunnel-vault; long transepts; chancel with ambulatory and radiating chapels. St S.'s tower, diminishing in stages like a telescope, is unusual. The chancel contains stone relief panels of Christ and Saints which mark the beginning of large-scale Romanesque figure sculpture.

SS Giovanni e Paolo. One of the 2 great friars' churches of Venice, begun in 1234; its basic features are the same as the Frari. It is notable for its series of Doges' tombs and for Verrocchio's Colleoni monument, which stands outside.

Saint-Simon Claude-Henri de Rouvroy, comte de (1760–1825). French writer who evolved the form of Socialism known as Saint-Simonism.

Saint-Simon Louis de Rouvroy, duc de (1675–1755). French writer of memoirs. An inherited sense of his own importance and his innate pride antagonized the king, Louis XIV, prevented his preferment and embittered his judgement. He retired from court when the regent, his patron, died in 1723. Having kept records of court life continuously from the age of 19, when he acquired (*c.* 1730) the journal of a contemporary courtier, Dangeau, he had materials for a detailed and exhaustive commentary on the age. The *Mémoires* (publ. 1829/30; 1857) are conspicuously brilliant in description and malicious portraiture.

St Sophia Constantinople. The greatest achievement of Byzantine architecture and the most important single influence on later Islamic. Built in 5 years (532–7) for Justinian by Anthemius of Tralles and Isidorus of Miletus. It consists basically of a square space of 107 ft bounded by 4 huge arches and covered by a shallow dome (180 ft above the ground) which is pierced by a ring of small windows and rests on pendentives. To N. and S. the sides are solid; on the outside massive buttresses carry the thrust of the dome. To E. and W. the space opens out into semi-domes (which provide support for the dome in these directions). At the end of the E. semi-dome is the altar, at the end of the W. the entrance. The church thus combines a centralized ground-plan with a basilican W.–E. movement. Its material is brick with facings of marble veneer and (originally) mosaic. The marble columns of the interior come from Hellenistic and Roman buildings (Baalbek, Ephesus, etc.). After the fall of Constantinople in 1453 St S. became a mosque and was given 4 minarets.

St Sophia Kiev. The 1st great achievement of Russian architecture after the conversion of the kingdom of Kiev to Christianity in the 10th c. It was based on Byzantine models, probably begun in 1018 and had a nave, transept and 6 aisles, 3 on each side; it was roofed by numerous small domes on drums. In succeeding cs it was added to, wrecked by the Tartars, abandoned as a ruin and restored in 18th-c. baroque, so that little of its original appearance remains.

SS Sergius and Bacchus Constantinople. Byzantine church (A.D. 527). Its plan is a central octagon covered by a dome and surrounded by a square ambulatory.

St Stephen. Cathedral of Vienna, the most notable Gothic church there. Built throughout the 14th c. and never finished, it is a hall-church, dominated outside by a tall tower and spire over the S. transept.

St Trophîme Arles, France. Provençal Romanesque church (*c.* 1150) with the 2-storey elevation and pointed tunnel-vault normal in that district. The W. front shows marked Roman influence in its sculpture and architecture (fluted pilasters, straight entablature, etc.). The cloister is notable for its twin columns with elaborate figured capitals.

St Sernin

Saint-Saëns

The duc de Saint-Simon

St Sophia, Kiev

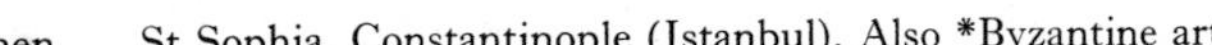

St Stephen

St Sophia, Constantinople (Istanbul). Also *Byzantine art

St Trophîme: the porch

S. Vitale. Also *Byzantine art

Antonio Salieri

S. Vitale Ravenna. Byzantine church (A.D. 526–47). Its plan is a central octagon surrounded by an octagonal ambulatory. Between the arches of the inner octagon columns carry a curved entablature, making each opening into an open niche extending from the ground to the dome. The chancel, an apsed extension at the E. end, contains the famous mosaics of Old Testament subjects and of Justinian and Theodora with their court.

S. Zeno Verona. One of the largest of Italian Romanesque churches (mid 12th c.). It has alternating supports in the nave, a raised E. end with a crypt open to the nave on arches, and a wooden roof. The bronze doors, and stone reliefs round them showing Biblical scenes, are among the finest works of Italian Romanesque sculpture.

S. Zeno. Bronze reliefs

Saison en enfer, Une (1873). Poetic work by *Rimbaud.

Saki: H. H. *Munro

Salacrou Armand (1899–). French playwright. His works, always skilfully composed, have great variety of subject and treatment. They include *Tour à Terre* (1925); *L'Inconnue d'Arras* (1935); *Les Nuits de la colère* (1946) and *Boulevard Durand* (1960).

Salammbô (1863). Novel by *Flaubert.

Salieri Antonio (1750–1825). Italian composer and renowned teacher under whom both Beethoven and Schubert studied. His operas include: *Europa riconosciuta* for the opening of La Scala, Milan (1778); *Les Danaïdes,* performed (1784) when S. was Gluck's pupil in Paris; and the *opera buffa, La grotta di Trofonio* (1785), which rivalled Mozart's successes. The legend that S. poisoned Mozart inspired Pushkin's 1-act verse play *Mozart and S.*, and the opera by Rimsky-Korsakov, based on this.

Salinas Pedro (1892–1951). Spanish poet. S.'s poems mainly deal with love and show an extraordinary unity of style throughout his career; they are distinguished by extremely subtle, delicate language and metre.

Salinger J(erome) D(avid) (1919–). U.S. novelist and short-story writer. S. made his reputation with a short novel, *The Catcher in the Rye* (1951), whose protagonist is a quasi-sophisticated adolescent whose observations on his relationship to society are subtly conveyed in a precise, colloquial style. S.'s works include *Nine Stories* (1953; also called *For Esmé–with Love and Squalor*) and the series about the Glass family, *Franny and Zooey* (1961) and *Raise High the Roof Beam, Carpenters* (1963).

Salisbury cathedral: aerial view. Also *Farleigh

Salisbury cathedral: interior

Salisbury cathedral. *Early English cathedral, remarkable for the consistency of its style. It was built (apart from the tower) between 1220 and 1260 on a completely fresh site. The quadripartite vault and absence of ridge-rib show French influence, but most of its features are typically English: the plan, with long nave and double transepts; use of Purbeck marble, absence of tracery (lancet windows throughout); and the W. front, which is a mere screen, unrelated to the interior. The tower and spire, the highest in England, were built by Richard of *Farleigh in the mid 14th c.

Sallust (86–*c.* 34 B.C.). Roman pamphleteer. Gaius Sallustius Crispus, born at Amiternum of plebeian family, entered on a senatorial career and became a partisan of Caesar, who rewarded him with the governorship of Numidia. He made enough money out of his province to buy a luxurious estate at Rome, and retired from politics to devote himself to writing–2 historical monographs and 5 (lost) books of histories. Both the *Catiline* and the *Jugurthine War*, under the guise of philosophic impartiality, are propaganda for the Caesarian party. Sallust's style is terse, epigrammatic and archaic, deliberately modelled on *Thucydides. He uses his historical material as a vehicle for moral reflection and character drawing: according to one ancient authority 'he should be read as an orator, not as an historian'.

Salmagundi: or, The Whim-Whams and Opinions of Launcelot Langstaff, Esq., . . . (1807–8). Humorous magazine publ. by Washington Irving, his brother William, and James Kirke Paulding; revived for a time (1819) by Paulding.

Salmon André (1881–). French poet and novelist profoundly influenced by cubism. He was one of the group round Apollinaire and Picasso.

Salome (1896). Play by Oscar *Wilde, the basis of a 1-act opera by R. *Strauss.

Salomon Johann Peter (1745–1815). German violinist and conductor. He settled in London in 1781 and organized the 2 visits to that city of his great friend Haydn, who dedicated his last 12 symphonies to him.

salon. A number of friends, forming a more or less stable group, who meet regularly at a private house; the lady of the house usually presides. The intellectual s. originated in 17th-c. France and has since always played an important role in the literary and artistic life of the country. The Hôtel de *Rambouillet was the most famous of the early s.s.

Salon des Indépendants. Founded, in Paris, in 1884 in opposition to the official annual Salon, by artists who disagreed with academic art.

Salon des Refusés. Special exhibition held in Paris in 1863 of the works refused by the Salon of that year. The exhibition was ordered by Napoleon III after the outcry caused by the number of rejections. One of the principal exhibits was Manet's *Le Déjeuner sur l'Herbe* while other artists exhibiting were Boudin, Cézanne, Fantin-Latour, Jongkind, Pissarro and Whistler. The paintings exhibited were attacked by critics and public and no such exhibition was held again.

salt. In the middle ages large ceremonial table salts were the most impressive pieces of domestic silver. Lavishly embellished, they were frequently in the form of ships, hourglasses, animals or even men. Only in the 17th c. did the small individual salt-cellar replace the large standing-salt (also *centre-piece).

salt-glaze. A glaze used on stoneware. It is made by throwing common salt into the fire-grates during the finishing period of the firing process. A thin, transparent and colourless glaze forms on the stoneware surface and the colour of the pot is dependent on the colour of the body.

Saltus Edgar (Evertson) (1855–1921). U.S. writer. S.'s novels and other books exploited the exotic and erotic, achieving a temporary popularity. They include the histories *The Imperial Purple* (1892) and *The Imperial Orgy* (1927).

Saltykov Mikhail Evgrafovich (1826–89). Russian writer. S. used the pseud. 'N. Shchedrin' and is often called SALTYKOV-SHCHEDRIN. He wrote a large number of splendid satirical sketches, but is best known in the West for *The Golovlyov Family* (1876–80; 1916), a masterly but unrelievedly gloomy novel describing the brutal life of the provincial gentry.

Salutati Coluccio (1331–1406). Italian humanist scholar and author of many moral and political treatises. He was regarded as one of the finest letter writers of his age.

Salvatore Giuliano (1961). Film directed by F. *Rosi.

Salvi Nicola (1697–1751). Italian architect who designed the Fontana Trevi in Rome (begun 1732). It consists of a cascade over rocks, with Neptune standing on a shell drawn by horses, in front of an unexpectedly sober and classical palace-façade. After S.'s death it was finished by Giuseppe Pannini.

Salviati Francesco de' Rossi, called (1510–63). Florentine mannerist painter and designer, pupil of Andrea del Sarto and friend of Vasari. He worked in Florence, Venice and Rome and from 1554 to 1556 in Paris. His paintings include *Justice* (Bargello, Florence) and *Story of Psyche* (Palazzo Grimani, Venice).

Samain Albert (1858–1900). French poet. S. helped to found the *Mercure de France.* His verse, which shows the influence of symbolism, includes the coll. *Au jardin de l'infante* (1893).

Samian ware: *terra sigillata

Sammartini Giovanni Battista (1700/1–75). Italian composer, famous throughout Europe for his instrumental music. This included symphonies (the earliest date from the 1730s) and chamber music. Haydn hotly denied the contemporary assertion that S. had influenced him but unquestionably S. played an important role in the development of sonata form. Gluck was a pupil (1737–41).

Samson Joseph-Isidore (1793–1871). French actor who spent most of his career at the Comédie-Française. He was also the teacher of *Rachel, through her contributing to the revival of French tragedy.

Samson Agonistes (1671). Dramatic poem by *Milton.

Salon. A *soirée* at Mme Geoffrin's (d'Alembert lecturing)

Salviate. *Charity*

Silver-gilt salt; London, 1581

Salvi. Fontana Trevi

George Sand: painting (1834) by Delacroix and photograph (1870) by Nadar

Carl Sandburg

Sandby. *Bishopsgate Entrance to Windsor Great Park*

Sanctuary knocker, Durham cathedral

De Sanctis. The Spanish Steps

Samson and Delilah (1877). Opera by *Saint-Saëns.

Samsonov Sergei. Soviet film director. His adaptation of Chekhov, *The Grasshopper* (1955), is one of the better post-war Russian films; but *The Optimistic Tragedy* (1962), in 70-mm. monochrome, is a throwback to the epics of the Stalin era.

Samuel. One of the books of the *Bible (Old Testament), in Christian versions usually regarded as the 1st 2 books of *Kings; it describes the lives of Samuel, Saul and David.

Sanctis Francesco De (1693–1740). Italian architect who designed the Spanish Steps in Rome (1723), one of the most flamboyant and successful pieces of baroque town planning.

Sanctuary (1931). Novel by William *Faulkner.

sanctuary knocker. Ornamental knocker on the door of a church; if a fugitive touched it he was entitled under medieval ecclesiastical law to sanctuary (i.e. immunity from arrest).

sanctus: *mass

Sand George. Pseud. of Aurore Dupin, baronne Dudevant (1804–76). French novelist born in Paris; brought up in her grandmother's household at Nohant on Rousseauesque lines and convent educated in Paris. She married a retired army officer (1822), bore him 2 children, left him for literature (1831) and was legally separated in 1840. A liaison with Alfred de Musset influenced her early work, e.g. the romantic novels *Lélia* (1833) and *Mauprat* (1837). From 1837 to 1847 she lived with Chopin, for a brief period on Majorca. Later she began to incorporate second-hand philosophy into her work, as in *Spiridion* (1839), *Le Compagnon du Tour de France* (1840), and the novel *Consuelo* (1842; 1847). In the 1848 Revolution she took a hand as a journalist, but after this retired to her estate. From the 1840s her work dealt mainly with pastoral and peasant themes; it includes the masterly village novels *La Mare au diable* (1846; *The Haunted Marsh*, 1847), *La Petite Fadette* (1848; 1850) and *François le champi* (1850; *Francis the Waif*, 1889); *Les Maîtres Sonneurs* (1852); *L'Homme de neige* (1856); *Les Beaux Messieurs de Bois-Doré* (1858); *Le Marquis de Villemer* (1860); and *Mademoiselle de Quintinie* (1863). She also wrote several unsuccessful plays, autobiographical pieces like *Lettres d'un voyageur* (1836), *Un Hiver à Majorque* (1841), and *Histoire de ma Vie* (1854/5), and letters to many correspondents including Sainte-Beuve and Flaubert.

Sandburg Carl (1878–). U.S. poet. His poems first made an impact when he created a stance and a theme out of his Middle West and populist experiences and made a style out of personal rhetoric and popular idiom, affected by current imagism: the result was *Chicago Poems* (1916). His poetry includes *Good Morning America* (1928) and the tribute to the American folk, *The People, Yes* (1936), after which his energies went into a monumental biography of his hero Lincoln (1926–39).

Sandby Paul (1725–1809). English landscape painter and engraver. He did some of his best work in and around Windsor Great Park and discovered the artistic potentialities of Welsh scenery. Besides watercolour he worked in gouache and was also the first to use aquatint engraving creatively. He gave an unidealized though sometimes over-detailed rendering of his subject.

Sandeau Jules (1811–83). French novelist and playwright. S. wrote the novels *Mademoiselle de la Seiglière* (1848) and, in collaboration with George Sand, *Rose et Blanche ou la comédienne et la religieuse* (1831); with Augier he wrote the play *Le Gendre de Monsieur Poirier* (1854).

Sanders Denis (1929–) and Terry (1931–). The producer/director team of the S. brothers came to notice with a brilliant short film *A Time out of War* (1953). Working with intelligence on a low budget, they have since made *Crime and Punishment U.S.A.* (1958; derived from Dostoyevsky) and *War Hunt* (1961).

Sanders George (1906–). British-born U.S. film actor. Typed as a smooth, somewhat caddish man of the world; his effortless style is seen in *Moonfleet* and many other films.

Sandrart Joachim von (1606–88). German painter and art historian widely travelled in Germany and Italy. He is important as the author of *Teutsche Academie . . .* (1675–79), a valuable source of information on 17th-c. art and artists.

Sandys Frederick (1829–1904). English illustrator, subject painter and portraitist associated with later Pre-Raphaelitism.

Sandys George (1578–1644). English poet and trs., secretary of the London Virginia Company. S. worked in the colony between 1621 and 1631. His *Ovid's Metamorphosis Englished by G. S.* (1626) was the 1st trs. of a classic made in America.

Sanfelice Ferdinando (1675–1750). Italian architect, the greatest of late baroque architects in Naples. He designed many churches and palaces in and around Naples, but his fame rests on his monumental staircases. 2 of the most spectacular are those of the Palazzo Sanfelice and the Palazzo di Bartolomeo di Majo.

San Francisco (1936). Film directed by W. S. *Van Dyke.

Sangallo Antonio da, the Elder (1455–1534). Italian architect. He designed S. Maria di Loreto, Rome–the lower parts only–and S. Biagio, Montepulciano, both important central-spaced churches developed from his brother Guiliano's S. Maria delle Carceri.

Sangallo Antonio da, the Younger (1485–1546). Italian high Renaissance architect, nephew of Antonio the Elder. He was an orthodox classical architect with a strong but not strikingly original style. He is best known for the Farnese Palace, Rome (begun 1530); it has a plain façade without rustication; a courtyard elevation based on the Theatre of Marcellus; a top-storey and cornice added by Michelangelo. From 1536 he was in charge of St Peter's and put forward a modified longitudinal plan.

Sangallo Giuliano da (1445-1516). Italian architect, brother of Antonio da S. the Elder. He is best known for his church of S. Maria delle Carceri, Prato, a central-spaced building closely modelled on Brunelleschi's Pazzi chapel, but bigger. He was for a short time partly in charge of the rebuilding of St Peter's.

Sang des Bêtes, Le (1949). Short film directed by G. *Franju.

Sang d'un Poète, Le (1930). Film directed by Jean *Cocteau.

San Michele, The Story of (1929). Autobiographical book by Axel *Munthe.

Sanmicheli Michele (1484–1559). Italian architect and military engineer. He spent most of his life at Verona, building there the walls and 2 gates, and several palaces, e.g. Palazzo Pompeii (*c.* 1530) and Palazzo Bevilaqua (*c.* 1530)–important as an early example of *mannerism with complicated rhythms and wilful contradictions in the detail. He also built the Palazzo Grimani at Venice. S.'s work is distinguished by a massive, stony quality; he thought in terms of masonry rather than the drawing-board.

Sannazzaro Jacopo (1456–1530). Italian poet, member of the Neapolitan Academy of Humanities in which he was known as 'Actius Syncerus'. He passed most of his life in Naples at the Aragonese court, and when King Frederick was sent in exile to France, S. followed him, returning to Naples on the king's death. His famous *Arcadia* (1504), in prose and verse, sings the praises of an idealized rural life and was the first of a new literature of Arcadia. S. also wrote Petrarchan sonnets and canzoni, Latin eclogues, elegies and epigrams.

Sano di Pietro (1406–81). Sienese painter, pupil and follower of Sassetta. He painted many scenes from the life of St Bernard, including *St Bernard Preaching* in Siena cathedral.

Sansho Dayu (1954). Film directed by K. *Mizoguchi.

Sansom William (1912–). English novelist and short-story writer. His works are distinguished by sensuous descriptions of great symbolic power; they include the short-story colls *The Passionate North* (1950) and *A Contest of Ladies* (1956), and the novel *The Body* (1949).

Sansovino Il (Andrea Contucci) (1460–1529). Italian sculptor. He was trained in Florence but worked mainly in Portugal (Lisbon and Coimbra) and Rome. His style is that of the high Renaissance, though the early influence from Donatello always remained strong. Works include the tomb of Cardinal Sforza, Rome; *The Baptism*, over the door of the

Giuliano da Sangallo. S. Maria delle Carceri

Antonio da Sangallo the Younger. The Farnese Palace

Sanmicheli. The Palazzo Bevilaqua

George Santayana

Jacopo da Sansovino. The Old Library

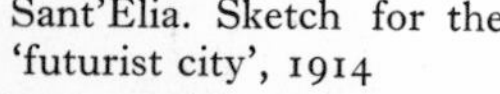

Sant'Elia. Sketch for the 'futurist city', 1914

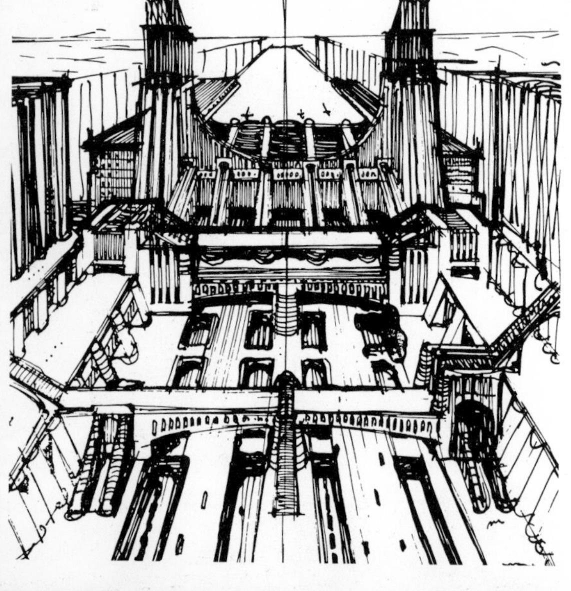

Santi. *Madonna and Saints*

Santiago de Compostela

Santomaso. *Wedding in Venice* (1953)

Baptistery, Florence; and a *Madonna* for Genoa cathedral.

Sansovino Jacopo da. Name used by Jacopo Tatti (1486–1570). Italian architect who worked mostly in Venice. He assimilated the influence of Bramante and Peruzzi and helped to create the style of the Renaissance in Venice (where it arrived later than in Florence and Rome). His style is flamboyant and grandiose, with lavish use of statues, reliefs, etc. His chief works include: the Old Library, opposite the Doge's Palace; the Loggia of St Mark's Campanile; the Palazza Corner della Ca' Grande, a big palace on the Grand Canal; and La Zecca (the Mint), whose wildly exaggerated rustication seems to point forward to *mannerism.

Santayana George (1863–1952). U.S. philosopher and writer born in Spain; his parents brought him to the U.S. in 1872. Most of his later life was spent in Europe. S.'s fame rests on his limpid, precise prose, shrewd insights and self-exploration, rather than on a coherent philosophical system. In *The Life of Reason* (1905–6) he adopted a materialist position subsequently modified in *Scepticism and Animal Faith* (1923) and later works. S.'s literary works include poems, a novel, *The Last Puritan* (1935), and criticism, e.g. *Three Philosophical Poets* (1910).

Sant'Elia Antonio (1880–1916). The architect of *futurism, delighting in the movement of people and vehicles, S. built no buildings, but worked on projects for a new city of skyscrapers linked with bridges.

Santi Giovanni (d. 1494). Italian painter of the Umbrian school, father of Raphael and author of a rhymed chronicle which refers to various 15th-c. artists. His paintings include frescoes in S. Domenico, Cagli and *Virgin and Child* in the N.G., London.

Santiago de Compostela Spain. Romanesque cathedral housing a body reputed to be that of St James, and one of the chief places of pilgrimage during the middle ages. It was begun in 1075, on the same lines as the French pilgrimage churches (*St Sernin, Toulouse). The figures of the W. front, the *Portico de la Gloria* (late 12th c.) form one of the masterpieces of Romanesque sculpture. In the 18th c. it was given a new baroque façade.

Santillana Iñigo López de Mendoza Marqués de (1398–1458). Spanish poet, scholar and warrior. One of the earliest literary figures of the Spanish Renaissance and the first to adapt Italian sonnets and metrical forms into Spanish. In his Italianate poems he made great use of allegory, was influenced by Dante, Petrarch and Boccaccio, and aimed to create a latinized style in Spanish, full of erudite allusions and philosophic content. He wrote 42 sonnets in the Italian style, a coll. of proverbs and a number of delightful *serranillas*, poems on pastoral encounters with country girls.

Santis Giuseppe de (1917–). Italian film director, a polemical film critic who worked on *Ossessione*, and made his 1st film, *Caccia tragica* (1947), in the post-war neo-realist phase. The melodramatic tendencies of this film found full and very lucrative expression in his 2nd film, *Bitter Rice* (1949), a peasant-and-sex drama.

Santomaso Giuseppe (1907–). Italian painter, a founder of the *fronte nuova delle arti. He developed his own colouristic style of abstraction after World War II in compositions which remained indirectly related to his surroundings.

Sappho (7th/6th c. B.C.). Greek poet born at Mytilene in Lesbos of aristocratic family. She suffered along with her friend Alcaeus in the political upheavals of her time and was exiled, perhaps to Syracuse. Most of her poems were written for her friends, members of a cult-fellowship she established for the worship of Aphrodite. Not even one poem is complete and her reputation rests on the high estimate held of her by ancient scholars and poets such as Horace, as well as on the quality of the surviving fragments. She writes simply, almost colloquially, in her own native dialect. Her lyrics are the earliest personal expressions of romantic love in poetry.

saraband(e). Dance in a stately 3-in-a-bar time. It was of ancient origin, probably Spanish, and formed a movement in the *suite.

Sarbiewski Maciej Kazimierz (1595–1640). Polish baroque Latin poet and Jesuit priest. His works, which won him European fame, went through 58 editions between 1625 and 1892. Of particular interest is the long poem *Silviludia.*

Sardou Victorien (1831–1908). French playwright, very popular in his lifetime. His plays, though skilfully constructed in the manner of *Scribe, were superficial. His melodrama *La Tosca* (1887) was the basis of Puccini's opera.

Sargent John Singer (1856–1952). Painter of the English school, but of U.S. origin. S. studied in Paris, arriving in London (1884) as an 'impressionist', although influenced by the work of Frans Hals and Velazquez. Famous after the acquisition by the Chantrey Trustees of *Carnation, Lily, Lily, Rose*, S. became a prolific and fashionable portrait painter. His technical dexterity and ability to flatter the sitter were offset by a bravura brushwork, sometimes degenerating into the slipshod, which earned him and his followers the nickname of 'the Slashing School'.

Sargent Sir (Harold) Malcolm (Watts) (1895–). English conductor of the B.B.C. Symphony Orchestra from 1950 to 1957, remaining chief conductor of the Promenade Concerts after that date.

Sargeson Frank (1903–). New Zealand short-story writer who, indebted to Sherwood Anderson and Hemingway, has in turn influenced later New Zealand writers. His bare, 'tough-guy' technique now seems distinctive of the 1930s, but his concern for technique was new and important.

Saroyan William (1908–). U.S. short-story writer, novelist and playwright, a prolific, exuberant and colourful writer. S.'s work is an original combination of bravado, lyricism and sentimentality. It includes *The Daring Young Man on the Flying Trapeze* (1934); *My Name is Aram* (1940); *The Human Comedy* (1943) and the play *The Time of Your Life* (1939).

Sarraute Nathalie (1900–). French novelist. S. was born in Russia, which she left in 1904. Her novels include *Tropismes* (1938) and *Portrait d'un inconnu* (1949; *Portrait of a Man Unknown*, 1959).

sarrusophone. Brass musical instrument played with a double reed like the bassoon. It was patented (1856) by the French army bandmaster Sarrus, as a substitute for oboes and bassoons in military bands, but the contrabass version has been used by Saint-Saëns, Delius and Ravel in the orchestra.

Sarti Giuseppe (1729–1802). Italian opera composer who worked in Copenhagen, Italy and Russia. Mozart, an acquaintance, used a theme by S. in the 2nd finale of *Don Giovanni*.

Sartoris (1929). Novel by William *Faulkner.

Sartor Resartus: The Life and Opinions of Herr Teufelsdrockh (1836). Book by Carlyle.

Sartre Jean-Paul (1905–). French philosopher who has written novels, plays, film scenarios and polemical and critical works. He taught philosophy intermittently and has been active in left-wing politics since the time of the Resistance movement, in which he took part. In recent years he has tried to produce an existentialist ethical system and to combine Marxism with existentialism; the evolution of his post-war thought may be studied in his writings in his periodical *Les Temps Modernes*. S.'s imaginative works are expositions of his philosophy, and their didactic and purposive nature gives them force, since the philosophic themes are dramatic–man's 'abandonment' by God, his consequent anguish in exercising his freedom in making choices, and the final nature of all action, intentions going for nothing. S.'s plays have been his most effective works, e.g. *Les Mouches* (1943; *The Flies*, 1946), *Huis clos* (1944; *In Camera*, 1946), *Les Mains sales* (1948; *Crime Passionel* or *Dirty Hands*, 1949), *Le Diable et le Bon Dieu* (1951; *Lucifer and the Lord*, 1952), *Les Séquestres d'Altona* (1959; 1960). Also important are the early novel *La Nausée* (1938; *The Diary of Antoine Roquentin*, 1949), portraying a man so completely alienated that objects overwhelm and disgust him; the unfinished series of novels about pre-war and Occupied France *Les Chemins de la liberté* (3 completed vols 1946–9; *The Age of Reason, The Reprieve, Iron in the Soul*, 1947–50) which S. abandoned because the relatively simple choices of the period were no longer relevant to complex modern problems of commitment; the short-story coll. *Le Mur* (1939; *Intimacy*, 1960); and such philosophical works as *L'Être et le Néant* (1943; *Being and Nothingness*, 1957).

Saryan Martiros (1880–). Armenian painter. He studied at Moscow School of Art under Leonid Pasternak and Serov. He was a prominent member of the *Blue Rose group, and his work is closely related to that of Kusnetsov in his interest in Middle Eastern traditions, particularly Kirghiz Mongol painting, which

Sappho and Alcaeus: Greek vase painting, school of the Brygos painter (*c.* 480 B.C.)

Sargent. *Vernon Lee.*
Also *James, *Patmore

Jean-Paul Sartre

Saryan. *Man with gazelles* (detail)

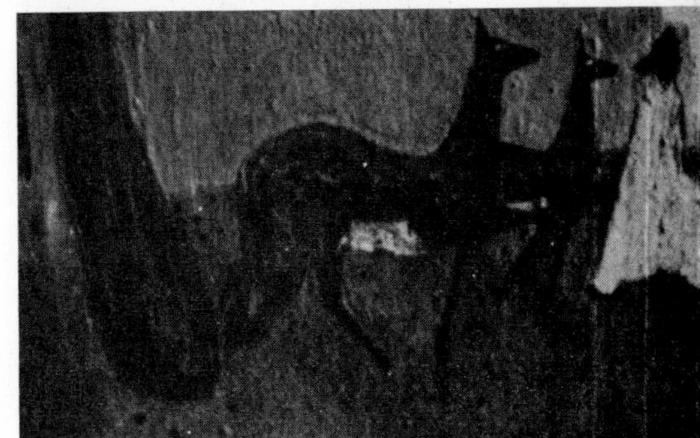

Siegfried Sassoon

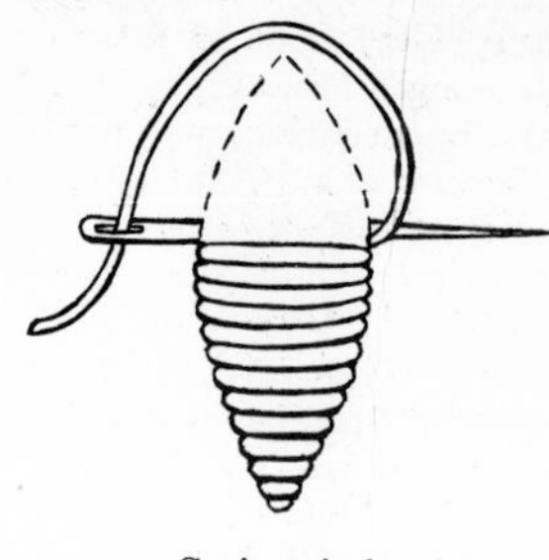

Satin stitch

Sassetta. *The Whim of the young St Francis to become a soldier*

Satie: drawing by Picasso

Satyr play. Satyrs on a Greek vase (*psykter*) by Douris

together with the work of Matisse played an important part in forming his style.

Sassetta Stefano di Giovanni (*c.* 1392–1450). Sienese painter of great power and invention; he combined naïvety with the courtly sophistication of the international Gothic style. His most important work consists of a series of 8 panels dealing with the life of St Francis, painted for the town of Borgo San Sepolcro (1437–44). 7 panels are in the N.G., London.

Sassoferrato Giovanni Battista Salvi, called (1605–85). Italian painter of Raphaelesque Madonnas. He worked mainly in Urbino and was probably a pupil of Domenichino.

Sassoon Siegfried (1886–). English poet and author of the autobiographical novels *Memoirs of a Fox-Hunting Man* (1928), *Memoirs of an Infantry Officer* (1930), *Sherston's Progress* (1936) and the autobiography *Siegfried's Journey* (1945). S.'s best-known poems, especially the coll. *Counter-Attack* (1918), reflect the disgust inspired in him by World War I.

Satie Erik (Alfred Leslie) (1866–1925). French composer. He abandoned his studies at the Paris Conservatoire to work as a café pianist. About 1890, after his 1st piano works had been publ., he became a friend of Debussy; and during this period he was involved with the Rosicrucians. In 1898 he settled at Arceuil, near Paris, which was to become a centre of the French *avant-garde* of the early 20th c., S. being visited there by Diaghilev, Cocteau and Picasso among others. From 1905 to 1908 he studied at the Schola Cantorum under d'Indy and Roussel. S. was legendary for his humorous eccentricity; he treated all the musical material he employed with equal detachment; his work was at first influenced by his interest in mysticism and medieval music. Normal chords and progressions he placed starkly to uncover the abnormality of their associations. Debussy, The *Six, Ravel and Stravinsky each learned something. His works include: the chamber oratorio *Socrate* on texts from Plato's dialogues (1918); the ballet *Parade* (1917) with Cocteau, Massine and Picasso; for piano, *Trois Sarabandes* (1887), *Trois Gymnopédies* (1888) and 10 important suites between 1912 and 1915.

satin stitch. In its simplest form a close embroidery stitch used not for decoration or making an outline, but to fill in areas of colour. The name is derived from its resemblance to the close, even stitch of woven satin.

satire. From Latin *satira*, 'a medley', applied to poems; in modern usage any literary work ridiculing contemporary vices and follies.

Satta Sebastiano (1867–1914). Italian (Sardinian) poet whose work is full of profound humanity, compassion and understanding of his poverty-stricken fellow-islanders and fierce, rebellious indignation against social injustice.

satyr play. In classical Greek drama, bawdy boisterous plays with a mythical hero in some absurd situation and featuring choruses of satyrs (half-human, half-animal); for dramatic competitions the dramatist submitted 3 tragedies and a s. p. which were given at 1 performance. Euripides' *Cyclops* and parts of Sophocles' *Ichneutae* survive.

Saul. Oratorio by *Handel; 1st performed at London in 1739.

Saura Carlos. Spanish film director. S. is the best known of the youngest generation of Spanish directors, who have become known in the past 5 years. *Los Golfos* (1959) used bull-fighting as the focus of a treatment of juvenile delinquency.

Savage James (1779–1852). English architect who designed the church of St Luke, Chelsea (1820), one of the 1st and most influential churches of the *Gothic revival.

Savage Richard (*c.* 1697–1743). Mediocre English poet and playwright remembered because his friend Samuel Johnson wrote *An Account of the Life of Mr Richard Savage* (1744) which he included in his *Lives of the Poets.*

Savage Eye, The (1959). Film directed by J. *Strick.

Savery Roelandt (1576?–1639). Flemish painter of landscapes, animals and flowers, trained in Amsterdam. He worked in Prague and Vienna in the service of the Emperors Rudolf II and Mathias, but later settled in Utrecht. Favourite subjects were the Garden of Eden and Orpheus enchanting the wild beasts, e.g. versions of *Orpheus* in the N.G., London and Fitzwilliam Mus., Cambridge.

Savile George, 1st Marquess of Halifax (1633–95). English statesman and author of ably written pamphlets and essays, especially his *Character of a Trimmer* (1688) and *Character of King Charles II* (1750).

Savinio Alberto. The pseud. of Andrea de Chirico (1891–1952). Italian writer, painter and concert pianist, brother of the painter Giorgio de Chirico. Most of S.'s novels and plays are fantasies, products of the unconscious which show the influence of surrealism. His novels include *Angelica o la notte di maggio* (1927).

Savoldo Giovanni Girolamo (*c.* 1480–*c.* 1550). Italian painter of religious subjects and portraits influenced by the Venetian school and Leonardo da Vinci. He anticipated Caravaggio in his realism and Elsheimer in his use of strange lighting effects.

Savona faïence. The portmanteau name for faïence and maiolica produced during the 17th and 18th cs at the neighbouring Italian towns of Genoa, Savona and Albissola.

Savoy Theatre London. Built by the D'Oyly Carte Co. in 1881 for the performance of the *Gilbert and Sullivan light operas; these became known as the SAVOY OPERAS.

saxhorns. A family of brass instruments evolved (*c.* 1845) by the Belgian instrument maker Adolphe Sax. The instruments are played with a cup mouthpiece, as is the trumpet, and have a conical tube like the cornet; the s.s are virtually indistinguishable from the flugelhorns.

Saxo Grammaticus (*fl.* 1200). Danish writer whose *Gesta Danorum* is written in a turgid Latin but records many pre-Christian myths and the legend of Amleth, which Shakespeare used in *Hamlet.*

saxophones. A family of musical instruments evolved (*c.* 1844) by the Belgian instrument maker Adolphe Sax, primarily as a powerful supplement to the woodwind section of the military band. The instruments are made of brass, have a single reed (like the clarinet) and a conical tube. S.s are occasionally used in the symphony orchestra but are now mainly associated with jazz. The most common of the numerous sizes are the soprano, alto, tenor and baritone.

Sayers Dorothy (Leigh) (1893–1963). English writer best known for her stories about the amateur detective Lord Peter Wimsey. Her other works include a trs. of Dante and the series of plays on the life of Christ *Man Born to be King.*

Sbarbaro Camillo (1888–). Italian poet and prose writer, one of the most personal and sensitive of modern Italian writers; his style is intimate and delicate.

scagliola. Plaster-work of Italian origin made to resemble marble and other ornamental stones. It could be highly polished and was particularly popular in the 18th c.

Scala, Teatro alla or **La Scala, Milan.** The world's greatest opera house. It was opened in 1778 with an opera by *Salieri, was the centre for frequent patriotic demonstrations for Italian unity in the 19th c. and after destruction (1943) in World War II was fully restored and reopened in 1946.

scalds: *skalds

scale. A theoretical construction containing all the notes available for composition in a particular kind of music. Innumerable s.s have been used at different times and in different places, ranging from the pentatonic s. containing only 5 notes and used in folk-song from China to Scotland to the extremely complex and sophisticated s.s of Indian music, containing as many as 22 notes. The s. used determines the 'atmosphere' of the music. The DIATONIC major s. proceeds up the 8ve by step, having in all 5 tones and 2 semitones; there are 3 forms of the diatonic minor s., the essential difference between them all and the majors being that all have the 3rd degree flattened; thus the major s. of C begins CDE; and the minor s.s of C begin DCE♭. The DEGREES of the s. have names: the first is the tonic or keynote, so called because it is the reference note for the tonality of the key; there follow the supertonic; mediant; subdominant; dominant, the most important after the tonic; submediant and *leading note. Other s.s used in European music are the chromatic s. of 12-semitone intervals; the *twelve-note s. (i.e. the chromatic s. outside any harmonic context); the blues s. (*jazz) and the whole-tone s. of *Debussy.

Savoldo. *Madonna with SS Peter, Dominic, Paul and Jerome*

Saxophones: soprano (*left*) and alto

La Scala in 1840

Scenery. *Romeo and Juliet*: Royal Ballet production designed by Georgiadis

Scallop

Alessandro Scarlatti

Domenico Scarlatti

Scaliger Joseph (1540–1609). Italian classical scholar and son of Julius S. He revolutionized textual criticism and emendation by his ed. of the classics and wrote an extremely important work on comparative chronology, *De emendatione temporum* (1583).

Scaliger Julius Caesar (1484–1558). Italian humanist scholar renowned throughout Europe for his erudition. He is now chiefly remembered for his *Poetices libri septem*, an interpretation of Aristotelean literary theories which had a great influence on French classical literature.

scallop. An ornamental edge to material cut in rising and falling curves in imitation of the scallop shell. When used in embroidery, this edge is finished with some form of binding stitch.

Scannell Vernon (1922–). English novelist and poet. His novels are *The Fight* (1953), *The Shadowed Place* (1961), *The Face of the Enemy* (1961); his poems include *A Mortal Pitch*, *The Masks of Love* and *A Sense of Danger*.

Scapegoat, The (1856). Painting by Holman *Hunt.

scarab. An Egyptian symbol in the form of a dung beetle, sacred to the sun god and also used in funeral rites. An important class of s.s have engraved designs on their bases for seals, and often have a hole for threading as a bead.

Scaramouche. Character in the Italian **commedia dell'arte*.

Scarface (1932). Film directed by H. *Hawks.

Scarlatti (Pietro) Alessandro (Gaspare) (1660–1725). Italian composer born in Sicily. He went to Rome (1672), where he met Pasquini and Corelli and served Queen Christina of Sweden; from 1684 to 1702 he was music director at Naples and again from 1709 to 1717, working also at Rome. His pupils included his son Domenico and J. A. Hasse. S. established the Neapolitan *opera seria*, developing from Venetian influence to a style in which the da capo *aria predominated; few vocal ensembles larger than the duet were used, a fine melodic gift was matched with instrumental colour and a use of tonal centres. S.'s operas frequently have the 3-movement 'Italian' *Sinfonia* or overture, a forebear of the classical *symphony. Among his greatest operas are *Il Mitridate Eupatore* (1707) and *Griselda* (1721); he also wrote oratorios and masses.

Scarlatti Domenico (1685–1757). Italian composer and keyboard virtuoso; son and pupil of the above. He worked and studied in Naples, Venice and Rome having a keyboard contest there with Handel in 1709 (drawn match on the harpsichord, win to Handel on the organ). From 1729 he worked for the Spanish court. S. was employed primarily as an opera and church music composer but is now known for his keyboard *Esercizi* (about 500, mostly written in Spain). These miniatures, in turn brilliant, delicate, violent or melancholy, are in effect 1-movement *sonatas in binary form; they demonstrate not only immense virtuosity but a wide range of mood and perfectly controlled contrasts. Characteristic are powerful and sudden changes of mood, key, tempo, etc. Inspired no doubt by Spanish guitar playing he makes use of strong discord and exploits the possibilities of dual-keyboards to the fullest extent.

Scarlet and Black (1831). Novel by *Stendhal.

Scarlet Letter, The (1850). Novel by Nathaniel *Hawthorne.

Scarlet Street (1945). Film directed by F. *Lang.

Scarpazza Vittore: Vittore *Carpaccio

Scarron Paul (1610–60). French writer of burlesques and parodies of Virgil and classical mythology. He also wrote one of the few realistic novels of the period, *Le Roman comique* (1651–7).

Sceaux. French porcelain and faïence factory (*c.* 1748–94) particularly noted for its enamel-painted faïence ware (*muffle kiln).

scena. An Italian word used in English musical terminology for an operatic composition, usually for solo voice, designed for concert performance. The term is sometimes applied to passages from true operas.

scenario. Originally used to describe the synopsis of a *commedia dell'arte* plot, now the name of a film script, which includes dialogue, camera shots, etc.

Scenery. Wotruba, set for *Oedipus Rex* (1960)

Scenery. Set for the Théâtre National Populaire production of *Nucléa* (1952)

Schadow. *Two Princesses*

scenery. This provides the visual background or setting for a play, opera, or ballet, and is usually constructed from a *backdrop and *flats. In the classical Greek and Roman theatre, the acting area (Greek *skena*) was backed by a wall in which 3 doorways were used for entrances and exits. Exteriors of buildings also provided the settings in medieval times, but during the Renaissance there was a move to perform plays indoors and the development of perspective painting made it possible to create the illusion of greater space. Scenery construction began in 16th-c. Italy; G. *Torelli was one of the first scene painters and probably introduced the painted backdrop. On the Elizabethan stage virtually no scenery was used – the setting was simply an *apron stage with a balcony above – but shortly afterwards Inigo *Jones helped to develop scenic design, and in the mid 17th c. Sir William Davenant further developed set construction. By the 1830s transparent scenery and cut-outs (i.e. scenic effects additional to the backdrop and flats, cut to the shape of the object depicted) were introduced; the increasing desire for realistic pictorial representation led to the introduction of the *box-set and the use of furniture and stage properties. Gordon *Craig reacted against the ultra-realism of the late 19th c. (represented e.g. by *Irving), advocating the use of skilful lighting (made possible by the discovery of electricity) to obtain a 3-dimensional effect. At present scenic effects vary greatly and depend on the type of play, and the visual background is produced by realistically constructed sets with furniture and lighting, lighting alone, by symbolic objects, or by any other suitable or feasible means.

Scenes from Clerical Life (1858). Book by George *Eliot.

Scève Maurice (*c.* 1510–*c.* 64). French poet. S. discovered the tomb of Petrarch's Laura at Avignon. His long poem *Délie, object de plus haulte vertu* (1544) was perhaps inspired by the woman poet Pernette du Guillet.

Schack Adolf Friedrich, Graf von (1815–94). German art patron who built up an important coll. of paintings (Schack Gal., Munich). S. was also a poet and novelist; his house was a literary centre in Munich, and he made influential trs from Spanish and other literatures.

Schadow Johann Gottfried (1764–1850). German sculptor and art theorist, one of the leading exponents of neo-classicism in Germany. He studied in Rome (1785–7). His works include the Quadriga of the Brandenburg Gate, Berlin and monuments to Frederick the Great (Stettin) and Luther (Wittenberg). His group of the princesses Louise and Frederike of Prussia (Berlin) is a good example of his earlier work. His son FRIEDRICH WILHELM von Schadow-Godenhaus (1788–1862), a painter and writer, joined the *nazarenes group in Rome (1811). He was director of the Düsseldorf Academy (1826–59).

Schaffner Martin (late 15th–early 16th c.). German late Gothic/early Renaissance painter of religious subjects and portraits, active in Ulm. His masterpiece is the *Wettenhausen altarpiece* (Alte Pina., Munich).

Schalcken Godfried (1643–1706). Dutch genre and portrait painter best known for his genre scenes by candlelight. He studied under van Hoogstraten, then under Dou, whom he imitated closely in his earlier works.

Scharff Edwin (1887–1955). German sculptor. He first studied painting but took up sculpture while in France (1911–13). He was a founder-member of the Neue *Sezession group and was twice dismissed from teaching posts by the Nazis. His work has a monumental quality indicative of the influence of Rodin and Maillol.

Scharoun Hans (1893–). German architect. The continuity of his stylistic development was not broken by enforced inactivity under the Nazi régime. Before 1933 he designed free and undogmatic housing in Berlin; after 1945 he did similar work and built the Berlin Philharmonic Concert Hall (1963); its complex seating plan is divided into small areas so that the listener is not overawed.

Schary Dore (1905–). U.S. film producer, a script writer before becoming a producer. At R.K.O. in the late 1940s he instituted the policy, carried out by J. Houseman, of making low-budget films with new directors, a policy whose significant result was *They Live By Night*. In 1948 he became a producer and supervisor of all production at M.G.M., first under L. B. *Mayer and then alone. Now he is an independent producer and director.

Scharoun. Apartment House at the Home and Work Exhibition, Breslau (1928)

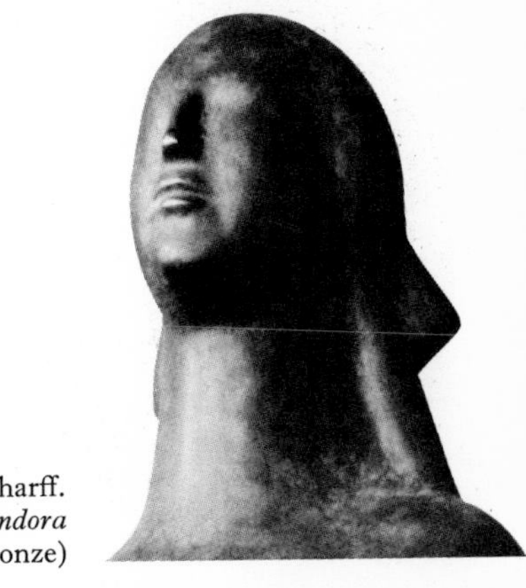

Scharff. *Pandora* (1952–3; bronze)

Schauffelin. *Agony in the Garden*

Schiavone. *St Catherine*; polyptych panel, N.G., London

Scheemakers. The Shakespeare monument, Westminster Abbey

Schiele. *Paris von Gütersloh, the Painter's Biographer* (1914; detail)

Schauffel(e)in Hans Leonhard (*c.* 1480–1538/40). German painter of portraits and religious subjects, and a woodcut designer, pupil and follower of Dürer.

Scheemakers Henry (d. 1748). Flemish sculptor, brother of Peter S. He worked in England (*c.* 1720–33) sometimes as assistant to his brother.

Scheemakers Peter (1691–1781). Flemish sculptor. After studying in Rome he worked in England almost continuously from *c.* 1716 to 1771, first assisting Francis Bird, then in partnership with Laurent Delvaux. He executed the Shakespeare monument in Westminster Abbey and many tombs in the Abbey and in country churches. His work is highly competent but lacking in character. His son THOMAS (1740–1808) was also a sculptor and worked in England.

Scheffel Josef Viktor von (1826–86). German poet, author of the narrative poem *Der Trompeter von Säkkingen* (1854; *The Trumpeter*, 1877), the well-known coll. of student-songs *Gaudeamus* (1869), and an historical novel set in the 10th c., *Ekkehard* (1862).

Scheffler Johann: *Angelus Silesius

Schéhérazade. 1-act ballet with choreography by Fokine, music from Rimsky-Korsakov and décor by Bakst; 1st performance 1910.

Scheidt Samuel (1587–1654). German composer and organist; a close friend of *Schein. S.'s study under *Sweelinck (1608–9) in Amsterdam was decisively influential on his style. He held successively more important posts in the town of Halle until his dismissal in 1630; during the following troubled war years he lived in poor circumstances, dying in obscurity. His organ chorales and variations were of great importance in the history of German organ music but he also publ. motets, dance suites and sacred concertos.

Schein Johann Hermann (1586–1630). German composer, a close friend of Schütz; they, together with Scheidt, are three of the greatest of 17th-c. German composers. After a year as musical director at the court of Weimar he became cantor of St Thomas's, Leipzig (1616). S. was particularly important in the history of the sacred choral song and the continuo-bass song. His works include: *Venus Kräntzlein* (1609), containing 17 five-part *Lieder*; Latin and German motets; and 20 dance suites.

Schelling Friedrich Wilhelm Joseph von (1775–1854). German philosopher who gave art the most important place in human activity; he exercised an important influence on romantic writers.

Schenkendorf (Gottlob Ferdinand) Max (Gottfried) von (1783–1817). German poet whose verse celebrated the glories of medieval Germany and looked forward to German liberation.

Scherchen Hermann (1891–). German conductor; distinguished among other things as an interpreter and sponsor of modern music above all that of Schoenberg and his school.

scherzo (Italian, 'joke'). A fast, not necessarily lighthearted movement of the symphony.

Schiavone Giorgio Chiulinović, called (1436–1504). Dalmatian painter trained in Squarcione's workshop in Padua. The N.G., London has a signed polyptych and an attributed *Virgin and Child.*

Schiavone Andrea Meldolla, called (d. 1563). Dalmatian painter and engraver who worked in Venice in a style derived from Parmigianino and Titian.

Schiele Egon (1890–1918). Austrian painter and graphic artist; with Klimt, who influenced him, and Kokoschka, one of the great expressionist artists of early 20th-c. Vienna. S.'s most powerful work is in his male and female nudes in pencil, gouache, watercolour, etc.; the figures express in their postures the emotions from despair to passion–and the female nudes are often unashamedly erotic. S. was primarily a draughtsman, and the angularities of his line and its nervous precision pervade all his work. His 1st real success came in the last year of his life, but full recognition was not accorded his work until the 1950s.

Schiller (Johann Christoph) Friedrich von (1759–1805). German dramatist and thinker born in Marbach (Württemberg). In 1773 S. reluctantly entered the Ducal Military Academy near Stuttgart; despite the stifling correctitude of his environment he began to read *storm and stress drama. In 1780 he was relegated to an inferior post as regimental doctor, from which he fled to Mannheim in 1782 to devote himself to the stage; he was later the guest of various well-wishers in Bauerbach, Leipzig, Dresden (with C. G. Körner) and Weimar. In 1789 he was appointed professor of history in Jena, and a year later married Charlotte von Lengefeld. His fruitful friendship with Goethe dates only from 1794; 10 years of creative co-operation followed, S. moving to Weimar in 1799.

In Germany S. has always ranked with, and been more popular than Goethe; English readers feel less at home with his characteristic combination of intellectual idealism and rhetorical pathos, seeing in him a profounder Corneille, exciting admiration, not affection. Yet there is warmth as well as brilliance in his fire.

As Goethe observed, S.'s constant theme is freedom, and he has always inspired progressives. The expression of this theme is crudest in *Die Räuber* (1782; *The Robbers*, 1792), most homely in *Wilhelm Tell* (1804; *William Tell*, 1825), most poignant in *Wallenstein* (trilogy, 1798–9; 1800–30) dealing with the German commander in the Thirty Years War, and *Maria Stuart* (1800; *Mary Stuart*, 1801), dealing with Mary Queen of Scots, and most cogent in his philosophical writings. His dramas move from storm and stress violence of plot and language – *Die Räuber* and *Die Verschwörung des Fiesko zu Genua* (1784; *Fiesco*, 1796) – through a transitional, not entirely homogeneous work – *Don Carlos* (1787; 1795), the basis of Verdi's opera – to the thematic, linguistic and structural restraint of Weimar classicism (*Goethe) in historical subjects – *Wallenstein*, *Maria Stuart*, *Die Jungfrau von Orleans* (1801; *The Maid of Orleans*, 1824), *Wilhelm Tell* – and in the latter-day fate-tragedy complete with chorus *Die Braut von Messina* (1803; *The Bride of Messina*, 1837). In the early plays, in prose, the freedom sought is freedom from familial, social or political oppression; in the later ones, in blank verse, the individual finds freedom through an ethical decision which triumphs over the dictates of fate. *Wallenstein*, the least didactic of his plays and the closest to experience, stands somewhat apart and has seemed the most satisfying and the most Shakespearian; *Maria Stuart*, more typical, is also enthralling. In all his plays, S. shows a mastery of dramatic effects through language and plotting.

S.'s philosophical verse, including *An Die Freude* (1786), used by Beethoven in his 'Choral' symphony, appeals rather to German taste. His ballads, more persuasive, have tension and drive, but leave little unsaid. These and other short works appeared in periodicals he ed., including *Anthologie auf das Jahr 1782*; *Die Rheinische Thalia* (1787–91); *Die Horen* (1795–7); and the *Musenalmanach* (1796–1800). More important are his philosophical works on ethics and aesthetics. *Über Anmut und Würde* (1793) establishes his concept of the 'beautiful soul' in whom impulse and volition are one. *Briefe über die ästhetische Erziehung des Menschen* (1795; *Letters upon the Aesthetic Education of Man*, 1844) sees art as a pedagogic means of producing such characters. *Über naïve und sentimentalische Dichtung* (1795; 1849) distinguishes 2 types of poet, one (*naïv*) reproducing reality, the other (*sentimentalisch*) representing ideals. Based on his observation of Goethe and himself, it offers a self-assessment which later critics have needed only to refine.

Schiller: bust by Dannecker

Schimmel Hendrik Jan (1823–1906). Dutch writer remembered for his historical novels, but important in his lifetime as a playwright and theatrical organizer.

Schindler Anton (1798–1864). German musician and Beethoven's 1st biographer. During the last 12 years of Beethoven's life S. was his true, if sometimes infuriating friend, his secretary and nurse.

Schindler Kurt (1882–1935). German musician who settled in the U.S. He made studies of folk-music and founded what came to be known as the Schola Cantorum in New York.

Schinkel Karl Friedrich (1781–1841). German architect. S. began as a painter and designer of theatre sets, with a special fondness for vast imaginary Gothic buildings. His actual architecture, however, is nearly all classical: most notable are the Neue Wache Gate, the Schauspielhaus and the Altes Museum, all at Berlin. Using the elements of Greek architecture, S. built up an austere and personal style, somewhat as Soane did in England. His versatility is shown by works like the war memorial, Berlin, a Gothic shrine over 100 ft high and made entirely of cast iron, and the Zivilcasino, Potsdam, an experiment in extreme

Schinkel. Stage design from Kleist's *Käthchen von Heilbronn*

Schinkel. The Schauspielhaus, Berlin

Friedrich von Schlegel

August Wilhelm von Schlegel

Schmidt-Rottluff. *The Road to Emmaus* (1918; woodcut)

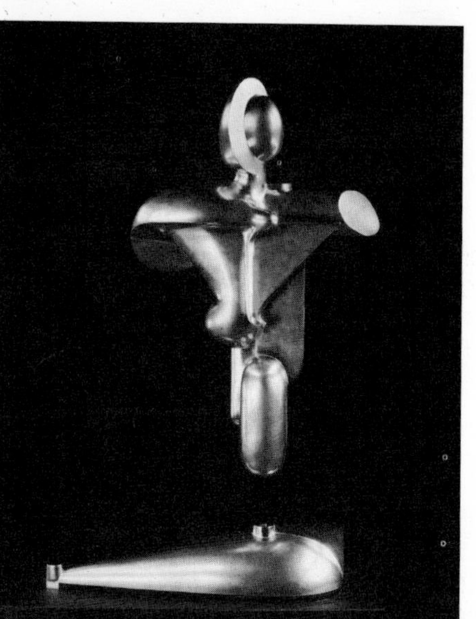

Schlemmer. *Abstrakte Rindplastik* (1921)

Schlemmer. *Bauhaus Stairway* (1932). Also *Bauhaus

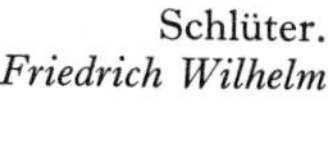

Schlüter. *Friedrich Wilhelm*

asymmetry of massing. His influence dominated German (especially Prussian) architecture until the end of the 19th c.

Schlegel August Wilhelm von (1767–1845). German critic, with his brother F. von S. a major theorist of the German romantic movement, and author of the 1st great German trs. of Shakespeare (1797–1810). S. was a close friend of Mme de Staël, knew Goethe and wrote for Schiller's journal *Die Horen*; he was also in contact with Coleridge and the English romantics. His works include *Über dramatische Kunst und Literatur* (1809–11; . . . *Lectures on Dramatic Art and Literature*, 1815); trs of Calderon, *Spanisches Theater* (1803–9); and a trs. of the *Bhagavad-Gita*.

Schlegel Friedrich von (1772–1829). German critic and poet who enunciated most clearly the principles of German romanticism. With his brother (the above) he ed. the periodical *Das Athenäum* (1798–1800), contributing to it pregnant yet fragmentary articles. S.'s major works were *Die Griechen und Römer* (1797), *Geschichte der Poesie der Griechen und Römer* (1798) and *Geschichte der alten und neuen Literatur* (1815).

Schlemmer Oscar (1888–1943). German sculptor who studied at the Stuttgart Academy under Hoelzel (1909–14, 1918–19). He exhibited at the Sturm Gallery, Berlin in 1919 and from 1920 to 1928 was at the *Bauhaus teaching stone carving. His paintings, mural reliefs and sculpture run through a wide range of media in reducing the figure to a rhythmic play between convex, concave and flat surfaces. His *Triadic Ballet* produced at the Bauhaus (1922) simply extended this field by the introduction of time, movement and changing light. Under Nazi suppression he virtually retired in 1937.

Schlumberger Jean (1877–). French novelist and critic, one of the founders of the *Nouvelle Revue Française*. His novels include *Saint-Saturnin* (1931).

Schlüter Andreas (*c*. 1664–1714). German sculptor and architect. In 1694 he was appointed court sculptor at Berlin (producing, e.g., an equestrian statue of Friedrich Wilhelm). He visited Rome and his chief work, the Royal Palace, Berlin (1698–1706) shows the influence of Bernini. In 1713 he became chief architect to the Russian court; he died at St Petersburg.

Schmidt-Rottluff. *Nude* (1912)

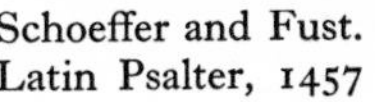

Schoeffer and Fust. Latin Psalter, 1457

Arnold Schoenberg

Schmidt-Rottluff Karl (1884–). German artist born at Rottluff, near Chemnitz. He, Heckel and Kirchner founded Die *Brücke group in Dresden in 1906 and were joined by Nolde and Pechstein. He stayed with the group until its dissolution in 1913. His (and the rest of the group's) fervent belief in a new world and a new élite society was fundamentally inspired by Nietzsche. He served in the army (1915–18) then returned to Berlin. Like the other progressive German artists he was dismissed as 'degenerate' from the Prussian Academy in 1933 and in 1944, like Nolde, was forbidden to paint by the Nazis. Since 1947 he has taught at the Berlin Academy. S.-R. was one of the most brutally violent of the German expressionists, aggressively stark in drawing and raw in colour, e.g. *Two Women* (1912; Tate).

In Berlin (from 1910) he was deeply influenced by Negro sculpture and produced several carvings, often brightly coloured, e.g. *Head* (1917; Tate) and woodcuts, e.g. *The Way to Emmaus* (1918; Philadelphia). His later work is less intense, more lyrical, but retains a monumental simplicity and directness.

Schmitt Florent (1870–1958). French composer; taught at the Conservatoire by Fauré among others, and a winner of the Rome prize. S.'s music shows more than that of most other French composers the influence of the German romantics, as in his use of monumental form, though he inevitably drew also on Debussy's impressionistic methods. His works include: *Psaume XLVII* for soprano, chorus, orchestra and organ (1904); ballets, orchestral works, film music, etc.

Schnabel Artur (1882–1951). Austrian pianist, one of the great masters in the power and poetry of his deeply considered interpretations, above all of Beethoven, Schubert and Brahms. His own compositions, in a modernistic idiom, include a symphony and a piano concerto.

Schnabel Johann Gottfried (*c.* 1692–1750). German author of *Die Insel Felsenburg* (1731–43), the most long lived of the many 18th-c. German books prompted by *Robinson Crusoe*. Its hero establishes a utopia on his island.

Schneider Gérard (1896–). Swiss painter in an abstract calligraphic style which links him with Hartung and Soulages. His broad fierce brush-strokes and use of a dominant black imbue his paintings with a threatening force.

Schnitger Arp (1648–1720). One of the greatest German baroque organ builders, the founder of a family and a school of builders. He worked mostly in N. Germany and the Netherlands; 2 of his finest surviving instruments are at St Jacobi church, Hamburg and at Cappel (originally in St Johannis, Hamburg).

Schnitzler Arthur (1862–1931). Austrian playwright, novelist and short-story writer. S.'s works are *fin de siècle* in mood, mainly ironic, melancholy studies of love. Plays include *Anatol* (1893; 1911); *Liebelei* (1896; *The Reckoning*, 1907) and *Reigen* (1900; *Hands Around*, 1920), which has twice been successfully filmed as *La Ronde*.

Schobert Johann (1720–67). German harpsichordist and pianist and composer; in 1760 he settled in Paris. His compositions influenced the young Mozart.

Schoeffer Peter (*c.* 1430–1503). German printer who worked for Gutenberg and later Johann Fust when the latter took over the business. S. started his career in Paris as a copyist and went on to become one of the foremost printer/typographers of his day. S. was the 1st printer to use copper for his matrices, the inventor of 'leads' for spacing, the 1st to design a real title-page, and the 1st to employ a colophon in his productions. Publs include a 48-line Bible and a *Psalter* (1457) in which he made the 1st attempt to print in more than one colour.

Schoenberg Arnold (1874–1951). Austrian composer, largely self-taught. From 1901 to 1903 he was in Berlin, where he received the Liszt prize at the instigation of Richard Strauss. In Vienna (1903–4) he was a friend of Mahler and the teacher of Webern and Berg; S. also painted during this period, Kandinsky including pictures by him in Blaue Reiter exhibitions. He toured as a conductor, served in World War I, continued a successful career in Vienna, was called to the Prussian Academy of Art in Berlin but in 1933 left Germany for France and the U.S., becoming professor of music at the Univ. of California. S.'s work, the most important corpus by a 20th-c. composer, has been fully recognized only since 1945. He is in fact the founder of the *12-note school of composition. S.'s radical atonal style sprang from his study of the structure of harmony, both as a theorist and experimental composer, at the time when the classic diatonic structure was already collapsing after the extreme chromaticism of Wagner and his successors. In common with certain other theorists he extended harmonic theory to include certain chords and intervals used by composers from the 18th c. but excluded from theoretical classifications; he experimented with the whole-tone scale and polytonal techniques and introduced strict contrapuntal procedures to his music. His work divides into 3 phases: a basically tonal period showing the influences of Brahms and Wagner up to *c.* 1907; the development towards atonality up to the early 1920s; and the final establishment and exploitation of the 12-note system, occasionally used in conjunction with a tonal idiom. The following are his main works: the string sextet *Verklärte Nacht* (1899; string orchestra 1917), on a poem by R. Dehmel; *Gurrelieder* for soloists, choruses and orchestra (1900; orchestrated 1911) based on a 14th-c. Danish legend; the symphonic poem *Pelleas und Melisande* (1903); 2 chamber symphonies, in E (1906) and No 2 in 1939; *Erwartung* (1909), a monodrama in which a woman finds her lover's body – it is for orchestra and 'speech-voice', i.e. a soloist part speaking, part singing (S.'s name for this was '*Sprechgesang*'); *Pierrot lunaire* (1912) for speech-voice, piano and flute; 5 pieces for piano (1920–3) which marks the transition to 12-note methods; *Variations for orchestra* (1928); an *Ode to Napoleon* for speaker, string quartet and piano (1942); *A Survivor from Warsaw* for speaker, male chorus and orchestra (1947); *De Profundis* for a capella choir (1950). Rapidly gaining recognition as S.'s greatest work is the opera *Moses and Aaron* (acts 1 and 2 completed 1930–2), libretto by the composer.

Scholemaster, The (1570). Educational treatise by Roger *Ascham.

Schonbroeck Pieter (*c.* 1570–1607). Landscape painter born at Frankenthal, Germany where his Flemish Protestant parents fled to escape religious persecution. There he was a pupil of G. van Coninxloo. He later worked in Nuremberg. Characteristic paintings are of mountain scenery with small figures.

Schongauer Martin (*c.* 1430–91). German painter, influenced by R. van der Weyden, and

Schongauer. *Madonna of the Rose Bower*

Schongauer. *Temptation of St Anthony*; engraving

Arthur Schopenhauer

engraver. He worked mainly in Colmar and his only authenticated work, *Madonna of the Rose Bower* (1473), is in St Martin's church, Colmar. A number of other paintings, mainly of Madonnas and Nativity scenes, are attributed to him. His engravings exercised a powerful influence on Dürer and on the development of the medium in Germany. H. Burgkmair was his pupil.

School for Scandal, The (1777). Comedy by *Sheridan.

School of Athens, The (1509–12). Fresco by *Raphael.

school of night. English literary coterie of the last decade of the 16th c. based on Sir Walter Raleigh's estate near Sherborne, Dorset. Members included Thomas Hariot, mathematician and astronomer; Dr John Dee, mathematician and alchemist; the earl of Northumberland; the playwright Christopher Marlowe, and the poet George Chapman. Free speculation and criticism gained them a reputation for atheism and worse.

Schopenhauer Arthur (1788–1860). German philosopher. S. was profoundly influenced by the Hindu and Buddhist scriptures and in *Die Welt als Wille und Vorstellung* (1818; *The World as Will and Idea*, 1883) emphasizes the primacy of a blind will, of which the intellect is a slave. The operation of this insatiable will causes endless suffering which only the artist, the philosopher and the saint can overcome (by negating the will). S. was the first of a long line of modern philosophers and psychologists who have emphasized the non-rational aspects of existence.

Schreiner Olive (1859–1922). South African-born writer of German, English and Jewish descent. *The Story of an African Farm* (1883) is a still readable description of the bush done by one who saw it as her homeland. In later life, despite poor health, she campaigned for and wrote about racial and sexual equality.

Schreker Franz (1878–1934). Austrian composer, director of the Berlin Music Academy (1920–32) and teacher of Haba and Krenek among others. His reputation rests on operas such as *Der ferne Klang* (1912), *Der Schatzgräber* (1920) and *Irrelohe* (1924). Like Wagner he wrote his own librettos and he used a Wagnerian orchestra; but his style is essentially post-impressionist and the atmosphere of heavy eroticism in his operas, unique.

Schröder Friedrich Ludwich (1744–1816). German actor who enjoyed great success at the National Theatre in Hamburg, eventually becoming its manager. He also spent 4 years in Vienna, where he exercised a refining influence on the theatre. S. encouraged *storm and stress writers and was the first to produce Goethe's play *Götz von Berlichingen*. His greatest achievement was to introduce Shakespeare (albeit cut and altered) to the German stage.

Schubert Franz Peter (1797–1828). Austrian composer, the son of a schoolmaster in Liechtenthal, near Vienna. From 1808 to 1813 he was a member of the choir of the Imperial Chapel and studied at the school attached, where his immense musical talent was remarked by his teachers – among them Salieri. However, when his voice broke and he had to leave the choir, S. returned to help his father as a teacher; and although by his 17th year he had completed many compositions, among them a mass, a symphony and an opera, it was not until 1818 that he was able to devote himself to composition. During the following years he endeavoured to produce the opera, then so important for the career of a young composer, but never had success on the stage. He worked occasionally for the Esterhazy family and also as a recitalist but he relied heavily upon the patronage of his friends, among them Franz von Schober, and composed and performed much for the 'Schubertiaden', musical-social gatherings of his friends. His chamber works and songs began to be publ. from the early 1820s and his songs reached a wide public through a famous tenor, J. M. Vogl; his 1st public concert, a great success, was not until 1828. S.'s music clearly devolves from his great Viennese predecessors, above all Beethoven, but equally clearly does it anticipate features in subsequent romantic music from Liszt to Mahler. The mere length of S.'s ('Great') C maj. symphony was a significant pointer to the scale of later romantic works, but more important is the developing chromaticism and the free modulation and transforming key changes. S. viewed chamber music as the preparation ground of the symphonist but in fact some of his finest work is found in such pieces as the

Franz Schubert (*far left*); *The Schubert Soirée*: drawing by Moritz von Schwind

great C maj. string quintet. S.'s unique achievement was his songs (more than 600) which established the main lines of the 19th-c. German *Lied*. In both the strophic and 'through composed' song S. combined an inspired gift for lyrical melody with an expressive and integrated piano accompaniment; his settings of the great German lyric poets–Klopstock, Novalis, Goethe, Schiller and Heine–achieve a seemingly inevitable synthesis of music and words. S was immensely prolific; his main works include the following. Symphonies: no. 1 in D maj. (1813); no. 2 in B♭ (1815); no. 3 in D maj. (1815); no. 4 in C min. (1816) called by S. *The Tragic*; no. 5 in B♭ maj. (1816); no. 6 in C maj. (1818) the 'Little'; no. 8 in B min. (1822), the 'Unfinished'–2 movements being completed and a sketch for a scherzo; the 'Great' in C maj. (1828), called no. 7 or 9. A German and 6 Latin masses. Stage music: the *Singspiel*, *Die Zwillings brüder* (1819); the opera *Alfonso and Estretta* (1822); the *Rosamunde overture* (1823). Piano music: many dances including 12 *Valses nobles*, the '*Wanderer' Fantasy* (1816), which uses material from a song 'The Wanderer'; many works for piano duet including the famous *Marche Militaire*, first of a group of 3. S.'s chamber music includes: 15 string quartets, among them *Death and the Maiden* (1826) in D min., using material from the song, and a quartet movement in C min. (1820); *The Trout* piano quintet (1819) in A maj. whose 4th movement is variations on his song of that name; and the superb string quintet in C maj. Among S.'s best-known songs are: 'Gretchen and the Spinning Wheel' (1814), 'Erl King' (1815), 'The Fisher' (1815) with texts from Goethe; the song cycles *Winterreise* (*Winter's Journey*) (1827) and *Die schöne Müllerin* (*The Pretty Miller Maid*) (1823) to texts by W. Müller.

Schufftan Eugen (1893–). German-born cameraman. The inventor of the S. process for integrating live figures into still photographic backgrounds–first used in *Metropolis* and the British Museum sequences of *Blackmail*. S. also worked with distinction as a director of photography in a number of countries over a period of many years, e.g. in *Menschen am Sonntag*, *La Tête Contre les Murs*, *Les Yeux Sans Visage* and *The Hustler*, for which he won an Academy Award.

Schulberg Budd (1914–). U.S. novelist. S.'s works include the novels *What Makes Sammy Run?* (1941), a story of careerism in Hollywood; *The Harder They Fall* (1947), about boxing; and a semi-biographical work about F. Scott Fitzgerald, *The Disenchanted* (1950). He also wrote the film script **On the Waterfront* (1954).

Schulhoff Erwin (1894–1942). Czech composer and pianist, a teacher at the Prague Conservatory. He experimented freely in the new musical idioms of the 20th c. and produced a ballet, operas, a jazz oratorio and other works.

Schulz Bruno (1892–1942). Polish prose writer of Jewish origin, killed by the Nazis. In his coll. of tales *Sklepy cynamonowe* (1933; *Cinnamon Shops*, 1963) he transforms the reality of a small Polish provincial town into a grotesque and irrational dream landscape. His writing shows certain affinities with the work of Kafka, whose *Trial* he trs.

Schumacher Emil (1912–). German painter, exponent of a romantic, peculiarly German type of abstract *expressionism which through Wols has affected the school of Paris. Himself influenced by Wols, S. paints with more control than *action painters, but has a free improvisatory quality of line that can be traced back to the work of Klee.

Emil Schumacher. *Gonza* (1958)

Schumann Clara Josephine (née Wieck) (1819–96). German pianist, wife of Robert S. and the 1st exponent of his music. After her husband's death she became a close friend of Brahms, bringing his compositions before a wider public. S. was also a composer.

Schumann Elisabeth (1885–1952). German-born singer who left Austria in 1938. She was distinguished above all for her interpretations of Strauss operatic parts, but also in Mozart.

Schumann Robert (Alexander) (1810–56). German romantic composer. His father being a bookseller, S. developed a literary interest which was to affect his work as a composer. As a law student at Leipzig he began taking piano lessons from Wieck and soon abandoned his legal studies. A mechanical aid to practice damaged his hand and ended his hopes of a concert career. As a journalist he hailed the young Chopin and Brahms; in 1834 he founded the journal *Neue Zeitschrift für Musik*, the organ of the Davids bündler, i.e. 'David's confederates', enemies of all philistines. In 1840

Robert and Clara Schumann

Schwind. *The Faithful Sister and the King's Son.* Also *Schubert

Heinrich Schütz

Albert Schweitzer

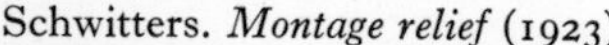

Schwitters. *Montage relief* (1923)

Schwitters. Hanover *Merzbau*

he married Clara Wieck (C. J. *Schumann). A hereditary mental disease and failure as a conductor led to attempted suicide in 1854; he died in an asylum. S.'s finest music is found in his piano works, e.g. the ABEGG variations (1830); *Papillons* (1828–32), inspired by a novel by Jean Paul; *Carnaval Scenes mignonnes* (1835) on the 4 notes ASCH which spell the home town of his 1st fiancée, Ernestine von Fricken; *Fantasiestücke* (1837) and *Kreisleriana* (1838), both based on E. T. A. Hoffmann; *Kinderszenen* (1838) and the song cycle *Dichterliebe* (1840), settings of Heine. His other works include: 4 symphonies, no. 1 in B maj. (1841) being called 'The Spring'; the magnificent piano concerto in A min. (1st movement in 1841; 2 further movements added in 1845); a cello concerto in A maj. (1850); the opera *Genoveva* (1850); the choral work *Das Paradies und die Peri* (1843); the overture *Manfred* and chamber music.

Schütz Heinrich (1585–1672). German composer. He was a choirboy at Kassel; in 1609 the Landgrave sent him to study in Venice under G. Gabrieli. He returned in 1613, becoming court organist at Kassel and then in 1617 Kapellmeister at Dresden to the Elector of Saxony. In 1628 he revisited Venice to study new developments, especially the work of Monteverdi. During the worst period of the Thirty Years War S. worked for a time in Copenhagen. After the war he returned to Saxony but lived in increasing retirement in his house Weissenfels.

S. was the major composer of 17th-c. Germany. He made the new 'concertato' style of N. Italy part of the German tradition; yet his mastery of the Italian style in writing for soloists and chorus, of the Italian instrumental style and the basso continuo was deployed in a fully German context; the music of Gabrieli and Monteverdi's 'stil concitato' for example were important influences but did not dominate. S.'s output consists entirely of vocal music. He wrote the 1st German opera, *Dafne* (1627), but it is lost. Virtually all of the remainder is religious. His fervour is expressed by a characteristically German straightforwardness to the point of apparent naïvety. In his earlier works he deploys mass forces, choirs from all parts of the building, several organs and instrumental groups after the Venetian manner, highly decorated solo singing and florid violin accompaniments. His last works (the Passion stories) are austere and bare; there are pages of unaccompanied recitative interrupted by brief unadorned and comparatively unmelodious choruses. His whole oeuvre is marked by dramatic and vivid characterization. His works include: the choral *History of the . . . Resurrection . . . of our only Redeemer . . . Jesus Christ* (1623); *Christmas Story* (1664); 3 sets of *Symphoniae sacrae* (1629, 1647, 1650), Latin and German motets for 3–6 voices and 2 solo instruments and continuo; *The Seven Words of Jesus on the Cross* (*c.* 1645); settings of the Psalms; and madrigals.

Schwab Gustav (1792–1850). German poet, writer and trs. best known for his retelling of German and classical legends, e.g. *Deutsche Volksbücher* (1836) and *Die schönsten Sagen des klassischen Alterthums* (1838–9). S. was a friend of Uhland, who heavily influenced his poetry, and of Chamisso.

Schwarzkopf Elisabeth (1915–). German soprano; she made her début in 1938. She is particularly celebrated for her performance as Marschallin in *Der Rosenkavalier*.

Schweitzer Albert (1875–1965). Born in Alsace. He achieved world-wide fame as a humanitarian by his work as a doctor in his hospital at Lambarene in Gabon. Before going to Africa he had achieved distinction as a theologian and a great reputation for his performances of Bach's organ works. He wrote a biography of Bach (1st publ. in French 1905; English trs. 1911) in which he advanced the theory that Bach used an exact symbolic musical code to represent the emotions.

Schwind Moritz von (1804–71). Austrian painter and graphic artist, a representative of late German romanticism; pupil of Cornelius. He attempted monumental murals but was more successful with smaller paintings such as *Des Knaben Wunderhorn* and *The Morning Hour* (both Schackgal., Munich) and book illustrations.

Schwitters Kurt (1887–1948). German painter. He started painting in a cubist idiom *c.* 1917. In 1919 he was the founder of the dada group in Hanover. He lived in Norway from 1930 to 1937 and then in England. His 2 principal media were constructions and collage in which he used broken and discarded rubbish to create works of remarkable sensitivity, e.g. *Opened by Customs* (1937–9; Tate).

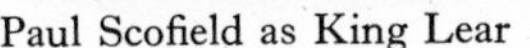

Paul Scofield as King Lear

Cyril Scott

He extended these ideas with the 3 *Merzbaue*, Hanover (1920–2; destroyed 1943), Oslo (1930–7; burnt 1953) and Langdale, Westmorland (1947–8), constructions which filled a whole building.

Schwob Marcel (1867–1905). French scholar and essayist. He was connected with the *Mercure de France* when it was a symbolist organ, and some of his prose has the brooding, exotic quality characteristic of the school. His most important contribution to literature was perhaps in the field of trs., e.g. Defoe's *Moll Flanders* (1895), but his short poetical biographies, *Les Vies imaginaires* (1896), are still occasionally referred to.

Sciuscia (1946). Film directed by V. de *Sica.

Scofield Paul (1922–). English actor who after his performances at Birmingham Repertory Theatre (1941–6) quickly made a reputation. He has often played in Shakespeare, most notably as King Lear (Stratford and London (1963), and abroad); also in modern plays, e.g. in the musical *Expresso Bongo* (1958) and *A Man For All Seasons* (1960).

Scopas (mid 4th c. B.C.). Greek sculptor of the early *Hellenistic period. The tendency towards violent action and pathos in his work became typical of much Hellenistic sculpture. He worked on the famous Mausoleum at Halicarnassus.

scordatura (Italian, 'false tuning'). The tuning of a stringed musical instrument in an unusual way; it may be done for special effects of tone, to extend the instrument's range (by tuning the bottom lower than in standard tuning) or to facilitate the fingering in a certain key.

score. A full musical s. carries all the parts of a composition laid out one above the other. The name derives from the practice of scoring the bar lines across the music staves on the music paper preparatory to setting down the notes. A 'vocal' s. sets out the voice parts in full but gives a piano version of the instrumental parts. A 'short' s. is either a sketch of a composer's intentions or a condensed version of a full s. A work normally scored like piano music with all the parts on 2 staves is said to be in 'open' s. when the parts are laid out on individual lines. SCORING means laying out the parts in open s.

Scorel Jan van (1495–1562). The first Dutch painter of importance to study in Italy and responsible for introducing the Italian high Renaissance to the Netherlands. He was widely travelled and was appointed by Pope Hadrian VI superintendent of the Vatican Coll. In Rome he was influenced by Michelangelo and Raphael, particularly the latter. He returned to the Netherlands in 1524. His works include *Pilgrims to Jerusalem* (Utrecht Mus.), *St Mary Magdalene* (Rijksmus., Amsterdam) and *Holy Kinship* (Utrecht).

scorper. A small chisel or gouging instrument used for engraving in metalwork.

Scotch snap. Musical term for a rhythmic figure in which a short note, usually a semiquaver, on the beat is followed by a dotted note, usually a quaver, e.g.

It is a feature of the 'Strathspey Reel'.

scotia. A concave half-round moulding, used in room decoration and panelling, which projects a deep shadow on itself, giving the effect of a dark line. Used mainly in base mouldings.

Scott Cyril (Meir) (1879–). English composer. He studied at Frankfurt, has been influenced by the ideas of his friend, the poet George, and has written poetry himself. His individual if limited style shows similarities to Debussy. His music includes: the opera *The Alchemist* (Essen, 1925), 3 symphonies, much chamber and piano music. He has also written the book *An Outline of Modern Occultism* (1935).

Scott Duncan Campbell (1862–1947). Canadian poet whose work, such as *The Piper of Arll* began in the spirit of romanticism. However, it moved on, while using traditional techniques of versification, to a realistic portrayal of North Canadian life.

Scott Evelyn (1893–). U.S. novelist; works include *The Wave* (1929), an exploration in depth of the U.S. Civil War, which is presented as a collective phenomenon.

Scott Sir George Gilbert (1811–78). English architect. In 1844 he won a competition to

Scorel. *Holy Kinship*

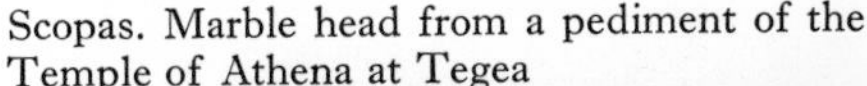

Scopas. Marble head from a pediment of the Temple of Athena at Tegea

Sir George Gilbert Scott. The Nikolaikirche, Hamburg

Sir Walter Scott

design the Nikolaikirche in Hamburg, thus establishing his own career and the English Gothic revival as an influence on the Continent. Among his best-known works are the Albert Memorial, Kensington; the Foreign Office, Whitehall; St Pancras Station; and the chapels of Exeter College, Oxford (a copy of Sainte-Chapelle, Paris) and St John's College, Cambridge; he also 'restored' medieval cathedrals. His 2 sons George Gilbert (1837–97) and John Oldrid (1841–1913) were also architects. Sir Giles Gilbert S. (1880–1960) designed Liverpool cathedral (begun in 1903 and still in progress).

Scott Randolph (1903–). U.S. film actor, particularly known for western roles, e.g. *Ride Lonesome* (1958).

Scott Samuel (*c.* 1702–72). English marine and topographical painter. In his early work he followed W. van de Velde the Elder and the Younger but later, inspired by Canaletto's success in London, turned to views of the City and the river Thames.

Scott Sir Walter (1771–1832). Scottish novelist and poet. S. was educated at Edinburgh High School and Univ., called to the Bar in 1792 and became sheriff-depute of Selkirkshire in 1799. He went into partnership with Ballantyne in a bookselling business (1809); he also helped to found *The Quarterly Review*. Meanwhile, he became famous as a poet, publ. *Minstrelsy of the Scottish Border* (1802–3), a ballad coll. with S.'s imitations appended; *The Lay of the Last Minstrel* (1805), a poem based on Border legend; *Marmion: A Tale of Flodden Field* (1808), and *The Lady of the Lake* (1810). In 1813 he refused the laureateship (recommending Southey) and, feeling that he had been eclipsed as a poet by Byron, turned to writing historical novels, of which he acknowledged his authorship only in 1827. In 1826 the bookseller's failed and S. worked hard for the rest of his life to pay the creditors.
S. was influenced by Border stories, songs and ballads, Percy's *Reliques*, ancient European lore and the continental romantics, notably Goethe; in turn his novels influenced a new generation of romantics, including Balzac, Dumas and Alexis, creating the vogue for the historical novel and stimulating interest in the middle ages. Although diffuse, the novels are absorbing stories with many vivid characters. *Waverley* (1814), which is set during the Jacobite Rebellion of 1745, *Guy Mannering* (1815), *The Antiquary* (1816), *Old Mortality* (1816) and *The Heart of Midlothian* (1818), often considered S.'s best novel, treated quite recent history. S. described the period of Richard I in *Ivanhoe* (1819) and *The Talisman* (1825); 15th-c. France in *Quentin Durward* (1823); and 16th-c. England and Scotland in *Kenilworth* (1821) and *The Abbot* (1820). His other novels include *Rob Roy* (1817); *The Bride of Lammermoor* (1819), the basis of Donizetti's opera *Lucia di Lammermoor*; *The Fortunes of Nigel* (1822); *Redgauntlet* (1824); *Woodstock* (1826); *St Valentine's Day, or The Fair Maid of Perth* (1828); and *Count Robert of Paris* (1832). He also wrote plays, criticism, history and antiquarian works.

Scott William Bell (1811–90). Scottish poet and painter, friend of D. G. Rossetti and Swinburne. His *Autobiographical Notes . . .* (1892) gives an idea of 19th-c. literary and artistic circles. It has lately been revealed that an unsatisfied love for S. motivated the intensely sad love-poems of Christina Rossetti.

Scottish (or Scotch) symphony. *Mendelssohn's 3rd symphony.

Scriabin Alexander Nikolayevich (1872–1915). Russian composer and concert pianist. He studied at the Moscow Conservatory, toured Europe as a performer and was teacher of the piano at the Conservatory. S.'s works, predominantly for the piano, show the influence of Chopin and Liszt; gradually, however, he adopted new harmonic procedures devised on the basis of his own theorizings, and his music became increasingly complex rhythmically. His work reflects his mystical theories of art and religion and includes 4 symphonies, among them *The Divine Poem* (1905); the orchestral *Prometheus*; and very many works for piano.

Scribe Eugène (1791–1861). French playwright. S.'s 'well-made plays' influenced many later writers; they excelled in plot, construction and effective dialogue, although their treatment of subject and character was superficial.

scroll-work. A decorative motif derived from the volute of the classical Ionic capital (*orders). Used extensively and in every

Samuel Scott. *Old London Bridge*

Alexander Scriabin

Scroll-work by Hans Vredeman de Vries (*c.* 1560–70)

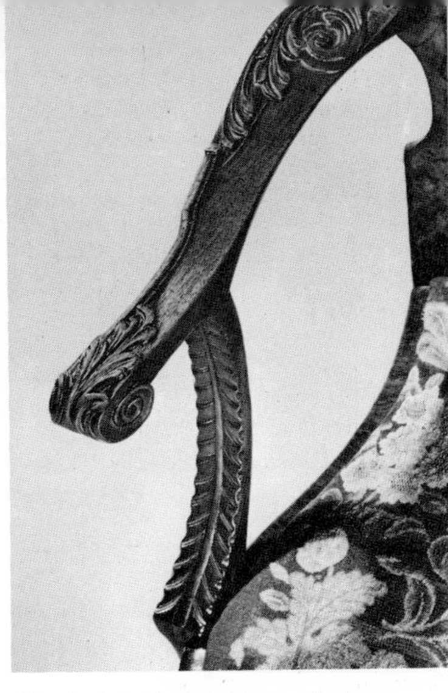

Scroll-work. Arm and support of a chair

possible variety in all the decorative arts, particularly during the 16th c.

Scrutiny. English magazine; F. R. *Leavis.

Scudéry Georges de (1601–67). French playwright. S. was the brother of Madeleine de S., and took an undetermined part in the composition of her romances. His works include *L'Amour tyrannique* (*c.* 1638) and the essay *Observations sur le Cid* (1637), which persuaded the Academy to condemn Corneille's *Le Cid.*

Scudéry Madeleine de (1607–1701). French novelist. She wrote a number of very popular long romances, notably *Artamène, ou le Grand Cyrus* (1649–53; *Artamenes. . .* , 1653–5) and *Clélie* (1654–60; *Clelia,* 1656–61), which were publ. under the name of Georges de S., her brother; they contained incredible adventures, sentimental love-stories and portraits of contemporaries placed in pseudo-historical settings. From about 1650, S.'s *salon* was the most important in France.

scumbling. In oil painting, the technique of working a layer of opaque colour over an existing colour in such a way that the latter is only partially obliterated and a broken effect obtained.

Sea Drift (1903). Work by Delius for voices and orchestra based on Walt Whitman.

Seagram Building New York (1958). Architects *Mies van der Rohe and Philip Johnson.

Sealsfield Charles. Chief pseud. of Karl Anton Postl (1793–1864), U.S. novelist and travel writer born in Moravia, where he was a monk until he fled his monastery. S. wrote his works in German, himself trs. them into English; they include the novel *Tokeah: or the White Rose* (1828).

Searle Humphrey (1915–). English composer, influenced by his teacher, Webern. His works include: a 1-act opera, *Tagebuch eines Irren* (Berlin, 1958); the trilogy for speaker and orchestra *Gold Coast Customs* (1949, his 1st important 12-note composition), *The River run* (1951) and *The Shadow of Cain* (1952), with texts by Edith Sitwell and James Joyce; the ballet *Noctambules* (1956); *Put Away the Flutes* (1947) on a poem by W. R. Rodgers and *Poem for Twenty-two strings* (1950).

Season in Hell, A (1873). Poetic work by *Rimbaud.

Seasons, The (1726–30). Poem by James *Thomson; it inspired *Haydn's oratorio. Vivaldi's set of concertos (*The Four Seasons*) is not connected.

Sebastiano del Piombo (1485–1547). Venetian painter of religious subjects and portraits, born Sebastiano Luciani but known as 'del Piombo' (Italian, 'seal') after his appointment as keeper of the Papal seal. His early style was in the manner of Giorgione, some of whose work he completed. In 1511 he went to Rome to work at the Villa Farnesina, where he met and was influenced by Raphael. Later he became a friend and follower of Michelangelo, who supplied the drawings for some of S.'s paintings such as the *Flagellation* in S. Pietro in Montorio, Rome. S.'s late work forms a link between the Venetian school and the high Renaissance in Rome.

Seberg Jean (1938–). U.S. film actress who was still at drama school when Preminger starred her in *St Joan* (1957). The lead in *Bonjour Tristesse* (1957) followed. She reappeared in France, playing a kind of moll in *À Bout de Souffle* (1960), and her boyish, cropped beauty has since personified young America for the French.

Secession, New Secession: *Sezession

second. A musical *interval.

Second Mrs Tanqueray, The (1893). Play by *Pinero.

Secret Agent, The (1907). Novel by *Conrad.

Secret Life of Walter Mitty, The. Short story by James *Thurber.

Secret Marriage, The (Italian *Il Matrimonio Segreto*). Opera by *Cimarosa on a libretto by Bertati after a play by George Colman and Garrick; 1st performance at Vienna in 1792.

Section: Rock-Drill 85–95 de los Cantares (1956). Section of the *Cantos* of Ezra *Pound.

Sedaine Michel-Jean (1719–97). French playwright and librettist. His plays include the comedy *Le Philosophe sans le savoir* (1765).

Madeleine de Scudéry

Sebastiano del Piombo. *Flagellation*

Hercules Pietersz Seghers. *Landscape*

Segonzac. *River Landscape*

George Seferis

Andrés Segovia

Doric Temple at Segesta

Sedding John Dando (1838–91). English architect, working mostly in the neo-Gothic style. He designed several churches of merit e.g. at Netley, Hants. and Holy Trinity, Chelsea, paying special attention to detail and trying to revive the idea of craftsmanship.

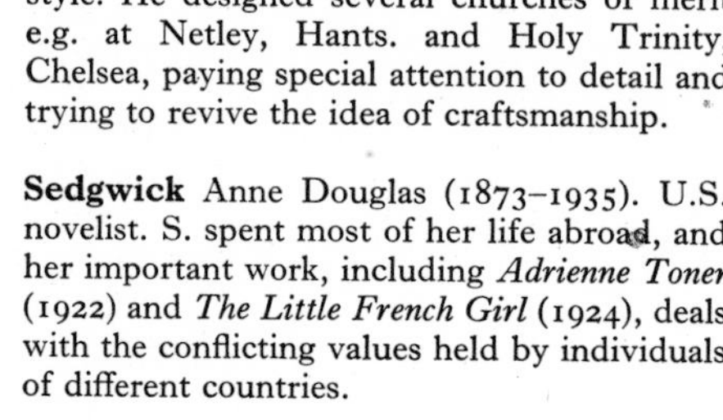

Sedgwick Anne Douglas (1873–1935). U.S. novelist. S. spent most of her life abroad, and her important work, including *Adrienne Toner* (1922) and *The Little French Girl* (1924), deals with the conflicting values held by individuals of different countries.

Sedgwick Catherine Maria (1789–1867). U.S novelist, a member of a prominent New England family. S.'s historical romances include *Redwood* (1824) and *Hope Leslie* (1827).

Sedley Sir Charles (1639–1701). English playwright, author of *The Mulberry Garden* (1668) and *Bellamira* (1687), based on comedies by Molière and Terence.

Seefried Irmgard (1919–). German soprano, an outstanding performer in Mozart roles.

Seferis George (1900–). Greek poet. S. spent many years in the diplomatic service and was an official of the Greek government-in-exile during World War II. S. is steeped in the Greek past, and his verse is shot through with mythological allusions; yet it returns constantly to the themes of loss and exile, and the poet repeatedly identifies with the wanderer and exile Odysseus. S.'s works include the linked poems of *Mythical Story* and the well-known *The King of Asine*.

Segesta Sicily. Greek town, site of a famous Doric temple (late 5th c. B.C.). It was never completed but is extremely well preserved.

Seghers Anna. Pseud. of Netty Radvanyi (1900–). German novelist; she has written many novels of social and political protest, including *Aufstand der Fischer von St Barbara* (1928; *The Revolt of the Fisherman*, 1929) and *Das siebte Kreuz* (1939; *The Seventh Cross*, 1943).

Seghers Daniel (1590–1661). Early Flemish flower painter, pupil of Jan Bruegel the Elder. He specialized in floral garlands surrounding religious paintings and portraits often by another artist.

Seghers Hercules Pietersz (1589/90–after 1633). Dutch landscape painter and etcher, a pupil of G. van Coninxloo; he may have visited Italy and come into contact with Elsheimer there. His rocky landscapes with dramatic lighting effects were expressive of awe at the sublimity of nature; they considerably influenced Rembrandt's landscapes. S. produced powerfully imaginative experimental etchings using inks of different colours and printing on coloured paper and canvas.

Segonzac André Dunoyer de (1884–). French landscape, still-life and figure painter in a personal style influenced by Cézanne and the fauves, graphic artist and theatrical designer. Many of his paintings are in water-colour. Among the books he has illustrated are Colette's *La Treille Muscate* and Virgil's *Georgics*.

Segovia Andrés (1893–). Spanish guitar virtuoso. Self-taught and using a style marking a break with the classic Spanish tradition, S. has established the guitar as a concert instrument. Roussel and Castelnuovo-Tedesco are among composers who have written works for him.

Segrais Jean Regnault de (1624–1701). French poet. He was a friend of Mme de Lafayette, 2 of whose books, *La Princesse de Clèves* and *Zaÿde*, were publ. under his name.

Sehna knot. From Sinna, a town in Persia. A knot used in hand-made pile carpet weaving in the majority of Persian, Central Asiatic, Indian and Chinese carpets. It is tied on 2 adjacent warp threads; successive rows of knots, separated generally by a line of weft, are tied to the same pairs of warp threads. Also called the 'Persian knot'.

Seiber Mátyás (1905–60). Hungarian composer, a pupil of Kodály, living in Britain from 1935. He worked as conductor, composer and teacher, his pupils including P. R. Fricker. As S. developed he combined Hungarian elements into an individual style; later works used 12-note techniques. Works include: the cantata *Ulysses* (1947), based on Joyce; 3 string quartets; and *Tre pezzi* for cello and orchestra (1956).

Seidel Heinrich (1842–1906). German humorous writer, author of series of stories so popular that they were combined and issued as a novel about 'Leberecht Hünnchen'. S. also wrote children's verse, short stories and his autobiography, *Von Perlin nach Berlin* (1894).

Seidler Harry (1923–). Viennese-born architect trained by Gropius and Breuer at Harvard. S. went to Australia and by the early 1950s had built a series of houses which made him the 1st Australian architect to win world fame. Other work includes the Melbourne Olympic Stadium.

Sekles Bernhard (1872–1934). German composer and teacher of harmony; Hindemith was one of his pupils. S.'s best music was in an 'oriental' style.

Selden John (1584–1654). English scholar whose weighty utterances were preserved by his secretary, Richard Milward, and publ. (1689, after both were dead) as *Table-Talk*. . . .

Seligmann Kurt (1900–62). Swiss painter, graphic artist and theatrical designer in the surrealist tradition. In 1939 he settled in the U.S.

Sellaio Jacopo del (*c.* 1441–93). Florentine painter, pupil of Fra Filippo Lippi and strongly influenced by Botticelli. His only fully authenticated work is a *Pietà* (Berlin) from S. Frediano, Florence.

Sellers Peter (1925–). English actor. After experience in theatre and variety, S. caught the public's attention in the zany radio series *The Goon Show*. He has starred in Britain and Hollywood in a run of popular films since *I'm All Right Jack* (1959), almost all comedies. Notable are *Lolita* (1962) and *Dr Strangelove* (1963).

Selznick David O. (1902–65). Film producer. S. became a producer at R.K.O. (1932) and then at M.G.M. (1933). In 1936 he started Selznick International Pictures, which mainly specialized in extravagant melodramas often, like *Ruby Gentry* and *Duel in the Sun*, built round his wife Jennifer Jones. S. brought Hitchcock to Hollywood to make *Rebecca* (1940). The most famous S. film is *Gone with the Wind*, which made more money than any other film up to 1962.

semibreve. The note with longest time value commonly used in modern *notation; its German name, '*ganze Note*', means 'whole note', the U.S. term. The s. is notated, 𝅝; its rest 𝄻.

semiquaver. In music, a note with a time value half that of a *quaver, called 'sixteenth note' in the U.S. It is notated 𝅘𝅥𝅯 or ♬; its rest 𝄿.

semitone. Musical *interval.

Semper Gottfried (1803–79). German architect who began his career at Dresden, building the Opera House and the Art Gallery. In Austria (in partnership with Karl von Hasenauer) he designed the Burgtheater and the Museums of Art History and Natural History, Vienna. S. developed from an eclectic imitation of Gothic (Cholera Fountain, Dresden) and Renaissance forms to a warm and lavish Second Empire style.

Senancour Étienne Pivert de (1770–1846). French author born in Paris; he left home as a young man for Switzerland, where the scenery, coupled with his early reading of Rousseau and Goethe's *Werther*, kindled his characteristically disillusioned melancholy and love of nature. His life was clouded by his neurotic temperament, an unhappy marriage and experiments with drugs. He earned a precarious living by hack-work until 1833, when he received a pension. His epistolary novel *Obermann* (1804), the introspective letters of a melancholy young man living with his ennui in the Alps, was a precursor of French romanticism.

Sender Ramón José (1902–). Spanish novelist and playwright. S. fought in the Civil War; his wife was executed and when the Republic fell he went into exile. The novels of S.'s maturity portray Spain's unstable political life in many ways–through realistic and horrific description and through fantasy; they include *Imán* (1930; *Earmarked for Hell*, 1934), *Siete domingos rojos* (1932; *Seven Red Sundays*, 1936) and *La Noche de las cien cabezas–novela del tiempo en delirio* (1934).

Seneca Lucius Annaeus, the Younger (*c.* 5 B.C.–A.D. 65). Roman essayist and playwright born at Cordoba, the son of a most discerning critic of rhetoric, SENECA THE ELDER (*c.* 55 B.C.–*c.* A.D. 40). He soon made his mark in the rhetorical schools at Rome where he was

Seidler. Lend Lease House, Sydney

Seligmann. *Sabbath Phantoms* (1939)

Sehna knot

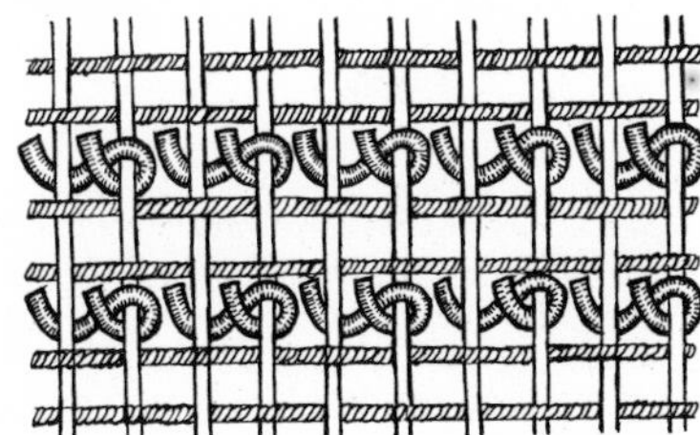

Semper. The Opera House, Dresden

Sennett. The Keystone Cops

Sens cathedral: the nave

educated. By 37 he was recognized as one of the first writers and speakers at Rome. Exiled in 41, he returned in 49 as tutor to the young Nero, to whom he became chief minister on his accession in 54, retiring in 61 when Nero's vices began to get out of hand. Even the offer of all his wealth to the emperor, however, did not spare him when he was accused in the conspiracy of 65 and obliged to commit suicide. Seneca professed Stoicism: a dozen treatises on various moral themes and 124 of the moral epistles in 20 books survive, the scabrous and slanderous skit on the deification of Claudius called *Apocolocyntosis*, and 10 tragedies, inflated and bombastic adaptations of Euripides and other Greek authors, which exercised a great influence over the Elizabethan and Jacobean theatre. His high-mindedness, most happily exemplified in the *Epistles*, written to a friend towards the end of his life, recommended him to the Fathers of the Church, but modern critics observe that it was belied by his great wealth, his flattery of those in power, his connivance at Nero's matricide.

Senefelder Aloys (1771–1834). German dramatist and inventor of *lithography as a cheap means of printing his own writings. He publ. an account of his experiments in *Vollständiges Lehrbuch der Steindruckerey . . .* (1818; *A Complete Course of Lithography*, 1819).

Senesino. Stage-name used by the great Italian castrato mezzo-soprano singer, Francesco Bernardi (*c.* 1680–*c.* 1750); he sang in several of Handel's London operas.

Senfl Ludwig (*c.* 1490–1543). German-Swiss composer, a pupil of H. Isaac and his successor (1517–19) as music director of the Emperor Maximilian's chapel. He was admired for his polyphonic motets and above all for his masterly German *Lieder* (about 250) which exhibit the full range of this genre (e.g. court songs and folk-songs).

Sennett Mack (1880–1960). Film producer. S. worked for D. W. Griffith before setting up his own Keystone Studios in 1912–at Los Angeles rather than New York, which was still the American production centre. S.'s output, which continued with diminishing returns until 1935, when he retired, consisted entirely of short slapstick comedies and satires. He started Chaplin in the cinema and developed a co. of stars including Mabel Normand, Fatty Arbuckle and Ben Turpin as well as the Keystone Cops. Apart from Keaton and Laurel and Hardy, all the leading silent comedians worked for him.

Sens cathedral (begun *c.* 1140). One of the 12th-c. cathedrals of the Île de France which produced the mature Gothic style. S. has pointed arches, sexpartite vaulting and flying buttresses. An unusual feature is the coupled columns used in alternation with piers in the nave.

Sense and Sensibility (1811). Novel by Jane *Austen.

Senso (1954). Film directed by L. *Visconti.

Sentimental Education, A (1870). Novel by *Flaubert.

Sentimental Journey through France and Italy, A (1768). Book by *Sterne.

Separate Tables (1954). Play by Terence Rattigan.

sepia. A brown pigment prepared from the inky secretion of the cuttle-fish and used in watercolour and ink, often in monochrome. It was not much used until the 19th c. and should not be confused with bistre.

Sep-Szarzyński Mikołaj (*c.* 1550–81). Polish poet. His love-poetry and religious poetry, including some exceptionally fine sonnets, is in forceful, stringent language akin to the English metaphysical poets.

septet. Musical combination of 7 instruments or a composition for such a group. There is a famous s. by Beethoven, for violin, viola, cello, double-bass, clarinet, bassoon and horn.

Septuagint: *Bible

septuplet. In music a group of 7 equal notes, which are to be performed in the time allowed by the *time signature of the piece to a smaller number of notes.

sequence. A hymn which followed the alleluia and gradual in the Roman Catholic service of mass; from the 11th to 13th cs a number of these monodic liturgical pieces were produced. The Council of Trent limited the number permitted to 5.

Seraglio, The (full English title, *The Abduction from the Seraglio*). *Singspiel* by *Mozart; 1st performance at Vienna in 1782.

Serao Matilde (1856–1927). Prolific and popular novelist who usually wrote about Neapolitan life. Her works include *Il Romanzo della Fanciulla* (1886) and *Il Paese de Cuccagua* (1891).

Sercambi Giovanni (1347–1424). Italian chronicler and short-story writer. He wrote a history of his native city of Lucca and more than 150 *novelle* on various themes.

serenade. Originally music performed by a lover under his mistress's window at evening. Commonly used from the 18th c. for a type of suite with an opening movement in sonata form.

Sereni Vittorio (1913–). Italian poet and critic. His works include *Diario d'Algeria* (1947), based upon his military experiences in Greece and North Africa.

Sergeant York (1941). Film directed by H. *Hawks.

serial music. An extension of the technique applied in *twelve-note music whereby not only the notes are arranged in a set order but also, for example, the duration of the notes, their dynamics, the kind of attack (i.e. staccato, tenuto, etc.). Also involved is the idea of permutations of the basic series (or 'row')– i.e. not merely repetition 1–12 but continually varying mathematical patterns. The sources of this technique are to be found in certain works of Webern's last period, e.g. the 1st movement

of his symphony, which moves from set 8ves in the exposition to 'free' ones in the development section, and in Messiaen (especially *Modes de Valeurs et Intensités* which lays down certain combinations of notes, durations and dynamics–though they are not 'serialized'. They were used as the series for Boulez's *Structures*, the work which makes the most extensive use of serial methods.) The term is often used loosely to include 12-note music and of *avant-garde* music in general.
The aim is not necessarily that the series be heard but that it should provide the means for deriving textures. In other words the notes matter less in this music than in 'classical' music and various elements which were secondary or even haphazard in classical music have taken on an importance of their own. Some of the composers who have used serial methods are: Boulez, Stockhausen, Nono, Berio, Maderna, Maxwell-Davies and Pousseur.

series. A sequence of notes used as the basis of a musical composition: hence the term SERIAL TECHNIQUE. Also *twelve-note music.

Serlio Sebastiano (1475–1554). Italian architect, a pupil of Peruzzi. In 1540 he settled in France. His only buildings are: La Grande Ferrare, Fontainebleau (1544), whose plan became standard for French hôtels; and Ancy-le-Franc (*c.* 1546). His book, or rather series of books, *Tutte l'opere d'architettura* (1st complete ed. 1584), was trs. into most European languages and had an enormous influence, especially in France; it provided a copy-book of Italian examples, capable of being adapted to all tastes.

Sermini Gentile (15th-c.). Italian (Sienese) short-story writer. His stories are vulgar, but are written in good Tuscan.

Serov Alexander Nikolayevich (1820–71). Russian composer. After a visit to Germany in 1858 he introduced Wagner's music to Russia, writing polemics against the Russian nationalist school. His opera *Judith* (1863) showed the influence of Wagner and Meyerbeer, but in *Rogneda* (1865) Russian folk influences were in fact apparent.

Serov Valentin (1865–1911). Russian painter, an influential teacher at the Moscow School of Art (1897–1909) and a contributor to the *World of Art* magazine and exhibitions. S. was largely brought up on *Mamontov's estate and taught at the *Abramtsevo Colony. He painted portraits of all the famous men of his day, but one of his most famous works is *The Girl with Peaches* (1887), depicting Mamontov's daughter. He was also a talented landscape painter.

Serpan Iaroslav (1922–). Czech painter and theorist of the school of Paris.

serpent. Musical wind instrument of conical bore. It was made of wood bound with leather (or of brass) played with a cup mouthpiece like a trombone, and had keys and finger-holes like a bassoon. It was gradually displaced in the 19th c. by the ophicleide and tuba.

Serra Jaime (d. before 1395) and Pedro (d. after 1405). The most important Catalonian painters of the late 14th c. They continued the Sienese tradition introduced by Ferrer Bassa. Pedro's altarpiece *The Holy Spirit* in Manresa cathedral is a fine example of their work.

Serra Renato (1884–1915). Italian writer and critic. S.'s *Esame di coscienza di un letterato* is a kind of spiritual and literary testament written on the eve of his departure for the war in 1915.

Sert José Luis (1902–). Barcelona architect who emigrated to the U.S. with the advent of Fascism. S. has become the leading U.S. exponent of the architecture of Le Corbusier, and has built several heavy concrete structures for Harvard Univ.

Sérusier Paul (1865–1927). French painter, founder of the *nabis group in 1889 under the influence of Gauguin.

Servant, The (1963). Film directed by J. *Losey.

serventois. French term for *sirventés; later applied particularly to poems praising the Virgin Mary.

Service Robert W(illiam) (1874–1958). English poet and novelist who lived for long periods in Canada and France. S. arrived in the Klondike at the tail-end of the gold rush, whose hairy-chested ethos he sought to capture in his many ballads, including the famous *The Shooting of Dan McGrew* (1907).

Servranckz Victor (1897–). Belgian painter and industrial designer, an early propagandist for abstract art in Belgium. His work has been varied in style, being related to several modern movements–futurism, surrealism, neo-plasticism, tachisme–but he has given strongly personal interpretation to each.

Sessions Roger Huntington (1896–). U.S. composer. He studied under Bloch and worked from 1926 to 1933 in Europe; he has held teaching posts at Princeton Univ. and the Univ. of California. His works, freely atonal and contrapuntal in idiom, include: the opera

Pedro Serra. *The Holy Spirit*; part of the Manresa cathedral altarpiece

Sérusier. *Landscape, Pont-Aven*

Servranckz. *Opus 47* (1923)

Serov. *The Girl with Peaches.* Also *Dostoyevsky

Serpent; London, early 19th c.

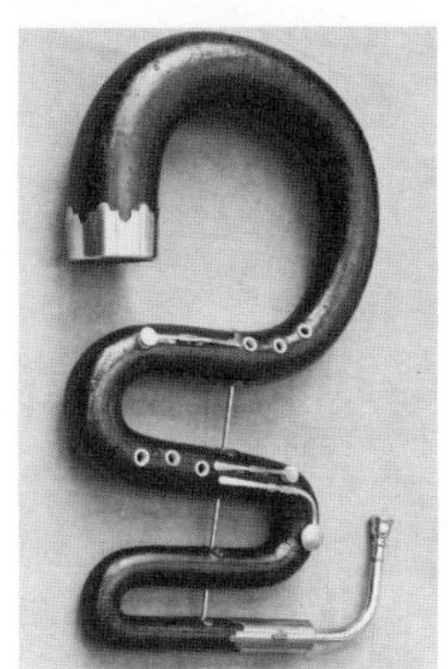

Serlio. Woodcut illustration of the Tuscan, Doric, Ionic, Corinthian and Composite orders

Severini. *Black Cat* (1911)

Severn. *John Keats*

The Trial of Lucullus (1947), after Brecht, 4 symphonies and a mass for chorus and organ (1956).

sestina. Verse form consisting of 6 stanzas of 6 lines and 1 of 3 lines; the last word of each of the 1st 6 lines reappears as the last word of a line in each of the subsequent stanzas. In the last stanza, 3 of the terminal words are placed at the ends, 3 in the middle of the lines.

set. Term used to describe the entire material background used in a play production. It is a composite term, including the *scenery, furniture and properties. The name originated from 'set scene' when one set of scenery was placed behind another and only revealed when the front set had been dispensed with.

Settignano Desiderio da: *Desiderio da Settignano

Settle Elkanah (1648–1724). English playwright. His *Empress of Morocco* gave rise to a prolonged and venomous controversy between S. and Dryden.

Seurat Georges (1859–91). French painter born in Paris. S. studied at the École des Beaux-Arts (1878–9) where he was a model academic student. Early drawings show a complete absorption of Ingres's classical discipline and his careful preparation in sketches and colour studies for each of his 7 large paintings was thoroughly traditional. His successive investigations of form, colour and line were part of a lifelong search for a sense of order in painting.

Most of his early independent works were conté drawings reflecting Millet in subject, in which a monumentality of form was realized by gradual tonal gradation.

The *Baignade* (1883–4; N.G., London) shows the simplicity of his early works enforced by the carefully calculated composition and by a palette of primary colours. His study of colour was based not on the empirical observation of the impressionists, but on research into the writings of Chevreul, Blanc, Superville and Delacroix. In his theory of 'divisionism' (later called 'neo-impressionism') each local colour is composed of tiny particles of pure colour which not only represent the colour of the object, but also the colour of light, reflected local colours and complementaries. These are blended at a distance by the eye. The purest example of this is *Un Dimanche d'Été à l'Île de la Grande Jatte* (1884–6; A. Inst., Chicago).

His later works–*Poseuses* (1886–7; Barnes Foundation, Philadelphia), *Parade* (1887–8; Clark Coll., New York), *La Poudreuse* (1889; Courtauld Gal., London), *Le Chahut* (1889–90; Kröller-Müller, Otterlo) and *Le Cirque* (1890; Louvre)–become increasingly linear and decorative, reflecting both the curvilinear arabesques of art nouveau and his own lifelong interest in popular art (posters, prints, etc.). The widespread use of his divisionist technique illustrates his superficial influence on almost all painters. Of a more long-term significance were his liberation of pure colour and his reaction against impressionism's formlessness, which–like Cézanne–foreshadows the structural discipline of later abstract art.

Seven against Thebes, The (467 B.C.). Tragedy by *Aeschylus.

Seven Brides for Seven Brothers (1954). Film directed by S. *Donen.

Seven Lamps of Architecture, The (1849). Book by John *Ruskin.

Seven Pillars of Wisdom (1926). Book by T. E. *Lawrence.

Seven Samurai, The (1954). Film directed by A. *Kurosawa.

Seventh Seal, The (1956). Film directed by I. *Bergman.

Severini Gino (1883–1966). Italian painter who signed the futurist manifesto (1910) and was one of the most significant members of the movement; from 1906 he lived chiefly in Paris. His futurist paintings include *Dance of Pan Pan* (1911; Coll. Walden, Berlin) and *Dynamic Hieroglyph of the Bal Tabarin* (1912; M.M.A., New York). He later allied himself with the cubists and as a result of his theoretical studies publ. *Du Cubisme au Classicisme* (1921). This was followed by a period of representational, almost academic painting; more recently he has returned to a non-figurative idiom. His works include murals and mosaics.

Severn Joseph (1793–1879). English portrait and subject painter, a friend of Keats. He accompanied the poet to Italy in 1820 and was with him at his death. One of his many portraits of Keats is in the N.P.G., London.

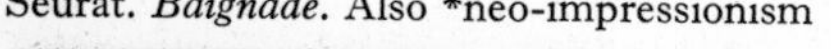

Seurat. *Baignade*. Also *neo-impressionism

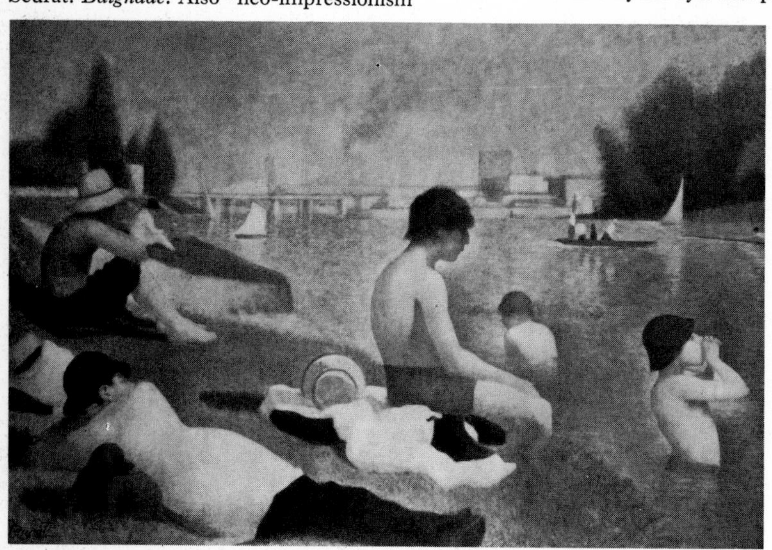

Seurat. *Un Dimanche d'Été à l'Île de la Grand Jatte*

Mme de Sévigné

Sèvres cabaret (1767)

Seymour. Illustration for *The Pickwick Papers*

sévigné. An ornament, jewelled or enamelled, in the shape of a three-dimensional bow of ribbon. First popular in the late 17th c. and associated with Mme de Sévigné.

Sévigné Marie, marquise de (1626–96). French writer. The fame of Mme de S. rests solely upon her correspondence (1726; 1764). Most of her letters were written to her favourite child, the comtesse de Grignan, and were designed to alleviate the distress and inconvenience of prolonged separation. They contain literary comments, moral reflections, natural descriptions, anecdotes and reports of contemporary events. Void of sentimentality and even lacking in sensibility, their charm lives in their natural spontaneity and in their revelation of a personality in which characteristic intellectualism was combined with unique powers of imagination and verbal invention. The direct simplicity of Mme de S.'s style contrasts strongly with the preciosity common in fashionable literature in the early 17th c.

Seville cathedral Spain. The last and largest medieval cathedral in Europe. It occupies the site of a mosque (of which the tower is retained) and has wide spacious proportions.

Sèvres. French porcelain factory which took over European leadership from Meissen; it moved to S. (1756) from Vincennes (founded *c.* 1738). The patronage and financial interest of Louis XV and Mme de Pompadour gave S. a fashionable (and semi-monopolistic) position; outstanding artistic figures were the art director Jean-Jacques Bachelier and the goldsmith and sculptor Duplessis. Flower paintings were the predominant decorative motifs; rich deep ground colours (e.g. the famous '*gros bleu*') were introduced, and elaborate gilding was used. In 1768 production in hard-paste *porcelain began. S. productions of the 1770s, when rococo was giving way to the neo-classical style, were less successful; and in the 19th c. little original work was produced.

Sewall Samuel (1652–1730). English-born American jurist, one of the commissioners in the Salem witchcraft trials; he left a valuable *Diary* (1878–82).

Sewell Anna (1820–78). English writer, author of the children's classic *Black Beauty* (1877), the 'autobiography' of a horse.

sextet. Musical combination of 6 instruments or a composition for such a group. Brahms wrote a s. for strings and Beethoven one for strings and 2 horns and one for wind instruments.

sextolet: *sextuplet

sextuplet. Musical term to describe 6 in the time (usually) of 4; e.g. [four notes] and [six notes, marked 6] are of the same length.

Seymour James (1702–52). English painter, with Wootton a pioneer of sporting art in England. He specialized in hunting and racing subjects and was noted for his horse portraiture.

Seymour Robert (1798–1836). English illustrator, caricaturist, engraver and painter whose fame rests on his illustrations for *The Pickwick Papers* by Dickens, one of his last commissions before he committed suicide.

Sezession (German, 'secession'). Term for the groups of German and Austrian artists who in the 1890s resigned from the recognized academic organizations in order to further the modern (mainly *impressionist and *art nouveau) movement. The most important were the S.s of Munich (1892), Vienna (1897) and Berlin (1899). The most *avant-garde*, the Berlin S., evolved from the rejection of Munch's paintings in the Berlin Artists' Association (1892). In 1910 the Berlin S. split and the NEUE SEZESSION was formed; its members included Nolde, Pechstein and other artists who later formed Die *Brücke, as well as Kandinsky and Jawlensky.

sforzando. The Italian word for 'strengthened' used as a musical direction (abbreviated to '*sf.*'). The note so marked is to be played with special, usually harsh, emphasis.

sfumato (Italian, 'evaporated'). The rendering of form by means of subtle tonal gradations so as to eliminate any sharply defined contours. The work of Leonardo is an example.

Sgambati Giovanni (1841–1914). Italian composer, conductor and pianist, a pupil of Liszt; in 1877 he became piano professor at the Academy of St Cecilia in Rome. His compositions are in a Wagnerian tradition.

Seville. The cathedral tower

Indonesian shadow theatre

Shadbolt. *Medieval Landscape*

Shahn. *Cherubs and Children* (*above*) and *The Passion of Sacco and Vanzetti* (1931–2)

Partly finished sgraffito being prepared for further work

Finished sgraffito with coats of arms painted on to the fresh plaster

sgraffito (Italian, 'scratched'). Method of decorating a stuccoed building by incising a design through the still wet top layer of plaster on to the undercoat. The term is also used of the similar practice in pottery.

Shadbolt Jack (1909–). English-born Canadian painter. He studied in London, Paris and New York, but his expressionistic paintings derive from the countryside of British Columbia; in recent years they have become increasingly abstract.

Shadows (1960). Film directed by J. *Cassavetes.

shadow theatre. A kind of puppet show, using flat figures which, by means of a light cast from behind, throw silhouettes on to a screen. This entertainment originated in China, Bali and Java, and puppets from those regions, with their intricate carving, are works of art in themselves. The shadow convention gradually spread eastwards and was very popular in France during the 18th c. and shadow plays were presented in England until the end of the 19th c.

Shadwell Thomas (*c.* 1642–92). English playwright whose works include *Epsom Wells* (1672), *The Squire of Alsatia* (1688) and *Bury Fair* (1689). From 1682 S. and Dryden attacked each other mercilessly; S. appears in Dryden's *Absalom and Achitophel* and is the chief target of his *Mac Flecknoe*. S. became poet laureate in 1688.

shaft. Architectural term for the main, cylindrical part of a column between base and capital; also used of a thin vertical support of an arch, usually attached to a wall or pier.

Shahn Ben (1898–). Russian-born U.S. painter. After study in New York he travelled in Europe and Africa (1927–9). He collaborated with Rivera on the Rockefeller Center murals (1933) and became one of the major figures in the wave of American realist painting in the 1930s. His tightly drawn, slightly caricatured realism often has a satirical element reminiscent of late German expressionism (Dix, Grosz, etc.). He painted several public murals under the *W.P.A. Art Project.

shake or trill. A musical *ornament.

Shakespeare William (1564–1616). English poet and playwright, the son of a Stratford-upon-Avon tradesman who had at one time been high bailiff of the town. In 1582 S. married Anne Hathaway: their 1st child, Susanna, was born 6 months later and in 1585 Anne gave birth to twins, Hamnet and Judith. S. is next heard of as a London actor-dramatist, already well enough known to be the object of an attack by Greene in his *Groatsworth of Wit*. The narrative poems *Venus and Adonis* (1593) and *The Rape of Lucrece* (1594) were dedicated to S.'s patron, the earl of Southampton. S.'s son Hamnet died in 1596, and in 1597 S. bought a fine house, New Place, in Stratford, to which he eventually retired. He became a shareholder in The Globe Theatre in 1599. Little else is known for certain about Shakespeare's life, though numerous ingenious theories have been evolved to fill the gaps. The sonnets, already circulating among friends in 1598 although not publ. until 1609, are addressed, some to a young man, others to the famous 'Dark Lady'; their identity and S.'s relationship to them remains a mystery.

S. wrote for the commercial theatre. He was consummate in manipulating the conventions of the Elizabethan stage; created characters which in the theatre have the authenticity of life; completely and successfully disregarded the *unities which were coming to shape European theatre and had an intuitive stage-sense which enabled him to juxtapose, in a single play, high tragedy and farce. His dramatis personae are kings and noblemen, yet he so handles their conflict with their ambitions, jealousies and weaknesses that the plays have a universal human validity. The plays do not give a clear picture of the personality of their author, but they do show recurrent themes. The confusion of being and seeming, playfully used in the comedies, is explored with anguished intensity in *Hamlet*, *Troilus and Cressida* and *Measure for Measure*; betrayal by those to be most trusted is often of critical importance: Duncan by Macbeth, Othello by Iago, Lear by his daughters, the old Hamlet by his wife and brother; the divinity of kingship, the theme of the histories, recurs in *Macbeth* and *King Lear*.

In his early poetry and plays S. made use of the wordy, 'conceited' poetry admired at the time, and of passages of dialogue bristling with obscure puns and topical allusions. In *Romeo and Juliet* and *Richard II* the poetry is already freeing itself of affectations, while in the comedies of this period the humour ceases to be predominantly verbal and has become the more enduring comedy of character. The 2 parts of *Henry IV* contain some of Shakespeare's richest and most mature comic writing, displaying a complementary subtlety and power in the use of prose. In the great tragedies the verse is completely the dramatist's tool, whether its cadences are used to create character, as in *Antony and Cleopatra*, or to build up a climate of evil doom by the cumulative effect of its imagery, as in *Macbeth*. In *King Lear* the verse is tauter and more elliptical, carrying a great weight of compressed meaning.

S.'s influence and reputation in Europe, first felt in Germany in the 1st half of the 18th c., became immense with the advent of romanticism–his disregard for the unities and the burning passion and vigour of his tragic heroes being obviously sympathetic to the romantic ethos. The immensity of his achievement is now accepted without question in all countries importantly affected by European culture.

The plays cannot be dated with any certainty, but they can be arranged in approximate sequence. The earliest, written when Shakespeare was learning his craft and probably refurbishing old plays as well as writing new, are *The Comedy of Errors*, *The Two Gentlemen of Verona*, *The Taming of the Shrew* and *Love's Labour's Lost*, comedies which vary from knockabout farce to exquisitely artificial verbal wit; the tragedy *Titus Andronicus* and the histories *Henry VI* (in 3 parts) and *Richard III*. Next came *Richard II*, the romantic tragedy of *Romeo and Juliet*, young lovers destroyed by their passion, which cuts across, but after their deaths finally heals, their families' enmity. The mature histories, *Henry IV* (parts I and II) and *Henry V*, contain S.'s greatest comic creation, Sir John Falstaff–with *The Merry Wives of Windsor* as a sequel showing him in love. There followed the 5 great comedies: *A Midsummer Night's Dream*, a pastoral fantasy of ancient Greece, *The Merchant of Venice*, the tragi-comedy of Shylock the Jew set in 16th-c. Venice, *Much Ado About Nothing*, and 2 sparkling comedies of mistaken identities *As You Like It* and *Twelfth Night*. About 1600 begins the period of the great tragedies of *Hamlet*, a sensitive, noble yet indecisive man, obliged to revenge his father's death; *Macbeth*, a noble man made ruthless and savage by driving ambition; *Othello*, a noble man who destroys himself and his beloved wife, driven by self-torturing jealousy; *King Lear*, a noble king betrayed by his family and his own reason and judgement. The works of this later period include: the 'problem plays' *Timon of Athens*, *Troilus and Cressida*, *Measure for Measure* and *All's Well that Ends Well*; *Pericles Prince of Tyre*; and the Roman plays *Julius Caesar*, *Coriolanus* and *Antony and Cleopatra*. The serene, mysterious last plays include *Cymbeline*, *The Winter's Tale* and *The Tempest*, in which the magician Duke Prospero manipulates his enemies and returns to his inheritance. It is probable that S. collaborated with John Fletcher in *Henry VIII* and *The Two Noble Kinsmen*. The various sources S. used for his plays and their dates of publ., etc. will be found in the brief entries on each individual play.

Shakespeare. The 'Chandos' portrait, perhaps the best known of portraits traditionally supposed to be of Shakespeare

Shane (1953). Film directed by G. *Stevens.

Shanghai Gesture, The (1941). Film directed by J. von *Sternberg.

shanty (suggested derivation from the French *chantez*, 'sing!'). Formerly a work-song used by sailors; there are 2 main categories of s., 'hauling', e.g. 'What shall we do with the drunken sailor' and 'capstan'.

Shapiro Karl (Jay) (1913–). U.S. poet and critic. S. was the ed. of *Poetry* (1950–6) and is now ed. of *The Schooner*. His works include *V-Letter and Other Poems* (1944), reflecting his war experiences, and the verse *Essay on Rime* (1945).

sharp. In music the sign ♯, which indicates that the note before which it stands is to be raised a semitone on every occurrence within the bar unless the s. is cancelled by a *natural. (Also *key signature.) In a performance a note is said to be sharp when it is a shade higher in pitch than it should be.

Sharp Cecil (James) (1859–1924). English folk-lorist, a prime mover in the revival of interest in English folk-music. He coll. and ed. songs, and founded The English Folk Dance Society (1911).

Shaw George Bernard (1856–1950). Irish playwright born in Dublin, of English Protestant stock. S. worked as a clerk in a land agency until 1876, when he joined his mother

Shakespeare's signature (on his will, 1616)

A PLEASANT
Conceited Comedie
CALLED,
Loues labors lost.
As it vvas presented before her Highnes this last Christmas.
Newly corrected and augmented By W. Shakespere.
Imprinted at London by W.W. for Cutbert Burby.
1598.

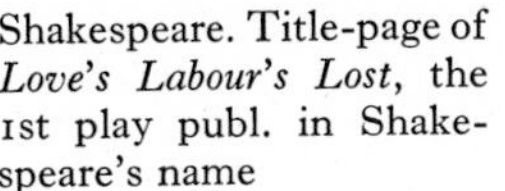

Shakespeare. Title-page of *Love's Labour's Lost*, the 1st play publ. in Shakespeare's name

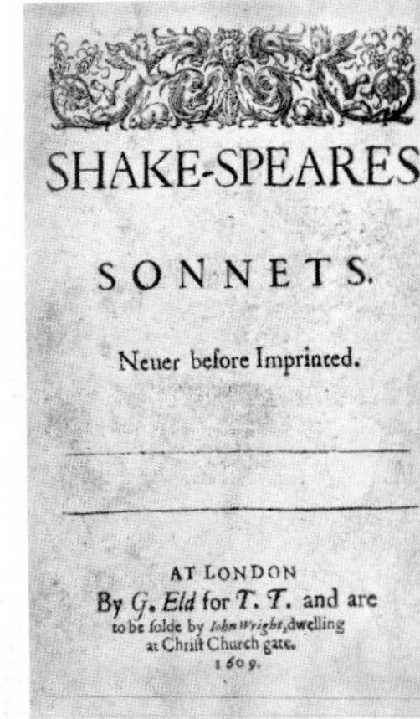

SHAKE-SPEARES
SONNETS.
Neuer before Imprinted.
AT LONDON
By G. Eld for T. T. and are to be solde by John Wright, dwelling at Christ Church gate.
1609.

Shakespeare. The *Sonnets*; 1609 ed. Also *Sonnets

Shakespeare. Life-size memorial bust (before 1623). Thi and Droeshout's engraving (*Blount) are the best authenticated portraits

George Bernard Shaw in 1901

George Bernard Shaw at a debate (1927) with Belloc and Chesterton. Also *Abbey Theatre

Norman Shaw. Old Swan House, London

Shawms

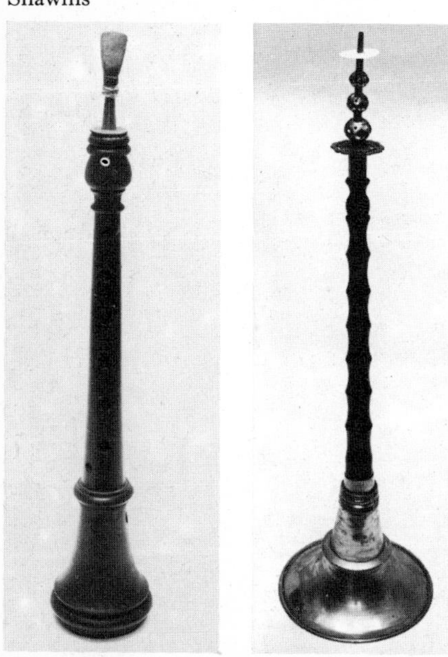

in London. He publ. 4 novels without much success, became a Fabian (1884), and from 1885 worked as a critic of music and (later) drama. He wrote his 1st play in 1891, but became widely popular, frequently performed and ultimately recognized as the greatest British playwright of his time only after the repertory seasons at the Court Theatre (1904–7).

S.'s comedies have 4 outstanding merits: brilliant wit and a strong sense of fun; a gallery of closely observed contemporary types whose foibles are exaggerated in the comedic tradition which includes Jonson, Sheridan and Wilde; a simple, lucid, forceful prose; and clear-cut, well-thought-out ideas, often expressed as paradoxes, which give direction and cogency to the comedy. Many of the plays have prefaces of pamphlet length which discuss the ideas behind the play. The early comedies like *Widowers' Houses* (1892) and *Mrs Warren's Profession* (written 1893; U.S. performance 1905) deal with social abuses; the latter, a study of prostitution, was banned from the English public stage until 1925. But it became clear that S.'s Socialism was only part of a larger, ultimately religious vision, a *vitalism which held that men would eventually become as gods. This philosophy was first expounded at length in the play-within-a-play (*Don Juan in Hell*) in *Man and Superman* (1903) and more fully (though artistically less successfully) in the 5 plays of *Back to Methusalah* (1922). The most successful non-comic character S. portrayed was the type of the man of action with a religious purpose, the warrior-saint, an ideal of human greatness most convincingly set forth in *Caesar and Cleopatra* (1899) and *St Joan* (1923), which is generally considered his greatest play. *Candida* (1895) and *The Devil's Disciple* (1897) describe the crises during which the heroes realize their destiny and relinquish ordinary human affections and aims. In *Heartbreak House* (1920), however, the mood is close to despair–a reaction to the catastrophe of World War I, the stupidity of the ruling classes and the feebleness of the intelligentsia. *Pygmalion* (1914) remains extremely popular as a modern Cinderella story, relating how the irascible Professor Higgins teaches Eliza, a flower-girl, to speak correctly and triumphantly enter society. Works include *Arms and the Man* (1894), which satirizes the romantic conception of war; *You Never Can Tell* (1898); *Captain Brassbound's Conversion* (1899); *John Bull's Other Island* (1904); *Major Barbara* (1905), a discussion of the use of power; *Androcles and the Lion* (1913); *The Doctor's Dilemma* (1906); *The Millionairess* (1936); and correspondence with Ellen Terry and Mrs Patrick Campbell.

Shaw Glen Byam (1904–). English actor and director. He was co-director of the Stratford Theatre (1953–6) and then sole director until 1959. In 1960 he directed Charles Laughton as King Lear and also Alec Guinness in the title-role of Terence Rattigan's *Ross*.

Shaw Henry Wheeler: Josh *Billings

Shaw Irwin (1913–). U.S. novelist and playwright. S.'s early works show a pre-occupation with social and political ideas which he has never completely abandoned; they include the plays *Bury the Dead* (1936) and *The Gentle People: A Brooklyn Fable* (1939). *The Young Lions* (1948), a novel set in World War II, made him famous. S.'s novels include *Lucy Crown* (1956) and *Two Weeks in Another Town* (1960).

Shaw Martin (1875–). English composer and ed., one of the most active figures in the early 20th-c. English nationalistic school of music, using English folk-music and forwarding the revival of Purcell's music. His brother Geoffrey (1879–1943) held a similar position in English musical life.

Shaw (Richard) Norman (1831–1912). Scottish architect who introduced the vogue for the Queen Anne style–brick walls, stone quoins, regular sash-windows–as in his Bryanston House, Dorset (1890). He also built in the free English domestic style, e.g. his Bedford Park suburb (1876–80) which was so influential on the Continent through Muthesius. His later work was thoroughly academic, e.g. the Piccadilly Hotel, London (1905).

shawm. Woodwind musical instrument. It is now used in folk-music but from the 13th c., when it was introduced to Europe from the East, to the 16th, it was important in art music. It is played with a double reed, as is the oboe, has a rapidly widening conical bore and a flaring bell. Its tone is powerful and heavily reedy.

Shchedrin Nikolay Evgrafovich: Saltykov.

Moira Shearer in *Les Patineurs*

Sheeler. *River Rouge Plant* (1932). Also *cubist-realism

Sheffield plate. Soup-tureen (*c.* 1810)

Shearer Moira (1926–). English ballerina and actress; she danced at Sadler's Wells and then at Covent Garden (1946–52). In 1948 she starred in the ballet film *The Red Shoes.* She also danced in New York and Paris, but in 1954 retired from ballet to make her career as an actress.

Shearer Norma (1904–). U.S. film actress. Sweet but volatile star of romantic sacrifice, S. had her first success in V. Sjöström's *He Who Gets Slapped* (1925). She won an Oscar for *The Divorce* (1930). Her later films included I. Thalberg's *Romeo and Juliet* (1936) and *The Women* (1939). She became one of America's richest women and retired in 1942.

She Done Him Wrong (1933). Film directed by Lowell Sherman, with Mae West.

Sheeler Charles (1883–). U.S. painter of industrial architecture and machinery, a leading exponent of cubist-realism (or precisionism) exemplified in *New England Irrelevancy* (Downtown Gal., New York). In the 1930s, beginning with scenes of the River Rouge Plant for Ford, he worked in a style of straight realism, influenced by his work as a photographer.

Sheffield John, Earl of Mulgrave (1648–1721). English statesman and writer, a patron of Dryden and arbiter of taste. His works include an *Essay on Satire.*

Sheffield plate. A form of silver-coated plate. A thin sheet of silver is soldered to a thicker one of copper and the 2 are then rolled. Discovered by Thomas Boulsover in 1742, it was taken up by Matthew Boulton on a large scale. He produced the whole range of domestic articles at a much lower cost than silver. S. p. was gradually replaced in the 1830s by electroplate.

Sheldon Edward Brewster (1886–1946). U.S. popular playwright. His works include *The Nigger* (1909), which dealt with the status of Negroes in the South; *Salvation Nell* (1908); *The Boss* (1911); and *Romance* (1913).

Shelley Mary Wollstonecraft (1797–1851). English writer, daughter of the utopian political theorist William Godwin and wife of Percy Bysshe S. Her novels include *Frankenstein, or the Modern Prometheus* (1818). The scientist Frankenstein discovers a method of creating life; the result is a monster whose loathsome appearance cuts him off from human society and drives him to crime.

Shelley Percy Bysshe (1792–1822). English romantic poet, son of a baronet. Inspired by W. Godwin's *Political Justice,* S. publ. *The Necessity of Atheism* (1818), for which he was expelled from Oxford. He campaigned ineffectually for political liberty in Dublin and Wales, and attacked 'kings, priests and statesmen' in the long poem *Queen Mab* (1813). He married Harriet Westbrook in 1811; after they separated, he went abroad with Godwin's daughter, Mary, whom S. married after Harriet's suicide (1816). From 1818 he lived in Italy. He was drowned while sailing in the Gulf of Spezzia.

S.'s poems treat ideals and ideas–often the idea of revolution (Europe had been in the grip of reaction since the fall of Napoleon). But they usually employ allegory or parable; and their imagery is abstract or general, symbolic rather than descriptive. The result is a peculiarly ethereal beauty. *Alastor* (1816) condemns the self-absorbed idealist who can be destroyed by contact with reality. *The Revolt of Islam* (1818, the revised version of *Laon and Cynthia*) and the verse drama *Prometheus Unbound* (1820) predict the eventual triumph of revolution. *Epipsychidion* (1821) defends free love between complementary souls. *Adonais* (1821) is an elegy on the death of Keats, which S. blames on the savage reviews of magazines like *Blackwood's.* The essay *A Defence of Poetry* (1821) argued the necessity of imaginative art and describes the poet as the world's unacknowledged legislator. S.'s works include the play *The Cenci* (1819), an imitation of Shakespeare dealing with incest; *Julian and Maddalo,* an account of one of S.'s meetings with Byron; *Lines written in the Euganean Hills*; *Stanzas written in dejection, near Naples*; the unfinished *Triumph of Life*; *Ozymandias*; and the famous lyrics *Ode to the West Wind, Ode to a Skylark* and *The Cloud.*

Shenstone William (1714–63). English poet, author of *The Schoolmistress* and *Pastoral Ballad.*

Shepheard's Calendar, The (1579). Poem by *Spenser. John Clare wrote *The Shepherd's Calendar* (1827).

Mary Wollstonecraft Shelley

Percy Bysshe Shelley

Shinn. *Revue* (1908)

Shoedsack. *King Kong*

Sheraton. Illustration from *The Cabinet-Maker and Upholsterer's Drawing Book*

Sheridan

Shepherd Arthur (1880–1958). U.S. composer of 2 symphonies, no. 1, *Horizons* (1927), containing cowboy themes; *Triptychon* for voice and string quartet to poems by Tagore, etc.

Shepherd John. Mid-16th-c. English composer. He wrote much church music for both the English and Latin rites.

Sheraton Thomas (*c.* 1751–1806). English furniture designer. Very little is known of his life, and it is not even clear how far he himself was active as a craftsman. He influenced a generation of furniture design through his important *The Cabinet-Maker and Upholsterer's Drawing Book* (1791). The S. style is characterized by slender elegance, graceful curves and a preference for woods capable of a high polish, e.g. satin-wood. Subsequent publs by S. carried designs increasingly affected by the taste for bizarre and exotic effects of the early 19th-c. 'picturesque' style.

Sheridan Ann (1915–). U.S. film star, mainly in light-comedy roles, e.g. *I Married a Male War Bride*

Sheridan Richard Brinsley Butler (1751–1816). Irish playwright, a famous wit and able orator, the son of an actor and of the writer Mrs Frances S. (1724–66). S. succeeded Garrick as the manager of Drury Lane; he became an M.P. in 1780 and was Treasurer of the Navy in 1806–7.
S.'s plays are among the supreme examples of the comedy of manners, gracefully and wittily castigating the vices and follies of the age. His masterpiece, *The School for Scandal* (1777), contrasts the Surface brothers, the hypocritical and intriguing Joseph, ultimately exposed, and the feckless but warm-hearted Charles. *The Rivals* (1775) satirizes Lydia Languish's novel-bred romanticism, which forces the well-born Captain Absolute to pose as a half-pay ensign willing to elope; it also contains Mrs Malaprop, a character whose use of long, wrong words has immortalized her. S.'s works include the comic opera *The Duenna* (1775) and the farcical play *The Critic* (1779), which sends up critics and playwrights alike.

Sherlock Holmes, The Adventures of (1891). Coll. of detective stories by Conan *Doyle.

Sherriff R(obert) C(edric) (1896–). English playwright and novelist, author of *Journey's End* (1928), the most successful play about World War I; it portrays the reactions of a group of British soldiers in a dug-out.

Sherwood Robert E(mmet) (1896–1955). U.S. playwright whose most important works defend democracy and attack Fascism and militarism. They include *The Road to Rome* (1927); *Idiot's Delight* (1936); *Abe Lincoln in Illinois* (1938); and *There Shall Be No Night* (1940). *The Petrified Forest* (1935) demonstrates S.'s social conscience. Works include the film scripts *Rebecca* and *The Best Years of Our Lives.*

She Stoops to Conquer, or The Mistakes of a Night (1773). Comedy by *Goldsmith.

She Wore a Yellow Ribbon (1949). Film directed by J. *Ford.

Shields Frederic James (1833–1911). English painter and illustrator influenced by Rossetti.

Shiels George (1886–1949). Irish dramatist; his best-known plays are *The New Gossoon* (1930), *The Rugged Path* (1940) and *The Summit* (1941).

Shindo Kaneto (1912–). Japanese film director of *The Children of Hiroshima* (his birthplace) in 1952. This received a wide, often non-theatrical showing for its depiction of the aftermath of bombing. Half a dozen films later, *The Island* (1961) gained attention for its extremely austere treatment of the theme of man against nature.

Shinn Everett (1876–1953). U.S. painter, member of The Eight. Influenced by Degas, he abandoned urban realism for subjects from the theatre and theatrical decoration.

Shirley (1849). Novel by Charlotte *Brontë.

Shirley James (1596–1666). English playwright. S. wrote some good lyrics and a large number of plays, including the tragedies *The Maid's Revenge* (1626), *Love's Cruelty* (1631) and *The Cardinall* (1641), and the comedies *The Gamester* (1633) and *The Lady of Pleasure* (1635).

Shoedsack E(rnest) B(eaumont) (1893–). U.S. film director. S. and M. C. Cooper made a famous long documentary, *Grass* (1925), about the migrations of a Persian tribe. *Chang* (1927) was shot in Siam, but *The Four Feathers* (1929) was a fiction film. They also made the famous monster movie *King Kong* (1933). S.'s *The Most Dangerous Game* or *The Hounds of Zaroff* (1932, co-directed by Irving Pichel) is known for its refined sado-masochistic fantasies.

Shoemaker's Holiday, The, or A pleasant comedy of the Gentle Craft (publ. 1600). Comedy by *Dekker.

Sholokhov Mikhail Alexandrovich (1905–). Soviet novelist. S.'s works are in the tradition of 19th-c. realism; his masterpiece *The Quiet Don* (1928–40; trs. as 2 books, *And Quiet Flows the Don*, 1934, and *The Don Flows Home to the Sea*, 1940) is an epic account of the Don Cossacks during the 1917 Revolution and the Civil War. S. portrays existence as a savage, brutal and destructive struggle, redeemed only by nature's power to create new life. His works include the story colls *Tales of the Don* (1925) and *The Azure Steppe* (1926), and the novel about collectivization during the first 5-year plan, *Virgin Soil Upturned* (1932–3; 1935; also called *Seeds of Tomorrow*).

Shors (1939). Film directed by A. *Dovzhenko.

Shortest Way with the Dissenters, The (1702). Pamphlet by *Defoe.

Shorthouse Joseph Henry (1834–1903). English novelist, author of *John Inglesant* (1880), an historical novel set in the time of Charles I and Cromwell.

short octave. An arrangement frequent on keyboard instruments, especially organs, up to the 19th c. Certain notes, unusable as key-notes on an untempered instrument (*temperament), were omitted from the bottom 8ve of the instrument to bring the bass key-notes of the other keys within reach of the player's hand.

Shostakovich Dmitri (1906–). Soviet composer. Born in St Petersburg (Leningrad), he studied there at the Conservatory, where Glazunov was among his teachers. While still a student, he achieved wide acclaim for his 1st symphony (1926), a work of Mahlerian proportions, exhibiting embryonically characteristic traits–grandeur, mock-gaiety, nostalgia and a sarcasm and harshness which were to make him the centre of many controversies, e.g. with his 2nd symphony (1927) which celebrated the 10th anniversary of the October Revolution in the most dissonant terms, with his opera *The Nose* (1930), after *Gogol's satire against bureaucracy, with the ballet *The Golden Age* (1930), a sarcastic attack on bourgeois culture and Fascism, and the more personal *Lady Macbeth of Minsk* (1934), a near-pornographic tragic opera on the Leskov story of an ambitious woman who murders her husband. It received stormy receptions in the U.S. and in the U.S.S.R. and S. was criticized for failing to conform to the standards of *socialist realism. In 1937 he was made professor at the Leningrad Conservatory, and his 5th symphony was an international success. On this occasion Soviet critics praised S.'s heroic optimism and formal clarity. The idea of giving an extra-musical interpretation, even a propagandist one was not foreign to S., who once said that all composers uphold a political theory whether they know it or not. S. certainly did this fully consciously; his 7th symphony (1941) was written during and about the siege of Leningrad, his 11th (1957) about the 1905 Revolution, and the 12th (1961) about the Revolution of 1917. The 10th (1953) also has a conscious epic quality which is almost programmatic. His 9th symphony on the other hand, was short and almost neo-classical. Other works include the concertos: for piano and trumpet (1933), a satirical piece, for violin (1955), possibly his most pleasing work, and for cello (1959). Piano works: 3 fantastic dances (1922), 24 preludes (1933), 24 preludes and fugues (1951). He has also written much chamber music and scores for many films.

Shoulder Arms (1918). Short film directed by *Chaplin.

Showboat. In the U.S., throughout the 19th c. and even up to the 1930s, riverboats plied on the Mississippi and Ohio rivers, carrying plays and actors to outlying, originally pioneer districts. There was often a theatre on the boat itself.

Shropshire Lad, A (1896). Book of poems by A. E. *Housman.

Shudi Burkhardt: *Broadwood

shuttering. In building, the use of wooden boards as a mould for concrete; when the concrete has set they are removed.

Showboat. The *Mark Twain*, a reproduction of a typical showboat

Shuttering used as a decorative motif. Le Corbusier, Unité d'Habitation, Marseille

Dmitri Shostakovich

Mikhail Sholokhov

Sickert. *The Old Bedford.* Also George *Moore

AN
APOLOGIE
for Poetrie.
Written by the right noble, vertuous, and learned, Sir Phillip Sidney, Knight.
Odi profanum vulgus, et arceo.
AT LONDON,
Printed for Henry Olney, and are to be sold at his shop in Paules Church-yard, at the signe of the George, neere to Cheap-gate.
Anno. 1595.

Sir Philip Sidney (anon. portrait, *c.* 1577); and title-page of the 1st ed. of *An Apologie for Poetrie*

Jean Sibelius

Sibelius Jean (1865–1957). Finnish composer. He studied at the Helsinki Conservatory, and in Berlin and Vienna. In 1892 came his 1st concert and in 1897 he received a government pension to devote himself to composition. S. worked towards a Finnish national-romantic style, e.g. the symphonic poem *Kullervo* (1892) is based on the **Kalevala*. His romanticism is economic in expression and his later work in particular is tautly constructed; outstanding is his use of orchestral colour and the frequent changes of mood within a piece.
S.'s greatest work is in the symphonies: no. 1 in E min. (1899), no. 2 in D (1902), no. 3 in C (1907), no. 4 in A min. (1911), no. 5 in E♭ (1919), no. 6 in D min. (1923) and no. 7 in C (1924). His best-known symphonic poems are: *A Saga* (1892), *The Swan of Tuonela* (1893), *Finlandia* (1899), *Pohjola's Daughter* (1906) and *Tapiola* (1925); his other works include a violin concerto in D min. (1903), the orchestral suite *Karelia* (1893) and *Valse triste* for orchestra (1904).

Siberechts Jan (1627–*c.* 1700). Antwerp landscape painter who settled in England and was one of the earliest interpreters of the English landscape and country-houses.

De Sica. *Bicycle Thieves*

Sica Vittorio de (1902–). Italian film actor and director. S. has acted in films since 1928 and directed since 1940. Apart from *I Bambini ci guardano* (1943), which acquired a retrospective reputation, his 1st important film is *Sciuscia* (1946) which with **Roma Città Aperta* introduced to the world Italian neo-realism, a trend produced by economic necessity, which dictated real locations and minimal resources, as well as conviction. His most successful films are: *Bicycle Thieves* (1948), *Umberto D* (1952), *Il Tetto* (1956). Although sometimes generalized and sentimental, they are for the most part honest and moving, observant about people and their problems.

Siegel. *Riot in Cell Block 11*

siciliano or **siciliana.** 17th-c. dance form in a moderate tempo and nostalgic in mood; it sometimes figured in the *suite, or took the place of an adagio in earlier forms of the sonata and concerto.

Sickert Walter (1860–1942). English artist, the leading British impressionist painter. S. studied under Whistler and was much influenced by his friend Degas, whose wit and meticulous draughtsmanship he appreciated fully. He employed impressionist techniques to portray interiors, often of the theatre, using, however, sombre tones to express the nuances of colour rather than light. S. also painted landscapes and townscapes in London, Dieppe and Venice. In 1911 he helped to found the Camden Town Group and was also a member of the New English Art Club and the London Group. In London, after 1905, he was associated with Spencer Gore, Lucien Pissarro and Harold Gilman. The coll. *A Free House!* (1947) reveals that S. was a fluent writer on artistic subjects.

Sickness unto Death, The (1848). Book by Kierkegaard.

Siddons Mrs (Sarah) (1755–1831). English actress and sister of the actor J. P. *Kemble; she married the actor William Siddons in 1773. Her 1st London success was at Drury Lane in 1782. She then quickly established herself as a great tragic actress. Her most famous parts were Lady Macbeth, Queen Katherine in *Henry VIII*, Desdemona and Volumnia in *Coriolanus*. She was the subject of Reynolds's painting *The Tragic Muse*.

Sidney Sir Philip (1554–86). English poet and prose writer, a courtier, diplomat and soldier highly regarded by contemporaries; he was killed at the battle of Zutphen. S.'s works circulated but were not publ. during his lifetime. His *Astrophel and Stella* (1591), the 1st sonnet sequence in English, operates on 2 levels, the personal–it is apparently addressed to Penelope Devereux, daughter of the earl of Essex–and the symbolic, in which the poet explores the nature of love. S. also wrote *The Arcadia* (1590), a prose romance of knightly love and adventure, and *An Apologie for Poetrie* (1595), which defends poetry, analyses English prosody, and discusses contemporary styles.

Siegel Donald (1912–). U.S. film director. S. was an editor who started directing in 1945. Many of his best films have been crime pictures, like *Baby-face Nelson* (1957). He has also succeeded with a science-fiction film, *Invasion of the Body Snatchers* (1955) and a prison exposé, *Riot in Cell Block 11* (1954). Since a thriller, *Edge of Eternity* (1959), he has worked well on larger budgets especially in a war film, *Hell is for Heroes* (1962).

Mrs Siddons as the Tragic Muse: mezzotint after Reynolds

Signac. *Palace of the Popes, Avignon*

Siegfried–die Nibelungen part 1 (1924). Film directed by F. *Lang.

Siegfried Idyll. Orchestral work by Wagner performed (1870) for his wife Cosima to commemorate the birth (1869) of their son, Siegfried.

Siena, school of. School of Italian painting which flourished between the 13th and 15th cs and for a time rivalled Florence, though it was more conservative, being inclined towards the decorative beauty and elegant grace of late Gothic art. Its most important representatives include Duccio, whose work shows Byzantine influence; his pupil Simone Martini; Pietro and Ambrogio Lorenzetti; Taddeo and Domenico Bartolo; Sassetta; and Matteo di Giovanni. In the 16th c. the mannerists Beccafumi and Sodoma worked there.

Siena cathedral Italy. One of the few outstanding examples of Gothic ecclesiastical architecture in Italy, begun early in the 13th c. Its most notable features are the hexagonal dome over the crossing (which takes in the aisle space as well), its horizontal bands of light and dark marble, and the prevailing use of the round arch, a continuation of Romanesque traditions. The W. front (lower part 1284–1300; upper 1377–80) reflects French models (3 portals and gables) in a thoroughly Italian way: it is lavishly covered with mosaic and sculpture. To the S. of the church the half-finished nave of a yet larger church remains, the intention being to convert the whole of the present cathedral into a transept. S. cathedral contains famous works by Nicolo *Pisano and Pinturicchio; *Duccio's *Maestà* originally stood as its altarpiece.

Sienkiewicz Henryk (Adam Aleksander Pius) (1846–1916). Polish novelist awarded the Nobel prize in 1905. In Poland S.'s most admired works are novels of the Polish past, but in the West he is known as the author of *Quo Vadis?* (1895; 1896), a best-selling novel, 3 times made into successful films, about the Roman Christians under Nero.

sight reading. The performance of a musical score 'at sight', an essential ability for a professional musician.

Signac Paul (1863–1935). French painter who joined Seurat and with him worked out the theoretical principles of *neo-impressionism which he defined in *D'Eugène Delacroix au néo-impressionnisme* (1899). He was the most rigid exponent of divisionism.

Signorelli Luca (1441–1523). Italian painter, pupil of Piero della Francesca. S. anticipated Michelangelo in his interest in nude figures in action, though he was not entirely successful in his attempts to depict movement. His work finds its most complete expression in the famous fresco cycle at Orvieto cathedral (1499–1503), a series of semicircular compositions conveying his vision of life, death, damnation and resurrection. The story is told in a harsh, brutal manner which emphasizes the solemnity and horror of the subject. S.'s interest in the formal qualities of dramatic action pervades his religious compositions and portraits. S. worked on the frescoes in the Sistine Chapel in the 1480s.

Signoret Simone (1921–). French actress of warm beauty, ability and experience; she manages to survive frequent casting in bitchy roles. Some of her best performances have been in *Casque d'Or* (1952), *Les Diaboliques* (1954) and *Room at the Top* (1959).

Sigtenhorst Meyer Bernhard van de (1888–1953). Dutch composer whose music, in a nationalistic idiom, includes a *Stabat Mater* (1918) for a capella choir; he also ed. Sweelinck's keyboard music.

Sikelianos Angelos (1884–1951). Greek poet. All S.'s verse reflects his absorption with the Greek tradition, his study of the earliest Greek history and philosophy, and his struggle to deduce from them a meaningful and fruitful way of life. Works include *Hymn to Artemis Orthia* and *The Sacred Way*.

Silbermann Gottfried (1683–1753). The outstanding member of a brilliant family of German instrument builders. Besides superb organs (1 survives in Freiberg cathedral) he built clavichords and the 1st German pianos.

Silcher Philipp Friedrich (1789–1860). German composer best known for his composed 'folk' songs, particularly 'Loreley' (to Heine's words), and as an important collector and ed. of true folk-songs.

Si le grain ne meurt (1924). Autobiographical book by André Gide.

Signorelli. *The Damned* (Orvieto)

Siena cathedral

Ignazio Silone

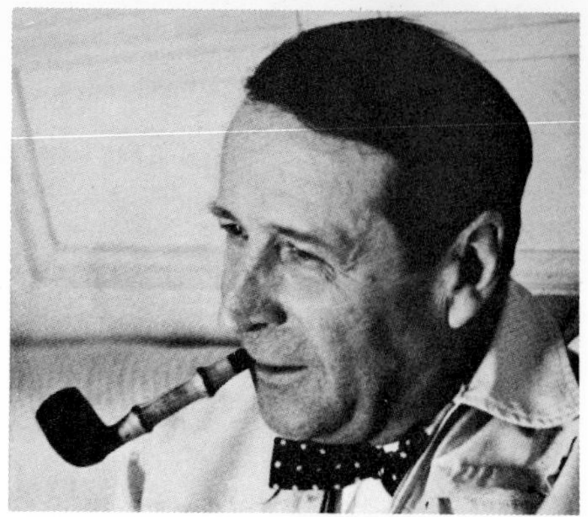

Georges Simenon

Silhouette of Caspar Friedrich Wolff

Silence, The (1963). Film directed by I. *Bergman.

Silence de la Mer, Le (1947). Film directed by J.-P. *Melville.

Silence est d'Or, Le (1947). Film directed by R. *Clair.

Silences de Colonel Bramble, Les (1918). Novel by André Maurois.

silhouette. A profile outline of a face, cut out of black paper or painted or drawn from shadow. The medium was at its most popular in the 18th c. and early 19th c. and derives its name from Étienne de Silhouette (d. 1767), an unpopular French finance minister, whose hobby was cut-out portraiture.

Silius Italicus Titus Catius Asconius (*c.* 25–101). Roman poet, for some years an important if time-serving politician; his epic the *Punica* is poetically correct and pure in language (and therefore of scholarly interest) but derivative and uninspired.

Silver point. Detail of Dürer's *Caspar Sturm*

Sill Edward Rowland (1841–87). U.S. poet. S. had a delicate lyrical style; his poems often reflect his religious doubts. Among his works are *The Hermitage and Other Poems* (1868) and *The Venus of Milo and Other Poems* (1883).

Sillanpää Frans Eemil (1888–1964). Finnish novelist, awarded the Nobel prize in 1939. His novels of peasant life include *Hurskas kurjuus* (1919; *Meek Heritage,* 1939) and *Nuorena Nukkunut* (1931; *Fallen Asleep While Young,* 1933).

Sillitoe Alan (1928–). English novelist, author of the best-selling *Saturday Night and Sunday Morning* (1958), about working-class life in Nottingham. Like the short story *The Loneliness of the Long-Distance Runner* (1959) it describes anarchical and resentful feelings in revolt against smooth and omnipresent authority.

Silone Ignazio (1900–). Italian novelist widely known since his 1st novel, *Fontamara* (1930–6), an acute and moving study of the impact of Fascism on a simple peasant community. Most of S.'s novels deal with problems of political engagement and personal morality in a world in which man's freedom and spiritual integrity are constantly threatened.

Silva Antonio José da (1705–39). Portuguese playwright born in Brazil, a victim of the Inquisition (he was strangled and burnt). He wrote comedies, also called operas, since the dialogue was interspersed with music and singing.

Silva Feliciano de (1492?–1558?). Spanish poet and novelist, the author of several high-flown romances including *Amadis de Grecia* (1530?) and *Don Florisel* (1532); they had an immense success all over Europe and were read by Sidney, Spenser and Shakespeare, who borrowed ideas and themes from them.

silver. The aesthetic qualities of the metal and the relative easiness of working it, were early appreciated by man, and it was used either for jewellery or for drinking-vessels, and was the mark of riches and power. By the time of the Romans, it had become so plentiful that it was even used for furniture. In the middle ages, with the decline in living conditions, the chief user was the Church, and not until the 16th c. was there a substantial output for secular purposes, thanks to the enormous supplies from the Americas. From then, and especially in the 18th c., every European country made great quantities of s. ware, France and England setting the fashion and producing the finest examples.

Silver Age. Term used of Latin literature of the 1st c. A.D. covering such names as Livy and Tacitus. Very broadly speaking, writers of this period show grammatical idiosyncrasies and love of epigram.

silver point. 15th–16th-c. drawing technique; Dürer was a master of the medium. A silver pointed pencil (sometimes gold or lead) was used on paper, often tinted, prepared with an abrasive compound. Although heightened effects were obtained with opaque white, s. p. depended fundamentally on line; shading for example was possible only by hatching. The s.-p. line was indelible.

Simenon Georges (1903–). French-speaking Belgian writer, born in Liège, now living in Switzerland, after spending a number of years in America. One of the most prolific writers of the 20th c., he can complete a short novel in 11 days. His crime fiction has made him world famous. At first, he was considered as a purely commercial writer, but his sense of

Upton Sinclair

Singier. *Dutch Town* (1952–3)

Frank Sinatra in *Johnny Concho*

atmosphere and his tragic vision have won him critical respect. He is the creator of the detective hero Maigret, as well known in the English-speaking countries as in France.

Simmons Jean (1929–). English actress whose film career began with *Caesar and Cleopatra* (1945). Although now working in America, she remains a 'nice English girl'; playing on stage and screen, she has progressed and steadily matured. Her pictures include *Great Expectations* (1946), *Hamlet* (1948), *The Robe* (1953) and *Spartacus* (1960).

Simms William Gilmore (1806–70). U.S. novelist. A prolific author of Southern romances, G. exploited the traditions of his region in the manner of Scott and Fenimore Cooper. His works include *Guy Rivers* (1834); *The Partisan* (1835); *Beauchampe* (1842) and *History of South Carolina* (1840).

Simoni Renato (1875–1952). Italian playwright and a leading dramatic critic. He wrote only 5 plays; they have some interesting affinities with Pirandello's work.

Simonides (*c*. 556–*c*. 468 B.C.). Greek lyric poet born in Ceos, a highly paid professional writer famous for his *epigrams, especially the epitaph on the Three Hundred who fought and died at Thermopylae.

Simplicissimus. Common abbreviation of the title of a novel by *Grimmelshausen.

Simpson N(orman) F(rederick) (1919–). English playwright. Plays such as *A Resounding Tinkle* (1958) and *One Way Pendulum* (1960) present ordinary people in absurd situations and use dialogue of topsy-turvy logic rich with implied satire as well as extremely funny.

simultanéisme. Robert *Delaunay's name for orphism. Also a literary movement: H.-M. *Barzun.

Sinatra Frank (1915–). U.S. singer (the 1st crooner to elicit screams) and film actor whose style is adaptable to very diverse roles – drama, e.g. *From Here to Eternity*, comedy, e.g. *A Hole in the Head* (1959) and musicals, e.g. *Pal Joey* (1957), *On The Town* (1950).

Sinclair Upton (Beall) (1878–). U.S. novelist. S.'s most important works are novels of protest written from a Socialist viewpoint, especially *The Jungle* (1906), a best-seller which attacked the degradation of unskilled labour in Chicago's meat-packing industry. *King Coal* (1917) and *Oil!* (1927) have similar plots. *Boston* (1928) is a version of the Sacco-Vanzetti case. S. has also written the *Lanny Budd* novels, from *World's End* (1940) to *O Shepherd Speak!* (1949), a panoramic sequence which depicts 20th-c. Western society; and also an autobiography (1962).

Sindbad of the Sea. The tale of Sindbad the Sailor, one of *The *Arabian Nights' Entertainments.*

Sinding Christian (1856–1941). Norwegian composer whose piano piece *Rustle of Spring* is very popular. He also wrote operas, violin concertos, etc.

sinfonia or *symphony. A musical term used in the 17th and 18th c. to designate an instrumental passage in an opera or oratorio; e.g. the pastoral symphony in Handel's *Messiah*, or what is now called 'the overture'. A SINFONIA CONCERTANTE is a work in symphonic form with 1 or more solo instruments.

Sinfonia Antartica (1953). *Vaughan Williams's 7th symphony.

sinfonietta. A short or unelaborate symphony.

Singer Alexander (1932–). U.S. film director. His 1st film, *A Cold Wind in August* (1960), about an affair between a stripper and an adolescent, was made quickly in New York, and had a good critical and financial success.

Singier Gustave (1909–). Belgian-born French painter, of the school of Paris. Like Manessier, Bazaine, Le Moal and others he is concerned with abstracting shapes, colours and associations from his subjects and blending them into a non-figurative design of unified texture. He has also produced tapestry, stained glass and stage designs.

Singin' in the Rain (1952). Film directed by S. *Donen and G. *Kelly.

single warp knot. A knot used in hand-made pile carpet weaving in most Spanish and some medieval European wall carpets. Knots are tied on alternate warp threads; successive rows,

Single warp knot

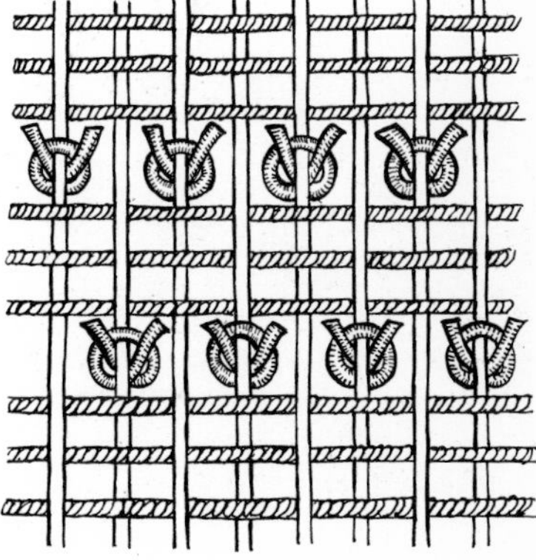

Sintenis. *The Young Ox*

Siqueiros. *Echo of a Scream* (1937)

Sisley. *The Flood* (Louvre). Also *impressionism

The *Sistine Madonna*

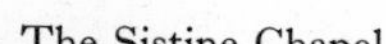

The Sistine Chapel

separated by several lines of weft, are tied on the intervening alternate warp.

Singspiel. German stage entertainment similar to the English ballad opera. In the late 16th c. (J. *Ayrer) it was stimulated by the *jigs of English strolling players. The form, essentially a light opera with much spoken dialogue, was fully developed during the 18th c., again influenced by the English ballad opera; Mozart's *Il Seraglio* is the greatest example.

Sinigaglia Leone (1868–1944). Italian composer much of whose early work is in a style reminiscent of Brahms and Dvořák. His popularity rested on the 6 colls of Piedmontese folk-melodies he publ.

Sintenis Renée (1888–). German sculptor of small bronzes of animals in movement and portrait heads.

Siodmak Robert (1900–). U.S.-born German film director. S. was the director of *Menschen am Sonntag* (1929), a dramatized documentary on which Wilder, Schufftan, Ulmer and Zinnemann worked. He made one more German film and some in Paris before moving to Hollywood (1940) and making ornate thrillers like *Phantom Lady* (1944) and *The Spiral Staircase* (1946) and more realistic ones like *The Killers* (1946) and *Cry of the City* (1948). After a burlesque, *The Crimson Pirate* (1952), he returned to work in Europe. His films are unambitious in subject-matter but have flair and solid craftsmanship.

Siqueiros David Alfaro (1896–). Mexican painter. He fought in the Mexican Revolutionary army and his left-wing political and trade union activities have led to frequent periods of imprisonment and exile; as a result he has worked all over the Americas. In Europe (1919) he and Diego Rivera were able to agree on principles, both being determined to create a public art derived from *Pre-Columbian tradition. Since 1922 S. has painted many huge, turbulent, crowded murals, e.g. *The Mexican Revolution* (Mus. of Anthropology and History, Mexico).

Sirk Douglas (1900–). Danish-born film director. S. made films in Germany, etc., then a Hollywood anti-Nazi film, *Hitler's Madman* (1943). After 10 years of smallish projects S. remade J. Stahl's *Magnificent Obsession* (1954) –suitably enough, for S., like Stahl, has built his career above all on lush melodramas. Perhaps his work reached its peak in 1958 in *Pylon* or *The Tarnished Angels* (1958), the only good film made from a Faulkner novel. *A Time to Love and a Time to Die* (1958), from Remarque, had a baroque symbolism.

sirventés. Medieval Provençal verse form used to treat serious subjects.

Sisley Alfred (1839/40–99). Painter born in Paris of English parents. While a student under Gleyre (1863–4) he met Monet, Renoir and Bazille and painted with them near Fontainebleau. He made 4 visits to England (1871–97); from 1880 he lived at Moret-sur-Loing. Influenced at first by Corot, he became a central figure of the impressionist group, exhibiting with them (1874, 1876, 1877, 1883). The paintings of the floods at Marly (examples at the Tate and Courtauld Gal., London) are paramount examples of impressionism, freshly painted in clear colour, but his landscapes are mostly of the Île de France.

Sister Carrie (1900). Novel by Theodore *Dreiser.

Sistine Chapel. A private chapel of the Pope, also used for Papal elections. It is a long plain room covered with a tunnel-vault pierced by windows. Built in 1473 for Sixtus IV (whence the name) it was decorated (1481–3) with large frescoes by *Pinturicchio, *Botticelli, *Signorelli, *Ghirlandaio, *Perugino and *Rosselli. Between 1508 and 1512 the ceiling was painted by *Michelangelo in 9 main scenes (from the Creation to Noah) surrounded by Prophets, Sybils and nude youths. In 1536–41 Michelangelo returned to paint *The Last Judgement* on the E. wall behind the altar.

Sistine Madonna (*c.* 1513). Painting by *Raphael.

Sitwell Dame Edith (1887–1964). English poet and critic. Her poetry depends for its appeal on metrical skill, arresting images, and sound, and an initiated audience. The 'meaning' she attaches to sound is arbitrary, however, depending on accent and association. Music has helped to fix both more firmly, e.g. **Façade*. Her later *Three poems of the Atomic Age* succeed in communicating the significance of a 'universal moment'. Although she has had no direct influence on today's poets, her earlier radical examination of poetic technique was important.

Sitwell Sir Osbert (1893–). English satirical novelist and autobiographical writer, brother of the above; works include the autobiographical series beginning with *Left Hand, Right Hand!* (1944) and *The Scarlet Tree* (1945).

Sitwell Sacheverell (1897–). English writer, brother of Edith and Osbert S. His poetry often treats mystical or exotic subjects, but his most important books are perhaps the prose descriptions or evocations of places and works of art.

Six, The (French, 'Groupe des Six'). The 6 musicians Auric, Durey, Honegger, Milhaud, Poulenc and Tailleferre who in the early 1920s were loosely associated in a general acceptance of an aesthetic programme laid down by Cocteau, and a respect for the music of Satie.

Six Characters in Search of an Author (1921). Play by *Pirandello.

sixteen-foot stop: *organ

sixteenth note. U.S. musical term for *quaver.

sixth. A musical *interval.

Sjöberg Alf (1903–). Swedish film and theatre director. His main film output began in 1940. *The Road to Heaven* (1942) was a fine film equivalent of a religious folk-legend. On the other hand, *Frenzy* (1944), script by Ingmar Bergman, was a masochistic story of classroom victimization and tragic adolescent love. If there is little personal similarity between his films, they are all characterized by great technical expertise, and none more so than his famous adaptation of Strindberg's *Miss Julie* (1951) in which he even manages to combine present and past in a single shot. After a disastrous adaptation of Pär Lagerkvist's *Barabbas* (1953), his most notable films have been a historical tragedy, *Karin Mansdotter* (1954) and another Bergman-scripted film, *Sista paret ut* (1956).

Sjöström Victor (1879–1960). Swedish film director and actor. S. started acting and directing in the cinema in 1912 and with *Stiller was responsible for making the Swedish cinema of the next 10 years among the most important of the time. His films were very national in content, a number being taken from novels of Selma Lagerlöf. His most notable films from this period include *Ingeborg Holm* (1913), *Terje Vigen* (1916) and *The Phantom Carriage* (1920). In Hollywood from 1925, he made among others 2 films with Lillian Gish, *The Scarlet Letter* (1926) and *The Wind* (1928), and one with Garbo, *Divine Woman* (1927). He returned to Sweden in 1931 and directed 1 film there. Thereafter he worked as an actor, although he directed *Under the Red Robe* (1936) in Britain. His last film as an actor was *Wild Strawberries* (1957).

skalds. Scandinavian poets of courtly verse flourishing chiefly in Norway and Iceland between the 9th and 11th cs. Owing to the employment of *kenning and complex alliteration, metre and word order, skaldic verse was frequently esoteric and artificial. If fell into 2 main groups: the '*drápur*' and '*flokkar*', long poems for recitation to kings and chiefs, and the '*lausavísur*', single epigrammatic stanzas.

Skalkottas Nikos (1904–49). Greek composer. He studied at Berlin under Weill, Jarnach and Schoenberg. His music, given little recognition during his lifetime, consists mostly of 12-note works. It is predominantly instrumental and includes: Greek dances for orchestra; 3 piano concertos and concertos for violin and for violin and viola; and piano pieces.

Skeat Walter William (1835–1912). English scholar of Old English and Middle English. His ed. of Chaucer long remained the standard text.

Skelton John (*c.* 1460–1529). English poet, tutor of Henry VIII, rector of Diss (Norfolk) and in old age a bitter opponent of Wolsey, whom he attacked in such poems as *Colin Clout* (1522) and *Why Come Ye Not to Court?*. His characteristic verse ('Skeltonic') has short jingling irregular (basically 3-stress) lines, often dismissed as rhymed doggerel but admired by such modern poets as Robert Graves and W. H. Auden. S.'s poems include *Philip Sparrow* and *The Tunning of Elinor Rumming*, and he wrote a long morality play, *Magnificence* (1516).

skene: *Greek drama

Sjöberg. Anita Bjork in *Miss Julie*

Sjöström. Greta Garbo in *Divine Woman*

Dame Edith Sitwell:
painting by Wyndham Lewis

Sloan. *Greenwich Village Backyards.* Also *social realism

Sketch by Rubens for *Coronation of Marie de Médicis*

Slevogt. *D'Andrade in the role of Don Giovanni*

Slipware. Oven and baking dish; Staffordshire, 18th c.

Skidmore, Owings and Merrill. Inland Steel Co. Building (1954). Also *Lever House

sketch. Quick drawing or painting made as an aid to memory or a rough draught of a painting made to give the artist some idea of what the completed work will look like. Some of the s.s of artists such as Constable have a spontaneity which is lost in their finished paintings. In the case of Rubens, the full-scale compositions were frequently the work of pupils whereas his s.s were his own.

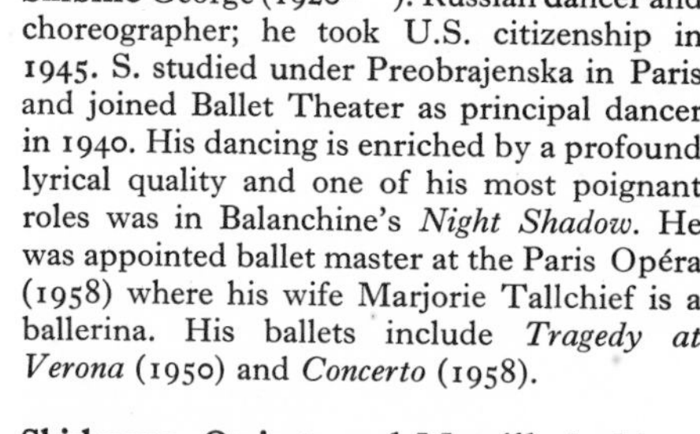

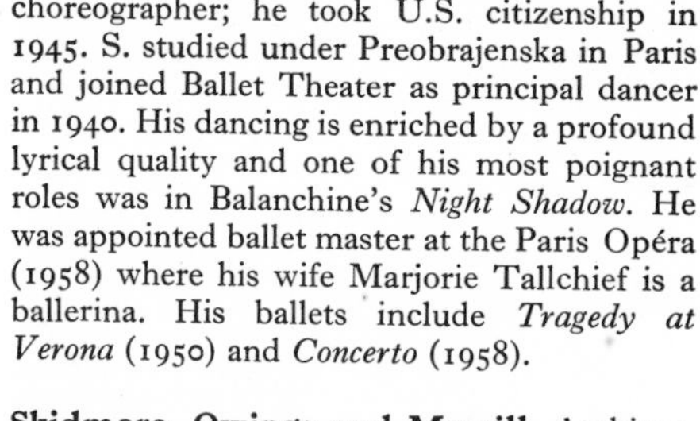

Skibine George (1920–). Russian dancer and choreographer; he took U.S. citizenship in 1945. S. studied under Preobrajenska in Paris and joined Ballet Theater as principal dancer in 1940. His dancing is enriched by a profound lyrical quality and one of his most poignant roles was in Balanchine's *Night Shadow.* He was appointed ballet master at the Paris Opéra (1958) where his wife Marjorie Tallchief is a ballerina. His ballets include *Tragedy at Verona* (1950) and *Concerto* (1958).

Skidmore, Owings and Merrill. Architectural partnership founded in 1935; it now contains some of the best architects working in America–Gordon *Bunshaft, Walter Netsch, Charles Bassett, Myron Goldsmith and others. S. O. M. built Lever House in New York in 1952, the most influential post-war building. They have refined the Lever House idea–austere machine-age luxury for big business–in a series of office buildings, culminating in the Chase Manhattan Bank (1961).

Their most recent work shows a break with their glossy, metallic tradition; most of their new buildings are concrete, sometimes, as in the Oakland Coliseum, of magnificent logic, but more often, as in the Yale Library, the designs seem wilful and confined.

Skinner Otis (1858–1942). U.S. actor; he had a long and varied career and was famous for his performance in romantic roles and in *Kismet.* S. was the father of CORNELIA OTIS S. (1901–), singer and author of several books of reminiscences.

Skin of Our Teeth, The (1942). Play by Thornton *Wilder.

Slaveykov Pencho (1866–1912). Bulgarian poet, son of PETKO (1827–95) whose trs. of the Bible (1862) was formative in the development of modern Bulgarian. Pencho's sophisticated and polished 'individualist' style was the main rival to that of I. Vázov.

Sleeping Beauty, The (*The Sleeping Princess; La Belle au Bois Dormant*). A 4-act ballet with music by Tchaikovsky and original choreography by Petipa; it was first produced in St Petersburg in 1890. One of the most lavish show pieces on the ballet stage, it has been revived by many cos. Most notable recent productions are the Royal Ballet's 1946 version and the Nijinska-Helpmann arrangement for the Cuevas Ballet (1960).

Sleepy Hollow, The Legend of (1820). Story by Washington *Irving.

Slessor Kenneth (1901–). Australian poet, journalist and critic, whose reputation as a poet who offers technical innovation and something worth saying rests mainly on work done before 1944, when *One Hundred Poems* appeared. Influenced at different times by Flecker, Yeats and Eliot, his best poetry is an original amalgam of sensuousness and irony.

Slevogt Max (1868–1932). German impressionist painter, illustrator and theatrical designer trained in Munich (1885–9) and Paris (1889). He developed a vigorous excited style which often came close to expressionism and was appropriate to the violent and erotic scenes which form a large part of his work. He also made many paintings and drawings of opera singers and musicians which owe their vitality to his ability to record a characteristic, passing gesture.

slip. In potters' terms, clay in a liquid form; used for making, coating or decorating pottery articles. If used as a medium of decoration by painting or piping, the resultant articles are called SLIPWARE.

Sloan John (1871–1951). U.S. realist painter, illustrator for newspapers in Philadelphia and New York, and cartoonist, one of the most important members of The Eight. His city scenes include *Greenwich Village Backyards* (1914; Whitney Mus., New York). His later studies of nudes show an interest in formal problems.

Slonimsky Nicolas (1894–). Russian-born U.S. musicologist, teacher, composer and conductor, in the last capacity a proponent of modern works.

Juliusz Słowacki

Christopher Smart

Bedřich Smetana

Smibert. *Mrs Elizabeth Ferne*

Słowacki Juliusz (1809–49). Polish romantic poet and dramatist, an exile after 1831, eventually settling in Paris. His great poetic achievement was recognized only at the end of the 19th c. when it exerted an enormous influence on the nascent Young Poland movement. Works include the poetical drama *Kordian* (1834) which examined the psychology of S.'s generation on the eve of the 1830 Rising; *Anhelli* (1838; 1930), a symbolic poem in impressive Biblical prose; *W Szwajcarii* (1839; *In Switzerland*, 1953), a love idyll; *Ojciec zadżumionych* (1839; *The Father of the Plague-Stricken*, 1930), a romantic tale in verse; 2 poetical dramas, *Balladyna* (1839) and *Lilla Weneda* (1840); an epic satire, *Beniowski* (1841), mystical plays and many lyrics.

Sluchevsky Konstantin Konstantinovich (1837–1904). Russian poet of some talent and originality, hampered by poor technique; the only important poet of the generation after that of Nekrassov and Fet. S. wrote mainly on philosophical and metaphysical themes.

slur. In musical notation, a sign which indicates that a group of separate notes are to be played in a smoothly connected manner. A s., like a *tie, is a curved line.

Sluter Claus (died *c.* 1405). Netherlands sculptor in the service of Philip the Bold of Burgundy. He assisted Jean de Marville in constructing the portal of the Carthusian monastery at Champmol, completing it in 1400 with the addition of 4 figures. The duke's tomb (Dijon Mus.), begun in 1384, was only completed in 1411 after S.'s death. Carved in black and white marble, the duke's effigy was placed on a slab surmounting a rectangular base flanked by figures in different attitudes of grief. This tomb and the well-head, *The Well of Moses* (1395–1406), with its powerful figures of the Prophets, anticipating Michelangelo, were influential well into the 16th c. S. was a great innovator in the expressive handling of drapery, realism of gesture and rendering of character type. He can be regarded as the founder of the Burgundian school.

Smart Christopher (1722–71). English poet. S. became a fellow of Pembroke College, Cambridge (1745). He went to London (*c.* 1749) where he earned a living by writing for periodicals, was confined in a lunatic asylum (1756–8), and at last died in a debtors' prison. S.'s best work–poems in praise of God strongly influenced by Hebrew poetry–was written in the asylum; it includes the ardent and sustained *A Song to David* (1763) and the long religious poem *Jubilate Agno* (publ. only in 1939).

Smart John (1741–1811). English portrait painter and miniaturist, friend of Cosway. He worked in India from 1784 to 1797.

Smet Gustave de (1877–1943). Belgian expressionist painter. During World War I he stayed with Van den Berghe in Holland, where he came into contact with German expressionism. After the war he worked with Permeke and other expressionists at Laethem-Saint-Martin. He painted many scenes of rural life, stylized in a manner reminiscent of child art.

Smet. *Girl in Blue* (1935)

Smetana Bedřich (1824–84). Czech composer; a fierce patriot (taking part in the 1848 Revolution) and the 1st composer of the Czech national school. He was a gifted musician from childhood; he ran his own music school in Prague, for a time worked as teacher and conductor in Sweden, and finally settled in Prague in 1861, later opening another school there. At the age of 50 he became deaf and in the last years insane. S.'s music, particularly the early symphonic poems, proclaims his allegiance to the school of Liszt; but increasingly the monumental forms of his symphonic idiom were affected by the spirit of Czech folk-music. His works include: 10 operas, among them the world-famous *The Bartered Bride* (1866), about a village romance, and *The Kiss* (1876); 4 symphonic poems, including *My Country* (1879) in 6 sections; choral works, etc., and 2 string quartets, no. 1 being subtitled 'From my Life' (1876).

Smibert John (1688–1751?). Scottish portrait painter, a follower of Kneller, who worked in Italy and London before going to America in 1728 and settling in Boston. He established the New England tradition of portrait painting.

Smiles Samuel (1812–1904). Scottish writer, author of a number of biographies including *Self-help* (1859), intended to demonstrate that the humblest person could rise in the world and accomplish great deeds. S.'s *Lives of the Great Engineers* (1861–2) is still an important source-book.

Smiles of a Summer Night (1955). Film directed by I. *Bergman.

Sluter. *The Well of Moses.* Also *drapery

Sir Matthew Smith. *Model Waking* (1924–5)

Sir Matthew Smith. *Fitzroy Street Nude No. 1* (1916)

Smirke Sir Robert (1781–1867). English architect. He held several important official posts and was extremely successful. His style is usually a dignified but uninspired neo-classical, e.g. the main front of the British Museum, King's College, London (an extension of Somerset House) and much of the Inner Temple, London.

Smith Adam (1723–90). Scottish economist, author of *The Wealth of Nations* (1776), which was the 1st complete exposition of economics and contains the essential doctrine of 19th-c. economic individualism.

Smith A(rthur) J(ames) M(arshall) (1902–). Canadian poet who used new techniques to express attitudes radically different from prevailing late Victorianism. Dilemmas of social man, particularly urban man, replaced nature as the poet's concern. *A Sort of Ecstasy* expresses a belief in lonely integrity.

Smith Alexander (1830–67). Scottish poet; his *City Poems* (1857) give a gloomy picture of mid-19th-c. Glasgow.

Smith Bessie (*c.* 1900–37). U.S. blues singer, generally considered the greatest jazz singer before Billie Holiday. Her majestic voice and mastery of vocal inflection are displayed in the many recordings she made at the peak of her success between 1924 and 1927.

Smith Charles Henry (1826–1903). U.S. writer; as 'Bill Arp' he for many years contributed humorous dialect 'letters' to Georgia newspapers.

Smith David (1906–65). U.S. sculptor, a pioneer in the field of metal sculpture. Originally a painter, he turned to reliefs and free-standing structures in the mid 1930s; he held his 1st one-man exhibition in 1938. His work ranges from the semi-representational, sometimes almost surrealist, to a monumental abstraction in his last years.

Smith Edward Tyrrell (1804–77). English theatre manager. He owned several theatres presenting a diversity of programmes. S. instituted the morning performance, which later became the modern matinée.

Smith, 'Father'. The name given to Bernhard Schmidt (*c.* 1630–1708), a German organ builder who worked in England from 1660.

Smith F(rancis) Hopkinson (1838–1915). U.S. novelist. His works, realistic stories using local colour, include *Colonel Carter of Cartersville* (1891), *Tom Grogan* (1896) and *The Tides of Barnegat* (1906).

Smith John (1580–1631). English explorer and soldier of fortune who publicized the settlement of the American colonies. In his *General Historie of Virginia . . .* (1624) S. describes his rescue from the Red Indians by their princess, Pocahontas.

Smith John Christopher (originally Johann Christoph Schmid) (1712–95). German-born composer, brought to England by his father, a friend of Handel. S. was Handel's pupil and amanuensis in his blindness.

Smith Logan Pearsall (1865–1946). U.S. critic and essayist who became a British national in 1913. S. made an international reputation for his fastidious and witty use of language. His works include *All Trivia* (1934); his autobiography, *Unforgotten Years* (1938); and 2 books on language, *The English Language* (1912) and *Words and Idioms* (1925).

Smith Sir Matthew (1879–1959). English painter who studied at Manchester School of Art (1900–4) and the Slade School, London (1905–7), worked at Pont-Aven, Brittany (1908) and studied in Matisse's studio (1910). *Fitzroy Street Nude No. 1* (1916; Tate) in its strong colour and simplified forms, shows the extent of S.'s absorption of fauvism, which was also brilliantly expressed in his early Cornish landscapes. In his later nudes, landscapes and flower paintings form suffered from an expressive flamboyance of paint and colour. There was a big retrospective exhibition at the Tate in 1953.

Smith Richard Penn (1799–1854). U.S. playwright. S. helped to carry American drama through a transitional phase, drawing heavily on French originals in his plays. He is also said to have ghost-written Davy Crockett's autobiography.

Smith Seba (1792–1868). U.S. humorist. As 'Major Jack Downing' S. contributed gently satirical letters on U.S. politics to his own newspaper; the rustic Downing was the first 'homespun philosopher' commenting shrewdly on public affairs, a type which has become a

David Smith. *Royal Bird* (1948)

Smirke. The British Museum

Alison and Peter Smithson. The Economist Group Building. Also *brutalism

Tobias Smollett

U.S. tradition. The letters were reprinted everywhere in the U.S. and widely imitated.

Smith Stevie, properly Florence Margaret (1902–). English poet who has produced complex and highly allusive verse showing great command of rhythm and assonance; her themes, however, are basic, and express a straightforward idealism. Works include the coll. *Not Waving but Drowning* (1957) and *Novel on Yellow Paper* (1936), a novel whose highly experimental form aroused great interest.

Smithson Alison (1928–) and Peter (1923–). English architects. Their Hunstanton School, Norfolk (1954) is a highly formal, Miesian building, one of the most serious works of architecture in post-war Britain. Their proposed house in Colville Street, London (1953) initiated the *brutalist movement and their entries to the architectural competitions of the 1950s had a considerable influence, e.g. the street decks for their Golden Lane project which became an accepted solution to British high rise housing by 1960. The Economist Group Building, St James's (1964), are simple buildings set in an elaborate pedestrian space.

Smithson Harriet (1800–54). English actress who after being leading lady to Edmund Kean in London, went to Paris with Macready's co. where she enjoyed enormous success. She married the composer *Berlioz.

Smoke (1867). Novel by Turgenev.

Smollett Tobias (1721–71). Scottish novelist. Educated at Glasgow Univ. and apprenticed to a doctor-apothecary, S. sailed as a surgeon's mate on the Carthagena Expedition of 1741, an experience which provided him with material for his novel *Roderick Random* (1748).
S.'s novels are picaresque masterpieces which bear a superficial resemblance to those of Fielding, though S.'s characters elicit less sympathy. His merits lie in the pace and inventiveness of his plots and his lively and boisterous, bawdy humour, and in the unusual scenes and types that fill his pages. In *Humphry Clinker* (1700), a novel in letters, the description of events from several points of view achieves vivid characterization and a subtle relativism. Other works include the novel *Peregrine Pickle* (1751); trs of Le Sage's *Gil Blas*, Cervantes' *Don Quixote* and the works of Voltaire; and a history of England.

Smyth Dame Ethel Mary (1858–1944). English composer also active as suffragette. She studied in Germany and her music shows the strong influence of German late romanticism; her string quartets and quintets follow Brahms almost slavishly but other music shows individuality. She is best known for such operas as *The Wreckers* (Leipzig, 1906) and *The Boatswain's Mate* (London, 1916).

Dame Ethel Smyth

Snorri Sturluson (1178–1241). Icelandic poet and historian, the most famous of the Norse chroniclers; an important and powerful man ultimately killed as a rebel against the king of Norway. He saved much Scandinavian folklore from extinction in his great prose **Edda*, a valuable account of Northern mythology written as a handbook for poets (to explain *kennings, etc.). He was also one of the most critical historians of the middle ages, drawing psychologically convincing portraits in his sequence of *sagas of the Norwegian kings, the *Heimskringla*.

Snow C(harles) P(ercy) (Lord) (1905–). English novelist, scientist and civil servant who has expressed concern at the lack of contact between the '2 cultures' of art and science (e.g. his lecture *The Two Cultures and the Scientific Revolution*, 1959). His novels include *The Masters* (1951) and *The Affair* (1960), both successfully dramatized, and *Corridors of Power* (1964).

Snuff-box; Staffordshire, *c.* 1770

Snows of Kilimanjaro, The (1936). Short story by Hemingway.

snuff-box. An essential article of every 18th-c. gentleman's equipment, when the habit of snuff-taking was ubiquitous. The materials employed were various: porcelain, hardstones, silver and gold frequently set with precious stones and decorated with enamel. In spite of their small size much time and money was expended on them.

Snyder Gary (1930–). U.S. poet, one of the *beats, strongly influenced by his study of Chinese and Japanese poetry. His verse includes *Myths and Texts* (1960).

Snyders Frans (1579–1657). Flemish painter of still-life subjects, animals and hunting scenes, pupil of P. Bruegel the Younger and H. van Balen. He worked in Antwerp, often collaborating with Rubens, in whose pictures

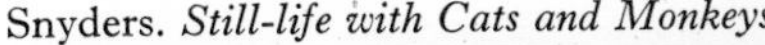

Snyders. *Still-life with Cats and Monkeys*

Soane. Sketch for a church in 3 different styles

he painted the flowers and fruit. One of his best-known paintings is *The Kitchen Table* (Alte Pina., Munich).

Soane Sir John (1753–1837). English architect. His 1st and most important commission was the Bank of England (1792 onwards); only the exterior, the present ground-storey, remains. In 1812 he built his own house, filling it with his coll. of sculpture, antiques and pictures; it is now the Soane Museum. Inspired by Greek architecture, S. evolved a completely personal idiom characterized by shallow domes, segmental arches, ingenious spatial vistas, clerestory lighting and an absence of decorative features. Although many of his designs were publ., S. had little influence; his work, however, interests modern architects.

Social realism. Jack Smith, *Child Walking* (1953)

Social realism. Sloan, *Roofs, Summer Night* (1906)

socialist realism. Pronounced as a dogma for all Soviet artists in all fields of art in 1934. It aimed to produce art comprehensible to the masses, and inspire the people with admiration for the dignity of the working man and his task of building Communism. Heroic idealization of work and the worker was the required theme, and the guiding hand of the Communist party and its discipline was to mould and prune artists, in order to create, in Stalin's words, worthy 'engineers of souls'. The approved techniques were derived from the realistic and naturalistic traditions.

social realism. A term used to describe paintings of the life and environment of the lower middle and working classes in the 20th c. The 2 main groups generally identified as s.-r. painters are The Eight, painting after 1900 in the U.S., and an English group (kitchen sink school), working in the 1950s, among them Jack Smith, John Bratby, Edward Middleditch and Derrick Greaves.

Socialist realism. Deineka, *The Tractor-Driver*

Socrates (469–399 B.C.). Athenian philosopher, the first to concentrate on ethical questions, using the reason and casting doubt on accepted beliefs by a technique of question-and-answer which revealed the inconsistency of the speaker's statements. S.'s life and thought are known only through the writings of Xenophon, Aristotle and (most fully) *Plato (though the extent to which Plato uses S. as a mouthpiece for his own ideas is uncertain). S. was accused of corrupting Athenian youth and denying the city's gods; he was tried and, having rejected the opportunity to escape, put to death (he drank a cup of hemlock).

Socrates: marble bust, copy of a 4th-c. B.C. Greek original

soda glass. The essential ingredients of glass are silica and an alkaline flux; the alkali first used in glass making was soda. Egyptian, Roman (Syrian and Rhenish), Spanish and Venetian glass were made with soda but the Northern countries, including England, took to using potash. Today both are used.

Söderberg Hjalmar (1869–1941). Swedish novelist and short-story writer, an outstanding stylist and a subtle, sceptical intelligence; most of his works are set in Stockholm. Works include the partly autobiographical *Martin Birks ungdom* (1901; *Martin Birck's Youth*, 1930), *Doktor Glas* (1905), and the short stories of *Historietter* (1898).

Sodoma Giovanni Antonio Bazzi, called Il (1477–1549). Italian painter who worked chiefly in Siena in an elegant mannered style. According to Vasari, who disliked him, he got his nickname on account of his homosexuality. However, he used it himself in his signature. In 1498 he went to Milan, where he was strongly influenced by Leonardo da Vinci, and in 1501 to Siena. His work there included the completion of a series of frescoes begun by Signorelli in the monastery of Monte Oliveto and the notable *Vision of St Catherine* in S. Domenico. He was employed in the Vatican and the Villa Farnesina, Rome.

Sodome et Gomorrhe (1921–2). Novel by *Proust.

Soest Gerard (d. 1681). Portrait painter, either from Germany or the Netherlands, who worked in England from 1656. He painted fine male portraits but never rivalled Lely as a fashionable portraitist because his rough manners made women dislike sitting to him.

Soffici Ardengo (1879–). Italian artist and writer. After taking part in the cubist movement in Paris S. became one of the most vociferous members of Marinetti's futurist group and wrote violent but brilliant polemics and poems.

soft paste: *porcelain

Sohrab and Rustum (1853). Poem by Matthew *Arnold.

Soirées de Médan, Les (1880). Coll. of short stories by Zola and 5 disciples, including Paul Alexis, Huysmans, and Guy de Maupassant. It contained Maupassant's *Boule-de-suif*. Zola's country-house, where his friends met, was at Médan.

Sokolova Lydia. Stage-name of Hilda Munnings (1896–). The 1st English dancer to join the Diaghilev co. (1913). She showed fine dramatic sensitivity and developed as a character dancer.

Solari(o) Andrea (d. *c.* 1520). Milanese painter who was influenced by the work of Antonello da Messina on a visit to Venice and by Leonardo da Vinci in Milan. One of his finest paintings is *Madonna with the Green Cushion* (Louvre). His brother CRISTOFORO (d. 1527), called 'Il Gobbo', was an architect and sculptor.

Solari(o) Antonio da (*fl.* 1502–18). Italian painter nicknamed 'Lo Zingaro' ('The Gipsy'). He was a follower of Giovanni Bellini and Carpaccio and worked mainly in Naples. He is best known for his frescoes of the life of St Benedict in S. Severino, Naples.

Soldati Atanasio (1887–1953). Italian painter who developed a purely abstract style after World War II and gathered round him in Milan the 1st group of Italian abstractionists.

Soldati Mario (1906–). Italian author and film director. S.'s novels include the complex but inventive *Le lettere da Capri* (1954). His most famous films are *Euga in Francia* (1948), *La Provinciale* (1953) from Moravia, and *War and Peace*, of which he directed the battle scenes.

Soldiers Three (1888). Coll. of linked stories by Kipling.

Soledades, Las (1627). Poem by Góngora.

Solesmes. French monastery where researchers established the basis of a reformed *plainsong.

sol-fa: *tonic sol-fa

solfège. French term for (1) a method for sight reading music, similar to tonic sol-fa; synonymous with the Italian '*solfeggio*'; (2) a course in the elements of music at the Paris Conservatoire, etc.

Solimena Francesco (1657–1747). Italian painter who worked mainly in Naples; one of the most famous exponents of late baroque decorative painting. The chief formative influence on S.'s style was that of Giordano but tempered with elements borrowed from Maratta's classicism. Representative paintings are in the churches of S. Paolo Maggiore and Gesù Nuovo, both Naples. His many pupils included S. Conca and A. Ramsay.

solmization. The designation of musical notes by a nomenclature of syllables, designed to assist learners to read music as in *tonic sol-fa.

solo (Italian, 'alone'). Used in music of unaccompanied instrumental parts, or of parts played by only 1 instrument; thus one speaks of the 's'. part in a concerto.

Sologub Fyodor. Pseud. of Fyodor Kuzmich Teternikov (1863–1927). Russian symbolist poet, novelist and playwright. S.'s work is 'decadent' and fascinated by the morbid and perverse, part of the late 19th-c. reaction against realism. His poetry is wonderfully musical, but his fame outside Russia rests on the novel *The Little Demon* (1907; 1916), the story of a sadistic schoolmaster and the demon who finally drives him insane.

Solomon. Stage-name of Solomon Cutner (1902–). English pianist. At the age of 8 he publicly performed Tchaikovsky's 1st piano concerto and became internationally known for his virtuosity and sense of style.

Solomon Erich (1886–1944). German photographer who took advantage of the introduction of high-speed miniature cameras to do the first indoor candid photography. His mastery of the available light technique (as opposed to the obtrusive and disrupting flash system of the day) opened new possibilities to photography. S.'s picture essays of court trials and the confidential meetings of diplomats and heads of state added a new dimension to photo-journalism.

Soloviev Vladimir Sergeyevich (1853–1900). Russian poet, mystic and philosopher; his influence developed the cult of Sophia, the divine principle of wisdom, among the symbolists. His dialogue *Three Conversations on War, Progress and the End of Human History* . . .

Sodoma. *St Sebastian*

Lydia Sokolova (right) in *Chout* (1921)

Soffici. *Still-life* (collage; 1913)

Somer. *Queen Anne of Denmark*

(1900; 1915) advocated an active Christianity and attacked Tolstoy's doctrines of non-resistance and anarchism.

Solzhenitsyn Alexander Isayevich (1918–). Soviet writer, author of the short novels *One Day in the Life of Ivan Denisovich* (1962; 1963), which describes the life of prisoners in Stalin's labour camps, and *For the Good of the Cause* (1964), satirizing bureaucratic delays to a building project.

Some Like it Hot (1959). Film directed by B. *Wilder.

Somer Paul van (1577/8–1621/2). Flemish portrait painter, possibly trained in Italy, who worked in the Netherlands and from 1616 in London where he was patronized by the court. His most important painting is a full-length portrait of Queen Anne of Denmark (1617; Royal Coll.).

Somes Michael (1917–). English dancer who was the 1st male dancer to be produced through the Sadler's Wells school and co. As leading dancer when Helpmann left the co. in 1950, S. partnered Fonteyn, creating roles in many ballets, e.g. Ashton's *La Peri* (1956), as well as interpreting the established classical roles with distinction. No longer a performer, he is now assistant director of the Royal Ballet.

Michael Somes in *La Peri*

sonata (from the Italian 'to sound'). A musical term used loosely in the early 17th c. to denote a piece for instruments as opposed to one for voices. There developed the '*sonata da camera*', a suite of several movements for 2 or more instruments and continuo bass, and the graver '*sonata da chiesa*'. The classical s. as developed in the mid 18th c. and familiar in the works of composers from Haydn to Brahms, is in 3 or 4 movements, the 1st and sometimes one other in sonata form. The term s. is now given only to pieces for 1 or 2 instruments; other pieces in the same form are called trio, quartet, etc.

sonata form. Predominant musical form of the classical period, used not merely in sonatas but also in symphonies, quartets, etc., almost invariably in 1st movements and often in other movements. It arose from the common binary form in which a piece was divided into 2 halves, the 1st half ending in the *dominant key-region, and the 2nd half in the *tonic. Later, with the breaking-up of movements into various sections, themes, and motifs, the following schema tended to be adopted: 1st group of themes, establishing the original key and moving towards the dominant, 2nd group in the dominant, the groups known together as the 'exposition' section, followed by a short 'development' section (free) and finally a repeat of the exposition of both groups ('recapitulation' in the tonic). This sequence of key is, in classical s. f., often followed by a coda. Beethoven lengthened the development section and wrote extended codas, thus creating in effect a 4-section movement.

sonatina. A 'little sonata'.

Sonderborg. *Composition* (1954)

Sonderborg K. R. H. (born Kurt R. Hofmann) (1923–). Danish abstract expressionist painter. He worked in Germany, then moved to Paris; now lives in Paris and New York.

song. Musical form for a single voice with or without accompaniment. In the strophic s. the verses of the poem are set each to the same tune and the same basic accompaniment; a s. is said to be 'through composed' (from German '*durchkomponiert*') when the melodic line and accompaniment develop continuously throughout the piece.

Song of Bernadette, The (1944). Film directed by H. *King.

Song of Ceylon (1934). Short film directed by B. *Wright.

Song of Hiawatha (1855). Narrative poem by *Longfellow.

Song of Myself (1855). Poem by Walt Whitman.

Song of Solomon, The or **Song of Songs.** One of the poetical books of the Bible. It is still sometimes argued that its erotic content is in fact an expression of mystical experience.

Songs of Innocence (1789) and **Songs of Experience** (1794). Colls of poems by *Blake.

Songs Without Words (German *Lieder ohne Worte*). Piano compositions by *Mendelssohn.

Sonnambula, La. Opera by *Bellini with libretto by F. Romani; 1st produced at Milan in 1831.

sonnet. Enduringly popular and extremely flexible verse form with 14 lines, originating in 13th-c. Italy and standardized for that language by *Petrarch with the rhyme scheme *abba abba cdc dcd*. Wyatt first practised it in English, where it usually ends with a rhyming couplet, incisively concluding and summarizing the poem; thus the Shakespearian or English s., which rhymes *abab cdcd efef gg*. The s. has normally been written in the characteristic metre of the poet's language–i.e. with 11 syllables in Italian, 12 in French, 10 in English. Shakespeare, Milton and Wordsworth are regarded as the English masters of the form; there are also famous s. sequences by Sir Philip Sidney, Spenser and Elizabeth Browning.

Sonnets, Shakespeare's (1609). Sequence of 154 sonnets. There is still controversy about their date and meaning, the identity of 'Mr W. H.' to whom they are dedicated as their 'onlie begetter', and that of 'the Dark Lady' Shakespeare addresses as his mistress.

Sons and Lovers (1913). Novel by D. H. *Lawrence.

Sophocles (*c.* 496–406 B.C.). Athenian dramatist. S. was born at Colonus near Athens and was the son of an armourer. He was of conspicuous beauty and of an even temper, so that he became universally popular. At 15 he led the chorus of boys in the paean to celebrate the victory over the Persians at Salamis. He acted himself in his early plays–his performance as Nausicaa being particularly celebrated–but his voice proved too weak for the demands of the theatre. At his first appearance in 468 he defeated Aeschylus and thereafter won 20 or more dramatic victories. He was steward of the treasury in 442, general in 440 and on another occasion. He introduced the 3rd actor and painted scenery into tragedy. He died shortly after Euripides and just before the collapse of Athens' glory. 7 plays survive out of 123. His plots are the most strongly constructed in ancient drama and his style the smoothest example of Attic purity. Using the assumptions of orthodox piety, he masks his own beliefs. *Ajax* (448?) and *Antigone* (441) deal with the demands of natural piety. Ajax, vowing vengeance on the Greeks for cheating him out of Achilles' armour, is driven mad by Athene and kills only some sheep. Recovering his senses he commits suicide in remorse. Teucer and Menelaus discuss his right to burial; only the intervention of his enemy Odysseus, prompted by Athene, secures for Ajax a funeral with full heroic honours. In his **Antigone* both Antigone and Creon are intransigent and both are justified. In the catastrophe Creon suffers as well as Antigone. **Oedipus Tyrannus* (428?) earned Aristotle's repeated commendation for its plot, of which the crisis exhibits the perfect example of 'reversal', i.e. an event which has the contrary result to that intended by its author. Oedipus' insistent interrogation of the messenger, instead of proving his innocence as he expects, reveals his guilt. *Trachiniae* (425?) deals with part of the story of Hercules. Like *Ajax* and *Antigone* it falls into 2 parts, but more conspicuously in that the 2 principal personages, Deianeira and Hercules, never encounter one another on the stage. **Electra* (*c.* 413?) is closely linked with Euripides' play of the same name, but which was written first is still in dispute. Sophocles withdraws attention from the horrors of the story to the relationship between Electra and her brother Orestes. In presenting this he uses most poignantly the device of dramatic irony, where Electra receives from Orestes in disguise the urn containing Orestes' supposed ashes. *Philoctetes* (409) presents another moral conflict, between patriotism, meanly represented by Odysseus, and honesty, nobly represented by Neoptolemus. Uniquely for S., a *deus ex machina resolves the plot. The last play, *Oedipus at Colonus*, was produced posth.; it has an exiguous plot but contains some of S.'s finest lyrics, particularly one in praise of his native village, from which the play takes its title. The austere beauty of his language and the taut construction of his plots make S. the finest craftsman and his uncommitted awareness of all the contradictory currents of contemporary thought make him seem the profoundest thinker of the Attic theatre.

soprano. The high female voice with an approximate range of two 8ves upwards from middle C. The term is also used to describe the high members of families of instruments; the s. *clef is a C clef resting on the bottom line of the staff. The diminutive of s., SOPRANINO is used of the very highest members of some instrumental families.

Sorabji Kaikosru (1892–). Composer, the son of an Indian father and Spanish mother, born in England and christened Leon Dudley. His works include the very lengthy *Opus*

Songs of Innocence: illustration by Blake

TO.THE.ONLIE.BEGETTER.OF.
THESE.INSVING.SONNETS.
M^r.W.H. ALL.HAPPINESSE.
AND.THAT.ETERNITIE.
PROMISED.
BY.
OVR.EVER-LIVING.POET.
WISHETH.
THE.WELL-WISHING.
ADVENTVRER.IN.
SETTING.
FORTH.

T. T.

Shakespeare's *Sonnets*: the dedication

Greek portrait bust, thought to be of Sophocles

Sotto in sù. Ceiling by Mantegna

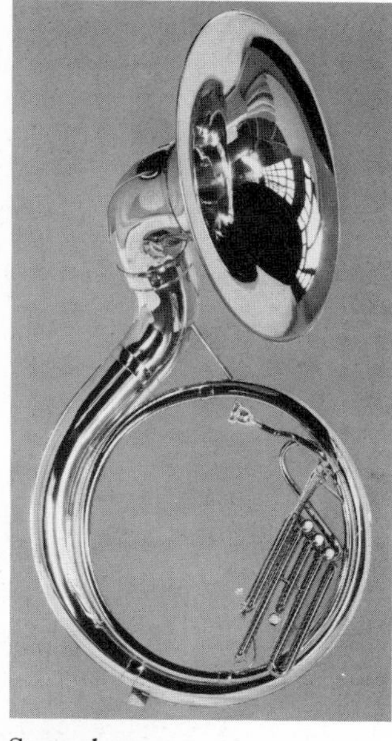

Sousaphone

Soufflot. Ste Geneviève

Soulages. *Painting* (1958)

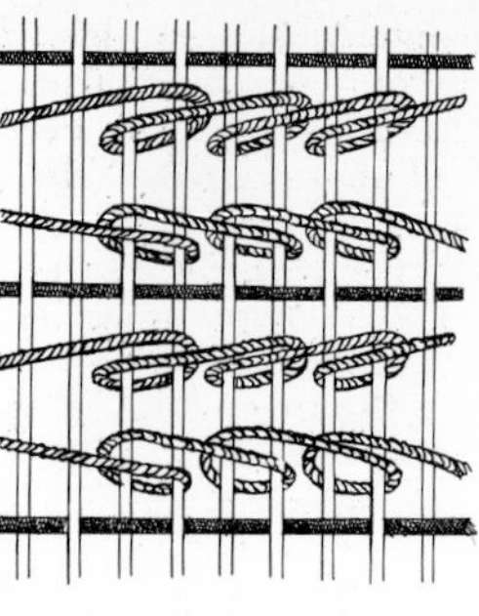

Soumak carpet weave

clavicembalisticum, which S. claims is vastly important.

Sorcerer's Apprentice, The (1897). English name for a symphonic poem by Dukas.

Sordello di Goito (*c.* 1200–70). Italian troubadour poet who wrote in Provençal. His most famous and moving work is his lament on the death of his patron Blacas. S. is the hero of a poem by Browning and also figures in Dante's *Purgatorio.*

Sorel Charles (1597–1674). French novelist. S. wrote a picaresque novel, *Le Vrai histoire comique de Francion* (1622) and *Le Berger extravagant* (1627), which satirizes the pastoral novel; its framework is similar to that of *Don Quixote.*

Sothern Edward Askew (1826–81). English comic actor who created and made his own the part of Lord Dundreary in *Our American Cousin* (New York, 1858). His son EDWARD HUGH S. (1859–1933), also an actor, worked in the U.S. from 1879 onwards; his Malvolio was highly praised.

sotto in sù (Italian, 'from below upward'). Term applied to foreshortening in a ceiling painting so that from below the figures have the appearance of floating in space. It was used by Mantegna (Camera degli Sposi frescoes, Mantua) and reached its highest point of development in the baroque period.

Soufflot Jacques-Germain (1713–80). French architect who designed the very large church of Ste Geneviève (now the Panthéon), Paris, in 1755. It is cruciform, with a large dome over the crossing, a coldly neo-classical version of St Peter's. S. also did some work in Gothic and in iron construction.

Soulages Pierre (1919–). French painter principally self-taught under the inspiration of prehistoric and medieval art. His mature style did not fully develop until, after his military service (1940–5), he emerged as one of the leading members of the post-war school of Paris. He first exhibited in 1947. His abstract images have an ambiguous icon-like significance and are painted intuitively with no preconceptions. This type of art, and the structural strength of his dark shapes, are directly comparable to U.S. painters like Kline. *23 May 1953* (Tate) is a typical work.

Soulier de Satin, Le (1930). Poetic drama by *Claudel.

Soumak. Probably derived from Shemakha (Azerbaijan, U.S.S.R.). A complicated stitch-woven carpet. The weft thread passes in front of 4 warp threads, and is then taken back behind the last 2. In the next stitch these 2 form the first of the next group of 4 threads. A plain weft thread is put through after every line or 2 lines. The pairing of the same warp threads is kept throughout. The patterns are generally of geometric form. Many Caucasian carpets are so made.

Sound and the Fury, The (1929). Novel by William Faulkner.

sound hole. In the *violin called the 'f-holes' and in the *lute called the 'rose'.

Soupault Philippe (1897–). French poet, novelist and critic, member of the Paris dada group, then of the surrealist movement.

Sousa John (1854–1932). U.S. composer and band-master of the U.S. Marines Band and 'Sousa's Band'. He wrote about 100 marches, e.g. *The Washington Post* and *Stars and Stripes for Ever* and several operettas, and had designed a form of tuba (the SOUSAPHONE) which coils round the player's body, the bell projecting over the shoulder; it is easier to carry on the march than the normal tuba.

Sous les Toits de Paris (1929). Film directed by R. *Clair.

Southern Review, The. Name of several U.S. magazines, notably the influential *S. R.* of 1935–42; Robert Penn Warren ed. it for a time.

Southey Robert (1774–1843). English poet. In his youth S. shared the Revolutionary sentiments of his friend and brother-in-law Coleridge, with whom he planned to set up a utopian settlement ('Pantisocracy') in America. His growing conservatism (he became poet laureate in 1813) made him the target of Byron's ferocious satire, especially *The Vision of Judgement*, parodying S.'s *A Vision of Judgement* (1821), which describes the lately dead George III entering heaven. S. wrote voluminously, but his epic long poems are forgotten and only a few lyrics are read. He also produced many biographies, including a well-known *Life of Nelson* (1813).

Southwell Robert (*c.* 1561–95). English poet. S., a Jesuit, was imprisoned (1592), tortured and executed. His religious poems include *The Burning Babe* and *St Peter's Complaint.*

Southwell Minster England. English church, notable for its 12th-c. nave and transepts and its chapter-house in the decorated style (1290–1300), which contains beautifully carved naturalistic foliage, the 'Leaves of Southwell'.

South Wind (1917). Novel by Norman *Douglas.

Soutine Chaim (1894–1943). Russian painter. He moved to Paris (1913), living in desperate poverty; there he met Chagall and Modigliani. Like theirs, his work was only tenuously connected with the current Parisian mainstream. S.'s art is closer to other isolated expressionists like Nolde and Kokoschka. Under the influence of the fauves and Van Gogh, the haunted melancholy of his early work gave way to the volcanic violence of colour and technique in the landscapes painted at Céret (1919–22), e.g. *Gnarled Trees* (Colin Coll., New York) whose crude brushwork witnesses furiously expended energy. These are some of the most extreme examples of expressionism.
With a growing patronage from 1923 (most of his works are still in private colls) his financial hardship was over, but the disturbing images persisted, painted in the colour and texture of raw flesh, e.g. the Rembrandt-inspired *Carcass of Beef* (Albright-Knox A. Gall., Buffalo). Only in his last works, e.g. *Windy Day, Auxerres* (1939; Phillips Coll., Washington), does a lyrical decorative quality appear.

Souza Mme de (1761–1836). French novelist. Her books are sentimental stories about 18th-c. aristocratic society.

Soyinka Wole (1934–). Nigerian dramatist, whose work has been seen in England, where he lived for a short time. *The Lion and the Jewel, The Swamp Dwellers, The Trials of Brother Jess,* and his major work, *A Dance of the Forests,* display in rigorous style his imaginative refashioning of Yoruba legends.

Spada Leonello (1576–1622). Bolognese painter of religious and genre subjects who studied at the Carracci Academy before entering Caravaggio's studio in Rome. He accompanied Caravaggio to Naples and Malta and became a close follower of his style. He ended his career in Parma, softening his style under the influence of Correggio.

Spagna Giovanni di Pietro called Lo (d. 1528). Spanish painter who worked in and around Perugia. He was a follower of Perugino and Raphael.

Spalato: *Diocletian's palace

spandrel. Architectural term for the roughly triangular, often richly carved area between 2 arches or between an arch and a wall.

Spanish Bawd, The. English title of de Rojas's *La *Celestina.*

Spanish or **rose point lace.** Needle-point lace of elaborate raised floral patterns closely based on Venetian laces; at its best in the late 17th c. The term sometimes denotes gold or silver wire bordered lace.

Spanish Tragedy, The (*c.* 1585). Play by Thomas *Kyd.

spasmodic school. Term coined by W. E. Aytoun, applied to a group of British poets including P. J. Bailey, Sidney Dobell and Alexander Smith.

Spectator, The (1711–12). Periodical ed. and largely written by *Addison and *Steele.

Spee von Lagenfeld Friedrich (1591–1635). German poet. S. von L. became a Jesuit and (in 1627) confessor to those condemned as witches; he attacked belief in witchcraft in his *Cautio Criminalis* (1631). His religious poetry was publ. posth. as *Trutz-Nachtigall, oder geistlichs-poetisch Lust-Waldlein* (1649).

Spellbound (1945). Film directed by *Hitchcock.

Spence Sir Basil (1907–). English architect, famous for his Coventry cathedral (1962), a compromise building in terms of new thinking in both architecture and liturgy; it was none the less a great popular success. His Sussex

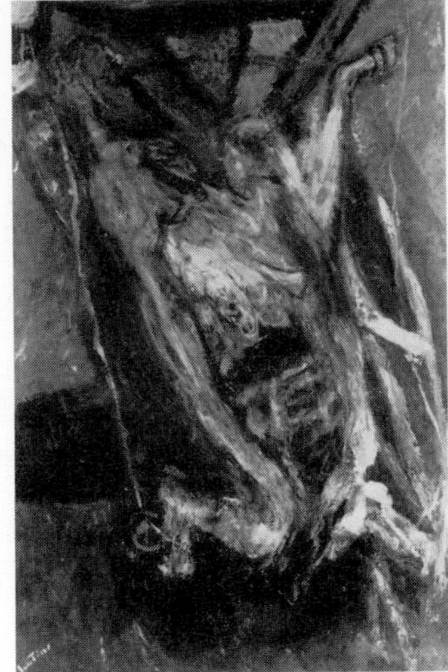

Soutine. *Flayed Ox.*
Also *expressionism

Soutine. *Portrait of a Boy* (1928)

Robert Southey

Southwell Minster wall arcade decorated with leaves

Stanley Spencer. *The Betrayal* (1922)

Stanley Spencer. E. wall of the Burghclere chapel

Univ. is a romantic design in brick with concrete vaults and his housing in the Gorbals, Glasgow may be the first to embody Le Corbusier's superimposed villas, each with a garden in the air.

Spencer Bernard (1909–). English poet who in the late 1930s helped Geoffrey Grigson ed. *New Verse*, with which magazine his poetry is identifiable in its close combination of intelligence and feeling. The coll. *Aegean Islands* (1946) illustrates this quietly persistent quality.

Spencer Sir Stanley (1891–1959). English painter born in Cookham, Berkshire, where he spent most of his life. He studied at the Slade School, London (1908–12). Untouched by modern art and a meticulously dry craftsman, he was the isolated eccentric of British 20th-c. art. He was gifted with an extraordinary visual imagination; most of his paintings were of religious subjects poetically interpreted in the context of Cookham Village, e.g. *Resurrection Cookham* (1923–7; Tate). After 1932 he felt that his visionary power had left him and that all subsequent works were uncertain and incomplete. He decorated the Burghclere chapel (*Soldiers Resurrecting*, 1926–32) and was an official war artist (1940–1). He was made an O.B.E. and R.A. in 1950.

Spender Stephen (1909–). English poet, one of the Marxists of the 1930s closely associated with W. H. Auden and C. Day Lewis. His best verse, however, has always been private and lyrical. S. was co-founder and ed. of the magazine *Horizon* (1940–1) and has co-ed. *Encounter* since 1953.

Spengler Oswald (1880–1936). German historian, a schoolteacher whose massive synthesizing work *Der Untergang des Abendlandes . . .* (1918–23; *The Decline of the West*, 1926–9) fortuitously appeared when Germany was crashing to defeat in World War I, and became a best-seller. S. analysed and compared previous civilizations, concluding that they were organisms which obeyed a common life-pattern; Western civilization, he believed, was ending its life-span. Works include *Der Mensch und die Technik* (1931; *Man and Technics*, 1932).

Spenser Edmund (1552–99). English poet. S. began writing very early and was a member of Sir Philip Sidney's circle; *The Shepheard's Calendar*, a poem in 12 eclogues, was dedicated to Sidney in 1579. In 1580 he went to Ireland as secretary to Lord Grey of Wilton and began writing *The Faerie Queene*. His lament *Astrophel* was written on Sidney's death in 1586, and the first 3 books of *The Faerie Queene* were publ. in 1590. On his return to Ireland after a visit to England made at Raleigh's instigation he wrote a satirical poem, *Colin Clout's Come Home Again*. For his marriage in 1594 to Elizabeth Boyle, whom he had courted in the sonnet sequence *Amoretti*, he wrote the *Epithalamion*, his most perfect and most approachable poem. Another 3 books of *The Faerie Queene* were publ. in England in 1596. He was appointed sheriff of Cork in 1598, but his castle was destroyed and his youngest child killed in the Tyrone Rebellion, a tragedy from which he never recovered. When S. died he had composed only 6 of the projected 12 books of his great poem *The Faerie Queen*. The poem shows the influence of Ariosto in its use of the stories of medieval chivalry for complex symbolic purposes; there is no means of telling how S. proposed to complete its many stories or exactly how the elaborate allegorical structure was to be resolved, but S. probably had in mind an underlying moral concept as well as the more obvious application of the various figures to personages at court or in the army (e.g. the 'Queen' is, on one level, Queen Elizabeth). S.'s verse is lush and sensual, displaying incomparable technical skill, which is placed at the service of the narrative rather than used for virtuoso effects. The adept modulation of the strict ('Spenserian') *stanza form, the meticulous attention to rhythm and metre, and the frequent use of alliteration to establish atmosphere and as a linking device, combine to create a rare and sustained melodic harmony impressive in all S.'s poetry and outweighing the lack of pace and direction in *The Faerie Queen*.

Sperling Milton (1912–). U.S. film producer. An independent producer with an unusually good record. His productions include *The Rise and Fall of Legs Diamond* as well as films by Lang, Walsh, Fregonese, Preminger and Fuller.

Speroni Sperone (1500–88). Italian humanist. A noted philologist, S. wrote a treatise on language, *Dialogho delle lingue*, which inspired much of Du Bellay's own work on the French language. He was also the author of *Canace*

Spence.
Coventry cathedral

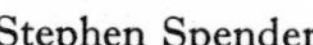

Stephen Spender

Edmund Spenser

Olga Spessivtseva in *La Chatte*

Spinello. *Madonna*

Spinoza

(publ. 1546), a horrific drama of incest, in which he tried to apply Aristotle's dramatic precepts.

'Spervogel': *Spruch

Spessivtseva Olga (Spessiva) (1895–). Russian dancer of the Imperial School, St Petersburg. She became one of the greatest Giselles at a time when Pavlova's popularity was at its peak. After occasional guest appearances with Diaghilev, she went to the Paris Opéra as *étoile (1924) and retired in 1933.

Speyer cathedral. One of the formative buildings of Rhineland Romanesque. It was begun in 1030 with nave, transepts, crossing and towers at E. and W. ends. The nave was groin-vaulted in 1080–90, the earliest major groin-vault in Europe. Dwarf-galleries round the exterior are after 1100, the present W. front a 19th-c. reconstruction.

Sphinx, The Great (*c.* 2900 B.C.; Giza). Colossal sphinx with the body of a lion and the head of King Chephren, the builder of the 2nd pyramid of Giza before which it stands. It is 240 ft long and 66 ft high. The head and body were carved out of a ridge of limestone, the legs and paws being built of stone blocks.

spiccato (Italian, 'detached'). A type of bowing (*bow) on instruments of the violin family in which a series of rapid notes are played with a bouncing bow.

Spiegel Henric Laurens (1549–1612). Dutch poet, an important member of the Eglantier chamber of rhetoric (*rederijkers); he played the leading part in producing their Dutch grammar, which aimed to purify the language. His chief poem is the philosophical *Hert spiegel.*

Spiegel Sam (1903–). Polish-born U.S. film producer for Universal in Berlin, and later elsewhere in Europe until his departure in 1940 for the U.S. Thanks to the great success of some of his films (*The African Queen*, *The Bridge on the River Kwai*, *Lawrence of Arabia*), he has retained the most complete independence, which he uses to indulge his taste for 'big' subjects.

Spielhagen Friedrich (1829–1911). German novelist, critic and journalist active in left-wing politics. He attempted to expound contemporary problems in such novels as *Problematische Naturen* (1861) and *Durch Nacht Zum Licht* (1862; *Through Night to Light*, 1870).

spindle and bead. A decorative relief moulding made up of alternate spindle and bead shapes used in classical architecture to enrich the scotia moulding at the base of a column. Revived in the decoration of neo-classical furniture.

Spinello Aretino (*fl.* 1373–1410). Italian painter of the early Florentine school who in his late work anticipated Masaccio in reviving the tradition of Giotto. He worked in Arezzo, Florence, Pisa and Siena, painting frescoes and altarpieces.

spinet. A small *harpsichord. It has only 1 keyboard, but is wing-shaped like the harpsichord, not square like the *virginals.

Spinoza Benedictus de, originally Baruch (1632–77). Dutch philosopher excommunicated from the Jewish church (1656) for his unorthodoxy. His *Ethica* (posth. 1677) contains a systematized coll. of definitions, axioms and theorems dividing the cosmos into substance–there is only one, God–and attributes, including the minds and bodies of men. God, therefore, is immanent in nature (S.'s formula was '*Deus sive Natura*') and good and evil become relative concepts only of concern to man; knowledge becomes the key to salvation. S.'s writings include the *Tractatus Theologico–Politicus* (1670), advocating religious toleration.

spire. Architectural term for a long, usually pyramidical-conical structure on top of a tower.

Spitta Julius August Philipp (1841–94). German music historian; author of the standard biography of J. S. Bach (1873; 1880) and ed. of the works of Schütz.

Spitteler Carl (1845–1924). Swiss writer. S. studied theology, worked as a teacher, then publ. *Prometheus und Epimetheus* (1880–1), a poetic prose epic. His career as poet, novelist and essayist was crowned by another epic, *Olympischer Frühling* (1900), for which he was awarded the Nobel prize (1919).

The Great Sphinx

Speyer cathedral

Louis Spohr

Spitzweg. *The Poor Poet*

Split stitch

Spode centre dish

Spode plate (1826)

Spitzweg Carl (1808–85). German painter of delicate romantic landscapes and anecdotal pictures of eccentric small-town characters such as *The Poor Poet* (1839; Alte Pina., Munich).

split stitch. An embroidery stitch in which the needle is brought through from the back, passing through and splitting the thread of the previous stitch; it has the appearance of a fine chain stitch. It enables colours to be blended skilfully and is particularly useful in modelling draperies or features; it was much used in *Opus Anglicanum.

Spode. Family of Staffordshire potters working at Stoke-on-Trent. The 1st JOSIAH S. (1733–97) in 1770 established a pottery which became increasingly prosperous under his son and grandson (d. 1829) and was bought in 1833 by the Copeland family (already partners). The 2nd Josiah S. (d. 1827) evolved what became a standard recipe for English bone porcelain. The S.s were also well known as early makers of under-glaze blue printed earthenwares.

Spofford Harriet (Elizabeth) Prescott (1835–1921). U.S. novelist and short-story writer, one of the most productive and popular writers of romances in the later 19th c. Her novels include *Azarian* (1864).

Spohr Louis (1784–1859). German composer, conductor and virtuoso violinist, considered 2nd only to Paganini. As a composer he enjoyed a fantastic contemporary reputation but his music, showing affinities to Mendelssohn's, loses strength from his preference for minor keys and over-frequent chromaticism. His works include 10 operas; oratorios; 9 symphonies; 15 violin concertos, etc.; but his chamber works, among them a famous nonet for woodwind, horn and strings, are now most admired. A Spohr Society was founded in 1954.

Spoils of Poynton, The (1897). Novel by Henry James.

Spolverini Giambattista (1695–1762). Italian poet whose main work was a long didactic poem on the cultivation of rice, *La coltivazione del riso* (1758), in the manner of Virgil's *Georgics*. This was a peculiarly Veronese literary genre which allowed a great deal of digression from the ostensible theme.

Sponde Jean de (1557–95). French poet. His most important works are religious poems, especially *Stances du sacré banquet et convive de Jésus-Christ* and *Méditations sur les Pseaumes.*

spondee: *metre in verse

Spontini Gasparo (1774–1851). Italian opera composer who from 1805 served the court of Napoleon and then that of Louis XVIII; from 1819 to 1841 he was musical director at Berlin. S. was also important as a conductor, e.g. he introduced the authentic version of Mozart's *Don Giovanni* to the Paris stage. Berlioz much admired his work, above all the opera *Il Vestale* (1807), for its dramatic force and bold originality.

Spoon River Anthology, The (1915). Coll. of poems by Edgar Lee *Masters.

Sportsman's Sketches, A (1852). Coll. of stories by *Turgenev.

Spranger Bartholomeus (1546–*c.* 1627). Flemish painter of religious and allegorical subjects who worked in Rome, Vienna and Prague. He followed the rhetorical style of late Italian mannerism derived from Correggio and Parmigianino.

Sprechgesang. Term used by *Schoenberg.

Spring Howard (1899–1965). English novelist, author of the popular successes *O Absalom!* (1938; also called *My Son, My Son!*) and *Fame is the Spur* (1940).

Springer Ferdinand (1907–). German-born artist who settled in Paris in 1928, later becoming a French citizen. At first a graphic artist, he worked under Bissière in Paris and at S. W. Hayter's Atelier 17. He has produced several fine book illustrations, designs for tapestries and abstract painting.

springing-line. The level at which an arch begins, i.e. curves inward. The SPRINGER is the lowest *voussoir of the arch; its underside is on the s.-l.

Spring's Awakening (1906). Play by Frank *Wedekind.

Spring symphony. Name for (1) *Schumann's 1st symphony and (2) for a work by *Britten

Spranger. *Allegory of Rudolph II*

Squarcione. *Madonna and Child*

Mme de Staël

for solo voices, chorus and orchestra, on the theme of spring.

Spruch. Medieval German verse form, short and aphoristic, and normally satirical or didactic in intention. The oldest colls (late 12th c.) appear under the names of 'Herger' and 'Spervogel'.

sprung rhythm: Gerard Manley *Hopkins

Squarcialupi Antonio (1416–80). Italian organist and composer patronized by Lorenzo de' Medici, who was also perhaps a pupil; his most important was the German composer H. Isaac. S. owned and possibly copied the important musical ms., the *S.-codex.*

Squarcione Francesco (1397–1468). Italian painter, teacher and antiquarian, founder of the school of Padua. He travelled in Greece and Italy coll. antique works. These influenced his own work and that of his pupils who included Mantegna, Cosimo Tura and Crivelli.

Squaw Man, The (1914, 1919, 1931). Films directed by C. B. *De Mille.

squint. Small opening in the wall of a church which enables the worshipper to see the altar; also called a 'hagioscope'.

Stabat Mater ('The mother was standing'). Latin hymn by the 13th-c. Franciscan Jacopone da Todi, about the Virgin Mary standing in grief by the Cross; the most famous musical setting is by *Pergolesi.

staccato (Italian, 'detached'). In musical performance, the playing of notes in a markedly detached manner.

Staël Anne-Louise-Germaine Necker, Mme de (1766–1817). French publicist and critic, daughter of the Swiss banker Jacques Necker, and of Gibbon's quondam fiancée, Suzanne Curchod. She married (1786) the Swedish ambassador to Paris, bore him 3 children and in 1798 obtained a separation. Thereafter at her *salon* in Paris, or in the intervals of exile decreed by Napoleon at her house at Coppet on Lake Geneva, or travelling in Europe, she cultivated the literary, cultured and intellectual lions of her time, and enjoyed the vagaries of a liaison with Benjamin Constant until in 1811 she secretly married a young Swiss officer, Albert de Rocca. 2 novels, *Delphine* (1802) and *Corinne* (1807), depict the solitude of the emancipated woman. *De la littérature . . .* (1800) and *De l'Allemagne* (1810), contain her critical doctrine, which influenced French romanticism–the use of relativism of judgement, the superiority of natural sentiment over conventional form, the distinction between the classical literature of the South and the romantic literature of the North and the superiority of the latter, particularly of the vigorously instinctual Germans.

Nicholas de Stael. *The Roofs*

Stael Nicholas de (1914–55). Russian painter who studied at the Académie des Beaux-Arts in Brussels, and settled in Paris in 1932; he was influenced by Braque, whom he met in 1940, and also by the spirit generated by the Bauhaus. His abstract and lyrical style is characterized by use of boldly defined masses, painted in rich contrasting tones. He slowly gravitated towards representational paintings, with his colour becoming more subdued and neutral. He committed suicide.

staff (plural, staves). In musical notation the name for the 5-line 'grid' on which the notes are written; the pitch of the notes is indicated by the *clef.

Staff Leopold (1878–1957). Polish lyrical poet, playwright and trs., linked with the Young Poland movement. In his youth he was powerfully influenced by Nietzsche; in later life no less powerfully by the Christian mystics.

staffage. French term used in English for the figures, human and animal, in a landscape. Often landscape painters, particularly Dutch 17th- and 18th-c. masters, employed a second painter to add the s.

Stagecoach (1939). Film directed by J. *Ford.

Stagnelius Erik Johan (1793–1823). Swedish romantic poet and playwright, an isolated, neurotic figure who publ. little during his lifetime but exerted considerable posth. influence. Works include the poetic drama *Bacchanterna* (publ. 1822).

Stahl John M. (1886–1950). U.S. film director. S. started directing about 1914 and continued until 1947. There is little critical following for the Hollywood romantic melodrama except when treated in the Sternberg-Dietrich manner,

Squint

Stained glass. The Prophet Hosea; from Augsburg cathedral (beginning of the 12th c.)

Stained glass. Window for Metz cathedral by Chagall

Stained glass. The Emperor Henry II; detail from Strassburg Minster (*c.* 1260). See also colour plate 34

Standish; London, 1697

Standish; London, 1723–4

but S. was one of the best workers in the genre, e.g. *Back Street* (1932), *Imitation of Life* (1934) and *Magnificent Obsession* (1935).

stained glass. Pieces of glass stained with metal oxides are joined together with leading, and details can be painted on. Unique among the visual arts, s. g. is illuminated by diaphanous rather than reflected light. It probably originated in the Near East with coloured glass set in a plaster framework; in Europe it was used for representational art. The finest examples are in the churches of France, England and Germany. The successful use of s. g. depends not only on the manipulation of the richly coloured glass pieces but also on the use of the heavy leads to create a satisfactory pattern. From the 17th c. onwards a facile technique of enamel painting on clear glass was gradually substituted for grisaille painting on s. g. In the 20th c. s. g. has been used by expressionist artists and a new technique has been developed in Denmark, involving thick glass pieces joined by reinforced concrete. In recent years the medieval techniques have been revived in England, notably for the cathedral at Coventry.

Stainer Sir John (1840–1901). English organist, music ed. and composer. His church music such as *The Crucifixion* (1887) is over-sentimental, but *Dufay and his Contemporaries* (1898) and *Early Bodleian Music* (1901) were valuable publs in the field of medieval music.

Stalky & Co. (1899). Boys' book by Kipling.

Stamitz Johann Wenzel Anton (1717–57). German (Bohemian) composer and violinist working at Mannheim from 1741, music director from 1748, and founder of the Mannheim school. S.'s chamber symphonies established the classic 4-movement form of the symphony, the 3rd movement being a minuet; his music is fresh, uses dramatic contrasts of tempo and dynamics, and gives a new independence to the wind instruments. S. was much admired in Paris, and his son Carl (1745–1801), composer of 80 symphonies and concert violinist, worked there as well as in other European centres.

Stampa Gaspara (1523–54). Italian poet. Her *Rime* are entirely inspired by her desperate passion for a rich nobleman who abandoned her. Her verse is genuinely tragic and passionate, and often extremely moving.

standish. Until the early 19th c. this was the name for an inkstand. In the 18th c. inkstands in the shape of a box with 3 compartments were replaced by a tray with 3 separate sockets for inkpot, pounce-box and wafer-box, or 2 sockets and a bell.

Stanfield Clarkson (1793–1867). English marine painter admired by Ruskin.

Stanford Sir Charles Villiers (1852–1924). Irish composer, conductor and teacher. He studied in Germany, influenced by Brahms, and taught at Cambridge Univ. and at the R.C.M. (1883–1924), his pupils including Vaughan Williams and Bliss. His works include: the operas *Shamus O'Brien* (1896) and *The Critic* (1916), after Sheridan; 6 symphonies; *Irish Rhapsodies* for orchestra; chamber music and settings of Irish songs, e.g. *Songs of Erin* (1900).

Stanislavsky Konstantin Sergeyevich (1863–1938). Russian actor, producer and teacher who was the founder of the Moscow Art Theatre (1898). The system of acting which he taught has come to be called the *method; it had its source, according to S., in the amateur plays performed at *Abramtsevo. He was a great actor himself, excelling in the plays of Chekhov, and publ. several books about his art, notably *My Life In Art* (1924) and *An Actor Prepares* (1936).

Stanley John (1713–86). English composer and organist blind from early childhood but a professional musician by 11. He was a pupil of M. Greene and composed oratorios and stage and instrumental music.

Stanwyck Barbara (1902–). U.S. film star, who in her career of over 30 years has played with skill a great variety of roles, but especially the hard-boiled heroine, e.g. *Clash by Night*.

stanza (Italian, 'station'). Group of lines of verse arranged according to a regular metrical and rhyming pattern; usually a poem will be composed of a number of s.s. The most famous English example is the SPENSERIAN s. which has 8 10-syllable lines followed by 1 12-syllable line, and rhymes *ababbcbcc*.

Star is Born, A. Film (1937) directed by W. *Wellman. Film (1954) directed by G. *Cukor.

state. Used as a technical term to describe the various stages through which an *engraving or etching may pass. The 1st s. is the 1st proof pulled from the plate. The artist may decide on some improvement and alter lines on the plate; the proof from the altered plate is the 2nd s. This process may be repeated a number of times until the artist is fully satisfied with the work.

Statius Publius Papinius (*c.* A.D. 40–*c.* 96). Roman poet born at Naples, author of the *Silvae*, a coll. of poems, and an epic poem, the *Thebaïs*.

Staudte Wolfgang (1906–). German film director. He worked in the theatre with Reinhardt and Piscator, and directed his 1st feature in 1943. After the war, in East Germany, he made films set during the Nazi régime, including *Murderers Are Among Us* (1946) and *The Underdog* (1951). His most celebrated later film is *Roses for the Prosecutor* (1960), made in West Germany.

Stavenhagen Fritz (1876–1906). Low German writer of naturalistic plays including the well-known *Mudder Mews* (1904).

Stedman Edmund Clarence (1833–1908). U.S. critic and anthologist, a leader of New York literary society. S. was one of the first to recognize Walt Whitman's merits. His reputation rests on *The Poets of America* (1885) and 2 anthologies, *A Library of American Literature* (1888–90) and *An American Anthology* (1900).

Steele Sir Richard (1672–1729). English writer. After education at Charterhouse, where he met Addison, and Oxford, S. became an officer in the Life Guards. His subsequent career in politics was generally successful though for a time damaged by pro-Hanoverian sympathies. S.'s moral purpose was clear with the publ. *The Christian Hero* (1701), a treatise on morals originally intended for his own guidance. In 1709, with *Addison's help and collaboration, he began to publ. *The Tatler*, the 1st periodical of the age; this was succeeded in 1711 by *The Spectator* and in 1713 by *The Guardian*. S.'s reputation as a writer rests on the essays–often of a didactic nature and designed to raise the moral tone of society–which he wrote for these journals. His 3 comedies had little success.

steel engraving. Copper, the metal generally used in *engraving, was too soft to allow a large number of reprints. In the 19th c. some workers began to engrave on steel, which was durable but also hard to work; a further refinement was STEEL FACING in which a fine steel film was laid on the copper plate by electrolysis.

steel-frame. Architectural term for the skeleton of steel girders which provides the structurally essential framework of a building.

Steell Sir John (1804–91). Scottish sculptor of the statue of Sir Walter Scott in the Scott Monument, Edinburgh.

Steen Jan Havicksz (1625/6–79). Dutch genre painter, pupil of A. van Ostade and J. van Goyen. He worked at Leyden, The Hague, Delft and Haarlem, producing a great number of paintings, often of tavern scenes and social gatherings. There is a wide range of humour and anecdotal interest in his work. He is noted for his rich colour harmonies and sense of composition.

steeple. Architectural term for the tower and spire of a church.

Steer Philip Wilson (1860–1942). English painter who studied in Paris under Bougereau and Cabanel. S.'s work was strongly influenced by neo-impressionism, but in the 1890s he turned to a style derived from Turner and Constable. He became widely known only when the Tate accepted *Chepstow Castle*, an oil painting, in 1909. S.'s fresh, light, breezy landscapes in oil were matched by watercolours of great liquidity and economy of statement, with large skies and a strong sense of atmosphere.

Stefano da Zevio (or da Verona) (*c.* 1375–1451). Veronese painter in the international Gothic style. Antonio Pisanello was probably his pupil.

Steffani Agostino (1654–1728). Italian composer, diplomat and churchman. Most of his working life was spent in Germany; Handel, who met S. at Hanover, admired his cantabile style.

Steichen Edward (1879–). U.S. photographer whose lifetime has spanned the historical and technological development of

Sir Richard Steele: painting by Kneller

Konstantin Stanislavsky

Steen. *Wedding*

Steer. *The Horseshoe Bend of the Severn*

Stefano da Zevio. *Adoration of the Magi*

Gertrude Stein: painting by Picasso

John Steinbeck

Stella. *Brooklyn Bridge*

Steinlen. *Vagabonds in the Snow*; lithograph

photography. In 1902 he and Steiglitz formed the Photo-Secession Gallery, in an effort to provide photographers with an outlet and a place to be seen. During World War II S. was in charge of Naval War Photography and during his tenure as head of the photography department of the Mus. of Modern Art was responsible for organizing the international 'Family of Man' Exhibition.

Stein Gertrude (1874–1946). U.S. writer, one of America's most influential expatriates and linguistic experimentalists. Her earliest work (1896) was a paper on automatism in writing, a subject affecting her own later works. She settled in France in 1902 and in the 1920s became the centre of a Paris group which included Hemingway, Pound and Anderson. She was in France during the German Occupation (*Wars I Have Known*, 1945). *Three Lives* (1909) is her straightforward and moving story of 3 servant-girls; *Tender Buttons* (1914) is radically, cubistically experimental; and *The Autobiography of Alice B. Toklas* (1933) is in fact her own life story. She wrote the libretto for an opera, *Four Saints in Three Acts* (1934), with music by Virgil Thompson.

Steinbeck John (1902–). U.S. novelist who was awarded the Nobel prize in 1962. The scene of most of S.'s best-known work is the Salinas area of California where he was born. He began writing while acting as caretaker in a snowbound resort (one of his many earlier jobs) but recognition only came with his 3rd novel, *Tortilla Flat* (1935), an amusing series of linked episodes about the people (*paisanos* and others) of Monterey, of whom he again wrote in *Cannery Row* (1945) and *Sweet Thursday* (1954). *In Dubious Battle* (1936) concerns the move towards Communism of a young San Franciscan among West Coast itinerant labourers. *The Grapes of Wrath* (1939), S.'s realistic masterpiece, describes the plight of an Oklahoma farming family who leave the Dust Bowl and seek a better life in California. *Of Mice and Men* (1937) is a brief and tragic story of an intelligent ranch labourer and his strong, half-witted companion. S.'s novels include *The Pearl* (1947), *East of Eden* (1952), a symbolic transference of Biblical themes to the Salinas Valley, and *The Winter of Our Discontent* (1961).

Steinberg Maximilian Osseyevich (1883–1946). Russian composer; a pupil of Glazunov and Rimsky-Korsakov (his father-in-law). S. himself taught at the St Petersburg (later Leningrad) Conservatory, becoming its director in 1934. For a time his music showed the influence of Rimsky-Korsakov; this was followed by a mystical phase inspired by Scriabin and later tendencies to impressionism.

Steinlen Théophile-Alexandre (1859–1923). Swiss-born French painter and graphic artist, a vigorous impassioned critic of social misery and human exploitation. His poster designs of the 1890s were executed in the bold, flat style, influenced by the Japanese print, which is best exemplified in the work of Toulouse-Lautrec.

Steinway and Sons. New York piano makers with branches in London and Hamburg. The firm was founded by H. E. Steinway (originally Steinweg) (1797–1871) who settled in the U.S. in 1850.

Stella Joseph (1870/80–1946). Italian-born painter who emigrated to the U.S. in 1896. He was later deeply affected by contact with the Italian futurists, and produced many works celebrating urban America, e.g. *Brooklyn Bridge* (1917–18).

stem. The stem is the length of glass which joins the bowl of a glass to its foot. Stems can be decorated in a variety of ways–with air and colour twists, with faceting or most often with swellings of various shapes known as *knops.

Stendhal. Pseud. of Henri-Marie Beyle (1783–1842). French novelist, born at Grenoble. S. escaped from his devout, Royalist father to Paris (1799) and in 1800 procured an army commission. Posted to Milan, he fell in love with Italy and also began to learn English (much later he visited England and contributed to English reviews). He resigned in 1802 and settled in Paris until shortage of funds drove him into the army again (1806). He served as a Commissariat officer, following Napoleon's armies through Germany, Austria and Russia, but in 1813, owing to ill-health, resigned and made for Milan. He spent 7 years there, without prospect of employment in Restoration France because of his service under Napoleon, and publ. *Vie de Haydn, de Mozart et de Métastase* (1814), *Histoire de la Peinture en Italie* (1817), both cribbed from other authors but including some original insights, and *Rome, Naples et Florence en 1817* (1817; revised ed.

1827). Returning to Paris, where he frequented the *salons* (especially Mme Ancelot's), he publ. *De l'amour* (1822), a profound analysis of passion based on the succession of unhappy love-affairs which had absorbed–and continued to absorb–his private life; *La Vie de Rossini* (1823); *Racine et Shakespeare* (1823; 1825), 2 tracts in defence of romanticism; *Armance* (1827), his 1st novel; *Promenades dans Rome* (1829); and his great novel *Le Rouge et le Noir* (1830). This psychological study of intrigue deals with the ambitious career, ending on the scaffold, of Julien Sorel, a carpenter's son, and is a bitter description of Restoration society; its climax is based on an attempted murder of 1827. *Le Rouge* is either the life of military glory or the spirit of Republicanism; *le Noir* the career offered by the Church or the force of clerical reaction. When the Orleanist Louis-Philippe became king, S. was appointed consul at Trieste (1831), but soon transferred to Civitavecchia, where he remained with spells abroad until his death in Paris (from apoplexy). *Mémoires d'un touriste* (1838) are travel impressions interspersed with criticism. *La Chartreuse de Parme* (1839), his other great novel, is based on the 16th-c. annals of the ducal House of Parma, but describes Italian society in the period 1815–30. Like *Le Rouge et le Noir* it is a profoundly analytical presentation of a tale of passion and intrigue; Balzac praised it enthusiastically. The last novel publ. in S.'s lifetime was *L'Abbesse de Castro* (1839). S. said that he wrote for 'the happy few' and accurately predicted that he would not be widely appreciated until the end of the 19th c.–not surprisingly, since his works appeared when romanticism was at its height; and although S.'s subject was passion, his method was analytical and his style plain, dry and concise. Posth. publ. works: *Vie de Napoléon* (1876); *Lamiel* (1889) and *Lucien Leuwen* (1894), 2 fragmentary novels; *Journal 1801–18* (1888); *La Vie de Henri Brulard* (1890), a moving, simple and honest description of his childhood and early youth; and *Souvenirs d'égotisme* (1892).

Stephen Sir Leslie (1832–1904). English writer, ed. of *The Cornhill Magazine* (1871–82) and of *The Dictionary of National Biography*, to which he also contributed many articles. S. was the father of Virginia Woolf.

Stephen Hero. Early draft of James Joyce's *Portrait of the Artist as a Young Man.*

Stephens A(lfred) G(eorge) (1865–1933). Australian critic associated with the early *Sydney Bulletin* magazine and for long regarded as the father of Australian criticism. He befriended many writers, encouraged Furphy and Neilson, but in criticism, e.g. of Brennan, was often unjust through provincial arrogance.

Stephens Frederick George (1828–1907). English painter and writer on art, a member of the Pre-Raphaelite Brotherhood.

Stephens James (1882–1950). Irish novelist and poet best known for the fairy-story *The Crock of Gold* (1912).

Sterling George (1869–1926). U.S. poet whose overblown long poems (e.g. *A Wine of Wizardry*, 1909) enjoyed some popularity. He committed suicide.

Stern Isaac (1920–). One of the world's leading violinists; of U.S. citizenship. He has frequently appeared with Casals at the Prades and Perpignan festivals.

Sternberg Josef von (1894–). Austrian-born U.S. film director. S. moved to the U.S. after World War I, and started in films in 1923 as writer and cinematographer–most of his features were actually photographed by him. His 1st, experimental film as director was *The Salvation Hunters* (1925), almost entirely composed of shots which were completely motionless. *The Seagull* (1926) was made for Chaplin. S.'s 1st big success was *Underworld* (1927), written by B. *Hecht, which attempted a more truthful description of the criminal classes. After 3 more films, including *Docks of New York* (1928), he accepted the invitation of Emil Jannings to direct *Der Blaue Engel* (1930), the 1st important film with Marlene Dietrich, who appeared in S.'s next 6 films. S.'s subject in the Dietrich films is the deception of men by women, the seductive lie, the desperate snatching at illusion. As befitted the subject, the films have a rich and alluring surface like a thin veneer over depths of corruption only made at all explicit in *The Blue Angel*, and in a later echo of these films, *The Shanghai Gesture* (1941). In *Morocco* (1930) and *Dishonored* (1931), deception of the male was also self-deception and had to be paid for. Far more soberly treated were *An American Tragedy* (1931) and *Crime and Punishment* (1935). From the late 1930s he made films less frequently. *Macao* (1952) and *Jet Pilot* (shot

Stendhal

Isaac Stern

Sternberg. Emil Jannings and Marlene Dietrich in *The Blue Angel*

Stevens. James Dean and Elizabeth Taylor in *Giant*

Laurence Sterne: contemporary painting

Wallace Stevens

Stettheimer. Choir of the Franciscan church, Salzburg.

1950, released 1957) bear almost as many signs of production by Howard Hughes as they do of direction by S. His last film, *The Saga of Anatahan* (1953), was shot in Japan.

Sterne Laurence (1713–68). English novelist. From 1738 to 1759 S. lived in Yorkshire, taking his duties as vicar of Stillington and Coxwold lightly. He began writing *Tristram Shandy* in 1758, to relieve the depression he felt after his wife's illness. Privately printed in 1759, the first 2 vols created an immediate sensation and ensured S.'s fame and welcome in London social life. Subsequent vols followed at intervals until 1767, when *A Sentimental Journey* (1768), written to commemorate a trip to France and Italy made on medical advice in 1765, was also publ. The *Journal to Eliza* was written for the last of his many loves.
A totally amoral writer, S. gave the English language the word 'sentimental' and was the first to find a source of pride and pleasure in the exquisite play of his own sensations. With intense sensitivity, probably made more acute by his tubercular condition, he extracted from every situation the maximum of emotion or innuendo, and was sometimes guilty of bad taste in the process. *Tristram Shandy* is nevertheless a classic of comic literature. In it S. drew on his experiences of military life as a boy in his father's barracks for the characters of Uncle Toby, Corporal Trim and Le Fever; the fantastical Parson Yorick is a self-portrait and several of his parishioners were drawn from S.'s neighbours in Yorkshire.
Its rambling, digressive, impressionistic style, which influenced Virginia Woolf in her contribution to the stream-of-consciousness novel, would be enough in itself to make it an eccentric achievement; but in addition S. has created in Toby and Trim characters who are both comical and warmly alive, and in the story of Le Fever and a few other passages he rises above the general level of forced and hectic emotion to distil a piercing and simple pathos.

Stettheimer Hans the Elder (*c.* 1355–1432). German architect, one of the best-known masters of S. German late Gothic. He designed several hall-churches, including St Martin, Landshut, and the choir of the Franciscan church, Salzburg.

Stevens George (1905–). U.S. film director. Even his early films (1st feature in 1933) like *Alice Adams* (1935) and *Annie Oakley* (1935) were technically very assured, and he succeeded with an Astaire-Rogers musical, *Swing Time* (1936), and a period film, *Quality Street* (1937). *Woman of the Year* (1942) and particularly *The More the Merrier* (1943), which was inspired by the housing shortage in wartime Washington, were hilarious comedies. But the mutation of *Talk of the Town* (1942) from comedy to anti-lynch film revealed aspirations towards a high seriousness for which S. seemed unequipped. After the touching nostalgia of *I Remember Mama* (1948), he made perhaps the most successful of his big pictures with *A Place in the Sun* (1951), from T. Dreiser. *Shane* (1952) is a western, calculated in effect down to the last meteorological detail, which attempts to combine western action with social history. Some of the same preoccupations are to be found in *Giant* (1956). *The Diary of Anne Frank* (1959) although obviously made with complete sincerity, never rose above the level of relentless cliché. His only film since is *The Greatest Story Ever Told* (1965).

Stevens Wallace (1879–1955), U.S. poet. An executive in a Connecticut insurance co., he wrote in his spare time some of the most remarkable poetry produced by the experimental generation of the 1920s. His poetic manner has always been modern, colourful, stylish; a rhetorical comic diction using recondite words and amazing symbolistic inventions makes the first impact. 'Unsack your snood, Madonna . . .' begins one poem. He shows how things resist identity and meaning and how poetry and imagination, 'the supreme fiction' are primary and truthful instruments, constituting the highest way of knowing. Many of his poems concern writing poetry and the supersession of Christian faith by the clarity of the unencumbered imagination. Yet reality constantly changes, and it is the truthfulness and seriousness of his search and his discipline over an extended oeuvre that makes him a major poet. His chief works are *Harmonium* (1923), *Ideas of Order* (1935), *Owl's Clover* (1936), *The Man with the Blue Guitar* (1937), *Parts of a World* (1942), *Notes towards a Supreme Fiction* (1942), *Esthétique du Mal* (1945) and *The Auroras of Autumn* (1947), showing a continuous development. Colls include *Collected Poems* and *Opus Posthumous*, and *The Necessary Angel* (1951), essays concerned with the imagination and revealing his affinity with Coleridge and the romantics.

Stevenson Robert Louis (1850–94). Scottish writer. S.'s poor health induced him to travel widely; he at last settled in the South Seas, where he died. S. wrote successfully in a number of genres, his style is graceful and flexible, yet unobtrusive. His most popular works have always been the novels of adventure–*Treasure Island* (1883), *Kidnapped* (1886) and its sequel *Catriona* (1893), and *The Master of Ballantrae* (1888)–and *The Strange Case of Dr. Jekyll and Mr Hyde* (1886). In this the protagonist acquires 2 separate personalities, gradually succumbing to the evil one, Mr Hyde. S. also wrote the unfinished *Weir of Hermiston* (1896), many travel books and essays, including *Travels with a Donkey in the Cevennes* (1879) and *Virginibus Puerisque* (1881), and some fine lyric poems.

Stewart Douglas (1913–). New Zealand-born writer working in Australia. His poetry, traditional in technique, yet allows full use of colloquial speech rhythms and whimsy that becomes sardonic. He has also written criticism and verse plays, e.g. *The Fire on the Snow* (1944).

Stewart James (1908–). U.S. film actor who has since 1934 made westerns, comedies, mysteries and romances to continued popular and critical acclaim. Among his films are *Mr Smith Goes to Washington* (1939), *Philadelphia Story* (1940), *Winchester '73* (1950), *Vertigo* (1958) and *How the West Was Won* (1962). His hesitant drawl remains, but he has matured from gentle young charmers to more forthright roles.

Stieglitz Alfred (1864–1946). U.S. photographer who has been called the father of modern photography. He pioneered the use of hand cameras for serious photography and founded the revolutionary Photo-Secession group (with *Steichen) and its periodical *Camera Work*. S. discovered and influenced many of the best 20th-c. photographers, including Strand and Steichen. His work is best represented by the series of New York scenes carried out over a period of 40 years. His gallery was important in publicizing modern painting.

Stifter Adalbert (1805–68). Austrian novelist. The preface to *Bunte Steine* (coll. stories 1853) summarizes his literary philosophy: to use subjects from everyday, small-scale life, exemplifying the 'gentle law' that constructive forces, appearances notwithstanding, are greater than destructive ones in nature and human life. These principles are illustrated by the stories, set in remote rural settings minutely described, composing *Studien* (1844–50)–including *Abdias* (1843; 1850) and *Brigitta* (1840; 1957)–and *Bunte Steine*, including *Bergkristall* (1845; 1857) and *Kalkstein* (1848), as by the late novels *Der Nachsommer* (1857) and *Witiko* (1865–7).

Still Clyfford (1904–). U.S. painter. His style, which is highly individualistic, owes little or nothing to contemporary European movements. He employs large monochrome masses, and predominant colours are red and black.

Still William Grant (1895–). U.S. Negro composer and conductor; his teachers included Varèse. S.'s music includes *Afro-American Symphony* (1931); the opera *Blue Steel* (1935); and *And They Lynched Him on a Tree* for narrator, chorus and orchestra (1940).

Stiller Mauritz (1883–1928). Finnish-born Swedish film director. S. started directing in 1912. Like Sjöström, S. took stylistic inspiration from the work of Griffith and particularly Ince with his use of landscape. The subjects were, however, completely native, often from novels, like *Sir Arne's Treasure* (1919). His *Gösta-Berlings Saga* (1923) was the 1st important film with Greta Garbo. Like Sjöström, he went to Hollywood in the great mid-1920s talent importation, and made a few films of which the most ambitious was *Hotel Imperial* (1927).

still-life. Painting containing only objects (most often domestic–tableware, flowers, books –but sometimes skulls, dead game, etc.) viewed close up. S.-l. was early of importance in oriental art, and is approached in Greek and Roman mosaics; but it emerged as an independent subject in the West only in the 16th c., e.g. practised by Caravaggio, and flowering in 17th-c. Flanders. It was often used symbolically and allusively. Chardin was the 1st notable French s.-l. painter. Since the 18th c. it has been widely used, receiving impetus from the 19th-c. discovery of the Japanese colour print; with Cézanne and others the s.-l. has been a stage in a development towards non-representational art.

Robert Louis Stevenson: oil sketch

Still-life from Pompeii

Still-life. Caravaggio, *Supper at Emmaus* (detail)

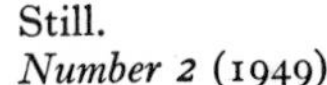

Still.
Number 2 (1949)

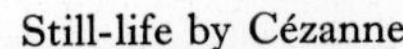

Still-life by Cézanne

Stieglitz.
In Steerage

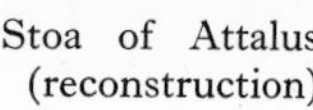

Stoa of Attalus (reconstruction)

Karlheinz Stockhausen

Stokowski

Stomer. *Miracle of St Isadore*

Stirling and Gowan. Engineering Laboratories, Leicester

stippling. In drawing or painting, modelling form by means of small dots or short strokes instead of lines or areas of colour.

Stirling and Gowan. London architectural partnership (1956–63) producing tough and influential designs. Their Ham Common Flats (1958) brought to England the style of Le Corbusier's Jaoul Houses, and their Engineering Laboratories at Leicester Univ. (1959–63) achieve powerful plastic effects by visually separating all the elements (staircase, auditoria, etc.) of the building.

stoa. Colonnaded walk, built round or near the '*agora*' ('public square') of a Greek town, as a meeting-place and protection from the weather. The best known is the Stoa of Attalus, Athens (*c.* 150 B.C.), now carefully reconstructed by the American School of Classical Studies.

Stockhausen Karlheinz (1928–). One of the foremost *avant-garde* German composers, and a major theorist of *serialism. After studying at the Cologne School of Music (with Frank *Martin), he went to Paris in 1952, studying with Milhaud and Messiaen and making experimental *musique concrète recordings. His theories on music owe much to his studies of information-theory (at Bonn in 1953). He divides music into 5 parameters, or basic elements: duration, frequency, tone-colour, intensity, and the position of the sound-sources in space. S. seeks to establish within and between these elements mathematical relationships as sophisticated as classical *12-note technique did for one of them (frequency: i.e. the notes). He wishes composers to devise techniques suitable for each of the numerous media now available to them. A composer writing for radio should think in that medium, e.g. *Carrée* ('Square') (1959–60) for orchestras and 4 choirs, should be broadcast on 4 channels, i.e. stereophonically. When writing for instruments, however, the composer should allow more scope for the artistic judgement of the performer, e.g. in *Klavierstück XI* (1956), various fragments–'groups'–can be played in a variety of orders, in various manners. Other works include: *Kontrapunkte* ('Counterpoints') for 10 instruments (1952), *Zeitmasse* ('Tempos') (1955–6) for 5 wind instruments, *Gruppen* ('Groups') for 3 orchestras (1955–7), *Kontakte* ('Contacts') for electronic sounds, percussion and piano (1960), and *Momente* ('Moments') for soprano, 4 choirs and 13 instruments (1961–2).

Stockton Frank R. (1834–1902). U.S. novelist and short-story writer. S. was the forerunner of O. Henry in his use of the surprise ending. His writing was characterized by humour and narrative ability. His works include the famous story *The Lady or The Tiger?* (1882), and the novel *The Casting Away of Mrs Lecks and Mrs Aleshine* (1886).

Stoddard Charles Warren (1843–1909). U.S. writer. S.'s travel book *South-Sea Idylls* (1873) created the literary fashion for Polynesian subjects (R. L. Stevenson read it).

Stoddard Richard Henry (1825–1903). U.S. poet and critic. His best poem is perhaps *Abraham Lincoln: An Horatian Ode* (1865).

Stoic, The (1947). Novel by Dreiser.

Stoker Bram (1847–1912). Irish writer, for years Sir Henry Irving's manager. He also wrote horror novels, notably the enduringly popular *Dracula* (1897), about the Transylvanian vampire Count Dracula; characteristic is a peculiar mixture of the horrific and the Victorian-sentimental.

Stokowski (originally Boleslowowicz, Stanislaw Antoni–for a time Stokes) Leopold (1882–). British-born U.S. conductor, notably of the Philadelphia Orchestra (1912–36). He gave the 1st U.S. performance of *Wozzeck* (1931), was the conductor in Walt Disney's film *Fantasia* and has produced dramatic and ponderous orchestral versions of organ works by J. S. Bach.

Stolberg brothers. The German poets and writers Count Christian S. (1748–1821) and Count Friedrich Leopold S. (1750–1819) toured Switzerland with Goethe in 1775 and were friends of other important contemporaries and members of the Hainbund, a romantic-nationalist group of writers. They publ. a vol. of poems (1779) and *Schauspiele mit chören* (1787), which aimed to revive an interest in Greek drama. Friedrich also publ. *Geschichte der Religion Jesu Christi* (1806–18).

Stomer Matthias (17th c.). Dutch Caravaggesque painter of religious subjects who settled in Italy; pupil of Honthorst.

Stone Andrew L. (1902–). U.S. film director who started in films in 1918. He now works as an independent writer/producer/director with

Edward Durrell Stone. U.S. Pavilion, Brussels

Theodor Storm

his wife Virginia as co-producer and editor. Natural locations play an essential part in his recent thrillers, where ordinary people become victims of circumstance: gangsters (*Cry Terror*, 1958), shipwreck (*The Last Voyage*, 1959), or forest fire (*Ring of Fire*, 1961).

Stone Edward Durrell (1902–). U.S. architect and a pioneer of the international style in America in the 1930s (he designed the M.M.A., New York (1939), in collaboration with Philip Goodwin). S.'s work became more personal in the 1950s with his use of pierced screens to almost all his buildings, as at the U.S. Embassy in New Delhi and the U.S. Pavilion at the 1958 Brussels Exhibition.

Stone Sir John (1804–91). Scottish sculptor. After several years of study in Rome he established himself as the leading sculptor in Scotland. In Edinburgh he executed statues of Sir Walter Scott, the Duke of Wellington, Queen Victoria and the Prince Consort.

Stone Nicholas (1586–1647). English mason-sculptor and architect, trained under Hendrick de Keyser in Amsterdam (1606–13) and appointed master mason to James I (1619). He worked on the Banqueting House, Whitehall, where he began an association with Inigo Jones. He is best known for his tombs, which include that of Francis Holles (Westminster Abbey), based on Michelangelo's tomb of Giuliano de' Medici. His son NICHOLAS (d. 1647) was a sculptor who worked under Bernini in Italy, and another son HENRY (d. 1653) was a painter noted as a copyist of Van Dyck.

Stones of Venice, The (1851–3). Book by John *Ruskin.

stoneware. Term used of types of highly fired earthenware. Glaze is not necessary in so far as the clay is in effect vitrified by its high-temperature firing, but glazes are occasionally used; lead and salt *glazes being most common. *Wedgwood's jasperware is a fine example of s.

Stong Phil(ip Duffield) (1899–1957). U.S. novelist who wrote humorous tales of Middle Western American life. His best-known novel is *State Fair* (1932).

Storace Stephen (1763–96). English composer of Italian parentage; he produced a number of light operas including *No Song, No Supper*. Studying in Vienna, he and his sister NANCY (1766–1817) were friends of Mozart, who wrote the part of Susanna in *The Marriage of Figaro* for Nancy.

Storey David (1933–). English novelist. He studied art at the Slade School, then became a rugby footballer, which provided the background for his best-selling novel *This Sporting Life* (1960). Works include *Flight into Camden* (1960) and *Radcliffe* (1963).

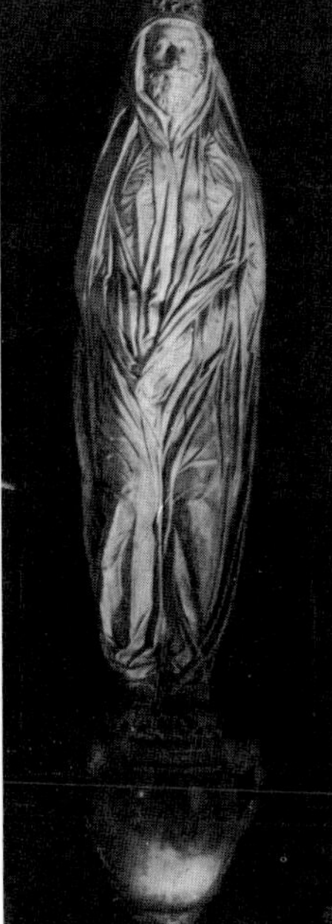

Nicholas Stone. Tomb of John Donne

Storm (Hans) Theodor (Woldsen) (1817–88). German writer. Studied law in Kiel; voluntary exile from his native Husum (1853) when Denmark annexed Holstein; became Prussian magistrate; recalled 1864. By temperament a lyric poet, e.g. *Liederbuch dreier Freunde*, in collaboration with the Mommsen brothers, (1843), *Gedichte* (1852). A master of word music and rhythm; he writes best about passion and marriage, especially in relation to transience; about dying; his native coast; and humorous genre scenes. His early stories, too, convey mood rather than plot; the best known, *Immensee* (1849; 1858), once immensely popular, is now thought sentimental, and his later *Novellen*, with their stronger plot, starker setting and characters, and psychological, occasionally social problems, are preferred. They include: *Viola tricolor* (1874; 1956), *Aquis submersus* (1876; 1910), *Renate* (1878; 1909), *Hans und Heinz Kirch* (1882), *Zur Chronik von Grieshuus* (1884; *A Chapter in the History of Grieshuus*, 1908), *Ein Doppelgänger* (1886), and *Der Schimmelreiter* (1888; *Rider on a White Horse*, 1913).

Stoneware bust of Prince Rupert by Dwight of Fulham (*c.* 1680)

Storm, The (1859). Play by *Ostrovsky.

storm and stress (from German '*Sturm und Drang*'). German literary movement, first known as the '*Geniezeit*' ('period of geniuses'), flourishing in the 1770s; it was characterized by extreme romanticism and inspired by J.-J. Rousseau. The main German critic involved was Herder; its major figure was the young Goethe of *Goetz von Berlichingen* and *Die Leiden des jungen Werthers*; others were Schiller, Klinger, Lenz, H. L. Wagner and Mahler Müller.

Storm Over Asia (1928; sound version 1952). Film directed by V. I. *Pudovkin.

Stoneware jugs by Spode

Stradivarius, dated 1699

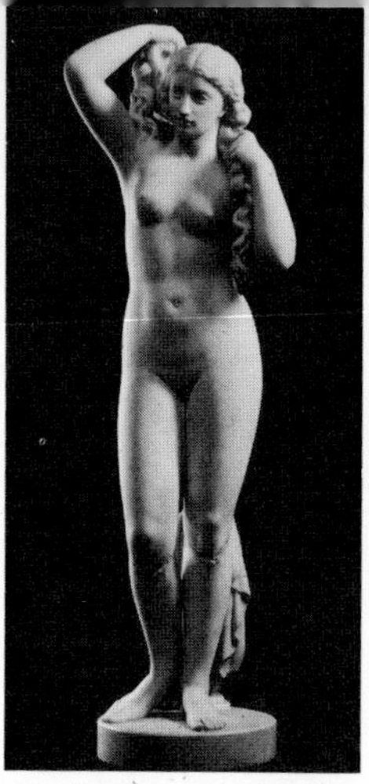

William Wetmore Story. *Venus*

Strapwork, Wollaston Hall, Nottinghamshire

Lytton Strachey: painting by Henry Lamb

Stoss. High Altar, the church of Our Lady, Cracow

Story William Wetmore (1819–95). U.S. lawyer, sculptor and poet who spent most of his life in Italy. In *William Wetmore Story and His Friends* (1903), Henry James explored the motivation of early 19th-c. expatriates.

Story of an African Farm, The (1883). Book by Olive *Schreiner.

Story of G.I. Joe, The (1945). Film directed by W. *Wellman.

Story of My Heart, The (1883). Book by Richard *Jefferies.

Stoss Veit (d. 1533). German late Gothic sculptor, painter and engraver active in Cracow and Nuremberg. His masterpiece is the huge high altar in carved and painted wood in the church of Our Lady, Cracow. Other important works include the tomb of King Casimir IV (Cracow cathedral), *Annunciation* (St Lorenz, Nuremberg) and the high altar of Bamberg cathedral.

Stothard Thomas (1755–1834). English painter, and a book illustrator and embellisher of considerable charm. His best-known painting is *Canterbury Pilgrims* (Tate) which caused a quarrel between him and Blake, who was already working on the same subject.

Stourbridge glass. In 1612 emigrant glass makers from Lorraine are recorded as working in the Stourbridge area, and from that date this town remained one of the most important glass-making centres in England. At first it only produced window-glass but by the 18th c. fine glasses were being made.

Stout Rex (Todhunter) (1886–). U.S. detective-story writer, creator of the famous character Nero Wolfe.

Stow John (1525?–1605). English chronicler and antiquary. He wrote *The Chronicles of England* (1580), now better known as *The Annales of England.*

Stowe Harriet (Elizabeth) Beecher (1811–96). U.S. novelist, the wife of a Congregationalist clergyman. Her *Uncle Tom's Cabin, or, Life Among the Lowly* (1852), one of the most widely circulated books in history, denounced the evils of slavery and strongly influenced public opinion.

Strachey (Giles) Lytton (1880–1932). English biographer. The 4 short studies in *Eminent Victorians* (1918) made S. famous, and his sceptical investigation of the motives of respected historical figures had many imitators. S.'s style is elegant and urbane, and his attacks are conducted with irony rather than violence. He also wrote *Queen Victoria* (1921) and *Elizabeth and Essex* (1928).

Strada, La (1954). Film directed by F. *Fellini.

Stradella Alessandro (*c.* 1642–82). Italian composer important in the development of the accompanied aria and in the concerto grosso; he wrote operas, oratorios, etc. His life is obscure but he was the victim of 2 murder attempts and he died by murder; his romantic elopement was the subject of an opera by Flotow.

Stradivarius. Latinized form of Stradivari, a family of Cremonese violin makers; ANTONIO (*c.* 1644–1737) is the most famous of all violin makers. He was a pupil of N. Amati whose influence is apparent up to about 1685. Years of experiment (1685–1700) produced the characteristic S. violin–exquisitely proportioned, with a rich golden brown varnish and a brilliant 'oboe' tone. S. produced about 1,100 instruments, of which about 540 violins, 12 violas and 50 cellos are known today.

Straight is the Gate (1909). Novel by André Gide.

Strand Paul (1890–). U.S. photographer strongly influenced by Stieglitz. Concerned with what he called 'the spirit of place', S. worked at a leisurely pace using a large camera and heavy equipment in contrast with the modern trend. S.'s long career has included work on documentary films and the publ. of humorous books which have become photographic classics.

Strand Theatre. A theatre was built on the site in 1832 but the present building went up in 1905, taking its present name in 1910. Despite serious bombing during World War II performances continued, notably lunchtime Shakespeare recitals given by Sir Donald Wolfit.

Strange Sir Robert (1721–92). Scottish engraver, noted for line engravings after Van Dyck; rival of Bartolozzi.

Strange Incident: *The *Ox-Bow Incident*

Strange Meeting. Poem by Wilfred Owen.

Stranger, The (1942). Novel by Albert *Camus.

Straparola Gian Francesco (*c.* 1480–1557). Italian writer. His best-known work is his coll. of short stories or *novelle*, *Le Piacevoli notti*, which often show great power of imagination and a talent for fairy-tales; they were extremely popular.

strapwork. 16th-c. ornamental style in architecture, originating in the Netherlands and popular in England and W. Europe, of which the main feature was a pattern of interlacing strap-like bands.

Strasberg Lee (1901–). American director, one of the founders of *Group Theater and artistic director of the New York Actors' Studio, a school for experienced actors and modern home of the *method.

Strassburg. Important 18th-c. faïence factory in Alsace, controlled by the Hannong family–notably Charles-François (*c.* 1669–1739) and his son Paul-Antoine (1700–60); the latter introduced enamel-painted faïence (revolutionizing French and German production) just before 1750, as well as opening the porcelain factory at Frankenthal. The family also controlled the Hagenau factory, which probably made the faïence, the decorating being done at S. In style S. work followed the porcelain style developed by Meissen, and 'S. flowers' became particularly well known.

Strassburg cathedral. One of the most spectacular Gothic cathedrals. Choir and transepts (*c.* 1180) are Romanesque but the nave (1250–90) was added in the mature style of Île de France Gothic. In the 14th and early 15th cs the W. front was continued with a lattice of tracery and 2 towers with open-work spires (only 1 was finished).

Stratford-on-Avon. The place where William Shakespeare was born (and buried) and consequently a centre of pilgrimage, cultural activity and commercial exploitation. The 1st Shakespeare Memorial Theatre went up in 1879 and was of such ugliness that when it was burned down in 1926, Bernard Shaw sent a telegram of congratulation to the governors. The new theatre, opened in 1932, also received much criticism and was nicknamed 'the jam factory'. This building is now called the Royal Shakespeare Theatre.

Stratford Ontario Theatre. Canadian theatre opened in 1953 with productions of *All's Well That Ends Well* and *Richard III* by Sir Tyrone *Guthrie who has often worked there. This theatre has produced many excellent actors, notably Christopher Plummer, and in 1964 played a season at *Chichester, England.

Straub Johann Baptist (1704–84). Bavarian rococo sculptor, from 1737 court sculptor in Munich. His works include the high altar, St Michael's church, Berg-am-Laim, Munich and altars in the monastic churches of Ettal and Schäftlarn. Ignaz Günther was his pupil.

Straube Karl (1873–1950). German organist, also important as ed. of works by Bach and Handel.

Straus Oscar (1870–1954). Austrian composer of the operettas *A Waltz Dream* (1907) and *The Chocolate Soldier* (1908; based on Bernard Shaw's *Arms and the Man*) and much film music, including *La Ronde*.

Strauss Johann the Elder (1804–49). Viennese dance composer and violinist. He at first played under Lanner but founded his own band in 1825, rapidly gaining immense popularity with his waltzes (over 150), galops, marches, including the *Radetsky March*, and polkas. His sons Johann (the following), EDUARD (1835–1916) and JOSEF (1827–70) were also composers.

Strauss Johann the Younger (1825–99). The 'Waltz King'; son of the above, in 1844 founding a band which rivalled his father's. Above all S. is famed for his waltzes, admired, indeed envied, by Brahms and other composers and known throughout the Western world; they include *The Blue Danube* (1867), *Tales from the Vienna Woods* (1868), *Vienna Blood*. S. also wrote the operettas *Die Fledermaus* (1874; 'The Bat'); *The Gipsy Baron* (1885); and *A Night in Venice* (1883).

Strauss Richard (1864–1949). German composer. Son of a musical father violently opposed to Wagner, S. as assistant to Bülow at Meiningen (1885) nevertheless became a convert to

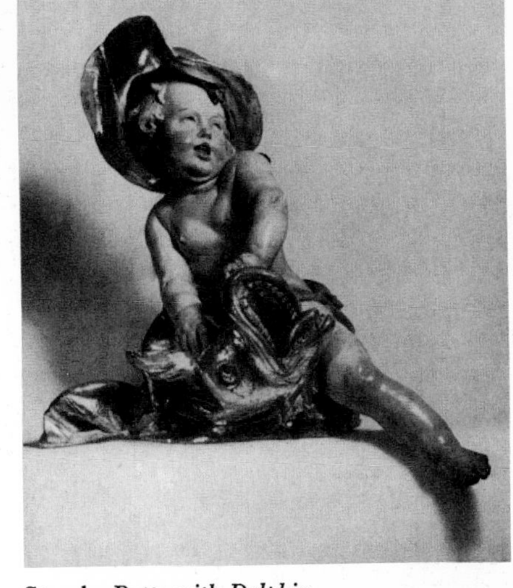

Straub. *Putto with Dolphin*

Strassburg faïence (late 18th c.)

Johann Strauss the Elder

Johann Strauss the Younger

Richard Strauss: lithograph by Max Liebermann. Also *Hofmannsthal

Strassburg cathedral, W. front. See also colour plate 32

Stravinsky: drawing by Picasso. Also *Avedon

Stravinsky, seated, with (left to right) Massine, Goncharova, Larionov and Bakst

the New German school. He worked subsequently as conductor, musical director or teacher at Munich, the Berlin Academy and the Vienna opera; after 1924 he lived by composition and guest conducting. S.'s music, classed as neo-romantic, displays immense virtuosity in orchestration; his early work is clearly influenced by Wagner but he developed an unmistakable style of scintillating and richly colourful harmony, combined with long, striding melody. He was important as a major composer continuing the main tradition of European music. His operas include: *Salome* (1905), after Oscar Wilde; *Elektra* (1909), libretto by Hofmannsthal after Sophocles; *Der Rosenkavalier* (1910), librettist Hofmannsthal, in which the Rose Cavalier (played by mezzo soprano), bearing a love-token from a boorish old man to his young fiancée, in fact wins the girl; the chamber opera *Ariadne auf Naxos* (1912 version to follow a performance of Molière's *Le Bourgeois gentilhomme* with S.'s music; independent version 1916); *The Love of Danaë* (written 1940; 1st performance at Salzburg in 1952); and the conversation piece for music *Capriccio* (1941). His other works include: the ballet *The Legend of Joseph* (1914) for Diaghilev with Massine and Bakst; *Metamorphoses*, a study for 23 strings (1945); *Four Last Songs* with orchestra, settings of Hesse and Eichendorff (1949). His important symphonic poems are *Don Juan* (1888), *Death and Transfiguration* (1890; German *Tod und Verklärung*), *Till Eulenspiegel* (1895), *Also sprach Zarathustra* (1896) based on Nietzsche, *Ein Heldenleben* ('A Hero's Life', 1898); his other major orchestral works are the fantasy variations *Don Quixote* (1897), the *Sinfonia Domestica* (1904) and *An Alpine Symphony* (1915).

Stravinsky Igor (1882–). Russian-born composer. Although his father was a distinguished singer, S. was entered as a law student, completing his course; but lessons with Rimsky-Korsakov (1902) decided him on music. In 1910 began his fruitful collaboration with Diaghilev's ballet co. in Paris. After the Revolution of 1917 S. decided not to return to Russia, living in Paris from 1920 and taking French citizenship in 1934, and living in the U.S. from 1939 and taking U.S. citizenship in 1945.
S.'s music can be divided into 4 periods: the period when late 19th-c. and Russian influences are apparent; from 1920 to about 1940–the period of *neo-classicism and eclecticism; followed by compositions in which eclecticism plays a small part; and then further experimentation from about 1952, when he adapted 12-note serial methods to his still essentially tonal music. S. is no innovator, but his own unmistakable style has been influential. Driving yet disciplined, often asymmetric rhythms are combined into complex polyrhythmic patterns; melodic elements are characteristically brief; harmonically his music ranges from the wildest dissonance and freely used polytonality to the most simple and ancient effects given new vigour of expression by masterly placing in an alien structure. After the vast orchestra of early works S. developed a characteristic handling of individual instruments, distinct in a clearly organized structure.
The music to *The Rite of Spring* (1913), the enactment of a ritual sacrifice of a virgin, summed up the obsession of early 20th-c. art with the primitive; its barbaric, violent expression of savage atavism and its evocation of instincts suppressed in civilized society is still disturbing and caused a riot at the 1st performance. In strong contrast the ballet *Pulcinella* (1920) with its proclaimed use of 18th-c. material is regarded as the inspiration of neo-classicism. With the opera-oratorio *Oedipus Rex* (1927) S. achieved a masterpiece; all the elements of his style combine to produce a powerful and tragic drama. Cocteau's text derived from Sophocles was trs. into Latin, and the staging is in tableaux, the chorus and actors masked and stationary; the action is expounded in the vernacular by a narrator, outside the action.
S.'s numerous important works include: the opera *The Rake's Progress* (1951), libretto by Auden and Kallman; the ballets *Firebird* (1910), choreographer Fokine, *Petrushka* (1911), choreographer Benois, *Les Noces* (1923) in which the early primitivism is tempered by his neo-classical style, *Apollon-Musagète* (1928), choreographer Balanchine, and *A Card Game* (1937); for orchestra, *Symphonies for Wind Instruments: In Memoriam Claude Debussy* (1920); concerto for piano and wind instruments (1924); violin concerto in D (1931); *Dumbarton Oaks* concerto in E♭ for chamber orchestra (1938); *Symphony in C* (1940); *Symphony in Three Movements* (1945). Other works include: *Symphony of Psalms* (1930); a mass for choir and double wind quintet (1948); *Threni* (i.e. 'The Lamentations of Jeremiah', 1958) for voices and orchestra and *In Memoriam Dylan Thomas* for voice and instruments (1954). S. has also written aggressively on his work and on music, e.g. *Chronique de ma vie* (1935; *Chronicles of my Life*, 1936) and *Poètique Musicale* (1946; *Poetics of Music*, 1948).

stream-of-consciousness. Method of novel or short-story writing which attempts to convey directly the fragmentary and incoherent nature of characters' thought processes, as opposed to the ordered accounts given by writers until the 20th c. Notable exponents of s.-of-c. techniques include Dorothy Richardson, James Joyce and Virginia Woolf.

Street George Edmund (1824–81). English architect, one of the leaders of the high Victorian Gothic revival, and associated with the Pre-Raphaelites. He designed a number of churches but his best-known work is the Royal Courts of Justice (Strand, London), one of the largest and most successful (though functionally inconvenient) applications of neo-Gothic to a public building.

Streetcar Named Desire, A (1947). Play by Tennessee *Williams, made into a film (1950) directed by Elia *Kazan.

Streeter (Streater) Robert (1624–80). English decorative painter, best known for the ceiling (1669) of the Sheldonian Theatre, Oxford, the nearest approach to baroque decoration by an Englishman before Sir J. Thornhill.

stretcher. The frame on which canvas is stretched for painting.

Streuvels Stijn. Pseud. of Frank Lateur (1871–). Dutch novelist and short-story writer. S. writes about rural Flanders; his theme is the struggle between man and nature. Works include *De Vlaschaard* (1908).

striation. Decoration by making narrow, parallel grooves, e.g. *fluting in architecture; either the groove or ridge may be called a STRIA.

Stribling T(homas) S(igismund) (1881–). U.S. novelist. Many of his books are set in the South, including the historical trilogy *The Forge* (1931), *The Store* (1932) and *Unfinished Cathedral* (1934).

Strick Joseph. U.S. film director. S. co-directed *The Savage Eye* (1959), a pretentious

Strindberg: contemporary painting

Streeter. Ceiling of the Sheldonian Theatre, Oxford

jaundiced view of Los Angeles through the eyes of a recent divorcée. The film was made independently by S., Ben Maddow and Sidney Meyers. S. directed an excellent Maddow adaptation of a Genet play, *The Balcony* (1963), which was a low-budget studio-made movie of some skill, with an accomplished performance by Shelley Winters.

Strickland William (1788–1854). U.S. architect, a pupil of Latrobe. His major buildings are in Philadelphia: the Masonic Hall (neo-Gothic), the Branch Bank of the United States (a replica of the Parthenon), and the Merchants' Exchange (elegant neo-classical with carved façade).

Strike (1924). Film directed by S. M. *Eisenstein.

Strindberg (Johan) August (1849–1912). Swedish playwright and novelist, an extraordinarily prolific writer with a tormented, neurotic personality. S. studied in desultory fashion at Uppsala Univ. and worked as tutor, journalist and librarian before settling to writing. His childhood was unhappy and his 3 marriages ended in divorce. From them he acquired a persecution mania, which culminated in the mental crisis so brilliantly described in *Inferno* (1897; 1912), and a conviction of the voracity of women and the inevitability of merciless struggle between the sexes. Both elements appear in his most famous plays, *Fadren* (1887; *The Father*, 1899), in which the protagonist is driven mad by the suspicion–implanted by his wife–that he is not the real father of his beloved daughter; and *Fröken Julie* (1888; *Miss Julie*, 1912), nominally a naturalistic drama, in which, typically, the conditions determining the action are such as to give a macabre poetry to the seduction and suicide of the heroine. S.'s masterpiece is perhaps *Dödsdansen* (1901; *The Dance of Death*, 1900), like *The Father* a harrowing dissection of marriage. However, the bulk and variety of his writings is scarcely appreciated outside Sweden. They include historical plays, e.g. *Mäster Olof* (1874; 1914), *Gustav Vasa* (1899; 1929) and *Gustav Adolf* (1900); novels, e.g. the satirical *Röda Rummet* (1879; *The Red Room*, 1913) and the boisterous *Hemsöborna* (1887; *The People of Hemsö*, 1959); many symbolic plays, e.g. *Ett Drömspell* (1902; *A Dream Play*, 1902), and the great religious drama *Till Damascus* (1898–1904; *To Damascus*, 1913);

Street. The Royal Courts of Justice, Strand, London

Strickland. Merchants' Exchange, Philadelphia

String-course: the tower of Earls Barton Saxon church

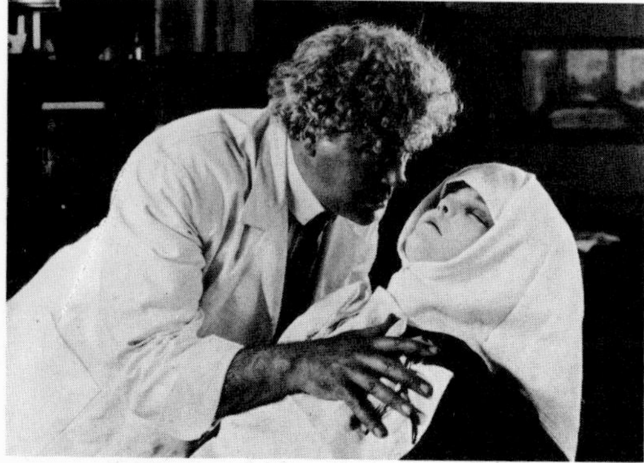

Von Stroheim. Jean Hersholt and Zasu Pitts in *Greed*

Strozzi. Allegorical figure of Sculpture

'chamber plays' like *Spöksonaten* (1908; *The Ghost Sonata*, 1929), written for the 'intimate theatre' he founded in Stockholm; and many directly autobiographical writings.

string-course. Architectural term for a projecting or moulded horizontal band of brick or stone running across the face of a building.

Stroheim Erich von (1885–1957). Austrian-born U.S. film actor and director. S. was actor, assistant and military adviser for D. W. Griffith before directing and acting in *Blind Husbands* (1918). This and the later typical S. movies, *The Devil's Passkey* (1919), *Foolish Wives* and *Merry-Go-Round* (1922), *The Merry Widow* (1925), *The Wedding March* and *Queen Kelly* (1928), are set in an aggressively voluptuous Austro-Hungarian dreamland, in which aristocrats of unbelievable depravity disport themselves, enjoying the corruption of the pure and simple. Among the spike-belted Negroes and blindfolded orchestras, masquerading as subtle suggestions of sexual depravity, lies a talent for a disarming literalness of statement, which applied equally to all aspects of his minutely detailed world, the carnal as well as the decorative. *Greed* (1925) applies the same meticulousness to a contemporary realist subject with much less success. At least in its released form, heavily truncated by its producers, the most successful moments are the most extravagantly strange. *Walking Down Broadway* (1932), S.'s last, uncredited film, and his only one in sound, was mutilated and partly reshot when its producers discovered that S. had made it into a film about lesbianism. He continued in films as an actor, most notably in *La Grande Illusion* and *Sunset Boulevard.*

Strong George Templeton (1856–1948). U.S. composer who studied in Europe, being a member of Liszt's circle at Weimar. After a year teaching at the Conservatory in Boston, he settled (1892) in Switzerland; his works include the symphonic poem *Le Roi Arthur*. S. was also a watercolourist.

Strozzi Bernardo (1581–1644) called 'Il Cappuccino'. Genoese painter of religious subjects who was for a time a Franciscan friar. From 1630 he worked in Venice. His painting was influenced by Rubens, later by the Venetian school.

Struchkova Raissa (1925–). Soviet dancer of the Bolshoi Co. since 1944. She is one of the principal ballerinas in Russia today and has become popular in such different ballets as *Giselle* and the *Fountains of Bakhchisarai.* Since Ulanova's retirement, S. with Plisetskaya has taken over many of her roles.

Stryker Roy E. U.S. photographic editor and administrator. As director of the Farm Security Administration's photographic section during the Depression, he encouraged such photographers as Dorothea Lange and Walker Evans to put together a classic document of rural America undergoing economic and social upheaval. More recently, S. has administered photographic projects for the oil and steel industries.

Stuart Gilbert (1755–1828). Outstanding U.S. portrait painter. He studied in London under B. West although the development of his style owed more to Gainsborough and Reynolds. He worked in London and Dublin before returning to the U.S., acquiring a great reputation for the honesty and psychological insight of his work. He painted the best-known portraits of Washington including the unfinished 'Athenaeum' head (M. of Fine A., Boston).

Stuart James (1713–88). English architect, the originator and arbiter of the Greek revival. In 1762 with N. Revett he publ. *The Antiquities of Athens*. It made S. famous (he was called the 'Athenian S.') though in fact Revett had done all the measured drawings.

Stuart Jesse (Hilton) (1907–). U.S. poet and novelist writing about his native Kentucky, e.g. in the verse coll. *Kentucky is My Land* (1952).

Stubbs George (1724–1806). English painter. He studied anatomy at York and then made a perfunctory visit to Italy in 1754. S. lived and worked in Lincolnshire and London, making anatomical drawings, especially of horses, publ. the *Anatomy of the Horse* (1766). He became a popular painter of racehorses for the aristocracy, but his animal paintings are not mere records; they are elegant and dignified in design. He is a master of composition and also painted brilliant conversation pieces and portraits. S. also painted genre paintings of rural life and some enamelled earthenware panels for Josiah Wedgwood.

Stuart. *William Grant Skating*

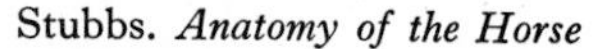

Stubbs. *Anatomy of the Horse*

Stubbs. *The Prince of Wales's Phaeton*

Stucco by Pietro da Cortona in the Pitti Palace, Florence.

Sir John Suckling: contemporary painting

stucco. Originally the lime-plaster used as a ground in fresco painting and in the decoration of buildings; the term is now used loosely to describe any plaster or cement used on exteriors.

Sturges John. U.S. film director. Although he started directing features in 1946, his critical reputation dates from *Bad Day at Black Rock* (1954), a modern western. His commercial successes have been with westerns like *Gunfight at the O.K. Corral* (1957) and *The Magnificent Seven* (1960).

Sturges Preston (1898–1959). U.S. film writer/director. S. was a playwright who from 1933 wrote film scripts and from 1940 to 1949 directed in Hollywood. His only later film was *Les Carnets du Major Thompson* (1955) in France. His genre was the satirical comedy intimately related to the current American scene: e.g. *The Great McGinty* (1940), on political corruption, or *Hail the Conquering Hero* (1944).

Sturm, Der. The magazine (inaugurated in 1910) of the German expressionist movement. In its pages appeared illustrations by members of the Brücke and Blaue Reiter groups and articles expounding the new aesthetic.

Sturm und Drang: *storm and stress

style. Term for the manner of execution in writing, painting, etc. as opposed to subject-matter or its organization (i.e. *form); (2) the common characteristics of the arts in a given period–e.g. *Louis XIV s.–or of a school or movement.

stylobate. Architectural term for a platform on which a colonnade stands.

subdominant. The 4th degree of the major or minor *scale.

subject. A theme or motif of a piece in *sonata form, or of a *fugue.

Sublime and Beautiful, A Philosophical Enquiry into the Origin of our Ideas of the (1756). Treatise by Edmund *Burke.

submediant. The 6th degree of the major and minor *scale.

Suckling Sir John (1609–42). English poet and playwright. S. is said to have fought in the Thirty Years War. He was a courtier and leading Royalist until 1642, when he fled to France; according to John Aubrey he committed suicide. S.'s best works are his lyrics, of which the best known is *Why so pale and wan, fond lover?*. His plays include *Aglaura* (1637).

Sucksdorff Arne (1917–). Swedish film maker. S. made short documentaries including *Rhythm of a City* (1947), but mainly about the country–*A Divided World* (1948). *The Wind and the River* (1950) was shot in India. His 1st feature, *The Great Adventure* (1953), was a remarkably photographed (especially animals) unsentimental account of life on a Swedish farm. His 2nd, which did not have the same success, was set again in India: *The Flute and the Arrow* (1958).

Suddenly, Last Summer (1958). Play by Tennessee Williams.

Sue Eugène, originally called Marie-Joseph S. (1804–75). French novelist. S. wrote several novels about seafaring life; but he became tremendously popular when he turned to melodramatic plots of low life spiced with Socialist and anti-clerical propaganda. They include *Les Mystères de Paris* (1842–3; *The Mysteries of Paris*, 1844) and *Le Juif errant* (1844–5; *The Wandering Jew*, 1844–5).

Suetonius (*c.* A.D. 69–*c.* 140). Gaius Suetonius Tranquillus, Roman biographer born at Rome. He became one of the secretaries of state to the Emperor Hadrian, but after his dismissal for some breach of court etiquette he devoted himself to letters. Of the *Lives of Famous Men* only a few survive–Terence, Horace and Lucan. His *Lives of the Caesars*, all but complete, catalogues indiscriminately the achievements and vices of the 12 Caesars from Julius to Domitian. Since Suetonius had access to official records lost to us, his accounts of political events must be treated with respect, but his work has been discredited by the coldly prurient relish with which he records the nastiest manifestations of imperial lust.

Suger (1081–1151). Abbot of *St Denis, near Paris, who commissioned the new church, considered as the 1st example of the Gothic style. S. was also regent for Louis VII of France during the Second Crusade in 1146.

Der Sturm. Book-plate by Campendonk

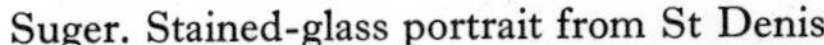

Suger. Stained-glass portrait from St Denis

Sumer is icumen in: opening lines of the ms.

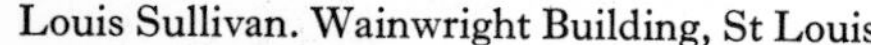

Louis Sullivan. Wainwright Building, St Louis

Sully. Study for a portrait of Queen Victoria in 1838

Sung. White Ting ware ewer

He wrote a life of Louis VI and began one of Louis VII, and several works on the administration and rebuilding of St Denis.

suite. A piece of music, in several movements, for instruments or keyboard but not for voices. In the 17th and 18th cs the movements were dances, such as *allemande, *sarabande, contrasting in mood. At first they were in no fixed order but later the sequence allemande, courante, sarabande, gigue was common.

Suk Josef (1874–1935). Czech composer and violinist; successively professor of composition and rector of the Prague Conservatory and from 1892 in the Bohemian String Quartet. He was Dvořák's son-in-law and his style developed from that of Dvořák towards an increasingly independent and more modern idiom. He wrote much instrumental music.

Sullivan Sir Arthur Seymour (1842–1900). English composer whose reputation rests on the comic operas he composed to the librettos of W. S. *Gilbert. They show an outstanding talent for the genre and S.'s numerous serious compositions, e.g. the cantata *The Golden Legend* (1886) and the grand opera *Ivanhoe* (1891), are not so successful. S. also wrote the song 'The Lost Chord' (1877).

Sullivan Louis (1856–1924). U.S. architect. When Chicago was rebuilt after the fire of 1871, salesmen from Carnegie Steel and Otis Elevators gave architects the tools for skyscraper buildings. Architects fumbled with the problem of adapting historical styles, until S., understanding the repetitious nature of the steel-frame, solved the difficulties and designed magnificent high buildings which owed little to the styles of the past, and form one of the bases of modern architecture.

Sully Thomas (1783–1872). U.S. portrait painter. He studied under Benjamin West in London. There he was influenced by Sir Thomas Lawrence, particularly in his portrayal of women and children. He settled in Philadelphia, where he had no rivals after the deaths of C. W. Peale and G. Stuart. He also produced a large number of subject paintings.

Sully-Prudhomme René-François-Armand (1839–1907). French poet, a leading *Parnassian. S., who excelled in short, philosophical poems, was awarded the Nobel prize (1901).

Sumer is icumen in also called the *Reading Rota*. A famous part song of the mid 13th c., a remarkably early example of contrapuntal writing. It is used by Britten in his *Spring Symphony* and in 1964 appeared in a mutilated form as a pop song.

summation tone: *resultant tone

Summer and Smoke (1948). Play by Tennessee Williams.

Sun Also Rises, The (1926). Novel by Hemingway.

Sunday painter. One who paints for pleasure in his spare time. The term is often used in a derogatory sense but is also associated with modern primitive painters who usually began as self-taught amateurs.

Sung. Chinese dynasty (960–1279) famous for its ultra-refined and delicately incised pottery and for its paintings of landscapes and flowers-and-birds. Perhaps its finest pots are the white Ting wares but better known are the *celadon wares. From the Ching-dê-chên kilns in Kiangsi province the bluish-glazed Ch'ing-pai wares were exported, but the Tz'û-chou and Chun stonewares, the former painted, the latter incised and painted with vigorous floral designs, are equally impressive. Under the Academy of the Emperor Hui-tsung (1802–1135) painting in this dynasty came closest in Chinese history to becoming a full-time professional occupation. The attention given to the minutiae of animals, birds and landscapes reflects the current philosophical doctrine of investigating the inner life of things.

Sunrise (1927). Film directed by F. W. *Murnau.

Sunset Boulevard (1950). Film directed by B. *Wilder.

Supervielle Jules (1884–1960). French poet. S. was born and lived for long periods in Uruguay; desert and pampas are reflected in his work but it otherwise displays nothing of the exotic. The coll. *Gravitations* (1925) was the 1st important manifestation of this quiet, fresh, tender lyric gift. S. also wrote novels, including *Le Voleur d'enfants* (1926; *The Colonel's Children*, 1950), and short stories and plays for children.

supertonic (i.e. above the tonic). In music the name for the 2nd degree of the major or minor *scale.

Suppé Franz von (1819–95). Austrian composer (born Francesco Suppé Demelli) of operettas, e.g. *The Beautiful Galatea* and the famous *Poet and Peasant* overture.

Suppliants, The. Tragedy by *Aeschylus.

suprematism. The 1st system of purely abstract pictorial composition, based on geometric figures. Its founder was the Russian artist *Malevich whose 1st suprematist work was a black square on a white ground painted in 1913; he himself described this as 'no empty square, but rather the experience of non-objectivity . . . the supremacy of pure feeling. . .'. Malevich's early suprematist works were 2-dimensional simple geometric studies using chiefly primary colours; from *c.* 1915 greater complexity appears, 2 or more interrelated groups of shapes overlapping or in receding succession, thus introducing the 3rd dimension.

Surikov Vassily (1848–1916). Russian painter, a member of the *Wanderers. His subjects, however, were chiefly historical; one of the most famous is the colossal canvas *The Boyarina Morosova* (1887). He was fascinated by Russian medieval art and architecture; Veronese, Titian and other monumental Italian painters played a part in forming his style which was the earliest attempt to marry the ideals of the Wanderers with national artistic traditions.

surrealism. Movement begun in 1924 (when the *dada movement split) with a manifesto written by André Breton, in which it is described as 'pure automatism'. This fitted surrealist literature better than surrealist painting, but surrealist art has become better known than surrealist writing, especially in the work of Hans Arp, Max Ernst, Salvador Dali and Joan Miró. Paintings are of 2 main sorts: Dali has called the one 'hand-painted dream objects'–conventional techniques are used to depict a fantastic image like Giorgio de Chirico's enigmatic townscapes or the soft watches in Dali's *Persistence of Memory*; the other is inventive in technique, as in rubbings ('frottage') by Max Ernst, the decalcomania (a sort of monotype) invented by Dominguez, and the informal abstract painting of an artist like Masson. In both sorts of painting the surrealists aimed to mingle reason with unreason, using dreams, chance effects, the automatism uncontrolled by aesthetic or moral consideration, to create a new reality. Surrealist poetry by writers like Paul Éluard and René Crevel had the same aim, and so had the 2 important surrealist films *Un Chien Andalou* and *L'Âge d'Or.* The zenith of the movement was in the 1930s, surrealist groups having been formed in Britain, the U.S., Japan, Scandinavia and elsewhere. During the war many surrealists were in the U.S., where their art and ideas had a liberating influence on American art. There has been some surrealist activity in Paris since 1945, but the major surrealist artists have worked and developed independently. The term s. is more loosely used of fantastic, weird or horrific imagery in the art of any period. The word was coined in 1917 by Apollinaire for the work of certain artists, in particular Marc Chagall.

Surrender of Breda, The (*c.* 1643). Painting by *Velazquez.

Surrey Henry Howard, Earl of (1517?–47). English poet, companion of Henry VIII's illegitimate son, the duke of Richmond. He was accused on a trifling charge and beheaded for high treason. His trs. of the *Aeneid* (1557) was the first deliberate use of blank verse in English. Moreover, S. and Wyatt introduced the sonnet into the language from Italian, particularly Petrarchan, poetry. He established the Shakespearean form of sonnet and the 'poulter's measure' (alternate 12- and 14-line iambic couplets). His courtly, sensitive poetry first appeared in 1557 in 'Tottel's Miscellany' (*Book of Songs and Sonnets*).

Surtees Robert Smith (1803–64). English author of *Jorrocks's Jaunts and Jollities* (1838), *Handley Cross* (1843) and *Mr Sponge's Sporting Tour* (1853), comic novels about fox-hunting.

Survage Léopold (1879–). Russian painter and theatrical designer who settled in Paris (1908) and joined the cubists. Before World War I he made studies ('*rhythmes colorés*') for an abstract film which were encouraged by Apollinaire but were not continued after the latter's death. A number of decorative works by S. include *Peace* (1958–9), fresco for the Palais des Congrès Européens, Liège.

Surrealism. Max Ernst, *Woman, Grey and Blue* (1924)

Suprematism. Malevich, *House under construction 1914–15*

Surikov. *The Boyarina Morosova*

Survage. *Landscape* (1921)

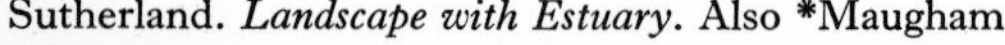

Sutherland. Tapestry, Coventry cathedral

Susanna. One of the books of the *Apocrypha. S. is accused of immorality by 2 elders she has repulsed; she is saved by the young Daniel, who examines the elders and exposes their false testimony.

Suso (also Seuse) Heinrich (*c.* 1300–66). German Dominican mystic, canonized in 1831, a pupil of Meister Eckhart. His mystical work, *Büchlein der ewigen Weisheit* which he later trs. and modified as *Horologium Sapientiae* is an important example of early German prose. S. also wrote the earliest German prose autobiography.

suspension. Term used in musical analysis to describe the effect when a note essential to the harmony of one chord is held over (suspended) into the succeeding chord so as to cause a moment of dissonance (*harmony).

Süss von Kulmbach Hans: Hans Süss von *Kulmbach.

Susterman(s) or Sutterman, Justus (1597–1681). Flemish portrait painter in the tradition of Van Dyck. He was court painter for a time in Florence. One of his finest portraits is that of Galileo in the Uffizi.

Sutermeister Heinrich (1910–). Swiss composer. While studying philosophy in Paris (1929–30) he was impressed by the music of Debussy, Milhaud and Honegger; other important influences are Verdi and Puccini. His opera *Romeo and Juliet* (1940) has been very widely successful; he has also written 2 piano concertos.

Sutherland Graham (1930–). English painter; he studied graphic art at Goldsmiths' College (1921–6). S. started painting in earnest in 1935 and contributed to the 1936 Surrealist Exhibition, London. His pre-war landscapes, e.g. *Entrance to Lane* (1939; Tate), moved from Palmer's formalizations towards a freer organic language. As a war artist (1940–5) S. withdrew, like Piper, Vaughan and others, into the English romantic tradition, e.g. *Tapping a Steel Furnace* (1941; Ferens Gal., Hull); but following an important visit to the Mediterranean seaboard (1947) he has developed a spiky language of expressive abstract forms, surrealist in mood, e.g. *Head III* (1953; Tate). He has also painted a series of portraits and in 1957 completed the design for the altar tapestry for Coventry cathedral.

Sutherland Joan (1928–). Australian-born operatic singer who, since joining the Covent Garden Opera Co. in 1952, has gained a world reputation as a coloratura soprano.

Suttner Bertha von (1843–1914). German novelist whose novel *Die Waffen nieder* (1889; *Lay down your Arms*, 1892) prompted Alfred Nobel to found his Peace prize.

Svendsen Johan Severin (1840–1911). One of the leading Norwegian composers of his generation; he studied in Leipzig (1863–7) and worked in Germany, Rome, London and Paris before settling at Oslo. He wrote 2 symphonies, a violin and a cello concerto and *4 Norwegian Rhapsodies* for orchestra.

Svevo Italo. Pseud. of Ettore Schmitz (1861–1928), Italian novelist, partly Austrian-Jewish in origin. S. worked in a bank until 1897, then became a manufacturer. His novels explore the aimless, unheroic existence of the urban middle class, often employing stream-of-consciousness techniques. S.'s broad humour does not conceal his fundamental pessimism. His early novels, *Una Vita* (1893) and *Senilità* (1898; *As a Man Grows Older*, 1949) were ignored, and he publ. nothing until *La Coscienza di Zeno* (1923; *The Confessions of Zeno*, 1930), which the support of James Joyce made famous in France and only thereafter in Italy.

swag. Ornamental festoon of fruit or flowers in wood, plaster, etc.

Swan John Macallan (1847–1910). English painter and sculptor, chiefly of animals. He was a considerable draughtsman and worked in the London Zoo and Jardin des Plantes, Paris, producing fine unsentimental work.

Swan Lake (*Le Lac des Cygnes*). A 4-act ballet with music by Tchaikovsky. It was an utter failure when first produced in Moscow in 1877 but since its revival in St Petersburg in full in 1895, with choreography by Petipa and Lev Ivanov, it has become established as one of the great classical ballets. It is now in the repertoire of most leading cos and notable modern

Sutherland. *Landscape with Estuary*. Also *Maugham

Swags around the tomb of Ilaria del Carretto; by Jacopo della Quercia

Swan Lake

Swedenborg

Sweelinck

arrangements are Cranko's for the Stuttgart ballet (1960) and the Ashton-Helpmann version for the Royal Ballet (1963).

Swann's Way (1913). Novel by *Proust.

Swansea. In the late 18th and the 19th c. this Welsh town was the centre of a large high-quality soft-paste *porcelain industry. The wares were often bought, unpainted, by London dealers, who had them decorated.

Swanson Gloria (1899–). U.S. star in silent films, playing in the grand manner; films included *Bluebeard's 8th Wife* (1923), *Sadie Thompson* (1927) and *Queen Kelly* (1928). Her style was epitomized in *Sunset Boulevard* (1950), in which she returned to the screen to play a silent-movie queen living on her memories.

Swan Theatre. London theatre which was probably built in 1595 and at which Shakespeare's co. almost certainly performed. It is recorded in a famous picture by De Witt, a fundamental document in the study of the *Elizabethan stage.

Swedenborg Emmanuel (1688–1722). Swedish mystical writer, and in earlier years an important engineer and scientific worker. He underwent a series of visions, claimed to hold extended conversations with angels, and wrote books of prophecy and expositions of Scripture which have had a slight but persistent influence, affecting a few artists or thinkers in each generation, e.g. Balzac when he wrote *Seraphita* and *Louis Lambert*.

Sweelinck Jan Pieterszoon (1562–1621). Dutch composer and organist (from *c.* 1580 at the Oudekerk, Amsterdam), the last of the great polyphonic composers of the Low Countries. S. was above all famous as an organist and organ composer; his style had affinities with the English and Spanish keyboard schools and through his German pupils, e.g. Scheidt and Praetorius, was powerfully influential in N. Germany; the chorale prelude, perfected by J. S. Bach, has its forerunners in the work of S. Besides his ricercars, toccatas and fantasies for organ S. also wrote vocal works, e.g. the motets with basso continuo *Cantiones sacrae* (1619).

Sweeney Agonistes (1926–7). 2 fragments of an unfinished verse play by T. S. Eliot; the character Sweeney also appears in several of Eliot's poems.

Sweerts Michiel (1624–64). Flemish genre and portrait painter, in Rome from 1642 to 1652/4. He went to India as a missionary and died in Goa.

Sweet Bird of Youth (1959). Play by Tennessee Williams.

swell. Device used on the organ to gradually increase or diminish the volume of sound; and also the name for one of the 3 main divisions of the *organ.

Swift Jonathan (1667–1745). Irish prose writer. After taking a degree at Trinity College, Dublin, S. became secretary to Sir William Temple at Moor Park in England. In Temple's household he met Esther Johnson, who became his closest and lifelong friend; he named her 'Stella'. In 1694 he quarrelled with Temple and returned to Ireland to take orders, but the breach was healed and he went back to Moor Park, where he wrote *The Battle of the Books*, a satire on the Ancients and Moderns Controversy (*Temple) in which books in a library do mock-Homeric battle. It was publ. with *A Tale of a Tub* in 1704. After Temple's death S. persuaded Stella to settle in Ireland and from 1700 to 1713 divided his time between his Irish livings and literary life in London. During this time he had some sort of liaison with Esther Vanhomrigh, the Vanessa of *Cadenus and Vanessa* (1726). In 1710 he left the Whigs and worked as a pamphleteer for Bolingbroke's party: these 3 years are covered in the *Journal to Stella*. Appointed dean of St Patrick's in 1713, he returned to Ireland and interested himself in Irish affairs, publ. the series *Drapier's Letters* which made him a popular hero. He visited England again in 1726 and 1727, publ. *Miscellanies* with Pope and Arbuthnot, and *Gulliver's Travels* (1726). After Stella's death in 1728 he wrote a few more pieces, including *A Modest Proposal*, one of his most biting satires, but his mind gradually gave way and he died in the madness he had always dreaded. S. is the most savage and powerful satirist in English, and the one with the greatest scope. The early satires, dealing with current controversies, are remarkable for their abundant inventiveness and the terseness and pungency of their language. In *Gulliver's Travels* his target is the pride and

Sweerts. *Studio of a Painter*

Swansea porcelain (*c.* 1815)

Jonathan Swift: engraving from a contemporary painting

Marie Taglioni in *La Sylphide*

Pavlova in *Les Sylphides*

pretensions of all humankind. In Lilliput Gulliver learns that his people are clumsy and their politics vicious, in Brobdingnag that they are puny and contemptible. His adventures among the philosophers teach him that learning and science are pedantry and affectation, and the wisdom of old age a hideous myth. Among the Houyhnhnms he discovers that, compared with the philosophical, temperate and virtuous horses, man is a greedy, filthy, lecherous brute, fit only to be a slave. S.'s inventiveness and the force of disgust in his scatological imagination drive his ideas home with terrible force. In *A Modest Proposal* he draws attention to the distress in Ireland by an apparently bland suggestion for alleviating it: let the superfluous children be slaughtered for food.

Swinburne: painting by G. F. Watts

Swinburne Algernon Charles (1837–1909). English poet, educated at Eton and Oxford, an intimate of D. G. Rossetti and Meredith. In 1860 he publ. 2 blank-verse plays, *The Queen Mother* and *Rosamond*; but *Atalanta in Calydon* (1865), modelled on Hellenic dramas, made him famous. Its atheistic sentiments gained him a notoriety increased by the sensual and pagan themes of *Poems and Ballads: First Series* (1866); this 'paganism', then thought a dangerous manifestation, now seems artificial. More acceptable was his enthusiasm for Italian independence (*A Song of Italy*, 1867; and *Songs Before Sunrise*, 1871). His health deteriorated prematurely (partly a result of sexual and alcoholic excesses); from 1879 he lived in seclusion at Putney, looked after by T. Watts-Dunton, gradually adopting more conservative views. S.'s verse displays great fluency, sonority and metrical virtuosity, though its tone is somewhat monotonous; he absorbed many influences, among them Hugo and Baudelaire. Much of his later work (including the dramas *Bothwell* and *Mary Stuart*; *Tristram of Lyonesse*, *Astrophel* and additional *Poems and Ballads*) is impressive, though it does not extend its range.

Swinton vases

swing: *jazz

Swinton. Town in Yorkshire, England. In the late 18th and the 19th c. the site of a number of important pottery and porcelain manufactories, among them the famous Rockingham works. This gave its name to a characteristic manganese-brown glaze; its fine wares in the 1820s and 1830s were in a florid, almost rococo style.

sword dance. English folk-dance in which each dancer is equipped with a sword, now a wooden substitute. The dance is a series of involved movement patterns and often culminates with 'swords' being interlocked in an open lattice shape and brandished by one of the dancers.

Sybil, or The Two Nations (1845). Novel by *Disraeli.

Sylphide, La. 2-act ballet with choreography by Filippo *Taglioni, music by Schneitzhöffer, scenery by Ciceri and costumes by Lormier.

Sylphides, Les. 1-act ballet with choreography by Fokine, music by Chopin and décor by Benois; 1st performance 1909.

Sylvester Joshuah: Guillaume du *Bartas

Sylvia. 3-act ballet about the mythological court of Diana, first produced to Delibes's music in 1876. It has remained a favourite and was revived by the Sadler's Wells Ballet (1952) with choreography by Ashton and décor by Robin and Christopher Ironside.

Sylvie (1854). Story by Gérard de *Nerval.

symbolism. Literary movement in reaction against *realism and *naturalism, originating in late 19th-c. France; the term can be applied, e.g., to the poetry of Verlaine and Rimbaud, but the true father of s. is probably Mallarmé. Symbolist poets used external objects to convey inner reality; but in practice s. made poetry less accessible to the public, since the chosen symbols were usually private and therefore difficult to interpret. Great musicality and increased freedom of form were characteristic of s.; its poets include Yeats, Blok and Maeterlinck, and many 20th-c. poets show affinities with the movement.

Symonds John Addington (1840–93). English writer. His works include a *History of the Renaissance in Italy* (1875–86), many studies, and a number of trs, notably the sonnets of Michelangelo (1878) and *The Autobiography of Benvenuto Cellini* (1887).

sympathetic strings. Certain old stringed instruments, e.g. the viola d'amore, had a set of strings which, running beneath the fingerboard, were not stopped by the fingers, but were left to vibrate in sympathy with the strings sounded by the bow.

symphonic poem. A genre of *programme music rather less strict in form than the symphony but using a full orchestra and of symphonic dimensions. The name and, in effect, the genre was introduced by *Liszt.

Symphonic Variations. 1-act ballet with choreography by Ashton, music by César Franck and décor by Fedorovitch; 1st performance 1946.

symphony. A musical form. The classical orchestral s. has 4 movements: the first, an allegro in *sonata form with sometimes a grave introduction, the second a slow movement, the third a *minuet and trio and the finale a fast movement. This basic form evolved from the late 17th c., the sinfonias or 3-movement overtures of A. Scarlatti's operas being generally regarded as the beginnings, the *Mannheim school introducing the minuet; the s. became a major form with Haydn. Modifications include the substitution of the vigorous scherzo for the more stately minuet by Beethoven; the introduction of choral parts when desired (also first by Beethoven) and the 1-movement s. developed by Liszt.

Symposium, The. Dialogue by *Plato.

syncopation. In music, the emphasizing of a beat outside the regular pattern of accented beats, or slightly displacing the accented beat itself. For the device to be effective, the strict rhythmic beat must either be maintained in another part, or the s. must be so written that the listener is aware of the conflicting rhythms, feeling though not hearing the original 'correct' pattern of accents.

Syndics, The (1662). Painting by *Rembrandt.

Synge J(ohn) M(illington) (1871–1909). Irish playwright. S. spent some years on the Continent before returning to Ireland and studying the speech and ways of the peasant. He gradually elaborated the rich (English-Irish) dialect which gives his plays their life. In 1904 he became a director of the *Abbey Theatre, which the fame of his *The Playboy of the Western World* (1907) did much to establish. His plays include the 1-act plays *The Shadow of the Glen* (1903) and *Riders to the Sea* (1904); *The Well of Saints* (1905); and *Deirdre of the Sorrows* (posth. 1910). S. also wrote poetry, and the coll. of sketches *The Aran Islands* (1907).

synthetism or cloissonism. A style of painting in the 1890s by Gauguin, Émile Bernard and other artists at Pont-Aven in Brittany. Flat areas of colour are surrounded with black lines (inspired by the work of an artist called Anquetin): the young Bernard seems to have influenced Gauguin to use this technique.

Szinyei Merse Pál (1845–1920). Hungarian painter who evolved an impressionist technique akin to that of Manet and exerted an important influence on Hungarian painting before World War II. He was trained under Piloty in Munich but his development owed more to the influence of Courbet. His subjects were chiefly figures in landscape, the most famous being *Májalis* (*Picnic in May*) (1873; M. of Fine A., Budapest).

Szymanowski Karol (1882–1937). Polish late romantic composer. He studied in Berlin, Warsaw and Paris. His style, besides a debt to R. Strauss, was influenced by Debussy and Chopin, later developing towards atonalism. His numerous works include: the opera *King Roger* (1926), about 12th-c. Sicily; 3 symphonies; a symphonia concertante for piano and orchestra; 2 violin concertos; song settings including texts by Tagore; and 4 Polish dances and 20 mazurkas (1924–6) for piano, deriving inspiration from Polish folk-music.

J. M. Synge: Indian ink wash drawing by J. B. Yeats

Synthetism. Émile Bernard, *Breton Women*

The Syndics by Rembrandt

Rabindranath Tagore

Hippolyte Taine

Taeuber-Arp. *Elemental forms* (embroidery; 1917)

Marie Taglioni in *Le Dieu et la Bayadère* (1830) Also *Cerrito, *La *Sylphide*

Talashkino. Table designed (*c.* 1905) by A. Zinoviev

T

Tabb John B(annister) (1845–1909). U.S. poet, a Confederate blockade runner, converted (1872) and ultimately ordained in the Roman Catholic Church; his poems are generally short and intense pieces on religious themes.

tablature. A method of musical *notation for such instruments as the lute and guitar (in 15th- and 16th-c. Germany also for some organ music). The player is presented not with a series of notes but, in effect, with a series of instructions as to where to place his fingers so as to obtain the notes.

tabor. A small drum: *pipe and tabor.

Tabu (1931). Film directed by F. W. *Murnau and R. *Flaherty.

tachisme: *action painting

Tacitus Publius Cornelius (*c.* A.D. 55–*c.* 117). Roman historian, praetor in 83 and consul suffectus in 97. T.'s style is incisive and compressed, his tone elevated; his surviving works are the *Dialogus de Oratoribus*, lamenting the decline of oratory under the empire; the *Vita Agricolae*, a biography of his father-in-law Agricola, the conqueror of Britain; *De Origine et Situ Germaniae*, an account of the Germanic peoples contrasting their simple manners and rigorous morality with declining Roman standards; and 2 records of the more recent past, both incomplete in their present form, the *Historiae* (from the death of Nero to 96) and the *Annales*, T.'s masterpiece, dealing with the period from the death of Augustus to that of Nero.

Taddeo di Bartolo (Taddeo Bartoli) 14th–15th-c. Sienese painter, follower of the Lorenzetti brothers.

Taeuber-Arp Sophie (1889–1943). Swiss painter and designer, member of the Zürich dada group and the Cercle et Carré and Abstraction-Création groups; wife of Hans Arp. Some of her earliest paintings (1916) were geometric abstractions. In 1928 she collaborated with van Doesburg and Arp on the interior decoration of the Aubette Café, Strassburg (since destroyed).

Taglioni Filippo (1778–1871). Italian dancer and choreographer who arranged many ballets, the most famous being *La Sylphide* (1832) in which his daughter Marie created the leading role. This is regarded as the beginning of the romantic movement in dancing and changed the concept of ballet in content, costume and construction.

Taglioni Marie (1804–84). Italian-Swedish dancer who made her début in Vienna in 1822. T. was the 1st dancer to become internationally famous and, with her father's *La Sylphide* (1832), brought ballet into the romantic movement. She also introduced into ballet the calf-length dress. Giselle was another of her greatest roles and she used point work more fully than had ever been attempted before. Endowed with a perfect dancer's physique, she achieved a lightness and ethereal quality that has become legendary.

Tagore Rabindranath (1861–1941). Indian writer, Nobel prizewinner (1913) and philosopher. T. enjoyed a great vogue in England, Yeats writing an introduction to his *Gitanjali* (1912), T.'s trs. of his own Bengali prose lyrics. He and others trs. more of his poems, plays, stories and novels but it is said the English versions are shadows of the originals. Everything he wrote is alive with religious feeling.

Taine Hippolyte (Adolphe) (1828–93). French writer on philosophy, history and literature, an important literary figure whose formula of '*la race, le milieu, et le moment*' amounted to a complex determinist theory which T. used to explain races and individuals; it was in effect the philosophy of *naturalism and clearly and strongly influenced Zola. Works include *L'Histoire de la littérature anglaise* (1863; 1871) and *Les Origines de la France contemporaine* (1876–94).

Talashkino. A centre for artists and a school for children, founded for the encouragement of Russian arts and crafts by the Princess Tenishevo on her estate near Smolensk in the 1890s. In many ways it was based on a continuation of Mamontov's *Abramtsevo Colony. Artists such as Vrubel and Roerich, and the theatre designer Alexander Golovin worked there. These centres created the 'Russian style' of interior design and were influential also in theatre design.

Talbot (William Henry) Fox (1800–71). English photographer who first developed a practical method for producing photographic

Fox Talbot

Portable camera obscura of the type used by Fox Talbot

François-Joseph Talma

negatives on oiled paper. His process, known as the 'Calotype', was patented in 1841.

Tale of a Tub, A (1704). Satire by *Swift; also the title of a comedy by Ben Jonson.

Tale of Two Cities, A (1859). Historical novel by *Dickens.

Tales from the Vienna Woods. A waltz by J. *Strauss the Younger.

Taliesin, The Book of. 14th-c. coll. of Welsh poems written at different dates; they were ascribed to T., a legendary 6th-c. poet.

Talisman, The (1825). Historical novel by Sir Walter *Scott.

tallboy: *lowboy

Tallchief Maria (1925–). American-Indian dancer and sister of Marjorie T. A pupil of Nijinska and Lichine, T. danced with the Ballet Russe de Monte Carlo in 1942 and is now leading dancer with the New York City Ballet. T. symbolizes the modern American ballerina with her faultless technique and almost acrobatic precision.

Tallchief Marjorie (1927–). American-Indian dancer whose training followed a similar pattern to that of her sister, Maria T. Her husband, George Skibine, has defined her talent in the lyrical parts he has created for her in his ballets, e.g. *Annabel Lee* (1951). T.'s interpretation of the Sleepwalker in Balanchine's *Night Shadow* (1946) was a landmark in the modern romantic ballet.

Tallis Thomas (*c.* 1505–85). English composer and organist. He began his career as organist at Waltham abbey in Essex but from 1542 worked in the Chapel Royal. With Byrd he received a monopoly of printing music (1575). T. wrote much church music including masses, motets, among them the magnificent 40-part *Spem in alium*, and Psalm settings, one of them being used by *Vaughan Williams; T.'s instrumental music includes several works for organ.

Tall Men, The (1955). Film directed by R. *Walsh.

Talma François-Joseph (1763–1826). French tragic actor who made his début at the Comédie-Française in 1787. He was the first to play Roman parts in a toga instead of in contemporary dress, and to try to make more of the sense than the metre in poetic drama.

Talman William (1650–1719). English architect of country-houses (Uppark, Sussex), though his best works have been demolished. He was Comptroller of the King's Works before Vanbrugh.

Talmud, The. Jewish coll., originally oral, of civic and religious decisions (the *Mishnah*, codified *c.* A.D. 200) and commentaries (the *Gemara*, 5th c. A.D.) made by the great rabbis.

Tamayo Rufino (1899–). Important Mexican painter who has settled in New York. Although more influenced than the other Mexicans, Rivera and Orozco, by modern European painters, particularly Picasso and Braque, his work (including murals for the National Conservatory, Mexico City and for Smith College, Northampton, Mass.) retains a distinctively Mexican character.

Tamayo y Baus Manuel (1829–98). Spanish playwright. He wrote a number of successful historical plays, of which the most original was *Un drama nuevo* (1867); in it he used the device of the 'play-within-a-play'. T. and López de Ayala brought a new freedom and realism to the Spanish stage.

tambourine. A percussion instrument. It consists of a circular wooden frame about 10 ins in diameter and 4 ins deep; a vellum head is stretched over one side of the frame and in the frame are slits with metal discs set in them so as to jingle when the head is struck with the hand.

Tamburlaine the Great (publ. 1590). Play by *Marlowe.

Taming of the Shrew, The (1594; publ. 1623). Comedy by *Shakespeare, written *c.* 1593. Its source was perhaps the anonymous play *The Taming of a Shrew* (*c.* 1589). It has been filmed several times, notably in 1908, directed by D. W. Griffith.

Taneyev Sergei Ivanovich (1856–1915). Russian composer and pianist, a pupil of N. Rubinstein and Tchaikovsky. He held several professorial posts at the Moscow Conservatory,

Thomas Tallis

Maria Tallchief in *Firebird*

Rufino Tamayo. *Women of Tehuantepec*

T'ang. *Dancer*; unglazed pottery

T'ang. *Horse*; unglazed pottery

T'ang. Tripod jar

Tange. Kagawa Prefectural Office (1958)

eventually becoming director (1885–9). His compositions reflect his interest in contrapuntal theory and his opposition to the ideals of the nationalist composers.

T'ang. Chinese dynasty (618–906) during which the famous Buddhist pilgrim Hsüan Tsang (*Monkey) returned to China from India (A.D. 645) bringing with him statues of the Indian Gupta period which stimulated the climax of Chinese Buddhist achievement: the sculpture and wall paintings of the cave-shrines. Ch'ang-an (now Sian), capital of T. China, was the richest and most cosmopolitan city in the world and T. artistic development was an assimilation and Sinification of such widespread foreign influences as the semi-naturalistic floral motifs from Sassanid Persian metalwork which were to become characteristic of Chinese pottery decoration. The influence of Syrian and Seine-Rhine Roman glassware is also evident in the shapes of some T. pottery. The grey-green T. Yüeh porcelain is a forerunner of Sung dynasty (960–1279) *celadons. But the best-known T. pottery products are the statuettes of horses, court dancers, Middle Eastern merchants, etc., the culmination of a Han dynasty (206 B.C.–A.D. 220) tradition of pottery tomb furnishings – the most lively branch of Chinese sculptural art and one which is continued perhaps in Ming dynasty (1368–1644) *blanc-de-chine figures and, up to modern times, in the clay figures on Chinese roofs.

Tange Kenzo (1913–). Leading Japanese architect who builds vigorous buildings of heavily shuttered concrete in the late manner of Le Corbusier. His Memorial Hall at Hiroshima (1950) was followed by Tokyo city hall (1956), then, with full mastery of concrete, by the Sogetsu Flower School (1957) and the Kurashiki town hall (1958). His project for housing 5 million people on buildings built over Tokyo Bay is one of the most powerful examples of post-war planning.

tangent: *clavichord

Tanglewood Tales (1853). Coll. of children's stories by Nathaniel *Hawthorne.

tango. Argentinian dance, introduced as a ballroom dance in the 1910s.

Tanguy Yves (1900–55). French painter living in the U.S. from 1939. Self-taught, he began to paint in 1922 and was influenced at first by de Chirico's scuola metafisica. In 1930 with Ernst and Dali he contributed to Breton's Communist periodical *La Surréalisme au Service de la Révolution*. The barren desert-like lunar landscapes of his paintings shared with much surrealist imagery an hallucinatory stillness and silence, but the strange organisms which inhabit them were his peculiar invention and foreshadowed similar forms in Picasso's paintings and Moore's carvings of the 1930s. *Jours de Lenteur* (1937; M.M.A., Paris) is a typical example of his work.

Tannhäuser. A 13th-c. German *minnesinger whose life was surrounded by legends. Love was the subject of his verse but he also wrote *Song of Repentance*. T. is said to have passed a year of debauch with Venus in the Venusberg. He returned to earth to seek absolution from the Pope; the reply was that he would be pardoned when the Pope's staff broke into leaf. The miracle occurred but T. had returned to Venus. *Wagner wrote an opera on the subject.

Tansillo Luigi (1510–68). Italian poet remembered for his sonnets dealing with love and with nature, which he described with a degree of realism. He also wrote a Christian epic, *Le lagrime di San Pietro*.

Tansman Alexandre (1897–). Polish-born composer and pianist (he took French nationality). His numerous works show a preference for the neo-classical idiom; the influences of Richard Strauss, Stravinsky and Ravel are also apparent and Polish folk-music has provided material.

taperstick. Used to hold a taper for melting sealing-wax and often found on inkstands. Silver examples occur from the later 17th c.; their development exactly parallels that of candlesticks, of which they were usually miniature reproductions.

tapestry. A textile woven into designs by shorter or longer weft stitches across the warp. The term usually denotes a hand-woven fabric in which a spindle is used instead of a shuttle. It has been loosely and inaccurately used to describe embroidery.
There are 2 subdivisions of t. weaving, (1) 'high warp' or '*haute lisse*', where the warp threads are held vertically between beams and the design is worked in the reverse sense from the

Tanguy. *Lazy Days*

French tapestry (15th c.). See also colour plate 50

cartoon or design; and (2) 'low warp', in which threads are held horizontally on beams, and the work is rolled as completed; it is worked above the design, and is therefore in the same sense as it. It is more quickly made than high warp, but may appear more mechanical.

The golden age of tapestry was in the middle ages, when the weavers of France and Flanders led Europe. High warp was thought to be the superior process, but in the late 17th and the 18th c. the expert weavers of the Gobelins Factory caused the low-warp technique to be considered the superior process.

Tapies Antonio (1923–). Spanish painter; he took up painting with no formal training after studying law. Influenced by Miró and Dubuffet, he has developed a profoundly dramatic style with a mysterious 'ritual' quality.

tarantella. Italian dance. The bite of the tarantula spider was said to induce a frenzy; there are 2 theories concerning the dance, (1) that it is the result of the bite; (2) that it cures it.

Taras Bulba (1835). Novel by *Gogol.

Tarchetti Iginio Ugo (1841–69). Italian poet and novelist. He was an ardent admirer of Ugo Foscolo and his lyrics show the influence of French romanticism. His novel *Una nobile follia* (1867) is a passionate attack on war.

Tarkington Newton Booth (1869–1946). U.S. novelist born in Indianapolis, Indiana; most of his novels have a Middle Western setting. Early works were the semi-autobiographical *Gentleman from Indiana* (1899) and the popular success, *Monsieur Beaucaire* (1900). T.'s best-known novel is *The Magnificent Ambersons* (1918), the chronicle of 3 generations at the turn of the century, documenting the clash of established fortunes with early 20th-c. technology. It is the centre of the *Growth* trilogy which includes *The Turmoil* (1915) and *The Midlander* (1923). T.'s novels include *Alice Adams* (1921) and the humorous series about the boy Penrod Schofield, including *Penrod* (1914), *Penrod and Sam* (1916) and *Penrod Jashber* (1929).

Tarlton Richard (d. 1588). English comic actor and royal jester. It is thought that Shakespeare had him in mind when he wrote of the jester Yorick in *Hamlet*.

Tarnished Angels, The (1958). Film directed by D. *Sirk.

Tarr (1918). Novel by Wyndham *Lewis.

Tartarin de Tarascon (1872). Novel by *Daudet.

Tartini Giuseppe (1692–1770). Italian violinist and composer; his very numerous violin pupils included Pugnani. T. made important developments in bowing technique and was noted for his musicianly treatment of ornamentation. T.'s instrumental compositions not only show formal and melodic elegance and rich harmonic invention but are also a bridge between the high baroque and pre-classic periods.

Tartuffe, Le (1664). Comedy by *Molière.

Tashlin Frank (1913–). U.S. film director and writer. He worked as gagman for Harpo Marx on *A Night in Casablanca* (1945) and wrote scripts including *The Paleface* (1948) before starting to direct in 1951. *Son of Paleface* (1952) is the funniest of all spoof westerns. His world includes juvenile delinquency (*Susan Slept Here*, 1954), horror comics (*Artists and Models*, 1955), rock'n roll (*The Girl Can't Help It*, 1956) and advertising (*Will Success Spoil Rock Hunter?*, 1957). T. views with distaste an increasingly synthetic world, in which form has become artificially separated from function. T. has been the mentor and most frequent director of Jerry *Lewis, with whom he made *The Disorderly Orderly* (1964) among others.

Task, The (1785). Poem by William *Cowper.

Tassel Richard (1588–1666 or 68). French painter who worked at Langres in an eclectic style derived from contemporary Italian painting. He was a pupil of Reni at Bologna and was later in Rome. His masterpiece is a portrait of the foundress of the Ursuline convent at Dijon (Dijon Mus.).

Tasso Bernardo (1493–1569). Italian poet and father of Torquato T. His lyrics are varied in quality and show the influence of Bembo, Horace and Ovid. He wrote a version of the epic romance *Amadis de Gaula*, *Amadigi di Gaula* (1560).

Tasso Torquato (1544–95). Italian poet. T. was educated by the Jesuits at Naples and then

Tapies. *Green and Black*

Giuseppe Tartini

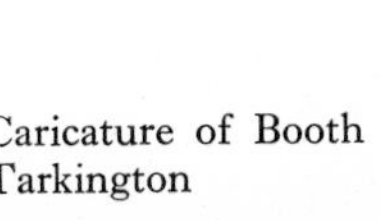

Caricature of Booth Tarkington

Tashlin. Dick Powell in *Susan Slept Here*

Tapestry, high-warp technique; 18th-c. French engraving

Tapestry, low-warp technique

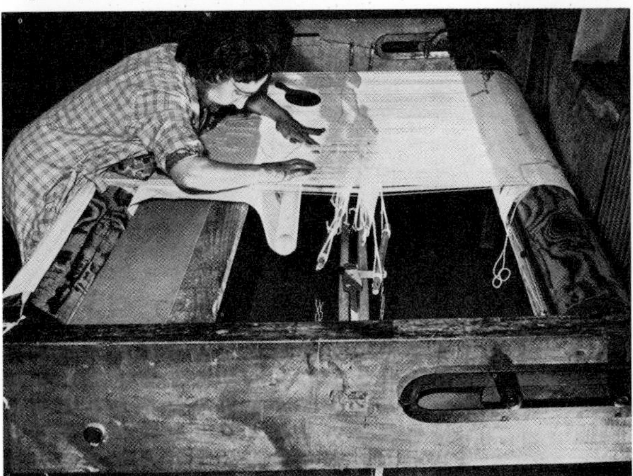

Torquato Tasso

at the Univ. of Padua; there, in 1562, he publ. his 1st epic poem, *Rinaldo*. In 1565 he entered the service of the d'Este family at Ferrara; his pastoral play *Aminta* was 1st performed before the court (1573). It was soon trs. and influenced English and French work in the genre. T. completed his masterpiece, *Gerusalemme Liberata*, in 1575; in the same year he began to show signs of the persecution complex which ultimately led to his confinement in the asylum of Sant'Anna (1579–86). On his release T. rewrote his epic and publ. it (1593) as *Gerusalemme Conquistata*; but it is much inferior to the original. T.'s last years were spent wandering restlessly over Italy, producing little work of value.

Gerusalemme Liberata (publ. 1581; partly trs. 1594, in full as *Godfrey of Buloigne* 1600) is a heroic poem modelled on the classical epic (Virgil in particular). Its theme is the liberation of Jerusalem in the First Crusade, but much of the interest is concentrated on love-stories. Rinaldo, Prince of Este, falls under the spell of the Saracen enchantress Armida, and lives happily with her until summoned to help the army; he then plays the leading role in the capture of Jerusalem. Another love-story is that of Tancredi, who in combat unwittingly kills Clorinda, the Saracen maiden he loves. In each case the heroine is converted to Christianity. T. also wrote *Dialoghi*; the tragedy *Torrismondo*; letters; and a very large number of lyrics, many of them written in Sant'Anna.

Tassoni Alessandro (1565–1635). Italian poet, best known for his poetic satire in the mock-heroic style, *La Secchia Rapita* (1622; *The Rape of the Bucket*, 1825).

Allen Tate

Tate (John Oxley) Allen (1899–). U.S. poet, critic and novelist. T. was educated at Vanderbilt Univ., Tennessee and became ed. of *The Fugitive*, championing the *new criticism and the Old South. *Stonewall Jackson* (1928) describes the South before the Civil War and its unified culture – a myth which is the basis of essays like *The Man of Letters in the Modern World* (1955) and of his finest poem, *Ode to the Confederate Dead*. His nostalgic, ironic, didactic poems are supported by an important body of criticism in *Reactionary Essays on Poetry and Ideas* (1936) and *On the Limits of Poetry* (1948). T. has also written a novel, *The Fathers* (1938).

Tate Nahum (1652–1715). English poet. T. wrote the 2nd part of his friend Dryden's *Absalom and Achitophel*; he also wrote the libretto for Purcell's opera *Dido and Aeneas*. He was poet laureate from 1692.

Tati in *Monsieur Hulot's Holiday*

Tati Jacques (1908–). French film director and actor, one of the great screen comedians, alongside Chaplin and Keaton. Like theirs, his comedy depends on appearance, mannerisms, gags involving physical action; like them he has a considerable streak of melancholy. T. became famous with *Jour de Fête* (1949), about the misadventures of a village postman. He followed this with *Monsieur Hulot's Holiday* (1953), a brilliant succession of gags and a few elegiac moments. The mood of detached sadness became even more apparent in *Mon Oncle* (1958), a protest against the dehumanizing influence of the modern consumer society. T. is a very slow worker who pays infinite attention to detail, a trait reflected in the remarkable atmosphere and realism of the locations in his films.

Tatler, The (1709–11). Periodical ed. by Sir Richard *Steele.

Tatlin Vladimir (1885–1953). Soviet painter, born in Kharkov. T. studied at the Penza School of Art (1902–9) and the College of Painting, Sculpture and Architecture at Moscow (1909–11). He became the pupil and protégé of Larionov and Goncharova. In 1911 his 1st designs for the theatre were used in a production in Moscow. He visited Paris (1913) where he was much impressed by Picasso's work; he produced his 1st semi-abstract 'Relief Construction' in Moscow in the winter of 1913–14. He continued to make reliefs of such materials as glass, iron, wood, now entirely abstract; by 1915 these had developed into free-hanging 'Corner Constructions'. In 1917 T. was invited by Georgy Yakulov to help him to decorate the Café Pittoresque in Moscow with constructions – their first practical application and generally regarded as the beginning of constructivism. After the Bolshevik Revolution T. emerged as an important figure in the artistic reorganization of the country undertaken by the former futurist, now 'leftist' artists; he was appointed head of the Moscow Department of Fine Arts. His growing group of followers gradually became known as constructivists. He lived in Petrograd (1920–5), building his *Monument to the Third International* and working on practical projects, designing stoves, workers' clothes, etc.

Tatlin. *Self-portrait as a sailor*

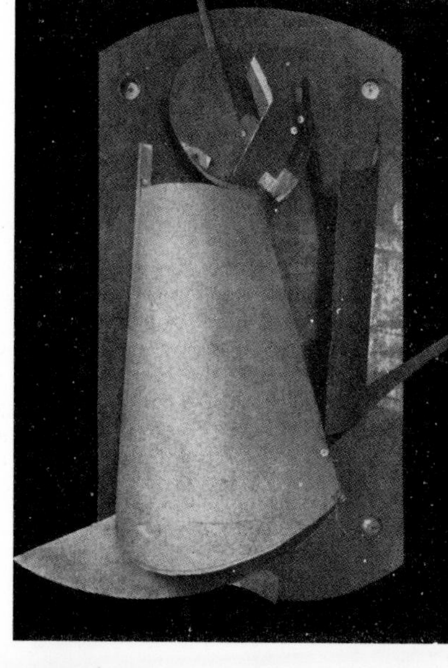
Tatlin. *Relief* (1917)

Tatlin. *Nude* (1913). Also *constructivism

Jeremy Taylor

with economy and sensitivity to the nature of the materials used. T. called this system of design 'culture of materials'. He directed the ceramic faculty in the reorganized Moscow Art School, Vkhutein, continuing to develop 'culture of materials'. He also became known as a glider designer. Between 1933 and 1952 he worked as theatrical designer, continuing to paint, mostly still-life subjects and nudes, using icon preparation on wooden panels.

Tatum Art (1910–). U.S. pianist, acknowledged as a leading jazz pianist. His harmonic command and extraordinary left-hand technique placed him ahead of all his contemporaries, and have still not been equalled.

Taurog Norman (1899–). U.S. film director. A very prolific veteran who directed silent comedies and had a reputation in the 1930s as a director of children–Mickey Rooney, Freddie Bartholomew and Judy Garland (*Little Nellie Kelly*, 1940). Later he directed musicals, including *Words and Music* (1948), about Rodgers and Hart, as well as poorer films with Jerry Lewis and Elvis Presley.

Tausig Carl (1841–71). Polish pianist resident in Germany; he was a pupil of Liszt, acquiring a similar astonishing technique. His early death was caused by typhoid.

Taut Bruno (1880–1938). German architect. His early exhibition building (Leipzig, 1913; Cologne, 1914) showed imaginative use of steel and glass. During the 1920s he was a leading German practitioner of the international style, but is perhaps best known for introducing traditional Japanese architecture to European architects.

Taverner John (*c.* 1495–1545). English composer, the last great master before the Reformation. His church music includes *cantus firmus masses (8, including the famous *Westron Wind*) and motets and is distinguished by its masterly and beautiful use of *imitation. He was inadvertently composer of the 1st *In nomine and also 3 secular pieces by him appeared in Wynkyn de Worde's *Song Book*.

Taylor (James) Bayard (1825–78). U.S. writer of once very popular travel books, and a poet remembered for the lyric *Bedouin Song*.

Taylor Elizabeth (1932–). English-born film star, beginning in child parts in the U.S. (*Lassie Come Home*, 1943). In the 1950s her great beauty and widely publicized life led to major roles, e.g. in *A Place in the Sun* (1951), *Cat on a Hot Tin Roof* (1958) and *Cleopatra* (1963).

Taylor Jeremy (1613–67). English clergyman (he became bishop of Dromore) and prose writer, famous for the simplicity, eloquence and at moments, grandeur of his sermons, especially *The Rule and Exercises of Holy Living* (1650) and . . . *of Holy Dying* (1651). T. also wrote *A Discourse of the Liberty of Prophesying* (1646), a plea for toleration.

Taylor John (1580–1653). English poet and (among other things) Thames waterman. His outlandish adventures and travels colour his publ. *All the Workes of John Taylor the Water Poet* (1630).

Taylor Joseph Deems (1885–). U.S. composer and music critic. His works, in a melodic idiom, include the opera *The King's Henchman* (1927), with libretto by Edna St Vincent Millay.

Taylor Sir Robert (1714–88). English architect. Beginning as a monumental sculptor (pediment of the Mansion House), he became the most successful architect of his day. His style shows little originality, faithfully reflecting the change in taste from the Palladianism of the 1740s to the Adam brothers' style of the 1780s. His work includes the Council House, Salisbury and Stone Buildings, Lincoln's Inn.

Taylor Robert (1911–). U.S. film star; he played opposite Garbo in *Camille* (1936) and has had a long and successful career including *Quo Vadis?* (1951).

Taylor Tom (1817–80). English playwright, an ed. of *Punch* (1874–80). His plays include *Our American Cousin* (1858).

Tchaikovsky Piotr Ilyich (1840–93). Russian composer. From 1866 he taught theory at the Moscow Conservatory; in 1877 he married one of his pupils but, unable to overcome his homosexuality, left her after a few weeks. From 1878 he received an annual pension from the wealthy widow Nadezhda von Meck; by design they never met, but in his numerous letters to

Sir Robert Taylor's Bank of England, since destroyed

Tchaikovsky

Taut. Building for the Cologne Werkbund Exhibition

Tecton, Penguin Pool, London Zoo (1934)

Tecton. Finsbury Health Centre, London (1939)

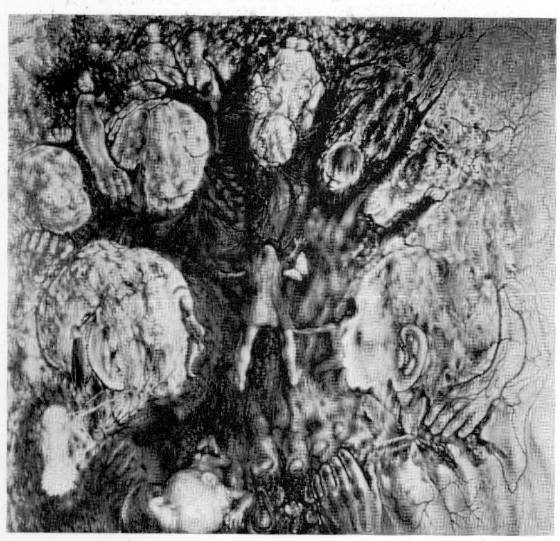
Tchelitchew. *Hide and Seek*

her T. reveals his personality and discusses his work at length.

T.'s work has little contact with the contemporary nationalist movement, being inspired as much by the German romantics and the 19th-c. Italian and French schools as by Russian folk-music. His music is romantic, ranging from sensitive sweetness to passionate statement; often pervaded by nostalgia and melancholy, sometimes brash, but always elegant beneath the surface. His symphonies, programmatic by nature, are: no. 1 in G min. (1868; revised 1874), called 'Winter Dreams'; no. 2 in C min. (1873; revised 1881), called the 'Little Russian'; no. 3 in D maj. (1875), called the 'Polish'; no. 4 in F min. (1878); no. 5 in E min. (1888); no. 6 in B min. (1893), called the *Pathétique*. T. wrote 11 operas, among them *Eugene Onegin* (1879), on Pushkin's poem; **Mazeppa* (1884); *The Queen of Spades* (1890), also after Pushkin; and *Iolanta* (1890), with an original libretto by his brother Modest T. His ballets include *Swan Lake* (1877), *The Sleeping Beauty* (1892) and *The Nutcracker* (1892). T. also wrote the orchestral works *Francesca di Rimini* (1874); *Romeo and Juliet*; the *1812 Overture* celebrating Napoleon's defeat by the Russians; the *Manfred* symphony (1885); 3 piano concertos (no. 1 in B min., 1875); and a violin concerto.

Tchelitchew Pavel (1898–1957). Russian neo-romantic painter and stage designer; he worked in Berlin and Paris before settling in the U.S. He made use of perspective distortion and multiple images in the late 1920s, and at that time he also began to develop his interest in metamorphic forms; the surrealist practice of *automatism played a significant part in his metamorphic compositions, of which the most famous is *Hide and Seek* (1942; M.M.A., New York).

Tcherepnin Nikolay (1873–1945). Russian composer and conductor. He held teaching posts at the St Petersburg Conservatory but in 1909, 1911 and 1912 toured with Diaghilev's ballet co. as conductor, and in 1921 settled in Paris. His music reflects his sympathy with the nationalist Russian composers. His son ALEXANDER (1899–) is also a pianist and composer, working in the U.S. from 1949.

Teagarden Jack (1905–64). U.S. jazz trombonist, leader of a famous big band in the 1930s and 1940s.

teapoy. Derives from the Hindi *tipai*, a 3-footed table, but often incorrectly used to describe a small table incorporating a tea-caddy.

Tearle Godfrey (1884–). English actor, who made his 1st appearance in the company run by his father, GEORGE OSMOND T. (1852–1901). He played many Shakespearian parts on stage and appeared in many films.

Teasdale Sarah (1884–1933). U.S. poet, a writer of quiet craftsmanship; her works include the popular coll. *Love Songs* (1917).

Tebaldeo Antonio Tebalde, called (1463–1537). Italian poet. Most of his works are over-elaborate imitations of Petrarch.

Tecchi Bonaventura (1896–). Italian novelist. His psychological novels, including *Il nome sulla sabbia* (1924), *I Villatauri* (1935), *Giovani amici* (1941) and *Valentina Velier* (1950), are developed with considerable insight and skill.

Tecton. British architectural partnership under the leadership of Berthold Lubetkin (1901–), a Russian who had previously practised in Paris. Their work in the 1930s is a lyrical version of the international style, and Highpoint I, Highgate (1933) and the Penguin Pool, London Zoo (1934) are among the masterpieces of modern English architecture.

te deum laudamus (English, 'we praise thee, O God'). A hymn of thanksgiving dating from the 5th c.; it has a plainsong melody and has been set by many composers both Roman Catholic and Protestant.

Tegnér Esaias (1782–1846). Swedish poet, an outstanding scholar, orator, wit and influence on contemporaries; bishop of Växjö from 1824, although his career in the Church was dictated by financial considerations rather than vocation. T. remained aloof from the literary quarrels of the period, and although his work shows the influence of romanticism, he condemned much romantic poetry. His epic cycle on Icelandic themes, *Frithjofs Saga* (1820), won tremendous popularity; he also wrote the long poems *Nattvardsbarnen* (1820; 1833) and *Axel* (1822; 1838); 2 unfinished epics, shorter philosophical poems and love-poems, and many fine letters.

Tel-el-Amarna: *Amarna

Esaias Tegnér

Telford. Menai suspension bridge

Telemann Georg Philipp (1681–1767). German composer. He worked mainly in Germany, notably at Leipzig, where he founded a Collegium musicum, and Hamburg where, from 1721, he directed much of the city's church music and gave the opera a last period of brilliance. His music, anticipating the *galante style, looks forward to Haydn and has rhythmic elements derived from an acquaintance with Polish music. Such was his international reputation that the board of St Thomas's, Leipzig felt they had a second-best in J. S. Bach. His incredibly large output includes operas, oratorios and about 1,000 instrumental suites.

Telesio Antonio (1482–1534). Italian humanist; in Latin called 'Thylesius'. He wrote Latin lyrics, commentaries and letters, and a tragedy, *Imber Aureus* (1529).

Telesio Bernardino (1509–88). Italian philosopher, nephew of the above; his works rejected the authority of Aristotle and Plato in favour of free investigation.

Telford Thomas (1757–1834). English engineer, the leading European engineer of his age. In 1793 he was put in charge of the Ellesmere Canal, and from that time worked mainly on canals, bridges and roads. Many of these utilitarian works are of outstanding beauty, e.g. his great viaduct of Pont-y-Cysyllte over the Dee Valley and his bridges at Conway and over the Menai Straits.

Tell-Tale Heart, The (1843). Story by Edgar Allan *Poe.

tempera. Painting technique in which powder colour is mixed with a binder, normally the yolk of an egg or both white and yolk together, thinned with water and applied to a *gesso ground. It is opaque, permanent and fast drying, though the colours dry lighter than they appear when wet. Modelling is achieved by *hatching. T. was the usual technique for panel painting until the 15th c. From the early 14th c. and lasting into the 16th c. a mixed technique was also common, i.e. an oil glaze applied over tempera. From this the technique of oil painting developed and superseded t. because of its greater range of possibilities, particularly *impasto. T. has been considerably revived in the 20th c.

temperament. In musical terminology a keyboard instrument is said to have 'equal temperament' tuning when the notes are so tuned that all keys can be played without retuning. There is in fact a difference of pitch between G♯ and A♭, C♯ and D♭, etc. only fractional but enough to mean that a pure G♯, etc. could not be used in the flat keys without producing fearful dissonance. A keyboard instrument tuned perfectly for a given key and its related keys restricted composers from modulating into remote keys; as the 17th c. progressed the practice of 'equal t.' became common. One string is used for *enharmonic pairs of notes such as G♯ and A♭. The slight impurities of intonation permit greater harmonic mobility.

Tempest Marie. Stage-name of Mary Susan Etherington (1864–1942), English actress in light opera and musical comedy into her 30s, but appearing thereafter in comedy.

Tempest, The (*c.* 1503). Painting by *Giorgione.

Tempest, The (publ. 1623). Play by *Shakespeare performed at court in 1611. It was based on Jakob *Ayrer's play *Die Schöne Sidea* or a source common to both.

Temple Shirley (1928–). U.S. film actress famous as a child star, e.g. *Now and Forever* (1934).

Temple Sir William (1628–99). English statesman and essayist, friend of Swift, who became his secretary. T.'s *Of Ancient and Modern Learning* (1690), denying that any advance had been made on classical literature, gave rise to a prolonged controversy in which R. *Bentley and Swift's *Battle of the Books* featured. T. wrote a direct, agreeable prose, though most of his subjects are of historical interest only.

Temple, Le Paris. Lodge of the Knights Templars (built 12th c.); a centre of free-thinking society at the end of the 17th c., and in the 18th c. the *salon* of the prince de Conti, where many men of letters gathered.

tempo (Italian, 'time'). Musical term meaning 'speed'; thus 'fast t.' or a 'control of t.' when speaking of a piece or a performer.

Georg Philipp Telemann

Sir William Temple

Teniers the Elder. *Playing at Bowls*

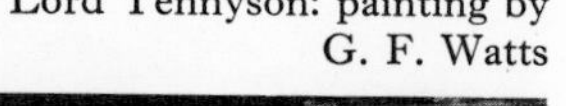

Lord Tennyson: painting by G. F. Watts

Teniers the Younger. *Boors carousing*

Teniers the Younger. *Archduke Leopold Wilhelm in his Gallery in Brussels*

Tenniel. The White Knight; from *Through the Looking Glass*

Temps Modernes, Les (1941–). Periodical founded and ed. by Jean-Paul *Sartre.

Tencin Claudine-Alexandrine Guérin, marquise de (1685?–1749). French society woman, the mother of d'Alembert. T.'s *salon* was attended by Montesquieu, Fontenelle, Marivaux and other writers. She also wrote novels, including *Mémoires du comte de Comminges* (1735).

Ten Commandments, The (1923, 1956). Films directed by C. B. *De Mille.

Tender is the Night (1934). Novel by F. Scott *Fitzgerald.

tenebrae: *lamentations

Ténébreuse Affaire, Une (1841). Novel by Balzac.

tenebrist (pl. tenebristi) (Italian *tenebroso*, 'dark'). Name given to 17th-c. painters in Naples, the Netherlands and Spain who painted in a low key and emphasized light-shade contrasts in imitation of Caravaggio.

Teniers the Elder, David (1582–1649). Antwerp painter who studied under Rubens and in Rome under Elsheimer. He painted mainly religious subjects but his reputation rests on such landscapes and genre scenes as *Playing at Bowls* (N.G., London).

Teniers the Younger, David (1610–90). Flemish painter, chiefly of peasant genre scenes. He was taught by his father (the above) but in the development of his style owed more to Brouwer. He became court painter to the Archduke Leopold Wilhelm in Brussels and keeper of his art coll., which included works by Titian, Giorgione and Veronese. T.'s copies of these pictures (engraved *Theatrum Pictorium*, 1660) and his paintings of the interior of the gal. provide valuable evidence for art historians. His peasant scenes were fantastically popular and gained T. his fashionable reputation.

Tenniel Sir John (1820–1914). English artist and draughtsman; best remembered for his political cartoons for *Punch* (1850–1901) and his illustrations for Lewis *Carroll's *Alice* books (1866 and 1870).

Tennyson Alfred, Lord (1809–92). English poet. The son of a Lincolnshire parson, T. came from a morbidly eccentric family. He attended Louth Grammar School and Trinity College, Cambridge; here his circle included A. H. Hallam, who became his intimate friend and was later engaged to T.'s sister. Some of T.'s juvenilia appeared in *Poems by Two Brothers* (1827). *Poems, chiefly Lyrical* (1830) and *Poems* (1832, dated 1833) contain important work; but T. only became established as the leading English poet–excepting the aged Wordsworth–after the publ. of the coll. of 1842. He received a government pension in 1845 and in 1850 became poet laureate. He wrote a number of poems on national themes, including the famous *Ode on the Death of Wellington* (1852) and *The Charge of the Light Brigade* (1854). His unique position was recognized by a peerage (1884) and interment in Westminster Abbey.

T.'s longer works include *Maud* (1855); *Morte d'Arthur* (1842) and other poems of the Arthurian cycle *Idylls of the King*; *In Memoriam A.H.H.* (1850), an elegy publ. anonymously (although the author's identity was quickly divined) which recounts T.'s religious perplexities after Hallam's death (1833); and *Enoch Arden* (1864). They all contain passages of great beauty which illustrate the tremendous lyrical gifts and metrical dexterity he had already revealed in poems like *Mariana*, *Oenone*, *The Lotos-Eaters*, *The Lady of Shalott* and *Ulysses*, gifts which outweigh faults in construction and occasional banality of sentiment. Neglected after the reaction against Victorian taste and standards–and especially against the belief in progress expressed in such poems as *Locksley Hall*–T. has regained much of his former stature.

Tennyson Charles: Charles Tennyson *Turner.

Tennyson Frederick (1807–98). English poet, brother of Charles and Alfred T. His verse includes 4 pieces for *Poems by Two Brothers* (1827).

tenor (from Latin *tenere*, 'to hold'). A musical term, originally (in the middle ages) for the part, whether high or low, which held the plainsong or other *cantus firmus; now the term is used of high male voice with an approximate range of an 8ve and a 5th from the C below middle C. By transference the

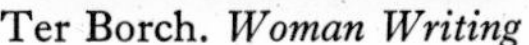

Ter Borch. *Woman Writing*

Terbrugghen. *Duet*

term is used of instruments in the same relation to their families as the t. voice is to the other voices. The t. *clef is a C clef.

tentstitch. An embroidery stitch used for very fine work. Frequently used to describe a diagonal stitch worked in single thread canvas over a single intersection. It is then also called *'petit point'. The term may also be used to describe all forms of cross stitch on canvas.

Tepl Johann von (or Saaz) (*c.* 1350–1414). German writer and author of the poem *Ackermann aus Böhmen* (1399; *Death and the Ploughman*, 1917), in which a peasant reproaches Death for having robbed him of his wife. It is remarkable both for the logic and yet compassion of its argument and the sustained power and effectiveness of the writing.

Ter Borch (Terborch, Terburg) Gerard (1617–81). Dutch genre and portrait painter. He travelled widely as a young man, making his reputation with the group portrait *Signing of the Peace of Munster, May 15, 1648* (N.G., London). His early paintings were guardroom scenes similar to those of Codde and Duyster but he later specialized in a distinctive type of interior genre, elegant and serene. Examples include *The Letter* (Royal Coll.), *The Singing Lesson* (Louvre) and *Woman Writing* (Mauritshuis, The Hague).

Terbrugghen Hendrick (1588–1629). Dutch painter of religious and genre subjects, a leading member of the Utrecht school. After studying under Bloemaert he went to Italy (1604–14), then settled in Utrecht. He was a follower of Caravaggio and Manfredi; the influence of the latter in particular is apparent in his half-lengths of figures playing musical instruments, singing, drinking, etc. In his later works, e.g. *Jacob, Laban and Leah* (1627; N.G., London), T. came closer to Vermeer.

Terence (*c.* 185–159 B.C.). Publius Terentius Afer, Roman comic dramatist; an African slave, educated and liberated by his master and taken up by the younger Scipio's literary circle. His rivals averred, perhaps with some truth, that his plays were the work of his patrons and accused him of plagiarism, that is, taking plays that had already been done into Latin. Terence in his prologues defends himself against both charges. He pleads guilty, however, to the charge of doubling his plots, that is, borrowing material from 2 Greek plays to make one of his own. He was most admired by posterity for the purity of his language; Julius Caesar in an epigram admits this virtue, but complains that he lacks 'comic force'. He is certainly less rumbustious than Plautus but exercised more influence over the development of drama in W. Europe because he was better known. He is the source of the modern comedy of manners. His 6 plays, like those of Plautus and his contemporaries, were drawn from the *new comedy of Athens; they were *Andria* (166), *Hecyra* (165), *Hauton Timorumenos* (163), *Eunuchus* (161), *Phormio* (161), *Adelphoe* (160).

Teresa of Avila, St (1515–82). Spanish mystic and reformer and mentor of St John of the Cross. She became a Carmelite nun at Avila in 1534, founding a convent in that city in 1562. She attacked the laxity of her order and together with St John initiated a reforming movement. Her autobiography reveals and analyses her innermost feelings and describes her mystical experiences with great frankness in a lively and spontaneous style; it and her vividly written letters are more generally interesting than her numerous treatises.

ternary form. A musical form in 3 self-contained sections in the pattern ABA, although the 1st section may be repeated before the 2nd section is given (i.e. AABA) and the 3rd section may be a slight variant of the 1st. The 2nd section is in a key related to that used by the 1st and 3rd.

terracotta (Italian, 'baked earth'). A hard baked clay used for statuary or decoratively in architecture.

Terragni Giuseppe (1904–42). A leading Italian architect, evaluation of whose work has always been clouded by his Fascist sympathies. However, his Novocomum Flats (1927) brought Italian architecture into the mainstream of European development, and the Casa del Fascio at Como (1936), a rectangular building with the structural frame revealed, is a building of extraordinary perfection and simplicity.

terra sigillata. Mass-produced bright red clay pottery in common use, largely as tableware, throughout the Roman empire from the 1st c. B.C. to the 3rd c. A.D. The name derives from the moulded reliefs ('sigilla') with which much of the ware was decorated. 'Samian'

Greek Terracotta: slave and boy reading. See also colour plate 10

Terra sigillata. Late 1st-c. B.C. mould for a Roman Arretine vase

Terragni. Novocomum Flats

Ellen Terry

Theatre Workshop production of *Uranium 235*

William Makepeace Thackeray

ware is another name used for it although the connection with Samos is obscure. It was first manufactured in Italy and the Italian fabric in general is called 'Arretine' after the chief centre of production, Arretium (Arezzo) in Etruria. From the end of the 1st c. A.D. production centred in Gaul. The shapes originally imitated metal vessels. The bodies, adorned in relief with a large repertoire of figurative scenes and decorative motifs, were cast complete in moulds, and often had makers' marks.

Terra Trema, La (1948). Film directed by L. *Visconti.

Terre, La (1887). Novel by *Zola.

terre à terre. A term in ballet describing steps forward on the ground, as opposed to *en l'air.

terribilità (Italian, 'terribleness'). The effect or expression of awesome grandeur in art, used by contemporaries of the work of *Michelangelo.

Tester bed (*c.* 1575)

Terris William (1847–97). English actor who after playing with Irving's co., established himself as a favourite in melodrama at the Adelphi; outside which theatre he was murdered by a lunatic. The actress ELLALINE T. (1871–) is his daughter.

Terry Charles Sanford (1864–1936). English professor of history who gained European fame as a music scholar for his work on J. S. Bach's music and life.

Terry Ellen (1847–1928). English actress who after beginning her career as a child in boys' parts subsequently became, in 1878, Sir Henry *Irving's leading lady at the Lyceum. Here and in America she played all the leading Shakespearian parts, achieving her greatest success as Portia in *The Merchant of Venice.* Her last major appearance was in 1919 as the nurse in *Romeo and Juliet.* She could also write with charm and force, e.g. her correspondence with G. B. Shaw.

Tertis Lionel (1876–). English viola player who established the viola as a major solo instrument. His virtuosity prompted a series of works from English composers and T. himself arranged violin and cello classics for viola and developed an improved model of viola.

Nicodemus Tessin the Elder. Drottningholm Castle

terza rima. Verse form, Italian in origin, consisting of groups of 3 lines rhyming *aba, bcb, cdc, ded,* etc.; Dante's *Divine Comedy* is written in t. r.

Tessin. Family of Swedish architects active in the 17th and 18th cs. Nicodemus the Elder (1615–81) was the royal architect under Oxenstierna, building Drottningholm Castle and the cathedral of Kalmar. His son Nicodemus the Younger, (1654–1728) travelled widely in Europe, acquiring an eclectic late Renaissance style which became standard in his own country. His chief work is the royal castle of Stockholm (begun 1690), a large building based on Roman *palazzi.*

tessitura (Italian, 'texture'). Musical term for the average range of pitches in a vocal or instrumental part. Thus a piece in which high notes predominate is said to have a 'high t.'.

Tess of the D'Urbervilles, A Pure Woman (1891). Novel by Thomas *Hardy.

Testa Arrigo (*c.* 1194–1247). Italian poet of the Sicilian school of whom only 1 canzone, on the theme of courtly love, survives.

Testament d'Orphée, Le (1959). Film directed by J. *Cocteau.

Testament of Beauty, The (1929). Poem by Robert *Bridges.

Testament of Cresseid. Poem by *Henryson.

tester (from Old French *testre,* 'head'). The word may be used to describe various sorts of canopy, including portable, but usually denotes the wooden canopy supported on the posts of a bed; it is also used of the sounding-board of a pulpit; also of a piece of head-armour.

Testi Fulvio (1593–1646). Italian poet. Many of his poems were imitations of Horace and Pindar but he had a natural lyrical gift admired by Leopardi. Most of his lyrics are either protests against the artificiality and hypocrisy of society, or in praise of country life; he also wrote some fine patriotic verse.

Tête Contre les Murs, La (1958). Film directed by G. *Franju.

Théâtre National Populaire performance of Giraudoux's *Tiger at the Gates*

Theophanes the Greek. Icon of the Saviour, in the cathedral of the Annunciation, Moscow (detail)

Theodoric of Prague. *St Theodore*

Tetmajer Kazimierz (1865–1940). Polish poet, playwright, novelist and short-story writer. He wrote modishly decadent love-lyrics and a cycle of brilliant short stories about Polish highland life, *Na Skalnym Podhalu* (1903–12; selected trs. *Tales of the Tatras*, 1941).

Tetrazzini Luisa (1871–1940). Italian coloratura opera singer whose London début (1907) led to a New York season and world fame.

Thackeray William Makepeace (1811–63). Educated at Charterhouse and Cambridge, T. left the university without a degree, and after abortive legal and artistic careers, embarked on journalism, contributing to *Fraser's Magazine* and *Punch* among others; *The Book of Snobs* (1848) was originally a series of articles in *Punch*. Later T. ed. *The Cornhill Magazine*. Even the best of T.'s novels can be tedious, and the blend of detached irony and involved sentimentality sometimes grates, but his novels endure for the clarity and coherence of his view of humanity, his assured style, and the careful artistry that he shows in construction. His 1st and greatest novel, *Vanity Fair* (issued in serial form 1847–8), compares the fortunes of the penniless but strong-willed and resourceful Becky Sharp with those of her weak and dependent school-friend, Amelia Sedley. T. depicts English society in the early 19th c., and exposes the pretensions, deceptions and self-interest of his characters. *Pendennis* (1848–50), a semi-autobiography, charts a young man's follies and redemption; *Henry Esmond* (1852) is an accomplished romantic novel set in the 18th c.; *The Newcomes* (1853–5) is the sentimental chronicle of a family. *The Virginians* (1857–9), a sequel to *Esmond*, is set in America during the War of Independence.

Thalberg Irving (1899–1936). U.S. film producer who became vice-president of M.G.M. at the age of 25. Such box-office successes as *The Big Parade*, Victor *Sjöstrom's *He Who Gets Slapped* (1926), and *Flesh and the Devil*, gave him a reputation for accurate prediction of public taste. In 1935 he teamed Nelson Eddy and Jeanette MacDonald in *Naughty Marietta*, first of a long line of romantic operettas. *A Night at the Opera* owed much to his supervision. T. came nearest to making a commercial success of Shakespeare with Cukor's *Romeo and Juliet* (1936), which starred his wife, Norma Shearer.

Thalberg Sigismund (1812–71). Austrian pianist whose virtuosity was so great that a contest with Liszt was arranged at Paris in 1837; in fact Liszt won but T.'s reputation was nevertheless European wide. His compositions were show pieces.

Theater Guild. New York society formed in 1919 for the presentation of unusual modern plays which would not be performed commercially. A progressive and influential movement in America; its own Guild Theater was built in 1925.

Theatre, The. The first permanent English playhouse. It was built by James Burbage in 1576 and all the leading cos of the time seem to have played in it. It was a roofless circular building of wood. The Globe Theatre was built from its timbers in 1599.

theatre-in-the-round. Much favoured in recent years, this method of play production uses an open stage with no proscenium and has the audience either on 3 or all 4 sides of the stage. This makes for intimate contact between actor and audience.

Théâtre Libre. Founded in 1887 by André Antoine in Paris, for the production of the new realistic drama. The 1st production was *Ghosts* in 1890 and this was followed by other Ibsen plays, and plays by Hauptmann, Strindberg and others. It also introduced naturalistic acting and stage design. Die *Freie Bühne and the Independent Theatre in London were directly influenced by the T. L.

Théâtre National Populaire. French theatre co. begun in 1920. It is a state-subsidized group based in Paris, but makes many tours and also plays at the Avignon Festival. As well as plays, lectures, talks and musical concerts are arranged by the T. N. P. It is a popular theatre and aims at a wider audience than, for example, the Comédie-Française. It has gained an increasing reputation under the directorship of Jean *Vilar since 1951.

Theatre of the Revolution. Moscow theatre founded in 1922 to present plays which dealt with the immediate problems of the day. For a while it became something comparable to a news cinema, but then flourished in its own right under the direction of A. *Popov.

Theatre Workshop. A group, formed in 1946, of actors and writers opposed to the commercial theatre on artistic and political grounds. One of the founders was Joan *Littlewood. The co. has never had financial help from outside sources and any money that has been made has been shared among the members. For years they toured but finally settled at the Theatre Royal, Stratford East, London (1953). Left-wing and experimental, the T. W. has had a great influence in recent years, encouraging new writers and always crying out against the staid and conventional West End commercial theatre.

theme. In music, a usually melodic figure which forms the basic material from which the piece is built, recurring in various forms, in fragments and in different moods. The t. of a 'theme and variations' is complete in itself and not merely a figure with possibilities of development.

Theobald Lewis (1688–1744). English writer, an able ed. of Shakespeare. His exposure of the mistakes in Pope's ed. caused Pope to make T. the 1st hero of *The Dunciad*.

Theocritus (3rd c. B.C.). Alexandrian poet, the inventor of pastoral poetry. He was born at Syracuse but travelled to Cos in the Aegean and *c.* 275 to Egypt, where Ptolemy II apparently patronized him. He wrote epyllia or miniature epics and a number of epigrams but his principal work is the pastoral idylls. These are brief dramatic sketches mostly dealing with shepherds and their swains, their competitions in story-telling and their loves and sorrows. In spite of their artificial subject-matter, the idylls are naturally written (the Doric dialect T. uses seems to be his own native speech, not a literary dialect, apart from the quotation of epic phraseology) and breathe a living air of the countryside, as well as being exceptionally rich in landscape, rare in Greek verse. They take pride of place in Alexandrian literature and provided Virgil with a model for his *Eclogues* and later European poets with a model for pastoral verse.

Theodoric of Prague. 14th-c. Bohemian painter whose naturalistic style influenced later German painting. He worked at the court of the Emperor Charles IV and executed religious paintings in the royal chapel at Burg Karlstein.

Theophanes the Greek (*fl.* late 14th c.). Greek icon and fresco painter in the Byzantine

The Theseion

Charles-Louis-Ambroise Thomas

The Thinker

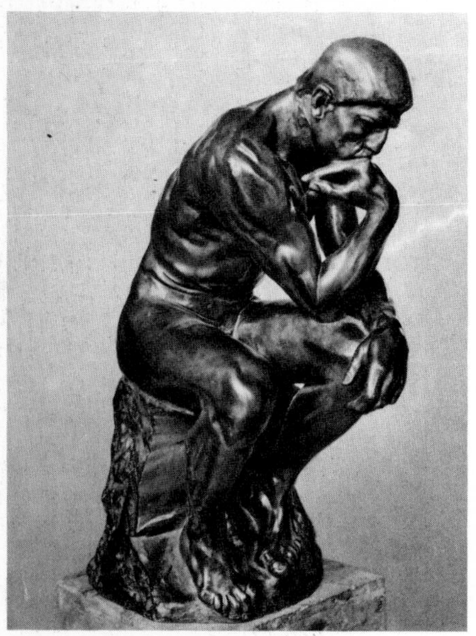

tradition who worked in Russia in Novgorod and Moscow. His surviving paintings include frescoes in the church of the Transfiguration, Novgorod.

Théophile de Viau (1590–1626). French poet and playwright, twice banished as a Protestant and author of licentious poems–on the 2nd occasion for his contributions to the coll. *Le Parnasse satyrique* (1622).

Theophrastus of Eresus (*c.* 370–*c.* 287 B.C.). Greek philosopher, the favourite pupil of Aristotle, author of important works on botany and the *Characters*, a book of sketches of bad and weak human types, the 1st known example of the genre. It inspired (among others) Overbury and La Bruyère.

Thérémin Leon (1896–). Russian scientist who in 1920 demonstrated an electronic musical instrument now named after him. The instrument has a charged metal antenna and the performer can alter the charge and hence the note by holding his hand at different distances from the antenna.

Thérèse Desqueyroux (1962). Film directed by G. *Franju.

thermae. Roman public *baths.

Theseion Athens. Doric temple (449–444 B.C.) thought to have been dedicated to Hephaestus. It coincides in date with the *Parthenon and shows all the latter's basic features, though lacking its special refinements.

They Live by Night (1948). Film directed by N. *Ray.

Thibaud de Champagne (1201–53). French noble who became king of Navarre (1234–53). His poems deal with courtly love in the manner of the Provençal troubadours.

Thibault, Les (1922–40). Cycle of novels by Roger *Martin du Gard.

Thief of Bagdad, The (1924). Film directed by R. *Walsh.

Thief's Journal, The (1949). Autobiographical book by Jean *Genet.

Thinker, The (*Le Penseur*; 1894). Sculpture by *Rodin.

Thoma. *Sunday Peace*

Thin Man, The (1934). Detective novel by Dashiell *Hammett.

third. A musical *interval of determinative importance in the major and minor *scale.

Third Man, The (1949). Film directed by C. *Reed.

Thirty-Nine Steps, The (1915). Novel by John *Buchan; also made into a film (1935), directed by *Hitchcock.

thirty second note: *demisemiquaver

This Side of Paradise (1920). Novel by F. Scott *Fitzgerald.

Thoma Hans (1839–1924). German painter in the tradition of late German romanticism modified by the influence of Courbet. His work is very uneven in quality; his most successful paintings are landscapes and portraits of his family and friends.

Thoma Ludwig (1867–1921). German playwright, journalist and poet, a humorous writer in the Bavarian idiom.

Thomas Augustus (1857–1934). U.S. playwright, a professional who wrote or adapted more than 50 plays. Works include *The Witching Hour* (1907) and *In Mizzoura* (1893).

Thomas Charles-Louis-Ambroise (1811–96). French composer; in 1871 he succeeded Auber as head of the Conservatoire. His stage works, elegant and gracious but sometimes oversentimental, include the operas *Mignon* (1866) and *Hamlet* (1868).

Thomas Dylan (1914–53). Welsh poet. Excessively praised during his lifetime, T. suffered an abrupt eclipse after his early death and a balanced assessment of his stature as a poet has yet to be made. To the sensuous yet Puritanical Welsh tradition humorously portrayed in his fictional autobiography *Portrait of the Artist as a Young Dog* (1940) and the radio play *Under Milk Wood* (1953) he united an exuberant delight in language. At their worst his poems degenerate into wordy rhetoric and obscurity; at their best, in *Fern Hill, Do not go gentle*, or *After the Funeral* they attain rare dignity and humanity.

Dylan Thomas: painting by Augustus John

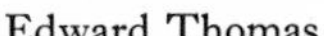

Edward Thomas

Virgil Thomson

James Thomson: painting (1746) by James Patoun

Thomas Edward (1878–1917). English poet. Known during his life as a miscellaneous prose writer and a severe critic of verse, he was encouraged to write poetry by his friend Robert Frost, *Poems* ('by Philip Eastaway') appearing (1917) after his death as a soldier in France, and *Last Poems* in 1918. His verse, quiet, fastidious in style, delicate in rhythm, interprets life by way of nature and the seasons, compassionate–as in *The Owl*–for the 'Helpless among the living and the dead'.

Thomas Helen (1877–). English writer, wife of the above; her autobiographies, *As it Was* (1926) and *World Without End* (1931), record her life with him.

Thomas R(onald) S(tuart) (1913–). A priest and poet who, born in Wales, has returned there. These 2 roles in their relationship with audience and flock form the subject of most of Thomas's poetry in *Song at the Year's Turning* (1956) and *Poetry for Supper* (1958). Expressed in traditional forms, the poetry's tenseness comes from singular honesty and clarity of perception.

Thomas Theodore (1835–1905). U.S. conductor who founded what is now known as the Chicago Symphony Orchestra.

Thomas à Kempis originally Thomas Hämmerken (1380–1471). Dutch writer of mystical works and poems, an Augustinian monk. His book *The Imitation of Christ* (in Latin; trs. into English in the 15th c.) describes the progress of the soul towards union with God; its simplicity, fervour and lyrical qualities have ensured its enduring popularity (it is said to have been read by more people than any religious book but the Bible).

Thomas of Celano: *dies irae

Thompson Daniel Pierce (1795–1868). U.S. novelist, author of many popular historical adventure novels, usually with a basis of fact, of New England frontier life, including *The Green Mountain Boys* (1839).

Thompson Francis (1859–1907). English poet, author of *The Hound of Heaven* (1891), a mystical religious poem describing the poet's flight from and pursuit by God.

Thompson Randall (1899–). U.S. composer, particularly admired for his choral works, e.g. *The Testament of Freedom* for male chorus (1943); his teachers included Bloch.

Thomson Alexander (1817–75). Scottish architect, known as 'Greek Thomson'. He designed several churches and terraces in Glasgow, using a personal Greek style influenced by Schinkel and Soane.

Thomson James (1700–48). English poet. In 1725 he went to London, where he became a member of Pope's circle. He publ. his 1st blank-verse poem *Winter* in 1726; *Summer*, *Spring* and *Autumn* followed at intervals until 1730, when the series was coll. as *The Seasons*. His plays had only limited success, but *The Castle of Indolence* (1748), a poem in Spenserian stanzas, was popular. T.'s blank verse is musical and his scenes have a quiet idyllic charm. He was the 1st writer to make descriptions of nature his subject rather than an incidental embellishment, and his model was followed by writers in England and on the Continent; *The Seasons* thus marks an important stage in the development towards romanticism.

Thomson James (1834–82). Scottish poet, author of *The City of Dreadful Night* (1874), a poem of extreme pessimism and nightmarish despair which appealed to Victorian morbidity. T. himself died of melancholia and drinking.

Thomson Mortimer Neal (1831–75). U.S. humorist using the pseud. 'Q.K.', author of the satirical sketches *Doesticks What He Says* (1855).

Thomson Tom (Thomas John) (1877–1917). Canadian painter, closely associated with the group of painters who in 1919 formed the *Group of Seven.

Thomson Virgil (1896–). U.S. composer and important critic, one of the most notable figures in American music. In Paris in the 1920s he was a member of Gertrude Stein's circle and a pupil of N. Boulanger, persuading other U.S. composers to study under her. Important works by T. are the operas *Four Saints in Three Acts* (1934) and *The Mother of Us All* (1947), with librettos by Stein, and *Symphony on a Hymn Tune* (1928); he has written church music and also song cycles, chamber works, etc.

Alexander Thomson. Oakfield Avenue, Glasgow

Thornhill. Part of the ceiling of the Painted Hall

Thoreau Henry David (1817–62). U.S. writer born in Concord, Mass., where he was educated and spent most of his life. He graduated from Harvard, taught for 3 years (1839–41), then lived (1841–3) at the home of his friend and mentor R. W. *Emerson, whose *transcendentalism profoundly influenced him. In 1844 he cleared the land, built a cabin and lived (1845–7) next to Walden Pond, Concord, practising his doctrines of self-sufficiency and closeness to nature. These were the most fruitful years of his life: he wrote *A Week on the Concord and Merrimack Rivers* (1849), recording a trip with his brother; spent a night in jail for refusing to pay his taxes (he opposed the Mexican War); and elaborated his influential theory of passive resistance and belief in the superiority of the individual conscience to the majority or the state (recorded in the famous essay *Civil Disobedience*, 1849). His life and meditations during this period provided the material for his masterpiece, *Walden, or Life in the Woods* (1854), the fullest and stylistically finest exposition of his individualism, love of nature and belief in living simply, naturally and without ties. In his later years T. worked as a day-labourer, became a skilful surveyor, and made a series of excursions, which are described in *The Maine Woods* (1864), *Cape Cod* (1865), *A Yankee in Canada* (1866) and other books. T.'s *Journal* (kept from 1837) is a 2-million word record of his inner life, and the source of all his works. He also wrote poetry.

Thorild originally Thoren, Thomas (1759–1808). Swedish poet and critic who engaged in controversy with *Kellgren; his works, upholding the autonomy of the individual genius, anticipate romanticism.

Thorndike Dame Sybil (1882–). English actress. During World War I she led the co. at the Old Vic, playing Lady Macbeth, Portia in *The Merchant of Venice* and also several male parts including Prince Hal in *Henry IV* and the Fool in *King Lear*. She played the title-role in the 1st production of Shaw's *Saint Joan* (1924). Other distinguished parts have been Volumnia in *Coriolanus* with Laurence Olivier (1938) and Aase in *Peer Gynt* with Ralph Richardson (1944). Her husband is the actor Lewis *Casson.

Henry David Thoreau

Sybil Thorndike as St Joan (1924)

Thornhill Sir James (1675–1734). English painter of portraits and, more notably, the 1st English fresco painter in the baroque manner. Master of the Painters' Co. (1720), he was also a fellow of the Royal Society (1723), M.P. (1722–34) and history painter to George I and George II. T. decorated the dome of St Paul's cathedral (1716–19) and the Painted Hall at Greenwich (1708–27). He also worked on ceilings at Hampton Court, Blenheim Palace and Chatsworth. Apart from portraits of notable people such as Steele and Newton, he painted altarpieces for several Oxford colleges.

Thoroddsen Jón Thordarson (1819–68). The 1st important figure in the Icelandic novel. His works are realistic, with a strong vein of humour; they include *Piltur og stúlka* (1850; *Lad and Lass*, 1890).

thorough bass: *continuo

Thorpe Richard (1896–). U.S. film director, one of the most versatile and among the most prolific of A-feature directors. Apart from the 1st version of *Night Must Fall* (1937), his best films have been musicals like *Three Little Words* (1950) and *Athena* (1954) and particularly 'historical' films like *The Adventures of Quentin Durward* (1955).

Thorwaldsen Bertel Alberto (*c.* 1770–1844). Danish neo-classic sculptor who worked much in Italy. Although a rather superficial imitator of antiquity, he was greatly admired by his contemporaries and became the most influential sculptor of his time. He established his fame with the huge frieze *Alexander the Great entering Babylon* for a room of the Quirinal Palace. There is a Thorwaldsen Mus. in Copenhagen.

Those Barren Leaves (1925). Novel by Aldous Huxley.

Thrale Mrs Hester Lynch (1741–1821). English writer of *Anecdotes of the late Samuel Johnson* (1786). She was for a long time a close friend of Johnson, as was her 1st husband, Henry Thrale.

Three Choirs Festival. Annual English music festival held in turn at the cathedral cities of Gloucester, Hereford and Worcester; it can be traced back to 1715.

Three-Cornered Hat, The. 1-act ballet with choreography by Massine, music by de Falla and décor by Picasso; 1st performance 1919.

Three Musketeers, The (1844). Historical novel by Alexandre *Dumas.

Threepenny Novel, The (1934). Novel by Brecht.

Threepenny Opera, The (1929). Stage work by *Brecht and *Weill.

3.10 to Yuma (1957). Film directed by D. *Daves.

threnody. Song for the dead.

through-composed. Musical term describing a work composed on the basis of *continuo. THROUGH-BASS and 'thorough bass' are the English terms for *continuo.

Through the Looking-Glass (1872). Children's story by Lewis *Carroll.

Thucydides (460/55–*c.* 400 B.C.). Greek historian. He was born of one of the best families at Athens allied to the princes of Thrace. He commanded one of the campaigns of 424 B.C., was exiled for being defeated, returned when the Peloponnesian War was over 20 years later and died soon afterwards.

'Thucydides the Athenian wrote up the war which the Peloponnesians and the Athenians waged against each other, beginning as soon as hostilities started, because he expected it to be important and more remarkable than any that had gone before, judging from the fact that both parties were at the peak of all their preparations and seeing that the rest of the Greek world was either taking sides at once or preparing to do so.' (The opening of T.'s *History*.) Apart from a bias in favour of Pericles, and animosity against Cleon, T. is uniquely impartial. He coll. material from both sides and was scrupulously diligent to obtain an accurate report. The speeches represent the substance of what was said or what the circumstances demanded. His meticulous care for truth grows from his belief that his work will be an 'everlasting possession'. T.'s *History of the Peloponnesian War* is in 5 sections: the introductory survey of earlier history, the Ten Years' War (431–421), the truce (420–416), the Sicilian expedition (415–413), later events (411); he seems to have added to and corrected the work continuously so that it is impossible to trace the course of its composition. Xenophon continued and perhaps ed. his unfinished work. His style is archaic and poetic, rough, crabbed, swift at need, and compressed. Writers of the 4th c. admired it but imitated all its idiosyncrasies sparingly.

Thumb. Family of Swiss-Austrian architects, flourishing in the late 17th and early 18th cs. The most famous member is PETER (1681–1766), architect of Birnau and (with others) of St Gall, Switzerland.

Thurber James (Grove) (1894–1961). U.S. humorous writer and cartoonist. T. lost an eye in a boyhood accident and in later life became almost blind. His long connection with *The New Yorker* is recorded in the memoir *The Years With Ross* (1959). Much of T.'s humour depends on the contrast between the fantasies of men and the realities of a society dominated by women, notably in the famous story *The Secret Life of Walter Mitty*. T.'s books include *Is Sex Necessary? or Why You Feel the Way You Do* (1929, with E. B. White); *Fables for Our Time* (1940); and *The Beast in Me and Other Animals* (1948).

Tibaldi Pellegrine (1527–96). Italian painter and architect. From 1547 to 1550 he lived in Rome, coming mainly under the influence of Michelangelo and Daniele da Volterra. He later worked at Bologna (his home town), Milan, Ferrara and in Spain (for Philip II). His style is typically mannerist–characterized in his painting by violent gestures, strained poses and sharp contrast of light and shade (e.g. *Adoration of the Shepherds*, Borghese Gal., Rome), and in his architecture by arbitrarily combined classical motifs, multiplication of planes and awkward proportions (e.g. façade of S. Fedele, Milan). He is an important figure in the spread of mannerism outside Rome.

Tibullus Albius (55?–19 B.C.). Roman elegist. Owner of a small property between Palestrina and Tivoli, he was perhaps dispossessed in the Civil Wars, but Horace calls him rich. His 2 books of elegies, terse and polished, are mostly amatory: they treat of his passion for his mistress Delia or of his other affairs. They are smooth and clear in versification and language, showing a tender melancholy and a strong love of country life. The other 2 books preserved with T.'s poems are the work of friends.

Tickell Thomas (1686–1740). English poet, author of the ballad *Colin and Lucy* and ed. of the works of his friend Addison.

Thorwaldsen. *St Paul.* Also *neo-classicism

Mrs Hester Lynch Thrale

The Three-Cornered Hat: study by Picasso

James Thurber

Tibaldi. *Adoration of the Shepherds*

Tibaldi. The Sanctuary of Saronno

An evening at Tieck's: Tieck (seated, right) reading

Tiepolo. *The Institution of the Rosary*

tie or bind. A sign used in musical notation when a single note has to be represented by 2 symbols; when a note of 4 beats begins on the 3rd beat of a bar in 4:4 time it can only be represented by 2 minims, one on either side of the bar line, the curved tie line showing that they are to be played as one note.

tie-beam. Architectural term for the horizontal beam connecting the 2 slopes of a roof at its base.

Tieck Johann Ludwig (1773–1853). German writer and critic, prolific if not profound; until about 1816 he was a leader of early (Jena) romanticism but later evolved a more realistic manner. His works include: poems, *Gedichte* (1821–3, 2nd ed. 1841); plays, *Der gestiefelte Kater* (1799) and . . . *Genoveva* (1799); novels, *William Lovell* (1795–6), *Franz Sternbalds Wanderungen* (1798)–an influential **Künstler- und-*Bildungsroman*–and *Vittoria Accorombona* (1840); and especially stories: early *Märchen*, e.g. *Der blonde Eckbert* (1796) and *Der Runenberg* (1802); and later *Novellen*, e.g. *Der fünfzehnte November* (1827) and *Des Lebens Ueberfluss* (1837). Important also as a critic, T. wrote *Herzensergiessungen eines kunstliebenden Klosterbruders* (with *Wackenroder, 1796), and was an ed. and trs. His revision (1825–33) of A. W. von Schlegel's trs. of Shakespeare became the standard German 19th-c. version.

Tiepolo Giovanni Battista (Giambattista Chiepoletto) (1692–1770). Venetian mural, genre and historical painter, draughtsman and etcher. An artist of immense industry and invention, he travelled to many parts of Europe to carry out his numerous commissions. His sons Domenico and Lorenzo worked as his assistants on many of his mural decorations. In 1737 he was active near Vienna, 3 years later in Milan, and from 1750 to 1753 he painted his most important works in the palace of the archbishop at Würzburg. He was called by Charles III to Madrid in 1761 to decorate the new royal palace and died whilst working on this monumental commission.
A typical example of T.'s work carried out for the merchant princes of Venice are the frescoes on the ceilings of the Ca' Rezzonico Palace. These decorations convey a feeling of luxury and splendour transporting the spectator into a world of heightened energy. T. was a draughtsman of genius and he introduced into his drawings and etchings a light touch which foreshadowed the achievements of the impressionists.
T. liberated Venetian art from the academic baroque style into which it had degenerated. He was strongly influenced by Paolo Veronese, but his colours were more brilliant, the foreshortening bolder, the compositions more dramatic yet ordered with tonal clarity and the effect of atmosphere. Life is portrayed with humour, sympathy and heroic exaggeration and his influence on 18th- and 19th-c. painters was inevitable and decisive.

tierce de picardie (French, 'Picardy third'). A maj. 3rd (*intervals), used as a cadence in a piece in a min. key. This was a common practice in 17th- and 18th-c. music. The theory has been put forward that this was because the maj. 3rd, being the 5th harmonic of the fundamental, would sound faintly and thus clash with a min. 3rd held at the end of a phrase or a piece.

tierceron. Architectural term for a rib that springs from the wall-shaft and meets the ridge of the vault.

Tierney Gene (1920–). U.S. film actress; her cold and exquisite passion was revealed in *Laura* (1944).

Tikhonov Nikolay Semyonovich (1896–). Soviet poet and short-story writer whose verse blends a personal romanticism with an accurate record of his experiences as a soldier and traveller.

tiles. Flat thin pieces of earthenware used to cover surfaces inside or on a building. Decorative t. have been used since antiquity but reached the highest general level of excellence in medieval Islam–in Persia (flower-and-leaf patterned) and Spain (geometrical), notably the Alhambra (*azulejos). The maiolica tile came to Europe from Renaissance Italy. Richly ornamented t. (in relief, and mainly for stoves) were produced in Germany, but the most important N. European t. were made at Delft and were widely imitated; they were mainly blue and white (Chinese influence) and painted with great delicacy, a group of t. making a picture.

Tiller Terence (1916–). English poet. Much of his early work, written in Cairo, deals with exile and isolation, and communicates a

Tiepolo. *Apollo conducting Beatrice of Burgundy*. Also *modello

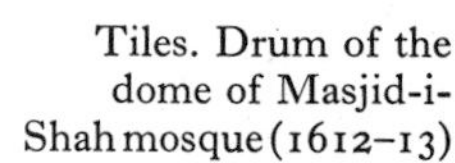

Tiles. Drum of the dome of Masjid-i-Shah mosque (1612–13)

plangent melancholy. Later work, keeping earlier economy of vocabulary and intention, relies on richer experience to produce a sense of urgency and struggle. His books include: *The Inward Animal* (1943) and *Reading a Medal* (1957).

Till Eulenspiegel. Symphonic poem by R. *Strauss.

Timaeus. Dialogue by *Plato.

timbre. French word used also in English as a musical term to mean *tone colour.

time; time signature. Time is the musical term for the number of beats in a bar. The time signature is the sign used for the particular piece. For example a march is usually in 4:4 time (i.e. has 4 crotchet beats in the bar), a waltz in 3:4, a gigue in 6:8 (i.e. 6 quaver beats). Though in actual length 3:4 and 6:8 are identical, 3:4 consists of three long beats and hence is called 'triple'; 6:8 is of 6 short beats divided into 2 beats, each of 3 quavers, and is hence called 'duple'. The actual speed of each beat is conveyed by an indication of *tempo.

Time Machine, The (1895). Story by H. G. *Wells.

Time of Your Life, The (1939). Play by William Saroyan.

Time Out of War, A (1954). Short film directed by Dennis and Terry Sanders.

Timomachos of Byzantium (1st c. B.C.). Greek painter. Copies of his *Medea* were found at Pompeii and Herculaneum.

Timon of Athens (publ. 1623). Tragedy by *Shakespeare, written *c.* 1604. Its sources include Sir Thomas *North's trs. of Plutarch, and an earlier play.

Timotheus of Miletus (d. 357 B.C.). Greek lyric poet; his *Persians*, full of extravagant metaphors and neologisms, was a symptom of the decline of Greek poetry.

timpani. Italian term in common usage for the kettledrums. These are tuned drums and consist of a copper 'kettle' or shell, supported on a pedestal, from about 3 ft to 2 ft in diameter across the top and about 2 ft to 18 ins deep. A head of vellum, or a plastic substitute, stretched over the shell can be 'tensioned' by screws acting on a rim which holds the head in place; the higher the tension, the higher the note. Differently covered drum-sticks produce different tone qualities. The 18th-c. orchestra usually had 2 t.; from the 1830s 3 or more were used and recently concertos have been written. The 'machine' drum, now very common, has a pedal mechanism which tunes the drum-head almost instantaneously; this permits rapid changes of note and *glissando effects.

Timrod Henry (1828–67). U.S. poet and war correspondent, 'the laureate of the Confederacy', a skilful and restrained writer now chiefly remembered for his war poems.

Tinctoris Johannes (*c.* 1435–1511). Flemish music theorist and composer and the leading teacher of his generation; his writings, which include a dictionary (publ. 1473/4), are valuable historical documents, particularly on instruments.

tin-glaze. A glaze or enamel whitened and made opaque by tin oxide; made in Syria, Egypt and Asia Minor as early as the 6th c. It was introduced by the Moors into Spain and spread into Europe. In England tin-enamel was used from the end of the 16th c. to the early 19th c.

Tino di (da) Camaino (*c.* 1285–1337). Sienese sculptor, pupil of Giovanni Pisano. He worked in Pisa cathedral, then in Siena and Florence. In 1323 he settled in Naples, where he executed the series of tombs (for the Angevin rulers) for which he is chiefly remembered.

Tintern Abbey, Lines written above (1798). Poem by *Wordsworth.

Tintoretto Jacopo Robusti (1518–94). Venetian painter. Though accounts of his life and work were written in his lifetime, little is known of the man. His origins and training are obscure; the 1st document (1539) refers to T. as a master. He married in 1550 and had a daughter, Marietta, and 2 sons, Domenico and Marco; all 3 were active as painters. After T.'s death Domenico carried on in charge of the workshop. In 1565 T. became a member of the charitable Brotherhood of St Rochus and

Timpani

Tino di Camaino. *Madonna*; from the Orso monument

Tintoretto. *Self-portrait*

Tiles. 17th-c. Dutch tile picture and Swiss stove

Tintoretto. *Temptation of Christ* (detail); and *The Last Supper* (1592–4)

Michael Tippett

Tischbein. *Goethe in the Campagna*

Tiryns. Gallery with corbelled arching

eventually its official painter. He seems to have led the life of a prosperous Venetian, outwardly unadventurous but of tremendous industry and an iron will to succeed. This is clear from contemporary evidence. In his relations with his patrons he used any means to secure a commission; for example, during a competition for one of the ceiling decorations of the Scuola di S. Rocco (1564) he broke the rules by finishing the painting and displaying it on the ceiling. These practices made him unpopular with many of his contemporaries.

T.'s creative development was more complex than his alleged statement about his own work, 'Michelangelo's drawing, the colour of Titian', implies. In his youth he seems to have worked briefly with Titian, for whom he professed a lifelong admiration, though Titian never concealed his aversion to T. Not only did he assimilate the gigantic forms of Michelangelo, but his starting-point could have been Paris Bordone, and all his life he remained sensitive to outside influences to enrich his art. T. had a highly organized workshop capable of dealing with the most varied commissions, from *cassoni* panels to portraits, monumental compositions on canvas for official commissions and private patrons. He kept the best work for his native Venice, whilst studio productions found their way abroad. To keep up with the demand he developed a method of work which was swift, energetic and sure, based on study, observation and analysis. He often worked from models of his own, so as to be able to experiment with effects of light, then returned to the human figure for detailed action studies. The final, full-scale painting was made on the site when and if its relationship with the prevailing architecture and light was satisfactory. Thus he achieved a seeming spontaneity and blended the subject with its environment with much labour. A number of his action studies, drawn with a nervous, summary line, have been preserved. From one of the earliest signed and dated paintings, *The Last Supper* (1547; S. Marcuola) to *The Last Supper* of 1592–4 (S. Giorgio, Venice) his work constantly gained greater depth of feeling, mastery of form, and above all, effective use of light. His influence is most apparent in El Greco's work.

T.'s gift for dramatic story-telling is brought to its height in his vast painting cycle at the Scuola di S. Rocco. Here, unhampered by the exigencies of patrons, he composed a series of deeply tragic visual meditations on the life of Christ. The *Crucifixion* is perhaps the most powerful and moving composition. Painted with bold brush-strokes in a low tonal scale, it has the freedom and pathos of an elemental statement of faith. His *Last Supper* (1592) transformed an earthly scene into a superhuman vision.

Tippett Michael (Kemp) (1905–). English composer, head of music at Morley College, London (1940–51) although he spent some of that time in prison for pacificist views. His music is robust, typically using harmony at the 2nd or 4th, and basically contrapuntal–close canon is a common feature of his style. He makes great use of the most complex rhythmic patterns. His works include: the opera *The Midsummer Marriage* (1955) to his own libretto (which includes the well-known 4 ritual dances); the oratorio *A Child of our Time* (1944) for which he based his text on an actual account of a young man killed by Nazis–in this piece, Negro spirituals are used as chorales were in earlier oratorios; concerto for double string orchestra (1943); 2 symphonies; a piano concerto (1956); string quartets and a work for 4 horns, and the opera *King Priam* (1962).

Tiraboschi Girolamo (1731–94). Italian writer, author of *Storia della Letteratura Italiana* (1772–81) which contains valuable biographical information on various authors.

Tire au Flanc (1929). Film directed by J. *Renoir.

Tirez sur le Pianiste (1960). Film directed by F. *Truffaut.

tiring-house: *Elizabethan stage

Tirso de Molina. Pseud. of Gabriel Téllez (1571?–1648). Spanish playwright and novelist. He became a friar in 1601 and was ordered to abandon playwriting after an official rebuke for his frank treatment of vice. His large output included 'cloak-and-sword' comedies full of rapid action and realistic dialogue, beautiful religious dramas, and prose works including stories somewhat in the manner of Boccaccio; but he is inevitably remembered as the creator of Don Juan in his play *El burlador de Sevilla y convidado de piedra* (publ. 1630). His hero Don Juan de Tenorio is a libertine but also a man of courage who chooses damnation rather than be untrue to himself; he is finally dragged down to hell by the stone statue of a man he has murdered, the father of Doña Anna, one of his intended conquests.

Tiryns. One of the 3 notable Mycenaean sites; the others being *Mycenae and Pylos.

Tischbein. Family of German artists including the following. JOHANN FRIEDRICH AUGUST (1750–1812). Portrait painter influenced by Gainsborough and other English portraitists, nephew of J. H. T. the Elder and cousin of J. H. W. T. JOHANN HEINRICH the Elder (1722–89). Rococo painter of portraits, historical and mythological subjects. JOHANN HEINRICH WILHELM, called 'Goethe' T. (1751–1829). Nephew of J. H. T. the Elder and painter of the famous portrait of Goethe in the Campagna (Staedelsches K. Inst., Frankfurt). This shows the poet unnaturally posed among classical remains and typifies the romantic element in neo-classicism.

Tis Pitty Shees a Whore (publ. 1633). Play by John *Ford.

Tissot James (1836–1902). French painter and illustrator. Working in London he painted delightful genre scenes from fashionable life, e.g. *The Picnic* and *The Ball on Shipboard* (both Tate), influenced by Manet and A. Stevens. Later he concentrated on Biblical subjects, staying for a time in Palestine.

Titan, The (1914). Novel by Dreiser.

Tite Sir William (1798–1873). English architect who designed the Royal Exchange, London (1841–4).

Titelouze Jehan (1563–1633). French organist and composer. His work shows sensitive awareness of developments in Spanish and English *keyboard music and the fantasies of Frescobaldi and are important in the history of French keyboard style.

Titian (Tiziano Vecellino) (*c.* 1477–1576). Venetian painter, the most important of the 16th c. He was born in the region of the Dolomites and brought with him to Venice, where he was apprenticed to Giovanni and Gentile Bellini, the elemental vitality and the toughness of his childhood. For some years he worked with Giorgione, a few years his senior. In 1510 he worked in Padua and returned to Venice in 1512. He became the painter of the wealthy Venetian intellectual circles and the close friend of Pietro Aretino, the writer and publicist, who did much towards establishing T.'s fame during his lifetime. The kings and princes of Europe competed for his services and his stature was as great as Michelangelo's. In 1516, after Bellini's death, he was appointed painter to the Venetian Republic. In the same year he was commissioned to paint a series of mythological subjects, the *Bacchanals*, for the duke of Ferrara, Alfonso d'Este, and in 1523 painted the portraits of the Gonzagas at Mantua. His wife died in 1523, an event which affected T. deeply. At this time Charles V commanded him to paint his portrait and in 1533 he ennobled T. as Count Palatine. In 1543 he painted the portrait of Pope Paul III and 2 years after was called to the Vatican and received with great splendour. In Rome he met Michelangelo. After 1553 he began his paintings for Philip II of Spain. T. died at the age of 99 during a plague epidemic in Venice. T.'s creative development was as meteoric as his life. From the poetic style of Giorgione he developed an unparalleled expressiveness. The feelings of the courtier, the cosmic powers of the universe, the mystery of life and death, the joys of sacred and profane love, were themes which occupied him during his long creative life. He had developed a technique which became more complex and free with maturity and foreshadowed in his last years the achievements of the impressionists. Over an underpainting, often on coarse-textured canvas, he applied a great many glazes and brilliant colours. T.'s use of colour was an achievement both of an emotional and intellectual nature; he influenced generations of painters of all schools.

T.'s vast work is best discussed from the point of view of his subject-matter, religious paintings, mythological and historical subjects and portraits. In each field his contribution was original and decisive for the future development of art. The portraits temper a searching realism with lyricism and compassion, and they range from the famous men of his time to the beauties of Venice. The portrait of Charles V (1548; Alte Pina., Munich) is typical in showing the tragedy of a lonely man beneath the trappings of power, the *Flora* (*c.* 1515; Uffizi) the ideal beauty of a satiated society.

His mythological paintings, e.g. the *Bacchanal* (1518; Prado) and the later *Venus* paintings, are in praise of the ideal, celebrating the beauty and richness of life. T.'s religious paintings

Titian. *Bacchanal*

Titian. *Charles V*

Tissot. *The Captain's Daughter*

Titian. *Danaë*. Also *Aretino

Tobey. *Northwest Drift*

Tobey. *Canals* (1954)

Ernst Toch

Tocqué. *The Marquis de Marigny*

Toft slipware dish with the Royal Arms of England (*c.* 1675)

Toledo cathedral

vary from the sensuality of the *Mary Magdalene* (*c.* 1530; Hermitage) to the horror and tragedy of the unfinished *Pietà* (Ac., Venice).

Titus Andronicus (1592; publ. 1594). Tragedy attributed to *Shakespeare, perhaps written *c.* 1592. Its sources were the *Thyestes* and *Troades* of Seneca and Ovid's *Metamorphoses*.

Tobacco Road (1932). Novel by Erskine Caldwell.

Tobey Mark (1890–). U.S. painter; in 1960 he settled in Switzerland. The main formative influence upon his painting was his visit (1934–5), with the English potter Bernard Leach, to China and Japan, where he spent some time in a Zen monastery. His technique in the 1940s (sometimes called 'white writing') bore a formal resemblance to oriental calligraphy, but more important was his intention to create, like Rothko, abstract images for meditation. His *Northwest Drift* (1958) is in the Tate.

Tobit. One of the books of the *Apocrypha, the story of Tobit's son Tobias, who marries Sara and exorcizes the demon who has killed her 7 previous husbands on their wedding-nights.

toccata. A term common in 17th-c. music, notably keyboard music, denoting a piece in free form usually suitable for a display of technical virtuosity; early in the c. it was sometimes used to describe a trumpet fanfare.

Toch Ernst (1887–). Austrian composer; a naturalized U.S. citizen since 1940. His music, generally classical-romantic in tone, reveals T.'s strong formal sense; it includes: 4 symphonies (1950–7); the variations-fantasy for orchestra, *Big Ben* (1933); 8 string quartets and the *Geographical Fugue* for a choir of speaking voices pronouncing a series of place-names.

Tocqué Louis (1696–1772). French portrait painter of the rococo period, pupil and son-in-law of J.-M. Nattier.

Tocqueville Alexis, comte de (1805–59). French writer, author of the classic sociological-historical studies *La Démocratie en Amérique* and *L'Ancien Régime*.

Todd Michael (1907–58). A Broadway producer of girlie shows and one of the original backers of *Cinerama. Dissatisfied with its complexity, he pioneered a simplified wide-screen process known as Todd-AO. Rodgers and Hammerstein's *Oklahoma!* (1955) was the 1st film made with the process. T.'s only production was *Around the World in 80 Days* (1956), from the book by Jules Verne.

Toft. 17th- and 18th-c. Staffordshire family of potters and designers whose slipware was so famous and widespread that their name has sometimes loosely been used to describe any Staffordshire slipware. Typical of T. ware are the vigorous bold, 'primitive' designs.

To Have and Have Not (1937). Novel by Hemingway.

Tokyo Story (1953). Film directed by Y. *Ozu.

Tol'able David (1921). Film directed by H. *King.

Toland Gregg (1904–48). U.S. cinematographer. From the time he became a director of photography in 1931 until his death, T. was under contract to Goldwyn. Although he photographed a number of films for John Ford, including *The Grapes of Wrath,* he became famous for providing the technical expertise behind the deep focus of *Citizen Kane* and the shifting compositions within the frame in *The Best Years of Our Lives.*

Toledo Juan Bautista de (d. 1567). Spanish architect who conceived and began the Escorial, Madrid. His work was taken over by Juan de Herrera.

Toledo cathedral Spain. It was begun in 1227; the nave was finished by about 1300. Its style follows French Gothic very closely, with double aisles and non-projecting transepts, but there is also Islamic influence in the decoration. It retains most of its original stained glass and in the ambulatory is the famous *transparente* by *Tomé.

Toller Ernst (1893–1939). German expressionist playwright. His work reflects fierce Socialist convictions and uses all the devices of expressionist theatre–film, music, e.g. jazz, brutal and horrific symbolism–to protest against a society ruled by callousness and money and maintained by sweat and stupidity. His works include: *Die Wandlung* (1919; *Transfiguration,* 1935); *Masse Mensch* (1921; *Masses and Man,* 1924); *Die Maschinenstürmer* (1922), on a Luddite rebellion in Nottingham; *Hoppla, wir leben!* (1927; *Hoppla, such is life,* 1928) and *Feuer aus den Kesseln* (1930; *Draw the Fires,* 1935).

Tolstoy Count Alexey Konstantinovich (1817–75). Russian poet, a distant cousin of Leo T. He was successful in several genres–nonsense poetry, lyrics, and ballads on themes inspired by folk-legends.

Tolstoy Alexey Nikolayevich (1883–1945). Soviet novelist, a distant relative of Leo T. He emigrated in 1919, but returned in 1923. His works were extremely popular; they include *The Road to Calvary* (1921–41; 1923–46), a trilogy about the Revolution and its aftermath, and historical novels and plays which reflect the resurgence of Russian patriotism under Stalin, emphasizing the creative role of the great Tsars, e.g. the novel *Peter the Great* (1929–45; from 1932) and 2 plays about Ivan the Terrible.

Tolstoy Count Leo Nikolayevich (1828–1910). Russian novelist and playwright. T.'s parents died when he was a boy, and relatives and foreign tutors brought him up. At the Univ. of Kazan (1844–7) he studied law, transferred to oriental languages, but left without taking a degree. T. led the wild life of a young aristocrat, yet had already begun a journal which shows him trying to overcome his vices; and during this period he attempted to help his serfs, though he failed to overcome their suspicions. In 1857 he joined the army, was commissioned, and served in the prolonged war against the Caucasian mountain tribes; at the same time he enjoyed his 1st literary success with *Childhood.* In the Crimean War T. fought in besieged Sevastopol. Leaving the army, he travelled widely in Europe (1857 and 1860–1), where he was disgusted by Western materialism. In 1859 he set up a school for peasant children on his estate at Yasnaya Polyana; 3 years later he was arguing that the intelligentsia should learn from the peasantry. In marriage with Sophia Andreyevna Behrs (1862) T. found a peace which helped him to write his greatest novels; but by 1880 he had undergone a religious conversion which gradually estranged him from his family. He preached a Christianity which stressed its moral rather than doctrinal or ritual elements, and T.'s interpretation of the social consequences–communal ownership of property, non-violence and agrarian anarchism. These doctrines attracted many disciples, and T. became a moral force throughout Europe. At last, in 1910, feeling that his family life had become intolerable, T. fled dramatically; he reached Astapovo Junction and died in the stationmaster's house.

T.'s power of observation and ear for dialogue mark the great realist; but his novels so successfully create the illusion that they record actual events because artificial construction is avoided (though *Anna Karenina* in particular possesses notable formal qualities), the characters have credible backgrounds and motives ('villains' almost never appear), and the style is easy, natural and unobtrusive. Most of T.'s works contain a strong autobiographical element, benefiting from the breadth of his experience and intensity of his inner life. *An Account of Yesterday,* the fragment which was T.'s earliest imaginative work, shows the same interest in the process of consciousness as *Childhood* (1852; 1862), *Boyhood* (1854; 1862) and *Youth* (1857; 1862). Like *Tales of Sevastopol* (1855–6; 1887), unromantic accounts of war, they owe much to Stendhal. But T.'s moral preoccupations gradually became evident: civilization, he felt, created a self-doubting, unspontaneous man, burdened with superfluous needs; stories like *Two Hussars* reveal the superiority of the 'natural man' (a concept derived from Rousseau). This phase culminated in the novel *The Cossacks* (1863; 1878). *War and Peace* (1869; 1886), set during the Napoleonic Wars, took over 4 years to write and is the supreme novel of Russian realism. It contains all the features of T.'s previous work, presented on a vast scale and unified by the glorification of life's endless creativity; in it T. expounds a philosophy of history which stresses the tidal movements of the masses, who bear along those, like Napoleon, thought to control them. *Anna Karenina* (1875–7; 1886) sounds a more tragic note. Anna, married to a desiccated civil servant, commits adultery with Vronsky, an army officer; at last, unable to endure her false position, she throws herself under a train. Whatever T.'s intentions, he so describes all the characters that they seem victims, and such guilt as exists is that of society and its hypocrisies. In the sub-plot, Levin, tormented like T. himself by the problem of the meaning of existence, finds salvation in family life–a solution which, however, carries less conviction than at comparable

Alexey Nikolayevich Tolstoy

Leo Tolstoy; from a painting of 1873

Leo Tolstoy and Maxim Gorky in 1900. Also *Goncharov

Tomaso da Modena. *A Saint of the Dominican Order*

Tomé. *Transparente* at Toledo cathedral

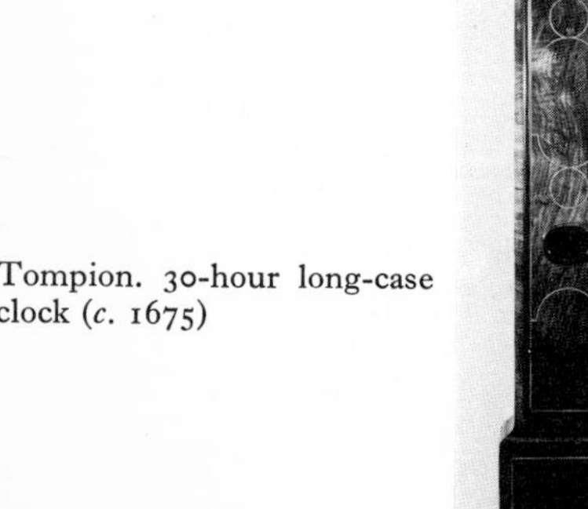
Tompion. 30-hour long-case clock (*c.* 1675)

Tomlin. *Still-life* (1939)

points in *War and Peace*–a reflection, perhaps, of the religious crisis T. was undergoing. His conversion, recorded in *A Confession* (1880; 1885) and re-created in the stories *The Death of Ivan Ilyich*, *Notes of a Madman* and *Master and Man*, led him to a new theory of literature, expounded in *What Is Art?*. He condemned the realistic detail of his previous work and used a simpler style to achieve universal appeal. His later works include the novels *Resurrection* (1899; 1900) and *Hadji Murad* (posth. 1911); the plays *The Fruits of Enlightenment* (1886; 1890), *The Power of Darkness* (Paris, 1888; 1888), *The Living Corpse* and the unfinished *The Light Shines in Darkness*; didactic books (*What then must we Do?*) and stories like *Evil Allures, but Good Endures* and *God Sees the Truth but Waits*; fairy-tales; and *The Devil*, *The Kreutzer Sonata* and the stories of conversion.

Tomášek Vaclav Jan (1774–1850). Czech composer and pianist and from 1820 teacher at a school founded by himself. He was a friend of Goethe's and his works include 9 vols of settings of songs by Goethe.

Tom(m)aso da Modena (14th–15th c.). Italian painter, son of the painter Barisino dei Barisini (d. 1343). His paintings include 40 figures of monks of the Dominican order for the Chapter-House, S. Nicolò, Treviso, painted in a flat linear style with interesting individual characterization, and an altarpiece, *Madonna with SS Wenceslaus and Dalmasius* and panels in Burg Karlstein, Bohemia, where he worked with Theodoric of Prague. He had many followers among minor Bohemian painters.

Tom Brown's Schooldays (1857). Novel by Thomas *Hughes.

Tomé Narciso (*fl.* 1715–42). Spanish architect, famous as the designer of the *transparente* at Toledo cathedral, an exuberantly baroque chapel cunningly inserted into the space behind the Gothic choir, and lit (invisibly from the ground) by the removal of one whole bay of the original ambulatory vault.

Tom Jones, a Foundling (1749). Novel by Henry *Fielding; made into a film (1963) directed by Tony Richardson.

Tomkins Thomas (1572–1656). English composer and organist; a pupil of Byrd and the last great member of the English polyphonic school. His powerful and original style is apparent in church music (publ. by his son as *Musica deo sacra*, 1668) and such a great and moving piece as the madrigal *When David heard that Absalom was slain*. T. also wrote music for viols and publ. a set of madrigals (1622).

Tomlin Bradley Walker (1899–1953). U.S. painter, for a long time of cubist still-lifes, in the last few years of his life of abstract expressionist canvases filled with symbols (geometrical forms, letters, etc.).

Tommaseo Niccolò (1802–74). Italian writer. His works include *Una Serva*, a long, romantic and deeply religious epic poem, and *Fede e Bellezza* (1840), a novel, considered one of the finest naturalistic works of the time.

Tommasini Vincenzo (1878–1950). Italian composer; commissioned by Diaghilev, he arranged the ballet music *The Good-Humoured Ladies* (1917) from piano sonatas by D. Scarlatti.

Tompion Thomas (1639–1713). Perhaps the best known and finest of the English clock and watch makers. The theories of scientists and mathematicians in and around the Royal Society were converted by Tompion into mechanical fact, and ensured the supremacy of his timepieces which made English clocks the finest in the world.

Tom Sawyer (1876). Comic novel by Mark *Twain.

tonality. The system of music which uses *keys. Out of the use of t. various tonal forms arose, notably *sonata form, which depended on the movement of keys around a basic key giving the listener a perspective of the overall form; e.g. in moving from the *tonic for the 1st group of themes to the dominant, a tension was created which was not to be resolved until the return of the original key. Polytonality is the use of more than 1 key at a time; atonality the deliberate avoidance of key: both have been used increasingly freely during the 20th c. Polytonal music derives its effects, in part, from exploiting the listener's familiarity with the system of keys to achieve startling or new effects by contradicting that system. Atonal music rejects the idea of key altogether, seeking other methods of organizing sound (*twelve-note music, *serial music).

tone. A musical *interval; also the U.S. term for *note.

tone cluster. In piano technique, the playing of a group of adjacent notes with the open hand, fist or forearm. It was invented by the U.S. composer H. D. Cowell. The English term is 'note cluster'.

tone colour. Musical term using the analogy of colour in painting to describe the effect of the different qualities of sounds of instruments used separately and in combination.

tonguing. In the technique of wind instruments the tongue determines the attack on a note and the various methods of t., e.g. single-, double-, triple-, and flutter-t., affect the musical phrasing, as well as aiding rapid execution.

Toni (1935). Film directed by J. *Renoir.

tonic. The 1st degree of the major or minor *scale; it is also called the keynote. The scale receives its name from the tonic, e.g. the scale of C begins on C (also *harmony).

tonic sol-fa. A system of musical notation, evolved by John Curwen (1816–80) to simplify sight reading for singers with little musical education. It was an important factor in the growth of the 19th-c. English choral society movement, being in this a rival to John Pyke *Hullah's work. The degrees of the maj. scale are named as follows: doh, ray, me, fah, soh, lah, te; doh is the keynote of the scale and is fixed to the keynote of the piece. Thus the singer has only to contend with a single pattern of relationships and is not troubled with the absolute pitch of the notes. As an example: the simple run d:r:m:f will be sung at sight, once the keynote is given, whether it represents

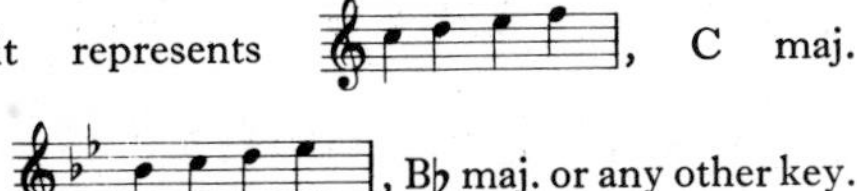

C maj., B♭ maj. or any other key.

Tonks Henry (1862–1937). English figure painter, notably of conversation pieces, Slade Professor of Fine Art, Univ. of London (1918–30) and a leading member of the N.E.A.C.

Torah: *Bible

torchon lace. A coarse bobbin lace with a loose net ground, made in most parts of Europe.

Torelli Giacomo (1608–78). Italian scene painter and designer, the 1st professional designer and one of the most expert in devising machinery and effects. He worked in Venice and then Paris, where he introduced many innovations.

Torelli Giuseppe (1658–1709). Italian violinist and composer of some of the earliest examples of the concerto grosso and of the solo violin concerto.

Torr Cecil (1857–1928). English scholar and miscellaneous writer (books on portraits of Christ, triremes, Hannibal's crossing the Alps, etc.), whose 3 vols of causerie, *Small Talk at Wreyland* (1918, 21, 23), have established themselves as a minor classic, at once witty and urbane and an unconscious portrait of their author.

Torre Nilsson Leopoldo (1924–). Argentinian film director. After making 2 films in collaboration with his father, also a director, and making 4 alone, he directed *La Casa del Angel* (1956) from a novel by his wife, Beatriz Guido. This and later films like *La Caida* (1959) and *The Hand in the Trap* (1960) were admired for their attempts at a Gothic style of narrative.

Torrès-Garcia Joaquín (1874–1949). Uruguayan painter; he worked in Paris (1924–34), where he was influenced by abstract art, though his work has always retained figurative elements–owing much formally to Pre-Columbian art.

Torres Naharro Bartolome de (d. *c.* 1524). Spanish playwright who lived in Rome and Naples. T.'s *Himenea* was the 1st Spanish 'cloak-and-sword' play.

Torres Villarroel Diego de (1693–1770). Spanish writer who describes his turbulent and adventurous career in *Vida* (1743), an autobiography written in the picaresque manner and influenced by Quevedo.

Tonks. *An Evening in the Vale* (1929)

Torre Nilsson. *The Hand in the Trap*

Torrès-Garcia. *Symmetrical Composition* (1931)

Giacomo Torelli. Décor for the opera *Marriage of Thetis and Peleus*

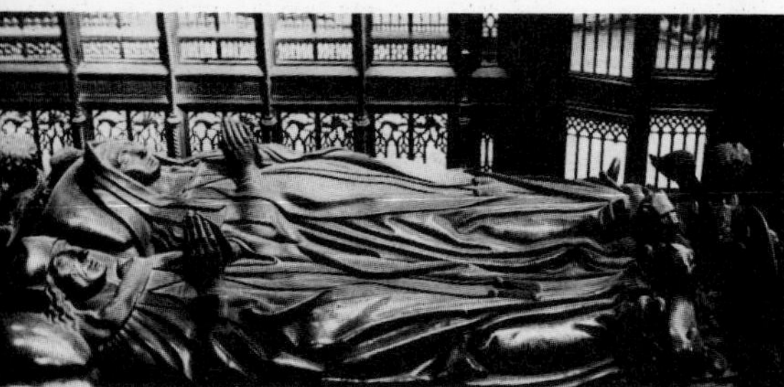

Torrigiano. Tomb of Henry VII and Elizabeth of York

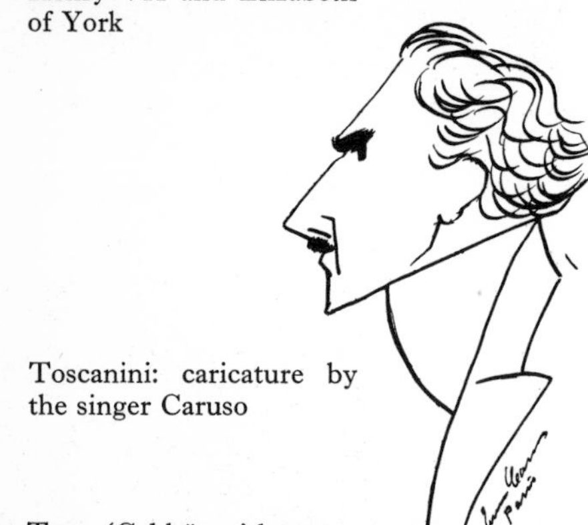

Toscanini: caricature by the singer Caruso

Tory. 'Caldaïque' letters

LETTRES CALDAIQVES.

Et ainsi des sequentes. Gimel. Beth. Aleph.

Torroja. Grandstand, Zarzuela racecourse

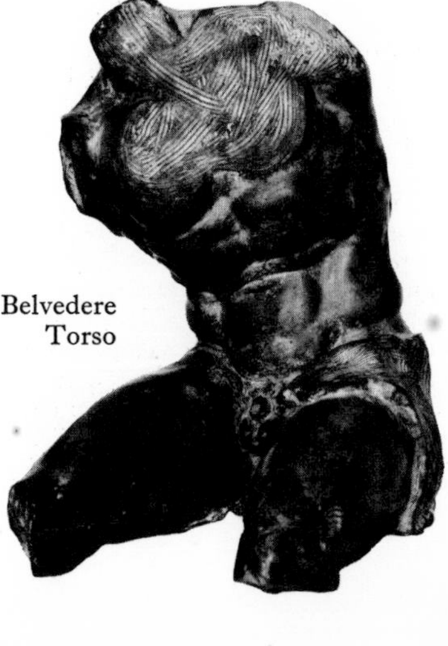

Belvedere Torso

Torrigiano Pietro (1472–1528). Florentine sculptor, the most important Italian Renaissance artist to work in England. He studied under Bertoldo di Giovanni in Florence but was exiled after a fight in which he broke Michelangelo's nose. He died in Spain while imprisoned by the Inquisition. His masterpiece is the joint tomb of Henry VII and Elizabeth of York (1512–18; Westminster Abbey). Of his work in Spain only the statues *St Jerome* and *Virgin and Child* (both Seville Mus.) have been preserved.

Torroja Eduardo (1899–1961). Spanish engineer. Like Nervi, Maillart and Candela, he made a powerful contribution to contemporary architecture by building great structures of clear logic and magnificence. His most famous work is the grandstand for the Zarzuela racecourse, Madrid (1935), with concrete shell-vaults cantilevering 42 ft over the spectators.

torso. The trunk of the human body and hence a statue which by accident or design is without head, arms and legs. Modern sculptors often use this depersonalized human form to express abstract concepts of line and pose.

Tortilla Flat (1935). Book by John *Steinbeck.

Tory Geoffroi (1480–1533). French printer. He re-drew the alphabet and attempted to reform the French language, also designing letters and decorations much admired for their delicacy of treatment. With *Garamond he helped to bring about the final break between printing and the manuscript and its letter form. His works, distinguished by the simplicity and clarity of their page layout, include *A Book of Hours* (1525) and the 1st theoretical treatise on the designing of types, written by T. himself (1529).

Tosca. Opera by *Puccini; 1st performance at Rome in 1900.

Toscanini Arturo (1867–1957). Italian conductor, at first a professional cellist; he made his début as a conductor in 1886. His brilliant career included the 1st Italian performance of Wagner's *Götterdämmerung*, the 1st performance of Puccini's *La Bohème* and *Turandot*, appointments at La Scala, Milan, at the Metropolitan Opera House, New York (1908–15), as conductor of the New York Philharmonic Society, and of the N.B.C.'s orchestra, New York (1937–54).

Toth Andre de (1910–). Hungarian-born film director. In Hollywood from 1943 he made mainly westerns, including the excellent *The Indian Fighter* (1955) and a uniquely gloomy western, *Day of the Outlaw* (1959). He has also succeeded with a 3-D horror movie, *House of Wax* (1953), a thriller, *The City Is Dark* (1953), and a spectacular, *I Mongoli* (with *Freda, 1961), made in Italy where he now works.

To the Finland Station (1940). Book by Edmund *Wilson.

To the Lighthouse (1927). Novel by Virginia Woolf.

Totheroh Dan (1895–). U.S. playwright and novelist; his plays include *Distant Drums* (1932) and the study of the Brontë family, *Moor Born* (1934).

Touch of Evil (1957). Film directed by O. *Welles.

Toulet Paul-Jean (1867–1920). French poet and novelist remembered for the verse coll. *Les Contrerimes* (posth. 1921).

Toulouse-Lautrec Henri de (1864–1901). French painter born at Albi into an aristocratic family. Physically frail, he broke both legs in accidents of 1878–9, after which he remained crippled. He studied in Paris (1882–5) under Bonnat and Cormon, was a student with Émile Bernard and met Van Gogh in 1886. He was aware of impressionism, but his 1st important work *Le Cirque Fernando* (1888; A. Inst., Chicago) is formally closer to Manet, Degas and the poster artist Jules Cheret. In studying the same aspects of contemporary life as Degas–racecourses, music- and dance-halls, cabarets, etc.–T.-L. foreshadowed Seurat and the nabis in his flat treatment of forms enlivened by curvilinear contours. This interest in exotic silhouettes predominates in his studies of the Moulin Rouge and the Cabaret Aristide Bruant of the late 1880s and early 1890s.
Jane Avril Entering the Moulin Rouge (1892; Courtauld Gal., London) is typical in its strident colour, theatrical lighting and strong contours. A personal friend of the singers and dancers, T.-L. was a central figure of the society he depicted and the intimacy of a painting like *Les Deux Amies* (1894; Tate) is characteristic.

Tamara Toumanova in *Cotillon*

Tournay group (*c.* 1765)

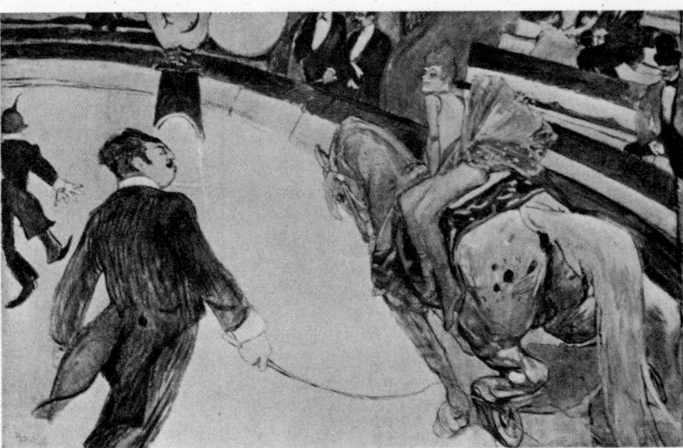

Toulouse-Lautrec. *Le Cirque Fernando*

Like Degas he worked in a wide range of media often freely mixed: his reputation as a graphic artist was established with his earliest posters and lithographs (1891–2).

His prolific output shrank with his deteriorating health (*c.* 1896) and his last painting, the *Examination Board* (1901; Lautrec Mus., Albi), an uncomfortable attempt to reorientate his art, betrays his spiritual and physical exhaustion.

His work inspired Van Gogh, Seurat, Rouault and others and his brief career was an important manifestation of the *fin de siècle* intensity and exoticism (he admired Wilde enormously) which swept Europe and which can be seen for example in the early work of Picasso.

Toumanova Tamara (1919–). Russian dancer who studied with Preobrajenska in Paris and became one of the de Basil *baby ballerinas. She developed into a dancer of great lyrical quality and has danced all the classical roles with many of the world's leading cos, particularly identifying herself with Giselle, and has appeared in films and musicals.

Tourgée Albion W(inegar) (1838–1905). U.S. novelist. T. fought for the North in the Civil War, settled in N. Carolina and played a doubtful role as judge and newspaper ed. during the Reconstruction period. His novels, including the semi-autobiographical *A Fool's Errand* (1879) and its sequel *Bricks Without Straw* (1880), sought to combat the growth of glamorous notions about the South, describing in particular the plight of the Southern Negro.

Tournay. French soft-paste *porcelain factory founded in 1751. In style it shows slight affinities with English work, but decorative motifs were often copied from Meissen or Sèvres; the largest part of the factory's output was in blue-and-white ware; also much ware was sold undecorated to be painted elsewhere.

Tourneur Cyril (1575?–1626). English playwright; virtually nothing is known of his career. Apart from some panegyric poems, the only works to survive are 2 plays, *The Revenger's Tragedie* (1607) and *The Atheist's Tragedie* (1611). Both are marred by contrived melodramatic plots, implausibly handled, and an atmosphere of hectic moral pollution. *The Revenger's Tragedie*, however, attains stature through its vitality and the vigour of its protagonist, who has a sombre integrity in his single-minded pursuit of vengeance. Theatrically extremely effective, it has flashes of poetry of astonishing power and resonance.

Tourneur Jacques (1904–). French-born U.S. film director, son of Maurice *T. His 1st notable film was a horror picture, *Cat People* (1942), produced by Lewton. T. has always been the most anonymous of good directors. Never totally responsible for a film he makes good and meaningful films even from quite bad scripts. The best of his films are *Canyon Passage* (1946), *Out of the Past* (or *Build My Gallows High*, 1947), *Stars in My Crown* (1950), *Way of a Gaucho* (1952), *Stranger on Horseback* (1955), *Nightfall* (1956), and *Curse of the Demon* (1957), a low-budget British horror film.

Tourneur Maurice (1878–1961). French film director. T. made his first films in France (1912–13) but in 1914 went to the U.S., where he directed mainly adaptations like *Trilby* (1916), *The Blue Bird* (1918), *The Doll's House* (1918), *Treasure Island* (1920), *The Last of the Mohicans* (1922), etc. He returned to France in 1927 and made occasional films until 1948.

Tournier Nicolas (late 16th–17th c.). French painter, chiefly of religious subjects, in a Caravaggesque style, pupil of Valentin in Rome. He worked in Toulouse and many of his paintings are there.

Tournus France. St Philibert, early Romanesque church (1st quarter of 11th c.) of key importance in the history of vaulting. It includes a longitudinal tunnel-vault (upper floor of the ante-church) and groin-vaults (lower floor of ante-church); the nave itself has a series of transverse tunnel-vaults (i.e. running *across* the nave) supported on arches.

Tourte François (1747–1835). French bow maker whose work essentially decided the form of the modern violin bow.

Toute la Mémoire du Monde (1956). Short film directed by A. *Resnais.

Tovey Sir Donald Francis (1875–1940). English composer, conductor and writer on music. His many books include *Essays in Musical Analysis* (1935–9) and he publ. an ed. of J. S. Bach's *Art of Fugue* containing one of the best attempts at concluding the final fugue.

Toulouse-Lautrec. *Jane Avril Entering the Moulin Rouge*. Also *lithography, *Moulin Rouge, *poster

St Philibert, Tournus

Towne. *The Source of the Arveiron*

Toy Theatre

Tracery

tower weight. The tower pound of 5400 grains *troy was replaced by the troy pound in 1527. It was of Saxon origin.

Town Harold (1924–). Canadian artist who has produced brilliant and disturbing abstracts in 'single autographic prints' (lithographic monotypes), collages and oil paintings. He has also painted murals and sculpted.

Towne Francis (1740–1816). English water-colourist chiefly inspired by the mountainous districts of Italy, Switzerland and the Lake District. His best work is notable for its bold simplification of natural forms, e.g. *The Source of the Arveiron* (V. and A.).

'Towneley Plays', The (or 'Wakefield Plays'). Cycle of 15th-c. English *miracle plays.

Toynbee Arnold (Joseph) (1889–). English historian, author of *A Study of History* (1934–60), a massive work which analyses all known civilizations and attempts to find in them a common pattern.

toy theatre. A type of cardboard cut-out theatre (very popular in the 19th c.) for which could be bought cut-outs ('penny plain, twopence coloured') of famous actors in scenes from their plays. These give a good idea of what Victorian actors and settings looked like.

Tozzi Federigo (1883–1920). Italian novelist. His finest novel is considered to be *Tre Croci* (1920; *Three Crosses*, 1921), a study of 3 brothers.

trabeated. Architectural term for the use of beams (as, e.g., in Greek architecture) rather than arches (as, e.g., in Gothic architecture).

tracery. Term used in Gothic architecture of the elaborately patterned work executed in the upper (curving) section of a pointed window with stone ribbing.

Trachiniae (425). Play by *Sophocles.

tracker action. In older organs a system of articulated rods ('trackers' and 'stickers') connecting the keys operated by the player to the 'pallets' which control the air flow into the individual organ pipes. Modern organ actions are either electric or electro-pneumatic.

tracking: *film techniques

Tracy Spencer (1900–). U.S. film actor. Landmarks are his Oscars for his seadog in *Captains Courageous* (1937) and his priest in *Boys' Town* (1938), and the series of comedies he made opposite Katharine Hepburn.

tragedy. In essence, classical t. related the fall of a great man, a fall preordained by Fate or Necessity (though often brought about by the sins of previous members of the hero's House). The action concentrated on the stages of this calamity to the exclusion of all else, strictly observing the *unities. T. originated in religious ritual–in the choral song in honour of Dionysus–and the chorus was therefore its earliest element. Aeschylus' *The Suppliants* is the 1st t. preserved. Since the classical period the constituents of t. have been modified, e.g. Shakespeare emphasized the importance of a single flaw in the hero's character which causes his downfall, abandoned the unities and introduced comic scenes; while Corneille and Racine exploited the tragic possibilities of romantic love. Most 19th- and 20th-c. drama, which has generally focused on the details of living, and on people of middle or low station, cannot usefully be classified as t.

tragi-comedy. A play treated with the high seriousness of tragedy but which has a happy ending.

Tragic Overture. Orchestral work by *Brahms.

Tragic Sense of Life, The (1912). Book by *Unamuno.

Tragic symphony. *Schubert's 4th symphony.

Traherne Thomas (1637–74). English mystic, writer and poet, author of the prose works *Christian Ethicks* (1675) and *Centuries of Meditation*; his poems were discovered at the end of the 19th c. His writing is simple and clear, affirming the goodness of Creation and reflecting his search for the pure vision of childhood.

Trahison des Clercs, La (1927). Book by Julien *Benda.

Traini Francesco (*fl.* early 14th c.). Italian painter, follower of the Lorenzetti brothers and the Sienese school and known principally for

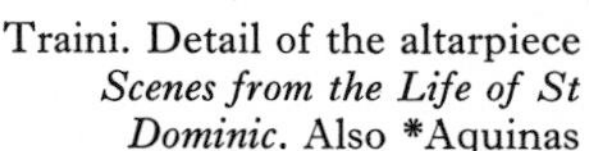

Traini. Detail of the altarpiece *Scenes from the Life of St Dominic*. Also *Aquinas

Georg Trakl

Transfer-printed decoration. Wedgwood, printed in Liverpool

his fresco *Triumph of Death* (*c.* 1350; destroyed in World War II) for the Campo Santo, Pisa.

Trajan's Column Rome. Roman memorial column, erected A.D. 113. It is 100 ft high and covered with a spiral band of reliefs (650 ft) illustrating Trajan's campaigns against the Dacians; it is the most complete surviving example of Roman narrative sculpture.

Trakl Georg (1887–1914). Austrian poet, one of the leaders of expressionism. Born in Salzburg, he studied pharmacology in Vienna and lived in Innsbruck (1912–14), contributing poems to the periodical *Der Brenner*. Called up in 1914, T. committed suicide in hospital at Cracow, appalled by the wounds he was treating. His poems, e.g. *Gedichte* (1912), *Sebastian im Traum* (1913), *Die Dichtungen* (1917), express in realistic images surrealistically deployed a pervasive, autumnal sense of disintegration in a lonely world bereft of the divine.

transcendentalism. Philosophical term, medieval in origin, adapted by Kant and the German idealists, whose thought was transmitted (partly via Coleridge and Carlyle) to a group of New England writers including Emerson and Thoreau. Their standpoint–rejecting merely empirical and materialist methods, and emphasizing individual intuition –is most clearly formulated in *The Transcendentalist* (1842), an essay by Emerson, who also ed. (1842–4) *The Dial* (1840–4), the magazine of the group. There was a Transcendental Club (founded 1836), and many of the group–and Nathaniel Hawthorne–became members of the utopian collectivist community set up at Brook Farm (1841–7).

transcribe. A musical term for the rewriting of a piece of music to be performed in a medium other than that prescribed by the composer; thus in the 19th c. piano transcriptions of orchestral works were common. Also scholars are said to transcribe a piece of early music when they write it out in modern notation.

transept. In a cruciform church, the arm running N.–S.; it is, however, common usage to refer to the 't.s', distinguishing between the 'north t.' and 'south t.' and meaning the areas N. and S. of the crossing. Hence there is in some cathedrals an area E. of the crossing which is called the 'eastern t.'.

transfer-printed decoration. The surface decoration of pottery by the use of prints from engraved copper plates using potters' colours. In mid-18th-c. England this was first achieved by 'bat-printing' with gelatine, and later, at the turn of the c., by use of transfer papers. It was used over glaze at Bow in 1756, but its most accomplished use was at Worcester. Here also under-glaze transfer-printing in blue was practised from *c.* 1759, and was to become one of the most popular forms of pottery decoration in England. Other colours came into the range during the 19th c., and this inexpensive method of producing highly decorated wares began to be used to commemorate important events and personalities.

transition. A passage of music which serves to link 2 sections. T. is also the term for a sudden change from one *key to another remote from it, without an intervening modulation.

transitional. Term sometimes applied to the English architecture of the period *c.* 1145–*c.* 1190, when the transition between Norman (English *Romanesque) and *Gothic was taking place.

transom. Architectural term for a horizontal bar of wood or stone which divides a window or other opening.

transpose. To perform or write a piece of music at a higher or lower pitch than the original one. Thus an accompanist may t. a piece down to a note to suit a singer's range; or music for one voice, e.g. tenor, may be publ. in a transposed ed. to suit it for another, e.g. a bass.

transposing instruments. Instruments whose parts are written at a different pitch from the actual sound produced. Thus a clarinet in B♭ given [music notation] will play what in fact sounds [music notation]. A horn in F, given [music notation] will play what in fact sounds [music notation]. The practice was introduced to facilitate playing in various keys in various pieces. For example, a player would not have

Trajan's Column: the 1st 4 bands of reliefs

Transitional. Glastonbury abbey

Sir Herbert Beerbohm Tree. Also *Furniss

Très Riches Heures du Duc de Berry: calendar page of October. Also *international Gothic, *Limbourg

to learn a new fingering each time he played in a new key: he could play in C on all occasions, and the actual sounds would suit the key of the piece. Nowadays, the practice is beginning to die out with the introduction of machinery that enables most instruments to play in any key with almost equal ease, and with the rise of all kinds of atonal music.

Trauberg Leonid (1902–). Soviet film director, collaborator of *Kozintzev; he has directed films alone since their collaboration ended.

Travels with a Donkey in the Cevennes (1879). Book by R. L. Stevenson.

Traven B., Ben or Bruno. Pseud. of Berick Traven Torsvan Torsvan (*c.* 1895–). U.S. novelist who has concealed the details of his life; he lives in Mexico, the scene of many of his novels. His outlook is anarchistic, a recurring theme the inhumanity of all organizations, most forcefully put in the expressionistic *The Death Ship* (Germany 1926; in English 1934). Works include *The Treasure of Sierra Madre* (1934; filmed 1947) and *The Rebellion of the Hanged* (1952).

Traviata, La. An opera by *Verdi to a libretto by F. M. Piave based on *La Dame aux Camélias* by Dumas fils.

Trdat (*fl.* late 10th c.). Armenian architect who designed the churches of Argin, Haghbat and Horomos, which show brilliant centralized planning, and the cathedral of Ani, where several features of Gothic architecture (e.g. clustered piers, pointed arches) are anticipated by 150 years. In 989 T. was called to Constantinople to repair the dome of St Sophia, damaged by an earthquake.

Treasure Island (1883). Adventure story by R. L. *Stevenson.

Treasure of Sierra Madre, The (1934). Novel by Ben *Traven; also made into a film (1947), directed by J. *Huston.

treble. Musical term used to denote a high, child's voice, and a high instrumental part; it is also used to distinguish the high-pitched members of some families of instruments. Also *clef.

Tree Sir Herbert Beerbohm (1852–1917). English actor-manager who in 1887 took control of the Haymarket Theatre and later (1897) Her Majesty's, where he produced and acted in many spectacular Shakespeare revivals. He concentrated on lavish presentation and had a voice of great beauty and remarkable range. He was the half-brother of Max Beerbohm.

Trefilova Vera (1875–1943). Russian dancer of the Imperial School, St Petersburg, who developed as a purely classical dancer; her interpretation of the Sleeping Beauty was unsurpassed. A refugee from the Revolution, she moved to Paris and opened a studio (1917) which became a centre of teaching in the classical tradition.

trefoil. A motif in the form of 3 leaves upon a common stem used in Gothic architecture and decoration and during subsequent periods of revival of the Gothic style. Similarly, a quatrefoil is made up of 4 leaves and a cinquefoil of 5.

Tregian Francis (1574–1619). English musician and copyist of the **Fitzwilliam Virginal Book*, which contains 4 pieces by him.

Treitschke Heinrich von (1834–96). German historian and masterly prose stylist. His works include: *Deutsche Geschichte im neunzehnten Jahrhundert* (1879–94; *Treitschke's History of Germany in the 19th c.*, 1915–19). Its theme is the destiny of Prussia.

tremolo. In stringed instrument technique, the rapid reiteration of a note by quick short strokes of the bow.

tremulant. Device on an organ which produces a marked *vibrato effect by causing interruptions in the air flow to the speaking pipes.

Trespasser, The (1912). Novel by D. H. Lawrence.

Très Riches Heures du Duc de Berry (15th c.; Musée Condé, Chantilly). French illuminated manuscript. Its outstanding feature is the series of 12 full-page calendar illustrations by the *Limbourg brothers which depict the signs of the zodiac and the occupations of the different months of the year. The duke's châteaux are all minutely depicted. The ms., left unfinished on the duke's death in 1416, was completed by Jean Colombe in 1485.

Trdat. Ani cathedral

Trefoil

Tressell Robert. Pseud. of Robert Noonan (1868–1911). English novelist, a house painter whose only work, the posth. publ. description of working-class life, *The Ragged Trousered Philanthropists* (1914), became a Socialist classic.

Trevelyan George Macaulay (1876–1962). English historian and son of a historian, Sir GEORGE OTTO T. (1838–1928). He wrote famous books on Garibaldi, and on English political and social history.

triad. The basic chord of traditional *harmony.

Trial, The (1925). Novel by Franz *Kafka; also made into a film (1962), directed by O. *Welles.

triangle. Percussion instrument consisting of a metal triangle, of round cross-section open at one of the corners. It is played with a metal striker.

tribrach: *metre in verse

Tribute Money, The. Painting by *Masaccio.

trichromie. Photographic process in which 3 separate negatives were produced with filters to separate the primary colours to produce the 1st successful colour photographs.

Trier Hann (1915–). German abstract painter. He studied at the School of Fine Arts, Düsseldorf and has travelled widely; a member of the Zen 49 group. His paintings are symbolic signs written in a highly personal, dynamic shorthand.

trifid spoon. A pattern developed from the square-end Puritan spoon. Of flat leaf shape, it has 2 notches at the end giving it 3 distinct lobes. It was popular from about 1660 to 1700 and often decorated with foliage in relief or engraving. Also called 'lobed-end', 'trefoil', 'split-end' or '*pied-de-biche*' from its resemblance to a hind's foot.

triforium. Architectural term for the middle storey of a medieval church between the arcade and clerestory; also called the blind storey.

triglyph. Architectural term for a block with 3 grooves on its face; the t.s and metopes make up a frieze of the Doric order.

Trilby (1894). Novel by George *Du Maurier.

trill: *ornament in music

Trilussa. Pseud. of Carlo Salustri (1871–1950). Italian poet who usually wrote in the Roman dialect. Much of his verse is satirical and he became famous for delightfully written fables inspired by Aesop.

trio. In music, a piece for 3 performers or the group of performers themselves; a common combination is a piano t.–i.e. a piano, a cello and a violin. Sometimes a keyboard work of 3 parts is called a t. (also *minuet).

triolet. Verse form originating in medieval France. Its 8 lines rhyme *abaaabab*; line 4 repeats line 1, lines 7 and 8 repeat lines 1 and 2.

trio sonata. A piece for 3 instruments, usually 2 violins and a cello with *continuo harpsichord, common in the late 17th and 18th cs, and also the name for organ compositions in 3 parts by J. S. Bach.

triplet. In music, 3 notes required to be played in the time occupied by 2 of the same denomination: thus ♪♪♪ (3) are to be played in the time allowed for ♪♪.

triptych. 3 painted panels, usually of wood, hinged together; the 2 outer wings can be closed over the central panel and may be decorated on the reverse side. Altarpieces were frequently in the form of a t., the central panel showing the Virgin and Child, the Crucifixion or some similar subject, the outer panels showing figures of Saints or the donor of the painting, etc.

Trissino Giangiorgio (1478–1550). Italian humanist, poet and playwright. He wrote a vast but unreadable epic in imitation of Homer, *La Italia Liberata dai Goti* (1547–8), and a tragedy, *La Sophonisba*, which kept the forms of Greek drama but none of its spirit.

Tristan and Isolde. Opera by *Wagner; 1st performance at Munich in 1865.

Tristan l'Hermite. Pseud. of François l'Hermite (1602–55). French playwright, poet and

Trier. *Nest Construction I* (1955)

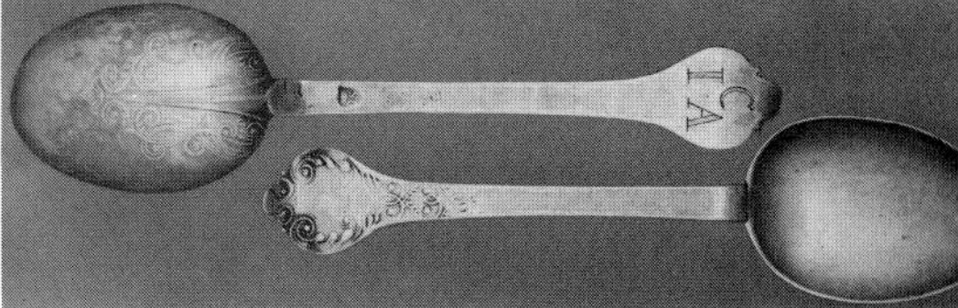

Trifid spoons; London, 1683

Triforium (above the arcade) of Mont-St-Michel

Triptych. Rogier van der Weyden, The Braque triptych

Tromba marina; from a painting by Memlinc

Trombones

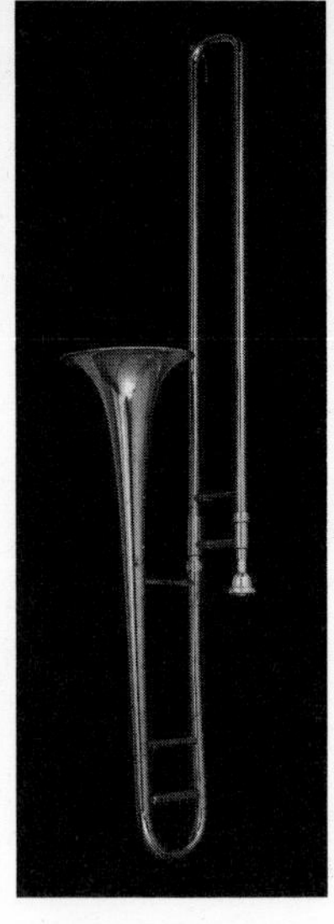

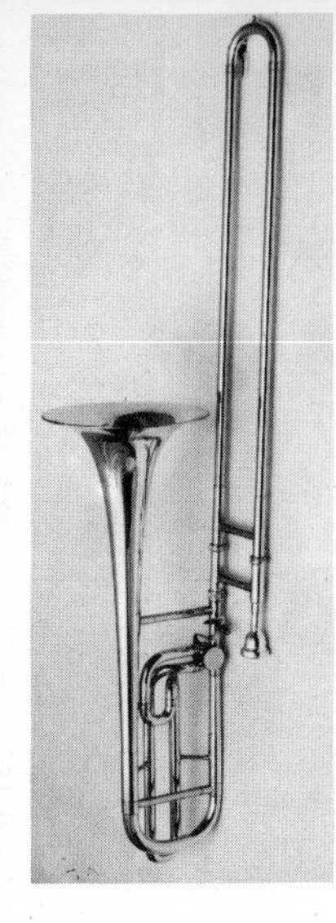

Anthony Trollope

Trnka. *Old Czech Legends*

17th-c. *trompe l'œil* fresco in the Palazzo Spada, Rome

novelist. T.'s best play is *La Mort de Sénèque* (1644); he also wrote an autobiographical novel, *Le Page disgracié* (1643) and the poems coll. as *Les Amours de Tristan*.

Tristram Shandy, The Life and Opinions of (1760–7). Comic novel by *Sterne.

tritone: *intervals

triumphal arch. Roman monument erected in honour of victorious emperors, normally with either 1 large opening, or 1 large plus 2 smaller ones, 1 on each side; it carried reliefs and inscriptions of the emperor's campaigns. The best known are those of Constantine (A.D. 312), which contains sculpture from a variety of earlier monuments; of Titus (A.D. 82), with reliefs of the taking of Jerusalem; and of Septimius Severus (A.D. 203); all are at Rome.

Triumph of the Will (1936). Film directed by L. *Riefenstahl.

trivium. The part of the medieval university curriculum containing grammar, rhetoric and logic, 3 of the 7 *liberal arts.

Trnka Jiři (1910–). Czechoslovak cartoon and puppet-film director. His greatest achievement is *Old Czech Legends* (1951), a remarkable re-creation of heroic legend, in which the puppets have extraordinary emotional power. A version of *The Good Soldier Schweik* (1955) is also noteworthy. T.'s work has great delicacy of movement; naturalistic settings, elaborate composition and stylized puppets create a world both intimate and exalted.

trochee: *metre in verse

Troilus and Cressida (publ. 1609). Play by *Shakespeare, written *c.* 1601. Its sources include Chaucer's *Troilus and Criseyde*, Caxton's *Recuyell of the Historyes of Troye* and a trs. of Homer.

Trojans, The (French *Les Troyens à Carthage*). Opera by *Berlioz, who also wrote the libretto after Virgil; 1st performance at Paris in 1863.

Trojan Women, The (415 B.C.). Play by *Euripides.

Trökes Heinz (1915–). German painter. Surrealist elements feature prominently in his highly inventive abstractions; his work is reminiscent of the work of Klee.

Trollope Anthony (1815–82). English novelist. A Post Office official, T. first attracted attention with *The Warden* (1855), followed by 5 other 'Barsetshire' novels, including *Barchester Towers* (1857) and *Framley Parsonage* (1861), which describe clerical circles in a provincial town. T.'s *Autobiography* (1883) describes his methodical habits of composition, which enabled him to write over 50 novels. They tend to be diffuse, but are notable for their quiet humour, reflection of the even tenor of Victorian middle-class life, and neatly delineated characters whose intellectual and spiritual values are rarely probed.

tromba marina (Italian, 'marine trumpet'). An obsolete musical instrument. A 1-stringed instrument, about 5 ft long, it was in fact a bowed monochord.

trombone. *Brass musical instrument played with a cup mouthpiece (a conical one is often used on the Continent) and with a cylindrical bore. The difficulties created by the fact that a tube of given length has available only certain notes (*harmonic series) are obviated by the slide mechanism of the trombone whose 7 separate positions of extension lengthen the instrument and in effect make it 7 tubes of differing length. Invented in the 15th c. (*sackbut), the t. was used primarily in church music until in the late 18th c. it was introduced into the opera and then (19th c.) into the symphony orchestra. Most common is the tenor t. with a chromatic range of about three 8ves up from the E below the bass staff; but alto and bass models are frequent and soprano and double bass ones exist. A valve t. has been developed to facilitate the performance of very rapid passages, as in modern jazz.

trompe l'œil (French, 'deceive the eye'). In painting a type of illusionism designed to trick the onlooker into accepting what is painted as real.

Tropic of Cancer (1931) and **Tropic of Capricorn** (1938). Novels by Henry *Miller.

Trou, Le (1960). Film directed by J. *Becker.

troubadour: *Provençal culture

Trouble in Paradise (1932). Film directed by E. *Lubitsch.

Trumbull. *The Battle of Bunker's Hill*

Troy. *The Alarm*

Trouble with Harry, The (1955). Film directed by *Hitchcock.

Trout quintet: *Schubert

trouvères. French medieval poets, e.g. Thibaud de Champagne, writing in the langue d'oïl of N. France; their compositions–**chansons de geste*, **romans bretons*, poems of courtly love, etc.–show the influence of the *Provençal troubadours (the word means the same as t.) writing in the langue d'oc.

Trovatore, Il. Opera by *Verdi, libretto by S. Cammarano after Gutiérrez; 1st performance at Rome in 1853.

Troy François de (1645–1730). French portrait painter influenced by the portraiture of Rubens and Van Dyck.

Troy Jean-François de (1679–1752). French rococo painter and designer for Gobelins tapestries, pupil of his father François de T. He specialized in light, charming genre scenes of upper-class life and large decorative compositions.

Troyon Constant (1810–65). French landscape and animal painter, at first associated with the *Barbizon school but later influenced by A. Cuyp and P. Potter. His mature work consists chiefly of very large paintings of cattle. His attempt to treat animals in the grand manner was developed in later 19th-c. animal painting.

troy weight. The standard system of weights used for precious metals and stones. The troy pound is divided into 12 ounces and contains 5760 grains. It replaced the tower pound in 1527, and was replaced commercially by the avoirdupois pound of 7000 grains in 1878. The name is said to have been current in England by 1350, and no doubt derives from the French town of Troyes.

Trubetskoi Pavel (1866–1938). Russian symbolist sculptor, known as the 'Russian Rodin'. Of aristocratic family, he grew up in Milan, where he studied sculpture with Bazarro. He made likenesses of many celebrities of his day, e.g. Leo Tolstoy (1899), Tsar Alexander III (1909), and also taught in the Moscow College; Goncharova was among his pupils.

Truffaut François (1932–). French film director. Like Chabrol and Godard, T. wrote for *Cahiers du Cinéma*. His 1st film was a short, *Les Mistons* (1957). Commercially the most successful of his group (the *nouvelle vague), T. makes films less demanding on audiences than those of Godard or Chabrol. In *Les 400 Coups* (1958) he seemed to be on a much simpler level, the Rossellini of the nouvelle vague, but he changed approach for his 2nd film, *Tirez sur le pianiste* (1960), a scatty, touching American thriller transposed to look incongruous in a French setting. By virtue of its obviously excellent period reconstruction and chic camera-work, *Jules et Jim* (1961) was a great success in spite of doing little justice to H.-P. Roche's novel. T. followed with the bitterly misogynist comic melodramatics of *La Peau Douce* (1964).

Trumbull John (1750–1831). U.S. satirical and burlesque poet, author of *M'Fingal* (1775, 82), modelled on Samuel Butler's *Hudibras*, the popular satire on American Loyalists (those who opposed the War of Independence). T. became leader of the *Hartford Wits, having some part in the authorship of the satires they produced.

Trumbull John (1756–1843). U.S. painter, the pictorial chronicler of the American Revolution in which he took part, for a time as aide-de-camp to Washington. He later studied under Benjamin West in London. He executed 4 large panels (completed 1824)–*Declaration of Independence, Surrender of Burgoyne, Surrender of Cornwallis* and *Resignation of Washington at Annapolis*–for the rotunda of the Capitol, Washington, based on small earlier versions.

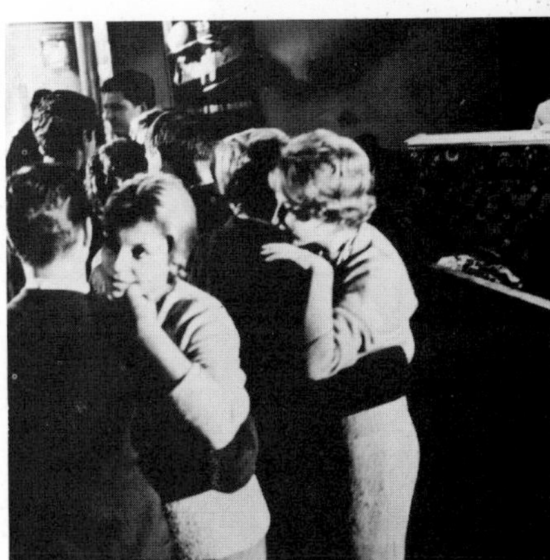
Truffaut. Charles Aznavour (at the piano) in *Tirez sur le pianiste*

trumpet. A valved *brass instrument of cylindrical bore and played with a cup mouthpiece with a compass of about three 8ves upwards from the E or F♯ below middle C. T.s of some sort have been known since antiquity; from the middle ages till the late 17th c. t.s and drums were a very important ensemble combination in ceremonial music; trumpeters could could be divided into *clarino and principale players until the introduction of valved brass instruments removed the need for specialization. Earlier attempts at a chromatic compass included the SLIDE T. using a principle similar to the trombone and the KEYED T. with keys like a saxophone; for this instrument Haydn wrote his concerto. For Bach t. *clarino.

Trumpet; from a painting by Memlinc

Trumpet Voluntary. A famous piece of music, not originally for trumpet, variously ascribed to Purcell and J. *Clarke–it was

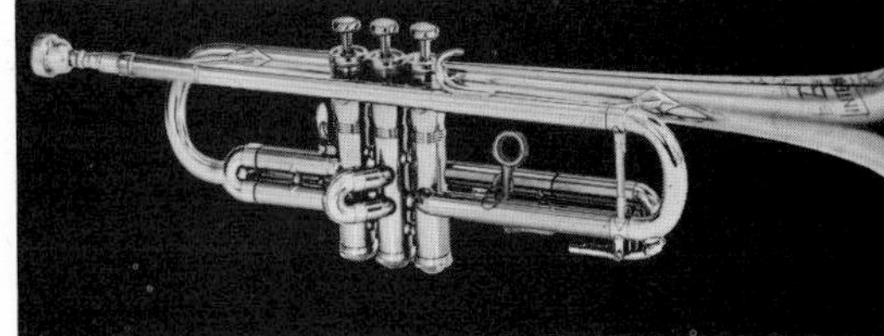
Modern trumpet

Tura. *St Jerome*

Tuba

Antony Tudor. *Jardin aux Lilas*

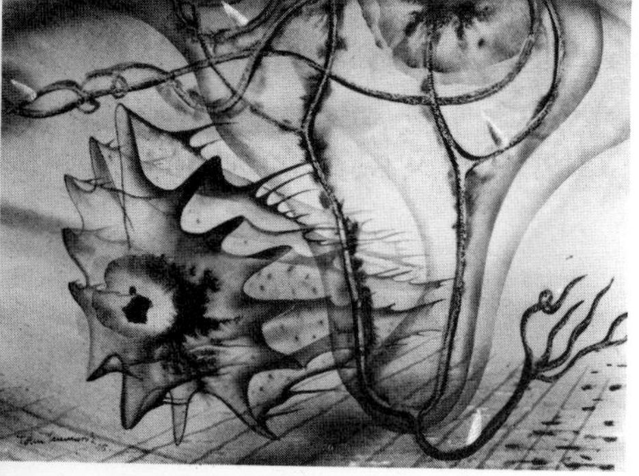

Tunnard. *Sea Flower* (1955)

Tudor style. Hardwick Hall, Derbyshire

arranged by Henry Wood for organ, brass and drums.

Tsvetayeva Marina Ivanovna (1892–1941). Russian poet. T. left the Soviet Union in 1922, returned in 1939 but, failing to adjust or win favour for her work, committed suicide. Much of her verse was inspired by folk-tales.

tuba. A low-pitched, valved brass instrument of wide conical bore and played with a cup mouthpiece. There are many systems of nomenclature for the tubas. 3 important members of the family are: the euphonium or tenor B♭ t. with the same range as a tenor trombone; the E♭ tuba, a 4th lower in pitch, and the bass B♭ t., an 8ve below the tenor. T.s were developed in the mid 19th c. and Wagner had 2 instruments built to form a bass to the horns and with a similar narrow bore.

Tucholsky Kurt (1890–1935). German satirical journalist, who wrote in particular for the weekly *Die Weltbühne*, using several pseuds. Colls of articles and poems include *Zwischen Gestern und Morgen* (1952) and *Panter, Tiger & Co.* (1954). T. also wrote 2 lighthearted love-stories, *Rheinsberg* (1912) and *Schloss Gripsholm* (1931). A brilliant wit, versatile and outspoken, an impassioned pacificist and Socialist, he has dated remarkably little.

Tudor Antony (1909–). British choreographer who contributed to the development of English ballet in the early 1930s when he was a member of Marie Rambert's co. For the past 25 years T. has worked in the U.S. with Ballet Theater and the Ballet School at the Metropolitan Opera House. His *Jardin aux Lilas* (1936) was the 1st example of English choreography to shed fantasy and tell a tale of human emotions. *Pillar of Fire* (1942) for Ballet Theater has remained his most outstanding work and together with *Undertow* (1945) it continued T.'s explorations in psychology. Later work includes *Echo of Trumpets* (1963) for the Royal Swedish Ballet.

Tudor style. Term applied in architecture to 16th-c. English building; it was characterized by the development of a decorative use of Renaissance style (derived from study of the classical orders) superimposed on the native late perpendicular.

tuning-fork. A device which gives a pure note, i.e. free from secondary *harmonics, of a precise frequency. It is in the form of a 2-pronged fork and is sounded by striking the prongs on the hand and holding the handle down on some resonating surface such as a table or a violin.

Tunnard John (1900–). English painter particularly well known in the late 1940s and early 1950s for rather spiky semi-abstract landscapes and figure paintings. He was also a surrealist for a time.

Tupper Martin (Farquhar) (1810–89). English author of *Proverbial Philosophy* (1838), an immensely popular book of maxims in verse form, but without rhyme or rhythm, which was Queen Victoria's favourite book.

Tura Cosimo (*c.* 1431–95). Court painter to the d'Este family at Ferrara and founder of the Ferrarese school; he was eventually eclipsed by Ercole Roberti. He is best known for his series of wall paintings commissioned by Duke Borso d'Este for the Palazzo Schifanoia at Ferrara to record the splendour of court life. These are rich compositions full of pattern and gaiety. A more dramatic aspect of his talent is revealed in *St Jerome* (N.G., London) where the influence of Mantegna is apparent in the sculpturesque treatment of the figure.

Turandot. *Puccini's last opera; 1st performance at Milan in 1926.

Turberville George (1540–98). English poet, author of *Epitaphs, Epigrams, Songs and Sonets* (1567). He also wrote books about falconry and hunting.

Turgenev Ivan Sergeyevich (1818–83). Novelist and playwright, the first Russian writer widely recognized in Europe. As a student T. became an admirer of Western ideals and institutions. He began as a poet, but the *Sportsman's Sketches* (publ. from 1847, issued in book form in 1852; 1885) made him famous. These stories of country life were interpreted as a protest against serfdom, and T.'s identification with the progressives was completed by his enthusiastic obituary of Gogol (1852), for which he was exiled to his estates. But later works, especially *Fathers and Sons* (1862; 1867) with its portrait of the Nihilist Bazarov, offended the radical Press; and T. became politically unpopular on all sides. This, and his attachment to the opera singer Pauline Viardot, led him to settle abroad. Mme Viardot never became his mistress, but allowed him to live with her and her family; and the peculiar nature of their relations had a strong influence on his work especially clear in *A Month in the Country*, his most famous play. Where Russians considered the political implications of T.'s books, the French appreciated them solely as works of art. He became an intimate of Flaubert and his circle, although his realism was more lyrical and melancholy than theirs, featuring 'superfluous men' whose talents are dissipated through weakness of will, as in his novel *Rudin* (1856; 1873). His female characters either dominate and destroy the men or are let down by them. Political and personal themes are carefully blended: T. portrayed a new generation of Revolutionists, crude and often foolish in their ideas; but, conscious that his moderate, liberal outlook had proved ineffective, he was impressed by their ruthless determination. Perhaps the greatest Russian prose stylist, T. excelled in descriptions of nature. His works include the novels *A Nest of Gentlefolk* (1858; 1869), *On the Eve* (1860; 1871), *Smoke* (1867; 1868), and *Virgin Soil* (1877; 1877); and the short novels *Asya*, *First Love* and *Torrents of Spring*.

Turina Joaquín (1882–1949). Spanish composer. He was in Paris from 1905 to 1914; there he studied under d'Indy at the Schola Cantorum and also was in contact with Debussy, Ravel and Dukas. Returned to Madrid he became a principal figure in the 20th-c. Spanish nationalist school, both by his compositions, which draw on folk-music, and as a journalist.

Turkeywork. An upholstery textile in imitation of the texture of Turkey carpets; stylized flower designs were the most usual. The material, manufactured mainly in England and by English settlers in American colonies, was used extensively in the late 16th–early 17th cs.

turn: *ornament in music

Turner Charles Tennyson (1808–79). English poet and cleric, elder brother of Alfred, Lord Tennyson. He changed his name as heir to a great-uncle Turner. Though he collaborated with Alfred in *Poems by Two Brothers* (1827), his distinctive work was a long series of country sonnets on subjects from stars, landscapes, weather and village life to the new farm machinery.

Turner Harold (1909–62). English dancer who studied under Marie Rambert and was one of the first leading dancers to be produced in England. With the Royal Ballet he excelled in roles, such as the Miller in *The Three-Cornered Hat*, which require stamina and attack.

Turner Joseph Mallord William (1775–1851). English painter in oils and watercolour, mainly of landscape, historical and seascape subjects; he was born in London, the son of a barber. He was taught by Thomas Malton but his precocious talent took him to the R. A. Schools (1789) and he exhibited at the R.A. for the first time in 1790; he became a full Academician in 1802. Contact with Dr Monro's circle led him to be influenced by J. R. Cozens, Richard Wilson and Thomas Girtin, and his work gained greatly in imagination and technical expertise. The death of Girtin (1802) left T. master of the architectural and topographical field, but already his interests had broadened. In 1802 he made studies in the Louvre and was showing the influence of the Dutch marine artists and the Venetian painters. A journey to Switzerland, via Lyon, returning through Schaffhausen and Strassburg, resulted in 400 sketches, many later worked up into pictures. This was a culmination of earlier sketching tours to North Wales, Yorkshire and Scotland. After 1802 T. produced a large number of historical works such as *Hannibal Crossing the Alps* (1812; N.G., London). Influence of Claude Lorrain is seen in several idyllic landscapes, including *Dido Building Carthage* (1815; N.G., London). Between 1810 and 1835, the 'middle period', T. produced many large-scale works for rich or aristocratic patrons. He also did engravings for a number of books, including the *Liber Studiorum* (1807–19), a series of landscapes and intended to rival *Claude's *Liber veritatis*. After a visit to Italy (1819), Italian and especially Venetian scenes formed the subject-matter of many hundreds of works. T.'s late period, beginning in the early 1830s, was concerned with the painting of light, to which the ostensible subject-matter was almost secondary. Forms and details were suggested and painted on previously prepared broad areas of yellows, whites, pinks and reds, or cool greys and blues. Petworth, the home of T.'s friend and patron Lord Egremont, figured in many of these works. Among major late paintings were *The Fighting Téméraire*, *A Fire at Sea*, *Interior at Petworth*, and *Rain, Steam and Speed* (all N.G., London), and *Rockets and Blue Lights* (Clark A. Inst., Williamstown, Mass., U.S.). Although T. had become successful as a painter by 1801 and remained so for many of his formal Academy paintings, the advocacy of John Ruskin in

Ivan Turgenev. Also *Goncharov

Turner. *The Fighting Téméraire*

Turner. *Ben Arthur, Scotland*; from the *Liber Studiorum*

Turner. *Hannibal Crossing the Alps*. Also *coulisse, *romanticism

Turner. *Rain, Steam and Speed*

Marie Taglioni in a tutu

Modern tutu

Amos Tutuola

Modern Painters (vol. 1, 1843) helped greatly in the public appreciation of his later works. His painting of light influenced the impressionists, especially Monet and Pissarro, who saw his work in London in 1870. After the T. exhibition at the Venice Biennale (1948) there was a second wave of influence, on non-figurative painters.

Turner Lana (1921–). U.S. film actress, blonde 'sweater girl' in *Ziegfeld Girl* (1941); later mainly in women's magazine dramas, e.g. *Peyton Place* (1957).

Turn of the Screw, The (1898). Short story by Henry *James.

Tutankhamen (d. *c.* 1350 B.C., Thebes). A young Pharaoh whose tomb, with its original magnificent contents almost intact, was discovered in the Valley of the Kings at Thebes by Howard Carter and the earl of Carnarvon in 1922. The contents are now in Cairo Mus.

tutti (Italian, 'all'). Direction on musical scores that all the instruments shall play; hence the term 't. passages' is sometimes used to distinguish passages in concertos not for solo instrument.

tutu. The short ballet skirt which has evolved from the long dress of the 18th c., through the shorter romantic style of the middle 19th c., first worn by *Taglioni, to the Zucchi knee-length fashion of the late 19th c. From the late 1940s it became shorter and is now little more than hip-length. The modern t. consists of layers of frills, usually made of tarlatan. The longer, calf-length skirt is also sometimes called a t.

Tutuola Amos (1920–). West African writer who has brought to English the vitality of African legend and speech. Of his novels, *Palm Wine Drinkard* (1952) is a fearsome magical tale of a man's journey to the town of the 'Deads'. Other books include *The Brave African Huntress* (1958).

Tuwim Julian (1894–1953). Polish poet and satirist, the foremost representative of the Skamander group. He wrote dynamic, strongly rhythmic lyrics full of daring juxtapositions and associations. He was a consummate trs. of Russian poetry, especially Pushkin.

Twain Mark. Pseud. of Samuel Langhorne Clemens (1835–1910). U.S. humorous writer whose boyhood in Hannibal, Missouri provided him with much of his material. T. was apprenticed to a printer, worked as a journalist, then (1857) became a riverboat pilot; his experiences are recorded in *Life on the Mississippi* (1883). He spent the Civil War years as miner and journalist in Nevada; this is described in *Roughing It* (1871). Already known as a sketch writer, lecturer and wit, T. became famous after the publ. of *The Innocents Abroad or The New Pilgrims Progress* (1869), 'letters' about his newspaper-financed trip abroad. Thereafter he wrote prolifically and became a recognized classic in his lifetime.
T. drew upon dialect writers, Frontier humorists and, to a lesser extent, on the orthographical humour of Artemus Ward and Seba Smith; but he brought to this thoroughly American tradition a conscious artistry and sense of style which give his novels and stories universal appeal. His great character creations are 2 boys, both scamps, Huckleberry Finn, an outcast resisting well-meaning efforts to civilize him, and Tom Sawyer, a harum-scarum constantly escaping from the demands of his respectability. In *The Adventures of Huckleberry Finn* (1884) Huck narrates his flight down the Mississippi with Jim, the escaped Negro slave; he also appears in *The Adventures of Tom Sawyer* (1876) and its 2 sequels. T.'s humour can be bitterly satirical, e.g. the story *The Man That Corrupted Hadleyburg*, depicting small-town corruption and hypocrisy; but the books he publ. during his lifetime never revealed the full extent of his misanthropy. Works include *The Tragedy of Pudd'nhead Wilson* (1894), analysing problems of racial prejudice and miscegenation and describing the eccentric Pudd'nhead's detective feats, and the fantastic *A Connecticut Yankee in King Arthur's Court* (1889).

Twelfth Night, or What You Will (publ. 1623). Comedy by *Shakespeare, written *c.* 1599 and said to have been performed before the court on Twelfth Night, 1601. The main source was Barnabe Rich's *Riche his Farewell to Militarie Profession* (1581). It was filmed in the U.S.S.R. (1955).

Twelve, The (1918). Poem by Alexander *Blok.

Twelve Angry Men (1957). Film directed by S. *Lumet.

twelve-note music. Name given to a technique of composition, associated primarily with

Mark Twain: from a poster advertising one of his lectures

The gold coffin of Tutankhamen

Tympana. Porte Royale, W. façade of Chartres

*Schoenberg. The basic assumption of 12-note music is that the 12 notes of the chromatic scale are of equal 'weight'. In the major-minor tonal system the notes of the diatonic *scale are felt to be related to one another in relationships of subordinance and superiority; *keys are 'related' or 'remote' and the music derives its basic shape from this pattern of key and note relationships. In 12-note music this ordering pattern is replaced by a note-row, i.e. the 12 notes arranged in a sequence or 'series' (*serial music). It is this note-row, decided by the composer, sometimes stated at the beginning of the piece, which dictates the relationships of the notes throughout that piece. The row, or any fragment of it can be *inverted, given backwards (i.e. retrograde), or both–although the sequence may be thus distorted, it is not dislocated.

Twentieth Century (1934). Film directed by H. *Hawks.

Two Gentlemen of Verona, The (before 1598; publ. 1623). Comedy by *Shakespeare, written *c.* 1594. Its source was Jorge de Montemayor's *La Diana Enamorada.*

Two Noble Kinsmen, The (publ. 1634). Play of uncertain authorship (perhaps by Shakespeare and *Fletcher), based on Chaucer's *The Knight's Tale.* It may have been performed at court in 1619.

Two Years Before the Mast (1840). Book by R. H. *Dana.

T(h)yard Pontus de (1521–1605). French poet, bishop of Chalon-sur-Saône (1578–89), one of the *Pléiade. He wrote a sonnet sequence, *Les Erreurs amoureuses* (1549–55), and the prose *Discours philosophiques* (1587).

Tye Christopher (*c.* 1500–73). English composer and cleric; possibly the music teacher to Henry VIII's children. His most important works were masses and music for the Reformed English service, but he also wrote keyboard music.

Tyler Royall (1757–1826). Distinguished U.S. lawyer and writer; his *The Contrast* (1787) was the 1st U.S. comedy. Other works, including the novel *The Algerine Captive* (1797), contributed towards the development of a distinctively American literature.

tympanum. Architectural term for the triangular area within a classical *pediment, or for the area enclosed by an arch over the *lintel of a doorway.

Tyndale William (d. 1536). Religious Reformer whose English trs. of the New Testament was the 1st printed (1526, smuggled into the country; revised 1534; printed in England 1536). It was extremely accurate; T.'s purpose was to reach the widest possible audience, and his strong, simple prose was the model for subsequent trs, including the Authorized Version. He also trs. the Pentateuch (*c.* 1530) and the Book of Job (1531). Most of T.'s working life was spent in Germany and the Low Countries, where he was burned as a heretic.

Tynyanov Yuri Nikolayevich (1894–1943). Soviet novelist and literary historian who wrote fictional but scholarly literary biographies of Küchelbecker, Griboyedov and Pushkin. As a result, this genre became very popular during the 1920s and 1930s.

Typee: A Peep at Polynesian Life (1846). Novel by Herman *Melville.

Tyrwhitt Thomas (1730–86). English scholar. T. proved that the 'Rowley Poems' were a forgery by Chatterton. He ed. *The Canterbury Tales* and helped to establish the Chaucer canon.

Tyutchev Fyodor Ivanovich (1803–73). Russian poet. T. spent much of his life in the diplomatic service in Germany and Italy. He publ. his verse anonymously and remained unknown until 1850, when Nekrasov, later joined by Turgenev, used his prestige to make him famous. T.'s best poems are nature lyrics in which his apprehension of beauty (especially the beauty of the night) is transformed into a sense of the chaos at the heart of the universe which day conceals. When middle-aged he wrote a series of great love-lyrics inspired by his tortured love-affair with his children's governess.

Tzara Tristan (1896–1963). Rumanian poet who founded the *dada group in Zürich (1916) and ed. the periodical *Dada.* He later became leader of the Paris group. In addition to numerous writings on the dada movement, his own dada works include *Vingt-Cinq poèmes* (1918) and the play *La Cœur à Gaz* (1923).

William Tyndale

Fyodor Ivanovich Tyutchev

Tristan Tzara

Uccello. *Self-portrait.* Also *The *Rout of San Romano*

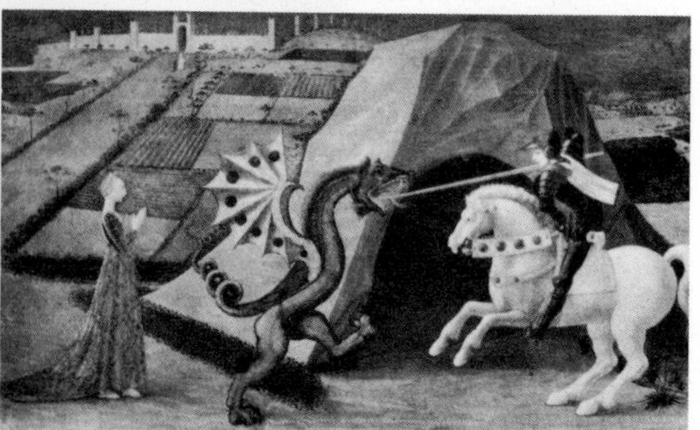
Uccello. *St George and the Dragon* (Mus. Jacquemart-André)

Uccello. *St George and the Dragon* (N.G.)

Ugolino di Nerio. *Deposition*

U

Ubac Raoul (1911–). Belgian painter and graphic artist. He was a member of the surrealist group in Paris in the 1930s and produced some interesting photographic collages. He later turned to abstract painting.

Uberti Fazio degli (*c.* 1305–*c.* 68). Italian poet. U.'s long allegorical narrative the *Dittamondo* was inspired by Dante's *Divina Commedia*; it describes the author's imaginary travels around the world in search of virtue.

Ubu Roi (1896). Play by Alfred *Jarry.

Uccello Paolo (*c.* 1396–1479). Florentine painter apprenticed to Ghiberti. At first successful, he fell out of favour with his patrons, due it is believed to his uncompromising interest in the problems of perspective. Vasari relates how according to his daughter . . . 'Paolo would stand the whole night through beside his writing-desk seeking new terms for the expression of his rules in perspective. . . .' Vasari also refers to the reason for his nickname 'Uccello' (Italian, 'bird'). As he was very fond of animals but could not afford to keep any, he surrounded himself with paintings of birds and other animals in his house.
Belonging to Donatello's circle, U. threw himself wholeheartedly into the new scientific-painterly problems of representing 3-dimensional reality on a 2-dimensional surface by means of perspective. After his death he was forgotten but 20th-c. concern with formal problems has caused a revival of interest in his work.
It is interesting to compare 2 early paintings, versions of *St George and the Dragon* (Mus. Jacquemart-André, Paris and N.G. London), the first flat and decorative, the second with a passionate concern for space and form. The pattern of circles on the dragon's wings becomes an excuse for showing them in perspective, the treatment of the prancing horse and knight's armour is identical. The upright figure of the princess is composed with severity. The lines of central perspective are accentuated by the diagonals of the knight's lance and the dragon's leg. All the essential elements of U.'s later paintings are here clearly and uncompromisingly stated.
His best-known works are the fresco *The Flood* (Chiostro Verde, S. Maria Novella, Florence) and the 3 panels of *The Rout of San Romano* (1454–7), painted decorations for the Medici Palace in Florence and now in the N.G., London, the Louvre and the Uffizi. They are further examples of his highly original and imaginative approach. Scientific perspective is blended with a poetical interpretation of reality. The trappings of horses and armour are turned into fantastic forms and the colour scheme is rich and unexpected. His last important work, *The Hunt* (1468; Ashmolean, Oxford), is a night scene. Perspective is used here to create a superb, varied pattern of diminishing forms.

Udall Nicholas (1505–56). English playwright, a headmaster of Eton. U.'s *Ralph Roister Doister* (*c.* 1552) is the earliest English comedy known.

Udine Giovanni da (Giovanni Nanni) (1487–1546). Italian painter, one of the foremost decorative artists of his time, notable for his grotesque ornamentation and responsible for reviving and popularizing stucco as a form of decoration. He studied under Giorgione in Venice, then entered Raphael's workshop in Rome; on the Sack of Rome (1527) he fled to Florence.

Ugetsu Monogatari (1953). Film directed by K. *Mizoguchi.

Ugolino di Nerio (da Siena) (*fl.* 1317–27). Italian painter of the Sienese school, follower of Duccio. His only authenticated painting was the high altar of S. Croce, Florence, a polyptych, only fragments of which now exist, some in the N.G., London. Many other paintings are attributed to him.

Uhland Johann Ludwig (1787–1862). German poet and scholar. After a period as a lawyer he became, in 1830, professor of German at Tübingen. Influenced by Arnim and Brentano's folk-song coll. *Des Knaben Wunderhorn* (1806) and the romantic interest in older literature, he initiated the Swabian school of down-to-earth romanticism. His much-loved poems were written early in life (*Gedichte*, 1815): they follow the folk-song's simple lines and include many ballads. U. influenced many poets, e.g. G. Schwab and other Swabians, Chamisso, Hebbel and Storm; but for modern taste his poetic language is too thin. He also wrote plays and produced an ed. of German folk-songs (1845).

Ukelele

Ulanova in *The Fountain of Bakhchisarai*

Ulmer. *The Naked Dawn*

Unamuno

ukelele (ukulele). Small plucked musical instrument, of Hawaian origins, similar to the guitar. There is also a 'banjo-u.'.

Ulanova Galina (1910–). Soviet dancer trained at the Imperial School, Leningrad but joined the Bolshoi Co. in Moscow (1944) and has danced all the leading classical roles in the repertoire as well as creating new characters in works of contemporary Soviet composers (*Fountain of Bakhchisarai* (1934), etc.). Her technical skill and dramatic sensitivity are astonishing and she is recognized as one of the greatest dancers in ballet history.

Ulfilas or **Wulfila.** 4th-c. Gothic Arian bishop whose trs. of the Bible into Gothic is the 1st great literary work in a Germanic language. Part of the trs. of the Gospels survives in the *Codex argenteus* at Uppsala, written in silver on purple vellum.

Ulm cathedral Germany. Built as the parish church during the 15th c., the cathedral is famous for its huge W. tower and open-work spire, 529 ft high, the culmination of a wide-spread late Gothic fashion in Germany. It was only completed (though to the original designs) in the 19th c.

Ulmer Edgar G. (1904–). Austrian-born film director. U. was a stage actor and set designer (for M. Reinhardt), a film designer and assistant to Murnau on his last 7 films. He worked on *Menschen am sonntag* and went to the U.S., where he worked as a designer before directing (1933). Most of his films were shot on extremely low budgets. *The Naked Dawn* (1955), about Mexican peasants, a bandit and the police, is his most personal work.

Ulrich von Lichtenstein. 13th-c. Styrian aristocrat and poet. Besides numerous lyrics he wrote the ostensibly autobiographical *Frauendienst*, containing numerous improbable knightly and amorous adventures, and *Frauenbuch*, discussing the reasons for the decline of chivalry.

Ulysses (1922). Novel by James *Joyce.

Umberto D (1952). Film directed by V. de *Sica.

Umbria, school of. Central Italian school of painting of the 15th–16th c. based on Perugia and represented by Perugino, Pinturicchio and Raphael.

Unamuno y Jugo Miguel de (1864–1936). Spanish philosopher, novelist and poet; the eldest of the *generation of '98 and one of the most powerful and influential Spanish thinkers of his time. He was deported (1924–30) for opposing the dictatorship of Primo de Rivera; when the Civil War broke out in 1936 he at first supported the Nationalists but later denounced both sides and died broken-hearted. In his masterpieces *Del Sentimiento trágico de la vida* (1913; *The Tragic Sense of Life*, 1921) and *The Agony of Christianity* (publ. in French 1925; English trs. 1928) U. expresses his preoccupation with death, his passionate longing for personal immortality, and his feelings of anguish and doubt with regard to religion and the human condition.

unanimism. French literary movement founded by Jules *Romains and first set out in his coll. of poems *Vie unanime* (1908). It held that the collectivity has an existence over and above those of the individuals composing it; the task of poets and novelists was to portray this group soul. Duhamel and other members of the *Abbaye group were associated with u.

Uncle Remus, His Songs and His Sayings (1880). Coll. of stories by Joel Chandler *Harris.

Uncle Tom's Cabin (1851). Novel by Harriet Beecher *Stowe.

Uncle Vanya (1899). Play by *Chekhov.

Under Milk Wood: a Play for Voices (1953). Radio play by Dylan *Thomas.

underpainting. Painting of a composition in monochrome before the addition of colour glazes, which was the initial stage in the traditional method of oil painting. The word can also be applied to a layer of colour which is to be glazed or scumbled.

Under the Greenwood Tree (1872). Novel by Thomas *Hardy.

Undertones of War (1928). Book by Edmund *Blunden.

Under Western Eyes (1911). Novel by *Conrad.

Ulfilas. Page from the *Codex argenteus*

Ulm cathedral

Upjohn. Trinity church, New York City

The Ducal Palace of Urbino

Giuseppe Ungaretti

Undset Sigrid (1882–1949). Norwegian novelist. U.'s first novels were such realistic studies as *Jenny* (1912; 1920), dealing frankly with the problems of young women and often reflecting her 10 years' experiences as an office worker. But her best work was a series of historical novels revealing profound insight and fine historical imagination, e.g. *Kristin Lavransdatter* (1920–22; 1923–30), set in the 14th c.

Unfinished symphony. Nickname for *Schubert's symphony in B min. (1822), of which only 2 completed movements survive.

Unfortunate Traveller, or the life of Jacke Wilton, The (1594). Picaresque novel by Thomas *Nashe.

Ungaretti Giuseppe (1888–). Most influential modern Italian poet, the founder of the 'hermetic' school (*hermetic tradition). U. studied in Paris, where he acquired an admiration for Rimbaud and Mallarmé which deeply influenced his work. He taught at the univ. of São Paolo, Brazil (1936–42) and has since been a professor at the Univ. of Rome. U.'s lyrics are simple, intense and concentrated, using short lines and an unrhetorical style. The best coll.–poems written during U.'s army service in World War I–is perhaps *Allegria di naufraghi* (1919, called *L'allegria* in later eds). Others include *Il sentimento del tempo* (1933), *Il dolore* (1947), *La terra promessa* (1950), *Il taccuino del vecchio* (1960) and *Il deserto e dopo* (1961).

unison. In music 2 voices are said to be in u. when they are singing the same part at the same pitch–the term is also used loosely of a group of singers and instrumentalists all singing and playing the same line of music, thus giving no harmonies but possibly separated by many *octaves.

Unité d'Habitation, Marseille (1947–52). Architect *Le Corbusier.

unities, the 3 dramatic. A rigid theory of tragedy developed by Italian and French Renaissance writers claiming Aristotle as their authority. The u.s are: unity of action, i.e. coherent integration of the parts of the drama; of time, i.e. the events described in the play do not extend over a longer period than the play itself; of place, i.e. the action does not take place over a larger area than the theatre.

Unit One. Group of British artists formed in 1933 and including Henry Moore, Ben Nicholson, Barbara Hepworth and Paul Nash; Herbert Read was its spokesman. The group organized the International Surrealist Exhibition (1936), important in renewing contact between British and continental art.

Unity Theatre. London theatre founded in 1936 and largely run by amateurs. It is politically left-wing and often presents plays with political themes. Many famous professional actors and producers have begun their careers there.

University Wits. Name given to a group of Elizabethan writers, including Greene, Lodge, Lyly, Nashe and Peele, who derided writers without a univ. education, as in Nashe's preface to Greene's *Menaphon.*

Unknown Political Prisoner, The. Subject of many sculptures for an international competition (1953); the winning entry was by Reg *Butler.

Unnameable, The (1958). Novel by Samuel Beckett.

Unquiet Grave, The (1944). Book by 'Palinurus', pseud. of Cyril *Connolly.

Untermeyer Louis (1885–). U.S. poet, author of such colls as *Burning Bush* (1928), and an influential verse anthologist. His *The Letters of Robert Frost to Louis Untermeyer* (1963) was the fruit of U.'s lifelong friendship with the poet.

Upanishads: *Vedas

up-beat. In music the name for the final beat in a bar, i.e. the beat immediately before the main beat and indicated by the conductor by an upward movement of the baton. Thus a piece which begins on the u.-b. begins on an unaccented beat.

Updike John (Hoyer) (1932–). U.S. novelist, author of *The Poorhouse Fair* (1959) and the very successful *Rabbit, run* (1961), plotting the disintegration of a man unable to master his oppressive environment.

Upjohn Richard (1802–78). English-born architect. As a young man he settled in the U.S., where after a period in Bulfinch's office he became an important exponent of the Gothic revival.

Urbino, Ducal Palace of. Home of Federigo and Guidobaldo da Montefeltro, humanists, patrons and connoisseurs; one of the finest early Renaissance palaces. It was enlarged and rebuilt (1466–79) by Luciano Laurana, whose work includes an exterior tier of balconies between towers, an arcaded courtyard and a series of state rooms distinguished by their pure classical decoration and perfect proportions.

Urfé Honoré d' (1567–1625). French writer, author of a very long unfinished romance, *L'Astrée* (1607–27), which created a fashion. Balthazar Baro added a conclusion (1628) based on U.'s notes.

Urn Burial or **Hydriotaphia** (1658). Essay by Sir Thomas *Browne.

Urquhart Sir Thomas (1611–60?). Scottish writer best known for his trs. of the first 3 books of Rabelais (1653).

U.S.A. (1930–6). Trilogy of novels by John *Dos Passos.

Usk Thomas (d. 1388). English writer, author of the prose allegory *The Testament of Love.*

Uspensky Gleb Ivanovich (1843–1902). Russian writer of realistic stories. His sketches of rural life, including *The Power of the Soil* (1882), attacked the radicals' idealization of the peasant.

Ustinov Peter (1921–). English actor, director, conversationalist and author who has written many successful plays including *The Love of Four Colonels* (1951), *Romanoff and Juliet* (1956) and *Photo Finish* (1962). Essentially a comic actor, he has appeared in most of his own plays and in several films.

Utamaro (1753–1806). Japanese master of the wood-block colour print, the 1st Japanese artist to become known in the West.

utility music (German *Gebrauchsmusik*). Term introduced by *Hindemith.

Utopia (1516). Latin work by Sir Thomas *More.

Utrecht Psalter (9th c.; University Library, Utrecht). Carolingian Psalter from the Rheims school, almost certainly a copy of a much older codex. Each Psalm has an illustrative ink drawing in a sketchy, agitated freehand style totally unlike the usual Carolingian style. The Psalter was brought to England in the late 10th c. and strongly influenced the English school.

Utrecht school. Group of Dutch painters including Terbrugghen, Honthorst and Baburen who were influenced in Rome (*c.* 1610–20) by the realism of Caravaggio and his follower Manfredi, and later worked in Utrecht painting religious and genre subjects. Frans Hals, Rembrandt and Vermeer, as well as lesser artists, were all to some extent affected.

Utrillo Maurice (1883–1955). French painter, son of the painter Suzanne Valadon. An habitual drinker from his youth, he reputedly began to paint as a therapeutic distraction between sanatorium confinements, often copying his views of Paris streets from picture postcards, e.g. *Place du Tertre* (1912; Tate). Influenced by impressionism at first, he developed a more personal style of freely impasted paint and very high-keyed pale colours, which by the 1920s enjoyed a popular success. His poetic interpretation of the streets and squares of Montmartre helped to create the locality's popular romantic image.

Utzon Jørn (1918–). Danish architect, designer of some exquisite houses, who became internationally known in 1956 by winning the competition for Sydney Opera House; the design, now being built on a peninsula next to the harbour bridge, is very sensitively planned, and roofed with a wild array of shell-vaults.

Uz Johann Peter (1720–96). The outstanding poetic talent of the Prussian Anacreontic school. His verse, influenced by French and Latin models, is at its best in *Lyrische Gedichte* (1749).

Page from the *Utrecht Psalter*

Utrecht school. Baburen, *The Procuress*

Peter Ustinov in the film *Lady L* (1965), which he directed

Utamaro. Wood-block colour print

Utrillo. *L'Impasse Cottin* (*c.* 1910)

Utzon. Sydney Opera House (model)

V

Vadim. Jane Fonda in *La Ronde*

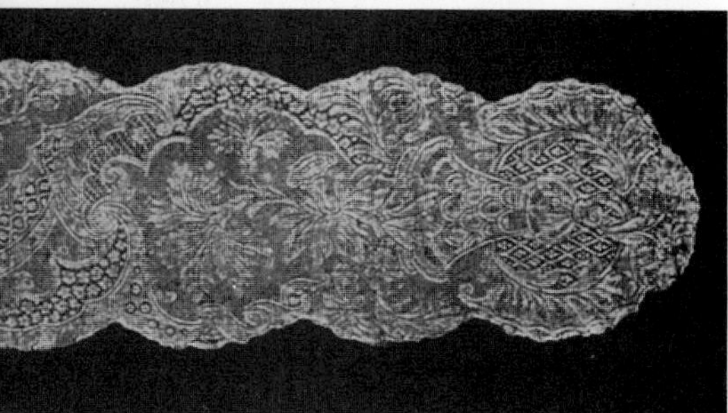
Valenciennes lace

Valadon. *Adam and Eve*

Rudolph Valentino in *Son of the Sheik*

Vadim Roger (1928–). French film director. V. worked as a journalist and wrote scripts (for M. Allegret, etc.) before making *Et Dieu . . . Créa la Femme* (1956) which anticipated the first nouvelle vague films in its independence, its morality, its Americanism and its commercial success (at first outside France), which in turn came from its definitive launching of *Bardot. *Sait-on jamais* (1957) was an elegant thriller. Since then his work has declined, although *Les Liaisons Dangereuses* (1959) is an interesting modern adaptation of Laclos and the vampire scenes of *Et mourir de plaisir* (1960) are very beautiful. *La Ronde* (1965), from Schnitzler, shows V.'s mastery of sex-comedy.

Vaillant Wallerant (1623–77). Portrait and genre painter of the Dutch school and an early practitioner of mezzotint engraving. He worked in Holland, Germany and Paris.

Vakhtangov Eugene (1883–1922). Soviet actor and director who was a great friend and associate of Stanislavsky. He was a beneficial and powerful force in Russian theatre. A theatre in Moscow bears his name.

Valadon Suzanne (Marie-Clémentine Valadon) (1867–1938). French painter and mother of Utrillo. She began as a model posing for Puvis de Chavannes, Renoir and Toulouse-Lautrec, who encouraged her to draw. She took up painting in 1909 but her interpretation of still-life and figure subjects remained strongly linear. Both her drawings and paintings, particularly of the female nude, are characterized by a merciless objectivity.

Valckenborch Lucas (d. 1597) and Marten (1535–1612). Flemish landscape painters who settled in Frankfurt to avoid religious persecution. They both painted panoramic views with small figures. Lucas imposed an atmospheric unity on his work by his use of subtly graded shades of grey, green and blue.

Valdés Juan de (*c.* 1490–1541). Spanish humanist, strongly influenced by Erasmus. His *Dialogo de la lengua* on style and vocabulary was the 1st important treatise on the Spanish language; V.'s own prose was elegant and unaffected. His twin brother ALFONSO (d. 1532) was also an Erasmian humanist; he was, however, the Emperor Charles V's secretary, and wrote a treatise defending the Sack of Rome of 1527.

Valdés-Leal Juan de (1622–90). Spanish baroque painter and engraver of Portuguese origin who worked in Seville from 1656. He was a pupil of A. del Castillo. His most famous paintings are those on *vanitas* themes such as *Finis Gloriae Mundi* and *Triumph of Death* (both Caridad, Seville).

Valdivielso José de (1560–1638). Spanish poet and playwright. He wrote charming poetry in the form of *romances* or *villancicos*, among the finest being his *Ensaladilla del Retablo.*

Valen Olav Fartein (1887–1952). Norwegian composer who used modified 12-note techniques.

Valenciennes lace. From the town of that name, originally part of Flanders, but ceded to France in the late 17th c., and thereafter encouraged by France in rivalry to the Flemish laces. A very fine, rich and even bobbin lace of floral design, made originally in damp cellars to discourage the breaking of the threads. Its manufacture was laborious, a pair of men's ruffles taking 12 months to complete, and lace 2 ins wide needing at least 300 bobbins.

Valentin, Le (Moïse) (*c.* 1591–1632). French painter of religious and genre subjects who spent most of his working life in Rome where he came under the influence of Manfredi and through him of Caravaggio. Various paintings in a Caravaggesque style such as *Brawling Soldiers* (Alte Pina., Munich) and *Tavern* (Louvre) are attributed to him. His only documented work, *Martyrdom of SS Processus and Martinian* (Vatican) shows the influence of his friend N. Poussin.

Valentino Rudolph (1895–1926). Italian-born Hollywood film star, the 'Great Lover' of the 1920s. V. had a startling success in *Four Horsemen of the Apocalypse* (1921). Hot, romantic dramas like *The Sheik* (1921) and *The Eagle* (1925) were lapped up by his adoring feminine public, and his sudden death caused global hysteria.

Vale Press. One of the great English private presses. It was directed by the artist Charles Ricketts who also designed the type-faces; the press operated from 1896 to 1904, its masterpiece being a 39-vol. ed. of *The Works of Shakespeare* (1900–3).

Valera Juan (1824–1905). Spanish novelist. A man of very wide culture and cosmopolitan tastes, reflected in his writings, he began his career as a diplomat. He attached great importance to form and style, and mainly wrote about love. His best-known novel is *Pepita Jiménez* (1874; 1891).

Valéry Paul (Ambroise Toussaint Jules) (1871–1945). French poet. V. studied law at Montpellier, then came to Paris (1892), where he was influenced by the symbolists, especially Mallarmé. Some of the poems he wrote during this period were coll. as the *Album de vers anciens* (1920); 2 prose works, however, made his reputation, the *Introduction à la méthode de Léonard de Vinci* (1895; *Introduction to the Method of Leonardo da Vinci*, 1929), which examines genius and the creative process, and *La Soirée avec Monsieur Teste* (1896; *An Evening with Monsieur Teste*, 1925), which introduces the famous character who embodies intellect to the exclusion of all other qualities. Philosophical speculation occupied V. for years, and he publ. nothing until 1917, when *La Jeune Parque* appeared. It was followed by the coll. *Charmes* (1922), which contains the famous *Cimetière Marin* (*The Graveyard by the Sea*, 1932). These established V. as the leading French poet. His verse is vivid and musical, but difficult: his thought is concentrated and elliptical, proceeding within severely traditional forms and freely mixing abstract speculation with concrete imagery. He also wrote much critical and imaginative prose, including 3 further pieces about Teste, *Lettre d'un ami*, *Lettre de Madame Émilie Teste* and *Extraits du Logbook de Monsieur Teste*.

Paul Valéry

Valla Lorenzo (1407–57). The greatest Italian humanist scholar of his age. He initiated the scientific study of classical and religious texts and was one of the 1st to stress the importance of philology in literary studies. One of the foremost champions of the revival of learning, V. made his greatest scholarly contribution to the Italian Renaissance in his treatise on Latin style and grammar, the *De Elegantia Latinae Linguae* (1444).

Laurentii Vallenſis Viri Clariſſimi:& De Lingua Latina Benemerentis Ad Ioãnem Tortelliũ Arretinum:Cui Opus Elegantiarum Linguæ Latinæ Dedicat Epiſtola:

AVRENTIVS Vallenſis Ioanni Tortellio Aretio cubiculario apoſtolico theologoq; facundiſſimo ſalutem.P.D. Libros de linguæ latinæ elegantia mi Ioannes unicum amiciciæ ſpecimẽ & omnis ſcientiæ decus olim iam tibi debitos:totiensq; abſ te efflagitatos: & tanquam creditore repetitos tandem exhibeo:nominiq; tuo dedico:ac uelut æs alienum perſoluo:Et ut longioris moræ dem pœnas etiam cum fœnore:eoq; tanto ut ſorti par ſit.Nam cum ſex eſſent libri quos tibi:cui omnia debeo repromiſeram:nũc totidem ad illos accedunt eiuſdẽ germanæq; materiæ: & quaſi ſemiſſi ſemis addita explet aſſem lucri.Feciſti itaq; tu lõgam quidem expectationem. Verum ipſius expectationis non negligentia mea:ſed conſilium extitit cauſa. Nolo enim fraudare beneficium meũ gratia ſua. Siquidem nullã aliam inire rationem poterã: qua libros iiuſſu meo:ut ſcis:editos:& in plurima exemplaria tranſcriptos tibi dicarem:niſi & repurgarem diligẽtius: & (quod maius eſt) aliorum ueluti:reliqui corporis acceſſione perfectos me emittere teſtarer:ut nemo niſi ab hoc fonte & eius riuis noſtrarum elegantiarum aquas ſibi hauriẽdas exiſtimaret non ſolum uberiore gurgite:ſed etiam nitidiore. Quo magis & ſpero:& opto libros hos abſ te in ſũmi Pontificis bibliotheca repoſitum iri:teq; curaturum ut ille:cuius cõtubernalis es:& ſtudiorum intimus comes nonnunquam eos euoluat:& quemadmodum de parte iam fecit totum opus laudet:eximium profecto ac maximi laboris mei fructum ac præmium. Nam quis uberior fructus: aut quod magis optimum præmium generoſo animo contingere poteſt:q̃ laudari a laudato uiro:ut ille apud Acci-

Valla. Dedication of *De Elegantia Latinae Linguae*

Valle-Inclán Ramón Maria del (1866–1936). Spanish novelist, dramatist and poet, a flamboyant and eccentric figure in Spanish literary circles; his style, influenced at first by the French 'decadent' and symbolist writers, finally evolved into a highly individual modern expressiveness. His 4 long stories publ. as *Sonatas* (1902–5) deal with the amorous adventures of a Galician marquis. *Flor de Santidad* (1904) was in complete contrast, being the story of a peasant girl's love for a pilgrim she believes to be God. His best novels are considered to be *La Corte de los Milagros* (1927) and *Viva mi dueño* (1928); he also wrote a series of satirical essays known as '*asperpentos*'.

Vallejo César (1895–1937). Peruvian poet. V. was politically on the left (reflecting, among other things, his sympathy with the plight of the indigenous Indian population) and spent his manhood in France, where he was for long preoccupied with political activity. He died from tuberculosis. His poetry is uneven, often unsuccessful in attempting to absorb the new European influences (e.g. dadaism), but profoundly moving at its best, e.g. in *Poemas humanos* (posth. 1939), an affirmation of human solidarity inspired by the approach of death and the cause of the Republic in the Spanish Civil War.

César Vallejo

Vallès Jules (1833–85). French novelist. V.'s autobiographical trilogy *Jacques Vingtras* (*L'Enfant*, 1879; *Le Bachelier*, 1881; *L'Insurgé*, 1886) is a bitter description of a life of poverty and struggle.

Vallotton Félix (1865–1925). Swiss painter, woodcut artist and writer who became a naturalized French subject in 1900. He went to Paris in 1882 and joined the nabis but later adopted a more detailed and objective style reminiscent of the German and Swiss schools. His use of the woodcut was influential in reviving that medium.

Vallotton. *Le Bon Marché*

Valmouth (1918). Novel by Ronald *Firbank.

valve instruments: *brass instruments

vamp. To provide on the piano a chord accompaniment, usually of the 'oom-cha-cha' variety, to a song.

Vampires, Les (1915). Film serial directed by L. *Feuillade.

Vanbrugh Sir John (1664–1726). English playwright and architect, of Flemish descent. He served as an officer in the army but was arrested in France as a spy in 1690 and spent

Valdés-Leal.
Triumph of Death

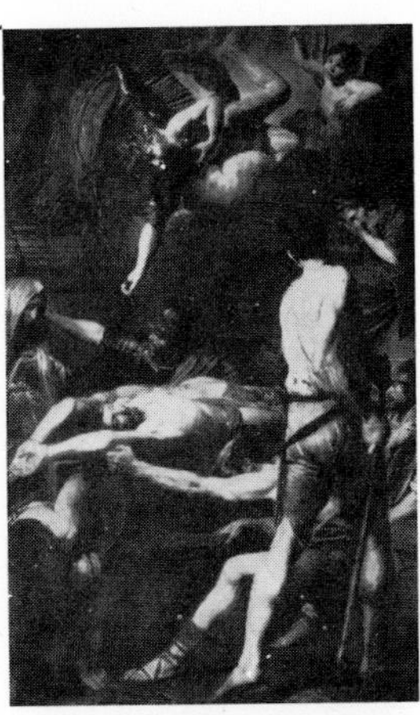

Valentin. *Martydom of SS Processus and Martinian*

Sir John Vanbrugh

Vanbrugh. Castle Howard

Van de Velde. Werkbund Theater

18 months in the Bastille. He remained in the army until 1702, but had meanwhile become famous by his comedies *The Relapse* (1696) and *The Provok'd Wife* (1697), characteristic examples of *Restoration comedy. He went on writing for the stage until 1705 but never repeated his early success. His career as an architect dates from 1699, when he designed Castle Howard. Blenheim, commissioned in 1704 as a national tribute to the duke of Marlborough, occupied him for 12 years, during which he quarrelled continuously with the duchess; he was dismissed in 1716 while it was still unfinished. Seaton Delaval, another large country-house, was begun in 1720. V. belongs to the small band of English baroque architects, owing little to any foreign influence. His style, often called masculine, excels at massive effects of grouping, extreme projection and recession of surfaces, and large-scale, often bizarre decorative treatment. He often anticipates the romantic movement, especially in such less important works as his house at Maze Hill, Greenwich (a castellated mansion built for himself) and the Garden buildings (temples, pyramid, etc.), at Stowe. At Castle Howard and Blenheim V. was assisted by Hawksmoor and the proportion of work to be attributed to each architect is still a matter of dispute.

Vanbrugh Violet (1867–1942). English actress who was at various times leading lady with Sir Henry Irving and Beerbohm Tree. Her major work, however, was done in the company of her husband, the actor-manager Arthur Bourchier. Her sister IRENE (1872–1949) was also an actress.

Vanderlyn John (1775–1852). U.S. neo-classical history and portrait painter. From 1796 to 1815 he lived chiefly in Paris, where he built up a considerable reputation with *Marius amid the Ruins of Carthage* (1807; H. M. de Young Memorial Mus., San Francisco) and *Ariadne* (1812; Pennsylvania Ac. of Fine A.). On his return to America his work met with little success.

Van de Velde Henri (1863–1957). Belgian art nouveau architect, designer and teacher. His 1st house (1895), completely decorated and furnished by him, was influenced by William Morris and the arts and crafts movement in England. V. moved to Berlin in 1899; in 1905 he built the new School of Applied Arts at Dessau, an undecorated building influenced more by Mackintosh's Glasgow Art School than European art nouveau; as head of the school he introduced modern design theories and recommended Gropius as his successor. His last significant building was the Werkbund Theater, Cologne (1914).

Van Doren Mark (1894–). U.S. poet, novelist and critic. He has written criticism of importance, especially on Dryden; other critical and biographical works include studies of Thoreau, Shakespeare and Hawthorne; his *Collected Poems* (1939) won the 1940 Pulitzer prize.

Van Dyk Christoffel (1601–69/70). Dutch type-cutter and designer for the *Elzevirs who cut several pleasing roman and Hebrew founts; the leading letter-founder of his period. Some types ascribed to him were used by the Cambridge Univ. Press.

Van Dyke Willard (1906–). U.S. film maker. One of the same group of U.S. documentarists as Pare Lorentz, he made (with Ralph Steiner) *The City* (1939) to illustrate the theories of Lewis Mumford. From 1950 he worked in Puerto Rico, where he founded a school of documentarists.

Van Dyke W. S. or 'Woody' (1899–). U.S. film director. During the 1920s and early 1930s he specialized in action pictures, e.g. *Trader Horn* (1931) and *Tarzan the Ape Man* (1932), with Weissmuller, the most famous of that series. After his great success with a comedy thriller, *The Thin Man* (1934), his work included big pictures like *San Francisco* (1936) with its spectacular earthquake sequence, and *Marie Antoinette* (1938).

Vanity Fair (1847–8). Novel by *Thackeray.

Vanity of Human Wishes, The (1749). Poem by Dr Johnson.

Van Loo Charles-André called Carle (1705–65). French painter of religious and mythological subjects and portraits, brother and pupil of Jean-Baptiste V. L. He lived in Italy (1727–34), then settled in Paris and later became court painter to Louis XV. His work was elegant and superficial, typical of its age. His son JULES-CÉSAR (1743–1821) was a landscape painter.

Van Loo Jean-Baptiste (1684–1745). French portrait and decorative painter. He worked in England (1737–42) where he became the leading portraitist in succession to Jonathan Richardson the Elder and Dahl. He acquired an inflated contemporary reputation because he brought a certain elegance to English portraiture. His sons CHARLES-AMÉDÉE (1719–95) and LOUIS-MICHEL (1707–71) were also painters.

Van de Velde. Writing-table (1899)

Jean-Baptiste Van Loo. *The Rt Hon. Thomas Winnington*

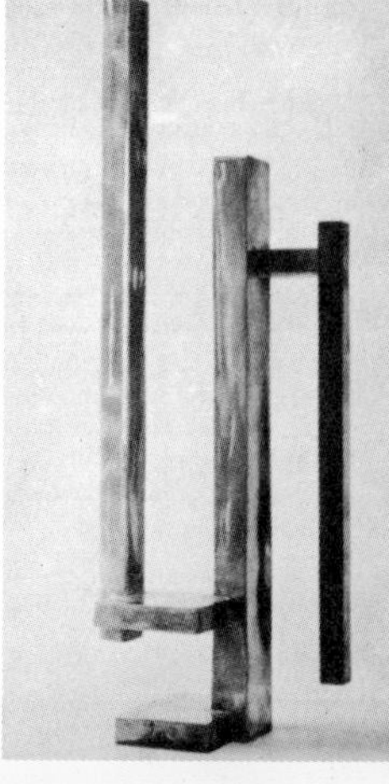
Vantongerloo. *Sculpture in Space:* $y=ax^3-bx^3$ (1935)

Vanvitelli. Royal Palace, Caserta

Van Loon Hendrik Willem (1882–1944). Dutch-born historian and popularizer of history, author of the best-selling *The Story of Mankind* (1921).

Vanni Andrea (*fl.* 1350–75). Sienese painter, follower of Simone Martini.

Vantongerloo Georges (1886–). Belgian sculptor, painter and writer on art theory, one of the most important members of the de stijl group and co-founder of the Abstraction-Création group. He was one of the earliest abstract sculptors, following in his sculpture as well as his painting the horizontal-vertical principle of de stijl. He began to make use of the curve in the mid 1930s.

Van Vechten Carl (1880–). U.S. writer, a critic until 1922, novelist from 1922 to 1930, and thereafter a photographer. His urbane, elegant novels, e.g. *The Blind Bow-Boy* (1923), reflect the life of sophisticates in the 1920s, though in *Nigger Heaven* (1926) he produced a realistic picture of life in Harlem.

Vanvitelli Luigi (1700–73). Italian architect, son of the painter Gaspar van Wittel. In Rome he remodelled Michelangelo's S. Maria degli Angeli. His chief work (begun in 1752) is the Royal Palace at Caserta–a huge rectangle 600 by 500 ft, with wings connecting the centres of all 4 sides to a big central octagon. Built as a rival to Versailles and the Escorial, it has 1200 rooms and is set in an immense formal park. Each of the main elevations has pavilions at either end and a 'temple' motif with pillars and pediment in the middle. The palace was never finished, and the effect now is more austere than was intended. 2 other purely utilitarian works by V., a cavalry barracks and an aqueduct, have had an influence on 20th-c. Italian architecture.

Varchi Benedetto (1503–65). Italian humanist writer and scholar. He wrote a political history of Florence at the request of Cosimo I, the *Storia Fiorentina*. His reputation as a scholar is based on his outstanding philological treatises, including a Provençal grammar, and his *L'Ercolano*, in which he defended the choice of Tuscan as the Italian national language.

Varda Agnès (1928–). French film director: intellectual, occasionally at the expense of her directorial judgement. She was a still photographer before making a feature, *La Pointe Courte* (1954–5), which used the shooting methods of the nouvelle vague 4 years in advance. Its style influenced Resnais who edited it in *Hiroshima mon amour*. She made 4 shorts, 2 of exceptional preciousness, before making a feature, *Cléo de 5 à 7* (1961).

Varèse Edgar(d) (1885–). French-born composer, a naturalized U.S. citizen since 1915. V., whose 1st compositions date from the age of Mahler, has followed the theory that the modern industrial world demands a music as harsh and alienated as itself, music in which noise should be an important element (*vide* Henry Miller's *Journey through the desert with E. V.*). His music is brutal, extreme, dry and dissonant–in the inter-war years primitive and repetitive, stretching the technique and spirit of e.g. Stravinsky's *Rite of Spring*; later, with the advent of electronic music in particular, completely individual in style, owing little to any other music. His music with electronic sounds is among the most vivid and imaginative of its kind–indeed V.'s understanding of acoustic principles has always been unparalleled (e.g. wind instruments strained to their uppermost limits, with double-bass harmonics, producing 'resultant notes' below). Works include: *Hyperprism* (1923), for wind and percussion, *Octandre* (1924), for wind and double bass, *Arcana* (1927) for orchestra, *Ionisation* (1931) for 41 percussion instruments including police whistles and siren, and *Déserts* (1954) for wind, percussion and electronic sounds.

Vargas Luis de (1502–68). Spanish painter who spent many years in Italy, where he was influenced by the followers of Raphael. He worked in Seville, where his greatest achievement is the altarpiece of the Nativity in the cathedral. He is credited with introducing the art of fresco to Seville.

variation. Form in music which takes a melodic theme or harmonic sequence as the basis for a number of movements related in material but contrasting in mood. The form was well developed in the works of vihuelista (*vihuela) composers of 16th-c. Spain and was used by the English virginalists. It has produced such masterpieces as Bach's 'Goldberg' v.s and Beethoven's 'Diabelli' v.s.

Varieties of Religious Experience, The (1902). Book by William *James.

Varda. Jean-Luc Godard and Anna Karina in *Cléo de 5 à 7*

Edgar Varèse

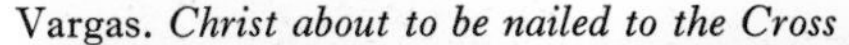

Vargas. *Christ about to be nailed to the Cross*

John Varley. *Chiswick from Barnes*

Vasari. *Temptation of St Jerome*

Vasarely. *100 F* (1957). Also *op art

Vaughan Williams

variety. A form of light entertainment which consists of individual items given by different performers. These can be musicians, singers, comedians, etc. V. is derived from the entertainments in 18th-c. taverns. Also *music-hall and *vaudeville.

Varley F(rederick) H(orsman) (1881–). English-born Canadian painter; he settled in Canada in 1912. V. was known mainly for his portrait and figure painting, and his powerful work as a war artist (1918); but he was also a member of the *Group of Seven.

Varley John (1778–1842). English watercolourist. He worked with an architectural draughtsman before being taken up by Dr Monro, in whose house he met Turner and Girtin; he was also a friend of Blake. Much of his work was hasty and inferior, but he was popular as a teacher, his pupils including David Cox, Palmer, Linnell, Mulready and Holman Hunt. He wrote treatises on drawing, composition and perspective.

Varnhagen von Ense Karl August (1785–1858). German diplomat and diarist; the Berlin *salon* of V. von E. and his wife Rahel (née Levin) was a centre of the romantics.

varnish. Resinous transparent substance applied by painters to their works in order to preserve them–as distinct from glazing.

Varro Marcus Terentius (116–27 B.C.). Roman man of letters and antiquary, an extraordinarily voluminous writer. His work, however, survives only in fragments apart from the grammatical work *De Lingua Latina* and (written in his 80th year) *Rerum Rusticarum.*

Vasarely Victor de (1908–). Hungarian painter. V. studied medicine in Budapest until 1928, when he gave it up and studied art at the Academy. He was tutored by Moholy-Nagy, and through him was introduced to the work of Kandinsky, Gropius, Mondrian and Le Corbusier. Since 1930 he has lived in Paris. He was profoundly influenced by the functionalism of the Bauhaus, and set himself the task of relating the experiments going on in the material world around him, to painting. His abstractions, painted in contrasting colours, are composed of clean-cut geometric forms in such a way as to effect a feeling of harmony out of the apparent discord of shape and colour. Also *op art.

Vasari Giorgio (1511–74). Italian mannerist painter and architect of the Uffizi Gal. but important as an art historian. His *Le Vite de'più eccelenti Architetti, Pittori, et Scultori Italiani*, a coll. of nearly 200 biographies dedicated to Cosimo de' Medici was first publ. in 1550 and carefully revised and enlarged in 1568. V.'s appreciation of Venetian art is coloured by his great love for all things Florentine and his worship of Michelangelo blinds him to the ability of others. But in spite of some inaccuracies V.'s book is an all-important source of information relating to the history of Renaissance art. The 1st complete English trs. appeared in 1850.

vase carpets. A well-known class of Persian carpet in which flowers, palmettes and vases of flowers play a prominent part in the design and in which no animals or birds are included.

Vasiliev Vladimir (1940–). Soviet dancer of the Bolshoi Co. His elevation and ballon have enhanced his style, making him a fine soloist. He is married to Ekatrina Maximova.

Vassiliev Serge (1900–59) and Grigori (1899–1946). Russian film directors. They worked as the 'V. Brothers' (though unrelated) from 1928 with documentaries and then (1929) features. Their *Chapayev* (1934) was a great success with its story of a Bolshevik guerilla in the Civil War, and formed a pattern for the big Russian films of the late 1930s.

Vathek, An Arabian Tale (1786). Novel by William *Beckford.

Vatican Rome. Works of art in the Vatican Palace, in addition to the works by Raphael, artists of the Venetian school and of the 17th-c. Roman school contained in the picture gallery founded by Pius VII, include the paintings by Michelangelo and other artists in the *Sistine Chapel, the paintings by Raphael and his assistants and pupils in the Stanze and Loggie, the paintings by Pinturicchio in the Borgia Apartments and the Raphael tapestries. The chapel of Nicholas V contains frescoes by Fra Angelico.

vaudeville. A term of French origin which at first applied to light plays and operas. In America the word is used to describe what the English would call *variety.

Vaughan Henry (1622–95). Welsh poet, sometimes called 'the Silurist'. V. studied at Oxford, perhaps took part in the Civil War as a Royalist, and spent his last 20 years practising as a doctor in his native Brecon. V.'s significant work is the religious poetry of the coll. *Silex Scintillans* (1650, 55), in which he admits his debt to George Herbert. It sets forth a simple, personal religious feeling (with neither the intellectuality nor the over-elaboration of the *metaphysical poets) which often turns to memories of childhood. His well-known poems include *I saw Eternity the other night* and *They are all gone into the world of light.*

Vaughan Keith (1912–). English painter specializing in studies of the male nude.

Vaughan Williams Ralph (1872–1958). English composer taught by Parry and Stanford. Brief periods of study with Max Bruch and Ravel had no discernible effects on his style, which derived essentially from his study of English folk-music and church music of the 16th and 17th cs. From the beginning V. W. developed a highly personal style which, particularly in its lyrical moods, is nevertheless fairly called 'typically English'; in earlier works he sometimes took his inspiration from the medieval system of *modes and later made extensive and dramatic use of dissonance. His works include: 6 operas, e.g. *Sir John in Love* (1929) and *The Pilgrim's Progress* (1951); the 'masque for dancing' *Job* (1930); 9 symphonies, including *Sea Symphony* (1910) with voices, text from Walt Whitman, *London* (1914), *Pastoral Symphony* (1922), the powerful 4th symphony in F min. (1935), the idyllic 5th in D (1943), the threatening and ominous 6th in E min. (1948) and *Sinfonia Antartica* (1953),

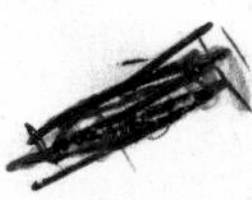

taken from his film music for *Scott of the Antarctic*; numerous choral works, e.g. *Flos campi* (1925) and the Christmas cantata *This Day* (*Hodie*, 1954); *Fantasia on a Theme by Thomas Tallis* for string orchestra (1910); the incidental music *The Wasps* (1909) and the song cycle (from A. E. Housman) *On Wenlock Edge* (1909).

vault. Architectural term for a ceiling of stone or brick, especially one with a curved surface which is supported in much the same way as an arch. Important types are the BARREL- or TUNNEL-v., which rests on 2 continuous supporting walls, i.e. like a continuous arch; the GROIN- or CROSS-v., 2 barrel-v.s intersecting at right angles, the lines of intersection being the groins; the RIB-v., which has stone ribs running along the lines of the groins; the FAN-v., an ornamental rib-v. in which the ribs spring from the wall-shafts in fan-shapes, meeting or overlapping in the centre; and the CORBEL-v., which is constructed on the same principle as the *corbel arch. When the v. is divided into 4 compartments, it is called a QUADRIPARTITE v. (e.g. in the groin-v.); when there are 6 compartments, it is a SEXPARTITE v.

Vauvenargues Luc de Clapiers, marquis de (1715–47). French writer, notable for the essays and maxims in his *Introduction à la connaissance de l'ésprit humain . . .* (1746).

Vázov Iván (1850–1921). Between 1890 and 1920 the dominant Bulgarian writer. Writers in the 'V. period' aimed at expressing the collective experience and sufferings of the Bulgarian people in down-to-earth, simple language. V. excelled in all forms of literature but his outstanding work is the novel *Pod Igoto* (1893; *Under the Yoke*, 1894).

Veblen Thorstein (Bunde) (1857–1929). U.S. economist and social philosopher, author of the ironic yet vigorous denunciation of business – regarded as a parasitical growth feeding on industry – *The Theory of the Leisure Class* (1899).

Vecchi Orazio (1550–1605). Italian composer, one of the outstanding madrigalists of his generation. In his music drama *Amfiparnaso* (1594) the dramatic dialogue is conducted between madrigal choirs rather than solo voices as were being introduced by the monodists (*opera).

Vecchietta Lorenzo di Pietro called Il (1412–80). Sienese painter and sculptor probably trained as a painter by Sassetta; his masterpiece is *Assumption of the Virgin* (Pienza cathedral). His sculptural work, which shows Florentine influence, includes the statue *Risen Christ* (Chiesa dell'Ospedale, Siena) and the bronze ciborium on the high altar of Siena cathedral.

Vedas (*Veda*, 'knowledge'). Hindu religious books of great antiquity (*c.* 2500 B.C.). There are 4 *V.* – the *Rig*, the *Sama*, the *Yajura* and the *Atharva* – consisting of hymns and 'Brahmanas' ('precepts'). The *Upanishads* (*c.* 800–600 B.C.), appended to the *V.*, are metaphysical documents, representing a spiritualization of the *V.*, which describe the path to knowledge of the Godhead.

Fan-vaulting, Bath abbey, Somerset; and groin-vaulting, Speyer cathedral

Barrel-vault. Bernini's Scala Regia, Vatican

Sexpartite vaulting. St-Étienne, Caen

Ribbed vault

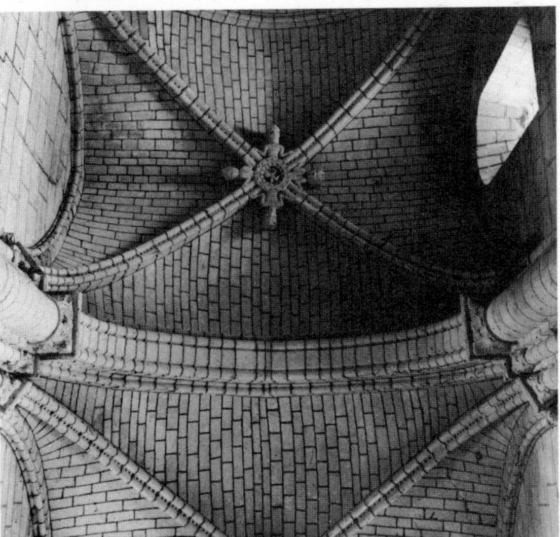

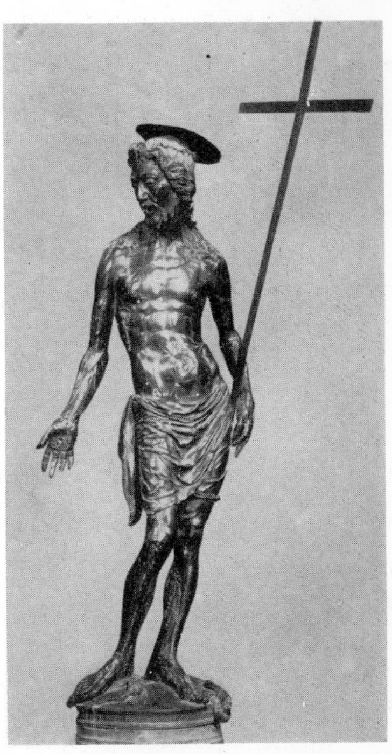

Vecchietta. *Risen Christ*

Velazquez. *The Water Carrier of Seville*

Velazquez. *Pope Innocent X*

Velazquez. *King Philip IV*

Velazquez. *The Surrender of Breda.* Also *bodegón, *Las *Meninas, The *Rokeby Venus*

Esaias van de Velde. *Winter Landscape*

Willem van de Velde the Younger. *Coast Scene, Calm*

Vedder Elihu (1836–1923). U.S. painter of imaginative subjects famous for his series of over 50 illustrations to Edward Fitzgerald's *Rubá'iyát of Omar Khayyám.*

Vedova Emilio (1919–). Italian painter; he has passed through several phases, emerging as an abstract painter of canvases full of conflict.

Veen (Vaenius) Otto van (1556–1629). Dutch painter of portraits and religious subjects who worked mainly in Antwerp and Brussels but also in Italy under Zuccaro. He adopted an Italianate style.

vehicle: *medium

Veidt Conrad (1893–1943). German film actor who began in the classic expressionist thriller *The Cabinet of Dr Caligari* (1919); his tall, spare, haughty brutality thrust him always into parts of sinister villainy. After playing Metternich in *Congress Dances* (1931) and, in Britain, *Jew Süss* (1933), his American career was confined and insignificant.

Velazquez Diego Rodriguez de Silva (1599–1660). Spanish painter, pupil of Francisco de Herrera and Don Francisco Pacheco. In 1617 he graduated from Pacheco's workshop-academy as a master painter and married his daughter in 1618. 4 years later V. left his native Seville for Madrid; his hope of admission to the royal court was disappointed, but the following year his portrait of his friend the courtier Juan de Fonseca was seen by the king, and this secured V. the commission to paint the king's own portrait. V. became Philip IV's close companion at the Alcazar Palace and remained in his service until his death. Rubens visited the court in 1628 and on his advice V. obtained the king's consent to travel. He left for Italy in 1629 and studied the Italian masters. 20 years passed before he was able to visit Italy again, when he not only studied but also bought paintings by Tintoretto, Veronese and Titian for the Royal College. In 1650 he painted the portrait of Pope Innocent X in Rome. In 1659 he was ennobled as a Knight of the Order of Santiago.

V.'s greatest achievement is seen not in his splendid representations of Spanish court life but in the profound feeling for humanity which underlies all his work. In the midst of the glitter and artificiality of his daily life he was keenly concerned with human tragedy and suffering, and the deformed, the dwarfs and the poor were of as much interest as a pope, king or courtier. As an artist he preferred Titian to Raphael. The art of V., like that of Titian, was concerned with movement, the movement of light over objects, dissolving static forms into a summary statement of a visual impression. The paintings of V. show a development in their means–but the end, painting life as it appeared to him, remained constant.

His earliest paintings such as *The Water Carrier of Seville* (*c.* 1618; Apsley House, London) show a deep concern for everyday reality, uncompromising in subject-matter and unpretentious in presentation. The jar in the foreground is just as important as the figures. Material existence is shown here as essence, the trivial becomes eternal.

The royal portraits needed to be treated differently. Form is here partly monumental, partly psychologically conditioned, as in the *King Philip IV* (Prado). The psychological interest increases, as in the later portrait (N.G., London). The famous *Las Meninas* (1656; Prado) contains a number of figures, puppet-like and including the artist at his easel, ladies' maids and a dwarf, and reveals the atmosphere of life at the court as seen by a detached and critical man. Forms are suggested with the minimum amount of brushwork and controlled with a superb economy of means.

During his life V. continued to be intrigued by the depth of the human mind and in his paintings of dwarfs and court jesters he created a series of tragic and revealing documents, meditations on fate painted in sombre colours. The *Pope Innocent X* portrait (1650) is one of V.'s greatest. The colour of the papal purple sets the key for a representation of the all-too-human in a monumental setting.

2 landscapes, views of the Villa Medici, Rome, date from about the same time. V. here foreshadows impressionism in his glimpse of the fleeting atmosphere of day and dusk. *The Surrender of Breda* (*c.* 1634; Prado) turns the 'historical' into a composition with light, where the human drama becomes an element of nature. *The Rokeby Venus* (1658; N.G., London), painted with superb restraint, is the only surviving nude by V.; at the time the subject was virtually forbidden in Spain. V.'s fame suffered an eclipse after his death, but during the 2nd half of the 19th c. he was hailed as the 'greatest painter'. The formalists of today have been studying his work for his mastery over formal problems of colour and relationship.

Velde Adriaen van de (1636–72). Dutch painter of landscapes with figures and animals, portraits and genre and religious subjects. He studied under his father, Willem van de V. the Elder, and J. Wynants. He was influenced by the Italianate manner of Berchem. He frequently painted the animals in landscapes by other artists such as Jacob van Ruisdael and Wynants.

Velde Bram van (1895–). Dutch painter of the school of Paris whose informal abstracts are characterized by immensely supple forms in a state of continuous metamorphosis in relation to the surrounding atmosphere.

Velde Esaias van de (*c.* 1590–1630). Dutch landscape and genre painter who contributed towards the development of realism in Dutch landscape painting. He was influenced by Buytewech and worked in Haarlem and The Hague. His most notable paintings are small landscapes with figures. J. van Goyen was his pupil.

Velde Geer van (1898–). Dutch painter of the school of Paris; brother of Bram van V. His compositions, which are of great colouristic sensitivity, relate to exterior reality but transform it spatially within a geometrical framework.

Velde the Elder, Willem van de (1611–93). Dutch marine painter, brother of Esais van de V. In 1672 he settled in England with his son Willem the Younger and together they entered the service of Charles II. He is known for his grisaille drawings, though it is probable that he also painted in oils. He collaborated with his son.

Velde the Younger, Willem van de (1633–1707). Dutch marine painter, son of Willem the Elder. He studied under his father and S. de Vlieger. His early paintings were seascapes influenced by de Vlieger, but after settling in England he concentrated on shipping and naval events. In the work which he produced with his father he is reputed to have been responsible for the colouring, his father for the draughtsmanship. He had many English imitators.

Vélez de Guevara Luis de (1579–1644). Spanish playwright and novelist. His tedious and affected satirical novel *El Diablo Cojuelo* (1641) was to inspire Le Sage's *Diable Boiteux*. He wrote nearly 400 plays, the finest being his *Reinar después de morir*, a beautiful adaptation of the tragic story of Inés de Castro.

veneer. A thin layer of one or more woods, brass, tortoiseshell, silver, ivory or other decorative material, either by itself or in various combinations, attached by gluing to a base of inferior wood. Used in furniture, especially in late 17th- and 18th-c. France.

Venetian glass. By the 11th c. glass was being made in Venice in a tradition deriving from Roman times. By the 13th c. the main centre of production was Murano, an island in the Venetian lagoon. In the 15th c. a 'crystal' glass material had been perfected, based on a soda-lime recipe decolourized by manganese, and also coloured glass of much variety. At the end of the c. Islamic enamel painting had been rediscovered and this was used for decoration, as were gilding and engraving. Venetian skill and ingenuity were at their height in the 16th c., when vessels were waved, crumpled and covered with loops and trails of glass in designs of great extravagance and fantasy. Crackle glass was made and the body of vessels was often made of interlacing spiral rods of white or coloured glass known as '*latticino*'. Much glass of this kind is still made at Murano.

Venetian lace ('Point de Venise'). Venice was probably the first place in which needlepoint lace was produced in Europe; according to tradition the technique was learned from the East. The term V. l. usually denotes a rich needlepoint lace of bold floral design and few background brides; the best period was during the 16th and 17th cs. Bobbin or bone lace was also made in Venice.

Venevitinov Dmitry Vladimirovich (1805–27). Russian poet. Before his death at 22 V. produced poetry of remarkable maturity and technical assurance.

Veneziano Domenico: *Domenico Veneziano

Venice, school of. School of Italian painting which flourished in the 16th and 18th cs. In the 16th c. it developed under the influences of the school of Padua and Antonello da Messina,

Veneer. Part of a walnut side-table (*c.* 1690)

Venetian glass. Late 15th-c. jug in polychrome enamels (*above, left*); mid-16th-c. ampulla (*above, right*); late 16th-c. winged goblet (*below, left*); late 19th-c. vase (*below, right*)

Venetian lace chalice veil

Vereshchagin. *Apotheosis of War*

The Venus de Milo

who introduced the oil-painting technique of the van Eycks. Rich and painterly use of colour characterized Venetian painting. Early masters were the Bellini and Vivarini families, followed by Giorgione and Titian, then Tintoretto and Veronese. In the 18th c. the decorative art of Tiepolo and the views of Canaletto and Guardi revived Venetian painting.
In music Venice was, during the 16th and 17th cs, one of the greatest European centres. From the time of *Willaert the musical directors of St Mark's were often among the greatest of European masters; e.g. Andrea and Giovanni *Gabrieli, *Monteverdi, Corelli and Vivaldi.

Venice Preserved (1682). Play by *Otway.

Venus and Adonis (1593). Narrative poem by *Shakespeare, dedicated to his patron, the earl of Southampton.

Venus de Milo (late 2nd c. B.C.; Louvre). This late Hellenistic Aphrodite, probably the most famous statue in the world, has been accepted as the embodiment of the ideal of feminine beauty since its discovery on the island of Melos (French *Milo*) in 1820.

Veracini Francesco Maria (1690–*c.* 1750). Italian violinist and composer, nephew of ANTONIO V., who worked in London (1714 and 1736–45); his works include 5 operas and 24 violin sonatas.

Vercelli Book. 11th-c. ms. of Anglo-Saxon poems in the cathedral library of Vercelli, Piedmont.

Verdelot Philippe (d. before 1567). Franco-Flemish composer working in Italy (in Venice for a period); he was one of the creators of the *madrigal. His early madrigals are predominantly homophonic but independent movement of parts appears in later works. V. also wrote motets.

Giuseppe Verdi

Verdi Giuseppe (1813–1901). Italian composer born near Busseto of a poor family. His musical education was financed by a friend after V.'s rejection from Milan Conservatory. His 1st opera, *Oberto* (1839), at Milan with the prima donna Giuseppina Strepponi (who became his 2nd wife) was successful, but his 3rd opera *Nabucco*, based on the story of Nebuchadnezzar's invasion of Judea, launched V.'s

Sándor Veress

Émile Verhaeren

Paul Verlaine. Also *Rimbaud

career. There followed a number of works, some bringing V. under police suspicion for their unconcealed sympathy with the patriot cause. In 1874 was performed V.'s magnificent *Requiem* written on the death of the writer, Manzoni: V. also wrote other church works, a *Stabat Mater*, a *Te Deum Laudi alla Vergine* and an *Ave Maria* forming collectively the *Quattro pezzi sacri*. V.'s music grew from its roots in the style of Rossini, Bellini and Donizetti into a medium of great tragic drama; his reading of Shakespeare was important in this development. The high point of Italian 19th-c. opera, V.'s work represents a development of romantic opera in Italy similar to Wagner's achievement in Germany. As his style matured V. gained increasing mastery of the orchestra and its possibilities and came increasingly to control his librettists and the dramatic shape of the opera. There are obvious parallels in Wagner's evolution of the 'music-drama'; but V. transformed the traditional Italian operatic style rather than rejected it. His great strength lies in his mastery of the grand melodic line, and the ensemble scenes of his mature works are virtuoso displays of 'polymelodic' composition.

V.'s operas include the following. *Ernani* (1844), libretto by F. Piave after Hugo. *Macbeth* (1847; later revised) based on Shakespeare. *Luisa Miller* (1849) with libretto by S. Cammarano after Schiller, a tale of 'Love, Intrigue and Poison'. *Rigoletto* (1851) with libretto by Piave after Hugo. *Il Trovatore* (1853) with libretto by Cammarano after Gutiérrez; set in medieval Spain, a tragic story of confused identity, it has for its hero a prince brought up as a gipsy's son ('the troubadour'). *La Traviata* (1853), libretto by Piave after Dumas's *La Dame aux camélias*; Violetta, a courtesan, falls in love with a young man but their romance is destroyed by his family and his insensitivity; finally, after a reconciliation, Violetta dies. *Les Vêpres Siciliennes* (1855), libretto by Scribe and C. Duveysier, set during the Sicilian Vespers of 1282, the revolt of Palermo against Charles of Anjou. *Simone Boccanegra* (1857), libretto by Piave after Gutiérrez; the opera is set in 15th-c. Genoa (Boccanegra was doge). *Un Ballo in Maschera* (1859), libretto by A. Somma after Scribe, the original libretto based on a plot to kill Gustavus III of Sweden at a masked ball, was changed, because of censorship, and set in 17th-c. Boston, Mass. *La Forza del Destino* (1862) libretto by Piave; a romantic tragedy set in 18th-c. Peru. *Don Carlos* (1867), libretto after Schiller; the tragedy concerns the love of Don Carlos (the son of Philip II of Spain) for Elisabeth of Valois, married to Philip for political reasons, and his involvement with the revolt in Flanders. *Aida* (1871), libretto by Ghislanzoni, commissioned for the inauguration of the Cairo Opera House; it is set in ancient Egypt. *Otello* (1887), libretto by Boito after Shakespeare; and *Falstaff* (1893), libretto by Boito after Shakespeare.

Verelst Simon (1644–1721). Dutch flower and portrait painter who settled in London (1669) where his highly finished naturalistic flower pieces became very popular. He started a vogue for portraits with floral surrounds. His brother HARMEN (1643?–1700?), also a painter, worked in London from 1683.

Vereshchagin Vasily Vasilevich (1843–1904). Russian painter who enjoyed an international reputation based chiefly on his military paintings, which exposed the grim reality of war as he had seen it as a war correspondent. His historical paintings of Napoleon's invasion of Russia in 1812 were popular as illustrations to Tolstoy's *War and Peace*.

Veress Sándor (1907–). Hungarian composer, pupil of Bartók and Kodály. Since 1949 he has worked in Switzerland; in the 1930s he introduced neo-classicism into Hungary but later developed a nationalistic style, using folk-music.

Veretti Antonio (1900–). Italian composer and director of the Rome Conservatory since 1941. Post-war compositions have shown tendencies towards 12-note technique.

Verga Giovanni (1840–1922). Italian novelist. V.'s early novels include *I carbonari della montagna* (1861), *Una Peccatrice* (1866) and the sentimental, very popular epistolary novel, *Storia di una capinera* (1870). Residence in Milan produced *Eva* (1873), *Tigre reale* (1875) and *Eros* (1875), sophisticated, rather melodramatic stories of life among the rich of Northern Italy. After this V. found his true vein–realistic descriptions of peasant life in his native Sicily in which individuals are controlled by social and economic forces. *Malavoglia* (1881; *The House by the Medlar-tree*, 1890) chronicles the life of toil and endurance of a poor family of fishermen. *Mastro Don Gesualdo* (1893; *Master Don Gesualdo*, 1893) narrates the life of an ambitious peasant who sacrifices everything of value to achieve wealth and position. V. never pursued his intention to write further novels (the whole was to be a series showing progress at work). His many long stories, striking in their simplicity and concentration, are perhaps his best works. They include the famous *Cavalleria rusticana* (1880; 1893), which V. later rewrote as a 1-act play; its successful production introduced realism to the Italian stage, and it was the basis of *Mascagni's opera. D. H. Lawrence trs. several of V.'s books.

Vergós. Family of Spanish painters of the 15th c. who worked in Barcelona.

Verhaeren Émile (Adolphe-Gustave) (1855–1916). Belgian poet. V. and Maeterlinck were the leading figures of the important generation of writers associated with the magazine *La Jeune Belgique*. V. wrote in many styles, but his most typical verse is perhaps displayed in the rugged, heady optimism of *Les Forces tumultueuses* (1902) and the descriptions of his native Flanders in the 5 vols of lyrics *Tout la Flandre* (1904–11).

verismo (from Italian, 'truth'). Term used in music of Italian operas of the early 20th c. set in the contemporary scene, sometimes in sordid surroundings, and usually having violently dramatic plots. Puccini's *La Bohème*, with its poor setting (a student quarter) and Mimi's cruel and tragic death, is an example.

Verklärte Nacht. Work for strings by *Schoenberg.

Verlaine Paul (1844–96). French poet, the son of an army officer and, for a time, a minor civil servant. While still a young man he became an alcoholic, and thereafter led an erratic, and finally precarious existence. He married in 1870, but soon left his wife to go wandering in England and Belgium with *Rimbaud who, although several years his junior, seems to have dominated and corrupted him. Their association came to an end when V. was imprisoned in Belgium for having fired on Rimbaud during a drunken brawl. The shock of this experience turned V. into a fervent Catholic, although he never achieved stability. After further wanderings in England and elsewhere, he eventually settled again in Paris as a living

Vermeer. *Christ in the House of Martha and Mary*

Vermeer. *The Love Letter*

embodiment of the '*poète maudit*', having himself launched the expression by using it as the title for a book of essays on poets who failed to come to terms with society.

In spite of his dissolute life, V. wrote some of the most delicate and controlled poetry in the language. He was associated with 3 successive schools: the Parnassians, the decadents and the symbolists, but his characteristic verse is always recognizably his own through its apparently effortless musicality and suppleness of rhythm. He gave an admirable definition of his poetic ideal of lyrical freedom in *Art poétique*, publ. in *Jadis et naguère* (1884). His homosexual tendencies did not prevent him from writing some perfect love-poems addressed to his fiancée in *La Bonne Chanson* (1870; in *Poems of Paul Verlaine*, 1895). While in prison after the shooting episode, he composed the pure and immortal lyric:

> Le ciel est, par-dessus le toit
> Si bleu, si calme . . .

Not all his work is on the same level; some of his later, Catholic verse is rather maudlin in tone but, generally speaking, he is the most accessible, and one of the most gifted, of all French poets.

Vermeer Jan, of Delft (Joannes van der Meer) (1632–75). Dutch painter mainly active as an art dealer; a member and eventual president of the Painters' Guild at Delft. It is thought that he did not sell one of his own paintings; there survive few contemporary references to his work and he seems to have died in poverty; over half the paintings attributed to him were noted at the time in his house and studio. A contemporary of the painter Carel Fabritius, a pupil of Rembrandt, it is likely that he came under both his and Caravaggio's influence. After the death of Fabritius, V.'s own style began to develop: classical, timeless and monumental–reality in its everyday aspect observed by a passionate and detached intelligence. Domestic life is raised to the level of poetry. V. is acknowledged in our time as one of the great masters and his influence on the 'tonal' painters has been enormous.

V.'s striving towards the fullest possible representation of reality was achieved with a number of mechanical and pictorial means: the *camera obscura, mirrors, smooth and lean paint whose texture does not destroy the illusion of the counterfeit, sculpturesque modelling, the tonal and geometric organization of pictorial space, all these were used ruthlessly to emphasize the visual process. This is now recognized as V.'s unique achievement. A tentative chronology, the result of 50 years' scholarship, permits the following outline of V.'s development.

The *Girl asleep at a table* (*c.* 1656; Met. Mus.) shows a growing realization of creative problems and points towards possible solutions. The conventional genre subject is treated quite differently from the average stage-like representation by his contemporaries. As in a landscape, the eye is compelled to travel over a number of clearly defined forms of the foreground, such as a table and chair, before it can reach the figure of the middle distance and see into the room at the far end of the interior. This visual intent is reinforced by cutting into the visual field of the foreground and projecting beyond the picture frame part of the table and the chair, so that the space of the painting is extended into the real space of the spectator. The *Maidservant pouring milk* (*c.* 1658; Rijksmus., Amsterdam) carries the intensification of the visual a stage further. Objects are seen as eternal forms placed in an ideal space; a silvery light plays over objects and figures with the same cool detachment. *The Love Letter* (*c.* 1670; Rijksmus., Amsterdam) is the most profound example of V.'s visual philosophy.

Other famous paintings by V. are *View of Delft* and *The Head of a Young Girl* (both Mauritshuis), *The Artist's Studio* (K. Mus., Vienna) and *Christ in the House of Martha and Mary* (N.G., Edinburgh).

Vermeer van Haarlem Jan (1628–91). Dutch landscape painter. His son JAN (1656–1705) painted Italianate landscapes and his younger son BARENT (1659–*c.* 1700) still-life subjects.

Vermeyen Jan Cornelisz (*c.* 1500–59). Dutch painter, mainly of portraits, influenced by Mabuse and J. van Scorel. Travels in Spain and Tunis gave him themes for some historical paintings and a series of tapestries designed for Mary of Hungary.

Verne Jules (1828–1905). French novelist. V.'s adventure stories, set in the future and based on credible developments of scientific knowledge, popularized a new genre. They include *Cinq Semaines en ballon* (1863; *Five Weeks in a Balloon*, 1870); *Voyage au centre de la terre* (1864; *Journey to the Centre of the*

Vermeer. *View of Delft*. See also colour plate 61

Vernet. *Italian Landscape*

Veronese. *Feast in the House of Levi*

Veronese. *Self-portrait*

Earth, 1872); *Vingt mille lieues sous les mers* (1870; *Twenty Thousand Leagues Under the Sea*, 1873); and *Le Tour de monde en quatre-vingts jours* (1873; *Around the World in Eighty Days*, 1874).

Vernet Carle (1758–1836). French painter of horses and Napoleonic battle scenes; son of Claude-Joseph V. Carle's son, HORACE (1789–1863), also a painter and illustrator, decorated the Gallery of Battles at Versailles for Louis-Philippe.

Vernet Claude-Joseph (1714–89). French painter who spent many years in Italy. He painted chiefly classical landscapes after the manner of Claude Lorrain and over-dramatized marine subjects. For Louis XV he completed the 16 paintings the *Ports of France* (Louvre).

Veronese. The name used by Paolo Caliari (*c.* 1528–88). One of the greatest painters of the 16th-c. Venetian school, named after his birthplace, Verona, then within the Venetian cultural and political orbit. Although the son of a stonebreaker and trained by minor mannerist painters, V. shows an extraordinary assurance of style from the beginning, from which he hardly developed or varied. His first frescoes in the Doge's Palace (*c.* 1553) and the St Mark's Library, Venice, won him acclaim in Venice and even the respect of Titian. After Titian's semi-retirement V. shared with Tintoretto the most important commissions, and his chief patrons were the religious foundations in Venice. In 1573, however, V. was in serious trouble with the Inquisition for his manner of representing traditional religious scenes in the spirit of high-festival, e.g. *Marriage at Cana* (Louvre), *Feast in the House of Levi* (Ac., Venice). Although he was censured, his reputation did not suffer permanently. Like Tintoretto's, V.'s art was enormously influential throughout the 17th and even 18th c., especially with the artists of Spain and Flanders and with Tiepolo and other painters of large-scale decorative schemes. V.'s style shows his delight in elegance, opulence and the splendour of surfaces. This is saved from appearing simply mundane or too facile by high technical skill and a superb colour sense. It would be impossible to list more than a fraction of the paintings of this prolific and consistently fine artist, but nowhere is his colour sense better illustrated than in the painting of the golden hair of St Barbara cascading down a dress of gold and black thread in *Holy Family with St Barbara* (Uffizi). V.'s very personal conception of aristocratic grandeur appears in *The Family of Darius before Alexander* (N.G., London). Other fine works are: *Feast in the House of Simon* (Brera), *The Finding of Moses* (2 versions –Prado and G.-Gal., Dresden), *A Lady with Her Small Daughter* (Walters A. Gal., Baltimore), and *Rebecca at the Well* (N.G., Washington). That V. could, on occasion, bring a note of tragedy into his painting is shown in the figures on their high crosses against the dark storm-torn sky in the *Crucifixion* (Louvre).

Verri Alessandro (1741–1816). Italian novelist and playwright. His chief work was *Le notti Romane* (1792–1804), a series of imaginary conversations with ancient Romans, and a play, *Congiura di Milano*, a precursor of the romantic school of drama.

Verrio Antonio (d. 1707). Neapolitan decorative painter who settled in England in 1671 and was appointed court painter in 1684. In spite of his mediocrity he achieved great success because of the comparative novelty of his late baroque style in England. He worked at Windsor Castle, Hampton Court and elsewhere.

Verrocchio Andrea del (*c.* 1435–88). Florentine goldsmith, sculptor and painter. Very little is known of V.'s life, none of his works as a goldsmith have survived and few sculptures can be definitely attributed to him. He worked in Florence at the court of Lorenzo de' Medici 'the Magnificent'. V. is regarded as the most influential Florentine painter of the 2nd half of the 15th c. The achievement of V. and his relationship with his young apprentice Leonardo da Vinci have been debated; his profound influence on Leonardo, Lorenzo da Credi and others of the Florentine school is indisputable. In the bronze statue *David* (*c.* 1476) V.'s style is clearly expressive of the new trends in Florentine art. In the quest for naturalism, the mastery of the figure is extended into an understanding of the psychological; the youthful, victorious David is seen as an adolescent full of conceit and self-confidence. This striving after psychological truth expressed by plastic means is carried further in the group on the outside of Or San Michele, Florence (1476–83) representing *The Unbelief of St Thomas*. The Colleoni monument in Venice, begun in 1479 and

Verrocchio. *David*

Verrocchio. The Colleoni monument

Verzelini goblet (1581)

Verrocchio. *The Baptism of Christ*

Versailles

Vertue. *Self-portrait*

Gaetan Vestris in *Plaisir*

Auguste Vestris: anon. caricature (1779)

Mme Vestris

only completed after his death, is perhaps his best-known work. Compared with Donatello's earlier Gattamelata, it shows the individuality of V.'s achievement at its height. The condottiere and his horse have become the embodiment of will-power, a purposeful and ruthless machine.
Of V.'s painting only the much-disputed *The Baptism of Christ* (Uffizi) remains. On the suggestion of Vasari, the head of one of the kneeling angels is attributed to the young Leonardo da Vinci.

Versailles France. The grandest of European royal palaces and the object of more jealous imitation than perhaps any other building in the world. The original château (*c.* 1624) was enlarged from 1664 by *Le Vau into a 3-sided court with classical façades. From 1678 this was further extended on each side by J.-H. *Mansart until the finished building was over a quarter of a mile long.

verse: *anthem

verse. Writing organized in metrical lines; the term is distinct from 'poetry', which is a qualitative term applied to v. and occasionally prose. 'Jack and Jill went up the hill' is, e.g., v. but is not poetry. Other meanings of the term v. are (1) one such metrical line (strictly speaking, the only correct meaning); and (2) a group of lines, stanza. It is also used to describe the short sections into which each chapter of the Bible is divided.

verset. In the Roman Catholic service, a verse of a Psalm during which there is no singing, the worshippers meditating on the words. The organist may play the music of the Psalm, extemporize or perform a specially composed piece, a v.

vers libre: *free verse

Verspronck Jan Cornelisz (1597–1662). Dutch portrait painter noted for his portraits of children. He was a pupil of Hals and worked in Haarlem.

Vertue George (1684–1756). English engraver and antiquary whose notebooks on English art from about 1700 to 1750, although disorderly and mainly unreflective, are the principal source for the period. On them H. Walpole based his *Anecdotes of Painting in England.*

Verwey Albert (1865–1937). Dutch poet, an important ed. of literary magazines, one of the chief figures in the Dutch literary revival of the 1880s and 1890s. His early verse was melodious and colourful; later it became more restrained and reflective.

Very Jones (1813–80). U.S. poet, a Unitarian minister; a friend of Emerson. V.'s lyrics describe his profound and ecstatic religious experiences.

Verzelini Jacopo (1522–1606). A Venetian who probably came to England from Antwerp in 1571. In 1575 he obtained from Queen Elizabeth a privilege to make Venetian glass in London and to teach the art to Englishmen. 8 glasses attributed to him have survived. They are all large goblets of various proportions with moulded, hollow knops, diamond-engraved with initials, names and hunting scenes.

Vestris family. Italian dancers and actors who appeared both in Paris and London. The 1st to achieve fame was Gaetan (1728–1808) who on one occasion danced at the Paris Opéra with both his son Auguste (1760–1842) and his grandson Auguste-Armand (1788–1825). This grandson married Elizabeth (1797–1856), granddaughter of the engraver F. *Bartolozzi. As Madame Vestris, she became an actress and later manageress of the Olympic, London; she was the 1st female lessee in the history of the stage. She and her 2nd husband, the actor C. J. Mathews, were the 1st managers to use the *box-set.

Vézelay France. La Madeleine, Romanesque church (Gothic E. end added later) notable both for its architecture and sculpture of *c.* 1130, one of the great series of French Romanesque tympana with elongated figures, dramatic gesture, and drapery shown by thin linear folds.

Viadana Lodovico (1564–1645). Italian composer. *Cento concerti ecclesiastici* (1602) for voice and organ are an important landmark in the development of the basso *continuo.

Viani Albert (1906–). Italian sculptor, a pupil of A. Martini and a member of the fronte nuovo delle arte group. His style follows that of Arp but is less purely abstract. The female form is usually the basis of his work.

vibraphone. Musical instrument similar to a xylophone. The keys of a v. are metal and below each hangs a tubular bell resonator–within the top of each resonator there is a rotating disc driven by an electric motor. The rotating disc disturbs the air column of the resonator and causes a vibrato effect.

vibrato. Musical term for the throbbing effect achieved in a note by singers and instrumentalists by slightly varying the pitch. String players produce v. by rocking the finger-tip pad on the string and singers and wind instrumentalists by variations in wind pressure and other means; artistically used v. gives expressiveness to a performance. The technique was developed from the mid 18th c. and is out of place in performances of earlier music.

Vicar of Wakefield, The (1766). Novel by Oliver *Goldsmith.

Vicente Gil (*c.* 1465–*c.* 1536). Poet and playwright, one of the greatest figures in Portuguese literature. Little is known of his life. V. took up writing in early middle age and produced exclusively for the court. Besides his beautiful *romances* and *villancicos*, he wrote 43 plays in both Portuguese and Spanish. Many are bilingual and incorporate peasant and gipsy dialect, slang and scraps of Latin and other languages. They include farces; *autos* for performance on religious occasions, notably the *Auto da Sibila Cassandra*; and tragic comedies, e.g. *Amadís de Gaula* and *Dom Duardos*, based on romances of chivalry. V. had magnificent lyrical gifts, and a rich, warm humanity animates his characters. Although he wrote for a noble audience he was free from artificiality or affectation, and his pungent wit and frank social comments more than once provoked the intervention of the Inquisition.

Vickers Jon (1926–). Canadian tenor known for his performances in Wagner and Verdi operas.

Vico Giambattista (1668–1744). Italian philosopher. V.'s thought, finalized in *La Scienza nuova* (1725, 1729–30; revised 1744) anticipated later historical studies in attempting to formulate laws of recurring cycles; he also elaborated valuable aesthetic–particularly literary–theories. V.'s work had little immediate influence and was reassessed only in the 19th c.

Victoria Tomás Luis de (*c.* 1550–1611). The greatest of the Spanish polyphonic composers. In Rome (from 1565) he was a friend of Palestrina and held various posts before returning to Madrid in 1585, serving the Empress Maria and then her daughter, in retirement in a nunnery. His austere and deeply religious music, while showing the inevitable impact of Palestrina, is a natural product of the Spanish school, and with an economy of resource similar to Morales achieves the most powerful, moving and sometimes dramatic effects. V.'s works include: 20 masses, 44 motets, a requiem mass (1603) for the death of the Empress Maria and the *Officium Hebdomadae Sanctae*.

Victory of Samothrace: *Winged Victory of Samothrace.

Vida Marco Girolamo (1485–1566). Italian humanist and poet, and a cleric. V. was encouraged by Pope Leo X to use his poetic talent for Christian purposes, and his chief work was an epic poem in Latin verse, *La Cristiade* (1535).

Vidor Charles (1900–59). Hungarian-born U.S. film director. He went from Berlin to Hollywood and started directing in 1932. He made 2 key Rita Hayworth movies, *Cover Girl* (1944) and *Gilda* (1946), and the Hollywood biographies of Chopin (*A Song to Remember*, 1945) and Liszt (*Song Without End*, 1959, finished by Cukor).

Vidor King (1896–). U.S. film director. V. started in films at the age of 18 as a newsreel cameraman and made his 1st feature in 1918. His 1st major success was an expensive war film, *The Big Parade* (1925), and he followed this with one of the greatest of all silent pictures, *The Crowd*, in which he showed an almost unique ability to catch in its most intimate details the feeling of happy family life, a success which he repeated with *H. M. Pulham, Esq.* (1941). *Hallelujah!* (1929) brings feelings of social responsibility and respect for the participants to an all-Negro picture, and *Our Daily Bread* (1934), in a sense a sequel to *The Crowd*, shows urban unemployed forming a farming co-operative. This film, the peak achievement of V.'s humanist period, is by way of being an apologia for a rather utopian Communism. *Stella Dallas* (1937) and *Northwest Passage* (1939), respectively a weepie and a big historical movie which was released in uncompleted form, are V.'s other famous 1930s

Vézelay. Portal of the W. vestibule

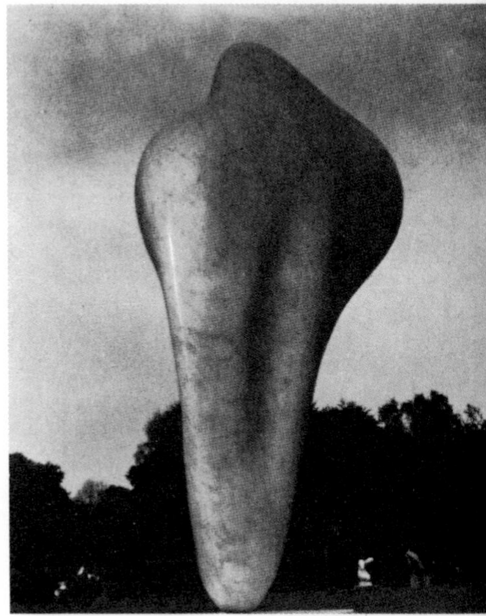

Viani. *Torso* (1956–62)

Vibraphone

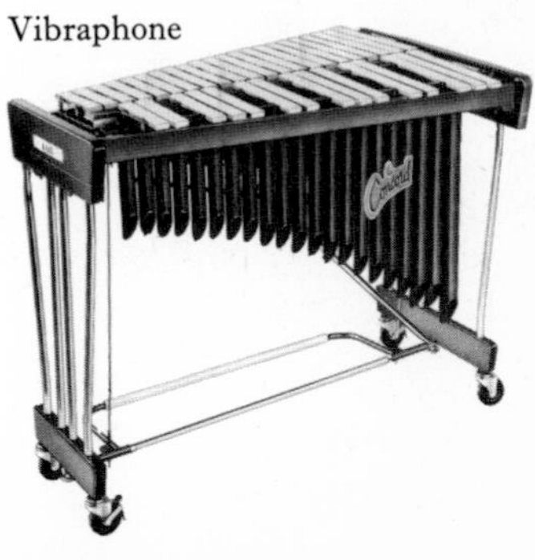

Vienna. Pear-shaped tankard (*c.* 1720)

Vienna. Octagonal plate (*c.* 1750)

Vignola. Il Gesù

King Vidor. Jennifer Jones in *Ruby*

Vignettes by Fournier

Vigée-Lebrun. *The Artist and her Daughter*

Vieira da Silva. *Painting* (1953)

films. Starting with *Duel in the Sun* (1947), V. launched into his big melodramatic period of Freudian symbolism and often highly erotic violence. Its successors in the genre were *The Fountainhead* (1949) taken from a novel by Ayn Rand, *Beyond the Forest* (1949) and *Ruby Gentry* (1952). Echoes of this and of the physical exhilaration generated by *Duel in the Sun* are found in a western, *Man Without a Star* (1955), and more dimly in *Solomon and Sheba* (1959). Between these he made an adaptation of *War and Peace* (1956), with battle sequences directed by M. Soldati.

Vieira da Silva Maria Elena (1908–). Portuguese painter of abstract compositions of great sensitivity. She settled in Paris in 1920 and in 1930 married the Hungarian painter Arpad Szenes. The theme recurrent in her work is that of the city, which she invests with an insubstantial dream-like quality.

Vien Joseph (1716–1809). French painter working at Rome for a period and influenced by the neo-classicism of the later 18th c. He achieved a great contemporary reputation both as artist and teacher; J.-L. David was a pupil.

Vienna porcelain. The 2nd factory producing hard-paste *porcelain in Europe was founded, with help from Meissen workmen, by C. I. du Paquier in 1719 at Vienna. From 1744 it was run by the state until its closure in 1864. In the du Paquier period the factory was not a business success but the ware enjoyed great fame; the designs, based on silver-work, were frequently reminiscent of Böttger's work at Meissen. In the period 1744–84 the best work included the figures modelled by Josef Niedermayer. In 1784 the running of the factory was undertaken by Konrad von Sorgenthal, under whom highly wrought gilded ware inspired by neo-classical design brought the factory new fame.

Vierne Louis-Victor-Jules (1870–1937). French organist, a pupil of Franck and Widor, with whom he worked for a time at St Sulpice. V. himself had numerous distinguished pupils, among them M. Dupré and N. Boulanger. His compositions, following the style of his 2 great teachers, include 6 organ symphonies and other pieces.

Vierzehnheiligen. German baroque church; architect Balthasar *Neumann.

Vieuxtemps Henri (1820–81). Belgian violinist, composer and important teacher of his instrument. He taught in Russia and later at the Brussels Conservatory; his compositions include 6 violin concertos.

View from the Bridge, A (1955). Play by Arthur *Miller.

Vigée-Lebrun Marie-Elisabeth-Louise (1755–1842). French portraitist of the rococo period, pupil of her father the pastellist Louis V. (1715–67) and wife of Jean-Baptiste-Pierre Lebrun (1748–1813), painter and art dealer. She painted attractive, flattering portraits which brought her the patronage of Queen Marie-Antoinette and, during the years of the Revolution, of royalty elsewhere in Europe. Her memoirs were publ. under the title *Souvenirs* (1835–7; *Souvenirs. . .*, 1879).

Vigeland Gustav (1869–1943). Norwegian sculptor. He studied in Oslo and Copenhagen, and then in Paris under Rodin (1892). His major work, begun *c.* 1906, is the group of sculptures in the Frognerpark, Oslo, conceived as an open-air chapel and culminating in a massive column of interwoven nude figures which is medieval in spirit and complexity.

vignette. Term originally applied to the decorative borders of medieval mss, later to the small decorative motifs appearing at the end of the chapters of 18th- and 19th-c. books.

Vignola Giacomo Barozzi da (1507–73). Leading Italian mannerist architect. His chief works are: the villa of Pope Julius, near Rome (1550), a complex of eccentric architecture and labyrinthine gardens (one façade is a single huge niche); Castello Farnese, Caprarola (1559), a huge palace on a pentagonal plan, with circular internal courtyard; Il Gesù, Rome (1568), the mother church of the Jesuits –L. B. Alberti's S. Andrea reinterpreted in mannerist terms (façade not by V.); and S. Anna dei Palafrenieri (1572; demolished), the 1st use of an oval plan.

Vignon Claude (1593–1670). French painter and etcher who worked for Louis XIII and Richelieu. He studied in Rome (*c.* 1616–24), where he was influenced by the followers of Caravaggio and Elsheimer, developing a style strikingly similar to that of the young

Vigeland. Group in the Frognerpark

Vigo. *L'Atalante*

Heitor Villa-Lobos

Rembrandt. The 2 artists were acquainted with one another and V. sold some works by Rembrandt in Paris.

Vigny Alfred (Victor) de (1797–1863). French poet, novelist, dramatist and essayist, and one of the outstanding representatives of the romantic movement. His aristocratic origins and training as an officer emphasized the natural haughtiness and severity of his manner. In 1825 he had married an Englishwoman, partly in the mistaken hope that her father's fortune would relieve him of financial worry. V. was continuously afflicted with a sense of spiritual isolation and of the uselessness of life. He is the foremost stoical pessimist in French literature.
In his vol. *Poèmes antiques et modernes* (1826), his literary personality is already fully developed. He usually illustrates a simple idea by means of a symbol: e.g. in *Moïse*, the Hebrew prophet represents the bitter solitude of the great or dedicated man, a theme which is further developed in the play *Chatterton* (publ. 1835), and the prose tales of *Stello* (1832) and *Servitude et grandeur militaires* (1835; trs. in *Lights and Shades of Military Life*, 1840). A curiously optimistic belief in the possibilities of knowledge or science appears in some of the later verse, publ. in *Les Destinées* (1864), and is not properly reconciled with the accompanying pessimism. V. also left a bleak but interesting diary, *Journal d'un poète* (1867).

Vigo Jean (1905–34). French film director. V. was an anarchist by political conviction. He made only 4 films; one was a documentary about a swimmer, *Taris* (1932), and one, *À Propos de Nice* (1929), a documentary of social contrasts between rich holidaymakers and poor residents. *Zéro de Conduite* (1933), set in a boarding-school, has the surrealism of extreme subjectivity in its combination of the grotesque in the treatment of the staff and the lyrical handling in slow motion of a pillow fight. This film's wide sphere of influence includes the work 30 years later of Godard and Demy, while that of his only full-length feature, *L'Atalante* (1934), was evident much earlier, even in the early work of Carné. A melancholy story of a young couple who own a river barge, it derives much of its feeling from the desolation of industrial landscapes. The film was mutilated by its distributors just before V.'s death from tuberculosis.

vihara. A Buddist monastery or monastic hall.

vihuela. A musical instrument peculiar to Spain, similar to a guitar but tuned like a lute. In 16th-c. Spain the vihuelista composers, e.g. Luis de *Milan, produced sophisticated fantasias, trentos and variations.

Vilar Jean (1912–). French actor and director who in 1947 founded the open-air festival at Avignon and from 1951 to 1963 was director of the *Théâtre National Populaire, a co. with which he did much excellent experimental work.

Vile Bodies (1930). Novel by Evelyn Waugh.

Village, The (1783). Poem by Crabbe.

Villa-Lobos Heitor (1887–1959). Brazilian composer and folk-lorist. In the 1920s he visited Europe; from 1930 he held influential teaching posts in Brazil and toured internationally conducting his own works. V.-L.'s music, predominantly romantic in mood, has besides Brazilian folk elements stylistic similarities to European impressionism and neo-classicism. His works include: 4 operas; ballets, including *Emperor Jones* (1955); 13 programmatic symphonies (1916–57); 9 *Bachianas Brasileiras* (1932–41), no. 1 for 8 cellos, no. 2 for cellos and soprano, based on V.-L.'s belief that Bach's music was rooted in folk-music; 14 *Chôros* claimed as a new type of work and in which Brazilian folk-music and folk-instruments are combined with traditional orchestral methods.

villanella. A 15th–16th-c. Italian style of part song–a kind of 'rustic' madrigal.

villanelle. Verse form consisting of 5 3-line stanzas rhyming *aba* and a final quatrain *abaa*. Lines 1, 6, 12 and 18 are identical, as are lines 3, 9, 15 and 19; i.e. lines 1 and 3 alternately form the refrain of the middle 4 stanzas and together end the poem.

Villani Giovanni (*c.* 1276–1348). Italian historian of the city of Florence: his *Nuova Cronica* is one of the finest historical documents of the 14th c.

Villanueva Carlos Raul (1900–). The leading architect of Venezuela. V.'s architecture is based on a love of structure and its expression.

Alfred de Vigny

Villanueva. Hall for Faculty of Architecture and Town Planning, Caracas

Villard de Honnecourt. Apse designs from the sketch-book

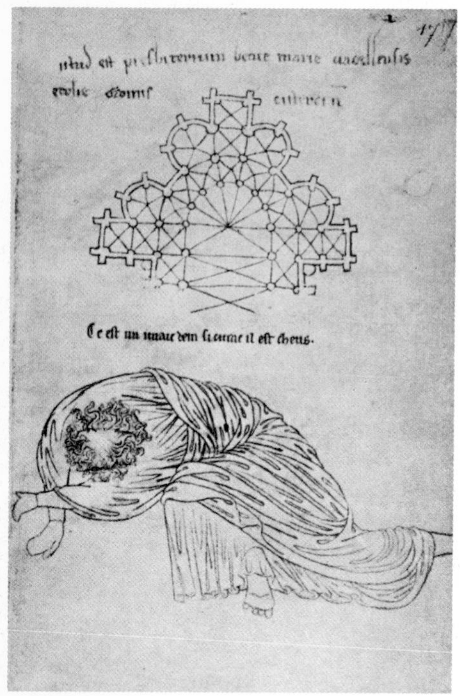

Villard de Honnecourt. Designs from the sketch-book

Villiers de L'Isle Adam

Jacques Villon. *Young Girl* (1912)

Viol

Apart from housing developments his best-known work is Caracas Univ., with its great hall (1953) with pendant sounding-boards designed by Alexander Calder, and a lobby housing the work of Léger and Arp.

Villard de Honnecourt. 13th-c. French master mason, known to posterity only through his sketch-book. It contains plans and elevations of buildings then in course of construction (e.g. Rheims, Chartres), projects for his own work, some elementary geometry, and some notes for sculptors on stock subjects like apostles, angels, lions, etc. As a document showing how a medieval architect worked it is unique. H. travelled widely (as far as Hungary).

Villehardouin Geoffroy de (d. 1212?). French nobleman, one of the leaders of the 4th Crusade. V.'s *Conquête de Constantinople*, an apologia for the Crusade, is an early example of French prose.

Villette (1853). Novel by Charlotte *Brontë.

Villiers de L'Isle-Adam (Jean-Marie-Mathias) Philippe-Auguste, comte de (1838–89). French writer, a member of a celebrated impoverished Breton aristocratic family. He tried, unsuccessfully, to live by his writings, which express post-romantic cynical dandyism mixed with symbolist idealism. In spite of the aristocratic tone of his works, he had an unhappy, poverty-stricken existence. Two colls of stories, *Contes cruels* (1883) and *Nouveaux Contes cruels* (1889), are still occasionally read, and the drama, *Axël* (1894, publ. 1890; *Axël* 1925), has remained famous as an expression of post-romantic feeling. V. is now chiefly remembered for his remark: 'As for living, our servants will do that for us.'

Villon François (1431–63?). French poet, one of the most striking literary personalities of the middle ages. V. was born in Paris and brought up by a priest who gave him his own name. As a student at the Univ. of Paris, he fell into a vicious mode of life which soon led him into crime. Much of his life was spent in prison and in 1463 he was under sentence of death, but was pardoned and banished; at this point he disappears from history. He uses the conventional forms with ease, but not to conventional effects: his ballades, for example, deal with the sordid realities of his own experience, as titles such as the *Ballade des Pendus* indicate. The grossly realistic was not something new in medieval literature; what singles V. out is that in him these aspects of human experience are not part of an attitudinizing stance. It is, at one and the same time, the personal quality of his response, and the objectiveness of his vision which make his work memorable; his grossness, bitterness, and occasional tenderness, even sentimentality, are not poses. His thought is generally conventional, and the moralizing about the state of man exemplified in his masterpiece, *Le Grand Testament* (1461–2) includes the artistic commonplaces of the 15th c. It is the personal quality of his apprehension of the physical horrors of death and age which stand out, at the cost of much ephemeral personal material.

Villon Jacques, real name Gaston Duchamp (1875–1963). French painter, half-brother of Marcel Duchamp and Raymond Duchamp-Villon. In 1911 he became a cubist, for a time the leader of a faction including Léger, Gleyre and Gleizes. In 1919 he began painting abstracts, and his work passed through several phases, all however marked by command of proportion and line.

Vincennes or **Vincennes-Sèvres.** Porcelain factory opened *c.* 1738; in 1756 it was transferred to *Sèvres.

Vinci Leonardo (1690–1730). Italian opera composer, one of the more important of the Neapolitan school (*opera).

viol. A family of stringed instruments prominent in European music from the middle ages to the late 17th c., being then gradually displaced by the violins. The v.s are differentiated from the violins in that they are fretted (*frets), are lighter in construction and have lighter, less tensioned strings; they also have sloping shoulders and a flat back. The tone is more 'reedy' and less incisive than the violin's. The treble, tenor and bass v.s are all played rested on or between the legs (*gamba); the VIOLONE rests on the ground like the double bass. The bass v. was a very popular solo instrument (K. F. *Abel) and smaller versions of it such as the DIVISION V. and the LYRA V. were also used.

viola. The tenor member of the violin family with a range of about three 8ves up from the C below middle C; its modern status as a solo instrument is largely due to Lionel *Tertis.

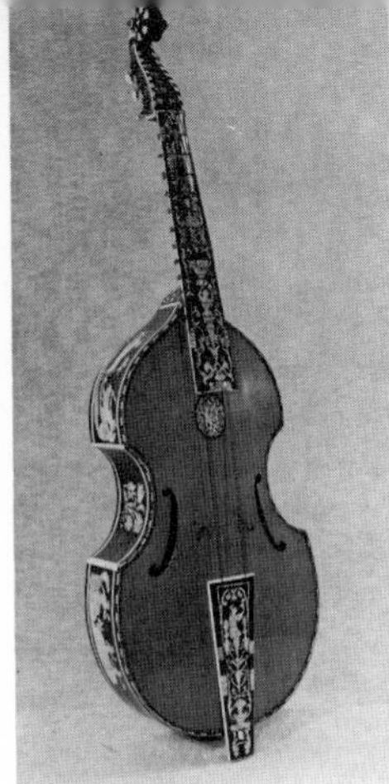
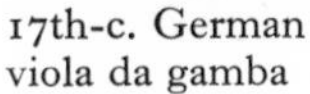

17th-c. German viola da gamba

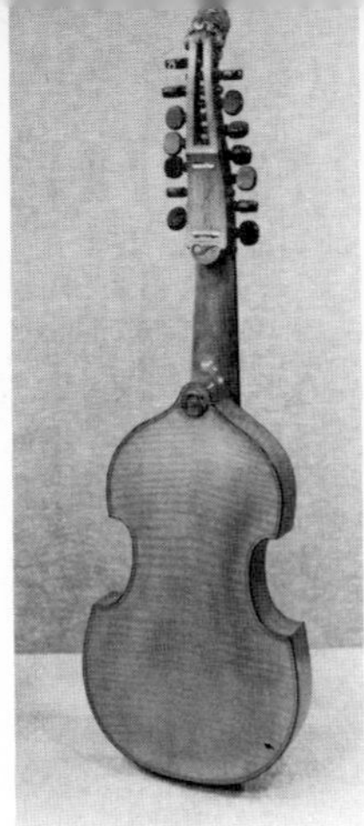

17th-c. Italian viola d'amore

Violin by Nicolo Amati

viola d'amore. Obsolete member of the violin family which had *sympathetic strings.

violin. Stringed musical instrument developed in the early 16th c. by the Amati family of *Cremona. The v.s differ from the *viols which they displaced in the late 17th c. in many respects. The body has a convex back and high shoulders, the strings are under greater tension and the finger-board is unfretted; all these characteristics combine to give the v. its bright, powerful tone. The modern v. differs from the early v.s in having a more sharply convex bridge and in using a concave rather than convex *bow. The members of the v. family, which forms the basis of the modern orchestra, are the v., the viola (a tenor instrument), the cello and the double bass.

Viollet-le-Duc Eugène (1814–79). French architect. His fame chiefly rests on his restorations of Gothic cathedrals (e.g. Notre-Dame, Paris), castles (Pierrefonds) and even whole towns (Carcassonne), but in his books he advocated a functional theory of architecture which had some influence on the pioneers of the modern style.

violone: *viol

Viotti Giovanni Battista (1755–1824). Italian violinist, a pupil of Pugnani, and composer. He worked much in London and performed some of his concertos at the *Salomon Concerts (1794). His compositions, distinguished by a fine musical instinct and important technical innovations, include 29 violin concertos.

Virgil (70–19 B.C.). Publius Vergilius Maro, Roman poet, was born at Mantua and educated for the Bar at Cremona, Milan and Rome. But he appeared in court only once, being too shy and awkward to succeed in a public career, and retired to Naples to study with the Epicurean philosopher Siro. In 41 B.C. Octavian (the future emperor Augustus), after defeating the Republicans at Philippi, seized land around Cremona, including V.'s, for distribution among his soldiers. V. apparently appealed to Octavian himself for compensation, succeeded, and (according to the usual interpretation) incorporated the incident by way of compliment to Octavian in the first of the *Eclogues*, publ. *c.* 37 B.C. He then received the patronage of Maecenas, who suggested to him the subject of the *Georgics* and perhaps of the *Aeneid*. The *Eclogues*, addressed to several friends, are pastorals in the manner of Theocritus dealing with contemporary events under a disguise that cannot now be penetrated. The language shows the influence of Lucretius but the feeling of the poems is Virgil's own melancholy romanticism. The *Georgics*–books of didactic verse dealing with crops, the vine and olive, stock-breeding and bee-keeping respectively–were publ. *c.* 29 B.C. after 7 years' labour. They are V.'s most perfect work, completely finished and polished, and delivered to the world under his own authority. He treats the conventional subject-matter drawn from Hellenistic handbooks and the Greek didactic poet Hesiod, in language unique for its purity and originality, ease and harmony, influenced again by Lucretius and infused with his own love for the Italian countryside and its pursuits.
The *Aeneid*, which occupied the last 11 years of his life, was left unfinished, and V. gave instructions on his death-bed that it should be burned unread. Augustus intervened and ordered the work to be publ. with no more than minor necessary corrections. It still contains inconsistencies and unfinished lines which the eds were too scrupulous to correct. Almost at once it was received as a classic. Drawing on a wide reading of the early legendary history of Rome and of its later development, V. used what had come to be the generally accepted account of the foundation of the Roman state by Aeneas and his band of fugitives from ruined Troy. The hero, having to stand as a paragon of the ideal Roman virtues, is not a convincing character, nor does V. relish the blood and violence which his subject demands, but the detrimental comparison with Homer's *Iliad* is misleading. The narrative is less important than V.'s reflection on the destiny of power as embodied in his country's history. It is an erudite and allusive work, but deliberately solemn, the language always grave and correct, carrying with it the music of the poet's wan melancholy.

virginals. A keyboard instrument of the 16th and 17th cs using exactly the same mechanism as the *harpsichord but differing from it in being smaller, oblong in shape, and with the keyboard on the long-side, not at the end. The name probably derives from the Latin *virga*, 'rod', i.e. the quill which plucks the string.

Virginians, The (18579–). Historical novel by *Thackeray.

Viollet-le-Duc. Assembly Hall (project; *above*) and Pierrefonds (*below*)

Italian virginals which belonged to Queen Elizabeth I

Peter Vischer the Younger. *Hercules*

Vittone. S. Chiara

Peter Vischer the Elder. *King Arthur*; from the tomb of Maximilian

Visconti. Spiros Focas and Claudia Cardinale in *Rocco e i suoi fratelli*

Virginibus Puerisque (1881). Coll. of essays by R. L. Stevenson.

Virgin of the Rocks. Painting by *Leonardo of which 2 versions exist (N.G., London and Louvre).

Viridiana (1961). Film directed by L. *Buñuel.

Vischer. Family of German sculptors and metal-founders (*fl.* mid 15th–mid 16th c.). The family workshop in Nuremberg was established by HERMANN (d. 1488) and taken over by his son PETER the Elder (d. 1529) and his sons PETER the Younger (1487–1528), HERMANN the Younger (1486–1517) and HANS (d. 1550). Between them they were responsible for the tomb of Archbishop Ernst of Saxony (Magdeburg cathedral), the statues of Theodoric and Artus for the tomb of the Emperor Maximilian (Hofkirche, Innsbruck) and the tomb of St Sebald (St Sebald's church, Nuremberg), a fine example of German Renaissance art.

Vischer Friedrich Theodor (1807–87). German writer, an important theorist on aesthetics and author of the satirical novel *Auch Einer* (1879).

Visconti Luchino (1906–). Italian film director, also a distinguished opera director. V. was first a set designer, and was an assistant on Renoir's *Une Partie de Campagne* and on the version of *Tosca* which he began in Italy in 1940. V.'s *Ossessione* (1942) was a wartime antecedent (*Rossellini) of neo-realism. It was a transposition to Italy of James M. Cain's *The Postman Always Rings Twice*. *La Terra Trema* (1948), set among and acted by Sicilian fishermen, tries to tell a social story of the undermining of a fisherman's co-operative by capitalistic dealers, but the motive force seems to be fate rather than capitalism, and the shots have a posed deadness. *Senso* (1954) was a failure, but the studio setting and romantic story of *Le notti bianche* (1957) were better suited to V.'s talents. The tragedy of *Rocco e i suoi fratelli* (1960), about Sicilians who have moved to Milan, suffers from some of the defects of *La Terra Trema* but had a slickness which made it more watchable. V.'s look at Italy's decadent aristocracy in his episode of *Boccaccio '70* (1962) heralded his 1st great film, *The Leopard* (1963), from the *Lampedusa novel. The film is autobiographical in feeling; it shows the predicament of the traditional aristocrat with progressive convictions.

Vision of Judgement, The (1822). Poem by *Byron.

Visiteurs du Soir, Les (1942). Film directed by M. *Carné.

Vitale da Bologna Vitale d'Aimo de'Cavalli, known as (*fl.* 1334–59). Italian painter, founder of the Bolognese school. His early work, in which there is a strong decorative element, shows Sienese influence; he later adopted a broader, more simplified treatment. His paintings include *Madonnas* in Bologna Gal. and the Vatican Mus., and a polyptych in S. Salvatore, Bologna.

Vitali Giovanni Battista (*c.* 1644–92). Italian composer of chamber music, one of Corelli's most distinguished predecessors; his son TOMMASO ANTONIO (b. *c.* 1665) composed a still famous chaconne for violin and continuo.

vitalism. Term loosely used to describe writers (e.g. Bernard *Shaw) and philosophers (e.g. *Bergson) who believe in a vital principle or life-force distinct from matter and manifesting itself in human activity; sometimes applied still more loosely to those (e.g. D. H. *Lawrence) who celebrate the animal, spontaneous, non-rational side of man.

Vita nuova, La. Coll. of poems and prose commentaries by *Dante.

Vitelloni, I (1953). Film directed by F. *Fellini.

Viti Timoteo (1469/70–1523) called 'Timoteo da Urbino'. Italian painter trained as a goldsmith, then as a painter under Francia in Bologna. He worked in Urbino where he was Raphael's master.

Vitruvius Pollio (*fl.* late 1st c. B.C.). Roman architect and writer. His treatise *De Architectura* is the only ancient work on architecture to have survived. It covers systematically town planning; building materials; temples; basilicas and baths; houses; surveying; astronomy; and engines of war. The text was rediscovered during the Renaissance, publ. in 1486 (Italian trs. 1521) and had an immense influence on humanist architectural theory (especially L. B. Alberti).

Vitry Philippe de (1291–1361). French poet, philosopher, mathematician and leading ars

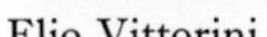

Elio Vittorini

Vivaldi (presumed portrait)

nova composer; bishop of Meaux from 1351. Very little of his work has survived, but his friend Petrarch revered him as man and as poet and V. may have invented the poetic forms of ballade, rondeau and lay. Only 14 motets are known to be his; the earliest (*c.* 1316) already show the isorhythmic structure which V., although not its inventor, was to develop.

Vitti Monica (1933–). Italian film actress, especially associated with Antonioni, in whose films her grave beauty and psychological perception are used to advantage.

Vittone Bernardo (1704/5–70). Italian baroque architect who spent all his working life in Piedmont, building mainly churches. His style derives from Guarini and Juvarra and is marked by a fondness for ingenious centralized plans – circles, hexagons, ovals, etc. – and complicated ribbed domes. Among his chief works are the Sanctuary at Vallinotto, S. Chiara at Brà, S. Croce at Villanova di Mondovì, and S. Maria di Piazza at Turin. V. was a brilliant architect, though the fact that his works were in such unfrequented places made his subsequent influence negligible.

Vittorini Elio (1908–). Italian novelist, one of the initiators of the 'new realist' school after World War II. Most of V.'s novels deal with poverty and reflect his position as a politically engaged writer; the best, including *Conversazione in Sicilia* (1941; *Conversation in Sicily*, 1948), are subtle in treatment and formally satisfying. Other works include the short novels (publ. together) *Erica* and *La Garibaldina* (1956; 1961).

Vittorino da Feltre V. de' Rambaldoni called (*c.* 1378–1446). Italian humanist, a famous educator who anticipated later methods by employing classical literature as a means of educating rather than an end of knowledge, and as a discipline complementary and not hostile to religious study.

Vivaldi Antonio (*c.* 1678–1741). Italian composer and violinist; known as the 'red priest', from his hair colour, although he early had to abandon his duties at the altar because of an illness (probably asthma). As composer and conductor to the Ospedale della Pietà, Venice (from 1703) he ran concerts which soon acquired a European reputation; he travelled widely in Europe and produced operas in many Italian towns; his vast output (he reputedly claimed to compose faster than a copyist could copy) influenced every important contemporary, e.g. J. S. Bach, Tartini and Telemann, and effected major advances in violin technique; yet his work, criticized in his own lifetime, was virtually forgotten until its revival in the 1930s. His powerful style is characterized by dramatic and passionate effects of dynamics and harmony and by a lyricism new in instrumental music; but above all he established the form of the solo *concerto of the high baroque period. Of his 49 operas, 19 survive complete; his church music, in an operatic idiom, includes motets and mass settings and the oratorio *Judith* (1716), remarkable for its colourful orchestration. Over 400 concertos include more than 200 for violin, others for flute, recorder, clarinet, oboe, bassoon and trumpet. Among his best-known works are the suites of concertos *The Four Seasons* (*c.* 1725), the 1st part of *The Challenge of Harmony and Invention*, and *Estro armonico* (publ. 1712).

Vivarini. Family of Venetian painters who contributed to the development of the Venetian school. ANTONIO (*fl.* 1440–76) worked until 1450 with his brother-in-law Giovanni d'Alemagna in a Gothic style chiefly derived from G. da Fabriano. He later collaborated with his brother BARTOLOMMEO (*fl.* 1450–99) who in the 1460s developed a style strongly influenced by Mantegna. His work makes the transition from Gothic to Renaissance. ALVISE (d. 1503/5), son of Antonio, was strongly influenced by Antonella da Messina and Giovanni Bellini. He painted altarpieces and portraits.

Vives Juan Luis (1492–1540). The greatest Spanish humanist, a disciple of Erasmus; he spent some time in England. V.'s most interesting writings are on such practical topics as politics, psychology and education.

Vivin Louis (1861–1936). French 'primitive' painter, a Post Office employee and 'Sunday painter' until his retirement from the Post Office in 1922, when he was able to devote all his time to painting. He is best known for his paintings of the buildings of Paris.

Vkhutemas. 'Higher Technical-Artistic Studios' set up by the Soviet government in Moscow (1920) and Petrograd and Vitebsk (1921); they ran their own affairs and were

Antonio Vivarini. Polyptych with *imago pietatis* and saints

Bartolommeo Vivarini. *St Martin triptych*

Alvise Vivarini. *Madonna*

Vivin. *Notre-Dame* (*c.* 1933)

Vlaminck. *Self-portrait*

Vlaminck. *Paysage aux Arbres Rouges*. Also *fauvism

Vlieger. *View of an Estuary*

Vollard: drawing by Picasso

Voltaire: bust by Houdon

important and more or less open centres of teaching, theoretical development (especially of *constructivism) and discussion for Malevich, Kandinsky, Antoine Pevsner and Tatlin.

Vlaminck Maurice de (1876–1958). Painter, born in Paris of Flemish parents. He was untrained and claimed to have never been inside the Louvre; the only debt he acknowledged was to Van Gogh, whose expressive use of colour and execution was the foundation of V.'s fauvism. With Derain, he was one of the 1st painters to collect African masks (*c.* 1905) and his fauve paintings have a more savage intensity than those of his Parisian contemporaries, e.g. *Paysage aux Arbres Rouges* (1906; M.M.A., Paris). He believed that 'instinct is the foundation of art. I try to paint with my heart and my loins.' He was influenced by Cézanne in 1907 and his later works, though often wildly painted, are more subdued in colour.

Vlieger Simon de (*c.* 1600–53). Dutch painter, principally of marine subjects, and etcher whose style was based on that of Porcellis. Willem van de Velde the Younger was his pupil and he also strongly influenced van de Capelle.

Vogel Vladimir (1896–). Swiss composer of Russo-German origins. Friendship with Scriabin prompted V. to start composing and for 4 years (1920–4) he was a pupil of Busoni. In the 1930s he began to study and use 12-note techniques. Recent works include the *Arpiade* (1955) to verses by Jean Arp.

Vogler Georg Joseph (1749–1814). German composer, ordained as a priest and known as the Abbé V. His pupils included Weber and Meyerbeer.

voice leading. A U.S. musical term being a literal trs. of the German '*Stimmeführung*', meaning *part writing.

voicing. The final adjustment of an organ pipe, by the instrument maker, to perfect its tonal quality.

voiding. A method of working embroidery in which the details of a figure or flower are left unworked, or voided.

Voiture Vincent (1598–1648). French poet and letter writer, one of the circle at the Hôtel de Rambouillet.

Vol de Nuit (1931). Novel by *Saint-Exupéry.

Vollard Ambroise (1865–1939). French art dealer and collector, an extremely important figure in modern art through his encouragement of painters of the school of *Paris; he arranged the 1st exhibitions of the work of Cézanne (1895), Picasso (1901) and Matisse (1904). He also publ. many works which included advanced examples of graphic design (notably by Picasso); these played a great part in the modern development of that art.

Volpone, or The Fox (1606). Comedy by Ben *Jonson.

volta (Italian, 'jump'). Old Italian dance, one of the steps of which is a jump; an English name was 'Lavolta'.

Voltaire. Pseud. of François-Marie Arouet (1694–1778). French writer born in Paris and educated by the Jesuits at the Collège Louis-le-Grand. V. lived in constant conflict with authority: twice imprisoned in the Bastille, exiled in England (1726–9), hiding in retirement under Mme de Chatelet's protection (1734–44), at the court of Frederick II (1750–3), in Switzerland (1753–60) and driven thence to take refuge again on French soil at Ferney, V. ceaselessly wrote, talked and campaigned for clarity and justice. He was adulated and execrated by turns for his wit and intelligence, but although a malicious controversialist, he often displayed great humanity and generosity, particularly in rehabilitating the victims of unjust oppression.

V. achieved a unique position as an intellectual force in Europe, and his career gave the practice of literature a new prestige. The lucidity, brevity, economy and elegance of his style reflect the attitudes of the Enlightenment, which he in many respects epitomized. He was a prolific writer – a skilful playwright who wrote over 20 tragedies, including *Zaïre* (1732; *The Tragedy of Zara*, 1736) and *Mérope* (1743; 1744); a poet, e.g. the epic *La Henriade* (1728; 1732); a philosopher who produced a *Dictionnaire philosophique* (1764; 1765); and a historian who wrote the *Histoire de Charles XII* (1731; 1732) and *Siècle de Louis XIV* (1751; *The Age of Louis XIV*, 1752). But he is most

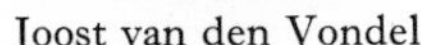

Joost van den Vondel

Vörösmarty: contemporary engraving

Volute from a book-case. For use in architecture *orders

famous for his philosophical tales – *Zadig* (1747; 1749), *Micromégas* (1759) and, above all, *Candide, ou l'Optimisme* (1759; 1759). This last relates the comic, outlandish and gruesome adventures which finally disillusion Candide with the Leibnitzian philosophical optimism of his tutor, Dr Pangloss ('all is for the best in this best of all possible worlds'); the moral is that we must 'cultivate our garden' and forget metaphysics. V. also wrote: contributions to the **Encyclopédie*; influential criticism which helped to popularize Shakespeare in Europe (though V. later attacked him); and *Lettres philosophiques* (1734; *Letters Concerning the English Nation*, 1733), consisting of reflections (by implication critical of French institutions) arising from his visit to England.

Volterra Daniele Ricciarelli called Daniele da (1509–66). Italian mannerist painter, follower of Michelangelo. He is sometimes known as 'the breeches painter' because in obedience to an order from Pope Paul IV he painted draperies to cover the nudity of some of the figures in Michelangelo's *Last Judgement*. *Descent from the Cross* (Trinità dei Monti, Rome) is the most famous of his paintings.

voluntary. An organ piece usually given before or after a church service; originally and occasionally still, these pieces were improvised at the will of the performer (hence 'voluntary').

volute. The spiral scroll of an Ionic capital; used in room decoration and furniture from the Renaissance onwards. Also *order.

Vondel Joost van den (1587–1679). The greatest Dutch poet in a period of literary greatness. V.'s parents were Anabaptists who fled with him from Cologne to Amsterdam when he was still a child. He was a prolific writer, excelling in all forms. He wrote 24 plays, including *Palamedes* (1625), *Maeghden* (1639) and *Jeptha* (1659), considered by V. and many contemporaries his most important works; satirical and didactic poems on religious and political subjects; melancholy lyrics suggested by the death of his wife and 2 of his children; songs celebrating the Republic and the House of Orange, e.g. *Geboortklock van Willem van Nassau*; and long poems in defence of Catholicism after his conversion (*c.* 1640).

Von Rosen Elsa Marianne (1927–). Swedish dancer of the Swedish Ballet School. V. R. has developed in the modern idiom and time spent with cos outside Sweden has added technical strength to her style. She created the role of *Miss Julie* (1950; after Strindberg) and formed the Scandinavian Ballet in 1960.

Vörösmarty Mihály (1800–55). One of the greatest Hungarian romantic poets; he emancipated patriotic poetry from purely declamatory features. As an ed. of the journal *Tudományos Gyüjtemény* he exerted influence on the development of contemporary Hungarian literature. Of his plays *Csongor és Tünde* (1831) is the most significant; the romantic splendour of its language is unparalleled. The failure of the War of Independence in 1849 drove V. to the verge of insanity; nevertheless his later poems contain some of his greatest achievements.

vorticism. A British art movement deriving inspiration partly from cubism and futurism. The name was invented by Ezra Pound in 1913; but in 1912 Wyndham *Lewis had made vorticist drawings. The group's only exhibition took place in 1915, and included works by William Roberts, Edward Wadsworth, C. R. W. Nevinson and Gaudier-Brzeska.

Vos Cornelis de (1584–1651). Flemish painter of portraits and historical, allegorical and religious subjects; also an art dealer. He worked in Antwerp. His style of portraiture follows Rubens and Van Dyck and his paintings have sometimes been confused with theirs. *Portrait of the Artist and his Family* (1621; M.R. des B.-A., Brussels) is a good example of his work.

Vos Marten de (1531/2–1603). Flemish mannerist painter who studied under Floris, then went to Italy and worked in Venice under Tintoretto. On his return to the Netherlands the novelty of his style made him popular as a painter of religious subjects and portraits.

Vos Paul de (1596–1678). Flemish painter of hunting scenes, animals and still-life subjects, brother of Cornelis de V. He collaborated with Rubens and Snyders.

Voss (1957). Novel by Patrick *White.

Voss Johann Heinrich (1751–1826). German writer, leader of the Göttinger Dichterbund, noted for his original works, e.g. 'idylls' and *Luise* (1784), a narrative poem, and for his

Cornelis de Vos. *Family group*

Marten de Vos. *Christ on the Sea of Tiberias*

Paul de Vos. *Stag Hunt*

Vouet. *Wealth*

Vrubel. Egyptian costume design of the 1890s

outstanding trs; these include *Homers Odüssee* (1781), still one of the best German versions of Homer.

Vouet Simon (1590–1649). Leading French baroque painter and a director of taste for almost 20 years. The son of an artist, V. settled in Italy (1613), living chiefly in Rome, with periods in Genoa, Venice and Naples. His style shows an individual talent and a profound study of Italian painters, especially Veronese. V. soon enjoyed high favour, including the patronage of Pope Urban VIII. In 1627 he was invited back to France, where he became First Painter, a position challenged only once, in 1640–2, when he was brought into an artificial rivalry with Poussin. V. taught or collaborated with almost all the painters of the next generation in France, notably Lebrun, Le Sueur and Mignard. His portraits of the court of Louis XIII and most of his large-scale decorative schemes for Parisian houses and country châteaux have been destroyed. Among surviving pictures are: *Wealth* (Louvre), *Time Vanquished* (Prado) and *Ceres* (N.G., London).

voussoir. Architectural term for one of the wedge-shaped blocks of which an arch is composed.

vox celeste. Organ stop which when drawn brings into action 2 ranks of pipes, one tuned intentionally a little sharp or flat; a *beat results, giving a vibrato effect. The VOX HUMANA is a crude version of the same effect.

Voyage au bout de la nuit (1932). Novel by L.-F. *Céline.

Voysey Charles Francis Annesley (1857–1941). British architect whose houses, e.g. Broadleys, Lake Windermere (1899), were in a craftsmanly cottage style, with heavy slate roofs and roughcast walls. These houses were publ. in Germany by Muthesius, and had a great influence on German architecture at that time.

Vranckz (Vranx) Sebastian (1573–1647). Flemish painter of lively episodic scenes depicting genre subjects or military skirmishes. He was influenced by contemporary Italian painting and the work of Pieter Bruegel the Elder.

Vrubel Mikhail (1856–1910). Russian painter, theatrical designer and craftsman. He suffered from schizophrenia and ended his life in a mental asylum. Before graduating he was commissioned to work on the restoration of Byzantine frescoes in Kiev. This work prompted the artist to begin his important and persistent researches into pictorial analysis; many of his drawings, such as those for *Demon* (1890), anticipate cubist and futurist work. He was connected with the *Abramtsevo and *Talashkino colonies and the World of Art.

Vuillard Édouard (1876–1953). French painter. V. studied at the Lycée Condorcet, the École des Beaux-Arts, Paris and the Académie Julian where he met the other future nabis, including Bonnard, with whom he shared a studio. *Au Lit* (1891; M.M.A., Paris), evenly painted in flat areas, shows his current proximity to Denis's ideas. He usually painted homely interior scenes – *The Mantelpiece* (1905; Tate) – richly coloured but often low-toned and creating a strong surface pattern. Their form and content influenced Sickert and thence the Camden Town Group in London. V. lived a withdrawn life and seldom exhibited after 1914.

Vulgate: *Bible

Vyroubova Nina (1921–). Russian dancer, now French-domiciled, trained by Trefilova; she has developed in the classical tradition. Because of her command of both technique and dramatic artistry, she has become one of the memorable contemporary Giselles. Another of her great roles is the title-role of Taglioni's *La Sylphide* which she re-created in a revival by the Ballets des Champs-Élysées (1946).

Voysey. *Serpent d'Eau* (*c.* 1890)

Voysey. Perrycroft House, Colwall (1893)

Vuillard. *Interior at l'Étang-la-Ville.* Also *nabis

Wachsmann. Structural system for halls (model; 1950–3)

W

Wace Robert (*c.* 1100–after 1174). French writer, author of the verse *Roman de Brut*, a history of the Britons based on Geoffrey of Monmouth; it contains the 1st reference to King Arthur's Round Table and was one of the sources of Layamon's *Brut*. He also wrote a *Roman de Rou* about the history of the Normans.

Wachsmann Konrad (1901–). German-U.S. architect who is the leading theoretician of industrialized building. The General Panel House (1948) by Gropius and W. is one of the 1st designs for an adaptable prefabrication system to be put into production. His research into space frames led to the 'Mobilar' system for building hangars, never built but very impressive in model form.

Wackenroder Wilhelm Heinrich (1773–98). German romantic writer, author of the influential vol. of critical essays *Herzensergiessungen eines kunstliebenden Klosterbruders* (1797), a landmark in the romantics' elevation of art into a religion; a small part is by Tieck, who was W.'s intimate friend and was deeply influenced by him.

Waddell Helen (Jane) (1889–). Irish writer and a distinguished scholar, best known for her trs of medieval Latin lyrics and folk-tales; for *The Wandering Scholars* (1927), an account of the Vagantes (late medieval Latin poets); and for the novel *Peter Abelard* (1933).

Wagenaar Johan (1862–1941). Netherlands composer and teacher; director of the Dutch Conservatory in The Hague from 1919 to 1937. Among his pupils was W. Pijper. In his compositions, W. took Strauss and Berlioz as his models. His son BERNARD (1894–) is a composer and violinist; he has lived in the U.S. since 1920, and became teacher in composition at the Juillard School, New York, in 1927.

Wages of Fear, The (1953). Film directed by H.-G. *Clouzot.

Wagner Heinrich Leopold (1747–79). German playwright, for a time a friend of Goethe. Works include the tragedies *Die Reue nach der That* (1775) and *Die Kindermörderinn*, and the verse satire *Prometheus, Deukalion und seine Recensenten* (1775).

Wagner Otto (1841–1918). Viennese architect who was very academic until in the 1890s he became interested in art nouveau; his Karlsplatz Station and Majolika Haus (1899) are the leading Viennese examples of this style. After 1900 he abandoned art nouveau, and his Post Office Savings Bank (1906) is a 'machine aesthetic' building.

Wagner Richard (1813–83). German composer born in Leipzig. His life was troubled and restless; musical director to a theatre in Riga (1837), he was forced to take ship to avoid his creditors. In Paris (1839–42), where he met Berlioz and Liszt, he completed *Rienzi* and *The Flying Dutchman*, his 1st great successes. As music director at the Dresden opera (1843–8) he gained a great reputation as a conductor but had to flee after involvement in the 1848 Revolution, living in exile in Zürich until 1858. A love-affair there with Mathilde Wesendonck produced settings of 5 of her poems; during this period W. publ. important prose works. In 1861 he divorced his 1st wife, Minna. In 1864 Ludwig II of Bavaria summoned W. to Munich; there he became intimate with Cosima von Bülow (Liszt's daughter). Opposition from various quarters forced W. to leave Munich in 1865. In 1869 Siegfried, his son by Cosima, was born (W. composed the **Siegfried Idyll* for him) and following Cosima's divorce, W. married her in 1870. This period saw also the friendship between W., Cosima and Nietzsche. In 1872 W. settled in Bayreuth; here he founded the Festival Theatre for the performance of his works; it was officially opened in 1876. His many writings include important works of music criticism, an autobiography (*Newman), politico-philosophical works and anti-Semitic treatises. W.'s mature music is the high point of German romanticism and affected everything of importance which followed. His harmonic procedures became increasingly chromatic and contributed to the collapse of diatonic harmony, a collapse completed in the music of Mahler and Schoenberg.

W.'s technique of organic theme development, approach to orchestration and brilliant expressive use of instrumental colour were also profoundly influential; in opera he effected a near-revolution. Inspired by Beethoven's symphonic music, W. created a 'symphonic opera'. The *Gesammtkunstwerk*, a 'general work of art', should be an integrated composite of all the arts–music, drama and the visual arts. A necessary corollary of this was that the traditional operatic pattern–of arias, recitatives,

Otto Wagner. Post Office Savings Bank, Vienna

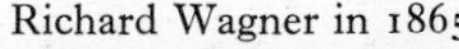

Richard Wagner in 1865

Wajda. *Ashes and Diamonds*

Arthur Waley

Edmund Waller

Wagner. *Parsifal* at Bayreuth, 1882

Wagner. *Parsifal* at Bayreuth, 1951

ensembles and choruses accompanied by a subordinate instrumental commentary and treated as distinct elements–must go. Gluck had restored the dramatic plot to the centre of *opera but W. went further, and by using *Leitmotivs* made the music itself capable of carrying and revealing the developing dramatic situation as opposed to merely illustrating it; the orchestra became equal in importance with the voices. Dramatis personae, moods, ideas and objects–each has a *Leitmotiv*, a significant fragment of melody which by recurrence and modification brings its subject immediately before the audience and at the same time conveys new aspects or emotions of the subject. The resulting complex web of music is a composition of 'endless melody', W.'s own term. W.'s work, though a continuous development, passed through 3 phases. The youthful period ending with *Rienzi* shows the influence of Meyerbeer and Parisian grand opera; the middle period ending with *Lohengrin* is romantic opera in the tradition of Weber; the final period is the full working-out of W.'s 'music-drama'. Throughout W. wrote his own librettos. The main operas follow. *Rienzi* (1842), based on Bulwer-Lytton's novel *Rienzi, the Last of the Tribunes*, on the life of Cola di Rienzi (1313–54). *The Flying Dutchman* (1843), based on Heine's version of the legend of a Dutch sea-captain doomed to voyage till Judgement Day unless he finds a maiden faithful unto death. *Tannhäuser* (1845), based on the legend surrounding the 13th-c. poet *Tannhäuser. *Lohengrin* (1850), one of the knights of the Grail, champions a maligned princess. The opera cycle *The Ring of the Nibelungs* uses the apparatus of German mythology to present symbolically the corruption of human society dominated by a lust for power. The 4 parts of 'the Ring' are *The Rhinegold* (1869), *The Valkyrie* (1870), *Siegfried* (1876) and *Götterdämmerung* (1876), 'The Twilight of the Gods'. *Tristan und Isolde* (1865), on the Celtic legend of lovers united in death. *The *Mastersingers of Nuremberg* (1868), set in medieval Germany–the story of rivalry in romance decided by victory in a singing contest. *Parsifal* (1882), a religious festival music-drama, using the legend of the Holy Grail.

Wagonmaster (1950). Film directed by J. *Ford.

Wain John (Barrington) (1925–). English novelist and poet, author of the novel *Hurry On Down* (1953), which describes its hero's adventures in search of a place outside a competitive society. It was considered one of the important works of the *angry young men.

Waiting for Godot (1957). Play by Samuel *Beckett.

Waiting for Lefty (1935). Play by Clifford *Odets.

waits or **waytes.** English town musicians. From the middle ages each important town had its band of musicians who performed at civic and ceremonial occasions and gave public performances at Christmas.

Wajda Andrzej (1926–). Polish film director. W. was assistant to A. Ford before making his famous trilogy about the war: *A Generation* (1954), *Kanal* (1957) and *Ashes and Diamonds* (1958). W. has attempted increasingly in these 3 films to achieve an elaborate and flamboyant style, at the expense of directness. *Lotna* (1959) and *Siberian Lady Macbeth* (1962) have similar tendencies.

'Wakefield Plays', The (or 'Towneley plays'). Cycle of 15th-c. English *miracle plays.

Walbaum Justus Erich (1768–1837). German type-cutter and designer whose designs were much influenced by the work of Firmin Didot. A modern fount bears his name.

Walch Jacob: Jacopo de *Barbari

Walcha Helmut (1907–). German organist, blind from the age of 16. W. is known for his scholarly and musicianly interpretations of J. S. Bach's organ works.

Walcott Derek (1930–). Poet from St Lucia; his *Twenty-Five Poems* (1948), dealing with social and racial difficulties, and verse dramas *The Sea at Dauphin* (1954), *Henri Christophe* (1955) and *Lone* (1957), and especially recent poems, *In a Green Night* (1962), undoubtedly make him the West Indies' outstanding poet.

Wald Jerry (1911–62). U.S. film producer. As an executive producer his ambitions were rarely equalled in courage or achievement by the final results. Apart from 2 films co-produced with Norman Krasna (*Clash by Night*, *The Lusty Men*), his greatest successes were among the less 'ambitious'–*An Affair to Remember* and *Pushover*.

Walden, or, Life in the Woods (1854). Book by H. D. *Thoreau.

Waldis Burkard (*c.* 1490–*c.* 1556). German fabulist and playwright, a friar who became a Lutheran; his working life was spent in Riga. W. wrote vivid fables and the *Fastnachtsspiel* ('Shrovetide play') *De Parabell vam vorlorn Szohn* (publ. 1527).

Waley Arthur (1889–). English trs. of Chinese and Japanese literature, and for the most part of Chinese poetry of the T'ang dynasty. Apparently galvanized by Ezra Pound's paraphrases of trs from the Chinese into English poetry in *Cathay* (1915), W. applied his Chinese scholarship and his own talent for the then current imagist poetry to make genuine trs, preserving the imagery of the Chinese poems but rejecting all possibility of reproducing their very strict systems of rhyme and metre. Works include *The Book of Songs* (1937), trs from the ancient classic of poetry; *Monkey* (1942); *The Poetry and Career of Li Po* (1950); *The Tale of Genji* (1939).

Walker Emery (1851–1933). English typographer, who was adviser and type-designer to the *Kelmscott Press of William Morris, the *Doves Press and the *Ashendene Press. He designed a number of types based closely on those of *Jenson. His lecture given at the Arts and Crafts Exhibition in 1888, allied to his close friendship with Morris, was the starting-point of a new movement in typography.

Walker Robert (d. 1656/8). English portrait painter famous for his portraits of Oliver Cromwell and other important Parliamentarians.

Walking Down Broadway (1932). The only sound film of E. von *Stroheim.

Walk in the Sun, A (1946). Film directed by L. *Milestone.

Wallace (Richard Horatio) Edgar (1875–1932). English novelist and playwright, an amazingly prolific and popular writer of thriller stories; examples are the play *The Ringer* (1926) and the novels *The Four Just Men* (1906) and *Sanders of the River* (1911).

Wallace Lew(is) (1827–1905). U.S. novelist, also a major-general in the Civil War, diplomat and state governor. His *Ben Hur: A Tale of the Christ* (1880), the story of the enmity between a Jewish prince and his childhood friend, a Roman, has sold millions of copies and twice (1926 and 1959) been successfully filmed. W. also wrote *The Fair God* (1873), *The Prince of India* (1893) and an autobiography.

Wallack family. English actors who spent much of their time in the U.S.A. and left their mark on the theatre of that country. Notable among them were Henry John (1790–1870), his brother James William (1791–1864), who is said to have crossed the Atlantic 35 times, and his nephew James William (1818–73).

Wallenstein. Dramatic trilogy by *Schiller.

Waller Edmund (1606–87). English poet. W.'s lucid, polished style became the model for the 18th-c. Augustan poets. His poems include the famous *Go, lovely Rose.*

Waller Fats (1904–43). U.S. jazz pianist and a popular entertainer as a humorous singer.

Waller Fred: *Cinerama

Wallis Alfred (1855–1942). English primitive painter. He worked as a fisherman in St Ives, Cornwall from 1892, starting to paint (St Ives and the sea) only in 1928. Ben Nicholson and the painter Christopher Wood were chiefly responsible for discovering him.

Wallis Hal B. (1899–). Film producer. W. entered films in 1922 via Warners' publicity department. His first films as a producer were *Little Caesar* and *I Am a Fugitive from a Chain Gang*. After these social message films, and romantic melodramas in the 1940s, he has settled down to a steady mixture of stage adaptations (like *Come Back, Little Sheba*) and comedies with Presley and Lewis.

Wallis Henry (1830–1916). English painter and authority on Persian ceramics, known for his *Death of Chatterton* (1856; Tate), for which the model was George Meredith. W.'s career was interrupted by the scandal of his elopement with Meredith's wife (1858). Other works, including *The Stonebreaker* (1858), are at Birmingham.

Robert Walker. *Cromwell*

Wallis. *The Stonebreaker*. Also *Chatterton

Alfred Wallis. *Cornish Port*

Horace Walpole.
Also *'Gothick'

Thomas Ustick Walter. Girard College

Izaak Walton: etching and poem by Joseph Crawhall. Also **Compleat Angler*

Bruno Walter conducting

Walsh. Agnes Moorehead and Jane Russell in *The Revolt of Mamie Stover*

Walpole Horace, 4th Earl of Orford (1717–97). English author, the son of Sir Robert Walpole. W.'s reputation rests on his witty and informative letters and *The Castle of Otranto* (1764), which started the vogue of the *Gothic novel. In 1747 he acquired a house at Strawberry Hill, Twickenham, which he gradually turned into a small 'Gothick' castle and made a storehouse of picturesque *objets d'art*.

Walpole Sir Hugh (Seymour) (1884–1941). English novelist. His works include *Rogue Herries* (1930) and subsequent books of the *Herries Chronicle*.

Walsh Raoul (1892–). U.S. film director. At first an actor, in 1912 he became assistant to Griffith, who sent him to Mexico to shoot his 1st film, *Life of Villa* (1912). He played John Wilkes Booth in *Birth of a Nation*, and continued acting until he lost an eye in an accident. His silent films include the Douglas Fairbanks *Thief of Bagdad* (1924) and the Gloria Swanson *Sadie Thompson* (1928). Although the vast list of his films includes almost every genre, his favourite has always been the adventure film. At the beginning of World War II he made thrillers about usually psychopathic criminals: *The Roaring Twenties* (1939), *They Drive By Night* (1940), *High Sierra* (1941) and later, *White Heat* (1949). His films of the 1940s were tough and unsentimental: *They Died With Their Boots On* (1941), *Objective Burma* (1945), *Pursued* (1947); those of the 1950s were more mellow–a typical hero is Clark Gable in *The Tall Men* (1955), *A King and Four Queens* (1956) and *Band of Angels* (1957), a good-humoured adventurer. But *Battle Cry* (1955) and his version of Norman Mailer's *The Naked and the Dead* (1958) are uncompromisingly hard.

Walter Bruno (1876–1962). German-born conductor (full name B. W. Schlesinger) who took successively French and then U.S. nationality. He was a close friend of Mahler and specialized also in Mozart's music; W. also composed.

Walter Thomas Ustick (1804–87). U.S. architect. He completed the Capitol, Washington by adding wings and a huge cast-iron dome (1855–65) mainly Renaissance in inspiration. His other buildings are mostly more Greek, e.g. Girard College, Philadelphia.

Walters Charles. U.S. film director who started in films as a choreographer at M.G.M. (1942) where he has worked ever since. He choreographed *Meet Me in St Louis* and his forte as a director (since 1947) has been musicals, e.g. *Summer Stock* (1950), *Easter Parade* (1948), and *High Society* (1956).

Walther Johann (1496–1570). German religious composer, a friend of Luther, with whom he collaborated on several books of hymns. He also wrote the 1st setting in German of the Passion story.

Walther Johann Gottfried (1684–1748). German organist and composer; at Weimar (1708–14) a friend of J. S. Bach, who received a large notice in W.'s *Musicalisches Lexicon* (1732), the 1st biographical music dictionary.

Walther von der Vogelweide (*c.* 1170–*c.* 1228). German poet, greatest of the *minnesingers; he was born in S. Germany and wrote in the 'Bavarian' (S. German) dialect. He worked in Vienna at the court of Duke Leopold V until 1198, when he lost the favour of Leopold's successor. He was the most versatile exponent of *Minnesang*, the narrow appeal of which he transcends. He was also the effective creator of the German political and patriotic poem, which he used for propaganda purposes in the long struggles over the succession to the Holy Roman Empire and in the quarrel between Frederick II and the Pope.

Walton Henry (1746–1813). English painter remembered for his rare genre scenes such as *Girl Plucking a Turkey* (*c.* 1776; Tate). These scenes are strongly influenced by Greuze's treatment of similar themes but they also show (unusual in England) the influence of Chardin.

Walton Sir Izaak (1593–1683). English writer. Although simply a fishing handbook, W.'s *The Compleat Angler, or the Contemplative Man's Recreation* (1653) has become an English classic because of the charm of its style and tone. The 5th ed. contained a continuation by Charles *Cotton. W. also wrote biographies of Donne, Wotton, Hooker and Herbert.

Walton Sir William (Turner) (1902–). English composer. An early string quartet (1923) showed an interest in Schoenberg and Bartók; and *Façade* (1923; ballet 1931) to words for speaker by Edith Sitwell, brilliantly and wittily set, used jazz elements to heighten the effect;

James Ward. *Gordale Scar*

The Wanderers. Kramskoy, *Portrait of a Miller*

Sir William Walton

but W.'s style developed into a form of romanticism. His works include: the opera *Troilus and Cressida* (1954), based on Chaucer; the oratorio *Belshazzar's Feast* (1931); 2 symphonies (1935; 1960); *Sinfonia Concertante* for piano and orchestra; a viola concerto (1929), 1st performance by Hindemith; the overture *Portsmouth Point*; 2 further string quartets (1937 and 1947) and film music.

waltz. Dance in a lilting 3-in-a-bar time; originating in Germany in the mid 18th c., probably from the **Ländler*, and enjoying a European vogue in the early 19th c. The most famous examples of the w. are the Viennese w.s of the *Strauss family; the w. has often been used as a movement or section of larger works by Haydn, Weber, Berlioz, R. *Strauss and others.

Wanderers, The. Group of itinerant Russian artists who revolted from the Imperial Academy of Arts in St Petersburg in 1863. In 1870 they were formally established. Like their friends the writers Turgenev and Tolstoy, they were fired by ideas of bringing art to the people and organized exhibitions throughout the countryside; their themes were taken from peasant life and were strictly didactic in aim, scorning technical preoccupations.

Wanger Walter (1894–). U.S. film producer. Since 1933 he has been among the most ambitious and intelligent producers in Hollywood, working either as a studio executive or as an independent. Producer of *Cleopatra*.

War and Peace (1869). Novel by *Tolstoy; made into a film (1956), directed by K. *Vidor and M. *Soldati.

Ward Artemus. Pseud. of Charles Farrar Browne (1834–67). U.S. humorous writer who won fame by contributing 'letters' by an illiterate showman, W., to the Cleveland *Plain Dealer*; thereafter the real author was best known by the name of his character. W.'s humour, derived from Seba *Smith and itself long and widely imitated, leaned strongly on bad grammar and misspellings, and on the incongruities produced by dialect speech when it attempts to cope with unfamiliar situations. Colls include *Artemus Ward, His Book* (1862).

Ward Edward (1667–1731). English writer, author of *The London Spy* (1698–1703), a humorous description of London life.

Ward Elizabeth Stuart Phelps (1844–1911). U.S. novelist, author of such elevating, sentimental religious fiction as *The Gates Ajar* (1868).

Ward Mrs Humphry (1851–1920). English novelist, author of *Robert Elsmere* (1888), a once-famous novel which emphasized the social mission of Christianity.

Ward James (1769–1859). English romantic painter and engraver. His early paintings were genre subjects influenced by his brother-in-law George Morland. But he was a far more robust artist and developed into a romantic realist of considerable power, much influenced by Rubens's landscapes. He painted the combat of powerful animals, portraits (including portraits of madmen), wild allegories, and sporting subjects. His masterpiece is the huge sombre landscape *Gordale Scar* (Tate). Géricault admired and was influenced by his work.

Warden, The (1855). Novel by *Trollope.

Warlock Peter. Pseud. of Philip Heseltine (1894–1930). English composer. Under his own name he publ. eds of Elizabethan songs, etc. and acted as Delius's amanuensis; as W. ('male witch') he composed music in a contemporary idiom reminiscent of Delius. He committed suicide. Works include: many songs; *The Curlew*, a lengthy song cycle from W. B. Yeats, for tenor, flute, cor anglais and string quartet, and *Capriol Suite* for string orchestra, an adaptation of Elizabethan tunes.

Warner Charles Dudley (1829–1900). U.S. satirical novelist and essayist, chiefly remembered as Mark Twain's collaborator in writing *The Gilded Age* (1873), a Dickensian concoction mixing sentiment with exposure of political and social abuses.

Warner Rex (1905–). English novelist and poet, author of semi-surrealist novels (e.g. *The Kite*, 1936; *The Professor*, 1938; *The Aerodrome*, 1941) in which the influence of Kafka is apparent, and the skilful 'autobiographies' *The Young Caesar* (1958) and *Imperial Caesar* (1960).

Warner Sylvia Townsend (1893–). English novelist and short-story writer, witty and sharp; her subject-matter is fanciful. Works include *Lolly Willowes* (1926) and *Mr Fortune's Maggot* (1927).

Warner William (1558?–1609). English writer once greatly admired, author of *Albion's England* (1586–1612), a verse history.

War of the Worlds, The (1898). Science-fiction novel by H. G. *Wells.

Warren Robert Penn (1905–). U.S. novelist and poet. W. championed the *new criticism, notably in *Understanding Poetry* (1939, written in collaboration with C. Brooks) and his editorship of *The Southern Review*. W.'s most famous novel is *All the King's Men* (1946), which describes the career of a Southern governor said to have been modelled on Huey Long.

Warren Samuel (1807–77). English writer, author of *Passages from the Diary of a Late Physician* (1831) and the popular novel *Ten Thousand a Year* (1839–41).

War Requiem (1963). Work by Benjamin *Britten.

Warton Thomas (1728–90). English poet and poet laureate from 1785. His verse in many respects anticipated that of the romantics in its attitude to nature. His brother Joseph (1722–1800) attacked earlier 18th-c. notions of correctness in poetry.

Washington Booker (Taliaferro) (1856–1915). U.S. Negro writer and outstanding educationalist; his father was a white man. Works include the autobiography *Up from Slavery* (1901).

Washington George (1732–99). 1st U.S. president, the colonists' leader in the War of Independence. His famous *Farewell Address*, publ., not spoken (1796), was written with the help of friends.

Washington Square (1880). Novel by Henry James.

Wasps, The (422 B.C.). Comedy by *Aristophanes.

Wasserman Jacob (1873–1934). German novelist whose books, blending the sensational with the metaphysical, enjoyed a great reputation in the 1920s and 1930s. They include *Die Juden von Zirndorf* (1897; *The Jews of Zirndorf*, 1933) and *Der Fall Maurizius* (1928; *The Maurizius Case*, 1930).

Waterhouse. The Town Hall, Manchester

Waste Land, The (1922). Poem by T. S. *Eliot.

Water Babies, The (1863). Children's book by *Kingsley.

watercolour. Painting in colours which are soluble in water (bound with gum-arabic or similar substances) on white or tinted paper. W.s were known in 2nd-c. A.D. Egypt, but became an important art with Dürer; a tradition of w. painting was created by English painters from the 19th c.

Waterford: *Irish glass

Waterhouse Alfred (1830–1905). English architect, prolific but undistinguished. His best building is the Natural History Mus., Kensington, an enthusiastic exercise in Romanesque. His other works, mostly rather coarse neo-Gothic, include the Prudential Building, Holborn; Town Hall, Manchester; Eaton Hall, Cheshire; and additions to Gonville and Caius College, Cambridge.

Watteau. *Mezzetino with a Guitar*

waterleaf. A decorative motif of leaf shape, usually ribless, used on gold and silver plate during the neo-classical period (1770–1830).

Water Music, The (1715). Suite of instrumental pieces by *Handel.

Watson Thomas (1557?–92). English poet. His works include . . . *Passionate Centurie of Love* (1582) and *The First Sett of Italian Madrigals Englished* (1590).

Watt (1953). Novel by Samuel Beckett.

Watt Harry (1906–). Scottish film director. W. assisted Flaherty on *Man of Aran* before writing and directing a number of 1930s documentaries including *Night Mail* (1936, with B. Wright) and *North Sea* (1938). His 1st feature, *Target for Tonight* (1941), was a dramatized documentary on a bombing raid, and there is a strong documentary background in later fiction films, e.g. *The Overlanders* (1946).

Watteau Jean-Antoine (1684–1721). French painter, draughtsman and etcher. His life is well documented since both his dealer Gersaint and his friends wrote his biography. From his provincial home in Valenciennes and an apprenticeship to obscure master painters, W. made his way to Paris, where he at first worked as a hack copyist. From 1703 for 5 years he was assistant to Gillot, the leading painter of fashionable Italian theatrical scenes, painter of the *commedia dell'arte*. W. now joined Audran the court painter, who was charged with decorations of the royal châteaux. His artistic training was now complete and his social ascendancy just beginning. He became a recorder of the social life of his times, a celebrated painter whose patrons were the richest men of France. He was invited to join the French Academy and in 1717 became a full member.
W.'s work was 'the deification of the ideals of the 18th c., the spirit of the period . . .'. His world of reality was the reality of the fairy-story, where women became goddesses and men satyrs in fashionable clothes. He transformed the coarse and earthly into dreams and fantasy.
W. was deeply imbued with the spirit of the great colourists of the past. He had ample opportunity to study the paintings of the masters in the colls of his patrons, and he copied avidly. Rubens and the painters of the Venetian school were the greatest influences on his development. The *Harlequin and Columbine* (*c.* 1715; Wallace Coll., London) shows this influence clearly, but the exquisite delicacy of the draughtsmanship and the dream-like sentiment is that of the mature W. His Academy presentation piece, and perhaps his most famous painting, the *Embarkation for Cythera* (Louvre) was painted in 1717. Here the spirit of the French rococo found its 1st full expression. Elegant courtiers wend their way to a landing-stage, where cherubs wait to conduct them to the island. One of the last and greatest paintings is the sign of the picture dealer Gersaint. Painted in 1720, it is said in a matter of 8 days, it was a triumph of observation, composition and draughtsmanship. The execution and treatment of colour foreshadows the impressionists.

Watts George Frederick (1817–1904). English painter. He supported himself by painting portraits now considered among his best works, though W. thought them unimportant compared with his allegorical compositions; in these, e.g. *Hope* (Tate), he aimed to deliver a timeless and universal message based on his own vague moral idealism. W. was also a sculptor, e.g. the huge equestrian statue *Physical Energy* in Kensington Gardens.

Watteau. *Embarkation for Cythera*

G. F. Watts. *Hope*. Also *Browning, *Meredith, *Swinburne, *Tennyson

Philip Webb. The 'Red House'

Watts Isaac (1674–1748). English hymn writer and poet, a Nonconformist pastor. W.'s *Divine Songs for Children* (1715) was required reading for generations of children, and in spite of absurdities has simple, skilful and moving passages, many of which have become proverbial, e.g. 'Satan finds some mischief still for idle hands to do'. W.'s hymns include the enduringly popular 'When I survey the wondrous Cross' and 'O God, our help in ages past'.

Watts-Dunton (Walter) Theodore (1832–1914). English critic. Swinburne spent his last 30 years (1879–1909) under W.-D.'s care and control.

Waugh Evelyn (1903–1966). English novelist, author of many very popular satirical works, including *Decline and Fall* (1928), *Vile Bodies* (1930) and *Put Out More Flags* (1942), which comment scathingly on English society in the 1920s and 1930s. W.'s belief in aristocracy and Catholicism (he became a convert in 1930) is expressed more positively in the serious *Brideshead Revisited* (1945) and the biographies *Edmund Campion* (1935) and *Ronald Knox* (1959).

Waverley (1814). Historical novel by Sir Walter *Scott.

Waves, The (1931). Novel by Virginia Woolf.

Waxworks (1924). Film directed by P. *Leni.

Way Down East (1920). Film directed by D. W. *Griffith.

Wayne John (1907–). U.S. film actor, producer and director. A long association with John Ford brought W. stardom in *Stagecoach* (1939). He has become the image of the wry, slow-talking, but rugged and hard-fighting frontiersman or officer of western and war pictures. W.'s co., Batjac Productions, have made such films as *Seven Men from Now* and W. directed and starred in *The Alamo* (1960).

Way of All Flesh, The (1903). Novel by Samuel *Butler.

Way of the World, The (1699). Comedy by *Congreve.

Wealth of Nations, The (1776). Book by Adam *Smith.

Webb Sir Aston (1849–1930). English architect of mediocre talents, though his works are conspicuous. They include the main front of the Victoria and Albert Museum, Kensington; the façade of Buckingham Palace (a mere facing applied to Blore's earlier E. wing) and the Admiralty Arch, London.

Webb Jack (1920–). U.S. film actor and director. W. directed 2 very successful radio, then TV series which he used as the basis of films: *Dragnet* (1954), a thriller, and *Pete Kelly's Blues* (1955), about a jazz musician during Prohibition, which became an elaborate and baroque film.

Webb John (1611–72). English architect trained by Inigo Jones. The Civil War deprived him of the Surveyorship, and after the Restoration he was passed over in favour of more devoted Royalists. His chief work is the King Charles Block of Greenwich Hospital, a design followed by later architects.

Webb Philip (1831–1915). Victorian architect, best known as architect of the 'Red House' at Bexleyheath, Kent for his friend William Morris. The style of the house is simple, relaxed and slightly medieval, but W.'s later work is more formal. His connection with Morris was close, and he was responsible for much of the architectural work and furniture design of Morris and Co.

Weber Carl Maria von (1786–1826). German composer; his teachers were Michael Haydn and the Abbé Vogler. He was director of the German opera at Dresden from 1817 and later went to London where he conducted the première of his opera *Oberon* (1826); he died 2 months later. In 1844 his body was brought back to Dresden at the instigation of Wagner, who composed a funeral march for the re-interment. W.'s music, which to his countrymen seemed to embody the patriotic fervour of the times (he set T. *Körner's *Leyer und Schwert*), is of prime importance in the development of romanticism in music. In his opera *Der Freischütz* (1820) the forces of nature are portrayed and used as symbols of the forces of good and evil and W.'s orchestral techniques in the exploitation of instrumental tone colours prepare the way for the work of later romantics. His other works include the opera *Euryanthe* (1823); incidental music including the *Preciosa* and *Turandot* overtures; a concert piece for

Evelyn Waugh

Carl Maria von Weber

Weber. *The Geranium* (1911)

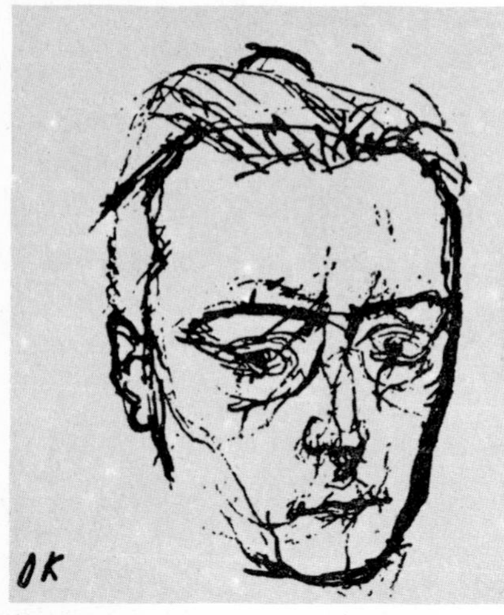

Anton Webern: drawing by Kokoschka

piano and orchestra; a concertino and 2 concertos for clarinet; chamber music including a clarinet quintet, and piano music including *Invitation to the Dance* (1819), orchestrated by Berlioz.

Weber Max (1881–1961). Russian-born U.S. painter who studied in Paris (1905–8), for a time under Matisse, and was a pioneer of *avant-garde* European art movements in the U.S. before World War I. From fauvism he turned to cubism and in *The Geranium* (1911; M.M.A., New York) began to evolve a style which combined cubism and expressionism. He attained complete cubist abstraction in *Chinese Restaurant* (1915; Whitney Mus., New York). From 1918 he painted in a representational expressionist idiom.

Webern Anton (1883–1945). Austrian composer, also a distinguished conductor and a musicologist. At Vienna Univ. in the early 1900s he met Schoenberg, becoming his 1st pupil and a close friend. From 1922 to 1934 he directed the Vienna Workmen's Symphony Orchestra and later worked for the Austrian Radio Corporation. He died at a village near Salzburg, shot by a U.S. soldier.
W. adopted the *twelve-note method of Schoenberg and was with him and Berg a founder of the school of composers in this idiom; after World War II W.'s music served as the starting-point for a major group of young *avant-garde* continental composers. W.'s studies in medieval music and its complex rhythms, closed forms and canonic procedures is to be found reflected in his music. Characteristically his pieces are short (sometimes a matter of seconds), concise and intense, often without repetition of themes; the parts move in wide interval leaps, the instrumentation produces unique effects of tone colour, sound quality and pitch are seen as related. His works include: the tonal, almost Brahmsian, *Passacaglia* for orchestra (1908); *Six Pieces* for large orchestra (1909); *Two songs after poems by R. M. Rilke* (1912); *Five Pieces* for orchestra; *Concerto* for 9 instruments (1934); *Variations* for orchestra (1940); an orchestration of the *Ricercare* of Bach's *Musical Offering* which uses instrumental colour to emphasize structural features of the work. W. also wrote many sets of songs, and a symphony.

Webster John (1580?–1625?). English playwright. In 1602 W. began work as a collaborator-dramatist for Philip Henslowe's co. Superficially similar to *Tourneur's, his 2 best plays, *The White Devil* (1612) and *The Duchess of Malfi* (1623) are distinguished by their moral stature and their deeper realization of character, the subtlety with which W. uses the horrible incidents of his plots, both taken from Italian history, and his death-obsessed poetry, at its height in the scene where the radiant and tender duchess of Malfi is murdered. Shakespeare's heir and debtor, W. had learned from him the power of simple utterance in moments of unbearable dramatic stress.

Webster Noah (1758–1843). U.S. lexicographer. W. took part in the War of Independence and later tackled many subjects as educator, pamphleteer and journalist, always emphasizing the duty of the U.S. to create a national (in particular, non-British) culture. To this end he compiled *The American Dictionary of the English Language* (1828) which, issued in a one-vol. ed. (1847), became a best-seller. *Webster's Dictionary*, frequently revised, has become a standard authority.

Webster Thomas (1800–86). English painter of scenes of school and village life, e.g. *A Village Choir* (V. and A.).

Weckmann Mathias (*c.* 1619–74). German organist and composer who worked at Dresden with *Schütz and from 1655 in Hamburg, where he inaugurated an important series of concerts. His compositions unite the styles of Sweelinck and Schütz and also show the influence of Froberger, whom W. once defeated in a keyboard contest.

Wedderburn John (*c.* 1495–1553). Scottish poet, probably the author of *The Gude and Godlie Ballatis* (1567), a coll. of verses, popular songs, etc. adapted to religious themes.

Wedding March, The (1928). Film directed by E. von *Stroheim.

Wedekind Frank (1864–1918). German playwright, notably of tragedies of sex combining expressionist and symbolist elements, e.g. *Frühlings Erwachen* (1891; *Spring's Awakening*, 1923), the tragedy resulting from repression and hypocrisy. W.'s work had an enduring influence on the post-war German expressionist drama.

Wedgwood Josiah (1730–95). English potter. The ware produced by him and his successors to the present day is called 'Wedgwood'. By his refinement of cream-coloured earthenware ('creamware') and basaltes, and his invention of other bodies such as jasperware W. revolutionized the English pottery industry, making its products for the 1st time available to a large public. His perfection of creamware followed innovations made earlier in the 18th c. by such potters as John Astbury, Enoch Booth and Thomas Whieldon. In 1763 W. bought from the inventors the right to do transfer printing on pottery, a process that drastically reduced the time and cost of producing decorated creamware. The most ambitious example of this 'Queen's ware' (so called by W. after he had obtained royal patronage in 1765) is the service of 952 pieces made in 1774 for the Empress Catherine of Russia, decorated with 1244 views of English estates. Tableware of high quality supplied a large market in England and abroad; this 'useful ware' was the real basis of the W. industry. Its commercial success enabled W. to develop at the same time his 'ornamental ware' which supplied the quite different demands of the neo-classical taste; it was made at W.'s factory 'Etruria' (opened 1769) in Burslem, Staffs. (so called after the vases being excavated in Etruria; it was only later realized that they were Greek). He evolved BASALTES, a fine-grained, unglazed black stoneware made by staining the body with manganese oxide, from *Egyptian Black. He used it to imitate Greek vases, antique busts and gems, of which he made many copies, employing artists who included Flaxman and Reynolds and gem engravers such as the Tassie brothers. Plaques, seals, etc. of original design were also made. Highly durable and capable of bearing a stronger fire than natural basalt, W. basaltes produces sparks when struck by steel. Jewellers, goldsmiths and silversmiths use it as a touchstone for testing metals. He invented JASPERWARE, a white porcellaneous stoneware with a perfectly white, extremely hard body which could be high fired to the point of semi-vitrification and required no glazing; it contained sulphate of barium and could be stained to many colours with metallic oxide (*c.* 1774). It could receive colour throughout its substance by mixing (solid jasper) or be dipped in colour (jasper dip). The range comprised 3 blacks, 4 whites, 5 blues, 6 greens, 3 reds, 2 yellows, as well as lilac, rose, plum, chocolate, buff and cane. Combinations, especially of a cameo, were used. Relief decoration in white was moulded separately and applied.

Weelkes Thomas (1575–1623). English madrigal composer. His work, among the boldest harmonically of the English school, shows the influence of Marenzio; his publs include *Madrigals of 5 and 6 parts, apt for the viol and voices* (1600) and *Ayres or Phantasticke Spirites for 3 voices* (1608). W. also contributed to Morley's *The Triumphs of Oriana* and wrote about 10 services and 40 anthems.

Weenix Jan (d. 1719). Dutch still-life and landscape painter, son and pupil of Jan Baptist W. He worked in Amsterdam and at the court of the Elector Palatine, for whom he executed a series of paintings of live and dead game.

Weenix Jan Baptist (1621–60). Dutch painter who studied under A. Bloemaert, then in Italy. In addition to Italianate landscapes he painted still-life subjects and portraits.

Weigel Helene (1900–). German actress; she married Bertolt Brecht in 1928, played principal roles in many of his plays at their 1st performance and with him founded and has continued to work in the *Berliner Ensemble; her most famous part is that of Mother Courage.

Weil Simone (1909–43). French Jewish writer on religious, social and political questions. Works include *L'Attente de Dieu* (1950), a spiritual autobiography relating her progress towards a form of Christian belief.

Weill Kurt (1900–50). German composer; he settled in the U.S. in 1935, becoming naturalized in 1943. His teachers included Busoni, and W. wrote instrumental works, e.g. 2 symphonies and a concerto for wind instruments; but already in 1926 he was producing stage music, for Georg Kaiser, and in 1928 collaboration with *Brecht produced *Die Dreigroschenoper*. Both in this and the opera *Mahagonny* (1930), reworked from an earlier version (1927), W.'s witty, spiky music, using jazz elements, with emotive as well as satiric effects, became inseparable from Brecht's words. Later works in the U.S. included music (e.g. 'September Song') for such Broadway musicals as *Knickerbocker Holiday* (1938).

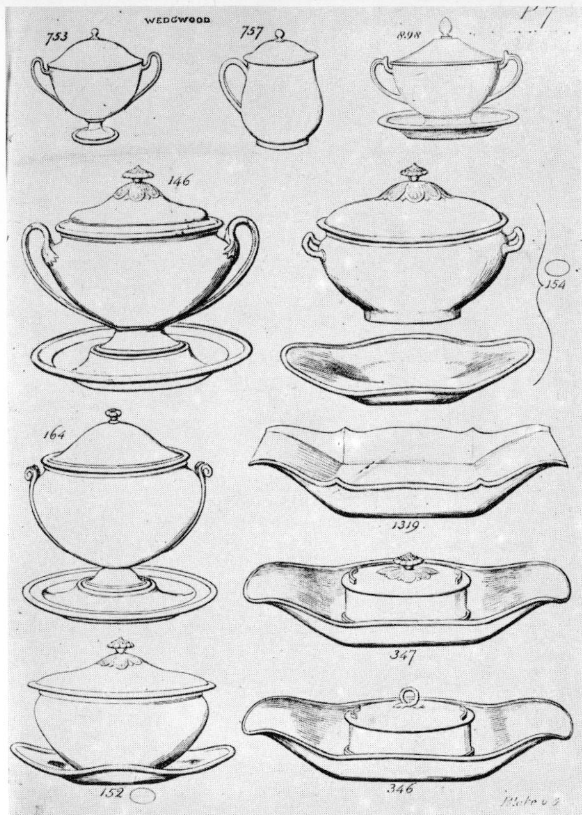

Wedgwood catalogue page of the early 19th c.

Jan Weenix. *Still-life with dead Hare*

Helene Weigel: painting by Rudolf Schlichter

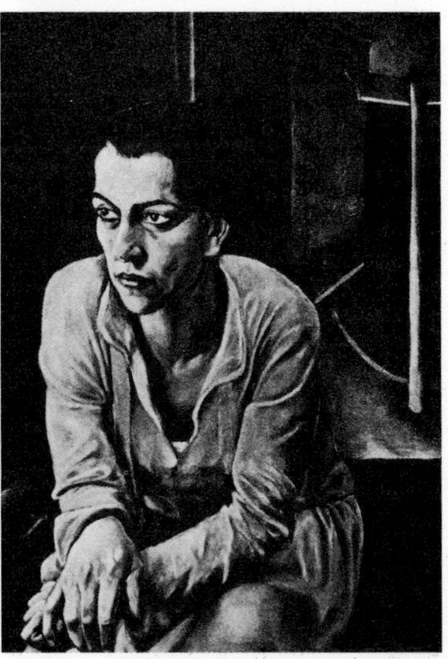

Wedgwood. The Portland Vase. Also *Homeric Vase, *Queen's ware

Wedgwood. One of the vases (black basalt with red-painted figures) thrown on the 1st day at Etruria

Wedgwood. Slave Medallion: 'Am I not a man and a brother?'

Kurt Weill

Orson Welles in *Citizen Kane*

Weis. Donald O'Connor and Debbie Reynolds in *I Love Melvin*

Wellman. Janet Gaynor, Fredric March and Adolphe Menjou in *A Star is Born*

Weinberger Jaromir (1896–). Czech composer known for his opera *Svanda the Bagpiper* (1927), which uses folk themes. He has written 4 more operas, *8 Préludes Réligieux et Profanes* (1952), and other works.

Weingartner Felix Paul von (1863–1942). Austrian conductor, Mahler's successor at the Vienna court opera, and composer–at first composing in a Wagnerian idiom but developing an individual style.

Weis Don (1922–). U.S. film director. W. made 9 films between 1950 and 1954, when political troubles made him move to TV. From this period, a musical, *I Love Melvin* (1952), a comedy thriller, *Remains to be Seen* (1953), and *The Adventures of Hajji Baba* (1954) are outstanding. He has since made *The Gene Krupa Story* (1960) and a comedy, *Critic's Choice* (1962).

Weiss Peter (1916–). German artist and writer living mainly in Sweden since 1939. In form his play *Der Verfolgung und Ermordung Jean Paul Marat* (1964; *The Death of Marat*, 1964) is a reconstruction of an imaginative play written and produced in the Charenton Asylum by de *Sade.

Orson Welles in *Touch of Evil*

Welch Denton (1917–48). English novelist; trained as a painter. Most of W.'s fiction is autobiographical. He was involved in a road accident and never recovered from the injuries, though it was years before he died; the story is told in *A Voice Through a Cloud* (1950).

well. In architecture, the space round which a circular staircase winds, or any similar shaft-like space (e.g. a lift-w.) in the middle of a building.

Welles Orson (1915–). U.S. film director and actor. W. started acting at the Gate Theatre, Dublin at the age of 16, and 5 years later was directing for the Federal Theater and for Mercury Theater, which he founded in 1937. He also directed, wrote and acted for radio–his realistic production of H. G. Wells's *War of the Worlds* caused a panic–and made his 1st film, *Citizen Kane*, in 1941. This instantly received and has kept an enormous reputation for its complex narrative, formed by the memories of a series of narrators, and particularly for its use of wide-angle, deep-focus photography, which W. and his cinematographer G. *Toland used–not for the 1st time, but more strikingly than ever before. The technique allowed W. to shoot complex scenes using camera movements and movements of the actors within the frame instead of conventional cutting. He carried the technique even further in *The Magnificent Ambersons* (1942), combining its use with overlapping conversations as the camera and microphone pick up successive couples in the ball scene. *The Stranger* (1946) was an attempt at a conventional thriller, but it was little more conventional than the extraordinary *Lady from Shanghai* (1947). His 2 Shakespeare adaptations take great liberties with the text, but *Othello* (1952) and to a lesser extent *Macbeth* (1947) are remarkable pictures. In them W. plays the part which was identifiable in embryo in *Kane* but already developed in *Journey into Fear* (1942, finished by and credited to Norman Foster): the flawed genius, the man corrupted and finally destroyed by his own power. In a modern setting, stylized and baroque–full of low-angle deep-focus shots of the looming W.–the W. hero reached his apotheosis in *Confidential Report* (or *Mr Arkadin*, 1955) and *Touch of Evil* (1957). After a still uncompleted *Don Quixote* (1957), he shot an adaptation of *The Trial* (1962) in which his view of the world proves to be incompatible with Kafka's. He returns to Shakespeare in *Chimes at Midnight* (1965), from *Henry IV*.

Wellesz Egon (1885–). Austrian composer and musicologist making major contributions to the study of Byzantine music; he settled in England in 1938. He studied composition under Schoenberg and Mahler; W.'s music, showing at first the influence of Schoenberg, but later returning to a less advanced idiom, includes: the operas *Alcestis* (1924) and *Incognita* (1951); 5 symphonies; church music and chamber works.

Wellington's Victory. Alternative name for *Beethoven's 'Battle Symphony'.

Wellman William (1896–). U.S. film director who has made a number of outstanding films in widely differing genres. He has no very personal idiom but his work is always craftsmanlike. Films include: *Wings* (1927), with superb flying sequences; *Public Enemy* (1931) a vivid gangster drama with James Cagney and Jean Harlow; *Nothing Sacred* (1937), with

Egon Wellesz: painting by Kokoschka

Wendkos. *Angel Baby*

H. G. Wells

Franz Werfel

a deliciously absurd Hecht script; *A Star is Born* (1937), the archetypal rags-to-riches woman's picture; *Ox-Bow Incident* (1943), a sombre drama in western setting about lynching; and *The Story of G.I. Joe* (1945).

Wells H(erbert) G(eorge) (1866–1946). English writer. He was apprenticed first to a draper and then to a chemist. He gained a scholarship to the Royal College of Science, and then obtained a science degree through the Univ. Correspondence College, and became a science instructor in 1890. When his 1st marriage ended in divorce in 1895 he married one of his pupils, Catherine Roberts; this situation is reflected in *Ann Veronica* (1909).
When ill-health interrupted his scientific work he turned to 'science fiction', producing works of great imagination–*The Time Machine* (1895), *The Invisible Man* (1897), *The War of the Worlds* (1898), *The First Men in the Moon* (1901). From 1900 to 1908 he wrote 4 outlines of an ideal society to be ruled by the intellectually gifted; this interest in sociology was more creatively used in his novels of lower-middle-class life; e.g. *Kipps* (1905) and *Tono-Bungay* (1909), drawing on the experiences of his apprenticeship, *The History of Mr Polly* (1910) and *Love and Mr Lewisham* (1900). They combine a warm sense of humour with a profound faith in science and progress. Later novels became increasingly doctrinaire, and he abandoned the novel for philosophical works, including his extremely popular *Outline of History* (1920). 2 World Wars and the beginning of the Atomic age destroyed his faith in human destiny, and his last writings are very pessimistic.

Wells Reginald (1877–1951). English artist potter (up to 1909), the 1st important figure to turn to the English tradition for inspiration.

Wells cathedral Somerset (begun *c.* 1180). Chancel, transepts and nave form one of the outstanding examples of Early English architecture. In the decorated period (*c.* 1330) the tower was heightened, necessitating the extraordinary strainer arches across the nave and transepts, the beautiful octagonal chapter-house was built and the W. front finished (not according to the original intention) with 2 low towers.

Well Tempered Clavier. English name for 2 sets of 24 preludes (commonly called 'The Forty Eight') by J. S. Bach.

Wendkos Paul. U.S. film director. W. first made independently a striking low-budget thriller, *The Burglar* (1957). His taste for cathartic violence has run through all his best films, whether western (*Face of a Fugitive*, 1959) or crime picture (*The Case Against Brooklyn*, 1958). *Angel Baby* (1961) deals with the relationship between religion and sex.

Werfel Franz (1890–1945). Austrian expressionist novelist, playwright and poet. W. was born in Prague, settled in Vienna, fled (1938) to France, and after the fall of France to the U.S., where he died. W.'s work is often bitter and denunciatory, condemning man's guilt; but behind all of it lies a conviction of human worth and of the necessity of solidarity. Works include the dramatic trilogy *Der Spiegelmensch* (1920), a reworking of the Faust theme; and the novels *Barbara oder die Frömmigkeit* (1929; *The Pure in Heart*, 1931) and *Das veruntreute Himmel* (1939; *Embezzled Heaven*, 1940).

Werff Adriaen van der (1659–1722). Dutch painter of portraits and religious, mythological and genre subjects; also an architect. In his early paintings he followed the style of his master, van der Neer, but he was later influenced by contemporary French classicism. His mature work has an exceptionally high finish.

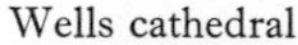

Werff Pieter van der (1665–1722). Dutch painter of portraits and Biblical and mythological subjects, brother and imitator of the above.

Wergeland Henrik Arnold (1808–45). Norwegian romantic poet, the son of a clergyman. W. was the leading figure of his generation, prolific as a republican and democratic journalist and as a playwright. In spite of rhetorical extravagances and carelessness, he produced many important poems–short lyrics and longer poems like *Den engelske Lods* (1845).

Werner Friedrich Ludwig Zacharias (1768–1823). German romantic playwright. W.'s life was restless and dissolute–with bursts of piety –until his 40s, when he was converted to Catholicism and ultimately became a priest. His works have elements of crudity, but are theatrically effective and mark an advance in the romantic drama. They include *Martin Luther, oder die Wiehe der Kraft* (1807), *Attila, König der Hunnen* (1808) and *Wanda, Königen der Sarmaten* (1810).

Wells cathedral

Werner. *Astral Flowers* (1951)

Benjamin West. *Death of Wolfe*

Werner Theodor (1886–). German abstract expressionist painter. He studied at Stuttgart Academy (1908–9) and lived in Paris from 1930 to 1935; member of the Zen 49 group. He came to abstraction in the 1930s after study of Cézanne and the cubists. He gives metaphysical significance to his free rhythmic compositions.

Wert Giaches de (1535–96). Flemish composer working in Italy from boyhood and becoming music director to the court of Mantua. His contemporary admirers included Monteverdi, one of his pupils.

Nathanael West

Werther, The Sorrows of Young (1774). Epistolary novel by *Goethe.

Wescott Glenway (1901–). U.S. novelist and poet. Works include the novel *The Grandmothers* (1927), an examination of the lives of 2 generations of a family.

Wesker Arnold (1932–). English playwright. W. became famous with *Chicken Soup with Barley* (1959), *Roots* (1959) and *I'm Talking about Jerusalem* (1960), the 'Wesker trilogy' about the idealism and disillusion of an East End Jewish family. W.'s plays include *The Kitchen* (1959) and *Chips with Everything* (1962).

Wesley Charles (1707–88). English hymn writer. W.'s hymns combine considerable poetic merit with significant theological content. His brother JOHN (1703–91), the founder of Methodism, wrote a well-known *Journal* (1827).

Wesley Samuel (1766–1837). English organist and composer; son of Charles Wesley the Elder. He is important for his prominent part in the *Bach revival, publ. an ed. (1810) of the *Well Tempered Clavier*. W. was a convert to Roman Catholicism and his works include masses and motets.

Wesley Samuel Sebastian (1810–76). English composer and organist, natural son of the above; he campaigned for reforms in English cathedral music.

West Benjamin (1738–1820). American portrait and history painter who settled in London, having studied in Italy, where he was influenced by the neo-classicism of Mengs. He was much favoured by George III, was a founder-member of the R.A. and became its president on the death of Reynolds. His history picture *Death of Wolfe* is a typical and well-known work.

West Mae (1893–). U.S. film star, the junoesque siren who put curves back on the screen: W. became notorious for her vulgar but very amusing sexy innuendo in *She Done Him Wrong* (1933). Sections of the public were shocked by her, and her retirement in 1943 was virtually forced.

West Nathanael. Pseud. of Nathan Wallenstein Weinstein (1902–40). U.S. novelist who produced only 4 short novels combining bitter humour with horror, and dissecting the ugly realities behind the meretricious values and sentimentality of much American life. *Miss Lonelyhearts* (1933) describes the failure in action and death of a reporter who writes a lonelyhearts column; in *The Day of the Locust* (1939) Hollywood is presented as a landscape of material and moral falsehoods. Other works are the surrealistic *The Dream Life of Balso Snell* (1931) and *A Cool Million* (1934). W. was killed in a motor accident.

West Coast or 'cool' jazz. A movement based on the U.S. Pacific coast in which mostly white musicians were involved, although Miles Davis provided the lead with his 9-piece group of 1949–50. The cool musicians eschewed the angular melodic lines and rhythmic complexity of the Parker-Gillespie school, and developed a more smoothly contoured style, concentrating on achieving the utmost degree of relaxation in their playing. Their debt to Lester *Young was considerable.

Westfront 1918 (1930). Film directed by G. W. *Pabst.

Westmacott Sir Richard (1775–1856). English neo-classical sculptor. He studied under his father, RICHARD (1747–1808) and in Rome under Canova. His work includes the bronze *Achilles* (1822) in Hyde Park, the memorial to Charles James Fox (1810) in Westminster Abbey and the figures on the pediment of the British Museum. His son RICHARD (1799–1872) was also a sculptor.

Westminster Abbey London. The royal coronation cathedral of England. The present building dates from 3 main periods: (1) E.

Westminster Abbey. Henry VII's chapel

Westmacott. Memorial to Charles James Fox

Weston. *Halved Cabbage* (1930)

Weyden. *Descent from the Cross*. Also *triptych and colour plate 40

end, transepts and chapter-house (1245–60), strongly influenced by *Rheims (whence the architect probably came), with very high proportions, French-type chevet, bar-tracery (first used at Rheims 1210) and 'spherical triangles' (first used at Ste-Chapelle 1248); (2) nave, continued in basically the same style by Henry *Yevele in the late 14th c.; (3) Henry VII's chapel (1503–9), the last major example of Gothic architecture in England–fan-vault with heavy pendants, lavish use of sculpture (still surviving), a restless wavy surface all round the exterior, and Renaissance tomb of Henry VII by *Torrigiano.

Westminster Hall: Hugh *Herland

Weston Edward (1886–1958). U.S. photographer. W. produced abstract photographs out of the forms of nature, the sand dunes and rock formations of the American South-West, and the textures and surfaces of shells and vegetables. In 1931 he founded the Group F 64 with Ansel Adams. The group used large cameras, natural light conditions and deep focus to produce photographs noted for their definition and dramatic tonal contrasts.

Westward Ho! (1855). Novel by Kingsley. Dekker and Webster wrote a comedy called *Westward Hoe*.

Weyden Rogier van der, or Rogier de la Pasture (*c.* 1400–64). The most important early Netherlands painter after the death of van Eyck. The identity of his work is disputed and he may be identical with Rogelet, Roger of Bruges and others. No signed paintings have survived and very little is known about his life. He is believed to have been apprenticed to Roger Campin and is known to have lived in Brussels from 1435 to 1449, when he was appointed painter to the city. A probable visit to Italy in 1450 resulted in the *Entombment* (Uffizi) which shows Italian influence, and the *Madonna with Four Saints* (Frankfurt) which carries the Medici arms and patron saints. He painted for several members of the Burgundian court including Chancellor Rolin, for whose foundation he painted the *Last Judgement* (Beaune). The *Descent from the Cross* is stylistically his most important work. The action has the quality of a relief set against a flat background, and conveys the deep pathos of suffering. His works show a feeling for the significance of the action rather than realistic representation. A fine example of this is the *Adoration of the Magi* (Munich), known as the *St Columba altarpiece*, and such portraits as *Portrait of a Lady* (Washington) and *Le Grand Bâtard* (Brussels), which skilfully capture the subjects' emotions.

Weyse Christopher Ernst Friedrich (1774–1842). Danish composer and both by his works and his teaching (J. P. E. Hartmann and Gade were his pupils) a founder of the Danish national school.

Weyssenhoff Józef (1860–1932). Polish novelist, whose reputation rests on 2 works: the satirical novel *Żywot i myśli Zygmunta Podfilipskiego* (1898) and the coll. of deeply poetical hunting sketches *Soból i panna* (1911; *The Sable and the Girl*, 1929). Both works reveal his nostalgia for the past.

Whalen Phil (1923–). U.S. poet, one of the *beats. His verse, much of it humorous, includes the coll. *Memoirs of an Interglacial Age* (1960).

Wharton Edith (Newbold Jones) (1862–1937). U.S. novelist. W., a society woman, was deeply influenced by Henry James (though her temperament was more melodramatic than his) and typical works are such psychological-ethical studies of society as *The House of Mirth* (1905) and *The Age of Innocence* (1920). Best known, however, is *Ethan Frome* (1911), a grim story of life in a New England village.

What Maisie Knew (1897). Novel by Henry *James.

Wheatley Francis (1747–1801). English painter, famous for his *Cries of London* series (engraved 1795). He painted genre subjects with a forced sentiment akin to that of Greuze.

When Lilacs Last in the Dooryard Bloom'd (1865–6). Poem by Walt *Whitman.

Where Angels Fear to Tread (1905). Novel by E. M. *Forster.

Whetstone George (1544?–82). English poet and playwright. His verse play *Promos and Cassandra* (1578) was the basis of Shakespeare's *Measure for Measure*.

Whieldon Thomas (1719–95). One of the most famous and versatile of the Staffordshire

Weyden. *St Columba altarpiece* (detail)

Wheatley. *The Return from Market*

Edith Wharton

Whistler. Butterfly emblem, which he used to 'sign' many of his works

John White. *Indian Village of Pomeiooc, Virginia*; watercolour

Whistler. *Nocturne in Blue and Silver: Old Battersea Bridge*

Whistler. *Portrait of the Artist's Mother (Arrangement in Black and Gray)*

potters–Wedgwood was his partner for 5 years. He produced examples of all the main styles of Staffordshire pottery, especially that linked with his name, marbled ware figures, etc. given their characteristic appearance by the use of coloured clays and glazes.

Whistler James Abbott McNeill (1834–1903). U.S. painter, a notable dandy and wit. W. was a cadet at West Point (1851–4), failed to qualify for the army and came to Europe, studying painting in Paris under Gleyre. He settled in London (1859), introducing the cult of the Japanese, which had already arrived in Paris. The famous libel action against Ruskin (1878) ruined W. and he lived abroad for some years. His painting theories and doctrine of 'Art for Art's sake' found expression in the witty and vitriolic *Ten O'Clock Lecture* (1885) and *The Gentle Art of Making Enemies* (1890). The early influence of Courbet was later modified by a greater emphasis on surface arrangement, abstract harmonies, and close colour and tonal relationships. In the 1860s W. sought greater delicacy of colour and form, e.g. 'The white girl' (*Symphony in White Number 2*; 1864, Tate); in the 1870s the influence of Velazquez led to greater robustness, as in the *Portrait of the Artist's Mother* (1872; Louvre) and *Thomas Carlyle*. The *Nocturnes* depicting the blurred atmosphere of London fuse Japanese decorative qualities with the ideas of the French impressionists. W. was also a fine engraver.

White Henry Kirke (1785–1806). English poet encouraged by Southey; his work enjoyed a vogue perhaps stimulated by his early death. W. wrote the hymn 'Oft in danger, oft in woe'.

White John (*fl.* 1585–93). English painter who sailed to N. America with Sir Richard Grenville and was one of the 1st settlers in Virginia. His were the 1st watercolours of N. American subjects, the native inhabitants, the flora and fauna; the large coll. in the British Museum reveals a delicate and observant artist.

White Joseph Blanco (1775–1841). English writer, author of *Night and Death* (1828), a sonnet highly praised by Coleridge.

White Patrick (1912–). Australian writer of novels, short stories and plays, living mostly abroad. His settings are Australian, his techniques international, his concerns universal. He uses stream-of-consciousness, colloquial speech and commonplace people in novels charged with meaningful symbolism, as in *Happy Valley* (1938) and *The Tree of Man* (1955); uncommon people become epic heroes in *Voss* (1957), while in *Riders in the Chariot* (1961) Australian civilization is satirized by being contrasted with personal vision. Whether in the serious psychological analysis of *The Aunt's Story* (1948) or comedy in *The Tree of Man*, W. is a most significant writer of English fiction.

White Robert (*c.* 1530–74). English composer of church music including a magnificent, austere and moving setting of the Lamentations.

White T(erence) H(anbury) (1906–64). English writer, author of *The Once and Future King*, a cycle of 4 novels about a romanticized King Arthur and his court including *The Sword in the Stone* (1938).

White William Hale: Mark *Rutherford

White Devil or Vittoria Corombona, The (*c.* 1608). Tragedy by *Webster.

White Fang (1906). Novel by Jack *London.

White Goddess, The (1948). Book by Robert *Graves.

White Jacket, or The World in a Man-of-War (1850). Novel by Herman Melville.

Whiteley Brett (1939–). Australian painter, the outstanding abstract artist of his generation and, for an Australian, markedly influenced by American art.

White Peacock, The (1911). Novel by D. H. Lawrence.

Whithorne Emerson (1884–1958). U.S. composer and pianist; he studied under Schnabel in Berlin (1905–7). His works include: *The Rain* and *The Aeroplane* symphonies.

Whiting John (Robert) (1917–63). English playwright who became widely known before his death with *The Devils* (1961), based on a book by Aldous Huxley, about religious hysteria and persecution in 17th-c. France.

Whitman Walt (1819–92). U.S. poet. W. spent his childhood on Long Island and in

Brooklyn. At 14 he was apprenticed to a printer and his early career in printing, ed. and contributing to newspapers was temporarily interrupted by schoolteaching. Nominally a Democrat, W. showed too early his opposition to the extension of slavery and lost his ed. of the Brooklyn *Eagle*. He then journeyed to New Orleans in 1848, the first important experience to give him the sense of America's size and diversity of peoples which dominates his later poetry. W.'s early verse was conventional in form, politically indignant and not very interesting: meanwhile, he extended his cultural experience and business acumen in New York. But with *Leaves of Grass* (1855) he became, with apparent suddenness, the great, original, prophetic poet of America, the first indigenous and unmistakably national poet since the Independence. His poems seek to embody the spirit of America; they are spoken by Walt, the celebrator of the open road, the un-European bard of the people wearing working-class dress, whose theme of freedom embraced cosmic, sexual and philosophical liberties and who aimed to encompass death as part of the affirmation of all of life. W.'s poetry was always experiential in outlook: 'I am the man, I suffered, I was there'. The sexuality, the 'barbaric yawp', the huge roll-calls of activities and the long lines and free rhythms are only part of his enormous influence on American and European poets since his death. The most important single poem was *Song of Myself*. At 35 W. became the legend he has remained. In 1857 economic depression left him poor but before the Civil War he expanded *Leaves* with such poems as *Out of the Cradle Endlessly Rocking*, *Bardic Symbols*, and the *Calamus* sequences of intimate love. During the war his buoyant optimism modified as he nursed the wounded in camp hospitals (*Hospital Visits*) and composed his *Drum Taps*, war poems later added to *Leaves*, as most of his poetry eventually was. Lincoln's murder prompted the fine elegy *When Lilacs Last in the Dooryard Bloom'd*, but there was little appreciation of W.'s work except from England. He was only too conscious of his declining capacity but publ. the essays in *Democratic Vistas* (1871) and added *Passage to India* (1870) to *Leaves*.

Whittier John Greenleaf (1807–92). U.S. poet born in Massachusetts. W. had a long career as a political journalist, especially as an anti-slavery agitator, but his reputation now rests on a few good, popular poems, *The Barefoot Boy*, *Telling the Bees*, *Skipper Ireson's Ride*, *Snow-Bound* and *The Tent on the Beach* (1867), a narrative verse cycle. A number of his poems have become well known as hymns. W.'s novel, *Leaves from Margaret Smith's Journal . . .* (1849), describes the Salem witch-craft trials.

Whittingham Charles the Younger (1795–1876). English printer who inherited the Chiswick Press from his uncle in 1840. He was responsible for several 'revivals', one of these being an original *Caslon 'old style' type, also an 'ancient' type known as 'Basle', and the use of layout and decoration in 15th–17th-c. styles. His later work was extremely rich and its influence over his contemporaries in England and America widely felt.

Widmark Richard (1915–). U.S. film star alternating between parts as psychopath (*Kiss of Death*, 1947) and hero (*Panic in the Streets*, 1950, *The Alamo*, 1960).

Widor Charles-Marie Jean Albert (1844–1937). French composer and organist at St Sulpice, Paris from 1870 to 1934. He introduced the organ works of Bach to Paris, was teacher of Vierne, Dupré and Schweitzer, and was renowned for his improvisations. He composed in all genres and also produced 10 works of a new kind, organ symphonies.

Widsith. Anglo-Saxon poem, of which parts date from the 7th c., about the adventures of W., a wandering minstrel; it is included in *The Exeter Book*.

Wied Gustav Johannes (1858–1914). Danish novelist and playwright, author of many humorous works full of bitterness and malice, including the play *Ranke Viljer* (1907; *2 × 2 = 5*, 1923). He committed suicide.

Wieland Christoph Martin (1733–1813). German writer. Influential in preparing the way for the Age of Goethe, but now a neglected monument; perhaps because his language, though elegant, lacks overtones; and his ideas, though lively, lack intensity. His work straddles, rather uncomfortably, the Enlightenment and pre-romanticism, rococo and classicism. W. wrote didactic poems and plays, narrative works in verse, e.g. *Oberon* (1780; 1798), the basis of Weber's opera, and especially in prose. His novels include: . . . *Don*

Walt Whitman: photograph by Brady

Wieland

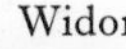

Widor

I. THE TEMPLE

The Dedication.

Lord, my first fruits present themselves to thee;
Yet not mine neither: for from thee they came,
And must return. Accept of them and me,
And make us strive, who shall sing best thy name.
Turn their eyes hither, who shall make a gain
Theirs, who shall hurt themselves or me, refrain.

1. The Church-porch.

Perirrhanterium.

THOU, whose sweet youth and early hopes inhance
Thy rate and price, and mark thee for a treasure,
Hearken unto a Verser, who may chance
Ryme thee to good, and make a bait of pleasure.
A verse may finde him, who a sermon flies,
And turn delight into a sacrifice.

Whittingham. Caslon 'old style'

Wiene.
The Cabinet of Doctor Caligari

Billy Wilder. Tony Curtis and Marilyn Monroe in *Some Like it Hot*

Oscar Wilde at the Private View at the Royal Academy: painting by Frith

Oscar Wilde in 1894–5. Also *aestheticism

Sylvio von Rosalva (1764; 1773) in the style of *Don Quixote*; . . . *Agathon* (1766–7; *The History of Agathon*, 1773), an account, in a classical Greek setting, of an individual's development, which initiated the **Bildungsroman*; *Der goldene Spiegel* (1772; *The Golden Mirror*, 1798), a fictional 'manual for princes' which brought him a court appointment in Weimar; and *Die Abderiten* (1774–80; *The Republic of Fools*, 1861), a loosely constructed satire. W. also ed. the important periodical *Der Teutsche Merkur* (1773–89), and trs. the 1st coll. in German of Shakespeare's plays (22 plays, 1762–6), a prose version that made Shakespeare available to the young writers of the *storm and stress.

Wiene Robert (1881–1938). Czech-born German film director, prolific and commercially successful. He was the director of the expressionist classic *The Cabinet of Doctor Caligari* (1919), but the film's power and imaginative qualities derive from its writers, particularly C. *Meyer, and its designers, 3 members of Der *Sturm.

Wiertz Antoine-Joseph (1806–65). Belgian painter of banal, melodramatic compositions such as *Triumph of Christ* (1848; Wiertz Mus.) in which he aimed to combine the characteristics of Michelangelo and Rubens. He also painted portraits and morbid scenes depicting premature burial, suicide, madness, etc. After his death his studio in Brussels was turned into a mus. of his work.

Wihtol Joseph (1863–1948). Latvian composer. He followed his teacher Rimsky-Korsakov as leader of the composition class at St Petersburg Conservatory; his pupils included Prokofiev and Miaskovsky. W.'s compositions included a symphony and a fantasy on Lettish folk-songs.

Wilbye John (1574–1638). English madrigal composer; house musician to an English country family. The inventiveness and beauty of W.'s madrigals (publ. 1598, 1609) place him at the fore of the English madrigal school.

Wilcox Ella Wheeler (1850–1919). U.S. poet and novelist famous for pseudo-passionate sentimental verse colls, e.g. *Poems of Passion* (1876), which sold in vast quantities.

Wilcox Fred McLeod. U.S. film director. W. was an M.G.M. contract director (e.g. *Lassie Come Home*, 1943). His best film is *Forbidden Planet* (1956), imaginative science fiction.

Wild Duck, The (1884). Play by *Ibsen.

Wilde Oscar (Fingall O'Flahertie Wills) (1854–1900). Irish playwright. W.'s childhood was spent in Dublin: he began writing at Oxford, publ. a 1st book of poems in 1881. He was an exponent of 'Art for Art's sake' – the doctrine that beauty of form and style alone can justify art, independently of content or purpose. From 1879 onwards he lived mainly in London, marrying in 1884. The zenith of his fame as a writer was reached with the production in 1895 of *The Importance of Being Earnest*; in the same year he brought a misguided libel action against Lord Queensberry, the father of his friend Lord Alfred Douglas. Loss of the action led to his trial and conviction for homosexual offences and in May 1895 he was sentenced to 2 years' imprisonment. After his release he publ. *The Ballad of Reading Gaol*, a movingly rhetorical poem based on his prison experiences. *De Profundis*, an apologia for his life written in prison, was posth. publ. in 1905.
A great wit and conversationalist as well as a writer, W. summed up in his vain, kindly, glittering personality the spirit of an era which, reacting against the moral fervour of the Victorians, sought its gratification in hedonism and the cult of beauty.
W.'s plays, in particular *The Importance of Being Earnest*, display the style and wit for which his conversation was famous and occasionally, in their plots, a touch of the absurdity of which he was capable. His tales are highly wrought extravagant fables which leave an aftertaste of morbidity, as does his only novel, *The Portrait of Dorian Gray* (1891), in which the picture reflects the debauches of the man who remains young and handsome. In the prison writings he touches a deeper level of feeling: self-pity and posing are not entirely absent, but the emotions are genuine and raw. Works include the plays *Lady Windermere's Fan* (1892), *A Woman of No Importance* (1893) and *An Ideal Husband* (1895).

Wilder Billy (1906–). Austrian-born U.S. film director. W. was involved on Siodmak's *Menschen am sonntag*. He wrote scripts for a large number of silent and sound German films, and co-directed a feature in Paris in

1933. He worked as a script writer in Hollywood from 1934, working notably for Lubitsch, e.g. on *Ninotchka*. He has been a writer-director, and often a producer, since 1942. He had his 1st big success with a remarkably seedy version of James M. Cain's *Double Indemnity* (1945) and followed this with a film on alcoholism, *The Lost Weekend* (1945). Since *A Foreign Affair* (1948) he has become Hollywood's leading cynic, for whom no subject is unsuitable for comedy treatment–prisoner of war camps (*Stalag 17*, 1952), the cold war (*One, Two, Three*, 1961) and prostitution (*Irma la Douce*, 1963). His most famous films are *Sunset Boulevard* (1950), a hard drama of a retired Hollywood star (Gloria Swanson); a heavily handled comedy *The Seven Year Itch* (1955); a burlesque of 1920s violence with comic transvestism, *Some Like It Hot* (1959); and a comedy of sex in the business world, *The Apartment* (1960). Less well known but very highly regarded by some is *Love in the Afternoon* (1957), a romantic comedy of a young woman and an older man.

Wilder Thornton (1897–). U.S. novelist and playwright. W. was a schoolteacher until 1928; he became a professional writer after the success of *The Cabala* (1926) and *The Bridge of San Luis Rey* (1927), a novel which describes the lives of characters whose destinies meet in death when a bridge collapses. W.'s plays include *Our Town* (1938) and *The Skin of Our Teeth* (1942), a satirical comedy about the history of man. They were mainly humorous in intention but, at the time, technically advanced: they range freely over time and space, and their characters often comment on the action to the audience. *The Ides of March* (1948) is an epistolary novel about the last weeks of Caesar's life.

Wildfell Hall, The Tenant of (1848). Novel by Anne *Brontë.

Wild Strawberries (1957). Film directed by I. *Bergman.

Wilhelmj August (1845–1908). German violinist and arranger, e.g. the air from Bach's orchestral suite in D. maj. as *Air on the G string*.

Wilhelm Meisters Lehrjahre (1795–6) and **Wilhelm Meisters Wunderjahre, oder die Entsagenden** (1821–9). Novels by *Goethe.

Wilkes John (1727–97). English politician and journalist who publ. the newspaper *The North Briton* (1762), attacking George III's government, was prosecuted for publ. the obscene poem *Essay on Woman* and had a chequered career (including exile and outlawry) as a popular hero and martyr for liberty.

Wilkie Sir David (1785–1841). Scottish painter. He made his reputation with scenes of village life in the style of Teniers the Younger and van Ostade, e.g. *Blind Man's Buff* (R. Coll.); influenced by Spanish painting (he visited Italy and Spain) he developed a looser technique and turned to historical subjects such as *Sir David Baird discovering the body of Tippoo Sahib* (Edinburgh Castle).

Wilkins William (1778–1839). English architect. He spent 4 years travelling in Italy, Greece and Asia Minor, and became one of the leading figures of the Greek revival. His chief works are Downing College, Cambridge; the N.G., London; Univ. College, London (all in Greek style); and the screen along the E. side of King's College, Cambridge–a charming essay in Gothic.

Willaert Adrian (1480/90–1562). Flemish composer working primarily in Italy and of immense importance to Italian music. He was appointed musical director of St Mark's, Venice (1527), and established it as a major musical centre. W.'s great achievement was to integrate the techniques of Flemish polyphony into Italian style; his use of antiphonal choirs, *Salmi spezzati* (1550), held great potentialities developed by his pupil A. *Gabrieli; he composed fine 4-part motets and powerfully expressive madrigals using chromatic harmonies extensively, an important precedent.

William of Malmesbury (*c.* 1090–1143?). English chronicler, author of *Gesta Regum Anglorum, Historia Novella* and *Gesta Pontificum Anglorum.*

William of Sens (*fl.* 1174–8). French architect, but known only for his rebuilding of the choir of Canterbury cathedral (after the fire of 1170) which marks the introduction of the French Gothic style into England. W.'s design retained the old Romanesque walls but the interior was entirely new, with pointed arches, sexpartite vaults and concealed flying buttresses over the aisle roofs.

Thornton Wilder

Wilkins. The National Gallery

William of Sens. The choir of Canterbury cathedral

Wilkie. *Waterloo Dispatch*

Tennessee Williams

William Carlos Williams

Edmund Wilson

Spode willow-pattern plate

William of Wykeham (1323–1404). Bishop of Winchester and Lord Chancellor of England. He was keenly interested in architecture, becoming the friend and patron of the master mason *William of Wynford.

William of Wynford (*fl.* 1360–1403). English medieval architect. In 1365 he was appointed master mason of Wells cathedral, where *William of Wykeham (his patron) was provost. He stayed with Wykeham for the rest of his life, going with him to Winchester. Together they were responsible for the W. towers of Wells cathedral; the 2 colleges which Wykeham founded, Winchester College and New College, Oxford (which set the pattern for later college architecture at Oxford and Cambridge); and the rebuilding of the nave of Winchester cathedral in perpendicular style (begun *c.* 1394).

Williams Alberto (1862–1952). Argentinian composer, of English and Basque parentage, called 'The father of Argentinian music.' From 1893 to 1940 he was director of the Buenos Aires Conservatory, which he founded. His works, showing affinities with those of his teacher, César Franck, and with Argentinian folk-music, include: 9 symphonies, a symphonic poem, overtures, orchestral suites and chamber music.

Williams Bransby (1870–1963). English character actor and mimic famous for his solo performances from the works of Dickens.

Williams Emlyn (1905–). Welsh actor and author who has played in classical and modern works and also in most of his own plays, the most famous of which are *Night Must Fall* (1935) and *The Corn is Green* (1938). He tours giving solo performances from the works of Charles Dickens.

Williams Harcourt (1880–1957). English actor and director at the Old Vic, from 1929 to 1934. In his interpretation of Shakespeare he closely followed the principles of his friend *Granville-Barker.

Williams Tennessee, originally Thomas Lanier W. (1914–). U.S. playwright. W. was born in Mississippi, and most of his works are set in the American South. He uses poetic language, symbolism and expressionistic staging to convey the frustration and loneliness of human beings, their attempts to communicate with each other and the resultant tensions, which are often released in violence. *The Glass Menagerie* (1945) and *A Streetcar Named Desire* (1947) gave W. an international reputation; both depict the vulnerability of defensive fantasies to the intrusions of a brutal reality. W.'s works include the plays *Summer and Smoke* (1948); *The Rose Tattoo* (1950); *Camino Real* (1953); *Cat on a Hot Tin Roof* (1955); *Orpheus Descending* (1957), a reworking of the earlier *Battle of Angels* (1945); *Suddenly Last Summer* (1958); *Sweet Bird of Youth* (1959); *Period of Adjustment* (1960); *The Night of the Iguana* (1961) and *The Milk Train Doesn't Stop Here Any More* (1963); the film script *Baby Doll* (1956); and the short novel *The Roman Spring of Mrs Stone* (1950).

Williams William Carlos (1883–1963). U.S. poet and also novelist; he practised most of his life as a small-town doctor in Rutherford, New Jersey. His most ambitious work, the 5-book poem *Paterson* (1946–58), embodies the results of a lifetime's experimental technique and expresses W.'s generous, humanitarian vision. Other fine shorter poems, e.g. *The Red Wheelbarrow* and *The Yachts*, reveal the development of his personal style of imitative images. Other works by W. include critical essays, an *Autobiography* (1951), and a novel trilogy.

Williamson Henry (1897–). English novelist, author of *Tarka the Otter* (1927), an animal story, and many novels of country life.

William Tell. Opera by *Rossini based on Schiller; 1st performance at Paris in 1829.

Willis Nathaniel Parker (1806–67). U.S. poet, playwright, travel and general writer, and an influential editor; a versatile figure once highly considered, and popular for his sentimental verse.

willow pattern. A motif on English blue-printed earthenware of the 1800s which was derived from Chinese landscape paintings. Examples of this ware were sent to Chinese factories with orders for copies to be made, thus effecting a curious stylistic ricochet with China reproducing chinoiserie for the European market.

Wilson Angus (Frank Johnstone) (1913–). English novelist, short-story writer and playwright whose books contain acid, ironical portraits of contemporary society and its types, and investigate complex problems of conduct. His works include the novels *Hemlock and After* (1952), *Anglo-Saxon Attitudes* (1956), *The Middle Age of Mrs Eliot* (1958) and *The Old Men at the Zoo* (1961); several story colls and a play *The Mulberry Bush* (1956).

Wilson Colin (1931–). English writer, author of *The Outsider* (1956), a best-selling study of individuals (mainly writers and artists) alienated from society by superior insight. W.'s works include *Religion and the Rebel* (1957) and the novel *Ritual in the Dark* (1960).

Wilson Edmund (1895–). U.S. critic and man of letters, a contemporary and friend of F. Scott Fitzgerald at Princeton. W., a polymath and polyglot, has written prolifically and on many subjects, e.g. his *The Scrolls of the Dead Sea* (1955), while regularly producing review criticism. His politico-social awareness and changing commitments (like those of Mary McCarthy, to whom he was married) typify the American intelligentsia of his generation. His best-known works are *Axel's Castle* (1931), a critical, synthesizing discussion of European symbolism, and *To the Finland Station* (1940), which studies the interaction of theories and events in the Revolutionary tradition of Europe. W. was also married to Edna St Vincent Millay.

Wilson John (1626–96). English playwright. His works include the comedies *The Cheats* (1663) and *The Projectors* (1665), modelled on Jonson, and the tragedy *Andronicus Comnenius*.

Wilson John (1785–1854): Christopher *North

Wilson Richard (1714–82). Landscape painter of the English school, born in Wales. In 1729 he was a pupil of Thomas Wright in London and from 1735 was working on his own. He had turned to landscape before going to Italy (1750–*c.* 57) where he was influenced by the work of Poussin and Claude, and the picturesque landscapes of Vernet and Zuccarelli. He later painted landscapes in England and Wales, and reminiscences of Italian scenes, works full of serenity, light and the nuances of atmosphere. Although his work was not popular, he had considerable influence on Turner, Cotman, Constable and Crome, and started the cult for Welsh mountain landscapes.

Wilson Richard (1915–). U.S. film director. W. was a script writer and worked as a producer on some of Welles's films, before directing a western, *Trouble Shooter* (1955). He was praised by critics for his reportage-style thriller *Al Capone* (1959), about the Chicago gangster, which he bettered with the similar *Pay or Die!* (1960).

Wilson Thomas (*c.* 1525–81). English writer, author of *The Art of Rhetorique* (1553), a textbook of composition which argued that the English language could suitably be used to treat any subject.

Wilson Sir William (1641–1710). English architect who designed the nave and part of the tower of St Mary's, Warwick, an example of the persistence (not revival) of the Gothic tradition as late as 1698.

Wilton Joseph (1722–1803). English sculptor, founder-member of the R.A. He studied in the Netherlands, Paris, Rome and Florence. His monumental works include General Wolfe's tomb in Westminster Abbey. He is also known for his portrait busts and decorative carving.

Wilton carpet: *Brussels carpet

Wilton diptych (N.G., London). Formerly attributed to the Parisian school, it appears likely now that this charming work, a major example of international Gothic art, was painted in England *c.* 1395–9. The theme is the presentation of King Richard II to the Virgin and Child by his patron saints, Edmund, Edward the Confessor and John the Baptist.

Winchester cathedral England. English cathedral with the longest nave in Europe; basically Norman in structure but substantially remodelled in the perpendicular style by *William of Wynford.

Winchilsea Anne Finch, Countess of (1661–1720). English poet, a friend of Pope. *Fanscomb Barn* and *A Nocturnal Reverie* (in *Miscellany Poems*, 1713) embody a mood and an attitude to nature which were to underlie romanticism in one of its aspects.

Winckelmann Johann Joachim (1717–68). German writer on archaeology, in which his attempt to classify and interpret styles of antique art was extremely important. His *Gedancken über die Nachahmung der Griechischen*

Richard Wilson.
Lake Albano and Castelgandolfo

Richard Wilson. Rod Steiger (left) in *Al Capone*

The *Wilton diptych*

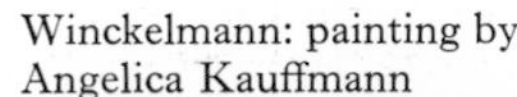

Winckelmann: painting by Angelica Kauffmann

Winchester cathedral

Robert Wise and Jerome Robbins. *West Side Story*

Witte. *Interior of Amsterdam Church*

Werke . . . (1755) formulated a long unchallenged interpretation of Greek art which stressed its 'noble simplicity' and 'tranquil grandeur'; these ideas, expanded in W.'s major work, the *Geschichte der Kunst des Alterthums* (1764; *History of Ancient Art among the Greeks*, 1850), were extremely influential in the development of *neo-classicism. W., a homosexual, was killed in an encounter in Trieste.

The Winged Victory of Samothrace

Windgassen Wolfgang (1914–). German tenor who has played all the important Wagner tenor roles.

Wind in the Willows, The (1908). Children's book by Kenneth *Grahame.

Winesburg, Ohio (1919). Coll. of stories by Sherwood *Anderson.

Winged Victory of Samothrace (*c.* 180 B.C.; Louvre). Hellenistic statue (discovered on the Greek island of Samothrace in 1863) of Nike, the goddess of victory. Erected after a naval victory over Antiochus III of Syria, it depicts the goddess alighting on the prow of a victorious ship. The sculptor was probably from Rhodes. This statue is the best-known representation of the goddess–a subject popular in Greek art from the archaic period.

wings. In the theatre, the area concealed from the audience by *flats.

Wings of the Dove, The (1902). Novel by Henry *James.

Winnie-the-Pooh (1926). Children's book by A. A. *Milne.

Winslow Boy, The (1946). Play by Terence Rattigan.

Fritz Winter. *Earthbound* (1952)

Winter Fritz (1905–). German abstract expressionist painter. He studied (1927–30) at the Dessau Bauhaus under Schlemmer, Kandinsky and Klee; his work was condemned as 'decadent' by the Nazis and he was forbidden to paint. He served in the German army in World War II and was a prisoner-of-war in Russia until 1949. His sombre paintings convey a romantic sense of awe before the forces of nature.

Winterhalter Franz Xaver (1806–73). German portrait painter famous as the portrayer of European royalty, including Queen Victoria, Prince Albert and their children.

Winterreise, Die (i.e. 'The Winter Journey'). Song cycle by *Schubert.

Winters Shelley (1922–). U.S. film actress built up as another voluptuous blonde, tempestuous and brassy, but also an actress of talent and sensibility. 10 years brought her not much better than *A Place in the Sun* (1951), so she abandoned her figure for 'drab' parts, e.g. *Night of the Hunter* (1955). Her best role has been in *The Diary of Anne Frank* (1958).

Winters (Arthur) Yvor (1900–). U.S. critic and also a poet, who has stressed the importance of moral intention in works of art. He has championed literary 'reaction' and classical severity, and has been the centre of much discussion.

Winter's Tale, The (publ. 1623). Play by *Shakespeare, written *c.* 1610, performed at court in 1611, and evidently a favourite there. Its source was Robert Greene's *Pandosto or the Triumph of Time.*

wipe: *film techniques

Wisdom of Solomon, The. One of the books of the *Apocrypha.

Wise Robert (1914–). U.S. film director. He started as an editor at R.K.O. (1933) and edited *Citizen Kane* and *The Magnificent Ambersons.* He started directing in 1944. He has made the occasional good film, *The Set-Up* (1949), *Executive Suite* (1954) and a prestige success *I Want to Live* (1958). He co-directed the musical *West Side Story* (1961) with Jerome Robbins.

Wise Thomas James (1859–1937). English book collector, founder of the Ashley Library, notorious for his literary forgeries.

Witch of Edmonton, The (1623?). Tragicomedy by Dekker, Ford and Rowley.

Wither George (1588–1667). English poet. His works include the satires *Abuses stript and whipt* (1613) and the pastoral poems *The Shepherd's Hunting* (1615).

Witkiewicz Stanisław Ignacy (1885–1939). Polish painter, philosopher, playwright and novelist. He pioneered modernistic trends in literature and painting. His experimental dramas foreshadow the contemporary French *avant-garde* theatre. In his 2 novels he gave a terrifying vision of the passing of Western civilization. He committed suicide in September 1939.

Witte Emanuel de (1615/17–92). Dutch painter, chiefly of church interiors such as *Interior of the Oudekerk, Amsterdam, during a Sermon* in the N.G., London.

Witten Hans. 15th–16th-c. German sculptor in wood and stone. His works include the statue *St Helen* (Town Hall, Halle), the tulip pulpit in Freiberg cathedral, and a *Scourging of Christ* group (Schlosskirche, Chemnitz).

Wittgenstein Ludwig Josef Johann (1899–1951). Austrian philosopher who became a British citizen; a major influence on modern philosophy through his *Tractatus Logico-Philosophicus* (1921, in German; 1922). W. argued that many philosophical problems are embedded in linguistic confusion, and that the function of language (inefficiently performed in practice) is to picture the facts of the world. He later modified his views, recognizing the subtlety and variety of the social functions of language.

Witz Conrad. 15th-c. painter mainly active in Basle. Rediscovered in 1901, his paintings were until then attributed to various painters. His work is characterized by great strength and simplicity and a searching realism. His paintings include the *St Bartholomew* (K. Mus., Basle), a monumental free-standing figure, and the *Draught of Fishes* (1444) at Geneva.

Wodehouse P(elham) G(renville) (1881–). English humorous novelist and a considerable stylist. The most popular of his stories, set in an idyllic, vaguely Edwardian England, feature the master-mind Jeeves, butler to the dim, engaging man-about-town Bertie Wooster. Works include his autobiography, *Performing Flea*, and the novels *Carry on, Jeeves* (1925), *The Code of the Woosters* (1938), *Uncle Fred in the Springtime* (1939) and, most recently, *Frozen Assets* (1964).

Woe from Wit. Play by *Griboyedov.

Woestijne Karel van de (1878–1929). Dutch symbolist poet whose verse is in effect a long spiritual autobiography revealing W.'s feelings of inadequacy, torment and melancholy. His florid prose stories deal with Biblical and legendary subjects.

Woffington Peg (*c.* 1714–60). Dublin-born English comedy actress, notably in Congreve and Shakespeare. She was regarded as the most beautiful woman of her day and was a member of the literary as well as the social world. She was for some years Garrick's mistress.

Wolf Hugo (1860–1903). Austrian song composer, an ardent Wagnerian; he made intemperate attacks on other composers such as Brahms during 3 years as a music critic (1884–7). In 1897 and permanently in 1898 W. was confined to a mental home where he died. Despite his admiration for Wagner, W.'s greatest inspiration was Schumann's songs; he would not set a text used by Schumann, and his own are considered a natural continuation of Schumann's work. His song cycles included: *Mörike Lieder* (1888), 53 songs; *Gedichte von Goethe* (1890), 51 songs; *Spanish Song book* (1891) and *Italian Song book* (1892; 1896).

Wolfe Thomas (Clayton) (1900–38). U.S. novelist, the son of a stone-cutter. W. studied at the Univ. of N. Carolina and at G. P. *Baker's Workshop 47, and worked intermittently as English instructor at New York Univ. Maxwell Perkins of Scribner's the publishers played a considerable part in the success of W.'s first 2 novels, *Look Homeward, Angel: A Story of the Buried Life* (1929) and *Of Time and the River* (1935), helping to ed., cut and reorganize W.'s sprawling mss. Their rushing, rhetorical style, panoramic descriptions, romantic and autobiographical attack on experience and fundamental optimism gave W.'s books a great reputation; at present, however, their stock is relatively low. Works include the posth. ed. and publ. *The Web and the Rock* (1939), *You Can't Go Home Again* (1940) and *The Hills Beyond* (1941).

Wolf-Ferrari Ermanno (1876–1948). Italian composer (his father was German), a pupil of Rheinberger. In an individual lyrical idiom he achieved his best work in his operas, especially comic operas re-presenting the traditional form of the *opera buffa*. His works include: *I quattro rusteghi* ('School for Fathers', 1906), *La Dama boba* (1939) and the 'folk' opera *I Giojelli della Madonna* (1911, reworked 1933).

Thomas Wolfe

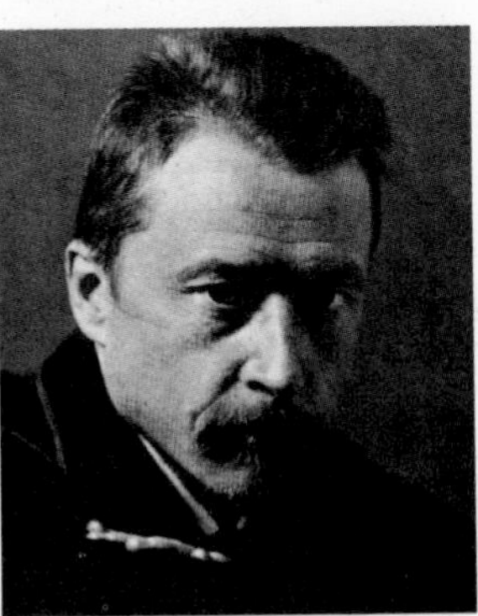

Hugo Wolf

P. G. Wodehouse

Witz. *Draught of Fishes*

John Wood the Elder. Queen Square, Bath. For Wood the Younger *Bath

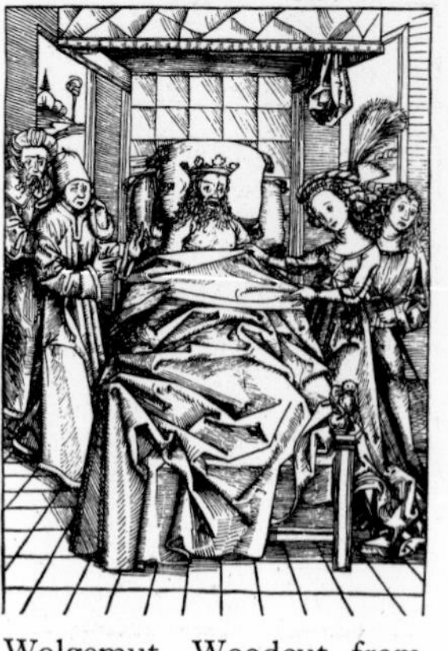

Wolgemut. Woodcut from the *Schatzbehalter*

Sir Donald Wolfit

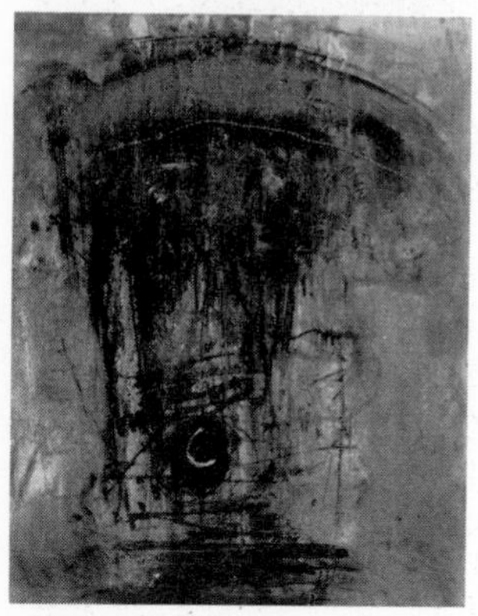

Wols. *Composition* (1947)

Grant Wood. *American Gothic*

Wolfit Sir Donald (1902–). English actor-manager who of all the great modern actors most retains the influences of the last c.; hence, perhaps, the frequency with which he is cast in films and on television as a sidewhiskered villain. For a long time he ran his own co. after the manner of the Victorian actor-managers, but he has also appeared often at the Old Vic and at Stratford. His great performances include the title-roles in Jonson's *Volpone* (1938), and Marlowe's *Tamburlaine* (1951) and Shakespeare's *King Lear*. His versatility has led him into a revival of music-hall.

Wolfram von Eschenbach (*c.* 1170–*c.* 1220). The greatest medieval German poet, author of *Parzival* (*c.* 1200–12), an Arthurian epic drawing on *Chrétien de Troyes and (perhaps) lost sources, describing the trials and ultimate purification of Parzival, and his quest for the Holy Grail (in this version a miraculous stone). W. von E.'s diction was more vigorous, his imagery more florid and his humour broader than was usual in the court epic poet; these qualities, and his obscurity, were censured by contemporaries, e.g. Gottfried von Strassburg. He also wrote *Willehalm*, *Titurel* and a number of outstanding lyrics.

Wolgemut Michael (1434–1519). German painter and master of Dürer. He was head of a workshop in Nuremberg which produced painted and carved altarpieces and designer of the woodcut illustrations to the famous 15th-c. books, the *Schatzbehalter* and Hartmann Schedel's *Weltchronik* (known as the *Nuremberg Chronicle*, 1493).

Wollaston John. 18th-c. English portrait painter who went to work in the American colonies.

Wollstonecraft Mary. Wife of William *Godwin.

Wols Alfred Otto Wolfgang Schulze called (1913–51). German painter and poet who studied at the Dessau Bauhaus under Mies van der Rohe and Moholy-Nagy, moved to Paris in 1932 and became with Fautrier a pioneer of abstract expressionism. He illustrated with engravings works by Kafka and Sartre.

Woman in White, The (1860). Novel by Wilkie *Collins.

Woman Kilde with Kindnesse, A (1603). Play by Thomas Heywood.

Woman of No Importance, A (1893). Play by Oscar Wilde.

Woman of Paris, A (1923). Film directed by *Chaplin, the only film he directed without acting a leading role.

Woman of Rome, The (1947). Novel by Alberto *Moravia.

Women beware Women (1621?). Play by Thomas *Middleton.

Wood. Leading family of Staffordshire potters of whom the most important members were: AARON (1717–85), the outstanding mould cutter in Staffordshire, his brother RALPH (1715–72) and his son ENOCH (1759–1840).

Wood Anthony à (1632–95). English writer, author of *Historia et antiquitates Universitatis Oxoniensis* (1674), later publ. as *Athenae Oxoniensis* (1691–2), which represents his extensive researches into the archives of Oxford colleges. He drew heavily on work done by John Aubrey.

Wood Grant (1892–1942). U.S. regionalist painter of Iowa. His development was influenced on visits to Europe in the 1920s, by 15th- and 16th-c. Flemish and German painting and the Neue Sachlichkeit movement. The technical precision and stylization which characterize his work are also reminiscent of U.S. folk-art. His best-known paintings are *American Gothic* (A. Inst. of Chicago) and *Daughters of the Revolution* (private coll.) in which there is a strong element of satire.

Wood Haydn (1882–1959). Popular English composer; his songs include 'Roses of Picardy'.

Wood Mrs Henry (1814–87). English novelist, author of temperance novels and *East Lynne* (1861), which achieved great success in its dramatized form.

Wood Sir Henry (Joseph) (1869–1944). English conductor, the founder of the 'Henry Wood' Promenade Concerts which began with a series at the Queen's Hall, London in 1895. W.'s aim was to introduce good music and modern controversial music to the British public. W. also composed under the pseud.

Venetian woodcut of 1497

Woodcut. Heckel, *The Crouching One* (1914)

Woodcut. Dürer, *Demonstration of Perspective Drawing of a Lute*

'Paul Klenovsky', and publ. several books on music.

Wood John the Elder (1704–54). English architect, born and practising in *Bath. In 1725 he drew up elaborate proposals for the improvement of the city. Queen Square was begun in 1729–the 1st square in England to treat all 4 sides as palace-façades planned on one consistent scheme; the interiors were left to sub-contractors–W. was concerned only with the façades. The Circus, begun 1754, is the first in England; it is a circle of 3-storey houses with identical façades of coupled columns in 3 orders, Tuscan, Ionic and Corinthian. Prior Park, Ralph Allen's mansion, was designed by W. in close imitation of Palladio's villas. Most of W.'s work is in a chastely Palladian style, dignified, ordered and disciplined. His son, JOHN W. the Younger (1728–81), continued in the same tradition, building, among many others, Russell Street, George Street, and the Royal Crescent (1764–74)–a large half-ellipse facing open country and using a giant Ionic order instead of his father's superimposed orders. He also designed the New Assembly Rooms and even experimented in neo-Gothic (Margaret chapel, Brock Street).

Wood Sam (1883–1949). U.S. film director. W. was one of the top prestige directors in Hollywood around 1940. He made *A Night at the Opera* (1935) with the Marx Brothers, *Goodbye Mr Chips* (1939), *Our Town* (1940) from Thornton Wilder, *Pride of the Yankees* (1942) and *For Whom the Bell Tolls* (1943) from Hemingway.

woodcut. Relief printing technique in which the design is drawn on the plank surface of the wood (usually pear or alder) and that part of it which is to be white is cut away with a gouge or knife, leaving the remainder to print black. The w. came into use in the late 14th c. for the printing of playing-cards and block-books and had become an artistic medium by the mid 15th c., culminating in the work of Dürer. Displaced by the line engraving, it was revived in the 19th c. by William Morris and others. The medium is ideally suited to subjective expression and was widely exploited in the 1st quarter of the 20th c. by the German expressionists, e.g. Kirchner and Heckel, who used it with a power and originality not attained since Dürer.

wood engraving. Relief technique of printing which differs from the woodcut in that the block is made of boxwood cut across the grain, and a burin instead of a gouge is used for cutting. This makes very fine lines possible, so that effects similar to those of line engraving can be achieved. W. e. was developed in the mid 18th c. and was beautifully handled by Bewick (1753–1828). In the mid 19th c. it was used as a reproduction technique by the Dalziel brothers and others but was revived as a medium for original work just after World War I. The major exponents of w. e., including Bewick and Gwen Raverat, have used the white-line method, i.e. the lines are cut into the block and therefore print white in contrast with both the woodcut and the line engraving.

woodwind musical instruments. Generic term for those musical instruments traditionally made of wood (flutes and clarinets are now often made of metal) with the air column activated by either a reed or by a *fipple or lip (*flute). The reed instruments are in 2 main groups: those with double reed such as the krumhorn, oboe and bassoon, and those with single beating reed such as the clarinet. In all these instruments the length of the air column, and hence the pitch of the notes, is varied by opening holes in the tube either by the fingers closing directly (e.g. the descant recorder) or by keys operated by the fingers.

Woolf Virginia (1882–1941). English writer, educated by her father, Leslie Stephen, and from about 1901, with her sister, the centre of the brilliant circle known as the 'Bloomsbury Group'. In 1914 she married Leonard Woolf and between 1915 and 1941 publ. 7 novels, besides critical essays, a biography of Roger Fry and the historical fantasies *Orlando* and *Flush*. Nervous instability resulted in repeated breakdowns, the last of them culminating in her suicide.
W. developed the stream-of-consciousness novel which brings its characters to life through a kind of eavesdropping upon the thoughts, often fragmentary and disorganized, which run through their minds, persisting beneath their concern with daily life. Her theme is the perpetual involvement and inevitable separateness of human beings, most ambitiously worked out in *The Waves*. Rarely writing directly of the larger human disasters, which form a kind of parenthetic threatening background to the novels, she excels in

Wood engraving. Bewick, *Sea Eagle*

Wood engraving by Dalziel: The Walrus and the Carpenter, from *Through the Looking-Glass*

Virginia Woolf

Wordsworth: painting by Haydon (detail)

Wootton. *Members of the Beaufort Hunt*

Worcester ware (1770–80)

Worcester. Sucrier and stand (1765–70); based on Imari ware

displaying the small hurts, petty fears and secret humiliations of raw sensibilities. Because she shows human personality stripped of its self-consciousness and self-protecting public front, her most satisfying portraits are of children. Her best-known novels are *Mrs Dalloway* (1925), *To the Lighthouse* (1927) and *The Waves* (1931); she also wrote *Jacob's Room* (1922), *The Years* (1937) and *Between the Acts* (1941).

Woolman John (1720–72). Leading U.S. Quaker, anti-slave-trade agitator and writer of religious and social tracts. His *Journal* (1774) records his spiritual life.

Wootton John (*c.* 1686–1765). English painter of hunting and racing scenes, pupil of J. Wyck and the 1st important sporting artist in England. He was also one of the first English artists to follow the landscape style of Claude and G. Poussin.

Worcester Royal Porcelain Co. One of the largest and most important English producers of fine (soft-paste) *porcelain; the firm, established in Bristol in 1748, moved to Worcester (1751–2). The early styles were influenced by contemporary English silverwork or by Chinese porcelain; later such continental centres as Meissen and Sèvres provided models. Work in the fashionable Japanese Kakiemon and Imari styles was also produced, but other decorations included the scale-blue pattern, i.e. overlapping scale shapes in light blue outlined in dark blue. Although often derivative in design, early Worcester porcelain is of the very highest quality. The factory continues to produce high-quality porcelain.

Wordsworth William (1770–1850). English romantic poet whose parents died when he was a boy. W. grew up in the English Lake District where, largely left to his own devices, he formed his strongest relationships with mountains and lakes, and knew the mystical experiences that later haunted him and inspired his finest poetry. He was indifferent to life at Cambridge (1787–91), but the ideals of the Revolution moved him profoundly when he visited France (1790, 1791–2). There he became attached to Annette Vallon, who bore him a daughter. He was forced to return to England by lack of money, but a legacy from a friend enabled him to devote himself to poetry (1795), S. T. Coleridge becoming his close friend. In 1799 W. settled at Grasmere with his sister, Dorothy. In 1802 he married Mary Hutchinson. He grew steadily more conservative in his religious and political views. After 1807, though he produced some fine verse–including *The White Doe of Rylestone* (1815) and *The River Duddon* (1820)–it lacked the inspired quality of his early work. But his reputation continued to grow, and in 1843 he was appointed poet laureate.

W. was a typical romantic in his preoccupation with his feelings and experiences, his nostalgia for childhood and love of nature; but in his best poetry they become part of a coherent philosophy. The operations of the intellect, which separates and analyses, have obscured the fact that man is part of nature; hence the small child has a relationship with nature which the adult has lost (the ode *Intimations of Immortality*), though he may come to understand its healing power (*Lines written above Tintern Abbey*). Because of this pantheistic attitude, W. tended, like Rousseau, to equate the natural with the good. He wrote the conventional *Descriptive Sketches* and *An Evening Walk* (both 1793); but his first important poetry appeared in the *Lyrical Ballads* (1798; enlarged, with W.'s important preface, *Observations*, 1800; with the essay on *Poetical Diction*, 1802), produced in collaboration with Coleridge. W.'s aim was to treat ordinary, usually rustic life in language carefully selected from every day. This was a fruitful break with 18th-c. conventions of diction and subject, though it occasionally led to banality and strained simplicity, as in *The Idiot Boy*. *The Prelude* (begun 1799; completed 1805; publ. posth. 1850) is a long autobiographical poem, the first of its kind. Addressed to Coleridge, it describes the development of the poet's abilities and the growth of his love for mankind. It was intended to be a stocktaking before W. wrote a great philosophical poem, *The Recluse*; but of this only the middle section, *The Excursion* (begun 1797; publ. 1814), was completed. Among W.'s notable works are *Michael*; the tragedy *The Borderers*; the *Lucy* poems; *Peter Bell*; *The Waggoner*; and many sonnets–including the lines *Composed on Westminster Bridge*–in which form W. was one of the English masters.

Wordsworth William (Brocklesby) (1908–). English composer working in a basically tonal idiom. His best music is in the 4 symphonies but he has also written the oratorio *Dies Domini* (1953), concertos and chamber music.

Work Henry Clay (1832–84). U.S. song writer; his many successful compositions include the Civil War song 'Marching Through Georgia'.

World as Will and Idea, The (1819). Philosophical work by *Schopenhauer.

World of Apu, The (1958). Film directed by S. *Ray.

World of Art, The. The name for a society, exhibiting organization and a magazine, founded in St Petersburg in the early 1890s, similar to the *nabi group. It brought together artists chiefly, but also poets and musicians; prominent members were Benois, Diaghilev and Bakst. They were in revolt against the 'provincial nationalism' of the *Wanderers and in contrast declared for 'Art for Art's sake' and close ties with Western European ideas. The magazine was ed. (1899–1904) by Diaghilev and his Ballet Russe is the group's most notable production, to which most of its members contributed.

Worms cathedral Germany. One of the most notable Rhineland Romanesque churches, dating from the 12th to the 13th c. It has the characteristics of its type: apse at both ends, 4 round towers, and dwarf-galleries. The interior (with alternating supports) originally had a groin-vault; now ribbed.

Worringer Wilhelm (1881–). German writer on aesthetics. His *Abstraktion und Einfühlung* (1908; *Abstraction and Empathy*, 1953) recognized the role of abstraction in the history of art; and *Formprobleme der Gothik* (1912; *Form in Gothic*, 1927)–arguing the existence and continuity of a non-classical Northern tradition of spiritual unrest expressing itself by distorting reality–profoundly influenced the development of expressionism.

Wotruba Fritz (1907–). The leading contemporary Austrian sculptor, trained as a stonemason. His first exhibition was in Vienna in 1930. Since 1945 he has been director of the sculpture school at the Vienna Academy. Most of W.'s works since 1928 are directly carved in stone. They are mostly figure-images, but their character is determined largely by the nature of the stone's mass, shape and texture, as in *Standing Figure* (1949–50; Tate) or *Figure* (1959; Municipal Hall, Vienna). In this and in its proximity to primitive and archaic traditions, W.'s sculpture lies well within the European mainstream.

Wotton Sir Henry (1568–1639). English lyric poet, e.g. *On His Mistress the Queen of Bohemia* (*Reliquiae Wottonianae*, 1651); also ambassador to Venice (1604–24) and author of *Elements of Architecture* (1624).

Wouk Herman (1915–). U.S. novelist, author of the best-selling *The Caine Mutiny* (1951), which describes and investigates the ethics of a crew's mutiny against their despicable commander during World War II. Works include *Aurora Dawn* (1947), *City Boy* (1948) and *Marjorie Morningstar* (1955).

Wouters Frans (1612–59). Flemish painter of landscapes with figures and religious and allegorical subjects, pupil of Rubens. He worked in England (1637–*c.* 1641).

Wouwerman(s) Philips (1619–68). Dutch painter of landscapes with battle and hunting scenes and genre scenes of soldiers in camp reminiscent of the work of P. van Laer. His canvases usually contain a white horse and often large numbers of tiny figures. His brother JAN (1629–66) worked in a similar style.

Woytowicz Bolesław (1899–). Polish national romantic composer and pianist; a pupil of N. Boulanger. Works include: *Cantata in Praise of Labour.*

Wozzeck. Opera by *Berg with libretto by the composer from the play *Woyzek* by *Büchner; 1st performance at Berlin in 1925.

W.P.A. The Works Progress (later called Projects) Administration, an agency set up by the U.S. government in 1935. It organized a great number of projects which provided employment during the Depression. Artists of all kinds were among those employed, the emphasis being on public service (writers produced the 'American Guides', painters decorated public buildings, there was a *Federal Theater, etc.); but from 1939 the artistic projects were wound up.

Wreck of the Deutschland, The (1918). Poem by Gerard Manley *Hopkins.

Wren Sir Christopher (1632–1723). English architect. His early interests were scientific; as

Wotruba. *Figure with Raised Arms* (1956–7)

Wouwerman. *Courtyard with a Farrier*

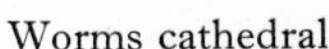

Worms cathedral

World of Art. Bakst, set and costumes for *L'Après-Midi d'un Faune*

Wren. St Paul's

Wren. St Mary-le-Bow. Also *Pearce

a young man he contributed to geometry, scientific-instrument making, astronomy, physics and physiology. He was Gresham Professor of Astronomy at 25, and a founder-member of the Royal Society. His architecture was at first dilettante, beginning with the chapel of Pembroke College, Cambridge (done for his uncle) and the Sheldonian Theatre, Oxford (where his main interest was in the mechanics of the roof). In 1665–6 he visited Paris–his only trip abroad–saw the new domed churches there (Val-de-Grâce and the Sorbonne) and was introduced to Bernini. From this time he devoted himself more and more seriously to architecture. In 1669 he was appointed Surveyor-General with the task of rebuilding St Paul's and the City churches after the fire of 1666. W. designed, or had a main hand in, over 50 churches. They can be divided by plan into several types–basilican, the traditional Gothic parish-church plan, classically interpreted (e.g. St Bride's, St Mary-le-Bow); basilican with galleries (St James, Piccadilly); dome over a square (St Mary Abchurch); Greek cross (St Mary-at-Hill) and other variants. Many of their irregularities (few corners in a W. church, for instance, are right angles) are due to the old medieval sites that he was compelled to use. The greatest of them is St Stephen Walbrook, a combination of the Greek plan with the dome over a square, resulting in a fascinating yet lucid complex of rhythms and spaces. The exteriors are mostly undistinguished except for their spires, where W. allowed his imagination more licence than normally (e.g. St Mary-le-Bow, St Vedast, St Bride's and St Dunstan-in-the-East). At the same time W. was designing the Library of Trinity Coll., Cambridge; Chelsea Hospital; the east and south wings of Hampton Court; and part of Greenwich Hospital. His work on St Paul's began even before the fire, when its precarious condition was thought to make the demolition of the central tower necessary. W. submitted designs for a big central space (possibly suggested to him by the octagon at Ely) covered by a dome on a circular colonnade and topped by a huge elongated pineapple. Plans for the complete rebuilding of the cathedral after the fire went through several versions–the 'First Model' (1670), a fairly small church with superimposed orders; then the 'Great Model' (1673), a bold design with 4 equal arms connected on the exterior by concave walls and surmounted by a big dome (this was W.'s preferred version and it is regrettable that it was never built); and then the 'Warrant Design' (1675), a return to the longitudinal plan, with a grotesque and practically indescribable dome over the crossing. This last design was officially approved, but W. seems to have changed his mind again. The cathedral as built is traditional in plan and structure–nave, choir and transepts lit by a clerestory; but the clerestory is concealed from the outside by screen walls. To support the dome W. wanted 8 arches of equal span (as he had at St Stephen Walbrook) but was unable to achieve this for various structural reasons; he compromised by trying to disguise the inequalities, a rather uncomfortable effect. The dome is triple–first the interior dome of plaster; then a brick cone supporting the lantern; then the exterior dome of wood and lead. W.'s scheme for replanning the whole City of London (influenced by Le Nôtre's garden plans for Versailles) was never used.

Wren P(ercival) C(hristopher) (1885–1941). English writer, author of *Beau Geste* (1924), about Englishmen in the Foreign Legion, *Beau Sabreur* (1926) and *Beau Ideal* (1928).

Wright Basil (1907–). English film director. W. worked with Grierson and directed documentaries like *Song of Ceylon* (1934), highly praised for its lyricism, and *Night Mail* (1936, with H. *Watt). Since a feature-length documentary, *World Without End* (1952, with P. Rotha), for the U.N., he has made only art documentaries.

Wright Frank Lloyd (1869–1959). U.S. architect and one of the most famous modern architects. He grew up and practised in the American Middle West; thus isolated from the mainstream of modern architecture, he developed largely on his own. Raised on a farm, he always respected the land and called his architecture 'organic' to imply that each building grew out of its site as a natural thing. This places him at the other extreme to Le Corbusier and Mies, urban men whose designs are in contrast with nature.
W. is immensely admired but little imitated, and even his own students have found difficulty in developing along the directions he pointed out. A profuse writer, as well as architect to over 1,000 buildings, he is too much an individualist to be neatly put in any category or movement.
Trained in engineering, W. worked in the Chicago office of Adler and Sullivan and learned much from Sullivan. In 1893 he

Wren. St Bride's

Basil Wright and H. Watt. *Night Mail*

Frank Lloyd Wright. Drawing for the Solomon R. Guggenheim Museum

Frank Lloyd Wright. Kaufmann House

opened his own office and until 1910 his creativity was incredible. Most of his buildings were suburban houses in what he called the 'Prairie' style because they were long and low and hugged the land; partly influenced by Bruce Price and the 'shingle style' of the East Coast, they were none the less profoundly original: their plan opened the interior spaces to one another in a magnificent free flow of space, and the best examples–the Willits House (1902), the Coonley House (1908), and the Robie House (1909)–are among the greatest buildings of the 20th c. In addition to houses there were larger structures of equal originality. His work was widely publ. in Germany and thus had international interest and acclaim.

Personal problems and economic depression made his middle years much less productive, but important buildings were built in Japan, Los Angeles and elsewhere, often influenced by his interest in Mayan architecture.

The late 1930s saw renewed activity, and he was busy until his death. He was head of the Taliesin Fellowship, a mixture of art colony, farm, school of architecture and architect's office, which summered in Taliesin East, Wisconsin, and wintered in Taliesin West, Arizona, both in splendid, sprawling buildings designed by W. and largely built by the Fellowship. W. was for a few years influenced by European modern architecture, especially Mies, as in the Winkler-Goetsch House. His Kaufmann House (1936–9), hovering over a waterfall, marks his return to a full mastery not shown since his 1st period of practice, and the contemporary Johnson Wax Building marks his departure from a rectangular-based geometry to a circle, a development carried on through many buildings to the spiral of the Guggenheim Mus., New York; other buildings of this period are based on hexagons, for W. experimented until the end, though rarely exhibiting the sure touch of his 1st practice.

Wright John Michael (d. 1700). British portrait painter, a lesser contemporary of Lely. He studied under George Jamesone in Edinburgh, then spent several years in Italy. He worked as antiquary to the Archduke Leopold Wilhelm in Brussels before settling in England.

Wright Joseph ('Wright of Derby') (1734–97). English painter, almost the earliest to take his subjects from the Industrial Revolution. He visited Italy (1773–5), tried his fortune at Bath but, failing to oust Gainsborough as a portrait painter there, returned to Derby, where he spent most of the rest of his life. Apart from a few portraits and night landscapes, his main work was in depicting the domestic and workshop interiors at the time of the Industrial Revolution, where, by the light of a candle or furnace, the figures are thrown into relief and dramatically presented.

Wright Judith (1915–). Australia's most accomplished living poet; her command of precise imagery and, latterly, of introspective analysis, combined with rhythmic and tonal technique, make her one of the finest living poets in English. Her books include: *The Moving Image* (1946), *Woman to Man* (1949), *The Gateway* (1953) and *The Two Fires* (1955).

Wright Richard (Nathaniel) (1908–60). U.S. novelist, the outstanding Negro spokesman of his generation. His best-known novels are *Native Son* (1940), a bitter description of how society can make the Negro a hoodlum, and the autobiographical *Black Boy* (1945).

Wulfila: *Ulfilas

Wullner Franz (1832–1920). German conductor and also composer. He worked for more than 20 years in Munich, where he conducted the 1st performances of Wagner's *Rhinegold* and *Valkyrie*.

Wunderhorn, Des Knaben (1805–8): Achim von *Arnim.

Wu Tao-tzu (8th c. A.D.). One of the most renowned of Chinese painters, considered the greatest master of the T'ang dynasty although now his paintings can only be judged from copies, as none of the originals survive.

Wuthering Heights (1847). Novel by Emily *Brontë; also made into a film (1939), directed by W. *Wyler.

Wyant Alexander Helwig (1836–92). U.S. landscape painter. His early work was in the Hudson River school tradition, but influenced by Inness and by the work of Constable and Turner, which he studied on a visit to England, he developed a more atmospheric interpretation of nature. Much of his work was done in the Catskill Mountains.

Frank Lloyd Wright. Taliesin West. Also *Johnson Wax, *Robie House

Judith Wright

Joseph Wright of Derby. *Iron Forge*. Also *Darwin

James Wyatt. N.-W. view of Ashridge; drawing by J. C. Buckler

Page of a Wycliffe Bible of *c.* 1380

James Wyatt. Study for Fonthill

Wyatt James (1747–1813). English architect. He travelled in Italy for 6 years. From 1770 he designed the Pantheon, Oxford Street, London, based on St Sophia, Constantinople, dozens of country-houses in any style specified by the patron, and in 1796 began Fonthill Abbey for William Beckford. It was in a fantastically extravagant Gothic but was a landmark of the Gothic revival; the plan consisted of 4 arms spreading from an octagonal tower 225 ft high. It collapsed in 1825. W. also specialized in restoring and 'improving' medieval cathedrals by clearing away screens and tombs and 'opening out the vista'. His eldest son, BENJAMIN DEAN W. (1775–1850), also practised architecture and designed Drury Lane Theatre in 1811.

Wyatt Sir Thomas (1503–42). English poet, and a diplomat, courtier and soldier. W. was an admirer of Anne Boleyn before she married, was imprisoned when she was disgraced, restored to favour and knighted in 1537, and was again briefly imprisoned when his patron, Thomas Cromwell, was executed (1540).

W. is often called the 1st English Renaissance poet; his embassies to Italy, France and Spain made him familiar with foreign models, and he introduced and adapted to English the *sonnet. His best poems, however, take considerable (usually justified) liberties with metre ('corrected' in Tottel's famous miscellany, 1557) and, using simple means, express alternating moods of passion and pride; his love-poems are attractively manly and unaffected, yet free from cynicism. W.'s best-known lyric is *They flee from me that sometime did me seek.*

Sir Thomas Wyatt by Hans Holbein

Wycherley: mezzotint after Lely

Wyatville Sir Jeffry (1766–1840). English architect, nephew of James Wyatt. He took the name Wyatville in 1824 partly to distinguish himself from his uncle. His chief work is at Windsor Castle; he built most of the present state apartments and added 33 ft to the Round Tower (1824 onwards).

Wycherley William (1640–1716). English playwright. His early career was spent partly in the army, partly as an actor and theatrical producer. Influenced both in attitude and technique by Molière, W. probably intended to satirize the degeneracy of Restoration society and his manner was as bawdy as other writers of the Restoration comedy. In such plays as *The Country Wife* (1672 or 3) and *The Plain*

Wynants. *Landscape with a dead Tree*

Wynter. *Source*

Dealer (1674) he succeeded in deploying contemporary types in lively and complex plots hingeing upon their lusts and jealousies, but he lacked the human sympathy necessary to bring his characters to individual life and make his satire more than ephemeral.

Wyck Jan (*c.* 1640–*c.* 1700). Dutch painter who worked mainly in England. His hunting scenes foreshadowed those of J. Wootton. He also painted battle scenes, landscapes and small military equestrian portraits of a type which gained popularity in the 18th c.

Wycliffe John (1324?–84). English theologian, briefly master of Balliol College, Oxford. Most of his work was written in Latin, but he inspired and participated in the 1st complete trs. of the Bible into English. After his popular attacks on clerical privilege W. elaborated heretical views (including a denial of transubstantiation) which fired the Lollards, influenced the Bohemian reformer Huss and, in their appeal to Scripture, anticipated the Reformation.

Wyeth Andrew (Newell) (1917–). U.S. painter of genre subjects. He works in a meticulously detailed style but invests his paintings with an enigmatic, visionary quality which raises them above photographic naturalism.

Wyler William (1902–). French-born U.S. film director. W. started in films as a publicist for Universal in Paris in 1919 and was working in Hollywood from 1920. In the late 1930s he made a famous series of dramas for Sam Goldwyn: *Dodsworth* (1936), *Dead End* (1937), *Wuthering Heights* (1939) and *The Little Foxes* (1941). He also made *The Westerner* (1940), for Goldwyn, and saluted the courage of the British with the very successful *Mrs Miniver* (1942). Mobilized during the war, he shot documentaries for the U.S. Air Force. *The Best Years of Our Lives* (1946) showed the rehabilitation of demobilized servicemen. W., who had always made great use of camera movement, shot this film with the deep-focus techniques pioneered by *Welles and *Toland; but W., unlike Welles, used the techniques of movement within the frame, rather than montage, as a way of presenting a naturalistic subject. The best of his films since then is *Carrie* (1952) from the novel by Dreiser. Innumerable takes to get the right effect in each shot has made his other films over-calculated and lifeless. Commercially the most successful pictures were a 'serious' western, *The Big Country* (1958), and a remake of *Ben Hur* (1959, credited to him, but contributed to by other directors – the famous chariot race was directed by Andrew Marton).

Wynants (Wijnants) Jan (d. 1684). Dutch landscape painter who worked in Haarlem and later Amsterdam. Most of his pictures are similar, showing a sandy track winding through dune scenery with small figures often painted by P. Wouwerman or A. van de Velde.

Wyndham Sir Charles (1837–1919). English actor and manager, who in 1899 built and subsequently managed the New Theatre and Wyndham's Theatre, London.

Wyndham John. Pseud. of John Benyon Harris (1903–). English novelist, author of such best-selling science-fiction novels as *The Day of the Triffids* (1951), *The Kraken Wakes* (1953), *The Chrysalids* (1955) and *The Midwich Cuckoos* (1957).

Wynter Bryan (1916–). English abstract painter. His complex darting images and thick interweaving textures almost always resolve themselves into simple vertical and horizontal planes beneath the surface.

Wynyard Diana (1906–64). English actress of great beauty whose career was mainly in modern plays and films. She played in Shakespeare, however, notably as Beatrice in *Much Ado About Nothing* (1948) and as Hermione in *The Winter's Tale* (1951). She played Gertrude in *Hamlet* in the 1st production of the National Theatre (1963).

Wyspiański Stanisław (1869–1907). Polish verse dramatist, and a painter in art nouveau style. W. created a poetic theatre which continued the traditions of Polish romantic drama but made full use of the techniques of symbolism. In his masterpiece, *Wesele* (1901), W. infused the framework of a popular Nativity play with topicality and cruel historical symbols. His visionary drama *Wyzwolenie* (1903) indicts Polish political romanticism. His many works include *Protesilas i Laodamia* (1898; 1933).

Wyler. Dana Andrews and Fredric March in *The Best Years of Our Lives*

Stanisław Wyspiański; self-portrait

X Y

W. B. Yeats

Xylophone

Xenophon (*c.* 430–*c.* 354 B.C.). Greek author born at Athens and a disciple of Socrates. He joined Cyrus the Persian's expedition against his brother the king. X.'s *Anabasis* describes the expedition and its retreat, led by X. himself. Exiled from Athens, he settled at Olympia and died at Corinth. The *Hellenica* continues Thucydides' history, the *Cyropaedia* romantically describes the raising of Cyrus the Great, 1st king of Persia, the *Memorabilia* (memoirs) and the *Apology* vindicate Socrates' reputation, the *Oeconomicus* deals with estate management and the *Cynegeticus* with hunting. Smaller handbooks deal with cavalry command, horsemanship and Athenian finance. X.'s style is simple but undistinguished.

xylophone. Musical percussion instrument, used in Western Europe only since the late 19th c., being a row of tuned wooden blocks struck with hard sticks. It has a chromatic range of about three 8ves from middle C upwards.

Yamasaki. Century 21 Exposition (model)

Yamasaki Minoru (1912–). American architect of Japanese descent practising in Detroit. His work is characterized by decorative richness and frequent historical allusions, as in the precast concrete, rather Gothic style of Wayne Univ. and the Century 21 Exposition at Seattle.

Yang Kwei Fei (1955). Film directed by K. *Mizoguchi.

Years, The (1937). Novel by Virginia Woolf.

Jack Butler Yeats. *The Two Travellers* (1942). Also *Synge

Yeats Jack Butler (1871–1957). Irish painter, graphic artist and writer, brother of W. B. Y.; he studied at the Westminster School of Art. Y. sought to capture the Irish scene in pen, watercolour and, late in life (from the 1930s), oil painting; he always tried to convey mood rather than describe in detail, and the increasing violence of his colours brought his style close to *expressionism. He was recognized as a great national painter only after World War II.

Yeats William Butler (1865–1939). Irish poet and playwright born of a Protestant family. Y. spent much of his childhood in London, and in 1887 became one of the group of 'decadent' writers associated with the magazine *The Yellow Book*. He founded the Rhymers Club with Ernest Dowson and Lionel Johnson. He publ. the narrative poem *The Wanderings of Oisin* (1889) and 2 verse plays, *The Countess Cathleen* (1892; performed 1899) and *The Land of Heart's Desire* (1894; performed 1899). In 1896 he returned to Ireland and became a leader of the *Irish literary renaissance, founding the *Abbey Theatre with Lady Gregory in 1899. During this period he fell deeply and unhappily in love with the actress Maude Gonne. In 1917 he married Georgina Hyde Lees, a spiritualist medium, and settled in a tower on the Irish coast. The poetry of the ensuing years, *The Wild Swans at Coole* (1917), *The Tower* (1928) and *The Winding Stair* (1929), which includes the poem *Byzantium*, is among his finest. He was awarded the Nobel prize in 1923 and was a member of the Irish Senate from 1922 to 1928.
Y.'s poetry shows successive attempts to find a set of symbolic equivalents which would contain its turbulent emotional content and reduce it to the formal, intricate and timeless state he sought. He abandoned the Celtic mythology and *fin de siècle* mannerisms of his early poetry in favour of a more personal imagery, drawing upon stories of his ancestors and his Irish contemporaries; e.g. the famous poem *The Lake Isle of Innisfree*. Some of the poems of this period, high romantic elegies for an Irish civilization which he felt was disappearing, are among his loveliest, most technically assured and daring. Byzantine civilization, its violence expressed in gorgeous traditional patterns, provided one image of the art he aimed at; this was paralleled by the influence of the Japanese Nō drama on his theatrical work, e.g. the *4 Plays for Dancers*. An increasing preoccupation with the occult threatened to divorce his poetry from ordinary

Yevgeny Yevtushenko

Yevele. North aisle of the nave of Westminster Abbey

human experience, but Y. came to realize that the symbol was becoming a substitute for reality and his final poems were works of great richness and complexity. Y.'s plays include *Kathleen ni Houlihan* (1902) and *The Pot of Broth* in prose; and *Deirdre* (1907) and *On Baile's Strand* (1904) in verse.

Yellow Book, The (1894–7). Illustrated periodical to which many distinguished writers and artists–e.g. Henry James and Max Beerbohm–contributed, but particularly associated with the 'decadents' and 'aesthetes' of the period, e.g. Beardsley, Oscar Wilde and Rolfe.

Yeomen of the Guard, The. Operetta by W. S. *Gilbert and A. Sullivan; 1st performance at London in 1888.

Yerma (1934). Play by *Lorca.

Yeux Sans Visage, Les (1959). Film directed by G. *Franju.

Yevele Henry (*c.* 1320–1400). English architect. In 1360 he was appointed 'disposer of the King's works pertaining to the art of masonry', i.e. in effect chief architect of the country. He worked extensively on the royal palaces, defence-works, bridges, etc. but is chiefly remembered as the designer of the naves of Canterbury cathedral and Westminster Abbey. Both replaced earlier Romanesque structures. At Canterbury (1377 onwards) Y. built in the contemporary perpendicular style. But at Westminster (1362 onwards) he took the remarkable decision to imitate the 13th-c. Early English style of the choir and transepts.

Yevtushenko Yevgeny (1933–). Soviet poet regarded as typical of the post-Stalin generation; his verse expresses a generous idealism and a confidence in the Soviet future which has not prevented him from criticizing the present, e.g. *Winter Station, Consider Me a Communist!* and *Babi Yar*. He has also publ. *A Premature Autobiography* (1963; 1963).

yodel or **jodel.** A style of wordless singing common in the Tyrolean Alps; it is distinguished by characteristic rapid alternations, involving big leaps, between the *chest and *falsetto voice.

Yon Pietro Alessandro (1886–1943). Italian-born U.S. organist and composer; his works include the oratorio *The Triumph of St Patrick* (1934).

Yonge Charlotte Mary (1823–1901). English novelist. Her moralizing romances, once very popular, include *The Heir of Redclyffe* (1853) and *Heartsease* (1854).

Yonge Nicholas (d. 1619). English musician whose *Musica Transalpina* (1588–97), a coll. of Italian madrigals, had a tremendous impact on English composers, above all of the madrigal.

Yorke F(rancis) R(eginald) S(tevens) (1906–62). Pioneer British architect of the 1930s, partner of Breuer and member of the MARS group. Y. designed some of the best British houses of that period. After the war he headed a large organization, Yorke, Rosenberg and Mardall, who were responsible for Gatwick Airport (1958) and their own elegant offices in Greystoke Place, London (1961).

York Minster England. Cathedral with examples of all 3 English Gothic styles. The transepts, begun in 1242, are Early English, with huge lancets (the 'Five Sisters') and round windows, predating the introduction of tracery. The octagonal chapter-house and most of the nave and chancel are decorated and have wooden 'vaults' in imitation of stone. The 2-tower W. front (perpendicular) is perhaps the most successful English solution to this problem.

'York Plays', The. Cycle of 14th-c. English *miracle plays.

Yoshimura Kimisaburo (1911–). Japanese film director. Very versatile, he is particularly known for his handling of films about women. *The Fellows who ate the Elephant* (1947) is a satire, and *The Naked Face of Night* (1958) an outspoken study of classical dance.

Yorke, Rosenberg and Mardall. Gatwick Airport: Terminal Building and Central Pier

York Minster. Also *Gothic

Edward Young

Lester Young

Eugène Ysaÿe

You Know me, Al; A Busher's Letters (1916). Book by Ring *Lardner.

Young Edward (1683–1765). English poet and clergyman. His popular blank-verse poem in 9 books, *The Complaint, or Night Thoughts on Life, Death and Immortality* (1742–5), is didactic and sententious; but its gloomy setting and air of sorrow and mystery–anticipating romantic attitudes–gained it European fame. In *Conjectures on Original Composition* (1759) Y. held that genius was justified in breaking literary rules.

Young Lester (1909–59). U.S. tenor saxophonist. His light-toned, relaxed and linear approach made him the most influential jazz musician on his instrument after Coleman Hawkins, and anticipated many of the developments of modern jazz. He made a classic series of recordings in the late 1930s and early 1940s with Billie Holiday and Count Basie.

Young William (d. 1671). English musician working in the 1650s at Innsbruck, where he publ. a set of instrumental sonatas with continuo, the earliest known by an Englishman. After the Restoration Y. came to the court of Charles II.

Young France. Group of 20th-c. composers, Jolivet, Baudrier, Daniel-Lesur and Messiaen, opposed to the classicism of Stravinsky.

Young Germany. Term applied to a group of politically minded liberal German writers *c.* 1835–48, especially Börne, Büchner and Gutzkow; Heine is sometimes considered a Young German.

Young Person's Guide to the Orchestra. (1946). Work by Benjamin *Britten.

Young Törless (1906). Novel by Robert *Musil.

Youth (1857). Novel by Tolstoy; also the title of a short story by Conrad.

Yóvkov Yordan (1880–1937). The greatest of his generation of Bulgarian realist writers; his work, for all its simplicity of means, achieves epic effects.

Ysaÿe Eugène (1858–1931). Belgian violinist and conductor, professor of the violin at Brussels Conservatory. He toured Europe and the U.S., led a string quartet, and was one of the most important teachers in the history of modern violin technique. His compositions include 2 operas in Walloon and 6 violin concertos.

Ysenbrandt Adriaen: Adriaen *Isenbrandt

Yusskevich Igor (1912–). Russian dancer trained in Paris under Preobrajenska and since 1946 one of the most prominent male dancers in the U.S. In his years as leading dancer with Ballet Theater he has shown himself a great soloist and danseur noble.

Yutkevich Sergei (1904–). Russian film director. Y. was a co-founder of FEKS with *Kozintzev and Trauberg. He started directing in 1928 and his work includes documentaries as well as a 2-part *Adventures of the Good Soldier Schweik* (1941–3). He is best known in the West for his version of *Othello* (1956).

Yutkevich. *Othello*

Z

Zadkine. Maquette for *The Destroyed City*. Also *expressionism

Zadkine. *Orpheus*

Zacconi Lodovico (1555–1627). Italian musician and theorist whose treatise *Prattica di musica . . .* (part 1 1592; part 2 1619) gives information on contemporary instrumental techniques and the method of performing polyphonic choral works.

Zachow (Zachau) Friedrich Wilhelm (1663–1712). German composer and organist, Handel's teacher at Halle.

Zadig (1748). Philosophical tale by Voltaire.

Zadkine Ossip (1890–). Sculptor born in Smolensk, studied in Sunderland, in London at the Regent Street Polytechnic and then in 1909 at the École des Beaux-Arts, Paris. In Paris he formed a deep and lifelong admiration for Rodin, but the most immediate impact upon him was that of cubism. For a few years he experimented–like Lipchitz, Laurens and Archipenko–with a disciplined analysis of the figure into an austere geometric arrangement of solids. For him cubism was an important transitional period and in the 1920s his forms opened into curvilinear rhythms and were given an essentially expressive significance. The liberating experience of cubism allowed him, in his own words, 'to create an allegorical form that is complete in itself, no longer requiring an attribute'. Thus his *Prometheus* is a fusion of figure and flame, and the torso of *Orpheus* (1949; Marl, Westphalia) opens into the form of a lyre. *The Destroyed City* (1951–3; Rotterdam) is the best example of the formal freedom of cubism being used to create a violently expressionist image. Z. still lives in Paris, where he exerts a considerable influence as both artist and teacher.

Zadok the Priest. Anthem by *Handel for the coronation (1727) of George II.

Zamora Antonio de (*c.* 1662–1728). Spanish playwright; author of a play about Don Juan, *No hay plazo que no se cumpla.*

Zampa. Opera by *Hérold; 1st performance at Paris in 1831.

Zampa Luigi (1905–). Italian film director. Z. is one of the minor figures of Italian neo-realism. He is famous for the war film *Vivere in pace* (1946), a plea for tolerance.

Zamyatin Yevgeny Ivanovich (1884–1937). Soviet novelist, author of *We* (1924, in an English trs.; it has never appeared in the Soviet Union). This novel, set in the future, describes the regimented life of individuals in a totalitarian state where even thought is finally controlled. *We* anticipated George Orwell's *1984* in most respects. Z. was allowed to leave the U.S.S.R. in 1931.

Zanella Giacomo (1820–88). Italian poet. His work, including the well-known ode *Sopra una conchiglia fossile nel mio studio,* is distinguished by its delicacy of feeling and graceful expression.

Zangwill Israel (1864–1926). English novelist. His works, once very popular, include *Children of the Ghetto* (1892, successfully dramatized 1899).

Zanuck Darryl Francis (1902–). Film producer; co-founder of 20th Century Productions in 1933. He became an independent producer in 1952, but after the Fox crisis with *Cleopatra* in 1962 took over the running of the studio. Unlike most studio heads he has since 1933 personally produced many films. As a producer he is among the most courageous in America. His work includes *The Grapes of Wrath,* as well as other films by John Ford, Lang, Kazan and Mankiewicz.

Zao-Wou-Ki (1920–). Chinese abstract painter, resident in Paris. He has combined the decorative precision of Chinese calligraphy with dramatic hazy images of destruction.

Zarathustra. German rendering of Zoroaster, a Persian prophet who founded the Zoroastrian religion. Z. is the mouthpiece for *Nietzsche's views in *Also Sprach Zarathustra.*

Zarlino Gioseffo (1517–90). Italian composer and theorist whose *Institutioni harmoniche* (1558) on the modes, harmony and counterpoint has been called the 1st modern musical treatise. It was an exhaustive and scientific defence of the current musical establishment.

Zao-Wou-Ki. *Cathedral and its Surroundings* (1955)

Ziggurat. 3rd Dynasty, Ur (reconstruction)

Stefan Żeromski

Januarius Zick. *St Charles Borromeo giving Communion to the Plague-stricken*

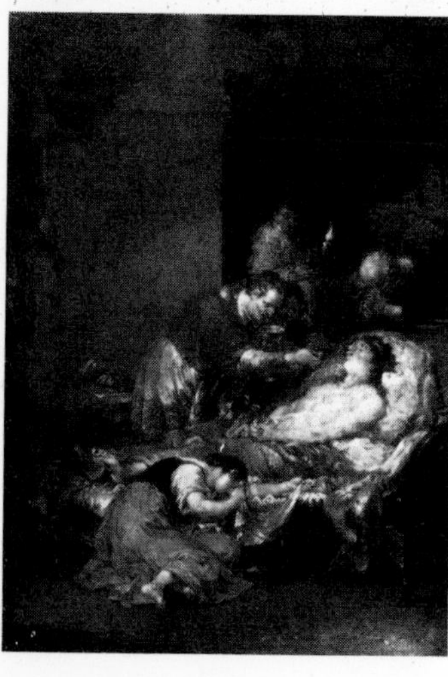

zarzuela. Spanish stage entertainment with music; like the *Singspiel in having spoken dialogue and like the *ballad opera in that the music is often based on traditional national airs. The manner is usually satirical and the libretto occasionally has improvised sections.

Zavattini Cesare (1902–). Italian film writer. Z. is one of the key figures in neo-realism as its most convinced propagandist and as script writer of de Sica's films from 1942.

Zecchi Adone (1904–). Italian composer and conductor. He founded the Bolognese da Camera Orchestra and has taught at the music Liceo in Bologna. Recent compositions have used 12-note techniques.

Zechariah. One of the minor prophetic books of the *Bible (Old Testament).

Zelenka Jan Dismas (1679–1745). Czech baroque composer whose instrumental music has recently been 'rediscovered'. J. J. Quantz was a pupil of his in Vienna.

Żeleński Tadeusz (1874–1941). Polish writer using the pseud. 'Boy'. He wrote gay, satirical verses which enjoyed immense popularity, and trs. into Polish more than 100 classics, providing the 1st outstanding trs of the major figures of French literature. In his critical writings he systematically 'debunked' literary idols. He was also an outstanding theatre critic.

Zelter Carl Friedrich (1758–1832). German composer and music pedagogue. In 1791 he became a member of the Berlin Singakademie and in 1800 its director, frequently producing performances of works by J. S. Bach. Z. was in effect the founder of Prussian musical education; his pupils included Mendelssohn, Nicolai, and Meyerbeer; he was a lifelong friend of Goethe.

Zeman Karel (1910–). Czech film director. Z. made from 1946 short puppet films and cartoons. Of his features, the last 2, *An Invention of Destruction* (1957) and *Baron Munchausen* (1962), combine actors with animation and model work, in a vein of imaginative, free-wheeling fantasy.

Zenale Bernardino (d. 1526). Italian painter and architect, pupil of Foppa in Milan. He was a friend of Leonardo da Vinci and to some extent influenced by him. He frequently collaborated with Butinone.

Zeno Apostolo (1668–1750). Italian librettist, court poet at the imperial court in Vienna, author of a large number of operatic librettos (on classical themes) and oratorios.

Zephaniah. One of the minor prophetic books of the *Bible (Old Testament).

Zéro de Conduite (1933). Short film directed by J. *Vigo.

Żeromski Stefan (1864–1925). Polish writer whose intense, poetic prose conceals any structural weaknesses in his works. He made his reputation writing on social themes, but is known in the West for *Popioły* (1904; *The Ashes*, 1928), a novel of the Napoleonic period which balances the glories with the pity and horror of war, and *Wierna rzeka* (1912; *The Faithful River*, 1943) a short novel of the 1863 Rising.

Zeuxis (*fl.* late 5th c. B.C.). Greek painter, pupil of Apollodoros and particularly renowned for a painting of Helen for the city of Crotona in which he combined the best features of several young girls. He was reputed to have painted a bunch of grapes with such naturalism that the birds flew to peck at it.

Zhukovsky Vasily Andreyevich (1783–1852). Russian poet, one of the founders of the *Arzamas group. Z.'s trs of English and German poets played an important role in the development of romanticism in Russia and his forms and vocabulary dominated subsequent 19th-c. Russian poetry.

Zick Januarius Johann Rasso (1730–97). German painter and architect who studied under his father JOHANN Z. (1702–62), a painter of religious subjects, and in Rome under

Ziggurat. Yucatan, Mexico

Mengs. He produced many large-scale frescoes. He also painted portraits and genre scenes which showed the combined influences of Mengs and Rembrandt.

Ziegfeld Florenz (1867–1932). U.S. theatre manager whose name is synonymous with the 'Ziegfeld Follies', a form of *revue modelled on the Folies-Bergère in Paris; it was noted for its lavish scenery and costumes and beautiful girls.

ziggurat. In ancient Mesopotamian and Mexican architecture, a pyramid-shaped construction built in tiers and supporting a temple or altar.

Zilahy Lajos (1891–). Hungarian novelist and playwright, one of the best-known contemporary Hungarian authors abroad. Z. exhibits traits which in style, plot and characterization appeal to a large segment of the public. His *Két fogoly* (1927; *Two Prisoners*, 1931), *A szökevény* (1930; *The Deserter*, 1932) *A fegyverek visszanéznek* (1936; *The Guns Look Back*, 1938), *The Dukays* (1950) and *The Angry Angel* (1954) were popular in England.

Zillig Winfried (1905–). German composer, a pupil of Schoenberg, and conductor; in the latter capacity he has favoured the music of Schoenberg and Mahler.

Zimmerman Bernd Alois (1918–). German composer, one of the most *avant-garde* of his generation. Stravinsky's music was an early model, e.g. the oboe concerto (1952), but subsequently Z. has been associated with the Webern school and has throughout been affected by the jazz idiom, e.g. the trumpet concerto *Nobody Knows de trouble I see* (1954). Z. has also written a 1-movement symphony (1953) and the ballet *Contrasts* (1954).

Zimmerman Mac (1912–). German surrealist painter and graphic artist.

Zimmermann Dominikus (1685–1766). S. German rococo architect. He was one of a large and poor family and began life as an artist in stucco. Later he learned to work as a mason, but never had any academic training. He built 3 famous churches: Steinhausen, Günzburg and 'Die Wies'. All show a striking unity of design and make probably the most immediate and dramatic impact on the spectator of any architecture anywhere; Z. combined spatial complexity with lavish stucco decoration (using gold and imitation marble), statuary, fresco (often by his brother JOHANN BAPTIST: 1680–1758), woodwork, metalwork, and subtle effects of lighting. The total effect, however, is one of extreme lightness and elegance. In spite of his sophistication Z. remained in many ways a simple craftsman and often indulges in an attractive whimsicality – insects, birds and cherubs creeping round in solemn surroundings.

Zingarelli Nicola Antonio (1752–1837). Italian composer, immensely popular for his operas. As director of the Naples Conservatory he had Bellini as a pupil.

Zingaro, Lo: Antonio da *Solario

Zinnemann Fred (1907–). Austrian-born U.S. film director. Z. was assistant to *Schufftan on *Menschen am Sonntag* before going to America; in Mexico he made *The Wave* (1934) with Paul Strand. From 1937 to 1942 he made shorts for M.G.M., then features. Apart from *The Seventh Cross* (1944), his 1st important picture was *The Search* (1948); since then all his pictures have had great prestige, and occasionally as in *High Noon* (1952), *From Here to Eternity* (1953) and *The Nun's Story* (1959) great commercial success. Z. is a very serious director who does not feel equipped to tackle comedy, but his seriousness is weighty rather than exciting.

zither. Stringed musical instrument of Central European origins. It consists of strings stretched over a flat sound-box rested on the knees or on a table; the strings are plucked and the upper ones can be stopped by the fingers to produce different notes.

Zoffany John (Johann Zoffani) (1733–1810). German painter who studied in Rome before

Dominikus Zimmermann. 'Die Wies'. Also *rococo and colour plate 64

Zinnemann. Gary Cooper in *High Noon*

Zithers

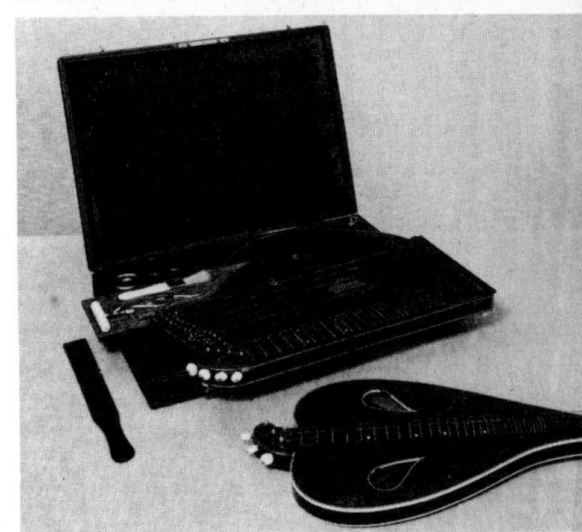

Zoppo. *Madonna and Four Saints*

Zorach. *The Artist's Daughter* (1930–46)

Mikhail Zoshchenko

Zola: painting by Manet. Also *Fantin-Latour

Cinq Centimes

ERNEST VAUGHAN

L'AURORE

Littéraire, Artistique, Sociale

J'Accuse...!

TRE AU PRÉSIDENT DE LA RÉPUBLIQUE

Par ÉMILE ZOLA

Zola. Headline of *J'accuse*; the letter was publ. in the newspaper *L'Aurore*

he settled in England *c.* 1760. One of the founder-members of the R.A. his patrons were Garrick's circle and the Royal Family. Some of his best paintings deal with the theatre, but he also painted a number of hack portraits and domestic scenes. During a stay in India (1783–90) Z. produced a great deal of work. *Queen Charlotte with the Prince of Wales and Duke of York* (N.P.G., London) is one of his typical paintings.

Zola Émile (1840–1902). French novelist, of Italian origin on his father's side. For a time he worked for the publ. Hachette, and then lived entirely by his pen. His career was uneventful, apart from 2 episodes: he had, in addition to his wife, a mistress and 2 illegitimate children, and he played a prominent part in the Dreyfus Affair by writing the famous open letter, *J'accuse* (1898), condemning the government and institutions of France for conniving at injustice; he was forced to flee to England, where he remained for a year.
Z. was the principal exponent of *naturalism, and his works are all carefully documented. The use of the novel to investigate social conditions, organizations and professions is foreshadowed in Dickens and Balzac, but achieves its modern form in Z. His influence has been widespread, notably among 20th-c. U.S. writers. The 20 novels of the cycle *Les Rougon-Macquart* (1871–93) depict all classes of society under the Second Empire, describing the fortunes of a family tainted with insanity and drunkenness. Z.'s theories emphasized the importance of heredity, but the novels increasingly imply that bad social conditions bring hereditary vices to the surface, e.g. in *L'Assommoir* (1877; *The Dram Shop*, 1884) Gervaise's attempts to achieve respectability are frustrated by circumstances and she at last turns to alcohol. Although the mass of detail is sometimes tedious, it often has a cumulative effect, as e.g. in *Nana* (1880; 1880), where the life of a courtesan comes to symbolize the corruption of the Second Empire; at the end of the book she is horribly disfigured, dying of smallpox as the Empire moves towards destruction. The many powerful scenes of sex and violence in Z.'s novels shocked contemporaries. They undoubtedly spring in part from Z.'s personal obsessions, but also from his love of truth and crusading zeal, e.g. the description in *La Joie de vivre* (1884; *How Jolly Life Is*, 1886; also called *Zest for Life*), of a young girl's terror–the result of ignorance and prudishness–when she first menstruates. Z. could also be lyrical, e.g. the descriptions of Paris in *Une Page d'amour* (1878; *A Love Episode*, 1887) and the idyll in an overgrown, paradisical garden in *La Faute de l'abbé Mouret* (1875; 1886). Other novels include *Germinal* (1885, *Germinal* or *Master and Man*, 1901), which exposes mining conditions; a lurid description of the bestiality of the peasants, *La Terre* (1887; *The Soil*, 1888); *La Bête humaine* (1890; *The Human Beast*, 1901), set among railway workers; and (not in the *Rougon-Macquart* series) *Thérèse Raquin* (1867; 1886).

zoom: *film techniques

Zoppo Marco (*c.* 1432–*c.* 78). Italian painter, pupil of Squarcione at Padua but more strongly influenced by Cosimo Tura. He worked mainly in Venice.

Zorach William (1887–). Lithuanian-born U.S. sculptor and painter. He began as a painter, studying in the U.S. and in Paris where he came under the influence of cubism. On his return to the U.S. he exhibited at the Armory Show. He devoted himself to sculpture in the early 1920s. As a sculptor he is a traditionalist both in his choice of subjects and his mode of expression.

Zorn Anders Leonard (1860–1920). Swedish genre and portrait painter in a vigorous impressionistic style, and etcher. He worked in England, France and the U.S. before settling in Mora, his birthplace.

Zorrilla José (1817–93). Spanish romantic poet and playwright who wrote a popular Don Juan play, *Don Juan Tenorio*.

Zuccarelli. *Landscape with Figures bathing and fishing below a Waterfall*

Federico Zuccaro. *Barbarossa and Alexander III*

Taddeo Zuccaro. *Conversion of St Paul*

Zoshchenko Mikhail Mikhailovich (1895–1958). Soviet humorous writer. Z.'s best works are short stories distinguished by their use of the pretentious, would-be-cultured jargon of contemporary townspeople. He was most popular and artistically successful in the 1920s and early 1930s, when his stories reflected the poverty of the masses and contained much implied criticism of the régime. From this time his works became less acceptable to the authorities; in 1946 he was expelled from the Writers' Union and publ. of his works was only allowed in the last few years of his life.

Zuccalli Enrico (1642–1724). Italian architect who worked mostly in S. Germany. He contributed to the Theatinerkirche and the Palace of Nymphenburg, both at Munich. His masterpiece is the Palace of Schleissheim, just outside Munich, a very long frontage showing influence from Versailles but more lively.

Zuccarelli Francesco (1702–88). Italian painter of light pastoral, chiefly riverside, scenes after the manner of M. Ricci. He worked mainly in Venice but made 2 visits to England where he received court patronage and became a founder-member of the R.A.

Zuccaro (Zuccari, Zuccheri) Federico (1543–1609). Italian painter in the mannerist tradition; brother of Taddeo Z. He visited England (1574–5) where he made chalk drawings of Queen Elizabeth I and the earl of Leicester and possibly painted some of the many portraits attributed to him. On his return to Italy he finished Vasari's frescoes in the dome of Florence cathedral. He later worked in the Escorial, Madrid for Philip II. He was a founder of the Academy of St Luke, Rome and in 1607 publ. the theoretical work *L'Idea de' Pittori, Scultori et Architetti.*

Zuccaro (Zuccari, Zuccheri) Taddeo (1529–66). Italian mannerist painter active chiefly in Rome. His most important works were decorative frescoes in the Palazzo Farnese at Caprarola and in the Sala Regia in the Vatican.

Zucchi Antonio (1726–95). Venetian decorative painter who worked in England for R. Adam. In 1781 he married Angelica Kauffmann and settled with her in Rome.

Zucchi Virginia (1847–1930). Italian dancer who studied under Blasis and later joined the Bolshoi Theatre (1885). She had a dazzling technique and fine dramatic capabilities and became extremely popular with Russian audiences. She started the fashion for the shorter *tutu and spent her retirement from the stage teaching in Monte Carlo.

Zuckmayer Carl (1896–). German playwright whose comedies were frequently performed in the 1920s, the most famous being *Der Hauptmann von Kopenick* (1931; *The Captain of Kopenick*, 1932), a satire on German officialdom.

Zuleika Dobson (1911). Fantasy by Max *Beerbohm.

Zuloaga (y Zabaleta) Ignacio (1870–1945). Spanish portrait and genre painter who worked in France as well as Spain. As a young man he was friendly with *avant-garde* painters and writers in Paris but nevertheless remained aloof from modern movements. He painted Spanish scenes and typical national types in a decorative, highly coloured style.

Zurbarán Francisco de (1598–1664). Spanish painter of portraits and religious subjects. At the request of Seville, then one of the most important art centres in Spain, he moved to the city as official painter. The commission to decorate the new royal palace, Buen Retiro in Madrid, with a series of paintings, *The Labours of Hercules* (1624), probably came through his good friend Velazquez. From 1628 to 1640 he was working on a great many paintings for the Jeronymite monastery at Guadalupe. From 1640 onwards his fortunes changed and he died in poverty and obscurity. A characteristic feature of his paintings is flat

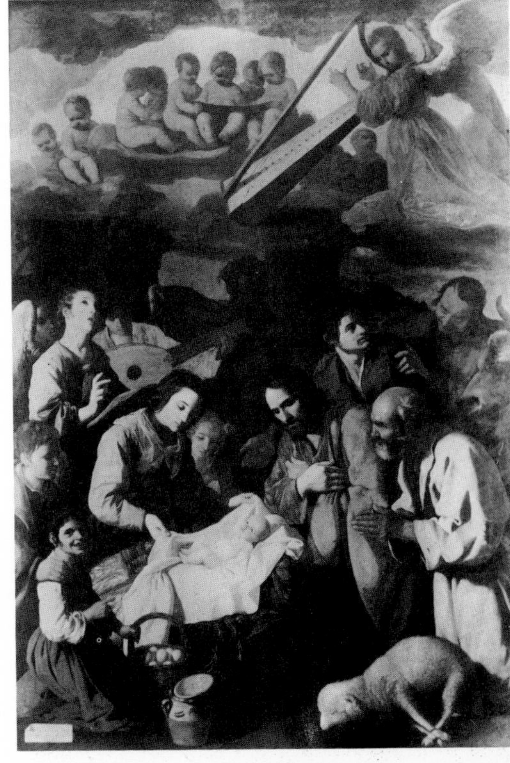
Zurbarán. *Adoration of the Shepherds*

Zurbarán. *St Serapion*

areas of pure colour and clashing dissonances of yellow, crimson and blue. A change took place, however, towards the end of his life, as his colours became less harsh and their tonal relationship more subtle. This could have been partly due to the necessity of pleasing his patrons the religious orders. Living a life close to theirs, he came to produce work which was the embodiment of mysticism and spiritual composition. He influenced the work of Spanish painters and the artists of the Spanish South American colonies. The realists in 19th-c. France owed him a great deal.

Stefan Zweig

Zurlini Valerio (1926–). Italian film director. Z. made a lot of shorts before directing his 1st feature in 1954. Before his *Cronaca familiare* won the main prize at Venice in 1962, he had already attracted attention with *Estate violenta* (1959) and *La ragazza con la valigia* (1960). *Cronaca* is marked by its meticulous use of colour and setting for dramatic effect.

Zvenigora (1928). Film directed by A. *Dovzhenko.

Zweig Arnold (1887–). German novelist. After World War I his work–until then sensitive, ironic, psychological–was concerned with the individual's relationship with the community, with the military and social machines; the most impressive result was the war novel *Der Streit um den Sergeanten Grischa* (1927; *The Case of Sergeant Grischa*, 1928). Z. left Nazi Germany and settled in Palestine. Works include *Erziehung vor Verdun* (1935; *Education before Verdun*, 1936) and *Einsetzung eines Königs* (1937; *The Crowning of a King*, 1938).

Zweig Stefan (1881–1942). Austrian writer, much travelled, an émigré in 2 World Wars; he committed suicide in Brazil. Z. wrote trs, poems and plays, but was more successful in his psychological probing of life's victims in such stories as *Erstes Erlebnis* (1911), *Amok* (1922) and *Verwirrung der Gefühle* (1927) and in his biographical studies of creativity, notably 12 essays (1919–31) coll. as *Baumeister der Welt* (1936), and *Sternstunden der Menschheit* (1927).

LIST OF COLOUR PLATES

23 Visigothic eagle brooches from Estramadura
Early sixth century
Walters Art Gallery, Baltimore

24 The sandal of St Andrew
Reliquary from the Ottonian court at Trier
Late tenth century
Domschatz, Trier

25 The Bayeux Tapestry
Detail from scenes of the Battle of Hastings
Late eleventh century
Bayeux Museum

26 Otto III enthroned
Illustration from the *Gospel Book of Otto III*
c. 998
Staatsbibliothek, Munich

27 The abbey church of La Madeleine, Vézelay
Interior, looking east (the nave)
c. 1104–32

28 Martinus Presbyter
Virgin and Child
1199
Staatliche Museum, Berlin

29 Christ in Glory
Book-cover of Limoges enamel
Late twelfth century
Musée de Cluny, Paris

30 Amiens cathedral
Interior, looking east
First half of the thirteenth century

31 St John the Baptist
Statue on the north transept of Chartres cathedral
c. 1220

32 Strassburg cathedral
Rose-window on the west front
1360

33 Gloucester cathedral
Walk in the cloister
c. 1350

34 A Sower
Detail of a stained-glass window in Canterbury cathedral
Early thirteenth century

35 Façade of Orvieto cathedral
Begun in 1309

36 Giotto
Lamentation over the Dead Christ
Fresco in the Scrovegni Chapel, Padua
c. 1306

37 Simone Martini
The Annunciation
Early fourteenth century
Galleria degli Uffizi, Florence

38 Jan van Eyck
The Arnolfini Marriage Group
1434
National Gallery, London

39 The Master of Flémalle
St Barbara
1438
Museo Nacional del Prado, Madrid

40 Rogier van der Weyden
Portrait of a Lady
Mid-fifteenth century
National Gallery, London

41 Ghiberti
Detail from the *Gates of Paradise*
Gates of the Baptistery, Florence
1430–47

42 Piero della Francesca
The Triumph of Federigo da Montefeltro
1465–6
Galleria degli Uffizi, Florence

43 Botticelli
The Annunciation
1489–90
Galleria degli Uffizi, Florence

44 Leonardo da Vinci
The Virgin of the Rocks
c. 1483
National Gallery, London

45 Giorgione
The Tempest
1505
Gallerie dell'Accademia, Venice

46 Michelangelo
The Holy Family
1504
Galleria degli Uffizi, Florence

47 Michelangelo
The Palazzo dei Conservatori, on the Capitol, Rome
Begun in 1546

48 Palladio
Palazzo Chiericati, Vicenza
1550–7

49 Intarsia panelling in the private study of Federigo da Montefeltro in the Ducal Palace, Gubbio
1479–82
Metropolitan Museum, New York

50 *The Garden of Love*
Tapestry from Touraine
c. 1503
Musée des Gobelins, Paris

51 Dürer
Self-portrait
1498
Museo Nacional del Prado, Madrid

52 Cranach
Venus and Cupid stung by a bee
1531
Musées Royaux des Beaux-Arts, Brussels

53 El Greco
St Martin and the Beggar
1597–9
Museo Nacional del Prado, Madrid

54 Caravaggio
The Musical Party
1594–5
Metropolitan Museum, New York

55 Celestial and terrestrial globe
Made at Augsburg for Rudolf II
1588
Kunsthistorisches Museum, Vienna

56 Benvenuto Cellini
Gold salt-cellar
1570
Kunsthistorisches Museum, Vienna

57 Wine-cooler
Made for the Duke of Urbino in the studio of Fontana
1565–71
Museo Nazionale (Bargello), Florence

58 Poussin
Bacchanalian Revel before a Term of Pan
c. 1635
National Gallery, London

59 Rubens
Hélène Fourment in a Fur Coat
After 1630
Kunsthistorisches Museum, Vienna

60 Rembrandt
Titus Reading
c. 1656
Kunsthistorisches Museum, Vienna

61 Vermeer
The Artist's Studio
1665–70
Kunsthistorisches Museum, Vienna

62 Heda
Still-life
1637
Musée du Louvre, Paris

63 Salon in the Château de Champs
Eighteenth century

64 Dominikus Zimmermann
Pilgrimage church 'In der Wies' (Wieskirche)
1746–54

65 Franz Ignaz Günther
The Guardian Angel
Painted wood sculpture
1763
Burgersaal, Vienna

66 François de Cuvilliès
The old Residence Theatre, Munich
1751–3

67 Gainsborough
The Morning Walk
c. 1785
National Gallery, London

68 Ingres
La Grande Odalisque
1819
Musée du Louvre, Paris

69 Delacroix
Arab on Horseback attacked by a Lion (detail)
1849
Art Institute of Chicago

70 Monet
Field of Poppies
1873
Musée du Louvre, Paris

71 Van Gogh
Road with Cypresses (detail)
1889
Kröller-Müller Rijksmuseum, Otterlo

72 Cézanne
Mont-Ste-Victoire (detail)
1904–6
Tyson Collection, Philadelphia Museum of Art

73 Picasso
Les Demoiselles d'Avignon
1907
Museum of Modern Art, New York

74 Kokoschka
Windsbraut
1914
Kunstmuseum, Basle

75 Jackson Pollock
Painting
1948
Paul Facchetti Collection, Paris

76 Mondrian
Rhythm of Straight Lines
c. 1936
Henry Clifford Collection

77 Eero Saarinen
TWA building, Kennedy Airport, New York
1956–61

78 Mies van der Rohe
Seagram Building, New York
1958

79 Henry Moore
Seated Figure
1962
Collection the artist

SOURCES OF ILLUSTRATIONS

The following plates are reproduced by gracious permission of Her Majesty the Queen: pages 32 (Coninxloo), 47 (Aubrey), 55 (Baglione), 91 (Bernini, self-portrait), 144 (Byron), 187 (Cignani), 205 (Zoffany), 406 (Hoppner), 420 (Gentile), 528 (Kneller), 572 (Lotto), 676 (Oliver, Unknown Man), 692 (Pantoja de la Cruz), 704 (Perréal), 763 (M. Ricci and S. and M. Ricci), 766 (Riley), 796 (Sandby), 838 (Somer), 858 (Stubbs, *The Prince of Wales' Phaeton*), 965 (Zuccarelli).

The publishers wish to thank all the museums and galleries whose works are reproduced in this book: Aberdeen Art Gallery: 658 (Nash, *Northern Adventure*), 763 (Richards), 847 (Steer); Marischal College 761 (Reynolds, *The Triumph of Truth*). Akron (Ohio): Art Institute 51 (Baburen). Amsterdam: Gemeente Museum 243, 424 (Israëls); Rijksmuseum 45 (Asselyn), 108 (Bol), 115 (Both), 126 (Bril), 332 (Gelder), 369 (Rembrandt), 390 (Helst), 395 (Heyden), 521 (Key), 608 (Master of the Virgo inter Virgines), 621 (Metsu), 755 (Rembrandt, *The Night Watch*), 785 (Ruisdael), 865 (Rembrandt), 916 (Vermeer, *The Love-letter*), 927 (Vondel), Prentenkabinett 608 (Master of the Housebook); Stedelijk Museum 173 (Chagall), 194 (Corneille), 243 (Mondrian), 323 (Malevich), 766, 841 (Soutine, *Flayed Ox*). Antwerp: Musée Royal des Beaux-Arts 282 (Ensor, *Rower*), 366 (Van Eyck); Museum Mayer van den Bergh 133 (Brueghel, *Dulle Griet*). Arras: Bibliothèque de la Ville 7. Athens: Acropolis Museum 36; Ceramikos Museum 26; National Museum 811 (Scopas). Baghdad: Iraq Museum 188. Baltimore (Md): Museum of Art 527 (Kline), 609 (Matisse, *Seated Nude*); The Walters Art Gallery 563, 692 (Panini). Barcelona: Museum of Ancient Art 410 (Huguet); Museum of Modern Art 313 (Fortuny); Museo di Arte di Cataluna 225 (Dalmau). Barnard Castle, Bowes Museum 709 (Robert). Basle: Öffentliche Kunstsammlung 3 (Gris), 105 (Böcklin), 87 (Van den Berghe), 123 (Braque, *Violin and Jug*), 358 (Graf), 524 (Kirchner, *Amselfluh*), 595 (Manuel), 787 (Russolo), 908 (Vantongerloo). Belfast: Ulster Museum and Art Gallery 842 (Spencer, *The Betrayal*). Belgrade: Gallery of Contemporary Art 575 (Lubarda). Bergamo: Accademia Carrara 326 (Galgario), 925 (B. Vivarini). Berlin: Deutsche Staatsbibliothek 53; Staatliche Museen 24 (Amarna and Amberger), 107 (Bohemian Master), 125 (Breu), 177, 185 (Petrus Christus, *Portrait of a Lady*), 319, 362, 370 (Guardi), 377 (Hals), 546 (Lastman), 630 (Mino da Fiesole), 635 (Molenaer), 644 (Moretto), 651 (Multscher), 660, 685 (Ouwater), 750 (Rayski), 803 (Schadow), 845 (Squarcione), 927 (M. de Vos), 962 (Zick), 964 (Zoppo); Kupferstichkabinett 408 (Huber); Verwaltung der Staatlichen Schlösser und Gärten 300 (Lancret), 775 (Friedrich). Berne: Paul Klee Stiftung 526 (Klee, *Kinderspiel*, *Family Walk*); Kunstmuseum 399 (Hodler). Birmingham: Barber Institute of Fine Arts 190 (Claude), 329 (Zoffany, *Garrick in 'Lethe'*); City Museum and Art Gallery 63 (Diaz), 140 (Burne-Jones), 158 (Carlevaris), 164 (Castiglione), 717 (Pissarro, *Rouen*), 910 (Varley), 931 (H. Walters). Bologna: Liceo Musicale 52 (J. C. Bach), 802 (A. Scarlatti). Bonn: Rheinisches Landesmuseum 713. Boston: Museum of Fine Arts 621 (Metzinger), 854 (Storey), 905 (Baburen). Bremen: Kunsthalle 348 (Van Gogh, *Starry Night*), 605 (Masolino). Bristol: City Art Gallery 651 (Muller), 718 (Pissarro). The Brooklyn Museum 506 (E. Johnson). Bruges: City Museum 231 (G. David). Brunswick: Herzog Anton Ulrich-Museum 304 (Finson), 538 (Laer). Brussels: Bibliothèque Royale de Belgique 395; Musée du Conservatoire 57, 219; Musées Royaux des Beaux-Arts 93 (Beuckelaer), 290 (Permeke), 607 (Massys), 678 (Opsomer), 681 (Orley), 728 (Pourbus), 833 (Smet), 927 (P. de Vos). Buffalo (N.Y.): Albright-Knox Art Gallery 3 (Mondrian), 240 (Demuth), 290 (de Kooning), 529 (Kokoschka, *Thames Landscape*), 631 (Miró, *Harlequinade*), 867 (Tamayo). Cambridge: Fitzwilliam Museum (reproduced by kind permission of the Syndics) 7, 15, 56, 242, 387 (Heemskerck). Cambridge (Mass.): Harvard University 276 (Wyndham Lewis). Cardiff: National Museum of Wales 419 (Innes), 637 (Monet, *Waterlilies*). Chatsworth: Devonshire Collection (by permission of the Trustees of the Chatsworth Settlement) 508 (Jones, designs for Chlorida and the

Masque of Blackness). Chantilly: Musée Condé 420, 563, 598 (F. Clouet), 774, 894. Chicago: Art Institute 159 and 265 (Stieglitz Collection), 290 (Van Gogh), 610 (Matta), 710 (Picabia and Picasso, *The Old Guitarist*), 818 (Seurat, *Grande Jatte*), 891 (Toulouse-Lautrec, *Le Cirque Fernando*), 950 (Wood). Cleveland: Museum of Art 83 (Bellows), 787 (Ryder). Cluny: Musée Ochier 193. Colmar: Musée 369 (Grünewald, *Ascension of Christ*), 423 (Grünewald, *Crucifixion*). Colchester and Essex Museum 63. Cologne: Stadtmuseum 132 (Kirchner, Brücke painters), 668 (Nolde); Wallraf-Richartz Museum 72 (Baumeister), 207 (Corinth), 501 (Jawlensky, *Still-life*), 509 (Joos van Cleve), 710 (Piazetta). Copenhagen: Nationalmuseet 30, 287; Statens Museum 70 (Batoni), 287 (Euripides). Darmstadt: Hessisches Landesmuseum 297 (L. Feininger, *Grützturm*). Delphi Museum 176. Detroit: Institute of Arts 96 (Bingham), 863 (Sweerts). Dijon: Musée 128 (Broederlam), 258 (Sluter), 334 (Géricault, *The Madwoman*). Douai: Musée 81 (Bellegambe). Dresden: Gemäldegalerie 57 (Baldung), 161 (Carriera), 189 (Claesz), 203 (Coninxloo), 209 (Correggio), 215 (Cranach, *Henry of Saxony*), 217 (Crespi), 340 (Giorgione, *Sleeping Venus*), 718 (Pittoni), 830 (Raphael). Dublin: National Gallery of Ireland 195 (Coello), 405 (Hone); Trinity College 520. Duisburg: Städelsches Kunstmuseum 37 (Archipenko). Düsseldorf: Kunstmuseum 659 (Cornelius). Edinburgh: National Gallery of Scotland 21 (Allan), 105 (Velasquez), 157 (Carducci), 288 (Ferguson), 330 (Gauguin, *Jacob Wrestling with the Angel*), 363 (Greuze), 637 (Monet, *Poplars*), 655 (Mytens), 745 (Raeburn), 747 (Ramsay), 776 (Romney, *Mrs Wilbraham Bootle*), 916 (Vermeer, *Christ in the House of Martha and Mary*); Scottish National Portrait Gallery 411 (Ramsay, *Hume*). Eisenach: Bach Museum 52, 53. Essen: Folkwang Museum 633 (Modersohn-Becker), 757 (Renoir, *Lise*). Exeter: Royal Albert Memorial Museum 669 (Northcote). Florence, Accademia 843 (Spinello); Bargello 242 (Desiderio, bust), 252 (Donatello), 778 (A. Rossellino), 795 (Salviati), 883 (Tino), 917 (Verrocchio, *David*); Museo Nazionale 301; Museo dell'Opera del Duomo 253 (Donatello), 769 (Luca della Robbia); Museo di S. Marco 29 (Fra Angelico, *Deposition*); Palazzo Vecchio 205 (Michelangelo), 582 (Machiavelli); Pitti Palace 22 (Allori), 837 (Sodoma), 910 (Vasari); Uffizi 16 (Albertinelli), 28 (Andrea del Sarto), 65 (Barocci), 100, 104 (Boccaccino), 115 (Botticelli), 156 (Caravaggio, *Bacchus*), 187 (Cimabue), 261 (Duccio), 333 (Gentile), 341 (Giotto, *Madonna*), 347 (van der Goes, Portinari), 419 (Ingres, *Self-portrait*), 557 (Leonardo, *Adoration*), 565 (Liotard), 604 (Masaccio, *Madonna and Child with St Anne . . .*), 635 (Monaco), 694 (Parmigianino, *Madonna of St Zacchary*), 780 (Rosso), 789 (Domenico), 918 (Verrocchio). Frankfurt: Museum für Kunsthandwerke 359; Städelsches Kunstinstitut 884 (Tischbein). Geneva: Musée d'Art et d'Histoire 949 (Witz). Glasgow Art Gallery and Museum 515 (Kalf), 558 (Lepine), 762 (Ribena, *St Peter*), 777 (Rosa). Grenoble: Musée de Peinture et de Sculpture 544 (Largillière), 965 (Zurbarán). Haarlem: Frans Hals Museum 376 (Frans Hals). The Hague: Gemeentemuseum 251 (Doesburg), 636 (Mondrian, *Still-life with Gingerpot*); Mauritshuis 256 (Dou, *Young Mother*), 727 (Potter), 755 (Rembrandt, *The Anatomy Lesson*), 863 (Sweelinck), 875 (Ter Borch), 916 (Vermeer, *View of Delft*). Hamburg: Ernst Barlach-Gesellschaft 64; Kunsthalle 76 (Beckmann), 304, 315 (Francken), 319 (Friedrich), 533 (Leibl), 607 (Master Francke), 667 (Nolde, *Aegyptiaca*), 786 (Runge), 878 (Thoma), 950 (Wols). Hanover: Niedersächsische Landesgalerie 250 (Dix), 583 (Macke). Hartford (Conn.): Wadsworth Athenaeum 156 (Caracciolo), 271 (Earle), 409 (Cole), 966 (Zurbarán). Heidelberg: Universitätsbibliothek 630. Istanbul: Archaeological Museum 579 (Lysippus). University of Kansas: Lawrence Museum of Art 775 (Rombouts). Karlsruhe: Kunsthalle 307 (Flegel), 369 (Grünewald, *Crucifixion*). Burg Karlstein: 877 (Theodoric). Krefeld: Kaiser-Wilhelm Museum 152 (Campendonk). Laren: Van Gogh Collection 348 (Van Gogh, *Potato Eaters*). Leamington Spa Museum: 101 (Bloemart). Leeds: City Art Gallery, Temple Newsam House 181 (Wilson), 641 (Moore, *Reclining Figure*), 834 (Smith, *Model Waking*), 941 (Wheatley). Leningrad: State Hermitage Museum 3 (Kandinsky), 220 (Picasso, *Nude in the Forest*), 609 (Matisse, *Mme Matisse*); Pushkin Museum 533 (Chernetsov); Russian Museum 204, 344, 589 (Malevich, *Black Square*), 707 (Petrov-Vodkin), 870 (Tatlin, *Sailor*); Theatrical Museum 589 (Malevich, *Victory over the Sun*). Leyden: Lakenthal Museum 575 (van Leyden, *Last Judgement*). Liège: Musée des Beaux-Arts 282 (Ensor, *Death and Masks*). Lisbon: Museo Nacional di Arte Antiga 35 (Gonçalves). Liverpool: Walker Art Gallery 323 (Fuseli, *Death of Oedipus*), 339 (Gilman), 506 (C. Johnson), 647 (Mostaert), 732 (Millais), 769 (Roberti). London: The Wellington Museum, Apsley House 187 (Cicero), 683 (Ostade), 847 (Steen), 912 (Velasquez, *Water-carrier*), 945 (Wilkie); The Arts Council of Great Britain 124 (Bratby), 198 (Colquhoun), 693 (Paolozzi); The British Council 39 (Armitage), 173 (Chadwick), 862 (Sutherland, *Landscape with Estuary*); British Museum (reproduced by courtesy of the Trustees) 10, 12, 17, 42, 45, 54, 77, 84, 93, 99, 119, 122, 134, 138, 147, 149, 154, 179, 200, 201, 226, 227, 281, 283, 301, 320, 339, 342, 360, 373, 376, 380, 381, 386, 401, 403, 415, 424, 498, 504, 519, 522, 532, 556, 564, 575, 578, 612, 669, 693, 695, 708, 716, 719, 727, 739, 742, 777, 799, 836, 839, 860, 899, 942, 956; Courtauld Institute of Art, Witt Library 62, 79, 94, 158, 163, 249, 321; Courtauld Institute Galleries 77 (Beechey), 289 (Eworth), 330 (Gauguin, *Nevermore*), 348 (Van Gogh, *Self-portrait*), 554 (Lely), 592 (Manet, *Folies-Bergères*), 634 (Modigliani, *Nude*), 717 (Pissarro, *Penge Station*), 758 (Renoir, *La Loge*), 891 (Toulouse-Lautrec, *Jane Avril*); Dulwich College Picture Gallery 21 (Alleyn), 54 (Backhuysen), 138 (Burbage), 409 (Hudson), 916 (Vernet), 953 (Wouwerman); Guildhall Museum 186 (Cibber, *Madness*), 678 (Opie); Horniman Museum 751; Imperial War Museum 109 (Bone); Kenwood, the Iveagh Bequest 668 (Nollekens); National Gallery (by permission of the Trustees) 1 (Abbate), 25 (Amico), 52 (Bacchiacca), 64 (Barnaba), 68 (Basaiti and Bartolommeo), 81 (Berchem and Berckheyde), 108 (Reni), 109 (Boltraffio), 110 (Bono da Ferrara), 111 (Bordone), 116 (Boucher), 129

(Bronzino), 149 (Callot), 153 (Canaletto), 154 (Capelle), 156 (Caravaggio, *Supper at Emmaus*), 162 (Leonardo), 165 (Catena), 203 (Constable, *Hay Wain*), 205 (Giovanni di Paolo), 210 (Costa), 211 (Claude), 215 (Cranach, *Charity*), 218 (Crivelli), 223 (Cuyp), 256 (Dou, *Man with Pipe*), 263 (Dujardin), 272 (Eeckhout), 289 (Everdingen), 291 (Van Eyck, *Man in red Turban*), 308 (Flinck), 311 (Foppa), 315 (Franciabigio), 325 (Gainsborough, *Cornard Wood* and *Mr and Mrs Andrews*), 329 (Garofalo), 332 (Dou), 333 (Chardin), 335 (Gerolamo), 352 (E. Gonzales), 357 (Goyen), 376 (Dirck Hals), 399 (Hobbema), 400 (Hogarth, *Marriage à la Mode, The Artist's Servants*), 401 (Holbein, *The Ambassadors*), 405 (Honthorst and Hoogh), 417 (Pissarro), 510 (Jordaens), 521 (Kessel), 522 (Keyser), 530 (Koninck), 541 (Lancret), 555 (Le Nain), 563 (Lievensz), 565 (Filippino Lippi), 569 (Longhi), 580 (Mabuse), 586 (Maes), 595 (Mantegna, *The Agony in the Garden*), 601 (Hogarth), 604 (Masaccio, *Madonna and Child*), 607 (Master of St Giles), 624 (Miereveld), 625 (Mignard), 645 (Moroni), 660 (Neer), 674 (Ochtervelt), 680 (Memlinc), 705 (Pesellino), 713 (Piero di Cosimo), 716 (Pisanello), 722 (Pollaiuolo), 726 (Memlinc), 728 (Poussin, *Annunciation*), 736 (Memlinc), 747 (Raphael), 755 (Rembrandt, *Flora* and *Françoise von Wassenhove*), 756 (Rembrandt, *Woman Bathing*), 758 (Renoir, *Les Parapluies*), 762 (Ribalta, *Fr Simon*), 765 (Richelieu), 773 (Velasquez), 782 (Uccello), 784 (Rubens, *Le Chapeau de Paille*, and *War and Peace*), 789 (Schiavone), 818 (Seurat, *Baignade*), 851 (Caravaggio), 874 (Teniers, *Playing at Bowls*), 898 (Tura), 899 (Turner, *Rain, Steam and Speed*), 902 (Uccello, *St George and the Dragon*), 902 (Ugolino), 912 (E. and W. van de Velde), 925 (Alvise Vivarini), 926 (Vlieger), 947 (Wilton), 948 (Witte), 957 (Wynants); National Maritime Museum, Greenwich (by permission of the Trustees) 363 (Greenhill); National Portrait Gallery 1 (Nelson), 8 (Addison), 15 (Albert), 22 (Coleridge), 85 (Bentham), 88 (Berkeley), 114 (Boswell), 129 (C. and E. Brontë), 131 (R. Browning), 140 (F. Burney), 141 (Burns), 143 (Samuel Butler), 186 (Roubiliac), 194 (Cobbett), 196 (Coleridge), 214 (Cowper), 216 (Cranmer), 224 (Dahl), 234 (Defoe), 241 (De Quincey), 259 (Drayton), 261 (Dryden), 276 (G. Eliot), 277 (Elizabeth I), 308 (Fletcher), 322 (Furniss), 329 (Gaskell), 337 (Gibbon), 354 (Gosse), 360 (Gray), 377 (Hardy), 399 (Hobbes), 406 (Hopkins), 411 (Leigh Hunt), 498 (Henry James), 499 (James I), 506 (Dr Johnson), 508 (Jonson), 511 (Joyce), 519 (Kean and Keats), 520 (Kemble), 523 (Killigrew), 524 (Kingsley), 540 (Lamb), 548 (T. E. Lawrence), 568 (Locke), 580 (Lord Macaulay), 603 (Marvell), 619 (Meredith), 626 (J. S. Mill), 643 (More), 663 (Cardinal Newman), 702 (Pepys), 741 (Quarles), 746 (Raleigh), 764 (S. Richardson and Vertue), 787 (Rysbrack), 813 (Walter Scott), 818 (Severn), 821 (Shakespeare, Chandos portrait), 823 (Shelley), 826 (Sidney), 833 (Smart), 835 (Smollett), 841 (Southey), 847 (Steele), 850 (Sterne), 851 (Stevenson), 859 (Suckling), 863 (Swift), 864 (Swinburne), 873 (Temple), 874 (Tennyson), 879 (J. Thomson), 880 (Thrale), 894 (Tree), 896 (Trollope), 908 (Vanbrugh), 918 (Vertue and Mme Vestris), 930 (Waller), 932 (Walpole), 952 (Wordsworth), 956 (Wyatt), 960 (E. Young); Royal Academy of Art 66 (Barry), 325 (Gainsborough, *Self-portrait*), 341 (Gilpin), 401 (Holbein, *Anne Boleyn*), 858 (Stubbs, *Flayed Horse*); Royal College of Music 10, 183, 190, 208, 673; Royal Institute of British Architects 956 (Wyatt, Ashbridge); Sir John Soane's Museum (by permission of the Trustees) 746 (Hogarth); Tate Gallery (by permission of the Trustees) 9 (Adler), 34 (Appel), 56 (Rodin), 71 (Bauchant), 99 (Blake, *Satan Smiting Job*), 110 (Bonington), 136 (Buffet), 179 (Wallis), 204 (Gabo), 210 (Cotes), 211 (Turner), 218 (Crome), 225 (Dalou), 235 (Degas, *The Little Dancer*, *Young Spartans*), 241 (Derain), 243 (Despiau), 250 (Dobson), 268 (Dyce), 271 (Eastlake), 272 (Egg), 311 (Forain), 319 (Frith), 353 (Gore), 360 (Greaves), 361 (Emilio Greco), 366 (Gris, *Still life with Newspaper*), 368 (Grosz, *Man and Wife*), 386 (Haydon), 396 (Highmore), 398 (Hitchens), 399 (Hodgkins), 409 (Arthur Hughes), 505 (A. and G. John), 515 (Kandinsky, *Battle*), 519 (Keene), 526 (Klee, *A Young Lady's Adventure*), 545 (Laroon), 553 (Leighton), 561 (W. Lewis), 562 (Liebermann), 587 (Maillot, *Torso*), 596 (Manzu), 611 (Sutherland), 627 (Millais), 628 (Milles), 632 (Chadwick), 643 (Morandi), 645 (Morland), 646 (Morris, *Iseult*), 657 (Martineau), 658 (Nash, *Pillar and Moon*), 662 (Nevinson), 664 (Nicholson, *White Relief*), 716 (Piper), 722 (Poliakoff), 743 (Hogarth), 771 (Rodin), 779 (D. G. Rossetti), 780 (Rothko), 799 (Sargent), 826 (Sickert), 831 (W. Lewis), 834 (Smith, *Nude*), 869 (Tapiès), 878 (John), 886 (Tobey, *North-west Drift*), 899 (Turner, *Hannibal* and *The Fighting Téméraire*), 933 (Ward), 934 (Watts), 942 (Whistler, *Nocturne*), 953 (Wootton), 958 (J. B. Yeats); Victoria and Albert Museum (Crown Copyright reserved) 13, 18, 29, 56, 60, 69, 79, 83, 84, 85 (Benois), 89, 94, 104, 105, 107, 108 (G. da Bologna), 116, 117, 127, 141 (Burra), 150 (Calvert), 152, 157, 160, 171 (Cesti), 175 (Chantrey), 183, 190, 191, 196, 203 (Constable, *Brighton Beach*, *Colliers*), 211 (Cotman, *Chirk Aqueduct*), 214 (Cox and Cozens), 226 (Danby), 237, 240, 241, 244, 247, 250, 259, 267, 271, 275, 280, 283, 287 (Etty), 295 (Farington), 306, 309, 316, 321, 336, 362, 365, 377, 381, 386 (Hayman), 397 (Hilliard), 398, 404, 405, 410, 412, 422, 497, 520, 525, 536, 537, 540, 548, 549, 551, 570, 574, 584, 588, 601, 602, 613, 647, 653, 660, 662, 663, 665, 670, 677, 679, 691 (Palmer, *Ruth*), 709, 713, 721, 725, 726, 736, 740, 760, 763, 776, 781, 785, 817, 853, 854, 855, 863, 864, 876, 882, 886, 891, 892 (Towne), 893, 897 (Troy), 906, 913, 918, 923, 963; Wallace Collection (by permission of the Trustees) 27, 48 (Augustin), 53 (Backer), 100 (Lawrence), 175, 208 (Corneille de Lyon), 210 (Cosway), 213 (Couture), 214 (Coysevox), 215, 266 (Dupré), 273, 314 (Fragonard), 323 (Fyt), 405 (Hondecoeter), 521 (Heyden), 547 (Hals), 874 (Teniers, *Boors Carousing*); Wellcome Foundation Historical Medical Museum 92; William Morris Gallery 240. Lugano: Thyssen-Bornemisza Collection 229 (Daret). Lund: Tegnerhuset 800. Madrid: Academia de San Fernando 643 (Morales); Biblioteca Nacional 19; Prado 72 (Goya), 92 (P. Berruguete), 114 (Bosch), 269 (Van Dyck, *Self-portrait*), 326 (Gallego), 356 (all Goya paintings), 512 (Juan de Flandes), 599 (Marinus), 618 (Velasquez), 642

830 (Sisley), 883 (Tintoretto), 895 (Weyden), 902 (Uccello, *Self-portrait*), 914 (Venus), 920 (Vigée-Lebrun), 928 (Vouet), 934 (Watteau, *Embarkation*), 942 (Whistler, *The Artist's Mother*), 948 (Winged Victory), 964 (Manet); Luxembourg 335 (Gérôme); Musée Marmottan 417 (Monet); Musée National d'Art Moderne 90 (Bernard), 109 (Bombois), 237 (Delaunay-Terk), 240 (Denis), 243 (Desnoyer), 263 (Dufy, Dufresne), 296 (Vlaminck, Marquet), 382 (Hartung), 525 (Kisling), 547 (Laurens and Laurencin), 554 (Le Moal), 561 (Lhote), 587 (Maillol, *Air*), 590 (Manessier), 597 (Marcoussis), 600 (Marquet), 610 (Matisse), 827 (Signac), 845 (Staël), 868 (Tanguy), 905 (Utrillo), 906 (Valadon), 925 (Vivin), 926 (Vlaminck, *Paysage*); Petit Palais 334 (Gérard), 367 (Gromaire). Philadelphia: The Barnes Foundation 609 (Matisse, *Joie de Vivre*); Historical Society of Pennsylvania 316 (Peale); Museum of Art 183 (de Chirico), 225 (Dali), 262 (Duchamp), 281 (Goya), 404 (Homer), 552 (Léger, *The City*), 806 (Schmidt-Rottluff), 909 (Vargas), 922 (Villon), 927 (C. de Vos). Lady Lever Art Gallery, Port Sunlight (by permission of the Trustees) 411 (Holman Hunt), 947 (R. Wilson). Prague: National Gallery 608 (Master of Wittingau); State Library of the Czechoslovak S.S.R. 412. Providence (R.I.): School of Design 614 (Medina). Ravenna: Archiepiscopal Museum 424. Rome: Borghese 149 (Calvaert), 154 (Canova), 875 (Terbrugghen), 881 (Tibaldi, *Adoration*); Palazzo Chigi 37 (Titian); Palazzo dei Conservatori 41 (Arnolfo di Cambio); Galleria Corsini 652 (Murillo, *Madonna*); Gab. Naz. delle Stampe 121; Gall. Doria-Pamphilj 161 (Carracci), 912 (Velasquez, *Innocent X*); Gall. Nazionale 337 (Giambono); Museo delle Terme 655 (Myron). Rotterdam: Boymans-van-Beuningen Museum 10 (Aertsen), 150 (Calvin), 292 (Fabritius, *Self-portrait*), 814 (Seghers). Rouen: Musée des Beaux-Arts 795 (Lemonnier). Salzburg: Mozarteum 603. San Diego (Calif.): Fine Arts Gallery 210 (Cotán). San Francisco: Art Institute 768 (Rivera). San Marino (Calif.): Huntingdon Library and Museum 168, 325 (Gainsborough, *The Blue Boy*), 353. St Quentin: Musée Lecuyer 546 (M.-Q. de La Tour). Birgo S. Sepolcro: Pal. Communale 712 (Piero, *Madonna of Mercy*). Sarasota (Fla.): John and Mabel Ringling Museum of Art 835 (Snyders). Schwerin: Staatliches Museum 385 (Haydn), 413 (Huysum). Seattle Art Museum 886 (Tobey, *Canals*). Seville Museum 772 (Roelas). Siena: Accademia 75 (Beccafumi); Biblioteca Piccolomini 715 (Pinturicchio); Pal. Pubblico 603 (Martini). Southampton Gallery 602 (John Martin), 885 (Tissot). Stockholm: Kungl. Husgeradskammaren 75; Nationalmuseum 561 (Leyster), 778 (Roslin). Stuttgart: Landesgewerbemuseum 590; Württembergische Staatsgalerie 300 (Feuerbach), 529 (Kokoschka, *Woman in Blue*), 805 (Danneker), 832 (Slevogt). Toledo (Ohio): Museum of Art 381 (Harpignies), 757 (Renoir, *Baigneuse*). Toronto: Art Gallery 937 (Weenix). Tours: Musée 60 (Boulanger). Uppsala: University Library 903. Urbana: University of Illinois 360 (M. Graves). Urbino: Gall. Nazionale 712 (Piero, *Flagellation*). Utrecht: Centraal Museum 144 (Bylert); University Library 905. Vaduz: Liechtenstein Collection 333 (Gentileschi). Valladolid: Museo Nacional de Escultura 92 (A. Berruguete), 299 (Fernández). Vancouver: Art Gallery 820 (Shadbolt). Vatican Museums and Galleries 17, 29 (Fra Angelico, *St Lorenzo*), 33 (Cnidian Aphrodite), 34 (Apollo Belvedere), 288, 543 (*Laocöon*), 615 (Melozzo), 907 (Valentin), 925 (Ant. Vivarini); Museo Gregoriano Etrusco 289. Venice: Accademia 81 (Gent. Bellini), 160 (Carpaccio), 917 (Veronese, *Feast* and self-portrait); Casa Goldoni 350 (Longhi); Museo Correr 160 (Carpaccio), 259; Pal. Ducale 965 (F. Zuccaro). Versailles: Musée 91 (Bernini, *Louis XIV*), 639, 744, 886 (Tocqué). Verulamium Excavation Committee 63. Vicenza: Museo Civico 638 (Montagna). Vienna: Akademie der Bildenden Künste 113 (Bosch); Albertina 267 (Dürer, *Large tuft of grass*), 269 (Van Dyck, *Sir K. Digby*); Barockmuseum 611 (Maulpertsch); Kunsthistorisches Museum 37 (Arcimboldo), 82 (Bellotto), 133 (J. Brueghel, P. Brueghel, *Peasant Wedding, Massacre of the Innocents*), 135, 170, 275, 331 (Geertgen), 341 (Giorgione), 345 (Duplessis, *Gluck*), 347 (Van der Goes, *Fall of Adam*), 424, 845 (Spranger), 874 (Teniers, *Archduke Leopold Wilhelm*); Museum des 20 Jahrhunderts 908; Nationalbibliothek 223; Österreichisches Galerie 321 (Frueauf the Elder), 527 (Klimt); Österreichisches Museum für angewandte Kunst 13. Volterra: Gall. Civico 594 (Rosso). Waddesdon Manor Collections 699. Washington: National Gallery 81 (Giov. Bellini, *Feast of the Gods*), 163 (Cassatt), 252 (Dom. Veneziano), 255 (Dosso), 419 (Inness), 593 (El Greco), 758 (Renoir, *Diana*), 841 (Soutine, *Portrait of a Boy*), 858 (Stuart); Phillips Collection 110 (Bonnard), 178 (Chase), 212 (Courbet, *Rocks at Ornans*), 230 (Daumier, *Painter before his Easel, For the Defence*), 257 (Dove), 290 (Soutine), 373 (Guys, *La Promenade*), 383 (Hassam), 396 (Hicks), 417 (Renoir), 598 (Marin); Smithsonian Institution 363 (Greenough). Williamstown (Mass.): Williams College Museum of Art 687 (Pacheco). Worcester (Mass.): Art Museum 833 (Smibert). Würzburg: Martin von Wagner Museum der Universität 362; Residenz 882 (Tiepolo, *Apollo*). Zürich: Kunsthaus 400 (Hoflehner), 567 (Lipchitz), 771 (Rodin, *Gates of Hell*), 947 (Kauffman).

The publishers wish to acknowledge the kind co-operation of the following in providing illustrations for this book: Ansel Adams, San Francisco; Ateliers, Bernes; Ballet des Champs-Elysées, Paris; George Eastman House, Rochester N.Y.; Hachette, Paris; Hirschl and Adler Galleries, New York; Inter Nationes, Bonn; Galerie Iolas, Paris; Martha Jackson Gallery, New York; Micheal Mac Liammoir, Dublin; New York City Ballet; Galleria Odyssia, Rome; Govt of Ontario; Oxford, Master and Fellows of Pembroke College; Parke-Bernet Galleries, New York; Dr Alistair Rowan, Belfast; Société française de photographie, Paris; Standard Oil of New Jersey; Karlheinz Stockhausen, Hamburg; Théâtre de France, Paris; Universal-Edition A.G., Vienna; Josiah Wedgwood & Sons,

Ltd., Barlaston, Staffs. In London: Arup Associates; the Austrian Institute; Ballet Rambert; Cyril Beaumont; Belgian Tourist Office; The Bodley Head; Boosey & Hawkes Ltd; John Broadwood Ltd; Brown, Lenox & Co. Ltd; the Canadian High Commission; Jonathan Cape Ltd; the Chilean Embassy; Christie Manson & Woods Ltd; John Constable & Sons Ltd; Royal Opera House, Covent Garden; Peter Coviello; the Czechoslovak Embassy; the Danish Embassy; John Dewar & Sons; the Dickens Fellowship; Doulton & Co. Ltd; Faber & Faber Ltd; the Finnish Embassy; I. Freeman Ltd; the French Embassy; Garrard Ltd; the German Institute; Gimpel Fils; the Greek Embassy; Mariane Haile; Hamish Hamilton Ltd; Hanover Gallery; Wm. Heinemann Ltd; the Hispanic Institute, Canning House; Hohner Ltd; the Italian Institute; the Japanese Embassy; Herbert Jenkins Ltd; Michael Joseph Ltd; The Design Development Studio; Denys Lasdun & Partners; Little Angel Marionette Theatre; Marlborough Fine Art; *Melody Maker*; Yehudi Menuhin; The Mermaid Theatre; Methuen & Co. Ltd; the Royal Netherlands Embassy; Novello & Co. Ltd; Orbis Ltd, Publishers; Peter Owen Ltd; Oxford University Press; Penguin Books; Perez (London) Ltd; Phillips Records; the Polish Cultural Institute; Premier Musical Instruments Ltd; *Punch*; *The Reader's Digest*; Ricordi Ltd; The Royal College of Surgeons; St Bride's Institute; The St Giles Music Centre; Schotts Ltd; Sotheby & Co; The Peter Stuyvesant Foundation; the Swedish Embassy; Swiss National Tourist Office; United Music Publishers; United States Information Service; Royal Worcester Porcelain Co.; the Yugoslav Embassy.

Photo credits: Aerofilms, London; Agraci, Paris; Alinari Anderson, Florence; Derek Allen, London; Gordon Anthony, London; *Architectural & Building News*; ACL Brussels; Arch. Fotografico Gall. Mus. Vaticani; Archives Photographiques, Paris; Arts Council of Great Britain; Associated Press; Austrian Archaeological Institute (Ephesus Museum); Lala Aufsberg; G. Bakker; Roloff Beny; Henri Berthault; Osvaldo Böhm, Venice; Arnold von Borsig; Bulloz, Paris; F. Cali; Camera Press, London; P. Cannon Brookes; J. Allan Cash, London; Canvin, Paris; Central Press Photos, London; Allan Chappelow, London; Chatto & Windus, London; Bodo Cichy, Stuttgart; Courtauld Institute of Art; *Country Life*; Anthony Crickmay, London; E. Cruikshank; Culver Service; Mike Davis, London; Gerti Deutsch; Deutsches Archeologisches Institut, Athens; Robert Doisneau, Paris (Agence Rapho); Dominic, London; Walter Drayer, Zürich; Eliot Elisofon, New York; Elliot & Fry (Bassano, London); Exclusive News Agency; David Farrell, Gloucester; Festival Ballet, London; Fotocielo, Rome; Francesci; Gabinetto Fotografico Nazionale, Rome; Gasilov, Leningrad; Gernsheim Collection, University of Texas, Austin, USA; Noel Gibson, London; Photographie Giraudon, Paris; Gordon Goode, Stratford-upon-Avon; Henry Grant, London; Ara Güler ,Turkey; F. E. Halliday (reconstruction); Max Hirmer, Munich; John Hopkins (Powell & Moya); Hungarian Information Service, London; Martin Hürlimann, Zürich; Interiors International, London; Karsh, Ottawa (Cam. Press); F. E. Kersting; Keystone, London; Stanislaw Kolowca, Cracow; Kunstgewerbe Museum, Zürich; Alfred Lammer; Landbildstelle Salzburg (photo Puschej); Landbildstelle Württemberg, Stuttgart; Landesgalerie, Hanover; Richard Lannoy; Lidbrooke, London; *Life Magazine*, Copyright Time, Inc.; Lipnitzki, Paris; Angus McBean, London; Magnum; Mander & Mitchenson Theatre Collection; Mansell Collection; Bildarchiv Foto Marburg; Eric de Mare; MAS, Barcelona; Georgina Masson, Rome; D. Mazonowicz, Editions Alecto; Lotte Meidner-Graf, London; Ministry of Works (Crown copyright); Sheila Muir, London; Service Photographique des Musées Nationaux, Versailles; Hans Namuth, N.Y.; National Monuments Record; National Theatre, London; Morris Newcombe, London; Nordisk Pressphoto; Novosti Press Agency, London; *The Observer*; U. Pfistermeister; Photo Pic, Paris; Photopress Zürich; Rosemarie Pierer, Hamburg; Paul Popper Ltd, London; Radio Times Hulton Picture Library, London; David Redfern, London; Galerie Denise René, Paris; Reuters/P.A.; Houston Rogers, London; Roger-Viollet, Paris; Fotoatelier Rossmann, Innsbruck; Jean Roubier, Paris; Royal Academy of Arts, London; Royal Commission on Historical Monuments, London; Helga Schmidt-Glassner, Stuttgart; Walter Scott, Bradford; Jack Skeel; Edwin Smith; Malcolm Smith; P. E. C. Smith, London; Henk Snoek, London; Society for Cultural Relations with the Soviet Union, London; Soprintendenza alle Galerie, Florence; Walter Suschitzky, London; *The Times*, London; Eileen Tweedy, Paris; Ullstein, Berlin; John Vickers, London; Vrijhof, Rotterdam; Warburg Institute, London; Walter Wellek; Westermann Verlag; Edmund Weston; Edward Weston, Carmel, California; Colin Westwood, Weybridge, Surrey; Harold White, Gt Yarmouth; Hans Wild, London; Edmund Wilford; Reg Wilson, London; Roger Wood, London.

Film stills appear in this book by courtesy of the following: Allied Artists; Anglo-Amalgamated; Associated British Picture Corporation; Bargate Films; British Lion Films; Columbia Pictures Corporation; Contemporary Films; Cross-Channel Film Distributors; Curzon Film Distributors; Film Polski; Gala Film Distributors; Metro-Goldwyn-Mayer Pictures; Miracle Films; National Film Archive; National Film Board of Canada; Paramount Pictures; The Rank Organization; Sebricon Productions; Soviet Film Agency; Supreme Film Distributors; Twentieth-Century Fox; Unifrance; United Artists Corporation; Universal International; Warner Brothers.

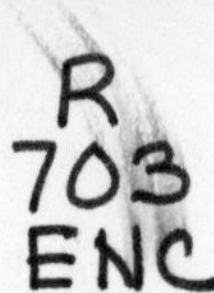

Encyclopedia of the arts :
Read, Herbert,
Goshen Public Lib.
72632